ESV
DAILY
READING
BIBLE

ESV

DAILY

READING

BIBLE

Through the Bible in 365 Days

based on the popular

M'Cheyne Bible Reading Plan

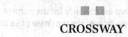

CROSSWAY

WHEATON, ILLINOIS — WWW.ESVBIBLE.ORG

ESV® Bible, The Daily Reading Edition

The Holy Bible, English Standard Version® (ESV®)
Copyright © 2001 by Crossway,
a publishing ministry of Good News Publishers.
All rights reserved.

ESV Text Edition: 2011

Library of Congress Catalog Card Number 2012022685

Printed in the United States of America
Published by Crossway
Wheaton, Illinois 60187, U.S.A.
www.Crossway.org

Crossway is a not-for-profit publishing ministry that exists solely for the purpose of publishing the Good News of the Gospel and the Truth of God's Word, the Bible. A portion of the purchase price of every ESV Bible is donated to help support Bible distribution ministry around the world.

| D P | 2 0 | 1 9 | 1 8 | 1 7 | 1 6 | 1 5 | 1 4 | 1 3 | 1 2 |
| 1 3 | 1 2 | 1 1 | 1 0 | 9 | 8 | 7 | 6 | 5 | 4 | 3 | 2 | 1 |

TABLE OF CONTENTS

Books of the Bible in Alphabetical Order

PUBLISHER'S PREFACE

The Daily Reading Bible is a unique edition of the English Standard Version of the Bible (ESV). The strategic contribution of the Daily Reading Bible is that it presents the Bible text according to one of the world's most beloved Bible reading plans, prepared by Robert Murray M'Cheyne. In this way the reader finds the daily texts for each day organized in sequence, ready for reflection and meditation.

Robert Murray M'Cheyne (1813–1843) was a Scottish pastor who, despite his short life, had a profound impact on the spiritual state of Scotland through his preaching and personal holiness. He is probably best known, however, for his Bible reading calendar that has become widely used throughout the world.

The M'Cheyne's calendar for daily Bible reading takes the reader through the entire Bible once each year, and through the Psalms and the New Testament twice. This is done by the careful selection of four different Scripture portions to be read each day—or, if the reader prefers, two readings may be done in the morning and two in the evening. The genius of this plan is that readers are exposed to different parts of Scripture on a daily basis and to the entire Bible throughout the year—an excellent way to rapidly gain deep appreciation for the full scope and message of the Bible.

The ESV Bible carries forward the classic principles of essentially literal Bible translation exemplified by the King James Version and subsequent translations that have followed its lead. As such, the ESV translates the original text with word-for-word accuracy into simple, beautiful, and readable English for our day, whether in private study or public reading.

We invite you to enrich your own personal walk with the Lord through the Daily Reading Bible. May you find deep encouragement and strengthening as you grow in your knowledge and understanding of Scripture, and of the God who has given his Word to us.

ESV PREFACE

The Bible

"This Book [is] the most valuable thing that this world affords. Here is Wisdom; this is the royal Law; these are the lively Oracles of God." With these words the Moderator of the Church of Scotland hands a Bible to the new monarch in Britain's coronation service. These words echo the King James Bible translators, who wrote in 1611: "God's sacred Word . . . is that inestimable treasure that excelleth all the riches of the earth." This assessment of the Bible is the motivating force behind the publication of the English Standard Version.

Translation Legacy

The English Standard Version (ESV) stands in the classic mainstream of English Bible translations over the past half-millennium. The fountainhead of that stream was William Tyndale's New Testament of 1526; marking its course were the King James Version of 1611 (KJV), the English Revised Version of 1885 (RV), the American Standard Version of 1901 (ASV), and the Revised Standard Version of 1952 and 1971 (RSV). In that stream, faithfulness to the text and vigorous pursuit of accuracy were combined with simplicity, beauty, and dignity of expression. Our goal has been to carry forward this legacy for a new century.

To this end each word and phrase in the ESV has been carefully weighed against the original Hebrew, Aramaic, and Greek, to ensure the fullest accuracy and clarity and to avoid undertranslating or overlooking any nuance of the original text. The words and phrases themselves grow out of the Tyndale–King James legacy, and most recently out of the RSV, with the 1971 RSV text providing the starting point for our work. Archaic language has been brought to current usage and significant corrections have been made in the translation of key texts. But throughout, our goal has been to retain the depth of meaning and enduring language that have made their indelible mark on the English-speaking world and have defined the life and doctrine of the church over the last four centuries.

Translation Philosophy

The ESV is an "essentially literal" translation that seeks as far as possible to capture the precise wording of the original text and the personal style of each Bible writer. As such, its emphasis is on "word-for-word" correspondence, at the same time taking into account differences of grammar, syntax, and idiom between current literary English and the original languages. Thus it seeks to be transparent to the original text, letting the reader see as directly as possible the structure and meaning of the original.

In contrast to the ESV, some Bible versions have followed a "thought-for-thought" rather than "word-for-word" translation philosophy, emphasizing "dynamic equivalence" rather than the "essentially literal" meaning of the original. A "thought-for-thought" translation is of necessity more inclined to reflect the interpretive opinions of the translator and the influences of contemporary culture.

Every translation is at many points a trade-off between literal precision and readability, between "formal equivalence" in expression and "functional equivalence" in communication, and the ESV is no exception. Within this framework we have sought to be "as literal as possible" while maintaining clarity of expression and literary excellence. Therefore, to the extent that plain English permits and the meaning in each case allows, we have sought to use the same English word for important recurring words in the original; and, as far as grammar and syntax allow, we have rendered Old Testament passages cited in the New in ways that show their correspondence. Thus in each of these areas, as well as throughout the Bible as a whole, we have sought to capture the echoes and overtones of meaning that are so abundantly present in the original texts.

As an essentially literal translation, then, the ESV seeks to carry over every possible nuance of meaning in the original words of Scripture into our own language. As such, the ESV is ideally suited for in-depth study of the Bible. Indeed, with its emphasis on literary excellence, the ESV is equally suited for public reading and preaching, for private reading and reflection, for both academic and devotional study, and for Scripture memorization.

Translation Principles and Style

The ESV also carries forward classic translation principles in its literary style. Accordingly it retains theological terminology—words such as grace, faith, justification, sanctification, redemption, regeneration, reconciliation, propitiation—because of their central importance for Christian doctrine and also because the underlying Greek words were already becoming key words and technical terms in New Testament times.

The ESV lets the stylistic variety of the biblical writers fully express itself—from the exalted prose that opens Genesis, to the flowing narratives of the historical books, to the rich metaphors and dramatic imagery of the poetic books, to the ringing rhetorical indictments in the prophetic books, to the smooth elegance of Luke, to the profound simplicities of John, and the closely reasoned logic of Paul.

In punctuating, paragraphing, dividing long sentences, and rendering connectives, the ESV follows the path that seems to make the ongoing flow of thought clearest in English. The biblical languages regularly connect sentences by frequent repetition of words such as "and," "but," and "for," in a way that goes beyond the conventions of literary English. Effective translation, however, requires that these links in the original be reproduced so that the flow of the argument will be transparent to the reader. We have therefore normally translated these connectives, though occasionally we have varied the rendering by using alternatives (such as "also," "however," "now," "so," "then," or "thus") when they better capture the sense in specific instances.

In the area of gender language, the goal of the ESV is to render literally what is in the original. For example, "anyone" replaces "any man" where there is no word corresponding to "man" in the original languages, and "people" rather than "men" is regularly used where the original languages refer to both men and women. But the words "man" and "men" are retained where a male meaning component is part of the original Greek or Hebrew. Likewise, the word "man" has been retained where the original text intends to convey a clear contrast between "God" on the one hand and "man" on the other hand, with "man" being used in the collective sense of the whole human race (see Luke 2:52). Similarly, the English word "brothers" (translating the Greek word *adelphoi*) is retained as an important familial form of address between fellow-Jews and fellow-Christians in the first century. A recurring note is included to indicate that the term "brothers" (*adelphoi*) was often used in Greek to refer to both men and women, and to indicate the specific instances in the text where this is the case. In addition, the English word "sons" (translating the Greek word *huioi*) is retained in specific instances because the underlying Greek term usually includes a male meaning component and it was used as a legal term in the adoption and inheritance laws of first-century Rome. As used by the apostle Paul, this term refers to the status of all Christians, both men and women, who, having been adopted into God's family, now enjoy all the privileges, obligations, and inheritance rights of God's children.

The inclusive use of the generic "he" has also regularly been retained, because this is consistent with similar usage in the original languages and because an essentially literal translation would be impossible without it.

In each case the objective has been transparency to the original text, allowing the reader to understand the original on its own terms rather than on the terms of our present-day culture.

The Translation of Specialized Terms

In the translation of biblical terms referring to God, the ESV takes great care to convey the specific nuances of meaning of the original Hebrew and Greek terms. First, concerning terms that refer to God in the Old Testament: God, the Maker of heaven and earth, introduced himself to the people of Israel with a special personal name, the consonants for which are YHWH (see Exodus 3:14–15). Scholars call this the "Tetragrammaton," a Greek term referring to the four Hebrew letters YHWH. The exact pronunciation of YHWH is uncertain, because the Jewish people considered the personal name of God to be so holy that it should never be spoken aloud. Instead of reading the word YHWH, they would normally read the Hebrew word 'adonay ("Lord"), and the ancient translations into Greek, Syriac, and Aramaic also followed this practice. When the vowels of the word 'adonay are placed with the consonants of YHWH, this results in the familiar word Jehovah that was used in some earlier English Bible translations. As is common among English translations today, the ESV usually renders the personal name of God (YHWH) with the word LORD (printed in small capitals). An exception to this is when the Hebrew word 'adonay appears together with YHWH, in which case the two words are rendered together as "the Lord [in lower case] GOD [in small capitals]." In contrast to the personal name for God (YHWH), the more general name for God in Old Testament Hebrew is 'elohim and its related forms of 'el or 'eloah, all of which are normally translated "God" (in lower case letters). The use of these different ways to translate the Hebrew words for God is especially beneficial to the English reader, enabling the reader to see and understand the different ways that the personal name and the general name for God are both used to refer to the One True God of the Old Testament.

Second, in the New Testament, the Greek word Christos has been translated consistently as "Christ." Although the term originally meant "anointed," among Jews in New Testament times the term came to designate the Messiah, the great Savior that God had promised to raise up. In other New Testament contexts, however, especially among Gentiles, Christos ("Christ") was on its way to becoming a proper name. It is important, therefore, to keep the context in mind in understanding the various ways that Christos ("Christ") is used in the New Testament. At the same time, in accord with its "essentially literal" translation philosophy, the ESV has retained consistency and concordance in the translation of Christos ("Christ") throughout the New Testament.

Third, a particular difficulty is presented when words in biblical Hebrew and Greek refer to ancient practices and institutions that do not correspond directly to those in the modern world. Such is the case in the translation of 'ebed (Hebrew) and doulos (Greek), terms which are often rendered "slave." These terms, however, actually cover a range of relationships that require a range of renderings — either "slave," "bondservant," or "servant" — depending on the context. Further, the word "slave" currently carries associations with the often brutal and dehumanizing institution of slavery in nineteenth-century America. For this reason, the ESV translation of the words 'ebed and doulos has been undertaken with particular attention to their meaning in each specific context. Thus in Old Testament times, one might enter slavery either voluntarily (e.g., to escape poverty or to pay off a debt) or involuntarily (e.g., by birth, by being captured in battle, or by judicial sentence). Protection for all in servitude in ancient Israel was provided by the Mosaic Law. In New Testament times, a doulos is often best described as a "bondservant" — that is, as someone bound to serve his master for a specific (usually lengthy) period of time, but also as someone who might nevertheless own property, achieve social advancement, and even be released or purchase his freedom. The ESV usage thus seeks to express the nuance of meaning in each context. Where absolute ownership by a master is in view (as in Romans 6), "slave" is used; where a more limited form of servitude is in view, "bondservant" is used (as in 1 Corinthians 7:21–24); where the context indicates a wide range of freedom (as in John 4:51), "servant" is preferred. Footnotes are generally provided to identify the Hebrew or Greek and the range of meaning that these terms may carry in each case.

Fourth, it is sometimes suggested that Bible translations should capitalize pronouns referring to deity. It has seemed best not to capitalize deity pronouns in the ESV, however, for the following reasons: first, there is nothing in the original Hebrew and Greek manuscripts that corresponds to such capitalization; second, the practice of capitalizing deity pronouns in English Bible translations is a recent innovation, which began only in the mid-twentieth century; and, third, such capitalization is absent from the KJV Bible and the whole stream of Bible translations that the ESV seeks to carry forward.

A fifth specialized term, the word "behold," usually has been retained as the most common translation for the Hebrew word *hinneh* and the Greek word *idou*. Both of these words mean something like "Pay careful attention to what follows! This is important!" Other than the word "behold," there is no single word in English that fits well in most contexts. Although "Look!" and "See!" and "Listen!" would be workable in some contexts, in many others these words lack sufficient weight and dignity. Given the principles of "essentially literal" translation, it is important not to leave *hinneh* and *idou* completely untranslated, and so to lose the intended emphasis in the original languages. The older and more formal word "behold" has usually been retained, therefore, as the best available option for conveying the original sense of meaning.

Textual Basis and Resources

The ESV is based on the Masoretic text of the Hebrew Bible as found in *Biblia Hebraica Stuttgartensia* (2nd ed., 1983), and on the Greek text in the 1993 editions of the *Greek New Testament* (4th corrected ed.), published by the United Bible Societies (UBS), and *Novum Testamentum Graece* (27th ed.), edited by Nestle and Aland. The currently renewed respect among Old Testament scholars for the Masoretic text is reflected in the ESV's attempt, wherever possible, to translate difficult Hebrew passages as they stand in the Masoretic text rather than resorting to emendations or to finding an alternative reading in the ancient versions. In exceptional, difficult cases, the Dead Sea Scrolls, the Septuagint, the Samaritan Pentateuch, the Syriac Peshitta, the Latin Vulgate, and other sources were consulted to shed possible light on the text, or, if necessary, to support a divergence from the Masoretic text. Similarly, in a few difficult cases in the New Testament, the ESV has followed a Greek text different from the text given preference in the UBS/Nestle-Aland 27th edition. Throughout, the translation team has benefited greatly from the massive textual resources that have become readily available recently, from new insights into biblical laws and culture, and from current advances in Hebrew and Greek lexicography and grammatical understanding.

Textual Footnotes

The footnotes that accompany the ESV text are an integral part of the ESV translation, informing the reader of textual variations and difficulties and showing how these have been resolved by the ESV translation team. In addition to this, the footnotes indicate significant alternative readings and occasionally provide an explanation for technical terms or for a difficult reading in the text.

Publishing Team

The ESV publishing team includes more than a hundred people. The fourteen-member Translation Oversight Committee has benefited from the work of more than fifty biblical experts serving as Translation Review Scholars and from the comments of the more than fifty members of the Advisory Council, all of which has been carried out under the auspices of the Crossway Board of Directors. This hundred-plus-member team shares a common commitment to the truth of God's Word and to historic Christian orthodoxy and is international in scope, including leaders in many denominations.

To God's Honor and Praise

We know that no Bible translation is perfect or final; but we also know that God uses imperfect and inadequate things to his honor and praise. So to our triune God and to his people we offer what we have done, with our prayers that it may prove useful, with gratitude for much help given, and with ongoing wonder that our God should ever have entrusted to us so momentous a task.

Soli Deo Gloria!—To God alone be the glory!

*The Translation Oversight Committee**

*A complete list of the Translation Oversight Committee, the Translation Review Scholars, and the Advisory Council, is available upon request from Crossway.

FEATURES

The Daily Reading Edition of the ESV Bible includes a number of valuable features to encourage the reading and study of the Bible. A brief description is provided below explaining the purpose and use of these features.

TEXTUAL FOOTNOTES

Several kinds of footnotes related to the ESV text are provided throughout the ESV Bible to assist the reader. These footnotes appear at the bottom of the page and are indicated in the ESV text by a superscript *number* that *follows* the word or phrase to which the footnote applies (e.g., "Isaac²"). Superscript *letters* that *precede* a word indicate cross-references (see explanation on the following page).

The footnotes included in the ESV Bible are an integral part of the text and provide important information concerning the understanding and translation of the text. The footnotes fall mainly into four categories, as illustrated in the examples below.

Types of Textual Footnotes

(1) *Alternative Translations.* Footnotes of this kind provide alternative translations for specific words or phrases when there is a strong possibility that such words or phrases could be translated in another way, such as: "Or *keep awake*" (see Matt. 26:38); and "Or *down payment*" (see Eph. 1:14). In such cases, the translation deemed to have the stronger support is in the text while other possible renderings are given in the note.

(2) *Explanation of Greek and Hebrew Terms.* Notes of this kind relate primarily to the meaning of specific Greek or Hebrew terms, as illustrated by the following examples:

(a) Notes about the meaning of names in the original languages, such as: "*Isaac* means *he laughs*" (see Gen. 17:19); and "*Simeon* sounds like the Hebrew for *heard*" (see Gen. 29:33).

(b) Notes that give the literal translation of a Greek or Hebrew word or phrase deemed too awkward to be used in the English text, such as: "Greek *girding up the loins of your mind*" (see 1 Pet. 1:13).

(c) Notes indicating that absolute certainty of the meaning of a word or phrase is not possible given our best understanding of the original language (e.g., Hebrew words occurring so infrequently in the Old Testament that their meaning cannot be determined with certainty). Such words are identified with a note stating that "The meaning of the Hebrew is uncertain" (see, e.g., Josh. 17:11).

(d) Notes that indicate the specialized use of a Greek word, such as: "brothers," translating the Greek word *adelphoi* (see, e.g., the extended note on Rom. 1:13, corresponding to the first occurrence of *adelphoi* in any New Testament book, and the abbreviated note, e.g., on Rom. 7:1, corresponding to subsequent occurrences of *adelphoi* in any New Testament book); and "sons," translating the Greek word *huioi* (see, e.g., Rom. 8:14). See also the discussion of *adelphoi* and *huioi* in the Preface.

(3) *Other Explanatory Notes.* Footnotes of this kind provide clarifying information as illustrated by the following examples:

(a) Notes clarifying additional meanings that may not otherwise be apparent in the text, such as: "*Leprosy* was a term for several skin diseases; see Leviticus 13."

(b) Notes clarifying important grammatical points that would not otherwise be apparent in English, such as: "In Hebrew *you* is plural in verses 1–5" (see Gen. 3:1).

(c) Notes clarifying when the referent for a pronoun has been supplied in the English text, such as: "Greek *he*" (see, e.g., Mark 1:43).

(d) Notes giving English equivalents for weights, measures, and monetary values.

(4) *Technical Translation Notes.* Footnotes of this kind indicate how decisions have been made in the translation of difficult Hebrew and Greek passages. Such notes occasionally include technical terms. For an explanation of these terms the reader is referred to standard Bible study reference works. See further the section in the Preface on "Textual Basis and Resources" for an explanation of the original-language texts used in the translation of the ESV Bible and how the translation of difficult passages has been resolved.

The
DAILY READING BIBLE

JANUARY 1

Genesis 1

In the beginning, God created the heavens and the earth. ²The earth was without form and void, and darkness was over the face of the deep. And the Spirit of God was hovering over the face of the waters.

³And God said, "Let there be light," and there was light. ⁴And God saw that the light was good. And God separated the light from the darkness. ⁵God called the light Day, and the darkness he called Night. And there was evening and there was morning, the first day.

⁶And God said, "Let there be an expanse[1] in the midst of the waters, and let it separate the waters from the waters." ⁷And God made[2] the expanse and separated the waters that were under the expanse from the waters that were above the expanse. And it was so. ⁸And God called the expanse Heaven.[3] And there was evening and there was morning, the second day.

⁹And God said, "Let the waters under the heavens be gathered together into one place, and let the dry land appear." And it was so. ¹⁰God called the dry land Earth,[4] and the waters that were gathered together he called Seas. And God saw that it was good.

¹¹And God said, "Let the earth sprout vegetation, plants[5] yielding seed, and fruit trees bearing fruit in which is their seed, each according to its kind, on the earth." And it was so. ¹²The earth brought forth vegetation, plants yielding seed according to their own kinds, and trees bearing fruit in which is their seed, each according to its kind. And God saw that it was good. ¹³And there was evening and there was morning, the third day.

¹⁴And God said, "Let there be lights in the expanse of the heavens to separate the day from the night. And let them be for signs and for seasons,[6] and for days and years, ¹⁵and let them be lights in the expanse of the heavens to give light upon the earth." And it was so. ¹⁶And God made the two great lights—the greater light to rule the day and the lesser light to rule the night—and the stars. ¹⁷And God set them in the expanse of the heavens to give light on the earth, ¹⁸to rule over the day and over the night, and to separate the light from the darkness. And God saw that it was good. ¹⁹And there was evening and there was morning, the fourth day.

²⁰And God said, "Let the waters swarm with swarms of living creatures, and let birds[7] fly above the earth across the expanse of the heavens." ²¹So God created the great sea creatures and every living creature that moves, with which the waters swarm, according to their kinds, and every winged bird according to its kind. And God saw that it was good. ²²And God blessed them, saying, "Be fruitful and multiply and fill the waters in the seas, and let birds multiply on the earth." ²³And there was evening and there was morning, the fifth day.

²⁴And God said, "Let the earth bring forth living creatures according to their kinds—livestock and creeping things and beasts of the earth according to their kinds." And it was so. ²⁵And God made the beasts of the earth according to their kinds and the livestock according to their kinds, and everything that creeps on the ground according to its kind. And God saw that it was good.

²⁶Then God said, "Let us make man[8] in our image, after our likeness. And let them have dominion over the fish of the sea and over the birds of the heavens and over the livestock and over all the earth and over every creeping thing that creeps on the earth."

²⁷   So God created man in his own image,
         in the image of God he created him;
         male and female he created them.

²⁸And God blessed them. And God said to them, "Be fruitful and multiply and fill the earth and subdue it, and have dominion over the fish of the sea and over the birds of the heavens and over every living thing that moves on the earth." ²⁹And God said, "Behold, I have given you every plant yielding seed that is on

¹ Or *a canopy*; also verses 7, 8, 14, 15, 17, 20 ² Or *fashioned*; also verse 16 ³ Or *Sky*; also verses 9, 14, 15, 17, 20, 26, 28, 30; 2:1 ⁴ Or *Land*; also verses 11, 12, 22, 24, 25, 26, 28, 30; 2:1 ⁵ Or *small plants*; also verses 12, 29 ⁶ Or *appointed times* ⁷ Or *flying things*; see Leviticus 11:19–20 ⁸ The Hebrew word for *man* (*adam*) is the generic term for mankind and becomes the proper name *Adam*

the face of all the earth, and every tree with seed in its fruit. You shall have them for food. [30]And to every beast of the earth and to every bird of the heavens and to everything that creeps on the earth, everything that has the breath of life, I have given every green plant for food." And it was so. [31]And God saw everything that he had made, and behold, it was very good. And there was evening and there was morning, the sixth day.

Matthew 1

[1]The book of the genealogy of Jesus Christ, the son of David, the son of Abraham.

[2]Abraham was the father of Isaac, and Isaac the father of Jacob, and Jacob the father of Judah and his brothers, [3]and Judah the father of Perez and Zerah by Tamar, and Perez the father of Hezron, and Hezron the father of Ram,[1] [4]and Ram the father of Amminadab, and Amminadab the father of Nahshon, and Nahshon the father of Salmon, [5]and Salmon the father of Boaz by Rahab, and Boaz the father of Obed by Ruth, and Obed the father of Jesse, [6]and Jesse the father of David the king.

And David was the father of Solomon by the wife of Uriah, [7]and Solomon the father of Rehoboam, and Rehoboam the father of Abijah, and Abijah the father of Asaph,[2] [8]and Asaph the father of Jehoshaphat, and Jehoshaphat the father of Joram, and Joram the father of Uzziah, [9]and Uzziah the father of Jotham, and Jotham the father of Ahaz, and Ahaz the father of Hezekiah, [10]and Hezekiah the father of Manasseh, and Manasseh the father of Amos,[3] and Amos the father of Josiah, [11]and Josiah the father of Jechoniah and his brothers, at the time of the deportation to Babylon.

[12]And after the deportation to Babylon: Jechoniah was the father of Shealtiel,[4] and Shealtiel the father of Zerubbabel, [13]and Zerubbabel the father of Abiud, and Abiud the father of Eliakim, and Eliakim the father of Azor, [14]and Azor the father of Zadok, and Zadok the father of Achim, and Achim the father of Eliud, [15]and Eliud the father of Eleazar, and Eleazar the father of Matthan, and Matthan the father of Jacob, [16]and Jacob the father of Joseph the husband of Mary, of whom Jesus was born, who is called Christ.

[17]So all the generations from Abraham to David were fourteen generations, and from David to the deportation to Babylon fourteen generations, and from the deportation to Babylon to the Christ fourteen generations.

[18]Now the birth of Jesus Christ[5] took place in this way. When his mother Mary had been betrothed[6] to Joseph, before they came together she was found to be with child from the Holy Spirit. [19]And her husband Joseph, being a just man and unwilling to put her to shame, resolved to divorce her quietly. [20]But as he considered these things, behold, an angel of the Lord appeared to him in a dream, saying, "Joseph, son of David, do not fear to take Mary as your wife, for that which is conceived in her is from the Holy Spirit. [21]She will bear a son, and you shall call his name Jesus, for he will save his people from their sins." [22]All this took place to fulfill what the Lord had spoken by the prophet:

23 "Behold, the virgin shall conceive and
        bear a son,
     and they shall call his name
        Immanuel"

(which means, God with us). [24]When Joseph woke from sleep, he did as the angel of the Lord commanded him: he took his wife, [25]but knew her not until she had given birth to a son. And he called his name Jesus.

Ezra 1

[1]In the first year of Cyrus king of Persia, that the word of the LORD by the mouth of Jeremiah might be fulfilled, the LORD stirred up the spirit of Cyrus king of Persia, so that he made a proclamation throughout all his kingdom and also put it in writing:

[2]"Thus says Cyrus king of Persia: The LORD, the God of heaven, has given me all the kingdoms of the earth, and he has charged me to build him a house at Jerusalem, which is in Judah. [3]Whoever is among you of all his people, may his God be with him, and let him go up to Jerusalem, which is in Judah, and rebuild the house of the LORD, the God of Israel—he is the God who is in Jerusalem. [4]And let each survivor, in whatever place he sojourns, be assisted by the men of his place with silver and gold, with goods and with beasts, besides freewill offerings for the house of God that is in Jerusalem."

[1] Greek Aram; also verse 4 [2] Asaph is probably an alternate spelling of Asa; some manuscripts Asa; also verse 8 [3] Amos is probably an alternate spelling of Amon; some manuscripts Amon; twice in this verse [4] Greek Salathiel; twice in this verse [5] Some manuscripts of the Christ [6] That is, legally pledged to be married

⁵Then rose up the heads of the fathers' houses of Judah and Benjamin, and the priests and the Levites, everyone whose spirit God had stirred to go up to rebuild the house of the LORD that is in Jerusalem. ⁶And all who were about them aided them with vessels of silver, with gold, with goods, with beasts, and with costly wares, besides all that was freely offered. ⁷Cyrus the king also brought out the vessels of the house of the LORD that Nebuchadnezzar had carried away from Jerusalem and placed in the house of his gods. ⁸Cyrus king of Persia brought these out in the charge of Mithredath the treasurer, who counted them out to Sheshbazzar the prince of Judah. ⁹And this was the number of them: 30 basins of gold, 1,000 basins of silver, 29 censers, ¹⁰30 bowls of gold, 410 bowls of silver, and 1,000 other vessels; ¹¹all the vessels of gold and of silver were 5,400. All these did Sheshbazzar bring up, when the exiles were brought up from Babylonia to Jerusalem.

Acts 1

In the first book, O Theophilus, I have dealt with all that Jesus began to do and teach, ²until the day when he was taken up, after he had given commands through the Holy Spirit to the apostles whom he had chosen. ³He presented himself alive to them after his suffering by many proofs, appearing to them during forty days and speaking about the kingdom of God. ⁴And while staying¹ with them he ordered them not to depart from Jerusalem, but to wait for the promise of the Father, which, he said, "you heard from me; ⁵for John baptized with water, but you will be baptized with² the Holy Spirit not many days from now."

⁶So when they had come together, they asked him, "Lord, will you at this time restore the kingdom to Israel?" ⁷He said to them, "It is not for you to know times or seasons that the Father has fixed by his own authority. ⁸But you will receive power when the Holy Spirit has come upon you, and you will be my witnesses in Jerusalem and in all Judea and Samaria, and to the end of the earth." ⁹And when he had said these things, as they were looking on, he was lifted up, and a cloud took him out of their sight. ¹⁰And while they were gazing into heaven as he went, behold, two men stood by them in white robes, ¹¹and said, "Men of Galilee, why do you stand looking into heaven? This Jesus, who was taken up from you into heaven, will come in the same way as you saw him go into heaven."

¹²Then they returned to Jerusalem from the mount called Olivet, which is near Jerusalem, a Sabbath day's journey away. ¹³And when they had entered, they went up to the upper room, where they were staying, Peter and John and James and Andrew, Philip and Thomas, Bartholomew and Matthew, James the son of Alphaeus and Simon the Zealot and Judas the son of James. ¹⁴All these with one accord were devoting themselves to prayer, together with the women and Mary the mother of Jesus, and his brothers.³

¹⁵In those days Peter stood up among the brothers (the company of persons was in all about 120) and said, ¹⁶"Brothers, the Scripture had to be fulfilled, which the Holy Spirit spoke beforehand by the mouth of David concerning Judas, who became a guide to those who arrested Jesus. ¹⁷For he was numbered among us and was allotted his share in this ministry." ¹⁸(Now this man acquired a field with the reward of his wickedness, and falling headlong⁴ he burst open in the middle and all his bowels gushed out. ¹⁹And it became known to all the inhabitants of Jerusalem, so that the field was called in their own language Akeldama, that is, Field of Blood.) ²⁰"For it is written in the Book of Psalms,

"'May his camp become desolate,
    and let there be no one to dwell in it';

and

"'Let another take his office.'

²¹So one of the men who have accompanied us during all the time that the Lord Jesus went in and out among us, ²²beginning from the baptism of John until the day when he was taken up from us—one of these men must become with us a witness to his resurrection." ²³And they put forward two, Joseph called Barsabbas, who was also called Justus, and Matthias. ²⁴And they prayed and said, "You, Lord, who know the hearts of all, show which one of these two you have chosen ²⁵to take the place in this ministry and apostleship from which Judas turned aside to go to his own place." ²⁶And they cast lots for them, and the lot fell on Matthias, and he was numbered with the eleven apostles.

¹ Or eating ² Or in ³ Or brothers and sisters. The plural Greek word adelphoi (translated "brothers") refers to siblings in a family. In New Testament usage, depending on the context, adelphoi may refer either to men or to both men and women who are siblings (brothers and sisters) in God's family, the church; also verse 15 ⁴ Or swelling up

JANUARY 2

Genesis 2

Thus the heavens and the earth were finished, and all the host of them. ²And on the seventh day God finished his work that he had done, and he rested on the seventh day from all his work that he had done. ³So God blessed the seventh day and made it holy, because on it God rested from all his work that he had done in creation.

4   These are the generations
    of the heavens and the earth when they
       were created,
    in the day that the LORD God made the
       earth and the heavens.

⁵When no bush of the field¹ was yet in the land² and no small plant of the field had yet sprung up—for the LORD God had not caused it to rain on the land, and there was no man to work the ground, ⁶and a mist³ was going up from the land and was watering the whole face of the ground— ⁷then the LORD God formed the man of dust from the ground and breathed into his nostrils the breath of life, and the man became a living creature. ⁸And the LORD God planted a garden in Eden, in the east, and there he put the man whom he had formed. ⁹And out of the ground the LORD God made to spring up every tree that is pleasant to the sight and good for food. The tree of life was in the midst of the garden, and the tree of the knowledge of good and evil.

¹⁰A river flowed out of Eden to water the garden, and there it divided and became four rivers. ¹¹The name of the first is the Pishon. It is the one that flowed around the whole land of Havilah, where there is gold. ¹²And the gold of that land is good; bdellium and onyx stone are there. ¹³The name of the second river is the Gihon. It is the one that flowed around the whole land of Cush. ¹⁴And the name of the third river is the Tigris, which flows east of Assyria. And the fourth river is the Euphrates. ¹⁵The LORD God took the man and put him in the garden of Eden to work it and keep it.

¹⁶And the LORD God commanded the man, saying, "You may surely eat of every tree of the garden, ¹⁷but of the tree of the knowledge of good and evil you shall not eat, for in the day that you eat⁴ of it you shall surely die."

¹⁸Then the LORD God said, "It is not good that the man should be alone; I will make him a helper fit for⁵ him." ¹⁹Now out of the ground the LORD God had formed⁶ every beast of the field and every bird of the heavens and brought them to the man to see what he would call them. And whatever the man called every living creature, that was its name. ²⁰The man gave names to all livestock and to the birds of the heavens and to every beast of the field. But for Adam⁷ there was not found a helper fit for him. ²¹So the LORD God caused a deep sleep to fall upon the man, and while he slept took one of his ribs and closed up its place with flesh. ²²And the rib that the LORD God had taken from the man he made⁸ into a woman and brought her to the man. ²³Then the man said,

"This at last is bone of my bones
    and flesh of my flesh;
  she shall be called Woman,
    because she was taken out of Man."⁹

²⁴Therefore a man shall leave his father and his mother and hold fast to his wife, and they shall become one flesh. ²⁵And the man and his wife were both naked and were not ashamed.

Matthew 2

Now after Jesus was born in Bethlehem of Judea in the days of Herod the king, behold, wise men¹⁰ from the east came to Jerusalem, ²saying, "Where is he who has been born king of the Jews? For we saw his star when it rose¹¹ and have come to worship him." ³When Herod the king heard this, he was troubled, and all Jerusalem with him; ⁴and assembling all the chief priests and scribes of the people, he inquired of them where the Christ

¹ Or open country ² Or earth; also verse 6 ³ Or spring ⁴ Or when you eat ⁵ Or corresponding to; also verse 20 ⁶ Or And out of the ground the LORD God formed ⁷ Or the man ⁸ Hebrew built ⁹ The Hebrew words for woman (ishshah) and man (ish) sound alike ¹⁰ Greek magi; also verses 7, 16 ¹¹ Or in the east; also verse 9

was to be born. ⁵They told him, "In Bethlehem of Judea, for so it is written by the prophet:

⁶ "'And you, O Bethlehem, in the land of Judah,
are by no means least among the rulers of Judah;
for from you shall come a ruler who will shepherd my people Israel.'"

⁷Then Herod summoned the wise men secretly and ascertained from them what time the star had appeared. ⁸And he sent them to Bethlehem, saying, "Go and search diligently for the child, and when you have found him, bring me word, that I too may come and worship him." ⁹After listening to the king, they went on their way. And behold, the star that they had seen when it rose went before them until it came to rest over the place where the child was. ¹⁰When they saw the star, they rejoiced exceedingly with great joy. ¹¹And going into the house they saw the child with Mary his mother, and they fell down and worshiped him. Then, opening their treasures, they offered him gifts, gold and frankincense and myrrh. ¹²And being warned in a dream not to return to Herod, they departed to their own country by another way.

¹³Now when they had departed, behold, an angel of the Lord appeared to Joseph in a dream and said, "Rise, take the child and his mother, and flee to Egypt, and remain there until I tell you, for Herod is about to search for the child, to destroy him." ¹⁴And he rose and took the child and his mother by night and departed to Egypt ¹⁵and remained there until the death of Herod. This was to fulfill what the Lord had spoken by the prophet, "Out of Egypt I called my son."

¹⁶Then Herod, when he saw that he had been tricked by the wise men, became furious, and he sent and killed all the male children in Bethlehem and in all that region who were two years old or under, according to the time that he had ascertained from the wise men. ¹⁷Then was fulfilled what was spoken by the prophet Jeremiah:

¹⁸ "A voice was heard in Ramah,
weeping and loud lamentation,
Rachel weeping for her children;
she refused to be comforted, because they are no more."

¹⁹But when Herod died, behold, an angel of the Lord appeared in a dream to Joseph in Egypt, ²⁰saying, "Rise, take the child and his mother and go to the land of Israel, for those who sought the child's life are dead." ²¹And he rose and took the child and his mother and went to the land of Israel. ²²But when he heard that Archelaus was reigning over Judea in place of his father Herod, he was afraid to go there, and being warned in a dream he withdrew to the district of Galilee. ²³And he went and lived in a city called Nazareth, so that what was spoken by the prophets might be fulfilled, that he would be called a Nazarene.

Ezra 2

Now these were the people of the province who came up out of the captivity of those exiles whom Nebuchadnezzar the king of Babylon had carried captive to Babylonia. They returned to Jerusalem and Judah, each to his own town. ²They came with Zerubbabel, Jeshua, Nehemiah, Seraiah, Reelaiah, Mordecai, Bilshan, Mispar, Bigvai, Rehum, and Baanah.

The number of the men of the people of Israel: ³the sons of Parosh, 2,172. ⁴The sons of Shephatiah, 372. ⁵The sons of Arah, 775. ⁶The sons of Pahath-moab, namely the sons of Jeshua and Joab, 2,812. ⁷The sons of Elam, 1,254. ⁸The sons of Zattu, 945. ⁹The sons of Zaccai, 760. ¹⁰The sons of Bani, 642. ¹¹The sons of Bebai, 623. ¹²The sons of Azgad, 1,222. ¹³The sons of Adonikam, 666. ¹⁴The sons of Bigvai, 2,056. ¹⁵The sons of Adin, 454. ¹⁶The sons of Ater, namely of Hezekiah, 98. ¹⁷The sons of Bezai, 323. ¹⁸The sons of Jorah, 112. ¹⁹The sons of Hashum, 223. ²⁰The sons of Gibbar, 95. ²¹The sons of Bethlehem, 123. ²²The men of Netophah, 56. ²³The men of Anathoth, 128. ²⁴The sons of Azmaveth, 42. ²⁵The sons of Kiriath-arim, Chephirah, and Beeroth, 743. ²⁶The sons of Ramah and Geba, 621. ²⁷The men of Michmas, 122. ²⁸The men of Bethel and Ai, 223. ²⁹The sons of Nebo, 52. ³⁰The sons of Magbish, 156. ³¹The sons of the other Elam, 1,254. ³²The sons of Harim, 320. ³³The sons of Lod, Hadid, and Ono, 725. ³⁴The sons of Jericho, 345. ³⁵The sons of Senaah, 3,630.

³⁶The priests: the sons of Jedaiah, of the house of Jeshua, 973. ³⁷The sons of Immer,

1,052. [38]The sons of Pashhur, 1,247. [39]The sons of Harim, 1,017.

[40]The Levites: the sons of Jeshua and Kadmiel, of the sons of Hodaviah, 74. [41]The singers: the sons of Asaph, 128. [42]The sons of the gatekeepers: the sons of Shallum, the sons of Ater, the sons of Talmon, the sons of Akkub, the sons of Hatita, and the sons of Shobai, in all 139.

[43]The temple servants: the sons of Ziha, the sons of Hasupha, the sons of Tabbaoth, [44]the sons of Keros, the sons of Siaha, the sons of Padon, [45]the sons of Lebanah, the sons of Hagabah, the sons of Akkub, [46]the sons of Hagab, the sons of Shamlai, the sons of Hanan, [47]the sons of Giddel, the sons of Gahar, the sons of Reaiah, [48]the sons of Rezin, the sons of Nekoda, the sons of Gazzam, [49]the sons of Uzza, the sons of Paseah, the sons of Besai, [50]the sons of Asnah, the sons of Meunim, the sons of Nephisim, [51]the sons of Bakbuk, the sons of Hakupha, the sons of Harhur, [52]the sons of Bazluth, the sons of Mehida, the sons of Harsha, [53]the sons of Barkos, the sons of Sisera, the sons of Temah, [54]the sons of Neziah, and the sons of Hatipha.

[55]The sons of Solomon's servants: the sons of Sotai, the sons of Hassophereth, the sons of Peruda, [56]the sons of Jaalah, the sons of Darkon, the sons of Giddel, [57]the sons of Shephatiah, the sons of Hattil, the sons of Pochereth-hazzebaim, and the sons of Ami.

[58]All the temple servants and the sons of Solomon's servants were 392.

[59]The following were those who came up from Tel-melah, Tel-harsha, Cherub, Addan, and Immer, though they could not prove their fathers' houses or their descent, whether they belonged to Israel: [60]the sons of Delaiah, the sons of Tobiah, and the sons of Nekoda, 652. [61]Also, of the sons of the priests: the sons of Habaiah, the sons of Hakkoz, and the sons of Barzillai (who had taken a wife from the daughters of Barzillai the Gileadite, and was called by their name). [62]These sought their registration among those enrolled in the genealogies, but they were not found there, and so they were excluded from the priesthood as unclean. [63]The governor told them that they were not to partake of the most holy food, until there should be a priest to consult Urim and Thummim.

[64]The whole assembly together was 42,360, [65]besides their male and female servants, of whom there were 7,337, and they had 200 male and female singers. [66]Their horses were 736, their mules were 245, [67]their camels were 435, and their donkeys were 6,720.

[68]Some of the heads of families, when they came to the house of the LORD that is in Jerusalem, made freewill offerings for the house of God, to erect it on its site. [69]According to their ability they gave to the treasury of the work 61,000 darics[1] of gold, 5,000 minas[2] of silver, and 100 priests' garments.

[70]Now the priests, the Levites, some of the people, the singers, the gatekeepers, and the temple servants lived in their towns, and all the rest of Israel[3] in their towns.

Acts 2

When the day of Pentecost arrived, they were all together in one place. [2]And suddenly there came from heaven a sound like a mighty rushing wind, and it filled the entire house where they were sitting. [3]And divided tongues as of fire appeared to them and rested[4] on each one of them. [4]And they were all filled with the Holy Spirit and began to speak in other tongues as the Spirit gave them utterance.

[5]Now there were dwelling in Jerusalem Jews, devout men from every nation under heaven. [6]And at this sound the multitude came together, and they were bewildered, because each one was hearing them speak in his own language. [7]And they were amazed and astonished, saying, "Are not all these who are speaking Galileans? [8]And how is it that we hear, each of us in his own native language? [9]Parthians and Medes and Elamites and residents of Mesopotamia, Judea and Cappadocia, Pontus and Asia, [10]Phrygia and Pamphylia, Egypt and the parts of Libya belonging to Cyrene, and visitors from Rome, [11]both Jews and proselytes, Cretans and Arabians—we hear them telling in our own tongues the mighty works of God." [12]And all were amazed and perplexed, saying to one another, "What does this mean?" [13]But others mocking said, "They are filled with new wine."

[14]But Peter, standing with the eleven, lifted up his voice and addressed them: "Men of Judea and all who dwell in Jerusalem, let this be known to you, and give ear to my words. [15]For these people are not drunk, as you suppose, since it is only the third hour of the day.[5]

[1] A daric was a coin weighing about 1/4 ounce or 8.5 grams [2] A mina was about 1 1/4 pounds or 0.6 kilogram [3] Hebrew all Israel [4] Or And tongues as of fire appeared to them, distributed among them, and rested [5] That is, 9 A.M.

[16] But this is what was uttered through the prophet Joel:

[17] "'And in the last days it shall be, God declares,
　　that I will pour out my Spirit on all flesh,
　　and your sons and your daughters shall prophesy,
　　and your young men shall see visions,
　　and your old men shall dream dreams;
[18] 　even on my male servants[1] and female servants
　　in those days I will pour out my Spirit,
　　and they shall prophesy.
[19] 　And I will show wonders in the heavens above
　　and signs on the earth below,
　　blood, and fire, and vapor of smoke;
[20] 　the sun shall be turned to darkness
　　and the moon to blood,
　　before the day of the Lord comes, the great and magnificent day.
[21] 　And it shall come to pass that everyone who calls upon the name of the Lord shall be saved.'

[22] "Men of Israel, hear these words: Jesus of Nazareth, a man attested to you by God with mighty works and wonders and signs that God did through him in your midst, as you yourselves know— [23] this Jesus,[2] delivered up according to the definite plan and foreknowledge of God, you crucified and killed by the hands of lawless men. [24] God raised him up, loosing the pangs of death, because it was not possible for him to be held by it. [25] For David says concerning him,

"'I saw the Lord always before me,
　　for he is at my right hand that I may not be shaken;
[26] 　therefore my heart was glad, and my tongue rejoiced;
　　my flesh also will dwell in hope.
[27] 　For you will not abandon my soul to Hades,
　　or let your Holy One see corruption.
[28] 　You have made known to me the paths of life;
　　you will make me full of gladness with your presence.'

[29] "Brothers, I may say to you with confidence about the patriarch David that he both died and was buried, and his tomb is with us to this day. [30] Being therefore a prophet, and knowing that God had sworn with an oath to him that he would set one of his descendants on his throne, [31] he foresaw and spoke about the resurrection of the Christ, that he was not abandoned to Hades, nor did his flesh see corruption. [32] This Jesus God raised up, and of that we all are witnesses. [33] Being therefore exalted at the right hand of God, and having received from the Father the promise of the Holy Spirit, he has poured out this that you yourselves are seeing and hearing. [34] For David did not ascend into the heavens, but he himself says,

"'The Lord said to my Lord,
　"Sit at my right hand,
[35] 　　until I make your enemies your footstool."'

[36] Let all the house of Israel therefore know for certain that God has made him both Lord and Christ, this Jesus whom you crucified."

[37] Now when they heard this they were cut to the heart, and said to Peter and the rest of the apostles, "Brothers, what shall we do?" [38] And Peter said to them, "Repent and be baptized every one of you in the name of Jesus Christ for the forgiveness of your sins, and you will receive the gift of the Holy Spirit. [39] For the promise is for you and for your children and for all who are far off, everyone whom the Lord our God calls to himself." [40] And with many other words he bore witness and continued to exhort them, saying, "Save yourselves from this crooked generation." [41] So those who received his word were baptized, and there were added that day about three thousand souls.

[42] And they devoted themselves to the apostles' teaching and the fellowship, to the breaking of bread and the prayers. [43] And awe[3] came upon every soul, and many wonders and signs were being done through the apostles. [44] And all who believed were together and had all things in common. [45] And they were selling their possessions and belongings and distributing the proceeds to all, as any had need. [46] And day by day, attending the temple together and breaking bread in their homes, they received their food with glad and generous hearts, [47] praising God and having favor with all the people. And the Lord added to their number day by day those who were being saved.

---

[1] Greek *bondservants*; twice in this verse　[2] Greek *this one*　[3] Or *fear*

JANUARY 3

Genesis 3

Now the serpent was more crafty than any other beast of the field that the LORD God had made.

He said to the woman, "Did God actually say, 'You[1] shall not eat of any tree in the garden'?" [2]And the woman said to the serpent, "We may eat of the fruit of the trees in the garden, [3]but God said, 'You shall not eat of the fruit of the tree that is in the midst of the garden, neither shall you touch it, lest you die.'" [4]But the serpent said to the woman, "You will not surely die. [5]For God knows that when you eat of it your eyes will be opened, and you will be like God, knowing good and evil." [6]So when the woman saw that the tree was good for food, and that it was a delight to the eyes, and that the tree was to be desired to make one wise,[2] she took of its fruit and ate, and she also gave some to her husband who was with her, and he ate. [7]Then the eyes of both were opened, and they knew that they were naked. And they sewed fig leaves together and made themselves loincloths.

[8]And they heard the sound of the LORD God walking in the garden in the cool[3] of the day, and the man and his wife hid themselves from the presence of the LORD God among the trees of the garden. [9]But the LORD God called to the man and said to him, "Where are you?"[4] [10]And he said, "I heard the sound of you in the garden, and I was afraid, because I was naked, and I hid myself." [11]He said, "Who told you that you were naked? Have you eaten of the tree of which I commanded you not to eat?" [12]The man said, "The woman whom you gave to be with me, she gave me fruit of the tree, and I ate." [13]Then the LORD God said to the woman, "What is this that you have done?" The woman said, "The serpent deceived me, and I ate."

[14]The LORD God said to the serpent,

"Because you have done this,
    cursed are you above all livestock
    and above all beasts of the field;

on your belly you shall go,
    and dust you shall eat
    all the days of your life.
[15] I will put enmity between you and the
        woman,
    and between your offspring[5] and her
        offspring;
he shall bruise your head,
    and you shall bruise his heel."

[16]To the woman he said,

"I will surely multiply your pain in
        childbearing;
    in pain you shall bring forth children.
Your desire shall be for[6] your husband,
    and he shall rule over you."

[17]And to Adam he said,

"Because you have listened to the voice of
        your wife
    and have eaten of the tree
of which I commanded you,
    'You shall not eat of it,'
cursed is the ground because of you;
    in pain you shall eat of it all the days
        of your life;
[18]   thorns and thistles it shall bring forth
        for you;
    and you shall eat the plants of the field.
[19] By the sweat of your face
        you shall eat bread,
    till you return to the ground,
    for out of it you were taken;
for you are dust,
    and to dust you shall return."

[20]The man called his wife's name Eve, because she was the mother of all living.[7] [21]And the LORD God made for Adam and for his wife garments of skins and clothed them.

[22]Then the LORD God said, "Behold, the man has become like one of us in knowing good and evil. Now, lest he reach out his hand and take also of the tree of life and eat, and live forever—" [23]therefore the LORD God sent

---

[1] In Hebrew you is plural in verses 1–5 [2] Or to give insight [3] Hebrew wind [4] In Hebrew you is singular in verses 9 and 11 [5] Hebrew seed; so throughout Genesis [6] Or against
[7] Eve sounds like the Hebrew for life-giver and resembles the word for living

him out from the garden of Eden to work the ground from which he was taken. [24]He drove out the man, and at the east of the garden of Eden he placed the cherubim and a flaming sword that turned every way to guard the way to the tree of life.

Matthew 3

In those days John the Baptist came preaching in the wilderness of Judea, [2]"Repent, for the kingdom of heaven is at hand." [3]For this is he who was spoken of by the prophet Isaiah when he said,

"The voice of one crying in the
  wilderness:
'Prepare[1] the way of the Lord;
  make his paths straight.'"

[4]Now John wore a garment of camel's hair and a leather belt around his waist, and his food was locusts and wild honey. [5]Then Jerusalem and all Judea and all the region about the Jordan were going out to him, [6]and they were baptized by him in the river Jordan, confessing their sins.

[7]But when he saw many of the Pharisees and Sadducees coming to his baptism, he said to them, "You brood of vipers! Who warned you to flee from the wrath to come? [8]Bear fruit in keeping with repentance. [9]And do not presume to say to yourselves, 'We have Abraham as our father,' for I tell you, God is able from these stones to raise up children for Abraham. [10]Even now the axe is laid to the root of the trees. Every tree therefore that does not bear good fruit is cut down and thrown into the fire.

[11]"I baptize you with water for repentance, but he who is coming after me is mightier than I, whose sandals I am not worthy to carry. He will baptize you with the Holy Spirit and fire. [12]His winnowing fork is in his hand, and he will clear his threshing floor and gather his wheat into the barn, but the chaff he will burn with unquenchable fire."

[13]Then Jesus came from Galilee to the Jordan to John, to be baptized by him. [14]John would have prevented him, saying, "I need to be baptized by you, and do you come to me?" [15]But Jesus answered him, "Let it be so now, for thus it is fitting for us to fulfill all righteousness." Then he consented. [16]And when Jesus was baptized, immediately he went up

from the water, and behold, the heavens were opened to him,[2] and he saw the Spirit of God descending like a dove and coming to rest on him; [17]and behold, a voice from heaven said, "This is my beloved Son,[3] with whom I am well pleased."

Ezra 3

When the seventh month came, and the children of Israel were in the towns, the people gathered as one man to Jerusalem. [2]Then arose Jeshua the son of Jozadak, with his fellow priests, and Zerubbabel the son of Shealtiel with his kinsmen, and they built the altar of the God of Israel, to offer burnt offerings on it, as it is written in the Law of Moses the man of God. [3]They set the altar in its place, for fear was on them because of the peoples of the lands, and they offered burnt offerings on it to the LORD, burnt offerings morning and evening. [4]And they kept the Feast of Booths, as it is written, and offered the daily burnt offerings by number according to the rule, as each day required, [5]and after that the regular burnt offerings, the offerings at the new moon and at all the appointed feasts of the LORD, and the offerings of everyone who made a freewill offering to the LORD. [6]From the first day of the seventh month they began to offer burnt offerings to the LORD. But the foundation of the temple of the LORD was not yet laid. [7]So they gave money to the masons and the carpenters, and food, drink, and oil to the Sidonians and the Tyrians to bring cedar trees from Lebanon to the sea, to Joppa, according to the grant that they had from Cyrus king of Persia.

[8]Now in the second year after their coming to the house of God at Jerusalem, in the second month, Zerubbabel the son of Shealtiel and Jeshua the son of Jozadak made a beginning, together with the rest of their kinsmen, the priests and the Levites and all who had come to Jerusalem from the captivity. They appointed the Levites, from twenty years old and upward, to supervise the work of the house of the LORD. [9]And Jeshua with his sons and his brothers, and Kadmiel and his sons, the sons of Judah, together supervised the workmen in the house of God, along with the sons of Henadad and the Levites, their sons and brothers.

[1] Or crying: Prepare in the wilderness [2] Some manuscripts omit to him [3] Or my Son, my (or the) Beloved

[10]And when the builders laid the foundation of the temple of the LORD, the priests in their vestments came forward with trumpets, and the Levites, the sons of Asaph, with cymbals, to praise the LORD, according to the directions of David king of Israel. [11]And they sang responsively, praising and giving thanks to the LORD,

"For he is good,
  for his steadfast love endures forever
    toward Israel."

And all the people shouted with a great shout when they praised the LORD, because the foundation of the house of the LORD was laid. [12]But many of the priests and Levites and heads of fathers' houses, old men who had seen the first house, wept with a loud voice when they saw the foundation of this house being laid, though many shouted aloud for joy, [13]so that the people could not distinguish the sound of the joyful shout from the sound of the people's weeping, for the people shouted with a great shout, and the sound was heard far away.

―――――――― Acts 3 ――――――――

Now Peter and John were going up to the temple at the hour of prayer, the ninth hour.[1] [2]And a man lame from birth was being carried, whom they laid daily at the gate of the temple that is called the Beautiful Gate to ask alms of those entering the temple. [3]Seeing Peter and John about to go into the temple, he asked to receive alms. [4]And Peter directed his gaze at him, as did John, and said, "Look at us." [5]And he fixed his attention on them, expecting to receive something from them. [6]But Peter said, "I have no silver and gold, but what I do have I give to you. In the name of Jesus Christ of Nazareth, rise up and walk!" [7]And he took him by the right hand and raised him up, and immediately his feet and ankles were made strong. [8]And leaping up he stood and began to walk, and entered the temple with them, walking and leaping and praising God. [9]And all the people saw him walking and praising God, [10]and recognized him as the one who sat at the Beautiful Gate of the temple, asking for alms. And they were filled with wonder and amazement at what had happened to him.

[11]While he clung to Peter and John, all the people, utterly astounded, ran together to them in the portico called Solomon's. [12]And when Peter saw it he addressed the people: "Men of Israel, why do you wonder at this, or why do you stare at us, as though by our own power or piety we have made him walk? [13]The God of Abraham, the God of Isaac, and the God of Jacob, the God of our fathers, glorified his servant[2] Jesus, whom you delivered over and denied in the presence of Pilate, when he had decided to release him. [14]But you denied the Holy and Righteous One, and asked for a murderer to be granted to you, [15]and you killed the Author of life, whom God raised from the dead. To this we are witnesses. [16]And his name—by faith in his name—has made this man strong whom you see and know, and the faith that is through Jesus[3] has given the man this perfect health in the presence of you all.

[17]"And now, brothers, I know that you acted in ignorance, as did also your rulers. [18]But what God foretold by the mouth of all the prophets, that his Christ would suffer, he thus fulfilled. [19]Repent therefore, and turn back, that your sins may be blotted out, [20]that times of refreshing may come from the presence of the Lord, and that he may send the Christ appointed for you, Jesus, [21]whom heaven must receive until the time for restoring all the things about which God spoke by the mouth of his holy prophets long ago. [22]Moses said, 'The Lord God will raise up for you a prophet like me from your brothers. You shall listen to him in whatever he tells you. [23]And it shall be that every soul who does not listen to that prophet shall be destroyed from the people.' [24]And all the prophets who have spoken, from Samuel and those who came after him, also proclaimed these days. [25]You are the sons of the prophets and of the covenant that God made with your fathers, saying to Abraham, 'And in your offspring shall all the families of the earth be blessed.' [26]God, having raised up his servant, sent him to you first, to bless you by turning every one of you from your wickedness."

―――――――――――――――――――――――――――――――――

[1] That is, 3 P.M. [2] Or child; also verse 26 [3] Greek him

JANUARY 4

Genesis 4

Now Adam knew Eve his wife, and she conceived and bore Cain, saying, "I have gotten[1] a man with the help of the LORD." [2]And again, she bore his brother Abel. Now Abel was a keeper of sheep, and Cain a worker of the ground. [3]In the course of time Cain brought to the LORD an offering of the fruit of the ground, [4]and Abel also brought of the firstborn of his flock and of their fat portions. And the LORD had regard for Abel and his offering, [5]but for Cain and his offering he had no regard. So Cain was very angry, and his face fell. [6]The LORD said to Cain, "Why are you angry, and why has your face fallen? [7]If you do well, will you not be accepted?[2] And if you do not do well, sin is crouching at the door. Its desire is for[3] you, but you must rule over it."

[8]Cain spoke to Abel his brother.[4] And when they were in the field, Cain rose up against his brother Abel and killed him. [9]Then the LORD said to Cain, "Where is Abel your brother?" He said, "I do not know; am I my brother's keeper?" [10]And the LORD said, "What have you done? The voice of your brother's blood is crying to me from the ground. [11]And now you are cursed from the ground, which has opened its mouth to receive your brother's blood from your hand. [12]When you work the ground, it shall no longer yield to you its strength. You shall be a fugitive and a wanderer on the earth." [13]Cain said to the LORD, "My punishment is greater than I can bear.[5] [14]Behold, you have driven me today away from the ground, and from your face I shall be hidden. I shall be a fugitive and a wanderer on the earth, and whoever finds me will kill me." [15]Then the LORD said to him, "Not so! If anyone kills Cain, vengeance shall be taken on him sevenfold." And the LORD put a mark on Cain, lest any who found him should attack him. [16]Then Cain went away from the presence of the LORD and settled in the land of Nod,[6] east of Eden.

[17]Cain knew his wife, and she conceived and bore Enoch. When he built a city, he called the name of the city after the name of his son, Enoch. [18]To Enoch was born Irad, and Irad fathered Mehujael, and Mehujael fathered Methushael, and Methushael fathered Lamech. [19]And Lamech took two wives. The name of the one was Adah, and the name of the other Zillah. [20]Adah bore Jabal; he was the father of those who dwell in tents and have livestock. [21]His brother's name was Jubal; he was the father of all those who play the lyre and pipe. [22]Zillah also bore Tubal-cain; he was the forger of all instruments of bronze and iron. The sister of Tubal-cain was Naamah.

[23]Lamech said to his wives:

"Adah and Zillah, hear my voice;
    you wives of Lamech, listen to what I say:
I have killed a man for wounding me,
    a young man for striking me.
24 If Cain's revenge is sevenfold,
    then Lamech's is seventy-sevenfold."

[25]And Adam knew his wife again, and she bore a son and called his name Seth, for she said, "God has appointed[7] for me another offspring instead of Abel, for Cain killed him." [26]To Seth also a son was born, and he called his name Enosh. At that time people began to call upon the name of the LORD.

Matthew 4

Then Jesus was led up by the Spirit into the wilderness to be tempted by the devil. [2]And after fasting forty days and forty nights, he was hungry. [3]And the tempter came and said to him, "If you are the Son of God, command these stones to become loaves of bread." [4]But he answered, "It is written,

"'Man shall not live by bread alone,
    but by every word that comes from
    the mouth of God.'"

[5]Then the devil took him to the holy city and set him on the pinnacle of the temple [6]and said to

[1] Cain sounds like the Hebrew for gotten [2] Hebrew will there not be a lifting up [of your face]? [3] Or against [4] Hebrew; Samaritan, Septuagint, Syriac, Vulgate add Let us go out to the field [5] Or My guilt is too great to bear [6] Nod means wandering [7] Seth sounds like the Hebrew for he appointed

him, "If you are the Son of God, throw yourself down, for it is written,

"'He will command his angels concerning you,'

and

"'On their hands they will bear you up,
    lest you strike your foot against a
    stone.'"

[7] Jesus said to him, "Again it is written, 'You shall not put the Lord your God to the test.'" [8] Again, the devil took him to a very high mountain and showed him all the kingdoms of the world and their glory. [9] And he said to him, "All these I will give you, if you will fall down and worship me." [10] Then Jesus said to him, "Be gone, Satan! For it is written,

"'You shall worship the Lord your God
    and him only shall you serve.'"

[11] Then the devil left him, and behold, angels came and were ministering to him.

[12] Now when he heard that John had been arrested, he withdrew into Galilee. [13] And leaving Nazareth he went and lived in Capernaum by the sea, in the territory of Zebulun and Naphtali, [14] so that what was spoken by the prophet Isaiah might be fulfilled:

[15]   "The land of Zebulun and the land of
            Naphtali,
        the way of the sea, beyond the Jordan,
            Galilee of the Gentiles—
[16]   the people dwelling in darkness
            have seen a great light,
        and for those dwelling in the region and
            shadow of death,
        on them a light has dawned."

[17] From that time Jesus began to preach, saying, "Repent, for the kingdom of heaven is at hand."

[18] While walking by the Sea of Galilee, he saw two brothers, Simon (who is called Peter) and Andrew his brother, casting a net into the sea, for they were fishermen. [19] And he said to them, "Follow me, and I will make you fishers of men."[1] [20] Immediately they left their nets and followed him. [21] And going on from there he saw two other brothers, James the son of Zebedee and John his brother, in the boat with Zebedee their father, mending their nets, and he called them. [22] Immediately they left the boat and their father and followed him.

[23] And he went throughout all Galilee, teaching in their synagogues and proclaiming the gospel of the kingdom and healing every disease and every affliction among the people. [24] So his fame spread throughout all Syria, and they brought him all the sick, those afflicted with various diseases and pains, those oppressed by demons, epileptics, and paralytics, and he healed them. [25] And great crowds followed him from Galilee and the Decapolis, and from Jerusalem and Judea, and from beyond the Jordan.

—— Ezra 4 ——

Now when the adversaries of Judah and Benjamin heard that the returned exiles were building a temple to the LORD, the God of Israel, [2] they approached Zerubbabel and the heads of fathers' houses and said to them, "Let us build with you, for we worship your God as you do, and we have been sacrificing to him ever since the days of Esarhaddon king of Assyria who brought us here." [3] But Zerubbabel, Jeshua, and the rest of the heads of fathers' houses in Israel said to them, "You have nothing to do with us in building a house to our God; but we alone will build to the LORD, the God of Israel, as King Cyrus the king of Persia has commanded us."

[4] Then the people of the land discouraged the people of Judah and made them afraid to build [5] and bribed counselors against them to frustrate their purpose, all the days of Cyrus king of Persia, even until the reign of Darius king of Persia.

[6] And in the reign of Ahasuerus, in the beginning of his reign, they wrote an accusation against the inhabitants of Judah and Jerusalem. [7] In the days of Artaxerxes, Bishlam and Mithredath and Tabeel and the rest of their associates wrote to Artaxerxes king of Persia. The letter was written in Aramaic and translated.[2] [8] Rehum the commander and Shimshai the scribe wrote a letter against Jerusalem to Artaxerxes the king as follows: [9] Rehum the commander, Shimshai the scribe, and the rest of their associates, the judges, the governors, the officials, the Persians, the men of Erech, the Babylonians, the men of Susa, that is, the

[1] The Greek word anthropoi refers here to both men and women [2] Hebrew written in Aramaic and translated in Aramaic, indicating that 4:8–6:18 is in Aramaic; another interpretation is The letter was written in the Aramaic script and set forth in the Aramaic language

Elamites, [10]and the rest of the nations whom the great and noble Osnappar deported and settled in the cities of Samaria and in the rest of the province Beyond the River. [11](This is a copy of the letter that they sent.) "To Artaxerxes the king: Your servants, the men of the province Beyond the River, send greeting. And now [12]be it known to the king that the Jews who came up from you to us have gone to Jerusalem. They are rebuilding that rebellious and wicked city. They are finishing the walls and repairing the foundations. [13]Now be it known to the king that if this city is rebuilt and the walls finished, they will not pay tribute, custom, or toll, and the royal revenue will be impaired. [14]Now because we eat the salt of the palace and it is not fitting for us to witness the king's dishonor, therefore we send and inform the king, [15]in order that search may be made in the book of the records of your fathers. You will find in the book of the records and learn that this city is a rebellious city, hurtful to kings and provinces, and that sedition was stirred up in it from of old. That was why this city was laid waste. [16]We make known to the king that if this city is rebuilt and its walls finished, you will then have no possession in the province Beyond the River."

[17]The king sent an answer: "To Rehum the commander and Shimshai the scribe and the rest of their associates who live in Samaria and in the rest of the province Beyond the River, greeting. And now [18]the letter that you sent to us has been plainly read before me. [19]And I made a decree, and search has been made, and it has been found that this city from of old has risen against kings, and that rebellion and sedition have been made in it. [20]And mighty kings have been over Jerusalem, who ruled over the whole province Beyond the River, to whom tribute, custom, and toll were paid. [21]Therefore make a decree that these men be made to cease, and that this city be not rebuilt, until a decree is made by me. [22]And take care not to be slack in this matter. Why should damage grow to the hurt of the king?"

[23]Then, when the copy of King Artaxerxes' letter was read before Rehum and Shimshai the scribe and their associates, they went in haste to the Jews at Jerusalem and by force and power made them cease. [24]Then the work on the house of God that is in Jerusalem stopped,

and it ceased until the second year of the reign of Darius king of Persia.

Acts 4

And as they were speaking to the people, the priests and the captain of the temple and the Sadducees came upon them, [2]greatly annoyed because they were teaching the people and proclaiming in Jesus the resurrection from the dead. [3]And they arrested them and put them in custody until the next day, for it was already evening. [4]But many of those who had heard the word believed, and the number of the men came to about five thousand.

[5]On the next day their rulers and elders and scribes gathered together in Jerusalem, [6]with Annas the high priest and Caiaphas and John and Alexander, and all who were of the high-priestly family. [7]And when they had set them in the midst, they inquired, "By what power or by what name did you do this?" [8]Then Peter, filled with the Holy Spirit, said to them, "Rulers of the people and elders, [9]if we are being examined today concerning a good deed done to a crippled man, by what means this man has been healed, [10]let it be known to all of you and to all the people of Israel that by the name of Jesus Christ of Nazareth, whom you crucified, whom God raised from the dead—by him this man is standing before you well. [11]This Jesus[1] is the stone that was rejected by you, the builders, which has become the cornerstone.[2] [12]And there is salvation in no one else, for there is no other name under heaven given among men[3] by which we must be saved."

[13]Now when they saw the boldness of Peter and John, and perceived that they were uneducated, common men, they were astonished. And they recognized that they had been with Jesus. [14]But seeing the man who was healed standing beside them, they had nothing to say in opposition. [15]But when they had commanded them to leave the council, they conferred with one another, [16]saying, "What shall we do with these men? For that a notable sign has been performed through them is evident to all the inhabitants of Jerusalem, and we cannot deny it. [17]But in order that it may spread no further among the people, let us warn them to speak no more to anyone in this name." [18]So they called them and charged them not to speak

[1] Greek *This one* [2] Greek *the head of the corner* [3] The Greek word *anthropoi* refers here to both men and women

or teach at all in the name of Jesus. [19] But Peter and John answered them, "Whether it is right in the sight of God to listen to you rather than to God, you must judge, [20] for we cannot but speak of what we have seen and heard." [21] And when they had further threatened them, they let them go, finding no way to punish them, because of the people, for all were praising God for what had happened. [22] For the man on whom this sign of healing was performed was more than forty years old.

[23] When they were released, they went to their friends and reported what the chief priests and the elders had said to them. [24] And when they heard it, they lifted their voices together to God and said, "Sovereign Lord, who made the heaven and the earth and the sea and everything in them, [25] who through the mouth of our father David, your servant,[1] said by the Holy Spirit,

> " 'Why did the Gentiles rage,
> and the peoples plot in vain?
> [26]   The kings of the earth set themselves,
> and the rulers were gathered together,
> against the Lord and against his
> Anointed'[2]—

[27] for truly in this city there were gathered together against your holy servant Jesus, whom you anointed, both Herod and Pontius Pilate, along with the Gentiles and the peoples of Israel, [28] to do whatever your hand and your plan had predestined to take place. [29] And now, Lord, look upon their threats and grant to your servants[3] to continue to speak your word with all boldness, [30] while you stretch out your hand to heal, and signs and wonders are performed through the name of your holy servant Jesus." [31] And when they had prayed, the place in which they were gathered together was shaken, and they were all filled with the Holy Spirit and continued to speak the word of God with boldness.

[32] Now the full number of those who believed were of one heart and soul, and no one said that any of the things that belonged to him was his own, but they had everything in common. [33] And with great power the apostles were giving their testimony to the resurrection of the Lord Jesus, and great grace was upon them all. [34] There was not a needy person among them, for as many as were owners of lands or houses sold them and brought the proceeds of what was sold [35] and laid it at the apostles' feet, and it was distributed to each as any had need. [36] Thus Joseph, who was also called by the apostles Barnabas (which means son of encouragement), a Levite, a native of Cyprus, [37] sold a field that belonged to him and brought the money and laid it at the apostles' feet.

JANUARY 5

Genesis 5

This is the book of the generations of Adam. When God created man, he made him in the likeness of God. [2] Male and female he created them, and he blessed them and named them Man[4] when they were created. [3] When Adam had lived 130 years, he fathered a son in his own likeness, after his image, and named him Seth. [4] The days of Adam after he fathered Seth were 800 years; and he had other sons and daughters. [5] Thus all the days that Adam lived were 930 years, and he died.

[6] When Seth had lived 105 years, he fathered Enosh. [7] Seth lived after he fathered Enosh 807 years and had other sons and daughters. [8] Thus all the days of Seth were 912 years, and he died. [9] When Enosh had lived 90 years, he fathered Kenan. [10] Enosh lived after he fathered Kenan 815 years and had other sons and daughters. [11] Thus all the days of Enosh were 905 years, and he died.

[12] When Kenan had lived 70 years, he fathered Mahalalel. [13] Kenan lived after he

fathered Mahalalel 840 years and had other sons and daughters. ¹⁴Thus all the days of Kenan were 910 years, and he died.

¹⁵When Mahalalel had lived 65 years, he fathered Jared. ¹⁶Mahalalel lived after he fathered Jared 830 years and had other sons and daughters. ¹⁷Thus all the days of Mahalalel were 895 years, and he died.

¹⁸When Jared had lived 162 years he fathered Enoch. ¹⁹Jared lived after he fathered Enoch 800 years and had other sons and daughters. ²⁰Thus all the days of Jared were 962 years, and he died.

²¹When Enoch had lived 65 years, he fathered Methuselah. ²²Enoch walked with God¹ after he fathered Methuselah 300 years and had other sons and daughters. ²³Thus all the days of Enoch were 365 years. ²⁴Enoch walked with God, and he was not,² for God took him.

²⁵When Methuselah had lived 187 years, he fathered Lamech. ²⁶Methuselah lived after he fathered Lamech 782 years and had other sons and daughters. ²⁷Thus all the days of Methuselah were 969 years, and he died.

²⁸When Lamech had lived 182 years, he fathered a son ²⁹and called his name Noah, saying, "Out of the ground that the LORD has cursed, this one shall bring us relief³ from our work and from the painful toil of our hands." ³⁰Lamech lived after he fathered Noah 595 years and had other sons and daughters. ³¹Thus all the days of Lamech were 777 years, and he died.

³²After Noah was 500 years old, Noah fathered Shem, Ham, and Japheth.

Matthew 5

Seeing the crowds, he went up on the mountain, and when he sat down, his disciples came to him. ²And he opened his mouth and taught them, saying:

³"Blessed are the poor in spirit, for theirs is the kingdom of heaven.

⁴"Blessed are those who mourn, for they shall be comforted.

⁵"Blessed are the meek, for they shall inherit the earth.

⁶"Blessed are those who hunger and thirst for righteousness, for they shall be satisfied.

⁷"Blessed are the merciful, for they shall receive mercy.

⁸"Blessed are the pure in heart, for they shall see God.

⁹"Blessed are the peacemakers, for they shall be called sons⁴ of God.

¹⁰"Blessed are those who are persecuted for righteousness' sake, for theirs is the kingdom of heaven.

¹¹"Blessed are you when others revile you and persecute you and utter all kinds of evil against you falsely on my account. ¹²Rejoice and be glad, for your reward is great in heaven, for so they persecuted the prophets who were before you.

¹³"You are the salt of the earth, but if salt has lost its taste, how shall its saltiness be restored? It is no longer good for anything except to be thrown out and trampled under people's feet.

¹⁴"You are the light of the world. A city set on a hill cannot be hidden. ¹⁵Nor do people light a lamp and put it under a basket, but on a stand, and it gives light to all in the house. ¹⁶In the same way, let your light shine before others, so that⁵ they may see your good works and give glory to your Father who is in heaven.

¹⁷"Do not think that I have come to abolish the Law or the Prophets; I have not come to abolish them but to fulfill them. ¹⁸For truly, I say to you, until heaven and earth pass away, not an iota, not a dot, will pass from the Law until all is accomplished. ¹⁹Therefore whoever relaxes one of the least of these commandments and teaches others to do the same will be called least in the kingdom of heaven, but whoever does them and teaches them will be called great in the kingdom of heaven. ²⁰For I tell you, unless your righteousness exceeds that of the scribes and Pharisees, you will never enter the kingdom of heaven.

²¹"You have heard that it was said to those of old, 'You shall not murder; and whoever murders will be liable to judgment.' ²²But I say to you that everyone who is angry with his brother⁶ will be liable to judgment; whoever insults⁷ his brother will be liable to the council; and whoever says, 'You fool!' will be liable to the hell⁸ of fire. ²³So if you are offering your gift at the altar and there remember that your brother has something against you, ²⁴leave your gift there before the altar and go. First be reconciled to your brother, and then

come and offer your gift. [25] Come to terms quickly with your accuser while you are going with him to court, lest your accuser hand you over to the judge, and the judge to the guard, and you be put in prison. [26] Truly, I say to you, you will never get out until you have paid the last penny.[1]

[27] "You have heard that it was said, 'You shall not commit adultery.' [28] But I say to you that everyone who looks at a woman with lustful intent has already committed adultery with her in his heart. [29] If your right eye causes you to sin, tear it out and throw it away. For it is better that you lose one of your members than that your whole body be thrown into hell. [30] And if your right hand causes you to sin, cut it off and throw it away. For it is better that you lose one of your members than that your whole body go into hell.

[31] "It was also said, 'Whoever divorces his wife, let him give her a certificate of divorce.' [32] But I say to you that everyone who divorces his wife, except on the ground of sexual immorality, makes her commit adultery, and whoever marries a divorced woman commits adultery.

[33] "Again you have heard that it was said to those of old, 'You shall not swear falsely, but shall perform to the Lord what you have sworn.' [34] But I say to you, Do not take an oath at all, either by heaven, for it is the throne of God, [35] or by the earth, for it is his footstool, or by Jerusalem, for it is the city of the great King. [36] And do not take an oath by your head, for you cannot make one hair white or black. [37] Let what you say be simply 'Yes' or 'No'; anything more than this comes from evil.[2]

[38] "You have heard that it was said, 'An eye for an eye and a tooth for a tooth.' [39] But I say to you, Do not resist the one who is evil. But if anyone slaps you on the right cheek, turn to him the other also. [40] And if anyone would sue you and take your tunic,[3] let him have your cloak as well. [41] And if anyone forces you to go one mile, go with him two miles. [42] Give to the one who begs from you, and do not refuse the one who would borrow from you.

[43] "You have heard that it was said, 'You shall love your neighbor and hate your enemy.' [44] But I say to you, Love your enemies and pray for those who persecute you, [45] so that you may be sons of your Father who is in heaven. For he makes his sun rise on the evil and on the good, and sends rain on the just and on the unjust. [46] For if you love those who love you, what reward do you have? Do not even the tax collectors do the same? [47] And if you greet only your brothers,[4] what more are you doing than others? Do not even the Gentiles do the same? [48] You therefore must be perfect, as your heavenly Father is perfect.

Ezra 5

Now the prophets, Haggai and Zechariah the son of Iddo, prophesied to the Jews who were in Judah and Jerusalem, in the name of the God of Israel who was over them. [2] Then Zerubbabel the son of Shealtiel and Jeshua the son of Jozadak arose and began to rebuild the house of God that is in Jerusalem, and the prophets of God were with them, supporting them.

[3] At the same time Tattenai the governor of the province Beyond the River and Shethar-bozenai and their associates came to them and spoke to them thus: "Who gave you a decree to build this house and to finish this structure?" [4] They[5] also asked them this: "What are the names of the men who are building this building?" [5] But the eye of their God was on the elders of the Jews, and they did not stop them until the report should reach Darius and then an answer be returned by letter concerning it.

[6] This is a copy of the letter that Tattenai the governor of the province Beyond the River and Shethar-bozenai and his associates, the governors who were in the province Beyond the River, sent to Darius the king. [7] They sent him a report, in which was written as follows: "To Darius the king, all peace. [8] Be it known to the king that we went to the province of Judah, to the house of the great God. It is being built with huge stones, and timber is laid in the walls. This work goes on diligently and prospers in their hands. [9] Then we asked those elders and spoke to them thus: 'Who gave you a decree to build this house and to finish this structure?' [10] We also asked them their names, for your information, that we might write down the names of their leaders.[6] [11] And this was their reply to us: 'We are the servants of the God of heaven and earth, and we are rebuilding the house that was built many years ago, which a great

king of Israel built and finished. ¹²But because our fathers had angered the God of heaven, he gave them into the hand of Nebuchadnezzar king of Babylon, the Chaldean, who destroyed this house and carried away the people to Babylonia. ¹³However, in the first year of Cyrus king of Babylon, Cyrus the king made a decree that this house of God should be rebuilt. ¹⁴And the gold and silver vessels of the house of God, which Nebuchadnezzar had taken out of the temple that was in Jerusalem and brought into the temple of Babylon, these Cyrus the king took out of the temple of Babylon, and they were delivered to one whose name was Sheshbazzar, whom he had made governor; ¹⁵and he said to him, "Take these vessels, go and put them in the temple that is in Jerusalem, and let the house of God be rebuilt on its site." ¹⁶Then this Sheshbazzar came and laid the foundations of the house of God that is in Jerusalem, and from that time until now it has been in building, and it is not yet finished.' ¹⁷Therefore, if it seems good to the king, let search be made in the royal archives there in Babylon, to see whether a decree was issued by Cyrus the king for the rebuilding of this house of God in Jerusalem. And let the king send us his pleasure in this matter."

Acts 5

But a man named Ananias, with his wife Sapphira, sold a piece of property, ²and with his wife's knowledge he kept back for himself some of the proceeds and brought only a part of it and laid it at the apostles' feet. ³But Peter said, "Ananias, why has Satan filled your heart to lie to the Holy Spirit and to keep back for yourself part of the proceeds of the land? ⁴While it remained unsold, did it not remain your own? And after it was sold, was it not at your disposal? Why is it that you have contrived this deed in your heart? You have not lied to man but to God." ⁵When Ananias heard these words, he fell down and breathed his last. And great fear came upon all who heard of it. ⁶The young men rose and wrapped him up and carried him out and buried him.

⁷After an interval of about three hours his wife came in, not knowing what had happened. ⁸And Peter said to her, "Tell me whether you¹ sold the land for so much." And she said,

"Yes, for so much." ⁹But Peter said to her, "How is it that you have agreed together to test the Spirit of the Lord? Behold, the feet of those who have buried your husband are at the door, and they will carry you out." ¹⁰Immediately she fell down at his feet and breathed her last. When the young men came in they found her dead, and they carried her out and buried her beside her husband. ¹¹And great fear came upon the whole church and upon all who heard of these things.

¹²Now many signs and wonders were regularly done among the people by the hands of the apostles. And they were all together in Solomon's Portico. ¹³None of the rest dared join them, but the people held them in high esteem. ¹⁴And more than ever believers were added to the Lord, multitudes of both men and women, ¹⁵so that they even carried out the sick into the streets and laid them on cots and mats, that as Peter came by at least his shadow might fall on some of them. ¹⁶The people also gathered from the towns around Jerusalem, bringing the sick and those afflicted with unclean spirits, and they were all healed.

¹⁷But the high priest rose up, and all who were with him (that is, the party of the Sadducees), and filled with jealousy ¹⁸they arrested the apostles and put them in the public prison. ¹⁹But during the night an angel of the Lord opened the prison doors and brought them out, and said, ²⁰"Go and stand in the temple and speak to the people all the words of this Life." ²¹And when they heard this, they entered the temple at daybreak and began to teach.

Now when the high priest came, and those who were with him, they called together the council, all the senate of the people of Israel, and sent to the prison to have them brought. ²²But when the officers came, they did not find them in the prison, so they returned and reported, ²³"We found the prison securely locked and the guards standing at the doors, but when we opened them we found no one inside." ²⁴Now when the captain of the temple and the chief priests heard these words, they were greatly perplexed about them, wondering what this would come to. ²⁵And someone came and told them, "Look! The men whom you put in prison are standing in the temple and teaching the people." ²⁶Then the captain with the officers went and brought them, but not by

¹ The Greek for you is plural here

force, for they were afraid of being stoned by the people.

²⁷And when they had brought them, they set them before the council. And the high priest questioned them, ²⁸saying, "We strictly charged you not to teach in this name, yet here you have filled Jerusalem with your teaching, and you intend to bring this man's blood upon us." ²⁹But Peter and the apostles answered, "We must obey God rather than men. ³⁰The God of our fathers raised Jesus, whom you killed by hanging him on a tree. ³¹God exalted him at his right hand as Leader and Savior, to give repentance to Israel and forgiveness of sins. ³²And we are witnesses to these things, and so is the Holy Spirit, whom God has given to those who obey him."

³³When they heard this, they were enraged and wanted to kill them. ³⁴But a Pharisee in the council named Gamaliel, a teacher of the law held in honor by all the people, stood up and gave orders to put the men outside for a little while. ³⁵And he said to them, "Men of Israel, take care what you are about to do with these men. ³⁶For before these days Theudas rose up, claiming to be somebody, and a number of men, about four hundred, joined him. He was killed, and all who followed him were dispersed and came to nothing. ³⁷After him Judas the Galilean rose up in the days of the census and drew away some of the people after him. He too perished, and all who followed him were scattered. ³⁸So in the present case I tell you, keep away from these men and let them alone, for if this plan or this undertaking is of man, it will fail; ³⁹but if it is of God, you will not be able to overthrow them. You might even be found opposing God!" So they took his advice, ⁴⁰and when they had called in the apostles, they beat them and charged them not to speak in the name of Jesus, and let them go. ⁴¹Then they left the presence of the council, rejoicing that they were counted worthy to suffer dishonor for the name. ⁴²And every day, in the temple and from house to house, they did not cease teaching and preaching that the Christ is Jesus.

JANUARY 6

Genesis 6

When man began to multiply on the face of the land and daughters were born to them, ²the sons of God saw that the daughters of man were attractive. And they took as their wives any they chose. ³Then the LORD said, "My Spirit shall not abide in¹ man forever, for he is flesh: his days shall be 120 years." ⁴The Nephilim² were on the earth in those days, and also afterward, when the sons of God came in to the daughters of man and they bore children to them. These were the mighty men who were of old, the men of renown.

⁵The LORD saw that the wickedness of man was great in the earth, and that every intention of the thoughts of his heart was only evil continually. ⁶And the LORD regretted that he had made man on the earth, and it grieved him to his heart. ⁷So the LORD said, "I will blot out man whom I have created from the face of the land, man and animals and creeping things and birds of the heavens, for I am sorry that I have made them." ⁸But Noah found favor in the eyes of the LORD.

⁹These are the generations of Noah. Noah was a righteous man, blameless in his generation. Noah walked with God. ¹⁰And Noah had three sons, Shem, Ham, and Japheth.

¹¹Now the earth was corrupt in God's sight, and the earth was filled with violence. ¹²And God saw the earth, and behold, it was corrupt, for all flesh had corrupted their way on the earth. ¹³And God said to Noah, "I have determined to make an end of all flesh,³ for the earth is filled with violence through them. Behold, I will destroy them with the earth. ¹⁴Make yourself an ark of gopher wood.⁴ Make rooms in

¹ Or My Spirit shall not contend with ² Or giants ³ Hebrew The end of all flesh has come before me ⁴ An unknown kind of tree; transliterated from Hebrew

the ark, and cover it inside and out with pitch. [15]This is how you are to make it: the length of the ark 300 cubits,[1] its breadth 50 cubits, and its height 30 cubits. [16]Make a roof[2] for the ark, and finish it to a cubit above, and set the door of the ark in its side. Make it with lower, second, and third decks. [17]For behold, I will bring a flood of waters upon the earth to destroy all flesh in which is the breath of life under heaven. Everything that is on the earth shall die. [18]But I will establish my covenant with you, and you shall come into the ark, you, your sons, your wife, and your sons' wives with you. [19]And of every living thing of all flesh, you shall bring two of every sort into the ark to keep them alive with you. They shall be male and female. [20]Of the birds according to their kinds, and of the animals according to their kinds, of every creeping thing of the ground, according to its kind, two of every sort shall come in to you to keep them alive. [21]Also take with you every sort of food that is eaten, and store it up. It shall serve as food for you and for them." [22]Noah did this; he did all that God commanded him.

Matthew 6

"**B**eware of practicing your righteousness before other people in order to be seen by them, for then you will have no reward from your Father who is in heaven.

[2]"Thus, when you give to the needy, sound no trumpet before you, as the hypocrites do in the synagogues and in the streets, that they may be praised by others. Truly, I say to you, they have received their reward. [3]But when you give to the needy, do not let your left hand know what your right hand is doing, [4]so that your giving may be in secret. And your Father who sees in secret will reward you.

[5]"And when you pray, you must not be like the hypocrites. For they love to stand and pray in the synagogues and at the street corners, that they may be seen by others. Truly, I say to you, they have received their reward. [6]But when you pray, go into your room and shut the door and pray to your Father who is in secret. And your Father who sees in secret will reward you.

[7]"And when you pray, do not heap up empty phrases as the Gentiles do, for they think that they will be heard for their many words. [8]Do not

be like them, for your Father knows what you need before you ask him. [9]Pray then like this:

> "Our Father in heaven,
> 　hallowed be your name.[3]
> [10]　Your kingdom come,
> 　your will be done,[4]
> 　　on earth as it is in heaven.
> [11]　Give us this day our daily bread,[5]
> [12]　and forgive us our debts,
> 　　as we also have forgiven our debtors.
> [13]　And lead us not into temptation,
> 　　but deliver us from evil.[6]

[14]For if you forgive others their trespasses, your heavenly Father will also forgive you, [15]but if you do not forgive others their trespasses, neither will your Father forgive your trespasses.

[16]"And when you fast, do not look gloomy like the hypocrites, for they disfigure their faces that their fasting may be seen by others. Truly, I say to you, they have received their reward. [17]But when you fast, anoint your head and wash your face, [18]that your fasting may not be seen by others but by your Father who is in secret. And your Father who sees in secret will reward you.

[19]"Do not lay up for yourselves treasures on earth, where moth and rust[7] destroy and where thieves break in and steal, [20]but lay up for yourselves treasures in heaven, where neither moth nor rust destroys and where thieves do not break in and steal. [21]For where your treasure is, there your heart will be also.

[22]"The eye is the lamp of the body. So, if your eye is healthy, your whole body will be full of light, [23]but if your eye is bad, your whole body will be full of darkness. If then the light in you is darkness, how great is the darkness!

[24]"No one can serve two masters, for either he will hate the one and love the other, or he will be devoted to the one and despise the other. You cannot serve God and money.[8]

[25]"Therefore I tell you, do not be anxious about your life, what you will eat or what you will drink, nor about your body, what you will put on. Is not life more than food, and the body more than clothing? [26]Look at the birds of the air: they neither sow nor reap nor gather into barns, and yet your heavenly Father feeds them. Are you not of more value than they? [27]And which of you by being anxious can add a single

[1] A cubit was about 18 inches or 45 centimeters [2] Or skylight [3] Or Let your name be kept holy, or Let your name be treated with reverence [4] Or Let your kingdom come, let your will be done [5] Or our bread for tomorrow [6] Or the evil one; some manuscripts add For yours is the kingdom and the power and the glory, forever. Amen [7] Or worm; also verse 20 [8] Greek mammon, a Semitic word for money or possessions

hour to his span of life? [1] [28] And why are you anxious about clothing? Consider the lilies of the field, how they grow: they neither toil nor spin, [29] yet I tell you, even Solomon in all his glory was not arrayed like one of these. [30] But if God so clothes the grass of the field, which today is alive and tomorrow is thrown into the oven, will he not much more clothe you, O you of little faith? [31] Therefore do not be anxious, saying, 'What shall we eat?' or 'What shall we drink?' or 'What shall we wear?' [32] For the Gentiles seek after all these things, and your heavenly Father knows that you need them all. [33] But seek first the kingdom of God and his righteousness, and all these things will be added to you.

[34] "Therefore do not be anxious about tomorrow, for tomorrow will be anxious for itself. Sufficient for the day is its own trouble.

Ezra 6

Then Darius the king made a decree, and search was made in Babylonia, in the house of the archives where the documents were stored. [2] And in Ecbatana, the citadel that is in the province of Media, a scroll was found on which this was written: "A record. [3] In the first year of Cyrus the king, Cyrus the king issued a decree: Concerning the house of God at Jerusalem, let the house be rebuilt, the place where sacrifices were offered, and let its foundations be retained. Its height shall be sixty cubits [2] and its breadth sixty cubits, [4] with three layers of great stones and one layer of timber. Let the cost be paid from the royal treasury. [5] And also let the gold and silver vessels of the house of God, which Nebuchadnezzar took out of the temple that is in Jerusalem and brought to Babylon, be restored and brought back to the temple that is in Jerusalem, each to its place. You shall put them in the house of God."

[6] "Now therefore, Tattenai, governor of the province Beyond the River, Shethar-bozenai, and your [3] associates the governors who are in the province Beyond the River, keep away. [7] Let the work on this house of God alone. Let the governor of the Jews and the elders of the Jews rebuild this house of God on its site. [8] Moreover, I make a decree regarding what you shall do for these elders of the Jews for the rebuilding of this house of God. The cost is to be paid to these men in full and without delay from the

royal revenue, the tribute of the province from Beyond the River. [9] And whatever is needed—bulls, rams, or sheep for burnt offerings to the God of heaven, wheat, salt, wine, or oil, as the priests at Jerusalem require—let that be given to them day by day without fail, [10] that they may offer pleasing sacrifices to the God of heaven and pray for the life of the king and his sons. [11] Also I make a decree that if anyone alters this edict, a beam shall be pulled out of his house, and he shall be impaled on it, and his house shall be made a dunghill. [12] May the God who has caused his name to dwell there overthrow any king or people who shall put out a hand to alter this, or to destroy this house of God that is in Jerusalem. I Darius make a decree; let it be done with all diligence."

[13] Then, according to the word sent by Darius the king, Tattenai, the governor of the province Beyond the River, Shethar-bozenai, and their associates did with all diligence what Darius the king had ordered. [14] And the elders of the Jews built and prospered through the prophesying of Haggai the prophet and Zechariah the son of Iddo. They finished their building by decree of the God of Israel and by decree of Cyrus and Darius and Artaxerxes king of Persia; [15] and this house was finished on the third day of the month of Adar, in the sixth year of the reign of Darius the king.

[16] And the people of Israel, the priests and the Levites, and the rest of the returned exiles, celebrated the dedication of this house of God with joy. [17] They offered at the dedication of this house of God 100 bulls, 200 rams, 400 lambs, and as a sin offering for all Israel 12 male goats, according to the number of the tribes of Israel. [18] And they set the priests in their divisions and the Levites in their divisions, for the service of God at Jerusalem, as it is written in the Book of Moses.

[19] On the fourteenth day of the first month, the returned exiles kept the Passover. [20] For the priests and the Levites had purified themselves together; all of them were clean. So they slaughtered the Passover lamb for all the returned exiles, for their fellow priests, and for themselves. [21] It was eaten by the people of Israel who had returned from exile, and also by every one who had joined them and separated himself from the uncleanness of the peoples of the land to worship the LORD, the God of Israel.

[1] Or a single cubit to his stature; a cubit was about 18 inches or 45 centimeters [2] A cubit was about 18 inches or 45 centimeters [3] Aramaic their

²²And they kept the Feast of Unleavened Bread seven days with joy, for the LORD had made them joyful and had turned the heart of the king of Assyria to them, so that he aided them in the work of the house of God, the God of Israel.

Acts 6

Now in these days when the disciples were increasing in number, a complaint by the Hellenists[1] arose against the Hebrews because their widows were being neglected in the daily distribution. ²And the twelve summoned the full number of the disciples and said, "It is not right that we should give up preaching the word of God to serve tables. ³Therefore, brothers,[2] pick out from among you seven men of good repute, full of the Spirit and of wisdom, whom we will appoint to this duty. ⁴But we will devote ourselves to prayer and to the ministry of the word." ⁵And what they said pleased the whole gathering, and they chose Stephen, a man full of faith and of the Holy Spirit, and Philip, and Prochorus, and Nicanor, and Timon, and Parmenas, and Nicolaus, a proselyte of Antioch. ⁶These they set before the apostles, and they prayed and laid their hands on them.

⁷And the word of God continued to increase, and the number of the disciples multiplied greatly in Jerusalem, and a great many of the priests became obedient to the faith.

⁸And Stephen, full of grace and power, was doing great wonders and signs among the people. ⁹Then some of those who belonged to the synagogue of the Freedmen (as it was called), and of the Cyrenians, and of the Alexandrians, and of those from Cilicia and Asia, rose up and disputed with Stephen. ¹⁰But they could not withstand the wisdom and the Spirit with which he was speaking. ¹¹Then they secretly instigated men who said, "We have heard him speak blasphemous words against Moses and God." ¹²And they stirred up the people and the elders and the scribes, and they came upon him and seized him and brought him before the council, ¹³and they set up false witnesses who said, "This man never ceases to speak words against this holy place and the law, ¹⁴for we have heard him say that this Jesus of Nazareth will destroy this place and will change the customs that Moses delivered to us." ¹⁵And gazing at him, all who sat in the council saw that his face was like the face of an angel.

JANUARY 7

Genesis 7

Then the LORD said to Noah, "Go into the ark, you and all your household, for I have seen that you are righteous before me in this generation. ²Take with you seven pairs of all clean animals,[3] the male and his mate, and a pair of the animals that are not clean, the male and his mate, ³and seven pairs[4] of the birds of the heavens also, male and female, to keep their offspring alive on the face of all the earth. ⁴For in seven days I will send rain on the earth forty days and forty nights, and every living thing[5] that I have made I will blot out from the face of the ground." ⁵And Noah did all that the LORD had commanded him.

⁶Noah was six hundred years old when the flood of waters came upon the earth. ⁷And Noah and his sons and his wife and his sons' wives with him went into the ark to escape the waters of the flood. ⁸Of clean animals, and of animals that are not clean, and of birds, and of everything that creeps on the ground, ⁹two and two, male and female, went into the ark with Noah, as God had commanded Noah. ¹⁰And after seven days the waters of the flood came upon the earth.

¹¹In the six hundredth year of Noah's life, in the second month, on the seventeenth day of the month, on that day all the fountains of the great deep burst forth, and the windows of

the heavens were opened. ¹²And rain fell upon the earth forty days and forty nights. ¹³On the very same day Noah and his sons, Shem and Ham and Japheth, and Noah's wife and the three wives of his sons with them entered the ark, ¹⁴they and every beast, according to its kind, and all the livestock according to their kinds, and every creeping thing that creeps on the earth, according to its kind, and every bird, according to its kind, every winged creature. ¹⁵They went into the ark with Noah, two and two of all flesh in which there was the breath of life. ¹⁶And those that entered, male and female of all flesh, went in as God had commanded him. And the Lᴏʀᴅ shut him in.

¹⁷The flood continued forty days on the earth. The waters increased and bore up the ark, and it rose high above the earth. ¹⁸The waters prevailed and increased greatly on the earth, and the ark floated on the face of the waters. ¹⁹And the waters prevailed so mightily on the earth that all the high mountains under the whole heaven were covered. ²⁰The waters prevailed above the mountains, covering them fifteen cubits¹ deep. ²¹And all flesh died that moved on the earth, birds, livestock, beasts, all swarming creatures that swarm on the earth, and all mankind. ²²Everything on the dry land in whose nostrils was the breath of life died. ²³He blotted out every living thing that was on the face of the ground, man and animals and creeping things and birds of the heavens. They were blotted out from the earth. Only Noah was left, and those who were with him in the ark. ²⁴And the waters prevailed on the earth 150 days.

———— *Matthew 7* ————

¹⁰"Judge not, that you be not judged. ²For with the judgment you pronounce you will be judged, and with the measure you use it will be measured to you. ³Why do you see the speck that is in your brother's eye, but do not notice the log that is in your own eye? ⁴Or how can you say to your brother, 'Let me take the speck out of your eye,' when there is the log in your own eye? ⁵You hypocrite, first take the log out of your own eye, and then you will see clearly to take the speck out of your brother's eye.

⁶"Do not give dogs what is holy, and do not throw your pearls before pigs, lest they trample them underfoot and turn to attack you.

⁷"Ask, and it will be given to you; seek, and you will find; knock, and it will be opened to you. ⁸For everyone who asks receives, and the one who seeks finds, and to the one who knocks it will be opened. ⁹Or which one of you, if his son asks him for bread, will give him a stone? ¹⁰Or if he asks for a fish, will give him a serpent? ¹¹If you then, who are evil, know how to give good gifts to your children, how much more will your Father who is in heaven give good things to those who ask him!

¹²"So whatever you wish that others would do to you, do also to them, for this is the Law and the Prophets.

¹³"Enter by the narrow gate. For the gate is wide and the way is easy² that leads to destruction, and those who enter by it are many. ¹⁴For the gate is narrow and the way is hard that leads to life, and those who find it are few.

¹⁵"Beware of false prophets, who come to you in sheep's clothing but inwardly are ravenous wolves. ¹⁶You will recognize them by their fruits. Are grapes gathered from thornbushes, or figs from thistles? ¹⁷So, every healthy tree bears good fruit, but the diseased tree bears bad fruit. ¹⁸A healthy tree cannot bear bad fruit, nor can a diseased tree bear good fruit. ¹⁹Every tree that does not bear good fruit is cut down and thrown into the fire. ²⁰Thus you will recognize them by their fruits.

²¹"Not everyone who says to me, 'Lord, Lord,' will enter the kingdom of heaven, but the one who does the will of my Father who is in heaven. ²²On that day many will say to me, 'Lord, Lord, did we not prophesy in your name, and cast out demons in your name, and do many mighty works in your name?' ²³And then will I declare to them, 'I never knew you; depart from me, you workers of lawlessness.'

²⁴"Everyone then who hears these words of mine and does them will be like a wise man who built his house on the rock. ²⁵And the rain fell, and the floods came, and the winds blew and beat on that house, but it did not fall, because it had been founded on the rock. ²⁶And everyone who hears these words of mine and does not do them will be like a foolish man who built his house on the sand. ²⁷And the rain fell, and the floods came, and the winds blew and

¹ A *cubit* was about 18 inches or 45 centimeters ² Some manuscripts *For the way is wide and easy*

beat against that house, and it fell, and great was the fall of it."

²⁸And when Jesus finished these sayings, the crowds were astonished at his teaching, ²⁹for he was teaching them as one who had authority, and not as their scribes.

Ezra 7

Now after this, in the reign of Artaxerxes king of Persia, Ezra the son of Seraiah, son of Azariah, son of Hilkiah, ²son of Shallum, son of Zadok, son of Ahitub, ³son of Amariah, son of Azariah, son of Meraioth, ⁴son of Zerahiah, son of Uzzi, son of Bukki, ⁵son of Abishua, son of Phinehas, son of Eleazar, son of Aaron the chief priest— ⁶this Ezra went up from Babylonia. He was a scribe skilled in the Law of Moses that the LORD, the God of Israel, had given, and the king granted him all that he asked, for the hand of the LORD his God was on him.

⁷And there went up also to Jerusalem, in the seventh year of Artaxerxes the king, some of the people of Israel, and some of the priests and Levites, the singers and gatekeepers, and the temple servants. ⁸And Ezra¹ came to Jerusalem in the fifth month, which was in the seventh year of the king. ⁹For on the first day of the first month he began to go up from Babylonia, and on the first day of the fifth month he came to Jerusalem, for the good hand of his God was on him. ¹⁰For Ezra had set his heart to study the Law of the LORD, and to do it and to teach his statutes and rules in Israel.

¹¹This is a copy of the letter that King Artaxerxes gave to Ezra the priest, the scribe, a man learned in matters of the commandments of the LORD and his statutes for Israel: ¹²"Artaxerxes, king of kings, to Ezra the priest, the scribe of the Law of the God of heaven. Peace.² And now ¹³I make a decree that anyone of the people of Israel or their priests or Levites in my kingdom, who freely offers to go to Jerusalem, may go with you. ¹⁴For you are sent by the king and his seven counselors to make inquiries about Judah and Jerusalem according to the Law of your God, which is in your hand, ¹⁵and also to carry the silver and gold that the king and his counselors have freely offered to the God of Israel, whose dwelling is in Jerusalem, ¹⁶with all the silver and gold that you shall find in the whole province

of Babylonia, and with the freewill offerings of the people and the priests, vowed willingly for the house of their God that is in Jerusalem. ¹⁷With this money, then, you shall with all diligence buy bulls, rams, and lambs, with their grain offerings and their drink offerings, and you shall offer them on the altar of the house of your God that is in Jerusalem. ¹⁸Whatever seems good to you and your brothers to do with the rest of the silver and gold, you may do, according to the will of your God. ¹⁹The vessels that have been given you for the service of the house of your God, you shall deliver before the God of Jerusalem. ²⁰And whatever else is required for the house of your God, which it falls to you to provide, you may provide it out of the king's treasury.

²¹"And I, Artaxerxes the king, make a decree to all the treasurers in the province Beyond the River: Whatever Ezra the priest, the scribe of the Law of the God of heaven, requires of you, let it be done with all diligence, ²²up to 100 talents³ of silver, 100 cors⁴ of wheat, 100 baths⁵ of wine, 100 baths of oil, and salt without prescribing how much. ²³Whatever is decreed by the God of heaven, let it be done in full for the house of the God of heaven, lest his wrath be against the realm of the king and his sons. ²⁴We also notify you that it shall not be lawful to impose tribute, custom, or toll on anyone of the priests, the Levites, the singers, the doorkeepers, the temple servants, or other servants of this house of God.

²⁵"And you, Ezra, according to the wisdom of your God that is in your hand, appoint magistrates and judges who may judge all the people in the province Beyond the River, all such as know the laws of your God. And those who do not know them, you shall teach. ²⁶Whoever will not obey the law of your God and the law of the king, let judgment be strictly executed on him, whether for death or for banishment or for confiscation of his goods or for imprisonment."

²⁷Blessed be the LORD, the God of our fathers, who put such a thing as this into the heart of the king, to beautify the house of the LORD that is in Jerusalem, ²⁸and who extended to me his steadfast love before the king and his counselors, and before all the king's mighty officers. I took courage, for the hand of the LORD my God was on me, and I gathered leading men from Israel to go up with me.

---

¹ Aramaic *he* ² Aramaic *Perfect* (probably a greeting) ³ A *talent* was about 75 pounds or 34 kilograms ⁴ A *cor* was about 6 bushels or 220 liters ⁵ A *bath* was about 6 gallons or 22 liters

Acts 7

And the high priest said, "Are these things so?" ²And Stephen said:

"Brothers and fathers, hear me. The God of glory appeared to our father Abraham when he was in Mesopotamia, before he lived in Haran, ³and said to him, 'Go out from your land and from your kindred and go into the land that I will show you.' ⁴Then he went out from the land of the Chaldeans and lived in Haran. And after his father died, God removed him from there into this land in which you are now living. ⁵Yet he gave him no inheritance in it, not even a foot's length, but promised to give it to him as a possession and to his offspring after him, though he had no child. ⁶And God spoke to this effect—that his offspring would be sojourners in a land belonging to others, who would enslave them and afflict them four hundred years. ⁷'But I will judge the nation that they serve,' said God, 'and after that they shall come out and worship me in this place.' ⁸And he gave him the covenant of circumcision. And so Abraham became the father of Isaac, and circumcised him on the eighth day, and Isaac became the father of Jacob, and Jacob of the twelve patriarchs.

⁹"And the patriarchs, jealous of Joseph, sold him into Egypt; but God was with him ¹⁰and rescued him out of all his afflictions and gave him favor and wisdom before Pharaoh, king of Egypt, who made him ruler over Egypt and over all his household. ¹¹Now there came a famine throughout all Egypt and Canaan, and great affliction, and our fathers could find no food. ¹²But when Jacob heard that there was grain in Egypt, he sent out our fathers on their first visit. ¹³And on the second visit Joseph made himself known to his brothers, and Joseph's family became known to Pharaoh. ¹⁴And Joseph sent and summoned Jacob his father and all his kindred, seventy-five persons in all. ¹⁵And Jacob went down into Egypt, and he died, he and our fathers, ¹⁶and they were carried back to Shechem and laid in the tomb that Abraham had bought for a sum of silver from the sons of Hamor in Shechem.

¹⁷"But as the time of the promise drew near, which God had granted to Abraham, the people increased and multiplied in Egypt ¹⁸until there arose over Egypt another king who did not know Joseph. ¹⁹He dealt shrewdly with our race and forced our fathers to expose their infants, so that they would not be kept alive. ²⁰At this time Moses was born; and he was beautiful in God's sight. And he was brought up for three months in his father's house, ²¹and when he was exposed, Pharaoh's daughter adopted him and brought him up as her own son. ²²And Moses was instructed in all the wisdom of the Egyptians, and he was mighty in his words and deeds.

²³"When he was forty years old, it came into his heart to visit his brothers, the children of Israel. ²⁴And seeing one of them being wronged, he defended the oppressed man and avenged him by striking down the Egyptian. ²⁵He supposed that his brothers would understand that God was giving them salvation by his hand, but they did not understand. ²⁶And on the following day he appeared to them as they were quarreling and tried to reconcile them, saying, 'Men, you are brothers. Why do you wrong each other?' ²⁷But the man who was wronging his neighbor thrust him aside, saying, 'Who made you a ruler and a judge over us? ²⁸Do you want to kill me as you killed the Egyptian yesterday?' ²⁹At this retort Moses fled and became an exile in the land of Midian, where he became the father of two sons.

³⁰"Now when forty years had passed, an angel appeared to him in the wilderness of Mount Sinai, in a flame of fire in a bush. ³¹When Moses saw it, he was amazed at the sight, and as he drew near to look, there came the voice of the Lord: ³²'I am the God of your fathers, the God of Abraham and of Isaac and of Jacob.' And Moses trembled and did not dare to look. ³³Then the Lord said to him, 'Take off the sandals from your feet, for the place where you are standing is holy ground. ³⁴I have surely seen the affliction of my people who are in Egypt, and have heard their groaning, and I have come down to deliver them. And now come, I will send you to Egypt.'

³⁵"This Moses, whom they rejected, saying, 'Who made you a ruler and a judge?'—this man God sent as both ruler and redeemer by the hand of the angel who appeared to him in the bush. ³⁶This man led them out, performing wonders and signs in Egypt and at the Red Sea and in the wilderness for forty years. ³⁷This is the Moses who said to the Israelites, 'God

will raise up for you a prophet like me from your brothers.' [38] This is the one who was in the congregation in the wilderness with the angel who spoke to him at Mount Sinai, and with our fathers. He received living oracles to give to us. [39] Our fathers refused to obey him, but thrust him aside, and in their hearts they turned to Egypt, [40] saying to Aaron, 'Make for us gods who will go before us. As for this Moses who led us out from the land of Egypt, we do not know what has become of him.' [41] And they made a calf in those days, and offered a sacrifice to the idol and were rejoicing in the works of their hands. [42] But God turned away and gave them over to worship the host of heaven, as it is written in the book of the prophets:

> "'Did you bring to me slain beasts and
> sacrifices,
> during the forty years in the
> wilderness, O house of Israel?
> [43] You took up the tent of Moloch
> and the star of your god Rephan,
> the images that you made to worship;
> and I will send you into exile beyond
> Babylon.'

[44] "Our fathers had the tent of witness in the wilderness, just as he who spoke to Moses directed him to make it, according to the pattern that he had seen. [45] Our fathers in turn brought it in with Joshua when they dispossessed the nations that God drove out before our fathers. So it was until the days of David, [46] who found favor in the sight of God and asked to find a dwelling place for the God of Jacob.[1] [47] But it was Solomon who built a house

for him. [48] Yet the Most High does not dwell in houses made by hands, as the prophet says,

> [49] "'Heaven is my throne,
> and the earth is my footstool.
> What kind of house will you build for
> me, says the Lord,
> or what is the place of my rest?
> [50] Did not my hand make all these things?'

[51] "You stiff-necked people, uncircumcised in heart and ears, you always resist the Holy Spirit. As your fathers did, so do you. [52] Which of the prophets did your fathers not persecute? And they killed those who announced beforehand the coming of the Righteous One, whom you have now betrayed and murdered, [53] you who received the law as delivered by angels and did not keep it."

[54] Now when they heard these things they were enraged, and they ground their teeth at him. [55] But he, full of the Holy Spirit, gazed into heaven and saw the glory of God, and Jesus standing at the right hand of God. [56] And he said, "Behold, I see the heavens opened, and the Son of Man standing at the right hand of God." [57] But they cried out with a loud voice and stopped their ears and rushed together[2] at him. [58] Then they cast him out of the city and stoned him. And the witnesses laid down their garments at the feet of a young man named Saul. [59] And as they were stoning Stephen, he called out, "Lord Jesus, receive my spirit." [60] And falling to his knees he cried out with a loud voice, "Lord, do not hold this sin against them." And when he had said this, he fell asleep.

JANUARY 8

Genesis 8

But God remembered Noah and all the beasts and all the livestock that were with him in the ark. And God made a wind blow over the earth, and the waters subsided. [2] The fountains of the deep and the windows of the

heavens were closed, the rain from the heavens was restrained, [3] and the waters receded from the earth continually. At the end of 150 days the waters had abated, [4] and in the seventh month, on the seventeenth day of the

[1] Some manuscripts *for the house of Jacob*   [2] Or *rushed with one mind*

month, the ark came to rest on the mountains of Ararat. ⁵And the waters continued to abate until the tenth month; in the tenth month, on the first day of the month, the tops of the mountains were seen.

⁶At the end of forty days Noah opened the window of the ark that he had made ⁷and sent forth a raven. It went to and fro until the waters were dried up from the earth. ⁸Then he sent forth a dove from him, to see if the waters had subsided from the face of the ground. ⁹But the dove found no place to set her foot, and she returned to him to the ark, for the waters were still on the face of the whole earth. So he put out his hand and took her and brought her into the ark with him. ¹⁰He waited another seven days, and again he sent forth the dove out of the ark. ¹¹And the dove came back to him in the evening, and behold, in her mouth was a freshly plucked olive leaf. So Noah knew that the waters had subsided from the earth. ¹²Then he waited another seven days and sent forth the dove, and she did not return to him anymore.

¹³In the six hundred and first year, in the first month, the first day of the month, the waters were dried from off the earth. And Noah removed the covering of the ark and looked, and behold, the face of the ground was dry. ¹⁴In the second month, on the twenty-seventh day of the month, the earth had dried out. ¹⁵Then God said to Noah, ¹⁶"Go out from the ark, you and your wife, and your sons and your sons' wives with you. ¹⁷Bring out with you every living thing that is with you of all flesh—birds and animals and every creeping thing that creeps on the earth—that they may swarm on the earth, and be fruitful and multiply on the earth." ¹⁸So Noah went out, and his sons and his wife and his sons' wives with him. ¹⁹Every beast, every creeping thing, and every bird, everything that moves on the earth, went out by families from the ark.

²⁰Then Noah built an altar to the LORD and took some of every clean animal and some of every clean bird and offered burnt offerings on the altar. ²¹And when the LORD smelled the pleasing aroma, the LORD said in his heart, "I will never again curse¹ the ground because of man, for the intention of man's heart is evil from his youth. Neither will I ever again strike down every living creature as I have done. ²²While the earth remains, seedtime and

harvest, cold and heat, summer and winter, day and night, shall not cease."

Matthew 8

When he came down from the mountain, great crowds followed him. ²And behold, a leper² came to him and knelt before him, saying, "Lord, if you will, you can make me clean." ³And Jesus³ stretched out his hand and touched him, saying, "I will; be clean." And immediately his leprosy was cleansed. ⁴And Jesus said to him, "See that you say nothing to anyone, but go, show yourself to the priest and offer the gift that Moses commanded, for a proof to them."

⁵When he had entered Capernaum, a centurion came forward to him, appealing to him, ⁶"Lord, my servant is lying paralyzed at home, suffering terribly." ⁷And he said to him, "I will come and heal him." ⁸But the centurion replied, "Lord, I am not worthy to have you come under my roof, but only say the word, and my servant will be healed. ⁹For I too am a man under authority, with soldiers under me. And I say to one, 'Go,' and he goes, and to another, 'Come,' and he comes, and to my servant,⁴ 'Do this,' and he does it." ¹⁰When Jesus heard this, he marveled and said to those who followed him, "Truly, I tell you, with no one in Israel⁵ have I found such faith. ¹¹I tell you, many will come from east and west and recline at table with Abraham, Isaac, and Jacob in the kingdom of heaven, ¹²while the sons of the kingdom will be thrown into the outer darkness. In that place there will be weeping and gnashing of teeth." ¹³And to the centurion Jesus said, "Go; let it be done for you as you have believed." And the servant was healed at that very moment.

¹⁴And when Jesus entered Peter's house, he saw his mother-in-law lying sick with a fever. ¹⁵He touched her hand, and the fever left her, and she rose and began to serve him. ¹⁶That evening they brought to him many who were oppressed by demons, and he cast out the spirits with a word and healed all who were sick. ¹⁷This was to fulfill what was spoken by the prophet Isaiah: "He took our illnesses and bore our diseases."

¹⁸Now when Jesus saw a crowd around him, he gave orders to go over to the other side. ¹⁹And a scribe came up and said to him, "Teacher, I will follow you wherever you go."

¹ Or dishonor ² Leprosy was a term for several skin diseases; see Leviticus 13 ³ Greek he ⁴ Greek bondservant ⁵ Some manuscripts not even in Israel

[20]And Jesus said to him, "Foxes have holes, and birds of the air have nests, but the Son of Man has nowhere to lay his head." [21]Another of the disciples said to him, "Lord, let me first go and bury my father." [22]And Jesus said to him, "Follow me, and leave the dead to bury their own dead."

[23]And when he got into the boat, his disciples followed him. [24]And behold, there arose a great storm on the sea, so that the boat was being swamped by the waves; but he was asleep. [25]And they went and woke him, saying, "Save us, Lord; we are perishing." [26]And he said to them, "Why are you afraid, O you of little faith?" Then he rose and rebuked the winds and the sea, and there was a great calm. [27]And the men marveled, saying, "What sort of man is this, that even winds and sea obey him?"

[28]And when he came to the other side, to the country of the Gadarenes,[1] two demon-possessed[2] men met him, coming out of the tombs, so fierce that no one could pass that way. [29]And behold, they cried out, "What have you to do with us, O Son of God? Have you come here to torment us before the time?" [30]Now a herd of many pigs was feeding at some distance from them. [31]And the demons begged him, saying, "If you cast us out, send us away into the herd of pigs." [32]And he said to them, "Go." So they came out and went into the pigs, and behold, the whole herd rushed down the steep bank into the sea and drowned in the waters. [33]The herdsmen fled, and going into the city they told everything, especially what had happened to the demon-possessed men. [34]And behold, all the city came out to meet Jesus, and when they saw him, they begged him to leave their region.

Ezra 8

These are the heads of their fathers' houses, and this is the genealogy of those who went up with me from Babylonia, in the reign of Artaxerxes the king: [2]Of the sons of Phinehas, Gershom. Of the sons of Ithamar, Daniel. Of the sons of David, Hattush. [3]Of the sons of Shecaniah, who was of the sons of Parosh, Zechariah, with whom were registered 150 men. [4]Of the sons of Pahath-moab, Eliehoenai the son of Zerahiah, and with him 200 men. [5]Of the sons of Zattu,[3] Shecaniah the son of Jahaziel, and with him 300 men. [6]Of the sons

of Adin, Ebed the son of Jonathan, and with him 50 men. [7]Of the sons of Elam, Jeshaiah the son of Athaliah, and with him 70 men. [8]Of the sons of Shephatiah, Zebadiah the son of Michael, and with him 80 men. [9]Of the sons of Joab, Obadiah the son of Jehiel, and with him 218 men. [10]Of the sons of Bani,[4] Shelomith the son of Josiphiah, and with him 160 men. [11]Of the sons of Bebai, Zechariah, the son of Bebai, and with him 28 men. [12]Of the sons of Azgad, Johanan the son of Hakkatan, and with him 110 men. [13]Of the sons of Adonikam, those who came later, their names being Eliphelet, Jeuel, and Shemaiah, and with them 60 men. [14]Of the sons of Bigvai, Uthai and Zaccur, and with them 70 men.

[15]I gathered them to the river that runs to Ahava, and there we camped three days. As I reviewed the people and the priests, I found there none of the sons of Levi. [16]Then I sent for Eliezer, Ariel, Shemaiah, Elnathan, Jarib, Elnathan, Nathan, Zechariah, and Meshullam, leading men, and for Joiarib and Elnathan, who were men of insight, [17]and sent them to Iddo, the leading man at the place Casiphia, telling them what to say to Iddo and his brothers and[5] the temple servants at the place Casiphia, namely, to send us ministers for the house of our God. [18]And by the good hand of our God on us, they brought us a man of discretion, of the sons of Mahli the son of Levi, son of Israel, namely Sherebiah with his sons and kinsmen, 18; [19]also Hashabiah, and with him Jeshaiah of the sons of Merari, with his kinsmen and their sons, 20; [20]besides 220 of the temple servants, whom David and his officials had set apart to attend the Levites. These were all mentioned by name.

[21]Then I proclaimed a fast there, at the river Ahava, that we might humble ourselves before our God, to seek from him a safe journey for ourselves, our children, and all our goods. [22]For I was ashamed to ask the king for a band of soldiers and horsemen to protect us against the enemy on our way, since we had told the king, "The hand of our God is for good on all who seek him, and the power of his wrath is against all who forsake him." [23]So we fasted and implored our God for this, and he listened to our entreaty.

[24]Then I set apart twelve of the leading priests: Sherebiah, Hashabiah, and ten of their

---

[1] Some manuscripts *Gergesenes*; some *Gerasenes* [2] Greek *daimonizomai*; also verse 33; elsewhere rendered *oppressed by demons* [3] Septuagint; Hebrew lacks *of Zattu* [4] Septuagint; Hebrew lacks *Bani* [5] Hebrew lacks *and*

kinsmen with them. ²⁵And I weighed out to them the silver and the gold and the vessels, the offering for the house of our God that the king and his counselors and his lords and all Israel there present had offered. ²⁶I weighed out into their hand 650 talents¹ of silver, and silver vessels worth 200 talents,² and 100 talents of gold, ²⁷20 bowls of gold worth 1,000 darics,³ and two vessels of fine bright bronze as precious as gold. ²⁸And I said to them, "You are holy to the LORD, and the vessels are holy, and the silver and the gold are a freewill offering to the LORD, the God of your fathers. ²⁹Guard them and keep them until you weigh them before the chief priests and the Levites and the heads of fathers' houses in Israel at Jerusalem, within the chambers of the house of the LORD." ³⁰So the priests and the Levites took over the weight of the silver and the gold and the vessels, to bring them to Jerusalem, to the house of our God.

³¹Then we departed from the river Ahava on the twelfth day of the first month, to go to Jerusalem. The hand of our God was on us, and he delivered us from the hand of the enemy and from ambushes by the way. ³²We came to Jerusalem, and there we remained three days. ³³On the fourth day, within the house of our God, the silver and the gold and the vessels were weighed into the hands of Meremoth the priest, son of Uriah, and with him was Eleazar the son of Phinehas, and with them were the Levites, Jozabad the son of Jeshua and Noadiah the son of Binnui. ³⁴The whole was counted and weighed, and the weight of everything was recorded.

³⁵At that time those who had come from captivity, the returned exiles, offered burnt offerings to the God of Israel, twelve bulls for all Israel, ninety-six rams, seventy-seven lambs, and as a sin offering twelve male goats. All this was a burnt offering to the LORD. ³⁶They also delivered the king's commissions to the king's satraps⁴ and to the governors of the province Beyond the River, and they aided the people and the house of God.

Acts 8

A nd Saul approved of his execution.
And there arose on that day a great persecution against the church in Jerusalem, and they were all scattered throughout the regions of Judea and Samaria, except the apostles. ²Devout men buried Stephen and made great lamentation over him. ³But Saul was ravaging the church, and entering house after house, he dragged off men and women and committed them to prison.

⁴Now those who were scattered went about preaching the word. ⁵Philip went down to the city⁵ of Samaria and proclaimed to them the Christ. ⁶And the crowds with one accord paid attention to what was being said by Philip when they heard him and saw the signs that he did. ⁷For unclean spirits, crying out with a loud voice, came out of many who had them, and many who were paralyzed or lame were healed. ⁸So there was much joy in that city.

⁹But there was a man named Simon, who had previously practiced magic in the city and amazed the people of Samaria, saying that he himself was somebody great. ¹⁰They all paid attention to him, from the least to the greatest, saying, "This man is the power of God that is called Great." ¹¹And they paid attention to him because for a long time he had amazed them with his magic. ¹²But when they believed Philip as he preached good news about the kingdom of God and the name of Jesus Christ, they were baptized, both men and women. ¹³Even Simon himself believed, and after being baptized he continued with Philip. And seeing signs and great miracles⁶ performed, he was amazed.

¹⁴Now when the apostles at Jerusalem heard that Samaria had received the word of God, they sent to them Peter and John, ¹⁵who came down and prayed for them that they might receive the Holy Spirit, ¹⁶for he had not yet fallen on any of them, but they had only been baptized in the name of the Lord Jesus. ¹⁷Then they laid their hands on them and they received the Holy Spirit. ¹⁸Now when Simon saw that the Spirit was given through the laying on of the apostles' hands, he offered them money, ¹⁹saying, "Give me this power also, so that anyone on whom I lay my hands may receive the Holy Spirit." ²⁰But Peter said to him, "May your silver perish with you, because you thought you could obtain the gift of God with money! ²¹You have neither part nor lot in this matter, for your heart is not right before God. ²²Repent, therefore, of this wickedness of yours, and pray to the Lord that, if possible, the intent of your heart may

---

¹ A talent was about 75 pounds or 34 kilograms ² Revocalization; the number is missing in the Masoretic Text ³ A daric was a coin weighing about 1/4 ounce or 8.5 grams
⁴ A satrap was a Persian official ⁵ Some manuscripts a city ⁶ Greek works of power

be forgiven you. [23] For I see that you are in the gall[1] of bitterness and in the bond of iniquity." [24] And Simon answered, "Pray for me to the Lord, that nothing of what you have said may come upon me."

[25] Now when they had testified and spoken the word of the Lord, they returned to Jerusalem, preaching the gospel to many villages of the Samaritans.

[26] Now an angel of the Lord said to Philip, "Rise and go toward the south[2] to the road that goes down from Jerusalem to Gaza." This is a desert place. [27] And he rose and went. And there was an Ethiopian, a eunuch, a court official of Candace, queen of the Ethiopians, who was in charge of all her treasure. He had come to Jerusalem to worship [28] and was returning, seated in his chariot, and he was reading the prophet Isaiah. [29] And the Spirit said to Philip, "Go over and join this chariot." [30] So Philip ran to him and heard him reading Isaiah the prophet and asked, "Do you understand what you are reading?" [31] And he said, "How can I, unless someone guides me?" And he invited Philip to come up and sit with him. [32] Now the passage of the Scripture that he was reading was this:

"Like a sheep he was led to the slaughter
   and like a lamb before its shearer is
      silent,
   so he opens not his mouth.
[33]   In his humiliation justice was denied
      him.
   Who can describe his generation?
   For his life is taken away from the
      earth."

[34] And the eunuch said to Philip, "About whom, I ask you, does the prophet say this, about himself or about someone else?" [35] Then Philip opened his mouth, and beginning with this Scripture he told him the good news about Jesus. [36] And as they were going along the road they came to some water, and the eunuch said, "See, here is water! What prevents me from being baptized?"[3] [38] And he commanded the chariot to stop, and they both went down into the water, Philip and the eunuch, and he baptized him. [39] And when they came up out of the water, the Spirit of the Lord carried Philip away, and the eunuch saw him no more, and went on his way rejoicing. [40] But Philip found himself at Azotus, and as he passed through he preached the gospel to all the towns until he came to Caesarea.

JANUARY 9

Genesis 9–10

And God blessed Noah and his sons and said to them, "Be fruitful and multiply and fill the earth. [2] The fear of you and the dread of you shall be upon every beast of the earth and upon every bird of the heavens, upon everything that creeps on the ground and all the fish of the sea. Into your hand they are delivered. [3] Every moving thing that lives shall be food for you. And as I gave you the green plants, I give you everything. [4] But you shall not eat flesh with its life, that is, its blood. [5] And for your lifeblood I will require a reckoning: from every beast I will require it and from man. From his fellow man I will require a reckoning for the life of man.

[6]   "Whoever sheds the blood of man,
      by man shall his blood be shed,
   for God made man in his own image.

[7] And you,[4] be fruitful and multiply, increase greatly on the earth and multiply in it."

[8] Then God said to Noah and to his sons with him, [9] "Behold, I establish my covenant with you and your offspring after you, [10] and with every living creature that is with you, the birds, the livestock, and every beast of the earth with you, as many as came out of the ark; it is for every beast of the earth. [11] I establish my covenant with you, that never again shall all flesh

be cut off by the waters of the flood, and never again shall there be a flood to destroy the earth." ¹²And God said, "This is the sign of the covenant that I make between me and you and every living creature that is with you, for all future generations: ¹³I have set my bow in the cloud, and it shall be a sign of the covenant between me and the earth. ¹⁴When I bring clouds over the earth and the bow is seen in the clouds, ¹⁵I will remember my covenant that is between me and you and every living creature of all flesh. And the waters shall never again become a flood to destroy all flesh. ¹⁶When the bow is in the clouds, I will see it and remember the everlasting covenant between God and every living creature of all flesh that is on the earth." ¹⁷God said to Noah, "This is the sign of the covenant that I have established between me and all flesh that is on the earth."

¹⁸The sons of Noah who went forth from the ark were Shem, Ham, and Japheth. (Ham was the father of Canaan.) ¹⁹These three were the sons of Noah, and from these the people of the whole earth were dispersed.¹

²⁰Noah began to be a man of the soil, and he planted a vineyard.² ²¹He drank of the wine and became drunk and lay uncovered in his tent. ²²And Ham, the father of Canaan, saw the nakedness of his father and told his two brothers outside. ²³Then Shem and Japheth took a garment, laid it on both their shoulders, and walked backward and covered the nakedness of their father. Their faces were turned backward, and they did not see their father's nakedness. ²⁴When Noah awoke from his wine and knew what his youngest son had done to him, ²⁵he said,

"Cursed be Canaan;
    a servant of servants shall he be to his
        brothers."

²⁶He also said,

"Blessed be the LORD, the God of Shem;
    and let Canaan be his servant.
²⁷   May God enlarge Japheth,³
        and let him dwell in the tents of Shem,
    and let Canaan be his servant."

²⁸After the flood Noah lived 350 years. ²⁹All the days of Noah were 950 years, and he died.

¹⁰:¹These are the generations of the sons of Noah, Shem, Ham, and Japheth. Sons were born to them after the flood.

²The sons of Japheth: Gomer, Magog, Madai, Javan, Tubal, Meshech, and Tiras. ³The sons of Gomer: Ashkenaz, Riphath, and Togarmah. ⁴The sons of Javan: Elishah, Tarshish, Kittim, and Dodanim. ⁵From these the coastland peoples spread in their lands, each with his own language, by their clans, in their nations.

⁶The sons of Ham: Cush, Egypt, Put, and Canaan. ⁷The sons of Cush: Seba, Havilah, Sabtah, Raamah, and Sabteca. The sons of Raamah: Sheba and Dedan. ⁸Cush fathered Nimrod; he was the first on earth to be a mighty man.⁴ ⁹He was a mighty hunter before the LORD. Therefore it is said, "Like Nimrod a mighty hunter before the LORD." ¹⁰The beginning of his kingdom was Babel, Erech, Accad, and Calneh, in the land of Shinar. ¹¹From that land he went into Assyria and built Nineveh, Rehoboth-Ir, Calah, and ¹²Resen between Nineveh and Calah; that is the great city. ¹³Egypt fathered Ludim, Anamim, Lehabim, Naphtuhim, ¹⁴Pathrusim, Casluhim (from whom⁵ the Philistines came), and Caphtorim.

¹⁵Canaan fathered Sidon his firstborn and Heth, ¹⁶and the Jebusites, the Amorites, the Girgashites, ¹⁷the Hivites, the Arkites, the Sinites, ¹⁸the Arvadites, the Zemarites, and the Hamathites. Afterward the clans of the Canaanites dispersed. ¹⁹And the territory of the Canaanites extended from Sidon in the direction of Gerar as far as Gaza, and in the direction of Sodom, Gomorrah, Admah, and Zeboiim, as far as Lasha. ²⁰These are the sons of Ham, by their clans, their languages, their lands, and their nations.

²¹To Shem also, the father of all the children of Eber, the elder brother of Japheth, children were born. ²²The sons of Shem: Elam, Asshur, Arpachshad, Lud, and Aram. ²³The sons of Aram: Uz, Hul, Gether, and Mash. ²⁴Arpachshad fathered Shelah; and Shelah fathered Eber. ²⁵To Eber were born two sons: the name of the one was Peleg,⁶ for in his days the earth was divided, and his brother's name was Joktan. ²⁶Joktan fathered Almodad, Sheleph, Hazarmaveth, Jerah, ²⁷Hadoram, Uzal, Diklah, ²⁸Obal, Abimael, Sheba, ²⁹Ophir, Havilah, and Jobab; all these were the sons of Joktan. ³⁰The territory in which they lived extended from Mesha in the direction of Sephar to the hill country of the east. ³¹These are the sons of Shem, by their

¹Or from these the whole earth was populated ²Or Noah, a man of the soil, was the first to plant a vineyard ³Japheth sounds like the Hebrew for enlarge ⁴Or he began to be a mighty man on the earth ⁵Or from where ⁶Peleg means division

clans, their languages, their lands, and their nations. [32] These are the clans of the sons of Noah, according to their genealogies, in their nations, and from these the nations spread abroad on the earth after the flood.

Matthew 9

And getting into a boat he crossed over and came to his own city. [2] And behold, some people brought to him a paralytic, lying on a bed. And when Jesus saw their faith, he said to the paralytic, "Take heart, my son; your sins are forgiven." [3] And behold, some of the scribes said to themselves, "This man is blaspheming." [4] But Jesus, knowing[1] their thoughts, said, "Why do you think evil in your hearts? [5] For which is easier, to say, 'Your sins are forgiven,' or to say, 'Rise and walk'? [6] But that you may know that the Son of Man has authority on earth to forgive sins"—he then said to the paralytic—"Rise, pick up your bed and go home." [7] And he rose and went home. [8] When the crowds saw it, they were afraid, and they glorified God, who had given such authority to men.

[9] As Jesus passed on from there, he saw a man called Matthew sitting at the tax booth, and he said to him, "Follow me." And he rose and followed him.

[10] And as Jesus[2] reclined at table in the house, behold, many tax collectors and sinners came and were reclining with Jesus and his disciples. [11] And when the Pharisees saw this, they said to his disciples, "Why does your teacher eat with tax collectors and sinners?" [12] But when he heard it, he said, "Those who are well have no need of a physician, but those who are sick. [13] Go and learn what this means, 'I desire mercy, and not sacrifice.' For I came not to call the righteous, but sinners."

[14] Then the disciples of John came to him, saying, "Why do we and the Pharisees fast,[3] but your disciples do not fast?" [15] And Jesus said to them, "Can the wedding guests mourn as long as the bridegroom is with them? The days will come when the bridegroom is taken away from them, and then they will fast. [16] No one puts a piece of unshrunk cloth on an old garment, for the patch tears away from the garment, and a worse tear is made. [17] Neither is new wine put into old wineskins. If it is, the skins burst and the wine is spilled and the skins are destroyed. But new wine is put into fresh wineskins, and so both are preserved."

[18] While he was saying these things to them, behold, a ruler came in and knelt before him, saying, "My daughter has just died, but come and lay your hand on her, and she will live." [19] And Jesus rose and followed him, with his disciples. [20] And behold, a woman who had suffered from a discharge of blood for twelve years came up behind him and touched the fringe of his garment, [21] for she said to herself, "If I only touch his garment, I will be made well." [22] Jesus turned, and seeing her he said, "Take heart, daughter; your faith has made you well." And instantly[4] the woman was made well. [23] And when Jesus came to the ruler's house and saw the flute players and the crowd making a commotion, [24] he said, "Go away, for the girl is not dead but sleeping." And they laughed at him. [25] But when the crowd had been put outside, he went in and took her by the hand, and the girl arose. [26] And the report of this went through all that district.

[27] And as Jesus passed on from there, two blind men followed him, crying aloud, "Have mercy on us, Son of David." [28] When he entered the house, the blind men came to him, and Jesus said to them, "Do you believe that I am able to do this?" They said to him, "Yes, Lord." [29] Then he touched their eyes, saying, "According to your faith be it done to you." [30] And their eyes were opened. And Jesus sternly warned them, "See that no one knows about it." [31] But they went away and spread his fame through all that district.

[32] As they were going away, behold, a demon-oppressed man who was mute was brought to him. [33] And when the demon had been cast out, the mute man spoke. And the crowds marveled, saying, "Never was anything like this seen in Israel." [34] But the Pharisees said, "He casts out demons by the prince of demons."

[35] And Jesus went throughout all the cities and villages, teaching in their synagogues and proclaiming the gospel of the kingdom and healing every disease and every affliction. [36] When he saw the crowds, he had compassion for them, because they were harassed and helpless, like sheep without a shepherd. [37] Then he said to his disciples, "The harvest is plentiful, but the laborers are few; [38] therefore pray

[1] Some manuscripts *perceiving* [2] Greek *he* [3] Some manuscripts add *much*, or *often* [4] Greek *from that hour*

earnestly to the Lord of the harvest to send out laborers into his harvest."

Ezra 9

After these things had been done, the officials approached me and said, "The people of Israel and the priests and the Levites have not separated themselves from the peoples of the lands with their abominations, from the Canaanites, the Hittites, the Perizzites, the Jebusites, the Ammonites, the Moabites, the Egyptians, and the Amorites. ²For they have taken some of their daughters to be wives for themselves and for their sons, so that the holy race¹ has mixed itself with the peoples of the lands. And in this faithlessness the hand of the officials and chief men has been foremost." ³As soon as I heard this, I tore my garment and my cloak and pulled hair from my head and beard and sat appalled. ⁴Then all who trembled at the words of the God of Israel, because of the faithlessness of the returned exiles, gathered around me while I sat appalled until the evening sacrifice. ⁵And at the evening sacrifice I rose from my fasting, with my garment and my cloak torn, and fell upon my knees and spread out my hands to the LORD my God, ⁶saying:

"O my God, I am ashamed and blush to lift my face to you, my God, for our iniquities have risen higher than our heads, and our guilt has mounted up to the heavens. ⁷From the days of our fathers to this day we have been in great guilt. And for our iniquities we, our kings, and our priests have been given into the hand of the kings of the lands, to the sword, to captivity, to plundering, and to utter shame, as it is today. ⁸But now for a brief moment favor has been shown by the LORD our God, to leave us a remnant and to give us a secure hold² within his holy place, that our God may brighten our eyes and grant us a little reviving in our slavery. ⁹For we are slaves. Yet our God has not forsaken us in our slavery, but has extended to us his steadfast love before the kings of Persia, to grant us some reviving to set up the house of our God, to repair its ruins, and to give us protection³ in Judea and Jerusalem.

¹⁰"And now, O our God, what shall we say after this? For we have forsaken your commandments, ¹¹which you commanded by your servants the prophets, saying, 'The land

that you are entering, to take possession of it, is a land impure with the impurity of the peoples of the lands, with their abominations that have filled it from end to end with their uncleanness. ¹²Therefore do not give your daughters to their sons, neither take their daughters for your sons, and never seek their peace or prosperity, that you may be strong and eat the good of the land and leave it for an inheritance to your children forever.' ¹³And after all that has come upon us for our evil deeds and for our great guilt, seeing that you, our God, have punished us less than our iniquities deserved and have given us such a remnant as this, ¹⁴shall we break your commandments again and intermarry with the peoples who practice these abominations? Would you not be angry with us until you consumed us, so that there should be no remnant, nor any to escape? ¹⁵O LORD, the God of Israel, you are just, for we are left a remnant that has escaped, as it is today. Behold, we are before you in our guilt, for none can stand before you because of this."

Acts 9

But Saul, still breathing threats and murder against the disciples of the Lord, went to the high priest ²and asked him for letters to the synagogues at Damascus, so that if he found any belonging to the Way, men or women, he might bring them bound to Jerusalem. ³Now as he went on his way, he approached Damascus, and suddenly a light from heaven shone around him. ⁴And falling to the ground he heard a voice saying to him, "Saul, Saul, why are you persecuting me?" ⁵And he said, "Who are you, Lord?" And he said, "I am Jesus, whom you are persecuting. ⁶But rise and enter the city, and you will be told what you are to do." ⁷The men who were traveling with him stood speechless, hearing the voice but seeing no one. ⁸Saul rose from the ground, and although his eyes were opened, he saw nothing. So they led him by the hand and brought him into Damascus. ⁹And for three days he was without sight, and neither ate nor drank.

¹⁰Now there was a disciple at Damascus named Ananias. The Lord said to him in a vision, "Ananias." And he said, "Here I am, Lord." ¹¹And the Lord said to him, "Rise and go to the street called Straight, and at the house

---

¹ Hebrew offspring ² Hebrew nail, or tent-pin ³ Hebrew a wall

of Judas look for a man of Tarsus named Saul, for behold, he is praying, [12] and he has seen in a vision a man named Ananias come in and lay his hands on him so that he might regain his sight." [13] But Ananias answered, "Lord, I have heard from many about this man, how much evil he has done to your saints at Jerusalem. [14] And here he has authority from the chief priests to bind all who call on your name." [15] But the Lord said to him, "Go, for he is a chosen instrument of mine to carry my name before the Gentiles and kings and the children of Israel. [16] For I will show him how much he must suffer for the sake of my name." [17] So Ananias departed and entered the house. And laying his hands on him he said, "Brother Saul, the Lord Jesus who appeared to you on the road by which you came has sent me so that you may regain your sight and be filled with the Holy Spirit." [18] And immediately something like scales fell from his eyes, and he regained his sight. Then he rose and was baptized; [19] and taking food, he was strengthened.

For some days he was with the disciples at Damascus. [20] And immediately he proclaimed Jesus in the synagogues, saying, "He is the Son of God." [21] And all who heard him were amazed and said, "Is not this the man who made havoc in Jerusalem of those who called upon this name? And has he not come here for this purpose, to bring them bound before the chief priests?" [22] But Saul increased all the more in strength, and confounded the Jews who lived in Damascus by proving that Jesus was the Christ.

[23] When many days had passed, the Jews[1] plotted to kill him, [24] but their plot became known to Saul. They were watching the gates day and night in order to kill him, [25] but his disciples took him by night and let him down through an opening in the wall,[2] lowering him in a basket.

[26] And when he had come to Jerusalem, he attempted to join the disciples. And they were all afraid of him, for they did not believe that he was a disciple. [27] But Barnabas took him and brought him to the apostles and declared to them how on the road he had seen the Lord, who spoke to him, and how at Damascus he had preached boldly in the name of Jesus. [28] So he went in and out among them at Jerusalem, preaching boldly in the name of the Lord. [29] And he spoke and disputed against the Hellenists.[3] But they were seeking to kill him. [30] And when the brothers learned this, they brought him down to Caesarea and sent him off to Tarsus.

[31] So the church throughout all Judea and Galilee and Samaria had peace and was being built up. And walking in the fear of the Lord and in the comfort of the Holy Spirit, it multiplied.

[32] Now as Peter went here and there among them all, he came down also to the saints who lived at Lydda. [33] There he found a man named Aeneas, bedridden for eight years, who was paralyzed. [34] And Peter said to him, "Aeneas, Jesus Christ heals you; rise and make your bed." And immediately he rose. [35] And all the residents of Lydda and Sharon saw him, and they turned to the Lord.

[36] Now there was in Joppa a disciple named Tabitha, which, translated, means Dorcas.[4] She was full of good works and acts of charity. [37] In those days she became ill and died, and when they had washed her, they laid her in an upper room. [38] Since Lydda was near Joppa, the disciples, hearing that Peter was there, sent two men to him, urging him, "Please come to us without delay." [39] So Peter rose and went with them. And when he arrived, they took him to the upper room. All the widows stood beside him weeping and showing tunics[5] and other garments that Dorcas made while she was with them. [40] But Peter put them all outside, and knelt down and prayed; and turning to the body he said, "Tabitha, arise." And she opened her eyes, and when she saw Peter she sat up. [41] And he gave her his hand and raised her up. Then calling the saints and widows, he presented her alive. [42] And it became known throughout all Joppa, and many believed in the Lord. [43] And he stayed in Joppa for many days with one Simon, a tanner.

[1] The Greek word Ioudaioi refers specifically here to Jewish religious leaders, and others under their influence, who opposed the Christian faith in that time [2] Greek through the wall [3] That is, Greek-speaking Jews [4] The Aramaic name Tabitha and the Greek name Dorcas both mean gazelle [5] Greek chiton, a long garment worn under the cloak next to the skin

JANUARY 10

Genesis 11

Now the whole earth had one language and the same words. ²And as people migrated from the east, they found a plain in the land of Shinar and settled there. ³And they said to one another, "Come, let us make bricks, and burn them thoroughly." And they had brick for stone, and bitumen for mortar. ⁴Then they said, "Come, let us build ourselves a city and a tower with its top in the heavens, and let us make a name for ourselves, lest we be dispersed over the face of the whole earth." ⁵And the LORD came down to see the city and the tower, which the children of man had built. ⁶And the LORD said, "Behold, they are one people, and they have all one language, and this is only the beginning of what they will do. And nothing that they propose to do will now be impossible for them. ⁷Come, let us go down and there confuse their language, so that they may not understand one another's speech." ⁸So the LORD dispersed them from there over the face of all the earth, and they left off building the city. ⁹Therefore its name was called Babel, because there the LORD confused[1] the language of all the earth. And from there the LORD dispersed them over the face of all the earth.

¹⁰These are the generations of Shem. When Shem was 100 years old, he fathered Arpachshad two years after the flood. ¹¹And Shem lived after he fathered Arpachshad 500 years and had other sons and daughters.

¹²When Arpachshad had lived 35 years, he fathered Shelah. ¹³And Arpachshad lived after he fathered Shelah 403 years and had other sons and daughters.

¹⁴When Shelah had lived 30 years, he fathered Eber. ¹⁵And Shelah lived after he fathered Eber 403 years and had other sons and daughters.

¹⁶When Eber had lived 34 years, he fathered Peleg. ¹⁷And Eber lived after he fathered Peleg 430 years and had other sons and daughters.

¹⁸When Peleg had lived 30 years, he fathered Reu. ¹⁹And Peleg lived after he fathered Reu 209 years and had other sons and daughters.

²⁰When Reu had lived 32 years, he fathered Serug. ²¹And Reu lived after he fathered Serug 207 years and had other sons and daughters.

²²When Serug had lived 30 years, he fathered Nahor. ²³And Serug lived after he fathered Nahor 200 years and had other sons and daughters.

²⁴When Nahor had lived 29 years, he fathered Terah. ²⁵And Nahor lived after he fathered Terah 119 years and had other sons and daughters.

²⁶When Terah had lived 70 years, he fathered Abram, Nahor, and Haran.

²⁷Now these are the generations of Terah. Terah fathered Abram, Nahor, and Haran; and Haran fathered Lot. ²⁸Haran died in the presence of his father Terah in the land of his kindred, in Ur of the Chaldeans. ²⁹And Abram and Nahor took wives. The name of Abram's wife was Sarai, and the name of Nahor's wife, Milcah, the daughter of Haran the father of Milcah and Iscah. ³⁰Now Sarai was barren; she had no child.

³¹Terah took Abram his son and Lot the son of Haran, his grandson, and Sarai his daughter-in-law, his son Abram's wife, and they went forth together from Ur of the Chaldeans to go into the land of Canaan, but when they came to Haran, they settled there. ³²The days of Terah were 205 years, and Terah died in Haran.

Matthew 10

And he called to him his twelve disciples and gave them authority over unclean spirits, to cast them out, and to heal every disease and every affliction. ²The names of the twelve apostles are these: first, Simon, who is called Peter, and Andrew his brother; James the son of Zebedee, and John his brother; ³Philip and Bartholomew; Thomas and Matthew the tax collector; James the son of Alphaeus, and

---

[1] Babel sounds like the Hebrew for confused

Thaddaeus;[1] [4]Simon the Zealot,[2] and Judas Iscariot, who betrayed him.

[5]These twelve Jesus sent out, instructing them, "Go nowhere among the Gentiles and enter no town of the Samaritans, [6]but go rather to the lost sheep of the house of Israel. [7]And proclaim as you go, saying, 'The kingdom of heaven is at hand.' [8]Heal the sick, raise the dead, cleanse lepers,[3] cast out demons. You received without paying; give without pay. [9]Acquire no gold or silver or copper for your belts, [10]no bag for your journey, or two tunics[4] or sandals or a staff, for the laborer deserves his food. [11]And whatever town or village you enter, find out who is worthy in it and stay there until you depart. [12]As you enter the house, greet it. [13]And if the house is worthy, let your peace come upon it, but if it is not worthy, let your peace return to you. [14]And if anyone will not receive you or listen to your words, shake off the dust from your feet when you leave that house or town. [15]Truly, I say to you, it will be more bearable on the day of judgment for the land of Sodom and Gomorrah than for that town.

[16]"Behold, I am sending you out as sheep in the midst of wolves, so be wise as serpents and innocent as doves. [17]Beware of men, for they will deliver you over to courts and flog you in their synagogues, [18]and you will be dragged before governors and kings for my sake, to bear witness before them and the Gentiles. [19]When they deliver you over, do not be anxious how you are to speak or what you are to say, for what you are to say will be given to you in that hour. [20]For it is not you who speak, but the Spirit of your Father speaking through you. [21]Brother will deliver brother over to death, and the father his child, and children will rise against parents and have them put to death, [22]and you will be hated by all for my name's sake. But the one who endures to the end will be saved. [23]When they persecute you in one town, flee to the next, for truly, I say to you, you will not have gone through all the towns of Israel before the Son of Man comes.

[24]"A disciple is not above his teacher, nor a servant[5] above his master. [25]It is enough for the disciple to be like his teacher, and the servant like his master. If they have called the master of the house Beelzebul, how much more will they malign[6] those of his household.

[26]"So have no fear of them, for nothing is covered that will not be revealed, or hidden that will not be known. [27]What I tell you in the dark, say in the light, and what you hear whispered, proclaim on the housetops. [28]And do not fear those who kill the body but cannot kill the soul. Rather fear him who can destroy both soul and body in hell.[7] [29]Are not two sparrows sold for a penny?[8] And not one of them will fall to the ground apart from your Father. [30]But even the hairs of your head are all numbered. [31]Fear not, therefore; you are of more value than many sparrows. [32]So everyone who acknowledges me before men, I also will acknowledge before my Father who is in heaven, [33]but whoever denies me before men, I also will deny before my Father who is in heaven.

[34]"Do not think that I have come to bring peace to the earth. I have not come to bring peace, but a sword. [35]For I have come to set a man against his father, and a daughter against her mother, and a daughter-in-law against her mother-in-law. [36]And a person's enemies will be those of his own household. [37]Whoever loves father or mother more than me is not worthy of me, and whoever loves son or daughter more than me is not worthy of me. [38]And whoever does not take his cross and follow me is not worthy of me. [39]Whoever finds his life will lose it, and whoever loses his life for my sake will find it.

[40]"Whoever receives you receives me, and whoever receives me receives him who sent me. [41]The one who receives a prophet because he is a prophet will receive a prophet's reward, and the one who receives a righteous person because he is a righteous person will receive a righteous person's reward. [42]And whoever gives one of these little ones even a cup of cold water because he is a disciple, truly, I say to you, he will by no means lose his reward."

Ezra 10

While Ezra prayed and made confession, weeping and casting himself down before the house of God, a very great assembly of men, women, and children, gathered to him out of Israel, for the people wept bitterly. [2]And Shecaniah the son of Jehiel, of the sons of Elam, addressed Ezra: "We have broken faith with our

---

[1] Some manuscripts *Lebbaeus*, or *Lebbaeus called Thaddaeus* [2] Greek *kananaios*, meaning *zealot* [3] *Leprosy* was a term for several skin diseases; see Leviticus 13 [4] Greek *chiton*, a long garment worn under the cloak next to the skin [5] Greek *bondservant*; also verse 25 [6] Greek lacks *will they malign* [7] Greek *Gehenna* [8] Greek *assarion*, Roman copper coin (Latin *quadrans*) worth about 1/16 of a *denarius* (which was a day's wage for a laborer)

God and have married foreign women from the peoples of the land, but even now there is hope for Israel in spite of this. [3]Therefore let us make a covenant with our God to put away all these wives and their children, according to the counsel of my lord[1] and of those who tremble at the commandment of our God, and let it be done according to the Law. [4]Arise, for it is your task, and we are with you; be strong and do it." [5]Then Ezra arose and made the leading priests and Levites and all Israel take an oath that they would do as had been said. So they took the oath.

[6]Then Ezra withdrew from before the house of God and went to the chamber of Jehohanan the son of Eliashib, where he spent the night,[2] neither eating bread nor drinking water, for he was mourning over the faithlessness of the exiles. [7]And a proclamation was made throughout Judah and Jerusalem to all the returned exiles that they should assemble at Jerusalem, [8]and that if anyone did not come within three days, by order of the officials and the elders all his property should be forfeited, and he himself banned from the congregation of the exiles.

[9]Then all the men of Judah and Benjamin assembled at Jerusalem within the three days. It was the ninth month, on the twentieth day of the month. And all the people sat in the open square before the house of God, trembling because of this matter and because of the heavy rain. [10]And Ezra the priest stood up and said to them, "You have broken faith and married foreign women, and so increased the guilt of Israel. [11]Now then make confession to the LORD, the God of your fathers and do his will. Separate yourselves from the peoples of the land and from the foreign wives." [12]Then all the assembly answered with a loud voice, "It is so; we must do as you have said. [13]But the people are many, and it is a time of heavy rain; we cannot stand in the open. Nor is this a task for one day or for two, for we have greatly transgressed in this matter. [14]Let our officials stand for the whole assembly. Let all in our cities who have taken foreign wives come at appointed times, and with them the elders and judges of every city, until the fierce wrath of our God over this matter is turned away from us." [15]Only Jonathan the son of Asahel and Jahzeiah the son of Tikvah opposed this, and Meshullam and Shabbethai the Levite supported them.

[16]Then the returned exiles did so. Ezra the priest selected men,[3] heads of fathers' houses, according to their fathers' houses, each of them designated by name. On the first day of the tenth month they sat down to examine the matter; [17]and by the first day of the first month they had come to the end of all the men who had married foreign women.

[18]Now there were found some of the sons of the priests who had married foreign women: Maaseiah, Eliezer, Jarib, and Gedaliah, some of the sons of Jeshua the son of Jozadak and his brothers. [19]They pledged themselves to put away their wives, and their guilt offering was a ram of the flock for their guilt.[4] [20]Of the sons of Immer: Hanani and Zebadiah. [21]Of the sons of Harim: Maaseiah, Elijah, Shemaiah, Jehiel, and Uzziah. [22]Of the sons of Pashhur: Elioenai, Maaseiah, Ishmael, Nethanel, Jozabad, and Elasah.

[23]Of the Levites: Jozabad, Shimei, Kelaiah (that is, Kelita), Pethahiah, Judah, and Eliezer. [24]Of the singers: Eliashib. Of the gatekeepers: Shallum, Telem, and Uri.

[25]And of Israel: of the sons of Parosh: Ramiah, Izziah, Malchijah, Mijamin, Eleazar, Hashabiah,[5] and Benaiah. [26]Of the sons of Elam: Mattaniah, Zechariah, Jehiel, Abdi, Jeremoth, and Elijah. [27]Of the sons of Zattu: Elioenai, Eliashib, Mattaniah, Jeremoth, Zabad, and Aziza. [28]Of the sons of Bebai were Jehohanan, Hananiah, Zabbai, and Athlai. [29]Of the sons of Bani were Meshullam, Malluch, Adaiah, Jashub, Sheal, and Jeremoth. [30]Of the sons of Pahathmoab: Adna, Chelal, Benaiah, Maaseiah, Mattaniah, Bezalel, Binnui, and Manasseh. [31]Of the sons of Harim: Eliezer, Isshijah, Malchijah, Shemaiah, Shimeon, [32]Benjamin, Malluch, and Shemariah. [33]Of the sons of Hashum: Mattenai, Mattattah, Zabad, Eliphelet, Jeremai, Manasseh, and Shimei. [34]Of the sons of Bani: Maadai, Amram, Uel, [35]Benaiah, Bedeiah, Cheluhi, [36]Vaniah, Meremoth, Eliashib, [37]Mattaniah, Mattenai, Jaasu. [38]Of the sons of Binnui:[6] Shimei, [39]Shelemiah, Nathan, Adaiah, [40]Machnadebai, Shashai, Sharai, [41]Azarel, Shelemiah, Shemariah, [42]Shallum, Amariah, and Joseph. [43]Of the sons of Nebo: Jeiel, Mattithiah, Zabad, Zebina, Jaddai, Joel, and Benaiah. [44]All these had married foreign women, and some of the women had even borne children.[7]

[1] Or of the Lord [2] Probable reading; Hebrew where he went [3] Syriac; Hebrew And there were selected Ezra. . . [4] Or as their reparation [5] Septuagint; Hebrew Malchijah [6] Septuagint; Hebrew Bani, Binnui [7] Or and they put them away with their children

Acts 10

At Caesarea there was a man named Cornelius, a centurion of what was known as the Italian Cohort, [2]a devout man who feared God with all his household, gave alms generously to the people, and prayed continually to God. [3]About the ninth hour of the day[1] he saw clearly in a vision an angel of God come in and say to him, "Cornelius." [4]And he stared at him in terror and said, "What is it, Lord?" And he said to him, "Your prayers and your alms have ascended as a memorial before God. [5]And now send men to Joppa and bring one Simon who is called Peter. [6]He is lodging with one Simon, a tanner, whose house is by the sea." [7]When the angel who spoke to him had departed, he called two of his servants and a devout soldier from among those who attended him, [8]and having related everything to them, he sent them to Joppa.

[9]The next day, as they were on their journey and approaching the city, Peter went up on the housetop about the sixth hour[2] to pray. [10]And he became hungry and wanted something to eat, but while they were preparing it, he fell into a trance [11]and saw the heavens opened and something like a great sheet descending, being let down by its four corners upon the earth. [12]In it were all kinds of animals and reptiles and birds of the air. [13]And there came a voice to him: "Rise, Peter; kill and eat." [14]But Peter said, "By no means, Lord; for I have never eaten anything that is common or unclean." [15]And the voice came to him again a second time, "What God has made clean, do not call common." [16]This happened three times, and the thing was taken up at once to heaven.

[17]Now while Peter was inwardly perplexed as to what the vision that he had seen might mean, behold, the men who were sent by Cornelius, having made inquiry for Simon's house, stood at the gate [18]and called out to ask whether Simon who was called Peter was lodging there. [19]And while Peter was pondering the vision, the Spirit said to him, "Behold, three men are looking for you. [20]Rise and go down and accompany them without hesitation,[3] for I have sent them." [21]And Peter went down to the men and said, "I am the one you are looking for. What is the reason for your coming?" [22]And they said, "Cornelius, a centurion, an

upright and God-fearing man, who is well spoken of by the whole Jewish nation, was directed by a holy angel to send for you to come to his house and to hear what you have to say." [23]So he invited them in to be his guests.

The next day he rose and went away with them, and some of the brothers from Joppa accompanied him. [24]And on the following day they entered Caesarea. Cornelius was expecting them and had called together his relatives and close friends. [25]When Peter entered, Cornelius met him and fell down at his feet and worshiped him. [26]But Peter lifted him up, saying, "Stand up; I too am a man." [27]And as he talked with him, he went in and found many persons gathered. [28]And he said to them, "You yourselves know how unlawful it is for a Jew to associate with or to visit anyone of another nation, but God has shown me that I should not call any person common or unclean. [29]So when I was sent for, I came without objection. I ask then why you sent for me."

[30]And Cornelius said, "Four days ago, about this hour, I was praying in my house at the ninth hour,[4] and behold, a man stood before me in bright clothing [31]and said, 'Cornelius, your prayer has been heard and your alms have been remembered before God. [32]Send therefore to Joppa and ask for Simon who is called Peter. He is lodging in the house of Simon, a tanner, by the sea.' [33]So I sent for you at once, and you have been kind enough to come. Now therefore we are all here in the presence of God to hear all that you have been commanded by the Lord."

[34]So Peter opened his mouth and said: "Truly I understand that God shows no partiality, [35]but in every nation anyone who fears him and does what is right is acceptable to him. [36]As for the word that he sent to Israel, preaching good news of peace through Jesus Christ (he is Lord of all), [37]you yourselves know what happened throughout all Judea, beginning from Galilee after the baptism that John proclaimed: [38]how God anointed Jesus of Nazareth with the Holy Spirit and with power. He went about doing good and healing all who were oppressed by the devil, for God was with him. [39]And we are witnesses of all that he did both in the country of the Jews and in Jerusalem. They put him to death by hanging him on a tree, [40]but God raised him on the third day and made him to

[1] That is, 3 P.M. [2] That is, noon [3] Or *accompany them, making no distinction* [4] That is, 3 P.M.

appear, [41] not to all the people but to us who had been chosen by God as witnesses, who ate and drank with him after he rose from the dead. [42] And he commanded us to preach to the people and to testify that he is the one appointed by God to be judge of the living and the dead. [43] To him all the prophets bear witness that everyone who believes in him receives forgiveness of sins through his name."

[44] While Peter was still saying these things, the Holy Spirit fell on all who heard the word.

[45] And the believers from among the circumcised who had come with Peter were amazed, because the gift of the Holy Spirit was poured out even on the Gentiles. [46] For they were hearing them speaking in tongues and extolling God. Then Peter declared, [47] "Can anyone withhold water for baptizing these people, who have received the Holy Spirit just as we have?" [48] And he commanded them to be baptized in the name of Jesus Christ. Then they asked him to remain for some days.

JANUARY 11

Genesis 12

Now the LORD said[1] to Abram, "Go from your country[2] and your kindred and your father's house to the land that I will show you. [2] And I will make of you a great nation, and I will bless you and make your name great, so that you will be a blessing. [3] I will bless those who bless you, and him who dishonors you I will curse, and in you all the families of the earth shall be blessed."[3]

[4] So Abram went, as the LORD had told him, and Lot went with him. Abram was seventy-five years old when he departed from Haran. [5] And Abram took Sarai his wife, and Lot his brother's son, and all their possessions that they had gathered, and the people that they had acquired in Haran, and they set out to go to the land of Canaan. When they came to the land of Canaan, [6] Abram passed through the land to the place at Shechem, to the oak[4] of Moreh. At that time the Canaanites were in the land. [7] Then the LORD appeared to Abram and said, "To your offspring I will give this land." So he built there an altar to the LORD, who had appeared to him. [8] From there he moved to the hill country on the east of Bethel and pitched his tent, with Bethel on the west and Ai on the east. And there he built an altar to the LORD and called upon the name of the LORD. [9] And Abram journeyed on, still going toward the Negeb.

[10] Now there was a famine in the land. So Abram went down to Egypt to sojourn there, for the famine was severe in the land. [11] When he was about to enter Egypt, he said to Sarai his wife, "I know that you are a woman beautiful in appearance, [12] and when the Egyptians see you, they will say, 'This is his wife.' Then they will kill me, but they will let you live. [13] Say you are my sister, that it may go well with me because of you, and that my life may be spared for your sake." [14] When Abram entered Egypt, the Egyptians saw that the woman was very beautiful. [15] And when the princes of Pharaoh saw her, they praised her to Pharaoh. And the woman was taken into Pharaoh's house. [16] And for her sake he dealt well with Abram; and he had sheep, oxen, male donkeys, male servants, female servants, female donkeys, and camels.

[17] But the LORD afflicted Pharaoh and his house with great plagues because of Sarai, Abram's wife. [18] So Pharaoh called Abram and said, "What is this you have done to me? Why did you not tell me that she was your wife? [19] Why did you say, 'She is my sister,' so that I took her for my wife? Now then, here is your wife; take her, and go." [20] And Pharaoh gave men orders concerning him, and they sent him away with his wife and all that he had.

[1] Or had said [2] Or land [3] Or by you all the families of the earth shall bless themselves [4] Or terebinth

--- **Matthew 11** ---

When Jesus had finished instructing his twelve disciples, he went on from there to teach and preach in their cities.

[2] Now when John heard in prison about the deeds of the Christ, he sent word by his disciples [3] and said to him, "Are you the one who is to come, or shall we look for another?" [4] And Jesus answered them, "Go and tell John what you hear and see: [5] the blind receive their sight and the lame walk, lepers[1] are cleansed and the deaf hear, and the dead are raised up, and the poor have good news preached to them. [6] And blessed is the one who is not offended by me."

[7] As they went away, Jesus began to speak to the crowds concerning John: "What did you go out into the wilderness to see? A reed shaken by the wind? [8] What then did you go out to see? A man[2] dressed in soft clothing? Behold, those who wear soft clothing are in kings' houses. [9] What then did you go out to see? A prophet?[3] Yes, I tell you, and more than a prophet. [10] This is he of whom it is written,

" 'Behold, I send my messenger before your face,
    who will prepare your way before you.'

[11] Truly, I say to you, among those born of women there has arisen no one greater than John the Baptist. Yet the one who is least in the kingdom of heaven is greater than he. [12] From the days of John the Baptist until now the kingdom of heaven has suffered violence,[4] and the violent take it by force. [13] For all the Prophets and the Law prophesied until John, [14] and if you are willing to accept it, he is Elijah who is to come. [15] He who has ears to hear,[5] let him hear.

[16] "But to what shall I compare this generation? It is like children sitting in the marketplaces and calling to their playmates,

[17]   " 'We played the flute for you, and you did not dance;
        we sang a dirge, and you did not mourn.'

[18] For John came neither eating nor drinking, and they say, 'He has a demon.' [19] The Son of Man came eating and drinking, and they say, 'Look at him! A glutton and a drunkard, a friend of tax collectors and sinners!' Yet wisdom is justified by her deeds."[6]

[20] Then he began to denounce the cities where most of his mighty works had been done, because they did not repent. [21] "Woe to you, Chorazin! Woe to you, Bethsaida! For if the mighty works done in you had been done in Tyre and Sidon, they would have repented long ago in sackcloth and ashes. [22] But I tell you, it will be more bearable on the day of judgment for Tyre and Sidon than for you. [23] And you, Capernaum, will you be exalted to heaven? You will be brought down to Hades. For if the mighty works done in you had been done in Sodom, it would have remained until this day. [24] But I tell you that it will be more tolerable on the day of judgment for the land of Sodom than for you."

[25] At that time Jesus declared, "I thank you, Father, Lord of heaven and earth, that you have hidden these things from the wise and understanding and revealed them to little children; [26] yes, Father, for such was your gracious will.[7] [27] All things have been handed over to me by my Father, and no one knows the Son except the Father, and no one knows the Father except the Son and anyone to whom the Son chooses to reveal him. [28] Come to me, all who labor and are heavy laden, and I will give you rest. [29] Take my yoke upon you, and learn from me, for I am gentle and lowly in heart, and you will find rest for your souls. [30] For my yoke is easy, and my burden is light."

--- **Nehemiah 1** ---

The words of Nehemiah the son of Hacaliah. Now it happened in the month of Chislev, in the twentieth year, as I was in Susa the citadel, [2] that Hanani, one of my brothers, came with certain men from Judah. And I asked them concerning the Jews who escaped, who had survived the exile, and concerning Jerusalem. [3] And they said to me, "The remnant there in the province who had survived the exile is in great trouble and shame. The wall of Jerusalem is broken down, and its gates are destroyed by fire."

[4] As soon as I heard these words I sat down and wept and mourned for days, and I continued fasting and praying before the God of heaven. [5] And I said, "O LORD God of heaven, the great and awesome God who keeps covenant and steadfast love with those who love him and keep his commandments, [6] let your

[1] Leprosy was a term for several skin diseases; see Leviticus 13 [2] Or Why then did you go out? To see a man. . . [3] Some manuscripts Why then did you go out? To see a prophet? [4] Or has been coming violently [5] Some manuscripts omit to hear [6] Some manuscripts children (compare Luke 7:35) [7] Or for so it pleased you well

ear be attentive and your eyes open, to hear the prayer of your servant that I now pray before you day and night for the people of Israel your servants, confessing the sins of the people of Israel, which we have sinned against you. Even I and my father's house have sinned. [7]We have acted very corruptly against you and have not kept the commandments, the statutes, and the rules that you commanded your servant Moses. [8]Remember the word that you commanded your servant Moses, saying, 'If you are unfaithful, I will scatter you among the peoples, [9]but if you return to me and keep my commandments and do them, though your outcasts are in the uttermost parts of heaven, from there I will gather them and bring them to the place that I have chosen, to make my name dwell there.' [10]They are your servants and your people, whom you have redeemed by your great power and by your strong hand. [11]O Lord, let your ear be attentive to the prayer of your servant, and to the prayer of your servants who delight to fear your name, and give success to your servant today, and grant him mercy in the sight of this man."

Now I was cupbearer to the king.

Acts 11

Now the apostles and the brothers[1] who were throughout Judea heard that the Gentiles also had received the word of God. [2]So when Peter went up to Jerusalem, the circumcision party[2] criticized him, saying, [3]"You went to uncircumcised men and ate with them." [4]But Peter began and explained it to them in order: [5]"I was in the city of Joppa praying, and in a trance I saw a vision, something like a great sheet descending, being let down from heaven by its four corners, and it came down to me. [6]Looking at it closely, I observed animals and beasts of prey and reptiles and birds of the air. [7]And I heard a voice saying to me, 'Rise, Peter; kill and eat.' [8]But I said, 'By no means, Lord; for nothing common or unclean has ever entered my mouth.' [9]But the voice answered a second time from heaven, 'What God has made clean, do not call common.' [10]This happened three times, and all was drawn up again into heaven. [11]And behold, at that very moment three men arrived at the house in which we were, sent to

me from Caesarea. [12]And the Spirit told me to go with them, making no distinction. These six brothers also accompanied me, and we entered the man's house. [13]And he told us how he had seen the angel stand in his house and say, 'Send to Joppa and bring Simon who is called Peter; [14]he will declare to you a message by which you will be saved, you and all your household.' [15]As I began to speak, the Holy Spirit fell on them just as on us at the beginning. [16]And I remembered the word of the Lord, how he said, 'John baptized with water, but you will be baptized with the Holy Spirit.' [17]If then God gave the same gift to them as he gave to us when we believed in the Lord Jesus Christ, who was I that I could stand in God's way?" [18]When they heard these things they fell silent. And they glorified God, saying, "Then to the Gentiles also God has granted repentance that leads to life."

[19]Now those who were scattered because of the persecution that arose over Stephen traveled as far as Phoenicia and Cyprus and Antioch, speaking the word to no one except Jews. [20]But there were some of them, men of Cyprus and Cyrene, who on coming to Antioch spoke to the Hellenists[3] also, preaching the Lord Jesus. [21]And the hand of the Lord was with them, and a great number who believed turned to the Lord. [22]The report of this came to the ears of the church in Jerusalem, and they sent Barnabas to Antioch. [23]When he came and saw the grace of God, he was glad, and he exhorted them all to remain faithful to the Lord with steadfast purpose, [24]for he was a good man, full of the Holy Spirit and of faith. And a great many people were added to the Lord. [25]So Barnabas went to Tarsus to look for Saul, [26]and when he had found him, he brought him to Antioch. For a whole year they met with the church and taught a great many people. And in Antioch the disciples were first called Christians.

[27]Now in these days prophets came down from Jerusalem to Antioch. [28]And one of them named Agabus stood up and foretold by the Spirit that there would be a great famine over all the world (this took place in the days of Claudius). [29]So the disciples determined, every one according to his ability, to send relief to the brothers[4] living in Judea. [30]And they did so, sending it to the elders by the hand of Barnabas and Saul.

---

[1] Or brothers and sisters [2] Or Jerusalem, those of the circumcision [3] Or Greeks (that is, Greek-speaking non-Jews) [4] Or brothers and sisters

JANUARY 12

—————————— *Genesis 13* ——————————

So Abram went up from Egypt, he and his wife and all that he had, and Lot with him, into the Negeb.

²Now Abram was very rich in livestock, in silver, and in gold. ³And he journeyed on from the Negeb as far as Bethel to the place where his tent had been at the beginning, between Bethel and Ai, ⁴to the place where he had made an altar at the first. And there Abram called upon the name of the LORD. ⁵And Lot, who went with Abram, also had flocks and herds and tents, ⁶so that the land could not support both of them dwelling together; for their possessions were so great that they could not dwell together, ⁷and there was strife between the herdsmen of Abram's livestock and the herdsmen of Lot's livestock. At that time the Canaanites and the Perizzites were dwelling in the land.

⁸Then Abram said to Lot, "Let there be no strife between you and me, and between your herdsmen and my herdsmen, for we are kinsmen.¹ ⁹Is not the whole land before you? Separate yourself from me. If you take the left hand, then I will go to the right, or if you take the right hand, then I will go to the left." ¹⁰And Lot lifted up his eyes and saw that the Jordan Valley was well watered everywhere like the garden of the LORD, like the land of Egypt, in the direction of Zoar. (This was before the LORD destroyed Sodom and Gomorrah.) ¹¹So Lot chose for himself all the Jordan Valley, and Lot journeyed east. Thus they separated from each other. ¹²Abram settled in the land of Canaan, while Lot settled among the cities of the valley and moved his tent as far as Sodom. ¹³Now the men of Sodom were wicked, great sinners against the LORD.

¹⁴The LORD said to Abram, after Lot had separated from him, "Lift up your eyes and look from the place where you are, northward and southward and eastward and westward, ¹⁵for all the land that you see I will give to you and to your offspring forever. ¹⁶I will make your offspring as the dust of the earth, so that if one

can count the dust of the earth, your offspring also can be counted. ¹⁷Arise, walk through the length and the breadth of the land, for I will give it to you." ¹⁸So Abram moved his tent and came and settled by the oaks² of Mamre, which are at Hebron, and there he built an altar to the LORD.

—————————— *Matthew 12* ——————————

At that time Jesus went through the grainfields on the Sabbath. His disciples were hungry, and they began to pluck heads of grain and to eat. ²But when the Pharisees saw it, they said to him, "Look, your disciples are doing what is not lawful to do on the Sabbath." ³He said to them, "Have you not read what David did when he was hungry, and those who were with him: ⁴how he entered the house of God and ate the bread of the Presence, which it was not lawful for him to eat nor for those who were with him, but only for the priests? ⁵Or have you not read in the Law how on the Sabbath the priests in the temple profane the Sabbath and are guiltless? ⁶I tell you, something greater than the temple is here. ⁷And if you had known what this means, 'I desire mercy, and not sacrifice,' you would not have condemned the guiltless. ⁸For the Son of Man is lord of the Sabbath."

⁹He went on from there and entered their synagogue. ¹⁰And a man was there with a withered hand. And they asked him, "Is it lawful to heal on the Sabbath?"—so that they might accuse him. ¹¹He said to them, "Which one of you who has a sheep, if it falls into a pit on the Sabbath, will not take hold of it and lift it out? ¹²Of how much more value is a man than a sheep! So it is lawful to do good on the Sabbath." ¹³Then he said to the man, "Stretch out your hand." And the man stretched it out, and it was restored, healthy like the other. ¹⁴But the Pharisees went out and conspired against him, how to destroy him.

¹⁵Jesus, aware of this, withdrew from there. And many followed him, and he healed them

¹ Hebrew *we are men, brothers* ² Or *terebinths*

all [16] and ordered them not to make him known. [17] This was to fulfill what was spoken by the prophet Isaiah:

[18]   "Behold, my servant whom I have chosen,
              my beloved with whom my soul is
                  well pleased.
         I will put my Spirit upon him,
              and he will proclaim justice to the
                  Gentiles.
[19]   He will not quarrel or cry aloud,
              nor will anyone hear his voice in the
                  streets;
[20]   a bruised reed he will not break,
              and a smoldering wick he will not
                  quench,
         until he brings justice to victory;
[21]   and in his name the Gentiles will
                  hope."

[22] Then a demon-oppressed man who was blind and mute was brought to him, and he healed him, so that the man spoke and saw. [23] And all the people were amazed, and said, "Can this be the Son of David?" [24] But when the Pharisees heard it, they said, "It is only by Beelzebul, the prince of demons, that this man casts out demons." [25] Knowing their thoughts, he said to them, "Every kingdom divided against itself is laid waste, and no city or house divided against itself will stand. [26] And if Satan casts out Satan, he is divided against himself. How then will his kingdom stand? [27] And if I cast out demons by Beelzebul, by whom do your sons cast them out? Therefore they will be your judges. [28] But if it is by the Spirit of God that I cast out demons, then the kingdom of God has come upon you. [29] Or how can someone enter a strong man's house and plunder his goods, unless he first binds the strong man? Then indeed he may plunder his house. [30] Whoever is not with me is against me, and whoever does not gather with me scatters. [31] Therefore I tell you, every sin and blasphemy will be forgiven people, but the blasphemy against the Spirit will not be forgiven. [32] And whoever speaks a word against the Son of Man will be forgiven, but whoever speaks against the Holy Spirit will not be forgiven, either in this age or in the age to come. [33] "Either make the tree good and its fruit good, or make the tree bad and its fruit bad, for the tree is known by its fruit. [34] You brood of vipers! How can you speak good, when you are evil? For out of the abundance of the heart the mouth speaks. [35] The good person out of his good treasure brings forth good, and the evil person out of his evil treasure brings forth evil. [36] I tell you, on the day of judgment people will give account for every careless word they speak, [37] for by your words you will be justified, and by your words you will be condemned."

[38] Then some of the scribes and Pharisees answered him, saying, "Teacher, we wish to see a sign from you." [39] But he answered them, "An evil and adulterous generation seeks for a sign, but no sign will be given to it except the sign of the prophet Jonah. [40] For just as Jonah was three days and three nights in the belly of the great fish, so will the Son of Man be three days and three nights in the heart of the earth. [41] The men of Nineveh will rise up at the judgment with this generation and condemn it, for they repented at the preaching of Jonah, and behold, something greater than Jonah is here. [42] The queen of the South will rise up at the judgment with this generation and condemn it, for she came from the ends of the earth to hear the wisdom of Solomon, and behold, something greater than Solomon is here.

[43] "When the unclean spirit has gone out of a person, it passes through waterless places seeking rest, but finds none. [44] Then it says, 'I will return to my house from which I came.' And when it comes, it finds the house empty, swept, and put in order. [45] Then it goes and brings with it seven other spirits more evil than itself, and they enter and dwell there, and the last state of that person is worse than the first. So also will it be with this evil generation."

[46] While he was still speaking to the people, behold, his mother and his brothers stood outside, asking to speak to him. [1] [48] But he replied to the man who told him, "Who is my mother, and who are my brothers?" [49] And stretching out his hand toward his disciples, he said, "Here are my mother and my brothers! [50] For whoever does the will of my Father in heaven is my brother and sister and mother."

——————— *Nehemiah 2* ———————

In the month of Nisan, in the twentieth year of King Artaxerxes, when wine was before him, I took up the wine and gave it to the king. Now I

---

[1] Some manuscripts insert verse 47: *Someone told him, "Your mother and your brothers are standing outside, asking to speak to you"*

had not been sad in his presence. [2]And the king said to me, "Why is your face sad, seeing you are not sick? This is nothing but sadness of the heart." Then I was very much afraid. [3]I said to the king, "Let the king live forever! Why should not my face be sad, when the city, the place of my fathers' graves, lies in ruins, and its gates have been destroyed by fire?" [4]Then the king said to me, "What are you requesting?" So I prayed to the God of heaven. [5]And I said to the king, "If it pleases the king, and if your servant has found favor in your sight, that you send me to Judah, to the city of my fathers' graves, that I may rebuild it." [6]And the king said to me (the queen sitting beside him), "How long will you be gone, and when will you return?" So it pleased the king to send me when I had given him a time. [7]And I said to the king, "If it pleases the king, let letters be given me to the governors of the province Beyond the River, that they may let me pass through until I come to Judah, [8]and a letter to Asaph, the keeper of the king's forest, that he may give me timber to make beams for the gates of the fortress of the temple, and for the wall of the city, and for the house that I shall occupy." And the king granted me what I asked, for the good hand of my God was upon me.

[9]Then I came to the governors of the province Beyond the River and gave them the king's letters. Now the king had sent with me officers of the army and horsemen. [10]But when Sanballat the Horonite and Tobiah the Ammonite servant heard this, it displeased them greatly that someone had come to seek the welfare of the people of Israel.

[11]So I went to Jerusalem and was there three days. [12]Then I arose in the night, I and a few men with me. And I told no one what my God had put into my heart to do for Jerusalem. There was no animal with me but the one on which I rode. [13]I went out by night by the Valley Gate to the Dragon Spring and to the Dung Gate, and I inspected the walls of Jerusalem that were broken down and its gates that had been destroyed by fire. [14]Then I went on to the Fountain Gate and to the King's Pool, but there was no room for the animal that was under me to pass. [15]Then I went up in the night by the valley and inspected the wall, and I turned back and entered by the Valley Gate, and so returned. [16]And the officials did not know where I had gone or what I was doing, and I had not yet told the Jews, the priests, the nobles, the officials, and the rest who were to do the work.

[17]Then I said to them, "You see the trouble we are in, how Jerusalem lies in ruins with its gates burned. Come, let us build the wall of Jerusalem, that we may no longer suffer derision." [18]And I told them of the hand of my God that had been upon me for good, and also of the words that the king had spoken to me. And they said, "Let us rise up and build." So they strengthened their hands for the good work. [19]But when Sanballat the Horonite and Tobiah the Ammonite servant and Geshem the Arab heard of it, they jeered at us and despised us and said, "What is this thing that you are doing? Are you rebelling against the king?" [20]Then I replied to them, "The God of heaven will make us prosper, and we his servants will arise and build, but you have no portion or right or claim[1] in Jerusalem."

Acts 12

About that time Herod the king laid violent hands on some who belonged to the church. [2]He killed James the brother of John with the sword, [3]and when he saw that it pleased the Jews, he proceeded to arrest Peter also. This was during the days of Unleavened Bread. [4]And when he had seized him, he put him in prison, delivering him over to four squads of soldiers to guard him, intending after the Passover to bring him out to the people. [5]So Peter was kept in prison, but earnest prayer for him was made to God by the church.

[6]Now when Herod was about to bring him out, on that very night, Peter was sleeping between two soldiers, bound with two chains, and sentries before the door were guarding the prison. [7]And behold, an angel of the Lord stood next to him, and a light shone in the cell. He struck Peter on the side and woke him, saying, "Get up quickly." And the chains fell off his hands. [8]And the angel said to him, "Dress yourself and put on your sandals." And he did so. And he said to him, "Wrap your cloak around you and follow me." [9]And he went out and followed him. He did not know that what was being done by the angel was real, but thought he was seeing a vision. [10]When they had passed the first and the second guard, they came to the iron gate leading into the city. It opened

[1] Or memorial

for them of its own accord, and they went out and went along one street, and immediately the angel left him. [11] When Peter came to himself, he said, "Now I am sure that the Lord has sent his angel and rescued me from the hand of Herod and from all that the Jewish people were expecting."

[12] When he realized this, he went to the house of Mary, the mother of John whose other name was Mark, where many were gathered together and were praying. [13] And when he knocked at the door of the gateway, a servant girl named Rhoda came to answer. [14] Recognizing Peter's voice, in her joy she did not open the gate but ran in and reported that Peter was standing at the gate. [15] They said to her, "You are out of your mind." But she kept insisting that it was so, and they kept saying, "It is his angel!" [16] But Peter continued knocking, and when they opened, they saw him and were amazed. [17] But motioning to them with his hand to be silent, he described to them how the Lord had brought him out of the prison. And he said, "Tell these things to James and to the brothers."[1] Then he departed and went to another place.

[18] Now when day came, there was no little disturbance among the soldiers over what had become of Peter. [19] And after Herod searched for him and did not find him, he examined the sentries and ordered that they should be put to death. Then he went down from Judea to Caesarea and spent time there.

[20] Now Herod was angry with the people of Tyre and Sidon, and they came to him with one accord, and having persuaded Blastus, the king's chamberlain,[2] they asked for peace, because their country depended on the king's country for food. [21] On an appointed day Herod put on his royal robes, took his seat upon the throne, and delivered an oration to them. [22] And the people were shouting, "The voice of a god, and not of a man!" [23] Immediately an angel of the Lord struck him down, because he did not give God the glory, and he was eaten by worms and breathed his last.

[24] But the word of God increased and multiplied.

[25] And Barnabas and Saul returned from[3] Jerusalem when they had completed their service, bringing with them John, whose other name was Mark.

JANUARY 13

Genesis 14

In the days of Amraphel king of Shinar, Arioch king of Ellasar, Chedorlaomer king of Elam, and Tidal king of Goiim, [2] these kings made war with Bera king of Sodom, Birsha king of Gomorrah, Shinab king of Admah, Shemeber king of Zeboiim, and the king of Bela (that is, Zoar). [3] And all these joined forces in the Valley of Siddim (that is, the Salt Sea). [4] Twelve years they had served Chedorlaomer, but in the thirteenth year they rebelled. [5] In the fourteenth year Chedorlaomer and the kings who were with him came and defeated the Rephaim in Ashteroth-karnaim, the Zuzim in Ham, the Emim in Shaveh-kiriathaim, [6] and the Horites in their hill country of Seir as far as El-paran on the border of the wilderness. [7] Then they turned back and came to En-mishpat (that is, Kadesh) and defeated all the country of the Amalekites, and also the Amorites who were dwelling in Hazazon-tamar.

[8] Then the king of Sodom, the king of Gomorrah, the king of Admah, the king of Zeboiim, and the king of Bela (that is, Zoar) went out, and they joined battle in the Valley of Siddim [9] with Chedorlaomer king of Elam, Tidal king of Goiim, Amraphel king of Shinar, and Arioch king of Ellasar, four kings against five. [10] Now the Valley of Siddim was full of bitumen pits, and as the kings of Sodom and Gomorrah fled, some fell into them, and the rest fled to the hill

[1] Or brothers and sisters [2] That is, trusted personal attendant [3] Some manuscripts to

country. [11] So the enemy took all the possessions of Sodom and Gomorrah, and all their provisions, and went their way. [12] They also took Lot, the son of Abram's brother, who was dwelling in Sodom, and his possessions, and went their way.

[13] Then one who had escaped came and told Abram the Hebrew, who was living by the oaks[1] of Mamre the Amorite, brother of Eshcol and of Aner. These were allies of Abram. [14] When Abram heard that his kinsman had been taken captive, he led forth his trained men, born in his house, 318 of them, and went in pursuit as far as Dan. [15] And he divided his forces against them by night, he and his servants, and defeated them and pursued them to Hobah, north of Damascus. [16] Then he brought back all the possessions, and also brought back his kinsman Lot with his possessions, and the women and the people.

[17] After his return from the defeat of Chedorlaomer and the kings who were with him, the king of Sodom went out to meet him at the Valley of Shaveh (that is, the King's Valley). [18] And Melchizedek king of Salem brought out bread and wine. (He was priest of God Most High.) [19] And he blessed him and said,

> "Blessed be Abram by God Most High,
>   Possessor[2] of heaven and earth;
> [20]   and blessed be God Most High,
>   who has delivered your enemies into
>   your hand!"

And Abram gave him a tenth of everything. [21] And the king of Sodom said to Abram, "Give me the persons, but take the goods for yourself." [22] But Abram said to the king of Sodom, "I have lifted my hand[3] to the LORD, God Most High, Possessor of heaven and earth, [23] that I would not take a thread or a sandal strap or anything that is yours, lest you should say, 'I have made Abram rich.' [24] I will take nothing but what the young men have eaten, and the share of the men who went with me. Let Aner, Eshcol, and Mamre take their share."

Matthew 13

That same day Jesus went out of the house and sat beside the sea. [2] And great crowds gathered about him, so that he got into a boat and sat down. And the whole crowd stood on

the beach. [3] And he told them many things in parables, saying: "A sower went out to sow. [4] And as he sowed, some seeds fell along the path, and the birds came and devoured them. [5] Other seeds fell on rocky ground, where they did not have much soil, and immediately they sprang up, since they had no depth of soil, [6] but when the sun rose they were scorched. And since they had no root, they withered away. [7] Other seeds fell among thorns, and the thorns grew up and choked them. [8] Other seeds fell on good soil and produced grain, some a hundredfold, some sixty, some thirty. [9] He who has ears,[4] let him hear."

[10] Then the disciples came and said to him, "Why do you speak to them in parables?" [11] And he answered them, "To you it has been given to know the secrets of the kingdom of heaven, but to them it has not been given. [12] For to the one who has, more will be given, and he will have an abundance, but from the one who has not, even what he has will be taken away. [13] This is why I speak to them in parables, because seeing they do not see, and hearing they do not hear, nor do they understand. [14] Indeed, in their case the prophecy of Isaiah is fulfilled that says:

> " "You will indeed hear but never
>   understand,
>   and you will indeed see but never
>   perceive."
> [15]   For this people's heart has grown dull,
>   and with their ears they can barely
>   hear,
>   and their eyes they have closed,
>   lest they should see with their eyes
>   and hear with their ears
>   and understand with their heart
>   and turn, and I would heal them.'

[16] But blessed are your eyes, for they see, and your ears, for they hear. [17] For truly, I say to you, many prophets and righteous people longed to see what you see, and did not see it, and to hear what you hear, and did not hear it.

[18] "Hear then the parable of the sower: [19] When anyone hears the word of the kingdom and does not understand it, the evil one comes and snatches away what has been sown in his heart. This is what was sown along the path. [20] As for what was sown on rocky ground, this is the one who hears the word and immediately receives it with joy, [21] yet he has no root in

---

[1] Or terebinths [2] Or Creator; also verse 22 [3] Or I have taken a solemn oath [4] Some manuscripts add here and in verse 43 to hear

himself, but endures for a while, and when tribulation or persecution arises on account of the
word, immediately he falls away.[1] 22As for what
was sown among thorns, this is the one who
hears the word, but the cares of the world and
the deceitfulness of riches choke the word, and
it proves unfruitful. 23As for what was sown on
good soil, this is the one who hears the word
and understands it. He indeed bears fruit and
yields, in one case a hundredfold, in another
sixty, and in another thirty."

24He put another parable before them, saying, "The kingdom of heaven may be compared
to a man who sowed good seed in his field,
25but while his men were sleeping, his enemy
came and sowed weeds[2] among the wheat and
went away. 26So when the plants came up and
bore grain, then the weeds appeared also.
27And the servants[3] of the master of the house
came and said to him, 'Master, did you not sow
good seed in your field? How then does it have
weeds?' 28He said to them, 'An enemy has done
this.' So the servants said to him, 'Then do you
want us to go and gather them?' 29But he said,
'No, lest in gathering the weeds you root up
the wheat along with them. 30Let both grow
together until the harvest, and at harvest time
I will tell the reapers, Gather the weeds first and
bind them in bundles to be burned, but gather
the wheat into my barn.'"

31He put another parable before them, saying, "The kingdom of heaven is like a grain of
mustard seed that a man took and sowed in his
field. 32It is the smallest of all seeds, but when it
has grown it is larger than all the garden plants
and becomes a tree, so that the birds of the air
come and make nests in its branches."

33He told them another parable. "The kingdom of heaven is like leaven that a woman took
and hid in three measures of flour, till it was
all leavened."

34All these things Jesus said to the crowds
in parables; indeed, he said nothing to them
without a parable. 35This was to fulfill what was
spoken by the prophet:[4]

> "I will open my mouth in parables;
> I will utter what has been hidden since
>   the foundation of the world."

36Then he left the crowds and went into the
house. And his disciples came to him, saying,
"Explain to us the parable of the weeds of the
field." 37He answered, "The one who sows
the good seed is the Son of Man. 38The field
is the world, and the good seed is the sons of
the kingdom. The weeds are the sons of the
evil one, 39and the enemy who sowed them
is the devil. The harvest is the end of the age,
and the reapers are angels. 40Just as the weeds
are gathered and burned with fire, so will it be
at the end of the age. 41The Son of Man will
send his angels, and they will gather out of his
kingdom all causes of sin and all law-breakers,
42and throw them into the fiery furnace. In that
place there will be weeping and gnashing of
teeth. 43Then the righteous will shine like the
sun in the kingdom of their Father. He who has
ears, let him hear.

44"The kingdom of heaven is like treasure
hidden in a field, which a man found and covered up. Then in his joy he goes and sells all
that he has and buys that field.

45"Again, the kingdom of heaven is like a
merchant in search of fine pearls, 46who, on
finding one pearl of great value, went and sold
all that he had and bought it.

47"Again, the kingdom of heaven is like a net
that was thrown into the sea and gathered fish
of every kind. 48When it was full, men drew it
ashore and sat down and sorted the good into
containers but threw away the bad. 49So it will
be at the end of the age. The angels will come
out and separate the evil from the righteous
50and throw them into the fiery furnace. In
that place there will be weeping and gnashing
of teeth.

51"Have you understood all these things?"
They said to him, "Yes." 52And he said to them,
"Therefore every scribe who has been trained
for the kingdom of heaven is like a master of a
house, who brings out of his treasure what is
new and what is old."

53And when Jesus had finished these parables, he went away from there, 54and coming to his hometown he taught them in their
synagogue, so that they were astonished, and
said, "Where did this man get this wisdom and
these mighty works? 55Is not this the carpenter's son? Is not his mother called Mary? And
are not his brothers James and Joseph and
Simon and Judas? 56And are not all his sisters
with us? Where then did this man get all these
things?" 57And they took offense at him. But
Jesus said to them, "A prophet is not without

---

[1] Or stumbles [2] Probably darnel, a wheat-like weed [3] Greek bondservants; also verse 28 [4] Some manuscripts Isaiah the prophet

honor except in his hometown and in his own household." ⁵⁸And he did not do many mighty works there, because of their unbelief.

Nehemiah 3

Then Eliashib the high priest rose up with his brothers the priests, and they built the Sheep Gate. They consecrated it and set its doors. They consecrated it as far as the Tower of the Hundred, as far as the Tower of Hananel. ²And next to him the men of Jericho built. And next to them¹ Zaccur the son of Imri built.

³The sons of Hassenaah built the Fish Gate. They laid its beams and set its doors, its bolts, and its bars. ⁴And next to them Meremoth the son of Uriah, son of Hakkoz repaired. And next to them Meshullam the son of Berechiah, son of Meshezabel repaired. And next to them Zadok the son of Baana repaired. ⁵And next to them the Tekoites repaired, but their nobles would not stoop to serve their Lord.²

⁶Joiada the son of Paseah and Meshullam the son of Besodeiah repaired the Gate of Yeshanah.³ They laid its beams and set its doors, its bolts, and its bars. ⁷And next to them repaired Melatiah the Gibeonite and Jadon the Meronothite, the men of Gibeon and of Mizpah, the seat of the governor of the province Beyond the River. ⁸Next to them Uzziel the son of Harhaiah, goldsmiths, repaired. Next to him Hananiah, one of the perfumers, repaired, and they restored Jerusalem as far as the Broad Wall. ⁹Next to them Rephaiah the son of Hur, ruler of half the district of⁴ Jerusalem, repaired. ¹⁰Next to them Jedaiah the son of Harumaph repaired opposite his house. And next to him Hattush the son of Hashabneiah repaired. ¹¹Malchijah the son of Harim and Hasshub the son of Pahath-moab repaired another section and the Tower of the Ovens. ¹²Next to him Shallum the son of Hallohesh, ruler of half the district of Jerusalem, repaired, he and his daughters.

¹³Hanun and the inhabitants of Zanoah repaired the Valley Gate. They rebuilt it and set its doors, its bolts, and its bars, and repaired a thousand cubits⁵ of the wall, as far as the Dung Gate.

¹⁴Malchijah the son of Rechab, ruler of the district of Beth-haccherem, repaired the Dung Gate. He rebuilt it and set its doors, its bolts, and its bars.

¹⁵And Shallum the son of Col-hozeh, ruler of the district of Mizpah, repaired the Fountain Gate. He rebuilt it and covered it and set its doors, its bolts, and its bars. And he built the wall of the Pool of Shelah of the king's garden, as far as the stairs that go down from the city of David. ¹⁶After him Nehemiah the son of Azbuk, ruler of half the district of Beth-zur, repaired to a point opposite the tombs of David, as far as the artificial pool, and as far as the house of the mighty men. ¹⁷After him the Levites repaired: Rehum the son of Bani. Next to him Hashabiah, ruler of half the district of Keilah, repaired for his district. ¹⁸After him their brothers repaired: Bavvai the son of Henadad, ruler of half the district of Keilah. ¹⁹Next to him Ezer the son of Jeshua, ruler of Mizpah, repaired another section opposite the ascent to the armory at the buttress.⁶ ²⁰After him Baruch the son of Zabbai repaired another section from the buttress to the door of the house of Eliashib the high priest. ²¹After him Meremoth the son of Uriah, son of Hakkoz repaired another section from the door of the house of Eliashib to the end of the house of Eliashib. ²²After him the priests, the men of the surrounding area, repaired. ²³After them Benjamin and Hasshub repaired opposite their house. After them Azariah the son of Maaseiah, son of Ananiah repaired beside his own house. ²⁴After him Binnui the son of Henadad repaired another section, from the house of Azariah to the buttress ²⁵ and to the corner. Palal the son of Uzai repaired opposite the buttress and the tower projecting from the upper house of the king at the court of the guard. After him Pedaiah the son of Parosh ²⁶ and the temple servants living on Ophel repaired to a point opposite the Water Gate on the east and the projecting tower. ²⁷After him the Tekoites repaired another section opposite the great projecting tower as far as the wall of Ophel.

²⁸Above the Horse Gate the priests repaired, each one opposite his own house. ²⁹After them Zadok the son of Immer repaired opposite his own house. After him Shemaiah the son of Shecaniah, the keeper of the East Gate, repaired. ³⁰After him Hananiah the son of Shelemiah and Hanun the sixth son of Zalaph repaired another section. After him Meshullam the son of Berechiah repaired opposite his chamber. ³¹After him Malchijah, one of the goldsmiths, repaired as far as the house of the

temple servants and of the merchants, opposite the Muster Gate,[1] and to the upper chamber of the corner. [32]And between the upper chamber of the corner and the Sheep Gate the goldsmiths and the merchants repaired.

Acts 13

Now there were in the church at Antioch prophets and teachers, Barnabas, Simeon who was called Niger,[2] Lucius of Cyrene, Manaen a lifelong friend of Herod the tetrarch, and Saul. [2]While they were worshiping the Lord and fasting, the Holy Spirit said, "Set apart for me Barnabas and Saul for the work to which I have called them." [3]Then after fasting and praying they laid their hands on them and sent them off.

[4]So, being sent out by the Holy Spirit, they went down to Seleucia, and from there they sailed to Cyprus. [5]When they arrived at Salamis, they proclaimed the word of God in the synagogues of the Jews. And they had John to assist them. [6]When they had gone through the whole island as far as Paphos, they came upon a certain magician, a Jewish false prophet named Bar-Jesus. [7]He was with the proconsul, Sergius Paulus, a man of intelligence, who summoned Barnabas and Saul and sought to hear the word of God. [8]But Elymas the magician (for that is the meaning of his name) opposed them, seeking to turn the proconsul away from the faith. [9]But Saul, who was also called Paul, filled with the Holy Spirit, looked intently at him [10]and said, "You son of the devil, you enemy of all righteousness, full of all deceit and villainy, will you not stop making crooked the straight paths of the Lord? [11]And now, behold, the hand of the Lord is upon you, and you will be blind and unable to see the sun for a time." Immediately mist and darkness fell upon him, and he went about seeking people to lead him by the hand. [12]Then the proconsul believed, when he saw what had occurred, for he was astonished at the teaching of the Lord.

[13]Now Paul and his companions set sail from Paphos and came to Perga in Pamphylia. And John left them and returned to Jerusalem, [14]but they went on from Perga and came to Antioch in Pisidia. And on the Sabbath day they went into the synagogue and sat down. [15]After the reading from the Law and the Prophets, the rulers of the synagogue sent a message to them, saying, "Brothers, if you have any word of encouragement for the people, say it." [16]So Paul stood up, and motioning with his hand said:

"Men of Israel and you who fear God, listen. [17]The God of this people Israel chose our fathers and made the people great during their stay in the land of Egypt, and with uplifted arm he led them out of it. [18]And for about forty years he put up with[3] them in the wilderness. [19]And after destroying seven nations in the land of Canaan, he gave them their land as an inheritance. [20]All this took about 450 years. And after that he gave them judges until Samuel the prophet. [21]Then they asked for a king, and God gave them Saul the son of Kish, a man of the tribe of Benjamin, for forty years. [22]And when he had removed him, he raised up David to be their king, of whom he testified and said, 'I have found in David the son of Jesse a man after my heart, who will do all my will.' [23]Of this man's offspring God has brought to Israel a Savior, Jesus, as he promised. [24]Before his coming, John had proclaimed a baptism of repentance to all the people of Israel. [25]And as John was finishing his course, he said, 'What do you suppose that I am? I am not he. No, but behold, after me one is coming, the sandals of whose feet I am not worthy to untie.'

[26]"Brothers, sons of the family of Abraham, and those among you who fear God, to us has been sent the message of this salvation. [27]For those who live in Jerusalem and their rulers, because they did not recognize him nor understand the utterances of the prophets, which are read every Sabbath, fulfilled them by condemning him. [28]And though they found in him no guilt worthy of death, they asked Pilate to have him executed. [29]And when they had carried out all that was written of him, they took him down from the tree and laid him in a tomb. [30]But God raised him from the dead, [31]and for many days he appeared to those who had come up with him from Galilee to Jerusalem, who are now his witnesses to the people. [32]And we bring you the good news that what God promised to the fathers, [33]this he has fulfilled to us their children by raising Jesus, as also it is written in the second Psalm,

"'You are my Son,
        today I have begotten you.'

---

[1] Or Hammiphkad Gate   [2] Niger is a Latin word meaning black, or dark   [3] Some manuscripts he carried (compare Deuteronomy 1:31)

³⁴And as for the fact that he raised him from the dead, no more to return to corruption, he has spoken in this way,

"'I will give you the holy and sure
    blessings of David.'

³⁵Therefore he says also in another psalm,

"'You will not let your Holy One see
    corruption.'

³⁶For David, after he had served the purpose of God in his own generation, fell asleep and was laid with his fathers and saw corruption, ³⁷but he whom God raised up did not see corruption. ³⁸Let it be known to you therefore, brothers, that through this man forgiveness of sins is proclaimed to you, ³⁹and by him everyone who believes is freed[1] from everything from which you could not be freed by the law of Moses. ⁴⁰Beware, therefore, lest what is said in the Prophets should come about:

⁴¹ "'Look, you scoffers,
    be astounded and perish;
    for I am doing a work in your days,
    a work that you will not believe, even
        if one tells it to you.'"

⁴²As they went out, the people begged that these things might be told them the next Sabbath. ⁴³And after the meeting of the synagogue broke up, many Jews and devout converts

to Judaism followed Paul and Barnabas, who, as they spoke with them, urged them to continue in the grace of God.

⁴⁴The next Sabbath almost the whole city gathered to hear the word of the Lord. ⁴⁵But when the Jews saw the crowds, they were filled with jealousy and began to contradict what was spoken by Paul, reviling him. ⁴⁶And Paul and Barnabas spoke out boldly, saying, "It was necessary that the word of God be spoken first to you. Since you thrust it aside and judge yourselves unworthy of eternal life, behold, we are turning to the Gentiles. ⁴⁷For so the Lord has commanded us, saying,

"'I have made you a light for the Gentiles,
    that you may bring salvation to the
        ends of the earth.'"

⁴⁸And when the Gentiles heard this, they began rejoicing and glorifying the word of the Lord, and as many as were appointed to eternal life believed. ⁴⁹And the word of the Lord was spreading throughout the whole region. ⁵⁰But the Jews[2] incited the devout women of high standing and the leading men of the city, stirred up persecution against Paul and Barnabas, and drove them out of their district. ⁵¹But they shook off the dust from their feet against them and went to Iconium. ⁵²And the disciples were filled with joy and with the Holy Spirit.

JANUARY 14

Genesis 15

After these things the word of the Lord came to Abram in a vision: "Fear not, Abram, I am your shield; your reward shall be very great." ²But Abram said, "O Lord God, what will you give me, for I continue[3] childless, and the heir of my house is Eliezer of Damascus?" ³And Abram said, "Behold, you have given me no offspring, and a member of my household will be my heir." ⁴And behold, the word of the Lord came to him: "This man

shall not be your heir; your very own son[4] shall be your heir." ⁵And he brought him outside and said, "Look toward heaven, and number the stars, if you are able to number them." Then he said to him, "So shall your offspring be." ⁶And he believed the Lord, and he counted it to him as righteousness.

⁷And he said to him, "I am the Lord who brought you out from Ur of the Chaldeans to give you this land to possess." ⁸But he said,

[1] Greek justified; twice in this verse [2] Greek Ioudaioi probably refers here to Jewish religious leaders, and others under their influence, in that time [3] Or I shall die [4] Hebrew what will come out of your own loins

"O Lord God, how am I to know that I shall possess it?" ⁹He said to him, "Bring me a heifer three years old, a female goat three years old, a ram three years old, a turtledove, and a young pigeon." ¹⁰And he brought him all these, cut them in half, and laid each half over against the other. But he did not cut the birds in half. ¹¹And when birds of prey came down on the carcasses, Abram drove them away.

¹²As the sun was going down, a deep sleep fell on Abram. And behold, dreadful and great darkness fell upon him. ¹³Then the Lord said to Abram, "Know for certain that your offspring will be sojourners in a land that is not theirs and will be servants there, and they will be afflicted for four hundred years. ¹⁴But I will bring judgment on the nation that they serve, and afterward they shall come out with great possessions. ¹⁵As for you, you shall go to your fathers in peace; you shall be buried in a good old age. ¹⁶And they shall come back here in the fourth generation, for the iniquity of the Amorites is not yet complete."

¹⁷When the sun had gone down and it was dark, behold, a smoking fire pot and a flaming torch passed between these pieces. ¹⁸On that day the Lord made a covenant with Abram, saying, "To your offspring I give¹ this land, from the river of Egypt to the great river, the river Euphrates, ¹⁹the land of the Kenites, the Kenizzites, the Kadmonites, ²⁰the Hittites, the Perizzites, the Rephaim, ²¹the Amorites, the Canaanites, the Girgashites and the Jebusites."

Matthew 14

At that time Herod the tetrarch heard about the fame of Jesus, ²and he said to his servants, "This is John the Baptist. He has been raised from the dead; that is why these miraculous powers are at work in him." ³For Herod had seized John and bound him and put him in prison for the sake of Herodias, his brother Philip's wife,² ⁴because John had been saying to him, "It is not lawful for you to have her." ⁵And though he wanted to put him to death, he feared the people, because they held him to be a prophet. ⁶But when Herod's birthday came, the daughter of Herodias danced before the company and pleased Herod, ⁷so that he promised with an oath to give her whatever she might ask. ⁸Prompted by her mother, she said,

"Give me the head of John the Baptist here on a platter." ⁹And the king was sorry, but because of his oaths and his guests he commanded it to be given. ¹⁰He sent and had John beheaded in the prison, ¹¹and his head was brought on a platter and given to the girl, and she brought it to her mother. ¹²And his disciples came and took the body and buried it, and they went and told Jesus.

¹³Now when Jesus heard this, he withdrew from there in a boat to a desolate place by himself. But when the crowds heard it, they followed him on foot from the towns. ¹⁴When he went ashore he saw a great crowd, and he had compassion on them and healed their sick. ¹⁵Now when it was evening, the disciples came to him and said, "This is a desolate place, and the day is now over; send the crowds away to go into the villages and buy food for themselves." ¹⁶But Jesus said, "They need not go away; you give them something to eat." ¹⁷They said to him, "We have only five loaves here and two fish." ¹⁸And he said, "Bring them here to me." ¹⁹Then he ordered the crowds to sit down on the grass, and taking the five loaves and the two fish, he looked up to heaven and said a blessing. Then he broke the loaves and gave them to the disciples, and the disciples gave them to the crowds. ²⁰And they all ate and were satisfied. And they took up twelve baskets full of the broken pieces left over. ²¹And those who ate were about five thousand men, besides women and children.

²²Immediately he made the disciples get into the boat and go before him to the other side, while he dismissed the crowds. ²³And after he had dismissed the crowds, he went up on the mountain by himself to pray. When evening came, he was there alone, ²⁴but the boat by this time was a long way³ from the land,⁴ beaten by the waves, for the wind was against them. ²⁵And in the fourth watch of the night he came to them, walking on the sea. ²⁶But when the disciples saw him walking on the sea, they were terrified, and said, "It is a ghost!" and they cried out in fear. ²⁷But immediately Jesus spoke to them, saying, "Take heart; it is I. Do not be afraid."

²⁸And Peter answered him, "Lord, if it is you, command me to come to you on the water." ²⁹He said, "Come." So Peter got out of the boat and walked on the water and came to Jesus. ³⁰But when he saw the wind,⁵ he was afraid,

¹ Or have given ² Some manuscripts his brother's wife ³ Greek many stadia, a stadion was about 607 feet or 185 meters ⁴ Some manuscripts was out on the sea ⁵ Some manuscripts strong wind

and beginning to sink he cried out, "Lord, save me." ³¹Jesus immediately reached out his hand and took hold of him, saying to him, "O you of little faith, why did you doubt?" ³²And when they got into the boat, the wind ceased. ³³And those in the boat worshiped him, saying, "Truly you are the Son of God."

³⁴And when they had crossed over, they came to land at Gennesaret. ³⁵And when the men of that place recognized him, they sent around to all that region and brought to him all who were sick ³⁶and implored him that they might only touch the fringe of his garment. And as many as touched it were made well.

—————— *Nehemiah 4*¹ ——————

Now when Sanballat heard that we were building the wall, he was angry and greatly enraged, and he jeered at the Jews. ²And he said in the presence of his brothers and of the army of Samaria, "What are these feeble Jews doing? Will they restore it for themselves?² Will they sacrifice? Will they finish up in a day? Will they revive the stones out of the heaps of rubbish, and burned ones at that?" ³Tobiah the Ammonite was beside him, and he said, "Yes, what they are building—if a fox goes up on it he will break down their stone wall!" ⁴Hear, O our God, for we are despised. Turn back their taunt on their own heads and give them up to be plundered in a land where they are captives. ⁵Do not cover their guilt, and let not their sin be blotted out from your sight, for they have provoked you to anger in the presence of the builders.

⁶So we built the wall. And all the wall was joined together to half its height, for the people had a mind to work.

^{7 3}But when Sanballat and Tobiah and the Arabs and the Ammonites and the Ashdodites heard that the repairing of the walls of Jerusalem was going forward and that the breaches were beginning to be closed, they were very angry. ⁸And they all plotted together to come and fight against Jerusalem and to cause confusion in it. ⁹And we prayed to our God and set a guard as a protection against them day and night.

¹⁰In Judah it was said,⁴ "The strength of those who bear the burdens is failing. There is too much rubble. By ourselves we will not be able to rebuild the wall." ¹¹And our enemies said, "They will not know or see till we come among them and kill them and stop the work." ¹²At that time the Jews who lived near them came from all directions and said to us ten times, "You must return to us."⁵ ¹³So in the lowest parts of the space behind the wall, in open places, I stationed the people by their clans, with their swords, their spears, and their bows. ¹⁴And I looked and arose and said to the nobles and to the officials and to the rest of the people, "Do not be afraid of them. Remember the Lord, who is great and awesome, and fight for your brothers, your sons, your daughters, your wives, and your homes."

¹⁵When our enemies heard that it was known to us and that God had frustrated their plan, we all returned to the wall, each to his work. ¹⁶From that day on, half of my servants worked on construction, and half held the spears, shields, bows, and coats of mail. And the leaders stood behind the whole house of Judah, ¹⁷who were building on the wall. Those who carried burdens were loaded in such a way that each labored on the work with one hand and held his weapon with the other. ¹⁸And each of the builders had his sword strapped at his side while he built. The man who sounded the trumpet was beside me. ¹⁹And I said to the nobles and to the officials and to the rest of the people, "The work is great and widely spread, and we are separated on the wall, far from one another. ²⁰In the place where you hear the sound of the trumpet, rally to us there. Our God will fight for us."

²¹So we labored at the work, and half of them held the spears from the break of dawn until the stars came out. ²²I also said to the people at that time, "Let every man and his servant pass the night within Jerusalem, that they may be a guard for us by night and may labor by day." ²³So neither I nor my brothers nor my servants nor the men of the guard who followed me, none of us took off our clothes; each kept his weapon at his right hand.⁶

—————— *Acts 14* ——————

Now at Iconium they entered together into the Jewish synagogue and spoke in such a way that a great number of both Jews and Greeks believed. ²But the unbelieving Jews

¹Ch 3:33 in Hebrew ²Or *Will they commit themselves to God?* ³Ch 4:1 in Hebrew ⁴Hebrew *Judah said* ⁵The meaning of the Hebrew is uncertain ⁶Probable reading; Hebrew *each his weapon the water*

stirred up the Gentiles and poisoned their minds against the brothers.[1] [3]So they remained for a long time, speaking boldly for the Lord, who bore witness to the word of his grace, granting signs and wonders to be done by their hands. [4]But the people of the city were divided; some sided with the Jews and some with the apostles. [5]When an attempt was made by both Gentiles and Jews, with their rulers, to mistreat them and to stone them, [6]they learned of it and fled to Lystra and Derbe, cities of Lycaonia, and to the surrounding country, [7]and there they continued to preach the gospel.

[8]Now at Lystra there was a man sitting who could not use his feet. He was crippled from birth and had never walked. [9]He listened to Paul speaking. And Paul, looking intently at him and seeing that he had faith to be made well,[2] [10]said in a loud voice, "Stand upright on your feet." And he sprang up and began walking. [11]And when the crowds saw what Paul had done, they lifted up their voices, saying in Lycaonian, "The gods have come down to us in the likeness of men!" [12]Barnabas they called Zeus, and Paul, Hermes, because he was the chief speaker. [13]And the priest of Zeus, whose temple was at the entrance to the city, brought oxen and garlands to the gates and wanted to offer sacrifice with the crowds. [14]But when the apostles Barnabas and Paul heard of it, they tore their garments and rushed out into the crowd, crying out, [15]"Men, why are you doing these things? We also are men, of like nature with you, and we bring you good news, that you should turn from these vain things to a living God, who made the heaven and the earth and the sea and all that is in them. [16]In past generations he allowed all the nations to walk in their own ways. [17]Yet he did not leave himself without witness, for he did good by giving you rains from heaven and fruitful seasons, satisfying your hearts with food and gladness." [18]Even with these words they scarcely restrained the people from offering sacrifice to them.

[19]But Jews came from Antioch and Iconium, and having persuaded the crowds, they stoned Paul and dragged him out of the city, supposing that he was dead. [20]But when the disciples gathered about him, he rose up and entered the city, and on the next day he went on with Barnabas to Derbe. [21]When they had preached the gospel to that city and had made many disciples, they returned to Lystra and to Iconium and to Antioch, [22]strengthening the souls of the disciples, encouraging them to continue in the faith, and saying that through many tribulations we must enter the kingdom of God. [23]And when they had appointed elders for them in every church, with prayer and fasting they committed them to the Lord in whom they had believed.

[24]Then they passed through Pisidia and came to Pamphylia. [25]And when they had spoken the word in Perga, they went down to Attalia, [26]and from there they sailed to Antioch, where they had been commended to the grace of God for the work that they had fulfilled. [27]And when they arrived and gathered the church together, they declared all that God had done with them, and how he had opened a door of faith to the Gentiles. [28]And they remained no little time with the disciples.

JANUARY 15

Genesis 16

Now Sarai, Abram's wife, had borne him no children. She had a female Egyptian servant whose name was Hagar. [2]And Sarai said to Abram, "Behold now, the LORD has prevented me from bearing children. Go in to my servant; it may be that I shall obtain children[3] by her." And Abram listened to the voice of Sarai. [3]So, after Abram had lived ten years in the land of Canaan, Sarai, Abram's wife, took Hagar the Egyptian, her servant, and gave her

[1] Or brothers and sisters [2] Or be saved [3] Hebrew be built up, which sounds like the Hebrew for children

to Abram her husband as a wife. **4**And he went in to Hagar, and she conceived. And when she saw that she had conceived, she looked with contempt on her mistress.[1] **5**And Sarai said to Abram, "May the wrong done to me be on you! I gave my servant to your embrace, and when she saw that she had conceived, she looked on me with contempt. May the LORD judge between you and me!" **6**But Abram said to Sarai, "Behold, your servant is in your power; do to her as you please." Then Sarai dealt harshly with her, and she fled from her.

7The angel of the LORD found her by a spring of water in the wilderness, the spring on the way to Shur. **8**And he said, "Hagar, servant of Sarai, where have you come from and where are you going?" She said, "I am fleeing from my mistress Sarai." **9**The angel of the LORD said to her, "Return to your mistress and submit to her." **10**The angel of the LORD also said to her, "I will surely multiply your offspring so that they cannot be numbered for multitude." **11**And the angel of the LORD said to her,

> "Behold, you are pregnant
> and shall bear a son.
> You shall call his name Ishmael,[2]
> because the LORD has listened to your
> affliction.
> **12** He shall be a wild donkey of a man,
> his hand against everyone
> and everyone's hand against him,
> and he shall dwell over against all his
> kinsmen."

13So she called the name of the LORD who spoke to her, "You are a God of seeing,"[3] for she said, "Truly here I have seen him who looks after me."[4] **14**Therefore the well was called Beer-lahai-roi;[5] it lies between Kadesh and Bered.

15And Hagar bore Abram a son, and Abram called the name of his son, whom Hagar bore, Ishmael. **16**Abram was eighty-six years old when Hagar bore Ishmael to Abram.

Matthew 15

Then Pharisees and scribes came to Jesus from Jerusalem and said, **2**"Why do your disciples break the tradition of the elders? For they do not wash their hands when they eat." **3**He answered them, "And why do you break the commandment of God for the sake of your tradition? **4**For God commanded, 'Honor your father and your mother,' and, 'Whoever reviles father or mother must surely die.' **5**But you say, 'If anyone tells his father or his mother, "What you would have gained from me is given to God,"[6] **6**he need not honor his father.' So for the sake of your tradition you have made void the word[7] of God. **7**You hypocrites! Well did Isaiah prophesy of you, when he said:

> **8** "'This people honors me with their lips,
> but their heart is far from me;
> **9** in vain do they worship me,
> teaching as doctrines the
> commandments of men.'"

10And he called the people to him and said to them, "Hear and understand: **11**it is not what goes into the mouth that defiles a person, but what comes out of the mouth; this defiles a person." **12**Then the disciples came and said to him, "Do you know that the Pharisees were offended when they heard this saying?" **13**He answered, "Every plant that my heavenly Father has not planted will be rooted up. **14**Let them alone; they are blind guides.[8] And if the blind lead the blind, both will fall into a pit." **15**But Peter said to him, "Explain the parable to us." **16**And he said, "Are you also still without understanding? **17**Do you not see that whatever goes into the mouth passes into the stomach and is expelled?[9] **18**But what comes out of the mouth proceeds from the heart, and this defiles a person. **19**For out of the heart come evil thoughts, murder, adultery, sexual immorality, theft, false witness, slander. **20**These are what defile a person. But to eat with unwashed hands does not defile anyone."

21And Jesus went away from there and withdrew to the district of Tyre and Sidon. **22**And behold, a Canaanite woman from that region came out and was crying, "Have mercy on me, O Lord, Son of David; my daughter is severely oppressed by a demon." **23**But he did not answer her a word. And his disciples came and begged him, saying, "Send her away, for she is crying out after us." **24**He answered, "I was sent only to the lost sheep of the house of Israel." **25**But she came and knelt before him, saying, "Lord, help me." **26**And he answered, "It is not right to take the children's bread and

[1] Hebrew *her mistress was dishonorable in her eyes*; similarly in verse 5 [2] *Ishmael* means *God hears* [3] Or *You are a God who sees me* [4] Hebrew *Have I really seen him here who sees me?* or *Would I have looked here for the one who sees me?* [5] *Beer-lahai-roi* means *the well of the Living One who sees me* [6] Or *is an offering* [7] Some manuscripts *law* [8] Some manuscripts add *of the blind* [9] Greek *is expelled into the latrine*

throw it to the dogs." [27] She said, "Yes, Lord, yet even the dogs eat the crumbs that fall from their masters' table." [28] Then Jesus answered her, "O woman, great is your faith! Be it done for you as you desire." And her daughter was healed instantly.[1]

[29] Jesus went on from there and walked beside the Sea of Galilee. And he went up on the mountain and sat down there. [30] And great crowds came to him, bringing with them the lame, the blind, the crippled, the mute, and many others, and they put them at his feet, and he healed them, [31] so that the crowd wondered, when they saw the mute speaking, the crippled healthy, the lame walking, and the blind seeing. And they glorified the God of Israel.

[32] Then Jesus called his disciples to him and said, "I have compassion on the crowd because they have been with me now three days and have nothing to eat. And I am unwilling to send them away hungry, lest they faint on the way." [33] And the disciples said to him, "Where are we to get enough bread in such a desolate place to feed so great a crowd?" [34] And Jesus said to them, "How many loaves do you have?" They said, "Seven, and a few small fish." [35] And directing the crowd to sit down on the ground, [36] he took the seven loaves and the fish, and having given thanks he broke them and gave them to the disciples, and the disciples gave them to the crowds. [37] And they all ate and were satisfied. And they took up seven baskets full of the broken pieces left over. [38] Those who ate were four thousand men, besides women and children. [39] And after sending away the crowds, he got into the boat and went to the region of Magadan.

Nehemiah 5

Now there arose a great outcry of the people and of their wives against their Jewish brothers. [2] For there were those who said, "With our sons and our daughters, we are many. So let us get grain, that we may eat and keep alive." [3] There were also those who said, "We are mortgaging our fields, our vineyards, and our houses to get grain because of the famine." [4] And there were those who said, "We have borrowed money for the king's tax on our fields and our vineyards. [5] Now our flesh is as the flesh of our brothers, our children are as their children. Yet we are forcing our sons and our daughters to be slaves, and some of our daughters have already been enslaved, but it is not in our power to help it, for other men have our fields and our vineyards."

[6] I was very angry when I heard their outcry and these words. [7] I took counsel with myself, and I brought charges against the nobles and the officials. I said to them, "You are exacting interest, each from his brother." And I held a great assembly against them [8] and said to them, "We, as far as we are able, have bought back our Jewish brothers who have been sold to the nations, but you even sell your brothers that they may be sold to us!" They were silent and could not find a word to say. [9] So I said, "The thing that you are doing is not good. Ought you not to walk in the fear of our God to prevent the taunts of the nations our enemies? [10] Moreover, I and my brothers and my servants are lending them money and grain. Let us abandon this exacting of interest. [11] Return to them this very day their fields, their vineyards, their olive orchards, and their houses, and the percentage of money, grain, wine, and oil that you have been exacting from them." [12] Then they said, "We will restore these and require nothing from them. We will do as you say." And I called the priests and made them swear to do as they had promised. [13] I also shook out the fold[2] of my garment and said, "So may God shake out every man from his house and from his labor who does not keep this promise. So may he be shaken out and emptied." And all the assembly said "Amen" and praised the LORD. And the people did as they had promised.

[14] Moreover, from the time that I was appointed to be their governor in the land of Judah, from the twentieth year to the thirty-second year of Artaxerxes the king, twelve years, neither I nor my brothers ate the food allowance of the governor. [15] The former governors who were before me laid heavy burdens on the people and took from them for their daily ration[3] forty shekels[4] of silver. Even their servants lorded it over the people. But I did not do so, because of the fear of God. [16] I also persevered in the work on this wall, and we acquired no land, and all my servants were gathered there for the work. [17] Moreover, there were at my table 150 men, Jews and officials, besides those who came to us from the nations that were around us. [18] Now what was prepared at

my expense[1] for each day was one ox and six choice sheep and birds, and every ten days all kinds of wine in abundance. Yet for all this I did not demand the food allowance of the governor, because the service was too heavy on this people. [19]Remember for my good, O my God, all that I have done for this people.

--------- *Acts 15* ---------

But some men came down from Judea and were teaching the brothers, "Unless you are circumcised according to the custom of Moses, you cannot be saved." [2]And after Paul and Barnabas had no small dissension and debate with them, Paul and Barnabas and some of the others were appointed to go up to Jerusalem to the apostles and the elders about this question. [3]So, being sent on their way by the church, they passed through both Phoenicia and Samaria, describing in detail the conversion of the Gentiles, and brought great joy to all the brothers.[2] [4]When they came to Jerusalem, they were welcomed by the church and the apostles and the elders, and they declared all that God had done with them. [5]But some believers who belonged to the party of the Pharisees rose up and said, "It is necessary to circumcise them and to order them to keep the law of Moses."

[6]The apostles and the elders were gathered together to consider this matter. [7]And after there had been much debate, Peter stood up and said to them, "Brothers, you know that in the early days God made a choice among you, that by my mouth the Gentiles should hear the word of the gospel and believe. [8]And God, who knows the heart, bore witness to them, by giving them the Holy Spirit just as he did to us, [9]and he made no distinction between us and them, having cleansed their hearts by faith. [10]Now, therefore, why are you putting God to the test by placing a yoke on the neck of the disciples that neither our fathers nor we have been able to bear? [11]But we believe that we will be saved through the grace of the Lord Jesus, just as they will."

[12]And all the assembly fell silent, and they listened to Barnabas and Paul as they related what signs and wonders God had done through them among the Gentiles. [13]After they finished speaking, James replied, "Brothers, listen to me. [14]Simeon has related how God first visited the Gentiles, to take from them a people for his name. [15]And with this the words of the prophets agree, just as it is written,

[16] "'After this I will return,
    and I will rebuild the tent of David that
        has fallen;
    I will rebuild its ruins,
        and I will restore it,
[17]   that the remnant[3] of mankind may seek
        the Lord,
      and all the Gentiles who are called by
        my name,
      says the Lord, who makes these things
        [18]known from of old.'

[19]Therefore my judgment is that we should not trouble those of the Gentiles who turn to God, [20]but should write to them to abstain from the things polluted by idols, and from sexual immorality, and from what has been strangled, and from blood. [21]For from ancient generations Moses has had in every city those who proclaim him, for he is read every Sabbath in the synagogues."

[22]Then it seemed good to the apostles and the elders, with the whole church, to choose men from among them and send them to Antioch with Paul and Barnabas. They sent Judas called Barsabbas, and Silas, leading men among the brothers, [23]with the following letter: "The brothers, both the apostles and the elders, to the brothers[4] who are of the Gentiles in Antioch and Syria and Cilicia, greetings. [24]Since we have heard that some persons have gone out from us and troubled you[5] with words, unsettling your minds, although we gave them no instructions, [25]it has seemed good to us, having come to one accord, to choose men and send them to you with our beloved Barnabas and Paul, [26]men who have risked their lives for the name of our Lord Jesus Christ. [27]We have therefore sent Judas and Silas, who themselves will tell you the same things by word of mouth. [28]For it has seemed good to the Holy Spirit and to us to lay on you no greater burden than these requirements: [29]that you abstain from what has been sacrificed to idols, and from blood, and from what has been strangled, and from sexual immorality. If you keep yourselves from these, you will do well. Farewell."

[30]So when they were sent off, they went down to Antioch, and having gathered the

[1] Or *prepared for me* [2] Or *brothers and sisters*; also verse 22 [3] Or *rest* [4] Or *brothers and sisters*; also verses 32, 33, 36 [5] Some manuscripts *some persons from us have troubled you*

congregation together, they delivered the letter. [31]And when they had read it, they rejoiced because of its encouragement. [32]And Judas and Silas, who were themselves prophets, encouraged and strengthened the brothers with many words. [33]And after they had spent some time, they were sent off in peace by the brothers to those who had sent them.[1] [35]But Paul and Barnabas remained in Antioch, teaching and preaching the word of the Lord, with many others also.

[36]And after some days Paul said to Barnabas, "Let us return and visit the brothers in every city where we proclaimed the word of the Lord, and see how they are." [37]Now Barnabas wanted to take with them John called Mark. [38]But Paul thought best not to take with them one who had withdrawn from them in Pamphylia and had not gone with them to the work. [39]And there arose a sharp disagreement, so that they separated from each other. Barnabas took Mark with him and sailed away to Cyprus, [40]but Paul chose Silas and departed, having been commended by the brothers to the grace of the Lord. [41]And he went through Syria and Cilicia, strengthening the churches.

JANUARY 16

Genesis 17

When Abram was ninety-nine years old the LORD appeared to Abram and said to him, "I am God Almighty;[2] walk before me, and be blameless, [2]that I may make my covenant between me and you, and may multiply you greatly." [3]Then Abram fell on his face. And God said to him, [4]"Behold, my covenant is with you, and you shall be the father of a multitude of nations. [5]No longer shall your name be called Abram,[3] but your name shall be Abraham,[4] for I have made you the father of a multitude of nations. [6]I will make you exceedingly fruitful, and I will make you into nations, and kings shall come from you. [7]And I will establish my covenant between me and you and your offspring after you throughout their generations for an everlasting covenant, to be God to you and to your offspring after you. [8]And I will give to you and to your offspring after you the land of your sojournings, all the land of Canaan, for an everlasting possession, and I will be their God."

[9]And God said to Abraham, "As for you, you shall keep my covenant, you and your offspring after you throughout their generations. [10]This is my covenant, which you shall keep, between me and you and your offspring after you: Every male among you shall be circumcised. [11]You shall be circumcised in the flesh of your foreskins, and it shall be a sign of the covenant between me and you. [12]He who is eight days old among you shall be circumcised. Every male throughout your generations, whether born in your house or bought with your money from any foreigner who is not of your offspring, [13]both he who is born in your house and he who is bought with your money, shall surely be circumcised. So shall my covenant be in your flesh an everlasting covenant. [14]Any uncircumcised male who is not circumcised in the flesh of his foreskin shall be cut off from his people; he has broken my covenant."

[15]And God said to Abraham, "As for Sarai your wife, you shall not call her name Sarai, but Sarah[5] shall be her name. [16]I will bless her, and moreover, I will give[6] you a son by her. I will bless her, and she shall become nations; kings of peoples shall come from her." [17]Then Abraham fell on his face and laughed and said to himself, "Shall a child be born to a man who is a hundred years old? Shall Sarah, who is ninety years old, bear a child?" [18]And Abraham said to God, "Oh that Ishmael might live before you!" [19]God said, "No, but Sarah your wife shall bear you a son, and you shall call his name Isaac.[7] I will establish my covenant with him as an everlasting

covenant for his offspring after him. ²⁰As for Ishmael, I have heard you; behold, I have blessed him and will make him fruitful and multiply him greatly. He shall father twelve princes, and I will make him into a great nation. ²¹But I will establish my covenant with Isaac, whom Sarah shall bear to you at this time next year."

²²When he had finished talking with him, God went up from Abraham. ²³Then Abraham took Ishmael his son and all those born in his house or bought with his money, every male among the men of Abraham's house, and he circumcised the flesh of their foreskins that very day, as God had said to him. ²⁴Abraham was ninety-nine years old when he was circumcised in the flesh of his foreskin. ²⁵And Ishmael his son was thirteen years old when he was circumcised in the flesh of his foreskin. ²⁶That very day Abraham and his son Ishmael were circumcised. ²⁷And all the men of his house, those born in the house and those bought with money from a foreigner, were circumcised with him.

Matthew 16

And the Pharisees and Sadducees came, and to test him they asked him to show them a sign from heaven. ²He answered them,¹ "When it is evening, you say, 'It will be fair weather, for the sky is red.' ³And in the morning, 'It will be stormy today, for the sky is red and threatening.' You know how to interpret the appearance of the sky, but you cannot interpret the signs of the times. ⁴An evil and adulterous generation seeks for a sign, but no sign will be given to it except the sign of Jonah." So he left them and departed.

⁵When the disciples reached the other side, they had forgotten to bring any bread. ⁶Jesus said to them, "Watch and beware of the leaven of the Pharisees and Sadducees." ⁷And they began discussing it among themselves, saying, "We brought no bread." ⁸But Jesus, aware of this, said, "O you of little faith, why are you discussing among yourselves the fact that you have no bread? ⁹Do you not yet perceive? Do you not remember the five loaves for the five thousand, and how many baskets you gathered? ¹⁰Or the seven loaves for the four thousand, and how many baskets you gathered?

¹¹How is it that you fail to understand that I did not speak about bread? Beware of the leaven of the Pharisees and Sadducees." ¹²Then they understood that he did not tell them to beware of the leaven of bread, but of the teaching of the Pharisees and Sadducees.

¹³Now when Jesus came into the district of Caesarea Philippi, he asked his disciples, "Who do people say that the Son of Man is?" ¹⁴And they said, "Some say John the Baptist, others say Elijah, and others Jeremiah or one of the prophets." ¹⁵He said to them, "But who do you say that I am?" ¹⁶Simon Peter replied, "You are the Christ, the Son of the living God." ¹⁷And Jesus answered him, "Blessed are you, Simon Bar-Jonah! For flesh and blood has not revealed this to you, but my Father who is in heaven. ¹⁸And I tell you, you are Peter, and on this rock² I will build my church, and the gates of hell³ shall not prevail against it. ¹⁹I will give you the keys of the kingdom of heaven, and whatever you bind on earth shall be bound in heaven, and whatever you loose on earth shall be loosed⁴ in heaven." ²⁰Then he strictly charged the disciples to tell no one that he was the Christ.

²¹From that time Jesus began to show his disciples that he must go to Jerusalem and suffer many things from the elders and chief priests and scribes, and be killed, and on the third day be raised. ²²And Peter took him aside and began to rebuke him, saying, "Far be it from you, Lord!⁵ This shall never happen to you." ²³But he turned and said to Peter, "Get behind me, Satan! You are a hindrance⁶ to me. For you are not setting your mind on the things of God, but on the things of man."

²⁴Then Jesus told his disciples, "If anyone would come after me, let him deny himself and take up his cross and follow me. ²⁵For whoever would save his life⁷ will lose it, but whoever loses his life for my sake will find it. ²⁶For what will it profit a man if he gains the whole world and forfeits his soul? Or what shall a man give in return for his soul? ²⁷For the Son of Man is going to come with his angels in the glory of his Father, and then he will repay each person according to what he has done. ²⁸Truly, I say to you, there are some standing here who will not taste death until they see the Son of Man coming in his kingdom."

¹ Some manuscripts omit the following words to the end of verse 3 ² The Greek words for *Peter* and *rock* sound similar ³ Greek *the gates of Hades* ⁴ Or *shall have been bound. . . shall have been loosed* ⁵ Or "[May God be] *merciful to you, Lord!*" ⁶ Greek *stumbling block* ⁷ The same Greek word can mean either *soul* or *life*, depending on the context; twice in this verse and twice in verse 26

—————— *Nehemiah 6* ——————

Now when Sanballat and Tobiah and Geshem the Arab and the rest of our enemies heard that I had built the wall and that there was no breach left in it (although up to that time I had not set up the doors in the gates), ²Sanballat and Geshem sent to me, saying, "Come and let us meet together at Hakkephirim in the plain of Ono." But they intended to do me harm. ³And I sent messengers to them, saying, "I am doing a great work and I cannot come down. Why should the work stop while I leave it and come down to you?" ⁴And they sent to me four times in this way, and I answered them in the same manner. ⁵In the same way Sanballat for the fifth time sent his servant to me with an open letter in his hand. ⁶In it was written, "It is reported among the nations, and Geshem[1] also says it, that you and the Jews intend to rebel; that is why you are building the wall. And according to these reports you wish to become their king. ⁷And you have also set up prophets to proclaim concerning you in Jerusalem, 'There is a king in Judah.' And now the king will hear of these reports. So now come and let us take counsel together." ⁸Then I sent to him, saying, "No such things as you say have been done, for you are inventing them out of your own mind." ⁹For they all wanted to frighten us, thinking, "Their hands will drop from the work, and it will not be done." But now, O God,[2] strengthen my hands.

¹⁰Now when I went into the house of Shemaiah the son of Delaiah, son of Mehetabel, who was confined to his home, he said, "Let us meet together in the house of God, within the temple. Let us close the doors of the temple, for they are coming to kill you. They are coming to kill you by night." ¹¹But I said, "Should such a man as I run away? And what man such as I could go into the temple and live?[3] I will not go in." ¹²And I understood and saw that God had not sent him, but he had pronounced the prophecy against me because Tobiah and Sanballat had hired him. ¹³For this purpose he was hired, that I should be afraid and act in this way and sin, and so they could give me a bad name in order to taunt me. ¹⁴Remember Tobiah and Sanballat, O my God, according to these things that they did, and also the prophetess

Noadiah and the rest of the prophets who wanted to make me afraid.

¹⁵So the wall was finished on the twenty-fifth day of the month Elul, in fifty-two days. ¹⁶And when all our enemies heard of it, all the nations around us were afraid and fell greatly in their own esteem, for they perceived that this work had been accomplished with the help of our God. ¹⁷Moreover, in those days the nobles of Judah sent many letters to Tobiah, and Tobiah's letters came to them. ¹⁸For many in Judah were bound by oath to him, because he was the son-in-law of Shecaniah the son of Arah: and his son Jehohanan had taken the daughter of Meshullam the son of Berechiah as his wife. ¹⁹Also they spoke of his good deeds in my presence and reported my words to him. And Tobiah sent letters to make me afraid.

—————— *Acts 16* ——————

Paul[4] came also to Derbe and to Lystra. A disciple was there, named Timothy, the son of a Jewish woman who was a believer, but his father was a Greek. ²He was well spoken of by the brothers[5] at Lystra and Iconium. ³Paul wanted Timothy to accompany him, and he took him and circumcised him because of the Jews who were in those places, for they all knew that his father was a Greek. ⁴As they went on their way through the cities, they delivered to them for observance the decisions that had been reached by the apostles and elders who were in Jerusalem. ⁵So the churches were strengthened in the faith, and they increased in numbers daily.

⁶And they went through the region of Phrygia and Galatia, having been forbidden by the Holy Spirit to speak the word in Asia. ⁷And when they had come up to Mysia, they attempted to go into Bithynia, but the Spirit of Jesus did not allow them. ⁸So, passing by Mysia, they went down to Troas. ⁹And a vision appeared to Paul in the night: a man of Macedonia was standing there, urging him and saying, "Come over to Macedonia and help us." ¹⁰And when Paul[6] had seen the vision, immediately we sought to go on into Macedonia, concluding that God had called us to preach the gospel to them.

¹¹So, setting sail from Troas, we made a direct voyage to Samothrace, and the following day to Neapolis, ¹²and from there to

—————————————————————

¹ Hebrew *Gashmu* ² Hebrew lacks *O God* ³ Or *would go into the temple to save his life* ⁴ Greek *He* ⁵ Or *brothers and sisters; also verse 40* ⁶ Greek *he*

Philippi, which is a leading city of the[1] district of Macedonia and a Roman colony. We remained in this city some days. [13]And on the Sabbath day we went outside the gate to the riverside, where we supposed there was a place of prayer, and we sat down and spoke to the women who had come together. [14]One who heard us was a woman named Lydia, from the city of Thyatira, a seller of purple goods, who was a worshiper of God. The Lord opened her heart to pay attention to what was said by Paul. [15]And after she was baptized, and her household as well, she urged us, saying, "If you have judged me to be faithful to the Lord, come to my house and stay." And she prevailed upon us.

[16]As we were going to the place of prayer, we were met by a slave girl who had a spirit of divination and brought her owners much gain by fortune-telling. [17]She followed Paul and us, crying out, "These men are servants[2] of the Most High God, who proclaim to you the way of salvation." [18]And this she kept doing for many days. Paul, having become greatly annoyed, turned and said to the spirit, "I command you in the name of Jesus Christ to come out of her." And it came out that very hour.

[19]But when her owners saw that their hope of gain was gone, they seized Paul and Silas and dragged them into the marketplace before the rulers. [20]And when they had brought them to the magistrates, they said, "These men are Jews, and they are disturbing our city. [21]They advocate customs that are not lawful for us as Romans to accept or practice." [22]The crowd joined in attacking them, and the magistrates tore the garments off them and gave orders to beat them with rods. [23]And when they had inflicted many blows upon them, they threw them into prison, ordering the jailer to keep them safely. [24]Having received this order, he put them into the inner prison and fastened their feet in the stocks.

[25]About midnight Paul and Silas were praying and singing hymns to God, and the prisoners were listening to them, [26]and suddenly there was a great earthquake, so that the foundations of the prison were shaken. And immediately all the doors were opened, and everyone's bonds were unfastened. [27]When the jailer woke and saw that the prison doors were open, he drew his sword and was about to kill himself, supposing that the prisoners had escaped. [28]But Paul cried with a loud voice, "Do not harm yourself, for we are all here." [29]And the jailer[3] called for lights and rushed in, and trembling with fear he fell down before Paul and Silas. [30]Then he brought them out and said, "Sirs, what must I do to be saved?" [31]And they said, "Believe in the Lord Jesus, and you will be saved, you and your household." [32]And they spoke the word of the Lord to him and to all who were in his house. [33]And he took them the same hour of the night and washed their wounds; and he was baptized at once, he and all his family. [34]Then he brought them up into his house and set food before them. And he rejoiced along with his entire household that he had believed in God.

[35]But when it was day, the magistrates sent the police, saying, "Let those men go." [36]And the jailer reported these words to Paul, saying, "The magistrates have sent to let you go. Therefore come out now and go in peace." [37]But Paul said to them, "They have beaten us publicly, uncondemned, men who are Roman citizens, and have thrown us into prison; and do they now throw us out secretly? No! Let them come themselves and take us out." [38]The police reported these words to the magistrates, and they were afraid when they heard that they were Roman citizens. [39]So they came and apologized to them. And they took them out and asked them to leave the city. [40]So they went out of the prison and visited Lydia. And when they had seen the brothers, they encouraged them and departed.

---

[1] Or that [2] Greek bondservants [3] Greek he

JANUARY 17

Genesis 18

And the Lord appeared to him by the oaks[1] of Mamre, as he sat at the door of his tent in the heat of the day. [2]He lifted up his eyes and looked, and behold, three men were standing in front of him. When he saw them, he ran from the tent door to meet them and bowed himself to the earth [3]and said, "O Lord,[2] if I have found favor in your sight, do not pass by your servant. [4]Let a little water be brought, and wash your feet, and rest yourselves under the tree, [5]while I bring a morsel of bread, that you may refresh yourselves, and after that you may pass on—since you have come to your servant." So they said, "Do as you have said." [6]And Abraham went quickly into the tent to Sarah and said, "Quick! Three seahs[3] of fine flour! Knead it, and make cakes." [7]And Abraham ran to the herd and took a calf, tender and good, and gave it to a young man, who prepared it quickly. [8]Then he took curds and milk and the calf that he had prepared, and set it before them. And he stood by them under the tree while they ate.

[9]They said to him, "Where is Sarah your wife?" And he said, "She is in the tent." [10]The Lord said, "I will surely return to you about this time next year, and Sarah your wife shall have a son." And Sarah was listening at the tent door behind him. [11]Now Abraham and Sarah were old, advanced in years. The way of women had ceased to be with Sarah. [12]So Sarah laughed to herself, saying, "After I am worn out, and my lord is old, shall I have pleasure?" [13]The Lord said to Abraham, "Why did Sarah laugh and say, 'Shall I indeed bear a child, now that I am old?' [14]Is anything too hard[4] for the Lord? At the appointed time I will return to you, about this time next year, and Sarah shall have a son." [15]But Sarah denied it,[5] saying, "I did not laugh," for she was afraid. He said, "No, but you did laugh."

[16]Then the men set out from there, and they looked down toward Sodom. And Abraham went with them to set them on their way. [17]The Lord said, "Shall I hide from Abraham what I am about to do, [18]seeing that Abraham shall surely become a great and mighty nation, and all the nations of the earth shall be blessed in him? [19]For I have chosen[6] him, that he may command his children and his household after him to keep the way of the Lord by doing righteousness and justice, so that the Lord may bring to Abraham what he has promised him." [20]Then the Lord said, "Because the outcry against Sodom and Gomorrah is great and their sin is very grave, [21]I will go down to see whether they have done altogether[7] according to the outcry that has come to me. And if not, I will know."

[22]So the men turned from there and went toward Sodom, but Abraham still stood before the Lord. [23]Then Abraham drew near and said, "Will you indeed sweep away the righteous with the wicked? [24]Suppose there are fifty righteous within the city. Will you then sweep away the place and not spare it for the fifty righteous who are in it? [25]Far be it from you to do such a thing, to put the righteous to death with the wicked, so that the righteous fare as the wicked! Far be that from you! Shall not the Judge of all the earth do what is just?" [26]And the Lord said, "If I find at Sodom fifty righteous in the city, I will spare the whole place for their sake."

[27]Abraham answered and said, "Behold, I have undertaken to speak to the Lord, I who am but dust and ashes. [28]Suppose five of the fifty righteous are lacking. Will you destroy the whole city for lack of five?" And he said, "I will not destroy it if I find forty-five there." [29]Again he spoke to him and said, "Suppose forty are found there." He answered, "For the sake of forty I will not do it." [30]Then he said, "Oh let not the Lord be angry, and I will speak. Suppose thirty are found there." He answered, "I will not do it, if I find thirty there." [31]He said, "Behold, I have undertaken to speak to the Lord. Suppose twenty are found there." He answered, "For the sake of twenty I will not destroy it." [32]Then he said, "Oh let not the Lord be angry, and I will speak again but this once. Suppose ten are found there." He answered, "For the sake of

[1] Or terebinths [2] Or My lord [3] A seah was about 7 quarts or 7.3 liters [4] Or wonderful [5] Or acted falsely [6] Hebrew known [7] Or they deserve destruction; Hebrew they have made a complete end

ten I will not destroy it." ³³And the LORD went his way, when he had finished speaking to Abraham, and Abraham returned to his place.

Matthew 17

And after six days Jesus took with him Peter and James, and John his brother, and led them up a high mountain by themselves. ²And he was transfigured before them, and his face shone like the sun, and his clothes became white as light. ³And behold, there appeared to them Moses and Elijah, talking with him. ⁴And Peter said to Jesus, "Lord, it is good that we are here. If you wish, I will make three tents here, one for you and one for Moses and one for Elijah." ⁵He was still speaking when, behold, a bright cloud overshadowed them, and a voice from the cloud said, "This is my beloved Son,¹ with whom I am well pleased; listen to him." ⁶When the disciples heard this, they fell on their faces and were terrified. ⁷But Jesus came and touched them, saying, "Rise, and have no fear." ⁸And when they lifted up their eyes, they saw no one but Jesus only.

⁹And as they were coming down the mountain, Jesus commanded them, "Tell no one the vision, until the Son of Man is raised from the dead." ¹⁰And the disciples asked him, "Then why do the scribes say that first Elijah must come?" ¹¹He answered, "Elijah does come, and he will restore all things. ¹²But I tell you that Elijah has already come, and they did not recognize him, but did to him whatever they pleased. So also the Son of Man will certainly suffer at their hands." ¹³Then the disciples understood that he was speaking to them of John the Baptist.

¹⁴And when they came to the crowd, a man came up to him and, kneeling before him, ¹⁵said, "Lord, have mercy on my son, for he is an epileptic and he suffers terribly. For often he falls into the fire, and often into the water. ¹⁶And I brought him to your disciples, and they could not heal him." ¹⁷And Jesus answered, "O faithless and twisted generation, how long am I to be with you? How long am I to bear with you? Bring him here to me." ¹⁸And Jesus rebuked the demon,² and it³ came out of him, and the boy was healed instantly.⁴ ¹⁹Then the disciples came to Jesus privately and said, "Why could we not cast it out?" ²⁰He said to them,

"Because of your little faith. For truly, I say to you, if you have faith like a grain of mustard seed, you will say to this mountain, 'Move from here to there,' and it will move, and nothing will be impossible for you."⁵

²²As they were gathering⁶ in Galilee, Jesus said to them, "The Son of Man is about to be delivered into the hands of men, ²³and they will kill him, and he will be raised on the third day." And they were greatly distressed.

²⁴When they came to Capernaum, the collectors of the two-drachma tax went up to Peter and said, "Does your teacher not pay the tax?" ²⁵He said, "Yes." And when he came into the house, Jesus spoke to him first, saying, "What do you think, Simon? From whom do kings of the earth take toll or tax? From their sons or from others?" ²⁶And when he said, "From others," Jesus said to him, "Then the sons are free. ²⁷However, not to give offense to them, go to the sea and cast a hook and take the first fish that comes up, and when you open its mouth you will find a shekel.⁷ Take that and give it to them for me and for yourself."

Nehemiah 7

Now when the wall had been built and I had set up the doors, and the gatekeepers, the singers, and the Levites had been appointed, ²I gave my brother Hanani and Hananiah the governor of the castle charge over Jerusalem, for he was a more faithful and God-fearing man than many. ³And I said to them, "Let not the gates of Jerusalem be opened until the sun is hot. And while they are still standing guard, let them shut and bar the doors. Appoint guards from among the inhabitants of Jerusalem, some at their guard posts and some in front of their own homes." ⁴The city was wide and large, but the people within it were few, and no houses had been rebuilt.

⁵Then my God put it into my heart to assemble the nobles and the officials and the people to be enrolled by genealogy. And I found the book of the genealogy of those who came up at the first, and I found written in it:

⁶These were the people of the province who came up out of the captivity of those exiles whom Nebuchadnezzar the king of Babylon had carried into exile. They returned to Jerusalem and Judah, each to his town. ⁷They came

¹ Or my Son, my (or the) Beloved ² Greek it ³ Greek the demon ⁴ Greek from that hour ⁵ Some manuscripts insert verse 21: But this kind never comes out except by prayer and fasting ⁶ Some manuscripts remained ⁷ Greek stater, a silver coin worth four drachmas or approximately one shekel

with Zerubbabel, Jeshua, Nehemiah, Azariah, Raamiah, Nahamani, Mordecai, Bilshan, Mispereth, Bigvai, Nehum, Baanah.

The number of the men of the people of Israel: [8] the sons of Parosh, 2,172. [9] The sons of Shephatiah, 372. [10] The sons of Arah, 652. [11] The sons of Pahath-moab, namely the sons of Jeshua and Joab, 2,818. [12] The sons of Elam, 1,254. [13] The sons of Zattu, 845. [14] The sons of Zaccai, 760. [15] The sons of Binnui, 648. [16] The sons of Bebai, 628. [17] The sons of Azgad, 2,322. [18] The sons of Adonikam, 667. [19] The sons of Bigvai, 2,067. [20] The sons of Adin, 655. [21] The sons of Ater, namely of Hezekiah, 98. [22] The sons of Hashum, 328. [23] The sons of Bezai, 324. [24] The sons of Hariph, 112. [25] The sons of Gibeon, 95. [26] The men of Bethlehem and Netophah, 188. [27] The men of Anathoth, 128. [28] The men of Beth-azmaveth, 42. [29] The men of Kiriath-jearim, Chephirah, and Beeroth, 743. [30] The men of Ramah and Geba, 621. [31] The men of Michmas, 122. [32] The men of Bethel and Ai, 123. [33] The men of the other Nebo, 52. [34] The sons of the other Elam, 1,254. [35] The sons of Harim, 320. [36] The sons of Jericho, 345. [37] The sons of Lod, Hadid, and Ono, 721. [38] The sons of Senaah, 3,930.

[39] The priests: the sons of Jedaiah, namely the house of Jeshua, 973. [40] The sons of Immer, 1,052. [41] The sons of Pashhur, 1,247. [42] The sons of Harim, 1,017.

[43] The Levites: the sons of Jeshua, namely of Kadmiel of the sons of Hodevah, 74. [44] The singers: the sons of Asaph, 148. [45] The gatekeepers: the sons of Shallum, the sons of Ater, the sons of Talmon, the sons of Akkub, the sons of Hatita, the sons of Shobai, 138.

[46] The temple servants: the sons of Ziha, the sons of Hasupha, the sons of Tabbaoth, [47] the sons of Keros, the sons of Sia, the sons of Padon, [48] the sons of Lebana, the sons of Hagaba, the sons of Shalmai, [49] the sons of Hanan, the sons of Giddel, the sons of Gahar, [50] the sons of Reaiah, the sons of Rezin, the sons of Nekoda, [51] the sons of Gazzam, the sons of Uzza, the sons of Paseah, [52] the sons of Besai, the sons of Meunim, the sons of Nephushesim, [53] the sons of Bakbuk, the sons of Hakupha, the sons of Harhur, [54] the sons of Bazlith, the sons of Mehida, the sons of Harsha, [55] the sons of Barkos, the sons of Sisera, the sons of Temah, [56] the sons of Neziah, the sons of Hatipha.

[57] The sons of Solomon's servants: the sons of Sotai, the sons of Sophereth, the sons of Perida, [58] the sons of Jaala, the sons of Darkon, the sons of Giddel, [59] the sons of Shephatiah, the sons of Hattil, the sons of Pochereth-hazzebaim, the sons of Amon.

[60] All the temple servants and the sons of Solomon's servants were 392.

[61] The following were those who came up from Tel-melah, Tel-harsha, Cherub, Addon, and Immer, but they could not prove their fathers' houses nor their descent, whether they belonged to Israel: [62] the sons of Delaiah, the sons of Tobiah, the sons of Nekoda, 642. [63] Also, of the priests: the sons of Hobaiah, the sons of Hakkoz, the sons of Barzillai (who had taken a wife of the daughters of Barzillai the Gileadite and was called by their name). [64] These sought their registration among those enrolled in the genealogies, but it was not found there, so they were excluded from the priesthood as unclean. [65] The governor told them that they were not to partake of the most holy food until a priest with Urim and Thummim should arise.

[66] The whole assembly together was 42,360, [67] besides their male and female servants, of whom there were 7,337. And they had 245 singers, male and female. [68] Their horses were 736,[1] their mules 245,[1] [69] their camels 435, and their donkeys 6,720.

[70] Now some of the heads of fathers' houses gave to the work. The governor gave to the treasury 1,000 darics[2] of gold, 50 basins, 30 priests' garments and 500 minas[3] of silver.[4] [71] And some of the heads of fathers' houses gave into the treasury of the work 20,000 darics of gold and 2,200 minas of silver. [72] And what the rest of the people gave was 20,000 darics of gold, 2,000 minas of silver, and 67 priests' garments.

[73] So the priests, the Levites, the gatekeepers, the singers, some of the people, the temple servants, and all Israel, lived in their towns.

And when the seventh month had come, the people of Israel were in their towns.

Acts 17

Now when they had passed through Amphipolis and Apollonia, they came to Thessalonica, where there was a synagogue of the Jews. [2] And Paul went in, as was his custom, and on three Sabbath days he reasoned with

---

[1] Compare Ezra 2:66 and the margins of some Hebrew manuscripts; Hebrew lacks *Their horses*. . . *245* [2] A *daric* was a coin weighing about 1/4 ounce or 8.5 grams [3] A *mina* was about 1 1/4 pounds or 0.6 kilogram [4] Probable reading; Hebrew lacks *minas of silver*

them from the Scriptures, [3]explaining and proving that it was necessary for the Christ to suffer and to rise from the dead, and saying, "This Jesus, whom I proclaim to you, is the Christ." [4]And some of them were persuaded and joined Paul and Silas, as did a great many of the devout Greeks and not a few of the leading women. [5]But the Jews[1] were jealous, and taking some wicked men of the rabble, they formed a mob, set the city in an uproar, and attacked the house of Jason, seeking to bring them out to the crowd. [6]And when they could not find them, they dragged Jason and some of the brothers before the city authorities, shouting, "These men who have turned the world upside down have come here also, [7]and Jason has received them, and they are all acting against the decrees of Caesar, saying that there is another king, Jesus." [8]And the people and the city authorities were disturbed when they heard these things. [9]And when they had taken money as security from Jason and the rest, they let them go.

[10]The brothers[2] immediately sent Paul and Silas away by night to Berea, and when they arrived they went into the Jewish synagogue. [11]Now these Jews were more noble than those in Thessalonica; they received the word with all eagerness, examining the Scriptures daily to see if these things were so. [12]Many of them therefore believed, with not a few Greek women of high standing as well as men. [13]But when the Jews from Thessalonica learned that the word of God was proclaimed by Paul at Berea also, they came there too, agitating and stirring up the crowds. [14]Then the brothers immediately sent Paul off on his way to the sea, but Silas and Timothy remained there. [15]Those who conducted Paul brought him as far as Athens, and after receiving a command for Silas and Timothy to come to him as soon as possible, they departed.

[16]Now while Paul was waiting for them at Athens, his spirit was provoked within him as he saw that the city was full of idols. [17]So he reasoned in the synagogue with the Jews and the devout persons, and in the marketplace every day with those who happened to be there. [18]Some of the Epicurean and Stoic philosophers also conversed with him. And some said, "What does this babbler wish to say?" Others said, "He seems to be a preacher of foreign divinities"—because he was preaching Jesus and the resurrection. [19]And they took him and brought him to the Areopagus, saying, "May we know what this new teaching is that you are presenting? [20]For you bring some strange things to our ears. We wish to know therefore what these things mean." [21]Now all the Athenians and the foreigners who lived there would spend their time in nothing except telling or hearing something new.

[22]So Paul, standing in the midst of the Areopagus, said: "Men of Athens, I perceive that in every way you are very religious. [23]For as I passed along and observed the objects of your worship, I found also an altar with this inscription, 'To the unknown god.' What therefore you worship as unknown, this I proclaim to you. [24]The God who made the world and everything in it, being Lord of heaven and earth, does not live in temples made by man,[3] [25]nor is he served by human hands, as though he needed anything, since he himself gives to all mankind life and breath and everything. [26]And he made from one man every nation of mankind to live on all the face of the earth, having determined allotted periods and the boundaries of their dwelling place, [27]that they should seek God, and perhaps feel their way toward him and find him. Yet he is actually not far from each one of us, [28]for

" 'In him we live and move and have our being';[4]

as even some of your own poets have said,

" 'For we are indeed his offspring.'[5]

[29]Being then God's offspring, we ought not to think that the divine being is like gold or silver or stone, an image formed by the art and imagination of man. [30]The times of ignorance God overlooked, but now he commands all people everywhere to repent, [31]because he has fixed a day on which he will judge the world in righteousness by a man whom he has appointed; and of this he has given assurance to all by raising him from the dead."

[32]Now when they heard of the resurrection of the dead, some mocked. But others said, "We will hear you again about this." [33]So Paul went out from their midst. [34]But some men joined him and believed, among whom also were Dionysius the Areopagite and a woman named Damaris and others with them.

[1] Greek *Ioudaioi* probably refers here to Jewish religious leaders, and others under their influence, in that time; also verse 13   [2] Or *brothers and sisters*; also verse 14   [3] Greek *made by hands*   [4] Probably from Epimenides of Crete   [5] From Aratus's poem "Phainomena"

JANUARY 18

Genesis 19

The two angels came to Sodom in the evening, and Lot was sitting in the gate of Sodom. When Lot saw them, he rose to meet them and bowed himself with his face to the earth ²and said, "My lords, please turn aside to your servant's house and spend the night and wash your feet. Then you may rise up early and go on your way." They said, "No; we will spend the night in the town square." ³But he pressed them strongly; so they turned aside to him and entered his house. And he made them a feast and baked unleavened bread, and they ate.

⁴But before they lay down, the men of the city, the men of Sodom, both young and old, all the people to the last man, surrounded the house. ⁵And they called to Lot, "Where are the men who came to you tonight? Bring them out to us, that we may know them." ⁶Lot went out to the men at the entrance, shut the door after him, ⁷and said, "I beg you, my brothers, do not act so wickedly. ⁸Behold, I have two daughters who have not known any man. Let me bring them out to you, and do to them as you please. Only do nothing to these men, for they have come under the shelter of my roof." ⁹But they said, "Stand back!" And they said, "This fellow came to sojourn, and he has become the judge! Now we will deal worse with you than with them." Then they pressed hard against the man Lot, and drew near to break the door down. ¹⁰But the men reached out their hands and brought Lot into the house with them and shut the door. ¹¹And they struck with blindness the men who were at the entrance of the house, both small and great, so that they wore themselves out groping for the door.

¹²Then the men said to Lot, "Have you anyone else here? Sons-in-law, sons, daughters, or anyone you have in the city, bring them out of the place. ¹³For we are about to destroy this place, because the outcry against its people has become great before the LORD, and the LORD has sent us to destroy it." ¹⁴So Lot went out and said to his sons-in-law, who were to marry his daughters, "Up! Get out of this place, for the LORD is about to destroy the city." But he seemed to his sons-in-law to be jesting.

¹⁵As morning dawned, the angels urged Lot, saying, "Up! Take your wife and your two daughters who are here, lest you be swept away in the punishment of the city." ¹⁶But he lingered. So the men seized him and his wife and his two daughters by the hand, the LORD being merciful to him, and they brought him out and set him outside the city. ¹⁷And as they brought them out, one said, "Escape for your life. Do not look back or stop anywhere in the valley. Escape to the hills, lest you be swept away." ¹⁸And Lot said to them, "Oh, no, my lords. ¹⁹Behold, your servant has found favor in your sight, and you have shown me great kindness in saving my life. But I cannot escape to the hills, lest the disaster overtake me and I die. ²⁰Behold, this city is near enough to flee to, and it is a little one. Let me escape there—is it not a little one?—and my life will be saved!" ²¹He said to him, "Behold, I grant you this favor also, that I will not overthrow the city of which you have spoken. ²²Escape there quickly, for I can do nothing till you arrive there." Therefore the name of the city was called Zoar.¹

²³The sun had risen on the earth when Lot came to Zoar. ²⁴Then the LORD rained on Sodom and Gomorrah sulfur and fire from the LORD out of heaven. ²⁵And he overthrew those cities, and all the valley, and all the inhabitants of the cities, and what grew on the ground. ²⁶But Lot's wife, behind him, looked back, and she became a pillar of salt.

²⁷And Abraham went early in the morning to the place where he had stood before the LORD. ²⁸And he looked down toward Sodom and Gomorrah and toward all the land of the valley, and he looked and, behold, the smoke of the land went up like the smoke of a furnace.

²⁹So it was that, when God destroyed the cities of the valley, God remembered Abraham and sent Lot out of the midst of the overthrow

¹ *Zoar* means *little*

when he overthrew the cities in which Lot had lived. ³⁰Now Lot went up out of Zoar and lived in the hills with his two daughters, for he was afraid to live in Zoar. So he lived in a cave with his two daughters. ³¹And the firstborn said to the younger, "Our father is old, and there is not a man on earth to come in to us after the manner of all the earth. ³²Come, let us make our father drink wine, and we will lie with him, that we may preserve offspring from our father." ³³So they made their father drink wine that night. And the firstborn went in and lay with her father. He did not know when she lay down or when she arose.

³⁴The next day, the firstborn said to the younger, "Behold, I lay last night with my father. Let us make him drink wine tonight also. Then you go in and lie with him, that we may preserve offspring from our father." ³⁵So they made their father drink wine that night also. And the younger arose and lay with him, and he did not know when she lay down or when she arose. ³⁶Thus both the daughters of Lot became pregnant by their father. ³⁷The firstborn bore a son and called his name Moab.¹ He is the father of the Moabites to this day. ³⁸The younger also bore a son and called his name Ben-ammi.² He is the father of the Ammonites to this day.

Matthew 18

At that time the disciples came to Jesus, saying, "Who is the greatest in the kingdom of heaven?" ²And calling to him a child, he put him in the midst of them ³and said, "Truly, I say to you, unless you turn and become like children, you will never enter the kingdom of heaven. ⁴Whoever humbles himself like this child is the greatest in the kingdom of heaven.

⁵"Whoever receives one such child in my name receives me, ⁶but whoever causes one of these little ones who believe in me to sin,³ it would be better for him to have a great millstone fastened around his neck and to be drowned in the depth of the sea.

⁷"Woe to the world for temptations to sin!⁴ For it is necessary that temptations come, but woe to the one by whom the temptation comes!

⁸And if your hand or your foot causes you to sin, cut it off and throw it away. It is better for you to enter life crippled or lame than with two hands or two feet to be thrown into the eternal fire. ⁹And if your eye causes you to sin, tear it out and throw it away. It is better for you to enter life with one eye than with two eyes to be thrown into the hell⁵ of fire.

¹⁰"See that you do not despise one of these little ones. For I tell you that in heaven their angels always see the face of my Father who is in heaven.⁶ ¹²What do you think? If a man has a hundred sheep, and one of them has gone astray, does he not leave the ninety-nine on the mountains and go in search of the one that went astray? ¹³And if he finds it, truly, I say to you, he rejoices over it more than over the ninety-nine that never went astray. ¹⁴So it is not the will of my⁷ Father who is in heaven that one of these little ones should perish.

¹⁵"If your brother sins against you, go and tell him his fault, between you and him alone. If he listens to you, you have gained your brother. ¹⁶But if he does not listen, take one or two others along with you, that every charge may be established by the evidence of two or three witnesses. ¹⁷If he refuses to listen to them, tell it to the church. And if he refuses to listen even to the church, let him be to you as a Gentile and a tax collector. ¹⁸Truly, I say to you, whatever you bind on earth shall be bound in heaven, and whatever you loose on earth shall be loosed⁸ in heaven. ¹⁹Again I say to you, if two of you agree on earth about anything they ask, it will be done for them by my Father in heaven. ²⁰For where two or three are gathered in my name, there am I among them."

²¹Then Peter came up and said to him, "Lord, how often will my brother sin against me, and I forgive him? As many as seven times?" ²²Jesus said to him, "I do not say to you seven times, but seventy-seven times.

²³"Therefore the kingdom of heaven may be compared to a king who wished to settle accounts with his servants.⁹ ²⁴When he began to settle, one was brought to him who owed him ten thousand talents.¹⁰ ²⁵And since he could not pay, his master ordered him to be sold, with his wife and children and all that he had, and payment to be made. ²⁶So the servant¹¹ fell on his knees, imploring him, 'Have patience with

¹ Moab sounds like the Hebrew for *from father* ² Ben-ammi means son of my people ³ Greek causes. . . to stumble; also verses 8, 9 ⁴ Greek stumbling blocks ⁵ Greek Gehenna ⁶ Some manuscripts add verse 11: For the Son of Man came to save the lost ⁷ Some manuscripts your ⁸ Or shall have been bound. ... shall have been loosed ⁹ Greek bondservants; also verses 28, 31 ¹⁰ A talent was a monetary unit worth about twenty years' wages for a laborer ¹¹ Greek bondservant; also verses 27, 28, 29, 32, 33

me, and I will pay you everything.' ²⁷And out of pity for him, the master of that servant released him and forgave him the debt. ²⁸But when that same servant went out, he found one of his fellow servants who owed him a hundred denarii,¹ and seizing him, he began to choke him, saying, 'Pay what you owe.' ²⁹So his fellow servant fell down and pleaded with him, 'Have patience with me, and I will pay you.' ³⁰He refused and went and put him in prison until he should pay the debt. ³¹When his fellow servants saw what had taken place, they were greatly distressed, and they went and reported to their master all that had taken place. ³²Then his master summoned him and said to him, 'You wicked servant! I forgave you all that debt because you pleaded with me. ³³And should not you have had mercy on your fellow servant, as I had mercy on you?' ³⁴And in anger his master delivered him to the jailers,² until he should pay all his debt. ³⁵So also my heavenly Father will do to every one of you, if you do not forgive your brother from your heart."

Nehemiah 8

A nd all the people gathered as one man into the square before the Water Gate. And they told Ezra the scribe to bring the Book of the Law of Moses that the Lord had commanded Israel. ²So Ezra the priest brought the Law before the assembly, both men and women and all who could understand what they heard, on the first day of the seventh month. ³And he read from it facing the square before the Water Gate from early morning until midday, in the presence of the men and the women and those who could understand. And the ears of all the people were attentive to the Book of the Law. ⁴And Ezra the scribe stood on a wooden platform that they had made for the purpose. And beside him stood Mattithiah, Shema, Anaiah, Uriah, Hilkiah, and Maaseiah on his right hand, and Pedaiah, Mishael, Malchijah, Hashum, Hashbaddanah, Zechariah, and Meshullam on his left hand. ⁵And Ezra opened the book in the sight of all the people, for he was above all the people, and as he opened it all the people stood. ⁶And Ezra blessed the Lord, the great God, and all the people answered, "Amen, Amen," lifting up their hands. And they bowed their heads and worshiped the Lord with their faces to the

ground. ⁷Also Jeshua, Bani, Sherebiah, Jamin, Akkub, Shabbethai, Hodiah, Maaseiah, Kelita, Azariah, Jozabad, Hanan, Pelaiah, the Levites,³ helped the people to understand the Law, while the people remained in their places. ⁸They read from the book, from the Law of God, clearly,⁴ and they gave the sense, so that the people understood the reading.

⁹And Nehemiah, who was the governor, and Ezra the priest and scribe, and the Levites who taught the people said to all the people, "This day is holy to the Lord your God; do not mourn or weep." For all the people wept as they heard the words of the Law. ¹⁰Then he said to them, "Go your way. Eat the fat and drink sweet wine and send portions to anyone who has nothing ready, for this day is holy to our Lord. And do not be grieved, for the joy of the Lord is your strength." ¹¹So the Levites calmed all the people, saying, "Be quiet, for this day is holy; do not be grieved." ¹²And all the people went their way to eat and drink and to send portions and to make great rejoicing, because they had understood the words that were declared to them.

¹³On the second day the heads of fathers' houses of all the people, with the priests and the Levites, came together to Ezra the scribe in order to study the words of the Law. ¹⁴And they found it written in the Law that the Lord had commanded by Moses that the people of Israel should dwell in booths⁵ during the feast of the seventh month, ¹⁵and that they should proclaim it and publish it in all their towns and in Jerusalem, "Go out to the hills and bring branches of olive, wild olive, myrtle, palm, and other leafy trees to make booths, as it is written." ¹⁶So the people went out and brought them and made booths for themselves, each on his roof, and in their courts and in the courts of the house of God, and in the square at the Water Gate and in the square at the Gate of Ephraim. ¹⁷And all the assembly of those who had returned from the captivity made booths and lived in the booths, for from the days of Jeshua the son of Nun to that day the people of Israel had not done so. And there was very great rejoicing. ¹⁸And day by day, from the first day to the last day, he read from the Book of the Law of God. They kept the feast seven days, and on the eighth day there was a solemn assembly, according to the rule.

¹ A *denarius* was a day's wage for a laborer   ² Greek *torturers*   ³ Vulgate; Hebrew *and the Levites*   ⁴ Or *with interpretation, or paragraph by paragraph*   ⁵ Or *temporary shelters*

Acts 18

After this Paul[1] left Athens and went to Corinth. [2]And he found a Jew named Aquila, a native of Pontus, recently come from Italy with his wife Priscilla, because Claudius had commanded all the Jews to leave Rome. And he went to see them, [3]and because he was of the same trade he stayed with them and worked, for they were tentmakers by trade. [4]And he reasoned in the synagogue every Sabbath, and tried to persuade Jews and Greeks.

[5]When Silas and Timothy arrived from Macedonia, Paul was occupied with the word, testifying to the Jews that the Christ was Jesus. [6]And when they opposed and reviled him, he shook out his garments and said to them, "Your blood be on your own heads! I am innocent. From now on I will go to the Gentiles." [7]And he left there and went to the house of a man named Titius Justus, a worshiper of God. His house was next door to the synagogue. [8]Crispus, the ruler of the synagogue, believed in the Lord, together with his entire household. And many of the Corinthians hearing Paul believed and were baptized. [9]And the Lord said to Paul one night in a vision, "Do not be afraid, but go on speaking and do not be silent, [10]for I am with you, and no one will attack you to harm you, for I have many in this city who are my people." [11]And he stayed a year and six months, teaching the word of God among them.

[12]But when Gallio was proconsul of Achaia, the Jews[2] made a united attack on Paul and brought him before the tribunal, [13]saying, "This man is persuading people to worship God contrary to the law." [14]But when Paul was about to open his mouth, Gallio said to the Jews, "If it were a matter of wrongdoing or vicious crime, O Jews, I would have reason to accept your complaint. [15]But since it is a matter of questions about words and names and your own law, see to it yourselves. I refuse to be a judge of these things." [16]And he drove them from the tribunal. [17]And they all seized Sosthenes, the ruler of the synagogue, and beat him in front of the tribunal. But Gallio paid no attention to any of this.

[18]After this, Paul stayed many days longer and then took leave of the brothers[3] and set sail for Syria, and with him Priscilla and Aquila. At Cenchreae he had cut his hair, for he was under a vow. [19]And they came to Ephesus, and he left them there, but he himself went into the synagogue and reasoned with the Jews. [20]When they asked him to stay for a longer period, he declined. [21]But on taking leave of them he said, "I will return to you if God wills," and he set sail from Ephesus.

[22]When he had landed at Caesarea, he went up and greeted the church, and then went down to Antioch. [23]After spending some time there, he departed and went from one place to the next through the region of Galatia and Phrygia, strengthening all the disciples.

[24]Now a Jew named Apollos, a native of Alexandria, came to Ephesus. He was an eloquent man, competent in the Scriptures. [25]He had been instructed in the way of the Lord. And being fervent in spirit,[4] he spoke and taught accurately the things concerning Jesus, though he knew only the baptism of John. [26]He began to speak boldly in the synagogue, but when Priscilla and Aquila heard him, they took him aside and explained to him the way of God more accurately. [27]And when he wished to cross to Achaia, the brothers encouraged him and wrote to the disciples to welcome him. When he arrived, he greatly helped those who through grace had believed, [28]for he powerfully refuted the Jews in public, showing by the Scriptures that the Christ was Jesus.

---

[1] Greek he [2] Greek *Ioudaioi* probably refers here to Jewish religious leaders, and others under their influence, in that time; also verses 14 (twice), 28 [3] Or *brothers and sisters*; also verse 27 [4] Or *in the Spirit*

JANUARY 19

Genesis 20

From there Abraham journeyed toward the territory of the Negeb and lived between Kadesh and Shur; and he sojourned in Gerar. ²And Abraham said of Sarah his wife, "She is my sister." And Abimelech king of Gerar sent and took Sarah. ³But God came to Abimelech in a dream by night and said to him, "Behold, you are a dead man because of the woman whom you have taken, for she is a man's wife." ⁴Now Abimelech had not approached her. So he said, "Lord, will you kill an innocent people? ⁵Did he not himself say to me, 'She is my sister'? And she herself said, 'He is my brother.' In the integrity of my heart and the innocence of my hands I have done this." ⁶Then God said to him in the dream, "Yes, I know that you have done this in the integrity of your heart, and it was I who kept you from sinning against me. Therefore I did not let you touch her. ⁷Now then, return the man's wife, for he is a prophet, so that he will pray for you, and you shall live. But if you do not return her, know that you shall surely die, you and all who are yours."

⁸So Abimelech rose early in the morning and called all his servants and told them all these things. And the men were very much afraid. ⁹Then Abimelech called Abraham and said to him, "What have you done to us? And how have I sinned against you, that you have brought on me and my kingdom a great sin? You have done to me things that ought not to be done." ¹⁰And Abimelech said to Abraham, "What did you see, that you did this thing?" ¹¹Abraham said, "I did it because I thought, 'There is no fear of God at all in this place, and they will kill me because of my wife.' ¹²Besides, she is indeed my sister, the daughter of my father though not the daughter of my mother, and she became my wife. ¹³And when God caused me to wander from my father's house, I said to her, 'This is the kindness you must do me: at every place to which we come, say of me, "He is my brother."'"

¹⁴Then Abimelech took sheep and oxen, and male servants and female servants, and gave them to Abraham, and returned Sarah his wife to him. ¹⁵And Abimelech said, "Behold, my land is before you; dwell where it pleases you." ¹⁶To Sarah he said, "Behold, I have given your brother a thousand pieces of silver. It is a sign of your innocence in the eyes of all[1] who are with you, and before everyone you are vindicated." ¹⁷Then Abraham prayed to God, and God healed Abimelech, and also healed his wife and female slaves so that they bore children. ¹⁸For the LORD had closed all the wombs of the house of Abimelech because of Sarah, Abraham's wife.

Matthew 19

Now when Jesus had finished these sayings, he went away from Galilee and entered the region of Judea beyond the Jordan. ²And large crowds followed him, and he healed them there.

³And Pharisees came up to him and tested him by asking, "Is it lawful to divorce one's wife for any cause?" ⁴He answered, "Have you not read that he who created them from the beginning made them male and female, ⁵and said, 'Therefore a man shall leave his father and his mother and hold fast to his wife, and the two shall become one flesh'? ⁶So they are no longer two but one flesh. What therefore God has joined together, let not man separate." ⁷They said to him, "Why then did Moses command one to give a certificate of divorce and to send her away?" ⁸He said to them, "Because of your hardness of heart Moses allowed you to divorce your wives, but from the beginning it was not so. ⁹And I say to you: whoever divorces his wife, except for sexual immorality, and marries another, commits adultery."[2]

¹⁰The disciples said to him, "If such is the case of a man with his wife, it is better not to marry." ¹¹But he said to them, "Not everyone can receive this saying, but only those to whom it is given. ¹²For there are eunuchs who have

[1] Hebrew *It is a covering of eyes for all* [2] Some manuscripts add *and whoever marries a divorced woman commits adultery*; other manuscripts *except for sexual immorality, makes her commit adultery, and whoever marries a divorced woman commits adultery*

been so from birth, and there are eunuchs who have been made eunuchs by men, and there are eunuchs who have made themselves eunuchs for the sake of the kingdom of heaven. Let the one who is able to receive this receive it."

[13] Then children were brought to him that he might lay his hands on them and pray. The disciples rebuked the people, [14] but Jesus said, "Let the little children come to me and do not hinder them, for to such belongs the kingdom of heaven." [15] And he laid his hands on them and went away.

[16] And behold, a man came up to him, saying, "Teacher, what good deed must I do to have eternal life?" [17] And he said to him, "Why do you ask me about what is good? There is only one who is good. If you would enter life, keep the commandments." [18] He said to him, "Which ones?" And Jesus said, "You shall not murder, You shall not commit adultery, You shall not steal, You shall not bear false witness, [19] Honor your father and mother, and, You shall love your neighbor as yourself." [20] The young man said to him, "All these I have kept. What do I still lack?" [21] Jesus said to him, "If you would be perfect, go, sell what you possess and give to the poor, and you will have treasure in heaven; and come, follow me." [22] When the young man heard this he went away sorrowful, for he had great possessions.

[23] And Jesus said to his disciples, "Truly, I say to you, only with difficulty will a rich person enter the kingdom of heaven. [24] Again I tell you, it is easier for a camel to go through the eye of a needle than for a rich person to enter the kingdom of God." [25] When the disciples heard this, they were greatly astonished, saying, "Who then can be saved?" [26] But Jesus looked at them and said, "With man this is impossible, but with God all things are possible." [27] Then Peter said in reply, "See, we have left everything and followed you. What then will we have?" [28] Jesus said to them, "Truly, I say to you, in the new world,[1] when the Son of Man will sit on his glorious throne, you who have followed me will also sit on twelve thrones, judging the twelve tribes of Israel. [29] And everyone who has left houses or brothers or sisters or father or mother or children or lands, for my name's sake, will receive a hundredfold[2] and will inherit eternal life. [30] But many who are first will be last, and the last first.

Nehemiah 9

Now on the twenty-fourth day of this month the people of Israel were assembled with fasting and in sackcloth, and with earth on their heads. [2] And the Israelites[3] separated themselves from all foreigners and stood and confessed their sins and the iniquities of their fathers. [3] And they stood up in their place and read from the Book of the Law of the LORD their God for a quarter of the day; for another quarter of it they made confession and worshiped the LORD their God. [4] On the stairs of the Levites stood Jeshua, Bani, Kadmiel, Shebaniah, Bunni, Sherebiah, Bani, and Chenani; and they cried with a loud voice to the LORD their God. [5] Then the Levites, Jeshua, Kadmiel, Bani, Hashabneiah, Sherebiah, Hodiah, Shebaniah, and Pethahiah, said, "Stand up and bless the LORD your God from everlasting to everlasting. Blessed be your glorious name, which is exalted above all blessing and praise.

[6][4] "You are the LORD, you alone. You have made heaven, the heaven of heavens, with all their host, the earth and all that is on it, the seas and all that is in them; and you preserve all of them; and the host of heaven worships you. [7] You are the LORD, the God who chose Abram and brought him out of Ur of the Chaldeans and gave him the name Abraham. [8] You found his heart faithful before you, and made with him the covenant to give to his offspring the land of the Canaanite, the Hittite, the Amorite, the Perizzite, the Jebusite, and the Girgashite. And you have kept your promise, for you are righteous.

[9] "And you saw the affliction of our fathers in Egypt and heard their cry at the Red Sea, [10] and performed signs and wonders against Pharaoh and all his servants and all the people of his land, for you knew that they acted arrogantly against our fathers. And you made a name for yourself, as it is to this day. [11] And you divided the sea before them, so that they went through the midst of the sea on dry land, and you cast their pursuers into the depths, as a stone into mighty waters. [12] By a pillar of cloud you led them in the day, and by a pillar of fire in the night to light for them the way in which they should go. [13] You came down on Mount Sinai and spoke with them from heaven and gave them right rules and true laws, good statutes and commandments, [14] and you made

---

[1] Greek *in the regeneration* [2] Some manuscripts *manifold* [3] Hebrew *the offspring of Israel* [4] Septuagint adds *And Ezra said*

known to them your holy Sabbath and commanded them commandments and statutes and a law by Moses your servant. [15] You gave them bread from heaven for their hunger and brought water for them out of the rock for their thirst, and you told them to go in to possess the land that you had sworn to give them.

[16] "But they and our fathers acted presumptuously and stiffened their neck and did not obey your commandments. [17] They refused to obey and were not mindful of the wonders that you performed among them, but they stiffened their neck and appointed a leader to return to their slavery in Egypt. But you are a God ready to forgive, gracious and merciful, slow to anger and abounding in steadfast love, and did not forsake them. [18] Even when they had made for themselves a golden[1] calf and said, 'This is your God who brought you up out of Egypt,' and had committed great blasphemies, [19] you in your great mercies did not forsake them in the wilderness. The pillar of cloud to lead them in the way did not depart from them by day, nor the pillar of fire by night to light for them the way by which they should go. [20] You gave your good Spirit to instruct them and did not withhold your manna from their mouth and gave them water for their thirst. [21] Forty years you sustained them in the wilderness, and they lacked nothing. Their clothes did not wear out and their feet did not swell.

[22] "And you gave them kingdoms and peoples and allotted to them every corner. So they took possession of the land of Sihon king of Heshbon and the land of Og king of Bashan. [23] You multiplied their children as the stars of heaven, and you brought them into the land that you had told their fathers to enter and possess. [24] So the descendants went in and possessed the land, and you subdued before them the inhabitants of the land, the Canaanites, and gave them into their hand, with their kings and the peoples of the land, that they might do with them as they would. [25] And they captured fortified cities and a rich land, and took possession of houses full of all good things, cisterns already hewn, vineyards, olive orchards and fruit trees in abundance. So they ate and were filled and became fat and delighted themselves in your great goodness.

[26] "Nevertheless, they were disobedient and rebelled against you and cast your law behind their back and killed your prophets, who had warned them in order to turn them back to you, and they committed great blasphemies. [27] Therefore you gave them into the hand of their enemies, who made them suffer. And in the time of their suffering they cried out to you and you heard them from heaven, and according to your great mercies you gave them saviors who saved them from the hand of their enemies. [28] But after they had rest they did evil again before you, and you abandoned them to the hand of their enemies, so that they had dominion over them. Yet when they turned and cried to you, you heard from heaven, and many times you delivered them according to your mercies. [29] And you warned them in order to turn them back to your law. Yet they acted presumptuously and did not obey your commandments, but sinned against your rules, which if a person does them, he shall live by them, and they turned a stubborn shoulder and stiffened their neck and would not obey. [30] Many years you bore with them and warned them by your Spirit through your prophets. Yet they would not give ear. Therefore you gave them into the hand of the peoples of the lands. [31] Nevertheless, in your great mercies you did not make an end of them or forsake them, for you are a gracious and merciful God.

[32] "Now, therefore, our God, the great, the mighty, and the awesome God, who keeps covenant and steadfast love, let not all the hardship seem little to you that has come upon us, upon our kings, our princes, our priests, our prophets, our fathers, and all your people, since the time of the kings of Assyria until this day. [33] Yet you have been righteous in all that has come upon us, for you have dealt faithfully and we have acted wickedly. [34] Our kings, our princes, our priests, and our fathers have not kept your law or paid attention to your commandments and your warnings that you gave them. [35] Even in their own kingdom, and amid your great goodness that you gave them, and in the large and rich land that you set before them, they did not serve you or turn from their wicked works. [36] Behold, we are slaves this day; in the land that you gave to our fathers to enjoy its fruit and its good gifts, behold, we are slaves. [37] And its rich yield goes to the kings whom you have set over us because of our sins. They rule over our bodies and over

---

[1] Hebrew *metal*

our livestock as they please, and we are in great distress.

38 ¹ "Because of all this we make a firm covenant in writing; on the sealed document are the names of² our princes, our Levites, and our priests.

Acts 19

And it happened that while Apollos was at Corinth, Paul passed through the inland³ country and came to Ephesus. There he found some disciples. ²And he said to them, "Did you receive the Holy Spirit when you believed?" And they said, "No, we have not even heard that there is a Holy Spirit." ³And he said, "Into what then were you baptized?" They said, "Into John's baptism." ⁴And Paul said, "John baptized with the baptism of repentance, telling the people to believe in the one who was to come after him, that is, Jesus." ⁵On hearing this, they were baptized in⁴ the name of the Lord Jesus. ⁶And when Paul had laid his hands on them, the Holy Spirit came on them, and they began speaking in tongues and prophesying. ⁷There were about twelve men in all.

⁸And he entered the synagogue and for three months spoke boldly, reasoning and persuading them about the kingdom of God. ⁹But when some became stubborn and continued in unbelief, speaking evil of the Way before the congregation, he withdrew from them and took the disciples with him, reasoning daily in the hall of Tyrannus.⁵ ¹⁰This continued for two years, so that all the residents of Asia heard the word of the Lord, both Jews and Greeks.

¹¹And God was doing extraordinary miracles by the hands of Paul, ¹²so that even handkerchiefs or aprons that had touched his skin were carried away to the sick, and their diseases left them and the evil spirits came out of them. ¹³Then some of the itinerant Jewish exorcists undertook to invoke the name of the Lord Jesus over those who had evil spirits, saying, "I adjure you by the Jesus whom Paul proclaims." ¹⁴Seven sons of a Jewish high priest named Sceva were doing this. ¹⁵But the evil spirit answered them, "Jesus I know, and Paul I recognize, but who are you?" ¹⁶And the man in whom was the evil spirit leaped on them, mastered all⁶ of them and overpowered them, so that they fled out of that house naked and

wounded. ¹⁷And this became known to all the residents of Ephesus, both Jews and Greeks. And fear fell upon them all, and the name of the Lord Jesus was extolled. ¹⁸Also many of those who were now believers came, confessing and divulging their practices. ¹⁹And a number of those who had practiced magic arts brought their books together and burned them in the sight of all. And they counted the value of them and found it came to fifty thousand pieces of silver. ²⁰So the word of the Lord continued to increase and prevail mightily.

²¹Now after these events Paul resolved in the Spirit to pass through Macedonia and Achaia and go to Jerusalem, saying, "After I have been there, I must also see Rome." ²²And having sent into Macedonia two of his helpers, Timothy and Erastus, he himself stayed in Asia for a while.

²³About that time there arose no little disturbance concerning the Way. ²⁴For a man named Demetrius, a silversmith, who made silver shrines of Artemis, brought no little business to the craftsmen. ²⁵These he gathered together, with the workmen in similar trades, and said, "Men, you know that from this business we have our wealth. ²⁶And you see and hear that not only in Ephesus but in almost all of Asia this Paul has persuaded and turned away a great many people, saying that gods made with hands are not gods. ²⁷And there is danger not only that this trade of ours may come into disrepute but also that the temple of the great goddess Artemis may be counted as nothing, and that she may even be deposed from her magnificence, she whom all Asia and the world worship."

²⁸When they heard this they were enraged and were crying out, "Great is Artemis of the Ephesians!" ²⁹So the city was filled with the confusion, and they rushed together into the theater, dragging with them Gaius and Aristarchus, Macedonians who were Paul's companions in travel. ³⁰But when Paul wished to go in among the crowd, the disciples would not let him. ³¹And even some of the Asiarchs,⁷ who were friends of his, sent to him and were urging him not to venture into the theater. ³²Now some cried out one thing, some another, for the assembly was in confusion, and most of them did not know why they had come together. ³³Some of the crowd

¹ Ch 10:1 in Hebrew ² Hebrew lacks *the names of* ³ Greek *upper* (that is, highland) ⁴ Or *into* ⁵ Some manuscripts add *from the fifth hour to the tenth* (that is, from 11 A.M. to 4 P.M.)
⁶ Or *both* ⁷ That is, high-ranking officers of the province of Asia

prompted Alexander, whom the Jews had put forward. And Alexander, motioning with his hand, wanted to make a defense to the crowd. [34]But when they recognized that he was a Jew, for about two hours they all cried out with one voice, "Great is Artemis of the Ephesians!"

[35]And when the town clerk had quieted the crowd, he said, "Men of Ephesus, who is there who does not know that the city of the Ephesians is temple keeper of the great Artemis, and of the sacred stone that fell from the sky?[1] [36]Seeing then that these things cannot be denied, you ought to be quiet and do nothing rash. [37]For you have brought these men here who are neither sacrilegious nor blasphemers of our goddess. [38]If therefore Demetrius and the craftsmen with him have a complaint against anyone, the courts are open, and there are proconsuls. Let them bring charges against one another. [39]But if you seek anything further,[2] it shall be settled in the regular assembly. [40]For we really are in danger of being charged with rioting today, since there is no cause that we can give to justify this commotion." [41]And when he had said these things, he dismissed the assembly.

JANUARY 20

Genesis 21

The LORD visited Sarah as he had said, and the LORD did to Sarah as he had promised. [2]And Sarah conceived and bore Abraham a son in his old age at the time of which God had spoken to him. [3]Abraham called the name of his son who was born to him, whom Sarah bore him, Isaac.[3] [4]And Abraham circumcised his son Isaac when he was eight days old, as God had commanded him. [5]Abraham was a hundred years old when his son Isaac was born to him. [6]And Sarah said, "God has made laughter for me; everyone who hears will laugh over me." [7]And she said, "Who would have said to Abraham that Sarah would nurse children? Yet I have borne him a son in his old age."

[8]And the child grew and was weaned. And Abraham made a great feast on the day that Isaac was weaned. [9]But Sarah saw the son of Hagar the Egyptian, whom she had borne to Abraham, laughing.[4] [10]So she said to Abraham, "Cast out this slave woman with her son, for the son of this slave woman shall not be heir with my son Isaac." [11]And the thing was very displeasing to Abraham on account of his son. [12]But God said to Abraham, "Be not displeased because of the boy and because of your slave woman. Whatever Sarah says to you, do as she tells you, for through Isaac shall your offspring be named. [13]And I will make a nation of the son of the slave woman also, because he is your offspring." [14]So Abraham rose early in the morning and took bread and a skin of water and gave it to Hagar, putting it on her shoulder, along with the child, and sent her away. And she departed and wandered in the wilderness of Beersheba.

[15]When the water in the skin was gone, she put the child under one of the bushes. [16]Then she went and sat down opposite him a good way off, about the distance of a bowshot, for she said, "Let me not look on the death of the child." And as she sat opposite him, she lifted up her voice and wept. [17]And God heard the voice of the boy, and the angel of God called to Hagar from heaven and said to her, "What troubles you, Hagar? Fear not, for God has heard the voice of the boy where he is. [18]Up! Lift up the boy, and hold him fast with your hand, for I will make him into a great nation." [19]Then God opened her eyes, and she saw a well of water. And she went and filled the skin with water and gave the boy a drink. [20]And God was with the boy, and he grew up. He lived in the wilderness and became an expert with the bow. [21]He lived in the wilderness of Paran, and his mother took a wife for him from the land of Egypt.

---

[1] The meaning of the Greek is uncertain [2] Some manuscripts seek about other matters [3] Isaac means he laughs [4] Possibly laughing in mockery

²²At that time Abimelech and Phicol the commander of his army said to Abraham, "God is with you in all that you do. ²³Now therefore swear to me here by God that you will not deal falsely with me or with my descendants or with my posterity, but as I have dealt kindly with you, so you will deal with me and with the land where you have sojourned." ²⁴And Abraham said, "I will swear."

²⁵When Abraham reproved Abimelech about a well of water that Abimelech's servants had seized, ²⁶Abimelech said, "I do not know who has done this thing; you did not tell me, and I have not heard of it until today." ²⁷So Abraham took sheep and oxen and gave them to Abimelech, and the two men made a covenant. ²⁸Abraham set seven ewe lambs of the flock apart. ²⁹And Abimelech said to Abraham, "What is the meaning of these seven ewe lambs that you have set apart?" ³⁰He said, "These seven ewe lambs you will take from my hand, that this¹ may be a witness for me that I dug this well." ³¹Therefore that place was called Beersheba,² because there both of them swore an oath. ³²So they made a covenant at Beersheba. Then Abimelech and Phicol the commander of his army rose up and returned to the land of the Philistines. ³³Abraham planted a tamarisk tree in Beersheba and called there on the name of the LORD, the Everlasting God. ³⁴And Abraham sojourned many days in the land of the Philistines.

Matthew 20

"For the kingdom of heaven is like a master of a house who went out early in the morning to hire laborers for his vineyard. ²After agreeing with the laborers for a denarius³ a day, he sent them into his vineyard. ³And going out about the third hour he saw others standing idle in the marketplace, ⁴and to them he said, 'You go into the vineyard too, and whatever is right I will give you.' ⁵So they went. Going out again about the sixth hour and the ninth hour, he did the same. ⁶And about the eleventh hour he went out and found others standing. And he said to them, 'Why do you stand here idle all day?' ⁷They said to him, 'Because no one has hired us.' He said to them, 'You go into the vineyard too.' ⁸And when evening came, the owner of the vineyard said to his foreman, 'Call the laborers and pay them their wages, beginning with the last, up to the first.' ⁹And when those hired about the eleventh hour came, each of them received a denarius. ¹⁰Now when those hired first came, they thought they would receive more, but each of them also received a denarius. ¹¹And on receiving it they grumbled at the master of the house, ¹²saying, 'These last worked only one hour, and you have made them equal to us who have borne the burden of the day and the scorching heat.' ¹³But he replied to one of them, 'Friend, I am doing you no wrong. Did you not agree with me for a denarius? ¹⁴Take what belongs to you and go. I choose to give to this last worker as I give to you. ¹⁵Am I not allowed to do what I choose with what belongs to me? Or do you begrudge my generosity?'⁴ ¹⁶So the last will be first, and the first last."

¹⁷And as Jesus was going up to Jerusalem, he took the twelve disciples aside, and on the way he said to them, ¹⁸"See, we are going up to Jerusalem. And the Son of Man will be delivered over to the chief priests and scribes, and they will condemn him to death ¹⁹and deliver him over to the Gentiles to be mocked and flogged and crucified, and he will be raised on the third day."

²⁰Then the mother of the sons of Zebedee came up to him with her sons, and kneeling before him she asked him for something. ²¹And he said to her, "What do you want?" She said to him, "Say that these two sons of mine are to sit, one at your right hand and one at your left, in your kingdom." ²²Jesus answered, "You do not know what you are asking. Are you able to drink the cup that I am to drink?" They said to him, "We are able." ²³He said to them, "You will drink my cup, but to sit at my right hand and at my left is not mine to grant, but it is for those for whom it has been prepared by my Father." ²⁴And when the ten heard it, they were indignant at the two brothers. ²⁵But Jesus called them to him and said, "You know that the rulers of the Gentiles lord it over them, and their great ones exercise authority over them. ²⁶It shall not be so among you. But whoever would be great among you must be your servant,⁵ ²⁷and whoever would be first among you must be your slave,⁶ ²⁸even as the Son of Man came not to be served but to serve, and to give his life as a ransom for many."

¹ Or you ² *Beersheba* means *well of seven* or *well of the oath* ³ A *denarius* was a day's wage for a laborer ⁴ Or *is your eye bad because I am good?* ⁵ Greek *diakonos* ⁶ Greek *bondservant* (*doulos*)

²⁹And as they went out of Jericho, a great crowd followed him. ³⁰And behold, there were two blind men sitting by the roadside, and when they heard that Jesus was passing by, they cried out, "Lord,[1] have mercy on us, Son of David!" ³¹The crowd rebuked them, telling them to be silent, but they cried out all the more, "Lord, have mercy on us, Son of David!" ³²And stopping, Jesus called them and said, "What do you want me to do for you?" ³³They said to him, "Lord, let our eyes be opened." ³⁴And Jesus in pity touched their eyes, and immediately they recovered their sight and followed him.

Nehemiah 10[2]

"On the seals are the names of[3] Nehemiah the governor, the son of Hacaliah, Zedekiah, ²Seraiah, Azariah, Jeremiah, ³Pashhur, Amariah, Malchijah, ⁴Hattush, Shebaniah, Malluch, ⁵Harim, Meremoth, Obadiah, ⁶Daniel, Ginnethon, Baruch, ⁷Meshullam, Abijah, Mijamin, ⁸Maaziah, Bilgai, Shemaiah; these are the priests. ⁹And the Levites: Jeshua the son of Azaniah, Binnui of the sons of Henadad, Kadmiel; ¹⁰and their brothers, Shebaniah, Hodiah, Kelita, Pelaiah, Hanan, ¹¹Mica, Rehob, Hashabiah, ¹²Zaccur, Sherebiah, Shebaniah, ¹³Hodiah, Bani, Beninu. ¹⁴The chiefs of the people: Parosh, Pahath-moab, Elam, Zattu, Bani, ¹⁵Bunni, Azgad, Bebai, ¹⁶Adonijah, Bigvai, Adin, ¹⁷Ater, Hezekiah, Azzur, ¹⁸Hodiah, Hashum, Bezai, ¹⁹Hariph, Anathoth, Nebai, ²⁰Magpiash, Meshullam, Hezir, ²¹Meshezabel, Zadok, Jaddua, ²²Pelatiah, Hanan, Anaiah, ²³Hoshea, Hananiah, Hasshub, ²⁴Hallohesh, Pilha, Shobek, ²⁵Rehum, Hashabnah, Maaseiah, ²⁶Ahiah, Hanan, Anan, ²⁷Malluch, Harim, Baanah.

²⁸"The rest of the people, the priests, the Levites, the gatekeepers, the singers, the temple servants, and all who have separated themselves from the peoples of the lands to the Law of God, their wives, their sons, their daughters, all who have knowledge and understanding, ²⁹join with their brothers, their nobles, and enter into a curse and an oath to walk in God's Law that was given by Moses the servant of God, and to observe and do all the commandments of the LORD our Lord and his rules and his statutes. ³⁰We will not give our daughters to the peoples of the land or take their daughters

for our sons. ³¹And if the peoples of the land bring in goods or any grain on the Sabbath day to sell, we will not buy from them on the Sabbath or on a holy day. And we will forego the crops of the seventh year and the exaction of every debt.

³²"We also take on ourselves the obligation to give yearly a third part of a shekel[4] for the service of the house of our God: ³³for the showbread, the regular grain offering, the regular burnt offering, the Sabbaths, the new moons, the appointed feasts, the holy things, and the sin offerings to make atonement for Israel, and for all the work of the house of our God. ³⁴We, the priests, the Levites, and the people, have likewise cast lots for the wood offering, to bring it into the house of our God, according to our fathers' houses, at times appointed, year by year, to burn on the altar of the LORD our God, as it is written in the Law. ³⁵We obligate ourselves to bring the firstfruits of our ground and the firstfruits of all fruit of every tree, year by year, to the house of the LORD; ³⁶also to bring to the house of our God, to the priests who minister in the house of our God, the firstborn of our sons and of our cattle, as it is written in the Law, and the firstborn of our herds and of our flocks; ³⁷and to bring the first of our dough, and our contributions, the fruit of every tree, the wine and the oil, to the priests, to the chambers of the house of our God; and to bring to the Levites the tithes from our ground, for it is the Levites who collect the tithes in all our towns where we labor. ³⁸And the priest, the son of Aaron, shall be with the Levites when the Levites receive the tithes. And the Levites shall bring up the tithe of the tithes to the house of our God, to the chambers of the storehouse. ³⁹For the people of Israel and the sons of Levi shall bring the contribution of grain, wine, and oil to the chambers, where the vessels of the sanctuary are, as well as the priests who minister, and the gatekeepers and the singers. We will not neglect the house of our God."

Acts 20

After the uproar ceased, Paul sent for the disciples, and after encouraging them, he said farewell and departed for Macedonia. ²When he had gone through those regions and had given them much encouragement, he

[1] Some manuscripts omit Lord [2] Ch 10:2 in Hebrew [3] Hebrew lacks the names of [4] A shekel was about 2/5 ounce or 11 grams

came to Greece. ³There he spent three months, and when a plot was made against him by the Jews¹ as he was about to set sail for Syria, he decided to return through Macedonia. ⁴Sopater the Berean, son of Pyrrhus, accompanied him; and of the Thessalonians, Aristarchus and Secundus; and Gaius of Derbe, and Timothy; and the Asians, Tychicus and Trophimus. ⁵These went on ahead and were waiting for us at Troas, ⁶but we sailed away from Philippi after the days of Unleavened Bread, and in five days we came to them at Troas, where we stayed for seven days.

⁷On the first day of the week, when we were gathered together to break bread, Paul talked with them, intending to depart on the next day, and he prolonged his speech until midnight. ⁸There were many lamps in the upper room where we were gathered. ⁹And a young man named Eutychus, sitting at the window, sank into a deep sleep as Paul talked still longer. And being overcome by sleep, he fell down from the third story and was taken up dead. ¹⁰But Paul went down and bent over him, and taking him in his arms, said, "Do not be alarmed, for his life is in him." ¹¹And when Paul had gone up and had broken bread and eaten, he conversed with them a long while, until daybreak, and so departed. ¹²And they took the youth away alive, and were not a little comforted.

¹³But going ahead to the ship, we set sail for Assos, intending to take Paul aboard there, for so he had arranged, intending himself to go by land. ¹⁴And when he met us at Assos, we took him on board and went to Mitylene. ¹⁵And sailing from there we came the following day opposite Chios; the next day we touched at Samos; and² the day after that we went to Miletus. ¹⁶For Paul had decided to sail past Ephesus, so that he might not have to spend time in Asia, for he was hastening to be at Jerusalem, if possible, on the day of Pentecost.

¹⁷Now from Miletus he sent to Ephesus and called the elders of the church to come to him. ¹⁸And when they came to him, he said to them:

"You yourselves know how I lived among you the whole time from the first day that I set foot in Asia, ¹⁹serving the Lord with all humility and with tears and with trials that happened to me through the plots of the Jews; ²⁰how I did not shrink from declaring to you anything that was profitable, and teaching you in public and from house to house, ²¹testifying both to Jews and to Greeks of repentance toward God and of faith in our Lord Jesus Christ. ²²And now, behold, I am going to Jerusalem, constrained by³ the Spirit, not knowing what will happen to me there, ²³except that the Holy Spirit testifies to me in every city that imprisonment and afflictions await me. ²⁴But I do not account my life of any value nor as precious to myself, if only I may finish my course and the ministry that I received from the Lord Jesus, to testify to the gospel of the grace of God. ²⁵And now, behold, I know that none of you among whom I have gone about proclaiming the kingdom will see my face again. ²⁶Therefore I testify to you this day that I am innocent of the blood of all, ²⁷for I did not shrink from declaring to you the whole counsel of God. ²⁸Pay careful attention to yourselves and to all the flock, in which the Holy Spirit has made you overseers, to care for the church of God,⁴ which he obtained with his own blood.⁵ ²⁹I know that after my departure fierce wolves will come in among you, not sparing the flock; ³⁰and from among your own selves will arise men speaking twisted things, to draw away the disciples after them. ³¹Therefore be alert, remembering that for three years I did not cease night or day to admonish every one with tears. ³²And now I commend you to God and to the word of his grace, which is able to build you up and to give you the inheritance among all those who are sanctified. ³³I coveted no one's silver or gold or apparel. ³⁴You yourselves know that these hands ministered to my necessities and to those who were with me. ³⁵In all things I have shown you that by working hard in this way we must help the weak and remember the words of the Lord Jesus, how he himself said, 'It is more blessed to give than to receive.'"

³⁶And when he had said these things, he knelt down and prayed with them all. ³⁷And there was much weeping on the part of all; they embraced Paul and kissed him, ³⁸being sorrowful most of all because of the word he had spoken, that they would not see his face again. And they accompanied him to the ship.

J A N U A R Y   21

Genesis 22

After these things God tested Abraham and said to him, "Abraham!" And he said, "Here I am." [2]He said, "Take your son, your only son Isaac, whom you love, and go to the land of Moriah, and offer him there as a burnt offering on one of the mountains of which I shall tell you." [3]So Abraham rose early in the morning, saddled his donkey, and took two of his young men with him, and his son Isaac. And he cut the wood for the burnt offering and arose and went to the place of which God had told him. [4]On the third day Abraham lifted up his eyes and saw the place from afar. [5]Then Abraham said to his young men, "Stay here with the donkey; I and the boy[1] will go over there and worship and come again to you." [6]And Abraham took the wood of the burnt offering and laid it on Isaac his son. And he took in his hand the fire and the knife. So they went both of them together. [7]And Isaac said to his father Abraham, "My father!" And he said, "Here I am, my son." He said, "Behold, the fire and the wood, but where is the lamb for a burnt offering?" [8]Abraham said, "God will provide for himself the lamb for a burnt offering, my son." So they went both of them together.

[9]When they came to the place of which God had told him, Abraham built the altar there and laid the wood in order and bound Isaac his son and laid him on the altar, on top of the wood. [10]Then Abraham reached out his hand and took the knife to slaughter his son. [11]But the angel of the LORD called to him from heaven and said, "Abraham, Abraham!" And he said, "Here I am." [12]He said, "Do not lay your hand on the boy or do anything to him, for now I know that you fear God, seeing you have not withheld your son, your only son, from me." [13]And Abraham lifted up his eyes and looked, and behold, behind him was a ram, caught in a thicket by his horns. And Abraham went and took the ram and offered it up as a burnt offering instead of his son. [14]So Abraham called the name of that place, "The LORD will provide";[2] as

it is said to this day, "On the mount of the LORD it shall be provided."[3]

[15]And the angel of the LORD called to Abraham a second time from heaven [16]and said, "By myself I have sworn, declares the LORD, because you have done this and have not withheld your son, your only son, [17]I will surely bless you, and I will surely multiply your offspring as the stars of heaven and as the sand that is on the seashore. And your offspring shall possess the gate of his[4] enemies, [18]and in your offspring shall all the nations of the earth be blessed, because you have obeyed my voice." [19]So Abraham returned to his young men, and they arose and went together to Beersheba. And Abraham lived at Beersheba.

[20]Now after these things it was told to Abraham, "Behold, Milcah also has borne children to your brother Nahor: [21]Uz his firstborn, Buz his brother, Kemuel the father of Aram, [22]Chesed, Hazo, Pildash, Jidlaph, and Bethuel." [23](Bethuel fathered Rebekah.) These eight Milcah bore to Nahor, Abraham's brother. [24]Moreover, his concubine, whose name was Reumah, bore Tebah, Gaham, Tahash, and Maacah.

Matthew 21

Now when they drew near to Jerusalem and came to Bethphage, to the Mount of Olives, then Jesus sent two disciples, [2]saying to them, "Go into the village in front of you, and immediately you will find a donkey tied, and a colt with her. Untie them and bring them to me. [3]If anyone says anything to you, you shall say, 'The Lord needs them,' and he will send them at once." [4]This took place to fulfill what was spoken by the prophet, saying,

[5] "Say to the daughter of Zion,
    'Behold, your king is coming to you,
      humble, and mounted on a donkey,
    on a colt,[5] the foal of a beast of
      burden.'"

[1] Or young man; also verse 12 [2] Or will see [3] Or he will be seen [4] Or their [5] Or donkey, and on a colt,

⁶ The disciples went and did as Jesus had directed them. ⁷ They brought the donkey and the colt and put on them their cloaks, and he sat on them. ⁸ Most of the crowd spread their cloaks on the road, and others cut branches from the trees and spread them on the road. ⁹ And the crowds that went before him and that followed him were shouting, "Hosanna to the Son of David! Blessed is he who comes in the name of the Lord! Hosanna in the highest!" ¹⁰ And when he entered Jerusalem, the whole city was stirred up, saying, "Who is this?" ¹¹ And the crowds said, "This is the prophet Jesus, from Nazareth of Galilee."

¹² And Jesus entered the temple¹ and drove out all who sold and bought in the temple, and he overturned the tables of the money-changers and the seats of those who sold pigeons. ¹³ He said to them, "It is written, 'My house shall be called a house of prayer,' but you make it a den of robbers."

¹⁴ And the blind and the lame came to him in the temple, and he healed them. ¹⁵ But when the chief priests and the scribes saw the wonderful things that he did, and the children crying out in the temple, "Hosanna to the Son of David!" they were indignant, ¹⁶ and they said to him, "Do you hear what these are saying?" And Jesus said to them, "Yes; have you never read,

"'Out of the mouth of infants and nursing babies
you have prepared praise'?"

¹⁷ And leaving them, he went out of the city to Bethany and lodged there.

¹⁸ In the morning, as he was returning to the city, he became hungry. ¹⁹ And seeing a fig tree by the wayside, he went to it and found nothing on it but only leaves. And he said to it, "May no fruit ever come from you again!" And the fig tree withered at once.

²⁰ When the disciples saw it, they marveled, saying, "How did the fig tree wither at once?" ²¹ And Jesus answered them, "Truly, I say to you, if you have faith and do not doubt, you will not only do what has been done to the fig tree, but even if you say to this mountain, 'Be taken up and thrown into the sea,' it will happen. ²² And whatever you ask in prayer, you will receive, if you have faith."

²³ And when he entered the temple, the chief priests and the elders of the people came up to him as he was teaching, and said, "By what authority are you doing these things, and who gave you this authority?" ²⁴ Jesus answered them, "I also will ask you one question, and if you tell me the answer, then I also will tell you by what authority I do these things. ²⁵ The baptism of John, from where did it come? From heaven or from man?" And they discussed it among themselves, saying, "If we say, 'From heaven,' he will say to us, 'Why then did you not believe him?' ²⁶ But if we say, 'From man,' we are afraid of the crowd, for they all hold that John was a prophet." ²⁷ So they answered Jesus, "We do not know." And he said to them, "Neither will I tell you by what authority I do these things.

²⁸ "What do you think? A man had two sons. And he went to the first and said, 'Son, go and work in the vineyard today.' ²⁹ And he answered, 'I will not,' but afterward he changed his mind and went. ³⁰ And he went to the other son and said the same. And he answered, 'I go, sir,' but did not go. ³¹ Which of the two did the will of his father?" They said, "The first." Jesus said to them, "Truly, I say to you, the tax collectors and the prostitutes go into the kingdom of God before you. ³² For John came to you in the way of righteousness, and you did not believe him, but the tax collectors and the prostitutes believed him. And even when you saw it, you did not afterward change your minds and believe him.

³³ "Hear another parable. There was a master of a house who planted a vineyard and put a fence around it and dug a winepress in it and built a tower and leased it to tenants, and went into another country. ³⁴ When the season for fruit drew near, he sent his servants² to the tenants to get his fruit. ³⁵ And the tenants took his servants and beat one, killed another, and stoned another. ³⁶ Again he sent other servants, more than the first. And they did the same to them. ³⁷ Finally he sent his son to them, saying, 'They will respect my son.' ³⁸ But when the tenants saw the son, they said to themselves, 'This is the heir. Come, let us kill him and have his inheritance.' ³⁹ And they took him and threw him out of the vineyard and killed him. ⁴⁰ When therefore the owner of the vineyard comes, what will he do to those tenants?" ⁴¹ They said to him, "He will put those wretches to a miserable death and let out the vineyard

¹ Some manuscripts add of God ² Greek bondservants; also verses 35, 36

to other tenants who will give him the fruits in their seasons."

[42] Jesus said to them, "Have you never read in the Scriptures:

"'The stone that the builders rejected
    has become the cornerstone;[1]
this was the Lord's doing,
    and it is marvelous in our eyes'?

[43] Therefore I tell you, the kingdom of God will be taken away from you and given to a people producing its fruits. [44] And the one who falls on this stone will be broken to pieces; and when it falls on anyone, it will crush him."[2]

[45] When the chief priests and the Pharisees heard his parables, they perceived that he was speaking about them. [46] And although they were seeking to arrest him, they feared the crowds, because they held him to be a prophet.

Nehemiah 11

Now the leaders of the people lived in Jerusalem. And the rest of the people cast lots to bring one out of ten to live in Jerusalem the holy city, while nine out of ten[3] remained in the other towns. [2] And the people blessed all the men who willingly offered to live in Jerusalem. [3] These are the chiefs of the province who lived in Jerusalem; but in the towns of Judah everyone lived on his property in their towns: Israel, the priests, the Levites, the temple servants, and the descendants of Solomon's servants. [4] And in Jerusalem lived certain of the sons of Judah and of the sons of Benjamin. Of the sons of Judah: Athaiah the son of Uzziah, son of Zechariah, son of Amariah, son of Shephatiah, son of Mahalalel, of the sons of Perez; [5] and Maaseiah the son of Baruch, son of Col-hozeh, son of Hazaiah, son of Adaiah, son of Joiarib, son of Zechariah, son of the Shilonite. [6] All the sons of Perez who lived in Jerusalem were 468 valiant men.

[7] And these are the sons of Benjamin: Sallu the son of Meshullam, son of Joed, son of Pedaiah, son of Kolaiah, son of Maaseiah, son of Ithiel, son of Jeshaiah, [8] and his brothers, men of valor, 928.[4] [9] Joel the son of Zichri was their overseer; and Judah the son of Hassenuah was second over the city.

[10] Of the priests: Jedaiah the son of Joiarib, Jachin, [11] Seraiah the son of Hilkiah, son of

Meshullam, son of Zadok, son of Meraioth, son of Ahitub, ruler of the house of God, [12] and their brothers who did the work of the house, 822; and Adaiah the son of Jeroham, son of Pelaliah, son of Amzi, son of Zechariah, son of Pashhur, son of Malchijah, [13] and his brothers, heads of fathers' houses, 242; and Amashsai, the son of Azarel, son of Ahzai, son of Meshillemoth, son of Immer, [14] and their brothers, mighty men of valor, 128; their overseer was Zabdiel the son of Haggedolim.

[15] And of the Levites: Shemaiah the son of Hasshub, son of Azrikam, son of Hashabiah, son of Bunni; [16] and Shabbethai and Jozabad, of the chiefs of the Levites, who were over the outside work of the house of God; [17] and Mattaniah the son of Mica, son of Zabdi, son of Asaph, who was the leader of the praise,[5] who gave thanks, and Bakbukiah, the second among his brothers; and Abda the son of Shammua, son of Galal, son of Jeduthun. [18] All the Levites in the holy city were 284.

[19] The gatekeepers, Akkub, Talmon and their brothers, who kept watch at the gates, were 172. [20] And the rest of Israel, and of the priests and the Levites, were in all the towns of Judah, every one in his inheritance. [21] But the temple servants lived on Ophel; and Ziha and Gishpa were over the temple servants.

[22] The overseer of the Levites in Jerusalem was Uzzi the son of Bani, son of Hashabiah, son of Mattaniah, son of Mica, of the sons of Asaph, the singers, over the work of the house of God. [23] For there was a command from the king concerning them, and a fixed provision for the singers, as every day required. [24] And Pethahiah the son of Meshezabel, of the sons of Zerah the son of Judah, was at the king's side[6] in all matters concerning the people.

[25] And as for the villages, with their fields, some of the people of Judah lived in Kiriath-arba and its villages, and in Dibon and its villages, and in Jekabzeel and its villages, [26] and in Jeshua and in Moladah and Beth-pelet, [27] in Hazar-shual, in Beersheba and its villages, [28] in Ziklag, in Meconah and its villages, [29] in En-rimmon, in Zorah, in Jarmuth, [30] Zanoah, Adullam, and their villages, Lachish and its fields, and Azekah and its villages. So they encamped from Beersheba to the Valley of Hinnom. [31] The people of Benjamin also lived from Geba onward, at Michmash, Aija, Bethel

---

[1] Greek *the head of the corner* [2] Some manuscripts omit verse 44 [3] Hebrew *nine hands* [4] Compare Septuagint; Hebrew *Jeshaiah, and after him Gabbai, Sallai, 928* [5] Compare Septuagint, Vulgate; Hebrew *beginning* [6] Hebrew *hand*

and its villages, [32]Anathoth, Nob, Ananiah, [33]Hazor, Ramah, Gittaim, [34]Hadid, Zeboim, Neballat, [35]Lod, and Ono, the valley of craftsmen. [36]And certain divisions of the Levites in Judah were assigned to Benjamin.

Acts 21

[1]And when we had parted from them and set sail, we came by a straight course to Cos, and the next day to Rhodes, and from there to Patara.[1] [2]And having found a ship crossing to Phoenicia, we went aboard and set sail. [3]When we had come in sight of Cyprus, leaving it on the left we sailed to Syria and landed at Tyre, for there the ship was to unload its cargo. [4]And having sought out the disciples, we stayed there for seven days. And through the Spirit they were telling Paul not to go on to Jerusalem. [5]When our days there were ended, we departed and went on our journey, and they all, with wives and children, accompanied us until we were outside the city. And kneeling down on the beach, we prayed [6]and said farewell to one another. Then we went on board the ship, and they returned home.

[7]When we had finished the voyage from Tyre, we arrived at Ptolemais, and we greeted the brothers[2] and stayed with them for one day. [8]On the next day we departed and came to Caesarea, and we entered the house of Philip the evangelist, who was one of the seven, and stayed with him. [9]He had four unmarried daughters, who prophesied. [10]While we were staying for many days, a prophet named Agabus came down from Judea. [11]And coming to us, he took Paul's belt and bound his own feet and hands and said, "Thus says the Holy Spirit, 'This is how the Jews[3] at Jerusalem will bind the man who owns this belt and deliver him into the hands of the Gentiles.'" [12]When we heard this, we and the people there urged him not to go up to Jerusalem. [13]Then Paul answered, "What are you doing, weeping and breaking my heart? For I am ready not only to be imprisoned but even to die in Jerusalem for the name of the Lord Jesus." [14]And since he would not be persuaded, we ceased and said, "Let the will of the Lord be done."

[15]After these days we got ready and went up to Jerusalem. [16]And some of the disciples from Caesarea went with us, bringing us to the house of Mnason of Cyprus, an early disciple, with whom we should lodge.

[17]When we had come to Jerusalem, the brothers received us gladly. [18]On the following day Paul went in with us to James, and all the elders were present. [19]After greeting them, he related one by one the things that God had done among the Gentiles through his ministry. [20]And when they heard it, they glorified God. And they said to him, "You see, brother, how many thousands there are among the Jews of those who have believed. They are all zealous for the law, [21]and they have been told about you that you teach all the Jews who are among the Gentiles to forsake Moses, telling them not to circumcise their children or walk according to our customs. [22]What then is to be done? They will certainly hear that you have come. [23]Do therefore what we tell you. We have four men who are under a vow; [24]take these men and purify yourself along with them and pay their expenses, so that they may shave their heads. Thus all will know that there is nothing in what they have been told about you, but that you yourself also live in observance of the law. [25]But as for the Gentiles who have believed, we have sent a letter with our judgment that they should abstain from what has been sacrificed to idols, and from blood, and from what has been strangled,[4] and from sexual immorality." [26]Then Paul took the men, and the next day he purified himself along with them and went into the temple, giving notice when the days of purification would be fulfilled and the offering presented for each one of them.

[27]When the seven days were almost completed, the Jews from Asia, seeing him in the temple, stirred up the whole crowd and laid hands on him, [28]crying out, "Men of Israel, help! This is the man who is teaching everyone everywhere against the people and the law and this place. Moreover, he even brought Greeks into the temple and has defiled this holy place." [29]For they had previously seen Trophimus the Ephesian with him in the city, and they supposed that Paul had brought him into the temple. [30]Then all the city was stirred up, and the people ran together. They seized Paul and dragged him out of the temple, and at once the gates were shut. [31]And as they were seeking to kill him, word came to the tribune of the cohort that all Jerusalem was in confusion. [32]He at

---

[1] Some manuscripts add *and Myra* [2] Or *brothers and sisters*; also verse 17 [3] Greek *Ioudaioi* probably refers here to Jewish religious leaders, and others under their influence, in that time [4] Some manuscripts omit *and from what has been strangled*

once took soldiers and centurions and ran down to them. And when they saw the tribune and the soldiers, they stopped beating Paul. [33]Then the tribune came up and arrested him and ordered him to be bound with two chains. He inquired who he was and what he had done. [34]Some in the crowd were shouting one thing, some another. And as he could not learn the facts because of the uproar, he ordered him to be brought into the barracks. [35]And when he came to the steps, he was actually carried by the soldiers because of the violence of the crowd, [36]for the mob of the people followed, crying out, "Away with him!"

[37]As Paul was about to be brought into the barracks, he said to the tribune, "May I say something to you?" And he said, "Do you know Greek? [38]Are you not the Egyptian, then, who recently stirred up a revolt and led the four thousand men of the Assassins out into the wilderness?" [39]Paul replied, "I am a Jew, from Tarsus in Cilicia, a citizen of no obscure city. I beg you, permit me to speak to the people." [40]And when he had given him permission, Paul, standing on the steps, motioned with his hand to the people. And when there was a great hush, he addressed them in the Hebrew language,[1] saying:

JANUARY 22

Genesis 23

Sarah lived 127 years; these were the years of the life of Sarah. [2]And Sarah died at Kiriath-arba (that is, Hebron) in the land of Canaan, and Abraham went in to mourn for Sarah and to weep for her. [3]And Abraham rose up from before his dead and said to the Hittites,[2] [4]"I am a sojourner and foreigner among you; give me property among you for a burying place, that I may bury my dead out of my sight." [5]The Hittites answered Abraham, [6]"Hear us, my lord; you are a prince of God[3] among us. Bury your dead in the choicest of our tombs. None of us will withhold from you his tomb to hinder you from burying your dead." [7]Abraham rose and bowed to the Hittites, the people of the land. [8]And he said to them, "If you are willing that I should bury my dead out of my sight, hear me and entreat for me Ephron the son of Zohar, [9]that he may give me the cave of Machpelah, which he owns; it is at the end of his field. For the full price let him give it to me in your presence as property for a burying place." [10]Now Ephron was sitting among the Hittites, and Ephron the Hittite answered Abraham in the hearing of the Hittites, of all who went in at the gate of his city, [11]"No, my lord,

hear me: I give you the field, and I give you the cave that is in it. In the sight of the sons of my people I give it to you. Bury your dead." [12]Then Abraham bowed down before the people of the land. [13]And he said to Ephron in the hearing of the people of the land, "But if you will, hear me: I give the price of the field. Accept it from me, that I may bury my dead there." [14]Ephron answered Abraham, [15]"My lord, listen to me: a piece of land worth four hundred shekels[4] of silver, what is that between you and me? Bury your dead." [16]Abraham listened to Ephron, and Abraham weighed out for Ephron the silver that he had named in the hearing of the Hittites, four hundred shekels of silver, according to the weights current among the merchants.

[17]So the field of Ephron in Machpelah, which was to the east of Mamre, the field with the cave that was in it and all the trees that were in the field, throughout its whole area, was made over [18]to Abraham as a possession in the presence of the Hittites, before all who went in at the gate of his city. [19]After this, Abraham buried Sarah his wife in the cave of the field of Machpelah east of Mamre (that is, Hebron) in the land of Canaan. [20]The field and the cave that is in it

[1] Or the Hebrew dialect (probably Aramaic) [2] Hebrew sons of Heth; also verses 5, 7, 10, 16, 18, 20 [3] Or a mighty prince [4] A shekel was about 2/5 ounce or 11 grams

were made over to Abraham as property for a burying place by the Hittites.

Matthew 22

And again Jesus spoke to them in parables, saying, [2]"The kingdom of heaven may be compared to a king who gave a wedding feast for his son, [3]and sent his servants[1] to call those who were invited to the wedding feast, but they would not come. [4]Again he sent other servants, saying, 'Tell those who are invited, "See, I have prepared my dinner, my oxen and my fat calves have been slaughtered, and everything is ready. Come to the wedding feast."' [5]But they paid no attention and went off, one to his farm, another to his business, [6]while the rest seized his servants, treated them shamefully, and killed them. [7]The king was angry, and he sent his troops and destroyed those murderers and burned their city. [8]Then he said to his servants, 'The wedding feast is ready, but those invited were not worthy. [9]Go therefore to the main roads and invite to the wedding feast as many as you find.' [10]And those servants went out into the roads and gathered all whom they found, both bad and good. So the wedding hall was filled with guests.

[11]"But when the king came in to look at the guests, he saw there a man who had no wedding garment. [12]And he said to him, 'Friend, how did you get in here without a wedding garment?' And he was speechless. [13]Then the king said to the attendants, 'Bind him hand and foot and cast him into the outer darkness. In that place there will be weeping and gnashing of teeth.' [14]For many are called, but few are chosen."

[15]Then the Pharisees went and plotted how to entangle him in his words. [16]And they sent their disciples to him, along with the Herodians, saying, "Teacher, we know that you are true and teach the way of God truthfully, and you do not care about anyone's opinion, for you are not swayed by appearances.[2] [17]Tell us, then, what you think. Is it lawful to pay taxes to Caesar, or not?" [18]But Jesus, aware of their malice, said, "Why put me to the test, you hypocrites? [19]Show me the coin for the tax." And they brought him a denarius.[3] [20]And Jesus said to them, "Whose likeness and inscription is this?" [21]They said, "Caesar's." Then he said

to them, "Therefore render to Caesar the things that are Caesar's, and to God the things that are God's." [22]When they heard it, they marveled. And they left him and went away.

[23]The same day Sadducees came to him, who say that there is no resurrection, and they asked him a question, [24]saying, "Teacher, Moses said, 'If a man dies having no children, his brother must marry the widow and raise up offspring for his brother.' [25]Now there were seven brothers among us. The first married and died, and having no offspring left his wife to his brother. [26]So too the second and third, down to the seventh. [27]After them all, the woman died. [28]In the resurrection, therefore, of the seven, whose wife will she be? For they all had her." [29]But Jesus answered them, "You are wrong, because you know neither the Scriptures nor the power of God. [30]For in the resurrection they neither marry nor are given in marriage, but are like angels in heaven. [31]And as for the resurrection of the dead, have you not read what was said to you by God: [32]'I am the God of Abraham, and the God of Isaac, and the God of Jacob'? He is not God of the dead, but of the living." [33]And when the crowd heard it, they were astonished at his teaching.

[34]But when the Pharisees heard that he had silenced the Sadducees, they gathered together. [35]And one of them, a lawyer, asked him a question to test him. [36]"Teacher, which is the great commandment in the Law?" [37]And he said to him, "You shall love the Lord your God with all your heart and with all your soul and with all your mind. [38]This is the great and first commandment. [39]And a second is like it: You shall love your neighbor as yourself. [40]On these two commandments depend all the Law and the Prophets."

[41]Now while the Pharisees were gathered together, Jesus asked them a question, [42]saying, "What do you think about the Christ? Whose son is he?" They said to him, "The son of David." [43]He said to them, "How is it then that David, in the Spirit, calls him Lord, saying,

[44] "'The Lord said to my Lord,
"Sit at my right hand,
    until I put your enemies under your
      feet"'?

[45]If then David calls him Lord, how is he his son?" [46]And no one was able to answer him a

---

[1] Greek bondservants; also verses 4, 6, 8, 10 [2] Greek for you do not look at people's faces [3] A denarius was a day's wage for a laborer

word, nor from that day did anyone dare to ask him any more questions.

Nehemiah 12

These are the priests and the Levites who came up with Zerubbabel the son of Shealtiel, and Jeshua: Seraiah, Jeremiah, Ezra, [2]Amariah, Malluch, Hattush, [3]Shecaniah, Rehum, Meremoth, [4]Iddo, Ginnethoi, Abijah, [5]Mijamin, Maadiah, Bilgah, [6]Shemaiah, Joiarib, Jedaiah, [7]Sallu, Amok, Hilkiah, Jedaiah. These were the chiefs of the priests and of their brothers in the days of Jeshua.

[8]And the Levites: Jeshua, Binnui, Kadmiel, Sherebiah, Judah, and Mattaniah, who with his brothers was in charge of the songs of thanksgiving. [9]And Bakbukiah and Unni and their brothers stood opposite them in the service. [10]And Jeshua was the father of Joiakim, Joiakim the father of Eliashib, Eliashib the father of Joiada, [11]Joiada the father of Jonathan, and Jonathan the father of Jaddua.

[12]And in the days of Joiakim were priests, heads of fathers' houses: of Seraiah, Meraiah; of Jeremiah, Hananiah; [13]of Ezra, Meshullam; of Amariah, Jehohanan; [14]of Malluchi, Jonathan; of Shebaniah, Joseph; [15]of Harim, Adna; of Meraioth, Helkai; [16]of Iddo, Zechariah; of Ginnethon, Meshullam; [17]of Abijah, Zichri; of Miniamin, of Moadiah, Piltai; [18]of Bilgah, Shammua; of Shemaiah, Jehonathan; [19]of Joiarib, Mattenai; of Jedaiah, Uzzi; [20]of Sallai, Kallai; of Amok, Eber; [21]of Hilkiah, Hashabiah; of Jedaiah, Nethanel.

[22]In the days of Eliashib, Joiada, Johanan, and Jaddua, the Levites were recorded as heads of fathers' houses; so too were the priests in the reign of Darius the Persian. [23]As for the sons of Levi, their heads of fathers' houses were written in the Book of the Chronicles until the days of Johanan the son of Eliashib. [24]And the chiefs of the Levites: Hashabiah, Sherebiah, and Jeshua the son of Kadmiel, with their brothers who stood opposite them, to praise and to give thanks, according to the commandment of David the man of God, watch by watch. [25]Mattaniah, Bakbukiah, Obadiah, Meshullam, Talmon, and Akkub were gatekeepers standing guard at the storehouses of the gates. [26]These were in the days of Joiakim the son of Jeshua son of Jozadak, and in the days of Nehemiah the governor and of Ezra, the priest and scribe.

[27]And at the dedication of the wall of Jerusalem they sought the Levites in all their places, to bring them to Jerusalem to celebrate the dedication with gladness, with thanksgivings and with singing, with cymbals, harps, and lyres. [28]And the sons of the singers gathered together from the district surrounding Jerusalem and from the villages of the Netophathites; [29]also from Beth-gilgal and from the region of Geba and Azmaveth, for the singers had built for themselves villages around Jerusalem. [30]And the priests and the Levites purified themselves, and they purified the people and the gates and the wall.

[31]Then I brought the leaders of Judah up onto the wall and appointed two great choirs that gave thanks. One went to the south on the wall to the Dung Gate. [32]And after them went Hoshaiah and half of the leaders of Judah, [33]and Azariah, Ezra, Meshullam, [34]Judah, Benjamin, Shemaiah, and Jeremiah, [35]and certain of the priests' sons with trumpets: Zechariah the son of Jonathan, son of Shemaiah, son of Mattaniah, son of Micaiah, son of Zaccur, son of Asaph; [36]and his relatives, Shemaiah, Azarel, Milalai, Gilalai, Maai, Nethanel, Judah, and Hanani, with the musical instruments of David the man of God. And Ezra the scribe went before them. [37]At the Fountain Gate they went up straight before them by the stairs of the city of David, at the ascent of the wall, above the house of David, to the Water Gate on the east.

[38]The other choir of those who gave thanks went to the north, and I followed them with half of the people, on the wall, above the Tower of the Ovens, to the Broad Wall, [39]and above the Gate of Ephraim, and by the Gate of Yeshanah,[1] and by the Fish Gate and the Tower of Hananel and the Tower of the Hundred, to the Sheep Gate; and they came to a halt at the Gate of the Guard. [40]So both choirs of those who gave thanks stood in the house of God, and I and half of the officials with me; [41]and the priests Eliakim, Maaseiah, Miniamin, Micaiah, Elioenai, Zechariah, and Hananiah, with trumpets; [42]and Maaseiah, Shemaiah, Eleazar, Uzzi, Jehohanan, Malchijah, Elam, and Ezer. And the singers sang with Jezrahiah as their leader. [43]And they offered great sacrifices that day and rejoiced, for God had made them

---

[1] Or of the old city

rejoice with great joy; the women and children also rejoiced. And the joy of Jerusalem was heard far away.

44On that day men were appointed over the storerooms, the contributions, the firstfruits, and the tithes, to gather into them the portions required by the Law for the priests and for the Levites according to the fields of the towns, for Judah rejoiced over the priests and the Levites who ministered. **45**And they performed the service of their God and the service of purification, as did the singers and the gatekeepers, according to the command of David and his son Solomon. **46**For long ago in the days of David and Asaph there were directors of the singers, and there were songs¹ of praise and thanksgiving to God. **47**And all Israel in the days of Zerubbabel and in the days of Nehemiah gave the daily portions for the singers and the gatekeepers; and they set apart that which was for the Levites; and the Levites set apart that which was for the sons of Aaron.

Acts 22

"**B**rothers and fathers, hear the defense that I now make before you."

2And when they heard that he was addressing them in the Hebrew language,² they became even more quiet. And he said:

3"I am a Jew, born in Tarsus in Cilicia, but brought up in this city, educated at the feet of Gamaliel³ according to the strict manner of the law of our fathers, being zealous for God as all of you are this day. **4**I persecuted this Way to the death, binding and delivering to prison both men and women, **5**as the high priest and the whole council of elders can bear me witness. From them I received letters to the brothers, and I journeyed toward Damascus to take those also who were there and bring them in bonds to Jerusalem to be punished.

6"As I was on my way and drew near to Damascus, about noon a great light from heaven suddenly shone around me. **7**And I fell to the ground and heard a voice saying to me, 'Saul, Saul, why are you persecuting me?' **8**And I answered, 'Who are you, Lord?' And he said to me, 'I am Jesus of Nazareth, whom you are persecuting.' **9**Now those who were with me saw the light but did not understand⁴ the voice of the one who was speaking to me. **10**And I said,

'What shall I do, Lord?' And the Lord said to me, 'Rise, and go into Damascus, and there you will be told all that is appointed for you to do.' **11**And since I could not see because of the brightness of that light, I was led by the hand by those who were with me, and came into Damascus.

12"And one Ananias, a devout man according to the law, well spoken of by all the Jews who lived there, **13**came to me, and standing by me said to me, 'Brother Saul, receive your sight.' And at that very hour I received my sight and saw him. **14**And he said, 'The God of our fathers appointed you to know his will, to see the Righteous One and to hear a voice from his mouth; **15**for you will be a witness for him to everyone of what you have seen and heard. **16**And now why do you wait? Rise and be baptized and wash away your sins, calling on his name.'

17"When I had returned to Jerusalem and was praying in the temple, I fell into a trance **18**and saw him saying to me, 'Make haste and get out of Jerusalem quickly, because they will not accept your testimony about me.' **19**And I said, 'Lord, they themselves know that in one synagogue after another I imprisoned and beat those who believed in you. **20**And when the blood of Stephen your witness was being shed, I myself was standing by and approving and watching over the garments of those who killed him.' **21**And he said to me, 'Go, for I will send you far away to the Gentiles.'"

22Up to this word they listened to him. Then they raised their voices and said, "Away with such a fellow from the earth! For he should not be allowed to live." **23**And as they were shouting and throwing off their cloaks and flinging dust into the air, **24**the tribune ordered him to be brought into the barracks, saying that he should be examined by flogging, to find out why they were shouting against him like this. **25**But when they had stretched him out for the whips,⁵ Paul said to the centurion who was standing by, "Is it lawful for you to flog a man who is a Roman citizen and uncondemned?" **26**When the centurion heard this, he went to the tribune and said to him, "What are you about to do? For this man is a Roman citizen." **27**So the tribune came and said to him, "Tell me, are you a Roman citizen?" And he said, "Yes." **28**The tribune answered, "I bought this citizenship for a large sum." Paul said, "But I am a

---

¹ Or leaders ² Or the Hebrew dialect (probably Aramaic) ³ Or city at the feet of Gamaliel, educated ⁴ Or hear with understanding ⁵ Or when they had tied him up with leather strips

citizen by birth." ²⁹So those who were about to examine him withdrew from him immediately, and the tribune also was afraid, for he realized that Paul was a Roman citizen and that he had bound him.

³⁰But on the next day, desiring to know the real reason why he was being accused by the Jews, he unbound him and commanded the chief priests and all the council to meet, and he brought Paul down and set him before them.

J A N U A R Y   2 3

Genesis 24

Now Abraham was old, well advanced in years. And the LORD had blessed Abraham in all things. ²And Abraham said to his servant, the oldest of his household, who had charge of all that he had, "Put your hand under my thigh, ³that I may make you swear by the LORD, the God of heaven and God of the earth, that you will not take a wife for my son from the daughters of the Canaanites, among whom I dwell, ⁴but will go to my country and to my kindred, and take a wife for my son Isaac." ⁵The servant said to him, "Perhaps the woman may not be willing to follow me to this land. Must I then take your son back to the land from which you came?" ⁶Abraham said to him, "See to it that you do not take my son back there. ⁷The LORD, the God of heaven, who took me from my father's house and from the land of my kindred, and who spoke to me and swore to me, 'To your offspring I will give this land,' he will send his angel before you, and you shall take a wife for my son from there. ⁸But if the woman is not willing to follow you, then you will be free from this oath of mine; only you must not take my son back there." ⁹So the servant put his hand under the thigh of Abraham his master and swore to him concerning this matter.

¹⁰Then the servant took ten of his master's camels and departed, taking all sorts of choice gifts from his master; and he arose and went to Mesopotamia[1] to the city of Nahor. ¹¹And he made the camels kneel down outside the city by the well of water at the time of evening, the time when women go out to draw water. ¹²And he said, "O LORD, God of my master Abraham, please grant me success today and show steadfast love to my master Abraham. ¹³Behold, I am standing by the spring of water, and the daughters of the men of the city are coming out to draw water. ¹⁴Let the young woman to whom I shall say, 'Please let down your jar that I may drink,' and who shall say, 'Drink, and I will water your camels'—let her be the one whom you have appointed for your servant Isaac. By this[2] I shall know that you have shown steadfast love to my master."

¹⁵Before he had finished speaking, behold, Rebekah, who was born to Bethuel the son of Milcah, the wife of Nahor, Abraham's brother, came out with her water jar on her shoulder. ¹⁶The young woman was very attractive in appearance, a maiden[3] whom no man had known. She went down to the spring and filled her jar and came up. ¹⁷Then the servant ran to meet her and said, "Please give me a little water to drink from your jar." ¹⁸She said, "Drink, my lord." And she quickly let down her jar upon her hand and gave him a drink. ¹⁹When she had finished giving him a drink, she said, "I will draw water for your camels also, until they have finished drinking." ²⁰So she quickly emptied her jar into the trough and ran again to the well to draw water, and she drew for all his camels. ²¹The man gazed at her in silence to learn whether the LORD had prospered his journey or not.

²²When the camels had finished drinking, the man took a gold ring weighing a half shekel,[4] and two bracelets for her arms weighing ten gold shekels, ²³and said, "Please tell me whose daughter you are. Is there room in your father's house for us to spend the night?" ²⁴She

¹ Hebrew *Aram-naharaim* ² Or *By her* ³ Or *a woman of marriageable age* ⁴ A shekel was about 2/5 ounce or 11 grams

said to him, "I am the daughter of Bethuel the son of Milcah, whom she bore to Nahor." ²⁵She added, "We have plenty of both straw and fodder, and room to spend the night." ²⁶The man bowed his head and worshiped the LORD ²⁷and said, "Blessed be the LORD, the God of my master Abraham, who has not forsaken his steadfast love and his faithfulness toward my master. As for me, the LORD has led me in the way to the house of my master's kinsmen." ²⁸Then the young woman ran and told her mother's household about these things.

²⁹Rebekah had a brother whose name was Laban. Laban ran out toward the man, to the spring. ³⁰As soon as he saw the ring and the bracelets on his sister's arms, and heard the words of Rebekah his sister, "Thus the man spoke to me," he went to the man. And behold, he was standing by the camels at the spring. ³¹He said, "Come in, O blessed of the LORD. Why do you stand outside? For I have prepared the house and a place for the camels." ³²So the man came to the house and unharnessed the camels, and gave straw and fodder to the camels, and there was water to wash his feet and the feet of the men who were with him. ³³Then food was set before him to eat. But he said, "I will not eat until I have said what I have to say." He said, "Speak on."

³⁴So he said, "I am Abraham's servant. ³⁵The LORD has greatly blessed my master, and he has become great. He has given him flocks and herds, silver and gold, male servants and female servants, camels and donkeys. ³⁶And Sarah my master's wife bore a son to my master when she was old, and to him he has given all that he has. ³⁷My master made me swear, saying, 'You shall not take a wife for my son from the daughters of the Canaanites, in whose land I dwell, ³⁸but you shall go to my father's house and to my clan and take a wife for my son.' ³⁹I said to my master, 'Perhaps the woman will not follow me.' ⁴⁰But he said to me, 'The LORD, before whom I have walked, will send his angel with you and prosper your way. You shall take a wife for my son from my clan and from my father's house. ⁴¹Then you will be free from my oath, when you come to my clan. And if they will not give her to you, you will be free from my oath.'

⁴²"I came today to the spring and said, 'O LORD, the God of my master Abraham,

if now you are prospering the way that I go, ⁴³behold, I am standing by the spring of water. Let the virgin who comes out to draw water, to whom I shall say, "Please give me a little water from your jar to drink," ⁴⁴and who will say to me, "Drink, and I will draw for your camels also," let her be the woman whom the LORD has appointed for my master's son.'

⁴⁵"Before I had finished speaking in my heart, behold, Rebekah came out with her water jar on her shoulder, and she went down to the spring and drew water. I said to her, 'Please let me drink.' ⁴⁶She quickly let down her jar from her shoulder and said, 'Drink, and I will give your camels drink also.' So I drank, and she gave the camels drink also. ⁴⁷Then I asked her, 'Whose daughter are you?' She said, 'The daughter of Bethuel, Nahor's son, whom Milcah bore to him.' So I put the ring on her nose and the bracelets on her arms. ⁴⁸Then I bowed my head and worshiped the LORD and blessed the LORD, the God of my master Abraham, who had led me by the right way¹ to take the daughter of my master's kinsman for his son. ⁴⁹Now then, if you are going to show steadfast love and faithfulness to my master, tell me; and if not, tell me, that I may turn to the right hand or to the left."

⁵⁰Then Laban and Bethuel answered and said, "The thing has come from the LORD; we cannot speak to you bad or good. ⁵¹Behold, Rebekah is before you; take her and go, and let her be the wife of your master's son, as the LORD has spoken."

⁵²When Abraham's servant heard their words, he bowed himself to the earth before the LORD. ⁵³And the servant brought out jewelry of silver and of gold, and garments, and gave them to Rebekah. He also gave to her brother and to her mother costly ornaments. ⁵⁴And he and the men who were with him ate and drank, and they spent the night there. When they arose in the morning, he said, "Send me away to my master." ⁵⁵Her brother and her mother said, "Let the young woman remain with us a while, at least ten days; after that she may go." ⁵⁶But he said to them, "Do not delay me, since the LORD has prospered my way. Send me away that I may go to my master." ⁵⁷They said, "Let us call the young woman and ask her." ⁵⁸And they called Rebekah and said to her, "Will you go with this man?" She said, "I will go." ⁵⁹So they sent away Rebekah their sister and her

¹ Or faithfully

nurse, and Abraham's servant and his men. [60]And they blessed Rebekah and said to her,

> "Our sister, may you become
> thousands of ten thousands,
> and may your offspring possess
> the gate of those who hate him!"[1]

[61]Then Rebekah and her young women arose and rode on the camels and followed the man. Thus the servant took Rebekah and went his way. [62]Now Isaac had returned from Beer-lahai-roi and was dwelling in the Negeb. [63]And Isaac went out to meditate in the field toward evening. And he lifted up his eyes and saw, and behold, there were camels coming. [64]And Rebekah lifted up her eyes, and when she saw Isaac, she dismounted from the camel [65]and said to the servant, "Who is that man, walking in the field to meet us?" The servant said, "It is my master." So she took her veil and covered herself. [66]And the servant told Isaac all the things that he had done. [67]Then Isaac brought her into the tent of Sarah his mother and took Rebekah, and she became his wife, and he loved her. So Isaac was comforted after his mother's death.

—— *Matthew 23* ——

Then Jesus said to the crowds and to his disciples, [2]"The scribes and the Pharisees sit on Moses' seat, [3]so do and observe whatever they tell you, but not the works they do. For they preach, but do not practice. [4]They tie up heavy burdens, hard to bear,[2] and lay them on people's shoulders, but they themselves are not willing to move them with their finger. [5]They do all their deeds to be seen by others. For they make their phylacteries broad and their fringes long, [6]and they love the place of honor at feasts and the best seats in the synagogues [7]and greetings in the marketplaces and being called rabbi[3] by others. [8]But you are not to be called rabbi, for you have one teacher, and you are all brothers.[4] [9]And call no man your father on earth, for you have one Father, who is in heaven. [10]Neither be called instructors, for you have one instructor, the Christ. [11]The greatest among you shall be your servant. [12]Whoever exalts himself will be humbled, and whoever humbles himself will be exalted.

[13]"But woe to you, scribes and Pharisees, hypocrites! For you shut the kingdom of heaven in people's faces. For you neither enter yourselves nor allow those who would enter to go in.[5] [15]Woe to you, scribes and Pharisees, hypocrites! For you travel across sea and land to make a single proselyte, and when he becomes a proselyte, you make him twice as much a child of hell[6] as yourselves.

[16]"Woe to you, blind guides, who say, 'If anyone swears by the temple, it is nothing, but if anyone swears by the gold of the temple, he is bound by his oath.' [17]You blind fools! For which is greater, the gold or the temple that has made the gold sacred? [18]And you say, 'If anyone swears by the altar, it is nothing, but if anyone swears by the gift that is on the altar, he is bound by his oath.' [19]You blind men! For which is greater, the gift or the altar that makes the gift sacred? [20]So whoever swears by the altar swears by it and by everything on it. [21]And whoever swears by the temple swears by it and by him who dwells in it. [22]And whoever swears by heaven swears by the throne of God and by him who sits upon it.

[23]"Woe to you, scribes and Pharisees, hypocrites! For you tithe mint and dill and cumin, and have neglected the weightier matters of the law: justice and mercy and faithfulness. These you ought to have done, without neglecting the others. [24]You blind guides, straining out a gnat and swallowing a camel!

[25]"Woe to you, scribes and Pharisees, hypocrites! For you clean the outside of the cup and the plate, but inside they are full of greed and self-indulgence. [26]You blind Pharisee! First clean the inside of the cup and the plate, that the outside also may be clean.

[27]"Woe to you, scribes and Pharisees, hypocrites! For you are like whitewashed tombs, which outwardly appear beautiful, but within are full of dead people's bones and all uncleanness. [28]So you also outwardly appear righteous to others, but within you are full of hypocrisy and lawlessness.

[29]"Woe to you, scribes and Pharisees, hypocrites! For you build the tombs of the prophets and decorate the monuments of the righteous, [30]saying, 'If we had lived in the days of our fathers, we would not have taken part with them in shedding the blood of the prophets.'

[1] Or *hate them* [2] Some manuscripts omit *hard to bear* [3] *Rabbi* means *my teacher,* or *my master;* also verse 8 [4] Or *brothers and sisters* [5] Some manuscripts add here (or after verse 12) verse 14: *Woe to you, scribes and Pharisees, hypocrites! For you devour widows' houses and for a pretense you make long prayers; therefore you will receive the greater condemnation* [6] Greek *Gehenna;* also verse 33

[31] Thus you witness against yourselves that you are sons of those who murdered the prophets. [32] Fill up, then, the measure of your fathers. [33] You serpents, you brood of vipers, how are you to escape being sentenced to hell? [34] Therefore I send you prophets and wise men and scribes, some of whom you will kill and crucify, and some you will flog in your synagogues and persecute from town to town, [35] so that on you may come all the righteous blood shed on earth, from the blood of righteous Abel to the blood of Zechariah the son of Barachiah,[1] whom you murdered between the sanctuary and the altar. [36] Truly, I say to you, all these things will come upon this generation.

[37] "O Jerusalem, Jerusalem, the city that kills the prophets and stones those who are sent to it! How often would I have gathered your children together as a hen gathers her brood under her wings, and you were not willing! [38] See, your house is left to you desolate. [39] For I tell you, you will not see me again, until you say, 'Blessed is he who comes in the name of the Lord.'"

Nehemiah 13

On that day they read from the Book of Moses in the hearing of the people. And in it was found written that no Ammonite or Moabite should ever enter the assembly of God, [2] for they did not meet the people of Israel with bread and water, but hired Balaam against them to curse them—yet our God turned the curse into a blessing. [3] As soon as the people heard the law, they separated from Israel all those of foreign descent.

[4] Now before this, Eliashib the priest, who was appointed over the chambers of the house of our God, and who was related to Tobiah, [5] prepared for Tobiah a large chamber where they had previously put the grain offering, the frankincense, the vessels, and the tithes of grain, wine, and oil, which were given by commandment to the Levites, singers, and gatekeepers, and the contributions for the priests. [6] While this was taking place, I was not in Jerusalem, for in the thirty-second year of Artaxerxes king of Babylon I went to the king. And after some time I asked leave of the king [7] and came to Jerusalem, and I then discovered the evil that Eliashib had done for Tobiah, preparing for him a chamber in the courts of the house of God. [8] And I was very angry, and I threw all the household furniture of Tobiah out of the chamber. [9] Then I gave orders, and they cleansed the chambers, and I brought back there the vessels of the house of God, with the grain offering and the frankincense.

[10] I also found out that the portions of the Levites had not been given to them, so that the Levites and the singers, who did the work, had fled each to his field. [11] So I confronted the officials and said, "Why is the house of God forsaken?" And I gathered them together and set them in their stations. [12] Then all Judah brought the tithe of the grain, wine, and oil into the storehouses. [13] And I appointed as treasurers over the storehouses Shelemiah the priest, Zadok the scribe, and Pedaiah of the Levites, and as their assistant Hanan the son of Zaccur, son of Mattaniah, for they were considered reliable, and their duty was to distribute to their brothers. [14] Remember me, O my God, concerning this, and do not wipe out my good deeds that I have done for the house of my God and for his service.

[15] In those days I saw in Judah people treading winepresses on the Sabbath, and bringing in heaps of grain and loading them on donkeys, and also wine, grapes, figs, and all kinds of loads, which they brought into Jerusalem on the Sabbath day. And I warned them on the day when they sold food. [16] Tyrians also, who lived in the city, brought in fish and all kinds of goods and sold them on the Sabbath to the people of Judah, in Jerusalem itself! [17] Then I confronted the nobles of Judah and said to them, "What is this evil thing that you are doing, profaning the Sabbath day? [18] Did not your fathers act in this way, and did not our God bring all this disaster[2] on us and on this city? Now you are bringing more wrath on Israel by profaning the Sabbath."

[19] As soon as it began to grow dark at the gates of Jerusalem before the Sabbath, I commanded that the doors should be shut and gave orders that they should not be opened until after the Sabbath. And I stationed some of my servants at the gates, that no load might be brought in on the Sabbath day. [20] Then the merchants and sellers of all kinds of wares lodged outside Jerusalem once or twice. [21] But I warned them and said to them, "Why do you lodge outside the wall? If you do so again, I will lay hands on you." From that time on they did

[1] Some manuscripts omit *the son of Barachiah* [2] The Hebrew word can mean *evil, harm,* or *disaster,* depending on the context

not come on the Sabbath. [22]Then I commanded the Levites that they should purify themselves and come and guard the gates, to keep the Sabbath day holy. Remember this also in my favor, O my God, and spare me according to the greatness of your steadfast love.

[23]In those days also I saw the Jews who had married women of Ashdod, Ammon, and Moab. [24]And half of their children spoke the language of Ashdod, and they could not speak the language of Judah, but only the language of each people. [25]And I confronted them and cursed them and beat some of them and pulled out their hair. And I made them take an oath in the name of God, saying, "You shall not give your daughters to their sons, or take their daughters for your sons or for yourselves. [26]Did not Solomon king of Israel sin on account of such women? Among the many nations there was no king like him, and he was beloved by his God, and God made him king over all Israel. Nevertheless, foreign women made even him to sin. [27]Shall we then listen to you and do all this great evil and act treacherously against our God by marrying foreign women?"

[28]And one of the sons of Jehoiada, the son of Eliashib the high priest, was the son-in-law of Sanballat the Horonite. Therefore I chased him from me. [29]Remember them, O my God, because they have desecrated the priesthood and the covenant of the priesthood and the Levites.

[30]Thus I cleansed them from everything foreign, and I established the duties of the priests and Levites, each in his work; [31]and I provided for the wood offering at appointed times, and for the firstfruits.

Remember me, O my God, for good.

Acts 23

And looking intently at the council, Paul said, "Brothers, I have lived my life before God in all good conscience up to this day." [2]And the high priest Ananias commanded those who stood by him to strike him on the mouth. [3]Then Paul said to him, "God is going to strike you, you whitewashed wall! Are you sitting to judge me according to the law, and yet contrary to the law you order me to be struck?" [4]Those who stood by said, "Would you revile God's high priest?" [5]And Paul said, "I did not know, brothers, that he was the high priest, for it is

written, 'You shall not speak evil of a ruler of your people.'"

[6]Now when Paul perceived that one part were Sadducees and the other Pharisees, he cried out in the council, "Brothers, I am a Pharisee, a son of Pharisees. It is with respect to the hope and the resurrection of the dead that I am on trial." [7]And when he had said this, a dissension arose between the Pharisees and the Sadducees, and the assembly was divided. [8]For the Sadducees say that there is no resurrection, nor angel, nor spirit, but the Pharisees acknowledge them all. [9]Then a great clamor arose, and some of the scribes of the Pharisees' party stood up and contended sharply, "We find nothing wrong in this man. What if a spirit or an angel spoke to him?" [10]And when the dissension became violent, the tribune, afraid that Paul would be torn to pieces by them, commanded the soldiers to go down and take him away from among them by force and bring him into the barracks.

[11]The following night the Lord stood by him and said, "Take courage, for as you have testified to the facts about me in Jerusalem, so you must testify also in Rome."

[12]When it was day, the Jews made a plot and bound themselves by an oath neither to eat nor drink till they had killed Paul. [13]There were more than forty who made this conspiracy. [14]They went to the chief priests and elders and said, "We have strictly bound ourselves by an oath to taste no food till we have killed Paul. [15]Now therefore you, along with the council, give notice to the tribune to bring him down to you, as though you were going to determine his case more exactly. And we are ready to kill him before he comes near."

[16]Now the son of Paul's sister heard of their ambush, so he went and entered the barracks and told Paul. [17]Paul called one of the centurions and said, "Take this young man to the tribune, for he has something to tell him." [18]So he took him and brought him to the tribune and said, "Paul the prisoner called me and asked me to bring this young man to you, as he has something to say to you." [19]The tribune took him by the hand, and going aside asked him privately, "What is it that you have to tell me?" [20]And he said, "The Jews have agreed to ask you to bring Paul down to the council tomorrow, as though they were going to inquire somewhat more closely about him. [21]But do not

be persuaded by them, for more than forty of their men are lying in ambush for him, who have bound themselves by an oath neither to eat nor drink till they have killed him. And now they are ready, waiting for your consent." ²²So the tribune dismissed the young man, charging him, "Tell no one that you have informed me of these things."

²³Then he called two of the centurions and said, "Get ready two hundred soldiers, with seventy horsemen and two hundred spearmen to go as far as Caesarea at the third hour of the night.¹ ²⁴Also provide mounts for Paul to ride and bring him safely to Felix the governor." ²⁵And he wrote a letter to this effect:

²⁶"Claudius Lysias, to his Excellency the governor Felix, greetings. ²⁷This man was seized by the Jews and was about to be killed by them when I came upon them with the soldiers and rescued him, having learned that he was a Roman citizen. ²⁸And desiring to know the charge for which they were accusing him, I brought him down to their council. ²⁹I found that he was being accused about questions of their law, but charged with nothing deserving death or imprisonment. ³⁰And when it was disclosed to me that there would be a plot against the man, I sent him to you at once, ordering his accusers also to state before you what they have against him."

³¹So the soldiers, according to their instructions, took Paul and brought him by night to Antipatris. ³²And on the next day they returned to the barracks, letting the horsemen go on with him. ³³When they had come to Caesarea and delivered the letter to the governor, they presented Paul also before him. ³⁴On reading the letter, he asked what province he was from. And when he learned that he was from Cilicia, ³⁵he said, "I will give you a hearing when your accusers arrive." And he commanded him to be guarded in Herod's praetorium.

JANUARY 24

Genesis 25

Abraham took another wife, whose name was Keturah. ²She bore him Zimran, Jokshan, Medan, Midian, Ishbak, and Shuah. ³Jokshan fathered Sheba and Dedan. The sons of Dedan were Asshurim, Letushim, and Leummim. ⁴The sons of Midian were Ephah, Epher, Hanoch, Abida, and Eldaah. All these were the children of Keturah. ⁵Abraham gave all he had to Isaac. ⁶But to the sons of his concubines Abraham gave gifts, and while he was still living he sent them away from his son Isaac, eastward to the east country.

⁷These are the days of the years of Abraham's life, 175 years. ⁸Abraham breathed his last and died in a good old age, an old man and full of years, and was gathered to his people. ⁹Isaac and Ishmael his sons buried him in the cave of Machpelah, in the field of Ephron the son of Zohar the Hittite, east of Mamre, ¹⁰the field that Abraham purchased from the Hittites. There Abraham was buried, with Sarah his wife. ¹¹After the death of Abraham, God blessed Isaac his son. And Isaac settled at Beer-lahai-roi.

¹²These are the generations of Ishmael, Abraham's son, whom Hagar the Egyptian, Sarah's servant, bore to Abraham. ¹³These are the names of the sons of Ishmael, named in the order of their birth: Nebaioth, the firstborn of Ishmael; and Kedar, Adbeel, Mibsam, ¹⁴Mishma, Dumah, Massa, ¹⁵Hadad, Tema, Jetur, Naphish, and Kedemah. ¹⁶These are the sons of Ishmael and these are their names, by their villages and by their encampments, twelve princes according to their tribes. ¹⁷(These are the years of the life of Ishmael: 137 years. He breathed his last and died, and was gathered to his people.) ¹⁸They settled from Havilah to Shur, which is opposite Egypt in the direction of Assyria. He settled² over against all his kinsmen.

¹ That is, 9 P.M. ² Hebrew *fell*

19These are the generations of Isaac, Abraham's son: Abraham fathered Isaac, 20and Isaac was forty years old when he took Rebekah, the daughter of Bethuel the Aramean of Paddan-aram, the sister of Laban the Aramean, to be his wife. 21And Isaac prayed to the LORD for his wife, because she was barren. And the LORD granted his prayer, and Rebekah his wife conceived. 22The children struggled together within her, and she said, "If it is thus, why is this happening to me?"1 So she went to inquire of the LORD. 23And the LORD said to her,

"Two nations are in your womb,
　and two peoples from within you2
　　shall be divided;
the one shall be stronger than the other,
　the older shall serve the younger."

24When her days to give birth were completed, behold, there were twins in her womb. 25The first came out red, all his body like a hairy cloak, so they called his name Esau. 26Afterward his brother came out with his hand holding Esau's heel, so his name was called Jacob.3 Isaac was sixty years old when she bore them.

27When the boys grew up, Esau was a skillful hunter, a man of the field, while Jacob was a quiet man, dwelling in tents. 28Isaac loved Esau because he ate of his game, but Rebekah loved Jacob.

29Once when Jacob was cooking stew, Esau came in from the field, and he was exhausted. 30And Esau said to Jacob, "Let me eat some of that red stew, for I am exhausted!" (Therefore his name was called Edom.4) 31Jacob said, "Sell me your birthright now." 32Esau said, "I am about to die; of what use is a birthright to me?" 33Jacob said, "Swear to me now." So he swore to him and sold his birthright to Jacob. 34Then Jacob gave Esau bread and lentil stew, and he ate and drank and rose and went his way. Thus Esau despised his birthright.

Matthew 24

Jesus left the temple and was going away, when his disciples came to point out to him the buildings of the temple. 2But he answered them, "You see all these, do you not? Truly, I say to you, there will not be left here one stone upon another that will not be thrown down."

3As he sat on the Mount of Olives, the disciples came to him privately, saying, "Tell us, when will these things be, and what will be the sign of your coming and of the end of the age?" 4And Jesus answered them, "See that no one leads you astray. 5For many will come in my name, saying, 'I am the Christ,' and they will lead many astray. 6And you will hear of wars and rumors of wars. See that you are not alarmed, for this must take place, but the end is not yet. 7For nation will rise against nation, and kingdom against kingdom, and there will be famines and earthquakes in various places. 8All these are but the beginning of the birth pains.

9"Then they will deliver you up to tribulation and put you to death, and you will be hated by all nations for my name's sake. 10And then many will fall away5 and betray one another and hate one another. 11And many false prophets will arise and lead many astray. 12And because lawlessness will be increased, the love of many will grow cold. 13But the one who endures to the end will be saved. 14And this gospel of the kingdom will be proclaimed throughout the whole world as a testimony to all nations, and then the end will come.

15"So when you see the abomination of desolation spoken of by the prophet Daniel, standing in the holy place (let the reader understand), 16then let those who are in Judea flee to the mountains. 17Let the one who is on the housetop not go down to take what is in his house, 18and let the one who is in the field not turn back to take his cloak. 19And alas for women who are pregnant and for those who are nursing infants in those days! 20Pray that your flight may not be in winter or on a Sabbath. 21For then there will be great tribulation, such as has not been from the beginning of the world until now, no, and never will be. 22And if those days had not been cut short, no human being would be saved. But for the sake of the elect those days will be cut short. 23Then if anyone says to you, 'Look, here is the Christ!' or 'There he is!' do not believe it. 24For false christs and false prophets will arise and perform great signs and wonders, so as to lead astray, if possible, even the elect. 25See, I have told you beforehand. 26So, if they say to you, 'Look, he is in the wilderness,' do not go out. If they say, 'Look, he is in the inner rooms,' do not believe it. 27For as the lightning comes from the east and shines as far as the west, so will be

1 Or why do I live? 2 Or from birth 3 Jacob means He takes by the heel, or He cheats 4 Edom sounds like the Hebrew for red 5 Or stumble

the coming of the Son of Man. [28]Wherever the corpse is, there the vultures will gather.

[29]"Immediately after the tribulation of those days the sun will be darkened, and the moon will not give its light, and the stars will fall from heaven, and the powers of the heavens will be shaken. [30]Then will appear in heaven the sign of the Son of Man, and then all the tribes of the earth will mourn, and they will see the Son of Man coming on the clouds of heaven with power and great glory. [31]And he will send out his angels with a loud trumpet call, and they will gather his elect from the four winds, from one end of heaven to the other.

[32]"From the fig tree learn its lesson: as soon as its branch becomes tender and puts out its leaves, you know that summer is near. [33]So also, when you see all these things, you know that he is near, at the very gates. [34]Truly, I say to you, this generation will not pass away until all these things take place. [35]Heaven and earth will pass away, but my words will not pass away.

[36]"But concerning that day and hour no one knows, not even the angels of heaven, nor the Son,[1] but the Father only. [37]For as were the days of Noah, so will be the coming of the Son of Man. [38]For as in those days before the flood they were eating and drinking, marrying and giving in marriage, until the day when Noah entered the ark, [39]and they were unaware until the flood came and swept them all away, so will be the coming of the Son of Man. [40]Then two men will be in the field; one will be taken and one left. [41]Two women will be grinding at the mill; one will be taken and one left. [42]Therefore, stay awake, for you do not know on what day your Lord is coming. [43]But know this, that if the master of the house had known in what part of the night the thief was coming, he would have stayed awake and would not have let his house be broken into. [44]Therefore you also must be ready, for the Son of Man is coming at an hour you do not expect.

[45]"Who then is the faithful and wise servant,[2] whom his master has set over his household, to give them their food at the proper time? [46]Blessed is that servant whom his master will find so doing when he comes. [47]Truly, I say to you, he will set him over all his possessions. [48]But if that wicked servant says to himself, 'My master is delayed,' [49]and begins to beat his fellow servants[3] and eats and drinks with drunkards, [50]the master of that servant will come on a day when he does not expect him and at an hour he does not know [51]and will cut him in pieces and put him with the hypocrites. In that place there will be weeping and gnashing of teeth.

Esther 1

Now in the days of Ahasuerus, the Ahasuerus who reigned from India to Ethiopia over 127 provinces, [2]in those days when King Ahasuerus sat on his royal throne in Susa, the citadel, [3]in the third year of his reign he gave a feast for all his officials and servants. The army of Persia and Media and the nobles and governors of the provinces were before him, [4]while he showed the riches of his royal glory and the splendor and pomp of his greatness for many days, 180 days. [5]And when these days were completed, the king gave for all the people present in Susa the citadel, both great and small, a feast lasting for seven days in the court of the garden of the king's palace. [6]There were white cotton curtains and violet hangings fastened with cords of fine linen and purple to silver rods[4] and marble pillars, and also couches of gold and silver on a mosaic pavement of porphyry, marble, mother-of-pearl and precious stones. [7]Drinks were served in golden vessels, vessels of different kinds, and the royal wine was lavished according to the bounty of the king. [8]And drinking was according to this edict: "There is no compulsion." For the king had given orders to all the staff of his palace to do as each man desired. [9]Queen Vashti also gave a feast for the women in the palace that belonged to King Ahasuerus.

[10]On the seventh day, when the heart of the king was merry with wine, he commanded Mehuman, Biztha, Harbona, Bigtha and Abagtha, Zethar and Carkas, the seven eunuchs who served in the presence of King Ahasuerus, [11]to bring Queen Vashti before the king with her royal crown,[5] in order to show the peoples and the princes her beauty, for she was lovely to look at. [12]But Queen Vashti refused to come at the king's command delivered by the eunuchs. At this the king became enraged, and his anger burned within him.

[13]Then the king said to the wise men who knew the times (for this was the king's

---

[1] Some manuscripts omit *nor the Son*   [2] Greek *bondservant*; also verses 46, 48, 50   [3] Greek *bondservants*   [4] Or *rings*   [5] Or *headdress*

procedure toward all who were versed in law and judgment, [14]the men next to him being Carshena, Shethar, Admatha, Tarshish, Meres, Marsena, and Memucan, the seven princes of Persia and Media, who saw the king's face, and sat first in the kingdom): [15]"According to the law, what is to be done to Queen Vashti, because she has not performed the command of King Ahasuerus delivered by the eunuchs?" [16]Then Memucan said in the presence of the king and the officials, "Not only against the king has Queen Vashti done wrong, but also against all the officials and all the peoples who are in all the provinces of King Ahasuerus. [17]For the queen's behavior will be made known to all women, causing them to look at their husbands with contempt, since they will say, 'King Ahasuerus commanded Queen Vashti to be brought before him, and she did not come.' [18]This very day the noble women of Persia and Media who have heard of the queen's behavior will say the same to all the king's officials, and there will be contempt and wrath in plenty. [19]If it please the king, let a royal order go out from him, and let it be written among the laws of the Persians and the Medes so that it may not be repealed, that Vashti is never again to come before King Ahasuerus. And let the king give her royal position to another who is better than she. [20]So when the decree made by the king is proclaimed throughout all his kingdom, for it is vast, all women will give honor to their husbands, high and low alike." [21]This advice pleased the king and the princes, and the king did as Memucan proposed. [22]He sent letters to all the royal provinces, to every province in its own script and to every people in its own language, that every man be master in his own household and speak according to the language of his people.

Acts 24

And after five days the high priest Ananias came down with some elders and a spokesman, one Tertullus. They laid before the governor their case against Paul. [2]And when he had been summoned, Tertullus began to accuse him, saying:

"Since through you we enjoy much peace, and since by your foresight, most excellent Felix, reforms are being made for this nation, [3]in every way and everywhere we accept this with all gratitude. [4]But, to detain[1] you no further, I beg you in your kindness to hear us briefly. [5]For we have found this man a plague, one who stirs up riots among all the Jews throughout the world and is a ringleader of the sect of the Nazarenes. [6]He even tried to profane the temple, but we seized him.[2] [8]By examining him yourself you will be able to find out from him about everything of which we accuse him." [9]The Jews also joined in the charge, affirming that all these things were so.

[10]And when the governor had nodded to him to speak, Paul replied:

"Knowing that for many years you have been a judge over this nation, I cheerfully make my defense. [11]You can verify that it is not more than twelve days since I went up to worship in Jerusalem, [12]and they did not find me disputing with anyone or stirring up a crowd, either in the temple or in the synagogues or in the city. [13]Neither can they prove to you what they now bring up against me. [14]But this I confess to you, that according to the Way, which they call a sect, I worship the God of our fathers, believing everything laid down by the Law and written in the Prophets, [15]having a hope in God, which these men themselves accept, that there will be a resurrection of both the just and the unjust. [16]So I always take pains to have a clear conscience toward both God and man. [17]Now after several years I came to bring alms to my nation and to present offerings. [18]While I was doing this, they found me purified in the temple, without any crowd or tumult. But some Jews from Asia— [19]they ought to be here before you and to make an accusation, should they have anything against me. [20]Or else let these men themselves say what wrongdoing they found when I stood before the council, [21]other than this one thing that I cried out while standing among them: 'It is with respect to the resurrection of the dead that I am on trial before you this day.'"

[22]But Felix, having a rather accurate knowledge of the Way, put them off, saying, "When Lysias the tribune comes down, I will decide your case." [23]Then he gave orders to the centurion that he should be kept in custody but have some liberty, and that none of his friends should be prevented from attending to his needs. [24]After some days Felix came with his wife

[1] Or weary [2] Some manuscripts add and we would have judged him according to our law. [7]But the chief captain Lysias came and with great violence took him out of our hands, [8]commanding his accusers to come before you.

Drusilla, who was Jewish, and he sent for Paul and heard him speak about faith in Christ Jesus. [25]And as he reasoned about righteousness and self-control and the coming judgment, Felix was alarmed and said, "Go away for the present. When I get an opportunity I will summon you."

[26]At the same time he hoped that money would be given him by Paul. So he sent for him often and conversed with him. [27]When two years had elapsed, Felix was succeeded by Porcius Festus. And desiring to do the Jews a favor, Felix left Paul in prison.

JANUARY 25

Genesis 26

Now there was a famine in the land, besides the former famine that was in the days of Abraham. And Isaac went to Gerar to Abimelech king of the Philistines. [2]And the LORD appeared to him and said, "Do not go down to Egypt; dwell in the land of which I shall tell you. [3]Sojourn in this land, and I will be with you and will bless you, for to you and to your offspring I will give all these lands, and I will establish the oath that I swore to Abraham your father. [4]I will multiply your offspring as the stars of heaven and will give to your offspring all these lands. And in your offspring all the nations of the earth shall be blessed, [5]because Abraham obeyed my voice and kept my charge, my commandments, my statutes, and my laws."

[6]So Isaac settled in Gerar. [7]When the men of the place asked him about his wife, he said, "She is my sister," for he feared to say, "My wife," thinking, "lest the men of the place should kill me because of Rebekah," because she was attractive in appearance. [8]When he had been there a long time, Abimelech king of the Philistines looked out of a window and saw Isaac laughing with[1] Rebekah his wife. [9]So Abimelech called Isaac and said, "Behold, she is your wife. How then could you say, 'She is my sister'?" Isaac said to him, "Because I thought, 'Lest I die because of her.'" [10]Abimelech said, "What is this you have done to us? One of the people might easily have lain with your wife, and you would have brought guilt upon us." [11]So Abimelech warned all the people, saying, "Whoever

touches this man or his wife shall surely be put to death."

[12]And Isaac sowed in that land and reaped in the same year a hundredfold. The LORD blessed him, [13]and the man became rich, and gained more and more until he became very wealthy. [14]He had possessions of flocks and herds and many servants, so that the Philistines envied him. [15](Now the Philistines had stopped and filled with earth all the wells that his father's servants had dug in the days of Abraham his father.) [16]And Abimelech said to Isaac, "Go away from us, for you are much mightier than we."

[17]So Isaac departed from there and encamped in the Valley of Gerar and settled there. [18]And Isaac dug again the wells of water that had been dug in the days of Abraham his father, which the Philistines had stopped after the death of Abraham. And he gave them the names that his father had given them. [19]But when Isaac's servants dug in the valley and found there a well of spring water, [20]the herdsmen of Gerar quarreled with Isaac's herdsmen, saying, "The water is ours." So he called the name of the well Esek,[2] because they contended with him. [21]Then they dug another well, and they quarreled over that also, so he called its name Sitnah.[3] [22]And he moved from there and dug another well, and they did not quarrel over it. So he called its name Rehoboth,[4] saying, "For now the LORD has made room for us, and we shall be fruitful in the land."

[23]From there he went up to Beersheba. [24]And the LORD appeared to him the same night and said, "I am the God of Abraham your father.

[1] Hebrew may suggest an intimate relationship [2] Esek means contention [3] Sitnah means enmity [4] Rehoboth means broad places, or room

Fear not, for I am with you and will bless you and multiply your offspring for my servant Abraham's sake." ²⁵So he built an altar there and called upon the name of the LORD and pitched his tent there. And there Isaac's servants dug a well.

²⁶When Abimelech went to him from Gerar with Ahuzzath his adviser and Phicol the commander of his army, ²⁷Isaac said to them, "Why have you come to me, seeing that you hate me and have sent me away from you?" ²⁸They said, "We see plainly that the LORD has been with you. So we said, let there be a sworn pact between us, between you and us, and let us make a covenant with you, ²⁹that you will do us no harm, just as we have not touched you and have done to you nothing but good and have sent you away in peace. You are now the blessed of the LORD." ³⁰So he made them a feast, and they ate and drank. ³¹In the morning they rose early and exchanged oaths. And Isaac sent them on their way, and they departed from him in peace. ³²That same day Isaac's servants came and told him about the well that they had dug and said to him, "We have found water." ³³He called it Shibah;¹ therefore the name of the city is Beersheba to this day.

³⁴When Esau was forty years old, he took Judith the daughter of Beeri the Hittite to be his wife, and Basemath the daughter of Elon the Hittite, ³⁵and they made life bitter² for Isaac and Rebekah.

Matthew 25

¹"Then the kingdom of heaven will be like ten virgins who took their lamps³ and went to meet the bridegroom.⁴ ²Five of them were foolish, and five were wise. ³For when the foolish took their lamps, they took no oil with them, ⁴but the wise took flasks of oil with their lamps. ⁵As the bridegroom was delayed, they all became drowsy and slept. ⁶But at midnight there was a cry, 'Here is the bridegroom! Come out to meet him.' ⁷Then all those virgins rose and trimmed their lamps. ⁸And the foolish said to the wise, 'Give us some of your oil, for our lamps are going out.' ⁹But the wise answered, saying, 'Since there will not be enough for us and for you, go rather to the dealers and buy for yourselves.' ¹⁰And while they were going to buy, the bridegroom came, and those who were ready went in with him to the marriage feast, and the door was shut. ¹¹Afterward the other virgins came also, saying, 'Lord, lord, open to us.' ¹²But he answered, 'Truly, I say to you, I do not know you.' ¹³Watch therefore, for you know neither the day nor the hour.

¹⁴"For it will be like a man going on a journey, who called his servants⁵ and entrusted to them his property. ¹⁵To one he gave five talents,⁶ to another two, to another one, to each according to his ability. Then he went away. ¹⁶He who had received the five talents went at once and traded with them, and he made five talents more. ¹⁷So also he who had the two talents made two talents more. ¹⁸But he who had received the one talent went and dug in the ground and hid his master's money. ¹⁹Now after a long time the master of those servants came and settled accounts with them. ²⁰And he who had received the five talents came forward, bringing five talents more, saying, 'Master, you delivered to me five talents; here I have made five talents more.' ²¹His master said to him, 'Well done, good and faithful servant.⁷ You have been faithful over a little; I will set you over much. Enter into the joy of your master.' ²²And he also who had the two talents came forward, saying, 'Master, you delivered to me two talents; here I have made two talents more.' ²³His master said to him, 'Well done, good and faithful servant. You have been faithful over a little; I will set you over much. Enter into the joy of your master.' ²⁴He also who had received the one talent came forward, saying, 'Master, I knew you to be a hard man, reaping where you did not sow, and gathering where you scattered no seed, ²⁵so I was afraid, and I went and hid your talent in the ground. Here you have what is yours.' ²⁶But his master answered him, 'You wicked and slothful servant! You knew that I reap where I have not sown and gather where I scattered no seed? ²⁷Then you ought to have invested my money with the bankers, and at my coming I should have received what was my own with interest. ²⁸So take the talent from him and give it to him who has the ten talents. ²⁹For to everyone who has will more be given, and he will have an abundance. But from the one who has not, even what he has will be taken away. ³⁰And cast the worthless servant into the outer darkness. In that place there will be weeping and gnashing of teeth.'

---

¹ *Shibah* sounds like the Hebrew for *oath* ² Hebrew *they were bitterness of spirit* ³ Or *torches* ⁴ Some manuscripts add *and the bride* ⁵ Greek *bondservants*; also verse 19 ⁶ A *talent* was a monetary unit worth about twenty years' wages for a laborer ⁷ Greek *bondservant*; also verses 23, 26, 30

[31] "When the Son of Man comes in his glory, and all the angels with him, then he will sit on his glorious throne. [32] Before him will be gathered all the nations, and he will separate people one from another as a shepherd separates the sheep from the goats. [33] And he will place the sheep on his right, but the goats on the left. [34] Then the King will say to those on his right, 'Come, you who are blessed by my Father, inherit the kingdom prepared for you from the foundation of the world. [35] For I was hungry and you gave me food, I was thirsty and you gave me drink, I was a stranger and you welcomed me, [36] I was naked and you clothed me, I was sick and you visited me, I was in prison and you came to me.' [37] Then the righteous will answer him, saying, 'Lord, when did we see you hungry and feed you, or thirsty and give you drink? [38] And when did we see you a stranger and welcome you, or naked and clothe you? [39] And when did we see you sick or in prison and visit you?' [40] And the King will answer them, 'Truly, I say to you, as you did it to one of the least of these my brothers,[1] you did it to me.'

[41] "Then he will say to those on his left, 'Depart from me, you cursed, into the eternal fire prepared for the devil and his angels. [42] For I was hungry and you gave me no food, I was thirsty and you gave me no drink, [43] I was a stranger and you did not welcome me, naked and you did not clothe me, sick and in prison and you did not visit me.' [44] Then they also will answer, saying, 'Lord, when did we see you hungry or thirsty or a stranger or naked or sick or in prison, and did not minister to you?' [45] Then he will answer them, saying, 'Truly, I say to you, as you did not do it to one of the least of these, you did not do it to me.' [46] And these will go away into eternal punishment, but the righteous into eternal life."

Esther 2

After these things, when the anger of King Ahasuerus had abated, he remembered Vashti and what she had done and what had been decreed against her. [2] Then the king's young men who attended him said, "Let beautiful young virgins be sought out for the king. [3] And let the king appoint officers in all the provinces of his kingdom to gather all the beautiful young virgins to the harem in Susa

the citadel, under custody of Hegai, the king's eunuch, who is in charge of the women. Let their cosmetics be given them. [4] And let the young woman who pleases the king be queen instead of Vashti." This pleased the king, and he did so.

[5] Now there was a Jew in Susa the citadel whose name was Mordecai, the son of Jair, son of Shimei, son of Kish, a Benjaminite, [6] who had been carried away from Jerusalem among the captives carried away with Jeconiah king of Judah, whom Nebuchadnezzar king of Babylon had carried away. [7] He was bringing up Hadassah, that is Esther, the daughter of his uncle, for she had neither father nor mother. The young woman had a beautiful figure and was lovely to look at, and when her father and her mother died, Mordecai took her as his own daughter. [8] So when the king's order and his edict were proclaimed, and when many young women were gathered in Susa the citadel in custody of Hegai, Esther also was taken into the king's palace and put in custody of Hegai, who had charge of the women. [9] And the young woman pleased him and won his favor. And he quickly provided her with her cosmetics and her portion of food, and with seven chosen young women from the king's palace, and advanced her and her young women to the best place in the harem. [10] Esther had not made known her people or kindred, for Mordecai had commanded her not to make it known. [11] And every day Mordecai walked in front of the court of the harem to learn how Esther was and what was happening to her.

[12] Now when the turn came for each young woman to go in to King Ahasuerus, after being twelve months under the regulations for the women, since this was the regular period of their beautifying, six months with oil of myrrh and six months with spices and ointments for women— [13] when the young woman went in to the king in this way, she was given whatever she desired to take with her from the harem to the king's palace. [14] In the evening she would go in, and in the morning she would return to the second harem in custody of Shaashgaz, the king's eunuch, who was in charge of the concubines. She would not go in to the king again, unless the king delighted in her and she was summoned by name.

[15] When the turn came for Esther the daughter

---
[1] Or brothers and sisters

of Abihail the uncle of Mordecai, who had taken her as his own daughter, to go in to the king, she asked for nothing except what Hegai the king's eunuch, who had charge of the women, advised. Now Esther was winning favor in the eyes of all who saw her. [16]And when Esther was taken to King Ahasuerus, into his royal palace, in the tenth month, which is the month of Tebeth, in the seventh year of his reign, [17]the king loved Esther more than all the women, and she won grace and favor in his sight more than all the virgins, so that he set the royal crown[1] on her head and made her queen instead of Vashti. [18]Then the king gave a great feast for all his officials and servants; it was Esther's feast. He also granted a remission of taxes to the provinces and gave gifts with royal generosity.

[19]Now when the virgins were gathered together the second time, Mordecai was sitting at the king's gate. [20]Esther had not made known her kindred or her people, as Mordecai had commanded her, for Esther obeyed Mordecai just as when she was brought up by him. [21]In those days, as Mordecai was sitting at the king's gate, Bigthan and Teresh, two of the king's eunuchs, who guarded the threshold, became angry and sought to lay hands on King Ahasuerus. [22]And this came to the knowledge of Mordecai, and he told it to Queen Esther, and Esther told the king in the name of Mordecai. [23]When the affair was investigated and found to be so, the men were both hanged on the gallows.[2] And it was recorded in the book of the chronicles in the presence of the king.

Acts 25

[ ]Now three days after Festus had arrived in the province, he went up to Jerusalem from Caesarea. [2]And the chief priests and the principal men of the Jews laid out their case against Paul, and they urged him, [3]asking as a favor against Paul[3] that he summon him to Jerusalem—because they were planning an ambush to kill him on the way. [4]Festus replied that Paul was being kept at Caesarea and that he himself intended to go there shortly. [5]"So," said he, "let the men of authority among you go down with me, and if there is anything wrong about the man, let them bring charges against him."

[6]After he stayed among them not more than eight or ten days, he went down to Caesarea. And the next day he took his seat on the tribunal and ordered Paul to be brought. [7]When he had arrived, the Jews who had come down from Jerusalem stood around him, bringing many and serious charges against him that they could not prove. [8]Paul argued in his defense, "Neither against the law of the Jews, nor against the temple, nor against Caesar have I committed any offense." [9]But Festus, wishing to do the Jews a favor, said to Paul, "Do you wish to go up to Jerusalem and there be tried on these charges before me?" [10]But Paul said, "I am standing before Caesar's tribunal, where I ought to be tried. To the Jews I have done no wrong, as you yourself know very well. [11]If then I am a wrongdoer and have committed anything for which I deserve to die, I do not seek to escape death. But if there is nothing to their charges against me, no one can give me up to them. I appeal to Caesar." [12]Then Festus, when he had conferred with his council, answered, "To Caesar you have appealed; to Caesar you shall go."

[13]Now when some days had passed, Agrippa the king and Bernice arrived at Caesarea and greeted Festus. [14]And as they stayed there many days, Festus laid Paul's case before the king, saying, "There is a man left prisoner by Felix, [15]and when I was at Jerusalem, the chief priests and the elders of the Jews laid out their case against him, asking for a sentence of condemnation against him. [16]I answered them that it was not the custom of the Romans to give up anyone before the accused met the accusers face to face and had opportunity to make his defense concerning the charge laid against him. [17]So when they came together here, I made no delay, but on the next day took my seat on the tribunal and ordered the man to be brought. [18]When the accusers stood up, they brought no charge in his case of such evils as I supposed. [19]Rather they had certain points of dispute with him about their own religion and about a certain Jesus, who was dead, but whom Paul asserted to be alive. [20]Being at a loss how to investigate these questions, I asked whether he wanted to go to Jerusalem and be tried there regarding them. [21]But when Paul had appealed to be kept in custody for the decision of the emperor, I ordered him to be held until I could send him to Caesar." [22]Then Agrippa said to

---

[1] Or headdress [2] Or suspended on a stake [3] Greek him

Festus, "I would like to hear the man myself." "Tomorrow," said he, "you will hear him."

[23] So on the next day Agrippa and Bernice came with great pomp, and they entered the audience hall with the military tribunes and the prominent men of the city. Then, at the command of Festus, Paul was brought in. [24] And Festus said, "King Agrippa and all who are present with us, you see this man about whom the whole Jewish people petitioned me, both in Jerusalem and here, shouting that he ought not to live any longer. [25] But I found that he had done nothing deserving death. And as he himself appealed to the emperor, I decided to go ahead and send him. [26] But I have nothing definite to write to my lord about him. Therefore I have brought him before you all, and especially before you, King Agrippa, so that, after we have examined him, I may have something to write. [27] For it seems to me unreasonable, in sending a prisoner, not to indicate the charges against him."

JANUARY 26

Genesis 27

When Isaac was old and his eyes were dim so that he could not see, he called Esau his older son and said to him, "My son"; and he answered, "Here I am." [2] He said, "Behold, I am old; I do not know the day of my death. [3] Now then, take your weapons, your quiver and your bow, and go out to the field and hunt game for me, [4] and prepare for me delicious food, such as I love, and bring it to me so that I may eat, that my soul may bless you before I die."

[5] Now Rebekah was listening when Isaac spoke to his son Esau. So when Esau went to the field to hunt for game and bring it, [6] Rebekah said to her son Jacob, "I heard your father speak to your brother Esau, [7] 'Bring me game and prepare for me delicious food, that I may eat it and bless you before the LORD before I die.' [8] Now therefore, my son, obey my voice as I command you. [9] Go to the flock and bring me two good young goats, so that I may prepare from them delicious food for your father, such as he loves. [10] And you shall bring it to your father to eat, so that he may bless you before he dies." [11] But Jacob said to Rebekah his mother, "Behold, my brother Esau is a hairy man, and I am a smooth man. [12] Perhaps my father will feel me, and I shall seem to be mocking him and bring a curse upon myself and not a blessing." [13] His mother said to him, "Let your curse be on me, my son; only obey my voice, and go, bring them to me."

[14] So he went and took them and brought them to his mother, and his mother prepared delicious food, such as his father loved. [15] Then Rebekah took the best garments of Esau her older son, which were with her in the house, and put them on Jacob her younger son. [16] And the skins of the young goats she put on his hands and on the smooth part of his neck. [17] And she put the delicious food and the bread, which she had prepared, into the hand of her son Jacob.

[18] So he went in to his father and said, "My father." And he said, "Here I am. Who are you, my son?" [19] Jacob said to his father, "I am Esau your firstborn. I have done as you told me; now sit up and eat of my game, that your soul may bless me." [20] But Isaac said to his son, "How is it that you have found it so quickly, my son?" He answered, "Because the LORD your God granted me success." [21] Then Isaac said to Jacob, "Please come near, that I may feel you, my son, to know whether you are really my son Esau or not." [22] So Jacob went near to Isaac his father, who felt him and said, "The voice is Jacob's voice, but the hands are the hands of Esau." [23] And he did not recognize him, because his hands were hairy like his brother Esau's hands. So he blessed him. [24] He said, "Are you really my son Esau?" He answered, "I am." [25] Then he said, "Bring it near to me, that I may eat of my son's

game and bless you." So he brought it near to him, and he ate; and he brought him wine, and he drank.

²⁶Then his father Isaac said to him, "Come near and kiss me, my son." ²⁷So he came near and kissed him. And Isaac smelled the smell of his garments and blessed him and said,

"See, the smell of my son
　　is as the smell of a field that the LORD
　　　has blessed!
²⁸　May God give you of the dew of heaven
　　and of the fatness of the earth
　　and plenty of grain and wine.
²⁹　Let peoples serve you,
　　and nations bow down to you.
　Be lord over your brothers,
　　and may your mother's sons bow
　　　down to you.
　Cursed be everyone who curses you,
　　and blessed be everyone who blesses
　　　you!"

³⁰As soon as Isaac had finished blessing Jacob, when Jacob had scarcely gone out from the presence of Isaac his father, Esau his brother came in from his hunting. ³¹He also prepared delicious food and brought it to his father. And he said to his father, "Let my father arise and eat of his son's game, that you may bless me." ³²His father Isaac said to him, "Who are you?" He answered, "I am your son, your firstborn, Esau." ³³Then Isaac trembled very violently and said, "Who was it then that hunted game and brought it to me, and I ate it all before you came, and I have blessed him? Yes, and he shall be blessed." ³⁴As soon as Esau heard the words of his father, he cried out with an exceedingly great and bitter cry and said to his father, "Bless me, even me also, O my father!" ³⁵But he said, "Your brother came deceitfully, and he has taken away your blessing." ³⁶Esau said, "Is he not rightly named Jacob?¹ For he has cheated me these two times. He took away my birthright, and behold, now he has taken away my blessing." Then he said, "Have you not reserved a blessing for me?" ³⁷Isaac answered and said to Esau, "Behold, I have made him lord over you, and all his brothers I have given to him for servants, and with grain and wine I have sustained him. What then can I do for you, my son?" ³⁸Esau said to his father, "Have you but one blessing, my father? Bless me, even

me also, O my father." And Esau lifted up his voice and wept.

³⁹Then Isaac his father answered and said to him:

"Behold, away from² the fatness of the
　　earth shall your dwelling be,
　　and away from³ the dew of heaven on
　　　high.
⁴⁰　By your sword you shall live,
　　and you shall serve your brother;
　but when you grow restless
　　you shall break his yoke from your
　　　neck."

⁴¹Now Esau hated Jacob because of the blessing with which his father had blessed him, and Esau said to himself, "The days of mourning for my father are approaching; then I will kill my brother Jacob." ⁴²But the words of Esau her older son were told to Rebekah. So she sent and called Jacob her younger son and said to him, "Behold, your brother Esau comforts himself about you by planning to kill you. ⁴³Now therefore, my son, obey my voice. Arise, flee to Laban my brother in Haran ⁴⁴and stay with him a while, until your brother's fury turns away— ⁴⁵until your brother's anger turns away from you, and he forgets what you have done to him. Then I will send and bring you from there. Why should I be bereft of you both in one day?"

⁴⁶Then Rebekah said to Isaac, "I loathe my life because of the Hittite women.⁴ If Jacob marries one of the Hittite women like these, one of the women of the land, what good will my life be to me?"

Matthew 26

W hen Jesus had finished all these sayings, he said to his disciples, ²"You know that after two days the Passover is coming, and the Son of Man will be delivered up to be crucified."

³Then the chief priests and the elders of the people gathered in the palace of the high priest, whose name was Caiaphas, ⁴and plotted together in order to arrest Jesus by stealth and kill him. ⁵But they said, "Not during the feast, lest there be an uproar among the people."

⁶Now when Jesus was at Bethany in the house of Simon the leper,⁵ ⁷a woman came up to him with an alabaster flask of very expensive ointment, and she poured it on his head

---

¹ Jacob means He takes by the heel, or He cheats ² Or Behold, of ³ Or and of ⁴ Hebrew daughters of Heth ⁵ Leprosy was a term for several skin diseases; see Leviticus 13

as he reclined at table. **8**And when the disciples saw it, they were indignant, saying, "Why this waste? **9**For this could have been sold for a large sum and given to the poor." **10**But Jesus, aware of this, said to them, "Why do you trouble the woman? For she has done a beautiful thing to me. **11**For you always have the poor with you, but you will not always have me. **12**In pouring this ointment on my body, she has done it to prepare me for burial. **13**Truly, I say to you, wherever this gospel is proclaimed in the whole world, what she has done will also be told in memory of her."

14Then one of the twelve, whose name was Judas Iscariot, went to the chief priests **15**and said, "What will you give me if I deliver him over to you?" And they paid him thirty pieces of silver. **16**And from that moment he sought an opportunity to betray him.

17Now on the first day of Unleavened Bread the disciples came to Jesus, saying, "Where will you have us prepare for you to eat the Passover?" **18**He said, "Go into the city to a certain man and say to him, 'The Teacher says, My time is at hand. I will keep the Passover at your house with my disciples.'" **19**And the disciples did as Jesus had directed them, and they prepared the Passover.

20When it was evening, he reclined at table with the twelve.[1] **21**And as they were eating, he said, "Truly, I say to you, one of you will betray me." **22**And they were very sorrowful and began to say to him one after another, "Is it I, Lord?" **23**He answered, "He who has dipped his hand in the dish with me will betray me. **24**The Son of Man goes as it is written of him, but woe to that man by whom the Son of Man is betrayed! It would have been better for that man if he had not been born." **25**Judas, who would betray him, answered, "Is it I, Rabbi?" He said to him, "You have said so."

26Now as they were eating, Jesus took bread, and after blessing it broke it and gave it to the disciples, and said, "Take, eat; this is my body." **27**And he took a cup, and when he had given thanks he gave it to them, saying, "Drink of it, all of you, **28**for this is my blood of the[2] covenant, which is poured out for many for the forgiveness of sins. **29**I tell you I will not drink again of this fruit of the vine until that day when I drink it new with you in my Father's kingdom."

30And when they had sung a hymn, they went out to the Mount of Olives. **31**Then Jesus said to them, "You will all fall away because of me this night. For it is written, 'I will strike the shepherd, and the sheep of the flock will be scattered.' **32**But after I am raised up, I will go before you to Galilee." **33**Peter answered him, "Though they all fall away because of you, I will never fall away." **34**Jesus said to him, "Truly, I tell you, this very night, before the rooster crows, you will deny me three times." **35**Peter said to him, "Even if I must die with you, I will not deny you!" And all the disciples said the same.

36Then Jesus went with them to a place called Gethsemane, and he said to his disciples, "Sit here, while I go over there and pray." **37**And taking with him Peter and the two sons of Zebedee, he began to be sorrowful and troubled. **38**Then he said to them, "My soul is very sorrowful, even to death; remain here, and watch[3] with me." **39**And going a little farther he fell on his face and prayed, saying, "My Father, if it be possible, let this cup pass from me; nevertheless, not as I will, but as you will." **40**And he came to the disciples and found them sleeping. And he said to Peter, "So, could you not watch with me one hour? **41**Watch and pray that you may not enter into temptation. The spirit indeed is willing, but the flesh is weak." **42**Again, for the second time, he went away and prayed, "My Father, if this cannot pass unless I drink it, your will be done." **43**And again he came and found them sleeping, for their eyes were heavy. **44**So, leaving them again, he went away and prayed for the third time, saying the same words again. **45**Then he came to the disciples and said to them, "Sleep and take your rest later on.[4] See, the hour is at hand, and the Son of Man is betrayed into the hands of sinners. **46**Rise, let us be going; see, my betrayer is at hand."

47While he was still speaking, Judas came, one of the twelve, and with him a great crowd with swords and clubs, from the chief priests and the elders of the people. **48**Now the betrayer had given them a sign, saying, "The one I will kiss is the man; seize him." **49**And he came up to Jesus at once and said, "Greetings, Rabbi!" And he kissed him. **50**Jesus said to him, "Friend, do what you came to do."[5] Then they came up and laid hands on Jesus and seized him. **51**And behold, one of those who were with Jesus stretched out his hand and drew his sword and

---

[1] Some manuscripts add *disciples* [2] Some manuscripts insert *new* [3] Or *keep awake*; also verses 40, 41 [4] Or *Are you still sleeping and taking your rest?* [5] Or *Friend, why are you here?*

struck the servant[1] of the high priest and cut off his ear. [52]Then Jesus said to him, "Put your sword back into its place. For all who take the sword will perish by the sword. [53]Do you think that I cannot appeal to my Father, and he will at once send me more than twelve legions of angels? [54]But how then should the Scriptures be fulfilled, that it must be so?" [55]At that hour Jesus said to the crowds, "Have you come out as against a robber, with swords and clubs to capture me? Day after day I sat in the temple teaching, and you did not seize me. [56]But all this has taken place that the Scriptures of the prophets might be fulfilled." Then all the disciples left him and fled.

[57]Then those who had seized Jesus led him to Caiaphas the high priest, where the scribes and the elders had gathered. [58]And Peter was following him at a distance, as far as the courtyard of the high priest, and going inside he sat with the guards to see the end. [59]Now the chief priests and the whole council[2] were seeking false testimony against Jesus that they might put him to death, [60]but they found none, though many false witnesses came forward. At last two came forward [61]and said, "This man said, 'I am able to destroy the temple of God, and to rebuild it in three days.'" [62]And the high priest stood up and said, "Have you no answer to make? What is it that these men testify against you?"[3] [63]But Jesus remained silent. And the high priest said to him, "I adjure you by the living God, tell us if you are the Christ, the Son of God." [64]Jesus said to him, "You have said so. But I tell you, from now on you will see the Son of Man seated at the right hand of Power and coming on the clouds of heaven." [65]Then the high priest tore his robes and said, "He has uttered blasphemy. What further witnesses do we need? You have now heard his blasphemy. [66]What is your judgment?" They answered, "He deserves death." [67]Then they spit in his face and struck him. And some slapped him, [68]saying, "Prophesy to us, you Christ! Who is it that struck you?"

[69]Now Peter was sitting outside in the courtyard. And a servant girl came up to him and said, "You also were with Jesus the Galilean." [70]But he denied it before them all, saying, "I do not know what you mean." [71]And when he went out to the entrance, another servant girl saw him, and she said to the bystanders,

"This man was with Jesus of Nazareth." [72]And again he denied it with an oath: "I do not know the man." [73]After a little while the bystanders came up and said to Peter, "Certainly you too are one of them, for your accent betrays you." [74]Then he began to invoke a curse on himself and to swear, "I do not know the man." And immediately the rooster crowed. [75]And Peter remembered the saying of Jesus, "Before the rooster crows, you will deny me three times." And he went out and wept bitterly.

Esther 3

After these things King Ahasuerus promoted Haman the Agagite, the son of Hammedatha, and advanced him and set his throne above all the officials who were with him. [2]And all the king's servants who were at the king's gate bowed down and paid homage to Haman, for the king had so commanded concerning him. But Mordecai did not bow down or pay homage. [3]Then the king's servants who were at the king's gate said to Mordecai, "Why do you transgress the king's command?" [4]And when they spoke to him day after day and he would not listen to them, they told Haman, in order to see whether Mordecai's words would stand, for he had told them that he was a Jew. [5]And when Haman saw that Mordecai did not bow down or pay homage to him, Haman was filled with fury. [6]But he disdained to lay hands on Mordecai alone. So, as they had made known to him the people of Mordecai, Haman sought to destroy all the Jews, the people of Mordecai, throughout the whole kingdom of Ahasuerus.

[7]In the first month, which is the month of Nisan, in the twelfth year of King Ahasuerus, they cast Pur (that is, they cast lots) before Haman day after day; and they cast it month after month till the twelfth month, which is the month of Adar. [8]Then Haman said to King Ahasuerus, "There is a certain people scattered abroad and dispersed among the peoples in all the provinces of your kingdom. Their laws are different from those of every other people, and they do not keep the king's laws, so that it is not to the king's profit to tolerate them. [9]If it please the king, let it be decreed that they be destroyed, and I will pay 10,000 talents[4] of silver into the hands of those who have charge of

the king's business, that they may put it into the king's treasuries." [10]So the king took his signet ring from his hand and gave it to Haman the Agagite, the son of Hammedatha, the enemy of the Jews. [11]And the king said to Haman, "The money is given to you, the people also, to do with them as it seems good to you."

[12]Then the king's scribes were summoned on the thirteenth day of the first month, and an edict, according to all that Haman commanded, was written to the king's satraps and to the governors over all the provinces and to the officials of all the peoples, to every province in its own script and every people in its own language. It was written in the name of King Ahasuerus and sealed with the king's signet ring. [13]Letters were sent by couriers to all the king's provinces with instruction to destroy, to kill, and to annihilate all Jews, young and old, women and children, in one day, the thirteenth day of the twelfth month, which is the month of Adar, and to plunder their goods. [14]A copy of the document was to be issued as a decree in every province by proclamation to all the peoples to be ready for that day. [15]The couriers went out hurriedly by order of the king, and the decree was issued in Susa the citadel. And the king and Haman sat down to drink, but the city of Susa was thrown into confusion.

Acts 26

[1]So Agrippa said to Paul, "You have permission to speak for yourself." Then Paul stretched out his hand and made his defense:

[2]"I consider myself fortunate that it is before you, King Agrippa, I am going to make my defense today against all the accusations of the Jews, [3]especially because you are familiar with all the customs and controversies of the Jews. Therefore I beg you to listen to me patiently.

[4]"My manner of life from my youth, spent from the beginning among my own nation and in Jerusalem, is known by all the Jews. [5]They have known for a long time, if they are willing to testify, that according to the strictest party of our religion I have lived as a Pharisee. [6]And now I stand here on trial because of my hope in the promise made by God to our fathers, [7]to which our twelve tribes hope to attain, as they earnestly worship night and day. And for this

hope I am accused by Jews, O king! [8]Why is it thought incredible by any of you that God raises the dead?

[9]"I myself was convinced that I ought to do many things in opposing the name of Jesus of Nazareth. [10]And I did so in Jerusalem. I not only locked up many of the saints in prison after receiving authority from the chief priests, but when they were put to death I cast my vote against them. [11]And I punished them often in all the synagogues and tried to make them blaspheme, and in raging fury against them I persecuted them even to foreign cities.

[12]"In this connection I journeyed to Damascus with the authority and commission of the chief priests. [13]At midday, O king, I saw on the way a light from heaven, brighter than the sun, that shone around me and those who journeyed with me. [14]And when we had all fallen to the ground, I heard a voice saying to me in the Hebrew language,[1] 'Saul, Saul, why are you persecuting me? It is hard for you to kick against the goads.' [15]And I said, 'Who are you, Lord?' And the Lord said, 'I am Jesus whom you are persecuting. [16]But rise and stand upon your feet, for I have appeared to you for this purpose, to appoint you as a servant and witness to the things in which you have seen me and to those in which I will appear to you, [17]delivering you from your people and from the Gentiles—to whom I am sending you [18]to open their eyes, so that they may turn from darkness to light and from the power of Satan to God, that they may receive forgiveness of sins and a place among those who are sanctified by faith in me.'

[19]"Therefore, O King Agrippa, I was not disobedient to the heavenly vision, [20]but declared first to those in Damascus, then in Jerusalem and throughout all the region of Judea, and also to the Gentiles, that they should repent and turn to God, performing deeds in keeping with their repentance. [21]For this reason the Jews seized me in the temple and tried to kill me. [22]To this day I have had the help that comes from God, and so I stand here testifying both to small and great, saying nothing but what the prophets and Moses said would come to pass: [23]that the Christ must suffer and that, by being the first to rise from the dead, he would proclaim light both to our people and to the Gentiles."

[1] Or the Hebrew dialect (probably Aramaic)

[24]And as he was saying these things in his defense, Festus said with a loud voice, "Paul, you are out of your mind; your great learning is driving you out of your mind." [25]But Paul said, "I am not out of my mind, most excellent Festus, but I am speaking true and rational words. [26]For the king knows about these things, and to him I speak boldly. For I am persuaded that none of these things has escaped his notice, for this has not been done in a corner. [27]King Agrippa, do you believe the prophets? I know that you believe." [28]And Agrippa said to Paul, "In a short time would you persuade me to be a Christian?"[1] [29]And Paul said, "Whether short or long, I would to God that not only you but also all who hear me this day might become such as I am—except for these chains."

[30]Then the king rose, and the governor and Bernice and those who were sitting with them. [31]And when they had withdrawn, they said to one another, "This man is doing nothing to deserve death or imprisonment." [32]And Agrippa said to Festus, "This man could have been set free if he had not appealed to Caesar."

J A N U A R Y   2 7

Genesis 28

Then Isaac called Jacob and blessed him and directed him, "You must not take a wife from the Canaanite women. [2]Arise, go to Paddan-aram to the house of Bethuel your mother's father, and take as your wife from there one of the daughters of Laban your mother's brother. [3]God Almighty[2] bless you and make you fruitful and multiply you, that you may become a company of peoples. [4]May he give the blessing of Abraham to you and to your offspring with you, that you may take possession of the land of your sojournings that God gave to Abraham!" [5]Thus Isaac sent Jacob away. And he went to Paddan-aram, to Laban, the son of Bethuel the Aramean, the brother of Rebekah, Jacob's and Esau's mother.

[6]Now Esau saw that Isaac had blessed Jacob and sent him away to Paddan-aram to take a wife from there, and that as he blessed him he directed him, "You must not take a wife from the Canaanite women," [7]and that Jacob had obeyed his father and his mother and gone to Paddan-aram. [8]So when Esau saw that the Canaanite women did not please Isaac his father, [9]Esau went to Ishmael and took as his wife, besides the wives he had, Mahalath the daughter of Ishmael, Abraham's son, the sister of Nebaioth.

[10]Jacob left Beersheba and went toward Haran. [11]And he came to a certain place and stayed there that night, because the sun had set. Taking one of the stones of the place, he put it under his head and lay down in that place to sleep. [12]And he dreamed, and behold, there was a ladder[3] set up on the earth, and the top of it reached to heaven. And behold, the angels of God were ascending and descending on it! [13]And behold, the LORD stood above it[4] and said, "I am the LORD, the God of Abraham your father and the God of Isaac. The land on which you lie I will give to you and to your offspring. [14]Your offspring shall be like the dust of the earth, and you shall spread abroad to the west and to the east and to the north and to the south, and in you and your offspring shall all the families of the earth be blessed. [15]Behold, I am with you and will keep you wherever you go, and will bring you back to this land. For I will not leave you until I have done what I have promised you." [16]Then Jacob awoke from his sleep and said, "Surely the LORD is in this place, and I did not know it." [17]And he was afraid and said, "How awesome is this place! This is none other than the house of God, and this is the gate of heaven."

[18]So early in the morning Jacob took the stone that he had put under his head and set it up for a pillar and poured oil on the top of it.

[1] Or In a short time you would persuade me to act like a Christian! [2] Hebrew El Shaddai [3] Or a flight of steps [4] Or beside him

[19]He called the name of that place Bethel,[1] but the name of the city was Luz at the first. [20]Then Jacob made a vow, saying, "If God will be with me and will keep me in this way that I go, and will give me bread to eat and clothing to wear, [21]so that I come again to my father's house in peace, then the LORD shall be my God, [22]and this stone, which I have set up for a pillar, shall be God's house. And of all that you give me I will give a full tenth to you."

Matthew 27

When morning came, all the chief priests and the elders of the people took counsel against Jesus to put him to death. [2]And they bound him and led him away and delivered him over to Pilate the governor.

[3]Then when Judas, his betrayer, saw that Jesus[2] was condemned, he changed his mind and brought back the thirty pieces of silver to the chief priests and the elders, [4]saying, "I have sinned by betraying innocent blood." They said, "What is that to us? See to it yourself." [5]And throwing down the pieces of silver into the temple, he departed, and he went and hanged himself. [6]But the chief priests, taking the pieces of silver, said, "It is not lawful to put them into the treasury, since it is blood money." [7]So they took counsel and bought with them the potter's field as a burial place for strangers. [8]Therefore that field has been called the Field of Blood to this day. [9]Then was fulfilled what had been spoken by the prophet Jeremiah, saying, "And they took the thirty pieces of silver, the price of him on whom a price had been set by some of the sons of Israel, [10]and they gave them for the potter's field, as the Lord directed me."

[11]Now Jesus stood before the governor, and the governor asked him, "Are you the King of the Jews?" Jesus said, "You have said so." [12]But when he was accused by the chief priests and elders, he gave no answer. [13]Then Pilate said to him, "Do you not hear how many things they testify against you?" [14]But he gave him no answer, not even to a single charge, so that the governor was greatly amazed.

[15]Now at the feast the governor was accustomed to release for the crowd any one prisoner whom they wanted. [16]And they had then a notorious prisoner called Barabbas. [17]So when they had gathered, Pilate said to them, "Whom do you want me to release for you: Barabbas, or Jesus who is called Christ?" [18]For he knew that it was out of envy that they had delivered him up. [19]Besides, while he was sitting on the judgment seat, his wife sent word to him, "Have nothing to do with that righteous man, for I have suffered much because of him today in a dream." [20]Now the chief priests and the elders persuaded the crowd to ask for Barabbas and destroy Jesus. [21]The governor again said to them, "Which of the two do you want me to release for you?" And they said, "Barabbas." [22]Pilate said to them, "Then what shall I do with Jesus who is called Christ?" They all said, "Let him be crucified!" [23]And he said, "Why, what evil has he done?" But they shouted all the more, "Let him be crucified!"

[24]So when Pilate saw that he was gaining nothing, but rather that a riot was beginning, he took water and washed his hands before the crowd, saying, "I am innocent of this man's blood;[3] see to it yourselves." [25]And all the people answered, "His blood be on us and on our children!" [26]Then he released for them Barabbas, and having scourged[4] Jesus, delivered him to be crucified.

[27]Then the soldiers of the governor took Jesus into the governor's headquarters,[5] and they gathered the whole battalion[6] before him. [28]And they stripped him and put a scarlet robe on him, [29]and twisting together a crown of thorns, they put it on his head and put a reed in his right hand. And kneeling before him, they mocked him, saying, "Hail, King of the Jews!" [30]And they spit on him and took the reed and struck him on the head. [31]And when they had mocked him, they stripped him of the robe and put his own clothes on him and led him away to crucify him.

[32]As they went out, they found a man of Cyrene, Simon by name. They compelled this man to carry his cross. [33]And when they came to a place called Golgotha (which means Place of a Skull), [34]they offered him wine to drink, mixed with gall, but when he tasted it, he would not drink it. [35]And when they had crucified him, they divided his garments among them by casting lots. [36]Then they sat down and kept watch over him there. [37]And over his head they put the charge against him, which read, "This is Jesus, the King of the Jews." [38]Then two robbers were crucified with him, one on the right

---

[1] Bethel means the house of God [2] Greek he [3] Some manuscripts this righteous blood, or this righteous man's blood [4] A Roman judicial penalty, consisting of a severe beating with a multi-lashed whip containing imbedded pieces of bone and metal [5] Greek the praetorium [6] Greek cohort; a tenth of a Roman legion, usually about 600 men

and one on the left. [39] And those who passed by derided him, wagging their heads [40] and saying, "You who would destroy the temple and rebuild it in three days, save yourself! If you are the Son of God, come down from the cross." [41] So also the chief priests, with the scribes and elders, mocked him, saying, [42] "He saved others; he cannot save himself. He is the King of Israel; let him come down now from the cross, and we will believe in him. [43] He trusts in God; let God deliver him now, if he desires him. For he said, 'I am the Son of God.'" [44] And the robbers who were crucified with him also reviled him in the same way.

[45] Now from the sixth hour[1] there was darkness over all the land[2] until the ninth hour.[3] [46] And about the ninth hour Jesus cried out with a loud voice, saying, "Eli, Eli, lema sabachthani?" that is, "My God, my God, why have you forsaken me?" [47] And some of the bystanders, hearing it, said, "This man is calling Elijah." [48] And one of them at once ran and took a sponge, filled it with sour wine, and put it on a reed and gave it to him to drink. [49] But the others said, "Wait, let us see whether Elijah will come to save him." [50] And Jesus cried out again with a loud voice and yielded up his spirit.

[51] And behold, the curtain of the temple was torn in two, from top to bottom. And the earth shook, and the rocks were split. [52] The tombs also were opened. And many bodies of the saints who had fallen asleep were raised, [53] and coming out of the tombs after his resurrection they went into the holy city and appeared to many. [54] When the centurion and those who were with him, keeping watch over Jesus, saw the earthquake and what took place, they were filled with awe and said, "Truly this was the Son[4] of God!"

[55] There were also many women there, looking on from a distance, who had followed Jesus from Galilee, ministering to him, [56] among whom were Mary Magdalene and Mary the mother of James and Joseph and the mother of the sons of Zebedee.

[57] When it was evening, there came a rich man from Arimathea, named Joseph, who also was a disciple of Jesus. [58] He went to Pilate and asked for the body of Jesus. Then Pilate ordered it to be given to him. [59] And Joseph took the body and wrapped it in a clean linen shroud [60] and laid it in his own new tomb, which he had cut in the rock. And he rolled a great stone to the entrance of the tomb and went away. [61] Mary Magdalene and the other Mary were there, sitting opposite the tomb.

[62] The next day, that is, after the day of Preparation, the chief priests and the Pharisees gathered before Pilate [63] and said, "Sir, we remember how that impostor said, while he was still alive, 'After three days I will rise.' [64] Therefore order the tomb to be made secure until the third day, lest his disciples go and steal him away and tell the people, 'He has risen from the dead,' and the last fraud will be worse than the first." [65] Pilate said to them, "You have a guard[5] of soldiers. Go, make it as secure as you can." [66] So they went and made the tomb secure by sealing the stone and setting a guard.

Esther 4

When Mordecai learned all that had been done, Mordecai tore his clothes and put on sackcloth and ashes, and went out into the midst of the city, and he cried out with a loud and bitter cry. [2] He went up to the entrance of the king's gate, for no one was allowed to enter the king's gate clothed in sackcloth. [3] And in every province, wherever the king's command and his decree reached, there was great mourning among the Jews, with fasting and weeping and lamenting, and many of them lay in sackcloth and ashes.

[4] When Esther's young women and her eunuchs came and told her, the queen was deeply distressed. She sent garments to clothe Mordecai, so that he might take off his sackcloth, but he would not accept them. [5] Then Esther called for Hathach, one of the king's eunuchs, who had been appointed to attend her, and ordered him to go to Mordecai to learn what this was and why it was. [6] Hathach went out to Mordecai in the open square of the city in front of the king's gate, [7] and Mordecai told him all that had happened to him, and the exact sum of money that Haman had promised to pay into the king's treasuries for the destruction of the Jews. [8] Mordecai also gave him a copy of the written decree issued in Susa for their destruction, that he might show it to Esther and explain it to her and command her to go to the king to beg his favor and plead with him on behalf of her people. [9] And Hathach went and told

---

[1] That is, noon [2] Or earth [3] That is, 3 P.M. [4] Or a son [5] Or Take a guard

Esther what Mordecai had said. [10]Then Esther spoke to Hathach and commanded him to go to Mordecai and say, [11]"All the king's servants and the people of the king's provinces know that if any man or woman goes to the king inside the inner court without being called, there is but one law—to be put to death, except the one to whom the king holds out the golden scepter so that he may live. But as for me, I have not been called to come in to the king these thirty days."

[12]And they told Mordecai what Esther had said. [13]Then Mordecai told them to reply to Esther, "Do not think to yourself that in the king's palace you will escape any more than all the other Jews. [14]For if you keep silent at this time, relief and deliverance will rise for the Jews from another place, but you and your father's house will perish. And who knows whether you have not come to the kingdom for such a time as this?" [15]Then Esther told them to reply to Mordecai, [16]"Go, gather all the Jews to be found in Susa, and hold a fast on my behalf, and do not eat or drink for three days, night or day. I and my young women will also fast as you do. Then I will go to the king, though it is against the law, and if I perish, I perish." [17]Mordecai then went away and did everything as Esther had ordered him.

Acts 27

And when it was decided that we should sail for Italy, they delivered Paul and some other prisoners to a centurion of the Augustan Cohort named Julius. [2]And embarking in a ship of Adramyttium, which was about to sail to the ports along the coast of Asia, we put to sea, accompanied by Aristarchus, a Macedonian from Thessalonica. [3]The next day we put in at Sidon. And Julius treated Paul kindly and gave him leave to go to his friends and be cared for. [4]And putting out to sea from there we sailed under the lee of Cyprus, because the winds were against us. [5]And when we had sailed across the open sea along the coast of Cilicia and Pamphylia, we came to Myra in Lycia. [6]There the centurion found a ship of Alexandria sailing for Italy and put us on board. [7]We sailed slowly for a number of days and arrived with difficulty off Cnidus, and as the wind did not allow us to go farther, we sailed under the lee of Crete off Salmone. [8]Coasting along it with difficulty, we came to a place called Fair Havens, near which was the city of Lasea.

[9]Since much time had passed, and the voyage was now dangerous because even the Fast[1] was already over, Paul advised them, [10]saying, "Sirs, I perceive that the voyage will be with injury and much loss, not only of the cargo and the ship, but also of our lives." [11]But the centurion paid more attention to the pilot and to the owner of the ship than to what Paul said. [12]And because the harbor was not suitable to spend the winter in, the majority decided to put out to sea from there, on the chance that somehow they could reach Phoenix, a harbor of Crete, facing both southwest and northwest, and spend the winter there.

[13]Now when the south wind blew gently, supposing that they had obtained their purpose, they weighed anchor and sailed along Crete, close to the shore. [14]But soon a tempestuous wind, called the northeaster, struck down from the land. [15]And when the ship was caught and could not face the wind, we gave way to it and were driven along. [16]Running under the lee of a small island called Cauda,[2] we managed with difficulty to secure the ship's boat. [17]After hoisting it up, they used supports to undergird the ship. Then, fearing that they would run aground on the Syrtis, they lowered the gear,[3] and thus they were driven along. [18]Since we were violently storm-tossed, they began the next day to jettison the cargo. [19]And on the third day they threw the ship's tackle overboard with their own hands. [20]When neither sun nor stars appeared for many days, and no small tempest lay on us, all hope of our being saved was at last abandoned.

[21]Since they had been without food for a long time, Paul stood up among them and said, "Men, you should have listened to me and not have set sail from Crete and incurred this injury and loss. [22]Yet now I urge you to take heart, for there will be no loss of life among you, but only of the ship. [23]For this very night there stood before me an angel of the God to whom I belong and whom I worship, [24]and he said, 'Do not be afraid, Paul; you must stand before Caesar. And behold, God has granted you all those who sail with you.' [25]So take heart, men, for I have faith in God that it will be exactly as I have been told. [26]But we must run aground on some island." [27]When the fourteenth night had come, as

---

[1] That is, the Day of Atonement   [2] Some manuscripts *Clauda*   [3] That is, the sea-anchor (or possibly the mainsail)

we were being driven across the Adriatic Sea, about midnight the sailors suspected that they were nearing land. [28] So they took a sounding and found twenty fathoms.[1] A little farther on they took a sounding again and found fifteen fathoms.[2] [29] And fearing that we might run on the rocks, they let down four anchors from the stern and prayed for day to come. [30] And as the sailors were seeking to escape from the ship, and had lowered the ship's boat into the sea under pretense of laying out anchors from the bow, [31] Paul said to the centurion and the soldiers, "Unless these men stay in the ship, you cannot be saved." [32] Then the soldiers cut away the ropes of the ship's boat and let it go.

[33] As day was about to dawn, Paul urged them all to take some food, saying, "Today is the fourteenth day that you have continued in suspense and without food, having taken nothing. [34] Therefore I urge you to take some food. For it will give you strength,[3] for not a hair is to perish from the head of any of you." [35] And when he had said these things, he took bread, and giving thanks to God in the presence of all he broke it and began to eat. [36] Then they all were encouraged and ate some food themselves. [37] (We were in all 276[4] persons in the ship.) [38] And when they had eaten enough, they lightened the ship, throwing out the wheat into the sea.

[39] Now when it was day, they did not recognize the land, but they noticed a bay with a beach, on which they planned if possible to run the ship ashore. [40] So they cast off the anchors and left them in the sea, at the same time loosening the ropes that tied the rudders. Then hoisting the foresail to the wind they made for the beach. [41] But striking a reef,[5] they ran the vessel aground. The bow stuck and remained immovable, and the stern was being broken up by the surf. [42] The soldiers' plan was to kill the prisoners, lest any should swim away and escape. [43] But the centurion, wishing to save Paul, kept them from carrying out their plan. He ordered those who could swim to jump overboard first and make for the land, [44] and the rest on planks or on pieces of the ship. And so it was that all were brought safely to land.

JANUARY 28

Genesis 29

Then Jacob went on his journey and came to the land of the people of the east. [2] As he looked, he saw a well in the field, and behold, three flocks of sheep lying beside it, for out of that well the flocks were watered. The stone on the well's mouth was large, [3] and when all the flocks were gathered there, the shepherds would roll the stone from the mouth of the well and water the sheep, and put the stone back in its place over the mouth of the well.

[4] Jacob said to them, "My brothers, where do you come from?" They said, "We are from Haran." [5] He said to them, "Do you know Laban the son of Nahor?" They said, "We know him." [6] He said to them, "Is it well with him?" They said, "It is well; and see, Rachel his daughter is coming with the sheep!" [7] He said, "Behold, it is still high day; it is not time for the livestock to be gathered together. Water the sheep and go, pasture them." [8] But they said, "We cannot until all the flocks are gathered together and the stone is rolled from the mouth of the well; then we water the sheep."

[9] While he was still speaking with them, Rachel came with her father's sheep, for she was a shepherdess. [10] Now as soon as Jacob saw Rachel the daughter of Laban his mother's brother, and the sheep of Laban his mother's brother, Jacob came near and rolled the stone from the well's mouth and watered the flock of Laban his mother's brother. [11] Then Jacob kissed Rachel and wept aloud. [12] And Jacob told Rachel that he was her father's kinsman,

[1] About 120 feet; a fathom (Greek *orguia*) was about 6 feet or 2 meters [2] About 90 feet (see previous note) [3] Or *For it is for your deliverance* [4] Some manuscripts *seventy-six*, or *about seventy-six* [5] Or *sandbank*, or *crosscurrent*; Greek *place between two seas*

and that he was Rebekah's son, and she ran and told her father. [13] As soon as Laban heard the news about Jacob, his sister's son, he ran to meet him and embraced him and kissed him and brought him to his house. Jacob told Laban all these things, [14] and Laban said to him, "Surely you are my bone and my flesh!" And he stayed with him a month.

[15] Then Laban said to Jacob, "Because you are my kinsman, should you therefore serve me for nothing? Tell me, what shall your wages be?" [16] Now Laban had two daughters. The name of the older was Leah, and the name of the younger was Rachel. [17] Leah's eyes were weak,[1] but Rachel was beautiful in form and appearance. [18] Jacob loved Rachel. And he said, "I will serve you seven years for your younger daughter Rachel." [19] Laban said, "It is better that I give her to you than that I should give her to any other man; stay with me." [20] So Jacob served seven years for Rachel, and they seemed to him but a few days because of the love he had for her.

[21] Then Jacob said to Laban, "Give me my wife that I may go in to her, for my time is completed." [22] So Laban gathered together all the people of the place and made a feast. [23] But in the evening he took his daughter Leah and brought her to Jacob, and he went in to her. [24] (Laban gave[2] his female servant Zilpah to his daughter Leah to be her servant.) [25] And in the morning, behold, it was Leah! And Jacob said to Laban, "What is this you have done to me? Did I not serve with you for Rachel? Why then have you deceived me?" [26] Laban said, "It is not so done in our country, to give the younger before the firstborn. [27] Complete the week of this one, and we will give you the other also in return for serving me another seven years." [28] Jacob did so, and completed her week. Then Laban gave him his daughter Rachel to be his wife. [29] (Laban gave his female servant Bilhah to his daughter Rachel to be her servant.) [30] So Jacob went in to Rachel also, and he loved Rachel more than Leah, and served Laban for another seven years.

[31] When the LORD saw that Leah was hated, he opened her womb, but Rachel was barren. [32] And Leah conceived and bore a son, and she called his name Reuben,[3] for she said, "Because the LORD has looked upon my affliction; for now my husband will love me." [33] She conceived again and bore a son, and said, "Because the LORD has heard that I am hated, he has given me this son also." And she called his name Simeon.[4] [34] Again she conceived and bore a son, and said, "Now this time my husband will be attached to me, because I have borne him three sons." Therefore his name was called Levi.[5] [35] And she conceived again and bore a son, and said, "This time I will praise the LORD." Therefore she called his name Judah.[6] Then she ceased bearing.

─────── *Matthew 28* ───────

N
ow after the Sabbath, toward the dawn of the first day of the week, Mary Magdalene and the other Mary went to see the tomb. [2] And behold, there was a great earthquake, for an angel of the Lord descended from heaven and came and rolled back the stone and sat on it. [3] His appearance was like lightning, and his clothing white as snow. [4] And for fear of him the guards trembled and became like dead men. [5] But the angel said to the women, "Do not be afraid, for I know that you seek Jesus who was crucified. [6] He is not here, for he has risen, as he said. Come, see the place where he[7] lay. [7] Then go quickly and tell his disciples that he has risen from the dead, and behold, he is going before you to Galilee; there you will see him. See, I have told you." [8] So they departed quickly from the tomb with fear and great joy, and ran to tell his disciples. [9] And behold, Jesus met them and said, "Greetings!" And they came up and took hold of his feet and worshiped him. [10] Then Jesus said to them, "Do not be afraid; go and tell my brothers to go to Galilee, and there they will see me."

[11] While they were going, behold, some of the guard went into the city and told the chief priests all that had taken place. [12] And when they had assembled with the elders and taken counsel, they gave a sufficient sum of money to the soldiers [13] and said, "Tell people, 'His disciples came by night and stole him away while we were asleep.' [14] And if this comes to the governor's ears, we will satisfy him and keep you out of trouble." [15] So they took the money and did as they were directed. And this story has been spread among the Jews to this day.

[16] Now the eleven disciples went to Galilee, to the mountain to which Jesus had directed them.

---

[1] Or soft [2] Or had given; also verse 29 [3] Reuben means See, a son [4] Simeon sounds like the Hebrew for heard [5] Levi sounds like the Hebrew for attached [6] Judah sounds like the Hebrew for praise [7] Some manuscripts the Lord

[17]And when they saw him they worshiped him, but some doubted. [18]And Jesus came and said to them, "All authority in heaven and on earth has been given to me. [19]Go therefore and make disciples of all nations, baptizing them in[1] the name of the Father and of the Son and of the Holy Spirit, [20]teaching them to observe all that I have commanded you. And behold, I am with you always, to the end of the age."

Esther 5

On the third day Esther put on her royal robes and stood in the inner court of the king's palace, in front of the king's quarters, while the king was sitting on his royal throne inside the throne room opposite the entrance to the palace. [2]And when the king saw Queen Esther standing in the court, she won favor in his sight, and he held out to Esther the golden scepter that was in his hand. Then Esther approached and touched the tip of the scepter. [3]And the king said to her, "What is it, Queen Esther? What is your request? It shall be given you, even to the half of my kingdom." [4]And Esther said, "If it please the king, let the king and Haman come today to a feast that I have prepared for the king." [5]Then the king said, "Bring Haman quickly, so that we may do as Esther has asked." So the king and Haman came to the feast that Esther had prepared. [6]And as they were drinking wine after the feast, the king said to Esther, "What is your wish? It shall be granted you. And what is your request? Even to the half of my kingdom, it shall be fulfilled." [7]Then Esther answered, "My wish and my request is: [8]If I have found favor in the sight of the king, and if it please the king to grant my wish and fulfill my request, let the king and Haman come to the feast that I will prepare for them, and tomorrow I will do as the king has said."

[9]And Haman went out that day joyful and glad of heart. But when Haman saw Mordecai in the king's gate, that he neither rose nor trembled before him, he was filled with wrath against Mordecai. [10]Nevertheless, Haman restrained himself and went home, and he sent and brought his friends and his wife Zeresh. [11]And Haman recounted to them the splendor of his riches, the number of his sons, all the promotions with which the king had honored him, and how he had advanced him above the

officials and the servants of the king. [12]Then Haman said, "Even Queen Esther let no one but me come with the king to the feast she prepared. And tomorrow also I am invited by her together with the king. [13]Yet all this is worth nothing to me, so long as I see Mordecai the Jew sitting at the king's gate." [14]Then his wife Zeresh and all his friends said to him, "Let a gallows[2] fifty cubits[3] high be made, and in the morning tell the king to have Mordecai hanged upon it. Then go joyfully with the king to the feast." This idea pleased Haman, and he had the gallows made.

Acts 28

After we were brought safely through, we then learned that the island was called Malta. [2]The native people[4] showed us unusual kindness, for they kindled a fire and welcomed us all, because it had begun to rain and was cold. [3]When Paul had gathered a bundle of sticks and put them on the fire, a viper came out because of the heat and fastened on his hand. [4]When the native people saw the creature hanging from his hand, they said to one another, "No doubt this man is a murderer. Though he has escaped from the sea, Justice[5] has not allowed him to live." [5]He, however, shook off the creature into the fire and suffered no harm. [6]They were waiting for him to swell up or suddenly fall down dead. But when they had waited a long time and saw no misfortune come to him, they changed their minds and said that he was a god.

[7]Now in the neighborhood of that place were lands belonging to the chief man of the island, named Publius, who received us and entertained us hospitably for three days. [8]It happened that the father of Publius lay sick with fever and dysentery. And Paul visited him and prayed, and putting his hands on him healed him. [9]And when this had taken place, the rest of the people on the island who had diseases also came and were cured. [10]They also honored us greatly,[6] and when we were about to sail, they put on board whatever we needed.

[11]After three months we set sail in a ship that had wintered in the island, a ship of Alexandria, with the twin gods[7] as a figurehead. [12]Putting in at Syracuse, we stayed there for three days. [13]And from there we made a circuit and arrived

[1] Or into [2] Or stake; twice in this verse [3] A cubit was about 18 inches or 45 centimeters [4] Greek barbaroi (that is, non–Greek speakers); also verse 4 [5] Or justice [6] Greek honored us with many honors [7] That is, the Greek gods Castor and Pollux

at Rhegium. And after one day a south wind sprang up, and on the second day we came to Puteoli. [14]There we found brothers[1] and were invited to stay with them for seven days. And so we came to Rome. [15]And the brothers there, when they heard about us, came as far as the Forum of Appius and Three Taverns to meet us. On seeing them, Paul thanked God and took courage. [16]And when we came into Rome, Paul was allowed to stay by himself, with the soldier who guarded him.

[17]After three days he called together the local leaders of the Jews, and when they had gathered, he said to them, "Brothers, though I had done nothing against our people or the customs of our fathers, yet I was delivered as a prisoner from Jerusalem into the hands of the Romans. [18]When they had examined me, they wished to set me at liberty, because there was no reason for the death penalty in my case. [19]But because the Jews objected, I was compelled to appeal to Caesar—though I had no charge to bring against my nation. [20]For this reason, therefore, I have asked to see you and speak with you, since it is because of the hope of Israel that I am wearing this chain." [21]And they said to him, "We have received no letters from Judea about you, and none of the brothers coming here has reported or spoken any evil about you. [22]But we desire to hear from you what your views are, for with regard to this sect we know that everywhere it is spoken against."

[23]When they had appointed a day for him, they came to him at his lodging in greater numbers. From morning till evening he expounded to them, testifying to the kingdom of God and trying to convince them about Jesus both from the Law of Moses and from the Prophets. [24]And some were convinced by what he said, but others disbelieved. [25]And disagreeing among themselves, they departed after Paul had made one statement: "The Holy Spirit was right in saying to your fathers through Isaiah the prophet:

[26] "'Go to this people, and say,
"You will indeed hear but never understand,
and you will indeed see but never perceive."
[27] For this people's heart has grown dull,
and with their ears they can barely hear,
and their eyes they have closed;
lest they should see with their eyes
and hear with their ears
and understand with their heart
and turn, and I would heal them.'

[28]Therefore let it be known to you that this salvation of God has been sent to the Gentiles; they will listen."[2]

[30]He lived there two whole years at his own expense,[3] and welcomed all who came to him, [31]proclaiming the kingdom of God and teaching about the Lord Jesus Christ with all boldness and without hindrance.

JANUARY 29

Genesis 30

When Rachel saw that she bore Jacob no children, she envied her sister. She said to Jacob, "Give me children, or I shall die!" [2]Jacob's anger was kindled against Rachel, and he said, "Am I in the place of God, who has withheld from you the fruit of the womb?" [3]Then she said, "Here is my servant Bilhah; go in to her, so that she may give birth on my behalf,[4] that even I may have children[5] through her." [4]So she gave him her servant Bilhah as a wife, and Jacob went in to her. [5]And Bilhah conceived and bore Jacob a son. [6]Then Rachel said, "God has judged me, and has also heard my voice and given me a son." Therefore she called his name Dan.[6] [7]Rachel's servant Bilhah conceived again and bore Jacob a second son.

[1] Or brothers and sisters; also verses 15, 21 [2] Some manuscripts add verse 29: And when he had said these words, the Jews departed, having much dispute among themselves [3] Or in his own hired dwelling [4] Hebrew on my knees [5] Hebrew be built up, which sounds like the Hebrew for children [6] Dan sounds like the Hebrew for judged

⁸Then Rachel said, "With mighty wrestlings¹ I have wrestled with my sister and have prevailed." So she called his name Naphtali.² ⁹When Leah saw that she had ceased bearing children, she took her servant Zilpah and gave her to Jacob as a wife. ¹⁰Then Leah's servant Zilpah bore Jacob a son. ¹¹And Leah said, "Good fortune has come!" so she called his name Gad.³ ¹²Leah's servant Zilpah bore Jacob a second son. ¹³And Leah said, "Happy am I! For women have called me happy." So she called his name Asher.⁴

¹⁴In the days of wheat harvest Reuben went and found mandrakes in the field and brought them to his mother Leah. Then Rachel said to Leah, "Please give me some of your son's mandrakes." ¹⁵But she said to her, "Is it a small matter that you have taken away my husband? Would you take away my son's mandrakes also?" Rachel said, "Then he may lie with you tonight in exchange for your son's mandrakes." ¹⁶When Jacob came from the field in the evening, Leah went out to meet him and said, "You must come in to me, for I have hired you with my son's mandrakes." So he lay with her that night. ¹⁷And God listened to Leah, and she conceived and bore Jacob a fifth son. ¹⁸Leah said, "God has given me my wages because I gave my servant to my husband." So she called his name Issachar.⁵

¹⁹And Leah conceived again, and she bore Jacob a sixth son. ²⁰Then Leah said, "God has endowed me with a good endowment; now my husband will honor me, because I have borne him six sons." So she called his name Zebulun.⁶ ²¹Afterward she bore a daughter and called her name Dinah.

²²Then God remembered Rachel, and God listened to her and opened her womb. ²³She conceived and bore a son and said, "God has taken away my reproach." ²⁴And she called his name Joseph,⁷ saying, "May the LORD add to me another son!"

²⁵As soon as Rachel had borne Joseph, Jacob said to Laban, "Send me away, that I may go to my own home and country. ²⁶Give me my wives and my children for whom I have served you, that I may go, for you know the service that I have given you." ²⁷But Laban said to him, "If I have found favor in your sight, I have learned by divination that⁸ the LORD has blessed me because of you. ²⁸Name your wages, and I will give it." ²⁹Jacob said to him, "You yourself know how I have served you, and how your livestock has fared with me. ³⁰For you had little before I came, and it has increased abundantly, and the LORD has blessed you wherever I turned. But now when shall I provide for my own household also?" ³¹He said, "What shall I give you?" Jacob said, "You shall not give me anything. If you will do this for me, I will again pasture your flock and keep it: ³²let me pass through all your flock today, removing from it every speckled and spotted sheep and every black lamb, and the spotted and speckled among the goats, and they shall be my wages. ³³So my honesty will answer for me later, when you come to look into my wages with you. Every one that is not speckled and spotted among the goats and black among the lambs, if found with me, shall be counted stolen." ³⁴Laban said, "Good! Let it be as you have said." ³⁵But that day Laban removed the male goats that were striped and spotted, and all the female goats that were speckled and spotted, every one that had white on it, and every lamb that was black, and put them in the charge of his sons. ³⁶And he set a distance of three days' journey between himself and Jacob, and Jacob pastured the rest of Laban's flock.

³⁷Then Jacob took fresh sticks of poplar and almond and plane trees, and peeled white streaks in them, exposing the white of the sticks. ³⁸He set the sticks that he had peeled in front of the flocks in the troughs, that is, the watering places, where the flocks came to drink. And since they bred when they came to drink, ³⁹the flocks bred in front of the sticks and so the flocks brought forth striped, speckled, and spotted. ⁴⁰And Jacob separated the lambs and set the faces of the flocks toward the striped and all the black in the flock of Laban. He put his own droves apart and did not put them with Laban's flock. ⁴¹Whenever the stronger of the flock were breeding, Jacob would lay the sticks in the troughs before the eyes of the flock, that they might breed among the sticks, ⁴²but for the feebler of the flock he would not lay them there. So the feebler would be Laban's, and the stronger Jacob's. ⁴³Thus the man increased greatly and had large flocks, female servants and male servants, and camels and donkeys.

¹ Hebrew *With wrestlings of God* ² *Naphtali* sounds like the Hebrew for *wrestling* ³ *Gad* sounds like the Hebrew for *good fortune* ⁴ *Asher* sounds like the Hebrew for *happy* ⁵ *Issachar* sounds like the Hebrew for *wages*, or *hire* ⁶ *Zebulun* sounds like the Hebrew for *honor* ⁷ *Joseph* means *May he add*, and sounds like the Hebrew for *taken away* ⁸ Or *have become rich and*

Mark 1

The beginning of the gospel of Jesus Christ, the Son of God.[1]

[2] As it is written in Isaiah the prophet,[2]

"Behold, I send my messenger before
  your face,
 who will prepare your way,
[3] the voice of one crying in the
    wilderness:
  'Prepare[3] the way of the Lord,
   make his paths straight,'"

[4] John appeared, baptizing in the wilderness and proclaiming a baptism of repentance for the forgiveness of sins. [5] And all the country of Judea and all Jerusalem were going out to him and were being baptized by him in the river Jordan, confessing their sins. [6] Now John was clothed with camel's hair and wore a leather belt around his waist and ate locusts and wild honey. [7] And he preached, saying, "After me comes he who is mightier than I, the strap of whose sandals I am not worthy to stoop down and untie. [8] I have baptized you with water, but he will baptize you with the Holy Spirit."

[9] In those days Jesus came from Nazareth of Galilee and was baptized by John in the Jordan. [10] And when he came up out of the water, immediately he saw the heavens being torn open and the Spirit descending on him like a dove. [11] And a voice came from heaven, "You are my beloved Son;[4] with you I am well pleased."

[12] The Spirit immediately drove him out into the wilderness. [13] And he was in the wilderness forty days, being tempted by Satan. And he was with the wild animals, and the angels were ministering to him.

[14] Now after John was arrested, Jesus came into Galilee, proclaiming the gospel of God, [15] and saying, "The time is fulfilled, and the kingdom of God is at hand; repent and believe in the gospel."

[16] Passing alongside the Sea of Galilee, he saw Simon and Andrew the brother of Simon casting a net into the sea, for they were fishermen. [17] And Jesus said to them, "Follow me, and I will make you become fishers of men."[5] [18] And immediately they left their nets and followed him. [19] And going on a little farther, he saw James the son of Zebedee and John his brother, who were in their boat mending the nets. [20] And immediately he called them, and they left their father Zebedee in the boat with the hired servants and followed him.

[21] And they went into Capernaum, and immediately on the Sabbath he entered the synagogue and was teaching. [22] And they were astonished at his teaching, for he taught them as one who had authority, and not as the scribes. [23] And immediately there was in their synagogue a man with an unclean spirit. And he cried out, [24] "What have you to do with us, Jesus of Nazareth? Have you come to destroy us? I know who you are—the Holy One of God." [25] But Jesus rebuked him, saying, "Be silent, and come out of him!" [26] And the unclean spirit, convulsing him and crying out with a loud voice, came out of him. [27] And they were all amazed, so that they questioned among themselves, saying, "What is this? A new teaching with authority! He commands even the unclean spirits, and they obey him." [28] And at once his fame spread everywhere throughout all the surrounding region of Galilee.

[29] And immediately he[6] left the synagogue and entered the house of Simon and Andrew, with James and John. [30] Now Simon's mother-in-law lay ill with a fever, and immediately they told him about her. [31] And he came and took her by the hand and lifted her up, and the fever left her, and she began to serve them.

[32] That evening at sundown they brought to him all who were sick or oppressed by demons. [33] And the whole city was gathered together at the door. [34] And he healed many who were sick with various diseases, and cast out many demons. And he would not permit the demons to speak, because they knew him.

[35] And rising very early in the morning, while it was still dark, he departed and went out to a desolate place, and there he prayed. [36] And Simon and those who were with him searched for him, [37] and they found him and said to him, "Everyone is looking for you." [38] And he said to them, "Let us go on to the next towns, that I may preach there also, for that is why I came out." [39] And he went throughout all Galilee, preaching in their synagogues and casting out demons.

[40] And a leper[7] came to him, imploring him, and kneeling said to him, "If you will, you can make me clean." [41] Moved with pity, he stretched out his hand and touched him and

---

[1] Some manuscripts omit *the Son of God* [2] Some manuscripts *in the prophets* [3] Or *crying: Prepare in the wilderness* [4] Or *my Son, my (or the) Beloved* [5] The Greek word *anthropoi* refers here to both men and women [6] Some manuscripts *they* [7] *Leprosy* was a term for several skin diseases; see Leviticus 13

said to him, "I will; be clean." [42]And immediately the leprosy left him, and he was made clean. [43]And Jesus[1] sternly charged him and sent him away at once, [44]and said to him, "See that you say nothing to anyone, but go, show yourself to the priest and offer for your cleansing what Moses commanded, for a proof to them." [45]But he went out and began to talk freely about it, and to spread the news, so that Jesus could no longer openly enter a town, but was out in desolate places, and people were coming to him from every quarter.

Esther 6

On that night the king could not sleep. And he gave orders to bring the book of memorable deeds, the chronicles, and they were read before the king. [2]And it was found written how Mordecai had told about Bigthana[2] and Teresh, two of the king's eunuchs, who guarded the threshold, and who had sought to lay hands on King Ahasuerus. [3]And the king said, "What honor or distinction has been bestowed on Mordecai for this?" The king's young men who attended him said, "Nothing has been done for him." [4]And the king said, "Who is in the court?" Now Haman had just entered the outer court of the king's palace to speak to the king about having Mordecai hanged on the gallows[3] that he had prepared for him. [5]And the king's young men told him, "Haman is there, standing in the court." And the king said, "Let him come in." [6]So Haman came in, and the king said to him, "What should be done to the man whom the king delights to honor?" And Haman said to himself, "Whom would the king delight to honor more than me?" [7]And Haman said to the king, "For the man whom the king delights to honor, [8]let royal robes be brought, which the king has worn, and the horse that the king has ridden, and on whose head a royal crown[4] is set. [9]And let the robes and the horse be handed over to one of the king's most noble officials. Let them dress the man whom the king delights to honor, and let them lead him on the horse through the square of the city, proclaiming before him: 'Thus shall it be done to the man whom the king delights to honor.'" [10]Then the king said to Haman, "Hurry; take the robes and the horse, as you have said, and do so to

Mordecai the Jew, who sits at the king's gate. Leave out nothing that you have mentioned." [11]So Haman took the robes and the horse, and he dressed Mordecai and led him through the square of the city, proclaiming before him, "Thus shall it be done to the man whom the king delights to honor."

[12]Then Mordecai returned to the king's gate. But Haman hurried to his house, mourning and with his head covered. [13]And Haman told his wife Zeresh and all his friends everything that had happened to him. Then his wise men and his wife Zeresh said to him, "If Mordecai, before whom you have begun to fall, is of the Jewish people, you will not overcome him but will surely fall before him."

[14]While they were yet talking with him, the king's eunuchs arrived and hurried to bring Haman to the feast that Esther had prepared.

Romans 1

Paul, a servant[5] of Christ Jesus, called to be an apostle, set apart for the gospel of God, [2]which he promised beforehand through his prophets in the holy Scriptures, [3]concerning his Son, who was descended from David[6] according to the flesh [4]and was declared to be the Son of God in power according to the Spirit of holiness by his resurrection from the dead, Jesus Christ our Lord, [5]through whom we have received grace and apostleship to bring about the obedience of faith for the sake of his name among all the nations, [6]including you who are called to belong to Jesus Christ,

[7]To all those in Rome who are loved by God and called to be saints:

Grace to you and peace from God our Father and the Lord Jesus Christ.

[8]First, I thank my God through Jesus Christ for all of you, because your faith is proclaimed in all the world. [9]For God is my witness, whom I serve with my spirit in the gospel of his Son, that without ceasing I mention you [10]always in my prayers, asking that somehow by God's will I may now at last succeed in coming to you. [11]For I long to see you, that I may impart to you some spiritual gift to strengthen you— [12]that is, that we may be mutually encouraged by each other's faith, both yours and mine. [13]I do not want you to be unaware, brothers,[7] that I have

---

[1] Greek he; also verse 45 [2] Bigthana is an alternate spelling of Bigthan (see 2:21) [3] Or suspended on a stake [4] Or headdress [5] Or slave (for the contextual rendering of the Greek word doulos, see Preface) [6] Or who came from the offspring of David. [7] Or brothers and sisters. The plural Greek word adelphoi (translated "brothers") refers to siblings in a family. In New Testament usage, depending on the context, adelphoi may refer either to men or to both men and women who are siblings (brothers and sisters) in God's family, the church

often intended to come to you (but thus far have been prevented), in order that I may reap some harvest among you as well as among the rest of the Gentiles. [14] I am under obligation both to Greeks and to barbarians,[1] both to the wise and to the foolish. [15] So I am eager to preach the gospel to you also who are in Rome.

[16] For I am not ashamed of the gospel, for it is the power of God for salvation to everyone who believes, to the Jew first and also to the Greek. [17] For in it the righteousness of God is revealed from faith for faith,[2] as it is written, "The righteous shall live by faith."[3]

[18] For the wrath of God is revealed from heaven against all ungodliness and unrighteousness of men, who by their unrighteousness suppress the truth. [19] For what can be known about God is plain to them, because God has shown it to them. [20] For his invisible attributes, namely, his eternal power and divine nature, have been clearly perceived, ever since the creation of the world,[4] in the things that have been made. So they are without excuse. [21] For although they knew God, they did not honor him as God or give thanks to him, but they became futile in their thinking, and their foolish hearts were darkened. [22] Claiming to be wise, they became fools, [23] and exchanged the glory of the immortal God for images resembling mortal man and birds and animals and creeping things.

[24] Therefore God gave them up in the lusts of their hearts to impurity, to the dishonoring of their bodies among themselves, [25] because they exchanged the truth about God for a lie and worshiped and served the creature rather than the Creator, who is blessed forever! Amen.

[26] For this reason God gave them up to dishonorable passions. For their women exchanged natural relations for those that are contrary to nature; [27] and the men likewise gave up natural relations with women and were consumed with passion for one another, men committing shameless acts with men and receiving in themselves the due penalty for their error.

[28] And since they did not see fit to acknowledge God, God gave them up to a debased mind to do what ought not to be done. [29] They were filled with all manner of unrighteousness, evil, covetousness, malice. They are full of envy, murder, strife, deceit, maliciousness. They are gossips, [30] slanderers, haters of God, insolent, haughty, boastful, inventors of evil, disobedient to parents, [31] foolish, faithless, heartless, ruthless. [32] Though they know God's righteous decree that those who practice such things deserve to die, they not only do them but give approval to those who practice them.

JANUARY 30

Genesis 31

Now Jacob heard that the sons of Laban were saying, "Jacob has taken all that was our father's, and from what was our father's he has gained all this wealth." [2] And Jacob saw that Laban did not regard him with favor as before. [3] Then the LORD said to Jacob, "Return to the land of your fathers and to your kindred, and I will be with you."

[4] So Jacob sent and called Rachel and Leah into the field where his flock was [5] and said to them, "I see that your father does not regard me with favor as he did before. But the God of my father has been with me. [6] You know that I have served your father with all my strength, [7] yet your father has cheated me and changed my wages ten times. But God did not permit him to harm me. [8] If he said, 'The spotted shall be your wages,' then all the flock bore spotted; and if he said, 'The striped shall be your wages,' then all the flock bore striped. [9] Thus God has taken away the livestock of your father and given them to me. [10] In the breeding season of the flock I lifted up my eyes and saw in a dream that the goats that mated with the flock

---

[1] That is, non-Greeks [2] Or beginning and ending in faith [3] Or The one who by faith is righteous shall live [4] Or clearly perceived from the creation of the world

were striped, spotted, and mottled. ¹¹Then the angel of God said to me in the dream, 'Jacob,' and I said, 'Here I am!' ¹²And he said, 'Lift up your eyes and see, all the goats that mate with the flock are striped, spotted, and mottled, for I have seen all that Laban is doing to you. ¹³I am the God of Bethel, where you anointed a pillar and made a vow to me. Now arise, go out from this land and return to the land of your kindred.' " ¹⁴Then Rachel and Leah answered and said to him, "Is there any portion or inheritance left to us in our father's house? ¹⁵Are we not regarded by him as foreigners? For he has sold us, and he has indeed devoured our money. ¹⁶All the wealth that God has taken away from our father belongs to us and to our children. Now then, whatever God has said to you, do."

¹⁷So Jacob arose and set his sons and his wives on camels. ¹⁸He drove away all his livestock, all his property that he had gained, the livestock in his possession that he had acquired in Paddan-aram, to go to the land of Canaan to his father Isaac. ¹⁹Laban had gone to shear his sheep, and Rachel stole her father's household gods. ²⁰And Jacob tricked[1] Laban the Aramean, by not telling him that he intended to flee. ²¹He fled with all that he had and arose and crossed the Euphrates,[2] and set his face toward the hill country of Gilead.

²²When it was told Laban on the third day that Jacob had fled, ²³he took his kinsmen with him and pursued him for seven days and followed close after him into the hill country of Gilead. ²⁴But God came to Laban the Aramean in a dream by night and said to him, "Be careful not to say anything to Jacob, either good or bad."

²⁵And Laban overtook Jacob. Now Jacob had pitched his tent in the hill country, and Laban with his kinsmen pitched tents in the hill country of Gilead. ²⁶And Laban said to Jacob, "What have you done, that you have tricked me and driven away my daughters like captives of the sword? ²⁷Why did you flee secretly and trick me, and did not tell me, so that I might have sent you away with mirth and songs, with tambourine and lyre? ²⁸And why did you not permit me to kiss my sons and my daughters farewell? Now you have done foolishly. ²⁹It is in my power to do you harm. But the God of your[3] father spoke to me last night, saying, 'Be careful not to say anything to Jacob, either good or bad.' ³⁰And now you have gone away because

you longed greatly for your father's house, but why did you steal my gods?" ³¹Jacob answered and said to Laban, "Because I was afraid, for I thought that you would take your daughters from me by force. ³²Anyone with whom you find your gods shall not live. In the presence of our kinsmen point out what I have that is yours, and take it." Now Jacob did not know that Rachel had stolen them.

³³So Laban went into Jacob's tent and into Leah's tent and into the tent of the two female servants, but he did not find them. And he went out of Leah's tent and entered Rachel's. ³⁴Now Rachel had taken the household gods and put them in the camel's saddle and sat on them. Laban felt all about the tent, but did not find them. ³⁵And she said to her father, "Let not my lord be angry that I cannot rise before you, for the way of women is upon me." So he searched but did not find the household gods.

³⁶Then Jacob became angry and berated Laban. Jacob said to Laban, "What is my offense? What is my sin, that you have hotly pursued me? ³⁷For you have felt through all my goods; what have you found of all your household goods? Set it here before my kinsmen and your kinsmen, that they may decide between us two. ³⁸These twenty years I have been with you. Your ewes and your female goats have not miscarried, and I have not eaten the rams of your flocks. ³⁹What was torn by wild beasts I did not bring to you. I bore the loss of it myself. From my hand you required it, whether stolen by day or stolen by night. ⁴⁰There I was: by day the heat consumed me, and the cold by night, and my sleep fled from my eyes. ⁴¹These twenty years I have been in your house. I served you fourteen years for your two daughters, and six years for your flock, and you have changed my wages ten times. ⁴²If the God of my father, the God of Abraham and the Fear of Isaac, had not been on my side, surely now you would have sent me away empty-handed. God saw my affliction and the labor of my hands and rebuked you last night."

⁴³Then Laban answered and said to Jacob, "The daughters are my daughters, the children are my children, the flocks are my flocks, and all that you see is mine. But what can I do this day for these my daughters or for their children whom they have borne? ⁴⁴Come now, let us make a covenant, you and I. And let it be a

[1] Hebrew stole the heart of; also verses 26, 27 [2] Hebrew the River [3] The Hebrew for your is plural here

witness between you and me." ⁴⁵So Jacob took a stone and set it up as a pillar. ⁴⁶And Jacob said to his kinsmen, "Gather stones." And they took stones and made a heap, and they ate there by the heap. ⁴⁷Laban called it Jegar-sahadutha,¹ but Jacob called it Galeed.² ⁴⁸Laban said, "This heap is a witness between you and me today." Therefore he named it Galeed, ⁴⁹and Mizpah,³ for he said, "The LORD watch between you and me, when we are out of one another's sight. ⁵⁰If you oppress my daughters, or if you take wives besides my daughters, although no one is with us, see, God is witness between you and me."

⁵¹Then Laban said to Jacob, "See this heap and the pillar, which I have set between you and me. ⁵²This heap is a witness, and the pillar is a witness, that I will not pass over this heap to you, and you will not pass over this heap and this pillar to me, to do harm. ⁵³The God of Abraham and the God of Nahor, the God of their father, judge between us." So Jacob swore by the Fear of his father Isaac, ⁵⁴and Jacob offered a sacrifice in the hill country and called his kinsmen to eat bread. They ate bread and spent the night in the hill country.

⁵⁵⁴ Early in the morning Laban arose and kissed his grandchildren and his daughters and blessed them. Then Laban departed and returned home.

--- Mark 2 ---

And when he returned to Capernaum after some days, it was reported that he was at home. ²And many were gathered together, so that there was no more room, not even at the door. And he was preaching the word to them. ³And they came, bringing to him a paralytic carried by four men. ⁴And when they could not get near him because of the crowd, they removed the roof above him, and when they had made an opening, they let down the bed on which the paralytic lay. ⁵And when Jesus saw their faith, he said to the paralytic, "Son, your sins are forgiven." ⁶Now some of the scribes were sitting there, questioning in their hearts, ⁷"Why does this man speak like that? He is blaspheming! Who can forgive sins but God alone?" ⁸And immediately Jesus, perceiving in his spirit that they thus questioned within themselves, said to them, "Why do you question these things in your hearts? ⁹Which

is easier, to say to the paralytic, 'Your sins are forgiven,' or to say, 'Rise, take up your bed and walk'? ¹⁰But that you may know that the Son of Man has authority on earth to forgive sins"—he said to the paralytic— ¹¹"I say to you, rise, pick up your bed, and go home." ¹²And he rose and immediately picked up his bed and went out before them all, so that they were all amazed and glorified God, saying, "We never saw anything like this!"

¹³He went out again beside the sea, and all the crowd was coming to him, and he was teaching them. ¹⁴And as he passed by, he saw Levi the son of Alphaeus sitting at the tax booth, and he said to him, "Follow me." And he rose and followed him.

¹⁵And as he reclined at table in his house, many tax collectors and sinners were reclining with Jesus and his disciples, for there were many who followed him. ¹⁶And the scribes of⁵ the Pharisees, when they saw that he was eating with sinners and tax collectors, said to his disciples, "Why does he eat⁶ with tax collectors and sinners?" ¹⁷And when Jesus heard it, he said to them, "Those who are well have no need of a physician, but those who are sick. I came not to call the righteous, but sinners."

¹⁸Now John's disciples and the Pharisees were fasting. And people came and said to him, "Why do John's disciples and the disciples of the Pharisees fast, but your disciples do not fast?" ¹⁹And Jesus said to them, "Can the wedding guests fast while the bridegroom is with them? As long as they have the bridegroom with them, they cannot fast. ²⁰The days will come when the bridegroom is taken away from them, and then they will fast in that day. ²¹No one sews a piece of unshrunk cloth on an old garment. If he does, the patch tears away from it, the new from the old, and a worse tear is made. ²²And no one puts new wine into old wineskins. If he does, the wine will burst the skins—and the wine is destroyed, and so are the skins. But new wine is for fresh wineskins."⁷

²³One Sabbath he was going through the grainfields, and as they made their way, his disciples began to pluck heads of grain. ²⁴And the Pharisees were saying to him, "Look, why are they doing what is not lawful on the Sabbath?" ²⁵And he said to them, "Have you never read what David did, when he was in need and was hungry, he and those who were with him:

¹ Aramaic the heap of witness ² Hebrew the heap of witness ³ Mizpah means watchpost ⁴ Ch 32:1 in Hebrew ⁵ Some manuscripts and ⁶ Some manuscripts add and drink ⁷ Some manuscripts omit But new wine is for fresh wineskins

[26]how he entered the house of God, in the time of[1] Abiathar the high priest, and ate the bread of the Presence, which it is not lawful for any but the priests to eat, and also gave it to those who were with him?" [27]And he said to them, "The Sabbath was made for man, not man for the Sabbath. [28]So the Son of Man is lord even of the Sabbath."

Esther 7

So the king and Haman went in to feast with Queen Esther. [2]And on the second day, as they were drinking wine after the feast, the king again said to Esther, "What is your wish, Queen Esther? It shall be granted you. And what is your request? Even to the half of my kingdom, it shall be fulfilled." [3]Then Queen Esther answered, "If I have found favor in your sight, O king, and if it please the king, let my life be granted me for my wish, and my people for my request. [4]For we have been sold, I and my people, to be destroyed, to be killed, and to be annihilated. If we had been sold merely as slaves, men and women, I would have been silent, for our affliction is not to be compared with the loss to the king." [5]Then King Ahasuerus said to Queen Esther, "Who is he, and where is he, who has dared[2] to do this?" [6]And Esther said, "A foe and enemy! This wicked Haman!" Then Haman was terrified before the king and the queen.

[7]And the king arose in his wrath from the wine-drinking and went into the palace garden, but Haman stayed to beg for his life from Queen Esther, for he saw that harm was determined against him by the king. [8]And the king returned from the palace garden to the place where they were drinking wine, as Haman was falling on the couch where Esther was. And the king said, "Will he even assault the queen in my presence, in my own house?" As the word left the mouth of the king, they covered Haman's face. [9]Then Harbona, one of the eunuchs in attendance on the king, said, "Moreover, the gallows[3] that Haman has prepared for Mordecai, whose word saved the king, is standing at Haman's house, fifty cubits[4] high." [10]And the king said, "Hang him on that." So they hanged Haman on the gallows that he had prepared for Mordecai. Then the wrath of the king abated.

Romans 2

Therefore you have no excuse, O man, every one of you who judges. For in passing judgment on another you condemn yourself, because you, the judge, practice the very same things. [2]We know that the judgment of God rightly falls on those who practice such things. [3]Do you suppose, O man—you who judge those who practice such things and yet do them yourself—that you will escape the judgment of God? [4]Or do you presume on the riches of his kindness and forbearance and patience, not knowing that God's kindness is meant to lead you to repentance? [5]But because of your hard and impenitent heart you are storing up wrath for yourself on the day of wrath when God's righteous judgment will be revealed.

[6]He will render to each one according to his works: [7]to those who by patience in well-doing seek for glory and honor and immortality, he will give eternal life; [8]but for those who are self-seeking[5] and do not obey the truth, but obey unrighteousness, there will be wrath and fury. [9]There will be tribulation and distress for every human being who does evil, the Jew first and also the Greek, [10]but glory and honor and peace for everyone who does good, the Jew first and also the Greek. [11]For God shows no partiality.

[12]For all who have sinned without the law will also perish without the law, and all who have sinned under the law will be judged by the law. [13]For it is not the hearers of the law who are righteous before God, but the doers of the law who will be justified. [14]For when Gentiles, who do not have the law, by nature do what the law requires, they are a law to themselves, even though they do not have the law. [15]They show that the work of the law is written on their hearts, while their conscience also bears witness, and their conflicting thoughts accuse or even excuse them [16]on that day when, according to my gospel, God judges the secrets of men by Christ Jesus.

[17]But if you call yourself a Jew and rely on the law and boast in God [18]and know his will and approve what is excellent, because you are instructed from the law; [19]and if you are sure that you yourself are a guide to the blind, a light to those who are in darkness, [20]an instructor of the foolish, a teacher of children, having in the

[1] Or in the passage about [2] Hebrew whose heart has filled him [3] Or stake; also verse 10 [4] A cubit was about 18 inches or 45 centimeters [5] Or contentious

law the embodiment of knowledge and truth— [21] you then who teach others, do you not teach yourself? While you preach against stealing, do you steal? [22] You who say that one must not commit adultery, do you commit adultery? You who abhor idols, do you rob temples? [23] You who boast in the law dishonor God by breaking the law. [24] For, as it is written, "The name of God is blasphemed among the Gentiles because of you."

[25] For circumcision indeed is of value if you obey the law, but if you break the law, your circumcision becomes uncircumcision. [26] So, if a man who is uncircumcised keeps the precepts of the law, will not his uncircumcision be regarded[1] as circumcision? [27] Then he who is physically[2] uncircumcised but keeps the law will condemn you who have the written code[3] and circumcision but break the law. [28] For no one is a Jew who is merely one outwardly, nor is circumcision outward and physical. [29] But a Jew is one inwardly, and circumcision is a matter of the heart, by the Spirit, not by the letter. His praise is not from man but from God.

JANUARY 31

Genesis 32

Jacob went on his way, and the angels of God met him. [2] And when Jacob saw them he said, "This is God's camp!" So he called the name of that place Mahanaim.[4]

[3] And Jacob sent[5] messengers before him to Esau his brother in the land of Seir, the country of Edom, [4] instructing them, "Thus you shall say to my lord Esau: Thus says your servant Jacob, 'I have sojourned with Laban and stayed until now. [5] I have oxen, donkeys, flocks, male servants, and female servants. I have sent to tell my lord, in order that I may find favor in your sight.'"

[6] And the messengers returned to Jacob, saying, "We came to your brother Esau, and he is coming to meet you, and there are four hundred men with him." [7] Then Jacob was greatly afraid and distressed. He divided the people who were with him, and the flocks and herds and camels, into two camps, [8] thinking, "If Esau comes to the one camp and attacks it, then the camp that is left will escape."

[9] And Jacob said, "O God of my father Abraham and God of my father Isaac, O LORD who said to me, 'Return to your country and to your kindred, that I may do you good,' [10] I am not worthy of the least of all the deeds of steadfast love and all the faithfulness that you have shown to your servant, for with only my staff I crossed this Jordan, and now I have become two camps. [11] Please deliver me from the hand of my brother, from the hand of Esau, for I fear him, that he may come and attack me, the mothers with the children. [12] But you said, 'I will surely do you good, and make your offspring as the sand of the sea, which cannot be numbered for multitude.'"

[13] So he stayed there that night, and from what he had with him he took a present for his brother Esau, [14] two hundred female goats and twenty male goats, two hundred ewes and twenty rams, [15] thirty milking camels and their calves, forty cows and ten bulls, twenty female donkeys and ten male donkeys. [16] These he handed over to his servants, every drove by itself, and said to his servants, "Pass on ahead of me and put a space between drove and drove." [17] He instructed the first, "When Esau my brother meets you and asks you, 'To whom do you belong? Where are you going? And whose are these ahead of you?' [18] then you shall say, 'They belong to your servant Jacob. They are a present sent to my lord Esau. And moreover, he is behind us.'" [19] He likewise instructed the second and the third and all who followed the droves, "You shall say the same thing to Esau when you find him, [20] and you shall say, 'Moreover, your servant Jacob is

behind us.'" For he thought, "I may appease him[1] with the present that goes ahead of me, and afterward I shall see his face. Perhaps he will accept me."[2] [21]So the present passed on ahead of him, and he himself stayed that night in the camp.

[22]The same night he arose and took his two wives, his two female servants, and his eleven children,[3] and crossed the ford of the Jabbok. [23]He took them and sent them across the stream, and everything else that he had. [24]And Jacob was left alone. And a man wrestled with him until the breaking of the day. [25]When the man saw that he did not prevail against Jacob, he touched his hip socket, and Jacob's hip was put out of joint as he wrestled with him. [26]Then he said, "Let me go, for the day has broken." But Jacob said, "I will not let you go unless you bless me." [27]And he said to him, "What is your name?" And he said, "Jacob." [28]Then he said, "Your name shall no longer be called Jacob, but Israel,[4] for you have striven with God and with men, and have prevailed." [29]Then Jacob asked him, "Please tell me your name." But he said, "Why is it that you ask my name?" And there he blessed him. [30]So Jacob called the name of the place Peniel,[5] saying, "For I have seen God face to face, and yet my life has been delivered." [31]The sun rose upon him as he passed Penuel, limping because of his hip. [32]Therefore to this day the people of Israel do not eat the sinew of the thigh that is on the hip socket, because he touched the socket of Jacob's hip on the sinew of the thigh.

Mark 3

Again he entered the synagogue, and a man was there with a withered hand. [2]And they watched Jesus,[6] to see whether he would heal him on the Sabbath, so that they might accuse him. [3]And he said to the man with the withered hand, "Come here." [4]And he said to them, "Is it lawful on the Sabbath to do good or to do harm, to save life or to kill?" But they were silent. [5]And he looked around at them with anger, grieved at their hardness of heart, and said to the man, "Stretch out your hand." He stretched it out, and his hand was restored. [6]The Pharisees went out and immediately held counsel with the Herodians against him, how to destroy him.

[7]Jesus withdrew with his disciples to the sea, and a great crowd followed, from Galilee and Judea [8]and Jerusalem and Idumea and from beyond the Jordan and from around Tyre and Sidon. When the great crowd heard all that he was doing, they came to him. [9]And he told his disciples to have a boat ready for him because of the crowd, lest they crush him, [10]for he had healed many, so that all who had diseases pressed around him to touch him. [11]And whenever the unclean spirits saw him, they fell down before him and cried out, "You are the Son of God." [12]And he strictly ordered them not to make him known.

[13]And he went up on the mountain and called to him those whom he desired, and they came to him. [14]And he appointed twelve (whom he also named apostles) so that they might be with him and he might send them out to preach [15]and have authority to cast out demons. [16]He appointed the twelve: Simon (to whom he gave the name Peter); [17]James the son of Zebedee and John the brother of James (to whom he gave the name Boanerges, that is, Sons of Thunder); [18]Andrew, and Philip, and Bartholomew, and Matthew, and Thomas, and James the son of Alphaeus, and Thaddaeus, and Simon the Zealot,[7] [19]and Judas Iscariot, who betrayed him.

[20]Then he went home, and the crowd gathered again, so that they could not even eat. [21]And when his family heard it, they went out to seize him, for they were saying, "He is out of his mind."

[22]And the scribes who came down from Jerusalem were saying, "He is possessed by Beelzebul," and "by the prince of demons he casts out the demons." [23]And he called them to him and said to them in parables, "How can Satan cast out Satan? [24]If a kingdom is divided against itself, that kingdom cannot stand. [25]And if a house is divided against itself, that house will not be able to stand. [26]And if Satan has risen up against himself and is divided, he cannot stand, but is coming to an end. [27]But no one can enter a strong man's house and plunder his goods, unless he first binds the strong man. Then indeed he may plunder his house. [28]"Truly, I say to you, all sins will be forgiven the children of man, and whatever blasphemies they utter, [29]but whoever blasphemes against the Holy Spirit never has forgiveness,

---

[1] Hebrew *appease his face* [2] Hebrew *he will lift my face* [3] Or *sons* [4] *Israel* means *He strives with God*, or *God strives* [5] *Peniel* means *the face of God* [6] Greek *him* [7] Greek *kananaios*, meaning *zealot*

but is guilty of an eternal sin"— [30] for they were saying, "He has an unclean spirit."

[31] And his mother and his brothers came, and standing outside they sent to him and called him. [32] And a crowd was sitting around him, and they said to him, "Your mother and your brothers[1] are outside, seeking you." [33] And he answered them, "Who are my mother and my brothers?" [34] And looking about at those who sat around him, he said, "Here are my mother and my brothers! [35] For whoever does the will of God, he is my brother and sister and mother."

Esther 8

On that day King Ahasuerus gave to Queen Esther the house of Haman, the enemy of the Jews. And Mordecai came before the king, for Esther had told what he was to her. [2] And the king took off his signet ring, which he had taken from Haman, and gave it to Mordecai. And Esther set Mordecai over the house of Haman.

[3] Then Esther spoke again to the king. She fell at his feet and wept and pleaded with him to avert the evil plan of Haman the Agagite and the plot that he had devised against the Jews. [4] When the king held out the golden scepter to Esther, [5] Esther rose and stood before the king. And she said, "If it please the king, and if I have found favor in his sight, and if the thing seems right before the king, and I am pleasing in his eyes, let an order be written to revoke the letters devised by Haman the Agagite, the son of Hammedatha, which he wrote to destroy the Jews who are in all the provinces of the king. [6] For how can I bear to see the calamity that is coming to my people? Or how can I bear to see the destruction of my kindred?" [7] Then King Ahasuerus said to Queen Esther and to Mordecai the Jew, "Behold, I have given Esther the house of Haman, and they have hanged him on the gallows,[2] because he intended to lay hands on the Jews. [8] But you may write as you please with regard to the Jews, in the name of the king, and seal it with the king's ring, for an edict written in the name of the king and sealed with the king's ring cannot be revoked."

[9] The king's scribes were summoned at that time, in the third month, which is the month of Sivan, on the twenty-third day. And an edict was written, according to all that Mordecai commanded concerning the Jews, to the satraps and the governors and the officials of the provinces from India to Ethiopia, 127 provinces, to each province in its own script and to each people in its own language, and also to the Jews in their script and their language. [10] And he wrote in the name of King Ahasuerus and sealed it with the king's signet ring. Then he sent the letters by mounted couriers riding on swift horses that were used in the king's service, bred from the royal stud, [11] saying that the king allowed the Jews who were in every city to gather and defend their lives, to destroy, to kill, and to annihilate any armed force of any people or province that might attack them, children and women included, and to plunder their goods, [12] on one day throughout all the provinces of King Ahasuerus, on the thirteenth day of the twelfth month, which is the month of Adar. [13] A copy of what was written was to be issued as a decree in every province, being publicly displayed to all peoples, and the Jews were to be ready on that day to take vengeance on their enemies. [14] So the couriers, mounted on their swift horses that were used in the king's service, rode out hurriedly, urged by the king's command. And the decree was issued in Susa the citadel.

[15] Then Mordecai went out from the presence of the king in royal robes of blue and white, with a great golden crown[3] and a robe of fine linen and purple, and the city of Susa shouted and rejoiced. [16] The Jews had light and gladness and joy and honor. [17] And in every province and in every city, wherever the king's command and his edict reached, there was gladness and joy among the Jews, a feast and a holiday. And many from the peoples of the country declared themselves Jews, for fear of the Jews had fallen on them.

Romans 3

Then what advantage has the Jew? Or what is the value of circumcision? [2] Much in every way. To begin with, the Jews were entrusted with the oracles of God. [3] What if some were unfaithful? Does their faithlessness nullify the faithfulness of God? [4] By no means! Let God be true though every one were a liar, as it is written,

"That you may be justified in your words,
    and prevail when you are judged."

---

[1] Other early manuscripts add *and your sisters* [2] Or *stake* [3] Or *headdress*

[5] But if our unrighteousness serves to show the righteousness of God, what shall we say? That God is unrighteous to inflict wrath on us? (I speak in a human way.) [6] By no means! For then how could God judge the world? [7] But if through my lie God's truth abounds to his glory, why am I still being condemned as a sinner? [8] And why not do evil that good may come?—as some people slanderously charge us with saying. Their condemnation is just.

[9] What then? Are we Jews[1] any better off?[2] No, not at all. For we have already charged that all, both Jews and Greeks, are under sin, [10] as it is written:

> "None is righteous, no, not one;
> [11]   no one understands;
>   no one seeks for God.
> [12]   All have turned aside; together they
>   have become worthless;
>   no one does good,
>   not even one."
> [13]   "Their throat is an open grave;
>   they use their tongues to deceive."
>   "The venom of asps is under their lips."
> [14]   "Their mouth is full of curses and
>   bitterness."
> [15]   "Their feet are swift to shed blood;
> [16]   in their paths are ruin and misery,
> [17]   and the way of peace they have not
>   known."
> [18]   "There is no fear of God before their
>   eyes."

[19] Now we know that whatever the law says it speaks to those who are under the law, so that every mouth may be stopped, and the whole world may be held accountable to God. [20] For by works of the law no human being[3] will be justified in his sight, since through the law comes knowledge of sin.

[21] But now the righteousness of God has been manifested apart from the law, although the Law and the Prophets bear witness to it— [22] the righteousness of God through faith in Jesus Christ for all who believe. For there is no distinction: [23] for all have sinned and fall short of the glory of God, [24] and are justified by his grace as a gift, through the redemption that is in Christ Jesus, [25] whom God put forward as a propitiation by his blood, to be received by faith. This was to show God's righteousness, because in his divine forbearance he had passed over former sins. [26] It was to show his righteousness at the present time, so that he might be just and the justifier of the one who has faith in Jesus.

[27] Then what becomes of our boasting? It is excluded. By what kind of law? By a law of works? No, but by the law of faith. [28] For we hold that one is justified by faith apart from works of the law. [29] Or is God the God of Jews only? Is he not the God of Gentiles also? Yes, of Gentiles also, [30] since God is one—who will justify the circumcised by faith and the uncircumcised through faith. [31] Do we then overthrow the law by this faith? By no means! On the contrary, we uphold the law.

---

[1] Greek Are we   [2] Or at any disadvantage?   [3] Greek flesh

FEBRUARY 1

Genesis 33

And Jacob lifted up his eyes and looked, and behold, Esau was coming, and four hundred men with him. So he divided the children among Leah and Rachel and the two female servants. ²And he put the servants with their children in front, then Leah with her children, and Rachel and Joseph last of all. ³He himself went on before them, bowing himself to the ground seven times, until he came near to his brother.

⁴But Esau ran to meet him and embraced him and fell on his neck and kissed him, and they wept. ⁵And when Esau lifted up his eyes and saw the women and children, he said, "Who are these with you?" Jacob said, "The children whom God has graciously given your servant." ⁶Then the servants drew near, they and their children, and bowed down. ⁷Leah likewise and her children drew near and bowed down. And last Joseph and Rachel drew near, and they bowed down. ⁸Esau said, "What do you mean by all this company¹ that I met?" Jacob answered, "To find favor in the sight of my lord." ⁹But Esau said, "I have enough, my brother; keep what you have for yourself." ¹⁰Jacob said, "No, please, if I have found favor in your sight, then accept my present from my hand. For I have seen your face, which is like seeing the face of God, and you have accepted me. ¹¹Please accept my blessing that is brought to you, because God has dealt graciously with me, and because I have enough." Thus he urged him, and he took it.

¹²Then Esau said, "Let us journey on our way, and I will go ahead of² you." ¹³But Jacob said to him, "My lord knows that the children are frail, and that the nursing flocks and herds are a care to me. If they are driven hard for one day, all the flocks will die. ¹⁴Let my lord pass on ahead of his servant, and I will lead on slowly, at the pace of the livestock that are ahead of me and at the pace of the children, until I come to my lord in Seir."

¹⁵So Esau said, "Let me leave with you some of the people who are with me." But he said, "What need is there? Let me find favor in the sight of my lord." ¹⁶So Esau returned that day on his way to Seir. ¹⁷But Jacob journeyed to Succoth, and built himself a house and made booths for his livestock. Therefore the name of the place is called Succoth.³

¹⁸And Jacob came safely⁴ to the city of Shechem, which is in the land of Canaan, on his way from Paddan-aram, and he camped before the city. ¹⁹And from the sons of Hamor, Shechem's father, he bought for a hundred pieces of money⁵ the piece of land on which he had pitched his tent. ²⁰There he erected an altar and called it El-Elohe-Israel.⁶

Mark 4

Again he began to teach beside the sea. And a very large crowd gathered about him, so that he got into a boat and sat in it on the sea, and the whole crowd was beside the sea on the land. ²And he was teaching them many things in parables, and in his teaching he said to them: ³"Listen! Behold, a sower went out to sow. ⁴And as he sowed, some seed fell along the path, and the birds came and devoured it. ⁵Other seed fell on rocky ground, where it did not have much soil, and immediately it sprang up, since it had no depth of soil. ⁶And when the sun rose, it was scorched, and since it had no root, it withered away. ⁷Other seed fell among thorns, and the thorns grew up and choked it, and it yielded no grain. ⁸And other seeds fell into good soil and produced grain, growing up and increasing and yielding thirtyfold and sixtyfold and a hundredfold." ⁹And he said, "He who has ears to hear, let him hear."

¹⁰And when he was alone, those around him with the twelve asked him about the parables. ¹¹And he said to them, "To you has been given the secret of the kingdom of God, but for those outside everything is in parables, ¹²so that

---

¹ Hebrew *camp* ² Or *along with* ³ *Succoth* means *booths* ⁴ Or *peacefully* ⁵ Hebrew *a hundred qesitah*; a unit of money of unknown value ⁶ *El-Elohe-Israel* means *God, the God of Israel*

"they may indeed see but not perceive,
and may indeed hear but not
understand,
lest they should turn and be forgiven."

[13]And he said to them, "Do you not understand this parable? How then will you understand all the parables? [14]The sower sows the word. [15]And these are the ones along the path, where the word is sown: when they hear, Satan immediately comes and takes away the word that is sown in them. [16]And these are the ones sown on rocky ground: the ones who, when they hear the word, immediately receive it with joy. [17]And they have no root in themselves, but endure for a while; then, when tribulation or persecution arises on account of the word, immediately they fall away.[1] [18]And others are the ones sown among thorns. They are those who hear the word, [19]but the cares of the world and the deceitfulness of riches and the desires for other things enter in and choke the word, and it proves unfruitful. [20]But those that were sown on the good soil are the ones who hear the word and accept it and bear fruit, thirtyfold and sixtyfold and a hundredfold."

[21]And he said to them, "Is a lamp brought in to be put under a basket, or under a bed, and not on a stand? [22]For nothing is hidden except to be made manifest; nor is anything secret except to come to light. [23]If anyone has ears to hear, let him hear." [24]And he said to them, "Pay attention to what you hear: with the measure you use, it will be measured to you, and still more will be added to you. [25]For to the one who has, more will be given, and from the one who has not, even what he has will be taken away."

[26]And he said, "The kingdom of God is as if a man should scatter seed on the ground. [27]He sleeps and rises night and day, and the seed sprouts and grows; he knows not how. [28]The earth produces by itself, first the blade, then the ear, then the full grain in the ear. [29]But when the grain is ripe, at once he puts in the sickle, because the harvest has come."

[30]And he said, "With what can we compare the kingdom of God, or what parable shall we use for it? [31]It is like a grain of mustard seed, which, when sown on the ground, is the smallest of all the seeds on earth, [32]yet when it is sown it grows up and becomes larger than all the garden plants and puts out large branches, so that the birds of the air can make nests in its shade."

[33]With many such parables he spoke the word to them, as they were able to hear it. [34]He did not speak to them without a parable, but privately to his own disciples he explained everything.

[35]On that day, when evening had come, he said to them, "Let us go across to the other side." [36]And leaving the crowd, they took him with them in the boat, just as he was. And other boats were with him. [37]And a great windstorm arose, and the waves were breaking into the boat, so that the boat was already filling. [38]But he was in the stern, asleep on the cushion. And they woke him and said to him, "Teacher, do you not care that we are perishing?" [39]And he awoke and rebuked the wind and said to the sea, "Peace! Be still!" And the wind ceased, and there was a great calm. [40]He said to them, "Why are you so afraid? Have you still no faith?" [41]And they were filled with great fear and said to one another, "Who then is this, that even the wind and the sea obey him?"

Esther 9–10

Now in the twelfth month, which is the month of Adar, on the thirteenth day of the same, when the king's command and edict were about to be carried out, on the very day when the enemies of the Jews hoped to gain the mastery over them, the reverse occurred: the Jews gained mastery over those who hated them. [2]The Jews gathered in their cities throughout all the provinces of King Ahasuerus to lay hands on those who sought their harm. And no one could stand against them, for the fear of them had fallen on all peoples. [3]All the officials of the provinces and the satraps and the governors and the royal agents also helped the Jews, for the fear of Mordecai had fallen on them. [4]For Mordecai was great in the king's house, and his fame spread throughout all the provinces, for the man Mordecai grew more and more powerful. [5]The Jews struck all their enemies with the sword, killing and destroying them, and did as they pleased to those who hated them. [6]In Susa the citadel itself the Jews killed and destroyed 500 men, [7]and also killed Parshandatha and Dalphon and

[1] Or stumble

Aspatha [8]and Poratha and Adalia and Aridatha [9]and Parmashta and Arisai and Aridai and Vaizatha, [10]the ten sons of Haman the son of Hammedatha, the enemy of the Jews, but they laid no hand on the plunder.

[11]That very day the number of those killed in Susa the citadel was reported to the king. [12]And the king said to Queen Esther, "In Susa the citadel the Jews have killed and destroyed 500 men and also the ten sons of Haman. What then have they done in the rest of the king's provinces! Now what is your wish? It shall be granted you. And what further is your request? It shall be fulfilled." [13]And Esther said, "If it please the king, let the Jews who are in Susa be allowed tomorrow also to do according to this day's edict. And let the ten sons of Haman be hanged on the gallows."[1] [14]So the king commanded this to be done. A decree was issued in Susa, and the ten sons of Haman were hanged. [15]The Jews who were in Susa gathered also on the fourteenth day of the month of Adar and they killed 300 men in Susa, but they laid no hands on the plunder.

[16]Now the rest of the Jews who were in the king's provinces also gathered to defend their lives, and got relief from their enemies and killed 75,000 of those who hated them, but they laid no hands on the plunder. [17]This was on the thirteenth day of the month of Adar, and on the fourteenth day they rested and made that a day of feasting and gladness. [18]But the Jews who were in Susa gathered on the thirteenth day and on the fourteenth, and rested on the fifteenth day, making that a day of feasting and gladness. [19]Therefore the Jews of the villages, who live in the rural towns, hold the fourteenth day of the month of Adar as a day for gladness and feasting, as a holiday, and as a day on which they send gifts of food to one another.

[20]And Mordecai recorded these things and sent letters to all the Jews who were in all the provinces of King Ahasuerus, both near and far, [21]obliging them to keep the fourteenth day of the month Adar and also the fifteenth day of the same, year by year, [22]as the days on which the Jews got relief from their enemies, and as the month that had been turned for them from sorrow into gladness and from mourning into a holiday; that they should make them days of feasting and gladness, days for sending gifts of food to one another and gifts to the poor.

[23]So the Jews accepted what they had started to do, and what Mordecai had written to them. [24]For Haman the Agagite, the son of Hammedatha, the enemy of all the Jews, had plotted against the Jews to destroy them, and had cast Pur (that is, cast lots), to crush and to destroy them. [25]But when it came before the king, he gave orders in writing that his evil plan that he had devised against the Jews should return on his own head, and that he and his sons should be hanged on the gallows.[2] [26]Therefore they called these days Purim, after the term Pur. Therefore, because of all that was written in this letter, and of what they had faced in this matter, and of what had happened to them, [27]the Jews firmly obligated themselves and their offspring and all who joined them, that without fail they would keep these two days according to what was written and at the time appointed every year, [28]that these days should be remembered and kept throughout every generation, in every clan, province, and city, and that these days of Purim should never fall into disuse among the Jews, nor should the commemoration of these days cease among their descendants.

[29]Then Queen Esther, the daughter of Abihail, and Mordecai the Jew gave full written authority, confirming this second letter about Purim. [30]Letters were sent to all the Jews, to the 127 provinces of the kingdom of Ahasuerus, in words of peace and truth, [31]that these days of Purim should be observed at their appointed seasons, as Mordecai the Jew and Queen Esther obligated them, and as they had obligated themselves and their offspring, with regard to their fasts and their lamenting. [32]The command of Queen Esther confirmed these practices of Purim, and it was recorded in writing.

[10:1] King Ahasuerus imposed tax on the land and on the coastlands of the sea. [2]And all the acts of his power and might, and the full account of the high honor of Mordecai, to which the king advanced him, are they not written in the Book of the Chronicles of the kings of Media and Persia? [3]For Mordecai the Jew was second in rank to King Ahasuerus, and he was great among the Jews and popular with the multitude of his brothers, for he sought the welfare of his people and spoke peace to all his people.

[1] Or stake [2] Or suspended on a stake

Romans 4

What then shall we say was gained by[1] Abraham, our forefather according to the flesh? [2] For if Abraham was justified by works, he has something to boast about, but not before God. [3] For what does the Scripture say? "Abraham believed God, and it was counted to him as righteousness." [4] Now to the one who works, his wages are not counted as a gift but as his due. [5] And to the one who does not work but believes in[2] him who justifies the ungodly, his faith is counted as righteousness, [6] just as David also speaks of the blessing of the one to whom God counts righteousness apart from works:

[7]   "Blessed are those whose lawless deeds
        are forgiven,
     and whose sins are covered;
[8]   blessed is the man against whom the
        Lord will not count his sin."

[9] Is this blessing then only for the circumcised, or also for the uncircumcised? For we say that faith was counted to Abraham as righteousness. [10] How then was it counted to him? Was it before or after he had been circumcised? It was not after, but before he was circumcised. [11] He received the sign of circumcision as a seal of the righteousness that he had by faith while he was still uncircumcised. The purpose was to make him the father of all who believe without being circumcised, so that righteousness would be counted to them as well, [12] and to make him the father of the circumcised who are not merely circumcised but who also walk in the footsteps of the faith that our father Abraham had before he was circumcised.

[13] For the promise to Abraham and his offspring that he would be heir of the world did not come through the law but through the righteousness of faith. [14] For if it is the adherents of the law who are to be the heirs, faith is null and the promise is void. [15] For the law brings wrath, but where there is no law there is no transgression.

[16] That is why it depends on faith, in order that the promise may rest on grace and be guaranteed to all his offspring—not only to the adherent of the law but also to the one who shares the faith of Abraham, who is the father of us all, [17] as it is written, "I have made you the father of many nations"—in the presence of the God in whom he believed, who gives life to the dead and calls into existence the things that do not exist. [18] In hope he believed against hope, that he should become the father of many nations, as he had been told, "So shall your offspring be." [19] He did not weaken in faith when he considered his own body, which was as good as dead (since he was about a hundred years old), or when he considered the barrenness[3] of Sarah's womb. [20] No unbelief made him waver concerning the promise of God, but he grew strong in his faith as he gave glory to God, [21] fully convinced that God was able to do what he had promised. [22] That is why his faith was "counted to him as righteousness." [23] But the words "it was counted to him" were not written for his sake alone, [24] but for ours also. It will be counted to us who believe in him who raised from the dead Jesus our Lord, [25] who was delivered up for our trespasses and raised for our justification.

FEBRUARY 2

Genesis 34

Now Dinah the daughter of Leah, whom she had borne to Jacob, went out to see the women of the land. [2] And when Shechem the son of Hamor the Hivite, the prince of the land, saw her, he seized her and lay with her and humiliated her. [3] And his soul was drawn to Dinah the daughter of Jacob. He loved the young woman and spoke tenderly to her. [4] So

[1] Some manuscripts say about [2] Or but trusts; compare verse 24 [3] Greek deadness

Shechem spoke to his father Hamor, saying, "Get me this girl for my wife." **5**Now Jacob heard that he had defiled his daughter Dinah. But his sons were with his livestock in the field, so Jacob held his peace until they came. **6**And Hamor the father of Shechem went out to Jacob to speak with him. **7**The sons of Jacob had come in from the field as soon as they heard of it, and the men were indignant and very angry, because he had done an outrageous thing in Israel by lying with Jacob's daughter, for such a thing must not be done.

8But Hamor spoke with them, saying, "The soul of my son Shechem longs for your[1] daughter. Please give her to him to be his wife. **9**Make marriages with us. Give your daughters to us, and take our daughters for yourselves. **10**You shall dwell with us, and the land shall be open to you. Dwell and trade in it, and get property in it." **11**Shechem also said to her father and to her brothers, "Let me find favor in your eyes, and whatever you say to me I will give. **12**Ask me for as great a bride price[2] and gift as you will, and I will give whatever you say to me. Only give me the young woman to be my wife."

13The sons of Jacob answered Shechem and his father Hamor deceitfully, because he had defiled their sister Dinah. **14**They said to them, "We cannot do this thing, to give our sister to one who is uncircumcised, for that would be a disgrace to us. **15**Only on this condition will we agree with you—that you will become as we are by every male among you being circumcised. **16**Then we will give our daughters to you, and we will take your daughters to ourselves, and we will dwell with you and become one people. **17**But if you will not listen to us and be circumcised, then we will take our daughter, and we will be gone."

18Their words pleased Hamor and Hamor's son Shechem. **19**And the young man did not delay to do the thing, because he delighted in Jacob's daughter. Now he was the most honored of all his father's house. **20**So Hamor and his son Shechem came to the gate of their city and spoke to the men of their city, saying, **21**"These men are at peace with us; let them dwell in the land and trade in it, for behold, the land is large enough for them. Let us take their daughters as wives, and let us give them our daughters. **22**Only on this condition will the men agree to dwell with us to become one people—when

every male among us is circumcised as they are circumcised. **23**Will not their livestock, their property and all their beasts be ours? Only let us agree with them, and they will dwell with us." **24**And all who went out of the gate of his city listened to Hamor and his son Shechem, and every male was circumcised, all who went out of the gate of his city.

25On the third day, when they were sore, two of the sons of Jacob, Simeon and Levi, Dinah's brothers, took their swords and came against the city while it felt secure and killed all the males. **26**They killed Hamor and his son Shechem with the sword and took Dinah out of Shechem's house and went away. **27**The sons of Jacob came upon the slain and plundered the city, because they had defiled their sister. **28**They took their flocks and their herds, their donkeys, and whatever was in the city and in the field. **29**All their wealth, all their little ones and their wives, all that was in the houses, they captured and plundered.

30Then Jacob said to Simeon and Levi, "You have brought trouble on me by making me stink to the inhabitants of the land, the Canaanites and the Perizzites. My numbers are few, and if they gather themselves against me and attack me, I shall be destroyed, both I and my household." **31**But they said, "Should he treat our sister like a prostitute?"

Mark 5

They came to the other side of the sea, to the country of the Gerasenes.[3] **2**And when Jesus[4] had stepped out of the boat, immediately there met him out of the tombs a man with an unclean spirit. **3**He lived among the tombs. And no one could bind him anymore, not even with a chain, **4**for he had often been bound with shackles and chains, but he wrenched the chains apart, and he broke the shackles in pieces. No one had the strength to subdue him. **5**Night and day among the tombs and on the mountains he was always crying out and cutting himself with stones. **6**And when he saw Jesus from afar, he ran and fell down before him. **7**And crying out with a loud voice, he said, "What have you to do with me, Jesus, Son of the Most High God? I adjure you by God, do not torment me." **8**For he was saying to him, "Come out of the man, you unclean spirit!" **9**And Jesus asked him, "What is your name?" He replied, "My name is Legion, for we are many." [10]And he begged him earnestly not to send them out of the country. [11]Now a great herd of pigs was feeding there on the hillside, [12]and they begged him, saying, "Send us to the pigs; let us enter them." [13]So he gave them permission. And the unclean spirits came out and entered the pigs; and the herd, numbering about two thousand, rushed down the steep bank into the sea and drowned in the sea.

[14]The herdsmen fled and told it in the city and in the country. And people came to see what it was that had happened. [15]And they came to Jesus and saw the demon-possessed[1] man, the one who had had the legion, sitting there, clothed and in his right mind, and they were afraid. [16]And those who had seen it described to them what had happened to the demon-possessed man and to the pigs. [17]And they began to beg Jesus[2] to depart from their region. [18]As he was getting into the boat, the man who had been possessed with demons begged him that he might be with him. [19]And he did not permit him but said to him, "Go home to your friends and tell them how much the Lord has done for you, and how he has had mercy on you." [20]And he went away and began to proclaim in the Decapolis how much Jesus had done for him, and everyone marveled.

[21]And when Jesus had crossed again in the boat to the other side, a great crowd gathered about him, and he was beside the sea. [22]Then came one of the rulers of the synagogue, Jairus by name, and seeing him, he fell at his feet [23]and implored him earnestly, saying, "My little daughter is at the point of death. Come and lay your hands on her, so that she may be made well and live." [24]And he went with him.

And a great crowd followed him and thronged about him. [25]And there was a woman who had had a discharge of blood for twelve years, [26]and who had suffered much under many physicians, and had spent all that she had, and was no better but rather grew worse. [27]She had heard the reports about Jesus and came up behind him in the crowd and touched his garment. [28]For she said, "If I touch even his garments, I will be made well." [29]And immediately the flow of blood dried up, and she felt in her body that she was healed of her disease. [30]And Jesus, perceiving in himself that power had gone out from

him, immediately turned about in the crowd and said, "Who touched my garments?" [31]And his disciples said to him, "You see the crowd pressing around you, and yet you say, 'Who touched me?'" [32]And he looked around to see who had done it. [33]But the woman, knowing what had happened to her, came in fear and trembling and fell down before him and told him the whole truth. [34]And he said to her, "Daughter, your faith has made you well; go in peace, and be healed of your disease."

[35]While he was still speaking, there came from the ruler's house some who said, "Your daughter is dead. Why trouble the Teacher any further?" [36]But overhearing[3] what they said, Jesus said to the ruler of the synagogue, "Do not fear, only believe." [37]And he allowed no one to follow him except Peter and James and John the brother of James. [38]They came to the house of the ruler of the synagogue, and Jesus[4] saw a commotion, people weeping and wailing loudly. [39]And when he had entered, he said to them, "Why are you making a commotion and weeping? The child is not dead but sleeping." [40]And they laughed at him. But he put them all outside and took the child's father and mother and those who were with him and went in where the child was. [41]Taking her by the hand he said to her, "Talitha cumi," which means, "Little girl, I say to you, arise." [42]And immediately the girl got up and began walking (for she was twelve years of age), and they were immediately overcome with amazement. [43]And he strictly charged them that no one should know this, and told them to give her something to eat.

Job 1

There was a man in the land of Uz whose name was Job, and that man was blameless and upright, one who feared God and turned away from evil. [2]There were born to him seven sons and three daughters. [3]He possessed 7,000 sheep, 3,000 camels, 500 yoke of oxen, and 500 female donkeys, and very many servants, so that this man was the greatest of all the people of the east. [4]His sons used to go and hold a feast in the house of each one on his day, and they would send and invite their three sisters to eat and drink with them. [5]And when the days of the feast had run their course,

[1] Greek daimonizomai; also verses 16, 18; elsewhere rendered oppressed by demons [2] Greek him [3] Or ignoring; some manuscripts hearing [4] Greek he

Job would send and consecrate them, and he would rise early in the morning and offer burnt offerings according to the number of them all. For Job said, "It may be that my children have sinned, and cursed[1] God in their hearts." Thus Job did continually.

⁶Now there was a day when the sons of God came to present themselves before the LORD, and Satan[2] also came among them. ⁷The LORD said to Satan, "From where have you come?" Satan answered the LORD and said, "From going to and fro on the earth, and from walking up and down on it." ⁸And the LORD said to Satan, "Have you considered my servant Job, that there is none like him on the earth, a blameless and upright man, who fears God and turns away from evil?" ⁹Then Satan answered the LORD and said, "Does Job fear God for no reason? ¹⁰Have you not put a hedge around him and his house and all that he has, on every side? You have blessed the work of his hands, and his possessions have increased in the land. ¹¹But stretch out your hand and touch all that he has, and he will curse you to your face." ¹²And the LORD said to Satan, "Behold, all that he has is in your hand. Only against him do not stretch out your hand." So Satan went out from the presence of the LORD.

¹³Now there was a day when his sons and daughters were eating and drinking wine in their oldest brother's house, ¹⁴and there came a messenger to Job and said, "The oxen were plowing and the donkeys feeding beside them, ¹⁵and the Sabeans fell upon them and took them and struck down the servants[3] with the edge of the sword, and I alone have escaped to tell you." ¹⁶While he was yet speaking, there came another and said, "The fire of God fell from heaven and burned up the sheep and the servants and consumed them, and I alone have escaped to tell you." ¹⁷While he was yet speaking, there came another and said, "The Chaldeans formed three groups and made a raid on the camels and took them and struck down the servants with the edge of the sword, and I alone have escaped to tell you." ¹⁸While he was yet speaking, there came another and said, "Your sons and daughters were eating and drinking wine in their oldest brother's house, ¹⁹and behold, a great wind came across the wilderness and struck the four corners of the house,

and it fell upon the young people, and they are dead, and I alone have escaped to tell you."

²⁰Then Job arose and tore his robe and shaved his head and fell on the ground and worshiped. ²¹And he said, "Naked I came from my mother's womb, and naked shall I return. The LORD gave, and the LORD has taken away; blessed be the name of the LORD."

²²In all this Job did not sin or charge God with wrong.

Romans 5

Therefore, since we have been justified by faith, we[4] have peace with God through our Lord Jesus Christ. ²Through him we have also obtained access by faith[5] into this grace in which we stand, and we[6] rejoice[7] in hope of the glory of God. ³Not only that, but we rejoice in our sufferings, knowing that suffering produces endurance, ⁴and endurance produces character, and character produces hope, ⁵and hope does not put us to shame, because God's love has been poured into our hearts through the Holy Spirit who has been given to us.

⁶For while we were still weak, at the right time Christ died for the ungodly. ⁷For one will scarcely die for a righteous person—though perhaps for a good person one would dare even to die— ⁸but God shows his love for us in that while we were still sinners, Christ died for us. ⁹Since, therefore, we have now been justified by his blood, much more shall we be saved by him from the wrath of God. ¹⁰For if while we were enemies we were reconciled to God by the death of his Son, much more, now that we are reconciled, shall we be saved by his life. ¹¹More than that, we also rejoice in God through our Lord Jesus Christ, through whom we have now received reconciliation.

¹²Therefore, just as sin came into the world through one man, and death through sin, and so death spread to all men[8] because all sinned— ¹³for sin indeed was in the world before the law was given, but sin is not counted where there is no law. ¹⁴Yet death reigned from Adam to Moses, even over those whose sinning was not like the transgression of Adam, who was a type of the one who was to come.

¹⁵But the free gift is not like the trespass. For if many died through one man's trespass,

---

[1] The Hebrew word bless is used euphemistically for curse in 1:5, 11; 2:5, 9 [2] Hebrew the Accuser or the Adversary; so throughout chapters 1–2 [3] Hebrew the young men; also verses 16, 17 [4] Some manuscripts let us [5] Some manuscripts omit by faith [6] Or let us; also verse 3 [7] Or boast; also verses 3, 11 [8] The Greek word anthropoi refers here to both men and women; also twice in verse 18

much more have the grace of God and the free gift by the grace of that one man Jesus Christ abounded for many. ¹⁶And the free gift is not like the result of that one man's sin. For the judgment following one trespass brought condemnation, but the free gift following many trespasses brought justification. ¹⁷For if, because of one man's trespass, death reigned through that one man, much more will those who receive the abundance of grace and the free gift of righteousness reign in life through the one man Jesus Christ.

¹⁸Therefore, as one trespass[1] led to condemnation for all men, so one act of righteousness[2] leads to justification and life for all men. ¹⁹For as by the one man's disobedience the many were made sinners, so by the one man's obedience the many will be made righteous. ²⁰Now the law came in to increase the trespass, but where sin increased, grace abounded all the more, ²¹so that, as sin reigned in death, grace also might reign through righteousness leading to eternal life through Jesus Christ our Lord.

FEBRUARY 3

Genesis 35–36

God said to Jacob, "Arise, go up to Bethel and dwell there. Make an altar there to the God who appeared to you when you fled from your brother Esau. ²So Jacob said to his household and to all who were with him, "Put away the foreign gods that are among you and purify yourselves and change your garments. ³Then let us arise and go up to Bethel, so that I may make there an altar to the God who answers me in the day of my distress and has been with me wherever I have gone." ⁴So they gave to Jacob all the foreign gods that they had, and the rings that were in their ears. Jacob hid them under the terebinth tree that was near Shechem.

⁵And as they journeyed, a terror from God fell upon the cities that were around them, so that they did not pursue the sons of Jacob. ⁶And Jacob came to Luz (that is, Bethel), which is in the land of Canaan, he and all the people who were with him, ⁷and there he built an altar and called the place El-bethel,[3] because there God had revealed himself to him when he fled from his brother. ⁸And Deborah, Rebekah's nurse, died, and she was buried under an oak below Bethel. So he called its name Allon-bacuth.[4]

⁹God appeared[5] to Jacob again, when he came from Paddan-aram, and blessed him. ¹⁰And God said to him, "Your name is Jacob; no longer shall your name be called Jacob, but Israel shall

be your name." So he called his name Israel. ¹¹And God said to him, "I am God Almighty:[6] be fruitful and multiply. A nation and a company of nations shall come from you, and kings shall come from your own body.[7] ¹²The land that I gave to Abraham and Isaac I will give to you, and I will give the land to your offspring after you." ¹³Then God went up from him in the place where he had spoken with him. ¹⁴And Jacob set up a pillar in the place where he had spoken with him, a pillar of stone. He poured out a drink offering on it and poured oil on it. ¹⁵So Jacob called the name of the place where God had spoken with him Bethel.

¹⁶Then they journeyed from Bethel. When they were still some distance[8] from Ephrath, Rachel went into labor, and she had hard labor. ¹⁷And when her labor was at its hardest, the midwife said to her, "Do not fear, for you have another son." ¹⁸And as her soul was departing (for she was dying), she called his name Ben-oni;[9] but his father called him Benjamin.[10] ¹⁹So Rachel died, and she was buried on the way to Ephrath (that is, Bethlehem), ²⁰and Jacob set up a pillar over her tomb. It is the pillar of Rachel's tomb, which is there to this day. ²¹Israel journeyed on and pitched his tent beyond the tower of Eder.

²²While Israel lived in that land, Reuben

¹ Or the trespass of one ² Or the act of righteousness of one ³ El-bethel means God of Bethel ⁴ Allon-bacuth means oak of weeping ⁵ Or had appeared ⁶ Hebrew El Shaddai ⁷ Hebrew from your loins ⁸ Or about two hours' distance ⁹ Ben-oni could mean son of my sorrow, or son of my strength ¹⁰ Benjamin means son of the right hand

went and lay with Bilhah his father's concubine. And Israel heard of it.

Now the sons of Jacob were twelve. ²³The
sons of Leah: Reuben (Jacob's firstborn),
Simeon, Levi, Judah, Issachar, and Zebulun.
²⁴The sons of Rachel: Joseph and Benjamin.
²⁵The sons of Bilhah, Rachel's servant: Dan and
Naphtali. ²⁶The sons of Zilpah, Leah's servant:
Gad and Asher. These were the sons of Jacob
who were born to him in Paddan-aram.

²⁷And Jacob came to his father Isaac at
Mamre, or Kiriath-arba (that is, Hebron), where
Abraham and Isaac had sojourned. ²⁸Now
the days of Isaac were 180 years. ²⁹And Isaac
breathed his last, and he died and was gathered
to his people, old and full of days. And his sons
Esau and Jacob buried him.

36:1 These are the generations of Esau (that
is, Edom). ²Esau took his wives from the Canaanites: Adah the daughter of Elon the Hittite,
Oholibamah the daughter of Anah the daugh-
ter¹ of Zibeon the Hivite, ³and Basemath, Ishmael's daughter, the sister of Nebaioth. ⁴And
Adah bore to Esau, Eliphaz; Basemath bore
Reuel; ⁵and Oholibamah bore Jeush, Jalam,
and Korah. These are the sons of Esau who were
born to him in the land of Canaan.

⁶Then Esau took his wives, his sons, his
daughters, and all the members of his household, his livestock, all his beasts, and all his
property that he had acquired in the land of
Canaan. He went into a land away from his
brother Jacob. ⁷For their possessions were
too great for them to dwell together. The land
of their sojournings could not support them
because of their livestock. ⁸So Esau settled in
the hill country of Seir. (Esau is Edom.)

⁹These are the generations of Esau the
father of the Edomites in the hill country of
Seir. ¹⁰These are the names of Esau's sons:
Eliphaz the son of Adah the wife of Esau, Reuel
the son of Basemath the wife of Esau. ¹¹The
sons of Eliphaz were Teman, Omar, Zepho,
Gatam, and Kenaz. ¹²(Timna was a concubine of Eliphaz, Esau's son; she bore Amalek
to Eliphaz.) These are the sons of Adah, Esau's
wife. ¹³These are the sons of Reuel: Nahath,
Zerah, Shammah, and Mizzah. These are the
sons of Basemath, Esau's wife. ¹⁴These are
the sons of Oholibamah the daughter of Anah
the daughter of Zibeon, Esau's wife: she bore
to Esau Jeush, Jalam, and Korah.

¹⁵These are the chiefs of the sons of Esau.
The sons of Eliphaz the firstborn of Esau: the
chiefs Teman, Omar, Zepho, Kenaz, ¹⁶Korah,
Gatam, and Amalek; these are the chiefs of
Eliphaz in the land of Edom; these are the sons
of Adah. ¹⁷These are the sons of Reuel, Esau's
son: the chiefs Nahath, Zerah, Shammah, and
Mizzah; these are the chiefs of Reuel in the land
of Edom; these are the sons of Basemath, Esau's
wife. ¹⁸These are the sons of Oholibamah,
Esau's wife: the chiefs Jeush, Jalam, and Korah;
these are the chiefs born of Oholibamah the
daughter of Anah, Esau's wife. ¹⁹These are the
sons of Esau (that is, Edom), and these are their
chiefs.

²⁰These are the sons of Seir the Horite, the
inhabitants of the land: Lotan, Shobal, Zibeon,
Anah, ²¹Dishon, Ezer, and Dishan; these are the
chiefs of the Horites, the sons of Seir in the land
of Edom. ²²The sons of Lotan were Hori and
Hemam; and Lotan's sister was Timna. ²³These
are the sons of Shobal: Alvan, Manahath, Ebal,
Shepho, and Onam. ²⁴These are the sons of
Zibeon: Aiah and Anah; he is the Anah who
found the hot springs in the wilderness, as
he pastured the donkeys of Zibeon his father.
²⁵These are the children of Anah: Dishon and
Oholibamah the daughter of Anah. ²⁶These are
the sons of Dishon: Hemdan, Eshban, Ithran,
and Cheran. ²⁷These are the sons of Ezer:
Bilhan, Zaavan, and Akan. ²⁸These are the sons
of Dishan: Uz and Aran. ²⁹These are the chiefs
of the Horites: the chiefs Lotan, Shobal, Zibeon,
Anah, ³⁰Dishon, Ezer, and Dishan; these are the
chiefs of the Horites, chief by chief in the land
of Seir.

³¹These are the kings who reigned in the
land of Edom, before any king reigned over
the Israelites. ³²Bela the son of Beor reigned
in Edom, the name of his city being Dinhabah.
³³Bela died, and Jobab the son of Zerah of
Bozrah reigned in his place. ³⁴Jobab died, and
Husham of the land of the Temanites reigned
in his place. ³⁵Husham died, and Hadad the son
of Bedad, who defeated Midian in the country
of Moab, reigned in his place, the name of his
city being Avith. ³⁶Hadad died, and Samlah
of Masrekah reigned in his place. ³⁷Samlah
died, and Shaul of Rehoboth on the Euphrates²
reigned in his place. ³⁸Shaul died, and Baal-
hanan the son of Achbor reigned in his place.
³⁹Baal-hanan the son of Achbor died, and

¹ Hebrew; Samaritan, Septuagint, Syriac *son*; also verse 14 ² Hebrew *the River*

Hadar reigned in his place, the name of his city being Pau; his wife's name was Mehetabel, the daughter of Matred, daughter of Mezahab.

⁴⁰These are the names of the chiefs of Esau, according to their clans and their dwelling places, by their names: the chiefs Timna, Alvah, Jetheth, ⁴¹Oholibamah, Elah, Pinon, ⁴²Kenaz, Teman, Mibzar, ⁴³Magdiel, and Iram; these are the chiefs of Edom (that is, Esau, the father of Edom), according to their dwelling places in the land of their possession.

----------- *Mark 6* -----------

He went away from there and came to his hometown, and his disciples followed him. ²And on the Sabbath he began to teach in the synagogue, and many who heard him were astonished, saying, "Where did this man get these things? What is the wisdom given to him? How are such mighty works done by his hands? ³Is not this the carpenter, the son of Mary and brother of James and Joses and Judas and Simon? And are not his sisters here with us?" And they took offense at him. ⁴And Jesus said to them, "A prophet is not without honor, except in his hometown and among his relatives and in his own household." ⁵And he could do no mighty work there, except that he laid his hands on a few sick people and healed them. ⁶And he marveled because of their unbelief.

And he went about among the villages teaching.

⁷And he called the twelve and began to send them out two by two, and gave them authority over the unclean spirits. ⁸He charged them to take nothing for their journey except a staff—no bread, no bag, no money in their belts— ⁹but to wear sandals and not put on two tunics.[1] ¹⁰And he said to them, "Whenever you enter a house, stay there until you depart from there. ¹¹And if any place will not receive you and they will not listen to you, when you leave, shake off the dust that is on your feet as a testimony against them." ¹²So they went out and proclaimed that people should repent. ¹³And they cast out many demons and anointed with oil many who were sick and healed them.

¹⁴King Herod heard of it, for Jesus'[2] name had become known. Some[3] said, "John the Baptist[4] has been raised from the dead. That is why these miraculous powers are at work

in him." ¹⁵But others said, "He is Elijah." And others said, "He is a prophet, like one of the prophets of old." ¹⁶But when Herod heard of it, he said, "John, whom I beheaded, has been raised." ¹⁷For it was Herod who had sent and seized John and bound him in prison for the sake of Herodias, his brother Philip's wife, because he had married her. ¹⁸For John had been saying to Herod, "It is not lawful for you to have your brother's wife." ¹⁹And Herodias had a grudge against him and wanted to put him to death. But she could not, ²⁰for Herod feared John, knowing that he was a righteous and holy man, and he kept him safe. When he heard him, he was greatly perplexed, and yet he heard him gladly.

²¹But an opportunity came when Herod on his birthday gave a banquet for his nobles and military commanders and the leading men of Galilee. ²²For when Herodias's daughter came in and danced, she pleased Herod and his guests. And the king said to the girl, "Ask me for whatever you wish, and I will give it to you." ²³And he vowed to her, "Whatever you ask me, I will give you, up to half of my kingdom." ²⁴And she went out and said to her mother, "For what should I ask?" And she said, "The head of John the Baptist." ²⁵And she came in immediately with haste to the king and asked, saying, "I want you to give me at once the head of John the Baptist on a platter." ²⁶And the king was exceedingly sorry, but because of his oaths and his guests he did not want to break his word to her. ²⁷And immediately the king sent an executioner with orders to bring John's[5] head. He went and beheaded him in the prison ²⁸and brought his head on a platter and gave it to the girl, and the girl gave it to her mother. ²⁹When his disciples heard of it, they came and took his body and laid it in a tomb.

³⁰The apostles returned to Jesus and told him all that they had done and taught. ³¹And he said to them, "Come away by yourselves to a desolate place and rest a while." For many were coming and going, and they had no leisure even to eat. ³²And they went away in the boat to a desolate place by themselves. ³³Now many saw them going and recognized them, and they ran there on foot from all the towns and got there ahead of them. ³⁴When he went ashore he saw a great crowd, and he had compassion on them, because they were like sheep without a

---

[1] Greek *chiton*, a long garment worn under the cloak next to the skin [2] Greek *his* [3] Some manuscripts *He* [4] Greek *baptizer*; also verse 24 [5] Greek *his*

shepherd. And he began to teach them many things. **35**And when it grew late, his disciples came to him and said, "This is a desolate place, and the hour is now late. **36**Send them away to go into the surrounding countryside and villages and buy themselves something to eat." **37**But he answered them, "You give them something to eat." And they said to him, "Shall we go and buy two hundred denarii[1] worth of bread and give it to them to eat?" **38**And he said to them, "How many loaves do you have? Go and see." And when they had found out, they said, "Five, and two fish." **39**Then he commanded them all to sit down in groups on the green grass. **40**So they sat down in groups, by hundreds and by fifties. **41**And taking the five loaves and the two fish he looked up to heaven and said a blessing and broke the loaves and gave them to the disciples to set before the people. And he divided the two fish among them all. **42**And they all ate and were satisfied. **43**And they took up twelve baskets full of broken pieces and of the fish. **44**And those who ate the loaves were five thousand men.

45Immediately he made his disciples get into the boat and go before him to the other side, to Bethsaida, while he dismissed the crowd. **46**And after he had taken leave of them, he went up on the mountain to pray. **47**And when evening came, the boat was out on the sea, and he was alone on the land. **48**And he saw that they were making headway painfully, for the wind was against them. And about the fourth watch of the night[2] he came to them, walking on the sea. He meant to pass by them, **49**but when they saw him walking on the sea they thought it was a ghost, and cried out, **50**for they all saw him and were terrified. But immediately he spoke to them and said, "Take heart; it is I. Do not be afraid." **51**And he got into the boat with them, and the wind ceased. And they were utterly astounded, **52**for they did not understand about the loaves, but their hearts were hardened.

53When they had crossed over, they came to land at Gennesaret and moored to the shore. **54**And when they got out of the boat, the people immediately recognized him **55**and ran about the whole region and began to bring the sick people on their beds to wherever they heard he was. **56**And wherever he came, in villages, cities, or countryside, they laid the sick in the marketplaces and implored him that they might touch even the fringe of his garment. And as many as touched it were made well.

Job 2

Again there was a day when the sons of God came to present themselves before the LORD, and Satan also came among them to present himself before the LORD. **2**And the LORD said to Satan, "From where have you come?" Satan answered the LORD and said, "From going to and fro on the earth, and from walking up and down on it." **3**And the LORD said to Satan, "Have you considered my servant Job, that there is none like him on the earth, a blameless and upright man, who fears God and turns away from evil? He still holds fast his integrity, although you incited me against him to destroy him without reason." **4**Then Satan answered the LORD and said, "Skin for skin! All that a man has he will give for his life. **5**But stretch out your hand and touch his bone and his flesh, and he will curse you to your face." **6**And the LORD said to Satan, "Behold, he is in your hand; only spare his life."

7So Satan went out from the presence of the LORD and struck Job with loathsome sores from the sole of his foot to the crown of his head. **8**And he took a piece of broken pottery with which to scrape himself while he sat in the ashes.

9Then his wife said to him, "Do you still hold fast your integrity? Curse God and die." **10**But he said to her, "You speak as one of the foolish women would speak. Shall we receive good from God, and shall we not receive evil?"[3] In all this Job did not sin with his lips.

11Now when Job's three friends heard of all this evil that had come upon him, they came each from his own place, Eliphaz the Temanite, Bildad the Shuhite, and Zophar the Naamathite. They made an appointment together to come to show him sympathy and comfort him. **12**And when they saw him from a distance, they did not recognize him. And they raised their voices and wept, and they tore their robes and sprinkled dust on their heads toward heaven. **13**And they sat with him on the ground seven days and seven nights, and no one spoke a word to him, for they saw that his suffering was very great.

[1] A denarius was a day's wage for a laborer [2] That is, between 3 A.M. and 6 A.M. [3] Or disaster; also verse 11

--------- Romans 6 ---------

What shall we say then? Are we to continue in sin that grace may abound? ²By no means! How can we who died to sin still live in it? ³Do you not know that all of us who have been baptized into Christ Jesus were baptized into his death? ⁴We were buried therefore with him by baptism into death, in order that, just as Christ was raised from the dead by the glory of the Father, we too might walk in newness of life.

⁵For if we have been united with him in a death like his, we shall certainly be united with him in a resurrection like his. ⁶We know that our old self¹ was crucified with him in order that the body of sin might be brought to nothing, so that we would no longer be enslaved to sin. ⁷For one who has died has been set free² from sin. ⁸Now if we have died with Christ, we believe that we will also live with him. ⁹We know that Christ, being raised from the dead, will never die again; death no longer has dominion over him. ¹⁰For the death he died he died to sin, once for all, but the life he lives he lives to God. ¹¹So you also must consider yourselves dead to sin and alive to God in Christ Jesus.

¹²Let not sin therefore reign in your mortal body, to make you obey its passions. ¹³Do not present your members to sin as instruments for unrighteousness, but present yourselves to God as those who have been brought from death to life, and your members to God as instruments for righteousness. ¹⁴For sin will have no dominion over you, since you are not under law but under grace.

¹⁵What then? Are we to sin because we are not under law but under grace? By no means! ¹⁶Do you not know that if you present yourselves to anyone as obedient slaves,³ you are slaves of the one whom you obey, either of sin, which leads to death, or of obedience, which leads to righteousness? ¹⁷But thanks be to God, that you who were once slaves of sin have become obedient from the heart to the standard of teaching to which you were committed, ¹⁸and, having been set free from sin, have become slaves of righteousness. ¹⁹I am speaking in human terms, because of your natural limitations. For just as you once presented your members as slaves to impurity and to lawlessness leading to more lawlessness, so now present your members as slaves to righteousness leading to sanctification.

²⁰For when you were slaves of sin, you were free in regard to righteousness. ²¹But what fruit were you getting at that time from the things of which you are now ashamed? For the end of those things is death. ²²But now that you have been set free from sin and have become slaves of God, the fruit you get leads to sanctification and its end, eternal life. ²³For the wages of sin is death, but the free gift of God is eternal life in Christ Jesus our Lord.

FEBRUARY 4

--------- Genesis 37 ---------

Jacob lived in the land of his father's sojournings, in the land of Canaan.

²These are the generations of Jacob.

Joseph, being seventeen years old, was pasturing the flock with his brothers. He was a boy with the sons of Bilhah and Zilpah, his father's wives. And Joseph brought a bad report of them to their father. ³Now Israel loved Joseph more than any other of his sons, because he was the son of his old age. And he made him a robe of many colors.⁴ ⁴But when his brothers saw that their father loved him more than all his brothers, they hated him and could not speak peacefully to him.

⁵Now Joseph had a dream, and when he told it to his brothers they hated him even more.

¹ Greek man ² Greek has been justified ³ For the contextual rendering of the Greek word doulos, see Preface (twice in this verse and verse 19; also once in verses 17, 20)
⁴ See Septuagint, Vulgate; or (with Syriac) a robe with long sleeves. The meaning of the Hebrew is uncertain; also verses 23, 32

⁶He said to them, "Hear this dream that I have dreamed: ⁷Behold, we were binding sheaves in the field, and behold, my sheaf arose and stood upright. And behold, your sheaves gathered around it and bowed down to my sheaf." ⁸His brothers said to him, "Are you indeed to reign over us? Or are you indeed to rule over us?" So they hated him even more for his dreams and for his words.

⁹Then he dreamed another dream and told it to his brothers and said, "Behold, I have dreamed another dream. Behold, the sun, the moon, and eleven stars were bowing down to me." ¹⁰But when he told it to his father and to his brothers, his father rebuked him and said to him, "What is this dream that you have dreamed? Shall I and your mother and your brothers indeed come to bow ourselves to the ground before you?" ¹¹And his brothers were jealous of him, but his father kept the saying in mind.

¹²Now his brothers went to pasture their father's flock near Shechem. ¹³And Israel said to Joseph, "Are not your brothers pasturing the flock at Shechem? Come, I will send you to them." And he said to him, "Here I am." ¹⁴So he said to him, "Go now, see if it is well with your brothers and with the flock, and bring me word." So he sent him from the Valley of Hebron, and he came to Shechem. ¹⁵And a man found him wandering in the fields. And the man asked him, "What are you seeking?" ¹⁶"I am seeking my brothers," he said. "Tell me, please, where they are pasturing the flock." ¹⁷And the man said, "They have gone away, for I heard them say, 'Let us go to Dothan.'" So Joseph went after his brothers and found them at Dothan.

¹⁸They saw him from afar, and before he came near to them they conspired against him to kill him. ¹⁹They said to one another, "Here comes this dreamer. ²⁰Come now, let us kill him and throw him into one of the pits.¹ Then we will say that a fierce animal has devoured him, and we will see what will become of his dreams." ²¹But when Reuben heard it, he rescued him out of their hands, saying, "Let us not take his life." ²²And Reuben said to them, "Shed no blood; throw him into this pit here in the wilderness, but do not lay a hand on him"— that he might rescue him out of their hand to restore him to his father. ²³So when Joseph

came to his brothers, they stripped him of his robe, the robe of many colors that he wore. ²⁴And they took him and threw him into a pit. The pit was empty; there was no water in it.

²⁵Then they sat down to eat. And looking up they saw a caravan of Ishmaelites coming from Gilead, with their camels bearing gum, balm, and myrrh, on their way to carry it down to Egypt. ²⁶Then Judah said to his brothers, "What profit is it if we kill our brother and conceal his blood? ²⁷Come, let us sell him to the Ishmaelites, and let not our hand be upon him, for he is our brother, our own flesh." And his brothers listened to him. ²⁸Then Midianite traders passed by. And they drew Joseph up and lifted him out of the pit, and sold him to the Ishmaelites for twenty shekels² of silver. They took Joseph to Egypt.

²⁹When Reuben returned to the pit and saw that Joseph was not in the pit, he tore his clothes ³⁰and returned to his brothers and said, "The boy is gone, and I, where shall I go?" ³¹Then they took Joseph's robe and slaughtered a goat and dipped the robe in the blood. ³²And they sent the robe of many colors and brought it to their father and said, "This we have found; please identify whether it is your son's robe or not." ³³And he identified it and said, "It is my son's robe. A fierce animal has devoured him. Joseph is without doubt torn to pieces." ³⁴Then Jacob tore his garments and put sackcloth on his loins and mourned for his son many days. ³⁵All his sons and all his daughters rose up to comfort him, but he refused to be comforted and said, "No, I shall go down to Sheol to my son, mourning." Thus his father wept for him. ³⁶Meanwhile the Midianites had sold him in Egypt to Potiphar, an officer of Pharaoh, the captain of the guard.

Mark 7

Now when the Pharisees gathered to him, with some of the scribes who had come from Jerusalem, ²they saw that some of his disciples ate with hands that were defiled, that is, unwashed. ³(For the Pharisees and all the Jews do not eat unless they wash their hands properly,³ holding to the tradition of the elders, ⁴and when they come from the marketplace, they do not eat unless they wash.⁴ And there are many other traditions that they observe, such

¹ Or cisterns; also verses 22, 24　² A shekel was about 2/5 ounce or 11 grams　³ Greek unless they wash the hands with a fist, probably indicating a kind of ceremonial washing
⁴ Greek unless they baptize; some manuscripts unless they purify themselves

as the washing of cups and pots and copper vessels and dining couches.[1]) [5] And the Pharisees and the scribes asked him, "Why do your disciples not walk according to the tradition of the elders, but eat with defiled hands?" [6] And he said to them, "Well did Isaiah prophesy of you hypocrites, as it is written,

> " 'This people honors me with their lips,
>   but their heart is far from me;
> [7]   in vain do they worship me,
>   teaching as doctrines the
>   commandments of men.'

[8] You leave the commandment of God and hold to the tradition of men."

[9] And he said to them, "You have a fine way of rejecting the commandment of God in order to establish your tradition! [10] For Moses said, 'Honor your father and your mother'; and, 'Whoever reviles father or mother must surely die.' [11] But you say, 'If a man tells his father or his mother, "Whatever you would have gained from me is Corban" ' (that is, given to God)[2]— [12] then you no longer permit him to do anything for his father or mother, [13] thus making void the word of God by your tradition that you have handed down. And many such things you do."

[14] And he called the people to him again and said to them, "Hear me, all of you, and understand: [15] There is nothing outside a person that by going into him can defile him, but the things that come out of a person are what defile him."[3] [17] And when he had entered the house and left the people, his disciples asked him about the parable. [18] And he said to them, "Then are you also without understanding? Do you not see that whatever goes into a person from outside cannot defile him, [19] since it enters not his heart but his stomach, and is expelled?"[4] (Thus he declared all foods clean.) [20] And he said, "What comes out of a person is what defiles him. [21] For from within, out of the heart of man, come evil thoughts, sexual immorality, theft, murder, adultery, [22] coveting, wickedness, deceit, sensuality, envy, slander, pride, foolishness. [23] All these evil things come from within, and they defile a person."

[24] And from there he arose and went away to the region of Tyre and Sidon.[5] And he entered a house and did not want anyone to know, yet he could not be hidden. [25] But immediately a woman whose little daughter had an unclean spirit heard of him and came and fell down at his feet. [26] Now the woman was a Gentile, a Syrophoenician by birth. And she begged him to cast the demon out of her daughter. [27] And he said to her, "Let the children be fed first, for it is not right to take the children's bread and throw it to the dogs." [28] But she answered him, "Yes, Lord; yet even the dogs under the table eat the children's crumbs." [29] And he said to her, "For this statement you may go your way; the demon has left your daughter." [30] And she went home and found the child lying in bed and the demon gone.

[31] Then he returned from the region of Tyre and went through Sidon to the Sea of Galilee, in the region of the Decapolis. [32] And they brought to him a man who was deaf and had a speech impediment, and they begged him to lay his hand on him. [33] And taking him aside from the crowd privately, he put his fingers into his ears, and after spitting touched his tongue. [34] And looking up to heaven, he sighed and said to him, "Ephphatha," that is, "Be opened." [35] And his ears were opened, his tongue was released, and he spoke plainly. [36] And Jesus[6] charged them to tell no one. But the more he charged them, the more zealously they proclaimed it. [37] And they were astonished beyond measure, saying, "He has done all things well. He even makes the deaf hear and the mute speak."

Job 3

After this Job opened his mouth and cursed the day of his birth. [2] And Job said:

> [3]   "Let the day perish on which I was born,
>   and the night that said,
>   'A man is conceived.'
> [4]   Let that day be darkness!
>   May God above not seek it,
>   nor light shine upon it.
> [5]   Let gloom and deep darkness claim it.
>   Let clouds dwell upon it;
>   let the blackness of the day terrify it.
> [6]   That night—let thick darkness seize it!
>   Let it not rejoice among the days of
>   the year;
>   let it not come into the number of the
>   months.
> [7]   Behold, let that night be barren;
>   let no joyful cry enter it.

---

[1] Some manuscripts omit *and dining couches* [2] Or *an offering* [3] Some manuscripts add verse 16: *If anyone has ears to hear, let him hear* [4] Greek *goes out into the latrine*
[5] Some manuscripts omit *and Sidon* [6] Greek *he*

8 Let those curse it who curse the day,
　who are ready to rouse up Leviathan.
9 Let the stars of its dawn be dark;
　let it hope for light, but have none,
　nor see the eyelids of the morning,
10 because it did not shut the doors of my
　　mother's womb,
　nor hide trouble from my eyes.

11 "Why did I not die at birth,
　come out from the womb and expire?
12 Why did the knees receive me?
　Or why the breasts, that I should
　　nurse?
13 For then I would have lain down and
　　been quiet;
　I would have slept; then I would have
　　been at rest,
14 with kings and counselors of the earth
　who rebuilt ruins for themselves,
15 or with princes who had gold,
　who filled their houses with silver.
16 Or why was I not as a hidden stillborn
　　child,
　as infants who never see the light?
17 There the wicked cease from troubling,
　and there the weary are at rest.
18 There the prisoners are at ease together;
　they hear not the voice of the
　　taskmaster.
19 The small and the great are there,
　and the slave is free from his master.

20 "Why is light given to him who is in
　　misery,
　and life to the bitter in soul,
21 who long for death, but it comes not,
　and dig for it more than for hidden
　　treasures,
22 who rejoice exceedingly
　and are glad when they find the grave?
23 Why is light given to a man whose way
　　is hidden,
　whom God has hedged in?
24 For my sighing comes instead of[1] my
　　bread,
　and my groanings are poured out like
　　water.
25 For the thing that I fear comes upon me,
　and what I dread befalls me.
26 I am not at ease, nor am I quiet;
　I have no rest, but trouble comes."

Romans 7

Or do you not know, brothers[2]—for I am speaking to those who know the law—that the law is binding on a person only as long as he lives? [2] For a married woman is bound by law to her husband while he lives, but if her husband dies she is released from the law of marriage.[3] [3] Accordingly, she will be called an adulteress if she lives with another man while her husband is alive. But if her husband dies, she is free from that law, and if she marries another man she is not an adulteress.

[4] Likewise, my brothers, you also have died to the law through the body of Christ, so that you may belong to another, to him who has been raised from the dead, in order that we may bear fruit for God. [5] For while we were living in the flesh, our sinful passions, aroused by the law, were at work in our members to bear fruit for death. [6] But now we are released from the law, having died to that which held us captive, so that we serve in the new way of the Spirit and not in the old way of the written code.[4]

[7] What then shall we say? That the law is sin? By no means! Yet if it had not been for the law, I would not have known sin. For I would not have known what it is to covet if the law had not said, "You shall not covet." [8] But sin, seizing an opportunity through the commandment, produced in me all kinds of covetousness. For apart from the law, sin lies dead. [9] I was once alive apart from the law, but when the commandment came, sin came alive and I died. [10] The very commandment that promised life proved to be death to me. [11] For sin, seizing an opportunity through the commandment, deceived me and through it killed me. [12] So the law is holy, and the commandment is holy and righteous and good.

[13] Did that which is good, then, bring death to me? By no means! It was sin, producing death in me through what is good, in order that sin might be shown to be sin, and through the commandment might become sinful beyond measure. [14] For we know that the law is spiritual, but I am of the flesh, sold under sin. [15] For I do not understand my own actions. For I do not do what I want, but I do the very thing I hate. [16] Now if I do what I do not want, I agree with the law, that it is good. [17] So now it is no longer I who do it, but sin that dwells within me. [18] For

[1] Or like; Hebrew before　[2] Or brothers and sisters; also verse 4　[3] Greek law concerning the husband　[4] Greek of the letter

I know that nothing good dwells in me, that is, in my flesh. For I have the desire to do what is right, but not the ability to carry it out. ¹⁹For I do not do the good I want, but the evil I do not want is what I keep on doing. ²⁰Now if I do what I do not want, it is no longer I who do it, but sin that dwells within me.

²¹So I find it to be a law that when I want to do right, evil lies close at hand. ²²For I delight in the law of God, in my inner being, ²³but I see in my members another law waging war against the law of my mind and making me captive to the law of sin that dwells in my members. ²⁴Wretched man that I am! Who will deliver me from this body of death? ²⁵Thanks be to God through Jesus Christ our Lord! So then, I myself serve the law of God with my mind, but with my flesh I serve the law of sin.

FEBRUARY 5

Genesis 38

It happened at that time that Judah went down from his brothers and turned aside to a certain Adullamite, whose name was Hirah. ²There Judah saw the daughter of a certain Canaanite whose name was Shua. He took her and went in to her, ³and she conceived and bore a son, and he called his name Er. ⁴She conceived again and bore a son, and she called his name Onan. ⁵Yet again she bore a son, and she called his name Shelah. Judah¹ was in Chezib when she bore him.

⁶And Judah took a wife for Er his firstborn, and her name was Tamar. ⁷But Er, Judah's firstborn, was wicked in the sight of the LORD, and the LORD put him to death. ⁸Then Judah said to Onan, "Go in to your brother's wife and perform the duty of a brother-in-law to her, and raise up offspring for your brother." ⁹But Onan knew that the offspring would not be his. So whenever he went in to his brother's wife he would waste the semen on the ground, so as not to give offspring to his brother. ¹⁰And what he did was wicked in the sight of the LORD, and he put him to death also. ¹¹Then Judah said to Tamar his daughter-in-law, "Remain a widow in your father's house, till Shelah my son grows up"—for he feared that he would die, like his brothers. So Tamar went and remained in her father's house.

¹²In the course of time the wife of Judah, Shua's daughter, died. When Judah was comforted, he went up to Timnah to his sheepshearers, he and his friend Hirah the Adullamite. ¹³And when Tamar was told, "Your father-in-law is going up to Timnah to shear his sheep," ¹⁴she took off her widow's garments and covered herself with a veil, wrapping herself up, and sat at the entrance to Enaim, which is on the road to Timnah. For she saw that Shelah was grown up, and she had not been given to him in marriage. ¹⁵When Judah saw her, he thought she was a prostitute, for she had covered her face. ¹⁶He turned to her at the roadside and said, "Come, let me come in to you," for he did not know that she was his daughter-in-law. She said, "What will you give me, that you may come in to me?" ¹⁷He answered, "I will send you a young goat from the flock." And she said, "If you give me a pledge, until you send it—" ¹⁸He said, "What pledge shall I give you?" She replied, "Your signet and your cord and your staff that is in your hand." So he gave them to her and went in to her, and she conceived by him. ¹⁹Then she arose and went away, and taking off her veil she put on the garments of her widowhood.

²⁰When Judah sent the young goat by his friend the Adullamite to take back the pledge from the woman's hand, he did not find her. ²¹And he asked the men of the place, "Where is the cult prostitute² who was at Enaim at the roadside?" And they said, "No cult prostitute has been here." ²²So he returned to Judah and said, "I have not found her. Also, the men of the

¹ Hebrew *He* ² Hebrew *sacred woman*; a woman who served a pagan deity by prostitution; also verse 22

place said, 'No cult prostitute has been here.'" [23] And Judah replied, "Let her keep the things as her own, or we shall be laughed at. You see, I sent this young goat, and you did not find her."

[24] About three months later Judah was told, "Tamar your daughter-in-law has been immoral.[1] Moreover, she is pregnant by immorality."[2] And Judah said, "Bring her out, and let her be burned." [25] As she was being brought out, she sent word to her father-in-law, "By the man to whom these belong, I am pregnant." And she said, "Please identify whose these are, the signet and the cord and the staff." [26] Then Judah identified them and said, "She is more righteous than I, since I did not give her to my son Shelah." And he did not know her again.

[27] When the time of her labor came, there were twins in her womb. [28] And when she was in labor, one put out a hand, and the midwife took and tied a scarlet thread on his hand, saying, "This one came out first." [29] But as he drew back his hand, behold, his brother came out. And she said, "What a breach you have made for yourself!" Therefore his name was called Perez.[3] [30] Afterward his brother came out with the scarlet thread on his hand, and his name was called Zerah.

Mark 8

In those days, when again a great crowd had gathered, and they had nothing to eat, he called his disciples to him and said to them, [2] "I have compassion on the crowd, because they have been with me now three days and have nothing to eat. [3] And if I send them away hungry to their homes, they will faint on the way. And some of them have come from far away." [4] And his disciples answered him, "How can one feed these people with bread here in this desolate place?" [5] And he asked them, "How many loaves do you have?" They said, "Seven." [6] And he directed the crowd to sit down on the ground. And he took the seven loaves, and having given thanks, he broke them and gave them to his disciples to set before the people; and they set them before the crowd. [7] And they had a few small fish. And having blessed them, he said that these also should be set before them. [8] And they ate and were satisfied. And they took up the broken pieces left over, seven baskets full. [9] And there were about four thousand

people. And he sent them away. [10] And immediately he got into the boat with his disciples and went to the district of Dalmanutha.[4]

[11] The Pharisees came and began to argue with him, seeking from him a sign from heaven to test him. [12] And he sighed deeply in his spirit and said, "Why does this generation seek a sign? Truly, I say to you, no sign will be given to this generation." [13] And he left them, got into the boat again, and went to the other side.

[14] Now they had forgotten to bring bread, and they had only one loaf with them in the boat. [15] And he cautioned them, saying, "Watch out; beware of the leaven of the Pharisees and the leaven of Herod."[5] [16] And they began discussing with one another the fact that they had no bread. [17] And Jesus, aware of this, said to them, "Why are you discussing the fact that you have no bread? Do you not yet perceive or understand? Are your hearts hardened? [18] Having eyes do you not see, and having ears do you not hear? And do you not remember? [19] When I broke the five loaves for the five thousand, how many baskets full of broken pieces did you take up?" They said to him, "Twelve." [20] "And the seven for the four thousand, how many baskets full of broken pieces did you take up?" And they said to him, "Seven." [21] And he said to them, "Do you not yet understand?"

[22] And they came to Bethsaida. And some people brought to him a blind man and begged him to touch him. [23] And he took the blind man by the hand and led him out of the village, and when he had spit on his eyes and laid his hands on him, he asked him, "Do you see anything?" [24] And he looked up and said, "I see people, but they look like trees, walking." [25] Then Jesus[6] laid his hands on his eyes again; and he opened his eyes, his sight was restored, and he saw everything clearly. [26] And he sent him to his home, saying, "Do not even enter the village."

[27] And Jesus went on with his disciples to the villages of Caesarea Philippi. And on the way he asked his disciples, "Who do people say that I am?" [28] And they told him, "John the Baptist; and others say, Elijah; and others, one of the prophets." [29] And he asked them, "But who do you say that I am?" Peter answered him, "You are the Christ." [30] And he strictly charged them to tell no one about him.

[31] And he began to teach them that the Son of Man must suffer many things and be rejected

---

[1] Or has committed prostitution [2] Or by prostitution [3] Perez means a breach [4] Some manuscripts Magadan, or Magdala [5] Some manuscripts the Herodians [6] Greek he

by the elders and the chief priests and the scribes and be killed, and after three days rise again. [32]And he said this plainly. And Peter took him aside and began to rebuke him. [33]But turning and seeing his disciples, he rebuked Peter and said, "Get behind me, Satan! For you are not setting your mind on the things of God, but on the things of man."

[34]And calling the crowd to him with his disciples, he said to them, "If anyone would come after me, let him deny himself and take up his cross and follow me. [35]For whoever would save his life[1] will lose it, but whoever loses his life for my sake and the gospel's will save it. [36]For what does it profit a man to gain the whole world and forfeit his soul? [37]For what can a man give in return for his soul? [38]For whoever is ashamed of me and of my words in this adulterous and sinful generation, of him will the Son of Man also be ashamed when he comes in the glory of his Father with the holy angels."

Job 4

Then Eliphaz the Temanite answered and said:

[2] "If one ventures a word with you, will you
          be impatient?
      Yet who can keep from speaking?
[3]   Behold, you have instructed many,
          and you have strengthened the weak
          hands.
[4]   Your words have upheld him who was
          stumbling,
      and you have made firm the feeble
          knees.
[5]   But now it has come to you, and you are
          impatient;
      it touches you, and you are dismayed.
[6]   Is not your fear of God[2] your confidence,
      and the integrity of your ways your
          hope?
[7]   "Remember: who that was innocent ever
          perished?
      Or where were the upright cut off?
[8]   As I have seen, those who plow iniquity
      and sow trouble reap the same.
[9]   By the breath of God they perish,
      and by the blast of his anger they are
          consumed.

[10] The roar of the lion, the voice of the
          fierce lion,
      the teeth of the young lions are
          broken.
[11] The strong lion perishes for lack of prey,
      and the cubs of the lioness are
          scattered.

[12] "Now a word was brought to me
          stealthily;
      my ear received the whisper of it.
[13] Amid thoughts from visions of the night,
      when deep sleep falls on men,
[14] dread came upon me, and trembling,
      which made all my bones shake.
[15] A spirit glided past my face;
      the hair of my flesh stood up.
[16] It stood still,
      but I could not discern its appearance.
      A form was before my eyes;
      there was silence, then I heard a voice:
[17] 'Can mortal man be in the right before[3]
          God?
      Can a man be pure before his Maker?
[18] Even in his servants he puts no trust,
      and his angels he charges with error;
[19] how much more those who dwell in
          houses of clay,
      whose foundation is in the dust,
      who are crushed like the moth.
[20] Between morning and evening they are
          beaten to pieces;
      they perish forever without anyone
          regarding it.
[21] Is not their tent-cord plucked up within
          them,
      do they not die, and that without
          wisdom?'

Romans 8

There is therefore now no condemnation for those who are in Christ Jesus.[4] [2]For the law of the Spirit of life has set you[5] free in Christ Jesus from the law of sin and death. [3]For God has done what the law, weakened by the flesh, could not do. By sending his own Son in the likeness of sinful flesh and for sin,[6] he condemned sin in the flesh, [4]in order that the righteous requirement of the law might be fulfilled in us, who walk not according to the flesh but according to the Spirit. [5]For those who live according to the flesh set their minds on the things of the flesh, but those who live according to the Spirit set their minds on the things of the Spirit. [6] For to set the mind on the flesh is death, but to set the mind on the Spirit is life and peace. [7] For the mind that is set on the flesh is hostile to God, for it does not submit to God's law; indeed, it cannot. [8] Those who are in the flesh cannot please God.

[9] You, however, are not in the flesh but in the Spirit, if in fact the Spirit of God dwells in you. Anyone who does not have the Spirit of Christ does not belong to him. [10] But if Christ is in you, although the body is dead because of sin, the Spirit is life because of righteousness. [11] If the Spirit of him who raised Jesus from the dead dwells in you, he who raised Christ Jesus[1] from the dead will also give life to your mortal bodies through his Spirit who dwells in you.

[12] So then, brothers,[2] we are debtors, not to the flesh, to live according to the flesh. [13] For if you live according to the flesh you will die, but if by the Spirit you put to death the deeds of the body, you will live. [14] For all who are led by the Spirit of God are sons[3] of God. [15] For you did not receive the spirit of slavery to fall back into fear, but you have received the Spirit of adoption as sons, by whom we cry, "Abba! Father!" [16] The Spirit himself bears witness with our spirit that we are children of God, [17] and if children, then heirs—heirs of God and fellow heirs with Christ, provided we suffer with him in order that we may also be glorified with him.

[18] For I consider that the sufferings of this present time are not worth comparing with the glory that is to be revealed to us. [19] For the creation waits with eager longing for the revealing of the sons of God. [20] For the creation was subjected to futility, not willingly, but because of him who subjected it, in hope [21] that the creation itself will be set free from its bondage to corruption and obtain the freedom of the glory of the children of God. [22] For we know that the whole creation has been groaning together in the pains of childbirth until now. [23] And not only the creation, but we ourselves, who have the firstfruits of the Spirit, groan inwardly as we wait eagerly for adoption as sons, the redemption of our bodies. [24] For in this hope we were saved. Now hope that is seen is not hope. For who hopes for what he sees? [25] But if we hope for what we do not see, we wait for it with patience.

[26] Likewise the Spirit helps us in our weakness. For we do not know what to pray for as we ought, but the Spirit himself intercedes for us with groanings too deep for words. [27] And he who searches hearts knows what is the mind of the Spirit, because[4] the Spirit intercedes for the saints according to the will of God. [28] And we know that for those who love God all things work together for good,[5] for those who are called according to his purpose. [29] For those whom he foreknew he also predestined to be conformed to the image of his Son, in order that he might be the firstborn among many brothers. [30] And those whom he predestined he also called, and those whom he called he also justified, and those whom he justified he also glorified.

[31] What then shall we say to these things? If God is for us, who can be[6] against us? [32] He who did not spare his own Son but gave him up for us all, how will he not also with him graciously give us all things? [33] Who shall bring any charge against God's elect? It is God who justifies. [34] Who is to condemn? Christ Jesus is the one who died—more than that, who was raised—who is at the right hand of God, who indeed is interceding for us.[7] [35] Who shall separate us from the love of Christ? Shall tribulation, or distress, or persecution, or famine, or nakedness, or danger, or sword? [36] As it is written,

> "For your sake we are being killed all the day long;
> we are regarded as sheep to be slaughtered."

[37] No, in all these things we are more than conquerors through him who loved us. [38] For I am sure that neither death nor life, nor angels nor rulers, nor things present nor things to come, nor powers, [39] nor height nor depth, nor anything else in all creation, will be able to separate us from the love of God in Christ Jesus our Lord.

---

[1] Some manuscripts lack *Jesus* [2] Or *brothers and sisters*; also verse 29 [3] See discussion on "sons" in the Preface [4] Or *that* [5] Some manuscripts *God works all things together for good*, or *God works in all things for the good* [6] Or *who is* [7] Or *Is it Christ Jesus who died. . . for us?*

FEBRUARY 6

Genesis 39

Now Joseph had been brought down to Egypt, and Potiphar, an officer of Pharaoh, the captain of the guard, an Egyptian, had bought him from the Ishmaelites who had brought him down there. [2] The LORD was with Joseph, and he became a successful man, and he was in the house of his Egyptian master. [3] His master saw that the LORD was with him and that the LORD caused all that he did to succeed in his hands. [4] So Joseph found favor in his sight and attended him, and he made him overseer of his house and put him in charge of all that he had. [5] From the time that he made him overseer in his house and over all that he had, the LORD blessed the Egyptian's house for Joseph's sake; the blessing of the LORD was on all that he had, in house and field. [6] So he left all that he had in Joseph's charge, and because of him he had no concern about anything but the food he ate.

Now Joseph was handsome in form and appearance. [7] And after a time his master's wife cast her eyes on Joseph and said, "Lie with me." [8] But he refused and said to his master's wife, "Behold, because of me my master has no concern about anything in the house, and he has put everything that he has in my charge. [9] He is not greater in this house than I am, nor has he kept back anything from me except you, because you are his wife. How then can I do this great wickedness and sin against God?" [10] And as she spoke to Joseph day after day, he would not listen to her, to lie beside her or to be with her.

[11] But one day, when he went into the house to do his work and none of the men of the house was there in the house, [12] she caught him by his garment, saying, "Lie with me." But he left his garment in her hand and fled and got out of the house. [13] And as soon as she saw that he had left his garment in her hand and had fled out of the house, [14] she called to the men of her household and said to them, "See, he has brought among us a Hebrew to laugh at us. He came in to me

to lie with me, and I cried out with a loud voice. [15] And as soon as he heard that I lifted up my voice and cried out, he left his garment beside me and fled and got out of the house." [16] Then she laid up his garment by her until his master came home, [17] and she told him the same story, saying, "The Hebrew servant, whom you have brought among us, came in to me to laugh at me. [18] But as soon as I lifted up my voice and cried, he left his garment beside me and fled out of the house."

[19] As soon as his master heard the words that his wife spoke to him, "This is the way your servant treated me," his anger was kindled. [20] And Joseph's master took him and put him into the prison, the place where the king's prisoners were confined, and he was there in prison. [21] But the LORD was with Joseph and showed him steadfast love and gave him favor in the sight of the keeper of the prison. [22] And the keeper of the prison put Joseph in charge of all the prisoners who were in the prison. Whatever was done there, he was the one who did it. [23] The keeper of the prison paid no attention to anything that was in Joseph's charge, because the LORD was with him. And whatever he did, the LORD made it succeed.

Mark 9

And he said to them, "Truly, I say to you, there are some standing here who will not taste death until they see the kingdom of God after it has come with power."

[2] And after six days Jesus took with him Peter and James and John, and led them up a high mountain by themselves. And he was transfigured before them, [3] and his clothes became radiant, intensely white, as no one[1] on earth could bleach them. [4] And there appeared to them Elijah with Moses, and they were talking with Jesus. [5] And Peter said to Jesus, "Rabbi,[2] it is good that we are here. Let us make three tents, one for you and one for Moses and one

---

[1] Greek launderer (gnapheus)   [2] Rabbi means my teacher, or my master

for Elijah." [6]For he did not know what to say, for they were terrified. [7]And a cloud overshadowed them, and a voice came out of the cloud, "This is my beloved Son;[1] listen to him." [8]And suddenly, looking around, they no longer saw anyone with them but Jesus only.

[9]And as they were coming down the mountain, he charged them to tell no one what they had seen, until the Son of Man had risen from the dead. [10]So they kept the matter to themselves, questioning what this rising from the dead might mean. [11]And they asked him, "Why do the scribes say that first Elijah must come?" [12]And he said to them, "Elijah does come first to restore all things. And how is it written of the Son of Man that he should suffer many things and be treated with contempt? [13]But I tell you that Elijah has come, and they did to him whatever they pleased, as it is written of him."

[14]And when they came to the disciples, they saw a great crowd around them, and scribes arguing with them. [15]And immediately all the crowd, when they saw him, were greatly amazed and ran up to him and greeted him. [16]And he asked them, "What are you arguing about with them?" [17]And someone from the crowd answered him, "Teacher, I brought my son to you, for he has a spirit that makes him mute. [18]And whenever it seizes him, it throws him down, and he foams and grinds his teeth and becomes rigid. So I asked your disciples to cast it out, and they were not able." [19]And he answered them, "O faithless generation, how long am I to be with you? How long am I to bear with you? Bring him to me." [20]And they brought the boy to him. And when the spirit saw him, immediately it convulsed the boy, and he fell on the ground and rolled about, foaming at the mouth. [21]And Jesus asked his father, "How long has this been happening to him?" And he said, "From childhood. [22]And it has often cast him into fire and into water, to destroy him. But if you can do anything, have compassion on us and help us." [23]And Jesus said to him, "'If you can'! All things are possible for one who believes." [24]Immediately the father of the child cried out[2] and said, "I believe; help my unbelief!" [25]And when Jesus saw that a crowd came running together, he rebuked the unclean spirit, saying to it, "You mute and deaf spirit, I command you, come out of him and never enter him again." [26]And after crying out

and convulsing him terribly, it came out, and the boy was like a corpse, so that most of them said, "He is dead." [27]But Jesus took him by the hand and lifted him up, and he arose. [28]And when he had entered the house, his disciples asked him privately, "Why could we not cast it out?" [29]And he said to them, "This kind cannot be driven out by anything but prayer."[3]

[30]They went on from there and passed through Galilee. And he did not want anyone to know, [31]for he was teaching his disciples, saying to them, "The Son of Man is going to be delivered into the hands of men, and they will kill him. And when he is killed, after three days he will rise." [32]But they did not understand the saying, and were afraid to ask him.

[33]And they came to Capernaum. And when he was in the house he asked them, "What were you discussing on the way?" [34]But they kept silent, for on the way they had argued with one another about who was the greatest. [35]And he sat down and called the twelve. And he said to them, "If anyone would be first, he must be last of all and servant of all." [36]And he took a child and put him in the midst of them, and taking him in his arms, he said to them, [37]"Whoever receives one such child in my name receives me, and whoever receives me, receives not me but him who sent me."

[38]John said to him, "Teacher, we saw someone casting out demons in your name,[4] and we tried to stop him, because he was not following us." [39]But Jesus said, "Do not stop him, for no one who does a mighty work in my name will be able soon afterward to speak evil of me. [40]For the one who is not against us is for us. [41]For truly, I say to you, whoever gives you a cup of water to drink because you belong to Christ will by no means lose his reward.

[42]"Whoever causes one of these little ones who believe in me to sin,[5] it would be better for him if a great millstone were hung around his neck and he were thrown into the sea. [43]And if your hand causes you to sin, cut it off. It is better for you to enter life crippled than with two hands to go to hell,[6] to the unquenchable fire.[7] [45]And if your foot causes you to sin, cut it off. It is better for you to enter life lame than with two feet to be thrown into hell. [47]And if your eye causes you to sin, tear it out. It is better for you to enter the kingdom of God with one eye than with two eyes to be thrown into hell,

---

[1] Or my Son, my (or the) Beloved   [2] Some manuscripts add with tears   [3] Some manuscripts add and fasting   [4] Some manuscripts add who does not follow us   [5] Greek to stumble; also verses 43, 45, 47   [6] Greek Gehenna; also verse 47   [7] Some manuscripts add verses 44 and 46 (which are identical with verse 48)

48 'where their worm does not die and the fire is not quenched.' 49 For everyone will be salted with fire.[1] 50 Salt is good, but if the salt has lost its saltiness, how will you make it salty again? Have salt in yourselves, and be at peace with one another."

Job 5

1 "Call now; is there anyone who will answer you?
To which of the holy ones will you turn?

2 Surely vexation kills the fool,
and jealousy slays the simple.

3 I have seen the fool taking root,
but suddenly I cursed his dwelling.

4 His children are far from safety;
they are crushed in the gate,
and there is no one to deliver them.

5 The hungry eat his harvest,
and he takes it even out of thorns,[2]
and the thirsty pant[3] after his[4] wealth.

6 For affliction does not come from the dust,
nor does trouble sprout from the ground,

7 but man is born to trouble
as the sparks fly upward.

8 "As for me, I would seek God,
and to God would I commit my cause,

9 who does great things and unsearchable,
marvelous things without number:

10 he gives rain on the earth
and sends waters on the fields;

11 he sets on high those who are lowly,
and those who mourn are lifted to safety.

12 He frustrates the devices of the crafty,
so that their hands achieve no success.

13 He catches the wise in their own craftiness,
and the schemes of the wily are brought to a quick end.

14 They meet with darkness in the daytime
and grope at noonday as in the night.

15 But he saves the needy from the sword
of their mouth
and from the hand of the mighty.

16 So the poor have hope,
and injustice shuts her mouth.

17 "Behold, blessed is the one whom God reproves;
therefore despise not the discipline of the Almighty.

18 For he wounds, but he binds up;
he shatters, but his hands heal.

19 He will deliver you from six troubles;
in seven no evil[5] shall touch you.

20 In famine he will redeem you from death,
and in war from the power of the sword.

21 You shall be hidden from the lash of the tongue,
and shall not fear destruction when it comes.

22 At destruction and famine you shall laugh,
and shall not fear the beasts of the earth.

23 For you shall be in league with the stones of the field,
and the beasts of the field shall be at peace with you.

24 You shall know that your tent is at peace,
and you shall inspect your fold and miss nothing.

25 You shall know also that your offspring shall be many,
and your descendants as the grass of the earth.

26 You shall come to your grave in ripe old age,
like a sheaf gathered up in its season.

27 Behold, this we have searched out; it is true.
Hear, and know it for your good."[6]

Romans 9

1 I am speaking the truth in Christ—I am not lying; my conscience bears me witness in the Holy Spirit— 2 that I have great sorrow and unceasing anguish in my heart. 3 For I could wish that I myself were accursed and cut off from Christ for the sake of my brothers,[7] my kinsmen according to the flesh. 4 They are Israelites, and to them belong the adoption, the glory, the covenants, the giving of the law, the

---

[1] Some manuscripts add and every sacrifice will be salted with salt [2] The meaning of the Hebrew is uncertain [3] Aquila, Symmachus, Syriac, Vulgate; Hebrew could be read as and the snare pants [4] Hebrew their [5] Or disaster [6] Hebrew for yourself [7] Or brothers and sisters

worship, and the promises. ⁵To them belong the patriarchs, and from their race, according to the flesh, is the Christ, who is God over all, blessed forever. Amen.

⁶But it is not as though the word of God has failed. For not all who are descended from Israel belong to Israel, ⁷and not all are children of Abraham because they are his offspring, but "Through Isaac shall your offspring be named." ⁸This means that it is not the children of the flesh who are the children of God, but the children of the promise are counted as offspring. ⁹For this is what the promise said: "About this time next year I will return, and Sarah shall have a son." ¹⁰And not only so, but also when Rebekah had conceived children by one man, our forefather Isaac, ¹¹though they were not yet born and had done nothing either good or bad—in order that God's purpose of election might continue, not because of works but because of him who calls— ¹²she was told, "The older will serve the younger." ¹³As it is written, "Jacob I loved, but Esau I hated."

¹⁴What shall we say then? Is there injustice on God's part? By no means! ¹⁵For he says to Moses, "I will have mercy on whom I have mercy, and I will have compassion on whom I have compassion." ¹⁶So then it depends not on human will or exertion,¹ but on God, who has mercy. ¹⁷For the Scripture says to Pharaoh, "For this very purpose I have raised you up, that I might show my power in you, and that my name might be proclaimed in all the earth." ¹⁸So then he has mercy on whomever he wills, and he hardens whomever he wills.

¹⁹You will say to me then, "Why does he still find fault? For who can resist his will?" ²⁰But who are you, O man, to answer back to God? Will what is molded say to its molder, "Why have you made me like this?" ²¹Has the potter no right over the clay, to make out of the same lump one vessel for honorable use and another

for dishonorable use? ²²What if God, desiring to show his wrath and to make known his power, has endured with much patience vessels of wrath prepared for destruction, ²³in order to make known the riches of his glory for vessels of mercy, which he has prepared beforehand for glory— ²⁴even us whom he has called, not from the Jews only but also from the Gentiles? ²⁵As indeed he says in Hosea,

> "Those who were not my people I will call
> 'my people,'
>   and her who was not beloved I will call
>   'beloved.'"

26 "And in the very place where it was said
>   to them, 'You are not my people,'
>   there they will be called 'sons of the
>   living God.'"

²⁷And Isaiah cries out concerning Israel: "Though the number of the sons of Israel² be as the sand of the sea, only a remnant of them will be saved, ²⁸for the Lord will carry out his sentence upon the earth fully and without delay." ²⁹And as Isaiah predicted,

> "If the Lord of hosts had not left us
>   offspring,
>   we would have been like Sodom
>   and become like Gomorrah."

³⁰What shall we say, then? That Gentiles who did not pursue righteousness have attained it, that is, a righteousness that is by faith; ³¹but that Israel who pursued a law that would lead to righteousness³ did not succeed in reaching that law. ³²Why? Because they did not pursue it by faith, but as if it were based on works. They have stumbled over the stumbling stone, ³³as it is written,

> "Behold, I am laying in Zion a stone of
>   stumbling, and a rock of offense;
>   and whoever believes in him will not
>   be put to shame."

¹ Greek not of him who wills or runs ² Or children of Israel ³ Greek a law of righteousness

FEBRUARY 7

Genesis 40

Some time after this, the cupbearer of the king of Egypt and his baker committed an offense against their lord the king of Egypt. ²And Pharaoh was angry with his two officers, the chief cupbearer and the chief baker, ³and he put them in custody in the house of the captain of the guard, in the prison where Joseph was confined. ⁴The captain of the guard appointed Joseph to be with them, and he attended them. They continued for some time in custody.

⁵And one night they both dreamed—the cupbearer and the baker of the king of Egypt, who were confined in the prison—each his own dream, and each dream with its own interpretation. ⁶When Joseph came to them in the morning, he saw that they were troubled. ⁷So he asked Pharaoh's officers who were with him in custody in his master's house, "Why are your faces downcast today?" ⁸They said to him, "We have had dreams, and there is no one to interpret them." And Joseph said to them, "Do not interpretations belong to God? Please tell them to me."

⁹So the chief cupbearer told his dream to Joseph and said to him, "In my dream there was a vine before me, ¹⁰and on the vine there were three branches. As soon as it budded, its blossoms shot forth, and the clusters ripened into grapes. ¹¹Pharaoh's cup was in my hand, and I took the grapes and pressed them into Pharaoh's cup and placed the cup in Pharaoh's hand." ¹²Then Joseph said to him, "This is its interpretation: the three branches are three days. ¹³In three days Pharaoh will lift up your head and restore you to your office, and you shall place Pharaoh's cup in his hand as formerly, when you were his cupbearer. ¹⁴Only remember me, when it is well with you, and please do me the kindness to mention me to Pharaoh, and so get me out of this house. ¹⁵For I was indeed stolen out of the land of the Hebrews, and here also I have done nothing that they should put me into the pit."

¹⁶When the chief baker saw that the interpretation was favorable, he said to Joseph, "I also had a dream: there were three cake baskets on my head, ¹⁷and in the uppermost basket there were all sorts of baked food for Pharaoh, but the birds were eating it out of the basket on my head." ¹⁸And Joseph answered and said, "This is its interpretation: the three baskets are three days. ¹⁹In three days Pharaoh will lift up your head—from you!—and hang you on a tree. And the birds will eat the flesh from you."

²⁰On the third day, which was Pharaoh's birthday, he made a feast for all his servants and lifted up the head of the chief cupbearer and the head of the chief baker among his servants. ²¹He restored the chief cupbearer to his position, and he placed the cup in Pharaoh's hand. ²²But he hanged the chief baker, as Joseph had interpreted to them. ²³Yet the chief cupbearer did not remember Joseph, but forgot him.

Mark 10

And he left there and went to the region of Judea and beyond the Jordan, and crowds gathered to him again. And again, as was his custom, he taught them.

²And Pharisees came up and in order to test him asked, "Is it lawful for a man to divorce his wife?" ³He answered them, "What did Moses command you?" ⁴They said, "Moses allowed a man to write a certificate of divorce and to send her away." ⁵And Jesus said to them, "Because of your hardness of heart he wrote you this commandment. ⁶But from the beginning of creation, 'God made them male and female.' ⁷'Therefore a man shall leave his father and mother and hold fast to his wife,[1] ⁸and the two shall become one flesh.' So they are no longer two but one flesh. ⁹What therefore God has joined together, let not man separate."

¹⁰And in the house the disciples asked him again about this matter. ¹¹And he said to them, "Whoever divorces his wife and marries

[1] Some manuscripts omit *and hold fast to his wife*

another commits adultery against her, [12]and if she divorces her husband and marries another, she commits adultery."

[13]And they were bringing children to him that he might touch them, and the disciples rebuked them. [14]But when Jesus saw it, he was indignant and said to them, "Let the children come to me; do not hinder them, for to such belongs the kingdom of God. [15]Truly, I say to you, whoever does not receive the kingdom of God like a child shall not enter it." [16]And he took them in his arms and blessed them, laying his hands on them.

[17]And as he was setting out on his journey, a man ran up and knelt before him and asked him, "Good Teacher, what must I do to inherit eternal life?" [18]And Jesus said to him, "Why do you call me good? No one is good except God alone. [19]You know the commandments: 'Do not murder, Do not commit adultery, Do not steal, Do not bear false witness, Do not defraud, Honor your father and mother.'" [20]And he said to him, "Teacher, all these I have kept from my youth." [21]And Jesus, looking at him, loved him, and said to him, "You lack one thing: go, sell all that you have and give to the poor, and you will have treasure in heaven; and come, follow me." [22]Disheartened by the saying, he went away sorrowful, for he had great possessions.

[23]And Jesus looked around and said to his disciples, "How difficult it will be for those who have wealth to enter the kingdom of God!" [24]And the disciples were amazed at his words. But Jesus said to them again, "Children, how difficult it is[1] to enter the kingdom of God! [25]It is easier for a camel to go through the eye of a needle than for a rich person to enter the kingdom of God." [26]And they were exceedingly astonished, and said to him,[2] "Then who can be saved?" [27]Jesus looked at them and said, "With man it is impossible, but not with God. For all things are possible with God." [28]Peter began to say to him, "See, we have left everything and followed you." [29]Jesus said, "Truly, I say to you, there is no one who has left house or brothers or sisters or mother or father or children or lands, for my sake and for the gospel, [30]who will not receive a hundredfold now in this time, houses and brothers and sisters and mothers and children and lands, with persecutions, and in the age to come eternal life. [31]But many who are first will be last, and the last first."

[32]And they were on the road, going up to Jerusalem, and Jesus was walking ahead of them. And they were amazed, and those who followed were afraid. And taking the twelve again, he began to tell them what was to happen to him, [33]saying, "See, we are going up to Jerusalem, and the Son of Man will be delivered over to the chief priests and the scribes, and they will condemn him to death and deliver him over to the Gentiles. [34]And they will mock him and spit on him, and flog him and kill him. And after three days he will rise."

[35]And James and John, the sons of Zebedee, came up to him and said to him, "Teacher, we want you to do for us whatever we ask of you." [36]And he said to them, "What do you want me to do for you?" [37]And they said to him, "Grant us to sit, one at your right hand and one at your left, in your glory." [38]Jesus said to them, "You do not know what you are asking. Are you able to drink the cup that I drink, or to be baptized with the baptism with which I am baptized?" [39]And they said to him, "We are able." And Jesus said to them, "The cup that I drink you will drink, and with the baptism with which I am baptized, you will be baptized, [40]but to sit at my right hand or at my left is not mine to grant, but it is for those for whom it has been prepared." [41]And when the ten heard it, they began to be indignant at James and John. [42]And Jesus called them to him and said to them, "You know that those who are considered rulers of the Gentiles lord it over them, and their great ones exercise authority over them. [43]But it shall not be so among you. But whoever would be great among you must be your servant,[3] [44]and whoever would be first among you must be slave[4] of all. [45]For even the Son of Man came not to be served but to serve, and to give his life as a ransom for many."

[46]And they came to Jericho. And as he was leaving Jericho with his disciples and a great crowd, Bartimaeus, a blind beggar, the son of Timaeus, was sitting by the roadside. [47]And when he heard that it was Jesus of Nazareth, he began to cry out and say, "Jesus, Son of David, have mercy on me!" [48]And many rebuked him, telling him to be silent. But he cried out all the more, "Son of David, have mercy on me!" [49]And Jesus stopped and said, "Call him." And they called the blind man, saying to him, "Take heart. Get up; he is calling you." [50]And

[1] Some manuscripts add for those who trust in riches [2] Some manuscripts to one another [3] Greek diakonos [4] Greek bondservant (doulos)

throwing off his cloak, he sprang up and came to Jesus. [51]And Jesus said to him, "What do you want me to do for you?" And the blind man said to him, "Rabbi, let me recover my sight." [52]And Jesus said to him, "Go your way; your faith has made you well." And immediately he recovered his sight and followed him on the way.

Job 6

Then Job answered and said:

[2] "Oh that my vexation were weighed,
and all my calamity laid in the balances!
[3] For then it would be heavier than the sand of the sea;
therefore my words have been rash.
[4] For the arrows of the Almighty are in me;
my spirit drinks their poison;
the terrors of God are arrayed against me.
[5] Does the wild donkey bray when he has grass,
or the ox low over his fodder?
[6] Can that which is tasteless be eaten without salt,
or is there any taste in the juice of the mallow?[1]
[7] My appetite refuses to touch them;
they are as food that is loathsome to me.[2]

[8] "Oh that I might have my request,
and that God would fulfill my hope,
[9] that it would please God to crush me,
that he would let loose his hand and cut me off!
[10] This would be my comfort;
I would even exult[3] in pain unsparing,
for I have not denied the words of the Holy One.
[11] What is my strength, that I should wait?
And what is my end, that I should be patient?
[12] Is my strength the strength of stones, or is my flesh bronze?
[13] Have I any help in me,
when resource is driven from me?

[14] "He who withholds[4] kindness from a friend
forsakes the fear of the Almighty.
[15] My brothers are treacherous as a torrent-bed,
as torrential streams that pass away,
[16] which are dark with ice,
and where the snow hides itself.
[17] When they melt, they disappear;
when it is hot, they vanish from their place.
[18] The caravans turn aside from their course;
they go up into the waste and perish.
[19] The caravans of Tema look,
the travelers of Sheba hope.
[20] They are ashamed because they were confident;
they come there and are disappointed.
[21] For you have now become nothing;
you see my calamity and are afraid.
[22] Have I said, 'Make me a gift'?
Or, 'From your wealth offer a bribe for me'?
[23] Or, 'Deliver me from the adversary's hand'?
Or, 'Redeem me from the hand of the ruthless'?

[24] "Teach me, and I will be silent;
make me understand how I have gone astray.
[25] How forceful are upright words!
But what does reproof from you reprove?
[26] Do you think that you can reprove words,
when the speech of a despairing man is wind?
[27] You would even cast lots over the fatherless,
and bargain over your friend.

[28] "But now, be pleased to look at me,
for I will not lie to your face.
[29] Please turn; let no injustice be done.
Turn now; my vindication is at stake.
[30] Is there any injustice on my tongue?
Cannot my palate discern the cause of calamity?

Romans 10

Brothers,[5] my heart's desire and prayer to God for them is that they may be saved. [2]For I bear them witness that they have a zeal for God, but not according to knowledge. [3]For,

[1] The meaning of the Hebrew word is uncertain [2] The meaning of the Hebrew is uncertain [3] The meaning of the Hebrew word is uncertain [4] Syriac, Vulgate (compare Targum); the meaning of the Hebrew word is uncertain [5] Or Brothers and sisters

being ignorant of the righteousness of God, and seeking to establish their own, they did not submit to God's righteousness. [4]For Christ is the end of the law for righteousness to everyone who believes.[1]

[5]For Moses writes about the righteousness that is based on the law, that the person who does the commandments shall live by them. [6]But the righteousness based on faith says, "Do not say in your heart, 'Who will ascend into heaven?'" (that is, to bring Christ down) [7]"or 'Who will descend into the abyss?'" (that is, to bring Christ up from the dead). [8]But what does it say? "The word is near you, in your mouth and in your heart" (that is, the word of faith that we proclaim); [9]because, if you confess with your mouth that Jesus is Lord and believe in your heart that God raised him from the dead, you will be saved. [10]For with the heart one believes and is justified, and with the mouth one confesses and is saved. [11]For the Scripture says, "Everyone who believes in him will not be put to shame." [12]For there is no distinction between Jew and Greek; for the same Lord is Lord of all, bestowing his riches on all who call on him. [13]For "everyone who calls on the name of the Lord will be saved."

[14]How then will they call on him in whom they have not believed? And how are they to believe in him of whom they have never heard?[2] And how are they to hear without someone preaching? [15]And how are they to preach unless they are sent? As it is written, "How beautiful are the feet of those who preach the good news!" [16]But they have not all obeyed the gospel. For Isaiah says, "Lord, who has believed what he has heard from us?" [17]So faith comes from hearing, and hearing through the word of Christ.

[18]But I ask, have they not heard? Indeed they have, for

"Their voice has gone out to all the earth,
and their words to the ends of the
world."

[19]But I ask, did Israel not understand? First Moses says,

"I will make you jealous of those who are
not a nation;
with a foolish nation I will make you
angry."

[20]Then Isaiah is so bold as to say,

"I have been found by those who did not
seek me;
I have shown myself to those who did
not ask for me."

[21]But of Israel he says, "All day long I have held out my hands to a disobedient and contrary people."

FEBRUARY 8

Genesis 41

After two whole years, Pharaoh dreamed that he was standing by the Nile, [2]and behold, there came up out of the Nile seven cows attractive and plump, and they fed in the reed grass. [3]And behold, seven other cows, ugly and thin, came up out of the Nile after them, and stood by the other cows on the bank of the Nile. [4]And the ugly, thin cows ate up the seven attractive, plump cows. And Pharaoh awoke. [5]And he fell asleep and dreamed a second time. And behold, seven ears of grain, plump and good, were growing on one stalk. [6]And behold, after them sprouted seven ears, thin and blighted by the east wind. [7]And the thin ears swallowed up the seven plump, full ears. And Pharaoh awoke, and behold, it was a dream. [8]So in the morning his spirit was troubled, and he sent and called for all the magicians of Egypt and all its wise men. Pharaoh told them his dreams, but there was none who could interpret them to Pharaoh.

[1] Or end of the law, that everyone who believes may be justified [2] Or him whom they have never heard

[9]Then the chief cupbearer said to Pharaoh, "I remember my offenses today. [10]When Pharaoh was angry with his servants and put me and the chief baker in custody in the house of the captain of the guard, [11]we dreamed on the same night, he and I, each having a dream with its own interpretation. [12]A young Hebrew was there with us, a servant of the captain of the guard. When we told him, he interpreted our dreams to us, giving an interpretation to each man according to his dream. [13]And as he interpreted to us, so it came about. I was restored to my office, and the baker was hanged."

[14]Then Pharaoh sent and called Joseph, and they quickly brought him out of the pit. And when he had shaved himself and changed his clothes, he came in before Pharaoh. [15]And Pharaoh said to Joseph, "I have had a dream, and there is no one who can interpret it. I have heard it said of you that when you hear a dream you can interpret it." [16]Joseph answered Pharaoh, "It is not in me; God will give Pharaoh a favorable answer."[1] [17]Then Pharaoh said to Joseph, "Behold, in my dream I was standing on the banks of the Nile. [18]Seven cows, plump and attractive, came up out of the Nile and fed in the reed grass. [19]Seven other cows came up after them, poor and very ugly and thin, such as I had never seen in all the land of Egypt. [20]And the thin, ugly cows ate up the first seven plump cows, [21]but when they had eaten them no one would have known that they had eaten them, for they were still as ugly as at the beginning. Then I awoke. [22]I also saw in my dream seven ears growing on one stalk, full and good. [23]Seven ears, withered, thin, and blighted by the east wind, sprouted after them, [24]and the thin ears swallowed up the seven good ears. And I told it to the magicians, but there was no one who could explain it to me."

[25]Then Joseph said to Pharaoh, "The dreams of Pharaoh are one; God has revealed to Pharaoh what he is about to do. [26]The seven good cows are seven years, and the seven good ears are seven years; the dreams are one. [27]The seven lean and ugly cows that came up after them are seven years, and the seven empty ears blighted by the east wind are also seven years of famine. [28]It is as I told Pharaoh; God has shown to Pharaoh what he is about to do.

[29]There will come seven years of great plenty throughout all the land of Egypt, [30]but after them there will arise seven years of famine, and all the plenty will be forgotten in the land of Egypt. The famine will consume the land, [31]and the plenty will be unknown in the land by reason of the famine that will follow, for it will be very severe. [32]And the doubling of Pharaoh's dream means that the thing is fixed by God, and God will shortly bring it about. [33]Now therefore let Pharaoh select a discerning and wise man, and set him over the land of Egypt. [34]Let Pharaoh proceed to appoint overseers over the land and take one-fifth of the produce of the land[2] of Egypt during the seven plentiful years. [35]And let them gather all the food of these good years that are coming and store up grain under the authority of Pharaoh for food in the cities, and let them keep it. [36]That food shall be a reserve for the land against the seven years of famine that are to occur in the land of Egypt, so that the land may not perish through the famine."

[37]This proposal pleased Pharaoh and all his servants. [38]And Pharaoh said to his servants, "Can we find a man like this, in whom is the Spirit of God?"[3] [39]Then Pharaoh said to Joseph, "Since God has shown you all this, there is none so discerning and wise as you are. [40]You shall be over my house, and all my people shall order themselves as you command.[4] Only as regards the throne will I be greater than you." [41]And Pharaoh said to Joseph, "See, I have set you over all the land of Egypt." [42]Then Pharaoh took his signet ring from his hand and put it on Joseph's hand, and clothed him in garments of fine linen and put a gold chain about his neck. [43]And he made him ride in his second chariot. And they called out before him, "Bow the knee!"[5] Thus he set him over all the land of Egypt. [44]Moreover, Pharaoh said to Joseph, "I am Pharaoh, and without your consent no one shall lift up hand or foot in all the land of Egypt." [45]And Pharaoh called Joseph's name Zaphenath-paneah. And he gave him in marriage Asenath, the daughter of Potiphera priest of On. So Joseph went out over the land of Egypt.

[46]Joseph was thirty years old when he entered the service of Pharaoh king of Egypt. And Joseph went out from the presence of Pharaoh and went through all the land of Egypt. [47]During the seven plentiful years the

---

[1] Or (compare Samaritan, Septuagint) *Without God it is not possible to give Pharaoh an answer about his welfare*   [2] Or *over the land and organize the land*   [3] Or *of the gods*   [4] Hebrew *and according to your command all my people shall kiss the ground*   [5] *Abrek*, probably an Egyptian word, similar in sound to the Hebrew word meaning *to kneel*

earth produced abundantly, [48] and he gathered up all the food of these seven years, which occurred in the land of Egypt, and put the food in the cities. He put in every city the food from the fields around it. [49] And Joseph stored up grain in great abundance, like the sand of the sea, until he ceased to measure it, for it could not be measured.

[50] Before the year of famine came, two sons were born to Joseph. Asenath, the daughter of Potiphera priest of On, bore them to him. [51] Joseph called the name of the firstborn Manasseh. "For," he said, "God has made me forget all my hardship and all my father's house."[1] [52] The name of the second he called Ephraim, "For God has made me fruitful in the land of my affliction."[2]

[53] The seven years of plenty that occurred in the land of Egypt came to an end, [54] and the seven years of famine began to come, as Joseph had said. There was famine in all lands, but in all the land of Egypt there was bread. [55] When all the land of Egypt was famished, the people cried to Pharaoh for bread. Pharaoh said to all the Egyptians, "Go to Joseph. What he says to you, do."

[56] So when the famine had spread over all the land, Joseph opened all the storehouses[3] and sold to the Egyptians, for the famine was severe in the land of Egypt. [57] Moreover, all the earth came to Egypt to Joseph to buy grain, because the famine was severe over all the earth.

Mark 11

Now when they drew near to Jerusalem, to Bethphage and Bethany, at the Mount of Olives, Jesus[4] sent two of his disciples [2] and said to them, "Go into the village in front of you, and immediately as you enter it you will find a colt tied, on which no one has ever sat. Untie it and bring it. [3] If anyone says to you, 'Why are you doing this?' say, 'The Lord has need of it and will send it back here immediately.'" [4] And they went away and found a colt tied at a door outside in the street, and they untied it. [5] And some of those standing there said to them, "What are you doing, untying the colt?" [6] And they told them what Jesus had said, and they let them go. [7] And they brought the colt to Jesus and threw their cloaks on it, and he sat on it. [8] And many spread their cloaks

on the road, and others spread leafy branches that they had cut from the fields. [9] And those who went before and those who followed were shouting, "Hosanna! Blessed is he who comes in the name of the Lord! [10] Blessed is the coming kingdom of our father David! Hosanna in the highest!"

[11] And he entered Jerusalem and went into the temple. And when he had looked around at everything, as it was already late, he went out to Bethany with the twelve.

[12] On the following day, when they came from Bethany, he was hungry. [13] And seeing in the distance a fig tree in leaf, he went to see if he could find anything on it. When he came to it, he found nothing but leaves, for it was not the season for figs. [14] And he said to it, "May no one ever eat fruit from you again." And his disciples heard it.

[15] And they came to Jerusalem. And he entered the temple and began to drive out those who sold and those who bought in the temple, and he overturned the tables of the money-changers and the seats of those who sold pigeons. [16] And he would not allow anyone to carry anything through the temple. [17] And he was teaching them and saying to them, "Is it not written, 'My house shall be called a house of prayer for all the nations'? But you have made it a den of robbers." [18] And the chief priests and the scribes heard it and were seeking a way to destroy him, for they feared him, because all the crowd was astonished at his teaching. [19] And when evening came they[5] went out of the city.

[20] As they passed by in the morning, they saw the fig tree withered away to its roots. [21] And Peter remembered and said to him, "Rabbi, look! The fig tree that you cursed has withered." [22] And Jesus answered them, "Have faith in God. [23] Truly, I say to you, whoever says to this mountain, 'Be taken up and thrown into the sea,' and does not doubt in his heart, but believes that what he says will come to pass, it will be done for him. [24] Therefore I tell you, whatever you ask in prayer, believe that you have received[6] it, and it will be yours. [25] And whenever you stand praying, forgive, if you have anything against anyone, so that your Father also who is in heaven may forgive you your trespasses."[7]

[27] And they came again to Jerusalem. And

---

[1] Manasseh sounds like the Hebrew for making to forget [2] Ephraim sounds like the Hebrew for making fruitful [3] Hebrew all that was in them [4] Greek he [5] Some manuscripts he [6] Some manuscripts are receiving [7] Some manuscripts add verse 26: But if you do not forgive, neither will your Father who is in heaven forgive your trespasses

as he was walking in the temple, the chief priests and the scribes and the elders came to him, ²⁸ and they said to him, "By what authority are you doing these things, or who gave you this authority to do them?" ²⁹ Jesus said to them, "I will ask you one question; answer me, and I will tell you by what authority I do these things. ³⁰ Was the baptism of John from heaven or from man? Answer me." ³¹ And they discussed it with one another, saying, "If we say, 'From heaven,' he will say, 'Why then did you not believe him?' ³² But shall we say, 'From man'?"—they were afraid of the people, for they all held that John really was a prophet. ³³ So they answered Jesus, "We do not know." And Jesus said to them, "Neither will I tell you by what authority I do these things."

Job 7

"Has not man a hard service on earth,
and are not his days like the days of a
hired hand?
²   Like a slave who longs for the shadow,
and like a hired hand who looks for
his wages,
³   so I am allotted months of emptiness,
and nights of misery are apportioned
to me.
⁴   When I lie down I say, 'When shall I
arise?'
But the night is long,
and I am full of tossing till the dawn.
⁵   My flesh is clothed with worms and dirt;
my skin hardens, then breaks out
afresh.
⁶   My days are swifter than a weaver's
shuttle
and come to their end without hope.
⁷   "Remember that my life is a breath;
my eye will never again see good.
⁸   The eye of him who sees me will behold
me no more;
while your eyes are on me, I shall be
gone.
⁹   As the cloud fades and vanishes,
so he who goes down to Sheol does
not come up;
¹⁰ he returns no more to his house,
nor does his place know him
anymore.

¹¹ "Therefore I will not restrain my mouth;
I will speak in the anguish of my
spirit;
I will complain in the bitterness of my
soul.
¹² Am I the sea, or a sea monster,
that you set a guard over me?
¹³ When I say, 'My bed will comfort me,
my couch will ease my complaint,'
¹⁴ then you scare me with dreams
and terrify me with visions,
¹⁵ so that I would choose strangling
and death rather than my bones.
¹⁶ I loathe my life; I would not live forever.
Leave me alone, for my days are a
breath.
¹⁷ What is man, that you make so much of
him,
and that you set your heart on him,
¹⁸ visit him every morning
and test him every moment?
¹⁹ How long will you not look away from
me,
nor leave me alone till I swallow my
spit?
²⁰ If I sin, what do I do to you, you watcher
of mankind?
Why have you made me your mark?
Why have I become a burden to you?
²¹ Why do you not pardon my
transgression
and take away my iniquity?
For now I shall lie in the earth;
you will seek me, but I shall not be."

Romans 11

I ask, then, has God rejected his people? By no means! For I myself am an Israelite, a descendant of Abraham,[1] a member of the tribe of Benjamin. ² God has not rejected his people whom he foreknew. Do you not know what the Scripture says of Elijah, how he appeals to God against Israel? ³ "Lord, they have killed your prophets, they have demolished your altars, and I alone am left, and they seek my life." ⁴ But what is God's reply to him? "I have kept for myself seven thousand men who have not bowed the knee to Baal." ⁵ So too at the present time there is a remnant, chosen by grace. ⁶ But if it is by grace, it is no longer on the basis

---

¹ Or one of the offspring of Abraham

of works; otherwise grace would no longer be grace.

7 What then? Israel failed to obtain what it was seeking. The elect obtained it, but the rest were hardened, **8** as it is written,

"God gave them a spirit of stupor,
    eyes that would not see
    and ears that would not hear,
    down to this very day."

9 And David says,

"Let their table become a snare and a
        trap,
    a stumbling block and a retribution
        for them;
10   let their eyes be darkened so that they
        cannot see,
    and bend their backs forever."

11 So I ask, did they stumble in order that they might fall? By no means! Rather through their trespass salvation has come to the Gentiles, so as to make Israel jealous. **12** Now if their trespass means riches for the world, and if their failure means riches for the Gentiles, how much more will their full inclusion[1] mean!

13 Now I am speaking to you Gentiles. Inasmuch then as I am an apostle to the Gentiles, I magnify my ministry **14** in order somehow to make my fellow Jews jealous, and thus save some of them. **15** For if their rejection means the reconciliation of the world, what will their acceptance mean but life from the dead? **16** If the dough offered as firstfruits is holy, so is the whole lump, and if the root is holy, so are the branches.

17 But if some of the branches were broken off, and you, although a wild olive shoot, were grafted in among the others and now share in the nourishing root[2] of the olive tree, **18** do not be arrogant toward the branches. If you are, remember it is not you who support the root, but the root that supports you. **19** Then you will say, "Branches were broken off so that I might be grafted in." **20** That is true. They were broken off because of their unbelief, but you stand fast through faith. So do not become

proud, but fear. **21** For if God did not spare the natural branches, neither will he spare you. **22** Note then the kindness and the severity of God: severity toward those who have fallen, but God's kindness to you, provided you continue in his kindness. Otherwise you too will be cut off. **23** And even they, if they do not continue in their unbelief, will be grafted in, for God has the power to graft them in again. **24** For if you were cut from what is by nature a wild olive tree, and grafted, contrary to nature, into a cultivated olive tree, how much more will these, the natural branches, be grafted back into their own olive tree.

25 Lest you be wise in your own sight, I do not want you to be unaware of this mystery, brothers:[3] a partial hardening has come upon Israel, until the fullness of the Gentiles has come in. **26** And in this way all Israel will be saved, as it is written,

"The Deliverer will come from Zion,
    he will banish ungodliness from
        Jacob";
27   "and this will be my covenant with them
        when I take away their sins."

28 As regards the gospel, they are enemies for your sake. But as regards election, they are beloved for the sake of their forefathers. **29** For the gifts and the calling of God are irrevocable. **30** For just as you were at one time disobedient to God but now have received mercy because of their disobedience, **31** so they too have now been disobedient in order that by the mercy shown to you they also may now[4] receive mercy. **32** For God has consigned all to disobedience, that he may have mercy on all.

33 Oh, the depth of the riches and wisdom and knowledge of God! How unsearchable are his judgments and how inscrutable his ways!

34   "For who has known the mind of the Lord,
        or who has been his counselor?"
35   "Or who has given a gift to him
        that he might be repaid?"

36 For from him and through him and to him are all things. To him be glory forever. Amen.

---

[1] Greek *their fullness* [2] Greek *root of richness*; some manuscripts *richness* [3] Or *brothers and sisters* [4] Some manuscripts omit *now*

FEBRUARY 9

Genesis 42

When Jacob learned that there was grain for sale in Egypt, he said to his sons, "Why do you look at one another?" ²And he said, "Behold, I have heard that there is grain for sale in Egypt. Go down and buy grain for us there, that we may live and not die." ³So ten of Joseph's brothers went down to buy grain in Egypt. ⁴But Jacob did not send Benjamin, Joseph's brother, with his brothers, for he feared that harm might happen to him. ⁵Thus the sons of Israel came to buy among the others who came, for the famine was in the land of Canaan.

⁶Now Joseph was governor over the land. He was the one who sold to all the people of the land. And Joseph's brothers came and bowed themselves before him with their faces to the ground. ⁷Joseph saw his brothers and recognized them, but he treated them like strangers and spoke roughly to them. "Where do you come from?" he said. They said, "From the land of Canaan, to buy food." ⁸And Joseph recognized his brothers, but they did not recognize him. ⁹And Joseph remembered the dreams that he had dreamed of them. And he said to them, "You are spies; you have come to see the nakedness of the land." ¹⁰They said to him, "No, my lord, your servants have come to buy food. ¹¹We are all sons of one man. We are honest men. Your servants have never been spies."

¹²He said to them, "No, it is the nakedness of the land that you have come to see." ¹³And they said, "We, your servants, are twelve brothers, the sons of one man in the land of Canaan, and behold, the youngest is this day with our father, and one is no more." ¹⁴But Joseph said to them, "It is as I said to you. You are spies. ¹⁵By this you shall be tested: by the life of Pharaoh, you shall not go from this place unless your youngest brother comes here. ¹⁶Send one of you, and let him bring your brother, while you remain confined, that your words may be tested, whether there is truth in you. Or else, by the life of Pharaoh, surely you

are spies." ¹⁷And he put them all together in custody for three days.

¹⁸On the third day Joseph said to them, "Do this and you will live, for I fear God: ¹⁹if you are honest men, let one of your brothers remain confined where you are in custody, and let the rest go and carry grain for the famine of your households, ²⁰and bring your youngest brother to me. So your words will be verified, and you shall not die." And they did so. ²¹Then they said to one another, "In truth we are guilty concerning our brother, in that we saw the distress of his soul, when he begged us and we did not listen. That is why this distress has come upon us." ²²And Reuben answered them, "Did I not tell you not to sin against the boy? But you did not listen. So now there comes a reckoning for his blood." ²³They did not know that Joseph understood them, for there was an interpreter between them. ²⁴Then he turned away from them and wept. And he returned to them and spoke to them. And he took Simeon from them and bound him before their eyes. ²⁵And Joseph gave orders to fill their bags with grain, and to replace every man's money in his sack, and to give them provisions for the journey. This was done for them.

²⁶Then they loaded their donkeys with their grain and departed. ²⁷And as one of them opened his sack to give his donkey fodder at the lodging place, he saw his money in the mouth of his sack. ²⁸He said to his brothers, "My money has been put back; here it is in the mouth of my sack!" At this their hearts failed them, and they turned trembling to one another, saying, "What is this that God has done to us?"

²⁹When they came to Jacob their father in the land of Canaan, they told him all that had happened to them, saying, ³⁰"The man, the lord of the land, spoke roughly to us and took us to be spies of the land. ³¹But we said to him, 'We are honest men; we have never been spies. ³²We are twelve brothers, sons of our father.

One is no more, and the youngest is this day with our father in the land of Canaan.' ³³Then the man, the lord of the land, said to us, 'By this I shall know that you are honest men: leave one of your brothers with me, and take grain for the famine of your households, and go your way. ³⁴Bring your youngest brother to me. Then I shall know that you are not spies but honest men, and I will deliver your brother to you, and you shall trade in the land.'"

³⁵As they emptied their sacks, behold, every man's bundle of money was in his sack. And when they and their father saw their bundles of money, they were afraid. ³⁶And Jacob their father said to them, "You have bereaved me of my children: Joseph is no more, and Simeon is no more, and now you would take Benjamin. All this has come against me." ³⁷Then Reuben said to his father, "Kill my two sons if I do not bring him back to you. Put him in my hands, and I will bring him back to you." ³⁸But he said, "My son shall not go down with you, for his brother is dead, and he is the only one left. If harm should happen to him on the journey that you are to make, you would bring down my gray hairs with sorrow to Sheol."

Mark 12

And he began to speak to them in parables. "A man planted a vineyard and put a fence around it and dug a pit for the winepress and built a tower, and leased it to tenants and went into another country. ²When the season came, he sent a servant¹ to the tenants to get from them some of the fruit of the vineyard. ³And they took him and beat him and sent him away empty-handed. ⁴Again he sent to them another servant, and they struck him on the head and treated him shamefully. ⁵And he sent another, and him they killed. And so with many others: some they beat, and some they killed. ⁶He had still one other, a beloved son. Finally he sent him to them, saying, 'They will respect my son.' ⁷But those tenants said to one another, 'This is the heir. Come, let us kill him, and the inheritance will be ours.' ⁸And they took him and killed him and threw him out of the vineyard. ⁹What will the owner of the vineyard do? He will come and destroy the tenants and give the vineyard to others. ¹⁰Have you not read this Scripture:

" 'The stone that the builders rejected
    has become the cornerstone;²
¹¹ this was the Lord's doing,
    and it is marvelous in our eyes'?"

¹²And they were seeking to arrest him but feared the people, for they perceived that he had told the parable against them. So they left him and went away.

¹³And they sent to him some of the Pharisees and some of the Herodians, to trap him in his talk. ¹⁴And they came and said to him, "Teacher, we know that you are true and do not care about anyone's opinion. For you are not swayed by appearances,³ but truly teach the way of God. Is it lawful to pay taxes to Caesar, or not? Should we pay them, or should we not?" ¹⁵But, knowing their hypocrisy, he said to them, "Why put me to the test? Bring me a denarius⁴ and let me look at it." ¹⁶And they brought one. And he said to them, "Whose likeness and inscription is this?" They said to him, "Caesar's." ¹⁷Jesus said to them, "Render to Caesar the things that are Caesar's, and to God the things that are God's." And they marveled at him.

¹⁸And Sadducees came to him, who say that there is no resurrection. And they asked him a question, saying, ¹⁹"Teacher, Moses wrote for us that if a man's brother dies and leaves a wife, but leaves no child, the man⁵ must take the widow and raise up offspring for his brother. ²⁰There were seven brothers; the first took a wife, and when he died left no offspring. ²¹And the second took her, and died, leaving no offspring. And the third likewise. ²²And the seven left no offspring. Last of all the woman also died. ²³In the resurrection, when they rise again, whose wife will she be? For the seven had her as wife."

²⁴Jesus said to them, "Is this not the reason you are wrong, because you know neither the Scriptures nor the power of God? ²⁵For when they rise from the dead, they neither marry nor are given in marriage, but are like angels in heaven. ²⁶And as for the dead being raised, have you not read in the book of Moses, in the passage about the bush, how God spoke to him, saying, 'I am the God of Abraham, and the God of Isaac, and the God of Jacob'? ²⁷He is not God of the dead, but of the living. You are quite wrong."

¹ Greek bondservant; also verse 4 ² Greek the head of the corner ³ Greek you do not look at people's faces ⁴ A denarius was a day's wage for a laborer ⁵ Greek his brother

²⁸And one of the scribes came up and heard them disputing with one another, and seeing that he answered them well, asked him, "Which commandment is the most important of all?" ²⁹Jesus answered, "The most important is, 'Hear, O Israel: The Lord our God, the Lord is one. ³⁰And you shall love the Lord your God with all your heart and with all your soul and with all your mind and with all your strength.' ³¹The second is this: 'You shall love your neighbor as yourself.' There is no other commandment greater than these." ³²And the scribe said to him, "You are right, Teacher. You have truly said that he is one, and there is no other besides him. ³³And to love him with all the heart and with all the understanding and with all the strength, and to love one's neighbor as oneself, is much more than all whole burnt offerings and sacrifices." ³⁴And when Jesus saw that he answered wisely, he said to him, "You are not far from the kingdom of God." And after that no one dared to ask him any more questions.

³⁵And as Jesus taught in the temple, he said, "How can the scribes say that the Christ is the son of David? ³⁶David himself, in the Holy Spirit, declared,

"'The Lord said to my Lord,
"Sit at my right hand,
until I put your enemies under your
feet."'

³⁷David himself calls him Lord. So how is he his son?" And the great throng heard him gladly.

³⁸And in his teaching he said, "Beware of the scribes, who like to walk around in long robes and like greetings in the marketplaces ³⁹and have the best seats in the synagogues and the places of honor at feasts, ⁴⁰who devour widows' houses and for a pretense make long prayers. They will receive the greater condemnation."

⁴¹And he sat down opposite the treasury and watched the people putting money into the offering box. Many rich people put in large sums. ⁴²And a poor widow came and put in two small copper coins, which make a penny.[1] ⁴³And he called his disciples to him and said to them, "Truly, I say to you, this poor widow has put in more than all those who are contributing to the offering box. ⁴⁴For they all contributed out of their abundance, but she out of her poverty has put in everything she had, all she had to live on."

Job 8

Then Bildad the Shuhite answered and said:

2   "How long will you say these things,
    and the words of your mouth be a
      great wind?
3   Does God pervert justice?
    Or does the Almighty pervert the
      right?
4   If your children have sinned against him,
    he has delivered them into the hand of
      their transgression.
5   If you will seek God
    and plead with the Almighty for mercy,
6   if you are pure and upright,
    surely then he will rouse himself for
      you
    and restore your rightful habitation.
7   And though your beginning was small,
    your latter days will be very great.

8   "For inquire, please, of bygone ages,
    and consider what the fathers have
      searched out.
9   For we are but of yesterday and know
      nothing,
    for our days on earth are a shadow.
10   Will they not teach you and tell you
    and utter words out of their
      understanding?

11   "Can papyrus grow where there is no
      marsh?
    Can reeds flourish where there is no
      water?
12   While yet in flower and not cut down,
    they wither before any other plant.
13   Such are the paths of all who forget God;
    the hope of the godless shall perish.
14   His confidence is severed,
    and his trust is a spider's web.[2]
15   He leans against his house, but it does
      not stand;
    he lays hold of it, but it does not
      endure.
16   He is a lush plant before the sun,
    and his shoots spread over his garden.
17   His roots entwine the stone heap;
    he looks upon a house of stones.
18   If he is destroyed from his place,
    then it will deny him, saying, 'I have
      never seen you.'

[1] Greek two *lepta*, which make a *kodrantes*; a *kodrantes* (Latin *quadrans*) was a Roman copper coin worth about 1/64 of a *denarius* (which was a day's wage for a laborer)
[2] Hebrew *house*

¹⁹ Behold, this is the joy of his way,
   and out of the soil others will spring.

²⁰ "Behold, God will not reject a blameless man,
   nor take the hand of evildoers.

²¹ He will yet fill your mouth with laughter,
   and your lips with shouting.

²² Those who hate you will be clothed with shame,
   and the tent of the wicked will be no more."

--- *Romans 12* ---

I appeal to you therefore, brothers,[1] by the mercies of God, to present your bodies as a living sacrifice, holy and acceptable to God, which is your spiritual worship.[2] ²Do not be conformed to this world,[3] but be transformed by the renewal of your mind, that by testing you may discern what is the will of God, what is good and acceptable and perfect.[4]

³For by the grace given to me I say to everyone among you not to think of himself more highly than he ought to think, but to think with sober judgment, each according to the measure of faith that God has assigned. ⁴For as in one body we have many members,[5] and the members do not all have the same function, ⁵so we, though many, are one body in Christ, and individually members one of another.

⁶Having gifts that differ according to the grace given to us, let us use them: if prophecy, in proportion to our faith; ⁷if service, in our serving; the one who teaches, in his teaching; ⁸the one who exhorts, in his exhortation; the one who contributes, in generosity; the one who leads,[6] with zeal; the one who does acts of mercy, with cheerfulness.

⁹Let love be genuine. Abhor what is evil; hold fast to what is good. ¹⁰Love one another with brotherly affection. Outdo one another in showing honor. ¹¹Do not be slothful in zeal, be fervent in spirit,[7] serve the Lord. ¹²Rejoice in hope, be patient in tribulation, be constant in prayer. ¹³Contribute to the needs of the saints and seek to show hospitality.

¹⁴Bless those who persecute you; bless and do not curse them. ¹⁵Rejoice with those who rejoice, weep with those who weep. ¹⁶Live in harmony with one another. Do not be haughty, but associate with the lowly.[8] Never be wise in your own sight. ¹⁷Repay no one evil for evil, but give thought to do what is honorable in the sight of all. ¹⁸If possible, so far as it depends on you, live peaceably with all. ¹⁹Beloved, never avenge yourselves, but leave it[9] to the wrath of God, for it is written, "Vengeance is mine, I will repay, says the Lord." ²⁰To the contrary, "if your enemy is hungry, feed him; if he is thirsty, give him something to drink; for by so doing you will heap burning coals on his head." ²¹Do not be overcome by evil, but overcome evil with good.

FEBRUARY 10

--- *Genesis 43* ---

Now the famine was severe in the land. ²And when they had eaten the grain that they had brought from Egypt, their father said to them, "Go again, buy us a little food." ³But Judah said to him, "The man solemnly warned us, saying, 'You shall not see my face unless your brother is with you.' ⁴If you will send our brother with us, we will go down and buy you food. ⁵But if you will not send him, we will not go down, for the man said to us, 'You shall not see my face, unless your brother is with you.'" ⁶Israel said, "Why did you treat me so badly as to tell the man that you had another brother?" ⁷They replied, "The man questioned us carefully about ourselves and our kindred, saying, 'Is your father still alive? Do you have another brother?' What we told him was in answer to these questions. Could we in any way know that he would say, 'Bring your brother down'?" [8]And Judah said to Israel his father, "Send the boy with me, and we will arise and go, that we may live and not die, both we and you and also our little ones. [9]I will be a pledge of his safety. From my hand you shall require him. If I do not bring him back to you and set him before you, then let me bear the blame forever. [10]If we had not delayed, we would now have returned twice."

[11]Then their father Israel said to them, "If it must be so, then do this: take some of the choice fruits of the land in your bags, and carry a present down to the man, a little balm and a little honey, gum, myrrh, pistachio nuts, and almonds. [12]Take double the money with you. Carry back with you the money that was returned in the mouth of your sacks. Perhaps it was an oversight. [13]Take also your brother, and arise, go again to the man. [14]May God Almighty[1] grant you mercy before the man, and may he send back your other brother and Benjamin. And as for me, if I am bereaved of my children, I am bereaved."

[15]So the men took this present, and they took double the money with them, and Benjamin. They arose and went down to Egypt and stood before Joseph.

[16]When Joseph saw Benjamin with them, he said to the steward of his house, "Bring the men into the house, and slaughter an animal and make ready, for the men are to dine with me at noon." [17]The man did as Joseph told him and brought the men to Joseph's house. [18]And the men were afraid because they were brought to Joseph's house, and they said, "It is because of the money, which was replaced in our sacks the first time, that we are brought in, so that he may assault us and fall upon us to make us servants and seize our donkeys." [19]So they went up to the steward of Joseph's house and spoke with him at the door of the house, [20]and said, "Oh, my lord, we came down the first time to buy food. [21]And when we came to the lodging place we opened our sacks, and there was each man's money in the mouth of his sack, our money in full weight. So we have brought it again with us, [22]and we have brought other money down with us to buy food. We do not know who put our money in our sacks." [23]He replied, "Peace to

you, do not be afraid. Your God and the God of your father has put treasure in your sacks for you. I received your money." Then he brought Simeon out to them. [24]And when the man had brought the men into Joseph's house and given them water, and they had washed their feet, and when he had given their donkeys fodder, [25]they prepared the present for Joseph's coming at noon, for they heard that they should eat bread there.

[26]When Joseph came home, they brought into the house to him the present that they had with them and bowed down to him to the ground. [27]And he inquired about their welfare and said, "Is your father well, the old man of whom you spoke? Is he still alive?" [28]They said, "Your servant our father is well; he is still alive." And they bowed their heads and prostrated themselves. [29]And he lifted up his eyes and saw his brother Benjamin, his mother's son, and said, "Is this your youngest brother, of whom you spoke to me? God be gracious to you, my son!" [30]Then Joseph hurried out, for his compassion grew warm for his brother, and he sought a place to weep. And he entered his chamber and wept there. [31]Then he washed his face and came out. And controlling himself he said, "Serve the food." [32]They served him by himself, and them by themselves, and the Egyptians who ate with him by themselves, because the Egyptians could not eat with the Hebrews, for that is an abomination to the Egyptians. [33]And they sat before him, the firstborn according to his birthright and the youngest according to his youth. And the men looked at one another in amazement. [34]Portions were taken to them from Joseph's table, but Benjamin's portion was five times as much as any of theirs. And they drank and were merry[2] with him.

--- **Mark 13** ---

And as he came out of the temple, one of his disciples said to him, "Look, Teacher, what wonderful stones and what wonderful buildings!" [2]And Jesus said to him, "Do you see these great buildings? There will not be left here one stone upon another that will not be thrown down."

[3]And as he sat on the Mount of Olives opposite the temple, Peter and James and John and

[1] Hebrew *El Shaddai* [2] Hebrew *and became intoxicated*

Andrew asked him privately, ⁴ "Tell us, when will these things be, and what will be the sign when all these things are about to be accomplished?" ⁵ And Jesus began to say to them, "See that no one leads you astray. ⁶ Many will come in my name, saying, 'I am he!' and they will lead many astray. ⁷ And when you hear of wars and rumors of wars, do not be alarmed. This must take place, but the end is not yet. ⁸ For nation will rise against nation, and kingdom against kingdom. There will be earthquakes in various places; there will be famines. These are but the beginning of the birth pains.

⁹ "But be on your guard. For they will deliver you over to councils, and you will be beaten in synagogues, and you will stand before governors and kings for my sake, to bear witness before them. ¹⁰ And the gospel must first be proclaimed to all nations. ¹¹ And when they bring you to trial and deliver you over, do not be anxious beforehand what you are to say, but say whatever is given you in that hour, for it is not you who speak, but the Holy Spirit. ¹² And brother will deliver brother over to death, and the father his child, and children will rise against parents and have them put to death. ¹³ And you will be hated by all for my name's sake. But the one who endures to the end will be saved.

¹⁴ "But when you see the abomination of desolation standing where he ought not to be (let the reader understand), then let those who are in Judea flee to the mountains. ¹⁵ Let the one who is on the housetop not go down, nor enter his house, to take anything out, ¹⁶ and let the one who is in the field not turn back to take his cloak. ¹⁷ And alas for women who are pregnant and for those who are nursing infants in those days! ¹⁸ Pray that it may not happen in winter. ¹⁹ For in those days there will be such tribulation as has not been from the beginning of the creation that God created until now, and never will be. ²⁰ And if the Lord had not cut short the days, no human being would be saved. But for the sake of the elect, whom he chose, he shortened the days. ²¹ And then if anyone says to you, 'Look, here is the Christ!' or 'Look, there he is!' do not believe it. ²² For false christs and false prophets will arise and perform signs and wonders, to lead astray, if possible, the elect. ²³ But be on guard; I have told you all things beforehand.

²⁴ "But in those days, after that tribulation, the sun will be darkened, and the moon will not give its light, ²⁵ and the stars will be falling from heaven, and the powers in the heavens will be shaken. ²⁶ And then they will see the Son of Man coming in clouds with great power and glory. ²⁷ And then he will send out the angels and gather his elect from the four winds, from the ends of the earth to the ends of heaven.

²⁸ "From the fig tree learn its lesson: as soon as its branch becomes tender and puts out its leaves, you know that summer is near. ²⁹ So also, when you see these things taking place, you know that he is near, at the very gates. ³⁰ Truly, I say to you, this generation will not pass away until all these things take place. ³¹ Heaven and earth will pass away, but my words will not pass away.

³² "But concerning that day or that hour, no one knows, not even the angels in heaven, nor the Son, but only the Father. ³³ Be on guard, keep awake.¹ For you do not know when the time will come. ³⁴ It is like a man going on a journey, when he leaves home and puts his servants² in charge, each with his work, and commands the doorkeeper to stay awake. ³⁵ Therefore stay awake—for you do not know when the master of the house will come, in the evening, or at midnight, or when the rooster crows,³ or in the morning— ³⁶ lest he come suddenly and find you asleep. ³⁷ And what I say to you I say to all: Stay awake."

Job 9

Then Job answered and said:

2   "Truly I know that it is so:
       But how can a man be in the right
          before God?
3   If one wished to contend with him,
       one could not answer him once in a
          thousand times.
4   He is wise in heart and mighty in
          strength
       —who has hardened himself against
          him, and succeeded?—
5   he who removes mountains, and they
          know it not,
       when he overturns them in his anger,
6   who shakes the earth out of its place,
       and its pillars tremble;

¹ Some manuscripts add *and pray* ² Greek *bondservants* ³ That is, the third watch of the night, between midnight and 3 A.M.

7 who commands the sun, and it does not
   rise;
   who seals up the stars;
8 who alone stretched out the heavens
   and trampled the waves of the sea;
9 who made the Bear and Orion,
   the Pleiades and the chambers of the
   south;
10 who does great things beyond searching
   out,
   and marvelous things beyond
   number.
11 Behold, he passes by me, and I see him
   not;
   he moves on, but I do not perceive
   him.
12 Behold, he snatches away; who can turn
   him back?
   Who will say to him, 'What are you
   doing?'
13 "God will not turn back his anger;
   beneath him bowed the helpers of
   Rahab.
14 How then can I answer him,
   choosing my words with him?
15 Though I am in the right, I cannot
   answer him;
   I must appeal for mercy to my
   accuser.[1]
16 If I summoned him and he answered me,
   I would not believe that he was
   listening to my voice.
17 For he crushes me with a tempest
   and multiplies my wounds without
   cause;
18 he will not let me get my breath,
   but fills me with bitterness.
19 If it is a contest of strength, behold, he is
   mighty!
   If it is a matter of justice, who can
   summon him?[2]
20 Though I am in the right, my own
   mouth would condemn me;
   though I am blameless, he would
   prove me perverse.
21 I am blameless; I regard not myself;
   I loathe my life.
22 It is all one; therefore I say,
   'He destroys both the blameless and
   the wicked.'

23 When disaster brings sudden death,
   he mocks at the calamity[3] of the
   innocent.
24 The earth is given into the hand of the
   wicked;
   he covers the faces of its judges—
   if it is not he, who then is it?
25 "My days are swifter than a runner;
   they flee away; they see no good.
26 They go by like skiffs of reed,
   like an eagle swooping on the prey.
27 If I say, 'I will forget my complaint,
   I will put off my sad face, and be of
   good cheer,'
28 I become afraid of all my suffering,
   for I know you will not hold me
   innocent.
29 I shall be condemned;
   why then do I labor in vain?
30 If I wash myself with snow
   and cleanse my hands with lye,
31 yet you will plunge me into a pit,
   and my own clothes will abhor me.
32 For he is not a man, as I am, that I might
   answer him,
   that we should come to trial together.
33 There is no[4] arbiter between us,
   who might lay his hand on us both.
34 Let him take his rod away from me,
   and let not dread of him terrify me.
35 Then I would speak without fear of him,
   for I am not so in myself.

Romans 13

Let every person be subject to the governing authorities. For there is no authority except from God, and those that exist have been instituted by God. [2]Therefore whoever resists the authorities resists what God has appointed, and those who resist will incur judgment. [3]For rulers are not a terror to good conduct, but to bad. Would you have no fear of the one who is in authority? Then do what is good, and you will receive his approval, [4]for he is God's servant for your good. But if you do wrong, be afraid, for he does not bear the sword in vain. For he is the servant of God, an avenger who carries out God's wrath on the wrongdoer. [5]Therefore one must be in subjection, not only to avoid God's wrath but also for the sake of conscience.

[1] Or to my judge [2] Compare Septuagint; Hebrew me [3] The meaning of the Hebrew word is uncertain [4] Or Would that there were an

⁶For because of this you also pay taxes, for the authorities are ministers of God, attending to this very thing. ⁷Pay to all what is owed to them: taxes to whom taxes are owed, revenue to whom revenue is owed, respect to whom respect is owed, honor to whom honor is owed.

⁸Owe no one anything, except to love each other, for the one who loves another has fulfilled the law. ⁹For the commandments, "You shall not commit adultery, You shall not murder, You shall not steal, You shall not covet," and any other commandment, are summed up in this word: "You shall love your neighbor as yourself." ¹⁰Love does no wrong to a neighbor; therefore love is the fulfilling of the law.

¹¹Besides this you know the time, that the hour has come for you to wake from sleep. For salvation is nearer to us now than when we first believed. ¹²The night is far gone; the day is at hand. So then let us cast off the works of darkness and put on the armor of light. ¹³Let us walk properly as in the daytime, not in orgies and drunkenness, not in sexual immorality and sensuality, not in quarreling and jealousy. ¹⁴But put on the Lord Jesus Christ, and make no provision for the flesh, to gratify its desires.

FEBRUARY 11

Genesis 44

Then he commanded the steward of his house, "Fill the men's sacks with food, as much as they can carry, and put each man's money in the mouth of his sack, ²and put my cup, the silver cup, in the mouth of the sack of the youngest, with his money for the grain." And he did as Joseph told him.

³As soon as the morning was light, the men were sent away with their donkeys. ⁴They had gone only a short distance from the city. Now Joseph said to his steward, "Up, follow after the men, and when you overtake them, say to them, 'Why have you repaid evil for good?¹ ⁵Is it not from this that my lord drinks, and by this that he practices divination? You have done evil in doing this.'"

⁶When he overtook them, he spoke to them these words. ⁷They said to him, "Why does my lord speak such words as these? Far be it from your servants to do such a thing! ⁸Behold, the money that we found in the mouths of our sacks we brought back to you from the land of Canaan. How then could we steal silver or gold from your lord's house? ⁹Whichever of your servants is found with it shall die, and we also will be my lord's servants." ¹⁰He said, "Let it be as you say: he who is found with it shall be my servant, and the rest of you shall be innocent."

¹¹Then each man quickly lowered his sack to the ground, and each man opened his sack. ¹²And he searched, beginning with the eldest and ending with the youngest. And the cup was found in Benjamin's sack. ¹³Then they tore their clothes, and every man loaded his donkey, and they returned to the city.

¹⁴When Judah and his brothers came to Joseph's house, he was still there. They fell before him to the ground. ¹⁵Joseph said to them, "What deed is this that you have done? Do you not know that a man like me can indeed practice divination?" ¹⁶And Judah said, "What shall we say to my lord? What shall we speak? Or how can we clear ourselves? God has found out the guilt of your servants; behold, we are my lord's servants, both we and he also in whose hand the cup has been found." ¹⁷But he said, "Far be it from me that I should do so! Only the man in whose hand the cup was found shall be my servant. But as for you, go up in peace to your father."

¹⁸Then Judah went up to him and said, "Oh, my lord, please let your servant speak a word in my lord's ears, and let not your anger burn against your servant, for you are like Pharaoh himself. ¹⁹My lord asked his servants, saying, 'Have you a father, or a brother?' ²⁰And we said

¹ Septuagint (compare Vulgate) adds *Why have you stolen my silver cup?*

to my lord, 'We have a father, an old man, and a young brother, the child of his old age. His brother is dead, and he alone is left of his mother's children, and his father loves him.' [21]Then you said to your servants, 'Bring him down to me, that I may set my eyes on him.' [22]We said to my lord, 'The boy cannot leave his father, for if he should leave his father, his father would die.' [23]Then you said to your servants, 'Unless your youngest brother comes down with you, you shall not see my face again.'

[24]"When we went back to your servant my father, we told him the words of my lord. [25]And when our father said, 'Go again, buy us a little food,' [26]we said, 'We cannot go down. If our youngest brother goes with us, then we will go down. For we cannot see the man's face unless our youngest brother is with us.' [27]Then your servant my father said to us, 'You know that my wife bore me two sons. [28]One left me, and I said, "Surely he has been torn to pieces," and I have never seen him since. [29]If you take this one also from me, and harm happens to him, you will bring down my gray hairs in evil to Sheol.'

[30]"Now therefore, as soon as I come to your servant my father, and the boy is not with us, then, as his life is bound up in the boy's life, [31]as soon as he sees that the boy is not with us, he will die, and your servants will bring down the gray hairs of your servant our father with sorrow to Sheol. [32]For your servant became a pledge of safety for the boy to my father, saying, 'If I do not bring him back to you, then I shall bear the blame before my father all my life.' [33]Now therefore, please let your servant remain instead of the boy as a servant to my lord, and let the boy go back with his brothers. [34]For how can I go back to my father if the boy is not with me? I fear to see the evil that would find my father."

Mark 14

It was now two days before the Passover and the Feast of Unleavened Bread. And the chief priests and the scribes were seeking how to arrest him by stealth and kill him, [2]for they said, "Not during the feast, lest there be an uproar from the people."

[3]And while he was at Bethany in the house of Simon the leper,[1] as he was reclining at table, a woman came with an alabaster flask of ointment of pure nard, very costly, and she broke the flask and poured it over his head. [4]There were some who said to themselves indignantly, "Why was the ointment wasted like that? [5]For this ointment could have been sold for more than three hundred denarii[2] and given to the poor." And they scolded her. [6]But Jesus said, "Leave her alone. Why do you trouble her? She has done a beautiful thing to me. [7]For you always have the poor with you, and whenever you want, you can do good for them. But you will not always have me. [8]She has done what she could; she has anointed my body beforehand for burial. [9]And truly, I say to you, wherever the gospel is proclaimed in the whole world, what she has done will be told in memory of her."

[10]Then Judas Iscariot, who was one of the twelve, went to the chief priests in order to betray him to them. [11]And when they heard it, they were glad and promised to give him money. And he sought an opportunity to betray him.

[12]And on the first day of Unleavened Bread, when they sacrificed the Passover lamb, his disciples said to him, "Where will you have us go and prepare for you to eat the Passover?" [13]And he sent two of his disciples and said to them, "Go into the city, and a man carrying a jar of water will meet you. Follow him, [14]and wherever he enters, say to the master of the house, 'The Teacher says, Where is my guest room, where I may eat the Passover with my disciples?' [15]And he will show you a large upper room furnished and ready; there prepare for us." [16]And the disciples set out and went to the city and found it just as he had told them, and they prepared the Passover.

[17]And when it was evening, he came with the twelve. [18]And as they were reclining at table and eating, Jesus said, "Truly, I say to you, one of you will betray me, one who is eating with me." [19]They began to be sorrowful and to say to him one after another, "Is it I?" [20]He said to them, "It is one of the twelve, one who is dipping bread into the dish with me. [21]For the Son of Man goes as it is written of him, but woe to that man by whom the Son of Man is betrayed! It would have been better for that man if he had not been born."

[22]And as they were eating, he took bread, and after blessing it broke it and gave it to them, and said, "Take; this is my body." [23]And he took a

---

[1] Leprosy was a term for several skin diseases; see Leviticus 13 [2] A denarius was a day's wage for a laborer

cup, and when he had given thanks he gave it to them, and they all drank of it. ²⁴And he said to them, "This is my blood of the¹ covenant, which is poured out for many. ²⁵Truly, I say to you, I will not drink again of the fruit of the vine until that day when I drink it new in the kingdom of God."

²⁶And when they had sung a hymn, they went out to the Mount of Olives. ²⁷And Jesus said to them, "You will all fall away, for it is written, 'I will strike the shepherd, and the sheep will be scattered.' ²⁸But after I am raised up, I will go before you to Galilee." ²⁹Peter said to him, "Even though they all fall away, I will not." ³⁰And Jesus said to him, "Truly, I tell you, this very night, before the rooster crows twice, you will deny me three times." ³¹But he said emphatically, "If I must die with you, I will not deny you." And they all said the same.

³²And they went to a place called Gethsemane. And he said to his disciples, "Sit here while I pray." ³³And he took with him Peter and James and John, and began to be greatly distressed and troubled. ³⁴And he said to them, "My soul is very sorrowful, even to death. Remain here and watch."² ³⁵And going a little farther, he fell on the ground and prayed that, if it were possible, the hour might pass from him. ³⁶And he said, "Abba, Father, all things are possible for you. Remove this cup from me. Yet not what I will, but what you will." ³⁷And he came and found them sleeping, and he said to Peter, "Simon, are you asleep? Could you not watch one hour? ³⁸Watch and pray that you may not enter into temptation. The spirit indeed is willing, but the flesh is weak." ³⁹And again he went away and prayed, saying the same words. ⁴⁰And again he came and found them sleeping, for their eyes were very heavy, and they did not know what to answer him. ⁴¹And he came the third time and said to them, "Are you still sleeping and taking your rest? It is enough; the hour has come. The Son of Man is betrayed into the hands of sinners. ⁴²Rise, let us be going; see, my betrayer is at hand."

⁴³And immediately, while he was still speaking, Judas came, one of the twelve, and with him a crowd with swords and clubs, from the chief priests and the scribes and the elders. ⁴⁴Now the betrayer had given them a sign, saying, "The one I will kiss is the man. Seize him and lead him away under guard." ⁴⁵And when he came, he went up to him at once and said, "Rabbi!" And he kissed him. ⁴⁶And they laid hands on him and seized him. ⁴⁷But one of those who stood by drew his sword and struck the servant³ of the high priest and cut off his ear. ⁴⁸And Jesus said to them, "Have you come out as against a robber, with swords and clubs to capture me? ⁴⁹Day after day I was with you in the temple teaching, and you did not seize me. But let the Scriptures be fulfilled." ⁵⁰And they all left him and fled.

⁵¹And a young man followed him, with nothing but a linen cloth about his body. And they seized him, ⁵²but he left the linen cloth and ran away naked.

⁵³And they led Jesus to the high priest. And all the chief priests and the elders and the scribes came together. ⁵⁴And Peter had followed him at a distance, right into the courtyard of the high priest. And he was sitting with the guards and warming himself at the fire. ⁵⁵Now the chief priests and the whole council⁴ were seeking testimony against Jesus to put him to death, but they found none. ⁵⁶For many bore false witness against him, but their testimony did not agree. ⁵⁷And some stood up and bore false witness against him, saying, ⁵⁸"We heard him say, 'I will destroy this temple that is made with hands, and in three days I will build another, not made with hands.'" ⁵⁹Yet even about this their testimony did not agree. ⁶⁰And the high priest stood up in the midst and asked Jesus, "Have you no answer to make? What is it that these men testify against you?"⁵ ⁶¹But he remained silent and made no answer. Again the high priest asked him, "Are you the Christ, the Son of the Blessed?" ⁶²And Jesus said, "I am, and you will see the Son of Man seated at the right hand of Power, and coming with the clouds of heaven." ⁶³And the high priest tore his garments and said, "What further witnesses do we need? ⁶⁴You have heard his blasphemy. What is your decision?" And they all condemned him as deserving death. ⁶⁵And some began to spit on him and to cover his face and to strike him, saying to him, "Prophesy!" And the guards received him with blows.

⁶⁶And as Peter was below in the courtyard, one of the servant girls of the high priest came, ⁶⁷and seeing Peter warming himself, she looked at him and said, "You also were with the Nazarene, Jesus." ⁶⁸But he denied it,

¹ Some manuscripts insert new ² Or keep awake; also verses 37, 38 ³ Greek bondservant ⁴ Greek Sanhedrin ⁵ Or Have you no answer to what these men testify against you?

saying, "I neither know nor understand what you mean." And he went out into the gateway[1] and the rooster crowed.[2] [69]And the servant girl saw him and began again to say to the bystanders, "This man is one of them." [70]But again he denied it. And after a little while the bystanders again said to Peter, "Certainly you are one of them, for you are a Galilean." [71]But he began to invoke a curse on himself and to swear, "I do not know this man of whom you speak." [72]And immediately the rooster crowed a second time. And Peter remembered how Jesus had said to him, "Before the rooster crows twice, you will deny me three times." And he broke down and wept.[3]

------------------ *Job 10* ------------------

"I loathe my life;
I will give free utterance to my
complaint;
I will speak in the bitterness of my
soul.
[2] I will say to God, Do not condemn me;
let me know why you contend against
me.
[3] Does it seem good to you to oppress,
to despise the work of your hands
and favor the designs of the wicked?
[4] Have you eyes of flesh?
Do you see as man sees?
[5] Are your days as the days of man,
or your years as a man's years,
[6] that you seek out my iniquity
and search for my sin,
[7] although you know that I am not guilty,
and there is none to deliver out of
your hand?
[8] Your hands fashioned and made me,
and now you have destroyed me
altogether.
[9] Remember that you have made me like
clay;
and will you return me to the dust?
[10] Did you not pour me out like milk
and curdle me like cheese?
[11] You clothed me with skin and flesh,
and knit me together with bones and
sinews.
[12] You have granted me life and steadfast
love,
and your care has preserved my spirit.

[13] Yet these things you hid in your heart;
I know that this was your purpose.
[14] If I sin, you watch me
and do not acquit me of my iniquity.
[15] If I am guilty, woe to me!
If I am in the right, I cannot lift up my
head,
for I am filled with disgrace
and look on my affliction.
[16] And were my head lifted up,[4] you would
hunt me like a lion
and again work wonders against me.
[17] You renew your witnesses against me
and increase your vexation toward
me;
you bring fresh troops against me.
[18] "Why did you bring me out from the
womb?
Would that I had died before any eye
had seen me
[19] and were as though I had not been,
carried from the womb to the grave.
[20] Are not my days few?
Then cease, and leave me alone, that I
may find a little cheer
[21] before I go—and I shall not return—
to the land of darkness and deep
shadow,
[22] the land of gloom like thick darkness,
like deep shadow without any order,
where light is as thick darkness."

------------------ *Romans 14* ------------------

As for the one who is weak in faith, welcome him, but not to quarrel over opinions. [2]One person believes he may eat anything, while the weak person eats only vegetables. [3]Let not the one who eats despise the one who abstains, and let not the one who abstains pass judgment on the one who eats, for God has welcomed him. [4]Who are you to pass judgment on the servant of another? It is before his own master[5] that he stands or falls. And he will be upheld, for the Lord is able to make him stand.

[5]One person esteems one day as better than another, while another esteems all days alike. Each one should be fully convinced in his own mind. [6]The one who observes the day, observes it in honor of the Lord. The one who eats, eats

------

[1] Or forecourt [2] Some manuscripts omit *and the rooster crowed* [3] Or *And when he had thought about it, he wept* [4] Hebrew lacks *my head* [5] Or *lord*

in honor of the Lord, since he gives thanks to God, while the one who abstains, abstains in honor of the Lord and gives thanks to God. [7] For none of us lives to himself, and none of us dies to himself. [8] For if we live, we live to the Lord, and if we die, we die to the Lord. So then, whether we live or whether we die, we are the Lord's. [9] For to this end Christ died and lived again, that he might be Lord both of the dead and of the living.

[10] Why do you pass judgment on your brother? Or you, why do you despise your brother? For we will all stand before the judgment seat of God; [11] for it is written,

> "As I live, says the Lord, every knee shall
>   bow to me,
> and every tongue shall confess[1] to
>   God."

[12] So then each of us will give an account of himself to God.

[13] Therefore let us not pass judgment on one another any longer, but rather decide never to put a stumbling block or hindrance in the way of a brother. [14] I know and am persuaded in the Lord Jesus that nothing is unclean in itself, but it is unclean for anyone who thinks it unclean. [15] For if your brother is grieved by what you eat, you are no longer walking in love. By what you eat, do not destroy the one for whom Christ died. [16] So do not let what you regard as good be spoken of as evil. [17] For the kingdom of God is not a matter of eating and drinking but of righteousness and peace and joy in the Holy Spirit. [18] Whoever thus serves Christ is acceptable to God and approved by men. [19] So then let us pursue what makes for peace and for mutual upbuilding.

[20] Do not, for the sake of food, destroy the work of God. Everything is indeed clean, but it is wrong for anyone to make another stumble by what he eats. [21] It is good not to eat meat or drink wine or do anything that causes your brother to stumble.[2] [22] The faith that you have, keep between yourself and God. Blessed is the one who has no reason to pass judgment on himself for what he approves. [23] But whoever has doubts is condemned if he eats, because the eating is not from faith. For whatever does not proceed from faith is sin.[3]

FEBRUARY 12

Genesis 45

Then Joseph could not control himself before all those who stood by him. He cried, "Make everyone go out from me." So no one stayed with him when Joseph made himself known to his brothers. [2] And he wept aloud, so that the Egyptians heard it, and the household of Pharaoh heard it. [3] And Joseph said to his brothers, "I am Joseph! Is my father still alive?" But his brothers could not answer him, for they were dismayed at his presence.

[4] So Joseph said to his brothers, "Come near to me, please." And they came near. And he said, "I am your brother, Joseph, whom you sold into Egypt. [5] And now do not be distressed or angry with yourselves because you sold me here, for God sent me before you to preserve life. [6] For the famine has been in the land these two years, and there are yet five years in which there will be neither plowing nor harvest. [7] And God sent me before you to preserve for you a remnant on earth, and to keep alive for you many survivors. [8] So it was not you who sent me here, but God. He has made me a father to Pharaoh, and lord of all his house and ruler over all the land of Egypt. [9] Hurry and go up to my father and say to him, 'Thus says your son Joseph, God has made me lord of all Egypt. Come down to me; do not tarry. [10] You shall dwell in the land of Goshen, and you shall be near me, you and your children and your children's children, and your flocks, your herds, and all that you have. [11] There I

---

[1] Or *shall give praise* [2] Some manuscripts add *or be hindered or be weakened* [3] Some manuscripts insert here 16:25–27

will provide for you, for there are yet five years of famine to come, so that you and your household, and all that you have, do not come to poverty.' [12]And now your eyes see, and the eyes of my brother Benjamin see, that it is my mouth that speaks to you. [13]You must tell my father of all my honor in Egypt, and of all that you have seen. Hurry and bring my father down here." [14]Then he fell upon his brother Benjamin's neck and wept, and Benjamin wept upon his neck. [15]And he kissed all his brothers and wept upon them. After that his brothers talked with him.

[16]When the report was heard in Pharaoh's house, "Joseph's brothers have come," it pleased Pharaoh and his servants. [17]And Pharaoh said to Joseph, "Say to your brothers, 'Do this: load your beasts and go back to the land of Canaan, [18]and take your father and your households, and come to me, and I will give you the best of the land of Egypt, and you shall eat the fat of the land.' [19]And you, Joseph, are commanded to say, 'Do this: take wagons from the land of Egypt for your little ones and for your wives, and bring your father, and come. [20]Have no concern for[1] your goods, for the best of all the land of Egypt is yours.'"

[21]The sons of Israel did so: and Joseph gave them wagons, according to the command of Pharaoh, and gave them provisions for the journey. [22]To each and all of them he gave a change of clothes, but to Benjamin he gave three hundred shekels[2] of silver and five changes of clothes. [23]To his father he sent as follows: ten donkeys loaded with the good things of Egypt, and ten female donkeys loaded with grain, bread, and provision for his father on the journey. [24]Then he sent his brothers away, and as they departed, he said to them, "Do not quarrel on the way."

[25]So they went up out of Egypt and came to the land of Canaan to their father Jacob. [26]And they told him, "Joseph is still alive, and he is ruler over all the land of Egypt." And his heart became numb, for he did not believe them. [27]But when they told him all the words of Joseph, which he had said to them, and when he saw the wagons that Joseph had sent to carry him, the spirit of their father Jacob revived. [28]And Israel said, "It is enough; Joseph my son is still alive. I will go and see him before I die."

Mark 15

And as soon as it was morning, the chief priests held a consultation with the elders and scribes and the whole council. And they bound Jesus and led him away and delivered him over to Pilate. [2]And Pilate asked him, "Are you the King of the Jews?" And he answered him, "You have said so." [3]And the chief priests accused him of many things. [4]And Pilate again asked him, "Have you no answer to make? See how many charges they bring against you." [5]But Jesus made no further answer, so that Pilate was amazed.

[6]Now at the feast he used to release for them one prisoner for whom they asked. [7]And among the rebels in prison, who had committed murder in the insurrection, there was a man called Barabbas. [8]And the crowd came up and began to ask Pilate to do as he usually did for them. [9]And he answered them, saying, "Do you want me to release for you the King of the Jews?" [10]For he perceived that it was out of envy that the chief priests had delivered him up. [11]But the chief priests stirred up the crowd to have him release for them Barabbas instead. [12]And Pilate again said to them, "Then what shall I do with the man you call the King of the Jews?" [13]And they cried out again, "Crucify him." [14]And Pilate said to them, "Why, what evil has he done?" But they shouted all the more, "Crucify him." [15]So Pilate, wishing to satisfy the crowd, released for them Barabbas, and having scourged[3] Jesus, he delivered him to be crucified.

[16]And the soldiers led him away inside the palace (that is, the governor's headquarters),[4] and they called together the whole battalion.[5] [17]And they clothed him in a purple cloak, and twisting together a crown of thorns, they put it on him. [18]And they began to salute him, "Hail, King of the Jews!" [19]And they were striking his head with a reed and spitting on him and kneeling down in homage to him. [20]And when they had mocked him, they stripped him of the purple cloak and put his own clothes on him. And they led him out to crucify him.

[21]And they compelled a passerby, Simon of Cyrene, who was coming in from the country, the father of Alexander and Rufus, to carry his cross. [22]And they brought him to the place called Golgotha (which means Place of

[1] Hebrew Let your eye not pity [2] A shekel was about 2/5 ounce or 11 grams [3] A Roman judicial penalty, consisting of a severe beating with a multi-lashed whip containing imbedded pieces of bone and metal [4] Greek the praetorium [5] Greek cohort; a tenth of a Roman legion, usually about 600 men

a Skull). ²³And they offered him wine mixed with myrrh, but he did not take it. ²⁴And they crucified him and divided his garments among them, casting lots for them, to decide what each should take. ²⁵And it was the third hour[1] when they crucified him. ²⁶And the inscription of the charge against him read, "The King of the Jews." ²⁷And with him they crucified two robbers, one on his right and one on his left.[2] ²⁹And those who passed by derided him, wagging their heads and saying, "Aha! You who would destroy the temple and rebuild it in three days, ³⁰save yourself, and come down from the cross!" ³¹So also the chief priests with the scribes mocked him to one another, saying, "He saved others; he cannot save himself. ³²Let the Christ, the King of Israel, come down now from the cross that we may see and believe." Those who were crucified with him also reviled him.

³³And when the sixth hour[3] had come, there was darkness over the whole land until the ninth hour.[4] ³⁴And at the ninth hour Jesus cried with a loud voice, "Eloi, Eloi, lema sabachthani?" which means, "My God, my God, why have you forsaken me?" ³⁵And some of the bystanders hearing it said, "Behold, he is calling Elijah." ³⁶And someone ran and filled a sponge with sour wine, put it on a reed and gave it to him to drink, saying, "Wait, let us see whether Elijah will come to take him down." ³⁷And Jesus uttered a loud cry and breathed his last. ³⁸And the curtain of the temple was torn in two, from top to bottom. ³⁹And when the centurion, who stood facing him, saw that in this way he[5] breathed his last, he said, "Truly this man was the Son[6] of God!"

⁴⁰There were also women looking on from a distance, among whom were Mary Magdalene, and Mary the mother of James the younger and of Joses, and Salome. ⁴¹When he was in Galilee, they followed him and ministered to him, and there were also many other women who came up with him to Jerusalem.

⁴²And when evening had come, since it was the day of Preparation, that is, the day before the Sabbath, ⁴³Joseph of Arimathea, a respected member of the council, who was also himself looking for the kingdom of God, took courage and went to Pilate and asked for the body of Jesus. ⁴⁴Pilate was surprised to hear that he should have already died.[7] And summoning the centurion, he asked him whether he was already dead. ⁴⁵And when he learned from the centurion that he was dead, he granted the corpse to Joseph. ⁴⁶And Joseph[8] bought a linen shroud, and taking him down, wrapped him in the linen shroud and laid him in a tomb that had been cut out of the rock. And he rolled a stone against the entrance of the tomb. ⁴⁷Mary Magdalene and Mary the mother of Joses saw where he was laid.

Job 11

Then Zophar the Naamathite answered and said:

² "Should a multitude of words go
    unanswered,
       and a man full of talk be judged right?
³ Should your babble silence men,
    and when you mock, shall no one
       shame you?
⁴ For you say, 'My doctrine is pure,
    and I am clean in God's[9] eyes.'
⁵ But oh, that God would speak
    and open his lips to you,
⁶ and that he would tell you the secrets of
    wisdom!
    For he is manifold in understanding.[10]
Know then that God exacts of you less
    than your guilt deserves.

⁷ "Can you find out the deep things of God?
    Can you find out the limit of the
       Almighty?
⁸ It is higher than heaven[11]—what can
    you do?
    Deeper than Sheol—what can you
       know?
⁹ Its measure is longer than the earth
    and broader than the sea.
¹⁰ If he passes through and imprisons
    and summons the court, who can turn
       him back?
¹¹ For he knows worthless men;
    when he sees iniquity, will he not
       consider it?
¹² But a stupid man will get understanding
    when a wild donkey's colt is born a
       man!

¹³ "If you prepare your heart,
    you will stretch out your hands
       toward him.

---

¹ That is, 9 A.M. ² Some manuscripts insert verse 28: *And the Scripture was fulfilled that says, "He was numbered with the transgressors"* ³ That is, noon ⁴ That is, 3 P.M. ⁵ Some manuscripts insert *cried out and* ⁶ Or *a son* ⁷ Or *Pilate wondered whether he had already died* ⁸ Greek *he* ⁹ Hebrew *your* ¹⁰ The meaning of the Hebrew is uncertain ¹¹ Hebrew *The heights of heaven*

14 If iniquity is in your hand, put it far away,
and let not injustice dwell in your
tents.
15 Surely then you will lift up your face
without blemish;
you will be secure and will not fear.
16 You will forget your misery;
you will remember it as waters that
have passed away.
17 And your life will be brighter than the
noonday;
its darkness will be like the morning.
18 And you will feel secure, because there
is hope;
you will look around and take your
rest in security.
19 You will lie down, and none will make
you afraid;
many will court your favor.
20 But the eyes of the wicked will fail;
all way of escape will be lost to them,
and their hope is to breathe their last."

Romans 15

We who are strong have an obligation to bear with the failings of the weak, and not to please ourselves. [2] Let each of us please his neighbor for his good, to build him up. [3] For Christ did not please himself, but as it is written, "The reproaches of those who reproached you fell on me." [4] For whatever was written in former days was written for our instruction, that through endurance and through the encouragement of the Scriptures we might have hope. [5] May the God of endurance and encouragement grant you to live in such harmony with one another, in accord with Christ Jesus, [6] that together you may with one voice glorify the God and Father of our Lord Jesus Christ. [7] Therefore welcome one another as Christ has welcomed you, for the glory of God.

[8] For I tell you that Christ became a servant to the circumcised to show God's truthfulness, in order to confirm the promises given to the patriarchs, [9] and in order that the Gentiles might glorify God for his mercy. As it is written,

"Therefore I will praise you among the
Gentiles,
and sing to your name."

[10] And again it is said,

"Rejoice, O Gentiles, with his people."

[11] And again,

"Praise the Lord, all you Gentiles,
and let all the peoples extol him."

[12] And again Isaiah says,

"The root of Jesse will come,
even he who arises to rule the
Gentiles;
in him will the Gentiles hope."

[13] May the God of hope fill you with all joy and peace in believing, so that by the power of the Holy Spirit you may abound in hope.

[14] I myself am satisfied about you, my brothers,[1] that you yourselves are full of goodness, filled with all knowledge and able to instruct one another. [15] But on some points I have written to you very boldly by way of reminder, because of the grace given me by God [16] to be a minister of Christ Jesus to the Gentiles in the priestly service of the gospel of God, so that the offering of the Gentiles may be acceptable, sanctified by the Holy Spirit. [17] In Christ Jesus, then, I have reason to be proud of my work for God. [18] For I will not venture to speak of anything except what Christ has accomplished through me to bring the Gentiles to obedience—by word and deed, [19] by the power of signs and wonders, by the power of the Spirit of God—so that from Jerusalem and all the way around to Illyricum I have fulfilled the ministry of the gospel of Christ; [20] and thus I make it my ambition to preach the gospel, not where Christ has already been named, lest I build on someone else's foundation, [21] but as it is written,

"Those who have never been told of him
will see,
and those who have never heard will
understand."

[22] This is the reason why I have so often been hindered from coming to you. [23] But now, since I no longer have any room for work in these regions, and since I have longed for many years to come to you, [24] I hope to see you in passing as I go to Spain, and to be helped on my journey there by you, once I have enjoyed your company for a while. [25] At present, however,

[1] Or brothers and sisters; also verse 30

I am going to Jerusalem bringing aid to the saints. ²⁶For Macedonia and Achaia have been pleased to make some contribution for the poor among the saints at Jerusalem. ²⁷For they were pleased to do it, and indeed they owe it to them. For if the Gentiles have come to share in their spiritual blessings, they ought also to be of service to them in material blessings. ²⁸When therefore I have completed this and have delivered to them what has been collected,[1] I will leave for Spain by way of you.

²⁹I know that when I come to you I will come in the fullness of the blessing[2] of Christ.

³⁰I appeal to you, brothers, by our Lord Jesus Christ and by the love of the Spirit, to strive together with me in your prayers to God on my behalf, ³¹that I may be delivered from the unbelievers in Judea, and that my service for Jerusalem may be acceptable to the saints, ³²so that by God's will I may come to you with joy and be refreshed in your company. ³³May the God of peace be with you all. Amen.

FEBRUARY 13

Genesis 46

So Israel took his journey with all that he had and came to Beersheba, and offered sacrifices to the God of his father Isaac. ²And God spoke to Israel in visions of the night and said, "Jacob, Jacob." And he said, "Here I am." ³Then he said, "I am God, the God of your father. Do not be afraid to go down to Egypt, for there I will make you into a great nation. ⁴I myself will go down with you to Egypt, and I will also bring you up again, and Joseph's hand shall close your eyes."

⁵Then Jacob set out from Beersheba. The sons of Israel carried Jacob their father, their little ones, and their wives, in the wagons that Pharaoh had sent to carry him. ⁶They also took their livestock and their goods, which they had gained in the land of Canaan, and came into Egypt, Jacob and all his offspring with him, ⁷his sons, and his sons' sons with him, his daughters, and his sons' daughters. All his offspring he brought with him into Egypt.

⁸Now these are the names of the descendants of Israel, who came into Egypt, Jacob and his sons. Reuben, Jacob's firstborn, ⁹and the sons of Reuben: Hanoch, Pallu, Hezron, and Carmi. ¹⁰The sons of Simeon: Jemuel, Jamin, Ohad, Jachin, Zohar, and Shaul, the son of a Canaanite woman. ¹¹The sons of Levi: Gershon, Kohath, and Merari. ¹²The sons of Judah: Er, Onan, Shelah, Perez, and Zerah (but Er and Onan died in the land of Canaan); and the sons of Perez were Hezron and Hamul. ¹³The sons of Issachar: Tola, Puvah, Yob, and Shimron. ¹⁴The sons of Zebulun: Sered, Elon, and Jahleel. ¹⁵These are the sons of Leah, whom she bore to Jacob in Paddan-aram, together with his daughter Dinah; altogether his sons and his daughters numbered thirty-three.

¹⁶The sons of Gad: Ziphion, Haggi, Shuni, Ezbon, Eri, Arodi, and Areli. ¹⁷The sons of Asher: Imnah, Ishvah, Ishvi, Beriah, with Serah their sister. And the sons of Beriah: Heber and Malchiel. ¹⁸These are the sons of Zilpah, whom Laban gave to Leah his daughter; and these she bore to Jacob—sixteen persons.

¹⁹The sons of Rachel, Jacob's wife: Joseph and Benjamin. ²⁰And to Joseph in the land of Egypt were born Manasseh and Ephraim, whom Asenath, the daughter of Potiphera the priest of On, bore to him. ²¹And the sons of Benjamin: Bela, Becher, Ashbel, Gera, Naaman, Ehi, Rosh, Muppim, Huppim, and Ard. ²²These are the sons of Rachel, who were born to Jacob—fourteen persons in all.

²³The son[3] of Dan: Hushim. ²⁴The sons of Naphtali: Jahzeel, Guni, Jezer, and Shillem. ²⁵These are the sons of Bilhah, whom Laban gave to Rachel his daughter, and these she bore to Jacob—seven persons in all.

[1] Greek *sealed to them this fruit*   [2] Some manuscripts insert *of the gospel*   [3] Hebrew *sons*

²⁶All the persons belonging to Jacob who came into Egypt, who were his own descendants, not including Jacob's sons' wives, were sixty-six persons in all. ²⁷And the sons of Joseph, who were born to him in Egypt, were two. All the persons of the house of Jacob who came into Egypt were seventy.

²⁸He had sent Judah ahead of him to Joseph to show the way before him in Goshen, and they came into the land of Goshen. ²⁹Then Joseph prepared his chariot and went up to meet Israel his father in Goshen. He presented himself to him and fell on his neck and wept on his neck a good while. ³⁰Israel said to Joseph, "Now let me die, since I have seen your face and know that you are still alive." ³¹Joseph said to his brothers and to his father's household, "I will go up and tell Pharaoh and will say to him, 'My brothers and my father's household, who were in the land of Canaan, have come to me. ³²And the men are shepherds, for they have been keepers of livestock, and they have brought their flocks and their herds and all that they have.' ³³When Pharaoh calls you and says, 'What is your occupation?' ³⁴you shall say, 'Your servants have been keepers of livestock from our youth even until now, both we and our fathers,' in order that you may dwell in the land of Goshen, for every shepherd is an abomination to the Egyptians."

Mark 16

When the Sabbath was past, Mary Magdalene, Mary the mother of James, and Salome bought spices, so that they might go and anoint him. ²And very early on the first day of the week, when the sun had risen, they went to the tomb. ³And they were saying to one another, "Who will roll away the stone for us from the entrance of the tomb?" ⁴And looking up, they saw that the stone had been rolled back—it was very large. ⁵And entering the tomb, they saw a young man sitting on the right side, dressed in a white robe, and they were alarmed. ⁶And he said to them, "Do not be alarmed. You seek Jesus of Nazareth, who was crucified. He has risen; he is not here. See the place where they laid him. ⁷But go, tell his disciples and Peter that he is going before you to Galilee. There you will see him, just as he

told you." ⁸And they went out and fled from the tomb, for trembling and astonishment had seized them, and they said nothing to anyone, for they were afraid.

[SOME OF THE EARLIEST MANUSCRIPTS
DO NOT INCLUDE 16:9–20.][1]

⁹[[Now when he rose early on the first day of the week, he appeared first to Mary Magdalene, from whom he had cast out seven demons. ¹⁰She went and told those who had been with him, as they mourned and wept. ¹¹But when they heard that he was alive and had been seen by her, they would not believe it.

¹²After these things he appeared in another form to two of them, as they were walking into the country. ¹³And they went back and told the rest, but they did not believe them.

¹⁴Afterward he appeared to the eleven themselves as they were reclining at table, and he rebuked them for their unbelief and hardness of heart, because they had not believed those who saw him after he had risen. ¹⁵And he said to them, "Go into all the world and proclaim the gospel to the whole creation. ¹⁶Whoever believes and is baptized will be saved, but whoever does not believe will be condemned. ¹⁷And these signs will accompany those who believe: in my name they will cast out demons; they will speak in new tongues; ¹⁸they will pick up serpents with their hands; and if they drink any deadly poison, it will not hurt them; they will lay their hands on the sick, and they will recover."

¹⁹So then the Lord Jesus, after he had spoken to them, was taken up into heaven and sat down at the right hand of God. ²⁰And they went out and preached everywhere, while the Lord worked with them and confirmed the message by accompanying signs.]]

Job 12

Then Job answered and said:

²　"No doubt you are the people,
　　and wisdom will die with you.
³　But I have understanding as well as
　　　you;
　　I am not inferior to you.
　　Who does not know such things as
　　　these?

[1] Some manuscripts end the book with 16:8; others include verses 9–20 immediately after verse 8. At least one manuscript inserts additional material after verse 14; some manuscripts include after verse 8 the following: *But they reported briefly to Peter and those with him all that they had been told. And after this, Jesus himself sent out by means of them, from east to west, the sacred and imperishable proclamation of eternal salvation.* These manuscripts then continue with verses 9–20

4   I am a laughingstock to my friends;
     I, who called to God and he answered
       me,
     a just and blameless man, am a
       laughingstock.
5   In the thought of one who is at ease
     there is contempt for misfortune;
     it is ready for those whose feet slip.
6   The tents of robbers are at peace,
     and those who provoke God are
       secure,
     who bring their god in their hand.[1]
7   "But ask the beasts, and they will teach
     you;
     the birds of the heavens, and they will
       tell you;
8   or the bushes of the earth,[2] and they will
     teach you;
     and the fish of the sea will declare to
     you.
9   Who among all these does not know
     that the hand of the LORD has done
     this?
10   In his hand is the life of every living
     thing
     and the breath of all mankind.
11   Does not the ear test words
     as the palate tastes food?
12   Wisdom is with the aged,
     and understanding in length of days.
13   "With God[3] are wisdom and might;
     he has counsel and understanding.
14   If he tears down, none can rebuild;
     if he shuts a man in, none can open.
15   If he withholds the waters, they dry up;
     if he sends them out, they overwhelm
     the land.
16   With him are strength and sound
     wisdom;
     the deceived and the deceiver are his.
17   He leads counselors away stripped,
     and judges he makes fools.
18   He looses the bonds of kings
     and binds a waistcloth on their hips.
19   He leads priests away stripped
     and overthrows the mighty.
20   He deprives of speech those who are
     trusted
     and takes away the discernment of the
     elders.

21   He pours contempt on princes
     and loosens the belt of the strong.
22   He uncovers the deeps out of darkness
     and brings deep darkness to light.
23   He makes nations great, and he destroys
     them;
     he enlarges nations, and leads them
     away.
24   He takes away understanding from the
     chiefs of the people of the earth
     and makes them wander in a trackless
     waste.
25   They grope in the dark without light,
     and he makes them stagger like a
     drunken man.

Romans 16

I commend to you our sister Phoebe, a servant[4] of the church at Cenchreae, [2]that you may welcome her in the Lord in a way worthy of the saints, and help her in whatever she may need from you, for she has been a patron of many and of myself as well.

[3]Greet Prisca and Aquila, my fellow workers in Christ Jesus, [4]who risked their necks for my life, to whom not only I give thanks but all the churches of the Gentiles give thanks as well. [5]Greet also the church in their house. Greet my beloved Epaenetus, who was the first convert[5] to Christ in Asia. [6]Greet Mary, who has worked hard for you. [7]Greet Andronicus and Junia,[6] my kinsmen and my fellow prisoners. They are well known to the apostles,[7] and they were in Christ before me. [8]Greet Ampliatus, my beloved in the Lord. [9]Greet Urbanus, our fellow worker in Christ, and my beloved Stachys. [10]Greet Apelles, who is approved in Christ. Greet those who belong to the family of Aristobulus. [11]Greet my kinsman Herodion. Greet those in the Lord who belong to the family of Narcissus. [12]Greet those workers in the Lord, Tryphaena and Tryphosa. Greet the beloved Persis, who has worked hard in the Lord. [13]Greet Rufus, chosen in the Lord; also his mother, who has been a mother to me as well. [14]Greet Asyncritus, Phlegon, Hermes, Patrobas, Hermas, and the brothers[8] who are with them. [15]Greet Philologus, Julia, Nereus and his sister, and Olympas, and all the saints who are with them. [16]Greet one another with a holy kiss. All the churches of Christ greet you.

[1] The meaning of the Hebrew is uncertain [2] Or *speak to the earth* [3] Hebrew *him* [4] Or *deaconess* [5] Greek *firstfruit* [6] Or *Junias* [7] Or *messengers* [8] Or *brothers and sisters; also verse 17*

[17]I appeal to you, brothers, to watch out for those who cause divisions and create obstacles contrary to the doctrine that you have been taught; avoid them. [18]For such persons do not serve our Lord Christ, but their own appetites,[1] and by smooth talk and flattery they deceive the hearts of the naive. [19]For your obedience is known to all, so that I rejoice over you, but I want you to be wise as to what is good and innocent as to what is evil. [20]The God of peace will soon crush Satan under your feet. The grace of our Lord Jesus Christ be with you.

[21]Timothy, my fellow worker, greets you; so do Lucius and Jason and Sosipater, my kinsmen.

[22]I Tertius, who wrote this letter, greet you in the Lord.

[23]Gaius, who is host to me and to the whole church, greets you. Erastus, the city treasurer, and our brother Quartus, greet you.[2]

[25]Now to him who is able to strengthen you according to my gospel and the preaching of Jesus Christ, according to the revelation of the mystery that was kept secret for long ages [26]but has now been disclosed and through the prophetic writings has been made known to all nations, according to the command of the eternal God, to bring about the obedience of faith— [27]to the only wise God be glory forevermore through Jesus Christ! Amen.

FEBRUARY 14

Genesis 47

So Joseph went in and told Pharaoh, "My father and my brothers, with their flocks and herds and all that they possess, have come from the land of Canaan. They are now in the land of Goshen." [2]And from among his brothers he took five men and presented them to Pharaoh. [3]Pharaoh said to his brothers, "What is your occupation?" And they said to Pharaoh, "Your servants are shepherds, as our fathers were." [4]They said to Pharaoh, "We have come to sojourn in the land, for there is no pasture for your servants' flocks, for the famine is severe in the land of Canaan. And now, please let your servants dwell in the land of Goshen." [5]Then Pharaoh said to Joseph, "Your father and your brothers have come to you. [6]The land of Egypt is before you. Settle your father and your brothers in the best of the land. Let them settle in the land of Goshen, and if you know any able men among them, put them in charge of my livestock."

[7]Then Joseph brought in Jacob his father and stood him before Pharaoh, and Jacob blessed Pharaoh. [8]And Pharaoh said to Jacob, "How many are the days of the years of your life?" [9]And Jacob said to Pharaoh, "The days of the years of my sojourning are 130 years. Few and evil have been the days of the years of my life, and they have not attained to the days of the years of the life of my fathers in the days of their sojourning." [10]And Jacob blessed Pharaoh and went out from the presence of Pharaoh. [11]Then Joseph settled his father and his brothers and gave them a possession in the land of Egypt, in the best of the land, in the land of Rameses, as Pharaoh had commanded. [12]And Joseph provided his father, his brothers, and all his father's household with food, according to the number of their dependents.

[13]Now there was no food in all the land, for the famine was very severe, so that the land of Egypt and the land of Canaan languished by reason of the famine. [14]And Joseph gathered up all the money that was found in the land of Egypt and in the land of Canaan, in exchange for the grain that they bought. And Joseph brought the money into Pharaoh's house. [15]And when the money was all spent in the land of Egypt and in the land of Canaan, all the Egyptians came to Joseph and said, "Give us food. Why should we die before your eyes? For our money is gone." [16]And Joseph

[1] Greek *their own belly* [2] Some manuscripts insert verse 24: *The grace of our Lord Jesus Christ be with you all. Amen.*

answered, "Give your livestock, and I will give you food in exchange for your livestock, if your money is gone." [17] So they brought their livestock to Joseph, and Joseph gave them food in exchange for the horses, the flocks, the herds, and the donkeys. He supplied them with food in exchange for all their livestock that year. [18] And when that year was ended, they came to him the following year and said to him, "We will not hide from my lord that our money is all spent. The herds of livestock are my lord's. There is nothing left in the sight of my lord but our bodies and our land. [19] Why should we die before your eyes, both we and our land? Buy us and our land for food, and we with our land will be servants to Pharaoh. And give us seed that we may live and not die, and that the land may not be desolate."

[20] So Joseph bought all the land of Egypt for Pharaoh, for all the Egyptians sold their fields, because the famine was severe on them. The land became Pharaoh's. [21] As for the people, he made servants of them[1] from one end of Egypt to the other. [22] Only the land of the priests he did not buy, for the priests had a fixed allowance from Pharaoh and lived on the allowance that Pharaoh gave them; therefore they did not sell their land.

[23] Then Joseph said to the people, "Behold, I have this day bought you and your land for Pharaoh. Now here is seed for you, and you shall sow the land. [24] And at the harvests you shall give a fifth to Pharaoh, and four fifths shall be your own, as seed for the field and as food for yourselves and your households, and as food for your little ones." [25] And they said, "You have saved our lives; may it please my lord, we will be servants to Pharaoh." [26] So Joseph made it a statute concerning the land of Egypt, and it stands to this day, that Pharaoh should have the fifth; the land of the priests alone did not become Pharaoh's.

[27] Thus Israel settled in the land of Egypt, in the land of Goshen. And they gained possessions in it, and were fruitful and multiplied greatly. [28] And Jacob lived in the land of Egypt seventeen years. So the days of Jacob, the years of his life, were 147 years.

[29] And when the time drew near that Israel must die, he called his son Joseph and said to him, "If now I have found favor in your sight, put your hand under my thigh and promise to deal kindly and truly with me. Do not bury me in Egypt, [30] but let me lie with my fathers. Carry me out of Egypt and bury me in their burying place." He answered, "I will do as you have said." [31] And he said, "Swear to me"; and he swore to him. Then Israel bowed himself upon the head of his bed.[2]

——— *Luke 1:1–38* ———

Inasmuch as many have undertaken to compile a narrative of the things that have been accomplished among us, [2] just as those who from the beginning were eyewitnesses and ministers of the word have delivered them to us, [3] it seemed good to me also, having followed all things closely for some time past, to write an orderly account for you, most excellent Theophilus, [4] that you may have certainty concerning the things you have been taught.

[5] In the days of Herod, king of Judea, there was a priest named Zechariah,[3] of the division of Abijah. And he had a wife from the daughters of Aaron, and her name was Elizabeth. [6] And they were both righteous before God, walking blamelessly in all the commandments and statutes of the Lord. [7] But they had no child, because Elizabeth was barren, and both were advanced in years.

[8] Now while he was serving as priest before God when his division was on duty, [9] according to the custom of the priesthood, he was chosen by lot to enter the temple of the Lord and burn incense. [10] And the whole multitude of the people were praying outside at the hour of incense. [11] And there appeared to him an angel of the Lord standing on the right side of the altar of incense. [12] And Zechariah was troubled when he saw him, and fear fell upon him. [13] But the angel said to him, "Do not be afraid, Zechariah, for your prayer has been heard, and your wife Elizabeth will bear you a son, and you shall call his name John. [14] And you will have joy and gladness, and many will rejoice at his birth, [15] for he will be great before the Lord. And he must not drink wine or strong drink, and he will be filled with the Holy Spirit, even from his mother's womb. [16] And he will turn many of the children of Israel to the Lord their God, [17] and he will go before him in the spirit and power of Elijah, to turn the hearts of the fathers to the children, and the disobedient to

[1] Samaritan, Septuagint, Vulgate; Hebrew *he removed them to the cities* [2] Hebrew; Septuagint *staff* [3] Greek *Zacharias*

the wisdom of the just, to make ready for the Lord a people prepared."

[18]And Zechariah said to the angel, "How shall I know this? For I am an old man, and my wife is advanced in years." [19]And the angel answered him, "I am Gabriel. I stand in the presence of God, and I was sent to speak to you and to bring you this good news. [20]And behold, you will be silent and unable to speak until the day that these things take place, because you did not believe my words, which will be fulfilled in their time." [21]And the people were waiting for Zechariah, and they were wondering at his delay in the temple. [22]And when he came out, he was unable to speak to them, and they realized that he had seen a vision in the temple. And he kept making signs to them and remained mute. [23]And when his time of service was ended, he went to his home.

[24]After these days his wife Elizabeth conceived, and for five months she kept herself hidden, saying, [25]"Thus the Lord has done for me in the days when he looked on me, to take away my reproach among people."

[26] In the sixth month the angel Gabriel was sent from God to a city of Galilee named Nazareth, [27]to a virgin betrothed[1] to a man whose name was Joseph, of the house of David. And the virgin's name was Mary. [28]And he came to her and said, "Greetings, O favored one, the Lord is with you!"[2] [29]But she was greatly troubled at the saying, and tried to discern what sort of greeting this might be. [30]And the angel said to her, "Do not be afraid, Mary, for you have found favor with God. [31]And behold, you will conceive in your womb and bear a son, and you shall call his name Jesus. [32]He will be great and will be called the Son of the Most High. And the Lord God will give to him the throne of his father David, [33]and he will reign over the house of Jacob forever, and of his kingdom there will be no end."

[34]And Mary said to the angel, "How will this be, since I am a virgin?"[3] [35]And the angel answered her, "The Holy Spirit will come upon you, and the power of the Most High will overshadow you; therefore the child to be born[4] will be called holy— the Son of God. [36]And behold, your relative Elizabeth in her old age has also conceived a son, and this is the sixth month with her who was called barren. [37]For nothing will

be impossible with God." [38]And Mary said, "Behold, I am the servant[5] of the Lord; let it be to me according to your word." And the angel departed from her.

Job 13

[1] "Behold, my eye has seen all this,
    my ear has heard and understood it.
[2] What you know, I also know;
    I am not inferior to you.
[3] But I would speak to the Almighty,
    and I desire to argue my case with God.
[4] As for you, you whitewash with lies;
    worthless physicians are you all.
[5] Oh that you would keep silent,
    and it would be your wisdom!
[6] Hear now my argument
    and listen to the pleadings of my lips.
[7] Will you speak falsely for God
    and speak deceitfully for him?
[8] Will you show partiality toward him?
    Will you plead the case for God?
[9] Will it be well with you when he
    searches you out?
    Or can you deceive him, as one
    deceives a man?
[10] He will surely rebuke you
    if in secret you show partiality.
[11] Will not his majesty terrify you,
    and the dread of him fall upon you?
[12] Your maxims are proverbs of ashes;
    your defenses are defenses of clay.
[13] "Let me have silence, and I will speak,
    and let come on me what may.
[14] Why should I take my flesh in my teeth
    and put my life in my hand?
[15] Though he slay me, I will hope in him;[6]
    yet I will argue my ways to his face.
[16] This will be my salvation,
    that the godless shall not come before
    him.
[17] Keep listening to my words,
    and let my declaration be in your ears.
[18] Behold, I have prepared my case;
    I know that I shall be in the right.
[19] Who is there who will contend with me?
    For then I would be silent and die.
[20] Only grant me two things,
    then I will not hide myself from your
    face:

---

[1] That is, legally pledged to be married [2] Some manuscripts add *Blessed are you among women!* [3] Greek *since I do not know a man* [4] Some manuscripts add *of you*
[5] Greek *bondservant*; also verse 48 [6] Or *Behold, he will slay me; I have no hope*

21 withdraw your hand far from me,
    and let not dread of you terrify me.
22 Then call, and I will answer;
    or let me speak, and you reply to me.
23 How many are my iniquities and my
        sins?
    Make me know my transgression and
        my sin.
24 Why do you hide your face
    and count me as your enemy?
25 Will you frighten a driven leaf
    and pursue dry chaff?
26 For you write bitter things against me
    and make me inherit the iniquities of
        my youth.
27 You put my feet in the stocks
    and watch all my paths;
    you set a limit for[1] the soles of my feet.
28 Man[2] wastes away like a rotten thing,
    like a garment that is moth-eaten.

1 Corinthians 1

Paul, called by the will of God to be an apostle of Christ Jesus, and our brother Sosthenes, [2] To the church of God that is in Corinth, to those sanctified in Christ Jesus, called to be saints together with all those who in every place call upon the name of our Lord Jesus Christ, both their Lord and ours:

[3] Grace to you and peace from God our Father and the Lord Jesus Christ.

[4] I give thanks to my God always for you because of the grace of God that was given you in Christ Jesus, [5] that in every way you were enriched in him in all speech and all knowledge— [6] even as the testimony about Christ was confirmed among you— [7] so that you are not lacking in any gift, as you wait for the revealing of our Lord Jesus Christ, [8] who will sustain you to the end, guiltless in the day of our Lord Jesus Christ. [9] God is faithful, by whom you were called into the fellowship of his Son, Jesus Christ our Lord.

[10] I appeal to you, brothers,[3] by the name of our Lord Jesus Christ, that all of you agree, and that there be no divisions among you, but that you be united in the same mind and the same judgment. [11] For it has been reported to me by Chloe's people that there is quarreling among you, my brothers. [12] What I mean is that each one of you says, "I follow Paul," or "I follow Apollos," or "I follow Cephas," or "I follow Christ." [13] Is Christ divided? Was Paul crucified for you? Or were you baptized in the name of Paul? [14] I thank God that I baptized none of you except Crispus and Gaius, [15] so that no one may say that you were baptized in my name. [16] (I did baptize also the household of Stephanas. Beyond that, I do not know whether I baptized anyone else.) [17] For Christ did not send me to baptize but to preach the gospel, and not with words of eloquent wisdom, lest the cross of Christ be emptied of its power.

[18] For the word of the cross is folly to those who are perishing, but to us who are being saved it is the power of God. [19] For it is written,

"I will destroy the wisdom of the wise,
    and the discernment of the discerning
        I will thwart."

[20] Where is the one who is wise? Where is the scribe? Where is the debater of this age? Has not God made foolish the wisdom of the world? [21] For since, in the wisdom of God, the world did not know God through wisdom, it pleased God through the folly of what we preach[4] to save those who believe. [22] For Jews demand signs and Greeks seek wisdom, [23] but we preach Christ crucified, a stumbling block to Jews and folly to Gentiles, [24] but to those who are called, both Jews and Greeks, Christ the power of God and the wisdom of God. [25] For the foolishness of God is wiser than men, and the weakness of God is stronger than men.

[26] For consider your calling, brothers: not many of you were wise according to worldly standards,[5] not many were powerful, not many were of noble birth. [27] But God chose what is foolish in the world to shame the wise; God chose what is weak in the world to shame the strong; [28] God chose what is low and despised in the world, even things that are not, to bring to nothing things that are, [29] so that no human being[6] might boast in the presence of God. [30] And because of him[7] you are in Christ Jesus, who became to us wisdom from God, righteousness and sanctification and redemption, [31] so that, as it is written, "Let the one who boasts, boast in the Lord."

[1] Or you marked [2] Hebrew He [3] Or brothers and sisters. The plural Greek word adelphoi (translated "brothers") refers to siblings in a family. In New Testament usage, depending on the context, adelphoi may refer either to men or to both men and women who are siblings (brothers and sisters) in God's family, the church; also verses 11, 26 [4] Or the folly of preaching [5] Greek according to the flesh [6] Greek no flesh [7] Greek And from him

FEBRUARY 15

Genesis 48

After this, Joseph was told, "Behold, your father is ill." So he took with him his two sons, Manasseh and Ephraim. ²And it was told to Jacob, "Your son Joseph has come to you." Then Israel summoned his strength and sat up in bed. ³And Jacob said to Joseph, "God Almighty[1] appeared to me at Luz in the land of Canaan and blessed me, ⁴and said to me, 'Behold, I will make you fruitful and multiply you, and I will make of you a company of peoples and will give this land to your offspring after you for an everlasting possession.' ⁵And now your two sons, who were born to you in the land of Egypt before I came to you in Egypt, are mine; Ephraim and Manasseh shall be mine, as Reuben and Simeon are. ⁶And the children that you fathered after them shall be yours. They shall be called by the name of their brothers in their inheritance. ⁷As for me, when I came from Paddan, to my sorrow Rachel died in the land of Canaan on the way, when there was still some distance[2] to go to Ephrath, and I buried her there on the way to Ephrath (that is, Bethlehem)."

⁸When Israel saw Joseph's sons, he said, "Who are these?" ⁹Joseph said to his father, "They are my sons, whom God has given me here." And he said, "Bring them to me, please, that I may bless them." ¹⁰Now the eyes of Israel were dim with age, so that he could not see. So Joseph brought them near him, and he kissed them and embraced them. ¹¹And Israel said to Joseph, "I never expected to see your face; and behold, God has let me see your offspring also." ¹²Then Joseph removed them from his knees, and he bowed himself with his face to the earth. ¹³And Joseph took them both, Ephraim in his right hand toward Israel's left hand, and Manasseh in his left hand toward Israel's right hand, and brought them near him. ¹⁴And Israel stretched out his right hand and laid it on the head of Ephraim, who was the younger, and his left hand on the head of Manasseh, crossing his hands (for Manasseh was the firstborn). ¹⁵And he blessed Joseph and said,

"The God before whom my fathers
    Abraham and Isaac walked,
the God who has been my shepherd
    all my life long to this day,
¹⁶ the angel who has redeemed me from
    all evil, bless the boys;
and in them let my name be carried
    on, and the name of my fathers
    Abraham and Isaac;
and let them grow into a multitude[3] in
    the midst of the earth."

¹⁷When Joseph saw that his father laid his right hand on the head of Ephraim, it displeased him, and he took his father's hand to move it from Ephraim's head to Manasseh's head. ¹⁸And Joseph said to his father, "Not this way, my father; since this one is the firstborn, put your right hand on his head." ¹⁹But his father refused and said, "I know, my son, I know. He also shall become a people, and he also shall be great. Nevertheless, his younger brother shall be greater than he, and his offspring shall become a multitude[4] of nations." ²⁰So he blessed them that day, saying,

"By you Israel will pronounce blessings,
    saying,
'God make you as Ephraim and as
    Manasseh.'"

Thus he put Ephraim before Manasseh. ²¹Then Israel said to Joseph, "Behold, I am about to die, but God will be with you and will bring you again to the land of your fathers. ²²Moreover, I have given to you rather than to your brothers one mountain slope[5] that I took from the hand of the Amorites with my sword and with my bow."

Luke 1:39–80

In those days Mary arose and went with haste into the hill country, to a town in Judah, ⁴⁰and she entered the house of Zechariah and greeted Elizabeth. ⁴¹And when Elizabeth heard the

[1] Hebrew *El Shaddai* [2] *Or about two hours' distance* [3] Or *let them be like fish for multitude* [4] Hebrew *fullness* [5] *Or one portion of the land*; Hebrew *shekem*, which sounds like the town and district called *Shechem*

greeting of Mary, the baby leaped in her womb. And Elizabeth was filled with the Holy Spirit, [42] and she exclaimed with a loud cry, "Blessed are you among women, and blessed is the fruit of your womb! [43] And why is this granted to me that the mother of my Lord should come to me? [44] For behold, when the sound of your greeting came to my ears, the baby in my womb leaped for joy. [45] And blessed is she who believed that there would be[1] a fulfillment of what was spoken to her from the Lord."

[46] And Mary said,

"My soul magnifies the Lord,
[47]   and my spirit rejoices in God my
          Savior,
[48]   for he has looked on the humble estate
          of his servant.
      For behold, from now on all
          generations will call me blessed;
[49]   for he who is mighty has done great
          things for me,
      and holy is his name.
[50]   And his mercy is for those who fear
          him
      from generation to generation.
[51]   He has shown strength with his arm;
      he has scattered the proud in the
          thoughts of their hearts;
[52]   he has brought down the mighty from
          their thrones
      and exalted those of humble estate;
[53]   he has filled the hungry with good
          things,
      and the rich he has sent away empty.
[54]   He has helped his servant Israel,
      in remembrance of his mercy,
[55]   as he spoke to our fathers,
      to Abraham and to his offspring
          forever."

[56] And Mary remained with her about three months and returned to her home.

[57] Now the time came for Elizabeth to give birth, and she bore a son. [58] And her neighbors and relatives heard that the Lord had shown great mercy to her, and they rejoiced with her. [59] And on the eighth day they came to circumcise the child. And they would have called him Zechariah after his father, [60] but his mother answered, "No; he shall be called John." [61] And they said to her, "None of your relatives is called by this name." [62] And they made signs to his father, inquiring what he wanted him to be called. [63] And he asked for a writing tablet and wrote, "His name is John." And they all wondered. [64] And immediately his mouth was opened and his tongue loosed, and he spoke, blessing God. [65] And fear came on all their neighbors. And all these things were talked about through all the hill country of Judea, [66] and all who heard them laid them up in their hearts, saying, "What then will this child be?" For the hand of the Lord was with him.

[67] And his father Zechariah was filled with the Holy Spirit and prophesied, saying,

[68]   "Blessed be the Lord God of Israel,
      for he has visited and redeemed his
          people
[69]   and has raised up a horn of salvation
          for us
      in the house of his servant David,
[70]   as he spoke by the mouth of his holy
          prophets from of old,
[71]   that we should be saved from our
          enemies
      and from the hand of all who hate us;
[72]   to show the mercy promised to our
          fathers
      and to remember his holy covenant,
[73]   the oath that he swore to our father
          Abraham, to grant us
[74]   that we, being delivered from the
          hand of our enemies,
      might serve him without fear,
[75]   in holiness and righteousness before
          him all our days.
[76]   And you, child, will be called the
          prophet of the Most High;
      for you will go before the Lord to
          prepare his ways,
[77]   to give knowledge of salvation to his
          people
      in the forgiveness of their sins,
[78]   because of the tender mercy of our God,
      whereby the sunrise shall visit us[2]
          from on high
[79]   to give light to those who sit in darkness
          and in the shadow of death,
      to guide our feet into the way of
          peace."

[80] And the child grew and became strong in spirit, and he was in the wilderness until the day of his public appearance to Israel.

[1] Or believed, for there will be [2] Or when the sunrise shall dawn upon us; some manuscripts since the sunrise has visited us

Job 14

"Man who is born of a woman
is few of days and full of trouble.
2 He comes out like a flower and withers;
he flees like a shadow and continues
not.
3 And do you open your eyes on such a
one
and bring me into judgment with you?
4 Who can bring a clean thing out of an
unclean?
There is not one.
5 Since his days are determined,
and the number of his months is with
you,
and you have appointed his limits that
he cannot pass,
6 look away from him and leave him
alone,[1]
that he may enjoy, like a hired hand,
his day.

7 "For there is hope for a tree,
if it be cut down, that it will sprout
again,
and that its shoots will not cease.
8 Though its root grow old in the earth,
and its stump die in the soil,
9 yet at the scent of water it will bud
and put out branches like a young
plant.
10 But a man dies and is laid low;
man breathes his last, and where is he?
11 As waters fail from a lake
and a river wastes away and dries up,
12 so a man lies down and rises not again;
till the heavens are no more he will
not awake
or be roused out of his sleep.
13 Oh that you would hide me in Sheol,
that you would conceal me until your
wrath be past,
that you would appoint me a set time,
and remember me!
14 If a man dies, shall he live again?
All the days of my service I would
wait,
till my renewal[2] should come.
15 You would call, and I would answer you;
you would long for the work of your
hands.

16 For then you would number my steps;
you would not keep watch over my sin;
17 my transgression would be sealed up in
a bag,
and you would cover over my iniquity.

18 "But the mountain falls and crumbles
away,
and the rock is removed from its
place;
19 the waters wear away the stones;
the torrents wash away the soil of the
earth;
so you destroy the hope of man.
20 You prevail forever against him, and he
passes;
you change his countenance, and send
him away.
21 His sons come to honor, and he does not
know it;
they are brought low, and he perceives
it not.
22 He feels only the pain of his own body,
and he mourns only for himself."

1 Corinthians 2

And I, when I came to you, brothers,[3] did not come proclaiming to you the testimony[4] of God with lofty speech or wisdom. 2 For I decided to know nothing among you except Jesus Christ and him crucified. 3 And I was with you in weakness and in fear and much trembling, 4 and my speech and my message were not in plausible words of wisdom, but in demonstration of the Spirit and of power, 5 so that your faith might not rest in the wisdom of men[5] but in the power of God.

6 Yet among the mature we do impart wisdom, although it is not a wisdom of this age or of the rulers of this age, who are doomed to pass away. 7 But we impart a secret and hidden wisdom of God, which God decreed before the ages for our glory. 8 None of the rulers of this age understood this, for if they had, they would not have crucified the Lord of glory. 9 But, as it is written,

"What no eye has seen, nor ear heard,
nor the heart of man imagined,
what God has prepared for those who
love him"—

[1] Probable reading; Hebrew look away from him, that he may cease [2] Or relief [3] Or brothers and sisters [4] Some manuscripts mystery (or secret) [5] The Greek word anthropoi can refer to both men and women

[10]these things God has revealed to us through the Spirit. For the Spirit searches everything, even the depths of God. [11]For who knows a person's thoughts except the spirit of that person, which is in him? So also no one comprehends the thoughts of God except the Spirit of God. [12]Now we have received not the spirit of the world, but the Spirit who is from God, that we might understand the things freely given us by God. [13]And we impart this in words not taught by human wisdom but taught by the Spirit, interpreting spiritual truths to those who are spiritual.[1]

[14]The natural person does not accept the things of the Spirit of God, for they are folly to him, and he is not able to understand them because they are spiritually discerned. [15]The spiritual person judges all things, but is himself to be judged by no one. [16]"For who has understood the mind of the Lord so as to instruct him?" But we have the mind of Christ.

FEBRUARY 16

Genesis 49

Then Jacob called his sons and said, "Gather yourselves together, that I may tell you what shall happen to you in days to come.

2   "Assemble and listen, O sons of Jacob,
        listen to Israel your father.

3   "Reuben, you are my firstborn,
        my might, and the firstfruits of my
            strength,
        preeminent in dignity and preeminent
            in power.

4   Unstable as water, you shall not have
            preeminence,
        because you went up to your father's
            bed;
        then you defiled it—he went up to my
            couch!

5   "Simeon and Levi are brothers;
        weapons of violence are their swords.

6   Let my soul come not into their council;
        O my glory, be not joined to their
            company.
        For in their anger they killed men,
        and in their willfulness they
            hamstrung oxen.

7   Cursed be their anger, for it is fierce,
        and their wrath, for it is cruel!
        I will divide them in Jacob
        and scatter them in Israel.

8   "Judah, your brothers shall praise you;
        your hand shall be on the neck of your
            enemies;
        your father's sons shall bow down
            before you.

9   Judah is a lion's cub;
        from the prey, my son, you have gone
            up.
        He stooped down; he crouched as a lion
        and as a lioness; who dares rouse him?

10   The scepter shall not depart from Judah,
        nor the ruler's staff from between his
            feet,
        until tribute comes to him;[2]
        and to him shall be the obedience of
            the peoples.

11   Binding his foal to the vine
        and his donkey's colt to the choice
            vine,
        he has washed his garments in wine
        and his vesture in the blood of grapes.

12   His eyes are darker than wine,
        and his teeth whiter than milk.

13   "Zebulun shall dwell at the shore of the
            sea;
        he shall become a haven for ships,
        and his border shall be at Sidon.

14   "Issachar is a strong donkey,
        crouching between the sheepfolds.[3]

[1] Or interpreting spiritual truths in spiritual language, or comparing spiritual things with spiritual   [2] By a slight revocalization; a slight emendation yields (compare Septuagint, Syriac, Targum) until he comes to whom it belongs; Hebrew until Shiloh comes, or until he comes to Shiloh   [3] Or between its saddlebags

15 He saw that a resting place was good,
        and that the land was pleasant,
    so he bowed his shoulder to bear,
        and became a servant at forced labor.

16 "Dan shall judge his people
        as one of the tribes of Israel.
17 Dan shall be a serpent in the way,
        a viper by the path,
    that bites the horse's heels
        so that his rider falls backward.
18 I wait for your salvation, O Lord.

19 "Raiders shall raid Gad,[1]
        but he shall raid at their heels.

20 "Asher's food shall be rich,
        and he shall yield royal delicacies.

21 "Naphtali is a doe let loose
        that bears beautiful fawns.[2]

22 "Joseph is a fruitful bough,
        a fruitful bough by a spring;
        his branches run over the wall.[3]
23 The archers bitterly attacked him,
        shot at him, and harassed him
            severely,
24 yet his bow remained unmoved;
        his arms[4] were made agile
    by the hands of the Mighty One of Jacob
        (from there is the Shepherd,[5] the
            Stone of Israel),
25 by the God of your father who will help
            you,
        by the Almighty[6] who will bless you
    with blessings of heaven above,
    blessings of the deep that crouches
            beneath,
    blessings of the breasts and of the
            womb.
26 The blessings of your father
        are mighty beyond the blessings of my
            parents,
        up to the bounties of the everlasting
            hills.[7]
    May they be on the head of Joseph,
        and on the brow of him who was set
            apart from his brothers.

27 "Benjamin is a ravenous wolf,
        in the morning devouring the prey
        and at evening dividing the spoil."

[28]All these are the twelve tribes of Israel. This is what their father said to them as he blessed them, blessing each with the blessing suitable to him. [29]Then he commanded them and said to them, "I am to be gathered to my people; bury me with my fathers in the cave that is in the field of Ephron the Hittite, [30]in the cave that is in the field at Machpelah, to the east of Mamre, in the land of Canaan, which Abraham bought with the field from Ephron the Hittite to possess as a burying place. [31]There they buried Abraham and Sarah his wife. There they buried Isaac and Rebekah his wife, and there I buried Leah— [32]the field and the cave that is in it were bought from the Hittites." [33]When Jacob finished commanding his sons, he drew up his feet into the bed and breathed his last and was gathered to his people.

——————— *Luke 2* ———————

In those days a decree went out from Caesar Augustus that all the world should be registered. [2]This was the first registration when[8] Quirinius was governor of Syria. [3]And all went to be registered, each to his own town. [4]And Joseph also went up from Galilee, from the town of Nazareth, to Judea, to the city of David, which is called Bethlehem, because he was of the house and lineage of David, [5]to be registered with Mary, his betrothed,[9] who was with child. [6]And while they were there, the time came for her to give birth. [7]And she gave birth to her firstborn son and wrapped him in swaddling cloths and laid him in a manger, because there was no place for them in the inn.

[8]And in the same region there were shepherds out in the field, keeping watch over their flock by night. [9]And an angel of the Lord appeared to them, and the glory of the Lord shone around them, and they were filled with great fear. [10]And the angel said to them, "Fear not, for behold, I bring you good news of great joy that will be for all the people. [11]For unto you is born this day in the city of David a Savior, who is Christ the Lord. [12]And this will be a sign for you: you will find a baby wrapped in swaddling cloths and lying in a manger." [13]And suddenly there was with the angel a multitude of the heavenly host praising God and saying,

[1] Gad sounds like the Hebrew for raiders and raid [2] Or he gives beautiful words, or that bears fawns of the fold [3] Or Joseph is a wild donkey, a wild donkey beside a spring, his wild colts beside the wall [4] Hebrew the arms of his hands [5] Or by the name of the Shepherd [6] Hebrew Shaddai [7] A slight emendation yields (compare Septuagint) the blessings of the eternal mountains, the bounties of the everlasting hills [8] Or This was the registration before [9] That is, one legally pledged to be married

¹⁴ "Glory to God in the highest,
    and on earth peace among those with
      whom he is pleased!"[1]

¹⁵When the angels went away from them into heaven, the shepherds said to one another, "Let us go over to Bethlehem and see this thing that has happened, which the Lord has made known to us." ¹⁶And they went with haste and found Mary and Joseph, and the baby lying in a manger. ¹⁷And when they saw it, they made known the saying that had been told them concerning this child. ¹⁸And all who heard it wondered at what the shepherds told them. ¹⁹But Mary treasured up all these things, pondering them in her heart. ²⁰And the shepherds returned, glorifying and praising God for all they had heard and seen, as it had been told them.

²¹And at the end of eight days, when he was circumcised, he was called Jesus, the name given by the angel before he was conceived in the womb.

²²And when the time came for their purification according to the Law of Moses, they brought him up to Jerusalem to present him to the Lord ²³(as it is written in the Law of the Lord, "Every male who first opens the womb shall be called holy to the Lord") ²⁴and to offer a sacrifice according to what is said in the Law of the Lord, "a pair of turtledoves, or two young pigeons." ²⁵Now there was a man in Jerusalem, whose name was Simeon, and this man was righteous and devout, waiting for the consolation of Israel, and the Holy Spirit was upon him. ²⁶And it had been revealed to him by the Holy Spirit that he would not see death before he had seen the Lord's Christ. ²⁷And he came in the Spirit into the temple, and when the parents brought in the child Jesus, to do for him according to the custom of the Law, ²⁸he took him up in his arms and blessed God and said,

²⁹ "Lord, now you are letting your servant[2]
    depart in peace,
    according to your word;
³⁰ for my eyes have seen your salvation
³¹   that you have prepared in the
    presence of all peoples,
³² a light for revelation to the Gentiles,
    and for glory to your people Israel."

³³And his father and his mother marveled at what was said about him. ³⁴And Simeon blessed them and said to Mary his mother, "Behold, this child is appointed for the fall and rising of many in Israel, and for a sign that is opposed ³⁵(and a sword will pierce through your own soul also), so that thoughts from many hearts may be revealed."

³⁶And there was a prophetess, Anna, the daughter of Phanuel, of the tribe of Asher. She was advanced in years, having lived with her husband seven years from when she was a virgin, ³⁷and then as a widow until she was eighty-four.[3] She did not depart from the temple, worshiping with fasting and prayer night and day. ³⁸And coming up at that very hour she began to give thanks to God and to speak of him to all who were waiting for the redemption of Jerusalem.

³⁹And when they had performed everything according to the Law of the Lord, they returned into Galilee, to their own town of Nazareth. ⁴⁰And the child grew and became strong, filled with wisdom. And the favor of God was upon him.

⁴¹Now his parents went to Jerusalem every year at the Feast of the Passover. ⁴²And when he was twelve years old, they went up according to custom. ⁴³And when the feast was ended, as they were returning, the boy Jesus stayed behind in Jerusalem. His parents did not know it, ⁴⁴but supposing him to be in the group they went a day's journey, but then they began to search for him among their relatives and acquaintances, ⁴⁵and when they did not find him, they returned to Jerusalem, searching for him. ⁴⁶After three days they found him in the temple, sitting among the teachers, listening to them and asking them questions. ⁴⁷And all who heard him were amazed at his understanding and his answers. ⁴⁸And when his parents[4] saw him, they were astonished. And his mother said to him, "Son, why have you treated us so? Behold, your father and I have been searching for you in great distress." ⁴⁹And he said to them, "Why were you looking for me? Did you not know that I must be in my Father's house?"[5] ⁵⁰And they did not understand the saying that he spoke to them. ⁵¹And he went down with them and came to Nazareth and was submissive to them. And his mother treasured up all these things in her heart.

⁵²And Jesus increased in wisdom and in stature[6] and in favor with God and man.

[1] Some manuscripts peace, good will among men [2] Greek bondservant [3] Or as a widow for eighty-four years [4] Greek they [5] Or about my Father's business [6] Or years

Job 15

Then Eliphaz the Temanite answered and said:

2 "Should a wise man answer with windy knowledge,
and fill his belly with the east wind?
3 Should he argue in unprofitable talk,
or in words with which he can do no good?
4 But you are doing away with the fear of God[1]
and hindering meditation before God.
5 For your iniquity teaches your mouth,
and you choose the tongue of the crafty.
6 Your own mouth condemns you, and not I;
your own lips testify against you.

7 "Are you the first man who was born?
Or were you brought forth before the hills?
8 Have you listened in the council of God?
And do you limit wisdom to yourself?
9 What do you know that we do not know?
What do you understand that is not clear to us?
10 Both the gray-haired and the aged are among us,
older than your father.
11 Are the comforts of God too small for you,
or the word that deals gently with you?
12 Why does your heart carry you away,
and why do your eyes flash,
13 that you turn your spirit against God
and bring such words out of your mouth?
14 What is man, that he can be pure?
Or he who is born of a woman, that he can be righteous?
15 Behold, God[2] puts no trust in his holy ones,
and the heavens are not pure in his sight;
16 how much less one who is abominable and corrupt,
a man who drinks injustice like water!

17 "I will show you; hear me,
and what I have seen I will declare

18 (what wise men have told,
without hiding it from their fathers,
19 to whom alone the land was given,
and no stranger passed among them).
20 The wicked man writhes in pain all his days,
through all the years that are laid up for the ruthless.
21 Dreadful sounds are in his ears;
in prosperity the destroyer will come upon him.
22 He does not believe that he will return out of darkness,
and he is marked for the sword.
23 He wanders abroad for bread, saying, 'Where is it?'
He knows that a day of darkness is ready at his hand;
24 distress and anguish terrify him;
they prevail against him, like a king ready for battle.
25 Because he has stretched out his hand against God
and defies the Almighty,
26 running stubbornly against him
with a thickly bossed shield;
27 because he has covered his face with his fat
and gathered fat upon his waist
28 and has lived in desolate cities,
in houses that none should inhabit,
which were ready to become heaps of ruins;
29 he will not be rich, and his wealth will not endure,
nor will his possessions spread over the earth;[3]
30 he will not depart from darkness;
the flame will dry up his shoots,
and by the breath of his mouth he will depart.
31 Let him not trust in emptiness, deceiving himself,
for emptiness will be his payment.
32 It will be paid in full before his time,
and his branch will not be green.
33 He will shake off his unripe grape like the vine,
and cast off his blossom like the olive tree.
34 For the company of the godless is barren,
and fire consumes the tents of bribery.

---

[1] Hebrew lacks *of God* [2] Hebrew *he* [3] Or *nor will his produce bend down to the earth*

[35] They conceive trouble and give birth to
    evil,
    and their womb prepares deceit."

1 Corinthians 3

But I, brothers,[1] could not address you as
spiritual people, but as people of the flesh,
as infants in Christ. [2] I fed you with milk, not
solid food, for you were not ready for it. And
even now you are not yet ready, [3] for you are
still of the flesh. For while there is jealousy and
strife among you, are you not of the flesh and
behaving only in a human way? [4] For when
one says, "I follow Paul," and another, "I follow Apollos," are you not being merely human?
[5] What then is Apollos? What is Paul? Servants through whom you believed, as the Lord
assigned to each. [6] I planted, Apollos watered,
but God gave the growth. [7] So neither he who
plants nor he who waters is anything, but only
God who gives the growth. [8] He who plants and
he who waters are one, and each will receive
his wages according to his labor. [9] For we are
God's fellow workers. You are God's field, God's
building.
[10] According to the grace of God given to me,
like a skilled master builder I laid a foundation,
and someone else is building upon it. Let each
one take care how he builds upon it. [11] For no
one can lay a foundation other than that which
is laid, which is Jesus Christ. [12] Now if anyone
builds on the foundation with gold, silver, precious stones, wood, hay, straw— [13] each one's
work will become manifest, for the Day will disclose it, because it will be revealed by fire, and
the fire will test what sort of work each one has
done. [14] If the work that anyone has built on the
foundation survives, he will receive a reward.
[15] If anyone's work is burned up, he will suffer
loss, though he himself will be saved, but only
as through fire.
[16] Do you not know that you[2] are God's temple
and that God's Spirit dwells in you? [17] If anyone
destroys God's temple, God will destroy him. For
God's temple is holy, and you are that temple.
[18] Let no one deceive himself. If anyone
among you thinks that he is wise in this age,
let him become a fool that he may become wise.
[19] For the wisdom of this world is folly with
God. For it is written, "He catches the wise in
their craftiness," [20] and again, "The Lord knows
the thoughts of the wise, that they are futile."
[21] So let no one boast in men. For all things are
yours, [22] whether Paul or Apollos or Cephas or
the world or life or death or the present or the
future—all are yours, [23] and you are Christ's,
and Christ is God's.

FEBRUARY 17

Genesis 50

Then Joseph fell on his father's face and wept
over him and kissed him. [2] And Joseph commanded his servants the physicians to embalm
his father. So the physicians embalmed Israel.
[3] Forty days were required for it, for that is how
many are required for embalming. And the
Egyptians wept for him seventy days.
[4] And when the days of weeping for him were
past, Joseph spoke to the household of Pharaoh,
saying, "If now I have found favor in your eyes,
please speak in the ears of Pharaoh, saying,
[5] 'My father made me swear, saying, "I am about
to die: in my tomb that I hewed out for myself
in the land of Canaan, there shall you bury me."
Now therefore, let me please go up and bury
my father. Then I will return.'" [6] And Pharaoh
answered, "Go up, and bury your father, as he
made you swear." [7] So Joseph went up to bury
his father. With him went up all the servants
of Pharaoh, the elders of his household, and
all the elders of the land of Egypt, [8] as well as
all the household of Joseph, his brothers, and
his father's household. Only their children,
their flocks, and their herds were left in the

[1] Or brothers and sisters [2] The Greek for you is plural in verses 16 and 17

land of Goshen. ⁹And there went up with him both chariots and horsemen. It was a very great company. ¹⁰When they came to the threshing floor of Atad, which is beyond the Jordan, they lamented there with a very great and grievous lamentation, and he made a mourning for his father seven days. ¹¹When the inhabitants of the land, the Canaanites, saw the mourning on the threshing floor of Atad, they said, "This is a grievous mourning by the Egyptians." Therefore the place was named Abel-mizraim;¹ it is beyond the Jordan. ¹²Thus his sons did for him as he had commanded them, ¹³for his sons carried him to the land of Canaan and buried him in the cave of the field at Machpelah, to the east of Mamre, which Abraham bought with the field from Ephron the Hittite to possess as a burying place. ¹⁴After he had buried his father, Joseph returned to Egypt with his brothers and all who had gone up with him to bury his father.

¹⁵When Joseph's brothers saw that their father was dead, they said, "It may be that Joseph will hate us and pay us back for all the evil that we did to him." ¹⁶So they sent a message to Joseph, saying, "Your father gave this command before he died: ¹⁷'Say to Joseph, "Please forgive the transgression of your brothers and their sin, because they did evil to you."' And now, please forgive the transgression of the servants of the God of your father." Joseph wept when they spoke to him. ¹⁸His brothers also came and fell down before him and said, "Behold, we are your servants." ¹⁹But Joseph said to them, "Do not fear, for am I in the place of God? ²⁰As for you, you meant evil against me, but God meant it for good, to bring it about that many people² should be kept alive, as they are today. ²¹So do not fear; I will provide for you and your little ones." Thus he comforted them and spoke kindly to them.

²²So Joseph remained in Egypt, he and his father's house. Joseph lived 110 years. ²³And Joseph saw Ephraim's children of the third generation. The children also of Machir the son of Manasseh were counted as Joseph's own.³ ²⁴And Joseph said to his brothers, "I am about to die, but God will visit you and bring you up out of this land to the land that he swore to Abraham, to Isaac, and to Jacob." ²⁵Then Joseph made the sons of Israel swear, saying, "God will surely visit you, and you shall carry up my bones from here." ²⁶So Joseph died, being 110 years old. They embalmed him, and he was put in a coffin in Egypt.

Luke 3

In the fifteenth year of the reign of Tiberius Caesar, Pontius Pilate being governor of Judea, and Herod being tetrarch of Galilee, and his brother Philip tetrarch of the region of Ituraea and Trachonitis, and Lysanias tetrarch of Abilene, ²during the high priesthood of Annas and Caiaphas, the word of God came to John the son of Zechariah in the wilderness. ³And he went into all the region around the Jordan, proclaiming a baptism of repentance for the forgiveness of sins. ⁴As it is written in the book of the words of Isaiah the prophet,

"The voice of one crying in the
        wilderness:
    'Prepare the way of the Lord,⁴
        make his paths straight.
5   Every valley shall be filled,
        and every mountain and hill shall be
            made low,
    and the crooked shall become straight,
        and the rough places shall become
            level ways,
6   and all flesh shall see the salvation of
            God.'"

⁷He said therefore to the crowds that came out to be baptized by him, "You brood of vipers! Who warned you to flee from the wrath to come? ⁸Bear fruits in keeping with repentance. And do not begin to say to yourselves, 'We have Abraham as our father.' For I tell you, God is able from these stones to raise up children for Abraham. ⁹Even now the axe is laid to the root of the trees. Every tree therefore that does not bear good fruit is cut down and thrown into the fire."

¹⁰And the crowds asked him, "What then shall we do?" ¹¹And he answered them, "Whoever has two tunics⁵ is to share with him who has none, and whoever has food is to do likewise." ¹²Tax collectors also came to be baptized and said to him, "Teacher, what shall we do?" ¹³And he said to them, "Collect no more than you are authorized to do." ¹⁴Soldiers also asked him, "And we, what shall we do?" And he said to them, "Do not extort money from

¹ Abel-mizraim means mourning (or meadow) of Egypt ² Or a numerous people ³ Hebrew were born on Joseph's knees ⁴ Or crying, Prepare in the wilderness the way of the Lord
⁵ Greek chiton, a long garment worn under the cloak next to the skin

anyone by threats or by false accusation, and be content with your wages."

[15] As the people were in expectation, and all were questioning in their hearts concerning John, whether he might be the Christ, [16] John answered them all, saying, "I baptize you with water, but he who is mightier than I is coming, the strap of whose sandals I am not worthy to untie. He will baptize you with the Holy Spirit and fire. [17] His winnowing fork is in his hand, to clear his threshing floor and to gather the wheat into his barn, but the chaff he will burn with unquenchable fire."

[18] So with many other exhortations he preached good news to the people. [19] But Herod the tetrarch, who had been reproved by him for Herodias, his brother's wife, and for all the evil things that Herod had done, [20] added this to them all, that he locked up John in prison.

[21] Now when all the people were baptized, and when Jesus also had been baptized and was praying, the heavens were opened, [22] and the Holy Spirit descended on him in bodily form, like a dove; and a voice came from heaven, "You are my beloved Son;[1] with you I am well pleased."[2]

[23] Jesus, when he began his ministry, was about thirty years of age, being the son (as was supposed) of Joseph, the son of Heli, [24] the son of Matthat, the son of Levi, the son of Melchi, the son of Jannai, the son of Joseph, [25] the son of Mattathias, the son of Amos, the son of Nahum, the son of Esli, the son of Naggai, [26] the son of Maath, the son of Mattathias, the son of Semein, the son of Josech, the son of Joda, [27] the son of Joanan, the son of Rhesa, the son of Zerubbabel, the son of Shealtiel,[3] the son of Neri, [28] the son of Melchi, the son of Addi, the son of Cosam, the son of Elmadam, the son of Er, [29] the son of Joshua, the son of Eliezer, the son of Jorim, the son of Matthat, the son of Levi, [30] the son of Simeon, the son of Judah, the son of Joseph, the son of Jonam, the son of Eliakim, [31] the son of Melea, the son of Menna, the son of Mattatha, the son of Nathan, the son of David, [32] the son of Jesse, the son of Obed, the son of Boaz, the son of Sala, the son of Nahshon, [33] the son of Amminadab, the son of Admin, the son of Arni, the son of Hezron, the son of Perez, the son of Judah, [34] the son of Jacob, the son of Isaac, the son of Abraham, the son of Terah, the son of Nahor, [35] the son of Serug, the son of Reu, the

son of Peleg, the son of Eber, the son of She-lah, [36] the son of Cainan, the son of Arphaxad, the son of Shem, the son of Noah, the son of Lamech, [37] the son of Methuselah, the son of Enoch, the son of Jared, the son of Mahalaleel, the son of Cainan, [38] the son of Enos, the son of Seth, the son of Adam, the son of God.

Job 16–17

Then Job answered and said:

2   "I have heard many such things;
        miserable comforters are you all.
3   Shall windy words have an end?
        Or what provokes you that you
            answer?
4   I also could speak as you do,
        if you were in my place;
     I could join words together against you
        and shake my head at you.
5   I could strengthen you with my mouth,
        and the solace of my lips would
            assuage your pain.

6   "If I speak, my pain is not assuaged,
        and if I forbear, how much of it leaves
            me?
7   Surely now God has worn me out;
        he has[4] made desolate all my
            company.
8   And he has shriveled me up,
        which is a witness against me,
     and my leanness has risen up against
            me;
        it testifies to my face.
9   He has torn me in his wrath and hated
            me;
        he has gnashed his teeth at me;
     my adversary sharpens his eyes
            against me.
10   Men have gaped at me with their mouth;
        they have struck me insolently on the
            cheek;
        they mass themselves together
            against me.
11   God gives me up to the ungodly
        and casts me into the hands of the
            wicked.
12   I was at ease, and he broke me apart;
        he seized me by the neck and dashed
            me to pieces;

[1] Or my Son, my (or the) Beloved [2] Some manuscripts beloved Son; today I have begotten you [3] Greek Salathiel [4] Hebrew you have; also verse 8

he set me up as his target;
13   his archers surround me.
He slashes open my kidneys and does
       not spare;
he pours out my gall on the ground.
14   He breaks me with breach upon breach;
he runs upon me like a warrior.
15   I have sewed sackcloth upon my skin
and have laid my strength in the dust.
16   My face is red with weeping,
and on my eyelids is deep darkness,
17   although there is no violence in my
       hands,
and my prayer is pure.
18   "O earth, cover not my blood,
and let my cry find no resting place.
19   Even now, behold, my witness is in
       heaven,
and he who testifies for me is on
       high.
20   My friends scorn me;
my eye pours out tears to God,
21   that he would argue the case of a man
       with God,
as[1] a son of man does with his
       neighbor.
22   For when a few years have come
I shall go the way from which I shall
       not return.
17:1   "My spirit is broken; my days are extinct;
the graveyard is ready for me.
2   Surely there are mockers about me,
and my eye dwells on their
       provocation.
3   "Lay down a pledge for me with you;
who is there who will put up security
       for me?
4   Since you have closed their hearts to
       understanding,
therefore you will not let them
       triumph.
5   He who informs against his friends to
       get a share of their property—
the eyes of his children will fail.
6   "He has made me a byword of the
       peoples,
and I am one before whom men spit.
7   My eye has grown dim from vexation,
and all my members are like a
       shadow.

8   The upright are appalled at this,
and the innocent stirs himself up
       against the godless.
9   Yet the righteous holds to his way,
and he who has clean hands grows
       stronger and stronger.
10   But you, come on again, all of you,
and I shall not find a wise man among
       you.
11   My days are past; my plans are broken
       off,
the desires of my heart.
12   They make night into day:
'The light,' they say, 'is near to the
       darkness.'[2]
13   If I hope for Sheol as my house,
if I make my bed in darkness,
14   if I say to the pit, 'You are my father,'
and to the worm, 'My mother,' or 'My
       sister,'
15   where then is my hope?
Who will see my hope?
16   Will it go down to the bars of Sheol?
Shall we descend together into the
       dust?"

---

1 Corinthians 4

This is how one should regard us, as servants of Christ and stewards of the mysteries of God. [2]Moreover, it is required of stewards that they be found faithful. [3]But with me it is a very small thing that I should be judged by you or by any human court. In fact, I do not even judge myself. [4]For I am not aware of anything against myself, but I am not thereby acquitted. It is the Lord who judges me. [5]Therefore do not pronounce judgment before the time, before the Lord comes, who will bring to light the things now hidden in darkness and will disclose the purposes of the heart. Then each one will receive his commendation from God. [6]I have applied all these things to myself and Apollos for your benefit, brothers,[3] that you may learn by us not to go beyond what is written, that none of you may be puffed up in favor of one against another. [7]For who sees anything different in you? What do you have that you did not receive? If then you received it, why do you boast as if you did not receive it?

[8]Already you have all you want! Already you have become rich! Without us you have become

[1] Hebrew and   [2] The meaning of the Hebrew is uncertain   [3] Or brothers and sisters

kings! And would that you did reign, so that we might share the rule with you! [9]For I think that God has exhibited us apostles as last of all, like men sentenced to death, because we have become a spectacle to the world, to angels, and to men. [10]We are fools for Christ's sake, but you are wise in Christ. We are weak, but you are strong. You are held in honor, but we in disrepute. [11]To the present hour we hunger and thirst, we are poorly dressed and buffeted and homeless, [12]and we labor, working with our own hands. When reviled, we bless; when persecuted, we endure; [13]when slandered, we entreat. We have become, and are still, like the scum of the world, the refuse of all things. [14]I do not write these things to make you ashamed, but to admonish you as my beloved children. [15]For though you have countless[1] guides in Christ, you do not have many fathers. For I became your father in Christ Jesus through the gospel. [16]I urge you, then, be imitators of me. [17]That is why I sent[2] you Timothy, my beloved and faithful child in the Lord, to remind you of my ways in Christ,[3] as I teach them everywhere in every church. [18]Some are arrogant, as though I were not coming to you. [19]But I will come to you soon, if the Lord wills, and I will find out not the talk of these arrogant people but their power. [20]For the kingdom of God does not consist in talk but in power. [21]What do you wish? Shall I come to you with a rod, or with love in a spirit of gentleness?

FEBRUARY 18

Exodus 1

These are the names of the sons of Israel who came to Egypt with Jacob, each with his household: [2]Reuben, Simeon, Levi, and Judah, [3]Issachar, Zebulun, and Benjamin, [4]Dan and Naphtali, Gad and Asher. [5]All the descendants of Jacob were seventy persons; Joseph was already in Egypt. [6]Then Joseph died, and all his brothers and all that generation. [7]But the people of Israel were fruitful and increased greatly; they multiplied and grew exceedingly strong, so that the land was filled with them.

[8]Now there arose a new king over Egypt, who did not know Joseph. [9]And he said to his people, "Behold, the people of Israel are too many and too mighty for us. [10]Come, let us deal shrewdly with them, lest they multiply, and, if war breaks out, they join our enemies and fight against us and escape from the land." [11]Therefore they set taskmasters over them to afflict them with heavy burdens. They built for Pharaoh store cities, Pithom and Raamses. [12]But the more they were oppressed, the more they multiplied and the more they spread abroad. And the Egyptians were in dread of the people of Israel. [13]So they ruthlessly made the people of Israel work as slaves [14]and made their lives bitter with hard service, in mortar and brick, and in all kinds of work in the field. In all their work they ruthlessly made them work as slaves.

[15]Then the king of Egypt said to the Hebrew midwives, one of whom was named Shiphrah and the other Puah, [16]"When you serve as midwife to the Hebrew women and see them on the birthstool, if it is a son, you shall kill him, but if it is a daughter, she shall live." [17]But the midwives feared God and did not do as the king of Egypt commanded them, but let the male children live. [18]So the king of Egypt called the midwives and said to them, "Why have you done this, and let the male children live?" [19]The midwives said to Pharaoh, "Because the Hebrew women are not like the Egyptian women, for they are vigorous and give birth before the midwife comes to them." [20]So God dealt well with the midwives. And the people multiplied and grew very strong. [21]And because the midwives feared God, he gave them families. [22]Then Pharaoh commanded all his people, "Every son that is born to the

[1] Greek *you have ten thousand* [2] Or *am sending* [3] Some manuscripts add *Jesus*

Hebrews[1] you shall cast into the Nile, but you shall let every daughter live."

Luke 4

And Jesus, full of the Holy Spirit, returned from the Jordan and was led by the Spirit in the wilderness [2]for forty days, being tempted by the devil. And he ate nothing during those days. And when they were ended, he was hungry. [3]The devil said to him, "If you are the Son of God, command this stone to become bread." [4]And Jesus answered him, "It is written, 'Man shall not live by bread alone.'" [5]And the devil took him up and showed him all the kingdoms of the world in a moment of time, [6]and said to him, "To you I will give all this authority and their glory, for it has been delivered to me, and I give it to whom I will. [7]If you, then, will worship me, it will all be yours." [8]And Jesus answered him, "It is written,

"'You shall worship the Lord your God,
    and him only shall you serve.'"

[9]And he took him to Jerusalem and set him on the pinnacle of the temple and said to him, "If you are the Son of God, throw yourself down from here, [10]for it is written,

"'He will command his angels concerning
    you,
    to guard you,'

[11]and

"'On their hands they will bear you up,
    lest you strike your foot against a
    stone.'"

[12]And Jesus answered him, "It is said, 'You shall not put the Lord your God to the test.'" [13]And when the devil had ended every temptation, he departed from him until an opportune time.

[14]And Jesus returned in the power of the Spirit to Galilee, and a report about him went out through all the surrounding country. [15]And he taught in their synagogues, being glorified by all.

[16]And he came to Nazareth, where he had been brought up. And as was his custom, he went to the synagogue on the Sabbath day, and he stood up to read. [17]And the scroll of the prophet Isaiah was given to him. He unrolled the scroll and found the place where it was written,

[18] "The Spirit of the Lord is upon me,
    because he has anointed me
    to proclaim good news to the poor.
He has sent me to proclaim liberty to the
    captives
    and recovering of sight to the blind,
    to set at liberty those who are
    oppressed,
[19] to proclaim the year of the Lord's favor."

[20]And he rolled up the scroll and gave it back to the attendant and sat down. And the eyes of all in the synagogue were fixed on him. [21]And he began to say to them, "Today this Scripture has been fulfilled in your hearing." [22]And all spoke well of him and marveled at the gracious words that were coming from his mouth. And they said, "Is not this Joseph's son?" [23]And he said to them, "Doubtless you will quote to me this proverb, 'Physician, heal yourself.' What we have heard you did at Capernaum, do here in your hometown as well." [24]And he said, "Truly, I say to you, no prophet is acceptable in his hometown. [25]But in truth, I tell you, there were many widows in Israel in the days of Elijah, when the heavens were shut up three years and six months, and a great famine came over all the land, [26]and Elijah was sent to none of them but only to Zarephath, in the land of Sidon, to a woman who was a widow. [27]And there were many lepers[2] in Israel in the time of the prophet Elisha, and none of them was cleansed, but only Naaman the Syrian." [28]When they heard these things, all in the synagogue were filled with wrath. [29]And they rose up and drove him out of the town and brought him to the brow of the hill on which their town was built, so that they could throw him down the cliff. [30]But passing through their midst, he went away.

[31]And he went down to Capernaum, a city of Galilee. And he was teaching them on the Sabbath, [32]and they were astonished at his teaching, for his word possessed authority. [33]And in the synagogue there was a man who had the spirit of an unclean demon, and he cried out with a loud voice, [34]"Ha![3] What have you to do with us, Jesus of Nazareth? Have you come to destroy us? I know who you are—the Holy One of God." [35]But Jesus rebuked him,

---

[1] Samaritan, Septuagint, Targum; Hebrew lacks to the Hebrews [2] Leprosy was a term for several skin diseases; see Leviticus 13 [3] Or Leave us alone

saying, "Be silent and come out of him!" And when the demon had thrown him down in their midst, he came out of him, having done him no harm. ³⁶And they were all amazed and said to one another, "What is this word? For with authority and power he commands the unclean spirits, and they come out!" ³⁷And reports about him went out into every place in the surrounding region.

³⁸And he arose and left the synagogue and entered Simon's house. Now Simon's mother-in-law was ill with a high fever, and they appealed to him on her behalf. ³⁹And he stood over her and rebuked the fever, and it left her, and immediately she rose and began to serve them.

⁴⁰Now when the sun was setting, all those who had any who were sick with various diseases brought them to him, and he laid his hands on every one of them and healed them. ⁴¹And demons also came out of many, crying, "You are the Son of God!" But he rebuked them and would not allow them to speak, because they knew that he was the Christ.

⁴²And when it was day, he departed and went into a desolate place. And the people sought him and came to him, and would have kept him from leaving them, ⁴³but he said to them, "I must preach the good news of the kingdom of God to the other towns as well; for I was sent for this purpose." ⁴⁴And he was preaching in the synagogues of Judea.¹

Job 18

Then Bildad the Shuhite answered and said:

2 "How long will you hunt for words?
    Consider, and then we will speak.
3 Why are we counted as cattle?
    Why are we stupid in your sight?
4 You who tear yourself in your anger,
    shall the earth be forsaken for you,
    or the rock be removed out of its place?

5 "Indeed, the light of the wicked is put out,
    and the flame of his fire does not
        shine.
6 The light is dark in his tent,
    and his lamp above him is put out.
7 His strong steps are shortened,
    and his own schemes throw him
        down.

8 For he is cast into a net by his own feet,
    and he walks on its mesh.
9 A trap seizes him by the heel;
    a snare lays hold of him.
10 A rope is hidden for him in the ground,
    a trap for him in the path.
11 Terrors frighten him on every side,
    and chase him at his heels.
12 His strength is famished,
    and calamity is ready for his
        stumbling.
13 It consumes the parts of his skin;
    the firstborn of death consumes his
        limbs.
14 He is torn from the tent in which he
        trusted
    and is brought to the king of terrors.
15 In his tent dwells that which is none of
        his;
    sulfur is scattered over his habitation.
16 His roots dry up beneath,
    and his branches wither above.
17 His memory perishes from the earth,
    and he has no name in the street.
18 He is thrust from light into darkness,
    and driven out of the world.
19 He has no posterity or progeny among
        his people,
    and no survivor where he used to live.
20 They of the west are appalled at his day,
    and horror seizes them of the east.
21 Surely such are the dwellings of the
        unrighteous,
    such is the place of him who knows
        not God."

---

1 Corinthians 5

It is actually reported that there is sexual immorality among you, and of a kind that is not tolerated even among pagans, for a man has his father's wife. ²And you are arrogant! Ought you not rather to mourn? Let him who has done this be removed from among you.

³For though absent in body, I am present in spirit; and as if present, I have already pronounced judgment on the one who did such a thing. ⁴When you are assembled in the name of the Lord Jesus and my spirit is present, with the power of our Lord Jesus, ⁵you are to deliver this man to Satan for the destruction of the

¹ Some manuscripts *Galilee*

flesh, so that his spirit may be saved in the day of the Lord.[1]

[6] Your boasting is not good. Do you not know that a little leaven leavens the whole lump? [7] Cleanse out the old leaven that you may be a new lump, as you really are unleavened. For Christ, our Passover lamb, has been sacrificed. [8] Let us therefore celebrate the festival, not with the old leaven, the leaven of malice and evil, but with the unleavened bread of sincerity and truth.

[9] I wrote to you in my letter not to associate with sexually immoral people— [10] not at all meaning the sexually immoral of this world, or the greedy and swindlers, or idolaters, since then you would need to go out of the world. [11] But now I am writing to you not to associate with anyone who bears the name of brother if he is guilty of sexual immorality or greed, or is an idolater, reviler, drunkard, or swindler—not even to eat with such a one. [12] For what have I to do with judging outsiders? Is it not those inside the church[2] whom you are to judge? [13] God judges[3] those outside. "Purge the evil person from among you."

FEBRUARY 19

Exodus 2

Now a man from the house of Levi went and took as his wife a Levite woman. [2] The woman conceived and bore a son, and when she saw that he was a fine child, she hid him three months. [3] When she could hide him no longer, she took for him a basket made of bulrushes[4] and daubed it with bitumen and pitch. She put the child in it and placed it among the reeds by the river bank. [4] And his sister stood at a distance to know what would be done to him. [5] Now the daughter of Pharaoh came down to bathe at the river, while her young women walked beside the river. She saw the basket among the reeds and sent her servant woman, and she took it. [6] When she opened it, she saw the child, and behold, the baby was crying. She took pity on him and said, "This is one of the Hebrews' children." [7] Then his sister said to Pharaoh's daughter, "Shall I go and call you a nurse from the Hebrew women to nurse the child for you?" [8] And Pharaoh's daughter said to her, "Go." So the girl went and called the child's mother. [9] And Pharaoh's daughter said to her, "Take this child away and nurse him for me, and I will give you your wages." So the woman took the child and nursed him. [10] When the child grew older, she brought him to Pharaoh's daughter, and he became her son. She named him Moses, "Because," she said, "I drew him out of the water."[5]

[11] One day, when Moses had grown up, he went out to his people and looked on their burdens, and he saw an Egyptian beating a Hebrew, one of his people.[6] [12] He looked this way and that, and seeing no one, he struck down the Egyptian and hid him in the sand. [13] When he went out the next day, behold, two Hebrews were struggling together. And he said to the man in the wrong, "Why do you strike your companion?" [14] He answered, "Who made you a prince and a judge over us? Do you mean to kill me as you killed the Egyptian?" Then Moses was afraid, and thought, "Surely the thing is known." [15] When Pharaoh heard of it, he sought to kill Moses. But Moses fled from Pharaoh and stayed in the land of Midian. And he sat down by a well.

[16] Now the priest of Midian had seven daughters, and they came and drew water and filled the troughs to water their father's flock. [17] The shepherds came and drove them away, but Moses stood up and saved them, and watered their flock. [18] When they came home to their father Reuel, he said, "How is it that you have come home so soon today?" [19] They said, "An Egyptian delivered us out of the hand of the shepherds and even drew water for us

[1] Some manuscripts add *Jesus* [2] Greek *those inside* [3] Or *will judge* [4] Hebrew *papyrus reeds* [5] *Moses* sounds like the Hebrew for *draw out* [6] Hebrew *brothers*

and watered the flock." [20]He said to his daughters, "Then where is he? Why have you left the man? Call him, that he may eat bread." [21]And Moses was content to dwell with the man, and he gave Moses his daughter Zipporah. [22]She gave birth to a son, and he called his name Gershom, for he said, "I have been a sojourner[1] in a foreign land."

[23]During those many days the king of Egypt died, and the people of Israel groaned because of their slavery and cried out for help. Their cry for rescue from slavery came up to God. [24]And God heard their groaning, and God remembered his covenant with Abraham, with Isaac, and with Jacob. [25]God saw the people of Israel—and God knew.

Luke 5

On one occasion, while the crowd was pressing in on him to hear the word of God, he was standing by the lake of Gennesaret, [2]and he saw two boats by the lake, but the fishermen had gone out of them and were washing their nets. [3]Getting into one of the boats, which was Simon's, he asked him to put out a little from the land. And he sat down and taught the people from the boat. [4]And when he had finished speaking, he said to Simon, "Put out into the deep and let down your nets for a catch." [5]And Simon answered, "Master, we toiled all night and took nothing! But at your word I will let down the nets." [6]And when they had done this, they enclosed a large number of fish, and their nets were breaking. [7]They signaled to their partners in the other boat to come and help them. And they came and filled both the boats, so that they began to sink. [8]But when Simon Peter saw it, he fell down at Jesus' knees, saying, "Depart from me, for I am a sinful man, O Lord." [9]For he and all who were with him were astonished at the catch of fish that they had taken, [10]and so also were James and John, sons of Zebedee, who were partners with Simon. And Jesus said to Simon, "Do not be afraid; from now on you will be catching men."[2] [11]And when they had brought their boats to land, they left everything and followed him.

[12]While he was in one of the cities, there came a man full of leprosy.[3] And when he saw Jesus, he fell on his face and begged him, "Lord, if you will, you can make me clean." [13]And Jesus[4] stretched out his hand and touched him, saying, "I will; be clean." And immediately the leprosy left him. [14]And he charged him to tell no one, but "go and show yourself to the priest, and make an offering for your cleansing, as Moses commanded, for a proof to them." [15]But now even more the report about him went abroad, and great crowds gathered to hear him and to be healed of their infirmities. [16]But he would withdraw to desolate places and pray.

[17]On one of those days, as he was teaching, Pharisees and teachers of the law were sitting there, who had come from every village of Galilee and Judea and from Jerusalem. And the power of the Lord was with him to heal.[5] [18]And behold, some men were bringing on a bed a man who was paralyzed, and they were seeking to bring him in and lay him before Jesus, [19]but finding no way to bring him in, because of the crowd, they went up on the roof and let him down with his bed through the tiles into the midst before Jesus. [20]And when he saw their faith, he said, "Man, your sins are forgiven you." [21]And the scribes and the Pharisees began to question, saying, "Who is this who speaks blasphemies? Who can forgive sins but God alone?" [22]When Jesus perceived their thoughts, he answered them, "Why do you question in your hearts? [23]Which is easier, to say, 'Your sins are forgiven you,' or to say, 'Rise and walk'? [24]But that you may know that the Son of Man has authority on earth to forgive sins"—he said to the man who was paralyzed—"I say to you, rise, pick up your bed and go home." [25]And immediately he rose up before them and picked up what he had been lying on and went home, glorifying God. [26]And amazement seized them all, and they glorified God and were filled with awe, saying, "We have seen extraordinary things today."

[27]After this he went out and saw a tax collector named Levi, sitting at the tax booth. And he said to him, "Follow me." [28]And leaving everything, he rose and followed him.

[29]And Levi made him a great feast in his house, and there was a large company of tax collectors and others reclining at table with them. [30]And the Pharisees and their scribes grumbled at his disciples, saying, "Why do you eat and drink with tax collectors and sinners?" [31]And Jesus answered them, "Those who are well have no need of a physician, but those who

---

[1] Gershom sounds like the Hebrew for sojourner [2] The Greek word anthropoi refers here to both men and women [3] Leprosy was a term for several skin diseases; see Leviticus 13 [4] Greek he [5] Some manuscripts was present to heal them

are sick. ³²I have not come to call the righteous but sinners to repentance."

³³And they said to him, "The disciples of John fast often and offer prayers, and so do the disciples of the Pharisees, but yours eat and drink." ³⁴And Jesus said to them, "Can you make wedding guests fast while the bridegroom is with them? ³⁵The days will come when the bridegroom is taken away from them, and then they will fast in those days." ³⁶He also told them a parable: "No one tears a piece from a new garment and puts it on an old garment. If he does, he will tear the new, and the piece from the new will not match the old. ³⁷And no one puts new wine into old wineskins. If he does, the new wine will burst the skins and it will be spilled, and the skins will be destroyed. ³⁸But new wine must be put into fresh wineskins. ³⁹And no one after drinking old wine desires new, for he says, 'The old is good.'"[1]

Job 19

Then Job answered and said:

2   "How long will you torment me
          and break me in pieces with words?
3   These ten times you have cast reproach
              upon me;
          are you not ashamed to wrong me?
4   And even if it be true that I have erred,
          my error remains with myself.
5   If indeed you magnify yourselves
              against me
          and make my disgrace an argument
              against me,
6   know then that God has put me in the
              wrong
          and closed his net about me.
7   Behold, I cry out, 'Violence!' but I am
              not answered;
          I call for help, but there is no justice.
8   He has walled up my way, so that I
              cannot pass,
          and he has set darkness upon my
              paths.
9   He has stripped from me my glory
          and taken the crown from my head.
10   He breaks me down on every side, and I
              am gone,
          and my hope has he pulled up like a
              tree.

11   He has kindled his wrath against me
          and counts me as his adversary.
12   His troops come on together;
          they have cast up their siege ramp[2]
              against me
          and encamp around my tent.

13   "He has put my brothers far from me,
          and those who knew me are wholly
              estranged from me.
14   My relatives have failed me,
          my close friends have forgotten me.
15   The guests in my house and my
              maidservants count me as a
              stranger;
          I have become a foreigner in their
              eyes.
16   I call to my servant, but he gives me no
              answer;
          I must plead with him with my mouth
              for mercy.
17   My breath is strange to my wife,
          and I am a stench to the children of
              my own mother.
18   Even young children despise me;
          when I rise they talk against me.
19   All my intimate friends abhor me,
          and those whom I loved have turned
              against me.
20   My bones stick to my skin and to my
              flesh,
          and I have escaped by the skin of my
              teeth.
21   Have mercy on me, have mercy on me,
              O you my friends,
          for the hand of God has touched me!
22   Why do you, like God, pursue me?
          Why are you not satisfied with my
              flesh?

23   "Oh that my words were written!
          Oh that they were inscribed in a
              book!
24   Oh that with an iron pen and lead
          they were engraved in the rock
              forever!
25   For I know that my Redeemer lives,
          and at the last he will stand upon the
              earth.[3]
26   And after my skin has been thus
              destroyed,
          yet in[4] my flesh I shall see God,

---

¹ Some manuscripts *better* ² Hebrew *their way* ³ Hebrew *dust* ⁴ Or *without*

27   whom I shall see for myself,
     and my eyes shall behold, and not
       another.
     My heart faints within me!
28   If you say, 'How we will pursue him!'
     and, 'The root of the matter is found
       in him,'
29   be afraid of the sword,
     for wrath brings the punishment of
       the sword,
     that you may know there is a
       judgment."

1 Corinthians 6

When one of you has a grievance against another, does he dare go to law before the unrighteous instead of the saints? [2] Or do you not know that the saints will judge the world? And if the world is to be judged by you, are you incompetent to try trivial cases? [3] Do you not know that we are to judge angels? How much more, then, matters pertaining to this life! [4] So if you have such cases, why do you lay them before those who have no standing in the church? [5] I say this to your shame. Can it be that there is no one among you wise enough to settle a dispute between the brothers, [6] but brother goes to law against brother, and that before unbelievers? [7] To have lawsuits at all with one another is already a defeat for you. Why not rather suffer wrong? Why not rather be defrauded? [8] But you yourselves wrong and defraud—even your own brothers![1]

[9] Or do you not know that the unrighteous[2] will not inherit the kingdom of God? Do not be deceived: neither the sexually immoral, nor idolaters, nor adulterers, nor men who practice homosexuality,[3] [10] nor thieves, nor the greedy, nor drunkards, nor revilers, nor swindlers will inherit the kingdom of God. [11] And such were some of you. But you were washed, you were sanctified, you were justified in the name of the Lord Jesus Christ and by the Spirit of our God.

[12] "All things are lawful for me," but not all things are helpful. "All things are lawful for me," but I will not be dominated by anything. [13] "Food is meant for the stomach and the stomach for food"—and God will destroy both one and the other. The body is not meant for sexual immorality, but for the Lord, and the Lord for the body. [14] And God raised the Lord and will also raise us up by his power. [15] Do you not know that your bodies are members of Christ? Shall I then take the members of Christ and make them members of a prostitute? Never! [16] Or do you not know that he who is joined[4] to a prostitute becomes one body with her? For, as it is written, "The two will become one flesh." [17] But he who is joined to the Lord becomes one spirit with him. [18] Flee from sexual immorality. Every other sin[5] a person commits is outside the body, but the sexually immoral person sins against his own body. [19] Or do you not know that your body is a temple of the Holy Spirit within you, whom you have from God? You are not your own, [20] for you were bought with a price. So glorify God in your body.

FEBRUARY 20

Exodus 3

Now Moses was keeping the flock of his father-in-law, Jethro, the priest of Midian, and he led his flock to the west side of the wilderness and came to Horeb, the mountain of God. [2] And the angel of the LORD appeared to him in a flame of fire out of the midst of a bush. He looked, and behold, the bush was burning, yet it was not consumed. [3] And Moses said, "I will turn aside to see this great sight, why the bush is not burned." [4] When the LORD saw that he turned aside to see, God called to him out of the bush, "Moses, Moses!" And he said, "Here I am." [5] Then he said, "Do not come near; take your sandals off your feet, for the place on

[1] Or brothers and sisters [2] Or wrongdoers [3] The two Greek terms translated by this phrase refer to the passive and active partners in consensual homosexual acts [4] Or who holds fast (compare Genesis 2:24 and Deuteronomy 10:20); also verse 17 [5] Or Every sin

which you are standing is holy ground." ⁶And he said, "I am the God of your father, the God of Abraham, the God of Isaac, and the God of Jacob." And Moses hid his face, for he was afraid to look at God.

⁷Then the LORD said, "I have surely seen the affliction of my people who are in Egypt and have heard their cry because of their taskmasters. I know their sufferings, ⁸and I have come down to deliver them out of the hand of the Egyptians and to bring them up out of that land to a good and broad land, a land flowing with milk and honey, to the place of the Canaanites, the Hittites, the Amorites, the Perizzites, the Hivites, and the Jebusites. ⁹And now, behold, the cry of the people of Israel has come to me, and I have also seen the oppression with which the Egyptians oppress them. ¹⁰Come, I will send you to Pharaoh that you may bring my people, the children of Israel, out of Egypt." ¹¹But Moses said to God, "Who am I that I should go to Pharaoh and bring the children of Israel out of Egypt?" ¹²He said, "But I will be with you, and this shall be the sign for you, that I have sent you: when you have brought the people out of Egypt, you shall serve God on this mountain."

¹³Then Moses said to God, "If I come to the people of Israel and say to them, 'The God of your fathers has sent me to you,' and they ask me, 'What is his name?' what shall I say to them?" ¹⁴God said to Moses, "I AM WHO I AM."[1] And he said, "Say this to the people of Israel, 'I AM has sent me to you.'" ¹⁵God also said to Moses, "Say this to the people of Israel, 'The LORD,[2] the God of your fathers, the God of Abraham, the God of Isaac, and the God of Jacob, has sent me to you.' This is my name forever, and thus I am to be remembered throughout all generations. ¹⁶Go and gather the elders of Israel together and say to them, 'The LORD, the God of your fathers, the God of Abraham, of Isaac, and of Jacob, has appeared to me, saying, "I have observed you and what has been done to you in Egypt, ¹⁷and I promise that I will bring you up out of the affliction of Egypt to the land of the Canaanites, the Hittites, the Amorites, the Perizzites, the Hivites, and the Jebusites, a land flowing with milk and honey."' ¹⁸And they will listen to your voice, and you and the elders of Israel shall go to the king of Egypt and say to him, 'The LORD, the God of the Hebrews,

has met with us; and now, please let us go a three days' journey into the wilderness, that we may sacrifice to the LORD our God.' ¹⁹But I know that the king of Egypt will not let you go unless compelled by a mighty hand.[3] ²⁰So I will stretch out my hand and strike Egypt with all the wonders that I will do in it; after that he will let you go. ²¹And I will give this people favor in the sight of the Egyptians; and when you go, you shall not go empty, ²²but each woman shall ask of her neighbor, and any woman who lives in her house, for silver and gold jewelry, and for clothing. You shall put them on your sons and on your daughters. So you shall plunder the Egyptians."

Luke 6

On a Sabbath,[4] while he was going through the grainfields, his disciples plucked and ate some heads of grain, rubbing them in their hands. ²But some of the Pharisees said, "Why are you doing what is not lawful to do on the Sabbath?" ³And Jesus answered them, "Have you not read what David did when he was hungry, he and those who were with him: ⁴how he entered the house of God and took and ate the bread of the Presence, which is not lawful for any but the priests to eat, and also gave it to those with him?" ⁵And he said to them, "The Son of Man is lord of the Sabbath."

⁶On another Sabbath, he entered the synagogue and was teaching, and a man was there whose right hand was withered. ⁷And the scribes and the Pharisees watched him, to see whether he would heal on the Sabbath, so that they might find a reason to accuse him. ⁸But he knew their thoughts, and he said to the man with the withered hand, "Come and stand here." And he rose and stood there. ⁹And Jesus said to them, "I ask you, is it lawful on the Sabbath to do good or to do harm, to save life or to destroy it?" ¹⁰And after looking around at them all he said to him, "Stretch out your hand." And he did so, and his hand was restored. ¹¹But they were filled with fury and discussed with one another what they might do to Jesus.

¹²In these days he went out to the mountain to pray, and all night he continued in prayer to God. ¹³And when day came, he called his disciples and chose from them twelve, whom he

---

[1] Or I AM WHAT I AM, or I WILL BE WHAT I WILL BE [2] The word LORD, when spelled with capital letters, stands for the divine name, YHWH, which is here connected with the verb hayah, "to be" in verse 14 [3] Septuagint, Vulgate; Hebrew go, not by a mighty hand [4] Some manuscripts On the second first Sabbath (that is, on the second Sabbath after the first)

named apostles: [14] Simon, whom he named Peter, and Andrew his brother, and James and John, and Philip, and Bartholomew, [15] and Matthew, and Thomas, and James the son of Alphaeus, and Simon who was called the Zealot, [16] and Judas the son of James, and Judas Iscariot, who became a traitor.

[17] And he came down with them and stood on a level place, with a great crowd of his disciples and a great multitude of people from all Judea and Jerusalem and the seacoast of Tyre and Sidon, [18] who came to hear him and to be healed of their diseases. And those who were troubled with unclean spirits were cured. [19] And all the crowd sought to touch him, for power came out from him and healed them all.

[20] And he lifted up his eyes on his disciples, and said:

"Blessed are you who are poor, for yours is the kingdom of God.

[21] "Blessed are you who are hungry now, for you shall be satisfied.

"Blessed are you who weep now, for you shall laugh.

[22] "Blessed are you when people hate you and when they exclude you and revile you and spurn your name as evil, on account of the Son of Man! [23] Rejoice in that day, and leap for joy, for behold, your reward is great in heaven; for so their fathers did to the prophets.

[24] "But woe to you who are rich, for you have received your consolation.

[25] "Woe to you who are full now, for you shall be hungry.

"Woe to you who laugh now, for you shall mourn and weep.

[26] "Woe to you, when all people speak well of you, for so their fathers did to the false prophets.

[27] "But I say to you who hear, Love your enemies, do good to those who hate you, [28] bless those who curse you, pray for those who abuse you. [29] To one who strikes you on the cheek, offer the other also, and from one who takes away your cloak do not withhold your tunic[1] either. [30] Give to everyone who begs from you, and from one who takes away your goods do not demand them back. [31] And as you wish that others would do to you, do so to them. [32] "If you love those who love you, what benefit is that to you? For even sinners love those who love them. [33] And if you do good to those

who do good to you, what benefit is that to you? For even sinners do the same. [34] And if you lend to those from whom you expect to receive, what credit is that to you? Even sinners lend to sinners, to get back the same amount. [35] But love your enemies, and do good, and lend, expecting nothing in return, and your reward will be great, and you will be sons of the Most High, for he is kind to the ungrateful and the evil. [36] Be merciful, even as your Father is merciful.

[37] "Judge not, and you will not be judged; condemn not, and you will not be condemned; forgive, and you will be forgiven; [38] give, and it will be given to you. Good measure, pressed down, shaken together, running over, will be put into your lap. For with the measure you use it will be measured back to you."

[39] He also told them a parable: "Can a blind man lead a blind man? Will they not both fall into a pit? [40] A disciple is not above his teacher, but everyone when he is fully trained will be like his teacher. [41] Why do you see the speck that is in your brother's eye, but do not notice the log that is in your own eye? [42] How can you say to your brother, 'Brother, let me take out the speck that is in your eye,' when you yourself do not see the log that is in your own eye? You hypocrite, first take the log out of your own eye, and then you will see clearly to take out the speck that is in your brother's eye.

[43] "For no good tree bears bad fruit, nor again does a bad tree bear good fruit, [44] for each tree is known by its own fruit. For figs are not gathered from thornbushes, nor are grapes picked from a bramble bush. [45] The good person out of the good treasure of his heart produces good, and the evil person out of his evil treasure produces evil, for out of the abundance of the heart his mouth speaks.

[46] "Why do you call me 'Lord, Lord,' and not do what I tell you? [47] Everyone who comes to me and hears my words and does them, I will show you what he is like: [48] he is like a man building a house, who dug deep and laid the foundation on the rock. And when a flood arose, the stream broke against that house and could not shake it, because it had been well built.[2] [49] But the one who hears and does not do them is like a man who built a house on the ground without a foundation. When the stream broke against it, immediately it fell, and the ruin of that house was great."

[1] Greek *chiton*, a long garment worn under the cloak next to the skin [2] Some manuscripts *founded upon the rock*

Job 20

Then Zophar the Naamathite answered and said:

2 "Therefore my thoughts answer me,
    because of my haste within me.
3 I hear censure that insults me,
    and out of my understanding a spirit
        answers me.
4 Do you not know this from of old,
    since man was placed on earth,
5 that the exulting of the wicked is short,
    and the joy of the godless but for a
        moment?
6 Though his height mount up to the
        heavens,
    and his head reach to the clouds,
7 he will perish forever like his own dung;
    those who have seen him will say,
        'Where is he?'
8 He will fly away like a dream and not be
        found;
    he will be chased away like a vision of
        the night.
9 The eye that saw him will see him no
        more,
    nor will his place any more behold
        him.
10 His children will seek the favor of the
        poor,
    and his hands will give back his
        wealth.
11 His bones are full of his youthful vigor,
    but it will lie down with him in the
        dust.

12 "Though evil is sweet in his mouth,
    though he hides it under his tongue,
13 though he is loath to let it go
    and holds it in his mouth,
14 yet his food is turned in his stomach;
    it is the venom of cobras within him.
15 He swallows down riches and vomits
        them up again;
    God casts them out of his belly.
16 He will suck the poison of cobras;
    the tongue of a viper will kill him.
17 He will not look upon the rivers,
    the streams flowing with honey and
        curds.
18 He will give back the fruit of his toil
    and will not swallow it down;

from the profit of his trading
    he will get no enjoyment.
19 For he has crushed and abandoned the
        poor;
    he has seized a house that he did not
        build.

20 "Because he knew no contentment in his
        belly,
    he will not let anything in which he
        delights escape him.
21 There was nothing left after he had
        eaten;
    therefore his prosperity will not
        endure.
22 In the fullness of his sufficiency he will
        be in distress;
    the hand of everyone in misery will
        come against him.
23 To fill his belly to the full,
    God[1] will send his burning anger
        against him
    and rain it upon him into his body.
24 He will flee from an iron weapon;
    a bronze arrow will strike him
        through.
25 It is drawn forth and comes out of his
        body;
    the glittering point comes out of his
        gallbladder;
    terrors come upon him.
26 Utter darkness is laid up for his
        treasures;
    a fire not fanned will devour him;
    what is left in his tent will be
        consumed.
27 The heavens will reveal his iniquity,
    and the earth will rise up against him.
28 The possessions of his house will be
        carried away,
    dragged off in the day of God's[2] wrath.
29 This is the wicked man's portion from
        God,
    the heritage decreed for him by God."

1 Corinthians 7

Now concerning the matters about which you wrote: "It is good for a man not to have sexual relations with a woman." [2] But because of the temptation to sexual immorality, each man should have his own wife and

---

[1] Hebrew *he* [2] Hebrew *his*

each woman her own husband. ³The husband should give to his wife her conjugal rights, and likewise the wife to her husband. ⁴For the wife does not have authority over her own body, but the husband does. Likewise the husband does not have authority over his own body, but the wife does. ⁵Do not deprive one another, except perhaps by agreement for a limited time, that you may devote yourselves to prayer; but then come together again, so that Satan may not tempt you because of your lack of self-control.

⁶Now as a concession, not a command, I say this.¹ ⁷I wish that all were as I myself am. But each has his own gift from God, one of one kind and one of another.

⁸To the unmarried and the widows I say that it is good for them to remain single as I am. ⁹But if they cannot exercise self-control, they should marry. For it is better to marry than to burn with passion.

¹⁰To the married I give this charge (not I, but the Lord): the wife should not separate from her husband ¹¹(but if she does, she should remain unmarried or else be reconciled to her husband), and the husband should not divorce his wife.

¹²To the rest I say (I, not the Lord) that if any brother has a wife who is an unbeliever, and she consents to live with him, he should not divorce her. ¹³If any woman has a husband who is an unbeliever, and he consents to live with her, she should not divorce him. ¹⁴For the unbelieving husband is made holy because of his wife, and the unbelieving wife is made holy because of her husband. Otherwise your children would be unclean, but as it is, they are holy. ¹⁵But if the unbelieving partner separates, let it be so. In such cases the brother or sister is not enslaved. God has called you² to peace. ¹⁶For how do you know, wife, whether you will save your husband? Or how do you know, husband, whether you will save your wife?

¹⁷Only let each person lead the life³ that the Lord has assigned to him, and to which God has called him. This is my rule in all the churches. ¹⁸Was anyone at the time of his call already circumcised? Let him not seek to remove the marks of circumcision. Was anyone at the time of his call uncircumcised? Let him not seek circumcision. ¹⁹For neither circumcision counts for anything nor uncircumcision, but keeping the commandments of God. ²⁰Each one should remain in the condition in which he was called. ²¹Were you a bondservant⁴ when called? Do not be concerned about it. (But if you can gain your freedom, avail yourself of the opportunity.) ²²For he who was called in the Lord as a bondservant is a freedman of the Lord. Likewise he who was free when called is a bondservant of Christ. ²³You were bought with a price; do not become bondservants⁵ of men. ²⁴So, brothers,⁶ in whatever condition each was called, there let him remain with God.

²⁵Now concerning⁷ the betrothed,⁸ I have no command from the Lord, but I give my judgment as one who by the Lord's mercy is trustworthy. ²⁶I think that in view of the present⁹ distress it is good for a person to remain as he is. ²⁷Are you bound to a wife? Do not seek to be free. Are you free from a wife? Do not seek a wife. ²⁸But if you do marry, you have not sinned, and if a betrothed woman¹⁰ marries, she has not sinned. Yet those who marry will have worldly troubles, and I would spare you that. ²⁹This is what I mean, brothers: the appointed time has grown very short. From now on, let those who have wives live as though they had none, ³⁰and those who mourn as though they were not mourning, and those who rejoice as though they were not rejoicing, and those who buy as though they had no goods, ³¹and those who deal with the world as though they had no dealings with it. For the present form of this world is passing away.

³²I want you to be free from anxieties. The unmarried man is anxious about the things of the Lord, how to please the Lord. ³³But the married man is anxious about worldly things, how to please his wife, ³⁴and his interests are divided. And the unmarried or betrothed woman is anxious about the things of the Lord, how to be holy in body and spirit. But the married woman is anxious about worldly things, how to please her husband. ³⁵I say this for your own benefit, not to lay any restraint upon you, but to promote good order and to secure your undivided devotion to the Lord.

³⁶If anyone thinks that he is not behaving properly toward his betrothed,¹¹ if his¹² passions are strong, and it has to be, let him do as he wishes: let them marry—it is no sin. ³⁷But whoever is firmly established in his heart, being

¹ Or I say this: ² Some manuscripts us ³ Or each person walk in the way ⁴ Or slave; also twice in verse 22 (for the contextual rendering of the Greek word doulos, see Preface) ⁵ Or slaves (for the contextual rendering of the Greek word doulos, see Preface) ⁶ Or brothers and sisters; also verse 29 ⁷ The expression Now concerning introduces a reply to a question in the Corinthians' letter; see 7:1 ⁸ Greek virgins ⁹ Or impending ¹⁰ Greek virgin; also verse 34 ¹¹ Greek virgin; also verses 37, 38 ¹² Or her

under no necessity but having his desire under control, and has determined this in his heart, to keep her as his betrothed, he will do well. [38]So then he who marries his betrothed does well, and he who refrains from marriage will do even better.

[39]A wife is bound to her husband as long as he lives. But if her husband dies, she is free to be married to whom she wishes, only in the Lord. [40]Yet in my judgment she is happier if she remains as she is. And I think that I too have the Spirit of God.

FEBRUARY 21

Exodus 4

Then Moses answered, "But behold, they will not believe me or listen to my voice, for they will say, 'The LORD did not appear to you.'" [2]The LORD said to him, "What is that in your hand?" He said, "A staff." [3]And he said, "Throw it on the ground." So he threw it on the ground, and it became a serpent, and Moses ran from it. [4]But the LORD said to Moses, "Put out your hand and catch it by the tail"—so he put out his hand and caught it, and it became a staff in his hand— [5]"that they may believe that the LORD, the God of their fathers, the God of Abraham, the God of Isaac, and the God of Jacob, has appeared to you." [6]Again, the LORD said to him, "Put your hand inside your cloak."[1] And he put his hand inside his cloak, and when he took it out, behold, his hand was leprous[2] like snow. [7]Then God said, "Put your hand back inside your cloak." So he put his hand back inside his cloak, and when he took it out, behold, it was restored like the rest of his flesh. [8]"If they will not believe you," God said, "or listen to the first sign, they may believe the latter sign. [9]If they will not believe even these two signs or listen to your voice, you shall take some water from the Nile and pour it on the dry ground, and the water that you shall take from the Nile will become blood on the dry ground."

[10]But Moses said to the LORD, "Oh, my Lord, I am not eloquent, either in the past or since you have spoken to your servant, but I am slow of speech and of tongue." [11]Then the LORD said to him, "Who has made man's mouth? Who makes him mute, or deaf, or seeing, or blind? Is it not I, the LORD? [12]Now therefore go, and I will be with your mouth and teach you what you shall speak." [13]But he said, "Oh, my Lord, please send someone else." [14]Then the anger of the LORD was kindled against Moses and he said, "Is there not Aaron, your brother, the Levite? I know that he can speak well. Behold, he is coming out to meet you, and when he sees you, he will be glad in his heart. [15]You shall speak to him and put the words in his mouth, and I will be with your mouth and with his mouth and will teach you both what to do. [16]He shall speak for you to the people, and he shall be your mouth, and you shall be as God to him. [17]And take in your hand this staff, with which you shall do the signs."

[18]Moses went back to Jethro his father-in-law and said to him, "Please let me go back to my brothers in Egypt to see whether they are still alive." And Jethro said to Moses, "Go in peace." [19]And the LORD said to Moses in Midian, "Go back to Egypt, for all the men who were seeking your life are dead." [20]So Moses took his wife and his sons and had them ride on a donkey, and went back to the land of Egypt. And Moses took the staff of God in his hand.

[21]And the LORD said to Moses, "When you go back to Egypt, see that you do before Pharaoh all the miracles that I have put in your power. But I will harden his heart, so that he will not let the people go. [22]Then you shall say to Pharaoh, 'Thus says the LORD, Israel is my firstborn son, [23]and I say to you, "Let my son go that he may serve me." If you refuse to let him go, behold, I will kill your firstborn son.'"

[24]At a lodging place on the way the LORD met

[1] Hebrew *into your bosom*; also verse 7 [2] *Leprosy* was a term for several skin diseases; see Leviticus 13

him and sought to put him to death. ²⁵Then Zipporah took a flint and cut off her son's foreskin and touched Moses'[1] feet with it and said, "Surely you are a bridegroom of blood to me!" ²⁶So he let him alone. It was then that she said, "A bridegroom of blood," because of the circumcision.

²⁷The LORD said to Aaron, "Go into the wilderness to meet Moses." So he went and met him at the mountain of God and kissed him. ²⁸And Moses told Aaron all the words of the LORD with which he had sent him to speak, and all the signs that he had commanded him to do. ²⁹Then Moses and Aaron went and gathered together all the elders of the people of Israel. ³⁰Aaron spoke all the words that the LORD had spoken to Moses and did the signs in the sight of the people. ³¹And the people believed; and when they heard that the LORD had visited the people of Israel and that he had seen their affliction, they bowed their heads and worshiped.

Luke 7

After he had finished all his sayings in the hearing of the people, he entered Capernaum. ²Now a centurion had a servant[2] who was sick and at the point of death, who was highly valued by him. ³When the centurion[3] heard about Jesus, he sent to him elders of the Jews, asking him to come and heal his servant. ⁴And when they came to Jesus, they pleaded with him earnestly, saying, "He is worthy to have you do this for him, ⁵for he loves our nation, and he is the one who built us our synagogue." ⁶And Jesus went with them. When he was not far from the house, the centurion sent friends, saying to him, "Lord, do not trouble yourself, for I am not worthy to have you come under my roof. ⁷Therefore I did not presume to come to you. But say the word, and let my servant be healed. ⁸For I too am a man set under authority, with soldiers under me: and I say to one, 'Go,' and he goes; and to another, 'Come,' and he comes; and to my servant, 'Do this,' and he does it." ⁹When Jesus heard these things, he marveled at him, and turning to the crowd that followed him, said, "I tell you, not even in Israel have I found such faith." ¹⁰And when those who had been sent returned to the house, they found the servant well.

¹¹Soon afterward[4] he went to a town called Nain, and his disciples and a great crowd went with him. ¹²As he drew near to the gate of the town, behold, a man who had died was being carried out, the only son of his mother, and she was a widow, and a considerable crowd from the town was with her. ¹³And when the Lord saw her, he had compassion on her and said to her, "Do not weep." ¹⁴Then he came up and touched the bier, and the bearers stood still. And he said, "Young man, I say to you, arise." ¹⁵And the dead man sat up and began to speak, and Jesus[5] gave him to his mother. ¹⁶Fear seized them all, and they glorified God, saying, "A great prophet has arisen among us!" and "God has visited his people!" ¹⁷And this report about him spread through the whole of Judea and all the surrounding country.

¹⁸The disciples of John reported all these things to him. And John, ¹⁹calling two of his disciples to him, sent them to the Lord, saying, "Are you the one who is to come, or shall we look for another?" ²⁰And when the men had come to him, they said, "John the Baptist has sent us to you, saying, 'Are you the one who is to come, or shall we look for another?'" ²¹In that hour he healed many people of diseases and plagues and evil spirits, and on many who were blind he bestowed sight. ²²And he answered them, "Go and tell John what you have seen and heard: the blind receive their sight, the lame walk, lepers[6] are cleansed, and the deaf hear, the dead are raised up, the poor have good news preached to them. ²³And blessed is the one who is not offended by me."

²⁴When John's messengers had gone, Jesus[7] began to speak to the crowds concerning John: "What did you go out into the wilderness to see? A reed shaken by the wind? ²⁵What then did you go out to see? A man dressed in soft clothing? Behold, those who are dressed in splendid clothing and live in luxury are in kings' courts. ²⁶What then did you go out to see? A prophet? Yes, I tell you, and more than a prophet. ²⁷This is he of whom it is written,

"'Behold, I send my messenger before
        your face,
    who will prepare your way before you.'

²⁸I tell you, among those born of women none is greater than John. Yet the one who is least in the kingdom of God is greater than he." ²⁹(When all the people heard this, and the tax

¹ Hebrew *his* ² Greek *bondservant*; also verses 3, 8, 10 ³ Greek *he* ⁴ Some manuscripts *The next day* ⁵ Greek *he* ⁶ *Leprosy* was a term for several skin diseases; see Leviticus 13
⁷ Greek *he*

collectors too, they declared God just,[1] having been baptized with the baptism of John, [30]but the Pharisees and the lawyers rejected the purpose of God for themselves, not having been baptized by him.)

[31]"To what then shall I compare the people of this generation, and what are they like? [32]They are like children sitting in the marketplace and calling to one another,

"'We played the flute for you, and you did not dance;
  we sang a dirge, and you did not weep.'

[33]For John the Baptist has come eating no bread and drinking no wine, and you say, 'He has a demon.' [34]The Son of Man has come eating and drinking, and you say, 'Look at him! A glutton and a drunkard, a friend of tax collectors and sinners!' [35]Yet wisdom is justified by all her children."

[36]One of the Pharisees asked him to eat with him, and he went into the Pharisee's house and reclined at the table. [37]And behold, a woman of the city, who was a sinner, when she learned that he was reclining at table in the Pharisee's house, brought an alabaster flask of ointment, [38]and standing behind him at his feet, weeping, she began to wet his feet with her tears and wiped them with the hair of her head and kissed his feet and anointed them with the ointment. [39]Now when the Pharisee who had invited him saw this, he said to himself, "If this man were a prophet, he would have known who and what sort of woman this is who is touching him, for she is a sinner." [40]And Jesus answering said to him, "Simon, I have something to say to you." And he answered, "Say it, Teacher."

[41]"A certain moneylender had two debtors. One owed five hundred denarii, and the other fifty. [42]When they could not pay, he cancelled the debt of both. Now which of them will love him more?" [43]Simon answered, "The one, I suppose, for whom he cancelled the larger debt." And he said to him, "You have judged rightly." [44]Then turning toward the woman he said to Simon, "Do you see this woman? I entered your house; you gave me no water for my feet, but she has wet my feet with her tears and wiped them with her hair. [45]You gave me no kiss, but from the time I came in she has not ceased to kiss my feet. [46]You did not anoint my head with oil, but she has anointed my feet with ointment. [47]Therefore I tell you, her sins, which are many, are forgiven—for she loved much. But he who is forgiven little, loves little." [48]And he said to her, "Your sins are forgiven." [49]Then those who were at table with him began to say among[2] themselves, "Who is this, who even forgives sins?" [50]And he said to the woman, "Your faith has saved you; go in peace."

Job 21

Then Job answered and said:

2 "Keep listening to my words,
     and let this be your comfort.
3 Bear with me, and I will speak,
     and after I have spoken, mock on.
4 As for me, is my complaint against man?
     Why should I not be impatient?
5 Look at me and be appalled,
     and lay your hand over your mouth.
6 When I remember, I am dismayed,
     and shuddering seizes my flesh.
7 Why do the wicked live,
     reach old age, and grow mighty in power?
8 Their offspring are established in their presence,
     and their descendants before their eyes.
9 Their houses are safe from fear,
     and no rod of God is upon them.
10 Their bull breeds without fail;
     their cow calves and does not miscarry.
11 They send out their little boys like a flock,
     and their children dance.
12 They sing to the tambourine and the lyre
     and rejoice to the sound of the pipe.
13 They spend their days in prosperity,
     and in peace they go down to Sheol.
14 They say to God, 'Depart from us!
     We do not desire the knowledge of your ways.
15 What is the Almighty, that we should serve him?
     And what profit do we get if we pray to him?'
16 Behold, is not their prosperity in their hand?
     The counsel of the wicked is far from me.

[1] Greek they justified God [2] Or to

17 "How often is it that the lamp of the
        wicked is put out?
     That their calamity comes upon
        them?
     That God[1] distributes pains in his
        anger?
18 That they are like straw before the wind,
     and like chaff that the storm carries
        away?
19 You say, 'God stores up their iniquity for
        their children.'
     Let him pay it out to them, that they
        may know it.
20 Let their own eyes see their destruction,
     and let them drink of the wrath of the
        Almighty.
21 For what do they care for their houses
        after them,
     when the number of their months is
        cut off?
22 Will any teach God knowledge,
     seeing that he judges those who are
        on high?
23 One dies in his full vigor,
     being wholly at ease and secure,
24 his pails[2] full of milk
     and the marrow of his bones moist.
25 Another dies in bitterness of soul,
     never having tasted of prosperity.
26 They lie down alike in the dust,
     and the worms cover them.

27 "Behold, I know your thoughts
     and your schemes to wrong me.
28 For you say, 'Where is the house of the
        prince?
     Where is the tent in which the wicked
        lived?'
29 Have you not asked those who travel the
        roads,
     and do you not accept their testimony
30 that the evil man is spared in the day of
        calamity,
     that he is rescued in the day of wrath?
31 Who declares his way to his face,
     and who repays him for what he has
        done?

32 When he is carried to the grave,
     watch is kept over his tomb.
33 The clods of the valley are sweet to him;
     all mankind follows after him,
     and those who go before him are
        innumerable.
34 How then will you comfort me with
        empty nothings?
     There is nothing left of your answers
        but falsehood."

--------- *1 Corinthians 8* ---------

Now concerning[3] food offered to idols: we
know that "all of us possess knowledge."
This "knowledge" puffs up, but love builds up.
[2]If anyone imagines that he knows something,
he does not yet know as he ought to know. [3]But
if anyone loves God, he is known by God.[4]

[4]Therefore, as to the eating of food offered
to idols, we know that "an idol has no real existence," and that "there is no God but one." [5]For
although there may be so-called gods in heaven
or on earth—as indeed there are many "gods"
and many "lords"— [6]yet for us there is one
God, the Father, from whom are all things and
for whom we exist, and one Lord, Jesus Christ,
through whom are all things and through
whom we exist.

[7]However, not all possess this knowledge. But
some, through former association with idols, eat
food as really offered to an idol, and their conscience, being weak, is defiled. [8]Food will not
commend us to God. We are no worse off if we
do not eat, and no better off if we do. [9]But take
care that this right of yours does not somehow
become a stumbling block to the weak. [10]For
if anyone sees you who have knowledge eating[5] in an idol's temple, will he not be encouraged,[6] if his conscience is weak, to eat food
offered to idols? [11]And so by your knowledge
this weak person is destroyed, the brother for
whom Christ died. [12]Thus, sinning against your
brothers[7] and wounding their conscience when
it is weak, you sin against Christ. [13]Therefore, if
food makes my brother stumble, I will never eat
meat, lest I make my brother stumble.

---

[1] Hebrew *he* [2] The meaning of the Hebrew word is uncertain [3] The expression *Now concerning* introduces a reply to a question in the Corinthians' letter; see 7:1 [4] Greek *him*
[5] Greek *reclining at table* [6] Or *fortified*; Greek *built up* [7] Or *brothers and sisters*

FEBRUARY 22

Exodus 5

Afterward Moses and Aaron went and said to Pharaoh, "Thus says the LORD, the God of Israel, 'Let my people go, that they may hold a feast to me in the wilderness.'" ²But Pharaoh said, "Who is the LORD, that I should obey his voice and let Israel go? I do not know the LORD, and moreover, I will not let Israel go." ³Then they said, "The God of the Hebrews has met with us. Please let us go a three days' journey into the wilderness that we may sacrifice to the LORD our God, lest he fall upon us with pestilence or with the sword." ⁴But the king of Egypt said to them, "Moses and Aaron, why do you take the people away from their work? Get back to your burdens." ⁵And Pharaoh said, "Behold, the people of the land are now many,¹ and you make them rest from their burdens!" ⁶The same day Pharaoh commanded the taskmasters of the people and their foremen, ⁷"You shall no longer give the people straw to make bricks, as in the past; let them go and gather straw for themselves. ⁸But the number of bricks that they made in the past you shall impose on them, you shall by no means reduce it, for they are idle. Therefore they cry, 'Let us go and offer sacrifice to our God.' ⁹Let heavier work be laid on the men that they may labor at it and pay no regard to lying words."

¹⁰So the taskmasters and the foremen of the people went out and said to the people, "Thus says Pharaoh, 'I will not give you straw. ¹¹Go and get your straw yourselves wherever you can find it, but your work will not be reduced in the least.'" ¹²So the people were scattered throughout all the land of Egypt to gather stubble for straw. ¹³The taskmasters were urgent, saying, "Complete your work, your daily task each day, as when there was straw." ¹⁴And the foremen of the people of Israel, whom Pharaoh's taskmasters had set over them, were beaten and were asked, "Why have you not done all your task of making bricks today and yesterday, as in the past?"

¹⁵Then the foremen of the people of Israel came and cried to Pharaoh, "Why do you treat your servants like this? ¹⁶No straw is given to your servants, yet they say to us, 'Make bricks!' And behold, your servants are beaten; but the fault is in your own people." ¹⁷But he said, "You are idle, you are idle; that is why you say, 'Let us go and sacrifice to the LORD.' ¹⁸Go now and work. No straw will be given you, but you must still deliver the same number of bricks." ¹⁹The foremen of the people of Israel saw that they were in trouble when they said, "You shall by no means reduce your number of bricks, your daily task each day." ²⁰They met Moses and Aaron, who were waiting for them, as they came out from Pharaoh; ²¹and they said to them, "The LORD look on you and judge, because you have made us stink in the sight of Pharaoh and his servants, and have put a sword in their hand to kill us."

²²Then Moses turned to the LORD and said, "O Lord, why have you done evil to this people? Why did you ever send me? ²³For since I came to Pharaoh to speak in your name, he has done evil to this people, and you have not delivered your people at all."

Luke 8

Soon afterward he went on through cities and villages, proclaiming and bringing the good news of the kingdom of God. And the twelve were with him, ²and also some women who had been healed of evil spirits and infirmities: Mary, called Magdalene, from whom seven demons had gone out, ³and Joanna, the wife of Chuza, Herod's household manager, and Susanna, and many others, who provided for them² out of their means.

⁴And when a great crowd was gathering and people from town after town came to him, he said in a parable, ⁵"A sower went out to sow his seed. And as he sowed, some fell along the path and was trampled underfoot, and the birds of the air devoured it. ⁶And some fell on

¹ Samaritan *they are now more numerous than the people of the land* ² Some manuscripts *him*

the rock, and as it grew up, it withered away, because it had no moisture. [7]And some fell among thorns, and the thorns grew up with it and choked it. [8]And some fell into good soil and grew and yielded a hundredfold." As he said these things, he called out, "He who has ears to hear, let him hear."

[9]And when his disciples asked him what this parable meant, [10]he said, "To you it has been given to know the secrets of the kingdom of God, but for others they are in parables, so that 'seeing they may not see, and hearing they may not understand.' [11]Now the parable is this: The seed is the word of God. [12]The ones along the path are those who have heard; then the devil comes and takes away the word from their hearts, so that they may not believe and be saved. [13]And the ones on the rock are those who, when they hear the word, receive it with joy. But these have no root; they believe for a while, and in time of testing fall away. [14]And as for what fell among the thorns, they are those who hear, but as they go on their way they are choked by the cares and riches and pleasures of life, and their fruit does not mature. [15]As for that in the good soil, they are those who, hearing the word, hold it fast in an honest and good heart, and bear fruit with patience.

[16]"No one after lighting a lamp covers it with a jar or puts it under a bed, but puts it on a stand, so that those who enter may see the light. [17]For nothing is hidden that will not be made manifest, nor is anything secret that will not be known and come to light. [18]Take care then how you hear, for to the one who has, more will be given, and from the one who has not, even what he thinks that he has will be taken away."

[19]Then his mother and his brothers came to him, but they could not reach him because of the crowd. [20]And he was told, "Your mother and your brothers are standing outside, desiring to see you." [21]But he answered them, "My mother and my brothers are those who hear the word of God and do it."

[22]One day he got into a boat with his disciples, and he said to them, "Let us go across to the other side of the lake." So they set out, [23]and as they sailed he fell asleep. And a windstorm came down on the lake, and they were filling with water and were in danger. [24]And they went and woke him, saying, "Master, we are perishing!" And he awoke and rebuked the wind and the raging waves, and they ceased, and there was a calm. [25]He said to them, "Where is your faith?" And they were afraid, and they marveled, saying to one another, "Who then is this, that he commands even winds and water, and they obey him?"

[26]Then they sailed to the country of the Gerasenes,[1] which is opposite Galilee. [27]When Jesus[2] had stepped out on land, there met him a man from the city who had demons. For a long time he had worn no clothes, and he had not lived in a house but among the tombs. [28]When he saw Jesus, he cried out and fell down before him and said with a loud voice, "What have you to do with me, Jesus, Son of the Most High God? I beg you, do not torment me." [29]For he had commanded the unclean spirit to come out of the man. (For many a time it had seized him. He was kept under guard and bound with chains and shackles, but he would break the bonds and be driven by the demon into the desert.) [30]Jesus then asked him, "What is your name?" And he said, "Legion," for many demons had entered him. [31]And they begged him not to command them to depart into the abyss. [32]Now a large herd of pigs was feeding there on the hillside, and they begged him to let them enter these. So he gave them permission. [33]Then the demons came out of the man and entered the pigs, and the herd rushed down the steep bank into the lake and drowned.

[34]When the herdsmen saw what had happened, they fled and told it in the city and in the country. [35]Then people went out to see what had happened, and they came to Jesus and found the man from whom the demons had gone, sitting at the feet of Jesus, clothed and in his right mind, and they were afraid. [36]And those who had seen it told them how the demon-possessed[3] man had been healed. [37]Then all the people of the surrounding country of the Gerasenes asked him to depart from them, for they were seized with great fear. So he got into the boat and returned. [38]The man from whom the demons had gone begged that he might be with him, but Jesus sent him away, saying, [39]"Return to your home, and declare how much God has done for you." And he went away, proclaiming throughout the whole city how much Jesus had done for him.

[40]Now when Jesus returned, the crowd

[1] Some manuscripts *Gadarenes*; others *Gergesenes*; also verse 37 [2] Greek *he*; also verses 38, 42 [3] Greek *daimonizomai*; elsewhere rendered *oppressed by demons*

welcomed him, for they were all waiting for him. ⁴¹And there came a man named Jairus, who was a ruler of the synagogue. And falling at Jesus' feet, he implored him to come to his house, ⁴²for he had an only daughter, about twelve years of age, and she was dying.

As Jesus went, the people pressed around him. ⁴³And there was a woman who had had a discharge of blood for twelve years, and though she had spent all her living on physicians,¹ she could not be healed by anyone. ⁴⁴She came up behind him and touched the fringe of his garment, and immediately her discharge of blood ceased. ⁴⁵And Jesus said, "Who was it that touched me?" When all denied it, Peter² said, "Master, the crowds surround you and are pressing in on you!" ⁴⁶But Jesus said, "Someone touched me, for I perceive that power has gone out from me." ⁴⁷And when the woman saw that she was not hidden, she came trembling, and falling down before him declared in the presence of all the people why she had touched him, and how she had been immediately healed. ⁴⁸And he said to her, "Daughter, your faith has made you well; go in peace."

⁴⁹While he was still speaking, someone from the ruler's house came and said, "Your daughter is dead; do not trouble the Teacher any more." ⁵⁰But Jesus on hearing this answered him, "Do not fear; only believe, and she will be well." ⁵¹And when he came to the house, he allowed no one to enter with him, except Peter and John and James, and the father and mother of the child. ⁵²And all were weeping and mourning for her, but he said, "Do not weep, for she is not dead but sleeping." ⁵³And they laughed at him, knowing that she was dead. ⁵⁴But taking her by the hand he called, saying, "Child, arise." ⁵⁵And her spirit returned, and she got up at once. And he directed that something should be given her to eat. ⁵⁶And her parents were amazed, but he charged them to tell no one what had happened.

----------- Job 22 -----------

Then Eliphaz the Temanite answered and said:

2   "Can a man be profitable to God?
　　　Surely he who is wise is profitable to
　　　　himself.

3   Is it any pleasure to the Almighty if you
　　　are in the right,
　　　or is it gain to him if you make your
　　　　ways blameless?
4   Is it for your fear of him that he reproves
　　　you
　　　and enters into judgment with you?
5   Is not your evil abundant?
　　　There is no end to your iniquities.
6   For you have exacted pledges of your
　　　brothers for nothing
　　　and stripped the naked of their
　　　　clothing.
7   You have given no water to the weary to
　　　drink,
　　　and you have withheld bread from the
　　　　hungry.
8   The man with power possessed the land,
　　　and the favored man lived in it.
9   You have sent widows away empty,
　　　and the arms of the fatherless were
　　　　crushed.
10   Therefore snares are all around you,
　　　and sudden terror overwhelms you,
11   or darkness, so that you cannot see,
　　　and a flood of water covers you.
12   "Is not God high in the heavens?
　　　See the highest stars, how lofty they
　　　　are!
13   But you say, 'What does God know?
　　　Can he judge through the deep
　　　　darkness?
14   Thick clouds veil him, so that he does
　　　not see,
　　　and he walks on the vault of heaven.'
15   Will you keep to the old way
　　　that wicked men have trod?
16   They were snatched away before their
　　　time;
　　　their foundation was washed away.
17   They said to God, 'Depart from us,'
　　　and 'What can the Almighty do to us?'³
18   Yet he filled their houses with good
　　　things—
　　　but the counsel of the wicked is far
　　　　from me.
19   The righteous see it and are glad;
　　　the innocent one mocks at them,
20   saying, 'Surely our adversaries are cut off,
　　　and what they left the fire has
　　　　consumed.'

¹ Some manuscripts omit *and though she had spent all her living on physicians,* ² Some manuscripts add *and those who were with him* ³ Hebrew *them*

²¹ "Agree with God, and be at peace;
          thereby good will come to you.
²² Receive instruction from his mouth,
          and lay up his words in your heart.
²³ If you return to the Almighty you will be
              built up;
          if you remove injustice far from your
              tents,
²⁴ if you lay gold in the dust,
          and gold of Ophir among the stones of
              the torrent-bed,
²⁵ then the Almighty will be your gold
          and your precious silver.
²⁶ For then you will delight yourself in the
              Almighty
          and lift up your face to God.
²⁷ You will make your prayer to him, and
              he will hear you,
          and you will pay your vows.
²⁸ You will decide on a matter, and it will
              be established for you,
          and light will shine on your ways.
²⁹ For when they are humbled you say, 'It is
              because of pride';[1]
          but he saves the lowly.
³⁰ He delivers even the one who is not
              innocent,
          who will be delivered through the
              cleanness of your hands."

---
1 Corinthians 9

A m I not free? Am I not an apostle? Have I not seen Jesus our Lord? Are not you my workmanship in the Lord? ²If to others I am not an apostle, at least I am to you, for you are the seal of my apostleship in the Lord.

³This is my defense to those who would examine me. ⁴Do we not have the right to eat and drink? ⁵Do we not have the right to take along a believing wife,[2] as do the other apostles and the brothers of the Lord and Cephas? ⁶Or is it only Barnabas and I who have no right to refrain from working for a living? ⁷Who serves as a soldier at his own expense? Who plants a vineyard without eating any of its fruit? Or who tends a flock without getting some of the milk?

⁸Do I say these things on human authority? Does not the Law say the same? ⁹For it is written in the Law of Moses, "You shall not muzzle an ox when it treads out the grain." Is it for oxen that God is concerned? ¹⁰Does he not certainly speak for our sake? It was written for our sake, because the plowman should plow in hope and the thresher thresh in hope of sharing in the crop. ¹¹If we have sown spiritual things among you, is it too much if we reap material things from you? ¹²If others share this rightful claim on you, do not we even more?

Nevertheless, we have not made use of this right, but we endure anything rather than put an obstacle in the way of the gospel of Christ. ¹³Do you not know that those who are employed in the temple service get their food from the temple, and those who serve at the altar share in the sacrificial offerings? ¹⁴In the same way, the Lord commanded that those who proclaim the gospel should get their living by the gospel.

¹⁵But I have made no use of any of these rights, nor am I writing these things to secure any such provision. For I would rather die than have anyone deprive me of my ground for boasting. ¹⁶For if I preach the gospel, that gives me no ground for boasting. For necessity is laid upon me. Woe to me if I do not preach the gospel! ¹⁷For if I do this of my own will, I have a reward, but if not of my own will, I am still entrusted with a stewardship. ¹⁸What then is my reward? That in my preaching I may present the gospel free of charge, so as not to make full use of my right in the gospel.

¹⁹For though I am free from all, I have made myself a servant to all, that I might win more of them. ²⁰To the Jews I became as a Jew, in order to win Jews. To those under the law I became as one under the law (though not being myself under the law) that I might win those under the law. ²¹To those outside the law I became as one outside the law (not being outside the law of God but under the law of Christ) that I might win those outside the law. ²²To the weak I became weak, that I might win the weak. I have become all things to all people, that by all means I might save some. ²³I do it all for the sake of the gospel, that I may share with them in its blessings.

²⁴Do you not know that in a race all the runners run, but only one receives the prize? So run that you may obtain it. ²⁵Every athlete exercises self-control in all things. They do it to receive a perishable wreath, but we an imperishable. ²⁶So I do not run aimlessly; I do not box as one beating the air. ²⁷But I discipline my body and keep it under control,[3] lest after preaching to others I myself should be disqualified.

---

¹ Or you say, 'It is exaltation' ² Greek a sister as wife ³ Greek I pummel my body and make it a slave

FEBRUARY 23

Exodus 6

But the LORD said to Moses, "Now you shall see what I will do to Pharaoh; for with a strong hand he will send them out, and with a strong hand he will drive them out of his land."

²God spoke to Moses and said to him, "I am the LORD. ³I appeared to Abraham, to Isaac, and to Jacob, as God Almighty,[1] but by my name the LORD I did not make myself known to them. ⁴I also established my covenant with them to give them the land of Canaan, the land in which they lived as sojourners. ⁵Moreover, I have heard the groaning of the people of Israel whom the Egyptians hold as slaves, and I have remembered my covenant. ⁶Say therefore to the people of Israel, 'I am the LORD, and I will bring you out from under the burdens of the Egyptians, and I will deliver you from slavery to them, and I will redeem you with an outstretched arm and with great acts of judgment. ⁷I will take you to be my people, and I will be your God, and you shall know that I am the LORD your God, who has brought you out from under the burdens of the Egyptians. ⁸I will bring you into the land that I swore to give to Abraham, to Isaac, and to Jacob. I will give it to you for a possession. I am the LORD.'" ⁹Moses spoke thus to the people of Israel, but they did not listen to Moses, because of their broken spirit and harsh slavery.

¹⁰So the LORD said to Moses, ¹¹"Go in, tell Pharaoh king of Egypt to let the people of Israel go out of his land." ¹²But Moses said to the LORD, "Behold, the people of Israel have not listened to me. How then shall Pharaoh listen to me, for I am of uncircumcised lips?" ¹³But the LORD spoke to Moses and Aaron and gave them a charge about the people of Israel and about Pharaoh king of Egypt: to bring the people of Israel out of the land of Egypt.

¹⁴These are the heads of their fathers' houses: the sons of Reuben, the firstborn of Israel: Hanoch, Pallu, Hezron, and Carmi; these are the clans of Reuben. ¹⁵The sons of Simeon: Jemuel, Jamin, Ohad, Jachin, Zohar,

and Shaul, the son of a Canaanite woman; these are the clans of Simeon. ¹⁶These are the names of the sons of Levi according to their generations: Gershon, Kohath, and Merari, the years of the life of Levi being 137 years. ¹⁷The sons of Gershon: Libni and Shimei, by their clans. ¹⁸The sons of Kohath: Amram, Izhar, Hebron, and Uzziel, the years of the life of Kohath being 133 years. ¹⁹The sons of Merari: Mahli and Mushi. These are the clans of the Levites according to their generations. ²⁰Amram took as his wife Jochebed his father's sister, and she bore him Aaron and Moses, the years of the life of Amram being 137 years. ²¹The sons of Izhar: Korah, Nepheg, and Zichri. ²²The sons of Uzziel: Mishael, Elzaphan, and Sithri. ²³Aaron took as his wife Elisheba, the daughter of Amminadab and the sister of Nahshon, and she bore him Nadab, Abihu, Eleazar, and Ithamar. ²⁴The sons of Korah: Assir, Elkanah, and Abiasaph; these are the clans of the Korahites. ²⁵Eleazar, Aaron's son, took as his wife one of the daughters of Putiel, and she bore him Phinehas. These are the heads of the fathers' houses of the Levites by their clans.

²⁶These are the Aaron and Moses to whom the LORD said: "Bring out the people of Israel from the land of Egypt by their hosts." ²⁷It was they who spoke to Pharaoh king of Egypt about bringing out the people of Israel from Egypt, this Moses and this Aaron.

²⁸On the day when the LORD spoke to Moses in the land of Egypt, ²⁹the LORD said to Moses, "I am the LORD; tell Pharaoh king of Egypt all that I say to you." ³⁰But Moses said to the LORD, "Behold, I am of uncircumcised lips. How will Pharaoh listen to me?"

Luke 9

And he called the twelve together and gave them power and authority over all demons and to cure diseases, ²and he sent them out to proclaim the kingdom of God and to heal. ³And

[1] Hebrew El Shaddai

he said to them, "Take nothing for your journey, no staff, nor bag, nor bread, nor money; and do not have two tunics.[1] ⁴And whatever house you enter, stay there, and from there depart. ⁵And wherever they do not receive you, when you leave that town shake off the dust from your feet as a testimony against them." ⁶And they departed and went through the villages, preaching the gospel and healing everywhere.

⁷Now Herod the tetrarch heard about all that was happening, and he was perplexed, because it was said by some that John had been raised from the dead, ⁸by some that Elijah had appeared, and by others that one of the prophets of old had risen. ⁹Herod said, "John I beheaded, but who is this about whom I hear such things?" And he sought to see him.

¹⁰On their return the apostles told him all that they had done. And he took them and withdrew apart to a town called Bethsaida. ¹¹When the crowds learned it, they followed him, and he welcomed them and spoke to them of the kingdom of God and cured those who had need of healing. ¹²Now the day began to wear away, and the twelve came and said to him, "Send the crowd away to go into the surrounding villages and countryside to find lodging and get provisions, for we are here in a desolate place." ¹³But he said to them, "You give them something to eat." They said, "We have no more than five loaves and two fish—unless we are to go and buy food for all these people." ¹⁴For there were about five thousand men. And he said to his disciples, "Have them sit down in groups of about fifty each." ¹⁵And they did so, and had them all sit down. ¹⁶And taking the five loaves and the two fish, he looked up to heaven and said a blessing over them. Then he broke the loaves and gave them to the disciples to set before the crowd. ¹⁷And they all ate and were satisfied. And what was left over was picked up, twelve baskets of broken pieces.

¹⁸Now it happened that as he was praying alone, the disciples were with him. And he asked them, "Who do the crowds say that I am?" ¹⁹And they answered, "John the Baptist. But others say, Elijah, and others, that one of the prophets of old has risen." ²⁰Then he said to them, "But who do you say that I am?" And Peter answered, "The Christ of God."

²¹And he strictly charged and commanded them to tell this to no one, ²²saying, "The Son of Man must suffer many things and be rejected by the elders and chief priests and scribes, and be killed, and on the third day be raised."

²³And he said to all, "If anyone would come after me, let him deny himself and take up his cross daily and follow me. ²⁴For whoever would save his life will lose it, but whoever loses his life for my sake will save it. ²⁵For what does it profit a man if he gains the whole world and loses or forfeits himself? ²⁶For whoever is ashamed of me and of my words, of him will the Son of Man be ashamed when he comes in his glory and the glory of the Father and of the holy angels. ²⁷But I tell you truly, there are some standing here who will not taste death until they see the kingdom of God."

²⁸Now about eight days after these sayings he took with him Peter and John and James and went up on the mountain to pray. ²⁹And as he was praying, the appearance of his face was altered, and his clothing became dazzling white. ³⁰And behold, two men were talking with him, Moses and Elijah, ³¹who appeared in glory and spoke of his departure,[2] which he was about to accomplish at Jerusalem. ³²Now Peter and those who were with him were heavy with sleep, but when they became fully awake they saw his glory and the two men who stood with him. ³³And as the men were parting from him, Peter said to Jesus, "Master, it is good that we are here. Let us make three tents, one for you and one for Moses and one for Elijah"—not knowing what he said. ³⁴As he was saying these things, a cloud came and overshadowed them, and they were afraid as they entered the cloud. ³⁵And a voice came out of the cloud, saying, "This is my Son, my Chosen One;[3] listen to him!" ³⁶And when the voice had spoken, Jesus was found alone. And they kept silent and told no one in those days anything of what they had seen.

³⁷On the next day, when they had come down from the mountain, a great crowd met him. ³⁸And behold, a man from the crowd cried out, "Teacher, I beg you to look at my son, for he is my only child. ³⁹And behold, a spirit seizes him, and he suddenly cries out. It convulses him so that he foams at the mouth, and shatters him, and will hardly leave him. ⁴⁰And I begged your disciples to cast it out, but they could not." ⁴¹Jesus answered, "O faithless and twisted generation, how long am I to be with you and bear with you? Bring your son here."

[1] Greek *chiton*, a long garment worn under the cloak next to the skin [2] Greek *exodus* [3] Some manuscripts *my Beloved*

[42]While he was coming, the demon threw him to the ground and convulsed him. But Jesus rebuked the unclean spirit and healed the boy, and gave him back to his father. [43]And all were astonished at the majesty of God.

But while they were all marveling at everything he was doing, Jesus[1] said to his disciples, [44]"Let these words sink into your ears: The Son of Man is about to be delivered into the hands of men." [45]But they did not understand this saying, and it was concealed from them, so that they might not perceive it. And they were afraid to ask him about this saying.

[46]An argument arose among them as to which of them was the greatest. [47]But Jesus, knowing the reasoning of their hearts, took a child and put him by his side [48]and said to them, "Whoever receives this child in my name receives me, and whoever receives me receives him who sent me. For he who is least among you all is the one who is great."

[49]John answered, "Master, we saw someone casting out demons in your name, and we tried to stop him, because he does not follow with us." [50]But Jesus said to him, "Do not stop him, for the one who is not against you is for you."

[51]When the days drew near for him to be taken up, he set his face to go to Jerusalem. [52]And he sent messengers ahead of him, who went and entered a village of the Samaritans, to make preparations for him. [53]But the people did not receive him, because his face was set toward Jerusalem. [54]And when his disciples James and John saw it, they said, "Lord, do you want us to tell fire to come down from heaven and consume them?"[2] [55]But he turned and rebuked them.[3] [56]And they went on to another village.

[57]As they were going along the road, someone said to him, "I will follow you wherever you go." [58]And Jesus said to him, "Foxes have holes, and birds of the air have nests, but the Son of Man has nowhere to lay his head." [59]To another he said, "Follow me." But he said, "Lord, let me first go and bury my father." [60]And Jesus[4] said to him, "Leave the dead to bury their own dead. But as for you, go and proclaim the kingdom of God." [61]Yet another said, "I will follow you, Lord, but let me first say farewell to those at my home." [62]Jesus said to him, "No one who puts his hand to the plow and looks back is fit for the kingdom of God."

Job 23

Then Job answered and said:

[2] "Today also my complaint is bitter;[5]
    my hand is heavy on account of my groaning.
[3] Oh, that I knew where I might find him,
    that I might come even to his seat!
[4] I would lay my case before him
    and fill my mouth with arguments.
[5] I would know what he would answer me
    and understand what he would say to me.
[6] Would he contend with me in the greatness of his power?
    No; he would pay attention to me.
[7] There an upright man could argue with him,
    and I would be acquitted forever by my judge.

[8] "Behold, I go forward, but he is not there,
    and backward, but I do not perceive him;
[9] on the left hand when he is working, I do not behold him;
    he turns to the right hand, but I do not see him.
[10] But he knows the way that I take;
    when he has tried me, I shall come out as gold.
[11] My foot has held fast to his steps;
    I have kept his way and have not turned aside.
[12] I have not departed from the commandment of his lips;
    I have treasured the words of his mouth more than my portion of food.
[13] But he is unchangeable,[6] and who can turn him back?
    What he desires, that he does.
[14] For he will complete what he appoints for me,
    and many such things are in his mind.
[15] Therefore I am terrified at his presence;
    when I consider, I am in dread of him.
[16] God has made my heart faint;
    the Almighty has terrified me;

---

[1] Greek he   [2] Some manuscripts add as Elijah did   [3] Some manuscripts add and he said, "You do not know what manner of spirit you are of; for the Son of Man came not to destroy people's lives but to save them"   [4] Greek he   [5] Or defiant   [6] Or one

[17] yet I am not silenced because of the
     darkness,
          nor because thick darkness covers my
          face.

—— 1 Corinthians 10 ——

For I do not want you to be unaware, broth-ers,[1] that our fathers were all under the cloud, and all passed through the sea, [2] and all were baptized into Moses in the cloud and in the sea, [3] and all ate the same spiritual food, [4] and all drank the same spiritual drink. For they drank from the spiritual Rock that followed them, and the Rock was Christ. [5] Nevertheless, with most of them God was not pleased, for they were overthrown[2] in the wilderness.

[6] Now these things took place as examples for us, that we might not desire evil as they did. [7] Do not be idolaters as some of them were; as it is written, "The people sat down to eat and drink and rose up to play." [8] We must not indulge in sexual immorality as some of them did, and twenty-three thousand fell in a single day. [9] We must not put Christ[3] to the test, as some of them did and were destroyed by serpents, [10] nor grumble, as some of them did and were destroyed by the Destroyer. [11] Now these things happened to them as an example, but they were written down for our instruction, on whom the end of the ages has come. [12] Therefore let anyone who thinks that he stands take heed lest he fall. [13] No temp-tation has overtaken you that is not common to man. God is faithful, and he will not let you be tempted beyond your ability, but with the temp-tation he will also provide the way of escape, that you may be able to endure it.

[14] Therefore, my beloved, flee from idolatry. [15] I speak as to sensible people; judge for your-selves what I say. [16] The cup of blessing that we bless, is it not a participation in the blood of Christ? The bread that we break, is it not a par-ticipation in the body of Christ? [17] Because there is one bread, we who are many are one body, for we all partake of the one bread. [18] Consider the people of Israel:[4] are not those who eat the sacrifices participants in the altar? [19] What do I imply then? That food offered to idols is any-thing, or that an idol is anything? [20] No, I imply that what pagans sacrifice they offer to demons and not to God. I do not want you to be partici-pants with demons. [21] You cannot drink the cup of the Lord and the cup of demons. You cannot partake of the table of the Lord and the table of demons. [22] Shall we provoke the Lord to jeal-ousy? Are we stronger than he?

[23] "All things are lawful," but not all things are helpful. "All things are lawful," but not all things build up. [24] Let no one seek his own good, but the good of his neighbor. [25] Eat what-ever is sold in the meat market without rais-ing any question on the ground of conscience. [26] For "the earth is the Lord's, and the fullness thereof." [27] If one of the unbelievers invites you to dinner and you are disposed to go, eat whatever is set before you without raising any question on the ground of conscience. [28] But if someone says to you, "This has been offered in sacrifice," then do not eat it, for the sake of the one who informed you, and for the sake of conscience— [29] I do not mean your conscience, but his. For why should my liberty be deter-mined by someone else's conscience? [30] If I par-take with thankfulness, why am I denounced because of that for which I give thanks?

[31] So, whether you eat or drink, or whatever you do, do all to the glory of God. [32] Give no offense to Jews or to Greeks or to the church of God, [33] just as I try to please everyone in every-thing I do, not seeking my own advantage, but that of many, that they may be saved.

---

[1] Or brothers and sisters [2] Or were laid low [3] Some manuscripts the Lord [4] Greek Consider Israel according to the flesh

FEBRUARY 24

--- *Exodus 7* ---

And the Lord said to Moses, "See, I have made you like God to Pharaoh, and your brother Aaron shall be your prophet. [2] You shall speak all that I command you, and your brother Aaron shall tell Pharaoh to let the people of Israel go out of his land. [3] But I will harden Pharaoh's heart, and though I multiply my signs and wonders in the land of Egypt, [4] Pharaoh will not listen to you. Then I will lay my hand on Egypt and bring my hosts, my people the children of Israel, out of the land of Egypt by great acts of judgment. [5] The Egyptians shall know that I am the Lord, when I stretch out my hand against Egypt and bring out the people of Israel from among them." [6] Moses and Aaron did so; they did just as the Lord commanded them. [7] Now Moses was eighty years old, and Aaron eighty-three years old, when they spoke to Pharaoh.

[8] Then the Lord said to Moses and Aaron, [9] "When Pharaoh says to you, 'Prove yourselves by working a miracle,' then you shall say to Aaron, 'Take your staff and cast it down before Pharaoh, that it may become a serpent.'" [10] So Moses and Aaron went to Pharaoh and did just as the Lord commanded. Aaron cast down his staff before Pharaoh and his servants, and it became a serpent. [11] Then Pharaoh summoned the wise men and the sorcerers, and they, the magicians of Egypt, also did the same by their secret arts. [12] For each man cast down his staff, and they became serpents. But Aaron's staff swallowed up their staffs. [13] Still Pharaoh's heart was hardened, and he would not listen to them, as the Lord had said.

[14] Then the Lord said to Moses, "Pharaoh's heart is hardened; he refuses to let the people go. [15] Go to Pharaoh in the morning, as he is going out to the water. Stand on the bank of the Nile to meet him, and take in your hand the staff that turned into a serpent. [16] And you shall say to him, 'The Lord, the God of the Hebrews, sent me to you, saying, "Let my people go, that they may serve me in the wilderness." But so far, you have not obeyed. [17] Thus says the Lord, "By this you shall know that I am the Lord: behold, with the staff that is in my hand I will strike the water that is in the Nile, and it shall turn into blood. [18] The fish in the Nile shall die, and the Nile will stink, and the Egyptians will grow weary of drinking water from the Nile."'" [19] And the Lord said to Moses, "Say to Aaron, 'Take your staff and stretch out your hand over the waters of Egypt, over their rivers, their canals, and their ponds, and all their pools of water, so that they may become blood, and there shall be blood throughout all the land of Egypt, even in vessels of wood and in vessels of stone.'"

[20] Moses and Aaron did as the Lord commanded. In the sight of Pharaoh and in the sight of his servants he lifted up the staff and struck the water in the Nile, and all the water in the Nile turned into blood. [21] And the fish in the Nile died, and the Nile stank, so that the Egyptians could not drink water from the Nile. There was blood throughout all the land of Egypt. [22] But the magicians of Egypt did the same by their secret arts. So Pharaoh's heart remained hardened, and he would not listen to them, as the Lord had said. [23] Pharaoh turned and went into his house, and he did not take even this to heart. [24] And all the Egyptians dug along the Nile for water to drink, for they could not drink the water of the Nile.

[25] Seven full days passed after the Lord had struck the Nile.

--- *Luke 10* ---

After this the Lord appointed seventy-two[1] others and sent them on ahead of him, two by two, into every town and place where he himself was about to go. [2] And he said to them, "The harvest is plentiful, but the laborers are few. Therefore pray earnestly to the Lord of the harvest to send out laborers into his harvest. [3] Go your way; behold, I am sending you

---

[1] Some manuscripts *seventy*; also verse 17

out as lambs in the midst of wolves. [4]Carry no moneybag, no knapsack, no sandals, and greet no one on the road. [5]Whatever house you enter, first say, 'Peace be to this house!' [6]And if a son of peace is there, your peace will rest upon him. But if not, it will return to you. [7]And remain in the same house, eating and drinking what they provide, for the laborer deserves his wages. Do not go from house to house. [8]Whenever you enter a town and they receive you, eat what is set before you. [9]Heal the sick in it and say to them, 'The kingdom of God has come near to you.' [10]But whenever you enter a town and they do not receive you, go into its streets and say, [11]'Even the dust of your town that clings to our feet we wipe off against you. Nevertheless know this, that the kingdom of God has come near.' [12]I tell you, it will be more bearable on that day for Sodom than for that town.

[13]"Woe to you, Chorazin! Woe to you, Bethsaida! For if the mighty works done in you had been done in Tyre and Sidon, they would have repented long ago, sitting in sackcloth and ashes. [14]But it will be more bearable in the judgment for Tyre and Sidon than for you. [15]And you, Capernaum, will you be exalted to heaven? You shall be brought down to Hades.

[16]"The one who hears you hears me, and the one who rejects you rejects me, and the one who rejects me rejects him who sent me."

[17]The seventy-two returned with joy, saying, "Lord, even the demons are subject to us in your name!" [18]And he said to them, "I saw Satan fall like lightning from heaven. [19]Behold, I have given you authority to tread on serpents and scorpions, and over all the power of the enemy, and nothing shall hurt you. [20]Nevertheless, do not rejoice in this, that the spirits are subject to you, but rejoice that your names are written in heaven."

[21]In that same hour he rejoiced in the Holy Spirit and said, "I thank you, Father, Lord of heaven and earth, that you have hidden these things from the wise and understanding and revealed them to little children; yes, Father, for such was your gracious will.[1] [22]All things have been handed over to me by my Father, and no one knows who the Son is except the Father, or who the Father is except the Son and anyone to whom the Son chooses to reveal him."

[23]Then turning to the disciples he said privately, "Blessed are the eyes that see what you see! [24]For I tell you that many prophets and kings desired to see what you see, and did not see it, and to hear what you hear, and did not hear it."

[25]And behold, a lawyer stood up to put him to the test, saying, "Teacher, what shall I do to inherit eternal life?" [26]He said to him, "What is written in the Law? How do you read it?" [27]And he answered, "You shall love the Lord your God with all your heart and with all your soul and with all your strength and with all your mind, and your neighbor as yourself." [28]And he said to him, "You have answered correctly; do this, and you will live."

[29]But he, desiring to justify himself, said to Jesus, "And who is my neighbor?" [30]Jesus replied, "A man was going down from Jerusalem to Jericho, and he fell among robbers, who stripped him and beat him and departed, leaving him half dead. [31]Now by chance a priest was going down that road, and when he saw him he passed by on the other side. [32]So likewise a Levite, when he came to the place and saw him, passed by on the other side. [33]But a Samaritan, as he journeyed, came to where he was, and when he saw him, he had compassion. [34]He went to him and bound up his wounds, pouring on oil and wine. Then he set him on his own animal and brought him to an inn and took care of him. [35]And the next day he took out two denarii[2] and gave them to the innkeeper, saying, 'Take care of him, and whatever more you spend, I will repay you when I come back.' [36]Which of these three, do you think, proved to be a neighbor to the man who fell among the robbers?" [37]He said, "The one who showed him mercy." And Jesus said to him, "You go, and do likewise."

[38]Now as they went on their way, Jesus[3] entered a village. And a woman named Martha welcomed him into her house. [39]And she had a sister called Mary, who sat at the Lord's feet and listened to his teaching. [40]But Martha was distracted with much serving. And she went up to him and said, "Lord, do you not care that my sister has left me to serve alone? Tell her then to help me." [41]But the Lord answered her, "Martha, Martha, you are anxious and troubled about many things, [42]but one thing is necessary.[4] Mary has chosen the good portion, which will not be taken away from her."

[1] Or for so it pleased you well [2] A denarius was a day's wage for a laborer [3] Greek he [4] Some manuscripts few things are necessary, or only one

——————— *Job 24* ———————

"Why are not times of judgment kept by
the Almighty,
    and why do those who know him
        never see his days?
2 Some move landmarks;
    they seize flocks and pasture them.
3 They drive away the donkey of the
        fatherless;
    they take the widow's ox for a pledge.
4 They thrust the poor off the road;
    the poor of the earth all hide
        themselves.
5 Behold, like wild donkeys in the desert
    the poor[1] go out to their toil, seeking
        game;
    the wasteland yields food for their
        children.
6 They gather their[2] fodder in the field,
    and they glean the vineyard of the
        wicked man.
7 They lie all night naked, without
        clothing,
    and have no covering in the cold.
8 They are wet with the rain of the
        mountains
    and cling to the rock for lack of
        shelter.
9 (There are those who snatch the
        fatherless child from the breast,
    and they take a pledge against the
        poor.)
10 They go about naked, without clothing;
    hungry, they carry the sheaves;
11 among the olive rows of the wicked[3]
        they make oil;
    they tread the winepresses, but suffer
        thirst.
12 From out of the city the dying groan,
    and the soul of the wounded cries for
        help;
    yet God charges no one with wrong.
13 "There are those who rebel against the
        light,
    who are not acquainted with its ways,
    and do not stay in its paths.
14 The murderer rises before it is light,
    that he may kill the poor and needy,
    and in the night he is like a thief.

15 The eye of the adulterer also waits for
        the twilight,
    saying, 'No eye will see me';
    and he veils his face.
16 In the dark they dig through houses;
    by day they shut themselves up;
    they do not know the light.
17 For deep darkness is morning to all of
        them;
    for they are friends with the terrors of
        deep darkness.
18 "You say, 'Swift are they on the face of the
        waters;
    their portion is cursed in the land;
    no treader turns toward their
        vineyards.
19 Drought and heat snatch away the snow
        waters;
    so does Sheol those who have sinned.
20 The womb forgets them;
    the worm finds them sweet;
    they are no longer remembered,
    so wickedness is broken like a tree.'
21 "They wrong the barren, childless woman,
    and do no good to the widow.
22 Yet God[4] prolongs the life of the mighty
        by his power;
    they rise up when they despair of life.
23 He gives them security, and they are
        supported,
    and his eyes are upon their ways.
24 They are exalted a little while, and then
        are gone;
    they are brought low and gathered up
        like all others;
    they are cut off like the heads of grain.
25 If it is not so, who will prove me a liar
    and show that there is nothing in
        what I say?"

——————— *1 Corinthians 11* ———————

Be imitators of me, as I am of Christ.
²Now I commend you because you remember me in everything and maintain the traditions even as I delivered them to you. ³But I want you to understand that the head of every man is Christ, the head of a wife[5] is her husband, and the head of Christ is God. ⁴Every man who prays or prophesies with his head covered dishonors his head, ⁵but every wife[6]

[1] Hebrew *they* [2] Hebrew *his* [3] Hebrew *their olive rows* [4] Hebrew *he* [5] Greek *gunē*. This term may refer to a *woman* or a *wife*, depending on the context [6] In verses 5–13, the Greek word *gunē* is translated *wife* in verses that deal with wearing a veil, a sign of being married in first-century culture

who prays or prophesies with her head uncovered dishonors her head, since it is the same as if her head were shaven. [6]For if a wife will not cover her head, then she should cut her hair short. But since it is disgraceful for a wife to cut off her hair or shave her head, let her cover her head. [7]For a man ought not to cover his head, since he is the image and glory of God, but woman is the glory of man. [8]For man was not made from woman, but woman from man. [9]Neither was man created for woman, but woman for man. [10]That is why a wife ought to have a symbol of authority on her head, because of the angels.[1] [11]Nevertheless, in the Lord woman is not independent of man nor man of woman; [12]for as woman was made from man, so man is now born of woman. And all things are from God. [13]Judge for yourselves: is it proper for a wife to pray to God with her head uncovered? [14]Does not nature itself teach you that if a man wears long hair it is a disgrace for him, [15]but if a woman has long hair, it is her glory? For her hair is given to her for a covering. [16]If anyone is inclined to be contentious, we have no such practice, nor do the churches of God.

[17]But in the following instructions I do not commend you, because when you come together it is not for the better but for the worse. [18]For, in the first place, when you come together as a church, I hear that there are divisions among you. And I believe it in part,[2] [19]for there must be factions among you in order that those who are genuine among you may be recognized. [20]When you come together, it is not the Lord's supper that you eat. [21]For in eating, each one goes ahead with his own meal. One goes hungry, another gets drunk. [22]What! Do you not have houses to eat and drink in? Or do you despise the church of God and humiliate those who have nothing? What shall I say to you? Shall I commend you in this? No, I will not.

[23]For I received from the Lord what I also delivered to you, that the Lord Jesus on the night when he was betrayed took bread, [24]and when he had given thanks, he broke it, and said, "This is my body which is for[3] you. Do this in remembrance of me."[4] [25]In the same way also he took the cup, after supper, saying, "This cup is the new covenant in my blood. Do this, as often as you drink it, in remembrance of me." [26]For as often as you eat this bread and drink the cup, you proclaim the Lord's death until he comes.

[27]Whoever, therefore, eats the bread or drinks the cup of the Lord in an unworthy manner will be guilty concerning the body and blood of the Lord. [28]Let a person examine himself, then, and so eat of the bread and drink of the cup. [29]For anyone who eats and drinks without discerning the body eats and drinks judgment on himself. [30]That is why many of you are weak and ill, and some have died.[5] [31]But if we judged[6] ourselves truly, we would not be judged. [32]But when we are judged by the Lord, we are disciplined[7] so that we may not be condemned along with the world.

[33]So then, my brothers,[8] when you come together to eat, wait for[9] one another— [34]if anyone is hungry, let him eat at home—so that when you come together it will not be for judgment. About the other things I will give directions when I come.

FEBRUARY 25

Exodus 8[10]

Then the LORD said to Moses, "Go in to Pharaoh and say to him, 'Thus says the LORD, "Let my people go, that they may serve me. [2]But if you refuse to let them go, behold, I will plague all your country with frogs. [3]The Nile shall swarm with frogs that shall come up into your house and into your bedroom and on your bed and into the houses of your servants

[1] Or messengers, that is, people sent to observe and report [2] Or I believe a certain report [3] Some manuscripts broken for [4] Or as my memorial; also verse 25 [5] Greek have fallen asleep (as in 15:6, 20) [6] Or discerned [7] Or when we are judged we are being disciplined by the Lord [8] Or brothers and sisters [9] Or share with [10] Ch 7:26 in Hebrew

and your people,[1] and into your ovens and your kneading bowls. [4]The frogs shall come up on you and on your people and on all your servants.'"[2] [5][2]And the LORD said to Moses, "Say to Aaron, 'Stretch out your hand with your staff over the rivers, over the canals and over the pools, and make frogs come up on the land of Egypt!'" [6]So Aaron stretched out his hand over the waters of Egypt, and the frogs came up and covered the land of Egypt. [7]But the magicians did the same by their secret arts and made frogs come up on the land of Egypt.

[8]Then Pharaoh called Moses and Aaron and said, "Plead with the LORD to take away the frogs from me and from my people, and I will let the people go to sacrifice to the LORD." [9]Moses said to Pharaoh, "Be pleased to command me when I am to plead for you and for your servants and for your people, that the frogs be cut off from you and your houses and be left only in the Nile." [10]And he said, "Tomorrow." Moses said, "Be it as you say, so that you may know that there is no one like the LORD our God. [11]The frogs shall go away from you and your houses and your servants and your people. They shall be left only in the Nile." [12]So Moses and Aaron went out from Pharaoh, and Moses cried to the LORD about the frogs, as he had agreed with Pharaoh.[3] [13]And the LORD did according to the word of Moses. The frogs died out in the houses, the courtyards, and the fields. [14]And they gathered them together in heaps, and the land stank. [15]But when Pharaoh saw that there was a respite, he hardened his heart and would not listen to them, as the LORD had said.

[16]Then the LORD said to Moses, "Say to Aaron, 'Stretch out your staff and strike the dust of the earth, so that it may become gnats in all the land of Egypt.'" [17]And they did so. Aaron stretched out his hand with his staff and struck the dust of the earth, and there were gnats on man and beast. All the dust of the earth became gnats in all the land of Egypt. [18]The magicians tried by their secret arts to produce gnats, but they could not. So there were gnats on man and beast. [19]Then the magicians said to Pharaoh, "This is the finger of God." But Pharaoh's heart was hardened, and he would not listen to them, as the LORD had said.

[20]Then the LORD said to Moses, "Rise up early in the morning and present yourself to Pharaoh, as he goes out to the water, and say to him, 'Thus says the LORD, "Let my people go, that they may serve me. [21]Or else, if you will not let my people go, behold, I will send swarms of flies on you and your servants and your people, and into your houses. And the houses of the Egyptians shall be filled with swarms of flies, and also the ground on which they stand. [22]But on that day I will set apart the land of Goshen, where my people dwell, so that no swarms of flies shall be there, that you may know that I am the LORD in the midst of the earth.[4] [23]Thus I will put a division[5] between my people and your people. Tomorrow this sign shall happen."'" [24]And the LORD did so. There came great swarms of flies into the house of Pharaoh and into his servants' houses. Throughout all the land of Egypt the land was ruined by the swarms of flies.

[25]Then Pharaoh called Moses and Aaron and said, "Go, sacrifice to your God within the land." [26]But Moses said, "It would not be right to do so, for the offerings we shall sacrifice to the LORD our God are an abomination to the Egyptians. If we sacrifice offerings abominable to the Egyptians before their eyes, will they not stone us? [27]We must go three days' journey into the wilderness and sacrifice to the LORD our God as he tells us." [28]So Pharaoh said, "I will let you go to sacrifice to the LORD your God in the wilderness; only you must not go very far away. Plead for me." [29]Then Moses said, "Behold, I am going out from you and I will plead with the LORD that the swarms of flies may depart from Pharaoh, from his servants, and from his people, tomorrow. Only let not Pharaoh cheat again by not letting the people go to sacrifice to the LORD." [30]So Moses went out from Pharaoh and prayed to the LORD. [31]And the LORD did as Moses asked, and removed the swarms of flies from Pharaoh, from his servants, and from his people; not one remained. [32]But Pharaoh hardened his heart this time also, and did not let the people go.

Luke 11

[1]Now Jesus[6] was praying in a certain place, and when he finished, one of his disciples said to him, "Lord, teach us to pray, as John taught his disciples." [2]And he said to them, "When you pray, say:

---

[1] Or among your people [2] Ch 8:1 in Hebrew [3] Or which he had brought upon Pharaoh [4] Or that I the LORD am in the land [5] Septuagint, Vulgate; Hebrew set redemption [6] Greek he

"Father, hallowed be your name.
Your kingdom come.
3 Give us each day our daily bread,[1]
4 and forgive us our sins,
for we ourselves forgive everyone who
is indebted to us.
And lead us not into temptation."

[5]And he said to them, "Which of you who has a friend will go to him at midnight and say to him, 'Friend, lend me three loaves, [6]for a friend of mine has arrived on a journey, and I have nothing to set before him'; [7]and he will answer from within, 'Do not bother me; the door is now shut, and my children are with me in bed. I cannot get up and give you anything'? [8]I tell you, though he will not get up and give him anything because he is his friend, yet because of his impudence[2] he will rise and give him whatever he needs. [9]And I tell you, ask, and it will be given to you; seek, and you will find; knock, and it will be opened to you. [10]For everyone who asks receives, and the one who seeks finds, and to the one who knocks it will be opened. [11]What father among you, if his son asks for[3] a fish, will instead of a fish give him a serpent; [12]or if he asks for an egg, will give him a scorpion? [13]If you then, who are evil, know how to give good gifts to your children, how much more will the heavenly Father give the Holy Spirit to those who ask him!"

[14]Now he was casting out a demon that was mute. When the demon had gone out, the mute man spoke, and the people marveled. [15]But some of them said, "He casts out demons by Beelzebul, the prince of demons," [16]while others, to test him, kept seeking from him a sign from heaven. [17]But he, knowing their thoughts, said to them, "Every kingdom divided against itself is laid waste, and a divided household falls. [18]And if Satan also is divided against himself, how will his kingdom stand? For you say that I cast out demons by Beelzebul. [19]And if I cast out demons by Beelzebul, by whom do your sons cast them out? Therefore they will be your judges. [20]But if it is by the finger of God that I cast out demons, then the kingdom of God has come upon you. [21]When a strong man, fully armed, guards his own palace, his goods are safe; [22]but when one stronger than he attacks him and overcomes him, he takes away his armor in which he trusted and divides his spoil. [23]Whoever is not with me is against me, and whoever does not gather with me scatters.

[24]"When the unclean spirit has gone out of a person, it passes through waterless places seeking rest, and finding none it says, 'I will return to my house from which I came.' [25]And when it comes, it finds the house swept and put in order. [26]Then it goes and brings seven other spirits more evil than itself, and they enter and dwell there. And the last state of that person is worse than the first."

[27]As he said these things, a woman in the crowd raised her voice and said to him, "Blessed is the womb that bore you, and the breasts at which you nursed!" [28]But he said, "Blessed rather are those who hear the word of God and keep it!"

[29]When the crowds were increasing, he began to say, "This generation is an evil generation. It seeks for a sign, but no sign will be given to it except the sign of Jonah. [30]For as Jonah became a sign to the people of Nineveh, so will the Son of Man be to this generation. [31]The queen of the South will rise up at the judgment with the men of this generation and condemn them, for she came from the ends of the earth to hear the wisdom of Solomon, and behold, something greater than Solomon is here. [32]The men of Nineveh will rise up at the judgment with this generation and condemn it, for they repented at the preaching of Jonah, and behold, something greater than Jonah is here.

[33]"No one after lighting a lamp puts it in a cellar or under a basket, but on a stand, so that those who enter may see the light. [34]Your eye is the lamp of your body. When your eye is healthy, your whole body is full of light, but when it is bad, your body is full of darkness. [35]Therefore be careful lest the light in you be darkness. [36]If then your whole body is full of light, having no part dark, it will be wholly bright, as when a lamp with its rays gives you light."

[37]While Jesus[4] was speaking, a Pharisee asked him to dine with him, so he went in and reclined at table. [38]The Pharisee was astonished to see that he did not first wash before dinner. [39]And the Lord said to him, "Now you Pharisees cleanse the outside of the cup and of the dish, but inside you are full of greed and wickedness. [40]You fools! Did not he who made the outside make the inside also? [41]But give as alms those things that are within, and behold, everything is clean for you.

[1] Or our bread for tomorrow [2] Or persistence [3] Some manuscripts insert bread, will give him a stone; or if he asks for [4] Greek he

⁴²"But woe to you Pharisees! For you tithe mint and rue and every herb, and neglect justice and the love of God. These you ought to have done, without neglecting the others. ⁴³Woe to you Pharisees! For you love the best seat in the synagogues and greetings in the marketplaces. ⁴⁴Woe to you! For you are like unmarked graves, and people walk over them without knowing it."

⁴⁵One of the lawyers answered him, "Teacher, in saying these things you insult us also." ⁴⁶And he said, "Woe to you lawyers also! For you load people with burdens hard to bear, and you yourselves do not touch the burdens with one of your fingers. ⁴⁷Woe to you! For you build the tombs of the prophets whom your fathers killed. ⁴⁸So you are witnesses and you consent to the deeds of your fathers, for they killed them, and you build their tombs. ⁴⁹Therefore also the Wisdom of God said, 'I will send them prophets and apostles, some of whom they will kill and persecute,' ⁵⁰so that the blood of all the prophets, shed from the foundation of the world, may be charged against this generation, ⁵¹from the blood of Abel to the blood of Zechariah, who perished between the altar and the sanctuary. Yes, I tell you, it will be required of this generation. ⁵²Woe to you lawyers! For you have taken away the key of knowledge. You did not enter yourselves, and you hindered those who were entering."

⁵³As he went away from there, the scribes and the Pharisees began to press him hard and to provoke him to speak about many things, ⁵⁴lying in wait for him, to catch him in something he might say.

――――――― Job 25–26 ―――――――

Then Bildad the Shuhite answered and said:

² "Dominion and fear are with God;¹
   he makes peace in his high heaven.
³ Is there any number to his armies?
   Upon whom does his light not arise?
⁴ How then can man be in the right
   before God?
   How can he who is born of woman be
   pure?
⁵ Behold, even the moon is not bright,
   and the stars are not pure in his eyes;

⁶ how much less man, who is a maggot,
   and the son of man, who is a worm!"

²⁶:¹ Then Job answered and said:

² "How you have helped him who has no
   power!
   How you have saved the arm that has
   no strength!
³ How you have counseled him who has
   no wisdom,
   and plentifully declared sound
   knowledge!
⁴ With whose help have you uttered words,
   and whose breath has come out from
   you?
⁵ The dead tremble
   under the waters and their inhabitants.
⁶ Sheol is naked before God,²
   and Abaddon has no covering.
⁷ He stretches out the north over the void
   and hangs the earth on nothing.
⁸ He binds up the waters in his thick
   clouds,
   and the cloud is not split open under
   them.
⁹ He covers the face of the full moon³
   and spreads over it his cloud.
¹⁰ He has inscribed a circle on the face of
   the waters
   at the boundary between light and
   darkness.
¹¹ The pillars of heaven tremble
   and are astounded at his rebuke.
¹² By his power he stilled the sea;
   by his understanding he shattered
   Rahab.
¹³ By his wind the heavens were made fair;
   his hand pierced the fleeing serpent.
¹⁴ Behold, these are but the outskirts of his
   ways,
   and how small a whisper do we hear
   of him!
   But the thunder of his power who can
   understand?"

――――――― 1 Corinthians 12 ―――――――

Now concerning⁴ spiritual gifts,⁵ brothers,⁶ I do not want you to be uninformed. ²You know that when you were pagans you were led astray to mute idols, however you were led. ³Therefore I want you to understand that

¹ Hebrew him ² Hebrew him ³ Or his throne ⁴ The expression *Now concerning* introduces a reply to a question in the Corinthians' letter; see 7:1 ⁵ Or *spiritual persons* ⁶ Or *brothers and sisters*

no one speaking in the Spirit of God ever says "Jesus is accursed!" and no one can say "Jesus is Lord" except in the Holy Spirit.

⁴Now there are varieties of gifts, but the same Spirit; ⁵and there are varieties of service, but the same Lord; ⁶and there are varieties of activities, but it is the same God who empowers them all in everyone. ⁷To each is given the manifestation of the Spirit for the common good. ⁸For to one is given through the Spirit the utterance of wisdom, and to another the utterance of knowledge according to the same Spirit, ⁹to another faith by the same Spirit, to another gifts of healing by the one Spirit, ¹⁰to another the working of miracles, to another prophecy, to another the ability to distinguish between spirits, to another various kinds of tongues, to another the interpretation of tongues. ¹¹All these are empowered by one and the same Spirit, who apportions to each one individually as he wills.

¹²For just as the body is one and has many members, and all the members of the body, though many, are one body, so it is with Christ. ¹³For in one Spirit we were all baptized into one body—Jews or Greeks, slaves¹ or free—and all were made to drink of one Spirit.

¹⁴For the body does not consist of one member but of many. ¹⁵If the foot should say, "Because I am not a hand, I do not belong to the body," that would not make it any less a part of the body. ¹⁶And if the ear should say, "Because I am not an eye, I do not belong to the body," that would not make it any less a part of the body. ¹⁷If the whole body were an eye, where would be the sense of hearing? If the whole body were an ear, where would be the sense of smell? ¹⁸But as it is, God arranged the members in the body, each one of them, as he chose. ¹⁹If all were a single member, where would the body be? ²⁰As it is, there are many parts,² yet one body.

²¹The eye cannot say to the hand, "I have no need of you," nor again the head to the feet, "I have no need of you." ²²On the contrary, the parts of the body that seem to be weaker are indispensable, ²³and on those parts of the body that we think less honorable we bestow the greater honor, and our unpresentable parts are treated with greater modesty, ²⁴which our more presentable parts do not require. But God has so composed the body, giving greater honor to the part that lacked it, ²⁵that there may be no division in the body, but that the members may have the same care for one another. ²⁶If one member suffers, all suffer together; if one member is honored, all rejoice together.

²⁷Now you are the body of Christ and individually members of it. ²⁸And God has appointed in the church first apostles, second prophets, third teachers, then miracles, then gifts of healing, helping, administrating, and various kinds of tongues. ²⁹Are all apostles? Are all prophets? Are all teachers? Do all work miracles? ³⁰Do all possess gifts of healing? Do all speak with tongues? Do all interpret? ³¹But earnestly desire the higher gifts.

And I will show you a still more excellent way.

FEBRUARY 26

Exodus 9

Then the Lord said to Moses, "Go in to Pharaoh and say to him, 'Thus says the Lord, the God of the Hebrews, "Let my people go, that they may serve me. ²For if you refuse to let them go and still hold them, ³behold, the hand of the Lord will fall with a very severe plague upon your livestock that are in the field, the horses, the donkeys, the camels, the herds, and the flocks. ⁴But the Lord will make a distinction between the livestock of Israel and the livestock of Egypt, so that nothing of all that belongs to the people of Israel shall die."'" ⁵And the Lord set a time, saying, "Tomorrow the Lord will do this thing in the land." ⁶And

¹ Or *servants*; Greek *bondservants*   ² Or *members*; also verse 22

the next day the LORD did this thing. All the livestock of the Egyptians died, but not one of the livestock of the people of Israel died. [7] And Pharaoh sent, and behold, not one of the livestock of Israel was dead. But the heart of Pharaoh was hardened, and he did not let the people go.

[8] And the LORD said to Moses and Aaron, "Take handfuls of soot from the kiln, and let Moses throw them in the air in the sight of Pharaoh. [9] It shall become fine dust over all the land of Egypt, and become boils breaking out in sores on man and beast throughout all the land of Egypt." [10] So they took soot from the kiln and stood before Pharaoh. And Moses threw it in the air, and it became boils breaking out in sores on man and beast. [11] And the magicians could not stand before Moses because of the boils, for the boils came upon the magicians and upon all the Egyptians. [12] But the LORD hardened the heart of Pharaoh, and he did not listen to them, as the LORD had spoken to Moses.

[13] Then the LORD said to Moses, "Rise up early in the morning and present yourself before Pharaoh and say to him, 'Thus says the LORD, the God of the Hebrews, "Let my people go, that they may serve me. [14] For this time I will send all my plagues on you yourself,[1] and on your servants and your people, so that you may know that there is none like me in all the earth. [15] For by now I could have put out my hand and struck you and your people with pestilence, and you would have been cut off from the earth. [16] But for this purpose I have raised you up, to show you my power, so that my name may be proclaimed in all the earth. [17] You are still exalting yourself against my people and will not let them go. [18] Behold, about this time tomorrow I will cause very heavy hail to fall, such as never has been in Egypt from the day it was founded until now. [19] Now therefore send, get your livestock and all that you have in the field into safe shelter, for every man and beast that is in the field and is not brought home will die when the hail falls on them."'" [20] Then whoever feared the word of the LORD among the servants of Pharaoh hurried his slaves and his livestock into the houses, [21] but whoever did not pay attention to the word of the LORD left his slaves and his livestock in the field.

[22] Then the LORD said to Moses, "Stretch out your hand toward heaven, so that there may be hail in all the land of Egypt, on man and beast and every plant of the field, in the land of Egypt." [23] Then Moses stretched out his staff toward heaven, and the LORD sent thunder and hail, and fire ran down to the earth. And the LORD rained hail upon the land of Egypt. [24] There was hail and fire flashing continually in the midst of the hail, very heavy hail, such as had never been in all the land of Egypt since it became a nation. [25] The hail struck down everything that was in the field in all the land of Egypt, both man and beast. And the hail struck down every plant of the field and broke every tree of the field. [26] Only in the land of Goshen, where the people of Israel were, was there no hail.

[27] Then Pharaoh sent and called Moses and Aaron and said to them, "This time I have sinned; the LORD is in the right, and I and my people are in the wrong. [28] Plead with the LORD, for there has been enough of God's thunder and hail. I will let you go, and you shall stay no longer." [29] Moses said to him, "As soon as I have gone out of the city, I will stretch out my hands to the LORD. The thunder will cease, and there will be no more hail, so that you may know that the earth is the LORD's. [30] But as for you and your servants, I know that you do not yet fear the LORD God." [31] (The flax and the barley were struck down, for the barley was in the ear and the flax was in bud. [32] But the wheat and the emmer[2] were not struck down, for they are late in coming up.) [33] So Moses went out of the city from Pharaoh and stretched out his hands to the LORD, and the thunder and the hail ceased, and the rain no longer poured upon the earth. [34] But when Pharaoh saw that the rain and the hail and the thunder had ceased, he sinned yet again and hardened his heart, he and his servants. [35] So the heart of Pharaoh was hardened, and he did not let the people of Israel go, just as the LORD had spoken through Moses.

Luke 12

In the meantime, when so many thousands of the people had gathered together that they were trampling one another, he began to say to his disciples first, "Beware of the leaven of the Pharisees, which is hypocrisy. [2] Nothing is

[1] Hebrew *on your heart* [2] A type of wheat

covered up that will not be revealed, or hidden that will not be known. [3] Therefore whatever you have said in the dark shall be heard in the light, and what you have whispered in private rooms shall be proclaimed on the housetops.

[4] "I tell you, my friends, do not fear those who kill the body, and after that have nothing more that they can do. [5] But I will warn you whom to fear: fear him who, after he has killed, has authority to cast into hell.[1] Yes, I tell you, fear him! [6] Are not five sparrows sold for two pennies?[2] And not one of them is forgotten before God. [7] Why, even the hairs of your head are all numbered. Fear not; you are of more value than many sparrows.

[8] "And I tell you, everyone who acknowledges me before men, the Son of Man also will acknowledge before the angels of God, [9] but the one who denies me before men will be denied before the angels of God. [10] And everyone who speaks a word against the Son of Man will be forgiven, but the one who blasphemes against the Holy Spirit will not be forgiven. [11] And when they bring you before the synagogues and the rulers and the authorities, do not be anxious about how you should defend yourself or what you should say, [12] for the Holy Spirit will teach you in that very hour what you ought to say."

[13] Someone in the crowd said to him, "Teacher, tell my brother to divide the inheritance with me." [14] But he said to him, "Man, who made me a judge or arbitrator over you?" [15] And he said to them, "Take care, and be on your guard against all covetousness, for one's life does not consist in the abundance of his possessions." [16] And he told them a parable, saying, "The land of a rich man produced plentifully, [17] and he thought to himself, 'What shall I do, for I have nowhere to store my crops?' [18] And he said, 'I will do this: I will tear down my barns and build larger ones, and there I will store all my grain and my goods. [19] And I will say to my soul, "Soul, you have ample goods laid up for many years; relax, eat, drink, be merry."' [20] But God said to him, 'Fool! This night your soul is required of you, and the things you have prepared, whose will they be?' [21] So is the one who lays up treasure for himself and is not rich toward God."

[22] And he said to his disciples, "Therefore I tell you, do not be anxious about your life,

what you will eat, nor about your body, what you will put on. [23] For life is more than food, and the body more than clothing. [24] Consider the ravens: they neither sow nor reap, they have neither storehouse nor barn, and yet God feeds them. Of how much more value are you than the birds! [25] And which of you by being anxious can add a single hour to his span of life?[3] [26] If then you are not able to do as small a thing as that, why are you anxious about the rest? [27] Consider the lilies, how they grow: they neither toil nor spin,[4] yet I tell you, even Solomon in all his glory was not arrayed like one of these. [28] But if God so clothes the grass, which is alive in the field today, and tomorrow is thrown into the oven, how much more will he clothe you, O you of little faith! [29] And do not seek what you are to eat and what you are to drink, nor be worried. [30] For all the nations of the world seek after these things, and your Father knows that you need them. [31] Instead, seek his[5] kingdom, and these things will be added to you.

[32] "Fear not, little flock, for it is your Father's good pleasure to give you the kingdom. [33] Sell your possessions, and give to the needy. Provide yourselves with moneybags that do not grow old, with a treasure in the heavens that does not fail, where no thief approaches and no moth destroys. [34] For where your treasure is, there will your heart be also.

[35] "Stay dressed for action[6] and keep your lamps burning, [36] and be like men who are waiting for their master to come home from the wedding feast, so that they may open the door to him at once when he comes and knocks. [37] Blessed are those servants[7] whom the master finds awake when he comes. Truly, I say to you, he will dress himself for service and have them recline at table, and he will come and serve them. [38] If he comes in the second watch, or in the third, and finds them awake, blessed are those servants! [39] But know this, that if the master of the house had known at what hour the thief was coming, he[8] would not have left his house to be broken into. [40] You also must be ready, for the Son of Man is coming at an hour you do not expect."

[41] Peter said, "Lord, are you telling this parable for us or for all?" [42] And the Lord said, "Who then is the faithful and wise manager,

---

[1] Greek Gehenna [2] Greek two assaria; an assarion was a Roman copper coin worth about 1/16 of a denarius (which was a day's wage for a laborer) [3] Or a single cubit to his stature; a cubit was about 18 inches or 45 centimeters [4] Some manuscripts Consider the lilies; they neither spin nor weave [5] Some manuscripts God's [6] Greek Let your loins stay girded; compare Exodus 12:11 [7] Greek bondservants [8] Some manuscripts add would have stayed awake and

whom his master will set over his household, to give them their portion of food at the proper time? [43]Blessed is that servant[1] whom his master will find so doing when he comes. [44]Truly, I say to you, he will set him over all his possessions. [45]But if that servant says to himself, 'My master is delayed in coming,' and begins to beat the male and female servants, and to eat and drink and get drunk, [46]the master of that servant will come on a day when he does not expect him and at an hour he does not know, and will cut him in pieces and put him with the unfaithful. [47]And that servant who knew his master's will but did not get ready or act according to his will, will receive a severe beating. [48]But the one who did not know, and did what deserved a beating, will receive a light beating. Everyone to whom much was given, of him much will be required, and from him to whom they entrusted much, they will demand the more.

[49]"I came to cast fire on the earth, and would that it were already kindled! [50]I have a baptism to be baptized with, and how great is my distress until it is accomplished! [51]Do you think that I have come to give peace on earth? No, I tell you, but rather division. [52]For from now on in one house there will be five divided, three against two and two against three. [53]They will be divided, father against son and son against father, mother against daughter and daughter against mother, mother-in-law against her daughter-in-law and daughter-in-law against mother-in-law."

[54]He also said to the crowds, "When you see a cloud rising in the west, you say at once, 'A shower is coming.' And so it happens. [55]And when you see the south wind blowing, you say, 'There will be scorching heat,' and it happens. [56]You hypocrites! You know how to interpret the appearance of earth and sky, but why do you not know how to interpret the present time?

[57]"And why do you not judge for yourselves what is right? [58]As you go with your accuser before the magistrate, make an effort to settle with him on the way, lest he drag you to the judge, and the judge hand you over to the officer, and the officer put you in prison. [59]I tell you, you will never get out until you have paid the very last penny."[2]

Job 27

And Job again took up his discourse, and said:

[2] "As God lives, who has taken away my right,
    and the Almighty, who has made my soul bitter,
[3] as long as my breath is in me,
    and the spirit of God is in my nostrils,
[4] my lips will not speak falsehood,
    and my tongue will not utter deceit.
[5] Far be it from me to say that you are right;
    till I die I will not put away my integrity from me.
[6] I hold fast my righteousness and will not let it go;
    my heart does not reproach me for any of my days.

[7] "Let my enemy be as the wicked,
    and let him who rises up against me be as the unrighteous.
[8] For what is the hope of the godless when God cuts him off,
    when God takes away his life?
[9] Will God hear his cry
    when distress comes upon him?
[10] Will he take delight in the Almighty?
    Will he call upon God at all times?
[11] I will teach you concerning the hand of God;
    what is with the Almighty I will not conceal.
[12] Behold, all of you have seen it yourselves;
    why then have you become altogether vain?

[13] "This is the portion of a wicked man with God,
    and the heritage that oppressors receive from the Almighty:
[14] If his children are multiplied, it is for the sword,
    and his descendants have not enough bread.
[15] Those who survive him the pestilence buries,
    and his widows do not weep.
[16] Though he heap up silver like dust,
    and pile up clothing like clay,

---

[1] Greek bondservant; also verses 45, 46, 47   [2] Greek lepton, a Jewish bronze or copper coin worth about 1/128 of a denarius (which was a day's wage for a laborer)

17   he may pile it up, but the righteous will
      wear it,
    and the innocent will divide the silver.
18   He builds his house like a moth's,
    like a booth that a watchman makes.
19   He goes to bed rich, but will do so no
      more;
    he opens his eyes, and his wealth is
      gone.
20   Terrors overtake him like a flood;
    in the night a whirlwind carries him
      off.
21   The east wind lifts him up and he is
      gone;
    it sweeps him out of his place.
22   It[1] hurls at him without pity;
    he flees from its[2] power in headlong
      flight.
23   It claps its hands at him
    and hisses at him from its place.

1 Corinthians 13

If I speak in the tongues of men and of angels, but have not love, I am a noisy gong or a clanging cymbal. 2And if I have prophetic powers, and understand all mysteries and all knowledge, and if I have all faith, so as to remove mountains, but have not love, I am nothing. 3If I give away all I have, and if I deliver up my body to be burned,[3] but have not love, I gain nothing.

4Love is patient and kind; love does not envy or boast; it is not arrogant 5or rude. It does not insist on its own way; it is not irritable or resentful;[4] 6it does not rejoice at wrongdoing, but rejoices with the truth. 7Love bears all things, believes all things, hopes all things, endures all things.

8Love never ends. As for prophecies, they will pass away; as for tongues, they will cease; as for knowledge, it will pass away. 9For we know in part and we prophesy in part, 10but when the perfect comes, the partial will pass away. 11When I was a child, I spoke like a child, I thought like a child, I reasoned like a child. When I became a man, I gave up childish ways. 12For now we see in a mirror dimly, but then face to face. Now I know in part; then I shall know fully, even as I have been fully known.

13So now faith, hope, and love abide, these three; but the greatest of these is love.

FEBRUARY 27

Exodus 10

Then the LORD said to Moses, "Go in to Pharaoh, for I have hardened his heart and the heart of his servants, that I may show these signs of mine among them, 2and that you may tell in the hearing of your son and of your grandson how I have dealt harshly with the Egyptians and what signs I have done among them, that you may know that I am the LORD."

3So Moses and Aaron went in to Pharaoh and said to him, "Thus says the LORD, the God of the Hebrews, 'How long will you refuse to humble yourself before me? Let my people go, that they may serve me. 4For if you refuse to let my people go, behold, tomorrow I will bring locusts into your country, 5and they shall cover the face of the land, so that no one can see the land. And they shall eat what is left to you after the hail, and they shall eat every tree of yours that grows in the field, 6and they shall fill your houses and the houses of all your servants and of all the Egyptians, as neither your fathers nor your grandfathers have seen, from the day they came on earth to this day.'" Then he turned and went out from Pharaoh.

7Then Pharaoh's servants said to him, "How long shall this man be a snare to us? Let the men go, that they may serve the LORD their God. Do you not yet understand that Egypt is ruined?" 8So Moses and Aaron were brought back to Pharaoh. And he said to them, "Go,

[1] Or He (that is, God); also verse 23 [2] Or his; also verse 23 [3] Some manuscripts deliver up my body [to death] that I may boast [4] Greek irritable and does not count up wrongdoing

serve the LORD your God. But which ones are to go?" ⁹Moses said, "We will go with our young and our old. We will go with our sons and daughters and with our flocks and herds, for we must hold a feast to the LORD." ¹⁰But he said to them, "The LORD be with you, if ever I let you and your little ones go! Look, you have some evil purpose in mind.¹ ¹¹No! Go, the men among you, and serve the LORD, for that is what you are asking." And they were driven out from Pharaoh's presence.

¹²Then the LORD said to Moses, "Stretch out your hand over the land of Egypt for the locusts, so that they may come upon the land of Egypt and eat every plant in the land, all that the hail has left." ¹³So Moses stretched out his staff over the land of Egypt, and the LORD brought an east wind upon the land all that day and all that night. When it was morning, the east wind had brought the locusts. ¹⁴The locusts came up over all the land of Egypt and settled on the whole country of Egypt, such a dense swarm of locusts as had never been before, nor ever will be again. ¹⁵They covered the face of the whole land, so that the land was darkened, and they ate all the plants in the land and all the fruit of the trees that the hail had left. Not a green thing remained, neither tree nor plant of the field, through all the land of Egypt. ¹⁶Then Pharaoh hastily called Moses and Aaron and said, "I have sinned against the LORD your God, and against you. ¹⁷Now therefore, forgive my sin, please, only this once, and plead with the LORD your God only to remove this death from me." ¹⁸So he went out from Pharaoh and pleaded with the LORD. ¹⁹And the LORD turned the wind into a very strong west wind, which lifted the locusts and drove them into the Red Sea. Not a single locust was left in all the country of Egypt. ²⁰But the LORD hardened Pharaoh's heart, and he did not let the people of Israel go.

²¹Then the LORD said to Moses, "Stretch out your hand toward heaven, that there may be darkness over the land of Egypt, a darkness to be felt." ²²So Moses stretched out his hand toward heaven, and there was pitch darkness in all the land of Egypt three days. ²³They did not see one another, nor did anyone rise from his place for three days, but all the people of Israel had light where they lived. ²⁴Then Pharaoh called Moses and said, "Go, serve the LORD; your little ones also may go with you; only let

your flocks and your herds remain behind." ²⁵But Moses said, "You must also let us have sacrifices and burnt offerings, that we may sacrifice to the LORD our God. ²⁶Our livestock also must go with us; not a hoof shall be left behind, for we must take of them to serve the LORD our God, and we do not know with what we must serve the LORD until we arrive there." ²⁷But the LORD hardened Pharaoh's heart, and he would not let them go. ²⁸Then Pharaoh said to him, "Get away from me; take care never to see my face again, for on the day you see my face you shall die." ²⁹Moses said, "As you say! I will not see your face again."

Luke 13

There were some present at that very time who told him about the Galileans whose blood Pilate had mingled with their sacrifices. ²And he answered them, "Do you think that these Galileans were worse sinners than all the other Galileans, because they suffered in this way? ³No, I tell you; but unless you repent, you will all likewise perish. ⁴Or those eighteen on whom the tower in Siloam fell and killed them: do you think that they were worse offenders than all the others who lived in Jerusalem? ⁵No, I tell you; but unless you repent, you will all likewise perish."

⁶And he told this parable: "A man had a fig tree planted in his vineyard, and he came seeking fruit on it and found none. ⁷And he said to the vinedresser, 'Look, for three years now I have come seeking fruit on this fig tree, and I find none. Cut it down. Why should it use up the ground?' ⁸And he answered him, 'Sir, let it alone this year also, until I dig around it and put on manure. ⁹Then if it should bear fruit next year, well and good; but if not, you can cut it down.'"

¹⁰Now he was teaching in one of the synagogues on the Sabbath. ¹¹And behold, there was a woman who had had a disabling spirit for eighteen years. She was bent over and could not fully straighten herself. ¹²When Jesus saw her, he called her over and said to her, "Woman, you are freed from your disability." ¹³And he laid his hands on her, and immediately she was made straight, and she glorified God. ¹⁴But the ruler of the synagogue, indignant because Jesus had healed on the Sabbath, said to the people,

---

¹ Hebrew before your face

"There are six days in which work ought to be done. Come on those days and be healed, and not on the Sabbath day." [15] Then the Lord answered him, "You hypocrites! Does not each of you on the Sabbath untie his ox or his donkey from the manger and lead it away to water it? [16] And ought not this woman, a daughter of Abraham whom Satan bound for eighteen years, be loosed from this bond on the Sabbath day?" [17] As he said these things, all his adversaries were put to shame, and all the people rejoiced at all the glorious things that were done by him.

[18] He said therefore, "What is the kingdom of God like? And to what shall I compare it? [19] It is like a grain of mustard seed that a man took and sowed in his garden, and it grew and became a tree, and the birds of the air made nests in its branches."

[20] And again he said, "To what shall I compare the kingdom of God? [21] It is like leaven that a woman took and hid in three measures of flour, until it was all leavened."

[22] He went on his way through towns and villages, teaching and journeying toward Jerusalem. [23] And someone said to him, "Lord, will those who are saved be few?" And he said to them, [24] "Strive to enter through the narrow door. For many, I tell you, will seek to enter and will not be able. [25] When once the master of the house has risen and shut the door, and you begin to stand outside and to knock at the door, saying, 'Lord, open to us,' then he will answer you, 'I do not know where you come from.' [26] Then you will begin to say, 'We ate and drank in your presence, and you taught in our streets.' [27] But he will say, 'I tell you, I do not know where you come from. Depart from me, all you workers of evil!' [28] In that place there will be weeping and gnashing of teeth, when you see Abraham and Isaac and Jacob and all the prophets in the kingdom of God but you yourselves cast out. [29] And people will come from east and west, and from north and south, and recline at table in the kingdom of God. [30] And behold, some are last who will be first, and some are first who will be last."

[31] At that very hour some Pharisees came and said to him, "Get away from here, for Herod wants to kill you." [32] And he said to them, "Go and tell that fox, 'Behold, I cast out demons and perform cures today and tomorrow, and the

third day I finish my course. [33] Nevertheless, I must go on my way today and tomorrow and the day following, for it cannot be that a prophet should perish away from Jerusalem.' [34] O Jerusalem, Jerusalem, the city that kills the prophets and stones those who are sent to it! How often would I have gathered your children together as a hen gathers her brood under her wings, and you were not willing! [35] Behold, your house is forsaken. And I tell you, you will not see me until you say, 'Blessed is he who comes in the name of the Lord!' "

Job 28

"Surely there is a mine for silver,
and a place for gold that they refine.
2 Iron is taken out of the earth,
and copper is smelted from the ore.
3 Man puts an end to darkness
and searches out to the farthest limit
the ore in gloom and deep darkness.
4 He opens shafts in a valley away from
where anyone lives;
they are forgotten by travelers;
they hang in the air, far away from
mankind; they swing to and fro.
5 As for the earth, out of it comes bread,
but underneath it is turned up as by
fire.
6 Its stones are the place of sapphires,[1]
and it has dust of gold.
7 "That path no bird of prey knows,
and the falcon's eye has not seen it.
8 The proud beasts have not trodden it;
the lion has not passed over it.
9 "Man puts his hand to the flinty rock
and overturns mountains by the roots.
10 He cuts out channels in the rocks,
and his eye sees every precious thing.
11 He dams up the streams so that they do
not trickle,
and the thing that is hidden he brings
out to light.
12 "But where shall wisdom be found?
And where is the place of
understanding?
13 Man does not know its worth,
and it is not found in the land of the
living.

[1] Or lapis lazuli; also verse 16

14 The deep says, 'It is not in me,'
      and the sea says, 'It is not with me.'
15 It cannot be bought for gold,
      and silver cannot be weighed as its
        price.
16 It cannot be valued in the gold of Ophir,
      in precious onyx or sapphire.
17 Gold and glass cannot equal it,
      nor can it be exchanged for jewels of
        fine gold.
18 No mention shall be made of coral or of
        crystal;
      the price of wisdom is above pearls.
19 The topaz of Ethiopia cannot equal it,
      nor can it be valued in pure gold.

20 "From where, then, does wisdom come?
      And where is the place of
        understanding?
21 It is hidden from the eyes of all living
      and concealed from the birds of the air.
22 Abaddon and Death say,
      'We have heard a rumor of it with our
        ears.'
23 "God understands the way to it,
      and he knows its place.
24 For he looks to the ends of the earth
      and sees everything under the
        heavens.
25 When he gave to the wind its weight
      and apportioned the waters by
        measure,
26 when he made a decree for the rain
      and a way for the lightning of the
        thunder,
27 then he saw it and declared it;
      he established it, and searched it out.
28 And he said to man,
      'Behold, the fear of the Lord, that is
        wisdom,
      and to turn away from evil is
        understanding.'"

─────── 1 Corinthians 14 ───────

Pursue love, and earnestly desire the spiritual gifts, especially that you may prophesy. ²For one who speaks in a tongue speaks
not to men but to God; for no one understands
him, but he utters mysteries in the Spirit.
³On the other hand, the one who prophesies
speaks to people for their upbuilding and
encouragement and consolation. ⁴The one
who speaks in a tongue builds up himself, but
the one who prophesies builds up the church.
⁵Now I want you all to speak in tongues, but
even more to prophesy. The one who prophesies is greater than the one who speaks in
tongues, unless someone interprets, so that
the church may be built up.

⁶Now, brothers,¹ if I come to you speaking in
tongues, how will I benefit you unless I bring
you some revelation or knowledge or prophecy or teaching? ⁷If even lifeless instruments,
such as the flute or the harp, do not give distinct
notes, how will anyone know what is played?
⁸And if the bugle gives an indistinct sound, who
will get ready for battle? ⁹So with yourselves, if
with your tongue you utter speech that is not
intelligible, how will anyone know what is said?
For you will be speaking into the air. ¹⁰There
are doubtless many different languages in the
world, and none is without meaning, ¹¹but if I
do not know the meaning of the language, I will
be a foreigner to the speaker and the speaker a
foreigner to me. ¹²So with yourselves, since you
are eager for manifestations of the Spirit, strive
to excel in building up the church.

¹³Therefore, one who speaks in a tongue
should pray that he may interpret. ¹⁴For if I
pray in a tongue, my spirit prays but my mind
is unfruitful. ¹⁵What am I to do? I will pray
with my spirit, but I will pray with my mind
also; I will sing praise with my spirit, but I will
sing with my mind also. ¹⁶Otherwise, if you
give thanks with your spirit, how can anyone
in the position of an outsider² say "Amen" to
your thanksgiving when he does not know
what you are saying? ¹⁷For you may be giving
thanks well enough, but the other person is not
being built up. ¹⁸I thank God that I speak in
tongues more than all of you. ¹⁹Nevertheless,
in church I would rather speak five words with
my mind in order to instruct others, than ten
thousand words in a tongue.

²⁰Brothers, do not be children in your thinking. Be infants in evil, but in your thinking be
mature. ²¹In the Law it is written, "By people
of strange tongues and by the lips of foreigners
will I speak to this people, and even then they
will not listen to me, says the Lord." ²²Thus
tongues are a sign not for believers but for
unbelievers, while prophecy is a sign³ not for
unbelievers but for believers. ²³If, therefore,

¹ Or brothers and sisters; also verses 20, 26, 39 ² Or of him that is without gifts ³ Greek lacks a sign

the whole church comes together and all speak in tongues, and outsiders or unbelievers enter, will they not say that you are out of your minds? ²⁴But if all prophesy, and an unbeliever or outsider enters, he is convicted by all, he is called to account by all, ²⁵the secrets of his heart are disclosed, and so, falling on his face, he will worship God and declare that God is really among you.

²⁶What then, brothers? When you come together, each one has a hymn, a lesson, a revelation, a tongue, or an interpretation. Let all things be done for building up. ²⁷If any speak in a tongue, let there be only two or at most three, and each in turn, and let someone interpret. ²⁸But if there is no one to interpret, let each of them keep silent in church and speak to himself and to God. ²⁹Let two or three prophets speak, and let the others weigh what is said. ³⁰If a revelation is made to another sitting there, let the first be silent. ³¹For you can all prophesy one by one, so that all may learn and all be encouraged, ³²and the spirits of prophets are subject to prophets. ³³For God is not a God of confusion but of peace.

As in all the churches of the saints, ³⁴the women should keep silent in the churches. For they are not permitted to speak, but should be in submission, as the Law also says. ³⁵If there is anything they desire to learn, let them ask their husbands at home. For it is shameful for a woman to speak in church.

³⁶Or was it from you that the word of God came? Or are you the only ones it has reached? ³⁷If anyone thinks that he is a prophet, or spiritual, he should acknowledge that the things I am writing to you are a command of the Lord. ³⁸If anyone does not recognize this, he is not recognized. ³⁹So, my brothers, earnestly desire to prophesy, and do not forbid speaking in tongues. ⁴⁰But all things should be done decently and in order.

FEBRUARY 28

Exodus 11:1–12:21

The LORD said to Moses, "Yet one plague more I will bring upon Pharaoh and upon Egypt. Afterward he will let you go from here. When he lets you go, he will drive you away completely. ²Speak now in the hearing of the people, that they ask, every man of his neighbor and every woman of her neighbor, for silver and gold jewelry." ³And the LORD gave the people favor in the sight of the Egyptians. Moreover, the man Moses was very great in the land of Egypt, in the sight of Pharaoh's servants and in the sight of the people.

⁴So Moses said, "Thus says the LORD: 'About midnight I will go out in the midst of Egypt, ⁵and every firstborn in the land of Egypt shall die, from the firstborn of Pharaoh who sits on his throne, even to the firstborn of the slave girl who is behind the handmill, and all the firstborn of the cattle. ⁶There shall be a great cry throughout all the land of Egypt, such as there has never been, nor ever will be again. ⁷But not a dog shall growl against any of the people of Israel, either man or beast, that you may know that the LORD makes a distinction between Egypt and Israel.' ⁸And all these your servants shall come down to me and bow down to me, saying, 'Get out, you and all the people who follow you.' And after that I will go out." And he went out from Pharaoh in hot anger. ⁹Then the LORD said to Moses, "Pharaoh will not listen to you, that my wonders may be multiplied in the land of Egypt."

¹⁰Moses and Aaron did all these wonders before Pharaoh, and the LORD hardened Pharaoh's heart, and he did not let the people of Israel go out of his land.

^{12:1}The LORD said to Moses and Aaron in the land of Egypt, ²"This month shall be for you the beginning of months. It shall be the first month of the year for you. ³Tell all the congregation

of Israel that on the tenth day of this month every man shall take a lamb according to their fathers' houses, a lamb for a household. ⁴And if the household is too small for a lamb, then he and his nearest neighbor shall take according to the number of persons; according to what each can eat you shall make your count for the lamb. ⁵Your lamb shall be without blemish, a male a year old. You may take it from the sheep or from the goats, ⁶and you shall keep it until the fourteenth day of this month, when the whole assembly of the congregation of Israel shall kill their lambs at twilight.¹

⁷ "Then they shall take some of the blood and put it on the two doorposts and the lintel of the houses in which they eat it. ⁸They shall eat the flesh that night, roasted on the fire; with unleavened bread and bitter herbs they shall eat it. ⁹Do not eat any of it raw or boiled in water, but roasted, its head with its legs and its inner parts. ¹⁰And you shall let none of it remain until the morning; anything that remains until the morning you shall burn. ¹¹In this manner you shall eat it: with your belt fastened, your sandals on your feet, and your staff in your hand. And you shall eat it in haste. It is the LORD's Passover. ¹²For I will pass through the land of Egypt that night, and I will strike all the firstborn in the land of Egypt, both man and beast; and on all the gods of Egypt I will execute judgments: I am the LORD. ¹³The blood shall be a sign for you, on the houses where you are. And when I see the blood, I will pass over you, and no plague will befall you to destroy you, when I strike the land of Egypt.

¹⁴"This day shall be for you a memorial day, and you shall keep it as a feast to the LORD; throughout your generations, as a statute forever, you shall keep it as a feast. ¹⁵Seven days you shall eat unleavened bread. On the first day you shall remove leaven out of your houses, for if anyone eats what is leavened, from the first day until the seventh day, that person shall be cut off from Israel. ¹⁶On the first day you shall hold a holy assembly, and on the seventh day a holy assembly. No work shall be done on those days. But what everyone needs to eat, that alone may be prepared by you. ¹⁷And you shall observe the Feast of Unleavened Bread, for on this very day I brought your hosts out of the land of Egypt. Therefore you shall observe this day, throughout your generations, as a statute

forever. ¹⁸In the first month, from the fourteenth day of the month at evening, you shall eat unleavened bread until the twenty-first day of the month at evening. ¹⁹For seven days no leaven is to be found in your houses. If anyone eats what is leavened, that person will be cut off from the congregation of Israel, whether he is a sojourner or a native of the land. ²⁰You shall eat nothing leavened; in all your dwelling places you shall eat unleavened bread."

²¹Then Moses called all the elders of Israel and said to them, "Go and select lambs for yourselves according to your clans, and kill the Passover lamb."

Luke 14

One Sabbath, when he went to dine at the house of a ruler of the Pharisees, they were watching him carefully. ²And behold, there was a man before him who had dropsy. ³And Jesus responded to the lawyers and Pharisees, saying, "Is it lawful to heal on the Sabbath, or not?" ⁴But they remained silent. Then he took him and healed him and sent him away. ⁵And he said to them, "Which of you, having a son² or an ox that has fallen into a well on a Sabbath day, will not immediately pull him out?" ⁶And they could not reply to these things.

⁷Now he told a parable to those who were invited, when he noticed how they chose the places of honor, saying to them, ⁸"When you are invited by someone to a wedding feast, do not sit down in a place of honor, lest someone more distinguished than you be invited by him, ⁹and he who invited you both will come and say to you, 'Give your place to this person,' and then you will begin with shame to take the lowest place. ¹⁰But when you are invited, go and sit in the lowest place, so that when your host comes he may say to you, 'Friend, move up higher.' Then you will be honored in the presence of all who sit at table with you. ¹¹For everyone who exalts himself will be humbled, and he who humbles himself will be exalted."

¹²He said also to the man who had invited him, "When you give a dinner or a banquet, do not invite your friends or your brothers³ or your relatives or rich neighbors, lest they also invite you in return and you be repaid. ¹³But when you give a feast, invite the poor, the crippled, the lame, the blind, ¹⁴and you will be blessed,

¹ Hebrew *between the two evenings* ² Some manuscripts *a donkey* ³ Or *your brothers and sisters*. The plural Greek word *adelphoi* (translated "brothers") refers to siblings in a family. In New Testament usage, depending on the context, *adelphoi* may refer either to *brothers* or to *brothers and sisters*

because they cannot repay you. For you will be repaid at the resurrection of the just."

[15] When one of those who reclined at table with him heard these things, he said to him, "Blessed is everyone who will eat bread in the kingdom of God!" [16] But he said to him, "A man once gave a great banquet and invited many. [17] And at the time for the banquet he sent his servant[1] to say to those who had been invited, 'Come, for everything is now ready.' [18] But they all alike began to make excuses. The first said to him, 'I have bought a field, and I must go out and see it. Please have me excused.' [19] And another said, 'I have bought five yoke of oxen, and I go to examine them. Please have me excused.' [20] And another said, 'I have married a wife, and therefore I cannot come.' [21] So the servant came and reported these things to his master. Then the master of the house became angry and said to his servant, 'Go out quickly to the streets and lanes of the city, and bring in the poor and crippled and blind and lame.' [22] And the servant said, 'Sir, what you commanded has been done, and still there is room.' [23] And the master said to the servant, 'Go out to the highways and hedges and compel people to come in, that my house may be filled. [24] For I tell you,[2] none of those men who were invited shall taste my banquet.'"

[25] Now great crowds accompanied him, and he turned and said to them, [26] "If anyone comes to me and does not hate his own father and mother and wife and children and brothers and sisters, yes, and even his own life, he cannot be my disciple. [27] Whoever does not bear his own cross and come after me cannot be my disciple. [28] For which of you, desiring to build a tower, does not first sit down and count the cost, whether he has enough to complete it? [29] Otherwise, when he has laid a foundation and is not able to finish, all who see it begin to mock him, [30] saying, 'This man began to build and was not able to finish.' [31] Or what king, going out to encounter another king in war, will not sit down first and deliberate whether he is able with ten thousand to meet him who comes against him with twenty thousand? [32] And if not, while the other is yet a great way off, he sends a delegation and asks for terms of peace. [33] So therefore, any one of you who does not renounce all that he has cannot be my disciple.

[34] "Salt is good, but if salt has lost its taste, how shall its saltiness be restored? [35] It is of no use either for the soil or for the manure pile. It is thrown away. He who has ears to hear, let him hear."

Job 29

And Job again took up his discourse, and said:

2 "Oh, that I were as in the months of old,
      as in the days when God watched over me,
3 when his lamp shone upon my head,
      and by his light I walked through darkness,
4 as I was in my prime,[3]
      when the friendship of God was upon my tent,
5 when the Almighty was yet with me,
      when my children were all around me,
6 when my steps were washed with butter,
      and the rock poured out for me streams of oil!
7 When I went out to the gate of the city,
      when I prepared my seat in the square,
8 the young men saw me and withdrew,
      and the aged rose and stood;
9 the princes refrained from talking
      and laid their hand on their mouth;
10 the voice of the nobles was hushed,
      and their tongue stuck to the roof of their mouth.
11 When the ear heard, it called me blessed,
      and when the eye saw, it approved,
12 because I delivered the poor who cried for help,
      and the fatherless who had none to help him.
13 The blessing of him who was about to perish came upon me,
      and I caused the widow's heart to sing for joy.
14 I put on righteousness, and it clothed me;
      my justice was like a robe and a turban.
15 I was eyes to the blind
      and feet to the lame.

---

[1] Greek bondservant; also verses 21, 22, 23 [2] The Greek word for you here is plural [3] Hebrew my autumn days

16   I was a father to the needy,
      and I searched out the cause of him
         whom I did not know.
17   I broke the fangs of the unrighteous
      and made him drop his prey from his
         teeth.
18   Then I thought, 'I shall die in my nest,
      and I shall multiply my days as the
         sand,
19   my roots spread out to the waters,
      with the dew all night on my
         branches,
20   my glory fresh with me,
      and my bow ever new in my hand.'
21   "Men listened to me and waited
      and kept silence for my counsel.
22   After I spoke they did not speak again,
      and my word dropped upon them.
23   They waited for me as for the rain,
      and they opened their mouths as for
         the spring rain.
24   I smiled on them when they had no
         confidence,
      and the light of my face they did not
         cast down.
25   I chose their way and sat as chief,
      and I lived like a king among his
         troops,
      like one who comforts mourners.

1 Corinthians 15

Now I would remind you, brothers,[1] of the gospel I preached to you, which you received, in which you stand, [2] and by which you are being saved, if you hold fast to the word I preached to you—unless you believed in vain. [3] For I delivered to you as of first importance what I also received: that Christ died for our sins in accordance with the Scriptures, [4] that he was buried, that he was raised on the third day in accordance with the Scriptures, [5] and that he appeared to Cephas, then to the twelve. [6] Then he appeared to more than five hundred brothers at one time, most of whom are still alive, though some have fallen asleep. [7] Then he appeared to James, then to all the apostles. [8] Last of all, as to one untimely born, he appeared also to me. [9] For I am the least of the apostles, unworthy to be called an apostle, because I persecuted the church of God. [10] But by the grace of God I am what I am, and his grace toward me was not in vain. On the contrary, I worked harder than any of them, though it was not I, but the grace of God that is with me. [11] Whether then it was I or they, so we preach and so you believed.

[12] Now if Christ is proclaimed as raised from the dead, how can some of you say that there is no resurrection of the dead? [13] But if there is no resurrection of the dead, then not even Christ has been raised. [14] And if Christ has not been raised, then our preaching is in vain and your faith is in vain. [15] We are even found to be misrepresenting God, because we testified about God that he raised Christ, whom he did not raise if it is true that the dead are not raised. [16] For if the dead are not raised, not even Christ has been raised. [17] And if Christ has not been raised, your faith is futile and you are still in your sins. [18] Then those also who have fallen asleep in Christ have perished. [19] If in Christ we have hope[2] in this life only, we are of all people most to be pitied.

[20] But in fact Christ has been raised from the dead, the firstfruits of those who have fallen asleep. [21] For as by a man came death, by a man has come also the resurrection of the dead. [22] For as in Adam all die, so also in Christ shall all be made alive. [23] But each in his own order: Christ the firstfruits, then at his coming those who belong to Christ. [24] Then comes the end, when he delivers the kingdom to God the Father after destroying every rule and every authority and power. [25] For he must reign until he has put all his enemies under his feet. [26] The last enemy to be destroyed is death. [27] For "God[3] has put all things in subjection under his feet." But when it says, "all things are put in subjection," it is plain that he is excepted who put all things in subjection under him. [28] When all things are subjected to him, then the Son himself will also be subjected to him who put all things in subjection under him, that God may be all in all.

[29] Otherwise, what do people mean by being baptized on behalf of the dead? If the dead are not raised at all, why are people baptized on their behalf? [30] Why are we in danger every hour? [31] I protest, brothers, by my pride in you, which I have in Christ Jesus our Lord, I die every day! [32] What do I gain if, humanly speaking, I fought with beasts at Ephesus? If

---

[1] Or brothers and sisters; also verses 6, 31, 50, 58 [2] Or we have hoped [3] Greek he

the dead are not raised, "Let us eat and drink, for tomorrow we die." [33] Do not be deceived: "Bad company ruins good morals."[1] [34] Wake up from your drunken stupor, as is right, and do not go on sinning. For some have no knowledge of God. I say this to your shame.

[35] But someone will ask, "How are the dead raised? With what kind of body do they come?" [36] You foolish person! What you sow does not come to life unless it dies. [37] And what you sow is not the body that is to be, but a bare kernel, perhaps of wheat or of some other grain. [38] But God gives it a body as he has chosen, and to each kind of seed its own body. [39] For not all flesh is the same, but there is one kind for humans, another for animals, another for birds, and another for fish. [40] There are heavenly bodies and earthly bodies, but the glory of the heavenly is of one kind, and the glory of the earthly is of another. [41] There is one glory of the sun, and another glory of the moon, and another glory of the stars; for star differs from star in glory.

[42] So is it with the resurrection of the dead. What is sown is perishable; what is raised is imperishable. [43] It is sown in dishonor; it is raised in glory. It is sown in weakness; it is raised in power. [44] It is sown a natural body; it is raised a spiritual body. If there is a natural body, there is also a spiritual body. [45] Thus it is written, "The first man Adam became a living being";[2] the last Adam became a life-giving spirit. [46] But it is not the spiritual that is first but the natural, and then the spiritual. [47] The first man was from the earth, a man of dust; the second man is from heaven. [48] As was the man of dust, so also are those who are of the dust, and as is the man of heaven, so also are those who are of heaven. [49] Just as we have borne the image of the man of dust, we shall[3] also bear the image of the man of heaven.

[50] I tell you this, brothers: flesh and blood cannot inherit the kingdom of God, nor does the perishable inherit the imperishable. [51] Behold! I tell you a mystery. We shall not all sleep, but we shall all be changed, [52] in a moment, in the twinkling of an eye, at the last trumpet. For the trumpet will sound, and the dead will be raised imperishable, and we shall be changed. [53] For this perishable body must put on the imperishable, and this mortal body must put on immortality. [54] When the perishable puts on the imperishable, and the mortal puts on immortality, then shall come to pass the saying that is written:

"Death is swallowed up in victory."
[55]   "O death, where is your victory?
         O death, where is your sting?"

[56] The sting of death is sin, and the power of sin is the law. [57] But thanks be to God, who gives us the victory through our Lord Jesus Christ.

[58] Therefore, my beloved brothers, be steadfast, immovable, always abounding in the work of the Lord, knowing that in the Lord your labor is not in vain.

[1] Probably from Menander's comedy Thaïs [2] Greek a living soul [3] Some manuscripts let us

MARCH 1

Exodus 12:22–51

Take a bunch of hyssop and dip it in the blood that is in the basin, and touch the lintel and the two doorposts with the blood that is in the basin. None of you shall go out of the door of his house until the morning. ²³For the Lord will pass through to strike the Egyptians, and when he sees the blood on the lintel and on the two doorposts, the Lord will pass over the door and will not allow the destroyer to enter your houses to strike you. ²⁴You shall observe this rite as a statute for you and for your sons forever. ²⁵And when you come to the land that the Lord will give you, as he has promised, you shall keep this service. ²⁶And when your children say to you, 'What do you mean by this service?' ²⁷you shall say, 'It is the sacrifice of the Lord's Passover, for he passed over the houses of the people of Israel in Egypt, when he struck the Egyptians but spared our houses.'" And the people bowed their heads and worshiped.

²⁸Then the people of Israel went and did so; as the Lord had commanded Moses and Aaron, so they did.

²⁹At midnight the Lord struck down all the firstborn in the land of Egypt, from the firstborn of Pharaoh who sat on his throne to the firstborn of the captive who was in the dungeon, and all the firstborn of the livestock. ³⁰And Pharaoh rose up in the night, he and all his servants and all the Egyptians. And there was a great cry in Egypt, for there was not a house where someone was not dead. ³¹Then he summoned Moses and Aaron by night and said, "Up, go out from among my people, both you and the people of Israel; and go, serve the Lord, as you have said. ³²Take your flocks and your herds, as you have said, and be gone, and bless me also!"

³³The Egyptians were urgent with the people to send them out of the land in haste. For they said, "We shall all be dead." ³⁴So the people took their dough before it was leavened, their kneading bowls being bound up in their cloaks on their shoulders. ³⁵The people of Israel had

also done as Moses told them, for they had asked the Egyptians for silver and gold jewelry and for clothing. ³⁶And the Lord had given the people favor in the sight of the Egyptians, so that they let them have what they asked. Thus they plundered the Egyptians.

³⁷And the people of Israel journeyed from Rameses to Succoth, about six hundred thousand men on foot, besides women and children. ³⁸A mixed multitude also went up with them, and very much livestock, both flocks and herds. ³⁹And they baked unleavened cakes of the dough that they had brought out of Egypt, for it was not leavened, because they were thrust out of Egypt and could not wait, nor had they prepared any provisions for themselves.

⁴⁰The time that the people of Israel lived in Egypt was 430 years. ⁴¹At the end of 430 years, on that very day, all the hosts of the Lord went out from the land of Egypt. ⁴²It was a night of watching by the Lord, to bring them out of the land of Egypt; so this same night is a night of watching kept to the Lord by all the people of Israel throughout their generations.

⁴³And the Lord said to Moses and Aaron, "This is the statute of the Passover: no foreigner shall eat of it, ⁴⁴but every slave¹ that is bought for money may eat of it after you have circumcised him. ⁴⁵No foreigner or hired worker may eat of it. ⁴⁶It shall be eaten in one house; you shall not take any of the flesh outside the house, and you shall not break any of its bones. ⁴⁷All the congregation of Israel shall keep it. ⁴⁸If a stranger shall sojourn with you and would keep the Passover to the Lord, let all his males be circumcised. Then he may come near and keep it; he shall be as a native of the land. But no uncircumcised person shall eat of it. ⁴⁹There shall be one law for the native and for the stranger who sojourns among you."

⁵⁰All the people of Israel did just as the Lord commanded Moses and Aaron. ⁵¹And on that very day the Lord brought the people of Israel out of the land of Egypt by their hosts.

¹ Or *servant*; the Hebrew term *'ebed* designates a range of social and economic roles (see Preface)

——————— *Luke 15* ———————

Now the tax collectors and sinners were all drawing near to hear him. ²And the Pharisees and the scribes grumbled, saying, "This man receives sinners and eats with them."

³So he told them this parable: ⁴"What man of you, having a hundred sheep, if he has lost one of them, does not leave the ninety-nine in the open country, and go after the one that is lost, until he finds it? ⁵And when he has found it, he lays it on his shoulders, rejoicing. ⁶And when he comes home, he calls together his friends and his neighbors, saying to them, 'Rejoice with me, for I have found my sheep that was lost.' ⁷Just so, I tell you, there will be more joy in heaven over one sinner who repents than over ninety-nine righteous persons who need no repentance.

⁸"Or what woman, having ten silver coins,¹ if she loses one coin, does not light a lamp and sweep the house and seek diligently until she finds it? ⁹And when she has found it, she calls together her friends and neighbors, saying, 'Rejoice with me, for I have found the coin that I had lost.' ¹⁰Just so, I tell you, there is joy before the angels of God over one sinner who repents."

¹¹And he said, "There was a man who had two sons. ¹²And the younger of them said to his father, 'Father, give me the share of property that is coming to me.' And he divided his property between them. ¹³Not many days later, the younger son gathered all he had and took a journey into a far country, and there he squandered his property in reckless living. ¹⁴And when he had spent everything, a severe famine arose in that country, and he began to be in need. ¹⁵So he went and hired himself out to² one of the citizens of that country, who sent him into his fields to feed pigs. ¹⁶And he was longing to be fed with the pods that the pigs ate, and no one gave him anything.

¹⁷"But when he came to himself, he said, 'How many of my father's hired servants have more than enough bread, but I perish here with hunger! ¹⁸I will arise and go to my father, and I will say to him, "Father, I have sinned against heaven and before you. ¹⁹I am no longer worthy to be called your son. Treat me as one of your hired servants."' ²⁰And he arose and came to his father. But while he was still a long way off, his father saw him and felt compassion, and ran and embraced him and kissed him. ²¹And the son said to him, 'Father, I have sinned against heaven and before you. I am no longer worthy to be called your son.'³ ²²But the father said to his servants,⁴ 'Bring quickly the best robe, and put it on him, and put a ring on his hand, and shoes on his feet. ²³And bring the fattened calf and kill it, and let us eat and celebrate. ²⁴For this my son was dead, and is alive again; he was lost, and is found.' And they began to celebrate.

²⁵"Now his older son was in the field, and as he came and drew near to the house, he heard music and dancing. ²⁶And he called one of the servants and asked what these things meant. ²⁷And he said to him, 'Your brother has come, and your father has killed the fattened calf, because he has received him back safe and sound.' ²⁸But he was angry and refused to go in. His father came out and entreated him, ²⁹but he answered his father, 'Look, these many years I have served you, and I never disobeyed your command, yet you never gave me a young goat, that I might celebrate with my friends. ³⁰But when this son of yours came, who has devoured your property with prostitutes, you killed the fattened calf for him!' ³¹And he said to him, 'Son, you are always with me, and all that is mine is yours. ³²It was fitting to celebrate and be glad, for this your brother was dead, and is alive; he was lost, and is found.'"

——————— *Job 30* ———————

"But now they laugh at me,
    men who are younger than I,
whose fathers I would have disdained
    to set with the dogs of my flock.
2 What could I gain from the strength of
        their hands,
    men whose vigor is gone?
3 Through want and hard hunger
        they gnaw the dry ground by night in
        waste and desolation;
4 they pick saltwort and the leaves of
        bushes,
    and the roots of the broom tree for
        their food.⁵
5 They are driven out from human
        company;
    they shout after them as after a thief.

¹ Greek *ten drachmas*; a *drachma* was a Greek coin approximately equal in value to a Roman *denarius*, worth about a day's wage for a laborer ² Greek *joined himself to*
³ Some manuscripts add *treat me as one of your hired servants* ⁴ Greek *bondservants* ⁵ Or *warmth*

6 In the gullies of the torrents they must
dwell,
    in holes of the earth and of the rocks.
7 Among the bushes they bray;
    under the nettles they huddle
    together.
8 A senseless, a nameless brood,
    they have been whipped out of the
    land.
9 "And now I have become their song;
    I am a byword to them.
10 They abhor me; they keep aloof from me;
    they do not hesitate to spit at the sight
    of me.
11 Because God has loosed my cord and
    humbled me,
    they have cast off restraint[1] in my
    presence.
12 On my right hand the rabble rise;
    they push away my feet;
    they cast up against me their ways of
    destruction.
13 They break up my path;
    they promote my calamity;
    they need no one to help them.
14 As through a wide breach they come;
    amid the crash they roll on.
15 Terrors are turned upon me;
    my honor is pursued as by the wind,
    and my prosperity has passed away
    like a cloud.
16 "And now my soul is poured out within
    me;
    days of affliction have taken hold of
    me.
17 The night racks my bones,
    and the pain that gnaws me takes no
    rest.
18 With great force my garment is
    disfigured;
    it binds me about like the collar of my
    tunic.
19 God[2] has cast me into the mire,
    and I have become like dust and ashes.
20 I cry to you for help and you do not
    answer me;
    I stand, and you only look at me.
21 You have turned cruel to me;
    with the might of your hand you
    persecute me.

22 You lift me up on the wind; you make
    me ride on it,
    and you toss me about in the roar of
    the storm.
23 For I know that you will bring me to
    death
    and to the house appointed for all
    living.
24 "Yet does not one in a heap of ruins
    stretch out his hand,
    and in his disaster cry for help?[3]
25 Did not I weep for him whose day was
    hard?
    Was not my soul grieved for the
    needy?
26 But when I hoped for good, evil came,
    and when I waited for light, darkness
    came.
27 My inward parts are in turmoil and
    never still;
    days of affliction come to meet me.
28 I go about darkened, but not by the sun;
    I stand up in the assembly and cry for
    help.
29 I am a brother of jackals
    and a companion of ostriches.
30 My skin turns black and falls from me,
    and my bones burn with heat.
31 My lyre is turned to mourning,
    and my pipe to the voice of those who
    weep.

1 Corinthians 16

Now concerning[4] the collection for the
saints: as I directed the churches of Galatia, so you also are to do. [2] On the first day of
every week, each of you is to put something
aside and store it up, as he may prosper, so
that there will be no collecting when I come.
[3] And when I arrive, I will send those whom you
accredit by letter to carry your gift to Jerusalem.
[4] If it seems advisable that I should go also, they
will accompany me.
    [5] I will visit you after passing through Mace-
donia, for I intend to pass through Macedonia,
[6] and perhaps I will stay with you or even spend
the winter, so that you may help me on my journey, wherever I go. [7] For I do not want to see you
now just in passing. I hope to spend some time
with you, if the Lord permits. [8] But I will stay in

---

[1] Hebrew *the bridle* [2] Hebrew *He* [3] The meaning of the Hebrew is uncertain [4] The expression *Now concerning* introduces a reply to a question in the Corinthians' letter; see 7:1; also
verse 12

Ephesus until Pentecost, [9] for a wide door for effective work has opened to me, and there are many adversaries.

[10] When Timothy comes, see that you put him at ease among you, for he is doing the work of the Lord, as I am. [11] So let no one despise him. Help him on his way in peace, that he may return to me, for I am expecting him with the brothers.

[12] Now concerning our brother Apollos, I strongly urged him to visit you with the other brothers, but it was not at all his will[1] to come now. He will come when he has opportunity.

[13] Be watchful, stand firm in the faith, act like men, be strong. [14] Let all that you do be done in love.

[15] Now I urge you, brothers[2]—you know that the household[3] of Stephanas were the first converts in Achaia, and that they have devoted themselves to the service of the saints— [16] be subject to such as these, and to every fellow worker and laborer. [17] I rejoice at the coming of Stephanas and Fortunatus and Achaicus, because they have made up for your absence, [18] for they refreshed my spirit as well as yours. Give recognition to such people.

[19] The churches of Asia send you greetings. Aquila and Prisca, together with the church in their house, send you hearty greetings in the Lord. [20] All the brothers send you greetings. Greet one another with a holy kiss.

[21] I, Paul, write this greeting with my own hand. [22] If anyone has no love for the Lord, let him be accursed. Our Lord, come![4] [23] The grace of the Lord Jesus be with you. [24] My love be with you all in Christ Jesus. Amen.

MARCH 2

Exodus 13

The Lord said to Moses, [2] "Consecrate to me all the firstborn. Whatever is the first to open the womb among the people of Israel, both of man and of beast, is mine."

[3] Then Moses said to the people, "Remember this day in which you came out from Egypt, out of the house of slavery, for by a strong hand the Lord brought you out from this place. No leavened bread shall be eaten. [4] Today, in the month of Abib, you are going out. [5] And when the Lord brings you into the land of the Canaanites, the Hittites, the Amorites, the Hivites, and the Jebusites, which he swore to your fathers to give you, a land flowing with milk and honey, you shall keep this service in this month. [6] Seven days you shall eat unleavened bread, and on the seventh day there shall be a feast to the Lord. [7] Unleavened bread shall be eaten for seven days; no leavened bread shall be seen with you, and no leaven shall be seen with you in all your territory. [8] You shall tell your son on that day, 'It is because of what the Lord did for me when I came out of Egypt.'

[9] And it shall be to you as a sign on your hand and as a memorial between your eyes, that the law of the Lord may be in your mouth. For with a strong hand the Lord has brought you out of Egypt. [10] You shall therefore keep this statute at its appointed time from year to year.

[11] "When the Lord brings you into the land of the Canaanites, as he swore to you and your fathers, and shall give it to you, [12] you shall set apart to the Lord all that first opens the womb. All the firstborn of your animals that are males shall be the Lord's. [13] Every firstborn of a donkey you shall redeem with a lamb, or if you will not redeem it you shall break its neck. Every firstborn of man among your sons you shall redeem. [14] And when in time to come your son asks you, 'What does this mean?' you shall say to him, 'By a strong hand the Lord brought us out of Egypt, from the house of slavery. [15] For when Pharaoh stubbornly refused to let us go, the Lord killed all the firstborn in the land of Egypt, both the firstborn of man and the firstborn of animals. Therefore I sacrifice to the

[1] Or God's will for him [2] Or brothers and sisters; also verse 20 [3] Greek house [4] Greek Maranatha (a transliteration of Aramaic)

LORD all the males that first open the womb, but all the firstborn of my sons I redeem.' [16] It shall be as a mark on your hand or frontlets between your eyes, for by a strong hand the LORD brought us out of Egypt."

[17] When Pharaoh let the people go, God did not lead them by way of the land of the Philistines, although that was near. For God said, "Lest the people change their minds when they see war and return to Egypt." [18] But God led the people around by the way of the wilderness toward the Red Sea. And the people of Israel went up out of the land of Egypt equipped for battle. [19] Moses took the bones of Joseph with him, for Joseph[1] had made the sons of Israel solemnly swear, saying, "God will surely visit you, and you shall carry up my bones with you from here." [20] And they moved on from Succoth and encamped at Etham, on the edge of the wilderness. [21] And the LORD went before them by day in a pillar of cloud to lead them along the way, and by night in a pillar of fire to give them light, that they might travel by day and by night. [22] The pillar of cloud by day and the pillar of fire by night did not depart from before the people.

Luke 16

H e also said to the disciples, "There was a rich man who had a manager, and charges were brought to him that this man was wasting his possessions. [2] And he called him and said to him, 'What is this that I hear about you? Turn in the account of your management, for you can no longer be manager.' [3] And the manager said to himself, 'What shall I do, since my master is taking the management away from me? I am not strong enough to dig, and I am ashamed to beg. [4] I have decided what to do, so that when I am removed from management, people may receive me into their houses.' [5] So, summoning his master's debtors one by one, he said to the first, 'How much do you owe my master?' [6] He said, 'A hundred measures[2] of oil.' He said to him, 'Take your bill, and sit down quickly and write fifty.' [7] Then he said to another, 'And how much do you owe?' He said, 'A hundred measures[3] of wheat.' He said to him, 'Take your bill, and write eighty.' [8] The master commended the dishonest manager for his shrewdness. For the sons of this world[4] are more shrewd

in dealing with their own generation than the sons of light. [9] And I tell you, make friends for yourselves by means of unrighteous wealth,[5] so that when it fails they may receive you into the eternal dwellings.

[10] "One who is faithful in a very little is also faithful in much, and one who is dishonest in a very little is also dishonest in much. [11] If then you have not been faithful in the unrighteous wealth, who will entrust to you the true riches? [12] And if you have not been faithful in that which is another's, who will give you that which is your own? [13] No servant can serve two masters, for either he will hate the one and love the other, or he will be devoted to the one and despise the other. You cannot serve God and money."

[14] The Pharisees, who were lovers of money, heard all these things, and they ridiculed him. [15] And he said to them, "You are those who justify yourselves before men, but God knows your hearts. For what is exalted among men is an abomination in the sight of God.

[16] "The Law and the Prophets were until John; since then the good news of the kingdom of God is preached, and everyone forces his way into it.[6] [17] But it is easier for heaven and earth to pass away than for one dot of the Law to become void.

[18] "Everyone who divorces his wife and marries another commits adultery, and he who marries a woman divorced from her husband commits adultery.

[19] "There was a rich man who was clothed in purple and fine linen and who feasted sumptuously every day. [20] And at his gate was laid a poor man named Lazarus, covered with sores, [21] who desired to be fed with what fell from the rich man's table. Moreover, even the dogs came and licked his sores. [22] The poor man died and was carried by the angels to Abraham's side.[7] The rich man also died and was buried, [23] and in Hades, being in torment, he lifted up his eyes and saw Abraham far off and Lazarus at his side. [24] And he called out, 'Father Abraham, have mercy on me, and send Lazarus to dip the end of his finger in water and cool my tongue, for I am in anguish in this flame.' [25] But Abraham said, 'Child, remember that you in your lifetime received your good things, and Lazarus in like manner bad things; but now he is comforted here, and you are in anguish. [26] And besides all this, between us and

---

[1] Samaritan, Septuagint; Hebrew he [2] About 875 gallons or 3,200 liters [3] Between 1,000 and 1,200 bushels or 37,000 to 45,000 liters [4] Greek age [5] Greek mammon, a Semitic word for money or possessions; also verse 11; rendered money in verse 13 [6] Or everyone is forcefully urged into it [7] Greek bosom; also verse 23

you a great chasm has been fixed, in order that those who would pass from here to you may not be able, and none may cross from there to us.' ²⁷And he said, 'Then I beg you, father, to send him to my father's house— ²⁸for I have five brothers¹—so that he may warn them, lest they also come into this place of torment.' ²⁹But Abraham said, 'They have Moses and the Prophets; let them hear them.' ³⁰And he said, 'No, father Abraham, but if someone goes to them from the dead, they will repent.' ³¹He said to him, 'If they do not hear Moses and the Prophets, neither will they be convinced if someone should rise from the dead.'"

—————— Job 31 ——————

¹ "I have made a covenant with my eyes;
how then could I gaze at a virgin?
² What would be my portion from God
above
and my heritage from the Almighty
on high?
³ Is not calamity for the unrighteous,
and disaster for the workers of
iniquity?
⁴ Does not he see my ways
and number all my steps?

⁵ "If I have walked with falsehood
and my foot has hastened to deceit;
⁶ (Let me be weighed in a just balance,
and let God know my integrity!)
⁷ if my step has turned aside from the way
and my heart has gone after my eyes,
and if any spot has stuck to my hands,
⁸ then let me sow, and another eat,
and let what grows for me² be rooted
out.

⁹ "If my heart has been enticed toward a
woman,
and I have lain in wait at my
neighbor's door,
¹⁰ then let my wife grind for another,
and let others bow down on her.
¹¹ For that would be a heinous crime;
that would be an iniquity to be
punished by the judges;
¹² for that would be a fire that consumes as
far as Abaddon,
and it would burn to the root all my
increase.

¹³ "If I have rejected the cause of my
manservant or my maidservant,
when they brought a complaint
against me,
¹⁴ what then shall I do when God rises up?
When he makes inquiry, what shall I
answer him?
¹⁵ Did not he who made me in the womb
make him?
And did not one fashion us in the
womb?

¹⁶ "If I have withheld anything that the poor
desired,
or have caused the eyes of the widow
to fail,
¹⁷ or have eaten my morsel alone,
and the fatherless has not eaten of it
¹⁸ (for from my youth the fatherless³ grew
up with me as with a father,
and from my mother's womb I guided
the widow⁴),
¹⁹ if I have seen anyone perish for lack of
clothing,
or the needy without covering,
²⁰ if his body has not blessed me,⁵
and if he was not warmed with the
fleece of my sheep,
²¹ if I have raised my hand against the
fatherless,
because I saw my help in the gate,
²² then let my shoulder blade fall from my
shoulder,
and let my arm be broken from its
socket.
²³ For I was in terror of calamity from God,
and I could not have faced his majesty.

²⁴ "If I have made gold my trust
or called fine gold my confidence,
²⁵ if I have rejoiced because my wealth was
abundant
or because my hand had found much,
²⁶ if I have looked at the sun⁶ when it
shone,
or the moon moving in splendor,
²⁷ and my heart has been secretly enticed,
and my mouth has kissed my hand,
²⁸ this also would be an iniquity to be
punished by the judges,
for I would have been false to God
above.

¹ Or brothers and sisters ² Or let my descendants ³ Hebrew he ⁴ Hebrew her ⁵ Hebrew if his loins have not blessed me ⁶ Hebrew the light

29 "If I have rejoiced at the ruin of him who
     hated me,
        or exulted when evil overtook him
30   (I have not let my mouth sin
        by asking for his life with a curse),
31 if the men of my tent have not said,
        'Who is there that has not been filled
          with his meat?'
32 (the sojourner has not lodged in the
     street;
        I have opened my doors to the traveler),
33 if I have concealed my transgressions as
     others do[1]
        by hiding my iniquity in my heart,
34 because I stood in great fear of the
     multitude,
        and the contempt of families terrified
        me,
        so that I kept silence, and did not go
         out of doors—
35 Oh, that I had one to hear me!
     (Here is my signature! Let the
        Almighty answer me!)
     Oh, that I had the indictment written
        by my adversary!
36 Surely I would carry it on my shoulder;
     I would bind it on me as a crown;
37 I would give him an account of all my
     steps;
     like a prince I would approach him.

38 "If my land has cried out against me
     and its furrows have wept together,
39 if I have eaten its yield without payment
     and made its owners breathe their
        last,
40 let thorns grow instead of wheat,
     and foul weeds instead of barley."

The words of Job are ended.

--------- *2 Corinthians 1* ---------

Paul, an apostle of Christ Jesus by the will of God, and Timothy our brother,

To the church of God that is at Corinth, with all the saints who are in the whole of Achaia:

2 Grace to you and peace from God our Father and the Lord Jesus Christ.

3 Blessed be the God and Father of our Lord Jesus Christ, the Father of mercies and God of all comfort, **4** who comforts us in all our affliction, so that we may be able to comfort those who are in any affliction, with the comfort with which we ourselves are comforted by God. **5** For as we share abundantly in Christ's sufferings, so through Christ we share abundantly in comfort too.[2] **6** If we are afflicted, it is for your comfort and salvation; and if we are comforted, it is for your comfort, which you experience when you patiently endure the same sufferings that we suffer. **7** Our hope for you is unshaken, for we know that as you share in our sufferings, you will also share in our comfort.

8 For we do not want you to be unaware, brothers,[3] of the affliction we experienced in Asia. For we were so utterly burdened beyond our strength that we despaired of life itself. **9** Indeed, we felt that we had received the sentence of death. But that was to make us rely not on ourselves but on God who raises the dead. **10** He delivered us from such a deadly peril, and he will deliver us. On him we have set our hope that he will deliver us again. **11** You also must help us by prayer, so that many will give thanks on our behalf for the blessing granted us through the prayers of many.

12 For our boast is this, the testimony of our conscience, that we behaved in the world with simplicity[4] and godly sincerity, not by earthly wisdom but by the grace of God, and supremely so toward you. **13** For we are not writing to you anything other than what you read and understand and I hope you will fully understand— **14** just as you did partially understand us—that on the day of our Lord Jesus you will boast of us as we will boast of you.

15 Because I was sure of this, I wanted to come to you first, so that you might have a second experience of grace. **16** I wanted to visit you on my way to Macedonia, and to come back to you from Macedonia and have you send me on my way to Judea. **17** Was I vacillating when I wanted to do this? Do I make my plans according to the flesh, ready to say "Yes, yes" and "No, no" at the same time? **18** As surely as God is faithful, our word to you has not been Yes and No. **19** For the Son of God, Jesus Christ, whom we proclaimed among you, Silvanus and Timothy and I, was not Yes and No, but in him it is always Yes. **20** For all the promises of God find their Yes in him. That is why it is through him that we

---

[1] Or *as Adam did*   [2] Or *For as the sufferings of Christ abound for us, so also our comfort abounds through Christ*   [3] Or *brothers and sisters.* The plural Greek word *adelphoi* (translated "brothers") refers to siblings in a family. In New Testament usage, depending on the context, *adelphoi* may refer either to men or to both men and women who are siblings (brothers and sisters) in God's family, the church   [4] Some manuscripts *holiness*

utter our Amen to God for his glory. [21]And it is God who establishes us with you in Christ, and has anointed us, [22]and who has also put his seal on us and given us his Spirit in our hearts as a guarantee.[1]

[23]But I call God to witness against me—it was to spare you that I refrained from coming again to Corinth. [24]Not that we lord it over your faith, but we work with you for your joy, for you stand firm in your faith.

MARCH 3

Exodus 14

Then the LORD said to Moses, [2]"Tell the people of Israel to turn back and encamp in front of Pi-hahiroth, between Migdol and the sea, in front of Baal-zephon; you shall encamp facing it, by the sea. [3]For Pharaoh will say of the people of Israel, 'They are wandering in the land; the wilderness has shut them in.' [4]And I will harden Pharaoh's heart, and he will pursue them, and I will get glory over Pharaoh and all his host, and the Egyptians shall know that I am the LORD." And they did so.

[5]When the king of Egypt was told that the people had fled, the mind of Pharaoh and his servants was changed toward the people, and they said, "What is this we have done, that we have let Israel go from serving us?" [6]So he made ready his chariot and took his army with him, [7]and took six hundred chosen chariots and all the other chariots of Egypt with officers over all of them. [8]And the LORD hardened the heart of Pharaoh king of Egypt, and he pursued the people of Israel while the people of Israel were going out defiantly. [9]The Egyptians pursued them, all Pharaoh's horses and chariots and his horsemen and his army, and overtook them encamped at the sea, by Pi-hahiroth, in front of Baal-zephon.

[10]When Pharaoh drew near, the people of Israel lifted up their eyes, and behold, the Egyptians were marching after them, and they feared greatly. And the people of Israel cried out to the LORD. [11]They said to Moses, "Is it because there are no graves in Egypt that you have taken us away to die in the wilderness? What have you done to us in bringing us out of Egypt? [12]Is not this what we said to you in Egypt: 'Leave us alone that we may serve the Egyptians'? For it would have been better for us to serve the Egyptians than to die in the wilderness." [13]And Moses said to the people, "Fear not, stand firm, and see the salvation of the LORD, which he will work for you today. For the Egyptians whom you see today, you shall never see again. [14]The LORD will fight for you, and you have only to be silent."

[15]The LORD said to Moses, "Why do you cry to me? Tell the people of Israel to go forward. [16]Lift up your staff, and stretch out your hand over the sea and divide it, that the people of Israel may go through the sea on dry ground. [17]And I will harden the hearts of the Egyptians so that they shall go in after them, and I will get glory over Pharaoh and all his host, his chariots, and his horsemen. [18]And the Egyptians shall know that I am the LORD, when I have gotten glory over Pharaoh, his chariots, and his horsemen."

[19]Then the angel of God who was going before the host of Israel moved and went behind them, and the pillar of cloud moved from before them and stood behind them, [20]coming between the host of Egypt and the host of Israel. And there was the cloud and the darkness. And it lit up the night[2] without one coming near the other all night.

[21]Then Moses stretched out his hand over the sea, and the LORD drove the sea back by a strong east wind all night and made the sea dry land, and the waters were divided. [22]And the people of Israel went into the midst of the sea on dry ground, the waters being a wall to them on their right hand and on their left.

[1] Or down payment [2] Septuagint and the night passed

23 The Egyptians pursued and went in after them into the midst of the sea, all Pharaoh's horses, his chariots, and his horsemen. 24 And in the morning watch the LORD in the pillar of fire and of cloud looked down on the Egyptian forces and threw the Egyptian forces into a panic, 25 clogging[1] their chariot wheels so that they drove heavily. And the Egyptians said, "Let us flee from before Israel, for the LORD fights for them against the Egyptians."

26 Then the LORD said to Moses, "Stretch out your hand over the sea, that the water may come back upon the Egyptians, upon their chariots, and upon their horsemen." 27 So Moses stretched out his hand over the sea, and the sea returned to its normal course when the morning appeared. And as the Egyptians fled into it, the LORD threw[2] the Egyptians into the midst of the sea. 28 The waters returned and covered the chariots and the horsemen; of all the host of Pharaoh that had followed them into the sea, not one of them remained. 29 But the people of Israel walked on dry ground through the sea, the waters being a wall to them on their right hand and on their left.

30 Thus the LORD saved Israel that day from the hand of the Egyptians, and Israel saw the Egyptians dead on the seashore. 31 Israel saw the great power that the LORD used against the Egyptians, so the people feared the LORD, and they believed in the LORD and in his servant Moses.

Luke 17

And he said to his disciples, "Temptations to sin[3] are sure to come, but woe to the one through whom they come! 2 It would be better for him if a millstone were hung around his neck and he were cast into the sea than that he should cause one of these little ones to sin.[4] 3 Pay attention to yourselves! If your brother sins, rebuke him, and if he repents, forgive him, 4 and if he sins against you seven times in the day, and turns to you seven times, saying, 'I repent,' you must forgive him."

5 The apostles said to the Lord, "Increase our faith!" 6 And the Lord said, "If you had faith like a grain of mustard seed, you could say to this mulberry tree, 'Be uprooted and planted in the sea,' and it would obey you.

7 "Will any one of you who has a servant[5] plowing or keeping sheep say to him when he has come in from the field, 'Come at once and recline at table'? 8 Will he not rather say to him, 'Prepare supper for me, and dress properly,[6] and serve me while I eat and drink, and afterward you will eat and drink'? 9 Does he thank the servant because he did what was commanded? 10 So you also, when you have done all that you were commanded, say, 'We are unworthy servants;[7] we have only done what was our duty.'"

11 On the way to Jerusalem he was passing along between Samaria and Galilee. 12 And as he entered a village, he was met by ten lepers,[8] who stood at a distance 13 and lifted up their voices, saying, "Jesus, Master, have mercy on us." 14 When he saw them he said to them, "Go and show yourselves to the priests." And as they went they were cleansed. 15 Then one of them, when he saw that he was healed, turned back, praising God with a loud voice; 16 and he fell on his face at Jesus' feet, giving him thanks. Now he was a Samaritan. 17 Then Jesus answered, "Were not ten cleansed? Where are the nine? 18 Was no one found to return and give praise to God except this foreigner?" 19 And he said to him, "Rise and go your way; your faith has made you well."[9]

20 Being asked by the Pharisees when the kingdom of God would come, he answered them, "The kingdom of God is not coming in ways that can be observed, 21 nor will they say, 'Look, here it is!' or 'There!' for behold, the kingdom of God is in the midst of you."[10]

22 And he said to the disciples, "The days are coming when you will desire to see one of the days of the Son of Man, and you will not see it. 23 And they will say to you, 'Look, there!' or 'Look, here!' Do not go out or follow them. 24 For as the lightning flashes and lights up the sky from one side to the other, so will the Son of Man be in his day.[11] 25 But first he must suffer many things and be rejected by this generation. 26 Just as it was in the days of Noah, so will it be in the days of the Son of Man. 27 They were eating and drinking and marrying and being given in marriage, until the day when Noah entered the ark, and the flood came and destroyed them all. 28 Likewise, just as it was in the days of Lot—they were eating and drinking, buying and selling, planting and building, 29 but on the

---

[1] Or binding (compare Samaritan, Septuagint, Syriac); Hebrew removing [2] Hebrew shook off [3] Greek Stumbling blocks [4] Greek stumble [5] Greek bondservant; also verse 9 [6] Greek gird yourself [7] Greek bondservants [8] Leprosy was a term for several skin diseases; see Leviticus 13 [9] Or has saved you [10] Or within you, or within your grasp [11] Some manuscripts omit in his day

day when Lot went out from Sodom, fire and sulfur rained from heaven and destroyed them all— [30] so will it be on the day when the Son of Man is revealed. [31] On that day, let the one who is on the housetop, with his goods in the house, not come down to take them away, and likewise let the one who is in the field not turn back. [32] Remember Lot's wife. [33] Whoever seeks to preserve his life will lose it, but whoever loses his life will keep it. [34] I tell you, in that night there will be two in one bed. One will be taken and the other left. [35] There will be two women grinding together. One will be taken and the other left."[1] [37] And they said to him, "Where, Lord?" He said to them, "Where the corpse[2] is, there the vultures[3] will gather."

Job 32

So these three men ceased to answer Job, because he was righteous in his own eyes. [2] Then Elihu the son of Barachel the Buzite, of the family of Ram, burned with anger. He burned with anger at Job because he justified himself rather than God. [3] He burned with anger also at Job's three friends because they had found no answer, although they had declared Job to be in the wrong. [4] Now Elihu had waited to speak to Job because they were older than he. [5] And when Elihu saw that there was no answer in the mouth of these three men, he burned with anger.

[6] And Elihu the son of Barachel the Buzite answered and said:

"I am young in years,
   and you are aged;
therefore I was timid and afraid
   to declare my opinion to you.
[7] I said, 'Let days speak,
   and many years teach wisdom.'
[8] But it is the spirit in man,
   the breath of the Almighty, that makes him understand.
[9] It is not the old[4] who are wise,
   nor the aged who understand what is right.
[10] Therefore I say, 'Listen to me;
   let me also declare my opinion.'
[11] "Behold, I waited for your words,
   I listened for your wise sayings,
   while you searched out what to say.
[12] I gave you my attention,
   and, behold, there was none among you who refuted Job
   or who answered his words.
[13] Beware lest you say, 'We have found wisdom;
   God may vanquish him, not a man.'
[14] He has not directed his words against me,
   and I will not answer him with your speeches.
[15] "They are dismayed; they answer no more;
   they have not a word to say.
[16] And shall I wait, because they do not speak,
   because they stand there, and answer no more?
[17] I also will answer with my share;
   I also will declare my opinion.
[18] For I am full of words;
   the spirit within me constrains me.
[19] Behold, my belly is like wine that has no vent;
   like new wineskins ready to burst.
[20] I must speak, that I may find relief;
   I must open my lips and answer.
[21] I will not show partiality to any man
   or use flattery toward any person.
[22] For I do not know how to flatter,
   else my Maker would soon take me away.

---

2 Corinthians 2

For I made up my mind not to make another painful visit to you. [2] For if I cause you pain, who is there to make me glad but the one whom I have pained? [3] And I wrote as I did, so that when I came I might not suffer pain from those who should have made me rejoice, for I felt sure of all of you, that my joy would be the joy of you all. [4] For I wrote to you out of much affliction and anguish of heart and with many tears, not to cause you pain but to let you know the abundant love that I have for you.

[5] Now if anyone has caused pain, he has caused it not to me, but in some measure—not to put it too severely—to all of you. [6] For such a one, this punishment by the majority is enough, [7] so you should rather turn to forgive and comfort him, or he may be overwhelmed by excessive sorrow. [8] So I beg you to reaffirm

---

[1] Some manuscripts add verse 36: *Two men will be in the field; one will be taken and the other left* [2] Greek *body* [3] Or *eagles* [4] Hebrew *many* [in years]

your love for him. [9] For this is why I wrote, that I might test you and know whether you are obedient in everything. [10] Anyone whom you forgive, I also forgive. Indeed, what I have forgiven, if I have forgiven anything, has been for your sake in the presence of Christ, [11] so that we would not be outwitted by Satan; for we are not ignorant of his designs.

[12] When I came to Troas to preach the gospel of Christ, even though a door was opened for me in the Lord, [13] my spirit was not at rest because I did not find my brother Titus there. So I took leave of them and went on to Macedonia.

[14] But thanks be to God, who in Christ always leads us in triumphal procession, and through us spreads the fragrance of the knowledge of him everywhere. [15] For we are the aroma of Christ to God among those who are being saved and among those who are perishing, [16] to one a fragrance from death to death, to the other a fragrance from life to life. Who is sufficient for these things? [17] For we are not, like so many, peddlers of God's word, but as men of sincerity, as commissioned by God, in the sight of God we speak in Christ.

MARCH 4

Exodus 15

Then Moses and the people of Israel sang this song to the LORD, saying,

"I will sing to the LORD, for he has triumphed gloriously;
  the horse and his rider[1] he has thrown into the sea.
[2] The LORD is my strength and my song,
  and he has become my salvation;
this is my God, and I will praise him,
  my father's God, and I will exalt him.
[3] The LORD is a man of war;
  the LORD is his name.

[4] "Pharaoh's chariots and his host he cast into the sea,
  and his chosen officers were sunk in the Red Sea.
[5] The floods covered them;
  they went down into the depths like a stone.
[6] Your right hand, O LORD, glorious in power,
  your right hand, O LORD, shatters the enemy.
[7] In the greatness of your majesty you overthrow your adversaries;
  you send out your fury; it consumes them like stubble.

[8] At the blast of your nostrils the waters piled up;
  the floods stood up in a heap;
  the deeps congealed in the heart of the sea.
[9] The enemy said, 'I will pursue, I will overtake,
  I will divide the spoil, my desire shall have its fill of them.
  I will draw my sword; my hand shall destroy them.'
[10] You blew with your wind; the sea covered them;
  they sank like lead in the mighty waters.

[11] "Who is like you, O LORD, among the gods?
  Who is like you, majestic in holiness,
  awesome in glorious deeds, doing wonders?
[12] You stretched out your right hand;
  the earth swallowed them.

[13] "You have led in your steadfast love
  the people whom you have redeemed;
you have guided them by your strength to your holy abode.

[1] Or its chariot; also verse 21

14 The peoples have heard; they tremble;
    pangs have seized the inhabitants of
      Philistia.
15 Now are the chiefs of Edom dismayed;
    trembling seizes the leaders of Moab;
    all the inhabitants of Canaan have
      melted away.
16 Terror and dread fall upon them;
    because of the greatness of your arm,
      they are still as a stone,
    till your people, O LORD, pass by,
    till the people pass by whom you have
      purchased.
17 You will bring them in and plant them
    on your own mountain,
    the place, O LORD, which you have
      made for your abode,
    the sanctuary, O Lord, which your
      hands have established.
18 The LORD will reign forever and ever."

¹⁹ For when the horses of Pharaoh with his chariots and his horsemen went into the sea, the LORD brought back the waters of the sea upon them, but the people of Israel walked on dry ground in the midst of the sea. ²⁰ Then Miriam the prophetess, the sister of Aaron, took a tambourine in her hand, and all the women went out after her with tambourines and dancing. ²¹ And Miriam sang to them:

"Sing to the LORD, for he has triumphed
    gloriously;
the horse and his rider he has thrown
    into the sea."

²² Then Moses made Israel set out from the Red Sea, and they went into the wilderness of Shur. They went three days in the wilderness and found no water. ²³ When they came to Marah, they could not drink the water of Marah because it was bitter; therefore it was named Marah.¹ ²⁴ And the people grumbled against Moses, saying, "What shall we drink?" ²⁵ And he cried to the LORD, and the LORD showed him a log,² and he threw it into the water, and the water became sweet.

There the LORD³ made for them a statute and a rule, and there he tested them, ²⁶ saying, "If you will diligently listen to the voice of the LORD your God, and do that which is right in his eyes, and give ear to his commandments and keep all his statutes, I will put none of the diseases on you that I put on the Egyptians, for I am the LORD, your healer." ²⁷ Then they came to Elim, where there were twelve springs of water and seventy palm trees, and they encamped there by the water.

Luke 18

And he told them a parable to the effect that they ought always to pray and not lose heart. ² He said, "In a certain city there was a judge who neither feared God nor respected man. ³ And there was a widow in that city who kept coming to him and saying, 'Give me justice against my adversary.' ⁴ For a while he refused, but afterward he said to himself, 'Though I neither fear God nor respect man, ⁵ yet because this widow keeps bothering me, I will give her justice, so that she will not beat me down by her continual coming.'" ⁶ And the Lord said, "Hear what the unrighteous judge says. ⁷ And will not God give justice to his elect, who cry to him day and night? Will he delay long over them? ⁸ I tell you, he will give justice to them speedily. Nevertheless, when the Son of Man comes, will he find faith on earth?"

⁹ He also told this parable to some who trusted in themselves that they were righteous, and treated others with contempt: ¹⁰ "Two men went up into the temple to pray, one a Pharisee and the other a tax collector. ¹¹ The Pharisee, standing by himself, prayed⁴ thus: 'God, I thank you that I am not like other men, extortioners, unjust, adulterers, or even like this tax collector. ¹² I fast twice a week; I give tithes of all that I get.' ¹³ But the tax collector, standing far off, would not even lift up his eyes to heaven, but beat his breast, saying, 'God, be merciful to me, a sinner!' ¹⁴ I tell you, this man went down to his house justified, rather than the other. For everyone who exalts himself will be humbled, but the one who humbles himself will be exalted."

¹⁵ Now they were bringing even infants to him that he might touch them. And when the disciples saw it, they rebuked them. ¹⁶ But Jesus called them to him, saying, "Let the children come to me, and do not hinder them, for to such belongs the kingdom of God. ¹⁷ Truly, I say to you, whoever does not receive the kingdom of God like a child shall not enter it."

¹⁸ And a ruler asked him, "Good Teacher, what must I do to inherit eternal life?" ¹⁹ And

¹ Marah means bitterness ² Or tree ³ Hebrew he ⁴ Or standing, prayed to himself

Jesus said to him, "Why do you call me good? No one is good except God alone. ²⁰You know the commandments: 'Do not commit adultery, Do not murder, Do not steal, Do not bear false witness, Honor your father and mother.'" ²¹And he said, "All these I have kept from my youth." ²²When Jesus heard this, he said to him, "One thing you still lack. Sell all that you have and distribute to the poor, and you will have treasure in heaven; and come, follow me." ²³But when he heard these things, he became very sad, for he was extremely rich. ²⁴Jesus, seeing that he had become sad, said, "How difficult it is for those who have wealth to enter the kingdom of God! ²⁵For it is easier for a camel to go through the eye of a needle than for a rich person to enter the kingdom of God." ²⁶Those who heard it said, "Then who can be saved?" ²⁷But he said, "What is impossible with man is possible with God." ²⁸And Peter said, "See, we have left our homes and followed you." ²⁹And he said to them, "Truly, I say to you, there is no one who has left house or wife or brothers¹ or parents or children, for the sake of the kingdom of God, ³⁰who will not receive many times more in this time, and in the age to come eternal life."

³¹And taking the twelve, he said to them, "See, we are going up to Jerusalem, and everything that is written about the Son of Man by the prophets will be accomplished. ³²For he will be delivered over to the Gentiles and will be mocked and shamefully treated and spit upon. ³³And after flogging him, they will kill him, and on the third day he will rise." ³⁴But they understood none of these things. This saying was hidden from them, and they did not grasp what was said.

³⁵As he drew near to Jericho, a blind man was sitting by the roadside begging. ³⁶And hearing a crowd going by, he inquired what this meant. ³⁷They told him, "Jesus of Nazareth is passing by." ³⁸And he cried out, "Jesus, Son of David, have mercy on me!" ³⁹And those who were in front rebuked him, telling him to be silent. But he cried out all the more, "Son of David, have mercy on me!" ⁴⁰And Jesus stopped and commanded him to be brought to him. And when he came near, he asked him, ⁴¹"What do you want me to do for you?" He said, "Lord, let me recover my sight." ⁴²And Jesus said to him, "Recover your sight; your faith has made you well." ⁴³And immediately he recovered his sight and followed him, glorifying God. And all the people, when they saw it, gave praise to God.

Job 33

"But now, hear my speech, O Job,
    and listen to all my words.
2   Behold, I open my mouth;
        the tongue in my mouth speaks.
3   My words declare the uprightness of my
            heart,
        and what my lips know they speak
            sincerely.
4   The Spirit of God has made me,
        and the breath of the Almighty gives
            me life.
5   Answer me, if you can;
        set your words in order before me;
            take your stand.
6   Behold, I am toward God as you are;
        I too was pinched off from a piece of
            clay.
7   Behold, no fear of me need terrify you;
        my pressure will not be heavy upon
            you.
8   "Surely you have spoken in my ears,
        and I have heard the sound of your
            words.
9   You say, 'I am pure, without
            transgression;
        I am clean, and there is no iniquity in
            me.
10 Behold, he finds occasions against me,
        he counts me as his enemy,
11 he puts my feet in the stocks
        and watches all my paths.'
12 "Behold, in this you are not right. I will
            answer you,
        for God is greater than man.
13 Why do you contend against him,
        saying, 'He will answer none of man's²
            words'?³
14 For God speaks in one way,
        and in two, though man does not
            perceive it.
15 In a dream, in a vision of the night,
        when deep sleep falls on men,
        while they slumber on their beds,
16 then he opens the ears of men
        and terrifies them with warnings,

¹ Or wife or brothers and sisters ² Hebrew his ³ Or He will not answer for any of his own words

17 that he may turn man aside from his
        deed
    and conceal pride from a man;
18 he keeps back his soul from the pit,
        his life from perishing by the sword.

19 "Man is also rebuked with pain on his bed
        and with continual strife in his bones,
20 so that his life loathes bread,
        and his appetite the choicest food.
21 His flesh is so wasted away that it cannot
        be seen,
        and his bones that were not seen stick
        out.
22 His soul draws near the pit,
        and his life to those who bring death.
23 If there be for him an angel,
        a mediator, one of the thousand,
        to declare to man what is right for him,
24 and he is merciful to him, and says,
        'Deliver him from going down into the
        pit;
        I have found a ransom;
25 let his flesh become fresh with youth;
        let him return to the days of his
        youthful vigor';
26 then man[1] prays to God, and he accepts
        him;
        he sees his face with a shout of joy,
    and he restores to man his
        righteousness.
27 He sings before men and says:
    'I sinned and perverted what was right,
        and it was not repaid to me.
28 He has redeemed my soul from going
        down into the pit,
        and my life shall look upon the light.'

29 "Behold, God does all these things,
        twice, three times, with a man,
30 to bring back his soul from the pit,
        that he may be lighted with the light
        of life.
31 Pay attention, O Job, listen to me;
        be silent, and I will speak.
32 If you have any words, answer me;
        speak, for I desire to justify you.
33 If not, listen to me;
        be silent, and I will teach you
        wisdom."

──────── *2 Corinthians 3* ────────

Are we beginning to commend ourselves again? Or do we need, as some do, letters of recommendation to you, or from you? [2] You yourselves are our letter of recommendation, written on our[2] hearts, to be known and read by all. [3] And you show that you are a letter from Christ delivered by us, written not with ink but with the Spirit of the living God, not on tablets of stone but on tablets of human hearts.[3]

[4] Such is the confidence that we have through Christ toward God. [5] Not that we are sufficient in ourselves to claim anything as coming from us, but our sufficiency is from God, [6] who has made us sufficient to be ministers of a new covenant, not of the letter but of the Spirit. For the letter kills, but the Spirit gives life.

[7] Now if the ministry of death, carved in letters on stone, came with such glory that the Israelites could not gaze at Moses' face because of its glory, which was being brought to an end, [8] will not the ministry of the Spirit have even more glory? [9] For if there was glory in the ministry of condemnation, the ministry of righteousness must far exceed it in glory. [10] Indeed, in this case, what once had glory has come to have no glory at all, because of the glory that surpasses it. [11] For if what was being brought to an end came with glory, much more will what is permanent have glory.

[12] Since we have such a hope, we are very bold, [13] not like Moses, who would put a veil over his face so that the Israelites might not gaze at the outcome of what was being brought to an end. [14] But their minds were hardened. For to this day, when they read the old covenant, that same veil remains unlifted, because only through Christ is it taken away. [15] Yes, to this day whenever Moses is read a veil lies over their hearts. [16] But when one[4] turns to the Lord, the veil is removed. [17] Now the Lord[5] is the Spirit, and where the Spirit of the Lord is, there is freedom. [18] And we all, with unveiled face, beholding the glory of the Lord,[6] are being transformed into the same image from one degree of glory to another. For this comes from the Lord who is the Spirit.

---

[1] Hebrew *he* [2] Some manuscripts *your* [3] Greek *fleshly hearts* [4] Greek *he* [5] Or *this Lord* [6] Or *reflecting the glory of the Lord*

MARCH 5

Exodus 16

They set out from Elim, and all the congregation of the people of Israel came to the wilderness of Sin, which is between Elim and Sinai, on the fifteenth day of the second month after they had departed from the land of Egypt. ²And the whole congregation of the people of Israel grumbled against Moses and Aaron in the wilderness, ³and the people of Israel said to them, "Would that we had died by the hand of the LORD in the land of Egypt, when we sat by the meat pots and ate bread to the full, for you have brought us out into this wilderness to kill this whole assembly with hunger."

⁴Then the LORD said to Moses, "Behold, I am about to rain bread from heaven for you, and the people shall go out and gather a day's portion every day, that I may test them, whether they will walk in my law or not. ⁵On the sixth day, when they prepare what they bring in, it will be twice as much as they gather daily." ⁶So Moses and Aaron said to all the people of Israel, "At evening you shall know that it was the LORD who brought you out of the land of Egypt, ⁷and in the morning you shall see the glory of the LORD, because he has heard your grumbling against the LORD. For what are we, that you grumble against us?" ⁸And Moses said, "When the LORD gives you in the evening meat to eat and in the morning bread to the full, because the LORD has heard your grumbling that you grumble against him—what are we? Your grumbling is not against us but against the LORD."

⁹Then Moses said to Aaron, "Say to the whole congregation of the people of Israel, 'Come near before the LORD, for he has heard your grumbling.'" ¹⁰And as soon as Aaron spoke to the whole congregation of the people of Israel, they looked toward the wilderness, and behold, the glory of the LORD appeared in the cloud. ¹¹And the LORD said to Moses, ¹²"I have heard the grumbling of the people of Israel. Say to them, 'At twilight you shall eat meat, and in the morning you shall be filled

with bread. Then you shall know that I am the LORD your God.'"

¹³In the evening quail came up and covered the camp, and in the morning dew lay around the camp. ¹⁴And when the dew had gone up, there was on the face of the wilderness a fine, flake-like thing, fine as frost on the ground. ¹⁵When the people of Israel saw it, they said to one another, "What is it?"[1] For they did not know what it was. And Moses said to them, "It is the bread that the LORD has given you to eat. ¹⁶This is what the LORD has commanded: 'Gather of it, each one of you, as much as he can eat. You shall each take an omer,[2] according to the number of the persons that each of you has in his tent.'" ¹⁷And the people of Israel did so. They gathered, some more, some less. ¹⁸But when they measured it with an omer, whoever gathered much had nothing left over, and whoever gathered little had no lack. Each of them gathered as much as he could eat. ¹⁹And Moses said to them, "Let no one leave any of it over till the morning." ²⁰But they did not listen to Moses. Some left part of it till the morning, and it bred worms and stank. And Moses was angry with them. ²¹Morning by morning they gathered it, each as much as he could eat; but when the sun grew hot, it melted.

²²On the sixth day they gathered twice as much bread, two omers each. And when all the leaders of the congregation came and told Moses, ²³he said to them, "This is what the LORD has commanded: 'Tomorrow is a day of solemn rest, a holy Sabbath to the LORD; bake what you will bake and boil what you will boil, and all that is left over lay aside to be kept till the morning.'" ²⁴So they laid it aside till the morning, as Moses commanded them, and it did not stink, and there were no worms in it. ²⁵Moses said, "Eat it today, for today is a Sabbath to the LORD; today you will not find it in the field. ²⁶Six days you shall gather it, but on the seventh day, which is a Sabbath, there will be none."

[1] Or "It is manna." Hebrew man hu [2] An omer was about 2 quarts or 2 liters

[27] On the seventh day some of the people went out to gather, but they found none. [28] And the LORD said to Moses, "How long will you refuse to keep my commandments and my laws? [29] See! The LORD has given you the Sabbath; therefore on the sixth day he gives you bread for two days. Remain each of you in his place; let no one go out of his place on the seventh day." [30] So the people rested on the seventh day.

[31] Now the house of Israel called its name manna. It was like coriander seed, white, and the taste of it was like wafers made with honey. [32] Moses said, "This is what the LORD has commanded: 'Let an omer of it be kept throughout your generations, so that they may see the bread with which I fed you in the wilderness, when I brought you out of the land of Egypt.'" [33] And Moses said to Aaron, "Take a jar, and put an omer of manna in it, and place it before the LORD to be kept throughout your generations." [34] As the LORD commanded Moses, so Aaron placed it before the testimony to be kept. [35] The people of Israel ate the manna forty years, till they came to a habitable land. They ate the manna till they came to the border of the land of Canaan. [36] (An omer is the tenth part of an ephah.)[1]

Luke 19

He entered Jericho and was passing through. [2] And behold, there was a man named Zacchaeus. He was a chief tax collector and was rich. [3] And he was seeking to see who Jesus was, but on account of the crowd he could not, because he was small in stature. [4] So he ran on ahead and climbed up into a sycamore tree to see him, for he was about to pass that way. [5] And when Jesus came to the place, he looked up and said to him, "Zacchaeus, hurry and come down, for I must stay at your house today." [6] So he hurried and came down and received him joyfully. [7] And when they saw it, they all grumbled, "He has gone in to be the guest of a man who is a sinner." [8] And Zacchaeus stood and said to the Lord, "Behold, Lord, the half of my goods I give to the poor. And if I have defrauded anyone of anything, I restore it fourfold." [9] And Jesus said to him, "Today salvation has come to this house, since he also is a son of Abraham. [10] For the Son of Man came to seek and to save the lost."

[11] As they heard these things, he proceeded to tell a parable, because he was near to Jerusalem, and because they supposed that the kingdom of God was to appear immediately. [12] He said therefore, "A nobleman went into a far country to receive for himself a kingdom and then return. [13] Calling ten of his servants,[2] he gave them ten minas,[3] and said to them, 'Engage in business until I come.' [14] But his citizens hated him and sent a delegation after him, saying, 'We do not want this man to reign over us.' [15] When he returned, having received the kingdom, he ordered these servants to whom he had given the money to be called to him, that he might know what they had gained by doing business. [16] The first came before him, saying, 'Lord, your mina has made ten minas more.' [17] And he said to him, 'Well done, good servant![4] Because you have been faithful in a very little, you shall have authority over ten cities.' [18] And the second came, saying, 'Lord, your mina has made five minas.' [19] And he said to him, 'And you are to be over five cities.' [20] Then another came, saying, 'Lord, here is your mina, which I kept laid away in a handkerchief; [21] for I was afraid of you, because you are a severe man. You take what you did not deposit, and reap what you did not sow.' [22] He said to him, 'I will condemn you with your own words, you wicked servant! You knew that I was a severe man, taking what I did not deposit and reaping what I did not sow? [23] Why then did you not put my money in the bank, and at my coming I might have collected it with interest?' [24] And he said to those who stood by, 'Take the mina from him, and give it to the one who has the ten minas.' [25] And they said to him, 'Lord, he has ten minas!' [26] 'I tell you that to everyone who has, more will be given, but from the one who has not, even what he has will be taken away. [27] But as for these enemies of mine, who did not want me to reign over them, bring them here and slaughter them before me.'"

[28] And when he had said these things, he went on ahead, going up to Jerusalem. [29] When he drew near to Bethphage and Bethany, at the mount that is called Olivet, he sent two of the disciples, [30] saying, "Go into the village in front of you, where on entering you will find a colt tied, on which no one has ever yet sat. Untie it

[1] An *ephah* was about 3/5 bushel or 22 liters [2] Greek *bondservants*; also verse 15 [3] A *mina* was about three months' wages for a laborer [4] Greek *bondservant*; also verse 22

and bring it here. ³¹If anyone asks you, 'Why are you untying it?' you shall say this: 'The Lord has need of it.'" ³²So those who were sent went away and found it just as he had told them. ³³And as they were untying the colt, its owners said to them, "Why are you untying the colt?" ³⁴And they said, "The Lord has need of it." ³⁵And they brought it to Jesus, and throwing their cloaks on the colt, they set Jesus on it. ³⁶And as he rode along, they spread their cloaks on the road. ³⁷As he was drawing near—already on the way down the Mount of Olives—the whole multitude of his disciples began to rejoice and praise God with a loud voice for all the mighty works that they had seen, ³⁸saying, "Blessed is the King who comes in the name of the Lord! Peace in heaven and glory in the highest!" ³⁹And some of the Pharisees in the crowd said to him, "Teacher, rebuke your disciples." ⁴⁰He answered, "I tell you, if these were silent, the very stones would cry out."

⁴¹And when he drew near and saw the city, he wept over it, ⁴²saying, "Would that you, even you, had known on this day the things that make for peace! But now they are hidden from your eyes. ⁴³For the days will come upon you, when your enemies will set up a barricade around you and surround you and hem you in on every side ⁴⁴and tear you down to the ground, you and your children within you. And they will not leave one stone upon another in you, because you did not know the time of your visitation."

⁴⁵And he entered the temple and began to drive out those who sold, ⁴⁶saying to them, "It is written, 'My house shall be a house of prayer,' but you have made it a den of robbers."

⁴⁷And he was teaching daily in the temple. The chief priests and the scribes and the principal men of the people were seeking to destroy him, ⁴⁸but they did not find anything they could do, for all the people were hanging on his words.

Job 34

Then Elihu answered and said:

² "Hear my words, you wise men,
    and give ear to me, you who know;
³ for the ear tests words
    as the palate tastes food.

⁴ Let us choose what is right;
    let us know among ourselves what is
      good.
⁵ For Job has said, 'I am in the right,
    and God has taken away my right;
⁶ in spite of my right I am counted a liar;
    my wound is incurable, though I am
      without transgression.'
⁷ What man is like Job,
    who drinks up scoffing like water,
⁸ who travels in company with evildoers
    and walks with wicked men?
⁹ For he has said, 'It profits a man nothing
    that he should take delight in God.'

¹⁰ "Therefore, hear me, you men of
     understanding:
    far be it from God that he should do
     wickedness,
    and from the Almighty that he should
     do wrong.
¹¹ For according to the work of a man he
     will repay him,
    and according to his ways he will
     make it befall him.
¹² Of a truth, God will not do wickedly,
    and the Almighty will not pervert
     justice.
¹³ Who gave him charge over the earth,
    and who laid on him[1] the whole
     world?
¹⁴ If he should set his heart to it
    and gather to himself his spirit and his
     breath,
¹⁵ all flesh would perish together,
    and man would return to dust.

¹⁶ "If you have understanding, hear this;
    listen to what I say.
¹⁷ Shall one who hates justice govern?
    Will you condemn him who is
     righteous and mighty,
¹⁸ who says to a king, 'Worthless one,'
    and to nobles, 'Wicked man,'
¹⁹ who shows no partiality to princes,
    nor regards the rich more than the
     poor,
    for they are all the work of his hands?
²⁰ In a moment they die;
    at midnight the people are shaken and
     pass away,
    and the mighty are taken away by no
     human hand.

[1] Hebrew lacks *on him*

21   "For his eyes are on the ways of a man,
       and he sees all his steps.
22   There is no gloom or deep darkness
       where evildoers may hide themselves.
23   For God[1] has no need to consider a man
       further,
       that he should go before God in
       judgment.
24   He shatters the mighty without
       investigation
       and sets others in their place.
25   Thus, knowing their works,
       he overturns them in the night, and
       they are crushed.
26   He strikes them for their wickedness
       in a place for all to see,
27   because they turned aside from
       following him
       and had no regard for any of his ways,
28   so that they caused the cry of the poor to
       come to him,
       and he heard the cry of the afflicted—
29   When he is quiet, who can condemn?
       When he hides his face, who can
       behold him,
       whether it be a nation or a man?—
30   that a godless man should not reign,
       that he should not ensnare the people.

31   "For has anyone said to God,
       'I have borne punishment; I will not
       offend any more;
32   teach me what I do not see;
       if I have done iniquity, I will do it no
       more'?
33   Will he then make repayment to suit
       you,
       because you reject it?
       For you must choose, and not I;
       therefore declare what you know.[2]
34   Men of understanding will say to me,
       and the wise man who hears me will
       say:
35   'Job speaks without knowledge;
       his words are without insight.'
36   Would that Job were tried to the end,
       because he answers like wicked men.
37   For he adds rebellion to his sin;
       he claps his hands among us
       and multiplies his words against God."

2 Corinthians 4

Therefore, having this ministry by the mercy of God,[3] we do not lose heart. [2] But we have renounced disgraceful, underhanded ways. We refuse to practice[4] cunning or to tamper with God's word, but by the open statement of the truth we would commend ourselves to everyone's conscience in the sight of God. [3] And even if our gospel is veiled, it is veiled to those who are perishing. [4] In their case the god of this world has blinded the minds of the unbelievers, to keep them from seeing the light of the gospel of the glory of Christ, who is the image of God. [5] For what we proclaim is not ourselves, but Jesus Christ as Lord, with ourselves as your servants[5] for Jesus' sake. [6] For God, who said, "Let light shine out of darkness," has shone in our hearts to give the light of the knowledge of the glory of God in the face of Jesus Christ.

[7] But we have this treasure in jars of clay, to show that the surpassing power belongs to God and not to us. [8] We are afflicted in every way, but not crushed; perplexed, but not driven to despair; [9] persecuted, but not forsaken; struck down, but not destroyed; [10] always carrying in the body the death of Jesus, so that the life of Jesus may also be manifested in our bodies. [11] For we who live are always being given over to death for Jesus' sake, so that the life of Jesus also may be manifested in our mortal flesh. [12] So death is at work in us, but life in you.

[13] Since we have the same spirit of faith according to what has been written, "I believed, and so I spoke," we also believe, and so we also speak, [14] knowing that he who raised the Lord Jesus will raise us also with Jesus and bring us with you into his presence. [15] For it is all for your sake, so that as grace extends to more and more people it may increase thanksgiving, to the glory of God.

[16] So we do not lose heart. Though our outer self[6] is wasting away, our inner self is being renewed day by day. [17] For this light momentary affliction is preparing for us an eternal weight of glory beyond all comparison, [18] as we look not to the things that are seen but to the things that are unseen. For the things that are seen are transient, but the things that are unseen are eternal.

---

[1] Hebrew *he* [2] The meaning of the Hebrew in verses 29–33 is uncertain [3] Greek *as we have received mercy* [4] Greek *to walk in* [5] Greek *bondservants* [6] Greek *man*

MARCH 6

Exodus 17

All the congregation of the people of Israel moved on from the wilderness of Sin by stages, according to the commandment of the LORD, and camped at Rephidim, but there was no water for the people to drink. ²Therefore the people quarreled with Moses and said, "Give us water to drink." And Moses said to them, "Why do you quarrel with me? Why do you test the LORD?" ³But the people thirsted there for water, and the people grumbled against Moses and said, "Why did you bring us up out of Egypt, to kill us and our children and our livestock with thirst?" ⁴So Moses cried to the LORD, "What shall I do with this people? They are almost ready to stone me." ⁵And the LORD said to Moses, "Pass on before the people, taking with you some of the elders of Israel, and take in your hand the staff with which you struck the Nile, and go. ⁶Behold, I will stand before you there on the rock at Horeb, and you shall strike the rock, and water shall come out of it, and the people will drink." And Moses did so, in the sight of the elders of Israel. ⁷And he called the name of the place Massah¹ and Meribah,² because of the quarreling of the people of Israel, and because they tested the LORD by saying, "Is the LORD among us or not?"

⁸Then Amalek came and fought with Israel at Rephidim. ⁹So Moses said to Joshua, "Choose for us men, and go out and fight with Amalek. Tomorrow I will stand on the top of the hill with the staff of God in my hand." ¹⁰So Joshua did as Moses told him, and fought with Amalek, while Moses, Aaron, and Hur went up to the top of the hill. ¹¹Whenever Moses held up his hand, Israel prevailed, and whenever he lowered his hand, Amalek prevailed. ¹²But Moses' hands grew weary, so they took a stone and put it under him, and he sat on it, while Aaron and Hur held up his hands, one on one side, and the other on the other side. So his hands were steady until the going down of the sun. ¹³And Joshua overwhelmed Amalek and his people with the sword.

¹⁴Then the LORD said to Moses, "Write this as a memorial in a book and recite it in the ears of Joshua, that I will utterly blot out the memory of Amalek from under heaven." ¹⁵And Moses built an altar and called the name of it, The LORD Is My Banner, ¹⁶saying, "A hand upon the throne³ of the LORD! The LORD will have war with Amalek from generation to generation."

Luke 20

One day, as Jesus⁴ was teaching the people in the temple and preaching the gospel, the chief priests and the scribes with the elders came up ²and said to him, "Tell us by what authority you do these things, or who it is that gave you this authority." ³He answered them, "I also will ask you a question. Now tell me, ⁴was the baptism of John from heaven or from man?" ⁵And they discussed it with one another, saying, "If we say, 'From heaven,' he will say, 'Why did you not believe him?' ⁶But if we say, 'From man,' all the people will stone us to death, for they are convinced that John was a prophet." ⁷So they answered that they did not know where it came from. ⁸And Jesus said to them, "Neither will I tell you by what authority I do these things."

⁹And he began to tell the people this parable: "A man planted a vineyard and let it out to tenants and went into another country for a long while. ¹⁰When the time came, he sent a servant⁵ to the tenants, so that they would give him some of the fruit of the vineyard. But the tenants beat him and sent him away empty-handed. ¹¹And he sent another servant. But they also beat and treated him shamefully, and sent him away empty-handed. ¹²And he sent yet a third. This one also they wounded and cast out. ¹³Then the owner of the vineyard said, 'What shall I do? I will send my beloved son; perhaps they will respect him.' ¹⁴But when the tenants saw him, they said to themselves,

¹ *Massah* means *testing* ² *Meribah* means *quarreling* ³ A slight change would yield *upon the banner* ⁴ Greek *he* ⁵ Greek *bondservant*; also verse 11

'This is the heir. Let us kill him, so that the inheritance may be ours.' [15]And they threw him out of the vineyard and killed him. What then will the owner of the vineyard do to them? [16]He will come and destroy those tenants and give the vineyard to others." When they heard this, they said, "Surely not!" [17]But he looked directly at them and said, "What then is this that is written:

" 'The stone that the builders rejected
　　 has become the cornerstone'?[1]

[18]Everyone who falls on that stone will be broken to pieces, and when it falls on anyone, it will crush him."

[19]The scribes and the chief priests sought to lay hands on him at that very hour, for they perceived that he had told this parable against them, but they feared the people. [20]So they watched him and sent spies, who pretended to be sincere, that they might catch him in something he said, so as to deliver him up to the authority and jurisdiction of the governor. [21]So they asked him, "Teacher, we know that you speak and teach rightly, and show no partiality,[2] but truly teach the way of God. [22]Is it lawful for us to give tribute to Caesar, or not?" [23]But he perceived their craftiness, and said to them, [24]"Show me a denarius.[3] Whose likeness and inscription does it have?" They said, "Caesar's." [25]He said to them, "Then render to Caesar the things that are Caesar's, and to God the things that are God's." [26]And they were not able in the presence of the people to catch him in what he said, but marveling at his answer they became silent.

[27]There came to him some Sadducees, those who deny that there is a resurrection, [28]and they asked him a question, saying, "Teacher, Moses wrote for us that if a man's brother dies, having a wife but no children, the man[4] must take the widow and raise up offspring for his brother. [29]Now there were seven brothers. The first took a wife, and died without children. [30]And the second [31]and the third took her, and likewise all seven left no children and died. [32]Afterward the woman also died. [33]In the resurrection, therefore, whose wife will the woman be? For the seven had her as wife."

[34]And Jesus said to them, "The sons of this age marry and are given in marriage, [35]but those who are considered worthy to attain to that age and to the resurrection from the dead neither marry nor are given in marriage, [36]for they cannot die anymore, because they are equal to angels and are sons of God, being sons[5] of the resurrection. [37]But that the dead are raised, even Moses showed, in the passage about the bush, where he calls the Lord the God of Abraham and the God of Isaac and the God of Jacob. [38]Now he is not God of the dead, but of the living, for all live to him." [39]Then some of the scribes answered, "Teacher, you have spoken well." [40]For they no longer dared to ask him any question.

[41]But he said to them, "How can they say that the Christ is David's son? [42]For David himself says in the Book of Psalms,

" 'The Lord said to my Lord,
　"Sit at my right hand,
43　　 until I make your enemies your
　　　 footstool."'

[44]David thus calls him Lord, so how is he his son?"

[45]And in the hearing of all the people he said to his disciples, [46]"Beware of the scribes, who like to walk around in long robes, and love greetings in the marketplaces and the best seats in the synagogues and the places of honor at feasts, [47]who devour widows' houses and for a pretense make long prayers. They will receive the greater condemnation."

Job 35

And Elihu answered and said:

[2]　"Do you think this to be just?
　　 Do you say, 'It is my right before God,'
[3]　 that you ask, 'What advantage have I?
　　 How am I better off than if I had
　　　 sinned?'
[4]　 I will answer you
　　 and your friends with you.
[5]　 Look at the heavens, and see;
　　 and behold the clouds, which are
　　　 higher than you.
[6]　 If you have sinned, what do you
　　　 accomplish against him?
　　 And if your transgressions are
　　　 multiplied, what do you do to
　　　 him?

[1] Greek the head of the corner [2] Greek and do not receive a face [3] A denarius was a day's wage for a laborer [4] Greek his brother [5] Greek huioi; see Preface

7 If you are righteous, what do you give to
   him?
   Or what does he receive from your
   hand?
8 Your wickedness concerns a man like
   yourself,
   and your righteousness a son of man.
9 "Because of the multitude of oppressions
   people cry out;
   they call for help because of the arm
   of the mighty.[1]
10 But none says, 'Where is God my Maker,
   who gives songs in the night,
11 who teaches us more than the beasts of
   the earth
   and makes us wiser than the birds of
   the heavens?'
12 There they cry out, but he does not
   answer,
   because of the pride of evil men.
13 Surely God does not hear an empty cry,
   nor does the Almighty regard it.
14 How much less when you say that you
   do not see him,
   that the case is before him, and you
   are waiting for him!
15 And now, because his anger does not
   punish,
   and he does not take much note of
   transgression,[2]
16 Job opens his mouth in empty talk;
   he multiplies words without
   knowledge."

2 Corinthians 5

For we know that if the tent that is our
earthly home is destroyed, we have a building from God, a house not made with hands,
eternal in the heavens. [2]For in this tent we
groan, longing to put on our heavenly dwelling, [3]if indeed by putting it on[3] we may not
be found naked. [4]For while we are still in this
tent, we groan, being burdened—not that we
would be unclothed, but that we would be
further clothed, so that what is mortal may be
swallowed up by life. [5]He who has prepared us
for this very thing is God, who has given us the
Spirit as a guarantee.

[6]So we are always of good courage. We
know that while we are at home in the body
we are away from the Lord, [7]for we walk by
faith, not by sight. [8]Yes, we are of good courage, and we would rather be away from the
body and at home with the Lord. [9]So whether
we are at home or away, we make it our aim to
please him. [10]For we must all appear before the
judgment seat of Christ, so that each one may
receive what is due for what he has done in the
body, whether good or evil.

[11]Therefore, knowing the fear of the Lord,
we persuade others. But what we are is known
to God, and I hope it is known also to your conscience. [12]We are not commending ourselves to
you again but giving you cause to boast about
us, so that you may be able to answer those who
boast about outward appearance and not about
what is in the heart. [13]For if we are beside ourselves, it is for God; if we are in our right mind,
it is for you. [14]For the love of Christ controls
us, because we have concluded this: that one
has died for all, therefore all have died; [15]and
he died for all, that those who live might no
longer live for themselves but for him who for
their sake died and was raised.

[16]From now on, therefore, we regard no one
according to the flesh. Even though we once
regarded Christ according to the flesh, we
regard him thus no longer. [17]Therefore, if anyone is in Christ, he is a new creation.[4] The old
has passed away; behold, the new has come.
[18]All this is from God, who through Christ reconciled us to himself and gave us the ministry
of reconciliation; [19]that is, in Christ God was
reconciling[5] the world to himself, not counting
their trespasses against them, and entrusting to
us the message of reconciliation. [20]Therefore,
we are ambassadors for Christ, God making his
appeal through us. We implore you on behalf
of Christ, be reconciled to God. [21]For our sake
he made him to be sin who knew no sin, so
that in him we might become the righteousness of God.

[1] Or the many [2] Theodotion, Symmachus (compare Vulgate); the meaning of the Hebrew word is uncertain [3] Some manuscripts putting it off [4] Or creature [5] Or God was in Christ, reconciling

MARCH 7

───── *Exodus 18* ─────

Jethro, the priest of Midian, Moses' father-in-law, heard of all that God had done for Moses and for Israel his people, how the LORD had brought Israel out of Egypt. [2] Now Jethro, Moses' father-in-law, had taken Zipporah, Moses' wife, after he had sent her home, [3] along with her two sons. The name of the one was Gershom (for he said, "I have been a sojourner[1] in a foreign land"), [4] and the name of the other, Eliezer[2] (for he said, "The God of my father was my help, and delivered me from the sword of Pharaoh"). [5] Jethro, Moses' father-in-law, came with his sons and his wife to Moses in the wilderness where he was encamped at the mountain of God. [6] And when he sent word to Moses, "I,[3] your father-in-law Jethro, am coming to you with your wife and her two sons with her," [7] Moses went out to meet his father-in-law and bowed down and kissed him. And they asked each other of their welfare and went into the tent. [8] Then Moses told his father-in-law all that the LORD had done to Pharaoh and to the Egyptians for Israel's sake, all the hardship that had come upon them in the way, and how the LORD had delivered them. [9] And Jethro rejoiced for all the good that the LORD had done to Israel, in that he had delivered them out of the hand of the Egyptians.

[10] Jethro said, "Blessed be the LORD, who has delivered you out of the hand of the Egyptians and out of the hand of Pharaoh and has delivered the people from under the hand of the Egyptians. [11] Now I know that the LORD is greater than all gods, because in this affair they dealt arrogantly with the people."[4] [12] And Jethro, Moses' father-in-law, brought a burnt offering and sacrifices to God; and Aaron came with all the elders of Israel to eat bread with Moses' father-in-law before God.

[13] The next day Moses sat to judge the people, and the people stood around Moses from morning till evening. [14] When Moses' father-in-law saw all that he was doing for the people, he said, "What is this that you are doing for the people? Why do you sit alone, and all the people stand around you from morning till evening?" [15] And Moses said to his father-in-law, "Because the people come to me to inquire of God; [16] when they have a dispute, they come to me and I decide between one person and another, and I make them know the statutes of God and his laws." [17] Moses' father-in-law said to him, "What you are doing is not good. [18] You and the people with you will certainly wear yourselves out, for the thing is too heavy for you. You are not able to do it alone. [19] Now obey my voice; I will give you advice, and God be with you! You shall represent the people before God and bring their cases to God, [20] and you shall warn them about the statutes and the laws, and make them know the way in which they must walk and what they must do. [21] Moreover, look for able men from all the people, men who fear God, who are trustworthy and hate a bribe, and place such men over the people as chiefs of thousands, of hundreds, of fifties, and of tens. [22] And let them judge the people at all times. Every great matter they shall bring to you, but any small matter they shall decide themselves. So it will be easier for you, and they will bear the burden with you. [23] If you do this, God will direct you, you will be able to endure, and all this people also will go to their place in peace."

[24] So Moses listened to the voice of his father-in-law and did all that he had said. [25] Moses chose able men out of all Israel and made them heads over the people, chiefs of thousands, of hundreds, of fifties, and of tens. [26] And they judged the people at all times. Any hard case they brought to Moses, but any small matter they decided themselves. [27] Then Moses let his father-in-law depart, and he went away to his own country.

───── *Luke 21* ─────

Jesus[5] looked up and saw the rich putting their gifts into the offering box, [2] and he saw a poor widow put in two small copper coins.[6]

---

[1] *Gershom* sounds like the Hebrew word for *sojourner* [2] *Eliezer* means *My God is help* [3] Hebrew; Samaritan, Septuagint, Syriac *behold* [4] Hebrew *with them* [5] Greek *He* [6] Greek *two lepta; a lepton was a Jewish bronze or copper coin worth about 1/128 of a denarius* (which was a day's wage for a laborer)

³And he said, "Truly, I tell you, this poor widow has put in more than all of them. ⁴For they all contributed out of their abundance, but she out of her poverty put in all she had to live on."

⁵And while some were speaking of the temple, how it was adorned with noble stones and offerings, he said, ⁶"As for these things that you see, the days will come when there will not be left here one stone upon another that will not be thrown down." ⁷And they asked him, "Teacher, when will these things be, and what will be the sign when these things are about to take place?" ⁸And he said, "See that you are not led astray. For many will come in my name, saying, 'I am he!' and, 'The time is at hand!' Do not go after them. ⁹And when you hear of wars and tumults, do not be terrified, for these things must first take place, but the end will not be at once."

¹⁰Then he said to them, "Nation will rise against nation, and kingdom against kingdom. ¹¹There will be great earthquakes, and in various places famines and pestilences. And there will be terrors and great signs from heaven. ¹²But before all this they will lay their hands on you and persecute you, delivering you up to the synagogues and prisons, and you will be brought before kings and governors for my name's sake. ¹³This will be your opportunity to bear witness. ¹⁴Settle it therefore in your minds not to meditate beforehand how to answer, ¹⁵for I will give you a mouth and wisdom, which none of your adversaries will be able to withstand or contradict. ¹⁶You will be delivered up even by parents and brothers[1] and relatives and friends, and some of you they will put to death. ¹⁷You will be hated by all for my name's sake. ¹⁸But not a hair of your head will perish. ¹⁹By your endurance you will gain your lives.

²⁰"But when you see Jerusalem surrounded by armies, then know that its desolation has come near. ²¹Then let those who are in Judea flee to the mountains, and let those who are inside the city depart, and let not those who are out in the country enter it, ²²for these are days of vengeance, to fulfill all that is written. ²³Alas for women who are pregnant and for those who are nursing infants in those days! For there will be great distress upon the earth and wrath against this people. ²⁴They will fall by the edge of the sword and be led captive among all nations, and Jerusalem will be trampled underfoot by the Gentiles, until the times of the Gentiles are fulfilled.

²⁵"And there will be signs in sun and moon and stars, and on the earth distress of nations in perplexity because of the roaring of the sea and the waves, ²⁶people fainting with fear and with foreboding of what is coming on the world. For the powers of the heavens will be shaken. ²⁷And then they will see the Son of Man coming in a cloud with power and great glory. ²⁸Now when these things begin to take place, straighten up and raise your heads, because your redemption is drawing near."

²⁹And he told them a parable: "Look at the fig tree, and all the trees. ³⁰As soon as they come out in leaf, you see for yourselves and know that the summer is already near. ³¹So also, when you see these things taking place, you know that the kingdom of God is near. ³²Truly, I say to you, this generation will not pass away until all has taken place. ³³Heaven and earth will pass away, but my words will not pass away.

³⁴"But watch yourselves lest your hearts be weighed down with dissipation and drunkenness and cares of this life, and that day come upon you suddenly like a trap. ³⁵For it will come upon all who dwell on the face of the whole earth. ³⁶But stay awake at all times, praying that you may have strength to escape all these things that are going to take place, and to stand before the Son of Man."

³⁷And every day he was teaching in the temple, but at night he went out and lodged on the mount called Olivet. ³⁸And early in the morning all the people came to him in the temple to hear him.

Job 36

And Elihu continued, and said:

2   "Bear with me a little, and I will show you,
        for I have yet something to say on
            God's behalf.
3   I will get my knowledge from afar
        and ascribe righteousness to my
            Maker.
4   For truly my words are not false;
        one who is perfect in knowledge is
            with you.

---

[1] Or parents and brothers and sisters

5 "Behold, God is mighty, and does not
    despise any;
    he is mighty in strength of
      understanding.
6 He does not keep the wicked alive,
    but gives the afflicted their right.
7 He does not withdraw his eyes from the
    righteous,
    but with kings on the throne
    he sets them forever, and they are
      exalted.
8 And if they are bound in chains
    and caught in the cords of affliction,
9 then he declares to them their work
    and their transgressions, that they are
      behaving arrogantly.
10 He opens their ears to instruction
    and commands that they return from
      iniquity.
11 If they listen and serve him,
    they complete their days in prosperity,
    and their years in pleasantness.
12 But if they do not listen, they perish by
    the sword
    and die without knowledge.

13 "The godless in heart cherish anger;
    they do not cry for help when he
      binds them.
14 They die in youth,
    and their life ends among the cult
      prostitutes.
15 He delivers the afflicted by their
    affliction
    and opens their ear by adversity.
16 He also allured you out of distress
    into a broad place where there was no
      cramping,
    and what was set on your table was
      full of fatness.

17 "But you are full of the judgment on the
    wicked;
    judgment and justice seize you.
18 Beware lest wrath entice you into
    scoffing,
    and let not the greatness of the
      ransom turn you aside.
19 Will your cry for help avail to keep you
    from distress,
    or all the force of your strength?
20 Do not long for the night,
    when peoples vanish in their place.

21 Take care; do not turn to iniquity,
    for this you have chosen rather than
      affliction.
22 Behold, God is exalted in his power;
    who is a teacher like him?
23 Who has prescribed for him his way,
    or who can say, 'You have done wrong'?

24 "Remember to extol his work,
    of which men have sung.
25 All mankind has looked on it;
    man beholds it from afar.
26 Behold, God is great, and we know him
    not;
    the number of his years is
      unsearchable.
27 For he draws up the drops of water;
    they distill his mist in rain,
28 which the skies pour down
    and drop on mankind abundantly.
29 Can anyone understand the spreading of
    the clouds,
    the thunderings of his pavilion?
30 Behold, he scatters his lightning about
    him
    and covers the roots of the sea.
31 For by these he judges peoples;
    he gives food in abundance.
32 He covers his hands with the lightning
    and commands it to strike the mark.
33 Its crashing declares his presence;[1]
    the cattle also declare that he rises.

2 Corinthians 6

Working together with him, then, we
appeal to you not to receive the grace of
God in vain. [2] For he says,

"In a favorable time I listened to you,
    and in a day of salvation I have helped
      you."

Behold, now is the favorable time; behold, now
is the day of salvation. [3] We put no obstacle in
anyone's way, so that no fault may be found
with our ministry, [4] but as servants of God we
commend ourselves in every way: by great
endurance, in afflictions, hardships, calamities, [5] beatings, imprisonments, riots, labors,
sleepless nights, hunger; [6] by purity, knowledge, patience, kindness, the Holy Spirit, genuine love; [7] by truthful speech, and the power

---

[1] Hebrew *declares concerning him*

of God; with the weapons of righteousness for the right hand and for the left; [8]through honor and dishonor, through slander and praise. We are treated as impostors, and yet are true; [9]as unknown, and yet well known; as dying, and behold, we live; as punished, and yet not killed; [10]as sorrowful, yet always rejoicing; as poor, yet making many rich; as having nothing, yet possessing everything.

[11]We have spoken freely to you,[1] Corinthians; our heart is wide open. [12]You are not restricted by us, but you are restricted in your own affections. [13]In return (I speak as to children) widen your hearts also.

[14]Do not be unequally yoked with unbelievers. For what partnership has righteousness with lawlessness? Or what fellowship has light with darkness? [15]What accord has Christ with Belial?[2] Or what portion does a believer share with an unbeliever? [16]What agreement has the temple of God with idols? For we are the temple of the living God; as God said,

"I will make my dwelling among them
    and walk among them,
    and I will be their God,
    and they shall be my people.
[17]   Therefore go out from their midst,
    and be separate from them, says the
        Lord,
    and touch no unclean thing;
        then I will welcome you,
[18]   and I will be a father to you,
    and you shall be sons and daughters
        to me,
    says the Lord Almighty."

MARCH 8

Exodus 19

On the third new moon after the people of Israel had gone out of the land of Egypt, on that day they came into the wilderness of Sinai. [2]They set out from Rephidim and came into the wilderness of Sinai, and they encamped in the wilderness. There Israel encamped before the mountain, [3]while Moses went up to God. The LORD called to him out of the mountain, saying, "Thus you shall say to the house of Jacob, and tell the people of Israel: [4]You yourselves have seen what I did to the Egyptians, and how I bore you on eagles' wings and brought you to myself. [5]Now therefore, if you will indeed obey my voice and keep my covenant, you shall be my treasured possession among all peoples, for all the earth is mine; [6]and you shall be to me a kingdom of priests and a holy nation. These are the words that you shall speak to the people of Israel."

[7]So Moses came and called the elders of the people and set before them all these words that the LORD had commanded him. [8]All the people answered together and said, "All that the LORD has spoken we will do." And Moses reported the words of the people to the LORD. [9]And the LORD said to Moses, "Behold, I am coming to you in a thick cloud, that the people may hear when I speak with you, and may also believe you forever."

When Moses told the words of the people to the LORD, [10]the LORD said to Moses, "Go to the people and consecrate them today and tomorrow, and let them wash their garments [11]and be ready for the third day. For on the third day the LORD will come down on Mount Sinai in the sight of all the people. [12]And you shall set limits for the people all around, saying, 'Take care not to go up into the mountain or touch the edge of it. Whoever touches the mountain shall be put to death. [13]No hand shall touch him, but he shall be stoned or shot;[3] whether beast or man, he shall not live.' When the trumpet sounds a long blast, they shall come up to the mountain." [14]So Moses went down from the mountain to the people and consecrated the people; and they washed their garments. [15]And he said to

[1] Greek *Our mouth is open to you* [2] Greek *Beliar* [3] That is, shot with an arrow

the people, "Be ready for the third day; do not go near a woman."

¹⁶On the morning of the third day there were thunders and lightnings and a thick cloud on the mountain and a very loud trumpet blast, so that all the people in the camp trembled. ¹⁷Then Moses brought the people out of the camp to meet God, and they took their stand at the foot of the mountain. ¹⁸Now Mount Sinai was wrapped in smoke because the LORD had descended on it in fire. The smoke of it went up like the smoke of a kiln, and the whole mountain trembled greatly. ¹⁹And as the sound of the trumpet grew louder and louder, Moses spoke, and God answered him in thunder. ²⁰The LORD came down on Mount Sinai, to the top of the mountain. And the LORD called Moses to the top of the mountain, and Moses went up.

²¹And the LORD said to Moses, "Go down and warn the people, lest they break through to the LORD to look and many of them perish. ²²Also let the priests who come near to the LORD consecrate themselves, lest the LORD break out against them." ²³And Moses said to the LORD, "The people cannot come up to Mount Sinai, for you yourself warned us, saying, 'Set limits around the mountain and consecrate it.'" ²⁴And the LORD said to him, "Go down, and come up bringing Aaron with you. But do not let the priests and the people break through to come up to the LORD, lest he break out against them." ²⁵So Moses went down to the people and told them.

──────── Luke 22 ────────

Now the Feast of Unleavened Bread drew near, which is called the Passover. ²And the chief priests and the scribes were seeking how to put him to death, for they feared the people. ³Then Satan entered into Judas called Iscariot, who was of the number of the twelve. ⁴He went away and conferred with the chief priests and officers how he might betray him to them. ⁵And they were glad, and agreed to give him money. ⁶So he consented and sought an opportunity to betray him to them in the absence of a crowd.

⁷Then came the day of Unleavened Bread, on which the Passover lamb had to be sacrificed. ⁸So Jesus¹ sent Peter and John, saying, "Go and prepare the Passover for us, that we may eat it." ⁹They said to him, "Where will you have us prepare it?" ¹⁰He said to them, "Behold, when you have entered the city, a man carrying a jar of water will meet you. Follow him into the house that he enters ¹¹and tell the master of the house, 'The Teacher says to you, Where is the guest room, where I may eat the Passover with my disciples?' ¹²And he will show you a large upper room furnished; prepare it there." ¹³And they went and found it just as he had told them, and they prepared the Passover.

¹⁴And when the hour came, he reclined at table, and the apostles with him. ¹⁵And he said to them, "I have earnestly desired to eat this Passover with you before I suffer. ¹⁶For I tell you I will not eat it² until it is fulfilled in the kingdom of God." ¹⁷And he took a cup, and when he had given thanks he said, "Take this, and divide it among yourselves. ¹⁸For I tell you that from now on I will not drink of the fruit of the vine until the kingdom of God comes." ¹⁹And he took bread, and when he had given thanks, he broke it and gave it to them, saying, "This is my body, which is given for you. Do this in remembrance of me." ²⁰And likewise the cup after they had eaten, saying, "This cup that is poured out for you is the new covenant in my blood.³ ²¹But behold, the hand of him who betrays me is with me on the table. ²²For the Son of Man goes as it has been determined, but woe to that man by whom he is betrayed!" ²³And they began to question one another, which of them it could be who was going to do this.

²⁴A dispute also arose among them, as to which of them was to be regarded as the greatest. ²⁵And he said to them, "The kings of the Gentiles exercise lordship over them, and those in authority over them are called benefactors. ²⁶But not so with you. Rather, let the greatest among you become as the youngest, and the leader as one who serves. ²⁷For who is the greater, one who reclines at table or one who serves? Is it not the one who reclines at table? But I am among you as the one who serves.

²⁸"You are those who have stayed with me in my trials, ²⁹and I assign to you, as my Father assigned to me, a kingdom, ³⁰that you may eat and drink at my table in my kingdom and sit on thrones judging the twelve tribes of Israel.

³¹"Simon, Simon, behold, Satan demanded to have you,⁴ that he might sift you like wheat,

³²but I have prayed for you that your faith may not fail. And when you have turned again, strengthen your brothers." ³³Peter[1] said to him, "Lord, I am ready to go with you both to prison and to death." ³⁴Jesus[2] said, "I tell you, Peter, the rooster will not crow this day, until you deny three times that you know me."

³⁵And he said to them, "When I sent you out with no moneybag or knapsack or sandals, did you lack anything?" They said, "Nothing." ³⁶He said to them, "But now let the one who has a moneybag take it, and likewise a knapsack. And let the one who has no sword sell his cloak and buy one. ³⁷For I tell you that this Scripture must be fulfilled in me: 'And he was numbered with the transgressors.' For what is written about me has its fulfillment." ³⁸And they said, "Look, Lord, here are two swords." And he said to them, "It is enough."

³⁹And he came out and went, as was his custom, to the Mount of Olives, and the disciples followed him. ⁴⁰And when he came to the place, he said to them, "Pray that you may not enter into temptation." ⁴¹And he withdrew from them about a stone's throw, and knelt down and prayed, ⁴²saying, "Father, if you are willing, remove this cup from me. Nevertheless, not my will, but yours, be done." ⁴³And there appeared to him an angel from heaven, strengthening him. ⁴⁴And being in an agony he prayed more earnestly; and his sweat became like great drops of blood falling down to the ground.[3] ⁴⁵And when he rose from prayer, he came to the disciples and found them sleeping for sorrow, ⁴⁶and he said to them, "Why are you sleeping? Rise and pray that you may not enter into temptation."

⁴⁷While he was still speaking, there came a crowd, and the man called Judas, one of the twelve, was leading them. He drew near to Jesus to kiss him, ⁴⁸but Jesus said to him, "Judas, would you betray the Son of Man with a kiss?" ⁴⁹And when those who were around him saw what would follow, they said, "Lord, shall we strike with the sword?" ⁵⁰And one of them struck the servant[4] of the high priest and cut off his right ear. ⁵¹But Jesus said, "No more of this!" And he touched his ear and healed him. ⁵²Then Jesus said to the chief priests and officers of the temple and elders, who had come out against him, "Have you come out as against a robber, with swords and clubs? ⁵³When I was

with you day after day in the temple, you did not lay hands on me. But this is your hour, and the power of darkness."

⁵⁴Then they seized him and led him away, bringing him into the high priest's house, and Peter was following at a distance. ⁵⁵And when they had kindled a fire in the middle of the courtyard and sat down together, Peter sat down among them. ⁵⁶Then a servant girl, seeing him as he sat in the light and looking closely at him, said, "This man also was with him." ⁵⁷But he denied it, saying, "Woman, I do not know him." ⁵⁸And a little later someone else saw him and said, "You also are one of them." But Peter said, "Man, I am not." ⁵⁹And after an interval of about an hour still another insisted, saying, "Certainly this man also was with him, for he too is a Galilean." ⁶⁰But Peter said, "Man, I do not know what you are talking about." And immediately, while he was still speaking, the rooster crowed. ⁶¹And the Lord turned and looked at Peter. And Peter remembered the saying of the Lord, how he had said to him, "Before the rooster crows today, you will deny me three times." ⁶²And he went out and wept bitterly.

⁶³Now the men who were holding Jesus in custody were mocking him as they beat him. ⁶⁴They also blindfolded him and kept asking him, "Prophesy! Who is it that struck you?" ⁶⁵And they said many other things against him, blaspheming him.

⁶⁶When day came, the assembly of the elders of the people gathered together, both chief priests and scribes. And they led him away to their council, and they said, ⁶⁷"If you are the Christ, tell us." But he said to them, "If I tell you, you will not believe, ⁶⁸and if I ask you, you will not answer. ⁶⁹But from now on the Son of Man shall be seated at the right hand of the power of God." ⁷⁰So they all said, "Are you the Son of God, then?" And he said to them, "You say that I am." ⁷¹Then they said, "What further testimony do we need? We have heard it ourselves from his own lips."

Job 37

"At this also my heart trembles
and leaps out of its place.
2　Keep listening to the thunder of his voice
and the rumbling that comes from his mouth.

---
[1] Greek *He* [2] Greek *He* [3] Some manuscripts omit verses 43 and 44 [4] Greek *bondservant*

3   Under the whole heaven he lets it go,
     and his lightning to the corners of the
     earth.
4   After it his voice roars;
     he thunders with his majestic voice,
     and he does not restrain the
     lightnings[1] when his voice is
     heard.
5   God thunders wondrously with his
     voice;
     he does great things that we cannot
     comprehend.
6   For to the snow he says, 'Fall on the
     earth,'
     likewise to the downpour, his mighty
     downpour.
7   He seals up the hand of every man,
     that all men whom he made may
     know it.
8   Then the beasts go into their lairs,
     and remain in their dens.
9   From its chamber comes the whirlwind,
     and cold from the scattering winds.
10   By the breath of God ice is given,
     and the broad waters are frozen fast.
11   He loads the thick cloud with moisture;
     the clouds scatter his lightning.
12   They turn around and around by his
     guidance,
     to accomplish all that he commands
     them
     on the face of the habitable world.
13   Whether for correction or for his land
     or for love, he causes it to happen.

14   "Hear this, O Job;
     stop and consider the wondrous
     works of God.
15   Do you know how God lays his
     command upon them
     and causes the lightning of his cloud
     to shine?
16   Do you know the balancings[2] of the
     clouds,
     the wondrous works of him who is
     perfect in knowledge,
17   you whose garments are hot
     when the earth is still because of the
     south wind?
18   Can you, like him, spread out the skies,
     hard as a cast metal mirror?

19   Teach us what we shall say to him;
     we cannot draw up our case because
     of darkness.
20   Shall it be told him that I would speak?
     Did a man ever wish that he would be
     swallowed up?
21   "And now no one looks on the light
     when it is bright in the skies,
     when the wind has passed and cleared
     them.
22   Out of the north comes golden splendor;
     God is clothed with awesome majesty.
23   The Almighty—we cannot find him;
     he is great in power;
     justice and abundant righteousness he
     will not violate.
24   Therefore men fear him;
     he does not regard any who are wise
     in their own conceit."[3]

2 Corinthians 7

Since we have these promises, beloved, let us cleanse ourselves from every defilement of body[4] and spirit, bringing holiness to completion in the fear of God.

[2] Make room in your hearts[5] for us. We have wronged no one, we have corrupted no one, we have taken advantage of no one. [3] I do not say this to condemn you, for I said before that you are in our hearts, to die together and to live together. [4] I am acting with great boldness toward you; I have great pride in you; I am filled with comfort. In all our affliction, I am overflowing with joy.

[5] For even when we came into Macedonia, our bodies had no rest, but we were afflicted at every turn—fighting without and fear within. [6] But God, who comforts the downcast, comforted us by the coming of Titus, [7] and not only by his coming but also by the comfort with which he was comforted by you, as he told us of your longing, your mourning, your zeal for me, so that I rejoiced still more. [8] For even if I made you grieve with my letter, I do not regret it—though I did regret it, for I see that that letter grieved you, though only for a while. [9] As it is, I rejoice, not because you were grieved, but because you were grieved into repenting. For you felt a godly grief, so that you suffered no loss through us.

---

[1] Hebrew *them*   [2] Or *hoverings*   [3] Hebrew *in heart*   [4] Greek *flesh*   [5] Greek lacks *in your hearts*

[10] For godly grief produces a repentance that leads to salvation without regret, whereas worldly grief produces death. [11] For see what earnestness this godly grief has produced in you, but also what eagerness to clear yourselves, what indignation, what fear, what longing, what zeal, what punishment! At every point you have proved yourselves innocent in the matter. [12] So although I wrote to you, it was not for the sake of the one who did the wrong, nor for the sake of the one who suffered the wrong, but in order that your earnestness for us might be revealed to you in the sight of God. [13] Therefore we are comforted.

And besides our own comfort, we rejoiced still more at the joy of Titus, because his spirit has been refreshed by you all. [14] For whatever boasts I made to him about you, I was not put to shame. But just as everything we said to you was true, so also our boasting before Titus has proved true. [15] And his affection for you is even greater, as he remembers the obedience of you all, how you received him with fear and trembling. [16] I rejoice, because I have complete confidence in you.

MARCH 9

Exodus 20

And God spoke all these words, saying, [2] "I am the LORD your God, who brought you out of the land of Egypt, out of the house of slavery.

[3] "You shall have no other gods before[1] me.

[4] "You shall not make for yourself a carved image, or any likeness of anything that is in heaven above, or that is in the earth beneath, or that is in the water under the earth. [5] You shall not bow down to them or serve them, for I the LORD your God am a jealous God, visiting the iniquity of the fathers on the children to the third and the fourth generation of those who hate me, [6] but showing steadfast love to thousands[2] of those who love me and keep my commandments.

[7] "You shall not take the name of the LORD your God in vain, for the LORD will not hold him guiltless who takes his name in vain.

[8] "Remember the Sabbath day, to keep it holy. [9] Six days you shall labor, and do all your work, [10] but the seventh day is a Sabbath to the LORD your God. On it you shall not do any work, you, or your son, or your daughter, your male servant, or your female servant, or your livestock, or the sojourner who is within your gates. [11] For in six days the LORD made heaven and earth, the sea, and all that is in them, and rested on the seventh day. Therefore the LORD blessed the Sabbath day and made it holy.

[12] "Honor your father and your mother, that your days may be long in the land that the LORD your God is giving you.

[13] "You shall not murder.[3]

[14] "You shall not commit adultery.

[15] "You shall not steal.

[16] "You shall not bear false witness against your neighbor.

[17] "You shall not covet your neighbor's house; you shall not covet your neighbor's wife, or his male servant, or his female servant, or his ox, or his donkey, or anything that is your neighbor's."

[18] Now when all the people saw the thunder and the flashes of lightning and the sound of the trumpet and the mountain smoking, the people were afraid[4] and trembled, and they stood far off [19] and said to Moses, "You speak to us, and we will listen; but do not let God speak to us, lest we die." [20] Moses said to the people, "Do not fear, for God has come to test you, that the fear of him may be before you, that you may not sin." [21] The people stood far off, while Moses drew near to the thick darkness where God was.

[22] And the LORD said to Moses, "Thus you shall say to the people of Israel: 'You have seen

[1] Or besides [2] Or to the thousandth generation [3] The Hebrew word also covers causing human death through carelessness or negligence [4] Samaritan, Septuagint, Syriac, Vulgate; Masoretic Text *the people saw*

for yourselves that I have talked with you from heaven. [23] You shall not make gods of silver to be with me, nor shall you make for yourselves gods of gold. [24] An altar of earth you shall make for me and sacrifice on it your burnt offerings and your peace offerings, your sheep and your oxen. In every place where I cause my name to be remembered I will come to you and bless you. [25] If you make me an altar of stone, you shall not build it of hewn stones, for if you wield your tool on it you profane it. [26] And you shall not go up by steps to my altar, that your nakedness be not exposed on it.'

Luke 23

Then the whole company of them arose and brought him before Pilate. [2] And they began to accuse him, saying, "We found this man misleading our nation and forbidding us to give tribute to Caesar, and saying that he himself is Christ, a king." [3] And Pilate asked him, "Are you the King of the Jews?" And he answered him, "You have said so." [4] Then Pilate said to the chief priests and the crowds, "I find no guilt in this man." [5] But they were urgent, saying, "He stirs up the people, teaching throughout all Judea, from Galilee even to this place."

[6] When Pilate heard this, he asked whether the man was a Galilean. [7] And when he learned that he belonged to Herod's jurisdiction, he sent him over to Herod, who was himself in Jerusalem at that time. [8] When Herod saw Jesus, he was very glad, for he had long desired to see him, because he had heard about him, and he was hoping to see some sign done by him. [9] So he questioned him at some length, but he made no answer. [10] The chief priests and the scribes stood by, vehemently accusing him. [11] And Herod with his soldiers treated him with contempt and mocked him. Then, arraying him in splendid clothing, he sent him back to Pilate. [12] And Herod and Pilate became friends with each other that very day, for before this they had been at enmity with each other.

[13] Pilate then called together the chief priests and the rulers and the people, [14] and said to them, "You brought me this man as one who was misleading the people. And after examining him before you, behold, I did not find this man guilty of any of your charges against him. [15] Neither did Herod, for he sent him back to us.

Look, nothing deserving death has been done by him. [16] I will therefore punish and release him."[1]

[18] But they all cried out together, "Away with this man, and release to us Barabbas"— [19] a man who had been thrown into prison for an insurrection started in the city and for murder. [20] Pilate addressed them once more, desiring to release Jesus, [21] but they kept shouting, "Crucify, crucify him!" [22] A third time he said to them, "Why, what evil has he done? I have found in him no guilt deserving death. I will therefore punish and release him." [23] But they were urgent, demanding with loud cries that he should be crucified. And their voices prevailed. [24] So Pilate decided that their demand should be granted. [25] He released the man who had been thrown into prison for insurrection and murder, for whom they asked, but he delivered Jesus over to their will.

[26] And as they led him away, they seized one Simon of Cyrene, who was coming in from the country, and laid on him the cross, to carry it behind Jesus. [27] And there followed him a great multitude of the people and of women who were mourning and lamenting for him. [28] But turning to them Jesus said, "Daughters of Jerusalem, do not weep for me, but weep for yourselves and for your children. [29] For behold, the days are coming when they will say, 'Blessed are the barren and the wombs that never bore and the breasts that never nursed!' [30] Then they will begin to say to the mountains, 'Fall on us,' and to the hills, 'Cover us.' [31] For if they do these things when the wood is green, what will happen when it is dry?"

[32] Two others, who were criminals, were led away to be put to death with him. [33] And when they came to the place that is called The Skull, there they crucified him, and the criminals, one on his right and one on his left. [34] And Jesus said, "Father, forgive them, for they know not what they do."[2] And they cast lots to divide his garments. [35] And the people stood by, watching, but the rulers scoffed at him, saying, "He saved others; let him save himself, if he is the Christ of God, his Chosen One!" [36] The soldiers also mocked him, coming up and offering him sour wine [37] and saying, "If you are the King of the Jews, save yourself!" [38] There was also an inscription over him,[3] "This is the King of the Jews."

[39] One of the criminals who were hanged railed at him,[4] saying, "Are you not the Christ?

---

[1] Here, or after verse 19, some manuscripts add verse 17: *Now he was obliged to release one man to them at the festival* [2] Some manuscripts omit the sentence *And Jesus. . . what they do* [3] Some manuscripts add *in letters of Greek and Latin and Hebrew* [4] Or *blasphemed him*

Save yourself and us!" **40**But the other rebuked him, saying, "Do you not fear God, since you are under the same sentence of condemnation? **41**And we indeed justly, for we are receiving the due reward of our deeds; but this man has done nothing wrong." **42**And he said, "Jesus, remember me when you come into your kingdom." **43**And he said to him, "Truly, I say to you, today you will be with me in Paradise."

44It was now about the sixth hour,[1] and there was darkness over the whole land until the ninth hour,[2] **45**while the sun's light failed. And the curtain of the temple was torn in two. **46**Then Jesus, calling out with a loud voice, said, "Father, into your hands I commit my spirit!" And having said this he breathed his last. **47**Now when the centurion saw what had taken place, he praised God, saying, "Certainly this man was innocent!" **48**And all the crowds that had assembled for this spectacle, when they saw what had taken place, returned home beating their breasts. **49**And all his acquaintances and the women who had followed him from Galilee stood at a distance watching these things.

50Now there was a man named Joseph, from the Jewish town of Arimathea. He was a member of the council, a good and righteous man, **51**who had not consented to their decision and action; and he was looking for the kingdom of God. **52**This man went to Pilate and asked for the body of Jesus. **53**Then he took it down and wrapped it in a linen shroud and laid him in a tomb cut in stone, where no one had ever yet been laid. **54**It was the day of Preparation, and the Sabbath was beginning.[3] **55**The women who had come with him from Galilee followed and saw the tomb and how his body was laid. **56**Then they returned and prepared spices and ointments.

On the Sabbath they rested according to the commandment.

------ *Job 38* ------

Then the LORD answered Job out of the whirlwind and said:

2 "Who is this that darkens counsel by
words without knowledge?
3 Dress for action[4] like a man;
I will question you, and you make it
known to me.

4 "Where were you when I laid the
foundation of the earth?
Tell me, if you have understanding.
5 Who determined its measurements—
surely you know!
Or who stretched the line upon it?
6 On what were its bases sunk,
or who laid its cornerstone,
7 when the morning stars sang together
and all the sons of God shouted for
joy?

8 "Or who shut in the sea with doors
when it burst out from the womb,
9 when I made clouds its garment
and thick darkness its swaddling
band,
10 and prescribed limits for it
and set bars and doors,
11 and said, 'Thus far shall you come, and
no farther,
and here shall your proud waves be
stayed'?

12 "Have you commanded the morning
since your days began,
and caused the dawn to know its place,
13 that it might take hold of the skirts of
the earth,
and the wicked be shaken out of it?
14 It is changed like clay under the seal,
and its features stand out like a
garment.
15 From the wicked their light is withheld,
and their uplifted arm is broken.

16 "Have you entered into the springs of the
sea,
or walked in the recesses of the deep?
17 Have the gates of death been revealed to
you,
or have you seen the gates of deep
darkness?
18 Have you comprehended the expanse of
the earth?
Declare, if you know all this.

19 "Where is the way to the dwelling of light,
and where is the place of darkness,
20 that you may take it to its territory
and that you may discern the paths to
its home?
21 You know, for you were born then,
and the number of your days is great!

[1] That is, noon [2] That is, 3 P.M. [3] Greek *was dawning* [4] Hebrew *Gird up your loins*

22 "Have you entered the storehouses of the
       snow,
    or have you seen the storehouses of
       the hail,
23 which I have reserved for the time of
       trouble,
    for the day of battle and war?
24 What is the way to the place where the
       light is distributed,
    or where the east wind is scattered
       upon the earth?

25 "Who has cleft a channel for the torrents
       of rain
    and a way for the thunderbolt,
26 to bring rain on a land where no man is,
       on the desert in which there is no
       man,
27 to satisfy the waste and desolate land,
    and to make the ground sprout with
       grass?

28 "Has the rain a father,
    or who has begotten the drops of dew?
29 From whose womb did the ice come
       forth,
    and who has given birth to the frost of
       heaven?
30 The waters become hard like stone,
    and the face of the deep is frozen.

31 "Can you bind the chains of the Pleiades
    or loose the cords of Orion?
32 Can you lead forth the Mazzaroth¹ in
       their season,
    or can you guide the Bear with its
       children?
33 Do you know the ordinances of the
       heavens?
    Can you establish their rule on the
       earth?

34 "Can you lift up your voice to the clouds,
    that a flood of waters may cover you?
35 Can you send forth lightnings, that they
       may go
    and say to you, 'Here we are'?
36 Who has put wisdom in the inward
       parts²
    or given understanding to the mind?³
37 Who can number the clouds by
       wisdom?
    Or who can tilt the waterskins of the
       heavens,

38 when the dust runs into a mass
    and the clods stick fast together?

39 "Can you hunt the prey for the lion,
    or satisfy the appetite of the young
       lions,
40 when they crouch in their dens
    or lie in wait in their thicket?
41 Who provides for the raven its prey,
    when its young ones cry to God for
       help,
    and wander about for lack of food?

───────── *2 Corinthians 8* ─────────

We want you to know, brothers,⁴ about the grace of God that has been given among the churches of Macedonia, ²for in a severe test of affliction, their abundance of joy and their extreme poverty have overflowed in a wealth of generosity on their part. ³For they gave according to their means, as I can testify, and beyond their means, of their own accord, ⁴begging us earnestly for the favor⁵ of taking part in the relief of the saints— ⁵and this, not as we expected, but they gave themselves first to the Lord and then by the will of God to us. ⁶Accordingly, we urged Titus that as he had started, so he should complete among you this act of grace. ⁷But as you excel in everything—in faith, in speech, in knowledge, in all earnestness, and in our love for you⁶—see that you excel in this act of grace also.

⁸I say this not as a command, but to prove by the earnestness of others that your love also is genuine. ⁹For you know the grace of our Lord Jesus Christ, that though he was rich, yet for your sake he became poor, so that you by his poverty might become rich. ¹⁰And in this matter I give my judgment: this benefits you, who a year ago started not only to do this work but also to desire to do it. ¹¹So now finish doing it as well, so that your readiness in desiring it may be matched by your completing it out of what you have. ¹²For if the readiness is there, it is acceptable according to what a person has, not according to what he does not have. ¹³For I do not mean that others should be eased and you burdened, but that as a matter of fairness ¹⁴your abundance at the present time should supply their need, so that their abundance may supply

¹ Probably the name of a constellation ² Or *in the ibis* ³ Or *rooster* ⁴ Or *brothers and sisters* ⁵ The Greek word *charis* can mean *favor* or *grace* or *thanks*, depending on the context
⁶ Some manuscripts *in your love for us*

your need, that there may be fairness. ¹⁵As it is written, "Whoever gathered much had nothing left over, and whoever gathered little had no lack."

¹⁶But thanks be to God, who put into the heart of Titus the same earnest care I have for you. ¹⁷For he not only accepted our appeal, but being himself very earnest he is going¹ to you of his own accord. ¹⁸With him we are sending² the brother who is famous among all the churches for his preaching of the gospel. ¹⁹And not only that, but he has been appointed by the churches to travel with us as we carry out this act of grace that is being ministered by us, for the glory of the Lord himself and to show our good will. ²⁰We take this course so that no one should blame us about this generous gift that is being administered by us, ²¹for we aim at what is honorable not only in the Lord's sight but also in the sight of man. ²²And with them we are sending our brother whom we have often tested and found earnest in many matters, but who is now more earnest than ever because of his great confidence in you. ²³As for Titus, he is my partner and fellow worker for your benefit. And as for our brothers, they are messengers³ of the churches, the glory of Christ. ²⁴So give proof before the churches of your love and of our boasting about you to these men.

MARCH 10

Exodus 21

"Now these are the rules that you shall set before them. ²When you buy a Hebrew slave,⁴ he shall serve six years, and in the seventh he shall go out free, for nothing. ³If he comes in single, he shall go out single; if he comes in married, then his wife shall go out with him. ⁴If his master gives him a wife and she bears him sons or daughters, the wife and her children shall be her master's, and he shall go out alone. ⁵But if the slave plainly says, 'I love my master, my wife, and my children; I will not go out free,' ⁶then his master shall bring him to God, and he shall bring him to the door or the doorpost. And his master shall bore his ear through with an awl, and he shall be his slave forever.

⁷"When a man sells his daughter as a slave, she shall not go out as the male slaves do. ⁸If she does not please her master, who has designated her⁵ for himself, then he shall let her be redeemed. He shall have no right to sell her to a foreign people, since he has broken faith with her. ⁹If he designates her for his son, he shall deal with her as with a daughter. ¹⁰If he takes another wife to himself, he shall not diminish her food, her clothing, or her marital rights. ¹¹And if he does not do these three things for her, she shall go out for nothing, without payment of money.

¹²"Whoever strikes a man so that he dies shall be put to death. ¹³But if he did not lie in wait for him, but God let him fall into his hand, then I will appoint for you a place to which he may flee. ¹⁴But if a man willfully attacks another to kill him by cunning, you shall take him from my altar, that he may die.

¹⁵"Whoever strikes his father or his mother shall be put to death.

¹⁶"Whoever steals a man and sells him, and anyone found in possession of him, shall be put to death.

¹⁷"Whoever curses⁶ his father or his mother shall be put to death.

¹⁸"When men quarrel and one strikes the other with a stone or with his fist and the man does not die but takes to his bed, ¹⁹then if the man rises again and walks outdoors with his staff, he who struck him shall be clear; only he shall pay for the loss of his time, and shall have him thoroughly healed.

²⁰"When a man strikes his slave, male or female, with a rod and the slave dies under his

¹ Or he went ² Or we sent; also verse 22 ³ Greek apostles ⁴ Or servant; the Hebrew term 'ebed designates a range of social and economic roles; also verses 5, 6, 7, 20, 21, 26, 27, 32 (see Preface) ⁵ Or so that he has not designated her ⁶ Or dishonors; Septuagint reviles

hand, he shall be avenged. [21] But if the slave survives a day or two, he is not to be avenged, for the slave is his money.

[22] "When men strive together and hit a pregnant woman, so that her children come out, but there is no harm, the one who hit her shall surely be fined, as the woman's husband shall impose on him, and he shall pay as the judges determine. [23] But if there is harm,[1] then you shall pay life for life, [24] eye for eye, tooth for tooth, hand for hand, foot for foot, [25] burn for burn, wound for wound, stripe for stripe.

[26] "When a man strikes the eye of his slave, male or female, and destroys it, he shall let the slave go free because of his eye. [27] If he knocks out the tooth of his slave, male or female, he shall let the slave go free because of his tooth.

[28] "When an ox gores a man or a woman to death, the ox shall be stoned, and its flesh shall not be eaten, but the owner of the ox shall not be liable. [29] But if the ox has been accustomed to gore in the past, and its owner has been warned but has not kept it in, and it kills a man or a woman, the ox shall be stoned, and its owner also shall be put to death. [30] If a ransom is imposed on him, then he shall give for the redemption of his life whatever is imposed on him. [31] If it gores a man's son or daughter, he shall be dealt with according to this same rule. [32] If the ox gores a slave, male or female, the owner shall give to their master thirty shekels[2] of silver, and the ox shall be stoned.

[33] "When a man opens a pit, or when a man digs a pit and does not cover it, and an ox or a donkey falls into it, [34] the owner of the pit shall make restoration. He shall give money to its owner, and the dead beast shall be his.

[35] "When one man's ox butts another's, so that it dies, then they shall sell the live ox and share its price, and the dead beast also they shall share. [36] Or if it is known that the ox has been accustomed to gore in the past, and its owner has not kept it in, he shall repay ox for ox, and the dead beast shall be his.

--------- Luke 24 ---------

[B]ut on the first day of the week, at early dawn, they went to the tomb, taking the spices they had prepared. [2] And they found the stone rolled away from the tomb, [3] but when they went in they did not find the body of the

Lord Jesus. [4] While they were perplexed about this, behold, two men stood by them in dazzling apparel. [5] And as they were frightened and bowed their faces to the ground, the men said to them, "Why do you seek the living among the dead? [6] He is not here, but has risen. Remember how he told you, while he was still in Galilee, [7] that the Son of Man must be delivered into the hands of sinful men and be crucified and on the third day rise." [8] And they remembered his words, [9] and returning from the tomb they told all these things to the eleven and to all the rest. [10] Now it was Mary Magdalene and Joanna and Mary the mother of James and the other women with them who told these things to the apostles, [11] but these words seemed to them an idle tale, and they did not believe them. [12] But Peter rose and ran to the tomb; stooping and looking in, he saw the linen cloths by themselves; and he went home marveling at what had happened.

[13] That very day two of them were going to a village named Emmaus, about seven miles[3] from Jerusalem, [14] and they were talking with each other about all these things that had happened. [15] While they were talking and discussing together, Jesus himself drew near and went with them. [16] But their eyes were kept from recognizing him. [17] And he said to them, "What is this conversation that you are holding with each other as you walk?" And they stood still, looking sad. [18] Then one of them, named Cleopas, answered him, "Are you the only visitor to Jerusalem who does not know the things that have happened there in these days?" [19] And he said to them, "What things?" And they said to him, "Concerning Jesus of Nazareth, a man who was a prophet mighty in deed and word before God and all the people, [20] and how our chief priests and rulers delivered him up to be condemned to death, and crucified him. [21] But we had hoped that he was the one to redeem Israel. Yes, and besides all this, it is now the third day since these things happened. [22] Moreover, some women of our company amazed us. They were at the tomb early in the morning, [23] and when they did not find his body, they came back saying that they had even seen a vision of angels, who said that he was alive. [24] Some of those who were with us went to the tomb and found it just as the women had said, but him they did not see."

---

[1] Or so that her children come out and it is clear who was to blame, he shall be fined as the woman's husband shall impose on him, and he alone shall pay. If it is unclear who was to blame... [2] A shekel was about 2/5 ounce or 11 grams [3] Greek sixty stadia; a stadion was about 607 feet or 185 meters

²⁵And he said to them, "O foolish ones, and slow of heart to believe all that the prophets have spoken! ²⁶Was it not necessary that the Christ should suffer these things and enter into his glory?" ²⁷And beginning with Moses and all the Prophets, he interpreted to them in all the Scriptures the things concerning himself.

²⁸So they drew near to the village to which they were going. He acted as if he were going farther, ²⁹but they urged him strongly, saying, "Stay with us, for it is toward evening and the day is now far spent." So he went in to stay with them. ³⁰When he was at table with them, he took the bread and blessed and broke it and gave it to them. ³¹And their eyes were opened, and they recognized him. And he vanished from their sight. ³²They said to each other, "Did not our hearts burn within us while he talked to us on the road, while he opened to us the Scriptures?" ³³And they rose that same hour and returned to Jerusalem. And they found the eleven and those who were with them gathered together, ³⁴saying, "The Lord has risen indeed, and has appeared to Simon!" ³⁵Then they told what had happened on the road, and how he was known to them in the breaking of the bread.

³⁶As they were talking about these things, Jesus himself stood among them, and said to them, "Peace to you!" ³⁷But they were startled and frightened and thought they saw a spirit. ³⁸And he said to them, "Why are you troubled, and why do doubts arise in your hearts? ³⁹See my hands and my feet, that it is I myself. Touch me, and see. For a spirit does not have flesh and bones as you see that I have." ⁴⁰And when he had said this, he showed them his hands and his feet. ⁴¹And while they still disbelieved for joy and were marveling, he said to them, "Have you anything here to eat?" ⁴²They gave him a piece of broiled fish,¹ ⁴³and he took it and ate before them.

⁴⁴Then he said to them, "These are my words that I spoke to you while I was still with you, that everything written about me in the Law of Moses and the Prophets and the Psalms must be fulfilled." ⁴⁵Then he opened their minds to understand the Scriptures, ⁴⁶and said to them, "Thus it is written, that the Christ should suffer and on the third day rise from the dead, ⁴⁷and that repentance and² forgiveness of sins should be proclaimed in his name to all nations, beginning from Jerusalem. ⁴⁸You are witnesses of these things. ⁴⁹And behold, I am sending the promise of my Father upon you. But stay in the city until you are clothed with power from on high."

⁵⁰Then he led them out as far as Bethany, and lifting up his hands he blessed them. ⁵¹While he blessed them, he parted from them and was carried up into heaven. ⁵²And they worshiped him and returned to Jerusalem with great joy, ⁵³and were continually in the temple blessing God.

Job 39

"Do you know when the mountain goats give birth?
Do you observe the calving of the does?
² Can you number the months that they fulfill,
and do you know the time when they give birth,
³ when they crouch, bring forth their offspring,
and are delivered of their young?
⁴ Their young ones become strong; they grow up in the open;
they go out and do not return to them.

⁵ "Who has let the wild donkey go free?
Who has loosed the bonds of the swift donkey,
⁶ to whom I have given the arid plain for his home
and the salt land for his dwelling place?
⁷ He scorns the tumult of the city;
he hears not the shouts of the driver.
⁸ He ranges the mountains as his pasture,
and he searches after every green thing.

⁹ "Is the wild ox willing to serve you?
Will he spend the night at your manger?
¹⁰ Can you bind him in the furrow with ropes,
or will he harrow the valleys after you?
¹¹ Will you depend on him because his strength is great,
and will you leave to him your labor?
¹² Do you have faith in him that he will return your grain
and gather it to your threshing floor?

¹ Some manuscripts add *and some honeycomb* ² Some manuscripts *for*

13   "The wings of the ostrich wave proudly,
        but are they the pinions and plumage
        of love?[1]
14   For she leaves her eggs to the earth
        and lets them be warmed on the
        ground,
15   forgetting that a foot may crush them
        and that the wild beast may trample
        them.
16   She deals cruelly with her young, as if
        they were not hers;
        though her labor be in vain, yet she
        has no fear,
17   because God has made her forget
        wisdom
        and given her no share in
        understanding.
18   When she rouses herself to flee,[2]
        she laughs at the horse and his rider.

19   "Do you give the horse his might?
        Do you clothe his neck with a mane?
20   Do you make him leap like the locust?
        His majestic snorting is terrifying.
21   He paws[3] in the valley and exults in his
        strength;
        he goes out to meet the weapons.
22   He laughs at fear and is not dismayed;
        he does not turn back from the sword.
23   Upon him rattle the quiver,
        the flashing spear, and the javelin.
24   With fierceness and rage he swallows
        the ground;
        he cannot stand still at the sound of
        the trumpet.
25   When the trumpet sounds, he says
        'Aha!'
        He smells the battle from afar,
        the thunder of the captains, and the
        shouting.
26   "Is it by your understanding that the
        hawk soars
        and spreads his wings toward the
        south?
27   Is it at your command that the eagle
        mounts up
        and makes his nest on high?
28   On the rock he dwells and makes his
        home,
        on the rocky crag and stronghold.
29   From there he spies out the prey;
        his eyes behold it from far away.

30   His young ones suck up blood,
        and where the slain are, there is he."

2 Corinthians 9

Now it is superfluous for me to write to you about the ministry for the saints, [2]for I know your readiness, of which I boast about you to the people of Macedonia, saying that Achaia has been ready since last year. And your zeal has stirred up most of them. [3]But I am sending[4] the brothers so that our boasting about you may not prove empty in this matter, so that you may be ready, as I said you would be. [4]Otherwise, if some Macedonians come with me and find that you are not ready, we would be humiliated—to say nothing of you—for being so confident. [5]So I thought it necessary to urge the brothers to go on ahead to you and arrange in advance for the gift[5] you have promised, so that it may be ready as a willing gift, not as an exaction.[6]

[6]The point is this: whoever sows sparingly will also reap sparingly, and whoever sows bountifully[7] will also reap bountifully. [7]Each one must give as he has decided in his heart, not reluctantly or under compulsion, for God loves a cheerful giver. [8]And God is able to make all grace abound to you, so that having all sufficiency[8] in all things at all times, you may abound in every good work. [9]As it is written,

"He has distributed freely, he has given to
        the poor;
        his righteousness endures forever."

[10]He who supplies seed to the sower and bread for food will supply and multiply your seed for sowing and increase the harvest of your righteousness. [11]You will be enriched in every way to be generous in every way, which through us will produce thanksgiving to God. [12]For the ministry of this service is not only supplying the needs of the saints but is also overflowing in many thanksgivings to God. [13]By their approval of this service, they[9] will glorify God because of your submission that comes from your confession of the gospel of Christ, and the generosity of your contribution for them and for all others, [14]while they long for you and pray for you, because of the surpassing grace of God upon you. [15]Thanks be to God for his inexpressible gift!

[1] The meaning of the Hebrew is uncertain [2] The meaning of the Hebrew is uncertain [3] Hebrew *They paw* [4] Or *I have sent* [5] Greek *blessing*; twice in this verse [6] Or *a gift expecting something in return*; Greek *greed* [7] Greek *with blessings*; twice in this verse [8] Or *all contentment* [9] Or *you*

MARCH 11

Exodus 22[1]

"If a man steals an ox or a sheep, and kills it or sells it, he shall repay five oxen for an ox, and four sheep for a sheep. [2] If a thief is found breaking in and is struck so that he dies, there shall be no bloodguilt for him, [3] but if the sun has risen on him, there shall be bloodguilt for him. He shall surely pay. If he has nothing, then he shall be sold for his theft. [4] If the stolen beast is found alive in his possession, whether it is an ox or a donkey or a sheep, he shall pay double.

[5] "If a man causes a field or vineyard to be grazed over, or lets his beast loose and it feeds in another man's field, he shall make restitution from the best in his own field and in his own vineyard.

[6] "If fire breaks out and catches in thorns so that the stacked grain or the standing grain or the field is consumed, he who started the fire shall make full restitution.

[7] "If a man gives to his neighbor money or goods to keep safe, and it is stolen from the man's house, then, if the thief is found, he shall pay double. [8] If the thief is not found, the owner of the house shall come near to God to show whether or not he has put his hand to his neighbor's property. [9] For every breach of trust, whether it is for an ox, for a donkey, for a sheep, for a cloak, or for any kind of lost thing, of which one says, 'This is it,' the case of both parties shall come before God. The one whom God condemns shall pay double to his neighbor.

[10] "If a man gives to his neighbor a donkey or an ox or a sheep or any beast to keep safe, and it dies or is injured or is driven away, without anyone seeing it, [11] an oath by the LORD shall be between them both to see whether or not he has put his hand to his neighbor's property. The owner shall accept the oath, and he shall not make restitution. [12] But if it is stolen from him, he shall make restitution to its owner. [13] If it is torn by beasts, let him bring it as evidence. He shall not make restitution for what has been torn.

[14] "If a man borrows anything of his neighbor, and it is injured or dies, the owner not being with it, he shall make full restitution. [15] If the owner was with it, he shall not make restitution; if it was hired, it came for its hiring fee.[3]

[16] "If a man seduces a virgin[4] who is not betrothed and lies with her, he shall give the bride-price[5] for her and make her his wife. [17] If her father utterly refuses to give her to him, he shall pay money equal to the bride-price for virgins.

[18] "You shall not permit a sorceress to live.

[19] "Whoever lies with an animal shall be put to death.

[20] "Whoever sacrifices to any god, other than the LORD alone, shall be devoted to destruction.[6]

[21] "You shall not wrong a sojourner or oppress him, for you were sojourners in the land of Egypt. [22] You shall not mistreat any widow or fatherless child. [23] If you do mistreat them, and they cry out to me, I will surely hear their cry, [24] and my wrath will burn, and I will kill you with the sword, and your wives shall become widows and your children fatherless.

[25] "If you lend money to any of my people with you who is poor, you shall not be like a moneylender to him, and you shall not exact interest from him. [26] If ever you take your neighbor's cloak in pledge, you shall return it to him before the sun goes down, [27] for that is his only covering, and it is his cloak for his body; in what else shall he sleep? And if he cries to me, I will hear, for I am compassionate.

[28] "You shall not revile God, nor curse a ruler of your people.

[29] "You shall not delay to offer from the fullness of your harvest and from the outflow of your presses. The firstborn of your sons you shall give to me. [30] You shall do the same with your oxen and with your sheep: seven days it shall be with its mother; on the eighth day you shall give it to me.

[31] "You shall be consecrated to me. Therefore you shall not eat any flesh that is torn by beasts in the field; you shall throw it to the dogs.

[1] Ch 21:37 in Hebrew [2] Ch 22:1 in Hebrew [3] Or it is reckoned in (Hebrew comes into) its hiring fee [4] Or a girl of marriageable age; also verse 17 [5] Or engagement present; also verse 17 [6] That is, set apart (devoted) as an offering to the Lord (for destruction)

John 1

In the beginning was the Word, and the Word was with God, and the Word was God. [2] He was in the beginning with God. [3] All things were made through him, and without him was not any thing made that was made. [4] In him was life,[1] and the life was the light of men. [5] The light shines in the darkness, and the darkness has not overcome it.

[6] There was a man sent from God, whose name was John. [7] He came as a witness, to bear witness about the light, that all might believe through him. [8] He was not the light, but came to bear witness about the light.

[9] The true light, which gives light to everyone, was coming into the world. [10] He was in the world, and the world was made through him, yet the world did not know him. [11] He came to his own,[2] and his own people[3] did not receive him. [12] But to all who did receive him, who believed in his name, he gave the right to become children of God, [13] who were born, not of blood nor of the will of the flesh nor of the will of man, but of God.

[14] And the Word became flesh and dwelt among us, and we have seen his glory, glory as of the only Son from the Father, full of grace and truth. [15] (John bore witness about him, and cried out, "This was he of whom I said, 'He who comes after me ranks before me, because he was before me.'") [16] For from his fullness we have all received, grace upon grace.[4] [17] For the law was given through Moses; grace and truth came through Jesus Christ. [18] No one has ever seen God; the only God,[5] who is at the Father's side,[6] he has made him known.

[19] And this is the testimony of John, when the Jews sent priests and Levites from Jerusalem to ask him, "Who are you?" [20] He confessed, and did not deny, but confessed, "I am not the Christ." [21] And they asked him, "What then? Are you Elijah?" He said, "I am not." "Are you the Prophet?" And he answered, "No." [22] So they said to him, "Who are you? We need to give an answer to those who sent us. What do you say about yourself?" [23] He said, "I am the voice of one crying out in the wilderness, 'Make straight[7] the way of the Lord,' as the prophet Isaiah said."

[24] (Now they had been sent from the Pharisees.) [25] They asked him, "Then why are you baptizing, if you are neither the Christ, nor Elijah, nor the Prophet?" [26] John answered them, "I baptize with water, but among you stands one you do not know, [27] even he who comes after me, the strap of whose sandal I am not worthy to untie." [28] These things took place in Bethany across the Jordan, where John was baptizing.

[29] The next day he saw Jesus coming toward him, and said, "Behold, the Lamb of God, who takes away the sin of the world! [30] This is he of whom I said, 'After me comes a man who ranks before me, because he was before me.' [31] I myself did not know him, but for this purpose I came baptizing with water, that he might be revealed to Israel." [32] And John bore witness: "I saw the Spirit descend from heaven like a dove, and it remained on him. [33] I myself did not know him, but he who sent me to baptize with water said to me, 'He on whom you see the Spirit descend and remain, this is he who baptizes with the Holy Spirit.' [34] And I have seen and have borne witness that this is the Son of God."

[35] The next day again John was standing with two of his disciples, [36] and he looked at Jesus as he walked by and said, "Behold, the Lamb of God!" [37] The two disciples heard him say this, and they followed Jesus. [38] Jesus turned and saw them following and said to them, "What are you seeking?" And they said to him, "Rabbi" (which means Teacher), "where are you staying?" [39] He said to them, "Come and you will see." So they came and saw where he was staying, and they stayed with him that day, for it was about the tenth hour.[8] [40] One of the two who heard John speak and followed Jesus[9] was Andrew, Simon Peter's brother. [41] He first found his own brother Simon and said to him, "We have found the Messiah" (which means Christ). [42] He brought him to Jesus. Jesus looked at him and said, "You are Simon the son of John. You shall be called Cephas" (which means Peter[10]).

[43] The next day Jesus decided to go to Galilee. He found Philip and said to him, "Follow me." [44] Now Philip was from Bethsaida, the city of Andrew and Peter. [45] Philip found Nathanael and said to him, "We have found him of whom Moses in the Law and also the prophets wrote, Jesus of Nazareth, the son of Joseph." [46] Nathanael said to him, "Can anything good

[1] Or was not any thing made. That which has been made was life in him [2] Greek to his own things; that is, to his own domain, or to his own people [3] People is implied in Greek [4] Or grace in place of grace [5] Or the only One, who is God; some manuscripts the only Son [6] Greek in the bosom of the Father [7] Or crying out, 'In the wilderness make straight [8] That is, about 4 P.M. [9] Greek him [10] Cephas and Peter are from the word for rock in Aramaic and Greek, respectively

come out of Nazareth?" Philip said to him, "Come and see." ⁴⁷Jesus saw Nathanael coming toward him and said of him, "Behold, an Israelite indeed, in whom there is no deceit!" ⁴⁸Nathanael said to him, "How do you know me?" Jesus answered him, "Before Philip called you, when you were under the fig tree, I saw you." ⁴⁹Nathanael answered him, "Rabbi, you are the Son of God! You are the King of Israel!" ⁵⁰Jesus answered him, "Because I said to you, 'I saw you under the fig tree,' do you believe? You will see greater things than these." ⁵¹And he said to him, "Truly, truly, I say to you,¹ you will see heaven opened, and the angels of God ascending and descending on the Son of Man."

Job 40

And the LORD said to Job:

2　"Shall a faultfinder contend with the Almighty?
　　He who argues with God, let him answer it."

³Then Job answered the LORD and said:

4　"Behold, I am of small account; what shall I answer you?
　　I lay my hand on my mouth.
5　I have spoken once, and I will not answer;
　　twice, but I will proceed no further."

⁶Then the LORD answered Job out of the whirlwind and said:

7　"Dress for action² like a man;
　　I will question you, and you make it known to me.
8　Will you even put me in the wrong?
　　Will you condemn me that you may be in the right?
9　Have you an arm like God,
　　and can you thunder with a voice like his?
10　"Adorn yourself with majesty and dignity;
　　clothe yourself with glory and splendor.
11　Pour out the overflowings of your anger,
　　and look on everyone who is proud and abase him.

12　Look on everyone who is proud and bring him low
　　and tread down the wicked where they stand.
13　Hide them all in the dust together;
　　bind their faces in the world below.³
14　Then will I also acknowledge to you
　　that your own right hand can save you.

15　"Behold, Behemoth,⁴
　　which I made as I made you;
　　he eats grass like an ox.
16　Behold, his strength in his loins,
　　and his power in the muscles of his belly.
17　He makes his tail stiff like a cedar;
　　the sinews of his thighs are knit together.
18　His bones are tubes of bronze,
　　his limbs like bars of iron.

19　"He is the first of the works⁵ of God;
　　let him who made him bring near his sword!
20　For the mountains yield food for him
　　where all the wild beasts play.
21　Under the lotus plants he lies,
　　in the shelter of the reeds and in the marsh.
22　For his shade the lotus trees cover him;
　　the willows of the brook surround him.
23　Behold, if the river is turbulent he is not frightened;
　　he is confident though Jordan rushes against his mouth.
24　Can one take him by his eyes,⁶
　　or pierce his nose with a snare?

2 Corinthians 10

I, Paul, myself entreat you, by the meekness and gentleness of Christ—I who am humble when face to face with you, but bold toward you when I am away!— ²I beg of you that when I am present I may not have to show boldness with such confidence as I count on showing against some who suspect us of walking according to the flesh. ³For though we walk in the flesh, we are not waging war according to the flesh. ⁴For the weapons of our warfare are not of the flesh but have divine power to destroy strongholds. ⁵We destroy arguments and every lofty opinion raised against the knowledge of God, and take

¹ The Greek for you is plural; twice in this verse　² Hebrew Gird up your loins　³ Hebrew in the hidden place　⁴ A large animal, exact identity unknown　⁵ Hebrew ways　⁶ Or in his sight

every thought captive to obey Christ, [6]being ready to punish every disobedience, when your obedience is complete.

[7]Look at what is before your eyes. If anyone is confident that he is Christ's, let him remind himself that just as he is Christ's, so also are we. [8]For even if I boast a little too much of our authority, which the Lord gave for building you up and not for destroying you, I will not be ashamed. [9]I do not want to appear to be frightening you with my letters. [10]For they say, "His letters are weighty and strong, but his bodily presence is weak, and his speech of no account." [11]Let such a person understand that what we say by letter when absent, we do when present. [12]Not that we dare to classify or compare ourselves with some of those who are commending themselves. But when they measure themselves by one another and compare themselves with one another, they are without understanding.

[13]But we will not boast beyond limits, but will boast only with regard to the area of influence God assigned to us, to reach even to you. [14]For we are not overextending ourselves, as though we did not reach you. For we were the first to come all the way to you with the gospel of Christ. [15]We do not boast beyond limit in the labors of others. But our hope is that as your faith increases, our area of influence among you may be greatly enlarged, [16]so that we may preach the gospel in lands beyond you, without boasting of work already done in another's area of influence. [17]"Let the one who boasts, boast in the Lord." [18]For it is not the one who commends himself who is approved, but the one whom the Lord commends.

MARCH 12

Exodus 23

"You shall not spread a false report. You shall not join hands with a wicked man to be a malicious witness. [2]You shall not fall in with the many to do evil, nor shall you bear witness in a lawsuit, siding with the many, so as to pervert justice, [3]nor shall you be partial to a poor man in his lawsuit.

[4]"If you meet your enemy's ox or his donkey going astray, you shall bring it back to him. [5]If you see the donkey of one who hates you lying down under its burden, you shall refrain from leaving him with it; you shall rescue it with him.

[6]"You shall not pervert the justice due to your poor in his lawsuit. [7]Keep far from a false charge, and do not kill the innocent and righteous, for I will not acquit the wicked. [8]And you shall take no bribe, for a bribe blinds the clear-sighted and subverts the cause of those who are in the right. [9]"You shall not oppress a sojourner. You know the heart of a sojourner, for you were sojourners in the land of Egypt.

[10]"For six years you shall sow your land and gather in its yield, [11]but the seventh year you shall let it rest and lie fallow, that the poor of your people may eat; and what they leave the beasts of the field may eat. You shall do likewise with your vineyard, and with your olive orchard.

[12]"Six days you shall do your work, but on the seventh day you shall rest; that your ox and your donkey may have rest, and the son of your servant woman, and the alien, may be refreshed.

[13]"Pay attention to all that I have said to you, and make no mention of the names of other gods, nor let it be heard on your lips.

[14]"Three times in the year you shall keep a feast to me. [15]You shall keep the Feast of Unleavened Bread. As I commanded you, you shall eat unleavened bread for seven days at the appointed time in the month of Abib, for in it you came out of Egypt. None shall appear before me empty-handed. [16]You shall keep the Feast of Harvest, of the firstfruits of your labor, of what you sow in the field. You shall keep the Feast of Ingathering at the end of the year, when you gather in from the field the fruit

of your labor. ¹⁷Three times in the year shall all your males appear before the Lord GOD.

¹⁸"You shall not offer the blood of my sacrifice with anything leavened, or let the fat of my feast remain until the morning.

¹⁹"The best of the firstfruits of your ground you shall bring into the house of the LORD your God.

"You shall not boil a young goat in its mother's milk.

²⁰"Behold, I send an angel before you to guard you on the way and to bring you to the place that I have prepared. ²¹Pay careful attention to him and obey his voice; do not rebel against him, for he will not pardon your transgression, for my name is in him.

²²"But if you carefully obey his voice and do all that I say, then I will be an enemy to your enemies and an adversary to your adversaries.

²³"When my angel goes before you and brings you to the Amorites and the Hittites and the Perizzites and the Canaanites, the Hivites and the Jebusites, and I blot them out, ²⁴you shall not bow down to their gods nor serve them, nor do as they do, but you shall utterly overthrow them and break their pillars in pieces. ²⁵You shall serve the LORD your God, and he¹ will bless your bread and your water, and I will take sickness away from among you. ²⁶None shall miscarry or be barren in your land; I will fulfill the number of your days. ²⁷I will send my terror before you and will throw into confusion all the people against whom you shall come, and I will make all your enemies turn their backs to you. ²⁸And I will send hornets² before you, which shall drive out the Hivites, the Canaanites, and the Hittites from before you. ²⁹I will not drive them out from before you in one year, lest the land become desolate and the wild beasts multiply against you. ³⁰Little by little I will drive them out from before you, until you have increased and possess the land. ³¹And I will set your border from the Red Sea to the Sea of the Philistines, and from the wilderness to the Euphrates,³ for I will give the inhabitants of the land into your hand, and you shall drive them out before you. ³²You shall make no covenant with them and their gods. ³³They shall not dwell in your land, lest they make you sin against me; for if you serve their gods, it will surely be a snare to you."

John 2

On the third day there was a wedding at Cana in Galilee, and the mother of Jesus was there. ²Jesus also was invited to the wedding with his disciples. ³When the wine ran out, the mother of Jesus said to him, "They have no wine." ⁴And Jesus said to her, "Woman, what does this have to do with me? My hour has not yet come." ⁵His mother said to the servants, "Do whatever he tells you."

⁶Now there were six stone water jars there for the Jewish rites of purification, each holding twenty or thirty gallons.⁴ ⁷Jesus said to the servants, "Fill the jars with water." And they filled them up to the brim. ⁸And he said to them, "Now draw some out and take it to the master of the feast." So they took it. ⁹When the master of the feast tasted the water now become wine, and did not know where it came from (though the servants who had drawn the water knew), the master of the feast called the bridegroom ¹⁰and said to him, "Everyone serves the good wine first, and when people have drunk freely, then the poor wine. But you have kept the good wine until now." ¹¹This, the first of his signs, Jesus did at Cana in Galilee, and manifested his glory. And his disciples believed in him.

¹²After this he went down to Capernaum, with his mother and his brothers⁵ and his disciples, and they stayed there for a few days.

¹³The Passover of the Jews was at hand, and Jesus went up to Jerusalem. ¹⁴In the temple he found those who were selling oxen and sheep and pigeons, and the money-changers sitting there. ¹⁵And making a whip of cords, he drove them all out of the temple, with the sheep and oxen. And he poured out the coins of the money-changers and overturned their tables. ¹⁶And he told those who sold the pigeons, "Take these things away; do not make my Father's house a house of trade." ¹⁷His disciples remembered that it was written, "Zeal for your house will consume me."

¹⁸So the Jews said to him, "What sign do you show us for doing these things?" ¹⁹Jesus answered them, "Destroy this temple, and in three days I will raise it up." ²⁰The Jews then said, "It has taken forty-six years to build this temple,⁶ and will you raise it up in three days?" ²¹But he was speaking about the temple of his

¹ Septuagint, Vulgate I ² Or the hornet ³ Hebrew the River ⁴ Greek two or three measures (metrētas); a metrētēs was about 10 gallons or 35 liters ⁵ Or brothers and sisters. The plural Greek word adelphoi (translated "brothers") refers to siblings in a family. In New Testament usage, depending on the context, adelphoi may refer either to brothers or to brothers and sisters ⁶ Or This temple was built forty-six years ago

body. [22] When therefore he was raised from the dead, his disciples remembered that he had said this, and they believed the Scripture and the word that Jesus had spoken.

[23] Now when he was in Jerusalem at the Passover Feast, many believed in his name when they saw the signs that he was doing. [24] But Jesus on his part did not entrust himself to them, because he knew all people [25] and needed no one to bear witness about man, for he himself knew what was in man.

Job 41[1]

[1] "Can you draw out Leviathan[2] with a fishhook
     or press down his tongue with a cord?
[2] Can you put a rope in his nose
     or pierce his jaw with a hook?
[3] Will he make many pleas to you?
     Will he speak to you soft words?
[4] Will he make a covenant with you
     to take him for your servant forever?
[5] Will you play with him as with a bird,
     or will you put him on a leash for your girls?
[6] Will traders bargain over him?
     Will they divide him up among the merchants?
[7] Can you fill his skin with harpoons
     or his head with fishing spears?
[8] Lay your hands on him;
     remember the battle—you will not do it again!
[9][3] Behold, the hope of a man is false;
     he is laid low even at the sight of him.
[10] No one is so fierce that he dares to stir him up.
     Who then is he who can stand before me?
[11] Who has first given to me, that I should repay him?
     Whatever is under the whole heaven is mine.
[12] "I will not keep silence concerning his limbs,
     or his mighty strength, or his goodly frame.
[13] Who can strip off his outer garment?
     Who would come near him with a bridle?
[14] Who can open the doors of his face?
     Around his teeth is terror.
[15] His back is made of[4] rows of shields,
     shut up closely as with a seal.
[16] One is so near to another
     that no air can come between them.
[17] They are joined one to another;
     they clasp each other and cannot be separated.
[18] His sneezings flash forth light,
     and his eyes are like the eyelids of the dawn.
[19] Out of his mouth go flaming torches;
     sparks of fire leap forth.
[20] Out of his nostrils comes forth smoke,
     as from a boiling pot and burning rushes.
[21] His breath kindles coals,
     and a flame comes forth from his mouth.
[22] In his neck abides strength,
     and terror dances before him.
[23] The folds of his flesh stick together,
     firmly cast on him and immovable.
[24] His heart is hard as a stone,
     hard as the lower millstone.
[25] When he raises himself up the mighty[5] are afraid;
     at the crashing they are beside themselves.
[26] Though the sword reaches him, it does not avail,
     nor the spear, the dart, or the javelin.
[27] He counts iron as straw,
     and bronze as rotten wood.
[28] The arrow cannot make him flee;
     for him sling stones are turned to stubble.
[29] Clubs are counted as stubble;
     he laughs at the rattle of javelins.
[30] His underparts are like sharp potsherds;
     he spreads himself like a threshing sledge on the mire.
[31] He makes the deep boil like a pot;
     he makes the sea like a pot of ointment.
[32] Behind him he leaves a shining wake;
     one would think the deep to be white-haired.
[33] On earth there is not his like,
     a creature without fear.

---

[1] Ch 40:25 in Hebrew [2] A large sea animal, exact identity unknown [3] Ch 41:1 in Hebrew [4] Or His pride is in his [5] Or gods

34   He sees everything that is high;
          he is king over all the sons of pride."

——————— *2 Corinthians 11* ———————

I wish you would bear with me in a little foolishness. Do bear with me! **2** For I feel a divine jealousy for you, since I betrothed you to one husband, to present you as a pure virgin to Christ. **3** But I am afraid that as the serpent deceived Eve by his cunning, your thoughts will be led astray from a sincere and pure devotion to Christ. **4** For if someone comes and proclaims another Jesus than the one we proclaimed, or if you receive a different spirit from the one you received, or if you accept a different gospel from the one you accepted, you put up with it readily enough. **5** Indeed, I consider that I am not in the least inferior to these super-apostles. **6** Even if I am unskilled in speaking, I am not so in knowledge; indeed, in every way we have made this plain to you in all things.

7 Or did I commit a sin in humbling myself so that you might be exalted, because I preached God's gospel to you free of charge? **8** I robbed other churches by accepting support from them in order to serve you. **9** And when I was with you and was in need, I did not burden anyone, for the brothers who came from Macedonia supplied my need. So I refrained and will refrain from burdening you in any way. **10** As the truth of Christ is in me, this boasting of mine will not be silenced in the regions of Achaia. **11** And why? Because I do not love you? God knows I do!

12 And what I am doing I will continue to do, in order to undermine the claim of those who would like to claim that in their boasted mission they work on the same terms as we do. **13** For such men are false apostles, deceitful workmen, disguising themselves as apostles of Christ. **14** And no wonder, for even Satan disguises himself as an angel of light. **15** So it is no surprise if his servants, also, disguise themselves as servants of righteousness. Their end will correspond to their deeds.

16 I repeat, let no one think me foolish. But even if you do, accept me as a fool, so that I too may boast a little. **17** What I am saying with this boastful confidence, I say not as the Lord would[1] but as a fool. **18** Since many boast according to the flesh, I too will boast. **19** For you gladly bear with fools, being wise yourselves! **20** For you bear it if someone makes slaves of you, or devours you, or takes advantage of you, or puts on airs, or strikes you in the face. **21** To my shame, I must say, we were too weak for that!

But whatever anyone else dares to boast of—I am speaking as a fool—I also dare to boast of that. **22** Are they Hebrews? So am I. Are they Israelites? So am I. Are they offspring of Abraham? So am I. **23** Are they servants of Christ? I am a better one—I am talking like a madman—with far greater labors, far more imprisonments, with countless beatings, and often near death. **24** Five times I received at the hands of the Jews the forty lashes less one. **25** Three times I was beaten with rods. Once I was stoned. Three times I was shipwrecked; a night and a day I was adrift at sea; **26** on frequent journeys, in danger from rivers, danger from robbers, danger from my own people, danger from Gentiles, danger in the city, danger in the wilderness, danger at sea, danger from false brothers; **27** in toil and hardship, through many a sleepless night, in hunger and thirst, often without food,[2] in cold and exposure. **28** And, apart from other things, there is the daily pressure on me of my anxiety for all the churches. **29** Who is weak, and I am not weak? Who is made to fall, and I am not indignant?

30 If I must boast, I will boast of the things that show my weakness. **31** The God and Father of the Lord Jesus, he who is blessed forever, knows that I am not lying. **32** At Damascus, the governor under King Aretas was guarding the city of Damascus in order to seize me, **33** but I was let down in a basket through a window in the wall and escaped his hands.

[1] Greek *not according to the Lord* [2] Or *often in fasting*

MARCH 13

Exodus 24

Then he said to Moses, "Come up to the LORD, you and Aaron, Nadab, and Abihu, and seventy of the elders of Israel, and worship from afar. ²Moses alone shall come near to the LORD, but the others shall not come near, and the people shall not come up with him."

³Moses came and told the people all the words of the LORD and all the rules.¹ And all the people answered with one voice and said, "All the words that the LORD has spoken we will do." ⁴And Moses wrote down all the words of the LORD. He rose early in the morning and built an altar at the foot of the mountain, and twelve pillars, according to the twelve tribes of Israel. ⁵And he sent young men of the people of Israel, who offered burnt offerings and sacrificed peace offerings of oxen to the LORD. ⁶And Moses took half of the blood and put it in basins, and half of the blood he threw against the altar. ⁷Then he took the Book of the Covenant and read it in the hearing of the people. And they said, "All that the LORD has spoken we will do, and we will be obedient." ⁸And Moses took the blood and threw it on the people and said, "Behold the blood of the covenant that the LORD has made with you in accordance with all these words."

⁹Then Moses and Aaron, Nadab, and Abihu, and seventy of the elders of Israel went up, ¹⁰and they saw the God of Israel. There was under his feet as it were a pavement of sapphire stone, like the very heaven for clearness. ¹¹And he did not lay his hand on the chief men of the people of Israel; they beheld God, and ate and drank.

¹²The LORD said to Moses, "Come up to me on the mountain and wait there, that I may give you the tablets of stone, with the law and the commandment, which I have written for their instruction." ¹³So Moses rose with his assistant Joshua, and Moses went up into the mountain of God. ¹⁴And he said to the elders, "Wait here for us until we return to you. And behold, Aaron and Hur are with you. Whoever has a dispute, let him go to them."

¹⁵Then Moses went up on the mountain, and the cloud covered the mountain. ¹⁶The glory of the LORD dwelt on Mount Sinai, and the cloud covered it six days. And on the seventh day he called to Moses out of the midst of the cloud. ¹⁷Now the appearance of the glory of the LORD was like a devouring fire on the top of the mountain in the sight of the people of Israel. ¹⁸Moses entered the cloud and went up on the mountain. And Moses was on the mountain forty days and forty nights.

John 3

Now there was a man of the Pharisees named Nicodemus, a ruler of the Jews. ²This man came to Jesus² by night and said to him, "Rabbi, we know that you are a teacher come from God, for no one can do these signs that you do unless God is with him." ³Jesus answered him, "Truly, truly, I say to you, unless one is born again³ he cannot see the kingdom of God." ⁴Nicodemus said to him, "How can a man be born when he is old? Can he enter a second time into his mother's womb and be born?" ⁵Jesus answered, "Truly, truly, I say to you, unless one is born of water and the Spirit, he cannot enter the kingdom of God. ⁶That which is born of the flesh is flesh, and that which is born of the Spirit is spirit.⁴ ⁷Do not marvel that I said to you, 'You⁵ must be born again.' ⁸The wind⁶ blows where it wishes, and you hear its sound, but you do not know where it comes from or where it goes. So it is with everyone who is born of the Spirit."

⁹Nicodemus said to him, "How can these things be?" ¹⁰Jesus answered him, "Are you the teacher of Israel and yet you do not understand these things? ¹¹Truly, truly, I say to you, we speak of what we know, and bear witness to what we have seen, but you⁷ do not receive our testimony. ¹²If I have told you earthly things

---

¹ Or *all the just decrees*   ² Greek *him*   ³ Or *from above*; the Greek is purposely ambiguous and can mean both *again* and *from above*; also verse 7   ⁴ The same Greek word means both *wind and spirit*   ⁵ The Greek for *you* is plural here   ⁶ The same Greek word means both *wind and spirit*   ⁷ The Greek for *you* is plural here; also four times in verse 12

and you do not believe, how can you believe if I tell you heavenly things? [13] No one has ascended into heaven except he who descended from heaven, the Son of Man.[1] [14] And as Moses lifted up the serpent in the wilderness, so must the Son of Man be lifted up, [15] that whoever believes in him may have eternal life.[2]

[16] "For God so loved the world,[3] that he gave his only Son, that whoever believes in him should not perish but have eternal life. [17] For God did not send his Son into the world to condemn the world, but in order that the world might be saved through him. [18] Whoever believes in him is not condemned, but whoever does not believe is condemned already, because he has not believed in the name of the only Son of God. [19] And this is the judgment: the light has come into the world, and people loved the darkness rather than the light because their works were evil. [20] For everyone who does wicked things hates the light and does not come to the light, lest his works should be exposed. [21] But whoever does what is true comes to the light, so that it may be clearly seen that his works have been carried out in God."

[22] After this Jesus and his disciples went into the Judean countryside, and he remained there with them and was baptizing. [23] John also was baptizing at Aenon near Salim, because water was plentiful there, and people were coming and being baptized [24] (for John had not yet been put in prison).

[25] Now a discussion arose between some of John's disciples and a Jew over purification. [26] And they came to John and said to him, "Rabbi, he who was with you across the Jordan, to whom you bore witness—look, he is baptizing, and all are going to him." [27] John answered, "A person cannot receive even one thing unless it is given him from heaven. [28] You yourselves bear me witness, that I said, 'I am not the Christ, but I have been sent before him.' [29] The one who has the bride is the bridegroom. The friend of the bridegroom, who stands and hears him, rejoices greatly at the bridegroom's voice. Therefore this joy of mine is now complete. [30] He must increase, but I must decrease."[4]

[31] He who comes from above is above all. He who is of the earth belongs to the earth and speaks in an earthly way. He who comes from heaven is above all. [32] He bears witness to what he has seen and heard, yet no one receives his testimony. [33] Whoever receives his testimony sets his seal to this, that God is true. [34] For he whom God has sent utters the words of God, for he gives the Spirit without measure. [35] The Father loves the Son and has given all things into his hand. [36] Whoever believes in the Son has eternal life; whoever does not obey the Son shall not see life, but the wrath of God remains on him.

Job 42

Then Job answered the LORD and said:

[2]   "I know that you can do all things,
        and that no purpose of yours can be
          thwarted.
[3]   'Who is this that hides counsel without
          knowledge?'
      Therefore I have uttered what I did not
          understand,
        things too wonderful for me, which I
          did not know.
[4]   'Hear, and I will speak;
      I will question you, and you make it
          known to me.'
[5]   I had heard of you by the hearing of the
          ear,
      but now my eye sees you;
[6]   therefore I despise myself,
        and repent[5] in dust and ashes."

[7] After the LORD had spoken these words to Job, the LORD said to Eliphaz the Temanite: "My anger burns against you and against your two friends, for you have not spoken of me what is right, as my servant Job has. [8] Now therefore take seven bulls and seven rams and go to my servant Job and offer up a burnt offering for yourselves. And my servant Job shall pray for you, for I will accept his prayer not to deal with you according to your folly. For you have not spoken of me what is right, as my servant Job has." [9] So Eliphaz the Temanite and Bildad the Shuhite and Zophar the Naamathite went and did what the LORD had told them, and the LORD accepted Job's prayer.

[10] And the LORD restored the fortunes of Job, when he had prayed for his friends. And the LORD gave Job twice as much as he had before. [11] Then came to him all his brothers and sisters

[1] Some manuscripts add *who is in heaven* [2] Some interpreters hold that the quotation ends at verse 15 [3] Or *For this is how God loved the world* [4] Some interpreters hold that the quotation continues through verse 36 [5] Or *am comforted*

and all who had known him before, and ate bread with him in his house. And they showed him sympathy and comforted him for all the evil[1] that the LORD had brought upon him. And each of them gave him a piece of money[2] and a ring of gold.

[12] And the LORD blessed the latter days of Job more than his beginning. And he had 14,000 sheep, 6,000 camels, 1,000 yoke of oxen, and 1,000 female donkeys. [13] He had also seven sons and three daughters. [14] And he called the name of the first daughter Jemimah, and the name of the second Keziah, and the name of the third Keren-happuch. [15] And in all the land there were no women so beautiful as Job's daughters. And their father gave them an inheritance among their brothers. [16] And after this Job lived 140 years, and saw his sons, and his sons' sons, four generations. [17] And Job died, an old man, and full of days.

2 Corinthians 12

I must go on boasting. Though there is nothing to be gained by it, I will go on to visions and revelations of the Lord. [2] I know a man in Christ who fourteen years ago was caught up to the third heaven—whether in the body or out of the body I do not know, God knows. [3] And I know that this man was caught up into paradise—whether in the body or out of the body I do not know, God knows— [4] and he heard things that cannot be told, which man may not utter. [5] On behalf of this man I will boast, but on my own behalf I will not boast, except of my weaknesses— [6] though if I should wish to boast, I would not be a fool, for I would be speaking the truth; but I refrain from it, so that no one may think more of me than he sees in me or hears from me. [7] So to keep me from becoming conceited because of the surpassing greatness of the revelations,[3] a thorn was given me in the flesh, a messenger of Satan to harass me, to keep me from becoming conceited. [8] Three times I pleaded with the Lord about this, that it should leave me. [9] But he said

to me, "My grace is sufficient for you, for my power is made perfect in weakness." Therefore I will boast all the more gladly of my weaknesses, so that the power of Christ may rest upon me. [10] For the sake of Christ, then, I am content with weaknesses, insults, hardships, persecutions, and calamities. For when I am weak, then I am strong.

[11] I have been a fool! You forced me to it, for I ought to have been commended by you. For I was not at all inferior to these super-apostles, even though I am nothing. [12] The signs of a true apostle were performed among you with utmost patience, with signs and wonders and mighty works. [13] For in what were you less favored than the rest of the churches, except that I myself did not burden you? Forgive me this wrong!

[14] Here for the third time I am ready to come to you. And I will not be a burden, for I seek not what is yours but you. For children are not obligated to save up for their parents, but parents for their children. [15] I will most gladly spend and be spent for your souls. If I love you more, am I to be loved less? [16] But granting that I myself did not burden you, I was crafty, you say, and got the better of you by deceit. [17] Did I take advantage of you through any of those whom I sent to you? [18] I urged Titus to go, and sent the brother with him. Did Titus take advantage of you? Did we not act in the same spirit? Did we not take the same steps?

[19] Have you been thinking all along that we have been defending ourselves to you? It is in the sight of God that we have been speaking in Christ, and all for your upbuilding, beloved. [20] For I fear that perhaps when I come I may find you not as I wish, and that you may find me not as you wish—that perhaps there may be quarreling, jealousy, anger, hostility, slander, gossip, conceit, and disorder. [21] I fear that when I come again my God may humble me before you, and I may have to mourn over many of those who sinned earlier and have not repented of the impurity, sexual immorality, and sensuality that they have practiced.

[1] Or disaster [2] Hebrew a qesitah; a unit of money of unknown value [3] Or hears from me, even because of the surpassing greatness of the revelations. So to keep me from becoming conceited

MARCH 14

Exodus 25

The LORD said to Moses, [2]"Speak to the people of Israel, that they take for me a contribution. From every man whose heart moves him you shall receive the contribution for me. [3]And this is the contribution that you shall receive from them: gold, silver, and bronze, [4]blue and purple and scarlet yarns and fine twined linen, goats' hair, [5]tanned rams' skins, goatskins,[1] acacia wood, [6]oil for the lamps, spices for the anointing oil and for the fragrant incense, [7]onyx stones, and stones for setting, for the ephod and for the breastpiece. [8]And let them make me a sanctuary, that I may dwell in their midst. [9]Exactly as I show you concerning the pattern of the tabernacle, and of all its furniture, so you shall make it.

[10]"They shall make an ark of acacia wood. Two cubits[2] and a half shall be its length, a cubit and a half its breadth, and a cubit and a half its height. [11]You shall overlay it with pure gold, inside and outside shall you overlay it, and you shall make on it a molding of gold around it. [12]You shall cast four rings of gold for it and put them on its four feet, two rings on the one side of it, and two rings on the other side of it. [13]You shall make poles of acacia wood and overlay them with gold. [14]And you shall put the poles into the rings on the sides of the ark to carry the ark by them. [15]The poles shall remain in the rings of the ark; they shall not be taken from it. [16]And you shall put into the ark the testimony that I shall give you.

[17]"You shall make a mercy seat[3] of pure gold. Two cubits and a half shall be its length, and a cubit and a half its breadth. [18]And you shall make two cherubim of gold; of hammered work shall you make them, on the two ends of the mercy seat. [19]Make one cherub on the one end, and one cherub on the other end. Of one piece with the mercy seat shall you make the cherubim on its two ends. [20]The cherubim shall spread out their wings above, overshadowing the mercy seat with their wings, their faces one to another; toward the mercy seat shall the faces of the cherubim be. [21]And you shall put the mercy seat on the top of the ark, and in the ark you shall put the testimony that I shall give you. [22]There I will meet with you, and from above the mercy seat, from between the two cherubim that are on the ark of the testimony, I will speak with you about all that I will give you in commandment for the people of Israel.

[23]"You shall make a table of acacia wood. Two cubits shall be its length, a cubit its breadth, and a cubit and a half its height. [24]You shall overlay it with pure gold and make a molding of gold around it. [25]And you shall make a rim around it a handbreadth[4] wide, and a molding of gold around the rim. [26]And you shall make for it four rings of gold, and fasten the rings to the four corners at its four legs. [27]Close to the frame the rings shall lie, as holders for the poles to carry the table. [28]You shall make the poles of acacia wood, and overlay them with gold, and the table shall be carried with these. [29]And you shall make its plates and dishes for incense, and its flagons and bowls with which to pour drink offerings; you shall make them of pure gold. [30]And you shall set the bread of the Presence on the table before me regularly.

[31]"You shall make a lampstand of pure gold. The lampstand shall be made of hammered work: its base, its stem, its cups, its calyxes, and its flowers shall be of one piece with it. [32]And there shall be six branches going out of its sides, three branches of the lampstand out of one side of it and three branches of the lampstand out of the other side of it; [33]three cups made like almond blossoms, each with calyx and flower, on one branch, and three cups made like almond blossoms, each with calyx and flower, on the other branch—so for the six branches going out of the lampstand. [34]And on the lampstand itself there shall be four cups made like almond blossoms, with their calyxes and flowers, [35]and a calyx of one piece with it under each pair of the six branches going out from the lampstand. [36]Their calyxes and their

---
[1] Uncertain; possibly *dolphin skins*, or *dugong skins*; compare 26:14 [2] A *cubit* was about 18 inches or 45 centimeters [3] Or *cover* [4] A *handbreadth* was about 3 inches or 7.5 centimeters

branches shall be of one piece with it, the whole of it a single piece of hammered work of pure gold. [37] You shall make seven lamps for it. And the lamps shall be set up so as to give light on the space in front of it. [38] Its tongs and their trays shall be of pure gold. [39] It shall be made, with all these utensils, out of a talent[1] of pure gold. [40] And see that you make them after the pattern for them, which is being shown you on the mountain.

John 4

Now when Jesus learned that the Pharisees had heard that Jesus was making and baptizing more disciples than John [2] (although Jesus himself did not baptize, but only his disciples), [3] he left Judea and departed again for Galilee. [4] And he had to pass through Samaria. [5] So he came to a town of Samaria called Sychar, near the field that Jacob had given to his son Joseph. [6] Jacob's well was there; so Jesus, wearied as he was from his journey, was sitting beside the well. It was about the sixth hour.[2]

[7] A woman from Samaria came to draw water. Jesus said to her, "Give me a drink." [8] (For his disciples had gone away into the city to buy food.) [9] The Samaritan woman said to him, "How is it that you, a Jew, ask for a drink from me, a woman of Samaria?" (For Jews have no dealings with Samaritans.) [10] Jesus answered her, "If you knew the gift of God, and who it is that is saying to you, 'Give me a drink,' you would have asked him, and he would have given you living water." [11] The woman said to him, "Sir, you have nothing to draw water with, and the well is deep. Where do you get that living water? [12] Are you greater than our father Jacob? He gave us the well and drank from it himself, as did his sons and his livestock." [13] Jesus said to her, "Everyone who drinks of this water will be thirsty again, [14] but whoever drinks of the water that I will give him will never be thirsty again.[3] The water that I will give him will become in him a spring of water welling up to eternal life." [15] The woman said to him, "Sir, give me this water, so that I will not be thirsty or have to come here to draw water." [16] Jesus said to her, "Go, call your husband, and come here." [17] The woman answered him, "I have no husband." Jesus said to her, "You are right in saying, 'I have no husband'; [18] for you have had five husbands, and the one you now have is not your husband. What you have said is true." [19] The woman said to him, "Sir, I perceive that you are a prophet. [20] Our fathers worshiped on this mountain, but you say that in Jerusalem is the place where people ought to worship." [21] Jesus said to her, "Woman, believe me, the hour is coming when neither on this mountain nor in Jerusalem will you worship the Father. [22] You worship what you do not know; we worship what we know, for salvation is from the Jews. [23] But the hour is coming, and is now here, when the true worshipers will worship the Father in spirit and truth, for the Father is seeking such people to worship him. [24] God is spirit, and those who worship him must worship in spirit and truth." [25] The woman said to him, "I know that Messiah is coming (he who is called Christ). When he comes, he will tell us all things." [26] Jesus said to her, "I who speak to you am he."

[27] Just then his disciples came back. They marveled that he was talking with a woman, but no one said, "What do you seek?" or, "Why are you talking with her?" [28] So the woman left her water jar and went away into town and said to the people, [29] "Come, see a man who told me all that I ever did. Can this be the Christ?" [30] They went out of the town and were coming to him.

[31] Meanwhile the disciples were urging him, saying, "Rabbi, eat." [32] But he said to them, "I have food to eat that you do not know about." [33] So the disciples said to one another, "Has anyone brought him something to eat?" [34] Jesus said to them, "My food is to do the will of him who sent me and to accomplish his work. [35] Do you not say, 'There are yet four months, then comes the harvest'? Look, I tell you, lift up your eyes, and see that the fields are white for harvest. [36] Already the one who reaps is receiving wages and gathering fruit for eternal life, so that sower and reaper may rejoice together. [37] For here the saying holds true, 'One sows and another reaps.' [38] I sent you to reap that for which you did not labor. Others have labored, and you have entered into their labor."

[39] Many Samaritans from that town believed in him because of the woman's testimony, "He told me all that I ever did." [40] So when the Samaritans came to him, they asked him to stay with them, and he stayed there two days.

[1] A talent was about 75 pounds or 34 kilograms [2] That is, about noon [3] Greek forever

⁴¹And many more believed because of his word. ⁴²They said to the woman, "It is no longer because of what you said that we believe, for we have heard for ourselves, and we know that this is indeed the Savior of the world."

⁴³After the two days he departed for Galilee. ⁴⁴(For Jesus himself had testified that a prophet has no honor in his own hometown.) ⁴⁵So when he came to Galilee, the Galileans welcomed him, having seen all that he had done in Jerusalem at the feast. For they too had gone to the feast.

⁴⁶So he came again to Cana in Galilee, where he had made the water wine. And at Capernaum there was an official whose son was ill. ⁴⁷When this man heard that Jesus had come from Judea to Galilee, he went to him and asked him to come down and heal his son, for he was at the point of death. ⁴⁸So Jesus said to him, "Unless you¹ see signs and wonders you will not believe." ⁴⁹The official said to him, "Sir, come down before my child dies." ⁵⁰Jesus said to him, "Go; your son will live." The man believed the word that Jesus spoke to him and went on his way. ⁵¹As he was going down, his servants² met him and told him that his son was recovering. ⁵²So he asked them the hour when he began to get better, and they said to him, "Yesterday at the seventh hour³ the fever left him." ⁵³The father knew that was the hour when Jesus had said to him, "Your son will live." And he himself believed, and all his household. ⁵⁴This was now the second sign that Jesus did when he had come from Judea to Galilee.

Proverbs 1

The proverbs of Solomon, son of David, king of Israel:

² To know wisdom and instruction,
    to understand words of insight,
³   to receive instruction in wise dealing,
    in righteousness, justice, and equity;
⁴ to give prudence to the simple,
    knowledge and discretion to the youth—
⁵   Let the wise hear and increase in learning,
    and the one who understands obtain guidance,

⁶   to understand a proverb and a saying,
    the words of the wise and their riddles.

⁷   The fear of the Lᴏʀᴅ is the beginning of knowledge;
    fools despise wisdom and instruction.

⁸ Hear, my son, your father's instruction,
    and forsake not your mother's teaching,
⁹   for they are a graceful garland for your head
    and pendants for your neck.
¹⁰ My son, if sinners entice you,
    do not consent.
¹¹ If they say, "Come with us, let us lie in wait for blood;
    let us ambush the innocent without reason;
¹²   like Sheol let us swallow them alive,
    and whole, like those who go down to the pit;
¹³   we shall find all precious goods,
    we shall fill our houses with plunder;
¹⁴   throw in your lot among us;
    we will all have one purse"—
¹⁵   my son, do not walk in the way with them;
    hold back your foot from their paths,
¹⁶ for their feet run to evil,
    and they make haste to shed blood.
¹⁷ For in vain is a net spread
    in the sight of any bird,
¹⁸ but these men lie in wait for their own blood;
    they set an ambush for their own lives.
¹⁹ Such are the ways of everyone who is greedy for unjust gain;
    it takes away the life of its possessors.

²⁰ Wisdom cries aloud in the street,
    in the markets she raises her voice;
²¹ at the head of the noisy streets she cries out;
    at the entrance of the city gates she speaks:
²² "How long, O simple ones, will you love being simple?
    How long will scoffers delight in their scoffing
    and fools hate knowledge?

¹ The Greek for you is plural; twice in this verse ² Greek bondservants ³ That is, at 1 ᴘ.ᴍ.

23   If you turn at my reproof,[1]
        behold, I will pour out my spirit to you;
        I will make my words known to you.

24   Because I have called and you refused to
        listen,
        have stretched out my hand and no
        one has heeded,

25   because you have ignored all my
        counsel
        and would have none of my reproof,

26   I also will laugh at your calamity;
        I will mock when terror strikes you,

27   when terror strikes you like a storm
        and your calamity comes like a
        whirlwind,
        when distress and anguish come
        upon you.

28   Then they will call upon me, but I will
        not answer;
        they will seek me diligently but will
        not find me.

29   Because they hated knowledge
        and did not choose the fear of the
        LORD,

30   would have none of my counsel
        and despised all my reproof,

31   therefore they shall eat the fruit of their
        way,
        and have their fill of their own
        devices.

32   For the simple are killed by their turning
        away,
        and the complacency of fools destroys
        them;

33   but whoever listens to me will dwell
        secure
        and will be at ease, without dread of
        disaster."

2 Corinthians 13

This is the third time I am coming to you. Every charge must be established by the evidence of two or three witnesses. [2] I warned those who sinned before and all the others, and I warn them now while absent, as I did when present on my second visit, that if I come again I will not spare them— [3] since you seek proof that Christ is speaking in me. He is not weak in dealing with you, but is powerful among you. [4] For he was crucified in weakness, but lives by the power of God. For we also are weak in him, but in dealing with you we will live with him by the power of God.

[5] Examine yourselves, to see whether you are in the faith. Test yourselves. Or do you not realize this about yourselves, that Jesus Christ is in you?—unless indeed you fail to meet the test! [6] I hope you will find out that we have not failed the test. [7] But we pray to God that you may not do wrong—not that we may appear to have met the test, but that you may do what is right, though we may seem to have failed. [8] For we cannot do anything against the truth, but only for the truth. [9] For we are glad when we are weak and you are strong. Your restoration is what we pray for. [10] For this reason I write these things while I am away from you, that when I come I may not have to be severe in my use of the authority that the Lord has given me for building up and not for tearing down.

[11] Finally, brothers,[2] rejoice. Aim for restoration, comfort one another,[3] agree with one another, live in peace; and the God of love and peace will be with you. [12] Greet one another with a holy kiss. [13] All the saints greet you.

[14] The grace of the Lord Jesus Christ and the love of God and the fellowship of the Holy Spirit be with you all.

---

[1] Or Will you turn away at my reproof? [2] Or brothers and sisters [3] Or listen to my appeal

MARCH 15

Exodus 26

"Moreover, you shall make the tabernacle with ten curtains of fine twined linen and blue and purple and scarlet yarns; you shall make them with cherubim skillfully worked into them. [2] The length of each curtain shall be twenty-eight cubits,[1] and the breadth of each curtain four cubits; all the curtains shall be the same size. [3] Five curtains shall be coupled to one another, and the other five curtains shall be coupled to one another. [4] And you shall make loops of blue on the edge of the outermost curtain in the first set. Likewise you shall make loops on the edge of the outermost curtain in the second set. [5] Fifty loops you shall make on the one curtain, and fifty loops you shall make on the edge of the curtain that is in the second set; the loops shall be opposite one another. [6] And you shall make fifty clasps of gold, and couple the curtains one to the other with the clasps, so that the tabernacle may be a single whole.

[7] "You shall also make curtains of goats' hair for a tent over the tabernacle; eleven curtains shall you make. [8] The length of each curtain shall be thirty cubits, and the breadth of each curtain four cubits. The eleven curtains shall be the same size. [9] You shall couple five curtains by themselves, and six curtains by themselves, and the sixth curtain you shall double over at the front of the tent. [10] You shall make fifty loops on the edge of the curtain that is outermost in one set, and fifty loops on the edge of the curtain that is outermost in the second set.

[11] "You shall make fifty clasps of bronze, and put the clasps into the loops, and couple the tent together that it may be a single whole. [12] And the part that remains of the curtains of the tent, the half curtain that remains, shall hang over the back of the tabernacle. [13] And the extra that remains in the length of the curtains, the cubit on the one side, and the cubit on the other side, shall hang over the sides of the tabernacle, on this side and that side, to cover it. [14] And you shall make for the tent a covering of tanned rams' skins and a covering of goatskins on top.

[15] "You shall make upright frames for the tabernacle of acacia wood. [16] Ten cubits shall be the length of a frame, and a cubit and a half the breadth of each frame. [17] There shall be two tenons in each frame, for fitting together. So shall you do for all the frames of the tabernacle. [18] You shall make the frames for the tabernacle: twenty frames for the south side; [19] and forty bases of silver you shall make under the twenty frames, two bases under one frame for its two tenons, and two bases under the next frame for its two tenons; [20] and for the second side of the tabernacle, on the north side twenty frames, [21] and their forty bases of silver, two bases under one frame, and two bases under the next frame. [22] And for the rear of the tabernacle westward you shall make six frames. [23] And you shall make two frames for corners of the tabernacle in the rear; [24] they shall be separate beneath, but joined at the top, at the first ring. Thus shall it be with both of them; they shall form the two corners. [25] And there shall be eight frames, with their bases of silver, sixteen bases; two bases under one frame, and two bases under another frame.

[26] "You shall make bars of acacia wood, five for the frames of the one side of the tabernacle, [27] and five bars for the frames of the other side of the tabernacle, and five bars for the frames of the side of the tabernacle at the rear westward. [28] The middle bar, halfway up the frames, shall run from end to end. [29] You shall overlay the frames with gold and shall make their rings of gold for holders for the bars, and you shall overlay the bars with gold. [30] Then you shall erect the tabernacle according to the plan for it that you were shown on the mountain.

[31] "And you shall make a veil of blue and purple and scarlet yarns and fine twined linen. It shall be made with cherubim skillfully worked into it. [32] And you shall hang it on four pillars of acacia overlaid with gold, with hooks of gold, on four bases of silver. [33] And you shall hang the veil from the clasps, and bring the ark of

---

[1] A *cubit* was about 18 inches or 45 centimeters

the testimony in there within the veil. And the veil shall separate for you the Holy Place from the Most Holy. [34]You shall put the mercy seat on the ark of the testimony in the Most Holy Place. [35]And you shall set the table outside the veil, and the lampstand on the south side of the tabernacle opposite the table, and you shall put the table on the north side.

[36]"You shall make a screen for the entrance of the tent, of blue and purple and scarlet yarns and fine twined linen, embroidered with needlework. [37]And you shall make for the screen five pillars of acacia, and overlay them with gold. Their hooks shall be of gold, and you shall cast five bases of bronze for them.

John 5

After this there was a feast of the Jews, and Jesus went up to Jerusalem. [2]Now there is in Jerusalem by the Sheep Gate a pool, in Aramaic[1] called Bethesda,[2] which has five roofed colonnades. [3]In these lay a multitude of invalids—blind, lame, and paralyzed.[3] [5]One man was there who had been an invalid for thirty-eight years. [6]When Jesus saw him lying there and knew that he had already been there a long time, he said to him, "Do you want to be healed?" [7]The sick man answered him, "Sir, I have no one to put me into the pool when the water is stirred up, and while I am going another steps down before me." [8]Jesus said to him, "Get up, take up your bed, and walk." [9]And at once the man was healed, and he took up his bed and walked.

Now that day was the Sabbath. [10]So the Jews[4] said to the man who had been healed, "It is the Sabbath, and it is not lawful for you to take up your bed." [11]But he answered them, "The man who healed me, that man said to me, 'Take up your bed, and walk.'" [12]They asked him, "Who is the man who said to you, 'Take up your bed and walk'?" [13]Now the man who had been healed did not know who it was, for Jesus had withdrawn, as there was a crowd in the place. [14]Afterward Jesus found him in the temple and said to him, "See, you are well! Sin no more, that nothing worse may happen to you." [15]The man went away and told the Jews that it was Jesus who had healed him. [16]And this was why the Jews were persecuting Jesus, because he

was doing these things on the Sabbath. [17]But Jesus answered them, "My Father is working until now, and I am working."

[18]This was why the Jews were seeking all the more to kill him, because not only was he breaking the Sabbath, but he was even calling God his own Father, making himself equal with God.

[19]So Jesus said to them, "Truly, truly, I say to you, the Son can do nothing of his own accord, but only what he sees the Father doing. For whatever the Father[5] does, that the Son does likewise. [20]For the Father loves the Son and shows him all that he himself is doing. And greater works than these will he show him, so that you may marvel. [21]For as the Father raises the dead and gives them life, so also the Son gives life to whom he will. [22]The Father judges no one, but has given all judgment to the Son, [23]that all may honor the Son, just as they honor the Father. Whoever does not honor the Son does not honor the Father who sent him. [24]Truly, truly, I say to you, whoever hears my word and believes him who sent me has eternal life. He does not come into judgment, but has passed from death to life.

[25]"Truly, truly, I say to you, an hour is coming, and is now here, when the dead will hear the voice of the Son of God, and those who hear will live. [26]For as the Father has life in himself, so he has granted the Son also to have life in himself. [27]And he has given him authority to execute judgment, because he is the Son of Man. [28]Do not marvel at this, for an hour is coming when all who are in the tombs will hear his voice [29]and come out, those who have done good to the resurrection of life, and those who have done evil to the resurrection of judgment.

[30]"I can do nothing on my own. As I hear, I judge, and my judgment is just, because I seek not my own will but the will of him who sent me. [31]If I alone bear witness about myself, my testimony is not true. [32]There is another who bears witness about me, and I know that the testimony that he bears about me is true. [33]You sent to John, and he has borne witness to the truth. [34]Not that the testimony that I receive is from man, but I say these things so that you may be saved. [35]He was a burning and shining lamp, and you were willing to rejoice for a while in his light. [36]But the testimony that I have is

---

[1] Or Hebrew [2] Some manuscripts Bethsaida [3] Some manuscripts insert, wholly or in part, waiting for the moving of the water; [4]for an angel of the Lord went down at certain seasons into the pool, and stirred the water; whoever stepped in first after the stirring of the water was healed of whatever disease he had [4] The Greek word Ioudaioi refers specifically here to Jewish religious leaders, and others under their influence, who opposed Jesus in that time; also verses 15, 16, 18 [5] Greek he

greater than that of John. For the works that the Father has given me to accomplish, the very works that I am doing, bear witness about me that the Father has sent me. ³⁷And the Father who sent me has himself borne witness about me. His voice you have never heard, his form you have never seen, ³⁸and you do not have his word abiding in you, for you do not believe the one whom he has sent. ³⁹You search the Scriptures because you think that in them you have eternal life; and it is they that bear witness about me, ⁴⁰yet you refuse to come to me that you may have life. ⁴¹I do not receive glory from people. ⁴²But I know that you do not have the love of God within you. ⁴³I have come in my Father's name, and you do not receive me. If another comes in his own name, you will receive him. ⁴⁴How can you believe, when you receive glory from one another and do not seek the glory that comes from the only God? ⁴⁵Do not think that I will accuse you to the Father. There is one who accuses you: Moses, on whom you have set your hope. ⁴⁶For if you believed Moses, you would believe me; for he wrote of me. ⁴⁷But if you do not believe his writings, how will you believe my words?"

─────── Proverbs 2 ───────

My son, if you receive my words
  and treasure up my commandments
    with you,
² making your ear attentive to wisdom
  and inclining your heart to
    understanding;
³ yes, if you call out for insight
  and raise your voice for
    understanding,
⁴ if you seek it like silver
  and search for it as for hidden
    treasures,
⁵ then you will understand the fear of the
    LORD
  and find the knowledge of God.
⁶ For the LORD gives wisdom;
  from his mouth come knowledge and
    understanding;
⁷ he stores up sound wisdom for the
    upright;
  he is a shield to those who walk in
    integrity,

⁸ guarding the paths of justice
  and watching over the way of his saints.
⁹ Then you will understand righteousness
    and justice
  and equity, every good path;
¹⁰ for wisdom will come into your heart,
  and knowledge will be pleasant to
    your soul;
¹¹ discretion will watch over you,
  understanding will guard you,
¹² delivering you from the way of evil,
  from men of perverted speech,
¹³ who forsake the paths of uprightness
  to walk in the ways of darkness,
¹⁴ who rejoice in doing evil
  and delight in the perverseness of evil,
¹⁵ men whose paths are crooked,
  and who are devious in their ways.

¹⁶ So you will be delivered from the
    forbidden¹ woman,
  from the adulteress² with her smooth
    words,
¹⁷ who forsakes the companion of her youth
  and forgets the covenant of her God;
¹⁸ for her house sinks down to death,
  and her paths to the departed;³
¹⁹ none who go to her come back,
  nor do they regain the paths of life.

²⁰ So you will walk in the way of the good
  and keep to the paths of the righteous.
²¹ For the upright will inhabit the land,
  and those with integrity will remain
    in it,
²² but the wicked will be cut off from the
    land,
  and the treacherous will be rooted out
    of it.

─────── Galatians 1 ───────

Paul, an apostle—not from men nor through man, but through Jesus Christ and God the Father, who raised him from the dead— ²and all the brothers⁴ who are with me,
  To the churches of Galatia:
³Grace to you and peace from God our Father and the Lord Jesus Christ, ⁴who gave himself for our sins to deliver us from the present evil age, according to the will of our God and Father, ⁵to whom be the glory forever and ever. Amen.

¹ Hebrew *strange* ² Hebrew *foreign woman* ³ Hebrew *to the Rephaim* ⁴ Or *brothers and sisters*. The plural Greek word *adelphoi* (translated "brothers") refers to siblings in a family. In New Testament usage, depending on the context, *adelphoi* may refer either to men or to both men and women who are siblings (brothers and sisters) in God's family, the church; also verse 11

⁶I am astonished that you are so quickly deserting him who called you in the grace of Christ and are turning to a different gospel—⁷not that there is another one, but there are some who trouble you and want to distort the gospel of Christ. ⁸But even if we or an angel from heaven should preach to you a gospel contrary to the one we preached to you, let him be accursed. ⁹As we have said before, so now I say again: If anyone is preaching to you a gospel contrary to the one you received, let him be accursed.

¹⁰For am I now seeking the approval of man, or of God? Or am I trying to please man? If I were still trying to please man, I would not be a servant¹ of Christ.

¹¹For I would have you know, brothers, that the gospel that was preached by me is not man's gospel.² ¹²For I did not receive it from any man, nor was I taught it, but I received it through a revelation of Jesus Christ. ¹³For you have heard of my former life in Judaism, how I persecuted the church of God violently and tried

to destroy it. ¹⁴And I was advancing in Judaism beyond many of my own age among my people, so extremely zealous was I for the traditions of my fathers. ¹⁵But when he who had set me apart before I was born,³ and who called me by his grace, ¹⁶was pleased to reveal his Son to⁴ me, in order that I might preach him among the Gentiles, I did not immediately consult with anyone;⁵ ¹⁷nor did I go up to Jerusalem to those who were apostles before me, but I went away into Arabia, and returned again to Damascus.

¹⁸Then after three years I went up to Jerusalem to visit Cephas and remained with him fifteen days. ¹⁹But I saw none of the other apostles except James the Lord's brother. ²⁰(In what I am writing to you, before God, I do not lie!) ²¹Then I went into the regions of Syria and Cilicia. ²²And I was still unknown in person to the churches of Judea that are in Christ. ²³They only were hearing it said, "He who used to persecute us is now preaching the faith he once tried to destroy." ²⁴And they glorified God because of me.

MARCH 16

Exodus 27

¹"You shall make the altar of acacia wood, five cubits⁶ long and five cubits broad. The altar shall be square, and its height shall be three cubits. ²And you shall make horns for it on its four corners; its horns shall be of one piece with it, and you shall overlay it with bronze. ³You shall make pots for it to receive its ashes, and shovels and basins and forks and fire pans. You shall make all its utensils of bronze. ⁴You shall also make for it a grating, a network of bronze, and on the net you shall make four bronze rings at its four corners. ⁵And you shall set it under the ledge of the altar so that the net extends halfway down the altar. ⁶And you shall make poles for the altar, poles of acacia wood, and overlay them with bronze. ⁷And the poles shall be put through the rings, so that the poles are on the two sides of the altar when it is

carried. ⁸You shall make it hollow, with boards. As it has been shown you on the mountain, so shall it be made.

⁹"You shall make the court of the tabernacle. On the south side the court shall have hangings of fine twined linen a hundred cubits long for one side. ¹⁰Its twenty pillars and their twenty bases shall be of bronze, but the hooks of the pillars and their fillets shall be of silver. ¹¹And likewise for its length on the north side there shall be hangings a hundred cubits long, its pillars twenty and their bases twenty, of bronze, but the hooks of the pillars and their fillets shall be of silver. ¹²And for the breadth of the court on the west side there shall be hangings for fifty cubits, with ten pillars and ten bases. ¹³The breadth of the court on the front to the east shall be fifty cubits. ¹⁴The

¹ Or slave; Greek bondservant ² Greek not according to man ³ Greek set me apart from my mother's womb ⁴ Greek in ⁵ Greek with flesh and blood ⁶ A cubit was about 18 inches or 45 centimeters

hangings for the one side of the gate shall be fifteen cubits, with their three pillars and three bases. [15]On the other side the hangings shall be fifteen cubits, with their three pillars and three bases. [16]For the gate of the court there shall be a screen twenty cubits long, of blue and purple and scarlet yarns and fine twined linen, embroidered with needlework. It shall have four pillars and with them four bases. [17]All the pillars around the court shall be filleted with silver. Their hooks shall be of silver, and their bases of bronze. [18]The length of the court shall be a hundred cubits, the breadth fifty, and the height five cubits, with hangings of fine twined linen and bases of bronze. [19]All the utensils of the tabernacle for every use, and all its pegs and all the pegs of the court, shall be of bronze.

[20]"You shall command the people of Israel that they bring to you pure beaten olive oil for the light, that a lamp may regularly be set up to burn. [21]In the tent of meeting, outside the veil that is before the testimony, Aaron and his sons shall tend it from evening to morning before the LORD. It shall be a statute forever to be observed throughout their generations by the people of Israel.

John 6

After this Jesus went away to the other side of the Sea of Galilee, which is the Sea of Tiberias. [2]And a large crowd was following him, because they saw the signs that he was doing on the sick. [3]Jesus went up on the mountain, and there he sat down with his disciples. [4]Now the Passover, the feast of the Jews, was at hand. [5]Lifting up his eyes, then, and seeing that a large crowd was coming toward him, Jesus said to Philip, "Where are we to buy bread, so that these people may eat?" [6]He said this to test him, for he himself knew what he would do. [7]Philip answered him, "Two hundred denarii[1] worth of bread would not be enough for each of them to get a little." [8]One of his disciples, Andrew, Simon Peter's brother, said to him, [9]"There is a boy here who has five barley loaves and two fish, but what are they for so many?" [10]Jesus said, "Have the people sit down." Now there was much grass in the place. So the men sat down, about five thousand in number. [11]Jesus then took the loaves, and when he had given thanks, he distributed them to those who were seated. So also the fish, as much as they wanted. [12]And when they had eaten their fill, he told his disciples, "Gather up the leftover fragments, that nothing may be lost." [13]So they gathered them up and filled twelve baskets with fragments from the five barley loaves left by those who had eaten. [14]When the people saw the sign that he had done, they said, "This is indeed the Prophet who is to come into the world!"

[15]Perceiving then that they were about to come and take him by force to make him king, Jesus withdrew again to the mountain by himself.

[16]When evening came, his disciples went down to the sea, [17]got into a boat, and started across the sea to Capernaum. It was now dark, and Jesus had not yet come to them. [18]The sea became rough because a strong wind was blowing. [19]When they had rowed about three or four miles,[2] they saw Jesus walking on the sea and coming near the boat, and they were frightened. [20]But he said to them, "It is I; do not be afraid." [21]Then they were glad to take him into the boat, and immediately the boat was at the land to which they were going.

[22]On the next day the crowd that remained on the other side of the sea saw that there had been only one boat there, and that Jesus had not entered the boat with his disciples, but that his disciples had gone away alone. [23]Other boats from Tiberias came near the place where they had eaten the bread after the Lord had given thanks. [24]So when the crowd saw that Jesus was not there, nor his disciples, they themselves got into the boats and went to Capernaum, seeking Jesus.

[25]When they found him on the other side of the sea, they said to him, "Rabbi, when did you come here?" [26]Jesus answered them, "Truly, truly, I say to you, you are seeking me, not because you saw signs, but because you ate your fill of the loaves. [27]Do not work for the food that perishes, but for the food that endures to eternal life, which the Son of Man will give to you. For on him God the Father has set his seal." [28]Then they said to him, "What must we do, to be doing the works of God?" [29]Jesus answered them, "This is the work of God, that you believe in him whom he has sent." [30]So they said to him, "Then what sign

---

[1] A denarius was a day's wage for a laborer [2] Greek twenty-five or thirty stadia; a stadion was about 607 feet or 185 meters

do you do, that we may see and believe you? What work do you perform? [31]Our fathers ate the manna in the wilderness; as it is written, 'He gave them bread from heaven to eat.'" [32]Jesus then said to them, "Truly, truly, I say to you, it was not Moses who gave you the bread from heaven, but my Father gives you the true bread from heaven. [33]For the bread of God is he who comes down from heaven and gives life to the world." [34]They said to him, "Sir, give us this bread always."

[35]Jesus said to them, "I am the bread of life; whoever comes to me shall not hunger, and whoever believes in me shall never thirst. [36]But I said to you that you have seen me and yet do not believe. [37]All that the Father gives me will come to me, and whoever comes to me I will never cast out. [38]For I have come down from heaven, not to do my own will but the will of him who sent me. [39]And this is the will of him who sent me, that I should lose nothing of all that he has given me, but raise it up on the last day. [40]For this is the will of my Father, that everyone who looks on the Son and believes in him should have eternal life, and I will raise him up on the last day."

[41]So the Jews grumbled about him, because he said, "I am the bread that came down from heaven." [42]They said, "Is not this Jesus, the son of Joseph, whose father and mother we know? How does he now say, 'I have come down from heaven'?" [43]Jesus answered them, "Do not grumble among yourselves. [44]No one can come to me unless the Father who sent me draws him. And I will raise him up on the last day. [45]It is written in the Prophets, 'And they will all be taught by God.' Everyone who has heard and learned from the Father comes to me— [46]not that anyone has seen the Father except he who is from God; he has seen the Father. [47]Truly, truly, I say to you, whoever believes has eternal life. [48]I am the bread of life. [49]Your fathers ate the manna in the wilderness, and they died. [50]This is the bread that comes down from heaven, so that one may eat of it and not die. [51]I am the living bread that came down from heaven. If anyone eats of this bread, he will live forever. And the bread that I will give for the life of the world is my flesh."

[52]The Jews then disputed among themselves, saying, "How can this man give us his flesh to eat?" [53]So Jesus said to them, "Truly, truly, I say to you, unless you eat the flesh of the Son of Man and drink his blood, you have no life in you. [54]Whoever feeds on my flesh and drinks my blood has eternal life, and I will raise him up on the last day. [55]For my flesh is true food, and my blood is true drink. [56]Whoever feeds on my flesh and drinks my blood abides in me, and I in him. [57]As the living Father sent me, and I live because of the Father, so whoever feeds on me, he also will live because of me. [58]This is the bread that came down from heaven, not like the bread[1] the fathers ate, and died. Whoever feeds on this bread will live forever." [59]Jesus[2] said these things in the synagogue, as he taught at Capernaum.

[60]When many of his disciples heard it, they said, "This is a hard saying; who can listen to it?" [61]But Jesus, knowing in himself that his disciples were grumbling about this, said to them, "Do you take offense at this? [62]Then what if you were to see the Son of Man ascending to where he was before? [63]It is the Spirit who gives life; the flesh is no help at all. The words that I have spoken to you are spirit and life. [64]But there are some of you who do not believe." (For Jesus knew from the beginning who those were who did not believe, and who it was who would betray him.) [65]And he said, "This is why I told you that no one can come to me unless it is granted him by the Father."

[66]After this many of his disciples turned back and no longer walked with him. [67]So Jesus said to the Twelve, "Do you want to go away as well?" [68]Simon Peter answered him, "Lord, to whom shall we go? You have the words of eternal life, [69]and we have believed, and have come to know, that you are the Holy One of God." [70]Jesus answered them, "Did I not choose you, the Twelve? And yet one of you is a devil." [71]He spoke of Judas the son of Simon Iscariot, for he, one of the Twelve, was going to betray him.

Proverbs 3

My son, do not forget my teaching,
   but let your heart keep my
        commandments,
[2] for length of days and years of life
   and peace they will add to you.

---

[1] Greek lacks the bread   [2] Greek He

³ Let not steadfast love and faithfulness
    forsake you;
    bind them around your neck;
    write them on the tablet of your heart.
⁴ So you will find favor and good success¹
    in the sight of God and man.

⁵ Trust in the Lᴏʀᴅ with all your heart,
    and do not lean on your own
      understanding.
⁶ In all your ways acknowledge him,
    and he will make straight your paths.
⁷ Be not wise in your own eyes;
    fear the Lᴏʀᴅ, and turn away from
      evil.
⁸ It will be healing to your flesh²
    and refreshment³ to your bones.
⁹ Honor the Lᴏʀᴅ with your wealth
    and with the firstfruits of all your
      produce;
¹⁰ then your barns will be filled with
      plenty,
    and your vats will be bursting with
      wine.

¹¹ My son, do not despise the Lᴏʀᴅ's
      discipline
    or be weary of his reproof,
¹² for the Lᴏʀᴅ reproves him whom he
      loves,
    as a father the son in whom he
      delights.

¹³ Blessed is the one who finds wisdom,
    and the one who gets understanding,
¹⁴ for the gain from her is better than gain
      from silver
    and her profit better than gold.
¹⁵ She is more precious than jewels,
    and nothing you desire can compare
      with her.
¹⁶ Long life is in her right hand;
    in her left hand are riches and honor.
¹⁷ Her ways are ways of pleasantness,
    and all her paths are peace.
¹⁸ She is a tree of life to those who lay hold
      of her;
    those who hold her fast are called
      blessed.
¹⁹ The Lᴏʀᴅ by wisdom founded the earth;
    by understanding he established the
      heavens;

²⁰ by his knowledge the deeps broke open,
    and the clouds drop down the dew.

²¹ My son, do not lose sight of these—
    keep sound wisdom and discretion,
²² and they will be life for your soul
    and adornment for your neck.
²³ Then you will walk on your way securely,
    and your foot will not stumble.
²⁴ If you lie down, you will not be afraid;
    when you lie down, your sleep will be
      sweet.
²⁵ Do not be afraid of sudden terror
    or of the ruin⁴ of the wicked, when it
      comes,
²⁶ for the Lᴏʀᴅ will be your confidence
    and will keep your foot from being
      caught.
²⁷ Do not withhold good from those to
      whom it is due,⁵
    when it is in your power to do it.
²⁸ Do not say to your neighbor, "Go, and
      come again,
    tomorrow I will give it"—when you
      have it with you.
²⁹ Do not plan evil against your neighbor,
    who dwells trustingly beside you.
³⁰ Do not contend with a man for no
      reason,
    when he has done you no harm.
³¹ Do not envy a man of violence
    and do not choose any of his ways,
³² for the devious person is an
      abomination to the Lᴏʀᴅ,
    but the upright are in his confidence.
³³ The Lᴏʀᴅ's curse is on the house of the
      wicked,
    but he blesses the dwelling of the
      righteous.
³⁴ Toward the scorners he is scornful,
    but to the humble he gives favor.⁶
³⁵ The wise will inherit honor,
    but fools get⁷ disgrace.

――――――― *Galatians 2* ―――――――

Then after fourteen years I went up again to Jerusalem with Barnabas, taking Titus along with me. ²I went up because of a revelation and set before them (though privately before those who seemed influential) the gospel that I proclaim among the Gentiles, in

¹ Or *repute* ² Hebrew *navel* ³ Or *medicine* ⁴ Hebrew *storm* ⁵ Hebrew *Do not withhold good from its owners* ⁶ Or *grace* ⁷ The meaning of the Hebrew word is uncertain

order to make sure I was not running or had not run in vain. ³But even Titus, who was with me, was not forced to be circumcised, though he was a Greek. ⁴Yet because of false brothers secretly brought in—who slipped in to spy out our freedom that we have in Christ Jesus, so that they might bring us into slavery— ⁵to them we did not yield in submission even for a moment, so that the truth of the gospel might be preserved for you. ⁶And from those who seemed to be influential (what they were makes no difference to me; God shows no partiality)—those, I say, who seemed influential added nothing to me. ⁷On the contrary, when they saw that I had been entrusted with the gospel to the uncircumcised, just as Peter had been entrusted with the gospel to the circumcised ⁸(for he who worked through Peter for his apostolic ministry to the circumcised worked also through me for mine to the Gentiles), ⁹and when James and Cephas and John, who seemed to be pillars, perceived the grace that was given to me, they gave the right hand of fellowship to Barnabas and me, that we should go to the Gentiles and they to the circumcised. ¹⁰Only, they asked us to remember the poor, the very thing I was eager to do.

¹¹But when Cephas came to Antioch, I opposed him to his face, because he stood condemned. ¹²For before certain men came from James, he was eating with the Gentiles; but when they came he drew back and separated himself, fearing the circumcision party.¹ ¹³And the rest of the Jews acted hypocritically along with him, so that even Barnabas was led astray by their hypocrisy. ¹⁴But when I saw that their conduct was not in step with the truth of the gospel, I said to Cephas before them all, "If you, though a Jew, live like a Gentile and not like a Jew, how can you force the Gentiles to live like Jews?"

¹⁵We ourselves are Jews by birth and not Gentile sinners; ¹⁶yet we know that a person is not justified² by works of the law but through faith in Jesus Christ, so we also have believed in Christ Jesus, in order to be justified by faith in Christ and not by works of the law, because by works of the law no one will be justified.

¹⁷But if, in our endeavor to be justified in Christ, we too were found to be sinners, is Christ then a servant of sin? Certainly not! ¹⁸For if I rebuild what I tore down, I prove myself to be a transgressor. ¹⁹For through the law I died to the law, so that I might live to God. ²⁰I have been crucified with Christ. It is no longer I who live, but Christ who lives in me. And the life I now live in the flesh I live by faith in the Son of God, who loved me and gave himself for me. ²¹I do not nullify the grace of God, for if righteousness³ were through the law, then Christ died for no purpose.

MARCH 17

Exodus 28

"Then bring near to you Aaron your brother, and his sons with him, from among the people of Israel, to serve me as priests—Aaron and Aaron's sons, Nadab and Abihu, Eleazar and Ithamar. ²And you shall make holy garments for Aaron your brother, for glory and for beauty. ³You shall speak to all the skillful, whom I have filled with a spirit of skill, that they make Aaron's garments to consecrate him for my priesthood. ⁴These are the garments that they shall make: a breastpiece, an ephod, a robe, a coat of checker work, a turban, and a sash. They shall make holy garments for Aaron your brother and his sons to serve me as priests. ⁵They shall receive gold, blue and purple and scarlet yarns, and fine twined linen.

⁶"And they shall make the ephod of gold, of blue and purple and scarlet yarns, and of fine twined linen, skillfully worked. ⁷It shall have two shoulder pieces attached to its two

¹ Or fearing those of the circumcision ² Or counted righteous (three times in verse 16); also verse 17 ³ Or justification

edges, so that it may be joined together. ⁸And the skillfully woven band on it shall be made like it and be of one piece with it, of gold, blue and purple and scarlet yarns, and fine twined linen. ⁹You shall take two onyx stones, and engrave on them the names of the sons of Israel, ¹⁰six of their names on the one stone, and the names of the remaining six on the other stone, in the order of their birth. ¹¹As a jeweler engraves signets, so shall you engrave the two stones with the names of the sons of Israel. You shall enclose them in settings of gold filigree. ¹²And you shall set the two stones on the shoulder pieces of the ephod, as stones of remembrance for the sons of Israel. And Aaron shall bear their names before the Lord on his two shoulders for remembrance. ¹³You shall make settings of gold filigree, ¹⁴and two chains of pure gold, twisted like cords; and you shall attach the corded chains to the settings.

¹⁵"You shall make a breastpiece of judgment, in skilled work. In the style of the ephod you shall make it—of gold, blue and purple and scarlet yarns, and fine twined linen shall you make it. ¹⁶It shall be square and doubled, a span¹ its length and a span its breadth. ¹⁷You shall set in it four rows of stones. A row of sardius,² topaz, and carbuncle shall be the first row; ¹⁸and the second row an emerald, a sapphire, and a diamond; ¹⁹and the third row a jacinth, an agate, and an amethyst; ²⁰and the fourth row a beryl, an onyx, and a jasper. They shall be set in gold filigree. ²¹There shall be twelve stones with their names according to the names of the sons of Israel. They shall be like signets, each engraved with its name, for the twelve tribes. ²²You shall make for the breastpiece twisted chains like cords, of pure gold. ²³And you shall make for the breastpiece two rings of gold, and put the two rings on the two edges of the breastpiece. ²⁴And you shall put the two cords of gold in the two rings at the edges of the breastpiece. ²⁵The two ends of the two cords you shall attach to the two settings of filigree, and so attach it in front to the shoulder pieces of the ephod. ²⁶You shall make two rings of gold, and put them at the two ends of the breastpiece, on its inside edge next to the ephod. ²⁷And you shall make two rings of gold, and attach them in front to the lower part of the two shoulder pieces of the ephod, at its seam above the skillfully woven

band of the ephod. ²⁸And they shall bind the breastpiece by its rings to the rings of the ephod with a lace of blue, so that it may lie on the skillfully woven band of the ephod, so that the breastpiece shall not come loose from the ephod. ²⁹So Aaron shall bear the names of the sons of Israel in the breastpiece of judgment on his heart, when he goes into the Holy Place, to bring them to regular remembrance before the Lord. ³⁰And in the breastpiece of judgment you shall put the Urim and the Thummim, and they shall be on Aaron's heart, when he goes in before the Lord. Thus Aaron shall bear the judgment of the people of Israel on his heart before the Lord regularly.

³¹"You shall make the robe of the ephod all of blue. ³²It shall have an opening for the head in the middle of it, with a woven binding around the opening, like the opening in a garment,³ so that it may not tear. ³³On its hem you shall make pomegranates of blue and purple and scarlet yarns, around its hem, with bells of gold between them, ³⁴a golden bell and a pomegranate, a golden bell and a pomegranate, around the hem of the robe. ³⁵And it shall be on Aaron when he ministers, and its sound shall be heard when he goes into the Holy Place before the Lord, and when he comes out, so that he does not die.

³⁶"You shall make a plate of pure gold and engrave on it, like the engraving of a signet, 'Holy to the Lord.' ³⁷And you shall fasten it on the turban by a cord of blue. It shall be on the front of the turban. ³⁸It shall be on Aaron's forehead, and Aaron shall bear any guilt from the holy things that the people of Israel consecrate as their holy gifts. It shall regularly be on his forehead, that they may be accepted before the Lord.

³⁹"You shall weave the coat in checker work of fine linen, and you shall make a turban of fine linen, and you shall make a sash embroidered with needlework.

⁴⁰"For Aaron's sons you shall make coats and sashes and caps. You shall make them for glory and beauty. ⁴¹And you shall put them on Aaron your brother, and on his sons with him, and shall anoint them and ordain them and consecrate them, that they may serve me as priests. ⁴²You shall make for them linen undergarments to cover their naked flesh. They shall reach from the hips to the thighs; ⁴³and they

¹ A span was about 9 inches or 22 centimeters ² The identity of some of these stones is uncertain ³ The meaning of the Hebrew word is uncertain; possibly coat of mail

shall be on Aaron and on his sons when they go into the tent of meeting or when they come near the altar to minister in the Holy Place, lest they bear guilt and die. This shall be a statute forever for him and for his offspring after him.

John 7:1–52

After this Jesus went about in Galilee. He would not go about in Judea, because the Jews[1] were seeking to kill him. [2]Now the Jews' Feast of Booths was at hand. [3]So his brothers[2] said to him, "Leave here and go to Judea, that your disciples also may see the works you are doing. [4]For no one works in secret if he seeks to be known openly. If you do these things, show yourself to the world." [5]For not even his brothers believed in him. [6]Jesus said to them, "My time has not yet come, but your time is always here. [7]The world cannot hate you, but it hates me because I testify about it that its works are evil. [8]You go up to the feast. I am not[3] going up to this feast, for my time has not yet fully come." [9]After saying this, he remained in Galilee.

[10]But after his brothers had gone up to the feast, then he also went up, not publicly but in private. [11]The Jews were looking for him at the feast, and saying, "Where is he?" [12]And there was much muttering about him among the people. While some said, "He is a good man," others said, "No, he is leading the people astray." [13]Yet for fear of the Jews no one spoke openly of him.

[14]About the middle of the feast Jesus went up into the temple and began teaching. [15]The Jews therefore marveled, saying, "How is it that this man has learning,[4] when he has never studied?" [16]So Jesus answered them, "My teaching is not mine, but his who sent me. [17]If anyone's will is to do God's[5] will, he will know whether the teaching is from God or whether I am speaking on my own authority. [18]The one who speaks on his own authority seeks his own glory; but the one who seeks the glory of him who sent him is true, and in him there is no falsehood. [19]Has not Moses given you the law? Yet none of you keeps the law. Why do you seek to kill me?" [20]The crowd answered, "You have a demon! Who is seeking to kill you?" [21]Jesus answered them, "I did one work, and you all marvel at it. [22]Moses gave you circumcision (not that it

is from Moses, but from the fathers), and you circumcise a man on the Sabbath. [23]If on the Sabbath a man receives circumcision, so that the law of Moses may not be broken, are you angry with me because on the Sabbath I made a man's whole body well? [24]Do not judge by appearances, but judge with right judgment."

[25]Some of the people of Jerusalem therefore said, "Is not this the man whom they seek to kill? [26]And here he is, speaking openly, and they say nothing to him! Can it be that the authorities really know that this is the Christ? [27]But we know where this man comes from, and when the Christ appears, no one will know where he comes from." [28]So Jesus proclaimed, as he taught in the temple, "You know me, and you know where I come from. But I have not come of my own accord. He who sent me is true, and him you do not know. [29]I know him, for I come from him, and he sent me." [30]So they were seeking to arrest him, but no one laid a hand on him, because his hour had not yet come. [31]Yet many of the people believed in him. They said, "When the Christ appears, will he do more signs than this man has done?"

[32]The Pharisees heard the crowd muttering these things about him, and the chief priests and Pharisees sent officers to arrest him. [33]Jesus then said, "I will be with you a little longer, and then I am going to him who sent me. [34]You will seek me and you will not find me. Where I am you cannot come." [35]The Jews said to one another, "Where does this man intend to go that we will not find him? Does he intend to go to the Dispersion among the Greeks and teach the Greeks? [36]What does he mean by saying, 'You will seek me and you will not find me,' and, 'Where I am you cannot come'?"

[37]On the last day of the feast, the great day, Jesus stood up and cried out, "If anyone thirsts, let him come to me and drink. [38]Whoever believes in me, as[6] the Scripture has said, 'Out of his heart will flow rivers of living water.'" [39]Now this he said about the Spirit, whom those who believed in him were to receive, for as yet the Spirit had not been given, because Jesus was not yet glorified.

[40]When they heard these words, some of the people said, "This really is the Prophet." [41]Others said, "This is the Christ." But some said, "Is the Christ to come from Galilee? [42]Has not the Scripture said that the Christ comes

---

[1] Or Judeans; Greek Ioudaioi probably refers here to Jewish religious leaders, and others under their influence, in that time [2] Or brothers and sisters; also verses 5, 10 [3] Some manuscripts add yet [4] Or this man knows his letters [5] Greek his [6] Or let him come to me, and let him who believes in me drink. As

from the offspring of David, and comes from Bethlehem, the village where David was?" ⁴³So there was a division among the people over him. ⁴⁴Some of them wanted to arrest him, but no one laid hands on him.

⁴⁵The officers then came to the chief priests and Pharisees, who said to them, "Why did you not bring him?" ⁴⁶The officers answered, "No one ever spoke like this man!" ⁴⁷The Pharisees answered them, "Have you also been deceived? ⁴⁸Have any of the authorities or the Pharisees believed in him? ⁴⁹But this crowd that does not know the law is accursed." ⁵⁰Nicodemus, who had gone to him before, and who was one of them, said to them, ⁵¹"Does our law judge a man without first giving him a hearing and learning what he does?" ⁵²They replied, "Are you from Galilee too? Search and see that no prophet arises from Galilee."

Proverbs 4

Hear, O sons, a father's instruction,
  and be attentive, that you may gain[1]
    insight,
² for I give you good precepts;
    do not forsake my teaching.
³ When I was a son with my father,
    tender, the only one in the sight of my
      mother,
⁴ he taught me and said to me,
  "Let your heart hold fast my words;
    keep my commandments, and live.
⁵ Get wisdom; get insight;
    do not forget, and do not turn away
      from the words of my mouth.
⁶ Do not forsake her, and she will keep
      you;
    love her, and she will guard you.
⁷ The beginning of wisdom is this: Get
      wisdom,
    and whatever you get, get insight.
⁸ Prize her highly, and she will exalt you;
    she will honor you if you embrace her.
⁹ She will place on your head a graceful
      garland;
    she will bestow on you a beautiful
      crown."
¹⁰ Hear, my son, and accept my words,
    that the years of your life may be
      many.

¹¹ I have taught you the way of wisdom;
    I have led you in the paths of
      uprightness.
¹² When you walk, your step will not be
      hampered,
    and if you run, you will not stumble.
¹³ Keep hold of instruction; do not let go;
    guard her, for she is your life.
¹⁴ Do not enter the path of the wicked,
    and do not walk in the way of the evil.
¹⁵ Avoid it; do not go on it;
    turn away from it and pass on.
¹⁶ For they cannot sleep unless they have
      done wrong;
    they are robbed of sleep unless they
      have made someone stumble.
¹⁷ For they eat the bread of wickedness
    and drink the wine of violence.
¹⁸ But the path of the righteous is like the
      light of dawn,
    which shines brighter and brighter
      until full day.
¹⁹ The way of the wicked is like deep
      darkness;
    they do not know over what they
      stumble.

²⁰ My son, be attentive to my words;
    incline your ear to my sayings.
²¹ Let them not escape from your sight;
    keep them within your heart.
²² For they are life to those who find them,
    and healing to all their[2] flesh.
²³ Keep your heart with all vigilance,
    for from it flow the springs of life.
²⁴ Put away from you crooked speech,
    and put devious talk far from you.
²⁵ Let your eyes look directly forward,
    and your gaze be straight before you.
²⁶ Ponder[3] the path of your feet;
    then all your ways will be sure.
²⁷ Do not swerve to the right or to the left;
    turn your foot away from evil.

Galatians 3

O foolish Galatians! Who has bewitched you? It was before your eyes that Jesus Christ was publicly portrayed as crucified. ²Let me ask you only this: Did you receive the Spirit by works of the law or by hearing with faith? ³Are you so foolish? Having begun by the Spirit,

¹ Hebrew know ² Hebrew his ³ Or Make level

are you now being perfected by[1] the flesh? [4]Did you suffer[2] so many things in vain—if indeed it was in vain? [5]Does he who supplies the Spirit to you and works miracles among you do so by works of the law, or by hearing with faith— [6]just as Abraham "believed God, and it was counted to him as righteousness"?

[7]Know then that it is those of faith who are the sons of Abraham. [8]And the Scripture, foreseeing that God would justify[3] the Gentiles by faith, preached the gospel beforehand to Abraham, saying, "In you shall all the nations be blessed." [9]So then, those who are of faith are blessed along with Abraham, the man of faith.

[10]For all who rely on works of the law are under a curse; for it is written, "Cursed be everyone who does not abide by all things written in the Book of the Law, and do them." [11]Now it is evident that no one is justified before God by the law, for "The righteous shall live by faith."[4] [12]But the law is not of faith, rather "The one who does them shall live by them." [13]Christ redeemed us from the curse of the law by becoming a curse for us—for it is written, "Cursed is everyone who is hanged on a tree"— [14]so that in Christ Jesus the blessing of Abraham might come to the Gentiles, so that we might receive the promised Spirit[5] through faith.

[15]To give a human example, brothers:[6] even with a man-made covenant, no one annuls it or adds to it once it has been ratified. [16]Now the promises were made to Abraham and to his offspring. It does not say, "And to offsprings," referring to many, but referring to one, "And to your offspring," who is Christ. [17]This is what I mean: the law, which came 430 years afterward, does not annul a covenant previously ratified by God, so as to make the promise void. [18]For if the inheritance comes by the law, it no longer comes by promise; but God gave it to Abraham by a promise.

[19]Why then the law? It was added because of transgressions, until the offspring should come to whom the promise had been made, and it was put in place through angels by an intermediary. [20]Now an intermediary implies more than one, but God is one.

[21]Is the law then contrary to the promises of God? Certainly not! For if a law had been given that could give life, then righteousness would indeed be by the law. [22]But the Scripture imprisoned everything under sin, so that the promise by faith in Jesus Christ might be given to those who believe.

[23]Now before faith came, we were held captive under the law, imprisoned until the coming faith would be revealed. [24]So then, the law was our guardian until Christ came, in order that we might be justified by faith. [25]But now that faith has come, we are no longer under a guardian, [26]for in Christ Jesus you are all sons of God, through faith. [27]For as many of you as were baptized into Christ have put on Christ. [28]There is neither Jew nor Greek, there is neither slave[7] nor free, there is no male and female, for you are all one in Christ Jesus. [29]And if you are Christ's, then you are Abraham's offspring, heirs according to promise.

MARCH 18

Exodus 29

"Now this is what you shall do to them to consecrate them, that they may serve me as priests. Take one bull of the herd and two rams without blemish, [2]and unleavened bread, unleavened cakes mixed with oil, and unleavened wafers smeared with oil. You shall make them of fine wheat flour. [3]You shall put them in one basket and bring them in the basket, and bring the bull and the two rams. [4]You shall bring Aaron and his sons to the entrance of the tent of meeting and wash them with water. [5]Then you shall take the garments, and put on Aaron the coat and the robe of the ephod, and the ephod, and the breastpiece, and

[1] Or now ending with [2] Or experience [3] Or count righteous; also verses 11, 24 [4] Or The one who by faith is righteous will live [5] Greek receive the promise of the Spirit [6] Or brothers and sisters [7] Greek bondservant

gird him with the skillfully woven band of the ephod. ⁶And you shall set the turban on his head and put the holy crown on the turban. ⁷You shall take the anointing oil and pour it on his head and anoint him. ⁸Then you shall bring his sons and put coats on them, ⁹and you shall gird Aaron and his sons with sashes and bind caps on them. And the priesthood shall be theirs by a statute forever. Thus you shall ordain Aaron and his sons.

¹⁰"Then you shall bring the bull before the tent of meeting. Aaron and his sons shall lay their hands on the head of the bull. ¹¹Then you shall kill the bull before the Lord at the entrance of the tent of meeting, ¹²and shall take part of the blood of the bull and put it on the horns of the altar with your finger, and the rest of¹ the blood you shall pour out at the base of the altar. ¹³And you shall take all the fat that covers the entrails, and the long lobe of the liver, and the two kidneys with the fat that is on them, and burn them on the altar. ¹⁴But the flesh of the bull and its skin and its dung you shall burn with fire outside the camp; it is a sin offering.

¹⁵"Then you shall take one of the rams, and Aaron and his sons shall lay their hands on the head of the ram, ¹⁶and you shall kill the ram and shall take its blood and throw it against the sides of the altar. ¹⁷Then you shall cut the ram into pieces, and wash its entrails and its legs, and put them with its pieces and its head, ¹⁸and burn the whole ram on the altar. It is a burnt offering to the Lord. It is a pleasing aroma, a food offering² to the Lord.

¹⁹"You shall take the other ram, and Aaron and his sons shall lay their hands on the head of the ram, ²⁰and you shall kill the ram and take part of its blood and put it on the tip of the right ear of Aaron and on the tips of the right ears of his sons, and on the thumbs of their right hands and on the great toes of their right feet, and throw the rest of the blood against the sides of the altar. ²¹Then you shall take part of the blood that is on the altar, and of the anointing oil, and sprinkle it on Aaron and his garments, and on his sons and his sons' garments with him. He and his garments shall be holy, and his sons and his sons' garments with him.

²²"You shall also take the fat from the ram and the fat tail and the fat that covers the entrails, and the long lobe of the liver and the two kidneys with the fat that is on them, and the right thigh (for it is a ram of ordination), ²³and one loaf of bread and one cake of bread made with oil, and one wafer out of the basket of unleavened bread that is before the Lord. ²⁴You shall put all these on the palms of Aaron and on the palms of his sons, and wave them for a wave offering before the Lord. ²⁵Then you shall take them from their hands and burn them on the altar on top of the burnt offering, as a pleasing aroma before the Lord. It is a food offering to the Lord.

²⁶"You shall take the breast of the ram of Aaron's ordination and wave it for a wave offering before the Lord, and it shall be your portion. ²⁷And you shall consecrate the breast of the wave offering that is waved and the thigh of the priests' portion that is contributed from the ram of ordination, from what was Aaron's and his sons'. ²⁸It shall be for Aaron and his sons as a perpetual due from the people of Israel, for it is a contribution. It shall be a contribution from the people of Israel from their peace offerings, their contribution to the Lord.

²⁹"The holy garments of Aaron shall be for his sons after him; they shall be anointed in them and ordained in them. ³⁰The son who succeeds him as priest, who comes into the tent of meeting to minister in the Holy Place, shall wear them seven days.

³¹"You shall take the ram of ordination and boil its flesh in a holy place. ³²And Aaron and his sons shall eat the flesh of the ram and the bread that is in the basket in the entrance of the tent of meeting. ³³They shall eat those things with which atonement was made at their ordination and consecration, but an outsider shall not eat of them, because they are holy. ³⁴And if any of the flesh for the ordination or of the bread remain until the morning, then you shall burn the remainder with fire. It shall not be eaten, because it is holy.

³⁵"Thus you shall do to Aaron and to his sons, according to all that I have commanded you. Through seven days shall you ordain them, ³⁶and every day you shall offer a bull as a sin offering for atonement. Also you shall purify the altar, when you make atonement for it, and shall anoint it to consecrate it. ³⁷Seven days you shall make atonement for the altar and consecrate it, and the altar shall be most holy. Whatever touches the altar shall become holy.

¹ Hebrew *all* ² Or *an offering by fire*; also verses 25, 41

³⁸"Now this is what you shall offer on the altar: two lambs a year old day by day regularly. ³⁹One lamb you shall offer in the morning, and the other lamb you shall offer at twilight. ⁴⁰And with the first lamb a tenth measure[1] of fine flour mingled with a fourth of a hin[2] of beaten oil, and a fourth of a hin of wine for a drink offering. ⁴¹The other lamb you shall offer at twilight, and shall offer with it a grain offering and its drink offering, as in the morning, for a pleasing aroma, a food offering to the LORD. ⁴²It shall be a regular burnt offering throughout your generations at the entrance of the tent of meeting before the LORD, where I will meet with you, to speak to you there. ⁴³There I will meet with the people of Israel, and it shall be sanctified by my glory. ⁴⁴I will consecrate the tent of meeting and the altar. Aaron also and his sons I will consecrate to serve me as priests. ⁴⁵I will dwell among the people of Israel and will be their God. ⁴⁶And they shall know that I am the LORD their God, who brought them out of the land of Egypt that I might dwell among them. I am the LORD their God.

John 7:53–8:59

[THE EARLIEST MANUSCRIPTS DO NOT INCLUDE 7:53–8:11.][3]

[[They went each to his own house, ⁸:¹but Jesus went to the Mount of Olives. ²Early in the morning he came again to the temple. All the people came to him, and he sat down and taught them. ³The scribes and the Pharisees brought a woman who had been caught in adultery, and placing her in the midst ⁴they said to him, "Teacher, this woman has been caught in the act of adultery. ⁵Now in the Law Moses commanded us to stone such women. So what do you say?" ⁶This they said to test him, that they might have some charge to bring against him. Jesus bent down and wrote with his finger on the ground. ⁷And as they continued to ask him, he stood up and said to them, "Let him who is without sin among you be the first to throw a stone at her." ⁸And once more he bent down and wrote on the ground. ⁹But when they heard it, they went away one by one, beginning with the older ones, and Jesus was left alone with the woman standing before him. ¹⁰Jesus stood up and said to her, "Woman, where are they? Has no one condemned you?" ¹¹She said, "No one, Lord." And Jesus said, "Neither do I condemn you; go, and from now on sin no more."]]

¹²Again Jesus spoke to them, saying, "I am the light of the world. Whoever follows me will not walk in darkness, but will have the light of life." ¹³So the Pharisees said to him, "You are bearing witness about yourself; your testimony is not true." ¹⁴Jesus answered, "Even if I do bear witness about myself, my testimony is true, for I know where I came from and where I am going, but you do not know where I come from or where I am going. ¹⁵You judge according to the flesh; I judge no one. ¹⁶Yet even if I do judge, my judgment is true, for it is not I alone who judge, but I and the Father[4] who sent me. ¹⁷In your Law it is written that the testimony of two people is true. ¹⁸I am the one who bears witness about myself, and the Father who sent me bears witness about me." ¹⁹They said to him therefore, "Where is your Father?" Jesus answered, "You know neither me nor my Father. If you knew me, you would know my Father also." ²⁰These words he spoke in the treasury, as he taught in the temple; but no one arrested him, because his hour had not yet come.

²¹So he said to them again, "I am going away, and you will seek me, and you will die in your sin. Where I am going, you cannot come." ²²So the Jews said, "Will he kill himself, since he says, 'Where I am going, you cannot come'?" ²³He said to them, "You are from below; I am from above. You are of this world; I am not of this world. ²⁴I told you that you would die in your sins, for unless you believe that I am he you will die in your sins." ²⁵So they said to him, "Who are you?" Jesus said to them, "Just what I have been telling you from the beginning. ²⁶I have much to say about you and much to judge, but he who sent me is true, and I declare to the world what I have heard from him." ²⁷They did not understand that he had been speaking to them about the Father. ²⁸So Jesus said to them, "When you have lifted up the Son of Man, then you will know that I am he, and that I do nothing on my own authority, but speak just as the Father taught me. ²⁹And he who sent me is with me. He has not left me alone, for I always do the things that are pleasing to him." ³⁰As he was saying these things, many believed in him.

---

[1] Possibly an ephah (about 3/5 bushel or 22 liters) [2] A *hin* was about 4 quarts or 3.5 liters [3] Some manuscripts do not include 7:53–8:11; others add the passage here or after 7:36 or after 21:25 or after Luke 21:38, with variations in the text [4] Some manuscripts *he*

[31] So Jesus said to the Jews who had believed him, "If you abide in my word, you are truly my disciples, [32] and you will know the truth, and the truth will set you free." [33] They answered him, "We are offspring of Abraham and have never been enslaved to anyone. How is it that you say, 'You will become free'?"

[34] Jesus answered them, "Truly, truly, I say to you, everyone who practices sin is a slave[1] to sin. [35] The slave does not remain in the house forever; the son remains forever. [36] So if the Son sets you free, you will be free indeed. [37] I know that you are offspring of Abraham; yet you seek to kill me because my word finds no place in you. [38] I speak of what I have seen with my Father, and you do what you have heard from your father."

[39] They answered him, "Abraham is our father." Jesus said to them, "If you were Abraham's children, you would be doing the works Abraham did, [40] but now you seek to kill me, a man who has told you the truth that I heard from God. This is not what Abraham did. [41] You are doing the works your father did." They said to him, "We were not born of sexual immorality. We have one Father—even God." [42] Jesus said to them, "If God were your Father, you would love me, for I came from God and I am here. I came not of my own accord, but he sent me. [43] Why do you not understand what I say? It is because you cannot bear to hear my word. [44] You are of your father the devil, and your will is to do your father's desires. He was a murderer from the beginning, and does not stand in the truth, because there is no truth in him. When he lies, he speaks out of his own character, for he is a liar and the father of lies. [45] But because I tell the truth, you do not believe me. [46] Which one of you convicts me of sin? If I tell the truth, why do you not believe me? [47] Whoever is of God hears the words of God. The reason why you do not hear them is that you are not of God."

[48] The Jews answered him, "Are we not right in saying that you are a Samaritan and have a demon?" [49] Jesus answered, "I do not have a demon, but I honor my Father, and you dishonor me. [50] Yet I do not seek my own glory; there is One who seeks it, and he is the judge. [51] Truly, truly, I say to you, if anyone keeps my word, he will never see death." [52] The Jews said to him, "Now we know that you have a demon!

Abraham died, as did the prophets, yet you say, 'If anyone keeps my word, he will never taste death.' [53] Are you greater than our father Abraham, who died? And the prophets died! Who do you make yourself out to be?" [54] Jesus answered, "If I glorify myself, my glory is nothing. It is my Father who glorifies me, of whom you say, 'He is our God.'[2] [55] But you have not known him. I know him. If I were to say that I do not know him, I would be a liar like you, but I do know him and I keep his word. [56] Your father Abraham rejoiced that he would see my day. He saw it and was glad." [57] So the Jews said to him, "You are not yet fifty years old, and have you seen Abraham?"[3] [58] Jesus said to them, "Truly, truly, I say to you, before Abraham was, I am." [59] So they picked up stones to throw at him, but Jesus hid himself and went out of the temple.

--------- *Proverbs 5* ---------

My son, be attentive to my wisdom;
  incline your ear to my understanding,
[2]   that you may keep discretion,
      and your lips may guard knowledge.
[3]   For the lips of a forbidden[4] woman drip
        honey,
      and her speech[5] is smoother than oil,
[4]   but in the end she is bitter as
        wormwood,
      sharp as a two-edged sword.
[5]   Her feet go down to death;
      her steps follow the path to[6] Sheol;
[6]   she does not ponder the path of life;
      her ways wander, and she does not
        know it.

[7]   And now, O sons, listen to me,
      and do not depart from the words of
        my mouth.
[8]   Keep your way far from her,
      and do not go near the door of her
        house,
[9]   lest you give your honor to others
      and your years to the merciless,
[10] lest strangers take their fill of your
        strength,
      and your labors go to the house of a
        foreigner,
[11] and at the end of your life you groan,
      when your flesh and body are
        consumed,

---

[1] Greek *bondservant; also verse 35* [2] Some manuscripts *your God* [3] Some manuscripts *has Abraham seen you?* [4] Hebrew *strange; also verse 20* [5] Hebrew *palate* [6] Hebrew *lay hold of*

12   and you say, "How I hated discipline,
          and my heart despised reproof!
13   I did not listen to the voice of my
             teachers
          or incline my ear to my instructors.
14   I am at the brink of utter ruin
          in the assembled congregation."

15   Drink water from your own cistern,
          flowing water from your own well.
16   Should your springs be scattered abroad,
          streams of water in the streets?
17   Let them be for yourself alone,
          and not for strangers with you.
18   Let your fountain be blessed,
          and rejoice in the wife of your youth,
19   a lovely deer, a graceful doe.
      Let her breasts fill you at all times with
             delight;
          be intoxicated[1] always in her love.
20   Why should you be intoxicated, my son,
             with a forbidden woman
          and embrace the bosom of an
             adulteress?[2]
21   For a man's ways are before the eyes of
             the LORD,
          and he ponders[3] all his paths.
22   The iniquities of the wicked ensnare him,
          and he is held fast in the cords of his
             sin.
23   He dies for lack of discipline,
          and because of his great folly he is led
             astray.

――――――― *Galatians 4* ―――――――

I mean that the heir, as long as he is a child, is
no different from a slave,[4] though he is the
owner of everything, [2]but he is under guardians and managers until the date set by his
father. [3]In the same way we also, when we were
children, were enslaved to the elementary principles[5] of the world. [4]But when the fullness of
time had come, God sent forth his Son, born of
woman, born under the law, [5]to redeem those
who were under the law, so that we might
receive adoption as sons. [6]And because you are
sons, God has sent the Spirit of his Son into our
hearts, crying, "Abba! Father!" [7]So you are no
longer a slave, but a son, and if a son, then an
heir through God.
   [8]Formerly, when you did not know God, you

were enslaved to those that by nature are not
gods. [9]But now that you have come to know
God, or rather to be known by God, how can
you turn back again to the weak and worthless elementary principles of the world, whose
slaves you want to be once more? [10]You observe
days and months and seasons and years! [11]I am
afraid I may have labored over you in vain.
   [12]Brothers,[6] I entreat you, become as I am,
for I also have become as you are. You did me
no wrong. [13]You know it was because of a
bodily ailment that I preached the gospel to you
at first, [14]and though my condition was a trial
to you, you did not scorn or despise me, but
received me as an angel of God, as Christ Jesus.
[15]What then has become of your blessedness?
For I testify to you that, if possible, you would
have gouged out your eyes and given them to
me. [16]Have I then become your enemy by telling you the truth?[7] [17]They make much of you,
but for no good purpose. They want to shut
you out, that you may make much of them.
[18]It is always good to be made much of for a
good purpose, and not only when I am present
with you, [19]my little children, for whom I am
again in the anguish of childbirth until Christ
is formed in you! [20]I wish I could be present
with you now and change my tone, for I am
perplexed about you.
   [21]Tell me, you who desire to be under the
law, do you not listen to the law? [22]For it is
written that Abraham had two sons, one by a
slave woman and one by a free woman. [23]But
the son of the slave was born according to the
flesh, while the son of the free woman was
born through promise. [24]Now this may be
interpreted allegorically: these women are two
covenants. One is from Mount Sinai, bearing
children for slavery; she is Hagar. [25]Now Hagar
is Mount Sinai in Arabia;[8] she corresponds to
the present Jerusalem, for she is in slavery with
her children. [26]But the Jerusalem above is free,
and she is our mother. [27]For it is written,

    "Rejoice, O barren one who does not bear;
          break forth and cry aloud, you who
             are not in labor!
      For the children of the desolate one will
             be more
          than those of the one who has a
             husband."

[28]Now you,[9] brothers, like Isaac, are children

[1] Hebrew *be led astray;* also verse 20 [2] Hebrew *a foreign woman* [3] Or *makes level* [4] Greek *bondservant;* also verse 7 [5] Or *elemental spirits;* also verse 9 [6] Or *Brothers and sisters;* also
verses 28, 31 [7] Or *by dealing truthfully with you* [8] Some manuscripts *For Sinai is a mountain in Arabia* [9] Some manuscripts *we*

of promise. **29**But just as at that time he who was born according to the flesh persecuted him who was born according to the Spirit, so also it is now. **30**But what does the Scripture say? "Cast out the slave woman and her son, for the son of the slave woman shall not inherit with the son of the free woman." **31**So, brothers, we are not children of the slave but of the free woman.

MARCH 19

Exodus 30

"**Y**ou shall make an altar on which to burn incense; you shall make it of acacia wood. **2**A cubit[1] shall be its length, and a cubit its breadth. It shall be square, and two cubits shall be its height. Its horns shall be of one piece with it. **3**You shall overlay it with pure gold, its top and around its sides and its horns. And you shall make a molding of gold around it. **4**And you shall make two golden rings for it. Under its molding on two opposite sides of it you shall make them, and they shall be holders for poles with which to carry it. **5**You shall make the poles of acacia wood and overlay them with gold. **6**And you shall put it in front of the veil that is above the ark of the testimony, in front of the mercy seat that is above the testimony, where I will meet with you. **7**And Aaron shall burn fragrant incense on it. Every morning when he dresses the lamps he shall burn it, **8**and when Aaron sets up the lamps at twilight, he shall burn it, a regular incense offering before the LORD throughout your generations. **9**You shall not offer unauthorized incense on it, or a burnt offering, or a grain offering, and you shall not pour a drink offering on it. **10**Aaron shall make atonement on its horns once a year. With the blood of the sin offering of atonement he shall make atonement for it once in the year throughout your generations. It is most holy to the LORD."

11The LORD said to Moses, **12**"When you take the census of the people of Israel, then each shall give a ransom for his life to the LORD when you number them, that there be no plague among them when you number them. **13**Each one who is numbered in the census shall give this: half a shekel[2] according to the shekel of the sanctuary (the shekel is twenty gerahs),[3] half a shekel as an offering to the LORD. **14**Everyone who is numbered in the census, from twenty years old and upward, shall give the LORD's offering. **15**The rich shall not give more, and the poor shall not give less, than the half shekel, when you give the LORD's offering to make atonement for your lives. **16**You shall take the atonement money from the people of Israel and shall give it for the service of the tent of meeting, that it may bring the people of Israel to remembrance before the LORD, so as to make atonement for your lives."

17The LORD said to Moses, **18**"You shall also make a basin of bronze, with its stand of bronze, for washing. You shall put it between the tent of meeting and the altar, and you shall put water in it, **19**with which Aaron and his sons shall wash their hands and their feet. **20**When they go into the tent of meeting, or when they come near the altar to minister, to burn a food offering[4] to the LORD, they shall wash with water, so that they may not die. **21**They shall wash their hands and their feet, so that they may not die. It shall be a statute forever to them, even to him and to his offspring throughout their generations."

22The LORD said to Moses, **23**"Take the finest spices: of liquid myrrh 500 shekels, and of sweet-smelling cinnamon half as much, that is, 250, and 250 of aromatic cane, **24**and 500 of cassia, according to the shekel of the sanctuary, and a hin[5] of olive oil. **25**And you shall make of these a sacred anointing oil blended as by the perfumer; it shall be a holy anointing oil. **26**With it you shall anoint the tent of meeting and the ark of the testimony, **27**and the table and all its utensils, and the lampstand and its

---

[1] A *cubit* was about 18 inches or 45 centimeters [2] A *shekel* was about 2/5 ounce or 11 grams [3] A *gerah* was about 1/50 ounce or 0.6 gram [4] Or *an offering by fire* [5] A *hin* was about 4 quarts or 3.5 liters

utensils, and the altar of incense, ²⁸ and the altar of burnt offering with all its utensils and the basin and its stand. ²⁹ You shall consecrate them, that they may be most holy. Whatever touches them will become holy. ³⁰ You shall anoint Aaron and his sons, and consecrate them, that they may serve me as priests. ³¹ And you shall say to the people of Israel, 'This shall be my holy anointing oil throughout your generations. ³² It shall not be poured on the body of an ordinary person, and you shall make no other like it in composition. It is holy, and it shall be holy to you. ³³ Whoever compounds any like it or whoever puts any of it on an outsider shall be cut off from his people.'"

³⁴ The LORD said to Moses, "Take sweet spices, stacte, and onycha, and galbanum, sweet spices with pure frankincense (of each shall there be an equal part), ³⁵ and make an incense blended as by the perfumer, seasoned with salt, pure and holy. ³⁶ You shall beat some of it very small, and put part of it before the testimony in the tent of meeting where I shall meet with you. It shall be most holy for you. ³⁷ And the incense that you shall make according to its composition, you shall not make for yourselves. It shall be for you holy to the LORD. ³⁸ Whoever makes any like it to use as perfume shall be cut off from his people."

John 9

As he passed by, he saw a man blind from birth. ² And his disciples asked him, "Rabbi, who sinned, this man or his parents, that he was born blind?" ³ Jesus answered, "It was not that this man sinned, or his parents, but that the works of God might be displayed in him. ⁴ We must work the works of him who sent me while it is day; night is coming, when no one can work. ⁵ As long as I am in the world, I am the light of the world." ⁶ Having said these things, he spit on the ground and made mud with the saliva. Then he anointed the man's eyes with the mud ⁷ and said to him, "Go, wash in the pool of Siloam" (which means Sent). So he went and washed and came back seeing.

⁸ The neighbors and those who had seen him before as a beggar were saying, "Is this not the man who used to sit and beg?" ⁹ Some said, "It is he." Others said, "No, but he is like him." He kept saying, "I am the man." ¹⁰ So they said to him, "Then how were your eyes opened?" ¹¹ He answered, "The man called Jesus made mud and anointed my eyes and said to me, 'Go to Siloam and wash.' So I went and washed and received my sight." ¹² They said to him, "Where is he?" He said, "I do not know."

¹³ They brought to the Pharisees the man who had formerly been blind. ¹⁴ Now it was a Sabbath day when Jesus made the mud and opened his eyes. ¹⁵ So the Pharisees again asked him how he had received his sight. And he said to them, "He put mud on my eyes, and I washed, and I see." ¹⁶ Some of the Pharisees said, "This man is not from God, for he does not keep the Sabbath." But others said, "How can a man who is a sinner do such signs?" And there was a division among them. ¹⁷ So they said again to the blind man, "What do you say about him, since he has opened your eyes?" He said, "He is a prophet."

¹⁸ The Jews[1] did not believe that he had been blind and had received his sight, until they called the parents of the man who had received his sight ¹⁹ and asked them, "Is this your son, who you say was born blind? How then does he now see?" ²⁰ His parents answered, "We know that this is our son and that he was born blind. ²¹ But how he now sees we do not know, nor do we know who opened his eyes. Ask him; he is of age. He will speak for himself." ²² (His parents said these things because they feared the Jews, for the Jews had already agreed that if anyone should confess Jesus[2] to be Christ, he was to be put out of the synagogue.) ²³ Therefore his parents said, "He is of age; ask him."

²⁴ So for the second time they called the man who had been blind and said to him, "Give glory to God. We know that this man is a sinner." ²⁵ He answered, "Whether he is a sinner I do not know. One thing I do know, that though I was blind, now I see." ²⁶ They said to him, "What did he do to you? How did he open your eyes?" ²⁷ He answered them, "I have told you already, and you would not listen. Why do you want to hear it again? Do you also want to become his disciples?" ²⁸ And they reviled him, saying, "You are his disciple, but we are disciples of Moses. ²⁹ We know that God has spoken to Moses, but as for this man, we do not know where he comes from." ³⁰ The man answered, "Why, this is an amazing thing! You do not know where he comes from, and yet he opened my eyes. ³¹ We

¹ Greek *Ioudaioi* probably refers here to Jewish religious leaders, and others under their influence, in that time; also verse 22 ² Greek *him*

know that God does not listen to sinners, but if anyone is a worshiper of God and does his will, God listens to him. [32]Never since the world began has it been heard that anyone opened the eyes of a man born blind. [33]If this man were not from God, he could do nothing." [34]They answered him, "You were born in utter sin, and would you teach us?" And they cast him out.

[35]Jesus heard that they had cast him out, and having found him he said, "Do you believe in the Son of Man?"[1] [36]He answered, "And who is he, sir, that I may believe in him?" [37]Jesus said to him, "You have seen him, and it is he who is speaking to you." [38]He said, "Lord, I believe," and he worshiped him. [39]Jesus said, "For judgment I came into this world, that those who do not see may see, and those who see may become blind." [40]Some of the Pharisees near him heard these things, and said to him, "Are we also blind?" [41]Jesus said to them, "If you were blind, you would have no guilt;[2] but now that you say, 'We see,' your guilt remains.

Proverbs 6

M y son, if you have put up security for your neighbor,
　　have given your pledge for a stranger,
[2]　if you are snared in the words of your mouth,
　　caught in the words of your mouth,
[3]　then do this, my son, and save yourself,
　　for you have come into the hand of your neighbor:
　　go, hasten,[3] and plead urgently with your neighbor.
[4]　Give your eyes no sleep
　　and your eyelids no slumber;
[5]　save yourself like a gazelle from the hand of the hunter,[4]
　　like a bird from the hand of the fowler.

[6]　Go to the ant, O sluggard;
　　consider her ways, and be wise.
[7]　Without having any chief,
　　officer, or ruler,
[8]　she prepares her bread in summer
　　and gathers her food in harvest.
[9]　How long will you lie there, O sluggard?
　　When will you arise from your sleep?
[10]　A little sleep, a little slumber,
　　a little folding of the hands to rest,
[11]　and poverty will come upon you like a robber,
　　and want like an armed man.

[12]　A worthless person, a wicked man,
　　goes about with crooked speech,
[13]　winks with his eyes, signals[5] with his feet,
　　points with his finger,
[14]　with perverted heart devises evil,
　　continually sowing discord;
[15]　therefore calamity will come upon him suddenly;
　　in a moment he will be broken beyond healing.

[16]　There are six things that the LORD hates,
　　seven that are an abomination to him:
[17]　haughty eyes, a lying tongue,
　　and hands that shed innocent blood,
[18]　a heart that devises wicked plans,
　　feet that make haste to run to evil,
[19]　a false witness who breathes out lies,
　　and one who sows discord among brothers.

[20]　My son, keep your father's commandment,
　　and forsake not your mother's teaching.
[21]　Bind them on your heart always;
　　tie them around your neck.
[22]　When you walk, they[6] will lead you;
　　when you lie down, they will watch over you;
　　and when you awake, they will talk with you.
[23]　For the commandment is a lamp and the teaching a light,
　　and the reproofs of discipline are the way of life,
[24]　to preserve you from the evil woman,[7]
　　from the smooth tongue of the adulteress.[8]
[25]　Do not desire her beauty in your heart,
　　and do not let her capture you with her eyelashes;

[1] Some manuscripts the Son of God [2] Greek you would not have sin [3] Or humble yourself [4] Hebrew lacks of the hunter [5] Hebrew scrapes [6] Hebrew it; three times in this verse [7] Revocalization (compare Septuagint) yields from the wife of a neighbor [8] Hebrew the foreign woman

26 for the price of a prostitute is only a loaf of bread,[1]
    but a married woman[2] hunts down a precious life.
27 Can a man carry fire next to his chest
    and his clothes not be burned?
28 Or can one walk on hot coals
    and his feet not be scorched?
29 So is he who goes in to his neighbor's wife;
    none who touches her will go unpunished.
30 People do not despise a thief if he steals
    to satisfy his appetite when he is hungry,
31 but if he is caught, he will pay sevenfold;
    he will give all the goods of his house.
32 He who commits adultery lacks sense;
    he who does it destroys himself.
33 He will get wounds and dishonor,
    and his disgrace will not be wiped away.
34 For jealousy makes a man furious,
    and he will not spare when he takes revenge.
35 He will accept no compensation;
    he will refuse though you multiply gifts.

Galatians 5

For freedom Christ has set us free; stand firm therefore, and do not submit again to a yoke of slavery.

[2] Look: I, Paul, say to you that if you accept circumcision, Christ will be of no advantage to you. [3] I testify again to every man who accepts circumcision that he is obligated to keep the whole law. [4] You are severed from Christ, you who would be justified[3] by the law; you have fallen away from grace. [5] For through the Spirit, by faith, we ourselves eagerly wait for the hope of righteousness. [6] For in Christ Jesus neither circumcision nor uncircumcision counts for anything, but only faith working through love.

[7] You were running well. Who hindered you from obeying the truth? [8] This persuasion is not from him who calls you. [9] A little leaven leavens the whole lump. [10] I have confidence in the Lord that you will take no other view, and the one who is troubling you will bear the penalty, whoever he is. [11] But if I, brothers,[4] still preach[5] circumcision, why am I still being persecuted? In that case the offense of the cross has been removed. [12] I wish those who unsettle you would emasculate themselves!

[13] For you were called to freedom, brothers. Only do not use your freedom as an opportunity for the flesh, but through love serve one another. [14] For the whole law is fulfilled in one word: "You shall love your neighbor as yourself." [15] But if you bite and devour one another, watch out that you are not consumed by one another.

[16] But I say, walk by the Spirit, and you will not gratify the desires of the flesh. [17] For the desires of the flesh are against the Spirit, and the desires of the Spirit are against the flesh, for these are opposed to each other, to keep you from doing the things you want to do. [18] But if you are led by the Spirit, you are not under the law. [19] Now the works of the flesh are evident: sexual immorality, impurity, sensuality, [20] idolatry, sorcery, enmity, strife, jealousy, fits of anger, rivalries, dissensions, divisions, [21] envy,[6] drunkenness, orgies, and things like these. I warn you, as I warned you before, that those who do such things will not inherit the kingdom of God. [22] But the fruit of the Spirit is love, joy, peace, patience, kindness, goodness, faithfulness, [23] gentleness, self-control; against such things there is no law. [24] And those who belong to Christ Jesus have crucified the flesh with its passions and desires.

[25] If we live by the Spirit, let us also keep in step with the Spirit. [26] Let us not become conceited, provoking one another, envying one another.

MARCH 20

Exodus 31

The Lord said to Moses, [2] "See, I have called by name Bezalel the son of Uri, son of Hur, of the tribe of Judah, [3] and I have filled him with the Spirit of God, with ability and intelligence, with knowledge and all craftsmanship, [4] to devise artistic designs, to work in gold, silver, and bronze, [5] in cutting stones for setting, and in carving wood, to work in every craft. [6] And behold, I have appointed with him Oholiab, the son of Ahisamach, of the tribe of Dan. And I have given to all able men ability, that they may make all that I have commanded you: [7] the tent of meeting, and the ark of the testimony, and the mercy seat that is on it, and all the furnishings of the tent, [8] the table and its utensils, and the pure lampstand with all its utensils, and the altar of incense, [9] and the altar of burnt offering with all its utensils, and the basin and its stand, [10] and the finely worked garments,[1] the holy garments for Aaron the priest and the garments of his sons, for their service as priests, [11] and the anointing oil and the fragrant incense for the Holy Place. According to all that I have commanded you, they shall do."

[12] And the Lord said to Moses, [13] "You are to speak to the people of Israel and say, 'Above all you shall keep my Sabbaths, for this is a sign between me and you throughout your generations, that you may know that I, the Lord, sanctify you. [14] You shall keep the Sabbath, because it is holy for you. Everyone who profanes it shall be put to death. Whoever does any work on it, that soul shall be cut off from among his people. [15] Six days shall work be done, but the seventh day is a Sabbath of solemn rest, holy to the Lord. Whoever does any work on the Sabbath day shall be put to death. [16] Therefore the people of Israel shall keep the Sabbath, observing the Sabbath throughout their generations, as a covenant forever. [17] It is a sign forever between me and the people of Israel that in six days the Lord made heaven and earth, and on the seventh day he rested and was refreshed.'"

[18] And he gave to Moses, when he had finished speaking with him on Mount Sinai, the two tablets of the testimony, tablets of stone, written with the finger of God.

John 10

"Truly, truly, I say to you, he who does not enter the sheepfold by the door but climbs in by another way, that man is a thief and a robber. [2] But he who enters by the door is the shepherd of the sheep. [3] To him the gatekeeper opens. The sheep hear his voice, and he calls his own sheep by name and leads them out. [4] When he has brought out all his own, he goes before them, and the sheep follow him, for they know his voice. [5] A stranger they will not follow, but they will flee from him, for they do not know the voice of strangers." [6] This figure of speech Jesus used with them, but they did not understand what he was saying to them.

[7] So Jesus again said to them, "Truly, truly, I say to you, I am the door of the sheep. [8] All who came before me are thieves and robbers, but the sheep did not listen to them. [9] I am the door. If anyone enters by me, he will be saved and will go in and out and find pasture. [10] The thief comes only to steal and kill and destroy. I came that they may have life and have it abundantly. [11] I am the good shepherd. The good shepherd lays down his life for the sheep. [12] He who is a hired hand and not a shepherd, who does not own the sheep, sees the wolf coming and leaves the sheep and flees, and the wolf snatches them and scatters them. [13] He flees because he is a hired hand and cares nothing for the sheep. [14] I am the good shepherd. I know my own and my own know me, [15] just as the Father knows me and I know the Father; and I lay down my life for the sheep. [16] And I have other sheep that are not of this fold. I must bring them also, and they will listen to my voice. So there will be one flock, one shepherd. [17] For this reason the Father loves me, because I lay down my life that I may take it up again. [18] No one takes it from

---

[1] Or garments for worship

me, but I lay it down of my own accord. I have authority to lay it down, and I have authority to take it up again. This charge I have received from my Father."

¹⁹There was again a division among the Jews because of these words. ²⁰Many of them said, "He has a demon, and is insane; why listen to him?" ²¹Others said, "These are not the words of one who is oppressed by a demon. Can a demon open the eyes of the blind?"

²²At that time the Feast of Dedication took place at Jerusalem. It was winter, ²³and Jesus was walking in the temple, in the colonnade of Solomon. ²⁴So the Jews gathered around him and said to him, "How long will you keep us in suspense? If you are the Christ, tell us plainly." ²⁵Jesus answered them, "I told you, and you do not believe. The works that I do in my Father's name bear witness about me, ²⁶but you do not believe because you are not among my sheep. ²⁷My sheep hear my voice, and I know them, and they follow me. ²⁸I give them eternal life, and they will never perish, and no one will snatch them out of my hand. ²⁹My Father, who has given them to me,¹ is greater than all, and no one is able to snatch them out of the Father's hand. ³⁰I and the Father are one."

³¹The Jews picked up stones again to stone him. ³²Jesus answered them, "I have shown you many good works from the Father; for which of them are you going to stone me?" ³³The Jews answered him, "It is not for a good work that we are going to stone you but for blasphemy, because you, being a man, make yourself God." ³⁴Jesus answered them, "Is it not written in your Law, 'I said, you are gods'? ³⁵If he called them gods to whom the word of God came—and Scripture cannot be broken— ³⁶do you say of him whom the Father consecrated and sent into the world, 'You are blaspheming,' because I said, 'I am the Son of God'? ³⁷If I am not doing the works of my Father, then do not believe me; ³⁸but if I do them, even though you do not believe me, believe the works, that you may know and understand that the Father is in me and I am in the Father." ³⁹Again they sought to arrest him, but he escaped from their hands.

⁴⁰He went away again across the Jordan to the place where John had been baptizing at first, and there he remained. ⁴¹And many came to him. And they said, "John did no sign, but everything that John said about this man was true." ⁴²And many believed in him there.

——— *Proverbs 7* ———

My son, keep my words
  and treasure up my commandments
    with you;
2 keep my commandments and live;
    keep my teaching as the apple of your
      eye;
3 bind them on your fingers;
    write them on the tablet of your heart.
4 Say to wisdom, "You are my sister,"
    and call insight your intimate friend,
5 to keep you from the forbidden² woman,
    from the adulteress³ with her smooth
      words.

6 For at the window of my house
    I have looked out through my lattice,
7 and I have seen among the simple,
    I have perceived among the youths,
    a young man lacking sense,
8 passing along the street near her corner,
    taking the road to her house
9 in the twilight, in the evening,
    at the time of night and darkness.

10 And behold, the woman meets him,
    dressed as a prostitute, wily of heart.⁴
11 She is loud and wayward;
    her feet do not stay at home;
12 now in the street, now in the market,
    and at every corner she lies in wait.
13 She seizes him and kisses him,
    and with bold face she says to him,
14 "I had to offer sacrifices,⁵
    and today I have paid my vows;
15 so now I have come out to meet you,
    to seek you eagerly, and I have found
      you.
16 I have spread my couch with coverings,
    colored linens from Egyptian linen;
17 I have perfumed my bed with myrrh,
    aloes, and cinnamon.
18 Come, let us take our fill of love till
      morning;
    let us delight ourselves with love.
19 For my husband is not at home;
    he has gone on a long journey;
20 he took a bag of money with him;
    at full moon he will come home."

¹ Some manuscripts *What my Father has given to me* ² Hebrew *strange* ³ Hebrew *the foreign woman* ⁴ Hebrew *guarded in heart* ⁵ Hebrew *peace offerings*

²¹ With much seductive speech she
    persuades him;
    with her smooth talk she compels
    him.
²² All at once he follows her,
    as an ox goes to the slaughter,
    or as a stag is caught fast[1]
²³   till an arrow pierces its liver;
    as a bird rushes into a snare;
    he does not know that it will cost him
    his life.

²⁴ And now, O sons, listen to me,
    and be attentive to the words of my
    mouth.
²⁵ Let not your heart turn aside to her
    ways;
    do not stray into her paths,
²⁶ for many a victim has she laid low,
    and all her slain are a mighty throng.
²⁷ Her house is the way to Sheol,
    going down to the chambers of death.

Galatians 6

Brothers,[2] if anyone is caught in any transgression, you who are spiritual should restore him in a spirit of gentleness. Keep watch on yourself, lest you too be tempted. ²Bear one another's burdens, and so fulfill the law of Christ. ³For if anyone thinks he is something, when he is nothing, he deceives himself. ⁴But let each one test his own work, and then his reason to boast will be in himself alone and not in his neighbor. ⁵For each will have to bear his own load.

⁶Let the one who is taught the word share all good things with the one who teaches. ⁷Do not be deceived: God is not mocked, for whatever one sows, that he will also reap. ⁸For the one who sows to his own flesh will from the flesh reap corruption, but the one who sows to the Spirit will from the Spirit reap eternal life. ⁹And let us not grow weary of doing good, for in due season we will reap, if we do not give up. ¹⁰So then, as we have opportunity, let us do good to everyone, and especially to those who are of the household of faith.

¹¹See with what large letters I am writing to you with my own hand. ¹²It is those who want to make a good showing in the flesh who would force you to be circumcised, and only in order that they may not be persecuted for the cross of Christ. ¹³For even those who are circumcised do not themselves keep the law, but they desire to have you circumcised that they may boast in your flesh. ¹⁴But far be it from me to boast except in the cross of our Lord Jesus Christ, by which[3] the world has been crucified to me, and I to the world. ¹⁵For neither circumcision counts for anything, nor uncircumcision, but a new creation. ¹⁶And as for all who walk by this rule, peace and mercy be upon them, and upon the Israel of God.

¹⁷From now on let no one cause me trouble, for I bear on my body the marks of Jesus.

¹⁸The grace of our Lord Jesus Christ be with your spirit, brothers. Amen.

MARCH 21

Exodus 32

When the people saw that Moses delayed to come down from the mountain, the people gathered themselves together to Aaron and said to him, "Up, make us gods who shall go before us. As for this Moses, the man who brought us up out of the land of Egypt, we do not know what has become of him." ²So Aaron said to them, "Take off the rings of gold that are in the ears of your wives, your sons, and your daughters, and bring them to me." ³So all the people took off the rings of gold that were in their ears and brought them to Aaron. ⁴And he received the gold from their hand and fashioned it with a graving tool and made

[1] Probable reading (compare Septuagint, Vulgate, Syriac); Hebrew *as an anklet for the discipline of a fool* [2] Or *Brothers and sisters*; also verse 18 [3] Or *through whom*

a golden[1] calf. And they said, "These are your gods, O Israel, who brought you up out of the land of Egypt!" [5]When Aaron saw this, he built an altar before it. And Aaron made a proclamation and said, "Tomorrow shall be a feast to the Lord." [6]And they rose up early the next day and offered burnt offerings and brought peace offerings. And the people sat down to eat and drink and rose up to play.

[7]And the Lord said to Moses, "Go down, for your people, whom you brought up out of the land of Egypt, have corrupted themselves. [8]They have turned aside quickly out of the way that I commanded them. They have made for themselves a golden calf and have worshiped it and sacrificed to it and said, 'These are your gods, O Israel, who brought you up out of the land of Egypt!' [9]And the Lord said to Moses, "I have seen this people, and behold, it is a stiff-necked people. [10]Now therefore let me alone, that my wrath may burn hot against them and I may consume them, in order that I may make a great nation of you."

[11]But Moses implored the Lord his God and said, "O Lord, why does your wrath burn hot against your people, whom you have brought out of the land of Egypt with great power and with a mighty hand? [12]Why should the Egyptians say, 'With evil intent did he bring them out, to kill them in the mountains and to consume them from the face of the earth'? Turn from your burning anger and relent from this disaster against your people. [13]Remember Abraham, Isaac, and Israel, your servants, to whom you swore by your own self, and said to them, 'I will multiply your offspring as the stars of heaven, and all this land that I have promised I will give to your offspring, and they shall inherit it forever.'" [14]And the Lord relented from the disaster that he had spoken of bringing on his people.

[15]Then Moses turned and went down from the mountain with the two tablets of the testimony in his hand, tablets that were written on both sides; on the front and on the back they were written. [16]The tablets were the work of God, and the writing was the writing of God, engraved on the tablets. [17]When Joshua heard the noise of the people as they shouted, he said to Moses, "There is a noise of war in the camp." [18]But he said, "It is not the sound of shouting for victory, or the sound of the cry of defeat,

but the sound of singing that I hear." [19]And as soon as he came near the camp and saw the calf and the dancing, Moses' anger burned hot, and he threw the tablets out of his hands and broke them at the foot of the mountain. [20]He took the calf that they had made and burned it with fire and ground it to powder and scattered it on the water and made the people of Israel drink it.

[21]And Moses said to Aaron, "What did this people do to you that you have brought such a great sin upon them?" [22]And Aaron said, "Let not the anger of my lord burn hot. You know the people, that they are set on evil. [23]For they said to me, 'Make us gods who shall go before us. As for this Moses, the man who brought us up out of the land of Egypt, we do not know what has become of him.' [24]So I said to them, 'Let any who have gold take it off.' So they gave it to me, and I threw it into the fire, and out came this calf."

[25]And when Moses saw that the people had broken loose (for Aaron had let them break loose, to the derision of their enemies), [26]then Moses stood in the gate of the camp and said, "Who is on the Lord's side? Come to me." And all the sons of Levi gathered around him. [27]And he said to them, "Thus says the Lord God of Israel, 'Put your sword on your side each of you, and go to and fro from gate to gate throughout the camp, and each of you kill his brother and his companion and his neighbor.'" [28]And the sons of Levi did according to the word of Moses. And that day about three thousand men of the people fell. [29]And Moses said, "Today you have been ordained for the service of the Lord, each one at the cost of his son and of his brother, so that he might bestow a blessing upon you this day."

[30]The next day Moses said to the people, "You have sinned a great sin. And now I will go up to the Lord; perhaps I can make atonement for your sin." [31]So Moses returned to the Lord and said, "Alas, this people has sinned a great sin. They have made for themselves gods of gold. [32]But now, if you will forgive their sin—but if not, please blot me out of your book that you have written." [33]But the Lord said to Moses, "Whoever has sinned against me, I will blot out of my book. [34]But now go, lead the people to the place about which I have spoken to you; behold, my angel shall go before you.

[1] Hebrew cast metal; also verse 8

Nevertheless, in the day when I visit, I will visit their sin upon them."

³⁵ Then the LORD sent a plague on the people, because they made the calf, the one that Aaron made.

--------- *John 11* ---------

N ow a certain man was ill, Lazarus of Bethany, the village of Mary and her sister Martha. ² It was Mary who anointed the Lord with ointment and wiped his feet with her hair, whose brother Lazarus was ill. ³ So the sisters sent to him, saying, "Lord, he whom you love is ill." ⁴ But when Jesus heard it he said, "This illness does not lead to death. It is for the glory of God, so that the Son of God may be glorified through it."

⁵ Now Jesus loved Martha and her sister and Lazarus. ⁶ So, when he heard that Lazarus[1] was ill, he stayed two days longer in the place where he was. ⁷ Then after this he said to the disciples, "Let us go to Judea again." ⁸ The disciples said to him, "Rabbi, the Jews were just now seeking to stone you, and are you going there again?" ⁹ Jesus answered, "Are there not twelve hours in the day? If anyone walks in the day, he does not stumble, because he sees the light of this world. ¹⁰ But if anyone walks in the night, he stumbles, because the light is not in him." ¹¹ After saying these things, he said to them, "Our friend Lazarus has fallen asleep, but I go to awaken him." ¹² The disciples said to him, "Lord, if he has fallen asleep, he will recover." ¹³ Now Jesus had spoken of his death, but they thought that he meant taking rest in sleep. ¹⁴ Then Jesus told them plainly, "Lazarus has died, ¹⁵ and for your sake I am glad that I was not there, so that you may believe. But let us go to him." ¹⁶ So Thomas, called the Twin,[2] said to his fellow disciples, "Let us also go, that we may die with him."

¹⁷ Now when Jesus came, he found that Lazarus had already been in the tomb four days. ¹⁸ Bethany was near Jerusalem, about two miles[3] off, ¹⁹ and many of the Jews had come to Martha and Mary to console them concerning their brother. ²⁰ So when Martha heard that Jesus was coming, she went and met him, but Mary remained seated in the house. ²¹ Martha said to Jesus, "Lord, if you had been here, my brother would not have died. ²² But even now

I know that whatever you ask from God, God will give you." ²³ Jesus said to her, "Your brother will rise again." ²⁴ Martha said to him, "I know that he will rise again in the resurrection on the last day." ²⁵ Jesus said to her, "I am the resurrection and the life.[4] Whoever believes in me, though he die, yet shall he live, ²⁶ and everyone who lives and believes in me shall never die. Do you believe this?" ²⁷ She said to him, "Yes, Lord; I believe that you are the Christ, the Son of God, who is coming into the world."

²⁸ When she had said this, she went and called her sister Mary, saying in private, "The Teacher is here and is calling for you." ²⁹ And when she heard it, she rose quickly and went to him. ³⁰ Now Jesus had not yet come into the village, but was still in the place where Martha had met him. ³¹ When the Jews who were with her in the house, consoling her, saw Mary rise quickly and go out, they followed her, supposing that she was going to the tomb to weep there. ³² Now when Mary came to where Jesus was and saw him, she fell at his feet, saying to him, "Lord, if you had been here, my brother would not have died." ³³ When Jesus saw her weeping, and the Jews who had come with her also weeping, he was deeply moved[5] in his spirit and greatly troubled. ³⁴ And he said, "Where have you laid him?" They said to him, "Lord, come and see." ³⁵ Jesus wept. ³⁶ So the Jews said, "See how he loved him!" ³⁷ But some of them said, "Could not he who opened the eyes of the blind man also have kept this man from dying?"

³⁸ Then Jesus, deeply moved again, came to the tomb. It was a cave, and a stone lay against it. ³⁹ Jesus said, "Take away the stone." Martha, the sister of the dead man, said to him, "Lord, by this time there will be an odor, for he has been dead four days." ⁴⁰ Jesus said to her, "Did I not tell you that if you believed you would see the glory of God?" ⁴¹ So they took away the stone. And Jesus lifted up his eyes and said, "Father, I thank you that you have heard me. ⁴² I knew that you always hear me, but I said this on account of the people standing around, that they may believe that you sent me." ⁴³ When he had said these things, he cried out with a loud voice, "Lazarus, come out." ⁴⁴ The man who had died came out, his hands and feet bound with linen strips, and his face wrapped with a cloth. Jesus said to them, "Unbind him, and let him go."

[1] Greek *he*; also verse 17 [2] Greek *Didymus* [3] Greek *fifteen stadia*; a *stadion* was about 607 feet or 185 meters [4] Some manuscripts omit *and the life* [5] Or *was indignant*; also verse 38

45 Many of the Jews therefore, who had come with Mary and had seen what he did, believed in him, 46 but some of them went to the Pharisees and told them what Jesus had done. 47 So the chief priests and the Pharisees gathered the council and said, "What are we to do? For this man performs many signs. 48 If we let him go on like this, everyone will believe in him, and the Romans will come and take away both our place and our nation." 49 But one of them, Caiaphas, who was high priest that year, said to them, "You know nothing at all. 50 Nor do you understand that it is better for you that one man should die for the people, not that the whole nation should perish." 51 He did not say this of his own accord, but being high priest that year he prophesied that Jesus would die for the nation, 52 and not for the nation only, but also to gather into one the children of God who are scattered abroad. 53 So from that day on they made plans to put him to death.

54 Jesus therefore no longer walked openly among the Jews, but went from there to the region near the wilderness, to a town called Ephraim, and there he stayed with the disciples.

55 Now the Passover of the Jews was at hand, and many went up from the country to Jerusalem before the Passover to purify themselves. 56 They were looking for[1] Jesus and saying to one another as they stood in the temple, "What do you think? That he will not come to the feast at all?" 57 Now the chief priests and the Pharisees had given orders that if anyone knew where he was, he should let them know, so that they might arrest him.

Proverbs 8

Does not wisdom call?
Does not understanding raise her voice?
2 On the heights beside the way,
    at the crossroads she takes her stand;
3   beside the gates in front of the town,
    at the entrance of the portals she cries aloud:
4 "To you, O men, I call,
    and my cry is to the children of man.
5 O simple ones, learn prudence;
    O fools, learn sense.
6 Hear, for I will speak noble things,
    and from my lips will come what is right,

7 for my mouth will utter truth;
    wickedness is an abomination to my lips.
8 All the words of my mouth are righteous;
    there is nothing twisted or crooked in them.
9 They are all straight to him who understands,
    and right to those who find knowledge.
10 Take my instruction instead of silver,
    and knowledge rather than choice gold,
11 for wisdom is better than jewels,
    and all that you may desire cannot compare with her.

12 "I, wisdom, dwell with prudence,
    and I find knowledge and discretion.
13 The fear of the LORD is hatred of evil.
    Pride and arrogance and the way of evil
    and perverted speech I hate.
14 I have counsel and sound wisdom;
    I have insight; I have strength.
15 By me kings reign,
    and rulers decree what is just;
16 by me princes rule,
    and nobles, all who govern justly.[2]
17 I love those who love me,
    and those who seek me diligently find me.
18 Riches and honor are with me,
    enduring wealth and righteousness.
19 My fruit is better than gold, even fine gold,
    and my yield than choice silver.
20 I walk in the way of righteousness,
    in the paths of justice,
21 granting an inheritance to those who love me,
    and filling their treasuries.

22 "The LORD possessed[3] me at the beginning of his work,[4]
    the first of his acts of old.
23 Ages ago I was set up,
    at the first, before the beginning of the earth.
24 When there were no depths I was brought forth,
    when there were no springs abounding with water.

[1] Greek were seeking for [2] Most Hebrew manuscripts; many Hebrew manuscripts, Septuagint govern the earth [3] Or fathered; Septuagint created [4] Hebrew way

²⁵ Before the mountains had been shaped,
　　before the hills, I was brought forth,
²⁶ before he had made the earth with its
　　　fields,
　　or the first of the dust of the world.
²⁷ When he established the heavens, I was
　　　there;
　　when he drew a circle on the face of
　　　the deep,
²⁸ when he made firm the skies above,
　　when he established[1] the fountains of
　　　the deep,
²⁹ when he assigned to the sea its limit,
　　so that the waters might not
　　　transgress his command,
　　when he marked out the foundations of
　　　the earth,
³⁰ then I was beside him, like a master
　　　workman,
　　and I was daily his[2] delight,
　　rejoicing before him always,
³¹ rejoicing in his inhabited world
　　and delighting in the children of man.

³² "And now, O sons, listen to me:
　　blessed are those who keep my ways.
³³ Hear instruction and be wise,
　　and do not neglect it.
³⁴ Blessed is the one who listens to me,
　　watching daily at my gates,
　　waiting beside my doors.
³⁵ For whoever finds me finds life
　　and obtains favor from the LORD,
³⁶ but he who fails to find me injures
　　　himself;
　　all who hate me love death."

Ephesians 1

Paul, an apostle of Christ Jesus by the will of God,

To the saints who are in Ephesus, and are faithful[3] in Christ Jesus:

²Grace to you and peace from God our Father and the Lord Jesus Christ.

³Blessed be the God and Father of our Lord Jesus Christ, who has blessed us in Christ with every spiritual blessing in the heavenly places, ⁴even as he chose us in him before the foundation of the world, that we should be holy and blameless before him. In love ⁵he predestined us[4] for adoption as sons through Jesus Christ, according to the purpose of his will, ⁶to the praise of his glorious grace, with which he has blessed us in the Beloved. ⁷In him we have redemption through his blood, the forgiveness of our trespasses, according to the riches of his grace, ⁸which he lavished upon us, in all wisdom and insight ⁹making known[5] to us the mystery of his will, according to his purpose, which he set forth in Christ ¹⁰as a plan for the fullness of time, to unite all things in him, things in heaven and things on earth.

¹¹In him we have obtained an inheritance, having been predestined according to the purpose of him who works all things according to the counsel of his will, ¹²so that we who were the first to hope in Christ might be to the praise of his glory. ¹³In him you also, when you heard the word of truth, the gospel of your salvation, and believed in him, were sealed with the promised Holy Spirit, ¹⁴who is the guarantee[6] of our inheritance until we acquire possession of it,[7] to the praise of his glory.

¹⁵For this reason, because I have heard of your faith in the Lord Jesus and your love[8] toward all the saints, ¹⁶I do not cease to give thanks for you, remembering you in my prayers, ¹⁷that the God of our Lord Jesus Christ, the Father of glory, may give you the Spirit of wisdom and of revelation in the knowledge of him, ¹⁸having the eyes of your hearts enlightened, that you may know what is the hope to which he has called you, what are the riches of his glorious inheritance in the saints, ¹⁹and what is the immeasurable greatness of his power toward us who believe, according to the working of his great might ²⁰that he worked in Christ when he raised him from the dead and seated him at his right hand in the heavenly places, ²¹far above all rule and authority and power and dominion, and above every name that is named, not only in this age but also in the one to come. ²²And he put all things under his feet and gave him as head over all things to the church, ²³which is his body, the fullness of him who fills all in all.

---

[1] The meaning of the Hebrew is uncertain　[2] Or daily filled with　[3] Some manuscripts saints who are also faithful (omitting in Ephesus)　[4] Or before him in love, having predestined us　[5] Or he lavished upon us in all wisdom and insight, making known. . .　[6] Or down payment　[7] Or until God redeems his possession　[8] Some manuscripts omit your love

MARCH 22

Exodus 33

The LORD said to Moses, "Depart; go up from here, you and the people whom you have brought up out of the land of Egypt, to the land of which I swore to Abraham, Isaac, and Jacob, saying, 'To your offspring I will give it.' ²I will send an angel before you, and I will drive out the Canaanites, the Amorites, the Hittites, the Perizzites, the Hivites, and the Jebusites. ³Go up to a land flowing with milk and honey; but I will not go up among you, lest I consume you on the way, for you are a stiff-necked people."

⁴When the people heard this disastrous word, they mourned, and no one put on his ornaments. ⁵For the LORD had said to Moses, "Say to the people of Israel, 'You are a stiff-necked people; if for a single moment I should go up among you, I would consume you. So now take off your ornaments, that I may know what to do with you.'" ⁶Therefore the people of Israel stripped themselves of their ornaments, from Mount Horeb onward.

⁷Now Moses used to take the tent and pitch it outside the camp, far off from the camp, and he called it the tent of meeting. And everyone who sought the LORD would go out to the tent of meeting, which was outside the camp. ⁸Whenever Moses went out to the tent, all the people would rise up, and each would stand at his tent door, and watch Moses until he had gone into the tent. ⁹When Moses entered the tent, the pillar of cloud would descend and stand at the entrance of the tent, and the LORD¹ would speak with Moses. ¹⁰And when all the people saw the pillar of cloud standing at the entrance of the tent, all the people would rise up and worship, each at his tent door. ¹¹Thus the LORD used to speak to Moses face to face, as a man speaks to his friend. When Moses turned again into the camp, his assistant Joshua the son of Nun, a young man, would not depart from the tent.

¹²Moses said to the LORD, "See, you say to me, 'Bring up this people,' but you have not let me know whom you will send with me. Yet you have said, 'I know you by name, and you have also found favor in my sight.' ¹³Now therefore, if I have found favor in your sight, please show me now your ways, that I may know you in order to find favor in your sight. Consider too that this nation is your people." ¹⁴And he said, "My presence will go with you, and I will give you rest." ¹⁵And he said to him, "If your presence will not go with me, do not bring us up from here. ¹⁶For how shall it be known that I have found favor in your sight, I and your people? Is it not in your going with us, so that we are distinct, I and your people, from every other people on the face of the earth?"

¹⁷And the LORD said to Moses, "This very thing that you have spoken I will do, for you have found favor in my sight, and I know you by name." ¹⁸Moses said, "Please show me your glory." ¹⁹And he said, "I will make all my goodness pass before you and will proclaim before you my name 'The LORD.' And I will be gracious to whom I will be gracious, and will show mercy on whom I will show mercy. ²⁰But," he said, "you cannot see my face, for man shall not see me and live." ²¹And the LORD said, "Behold, there is a place by me where you shall stand on the rock, ²²and while my glory passes by I will put you in a cleft of the rock, and I will cover you with my hand until I have passed by. ²³Then I will take away my hand, and you shall see my back, but my face shall not be seen."

John 12

Six days before the Passover, Jesus therefore came to Bethany, where Lazarus was, whom Jesus had raised from the dead. ²So they gave a dinner for him there. Martha served, and Lazarus was one of those reclining with him at table. ³Mary therefore took a pound² of expensive ointment made from pure nard, and anointed the feet of Jesus and wiped his feet with her hair. The house was filled with the fragrance of the perfume. ⁴But Judas Iscariot,

¹ Hebrew *he* ² Greek *litra*; a *litra* (or Roman pound) was equal to about 11 1/2 ounces or 327 grams

one of his disciples (he who was about to betray him), said, **5** "Why was this ointment not sold for three hundred denarii[1] and given to the poor?" **6** He said this, not because he cared about the poor, but because he was a thief, and having charge of the moneybag he used to help himself to what was put into it. **7** Jesus said, "Leave her alone, so that she may keep it[2] for the day of my burial. **8** For the poor you always have with you, but you do not always have me."

9 When the large crowd of the Jews learned that Jesus[3] was there, they came, not only on account of him but also to see Lazarus, whom he had raised from the dead. **10** So the chief priests made plans to put Lazarus to death as well, **11** because on account of him many of the Jews were going away and believing in Jesus.

12 The next day the large crowd that had come to the feast heard that Jesus was coming to Jerusalem. **13** So they took branches of palm trees and went out to meet him, crying out, "Hosanna! Blessed is he who comes in the name of the Lord, even the King of Israel!" **14** And Jesus found a young donkey and sat on it, just as it is written,

15   "Fear not, daughter of Zion;
          behold, your king is coming,
              sitting on a donkey's colt!"

16 His disciples did not understand these things at first, but when Jesus was glorified, then they remembered that these things had been written about him and had been done to him. **17** The crowd that had been with him when he called Lazarus out of the tomb and raised him from the dead continued to bear witness. **18** The reason why the crowd went to meet him was that they heard he had done this sign. **19** So the Pharisees said to one another, "You see that you are gaining nothing. Look, the world has gone after him."

20 Now among those who went up to worship at the feast were some Greeks. **21** So these came to Philip, who was from Bethsaida in Galilee, and asked him, "Sir, we wish to see Jesus." **22** Philip went and told Andrew; Andrew and Philip went and told Jesus. **23** And Jesus answered them, "The hour has come for the Son of Man to be glorified. **24** Truly, truly, I say to you, unless a grain of wheat falls into the earth and dies, it remains alone; but if it dies, it bears much fruit. **25** Whoever loves his life loses it, and whoever hates his life in this world will keep it for eternal life. **26** If anyone serves me, he must follow me; and where I am, there will my servant be also. If anyone serves me, the Father will honor him.

27 "Now is my soul troubled. And what shall I say? 'Father, save me from this hour'? But for this purpose I have come to this hour. **28** Father, glorify your name." Then a voice came from heaven: "I have glorified it, and I will glorify it again." **29** The crowd that stood there and heard it said that it had thundered. Others said, "An angel has spoken to him." **30** Jesus answered, "This voice has come for your sake, not mine. **31** Now is the judgment of this world; now will the ruler of this world be cast out. **32** And I, when I am lifted up from the earth, will draw all people to myself." **33** He said this to show by what kind of death he was going to die. **34** So the crowd answered him, "We have heard from the Law that the Christ remains forever. How can you say that the Son of Man must be lifted up? Who is this Son of Man?" **35** So Jesus said to them, "The light is among you for a little while longer. Walk while you have the light, lest darkness overtake you. The one who walks in the darkness does not know where he is going. **36** While you have the light, believe in the light, that you may become sons of light."

When Jesus had said these things, he departed and hid himself from them. **37** Though he had done so many signs before them, they still did not believe in him, **38** so that the word spoken by the prophet Isaiah might be fulfilled:

"Lord, who has believed what he heard
      from us,
    and to whom has the arm of the Lord
        been revealed?"

39 Therefore they could not believe. For again Isaiah said,

40   "He has blinded their eyes
          and hardened their heart,
        lest they see with their eyes,
          and understand with their heart, and
            turn,
          and I would heal them."

41 Isaiah said these things because he saw his glory and spoke of him. **42** Nevertheless, many even of the authorities believed in him, but for fear of the Pharisees they did not confess it,

---

[1] A *denarius* was a day's wage for a laborer [2] Or *Leave her alone; she intended to keep it* [3] Greek *he*

so that they would not be put out of the synagogue; [43] for they loved the glory that comes from man more than the glory that comes from God.

[44] And Jesus cried out and said, "Whoever believes in me, believes not in me but in him who sent me. [45] And whoever sees me sees him who sent me. [46] I have come into the world as light, so that whoever believes in me may not remain in darkness. [47] If anyone hears my words and does not keep them, I do not judge him; for I did not come to judge the world but to save the world. [48] The one who rejects me and does not receive my words has a judge; the word that I have spoken will judge him on the last day. [49] For I have not spoken on my own authority, but the Father who sent me has himself given me a commandment— what to say and what to speak. [50] And I know that his commandment is eternal life. What I say, therefore, I say as the Father has told me."

Proverbs 9

Wisdom has built her house;
    she has hewn her seven pillars.
[2] She has slaughtered her beasts; she has
        mixed her wine;
    she has also set her table.
[3] She has sent out her young women to
        call
    from the highest places in the town,
[4] "Whoever is simple, let him turn in
        here!"
    To him who lacks sense she says,
[5] "Come, eat of my bread
    and drink of the wine I have mixed.
[6] Leave your simple ways,[1] and live,
    and walk in the way of insight."

[7] Whoever corrects a scoffer gets himself
        abuse,
    and he who reproves a wicked man
        incurs injury.
[8] Do not reprove a scoffer, or he will hate
        you;
    reprove a wise man, and he will love
        you.
[9] Give instruction[2] to a wise man, and he
        will be still wiser;
    teach a righteous man, and he will
        increase in learning.

[10] The fear of the LORD is the beginning of
        wisdom,
    and the knowledge of the Holy One is
        insight.
[11] For by me your days will be multiplied,
    and years will be added to your life.
[12] If you are wise, you are wise for yourself;
    if you scoff, you alone will bear it.

[13] The woman Folly is loud;
    she is seductive[3] and knows nothing.
[14] She sits at the door of her house;
    she takes a seat on the highest places
        of the town,
[15] calling to those who pass by,
    who are going straight on their way,
[16] "Whoever is simple, let him turn in here!"
    And to him who lacks sense she says,
[17] "Stolen water is sweet,
    and bread eaten in secret is pleasant."
[18] But he does not know that the dead[4] are
        there,
    that her guests are in the depths of
        Sheol.

Ephesians 2

And you were dead in the trespasses and sins [2] in which you once walked, following the course of this world, following the prince of the power of the air, the spirit that is now at work in the sons of disobedience— [3] among whom we all once lived in the passions of our flesh, carrying out the desires of the body[5] and the mind, and were by nature children of wrath, like the rest of mankind. [4] But[7] God, being rich in mercy, because of the great love with which he loved us, [5] even when we were dead in our trespasses, made us alive together with Christ—by grace you have been saved— [6] and raised us up with him and seated us with him in the heavenly places in Christ Jesus, [7] so that in the coming ages he might show the immeasurable riches of his grace in kindness toward us in Christ Jesus. [8] For by grace you have been saved through faith. And this is not your own doing; it is the gift of God, [9] not a result of works, so that no one may boast. [10] For we are his workmanship, created in Christ Jesus for good works, which God prepared beforehand, that we should walk in them. [11] Therefore remember that at one time you

[1] Or Leave the company of the simple   [2] Hebrew lacks instruction   [3] Or full of simpleness   [4] Hebrew Rephaim   [5] Greek flesh   [6] Greek like the rest   [7] Or And

Gentiles in the flesh, called "the uncircumcision" by what is called the circumcision, which is made in the flesh by hands— [12] remember that you were at that time separated from Christ, alienated from the commonwealth of Israel and strangers to the covenants of promise, having no hope and without God in the world. [13] But now in Christ Jesus you who once were far off have been brought near by the blood of Christ. [14] For he himself is our peace, who has made us both one and has broken down in his flesh the dividing wall of hostility [15] by abolishing the law of commandments expressed in ordinances, that he might create in himself one new man in place of the two, so making peace, [16] and might reconcile us both to God in one body through the cross, thereby killing the hostility. [17] And he came and preached peace to you who were far off and peace to those who were near. [18] For through him we both have access in one Spirit to the Father. [19] So then you are no longer strangers and aliens,[1] but you are fellow citizens with the saints and members of the household of God, [20] built on the foundation of the apostles and prophets, Christ Jesus himself being the cornerstone, [21] in whom the whole structure, being joined together, grows into a holy temple in the Lord. [22] In him you also are being built together into a dwelling place for God by[2] the Spirit.

MARCH 23

Exodus 34

The LORD said to Moses, "Cut for yourself two tablets of stone like the first, and I will write on the tablets the words that were on the first tablets, which you broke. [2] Be ready by the morning, and come up in the morning to Mount Sinai, and present yourself there to me on the top of the mountain. [3] No one shall come up with you, and let no one be seen throughout all the mountain. Let no flocks or herds graze opposite that mountain." [4] So Moses cut two tablets of stone like the first. And he rose early in the morning and went up on Mount Sinai, as the LORD had commanded him, and took in his hand two tablets of stone. [5] The LORD descended in the cloud and stood with him there, and proclaimed the name of the LORD. [6] The LORD passed before him and proclaimed, "The LORD, the LORD, a God merciful and gracious, slow to anger, and abounding in steadfast love and faithfulness, [7] keeping steadfast love for thousands,[3] forgiving iniquity and transgression and sin, but who will by no means clear the guilty, visiting the iniquity of the fathers on the children and the children's children, to the third and the fourth generation." [8] And Moses quickly bowed his head toward the earth and worshiped. [9] And he said, "If now I have found favor in your sight, O Lord, please let the Lord go in the midst of us, for it is a stiff-necked people, and pardon our iniquity and our sin, and take us for your inheritance." [10] And he said, "Behold, I am making a covenant. Before all your people I will do marvels, such as have not been created in all the earth or in any nation. And all the people among whom you are shall see the work of the LORD, for it is an awesome thing that I will do with you. [11] "Observe what I command you this day. Behold, I will drive out before you the Amorites, the Canaanites, the Hittites, the Perizzites, the Hivites, and the Jebusites. [12] Take care, lest you make a covenant with the inhabitants of the land to which you go, lest it become a snare in your midst. [13] You shall tear down their altars and break their pillars and cut down their Asherim [14] (for you shall worship no other god, for the LORD, whose name is Jealous, is a jealous God), [15] lest you make a covenant with the inhabitants of the land, and when they whore after their gods and sacrifice to their gods and you are invited, you eat of his sacrifice, [16] and you take of their daughters for your sons,

[1] Or sojourners [2] Or in [3] Or to the thousandth generation

and their daughters whore after their gods and make your sons whore after their gods. [17] "You shall not make for yourself any gods of cast metal.

[18] "You shall keep the Feast of Unleavened Bread. Seven days you shall eat unleavened bread, as I commanded you, at the time appointed in the month Abib, for in the month Abib you came out from Egypt. [19] All that open the womb are mine, all your male[1] livestock, the firstborn of cow and sheep. [20] The firstborn of a donkey you shall redeem with a lamb, or if you will not redeem it you shall break its neck. All the firstborn of your sons you shall redeem. And none shall appear before me empty-handed.

[21] "Six days you shall work, but on the seventh day you shall rest. In plowing time and in harvest you shall rest. [22] You shall observe the Feast of Weeks, the firstfruits of wheat harvest, and the Feast of Ingathering at the year's end. [23] Three times in the year shall all your males appear before the LORD God, the God of Israel. [24] For I will cast out nations before you and enlarge your borders; no one shall covet your land, when you go up to appear before the LORD your God three times in the year.

[25] "You shall not offer the blood of my sacrifice with anything leavened, or let the sacrifice of the Feast of the Passover remain until the morning. [26] The best of the firstfruits of your ground you shall bring to the house of the LORD your God. You shall not boil a young goat in its mother's milk."

[27] And the LORD said to Moses, "Write these words, for in accordance with these words I have made a covenant with you and with Israel." [28] So he was there with the LORD forty days and forty nights. He neither ate bread nor drank water. And he wrote on the tablets the words of the covenant, the Ten Commandments.[2]

[29] When Moses came down from Mount Sinai, with the two tablets of the testimony in his hand as he came down from the mountain, Moses did not know that the skin of his face shone because he had been talking with God.[3] [30] Aaron and all the people of Israel saw Moses, and behold, the skin of his face shone, and they were afraid to come near him. [31] But Moses called to them, and Aaron and all the leaders of the congregation returned to him, and Moses talked with them. [32] Afterward all the people of Israel came near, and he commanded them all

that the LORD had spoken with him in Mount Sinai. [33] And when Moses had finished speaking with them, he put a veil over his face. [34] Whenever Moses went in before the LORD to speak with him, he would remove the veil, until he came out. And when he came out and told the people of Israel what he was commanded, [35] the people of Israel would see the face of Moses, that the skin of Moses' face was shining. And Moses would put the veil over his face again, until he went in to speak with him.

John 13

Now before the Feast of the Passover, when Jesus knew that his hour had come to depart out of this world to the Father, having loved his own who were in the world, he loved them to the end. [2] During supper, when the devil had already put it into the heart of Judas Iscariot, Simon's son, to betray him, [3] Jesus, knowing that the Father had given all things into his hands, and that he had come from God and was going back to God, [4] rose from supper. He laid aside his outer garments, and taking a towel, tied it around his waist. [5] Then he poured water into a basin and began to wash the disciples' feet and to wipe them with the towel that was wrapped around him. [6] He came to Simon Peter, who said to him, "Lord, do you wash my feet?" [7] Jesus answered him, "What I am doing you do not understand now, but afterward you will understand." [8] Peter said to him, "You shall never wash my feet." Jesus answered him, "If I do not wash you, you have no share with me." [9] Simon Peter said to him, "Lord, not my feet only but also my hands and my head!" [10] Jesus said to him, "The one who has bathed does not need to wash, except for his feet,[4] but is completely clean. And you[5] are clean, but not every one of you." [11] For he knew who was to betray him; that was why he said, "Not all of you are clean."

[12] When he had washed their feet and put on his outer garments and resumed his place, he said to them, "Do you understand what I have done to you? [13] You call me Teacher and Lord, and you are right, for so I am. [14] If I then, your Lord and Teacher, have washed your feet, you also ought to wash one another's feet. [15] For I have given you an example, that you also should do just as I have done to you. [16] Truly,

---

[1] Septuagint, Theodotion, Vulgate, Targum; the meaning of the Hebrew is uncertain   [2] Hebrew *the ten words*   [3] Hebrew *him*   [4] Some manuscripts omit *except for his feet*   [5] The Greek words for *you* in this verse are plural

truly, I say to you, a servant[1] is not greater than his master, nor is a messenger greater than the one who sent him. [17]If you know these things, blessed are you if you do them. [18]I am not speaking of all of you; I know whom I have chosen. But the Scripture will be fulfilled,[2] 'He who ate my bread has lifted his heel against me.' [19]I am telling you this now, before it takes place, that when it does take place you may believe that I am he. [20]Truly, truly, I say to you, whoever receives the one I send receives me, and whoever receives me receives the one who sent me."

[21]After saying these things, Jesus was troubled in his spirit, and testified, "Truly, truly, I say to you, one of you will betray me." [22]The disciples looked at one another, uncertain of whom he spoke. [23]One of his disciples, whom Jesus loved, was reclining at table at Jesus' side,[3] [24]so Simon Peter motioned to him to ask Jesus[4] of whom he was speaking. [25]So that disciple, leaning back against Jesus, said to him, "Lord, who is it?" [26]Jesus answered, "It is he to whom I will give this morsel of bread when I have dipped it." So when he had dipped the morsel, he gave it to Judas, the son of Simon Iscariot. [27]Then after he had taken the morsel, Satan entered into him. Jesus said to him, "What you are going to do, do quickly." [28]Now no one at the table knew why he said this to him. [29]Some thought that, because Judas had the moneybag, Jesus was telling him, "Buy what we need for the feast," or that he should give something to the poor. [30]So, after receiving the morsel of bread, he immediately went out. And it was night.

[31]When he had gone out, Jesus said, "Now is the Son of Man glorified, and God is glorified in him. [32]If God is glorified in him, God will also glorify him in himself, and glorify him at once. [33]Little children, yet a little while I am with you. You will seek me, and just as I said to the Jews, so now I also say to you, 'Where I am going you cannot come.' [34]A new commandment I give to you, that you love one another: just as I have loved you, you also are to love one another. [35]By this all people will know that you are my disciples, if you have love for one another."

[36]Simon Peter said to him, "Lord, where are you going?" Jesus answered him, "Where I am going you cannot follow me now, but you will follow afterward." [37]Peter said to him, "Lord, why can I not follow you now? I will lay down my life for you." [38]Jesus answered, "Will you lay down your life for me? Truly, truly, I say to you, the rooster will not crow till you have denied me three times.

Proverbs 10

The proverbs of Solomon.

A wise son makes a glad father,
  but a foolish son is a sorrow to his
    mother.
2 Treasures gained by wickedness do not
     profit,
   but righteousness delivers from death.
3 The LORD does not let the righteous go
     hungry,
   but he thwarts the craving of the
     wicked.
4 A slack hand causes poverty,
   but the hand of the diligent makes
     rich.
5 He who gathers in summer is a prudent
     son,
   but he who sleeps in harvest is a son
     who brings shame.
6 Blessings are on the head of the
     righteous,
   but the mouth of the wicked conceals
     violence.
7 The memory of the righteous is a
     blessing,
   but the name of the wicked will rot.
8 The wise of heart will receive
     commandments,
   but a babbling fool will come to ruin.
9 Whoever walks in integrity walks
     securely,
   but he who makes his ways crooked
     will be found out.
10 Whoever winks the eye causes trouble,
    and a babbling fool will come to ruin.
11 The mouth of the righteous is a fountain
      of life,
    but the mouth of the wicked conceals
      violence.
12 Hatred stirs up strife,
    but love covers all offenses.
13 On the lips of him who has
      understanding, wisdom is found,
    but a rod is for the back of him who
      lacks sense.

---
[1] Greek bondservant [2] Greek But in order that the Scripture may be fulfilled [3] Greek in the bosom of Jesus [4] Greek lacks Jesus

14   The wise lay up knowledge,
    but the mouth of a fool brings ruin
      near.
15   A rich man's wealth is his strong city;
    the poverty of the poor is their ruin.
16   The wage of the righteous leads to life,
    the gain of the wicked to sin.
17   Whoever heeds instruction is on the
      path to life,
    but he who rejects reproof leads
      others astray.
18   The one who conceals hatred has lying
      lips,
    and whoever utters slander is a fool.
19   When words are many, transgression is
      not lacking,
    but whoever restrains his lips is
      prudent.
20   The tongue of the righteous is choice
      silver;
    the heart of the wicked is of little
      worth.
21   The lips of the righteous feed many,
    but fools die for lack of sense.
22   The blessing of the LORD makes rich,
    and he adds no sorrow with it.[1]
23   Doing wrong is like a joke to a fool,
    but wisdom is pleasure to a man of
      understanding.
24   What the wicked dreads will come upon
      him,
    but the desire of the righteous will be
      granted.
25   When the tempest passes, the wicked is
      no more,
    but the righteous is established forever.
26   Like vinegar to the teeth and smoke to
      the eyes,
    so is the sluggard to those who send
      him.
27   The fear of the LORD prolongs life,
    but the years of the wicked will be
      short.
28   The hope of the righteous brings joy,
    but the expectation of the wicked will
      perish.
29   The way of the LORD is a stronghold to
      the blameless,
    but destruction to evildoers.
30   The righteous will never be removed,
    but the wicked will not dwell in the
      land.
31   The mouth of the righteous brings forth
      wisdom,
    but the perverse tongue will be cut off.
32   The lips of the righteous know what is
      acceptable,
    but the mouth of the wicked, what is
      perverse.

Ephesians 3

For this reason I, Paul, a prisoner for Christ Jesus on behalf of you Gentiles— [2]assuming that you have heard of the stewardship of God's grace that was given to me for you, [3]how the mystery was made known to me by revelation, as I have written briefly. [4]When you read this, you can perceive my insight into the mystery of Christ, [5]which was not made known to the sons of men in other generations as it has now been revealed to his holy apostles and prophets by the Spirit. [6]This mystery is[2] that the Gentiles are fellow heirs, members of the same body, and partakers of the promise in Christ Jesus through the gospel.

[7]Of this gospel I was made a minister according to the gift of God's grace, which was given me by the working of his power. [8]To me, though I am the very least of all the saints, this grace was given, to preach to the Gentiles the unsearchable riches of Christ, [9]and to bring to light for everyone what is the plan of the mystery hidden for ages in[3] God who created all things, [10]so that through the church the manifold wisdom of God might now be made known to the rulers and authorities in the heavenly places. [11]This was according to the eternal purpose that he has realized in Christ Jesus our Lord, [12]in whom we have boldness and access with confidence through our faith in him. [13]So I ask you not to lose heart over what I am suffering for you, which is your glory.

[14]For this reason I bow my knees before the Father, [15]from whom every family[4] in heaven and on earth is named, [16]that according to the riches of his glory he may grant you to be strengthened with power through his Spirit in your inner being, [17]so that Christ may dwell in your hearts through faith—that you, being rooted and grounded in love, [18]may have strength to comprehend with all the saints what is the breadth and length and height and depth, [19]and to know the love of Christ that

---

[1] Or and toil adds nothing to it [2] The words This mystery is are inferred from verse 4 [3] Or by [4] Or fatherhood; the Greek word patria is closely related to the word for Father in verse 14

surpasses knowledge, that you may be filled with all the fullness of God. [20] Now to him who is able to do far more abundantly than all that we ask or think,

according to the power at work within us, [21] to him be glory in the church and in Christ Jesus throughout all generations, forever and ever. Amen.

MARCH 24

Exodus 35

Moses assembled all the congregation of the people of Israel and said to them, "These are the things that the LORD has commanded you to do. [2] Six days work shall be done, but on the seventh day you shall have a Sabbath of solemn rest, holy to the LORD. Whoever does any work on it shall be put to death. [3] You shall kindle no fire in all your dwelling places on the Sabbath day."

[4] Moses said to all the congregation of the people of Israel, "This is the thing that the LORD has commanded. [5] Take from among you a contribution to the LORD. Whoever is of a generous heart, let him bring the LORD's contribution: gold, silver, and bronze; [6] blue and purple and scarlet yarns and fine twined linen; goats' hair, [7] tanned rams' skins, and goatskins;[1] acacia wood, [8] oil for the light, spices for the anointing oil and for the fragrant incense, [9] and onyx stones and stones for setting, for the ephod and for the breastpiece.

[10] "Let every skillful craftsman among you come and make all that the LORD has commanded: [11] the tabernacle, its tent and its covering, its hooks and its frames, its bars, its pillars, and its bases; [12] the ark with its poles, the mercy seat, and the veil of the screen; [13] the table with its poles and all its utensils, and the bread of the Presence; [14] the lampstand also for the light, with its utensils and its lamps, and the oil for the light; [15] and the altar of incense, with its poles, and the anointing oil and the fragrant incense, and the screen for the door, at the door of the tabernacle; [16] the altar of burnt offering, with its grating of bronze, its poles, and all its utensils, the basin and its stand; [17] the hangings of the court, its pillars and its bases, and the screen

for the gate of the court; [18] the pegs of the tabernacle and the pegs of the court, and their cords; [19] the finely worked garments for ministering[2] in the Holy Place, the holy garments for Aaron the priest, and the garments of his sons, for their service as priests."

[20] Then all the congregation of the people of Israel departed from the presence of Moses. [21] And they came, everyone whose heart stirred him, and everyone whose spirit moved him, and brought the LORD's contribution to be used for the tent of meeting, and for all its service, and for the holy garments. [22] So they came, both men and women. All who were of a willing heart brought brooches and earrings and signet rings and armlets, all sorts of gold objects, every man dedicating an offering of gold to the LORD. [23] And every one who possessed blue or purple or scarlet yarns or fine linen or goats' hair or tanned rams' skins or goatskins brought them. [24] Everyone who could make a contribution of silver or bronze brought it as the LORD's contribution. And every one who possessed acacia wood of any use in the work brought it. [25] And every skillful woman spun with her hands, and they all brought what they had spun in blue and purple and scarlet yarns and fine twined linen. [26] All the women whose hearts stirred them to use their skill spun the goats' hair. [27] And the leaders brought onyx stones and stones to be set, for the ephod and for the breastpiece, [28] and spices and oil for the light, and for the anointing oil, and for the fragrant incense. [29] All the men and women, the people of Israel, whose heart moved them to bring anything for the work that the LORD had commanded by Moses to be done brought it as a freewill offering to the LORD.

[1] The meaning of the Hebrew word is uncertain; also verse 23; compare 25:5 [2] Or *garments for worship*; see 31:10

[30]Then Moses said to the people of Israel, "See, the LORD has called by name Bezalel the son of Uri, son of Hur, of the tribe of Judah; [31]and he has filled him with the Spirit of God, with skill, with intelligence, with knowledge, and with all craftsmanship, [32]to devise artistic designs, to work in gold and silver and bronze, [33]in cutting stones for setting, and in carving wood, for work in every skilled craft. [34]And he has inspired him to teach, both him and Oholiab the son of Ahisamach of the tribe of Dan. [35]He has filled them with skill to do every sort of work done by an engraver or by a designer or by an embroiderer in blue and purple and scarlet yarns and fine twined linen, or by a weaver—by any sort of workman or skilled designer.

John 14

"[1]Let not your hearts be troubled. Believe in God;[1] believe also in me. [2]In my Father's house are many rooms. If it were not so, would I have told you that I go to prepare a place for you?[2] [3]And if I go and prepare a place for you, I will come again and will take you to myself, that where I am you may be also. [4]And you know the way to where I am going."[3] [5]Thomas said to him, "Lord, we do not know where you are going. How can we know the way?" [6]Jesus said to him, "I am the way, and the truth, and the life. No one comes to the Father except through me. [7]If you had known me, you would have known my Father also.[4] From now on you do know him and have seen him."

[8]Philip said to him, "Lord, show us the Father, and it is enough for us." [9]Jesus said to him, "Have I been with you so long, and you still do not know me, Philip? Whoever has seen me has seen the Father. How can you say, 'Show us the Father'? [10]Do you not believe that I am in the Father and the Father is in me? The words that I say to you I do not speak on my own authority, but the Father who dwells in me does his works. [11]Believe me that I am in the Father and the Father is in me, or else believe on account of the works themselves.

[12]"Truly, truly, I say to you, whoever believes in me will also do the works that I do; and greater works than these will he do, because I am going to the Father. [13]Whatever you ask in my name, this I will do, that the Father may be glorified in the Son. [14]If you ask me[5] anything in my name, I will do it.

[15]"If you love me, you will keep my commandments. [16]And I will ask the Father, and he will give you another Helper,[6] to be with you forever, [17]even the Spirit of truth, whom the world cannot receive, because it neither sees him nor knows him. You know him, for he dwells with you and will be[7] in you.

[18]"I will not leave you as orphans; I will come to you. [19]Yet a little while and the world will see me no more, but you will see me. Because I live, you also will live. [20]In that day you will know that I am in my Father, and you in me, and I in you. [21]Whoever has my commandments and keeps them, he it is who loves me. And he who loves me will be loved by my Father, and I will love him and manifest myself to him." [22]Judas (not Iscariot) said to him, "Lord, how is it that you will manifest yourself to us, and not to the world?" [23]Jesus answered him, "If anyone loves me, he will keep my word, and my Father will love him, and we will come to him and make our home with him. [24]Whoever does not love me does not keep my words. And the word that you hear is not mine but the Father's who sent me.

[25]"These things I have spoken to you while I am still with you. [26]But the Helper, the Holy Spirit, whom the Father will send in my name, he will teach you all things and bring to your remembrance all that I have said to you. [27]Peace I leave with you; my peace I give to you. Not as the world gives do I give to you. Let not your hearts be troubled, neither let them be afraid. [28]You heard me say to you, 'I am going away, and I will come to you.' If you loved me, you would have rejoiced, because I am going to the Father, for the Father is greater than I. [29]And now I have told you before it takes place, so that when it does take place you may believe. [30]I will no longer talk much with you, for the ruler of this world is coming. He has no claim on me, [31]but I do as the Father has commanded me, so that the world may know that I love the Father. Rise, let us go from here.

Proverbs 11

[1]A false balance is an abomination to the LORD,
but a just weight is his delight.

---

[1] Or *You believe in God* [2] Or *In my Father's house are many rooms; if it were not so, I would have told you; for I go to prepare a place for you* [3] Some manuscripts *Where I am going you know, and the way you know* [4] Or *If you know me, you will know my Father also*, or *If you have known me, you will know my Father also* [5] Some manuscripts omit *me* [6] Or *Advocate, or Counselor; also 14:26; 15:26; 16:7* [7] Some manuscripts *and is*

2 When pride comes, then comes
disgrace,
but with the humble is wisdom.
3 The integrity of the upright guides
them,
but the crookedness of the
treacherous destroys them.
4 Riches do not profit in the day of wrath,
but righteousness delivers from
death.
5 The righteousness of the blameless
keeps his way straight,
but the wicked falls by his own
wickedness.
6 The righteousness of the upright
delivers them,
but the treacherous are taken captive
by their lust.
7 When the wicked dies, his hope will
perish,
and the expectation of wealth[1]
perishes too.
8 The righteous is delivered from trouble,
and the wicked walks into it instead.
9 With his mouth the godless man would
destroy his neighbor,
but by knowledge the righteous are
delivered.
10 When it goes well with the righteous,
the city rejoices,
and when the wicked perish there are
shouts of gladness.
11 By the blessing of the upright a city is
exalted,
but by the mouth of the wicked it is
overthrown.
12 Whoever belittles his neighbor lacks
sense,
but a man of understanding remains
silent.
13 Whoever goes about slandering reveals
secrets,
but he who is trustworthy in spirit
keeps a thing covered.
14 Where there is no guidance, a people
falls,
but in an abundance of counselors
there is safety.
15 Whoever puts up security for a stranger
will surely suffer harm,
but he who hates striking hands in
pledge is secure.

16 A gracious woman gets honor,
and violent men get riches.
17 A man who is kind benefits himself,
but a cruel man hurts himself.
18 The wicked earns deceptive wages,
but one who sows righteousness gets
a sure reward.
19 Whoever is steadfast in righteousness
will live,
but he who pursues evil will die.
20 Those of crooked heart are an
abomination to the LORD,
but those of blameless ways are his
delight.
21 Be assured, an evil person will not go
unpunished,
but the offspring of the righteous will
be delivered.
22 Like a gold ring in a pig's snout
is a beautiful woman without
discretion.
23 The desire of the righteous ends only in
good;
the expectation of the wicked in
wrath.
24 One gives freely, yet grows all the richer;
another withholds what he should
give, and only suffers want.
25 Whoever brings blessing will be
enriched,
and one who waters will himself be
watered.
26 The people curse him who holds back
grain,
but a blessing is on the head of him
who sells it.
27 Whoever diligently seeks good seeks
favor,[2]
but evil comes to him who searches
for it.
28 Whoever trusts in his riches will fall,
but the righteous will flourish like a
green leaf.
29 Whoever troubles his own household
will inherit the wind,
and the fool will be servant to the wise
of heart.
30 The fruit of the righteous is a tree of life,
and whoever captures souls is wise.
31 If the righteous is repaid on earth,
how much more the wicked and the
sinner!

[1] Or of his strength, or of iniquity [2] Or acceptance

Ephesians 4

I therefore, a prisoner for the Lord, urge you to walk in a manner worthy of the calling to which you have been called, ²with all humility and gentleness, with patience, bearing with one another in love, ³eager to maintain the unity of the Spirit in the bond of peace. ⁴There is one body and one Spirit—just as you were called to the one hope that belongs to your call—⁵one Lord, one faith, one baptism, ⁶one God and Father of all, who is over all and through all and in all. ⁷But grace was given to each one of us according to the measure of Christ's gift. ⁸Therefore it says,

"When he ascended on high he led a host of captives,
and he gave gifts to men."¹

⁹(In saying, "He ascended," what does it mean but that he had also descended into the lower regions, the earth?² ¹⁰He who descended is the one who also ascended far above all the heavens, that he might fill all things.) ¹¹And he gave the apostles, the prophets, the evangelists, the shepherds³ and teachers,⁴ ¹²to equip the saints for the work of ministry, for building up the body of Christ, ¹³until we all attain to the unity of the faith and of the knowledge of the Son of God, to mature manhood,⁵ to the measure of the stature of the fullness of Christ, ¹⁴so that we may no longer be children, tossed to and fro by the waves and carried about by every wind of doctrine, by human cunning, by craftiness in deceitful schemes. ¹⁵Rather, speaking the truth in love, we are to grow up in every way into him who is the head, into Christ, ¹⁶from whom the whole body, joined and held together by every joint with which it is equipped, when each part is working properly, makes the body grow so that it builds itself up in love.

¹⁷Now this I say and testify in the Lord, that you must no longer walk as the Gentiles do, in the futility of their minds. ¹⁸They are darkened in their understanding, alienated from the life of God because of the ignorance that is in them, due to their hardness of heart. ¹⁹They have become callous and have given themselves up to sensuality, greedy to practice every kind of impurity. ²⁰But that is not the way you learned Christ!— ²¹assuming that you have heard about him and were taught in him, as the truth is in Jesus, ²²to put off your old self,⁶ which belongs to your former manner of life and is corrupt through deceitful desires, ²³and to be renewed in the spirit of your minds, ²⁴and to put on the new self, created after the likeness of God in true righteousness and holiness.

²⁵Therefore, having put away falsehood, let each one of you speak the truth with his neighbor, for we are members one of another. ²⁶Be angry and do not sin; do not let the sun go down on your anger, ²⁷and give no opportunity to the devil. ²⁸Let the thief no longer steal, but rather let him labor, doing honest work with his own hands, so that he may have something to share with anyone in need. ²⁹Let no corrupting talk come out of your mouths, but only such as is good for building up, as fits the occasion, that it may give grace to those who hear. ³⁰And do not grieve the Holy Spirit of God, by whom you were sealed for the day of redemption. ³¹Let all bitterness and wrath and anger and clamor and slander be put away from you, along with all malice. ³²Be kind to one another, tenderhearted, forgiving one another, as God in Christ forgave you.

¹ The Greek word anthropoi can refer to both men and women ² Or the lower parts of the earth? ³ Or pastors ⁴ Or the shepherd-teachers ⁵ Greek to a full-grown man ⁶ Greek man; also verse 24

MARCH 25

Exodus 36

"Bezalel and Oholiab and every crafts-man in whom the LORD has put skill and intelligence to know how to do any work in the construction of the sanctuary shall work in accordance with all that the LORD has commanded."

²And Moses called Bezalel and Oholiab and every craftsman in whose mind the LORD had put skill, everyone whose heart stirred him up to come to do the work. ³And they received from Moses all the contribution that the people of Israel had brought for doing the work on the sanctuary. They still kept bringing him free-will offerings every morning, ⁴so that all the craftsmen who were doing every sort of task on the sanctuary came, each from the task that he was doing, ⁵and said to Moses, "The people bring much more than enough for doing the work that the LORD has commanded us to do." ⁶So Moses gave command, and word was proclaimed throughout the camp, "Let no man or woman do anything more for the contribution for the sanctuary." So the people were restrained from bringing, ⁷for the material they had was sufficient to do all the work, and more.

⁸And all the craftsmen among the workmen made the tabernacle with ten curtains. They were made of fine twined linen and blue and purple and scarlet yarns, with cherubim skillfully worked. ⁹The length of each curtain was twenty-eight cubits,[1] and the breadth of each curtain four cubits. All the curtains were the same size. ¹⁰He[2] coupled five curtains to one another, and the other five curtains he coupled to one another. ¹¹He made loops of blue on the edge of the outermost curtain of the first set. Likewise he made them on the edge of the outermost curtain of the second set. ¹²He made fifty loops on the one curtain, and he made fifty loops on the edge of the curtain that was in the second set. The loops were opposite one another. ¹³And he made fifty clasps of gold, and coupled the curtains one to the other with clasps. So the tabernacle was a single whole.

¹⁴He also made curtains of goats' hair for a tent over the tabernacle. He made eleven curtains. ¹⁵The length of each curtain was thirty cubits, and the breadth of each curtain four cubits. The eleven curtains were the same size. ¹⁶He coupled five curtains by themselves, and six curtains by themselves. ¹⁷And he made fifty loops on the edge of the outermost curtain of the one set, and fifty loops on the edge of the other connecting curtain. ¹⁸And he made fifty clasps of bronze to couple the tent together that it might be a single whole. ¹⁹And he made for the tent a covering of tanned rams' skins and goatskins.

²⁰Then he made the upright frames for the tabernacle of acacia wood. ²¹Ten cubits was the length of a frame, and a cubit and a half the breadth of each frame. ²²Each frame had two tenons for fitting together. He did this for all the frames of the tabernacle. ²³The frames for the tabernacle he made thus: twenty frames for the south side. ²⁴And he made forty bases of silver under the twenty frames, two bases under one frame for its two tenons, and two bases under the next frame for its two tenons. ²⁵For the second side of the tabernacle, on the north side, he made twenty frames ²⁶and their forty bases of silver, two bases under one frame and two bases under the next frame. ²⁷For the rear of the tabernacle westward he made six frames. ²⁸He made two frames for corners of the tabernacle in the rear. ²⁹And they were separate beneath but joined at the top, at the first ring. He made two of them this way for the two corners. ³⁰There were eight frames with their bases of silver: sixteen bases, under every frame two bases.

³¹He made bars of acacia wood, five for the frames of the one side of the tabernacle, ³²and five bars for the frames of the other side of the tabernacle, and five bars for the frames of the tabernacle at the rear westward. ³³And he made the middle bar to run from end to end halfway up the frames. ³⁴And he overlaid the

---

[1] A *cubit* was about 18 inches or 45 centimeters [2] Probably Bezalel (compare 35:30; 37:1)

frames with gold, and made their rings of gold for holders for the bars, and overlaid the bars with gold. ³⁵He made the veil of blue and purple and scarlet yarns and fine twined linen; with cherubim skillfully worked into it he made it. ³⁶And for it he made four pillars of acacia and overlaid them with gold. Their hooks were of gold, and he cast for them four bases of silver. ³⁷He also made a screen for the entrance of the tent, of blue and purple and scarlet yarns and fine twined linen, embroidered with needlework, ³⁸and its five pillars with their hooks. He overlaid their capitals, and their fillets were of gold, but their five bases were of bronze.

John 15

¹ "I am the true vine, and my Father is the vinedresser. ²Every branch in me that does not bear fruit he takes away, and every branch that does bear fruit he prunes, that it may bear more fruit. ³Already you are clean because of the word that I have spoken to you. ⁴Abide in me, and I in you. As the branch cannot bear fruit by itself, unless it abides in the vine, neither can you, unless you abide in me. ⁵I am the vine; you are the branches. Whoever abides in me and I in him, he it is that bears much fruit, for apart from me you can do nothing. ⁶If anyone does not abide in me he is thrown away like a branch and withers; and the branches are gathered, thrown into the fire, and burned. ⁷If you abide in me, and my words abide in you, ask whatever you wish, and it will be done for you. ⁸By this my Father is glorified, that you bear much fruit and so prove to be my disciples. ⁹As the Father has loved me, so have I loved you. Abide in my love. ¹⁰If you keep my commandments, you will abide in my love, just as I have kept my Father's commandments and abide in his love. ¹¹These things I have spoken to you, that my joy may be in you, and that your joy may be full. ¹²"This is my commandment, that you love one another as I have loved you. ¹³Greater love has no one than this, that someone lay down his life for his friends. ¹⁴You are my friends if you do what I command you. ¹⁵No longer do I call you servants,¹ for the servant² does not know what his master is doing; but I have called

you friends, for all that I have heard from my Father I have made known to you. ¹⁶You did not choose me, but I chose you and appointed you that you should go and bear fruit and that your fruit should abide, so that whatever you ask the Father in my name, he may give it to you. ¹⁷These things I command you, so that you will love one another.

¹⁸"If the world hates you, know that it has hated me before it hated you. ¹⁹If you were of the world, the world would love you as its own; but because you are not of the world, but I chose you out of the world, therefore the world hates you. ²⁰Remember the word that I said to you: 'A servant is not greater than his master.' If they persecuted me, they will also persecute you. If they kept my word, they will also keep yours. ²¹But all these things they will do to you on account of my name, because they do not know him who sent me. ²²If I had not come and spoken to them, they would not have been guilty of sin,³ but now they have no excuse for their sin. ²³Whoever hates me hates my Father also. ²⁴If I had not done among them the works that no one else did, they would not be guilty of sin, but now they have seen and hated both me and my Father. ²⁵But the word that is written in their Law must be fulfilled: 'They hated me without a cause.'

²⁶"But when the Helper comes, whom I will send to you from the Father, the Spirit of truth, who proceeds from the Father, he will bear witness about me. ²⁷And you also will bear witness, because you have been with me from the beginning.

Proverbs 12

Whoever loves discipline loves knowledge,
    but he who hates reproof is stupid.
2   A good man obtains favor from the LORD,
    but a man of evil devices he condemns.
3   No one is established by wickedness,
    but the root of the righteous will never be moved.
4   An excellent wife is the crown of her husband,
    but she who brings shame is like rottenness in his bones.

¹ Greek bondservants ² Greek bondservant; also verse 20 ³ Greek they would not have had sin; also verse 24

⁵ The thoughts of the righteous are just;
   the counsels of the wicked are
     deceitful.
⁶ The words of the wicked lie in wait for
   blood,
   but the mouth of the upright delivers
     them.
⁷ The wicked are overthrown and are no
   more,
   but the house of the righteous will
     stand.
⁸ A man is commended according to his
   good sense,
   but one of twisted mind is despised.
⁹ Better to be lowly and have a servant
   than to play the great man and lack
     bread.
¹⁰ Whoever is righteous has regard for the
   life of his beast,
   but the mercy of the wicked is cruel.
¹¹ Whoever works his land will have plenty
   of bread,
   but he who follows worthless pursuits
     lacks sense.
¹² Whoever is wicked covets the spoil of
   evildoers,
   but the root of the righteous bears
     fruit.
¹³ An evil man is ensnared by the
   transgression of his lips,
   but the righteous escapes from trouble.
¹⁴ From the fruit of his mouth a man is
   satisfied with good,
   and the work of a man's hand comes
     back to him.
¹⁵ The way of a fool is right in his own eyes,
   but a wise man listens to advice.
¹⁶ The vexation of a fool is known at once,
   but the prudent ignores an insult.
¹⁷ Whoever speaks[1] the truth gives honest
   evidence,
   but a false witness utters deceit.
¹⁸ There is one whose rash words are like
   sword thrusts,
   but the tongue of the wise brings
     healing.
¹⁹ Truthful lips endure forever,
   but a lying tongue is but for a
     moment.
²⁰ Deceit is in the heart of those who
   devise evil,
   but those who plan peace have joy.

²¹ No ill befalls the righteous,
   but the wicked are filled with trouble.
²² Lying lips are an abomination to the
   Lord,
   but those who act faithfully are his
     delight.
²³ A prudent man conceals knowledge,
   but the heart of fools proclaims folly.
²⁴ The hand of the diligent will rule,
   while the slothful will be put to forced
     labor.
²⁵ Anxiety in a man's heart weighs him
   down,
   but a good word makes him glad.
²⁶ One who is righteous is a guide to his
   neighbor,[2]
   but the way of the wicked leads them
     astray.
²⁷ Whoever is slothful will not roast his
   game,
   but the diligent man will get precious
     wealth.[3]
²⁸ In the path of righteousness is life,
   and in its pathway there is no death.

Ephesians 5

Therefore be imitators of God, as beloved children. ²And walk in love, as Christ loved us and gave himself up for us, a fragrant offering and sacrifice to God.

³But sexual immorality and all impurity or covetousness must not even be named among you, as is proper among saints. ⁴Let there be no filthiness nor foolish talk nor crude joking, which are out of place, but instead let there be thanksgiving. ⁵For you may be sure of this, that everyone who is sexually immoral or impure, or who is covetous (that is, an idolater), has no inheritance in the kingdom of Christ and God. ⁶Let no one deceive you with empty words, for because of these things the wrath of God comes upon the sons of disobedience. ⁷Therefore do not become partners with them; ⁸for at one time you were darkness, but now you are light in the Lord. Walk as children of light ⁹(for the fruit of light is found in all that is good and right and true), ¹⁰and try to discern what is pleasing to the Lord. ¹¹Take no part in the unfruitful works of darkness, but instead expose them. ¹²For it is shameful even to speak of the things that they do in secret. ¹³But when

[1] Hebrew breathes out [2] Or The righteous chooses his friends carefully [3] Or but diligence is precious wealth

anything is exposed by the light, it becomes visible, [14] for anything that becomes visible is light. Therefore it says,

"Awake, O sleeper,
    and arise from the dead,
    and Christ will shine on you."

[15] Look carefully then how you walk, not as unwise but as wise, [16] making the best use of the time, because the days are evil. [17] Therefore do not be foolish, but understand what the will of the Lord is. [18] And do not get drunk with wine, for that is debauchery, but be filled with the Spirit, [19] addressing one another in psalms and hymns and spiritual songs, singing and making melody to the Lord with your heart, [20] giving thanks always and for everything to God the Father in the name of our Lord Jesus Christ, [21] submitting to one another out of reverence for Christ.

[22] Wives, submit to your own husbands, as to the Lord. [23] For the husband is the head of the wife even as Christ is the head of the church,

his body, and is himself its Savior. [24] Now as the church submits to Christ, so also wives should submit in everything to their husbands.

[25] Husbands, love your wives, as Christ loved the church and gave himself up for her, [26] that he might sanctify her, having cleansed her by the washing of water with the word, [27] so that he might present the church to himself in splendor, without spot or wrinkle or any such thing, that she might be holy and without blemish.[1] [28] In the same way husbands should love their wives as their own bodies. He who loves his wife loves himself. [29] For no one ever hated his own flesh, but nourishes and cherishes it, just as Christ does the church, [30] because we are members of his body. [31] "Therefore a man shall leave his father and mother and hold fast to his wife, and the two shall become one flesh." [32] This mystery is profound, and I am saying that it refers to Christ and the church. [33] However, let each one of you love his wife as himself, and let the wife see that she respects her husband.

MARCH 26

Exodus 37

Bezalel made the ark of acacia wood. Two cubits[2] and a half was its length, a cubit and a half its breadth, and a cubit and a half its height. [2] And he overlaid it with pure gold inside and outside, and made a molding of gold around it. [3] And he cast for it four rings of gold for its four feet, two rings on its one side and two rings on its other side. [4] And he made poles of acacia wood and overlaid them with gold [5] and put the poles into the rings on the sides of the ark to carry the ark. [6] And he made a mercy seat of pure gold. Two cubits and a half was its length, and a cubit and a half its breadth. [7] And he made two cherubim of gold. He made them of hammered work on the two ends of the mercy seat, [8] one cherub on the one end, and one cherub on the other end. Of one piece with the mercy seat he made

the cherubim on its two ends. [9] The cherubim spread out their wings above, overshadowing the mercy seat with their wings, with their faces one to another; toward the mercy seat were the faces of the cherubim.

[10] He also made the table of acacia wood. Two cubits was its length, a cubit its breadth, and a cubit and a half its height. [11] And he overlaid it with pure gold, and made a molding of gold around it. [12] And he made a rim around it a handbreadth[3] wide, and made a molding of gold around the rim. [13] He cast for it four rings of gold and fastened the rings to the four corners at its four legs. [14] Close to the frame were the rings, as holders for the poles to carry the table. [15] He made the poles of acacia wood to carry the table, and overlaid them with gold. [16] And he made the vessels of pure gold that

---

[1] Or holy and blameless [2] A cubit was about 18 inches or 45 centimeters [3] A handbreadth was about 3 inches or 7.5 centimeters

were to be on the table, its plates and dishes for incense, and its bowls and flagons with which to pour drink offerings.

[17]He also made the lampstand of pure gold. He made the lampstand of hammered work. Its base, its stem, its cups, its calyxes, and its flowers were of one piece with it. [18]And there were six branches going out of its sides, three branches of the lampstand out of one side of it and three branches of the lampstand out of the other side of it; [19]three cups made like almond blossoms, each with calyx and flower, on one branch, and three cups made like almond blossoms, each with calyx and flower, on the other branch—so for the six branches going out of the lampstand. [20]And on the lampstand itself were four cups made like almond blossoms, with their calyxes and flowers, [21]and a calyx of one piece with it under each pair of the six branches going out of it. [22]Their calyxes and their branches were of one piece with it. The whole of it was a single piece of hammered work of pure gold. [23]And he made its seven lamps and its tongs and its trays of pure gold. [24]He made it and all its utensils out of a talent[1] of pure gold.

[25]He made the altar of incense of acacia wood. Its length was a cubit, and its breadth was a cubit. It was square, and two cubits was its height. Its horns were of one piece with it. [26]He overlaid it with pure gold, its top and around its sides and its horns. And he made a molding of gold around it, [27]and made two rings of gold on it under its molding, on two opposite sides of it, as holders for the poles with which to carry it. [28]And he made the poles of acacia wood and overlaid them with gold.

[29]He made the holy anointing oil also, and the pure fragrant incense, blended as by the perfumer.

John 16

[1]"I have said all these things to you to keep you from falling away. [2]They will put you out of the synagogues. Indeed, the hour is coming when whoever kills you will think he is offering service to God. [3]And they will do these things because they have not known the Father, nor me. [4]But I have said these things to you, that when their hour comes you may remember that I told them to you.

"I did not say these things to you from the beginning, because I was with you. [5]But now I am going to him who sent me, and none of you asks me, 'Where are you going?' [6]But because I have said these things to you, sorrow has filled your heart. [7]Nevertheless, I tell you the truth: it is to your advantage that I go away, for if I do not go away, the Helper will not come to you. But if I go, I will send him to you. [8]And when he comes, he will convict the world concerning sin and righteousness and judgment: [9]concerning sin, because they do not believe in me; [10]concerning righteousness, because I go to the Father, and you will see me no longer; [11]concerning judgment, because the ruler of this world is judged.

[12]"I still have many things to say to you, but you cannot bear them now. [13]When the Spirit of truth comes, he will guide you into all the truth, for he will not speak on his own authority, but whatever he hears he will speak, and he will declare to you the things that are to come. [14]He will glorify me, for he will take what is mine and declare it to you. [15]All that the Father has is mine; therefore I said that he will take what is mine and declare it to you.

[16]"A little while, and you will see me no longer; and again a little while, and you will see me." [17]So some of his disciples said to one another, "What is this that he says to us, 'A little while, and you will not see me, and again a little while, and you will see me'; and, 'because I am going to the Father'?" [18]So they were saying, "What does he mean by 'a little while'? We do not know what he is talking about." [19]Jesus knew that they wanted to ask him, so he said to them, "Is this what you are asking yourselves, what I meant by saying, 'A little while and you will not see me, and again a little while and you will see me'? [20]Truly, truly, I say to you, you will weep and lament, but the world will rejoice. You will be sorrowful, but your sorrow will turn into joy. [21]When a woman is giving birth, she has sorrow because her hour has come, but when she has delivered the baby, she no longer remembers the anguish, for joy that a human being has been born into the world. [22]So also you have sorrow now, but I will see you again, and your hearts will rejoice, and no one will take your joy from you. [23]In that day you will ask nothing of me. Truly, truly, I say to you, whatever

---

[1] A talent was about 75 pounds or 34 kilograms

you ask of the Father in my name, he will give it to you. [24]Until now you have asked nothing in my name. Ask, and you will receive, that your joy may be full.

[25]"I have said these things to you in figures of speech. The hour is coming when I will no longer speak to you in figures of speech but will tell you plainly about the Father. [26]In that day you will ask in my name, and I do not say to you that I will ask the Father on your behalf; [27]for the Father himself loves you, because you have loved me and have believed that I came from God.[1] [28]I came from the Father and have come into the world, and now I am leaving the world and going to the Father."

[29]His disciples said, "Ah, now you are speaking plainly and not using figurative speech! [30]Now we know that you know all things and do not need anyone to question you; this is why we believe that you came from God." [31]Jesus answered them, "Do you now believe? [32]Behold, the hour is coming, indeed it has come, when you will be scattered, each to his own home, and will leave me alone. Yet I am not alone, for the Father is with me. [33]I have said these things to you, that in me you may have peace. In the world you will have tribulation. But take heart; I have overcome the world."

Proverbs 13

A wise son hears his father's instruction,
but a scoffer does not listen to rebuke.
2 From the fruit of his mouth a man eats
what is good,
but the desire of the treacherous is for
violence.
3 Whoever guards his mouth preserves
his life;
he who opens wide his lips comes to
ruin.
4 The soul of the sluggard craves and gets
nothing,
while the soul of the diligent is richly
supplied.
5 The righteous hates falsehood,
but the wicked brings shame[2] and
disgrace.
6 Righteousness guards him whose way is
blameless,
but sin overthrows the wicked.

7 One pretends to be rich, yet has
nothing;
another pretends to be poor, yet has
great wealth.
8 The ransom of a man's life is his
wealth,
but a poor man hears no threat.
9 The light of the righteous rejoices,
but the lamp of the wicked will be put
out.
10 By insolence comes nothing but strife,
but with those who take advice is
wisdom.
11 Wealth gained hastily[3] will dwindle,
but whoever gathers little by little will
increase it.
12 Hope deferred makes the heart sick,
but a desire fulfilled is a tree of life.
13 Whoever despises the word brings
destruction on himself,
but he who reveres the
commandment will be rewarded.
14 The teaching of the wise is a fountain of
life,
that one may turn away from the
snares of death.
15 Good sense wins favor,
but the way of the treacherous is their
ruin.[4]
16 In everything the prudent acts with
knowledge,
but a fool flaunts his folly.
17 A wicked messenger falls into trouble,
but a faithful envoy brings healing.
18 Poverty and disgrace come to him who
ignores instruction,
but whoever heeds reproof is
honored.
19 A desire fulfilled is sweet to the soul,
but to turn away from evil is an
abomination to fools.
20 Whoever walks with the wise becomes
wise,
but the companion of fools will suffer
harm.
21 Disaster[5] pursues sinners,
but the righteous are rewarded with
good.
22 A good man leaves an inheritance to his
children's children,
but the sinner's wealth is laid up for
the righteous.

[1] Some manuscripts *from the Father* [2] Or *stench* [3] Or *by fraud* [4] Probable reading (compare Septuagint, Syriac, Vulgate); Hebrew *is rugged, or is an enduring rut* [5] Or *Evil*

23 The fallow ground of the poor would
yield much food,
but it is swept away through injustice.
24 Whoever spares the rod hates his son,
but he who loves him is diligent to
discipline him.[1]
25 The righteous has enough to satisfy his
appetite,
but the belly of the wicked suffers
want.

Ephesians 6

Children, obey your parents in the Lord,
for this is right. [2]"Honor your father and
mother" (this is the first commandment with
a promise), [3]"that it may go well with you and
that you may live long in the land." [4]Fathers, do
not provoke your children to anger, but bring
them up in the discipline and instruction of
the Lord.

[5]Bondservants,[2] obey your earthly masters[3]
with fear and trembling, with a sincere heart,
as you would Christ, [6]not by the way of eye-
service, as people-pleasers, but as bondservants
of Christ, doing the will of God from the heart,
[7]rendering service with a good will as to the
Lord and not to man, [8]knowing that whatever
good anyone does, this he will receive back
from the Lord, whether he is a bondservant[4]
or is free. [9]Masters, do the same to them, and
stop your threatening, knowing that he who is
both their Master[5] and yours is in heaven, and
that there is no partiality with him.

[10]Finally, be strong in the Lord and in the
strength of his might. [11]Put on the whole armor
of God, that you may be able to stand against
the schemes of the devil. [12]For we do not wrestle against flesh and blood, but against the rulers, against the authorities, against the cosmic
powers over this present darkness, against the
spiritual forces of evil in the heavenly places.
[13]Therefore take up the whole armor of God,
that you may be able to withstand in the evil
day, and having done all, to stand firm. [14]Stand
therefore, having fastened on the belt of truth,
and having put on the breastplate of righteousness, [15]and, as shoes for your feet, having put
on the readiness given by the gospel of peace.
[16]In all circumstances take up the shield of
faith, with which you can extinguish all the
flaming darts of the evil one; [17]and take the
helmet of salvation, and the sword of the Spirit,
which is the word of God, [18]praying at all times
in the Spirit, with all prayer and supplication.
To that end keep alert with all perseverance,
making supplication for all the saints, [19]and
also for me, that words may be given to me in
opening my mouth boldly to proclaim the mystery of the gospel, [20]for which I am an ambassador in chains, that I may declare it boldly, as
I ought to speak.

[21]So that you also may know how I am and
what I am doing, Tychicus the beloved brother
and faithful minister in the Lord will tell you
everything. [22]I have sent him to you for this
very purpose, that you may know how we are,
and that he may encourage your hearts.

[23]Peace be to the brothers,[6] and love with
faith, from God the Father and the Lord Jesus
Christ. [24]Grace be with all who love our Lord
Jesus Christ with love incorruptible.

MARCH 27

Exodus 38

He made the altar of burnt offering of acacia wood. Five cubits[7] was its length, and
five cubits its breadth. It was square, and three
cubits was its height. [2]He made horns for it on
its four corners. Its horns were of one piece
with it, and he overlaid it with bronze. [3]And
he made all the utensils of the altar, the pots,
the shovels, the basins, the forks, and the fire
pans. He made all its utensils of bronze. [4]And
he made for the altar a grating, a network of

---

[1] Or who loves him disciplines him early   [2] Or slaves; also verse 6 (for the contextual rendering of the Greek word doulos, see Preface)   [3] Or your masters according to the flesh   [4] Or slave (for the contextual rendering of the Greek word doulos, see Preface)   [5] Greek Lord   [6] Or brothers and sisters   [7] A cubit was about 18 inches or 45 centimeters

bronze, under its ledge, extending halfway down. [5]He cast four rings on the four corners of the bronze grating as holders for the poles. [6]He made the poles of acacia wood and overlaid them with bronze. [7]And he put the poles through the rings on the sides of the altar to carry it with them. He made it hollow, with boards.

[8]He made the basin of bronze and its stand of bronze, from the mirrors of the ministering women who ministered in the entrance of the tent of meeting.

[9]And he made the court. For the south side the hangings of the court were of fine twined linen, a hundred cubits; [10]their twenty pillars and their twenty bases were of bronze, but the hooks of the pillars and their fillets were of silver. [11]And for the north side there were hangings of a hundred cubits, their twenty pillars, their twenty bases were of bronze, but the hooks of the pillars and their fillets were of silver. [12]And for the west side were hangings of fifty cubits, their ten pillars, and their ten bases; the hooks of the pillars and their fillets were of silver. [13]And for the front to the east, fifty cubits. [14]The hangings for one side of the gate were fifteen cubits, with their three pillars and three bases. [15]And so for the other side. On both sides of the gate of the court were hangings of fifteen cubits, with their three pillars and their three bases. [16]All the hangings around the court were of fine twined linen. [17]And the bases for the pillars were of bronze, but the hooks of the pillars and their fillets were of silver. The overlaying of their capitals was also of silver, and all the pillars of the court were filleted with silver. [18]And the screen for the gate of the court was embroidered with needlework in blue and purple and scarlet yarns and fine twined linen. It was twenty cubits long and five cubits high in its breadth, corresponding to the hangings of the court. [19]And their pillars were four in number. Their four bases were of bronze, their hooks of silver, and the overlaying of their capitals and their fillets of silver. [20]And all the pegs for the tabernacle and for the court all around were of bronze.

[21]These are the records of the tabernacle, the tabernacle of the testimony, as they were recorded at the commandment of Moses, the responsibility of the Levites under the direction of Ithamar the son of Aaron the priest. [22]Bezalel the son of Uri, son of Hur, of the tribe of Judah, made all that the LORD commanded Moses; [23]and with him was Oholiab the son of Ahisamach, of the tribe of Dan, an engraver and designer and embroiderer in blue and purple and scarlet yarns and fine twined linen.

[24]All the gold that was used for the work, in all the construction of the sanctuary, the gold from the offering, was twenty-nine talents and 730 shekels,[1] by the shekel of the sanctuary. [25]The silver from those of the congregation who were recorded was a hundred talents and 1,775 shekels, by the shekel of the sanctuary: [26]a beka[2] a head (that is, half a shekel, by the shekel of the sanctuary), for everyone who was listed in the records, from twenty years old and upward, for 603,550 men. [27]The hundred talents of silver were for casting the bases of the sanctuary and the bases of the veil; a hundred bases for the hundred talents, a talent a base. [28]And of the 1,775 shekels he made hooks for the pillars and overlaid their capitals and made fillets for them. [29]The bronze that was offered was seventy talents and 2,400 shekels; [30]with it he made the bases for the entrance of the tent of meeting, the bronze altar and the bronze grating for it and all the utensils of the altar, [31]the bases around the court, and the bases of the gate of the court, all the pegs of the tabernacle, and all the pegs around the court.

John 17

When Jesus had spoken these words, he lifted up his eyes to heaven, and said, "Father, the hour has come; glorify your Son that the Son may glorify you, [2]since you have given him authority over all flesh, to give eternal life to all whom you have given him. [3]And this is eternal life, that they know you the only true God, and Jesus Christ whom you have sent. [4]I glorified you on earth, having accomplished the work that you gave me to do. [5]And now, Father, glorify me in your own presence with the glory that I had with you before the world existed.

[6]"I have manifested your name to the people whom you gave me out of the world. Yours they were, and you gave them to me, and they have kept your word. [7]Now they know that

---

[1] A talent was about 75 pounds or 34 kilograms; a shekel was about 2/5 ounce or 11 grams [2] A beka was about 1/5 ounce or 5.5 grams

everything that you have given me is from you. [8] For I have given them the words that you gave me, and they have received them and have come to know in truth that I came from you; and they have believed that you sent me. [9] I am praying for them. I am not praying for the world but for those whom you have given me, for they are yours. [10] All mine are yours, and yours are mine, and I am glorified in them. [11] And I am no longer in the world, but they are in the world, and I am coming to you. Holy Father, keep them in your name, which you have given me, that they may be one, even as we are one. [12] While I was with them, I kept them in your name, which you have given me. I have guarded them, and not one of them has been lost except the son of destruction, that the Scripture might be fulfilled. [13] But now I am coming to you, and these things I speak in the world, that they may have my joy fulfilled in themselves. [14] I have given them your word, and the world has hated them because they are not of the world, just as I am not of the world. [15] I do not ask that you take them out of the world, but that you keep them from the evil one.[1] [16] They are not of the world, just as I am not of the world. [17] Sanctify them[2] in the truth; your word is truth. [18] As you sent me into the world, so I have sent them into the world. [19] And for their sake I consecrate myself,[3] that they also may be sanctified[4] in truth.

[20] "I do not ask for these only, but also for those who will believe in me through their word, [21] that they may all be one, just as you, Father, are in me, and I in you, that they also may be in us, so that the world may believe that you have sent me. [22] The glory that you have given me I have given to them, that they may be one even as we are one, [23] I in them and you in me, that they may become perfectly one, so that the world may know that you sent me and loved them even as you loved me. [24] Father, I desire that they also, whom you have given me, may be with me where I am, to see my glory that you have given me because you loved me before the foundation of the world. [25] O righteous Father, even though the world does not know you, I know you, and these know that you have sent me. [26] I made known to them your name, and I will continue to make it known, that the love with which you have loved me may be in them, and I in them."

Proverbs 14

The wisest of women builds her house,
　　but folly with her own hands tears it
　　　　down.
2　Whoever walks in uprightness fears the
　　　　LORD,
　　but he who is devious in his ways
　　　　despises him.
3　By the mouth of a fool comes a rod for
　　　　his back,[5]
　　but the lips of the wise will preserve
　　　　them.
4　Where there are no oxen, the manger is
　　　　clean,
　　but abundant crops come by the
　　　　strength of the ox.
5　A faithful witness does not lie,
　　but a false witness breathes out lies.
6　A scoffer seeks wisdom in vain,
　　but knowledge is easy for a man of
　　　　understanding.
7　Leave the presence of a fool,
　　for there you do not meet words of
　　　　knowledge.
8　The wisdom of the prudent is to discern
　　　　his way,
　　but the folly of fools is deceiving.
9　Fools mock at the guilt offering,
　　but the upright enjoy acceptance.[6]
10　The heart knows its own bitterness,
　　and no stranger shares its joy.
11　The house of the wicked will be
　　　　destroyed,
　　but the tent of the upright will
　　　　flourish.
12　There is a way that seems right to a man,
　　but its end is the way to death.[7]
13　Even in laughter the heart may ache,
　　and the end of joy may be grief.
14　The backslider in heart will be filled
　　　　with the fruit of his ways,
　　and a good man will be filled with the
　　　　fruit of his ways.
15　The simple believes everything,
　　but the prudent gives thought to his
　　　　steps.
16　One who is wise is cautious[8] and turns
　　　　away from evil,
　　but a fool is reckless and careless.
17　A man of quick temper acts foolishly,
　　and a man of evil devices is hated.

---

[1] Or from evil [2] Greek Set them apart (for holy service to God) [3] Or I sanctify myself; or I set myself apart (for holy service to God) [4] Greek may be set apart (for holy service to God) [5] Or In the mouth of a fool is a rod of pride [6] Hebrew but among the upright is acceptance [7] Hebrew ways of death [8] Or fears [the LORD]

¹⁸ The simple inherit folly,
    but the prudent are crowned with
       knowledge.
¹⁹ The evil bow down before the good,
    the wicked at the gates of the
       righteous.
²⁰ The poor is disliked even by his
      neighbor,
    but the rich has many friends.
²¹ Whoever despises his neighbor is a
      sinner,
    but blessed is he who is generous to
      the poor.
²² Do they not go astray who devise evil?
    Those who devise good meet[1]
      steadfast love and faithfulness.
²³ In all toil there is profit,
    but mere talk tends only to poverty.
²⁴ The crown of the wise is their wealth,
    but the folly of fools brings folly.
²⁵ A truthful witness saves lives,
    but one who breathes out lies is
      deceitful.
²⁶ In the fear of the LORD one has strong
      confidence,
    and his children will have a refuge.
²⁷ The fear of the LORD is a fountain of life,
    that one may turn away from the
      snares of death.
²⁸ In a multitude of people is the glory of a
      king,
    but without people a prince is ruined.
²⁹ Whoever is slow to anger has great
      understanding,
    but he who has a hasty temper exalts
      folly.
³⁰ A tranquil[2] heart gives life to the flesh,
    but envy[3] makes the bones rot.
³¹ Whoever oppresses a poor man insults
      his Maker,
    but he who is generous to the needy
      honors him.
³² The wicked is overthrown through his
      evildoing,
    but the righteous finds refuge in his
      death.
³³ Wisdom rests in the heart of a man of
      understanding,
    but it makes itself known even in the
      midst of fools.[4]

³⁴ Righteousness exalts a nation,
    but sin is a reproach to any people.
³⁵ A servant who deals wisely has the
      king's favor,
    but his wrath falls on one who acts
      shamefully.

Philippians 1

Paul and Timothy, servants[5] of Christ Jesus,
To all the saints in Christ Jesus who are at Philippi, with the overseers[6] and deacons:[7] ²Grace to you and peace from God our Father and the Lord Jesus Christ.

³I thank my God in all my remembrance of you, ⁴always in every prayer of mine for you all making my prayer with joy, ⁵because of your partnership in the gospel from the first day until now. ⁶And I am sure of this, that he who began a good work in you will bring it to completion at the day of Jesus Christ. ⁷It is right for me to feel this way about you all, because I hold you in my heart, for you are all partakers with me of grace,[8] both in my imprisonment and in the defense and confirmation of the gospel. ⁸For God is my witness, how I yearn for you all with the affection of Christ Jesus. ⁹And it is my prayer that your love may abound more and more, with knowledge and all discernment, ¹⁰so that you may approve what is excellent, and so be pure and blameless for the day of Christ, ¹¹filled with the fruit of righteousness that comes through Jesus Christ, to the glory and praise of God.

¹²I want you to know, brothers,[9] that what has happened to me has really served to advance the gospel, ¹³so that it has become known throughout the whole imperial guard[10] and to all the rest that my imprisonment is for Christ. ¹⁴And most of the brothers, having become confident in the Lord by my imprisonment, are much more bold to speak the word[11] without fear.

¹⁵Some indeed preach Christ from envy and rivalry, but others from good will. ¹⁶The latter do it out of love, knowing that I am put here for the defense of the gospel. ¹⁷The former proclaim Christ out of selfish ambition, not sincerely but thinking to afflict me in my imprisonment. ¹⁸What then? Only that in every

[1] Or show [2] Or healing [3] Or jealousy [4] Wisdom rests quietly in the heart of a man of understanding, but makes itself known even in the midst of fools [5] Or slaves (for the contextual rendering of the Greek word doulos, see Preface) [6] Or bishops; Greek episkopoi [7] Or servants, or ministers; Greek diakonoi [8] Or you all have fellowship with me in grace [9] Or brothers and sisters. The plural Greek word adelphoi (translated "brothers") refers to siblings in a family. In New Testament usage, depending on the context, adelphoi may refer either to men or to both men and women who are siblings (brothers and sisters) in God's family, the church; also verse 14 [10] Greek in the whole praetorium [11] Some manuscripts add of God

way, whether in pretense or in truth, Christ is proclaimed, and in that I rejoice.

Yes, and I will rejoice, [19] for I know that through your prayers and the help of the Spirit of Jesus Christ this will turn out for my deliverance, [20] as it is my eager expectation and hope that I will not be at all ashamed, but that with full courage now as always Christ will be honored in my body, whether by life or by death. [21] For to me to live is Christ, and to die is gain. [22] If I am to live in the flesh, that means fruitful labor for me. Yet which I shall choose I cannot tell. [23] I am hard pressed between the two. My desire is to depart and be with Christ, for that is far better. [24] But to remain in the flesh is more necessary on your account. [25] Convinced of this, I know that I will remain and continue with you all, for your progress and joy in the faith, [26] so that in me you may have ample cause to glory in Christ Jesus, because of my coming to you again.

[27] Only let your manner of life be worthy[1] of the gospel of Christ, so that whether I come and see you or am absent, I may hear of you that you are standing firm in one spirit, with one mind striving side by side for the faith of the gospel, [28] and not frightened in anything by your opponents. This is a clear sign to them of their destruction, but of your salvation, and that from God. [29] For it has been granted to you that for the sake of Christ you should not only believe in him but also suffer for his sake, [30] engaged in the same conflict that you saw I had and now hear that I still have.

MARCH 28

Exodus 39

From the blue and purple and scarlet yarns they made finely woven garments,[2] for ministering in the Holy Place. They made the holy garments for Aaron, as the Lord had commanded Moses.

[2] He made the ephod of gold, blue and purple and scarlet yarns, and fine twined linen. [3] And they hammered out gold leaf, and he cut it into threads to work into the blue and purple and the scarlet yarns, and into the fine twined linen, in skilled design. [4] They made for the ephod attaching shoulder pieces, joined to it at its two edges. [5] And the skillfully woven band on it was of one piece with it and made like it, of gold, blue and purple and scarlet yarns, and fine twined linen, as the Lord had commanded Moses.

[6] They made the onyx stones, enclosed in settings of gold filigree, and engraved like the engravings of a signet, according to the names of the sons of Israel. [7] And he set them on the shoulder pieces of the ephod to be stones of remembrance for the sons of Israel, as the Lord had commanded Moses.

[8] He made the breastpiece, in skilled work, in the style of the ephod, of gold, blue and purple and scarlet yarns, and fine twined linen. [9] It was square. They made the breastpiece doubled, a span[3] its length and a span its breadth when doubled. [10] And they set in it four rows of stones. A row of sardius, topaz, and carbuncle was the first row; [11] and the second row, an emerald, a sapphire, and a diamond; [12] and the third row, a jacinth, an agate, and an amethyst; [13] and the fourth row, a beryl, an onyx, and a jasper. They were enclosed in settings of gold filigree. [14] There were twelve stones with their names according to the names of the sons of Israel. They were like signets, each engraved with its name, for the twelve tribes. [15] And they made on the breastpiece twisted chains like cords, of pure gold. [16] And they made two settings of gold filigree and two gold rings, and put the two rings on the two edges of the breastpiece. [17] And they put the two cords of gold in the two rings at the edges of the breastpiece. [18] They attached the two ends of the two cords to the two settings of filigree. Thus they attached it in front to the shoulder pieces of the ephod. [19] Then they made

[1] Greek *Only behave as citizens worthy* [2] Or *garments for worship* [3] A span was about 9 inches or 22 centimeters

two rings of gold, and put them at the two ends of the breastpiece, on its inside edge next to the ephod. ²⁰And they made two rings of gold, and attached them in front to the lower part of the two shoulder pieces of the ephod, at its seam above the skillfully woven band of the ephod. ²¹And they bound the breastpiece by its rings to the rings of the ephod with a lace of blue, so that it should lie on the skillfully woven band of the ephod, and that the breastpiece should not come loose from the ephod, as the LORD had commanded Moses.

²²He also made the robe of the ephod woven all of blue, ²³and the opening of the robe in it was like the opening in a garment, with a binding around the opening, so that it might not tear. ²⁴On the hem of the robe they made pomegranates of blue and purple and scarlet yarns and fine twined linen. ²⁵They also made bells of pure gold, and put the bells between the pomegranates all around the hem of the robe, between the pomegranates— ²⁶a bell and a pomegranate, a bell and a pomegranate around the hem of the robe for ministering, as the LORD had commanded Moses.

²⁷They also made the coats, woven of fine linen, for Aaron and his sons, ²⁸and the turban of fine linen, and the caps of fine linen, and the linen undergarments of fine twined linen, ²⁹and the sash of fine twined linen and of blue and purple and scarlet yarns, embroidered with needlework, as the LORD had commanded Moses.

³⁰They made the plate of the holy crown of pure gold, and wrote on it an inscription, like the engraving of a signet, "Holy to the LORD." ³¹And they tied to it a cord of blue to fasten it on the turban above, as the LORD had commanded Moses.

³²Thus all the work of the tabernacle of the tent of meeting was finished, and the people of Israel did according to all that the LORD had commanded Moses; so they did. ³³Then they brought the tabernacle to Moses, the tent and all its utensils, its hooks, its frames, its bars, its pillars, and its bases; ³⁴the covering of tanned rams' skins and goatskins, and the veil of the screen; ³⁵the ark of the testimony with its poles and the mercy seat; ³⁶the table with all its utensils, and the bread of the Presence; ³⁷the lampstand of pure gold and its lamps with the lamps set and all its utensils, and the oil for the light;

³⁸the golden altar, the anointing oil and the fragrant incense, and the screen for the entrance of the tent; ³⁹the bronze altar, and its grating of bronze, its poles, and all its utensils; the basin and its stand; ⁴⁰the hangings of the court, its pillars, and its bases, and the screen for the gate of the court, its cords, and its pegs; and all the utensils for the service of the tabernacle, for the tent of meeting; ⁴¹the finely worked garments for ministering in the Holy Place, the holy garments for Aaron the priest, and the garments of his sons for their service as priests. ⁴²According to all that the LORD had commanded Moses, so the people of Israel had done all the work. ⁴³And Moses saw all the work, and behold, they had done it; as the LORD had commanded, so had they done it. Then Moses blessed them.

───────── *John 18* ─────────

When Jesus had spoken these words, he went out with his disciples across the brook Kidron, where there was a garden, which he and his disciples entered. ²Now Judas, who betrayed him, also knew the place, for Jesus often met there with his disciples. ³So Judas, having procured a band of soldiers and some officers from the chief priests and the Pharisees, went there with lanterns and torches and weapons. ⁴Then Jesus, knowing all that would happen to him, came forward and said to them, "Whom do you seek?" ⁵They answered him, "Jesus of Nazareth." Jesus said to them, "I am he."¹ Judas, who betrayed him, was standing with them. ⁶When Jesus² said to them, "I am he," they drew back and fell to the ground. ⁷So he asked them again, "Whom do you seek?" And they said, "Jesus of Nazareth." ⁸Jesus answered, "I told you that I am he. So, if you seek me, let these men go." ⁹This was to fulfill the word that he had spoken: "Of those whom you gave me I have lost not one." ¹⁰Then Simon Peter, having a sword, drew it and struck the high priest's servant³ and cut off his right ear. (The servant's name was Malchus.) ¹¹So Jesus said to Peter, "Put your sword into its sheath; shall I not drink the cup that the Father has given me?"

¹²So the band of soldiers and their captain and the officers of the Jews⁴ arrested Jesus and bound him. ¹³First they led him to Annas, for he was the father-in-law of Caiaphas, who was

¹ Greek *I am*; also verses 6, 8 ² Greek *he* ³ Greek *bondservant*; twice in this verse ⁴ Greek *Ioudaioi* probably refers here to Jewish religious leaders, and others under their influence, in that time; also verses 14, 31, 36, 38

high priest that year. ¹⁴It was Caiaphas who had advised the Jews that it would be expedient that one man should die for the people.

¹⁵Simon Peter followed Jesus, and so did another disciple. Since that disciple was known to the high priest, he entered with Jesus into the courtyard of the high priest, ¹⁶but Peter stood outside at the door. So the other disciple, who was known to the high priest, went out and spoke to the servant girl who kept watch at the door, and brought Peter in. ¹⁷The servant girl at the door said to Peter, "You also are not one of this man's disciples, are you?" He said, "I am not." ¹⁸Now the servants¹ and officers had made a charcoal fire, because it was cold, and they were standing and warming themselves. Peter also was with them, standing and warming himself.

¹⁹The high priest then questioned Jesus about his disciples and his teaching. ²⁰Jesus answered him, "I have spoken openly to the world. I have always taught in synagogues and in the temple, where all Jews come together. I have said nothing in secret. ²¹Why do you ask me? Ask those who have heard me what I said to them; they know what I said." ²²When he had said these things, one of the officers standing by struck Jesus with his hand, saying, "Is that how you answer the high priest?" ²³Jesus answered him, "If what I said is wrong, bear witness about the wrong; but if what I said is right, why do you strike me?" ²⁴Annas then sent him bound to Caiaphas the high priest.

²⁵Now Simon Peter was standing and warming himself. So they said to him, "You also are not one of his disciples, are you?" He denied it and said, "I am not." ²⁶One of the servants of the high priest, a relative of the man whose ear Peter had cut off, asked, "Did I not see you in the garden with him?" ²⁷Peter again denied it, and at once a rooster crowed.

²⁸Then they led Jesus from the house of Caiaphas to the governor's headquarters.² It was early morning. They themselves did not enter the governor's headquarters, so that they would not be defiled, but could eat the Passover. ²⁹So Pilate went outside to them and said, "What accusation do you bring against this man?" ³⁰They answered him, "If this man were not doing evil, we would not have delivered him over to you." ³¹Pilate said to them, "Take him yourselves and judge him by your own law." The Jews said to him, "It is not lawful for us to put anyone to death." ³²This was to fulfill the word that Jesus had spoken to show by what kind of death he was going to die.

³³So Pilate entered his headquarters again and called Jesus and said to him, "Are you the King of the Jews?" ³⁴Jesus answered, "Do you say this of your own accord, or did others say it to you about me?" ³⁵Pilate answered, "Am I a Jew? Your own nation and the chief priests have delivered you over to me. What have you done?" ³⁶Jesus answered, "My kingdom is not of this world. If my kingdom were of this world, my servants would have been fighting, that I might not be delivered over to the Jews. But my kingdom is not from the world." ³⁷Then Pilate said to him, "So you are a king?" Jesus answered, "You say that I am a king. For this purpose I was born and for this purpose I have come into the world—to bear witness to the truth. Everyone who is of the truth listens to my voice." ³⁸Pilate said to him, "What is truth?"

After he had said this, he went back outside to the Jews and told them, "I find no guilt in him. ³⁹But you have a custom that I should release one man for you at the Passover. So do you want me to release to you the King of the Jews?" ⁴⁰They cried out again, "Not this man, but Barabbas!" Now Barabbas was a robber.³

Proverbs 15

1 A soft answer turns away wrath,
   but a harsh word stirs up anger.
2 The tongue of the wise commends knowledge,
   but the mouths of fools pour out folly.
3 The eyes of the LORD are in every place,
   keeping watch on the evil and the good.
4 A gentle⁴ tongue is a tree of life,
   but perverseness in it breaks the spirit.
5 A fool despises his father's instruction,
   but whoever heeds reproof is prudent.
6 In the house of the righteous there is much treasure,
   but trouble befalls the income of the wicked.
7 The lips of the wise spread knowledge;
   not so the hearts of fools.⁵

¹ Greek bondservants; also verse 26 ² Greek the praetorium ³ Or an insurrectionist ⁴ Or healing ⁵ Or the hearts of fools are not steadfast

8 The sacrifice of the wicked is an
    abomination to the LORD,
but the prayer of the upright is
    acceptable to him.

9 The way of the wicked is an
    abomination to the LORD,
but he loves him who pursues
    righteousness.

10 There is severe discipline for him who
    forsakes the way;
whoever hates reproof will die.

11 Sheol and Abaddon lie open before the
    LORD;
how much more the hearts of the
    children of man!

12 A scoffer does not like to be reproved;
he will not go to the wise.

13 A glad heart makes a cheerful face,
but by sorrow of heart the spirit is
    crushed.

14 The heart of him who has
    understanding seeks knowledge,
but the mouths of fools feed on folly.

15 All the days of the afflicted are evil,
but the cheerful of heart has a
    continual feast.

16 Better is a little with the fear of the
    LORD
than great treasure and trouble with
    it.

17 Better is a dinner of herbs where love is
than a fattened ox and hatred with it.

18 A hot-tempered man stirs up strife,
but he who is slow to anger quiets
    contention.

19 The way of a sluggard is like a hedge of
    thorns,
but the path of the upright is a level
    highway.

20 A wise son makes a glad father,
but a foolish man despises his mother.

21 Folly is a joy to him who lacks sense,
but a man of understanding walks
    straight ahead.

22 Without counsel plans fail,
but with many advisers they succeed.

23 To make an apt answer is a joy to a man,
and a word in season, how good it is!

24 The path of life leads upward for the
    prudent,
that he may turn away from Sheol
    beneath.

25 The LORD tears down the house of the
    proud
but maintains the widow's
    boundaries.

26 The thoughts of the wicked are an
    abomination to the LORD,
but gracious words are pure.

27 Whoever is greedy for unjust gain
    troubles his own household,
but he who hates bribes will live.

28 The heart of the righteous ponders how
    to answer,
but the mouth of the wicked pours out
    evil things.

29 The LORD is far from the wicked,
but he hears the prayer of the
    righteous.

30 The light of the eyes rejoices the heart,
and good news refreshes[1] the bones.

31 The ear that listens to life-giving reproof
will dwell among the wise.

32 Whoever ignores instruction despises
    himself,
but he who listens to reproof gains
    intelligence.

33 The fear of the LORD is instruction in
    wisdom,
and humility comes before honor.

Philippians 2

So if there is any encouragement in Christ, any comfort from love, any participation in the Spirit, any affection and sympathy, [2] complete my joy by being of the same mind, having the same love, being in full accord and of one mind. [3] Do nothing from selfish ambition or conceit, but in humility count others more significant than yourselves. [4] Let each of you look not only to his own interests, but also to the interests of others. [5] Have this mind among yourselves, which is yours in Christ Jesus,[2] [6] who, though he was in the form of God, did not count equality with God a thing to be grasped, [7] but emptied himself, by taking the form of a servant,[3] being born in the likeness of men. [8] And being found in human form, he humbled himself by becoming obedient to the point of death, even death on a cross. [9] Therefore God has highly exalted him and bestowed on him the name that is above every name, [10] so that at the name of Jesus

---
[1] Hebrew *makes fat* [2] Or *which was also in Christ Jesus* [3] Greek *bondservant*

every knee should bow, in heaven and on earth and under the earth, [11] and every tongue confess that Jesus Christ is Lord, to the glory of God the Father.

[12] Therefore, my beloved, as you have always obeyed, so now, not only as in my presence but much more in my absence, work out your own salvation with fear and trembling, [13] for it is God who works in you, both to will and to work for his good pleasure.

[14] Do all things without grumbling or disputing, [15] that you may be blameless and innocent, children of God without blemish in the midst of a crooked and twisted generation, among whom you shine as lights in the world, [16] holding fast to the word of life, so that in the day of Christ I may be proud that I did not run in vain or labor in vain. [17] Even if I am to be poured out as a drink offering upon the sacrificial offering of your faith, I am glad and rejoice with you all. [18] Likewise you also should be glad and rejoice with me.

[19] I hope in the Lord Jesus to send Timothy to you soon, so that I too may be cheered by news of you. [20] For I have no one like him, who will be genuinely concerned for your welfare. [21] For they all seek their own interests, not those of Jesus Christ. [22] But you know Timothy's[1] proven worth, how as a son[2] with a father he has served with me in the gospel. [23] I hope therefore to send him just as soon as I see how it will go with me, [24] and I trust in the Lord that shortly I myself will come also.

[25] I have thought it necessary to send to you Epaphroditus my brother and fellow worker and fellow soldier, and your messenger and minister to my need, [26] for he has been longing for you all and has been distressed because you heard that he was ill. [27] Indeed he was ill, near to death. But God had mercy on him, and not only on him but on me also, lest I should have sorrow upon sorrow. [28] I am the more eager to send him, therefore, that you may rejoice at seeing him again, and that I may be less anxious. [29] So receive him in the Lord with all joy, and honor such men, [30] for he nearly died for the work of Christ, risking his life to complete what was lacking in your service to me.

MARCH 29

Exodus 40

The LORD spoke to Moses, saying, [2] "On the first day of the first month you shall erect the tabernacle of the tent of meeting. [3] And you shall put in it the ark of the testimony, and you shall screen the ark with the veil. [4] And you shall bring in the table and arrange it, and you shall bring in the lampstand and set up its lamps. [5] And you shall put the golden altar for incense before the ark of the testimony, and set up the screen for the door of the tabernacle. [6] You shall set the altar of burnt offering before the door of the tabernacle of the tent of meeting, [7] and place the basin between the tent of meeting and the altar, and put water in it. [8] And you shall set up the court all around, and hang up the screen for the gate of the court.

[9] "Then you shall take the anointing oil and anoint the tabernacle and all that is in it, and consecrate it and all its furniture, so that it may become holy. [10] You shall also anoint the altar of burnt offering and all its utensils, and consecrate the altar, so that the altar may become most holy. [11] You shall also anoint the basin and its stand, and consecrate it. [12] Then you shall bring Aaron and his sons to the entrance of the tent of meeting and shall wash them with water [13] and put on Aaron the holy garments. And you shall anoint him and consecrate him, that he may serve me as priest. [14] You shall bring his sons also and put coats on them, [15] and anoint them, as you anointed their father, that they may serve me as priests. And their anointing shall admit them to a perpetual priesthood throughout their generations."

[1] Greek *his* [2] Greek *child*

[16] This Moses did; according to all that the Lord commanded him, so he did. [17] In the first month in the second year, on the first day of the month, the tabernacle was erected. [18] Moses erected the tabernacle. He laid its bases, and set up its frames, and put in its poles, and raised up its pillars. [19] And he spread the tent over the tabernacle and put the covering of the tent over it, as the Lord had commanded Moses. [20] He took the testimony and put it into the ark, and put the poles on the ark and set the mercy seat above on the ark. [21] And he brought the ark into the tabernacle and set up the veil of the screen, and screened the ark of the testimony, as the Lord had commanded Moses. [22] He put the table in the tent of meeting, on the north side of the tabernacle, outside the veil, [23] and arranged the bread on it before the Lord, as the Lord had commanded Moses. [24] He put the lampstand in the tent of meeting, opposite the table on the south side of the tabernacle, [25] and set up the lamps before the Lord, as the Lord had commanded Moses. [26] He put the golden altar in the tent of meeting before the veil, [27] and burned fragrant incense on it, as the Lord had commanded Moses. [28] He put in place the screen for the door of the tabernacle. [29] And he set the altar of burnt offering at the entrance of the tabernacle of the tent of meeting, and offered on it the burnt offering and the grain offering, as the Lord had commanded Moses. [30] He set the basin between the tent of meeting and the altar, and put water in it for washing, [31] with which Moses and Aaron and his sons washed their hands and their feet. [32] When they went into the tent of meeting, and when they approached the altar, they washed, as the Lord commanded Moses. [33] And he erected the court around the tabernacle and the altar, and set up the screen of the gate of the court. So Moses finished the work.

[34] Then the cloud covered the tent of meeting, and the glory of the Lord filled the tabernacle. [35] And Moses was not able to enter the tent of meeting because the cloud settled on it, and the glory of the Lord filled the tabernacle. [36] Throughout all their journeys, whenever the cloud was taken up from over the tabernacle, the people of Israel would set out. [37] But if the cloud was not taken up, then they did not set out till the day that it was taken up. [38] For the cloud of the Lord was on the tabernacle by day, and fire was in it by night, in the sight of all the house of Israel throughout all their journeys.

John 19

Then Pilate took Jesus and flogged him. [2] And the soldiers twisted together a crown of thorns and put it on his head and arrayed him in a purple robe. [3] They came up to him, saying, "Hail, King of the Jews!" and struck him with their hands. [4] Pilate went out again and said to them, "See, I am bringing him out to you that you may know that I find no guilt in him." [5] So Jesus came out, wearing the crown of thorns and the purple robe. Pilate said to them, "Behold the man!" [6] When the chief priests and the officers saw him, they cried out, "Crucify him, crucify him!" Pilate said to them, "Take him yourselves and crucify him, for I find no guilt in him." [7] The Jews[1] answered him, "We have a law, and according to that law he ought to die because he has made himself the Son of God." [8] When Pilate heard this statement, he was even more afraid. [9] He entered his headquarters again and said to Jesus, "Where are you from?" But Jesus gave him no answer. [10] So Pilate said to him, "You will not speak to me? Do you not know that I have authority to release you and authority to crucify you?" [11] Jesus answered him, "You would have no authority over me at all unless it had been given you from above. Therefore he who delivered me over to you has the greater sin."

[12] From then on Pilate sought to release him, but the Jews cried out, "If you release this man, you are not Caesar's friend. Everyone who makes himself a king opposes Caesar." [13] So when Pilate heard these words, he brought Jesus out and sat down on the judgment seat at a place called The Stone Pavement, and in Aramaic[2] Gabbatha. [14] Now it was the day of Preparation of the Passover. It was about the sixth hour.[3] He said to the Jews, "Behold your King!" [15] They cried out, "Away with him, away with him, crucify him!" Pilate said to them, "Shall I crucify your King?" The chief priests answered, "We have no king but Caesar." [16] So he delivered him over to them to be crucified.

So they took Jesus, [17] and he went out, bearing his own cross, to the place called The Place of a Skull, which in Aramaic is called Golgotha.

---

[1] Greek *Ioudaioi* probably refers here to Jewish religious leaders, and others under their influence, in that time; also verses 12, 14, 31, 38   [2] Or *Hebrew*; also verses 17, 20   [3] That is, about noon

[18]There they crucified him, and with him two others, one on either side, and Jesus between them. [19]Pilate also wrote an inscription and put it on the cross. It read, "Jesus of Nazareth, the King of the Jews." [20]Many of the Jews read this inscription, for the place where Jesus was crucified was near the city, and it was written in Aramaic, in Latin, and in Greek. [21]So the chief priests of the Jews said to Pilate, "Do not write, 'The King of the Jews,' but rather, 'This man said, I am King of the Jews.'" [22]Pilate answered, "What I have written I have written."

[23]When the soldiers had crucified Jesus, they took his garments and divided them into four parts, one part for each soldier; also his tunic.[1] But the tunic was seamless, woven in one piece from top to bottom, [24]so they said to one another, "Let us not tear it, but cast lots for it to see whose it shall be." This was to fulfill the Scripture which says,

> "They divided my garments among them,
>   and for my clothing they cast lots."

So the soldiers did these things, [25]but standing by the cross of Jesus were his mother and his mother's sister, Mary the wife of Clopas, and Mary Magdalene. [26]When Jesus saw his mother and the disciple whom he loved standing nearby, he said to his mother, "Woman, behold, your son!" [27]Then he said to the disciple, "Behold, your mother!" And from that hour the disciple took her to his own home.

[28]After this, Jesus, knowing that all was now finished, said (to fulfill the Scripture), "I thirst." [29]A jar full of sour wine stood there, so they put a sponge full of the sour wine on a hyssop branch and held it to his mouth. [30]When Jesus had received the sour wine, he said, "It is finished," and he bowed his head and gave up his spirit.

[31]Since it was the day of Preparation, and so that the bodies would not remain on the cross on the Sabbath (for that Sabbath was a high day), the Jews asked Pilate that their legs might be broken and that they might be taken away. [32]So the soldiers came and broke the legs of the first, and of the other who had been crucified with him. [33]But when they came to Jesus and saw that he was already dead, they did not break his legs. [34]But one of the soldiers pierced his side with a spear, and at once there came out blood and water. [35]He who saw it has borne witness—his testimony is true, and he knows

that he is telling the truth—that you also may believe. [36]For these things took place that the Scripture might be fulfilled: "Not one of his bones will be broken." [37]And again another Scripture says, "They will look on him whom they have pierced."

[38]After these things Joseph of Arimathea, who was a disciple of Jesus, but secretly for fear of the Jews, asked Pilate that he might take away the body of Jesus, and Pilate gave him permission. So he came and took away his body. [39]Nicodemus also, who earlier had come to Jesus[2] by night, came bringing a mixture of myrrh and aloes, about seventy-five pounds[3] in weight. [40]So they took the body of Jesus and bound it in linen cloths with the spices, as is the burial custom of the Jews. [41]Now in the place where he was crucified there was a garden, and in the garden a new tomb in which no one had yet been laid. [42]So because of the Jewish day of Preparation, since the tomb was close at hand, they laid Jesus there.

Proverbs 16

The plans of the heart belong to man,
    but the answer of the tongue is from the
    LORD.
2   All the ways of a man are pure in his
        own eyes,
    but the LORD weighs the spirit.
3   Commit your work to the LORD,
    and your plans will be established.
4   The LORD has made everything for its
        purpose,
    even the wicked for the day of trouble.
5   Everyone who is arrogant in heart is an
        abomination to the LORD;
    be assured, he will not go unpunished.
6   By steadfast love and faithfulness
        iniquity is atoned for,
    and by the fear of the LORD one turns
        away from evil.
7   When a man's ways please the LORD,
    he makes even his enemies to be at
        peace with him.
8   Better is a little with righteousness
    than great revenues with injustice.
9   The heart of man plans his way,
    but the LORD establishes his steps.
10 An oracle is on the lips of a king;
    his mouth does not sin in judgment.

---

[1] Greek *chiton*, a long garment worn under the cloak next to the skin [2] Greek *him* [3] Greek *one hundred litras; a litra* (or Roman pound) was equal to about 11 1/2 ounces or 327 grams

11 A just balance and scales are the LORD's;
  all the weights in the bag are his work.
12 It is an abomination to kings to do evil,
  for the throne is established by
   righteousness.
13 Righteous lips are the delight of a king,
  and he loves him who speaks what is
   right.
14 A king's wrath is a messenger of death,
  and a wise man will appease it.
15 In the light of a king's face there is life,
  and his favor is like the clouds that
   bring the spring rain.
16 How much better to get wisdom than
   gold!
  To get understanding is to be chosen
   rather than silver.
17 The highway of the upright turns aside
   from evil;
  whoever guards his way preserves his
   life.
18 Pride goes before destruction,
  and a haughty spirit before a fall.
19 It is better to be of a lowly spirit with the
   poor
  than to divide the spoil with the
   proud.
20 Whoever gives thought to the word[1] will
   discover good,
  and blessed is he who trusts in the
   LORD.
21 The wise of heart is called discerning,
  and sweetness of speech increases
   persuasiveness.
22 Good sense is a fountain of life to him
   who has it,
  but the instruction of fools is folly.
23 The heart of the wise makes his speech
   judicious
  and adds persuasiveness to his lips.
24 Gracious words are like a honeycomb,
  sweetness to the soul and health to
   the body.
25 There is a way that seems right to a man,
  but its end is the way to death.[2]
26 A worker's appetite works for him;
  his mouth urges him on.
27 A worthless man plots evil,
  and his speech[3] is like a scorching fire.
28 A dishonest man spreads strife,
  and a whisperer separates close
   friends.

29 A man of violence entices his neighbor
  and leads him in a way that is not
   good.
30 Whoever winks his eyes plans[4]
   dishonest things;
  he who purses his lips brings evil to
   pass.
31 Gray hair is a crown of glory;
  it is gained in a righteous life.
32 Whoever is slow to anger is better than
   the mighty,
  and he who rules his spirit than he
   who takes a city.
33 The lot is cast into the lap,
  but its every decision is from the LORD.

Philippians 3

Finally, my brothers,[5] rejoice in the Lord. To write the same things to you is no trouble to me and is safe for you.

[2] Look out for the dogs, look out for the evildoers, look out for those who mutilate the flesh. [3] For we are the circumcision, who worship by the Spirit of God[6] and glory in Christ Jesus and put no confidence in the flesh— [4] though I myself have reason for confidence in the flesh also. If anyone else thinks he has reason for confidence in the flesh, I have more: [5] circumcised on the eighth day, of the people of Israel, of the tribe of Benjamin, a Hebrew of Hebrews; as to the law, a Pharisee; [6] as to zeal, a persecutor of the church; as to righteousness under the law,[7] blameless. [7] But whatever gain I had, I counted as loss for the sake of Christ. [8] Indeed, I count everything as loss because of the surpassing worth of knowing Christ Jesus my Lord. For his sake I have suffered the loss of all things and count them as rubbish, in order that I may gain Christ [9] and be found in him, not having a righteousness of my own that comes from the law, but that which comes through faith in Christ, the righteousness from God that depends on faith— [10] that I may know him and the power of his resurrection, and may share his sufferings, becoming like him in his death, [11] that by any means possible I may attain the resurrection from the dead.

[12] Not that I have already obtained this or am already perfect, but I press on to make it my own, because Christ Jesus has made me his

---

[1] Or to a matter [2] Hebrew ways of death [3] Hebrew what is on his lips [4] Hebrew to plan [5] Or brothers and sisters; also verses 13, 17 [6] Some manuscripts God in spirit [7] Greek in the law

own. [13]Brothers, I do not consider that I have made it my own. But one thing I do: forgetting what lies behind and straining forward to what lies ahead, [14]I press on toward the goal for the prize of the upward call of God in Christ Jesus. [15]Let those of us who are mature think this way, and if in anything you think otherwise, God will reveal that also to you. [16]Only let us hold true to what we have attained.

[17]Brothers, join in imitating me, and keep your eyes on those who walk according to the example you have in us. [18]For many, of whom I have often told you and now tell you even with tears, walk as enemies of the cross of Christ. [19]Their end is destruction, their god is their belly, and they glory in their shame, with minds set on earthly things. [20]But our citizenship is in heaven, and from it we await a Savior, the Lord Jesus Christ, [21]who will transform our lowly body to be like his glorious body, by the power that enables him even to subject all things to himself.

MARCH 30

Leviticus 1

The Lord called Moses and spoke to him from the tent of meeting, saying, [2]"Speak to the people of Israel and say to them, When any one of you brings an offering to the Lord, you shall bring your offering of livestock from the herd or from the flock.

[3]"If his offering is a burnt offering from the herd, he shall offer a male without blemish. He shall bring it to the entrance of the tent of meeting, that he may be accepted before the Lord. [4]He shall lay his hand on the head of the burnt offering, and it shall be accepted for him to make atonement for him. [5]Then he shall kill the bull before the Lord, and Aaron's sons the priests shall bring the blood and throw the blood against the sides of the altar that is at the entrance of the tent of meeting. [6]Then he shall flay the burnt offering and cut it into pieces, [7]and the sons of Aaron the priest shall put fire on the altar and arrange wood on the fire. [8]And Aaron's sons the priests shall arrange the pieces, the head, and the fat, on the wood that is on the fire on the altar; [9]but its entrails and its legs he shall wash with water. And the priest shall burn all of it on the altar, as a burnt offering, a food offering[1] with a pleasing aroma to the Lord.

[10]"If his gift for a burnt offering is from the flock, from the sheep or goats, he shall bring a male without blemish, [11]and he shall kill it on the north side of the altar before the Lord, and Aaron's sons the priests shall throw its blood against the sides of the altar. [12]And he shall cut it into pieces, with its head and its fat, and the priest shall arrange them on the wood that is on the fire on the altar, [13]but the entrails and the legs he shall wash with water. And the priest shall offer all of it and burn it on the altar; it is a burnt offering, a food offering with a pleasing aroma to the Lord.

[14]"If his offering to the Lord is a burnt offering of birds, then he shall bring his offering of turtledoves or pigeons. [15]And the priest shall bring it to the altar and wring off its head and burn it on the altar. Its blood shall be drained out on the side of the altar. [16]He shall remove its crop with its contents[2] and cast it beside the altar on the east side, in the place for ashes. [17]He shall tear it open by its wings, but shall not sever it completely. And the priest shall burn it on the altar, on the wood that is on the fire. It is a burnt offering, a food offering with a pleasing aroma to the Lord.

John 20

Now on the first day of the week Mary Magdalene came to the tomb early, while it was still dark, and saw that the stone had been taken away from the tomb. [2]So she ran and

[1] Or an offering by fire; so throughout Leviticus [2] Or feathers

went to Simon Peter and the other disciple, the one whom Jesus loved, and said to them, "They have taken the Lord out of the tomb, and we do not know where they have laid him." [3] So Peter went out with the other disciple, and they were going toward the tomb. [4] Both of them were running together, but the other disciple outran Peter and reached the tomb first. [5] And stooping to look in, he saw the linen cloths lying there, but he did not go in. [6] Then Simon Peter came, following him, and went into the tomb. He saw the linen cloths lying there, [7] and the face cloth, which had been on Jesus'[1] head, not lying with the linen cloths but folded up in a place by itself. [8] Then the other disciple, who had reached the tomb first, also went in, and he saw and believed; [9] for as yet they did not understand the Scripture, that he must rise from the dead. [10] Then the disciples went back to their homes.

[11] But Mary stood weeping outside the tomb, and as she wept she stooped to look into the tomb. [12] And she saw two angels in white, sitting where the body of Jesus had lain, one at the head and one at the feet. [13] They said to her, "Woman, why are you weeping?" She said to them, "They have taken away my Lord, and I do not know where they have laid him." [14] Having said this, she turned around and saw Jesus standing, but she did not know that it was Jesus. [15] Jesus said to her, "Woman, why are you weeping? Whom are you seeking?" Supposing him to be the gardener, she said to him, "Sir, if you have carried him away, tell me where you have laid him, and I will take him away." [16] Jesus said to her, "Mary." She turned and said to him in Aramaic,[2] "Rabboni!" (which means Teacher). [17] Jesus said to her, "Do not cling to me, for I have not yet ascended to the Father; but go to my brothers and say to them, 'I am ascending to my Father and your Father, to my God and your God.'" [18] Mary Magdalene went and announced to the disciples, "I have seen the Lord"—and that he had said these things to her.

[19] On the evening of that day, the first day of the week, the doors being locked where the disciples were for fear of the Jews,[3] Jesus came and stood among them and said to them, "Peace be with you." [20] When he had said this, he showed them his hands and his side. Then the disciples were glad when they saw the Lord. [21] Jesus said to them again, "Peace be with you. As the Father has sent me, even so I am sending you." [22] And when he had said this, he breathed on them and said to them, "Receive the Holy Spirit. [23] If you forgive the sins of any, they are forgiven them; if you withhold forgiveness from any, it is withheld."

[24] Now Thomas, one of the Twelve, called the Twin,[4] was not with them when Jesus came. [25] So the other disciples told him, "We have seen the Lord." But he said to them, "Unless I see in his hands the mark of the nails, and place my finger into the mark of the nails, and place my hand into his side, I will never believe."

[26] Eight days later, his disciples were inside again, and Thomas was with them. Although the doors were locked, Jesus came and stood among them and said, "Peace be with you." [27] Then he said to Thomas, "Put your finger here, and see my hands; and put out your hand, and place it in my side. Do not disbelieve, but believe." [28] Thomas answered him, "My Lord and my God!" [29] Jesus said to him, "Have you believed because you have seen me? Blessed are those who have not seen and yet have believed."

[30] Now Jesus did many other signs in the presence of the disciples, which are not written in this book; [31] but these are written so that you may believe that Jesus is the Christ, the Son of God, and that by believing you may have life in his name.

Proverbs 17

B etter is a dry morsel with quiet
     than a house full of feasting[5] with strife.
2   A servant who deals wisely will rule over
         a son who acts shamefully
         and will share the inheritance as one
         of the brothers.
3   The crucible is for silver, and the furnace
         is for gold,
         and the LORD tests hearts.
4   An evildoer listens to wicked lips,
         and a liar gives ear to a mischievous
         tongue.
5   Whoever mocks the poor insults his
         Maker;
         he who is glad at calamity will not go
         unpunished.
6   Grandchildren are the crown of the aged,
         and the glory of children is their
         fathers.

---

[1] Greek *his*   [2] Or *Hebrew*   [3] Greek *Ioudaioi* probably refers here to Jewish religious leaders, and others under their influence, in that time   [4] Greek *Didymus*   [5] Hebrew *sacrifices*

7 Fine speech is not becoming to a fool;
  still less is false speech to a prince.
8 A bribe is like a magic stone in the eyes
    of the one who gives it;
  wherever he turns he prospers.
9 Whoever covers an offense seeks love,
  but he who repeats a matter separates
    close friends.
10 A rebuke goes deeper into a man of
     understanding
   than a hundred blows into a fool.
11 An evil man seeks only rebellion,
   and a cruel messenger will be sent
     against him.
12 Let a man meet a she-bear robbed of her
     cubs
   rather than a fool in his folly.
13 If anyone returns evil for good,
   evil will not depart from his house.
14 The beginning of strife is like letting out
     water,
   so quit before the quarrel breaks out.
15 He who justifies the wicked and he who
     condemns the righteous
   are both alike an abomination to the
     Lord.
16 Why should a fool have money in his
     hand to buy wisdom
   when he has no sense?
17 A friend loves at all times,
   and a brother is born for adversity.
18 One who lacks sense gives a pledge
   and puts up security in the presence
     of his neighbor.
19 Whoever loves transgression loves
     strife;
   he who makes his door high seeks
     destruction.
20 A man of crooked heart does not
     discover good,
   and one with a dishonest tongue falls
     into calamity.
21 He who sires a fool gets himself sorrow,
   and the father of a fool has no joy.
22 A joyful heart is good medicine,
   but a crushed spirit dries up the bones.
23 The wicked accepts a bribe in secret[1]
   to pervert the ways of justice.
24 The discerning sets his face toward
     wisdom,
   but the eyes of a fool are on the ends
     of the earth.

25 A foolish son is a grief to his father
   and bitterness to her who bore him.
26 To impose a fine on a righteous man is
     not good,
   nor to strike the noble for their
     uprightness.
27 Whoever restrains his words has
     knowledge,
   and he who has a cool spirit is a man
     of understanding.
28 Even a fool who keeps silent is
     considered wise;
   when he closes his lips, he is deemed
     intelligent.

——————— Philippians 4 ———————

Therefore, my brothers,[2] whom I love and
long for, my joy and crown, stand firm thus
in the Lord, my beloved.

2 I entreat Euodia and I entreat Syntyche to
agree in the Lord. 3 Yes, I ask you also, true companion,[3] help these women, who have labored
side by side with me in the gospel together
with Clement and the rest of my fellow workers, whose names are in the book of life.

4 Rejoice in the Lord always; again I will say,
rejoice. 5 Let your reasonableness be known
to everyone. The Lord is at hand; 6 do not be
anxious about anything, but in everything by
prayer and supplication with thanksgiving let
your requests be made known to God. 7 And the
peace of God, which surpasses all understanding, will guard your hearts and your minds in
Christ Jesus.

8 Finally, brothers, whatever is true, whatever
is honorable, whatever is just, whatever is pure,
whatever is lovely, whatever is commendable, if
there is any excellence, if there is anything worthy of praise, think about these things. 9 What
you have learned and received and heard and
seen in me—practice these things, and the God
of peace will be with you.

10 I rejoiced in the Lord greatly that now at
length you have revived your concern for me.
You were indeed concerned for me, but you
had no opportunity. 11 Not that I am speaking
of being in need, for I have learned in whatever
situation I am to be content. 12 I know how to
be brought low, and I know how to abound. In
any and every circumstance, I have learned the
secret of facing plenty and hunger, abundance

---

[1] Hebrew *a bribe from the bosom* [2] Or *brothers and sisters; also verses 8, 21* [3] Or *loyal Syzygus;* Greek *true yokefellow*

and need. [13] I can do all things through him who strengthens me.

[14] Yet it was kind of you to share[1] my trouble. [15] And you Philippians yourselves know that in the beginning of the gospel, when I left Macedonia, no church entered into partnership with me in giving and receiving, except you only. [16] Even in Thessalonica you sent me help for my needs once and again. [17] Not that I seek the gift, but I seek the fruit that increases to your credit.[2] [18] I have received full payment, and more. I am well supplied, having received from Epaphroditus the gifts you sent, a fragrant offering, a sacrifice acceptable and pleasing to God. [19] And my God will supply every need of yours according to his riches in glory in Christ Jesus. [20] To our God and Father be glory forever and ever. Amen.

[21] Greet every saint in Christ Jesus. The brothers who are with me greet you. [22] All the saints greet you, especially those of Caesar's household.

[23] The grace of the Lord Jesus Christ be with your spirit.

MARCH 31

Leviticus 2–3

[1] "When anyone brings a grain offering as an offering to the LORD, his offering shall be of fine flour. He shall pour oil on it and put frankincense on it [2] and bring it to Aaron's sons the priests. And he shall take from it a handful of the fine flour and oil, with all of its frankincense, and the priest shall burn this as its memorial portion on the altar, a food offering with a pleasing aroma to the LORD. [3] But the rest of the grain offering shall be for Aaron and his sons; it is a most holy part of the LORD's food offerings.

[4] "When you bring a grain offering baked in the oven as an offering, it shall be unleavened loaves of fine flour mixed with oil or unleavened wafers smeared with oil. [5] And if your offering is a grain offering baked on a griddle, it shall be of fine flour unleavened, mixed with oil. [6] You shall break it in pieces and pour oil on it; it is a grain offering. [7] And if your offering is a grain offering cooked in a pan, it shall be made of fine flour with oil. [8] And you shall bring the grain offering that is made of these things to the LORD, and when it is presented to the priest, he shall bring it to the altar. [9] And the priest shall take from the grain offering its memorial portion and burn this on the altar, a food offering with a pleasing aroma to the LORD. [10] But the rest of the grain offering shall be for Aaron and his sons; it is a most holy part of the LORD's food offerings.

[11] "No grain offering that you bring to the LORD shall be made with leaven, for you shall burn no leaven nor any honey as a food offering to the LORD. [12] As an offering of firstfruits you may bring them to the LORD, but they shall not be offered on the altar for a pleasing aroma. [13] You shall season all your grain offerings with salt. You shall not let the salt of the covenant with your God be missing from your grain offering; with all your offerings you shall offer salt.

[14] "If you offer a grain offering of firstfruits to the LORD, you shall offer for the grain offering of your firstfruits fresh ears, roasted with fire, crushed new grain. [15] And you shall put oil on it and lay frankincense on it; it is a grain offering. [16] And the priest shall burn as its memorial portion some of the crushed grain and some of the oil with all of its frankincense; it is a food offering to the LORD.

[3:1] "If his offering is a sacrifice of peace offering, if he offers an animal from the herd, male or female, he shall offer it without blemish before the LORD. [2] And he shall lay his hand on the head of his offering and kill it at the entrance of the tent of meeting, and Aaron's sons the priests shall throw the blood against the sides

[1] Or have fellowship in   [2] Or I seek the profit that accrues to your account

of the altar. **³**And from the sacrifice of the peace offering, as a food offering to the LORD, he shall offer the fat covering the entrails and all the fat that is on the entrails, **⁴**and the two kidneys with the fat that is on them at the loins, and the long lobe of the liver that he shall remove with the kidneys. **⁵**Then Aaron's sons shall burn it on the altar on top of the burnt offering, which is on the wood on the fire; it is a food offering with a pleasing aroma to the LORD.

⁶"If his offering for a sacrifice of peace offering to the LORD is an animal from the flock, male or female, he shall offer it without blemish. **⁷**If he offers a lamb for his offering, then he shall offer it before the LORD, **⁸**lay his hand on the head of his offering, and kill it in front of the tent of meeting; and Aaron's sons shall throw its blood against the sides of the altar. **⁹**Then from the sacrifice of the peace offering he shall offer as a food offering to the LORD its fat; he shall remove the whole fat tail, cut off close to the backbone, and the fat that covers the entrails and all the fat that is on the entrails **¹⁰**and the two kidneys with the fat that is on them at the loins and the long lobe of the liver that he shall remove with the kidneys. **¹¹**And the priest shall burn it on the altar as a food offering to the LORD.

¹²"If his offering is a goat, then he shall offer it before the LORD **¹³**and lay his hand on its head and kill it in front of the tent of meeting, and the sons of Aaron shall throw its blood against the sides of the altar. **¹⁴**Then he shall offer from it, as his offering for a food offering to the LORD, the fat covering the entrails and all the fat that is on the entrails **¹⁵**and the two kidneys with the fat that is on them at the loins and the long lobe of the liver that he shall remove with the kidneys. **¹⁶**And the priest shall burn them on the altar as a food offering with a pleasing aroma. All fat is the LORD's. **¹⁷**It shall be a statute forever throughout your generations, in all your dwelling places, that you eat neither fat nor blood."

John 21

After this Jesus revealed himself again to the disciples by the Sea of Tiberias, and he revealed himself in this way. **²**Simon Peter, Thomas (called the Twin), Nathanael of Cana in Galilee, the sons of Zebedee, and two others of his disciples were together. **³**Simon Peter said to them, "I am going fishing." They said to him, "We will go with you." They went out and got into the boat, but that night they caught nothing.

⁴Just as day was breaking, Jesus stood on the shore; yet the disciples did not know that it was Jesus. **⁵**Jesus said to them, "Children, do you have any fish?" They answered him, "No." **⁶**He said to them, "Cast the net on the right side of the boat, and you will find some." So they cast it, and now they were not able to haul it in, because of the quantity of fish. **⁷**That disciple whom Jesus loved therefore said to Peter, "It is the Lord!" When Simon Peter heard that it was the Lord, he put on his outer garment, for he was stripped for work, and threw himself into the sea. **⁸**The other disciples came in the boat, dragging the net full of fish, for they were not far from the land, but about a hundred yards¹ off.

⁹When they got out on land, they saw a charcoal fire in place, with fish laid out on it, and bread. **¹⁰**Jesus said to them, "Bring some of the fish that you have just caught." **¹¹**So Simon Peter went aboard and hauled the net ashore, full of large fish, 153 of them. And although there were so many, the net was not torn. **¹²**Jesus said to them, "Come and have breakfast." Now none of the disciples dared ask him, "Who are you?" They knew it was the Lord. **¹³**Jesus came and took the bread and gave it to them, and so with the fish. **¹⁴**This was now the third time that Jesus was revealed to the disciples after he was raised from the dead.

¹⁵When they had finished breakfast, Jesus said to Simon Peter, "Simon, son of John, do you love me more than these?" He said to him, "Yes, Lord; you know that I love you." He said to him, "Feed my lambs." **¹⁶**He said to him a second time, "Simon, son of John, do you love me?" He said to him, "Yes, Lord; you know that I love you." He said to him, "Tend my sheep." **¹⁷**He said to him the third time, "Simon, son of John, do you love me?" Peter was grieved because he said to him the third time, "Do you love me?" and he said to him, "Lord, you know everything; you know that I love you." Jesus said to him, "Feed my sheep. **¹⁸**Truly, truly, I say to you, when you were young, you used to dress yourself and walk wherever you wanted, but when you are old, you will stretch out your

¹ Greek *two hundred cubits*; a *cubit* was about 18 inches or 45 centimeters

hands, and another will dress you and carry you where you do not want to go." ¹⁹(This he said to show by what kind of death he was to glorify God.) And after saying this he said to him, "Follow me."

²⁰Peter turned and saw the disciple whom Jesus loved following them, the one who also had leaned back against him during the supper and had said, "Lord, who is it that is going to betray you?" ²¹When Peter saw him, he said to Jesus, "Lord, what about this man?" ²²Jesus said to him, "If it is my will that he remain until I come, what is that to you? You follow me!" ²³So the saying spread abroad among the brothers¹ that this disciple was not to die; yet Jesus did not say to him that he was not to die, but, "If it is my will that he remain until I come, what is that to you?"

²⁴This is the disciple who is bearing witness about these things, and who has written these things, and we know that his testimony is true.

²⁵Now there are also many other things that Jesus did. Were every one of them to be written, I suppose that the world itself could not contain the books that would be written.

Proverbs 18

Whoever isolates himself seeks his own desire;
  he breaks out against all sound judgment.
² A fool takes no pleasure in understanding,
  but only in expressing his opinion.
³ When wickedness comes, contempt comes also,
  and with dishonor comes disgrace.
⁴ The words of a man's mouth are deep waters;
  the fountain of wisdom is a bubbling brook.
⁵ It is not good to be partial to² the wicked
  or to deprive the righteous of justice.
⁶ A fool's lips walk into a fight,
  and his mouth invites a beating.
⁷ A fool's mouth is his ruin,
  and his lips are a snare to his soul.
⁸ The words of a whisperer are like delicious morsels;
  they go down into the inner parts of the body.

⁹ Whoever is slack in his work
  is a brother to him who destroys.
¹⁰ The name of the LORD is a strong tower;
  the righteous man runs into it and is safe.
¹¹ A rich man's wealth is his strong city,
  and like a high wall in his imagination.
¹² Before destruction a man's heart is haughty,
  but humility comes before honor.
¹³ If one gives an answer before he hears,
  it is his folly and shame.
¹⁴ A man's spirit will endure sickness,
  but a crushed spirit who can bear?
¹⁵ An intelligent heart acquires knowledge,
  and the ear of the wise seeks knowledge.
¹⁶ A man's gift makes room for him
  and brings him before the great.
¹⁷ The one who states his case first seems right,
  until the other comes and examines him.
¹⁸ The lot puts an end to quarrels
  and decides between powerful contenders.
¹⁹ A brother offended is more unyielding than a strong city,
  and quarreling is like the bars of a castle.
²⁰ From the fruit of a man's mouth his stomach is satisfied;
  he is satisfied by the yield of his lips.
²¹ Death and life are in the power of the tongue,
  and those who love it will eat its fruits.
²² He who finds a wife finds a good thing
  and obtains favor from the LORD.
²³ The poor use entreaties,
  but the rich answer roughly.
²⁴ A man of many companions may come to ruin,
  but there is a friend who sticks closer than a brother.

Colossians 1

Paul, an apostle of Christ Jesus by the will of God, and Timothy our brother,

²To the saints and faithful brothers³ in Christ at Colossae:

---

¹ Or *brothers and sisters* ² Hebrew to *lift the face of* ³ Or *brothers and sisters*. The plural Greek word *adelphoi* (translated "brothers") refers to siblings in a family. In New Testament usage, depending on the context, *adelphoi* may refer either to men or to both men and women who are siblings (brothers and sisters) in God's family, the church

Grace to you and peace from God our Father. ³We always thank God, the Father of our Lord Jesus Christ, when we pray for you, ⁴since we heard of your faith in Christ Jesus and of the love that you have for all the saints, ⁵because of the hope laid up for you in heaven. Of this you have heard before in the word of the truth, the gospel, ⁶which has come to you, as indeed in the whole world it is bearing fruit and increasing—as it also does among you, since the day you heard it and understood the grace of God in truth, ⁷just as you learned it from Epaphras our beloved fellow servant.¹ He is a faithful minister of Christ on your² behalf ⁸and has made known to us your love in the Spirit.

⁹And so, from the day we heard, we have not ceased to pray for you, asking that you may be filled with the knowledge of his will in all spiritual wisdom and understanding, ¹⁰so as to walk in a manner worthy of the Lord, fully pleasing to him, bearing fruit in every good work and increasing in the knowledge of God. ¹¹May you be strengthened with all power, according to his glorious might, for all endurance and patience with joy, ¹²giving thanks³ to the Father, who has qualified you⁴ to share in the inheritance of the saints in light. ¹³He has delivered us from the domain of darkness and transferred us to the kingdom of his beloved Son, ¹⁴in whom we have redemption, the forgiveness of sins.

¹⁵He is the image of the invisible God, the firstborn of all creation. ¹⁶For by⁵ him all things were created, in heaven and on earth, visible and invisible, whether thrones or dominions or rulers or authorities—all things were created through him and for him. ¹⁷And he is before all things, and in him all things hold together. ¹⁸And he is the head of the body, the church. He is the beginning, the firstborn from the dead, that in everything he might be preeminent. ¹⁹For in him all the fullness of God was pleased to dwell, ²⁰and through him to reconcile to himself all things, whether on earth or in heaven, making peace by the blood of his cross.

²¹And you, who once were alienated and hostile in mind, doing evil deeds, ²²he has now reconciled in his body of flesh by his death, in order to present you holy and blameless and above reproach before him, ²³if indeed you continue in the faith, stable and steadfast, not shifting from the hope of the gospel that you heard, which has been proclaimed in all creation⁶ under heaven, and of which I, Paul, became a minister.

²⁴Now I rejoice in my sufferings for your sake, and in my flesh I am filling up what is lacking in Christ's afflictions for the sake of his body, that is, the church, ²⁵of which I became a minister according to the stewardship from God that was given to me for you, to make the word of God fully known, ²⁶the mystery hidden for ages and generations but now revealed to his saints. ²⁷To them God chose to make known how great among the Gentiles are the riches of the glory of this mystery, which is Christ in you, the hope of glory. ²⁸Him we proclaim, warning everyone and teaching everyone with all wisdom, that we may present everyone mature in Christ. ²⁹For this I toil, struggling with all his energy that he powerfully works within me.

¹ Greek *fellow bondservant* ² Some manuscripts *our* ³ Or *patience, with joy giving thanks* ⁴ Some manuscripts *us* ⁵ That is, by means of; or *in* ⁶ Or *to every creature*

APRIL 1

Leviticus 4

And the LORD spoke to Moses, saying, [2] "Speak to the people of Israel, saying, If anyone sins unintentionally[1] in any of the LORD's commandments about things not to be done, and does any one of them, [3] if it is the anointed priest who sins, thus bringing guilt on the people, then he shall offer for the sin that he has committed a bull from the herd without blemish to the LORD for a sin offering. [4] He shall bring the bull to the entrance of the tent of meeting before the LORD and lay his hand on the head of the bull and kill the bull before the LORD. [5] And the anointed priest shall take some of the blood of the bull and bring it into the tent of meeting, [6] and the priest shall dip his finger in the blood and sprinkle part of the blood seven times before the LORD in front of the veil of the sanctuary. [7] And the priest shall put some of the blood on the horns of the altar of fragrant incense before the LORD that is in the tent of meeting, and all the rest of the blood of the bull he shall pour out at the base of the altar of burnt offering that is at the entrance of the tent of meeting. [8] And all the fat of the bull of the sin offering he shall remove from it, the fat that covers the entrails and all the fat that is on the entrails [9] and the two kidneys with the fat that is on them at the loins and the long lobe of the liver that he shall remove with the kidneys [10] (just as these are taken from the ox of the sacrifice of the peace offerings); and the priest shall burn them on the altar of burnt offering. [11] But the skin of the bull and all its flesh, with its head, its legs, its entrails, and its dung— [12] all the rest of the bull—he shall carry outside the camp to a clean place, to the ash heap, and shall burn it up on a fire of wood. On the ash heap it shall be burned up.

[13] "If the whole congregation of Israel sins unintentionally[2] and the thing is hidden from the eyes of the assembly, and they do any one of the things that by the LORD's commandments ought not to be done, and they realize their guilt,[3] [14] when the sin which they have committed becomes known, the assembly shall offer a bull from the herd for a sin offering and bring it in front of the tent of meeting. [15] And the elders of the congregation shall lay their hands on the head of the bull before the LORD, and the bull shall be killed before the LORD. [16] Then the anointed priest shall bring some of the blood of the bull into the tent of meeting, [17] and the priest shall dip his finger in the blood and sprinkle it seven times before the LORD in front of the veil. [18] And he shall put some of the blood on the horns of the altar that is in the tent of meeting before the LORD, and the rest of the blood he shall pour out at the base of the altar of burnt offering that is at the entrance of the tent of meeting. [19] And all its fat he shall take from it and burn on the altar. [20] Thus shall he do with the bull. As he did with the bull of the sin offering, so shall he do with this. And the priest shall make atonement for them, and they shall be forgiven. [21] And he shall carry the bull outside the camp and burn it up as he burned the first bull; it is the sin offering for the assembly.

[22] "When a leader sins, doing unintentionally any one of all the things that by the commandments of the LORD his God ought not to be done, and realizes his guilt, [23] or the sin which he has committed is made known to him, he shall bring as his offering a goat, a male without blemish, [24] and shall lay his hand on the head of the goat and kill it in the place where they kill the burnt offering before the LORD; it is a sin offering. [25] Then the priest shall take some of the blood of the sin offering with his finger and put it on the horns of the altar of burnt offering and pour out the rest of its blood at the base of the altar of burnt offering. [26] And all its fat he shall burn on the altar, like the fat of the sacrifice of peace offerings. So the priest shall make atonement for him for his sin, and he shall be forgiven.

[27] "If anyone of the common people sins unintentionally in doing any one of the things that by the LORD's commandments ought not

---

[1] Or *by mistake; so throughout Leviticus* [2] Or *makes a mistake* [3] Or *suffer for their guilt, or are guilty; also verses 22, 27, and chapter 5*

to be done, and realizes his guilt, ²⁸or the sin which he has committed is made known to him, he shall bring for his offering a goat, a female without blemish, for his sin which he has committed. ²⁹And he shall lay his hand on the head of the sin offering and kill the sin offering in the place of burnt offering. ³⁰And the priest shall take some of its blood with his finger and put it on the horns of the altar of burnt offering and pour out all the rest of its blood at the base of the altar. ³¹And all its fat he shall remove, as the fat is removed from the peace offerings, and the priest shall burn it on the altar for a pleasing aroma to the LORD. And the priest shall make atonement for him, and he shall be forgiven.

³²"If he brings a lamb as his offering for a sin offering, he shall bring a female without blemish ³³and lay his hand on the head of the sin offering and kill it for a sin offering in the place where they kill the burnt offering. ³⁴Then the priest shall take some of the blood of the sin offering with his finger and put it on the horns of the altar of burnt offering and pour out all the rest of its blood at the base of the altar. ³⁵And all its fat he shall remove as the fat of the lamb is removed from the sacrifice of peace offerings, and the priest shall burn it on the altar, on top of the LORD's food offerings. And the priest shall make atonement for him for the sin which he has committed, and he shall be forgiven.

Psalm 1–2

Blessed is the man[1]
who walks not in the counsel of the
wicked,
nor stands in the way of sinners,
nor sits in the seat of scoffers;
2 but his delight is in the law[2] of the LORD,
and on his law he meditates day and
night.

3 He is like a tree
planted by streams of water
that yields its fruit in its season,
and its leaf does not wither.
In all that he does, he prospers.
4 The wicked are not so,
but are like chaff that the wind drives
away.

5 Therefore the wicked will not stand in
the judgment,
nor sinners in the congregation of the
righteous;
6 for the LORD knows the way of the
righteous,
but the way of the wicked will perish.

Why do the nations rage[3]
and the peoples plot in vain?
2 The kings of the earth set themselves,
and the rulers take counsel together,
against the LORD and against his
Anointed, saying,
3 "Let us burst their bonds apart
and cast away their cords from us."

4 He who sits in the heavens laughs;
the Lord holds them in derision.
5 Then he will speak to them in his
wrath,
and terrify them in his fury, saying,
6 "As for me, I have set my King
on Zion, my holy hill."

7 I will tell of the decree:
The LORD said to me, "You are my Son;
today I have begotten you.
8 Ask of me, and I will make the nations
your heritage,
and the ends of the earth your
possession.
9 You shall break[4] them with a rod of
iron
and dash them in pieces like a potter's
vessel."

10 Now therefore, O kings, be wise;
be warned, O rulers of the earth.
11 Serve the LORD with fear,
and rejoice with trembling.
12 Kiss the Son,
lest he be angry, and you perish in the
way,
for his wrath is quickly kindled.
Blessed are all who take refuge in him.

Proverbs 19

Better is a poor person who walks in his
integrity
than one who is crooked in speech
and is a fool.

---

[1] The singular Hebrew word for *man* (ish) is used here to portray a representative example of a godly person; see Preface [2] Or *instruction* [3] Or *nations noisily assemble*
[4] Revocalization yields (compare Septuagint) *You shall rule*

² Desire¹ without knowledge is not good,
and whoever makes haste with his
feet misses his way.
³ When a man's folly brings his way to
ruin,
his heart rages against the LORD.
⁴ Wealth brings many new friends,
but a poor man is deserted by his
friend.
⁵ A false witness will not go unpunished,
and he who breathes out lies will not
escape.
⁶ Many seek the favor of a generous man,²
and everyone is a friend to a man who
gives gifts.
⁷ All a poor man's brothers hate him;
how much more do his friends go far
from him!
He pursues them with words, but does
not have them.³
⁸ Whoever gets sense loves his own soul;
he who keeps understanding will
discover good.
⁹ A false witness will not go unpunished,
and he who breathes out lies will
perish.
¹⁰ It is not fitting for a fool to live in luxury,
much less for a slave to rule over
princes.
¹¹ Good sense makes one slow to anger,
and it is his glory to overlook an
offense.
¹² A king's wrath is like the growling of a
lion,
but his favor is like dew on the grass.
¹³ A foolish son is ruin to his father,
and a wife's quarreling is a continual
dripping of rain.
¹⁴ House and wealth are inherited from
fathers,
but a prudent wife is from the LORD.
¹⁵ Slothfulness casts into a deep sleep,
and an idle person will suffer hunger.
¹⁶ Whoever keeps the commandment
keeps his life;
he who despises his ways will die.
¹⁷ Whoever is generous to the poor lends
to the LORD,
and he will repay him for his deed.
¹⁸ Discipline your son, for there is hope;
do not set your heart on putting him
to death.

¹⁹ A man of great wrath will pay the
penalty,
for if you deliver him, you will only
have to do it again.
²⁰ Listen to advice and accept instruction,
that you may gain wisdom in the
future.
²¹ Many are the plans in the mind of a man,
but it is the purpose of the LORD that
will stand.
²² What is desired in a man is steadfast
love,
and a poor man is better than a liar.
²³ The fear of the LORD leads to life,
and whoever has it rests satisfied;
he will not be visited by harm.
²⁴ The sluggard buries his hand in the dish
and will not even bring it back to his
mouth.
²⁵ Strike a scoffer, and the simple will learn
prudence;
reprove a man of understanding, and
he will gain knowledge.
²⁶ He who does violence to his father and
chases away his mother
is a son who brings shame and
reproach.
²⁷ Cease to hear instruction, my son,
and you will stray from the words of
knowledge.
²⁸ A worthless witness mocks at justice,
and the mouth of the wicked devours
iniquity.
²⁹ Condemnation is ready for scoffers,
and beating for the backs of fools.

Colossians 2

For I want you to know how great a struggle I have for you and for those at Laodicea and for all who have not seen me face to face, ² that their hearts may be encouraged, being knit together in love, to reach all the riches of full assurance of understanding and the knowledge of God's mystery, which is Christ, ³ in whom are hidden all the treasures of wisdom and knowledge. ⁴ I say this in order that no one may delude you with plausible arguments. ⁵ For though I am absent in body, yet I am with you in spirit, rejoicing to see your good order and the firmness of your faith in Christ.

¹ Or A soul ² Or of a noble ³ The meaning of the Hebrew sentence is uncertain

⁶Therefore, as you received Christ Jesus the Lord, so walk in him, ⁷rooted and built up in him and established in the faith, just as you were taught, abounding in thanksgiving.

⁸See to it that no one takes you captive by philosophy and empty deceit, according to human tradition, according to the elemental spirits¹ of the world, and not according to Christ. ⁹For in him the whole fullness of deity dwells bodily, ¹⁰and you have been filled in him, who is the head of all rule and authority. ¹¹In him also you were circumcised with a circumcision made without hands, by putting off the body of the flesh, by the circumcision of Christ, ¹²having been buried with him in baptism, in which you were also raised with him through faith in the powerful working of God, who raised him from the dead. ¹³And you, who were dead in your trespasses and the uncircumcision of your flesh, God made alive together with him, having forgiven us all our trespasses, ¹⁴by canceling the record of debt that stood against us with its legal demands. This he set aside, nailing it to the cross. ¹⁵He disarmed the rulers and authorities² and put them to open shame, by triumphing over them in him.³

¹⁶Therefore let no one pass judgment on you in questions of food and drink, or with regard to a festival or a new moon or a Sabbath. ¹⁷These are a shadow of the things to come, but the substance belongs to Christ. ¹⁸Let no one disqualify you, insisting on asceticism and worship of angels, going on in detail about visions,⁴ puffed up without reason by his sensuous mind, ¹⁹and not holding fast to the Head, from whom the whole body, nourished and knit together through its joints and ligaments, grows with a growth that is from God.

²⁰If with Christ you died to the elemental spirits of the world, why, as if you were still alive in the world, do you submit to regulations— ²¹"Do not handle, Do not taste, Do not touch" ²²(referring to things that all perish as they are used)— according to human precepts and teachings? ²³These have indeed an appearance of wisdom in promoting self-made religion and asceticism and severity to the body, but they are of no value in stopping the indulgence of the flesh.

APRIL 2

Leviticus 5

"If anyone sins in that he hears a public adjuration to testify, and though he is a witness, whether he has seen or come to know the matter, yet does not speak, he shall bear his iniquity; ²or if anyone touches an unclean thing, whether a carcass of an unclean wild animal or a carcass of unclean livestock or a carcass of unclean swarming things, and it is hidden from him and he has become unclean, and he realizes his guilt; ³or if he touches human uncleanness, of whatever sort the uncleanness may be with which one becomes unclean, and it is hidden from him, when he comes to know it, and realizes his guilt; ⁴or if anyone utters with his lips a rash oath to do evil or to do good, any sort of rash oath that people swear, and it is hidden from him, when he comes to know it, and he realizes his guilt in any of these; ⁵when he realizes his guilt in any of these and confesses the sin he has committed, ⁶he shall bring to the LORD as his compensation⁵ for the sin that he has committed, a female from the flock, a lamb or a goat, for a sin offering. And the priest shall make atonement for him for his sin.

⁷"But if he cannot afford a lamb, then he shall bring to the LORD as his compensation for the sin that he has committed two turtledoves or two pigeons,⁶ one for a sin offering and the other for a burnt offering. ⁸He shall bring them to the priest, who shall offer first the one for the sin offering. He shall wring its head from its neck but shall not sever it completely, ⁹and he shall sprinkle some of the blood of the sin offering on the side of the altar, while the rest of

¹ Or *elementary principles*; also verse 20 ² Probably demonic rulers and authorities ³ Or *in it* (that is, the cross) ⁴ Or *about the things he has seen* ⁵ Hebrew *his guilt penalty*; so throughout Leviticus ⁶ Septuagint *two young pigeons*; also verse 11

the blood shall be drained out at the base of the altar; it is a sin offering. ¹⁰Then he shall offer the second for a burnt offering according to the rule. And the priest shall make atonement for him for the sin that he has committed, and he shall be forgiven.

¹¹"But if he cannot afford two turtledoves or two pigeons, then he shall bring as his offering for the sin that he has committed a tenth of an ephah¹ of fine flour for a sin offering. He shall put no oil on it and shall put no frankincense on it, for it is a sin offering. ¹²And he shall bring it to the priest, and the priest shall take a handful of it as its memorial portion and burn this on the altar, on the LORD's food offerings; it is a sin offering. ¹³Thus the priest shall make atonement for him for the sin which he has committed in any one of these things, and he shall be forgiven. And the remainder² shall be for the priest, as in the grain offering."

¹⁴The LORD spoke to Moses, saying, ¹⁵"If anyone commits a breach of faith and sins unintentionally in any of the holy things of the LORD, he shall bring to the LORD as his compensation, a ram without blemish out of the flock, valued³ in silver shekels,⁴ according to the shekel of the sanctuary, for a guilt offering. ¹⁶He shall also make restitution for what he has done amiss in the holy thing and shall add a fifth to it and give it to the priest. And the priest shall make atonement for him with the ram of the guilt offering, and he shall be forgiven.

¹⁷"If anyone sins, doing any of the things that by the LORD's commandments ought not to be done, though he did not know it, then realizes his guilt, he shall bear his iniquity. ¹⁸He shall bring to the priest a ram without blemish out of the flock, or its equivalent for a guilt offering, and the priest shall make atonement for him for the mistake that he made unintentionally, and he shall be forgiven. ¹⁹It is a guilt offering; he has indeed incurred guilt before⁵ the LORD."

------ **Psalm 3–4** ------

A PSALM OF DAVID, WHEN HE FLED FROM ABSALOM HIS SON.

O LORD, how many are my foes!
Many are rising against me;
² many are saying of my soul,
there is no salvation for him in God. *Selah*⁶

³ But you, O LORD, are a shield about me,
my glory, and the lifter of my head.
⁴ I cried aloud to the LORD,
and he answered me from his holy hill. *Selah*

⁵ I lay down and slept;
I woke again, for the LORD sustained me.
⁶ I will not be afraid of many thousands of people
who have set themselves against me all around.

⁷ Arise, O LORD!
Save me, O my God!
For you strike all my enemies on the cheek;
you break the teeth of the wicked.

⁸ Salvation belongs to the LORD;
your blessing be on your people! *Selah*

TO THE CHOIRMASTER: WITH STRINGED INSTRUMENTS. A PSALM OF DAVID.

Answer me when I call, O God of my righteousness!
You have given me relief when I was in distress.
Be gracious to me and hear my prayer!

² O men,⁷ how long shall my honor be turned into shame?
How long will you love vain words and seek after lies? *Selah*
³ But know that the LORD has set apart the godly for himself;
the LORD hears when I call to him.

⁴ Be angry,⁸ and do not sin;
ponder in your own hearts on your beds, and be silent. *Selah*
⁵ Offer right sacrifices,
and put your trust in the LORD.

⁶ There are many who say, "Who will show us some good?
Lift up the light of your face upon us, O LORD!"
⁷ You have put more joy in my heart
than they have when their grain and wine abound.

¹ An *ephah* was about 3/5 bushel or 22 liters ² Septuagint; Hebrew *it* ³ Or *flock, or its equivalent* ⁴ A *shekel* was about 2/5 ounce or 11 grams ⁵ Or *he has paid full compensation to* ⁶ The meaning of the Hebrew word *Selah*, used frequently in the Psalms, is uncertain. It may be a musical or liturgical direction ⁷ Or *O men of rank* ⁸ Or *Be agitated*

8 In peace I will both lie down and sleep;
for you alone, O Lord, make me dwell
in safety.

Proverbs 20

Wine is a mocker, strong drink a brawler,
and whoever is led astray by it is not
wise.[1]
2 The terror of a king is like the growling
of a lion;
whoever provokes him to anger
forfeits his life.
3 It is an honor for a man to keep aloof
from strife,
but every fool will be quarreling.
4 The sluggard does not plow in the
autumn;
he will seek at harvest and have
nothing.
5 The purpose in a man's heart is like
deep water,
but a man of understanding will draw
it out.
6 Many a man proclaims his own
steadfast love,
but a faithful man who can find?
7 The righteous who walks in his
integrity—
blessed are his children after him!
8 A king who sits on the throne of
judgment
winnows all evil with his eyes.
9 Who can say, "I have made my heart
pure;
I am clean from my sin"?
10 Unequal[2] weights and unequal
measures
are both alike an abomination to the
Lord.
11 Even a child makes himself known by
his acts,
by whether his conduct is pure and
upright.[3]
12 The hearing ear and the seeing eye,
the Lord has made them both.
13 Love not sleep, lest you come to poverty;
open your eyes, and you will have
plenty of bread.
14 "Bad, bad," says the buyer,
but when he goes away, then he
boasts.

15 There is gold and abundance of costly
stones,
but the lips of knowledge are a
precious jewel.
16 Take a man's garment when he has put
up security for a stranger,
and hold it in pledge when he puts up
security for foreigners.[4]
17 Bread gained by deceit is sweet to a
man,
but afterward his mouth will be full of
gravel.
18 Plans are established by counsel;
by wise guidance wage war.
19 Whoever goes about slandering reveals
secrets;
therefore do not associate with a
simple babbler.[5]
20 If one curses his father or his mother,
his lamp will be put out in utter
darkness.
21 An inheritance gained hastily in the
beginning
will not be blessed in the end.
22 Do not say, "I will repay evil";
wait for the Lord, and he will deliver
you.
23 Unequal weights are an abomination to
the Lord,
and false scales are not good.
24 A man's steps are from the Lord;
how then can man understand his
way?
25 It is a snare to say rashly, "It is holy,"
and to reflect only after making vows.
26 A wise king winnows the wicked
and drives the wheel over them.
27 The spirit[6] of man is the lamp of the
Lord,
searching all his innermost parts.
28 Steadfast love and faithfulness preserve
the king,
and by steadfast love his throne is
upheld.
29 The glory of young men is their
strength,
but the splendor of old men is their
gray hair.
30 Blows that wound cleanse away evil;
strokes make clean the innermost
parts.

[1] Or will not become wise [2] Or Two kinds of; also verse 23 [3] Or Even a child can dissemble in his actions, though his conduct seems pure and upright [4] Or for an adulteress (compare 27:13) [5] Hebrew with one who is simple in his lips [6] Hebrew breath

Colossians 3

If then you have been raised with Christ, seek the things that are above, where Christ is, seated at the right hand of God. ²Set your minds on things that are above, not on things that are on earth. ³For you have died, and your life is hidden with Christ in God. ⁴When Christ who is your[1] life appears, then you also will appear with him in glory.

⁵Put to death therefore what is earthly in you:[2] sexual immorality, impurity, passion, evil desire, and covetousness, which is idolatry. ⁶On account of these the wrath of God is coming.[3] ⁷In these you too once walked, when you were living in them. ⁸But now you must put them all away: anger, wrath, malice, slander, and obscene talk from your mouth. ⁹Do not lie to one another, seeing that you have put off the old self[4] with its practices ¹⁰and have put on the new self, which is being renewed in knowledge after the image of its creator. ¹¹Here there is not Greek and Jew, circumcised and uncircumcised, barbarian, Scythian, slave,[5] free; but Christ is all, and in all.

¹²Put on then, as God's chosen ones, holy and beloved, compassionate hearts, kindness, humility, meekness, and patience, ¹³bearing with one another and, if one has a complaint

against another, forgiving each other; as the Lord has forgiven you, so you also must forgive. ¹⁴And above all these put on love, which binds everything together in perfect harmony. ¹⁵And let the peace of Christ rule in your hearts, to which indeed you were called in one body. And be thankful. ¹⁶Let the word of Christ dwell in you richly, teaching and admonishing one another in all wisdom, singing psalms and hymns and spiritual songs, with thankfulness in your hearts to God. ¹⁷And whatever you do, in word or deed, do everything in the name of the Lord Jesus, giving thanks to God the Father through him.

¹⁸Wives, submit to your husbands, as is fitting in the Lord. ¹⁹Husbands, love your wives, and do not be harsh with them. ²⁰Children, obey your parents in everything, for this pleases the Lord. ²¹Fathers, do not provoke your children, lest they become discouraged. ²²Bondservants,[6] obey in everything those who are your earthly masters,[7] not by way of eye-service, as people-pleasers, but with sincerity of heart, fearing the Lord. ²³Whatever you do, work heartily, as for the Lord and not for men, ²⁴knowing that from the Lord you will receive the inheritance as your reward. You are serving the Lord Christ. ²⁵For the wrongdoer will be paid back for the wrong he has done, and there is no partiality.

APRIL 3

Leviticus 6[8]

The Lord spoke to Moses, saying, ²"If anyone sins and commits a breach of faith against the Lord by deceiving his neighbor in a matter of deposit or security, or through robbery, or if he has oppressed his neighbor ³or has found something lost and lied about it, swearing falsely—in any of all the things that people do and sin thereby— ⁴if he has sinned and has realized his guilt and will restore what he took by robbery or what he got by oppression or the deposit that was committed to him or

the lost thing that he found ⁵or anything about which he has sworn falsely, he shall restore it in full and shall add a fifth to it, and give it to him to whom it belongs on the day he realizes his guilt. ⁶And he shall bring to the priest as his compensation to the Lord a ram without blemish out of the flock, or its equivalent for a guilt offering. ⁷And the priest shall make atonement for him before the Lord, and he shall be forgiven for any of the things that one may do and thereby become guilty."

[1] Some manuscripts our [2] Greek therefore your members that are on the earth [3] Some manuscripts add upon the sons of disobedience [4] Greek man; also as supplied in verse 10 [5] Greek bondservant [6] Or Slaves; also 4:1 (for the contextual rendering of the Greek word doulos, see Preface) [7] Or your masters according to the flesh [8] Ch 5:20 in Hebrew

⁸¹The LORD spoke to Moses, saying, ⁹"Command Aaron and his sons, saying, This is the law of the burnt offering. The burnt offering shall be on the hearth on the altar all night until the morning, and the fire of the altar shall be kept burning on it. ¹⁰And the priest shall put on his linen garment and put his linen undergarment on his body, and he shall take up the ashes to which the fire has reduced the burnt offering on the altar and put them beside the altar. ¹¹Then he shall take off his garments and put on other garments and carry the ashes outside the camp to a clean place. ¹²The fire on the altar shall be kept burning on it; it shall not go out. The priest shall burn wood on it every morning, and he shall arrange the burnt offering on it and shall burn on it the fat of the peace offerings. ¹³Fire shall be kept burning on the altar continually; it shall not go out.

¹⁴"And this is the law of the grain offering. The sons of Aaron shall offer it before the LORD in front of the altar. ¹⁵And one shall take from it a handful of the fine flour of the grain offering and its oil and all the frankincense that is on the grain offering and burn this as its memorial portion on the altar, a pleasing aroma to the LORD. ¹⁶And the rest of it Aaron and his sons shall eat. It shall be eaten unleavened in a holy place. In the court of the tent of meeting they shall eat it. ¹⁷It shall not be baked with leaven. I have given it as their portion of my food offerings. It is a thing most holy, like the sin offering and the guilt offering. ¹⁸Every male among the children of Aaron may eat of it, as decreed forever throughout your generations, from the LORD's food offerings. Whatever touches them shall become holy."

¹⁹The LORD spoke to Moses, saying, ²⁰"This is the offering that Aaron and his sons shall offer to the LORD on the day when he is anointed: a tenth of an ephah² of fine flour as a regular grain offering, half of it in the morning and half in the evening. ²¹It shall be made with oil on a griddle. You shall bring it well mixed, in baked³ pieces like a grain offering, and offer it for a pleasing aroma to the LORD. ²²The priest from among Aaron's sons, who is anointed to succeed him, shall offer it to the LORD as decreed forever. The whole of it shall be burned. ²³Every grain offering of a priest shall be wholly burned. It shall not be eaten."

²⁴The LORD spoke to Moses, saying, ²⁵"Speak to Aaron and his sons, saying, This is the law of the sin offering. In the place where the burnt offering is killed shall the sin offering be killed before the LORD; it is most holy. ²⁶The priest who offers it for sin shall eat it. In a holy place it shall be eaten, in the court of the tent of meeting. ²⁷Whatever touches its flesh shall be holy, and when any of its blood is splashed on a garment, you shall wash that on which it was splashed in a holy place. ²⁸And the earthenware vessel in which it is boiled shall be broken. But if it is boiled in a bronze vessel, that shall be scoured and rinsed in water. ²⁹Every male among the priests may eat of it; it is most holy. ³⁰But no sin offering shall be eaten from which any blood is brought into the tent of meeting to make atonement in the Holy Place; it shall be burned up with fire.

--- *Psalm 5–6* ---

TO THE CHOIRMASTER: FOR THE FLUTES.
A PSALM OF DAVID.

G ive ear to my words, O LORD;
  consider my groaning.
2   Give attention to the sound of my cry,
    my King and my God,
    for to you do I pray.
3   O LORD, in the morning you hear my
    voice;
    in the morning I prepare a sacrifice for
    you⁴ and watch.

4   For you are not a God who delights in
    wickedness;
    evil may not dwell with you.
5   The boastful shall not stand before your
    eyes;
    you hate all evildoers.
6   You destroy those who speak lies;
    the LORD abhors the bloodthirsty and
    deceitful man.

7   But I, through the abundance of your
    steadfast love,
    will enter your house.
  I will bow down toward your holy
    temple
    in the fear of you.
8   Lead me, O LORD, in your righteousness
    because of my enemies;
    make your way straight before me.

¹ Ch 6:1 in Hebrew ² An *ephah* was about 3/5 bushel or 22 liters ³ The meaning of the Hebrew is uncertain ⁴ Or *I direct my prayer to you*

9 For there is no truth in their mouth;
　　their inmost self is destruction;
　　their throat is an open grave;
　　they flatter with their tongue.
10 Make them bear their guilt, O God;
　　let them fall by their own counsels;
　　because of the abundance of their
　　　　transgressions cast them out,
　　for they have rebelled against you.

11 But let all who take refuge in you
　　　　rejoice;
　　let them ever sing for joy,
　　and spread your protection over them,
　　　that those who love your name may
　　　　exult in you.
12 For you bless the righteous, O Lord;
　　you cover him with favor as with a
　　　shield.

To the choirmaster: with stringed
instruments; according to The Sheminith.[1]
A Psalm of David.

O Lord, rebuke me not in your anger,
　　nor discipline me in your wrath.
2 Be gracious to me, O Lord, for I am
　　languishing;
　　heal me, O Lord, for my bones are
　　troubled.
3 My soul also is greatly troubled.
　　But you, O Lord—how long?

4 Turn, O Lord, deliver my life;
　　save me for the sake of your steadfast
　　love.
5 For in death there is no remembrance of
　　you;
　　in Sheol who will give you praise?

6 I am weary with my moaning;
　　every night I flood my bed with tears;
　　I drench my couch with my weeping.
7 My eye wastes away because of grief;
　　it grows weak because of all my foes.

8 Depart from me, all you workers of evil,
　　for the Lord has heard the sound of
　　my weeping.
9 The Lord has heard my plea;
　　the Lord accepts my prayer.
10 All my enemies shall be ashamed and
　　greatly troubled;
　　they shall turn back and be put to
　　shame in a moment.

——————— Proverbs 21 ———————

The king's heart is a stream of water in the
　　hand of the Lord;
　　he turns it wherever he will.
2 Every way of a man is right in his own
　　eyes,
　　but the Lord weighs the heart.
3 To do righteousness and justice
　　is more acceptable to the Lord than
　　sacrifice.
4 Haughty eyes and a proud heart,
　　the lamp[2] of the wicked, are sin.
5 The plans of the diligent lead surely to
　　abundance,
　　but everyone who is hasty comes only
　　to poverty.
6 The getting of treasures by a lying
　　tongue
　　is a fleeting vapor and a snare of
　　death.[3]
7 The violence of the wicked will sweep
　　them away,
　　because they refuse to do what is just.
8 The way of the guilty is crooked,
　　but the conduct of the pure is upright.
9 It is better to live in a corner of the
　　housetop
　　than in a house shared with a
　　quarrelsome wife.
10 The soul of the wicked desires evil;
　　his neighbor finds no mercy in his
　　eyes.
11 When a scoffer is punished, the simple
　　becomes wise;
　　when a wise man is instructed, he
　　gains knowledge.
12 The Righteous One observes the house
　　of the wicked;
　　he throws the wicked down to ruin.
13 Whoever closes his ear to the cry of the
　　poor
　　will himself call out and not be
　　answered.
14 A gift in secret averts anger,
　　and a concealed bribe[4] strong wrath.
15 When justice is done, it is a joy to the
　　righteous
　　but terror to evildoers.
16 One who wanders from the way of good
　　sense
　　will rest in the assembly of the dead.

[1] Probably a musical or liturgical term [2] Or the plowing [3] Some Hebrew manuscripts, Septuagint, Latin; most Hebrew manuscripts vapor for those who seek death [4] Hebrew a bribe in the bosom

17 Whoever loves pleasure will be a poor man;
he who loves wine and oil will not be rich.

18 The wicked is a ransom for the righteous,
and the traitor for the upright.

19 It is better to live in a desert land
than with a quarrelsome and fretful woman.

20 Precious treasure and oil are in a wise man's dwelling,
but a foolish man devours it.

21 Whoever pursues righteousness and kindness
will find life, righteousness, and honor.

22 A wise man scales the city of the mighty
and brings down the stronghold in which they trust.

23 Whoever keeps his mouth and his tongue
keeps himself out of trouble.

24 "Scoffer" is the name of the arrogant, haughty man
who acts with arrogant pride.

25 The desire of the sluggard kills him,
for his hands refuse to labor.

26 All day long he craves and craves,
but the righteous gives and does not hold back.

27 The sacrifice of the wicked is an abomination;
how much more when he brings it with evil intent.

28 A false witness will perish,
but the word of a man who hears will endure.

29 A wicked man puts on a bold face,
but the upright gives thought to[1] his ways.

30 No wisdom, no understanding, no counsel
can avail against the LORD.

31 The horse is made ready for the day of battle,
but the victory belongs to the LORD.

Colossians 4

Masters, treat your bondservants justly and fairly, knowing that you also have a Master in heaven. [2] Continue steadfastly in prayer, being watchful in it with thanksgiving. [3] At the same time, pray also for us, that God may open to us a door for the word, to declare the mystery of Christ, on account of which I am in prison— [4] that I may make it clear, which is how I ought to speak.

[5] Walk in wisdom toward outsiders, making the best use of the time. [6] Let your speech always be gracious, seasoned with salt, so that you may know how you ought to answer each person.

[7] Tychicus will tell you all about my activities. He is a beloved brother and faithful minister and fellow servant[2] in the Lord. [8] I have sent him to you for this very purpose, that you may know how we are and that he may encourage your hearts, [9] and with him Onesimus, our faithful and beloved brother, who is one of you. They will tell you of everything that has taken place here.

[10] Aristarchus my fellow prisoner greets you, and Mark the cousin of Barnabas (concerning whom you have received instructions—if he comes to you, welcome him), [11] and Jesus who is called Justus. These are the only men of the circumcision among my fellow workers for the kingdom of God, and they have been a comfort to me. [12] Epaphras, who is one of you, a servant of Christ Jesus, greets you, always struggling on your behalf in his prayers, that you may stand mature and fully assured in all the will of God. [13] For I bear him witness that he has worked hard for you and for those in Laodicea and in Hierapolis. [14] Luke the beloved physician greets you, as does Demas. [15] Give my greetings to the brothers[3] at Laodicea, and to Nympha and the church in her house. [16] And when this letter has been read among you, have it also read in the church of the Laodiceans; and see that you also read the letter from Laodicea. [17] And say to Archippus, "See that you fulfill the ministry that you have received in the Lord."

[18] I, Paul, write this greeting with my own hand. Remember my chains. Grace be with you.

---

[1] Or establishes [2] Greek fellow bondservant; also verse 12 [3] Or brothers and sisters

APRIL 4

Leviticus 7

"This is the law of the guilt offering. It is most holy. [2] In the place where they kill the burnt offering they shall kill the guilt offering, and its blood shall be thrown against the sides of the altar. [3] And all its fat shall be offered, the fat tail, the fat that covers the entrails, [4] the two kidneys with the fat that is on them at the loins, and the long lobe of the liver that he shall remove with the kidneys. [5] The priest shall burn them on the altar as a food offering to the LORD; it is a guilt offering. [6] Every male among the priests may eat of it. It shall be eaten in a holy place. It is most holy. [7] The guilt offering is just like the sin offering; there is one law for them. The priest who makes atonement with it shall have it. [8] And the priest who offers any man's burnt offering shall have for himself the skin of the burnt offering that he has offered. [9] And every grain offering baked in the oven and all that is prepared on a pan or a griddle shall belong to the priest who offers it. [10] And every grain offering, mixed with oil or dry, shall be shared equally among all the sons of Aaron.

[11] "And this is the law of the sacrifice of peace offerings that one may offer to the LORD. [12] If he offers it for a thanksgiving, then he shall offer with the thanksgiving sacrifice unleavened loaves mixed with oil, unleavened wafers smeared with oil, and loaves of fine flour well mixed with oil. [13] With the sacrifice of his peace offerings for thanksgiving he shall bring his offering with loaves of leavened bread. [14] And from it he shall offer one loaf from each offering, as a gift to the LORD. It shall belong to the priest who throws the blood of the peace offerings. [15] And the flesh of the sacrifice of his peace offerings for thanksgiving shall be eaten on the day of his offering. He shall not leave any of it until the morning. [16] But if the sacrifice of his offering is a vow offering or a freewill offering, it shall be eaten on the day that he offers his sacrifice, and on the next day what remains of it shall be eaten. [17] But what remains of the flesh of the sacrifice on the third day shall be burned up with fire. [18] If any of the flesh of the sacrifice of his peace offering is eaten on the third day, he who offers it shall not be accepted, neither shall it be credited to him. It is tainted, and he who eats of it shall bear his iniquity.

[19] "Flesh that touches any unclean thing shall not be eaten. It shall be burned up with fire. All who are clean may eat flesh, [20] but the person who eats of the flesh of the sacrifice of the LORD's peace offerings while an uncleanness is on him, that person shall be cut off from his people. [21] And if anyone touches an unclean thing, whether human uncleanness or an unclean beast or any unclean detestable creature, and then eats some flesh from the sacrifice of the LORD's peace offerings, that person shall be cut off from his people."

[22] The LORD spoke to Moses, saying, [23] "Speak to the people of Israel, saying, You shall eat no fat, of ox or sheep or goat. [24] The fat of an animal that dies of itself and the fat of one that is torn by beasts may be put to any other use, but on no account shall you eat it. [25] For every person who eats of the fat of an animal of which a food offering may be made to the LORD shall be cut off from his people. [26] Moreover, you shall eat no blood whatever, whether of fowl or of animal, in any of your dwelling places. [27] Whoever eats any blood, that person shall be cut off from his people."

[28] The LORD spoke to Moses, saying, [29] "Speak to the people of Israel, saying, Whoever offers the sacrifice of his peace offerings to the LORD shall bring his offering to the LORD from the sacrifice of his peace offerings. [30] His own hands shall bring the LORD's food offerings. He shall bring the fat with the breast, that the breast may be waved as a wave offering before the LORD. [31] The priest shall burn the fat on the altar, but the breast shall be for Aaron and his sons. [32] And the right thigh you shall give to the priest as a contribution from the sacrifice of your peace offerings. [33] Whoever among

the sons of Aaron offers the blood of the peace offerings and the fat shall have the right thigh for a portion. [34]For the breast that is waved and the thigh that is contributed I have taken from the people of Israel, out of the sacrifices of their peace offerings, and have given them to Aaron the priest and to his sons, as a perpetual due from the people of Israel. [35]This is the portion of Aaron and of his sons from the LORD's food offerings, from the day they were presented to serve as priests of the LORD. [36]The LORD commanded this to be given them by the people of Israel, from the day that he anointed them. It is a perpetual due throughout their generations."

[37]This is the law of the burnt offering, of the grain offering, of the sin offering, of the guilt offering, of the ordination offering, and of the peace offering, [38]which the LORD commanded Moses on Mount Sinai, on the day that he commanded the people of Israel to bring their offerings to the LORD, in the wilderness of Sinai.

Psalm 7–8

A SHIGGAION[1] OF DAVID, WHICH HE SANG TO THE LORD CONCERNING THE WORDS OF CUSH, A BENJAMINITE.

O LORD my God, in you do I take refuge;
   save me from all my pursuers and
     deliver me,
[2] lest like a lion they tear my soul apart,
   rending it in pieces, with none to
     deliver.

[3] O LORD my God, if I have done this,
   if there is wrong in my hands,
[4] if I have repaid my friend[2] with evil
   or plundered my enemy without cause,
[5] let the enemy pursue my soul and
     overtake it,
   and let him trample my life to the
     ground
   and lay my glory in the dust.   *Selah*

[6] Arise, O LORD, in your anger;
   lift yourself up against the fury of my
     enemies;
   awake for me; you have appointed a
     judgment.
[7] Let the assembly of the peoples be
     gathered about you;
   over it return on high.

[8] The LORD judges the peoples;
   judge me, O LORD, according to my
     righteousness
   and according to the integrity that is
     in me.
[9] Oh, let the evil of the wicked come to an
     end,
   and may you establish the righteous—
   you who test the minds and hearts,[3]
     O righteous God!
[10] My shield is with God,
   who saves the upright in heart.
[11] God is a righteous judge,
   and a God who feels indignation every
     day.

[12] If a man[4] does not repent, God[5] will
     whet his sword;
   he has bent and readied his bow;
[13] he has prepared for him his deadly
     weapons,
   making his arrows fiery shafts.
[14] Behold, the wicked man conceives evil
   and is pregnant with mischief
   and gives birth to lies.
[15] He makes a pit, digging it out,
   and falls into the hole that he has
     made.
[16] His mischief returns upon his own head,
   and on his own skull his violence
     descends.

[17] I will give to the LORD the thanks due to
     his righteousness,
   and I will sing praise to the name of
     the LORD, the Most High.

TO THE CHOIRMASTER: ACCORDING TO THE GITTITH.[6] A PSALM OF DAVID.

O LORD, our Lord,
   how majestic is your name in all the
     earth!
   You have set your glory above the
     heavens.
[2] Out of the mouth of babies and infants,
   you have established strength because
     of your foes,
   to still the enemy and the avenger.

[3] When I look at your heavens, the work
     of your fingers,
   the moon and the stars, which you
     have set in place,

---

[1] Probably a musical or liturgical term [2] Hebrew *the one at peace with me* [3] Hebrew *the hearts and kidneys* [4] Hebrew *he* [5] Hebrew *he* [6] Probably a musical or liturgical term

4   what is man that you are mindful of him,
         and the son of man that you care for
         him?

5   Yet you have made him a little lower
         than the heavenly beings[1]
     and crowned him with glory and
         honor.

6   You have given him dominion over the
         works of your hands;
     you have put all things under his feet,

7   all sheep and oxen,
         and also the beasts of the field,

8   the birds of the heavens, and the fish of
         the sea,
     whatever passes along the paths of
         the seas.

9   O LORD, our Lord,
     how majestic is your name in all the
         earth!

― *Proverbs 22* ―

A good name is to be chosen rather than
    great riches,
     and favor is better than silver or gold.

2   The rich and the poor meet together;
     the LORD is the maker of them all.

3   The prudent sees danger and hides
         himself,
     but the simple go on and suffer for it.

4   The reward for humility and fear of the
         LORD
     is riches and honor and life.[2]

5   Thorns and snares are in the way of the
         crooked;
     whoever guards his soul will keep far
         from them.

6   Train up a child in the way he should go;
         even when he is old he will not depart
         from it.

7   The rich rules over the poor,
         and the borrower is the slave of the
         lender.

8   Whoever sows injustice will reap
         calamity,
     and the rod of his fury will fail.

9   Whoever has a bountiful[3] eye will be
         blessed,
     for he shares his bread with the poor.

10   Drive out a scoffer, and strife will go out,
     and quarreling and abuse will cease.

11   He who loves purity of heart,
     and whose speech is gracious, will
         have the king as his friend.

12   The eyes of the LORD keep watch over
         knowledge,
     but he overthrows the words of the
         traitor.

13   The sluggard says, "There is a lion
         outside!
     I shall be killed in the streets!"

14   The mouth of forbidden[4] women is a
         deep pit;
     he with whom the LORD is angry will
         fall into it.

15   Folly is bound up in the heart of a child,
     but the rod of discipline drives it far
         from him.

16   Whoever oppresses the poor to increase
         his own wealth,
     or gives to the rich, will only come to
         poverty.

17   Incline your ear, and hear the words of
         the wise,
     and apply your heart to my
         knowledge,

18   for it will be pleasant if you keep them
         within you,
     if all of them are ready on your lips.

19   That your trust may be in the LORD,
     I have made them known to you today,
         even to you.

20   Have I not written for you thirty sayings
     of counsel and knowledge,

21   to make you know what is right and true,
     that you may give a true answer to
         those who sent you?

22   Do not rob the poor, because he is poor,
     or crush the afflicted at the gate,

23   for the LORD will plead their cause
     and rob of life those who rob them.

24   Make no friendship with a man given to
         anger,
     nor go with a wrathful man,

25   lest you learn his ways
     and entangle yourself in a snare.

26   Be not one of those who give pledges,
     who put up security for debts.

27   If you have nothing with which to pay,
     why should your bed be taken from
         under you?

[1] Or *than God; Septuagint than the angels* [2] Or *The reward for humility is the fear of the* LORD, *riches and honor and life* [3] Hebrew *good* [4] Hebrew *strange*

28　Do not move the ancient landmark
　　that your fathers have set.
29　Do you see a man skillful in his work?
　　He will stand before kings;
　　he will not stand before obscure
　　men.

1 Thessalonians 1

Paul, Silvanus, and Timothy,
　　To the church of the Thessalonians in God the Father and the Lord Jesus Christ:

Grace to you and peace.

[2] We give thanks to God always for all of you, constantly[1] mentioning you in our prayers, [3] remembering before our God and Father your work of faith and labor of love and steadfastness of hope in our Lord Jesus Christ. [4] For we know, brothers[2] loved by God, that he has chosen you, [5] because our gospel came to you not only in word, but also in power and in the Holy Spirit and with full conviction. You know what kind of men we proved to be among you for your sake. [6] And you became imitators of us and of the Lord, for you received the word in much affliction, with the joy of the Holy Spirit, [7] so that you became an example to all the believers in Macedonia and in Achaia. [8] For not only has the word of the Lord sounded forth from you in Macedonia and Achaia, but your faith in God has gone forth everywhere, so that we need not say anything. [9] For they themselves report concerning us the kind of reception we had among you, and how you turned to God from idols to serve the living and true God, [10] and to wait for his Son from heaven, whom he raised from the dead, Jesus who delivers us from the wrath to come.

A P R I L　5

Leviticus 8

The LORD spoke to Moses, saying, [2] "Take Aaron and his sons with him, and the garments and the anointing oil and the bull of the sin offering and the two rams and the basket of unleavened bread. [3] And assemble all the congregation at the entrance of the tent of meeting." [4] And Moses did as the LORD commanded him, and the congregation was assembled at the entrance of the tent of meeting.

[5] And Moses said to the congregation, "This is the thing that the LORD has commanded to be done." [6] And Moses brought Aaron and his sons and washed them with water. [7] And he put the coat on him and tied the sash around his waist and clothed him with the robe and put the ephod on him and tied the skillfully woven band of the ephod around him, binding it to him with the band.[3] [8] And he placed the breastpiece on him, and in the breastpiece he put the Urim and the Thummim. [9] And he set the turban on his head, and on the turban, in front, he set the golden plate, the holy crown, as the LORD commanded Moses.

[10] Then Moses took the anointing oil and anointed the tabernacle and all that was in it, and consecrated them. [11] And he sprinkled some of it on the altar seven times, and anointed the altar and all its utensils and the basin and its stand, to consecrate them. [12] And he poured some of the anointing oil on Aaron's head and anointed him to consecrate him. [13] And Moses brought Aaron's sons and clothed them with coats and tied sashes around their waists and bound caps on them, as the LORD commanded Moses.

[14] Then he brought the bull of the sin offering, and Aaron and his sons laid their hands on the head of the bull of the sin offering. [15] And he[4] killed it, and Moses took the blood, and with his finger put it on the horns of the altar around it and purified the altar

---

[1] Or without ceasing [2] Or brothers and sisters. The plural Greek word adelphoi (translated "brothers") refers to siblings in a family. In New Testament usage, depending on the context, adelphoi may refer either to men or to both men and women who are siblings (brothers and sisters) in God's family, the church [3] Hebrew with it [4] Probably Aaron or his representative; possibly Moses; also verses 16–23

and poured out the blood at the base of the altar and consecrated it to make atonement for it. ¹⁶And he took all the fat that was on the entrails and the long lobe of the liver and the two kidneys with their fat, and Moses burned them on the altar. ¹⁷But the bull and its skin and its flesh and its dung he burned up with fire outside the camp, as the LORD commanded Moses.

¹⁸Then he presented the ram of the burnt offering, and Aaron and his sons laid their hands on the head of the ram. ¹⁹And he killed it, and Moses threw the blood against the sides of the altar. ²⁰He cut the ram into pieces, and Moses burned the head and the pieces and the fat. ²¹He washed the entrails and the legs with water, and Moses burned the whole ram on the altar. It was a burnt offering with a pleasing aroma, a food offering for the LORD, as the LORD commanded Moses.

²²Then he presented the other ram, the ram of ordination, and Aaron and his sons laid their hands on the head of the ram. ²³And he killed it, and Moses took some of its blood and put it on the lobe of Aaron's right ear and on the thumb of his right hand and on the big toe of his right foot. ²⁴Then he presented Aaron's sons, and Moses put some of the blood on the lobes of their right ears and on the thumbs of their right hands and on the big toes of their right feet. And Moses threw the blood against the sides of the altar. ²⁵Then he took the fat and the fat tail and all the fat that was on the entrails and the long lobe of the liver and the two kidneys with their fat and the right thigh, ²⁶and out of the basket of unleavened bread that was before the LORD he took one unleavened loaf and one loaf of bread with oil and one wafer and placed them on the pieces of fat and on the right thigh. ²⁷And he put all these in the hands of Aaron and in the hands of his sons and waved them as a wave offering before the LORD. ²⁸Then Moses took them from their hands and burned them on the altar with the burnt offering. This was an ordination offering with a pleasing aroma, a food offering to the LORD. ²⁹And Moses took the breast and waved it for a wave offering before the LORD. It was Moses' portion of the ram of ordination, as the LORD commanded Moses.

³⁰Then Moses took some of the anointing oil and of the blood that was on the altar and sprinkled it on Aaron and his garments, and also on his sons and his sons' garments. So he consecrated Aaron and his garments, and his sons and his sons' garments with him.

³¹And Moses said to Aaron and his sons, "Boil the flesh at the entrance of the tent of meeting, and there eat it and the bread that is in the basket of ordination offerings, as I commanded, saying, 'Aaron and his sons shall eat it.' ³²And what remains of the flesh and the bread you shall burn up with fire. ³³And you shall not go outside the entrance of the tent of meeting for seven days, until the days of your ordination are completed, for it will take seven days to ordain you. ³⁴As has been done today, the LORD has commanded to be done to make atonement for you. ³⁵At the entrance of the tent of meeting you shall remain day and night for seven days, performing what the LORD has charged, so that you do not die, for so I have been commanded." ³⁶And Aaron and his sons did all the things that the LORD commanded by Moses.

Psalm 9¹

TO THE CHOIRMASTER: ACCORDING TO MUTH-LABBEN.² A PSALM OF DAVID.

I will give thanks to the LORD with my
  whole heart;
    I will recount all of your wonderful
      deeds.
2 I will be glad and exult in you;
    I will sing praise to your name, O Most
      High.

3 When my enemies turn back,
    they stumble and perish before³ your
      presence.
4 For you have maintained my just cause;
    you have sat on the throne, giving
      righteous judgment.

5 You have rebuked the nations; you have
      made the wicked perish;
    you have blotted out their name
      forever and ever.
6 The enemy came to an end in
      everlasting ruins;
    their cities you rooted out;
      the very memory of them has
        perished.

¹ Psalms 9 and 10 together follow an acrostic pattern, each stanza beginning with the successive letters of the Hebrew alphabet. In the Septuagint they form one psalm ² Probably a musical or liturgical term ³ Or *because of*

7 But the LORD sits enthroned forever;
   he has established his throne for
     justice,
8 and he judges the world with
     righteousness;
   he judges the peoples with
     uprightness.

9 The LORD is a stronghold for the
     oppressed,
   a stronghold in times of trouble.
10 And those who know your name put
     their trust in you,
   for you, O LORD, have not forsaken
     those who seek you.

11 Sing praises to the LORD, who sits
     enthroned in Zion!
   Tell among the peoples his deeds!
12 For he who avenges blood is mindful of
     them;
   he does not forget the cry of the
     afflicted.

13 Be gracious to me, O LORD!
   See my affliction from those who hate
     me,
   O you who lift me up from the gates of
     death,
14 that I may recount all your praises,
   that in the gates of the daughter of
     Zion
   I may rejoice in your salvation.

15 The nations have sunk in the pit that
     they made;
   in the net that they hid, their own foot
     has been caught.
16 The LORD has made himself known; he
     has executed judgment;
   the wicked are snared in the work of
     their own hands.   *Higgaion.*[1] *Selah*

17 The wicked shall return to Sheol,
   all the nations that forget God.

18 For the needy shall not always be
     forgotten,
   and the hope of the poor shall not
     perish forever.

19 Arise, O LORD! Let not man prevail;
   let the nations be judged before you!

20 Put them in fear, O LORD!
   Let the nations know that they are but
     men!   *Selah*

———————— *Proverbs 23* ————————

When you sit down to eat with a ruler,
   observe carefully what[2] is before you,
2 and put a knife to your throat
   if you are given to appetite.
3 Do not desire his delicacies,
   for they are deceptive food.
4 Do not toil to acquire wealth;
   be discerning enough to desist.
5 When your eyes light on it, it is gone,
   for suddenly it sprouts wings,
   flying like an eagle toward heaven.
6 Do not eat the bread of a man who is
     stingy;[3]
   do not desire his delicacies,
7 for he is like one who is inwardly
     calculating.[4]
   "Eat and drink!" he says to you,
   but his heart is not with you.
8 You will vomit up the morsels that you
     have eaten,
   and waste your pleasant words.
9 Do not speak in the hearing of a fool,
   for he will despise the good sense of
     your words.
10 Do not move an ancient landmark
   or enter the fields of the fatherless,
11 for their Redeemer is strong;
   he will plead their cause against you.
12 Apply your heart to instruction
   and your ear to words of knowledge.
13 Do not withhold discipline from a child;
   if you strike him with a rod, he will
     not die.
14 If you strike him with the rod,
   you will save his soul from Sheol.
15 My son, if your heart is wise,
   my heart too will be glad.
16 My inmost being[5] will exult
   when your lips speak what is right.
17 Let not your heart envy sinners,
   but continue in the fear of the LORD
     all the day.
18 Surely there is a future,
   and your hope will not be cut off.

[1] Probably a musical or liturgical term [2] Or *who* [3] Hebrew *whose eye is evil* [4] Or *for as he calculates in his soul, so is he* [5] Hebrew *My kidneys*

19 Hear, my son, and be wise,
  and direct your heart in the way.
20 Be not among drunkards[1]
  or among gluttonous eaters of meat,
21 for the drunkard and the glutton will
    come to poverty,
  and slumber will clothe them with
    rags.
22 Listen to your father who gave you life,
  and do not despise your mother when
    she is old.
23 Buy truth, and do not sell it;
  buy wisdom, instruction, and
    understanding.
24 The father of the righteous will greatly
    rejoice;
  he who fathers a wise son will be glad
    in him.
25 Let your father and mother be glad;
  let her who bore you rejoice.
26 My son, give me your heart,
  and let your eyes observe[2] my ways.
27 For a prostitute is a deep pit;
  an adulteress[3] is a narrow well.
28 She lies in wait like a robber
  and increases the traitors among
    mankind.
29 Who has woe? Who has sorrow?
  Who has strife? Who has
    complaining?
  Who has wounds without cause?
  Who has redness of eyes?
30 Those who tarry long over wine;
  those who go to try mixed wine.
31 Do not look at wine when it is red,
  when it sparkles in the cup
  and goes down smoothly.
32 In the end it bites like a serpent
  and stings like an adder.
33 Your eyes will see strange things,
  and your heart utter perverse things.
34 You will be like one who lies down in the
    midst of the sea,
  like one who lies on the top of a mast.[4]
35 "They struck me," you will say,[5] "but I was
    not hurt;
  they beat me, but I did not feel it.
  When shall I awake?
  I must have another drink."

——— 1 Thessalonians 2 ———

For you yourselves know, brothers,[6] that our coming to you was not in vain. [2]But though we had already suffered and been shamefully treated at Philippi, as you know, we had boldness in our God to declare to you the gospel of God in the midst of much conflict. [3]For our appeal does not spring from error or impurity or any attempt to deceive, [4]but just as we have been approved by God to be entrusted with the gospel, so we speak, not to please man, but to please God who tests our hearts. [5]For we never came with words of flattery,[7] as you know, nor with a pretext for greed—God is witness. [6]Nor did we seek glory from people, whether from you or from others, though we could have made demands as apostles of Christ. [7]But we were gentle[8] among you, like a nursing mother taking care of her own children. [8]So, being affectionately desirous of you, we were ready to share with you not only the gospel of God but also our own selves, because you had become very dear to us.

[9]For you remember, brothers, our labor and toil: we worked night and day, that we might not be a burden to any of you, while we proclaimed to you the gospel of God. [10]You are witnesses, and God also, how holy and righteous and blameless was our conduct toward you believers. [11]For you know how, like a father with his children, [12]we exhorted each one of you and encouraged you and charged you to walk in a manner worthy of God, who calls you into his own kingdom and glory.

[13]And we also thank God constantly[9] for this, that when you received the word of God, which you heard from us, you accepted it not as the word of men[10] but as what it really is, the word of God, which is at work in you believers. [14]For you, brothers, became imitators of the churches of God in Christ Jesus that are in Judea. For you suffered the same things from your own countrymen as they did from the Jews,[11] [15]who killed both the Lord Jesus and the prophets, and drove us out, and displease God and oppose all mankind [16]by hindering us from speaking to the Gentiles that they might be saved—so as always to fill up the measure of their sins. But wrath has come upon them at last![12]

[17]But since we were torn away from you,

[1] Hebrew those who drink too much wine [2] Or delight in [3] Hebrew a foreign woman [4] Or of the rigging [5] Hebrew lacks you will say [6] Or brothers and sisters; also verses 9, 14, 17 [7] Or with a flattering speech [8] Some manuscripts infants [9] Or without ceasing [10] The Greek word anthropoi can refer to both men and women [11] The Greek word Ioudaioi can refer to Jewish religious leaders and others under their influence, who opposed the Christian faith in that time [12] Or completely, or forever

brothers, for a short time, in person not in heart, we endeavored the more eagerly and with great desire to see you face to face, [18]because we wanted to come to you—I, Paul, again and again—but Satan hindered us. [19]For what is our hope or joy or crown of boasting before our Lord Jesus at his coming? Is it not you? [20]For you are our glory and joy.

APRIL 6

Leviticus 9

On the eighth day Moses called Aaron and his sons and the elders of Israel, [2]and he said to Aaron, "Take for yourself a bull calf for a sin offering and a ram for a burnt offering, both without blemish, and offer them before the LORD. [3]And say to the people of Israel, 'Take a male goat for a sin offering, and a calf and a lamb, both a year old without blemish, for a burnt offering, [4]and an ox and a ram for peace offerings, to sacrifice before the LORD, and a grain offering mixed with oil, for today the LORD will appear to you.'" [5]And they brought what Moses commanded in front of the tent of meeting, and all the congregation drew near and stood before the LORD. [6]And Moses said, "This is the thing that the LORD commanded you to do, that the glory of the LORD may appear to you." [7]Then Moses said to Aaron, "Draw near to the altar and offer your sin offering and your burnt offering and make atonement for yourself and for the people, and bring the offering of the people and make atonement for them, as the LORD has commanded."

[8]So Aaron drew near to the altar and killed the calf of the sin offering, which was for himself. [9]And the sons of Aaron presented the blood to him, and he dipped his finger in the blood and put it on the horns of the altar and poured out the blood at the base of the altar. [10]But the fat and the kidneys and the long lobe of the liver from the sin offering he burned on the altar, as the LORD commanded Moses. [11]The flesh and the skin he burned up with fire outside the camp.

[12]Then he killed the burnt offering, and Aaron's sons handed him the blood, and he threw it against the sides of the altar. [13]And they handed the burnt offering to him, piece by piece, and the head, and he burned them on the altar. [14]And he washed the entrails and the legs and burned them with the burnt offering on the altar.

[15]Then he presented the people's offering and took the goat of the sin offering that was for the people and killed it and offered it as a sin offering, like the first one. [16]And he presented the burnt offering and offered it according to the rule. [17]And he presented the grain offering, took a handful of it, and burned it on the altar, besides the burnt offering of the morning.

[18]Then he killed the ox and the ram, the sacrifice of peace offerings for the people. And Aaron's sons handed him the blood, and he threw it against the sides of the altar. [19]But the fat pieces of the ox and of the ram, the fat tail and that which covers the entrails and the kidneys and the long lobe of the liver— [20]they put the fat pieces on the breasts, and he burned the fat pieces on the altar, [21]but the breasts and the right thigh Aaron waved for a wave offering before the LORD, as Moses commanded.

[22]Then Aaron lifted up his hands toward the people and blessed them, and he came down from offering the sin offering and the burnt offering and the peace offerings. [23]And Moses and Aaron went into the tent of meeting, and when they came out they blessed the people, and the glory of the LORD appeared to all the people. [24]And fire came out from before the LORD and consumed the burnt offering and the pieces of fat on the altar, and when all the people saw it, they shouted and fell on their faces.

Psalm 10

Why, O LORD, do you stand far away?
    Why do you hide yourself in times of
      trouble?
2 In arrogance the wicked hotly pursue
      the poor;
    let them be caught in the schemes
      that they have devised.
3 For the wicked boasts of the desires of
      his soul,
    and the one greedy for gain curses[1]
      and renounces the LORD.
4 In the pride of his face[2] the wicked does
      not seek him;[3]
    all his thoughts are, "There is no God."
5 His ways prosper at all times;
    your judgments are on high, out of his
      sight;
    as for all his foes, he puffs at them.
6 He says in his heart, "I shall not be
      moved;
    throughout all generations I shall not
      meet adversity."
7 His mouth is filled with cursing and
      deceit and oppression;
    under his tongue are mischief and
      iniquity.
8 He sits in ambush in the villages;
    in hiding places he murders the
      innocent.
    His eyes stealthily watch for the
      helpless;
9 he lurks in ambush like a lion in his
      thicket;
    he lurks that he may seize the poor;
    he seizes the poor when he draws him
      into his net.
10 The helpless are crushed, sink down,
    and fall by his might.
11 He says in his heart, "God has forgotten,
    he has hidden his face, he will never
      see it."
12 Arise, O LORD; O God, lift up your hand;
    forget not the afflicted.
13 Why does the wicked renounce God
    and say in his heart, "You will not call
      to account"?
14 But you do see, for you note mischief
    and vexation,
    that you may take it into your hands;

to you the helpless commits himself;
    you have been the helper of the
      fatherless.
15 Break the arm of the wicked and
      evildoer;
    call his wickedness to account till you
      find none.
16 The LORD is king forever and ever;
    the nations perish from his land.
17 O LORD, you hear the desire of the
      afflicted;
    you will strengthen their heart; you
      will incline your ear
18 to do justice to the fatherless and the
      oppressed,
    so that man who is of the earth may
      strike terror no more.

Proverbs 24

Be not envious of evil men,
    nor desire to be with them,
2 for their hearts devise violence,
    and their lips talk of trouble.

3 By wisdom a house is built,
    and by understanding it is established;
4 by knowledge the rooms are filled
    with all precious and pleasant riches.
5 A wise man is full of strength,
    and a man of knowledge enhances his
      might,
6 for by wise guidance you can wage your
      war,
    and in abundance of counselors there
      is victory.
7 Wisdom is too high for a fool;
    in the gate he does not open his
      mouth.

8 Whoever plans to do evil
    will be called a schemer.
9 The devising[4] of folly is sin,
    and the scoffer is an abomination to
      mankind.

10 If you faint in the day of adversity,
    your strength is small.
11 Rescue those who are being taken away
    to death;
    hold back those who are stumbling to
      the slaughter.

[1] Or and he blesses the one greedy for gain   [2] Or of his anger   [3] Or the wicked says, "He will not call to account"   [4] Or scheming

¹² If you say, "Behold, we did not know
    this,"
    does not he who weighs the heart
      perceive it?
  Does not he who keeps watch over your
    soul know it,
    and will he not repay man according
      to his work?

¹³ My son, eat honey, for it is good,
    and the drippings of the honeycomb
      are sweet to your taste.
¹⁴ Know that wisdom is such to your soul;
    if you find it, there will be a future,
    and your hope will not be cut off.

¹⁵ Lie not in wait as a wicked man against
    the dwelling of the righteous;
  do no violence to his home;
¹⁶ for the righteous falls seven times and
    rises again,
  but the wicked stumble in times of
    calamity.

¹⁷ Do not rejoice when your enemy falls,
    and let not your heart be glad when he
    stumbles,
¹⁸ lest the LORD see it and be displeased,
    and turn away his anger from him.

¹⁹ Fret not yourself because of evildoers,
    and be not envious of the wicked,
²⁰ for the evil man has no future;
    the lamp of the wicked will be put
    out.

²¹ My son, fear the LORD and the king,
    and do not join with those who do
    otherwise,
²² for disaster will arise suddenly from
    them,
  and who knows the ruin that will
    come from them both?

²³These also are sayings of the wise.

Partiality in judging is not good.
²⁴ Whoever says to the wicked, "You are in
    the right,"
  will be cursed by peoples, abhorred by
    nations,
²⁵ but those who rebuke the wicked will
    have delight,
  and a good blessing will come upon
    them.

²⁶ Whoever gives an honest answer
    kisses the lips.

²⁷ Prepare your work outside;
    get everything ready for yourself in
      the field,
  and after that build your house.

²⁸ Be not a witness against your neighbor
    without cause,
  and do not deceive with your lips.
²⁹ Do not say, "I will do to him as he has
    done to me;
  I will pay the man back for what he
    has done."

³⁰ I passed by the field of a sluggard,
    by the vineyard of a man lacking sense,
³¹ and behold, it was all overgrown with
    thorns;
  the ground was covered with nettles,
  and its stone wall was broken down.
³² Then I saw and considered it;
    I looked and received instruction.
³³ A little sleep, a little slumber,
    a little folding of the hands to rest,
³⁴ and poverty will come upon you like a
    robber,
  and want like an armed man.

1 Thessalonians 3

Therefore when we could bear it no longer, we were willing to be left behind at Athens alone, ²and we sent Timothy, our brother and God's coworker[1] in the gospel of Christ, to establish and exhort you in your faith, ³that no one be moved by these afflictions. For you yourselves know that we are destined for this. ⁴For when we were with you, we kept telling you beforehand that we were to suffer affliction, just as it has come to pass, and just as you know. ⁵For this reason, when I could bear it no longer, I sent to learn about your faith, for fear that somehow the tempter had tempted you and our labor would be in vain.

⁶But now that Timothy has come to us from you, and has brought us the good news of your faith and love and reported that you always remember us kindly and long to see us, as we long to see you— ⁷for this reason, brothers,[2] in all our distress and affliction we have been comforted about you through your

¹ Some manuscripts servant ² Or brothers and sisters

faith. [8] For now we live, if you are standing fast in the Lord. [9] For what thanksgiving can we return to God for you, for all the joy that we feel for your sake before our God, [10] as we pray most earnestly night and day that we may see you face to face and supply what is lacking in your faith?

[11] Now may our God and Father himself, and our Lord Jesus, direct our way to you, [12] and may the Lord make you increase and abound in love for one another and for all, as we do for you, [13] so that he may establish your hearts blameless in holiness before our God and Father, at the coming of our Lord Jesus with all his saints.

APRIL 7

Leviticus 10

Now Nadab and Abihu, the sons of Aaron, each took his censer and put fire in it and laid incense on it and offered unauthorized[1] fire before the LORD, which he had not commanded them. [2] And fire came out from before the LORD and consumed them, and they died before the LORD. [3] Then Moses said to Aaron, "This is what the LORD has said: 'Among those who are near me I will be sanctified, and before all the people I will be glorified.'" And Aaron held his peace.

[4] And Moses called Mishael and Elzaphan, the sons of Uzziel the uncle of Aaron, and said to them, "Come near; carry your brothers away from the front of the sanctuary and out of the camp." [5] So they came near and carried them in their coats out of the camp, as Moses had said. [6] And Moses said to Aaron and to Eleazar and Ithamar his sons, "Do not let the hair of your heads hang loose, and do not tear your clothes, lest you die, and wrath come upon all the congregation; but let your brothers, the whole house of Israel, bewail the burning that the LORD has kindled. [7] And do not go outside the entrance of the tent of meeting, lest you die, for the anointing oil of the LORD is upon you." And they did according to the word of Moses.

[8] And the LORD spoke to Aaron, saying, [9] "Drink no wine or strong drink, you or your sons with you, when you go into the tent of meeting, lest you die. It shall be a statute forever throughout your generations. [10] You are to distinguish between the holy and the common,

and between the unclean and the clean, [11] and you are to teach the people of Israel all the statutes that the LORD has spoken to them by Moses."

[12] Moses spoke to Aaron and to Eleazar and Ithamar, his surviving sons: "Take the grain offering that is left of the LORD's food offerings, and eat it unleavened beside the altar, for it is most holy. [13] You shall eat it in a holy place, because it is your due and your sons' due, from the LORD's food offerings, for so I am commanded. [14] But the breast that is waved and the thigh that is contributed you shall eat in a clean place, you and your sons and your daughters with you, for they are given as your due and your sons' due from the sacrifices of the peace offerings of the people of Israel. [15] The thigh that is contributed and the breast that is waved they shall bring with the food offerings of the fat pieces to wave for a wave offering before the LORD, and it shall be yours and your sons' with you as a due forever, as the LORD has commanded."

[16] Now Moses diligently inquired about the goat of the sin offering, and behold, it was burned up! And he was angry with Eleazar and Ithamar, the surviving sons of Aaron, saying, [17] "Why have you not eaten the sin offering in the place of the sanctuary, since it is a thing most holy and has been given to you that you may bear the iniquity of the congregation, to make atonement for them before the LORD? [18] Behold, its blood was not brought into the inner part of the sanctuary. You certainly

---

[1] Or strange

ought to have eaten it in the sanctuary, as I commanded." [19]And Aaron said to Moses, "Behold, today they have offered their sin offering and their burnt offering before the LORD, and yet such things as these have happened to me! If I had eaten the sin offering today, would the LORD have approved?" [20]And when Moses heard that, he approved.

--------- *Psalm 11–12* ---------

To the choirmaster. Of David.

In the LORD I take refuge;
how can you say to my soul,
  "Flee like a bird to your mountain,
[2] for behold, the wicked bend the bow;
    they have fitted their arrow to the string
    to shoot in the dark at the upright in heart;
[3] if the foundations are destroyed,
    what can the righteous do?"[1]

[4] The LORD is in his holy temple;
    the LORD's throne is in heaven;
    his eyes see, his eyelids test the children of man.
[5] The LORD tests the righteous,
    but his soul hates the wicked and the one who loves violence.
[6] Let him rain coals on the wicked;
    fire and sulfur and a scorching wind
      shall be the portion of their cup.
[7] For the LORD is righteous;
    he loves righteous deeds;
    the upright shall behold his face.

To the choirmaster: according to The
Sheminith.[2] A Psalm of David.

Save, O LORD, for the godly one is gone;
  for the faithful have vanished from
    among the children of man.
[2] Everyone utters lies to his neighbor;
    with flattering lips and a double heart
      they speak.
[3] May the LORD cut off all flattering lips,
    the tongue that makes great boasts,
[4] those who say, "With our tongue we will prevail,
    our lips are with us; who is master over us?"

[5] "Because the poor are plundered, because
    the needy groan,
    I will now arise," says the LORD;
    "I will place him in the safety for which he longs."
[6] The words of the LORD are pure words,
    like silver refined in a furnace on the ground,
    purified seven times.

[7] You, O LORD, will keep them;
    you will guard us[3] from this generation forever.
[8] On every side the wicked prowl,
    as vileness is exalted among the children of man.

--------- *Proverbs 25* ---------

These also are proverbs of Solomon which
  the men of Hezekiah king of Judah copied.

[2] It is the glory of God to conceal things,
    but the glory of kings is to search things out.
[3] As the heavens for height, and the earth for depth,
    so the heart of kings is unsearchable.
[4] Take away the dross from the silver,
    and the smith has material for a vessel;
[5] take away the wicked from the presence of the king,
    and his throne will be established in righteousness.
[6] Do not put yourself forward in the king's presence
    or stand in the place of the great,
[7] for it is better to be told, "Come up here,"
    than to be put lower in the presence of a noble.

  What your eyes have seen
[8] do not hastily bring into court,
    for[4] what will you do in the end,
    when your neighbor puts you to shame?
[9] Argue your case with your neighbor himself,
    and do not reveal another's secret,
[10] lest he who hears you bring shame upon you,
    and your ill repute have no end.

[1] Or for the foundations will be destroyed; what has the righteous done? [2] Probably a musical or liturgical term [3] Or guard him [4] Hebrew or else

11 A word fitly spoken
        is like apples of gold in a setting of
            silver.
12 Like a gold ring or an ornament of gold
        is a wise reprover to a listening ear.
13 Like the cold of snow in the time of
            harvest
        is a faithful messenger to those who
            send him;
        he refreshes the soul of his masters.
14 Like clouds and wind without rain
        is a man who boasts of a gift he does
            not give.

15 With patience a ruler may be
            persuaded,
        and a soft tongue will break a bone.
16 If you have found honey, eat only
            enough for you,
        lest you have your fill of it and vomit it.
17 Let your foot be seldom in your
            neighbor's house,
        lest he have his fill of you and hate
            you.
18 A man who bears false witness against
            his neighbor
        is like a war club, or a sword, or a
            sharp arrow.
19 Trusting in a treacherous man in time of
            trouble
        is like a bad tooth or a foot that slips.
20 Whoever sings songs to a heavy heart
        is like one who takes off a garment on
            a cold day,
        and like vinegar on soda.
21 If your enemy is hungry, give him bread
            to eat,
        and if he is thirsty, give him water to
            drink,
22 for you will heap burning coals on his
            head,
        and the LORD will reward you.
23 The north wind brings forth rain,
        and a backbiting tongue, angry looks.
24 It is better to live in a corner of the
            housetop
        than in a house shared with a
            quarrelsome wife.
25 Like cold water to a thirsty soul,
        so is good news from a far country.
26 Like a muddied spring or a polluted
            fountain

        is a righteous man who gives way
            before the wicked.
27 It is not good to eat much honey,
        nor is it glorious to seek one's own
            glory.[1]
28 A man without self-control
        is like a city broken into and left
            without walls.

——— 1 Thessalonians 4 ———

Finally, then, brothers,[2] we ask and urge you in the Lord Jesus, that as you received from us how you ought to walk and to please God, just as you are doing, that you do so more and more. [2]For you know what instructions we gave you through the Lord Jesus. [3]For this is the will of God, your sanctification:[3] that you abstain from sexual immorality; [4]that each one of you know how to control his own body[4] in holiness and honor, [5]not in the passion of lust like the Gentiles who do not know God; [6]that no one transgress and wrong his brother in this matter, because the Lord is an avenger in all these things, as we told you beforehand and solemnly warned you. [7]For God has not called us for impurity, but in holiness. [8]Therefore whoever disregards this, disregards not man but God, who gives his Holy Spirit to you.

[9]Now concerning brotherly love you have no need for anyone to write to you, for you yourselves have been taught by God to love one another, [10]for that indeed is what you are doing to all the brothers throughout Macedonia. But we urge you, brothers, to do this more and more, [11]and to aspire to live quietly, and to mind your own affairs, and to work with your hands, as we instructed you, [12]so that you may walk properly before outsiders and be dependent on no one.

[13]But we do not want you to be uninformed, brothers, about those who are asleep, that you may not grieve as others do who have no hope. [14]For since we believe that Jesus died and rose again, even so, through Jesus, God will bring with him those who have fallen asleep. [15]For this we declare to you by a word from the Lord,[5] that we who are alive, who are left until the coming of the Lord, will not precede those who have fallen asleep. [16]For the Lord himself will descend from heaven with a cry of command, with the voice of an archangel, and with the sound of the trumpet of God. And

[1] The meaning of the Hebrew line is uncertain [2] Or brothers and sisters; also verses 10, 13 [3] Or your holiness [4] Or how to take a wife for himself; Greek how to possess his own vessel [5] Or by the word of the Lord

the dead in Christ will rise first. [17] Then we who are alive, who are left, will be caught up together with them in the clouds to meet the Lord in the air, and so we will always be with the Lord. [18] Therefore encourage one another with these words.

APRIL 8

Leviticus 11–12

And the LORD spoke to Moses and Aaron, saying to them, [2] "Speak to the people of Israel, saying, These are the living things that you may eat among all the animals that are on the earth. [3] Whatever parts the hoof and is cloven-footed and chews the cud, among the animals, you may eat. [4] Nevertheless, among those that chew the cud or part the hoof, you shall not eat these: The camel, because it chews the cud but does not part the hoof, is unclean to you. [5] And the rock badger, because it chews the cud but does not part the hoof, is unclean to you. [6] And the hare, because it chews the cud but does not part the hoof, is unclean to you. [7] And the pig, because it parts the hoof and is cloven-footed but does not chew the cud, is unclean to you. [8] You shall not eat any of their flesh, and you shall not touch their carcasses; they are unclean to you.

[9] "These you may eat, of all that are in the waters. Everything in the waters that has fins and scales, whether in the seas or in the rivers, you may eat. [10] But anything in the seas or the rivers that does not have fins and scales, of the swarming creatures in the waters and of the living creatures that are in the waters, is detestable to you. [11] You shall regard them as detestable; you shall not eat any of their flesh, and you shall detest their carcasses. [12] Everything in the waters that does not have fins and scales is detestable to you.

[13] "And these you shall detest among the birds;[1] they shall not be eaten; they are detestable: the eagle,[2] the bearded vulture, the black vulture, [14] the kite, the falcon of any kind, [15] every raven of any kind, [16] the ostrich, the nighthawk, the sea gull, the hawk of any kind, [17] the little owl, the cormorant, the short-eared owl, [18] the barn owl, the tawny owl, the carrion vulture, [19] the stork, the heron of any kind, the hoopoe, and the bat.

[20] "All winged insects that go on all fours are detestable to you. [21] Yet among the winged insects that go on all fours you may eat those that have jointed legs above their feet, with which to hop on the ground. [22] Of them you may eat: the locust of any kind, the bald locust of any kind, the cricket of any kind, and the grasshopper of any kind. [23] But all other winged insects that have four feet are detestable to you.

[24] "And by these you shall become unclean. Whoever touches their carcass shall be unclean until the evening, [25] and whoever carries any part of their carcass shall wash his clothes and be unclean until the evening. [26] Every animal that parts the hoof but is not cloven-footed or does not chew the cud is unclean to you. Everyone who touches them shall be unclean. [27] And all that walk on their paws, among the animals that go on all fours, are unclean to you. Whoever touches their carcass shall be unclean until the evening, [28] and he who carries their carcass shall wash his clothes and be unclean until the evening; they are unclean to you.

[29] "And these are unclean to you among the swarming things that swarm on the ground: the mole rat, the mouse, the great lizard of any kind, [30] the gecko, the monitor lizard, the lizard, the sand lizard, and the chameleon. [31] These are unclean to you among all that swarm. Whoever touches them when they are dead shall be unclean until the evening. [32] And anything on which any of them falls when they are dead shall be unclean, whether it is an article of wood or a garment or a skin or a sack, any

---

[1] Or things that fly; compare Genesis 1:20 [2] The identity of many of these birds is uncertain

article that is used for any purpose. It must be put into water, and it shall be unclean until the evening; then it shall be clean. ³³And if any of them falls into any earthenware vessel, all that is in it shall be unclean, and you shall break it. ³⁴Any food in it that could be eaten, on which water comes, shall be unclean. And all drink that could be drunk from every such vessel shall be unclean. ³⁵And everything on which any part of their carcass falls shall be unclean. Whether oven or stove, it shall be broken in pieces. They are unclean and shall remain unclean for you. ³⁶Nevertheless, a spring or a cistern holding water shall be clean, but whoever touches a carcass in them shall be unclean. ³⁷And if any part of their carcass falls upon any seed grain that is to be sown, it is clean, ³⁸but if water is put on the seed and any part of their carcass falls on it, it is unclean to you.

³⁹"And if any animal which you may eat dies, whoever touches its carcass shall be unclean until the evening, ⁴⁰and whoever eats of its carcass shall wash his clothes and be unclean until the evening. And whoever carries the carcass shall wash his clothes and be unclean until the evening.

⁴¹"Every swarming thing that swarms on the ground is detestable; it shall not be eaten. ⁴²Whatever goes on its belly, and whatever goes on all fours, or whatever has many feet, any swarming thing that swarms on the ground, you shall not eat, for they are detestable. ⁴³You shall not make yourselves detestable with any swarming thing that swarms, and you shall not defile yourselves with them, and become unclean through them. ⁴⁴For I am the Lord your God. Consecrate yourselves therefore, and be holy, for I am holy. You shall not defile yourselves with any swarming thing that crawls on the ground. ⁴⁵For I am the Lord who brought you up out of the land of Egypt to be your God. You shall therefore be holy, for I am holy."

⁴⁶This is the law about beast and bird and every living creature that moves through the waters and every creature that swarms on the ground, ⁴⁷to make a distinction between the unclean and the clean and between the living creature that may be eaten and the living creature that may not be eaten.

¹²:¹The Lord spoke to Moses, saying, ²"Speak to the people of Israel, saying, If a woman conceives and bears a male child, then she shall be unclean seven days. As at the time of her menstruation, she shall be unclean. ³And on the eighth day the flesh of his foreskin shall be circumcised. ⁴Then she shall continue for thirty-three days in the blood of her purifying. She shall not touch anything holy, nor come into the sanctuary, until the days of her purifying are completed. ⁵But if she bears a female child, then she shall be unclean two weeks, as in her menstruation. And she shall continue in the blood of her purifying for sixty-six days.

⁶"And when the days of her purifying are completed, whether for a son or for a daughter, she shall bring to the priest at the entrance of the tent of meeting a lamb a year old for a burnt offering, and a pigeon or a turtledove for a sin offering, ⁷and he shall offer it before the Lord and make atonement for her. Then she shall be clean from the flow of her blood. This is the law for her who bears a child, either male or female. ⁸And if she cannot afford a lamb, then she shall take two turtledoves or two pigeons,¹ one for a burnt offering and the other for a sin offering. And the priest shall make atonement for her, and she shall be clean."

Psalm 13–14

To the choirmaster. A Psalm of David.

How long, O Lord? Will you forget me forever?
How long will you hide your face from me?
2 How long must I take counsel in my soul
and have sorrow in my heart all the day?
How long shall my enemy be exalted over me?

3 Consider and answer me, O Lord my God;
light up my eyes, lest I sleep the sleep of death,
4 lest my enemy say, "I have prevailed over him,"
lest my foes rejoice because I am shaken.

5 But I have trusted in your steadfast love;
my heart shall rejoice in your salvation.
6 I will sing to the Lord,
because he has dealt bountifully with me.

¹ Septuagint two young pigeons

To the choirmaster. Of David.

The fool says in his heart, "There is no God."
  They are corrupt, they do abominable
     deeds;
     there is none who does good.
2 The LORD looks down from heaven on
     the children of man,
    to see if there are any who
     understand,[1]
    who seek after God.

3 They have all turned aside; together
     they have become corrupt;
    there is none who does good,
    not even one.

4 Have they no knowledge, all the
     evildoers
    who eat up my people as they eat
     bread
    and do not call upon the LORD?
5 There they are in great terror,
    for God is with the generation of the
     righteous.
6 You would shame the plans of the poor,
    but[2] the LORD is his refuge.

7 Oh, that salvation for Israel would come
    out of Zion!
    When the LORD restores the fortunes
     of his people,
    let Jacob rejoice, let Israel be glad.

Proverbs 26

Like snow in summer or rain in harvest,
  so honor is not fitting for a fool.
2 Like a sparrow in its flitting, like a
    swallow in its flying,
    a curse that is causeless does not alight.
3 A whip for the horse, a bridle for the
    donkey,
    and a rod for the back of fools.
4 Answer not a fool according to his folly,
    lest you be like him yourself.
5 Answer a fool according to his folly,
    lest he be wise in his own eyes.
6 Whoever sends a message by the hand
    of a fool
    cuts off his own feet and drinks
     violence.

7 Like a lame man's legs, which hang
    useless,
    is a proverb in the mouth of fools.
8 Like one who binds the stone in the
    sling
    is one who gives honor to a fool.
9 Like a thorn that goes up into the hand
    of a drunkard
    is a proverb in the mouth of fools.
10 Like an archer who wounds everyone
    is one who hires a passing fool or
     drunkard.[3]
11 Like a dog that returns to his vomit
    is a fool who repeats his folly.
12 Do you see a man who is wise in his own
    eyes?
    There is more hope for a fool than for
     him.
13 The sluggard says, "There is a lion in the
    road!
    There is a lion in the streets!"
14 As a door turns on its hinges,
    so does a sluggard on his bed.
15 The sluggard buries his hand in the dish;
    it wears him out to bring it back to his
     mouth.
16 The sluggard is wiser in his own eyes
    than seven men who can answer
     sensibly.
17 Whoever meddles in a quarrel not his
    own
    is like one who takes a passing dog by
     the ears.
18 Like a madman who throws firebrands,
    arrows, and death
19 is the man who deceives his neighbor
    and says, "I am only joking!"
20 For lack of wood the fire goes out,
    and where there is no whisperer,
     quarreling ceases.
21 As charcoal to hot embers and wood to
    fire,
    so is a quarrelsome man for kindling
     strife.
22 The words of a whisperer are like
    delicious morsels;
    they go down into the inner parts of
     the body.
23 Like the glaze[4] covering an earthen
    vessel
    are fervent lips with an evil heart.

[1] Or that act wisely [2] Or for [3] Or hires a fool or passersby [4] By revocalization; Hebrew silver of dross

24 Whoever hates disguises himself with
     his lips
   and harbors deceit in his heart;
25 when he speaks graciously, believe him
     not,
   for there are seven abominations in
     his heart;
26 though his hatred be covered with
     deception,
   his wickedness will be exposed in the
     assembly.
27 Whoever digs a pit will fall into it,
   and a stone will come back on him
     who starts it rolling.
28 A lying tongue hates its victims,
   and a flattering mouth works ruin.

---

1 Thessalonians 5

Now concerning the times and the seasons, brothers,[1] you have no need to have anything written to you. ²For you yourselves are fully aware that the day of the Lord will come like a thief in the night. ³While people are saying, "There is peace and security," then sudden destruction will come upon them as labor pains come upon a pregnant woman, and they will not escape. ⁴But you are not in darkness, brothers, for that day to surprise you like a thief. ⁵For you are all children[2] of light, children of the day. We are not of the night or of the darkness. ⁶So then let us not sleep, as others do, but let us keep awake and be sober. ⁷For those who sleep, sleep at night, and those who get drunk, are drunk at night. ⁸But since we belong to the day,

let us be sober, having put on the breastplate of faith and love, and for a helmet the hope of salvation. ⁹For God has not destined us for wrath, but to obtain salvation through our Lord Jesus Christ, ¹⁰who died for us so that whether we are awake or asleep we might live with him. ¹¹Therefore encourage one another and build one another up, just as you are doing.

¹²We ask you, brothers, to respect those who labor among you and are over you in the Lord and admonish you, ¹³and to esteem them very highly in love because of their work. Be at peace among yourselves. ¹⁴And we urge you, brothers, admonish the idle,[3] encourage the fainthearted, help the weak, be patient with them all. ¹⁵See that no one repays anyone evil for evil, but always seek to do good to one another and to everyone. ¹⁶Rejoice always, ¹⁷pray without ceasing, ¹⁸give thanks in all circumstances; for this is the will of God in Christ Jesus for you. ¹⁹Do not quench the Spirit. ²⁰Do not despise prophecies, ²¹but test everything; hold fast what is good. ²²Abstain from every form of evil.

²³Now may the God of peace himself sanctify you completely, and may your whole spirit and soul and body be kept blameless at the coming of our Lord Jesus Christ. ²⁴He who calls you is faithful; he will surely do it.

²⁵Brothers, pray for us.

²⁶Greet all the brothers with a holy kiss.

²⁷I put you under oath before the Lord to have this letter read to all the brothers.

²⁸The grace of our Lord Jesus Christ be with you.

APRIL 9

Leviticus 13

The LORD spoke to Moses and Aaron, saying, ²"When a person has on the skin of his body a swelling or an eruption or a spot, and it turns into a case of leprous[4] disease on the skin of his body, then he shall be brought to Aaron the priest or to one of his sons the priests, ³and

the priest shall examine the diseased area on the skin of his body. And if the hair in the diseased area has turned white and the disease appears to be deeper than the skin of his body, it is a case of leprous disease. When the priest has examined him, he shall pronounce him

---

[1] Or brothers and sisters; also verses 4, 12, 14, 25, 26, 27 [2] Or sons; twice in this verse [3] Or disorderly, or undisciplined [4] Leprosy was a term for several skin diseases

unclean. **4**But if the spot is white in the skin of his body and appears no deeper than the skin, and the hair in it has not turned white, the priest shall shut up the diseased person for seven days. **5**And the priest shall examine him on the seventh day, and if in his eyes the disease is checked and the disease has not spread in the skin, then the priest shall shut him up for another seven days. **6**And the priest shall examine him again on the seventh day, and if the diseased area has faded and the disease has not spread in the skin, then the priest shall pronounce him clean; it is only an eruption. And he shall wash his clothes and be clean. **7**But if the eruption spreads in the skin, after he has shown himself to the priest for his cleansing, he shall appear again before the priest. **8**And the priest shall look, and if the eruption has spread in the skin, then the priest shall pronounce him unclean; it is a leprous disease.

9"When a man is afflicted with a leprous disease, he shall be brought to the priest, **10**and the priest shall look. And if there is a white swelling in the skin that has turned the hair white, and there is raw flesh in the swelling, **11**it is a chronic leprous disease in the skin of his body, and the priest shall pronounce him unclean. He shall not shut him up, for he is unclean. **12**And if the leprous disease breaks out in the skin, so that the leprous disease covers all the skin of the diseased person from head to foot, so far as the priest can see, **13**then the priest shall look, and if the leprous disease has covered all his body, he shall pronounce him clean of the disease; it has all turned white, and he is clean. **14**But when raw flesh appears on him, he shall be unclean. **15**And the priest shall examine the raw flesh and pronounce him unclean. Raw flesh is unclean, for it is a leprous disease. **16**But if the raw flesh recovers and turns white again, then he shall come to the priest, **17**and the priest shall examine him, and if the disease has turned white, then the priest shall pronounce the diseased person clean; he is clean.

18"If there is in the skin of one's body a boil and it heals, **19**and in the place of the boil there comes a white swelling or a reddish-white spot, then it shall be shown to the priest. **20**And the priest shall look, and if it appears deeper than the skin and its hair has turned white, then the priest shall pronounce him unclean. It is a case

of leprous disease that has broken out in the boil. **21**But if the priest examines it and there is no white hair in it and it is not deeper than the skin, but has faded, then the priest shall shut him up seven days. **22**And if it spreads in the skin, then the priest shall pronounce him unclean; it is a disease. **23**But if the spot remains in one place and does not spread, it is the scar of the boil, and the priest shall pronounce him clean.

24"Or, when the body has a burn on its skin and the raw flesh of the burn becomes a spot, reddish-white or white, **25**the priest shall examine it, and if the hair in the spot has turned white and it appears deeper than the skin, then it is a leprous disease. It has broken out in the burn, and the priest shall pronounce him unclean; it is a case of leprous disease. **26**But if the priest examines it and there is no white hair in the spot and it is no deeper than the skin, but has faded, the priest shall shut him up seven days, **27**and the priest shall examine him the seventh day. If it is spreading in the skin, then the priest shall pronounce him unclean; it is a case of leprous disease. **28**But if the spot remains in one place and does not spread in the skin, but has faded, it is a swelling from the burn, and the priest shall pronounce him clean, for it is the scar of the burn.

29"When a man or woman has a disease on the head or the beard, **30**the priest shall examine the disease. And if it appears deeper than the skin, and the hair in it is yellow and thin, then the priest shall pronounce him unclean. It is an itch, a leprous disease of the head or the beard. **31**And if the priest examines the itching disease and it appears no deeper than the skin and there is no black hair in it, then the priest shall shut up the person with the itching disease for seven days, **32**and on the seventh day the priest shall examine the disease. If the itch has not spread, and there is in it no yellow hair, and the itch appears to be no deeper than the skin, **33**then he shall shave himself, but the itch he shall not shave; and the priest shall shut up the person with the itching disease for another seven days. **34**And on the seventh day the priest shall examine the itch, and if the itch has not spread in the skin and it appears to be no deeper than the skin, then the priest shall pronounce him clean. And he shall wash his clothes and be clean. **35**But if the itch spreads in the skin after his cleansing, [36]then the priest shall examine him, and if the itch has spread in the skin, the priest need not seek for the yellow hair; he is unclean. [37]But if in his eyes the itch is unchanged and black hair has grown in it, the itch is healed and he is clean, and the priest shall pronounce him clean.

[38]"When a man or a woman has spots on the skin of the body, white spots, [39]the priest shall look, and if the spots on the skin of the body are of a dull white, it is leukoderma that has broken out in the skin; he is clean.

[40]"If a man's hair falls out from his head, he is bald; he is clean. [41]And if a man's hair falls out from his forehead, he has baldness of the forehead; he is clean. [42]But if there is on the bald head or the bald forehead a reddish-white diseased area, it is a leprous disease breaking out on his bald head or his bald forehead. [43]Then the priest shall examine him, and if the diseased swelling is reddish-white on his bald head or on his bald forehead, like the appearance of leprous disease in the skin of the body, [44]he is a leprous man, he is unclean. The priest must pronounce him unclean; his disease is on his head.

[45]"The leprous person who has the disease shall wear torn clothes and let the hair of his head hang loose, and he shall cover his upper lip[1] and cry out, 'Unclean, unclean.' [46]He shall remain unclean as long as he has the disease. He is unclean. He shall live alone. His dwelling shall be outside the camp.

[47]"When there is a case of leprous disease in a garment, whether a woolen or a linen garment, [48]in warp or woof of linen or wool, or in a skin or in anything made of skin, [49]if the disease is greenish or reddish in the garment, or in the skin or in the warp or the woof or in any article made of skin, it is a case of leprous disease, and it shall be shown to the priest. [50]And the priest shall examine the disease and shut up that which has the disease for seven days. [51]Then he shall examine the disease on the seventh day. If the disease has spread in the garment, in the warp or the woof, or in the skin, whatever be the use of the skin, the disease is a persistent leprous disease; it is unclean. [52]And he shall burn the garment, or the warp or the woof, the wool or the linen, or any article made of skin that is diseased, for it is a persistent leprous disease. It shall be burned in the fire.

[53]"And if the priest examines, and if the disease has not spread in the garment, in the warp or the woof or in any article made of skin, [54]then the priest shall command that they wash the thing in which is the disease, and he shall shut it up for another seven days. [55]And the priest shall examine the diseased thing after it has been washed. And if the appearance of the diseased area has not changed, though the disease has not spread, it is unclean. You shall burn it in the fire, whether the rot is on the back or on the front.

[56]"But if the priest examines, and if the diseased area has faded after it has been washed, he shall tear it out of the garment or the skin or the warp or the woof. [57]Then if it appears again in the garment, in the warp or the woof, or in any article made of skin, it is spreading. You shall burn with fire whatever has the disease. [58]But the garment, or the warp or the woof, or any article made of skin from which the disease departs when you have washed it, shall then be washed a second time, and be clean."

[59]This is the law for a case of leprous disease in a garment of wool or linen, either in the warp or the woof, or in any article made of skin, to determine whether it is clean or unclean.

Psalm 15–16

A Psalm of David.

O Lord, who shall sojourn in your tent?
Who shall dwell on your holy hill?

2   He who walks blamelessly and does
        what is right
        and speaks truth in his heart;
3   who does not slander with his tongue
        and does no evil to his neighbor,
        nor takes up a reproach against his
            friend;
4   in whose eyes a vile person is despised,
        but who honors those who fear the
            Lord;
    who swears to his own hurt and does
        not change;
5   who does not put out his money at
        interest
        and does not take a bribe against the
            innocent.
    He who does these things shall never be
        moved.

[1] Or mustache

A Miktam[1] of David.

Preserve me, O God, for in you I take refuge.
2 I say to the Lord, "You are my Lord;
  I have no good apart from you."

3 As for the saints in the land, they are the
    excellent ones,
  in whom is all my delight.[2]

4 The sorrows of those who run after[3]
    another god shall multiply;
  their drink offerings of blood I will not
    pour out
  or take their names on my lips.

5 The Lord is my chosen portion and my
    cup;
  you hold my lot.
6 The lines have fallen for me in pleasant
    places;
  indeed, I have a beautiful inheritance.

7 I bless the Lord who gives me counsel;
  in the night also my heart instructs
    me.[4]
8 I have set the Lord always before me;
  because he is at my right hand, I shall
    not be shaken.

9 Therefore my heart is glad, and my
    whole being[5] rejoices;
  my flesh also dwells secure.
10 For you will not abandon my soul to
    Sheol,
  or let your holy one see corruption.[6]

11 You make known to me the path of life;
  in your presence there is fullness of joy;
  at your right hand are pleasures
    forevermore.

Proverbs 27

Do not boast about tomorrow,
  for you do not know what a day may
    bring.
2 Let another praise you, and not your
    own mouth;
  a stranger, and not your own lips.
3 A stone is heavy, and sand is weighty,
  but a fool's provocation is heavier
    than both.
4 Wrath is cruel, anger is overwhelming,
  but who can stand before jealousy?

5 Better is open rebuke
    than hidden love.
6 Faithful are the wounds of a friend;
    profuse are the kisses of an enemy.
7 One who is full loathes honey,
    but to one who is hungry everything
      bitter is sweet.
8 Like a bird that strays from its nest
    is a man who strays from his home.
9 Oil and perfume make the heart glad,
    and the sweetness of a friend comes
      from his earnest counsel.[7]
10 Do not forsake your friend and your
      father's friend,
    and do not go to your brother's house
      in the day of your calamity.
    Better is a neighbor who is near
      than a brother who is far away.
11 Be wise, my son, and make my heart
      glad,
    that I may answer him who
      reproaches me.
12 The prudent sees danger and hides
      himself,
    but the simple go on and suffer for it.
13 Take a man's garment when he has put
      up security for a stranger,
    and hold it in pledge when he puts up
      security for an adulteress.[8]
14 Whoever blesses his neighbor with a
      loud voice,
    rising early in the morning,
    will be counted as cursing.
15 A continual dripping on a rainy day
    and a quarrelsome wife are alike;
16 to restrain her is to restrain the wind
    or to grasp[9] oil in one's right hand.
17 Iron sharpens iron,
    and one man sharpens another.[10]
18 Whoever tends a fig tree will eat its
      fruit,
    and he who guards his master will be
      honored.
19 As in water face reflects face,
    so the heart of man reflects the man.
20 Sheol and Abaddon are never satisfied,
    and never satisfied are the eyes of
      man.
21 The crucible is for silver, and the furnace
      is for gold,
    and a man is tested by his praise.

---

[1] Probably a musical or liturgical term [2] Or To the saints in the land, the excellent in whom is all my delight, I say: [3] Or who acquire [4] Hebrew my kidneys instruct me [5] Hebrew my glory [6] Or see the pit [7] Or and so does the sweetness of a friend that comes from his earnest counsel [8] Hebrew a foreign woman; a slight emendation yields (compare Vulgate; see also 20:16) foreigners [9] Hebrew to meet with [10] Hebrew sharpens the face of another

22 Crush a fool in a mortar with a pestle
　　along with crushed grain,
　　yet his folly will not depart from him.
23 Know well the condition of your flocks,
　　and give attention to your herds,
24 for riches do not last forever;
　　and does a crown endure to all
　　generations?
25 When the grass is gone and the new
　　growth appears
　　and the vegetation of the mountains
　　is gathered,
26 the lambs will provide your clothing,
　　and the goats the price of a field.
27 There will be enough goats' milk for
　　your food,
　　for the food of your household
　　and maintenance for your girls.

2 Thessalonians 1

Paul, Silvanus, and Timothy,
To the church of the Thessalonians in God
our Father and the Lord Jesus Christ:

2 Grace to you and peace from God our Father
and the Lord Jesus Christ.

3 We ought always to give thanks to God for
you, brothers,[1] as is right, because your faith is
growing abundantly, and the love of every one
of you for one another is increasing. 4 Therefore
we ourselves boast about you in the churches
of God for your steadfastness and faith in all
your persecutions and in the afflictions that
you are enduring.

5 This is evidence of the righteous judgment
of God, that you may be considered worthy of
the kingdom of God, for which you are also suffering— 6 since indeed God considers it just to
repay with affliction those who afflict you, 7 and
to grant relief to you who are afflicted as well
as to us, when the Lord Jesus is revealed from
heaven with his mighty angels 8 in flaming fire,
inflicting vengeance on those who do not know
God and on those who do not obey the gospel
of our Lord Jesus. 9 They will suffer the punishment of eternal destruction, away from[2] the
presence of the Lord and from the glory of his
might, 10 when he comes on that day to be glorified in his saints, and to be marveled at among
all who have believed, because our testimony to
you was believed. 11 To this end we always pray
for you, that our God may make you worthy of
his calling and may fulfill every resolve for good
and every work of faith by his power, 12 so that
the name of our Lord Jesus may be glorified in
you, and you in him, according to the grace of
our God and the Lord Jesus Christ.

APRIL 10

Leviticus 14

The LORD spoke to Moses, saying, 2 "This
shall be the law of the leprous person for
the day of his cleansing. He shall be brought
to the priest, 3 and the priest shall go out of the
camp, and the priest shall look. Then, if the case
of leprous disease is healed in the leprous person, 4 the priest shall command them to take
for him who is to be cleansed two live[3] clean
birds and cedarwood and scarlet yarn and hyssop. 5 And the priest shall command them to kill
one of the birds in an earthenware vessel over
fresh[4] water. 6 He shall take the live bird with
the cedarwood and the scarlet yarn and the hyssop, and dip them and the live bird in the blood
of the bird that was killed over the fresh water.
7 And he shall sprinkle it seven times on him
who is to be cleansed of the leprous disease.
Then he shall pronounce him clean and shall
let the living bird go into the open field. 8 And
he who is to be cleansed shall wash his clothes
and shave off all his hair and bathe himself in
water, and he shall be clean. And after that he

[1] Or brothers and sisters. The plural Greek word adelphoi (translated "brothers") refers to siblings in a family. In New Testament usage, depending on the context, adelphoi may refer either to men or to both men and women who are siblings (brothers and sisters) in God's family, the church　[2] Or destruction that comes from　[3] Or wild　[4] Or running; Hebrew living; also verses 6, 50, 51, 52

may come into the camp, but live outside his tent seven days. [9]And on the seventh day he shall shave off all his hair from his head, his beard, and his eyebrows. He shall shave off all his hair, and then he shall wash his clothes and bathe his body in water, and he shall be clean. [10]"And on the eighth day he shall take two male lambs without blemish, and one ewe lamb a year old without blemish, and a grain offering of three tenths of an ephah[1] of fine flour mixed with oil, and one log[2] of oil. [11]And the priest who cleanses him shall set the man who is to be cleansed and these things before the LORD, at the entrance of the tent of meeting. [12]And the priest shall take one of the male lambs and offer it for a guilt offering, along with the log of oil, and wave them for a wave offering before the LORD. [13]And he shall kill the lamb in the place where they kill the sin offering and the burnt offering, in the place of the sanctuary. For the guilt offering, like the sin offering, belongs to the priest; it is most holy. [14]The priest shall take some of the blood of the guilt offering, and the priest shall put it on the lobe of the right ear of him who is to be cleansed and on the thumb of his right hand and on the big toe of his right foot. [15]Then the priest shall take some of the log of oil and pour it into the palm of his own left hand [16]and dip his right finger in the oil that is in his left hand and sprinkle some oil with his finger seven times before the LORD. [17]And some of the oil that remains in his hand the priest shall put on the lobe of the right ear of him who is to be cleansed and on the thumb of his right hand and on the big toe of his right foot, on top of the blood of the guilt offering. [18]And the rest of the oil that is in the priest's hand he shall put on the head of him who is to be cleansed. Then the priest shall make atonement for him before the LORD. [19]The priest shall offer the sin offering, to make atonement for him who is to be cleansed from his uncleanness. And afterward he shall kill the burnt offering. [20]And the priest shall offer the burnt offering and the grain offering on the altar. Thus the priest shall make atonement for him, and he shall be clean.

[21]"But if he is poor and cannot afford so much, then he shall take one male lamb for a guilt offering to be waved, to make atonement for him, and a tenth of an ephah of fine flour mixed with oil for a grain offering, and a log of oil; [22]also two turtledoves or two pigeons,

whichever he can afford. The one shall be a sin offering and the other a burnt offering. [23]And on the eighth day he shall bring them for his cleansing to the priest, to the entrance of the tent of meeting, before the LORD. [24]And the priest shall take the lamb of the guilt offering and the log of oil, and the priest shall wave them for a wave offering before the LORD. [25]And he shall kill the lamb of the guilt offering. And the priest shall take some of the blood of the guilt offering and put it on the lobe of the right ear of him who is to be cleansed, and on the thumb of his right hand and on the big toe of his right foot. [26]And the priest shall pour some of the oil into the palm of his own left hand, [27]and shall sprinkle with his right finger some of the oil that is in his left hand seven times before the LORD. [28]And the priest shall put some of the oil that is in his hand on the lobe of the right ear of him who is to be cleansed and on the thumb of his right hand and on the big toe of his right foot, in the place where the blood of the guilt offering was put. [29]And the rest of the oil that is in the priest's hand he shall put on the head of him who is to be cleansed, to make atonement for him before the LORD. [30]And he shall offer, of the turtledoves or pigeons, whichever he can afford, [31]one[3] for a sin offering and the other for a burnt offering, along with a grain offering. And the priest shall make atonement before the LORD for him who is being cleansed. [32]This is the law for him in whom is a case of leprous disease, who cannot afford the offerings for his cleansing."

[33]The LORD spoke to Moses and Aaron, saying, [34]"When you come into the land of Canaan, which I give you for a possession, and I put a case of leprous disease in a house in the land of your possession, [35]then he who owns the house shall come and tell the priest, 'There seems to me to be some case of disease in my house.' [36]Then the priest shall command that they empty the house before the priest goes to examine the disease, lest all that is in the house be declared unclean. And afterward the priest shall go in to see the house. [37]And he shall examine the disease. And if the disease is in the walls of the house with greenish or reddish spots, and if it appears to be deeper than the surface, [38]then the priest shall go out of the house to the door of the house and shut up the house seven days.

[1] An *ephah* was about 3/5 bushel or 22 liters [2] A *log* was about 1/3 quart or 0.3 liter [3] Septuagint, Syriac; Hebrew *afford*, [31]such as he can afford, one

39And the priest shall come again on the seventh day, and look. If the disease has spread in the walls of the house, **40**then the priest shall command that they take out the stones in which is the disease and throw them into an unclean place outside the city. **41**And he shall have the inside of the house scraped all around, and the plaster that they scrape off they shall pour out in an unclean place outside the city. **42**Then they shall take other stones and put them in the place of those stones, and he shall take other plaster and plaster the house.

43"If the disease breaks out again in the house, after he has taken out the stones and scraped the house and plastered it, **44**then the priest shall go and look. And if the disease has spread in the house, it is a persistent leprous disease in the house; it is unclean. **45**And he shall break down the house, its stones and timber and all the plaster of the house, and he shall carry them out of the city to an unclean place. **46**Moreover, whoever enters the house while it is shut up shall be unclean until the evening, **47**and whoever sleeps in the house shall wash his clothes, and whoever eats in the house shall wash his clothes.

48"But if the priest comes and looks, and if the disease has not spread in the house after the house was plastered, then the priest shall pronounce the house clean, for the disease is healed. **49**And for the cleansing of the house he shall take two small birds, with cedarwood and scarlet yarn and hyssop, **50**and shall kill one of the birds in an earthenware vessel over fresh water **51**and shall take the cedarwood and the hyssop and the scarlet yarn, along with the live bird, and dip them in the blood of the bird that was killed and in the fresh water and sprinkle the house seven times. **52**Thus he shall cleanse the house with the blood of the bird and with the fresh water and with the live bird and with the cedarwood and hyssop and scarlet yarn. **53**And he shall let the live bird go out of the city into the open country. So he shall make atonement for the house, and it shall be clean."

54This is the law for any case of leprous disease: for an itch, **55**for leprous disease in a garment or in a house, **56**and for a swelling or an eruption or a spot, **57**to show when it is unclean and when it is clean. This is the law for leprous disease.

Psalm 17

A Prayer of David.

Hear a just cause, O Lord; attend to my cry!
Give ear to my prayer from lips free of deceit!
2 From your presence let my vindication come!
Let your eyes behold the right!

3 You have tried my heart, you have visited me by night,
you have tested me, and you will find nothing;
I have purposed that my mouth will not transgress.
4 With regard to the works of man, by the word of your lips
I have avoided the ways of the violent.
5 My steps have held fast to your paths;
my feet have not slipped.

6 I call upon you, for you will answer me, O God;
incline your ear to me; hear my words.
7 Wondrously show[1] your steadfast love, O Savior of those who seek refuge
from their adversaries at your right hand.

8 Keep me as the apple of your eye;
hide me in the shadow of your wings,
9 from the wicked who do me violence,
my deadly enemies who surround me.
10 They close their hearts to pity;
with their mouths they speak arrogantly.
11 They have now surrounded our steps;
they set their eyes to cast us to the ground.
12 He is like a lion eager to tear,
as a young lion lurking in ambush.

13 Arise, O Lord! Confront him, subdue him!
Deliver my soul from the wicked by your sword,
14 from men by your hand, O Lord,
from men of the world whose portion is in this life.[2]

[1] Or *Distinguish me by* [2] Or *from men whose portion in life is of the world*

You fill their womb with treasure;[1]
    they are satisfied with children,
    and they leave their abundance to
        their infants.
15 As for me, I shall behold your face in
    righteousness;
    when I awake, I shall be satisfied with
        your likeness.

Proverbs 28

The wicked flee when no one pursues,
    but the righteous are bold as a lion.
2 When a land transgresses, it has many
    rulers,
    but with a man of understanding and
        knowledge,
    its stability will long continue.
3 A poor man who oppresses the poor
    is a beating rain that leaves no food.
4 Those who forsake the law praise the
    wicked,
    but those who keep the law strive
        against them.
5 Evil men do not understand justice,
    but those who seek the LORD
        understand it completely.
6 Better is a poor man who walks in his
    integrity
    than a rich man who is crooked in his
        ways.
7 The one who keeps the law is a son with
    understanding,
    but a companion of gluttons shames
        his father.
8 Whoever multiplies his wealth by
    interest and profit[2]
    gathers it for him who is generous to
        the poor.
9 If one turns away his ear from hearing
    the law,
    even his prayer is an abomination.
10 Whoever misleads the upright into an
    evil way
    will fall into his own pit,
    but the blameless will have a goodly
        inheritance.
11 A rich man is wise in his own eyes,
    but a poor man who has
        understanding will find him out.

12 When the righteous triumph, there is
    great glory,
    but when the wicked rise, people hide
        themselves.
13 Whoever conceals his transgressions
    will not prosper,
    but he who confesses and forsakes
        them will obtain mercy.
14 Blessed is the one who fears the LORD
    always,
    but whoever hardens his heart will fall
        into calamity.
15 Like a roaring lion or a charging bear
    is a wicked ruler over a poor people.
16 A ruler who lacks understanding is a
    cruel oppressor,
    but he who hates unjust gain will
        prolong his days.
17 If one is burdened with the blood of
    another,
    he will be a fugitive until death;[3]
    let no one help him.
18 Whoever walks in integrity will be
    delivered,
    but he who is crooked in his ways will
        suddenly fall.
19 Whoever works his land will have plenty
    of bread,
    but he who follows worthless pursuits
        will have plenty of poverty.
20 A faithful man will abound with
    blessings,
    but whoever hastens to be rich will
        not go unpunished.
21 To show partiality is not good,
    but for a piece of bread a man will do
        wrong.
22 A stingy man[4] hastens after wealth
    and does not know that poverty will
        come upon him.
23 Whoever rebukes a man will afterward
    find more favor
    than he who flatters with his tongue.
24 Whoever robs his father or his mother
    and says, "That is no transgression,"
    is a companion to a man who destroys.
25 A greedy man stirs up strife,
    but the one who trusts in the LORD
        will be enriched.
26 Whoever trusts in his own mind is a fool,
    but he who walks in wisdom will be
        delivered.

[1] Or As for your treasured ones, you fill their womb [2] That is, profit that comes from charging interest to the poor [3] Hebrew until the pit [4] Hebrew A man whose eye is evil

²⁷ Whoever gives to the poor will not
    want,
    but he who hides his eyes will get
    many a curse.
²⁸ When the wicked rise, people hide
    themselves,
    but when they perish, the righteous
    increase.

2 Thessalonians 2

Now concerning the coming of our Lord Jesus Christ and our being gathered together to him, we ask you, brothers,¹ ²not to be quickly shaken in mind or alarmed, either by a spirit or a spoken word, or a letter seeming to be from us, to the effect that the day of the Lord has come. ³Let no one deceive you in any way. For that day will not come, unless the rebellion comes first, and the man of lawlessness² is revealed, the son of destruction,³ ⁴who opposes and exalts himself against every so-called god or object of worship, so that he takes his seat in the temple of God, proclaiming himself to be God. ⁵Do you not remember that when I was still with you I told you these things? ⁶And you know what is restraining him now so that he may be revealed in his time. ⁷For the mystery of lawlessness is already at work. Only he who

now restrains it will do so until he is out of the way. ⁸And then the lawless one will be revealed, whom the Lord Jesus will kill with the breath of his mouth and bring to nothing by the appearance of his coming. ⁹The coming of the lawless one is by the activity of Satan with all power and false signs and wonders, ¹⁰and with all wicked deception for those who are perishing, because they refused to love the truth and so be saved. ¹¹Therefore God sends them a strong delusion, so that they may believe what is false, ¹²in order that all may be condemned who did not believe the truth but had pleasure in unrighteousness.

¹³But we ought always to give thanks to God for you, brothers beloved by the Lord, because God chose you as the firstfruits⁴ to be saved, through sanctification by the Spirit and belief in the truth. ¹⁴To this he called you through our gospel, so that you may obtain the glory of our Lord Jesus Christ. ¹⁵So then, brothers, stand firm and hold to the traditions that you were taught by us, either by our spoken word or by our letter.

¹⁶Now may our Lord Jesus Christ himself, and God our Father, who loved us and gave us eternal comfort and good hope through grace, ¹⁷comfort your hearts and establish them in every good work and word.

APRIL 11

Leviticus 15

The LORD spoke to Moses and Aaron, saying, ²"Speak to the people of Israel and say to them, When any man has a discharge from his body,⁵ his discharge is unclean. ³And this is the law of his uncleanness for a discharge: whether his body runs with his discharge, or his body is blocked up by his discharge, it is his uncleanness. ⁴Every bed on which the one with the discharge lies shall be unclean, and everything on which he sits shall be unclean. ⁵And anyone who touches his bed shall wash his clothes and bathe himself in water and be

unclean until the evening. ⁶And whoever sits on anything on which the one with the discharge has sat shall wash his clothes and bathe himself in water and be unclean until the evening. ⁷And whoever touches the body of the one with the discharge shall wash his clothes and bathe himself in water and be unclean until the evening. ⁸And if the one with the discharge spits on someone who is clean, then he shall wash his clothes and bathe himself in water and be unclean until the evening. ⁹And any saddle on which the one with the discharge rides shall

¹ Or brothers and sisters; also verses 13, 15 ² Some manuscripts sin ³ Greek the son of perdition (a Hebrew idiom) ⁴ Some manuscripts chose you from the beginning ⁵ Hebrew flesh; also verse 3

be unclean. [10]And whoever touches anything that was under him shall be unclean until the evening. And whoever carries such things shall wash his clothes and bathe himself in water and be unclean until the evening. [11]Anyone whom the one with the discharge touches without having rinsed his hands in water shall wash his clothes and bathe himself in water and be unclean until the evening. [12]And an earthenware vessel that the one with the discharge touches shall be broken, and every vessel of wood shall be rinsed in water.

[13]"And when the one with a discharge is cleansed of his discharge, then he shall count for himself seven days for his cleansing, and wash his clothes. And he shall bathe his body in fresh water and shall be clean. [14]And on the eighth day he shall take two turtledoves or two pigeons and come before the LORD to the entrance of the tent of meeting and give them to the priest. [15]And the priest shall use them, one for a sin offering and the other for a burnt offering. And the priest shall make atonement for him before the LORD for his discharge.

[16]"If a man has an emission of semen, he shall bathe his whole body in water and be unclean until the evening. [17]And every garment and every skin on which the semen comes shall be washed with water and be unclean until the evening. [18]If a man lies with a woman and has an emission of semen, both of them shall bathe themselves in water and be unclean until the evening.

[19]"When a woman has a discharge, and the discharge in her body is blood, she shall be in her menstrual impurity for seven days, and whoever touches her shall be unclean until the evening. [20]And everything on which she lies during her menstrual impurity shall be unclean. Everything also on which she sits shall be unclean. [21]And whoever touches her bed shall wash his clothes and bathe himself in water and be unclean until the evening. [22]And whoever touches anything on which she sits shall wash his clothes and bathe himself in water and be unclean until the evening. [23]Whether it is the bed or anything on which she sits, when he touches it he shall be unclean until the evening. [24]And if any man lies with her and her menstrual impurity comes upon him, he shall be unclean seven days, and every bed on which he lies shall be unclean.

[25]"If a woman has a discharge of blood for many days, not at the time of her menstrual impurity, or if she has a discharge beyond the time of her impurity, all the days of the discharge she shall continue in uncleanness. As in the days of her impurity, she shall be unclean. [26]Every bed on which she lies, all the days of her discharge, shall be to her as the bed of her impurity. And everything on which she sits shall be unclean, as in the uncleanness of her menstrual impurity. [27]And whoever touches these things shall be unclean, and shall wash his clothes and bathe himself in water and be unclean until the evening. [28]But if she is cleansed of her discharge, she shall count for herself seven days, and after that she shall be clean. [29]And on the eighth day she shall take two turtledoves or two pigeons and bring them to the priest, to the entrance of the tent of meeting. [30]And the priest shall use one for a sin offering and the other for a burnt offering. And the priest shall make atonement for her before the LORD for her unclean discharge.

[31]"Thus you shall keep the people of Israel separate from their uncleanness, lest they die in their uncleanness by defiling my tabernacle that is in their midst."

[32]This is the law for him who has a discharge and for him who has an emission of semen, becoming unclean thereby; [33]also for her who is unwell with her menstrual impurity, that is, for anyone, male or female, who has a discharge, and for the man who lies with a woman who is unclean.

Psalm 18

To THE CHOIRMASTER. A PSALM OF DAVID, THE SERVANT OF THE LORD, WHO ADDRESSED THE WORDS OF THIS SONG TO THE LORD ON THE DAY WHEN THE LORD RESCUED HIM FROM THE HAND OF ALL HIS ENEMIES, AND FROM THE HAND OF SAUL. HE SAID:

I love you, O LORD, my strength.
   [2]The LORD is my rock and my fortress and
      my deliverer,
   my God, my rock, in whom I take
      refuge,
   my shield, and the horn of my
      salvation, my stronghold.
[3]   I call upon the LORD, who is worthy to
      be praised,
   and I am saved from my enemies.

4   The cords of death encompassed me;
      the torrents of destruction assailed
      me;[1]
5   the cords of Sheol entangled me;
      the snares of death confronted me.

6   In my distress I called upon the LORD;
      to my God I cried for help.
    From his temple he heard my voice,
      and my cry to him reached his ears.

7   Then the earth reeled and rocked;
      the foundations also of the mountains
        trembled
      and quaked, because he was angry.
8   Smoke went up from his nostrils,[2]
      and devouring fire from his mouth;
      glowing coals flamed forth from him.
9   He bowed the heavens and came down;
      thick darkness was under his feet.
10 He rode on a cherub and flew;
      he came swiftly on the wings of the
        wind.
11 He made darkness his covering, his
        canopy around him,
      thick clouds dark with water.
12 Out of the brightness before him
      hailstones and coals of fire broke
        through his clouds.

13 The LORD also thundered in the
        heavens,
      and the Most High uttered his voice,
      hailstones and coals of fire.
14 And he sent out his arrows and
        scattered them;
      he flashed forth lightnings and routed
        them.
15 Then the channels of the sea were seen,
      and the foundations of the world were
        laid bare
    at your rebuke, O LORD,
      at the blast of the breath of your
        nostrils.

16 He sent from on high, he took me;
      he drew me out of many waters.
17 He rescued me from my strong enemy
      and from those who hated me,
      for they were too mighty for me.
18 They confronted me in the day of my
        calamity,
      but the LORD was my support.

19 He brought me out into a broad place;
      he rescued me, because he delighted
        in me.

20 The LORD dealt with me according to
        my righteousness;
      according to the cleanness of my
        hands he rewarded me.
21 For I have kept the ways of the LORD,
      and have not wickedly departed from
        my God.
22 For all his rules[3] were before me,
      and his statutes I did not put away
        from me.
23 I was blameless before him,
      and I kept myself from my guilt.
24 So the LORD has rewarded me according
        to my righteousness,
      according to the cleanness of my
        hands in his sight.

25 With the merciful you show yourself
        merciful;
      with the blameless man you show
        yourself blameless;
26 with the purified you show yourself pure;
      and with the crooked you make
        yourself seem tortuous.
27 For you save a humble people,
      but the haughty eyes you bring down.
28 For it is you who light my lamp;
      the LORD my God lightens my
        darkness.
29 For by you I can run against a troop,
      and by my God I can leap over a wall.
30 This God—his way is perfect;[4]
      the word of the LORD proves true;
      he is a shield for all those who take
        refuge in him.

31 For who is God, but the LORD?
      And who is a rock, except our God?—
32 the God who equipped me with strength
      and made my way blameless.
33 He made my feet like the feet of a deer
      and set me secure on the heights.
34 He trains my hands for war,
      so that my arms can bend a bow of
        bronze.
35 You have given me the shield of your
        salvation,
      and your right hand supported me,
      and your gentleness made me great.

[1] Or terrified me [2] Or in his wrath [3] Or just decrees [4] Or blameless

36 You gave a wide place for my steps
     under me,
   and my feet did not slip.
37 I pursued my enemies and overtook
     them,
   and did not turn back till they were
     consumed.
38 I thrust them through, so that they were
     not able to rise;
   they fell under my feet.
39 For you equipped me with strength for
     the battle;
   you made those who rise against me
     sink under me.
40 You made my enemies turn their backs
     to me,[1]
   and those who hated me I destroyed.
41 They cried for help, but there was none
     to save;
   they cried to the LORD, but he did not
     answer them.
42 I beat them fine as dust before the
     wind;
   I cast them out like the mire of the
     streets.
43 You delivered me from strife with the
     people;
   you made me the head of the nations;
   people whom I had not known served
     me.
44 As soon as they heard of me they
     obeyed me;
   foreigners came cringing to me.
45 Foreigners lost heart
   and came trembling out of their
     fortresses.
46 The LORD lives, and blessed be my rock,
   and exalted be the God of my
     salvation—
47 the God who gave me vengeance
   and subdued peoples under me,
48 who delivered me from my enemies;
   yes, you exalted me above those who
     rose against me;
   you rescued me from the man of
     violence.
49 For this I will praise you, O LORD, among
     the nations,
   and sing to your name.

50 Great salvation he brings to his king,
   and shows steadfast love to his
     anointed,
   to David and his offspring forever.

Proverbs 29

He who is often reproved, yet stiffens his
   neck,
   will suddenly be broken beyond
     healing.
2 When the righteous increase, the people
     rejoice,
   but when the wicked rule, the people
     groan.
3 He who loves wisdom makes his father
     glad,
   but a companion of prostitutes
     squanders his wealth.
4 By justice a king builds up the land,
   but he who exacts gifts[2] tears it
     down.
5 A man who flatters his neighbor
   spreads a net for his feet.
6 An evil man is ensnared in his
     transgression,
   but a righteous man sings and
     rejoices.
7 A righteous man knows the rights of the
     poor;
   a wicked man does not understand
     such knowledge.
8 Scoffers set a city aflame,
   but the wise turn away wrath.
9 If a wise man has an argument with a
     fool,
   the fool only rages and laughs, and
     there is no quiet.
10 Bloodthirsty men hate one who is
     blameless
   and seek the life of the upright.[3]
11 A fool gives full vent to his spirit,
   but a wise man quietly holds it back.
12 If a ruler listens to falsehood,
   all his officials will be wicked.
13 The poor man and the oppressor meet
     together;
   the LORD gives light to the eyes of
     both.
14 If a king faithfully judges the poor,
   his throne will be established forever.

[1] Or You gave me my enemies' necks [2] Or who taxes heavily [3] Or but the upright seek his soul

15 The rod and reproof give wisdom,
　　but a child left to himself brings
　　　shame to his mother.

16 When the wicked increase,
　　transgression increases,
　　but the righteous will look upon their
　　　downfall.

17 Discipline your son, and he will give you
　　rest;
　　he will give delight to your heart.

18 Where there is no prophetic vision the
　　people cast off restraint,[1]
　　but blessed is he who keeps the law.

19 By mere words a servant is not
　　disciplined,
　　for though he understands, he will not
　　　respond.

20 Do you see a man who is hasty in his
　　words?
　　There is more hope for a fool than for
　　　him.

21 Whoever pampers his servant from
　　childhood
　　will in the end find him his heir.[2]

22 A man of wrath stirs up strife,
　　and one given to anger causes much
　　　transgression.

23 One's pride will bring him low,
　　but he who is lowly in spirit will
　　　obtain honor.

24 The partner of a thief hates his own
　　life;
　　he hears the curse, but discloses
　　　nothing.

25 The fear of man lays a snare,
　　but whoever trusts in the LORD is
　　　safe.

26 Many seek the face of a ruler,
　　but it is from the LORD that a man
　　　gets justice.

27 An unjust man is an abomination to the
　　righteous,
　　but one whose way is straight is an
　　　abomination to the wicked.

---

2 Thessalonians 3

Finally, brothers,[3] pray for us, that the word of the Lord may speed ahead and be honored,[4] as happened among you, ²and that we may be delivered from wicked and evil men. For not all have faith. ³But the Lord is faithful. He will establish you and guard you against the evil one.[5] ⁴And we have confidence in the Lord about you, that you are doing and will do the things that we command. ⁵May the Lord direct your hearts to the love of God and to the steadfastness of Christ.

⁶Now we command you, brothers, in the name of our Lord Jesus Christ, that you keep away from any brother who is walking in idleness and not in accord with the tradition that you received from us. ⁷For you yourselves know how you ought to imitate us, because we were not idle when we were with you, ⁸nor did we eat anyone's bread without paying for it, but with toil and labor we worked night and day, that we might not be a burden to any of you. ⁹It was not because we do not have that right, but to give you in ourselves an example to imitate. ¹⁰For even when we were with you, we would give you this command: If anyone is not willing to work, let him not eat. ¹¹For we hear that some among you walk in idleness, not busy at work, but busybodies. ¹²Now such persons we command and encourage in the Lord Jesus Christ to do their work quietly and to earn their own living.[6]

¹³As for you, brothers, do not grow weary in doing good. ¹⁴If anyone does not obey what we say in this letter, take note of that person, and have nothing to do with him, that he may be ashamed. ¹⁵Do not regard him as an enemy, but warn him as a brother.

¹⁶Now may the Lord of peace himself give you peace at all times in every way. The Lord be with you all.

¹⁷I, Paul, write this greeting with my own hand. This is the sign of genuineness in every letter of mine; it is the way I write. ¹⁸The grace of our Lord Jesus Christ be with you all.

---

¹ Or *the people are discouraged* ² The meaning of the Hebrew word rendered *his heir* is uncertain ³ Or *brothers and sisters;* also verses 6, 13 ⁴ Or *glorified* ⁵ Or *evil* ⁶ Greek *to eat their own bread*

APRIL 12

Leviticus 16

The Lord spoke to Moses after the death of the two sons of Aaron, when they drew near before the Lord and died, ²and the Lord said to Moses, "Tell Aaron your brother not to come at any time into the Holy Place inside the veil, before the mercy seat that is on the ark, so that he may not die. For I will appear in the cloud over the mercy seat. ³But in this way Aaron shall come into the Holy Place: with a bull from the herd for a sin offering and a ram for a burnt offering. ⁴He shall put on the holy linen coat and shall have the linen undergarment on his body, and he shall tie the linen sash around his waist, and wear the linen turban; these are the holy garments. He shall bathe his body in water and then put them on. ⁵And he shall take from the congregation of the people of Israel two male goats for a sin offering, and one ram for a burnt offering.

⁶"Aaron shall offer the bull as a sin offering for himself and shall make atonement for himself and for his house. ⁷Then he shall take the two goats and set them before the Lord at the entrance of the tent of meeting. ⁸And Aaron shall cast lots over the two goats, one lot for the Lord and the other lot for Azazel.[1] ⁹And Aaron shall present the goat on which the lot fell for the Lord and use it as a sin offering, ¹⁰but the goat on which the lot fell for Azazel shall be presented alive before the Lord to make atonement over it, that it may be sent away into the wilderness to Azazel.

¹¹"Aaron shall present the bull as a sin offering for himself, and shall make atonement for himself and for his house. He shall kill the bull as a sin offering for himself. ¹²And he shall take a censer full of coals of fire from the altar before the Lord, and two handfuls of sweet incense beaten small, and he shall bring it inside the veil ¹³and put the incense on the fire before the Lord, that the cloud of the incense may cover the mercy seat that is over the testimony, so that he does not die. ¹⁴And he shall take some of the blood of the bull and sprinkle it with his finger on the front of the mercy seat on the east side, and in front of the mercy seat he shall sprinkle some of the blood with his finger seven times.

¹⁵"Then he shall kill the goat of the sin offering that is for the people and bring its blood inside the veil and do with its blood as he did with the blood of the bull, sprinkling it over the mercy seat and in front of the mercy seat. ¹⁶Thus he shall make atonement for the Holy Place, because of the uncleannesses of the people of Israel and because of their transgressions, all their sins. And so he shall do for the tent of meeting, which dwells with them in the midst of their uncleannesses. ¹⁷No one may be in the tent of meeting from the time he enters to make atonement in the Holy Place until he comes out and has made atonement for himself and for his house and for all the assembly of Israel. ¹⁸Then he shall go out to the altar that is before the Lord and make atonement for it, and shall take some of the blood of the bull and some of the blood of the goat, and put it on the horns of the altar all around. ¹⁹And he shall sprinkle some of the blood on it with his finger seven times, and cleanse it and consecrate it from the uncleannesses of the people of Israel.

²⁰"And when he has made an end of atoning for the Holy Place and the tent of meeting and the altar, he shall present the live goat. ²¹And Aaron shall lay both his hands on the head of the live goat, and confess over it all the iniquities of the people of Israel, and all their transgressions, all their sins. And he shall put them on the head of the goat and send it away into the wilderness by the hand of a man who is in readiness. ²²The goat shall bear all their iniquities on itself to a remote area, and he shall let the goat go free in the wilderness.

²³"Then Aaron shall come into the tent of meeting and shall take off the linen garments that he put on when he went into the Holy Place and shall leave them there. ²⁴And he shall bathe his body in water in a holy place and put on his

---

[1] The meaning of *Azazel* is uncertain; possibly the name of a place or a demon, traditionally a scapegoat; also verses 10, 26

garments and come out and offer his burnt offering and the burnt offering of the people and make atonement for himself and for the people. ²⁵And the fat of the sin offering he shall burn on the altar. ²⁶And he who lets the goat go to Azazel shall wash his clothes and bathe his body in water, and afterward he may come into the camp. ²⁷And the bull for the sin offering and the goat for the sin offering, whose blood was brought in to make atonement in the Holy Place, shall be carried outside the camp. Their skin and their flesh and their dung shall be burned up with fire. ²⁸And he who burns them shall wash his clothes and bathe his body in water, and afterward he may come into the camp.

²⁹"And it shall be a statute to you forever that in the seventh month, on the tenth day of the month, you shall afflict yourselves[1] and shall do no work, either the native or the stranger who sojourns among you. ³⁰For on this day shall atonement be made for you to cleanse you. You shall be clean before the Lord from all your sins. ³¹It is a Sabbath of solemn rest to you, and you shall afflict yourselves; it is a statute forever. ³²And the priest who is anointed and consecrated as priest in his father's place shall make atonement, wearing the holy linen garments. ³³He shall make atonement for the holy sanctuary, and he shall make atonement for the tent of meeting and for the altar, and he shall make atonement for the priests and for all the people of the assembly. ³⁴And this shall be a statute forever for you, that atonement may be made for the people of Israel once in the year because of all their sins." And Aaron[2] did as the Lord commanded Moses.

Psalm 19

To the choirmaster. A Psalm of David.

The heavens declare the glory of God,
 and the sky above[3] proclaims his
  handiwork.
² Day to day pours out speech,
  and night to night reveals knowledge.
³ There is no speech, nor are there words,
  whose voice is not heard.
⁴ Their voice[4] goes out through all the
   earth,
  and their words to the end of the
   world.

⁵ In them he has set a tent for the sun,
  which comes out like a bridegroom
   leaving his chamber,
  and, like a strong man, runs its course
   with joy.
⁶ Its rising is from the end of the heavens,
  and its circuit to the end of them,
  and there is nothing hidden from its
   heat.

⁷ The law of the Lord is perfect,[5]
  reviving the soul;
 the testimony of the Lord is sure,
  making wise the simple;
⁸ the precepts of the Lord are right,
  rejoicing the heart;
 the commandment of the Lord is pure,
  enlightening the eyes;
⁹ the fear of the Lord is clean,
  enduring forever;
 the rules[6] of the Lord are true,
  and righteous altogether.
¹⁰ More to be desired are they than gold,
  even much fine gold;
 sweeter also than honey
  and drippings of the honeycomb.
¹¹ Moreover, by them is your servant
   warned;
  in keeping them there is great reward.
¹² Who can discern his errors?
  Declare me innocent from hidden
   faults.
¹³ Keep back your servant also from
   presumptuous sins;
  let them not have dominion over me!
 Then I shall be blameless,
  and innocent of great transgression.

¹⁴ Let the words of my mouth and the
   meditation of my heart
  be acceptable in your sight,
  O Lord, my rock and my redeemer.

Proverbs 30

The words of Agur son of Jakeh. The oracle.[7]
 The man declares, I am weary, O God;
  I am weary, O God, and worn out.[8]
² Surely I am too stupid to be a man.
  I have not the understanding of a man.
³ I have not learned wisdom,
  nor have I knowledge of the Holy One.

¹ Or shall fast; also verse 31 ² Hebrew he ³ Hebrew the expanse; compare Genesis 1:6–8 ⁴ Or Their measuring line ⁵ Or blameless ⁶ Or just decrees ⁷ Or Jakeh, the man of Massa ⁸ Revocalization; Hebrew The man declares to Ithiel, to Ithiel and Ucal

⁴ Who has ascended to heaven and come
    down?
  Who has gathered the wind in his
    fists?
  Who has wrapped up the waters in a
    garment?
  Who has established all the ends of
    the earth?
  What is his name, and what is his son's
    name?
  Surely you know!

⁵ Every word of God proves true;
  he is a shield to those who take refuge
    in him.
⁶ Do not add to his words,
  lest he rebuke you and you be found a
    liar.

⁷ Two things I ask of you;
  deny them not to me before I die:
⁸ Remove far from me falsehood and lying;
  give me neither poverty nor riches;
  feed me with the food that is needful
    for me,
⁹ lest I be full and deny you
  and say, "Who is the LORD?"
  or lest I be poor and steal
  and profane the name of my God.

¹⁰ Do not slander a servant to his master,
  lest he curse you, and you be held
    guilty.

¹¹ There are those¹ who curse their fathers
  and do not bless their mothers.
¹² There are those who are clean in their
    own eyes
  but are not washed of their filth.
¹³ There are those—how lofty are their
    eyes,
  how high their eyelids lift!
¹⁴ There are those whose teeth are swords,
  whose fangs are knives,
  to devour the poor from off the earth,
  the needy from among mankind.

¹⁵ The leech has two daughters:
  Give and Give.²
  Three things are never satisfied;
  four never say, "Enough":
¹⁶ Sheol, the barren womb,
  the land never satisfied with water,
  and the fire that never says, "Enough."

¹⁷ The eye that mocks a father
  and scorns to obey a mother
  will be picked out by the ravens of the
    valley
  and eaten by the vultures.

¹⁸ Three things are too wonderful for me;
  four I do not understand:
¹⁹ the way of an eagle in the sky,
  the way of a serpent on a rock,
  the way of a ship on the high seas,
  and the way of a man with a virgin.

²⁰ This is the way of an adulteress:
  she eats and wipes her mouth
  and says, "I have done no wrong."

²¹ Under three things the earth trembles;
  under four it cannot bear up:
²² a slave when he becomes king,
  and a fool when he is filled with food;
²³ an unloved woman when she gets a
    husband,
  and a maidservant when she displaces
    her mistress.

²⁴ Four things on earth are small,
  but they are exceedingly wise:
²⁵ the ants are a people not strong,
  yet they provide their food in the
    summer;
²⁶ the rock badgers are a people not
    mighty,
  yet they make their homes in the
    cliffs;
²⁷ the locusts have no king,
  yet all of them march in rank;
²⁸ the lizard you can take in your hands,
  yet it is in kings' palaces.

²⁹ Three things are stately in their tread;
  four are stately in their stride:
³⁰ the lion, which is mightiest among
    beasts
  and does not turn back before any;
³¹ the strutting rooster,³ the he-goat,
  and a king whose army is with him.⁴

³² If you have been foolish, exalting
    yourself,
  or if you have been devising evil,
  put your hand on your mouth.
³³ For pressing milk produces curds,
  pressing the nose produces blood,
  and pressing anger produces strife.

¹ Hebrew *There is a generation*; also verses 12, 13, 14 ² Or *"Give, give," they cry* ³ Or *the magpie, or the greyhound*; Hebrew *girt-of-loins* ⁴ Or *against whom there is no rising up*

1 Timothy 1

Paul, an apostle of Christ Jesus by command of God our Savior and of Christ Jesus our hope,

²To Timothy, my true child in the faith:

Grace, mercy, and peace from God the Father and Christ Jesus our Lord.

³As I urged you when I was going to Macedonia, remain at Ephesus so that you may charge certain persons not to teach any different doctrine, ⁴nor to devote themselves to myths and endless genealogies, which promote speculations rather than the stewardship¹ from God that is by faith. ⁵The aim of our charge is love that issues from a pure heart and a good conscience and a sincere faith. ⁶Certain persons, by swerving from these, have wandered away into vain discussion, ⁷desiring to be teachers of the law, without understanding either what they are saying or the things about which they make confident assertions.

⁸Now we know that the law is good, if one uses it lawfully, ⁹understanding this, that the law is not laid down for the just but for the lawless and disobedient, for the ungodly and sinners, for the unholy and profane, for those who strike their fathers and mothers, for murderers, ¹⁰the sexually immoral, men who practice homosexuality, enslavers,² liars, perjurers, and whatever else is contrary to sound³ doctrine, ¹¹in accordance with the gospel of the glory of the blessed God with which I have been entrusted.

¹²I thank him who has given me strength, Christ Jesus our Lord, because he judged me faithful, appointing me to his service, ¹³though formerly I was a blasphemer, persecutor, and insolent opponent. But I received mercy because I had acted ignorantly in unbelief, ¹⁴and the grace of our Lord overflowed for me with the faith and love that are in Christ Jesus. ¹⁵The saying is trustworthy and deserving of full acceptance, that Christ Jesus came into the world to save sinners, of whom I am the foremost. ¹⁶But I received mercy for this reason, that in me, as the foremost, Jesus Christ might display his perfect patience as an example to those who were to believe in him for eternal life. ¹⁷To the King of the ages, immortal, invisible, the only God, be honor and glory forever and ever.⁴ Amen.

¹⁸This charge I entrust to you, Timothy, my child, in accordance with the prophecies previously made about you, that by them you may wage the good warfare, ¹⁹holding faith and a good conscience. By rejecting this, some have made shipwreck of their faith, ²⁰among whom are Hymenaeus and Alexander, whom I have handed over to Satan that they may learn not to blaspheme.

APRIL 13

Leviticus 17

And the LORD spoke to Moses, saying, ²"Speak to Aaron and his sons and to all the people of Israel and say to them, This is the thing that the LORD has commanded. ³If any one of the house of Israel kills an ox or a lamb or a goat in the camp, or kills it outside the camp, ⁴and does not bring it to the entrance of the tent of meeting to offer it as a gift to the LORD in front of the tabernacle of the LORD, bloodguilt shall be imputed to that man. He has shed blood, and that man shall be cut off from among his people. ⁵This is to the end that the people of Israel may bring their sacrifices that they sacrifice in the open field, that they may bring them to the LORD, to the priest at the entrance of the tent of meeting, and sacrifice them as sacrifices of peace offerings to the LORD. ⁶And the priest shall throw the blood on the altar of the LORD at the entrance of the tent of meeting and burn the fat for a pleasing aroma to the LORD. ⁷So they shall no more sacrifice their sacrifices to goat

¹ Or good order ² That is, those who take someone captive in order to sell him into slavery ³ Or healthy ⁴ Greek to the ages of ages

demons, after whom they whore. This shall be a statute forever for them throughout their generations.

⁸"And you shall say to them, Any one of the house of Israel, or of the strangers who sojourn among them, who offers a burnt offering or sacrifice ⁹and does not bring it to the entrance of the tent of meeting to offer it to the LORD, that man shall be cut off from his people.

¹⁰"If any one of the house of Israel or of the strangers who sojourn among them eats any blood, I will set my face against that person who eats blood and will cut him off from among his people. ¹¹For the life of the flesh is in the blood, and I have given it for you on the altar to make atonement for your souls, for it is the blood that makes atonement by the life. ¹²Therefore I have said to the people of Israel, No person among you shall eat blood, neither shall any stranger who sojourns among you eat blood.

¹³"Any one also of the people of Israel, or of the strangers who sojourn among them, who takes in hunting any beast or bird that may be eaten shall pour out its blood and cover it with earth. ¹⁴For the life of every creature[1] is its blood: its blood is its life.[2] Therefore I have said to the people of Israel, You shall not eat the blood of any creature, for the life of every creature is its blood. Whoever eats it shall be cut off. ¹⁵And every person who eats what dies of itself or what is torn by beasts, whether he is a native or a sojourner, shall wash his clothes and bathe himself in water and be unclean until the evening; then he shall be clean. ¹⁶But if he does not wash them or bathe his flesh, he shall bear his iniquity."

──── Psalm 20–21 ────

To the choirmaster. A Psalm of David.

May the LORD answer you in the day of trouble!
May the name of the God of Jacob protect you!
2 May he send you help from the sanctuary
and give you support from Zion!
3 May he remember all your offerings
and regard with favor your burnt sacrifices! *Selah*

4 May he grant you your heart's desire
and fulfill all your plans!
5 May we shout for joy over your salvation,
and in the name of our God set up our banners!
May the LORD fulfill all your petitions!

6 Now I know that the LORD saves his anointed;
he will answer him from his holy heaven
with the saving might of his right hand.
7 Some trust in chariots and some in horses,
but we trust in the name of the LORD our God.
8 They collapse and fall,
but we rise and stand upright.

9 O LORD, save the king!
May he answer us when we call.

To the choirmaster. A Psalm of David.

O LORD, in your strength the king rejoices,
and in your salvation how greatly he exults!
2 You have given him his heart's desire
and have not withheld the request of his lips. *Selah*
3 For you meet him with rich blessings;
you set a crown of fine gold upon his head.
4 He asked life of you; you gave it to him,
length of days forever and ever.
5 His glory is great through your salvation;
splendor and majesty you bestow on him.
6 For you make him most blessed forever;[3]
you make him glad with the joy of your presence.
7 For the king trusts in the LORD,
and through the steadfast love of the Most High he shall not be moved.

8 Your hand will find out all your enemies;
your right hand will find out those who hate you.
9 You will make them as a blazing oven when you appear.

[1] Hebrew *all flesh* [2] Hebrew *it is in its life* [3] Or *make him a source of blessing forever*

The LORD will swallow them up in his
    wrath,
    and fire will consume them.
10 You will destroy their descendants from
    the earth,
    and their offspring from among the
    children of man.
11 Though they plan evil against you,
    though they devise mischief, they will
    not succeed.
12 For you will put them to flight;
    you will aim at their faces with your
    bows.

13 Be exalted, O LORD, in your strength!
    We will sing and praise your power.

Proverbs 31

The words of King Lemuel. An oracle that
his mother taught him:

2 What are you doing, my son?[1] What are
    you doing, son of my womb?
    What are you doing, son of my vows?
3 Do not give your strength to women,
    your ways to those who destroy
    kings.
4 It is not for kings, O Lemuel,
    it is not for kings to drink wine,
    or for rulers to take strong drink,
5 lest they drink and forget what has been
    decreed
    and pervert the rights of all the
    afflicted.
6 Give strong drink to the one who is
    perishing,
    and wine to those in bitter distress;[2]
7 let them drink and forget their poverty
    and remember their misery no more.
8 Open your mouth for the mute,
    for the rights of all who are destitute.[3]
9 Open your mouth, judge righteously,
    defend the rights of the poor and
    needy.
10[4] An excellent wife who can find?
    She is far more precious than jewels.
11 The heart of her husband trusts in her,
    and he will have no lack of gain.
12 She does him good, and not harm,
    all the days of her life.

13 She seeks wool and flax,
    and works with willing hands.
14 She is like the ships of the merchant;
    she brings her food from afar.
15 She rises while it is yet night
    and provides food for her household
    and portions for her maidens.
16 She considers a field and buys it;
    with the fruit of her hands she plants
    a vineyard.
17 She dresses herself[5] with strength
    and makes her arms strong.
18 She perceives that her merchandise is
    profitable.
    Her lamp does not go out at night.
19 She puts her hands to the distaff,
    and her hands hold the spindle.
20 She opens her hand to the poor
    and reaches out her hands to the
    needy.
21 She is not afraid of snow for her
    household,
    for all her household are clothed in
    scarlet.[6]
22 She makes bed coverings for herself;
    her clothing is fine linen and purple.
23 Her husband is known in the gates
    when he sits among the elders of the
    land.
24 She makes linen garments and sells
    them;
    she delivers sashes to the merchant.
25 Strength and dignity are her clothing,
    and she laughs at the time to come.
26 She opens her mouth with wisdom,
    and the teaching of kindness is on her
    tongue.
27 She looks well to the ways of her
    household
    and does not eat the bread of idleness.
28 Her children rise up and call her
    blessed;
    her husband also, and he praises her:
29 "Many women have done excellently,
    but you surpass them all."
30 Charm is deceitful, and beauty is vain,
    but a woman who fears the LORD is to
    be praised.
31 Give her of the fruit of her hands,
    and let her works praise her in the
    gates.

[1] Hebrew *What, my son?* [2] Hebrew *those bitter in soul* [3] Hebrew *are sons of passing away* [4] Verses 10–31 are an acrostic poem, each verse beginning with the successive letters of the Hebrew alphabet [5] Hebrew *She girds her loins* [6] Or *in double thickness*

1 Timothy 2

First of all, then, I urge that supplications, prayers, intercessions, and thanksgivings be made for all people, [2] for kings and all who are in high positions, that we may lead a peaceful and quiet life, godly and dignified in every way. [3] This is good, and it is pleasing in the sight of God our Savior, [4] who desires all people to be saved and to come to the knowledge of the truth. [5] For there is one God, and there is one mediator between God and men, the man[1] Christ Jesus, [6] who gave himself as a ransom for all, which is the testimony given at the proper time. [7] For this I was appointed a preacher and an apostle (I am telling the truth, I am not lying), a teacher of the Gentiles in faith and truth.

[8] I desire then that in every place the men should pray, lifting holy hands without anger or quarreling; [9] likewise also that women should adorn themselves in respectable apparel, with modesty and self-control, not with braided hair and gold or pearls or costly attire, [10] but with what is proper for women who profess godliness—with good works. [11] Let a woman learn quietly with all submissiveness. [12] I do not permit a woman to teach or to exercise authority over a man; rather, she is to remain quiet. [13] For Adam was formed first, then Eve; [14] and Adam was not deceived, but the woman was deceived and became a transgressor. [15] Yet she will be saved through childbearing—if they continue in faith and love and holiness, with self-control.

APRIL 14

Leviticus 18

And the LORD spoke to Moses, saying, [2] "Speak to the people of Israel and say to them, I am the LORD your God. [3] You shall not do as they do in the land of Egypt, where you lived, and you shall not do as they do in the land of Canaan, to which I am bringing you. You shall not walk in their statutes. [4] You shall follow my rules[2] and keep my statutes and walk in them. I am the LORD your God. [5] You shall therefore keep my statutes and my rules; if a person does them, he shall live by them: I am the LORD.

[6] "None of you shall approach any one of his close relatives to uncover nakedness. I am the LORD. [7] You shall not uncover the nakedness of your father, which is the nakedness of your mother; she is your mother, you shall not uncover her nakedness. [8] You shall not uncover the nakedness of your father's wife; it is your father's nakedness. [9] You shall not uncover the nakedness of your sister, your father's daughter or your mother's daughter, whether brought up in the family or in another home. [10] You shall not uncover the nakedness of your son's daughter or of your daughter's daughter, for their nakedness is your own nakedness. [11] You shall not uncover the nakedness of your father's wife's daughter, brought up in your father's family, since she is your sister. [12] You shall not uncover the nakedness of your father's sister; she is your father's relative. [13] You shall not uncover the nakedness of your mother's sister, for she is your mother's relative. [14] You shall not uncover the nakedness of your father's brother, that is, you shall not approach his wife; she is your aunt. [15] You shall not uncover the nakedness of your daughter-in-law; she is your son's wife, you shall not uncover her nakedness. [16] You shall not uncover the nakedness of your brother's wife; it is your brother's nakedness. [17] You shall not uncover the nakedness of a woman and of her daughter, and you shall not take her son's daughter or her daughter's daughter to uncover her nakedness; they are relatives; it is depravity. [18] And you shall not take a woman as a rival wife to her sister, uncovering her nakedness while her sister is still alive.

[1] men and man render the same Greek word that is translated people in verses 1 and 4 [2] Or my just decrees; also verse 5

¹⁹ "You shall not approach a woman to uncover her nakedness while she is in her menstrual uncleanness. ²⁰And you shall not lie sexually with your neighbor's wife and so make yourself unclean with her. ²¹You shall not give any of your children to offer them¹ to Molech, and so profane the name of your God: I am the LORD. ²²You shall not lie with a male as with a woman; it is an abomination. ²³And you shall not lie with any animal and so make yourself unclean with it, neither shall any woman give herself to an animal to lie with it: it is perversion.

²⁴ "Do not make yourselves unclean by any of these things, for by all these the nations I am driving out before you have become unclean, ²⁵and the land became unclean, so that I punished its iniquity, and the land vomited out its inhabitants. ²⁶But you shall keep my statutes and my rules and do none of these abominations, either the native or the stranger who sojourns among you ²⁷(for the people of the land, who were before you, did all of these abominations, so that the land became unclean), ²⁸lest the land vomit you out when you make it unclean, as it vomited out the nation that was before you. ²⁹For everyone who does any of these abominations, the persons who do them shall be cut off from among their people. ³⁰So keep my charge never to practice any of these abominable customs that were practiced before you, and never to make yourselves unclean by them: I am the LORD your God."

Psalm 22

TO THE CHOIRMASTER: ACCORDING TO THE DOE OF THE DAWN. A PSALM OF DAVID.

My God, my God, why have you forsaken me?
Why are you so far from saving me,
from the words of my groaning?
² O my God, I cry by day, but you do not answer,
and by night, but I find no rest.
³ Yet you are holy,
enthroned on the praises² of Israel.
⁴ In you our fathers trusted;
they trusted, and you delivered them.
⁵ To you they cried and were rescued;
in you they trusted and were not put to shame.

⁶ But I am a worm and not a man,
scorned by mankind and despised by the people.
⁷ All who see me mock me;
they make mouths at me; they wag their heads;
⁸ "He trusts in the LORD; let him deliver him;
let him rescue him, for he delights in him!"

⁹ Yet you are he who took me from the womb;
you made me trust you at my mother's breasts.
¹⁰ On you was I cast from my birth,
and from my mother's womb you have been my God.
¹¹ Be not far from me,
for trouble is near,
and there is none to help.

¹² Many bulls encompass me;
strong bulls of Bashan surround me;
¹³ they open wide their mouths at me,
like a ravening and roaring lion.

¹⁴ I am poured out like water,
and all my bones are out of joint;
my heart is like wax;
it is melted within my breast;
¹⁵ my strength is dried up like a potsherd,
and my tongue sticks to my jaws;
you lay me in the dust of death.

¹⁶ For dogs encompass me;
a company of evildoers encircles me;
they have pierced my hands and feet³—
¹⁷ I can count all my bones—
they stare and gloat over me;
¹⁸ they divide my garments among them,
and for my clothing they cast lots.

¹⁹ But you, O LORD, do not be far off!
O you my help, come quickly to my aid!
²⁰ Deliver my soul from the sword,
my precious life from the power of the dog!
²¹ Save me from the mouth of the lion!
You have rescued⁴ me from the horns of the wild oxen!

²² I will tell of your name to my brothers;
in the midst of the congregation I will praise you:

¹ Hebrew to make them pass through [the fire] ² Or dwelling in the praises ³ Some Hebrew manuscripts, Septuagint, Vulgate, Syriac; most Hebrew manuscripts like a lion [they are at] my hands and feet ⁴ Hebrew answered

²³ You who fear the LORD, praise him!
    All you offspring of Jacob, glorify him,
    and stand in awe of him, all you
        offspring of Israel!
²⁴ For he has not despised or abhorred
    the affliction of the afflicted,
and he has not hidden his face from
        him,
    but has heard, when he cried to him.

²⁵ From you comes my praise in the great
        congregation;
    my vows I will perform before those
        who fear him.
²⁶ The afflicted¹ shall eat and be satisfied;
    those who seek him shall praise the
        LORD!
    May your hearts live forever!

²⁷ All the ends of the earth shall remember
        and turn to the LORD,
    and all the families of the nations
        shall worship before you.
²⁸ For kingship belongs to the LORD,
    and he rules over the nations.

²⁹ All the prosperous of the earth eat and
        worship;
    before him shall bow all who go down
        to the dust,
    even the one who could not keep
        himself alive.
³⁰ Posterity shall serve him;
    it shall be told of the Lord to the
        coming generation;
³¹ they shall come and proclaim his
        righteousness to a people yet
        unborn,
    that he has done it.

———— *Ecclesiastes 1* ————

The words of the Preacher,² the son of David,
king in Jerusalem.

² Vanity³ of vanities, says the Preacher,
    vanity of vanities! All is vanity.
³ What does man gain by all the toil
    at which he toils under the sun?
⁴ A generation goes, and a generation
        comes,
    but the earth remains forever.

⁵ The sun rises, and the sun goes down,
    and hastens⁴ to the place where it rises.
⁶ The wind blows to the south
    and goes around to the north;
around and around goes the wind,
    and on its circuits the wind returns.
⁷ All streams run to the sea,
    but the sea is not full;
to the place where the streams flow,
    there they flow again.
⁸ All things are full of weariness;
    a man cannot utter it;
the eye is not satisfied with seeing,
    nor the ear filled with hearing.
⁹ What has been is what will be,
    and what has been done is what will
        be done,
    and there is nothing new under the
        sun.
¹⁰ Is there a thing of which it is said,
    "See, this is new"?
It has been already
    in the ages before us.
¹¹ There is no remembrance of former
        things,⁵
    nor will there be any remembrance
of later things⁶ yet to be
    among those who come after.

¹²I the Preacher have been king over Israel in Jerusalem. ¹³And I applied my heart⁷ to seek and to search out by wisdom all that is done under heaven. It is an unhappy business that God has given to the children of man to be busy with. ¹⁴I have seen everything that is done under the sun, and behold, all is vanity⁸ and a striving after wind.⁹

¹⁵   What is crooked cannot be made straight,
        and what is lacking cannot be counted.

¹⁶I said in my heart, "I have acquired great wisdom, surpassing all who were over Jerusalem before me, and my heart has had great experience of wisdom and knowledge." ¹⁷And I applied my heart to know wisdom and to know madness and folly. I perceived that this also is but a striving after wind.

¹⁸   For in much wisdom is much vexation,
        and he who increases knowledge
        increases sorrow.

---

¹ Or *The meek* ² Or *Convener*, or *Collector*; Hebrew *Qoheleth* (so throughout Ecclesiastes) ³ The Hebrew term *hebel*, translated *vanity* or *vain*, refers concretely to a "mist," "vapor," or "mere breath," and metaphorically to something that is fleeting or elusive (with different nuances depending on the context). It appears five times in this verse and in 29 other verses in Ecclesiastes ⁴ Or *and returns panting* ⁵ Or *former people* ⁶ Or *later people* ⁷ The Hebrew term denotes the center of one's inner life, including mind, will, and emotions ⁸ The Hebrew term *hebel* can refer to a "vapor" or "mere breath" (see note on 1:2) ⁹ Or *a feeding on wind*; compare Hosea 12:1 (also in Ecclesiastes 1:17; 2:11, 17, 26; 4:4, 6, 16; 6:9)

1 Timothy 3

The saying is trustworthy: If anyone aspires to the office of overseer, he desires a noble task. ² Therefore an overseer[1] must be above reproach, the husband of one wife,[2] sober-minded, self-controlled, respectable, hospitable, able to teach, ³ not a drunkard, not violent but gentle, not quarrelsome, not a lover of money. ⁴ He must manage his own household well, with all dignity keeping his children submissive, ⁵ for if someone does not know how to manage his own household, how will he care for God's church? ⁶ He must not be a recent convert, or he may become puffed up with conceit and fall into the condemnation of the devil. ⁷ Moreover, he must be well thought of by outsiders, so that he may not fall into disgrace, into a snare of the devil.

⁸ Deacons likewise must be dignified, not double-tongued,[3] not addicted to much wine, not greedy for dishonest gain. ⁹ They must hold the mystery of the faith with a clear conscience.

¹⁰ And let them also be tested first; then let them serve as deacons if they prove themselves blameless. ¹¹ Their wives likewise must[4] be dignified, not slanderers, but sober-minded, faithful in all things. ¹² Let deacons each be the husband of one wife, managing their children and their own households well. ¹³ For those who serve well as deacons gain a good standing for themselves and also great confidence in the faith that is in Christ Jesus.

¹⁴ I hope to come to you soon, but I am writing these things to you so that, ¹⁵ if I delay, you may know how one ought to behave in the household of God, which is the church of the living God, a pillar and buttress of the truth. ¹⁶ Great indeed, we confess, is the mystery of godliness:

He[5] was manifested in the flesh,
    vindicated[6] by the Spirit,[7]
        seen by angels,
    proclaimed among the nations,
        believed on in the world,
            taken up in glory.

APRIL 15

Leviticus 19

And the LORD spoke to Moses, saying, ² "Speak to all the congregation of the people of Israel and say to them, You shall be holy, for I the LORD your God am holy. ³ Every one of you shall revere his mother and his father, and you shall keep my Sabbaths: I am the LORD your God. ⁴ Do not turn to idols or make for yourselves any gods of cast metal: I am the LORD your God.

⁵ "When you offer a sacrifice of peace offerings to the LORD, you shall offer it so that you may be accepted. ⁶ It shall be eaten the same day you offer it or on the day after, and anything left over until the third day shall be burned up with fire. ⁷ If it is eaten at all on the third day, it is tainted; it will not be accepted, ⁸ and everyone who eats it shall bear his iniquity, because he has profaned what is holy to

the LORD, and that person shall be cut off from his people.

⁹ "When you reap the harvest of your land, you shall not reap your field right up to its edge, neither shall you gather the gleanings after your harvest. ¹⁰ And you shall not strip your vineyard bare, neither shall you gather the fallen grapes of your vineyard. You shall leave them for the poor and for the sojourner: I am the LORD your God.

¹¹ "You shall not steal; you shall not deal falsely; you shall not lie to one another. ¹² You shall not swear by my name falsely, and so profane the name of your God: I am the LORD.

¹³ "You shall not oppress your neighbor or rob him. The wages of a hired worker shall not remain with you all night until the morning. ¹⁴ You shall not curse the deaf or put a

---

[1] Or bishop; Greek episkopos; a similar term occurs in verse 1 [2] Or a man of one woman; also verse 12 [3] Or devious in speech [4] Or Wives, likewise, must, or Women, likewise, must [5] Greek Who; some manuscripts God; others Which [6] Or justified [7] Or vindicated in spirit

stumbling block before the blind, but you shall fear your God: I am the LORD.

¹⁵ "You shall do no injustice in court. You shall not be partial to the poor or defer to the great, but in righteousness shall you judge your neighbor. ¹⁶You shall not go around as a slanderer among your people, and you shall not stand up against the life¹ of your neighbor: I am the LORD.

¹⁷ "You shall not hate your brother in your heart, but you shall reason frankly with your neighbor, lest you incur sin because of him. ¹⁸You shall not take vengeance or bear a grudge against the sons of your own people, but you shall love your neighbor as yourself: I am the LORD.

¹⁹ "You shall keep my statutes. You shall not let your cattle breed with a different kind. You shall not sow your field with two kinds of seed, nor shall you wear a garment of cloth made of two kinds of material.

²⁰ "If a man lies sexually with a woman who is a slave, assigned to another man and not yet ransomed or given her freedom, a distinction shall be made. They shall not be put to death, because she was not free; ²¹but he shall bring his compensation to the LORD, to the entrance of the tent of meeting, a ram for a guilt offering. ²²And the priest shall make atonement for him with the ram of the guilt offering before the LORD for his sin that he has committed, and he shall be forgiven for the sin that he has committed.

²³ "When you come into the land and plant any kind of tree for food, then you shall regard its fruit as forbidden.² Three years it shall be forbidden to you; it must not be eaten. ²⁴And in the fourth year all its fruit shall be holy, an offering of praise to the LORD. ²⁵But in the fifth year you may eat of its fruit, to increase its yield for you: I am the LORD your God.

²⁶ "You shall not eat any flesh with the blood in it. You shall not interpret omens or tell fortunes. ²⁷You shall not round off the hair on your temples or mar the edges of your beard. ²⁸You shall not make any cuts on your body for the dead or tattoo yourselves: I am the LORD.

²⁹ "Do not profane your daughter by making her a prostitute, lest the land fall into prostitution and the land become full of depravity. ³⁰You shall keep my Sabbaths and reverence my sanctuary: I am the LORD.

³¹ "Do not turn to mediums or necromancers; do not seek them out, and so make yourselves unclean by them: I am the LORD your God.

³² "You shall stand up before the gray head and honor the face of an old man, and you shall fear your God: I am the LORD.

³³ "When a stranger sojourns with you in your land, you shall not do him wrong. ³⁴You shall treat the stranger who sojourns with you as the native among you, and you shall love him as yourself, for you were strangers in the land of Egypt: I am the LORD your God.

³⁵ "You shall do no wrong in judgment, in measures of length or weight or quantity. ³⁶You shall have just balances, just weights, a just ephah, and a just hin:³ I am the LORD your God, who brought you out of the land of Egypt. ³⁷And you shall observe all my statutes and all my rules, and do them: I am the LORD."

Psalm 23–24

A PSALM OF DAVID.

The LORD is my shepherd; I shall not want.
²He makes me lie down in green pastures.
He leads me beside still waters.⁴
3   He restores my soul.
He leads me in paths of righteousness⁵
for his name's sake.

4   Even though I walk through the valley of
the shadow of death,⁶
I will fear no evil,
for you are with me;
your rod and your staff,
they comfort me.

5   You prepare a table before me
in the presence of my enemies;
you anoint my head with oil;
my cup overflows.

6   Surely⁷ goodness and mercy⁸ shall
follow me
all the days of my life,
and I shall dwell⁹ in the house of the
LORD
forever.¹⁰

A PSALM OF DAVID.

The earth is the LORD's and the fullness
thereof,¹¹
the world and those who dwell therein,

¹ Hebrew blood ² Hebrew as its uncircumcision ³ An ephah was about 3/5 bushel or 22 liters; a hin was about 4 quarts or 3.5 liters ⁴ Hebrew beside waters of rest ⁵ Or in right paths ⁶ Or the valley of deep darkness ⁷ Or Only ⁸ Or steadfast love ⁹ Or shall return to dwell ¹⁰ Hebrew for length of days ¹¹ Or and all that fills it

2   for he has founded it upon the seas
    and established it upon the rivers.

3   Who shall ascend the hill of the LORD?
    And who shall stand in his holy place?
4   He who has clean hands and a pure
      heart,
    who does not lift up his soul to what is
      false
    and does not swear deceitfully.
5   He will receive blessing from the LORD
    and righteousness from the God of his
      salvation.
6   Such is the generation of those who
      seek him,
    who seek the face of the God of Jacob.[1]
                         Selah

7   Lift up your heads, O gates!
    And be lifted up, O ancient doors,
    that the King of glory may come in.
8   Who is this King of glory?
    The LORD, strong and mighty,
    the LORD, mighty in battle!
9   Lift up your heads, O gates!
    And lift them up, O ancient doors,
    that the King of glory may come in.
10 Who is this King of glory?
    The LORD of hosts,
    he is the King of glory!   *Selah*

Ecclesiastes 2

I said in my heart, "Come now, I will test you with pleasure; enjoy yourself." But behold, this also was vanity.[2] [2]I said of laughter, "It is mad," and of pleasure, "What use is it?" [3]I searched with my heart how to cheer my body with wine—my heart still guiding me with wisdom—and how to lay hold on folly, till I might see what was good for the children of man to do under heaven during the few days of their life. [4]I made great works. I built houses and planted vineyards for myself. [5]I made myself gardens and parks, and planted in them all kinds of fruit trees. [6]I made myself pools from which to water the forest of growing trees. [7]I bought male and female slaves, and had slaves who were born in my house. I had also great possessions of herds and flocks, more than any who had been before me in Jerusalem. [8]I also gathered for myself silver and gold and the treasure of kings and provinces. I got singers, both men and women, and many concubines,[3] the delight of the sons of man.

[9]So I became great and surpassed all who were before me in Jerusalem. Also my wisdom remained with me. [10]And whatever my eyes desired I did not keep from them. I kept my heart from no pleasure, for my heart found pleasure in all my toil, and this was my reward for all my toil. [11]Then I considered all that my hands had done and the toil I had expended in doing it, and behold, all was vanity and a striving after wind, and there was nothing to be gained under the sun.

[12]So I turned to consider wisdom and madness and folly. For what can the man do who comes after the king? Only what has already been done. [13]Then I saw that there is more gain in wisdom than in folly, as there is more gain in light than in darkness. [14]The wise person has his eyes in his head, but the fool walks in darkness. And yet I perceived that the same event happens to all of them. [15]Then I said in my heart, "What happens to the fool will happen to me also. Why then have I been so very wise?" And I said in my heart that this also is vanity. [16]For of the wise as of the fool there is no enduring remembrance, seeing that in the days to come all will have been long forgotten. How the wise dies just like the fool! [17]So I hated life, because what is done under the sun was grievous to me, for all is vanity and a striving after wind.

[18]I hated all my toil in which I toil under the sun, seeing that I must leave it to the man who will come after me, [19]and who knows whether he will be wise or a fool? Yet he will be master of all for which I toiled and used my wisdom under the sun. This also is vanity. [20]So I turned about and gave my heart up to despair over all the toil of my labors under the sun, [21]because sometimes a person who has toiled with wisdom and knowledge and skill must leave everything to be enjoyed by someone who did not toil for it. This also is vanity and a great evil. [22]What has a man from all the toil and striving of heart with which he toils beneath the sun? [23]For all his days are full of sorrow, and his work is a vexation. Even in the night his heart does not rest. This also is vanity.

[24]There is nothing better for a person than that he should eat and drink and find enjoyment[4] in his toil. This also, I saw, is from the

---

[1] Septuagint, Syriac, and two Hebrew manuscripts; Masoretic Text *Jacob, who seek your face* [2] The Hebrew term *hebel* can refer to a "vapor" or "mere breath"; also verses 11, 15, 17, 19, 21, 23, 26 (see note on 1:2) [3] The meaning of the Hebrew word is uncertain [4] Or *and make his soul see good*

hand of God, ²⁵ for apart from him[1] who can eat or who can have enjoyment? ²⁶ For to the one who pleases him God has given wisdom and knowledge and joy, but to the sinner he has given the business of gathering and collecting, only to give to one who pleases God. This also is vanity and a striving after wind.

1 Timothy 4

Now the Spirit expressly says that in later times some will depart from the faith by devoting themselves to deceitful spirits and teachings of demons, ² through the insincerity of liars whose consciences are seared, ³ who forbid marriage and require abstinence from foods that God created to be received with thanksgiving by those who believe and know the truth. ⁴ For everything created by God is good, and nothing is to be rejected if it is received with thanksgiving, ⁵ for it is made holy by the word of God and prayer.

⁶ If you put these things before the brothers,[2] you will be a good servant of Christ Jesus, being trained in the words of the faith and of the good doctrine that you have followed. ⁷ Have nothing to do with irreverent, silly myths. Rather train yourself for godliness; ⁸ for while bodily training is of some value, godliness is of value in every way, as it holds promise for the present life and also for the life to come. ⁹ The saying is trustworthy and deserving of full acceptance. ¹⁰ For to this end we toil and strive,[3] because we have our hope set on the living God, who is the Savior of all people, especially of those who believe.

¹¹ Command and teach these things. ¹² Let no one despise you for your youth, but set the believers an example in speech, in conduct, in love, in faith, in purity. ¹³ Until I come, devote yourself to the public reading of Scripture, to exhortation, to teaching. ¹⁴ Do not neglect the gift you have, which was given you by prophecy when the council of elders laid their hands on you. ¹⁵ Practice these things, immerse yourself in them,[4] so that all may see your progress. ¹⁶ Keep a close watch on yourself and on the teaching. Persist in this, for by so doing you will save both yourself and your hearers.

APRIL 16

Leviticus 20

The LORD spoke to Moses, saying, ² "Say to the people of Israel, Any one of the people of Israel or of the strangers who sojourn in Israel who gives any of his children to Molech shall surely be put to death. The people of the land shall stone him with stones. ³ I myself will set my face against that man and will cut him off from among his people, because he has given one of his children to Molech, to make my sanctuary unclean and to profane my holy name. ⁴ And if the people of the land do at all close their eyes to that man when he gives one of his children to Molech, and do not put him to death, ⁵ then I will set my face against that man and against his clan and will cut them off from among their people, him and all who follow him in whoring after Molech.

⁶ "If a person turns to mediums and necromancers, whoring after them, I will set my face against that person and will cut him off from among his people. ⁷ Consecrate yourselves, therefore, and be holy, for I am the LORD your God. ⁸ Keep my statutes and do them; I am the LORD who sanctifies you. ⁹ For anyone who curses his father or his mother shall surely be put to death; he has cursed his father or his mother; his blood is upon him.

¹⁰ "If a man commits adultery with the wife of[5] his neighbor, both the adulterer and the adulteress shall surely be put to death. ¹¹ If a

---

[1] Some Hebrew manuscripts, Septuagint, Syriac; most Hebrew manuscripts *apart from me* [2] Or *brothers and sisters.* The plural Greek word *adelphoi* (translated "brothers") refers to siblings in a family. In New Testament usage, depending on the context, *adelphoi* may refer either to men or to both men and women who are siblings (brothers and sisters) in God's family, the church [3] Some manuscripts *and suffer reproach* [4] Greek *be in them* [5] Hebrew repeats *if a man commits adultery with the wife of*

man lies with his father's wife, he has uncovered his father's nakedness; both of them shall surely be put to death; their blood is upon them. ¹²If a man lies with his daughter-in-law, both of them shall surely be put to death; they have committed perversion; their blood is upon them. ¹³If a man lies with a male as with a woman, both of them have committed an abomination; they shall surely be put to death; their blood is upon them. ¹⁴If a man takes a woman and her mother also, it is depravity; he and they shall be burned with fire, that there may be no depravity among you. ¹⁵If a man lies with an animal, he shall surely be put to death, and you shall kill the animal. ¹⁶If a woman approaches any animal and lies with it, you shall kill the woman and the animal; they shall surely be put to death; their blood is upon them.

¹⁷"If a man takes his sister, a daughter of his father or a daughter of his mother, and sees her nakedness, and she sees his nakedness, it is a disgrace, and they shall be cut off in the sight of the children of their people. He has uncovered his sister's nakedness, and he shall bear his iniquity. ¹⁸If a man lies with a woman during her menstrual period and uncovers her nakedness, he has made naked her fountain, and she has uncovered the fountain of her blood. Both of them shall be cut off from among their people. ¹⁹You shall not uncover the nakedness of your mother's sister or of your father's sister, for that is to make naked one's relative; they shall bear their iniquity. ²⁰If a man lies with his uncle's wife, he has uncovered his uncle's nakedness; they shall bear their sin; they shall die childless. ²¹If a man takes his brother's wife, it is impurity.[1] He has uncovered his brother's nakedness; they shall be childless.

²²"You shall therefore keep all my statutes and all my rules and do them, that the land where I am bringing you to live may not vomit you out. ²³And you shall not walk in the customs of the nation that I am driving out before you, for they did all these things, and therefore I detested them. ²⁴But I have said to you, 'You shall inherit their land, and I will give it to you to possess, a land flowing with milk and honey.' I am the Lord your God, who has separated you from the peoples. ²⁵You shall therefore separate the clean beast from the unclean, and the unclean bird from the clean. You shall not make

yourselves detestable by beast or by bird or by anything with which the ground crawls, which I have set apart for you to hold unclean. ²⁶You shall be holy to me, for I the Lord am holy and have separated you from the peoples, that you should be mine.

²⁷"A man or a woman who is a medium or a necromancer shall surely be put to death. They shall be stoned with stones; their blood shall be upon them."

————— *Psalm 25*[2] —————

Of David.

To you, O Lord, I lift up my soul.
² O my God, in you I trust;
let me not be put to shame;
let not my enemies exult over me.
³ Indeed, none who wait for you shall be
put to shame;
they shall be ashamed who are
wantonly treacherous.

⁴ Make me to know your ways, O Lord;
teach me your paths.
⁵ Lead me in your truth and teach me,
for you are the God of my salvation;
for you I wait all the day long.

⁶ Remember your mercy, O Lord, and
your steadfast love,
for they have been from of old.
⁷ Remember not the sins of my youth or
my transgressions;
according to your steadfast love
remember me,
for the sake of your goodness, O Lord!

⁸ Good and upright is the Lord;
therefore he instructs sinners in the
way.
⁹ He leads the humble in what is right,
and teaches the humble his way.
¹⁰ All the paths of the Lord are steadfast
love and faithfulness,
for those who keep his covenant and
his testimonies.

¹¹ For your name's sake, O Lord,
pardon my guilt, for it is great.
¹² Who is the man who fears the Lord?
Him will he instruct in the way that he
should choose.

[1] Literally *menstrual impurity* [2] This psalm is an acrostic poem, each verse beginning with the successive letters of the Hebrew alphabet

13 His soul shall abide in well-being,
       and his offspring shall inherit the land.
14 The friendship[1] of the LORD is for those
       who fear him,
       and he makes known to them his
       covenant.
15 My eyes are ever toward the LORD,
       for he will pluck my feet out of the net.

16 Turn to me and be gracious to me,
       for I am lonely and afflicted.
17 The troubles of my heart are enlarged;
       bring me out of my distresses.
18 Consider my affliction and my trouble,
       and forgive all my sins.
19 Consider how many are my foes,
       and with what violent hatred they
       hate me.
20 Oh, guard my soul, and deliver me!
       Let me not be put to shame, for I take
       refuge in you.
21 May integrity and uprightness preserve
       me,
       for I wait for you.
22 Redeem Israel, O God,
       out of all his troubles.

────────── Ecclesiastes 3 ──────────

For everything there is a season, and a time
for every matter under heaven:
2   a time to be born, and a time to die;
    a time to plant, and a time to pluck up
       what is planted;
3   a time to kill, and a time to heal;
    a time to break down, and a time to
       build up;
4   a time to weep, and a time to laugh;
    a time to mourn, and a time to dance;
5   a time to cast away stones, and a time to
       gather stones together;
    a time to embrace, and a time to refrain
       from embracing;
6   a time to seek, and a time to lose;
    a time to keep, and a time to cast away;
7   a time to tear, and a time to sew;
    a time to keep silence, and a time to
       speak;
8   a time to love, and a time to hate;
    a time for war, and a time for peace.

9 What gain has the worker from his toil? [10] I have seen the business that God has given to the children of man to be busy with. [11] He has made everything beautiful in its time. Also, he has put eternity into man's heart, yet so that he cannot find out what God has done from the beginning to the end. [12] I perceived that there is nothing better for them than to be joyful and to do good as long as they live; [13] also that everyone should eat and drink and take pleasure in all his toil—this is God's gift to man.

[14] I perceived that whatever God does endures forever; nothing can be added to it, nor anything taken from it. God has done it, so that people fear before him. [15] That which is, already has been; that which is to be, already has been; and God seeks what has been driven away.[2]

[16] Moreover, I saw under the sun that in the place of justice, even there was wickedness, and in the place of righteousness, even there was wickedness. [17] I said in my heart, God will judge the righteous and the wicked, for there is a time for every matter and for every work. [18] I said in my heart with regard to the children of man that God is testing them that they may see that they themselves are but beasts. [19] For what happens to the children of man and what happens to the beasts is the same; as one dies, so dies the other. They all have the same breath, and man has no advantage over the beasts, for all is vanity.[3] [20] All go to one place. All are from the dust, and to dust all return. [21] Who knows whether the spirit of man goes upward and the spirit of the beast goes down into the earth? [22] So I saw that there is nothing better than that a man should rejoice in his work, for that is his lot. Who can bring him to see what will be after him?

────────── 1 Timothy 5 ──────────

Do not rebuke an older man but encourage him as you would a father, younger men as brothers, [2] older women as mothers, younger women as sisters, in all purity.

[3] Honor widows who are truly widows. [4] But if a widow has children or grandchildren, let them first learn to show godliness to their own household and to make some return to their parents, for this is pleasing in the sight of God. [5] She who is truly a widow, left all alone, has set her hope on God and continues in

[1] Or The secret counsel [2] Hebrew what has been pursued [3] The Hebrew term hebel can refer to a "vapor" or "mere breath" (see note on 1:2)

supplications and prayers night and day, [6]but she who is self-indulgent is dead even while she lives. [7]Command these things as well, so that they may be without reproach. [8]But if anyone does not provide for his relatives, and especially for members of his household, he has denied the faith and is worse than an unbeliever.

[9]Let a widow be enrolled if she is not less than sixty years of age, having been the wife of one husband,[1] [10]and having a reputation for good works: if she has brought up children, has shown hospitality, has washed the feet of the saints, has cared for the afflicted, and has devoted herself to every good work. [11]But refuse to enroll younger widows, for when their passions draw them away from Christ, they desire to marry [12]and so incur condemnation for having abandoned their former faith. [13]Besides that, they learn to be idlers, going about from house to house, and not only idlers, but also gossips and busybodies, saying what they should not. [14]So I would have younger widows marry, bear children, manage their households, and give the adversary no occasion for slander. [15]For some have already

strayed after Satan. [16]If any believing woman has relatives who are widows, let her care for them. Let the church not be burdened, so that it may care for those who are truly widows.

[17]Let the elders who rule well be considered worthy of double honor, especially those who labor in preaching and teaching. [18]For the Scripture says, "You shall not muzzle an ox when it treads out the grain," and, "The laborer deserves his wages." [19]Do not admit a charge against an elder except on the evidence of two or three witnesses. [20]As for those who persist in sin, rebuke them in the presence of all, so that the rest may stand in fear. [21]In the presence of God and of Christ Jesus and of the elect angels I charge you to keep these rules without prejudging, doing nothing from partiality. [22]Do not be hasty in the laying on of hands, nor take part in the sins of others; keep yourself pure. [23](No longer drink only water, but use a little wine for the sake of your stomach and your frequent ailments.) [24]The sins of some people are conspicuous, going before them to judgment, but the sins of others appear later. [25]So also good works are conspicuous, and even those that are not cannot remain hidden.

APRIL 17

Leviticus 21

And the LORD said to Moses, "Speak to the priests, the sons of Aaron, and say to them, No one shall make himself unclean for the dead among his people, [2]except for his closest relatives, his mother, his father, his son, his daughter, his brother, [3]or his virgin sister (who is near to him because she has had no husband; for her he may make himself unclean). [4]He shall not make himself unclean as a husband among his people and so profane himself. [5]They shall not make bald patches on their heads, nor shave off the edges of their beards, nor make any cuts on their body. [6]They shall be holy to their God and not profane the name of their God. For they offer the LORD's food offerings,

the bread of their God; therefore they shall be holy. [7]They shall not marry a prostitute or a woman who has been defiled, neither shall they marry a woman divorced from her husband, for the priest is holy to his God. [8]You shall sanctify him, for he offers the bread of your God. He shall be holy to you, for I, the LORD, who sanctify you, am holy. [9]And the daughter of any priest, if she profanes herself by whoring, profanes her father; she shall be burned with fire.

[10]"The priest who is chief among his brothers, on whose head the anointing oil is poured and who has been consecrated to wear the garments, shall not let the hair of his head hang loose nor tear his clothes. [11]He shall not go in

[1] Or a woman of one man

to any dead bodies nor make himself unclean, even for his father or for his mother. ¹²He shall not go out of the sanctuary, lest he profane the sanctuary of his God, for the consecration of the anointing oil of his God is on him: I am the LORD. ¹³And he shall take a wife in her virginity.[1] ¹⁴A widow, or a divorced woman, or a woman who has been defiled, or a prostitute, these he shall not marry. But he shall take as his wife a virgin[2] of his own people, ¹⁵that he may not profane his offspring among his people, for I am the LORD who sanctifies him."

¹⁶And the LORD spoke to Moses, saying, ¹⁷"Speak to Aaron, saying, None of your offspring throughout their generations who has a blemish may approach to offer the bread of his God. ¹⁸For no one who has a blemish shall draw near, a man blind or lame, or one who has a mutilated face or a limb too long, ¹⁹or a man who has an injured foot or an injured hand, ²⁰or a hunchback or a dwarf or a man with a defect in his sight or an itching disease or scabs or crushed testicles. ²¹No man of the offspring of Aaron the priest who has a blemish shall come near to offer the LORD's food offerings; since he has a blemish, he shall not come near to offer the bread of his God. ²²He may eat the bread of his God, both of the most holy and of the holy things, ²³but he shall not go through the veil or approach the altar, because he has a blemish, that he may not profane my sanctuaries, for I am the LORD who sanctifies them." ²⁴So Moses spoke to Aaron and to his sons and to all the people of Israel.

--------- *Psalm 26–27* ---------

OF DAVID.

Vindicate me, O LORD,
    for I have walked in my integrity,
    and I have trusted in the LORD
      without wavering.
2 Prove me, O LORD, and try me;
    test my heart and my mind.[3]
3 For your steadfast love is before my
      eyes,
    and I walk in your faithfulness.

4 I do not sit with men of falsehood,
    nor do I consort with hypocrites.
5 I hate the assembly of evildoers,
    and I will not sit with the wicked.

6 I wash my hands in innocence
    and go around your altar, O LORD,
7 proclaiming thanksgiving aloud,
    and telling all your wondrous deeds.

8 O LORD, I love the habitation of your
      house
    and the place where your glory
      dwells.
9 Do not sweep my soul away with
      sinners,
    nor my life with bloodthirsty men,
10 in whose hands are evil devices,
    and whose right hands are full of
      bribes.

11 But as for me, I shall walk in my
      integrity;
    redeem me, and be gracious to me.
12 My foot stands on level ground;
    in the great assembly I will bless the
      LORD.

OF DAVID.

The LORD is my light and my salvation;
    whom shall I fear?
    The LORD is the stronghold[4] of my life;
    of whom shall I be afraid?

2 When evildoers assail me
    to eat up my flesh,
    my adversaries and foes,
    it is they who stumble and fall.

3 Though an army encamp against me,
    my heart shall not fear;
    though war arise against me,
    yet[5] I will be confident.

4 One thing have I asked of the LORD,
    that will I seek after:
    that I may dwell in the house of the
      LORD
    all the days of my life,
    to gaze upon the beauty of the LORD
    and to inquire[6] in his temple.

5 For he will hide me in his shelter
    in the day of trouble;
    he will conceal me under the cover of
      his tent;
    he will lift me high upon a rock.

6 And now my head shall be lifted up
    above my enemies all around me,

---

[1] Or a young wife [2] Hebrew young woman [3] Hebrew test my kidneys and my heart [4] Or refuge [5] Or in this [6] Or meditate

and I will offer in his tent
    sacrifices with shouts of joy;
    I will sing and make melody to the LORD.

7 Hear, O LORD, when I cry aloud;
    be gracious to me and answer me!
8 You have said, "Seek[1] my face."
    My heart says to you,
    "Your face, LORD, do I seek."[2]
9   Hide not your face from me.
    Turn not your servant away in anger,
    O you who have been my help.
    Cast me not off; forsake me not,
    O God of my salvation!
10 For my father and my mother have
        forsaken me,
    but the LORD will take me in.

11 Teach me your way, O LORD,
    and lead me on a level path
    because of my enemies.
12 Give me not up to the will of my
        adversaries;
    for false witnesses have risen against
        me,
    and they breathe out violence.

13 I believe[3] that I shall look upon the
        goodness of the LORD
    in the land of the living!
14 Wait for the LORD;
    be strong, and let your heart take
        courage;
    wait for the LORD!

Ecclesiastes 4

Again I saw all the oppressions that are done under the sun. And behold, the tears of the oppressed, and they had no one to comfort them! On the side of their oppressors there was power, and there was no one to comfort them. ²And I thought the dead who are already dead more fortunate than the living who are still alive. ³But better than both is he who has not yet been and has not seen the evil deeds that are done under the sun.

⁴Then I saw that all toil and all skill in work come from a man's envy of his neighbor. This also is vanity[4] and a striving after wind. ⁵The fool folds his hands and eats his own flesh.

⁶Better is a handful of quietness than two hands full of toil and a striving after wind. ⁷Again, I saw vanity under the sun: ⁸one person who has no other, either son or brother, yet there is no end to all his toil, and his eyes are never satisfied with riches, so that he never asks, "For whom am I toiling and depriving myself of pleasure?" This also is vanity and an unhappy business.

⁹Two are better than one, because they have a good reward for their toil. ¹⁰For if they fall, one will lift up his fellow. But woe to him who is alone when he falls and has not another to lift him up! ¹¹Again, if two lie together, they keep warm, but how can one keep warm alone? ¹²And though a man might prevail against one who is alone, two will withstand him—a threefold cord is not quickly broken.

¹³Better was a poor and wise youth than an old and foolish king who no longer knew how to take advice. ¹⁴For he went from prison to the throne, though in his own kingdom he had been born poor. ¹⁵I saw all the living who move about under the sun, along with that[5] youth who was to stand in the king's[6] place. ¹⁶There was no end of all the people, all of whom he led. Yet those who come later will not rejoice in him. Surely this also is vanity and a striving after wind.

1 Timothy 6

Let all who are under a yoke as bondservants[7] regard their own masters as worthy of all honor, so that the name of God and the teaching may not be reviled. ²Those who have believing masters must not be disrespectful on the ground that they are brothers; rather they must serve all the better since those who benefit by their good service are believers and beloved.

Teach and urge these things. ³If anyone teaches a different doctrine and does not agree with the sound[8] words of our Lord Jesus Christ and the teaching that accords with godliness, ⁴he is puffed up with conceit and understands nothing. He has an unhealthy craving for controversy and for quarrels about words, which produce envy, dissension, slander, evil suspicions, ⁵and constant friction among people who are depraved

---

[1] The command (seek) is addressed to more than one person   [2] The meaning of the Hebrew verse is uncertain   [3] Other Hebrew manuscripts Oh! Had I not believed   [4] The Hebrew term hebel can refer to a "vapor" or "mere breath"; also verses 7, 8, 16 (see note on 1:2)   [5] Hebrew the second   [6] Hebrew his   [7] Or slaves (for the contextual rendering of the Greek word doulos, see Preface)   [8] Or healthy

in mind and deprived of the truth, imagining that godliness is a means of gain. ⁶But godliness with contentment is great gain, ⁷for we brought nothing into the world, and¹ we cannot take anything out of the world. ⁸But if we have food and clothing, with these we will be content. ⁹But those who desire to be rich fall into temptation, into a snare, into many senseless and harmful desires that plunge people into ruin and destruction. ¹⁰For the love of money is a root of all kinds of evils. It is through this craving that some have wandered away from the faith and pierced themselves with many pangs.

¹¹But as for you, O man of God, flee these things. Pursue righteousness, godliness, faith, love, steadfastness, gentleness. ¹²Fight the good fight of the faith. Take hold of the eternal life to which you were called and about which you made the good confession in the presence of many witnesses. ¹³I charge you in the presence of God, who gives life to all things, and of Christ Jesus, who in his testimony before² Pontius Pilate made the good confession, ¹⁴to

keep the commandment unstained and free from reproach until the appearing of our Lord Jesus Christ, ¹⁵which he will display at the proper time—he who is the blessed and only Sovereign, the King of kings and Lord of lords, ¹⁶who alone has immortality, who dwells in unapproachable light, whom no one has ever seen or can see. To him be honor and eternal dominion. Amen.

¹⁷As for the rich in this present age, charge them not to be haughty, nor to set their hopes on the uncertainty of riches, but on God, who richly provides us with everything to enjoy. ¹⁸They are to do good, to be rich in good works, to be generous and ready to share, ¹⁹thus storing up treasure for themselves as a good foundation for the future, so that they may take hold of that which is truly life.

²⁰O Timothy, guard the deposit entrusted to you. Avoid the irreverent babble and contradictions of what is falsely called "knowledge," ²¹for by professing it some have swerved from the faith.

Grace be with you.³

APRIL 18

Leviticus 22

And the LORD spoke to Moses, saying, ²"Speak to Aaron and his sons so that they abstain from the holy things of the people of Israel, which they dedicate to me, so that they do not profane my holy name: I am the LORD. ³Say to them, 'If any one of all your offspring throughout your generations approaches the holy things that the people of Israel dedicate to the LORD, while he has an uncleanness, that person shall be cut off from my presence: I am the LORD. ⁴None of the offspring of Aaron who has a leprous disease or a discharge may eat of the holy things until he is clean. Whoever touches anything that is unclean through contact with the dead or a man who has had an emission of semen, ⁵and whoever touches a swarming thing by which he may be made

unclean or a person from whom he may take uncleanness, whatever his uncleanness may be— ⁶the person who touches such a thing shall be unclean until the evening and shall not eat of the holy things unless he has bathed his body in water. ⁷When the sun goes down he shall be clean, and afterward he may eat of the holy things, because they are his food. ⁸He shall not eat what dies of itself or is torn by beasts, and so make himself unclean by it: I am the LORD.' ⁹They shall therefore keep my charge, lest they bear sin for it and die thereby when they profane it: I am the LORD who sanctifies them.

¹⁰"A lay person shall not eat of a holy thing; no foreign guest of the priest or hired worker shall eat of a holy thing, ¹¹but if a priest buys a slave⁴ as his property for money, the slave⁵ may

eat of it, and anyone born in his house may eat of his food. ¹²If a priest's daughter marries a layman, she shall not eat of the contribution of the holy things. ¹³But if a priest's daughter is widowed or divorced and has no child and returns to her father's house, as in her youth, she may eat of her father's food; yet no lay person shall eat of it. ¹⁴And if anyone eats of a holy thing unintentionally, he shall add the fifth of its value to it and give the holy thing to the priest. ¹⁵They shall not profane the holy things of the people of Israel, which they contribute to the LORD, ¹⁶and so cause them to bear iniquity and guilt, by eating their holy things: for I am the LORD who sanctifies them."

¹⁷And the LORD spoke to Moses, saying, ¹⁸"Speak to Aaron and his sons and all the people of Israel and say to them, When any one of the house of Israel or of the sojourners in Israel presents a burnt offering as his offering, for any of their vows or freewill offerings that they offer to the LORD, ¹⁹if it is to be accepted for you it shall be a male without blemish, of the bulls or the sheep or the goats. ²⁰You shall not offer anything that has a blemish, for it will not be acceptable for you. ²¹And when anyone offers a sacrifice of peace offerings to the LORD to fulfill a vow or as a freewill offering from the herd or from the flock, to be accepted it must be perfect; there shall be no blemish in it. ²²Animals blind or disabled or mutilated or having a discharge or an itch or scabs you shall not offer to the LORD or give them to the LORD as a food offering on the altar. ²³You may present a bull or a lamb that has a part too long or too short for a freewill offering, but for a vow offering it cannot be accepted. ²⁴Any animal that has its testicles bruised or crushed or torn or cut you shall not offer to the LORD; you shall not do it within your land, ²⁵neither shall you offer as the bread of your God any such animals gotten from a foreigner. Since there is a blemish in them, because of their mutilation, they will not be accepted for you."

²⁶And the LORD spoke to Moses, saying, ²⁷"When an ox or sheep or goat is born, it shall remain seven days with its mother, and from the eighth day on it shall be acceptable as a food offering to the LORD. ²⁸But you shall not kill an ox or a sheep and her young in one day. ²⁹And when you sacrifice a sacrifice of thanksgiving to the LORD, you shall sacrifice it so that you

may be accepted. ³⁰It shall be eaten on the same day; you shall leave none of it until morning: I am the LORD.

³¹"So you shall keep my commandments and do them: I am the LORD. ³²And you shall not profane my holy name, that I may be sanctified among the people of Israel. I am the LORD who sanctifies you, ³³who brought you out of the land of Egypt to be your God: I am the LORD."

Psalm 28–29

OF DAVID.

To you, O LORD, I call;
  my rock, be not deaf to me,
  lest, if you be silent to me,
    I become like those who go down to the pit.
2 Hear the voice of my pleas for mercy,
    when I cry to you for help,
  when I lift up my hands
    toward your most holy sanctuary.¹

3 Do not drag me off with the wicked,
    with the workers of evil,
  who speak peace with their neighbors
    while evil is in their hearts.
4 Give to them according to their work
    and according to the evil of their deeds;
  give to them according to the work of their hands;
    render them their due reward.
5 Because they do not regard the works of the LORD
    or the work of his hands,
  he will tear them down and build them up no more.

6 Blessed be the LORD!
    For he has heard the voice of my pleas for mercy.
7 The LORD is my strength and my shield;
    in him my heart trusts, and I am helped;
  my heart exults,
    and with my song I give thanks to him.

8 The LORD is the strength of his people;²
    he is the saving refuge of his anointed.
9 Oh, save your people and bless your heritage!
    Be their shepherd and carry them forever.

¹ Hebrew *your innermost sanctuary* ² Some Hebrew manuscripts, Septuagint, Syriac; most Hebrew manuscripts *is their strength*

A PSALM OF DAVID.

Ascribe to the LORD, O heavenly beings,[1]
ascribe to the LORD glory and strength.
2 Ascribe to the LORD the glory due his
name;
worship the LORD in the splendor of
holiness.[2]

3 The voice of the LORD is over the waters;
the God of glory thunders,
the LORD, over many waters.
4 The voice of the LORD is powerful;
the voice of the LORD is full of majesty.

5 The voice of the LORD breaks the cedars;
the LORD breaks the cedars of
Lebanon.
6 He makes Lebanon to skip like a calf,
and Sirion like a young wild ox.

7 The voice of the LORD flashes forth
flames of fire.
8 The voice of the LORD shakes the
wilderness;
the LORD shakes the wilderness of
Kadesh.

9 The voice of the LORD makes the deer
give birth[3]
and strips the forests bare,
and in his temple all cry, "Glory!"

10 The LORD sits enthroned over the flood;
the LORD sits enthroned as king
forever.
11 May the LORD give strength to his
people!
May the LORD bless[4] his people with
peace!

--- ***Ecclesiastes 5***[5] ---

Guard your steps when you go to the house
of God. To draw near to listen is better than
to offer the sacrifice of fools, for they do not
know that they are doing evil. 2 6 Be not rash
with your mouth, nor let your heart be hasty to
utter a word before God, for God is in heaven
and you are on earth. Therefore let your words
be few. 3 For a dream comes with much business, and a fool's voice with many words.
4 When you vow a vow to God, do not delay
paying it, for he has no pleasure in fools. Pay

what you vow. 5 It is better that you should not
vow than that you should vow and not pay. 6 Let
not your mouth lead you[7] into sin, and do not
say before the messenger[8] that it was a mistake. Why should God be angry at your voice
and destroy the work of your hands? 7 For when
dreams increase and words grow many, there
is vanity;[9] but[10] God is the one you must fear.

8 If you see in a province the oppression of the
poor and the violation of justice and righteousness, do not be amazed at the matter, for the
high official is watched by a higher, and there
are yet higher ones over them. 9 But this is gain
for a land in every way: a king committed to
cultivated fields.[11]

10 He who loves money will not be satisfied
with money, nor he who loves wealth with
his income; this also is vanity. 11 When goods
increase, they increase who eat them, and
what advantage has their owner but to see
them with his eyes? 12 Sweet is the sleep of a
laborer, whether he eats little or much, but the
full stomach of the rich will not let him sleep.

13 There is a grievous evil that I have seen
under the sun: riches were kept by their owner
to his hurt, 14 and those riches were lost in a
bad venture. And he is father of a son, but he
has nothing in his hand. 15 As he came from his
mother's womb he shall go again, naked as he
came, and shall take nothing for his toil that
he may carry away in his hand. 16 This also is
a grievous evil: just as he came, so shall he go,
and what gain is there to him who toils for the
wind? 17 Moreover, all his days he eats in darkness in much vexation and sickness and anger.

18 Behold, what I have seen to be good and
fitting is to eat and drink and find enjoyment[12]
in all the toil with which one toils under the sun
the few days of his life that God has given him,
for this is his lot. 19 Everyone also to whom God
has given wealth and possessions and power
to enjoy them, and to accept his lot and rejoice
in his toil—this is the gift of God. 20 For he will
not much remember the days of his life because
God keeps him occupied with joy in his heart.

--- ***2 Timothy 1*** ---

Paul, an apostle of Christ Jesus by the will
of God according to the promise of the life
that is in Christ Jesus,

[1] Hebrew *sons of God, or sons of might* [2] Or *in holy attire* [3] *Revocalization yields makes the oaks to shake* [4] Or *The LORD will give. . . The LORD will bless* [5] Ch 4:17 in Hebrew [6] Ch 5:1 in Hebrew [7] Hebrew *your flesh* [8] Or *angel* [9] The Hebrew term *hebel* can refer to a "vapor" or "mere breath"; also verse 10 (see note on 1:2) [10] Or *For when dreams and vanities increase, words also grow many; but* [11] The meaning of the Hebrew verse is uncertain [12] Or *and see good*

[2]To Timothy, my beloved child:

Grace, mercy, and peace from God the Father and Christ Jesus our Lord.

[3]I thank God whom I serve, as did my ancestors, with a clear conscience, as I remember you constantly in my prayers night and day. [4]As I remember your tears, I long to see you, that I may be filled with joy. [5]I am reminded of your sincere faith, a faith that dwelt first in your grandmother Lois and your mother Eunice and now, I am sure, dwells in you as well. [6]For this reason I remind you to fan into flame the gift of God, which is in you through the laying on of my hands, [7]for God gave us a spirit not of fear but of power and love and self-control.

[8]Therefore do not be ashamed of the testimony about our Lord, nor of me his prisoner, but share in suffering for the gospel by the power of God, [9]who saved us and called us to[1] a holy calling, not because of our works but because of his own purpose and grace, which he gave us in Christ Jesus before the ages began,[2] [10]and which now has been manifested through the appearing of our Savior Christ Jesus, who abolished death and brought life and immortality to light through the gospel, [11]for which I was appointed a preacher and apostle and teacher, [12]which is why I suffer as I do. But I am not ashamed, for I know whom I have believed, and I am convinced that he is able to guard until that Day what has been entrusted to me.[3] [13]Follow the pattern of the sound[4] words that you have heard from me, in the faith and love that are in Christ Jesus. [14]By the Holy Spirit who dwells within us, guard the good deposit entrusted to you.

[15]You are aware that all who are in Asia turned away from me, among whom are Phygelus and Hermogenes. [16]May the Lord grant mercy to the household of Onesiphorus, for he often refreshed me and was not ashamed of my chains, [17]but when he arrived in Rome he searched for me earnestly and found me— [18]may the Lord grant him to find mercy from the Lord on that Day!—and you well know all the service he rendered at Ephesus.

APRIL 19

Leviticus 23

The LORD spoke to Moses, saying, [2]"Speak to the people of Israel and say to them, These are the appointed feasts of the LORD that you shall proclaim as holy convocations; they are my appointed feasts.

[3]"Six days shall work be done, but on the seventh day is a Sabbath of solemn rest, a holy convocation. You shall do no work. It is a Sabbath to the LORD in all your dwelling places.

[4]"These are the appointed feasts of the LORD, the holy convocations, which you shall proclaim at the time appointed for them. [5]In the first month, on the fourteenth day of the month at twilight,[5] is the LORD's Passover. [6]And on the fifteenth day of the same month is the Feast of Unleavened Bread to the LORD; for seven days you shall eat unleavened bread. [7]On the first day you shall have a holy convocation; you shall not do any ordinary work. [8]But you shall present a food offering to the LORD for seven days. On the seventh day is a holy convocation; you shall not do any ordinary work."

[9]And the LORD spoke to Moses, saying, [10]"Speak to the people of Israel and say to them, When you come into the land that I give you and reap its harvest, you shall bring the sheaf of the firstfruits of your harvest to the priest, [11]and he shall wave the sheaf before the LORD, so that you may be accepted. On the day after the Sabbath the priest shall wave it. [12]And on the day when you wave the sheaf, you shall offer a male lamb a year old without blemish as a burnt offering to the LORD. [13]And the grain offering with it shall be two tenths of an ephah[6] of fine flour mixed with oil, a food offering to the LORD with a pleasing aroma, and the

[1] Or with [2] Greek before times eternal [3] Or what I have entrusted to him; Greek my deposit [4] Or healthy [5] Hebrew between the two evenings [6] An ephah was about 3/5 bushel or 22 liters

drink offering with it shall be of wine, a fourth of a hin.[1] [14]And you shall eat neither bread nor grain parched or fresh until this same day, until you have brought the offering of your God: it is a statute forever throughout your generations in all your dwellings.

[15]"You shall count seven full weeks from the day after the Sabbath, from the day that you brought the sheaf of the wave offering. [16]You shall count fifty days to the day after the seventh Sabbath. Then you shall present a grain offering of new grain to the LORD. [17]You shall bring from your dwelling places two loaves of bread to be waved, made of two tenths of an ephah. They shall be of fine flour, and they shall be baked with leaven, as firstfruits to the LORD. [18]And you shall present with the bread seven lambs a year old without blemish, and one bull from the herd and two rams. They shall be a burnt offering to the LORD, with their grain offering and their drink offerings, a food offering with a pleasing aroma to the LORD. [19]And you shall offer one male goat for a sin offering, and two male lambs a year old as a sacrifice of peace offerings. [20]And the priest shall wave them with the bread of the firstfruits as a wave offering before the LORD, with the two lambs. They shall be holy to the LORD for the priest. [21]And you shall make a proclamation on the same day. You shall hold a holy convocation. You shall not do any ordinary work. It is a statute forever in all your dwelling places throughout your generations.

[22]"And when you reap the harvest of your land, you shall not reap your field right up to its edge, nor shall you gather the gleanings after your harvest. You shall leave them for the poor and for the sojourner: I am the LORD your God."

[23]And the LORD spoke to Moses, saying, [24]"Speak to the people of Israel, saying, In the seventh month, on the first day of the month, you shall observe a day of solemn rest, a memorial proclaimed with blast of trumpets, a holy convocation. [25]You shall not do any ordinary work, and you shall present a food offering to the LORD."

[26]And the LORD spoke to Moses, saying, [27]"Now on the tenth day of this seventh month is the Day of Atonement. It shall be for you a time of holy convocation, and you shall afflict

yourselves[2] and present a food offering to the LORD. [28]And you shall not do any work on that very day, for it is a Day of Atonement, to make atonement for you before the LORD your God. [29]For whoever is not afflicted on that very day shall be cut off from his people. [30]And whoever does any work on that very day, that person I will destroy from among his people. [31]You shall not do any work. It is a statute forever throughout your generations in all your dwelling places. [32]It shall be to you a Sabbath of solemn rest, and you shall afflict yourselves. On the ninth day of the month beginning at evening, from evening to evening shall you keep your Sabbath."

[33]And the LORD spoke to Moses, saying, [34]"Speak to the people of Israel, saying, On the fifteenth day of this seventh month and for seven days is the Feast of Booths[3] to the LORD. [35]On the first day shall be a holy convocation; you shall not do any ordinary work. [36]For seven days you shall present food offerings to the LORD. On the eighth day you shall hold a holy convocation and present a food offering to the LORD. It is a solemn assembly; you shall not do any ordinary work.

[37]"These are the appointed feasts of the LORD, which you shall proclaim as times of holy convocation, for presenting to the LORD food offerings, burnt offerings and grain offerings, sacrifices and drink offerings, each on its proper day, [38]besides the LORD's Sabbaths and besides your gifts and besides all your vow offerings and besides all your freewill offerings, which you give to the LORD.

[39]"On the fifteenth day of the seventh month, when you have gathered in the produce of the land, you shall celebrate the feast of the LORD seven days. On the first day shall be a solemn rest, and on the eighth day shall be a solemn rest. [40]And you shall take on the first day the fruit of splendid trees, branches of palm trees and boughs of leafy trees and willows of the brook, and you shall rejoice before the LORD your God seven days. [41]You shall celebrate it as a feast to the LORD for seven days in the year. It is a statute forever throughout your generations; you shall celebrate it in the seventh month. [42]You shall dwell in booths for seven days. All native Israelites shall dwell in booths, [43]that your generations may know that I made the people of Israel dwell in booths when I

---

[1] A hin was about 4 quarts or 3.5 liters [2] Or shall fast; also verse 32 [3] Or tabernacles

brought them out of the land of Egypt: I am the LORD your God."

⁴⁴Thus Moses declared to the people of Israel the appointed feasts of the LORD.

Psalm 30

A PSALM OF DAVID. A SONG AT THE DEDICATION OF THE TEMPLE.

I will extol you, O LORD, for you have drawn me up
    and have not let my foes rejoice over me.
² O LORD my God, I cried to you for help,
    and you have healed me.
³ O LORD, you have brought up my soul from Sheol;
    you restored me to life from among those who go down to the pit.[1]

⁴ Sing praises to the LORD, O you his saints,
    and give thanks to his holy name.[2]
⁵ For his anger is but for a moment,
    and his favor is for a lifetime.[3]
Weeping may tarry for the night,
    but joy comes with the morning.

⁶ As for me, I said in my prosperity,
    "I shall never be moved."
⁷ By your favor, O LORD,
    you made my mountain stand strong;
you hid your face;
    I was dismayed.

⁸ To you, O LORD, I cry,
    and to the Lord I plead for mercy:
⁹ "What profit is there in my death,[4]
    if I go down to the pit?[5]
Will the dust praise you?
    Will it tell of your faithfulness?
¹⁰ Hear, O LORD, and be merciful to me!
    O LORD, be my helper!"

¹¹ You have turned for me my mourning into dancing;
    you have loosed my sackcloth
    and clothed me with gladness,
¹² that my glory may sing your praise and not be silent.
    O LORD my God, I will give thanks to you forever!

Ecclesiastes 6

There is an evil that I have seen under the sun, and it lies heavy on mankind: ²a man to whom God gives wealth, possessions, and honor, so that he lacks nothing of all that he desires, yet God does not give him power to enjoy them, but a stranger enjoys them. This is vanity;[6] it is a grievous evil. ³If a man fathers a hundred children and lives many years, so that the days of his years are many, but his soul is not satisfied with life's good things, and he also has no burial, I say that a stillborn child is better off than he. ⁴For it comes in vanity and goes in darkness, and in darkness its name is covered. ⁵Moreover, it has not seen the sun or known anything, yet it finds rest rather than he. ⁶Even though he should live a thousand years twice over, yet enjoy[7] no good—do not all go to the one place?

⁷All the toil of man is for his mouth, yet his appetite is not satisfied.[8] ⁸For what advantage has the wise man over the fool? And what does the poor man have who knows how to conduct himself before the living? ⁹Better is the sight of the eyes than the wandering of the appetite: this also is vanity and a striving after wind.

¹⁰Whatever has come to be has already been named, and it is known what man is, and that he is not able to dispute with one stronger than he. ¹¹The more words, the more vanity, and what is the advantage to man? ¹²For who knows what is good for man while he lives the few days of his vain[9] life, which he passes like a shadow? For who can tell man what will be after him under the sun?

2 Timothy 2

You then, my child, be strengthened by the grace that is in Christ Jesus, ²and what you have heard from me in the presence of many witnesses entrust to faithful men[10] who will be able to teach others also. ³Share in suffering as a good soldier of Christ Jesus. ⁴No soldier gets entangled in civilian pursuits, since his aim is to please the one who enlisted him. ⁵An athlete is not crowned unless he competes according to the rules. ⁶It is the hard-working farmer who ought to have the first share of the crops.

¹ Or to life, that I should not go down to the pit ² Hebrew to the memorial of his holiness (see Exodus 3:15) ³ Or and in his favor is life ⁴ Hebrew in my blood ⁵ Or to corruption ⁶ The Hebrew term hebel can refer to a "vapor" or "mere breath"; also verses 4, 9, 11 (see note on 1:2) ⁷ Or see ⁸ Hebrew filled ⁹ The Hebrew term hebel can refer to a "vapor" or "mere breath" (see note on 1:2) ¹⁰ The Greek word anthropoi can refer to both men and women, depending on the context

⁷Think over what I say, for the Lord will give you understanding in everything.

⁸Remember Jesus Christ, risen from the dead, the offspring of David, as preached in my gospel, ⁹for which I am suffering, bound with chains as a criminal. But the word of God is not bound! ¹⁰Therefore I endure everything for the sake of the elect, that they also may obtain the salvation that is in Christ Jesus with eternal glory. ¹¹The saying is trustworthy, for:

If we have died with him, we will also
    live with him;
¹² if we endure, we will also reign with him;
    if we deny him, he also will deny us;
¹³ if we are faithless, he remains faithful—

for he cannot deny himself.

¹⁴Remind them of these things, and charge them before God¹ not to quarrel about words, which does no good, but only ruins the hearers. ¹⁵Do your best to present yourself to God as one approved,² a worker who has no need to be ashamed, rightly handling the word of truth. ¹⁶But avoid irreverent babble, for it will lead people into more and more ungodliness, ¹⁷and their talk will spread like gangrene. Among them are Hymenaeus and Philetus, ¹⁸who have swerved from the truth, saying that the resurrection has already happened. They are upsetting the faith of some. ¹⁹But God's firm foundation stands, bearing this seal: "The Lord knows those who are his," and, "Let everyone who names the name of the Lord depart from iniquity."

²⁰Now in a great house there are not only vessels of gold and silver but also of wood and clay, some for honorable use, some for dishonorable. ²¹Therefore, if anyone cleanses himself from what is dishonorable,³ he will be a vessel for honorable use, set apart as holy, useful to the master of the house, ready for every good work. ²²So flee youthful passions and pursue righteousness, faith, love, and peace, along with those who call on the Lord from a pure heart. ²³Have nothing to do with foolish, ignorant controversies; you know that they breed quarrels. ²⁴And the Lord's servant⁴ must not be quarrelsome but kind to everyone, able to teach, patiently enduring evil, ²⁵correcting his opponents with gentleness. God may perhaps grant them repentance leading to a knowledge of the truth, ²⁶and they may come to their senses and escape from the snare of the devil, after being captured by him to do his will.

APRIL 20

Leviticus 24

The LORD spoke to Moses, saying, ²"Command the people of Israel to bring you pure oil from beaten olives for the lamp, that a light may be kept burning regularly. ³Outside the veil of the testimony, in the tent of meeting, Aaron shall arrange it from evening to morning before the LORD regularly. It shall be a statute forever throughout your generations. ⁴He shall arrange the lamps on the lampstand of pure gold⁵ before the LORD regularly.

⁵"You shall take fine flour and bake twelve loaves from it; two tenths of an ephah⁶ shall be in each loaf. ⁶And you shall set them in two piles, six in a pile, on the table of pure gold⁷ before the LORD. ⁷And you shall put pure frankincense on each pile, that it may go with the bread as a memorial portion as a food offering to the LORD. ⁸Every Sabbath day Aaron shall arrange it before the LORD regularly; it is from the people of Israel as a covenant forever. ⁹And it shall be for Aaron and his sons, and they shall eat it in a holy place, since it is for him a most holy portion out of the LORD's food offerings, a perpetual due."

¹⁰Now an Israelite woman's son, whose father was an Egyptian, went out among the people of Israel. And the Israelite woman's son and a man of Israel fought in the camp,

¹ Some manuscripts the Lord ² That is, one approved after being tested ³ Greek from these things ⁴ Greek bondservant ⁵ Hebrew the pure lampstand ⁶ An ephah was about 3/5 bushel or 22 liters ⁷ Hebrew the pure table

[11] and the Israelite woman's son blasphemed the Name, and cursed. Then they brought him to Moses. His mother's name was Shelomith, the daughter of Dibri, of the tribe of Dan. [12] And they put him in custody, till the will of the LORD should be clear to them.

[13] Then the LORD spoke to Moses, saying, [14] "Bring out of the camp the one who cursed, and let all who heard him lay their hands on his head, and let all the congregation stone him. [15] And speak to the people of Israel, saying, Whoever curses his God shall bear his sin. [16] Whoever blasphemes the name of the LORD shall surely be put to death. All the congregation shall stone him. The sojourner as well as the native, when he blasphemes the Name, shall be put to death.

[17] "Whoever takes a human life shall surely be put to death. [18] Whoever takes an animal's life shall make it good, life for life. [19] If anyone injures his neighbor, as he has done it shall be done to him, [20] fracture for fracture, eye for eye, tooth for tooth; whatever injury he has given a person shall be given to him. [21] Whoever kills an animal shall make it good, and whoever kills a person shall be put to death. [22] You shall have the same rule for the sojourner and for the native, for I am the LORD your God." [23] So Moses spoke to the people of Israel, and they brought out of the camp the one who had cursed and stoned him with stones. Thus the people of Israel did as the LORD commanded Moses.

Psalm 31

To THE CHOIRMASTER. A PSALM OF DAVID.

In you, O LORD, do I take refuge;
  let me never be put to shame;
    in your righteousness deliver me!
[2] Incline your ear to me;
    rescue me speedily!
  Be a rock of refuge for me,
    a strong fortress to save me!
[3] For you are my rock and my fortress;
    and for your name's sake you lead me
      and guide me;
[4] you take me out of the net they have
      hidden for me,
    for you are my refuge.

[5] Into your hand I commit my spirit;
    you have redeemed me, O LORD,
      faithful God.
[6] I hate[1] those who pay regard to
      worthless idols,
    but I trust in the LORD.
[7] I will rejoice and be glad in your
      steadfast love,
    because you have seen my affliction;
    you have known the distress of my
      soul,
[8] and you have not delivered me into the
      hand of the enemy;
    you have set my feet in a broad place.

[9] Be gracious to me, O LORD, for I am in
      distress;
    my eye is wasted from grief;
    my soul and my body also.
[10] For my life is spent with sorrow,
    and my years with sighing;
  my strength fails because of my
      iniquity,
    and my bones waste away.

[11] Because of all my adversaries I have
      become a reproach,
    especially to my neighbors,
  and an object of dread to my
      acquaintances;
    those who see me in the street flee
      from me.
[12] I have been forgotten like one who is
      dead;
    I have become like a broken vessel.
[13] For I hear the whispering of many—
      terror on every side!—
  as they scheme together against me,
    as they plot to take my life.

[14] But I trust in you, O LORD;
    I say, "You are my God."
[15] My times are in your hand;
    rescue me from the hand of my
      enemies and from my persecutors!
[16] Make your face shine on your servant;
    save me in your steadfast love!
[17] O LORD, let me not be put to shame,
    for I call upon you;
  let the wicked be put to shame;
    let them go silently to Sheol.

[1] Masoretic Text; one Hebrew manuscript, Septuagint, Syriac, Jerome You hate

18 Let the lying lips be mute,
which speak insolently against the
righteous
in pride and contempt.

19 Oh, how abundant is your goodness,
which you have stored up for those
who fear you
and worked for those who take refuge in
you,
in the sight of the children of mankind!

20 In the cover of your presence you hide
them
from the plots of men;
you store them in your shelter
from the strife of tongues.

21 Blessed be the LORD,
for he has wondrously shown his
steadfast love to me
when I was in a besieged city.

22 I had said in my alarm,[1]
"I am cut off from your sight."
But you heard the voice of my pleas for
mercy
when I cried to you for help.

23 Love the LORD, all you his saints!
The LORD preserves the faithful
but abundantly repays the one who
acts in pride.

24 Be strong, and let your heart take
courage,
all you who wait for the LORD!

Ecclesiastes 7

A good name is better than precious
ointment,
and the day of death than the day of
birth.

2 It is better to go to the house of
mourning
than to go to the house of feasting,
for this is the end of all mankind,
and the living will lay it to heart.

3 Sorrow is better than laughter,
for by sadness of face the heart is
made glad.

4 The heart of the wise is in the house of
mourning,
but the heart of fools is in the house of
mirth.

5 It is better for a man to hear the rebuke
of the wise
than to hear the song of fools.

6 For as the crackling of thorns under a
pot,
so is the laughter of the fools;
this also is vanity.[2]

7 Surely oppression drives the wise into
madness,
and a bribe corrupts the heart.

8 Better is the end of a thing than its
beginning,
and the patient in spirit is better than
the proud in spirit.

9 Be not quick in your spirit to become
angry,
for anger lodges in the heart[3] of fools.

10 Say not, "Why were the former days
better than these?"
For it is not from wisdom that you ask
this.

11 Wisdom is good with an inheritance,
an advantage to those who see the
sun.

12 For the protection of wisdom is like the
protection of money,
and the advantage of knowledge is that
wisdom preserves the life of him
who has it.

13 Consider the work of God:
who can make straight what he has
made crooked?

14 In the day of prosperity be joyful, and in
the day of adversity consider: God has made the
one as well as the other, so that man may not
find out anything that will be after him.

15 In my vain[4] life I have seen everything.
There is a righteous man who perishes in his
righteousness, and there is a wicked man who
prolongs his life in his evildoing. 16 Be not
overly righteous, and do not make yourself
too wise. Why should you destroy yourself?
17 Be not overly wicked, neither be a fool. Why
should you die before your time? 18 It is good
that you should take hold of this, and from that
withhold not your hand, for the one who fears
God shall come out from both of them.

19 Wisdom gives strength to the wise man
more than ten rulers who are in a city.

20 Surely there is not a righteous man on
earth who does good and never sins.

[1] Or in my haste [2] The Hebrew term hebel can refer to a "vapor" or "mere breath" (see note on 1:2) [3] Hebrew in the bosom [4] The Hebrew term hebel can refer to a "vapor" or "mere breath" (see note on 1:2)

²¹Do not take to heart all the things that people say, lest you hear your servant cursing you. ²²Your heart knows that many times you yourself have cursed others.

²³All this I have tested by wisdom. I said, "I will be wise," but it was far from me. ²⁴That which has been is far off, and deep, very deep; who can find it out?

²⁵I turned my heart to know and to search out and to seek wisdom and the scheme of things, and to know the wickedness of folly and the foolishness that is madness. ²⁶And I find something more bitter than death: the woman whose heart is snares and nets, and whose hands are fetters. He who pleases God escapes her, but the sinner is taken by her. ²⁷Behold, this is what I found, says the Preacher, while adding one thing to another to find the scheme of things— ²⁸which my soul has sought repeatedly, but I have not found. One man among a thousand I found, but a woman among all these I have not found. ²⁹See, this alone I found, that God made man upright, but they have sought out many schemes.

2 Timothy 3

But understand this, that in the last days there will come times of difficulty. ²For people will be lovers of self, lovers of money, proud, arrogant, abusive, disobedient to their parents, ungrateful, unholy, ³heartless, unappeasable, slanderous, without self-control, brutal, not loving good, ⁴treacherous, reckless, swollen with conceit, lovers of pleasure rather than lovers of God, ⁵having the appearance of godliness, but denying its power. Avoid such people. ⁶For among them are those who creep into households and capture weak women, burdened with sins and led astray by various passions, ⁷always learning and never able to arrive at a knowledge of the truth. ⁸Just as Jannes and Jambres opposed Moses, so these men also oppose the truth, men corrupted in mind and disqualified regarding the faith. ⁹But they will not get very far, for their folly will be plain to all, as was that of those two men.

¹⁰You, however, have followed my teaching, my conduct, my aim in life, my faith, my patience, my love, my steadfastness, ¹¹my persecutions and sufferings that happened to me at Antioch, at Iconium, and at Lystra—which persecutions I endured; yet from them all the Lord rescued me. ¹²Indeed, all who desire to live a godly life in Christ Jesus will be persecuted, ¹³while evil people and impostors will go on from bad to worse, deceiving and being deceived. ¹⁴But as for you, continue in what you have learned and have firmly believed, knowing from whom[1] you learned it ¹⁵and how from childhood you have been acquainted with the sacred writings, which are able to make you wise for salvation through faith in Christ Jesus. ¹⁶All Scripture is breathed out by God and profitable for teaching, for reproof, for correction, and for training in righteousness, ¹⁷that the man of God[2] may be complete, equipped for every good work.

APRIL 21

Leviticus 25

The LORD spoke to Moses on Mount Sinai, saying, ²"Speak to the people of Israel and say to them, When you come into the land that I give you, the land shall keep a Sabbath to the LORD. ³For six years you shall sow your field, and for six years you shall prune your vineyard and gather in its fruits, ⁴but in the seventh year there shall be a Sabbath of solemn rest for the land, a Sabbath to the LORD. You shall not sow your field or prune your vineyard. ⁵You shall not reap what grows of itself in your harvest, or gather the grapes of your undressed vine. It shall be a year of solemn rest for the land. ⁶The Sabbath of the land[3] shall provide food

---

[1] The Greek for *whom* is plural   [2] That is, a messenger of God (the phrase echoes a common Old Testament expression)   [3] That is, the Sabbath produce of the land

for you, for yourself and for your male and female slaves[1] and for your hired worker and the sojourner who lives with you, [7] and for your cattle and for the wild animals that are in your land: all its yield shall be for food.

[8] "You shall count seven weeks[2] of years, seven times seven years, so that the time of the seven weeks of years shall give you forty-nine years. [9] Then you shall sound the loud trumpet on the tenth day of the seventh month. On the Day of Atonement you shall sound the trumpet throughout all your land. [10] And you shall consecrate the fiftieth year, and proclaim liberty throughout the land to all its inhabitants. It shall be a jubilee for you, when each of you shall return to his property and each of you shall return to his clan. [11] That fiftieth year shall be a jubilee for you; in it you shall neither sow nor reap what grows of itself nor gather the grapes from the undressed vines. [12] For it is a jubilee. It shall be holy to you. You may eat the produce of the field.[3]

[13] "In this year of jubilee each of you shall return to his property. [14] And if you make a sale to your neighbor or buy from your neighbor, you shall not wrong one another. [15] You shall pay your neighbor according to the number of years after the jubilee, and he shall sell to you according to the number of years for crops. [16] If the years are many, you shall increase the price, and if the years are few, you shall reduce the price, for it is the number of the crops that he is selling to you. [17] You shall not wrong one another, but you shall fear your God, for I am the LORD your God.

[18] "Therefore you shall do my statutes and keep my rules and perform them, and then you will dwell in the land securely. [19] The land will yield its fruit, and you will eat your fill and dwell in it securely. [20] And if you say, 'What shall we eat in the seventh year, if we may not sow or gather in our crop?' [21] I will command my blessing on you in the sixth year, so that it will produce a crop sufficient for three years. [22] When you sow in the eighth year, you will be eating some of the old crop; you shall eat the old until the ninth year, when its crop arrives.

[23] "The land shall not be sold in perpetuity, for the land is mine. For you are strangers and sojourners with me. [24] And in all the country you possess, you shall allow a redemption of the land.

[25] "If your brother becomes poor and sells part of his property, then his nearest redeemer shall come and redeem what his brother has sold. [26] If a man has no one to redeem it and then himself becomes prosperous and finds sufficient means to redeem it, [27] let him calculate the years since he sold it and pay back the balance to the man to whom he sold it, and then return to his property. [28] But if he does not have sufficient means to recover it, then what he sold shall remain in the hand of the buyer until the year of jubilee. In the jubilee it shall be released, and he shall return to his property.

[29] "If a man sells a dwelling house in a walled city, he may redeem it within a year of its sale. For a full year he shall have the right of redemption. [30] If it is not redeemed within a full year, then the house in the walled city shall belong in perpetuity to the buyer, throughout his generations; it shall not be released in the jubilee. [31] But the houses of the villages that have no wall around them shall be classified with the fields of the land. They may be redeemed, and they shall be released in the jubilee. [32] As for the cities of the Levites, the Levites may redeem at any time the houses in the cities they possess. [33] And if one of the Levites exercises his right of redemption, then the house that was sold in a city they possess shall be released in the jubilee. For the houses in the cities of the Levites are their possession among the people of Israel. [34] But the fields of pastureland belonging to their cities may not be sold, for that is their possession forever.

[35] "If your brother becomes poor and cannot maintain himself with you, you shall support him as though he were a stranger and a sojourner, and he shall live with you. [36] Take no interest from him or profit, but fear your God, that your brother may live beside you. [37] You shall not lend him your money at interest, nor give him your food for profit. [38] I am the LORD your God, who brought you out of the land of Egypt to give you the land of Canaan, and to be your God.

[39] "If your brother becomes poor beside you and sells himself to you, you shall not make him serve as a slave: [40] he shall be with you as a hired worker and as a sojourner. He shall serve with you until the year of the jubilee. [41] Then he shall go out from you, he and his children with him, and go back to his own clan and return

[1] Or servants   [2] Or Sabbaths   [3] Or countryside

to the possession of his fathers. [42]For they are my servants,[1] whom I brought out of the land of Egypt; they shall not be sold as slaves. [43]You shall not rule over him ruthlessly but shall fear your God. [44]As for your male and female slaves whom you may have: you may buy male and female slaves from among the nations that are around you. [45]You may also buy from among the strangers who sojourn with you and their clans that are with you, who have been born in your land, and they may be your property. [46]You may bequeath them to your sons after you to inherit as a possession forever. You may make slaves of them, but over your brothers the people of Israel you shall not rule, one over another ruthlessly.

[47] "If a stranger or sojourner with you becomes rich, and your brother beside him becomes poor and sells himself to the stranger or sojourner with you or to a member of the stranger's clan, [48]then after he is sold he may be redeemed. One of his brothers may redeem him, [49]or his uncle or his cousin may redeem him, or a close relative from his clan may redeem him. Or if he grows rich he may redeem himself. [50]He shall calculate with his buyer from the year when he sold himself to him until the year of jubilee, and the price of his sale shall vary with the number of years. The time he was with his owner shall be rated as the time of a hired worker. [51]If there are still many years left, he shall pay proportionately for his redemption some of his sale price. [52]If there remain but a few years until the year of jubilee, he shall calculate and pay for his redemption in proportion to his years of service. [53]He shall treat him as a worker hired year by year. He shall not rule ruthlessly over him in your sight. [54]And if he is not redeemed by these means, then he and his children with him shall be released in the year of jubilee. [55]For it is to me that the people of Israel are servants.[2] They are my servants whom I brought out of the land of Egypt: I am the LORD your God.

Psalm 32

A MASKIL[3] OF DAVID.

Blessed is the one whose transgression is forgiven,
 whose sin is covered.

[2] Blessed is the man against whom the
 LORD counts no iniquity,
  and in whose spirit there is no deceit.

[3] For when I kept silent, my bones wasted
  away
 through my groaning all day long.
[4] For day and night your hand was heavy
  upon me;
 my strength was dried up[4] as by the
  heat of summer.   *Selah*

[5] I acknowledged my sin to you,
 and I did not cover my iniquity;
I said, "I will confess my transgressions
  to the LORD,"
 and you forgave the iniquity of my
  sin.   *Selah*

[6] Therefore let everyone who is godly
 offer prayer to you at a time when you
  may be found;
surely in the rush of great waters,
 they shall not reach him.
[7] You are a hiding place for me;
 you preserve me from trouble;
 you surround me with shouts of
  deliverance.   *Selah*

[8] I will instruct you and teach you in the
  way you should go;
 I will counsel you with my eye upon
  you.
[9] Be not like a horse or a mule, without
  understanding,
 which must be curbed with bit and
  bridle,
 or it will not stay near you.

[10] Many are the sorrows of the wicked,
 but steadfast love surrounds the one
  who trusts in the LORD.
[11] Be glad in the LORD, and rejoice,
 O righteous,
 and shout for joy, all you upright in
  heart!

Ecclesiastes 8

Who is like the wise?
 And who knows the interpretation of
  a thing?
A man's wisdom makes his face shine,
 and the hardness of his face is changed.

[1] Hebrew *slaves* [2] Or *slaves* [3] Probably a musical or liturgical term [4] Hebrew *my vitality was changed*

²I say:¹ Keep the king's command, because of God's oath to him.² ³Be not hasty to go from his presence. Do not take your stand in an evil cause, for he does whatever he pleases. ⁴For the word of the king is supreme, and who may say to him, "What are you doing?" ⁵Whoever keeps a command will know no evil thing, and the wise heart will know the proper time and the just way. ⁶For there is a time and a way for everything, although man's trouble³ lies heavy on him. ⁷For he does not know what is to be, for who can tell him how it will be? ⁸No man has power to retain the spirit, or power over the day of death. There is no discharge from war, nor will wickedness deliver those who are given to it. ⁹All this I observed while applying my heart to all that is done under the sun, when man had power over man to his hurt.

¹⁰Then I saw the wicked buried. They used to go in and out of the holy place and were praised⁴ in the city where they had done such things. This also is vanity.⁵ ¹¹Because the sentence against an evil deed is not executed speedily, the heart of the children of man is fully set to do evil. ¹²Though a sinner does evil a hundred times and prolongs his life, yet I know that it will be well with those who fear God, because they fear before him. ¹³But it will not be well with the wicked, neither will he prolong his days like a shadow, because he does not fear before God.

¹⁴There is a vanity that takes place on earth, that there are righteous people to whom it happens according to the deeds of the wicked, and there are wicked people to whom it happens according to the deeds of the righteous. I said that this also is vanity. ¹⁵And I commend joy, for man has nothing better under the sun but to eat and drink and be joyful, for this will go with him in his toil through the days of his life that God has given him under the sun.

¹⁶When I applied my heart to know wisdom, and to see the business that is done on earth, how neither day nor night do one's eyes see sleep, ¹⁷then I saw all the work of God, that man cannot find out the work that is done under the sun. However much man may toil in seeking, he will not find it out. Even though a wise man claims to know, he cannot find it out.

2 Timothy 4

I charge you in the presence of God and of Christ Jesus, who is to judge the living and the dead, and by his appearing and his kingdom: ²preach the word; be ready in season and out of season; reprove, rebuke, and exhort, with complete patience and teaching. ³For the time is coming when people will not endure sound⁶ teaching, but having itching ears they will accumulate for themselves teachers to suit their own passions, ⁴and will turn away from listening to the truth and wander off into myths. ⁵As for you, always be sober-minded, endure suffering, do the work of an evangelist, fulfill your ministry.

⁶For I am already being poured out as a drink offering, and the time of my departure has come. ⁷I have fought the good fight, I have finished the race, I have kept the faith. ⁸Henceforth there is laid up for me the crown of righteousness, which the Lord, the righteous judge, will award to me on that Day, and not only to me but also to all who have loved his appearing.

⁹Do your best to come to me soon. ¹⁰For Demas, in love with this present world, has deserted me and gone to Thessalonica. Crescens has gone to Galatia,⁷ Titus to Dalmatia. ¹¹Luke alone is with me. Get Mark and bring him with you, for he is very useful to me for ministry. ¹²Tychicus I have sent to Ephesus. ¹³When you come, bring the cloak that I left with Carpus at Troas, also the books, and above all the parchments. ¹⁴Alexander the coppersmith did me great harm; the Lord will repay him according to his deeds. ¹⁵Beware of him yourself, for he strongly opposed our message. ¹⁶At my first defense no one came to stand by me, but all deserted me. May it not be charged against them! ¹⁷But the Lord stood by me and strengthened me, so that through me the message might be fully proclaimed and all the Gentiles might hear it. So I was rescued from the lion's mouth. ¹⁸The Lord will rescue me from every evil deed and bring me safely into his heavenly kingdom. To him be the glory forever and ever. Amen.

¹⁹Greet Prisca and Aquila, and the household of Onesiphorus. ²⁰Erastus remained at Corinth, and I left Trophimus, who was ill, at Miletus. ²¹Do your best to come before winter. Eubulus

¹ Hebrew lacks *say* ² Or *because of your oath to God* ³ Or *evil* ⁴ Some Hebrew manuscripts, Septuagint, Vulgate; most Hebrew manuscripts *forgotten* ⁵ The Hebrew term *hebel* can refer to a "vapor" or "mere breath"; also twice in verse 14 (see note on 1:2) ⁶ Or *healthy* ⁷ Some manuscripts *Gaul*

sends greetings to you, as do Pudens and Linus and Claudia and all the brothers.[1]

[22] The Lord be with your spirit. Grace be with you.[2]

APRIL 22

Leviticus 26

[1] "You shall not make idols for yourselves or erect an image or pillar, and you shall not set up a figured stone in your land to bow down to it, for I am the LORD your God. [2] You shall keep my Sabbaths and reverence my sanctuary: I am the LORD.

[3] "If you walk in my statutes and observe my commandments and do them, [4] then I will give you your rains in their season, and the land shall yield its increase, and the trees of the field shall yield their fruit. [5] Your threshing shall last to the time of the grape harvest, and the grape harvest shall last to the time for sowing. And you shall eat your bread to the full and dwell in your land securely. [6] I will give peace in the land, and you shall lie down, and none shall make you afraid. And I will remove harmful beasts from the land, and the sword shall not go through your land. [7] You shall chase your enemies, and they shall fall before you by the sword. [8] Five of you shall chase a hundred, and a hundred of you shall chase ten thousand, and your enemies shall fall before you by the sword. [9] I will turn to you and make you fruitful and multiply you and will confirm my covenant with you. [10] You shall eat old store long kept, and you shall clear out the old to make way for the new. [11] I will make my dwelling[3] among you, and my soul shall not abhor you. [12] And I will walk among you and will be your God, and you shall be my people. [13] I am the LORD your God, who brought you out of the land of Egypt, that you should not be their slaves. And I have broken the bars of your yoke and made you walk erect.

[14] "But if you will not listen to me and will not do all these commandments, [15] if you spurn my statutes, and if your soul abhors my rules, so that you will not do all my commandments, but break my covenant, [16] then I will do this to you: I will visit you with panic, with wasting disease and fever that consume the eyes and make the heart ache. And you shall sow your seed in vain, for your enemies shall eat it. [17] I will set my face against you, and you shall be struck down before your enemies. Those who hate you shall rule over you, and you shall flee when none pursues you. [18] And if in spite of this you will not listen to me, then I will discipline you again sevenfold for your sins, [19] and I will break the pride of your power, and I will make your heavens like iron and your earth like bronze. [20] And your strength shall be spent in vain, for your land shall not yield its increase, and the trees of the land shall not yield their fruit.

[21] "Then if you walk contrary to me and will not listen to me, I will continue striking you, sevenfold for your sins. [22] And I will let loose the wild beasts against you, which shall bereave you of your children and destroy your livestock and make you few in number, so that your roads shall be deserted.

[23] "And if by this discipline you are not turned to me but walk contrary to me, [24] then I also will walk contrary to you, and I myself will strike you sevenfold for your sins. [25] And I will bring a sword upon you, that shall execute vengeance for the covenant. And if you gather within your cities, I will send pestilence among you, and you shall be delivered into the hand of the enemy. [26] When I break your supply[4] of bread, ten women shall bake your bread in a single oven and shall dole out your bread again by weight, and you shall eat and not be satisfied.

[27] "But if in spite of this you will not listen to me, but walk contrary to me, [28] then I will walk contrary to you in fury, and I myself will discipline you sevenfold for your sins. [29] You

---

[1] Or brothers and sisters. The plural Greek word adelphoi (translated "brothers") refers to siblings in a family. In New Testament usage, depending on the context, adelphoi may refer either to men or to both men and women who are siblings (brothers and sisters) in God's family, the church [2] The Greek for you is plural [3] Hebrew tabernacle [4] Hebrew staff

shall eat the flesh of your sons, and you shall eat the flesh of your daughters. ³⁰And I will destroy your high places and cut down your incense altars and cast your dead bodies upon the dead bodies of your idols, and my soul will abhor you. ³¹And I will lay your cities waste and will make your sanctuaries desolate, and I will not smell your pleasing aromas. ³²And I myself will devastate the land, so that your enemies who settle in it shall be appalled at it. ³³And I will scatter you among the nations, and I will unsheathe the sword after you, and your land shall be a desolation, and your cities shall be a waste.

³⁴"Then the land shall enjoy[1] its Sabbaths as long as it lies desolate, while you are in your enemies' land; then the land shall rest, and enjoy its Sabbaths. ³⁵As long as it lies desolate it shall have rest, the rest that it did not have on your Sabbaths when you were dwelling in it. ³⁶And as for those of you who are left, I will send faintness into their hearts in the lands of their enemies. The sound of a driven leaf shall put them to flight, and they shall flee as one flees from the sword, and they shall fall when none pursues. ³⁷They shall stumble over one another, as if to escape a sword, though none pursues. And you shall have no power to stand before your enemies. ³⁸And you shall perish among the nations, and the land of your enemies shall eat you up. ³⁹And those of you who are left shall rot away in your enemies' lands because of their iniquity, and also because of the iniquities of their fathers they shall rot away like them.

⁴⁰"But if they confess their iniquity and the iniquity of their fathers in their treachery that they committed against me, and also in walking contrary to me, ⁴¹so that I walked contrary to them and brought them into the land of their enemies—if then their uncircumcised heart is humbled and they make amends for their iniquity, ⁴²then I will remember my covenant with Jacob, and I will remember my covenant with Isaac and my covenant with Abraham, and I will remember the land. ⁴³But the land shall be abandoned by them and enjoy its Sabbaths while it lies desolate without them, and they shall make amends for their iniquity, because they spurned my rules and their soul abhorred my statutes. ⁴⁴Yet for all that, when they are in the land of their enemies, I will not spurn them,

neither will I abhor them so as to destroy them utterly and break my covenant with them, for I am the LORD their God. ⁴⁵But I will for their sake remember the covenant with their forefathers, whom I brought out of the land of Egypt in the sight of the nations, that I might be their God: I am the LORD."

⁴⁶These are the statutes and rules and laws that the LORD made between himself and the people of Israel through Moses on Mount Sinai.

Psalm 33

Shout for joy in the LORD, O you righteous!
Praise befits the upright.
² Give thanks to the LORD with the lyre;
make melody to him with the harp of ten strings!
³ Sing to him a new song;
play skillfully on the strings, with loud shouts.

⁴ For the word of the LORD is upright,
and all his work is done in faithfulness.
⁵ He loves righteousness and justice;
the earth is full of the steadfast love of the LORD.

⁶ By the word of the LORD the heavens were made,
and by the breath of his mouth all their host.
⁷ He gathers the waters of the sea as a heap;
he puts the deeps in storehouses.

⁸ Let all the earth fear the LORD;
let all the inhabitants of the world stand in awe of him!
⁹ For he spoke, and it came to be;
he commanded, and it stood firm.

¹⁰ The LORD brings the counsel of the nations to nothing;
he frustrates the plans of the peoples.
¹¹ The counsel of the LORD stands forever,
the plans of his heart to all generations.
¹² Blessed is the nation whose God is the LORD,
the people whom he has chosen as his heritage!

[1] Or *pay for*; twice in this verse; also verse 43

13 The LORD looks down from heaven;
   he sees all the children of man;
14 from where he sits enthroned he looks
   out
   on all the inhabitants of the earth,
15 he who fashions the hearts of them all
   and observes all their deeds.
16 The king is not saved by his great army;
   a warrior is not delivered by his great
   strength.
17 The war horse is a false hope for
   salvation,
   and by its great might it cannot
   rescue.
18 Behold, the eye of the LORD is on those
   who fear him,
   on those who hope in his steadfast
   love,
19 that he may deliver their soul from death
   and keep them alive in famine.
20 Our soul waits for the LORD;
   he is our help and our shield.
21 For our heart is glad in him,
   because we trust in his holy name.
22 Let your steadfast love, O LORD, be upon
   us,
   even as we hope in you.

--------- *Ecclesiastes 9* ---------

But all this I laid to heart, examining it all,
how the righteous and the wise and their
deeds are in the hand of God. Whether it is love
or hate, man does not know; both are before
him. ²It is the same for all, since the same event
happens to the righteous and the wicked, to the
good and the evil,¹ to the clean and the unclean,
to him who sacrifices and him who does not
sacrifice. As the good one is, so is the sinner,
and he who swears is as he who shuns an oath.
³This is an evil in all that is done under the sun,
that the same event happens to all. Also, the
hearts of the children of man are full of evil,
and madness is in their hearts while they live,
and after that they go to the dead. ⁴But he who
is joined with all the living has hope, for a living dog is better than a dead lion. ⁵For the living know that they will die, but the dead know
nothing, and they have no more reward, for the
memory of them is forgotten. ⁶Their love and
their hate and their envy have already perished,

and forever they have no more share in all that
is done under the sun.
   ⁷Go, eat your bread with joy, and drink your
wine with a merry heart, for God has already
approved what you do. ⁸Let your garments be always white. Let not
oil be lacking on your head. ⁹Enjoy life with the wife whom you love,
all the days of your vain² life that he has given
you under the sun, because that is your portion in life and in your toil at which you toil
under the sun. ¹⁰Whatever your hand finds to
do, do it with your might,³ for there is no work
or thought or knowledge or wisdom in Sheol,
to which you are going.
   ¹¹Again I saw that under the sun the race is
not to the swift, nor the battle to the strong,
nor bread to the wise, nor riches to the intelligent, nor favor to those with knowledge, but
time and chance happen to them all. ¹²For
man does not know his time. Like fish that
are taken in an evil net, and like birds that are
caught in a snare, so the children of man are
snared at an evil time, when it suddenly falls
upon them.
   ¹³I have also seen this example of wisdom
under the sun, and it seemed great to me.
¹⁴There was a little city with few men in it,
and a great king came against it and besieged
it, building great siegeworks against it. ¹⁵But
there was found in it a poor, wise man, and he
by his wisdom delivered the city. Yet no one
remembered that poor man. ¹⁶But I say that
wisdom is better than might, though the poor
man's wisdom is despised and his words are
not heard.
   ¹⁷The words of the wise heard in quiet are
better than the shouting of a ruler among fools.
¹⁸Wisdom is better than weapons of war, but
one sinner destroys much good.

--------- *Titus 1* ---------

Paul, a servant⁴ of God and an apostle of
Jesus Christ, for the sake of the faith of
God's elect and their knowledge of the truth,
which accords with godliness, ²in hope of eternal life, which God, who never lies, promised
before the ages began⁵ ³and at the proper time
manifested in his word through the preaching
with which I have been entrusted by the command of God our Savior;

¹ Septuagint, Syriac, Vulgate; Hebrew lacks *and the evil* ² The Hebrew term *hebel* can refer to a "vapor" or "mere breath" (see note on 1:2) ³ Or *finds to do with your might, do it*
⁴ Or *slave* (for the contextual rendering of the Greek word *doulos*, see Preface) ⁵ Greek *before times eternal*

[4] To Titus, my true child in a common faith:

Grace and peace from God the Father and Christ Jesus our Savior.

[5] This is why I left you in Crete, so that you might put what remained into order, and appoint elders in every town as I directed you— [6] if anyone is above reproach, the husband of one wife,[1] and his children are believers[2] and not open to the charge of debauchery or insubordination. [7] For an overseer,[3] as God's steward, must be above reproach. He must not be arrogant or quick-tempered or a drunkard or violent or greedy for gain, [8] but hospitable, a lover of good, self-controlled, upright, holy, and disciplined. [9] He must hold firm to the trustworthy word as taught, so that he may be able to give instruction in sound[4] doctrine and also to rebuke those who contradict it.

[10] For there are many who are insubordinate, empty talkers and deceivers, especially those of the circumcision party.[5] [11] They must be silenced, since they are upsetting whole families by teaching for shameful gain what they ought not to teach. [12] One of the Cretans,[6] a prophet of their own, said, "Cretans are always liars, evil beasts, lazy gluttons."[7] [13] This testimony is true. Therefore rebuke them sharply, that they may be sound in the faith, [14] not devoting themselves to Jewish myths and the commands of people who turn away from the truth. [15] To the pure, all things are pure, but to the defiled and unbelieving, nothing is pure; but both their minds and their consciences are defiled. [16] They profess to know God, but they deny him by their works. They are detestable, disobedient, unfit for any good work.

APRIL 23

Leviticus 27

The LORD spoke to Moses, saying, [2] "Speak to the people of Israel and say to them, If anyone makes a special vow to the LORD involving the valuation of persons, [3] then the valuation of a male from twenty years old up to sixty years old shall be fifty shekels[8] of silver, according to the shekel of the sanctuary. [4] If the person is a female, the valuation shall be thirty shekels. [5] If the person is from five years old up to twenty years old, the valuation shall be for a male twenty shekels, and for a female ten shekels. [6] If the person is from a month old up to five years old, the valuation shall be for a male five shekels of silver, and for a female the valuation shall be three shekels of silver. [7] And if the person is sixty years old or over, then the valuation for a male shall be fifteen shekels, and for a female ten shekels. [8] And if someone is too poor to pay the valuation, then he shall be made to stand before the priest, and the priest shall value him; the priest shall value him according to what the vower can afford.

[9] "If the vow[9] is an animal that may be offered as an offering to the LORD, all of it that he gives to the LORD is holy. [10] He shall not exchange it or make a substitute for it, good for bad, or bad for good; and if he does in fact substitute one animal for another, then both it and the substitute shall be holy. [11] And if it is any unclean animal that may not be offered as an offering to the LORD, then he shall stand the animal before the priest, [12] and the priest shall value it as either good or bad; as the priest values it, so it shall be. [13] But if he wishes to redeem it, he shall add a fifth to the valuation.

[14] "When a man dedicates his house as a holy gift to the LORD, the priest shall value it as either good or bad; as the priest values it, so it shall stand. [15] And if the donor wishes to redeem his house, he shall add a fifth to the valuation price, and it shall be his. [16] "If a man dedicates to the LORD part of the land that is his possession, then the valuation shall be in proportion to its seed. A homer[10] of barley seed shall be valued at fifty shekels of

---

[1] Or a man of one woman [2] Or are faithful [3] Or bishop; Greek episkopos [4] Or healthy; also verse 13 [5] Or especially those of the circumcision [6] Greek One of them [7] Probably from Epimenides of Crete [8] A shekel was about 2/5 ounce or 11 grams [9] Hebrew it [10] A homer was about 6 bushels or 220 liters

silver. [17] If he dedicates his field from the year of jubilee, the valuation shall stand, [18] but if he dedicates his field after the jubilee, then the priest shall calculate the price according to the years that remain until the year of jubilee, and a deduction shall be made from the valuation. [19] And if he who dedicates the field wishes to redeem it, then he shall add a fifth to its valuation price, and it shall remain his. [20] But if he does not wish to redeem the field, or if he has sold the field to another man, it shall not be redeemed anymore. [21] But the field, when it is released in the jubilee, shall be a holy gift to the LORD, like a field that has been devoted. The priest shall be in possession of it. [22] If he dedicates to the LORD a field that he has bought, which is not a part of his possession, [23] then the priest shall calculate the amount of the valuation for it up to the year of jubilee, and the man shall give the valuation on that day as a holy gift to the LORD. [24] In the year of jubilee the field shall return to him from whom it was bought, to whom the land belongs as a possession. [25] Every valuation shall be according to the shekel of the sanctuary: twenty gerahs[1] shall make a shekel.

[26] "But a firstborn of animals, which as a firstborn belongs to the LORD, no man may dedicate; whether ox or sheep, it is the LORD's. [27] And if it is an unclean animal, then he shall buy it back at the valuation, and add a fifth to it; or, if it is not redeemed, it shall be sold at the valuation.

[28] "But no devoted thing that a man devotes to the LORD, of anything that he has, whether man or beast, or of his inherited field, shall be sold or redeemed; every devoted thing is most holy to the LORD. [29] No one devoted, who is to be devoted for destruction[2] from mankind, shall be ransomed; he shall surely be put to death.

[30] "Every tithe of the land, whether of the seed of the land or of the fruit of the trees, is the LORD's; it is holy to the LORD. [31] If a man wishes to redeem some of his tithe, he shall add a fifth to it. [32] And every tithe of herds and flocks, every tenth animal of all that pass under the herdsman's staff, shall be holy to the LORD. [33] One shall not differentiate between good or bad, neither shall he make a substitute for it; and if he does substitute for it, then both it and the substitute shall be holy; it shall not be redeemed."

[34] These are the commandments that the LORD commanded Moses for the people of Israel on Mount Sinai.

Psalm 34[3]

OF DAVID, WHEN HE CHANGED HIS BEHAVIOR BEFORE ABIMELECH, SO THAT HE DROVE HIM OUT, AND HE WENT AWAY.

I will bless the LORD at all times;
his praise shall continually be in my mouth.
2 My soul makes its boast in the LORD;
let the humble hear and be glad.
3 Oh, magnify the LORD with me,
and let us exalt his name together!

4 I sought the LORD, and he answered me
and delivered me from all my fears.
5 Those who look to him are radiant,
and their faces shall never be
ashamed.
6 This poor man cried, and the LORD
heard him
and saved him out of all his troubles.
7 The angel of the LORD encamps
around those who fear him, and
delivers them.

8 Oh, taste and see that the LORD is good!
Blessed is the man who takes refuge
in him!
9 Oh, fear the LORD, you his saints,
for those who fear him have no lack!
10 The young lions suffer want and hunger;
but those who seek the LORD lack no
good thing.

11 Come, O children, listen to me;
I will teach you the fear of the LORD.
12 What man is there who desires life
and loves many days, that he may see
good?
13 Keep your tongue from evil
and your lips from speaking deceit.
14 Turn away from evil and do good;
seek peace and pursue it.

15 The eyes of the LORD are toward the
righteous
and his ears toward their cry.
16 The face of the LORD is against those
who do evil,
to cut off the memory of them from
the earth.

[1] A *gerah* was about 1/50 ounce or 0.6 gram [2] That is, set apart (devoted) as an offering to the Lord (for destruction) [3] This psalm is an acrostic poem, each verse beginning with the successive letters of the Hebrew alphabet

17 When the righteous cry for help, the Lord hears
and delivers them out of all their troubles.
18 The Lord is near to the brokenhearted
and saves the crushed in spirit.
19 Many are the afflictions of the righteous,
but the Lord delivers him out of them all.
20 He keeps all his bones;
not one of them is broken.
21 Affliction will slay the wicked,
and those who hate the righteous will be condemned.
22 The Lord redeems the life of his servants;
none of those who take refuge in him will be condemned.

Ecclesiastes 10

Dead flies make the perfumer's ointment give off a stench;
so a little folly outweighs wisdom and honor.
2 A wise man's heart inclines him to the right,
but a fool's heart to the left.
3 Even when the fool walks on the road, he lacks sense,
and he says to everyone that he is a fool.
4 If the anger of the ruler rises against you, do not leave your place,
for calmness[1] will lay great offenses to rest.

5 There is an evil that I have seen under the sun, as it were an error proceeding from the ruler: 6 folly is set in many high places, and the rich sit in a low place. 7 I have seen slaves on horses, and princes walking on the ground like slaves.

8 He who digs a pit will fall into it,
and a serpent will bite him who breaks through a wall.
9 He who quarries stones is hurt by them,
and he who splits logs is endangered by them.

10 If the iron is blunt, and one does not sharpen the edge,
he must use more strength,
but wisdom helps one to succeed.[2]
11 If the serpent bites before it is charmed,
there is no advantage to the charmer.
12 The words of a wise man's mouth win him favor,[3]
but the lips of a fool consume him.
13 The beginning of the words of his mouth is foolishness,
and the end of his talk is evil madness.
14 A fool multiplies words,
though no man knows what is to be,
and who can tell him what will be after him?
15 The toil of a fool wearies him,
for he does not know the way to the city.
16 Woe to you, O land, when your king is a child,
and your princes feast in the morning!
17 Happy are you, O land, when your king is the son of the nobility,
and your princes feast at the proper time,
for strength, and not for drunkenness!
18 Through sloth the roof sinks in,
and through indolence the house leaks.
19 Bread is made for laughter,
and wine gladdens life,
and money answers everything.
20 Even in your thoughts, do not curse the king,
nor in your bedroom curse the rich,
for a bird of the air will carry your voice,
or some winged creature tell the matter.

Titus 2

But as for you, teach what accords with sound[4] doctrine. 2 Older men are to be sober-minded, dignified, self-controlled, sound in faith, in love, and in steadfastness. 3 Older women likewise are to be reverent in behavior, not slanderers or slaves to much wine. They are to teach what is good, 4 and so train

[1] Hebrew healing [2] Or wisdom is an advantage for success [3] Or are gracious [4] Or healthy; also verses 2, 8

the young women to love their husbands and children, [5]to be self-controlled, pure, working at home, kind, and submissive to their own husbands, that the word of God may not be reviled. [6]Likewise, urge the younger men to be self-controlled. [7]Show yourself in all respects to be a model of good works, and in your teaching show integrity, dignity, [8]and sound speech that cannot be condemned, so that an opponent may be put to shame, having nothing evil to say about us. [9]Bondservants[1] are to be submissive to their own masters in everything; they are to be well-pleasing, not argumentative, [10]not pilfering, but showing all good faith, so that in everything they may adorn the doctrine of God our Savior.

[11]For the grace of God has appeared, bringing salvation for all people, [12]training us to renounce ungodliness and worldly passions, and to live self-controlled, upright, and godly lives in the present age, [13]waiting for our blessed hope, the appearing of the glory of our great God and Savior Jesus Christ, [14]who gave himself for us to redeem us from all lawlessness and to purify for himself a people for his own possession who are zealous for good works.

[15]Declare these things; exhort and rebuke with all authority. Let no one disregard you.

APRIL 24

Numbers 1

The LORD spoke to Moses in the wilderness of Sinai, in the tent of meeting, on the first day of the second month, in the second year after they had come out of the land of Egypt, saying, [2]"Take a census of all the congregation of the people of Israel, by clans, by fathers' houses, according to the number of names, every male, head by head. [3]From twenty years old and upward, all in Israel who are able to go to war, you and Aaron shall list them, company by company. [4]And there shall be with you a man from each tribe, each man being the head of the house of his fathers. [5]And these are the names of the men who shall assist you. From Reuben, Elizur the son of Shedeur; [6]from Simeon, Shelumiel the son of Zurishaddai; [7]from Judah, Nahshon the son of Amminadab; [8]from Issachar, Nethanel the son of Zuar; [9]from Zebulun, Eliab the son of Helon; [10]from the sons of Joseph, from Ephraim, Elishama the son of Ammihud, and from Manasseh, Gamaliel the son of Pedahzur; [11]from Benjamin, Abidan the son of Gideoni; [12]from Dan, Ahiezer the son of Ammishaddai; [13]from Asher, Pagiel the son of Ochran; [14]from Gad, Eliasaph the son of Deuel; [15]from Naphtali, Ahira the son of Enan." [16]These were the ones chosen from the congregation, the chiefs of their ancestral tribes, the heads of the clans of Israel.

[17]Moses and Aaron took these men who had been named, [18]and on the first day of the second month, they assembled the whole congregation together, who registered themselves by clans, by fathers' houses, according to the number of names from twenty years old and upward, head by head, [19]as the LORD commanded Moses. So he listed them in the wilderness of Sinai.

[20]The people of Reuben, Israel's firstborn, their generations, by their clans, by their fathers' houses, according to the number of names, head by head, every male from twenty years old and upward, all who were able to go to war: [21]those listed of the tribe of Reuben were 46,500.

[22]Of the people of Simeon, their generations, by their clans, by their fathers' houses, those of them who were listed, according to the number of names, head by head, every male from twenty years old and upward, all who were able to go to war: [23]those listed of the tribe of Simeon were 59,300.

[24]Of the people of Gad, their generations, by their clans, by their fathers' houses, according to the number of the names, from twenty years

[1] Or Slaves (for the contextual rendering of the Greek word doulos, see Preface)

old and upward, all who were able to go to war: ²⁵those listed of the tribe of Gad were 45,650.

²⁶Of the people of Judah, their generations, by their clans, by their fathers' houses, according to the number of names, from twenty years old and upward, every man able to go to war: ²⁷those listed of the tribe of Judah were 74,600.

²⁸Of the people of Issachar, their generations, by their clans, by their fathers' houses, according to the number of names, from twenty years old and upward, every man able to go to war: ²⁹those listed of the tribe of Issachar were 54,400.

³⁰Of the people of Zebulun, their generations, by their clans, by their fathers' houses, according to the number of names, from twenty years old and upward, every man able to go to war: ³¹those listed of the tribe of Zebulun were 57,400.

³²Of the people of Joseph, namely, of the people of Ephraim, their generations, by their clans, by their fathers' houses, according to the number of names, from twenty years old and upward, every man able to go to war: ³³those listed of the tribe of Ephraim were 40,500.

³⁴Of the people of Manasseh, their generations, by their clans, by their fathers' houses, according to the number of names, from twenty years old and upward, every man able to go to war: ³⁵those listed of the tribe of Manasseh were 32,200.

³⁶Of the people of Benjamin, their generations, by their clans, by their fathers' houses, according to the number of names, from twenty years old and upward, every man able to go to war: ³⁷those listed of the tribe of Benjamin were 35,400.

³⁸Of the people of Dan, their generations, by their clans, by their fathers' houses, according to the number of names, from twenty years old and upward, every man able to go to war: ³⁹those listed of the tribe of Dan were 62,700.

⁴⁰Of the people of Asher, their generations, by their clans, by their fathers' houses, according to the number of names, from twenty years old and upward, every man able to go to war: ⁴¹those listed of the tribe of Asher were 41,500.

⁴²Of the people of Naphtali, their generations, by their clans, by their fathers' houses, according to the number of names, from twenty years old and upward, every man able to go to war: ⁴³those listed of the tribe of Naphtali were 53,400.

⁴⁴These are those who were listed, whom Moses and Aaron listed with the help of the chiefs of Israel, twelve men, each representing his fathers' house. ⁴⁵So all those listed of the people of Israel, by their fathers' houses, from twenty years old and upward, every man able to go to war in Israel— ⁴⁶all those listed were 603,550.

⁴⁷But the Levites were not listed along with them by their ancestral tribe. ⁴⁸For the Lord spoke to Moses, saying, ⁴⁹"Only the tribe of Levi you shall not list, and you shall not take a census of them among the people of Israel. ⁵⁰But appoint the Levites over the tabernacle of the testimony, and over all its furnishings, and over all that belongs to it. They are to carry the tabernacle and all its furnishings, and they shall take care of it and shall camp around the tabernacle. ⁵¹When the tabernacle is to set out, the Levites shall take it down, and when the tabernacle is to be pitched, the Levites shall set it up. And if any outsider comes near, he shall be put to death. ⁵²The people of Israel shall pitch their tents by their companies, each man in his own camp and each man by his own standard. ⁵³But the Levites shall camp around the tabernacle of the testimony, so that there may be no wrath on the congregation of the people of Israel. And the Levites shall keep guard over the tabernacle of the testimony." ⁵⁴Thus did the people of Israel; they did according to all that the Lord commanded Moses.

Psalm 35

Of David.

Contend, O Lord, with those who contend with me;
    fight against those who fight against me!
² Take hold of shield and buckler
    and rise for my help!
³ Draw the spear and javelin[1]
    against my pursuers!
Say to my soul,
    "I am your salvation!"

⁴ Let them be put to shame and dishonor
    who seek after my life!
Let them be turned back and
    disappointed
    who devise evil against me!

[1] Or and close the way

5 Let them be like chaff before the wind,
  with the angel of the Lord driving
    them away!
6 Let their way be dark and slippery,
  with the angel of the Lord pursuing
    them!

7 For without cause they hid their net for
    me;
  without cause they dug a pit for my
    life.[1]
8 Let destruction come upon him when
    he does not know it!
  And let the net that he hid ensnare him;
  let him fall into it—to his destruction!

9 Then my soul will rejoice in the Lord,
  exulting in his salvation.
10 All my bones shall say,
  "O Lord, who is like you,
  delivering the poor
    from him who is too strong for him,
    the poor and needy from him who
      robs him?"

11 Malicious[2] witnesses rise up;
  they ask me of things that I do not
    know.
12 They repay me evil for good;
  my soul is bereft.[3]
13 But I, when they were sick—
  I wore sackcloth;
  I afflicted myself with fasting;
  I prayed with head bowed[4] on my chest.
14 I went about as though I grieved for
    my friend or my brother;
  as one who laments his mother,
  I bowed down in mourning.

15 But at my stumbling they rejoiced and
    gathered;
  they gathered together against me;
  wretches whom I did not know
    tore at me without ceasing;
16 like profane mockers at a feast,[5]
  they gnash at me with their teeth.

17 How long, O Lord, will you look on?
  Rescue me from their destruction,
    my precious life from the lions!
18 I will thank you in the great
    congregation;
  in the mighty throng I will praise you.

19 Let not those rejoice over me
    who are wrongfully my foes,
  and let not those wink the eye
    who hate me without cause.
20 For they do not speak peace,
  but against those who are quiet in the
    land
  they devise words of deceit.
21 They open wide their mouths against
    me;
  they say, "Aha, Aha!
  Our eyes have seen it!"

22 You have seen, O Lord; be not silent!
  O Lord, be not far from me!
23 Awake and rouse yourself for my
    vindication,
  for my cause, my God and my Lord!
24 Vindicate me, O Lord, my God,
  according to your righteousness,
  and let them not rejoice over me!
25 Let them not say in their hearts,
  "Aha, our heart's desire!"
  Let them not say, "We have swallowed
    him up."

26 Let them be put to shame and
    disappointed altogether
  who rejoice at my calamity!
  Let them be clothed with shame and
    dishonor
  who magnify themselves against me!

27 Let those who delight in my
    righteousness
  shout for joy and be glad
  and say evermore,
  "Great is the Lord,
  who delights in the welfare of his
    servant!"
28 Then my tongue shall tell of your
    righteousness
  and of your praise all the day long.

───────── *Ecclesiastes 11* ─────────

Cast your bread upon the waters,
  for you will find it after many days.
2 Give a portion to seven, or even to eight,
  for you know not what disaster may
    happen on earth.
3 If the clouds are full of rain,
  they empty themselves on the earth,

[1] The word pit is transposed from the preceding line; Hebrew For without cause they hid the pit of their net for me; without cause they dug for my life [2] Or Violent [3] Hebrew it is bereavement to my soul [4] Or my prayer shall turn back [5] The meaning of the Hebrew phrase is uncertain

and if a tree falls to the south or to the
    north,
  in the place where the tree falls, there
    it will lie.
4   He who observes the wind will not sow,
  and he who regards the clouds will
    not reap.

⁵As you do not know the way the spirit comes to the bones in the womb¹ of a woman with child, so you do not know the work of God who makes everything.

⁶In the morning sow your seed, and at evening withhold not your hand, for you do not know which will prosper, this or that, or whether both alike will be good.

⁷Light is sweet, and it is pleasant for the eyes to see the sun.

⁸So if a person lives many years, let him rejoice in them all; but let him remember that the days of darkness will be many. All that comes is vanity.²

⁹Rejoice, O young man, in your youth, and let your heart cheer you in the days of your youth. Walk in the ways of your heart and the sight of your eyes. But know that for all these things God will bring you into judgment.

¹⁰Remove vexation from your heart, and put away pain³ from your body, for youth and the dawn of life are vanity.

Titus 3

Remind them to be submissive to rulers and authorities, to be obedient, to be ready for every good work, ²to speak evil of no one, to avoid quarreling, to be gentle, and to show perfect courtesy toward all people. ³For we ourselves were once foolish, disobedient, led astray, slaves to various passions and pleasures, passing our days in malice and envy, hated by others and hating one another. ⁴But when the goodness and loving kindness of God our Savior appeared, ⁵he saved us, not because of works done by us in righteousness, but according to his own mercy, by the washing of regeneration and renewal of the Holy Spirit, ⁶whom he poured out on us richly through Jesus Christ our Savior, ⁷so that being justified by his grace we might become heirs according to the hope of eternal life. ⁸The saying is trustworthy, and I want you to insist on these things, so that those who have believed in God may be careful to devote themselves to good works. These things are excellent and profitable for people. ⁹But avoid foolish controversies, genealogies, dissensions, and quarrels about the law, for they are unprofitable and worthless. ¹⁰As for a person who stirs up division, after warning him once and then twice, have nothing more to do with him, ¹¹knowing that such a person is warped and sinful; he is self-condemned.

¹²When I send Artemas or Tychicus to you, do your best to come to me at Nicopolis, for I have decided to spend the winter there. ¹³Do your best to speed Zenas the lawyer and Apollos on their way; see that they lack nothing. ¹⁴And let our people learn to devote themselves to good works, so as to help cases of urgent need, and not be unfruitful.

¹⁵All who are with me send greetings to you. Greet those who love us in the faith.

Grace be with you all.

APRIL 25

Numbers 2

The LORD spoke to Moses and Aaron, saying, ²"The people of Israel shall camp each by his own standard, with the banners of their fathers' houses. They shall camp facing the tent of meeting on every side. ³Those to camp on the east side toward the sunrise shall be of the standard of the camp of Judah by their companies, the chief of the people of Judah being

---

¹ Some Hebrew manuscripts, Targum; most Hebrew manuscripts *As you do not know the way of the wind, or how the bones grow in the womb* ² The Hebrew term *hebel* can refer to a "vapor" or "mere breath"; also verse 10 (see note on 1:2) ³ Or *evil*

Nahshon the son of Amminadab, [4] his company as listed being 74,600. [5] Those to camp next to him shall be the tribe of Issachar, the chief of the people of Issachar being Nethanel the son of Zuar, [6] his company as listed being 54,400. [7] Then the tribe of Zebulun, the chief of the people of Zebulun being Eliab the son of Helon, [8] his company as listed being 57,400. [9] All those listed of the camp of Judah, by their companies, were 186,400. They shall set out first on the march.

[10] "On the south side shall be the standard of the camp of Reuben by their companies, the chief of the people of Reuben being Elizur the son of Shedeur, [11] his company as listed being 46,500. [12] And those to camp next to him shall be the tribe of Simeon, the chief of the people of Simeon being Shelumiel the son of Zurishaddai, [13] his company as listed being 59,300. [14] Then the tribe of Gad, the chief of the people of Gad being Eliasaph the son of Reuel, [15] his company as listed being 45,650. [16] All those listed of the camp of Reuben, by their companies, were 151,450. They shall set out second.

[17] "Then the tent of meeting shall set out, with the camp of the Levites in the midst of the camps; as they camp, so shall they set out, each in position, standard by standard.

[18] "On the west side shall be the standard of the camp of Ephraim by their companies, the chief of the people of Ephraim being Elishama the son of Ammihud, [19] his company as listed being 40,500. [20] And next to him shall be the tribe of Manasseh, the chief of the people of Manasseh being Gamaliel the son of Pedahzur, [21] his company as listed being 32,200. [22] Then the tribe of Benjamin, the chief of the people of Benjamin being Abidan the son of Gideoni, [23] his company as listed being 35,400. [24] All those listed of the camp of Ephraim, by their companies, were 108,100. They shall set out third on the march.

[25] "On the north side shall be the standard of the camp of Dan by their companies, the chief of the people of Dan being Ahiezer the son of Ammishaddai, [26] his company as listed being 62,700. [27] And those to camp next to him shall be the tribe of Asher, the chief of the people of Asher being Pagiel the son of Ochran, [28] his company as listed being 41,500. [29] Then the tribe of Naphtali, the chief of the people of Naphtali being Ahira the son of Enan, [30] his company as listed being 53,400. [31] All those listed of the camp of Dan were 157,600. They shall set out last, standard by standard."

[32] These are the people of Israel as listed by their fathers' houses. All those listed in the camps by their companies were 603,550. [33] But the Levites were not listed among the people of Israel, as the LORD commanded Moses.

[34] Thus did the people of Israel. According to all that the LORD commanded Moses, so they camped by their standards, and so they set out, each one in his clan, according to his fathers' house.

Psalm 36

To the choirmaster. Of David, the servant of the LORD.

Transgression speaks to the wicked
deep in his heart;[1]
 there is no fear of God
 before his eyes.
[2] For he flatters himself in his own eyes
 that his iniquity cannot be found out
 and hated.
[3] The words of his mouth are trouble and
 deceit;
 he has ceased to act wisely and do
 good.
[4] He plots trouble while on his bed;
 he sets himself in a way that is not
 good;
 he does not reject evil.

[5] Your steadfast love, O LORD, extends to
 the heavens,
 your faithfulness to the clouds.
[6] Your righteousness is like the
 mountains of God;
 your judgments are like the great deep;
 man and beast you save, O LORD.

[7] How precious is your steadfast love,
 O God!
 The children of mankind take refuge
 in the shadow of your wings.
[8] They feast on the abundance of your
 house,
 and you give them drink from the
 river of your delights.
[9] For with you is the fountain of life;
 in your light do we see light.

[1] Some Hebrew manuscripts, Syriac, Jerome (compare Septuagint); most Hebrew manuscripts *in my heart*

[10]   Oh, continue your steadfast love to those
          who know you,
          and your righteousness to the upright
          of heart!
[11]   Let not the foot of arrogance come upon
          me,
          nor the hand of the wicked drive me
          away.
[12]   There the evildoers lie fallen;
          they are thrust down, unable to rise.

Ecclesiastes 12

Remember also your Creator in the days of your youth, before the evil days come and the years draw near of which you will say, "I have no pleasure in them"; [2] before the sun and the light and the moon and the stars are darkened and the clouds return after the rain, [3] in the day when the keepers of the house tremble, and the strong men are bent, and the grinders cease because they are few, and those who look through the windows are dimmed, [4] and the doors on the street are shut—when the sound of the grinding is low, and one rises up at the sound of a bird, and all the daughters of song are brought low— [5] they are afraid also of what is high, and terrors are in the way; the almond tree blossoms, the grasshopper drags itself along,[1] and desire fails, because man is going to his eternal home, and the mourners go about the streets— [6] before the silver cord is snapped, or the golden bowl is broken, or the pitcher is shattered at the fountain, or the wheel broken at the cistern, [7] and the dust returns to the earth as it was, and the spirit returns to God who gave it. [8] Vanity[2] of vanities, says the Preacher; all is vanity.

[9] Besides being wise, the Preacher also taught the people knowledge, weighing and studying and arranging many proverbs with great care. [10] The Preacher sought to find words of delight, and uprightly he wrote words of truth.

[11] The words of the wise are like goads, and like nails firmly fixed are the collected sayings; they are given by one Shepherd. [12] My son, beware of anything beyond these. Of making many books there is no end, and much study is a weariness of the flesh.

[13] The end of the matter; all has been heard. Fear God and keep his commandments, for this is the whole duty of man.[3] [14] For God will bring every deed into judgment, with[4] every secret thing, whether good or evil.

Philemon 1

Paul, a prisoner for Christ Jesus, and Timothy our brother,

To Philemon our beloved fellow worker [2] and Apphia our sister and Archippus our fellow soldier, and the church in your house:

[3] Grace to you and peace from God our Father and the Lord Jesus Christ.

[4] I thank my God always when I remember you in my prayers, [5] because I hear of your love and of the faith that you have toward the Lord Jesus and for all the saints, [6] and I pray that the sharing of your faith may become effective for the full knowledge of every good thing that is in us for the sake of Christ.[5] [7] For I have derived much joy and comfort from your love, my brother, because the hearts of the saints have been refreshed through you.

[8] Accordingly, though I am bold enough in Christ to command you to do what is required, [9] yet for love's sake I prefer to appeal to you—I, Paul, an old man and now a prisoner also for Christ Jesus— [10] I appeal to you for my child, Onesimus,[6] whose father I became in my imprisonment. [11] (Formerly he was useless to you, but now he is indeed useful to you and to me.) [12] I am sending him back to you, sending my very heart. [13] I would have been glad to keep him with me, in order that he might serve me on your behalf during my imprisonment for the gospel, [14] but I preferred to do nothing without your consent in order that your goodness might not be by compulsion but of your own accord. [15] For this perhaps is why he was parted from you for a while, that you might have him back forever, [16] no longer as a bondservant[7] but more than a bondservant, as a beloved brother—especially to me, but how much more to you, both in the flesh and in the Lord.

[17] So if you consider me your partner, receive him as you would receive me. [18] If he has wronged you at all, or owes you anything, charge that to my account. [19] I, Paul, write this

[1] Or is a burden [2] The Hebrew term *hebel* can refer to a "vapor" or "mere breath" (three times in this verse); see note on 1:2 [3] Or the duty of all mankind [4] Or into the judgment on [5] Or for Christ's service [6] Onesimus means useful (see verse 11) or beneficial (see verse 20) [7] Or slave; twice in this verse (for the contextual rendering of the Greek word doulos, see Preface)

with my own hand: I will repay it—to say nothing of your owing me even your own self. ²⁰Yes, brother, I want some benefit from you in the Lord. Refresh my heart in Christ.

²¹Confident of your obedience, I write to you, knowing that you will do even more than I say. ²²At the same time, prepare a guest room for

me, for I am hoping that through your prayers I will be graciously given to you.

²³Epaphras, my fellow prisoner in Christ Jesus, sends greetings to you, ²⁴and so do Mark, Aristarchus, Demas, and Luke, my fellow workers. ²⁵The grace of the Lord Jesus Christ be with your spirit.

APRIL 26

Numbers 3

These are the generations of Aaron and Moses at the time when the LORD spoke with Moses on Mount Sinai. ²These are the names of the sons of Aaron: Nadab the firstborn, and Abihu, Eleazar, and Ithamar. ³These are the names of the sons of Aaron, the anointed priests, whom he ordained to serve as priests. ⁴But Nadab and Abihu died before the LORD when they offered unauthorized fire before the LORD in the wilderness of Sinai, and they had no children. So Eleazar and Ithamar served as priests in the lifetime of Aaron their father.

⁵And the LORD spoke to Moses, saying, ⁶"Bring the tribe of Levi near, and set them before Aaron the priest, that they may minister to him. ⁷They shall keep guard over him and over the whole congregation before the tent of meeting, as they minister at the tabernacle. ⁸They shall guard all the furnishings of the tent of meeting, and keep guard over the people of Israel as they minister at the tabernacle. ⁹And you shall give the Levites to Aaron and his sons; they are wholly given to him from among the people of Israel. ¹⁰And you shall appoint Aaron and his sons, and they shall guard their priesthood. But if any outsider comes near, he shall be put to death."

¹¹And the LORD spoke to Moses, saying, ¹²"Behold, I have taken the Levites from among the people of Israel instead of every firstborn who opens the womb among the people of Israel. The Levites shall be mine, ¹³for all the firstborn are mine. On the day that I struck down all the firstborn in the land of Egypt,

I consecrated for my own all the firstborn in Israel, both of man and of beast. They shall be mine: I am the LORD."

¹⁴And the LORD spoke to Moses in the wilderness of Sinai, saying, ¹⁵"List the sons of Levi, by fathers' houses and by clans; every male from a month old and upward you shall list." ¹⁶So Moses listed them according to the word of the LORD, as he was commanded. ¹⁷And these were the sons of Levi by their names: Gershon and Kohath and Merari. ¹⁸And these are the names of the sons of Gershon by their clans: Libni and Shimei. ¹⁹And the sons of Kohath by their clans: Amram, Izhar, Hebron, and Uzziel. ²⁰And the sons of Merari by their clans: Mahli and Mushi. These are the clans of the Levites, by their fathers' houses.

²¹To Gershon belonged the clan of the Libnites and the clan of the Shimeites; these were the clans of the Gershonites. ²²Their listing according to the number of all the males from a month old and upward was¹ 7,500. ²³The clans of the Gershonites were to camp behind the tabernacle on the west, ²⁴with Eliasaph, the son of Lael as chief of the fathers' house of the Gershonites. ²⁵And the guard duty of the sons of Gershon in the tent of meeting involved the tabernacle, the tent with its covering, the screen for the entrance of the tent of meeting, ²⁶the hangings of the court, the screen for the door of the court that is around the tabernacle and the altar, and its cords—all the service connected with these.

²⁷To Kohath belonged the clan of the

¹ Hebrew their listing was

Amramites and the clan of the Izharites and the clan of the Hebronites and the clan of the Uzzielites; these are the clans of the Kohathites. 28According to the number of all the males, from a month old and upward, there were 8,600, keeping guard over the sanctuary. 29The clans of the sons of Kohath were to camp on the south side of the tabernacle, 30with Elizaphan the son of Uzziel as chief of the fathers' house of the clans of the Kohathites. 31And their guard duty involved the ark, the table, the lampstand, the altars, the vessels of the sanctuary with which the priests minister, and the screen; all the service connected with these. 32And Eleazar the son of Aaron the priest was to be chief over the chiefs of the Levites, and to have oversight of those who kept guard over the sanctuary.

33To Merari belonged the clan of the Mahlites and the clan of the Mushites: these are the clans of Merari. 34Their listing according to the number of all the males from a month old and upward was 6,200. 35And the chief of the fathers' house of the clans of Merari was Zuriel the son of Abihail. They were to camp on the north side of the tabernacle. 36And the appointed guard duty of the sons of Merari involved the frames of the tabernacle, the bars, the pillars, the bases, and all their accessories; all the service connected with these; 37also the pillars around the court, with their bases and pegs and cords.

38Those who were to camp before the tabernacle on the east, before the tent of meeting toward the sunrise, were Moses and Aaron and his sons, guarding the sanctuary itself, to protect1 the people of Israel. And any outsider who came near was to be put to death. 39All those listed among the Levites, whom Moses and Aaron listed at the commandment of the LORD, by clans, all the males from a month old and upward, were 22,000.

40And the LORD said to Moses, "List all the firstborn males of the people of Israel, from a month old and upward, taking the number of their names. 41And you shall take the Levites for me—I am the LORD—instead of all the firstborn among the people of Israel, and the cattle of the Levites instead of all the firstborn among the cattle of the people of Israel." 42So Moses listed all the firstborn among the people of Israel, as the LORD commanded him. 43And all the firstborn males, according to the number of names, from a month old and upward as listed were 22,273.

44And the LORD spoke to Moses, saying, 45"Take the Levites instead of all the firstborn among the people of Israel, and the cattle of the Levites instead of their cattle. The Levites shall be mine: I am the LORD. 46And as the redemption price for the 273 of the firstborn of the people of Israel, over and above the number of the male Levites, 47you shall take five shekels2 per head; you shall take them according to the shekel of the sanctuary (the shekel of twenty gerahs3), 48and give the money to Aaron and his sons as the redemption price for those who are over." 49So Moses took the redemption money from those who were over and above those redeemed by the Levites. 50From the firstborn of the people of Israel he took the money, 1,365 shekels, by the shekel of the sanctuary. 51And Moses gave the redemption money to Aaron and his sons, according to the word of the LORD, as the LORD commanded Moses.

Psalm 37[4]

OF DAVID.

Fret not yourself because of evildoers;
   be not envious of wrongdoers!
2 For they will soon fade like the grass
      and wither like the green herb.

3 Trust in the LORD, and do good;
      dwell in the land and befriend
         faithfulness.[5]
4 Delight yourself in the LORD,
      and he will give you the desires of
         your heart.

5 Commit your way to the LORD;
      trust in him, and he will act.
6 He will bring forth your righteousness
         as the light,
      and your justice as the noonday.

7 Be still before the LORD and wait
         patiently for him;
      fret not yourself over the one who
         prospers in his way,
      over the man who carries out evil
         devices!

8 Refrain from anger, and forsake wrath!
      Fret not yourself; it tends only to evil.

1 Hebrew guard 2 A shekel was about 2/5 ounce or 11 grams 3 A gerah was about 1/50 ounce or 0.6 gram 4 This psalm is an acrostic poem, each stanza beginning with the successive letters of the Hebrew alphabet 5 Or and feed on faithfulness, or and find safe pasture

9 For the evildoers shall be cut off,
   but those who wait for the LORD shall
   inherit the land.

10 In just a little while, the wicked will be
   no more;
   though you look carefully at his place,
   he will not be there.

11 But the meek shall inherit the land
   and delight themselves in abundant
   peace.

12 The wicked plots against the righteous
   and gnashes his teeth at him,

13 but the Lord laughs at the wicked,
   for he sees that his day is coming.

14 The wicked draw the sword and bend
   their bows
   to bring down the poor and needy,
   to slay those whose way is upright;

15 their sword shall enter their own heart,
   and their bows shall be broken.

16 Better is the little that the righteous has
   than the abundance of many wicked.

17 For the arms of the wicked shall be
   broken,
   but the LORD upholds the righteous.

18 The LORD knows the days of the
   blameless,
   and their heritage will remain forever;

19 they are not put to shame in evil times;
   in the days of famine they have
   abundance.

20 But the wicked will perish;
   the enemies of the LORD are like the
   glory of the pastures;
   they vanish—like smoke they vanish
   away.

21 The wicked borrows but does not pay
   back,
   but the righteous is generous and
   gives;

22 for those blessed by the LORD[1] shall
   inherit the land,
   but those cursed by him shall be cut
   off.

23 The steps of a man are established by
   the LORD,
   when he delights in his way;

24 though he fall, he shall not be cast
   headlong,
   for the LORD upholds his hand.

25 I have been young, and now am old,
   yet I have not seen the righteous
   forsaken
   or his children begging for bread.

26 He is ever lending generously,
   and his children become a blessing.

27 Turn away from evil and do good;
   so shall you dwell forever.

28 For the LORD loves justice;
   he will not forsake his saints.
   They are preserved forever,
   but the children of the wicked shall be
   cut off.

29 The righteous shall inherit the land
   and dwell upon it forever.

30 The mouth of the righteous utters
   wisdom,
   and his tongue speaks justice.

31 The law of his God is in his heart;
   his steps do not slip.

32 The wicked watches for the righteous
   and seeks to put him to death.

33 The LORD will not abandon him to his
   power
   or let him be condemned when he is
   brought to trial.

34 Wait for the LORD and keep his way,
   and he will exalt you to inherit the
   land;
   you will look on when the wicked are
   cut off.

35 I have seen a wicked, ruthless man,
   spreading himself like a green laurel
   tree.[2]

36 But he passed away,[3] and behold, he was
   no more;
   though I sought him, he could not be
   found.

37 Mark the blameless and behold the
   upright,
   for there is a future for the man of
   peace.

38 But transgressors shall be altogether
   destroyed;
   the future of the wicked shall be cut off.

[1] Hebrew by him [2] The identity of this tree is uncertain [3] Or But one passed by

39 The salvation of the righteous is from
        the LORD;
    he is their stronghold in the time of
        trouble.
40 The LORD helps them and delivers them;
    he delivers them from the wicked and
        saves them,
    because they take refuge in him.

————— *Song of Solomon 1* —————

The Song of Songs, which is Solomon's.

SHE[1]

2 Let him kiss me with the kisses of his
        mouth!
    For your love is better than wine;
3   your anointing oils are fragrant;
    your name is oil poured out;
        therefore virgins love you.
4 Draw me after you; let us run.
    The king has brought me into his
        chambers.

OTHERS

We will exult and rejoice in you;
    we will extol your love more than wine;
    rightly do they love you.

SHE

5 I am very dark, but lovely,
    O daughters of Jerusalem,
    like the tents of Kedar,
    like the curtains of Solomon.
6 Do not gaze at me because I am dark,
    because the sun has looked upon me.
    My mother's sons were angry with me;
        they made me keeper of the vineyards,
        but my own vineyard I have not kept!
7 Tell me, you whom my soul loves,
    where you pasture your flock,
    where you make it lie down at noon;
    for why should I be like one who veils
        herself
    beside the flocks of your companions?

HE

8 If you do not know,
    O most beautiful among women,
    follow in the tracks of the flock,
    and pasture your young goats
    beside the shepherds' tents.

9 I compare you, my love,
    to a mare among Pharaoh's chariots.
10 Your cheeks are lovely with ornaments,
    your neck with strings of jewels.

OTHERS

11 We will make for you[2] ornaments of
        gold,
    studded with silver.

SHE

12 While the king was on his couch,
    my nard gave forth its fragrance.
13 My beloved is to me a sachet of myrrh
    that lies between my breasts.
14 My beloved is to me a cluster of henna
        blossoms
    in the vineyards of Engedi.

HE

15 Behold, you are beautiful, my love;
    behold, you are beautiful;
    your eyes are doves.

SHE

16 Behold, you are beautiful, my beloved,
        truly delightful.
    Our couch is green;
17   the beams of our house are cedar;
    our rafters are pine.

————— *Hebrews 1* —————

Long ago, at many times and in many ways,
God spoke to our fathers by the prophets,
[2]but in these last days he has spoken to us by his
Son, whom he appointed the heir of all things,
through whom also he created the world. [3]He
is the radiance of the glory of God and the exact
imprint of his nature, and he upholds the universe by the word of his power. After making
purification for sins, he sat down at the right
hand of the Majesty on high, [4]having become
as much superior to angels as the name he has
inherited is more excellent than theirs.

[5]For to which of the angels did God ever say,

    "You are my Son,
        today I have begotten you"?

Or again,

    "I will be to him a father,
        and he shall be to me a son"?

[1] The translators have added speaker identifications based on the gender and number of the Hebrew words [2] The Hebrew for *you* is feminine singular

⁶And again, when he brings the firstborn into the world, he says,

"Let all God's angels worship him."

⁷Of the angels he says,

"He makes his angels winds,
and his ministers a flame of fire."

⁸But of the Son he says,

"Your throne, O God, is forever and ever,
the scepter of uprightness is the
scepter of your kingdom.
⁹ You have loved righteousness and hated
wickedness;
therefore God, your God, has anointed
you
with the oil of gladness beyond your
companions."

¹⁰And,

"You, Lord, laid the foundation of the
earth in the beginning,
and the heavens are the work of your
hands;
¹¹ they will perish, but you remain;
they will all wear out like a garment,
¹² like a robe you will roll them up,
like a garment they will be changed.¹
But you are the same,
and your years will have no end."

¹³And to which of the angels has he ever said,

"Sit at my right hand
until I make your enemies a footstool
for your feet"?

¹⁴Are they not all ministering spirits sent out to serve for the sake of those who are to inherit salvation?

APRIL 27

Numbers 4

The LORD spoke to Moses and Aaron, saying, ²"Take a census of the sons of Kohath from among the sons of Levi, by their clans and their fathers' houses, ³from thirty years old up to fifty years old, all who can come on duty, to do the work in the tent of meeting. ⁴This is the service of the sons of Kohath in the tent of meeting: the most holy things. ⁵When the camp is to set out, Aaron and his sons shall go in and take down the veil of the screen and cover the ark of the testimony with it. ⁶Then they shall put on it a covering of goatskin² and spread on top of that a cloth all of blue, and shall put in its poles. ⁷And over the table of the bread of the Presence they shall spread a cloth of blue and put on it the plates, the dishes for incense, the bowls, and the flagons for the drink offering; the regular showbread also shall be on it. ⁸Then they shall spread over them a cloth of scarlet and cover the same with a covering of goatskin, and shall put in its poles. ⁹And they

shall take a cloth of blue and cover the lampstand for the light, with its lamps, its tongs, its trays, and all the vessels for oil with which it is supplied. ¹⁰And they shall put it with all its utensils in a covering of goatskin and put it on the carrying frame. ¹¹And over the golden altar they shall spread a cloth of blue and cover it with a covering of goatskin, and shall put in its poles. ¹²And they shall take all the vessels of the service that are used in the sanctuary and put them in a cloth of blue and cover them with a covering of goatskin and put them on the carrying frame. ¹³And they shall take away the ashes from the altar and spread a purple cloth over it. ¹⁴And they shall put on it all the utensils of the altar, which are used for the service there, the fire pans, the forks, the shovels, and the basins, all the utensils of the altar; and they shall spread on it a covering of goatskin, and shall put in its poles. ¹⁵And when Aaron and his sons have finished covering the sanctuary

¹ Some manuscripts omit *like a garment* ² The meaning of the Hebrew word is uncertain; compare Exodus 25:5

and all the furnishings of the sanctuary, as the camp sets out, after that the sons of Kohath shall come to carry these, but they must not touch the holy things, lest they die. These are the things of the tent of meeting that the sons of Kohath are to carry.

[16] "And Eleazar the son of Aaron the priest shall have charge of the oil for the light, the fragrant incense, the regular grain offering, and the anointing oil, with the oversight of the whole tabernacle and all that is in it, of the sanctuary and its vessels."

[17] The LORD spoke to Moses and Aaron, saying, [18] "Let not the tribe of the clans of the Kohathites be destroyed from among the Levites, [19] but deal thus with them, that they may live and not die when they come near to the most holy things: Aaron and his sons shall go in and appoint them each to his task and to his burden, [20] but they shall not go in to look on the holy things even for a moment, lest they die."

[21] The LORD spoke to Moses, saying, [22] "Take a census of the sons of Gershon also, by their fathers' houses and by their clans. [23] From thirty years old up to fifty years old, you shall list them, all who can come to do duty, to do service in the tent of meeting. [24] This is the service of the clans of the Gershonites, in serving and bearing burdens: [25] they shall carry the curtains of the tabernacle and the tent of meeting with its covering and the covering of goatskin that is on top of it and the screen for the entrance of the tent of meeting [26] and the hangings of the court and the screen for the entrance of the gate of the court that is around the tabernacle and the altar, and their cords and all the equipment for their service. And they shall do all that needs to be done with regard to them. [27] All the service of the sons of the Gershonites shall be at the command of Aaron and his sons, in all that they are to carry and in all that they have to do. And you shall assign to their charge all that they are to carry. [28] This is the service of the clans of the sons of the Gershonites in the tent of meeting, and their guard duty is to be under the direction of Ithamar the son of Aaron the priest.

[29] "As for the sons of Merari, you shall list them by their clans and their fathers' houses. [30] From thirty years old up to fifty years old, you shall list them, everyone who can come on duty, to do the service of the tent of meeting. [31] And

this is what they are charged to carry, as the whole of their service in the tent of meeting: the frames of the tabernacle, with its bars, pillars, and bases, [32] and the pillars around the court with their bases, pegs, and cords, with all their equipment and all their accessories. And you shall list by name the objects that they are required to carry. [33] This is the service of the clans of the sons of Merari, the whole of their service in the tent of meeting, under the direction of Ithamar the son of Aaron the priest."

[34] And Moses and Aaron and the chiefs of the congregation listed the sons of the Kohathites, by their clans and their fathers' houses, [35] from thirty years old up to fifty years old, everyone who could come on duty, for service in the tent of meeting; [36] and those listed by clans were 2,750. [37] This was the list of the clans of the Kohathites, all who served in the tent of meeting, whom Moses and Aaron listed according to the commandment of the LORD by Moses.

[38] Those listed of the sons of Gershon, by their clans and their fathers' houses, [39] from thirty years old up to fifty years old, everyone who could come on duty for service in the tent of meeting— [40] those listed by their clans and their fathers' houses were 2,630. [41] This was the list of the clans of the sons of Gershon, all who served in the tent of meeting, whom Moses and Aaron listed according to the commandment of the LORD.

[42] Those listed of the clans of the sons of Merari, by their clans and their fathers' houses, [43] from thirty years old up to fifty years old, everyone who could come on duty, for service in the tent of meeting— [44] those listed by clans were 3,200. [45] This was the list of the clans of the sons of Merari, whom Moses and Aaron listed according to the commandment of the LORD by Moses.

[46] All those who were listed of the Levites, whom Moses and Aaron and the chiefs of Israel listed, by their clans and their fathers' houses, [47] from thirty years old up to fifty years old, everyone who could come to do the service of ministry and the service of bearing burdens in the tent of meeting, [48] those listed were 8,580. [49] According to the commandment of the LORD through Moses they were listed, each one with his task of serving or carrying. Thus they were listed by him, as the LORD commanded Moses.

Psalm 38

A PSALM OF DAVID, FOR THE MEMORIAL OFFERING.

O LORD, rebuke me not in your anger,
  nor discipline me in your wrath!
2 For your arrows have sunk into me,
  and your hand has come down on me.

3 There is no soundness in my flesh
    because of your indignation;
  there is no health in my bones
    because of my sin.
4 For my iniquities have gone over my
      head;
    like a heavy burden, they are too
      heavy for me.

5 My wounds stink and fester
    because of my foolishness,
6 I am utterly bowed down and prostrate;
    all the day I go about mourning.
7 For my sides are filled with burning,
    and there is no soundness in my
      flesh.
8 I am feeble and crushed;
    I groan because of the tumult of my
      heart.

9 O Lord, all my longing is before you;
    my sighing is not hidden from you.
10 My heart throbs; my strength fails me,
    and the light of my eyes—it also has
      gone from me.
11 My friends and companions stand aloof
      from my plague,
    and my nearest kin stand far off.
12 Those who seek my life lay their snares;
    those who seek my hurt speak of ruin
    and meditate treachery all day long.

13 But I am like a deaf man; I do not hear,
    like a mute man who does not open
      his mouth.
14 I have become like a man who does not
      hear,
    and in whose mouth are no rebukes.

15 But for you, O LORD, do I wait;
    it is you, O Lord my God, who will
      answer.
16 For I said, "Only let them not rejoice
      over me,
    who boast against me when my foot
      slips!"

17 For I am ready to fall,
    and my pain is ever before me.
18 I confess my iniquity;
    I am sorry for my sin.
19 But my foes are vigorous, they are
      mighty,
    and many are those who hate me
      wrongfully.
20 Those who render me evil for good
    accuse me because I follow after
      good.

21 Do not forsake me, O LORD!
    O my God, be not far from me!
22 Make haste to help me,
    O Lord, my salvation!

Song of Solomon 2

I am a rose[1] of Sharon,
  a lily of the valleys.

HE

2 As a lily among brambles,
    so is my love among the young
      women.

SHE

3 As an apple tree among the trees of the
      forest,
    so is my beloved among the young
      men.
  With great delight I sat in his shadow,
    and his fruit was sweet to my taste.
4 He brought me to the banqueting
      house,[2]
    and his banner over me was love.
5 Sustain me with raisins;
    refresh me with apples,
    for I am sick with love.
6 His left hand is under my head,
    and his right hand embraces me!
7 I adjure you,[3] O daughters of Jerusalem,
    by the gazelles or the does of the field,
  that you not stir up or awaken love
      until it pleases.

8 The voice of my beloved!
    Behold, he comes,
  leaping over the mountains,
    bounding over the hills.
9 My beloved is like a gazelle
    or a young stag.

---

[1] Probably a bulb, such as a crocus, asphodel, or narcissus [2] Hebrew *the house of wine* [3] That is, I put you on oath; so throughout the Song

Behold, there he stands
  behind our wall,
gazing through the windows,
  looking through the lattice.
10 My beloved speaks and says to me:
  "Arise, my love, my beautiful one,
    and come away,
11 for behold, the winter is past;
  the rain is over and gone.
12 The flowers appear on the earth,
  the time of singing[1] has come,
and the voice of the turtledove
  is heard in our land.
13 The fig tree ripens its figs,
  and the vines are in blossom;
  they give forth fragrance.
Arise, my love, my beautiful one,
  and come away.
14 O my dove, in the clefts of the rock,
  in the crannies of the cliff,
let me see your face,
  let me hear your voice,
for your voice is sweet,
  and your face is lovely.
15 Catch the foxes[2] for us,
  the little foxes
that spoil the vineyards,
  for our vineyards are in blossom."

16 My beloved is mine, and I am his;
  he grazes[3] among the lilies.
17 Until the day breathes
  and the shadows flee,
turn, my beloved, be like a gazelle
  or a young stag on cleft mountains.[4]

Hebrews 2

Therefore we must pay much closer attention to what we have heard, lest we drift away from it. [2] For since the message declared by angels proved to be reliable, and every transgression or disobedience received a just retribution, [3] how shall we escape if we neglect such a great salvation? It was declared at first by the Lord, and it was attested to us by those who heard, [4] while God also bore witness by signs and wonders and various miracles and by gifts of the Holy Spirit distributed according to his will.

[5] For it was not to angels that God subjected the world to come, of which we are speaking. [6] It has been testified somewhere,

"What is man, that you are mindful of
  him,
  or the son of man, that you care for
    him?
7 You made him for a little while lower
  than the angels;
  you have crowned him with glory and
    honor,[5]
8   putting everything in subjection
    under his feet."

Now in putting everything in subjection to him, he left nothing outside his control. At present, we do not yet see everything in subjection to him. [9] But we see him who for a little while was made lower than the angels, namely Jesus, crowned with glory and honor because of the suffering of death, so that by the grace of God he might taste death for everyone.

[10] For it was fitting that he, for whom and by whom all things exist, in bringing many sons to glory, should make the founder of their salvation perfect through suffering. [11] For he who sanctifies and those who are sanctified all have one source.[6] That is why he is not ashamed to call them brothers,[7] [12] saying,

"I will tell of your name to my brothers;
  in the midst of the congregation I will
    sing your praise."

[13] And again,

"I will put my trust in him."

And again,

"Behold, I and the children God has
  given me."

[14] Since therefore the children share in flesh and blood, he himself likewise partook of the same things, that through death he might destroy the one who has the power of death, that is, the devil, [15] and deliver all those who through fear of death were subject to lifelong slavery. [16] For surely it is not angels that he helps, but he helps the offspring of Abraham. [17] Therefore he had to be made like his brothers in every respect, so that he might become a merciful and faithful high priest in the service of God, to make propitiation for the sins of the people. [18] For because he himself has suffered when tempted, he is able to help those who are being tempted.

[1] Or pruning [2] Or jackals [3] Or he pastures his flock [4] Or mountains of Bether [5] Some manuscripts insert and set him over the works of your hands [6] Greek all are of one [7] Or brothers and sisters. The plural Greek word adelphoi (translated "brothers") refers to siblings in a family. In New Testament usage, depending on the context, adelphoi may refer either to men or to both men and women who are siblings (brothers and sisters) in God's family, the church; also verse 12

APRIL 28

Numbers 5

The LORD spoke to Moses, saying, ²"Command the people of Israel that they put out of the camp everyone who is leprous¹ or has a discharge and everyone who is unclean through contact with the dead. ³You shall put out both male and female, putting them outside the camp, that they may not defile their camp, in the midst of which I dwell." ⁴And the people of Israel did so, and put them outside the camp; as the LORD said to Moses, so the people of Israel did.

⁵And the LORD spoke to Moses, saying, ⁶"Speak to the people of Israel, When a man or woman commits any of the sins that people commit by breaking faith with the LORD, and that person realizes his guilt, ⁷he shall confess his sin that he has committed.² And he shall make full restitution for his wrong, adding a fifth to it and giving it to him to whom he did the wrong. ⁸But if the man has no next of kin to whom restitution may be made for the wrong, the restitution for wrong shall go to the LORD for the priest, in addition to the ram of atonement with which atonement is made for him. ⁹And every contribution, all the holy donations of the people of Israel, which they bring to the priest, shall be his. ¹⁰Each one shall keep his holy donations: whatever anyone gives to the priest shall be his."

¹¹And the LORD spoke to Moses, saying, ¹²"Speak to the people of Israel, If any man's wife goes astray and breaks faith with him, ¹³if a man lies with her sexually, and it is hidden from the eyes of her husband, and she is undetected though she has defiled herself, and there is no witness against her, since she was not taken in the act, ¹⁴and if the spirit of jealousy comes over him and he is jealous of his wife who has defiled herself, or if the spirit of jealousy comes over him and he is jealous of his wife, though she has not defiled herself, ¹⁵then the man shall bring his wife to the priest and bring the offering required of her, a tenth of an ephah³ of barley flour. He shall pour no oil on it and put no frankincense on it, for it is a grain offering of jealousy, a grain offering of remembrance, bringing iniquity to remembrance.

¹⁶"And the priest shall bring her near and set her before the LORD. ¹⁷And the priest shall take holy water in an earthenware vessel and take some of the dust that is on the floor of the tabernacle and put it into the water. ¹⁸And the priest shall set the woman before the LORD and unbind the hair of the woman's head and place in her hands the grain offering of remembrance, which is the grain offering of jealousy. And in his hand the priest shall have the water of bitterness that brings the curse. ¹⁹Then the priest shall make her take an oath, saying, 'If no man has lain with you, and if you have not turned aside to uncleanness while you were under your husband's authority, be free from this water of bitterness that brings the curse. ²⁰But if you have gone astray, though you are under your husband's authority, and if you have defiled yourself, and some man other than your husband has lain with you, ²¹then' (let the priest make the woman take the oath of the curse, and say to the woman) 'the LORD make you a curse and an oath among your people, when the LORD makes your thigh fall away and your body swell. ²²May this water that brings the curse pass into your bowels and make your womb swell and your thigh fall away.' And the woman shall say, 'Amen, Amen.'

²³"Then the priest shall write these curses in a book and wash them off into the water of bitterness. ²⁴And he shall make the woman drink the water of bitterness that brings the curse, and the water that brings the curse shall enter into her and cause bitter pain. ²⁵And the priest shall take the grain offering of jealousy out of the woman's hand and shall wave the grain offering before the LORD and bring it to the altar. ²⁶And the priest shall take a handful of the grain offering, as its memorial portion, and burn it on the altar, and afterward shall make the woman drink the water. ²⁷And when he

---

¹ *Leprosy* was a term for several skin diseases; see Leviticus 13 ² Hebrew *they shall confess their sin that they have committed* ³ An *ephah* was about 3/5 bushel or 22 liters

has made her drink the water, then, if she has defiled herself and has broken faith with her husband, the water that brings the curse shall enter into her and cause bitter pain, and her womb shall swell, and her thigh shall fall away, and the woman shall become a curse among her people. **28** But if the woman has not defiled herself and is clean, then she shall be free and shall conceive children.

29 "This is the law in cases of jealousy, when a wife, though under her husband's authority, goes astray and defiles herself, **30** or when the spirit of jealousy comes over a man and he is jealous of his wife. Then he shall set the woman before the Lord, and the priest shall carry out for her all this law. **31** The man shall be free from iniquity, but the woman shall bear her iniquity."

——————— *Psalm 39* ———————

To the choirmaster: to Jeduthun. A Psalm of David.

I said, "I will guard my ways,
  that I may not sin with my tongue;
   I will guard my mouth with a muzzle,
    so long as the wicked are in my
     presence."
2 I was mute and silent;
   I held my peace to no avail,
  and my distress grew worse.
3   My heart became hot within me.
  As I mused, the fire burned;
   then I spoke with my tongue:

4 "O Lord, make me know my end
  and what is the measure of my days;
  let me know how fleeting I am!
5 Behold, you have made my days a few
    handbreadths,
  and my lifetime is as nothing before
    you.
  Surely all mankind stands as a mere
    breath!   *Selah*
6 Surely a man goes about as a shadow!
  Surely for nothing[1] they are in turmoil;
   man heaps up wealth and does not
    know who will gather!

7 "And now, O Lord, for what do I wait?
  My hope is in you.
8 Deliver me from all my transgressions.
  Do not make me the scorn of the fool!

[1] Hebrew *Surely as a breath*

9 I am mute; I do not open my mouth,
  for it is you who have done it.
10 Remove your stroke from me;
  I am spent by the hostility of your
    hand.
11 When you discipline a man
  with rebukes for sin,
  you consume like a moth what is dear to
    him;
   surely all mankind is a mere breath!
                   Selah

12 "Hear my prayer, O Lord,
  and give ear to my cry;
  hold not your peace at my tears!
  For I am a sojourner with you,
   a guest, like all my fathers.
13 Look away from me, that I may smile
    again,
  before I depart and am no more!"

——————— *Song of Solomon 3* ———————

On my bed by night
  I sought him whom my soul loves;
   I sought him, but found him not.
2 I will rise now and go about the city,
  in the streets and in the squares;
  I will seek him whom my soul loves.
   I sought him, but found him not.
3 The watchmen found me
  as they went about in the city.
  "Have you seen him whom my soul
    loves?"
4 Scarcely had I passed them
  when I found him whom my soul
    loves.
  I held him, and would not let him go
   until I had brought him into my
    mother's house,
  and into the chamber of her who
    conceived me.
5 I adjure you, O daughters of Jerusalem,
  by the gazelles or the does of the field,
  that you not stir up or awaken love
   until it pleases.

6 What is that coming up from the
    wilderness
  like columns of smoke,
  perfumed with myrrh and frankincense,
   with all the fragrant powders of a
    merchant?

7   Behold, it is the litter[1] of Solomon!
    Around it are sixty mighty men,
      some of the mighty men of Israel,
8   all of them wearing swords
      and expert in war,
    each with his sword at his thigh,
      against terror by night.
9   King Solomon made himself a
        carriage[2]
      from the wood of Lebanon.
10 He made its posts of silver,
      its back of gold, its seat of purple;
    its interior was inlaid with love
      by the daughters of Jerusalem.
11 Go out, O daughters of Zion,
      and look upon King Solomon,
    with the crown with which his mother
        crowned him
      on the day of his wedding,
      on the day of the gladness of his
        heart.

--- **Hebrews 3** ---

Therefore, holy brothers,[3] you who share in a heavenly calling, consider Jesus, the apostle and high priest of our confession, [2] who was faithful to him who appointed him, just as Moses also was faithful in all God's[4] house. [3] For Jesus has been counted worthy of more glory than Moses—as much more glory as the builder of a house has more honor than the house itself. [4] (For every house is built by someone, but the builder of all things is God.) [5] Now Moses was faithful in all God's house as a servant, to testify to the things that were to be spoken later, [6] but Christ is faithful over God's house as a son. And we are his house if indeed

we hold fast our confidence and our boasting in our hope.[5]
[7] Therefore, as the Holy Spirit says,

    "Today, if you hear his voice,
8   do not harden your hearts as in the
        rebellion,
      on the day of testing in the wilderness,
9   where your fathers put me to the test
      and saw my works for forty years.
10   Therefore I was provoked with that
        generation,
      and said, 'They always go astray in their
        heart;
      they have not known my ways.'
11   As I swore in my wrath,
      'They shall not enter my rest.'"

[12] Take care, brothers, lest there be in any of you an evil, unbelieving heart, leading you to fall away from the living God. [13] But exhort one another every day, as long as it is called "today," that none of you may be hardened by the deceitfulness of sin. [14] For we have come to share in Christ, if indeed we hold our original confidence firm to the end. [15] As it is said,

    "Today, if you hear his voice,
      do not harden your hearts as in the
        rebellion."

[16] For who were those who heard and yet rebelled? Was it not all those who left Egypt led by Moses? [17] And with whom was he provoked for forty years? Was it not with those who sinned, whose bodies fell in the wilderness? [18] And to whom did he swear that they would not enter his rest, but to those who were disobedient? [19] So we see that they were unable to enter because of unbelief.

APRIL 29

--- **Numbers 6** ---

And the Lord spoke to Moses, saying, [2] "Speak to the people of Israel and say to them, When either a man or a woman makes a special vow, the vow of a Nazirite,[6] to separate himself to the Lord, [3] he shall separate himself from wine and strong drink. He shall

[1] That is, the couch on which servants carry a king [2] Or *sedan chair* [3] Or *brothers and sisters*; also verse 12 [4] Greek *his*; also verses 5, 6 [5] Some manuscripts insert *firm to the end*
[6] *Nazirite* means *one separated*, or *one consecrated*

drink no vinegar made from wine or strong drink and shall not drink any juice of grapes or eat grapes, fresh or dried. [4]All the days of his separation[1] he shall eat nothing that is produced by the grapevine, not even the seeds or the skins.

[5] "All the days of his vow of separation, no razor shall touch his head. Until the time is completed for which he separates himself to the LORD, he shall be holy. He shall let the locks of hair of his head grow long.

[6] "All the days that he separates himself to the LORD he shall not go near a dead body. [7]Not even for his father or for his mother, for brother or sister, if they die, shall he make himself unclean, because his separation to God is on his head. [8]All the days of his separation he is holy to the LORD.

[9] "And if any man dies very suddenly beside him and he defiles his consecrated head, then he shall shave his head on the day of his cleansing; on the seventh day he shall shave it. [10]On the eighth day he shall bring two turtledoves or two pigeons to the priest to the entrance of the tent of meeting, [11]and the priest shall offer one for a sin offering and the other for a burnt offering, and make atonement for him, because he sinned by reason of the dead body. And he shall consecrate his head that same day [12]and separate himself to the LORD for the days of his separation and bring a male lamb a year old for a guilt offering. But the previous period shall be void, because his separation was defiled.

[13] "And this is the law for the Nazirite, when the time of his separation has been completed: he shall be brought to the entrance of the tent of meeting, [14]and he shall bring his gift to the LORD, one male lamb a year old without blemish for a burnt offering, and one ewe lamb a year old without blemish as a sin offering, and one ram without blemish as a peace offering, [15]and a basket of unleavened bread, loaves of fine flour mixed with oil, and unleavened wafers smeared with oil, and their grain offering and their drink offerings. [16]And the priest shall bring them before the LORD and offer his sin offering and his burnt offering, [17]and he shall offer the ram as a sacrifice of peace offering to the LORD, with the basket of unleavened bread. The priest shall offer also its grain offering and its drink offering. [18]And

the Nazirite shall shave his consecrated head at the entrance of the tent of meeting and shall take the hair from his consecrated head and put it on the fire that is under the sacrifice of the peace offering. [19]And the priest shall take the shoulder of the ram, when it is boiled, and one unleavened loaf out of the basket and one unleavened wafer, and shall put them on the hands of the Nazirite, after he has shaved the hair of his consecration, [20]and the priest shall wave them for a wave offering before the LORD. They are a holy portion for the priest, together with the breast that is waved and the thigh that is contributed. And after that the Nazirite may drink wine.

[21] "This is the law of the Nazirite. But if he vows an offering to the LORD above his Nazirite vow, as he can afford, in exact accordance with the vow that he takes, then he shall do in addition to the law of the Nazirite."

[22]The LORD spoke to Moses, saying, [23]"Speak to Aaron and his sons, saying, Thus you shall bless the people of Israel: you shall say to them,

[24]	The LORD bless you and keep you;
[25]	the LORD make his face to shine upon
	you and be gracious to you;
[26]	the LORD lift up his countenance[2] upon
	you and give you peace.

[27]"So shall they put my name upon the people of Israel, and I will bless them."

Psalm 40–41

To the choirmaster. A Psalm of David.

I waited patiently for the LORD;
  he inclined to me and heard my cry.
[2]   He drew me up from the pit of
     destruction,
    out of the miry bog,
  and set my feet upon a rock,
    making my steps secure.
[3]   He put a new song in my mouth,
    a song of praise to our God.
  Many will see and fear,
    and put their trust in the LORD.

[4]   Blessed is the man who makes
    the LORD his trust,
  who does not turn to the proud,
    to those who go astray after a lie!

[1] Or Naziriteship [2] Or face

5 You have multiplied, O Lᴏʀᴅ my God,
　　your wondrous deeds and your
　　　thoughts toward us;
　　none can compare with you!
　I will proclaim and tell of them,
　　yet they are more than can be told.

6 In sacrifice and offering you have not
　　delighted,
　　but you have given me an open ear.[1]
　Burnt offering and sin offering
　　you have not required.

7 Then I said, "Behold, I have come;
　　in the scroll of the book it is written of
　　me:

8 I delight to do your will, O my God;
　　your law is within my heart."

9 I have told the glad news of deliverance[2]
　　in the great congregation;
　behold, I have not restrained my lips,
　　as you know, O Lᴏʀᴅ.

10 I have not hidden your deliverance
　　within my heart;
　I have spoken of your faithfulness and
　　your salvation;
　I have not concealed your steadfast love
　　and your faithfulness
　　from the great congregation.

11 As for you, O Lᴏʀᴅ, you will not restrain
　　your mercy from me;
　your steadfast love and your faithfulness
　　will
　　ever preserve me!

12 For evils have encompassed me
　　beyond number;
　my iniquities have overtaken me,
　　and I cannot see;
　they are more than the hairs of my head;
　　my heart fails me.

13 Be pleased, O Lᴏʀᴅ, to deliver me!
　　O Lᴏʀᴅ, make haste to help me!

14 Let those be put to shame and
　　disappointed altogether
　　who seek to snatch away my life;
　let those be turned back and brought to
　　dishonor
　　who delight in my hurt!

15 Let those be appalled because of their
　　shame
　　who say to me, "Aha, Aha!"

16 But may all who seek you
　　rejoice and be glad in you;
　may those who love your salvation
　　say continually, "Great is the Lᴏʀᴅ!"

17 As for me, I am poor and needy,
　　but the Lord takes thought for me.
　You are my help and my deliverer;
　　do not delay, O my God!

ᴛᴏ ᴛʜᴇ ᴄʜᴏɪʀᴍᴀsᴛᴇʀ. A Psᴀʟᴍ ᴏғ Dᴀᴠɪᴅ.

Blessed is the one who considers the poor![3]
　In the day of trouble the Lᴏʀᴅ delivers
　　him;

2 the Lᴏʀᴅ protects him and keeps him
　　alive;
　he is called blessed in the land;
　you do not give him up to the will of
　　his enemies.

3 The Lᴏʀᴅ sustains him on his sickbed;
　in his illness you restore him to full
　　health.[4]

4 As for me, I said, "O Lᴏʀᴅ, be gracious
　　to me;
　heal me,[5] for I have sinned against
　　you!"

5 My enemies say of me in malice,
　"When will he die, and his name
　　perish?"

6 And when one comes to see me, he
　　utters empty words,
　while his heart gathers iniquity;
　when he goes out, he tells it abroad.

7 All who hate me whisper together about
　　me;
　　they imagine the worst for me.[6]

8 They say, "A deadly thing is poured out[7]
　　on him;
　he will not rise again from where he
　　lies."

9 Even my close friend in whom I trusted,
　　who ate my bread, has lifted his heel
　　against me.

10 But you, O Lᴏʀᴅ, be gracious to me,
　　and raise me up, that I may repay them!

11 By this I know that you delight in me:
　　my enemy will not shout in triumph
　　over me.

12 But you have upheld me because of my
　　integrity,
　and set me in your presence forever.

[1] Hebrew *ears you have dug for me* [2] Hebrew *righteousness; also verse 10* [3] Or *weak* [4] Hebrew *you turn all his bed* [5] Hebrew *my soul* [6] Or *they devise evil against me* [7] Or *has fastened*

13 Blessed be the Lord, the God of Israel,
from everlasting to everlasting!
     Amen and Amen.

——— *Song of Solomon 4* ———

HE

Behold, you are beautiful, my love,
behold, you are beautiful!
Your eyes are doves
    behind your veil.
Your hair is like a flock of goats
    leaping down the slopes of Gilead.
2 Your teeth are like a flock of shorn ewes
    that have come up from the washing,
all of which bear twins,
    and not one among them has lost its
      young.
3 Your lips are like a scarlet thread,
    and your mouth is lovely.
Your cheeks are like halves of a
     pomegranate
    behind your veil.
4 Your neck is like the tower of David,
    built in rows of stone;[1]
on it hang a thousand shields,
    all of them shields of warriors.
5 Your two breasts are like two fawns,
    twins of a gazelle,
    that graze among the lilies.
6 Until the day breathes
    and the shadows flee,
I will go away to the mountain of myrrh
    and the hill of frankincense.
7 You are altogether beautiful, my love;
    there is no flaw in you.
8 Come with me from Lebanon, my bride;
    come with me from Lebanon.
Depart[2] from the peak of Amana,
    from the peak of Senir and Hermon,
from the dens of lions,
    from the mountains of leopards.

9 You have captivated my heart, my sister,
     my bride;
you have captivated my heart with one
     glance of your eyes,
    with one jewel of your necklace.
10 How beautiful is your love, my sister, my
     bride!
How much better is your love than
     wine,

and the fragrance of your oils than
    any spice!
11 Your lips drip nectar, my bride;
    honey and milk are under your
     tongue;
the fragrance of your garments is like
    the fragrance of Lebanon.
12 A garden locked is my sister, my bride,
    a spring locked, a fountain sealed.
13 Your shoots are an orchard of
     pomegranates
    with all choicest fruits,
    henna with nard,
14 nard and saffron, calamus and
     cinnamon,
    with all trees of frankincense,
myrrh and aloes,
    with all choice spices—
15 a garden fountain, a well of living water,
    and flowing streams from Lebanon.

16 Awake, O north wind,
    and come, O south wind!
Blow upon my garden,
    let its spices flow.

SHE

Let my beloved come to his garden,
    and eat its choicest fruits.

——— *Hebrews 4* ———

Therefore, while the promise of entering his rest still stands, let us fear lest any of you should seem to have failed to reach it. [2]For good news came to us just as to them, but the message they heard did not benefit them, because they were not united by faith with those who listened.[3] [3]For we who have believed enter that rest, as he has said,

"As I swore in my wrath,
    'They shall not enter my rest,'"

although his works were finished from the foundation of the world. [4]For he has somewhere spoken of the seventh day in this way: "And God rested on the seventh day from all his works." [5]And again in this passage he said,

"They shall not enter my rest."

[6]Since therefore it remains for some to enter it, and those who formerly received the good

news failed to enter because of disobedience, [7] again he appoints a certain day, "Today," saying through David so long afterward, in the words already quoted,

> "Today, if you hear his voice,
>   do not harden your hearts."

[8] For if Joshua had given them rest, God[1] would not have spoken of another day later on. [9] So then, there remains a Sabbath rest for the people of God, [10] for whoever has entered God's rest has also rested from his works as God did from his.

[11] Let us therefore strive to enter that rest, so that no one may fall by the same sort of disobedience. [12] For the word of God is living and active, sharper than any two-edged sword, piercing to the division of soul and of spirit, of joints and of marrow, and discerning the thoughts and intentions of the heart. [13] And no creature is hidden from his sight, but all are naked and exposed to the eyes of him to whom we must give account.

[14] Since then we have a great high priest who has passed through the heavens, Jesus, the Son of God, let us hold fast our confession. [15] For we do not have a high priest who is unable to sympathize with our weaknesses, but one who in every respect has been tempted as we are, yet without sin. [16] Let us then with confidence draw near to the throne of grace, that we may receive mercy and find grace to help in time of need.

APRIL 30

Numbers 7

On the day when Moses had finished setting up the tabernacle and had anointed and consecrated it with all its furnishings and had anointed and consecrated the altar with all its utensils, [2] the chiefs of Israel, heads of their fathers' houses, who were the chiefs of the tribes, who were over those who were listed, approached [3] and brought their offerings before the LORD, six wagons and twelve oxen, a wagon for every two of the chiefs, and for each one an ox. They brought them before the tabernacle. [4] Then the LORD said to Moses, [5] "Accept these from them, that they may be used in the service of the tent of meeting, and give them to the Levites, to each man according to his service." [6] So Moses took the wagons and the oxen and gave them to the Levites. [7] Two wagons and four oxen he gave to the sons of Gershon, according to their service. [8] And four wagons and eight oxen he gave to the sons of Merari, according to their service, under the direction of Ithamar the son of Aaron the priest. [9] But to the sons of Kohath he gave none, because they were charged with the service of the holy things that had to be carried on the shoulder. [10] And the chiefs offered offerings for the dedication of the altar on the day it was anointed; and the chiefs offered their offering before the altar. [11] And the LORD said to Moses, "They shall offer their offerings, one chief each day, for the dedication of the altar."

[12] He who offered his offering the first day was Nahshon the son of Amminadab, of the tribe of Judah. [13] And his offering was one silver plate whose weight was 130 shekels,[2] one silver basin of 70 shekels, according to the shekel of the sanctuary, both of them full of fine flour mixed with oil for a grain offering; [14] one golden dish of 10 shekels, full of incense; [15] one bull from the herd, one ram, one male lamb a year old, for a burnt offering; [16] one male goat for a sin offering; [17] and for the sacrifice of peace offerings, two oxen, five rams, five male goats, and five male lambs a year old. This was the offering of Nahshon the son of Amminadab.

[18] On the second day Nethanel the son of Zuar, the chief of Issachar, made an offering. [19] He offered for his offering one silver plate whose weight was 130 shekels, one silver basin

---

[1] Greek he   [2] A shekel was about 2/5 ounce or 11 grams

of 70 shekels, according to the shekel of the sanctuary, both of them full of fine flour mixed with oil for a grain offering; [20] one golden dish of 10 shekels, full of incense; [21] one bull from the herd, one ram, one male lamb a year old, for a burnt offering; [22] one male goat for a sin offering; [23] and for the sacrifice of peace offerings, two oxen, five rams, five male goats, and five male lambs a year old. This was the offering of Nethanel the son of Zuar.

[24] On the third day Eliab the son of Helon, the chief of the people of Zebulun: [25] his offering was one silver plate whose weight was 130 shekels, one silver basin of 70 shekels, according to the shekel of the sanctuary, both of them full of fine flour mixed with oil for a grain offering; [26] one golden dish of 10 shekels, full of incense; [27] one bull from the herd, one ram, one male lamb a year old, for a burnt offering; [28] one male goat for a sin offering; [29] and for the sacrifice of peace offerings, two oxen, five rams, five male goats, and five male lambs a year old. This was the offering of Eliab the son of Helon.

[30] On the fourth day Elizur the son of Shedeur, the chief of the people of Reuben: [31] his offering was one silver plate whose weight was 130 shekels, one silver basin of 70 shekels, according to the shekel of the sanctuary, both of them full of fine flour mixed with oil for a grain offering; [32] one golden dish of 10 shekels, full of incense; [33] one bull from the herd, one ram, one male lamb a year old, for a burnt offering; [34] one male goat for a sin offering; [35] and for the sacrifice of peace offerings, two oxen, five rams, five male goats, and five male lambs a year old. This was the offering of Elizur the son of Shedeur.

[36] On the fifth day Shelumiel the son of Zurishaddai, the chief of the people of Simeon: [37] his offering was one silver plate whose weight was 130 shekels, one silver basin of 70 shekels, according to the shekel of the sanctuary, both of them full of fine flour mixed with oil for a grain offering; [38] one golden dish of 10 shekels, full of incense; [39] one bull from the herd, one ram, one male lamb a year old, for a burnt offering; [40] one male goat for a sin offering; [41] and for the sacrifice of peace offerings, two oxen, five rams, five male goats, and five male lambs a year old. This was the offering of Shelumiel the son of Zurishaddai.

[42] On the sixth day Eliasaph the son of Deuel, the chief of the people of Gad: [43] his offering was one silver plate whose weight was 130 shekels, one silver basin of 70 shekels, according to the shekel of the sanctuary, both of them full of fine flour mixed with oil for a grain offering; [44] one golden dish of 10 shekels, full of incense; [45] one bull from the herd, one ram, one male lamb a year old, for a burnt offering; [46] one male goat for a sin offering; [47] and for the sacrifice of peace offerings, two oxen, five rams, five male goats, and five male lambs a year old. This was the offering of Eliasaph the son of Deuel.

[48] On the seventh day Elishama the son of Ammihud, the chief of the people of Ephraim: [49] his offering was one silver plate whose weight was 130 shekels, one silver basin of 70 shekels, according to the shekel of the sanctuary, both of them full of fine flour mixed with oil for a grain offering; [50] one golden dish of 10 shekels, full of incense; [51] one bull from the herd, one ram, one male lamb a year old, for a burnt offering; [52] one male goat for a sin offering; [53] and for the sacrifice of peace offerings, two oxen, five rams, five male goats, and five male lambs a year old. This was the offering of Elishama the son of Ammihud.

[54] On the eighth day Gamaliel the son of Pedahzur, the chief of the people of Manasseh: [55] his offering was one silver plate whose weight was 130 shekels, one silver basin of 70 shekels, according to the shekel of the sanctuary, both of them full of fine flour mixed with oil for a grain offering; [56] one golden dish of 10 shekels, full of incense; [57] one bull from the herd, one ram, one male lamb a year old, for a burnt offering; [58] one male goat for a sin offering; [59] and for the sacrifice of peace offerings, two oxen, five rams, five male goats, and five male lambs a year old. This was the offering of Gamaliel the son of Pedahzur.

[60] On the ninth day Abidan the son of Gideoni, the chief of the people of Benjamin: [61] his offering was one silver plate whose weight was 130 shekels, one silver basin of 70 shekels, according to the shekel of the sanctuary, both of them full of fine flour mixed with oil for a grain offering; [62] one golden dish of 10 shekels, full of incense; [63] one bull from the herd, one ram, one male lamb a year old, for a burnt offering; [64] one male goat for a sin offering; [65] and for the sacrifice of peace offerings, two oxen, five rams, five male goats, and five male lambs a

year old. This was the offering of Abidan the son of Gideoni.

⁶⁶On the tenth day Ahiezer the son of Ammishaddai, the chief of the people of Dan: ⁶⁷his offering was one silver plate whose weight was 130 shekels, one silver basin of 70 shekels, according to the shekel of the sanctuary, both of them full of fine flour mixed with oil for a grain offering; ⁶⁸one golden dish of 10 shekels, full of incense; ⁶⁹one bull from the herd, one ram, one male lamb a year old, for a burnt offering; ⁷⁰one male goat for a sin offering; ⁷¹and for the sacrifice of peace offerings, two oxen, five rams, five male goats, and five male lambs a year old. This was the offering of Ahiezer the son of Ammishaddai.

⁷²On the eleventh day Pagiel the son of Ochran, the chief of the people of Asher: ⁷³his offering was one silver plate whose weight was 130 shekels, one silver basin of 70 shekels, according to the shekel of the sanctuary, both of them full of fine flour mixed with oil for a grain offering; ⁷⁴one golden dish of 10 shekels, full of incense; ⁷⁵one bull from the herd, one ram, one male lamb a year old, for a burnt offering; ⁷⁶one male goat for a sin offering; ⁷⁷and for the sacrifice of peace offerings, two oxen, five rams, five male goats, and five male lambs a year old. This was the offering of Pagiel the son of Ochran.

⁷⁸On the twelfth day Ahira the son of Enan, the chief of the people of Naphtali: ⁷⁹his offering was one silver plate whose weight was 130 shekels, one silver basin of 70 shekels, according to the shekel of the sanctuary, both of them full of fine flour mixed with oil for a grain offering; ⁸⁰one golden dish of 10 shekels, full of incense; ⁸¹one bull from the herd, one ram, one male lamb a year old, for a burnt offering; ⁸²one male goat for a sin offering; ⁸³and for the sacrifice of peace offerings, two oxen, five rams, five male goats, and five male lambs a year old. This was the offering of Ahira the son of Enan.

⁸⁴This was the dedication offering for the altar on the day when it was anointed, from the chiefs of Israel: twelve silver plates, twelve silver basins, twelve golden dishes, ⁸⁵each silver plate weighing 130 shekels and each basin 70, all the silver of the vessels 2,400 shekels according to the shekel of the sanctuary, ⁸⁶the twelve golden dishes, full of incense, weighing 10 shekels apiece according to the shekel of the sanctuary, all the gold of the dishes being 120 shekels; ⁸⁷all the cattle for the burnt offering twelve bulls, twelve rams, twelve male lambs a year old, with their grain offering; and twelve male goats for a sin offering; ⁸⁸and all the cattle for the sacrifice of peace offerings twenty-four bulls, the rams sixty, the male goats sixty, the male lambs a year old sixty. This was the dedication offering for the altar after it was anointed.

⁸⁹And when Moses went into the tent of meeting to speak with the LORD, he heard the voice speaking to him from above the mercy seat that was on the ark of the testimony, from between the two cherubim; and it spoke to him.

--------- *Psalm 42–43* ---------

To the choirmaster. A Maskil[1] of the Sons of Korah.

A s a deer pants for flowing streams,
　so pants my soul for you, O God.
2　My soul thirsts for God,
　　for the living God.
　When shall I come and appear before
　　God?[2]
3　My tears have been my food
　　day and night,
　while they say to me all the day long,
　　"Where is your God?"
4　These things I remember,
　　as I pour out my soul:
　how I would go with the throng
　　and lead them in procession to the
　　　house of God
　with glad shouts and songs of praise,
　　a multitude keeping festival.

5　Why are you cast down, O my soul,
　　and why are you in turmoil within me?
　Hope in God; for I shall again praise
　　him,
　　my salvation[3] 6and my God.

　My soul is cast down within me;
　　therefore I remember you
　from the land of Jordan and of Hermon,
　　from Mount Mizar.
7　Deep calls to deep
　　at the roar of your waterfalls;
　all your breakers and your waves
　　have gone over me.

---

[1] Probably a musical or liturgical term [2] Revocalization yields *and see the face of God* [3] Hebrew *the salvation of my face*; also verse 11 and 43:5

⁸ By day the Lord commands his
       steadfast love,
     and at night his song is with me,
     a prayer to the God of my life.
⁹ I say to God, my rock:
       "Why have you forgotten me?
     Why do I go mourning
       because of the oppression of the
         enemy?"
¹⁰ As with a deadly wound in my bones,
       my adversaries taunt me,
     while they say to me all the day long,
       "Where is your God?"

¹¹ Why are you cast down, O my soul,
       and why are you in turmoil within me?
     Hope in God; for I shall again praise
       him,
     my salvation and my God.

V indicate me, O God, and defend my cause
   against an ungodly people,
     from the deceitful and unjust man
       deliver me!
² For you are the God in whom I take
       refuge;
     why have you rejected me?
     Why do I go about mourning
       because of the oppression of the
         enemy?
³ Send out your light and your truth;
       let them lead me;
     let them bring me to your holy hill
       and to your dwelling!
⁴ Then I will go to the altar of God,
       to God my exceeding joy,
     and I will praise you with the lyre,
       O God, my God.

⁵ Why are you cast down, O my soul,
       and why are you in turmoil within me?
     Hope in God; for I shall again praise
       him,
     my salvation and my God.

––––––– Song of Solomon 5 –––––––

He

I came to my garden, my sister, my bride,
   I gathered my myrrh with my spice,
     I ate my honeycomb with my honey,
     I drank my wine with my milk.

Others

Eat, friends, drink,
   and be drunk with love!

She

² I slept, but my heart was awake.
     A sound! My beloved is knocking.
   "Open to me, my sister, my love,
       my dove, my perfect one,
     for my head is wet with dew,
       my locks with the drops of the
         night."
³ I had put off my garment;
       how could I put it on?
     I had bathed my feet;
       how could I soil them?
⁴ My beloved put his hand to the latch,
       and my heart was thrilled within me.
⁵ I arose to open to my beloved,
       and my hands dripped with myrrh,
     my fingers with liquid myrrh,
       on the handles of the bolt.
⁶ I opened to my beloved,
       but my beloved had turned and gone.
     My soul failed me when he spoke.
     I sought him, but found him not;
       I called him, but he gave no answer.
⁷ The watchmen found me
       as they went about in the city;
     they beat me, they bruised me,
       they took away my veil,
     those watchmen of the walls.
⁸ I adjure you, O daughters of Jerusalem,
       if you find my beloved,
     that you tell him
       I am sick with love.

Others

⁹ What is your beloved more than another
       beloved,
     O most beautiful among women?
     What is your beloved more than another
       beloved,
     that you thus adjure us?

She

¹⁰ My beloved is radiant and ruddy,
       distinguished among ten thousand.
¹¹ His head is the finest gold;
       his locks are wavy,
       black as a raven.
¹² His eyes are like doves
       beside streams of water,

bathed in milk,
    sitting beside a full pool.[1]
13 His cheeks are like beds of spices,
    mounds of sweet-smelling herbs.
His lips are lilies,
    dripping liquid myrrh.
14 His arms are rods of gold,
    set with jewels.
His body is polished ivory,[2]
    bedecked with sapphires.[3]
15 His legs are alabaster columns,
    set on bases of gold.
His appearance is like Lebanon,
    choice as the cedars.
16 His mouth[4] is most sweet,
    and he is altogether desirable.
This is my beloved and this is my friend,
    O daughters of Jerusalem.

Hebrews 5

For every high priest chosen from among men is appointed to act on behalf of men in relation to God, to offer gifts and sacrifices for sins. [2]He can deal gently with the ignorant and wayward, since he himself is beset with weakness. [3]Because of this he is obligated to offer sacrifice for his own sins just as he does for those of the people. [4]And no one takes this honor for himself, but only when called by God, just as Aaron was.

[5]So also Christ did not exalt himself to be made a high priest, but was appointed by him who said to him,

"You are my Son,
    today I have begotten you";

[6]as he says also in another place,

"You are a priest forever,
    after the order of Melchizedek."

[7]In the days of his flesh, Jesus[5] offered up prayers and supplications, with loud cries and tears, to him who was able to save him from death, and he was heard because of his reverence. [8]Although he was a son, he learned obedience through what he suffered. [9]And being made perfect, he became the source of eternal salvation to all who obey him, [10]being designated by God a high priest after the order of Melchizedek.

[11]About this we have much to say, and it is hard to explain, since you have become dull of hearing. [12]For though by this time you ought to be teachers, you need someone to teach you again the basic principles of the oracles of God. You need milk, not solid food, [13]for everyone who lives on milk is unskilled in the word of righteousness, since he is a child. [14]But solid food is for the mature, for those who have their powers of discernment trained by constant practice to distinguish good from evil.

[1] The meaning of the Hebrew is uncertain [2] The meaning of the Hebrew word is uncertain [3] Hebrew *lapis lazuli* [4] Hebrew *palate* [5] Greek *he*

MAY 1

Numbers 8

Now the LORD spoke to Moses, saying, [2] "Speak to Aaron and say to him, When you set up the lamps, the seven lamps shall give light in front of the lampstand." [3] And Aaron did so: he set up its lamps in front of the lampstand, as the LORD commanded Moses. [4] And this was the workmanship of the lampstand, hammered work of gold. From its base to its flowers, it was hammered work; according to the pattern that the LORD had shown Moses, so he made the lampstand.

[5] And the LORD spoke to Moses, saying, [6] "Take the Levites from among the people of Israel and cleanse them. [7] Thus you shall do to them to cleanse them: sprinkle the water of purification upon them, and let them go with a razor over all their body, and wash their clothes and cleanse themselves. [8] Then let them take a bull from the herd and its grain offering of fine flour mixed with oil, and you shall take another bull from the herd for a sin offering. [9] And you shall bring the Levites before the tent of meeting and assemble the whole congregation of the people of Israel. [10] When you bring the Levites before the LORD, the people of Israel shall lay their hands on the Levites, [11] and Aaron shall offer the Levites before the LORD as a wave offering from the people of Israel, that they may do the service of the LORD. [12] Then the Levites shall lay their hands on the heads of the bulls, and you shall offer the one for a sin offering and the other for a burnt offering to the LORD to make atonement for the Levites. [13] And you shall set the Levites before Aaron and his sons, and shall offer them as a wave offering to the LORD.

[14] "Thus you shall separate the Levites from among the people of Israel, and the Levites shall be mine. [15] And after that the Levites shall go in to serve at the tent of meeting, when you have cleansed them and offered them as a wave offering. [16] For they are wholly given to me from among the people of Israel. Instead of all who open the womb, the firstborn of all the people of Israel, I have taken them for myself. [17] For all the firstborn among the people of Israel are mine, both of man and of beast. On the day that I struck down all the firstborn in the land of Egypt I consecrated them for myself, [18] and I have taken the Levites instead of all the firstborn among the people of Israel. [19] And I have given the Levites as a gift to Aaron and his sons from among the people of Israel, to do the service for the people of Israel at the tent of meeting and to make atonement for the people of Israel, that there may be no plague among the people of Israel when the people of Israel come near the sanctuary."

[20] Thus did Moses and Aaron and all the congregation of the people of Israel to the Levites. According to all that the LORD commanded Moses concerning the Levites, the people of Israel did to them. [21] And the Levites purified themselves from sin and washed their clothes, and Aaron offered them as a wave offering before the LORD, and Aaron made atonement for them to cleanse them. [22] And after that the Levites went in to do their service in the tent of meeting before Aaron and his sons; as the LORD had commanded Moses concerning the Levites, so they did to them.

[23] And the LORD spoke to Moses, saying, [24] "This applies to the Levites: from twenty-five years old and upward they[1] shall come to do duty in the service of the tent of meeting. [25] And from the age of fifty years they shall withdraw from the duty of the service and serve no more. [26] They minister[2] to their brothers in the tent of meeting by keeping guard, but they shall do no service. Thus shall you do to the Levites in assigning their duties."

Psalm 44

TO THE CHOIRMASTER. A MASKIL[3] OF THE SONS OF KORAH.

O God, we have heard with our ears,
    our fathers have told us,
  what deeds you performed in their days,
    in the days of old:

[1] Hebrew *he*; also verses 25, 26 [2] Hebrew *He ministers* [3] Probably a musical or liturgical term

2 you with your own hand drove out the
    nations,
  but them you planted;
  you afflicted the peoples,
    but them you set free;
3 for not by their own sword did they win
    the land,
    nor did their own arm save them,
  but your right hand and your arm,
    and the light of your face,
    for you delighted in them.
4 You are my King, O God;
    ordain salvation for Jacob!
5 Through you we push down our foes;
    through your name we tread down
      those who rise up against us.
6 For not in my bow do I trust,
    nor can my sword save me.
7 But you have saved us from our foes
    and have put to shame those who hate
      us.
8 In God we have boasted continually,
    and we will give thanks to your name
      forever.   *Selah*
9 But you have rejected us and disgraced
    us
  and have not gone out with our
    armies.
10 You have made us turn back from the
    foe,
    and those who hate us have gotten
      spoil.
11 You have made us like sheep for
    slaughter
  and have scattered us among the
    nations.
12 You have sold your people for a trifle,
    demanding no high price for them.
13 You have made us the taunt of our
    neighbors,
    the derision and scorn of those
      around us.
14 You have made us a byword among the
    nations,
    a laughingstock[1] among the peoples.
15 All day long my disgrace is before me,
    and shame has covered my face
16 at the sound of the taunter and reviler,
    at the sight of the enemy and the
      avenger.

17 All this has come upon us,
    though we have not forgotten you,
    and we have not been false to your
      covenant.
18 Our heart has not turned back,
    nor have our steps departed from your
      way;
19 yet you have broken us in the place of
    jackals
    and covered us with the shadow of
      death.
20 If we had forgotten the name of our
    God
  or spread out our hands to a foreign
    god,
21 would not God discover this?
    For he knows the secrets of the heart.
22 Yet for your sake we are killed all the
    day long;
    we are regarded as sheep to be
      slaughtered.
23 Awake! Why are you sleeping, O Lord?
    Rouse yourself! Do not reject us
      forever!
24 Why do you hide your face?
    Why do you forget our affliction and
      oppression?
25 For our soul is bowed down to the dust;
    our belly clings to the ground.
26 Rise up; come to our help!
    Redeem us for the sake of your
      steadfast love!

——— *Song of Solomon 6* ———

OTHERS

Where has your beloved gone,
  O most beautiful among women?
Where has your beloved turned,
  that we may seek him with you?

SHE

2 My beloved has gone down to his
    garden
  to the beds of spices,
  to graze[2] in the gardens
    and to gather lilies.
3 I am my beloved's and my beloved is
    mine;
  he grazes among the lilies.

[1] Hebrew *a shaking of the head* [2] Or *to pasture his flock; also verse 3*

He

4 You are beautiful as Tirzah, my love,
     lovely as Jerusalem,
     awesome as an army with banners.
5 Turn away your eyes from me,
     for they overwhelm me—
   Your hair is like a flock of goats
     leaping down the slopes of Gilead.
6 Your teeth are like a flock of ewes
     that have come up from the washing;
   all of them bear twins;
     not one among them has lost its
       young.
7 Your cheeks are like halves of a
       pomegranate
     behind your veil.
8 There are sixty queens and eighty
       concubines,
     and virgins without number.
9 My dove, my perfect one, is the only
       one,
     the only one of her mother,
     pure to her who bore her.
   The young women saw her and called
       her blessed;
     the queens and concubines also, and
       they praised her.

10 "Who is this who looks down like the
       dawn,
     beautiful as the moon, bright as the
       sun,
     awesome as an army with banners?"

She

11 I went down to the nut orchard
     to look at the blossoms of the valley,
   to see whether the vines had budded,
     whether the pomegranates were in
       bloom.
12 Before I was aware, my desire set me
     among the chariots of my kinsman, a
       prince.[1]

Others

13 2 Return, return, O Shulammite,
     return, return, that we may look upon
       you.

He

Why should you look upon the
     Shulammite,
   as upon a dance before two armies?[3]

Hebrews 6

Therefore let us leave the elementary doctrine of Christ and go on to maturity, not laying again a foundation of repentance from dead works and of faith toward God, [2]and of instruction about washings,[4] the laying on of hands, the resurrection of the dead, and eternal judgment. [3]And this we will do if God permits. [4]For it is impossible, in the case of those who have once been enlightened, who have tasted the heavenly gift, and have shared in the Holy Spirit, [5]and have tasted the goodness of the word of God and the powers of the age to come, [6]and then have fallen away, to restore them again to repentance, since they are crucifying once again the Son of God to their own harm and holding him up to contempt. [7]For land that has drunk the rain that often falls on it, and produces a crop useful to those for whose sake it is cultivated, receives a blessing from God. [8]But if it bears thorns and thistles, it is worthless and near to being cursed, and its end is to be burned.

[9]Though we speak in this way, yet in your case, beloved, we feel sure of better things—things that belong to salvation. [10]For God is not unjust so as to overlook your work and the love that you have shown for his name in serving the saints, as you still do. [11]And we desire each one of you to show the same earnestness to have the full assurance of hope until the end, [12]so that you may not be sluggish, but imitators of those who through faith and patience inherit the promises.

[13]For when God made a promise to Abraham, since he had no one greater by whom to swear, he swore by himself, [14]saying, "Surely I will bless you and multiply you." [15]And thus Abraham,[5] having patiently waited, obtained the promise. [16]For people swear by something greater than themselves, and in all their disputes an oath is final for confirmation. [17]So when God desired to show more convincingly to the heirs of the promise the unchangeable character of his purpose, he guaranteed it with an oath, [18]so that by two unchangeable things, in which it is impossible for God to lie, we who have fled for refuge might have strong encouragement to hold fast to the hope set before us. [19]We have this as a sure and steadfast anchor of the soul, a hope that enters into the inner

---

[1] Or chariots of Ammi-Nadib [2] Ch 7:1 in Hebrew [3] Or dance of Mahanaim [4] Or baptisms (that is, cleansing rites) [5] Greek he

place behind the curtain, ²⁰where Jesus has gone as a forerunner on our behalf, having become a high priest forever after the order of Melchizedek.

MAY 2

Numbers 9

And the LORD spoke to Moses in the wilderness of Sinai, in the first month of the second year after they had come out of the land of Egypt, saying, ²"Let the people of Israel keep the Passover at its appointed time. ³On the fourteenth day of this month, at twilight, you shall keep it at its appointed time; according to all its statutes and all its rules you shall keep it." ⁴So Moses told the people of Israel that they should keep the Passover. ⁵And they kept the Passover in the first month, on the fourteenth day of the month, at twilight, in the wilderness of Sinai; according to all that the LORD commanded Moses, so the people of Israel did. ⁶And there were certain men who were unclean through touching a dead body, so that they could not keep the Passover on that day, and they came before Moses and Aaron on that day. ⁷And those men said to him, "We are unclean through touching a dead body. Why are we kept from bringing the LORD's offering at its appointed time among the people of Israel?" ⁸And Moses said to them, "Wait, that I may hear what the LORD will command concerning you."

⁹The LORD spoke to Moses, saying, ¹⁰"Speak to the people of Israel, saying, If any one of you or of your descendants is unclean through touching a dead body, or is on a long journey, he shall still keep the Passover to the LORD. ¹¹In the second month on the fourteenth day at twilight they shall keep it. They shall eat it with unleavened bread and bitter herbs. ¹²They shall leave none of it until the morning, nor break any of its bones; according to all the statute for the Passover they shall keep it. ¹³But if anyone who is clean and is not on a journey fails to keep the Passover, that person shall be cut off from his people because he did not bring the LORD's offering at its appointed time; that man

shall bear his sin. ¹⁴And if a stranger sojourns among you and would keep the Passover to the LORD, according to the statute of the Passover and according to its rule, so shall he do. You shall have one statute, both for the sojourner and for the native."

¹⁵On the day that the tabernacle was set up, the cloud covered the tabernacle, the tent of the testimony. And at evening it was over the tabernacle like the appearance of fire until morning. ¹⁶So it was always: the cloud covered it by day¹ and the appearance of fire by night. ¹⁷And whenever the cloud lifted from over the tent, after that the people of Israel set out, and in the place where the cloud settled down, there the people of Israel camped. ¹⁸At the command of the LORD the people of Israel set out, and at the command of the LORD they camped. As long as the cloud rested over the tabernacle, they remained in camp. ¹⁹Even when the cloud continued over the tabernacle many days, the people of Israel kept the charge of the LORD and did not set out. ²⁰Sometimes the cloud was a few days over the tabernacle, and according to the command of the LORD they remained in camp; then according to the command of the LORD they set out. ²¹And sometimes the cloud remained from evening until morning. And when the cloud lifted in the morning, they set out, or if it continued for a day and a night, when the cloud lifted they set out. ²²Whether it was two days, or a month, or a longer time, that the cloud continued over the tabernacle, abiding there, the people of Israel remained in camp and did not set out, but when it lifted they set out. ²³At the command of the LORD they camped, and at the command of the LORD they set out. They kept the charge of the LORD, at the command of the LORD by Moses.

¹ Septuagint, Syriac, Vulgate; Hebrew lacks *by day*

Psalm 45

TO THE CHOIRMASTER: ACCORDING TO LILIES.
A MASKIL[1] OF THE SONS OF KORAH; A LOVE SONG.

My heart overflows with a pleasing theme;
I address my verses to the king;
  my tongue is like the pen of a ready
    scribe.

2 You are the most handsome of the sons
    of men;
  grace is poured upon your lips;
    therefore God has blessed you forever.
3 Gird your sword on your thigh,
    O mighty one,
  in your splendor and majesty!

4 In your majesty ride out victoriously
  for the cause of truth and meekness
    and righteousness;
  let your right hand teach you
    awesome deeds!
5 Your arrows are sharp
  in the heart of the king's enemies;
  the peoples fall under you.

6 Your throne, O God, is forever and ever.
  The scepter of your kingdom is a
    scepter of uprightness;
7 you have loved righteousness and
    hated wickedness.
  Therefore God, your God, has anointed
    you
  with the oil of gladness beyond your
    companions;
8 your robes are all fragrant with myrrh
    and aloes and cassia.
  From ivory palaces stringed instruments
    make you glad;
9 daughters of kings are among your
    ladies of honor;
  at your right hand stands the queen in
    gold of Ophir.

10 Hear, O daughter, and consider, and
    incline your ear:
  forget your people and your father's
    house,
11 and the king will desire your beauty.
  Since he is your lord, bow to him.
12 The people[2] of Tyre will seek your
    favor with gifts,
  the richest of the people.[3]

13 All glorious is the princess in her
    chamber, with robes interwoven
    with gold.
14 In many-colored robes she is led to the
    king,
  with her virgin companions following
    behind her.
15 With joy and gladness they are led along
  as they enter the palace of the king.

16 In place of your fathers shall be your
    sons;
  you will make them princes in all the
    earth.
17 I will cause your name to be
    remembered in all generations;
  therefore nations will praise you
    forever and ever.

Song of Solomon 7

How beautiful are your feet in sandals,
O noble daughter!
  Your rounded thighs are like jewels,
    the work of a master hand.
2 Your navel is a rounded bowl
  that never lacks mixed wine.
  Your belly is a heap of wheat,
    encircled with lilies.
3 Your two breasts are like two fawns,
  twins of a gazelle.
4 Your neck is like an ivory tower.
  Your eyes are pools in Heshbon,
    by the gate of Bath-rabbim.
  Your nose is like a tower of Lebanon,
    which looks toward Damascus.
5 Your head crowns you like Carmel,
  and your flowing locks are like
    purple;
  a king is held captive in the tresses.

6 How beautiful and pleasant you are,
  O loved one, with all your delights![4]
7 Your stature is like a palm tree,
  and your breasts are like its clusters.
8 I say I will climb the palm tree
  and lay hold of its fruit.
  Oh may your breasts be like clusters of
    the vine,
  and the scent of your breath like
    apples,
9 and your mouth[5] like the best wine.

[1] Probably a musical or liturgical term [2] Hebrew daughter [3] Or The daughter of Tyre is here with gifts, the richest of people seek your favor [4] Or among delights [5] Hebrew palate

SHE

It goes down smoothly for my beloved,
    gliding over lips and teeth.[1]

10   I am my beloved's,
    and his desire is for me.

11   Come, my beloved,
    let us go out into the fields
    and lodge in the villages;[2]

12   let us go out early to the vineyards
    and see whether the vines have
        budded,
    whether the grape blossoms have opened
    and the pomegranates are in bloom.
    There I will give you my love.

13   The mandrakes give forth fragrance,
    and beside our doors are all choice
        fruits,
    new as well as old,
    which I have laid up for you, O my
        beloved.

Hebrews 7

For this Melchizedek, king of Salem, priest of the Most High God, met Abraham returning from the slaughter of the kings and blessed him, [2] and to him Abraham apportioned a tenth part of everything. He is first, by translation of his name, king of righteousness, and then he is also king of Salem, that is, king of peace. [3] He is without father or mother or genealogy, having neither beginning of days nor end of life, but resembling the Son of God he continues a priest forever.

[4] See how great this man was to whom Abraham the patriarch gave a tenth of the spoils! [5] And those descendants of Levi who receive the priestly office have a commandment in the law to take tithes from the people, that is, from their brothers,[3] though these also are descended from Abraham. [6] But this man who does not have his descent from them received tithes from Abraham and blessed him who had the promises. [7] It is beyond dispute that the inferior is blessed by the superior. [8] In the one case tithes are received by mortal men, but in the other case, by one of whom it is testified that he lives. [9] One might even say that Levi himself, who receives tithes, paid tithes through Abraham, [10] for he was still in the loins of his ancestor when Melchizedek met him.

[11] Now if perfection had been attainable through the Levitical priesthood (for under it the people received the law), what further need would there have been for another priest to arise after the order of Melchizedek, rather than one named after the order of Aaron? [12] For when there is a change in the priesthood, there is necessarily a change in the law as well. [13] For the one of whom these things are spoken belonged to another tribe, from which no one has ever served at the altar. [14] For it is evident that our Lord was descended from Judah, and in connection with that tribe Moses said nothing about priests.

[15] This becomes even more evident when another priest arises in the likeness of Melchizedek, [16] who has become a priest, not on the basis of a legal requirement concerning bodily descent, but by the power of an indestructible life. [17] For it is witnessed of him,

"You are a priest forever,
    after the order of Melchizedek."

[18] For on the one hand, a former commandment is set aside because of its weakness and uselessness [19] (for the law made nothing perfect); but on the other hand, a better hope is introduced, through which we draw near to God.

[20] And it was not without an oath. For those who formerly became priests were made such without an oath, [21] but this one was made a priest with an oath by the one who said to him:

"The Lord has sworn
    and will not change his mind,
  'You are a priest forever.'"

[22] This makes Jesus the guarantor of a better covenant.

[23] The former priests were many in number, because they were prevented by death from continuing in office, [24] but he holds his priesthood permanently, because he continues forever. [25] Consequently, he is able to save to the uttermost[4] those who draw near to God through him, since he always lives to make intercession for them.

[26] For it was indeed fitting that we should have such a high priest, holy, innocent, unstained, separated from sinners, and exalted above the heavens. [27] He has no need, like those high priests, to offer sacrifices daily, first for his own sins and then for those of

[1] Septuagint, Syriac, Vulgate; Hebrew *causing the lips of sleepers to speak*   [2] Or *among the henna plants*   [3] Or *brothers and sisters*   [4] That is, completely; or *at all times*

the people, since he did this once for all when he offered up himself. [28]For the law appoints men in their weakness as high priests, but the word of the oath, which came later than the law, appoints a Son who has been made perfect forever.

MAY 3

Numbers 10

The LORD spoke to Moses, saying, [2]"Make two silver trumpets. Of hammered work you shall make them, and you shall use them for summoning the congregation and for breaking camp. [3]And when both are blown, all the congregation shall gather themselves to you at the entrance of the tent of meeting. [4]But if they blow only one, then the chiefs, the heads of the tribes of Israel, shall gather themselves to you. [5]When you blow an alarm, the camps that are on the east side shall set out. [6]And when you blow an alarm the second time, the camps that are on the south side shall set out. An alarm is to be blown whenever they are to set out. [7]But when the assembly is to be gathered together, you shall blow a long blast, but you shall not sound an alarm. [8]And the sons of Aaron, the priests, shall blow the trumpets. The trumpets shall be to you for a perpetual statute throughout your generations. [9]And when you go to war in your land against the adversary who oppresses you, then you shall sound an alarm with the trumpets, that you may be remembered before the LORD your God, and you shall be saved from your enemies. [10]On the day of your gladness also, and at your appointed feasts and at the beginnings of your months, you shall blow the trumpets over your burnt offerings and over the sacrifices of your peace offerings. They shall be a reminder of you before your God: I am the LORD your God."

[11]In the second year, in the second month, on the twentieth day of the month, the cloud lifted from over the tabernacle of the testimony, [12]and the people of Israel set out by stages from the wilderness of Sinai. And the cloud settled down in the wilderness of Paran. [13]They set out for the first time at the command of the LORD by Moses. [14]The standard of the camp of the people of Judah set out first by their companies, and over their company was Nahshon the son of Amminadab. [15]And over the company of the tribe of the people of Issachar was Nethanel the son of Zuar. [16]And over the company of the tribe of the people of Zebulun was Eliab the son of Helon.

[17]And when the tabernacle was taken down, the sons of Gershon and the sons of Merari, who carried the tabernacle, set out. [18]And the standard of the camp of Reuben set out by their companies, and over their company was Elizur the son of Shedeur. [19]And over the company of the tribe of the people of Simeon was Shelumiel the son of Zurishaddai. [20]And over the company of the tribe of the people of Gad was Eliasaph the son of Deuel.

[21]Then the Kohathites set out, carrying the holy things, and the tabernacle was set up before their arrival. [22]And the standard of the camp of the people of Ephraim set out by their companies, and over their company was Elishama the son of Ammihud. [23]And over the company of the tribe of the people of Manasseh was Gamaliel the son of Pedahzur. [24]And over the company of the tribe of the people of Benjamin was Abidan the son of Gideoni.

[25]Then the standard of the camp of the people of Dan, acting as the rear guard of all the camps, set out by their companies, and over their company was Ahiezer the son of Ammishaddai. [26]And over the company of the tribe of the people of Asher was Pagiel the son of Ochran. [27]And over the company of the tribe of the people of Naphtali was Ahira the son of Enan. [28]This was the order of march of the

people of Israel by their companies, when they set out.

²⁹And Moses said to Hobab the son of Reuel the Midianite, Moses' father-in-law, "We are setting out for the place of which the LORD said, 'I will give it to you.' Come with us, and we will do good to you, for the LORD has promised good to Israel." ³⁰But he said to him, "I will not go. I will depart to my own land and to my kindred." ³¹And he said, "Please do not leave us, for you know where we should camp in the wilderness, and you will serve as eyes for us. ³²And if you do go with us, whatever good the LORD will do to us, the same will we do to you."

³³So they set out from the mount of the LORD three days' journey. And the ark of the covenant of the LORD went before them three days' journey, to seek out a resting place for them. ³⁴And the cloud of the LORD was over them by day, whenever they set out from the camp.

³⁵And whenever the ark set out, Moses said, "Arise, O LORD, and let your enemies be scattered, and let those who hate you flee before you." ³⁶And when it rested, he said, "Return, O LORD, to the ten thousand thousands of Israel."

Psalm 46–47

To the choirmaster. Of the Sons of Korah. According to Alamoth.[1] A Song.

God is our refuge and strength,
  a very present[2] help in trouble.
2   Therefore we will not fear though the
      earth gives way,
    though the mountains be moved into
      the heart of the sea,
3   though its waters roar and foam,
    though the mountains tremble at its
      swelling.   *Selah*

4   There is a river whose streams make
      glad the city of God,
    the holy habitation of the Most High.
5   God is in the midst of her; she shall not
      be moved;
    God will help her when morning
      dawns.
6   The nations rage, the kingdoms totter;
    he utters his voice, the earth melts.
7   The LORD of hosts is with us;
    the God of Jacob is our fortress.   *Selah*

8   Come, behold the works of the LORD,
      how he has brought desolations on
      the earth.
9   He makes wars cease to the end of the
      earth;
    he breaks the bow and shatters the
      spear;
    he burns the chariots with fire.
10 "Be still, and know that I am God.
    I will be exalted among the nations,
    I will be exalted in the earth!"
11 The LORD of hosts is with us;
    the God of Jacob is our fortress.   *Selah*

To the choirmaster. A Psalm of the Sons of Korah.

Clap your hands, all peoples!
  Shout to God with loud songs of joy!
2   For the LORD, the Most High, is to be
      feared,
    a great king over all the earth.
3   He subdued peoples under us,
    and nations under our feet.
4   He chose our heritage for us,
    the pride of Jacob whom he loves.*Selah*

5   God has gone up with a shout,
    the LORD with the sound of a trumpet.
6   Sing praises to God, sing praises!
    Sing praises to our King, sing praises!
7   For God is the King of all the earth;
    sing praises with a psalm![3]

8   God reigns over the nations;
    God sits on his holy throne.
9   The princes of the peoples gather
    as the people of the God of Abraham.
    For the shields of the earth belong to
      God;
    he is highly exalted!

Song of Solomon 8

Oh that you were like a brother to me
  who nursed at my mother's breasts!
    If I found you outside, I would kiss you,
    and none would despise me.
2   I would lead you and bring you
      into the house of my mother—
    she who used to teach me.
    I would give you spiced wine to drink,
      the juice of my pomegranate.

¹ Probably a musical or liturgical term ² Or *well proved* ³ Hebrew *maskil*

³ His left hand is under my head,
     and his right hand embraces me!
⁴ I adjure you, O daughters of Jerusalem,
     that you not stir up or awaken love
       until it pleases.

⁵ Who is that coming up from the
       wilderness,
     leaning on her beloved?

Under the apple tree I awakened you.
There your mother was in labor with
     you;
     there she who bore you was in labor.

⁶ Set me as a seal upon your heart,
     as a seal upon your arm,
for love is strong as death,
     jealousy¹ is fierce as the grave.²
Its flashes are flashes of fire,
     the very flame of the Lord.
⁷ Many waters cannot quench love,
     neither can floods drown it.
If a man offered for love
     all the wealth of his house,
he³ would be utterly despised.

OTHERS
⁸ We have a little sister,
     and she has no breasts.
What shall we do for our sister
     on the day when she is spoken for?
⁹ If she is a wall,
     we will build on her a battlement of
       silver,
but if she is a door,
     we will enclose her with boards of
       cedar.

SHE
¹⁰ I was a wall,
     and my breasts were like towers;
then I was in his eyes
     as one who finds⁴ peace.
¹¹ Solomon had a vineyard at Baal-hamon;
     he let out the vineyard to keepers;
     each one was to bring for its fruit a
       thousand pieces of silver.
¹² My vineyard, my very own, is before me;
     you, O Solomon, may have the
       thousand,
     and the keepers of the fruit two
       hundred.

HE
¹³ O you who dwell in the gardens,
     with companions listening for your
       voice;
     let me hear it.

SHE
¹⁴ Make haste, my beloved,
     and be like a gazelle
or a young stag
     on the mountains of spices.

Hebrews 8

Now the point in what we are saying is this: we have such a high priest, one who is seated at the right hand of the throne of the Majesty in heaven, ² a minister in the holy places, in the true tent⁵ that the Lord set up, not man. ³ For every high priest is appointed to offer gifts and sacrifices; thus it is necessary for this priest also to have something to offer. ⁴ Now if he were on earth, he would not be a priest at all, since there are priests who offer gifts according to the law. ⁵ They serve a copy and shadow of the heavenly things. For when Moses was about to erect the tent, he was instructed by God, saying, "See that you make everything according to the pattern that was shown you on the mountain." ⁶ But as it is, Christ⁶ has obtained a ministry that is as much more excellent than the old as the covenant he mediates is better, since it is enacted on better promises. ⁷ For if that first covenant had been faultless, there would have been no occasion to look for a second.

⁸ For he finds fault with them when he says:⁷

"Behold, the days are coming, declares
     the Lord,
     when I will establish a new covenant
       with the house of Israel
       and with the house of Judah,
⁹ not like the covenant that I made with
       their fathers
     on the day when I took them by the
       hand to bring them out of the land
       of Egypt.
For they did not continue in my
       covenant,
     and so I showed no concern for them,
       declares the Lord.

---

¹ Or *ardor*   ² Hebrew *as Sheol*   ³ Or *it*   ⁴ Or *brings out*   ⁵ Or *tabernacle; also verse 5*   ⁶ Greek *he*   ⁷ Some manuscripts *For finding fault with it he says to them*

10 For this is the covenant that I will make
    with the house of Israel
    after those days, declares the Lord:
  I will put my laws into their minds,
    and write them on their hearts,
  and I will be their God,
    and they shall be my people.
11 And they shall not teach, each one his
    neighbor
  and each one his brother, saying,
    'Know the Lord,'

for they shall all know me,
  from the least of them to the
    greatest.
12 For I will be merciful toward their
    iniquities,
  and I will remember their sins no
    more."

[13] In speaking of a new covenant, he makes the first one obsolete. And what is becoming obsolete and growing old is ready to vanish away.

MAY 4

Numbers 11

And the people complained in the hearing of the LORD about their misfortunes, and when the LORD heard it, his anger was kindled, and the fire of the LORD burned among them and consumed some outlying parts of the camp. [2] Then the people cried out to Moses, and Moses prayed to the LORD, and the fire died down. [3] So the name of that place was called Taberah,[1] because the fire of the LORD burned among them.

[4] Now the rabble that was among them had a strong craving. And the people of Israel also wept again and said, "Oh that we had meat to eat! [5] We remember the fish we ate in Egypt that cost nothing, the cucumbers, the melons, the leeks, the onions, and the garlic. [6] But now our strength is dried up, and there is nothing at all but this manna to look at."

[7] Now the manna was like coriander seed, and its appearance like that of bdellium. [8] The people went about and gathered it and ground it in handmills or beat it in mortars and boiled it in pots and made cakes of it. And the taste of it was like the taste of cakes baked with oil. [9] When the dew fell upon the camp in the night, the manna fell with it.

[10] Moses heard the people weeping throughout their clans, everyone at the door of his tent. And the anger of the LORD blazed hotly, and Moses was displeased. [11] Moses said to the LORD, "Why have you dealt ill with your servant? And why have I not found favor in your sight, that you lay the burden of all this people on me? [12] Did I conceive all this people? Did I give them birth, that you should say to me, 'Carry them in your bosom, as a nurse carries a nursing child,' to the land that you swore to give their fathers? [13] Where am I to get meat to give to all this people? For they weep before me and say, 'Give us meat, that we may eat.' [14] I am not able to carry all this people alone; the burden is too heavy for me. [15] If you will treat me like this, kill me at once, if I find favor in your sight, that I may not see my wretchedness."

[16] Then the LORD said to Moses, "Gather for me seventy men of the elders of Israel, whom you know to be the elders of the people and officers over them, and bring them to the tent of meeting, and let them take their stand there with you. [17] And I will come down and talk with you there. And I will take some of the Spirit that is on you and put it on them, and they shall bear the burden of the people with you, so that you may not bear it yourself alone. [18] And say to the people, 'Consecrate yourselves for tomorrow, and you shall eat meat, for you have wept in the hearing of the LORD, saying, "Who will give us meat to eat? For it was better for us in Egypt." Therefore the LORD will give you meat, and you shall eat. [19] You shall not eat just one day, or

---

[1] *Taberah* means *burning*

two days, or five days, or ten days, or twenty days, ²⁰but a whole month, until it comes out at your nostrils and becomes loathsome to you, because you have rejected the LORD who is among you and have wept before him, saying, "Why did we come out of Egypt?" ' " ²¹But Moses said, "The people among whom I am number six hundred thousand on foot, and you have said, 'I will give them meat, that they may eat a whole month!' ²²Shall flocks and herds be slaughtered for them, and be enough for them? Or shall all the fish of the sea be gathered together for them, and be enough for them?" ²³And the LORD said to Moses, "Is the LORD's hand shortened? Now you shall see whether my word will come true for you or not."

²⁴So Moses went out and told the people the words of the LORD. And he gathered seventy men of the elders of the people and placed them around the tent. ²⁵Then the LORD came down in the cloud and spoke to him, and took some of the Spirit that was on him and put it on the seventy elders. And as soon as the Spirit rested on them, they prophesied. But they did not continue doing it.

²⁶Now two men remained in the camp, one named Eldad, and the other named Medad, and the Spirit rested on them. They were among those registered, but they had not gone out to the tent, and so they prophesied in the camp. ²⁷And a young man ran and told Moses, "Eldad and Medad are prophesying in the camp." ²⁸And Joshua the son of Nun, the assistant of Moses from his youth, said, "My lord Moses, stop them." ²⁹But Moses said to him, "Are you jealous for my sake? Would that all the LORD's people were prophets, that the LORD would put his Spirit on them!" ³⁰And Moses and the elders of Israel returned to the camp.

³¹Then a wind from the LORD sprang up, and it brought quail from the sea and let them fall beside the camp, about a day's journey on this side and a day's journey on the other side, around the camp, and about two cubits¹ above the ground. ³²And the people rose all that day and all night and all the next day, and gathered the quail. Those who gathered least gathered ten homers.² And they spread them out for themselves all around the camp. ³³While the meat was yet between their teeth, before it was consumed, the anger of the LORD was kindled

against the people, and the LORD struck down the people with a very great plague. ³⁴Therefore the name of that place was called Kibroth-hattaavah,³ because there they buried the people who had the craving. ³⁵From Kibroth-hattaavah the people journeyed to Hazeroth, and they remained at Hazeroth.

Psalm 48

A SONG. A PSALM OF THE SONS OF KORAH.

Great is the LORD and greatly to be praised
in the city of our God!
His holy mountain, ²beautiful in elevation,
is the joy of all the earth,
Mount Zion, in the far north,
the city of the great King.
3 Within her citadels God
has made himself known as a fortress.

4 For behold, the kings assembled;
they came on together.
5 As soon as they saw it, they were astounded;
they were in panic; they took to flight.
6 Trembling took hold of them there,
anguish as of a woman in labor.
7 By the east wind you shattered
the ships of Tarshish.
8 As we have heard, so have we seen
in the city of the LORD of hosts,
in the city of our God,
which God will establish forever. Selah

9 We have thought on your steadfast love, O God,
in the midst of your temple.
10 As your name, O God,
so your praise reaches to the ends of the earth.
Your right hand is filled with righteousness.
11 Let Mount Zion be glad!
Let the daughters of Judah rejoice
because of your judgments!

12 Walk about Zion, go around her,
number her towers,
13 consider well her ramparts,
go through her citadels,
that you may tell the next generation
14 that this is God,

¹ A cubit was about 18 inches or 45 centimeters ² A homer was about 6 bushels or 220 liters ³ Kibroth-hattaavah means graves of craving

our God forever and ever.
  He will guide us forever.[1]

Isaiah 1

The vision of Isaiah the son of Amoz, which
he saw concerning Judah and Jerusalem in
the days of Uzziah, Jotham, Ahaz, and Hezekiah, kings of Judah.

2   Hear, O heavens, and give ear, O earth;
      for the LORD has spoken:
   "Children[2] have I reared and brought up,
      but they have rebelled against me.
3   The ox knows its owner,
      and the donkey its master's crib,
   but Israel does not know,
      my people do not understand."

4   Ah, sinful nation,
      a people laden with iniquity,
   offspring of evildoers,
      children who deal corruptly!
   They have forsaken the LORD,
      they have despised the Holy One of
        Israel,
      they are utterly estranged.

5   Why will you still be struck down?
      Why will you continue to rebel?
   The whole head is sick,
      and the whole heart faint.
6   From the sole of the foot even to the
        head,
      there is no soundness in it,
   but bruises and sores
      and raw wounds;
   they are not pressed out or bound up
      or softened with oil.

7   Your country lies desolate;
      your cities are burned with fire;
   in your very presence
      foreigners devour your land;
   it is desolate, as overthrown by
        foreigners.
8   And the daughter of Zion is left
      like a booth in a vineyard,
   like a lodge in a cucumber field,
      like a besieged city.
9   If the LORD of hosts
      had not left us a few survivors,

   we should have been like Sodom,
      and become like Gomorrah.

10   Hear the word of the LORD,
       you rulers of Sodom!
    Give ear to the teaching[3] of our God,
       you people of Gomorrah!
11   "What to me is the multitude of your
         sacrifices?
       says the LORD;
    I have had enough of burnt offerings of
         rams
       and the fat of well-fed beasts;
    I do not delight in the blood of bulls,
       or of lambs, or of goats.

12   "When you come to appear before me,
       who has required of you
       this trampling of my courts?
13   Bring no more vain offerings;
       incense is an abomination to me.
    New moon and Sabbath and the calling
         of convocations—
       I cannot endure iniquity and solemn
         assembly.
14   Your new moons and your appointed
         feasts
       my soul hates;
    they have become a burden to me;
       I am weary of bearing them.
15   When you spread out your hands,
       I will hide my eyes from you;
    even though you make many prayers,
       I will not listen;
       your hands are full of blood.
16   Wash yourselves; make yourselves clean;
       remove the evil of your deeds from
         before my eyes;
       cease to do evil,
17   learn to do good;
    seek justice,
       correct oppression;
    bring justice to the fatherless,
       plead the widow's cause.
18   "Come now, let us reason[4] together, says
         the LORD:
    though your sins are like scarlet,
       they shall be as white as snow;
    though they are red like crimson,
       they shall become like wool.
19   If you are willing and obedient,
       you shall eat the good of the land;

---

[1] Septuagint; another reading is (compare Jerome, Syriac) *He will guide us beyond death* [2] Or *Sons*; also verse 4 [3] Or *law* [4] Or *dispute*

²⁰ but if you refuse and rebel,
  you shall be eaten by the sword;
  for the mouth of the LORD has
    spoken."

²¹ How the faithful city
  has become a whore,¹
  she who was full of justice!
Righteousness lodged in her,
  but now murderers.
²² Your silver has become dross,
  your best wine mixed with water.
²³ Your princes are rebels
  and companions of thieves.
Everyone loves a bribe
  and runs after gifts.
They do not bring justice to the
    fatherless,
  and the widow's cause does not come
    to them.

²⁴ Therefore the Lord declares,
  the LORD of hosts,
  the Mighty One of Israel:
"Ah, I will get relief from my enemies
  and avenge myself on my foes.
²⁵ I will turn my hand against you
  and will smelt away your dross as with
    lye
  and remove all your alloy.
²⁶ And I will restore your judges as at the
    first,
  and your counselors as at the
    beginning.
Afterward you shall be called the city of
    righteousness,
  the faithful city."

²⁷ Zion shall be redeemed by justice,
  and those in her who repent, by
    righteousness.
²⁸ But rebels and sinners shall be broken
    together,
  and those who forsake the LORD shall
    be consumed.
²⁹ For they² shall be ashamed of the oaks
    that you desired;
  and you shall blush for the gardens
    that you have chosen.
³⁰ For you shall be like an oak
  whose leaf withers,
  and like a garden without water.

³¹ And the strong shall become tinder,
  and his work a spark,
  and both of them shall burn together,
  with none to quench them.

Hebrews 9

Now even the first covenant had regula-tions for worship and an earthly place of holiness. ²For a tent³ was prepared, the first section, in which were the lampstand and the table and the bread of the Presence.⁴ It is called the Holy Place. ³Behind the second curtain was a second section⁵ called the Most Holy Place, ⁴having the golden altar of incense and the ark of the covenant covered on all sides with gold, in which was a golden urn holding the manna, and Aaron's staff that budded, and the tablets of the covenant. ⁵Above it were the cherubim of glory overshadowing the mercy seat. Of these things we cannot now speak in detail.

⁶These preparations having thus been made, the priests go regularly into the first section, performing their ritual duties, ⁷but into the second only the high priest goes, and he but once a year, and not without taking blood, which he offers for himself and for the unin-tentional sins of the people. ⁸By this the Holy Spirit indicates that the way into the holy places is not yet opened as long as the first sec-tion is still standing ⁹(which is symbolic for the present age).⁶ According to this arrangement, gifts and sacrifices are offered that cannot per-fect the conscience of the worshiper, ¹⁰but deal only with food and drink and various wash-ings, regulations for the body imposed until the time of reformation.

¹¹But when Christ appeared as a high priest of the good things that have come,⁷ then through the greater and more perfect tent (not made with hands, that is, not of this creation) ¹²he entered once for all into the holy places, not by means of the blood of goats and calves but by means of his own blood, thus securing an eternal redemption. ¹³For if the blood of goats and bulls, and the sprinkling of defiled persons with the ashes of a heifer, sanctify⁸ for the purification of the flesh, ¹⁴how much more will the blood of Christ, who through the eter-nal Spirit offered himself without blemish to

¹ Or become unchaste ² Some Hebrew manuscripts you ³ Or tabernacle; also verses 11, 21 ⁴ Greek the presentation of the loaves ⁵ Greek tent; also verses 6, 8 ⁶ Or which is symbolic for the age then present ⁷ Some manuscripts good things to come ⁸ Or For if the sprinkling of defiled persons with the blood of goats and bulls and with the ashes of a heifer sanctifies

God, purify our[1] conscience from dead works to serve the living God.

¹⁵Therefore he is the mediator of a new covenant, so that those who are called may receive the promised eternal inheritance, since a death has occurred that redeems them from the transgressions committed under the first covenant.[2] ¹⁶For where a will is involved, the death of the one who made it must be established. ¹⁷For a will takes effect only at death, since it is not in force as long as the one who made it is alive. ¹⁸Therefore not even the first covenant was inaugurated without blood. ¹⁹For when every commandment of the law had been declared by Moses to all the people, he took the blood of calves and goats, with water and scarlet wool and hyssop, and sprinkled both the book itself and all the people, ²⁰saying, "This is the blood of the covenant that God commanded for you." ²¹And in the same way he sprinkled with the blood both the tent and all the vessels used in worship. ²²Indeed, under the law

almost everything is purified with blood, and without the shedding of blood there is no forgiveness of sins.

²³Thus it was necessary for the copies of the heavenly things to be purified with these rites, but the heavenly things themselves with better sacrifices than these. ²⁴For Christ has entered, not into holy places made with hands, which are copies of the true things, but into heaven itself, now to appear in the presence of God on our behalf. ²⁵Nor was it to offer himself repeatedly, as the high priest enters the holy places every year with blood not his own, ²⁶for then he would have had to suffer repeatedly since the foundation of the world. But as it is, he has appeared once for all at the end of the ages to put away sin by the sacrifice of himself. ²⁷And just as it is appointed for man to die once, and after that comes judgment, ²⁸so Christ, having been offered once to bear the sins of many, will appear a second time, not to deal with sin but to save those who are eagerly waiting for him.

MAY 5

Numbers 12–13

Miriam and Aaron spoke against Moses because of the Cushite woman whom he had married, for he had married a Cushite woman. ²And they said, "Has the LORD indeed spoken only through Moses? Has he not spoken through us also?" And the LORD heard it. ³Now the man Moses was very meek, more than all people who were on the face of the earth. ⁴And suddenly the LORD said to Moses and to Aaron and Miriam, "Come out, you three, to the tent of meeting." And the three of them came out. ⁵And the LORD came down in a pillar of cloud and stood at the entrance of the tent and called Aaron and Miriam, and they both came forward. ⁶And he said, "Hear my words: If there is a prophet among you, I the LORD make myself known to him in a vision; I speak with him in a dream. ⁷Not so with my servant Moses. He is faithful in all my house.

⁸With him I speak mouth to mouth, clearly, and not in riddles, and he beholds the form of the LORD. Why then were you not afraid to speak against my servant Moses?" ⁹And the anger of the LORD was kindled against them, and he departed.

¹⁰When the cloud removed from over the tent, behold, Miriam was leprous,[3] like snow. And Aaron turned toward Miriam, and behold, she was leprous. ¹¹And Aaron said to Moses, "Oh, my lord, do not punish us[4] because we have done foolishly and have sinned. ¹²Let her not be as one dead, whose flesh is half eaten away when he comes out of his mother's womb." ¹³And Moses cried to the LORD, "O God, please heal her—please." ¹⁴But the LORD said to Moses, "If her father had but spit in her face, should she not be shamed seven days? Let her be shut outside the camp seven days, and after

that she may be brought in again." [15] So Miriam was shut outside the camp seven days, and the people did not set out on the march till Miriam was brought in again. [16] After that the people set out from Hazeroth, and camped in the wilderness of Paran.

[13:1] The LORD spoke to Moses, saying, [2] "Send men to spy out the land of Canaan, which I am giving to the people of Israel. From each tribe of their fathers you shall send a man, every one a chief among them." [3] So Moses sent them from the wilderness of Paran, according to the command of the LORD, all of them men who were heads of the people of Israel. [4] And these were their names: From the tribe of Reuben, Shammua the son of Zaccur; [5] from the tribe of Simeon, Shaphat the son of Hori; [6] from the tribe of Judah, Caleb the son of Jephunneh; [7] from the tribe of Issachar, Igal the son of Joseph; [8] from the tribe of Ephraim, Hoshea the son of Nun; [9] from the tribe of Benjamin, Palti the son of Raphu; [10] from the tribe of Zebulun, Gaddiel the son of Sodi; [11] from the tribe of Joseph (that is, from the tribe of Manasseh), Gaddi the son of Susi; [12] from the tribe of Dan, Ammiel the son of Gemalli; [13] from the tribe of Asher, Sethur the son of Michael; [14] from the tribe of Naphtali, Nahbi the son of Vophsi; [15] from the tribe of Gad, Geuel the son of Machi. [16] These were the names of the men whom Moses sent to spy out the land. And Moses called Hoshea the son of Nun Joshua.

[17] Moses sent them to spy out the land of Canaan and said to them, "Go up into the Negeb and go up into the hill country, [18] and see what the land is, and whether the people who dwell in it are strong or weak, whether they are few or many, [19] and whether the land that they dwell in is good or bad, and whether the cities that they dwell in are camps or strongholds, [20] and whether the land is rich or poor, and whether there are trees in it or not. Be of good courage and bring some of the fruit of the land." Now the time was the season of the first ripe grapes.

[21] So they went up and spied out the land from the wilderness of Zin to Rehob, near Lebo-hamath. [22] They went up into the Negeb and came to Hebron. Ahiman, Sheshai, and Talmai, the descendants of Anak, were there. (Hebron was built seven years before Zoan in Egypt.) [23] And they came to the Valley of Eshcol

and cut down from there a branch with a single cluster of grapes, and they carried it on a pole between two of them; they also brought some pomegranates and figs. [24] That place was called the Valley of Eshcol,[1] because of the cluster that the people of Israel cut down from there.

[25] At the end of forty days they returned from spying out the land. [26] And they came to Moses and Aaron and to all the congregation of the people of Israel in the wilderness of Paran, at Kadesh. They brought back word to them and to all the congregation, and showed them the fruit of the land. [27] And they told him, "We came to the land to which you sent us. It flows with milk and honey, and this is its fruit. [28] However, the people who dwell in the land are strong, and the cities are fortified and very large. And besides, we saw the descendants of Anak there. [29] The Amalekites dwell in the land of the Negeb. The Hittites, the Jebusites, and the Amorites dwell in the hill country. And the Canaanites dwell by the sea, and along the Jordan."

[30] But Caleb quieted the people before Moses and said, "Let us go up at once and occupy it, for we are well able to overcome it." [31] Then the men who had gone up with him said, "We are not able to go up against the people, for they are stronger than we are." [32] So they brought to the people of Israel a bad report of the land that they had spied out, saying, "The land, through which we have gone to spy it out, is a land that devours its inhabitants, and all the people that we saw in it are of great height. [33] And there we saw the Nephilim (the sons of Anak, who come from the Nephilim), and we seemed to ourselves like grasshoppers, and so we seemed to them."

Psalm 49

To the choirmaster. A Psalm of the Sons of Korah.

Hear this, all peoples!
   Give ear, all inhabitants of the world,
[2]   both low and high,
      rich and poor together!
[3]   My mouth shall speak wisdom;
      the meditation of my heart shall be
      understanding.
[4]   I will incline my ear to a proverb;
      I will solve my riddle to the music of
      the lyre.

[1] *Eshcol means cluster*

5 Why should I fear in times of trouble,
   when the iniquity of those who cheat
     me surrounds me,
6 those who trust in their wealth
   and boast of the abundance of their
     riches?
7 Truly no man can ransom another,
   or give to God the price of his life,
8 for the ransom of their life is costly
   and can never suffice,
9 that he should live on forever
   and never see the pit.

10 For he sees that even the wise die;
   the fool and the stupid alike must
     perish
   and leave their wealth to others.
11 Their graves are their homes forever,[1]
   their dwelling places to all generations,
   though they called lands by their own
     names.
12 Man in his pomp will not remain;
   he is like the beasts that perish.

13 This is the path of those who have
     foolish confidence;
   yet after them people approve of their
     boasts.[2]   *Selah*
14 Like sheep they are appointed for Sheol;
   death shall be their shepherd,
   and the upright shall rule over them in
     the morning.
   Their form shall be consumed in
     Sheol, with no place to dwell.
15 But God will ransom my soul from the
     power of Sheol,
   for he will receive me.   *Selah*

16 Be not afraid when a man becomes rich,
   when the glory of his house increases.
17 For when he dies he will carry nothing
     away;
   his glory will not go down after him.
18 For though, while he lives, he counts
     himself blessed
   —and though you get praise when
     you do well for yourself—
19 his soul will go to the generation of his
     fathers,
   who will never again see light.
20 Man in his pomp yet without
     understanding is like the beasts
     that perish.

Isaiah 2

The word that Isaiah the son of Amoz saw concerning Judah and Jerusalem.

2 It shall come to pass in the latter days
   that the mountain of the house of the
     Lord
   shall be established as the highest of the
     mountains,
   and shall be lifted up above the hills;
   and all the nations shall flow to it,
3   and many peoples shall come, and
     say:
"Come, let us go up to the mountain of
     the Lord,
   to the house of the God of Jacob,
   that he may teach us his ways
   and that we may walk in his paths."
For out of Zion shall go the law,[3]
   and the word of the Lord from
     Jerusalem.
4 He shall judge between the nations,
   and shall decide disputes for many
     peoples;
   and they shall beat their swords into
     plowshares,
   and their spears into pruning hooks;
   nation shall not lift up sword against
     nation,
   neither shall they learn war anymore.

5 O house of Jacob,
   come, let us walk
   in the light of the Lord.

6 For you have rejected your people,
   the house of Jacob,
   because they are full of things from the
     east
   and of fortune-tellers like the
     Philistines,
   and they strike hands with the
     children of foreigners.
7 Their land is filled with silver and gold,
   and there is no end to their treasures;
   their land is filled with horses,
   and there is no end to their chariots.
8 Their land is filled with idols;
   they bow down to the work of their
     hands,
   to what their own fingers have made.

---

[1] Septuagint, Syriac, Targum; Hebrew *Their inward thought was that their homes were forever*   [2] Or *and of those after them who approve of their boasts*   [3] Or *teaching*

9   So man is humbled,
     and each one is brought low—
     do not forgive them!
10 Enter into the rock
     and hide in the dust
   from before the terror of the LORD,
     and from the splendor of his majesty.
11 The haughty looks of man shall be
     brought low,
   and the lofty pride of men shall be
     humbled,
   and the LORD alone will be exalted in
     that day.

12 For the LORD of hosts has a day
     against all that is proud and lofty,
     against all that is lifted up—and it
      shall be brought low;
13 against all the cedars of Lebanon,
     lofty and lifted up;
   and against all the oaks of Bashan;
14 against all the lofty mountains,
     and against all the uplifted hills;
15 against every high tower,
     and against every fortified wall;
16 against all the ships of Tarshish,
     and against all the beautiful craft.
17 And the haughtiness of man shall be
     humbled,
   and the lofty pride of men shall be
     brought low,
   and the LORD alone will be exalted in
     that day.
18 And the idols shall utterly pass away.
19 And people shall enter the caves of the
     rocks
   and the holes of the ground,[1]
   from before the terror of the LORD,
     and from the splendor of his majesty,
     when he rises to terrify the earth.

20 In that day mankind will cast away
     their idols of silver and their idols of
     gold,
   which they made for themselves to
     worship,
   to the moles and to the bats,
21 to enter the caverns of the rocks
     and the clefts of the cliffs,
   from before the terror of the LORD,
     and from the splendor of his majesty,
     when he rises to terrify the earth.

22 Stop regarding man
     in whose nostrils is breath,
     for of what account is he?

Hebrews 10

For since the law has but a shadow of the good things to come instead of the true form of these realities, it can never, by the same sacrifices that are continually offered every year, make perfect those who draw near. ²Otherwise, would they not have ceased to be offered, since the worshipers, having once been cleansed, would no longer have any consciousness of sins? ³But in these sacrifices there is a reminder of sins every year. ⁴For it is impossible for the blood of bulls and goats to take away sins.

⁵Consequently, when Christ[2] came into the world, he said,

"Sacrifices and offerings you have not
    desired,
  but a body have you prepared for me;
6 in burnt offerings and sin offerings
   you have taken no pleasure.
7 Then I said, 'Behold, I have come to do
    your will, O God,
  as it is written of me in the scroll of
    the book.'"

⁸When he said above, "You have neither desired nor taken pleasure in sacrifices and offerings and burnt offerings and sin offerings" (these are offered according to the law), ⁹then he added, "Behold, I have come to do your will." He does away with the first in order to establish the second. ¹⁰And by that will we have been sanctified through the offering of the body of Jesus Christ once for all.

¹¹And every priest stands daily at his service, offering repeatedly the same sacrifices, which can never take away sins. ¹²But when Christ[3] had offered for all time a single sacrifice for sins, he sat down at the right hand of God, ¹³waiting from that time until his enemies should be made a footstool for his feet. ¹⁴For by a single offering he has perfected for all time those who are being sanctified.

¹⁵And the Holy Spirit also bears witness to us; for after saying,

[1] Hebrew dust [2] Greek he [3] Greek this one

16 "This is the covenant that I will make
      with them
    after those days, declares the Lord:
  I will put my laws on their hearts,
    and write them on their minds,"

17 then he adds,

  "I will remember their sins and their
    lawless deeds no more."

18 Where there is forgiveness of these, there is
no longer any offering for sin.

19 Therefore, brothers,[1] since we have confidence to enter the holy places by the blood
of Jesus, 20 by the new and living way that he
opened for us through the curtain, that is,
through his flesh, 21 and since we have a great
priest over the house of God, 22 let us draw near
with a true heart in full assurance of faith,
with our hearts sprinkled clean from an evil
conscience and our bodies washed with pure
water. 23 Let us hold fast the confession of our
hope without wavering, for he who promised
is faithful. 24 And let us consider how to stir
up one another to love and good works, 25 not
neglecting to meet together, as is the habit of
some, but encouraging one another, and all the
more as you see the Day drawing near.

26 For if we go on sinning deliberately after
receiving the knowledge of the truth, there
no longer remains a sacrifice for sins, 27 but
a fearful expectation of judgment, and a fury
of fire that will consume the adversaries.
28 Anyone who has set aside the law of Moses

dies without mercy on the evidence of two or
three witnesses. 29 How much worse punishment, do you think, will be deserved by the one
who has trampled underfoot the Son of God,
and has profaned the blood of the covenant by
which he was sanctified, and has outraged the
Spirit of grace? 30 For we know him who said,
"Vengeance is mine; I will repay." And again,
"The Lord will judge his people." 31 It is a fearful
thing to fall into the hands of the living God.

32 But recall the former days when, after
you were enlightened, you endured a hard
struggle with sufferings, 33 sometimes being
publicly exposed to reproach and affliction,
and sometimes being partners with those so
treated. 34 For you had compassion on those in
prison, and you joyfully accepted the plundering of your property, since you knew that you
yourselves had a better possession and an abiding one. 35 Therefore do not throw away your
confidence, which has a great reward. 36 For you
have need of endurance, so that when you have
done the will of God you may receive what is
promised. 37 For,

  "Yet a little while,
    and the coming one will come and
      will not delay;
38   but my righteous one shall live by faith,
    and if he shrinks back,
      my soul has no pleasure in him."

39 But we are not of those who shrink back and
are destroyed, but of those who have faith and
preserve their souls.

MAY 6

Numbers 14

Then all the congregation raised a loud cry,
and the people wept that night. 2 And all the
people of Israel grumbled against Moses and
Aaron. The whole congregation said to them,
"Would that we had died in the land of Egypt!
Or would that we had died in this wilderness!
3 Why is the LORD bringing us into this land,

to fall by the sword? Our wives and our little
ones will become a prey. Would it not be better for us to go back to Egypt?" 4 And they said
to one another, "Let us choose a leader and go
back to Egypt."

5 Then Moses and Aaron fell on their faces
before all the assembly of the congregation

1 Or brothers and sisters

of the people of Israel. **6**And Joshua the son of Nun and Caleb the son of Jephunneh, who were among those who had spied out the land, tore their clothes **7**and said to all the congregation of the people of Israel, "The land, which we passed through to spy it out, is an exceedingly good land. **8**If the LORD delights in us, he will bring us into this land and give it to us, a land that flows with milk and honey. **9**Only do not rebel against the LORD. And do not fear the people of the land, for they are bread for us. Their protection is removed from them, and the LORD is with us; do not fear them." **10**Then all the congregation said to stone them with stones. But the glory of the LORD appeared at the tent of meeting to all the people of Israel.

11And the LORD said to Moses, "How long will this people despise me? And how long will they not believe in me, in spite of all the signs that I have done among them? **12**I will strike them with the pestilence and disinherit them, and I will make of you a nation greater and mightier than they."

13But Moses said to the LORD, "Then the Egyptians will hear of it, for you brought up this people in your might from among them, **14**and they will tell the inhabitants of this land. They have heard that you, O LORD, are in the midst of this people. For you, O LORD, are seen face to face, and your cloud stands over them and you go before them, in a pillar of cloud by day and in a pillar of fire by night. **15**Now if you kill this people as one man, then the nations who have heard your fame will say, **16**'It is because the LORD was not able to bring this people into the land that he swore to give to them that he has killed them in the wilderness.' **17**And now, please let the power of the Lord be great as you have promised, saying, **18**'The LORD is slow to anger and abounding in steadfast love, forgiving iniquity and transgression, but he will by no means clear the guilty, visiting the iniquity of the fathers on the children, to the third and the fourth generation.' **19**Please pardon the iniquity of this people, according to the greatness of your steadfast love, just as you have forgiven this people, from Egypt until now."

20Then the LORD said, "I have pardoned, according to your word. **21**But truly, as I live, and as all the earth shall be filled with the glory of the LORD, **22**none of the men who have seen my glory and my signs that I did in Egypt and in the wilderness, and yet have put me to the test these ten times and have not obeyed my voice, **23**shall see the land that I swore to give to their fathers. And none of those who despised me shall see it. **24**But my servant Caleb, because he has a different spirit and has followed me fully, I will bring into the land into which he went, and his descendants shall possess it. **25**Now, since the Amalekites and the Canaanites dwell in the valleys, turn tomorrow and set out for the wilderness by the way to the Red Sea."

26And the LORD spoke to Moses and to Aaron, saying, **27**"How long shall this wicked congregation grumble against me? I have heard the grumblings of the people of Israel, which they grumble against me. **28**Say to them, 'As I live, declares the LORD, what you have said in my hearing I will do to you: **29**your dead bodies shall fall in this wilderness, and of all your number, listed in the census from twenty years old and upward, who have grumbled against me, **30**not one shall come into the land where I swore that I would make you dwell, except Caleb the son of Jephunneh and Joshua the son of Nun. **31**But your little ones, who you said would become a prey, I will bring in, and they shall know the land that you have rejected. **32**But as for you, your dead bodies shall fall in this wilderness. **33**And your children shall be shepherds in the wilderness forty years and shall suffer for your faithlessness, until the last of your dead bodies lies in the wilderness. **34**According to the number of the days in which you spied out the land, forty days, a year for each day, you shall bear your iniquity forty years, and you shall know my displeasure.' **35**I, the LORD, have spoken. Surely this will I do to all this wicked congregation who are gathered together against me: in this wilderness they shall come to a full end, and there they shall die."

36And the men whom Moses sent to spy out the land, who returned and made all the congregation grumble against him by bringing up a bad report about the land— **37**the men who brought up a bad report of the land—died by plague before the LORD. **38**Of those men who went to spy out the land, only Joshua the son of Nun and Caleb the son of Jephunneh remained alive.

39When Moses told these words to all the people of Israel, the people mourned greatly.

⁴⁰And they rose early in the morning and went up to the heights of the hill country, saying, "Here we are. We will go up to the place that the LORD has promised, for we have sinned." ⁴¹But Moses said, "Why now are you transgressing the command of the LORD, when that will not succeed? ⁴²Do not go up, for the Lord is not among you, lest you be struck down before your enemies. ⁴³For there the Amalekites and the Canaanites are facing you, and you shall fall by the sword. Because you have turned back from following the LORD, the LORD will not be with you." ⁴⁴But they presumed to go up to the heights of the hill country, although neither the ark of the covenant of the LORD nor Moses departed out of the camp. ⁴⁵Then the Amalekites and the Canaanites who lived in that hill country came down and defeated them and pursued them, even to Hormah.

Psalm 50

A PSALM OF ASAPH.

The Mighty One, God the LORD,
  speaks and summons the earth
    from the rising of the sun to its
      setting.
² Out of Zion, the perfection of beauty,
    God shines forth.
³ Our God comes; he does not keep
    silence;¹
  before him is a devouring fire,
    around him a mighty tempest.
⁴ He calls to the heavens above
    and to the earth, that he may judge his
      people:
⁵ "Gather to me my faithful ones,
    who made a covenant with me by
      sacrifice!"
⁶ The heavens declare his righteousness,
    for God himself is judge!   Selah

⁷ "Hear, O my people, and I will speak;
    O Israel, I will testify against you.
    I am God, your God.
⁸ Not for your sacrifices do I rebuke you;
    your burnt offerings are continually
      before me.
⁹ I will not accept a bull from your house
    or goats from your folds.

¹⁰ For every beast of the forest is mine,
    the cattle on a thousand hills.
¹¹ I know all the birds of the hills,
    and all that moves in the field is mine.

¹² "If I were hungry, I would not tell you,
    for the world and its fullness are mine.
¹³ Do I eat the flesh of bulls
    or drink the blood of goats?
¹⁴ Offer to God a sacrifice of thanksgiving,²
    and perform your vows to the Most
      High,
¹⁵ and call upon me in the day of trouble;
    I will deliver you, and you shall glorify
      me."

¹⁶ But to the wicked God says:
  "What right have you to recite my
    statutes
  or take my covenant on your lips?
¹⁷ For you hate discipline,
    and you cast my words behind you.
¹⁸ If you see a thief, you are pleased with
      him,
    and you keep company with adulterers.

¹⁹ "You give your mouth free rein for evil,
    and your tongue frames deceit.
²⁰ You sit and speak against your brother;
    you slander your own mother's son.
²¹ These things you have done, and I have
      been silent;
    you thought that I³ was one like
      yourself.
  But now I rebuke you and lay the charge
    before you.

²² "Mark this, then, you who forget God,
    lest I tear you apart, and there be none
      to deliver!
²³ The one who offers thanksgiving as his
      sacrifice glorifies me;
    to one who orders his way rightly
    I will show the salvation of God!"

Isaiah 3–4

For behold, the Lord GOD of hosts
  is taking away from Jerusalem and from
    Judah
support and supply,⁴
  all support of bread,
  and all support of water;

¹ Or May our God come, and not keep silence ² Or Make thanksgiving your sacrifice to God ³ Or that the I AM ⁴ Hebrew staff

2   the mighty man and the soldier,
      the judge and the prophet,
      the diviner and the elder,
3   the captain of fifty
      and the man of rank,
   the counselor and the skillful magician
      and the expert in charms.
4   And I will make boys their princes,
      and infants[1] shall rule over them.
5   And the people will oppress one
       another,
      every one his fellow
      and every one his neighbor;
   the youth will be insolent to the elder,
      and the despised to the honorable.

6   For a man will take hold of his brother
      in the house of his father, saying:
   "You have a cloak;
      you shall be our leader,
   and this heap of ruins
      shall be under your rule";
7   in that day he will speak out, saying:
   "I will not be a healer;[2]
      in my house there is neither bread nor
       cloak;
   you shall not make me
      leader of the people."
8   For Jerusalem has stumbled,
      and Judah has fallen,
   because their speech and their deeds are
      against the LORD,
      defying his glorious presence.[3]
9   For the look on their faces bears witness
      against them;
   they proclaim their sin like Sodom;
      they do not hide it.
   Woe to them!
      For they have brought evil on
       themselves.
10   Tell the righteous that it shall be well
      with them,
      for they shall eat the fruit of their
       deeds.
11   Woe to the wicked! It shall be ill with
      him,
      for what his hands have dealt out shall
       be done to him.
12   My people—infants are their
       oppressors,
      and women rule over them.

   O my people, your guides mislead you
      and they have swallowed up[4] the
       course of your paths.

13   The LORD has taken his place to
       contend;
      he stands to judge peoples.
14   The LORD will enter into judgment
      with the elders and princes of his
       people:
   "It is you who have devoured[5] the
       vineyard,
      the spoil of the poor is in your houses.
15   What do you mean by crushing my
       people,
      by grinding the face of the poor?"
        declares the Lord GOD of hosts.

16   The LORD said:
   Because the daughters of Zion are
       haughty
      and walk with outstretched necks,
      glancing wantonly with their eyes,
   mincing along as they go,
      tinkling with their feet,
17   therefore the Lord will strike with a scab
      the heads of the daughters of Zion,
      and the LORD will lay bare their secret
       parts.

18 In that day the Lord will take away the finery of the anklets, the headbands, and the crescents; 19 the pendants, the bracelets, and the scarves; 20 the headdresses, the armlets, the sashes, the perfume boxes, and the amulets; 21 the signet rings and nose rings; 22 the festal robes, the mantles, the cloaks, and the handbags; 23 the mirrors, the linen garments, the turbans, and the veils.

24   Instead of perfume there will be
       rottenness;
      and instead of a belt, a rope;
   and instead of well-set hair, baldness;
      and instead of a rich robe, a skirt of
       sackcloth;
      and branding instead of beauty.
25   Your men shall fall by the sword
      and your mighty men in battle.
26   And her gates shall lament and mourn;
      empty, she shall sit on the ground.

4:1 And seven women shall take hold of one man in that day, saying, "We will eat our own

---

1 Or caprice   2 Hebrew binder of wounds   3 Hebrew the eyes of his glory   4 Or they have confused   5 Or grazed over; compare Exodus 22:5

bread and wear our own clothes, only let us be called by your name; take away our reproach."

²In that day the branch of the LORD shall be beautiful and glorious, and the fruit of the land shall be the pride and honor of the survivors of Israel. ³And he who is left in Zion and remains in Jerusalem will be called holy, everyone who has been recorded for life in Jerusalem, ⁴when the Lord shall have washed away the filth of the daughters of Zion and cleansed the bloodstains of Jerusalem from its midst by a spirit of judgment and by a spirit of burning.¹ ⁵Then the LORD will create over the whole site of Mount Zion and over her assemblies a cloud by day, and smoke and the shining of a flaming fire by night; for over all the glory there will be a canopy. ⁶There will be a booth for shade by day from the heat, and for a refuge and a shelter from the storm and rain.

--------- *Hebrews 11* ---------

Now faith is the assurance of things hoped for, the conviction of things not seen. ²For by it the people of old received their commendation. ³By faith we understand that the universe was created by the word of God, so that what is seen was not made out of things that are visible.

⁴By faith Abel offered to God a more acceptable sacrifice than Cain, through which he was commended as righteous, God commending him by accepting his gifts. And through his faith, though he died, he still speaks. ⁵By faith Enoch was taken up so that he should not see death, and he was not found, because God had taken him. Now before he was taken he was commended as having pleased God. ⁶And without faith it is impossible to please him, for whoever would draw near to God must believe that he exists and that he rewards those who seek him. ⁷By faith Noah, being warned by God concerning events as yet unseen, in reverent fear constructed an ark for the saving of his household. By this he condemned the world and became an heir of the righteousness that comes by faith.

⁸By faith Abraham obeyed when he was called to go out to a place that he was to receive as an inheritance. And he went out, not knowing where he was going. ⁹By faith he went to live in the land of promise, as in a foreign land, living in tents with Isaac and Jacob, heirs with him of the same promise. ¹⁰For he was looking forward to the city that has foundations, whose designer and builder is God. ¹¹By faith Sarah herself received power to conceive, even when she was past the age, since she considered him faithful who had promised. ¹²Therefore from one man, and him as good as dead, were born descendants as many as the stars of heaven and as many as the innumerable grains of sand by the seashore.

¹³These all died in faith, not having received the things promised, but having seen them and greeted them from afar, and having acknowledged that they were strangers and exiles on the earth. ¹⁴For people who speak thus make it clear that they are seeking a homeland. ¹⁵If they had been thinking of that land from which they had gone out, they would have had opportunity to return. ¹⁶But as it is, they desire a better country, that is, a heavenly one. Therefore God is not ashamed to be called their God, for he has prepared for them a city.

¹⁷By faith Abraham, when he was tested, offered up Isaac, and he who had received the promises was in the act of offering up his only son, ¹⁸of whom it was said, "Through Isaac shall your offspring be named." ¹⁹He considered that God was able even to raise him from the dead, from which, figuratively speaking, he did receive him back. ²⁰By faith Isaac invoked future blessings on Jacob and Esau. ²¹By faith Jacob, when dying, blessed each of the sons of Joseph, bowing in worship over the head of his staff. ²²By faith Joseph, at the end of his life, made mention of the exodus of the Israelites and gave directions concerning his bones.

²³By faith Moses, when he was born, was hidden for three months by his parents, because they saw that the child was beautiful, and they were not afraid of the king's edict. ²⁴By faith Moses, when he was grown up, refused to be called the son of Pharaoh's daughter, ²⁵choosing rather to be mistreated with the people of God than to enjoy the fleeting pleasures of sin. ²⁶He considered the reproach of Christ greater wealth than the treasures of Egypt, for he was looking to the reward. ²⁷By faith he left Egypt, not being afraid of the anger of the king, for he endured as seeing him who is invisible. ²⁸By faith he kept the Passover and sprinkled the

¹ Or *purging*

blood, so that the Destroyer of the firstborn might not touch them.

²⁹By faith the people crossed the Red Sea as on dry land, but the Egyptians, when they attempted to do the same, were drowned. ³⁰By faith the walls of Jericho fell down after they had been encircled for seven days. ³¹By faith Rahab the prostitute did not perish with those who were disobedient, because she had given a friendly welcome to the spies.

³²And what more shall I say? For time would fail me to tell of Gideon, Barak, Samson, Jephthah, of David and Samuel and the prophets— ³³who through faith conquered kingdoms, enforced justice, obtained promises, stopped the mouths of lions, ³⁴quenched the power of fire, escaped the edge of the sword, were made strong out of weakness, became mighty in war, put foreign armies to flight. ³⁵Women received back their dead by resurrection. Some were tortured, refusing to accept release, so that they might rise again to a better life. ³⁶Others suffered mocking and flogging, and even chains and imprisonment. ³⁷They were stoned, they were sawn in two,[1] they were killed with the sword. They went about in skins of sheep and goats, destitute, afflicted, mistreated— ³⁸of whom the world was not worthy—wandering about in deserts and mountains, and in dens and caves of the earth.

³⁹And all these, though commended through their faith, did not receive what was promised, ⁴⁰since God had provided something better for us, that apart from us they should not be made perfect.

MAY 7

Numbers 15

The LORD spoke to Moses, saying, ²"Speak to the people of Israel and say to them, When you come into the land you are to inhabit, which I am giving you, ³and you offer to the LORD from the herd or from the flock a food offering[2] or a burnt offering or a sacrifice, to fulfill a vow or as a freewill offering or at your appointed feasts, to make a pleasing aroma to the LORD, ⁴then he who brings his offering shall offer to the LORD a grain offering of a tenth of an ephah[3] of fine flour, mixed with a quarter of a hin[4] of oil; ⁵and you shall offer with the burnt offering, or for the sacrifice, a quarter of a hin of wine for the drink offering for each lamb. ⁶Or for a ram, you shall offer for a grain offering two tenths of an ephah of fine flour mixed with a third of a hin of oil. ⁷And for the drink offering you shall offer a third of a hin of wine, a pleasing aroma to the LORD. ⁸And when you offer a bull as a burnt offering or sacrifice, to fulfill a vow or for peace offerings to the LORD, ⁹then one shall offer with the bull a grain offering of three tenths of an ephah of fine flour, mixed with half a hin of oil. ¹⁰And you shall offer for the drink offering half a hin of wine, as a food offering, a pleasing aroma to the LORD.

¹¹"Thus it shall be done for each bull or ram, or for each lamb or young goat. ¹²As many as you offer, so shall you do with each one, as many as there are. ¹³Every native Israelite shall do these things in this way, in offering a food offering, with a pleasing aroma to the LORD. ¹⁴And if a stranger is sojourning with you, or anyone is living permanently among you, and he wishes to offer a food offering, with a pleasing aroma to the LORD, he shall do as you do. ¹⁵For the assembly, there shall be one statute for you and for the stranger who sojourns with you, a statute forever throughout your generations. You and the sojourner shall be alike before the LORD. ¹⁶One law and one rule shall be for you and for the stranger who sojourns with you."

¹⁷The LORD spoke to Moses, saying, ¹⁸"Speak to the people of Israel and say to them, When

---

[1] Some manuscripts add *they were tempted*   [2] Or *an offering by fire*; so throughout Numbers   [3] An *ephah* was about 3/5 bushel or 22 liters   [4] A *hin* was about 4 quarts or 3.5 liters

you come into the land to which I bring you [19] and when you eat of the bread of the land, you shall present a contribution to the LORD. [20] Of the first of your dough you shall present a loaf as a contribution; like a contribution from the threshing floor, so shall you present it. [21] Some of the first of your dough you shall give to the LORD as a contribution throughout your generations.

[22] "But if you sin unintentionally,[1] and do not observe all these commandments that the LORD has spoken to Moses, [23] all that the LORD has commanded you by Moses, from the day that the LORD gave commandment, and onward throughout your generations, [24] then if it was done unintentionally without the knowledge of the congregation, all the congregation shall offer one bull from the herd for a burnt offering, a pleasing aroma to the LORD, with its grain offering and its drink offering, according to the rule, and one male goat for a sin offering. [25] And the priest shall make atonement for all the congregation of the people of Israel, and they shall be forgiven, because it was a mistake, and they have brought their offering, a food offering to the LORD, and their sin offering before the LORD for their mistake. [26] And all the congregation of the people of Israel shall be forgiven, and the stranger who sojourns among them, because the whole population was involved in the mistake.

[27] "If one person sins unintentionally, he shall offer a female goat a year old for a sin offering. [28] And the priest shall make atonement before the LORD for the person who makes a mistake, when he sins unintentionally, to make atonement for him, and he shall be forgiven. [29] You shall have one law for him who does anything unintentionally, for him who is native among the people of Israel and for the stranger who sojourns among them. [30] But the person who does anything with a high hand, whether he is native or a sojourner, reviles the LORD, and that person shall be cut off from among his people. [31] Because he has despised the word of the LORD and has broken his commandment, that person shall be utterly cut off; his iniquity shall be on him."

[32] While the people of Israel were in the wilderness, they found a man gathering sticks on the Sabbath day. [33] And those who found him gathering sticks brought him to Moses and Aaron and to all the congregation. [34] They put him in custody, because it had not been made clear what should be done to him. [35] And the LORD said to Moses, "The man shall be put to death; all the congregation shall stone him with stones outside the camp." [36] And all the congregation brought him outside the camp and stoned him to death with stones, as the LORD commanded Moses.

[37] The LORD said to Moses, [38] "Speak to the people of Israel, and tell them to make tassels on the corners of their garments throughout their generations, and to put a cord of blue on the tassel of each corner. [39] And it shall be a tassel for you to look at and remember all the commandments of the LORD, to do them, not to follow[2] after your own heart and your own eyes, which you are inclined to whore after. [40] So you shall remember and do all my commandments, and be holy to your God. [41] I am the LORD your God, who brought you out of the land of Egypt to be your God: I am the LORD your God."

Psalm 51

TO THE CHOIRMASTER. A PSALM OF DAVID, WHEN NATHAN THE PROPHET WENT TO HIM, AFTER HE HAD GONE IN TO BATHSHEBA.

Have mercy on me,[3] O God,
   according to your steadfast love;
according to your abundant mercy
   blot out my transgressions.
[2] Wash me thoroughly from my iniquity,
   and cleanse me from my sin!

[3] For I know my transgressions,
   and my sin is ever before me.
[4] Against you, you only, have I sinned
   and done what is evil in your sight,
so that you may be justified in your
      words
   and blameless in your judgment.
[5] Behold, I was brought forth in iniquity,
   and in sin did my mother conceive me.
[6] Behold, you delight in truth in the
      inward being,
   and you teach me wisdom in the
      secret heart.

[7] Purge me with hyssop, and I shall be
      clean;
   wash me, and I shall be whiter than
      snow.

[1] Or by mistake; also verses 24, 27, 28, 29 [2] Hebrew to spy out [3] Or Be gracious to me

8 Let me hear joy and gladness;
    let the bones that you have broken
      rejoice.
9 Hide your face from my sins,
    and blot out all my iniquities.
10 Create in me a clean heart, O God,
    and renew a right[1] spirit within me.
11 Cast me not away from your presence,
    and take not your Holy Spirit from
      me.
12 Restore to me the joy of your salvation,
    and uphold me with a willing spirit.

13 Then I will teach transgressors your
      ways,
    and sinners will return to you.
14 Deliver me from bloodguiltiness, O God,
    O God of my salvation,
    and my tongue will sing aloud of your
      righteousness.
15 O Lord, open my lips,
    and my mouth will declare your
      praise.
16 For you will not delight in sacrifice, or I
      would give it;
    you will not be pleased with a burnt
      offering.
17 The sacrifices of God are a broken
      spirit;
    a broken and contrite heart, O God,
      you will not despise.

18 Do good to Zion in your good pleasure;
    build up the walls of Jerusalem;
19 then will you delight in right sacrifices,
    in burnt offerings and whole burnt
      offerings;
    then bulls will be offered on your
      altar.

Isaiah 5

Let me sing for my beloved
my love song concerning his vineyard:
My beloved had a vineyard
    on a very fertile hill.
2 He dug it and cleared it of stones,
    and planted it with choice vines;
he built a watchtower in the midst of it,
    and hewed out a wine vat in it;
and he looked for it to yield grapes,
    but it yielded wild grapes.

3 And now, O inhabitants of Jerusalem
    and men of Judah,
judge between me and my vineyard.
4 What more was there to do for my
      vineyard,
    that I have not done in it?
When I looked for it to yield grapes,
    why did it yield wild grapes?

5 And now I will tell you
    what I will do to my vineyard.
I will remove its hedge,
    and it shall be devoured;[2]
I will break down its wall,
    and it shall be trampled down.
6 I will make it a waste;
    it shall not be pruned or hoed,
    and briers and thorns shall grow up;
I will also command the clouds
    that they rain no rain upon it.

7 For the vineyard of the LORD of hosts
    is the house of Israel,
and the men of Judah
    are his pleasant planting;
and he looked for justice,
    but behold, bloodshed;[3]
for righteousness,
    but behold, an outcry![4]

8 Woe to those who join house to house,
    who add field to field,
until there is no more room,
    and you are made to dwell alone
    in the midst of the land.
9 The LORD of hosts has sworn in my
      hearing:
"Surely many houses shall be desolate,
    large and beautiful houses, without
      inhabitant.
10 For ten acres[5] of vineyard shall yield but
      one bath,
    and a homer of seed shall yield but an
      ephah."[6]

11 Woe to those who rise early in the
      morning,
    that they may run after strong drink,
who tarry late into the evening
    as wine inflames them!
12 They have lyre and harp,
    tambourine and flute and wine at
      their feasts,

[1] Or steadfast [2] Or grazed over; compare Exodus 22:5 [3] The Hebrew words for justice and bloodshed sound alike [4] The Hebrew words for righteous and outcry sound alike [5] Hebrew ten yoke, the area ten yoke of oxen can plow in a day [6] A bath was about 6 gallons or 22 liters; a homer was about 6 bushels or 220 liters; an ephah was about 3/5 bushel or 22 liters

but they do not regard the deeds of the
LORD,
or see the work of his hands.

13 Therefore my people go into exile
for lack of knowledge;[1]
their honored men go hungry,[2]
and their multitude is parched with
thirst.
14 Therefore Sheol has enlarged its
appetite
and opened its mouth beyond
measure,
and the nobility of Jerusalem[3] and her
multitude will go down,
her revelers and he who exults in her.
15 Man is humbled, and each one is
brought low,
and the eyes of the haughty[4] are
brought low.
16 But the LORD of hosts is exalted[5] in
justice,
and the Holy God shows himself holy
in righteousness.
17 Then shall the lambs graze as in their
pasture,
and nomads shall eat among the ruins
of the rich.

18 Woe to those who draw iniquity with
cords of falsehood,
who draw sin as with cart ropes,
19 who say: "Let him be quick,
let him speed his work
that we may see it;
let the counsel of the Holy One of Israel
draw near,
and let it come, that we may know it!"
20 Woe to those who call evil good
and good evil,
who put darkness for light
and light for darkness,
who put bitter for sweet
and sweet for bitter!
21 Woe to those who are wise in their own
eyes,
and shrewd in their own sight!
22 Woe to those who are heroes at drinking
wine,
and valiant men in mixing strong
drink,
23 who acquit the guilty for a bribe,
and deprive the innocent of his right!

24 Therefore, as the tongue of fire devours
the stubble,
and as dry grass sinks down in the
flame,
so their root will be as rottenness,
and their blossom go up like dust;
for they have rejected the law of the
LORD of hosts,
and have despised the word of the
Holy One of Israel.
25 Therefore the anger of the LORD was
kindled against his people,
and he stretched out his hand against
them and struck them,
and the mountains quaked;
and their corpses were as refuse
in the midst of the streets.
For all this his anger has not turned
away,
and his hand is stretched out still.

26 He will raise a signal for nations far away,
and whistle for them from the ends of
the earth;
and behold, quickly, speedily they come!
27 None is weary, none stumbles,
none slumbers or sleeps,
not a waistband is loose,
not a sandal strap broken;
28 their arrows are sharp,
all their bows bent,
their horses' hoofs seem like flint,
and their wheels like the whirlwind.
29 Their roaring is like a lion,
like young lions they roar;
they growl and seize their prey;
they carry it off, and none can rescue.
30 They will growl over it on that day,
like the growling of the sea.
And if one looks to the land,
behold, darkness and distress;
and the light is darkened by its clouds.

Hebrews 12

Therefore, since we are surrounded by so
great a cloud of witnesses, let us also lay
aside every weight, and sin which clings so
closely, and let us run with endurance the
race that is set before us, [2]looking to Jesus,
the founder and perfecter of our faith, who for
the joy that was set before him endured the

[1] Or without their knowledge [2] Or die of hunger [3] Hebrew her nobility [4] Hebrew high [5] Hebrew high

cross, despising the shame, and is seated at the right hand of the throne of God.

[3] Consider him who endured from sinners such hostility against himself, so that you may not grow weary or fainthearted. [4] In your struggle against sin you have not yet resisted to the point of shedding your blood. [5] And have you forgotten the exhortation that addresses you as sons?

> "My son, do not regard lightly the
> discipline of the Lord,
> nor be weary when reproved by him.
> [6] For the Lord disciplines the one he loves,
> and chastises every son whom he
> receives."

[7] It is for discipline that you have to endure. God is treating you as sons. For what son is there whom his father does not discipline? [8] If you are left without discipline, in which all have participated, then you are illegitimate children and not sons. [9] Besides this, we have had earthly fathers who disciplined us and we respected them. Shall we not much more be subject to the Father of spirits and live? [10] For they disciplined us for a short time as it seemed best to them, but he disciplines us for our good, that we may share his holiness. [11] For the moment all discipline seems painful rather than pleasant, but later it yields the peaceful fruit of righteousness to those who have been trained by it.

[12] Therefore lift your drooping hands and strengthen your weak knees, [13] and make straight paths for your feet, so that what is lame may not be put out of joint but rather be healed. [14] Strive for peace with everyone, and for the holiness without which no one will see the Lord. [15] See to it that no one fails to obtain the grace of God; that no "root of bitterness" springs up and causes trouble, and

by it many become defiled; [16] that no one is sexually immoral or unholy like Esau, who sold his birthright for a single meal. [17] For you know that afterward, when he desired to inherit the blessing, he was rejected, for he found no chance to repent, though he sought it with tears.

[18] For you have not come to what may be touched, a blazing fire and darkness and gloom and a tempest [19] and the sound of a trumpet and a voice whose words made the hearers beg that no further messages be spoken to them. [20] For they could not endure the order that was given, "If even a beast touches the mountain, it shall be stoned." [21] Indeed, so terrifying was the sight that Moses said, "I tremble with fear." [22] But you have come to Mount Zion and to the city of the living God, the heavenly Jerusalem, and to innumerable angels in festal gathering, [23] and to the assembly[1] of the firstborn who are enrolled in heaven, and to God, the judge of all, and to the spirits of the righteous made perfect, [24] and to Jesus, the mediator of a new covenant, and to the sprinkled blood that speaks a better word than the blood of Abel.

[25] See that you do not refuse him who is speaking. For if they did not escape when they refused him who warned them on earth, much less will we escape if we reject him who warns from heaven. [26] At that time his voice shook the earth, but now he has promised, "Yet once more I will shake not only the earth but also the heavens." [27] This phrase, "Yet once more," indicates the removal of things that are shaken—that is, things that have been made—in order that the things that cannot be shaken may remain. [28] Therefore let us be grateful for receiving a kingdom that cannot be shaken, and thus let us offer to God acceptable worship, with reverence and awe, [29] for our God is a consuming fire.

---

[1] Or church

MAY 8

Numbers 16

Now Korah the son of Izhar, son of Kohath, son of Levi, and Dathan and Abiram the sons of Eliab, and On the son of Peleth, sons of Reuben, took men. ²And they rose up before Moses, with a number of the people of Israel, 250 chiefs of the congregation, chosen from the assembly, well-known men. ³They assembled themselves together against Moses and against Aaron and said to them, "You have gone too far! For all in the congregation are holy, every one of them, and the LORD is among them. Why then do you exalt yourselves above the assembly of the LORD?" ⁴When Moses heard it, he fell on his face, ⁵and he said to Korah and all his company, "In the morning the LORD will show who is his,¹ and who is holy, and will bring him near to him. The one whom he chooses he will bring near to him. ⁶Do this: take censers, Korah and all his company; ⁷put fire in them and put incense on them before the LORD tomorrow, and the man whom the LORD chooses shall be the holy one. You have gone too far, sons of Levi!" ⁸And Moses said to Korah, "Hear now, you sons of Levi: ⁹is it too small a thing for you that the God of Israel has separated you from the congregation of Israel, to bring you near to himself, to do service in the tabernacle of the LORD and to stand before the congregation to minister to them, ¹⁰and that he has brought you near him, and all your brothers the sons of Levi with you? And would you seek the priesthood also? ¹¹Therefore it is against the LORD that you and all your company have gathered together. What is Aaron that you grumble against him?"

¹²And Moses sent to call Dathan and Abiram the sons of Eliab, and they said, "We will not come up. ¹³Is it a small thing that you have brought us up out of a land flowing with milk and honey, to kill us in the wilderness, that you must also make yourself a prince over us? ¹⁴Moreover, you have not brought us into a land flowing with milk and honey, nor given us inheritance of fields and vineyards. Will

you put out the eyes of these men? We will not come up." ¹⁵And Moses was very angry and said to the LORD, "Do not respect their offering. I have not taken one donkey from them, and I have not harmed one of them."

¹⁶And Moses said to Korah, "Be present, you and all your company, before the LORD, you and they, and Aaron, tomorrow. ¹⁷And let every one of you take his censer and put incense on it, and every one of you bring before the LORD his censer, 250 censers; you also, and Aaron, each his censer." ¹⁸So every man took his censer and put fire in them and laid incense on them and stood at the entrance of the tent of meeting with Moses and Aaron. ¹⁹Then Korah assembled all the congregation against them at the entrance of the tent of meeting. And the glory of the LORD appeared to all the congregation.

²⁰And the LORD spoke to Moses and to Aaron, saying, ²¹"Separate yourselves from among this congregation, that I may consume them in a moment." ²²And they fell on their faces and said, "O God, the God of the spirits of all flesh, shall one man sin, and will you be angry with all the congregation?" ²³And the LORD spoke to Moses, saying, ²⁴"Say to the congregation, Get away from the dwelling of Korah, Dathan, and Abiram."

²⁵Then Moses rose and went to Dathan and Abiram, and the elders of Israel followed him. ²⁶And he spoke to the congregation, saying, "Depart, please, from the tents of these wicked men, and touch nothing of theirs, lest you be swept away with all their sins." ²⁷So they got away from the dwelling of Korah, Dathan, and Abiram. And Dathan and Abiram came out and stood at the door of their tents, together with their wives, their sons, and their little ones. ²⁸And Moses said, "Hereby you shall know that the LORD has sent me to do all these works, and that it has not been of my own accord. ²⁹If these men die as all men die, or if they are visited by the fate of all mankind, then the LORD has not sent me. ³⁰But if the

¹ Septuagint *The LORD knows those who are his*

LORD creates something new, and the ground opens its mouth and swallows them up with all that belongs to them, and they go down alive into Sheol, then you shall know that these men have despised the LORD."

³¹And as soon as he had finished speaking all these words, the ground under them split apart. ³²And the earth opened its mouth and swallowed them up, with their households and all the people who belonged to Korah and all their goods. ³³So they and all that belonged to them went down alive into Sheol, and the earth closed over them, and they perished from the midst of the assembly. ³⁴And all Israel who were around them fled at their cry, for they said, "Lest the earth swallow us up!" ³⁵And fire came out from the LORD and consumed the 250 men offering the incense.

³⁶¹Then the LORD spoke to Moses, saying, ³⁷"Tell Eleazar the son of Aaron the priest to take up the censers out of the blaze, then scatter the fire far and wide, for they have become holy. ³⁸As for the censers of these men who have sinned at the cost of their lives, let them be made into hammered plates as a covering for the altar, for they offered them before the LORD, and they became holy. Thus they shall be a sign to the people of Israel." ³⁹So Eleazar the priest took the bronze censers, which those who were burned had offered, and they were hammered out as a covering for the altar, ⁴⁰to be a reminder to the people of Israel, so that no outsider, who is not of the descendants of Aaron, should draw near to burn incense before the LORD, lest he become like Korah and his company—as the LORD said to him through Moses.

⁴¹But on the next day all the congregation of the people of Israel grumbled against Moses and against Aaron, saying, "You have killed the people of the LORD." ⁴²And when the congregation had assembled against Moses and against Aaron, they turned toward the tent of meeting. And behold, the cloud covered it, and the glory of the LORD appeared. ⁴³And Moses and Aaron came to the front of the tent of meeting, ⁴⁴and the LORD spoke to Moses, saying, ⁴⁵"Get away from the midst of this congregation, that I may consume them in a moment." And they fell on their faces. ⁴⁶And Moses said to Aaron, "Take your censer, and put fire on it from off the altar and lay incense on it and carry it quickly

to the congregation and make atonement for them, for wrath has gone out from the LORD; the plague has begun." ⁴⁷So Aaron took it as Moses said and ran into the midst of the assembly. And behold, the plague had already begun among the people. And he put on the incense and made atonement for the people. ⁴⁸And he stood between the dead and the living, and the plague was stopped. ⁴⁹Now those who died in the plague were 14,700, besides those who died in the affair of Korah. ⁵⁰And Aaron returned to Moses at the entrance of the tent of meeting, when the plague was stopped.

Psalm 52–54

TO THE CHOIRMASTER. A MASKIL² OF DAVID, WHEN DOEG, THE EDOMITE, CAME AND TOLD SAUL, "DAVID HAS COME TO THE HOUSE OF AHIMELECH."

Why do you boast of evil, O mighty man?
    The steadfast love of God endures all
        the day.
2   Your tongue plots destruction,
        like a sharp razor, you worker of
            deceit.
3   You love evil more than good,
        and lying more than speaking what is
            right.   Selah
4   You love all words that devour,
        O deceitful tongue.

5   But God will break you down forever;
        he will snatch and tear you from your
            tent;
        he will uproot you from the land of
            the living.   Selah
6   The righteous shall see and fear,
        and shall laugh at him, saying,
7   "See the man who would not make
        God his refuge,
    but trusted in the abundance of his
        riches
        and sought refuge in his own
            destruction!"³

8   But I am like a green olive tree
        in the house of God.
    I trust in the steadfast love of God
        forever and ever.
9   I will thank you forever,
        because you have done it.
    I will wait for your name, for it is good,
        in the presence of the godly.

¹ Ch 17:1 in Hebrew ² Probably a musical or liturgical term ³ Or *in his work of destruction*

To the choirmaster: according to Mahalath. A Maskil[1] of David.

The fool says in his heart, "There is no God."
They are corrupt, doing abominable
iniquity;
there is none who does good.

2 God looks down from heaven
on the children of man
to see if there are any who understand,[2]
who seek after God.

3 They have all fallen away;
together they have become corrupt;
there is none who does good,
not even one.

4 Have those who work evil no
knowledge,
who eat up my people as they eat
bread,
and do not call upon God?

5 There they are, in great terror,
where there is no terror!
For God scatters the bones of him who
encamps against you;
you put them to shame, for God has
rejected them.

6 Oh, that salvation for Israel would come
out of Zion!
When God restores the fortunes of his
people,
let Jacob rejoice, let Israel be glad.

To the choirmaster: with stringed instruments. A Maskil[3] of David, when the Ziphites went and told Saul, "Is not David hiding among us?"

O God, save me by your name,
and vindicate me by your might.
2 O God, hear my prayer;
give ear to the words of my mouth.

3 For strangers[4] have risen against me;
ruthless men seek my life;
they do not set God before
themselves. *Selah*

4 Behold, God is my helper;
the Lord is the upholder of my life.
5 He will return the evil to my enemies;
in your faithfulness put an end to
them.

6 With a freewill offering I will sacrifice to
you;
I will give thanks to your name,
O Lord, for it is good.
7 For he has delivered me from every
trouble,
and my eye has looked in triumph on
my enemies.

————————— *Isaiah 6* —————————

In the year that King Uzziah died I saw the Lord sitting upon a throne, high and lifted up; and the train[5] of his robe filled the temple. ²Above him stood the seraphim. Each had six wings: with two he covered his face, and with two he covered his feet, and with two he flew. ³And one called to another and said:

"Holy, holy, holy is the Lord of hosts;
the whole earth is full of his glory!"[6]

⁴And the foundations of the thresholds shook at the voice of him who called, and the house was filled with smoke. ⁵And I said: "Woe is me! For I am lost; for I am a man of unclean lips, and I dwell in the midst of a people of unclean lips; for my eyes have seen the King, the Lord of hosts!"

⁶Then one of the seraphim flew to me, having in his hand a burning coal that he had taken with tongs from the altar. ⁷And he touched my mouth and said: "Behold, this has touched your lips; your guilt is taken away, and your sin atoned for."

⁸And I heard the voice of the Lord saying, "Whom shall I send, and who will go for us?" Then I said, "Here I am! Send me." ⁹And he said, "Go, and say to this people:

"'Keep on hearing,[7] but do not
understand;
keep on seeing,[8] but do not perceive.'
10 Make the heart of this people dull,[9]
and their ears heavy,
and blind their eyes;
lest they see with their eyes,
and hear with their ears,
and understand with their hearts,
and turn and be healed."
11 Then I said, "How long, O Lord?"
And he said:

¹ Probably musical or liturgical terms ² Or *who act wisely* ³ Probably a musical or liturgical term ⁴ Some Hebrew manuscripts and Targum *insolent men* (compare Psalm 86:14)
⁵ Or *hem* ⁶ Or *may his glory fill the whole earth* ⁷ Or *Hear indeed* ⁸ Or *see indeed* ⁹ Hebrew *fat*

"Until cities lie waste
without inhabitant,
and houses without people,
and the land is a desolate waste,
12   and the LORD removes people far away,
and the forsaken places are many in
the midst of the land.
13   And though a tenth remain in it,
it will be burned[1] again,
like a terebinth or an oak,
whose stump remains
when it is felled."
The holy seed[2] is its stump.

Hebrews 13

Let brotherly love continue. [2]Do not neglect to show hospitality to strangers, for thereby some have entertained angels unawares. [3]Remember those who are in prison, as though in prison with them, and those who are mistreated, since you also are in the body. [4]Let marriage be held in honor among all, and let the marriage bed be undefiled, for God will judge the sexually immoral and adulterous. [5]Keep your life free from love of money, and be content with what you have, for he has said, "I will never leave you nor forsake you." [6]So we can confidently say,

"The Lord is my helper;
I will not fear;
what can man do to me?"

[7]Remember your leaders, those who spoke to you the word of God. Consider the outcome of their way of life, and imitate their faith. [8]Jesus Christ is the same yesterday and today and forever. [9]Do not be led away by diverse and strange teachings, for it is good for the heart to be strengthened by grace, not by foods, which have not benefited those devoted to them. [10]We have an altar from which those who serve the tent have no right to eat. [11]For the bodies of those animals whose blood is brought into the holy places by the high priest as a sacrifice for sin are burned outside the camp. [12]So Jesus also suffered outside the gate in order to sanctify the people through his own blood. [13]Therefore let us go to him outside the camp and bear the reproach he endured. [14]For here we have no lasting city, but we seek the city that is to come. [15]Through him then let us continually offer up a sacrifice of praise to God, that is, the fruit of lips that acknowledge his name. [16]Do not neglect to do good and to share what you have, for such sacrifices are pleasing to God.

[17]Obey your leaders and submit to them, for they are keeping watch over your souls, as those who will have to give an account. Let them do this with joy and not with groaning, for that would be of no advantage to you.

[18]Pray for us, for we are sure that we have a clear conscience, desiring to act honorably in all things. [19]I urge you the more earnestly to do this in order that I may be restored to you the sooner.

[20]Now may the God of peace who brought again from the dead our Lord Jesus, the great shepherd of the sheep, by the blood of the eternal covenant, [21]equip you with everything good that you may do his will, working in us[3] that which is pleasing in his sight, through Jesus Christ, to whom be glory forever and ever. Amen.

[22]I appeal to you, brothers,[4] bear with my word of exhortation, for I have written to you briefly. [23]You should know that our brother Timothy has been released, with whom I shall see you if he comes soon. [24]Greet all your leaders and all the saints. Those who come from Italy send you greetings. [25]Grace be with all of you.

[1] Or purged [2] Or offspring [3] Some manuscripts you [4] Or brothers and sisters

MAY 9

Numbers 17¹–18

The LORD spoke to Moses, saying, ² "Speak to the people of Israel, and get from them staffs, one for each fathers' house, from all their chiefs according to their fathers' houses, twelve staffs. Write each man's name on his staff, ³ and write Aaron's name on the staff of Levi. For there shall be one staff for the head of each fathers' house. ⁴ Then you shall deposit them in the tent of meeting before the testimony, where I meet with you. ⁵ And the staff of the man whom I choose shall sprout. Thus I will make to cease from me the grumblings of the people of Israel, which they grumble against you." ⁶ Moses spoke to the people of Israel. And all their chiefs gave him staffs, one for each chief, according to their fathers' houses, twelve staffs. And the staff of Aaron was among their staffs. ⁷ And Moses deposited the staffs before the LORD in the tent of the testimony.

⁸ On the next day Moses went into the tent of the testimony, and behold, the staff of Aaron for the house of Levi had sprouted and put forth buds and produced blossoms, and it bore ripe almonds. ⁹ Then Moses brought out all the staffs from before the LORD to all the people of Israel. And they looked, and each man took his staff. ¹⁰ And the LORD said to Moses, "Put back the staff of Aaron before the testimony, to be kept as a sign for the rebels, that you may make an end of their grumblings against me, lest they die." ¹¹ Thus did Moses; as the LORD commanded him, so he did.

¹² And the people of Israel said to Moses, "Behold, we perish, we are undone, we are all undone. ¹³ Everyone who comes near, who comes near to the tabernacle of the LORD, shall die. Are we all to perish?"

¹⁸:¹ So the LORD said to Aaron, "You and your sons and your father's house with you shall bear iniquity connected with the sanctuary, and you and your sons with you shall bear iniquity connected with your priesthood. ² And with you bring your brothers also, the tribe of Levi, the tribe of your father, that they may join you and minister to you while you and your sons with you are before the tent of the testimony. ³ They shall keep guard over you and over the whole tent, but shall not come near to the vessels of the sanctuary or to the altar lest they, and you, die. ⁴ They shall join you and keep guard over the tent of meeting for all the service of the tent, and no outsider shall come near you. ⁵ And you shall keep guard over the sanctuary and over the altar, that there may never again be wrath on the people of Israel. ⁶ And behold, I have taken your brothers the Levites from among the people of Israel. They are a gift to you, given to the LORD, to do the service of the tent of meeting. ⁷ And you and your sons with you shall guard your priesthood for all that concerns the altar and that is within the veil; and you shall serve. I give your priesthood as a gift,² and any outsider who comes near shall be put to death."

⁸ Then the LORD spoke to Aaron, "Behold, I have given you charge of the contributions made to me, all the consecrated things of the people of Israel. I have given them to you as a portion and to your sons as a perpetual due. ⁹ This shall be yours of the most holy things, reserved from the fire: every offering of theirs, every grain offering of theirs and every sin offering of theirs and every guilt offering of theirs, which they render to me, shall be most holy to you and to your sons. ¹⁰ In a most holy place shall you eat it. Every male may eat it; it is holy to you. ¹¹ This also is yours: the contribution of their gift, all the wave offerings of the people of Israel. I have given them to you, and to your sons and daughters with you, as a perpetual due. Everyone who is clean in your house may eat it. ¹² All the best of the oil and all the best of the wine and of the grain, the firstfruits of what they give to the LORD, I give to you. ¹³ The first ripe fruits of all that is in their land, which they bring to the LORD, shall be yours. Everyone who is clean in your house may eat it. ¹⁴ Every devoted thing in Israel shall be yours. ¹⁵ Everything that opens the womb

¹ Ch 17:16 in Hebrew ² Hebrew *service of gift*

of all flesh, whether man or beast, which they offer to the LORD, shall be yours. Nevertheless, the firstborn of man you shall redeem, and the firstborn of unclean animals you shall redeem. [16]And their redemption price (at a month old you shall redeem them) you shall fix at five shekels[1] in silver, according to the shekel of the sanctuary, which is twenty gerahs. [17]But the firstborn of a cow, or the firstborn of a sheep, or the firstborn of a goat, you shall not redeem; they are holy. You shall sprinkle their blood on the altar and shall burn their fat as a food offering, with a pleasing aroma to the LORD. [18]But their flesh shall be yours, as the breast that is waved and as the right thigh are yours. [19]All the holy contributions that the people of Israel present to the LORD I give to you, and to your sons and daughters with you, as a perpetual due. It is a covenant of salt forever before the LORD for you and for your offspring with you." [20]And the LORD said to Aaron, "You shall have no inheritance in their land, neither shall you have any portion among them. I am your portion and your inheritance among the people of Israel.

[21]"To the Levites I have given every tithe in Israel for an inheritance, in return for their service that they do, their service in the tent of meeting, [22]so that the people of Israel do not come near the tent of meeting, lest they bear sin and die. [23]But the Levites shall do the service of the tent of meeting, and they shall bear their iniquity. It shall be a perpetual statute throughout your generations, and among the people of Israel they shall have no inheritance. [24]For the tithe of the people of Israel, which they present as a contribution to the LORD, I have given to the Levites for an inheritance. Therefore I have said of them that they shall have no inheritance among the people of Israel."

[25]And the LORD spoke to Moses, saying, [26]"Moreover, you shall speak and say to the Levites, 'When you take from the people of Israel the tithe that I have given you from them for your inheritance, then you shall present a contribution from it to the LORD, a tithe of the tithe. [27]And your contribution shall be counted to you as though it were the grain of the threshing floor, and as the fullness of the winepress. [28]So you shall also present a contribution to the LORD from all your tithes, which you receive from the people of Israel. And from it you shall give the LORD's contribution

to Aaron the priest. [29]Out of all the gifts to you, you shall present every contribution due to the LORD; from each its best part is to be dedicated.' [30]Therefore you shall say to them, 'When you have offered from it the best of it, then the rest shall be counted to the Levites as produce of the threshing floor, and as produce of the winepress. [31]And you may eat it in any place, you and your households, for it is your reward in return for your service in the tent of meeting. [32]And you shall bear no sin by reason of it, when you have contributed the best of it. But you shall not profane the holy things of the people of Israel, lest you die.'"

Psalm 55

TO THE CHOIRMASTER: WITH STRINGED INSTRUMENTS. A MASKIL[2] OF DAVID.

Give ear to my prayer, O God,
  and hide not yourself from my plea for
    mercy!
[2]   Attend to me, and answer me;
    I am restless in my complaint and I
      moan,
[3]   because of the noise of the enemy,
    because of the oppression of the
      wicked.
  For they drop trouble upon me,
    and in anger they bear a grudge
      against me.

[4]   My heart is in anguish within me;
    the terrors of death have fallen upon
      me.
[5]   Fear and trembling come upon me,
    and horror overwhelms me.
[6]   And I say, "Oh, that I had wings like a
      dove!
    I would fly away and be at rest;
[7]   yes, I would wander far away;
    I would lodge in the wilderness;   Selah
[8]   I would hurry to find a shelter
    from the raging wind and tempest."

[9]   Destroy, O Lord, divide their tongues;
    for I see violence and strife in the city.
[10] Day and night they go around it
      on its walls,
    and iniquity and trouble are within it;
[11] ruin is in its midst;
    oppression and fraud
      do not depart from its marketplace.

[1] A shekel was about 2/5 ounce or 11 grams [2] Probably a musical or liturgical term

12 For it is not an enemy who taunts me—
 then I could bear it;
 it is not an adversary who deals
 insolently with me—
 then I could hide from him.
13 But it is you, a man, my equal,
 my companion, my familiar friend.
14 We used to take sweet counsel together;
 within God's house we walked in the
 throng.
15 Let death steal over them;
 let them go down to Sheol alive;
 for evil is in their dwelling place and
 in their heart.

16 But I call to God,
 and the LORD will save me.
17 Evening and morning and at noon
 I utter my complaint and moan,
 and he hears my voice.
18 He redeems my soul in safety
 from the battle that I wage,
 for many are arrayed against me.
19 God will give ear and humble them,
 he who is enthroned from of old, *Selah*
 because they do not change
 and do not fear God.

20 My companion[1] stretched out his hand
 against his friends;
 he violated his covenant.
21 His speech was smooth as butter,
 yet war was in his heart;
 his words were softer than oil,
 yet they were drawn swords.

22 Cast your burden on the LORD,
 and he will sustain you;
 he will never permit
 the righteous to be moved.

23 But you, O God, will cast them down
 into the pit of destruction;
 men of blood and treachery
 shall not live out half their days.
 But I will trust in you.

Isaiah 7

In the days of Ahaz the son of Jotham, son of Uzziah, king of Judah, Rezin the king of Syria and Pekah the son of Remaliah the king of Israel came up to Jerusalem to wage war against

it, but could not yet mount an attack against it. [2]When the house of David was told, "Syria is in league with[2] Ephraim," the heart of Ahaz[3] and the heart of his people shook as the trees of the forest shake before the wind.

[3]And the LORD said to Isaiah, "Go out to meet Ahaz, you and Shear-jashub[4] your son, at the end of the conduit of the upper pool on the highway to the Washer's Field. [4]And say to him, 'Be careful, be quiet, do not fear, and do not let your heart be faint because of these two smoldering stumps of firebrands, at the fierce anger of Rezin and Syria and the son of Remaliah. [5]Because Syria, with Ephraim and the son of Remaliah, has devised evil against you, saying, [6]"Let us go up against Judah and terrify it, and let us conquer it[5] for ourselves, and set up the son of Tabeel as king in the midst of it," [7]thus says the Lord GOD:

 "'It shall not stand,
 and it shall not come to pass.
8 For the head of Syria is Damascus,
 and the head of Damascus is Rezin.
 And within sixty-five years
 Ephraim will be shattered from being
 a people.
9 And the head of Ephraim is Samaria,
 and the head of Samaria is the son of
 Remaliah.
 If you[6] are not firm in faith,
 you will not be firm at all.'"

[10]Again the LORD spoke to Ahaz, [11]"Ask a sign of the LORD your[7] God; let it be deep as Sheol or high as heaven." [12]But Ahaz said, "I will not ask, and I will not put the LORD to the test." [13]And he[8] said, "Hear then, O house of David! Is it too little for you to weary men, that you weary my God also? [14]Therefore the Lord himself will give you a sign. Behold, the virgin shall conceive and bear a son, and shall call his name Immanuel.[9] [15]He shall eat curds and honey when he knows how to refuse the evil and choose the good. [16]For before the boy knows how to refuse the evil and choose the good, the land whose two kings you dread will be deserted. [17]The LORD will bring upon you and upon your people and upon your father's house such days as have not come since the day that Ephraim departed from Judah—the king of Assyria."

[18]In that day the LORD will whistle for the

---

[1] Hebrew *He* [2] Hebrew *Syria has rested upon* [3] Hebrew *his heart* [4] *Shear-jashub* means *A remnant shall return* [5] Hebrew *let us split it open* [6] The Hebrew for *you* is plural in verses 9, 13, 14 [7] The Hebrew for *you* and *your* is singular in verses 11, 16, 17 [8] That is, Isaiah [9] *Immanuel* means *God is with us*

fly that is at the end of the streams of Egypt, and for the bee that is in the land of Assyria. ¹⁹And they will all come and settle in the steep ravines, and in the clefts of the rocks, and on all the thornbushes, and on all the pastures.¹

²⁰In that day the Lord will shave with a razor that is hired beyond the River—with the king of Assyria—the head and the hair of the feet, and it will sweep away the beard also.

²¹In that day a man will keep alive a young cow and two sheep, ²²and because of the abundance of milk that they give, he will eat curds, for everyone who is left in the land will eat curds and honey.

²³In that day every place where there used to be a thousand vines, worth a thousand shekels² of silver, will become briers and thorns. ²⁴With bow and arrows a man will come there, for all the land will be briers and thorns. ²⁵And as for all the hills that used to be hoed with a hoe, you will not come there for fear of briers and thorns, but they will become a place where cattle are let loose and where sheep tread.

James 1

James, a servant³ of God and of the Lord Jesus Christ,

To the twelve tribes in the Dispersion:

Greetings.

²Count it all joy, my brothers,⁴ when you meet trials of various kinds, ³for you know that the testing of your faith produces steadfastness. ⁴And let steadfastness have its full effect, that you may be perfect and complete, lacking in nothing.

⁵If any of you lacks wisdom, let him ask God, who gives generously to all without reproach, and it will be given him. ⁶But let him ask in faith, with no doubting, for the one who doubts is like a wave of the sea that is driven and tossed by the wind. ⁷For that person must not suppose that he will receive anything from the Lord; ⁸he is a double-minded man, unstable in all his ways.

⁹Let the lowly brother boast in his exaltation, ¹⁰and the rich in his humiliation, because like

a flower of the grass⁵ he will pass away. ¹¹For the sun rises with its scorching heat and withers the grass; its flower falls, and its beauty perishes. So also will the rich man fade away in the midst of his pursuits.

¹²Blessed is the man who remains steadfast under trial, for when he has stood the test he will receive the crown of life, which God has promised to those who love him. ¹³Let no one say when he is tempted, "I am being tempted by God," for God cannot be tempted with evil, and he himself tempts no one. ¹⁴But each person is tempted when he is lured and enticed by his own desire. ¹⁵Then desire when it has conceived gives birth to sin, and sin when it is fully grown brings forth death.

¹⁶Do not be deceived, my beloved brothers. ¹⁷Every good gift and every perfect gift is from above, coming down from the Father of lights with whom there is no variation or shadow due to change.⁶ ¹⁸Of his own will he brought us forth by the word of truth, that we should be a kind of firstfruits of his creatures.

¹⁹Know this, my beloved brothers: let every person be quick to hear, slow to speak, slow to anger; ²⁰for the anger of man does not produce the righteousness of God. ²¹Therefore put away all filthiness and rampant wickedness and receive with meekness the implanted word, which is able to save your souls.

²²But be doers of the word, and not hearers only, deceiving yourselves. ²³For if anyone is a hearer of the word and not a doer, he is like a man who looks intently at his natural face in a mirror. ²⁴For he looks at himself and goes away and at once forgets what he was like. ²⁵But the one who looks into the perfect law, the law of liberty, and perseveres, being no hearer who forgets but a doer who acts, he will be blessed in his doing.

²⁶If anyone thinks he is religious and does not bridle his tongue but deceives his heart, this person's religion is worthless. ²⁷Religion that is pure and undefiled before God, the Father, is this: to visit orphans and widows in their affliction, and to keep oneself unstained from the world.

---

¹ Or watering holes, or brambles ² A shekel was about 2/5 ounce or 11 grams ³ Or slave (for the contextual rendering of the Greek word doulos, see Preface) ⁴ Or brothers and sisters. The plural Greek word adelphoi (translated "brothers") refers to siblings in a family. In New Testament usage, depending on the context, adelphoi may refer either to men or to both men and women who are siblings (brothers and sisters) in God's family, the church; also verses 16, 19 ⁵ Or a wild flower ⁶ Some manuscripts variation due to a shadow of turning

MAY 10

Numbers 19

Now the LORD spoke to Moses and to Aaron, saying, ²"This is the statute of the law that the LORD has commanded: Tell the people of Israel to bring you a red heifer without defect, in which there is no blemish, and on which a yoke has never come. ³And you shall give it to Eleazar the priest, and it shall be taken outside the camp and slaughtered before him. ⁴And Eleazar the priest shall take some of its blood with his finger, and sprinkle some of its blood toward the front of the tent of meeting seven times. ⁵And the heifer shall be burned in his sight. Its skin, its flesh, and its blood, with its dung, shall be burned. ⁶And the priest shall take cedarwood and hyssop and scarlet yarn, and throw them into the fire burning the heifer. ⁷Then the priest shall wash his clothes and bathe his body in water, and afterward he may come into the camp. But the priest shall be unclean until evening. ⁸The one who burns the heifer shall wash his clothes in water and bathe his body in water and shall be unclean until evening. ⁹And a man who is clean shall gather up the ashes of the heifer and deposit them outside the camp in a clean place. And they shall be kept for the water for impurity for the congregation of the people of Israel; it is a sin offering. ¹⁰And the one who gathers the ashes of the heifer shall wash his clothes and be unclean until evening. And this shall be a perpetual statute for the people of Israel, and for the stranger who sojourns among them.

¹¹"Whoever touches the dead body of any person shall be unclean seven days. ¹²He shall cleanse himself with the water on the third day and on the seventh day, and so be clean. But if he does not cleanse himself on the third day and on the seventh day, he will not become clean. ¹³Whoever touches a dead person, the body of anyone who has died, and does not cleanse himself, defiles the tabernacle of the LORD, and that person shall be cut off from Israel; because the water for impurity was not thrown on him, he shall be unclean. His uncleanness is still on him.

¹⁴"This is the law when someone dies in a tent: everyone who comes into the tent and everyone who is in the tent shall be unclean seven days. ¹⁵And every open vessel that has no cover fastened on it is unclean. ¹⁶Whoever in the open field touches someone who was killed with a sword or who died naturally, or touches a human bone or a grave, shall be unclean seven days. ¹⁷For the unclean they shall take some ashes of the burnt sin offering, and fresh¹ water shall be added in a vessel. ¹⁸Then a clean person shall take hyssop and dip it in the water and sprinkle it on the tent and on all the furnishings and on the persons who were there and on whoever touched the bone, or the slain or the dead or the grave. ¹⁹And the clean person shall sprinkle it on the unclean on the third day and on the seventh day. Thus on the seventh day he shall cleanse him, and he shall wash his clothes and bathe himself in water, and at evening he shall be clean.

²⁰"If the man who is unclean does not cleanse himself, that person shall be cut off from the midst of the assembly, since he has defiled the sanctuary of the LORD. Because the water for impurity has not been thrown on him, he is unclean. ²¹And it shall be a statute forever for them. The one who sprinkles the water for impurity shall wash his clothes, and the one who touches the water for impurity shall be unclean until evening. ²²And whatever the unclean person touches shall be unclean, and anyone who touches it shall be unclean until evening."

Psalm 56–57

TO THE CHOIRMASTER: ACCORDING TO THE DOVE ON FAR-OFF TEREBINTHS. A MIKTAM² OF DAVID, WHEN THE PHILISTINES SEIZED HIM IN GATH.

Be gracious to me, O God, for man tramples on me;
    all day long an attacker oppresses me;

---

¹ Hebrew *living* ² Probably a musical or liturgical term

2 my enemies trample on me all day long,
  for many attack me proudly.
3 When I am afraid,
  I put my trust in you.
4 In God, whose word I praise,
  in God I trust; I shall not be afraid.
  What can flesh do to me?
5 All day long they injure my cause;[1]
  all their thoughts are against me for
    evil.
6 They stir up strife, they lurk;
  they watch my steps,
  as they have waited for my life.
7 For their crime will they escape?
  In wrath cast down the peoples, O God!
8 You have kept count of my tossings;[2]
  put my tears in your bottle.
  Are they not in your book?
9 Then my enemies will turn back
  in the day when I call.
  This I know, that[3] God is for me.
10 In God, whose word I praise,
   in the LORD, whose word I praise,
11 in God I trust; I shall not be afraid.
   What can man do to me?
12 I must perform my vows to you, O God;
   I will render thank offerings to you.
13 For you have delivered my soul from
     death,
   yes, my feet from falling,
   that I may walk before God
   in the light of life.

TO THE CHOIRMASTER: ACCORDING TO DO NOT
DESTROY. A MIKTAM[4] OF DAVID, WHEN HE FLED
FROM SAUL, IN THE CAVE.

Be merciful to me, O God, be merciful to me,
  for in you my soul takes refuge;
  in the shadow of your wings I will take
    refuge,
  till the storms of destruction pass by.
2 I cry out to God Most High,
  to God who fulfills his purpose for me.
3 He will send from heaven and save me;
  he will put to shame him who
    tramples on me.   Selah
  God will send out his steadfast love and
    his faithfulness!
4 My soul is in the midst of lions;
  I lie down amid fiery beasts—

the children of man, whose teeth are
    spears and arrows,
  whose tongues are sharp swords.
5 Be exalted, O God, above the heavens!
  Let your glory be over all the earth!
6 They set a net for my steps;
  my soul was bowed down.
  They dug a pit in my way,
  but they have fallen into it
    themselves.   Selah
7 My heart is steadfast, O God,
  my heart is steadfast!
  I will sing and make melody!
8 Awake, my glory![5]
  Awake, O harp and lyre!
  I will awake the dawn!
9 I will give thanks to you, O Lord, among
    the peoples;
  I will sing praises to you among the
    nations.
10 For your steadfast love is great to the
     heavens,
   your faithfulness to the clouds.
11 Be exalted, O God, above the heavens!
   Let your glory be over all the earth!

--- *Isaiah 8:1–9:7* ---

Then the LORD said to me, "Take a large tab-let and write on it in common characters,[6] 'Belonging to Maher-shalal-hash-baz.'[7] [2]And I will get reliable witnesses, Uriah the priest and Zechariah the son of Jeberechiah, to attest for me."

[3]And I went to the prophetess, and she conceived and bore a son. Then the LORD said to me, "Call his name Maher-shalal-hash-baz; [4]for before the boy knows how to cry 'My father' or 'My mother,' the wealth of Damascus and the spoil of Samaria will be carried away before the king of Assyria."

[5]The LORD spoke to me again: [6]"Because this people has refused the waters of Shiloah that flow gently, and rejoice over Rezin and the son of Remaliah, [7]therefore, behold, the Lord is bringing up against them the waters of the River, mighty and many, the king of Assyria and all his glory. And it will rise over all its channels and go over all its banks, [8]and it will sweep on into Judah, it will overflow and

[1] Or they twist my words [2] Or wanderings [3] Or because [4] Probably a musical or liturgical term [5] Or my whole being [6] Hebrew with a man's stylus [7] Maher-shalal-hash-baz means The spoil speeds, the prey hastens

pass on, reaching even to the neck, and its out-spread wings will fill the breadth of your land, O Immanuel."

9   Be broken,[1] you peoples, and be
          shattered;[2]
       give ear, all you far countries;
     strap on your armor and be shattered;
       strap on your armor and be shattered.
10   Take counsel together, but it will come
          to nothing;
       speak a word, but it will not stand,
          for God is with us.[3]

[11] For the LORD spoke thus to me with his strong hand upon me, and warned me not to walk in the way of this people, saying: [12] "Do not call conspiracy all that this people calls conspiracy, and do not fear what they fear, nor be in dread. [13] But the LORD of hosts, him you shall honor as holy. Let him be your fear, and let him be your dread. [14] And he will become a sanctuary and a stone of offense and a rock of stumbling to both houses of Israel, a trap and a snare to the inhabitants of Jerusalem. [15] And many shall stumble on it. They shall fall and be broken; they shall be snared and taken."

[16] Bind up the testimony; seal the teaching[4] among my disciples. [17] I will wait for the LORD, who is hiding his face from the house of Jacob, and I will hope in him. [18] Behold, I and the children whom the LORD has given me are signs and portents in Israel from the LORD of hosts, who dwells on Mount Zion. [19] And when they say to you, "Inquire of the mediums and the necromancers who chirp and mutter," should not a people inquire of their God? Should they inquire of the dead on behalf of the living? [20] To the teaching and to the testimony! If they will not speak according to this word, it is because they have no dawn. [21] They will pass through the land,[5] greatly distressed and hungry. And when they are hungry, they will be enraged and will speak contemptuously against[6] their king and their God, and turn their faces upward. [22] And they will look to the earth, but behold, distress and darkness, the gloom of anguish. And they will be thrust into thick darkness.

[9:1] [17] But there will be no gloom for her who was in anguish. In the former time he brought into contempt the land of Zebulun and the land of Naphtali, but in the latter time he has made glorious the way of the sea, the land beyond the Jordan, Galilee of the nations.[8]

2 9 The people who walked in darkness
          have seen a great light;
       those who dwelt in a land of deep
          darkness,
       on them has light shone.
3   You have multiplied the nation;
       you have increased its joy;
     they rejoice before you
       as with joy at the harvest,
       as they are glad when they divide the
          spoil.
4   For the yoke of his burden,
       and the staff for his shoulder,
       the rod of his oppressor,
     you have broken as on the day of
          Midian.
5   For every boot of the tramping warrior
          in battle tumult
       and every garment rolled in blood
       will be burned as fuel for the fire.
6   For to us a child is born,
       to us a son is given;
     and the government shall be upon[10] his
          shoulder,
       and his name shall be called[11]
     Wonderful Counselor, Mighty God,
       Everlasting Father, Prince of Peace.
7   Of the increase of his government and
          of peace
       there will be no end,
     on the throne of David and over his
          kingdom,
       to establish it and to uphold it
     with justice and with righteousness
       from this time forth and forevermore.
     The zeal of the LORD of hosts will do this.

――――――――――― *James 2* ―――――――――――

My brothers,[12] show no partiality as you hold the faith in our Lord Jesus Christ, the Lord of glory. [2] For if a man wearing a gold ring and fine clothing comes into your assembly, and a poor man in shabby clothing also comes in, [3] and if you pay attention to the one who wears the fine clothing and say, "You sit here in a good place," while you say to the poor man, "You stand over there," or, "Sit down at my feet," [4] have you not then made distinctions

[1] Or *Be evil* [2] Or *dismayed* [3] The Hebrew for *God is with us* is *Immanuel* [4] Or *law*; also verse 20 [5] Hebrew *it* [6] Or *speak contemptuously by* [7] Ch 8:23 in Hebrew [8] Or *of the Gentiles* [9] Ch 9:1 in Hebrew [10] Or *is upon* [11] Or *is called* [12] Or *brothers and sisters*; also verses 5, 14

among yourselves and become judges with evil thoughts? [5]Listen, my beloved brothers, has not God chosen those who are poor in the world to be rich in faith and heirs of the kingdom, which he has promised to those who love him? [6]But you have dishonored the poor man. Are not the rich the ones who oppress you, and the ones who drag you into court? [7]Are they not the ones who blaspheme the honorable name by which you were called?

[8]If you really fulfill the royal law according to the Scripture, "You shall love your neighbor as yourself," you are doing well. [9]But if you show partiality, you are committing sin and are convicted by the law as transgressors. [10]For whoever keeps the whole law but fails in one point has become accountable for all of it. [11]For he who said, "Do not commit adultery," also said, "Do not murder." If you do not commit adultery but do murder, you have become a transgressor of the law. [12]So speak and so act as those who are to be judged under the law of liberty. [13]For judgment is without mercy to one who has shown no mercy. Mercy triumphs over judgment.

[14]What good is it, my brothers, if someone says he has faith but does not have works? Can that faith save him? [15]If a brother or sister is poorly clothed and lacking in daily food, [16]and one of you says to them, "Go in peace, be warmed and filled," without giving them the things needed for the body, what good[1] is that? [17]So also faith by itself, if it does not have works, is dead.

[18]But someone will say, "You have faith and I have works." Show me your faith apart from your works, and I will show you my faith by my works. [19]You believe that God is one; you do well. Even the demons believe—and shudder! [20]Do you want to be shown, you foolish person, that faith apart from works is useless? [21]Was not Abraham our father justified by works when he offered up his son Isaac on the altar? [22]You see that faith was active along with his works, and faith was completed by his works; [23]and the Scripture was fulfilled that says, "Abraham believed God, and it was counted to him as righteousness"—and he was called a friend of God. [24]You see that a person is justified by works and not by faith alone. [25]And in the same way was not also Rahab the prostitute justified by works when she received the messengers and sent them out by another way? [26]For as the body apart from the spirit is dead, so also faith apart from works is dead.

MAY 11

Numbers 20

And the people of Israel, the whole congregation, came into the wilderness of Zin in the first month, and the people stayed in Kadesh. And Miriam died there and was buried there.

[2]Now there was no water for the congregation. And they assembled themselves together against Moses and against Aaron. [3]And the people quarreled with Moses and said, "Would that we had perished when our brothers perished before the Lord! [4]Why have you brought the assembly of the Lord into this wilderness, that we should die here, both we and our cattle? [5]And why have you made us come up out of Egypt to bring us to this evil place? It is no place for grain or figs or vines or pomegranates, and there is no water to drink." [6]Then Moses and Aaron went from the presence of the assembly to the entrance of the tent of meeting and fell on their faces. And the glory of the Lord appeared to them, [7]and the Lord spoke to Moses, saying, [8]"Take the staff, and assemble the congregation, you and Aaron your brother, and tell the rock before their eyes to yield its water. So you shall bring water out of the rock for them and give drink to the congregation and their cattle." [9]And Moses took the staff from before the Lord, as he commanded him.

[1] Or benefit

[10] Then Moses and Aaron gathered the assembly together before the rock, and he said to them, "Hear now, you rebels: shall we bring water for you out of this rock?" [11] And Moses lifted up his hand and struck the rock with his staff twice, and water came out abundantly, and the congregation drank, and their livestock. [12] And the LORD said to Moses and Aaron, "Because you did not believe in me, to uphold me as holy in the eyes of the people of Israel, therefore you shall not bring this assembly into the land that I have given them." [13] These are the waters of Meribah,[1] where the people of Israel quarreled with the LORD, and through them he showed himself holy.

[14] Moses sent messengers from Kadesh to the king of Edom: "Thus says your brother Israel: You know all the hardship that we have met: [15] how our fathers went down to Egypt, and we lived in Egypt a long time. And the Egyptians dealt harshly with us and our fathers. [16] And when we cried to the LORD, he heard our voice and sent an angel and brought us out of Egypt. And here we are in Kadesh, a city on the edge of your territory. [17] Please let us pass through your land. We will not pass through field or vineyard, or drink water from a well. We will go along the King's Highway. We will not turn aside to the right hand or to the left until we have passed through your territory." [18] But Edom said to him, "You shall not pass through, lest I come out with the sword against you." [19] And the people of Israel said to him, "We will go up by the highway, and if we drink of your water, I and my livestock, then I will pay for it. Let me only pass through on foot, nothing more." [20] But he said, "You shall not pass through." And Edom came out against them with a large army and with a strong force. [21] Thus Edom refused to give Israel passage through his territory, so Israel turned away from him.

[22] And they journeyed from Kadesh, and the people of Israel, the whole congregation, came to Mount Hor. [23] And the LORD said to Moses and Aaron at Mount Hor, on the border of the land of Edom, [24] "Let Aaron be gathered to his people, for he shall not enter the land that I have given to the people of Israel, because you rebelled against my command at the waters of Meribah. [25] Take Aaron and Eleazar his son and bring them up to Mount Hor. [26] And strip Aaron of his garments and put them on Eleazar his son. And Aaron shall be gathered to his people and shall die there." [27] Moses did as the LORD commanded. And they went up Mount Hor in the sight of all the congregation. [28] And Moses stripped Aaron of his garments and put them on Eleazar his son. And Aaron died there on the top of the mountain. Then Moses and Eleazar came down from the mountain. [29] And when all the congregation saw that Aaron had perished, all the house of Israel wept for Aaron thirty days.

Psalm 58–59

To the choirmaster: according to Do Not Destroy. A Miktam[2] of David.

Do you indeed decree what is right, you gods?[3]
> Do you judge the children of man uprightly?
[2] No, in your hearts you devise wrongs;
> your hands deal out violence on earth.

[3] The wicked are estranged from the womb;
> they go astray from birth, speaking lies.
[4] They have venom like the venom of a serpent,
> like the deaf adder that stops its ear,
[5] so that it does not hear the voice of charmers
> or of the cunning enchanter.

[6] O God, break the teeth in their mouths;
> tear out the fangs of the young lions, O LORD!
[7] Let them vanish like water that runs away;
> when he aims his arrows, let them be blunted.
[8] Let them be like the snail that dissolves into slime,
> like the stillborn child who never sees the sun.
[9] Sooner than your pots can feel the heat of thorns,
> whether green or ablaze, may he sweep them away![4]

[10] The righteous will rejoice when he sees the vengeance;
> he will bathe his feet in the blood of the wicked.

---

[1] Meribah means quarreling [2] Probably a musical or liturgical term [3] Or you mighty lords (by revocalization; Hebrew in silence) [4] The meaning of the Hebrew verse is uncertain

11 Mankind will say, "Surely there is a
   reward for the righteous;
   surely there is a God who judges on
      earth."

TO THE CHOIRMASTER: ACCORDING TO DO NOT
DESTROY. A MIKTAM[1] OF DAVID, WHEN SAUL SENT
MEN TO WATCH HIS HOUSE IN ORDER TO KILL HIM.

Deliver me from my enemies, O my God;
   protect me from those who rise up
      against me;
2 deliver me from those who work evil,
   and save me from bloodthirsty men.
3 For behold, they lie in wait for my life;
   fierce men stir up strife against me.
For no transgression or sin of mine,
   O LORD,
4 for no fault of mine, they run and
   make ready.
Awake, come to meet me, and see!
5 You, LORD God of hosts, are God of
   Israel.
Rouse yourself to punish all the nations;
   spare none of those who treacherously
      plot evil. *Selah*
6 Each evening they come back,
   howling like dogs
   and prowling about the city.
7 There they are, bellowing with their
      mouths
   with swords in their lips—
   for "Who," they think,[2] "will hear us?"
8 But you, O LORD, laugh at them;
   you hold all the nations in derision.
9 O my Strength, I will watch for you,
   for you, O God, are my fortress.
10 My God in his steadfast love[3] will meet
      me;
   God will let me look in triumph on my
      enemies.
11 Kill them not, lest my people forget;
   make them totter[4] by your power and
      bring them down,
   O Lord, our shield!
12 For the sin of their mouths, the words of
      their lips,
   let them be trapped in their pride.
For the cursing and lies that they utter,
13 consume them in wrath;
   consume them till they are no more,

that they may know that God rules over
      Jacob
   to the ends of the earth. *Selah*
14 Each evening they come back,
   howling like dogs
   and prowling about the city.
15 They wander about for food
   and growl if they do not get their fill.
16 But I will sing of your strength;
   I will sing aloud of your steadfast love
      in the morning.
For you have been to me a fortress
   and a refuge in the day of my distress.
17 O my Strength, I will sing praises to you,
   for you, O God, are my fortress,
   the God who shows me steadfast
      love.

Isaiah 9:8–10:4

The Lord has sent a word against Jacob,
   and it will fall on Israel;
9 and all the people will know,
   Ephraim and the inhabitants of
      Samaria,
   who say in pride and in arrogance of
      heart:
10 "The bricks have fallen,
   but we will build with dressed stones;
   the sycamores have been cut down,
   but we will put cedars in their place."
11 But the LORD raises the adversaries of
      Rezin against him,
   and stirs up his enemies.
12 The Syrians on the east and the
      Philistines on the west
   devour Israel with open mouth.
For all this his anger has not turned
      away,
   and his hand is stretched out still.
13 The people did not turn to him who
      struck them,
   nor inquire of the LORD of hosts.
14 So the LORD cut off from Israel head and
      tail,
   palm branch and reed in one day—
15 the elder and honored man is the head,
   and the prophet who teaches lies is
      the tail;

---

[1] Probably a musical or liturgical term [2] Hebrew lacks *they think* [3] Or *The God who shows me steadfast love* [4] Or *wander*

16 for those who guide this people have
    been leading them astray,
    and those who are guided by them are
    swallowed up.
17 Therefore the Lord does not rejoice over
    their young men,
    and has no compassion on their
    fatherless and widows;
for everyone is godless and an evildoer,
    and every mouth speaks folly.¹
For all this his anger has not turned away,
    and his hand is stretched out still.

18 For wickedness burns like a fire;
    it consumes briers and thorns;
it kindles the thickets of the forest,
    and they roll upward in a column of
    smoke.
19 Through the wrath of the Lord of hosts
    the land is scorched,
    and the people are like fuel for the fire;
    no one spares another.
20 They slice meat on the right, but are still
    hungry,
    and they devour on the left, but are
    not satisfied;
each devours the flesh of his own arm,
21 Manasseh devours Ephraim, and
    Ephraim devours Manasseh;
    together they are against Judah.
For all this his anger has not turned away,
    and his hand is stretched out still.

10:1 Woe to those who decree iniquitous
    decrees,
    and the writers who keep writing
    oppression,
2 to turn aside the needy from justice
    and to rob the poor of my people of
    their right,
that widows may be their spoil,
    and that they may make the fatherless
    their prey!
3 What will you do on the day of
    punishment,
    in the ruin that will come from afar?
To whom will you flee for help,
    and where will you leave your wealth?
4 Nothing remains but to crouch among
    the prisoners
    or fall among the slain.

For all this his anger has not turned away,
and his hand is stretched out still.

--- James 3 ---

Not many of you should become teachers, my brothers, for you know that we who teach will be judged with greater strictness. ²For we all stumble in many ways. And if anyone does not stumble in what he says, he is a perfect man, able also to bridle his whole body. ³If we put bits into the mouths of horses so that they obey us, we guide their whole bodies as well. ⁴Look at the ships also: though they are so large and are driven by strong winds, they are guided by a very small rudder wherever the will of the pilot directs. ⁵So also the tongue is a small member, yet it boasts of great things.

How great a forest is set ablaze by such a small fire! ⁶And the tongue is a fire, a world of unrighteousness. The tongue is set among our members, staining the whole body, setting on fire the entire course of life,² and set on fire by hell.³ ⁷For every kind of beast and bird, of reptile and sea creature, can be tamed and has been tamed by mankind, ⁸but no human being can tame the tongue. It is a restless evil, full of deadly poison. ⁹With it we bless our Lord and Father, and with it we curse people who are made in the likeness of God. ¹⁰From the same mouth come blessing and cursing. My brothers,⁴ these things ought not to be so. ¹¹Does a spring pour forth from the same opening both fresh and salt water? ¹²Can a fig tree, my brothers, bear olives, or a grapevine produce figs? Neither can a salt pond yield fresh water.

¹³Who is wise and understanding among you? By his good conduct let him show his works in the meekness of wisdom. ¹⁴But if you have bitter jealousy and selfish ambition in your hearts, do not boast and be false to the truth. ¹⁵This is not the wisdom that comes down from above, but is earthly, unspiritual, demonic. ¹⁶For where jealousy and selfish ambition exist, there will be disorder and every vile practice. ¹⁷But the wisdom from above is first pure, then peaceable, gentle, open to reason, full of mercy and good fruits, impartial and sincere. ¹⁸And a harvest of righteousness is sown in peace by those who make peace.

¹ Or *speaks disgraceful things* ² Or *wheel of birth* ³ Greek *Gehenna* ⁴ Or *brothers and sisters; also verse 12*

MAY 12

--- Numbers 21 ---

When the Canaanite, the king of Arad, who lived in the Negeb, heard that Israel was coming by the way of Atharim, he fought against Israel, and took some of them captive. **²**And Israel vowed a vow to the LORD and said, "If you will indeed give this people into my hand, then I will devote their cities to destruction."**¹ ³**And the LORD heeded the voice of Israel and gave over the Canaanites, and they devoted them and their cities to destruction. So the name of the place was called Hormah.**²**

⁴From Mount Hor they set out by the way to the Red Sea, to go around the land of Edom. And the people became impatient on the way. **⁵**And the people spoke against God and against Moses, "Why have you brought us up out of Egypt to die in the wilderness? For there is no food and no water, and we loathe this worthless food." **⁶**Then the LORD sent fiery serpents among the people, and they bit the people, so that many people of Israel died. **⁷**And the people came to Moses and said, "We have sinned, for we have spoken against the LORD and against you. Pray to the LORD, that he take away the serpents from us." So Moses prayed for the people. **⁸**And the LORD said to Moses, "Make a fiery serpent and set it on a pole, and everyone who is bitten, when he sees it, shall live." **⁹**So Moses made a bronze**³** serpent and set it on a pole. And if a serpent bit anyone, he would look at the bronze serpent and live.

¹⁰And the people of Israel set out and camped in Oboth. **¹¹**And they set out from Oboth and camped at Iye-abarim, in the wilderness that is opposite Moab, toward the sunrise. **¹²**From there they set out and camped in the Valley of Zered. **¹³**From there they set out and camped on the other side of the Arnon, which is in the wilderness that extends from the border of the Amorites, for the Arnon is the border of Moab, between Moab and the Amorites. **¹⁴**Therefore it is said in the Book of the Wars of the LORD,

"Waheb in Suphah, and the valleys of the
    Arnon,

¹⁵   and the slope of the valleys
    that extends to the seat of Ar,
    and leans to the border of Moab."

¹⁶And from there they continued to Beer;**⁴** that is the well of which the LORD said to Moses, "Gather the people together, so that I may give them water." **¹⁷**Then Israel sang this song:

"Spring up, O well!—Sing to it!—
¹⁸   the well that the princes made,
    that the nobles of the people dug,
    with the scepter and with their staffs."

And from the wilderness they went on to Mattanah, **¹⁹**and from Mattanah to Nahaliel, and from Nahaliel to Bamoth, **²⁰**and from Bamoth to the valley lying in the region of Moab by the top of Pisgah that looks down on the desert.**⁵**

²¹Then Israel sent messengers to Sihon king of the Amorites, saying, **²²**"Let me pass through your land. We will not turn aside into field or vineyard. We will not drink the water of a well. We will go by the King's Highway until we have passed through your territory." **²³**But Sihon would not allow Israel to pass through his territory. He gathered all his people together and went out against Israel to the wilderness and came to Jahaz and fought against Israel. **²⁴**And Israel defeated him with the edge of the sword and took possession of his land from the Arnon to the Jabbok, as far as to the Ammonites, for the border of the Ammonites was strong. **²⁵**And Israel took all these cities, and Israel settled in all the cities of the Amorites, in Heshbon, and in all its villages. **²⁶**For Heshbon was the city of Sihon the king of the Amorites, who had fought against the former king of Moab and taken all his land out of his hand, as far as the Arnon. **²⁷**Therefore the ballad singers say,

"Come to Heshbon, let it be built;
    let the city of Sihon be established.
²⁸   For fire came out from Heshbon,
    flame from the city of Sihon.

---

¹ That is, set apart (devote) as an offering to the Lord (for destruction); also verse 3 **²** *Hormah* means *destruction* **³** Or *copper* **⁴** *Beer* means *well* **⁵** Or *Jeshimon*

It devoured Ar of Moab,
and swallowed[1] the heights of the
Arnon.
29 Woe to you, O Moab!
You are undone, O people of
Chemosh!
He has made his sons fugitives,
and his daughters captives,
to an Amorite king, Sihon.
30 So we overthrew them;
Heshbon, as far as Dibon, perished;
and we laid waste as far as Nophah;
fire spread as far as Medeba."[2]

[31] Thus Israel lived in the land of the Amorites. [32] And Moses sent to spy out Jazer, and they captured its villages and dispossessed the Amorites who were there. [33] Then they turned and went up by the way to Bashan. And Og the king of Bashan came out against them, he and all his people, to battle at Edrei. [34] But the LORD said to Moses, "Do not fear him, for I have given him into your hand, and all his people, and his land. And you shall do to him as you did to Sihon king of the Amorites, who lived at Heshbon." [35] So they defeated him and his sons and all his people, until he had no survivor left. And they possessed his land.

Psalm 60–61

To the choirmaster: according to Shushan Eduth. A Miktam[3] of David; for instruction; when he strove with Aram-naharaim and with Aram-zobah, and when Joab on his return struck down twelve thousand of Edom in the Valley of Salt.

O God, you have rejected us, broken our defenses;
you have been angry; oh, restore us.
2 You have made the land to quake; you
have torn it open;
repair its breaches, for it totters.
3 You have made your people see hard
things;
you have given us wine to drink that
made us stagger.

4 You have set up a banner for those who
fear you,
that they may flee to it from the bow.[4]
Selah

5 That your beloved ones may be
delivered,
give salvation by your right hand and
answer us!

6 God has spoken in his holiness:[5]
"With exultation I will divide up
Shechem
and portion out the Vale of Succoth.
7 Gilead is mine; Manasseh is mine;
Ephraim is my helmet;
Judah is my scepter.
8 Moab is my washbasin;
upon Edom I cast my shoe;
over Philistia I shout in triumph."[6]

9 Who will bring me to the fortified city?
Who will lead me to Edom?
10 Have you not rejected us, O God?
You do not go forth, O God, with our
armies.
11 Oh, grant us help against the foe,
for vain is the salvation of man!
12 With God we shall do valiantly;
it is he who will tread down our foes.

To the choirmaster: with stringed instruments. Of David.

Hear my cry, O God,
listen to my prayer;
2 from the end of the earth I call to you
when my heart is faint.
Lead me to the rock
that is higher than I,
3 for you have been my refuge,
a strong tower against the enemy.

4 Let me dwell in your tent forever!
Let me take refuge under the shelter
of your wings!
Selah
5 For you, O God, have heard my vows;
you have given me the heritage of
those who fear your name.

6 Prolong the life of the king;
may his years endure to all
generations!
7 May he be enthroned forever before God;
appoint steadfast love and faithfulness
to watch over him!

8 So will I ever sing praises to your name,
as I perform my vows day after day.

---

[1] Septuagint; Hebrew the lords of [2] Compare Samaritan and Septuagint; Hebrew and we laid waste as far as Nophah, which is as far as Medeba [3] Probably musical or liturgical terms [4] Or that it may be displayed because of truth [5] Or sanctuary [6] Revocalization (compare Psalm 108:10); Masoretic Text over me, O Philistia, shout in triumph

Isaiah 10:5-34

Ah, Assyria, the rod of my anger;
   the staff in their hands is my fury!
6 Against a godless nation I send him,
   and against the people of my wrath I
      command him,
   to take spoil and seize plunder,
   and to tread them down like the mire
      of the streets.
7 But he does not so intend,
   and his heart does not so think;
   but it is in his heart to destroy,
   and to cut off nations not a few;
8 for he says:
   "Are not my commanders all kings?
9 Is not Calno like Carchemish?
   Is not Hamath like Arpad?
   Is not Samaria like Damascus?
10 As my hand has reached to the
      kingdoms of the idols,
   whose carved images were greater
      than those of Jerusalem and
      Samaria,
11 shall I not do to Jerusalem and her idols
   as I have done to Samaria and her
      images?"

[12] When the Lord has finished all his work on
Mount Zion and on Jerusalem, he[1] will punish
the speech of the arrogant heart of the king of
Assyria and the boastful look in his eyes. [13] For
he says:

   "By the strength of my hand I have done it,
      and by my wisdom, for I have
         understanding;
   I remove the boundaries of peoples,
      and plunder their treasures;
   like a bull I bring down those who sit
      on thrones.
14 My hand has found like a nest
      the wealth of the peoples;
   and as one gathers eggs that have been
      forsaken,
   so I have gathered all the earth;
   and there was none that moved a wing
      or opened the mouth or chirped."

15 Shall the axe boast over him who hews
      with it,
   or the saw magnify itself against him
      who wields it?

As if a rod should wield him who lifts it,
   or as if a staff should lift him who is
      not wood!
16 Therefore the Lord God of hosts
   will send wasting sickness among his
      stout warriors,
   and under his glory a burning will be
      kindled,
   like the burning of fire.
17 The light of Israel will become a fire,
   and his Holy One a flame,
   and it will burn and devour
   his thorns and briers in one day.
18 The glory of his forest and of his fruitful
      land
   the Lord will destroy, both soul and
      body,
   and it will be as when a sick man
      wastes away.
19 The remnant of the trees of his forest
      will be so few
   that a child can write them down.

[20] In that day the remnant of Israel and the
survivors of the house of Jacob will no more
lean on him who struck them, but will lean
on the Lord, the Holy One of Israel, in truth.
[21] A remnant will return, the remnant of Jacob,
to the mighty God. [22] For though your people
Israel be as the sand of the sea, only a remnant
of them will return. Destruction is decreed,
overflowing with righteousness. [23] For the Lord
God of hosts will make a full end, as decreed,
in the midst of all the earth.

[24] Therefore thus says the Lord God of hosts:
"O my people, who dwell in Zion, be not afraid
of the Assyrians when they strike with the
rod and lift up their staff against you as the
Egyptians did. [25] For in a very little while my
fury will come to an end, and my anger will be
directed to their destruction. [26] And the Lord of
hosts will wield against them a whip, as when
he struck Midian at the rock of Oreb. And his
staff will be over the sea, and he will lift it as
he did in Egypt. [27] And in that day his burden
will depart from your shoulder, and his yoke
from your neck; and the yoke will be broken
because of the fat."[2]

28   He has come to Aiath;
   he has passed through Migron;
   at Michmash he stores his baggage;

---

[1] Hebrew _I_   [2] The meaning of the Hebrew is uncertain

29   they have crossed over the pass;
       at Geba they lodge for the night;
    Ramah trembles;
       Gibeah of Saul has fled.
30   Cry aloud, O daughter of Gallim!
       Give attention, O Laishah!
       O poor Anathoth!
31   Madmenah is in flight;
       the inhabitants of Gebim flee for
         safety.
32   This very day he will halt at Nob;
       he will shake his fist
       at the mount of the daughter of Zion,
       the hill of Jerusalem.

33   Behold, the Lord GOD of hosts
       will lop the boughs with terrifying
         power;
    the great in height will be hewn down,
       and the lofty will be brought low.
34   He will cut down the thickets of the
         forest with an axe,
    and Lebanon will fall by the Majestic
         One.

James 4

What causes quarrels and what causes fights among you? Is it not this, that your passions[1] are at war within you?[2] 2 You desire and do not have, so you murder. You covet and cannot obtain, so you fight and quarrel. You do not have, because you do not ask. 3 You ask and do not receive, because you ask wrongly, to spend it on your passions. 4 You adulterous people![3] Do you not know that friendship with the world is enmity with God? Therefore whoever wishes to be a friend of the world makes himself an enemy of God. 5 Or do you suppose it is to no purpose that the Scripture says, "He yearns jealously over the spirit that he has made to dwell in us"? 6 But he gives more grace. Therefore it says, "God opposes the proud, but gives grace to the humble." 7 Submit yourselves therefore to God. Resist the devil, and he will flee from you. 8 Draw near to God, and he will draw near to you. Cleanse your hands, you sinners, and purify your hearts, you double-minded. 9 Be wretched and mourn and weep. Let your laughter be turned to mourning and your joy to gloom. 10 Humble yourselves before the Lord, and he will exalt you.

11 Do not speak evil against one another, brothers.[4] The one who speaks against a brother or judges his brother, speaks evil against the law and judges the law. But if you judge the law, you are not a doer of the law but a judge. 12 There is only one lawgiver and judge, he who is able to save and to destroy. But who are you to judge your neighbor?

13 Come now, you who say, "Today or tomorrow we will go into such and such a town and spend a year there and trade and make a profit"— 14 yet you do not know what tomorrow will bring. What is your life? For you are a mist that appears for a little time and then vanishes. 15 Instead you ought to say, "If the Lord wills, we will live and do this or that." 16 As it is, you boast in your arrogance. All such boasting is evil. 17 So whoever knows the right thing to do and fails to do it, for him it is sin.

MAY 13

Numbers 22

Then the people of Israel set out and camped in the plains of Moab beyond the Jordan at Jericho. 2 And Balak the son of Zippor saw all that Israel had done to the Amorites. 3 And Moab was in great dread of the people, because they were many. Moab was overcome with fear of the people of Israel. 4 And Moab said to the elders of Midian, "This horde will now lick up all that is around us, as the ox licks up the grass of the field." So Balak the son of Zippor, who

---
1 Greek *pleasures*; also verse 3   2 Greek *in your members*   3 Greek *You adulteresses!*   4 Or *brothers and sisters*

was king of Moab at that time, [5]sent messengers to Balaam the son of Beor at Pethor, which is near the River in the land of the people of Amaw,[1] to call him, saying, "Behold, a people has come out of Egypt. They cover the face of the earth, and they are dwelling opposite me. [6]Come now, curse this people for me, since they are too mighty for me. Perhaps I shall be able to defeat them and drive them from the land, for I know that he whom you bless is blessed, and he whom you curse is cursed."

[7]So the elders of Moab and the elders of Midian departed with the fees for divination in their hand. And they came to Balaam and gave him Balak's message. [8]And he said to them, "Lodge here tonight, and I will bring back word to you, as the LORD speaks to me." So the princes of Moab stayed with Balaam. [9]And God came to Balaam and said, "Who are these men with you?" [10]And Balaam said to God, "Balak the son of Zippor, king of Moab, has sent to me, saying, [11]'Behold, a people has come out of Egypt, and it covers the face of the earth. Now come, curse them for me. Perhaps I shall be able to fight against them and drive them out.'" [12]God said to Balaam, "You shall not go with them. You shall not curse the people, for they are blessed." [13]So Balaam rose in the morning and said to the princes of Balak, "Go to your own land, for the LORD has refused to let me go with you." [14]So the princes of Moab rose and went to Balak and said, "Balaam refuses to come with us."

[15]Once again Balak sent princes, more in number and more honorable than these. [16]And they came to Balaam and said to him, "Thus says Balak the son of Zippor: 'Let nothing hinder you from coming to me, [17]for I will surely do you great honor, and whatever you say to me I will do. Come, curse this people for me.'" [18]But Balaam answered and said to the servants of Balak, "Though Balak were to give me his house full of silver and gold, I could not go beyond the command of the LORD my God to do less or more. [19]So you, too, please stay here tonight, that I may know what more the LORD will say to me." [20]And God came to Balaam at night and said to him, "If the men have come to call you, rise, go with them; but only do what I tell you." [21]So Balaam rose in the morning and saddled his donkey and went with the princes of Moab.

[22]But God's anger was kindled because he went, and the angel of the LORD took his stand in the way as his adversary. Now he was riding on the donkey, and his two servants were with him. [23]And the donkey saw the angel of the LORD standing in the road, with a drawn sword in his hand. And the donkey turned aside out of the road and went into the field. And Balaam struck the donkey, to turn her into the road. [24]Then the angel of the LORD stood in a narrow path between the vineyards, with a wall on either side. [25]And when the donkey saw the angel of the LORD, she pushed against the wall and pressed Balaam's foot against the wall. So he struck her again. [26]Then the angel of the LORD went ahead and stood in a narrow place, where there was no way to turn either to the right or to the left. [27]When the donkey saw the angel of the LORD, she lay down under Balaam. And Balaam's anger was kindled, and he struck the donkey with his staff. [28]Then the LORD opened the mouth of the donkey, and she said to Balaam, "What have I done to you, that you have struck me these three times?" [29]And Balaam said to the donkey, "Because you have made a fool of me. I wish I had a sword in my hand, for then I would kill you." [30]And the donkey said to Balaam, "Am I not your donkey, on which you have ridden all your life long to this day? Is it my habit to treat you this way?" And he said, "No."

[31]Then the LORD opened the eyes of Balaam, and he saw the angel of the LORD standing in the way, with his drawn sword in his hand. And he bowed down and fell on his face. [32]And the angel of the LORD said to him, "Why have you struck your donkey these three times? Behold, I have come out to oppose you because your way is perverse[2] before me. [33]The donkey saw me and turned aside before me these three times. If she had not turned aside from me, surely just now I would have killed you and let her live." [34]Then Balaam said to the angel of the LORD, "I have sinned, for I did not know that you stood in the road against me. Now therefore, if it is evil in your sight, I will turn back." [35]And the angel of the LORD said to Balaam, "Go with the men, but speak only the word that I tell you." So Balaam went on with the princes of Balak.

[36]When Balak heard that Balaam had come, he went out to meet him at the city of Moab, on the border formed by the Arnon, at the

[1] Or the people of his kindred   [2] Or reckless

extremity of the border. ³⁷And Balak said to Balaam, "Did I not send to you to call you? Why did you not come to me? Am I not able to honor you?" ³⁸Balaam said to Balak, "Behold, I have come to you! Have I now any power of my own to speak anything? The word that God puts in my mouth, that must I speak." ³⁹Then Balaam went with Balak, and they came to Kiriath-huzoth. ⁴⁰And Balak sacrificed oxen and sheep, and sent for Balaam and for the princes who were with him.

⁴¹And in the morning Balak took Balaam and brought him up to Bamoth-baal, and from there he saw a fraction of the people.

Psalm 62–63

TO THE CHOIRMASTER: ACCORDING TO JEDUTHUN. A PSALM OF DAVID.

For God alone my soul waits in silence;
  from him comes my salvation.
² He alone is my rock and my salvation,
    my fortress; I shall not be greatly
      shaken.

³ How long will all of you attack a man
    to batter him,
    like a leaning wall, a tottering fence?
⁴ They only plan to thrust him down from
      his high position.
    They take pleasure in falsehood.
  They bless with their mouths,
    but inwardly they curse. Selah

⁵ For God alone, O my soul, wait in silence,
    for my hope is from him.
⁶ He only is my rock and my salvation,
    my fortress; I shall not be shaken.
⁷ On God rests my salvation and my glory;
    my mighty rock, my refuge is God.

⁸ Trust in him at all times, O people;
    pour out your heart before him;
  God is a refuge for us. Selah

⁹ Those of low estate are but a breath;
    those of high estate are a delusion;
  in the balances they go up;
    they are together lighter than a
      breath.
¹⁰ Put no trust in extortion;
    set no vain hopes on robbery;
  if riches increase, set not your heart
    on them.

¹¹ Once God has spoken;
    twice have I heard this:
  that power belongs to God,
¹²   and that to you, O Lord, belongs
      steadfast love.
  For you will render to a man
    according to his work.

A PSALM OF DAVID, WHEN HE WAS IN THE WILDERNESS OF JUDAH.

O God, you are my God; earnestly I seek you;
  my soul thirsts for you;
  my flesh faints for you,
    as in a dry and weary land where
      there is no water.
² So I have looked upon you in the
      sanctuary,
    beholding your power and glory.
³ Because your steadfast love is better
      than life,
    my lips will praise you.
⁴ So I will bless you as long as I live;
    in your name I will lift up my hands.

⁵ My soul will be satisfied as with fat and
      rich food,
    and my mouth will praise you with
      joyful lips,
⁶ when I remember you upon my bed,
    and meditate on you in the watches of
      the night;
⁷ for you have been my help,
    and in the shadow of your wings I will
      sing for joy.
⁸ My soul clings to you;
    your right hand upholds me.

⁹ But those who seek to destroy my life
    shall go down into the depths of the
      earth;
¹⁰ they shall be given over to the power of
      the sword;
    they shall be a portion for jackals.
¹¹ But the king shall rejoice in God;
    all who swear by him shall exult,
    for the mouths of liars will be stopped.

Isaiah 11–12

There shall come forth a shoot from the
  stump of Jesse,
    and a branch from his roots shall bear
      fruit.

2 And the Spirit of the Lord shall rest
  upon him,
  the Spirit of wisdom and
    understanding,
  the Spirit of counsel and might,
  the Spirit of knowledge and the fear of
    the Lord.
3 And his delight shall be in the fear of
    the Lord.
  He shall not judge by what his eyes see,
    or decide disputes by what his ears
    hear,
4 but with righteousness he shall judge
    the poor,
  and decide with equity for the meek
    of the earth;
  and he shall strike the earth with the
    rod of his mouth,
  and with the breath of his lips he shall
    kill the wicked.
5 Righteousness shall be the belt of his
    waist,
  and faithfulness the belt of his loins.

6 The wolf shall dwell with the lamb,
  and the leopard shall lie down with
    the young goat,
  and the calf and the lion and the
    fattened calf together;
  and a little child shall lead them.
7 The cow and the bear shall graze;
  their young shall lie down together;
  and the lion shall eat straw like the ox.
8 The nursing child shall play over the
    hole of the cobra,
  and the weaned child shall put his
    hand on the adder's den.
9 They shall not hurt or destroy
  in all my holy mountain;
  for the earth shall be full of the
    knowledge of the Lord
  as the waters cover the sea.

10 In that day the root of Jesse, who shall stand as a signal for the peoples—of him shall the nations inquire, and his resting place shall be glorious. 11 In that day the Lord will extend his hand yet a second time to recover the remnant that remains of his people, from Assyria, from Egypt, from Pathros, from Cush,[1] from Elam, from Shinar, from Hamath, and from the coastlands of the sea.

12 He will raise a signal for the nations
  and will assemble the banished of
    Israel,
  and gather the dispersed of Judah
  from the four corners of the earth.
13 The jealousy of Ephraim shall depart,
  and those who harass Judah shall be
    cut off;
  Ephraim shall not be jealous of Judah,
  and Judah shall not harass Ephraim.
14 But they shall swoop down on the
    shoulder of the Philistines in the
    west,
  and together they shall plunder the
    people of the east.
  They shall put out their hand against
    Edom and Moab,
  and the Ammonites shall obey them.
15 And the Lord will utterly destroy[2]
  the tongue of the Sea of Egypt,
  and will wave his hand over the River
  with his scorching breath,[3]
  and strike it into seven channels,
  and he will lead people across in
    sandals.
16 And there will be a highway from
    Assyria
  for the remnant that remains of his
    people,
  as there was for Israel
  when they came up from the land of
    Egypt.

12:1 You[4] will say in that day:
  "I will give thanks to you, O Lord,
  for though you were angry with me,
  your anger turned away,
    that you might comfort me.

2 "Behold, God is my salvation;
  I will trust, and will not be afraid;
  for the Lord God[5] is my strength and
    my song,
  and he has become my salvation."

3 With joy you[6] will draw water from the wells of salvation. 4 And you will say in that day:

"Give thanks to the Lord,
  call upon his name,
  make known his deeds among the
    peoples,
  proclaim that his name is exalted.

[1] Probably Nubia [2] Hebrew devote to destruction [3] Or wind [4] The Hebrew for you is singular in verse 1 [5] Hebrew for Yah, the Lord [6] The Hebrew for you is plural in verses 3, 4

5   "Sing praises to the LORD, for he has
       done gloriously;
       let this be made known[1] in all the
       earth.
6   Shout, and sing for joy, O inhabitant of
       Zion,
       for great in your[2] midst is the Holy
       One of Israel."

James 5

Come now, you rich, weep and howl for the miseries that are coming upon you. [2]Your riches have rotted and your garments are moth-eaten. [3]Your gold and silver have corroded, and their corrosion will be evidence against you and will eat your flesh like fire. You have laid up treasure in the last days. [4]Behold, the wages of the laborers who mowed your fields, which you kept back by fraud, are crying out against you, and the cries of the harvesters have reached the ears of the Lord of hosts. [5]You have lived on the earth in luxury and in self-indulgence. You have fattened your hearts in a day of slaughter. [6]You have condemned and murdered the righteous person. He does not resist you.

[7]Be patient, therefore, brothers,[3] until the coming of the Lord. See how the farmer waits for the precious fruit of the earth, being patient about it, until it receives the early and the late rains. [8]You also, be patient. Establish your hearts, for the coming of the Lord is at hand. [9]Do not grumble against one another, brothers, so that you may not be judged; behold,

the Judge is standing at the door. [10]As an example of suffering and patience, brothers, take the prophets who spoke in the name of the Lord. [11]Behold, we consider those blessed who remained steadfast. You have heard of the steadfastness of Job, and you have seen the purpose of the Lord, how the Lord is compassionate and merciful.

[12]But above all, my brothers, do not swear, either by heaven or by earth or by any other oath, but let your "yes" be yes and your "no" be no, so that you may not fall under condemnation.

[13]Is anyone among you suffering? Let him pray. Is anyone cheerful? Let him sing praise. [14]Is anyone among you sick? Let him call for the elders of the church, and let them pray over him, anointing him with oil in the name of the Lord. [15]And the prayer of faith will save the one who is sick, and the Lord will raise him up. And if he has committed sins, he will be forgiven. [16]Therefore, confess your sins to one another and pray for one another, that you may be healed. The prayer of a righteous person has great power as it is working.[4] [17]Elijah was a man with a nature like ours, and he prayed fervently that it might not rain, and for three years and six months it did not rain on the earth. [18]Then he prayed again, and heaven gave rain, and the earth bore its fruit.

[19]My brothers, if anyone among you wanders from the truth and someone brings him back, [20]let him know that whoever brings back a sinner from his wandering will save his soul from death and will cover a multitude of sins.

MAY 14

Numbers 23

And Balaam said to Balak, "Build for me here seven altars, and prepare for me here seven bulls and seven rams." [2]Balak did as Balaam had said. And Balak and Balaam offered on each altar a bull and a ram. [3]And Balaam said to Balak, "Stand beside your burnt offering, and I will go. Perhaps the LORD will

come to meet me, and whatever he shows me I will tell you." And he went to a bare height, [4]and God met Balaam. And Balaam said to him, "I have arranged the seven altars and I have offered on each altar a bull and a ram." [5]And the LORD put a word in Balaam's mouth and said, "Return to Balak, and thus you shall

[1] Or this is made known   [2] The Hebrew for your in verse 6 is singular, referring to the *inhabitant of Zion*   [3] Or *brothers and sisters;* also verses 9, 10, 12, 19   [4] Or *The effective prayer of a righteous person has great power*

speak." ⁶And he returned to him, and behold, he and all the princes of Moab were standing beside his burnt offering. ⁷And Balaam took up his discourse and said,

> "From Aram Balak has brought me,
>   the king of Moab from the eastern
>   mountains:
> 'Come, curse Jacob for me,
>   and come, denounce Israel!'
> ⁸   How can I curse whom God has not
>   cursed?
>   How can I denounce whom the LORD
>   has not denounced?
> ⁹   For from the top of the crags I see him,
>   from the hills I behold him;
>   behold, a people dwelling alone,
>   and not counting itself among the
>   nations!
> ¹⁰ Who can count the dust of Jacob
>   or number the fourth part¹ of Israel?
>   Let me die the death of the upright,
>   and let my end be like his!"

¹¹And Balak said to Balaam, "What have you done to me? I took you to curse my enemies, and behold, you have done nothing but bless them." ¹²And he answered and said, "Must I not take care to speak what the LORD puts in my mouth?"

¹³And Balak said to him, "Please come with me to another place, from which you may see them. You shall see only a fraction of them and shall not see them all. Then curse them for me from there." ¹⁴And he took him to the field of Zophim, to the top of Pisgah, and built seven altars and offered a bull and a ram on each altar. ¹⁵Balaam said to Balak, "Stand here beside your burnt offering, while I meet the LORD over there." ¹⁶And the LORD met Balaam and put a word in his mouth and said, "Return to Balak, and thus shall you speak." ¹⁷And he came to him, and behold, he was standing beside his burnt offering, and the princes of Moab with him. And Balak said to him, "What has the LORD spoken?" ¹⁸And Balaam took up his discourse and said,

> "Rise, Balak, and hear;
>   give ear to me, O son of Zippor:
> ¹⁹ God is not man, that he should lie,
>   or a son of man, that he should
>   change his mind.

> Has he said, and will he not do it?
>   Or has he spoken, and will he not
>   fulfill it?
> ²⁰ Behold, I received a command to bless:
>   he has blessed, and I cannot revoke it.
> ²¹ He has not beheld misfortune in Jacob,
>   nor has he seen trouble in Israel.
>   The LORD their God is with them,
>   and the shout of a king is among them.
> ²² God brings them out of Egypt
>   and is for them like the horns of the
>   wild ox.
> ²³ For there is no enchantment against
>   Jacob,
>   no divination against Israel;
>   now it shall be said of Jacob and Israel,
>   'What has God wrought!'
> ²⁴ Behold, a people! As a lioness it rises up
>   and as a lion it lifts itself;
>   it does not lie down until it has
>   devoured the prey
>   and drunk the blood of the slain."

²⁵And Balak said to Balaam, "Do not curse them at all, and do not bless them at all." ²⁶But Balaam answered Balak, "Did I not tell you, 'All that the LORD says, that I must do'?" ²⁷And Balak said to Balaam, "Come now, I will take you to another place. Perhaps it will please God that you may curse them for me from there." ²⁸So Balak took Balaam to the top of Peor, which overlooks the desert.² ²⁹And Balaam said to Balak, "Build for me here seven altars and prepare for me here seven bulls and seven rams." ³⁰And Balak did as Balaam had said, and offered a bull and a ram on each altar.

───────── *Psalm 64–65* ─────────

TO THE CHOIRMASTER. A PSALM OF DAVID.

Hear my voice, O God, in my complaint;
    preserve my life from dread of the enemy.
> 2   Hide me from the secret plots of the
>   wicked,
>   from the throng of evildoers,
> 3   who whet their tongues like swords,
>   who aim bitter words like arrows,
> 4   shooting from ambush at the blameless,
>   shooting at him suddenly and without
>   fear.
> 5   They hold fast to their evil purpose;
>   they talk of laying snares secretly,

¹ Or *dust clouds* ² Or *Jeshimon*

thinking, "Who can see them?"

6   They search out injustice,
     saying, "We have accomplished a
         diligent search."
     For the inward mind and heart of a
         man are deep.

7   But God shoots his arrow at them;
     they are wounded suddenly.

8   They are brought to ruin, with their own
         tongues turned against them;
     all who see them will wag their heads.

9   Then all mankind fears;
     they tell what God has brought about
     and ponder what he has done.

10   Let the righteous one rejoice in the
     Lord
     and take refuge in him!
     Let all the upright in heart exult!

To the choirmaster. A Psalm of David. A Song.

P raise is due to you,[1] O God, in Zion,
   and to you shall vows be performed.
2   O you who hear prayer,
     to you shall all flesh come.
3   When iniquities prevail against me,
     you atone for our transgressions.
4   Blessed is the one you choose and bring
         near,
     to dwell in your courts!
     We shall be satisfied with the goodness
         of your house,
     the holiness of your temple!

5   By awesome deeds you answer us with
         righteousness,
     O God of our salvation,
     the hope of all the ends of the earth
     and of the farthest seas;
6   the one who by his strength established
         the mountains,
     being girded with might;
7   who stills the roaring of the seas,
     the roaring of their waves,
     the tumult of the peoples,
8   so that those who dwell at the ends of
         the earth are in awe at your signs.
     You make the going out of the morning
     and the evening to shout for joy.

9   You visit the earth and water it;[2]
     you greatly enrich it;

     the river of God is full of water;
     you provide their grain,
     for so you have prepared it.
10   You water its furrows abundantly,
         settling its ridges,
     softening it with showers,
     and blessing its growth.
11   You crown the year with your bounty;
     your wagon tracks overflow with
         abundance.
12   The pastures of the wilderness
         overflow,
     the hills gird themselves with joy,
13   the meadows clothe themselves with
         flocks,
     the valleys deck themselves with
         grain,
     they shout and sing together for joy.

Isaiah 13

T he oracle concerning Babylon which Isaiah
   the son of Amoz saw.

2   On a bare hill raise a signal;
     cry aloud to them;
     wave the hand for them to enter
     the gates of the nobles.
3   I myself have commanded my
         consecrated ones,
     and have summoned my mighty men
         to execute my anger,
     my proudly exulting ones.[3]
4   The sound of a tumult is on the
         mountains
     as of a great multitude!
     The sound of an uproar of kingdoms,
     of nations gathering together!
     The Lord of hosts is mustering
     a host for battle.
5   They come from a distant land,
     from the end of the heavens,
     the Lord and the weapons of his
         indignation,
     to destroy the whole land.[4]

6   Wail, for the day of the Lord is near;
     as destruction from the Almighty[5] it
     will come!
7   Therefore all hands will be feeble,
     and every human heart will melt.

[1] Or *Praise waits for you in silence* [2] Or *and make it overflow* [3] Or *those who exult in my majesty* [4] Or *earth; also verse 9* [5] The Hebrew words for *destruction* and *almighty* sound alike

8 They will be dismayed:
pangs and agony will seize them;
they will be in anguish like a woman
in labor.
They will look aghast at one another;
their faces will be aflame.

9 Behold, the day of the LORD comes,
cruel, with wrath and fierce anger,
to make the land a desolation
and to destroy its sinners from it.

10 For the stars of the heavens and their
constellations
will not give their light;
the sun will be dark at its rising,
and the moon will not shed its light.

11 I will punish the world for its evil,
and the wicked for their iniquity;
I will put an end to the pomp of the
arrogant,
and lay low the pompous pride of the
ruthless.

12 I will make people more rare than fine
gold,
and mankind than the gold of Ophir.

13 Therefore I will make the heavens
tremble,
and the earth will be shaken out of its
place,
at the wrath of the LORD of hosts
in the day of his fierce anger.

14 And like a hunted gazelle,
or like sheep with none to gather them,
each will turn to his own people,
and each will flee to his own land.

15 Whoever is found will be thrust
through,
and whoever is caught will fall by the
sword.

16 Their infants will be dashed in pieces
before their eyes;
their houses will be plundered
and their wives ravished.

17 Behold, I am stirring up the Medes
against them,
who have no regard for silver
and do not delight in gold.

18 Their bows will slaughter[1] the young
men;
they will have no mercy on the fruit of
the womb;
their eyes will not pity children.

19 And Babylon, the glory of kingdoms,
the splendor and pomp of the
Chaldeans,
will be like Sodom and Gomorrah
when God overthrew them.

20 It will never be inhabited
or lived in for all generations;
no Arab will pitch his tent there;
no shepherds will make their flocks
lie down there.

21 But wild animals will lie down there,
and their houses will be full of
howling creatures;
there ostriches[2] will dwell,
and there wild goats will dance.

22 Hyenas[3] will cry in its towers,
and jackals in the pleasant palaces;
its time is close at hand
and its days will not be prolonged.

1 Peter 1

Peter, an apostle of Jesus Christ,
To those who are elect exiles of the Dispersion in Pontus, Galatia, Cappadocia, Asia, and Bithynia, [2] according to the foreknowledge of God the Father, in the sanctification of the Spirit, for obedience to Jesus Christ and for sprinkling with his blood:

May grace and peace be multiplied to you.

[3] Blessed be the God and Father of our Lord Jesus Christ! According to his great mercy, he has caused us to be born again to a living hope through the resurrection of Jesus Christ from the dead, [4] to an inheritance that is imperishable, undefiled, and unfading, kept in heaven for you, [5] who by God's power are being guarded through faith for a salvation ready to be revealed in the last time. [6] In this you rejoice, though now for a little while, if necessary, you have been grieved by various trials, [7] so that the tested genuineness of your faith—more precious than gold that perishes though it is tested by fire—may be found to result in praise and glory and honor at the revelation of Jesus Christ. [8] Though you have not seen him, you love him. Though you do not now see him, you believe in him and rejoice with joy that is inexpressible and filled with glory, [9] obtaining the outcome of your faith, the salvation of your souls.

[10] Concerning this salvation, the prophets who prophesied about the grace that was

---

[1] Hebrew dash in pieces [2] Or owls [3] Or foxes

to be yours searched and inquired carefully, ¹¹inquiring what person or time the Spirit of Christ in them was indicating when he predicted the sufferings of Christ and the subsequent glories. ¹²It was revealed to them that they were serving not themselves but you, in the things that have now been announced to you through those who preached the good news to you by the Holy Spirit sent from heaven, things into which angels long to look.

¹³Therefore, preparing your minds for action,¹ and being sober-minded, set your hope fully on the grace that will be brought to you at the revelation of Jesus Christ. ¹⁴As obedient children, do not be conformed to the passions of your former ignorance, ¹⁵but as he who called you is holy, you also be holy in all your conduct, ¹⁶since it is written, "You shall be holy, for I am holy." ¹⁷And if you call on him as Father who judges impartially according to each one's deeds, conduct yourselves with fear throughout the time of your exile, ¹⁸knowing that you were ransomed from the futile ways inherited from your forefathers,

not with perishable things such as silver or gold, ¹⁹but with the precious blood of Christ, like that of a lamb without blemish or spot. ²⁰He was foreknown before the foundation of the world but was made manifest in the last times for the sake of you ²¹who through him are believers in God, who raised him from the dead and gave him glory, so that your faith and hope are in God.

²²Having purified your souls by your obedience to the truth for a sincere brotherly love, love one another earnestly from a pure heart, ²³since you have been born again, not of perishable seed but of imperishable, through the living and abiding word of God; ²⁴for

> "All flesh is like grass
>   and all its glory like the flower of grass.
> The grass withers,
>   and the flower falls,
> 25 but the word of the Lord remains
>   forever."

And this word is the good news that was preached to you.

MAY 15

Numbers 24

When Balaam saw that it pleased the LORD to bless Israel, he did not go, as at other times, to look for omens, but set his face toward the wilderness. ²And Balaam lifted up his eyes and saw Israel camping tribe by tribe. And the Spirit of God came upon him, ³and he took up his discourse and said,

> "The oracle of Balaam the son of Beor,
>   the oracle of the man whose eye is opened,²
> 4   the oracle of him who hears the words of God,
>   who sees the vision of the Almighty,
>   falling down with his eyes uncovered:
> 5   How lovely are your tents, O Jacob,
>   your encampments, O Israel!

> 6   Like palm groves³ that stretch afar,
>   like gardens beside a river,
>   like aloes that the LORD has planted,
>   like cedar trees beside the waters.
> 7   Water shall flow from his buckets,
>   and his seed shall be in many waters;
>   his king shall be higher than Agag,
>   and his kingdom shall be exalted.
> 8   God brings him out of Egypt
>   and is for him like the horns of the wild ox;
>   he shall eat up the nations, his adversaries,
>   and shall break their bones in pieces
>   and pierce them through with his arrows.

¹ Greek girding up the loins of your mind ² Or closed, or perfect; also verse 15 ³ Or valleys

9 He crouched, he lay down like a lion
    and like a lioness; who will rouse him
        up?
   Blessed are those who bless you,
    and cursed are those who curse you."

¹⁰And Balak's anger was kindled against Balaam, and he struck his hands together. And Balak said to Balaam, "I called you to curse my enemies, and behold, you have blessed them these three times. ¹¹Therefore now flee to your own place. I said, 'I will certainly honor you,' but the LORD has held you back from honor." ¹²And Balaam said to Balak, "Did I not tell your messengers whom you sent to me, ¹³ 'If Balak should give me his house full of silver and gold, I would not be able to go beyond the word of the LORD, to do either good or bad of my own will. What the LORD speaks, that will I speak'? ¹⁴And now, behold, I am going to my people. Come, I will let you know what this people will do to your people in the latter days."

¹⁵And he took up his discourse and said,

   "The oracle of Balaam the son of Beor,
    the oracle of the man whose eye is
        opened,
16 the oracle of him who hears the words
        of God,
    and knows the knowledge of the Most
        High,
   who sees the vision of the Almighty,
    falling down with his eyes uncovered:
17 I see him, but not now;
    I behold him, but not near:
   a star shall come out of Jacob,
    and a scepter shall rise out of Israel;
   it shall crush the forehead¹ of Moab
    and break down all the sons of Sheth.
18 Edom shall be dispossessed;
    Seir also, his enemies, shall be
        dispossessed.
   Israel is doing valiantly.
19 And one from Jacob shall exercise
        dominion
    and destroy the survivors of cities!"

²⁰Then he looked on Amalek and took up his discourse and said,

   "Amalek was the first among the
        nations,
    but its end is utter destruction."

²¹And he looked on the Kenite, and took up his discourse and said,

   "Enduring is your dwelling place,
    and your nest is set in the rock.
22 Nevertheless, Kain shall be burned
    when Asshur takes you away captive."

²³And he took up his discourse and said,

   "Alas, who shall live when God does
        this?
24 But ships shall come from Kittim
   and shall afflict Asshur and Eber;
    and he too shall come to utter
        destruction."

²⁵Then Balaam rose and went back to his place. And Balak also went his way.

Psalm 66–67

TO THE CHOIRMASTER. A SONG. A PSALM.

Shout for joy to God, all the earth;
    ²sing the glory of his name;
    give to him glorious praise!
3   Say to God, "How awesome are your
        deeds!
   So great is your power that your
        enemies come cringing to you.
4   All the earth worships you
    and sings praises to you;
    they sing praises to your name." *Selah*

5   Come and see what God has done:
    he is awesome in his deeds toward the
        children of man.
6   He turned the sea into dry land;
    they passed through the river on foot.
   There did we rejoice in him,
7   who rules by his might forever,
   whose eyes keep watch on the nations—
    let not the rebellious exalt themselves.
                                            Selah

8   Bless our God, O peoples;
    let the sound of his praise be heard,
9   who has kept our soul among the living
    and has not let our feet slip.
10 For you, O God, have tested us;
    you have tried us as silver is tried.
11 You brought us into the net;
    you laid a crushing burden on our
        backs;

¹ Hebrew *corners* [of the head]

¹² you let men ride over our heads;
we went through fire and through
water;
yet you have brought us out to a place of
abundance.

¹³ I will come into your house with burnt
offerings;
I will perform my vows to you,
¹⁴ that which my lips uttered
and my mouth promised when I was
in trouble.
¹⁵ I will offer to you burnt offerings of
fattened animals,
with the smoke of the sacrifice of rams;
I will make an offering of bulls and
goats. *Selah*

¹⁶ Come and hear, all you who fear God,
and I will tell what he has done for my
soul.
¹⁷ I cried to him with my mouth,
and high praise was on[1] my tongue.[2]
¹⁸ If I had cherished iniquity in my heart,
the Lord would not have listened.
¹⁹ But truly God has listened;
he has attended to the voice of my
prayer.

²⁰ Blessed be God,
because he has not rejected my prayer
or removed his steadfast love from me!

To the choirmaster: with stringed
instruments. A Psalm. A Song.

May God be gracious to us and bless us
and make his face to shine upon us,
Selah
² that your way may be known on earth,
your saving power among all nations.
³ Let the peoples praise you, O God;
let all the peoples praise you!

⁴ Let the nations be glad and sing for joy,
for you judge the peoples with equity
and guide the nations upon earth.
Selah
⁵ Let the peoples praise you, O God;
let all the peoples praise you!

⁶ The earth has yielded its increase;
God, our God, shall bless us.
⁷ God shall bless us;
let all the ends of the earth fear him!

Isaiah 14

For the Lord will have compassion on Jacob and will again choose Israel, and will set them in their own land, and sojourners will join them and will attach themselves to the house of Jacob. ²And the peoples will take them and bring them to their place, and the house of Israel will possess them in the Lord's land as male and female slaves.[3] They will take captive those who were their captors, and rule over those who oppressed them.

³ When the Lord has given you rest from your pain and turmoil and the hard service with which you were made to serve, ⁴you will take up this taunt against the king of Babylon:

"How the oppressor has ceased,
the insolent fury[4] ceased!
⁵ The Lord has broken the staff of the
wicked,
the scepter of rulers,
⁶ that struck the peoples in wrath
with unceasing blows,
that ruled the nations in anger
with unrelenting persecution.
⁷ The whole earth is at rest and quiet;
they break forth into singing.
⁸ The cypresses rejoice at you,
the cedars of Lebanon, saying,
'Since you were laid low,
no woodcutter comes up against us.'
⁹ Sheol beneath is stirred up
to meet you when you come;
it rouses the shades to greet you,
all who were leaders of the earth;
it raises from their thrones
all who were kings of the nations.
¹⁰ All of them will answer
and say to you:
'You too have become as weak as we!
You have become like us!'
¹¹ Your pomp is brought down to Sheol,
the sound of your harps;
maggots are laid as a bed beneath you,
and worms are your covers.

¹² "How you are fallen from heaven,
O Day Star, son of Dawn!
How you are cut down to the ground,
you who laid the nations low!
¹³ You said in your heart,
'I will ascend to heaven;

[1] Hebrew *under* [2] Or *and he was exalted with my tongue* [3] Or *servants* [4] Dead Sea Scroll (compare Septuagint, Syriac, Vulgate); the meaning of the word in the Masoretic Text is uncertain

above the stars of God
  I will set my throne on high;
I will sit on the mount of assembly
  in the far reaches of the north;[1]
[14] I will ascend above the heights of the
  clouds;
I will make myself like the Most High.'
[15] But you are brought down to Sheol,
  to the far reaches of the pit.
[16] Those who see you will stare at you
  and ponder over you:
'Is this the man who made the earth
  tremble,
who shook kingdoms,
[17] who made the world like a desert
  and overthrew its cities,
who did not let his prisoners go
  home?'
[18] All the kings of the nations lie in glory,
  each in his own tomb;[2]
[19] but you are cast out, away from your
  grave,
like a loathed branch,
clothed with the slain, those pierced by
  the sword,
who go down to the stones of the pit,
like a dead body trampled underfoot.
[20] You will not be joined with them in
  burial,
because you have destroyed your land,
  you have slain your people.

"May the offspring of evildoers
  nevermore be named!
[21] Prepare slaughter for his sons
  because of the guilt of their fathers,
lest they rise and possess the earth,
  and fill the face of the world with
  cities."

[22] "I will rise up against them," declares the
Lord of hosts, "and will cut off from Babylon
name and remnant, descendants and posterity,"
declares the Lord. [23] "And I will make it a possession of the hedgehog,[3] and pools of water,
and I will sweep it with the broom of destruction," declares the Lord of hosts.

[24] The Lord of hosts has sworn:
"As I have planned,
  so shall it be,
and as I have purposed,
  so shall it stand,

[25] that I will break the Assyrian in my
  land,
and on my mountains trample him
  underfoot;
and his yoke shall depart from them,
  and his burden from their shoulder."

[26] This is the purpose that is purposed
  concerning the whole earth,
and this is the hand that is stretched out
  over all the nations.
[27] For the Lord of hosts has purposed,
  and who will annul it?
His hand is stretched out,
  and who will turn it back?

[28] In the year that King Ahaz died came this
oracle:

[29] Rejoice not, O Philistia, all of you,
  that the rod that struck you is broken,
for from the serpent's root will come
    forth an adder,
  and its fruit will be a flying fiery
    serpent.
[30] And the firstborn of the poor will graze,
  and the needy lie down in safety;
but I will kill your root with famine,
  and your remnant it will slay.
[31] Wail, O gate; cry out, O city;
  melt in fear, O Philistia, all of you!
For smoke comes out of the north,
  and there is no straggler in his ranks.

[32] What will one answer the messengers of
  the nation?
"The Lord has founded Zion,
  and in her the afflicted of his people
    find refuge."

——————— *1 Peter 2* ———————

So put away all malice and all deceit and
hypocrisy and envy and all slander. [2] Like
newborn infants, long for the pure spiritual
milk, that by it you may grow up into salvation— [3] if indeed you have tasted that the Lord
is good.
  [4] As you come to him, a living stone rejected
by men but in the sight of God chosen and
precious, [5] you yourselves like living stones
are being built up as a spiritual house, to be
a holy priesthood, to offer spiritual sacrifices

[1] Or *in the remote parts of Zaphon* [2] Hebrew *house* [3] Possibly *porcupine*, or *owl*

acceptable to God through Jesus Christ. **⁶**For it stands in Scripture:

> "Behold, I am laying in Zion a stone,
> a cornerstone chosen and precious,
> and whoever believes in him will not be
> put to shame."

⁷So the honor is for you who believe, but for those who do not believe,

> "The stone that the builders rejected
> has become the cornerstone,"¹

⁸and

> "A stone of stumbling,
> and a rock of offense."

They stumble because they disobey the word, as they were destined to do. **⁹**But you are a chosen race, a royal priesthood, a holy nation, a people for his own possession, that you may proclaim the excellencies of him who called you out of darkness into his marvelous light. **¹⁰**Once you were not a people, but now you are God's people; once you had not received mercy, but now you have received mercy. **¹¹**Beloved, I urge you as sojourners and exiles to abstain from the passions of the flesh, which wage war against your soul. **¹²**Keep your conduct among the Gentiles honorable, so that when they speak against you as evildoers, they may see your good deeds and glorify God on the day of visitation.

¹³Be subject for the Lord's sake to every human institution,² whether it be to the emperor³ as supreme, **¹⁴**or to governors as sent by him to punish those who do evil and to praise those who do good. **¹⁵**For this is the will of God, that by doing good you should put to silence the ignorance of foolish people. **¹⁶**Live as people who are free, not using your freedom as a cover-up for evil, but living as servants⁴ of God. **¹⁷**Honor everyone. Love the brotherhood. Fear God. Honor the emperor.

¹⁸Servants, be subject to your masters with all respect, not only to the good and gentle but also to the unjust. **¹⁹**For this is a gracious thing, when, mindful of God, one endures sorrows while suffering unjustly. **²⁰**For what credit is it if, when you sin and are beaten for it, you endure? But if when you do good and suffer for it you endure, this is a gracious thing in the sight of God. **²¹**For to this you have been called, because Christ also suffered for you, leaving you an example, so that you might follow in his steps. **²²**He committed no sin, neither was deceit found in his mouth. **²³**When he was reviled, he did not revile in return; when he suffered, he did not threaten, but continued entrusting himself to him who judges justly. **²⁴**He himself bore our sins in his body on the tree, that we might die to sin and live to righteousness. By his wounds you have been healed. **²⁵**For you were straying like sheep, but have now returned to the Shepherd and Overseer of your souls.

MAY 16

Numbers 25

While Israel lived in Shittim, the people began to whore with the daughters of Moab. **²**These invited the people to the sacrifices of their gods, and the people ate and bowed down to their gods. **³**So Israel yoked himself to Baal of Peor. And the anger of the LORD was kindled against Israel. **⁴**And the LORD said to Moses, "Take all the chiefs of the people and hang⁵ them in the sun before the LORD, that the fierce anger of the LORD may turn away from Israel." **⁵**And Moses said to the judges of Israel, "Each of you kill those of his men who have yoked themselves to Baal of Peor."

⁶And behold, one of the people of Israel came and brought a Midianite woman to his family, in the sight of Moses and in the sight of

---

¹ Greek *the head of the corner* ² Or *every institution ordained for people* ³ Or *king; also verse 17* ⁴ Greek *bondservants* ⁵ Or *impale*

the whole congregation of the people of Israel, while they were weeping in the entrance of the tent of meeting. **7** When Phinehas the son of Eleazar, son of Aaron the priest, saw it, he rose and left the congregation and took a spear in his hand **8** and went after the man of Israel into the chamber and pierced both of them, the man of Israel and the woman through her belly. Thus the plague on the people of Israel was stopped. **9** Nevertheless, those who died by the plague were twenty-four thousand.

10 And the LORD said to Moses, **11** "Phinehas the son of Eleazar, son of Aaron the priest, has turned back my wrath from the people of Israel, in that he was jealous with my jealousy among them, so that I did not consume the people of Israel in my jealousy. **12** Therefore say, 'Behold, I give to him my covenant of peace, **13** and it shall be to him and to his descendants after him the covenant of a perpetual priesthood, because he was jealous for his God and made atonement for the people of Israel.'"

14 The name of the slain man of Israel, who was killed with the Midianite woman, was Zimri the son of Salu, chief of a father's house belonging to the Simeonites. **15** And the name of the Midianite woman who was killed was Cozbi the daughter of Zur, who was the tribal head of a father's house in Midian.

16 And the LORD spoke to Moses, saying, **17** "Harass the Midianites and strike them down, **18** for they have harassed you with their wiles, with which they beguiled you in the matter of Peor, and in the matter of Cozbi, the daughter of the chief of Midian, their sister, who was killed on the day of the plague on account of Peor."

─────── *Psalm 68* ───────

TO THE CHOIRMASTER. A PSALM OF DAVID. A SONG.

G od shall arise, his enemies shall be scattered;
    and those who hate him shall flee
      before him!
2 As smoke is driven away, so you shall
      drive them away;
    as wax melts before fire,
      so the wicked shall perish before God!
3 But the righteous shall be glad;
    they shall exult before God;
    they shall be jubilant with joy!

4 Sing to God, sing praises to his name;
    lift up a song to him who rides
      through the deserts;
his name is the LORD;
    exult before him!
5 Father of the fatherless and protector of
    widows
    is God in his holy habitation.
6 God settles the solitary in a home;
    he leads out the prisoners to
      prosperity,
    but the rebellious dwell in a parched
      land.

7 O God, when you went out before your
    people,
    when you marched through the
      wilderness,   *Selah*
8 the earth quaked, the heavens poured
      down rain,
    before God, the One of Sinai,
    before God, the God of Israel.
9 Rain in abundance, O God, you shed
      abroad;
    you restored your inheritance as it
      languished;
10 your flock[1] found a dwelling in it;
    in your goodness, O God, you
      provided for the needy.

11 The Lord gives the word;
    the women who announce the news
      are a great host:
12 "The kings of the armies—they flee,
      they flee!"
The women at home divide the spoil—
13   though you men lie among the
      sheepfolds—
the wings of a dove covered with silver,
    its pinions with shimmering gold.
14 When the Almighty scatters kings there,
    let snow fall on Zalmon.

15 O mountain of God, mountain of
      Bashan;
    O many-peaked[2] mountain, mountain
      of Bashan!
16 Why do you look with hatred, O many-
      peaked mountain,
    at the mount that God desired for his
      abode,
    yes, where the LORD will dwell
      forever?

[1] Or *your congregation* [2] Or *hunch-backed*; also verse 16

17 The chariots of God are twice ten
    thousand,
    thousands upon thousands;
    the Lord is among them; Sinai is now
    in the sanctuary.
18 You ascended on high,
    leading a host of captives in your
    train
    and receiving gifts among men,
    even among the rebellious, that the
    LORD God may dwell there.
19 Blessed be the Lord,
    who daily bears us up;
    God is our salvation.   *Selah*
20 Our God is a God of salvation,
    and to GOD, the Lord, belong
    deliverances from death.
21 But God will strike the heads of his
    enemies,
    the hairy crown of him who walks in
    his guilty ways.
22 The Lord said,
    "I will bring them back from Bashan,
    I will bring them back from the depths
    of the sea,
23 that you may strike your feet in their
    blood,
    that the tongues of your dogs may
    have their portion from the foe."
24 Your procession is[1] seen, O God,
    the procession of my God, my King,
    into the sanctuary—
25 the singers in front, the musicians last,
    between them virgins playing
    tambourines:
26 "Bless God in the great congregation,
    the LORD, O you[2] who are of Israel's
    fountain!"
27 There is Benjamin, the least of them, in
    the lead,
    the princes of Judah in their throng,
    the princes of Zebulun, the princes of
    Naphtali.
28 Summon your power, O God,[3]
    the power, O God, by which you have
    worked for us.
29 Because of your temple at Jerusalem
    kings shall bear gifts to you.

30 Rebuke the beasts that dwell among the
    reeds,
    the herd of bulls with the calves of the
    peoples.
    Trample underfoot those who lust after
    tribute;
    scatter the peoples who delight in war.[4]
31 Nobles shall come from Egypt;
    Cush shall hasten to stretch out her
    hands to God.
32 O kingdoms of the earth, sing to God;
    sing praises to the Lord,   *Selah*
33 to him who rides in the heavens, the
    ancient heavens;
    behold, he sends out his voice, his
    mighty voice.
34 Ascribe power to God,
    whose majesty is over Israel,
    and whose power is in the skies.
35 Awesome is God from his[5] sanctuary;
    the God of Israel—he is the one who
    gives power and strength to his
    people.
    Blessed be God!

Isaiah 15

An oracle concerning Moab.

Because Ar of Moab is laid waste in a
    night,
    Moab is undone;
because Kir of Moab is laid waste in a
    night,
    Moab is undone.
2 He has gone up to the temple,[6] and to
    Dibon,
    to the high places[7] to weep;
over Nebo and over Medeba
    Moab wails.
On every head is baldness;
    every beard is shorn;
3 in the streets they wear sackcloth;
    on the housetops and in the squares
    everyone wails and melts in tears.
4 Heshbon and Elealeh cry out;
    their voice is heard as far as Jahaz;
    therefore the armed men of Moab cry
    aloud;
    his soul trembles.

[1] Or *has been* [2] The Hebrew *for you* is plural here [3] By revocalization (compare Septuagint); Hebrew *Your God has summoned your power* [4] The meaning of the Hebrew verse is uncertain [5] Septuagint; Hebrew *your* [6] Hebrew *the house* [7] Or *temple, even Dibon to the high places*

5 My heart cries out for Moab;
　　her fugitives flee to Zoar,
　　to Eglath-shelishiyah.
For at the ascent of Luhith
　　they go up weeping;
on the road to Horonaim
　　they raise a cry of destruction;
6 the waters of Nimrim
　　are a desolation;
the grass is withered, the vegetation fails,
　　the greenery is no more.
7 Therefore the abundance they have
　　　gained
　　and what they have laid up
they carry away
　　over the Brook of the Willows.
8 For a cry has gone
　　around the land of Moab;
her wailing reaches to Eglaim;
　　her wailing reaches to Beer-elim.
9 For the waters of Dibon[1] are full of blood;
　　for I will bring upon Dibon even more,
a lion for those of Moab who escape,
　　for the remnant of the land.

1 Peter 3

Likewise, wives, be subject to your own husbands, so that even if some do not obey the word, they may be won without a word by the conduct of their wives, [2]when they see your respectful and pure conduct. [3]Do not let your adorning be external—the braiding of hair and the putting on of gold jewelry, or the clothing you wear— [4]but let your adorning be the hidden person of the heart with the imperishable beauty of a gentle and quiet spirit, which in God's sight is very precious. [5]For this is how the holy women who hoped in God used to adorn themselves, by submitting to their own husbands, [6]as Sarah obeyed Abraham, calling him lord. And you are her children, if you do good and do not fear anything that is frightening.

[7]Likewise, husbands, live with your wives in an understanding way, showing honor to the woman as the weaker vessel, since they are heirs with you[2] of the grace of life, so that your prayers may not be hindered.

[8]Finally, all of you, have unity of mind, sympathy, brotherly love, a tender heart, and a humble mind. [9]Do not repay evil for evil or reviling for reviling, but on the contrary, bless, for to this you were called, that you may obtain a blessing. [10]For

"Whoever desires to love life
　　and see good days,
let him keep his tongue from evil
　　and his lips from speaking deceit;
11 let him turn away from evil and do good;
　　let him seek peace and pursue it.
12 For the eyes of the Lord are on the
　　　righteous,
　　and his ears are open to their prayer.
But the face of the Lord is against those
　　who do evil."

[13]Now who is there to harm you if you are zealous for what is good? [14]But even if you should suffer for righteousness' sake, you will be blessed. Have no fear of them, nor be troubled, [15]but in your hearts honor Christ the Lord as holy, always being prepared to make a defense to anyone who asks you for a reason for the hope that is in you; yet do it with gentleness and respect, [16]having a good conscience, so that, when you are slandered, those who revile your good behavior in Christ may be put to shame. [17]For it is better to suffer for doing good, if that should be God's will, than for doing evil.

[18]For Christ also suffered[3] once for sins, the righteous for the unrighteous, that he might bring us to God, being put to death in the flesh but made alive in the spirit, [19]in which[4] he went and proclaimed[5] to the spirits in prison, [20]because[6] they formerly did not obey, when God's patience waited in the days of Noah, while the ark was being prepared, in which a few, that is, eight persons, were brought safely through water. [21]Baptism, which corresponds to this, now saves you, not as a removal of dirt from the body but as an appeal to God for a good conscience, through the resurrection of Jesus Christ, [22]who has gone into heaven and is at the right hand of God, with angels, authorities, and powers having been subjected to him.

[1] Dead Sea Scroll, Vulgate (compare Syriac); Masoretic Text *Dimon*; twice in this verse [2] Some manuscripts *since you are joint heirs* [3] Some manuscripts *died* [4] Or *the Spirit, in whom* [5] Or *preached* [6] Or *when*

MAY 17

Numbers 26

After the plague, the LORD said to Moses and to Eleazar the son of Aaron, the priest, [2] "Take a census of all the congregation of the people of Israel, from twenty years old and upward, by their fathers' houses, all in Israel who are able to go to war." [3] And Moses and Eleazar the priest spoke with them in the plains of Moab by the Jordan at Jericho, saying, [4] "Take a census of the people,[1] from twenty years old and upward," as the LORD commanded Moses. The people of Israel who came out of the land of Egypt were:

[5] Reuben, the firstborn of Israel; the sons of Reuben: of Hanoch, the clan of the Hanochites; of Pallu, the clan of the Palluites; [6] of Hezron, the clan of the Hezronites; of Carmi, the clan of the Carmites. [7] These are the clans of the Reubenites, and those listed were 43,730. [8] And the sons of Pallu: Eliab. [9] The sons of Eliab: Nemuel, Dathan, and Abiram. These are the Dathan and Abiram, chosen from the congregation, who contended against Moses and Aaron in the company of Korah, when they contended against the LORD [10] and the earth opened its mouth and swallowed them up together with Korah, when that company died, when the fire devoured 250 men, and they became a warning. [11] But the sons of Korah did not die.

[12] The sons of Simeon according to their clans: of Nemuel, the clan of the Nemuelites; of Jamin, the clan of the Jaminites; of Jachin, the clan of the Jachinites; [13] of Zerah, the clan of the Zerahites; of Shaul, the clan of the Shaulites. [14] These are the clans of the Simeonites, 22,200.

[15] The sons of Gad according to their clans: of Zephon, the clan of the Zephonites; of Haggi, the clan of the Haggites; of Shuni, the clan of the Shunites; [16] of Ozni, the clan of the Oznites; of Eri, the clan of the Erites; [17] of Arod, the clan of the Arodites; of Areli, the clan of the Arelites. [18] These are the clans of the sons of Gad as they were listed, 40,500.

[19] The sons of Judah were Er and Onan; and Er and Onan died in the land of Canaan. [20] And the sons of Judah according to their clans were: of Shelah, the clan of the Shelanites; of Perez, the clan of the Perezites; of Zerah, the clan of the Zerahites. [21] And the sons of Perez were: of Hezron, the clan of the Hezronites; of Hamul, the clan of the Hamulites. [22] These are the clans of Judah as they were listed, 76,500.

[23] The sons of Issachar according to their clans: of Tola, the clan of the Tolaites; of Puvah, the clan of the Punites; [24] of Jashub, the clan of the Jashubites; of Shimron, the clan of the Shimronites. [25] These are the clans of Issachar as they were listed, 64,300.

[26] The sons of Zebulun, according to their clans: of Sered, the clan of the Seredites; of Elon, the clan of the Elonites; of Jahleel, the clan of the Jahleelites. [27] These are the clans of the Zebulunites as they were listed, 60,500.

[28] The sons of Joseph according to their clans: Manasseh and Ephraim. [29] The sons of Manasseh: of Machir, the clan of the Machirites; and Machir was the father of Gilead; of Gilead, the clan of the Gileadites. [30] These are the sons of Gilead: of Iezer, the clan of the Iezerites; of Helek, the clan of the Helekites; [31] and of Asriel, the clan of the Asrielites; and of Shechem, the clan of the Shechemites; [32] and of Shemida, the clan of the Shemidaites; and of Hepher, the clan of the Hepherites. [33] Now Zelophehad the son of Hepher had no sons, but daughters. And the names of the daughters of Zelophehad were Mahlah, Noah, Hoglah, Milcah, and Tirzah. [34] These are the clans of Manasseh, and those listed were 52,700.

[35] These are the sons of Ephraim according to their clans: of Shuthelah, the clan of the Shuthelahites; of Becher, the clan of the Becherites; of Tahan, the clan of the Tahanites. [36] And these are the sons of Shuthelah: of Eran, the clan of the Eranites. [37] These are the clans of the sons of Ephraim as they were listed, 32,500. These are the sons of Joseph according to their clans.

[38] The sons of Benjamin according to their

---

[1] *Take a census of the people* is implied (compare verse 2)

clans: of Bela, the clan of the Belaites; of Ashbel, the clan of the Ashbelites; of Ahiram, the clan of the Ahiramites; [39] of Shephupham, the clan of the Shuphamites; of Hupham, the clan of the Huphamites. [40] And the sons of Bela were Ard and Naaman: of Ard, the clan of the Ardites; of Naaman, the clan of the Naamites. [41] These are the sons of Benjamin according to their clans, and those listed were 45,600.

[42] These are the sons of Dan according to their clans: of Shuham, the clan of the Shuhamites. These are the clans of Dan according to their clans. [43] All the clans of the Shuhamites, as they were listed, were 64,400.

[44] The sons of Asher according to their clans: of Imnah, the clan of the Imnites; of Ishvi, the clan of the Ishvites; of Beriah, the clan of the Beriites. [45] Of the sons of Beriah: of Heber, the clan of the Heberites; of Malchiel, the clan of the Malchielites. [46] And the name of the daughter of Asher was Serah. [47] These are the clans of the sons of Asher as they were listed, 53,400.

[48] The sons of Naphtali according to their clans: of Jahzeel, the clan of the Jahzeelites; of Guni, the clan of the Gunites; [49] of Jezer, the clan of the Jezerites; of Shillem, the clan of the Shillemites. [50] These are the clans of Naphtali according to their clans, and those listed were 45,400.

[51] This was the list of the people of Israel, 601,730.

[52] The LORD spoke to Moses, saying, [53] "Among these the land shall be divided for inheritance according to the number of names. [54] To a large tribe you shall give a large inheritance, and to a small tribe you shall give a small inheritance; every tribe shall be given its inheritance in proportion to its list. [55] But the land shall be divided by lot. According to the names of the tribes of their fathers they shall inherit. [56] Their inheritance shall be divided according to lot between the larger and the smaller."

[57] This was the list of the Levites according to their clans: of Gershon, the clan of the Gershonites; of Kohath, the clan of the Kohathites; of Merari, the clan of the Merarites. [58] These are the clans of Levi: the clan of the Libnites, the clan of the Hebronites, the clan of the Mahlites, the clan of the Mushites, the clan of the Korahites. And Kohath was the father of Amram. [59] The name of Amram's wife was Jochebed the daughter of Levi, who was born to Levi in Egypt. And she bore to Amram Aaron and Moses and Miriam their sister. [60] And to Aaron were born Nadab, Abihu, Eleazar, and Ithamar. [61] But Nadab and Abihu died when they offered unauthorized fire before the LORD. [62] And those listed were 23,000, every male from a month old and upward. For they were not listed among the people of Israel, because there was no inheritance given to them among the people of Israel.

[63] These were those listed by Moses and Eleazar the priest, who listed the people of Israel in the plains of Moab by the Jordan at Jericho. [64] But among these there was not one of those listed by Moses and Aaron the priest, who had listed the people of Israel in the wilderness of Sinai. [65] For the LORD had said of them, "They shall die in the wilderness." Not one of them was left, except Caleb the son of Jephunneh and Joshua the son of Nun.

Psalm 69

TO THE CHOIRMASTER: ACCORDING TO LILIES. OF DAVID.

Save me, O God!
    For the waters have come up to my neck.[1]
2   I sink in deep mire,
        where there is no foothold;
    I have come into deep waters,
        and the flood sweeps over me.
3   I am weary with my crying out;
        my throat is parched.
    My eyes grow dim
        with waiting for my God.

4   More in number than the hairs of my
            head
        are those who hate me without cause;
    mighty are those who would destroy me,
        those who attack me with lies.
    What I did not steal
        must I now restore?
5   O God, you know my folly;
        the wrongs I have done are not hidden
            from you.

6   Let not those who hope in you be put to
            shame through me,
        O Lord GOD of hosts;
    let not those who seek you be brought to
            dishonor through me,
        O God of Israel.

---

[1] Or waters threaten my life

7 For it is for your sake that I have borne
     reproach,
   that dishonor has covered my face.
8 I have become a stranger to my brothers,
   an alien to my mother's sons.
9 For zeal for your house has consumed
     me,
   and the reproaches of those who
     reproach you have fallen on me.
10 When I wept and humbled[1] my soul
     with fasting,
   it became my reproach.
11 When I made sackcloth my clothing,
   I became a byword to them.
12 I am the talk of those who sit in the gate,
   and the drunkards make songs about
     me.

13 But as for me, my prayer is to you,
     O Lord.
   At an acceptable time, O God,
   in the abundance of your steadfast
     love answer me in your saving
     faithfulness.
14 Deliver me
   from sinking in the mire;
   let me be delivered from my enemies
   and from the deep waters.
15 Let not the flood sweep over me,
   or the deep swallow me up,
   or the pit close its mouth over me.

16 Answer me, O Lord, for your steadfast
     love is good;
   according to your abundant mercy,
     turn to me.
17 Hide not your face from your servant;
   for I am in distress; make haste to
     answer me.
18 Draw near to my soul, redeem me;
   ransom me because of my enemies!

19 You know my reproach,
   and my shame and my dishonor;
   my foes are all known to you.
20 Reproaches have broken my heart,
   so that I am in despair.
   I looked for pity, but there was none,
   and for comforters, but I found none.
21 They gave me poison for food,
   and for my thirst they gave me sour
     wine to drink.

22 Let their own table before them become
     a snare;
   and when they are at peace, let it
     become a trap.[2]
23 Let their eyes be darkened, so that they
     cannot see,
   and make their loins tremble
     continually.
24 Pour out your indignation upon them,
   and let your burning anger overtake
     them.
25 May their camp be a desolation;
   let no one dwell in their tents.
26 For they persecute him whom you have
     struck down,
   and they recount the pain of those
     you have wounded.
27 Add to them punishment upon
     punishment;
   may they have no acquittal from you.[3]
28 Let them be blotted out of the book of
     the living;
   let them not be enrolled among the
     righteous.
29 But I am afflicted and in pain;
   let your salvation, O God, set me on
     high!

30 I will praise the name of God with a song;
   I will magnify him with thanksgiving.
31 This will please the Lord more than
     an ox
   or a bull with horns and hoofs.
32 When the humble see it they will be
     glad;
   you who seek God, let your hearts
     revive.
33 For the Lord hears the needy
   and does not despise his own people
     who are prisoners.

34 Let heaven and earth praise him,
   the seas and everything that moves in
     them.
35 For God will save Zion
   and build up the cities of Judah,
   and people shall dwell there and possess
     it;
36 the offspring of his servants shall
     inherit it,
   and those who love his name shall
     dwell in it.

[1] Hebrew lacks *and humbled* [2] Hebrew; a slight revocalization yields (compare Septuagint, Syriac, Jerome) *a snare, and retribution and a trap* [3] Hebrew *may they not come into your righteousness*

Isaiah 16

Send the lamb to the ruler of the land,
    from Sela, by way of the desert,
        to the mount of the daughter of Zion.
2   Like fleeing birds,
        like a scattered nest,
    so are the daughters of Moab
        at the fords of the Arnon.

3   "Give counsel;
        grant justice;
    make your shade like night
        at the height of noon;
    shelter the outcasts;
        do not reveal the fugitive;
4   let the outcasts of Moab
        sojourn among you;
    be a shelter to them[1]
        from the destroyer.
    When the oppressor is no more,
        and destruction has ceased,
    and he who tramples underfoot has
            vanished from the land,
5   then a throne will be established in
            steadfast love,
        and on it will sit in faithfulness
            in the tent of David
    one who judges and seeks justice
        and is swift to do righteousness."

6   We have heard of the pride of Moab—
        how proud he is!—
    of his arrogance, his pride, and his
            insolence;
        in his idle boasting he is not right.
7   Therefore let Moab wail for Moab,
        let everyone wail.
    Mourn, utterly stricken,
        for the raisin cakes of Kir-hareseth.
8   For the fields of Heshbon languish,
        and the vine of Sibmah;
    the lords of the nations
        have struck down its branches,
    which reached to Jazer
        and strayed to the desert;
    its shoots spread abroad
        and passed over the sea.
9   Therefore I weep with the weeping of
            Jazer
        for the vine of Sibmah;

    I drench you with my tears,
        O Heshbon and Elealeh;
    for over your summer fruit and your
            harvest
        the shout has ceased.
10 And joy and gladness are taken away
            from the fruitful field,
    and in the vineyards no songs are sung,
        no cheers are raised;
    no treader treads out wine in the
            presses;
        I have put an end to the shouting.
11 Therefore my inner parts moan like a
            lyre for Moab,
        and my inmost self for Kir-hareseth.

12 And when Moab presents himself, when he wearies himself on the high place, when he comes to his sanctuary to pray, he will not prevail.

13 This is the word that the LORD spoke concerning Moab in the past. 14 But now the LORD has spoken, saying, "In three years, like the years of a hired worker, the glory of Moab will be brought into contempt, in spite of all his great multitude, and those who remain will be very few and feeble."

1 Peter 4

Since therefore Christ suffered in the flesh,[2] arm yourselves with the same way of thinking, for whoever has suffered in the flesh has ceased from sin, 2 so as to live for the rest of the time in the flesh no longer for human passions but for the will of God. 3 For the time that is past suffices for doing what the Gentiles want to do, living in sensuality, passions, drunkenness, orgies, drinking parties, and lawless idolatry. 4 With respect to this they are surprised when you do not join them in the same flood of debauchery, and they malign you; 5 but they will give account to him who is ready to judge the living and the dead. 6 For this is why the gospel was preached even to those who are dead, that though judged in the flesh the way people are, they might live in the spirit the way God does. 7 The end of all things is at hand; therefore be self-controlled and sober-minded for the sake of your prayers. 8 Above all, keep loving one another earnestly, since love covers a multitude of sins. 9 Show hospitality to one another

---

[1] Some Hebrew manuscripts, Septuagint, Syriac; Masoretic Text *let my outcasts sojourn among you; as for Moab, be a shelter to them* [2] Some manuscripts add *for us*; some *for you*

without grumbling. ¹⁰As each has received a gift, use it to serve one another, as good stewards of God's varied grace: ¹¹whoever speaks, as one who speaks oracles of God; whoever serves, as one who serves by the strength that God supplies—in order that in everything God may be glorified through Jesus Christ. To him belong glory and dominion forever and ever. Amen.

¹²Beloved, do not be surprised at the fiery trial when it comes upon you to test you, as though something strange were happening to you. ¹³But rejoice insofar as you share Christ's sufferings, that you may also rejoice and be glad when his glory is revealed. ¹⁴If you are insulted for the name of Christ, you are blessed, because the Spirit of glory¹ and of God rests upon you. ¹⁵But let none of you suffer as a murderer or a thief or an evildoer or as a meddler. ¹⁶Yet if anyone suffers as a Christian, let him not be ashamed, but let him glorify God in that name. ¹⁷For it is time for judgment to begin at the household of God; and if it begins with us, what will be the outcome for those who do not obey the gospel of God? ¹⁸And

> "If the righteous is scarcely saved,
> what will become of the ungodly and
>   the sinner?"²

¹⁹Therefore let those who suffer according to God's will entrust their souls to a faithful Creator while doing good.

MAY 18

Numbers 27

Then drew near the daughters of Zelophehad the son of Hepher, son of Gilead, son of Machir, son of Manasseh, from the clans of Manasseh the son of Joseph. The names of his daughters were: Mahlah, Noah, Hoglah, Milcah, and Tirzah. ²And they stood before Moses and before Eleazar the priest and before the chiefs and all the congregation, at the entrance of the tent of meeting, saying, ³"Our father died in the wilderness. He was not among the company of those who gathered themselves together against the LORD in the company of Korah, but died for his own sin. And he had no sons. ⁴Why should the name of our father be taken away from his clan because he had no son? Give to us a possession among our father's brothers."

⁵Moses brought their case before the LORD. ⁶And the LORD said to Moses, ⁷"The daughters of Zelophehad are right. You shall give them possession of an inheritance among their father's brothers and transfer the inheritance of their father to them. ⁸And you shall speak to the people of Israel, saying, 'If a man dies and has no son, then you shall transfer his inheritance to his daughter. ⁹And if he has no daughter, then you shall give his inheritance to his brothers. ¹⁰And if he has no brothers, then you shall give his inheritance to his father's brothers. ¹¹And if his father has no brothers, then you shall give his inheritance to the nearest kinsman of his clan, and he shall possess it. And it shall be for the people of Israel a statute and rule, as the LORD commanded Moses.'"

¹²The LORD said to Moses, "Go up into this mountain of Abarim and see the land that I have given to the people of Israel. ¹³When you have seen it, you also shall be gathered to your people, as your brother Aaron was, ¹⁴because you rebelled against my word in the wilderness of Zin when the congregation quarreled, failing to uphold me as holy at the waters before their eyes." (These are the waters of Meribah of Kadesh in the wilderness of Zin.) ¹⁵Moses spoke to the LORD, saying, ¹⁶"Let the LORD, the God of the spirits of all flesh, appoint a man over the congregation ¹⁷who shall go out before them and come in before them, who shall lead them out and bring them in, that the congregation of the LORD may not be as sheep that have no shepherd." ¹⁸So the LORD said to Moses, "Take

¹ Some manuscripts insert *and of power* ² Greek *where will the ungodly and sinner appear?*

Joshua the son of Nun, a man in whom is the Spirit, and lay your hand on him. ¹⁹Make him stand before Eleazar the priest and all the congregation, and you shall commission him in their sight. ²⁰You shall invest him with some of your authority, that all the congregation of the people of Israel may obey. ²¹And he shall stand before Eleazar the priest, who shall inquire for him by the judgment of the Urim before the LORD. At his word they shall go out, and at his word they shall come in, both he and all the people of Israel with him, the whole congregation." ²²And Moses did as the LORD commanded him. He took Joshua and made him stand before Eleazar the priest and the whole congregation, ²³and he laid his hands on him and commissioned him as the LORD directed through Moses.

Psalm 70–71

To the choirmaster. Of David, for the memorial offering.

Make haste, O God, to deliver me!
O LORD, make haste to help me!
² Let them be put to shame and confusion
   who seek my life!
   Let them be turned back and brought to
      dishonor
   who delight in my hurt!
³ Let them turn back because of their
      shame
   who say, "Aha, Aha!"

⁴ May all who seek you
   rejoice and be glad in you!
   May those who love your salvation
   say evermore, "God is great!"
⁵ But I am poor and needy;
   hasten to me, O God!
   You are my help and my deliverer;
   O LORD, do not delay!

In you, O LORD, do I take refuge;
let me never be put to shame!
² In your righteousness deliver me and
      rescue me;
   incline your ear to me, and save me!
³ Be to me a rock of refuge,
   to which I may continually come;
   you have given the command to save me,
   for you are my rock and my fortress.

⁴ Rescue me, O my God, from the hand of
      the wicked,
   from the grasp of the unjust and cruel
      man.
⁵ For you, O Lord, are my hope,
   my trust, O LORD, from my youth.
⁶ Upon you I have leaned from before my
      birth;
   you are he who took me from my
      mother's womb.
My praise is continually of you.

⁷ I have been as a portent to many,
   but you are my strong refuge.
⁸ My mouth is filled with your praise,
   and with your glory all the day.
⁹ Do not cast me off in the time of old age;
   forsake me not when my strength is
      spent.
¹⁰ For my enemies speak concerning me;
   those who watch for my life consult
      together
¹¹ and say, "God has forsaken him;
   pursue and seize him,
   for there is none to deliver him."

¹² O God, be not far from me;
   O my God, make haste to help me!
¹³ May my accusers be put to shame and
      consumed;
   with scorn and disgrace may they be
      covered
   who seek my hurt.
¹⁴ But I will hope continually
   and will praise you yet more and more.
¹⁵ My mouth will tell of your righteous acts,
   of your deeds of salvation all the day,
   for their number is past my
      knowledge.
¹⁶ With the mighty deeds of the Lord GOD
      I will come;
   I will remind them of your
      righteousness, yours alone.
¹⁷ O God, from my youth you have taught
      me,
   and I still proclaim your wondrous
      deeds.
¹⁸ So even to old age and gray hairs,
   O God, do not forsake me,
until I proclaim your might to another
      generation,
   your power to all those to come.

¹⁹ Your righteousness, O God,
　　reaches the high heavens.
　You who have done great things,
　　O God, who is like you?
²⁰ You who have made me see many
　　　troubles and calamities
　　will revive me again;
　from the depths of the earth
　　you will bring me up again.
²¹ You will increase my greatness
　　and comfort me again.

²² I will also praise you with the harp
　　for your faithfulness, O my God;
　I will sing praises to you with the lyre,
　　O Holy One of Israel.
²³ My lips will shout for joy,
　　when I sing praises to you;
　my soul also, which you have
　　redeemed.
²⁴ And my tongue will talk of your
　　　righteous help all the day long,
　for they have been put to shame and
　　disappointed
　　who sought to do me hurt.

Isaiah 17–18

An oracle concerning Damascus.

　Behold, Damascus will cease to be a city
　　and will become a heap of ruins.
² The cities of Aroer are deserted;
　　they will be for flocks,
　which will lie down, and none will
　　make them afraid.
³ The fortress will disappear from
　　Ephraim,
　　and the kingdom from Damascus;
　and the remnant of Syria will be
　　like the glory of the children of Israel,
　　　declares the LORD of hosts.

⁴ And in that day the glory of Jacob will be
　　　brought low,
　　and the fat of his flesh will grow lean.
⁵ And it shall be as when the reaper
　　　gathers standing grain
　　and his arm harvests the ears,
　and as when one gleans the ears of grain
　　in the Valley of Rephaim.
⁶ Gleanings will be left in it,
　　as when an olive tree is beaten—

two or three berries
　　in the top of the highest bough,
　four or five
　　on the branches of a fruit tree,
　　　declares the LORD God of Israel.

⁷In that day man will look to his Maker, and his eyes will look on the Holy One of Israel. ⁸He will not look to the altars, the work of his hands, and he will not look on what his own fingers have made, either the Asherim or the altars of incense.

⁹In that day their strong cities will be like the deserted places of the wooded heights and the hilltops, which they deserted because of the children of Israel, and there will be desolation.

¹⁰ For you have forgotten the God of your
　　　salvation
　　and have not remembered the Rock of
　　　your refuge;
　therefore, though you plant pleasant
　　　plants
　　and sow the vine-branch of a stranger,
¹¹ though you make them grow¹ on the
　　　day that you plant them,
　　and make them blossom in the
　　　morning that you sow,
　yet the harvest will flee away²
　　in a day of grief and incurable pain.

¹² Ah, the thunder of many peoples;
　　they thunder like the thundering of
　　　the sea!
　Ah, the roar of nations;
　　they roar like the roaring of mighty
　　　waters!
¹³ The nations roar like the roaring of
　　　many waters,
　　but he will rebuke them, and they will
　　　flee far away,
　chased like chaff on the mountains
　　before the wind
　　and whirling dust before the storm.
¹⁴ At evening time, behold, terror!
　　Before morning, they are no more!
　This is the portion of those who loot us,
　　and the lot of those who plunder us.

^{18:1} Ah, land of whirring wings
　　that is beyond the rivers of Cush,³
² which sends ambassadors by the sea,
　　in vessels of papyrus on the waters!

---

¹ Or *though you carefully fence them* ² Or *will be a heap* ³ Probably *Nubia*

Go, you swift messengers,
　to a nation tall and smooth,
to a people feared near and far,
　a nation mighty and conquering,
　whose land the rivers divide.

3　All you inhabitants of the world,
　　you who dwell on the earth,
　when a signal is raised on the
　　mountains, look!
　When a trumpet is blown, hear!
4　For thus the LORD said to me:
　"I will quietly look from my dwelling
　　like clear heat in sunshine,
　　like a cloud of dew in the heat of
　　　harvest."
5　For before the harvest, when the
　　blossom is over,
　　and the flower becomes a ripening
　　　grape,
　he cuts off the shoots with pruning
　　hooks,
　　and the spreading branches he lops
　　　off and clears away.
6　They shall all of them be left
　　to the birds of prey of the mountains
　　and to the beasts of the earth.
　And the birds of prey will summer on
　　them,
　　and all the beasts of the earth will
　　winter on them.

7 At that time tribute will be brought to the LORD of hosts

　from a people tall and smooth,
　　from a people feared near and far,
　a nation mighty and conquering,
　　whose land the rivers divide,

to Mount Zion, the place of the name of the LORD of hosts.

1 Peter 5

So I exhort the elders among you, as a fellow elder and a witness of the sufferings of Christ, as well as a partaker in the glory that is going to be revealed: ²shepherd the flock of God that is among you, exercising oversight,[1] not under compulsion, but willingly, as God would have you;[2] not for shameful gain, but eagerly; ³not domineering over those in your charge, but being examples to the flock. ⁴And when the chief Shepherd appears, you will receive the unfading crown of glory. ⁵Likewise, you who are younger, be subject to the elders. Clothe yourselves, all of you, with humility toward one another, for "God opposes the proud but gives grace to the humble."

⁶Humble yourselves, therefore, under the mighty hand of God so that at the proper time he may exalt you, ⁷casting all your anxieties on him, because he cares for you. ⁸Be soberminded; be watchful. Your adversary the devil prowls around like a roaring lion, seeking someone to devour. ⁹Resist him, firm in your faith, knowing that the same kinds of suffering are being experienced by your brotherhood throughout the world. ¹⁰And after you have suffered a little while, the God of all grace, who has called you to his eternal glory in Christ, will himself restore, confirm, strengthen, and establish you. ¹¹To him be the dominion forever and ever. Amen.

¹²By Silvanus, a faithful brother as I regard him, I have written briefly to you, exhorting and declaring that this is the true grace of God. Stand firm in it. ¹³She who is at Babylon, who is likewise chosen, sends you greetings, and so does Mark, my son. ¹⁴Greet one another with the kiss of love.

Peace to all of you who are in Christ.

[1] Some manuscripts omit *exercising oversight* [2] Some manuscripts omit *as God would have you*

MAY 19

Numbers 28

The LORD spoke to Moses, saying, [2]"Command the people of Israel and say to them, 'My offering, my food for my food offerings, my pleasing aroma, you shall be careful to offer to me at its appointed time.' [3]And you shall say to them, This is the food offering that you shall offer to the LORD: two male lambs a year old without blemish, day by day, as a regular offering. [4]The one lamb you shall offer in the morning, and the other lamb you shall offer at twilight; [5]also a tenth of an ephah[1] of fine flour for a grain offering, mixed with a quarter of a hin[2] of beaten oil. [6]It is a regular burnt offering, which was ordained at Mount Sinai for a pleasing aroma, a food offering to the LORD. [7]Its drink offering shall be a quarter of a hin for each lamb. In the Holy Place you shall pour out a drink offering of strong drink to the LORD. [8]The other lamb you shall offer at twilight. Like the grain offering of the morning, and like its drink offering, you shall offer it as a food offering, with a pleasing aroma to the LORD.

[9]"On the Sabbath day, two male lambs a year old without blemish, and two tenths of an ephah of fine flour for a grain offering, mixed with oil, and its drink offering: [10]this is the burnt offering of every Sabbath, besides the regular burnt offering and its drink offering.

[11]"At the beginnings of your months, you shall offer a burnt offering to the LORD: two bulls from the herd, one ram, seven male lambs a year old without blemish; [12]also three tenths of an ephah of fine flour for a grain offering, mixed with oil, for each bull, and two tenths of fine flour for a grain offering, mixed with oil, for the one ram; [13]and a tenth of fine flour mixed with oil as a grain offering for every lamb; for a burnt offering with a pleasing aroma, a food offering to the LORD. [14]Their drink offerings shall be half a hin of wine for a bull, a third of a hin for a ram, and a quarter of a hin for a lamb. This is the burnt offering of each month throughout the months of the year. [15]Also one male goat for a sin offering to the LORD; it shall be offered besides the regular burnt offering and its drink offering.

[16]"On the fourteenth day of the first month is the LORD's Passover, [17]and on the fifteenth day of this month is a feast. Seven days shall unleavened bread be eaten. [18]On the first day there shall be a holy convocation. You shall not do any ordinary work, [19]but offer a food offering, a burnt offering to the LORD: two bulls from the herd, one ram, and seven male lambs a year old; see that they are without blemish; [20]also their grain offering of fine flour mixed with oil; three tenths of an ephah shall you offer for a bull, and two tenths for a ram; [21]a tenth shall you offer for each of the seven lambs; [22]also one male goat for a sin offering, to make atonement for you. [23]You shall offer these besides the burnt offering of the morning, which is for a regular burnt offering. [24]In the same way you shall offer daily, for seven days, the food of a food offering, with a pleasing aroma to the LORD. It shall be offered besides the regular burnt offering and its drink offering. [25]And on the seventh day you shall have a holy convocation. You shall not do any ordinary work.

[26]"On the day of the firstfruits, when you offer a grain offering of new grain to the LORD at your Feast of Weeks, you shall have a holy convocation. You shall not do any ordinary work, [27]but offer a burnt offering, with a pleasing aroma to the LORD: two bulls from the herd, one ram, seven male lambs a year old; [28]also their grain offering of fine flour mixed with oil, three tenths of an ephah for each bull, two tenths for one ram, [29]a tenth for each of the seven lambs; [30]with one male goat, to make atonement for you. [31]Besides the regular burnt offering and its grain offering, you shall offer them and their drink offering. See that they are without blemish.

[1] An *ephah* was about 3/5 bushel or 22 liters [2] A *hin* was about 4 quarts or 3.5 liters

---
Psalm 72

OF SOLOMON.

Give the king your justice, O God,
and your righteousness to the royal son!
2   May he judge your people with
        righteousness,
        and your poor with justice!
3   Let the mountains bear prosperity for
        the people,
        and the hills, in righteousness!
4   May he defend the cause of the poor of
        the people,
        give deliverance to the children of the
            needy,
        and crush the oppressor!

5   May they fear you[1] while the sun
        endures,
        and as long as the moon, throughout
            all generations!
6   May he be like rain that falls on the
        mown grass,
        like showers that water the earth!
7   In his days may the righteous flourish,
        and peace abound, till the moon be no
            more!

8   May he have dominion from sea to sea,
        and from the River[2] to the ends of the
            earth!
9   May desert tribes bow down before him,
        and his enemies lick the dust!
10   May the kings of Tarshish and of the
        coastlands
        render him tribute;
        may the kings of Sheba and Seba
            bring gifts!
11   May all kings fall down before him,
        all nations serve him!

12   For he delivers the needy when he calls,
        the poor and him who has no helper.
13   He has pity on the weak and the needy,
        and saves the lives of the needy.
14   From oppression and violence he
        redeems their life,
        and precious is their blood in his sight.

15   Long may he live;
        may gold of Sheba be given to him!
        May prayer be made for him continually,
        and blessings invoked for him all the
            day!

16   May there be abundance of grain in the
        land;
        on the tops of the mountains may it
            wave;
        may its fruit be like Lebanon;
        and may people blossom in the cities
            like the grass of the field!
17   May his name endure forever,
        his fame continue as long as the sun!
        May people be blessed in him,
        all nations call him blessed!

18   Blessed be the LORD, the God of Israel,
        who alone does wondrous things.
19   Blessed be his glorious name forever;
        may the whole earth be filled with his
            glory!
            Amen and Amen!

20   The prayers of David, the son of Jesse,
        are ended.

Isaiah 19–20

An oracle concerning Egypt.

Behold, the LORD is riding on a swift
        cloud
        and comes to Egypt;
and the idols of Egypt will tremble at his
        presence,
        and the heart of the Egyptians will
            melt within them.
2   And I will stir up Egyptians against
        Egyptians,
        and they will fight, each against
            another
        and each against his neighbor,
        city against city, kingdom against
            kingdom;
3   and the spirit of the Egyptians within
        them will be emptied out,
        and I will confound[3] their counsel;
and they will inquire of the idols and the
        sorcerers,
        and the mediums and the
            necromancers;
4   and I will give over the Egyptians
        into the hand of a hard master,
and a fierce king will rule over them,
        declares the Lord GOD of hosts.

---

[1] Septuagint *He shall endure* [2] That is, the Euphrates [3] Or *I will swallow up*

5   And the waters of the sea will be dried
     up,
     and the river will be dry and parched,
6   and its canals will become foul,
     and the branches of Egypt's Nile will
        diminish and dry up,
     reeds and rushes will rot away.
7   There will be bare places by the Nile,
     on the brink of the Nile,
and all that is sown by the Nile will be
     parched,
     will be driven away, and will be no
        more.
8   The fishermen will mourn and lament,
     all who cast a hook in the Nile;
and they will languish
     who spread nets on the water.
9   The workers in combed flax will be in
        despair,
     and the weavers of white cotton.
10   Those who are the pillars of the land will
        be crushed,
     and all who work for pay will be
        grieved.

11   The princes of Zoan are utterly foolish;
     the wisest counselors of Pharaoh give
        stupid counsel.
How can you say to Pharaoh,
     "I am a son of the wise,
     a son of ancient kings"?
12   Where then are your wise men?
     Let them tell you
     that they might know what the Lord
        of hosts has purposed against
        Egypt.
13   The princes of Zoan have become fools,
     and the princes of Memphis are
        deluded;
those who are the cornerstones of her
     tribes
     have made Egypt stagger.
14   The Lord has mingled within her a
        spirit of confusion,
and they will make Egypt stagger in all
     its deeds,
     as a drunken man staggers in his
        vomit.
15   And there will be nothing for Egypt
     that head or tail, palm branch or reed,
     may do.

16 In that day the Egyptians will be like

women, and tremble with fear before the hand that the Lord of hosts shakes over them. 17And the land of Judah will become a terror to the Egyptians. Everyone to whom it is mentioned will fear because of the purpose that the Lord of hosts has purposed against them.

18 In that day there will be five cities in the land of Egypt that speak the language of Canaan and swear allegiance to the Lord of hosts. One of these will be called the City of Destruction.[1]

19 In that day there will be an altar to the Lord in the midst of the land of Egypt, and a pillar to the Lord at its border. 20It will be a sign and a witness to the Lord of hosts in the land of Egypt. When they cry to the Lord because of oppressors, he will send them a savior and defender, and deliver them. 21And the Lord will make himself known to the Egyptians, and the Egyptians will know the Lord in that day and worship with sacrifice and offering, and they will make vows to the Lord and perform them. 22And the Lord will strike Egypt, striking and healing, and they will return to the Lord, and he will listen to their pleas for mercy and heal them.

23 In that day there will be a highway from Egypt to Assyria, and Assyria will come into Egypt, and Egypt into Assyria, and the Egyptians will worship with the Assyrians. 24In that day Israel will be the third with Egypt and Assyria, a blessing in the midst of the earth, 25whom the Lord of hosts has blessed, saying, "Blessed be Egypt my people, and Assyria the work of my hands, and Israel my inheritance."

20:1 In the year that the commander in chief, who was sent by Sargon the king of Assyria, came to Ashdod and fought against it and captured it— 2at that time the Lord spoke by Isaiah the son of Amoz, saying, "Go, and loose the sackcloth from your waist and take off your sandals from your feet," and he did so, walking naked and barefoot.

3 Then the Lord said, "As my servant Isaiah has walked naked and barefoot for three years as a sign and a portent against Egypt and Cush,[2] 4so shall the king of Assyria lead away the Egyptian captives and the Cushite exiles, both the young and the old, naked and barefoot, with buttocks uncovered, the nakedness of Egypt. 5Then they shall be dismayed and ashamed because of Cush their hope and of

Egypt their boast. [6]And the inhabitants of this coastland will say in that day, 'Behold, this is what has happened to those in whom we hoped and to whom we fled for help to be delivered from the king of Assyria! And we, how shall we escape?'"

2 Peter 1

Simeon[1] Peter, a servant[2] and apostle of Jesus Christ,

To those who have obtained a faith of equal standing with ours by the righteousness of our God and Savior Jesus Christ:

[2]May grace and peace be multiplied to you in the knowledge of God and of Jesus our Lord.

[3]His divine power has granted to us all things that pertain to life and godliness, through the knowledge of him who called us to[3] his own glory and excellence,[4] [4]by which he has granted to us his precious and very great promises, so that through them you may become partakers of the divine nature, having escaped from the corruption that is in the world because of sinful desire. [5]For this very reason, make every effort to supplement your faith with virtue,[5] and virtue with knowledge, [6]and knowledge with self-control, and self-control with steadfastness, and steadfastness with godliness, [7]and godliness with brotherly affection, and brotherly affection with love. [8]For if these qualities[6] are yours and are increasing, they keep you from being ineffective or unfruitful in the knowledge of our Lord Jesus Christ. [9]For whoever lacks these qualities is so nearsighted that he is blind, having forgotten that he was cleansed from his former sins. [10]Therefore, brothers,[7] be all the more diligent to confirm your calling and election, for if you practice these qualities you will never fall. [11]For in this way there will be richly provided for you an entrance into the eternal kingdom of our Lord and Savior Jesus Christ.

[12]Therefore I intend always to remind you of these qualities, though you know them and are established in the truth that you have. [13]I think it right, as long as I am in this body,[8] to stir you up by way of reminder, [14]since I know that the putting off of my body will be soon, as our Lord Jesus Christ made clear to me. [15]And I will make every effort so that after my departure you may be able at any time to recall these things.

[16]For we did not follow cleverly devised myths when we made known to you the power and coming of our Lord Jesus Christ, but we were eyewitnesses of his majesty. [17]For when he received honor and glory from God the Father, and the voice was borne to him by the Majestic Glory, "This is my beloved Son,[9] with whom I am well pleased," [18]we ourselves heard this very voice borne from heaven, for we were with him on the holy mountain. [19]And we have the prophetic word more fully confirmed, to which you will do well to pay attention as to a lamp shining in a dark place, until the day dawns and the morning star rises in your hearts, [20]knowing this first of all, that no prophecy of Scripture comes from someone's own interpretation. [21]For no prophecy was ever produced by the will of man, but men spoke from God as they were carried along by the Holy Spirit.

MAY 20

Numbers 29

"On the first day of the seventh month you shall have a holy convocation. You shall not do any ordinary work. It is a day for you to blow the trumpets, [2]and you shall offer a burnt offering, for a pleasing aroma to the LORD: one bull from the herd, one ram, seven male lambs a year old without blemish; [3]also their grain offering of fine flour mixed with oil, three

[1] Some manuscripts Simeon [2] Or slave (for the contextual rendering of the Greek word doulos, see Preface) [3] Or by [4] Or virtue [5] Or excellence; twice in this verse [6] Greek these things; also verses 9, 10, 12 [7] Or brothers and sisters. The plural Greek word adelphoi (translated "brothers") refers to siblings in a family. In New Testament usage, depending on the context, adelphoi may refer either to men or to both men and women who are siblings (brothers and sisters) in God's family, the church [8] Greek tent; also verse 14 [9] Or my Son, my (or the) Beloved

tenths of an ephah[1] for the bull, two tenths for the ram, [4] and one tenth for each of the seven lambs; [5] with one male goat for a sin offering, to make atonement for you; [6] besides the burnt offering of the new moon, and its grain offering, and the regular burnt offering and its grain offering, and their drink offering, according to the rule for them, for a pleasing aroma, a food offering to the LORD.

[7] "On the tenth day of this seventh month you shall have a holy convocation and afflict yourselves.[2] You shall do no work, [8] but you shall offer a burnt offering to the LORD, a pleasing aroma: one bull from the herd, one ram, seven male lambs a year old: see that they are without blemish. [9] And their grain offering shall be of fine flour mixed with oil, three tenths of an ephah for the bull, two tenths for the one ram, [10] a tenth for each of the seven lambs: [11] also one male goat for a sin offering, besides the sin offering of atonement, and the regular burnt offering and its grain offering, and their drink offerings.

[12] "On the fifteenth day of the seventh month you shall have a holy convocation. You shall not do any ordinary work, and you shall keep a feast to the LORD seven days. [13] And you shall offer a burnt offering, a food offering, with a pleasing aroma to the LORD, thirteen bulls from the herd, two rams, fourteen male lambs a year old; they shall be without blemish; [14] and their grain offering of fine flour mixed with oil, three tenths of an ephah for each of the thirteen bulls, two tenths for each of the two rams, [15] and a tenth for each of the fourteen lambs; [16] also one male goat for a sin offering, besides the regular burnt offering, its grain offering and its drink offering.

[17] "On the second day twelve bulls from the herd, two rams, fourteen male lambs a year old without blemish, [18] with the grain offering and the drink offerings for the bulls, for the rams, and for the lambs, in the prescribed quantities; [19] also one male goat for a sin offering, besides the regular burnt offering and its grain offering, and their drink offerings.

[20] "On the third day eleven bulls, two rams, fourteen male lambs a year old without blemish, [21] with the grain offering and the drink offerings for the bulls, for the rams, and for the lambs, in the prescribed quantities; [22] also one male goat for a sin offering, besides the regular burnt offering and its grain offering and its drink offering.

[23] "On the fourth day ten bulls, two rams, fourteen male lambs a year old without blemish, [24] with the grain offering and the drink offerings for the bulls, for the rams, and for the lambs, in the prescribed quantities; [25] also one male goat for a sin offering, besides the regular burnt offering, its grain offering and its drink offering.

[26] "On the fifth day nine bulls, two rams, fourteen male lambs a year old without blemish, [27] with the grain offering and the drink offerings for the bulls, for the rams, and for the lambs, in the prescribed quantities; [28] also one male goat for a sin offering; besides the regular burnt offering and its grain offering and its drink offering.

[29] "On the sixth day eight bulls, two rams, fourteen male lambs a year old without blemish, [30] with the grain offering and the drink offerings for the bulls, for the rams, and for the lambs, in the prescribed quantities; [31] also one male goat for a sin offering; besides the regular burnt offering, its grain offering, and its drink offerings.

[32] "On the seventh day seven bulls, two rams, fourteen male lambs a year old without blemish, [33] with the grain offering and the drink offerings for the bulls, for the rams, and for the lambs, in the prescribed quantities; [34] also one male goat for a sin offering; besides the regular burnt offering, its grain offering, and its drink offering.

[35] "On the eighth day you shall have a solemn assembly. You shall not do any ordinary work, [36] but you shall offer a burnt offering, a food offering, with a pleasing aroma to the LORD: one bull, one ram, seven male lambs a year old without blemish, [37] and the grain offering and the drink offerings for the bull, for the ram, and for the lambs, in the prescribed quantities; [38] also one male goat for a sin offering; besides the regular burnt offering and its grain offering and its drink offering.

[39] "These you shall offer to the LORD at your appointed feasts, in addition to your vow offerings and your freewill offerings, for your burnt offerings, and for your grain offerings, and for your drink offerings, and for your peace offerings."

[40] [3] So Moses told the people of Israel everything just as the LORD had commanded Moses.

---

[1] An *ephah* was about 3/5 bushel or 22 liters [2] Or *and fast* [3] Ch 30:1 in Hebrew

Psalm 73

A PSALM OF ASAPH.

Truly God is good to Israel,
  to those who are pure in heart.
2 But as for me, my feet had almost
      stumbled,
    my steps had nearly slipped.
3 For I was envious of the arrogant
    when I saw the prosperity of the
      wicked.

4 For they have no pangs until death;
    their bodies are fat and sleek.
5 They are not in trouble as others are;
    they are not stricken like the rest of
      mankind.
6 Therefore pride is their necklace;
    violence covers them as a garment.
7 Their eyes swell out through fatness;
    their hearts overflow with follies.
8 They scoff and speak with malice;
    loftily they threaten oppression.
9 They set their mouths against the
      heavens,
    and their tongue struts through the
      earth.
10 Therefore his people turn back to them,
    and find no fault in them.[1]
11 And they say, "How can God know?
    Is there knowledge in the Most
      High?"
12 Behold, these are the wicked;
    always at ease, they increase in riches.
13 All in vain have I kept my heart clean
    and washed my hands in innocence.
14 For all the day long I have been stricken
    and rebuked every morning.
15 If I had said, "I will speak thus,"
    I would have betrayed the generation
      of your children.
16 But when I thought how to understand
      this,
    it seemed to me a wearisome task,
17 until I went into the sanctuary of God;
    then I discerned their end.

18 Truly you set them in slippery places;
    you make them fall to ruin.
19 How they are destroyed in a moment,
    swept away utterly by terrors!

20 Like a dream when one awakes,
    O Lord, when you rouse yourself, you
      despise them as phantoms.
21 When my soul was embittered,
    when I was pricked in heart,
22 I was brutish and ignorant;
    I was like a beast toward you.

23 Nevertheless, I am continually with you;
    you hold my right hand.
24 You guide me with your counsel,
    and afterward you will receive me to
      glory.
25 Whom have I in heaven but you?
    And there is nothing on earth that I
      desire besides you.
26 My flesh and my heart may fail,
    but God is the strength[2] of my heart
    and my portion forever.

27 For behold, those who are far from you
      shall perish;
    you put an end to everyone who is
      unfaithful to you.
28 But for me it is good to be near God;
    I have made the Lord GOD my refuge,
    that I may tell of all your works.

Isaiah 21

The oracle concerning the wilderness of the
  sea.

    As whirlwinds in the Negeb sweep on,
      it comes from the wilderness,
      from a terrible land.
2   A stern vision is told to me;
      the traitor betrays,
      and the destroyer destroys.
    Go up, O Elam;
      lay siege, O Media;
    all the sighing she has caused
      I bring to an end.
3   Therefore my loins are filled with
        anguish;
      pangs have seized me,
      like the pangs of a woman in labor;
    I am bowed down so that I cannot hear;
      I am dismayed so that I cannot see.
4   My heart staggers; horror has appalled
        me;
      the twilight I longed for
      has been turned for me into trembling.

---

[1] Probable reading; Hebrew *the waters of a full cup are drained by them*   [2] Hebrew *rock*

⁵ They prepare the table,
   they spread the rugs,[1]
   they eat, they drink.
Arise, O princes;
   oil the shield!

⁶ For thus the Lord said to me:
"Go, set a watchman;
   let him announce what he sees.
⁷ When he sees riders, horsemen in pairs,
   riders on donkeys, riders on camels,
let him listen diligently,
   very diligently."
⁸ Then he who saw cried out:[2]
"Upon a watchtower I stand, O Lord,
   continually by day,
and at my post I am stationed
   whole nights.
⁹ And behold, here come riders,
   horsemen in pairs!"
And he answered,
   "Fallen, fallen is Babylon;
and all the carved images of her gods
   he has shattered to the ground."
¹⁰ O my threshed and winnowed one,
   what I have heard from the LORD of
    hosts,
the God of Israel, I announce to you.

¹¹ The oracle concerning Dumah.

One is calling to me from Seir,
   "Watchman, what time of the night?
   Watchman, what time of the night?"
¹² The watchman says:
"Morning comes, and also the night.
   If you will inquire, inquire;
   come back again."

¹³ The oracle concerning Arabia.

In the thickets in Arabia you will lodge,
   O caravans of Dedanites.
¹⁴ To the thirsty bring water;
   meet the fugitive with bread,
   O inhabitants of the land of Tema.
¹⁵ For they have fled from the swords,
   from the drawn sword,
from the bent bow,
   and from the press of battle.

¹⁶ For thus the Lord said to me, "Within a year, according to the years of a hired worker, all the glory of Kedar will come to an end. ¹⁷ And the remainder of the archers of the mighty men

of the sons of Kedar will be few, for the LORD, the God of Israel, has spoken."

2 Peter 2

But false prophets also arose among the people, just as there will be false teachers among you, who will secretly bring in destructive heresies, even denying the Master who bought them, bringing upon themselves swift destruction. ²And many will follow their sensuality, and because of them the way of truth will be blasphemed. ³And in their greed they will exploit you with false words. Their condemnation from long ago is not idle, and their destruction is not asleep.

⁴ For if God did not spare angels when they sinned, but cast them into hell[3] and committed them to chains[4] of gloomy darkness to be kept until the judgment; ⁵ if he did not spare the ancient world, but preserved Noah, a herald of righteousness, with seven others, when he brought a flood upon the world of the ungodly; ⁶ if by turning the cities of Sodom and Gomorrah to ashes he condemned them to extinction, making them an example of what is going to happen to the ungodly;[5] ⁷ and if he rescued righteous Lot, greatly distressed by the sensual conduct of the wicked ⁸ (for as that righteous man lived among them day after day, he was tormenting his righteous soul over their lawless deeds that he saw and heard); ⁹ then the Lord knows how to rescue the godly from trials,[6] and to keep the unrighteous under punishment until the day of judgment, ¹⁰ and especially those who indulge[7] in the lust of defiling passion and despise authority.

Bold and willful, they do not tremble as they blaspheme the glorious ones, ¹¹ whereas angels, though greater in might and power, do not pronounce a blasphemous judgment against them before the Lord. ¹² But these, like irrational animals, creatures of instinct, born to be caught and destroyed, blaspheming about matters of which they are ignorant, will also be destroyed in their destruction, ¹³ suffering wrong as the wage for their wrongdoing. They count it pleasure to revel in the daytime. They are blots and blemishes, reveling in their deceptions,[8] while they feast with you. ¹⁴ They have eyes full of adultery, insatiable for sin. They entice unsteady souls. They have hearts trained in greed. Accursed children! [15]Forsaking the right way, they have gone astray. They have followed the way of Balaam, the son of Beor, who loved gain from wrongdoing, [16]but was rebuked for his own transgression; a speechless donkey spoke with human voice and restrained the prophet's madness.

[17]These are waterless springs and mists driven by a storm. For them the gloom of utter darkness has been reserved. [18]For, speaking loud boasts of folly, they entice by sensual passions of the flesh those who are barely escaping from those who live in error. [19]They promise them freedom, but they themselves are slaves[1] of corruption. For whatever overcomes a person, to that he is enslaved. [20]For if, after they have escaped the defilements of the world through the knowledge of our Lord and Savior Jesus Christ, they are again entangled in them and overcome, the last state has become worse for them than the first. [21]For it would have been better for them never to have known the way of righteousness than after knowing it to turn back from the holy commandment delivered to them. [22]What the true proverb says has happened to them: "The dog returns to its own vomit, and the sow, after washing herself, returns to wallow in the mire."

MAY 21

Numbers 30

Moses spoke to the heads of the tribes of the people of Israel, saying, "This is what the Lord has commanded. [2]If a man vows a vow to the Lord, or swears an oath to bind himself by a pledge, he shall not break his word. He shall do according to all that proceeds out of his mouth.

[3]"If a woman vows a vow to the Lord and binds herself by a pledge, while within her father's house in her youth, [4]and her father hears of her vow and of her pledge by which she has bound herself and says nothing to her, then all her vows shall stand, and every pledge by which she has bound herself shall stand. [5]But if her father opposes her on the day that he hears of it, no vow of hers, no pledge by which she has bound herself shall stand. And the Lord will forgive her, because her father opposed her.

[6]"If she marries a husband, while under her vows or any thoughtless utterance of her lips by which she has bound herself, [7]and her husband hears of it and says nothing to her on the day that he hears, then her vows shall stand, and her pledges by which she has bound herself shall stand. [8]But if, on the day that her husband comes to hear of it, he opposes her, then he makes void her vow that was on her, and the thoughtless utterance of her lips by which she bound herself. And the Lord will forgive her. [9](But any vow of a widow or of a divorced woman, anything by which she has bound herself, shall stand against her.) [10]And if she vowed in her husband's house or bound herself by a pledge with an oath, [11]and her husband heard of it and said nothing to her and did not oppose her, then all her vows shall stand, and every pledge by which she bound herself shall stand. [12]But if her husband makes them null and void on the day that he hears them, then whatever proceeds out of her lips concerning her vows or concerning her pledge of herself shall not stand. Her husband has made them void, and the Lord will forgive her. [13]Any vow and any binding oath to afflict herself,[2] her husband may establish,[3] or her husband may make void. [14]But if her husband says nothing to her from day to day, then he establishes all her vows or all her pledges that are upon her. He has established them, because he said nothing to her on the day that he heard of them. [15]But if he makes them null and void after he has heard of them, then he shall bear her iniquity."

[1] Greek bondservants [2] Or to fast [3] Or may allow to stand

[16]These are the statutes that the LORD commanded Moses about a man and his wife and about a father and his daughter while she is in her youth within her father's house.

--- *Psalm 74* ---

A MASKIL[1] OF ASAPH.

O God, why do you cast us off forever?
    Why does your anger smoke against the
        sheep of your pasture?
2 Remember your congregation, which
        you have purchased of old,
    which you have redeemed to be the
        tribe of your heritage!
    Remember Mount Zion, where you
        have dwelt.
3 Direct your steps to the perpetual ruins;
    the enemy has destroyed everything
        in the sanctuary!

4 Your foes have roared in the midst of
        your meeting place;
    they set up their own signs for signs.
5 They were like those who swing axes
        in a forest of trees.[2]
6 And all its carved wood
    they broke down with hatchets and
        hammers.
7 They set your sanctuary on fire;
    they profaned the dwelling place of
        your name,
    bringing it down to the ground.
8 They said to themselves, "We will utterly
        subdue them";
    they burned all the meeting places of
        God in the land.

9 We do not see our signs;
    there is no longer any prophet,
    and there is none among us who
        knows how long.
10 How long, O God, is the foe to scoff?
    Is the enemy to revile your name
        forever?
11 Why do you hold back your hand, your
        right hand?
    Take it from the fold of your garment[3]
        and destroy them!

12 Yet God my King is from of old,
    working salvation in the midst of the
        earth.

13 You divided the sea by your might;
    you broke the heads of the sea
        monsters[4] on the waters.
14 You crushed the heads of Leviathan;
    you gave him as food for the creatures
        of the wilderness.
15 You split open springs and brooks;
    you dried up ever-flowing streams.
16 Yours is the day, yours also the night;
    you have established the heavenly
        lights and the sun.
17 You have fixed all the boundaries of the
        earth;
    you have made summer and winter.

18 Remember this, O LORD, how the enemy
        scoffs,
    and a foolish people reviles your name.
19 Do not deliver the soul of your dove to
        the wild beasts;
    do not forget the life of your poor
        forever.

20 Have regard for the covenant,
    for the dark places of the land are full
        of the habitations of violence.
21 Let not the downtrodden turn back in
        shame;
    let the poor and needy praise your
        name.

22 Arise, O God, defend your cause;
    remember how the foolish scoff at you
        all the day!
23 Do not forget the clamor of your foes,
    the uproar of those who rise against
        you, which goes up continually!

--- *Isaiah 22* ---

The oracle concerning the valley of vision.

What do you mean that you have gone
        up,
    all of you, to the housetops,
2 you who are full of shoutings,
    tumultuous city, exultant town?
Your slain are not slain with the sword
    or dead in battle.
3 All your leaders have fled together;
    without the bow they were captured.
All of you who were found were captured,
    though they had fled far away.

[1] Probably a musical or liturgical term [2] The meaning of the Hebrew is uncertain [3] Hebrew *from your bosom* [4] Or *the great sea creatures*

⁴   Therefore I said:
    "Look away from me;
      let me weep bitter tears;
    do not labor to comfort me
      concerning the destruction of the
        daughter of my people."

⁵   For the Lord GOD of hosts has a day
      of tumult and trampling and
        confusion
    in the valley of vision,
    a battering down of walls
    and a shouting to the mountains.
⁶   And Elam bore the quiver
      with chariots and horsemen,
    and Kir uncovered the shield.
⁷   Your choicest valleys were full of
        chariots,
      and the horsemen took their stand at
        the gates.
⁸   He has taken away the covering of Judah.

In that day you looked to the weapons of the House of the Forest, ⁹and you saw that the breaches of the city of David were many. You collected the waters of the lower pool, ¹⁰and you counted the houses of Jerusalem, and you broke down the houses to fortify the wall. ¹¹You made a reservoir between the two walls for the water of the old pool. But you did not look to him who did it, or see him who planned it long ago.

¹² In that day the Lord GOD of hosts
      called for weeping and mourning,
      for baldness and wearing sackcloth;
¹³ and behold, joy and gladness,
      killing oxen and slaughtering sheep,
      eating flesh and drinking wine.
    "Let us eat and drink,
      for tomorrow we die."
¹⁴ The LORD of hosts has revealed himself
      in my ears:
    "Surely this iniquity will not be atoned
      for you until you die,"
    says the Lord GOD of hosts.

¹⁵Thus says the Lord GOD of hosts, "Come, go to this steward, to Shebna, who is over the household, and say to him: ¹⁶What have you to do here, and whom have you here, that you have cut out here a tomb for yourself, you who cut out a tomb on the height and carve a dwelling for yourself in the rock? ¹⁷Behold, the LORD will hurl you away violently, O you strong man.

He will seize firm hold on you ¹⁸and whirl you around and around, and throw you like a ball into a wide land. There you shall die, and there shall be your glorious chariots, you shame of your master's house. ¹⁹I will thrust you from your office, and you will be pulled down from your station. ²⁰In that day I will call my servant Eliakim the son of Hilkiah, ²¹and I will clothe him with your robe, and will bind your sash on him, and will commit your authority to his hand. And he shall be a father to the inhabitants of Jerusalem and to the house of Judah. ²²And I will place on his shoulder the key of the house of David. He shall open, and none shall shut; and he shall shut, and none shall open. ²³And I will fasten him like a peg in a secure place, and he will become a throne of honor to his father's house. ²⁴And they will hang on him the whole honor of his father's house, the offspring and issue, every small vessel, from the cups to all the flagons. ²⁵In that day, declares the LORD of hosts, the peg that was fastened in a secure place will give way, and it will be cut down and fall, and the load that was on it will be cut off, for the LORD has spoken."

2 Peter 3

This is now the second letter that I am writing to you, beloved. In both of them I am stirring up your sincere mind by way of reminder, ²that you should remember the predictions of the holy prophets and the commandment of the Lord and Savior through your apostles, ³knowing this first of all, that scoffers will come in the last days with scoffing, following their own sinful desires. ⁴They will say, "Where is the promise of his coming? For ever since the fathers fell asleep, all things are continuing as they were from the beginning of creation." ⁵For they deliberately overlook this fact, that the heavens existed long ago, and the earth was formed out of water and through water by the word of God, ⁶and that by means of these the world that then existed was deluged with water and perished. ⁷But by the same word the heavens and earth that now exist are stored up for fire, being kept until the day of judgment and destruction of the ungodly.

⁸But do not overlook this one fact, beloved, that with the Lord one day is as a thousand years, and a thousand years as one day. ⁹The

Lord is not slow to fulfill his promise as some count slowness, but is patient toward you,[1] not wishing that any should perish, but that all should reach repentance. [10]But the day of the Lord will come like a thief, and then the heavens will pass away with a roar, and the heavenly bodies[2] will be burned up and dissolved, and the earth and the works that are done on it will be exposed.[3]

[11]Since all these things are thus to be dissolved, what sort of people ought you to be in lives of holiness and godliness, [12]waiting for and hastening the coming of the day of God, because of which the heavens will be set on fire and dissolved, and the heavenly bodies will melt as they burn! [13]But according to his promise we are waiting for new heavens and a new earth in which righteousness dwells.

[14]Therefore, beloved, since you are waiting for these, be diligent to be found by him without spot or blemish, and at peace. [15]And count the patience of our Lord as salvation, just as our beloved brother Paul also wrote to you according to the wisdom given him, [16]as he does in all his letters when he speaks in them of these matters. There are some things in them that are hard to understand, which the ignorant and unstable twist to their own destruction, as they do the other Scriptures. [17]You therefore, beloved, knowing this beforehand, take care that you are not carried away with the error of lawless people and lose your own stability. [18]But grow in the grace and knowledge of our Lord and Savior Jesus Christ. To him be the glory both now and to the day of eternity. Amen.

MAY 22

Numbers 31

The LORD spoke to Moses, saying, [2]"Avenge the people of Israel on the Midianites. Afterward you shall be gathered to your people." [3]So Moses spoke to the people, saying, "Arm men from among you for the war, that they may go against Midian to execute the LORD's vengeance on Midian. [4]You shall send a thousand from each of the tribes of Israel to the war." [5]So there were provided, out of the thousands of Israel, a thousand from each tribe, twelve thousand armed for war. [6]And Moses sent them to the war, a thousand from each tribe, together with Phinehas the son of Eleazar the priest, with the vessels of the sanctuary and the trumpets for the alarm in his hand. [7]They warred against Midian, as the LORD commanded Moses, and killed every male. [8]They killed the kings of Midian with the rest of their slain, Evi, Rekem, Zur, Hur, and Reba, the five kings of Midian. And they also killed Balaam the son of Beor with the sword. [9]And the people of Israel took captive the women of Midian and their little ones, and they took as plunder

all their cattle, their flocks, and all their goods. [10]All their cities in the places where they lived, and all their encampments, they burned with fire, [11]and took all the spoil and all the plunder, both of man and of beast. [12]Then they brought the captives and the plunder and the spoil to Moses, and to Eleazar the priest, and to the congregation of the people of Israel, at the camp on the plains of Moab by the Jordan at Jericho.

[13]Moses and Eleazar the priest and all the chiefs of the congregation went to meet them outside the camp. [14]And Moses was angry with the officers of the army, the commanders of thousands and the commanders of hundreds, who had come from service in the war. [15]Moses said to them, "Have you let all the women live? [16]Behold, these, on Balaam's advice, caused the people of Israel to act treacherously against the LORD in the incident of Peor, and so the plague came among the congregation of the LORD. [17]Now therefore, kill every male among the little ones, and kill every woman who has known man by lying with him. [18]But all the young girls

[1] Some manuscripts *on your account* [2] Or *elements*; also verse 12 [3] Greek *found*; some manuscripts *will be burned up*

who have not known man by lying with him keep alive for yourselves. [19]Encamp outside the camp seven days. Whoever of you has killed any person and whoever has touched any slain, purify yourselves and your captives on the third day and on the seventh day. [20]You shall purify every garment, every article of skin, all work of goats' hair, and every article of wood."

[21]Then Eleazar the priest said to the men in the army who had gone to battle: "This is the statute of the law that the LORD has commanded Moses: [22]only the gold, the silver, the bronze, the iron, the tin, and the lead, [23]everything that can stand the fire, you shall pass through the fire, and it shall be clean. Nevertheless, it shall also be purified with the water for impurity. And whatever cannot stand the fire, you shall pass through the water. [24]You must wash your clothes on the seventh day, and you shall be clean. And afterward you may come into the camp."

[25]The LORD said to Moses, [26]"Take the count of the plunder that was taken, both of man and of beast, you and Eleazar the priest and the heads of the fathers' houses of the congregation, [27]and divide the plunder into two parts between the warriors who went out to battle and all the congregation. [28]And levy for the LORD a tribute from the men of war who went out to battle, one out of five hundred, of the people and of the oxen and of the donkeys and of the flocks. [29]Take it from their half and give it to Eleazar the priest as a contribution to the LORD. [30]And from the people of Israel's half you shall take one drawn out of every fifty, of the people, of the oxen, of the donkeys, and of the flocks, of all the cattle, and give them to the Levites who keep guard over the tabernacle of the LORD." [31]And Moses and Eleazar the priest did as the LORD commanded Moses.

[32]Now the plunder remaining of the spoil that the army took was 675,000 sheep, [33]72,000 cattle, [34]61,000 donkeys, [35]and 32,000 persons in all, women who had not known man by lying with him. [36]And the half, the portion of those who had gone out in the army, numbered 337,500 sheep, [37]and the LORD's tribute of sheep was 675. [38]The cattle were 36,000, of which the LORD's tribute was 72. [39]The donkeys were 30,500, of which the LORD's tribute was 61. [40]The persons were 16,000, of which the LORD's tribute was 32 persons. [41]And Moses

gave the tribute, which was the contribution for the LORD, to Eleazar the priest, as the LORD commanded Moses.

[42]From the people of Israel's half, which Moses separated from that of the men who had served in the army— [43]now the congregation's half was 337,500 sheep, [44]36,000 cattle, [45]and 30,500 donkeys, [46]and 16,000 persons— [47]from the people of Israel's half Moses took one of every 50, both of persons and of beasts, and gave them to the Levites who kept guard over the tabernacle of the LORD, as the LORD commanded Moses.

[48]Then the officers who were over the thousands of the army, the commanders of thousands and the commanders of hundreds, came near to Moses [49]and said to Moses, "Your servants have counted the men of war who are under our command, and there is not a man missing from us. [50]And we have brought the LORD's offering, what each man found, articles of gold, armlets and bracelets, signet rings, earrings, and beads, to make atonement for ourselves before the LORD." [51]And Moses and Eleazar the priest received from them the gold, all crafted articles. [52]And all the gold of the contribution that they presented to the LORD, from the commanders of thousands and the commanders of hundreds, was 16,750 shekels.[1] [53](The men in the army had each taken plunder for himself.) [54]And Moses and Eleazar the priest received the gold from the commanders of thousands and of hundreds, and brought it into the tent of meeting, as a memorial for the people of Israel before the LORD.

Psalm 75–76

TO THE CHOIRMASTER: ACCORDING TO DO NOT DESTROY. A PSALM OF ASAPH. A SONG.

We give thanks to you, O God;
  we give thanks, for your name is near.
  We[2] recount your wondrous deeds.

2 "At the set time that I appoint
    I will judge with equity.
3 When the earth totters, and all its
      inhabitants,
    it is I who keep steady its pillars. *Selah*
4 I say to the boastful, 'Do not boast,'
    and to the wicked, 'Do not lift up your
      horn;

[1] A *shekel* was about 2/5 ounce or 11 grams [2] Hebrew *They*

5 do not lift up your horn on high,
   or speak with haughty neck.'"

6 For not from the east or from the west
   and not from the wilderness comes
      lifting up,
7 but it is God who executes judgment,
   putting down one and lifting up
      another.
8 For in the hand of the LORD there is a
      cup
   with foaming wine, well mixed,
   and he pours out from it,
      and all the wicked of the earth
   shall drain it down to the dregs.

9 But I will declare it forever;
   I will sing praises to the God of Jacob.
10 All the horns of the wicked I will cut off,
   but the horns of the righteous shall be
      lifted up.

To THE CHOIRMASTER: WITH STRINGED
INSTRUMENTS. A PSALM OF ASAPH. A SONG.

In Judah God is known;
   his name is great in Israel.
2 His abode has been established in Salem,
   his dwelling place in Zion.
3 There he broke the flashing arrows,
   the shield, the sword, and the
      weapons of war.   Selah

4 Glorious are you, more majestic
   than the mountains full of prey.
5 The stouthearted were stripped of their
      spoil;
   they sank into sleep;
all the men of war
   were unable to use their hands.
6 At your rebuke, O God of Jacob,
   both rider and horse lay stunned.

7 But you, you are to be feared!
   Who can stand before you
   when once your anger is roused?
8 From the heavens you uttered judgment;
   the earth feared and was still,
9 when God arose to establish judgment,
   to save all the humble of the earth.
                                     Selah

10 Surely the wrath of man shall praise you;
   the remnant[1] of wrath you will put on
      like a belt.

11 Make your vows to the LORD your God
   and perform them;
   let all around him bring gifts
   to him who is to be feared,
12 who cuts off the spirit of princes,
   who is to be feared by the kings of the
      earth.

Isaiah 23

The oracle concerning Tyre.

   Wail, O ships of Tarshish,
      for Tyre is laid waste, without house
         or harbor!
   From the land of Cyprus[2]
      it is revealed to them.
2 Be still, O inhabitants of the coast;
   the merchants of Sidon, who cross the
      sea, have filled you.
3 And on many waters
   your revenue was the grain of Shihor,
   the harvest of the Nile;
      you were the merchant of the nations.
4 Be ashamed, O Sidon, for the sea has
      spoken,
   the stronghold of the sea, saying:
"I have neither labored nor given birth,
   I have neither reared young men
      nor brought up young women."
5 When the report comes to Egypt,
   they will be in anguish[3] over the
      report about Tyre.
6 Cross over to Tarshish;
   wail, O inhabitants of the coast!
7 Is this your exultant city
   whose origin is from days of old,
   whose feet carried her
      to settle far away?
8 Who has purposed this
   against Tyre, the bestower of crowns,
whose merchants were princes,
   whose traders were the honored of
      the earth?
9 The LORD of hosts has purposed it,
   to defile the pompous pride of all
      glory,[4]
   to dishonor all the honored of the
      earth.
10 Cross over your land like the Nile,
   O daughter of Tarshish;
   there is no restraint anymore.

[1] Or extremity [2] Hebrew Kittim; also verse 12 [3] Hebrew they will have labor pains [4] The Hebrew words for glory and hosts sound alike

11   He has stretched out his hand over the
         sea;
     he has shaken the kingdoms;
     the LORD has given command
         concerning Canaan
     to destroy its strongholds.
12   And he said:
     "You will no more exult,
         O oppressed virgin daughter of Sidon;
     arise, cross over to Cyprus,
         even there you will have no rest."

¹³Behold the land of the Chaldeans! This is
the people that was not;¹ Assyria destined it
for wild beasts. They erected their siege towers, they stripped her palaces bare, they made
her a ruin.

14   Wail, O ships of Tarshish,
         for your stronghold is laid waste.

¹⁵In that day Tyre will be forgotten for seventy
years, like the days² of one king. At the end of
seventy years, it will happen to Tyre as in the
song of the prostitute:

16   "Take a harp;
         go about the city,
         O forgotten prostitute!
     Make sweet melody;
         sing many songs,
         that you may be remembered."

¹⁷At the end of seventy years, the LORD will
visit Tyre, and she will return to her wages
and will prostitute herself with all the kingdoms of the world on the face of the earth.

¹⁸Her merchandise and her wages will be holy
to the LORD. It will not be stored or hoarded,
but her merchandise will supply abundant food
and fine clothing for those who dwell before
the LORD.

――――――― *1 John 1* ―――――――

That which was from the beginning, which
we have heard, which we have seen with
our eyes, which we looked upon and have
touched with our hands, concerning the word
of life— ²the life was made manifest, and we
have seen it, and testify to it and proclaim to
you the eternal life, which was with the Father
and was made manifest to us— ³that which we
have seen and heard we proclaim also to you, so
that you too may have fellowship with us; and
indeed our fellowship is with the Father and
with his Son Jesus Christ. ⁴And we are writing
these things so that our³ joy may be complete.
⁵This is the message we have heard from him
and proclaim to you, that God is light, and in
him is no darkness at all. ⁶If we say we have fellowship with him while we walk in darkness,
we lie and do not practice the truth. ⁷But if we
walk in the light, as he is in the light, we have
fellowship with one another, and the blood of
Jesus his Son cleanses us from all sin. ⁸If we
say we have no sin, we deceive ourselves, and
the truth is not in us. ⁹If we confess our sins,
he is faithful and just to forgive us our sins and
to cleanse us from all unrighteousness. ¹⁰If we
say we have not sinned, we make him a liar, and
his word is not in us.

MAY 23

――――――― *Numbers 32* ―――――――

Now the people of Reuben and the people
of Gad had a very great number of livestock. And they saw the land of Jazer and the
land of Gilead, and behold, the place was a
place for livestock. ²So the people of Gad and
the people of Reuben came and said to Moses
and to Eleazar the priest and to the chiefs of the
congregation, ³"Ataroth, Dibon, Jazer, Nimrah,
Heshbon, Elealeh, Sebam, Nebo, and Beon, ⁴the
land that the LORD struck down before the congregation of Israel, is a land for livestock, and
your servants have livestock." ⁵And they said,

¹ Or *that has become nothing* ² Or *lifetime* ³ Some manuscripts *your*

"If we have found favor in your sight, let this land be given to your servants for a possession. Do not take us across the Jordan." ⁶But Moses said to the people of Gad and to the people of Reuben, "Shall your brothers go to the war while you sit here? ⁷Why will you discourage the heart of the people of Israel from going over into the land that the LORD has given them? ⁸Your fathers did this, when I sent them from Kadesh-barnea to see the land. ⁹For when they went up to the Valley of Eshcol and saw the land, they discouraged the heart of the people of Israel from going into the land that the LORD had given them. ¹⁰And the LORD's anger was kindled on that day, and he swore, saying, ¹¹'Surely none of the men who came up out of Egypt, from twenty years old and upward, shall see the land that I swore to give to Abraham, to Isaac, and to Jacob, because they have not wholly followed me, ¹²none except Caleb the son of Jephunneh the Kenizzite and Joshua the son of Nun, for they have wholly followed the LORD.' ¹³And the LORD's anger was kindled against Israel, and he made them wander in the wilderness forty years, until all the generation that had done evil in the sight of the LORD was gone. ¹⁴And behold, you have risen in your fathers' place, a brood of sinful men, to increase still more the fierce anger of the LORD against Israel! ¹⁵For if you turn away from following him, he will again abandon them in the wilderness, and you will destroy all this people."

¹⁶Then they came near to him and said, "We will build sheepfolds here for our livestock, and cities for our little ones, ¹⁷but we will take up arms, ready to go before the people of Israel, until we have brought them to their place. And our little ones shall live in the fortified cities because of the inhabitants of the land. ¹⁸We will not return to our homes until each of the people of Israel has gained his inheritance. ¹⁹For we will not inherit with them on the other side of the Jordan and beyond, because our inheritance has come to us on this side of the Jordan to the east." ²⁰So Moses said to them, "If you will do this, if you will take up arms to go before the LORD for the war, ²¹and every armed man of you will pass over the Jordan before the LORD, until he has driven out his enemies from before him ²²and the land is subdued before the LORD; then after that you shall return and

be free of obligation to the LORD and to Israel, and this land shall be your possession before the LORD. ²³But if you will not do so, behold, you have sinned against the LORD, and be sure your sin will find you out. ²⁴Build cities for your little ones and folds for your sheep, and do what you have promised." ²⁵And the people of Gad and the people of Reuben said to Moses, "Your servants will do as my lord commands. ²⁶Our little ones, our wives, our livestock, and all our cattle shall remain there in the cities of Gilead, ²⁷but your servants will pass over, every man who is armed for war, before the LORD to battle, as my lord orders."

²⁸So Moses gave command concerning them to Eleazar the priest and to Joshua the son of Nun and to the heads of the fathers' houses of the tribes of the people of Israel. ²⁹And Moses said to them, "If the people of Gad and the people of Reuben, every man who is armed to battle before the LORD, will pass with you over the Jordan and the land shall be subdued before you, then you shall give them the land of Gilead for a possession. ³⁰However, if they will not pass over with you armed, they shall have possessions among you in the land of Canaan." ³¹And the people of Gad and the people of Reuben answered, "What the LORD has said to your servants, we will do. ³²We will pass over armed before the LORD into the land of Canaan, and the possession of our inheritance shall remain with us beyond the Jordan."

³³And Moses gave to them, to the people of Gad and to the people of Reuben and to the half-tribe of Manasseh the son of Joseph, the kingdom of Sihon king of the Amorites and the kingdom of Og king of Bashan, the land and its cities with their territories, the cities of the land throughout the country. ³⁴And the people of Gad built Dibon, Ataroth, Aroer, ³⁵Atroth-shophan, Jazer, Jogbehah, ³⁶Beth-nimrah and Beth-haran, fortified cities, and folds for sheep. ³⁷And the people of Reuben built Heshbon, Elealeh, Kiriathaim, ³⁸Nebo, and Baal-meon (their names were changed), and Sibmah. And they gave other names to the cities that they built. ³⁹And the sons of Machir the son of Manasseh went to Gilead and captured it, and dispossessed the Amorites who were in it. ⁴⁰And Moses gave Gilead to Machir the son of Manasseh, and he settled in it. ⁴¹And Jair the son of Manasseh

went and captured their villages, and called them Havvoth-jair.[1] [42]And Nobah went and captured Kenath and its villages, and called it Nobah, after his own name.

Psalm 77

TO THE CHOIRMASTER: ACCORDING TO JEDUTHUN. A PSALM OF ASAPH.

I cry aloud to God,
 aloud to God, and he will hear me.
[2] In the day of my trouble I seek the Lord;
  in the night my hand is stretched out
   without wearying;
  my soul refuses to be comforted.
[3] When I remember God, I moan;
  when I meditate, my spirit faints. *Selah*

[4] You hold my eyelids open;
  I am so troubled that I cannot speak.
[5] I consider the days of old,
  the years long ago.
[6] I said,[2] "Let me remember my song in
   the night;
  let me meditate in my heart."
  Then my spirit made a diligent
   search:
[7] "Will the Lord spurn forever,
  and never again be favorable?
[8] Has his steadfast love forever ceased?
  Are his promises at an end for all
   time?
[9] Has God forgotten to be gracious?
  Has he in anger shut up his
   compassion?" *Selah*

[10] Then I said, "I will appeal to this,
  to the years of the right hand of the
   Most High."[3]
[11] I will remember the deeds of the LORD;
  yes, I will remember your wonders of
   old.
[12] I will ponder all your work,
  and meditate on your mighty deeds.
[13] Your way, O God, is holy.
  What god is great like our God?
[14] You are the God who works wonders;
  you have made known your might
   among the peoples.
[15] You with your arm redeemed your
   people,
  the children of Jacob and Joseph. *Selah*

[16] When the waters saw you, O God,
  when the waters saw you, they were
   afraid;
  indeed, the deep trembled.
[17] The clouds poured out water;
  the skies gave forth thunder;
  your arrows flashed on every side.
[18] The crash of your thunder was in the
   whirlwind;
  your lightnings lighted up the world;
  the earth trembled and shook.
[19] Your way was through the sea,
  your path through the great waters;
  yet your footprints were unseen.[4]
[20] You led your people like a flock
  by the hand of Moses and Aaron.

Isaiah 24

Behold, the LORD will empty the earth[5]
 and make it desolate,
  and he will twist its surface and
   scatter its inhabitants.
[2] And it shall be, as with the people, so
   with the priest;
  as with the slave, so with his master;
  as with the maid, so with her
   mistress;
  as with the buyer, so with the seller;
  as with the lender, so with the
   borrower;
  as with the creditor, so with the
   debtor.
[3] The earth shall be utterly empty and
   utterly plundered;
  for the LORD has spoken this word.

[4] The earth mourns and withers;
  the world languishes and withers;
  the highest people of the earth
   languish.
[5] The earth lies defiled
  under its inhabitants;
  for they have transgressed the laws,
   violated the statutes,
   broken the everlasting covenant.
[6] Therefore a curse devours the earth,
  and its inhabitants suffer for their
   guilt;
  therefore the inhabitants of the earth
   are scorched,
  and few men are left.

[1] *Havvoth-jair* means *the villages of Jair* [2] Hebrew lacks *I said* [3] Or *This is my grief: that the right hand of the Most High has changed* [4] Hebrew *unknown* [5] Or *land*; also throughout this chapter

7　The wine mourns,
　　the vine languishes,
　　all the merry-hearted sigh.
8　The mirth of the tambourines is stilled,
　　the noise of the jubilant has ceased,
　　the mirth of the lyre is stilled.
9　No more do they drink wine with
　　　singing;
　　strong drink is bitter to those who
　　　drink it.
10　The wasted city is broken down;
　　every house is shut up so that none
　　　can enter.
11　There is an outcry in the streets for lack
　　　of wine;
　　all joy has grown dark;
　　the gladness of the earth is banished.
12　Desolation is left in the city;
　　the gates are battered into ruins.
13　For thus it shall be in the midst of the
　　　earth
　　among the nations,
　as when an olive tree is beaten,
　　as at the gleaning when the grape
　　　harvest is done.
14　They lift up their voices, they sing for joy;
　　over the majesty of the LORD they
　　　shout from the west.[1]
15　Therefore in the east[2] give glory to the
　　　LORD;
　　in the coastlands of the sea, give glory
　　　to the name of the LORD, the God
　　　of Israel.
16　From the ends of the earth we hear
　　　songs of praise,
　　of glory to the Righteous One.
　But I say, "I waste away,
　　I waste away. Woe is me!
　For the traitors have betrayed,
　　with betrayal the traitors have
　　　betrayed."
17　Terror and the pit and the snare[3]
　　are upon you, O inhabitant of the
　　　earth!
18　He who flees at the sound of the terror
　　shall fall into the pit,
　and he who climbs out of the pit
　　shall be caught in the snare.
　For the windows of heaven are opened,
　　and the foundations of the earth
　　　tremble.

19　The earth is utterly broken,
　　the earth is split apart,
　　the earth is violently shaken.
20　The earth staggers like a drunken man;
　　it sways like a hut;
　its transgression lies heavy upon it,
　　and it falls, and will not rise again.
21　On that day the LORD will punish
　　the host of heaven, in heaven,
　　and the kings of the earth, on the
　　　earth.
22　They will be gathered together
　　as prisoners in a pit;
　they will be shut up in a prison,
　　and after many days they will be
　　　punished.
23　Then the moon will be confounded
　　and the sun ashamed,
　for the LORD of hosts reigns
　　on Mount Zion and in Jerusalem,
　and his glory will be before his elders.

1 John 2

My little children, I am writing these things to you so that you may not sin. But if anyone does sin, we have an advocate with the Father, Jesus Christ the righteous. ²He is the propitiation for our sins, and not for ours only but also for the sins of the whole world. ³And by this we know that we have come to know him, if we keep his commandments. ⁴Whoever says "I know him" but does not keep his commandments is a liar, and the truth is not in him, ⁵but whoever keeps his word, in him truly the love of God is perfected. By this we may know that we are in him: ⁶whoever says he abides in him ought to walk in the same way in which he walked.

⁷Beloved, I am writing you no new commandment, but an old commandment that you had from the beginning. The old commandment is the word that you have heard. ⁸At the same time, it is a new commandment that I am writing to you, which is true in him and in you, because[4] the darkness is passing away and the true light is already shining. ⁹Whoever says he is in the light and hates his brother is still in darkness. ¹⁰Whoever loves his brother abides in the light, and in him[5] there is no cause for stumbling. ¹¹But whoever hates his brother is

[1] Hebrew *from the sea*　[2] Hebrew *in the realm of light*　[3] The Hebrew words for *terror, pit,* and *snare* sound alike　[4] Or *that*　[5] Or *it*

in the darkness and walks in the darkness, and does not know where he is going, because the darkness has blinded his eyes.

12   I am writing to you, little children,
     because your sins are forgiven for his
       name's sake.
13   I am writing to you, fathers,
     because you know him who is from
       the beginning.
     I am writing to you, young men,
     because you have overcome the evil
       one.
     I write to you, children,
     because you know the Father.
14   I write to you, fathers,
     because you know him who is from
       the beginning.
     I write to you, young men,
     because you are strong,
     and the word of God abides in you,
     and you have overcome the evil one.

15 Do not love the world or the things in the world. If anyone loves the world, the love of the Father is not in him. 16 For all that is in the world—the desires of the flesh and the desires of the eyes and pride of life[1]—is not from the Father but is from the world. 17 And the world is passing away along with its desires, but whoever does the will of God abides forever.

18 Children, it is the last hour, and as you have heard that antichrist is coming, so now many antichrists have come. Therefore we know that it is the last hour. 19 They went out from us, but they were not of us; for if they had been of us, they would have continued with us. But they went out, that it might become plain that they all are not of us. 20 But you have been anointed by the Holy One, and you all have knowledge.[2] 21 I write to you, not because you do not know the truth, but because you know it, and because no lie is of the truth. 22 Who is the liar but he who denies that Jesus is the Christ? This is the antichrist, he who denies the Father and the Son. 23 No one who denies the Son has the Father. Whoever confesses the Son has the Father also. 24 Let what you heard from the beginning abide in you. If what you heard from the beginning abides in you, then you too will abide in the Son and in the Father. 25 And this is the promise that he made to us[3]—eternal life.

26 I write these things to you about those who are trying to deceive you. 27 But the anointing that you received from him abides in you, and you have no need that anyone should teach you. But as his anointing teaches you about everything, and is true, and is no lie—just as it has taught you, abide in him.

28 And now, little children, abide in him, so that when he appears we may have confidence and not shrink from him in shame at his coming. 29 If you know that he is righteous, you may be sure that everyone who practices righteousness has been born of him.

MAY 24

Numbers 33

These are the stages of the people of Israel, when they went out of the land of Egypt by their companies under the leadership of Moses and Aaron. 2 Moses wrote down their starting places, stage by stage, by command of the LORD, and these are their stages according to their starting places. 3 They set out from Rameses in the first month, on the fifteenth day of the first month. On the day after the Passover, the people of Israel went out triumphantly in the sight of all the Egyptians, 4 while the Egyptians were burying all their firstborn, whom the LORD had struck down among them. On their gods also the LORD executed judgments.

5 So the people of Israel set out from Rameses and camped at Succoth. 6 And they set

[1] Or pride in possessions   [2] Some manuscripts you know everything   [3] Some manuscripts you

out from Succoth and camped at Etham, which is on the edge of the wilderness. [7]And they set out from Etham and turned back to Pi-hahiroth, which is east of Baal-zephon, and they camped before Migdol. [8]And they set out from before Hahiroth[1] and passed through the midst of the sea into the wilderness, and they went a three days' journey in the wilderness of Etham and camped at Marah. [9]And they set out from Marah and came to Elim; at Elim there were twelve springs of water and seventy palm trees, and they camped there. [10]And they set out from Elim and camped by the Red Sea. [11]And they set out from the Red Sea and camped in the wilderness of Sin. [12]And they set out from the wilderness of Sin and camped at Dophkah. [13]And they set out from Dophkah and camped at Alush. [14]And they set out from Alush and camped at Rephidim, where there was no water for the people to drink. [15]And they set out from Rephidim and camped in the wilderness of Sinai. [16]And they set out from the wilderness of Sinai and camped at Kibroth-hattaavah. [17]And they set out from Kibroth-hattaavah and camped at Hazeroth. [18]And they set out from Hazeroth and camped at Rithmah. [19]And they set out from Rithmah and camped at Rimmon-perez. [20]And they set out from Rimmon-perez and camped at Libnah. [21]And they set out from Libnah and camped at Rissah. [22]And they set out from Rissah and camped at Kehelathah. [23]And they set out from Kehelathah and camped at Mount Shepher. [24]And they set out from Mount Shepher and camped at Haradah. [25]And they set out from Haradah and camped at Makheloth. [26]And they set out from Makheloth and camped at Tahath. [27]And they set out from Tahath and camped at Terah. [28]And they set out from Terah and camped at Mithkah. [29]And they set out from Mithkah and camped at Hashmonah. [30]And they set out from Hashmonah and camped at Moseroth. [31]And they set out from Moseroth and camped at Bene-jaakan. [32]And they set out from Bene-jaakan and camped at Hor-haggidgad. [33]And they set out from Hor-haggidgad and camped at Jotbathah. [34]And they set out from Jotbathah and camped at Abronah. [35]And they set out from Abronah and camped at Ezion-geber. [36]And they set out from Ezion-geber and camped in the wilderness of Zin (that is, Kadesh). [37]And they set out from Kadesh and camped at Mount Hor, on the edge of the land of Edom.

[38]And Aaron the priest went up Mount Hor at the command of the LORD and died there, in the fortieth year after the people of Israel had come out of the land of Egypt, on the first day of the fifth month. [39]And Aaron was 123 years old when he died on Mount Hor.

[40]And the Canaanite, the king of Arad, who lived in the Negeb in the land of Canaan, heard of the coming of the people of Israel.

[41]And they set out from Mount Hor and camped at Zalmonah. [42]And they set out from Zalmonah and camped at Punon. [43]And they set out from Punon and camped at Oboth. [44]And they set out from Oboth and camped at Iye-abarim, in the territory of Moab. [45]And they set out from Iyim and camped at Dibon-gad. [46]And they set out from Dibon-gad and camped at Almon-diblathaim. [47]And they set out from Almon-diblathaim and camped in the mountains of Abarim, before Nebo. [48]And they set out from the mountains of Abarim and camped in the plains of Moab by the Jordan at Jericho; [49]they camped by the Jordan from Beth-jeshimoth as far as Abel-shittim in the plains of Moab.

[50]And the LORD spoke to Moses in the plains of Moab by the Jordan at Jericho, saying, [51]"Speak to the people of Israel and say to them, When you pass over the Jordan into the land of Canaan, [52]then you shall drive out all the inhabitants of the land from before you and destroy all their figured stones and destroy all their metal images and demolish all their high places. [53]And you shall take possession of the land and settle in it, for I have given the land to you to possess it. [54]You shall inherit the land by lot according to your clans. To a large tribe you shall give a large inheritance, and to a small tribe you shall give a small inheritance. Wherever the lot falls for anyone, that shall be his. According to the tribes of your fathers you shall inherit. [55]But if you do not drive out the inhabitants of the land from before you, then those of them whom you let remain shall be as barbs in your eyes and thorns in your sides, and they shall trouble you in the land where you dwell. [56]And I will do to you as I thought to do to them."

---

[1] Some manuscripts and versions Pi-hahiroth

Psalm 78:1-37

A Maskil[1] of Asaph.

G ive ear, O my people, to my teaching;
  incline your ears to the words of my
     mouth!
2 I will open my mouth in a parable;
    I will utter dark sayings from of old,
3 things that we have heard and known,
    that our fathers have told us.
4 We will not hide them from their
     children,
  but tell to the coming generation
the glorious deeds of the Lord, and his
     might,
  and the wonders that he has done.

5 He established a testimony in Jacob
    and appointed a law in Israel,
which he commanded our fathers
    to teach to their children,
6 that the next generation might know
     them,
  the children yet unborn,
and arise and tell them to their children,
7   so that they should set their hope in
     God
  and not forget the works of God,
    but keep his commandments;
8 and that they should not be like their
     fathers,
  a stubborn and rebellious generation,
a generation whose heart was not
     steadfast,
  whose spirit was not faithful to God.

9 The Ephraimites, armed with[2] the bow,
    turned back on the day of battle.
10 They did not keep God's covenant,
    but refused to walk according to his
     law.
11 They forgot his works
    and the wonders that he had shown
     them.
12 In the sight of their fathers he
     performed wonders
  in the land of Egypt, in the fields of
     Zoan.
13 He divided the sea and let them pass
     through it,
  and made the waters stand like a heap.
14 In the daytime he led them with a cloud,
  and all the night with a fiery light.

15 He split rocks in the wilderness
  and gave them drink abundantly as
     from the deep.
16 He made streams come out of the rock
  and caused waters to flow down like
     rivers.

17 Yet they sinned still more against him,
  rebelling against the Most High in the
     desert.
18 They tested God in their heart
  by demanding the food they craved.
19 They spoke against God, saying,
  "Can God spread a table in the
     wilderness?
20 He struck the rock so that water gushed
     out
  and streams overflowed.
Can he also give bread
  or provide meat for his people?"

21 Therefore, when the Lord heard, he was
     full of wrath;
  a fire was kindled against Jacob;
  his anger rose against Israel,
22 because they did not believe in God
  and did not trust his saving power.
23 Yet he commanded the skies above
  and opened the doors of heaven,
24 and he rained down on them manna to
     eat
  and gave them the grain of heaven.
25 Man ate of the bread of the angels;
  he sent them food in abundance.
26 He caused the east wind to blow in the
     heavens,
  and by his power he led out the south
     wind;
27 he rained meat on them like dust,
  winged birds like the sand of the seas;
28 he let them fall in the midst of their
     camp,
  all around their dwellings.
29 And they ate and were well filled,
  for he gave them what they craved.
30 But before they had satisfied their
     craving,
  while the food was still in their
     mouths,
31 the anger of God rose against them,
  and he killed the strongest of them
  and laid low the young men of Israel.

---

[1] Probably a musical or liturgical term   [2] Hebrew *armed and shooting*

32 In spite of all this, they still sinned;
despite his wonders, they did not
believe.

33 So he made their days vanish like[1] a
breath,[2]
and their years in terror.

34 When he killed them, they sought him;
they repented and sought God
earnestly.

35 They remembered that God was their
rock,
the Most High God their redeemer.

36 But they flattered him with their
mouths;
they lied to him with their tongues.

37 Their heart was not steadfast toward
him;
they were not faithful to his covenant.

--------- Isaiah 25 ---------

O LORD, you are my God;
I will exalt you; I will praise your name,
for you have done wonderful things,
plans formed of old, faithful and sure.

2 For you have made the city a heap,
the fortified city a ruin;
the foreigners' palace is a city no more;
it will never be rebuilt.

3 Therefore strong peoples will glorify
you;
cities of ruthless nations will fear you.

4 For you have been a stronghold to the
poor,
a stronghold to the needy in his
distress,
a shelter from the storm and a shade
from the heat;
for the breath of the ruthless is like a
storm against a wall,

5 like heat in a dry place.
You subdue the noise of the foreigners;
as heat by the shade of a cloud,
so the song of the ruthless is put
down.

6 On this mountain the LORD of hosts will
make for all peoples
a feast of rich food, a feast of well-
aged wine,
of rich food full of marrow, of aged
wine well refined.

7 And he will swallow up on this
mountain
the covering that is cast over all
peoples,
the veil that is spread over all nations.

8 He will swallow up death forever;
and the Lord GOD will wipe away tears
from all faces,
and the reproach of his people he will
take away from all the earth,
for the LORD has spoken.

9 It will be said on that day,
"Behold, this is our God; we have
waited for him, that he might save
us.
This is the LORD; we have waited for
him;
let us be glad and rejoice in his
salvation."

10 For the hand of the LORD will rest on
this mountain,
and Moab shall be trampled down in
his place,
as straw is trampled down in a
dunghill.[3]

11 And he will spread out his hands in the
midst of it
as a swimmer spreads his hands out
to swim,
but the LORD will lay low his pompous
pride together with the skill[4] of
his hands.

12 And the high fortifications of his walls
he will bring down,
lay low, and cast to the ground, to the
dust.

--------- 1 John 3 ---------

See what kind of love the Father has given
to us, that we should be called children of
God; and so we are. The reason why the world
does not know us is that it did not know him.
[2]Beloved, we are God's children now, and what
we will be has not yet appeared; but we know
that when he appears[5] we shall be like him,
because we shall see him as he is. [3]And everyone who thus hopes in him purifies himself as
he is pure.
[4]Everyone who makes a practice of sinning
also practices lawlessness; sin is lawlessness.
[5]You know that he appeared in order to take

---

[1] Hebrew in   [2] Or vapor   [3] The Hebrew words for dunghill and for the Moabite town Madmen (Jeremiah 48:2) sound alike   [4] Or in spite of the skill   [5] Or when it appears

away sins, and in him there is no sin. ⁶No one who abides in him keeps on sinning; no one who keeps on sinning has either seen him or known him. ⁷Little children, let no one deceive you. Whoever practices righteousness is righteous, as he is righteous. ⁸Whoever makes a practice of sinning is of the devil, for the devil has been sinning from the beginning. The reason the Son of God appeared was to destroy the works of the devil. ⁹No one born of God makes a practice of sinning, for God's¹ seed abides in him, and he cannot keep on sinning because he has been born of God. ¹⁰By this it is evident who are the children of God, and who are the children of the devil: whoever does not practice righteousness is not of God, nor is the one who does not love his brother.

¹¹For this is the message that you have heard from the beginning, that we should love one another. ¹²We should not be like Cain, who was of the evil one and murdered his brother. And why did he murder him? Because his own deeds were evil and his brother's righteous. ¹³Do not be surprised, brothers,² that the world hates you. ¹⁴We know that we have passed out of death into life, because we love the brothers. Whoever does not love abides in death. ¹⁵Everyone who hates his brother is a murderer, and you know that no murderer has eternal life abiding in him.

¹⁶By this we know love, that he laid down his life for us, and we ought to lay down our lives for the brothers. ¹⁷But if anyone has the world's goods and sees his brother in need, yet closes his heart against him, how does God's love abide in him? ¹⁸Little children, let us not love in word or talk but in deed and in truth.

¹⁹By this we shall know that we are of the truth and reassure our heart before him; ²⁰for whenever our heart condemns us, God is greater than our heart, and he knows everything. ²¹Beloved, if our heart does not condemn us, we have confidence before God; ²²and whatever we ask we receive from him, because we keep his commandments and do what pleases him. ²³And this is his commandment, that we believe in the name of his Son Jesus Christ and love one another, just as he has commanded us. ²⁴Whoever keeps his commandments abides in God,³ and God⁴ in him. And by this we know that he abides in us, by the Spirit whom he has given us.

MAY 25

Numbers 34

The LORD spoke to Moses, saying, ²"Command the people of Israel, and say to them, When you enter the land of Canaan (this is the land that shall fall to you for an inheritance, the land of Canaan as defined by its borders), ³your south side shall be from the wilderness of Zin alongside Edom, and your southern border shall run from the end of the Salt Sea on the east. ⁴And your border shall turn south of the ascent of Akrabbim, and cross to Zin, and its limit shall be south of Kadesh-barnea. Then it shall go on to Hazar-addar, and pass along to Azmon. ⁵And the border shall turn from Azmon to the Brook of Egypt, and its limit shall be at the sea.

⁶"For the western border, you shall have the Great Sea and its⁵ coast. This shall be your western border.

⁷"This shall be your northern border: from the Great Sea you shall draw a line to Mount Hor. ⁸From Mount Hor you shall draw a line to Lebo-hamath, and the limit of the border shall be at Zedad. ⁹Then the border shall extend to Ziphron, and its limit shall be at Hazar-enan. This shall be your northern border.

¹⁰"You shall draw a line for your eastern border from Hazar-enan to Shepham. ¹¹And the border shall go down from Shepham to Riblah on the east side of Ain. And the border shall go down and reach to the shoulder of the Sea of

¹ Greek *his* ² Or *brothers and sisters*. The plural Greek word *adelphoi* (translated "brothers") refers to siblings in a family. In New Testament usage, depending on the context, *adelphoi* may refer either to men or to both men and women who are siblings (brothers and sisters) in God's family, the church; also verses 14, 16 ³ Greek *him* ⁴ Greek *he* ⁵ Syriac; Hebrew lacks *its*

Chinnereth on the east. ¹²And the border shall go down to the Jordan, and its limit shall be at the Salt Sea. This shall be your land as defined by its borders all around."

¹³Moses commanded the people of Israel, saying, "This is the land that you shall inherit by lot, which the LORD has commanded to give to the nine tribes and to the half-tribe. ¹⁴For the tribe of the people of Reuben by fathers' houses and the tribe of the people of Gad by their fathers' houses have received their inheritance, and also the half-tribe of Manasseh. ¹⁵The two tribes and the half-tribe have received their inheritance beyond the Jordan east of Jericho, toward the sunrise."

¹⁶The LORD spoke to Moses, saying, ¹⁷"These are the names of the men who shall divide the land to you for inheritance: Eleazar the priest and Joshua the son of Nun. ¹⁸You shall take one chief from every tribe to divide the land for inheritance. ¹⁹These are the names of the men: Of the tribe of Judah, Caleb the son of Jephunneh. ²⁰Of the tribe of the people of Simeon, Shemuel the son of Ammihud. ²¹Of the tribe of Benjamin, Elidad the son of Chislon. ²²Of the tribe of the people of Dan a chief, Bukki the son of Jogli. ²³Of the people of Joseph: of the tribe of the people of Manasseh a chief, Hanniel the son of Ephod. ²⁴And of the tribe of the people of Ephraim a chief, Kemuel the son of Shiphtan. ²⁵Of the tribe of the people of Zebulun a chief, Elizaphan the son of Parnach. ²⁶Of the tribe of the people of Issachar a chief, Paltiel the son of Azzan. ²⁷And of the tribe of the people of Asher a chief, Ahihud the son of Shelomi. ²⁸Of the tribe of the people of Naphtali a chief, Pedahel the son of Ammihud. ²⁹These are the men whom the LORD commanded to divide the inheritance for the people of Israel in the land of Canaan."

Psalm 78:38–72

Yet he, being compassionate,
    atoned for their iniquity
        and did not destroy them;
    he restrained his anger often
        and did not stir up all his wrath.
³⁹   He remembered that they were but flesh,
        a wind that passes and comes not
            again.

⁴⁰   How often they rebelled against him in
            the wilderness
        and grieved him in the desert!
⁴¹   They tested God again and again
        and provoked the Holy One of Israel.
⁴²   They did not remember his power¹
        or the day when he redeemed them
            from the foe,
⁴³   when he performed his signs in Egypt
        and his marvels in the fields of Zoan.
⁴⁴   He turned their rivers to blood,
        so that they could not drink of their
            streams.
⁴⁵   He sent among them swarms of flies,
        which devoured them,
        and frogs, which destroyed them.
⁴⁶   He gave their crops to the destroying
            locust
        and the fruit of their labor to the locust.
⁴⁷   He destroyed their vines with hail
        and their sycamores with frost.
⁴⁸   He gave over their cattle to the hail
        and their flocks to thunderbolts.
⁴⁹   He let loose on them his burning anger,
        wrath, indignation, and distress,
        a company of destroying angels.
⁵⁰   He made a path for his anger;
        he did not spare them from death,
        but gave their lives over to the plague.
⁵¹   He struck down every firstborn in Egypt,
        the firstfruits of their strength in the
            tents of Ham.
⁵²   Then he led out his people like sheep
        and guided them in the wilderness
            like a flock.
⁵³   He led them in safety, so that they were
            not afraid,
        but the sea overwhelmed their enemies.
⁵⁴   And he brought them to his holy land,
        to the mountain which his right hand
            had won.
⁵⁵   He drove out nations before them;
        he apportioned them for a possession
        and settled the tribes of Israel in their
            tents.
⁵⁶   Yet they tested and rebelled against the
            Most High God
        and did not keep his testimonies,
⁵⁷   but turned away and acted treacherously
            like their fathers;
        they twisted like a deceitful bow.

¹ Hebrew hand

58 For they provoked him to anger with
   their high places;
   they moved him to jealousy with their
   idols.
59 When God heard, he was full of wrath,
   and he utterly rejected Israel.
60 He forsook his dwelling at Shiloh,
   the tent where he dwelt among
   mankind,
61 and delivered his power to captivity,
   his glory to the hand of the foe.
62 He gave his people over to the sword
   and vented his wrath on his heritage.
63 Fire devoured their young men,
   and their young women had no
   marriage song.
64 Their priests fell by the sword,
   and their widows made no
   lamentation.
65 Then the Lord awoke as from sleep,
   like a strong man shouting because of
   wine.
66 And he put his adversaries to rout;
   he put them to everlasting shame.
67 He rejected the tent of Joseph;
   he did not choose the tribe of
   Ephraim,
68 but he chose the tribe of Judah,
   Mount Zion, which he loves.
69 He built his sanctuary like the high
   heavens,
   like the earth, which he has founded
   forever.
70 He chose David his servant
   and took him from the sheepfolds;
71 from following the nursing ewes he
   brought him
   to shepherd Jacob his people,
   Israel his inheritance.
72 With upright heart he shepherded them
   and guided them with his skillful
   hand.

Isaiah 26

In that day this song will be sung in the land
of Judah:

"We have a strong city;
he sets up salvation
as walls and bulwarks.

2 Open the gates,
that the righteous nation that keeps
faith may enter in.
3 You keep him in perfect peace
whose mind is stayed on you,
because he trusts in you.
4 Trust in the LORD forever,
for the LORD GOD is an everlasting
rock.
5 For he has humbled
the inhabitants of the height,
the lofty city.
He lays it low, lays it low to the ground,
casts it to the dust.
6 The foot tramples it,
the feet of the poor,
the steps of the needy."

7 The path of the righteous is level;
you make level the way of the
righteous.
8 In the path of your judgments,
O LORD, we wait for you;
your name and remembrance
are the desire of our soul.
9 My soul yearns for you in the night;
my spirit within me earnestly seeks
you.
For when your judgments are in the
earth,
the inhabitants of the world learn
righteousness.
10 If favor is shown to the wicked,
he does not learn righteousness;
in the land of uprightness he deals
corruptly
and does not see the majesty of the
LORD.
11 O LORD, your hand is lifted up,
but they do not see it.
Let them see your zeal for your people,
and be ashamed.
Let the fire for your adversaries
consume them.
12 O LORD, you will ordain peace for us,
for you have indeed done for us all
our works.
13 O LORD our God,
other lords besides you have ruled
over us,
but your name alone we bring to
remembrance.

14 They are dead, they will not live;
    they are shades, they will not arise;
    to that end you have visited them with
        destruction
    and wiped out all remembrance of
        them.

15 But you have increased the nation,
    O LORD,
    you have increased the nation; you are
        glorified;
    you have enlarged all the borders of
        the land.

16 O LORD, in distress they sought you;
    they poured out a whispered prayer
    when your discipline was upon them.

17 Like a pregnant woman
    who writhes and cries out in her
        pangs
    when she is near to giving birth,
    so were we because of you, O LORD;

18   we were pregnant, we writhed,
    but we have given birth to wind.
  We have accomplished no deliverance
        in the earth,
    and the inhabitants of the world have
        not fallen.

19 Your dead shall live; their bodies shall
        rise.
    You who dwell in the dust, awake and
        sing for joy!
  For your dew is a dew of light,
    and the earth will give birth to the
        dead.

20 Come, my people, enter your chambers,
    and shut your doors behind you;
  hide yourselves for a little while
    until the fury has passed by.

21 For behold, the LORD is coming out
        from his place
    to punish the inhabitants of the earth
        for their iniquity,
  and the earth will disclose the blood
        shed on it,
  and will no more cover its slain.

1 John 4

Beloved, do not believe every spirit, but test the spirits to see whether they are from God, for many false prophets have gone out into the world. [2] By this you know the Spirit of God: every spirit that confesses that Jesus Christ has come in the flesh is from God, [3] and every spirit that does not confess Jesus is not from God. This is the spirit of the antichrist, which you heard was coming and now is in the world already. [4] Little children, you are from God and have overcome them, for he who is in you is greater than he who is in the world. [5] They are from the world; therefore they speak from the world, and the world listens to them. [6] We are from God. Whoever knows God listens to us; whoever is not from God does not listen to us. By this we know the Spirit of truth and the spirit of error.

[7] Beloved, let us love one another, for love is from God, and whoever loves has been born of God and knows God. [8] Anyone who does not love does not know God, because God is love. [9] In this the love of God was made manifest among us, that God sent his only Son into the world, so that we might live through him. [10] In this is love, not that we have loved God but that he loved us and sent his Son to be the propitiation for our sins. [11] Beloved, if God so loved us, we also ought to love one another. [12] No one has ever seen God; if we love one another, God abides in us and his love is perfected in us.

[13] By this we know that we abide in him and he in us, because he has given us of his Spirit. [14] And we have seen and testify that the Father has sent his Son to be the Savior of the world. [15] Whoever confesses that Jesus is the Son of God, God abides in him, and he in God. [16] So we have come to know and to believe the love that God has for us. God is love, and whoever abides in love abides in God, and God abides in him. [17] By this is love perfected with us, so that we may have confidence for the day of judgment, because as he is so also are we in this world. [18] There is no fear in love, but perfect love casts out fear. For fear has to do with punishment, and whoever fears has not been perfected in love. [19] We love because he first loved us. [20] If anyone says, "I love God," and hates his brother, he is a liar; for he who does not love his brother whom he has seen cannot[1] love God whom he has not seen. [21] And this commandment we have from him: whoever loves God must also love his brother.

[1] Some manuscripts *how can he*

MAY 26

Numbers 35

The LORD spoke to Moses in the plains of Moab by the Jordan at Jericho, saying, ² "Command the people of Israel to give to the Levites some of the inheritance of their possession as cities for them to dwell in. And you shall give to the Levites pasturelands around the cities. ³ The cities shall be theirs to dwell in, and their pasturelands shall be for their cattle and for their livestock and for all their beasts. ⁴ The pasturelands of the cities, which you shall give to the Levites, shall reach from the wall of the city outward a thousand cubits¹ all around. ⁵ And you shall measure, outside the city, on the east side two thousand cubits, and on the south side two thousand cubits, and on the west side two thousand cubits, and on the north side two thousand cubits, the city being in the middle. This shall belong to them as pastureland for their cities.

⁶ "The cities that you give to the Levites shall be the six cities of refuge, where you shall permit the manslayer to flee, and in addition to them you shall give forty-two cities. ⁷ All the cities that you give to the Levites shall be forty-eight, with their pasturelands. ⁸ And as for the cities that you shall give from the possession of the people of Israel, from the larger tribes you shall take many, and from the smaller tribes you shall take few; each, in proportion to the inheritance that it inherits, shall give of its cities to the Levites."

⁹ And the LORD spoke to Moses, saying, ¹⁰ "Speak to the people of Israel and say to them, When you cross the Jordan into the land of Canaan, ¹¹ then you shall select cities to be cities of refuge for you, that the manslayer who kills any person without intent may flee there. ¹² The cities shall be for you a refuge from the avenger, that the manslayer may not die until he stands before the congregation for judgment. ¹³ And the cities that you give shall be your six cities of refuge. ¹⁴ You shall give three cities beyond the Jordan, and three cities in the land of Canaan, to be cities of refuge. ¹⁵ These six cities shall be for refuge for the people of Israel, and for the stranger and for the sojourner among them, that anyone who kills any person without intent may flee there.

¹⁶ "But if he struck him down with an iron object, so that he died, he is a murderer. The murderer shall be put to death. ¹⁷ And if he struck him down with a stone tool that could cause death, and he died, he is a murderer. The murderer shall be put to death. ¹⁸ Or if he struck him down with a wooden tool that could cause death, and he died, he is a murderer. The murderer shall be put to death. ¹⁹ The avenger of blood shall himself put the murderer to death; when he meets him, he shall put him to death. ²⁰ And if he pushed him out of hatred or hurled something at him, lying in wait, so that he died, ²¹ or in enmity struck him down with his hand, so that he died, then he who struck the blow shall be put to death. He is a murderer. The avenger of blood shall put the murderer to death when he meets him.

²² "But if he pushed him suddenly without enmity, or hurled anything on him without lying in wait ²³ or used a stone that could cause death, and without seeing him dropped it on him, so that he died, though he was not his enemy and did not seek his harm, ²⁴ then the congregation shall judge between the manslayer and the avenger of blood, in accordance with these rules. ²⁵ And the congregation shall rescue the manslayer from the hand of the avenger of blood, and the congregation shall restore him to his city of refuge to which he had fled, and he shall live in it until the death of the high priest who was anointed with the holy oil. ²⁶ But if the manslayer shall at any time go beyond the boundaries of his city of refuge to which he fled, ²⁷ and the avenger of blood finds him outside the boundaries of his city of refuge, and the avenger of blood kills the manslayer, he shall not be guilty of blood. ²⁸ For he must remain in his city of refuge until the death of the high priest, but after the death of the high

¹ A *cubit* was about 18 inches or 45 centimeters

priest the manslayer may return to the land of his possession. ²⁹And these things shall be for a statute and rule for you throughout your generations in all your dwelling places.

³⁰"If anyone kills a person, the murderer shall be put to death on the evidence of witnesses. But no person shall be put to death on the testimony of one witness. ³¹Moreover, you shall accept no ransom for the life of a murderer, who is guilty of death, but he shall be put to death. ³²And you shall accept no ransom for him who has fled to his city of refuge, that he may return to dwell in the land before the death of the high priest. ³³You shall not pollute the land in which you live, for blood pollutes the land, and no atonement can be made for the land for the blood that is shed in it, except by the blood of the one who shed it. ³⁴You shall not defile the land in which you live, in the midst of which I dwell, for I the LORD dwell in the midst of the people of Israel."

Psalm 79

A PSALM OF ASAPH.

O God, the nations have come into your inheritance;
    they have defiled your holy temple;
    they have laid Jerusalem in ruins.
2 They have given the bodies of your servants
        to the birds of the heavens for food,
    the flesh of your faithful to the beasts of the earth.
3 They have poured out their blood like water
        all around Jerusalem,
    and there was no one to bury them.
4 We have become a taunt to our neighbors,
        mocked and derided by those around us.
5 How long, O LORD? Will you be angry forever?
    Will your jealousy burn like fire?
6 Pour out your anger on the nations that do not know you,
    and on the kingdoms that do not call upon your name!
7 For they have devoured Jacob and laid waste his habitation.

8 Do not remember against us our former iniquities;[1]
    let your compassion come speedily to meet us,
    for we are brought very low.
9 Help us, O God of our salvation,
    for the glory of your name;
    deliver us, and atone for our sins,
        for your name's sake!
10 Why should the nations say,
    "Where is their God?"
    Let the avenging of the outpoured blood of your servants
        be known among the nations before our eyes!
11 Let the groans of the prisoners come before you;
    according to your great power,
        preserve those doomed to die!
12 Return sevenfold into the lap of our neighbors
    the taunts with which they have taunted you, O Lord!
13 But we your people, the sheep of your pasture,
    will give thanks to you forever;
    from generation to generation we will recount your praise.

Isaiah 27

In that day the LORD with his hard and great and strong sword will punish Leviathan the fleeing serpent, Leviathan the twisting serpent, and he will slay the dragon that is in the sea.

2 In that day,
    "A pleasant vineyard,[2] sing of it!
3 I, the LORD, am its keeper;
    every moment I water it.
    Lest anyone punish it,
    I keep it night and day;
4 I have no wrath.
    Would that I had thorns and briers to battle!
    I would march against them,
    I would burn them up together.
5 Or let them lay hold of my protection,
    let them make peace with me,
    let them make peace with me."

[1] Or the iniquities of former generations [2] Many Hebrew manuscripts A vineyard of wine

6   In days to come[1] Jacob shall take root,
        Israel shall blossom and put forth
           shoots
        and fill the whole world with fruit.

7   Has he struck them as he struck those
           who struck them?
        Or have they been slain as their
           slayers were slain?

8   Measure by measure,[2] by exile you
           contended with them;
        he removed them with his fierce
           breath[3] in the day of the east wind.

9   Therefore by this the guilt of Jacob will
           be atoned for,
        and this will be the full fruit of the
           removal of his sin:[4]
        when he makes all the stones of the
           altars
        like chalkstones crushed to pieces,
        no Asherim or incense altars will
           remain standing.

10   For the fortified city is solitary,
        a habitation deserted and forsaken,
           like the wilderness;
        there the calf grazes;
        there it lies down and strips its
           branches.

11   When its boughs are dry, they are broken;
        women come and make a fire of them.
        For this is a people without discernment;
        therefore he who made them will not
           have compassion on them;
        he who formed them will show them
           no favor.

[12] In that day from the river Euphrates[5] to the Brook of Egypt the LORD will thresh out the grain, and you will be gleaned one by one, O people of Israel. [13] And in that day a great trumpet will be blown, and those who were lost in the land of Assyria and those who were driven out to the land of Egypt will come and worship the LORD on the holy mountain at Jerusalem.

--------- 1 John 5 ---------

Everyone who believes that Jesus is the Christ has been born of God, and everyone who loves the Father loves whoever has been born of him. [2] By this we know that we love the children of God, when we love God and obey his commandments. [3] For this is the love of God, that we keep his commandments. And his commandments are not burdensome. [4] For everyone who has been born of God overcomes the world. And this is the victory that has overcome the world—our faith. [5] Who is it that overcomes the world except the one who believes that Jesus is the Son of God?

[6] This is he who came by water and blood—Jesus Christ; not by the water only but by the water and the blood. And the Spirit is the one who testifies, because the Spirit is the truth. [7] For there are three that testify: [8] the Spirit and the water and the blood; and these three agree. [9] If we receive the testimony of men, the testimony of God is greater, for this is the testimony of God that he has borne concerning his Son. [10] Whoever believes in the Son of God has the testimony in himself. Whoever does not believe God has made him a liar, because he has not believed in the testimony that God has borne concerning his Son. [11] And this is the testimony, that God gave us eternal life, and this life is in his Son. [12] Whoever has the Son has life; whoever does not have the Son of God does not have life.

[13] I write these things to you who believe in the name of the Son of God that you may know that you have eternal life. [14] And this is the confidence that we have toward him, that if we ask anything according to his will he hears us. [15] And if we know that he hears us in whatever we ask, we know that we have the requests that we have asked of him.

[16] If anyone sees his brother committing a sin not leading to death, he shall ask, and God[6] will give him life—to those who commit sins that do not lead to death. There is sin that leads to death; I do not say that one should pray for that. [17] All wrongdoing is sin, but there is sin that does not lead to death.

[18] We know that everyone who has been born of God does not keep on sinning, but he who was born of God protects him, and the evil one does not touch him. [19] We know that we are from God, and the whole world lies in the power of the evil one. [20] And we know that the Son of God has come and has given us understanding, so that we may know him who is true; and we are in him who is true, in his Son Jesus Christ. He is the true God and eternal life. [21] Little children, keep yourselves from idols.

[1] Hebrew *In those to come* [2] Or *By driving her away; the meaning of the Hebrew word is uncertain* [3] Or *wind* [4] Septuagint *and this is the blessing when I take away his sin*
[5] Hebrew *from the River* [6] Greek *he*

MAY 27

Numbers 36

The heads of the fathers' houses of the clan of the people of Gilead the son of Machir, son of Manasseh, from the clans of the people of Joseph, came near and spoke before Moses and before the chiefs, the heads of the fathers' houses of the people of Israel. ²They said, "The LORD commanded my lord to give the land for inheritance by lot to the people of Israel, and my lord was commanded by the LORD to give the inheritance of Zelophehad our brother to his daughters. ³But if they are married to any of the sons of the other tribes of the people of Israel, then their inheritance will be taken from the inheritance of our fathers and added to the inheritance of the tribe into which they marry. So it will be taken away from the lot of our inheritance. ⁴And when the jubilee of the people of Israel comes, then their inheritance will be added to the inheritance of the tribe into which they marry, and their inheritance will be taken from the inheritance of the tribe of our fathers."

⁵And Moses commanded the people of Israel according to the word of the LORD, saying, "The tribe of the people of Joseph is right. ⁶This is what the LORD commands concerning the daughters of Zelophehad: 'Let them marry whom they think best, only they shall marry within the clan of the tribe of their father. ⁷The inheritance of the people of Israel shall not be transferred from one tribe to another, for every one of the people of Israel shall hold on to the inheritance of the tribe of his fathers. ⁸And every daughter who possesses an inheritance in any tribe of the people of Israel shall be wife to one of the clan of the tribe of her father, so that every one of the people of Israel may possess the inheritance of his fathers. ⁹So no inheritance shall be transferred from one tribe to another, for each of the tribes of the people of Israel shall hold on to its own inheritance.'"

¹⁰The daughters of Zelophehad did as the LORD commanded Moses, ¹¹for Mahlah, Tirzah, Hoglah, Milcah, and Noah, the daughters of Zelophehad, were married to sons of their father's brothers. ¹²They were married into the clans of the people of Manasseh the son of Joseph, and their inheritance remained in the tribe of their father's clan.

¹³These are the commandments and the rules that the LORD commanded through Moses to the people of Israel in the plains of Moab by the Jordan at Jericho.

Psalm 80

To THE CHOIRMASTER: ACCORDING TO LILIES. A TESTIMONY. OF ASAPH, A PSALM.

Give ear, O Shepherd of Israel,
   you who lead Joseph like a flock.
   You who are enthroned upon the
      cherubim, shine forth.
2   Before Ephraim and Benjamin and
      Manasseh,
   stir up your might
   and come to save us!

3   Restore us,[1] O God;
      let your face shine, that we may be
      saved!

4   O LORD God of hosts,
      how long will you be angry with your
      people's prayers?
5   You have fed them with the bread of
      tears
      and given them tears to drink in full
      measure.
6   You make us an object of contention for
      our neighbors,
      and our enemies laugh among
      themselves.

7   Restore us, O God of hosts;
      let your face shine, that we may be
      saved!

8   You brought a vine out of Egypt;
      you drove out the nations and planted
      it.

[1] Or Turn us again; also verses 7, 19

9   You cleared the ground for it;
  it took deep root and filled the land.
10 The mountains were covered with its
   shade,
  the mighty cedars with its branches.
11 It sent out its branches to the sea
  and its shoots to the River.[1]
12 Why then have you broken down its
   walls,
  so that all who pass along the way
   pluck its fruit?
13 The boar from the forest ravages it,
  and all that move in the field feed
   on it.

14 Turn again, O God of hosts!
  Look down from heaven, and see;
have regard for this vine,
15   the stock that your right hand planted,
  and for the son whom you made
   strong for yourself.
16 They have burned it with fire; they have
   cut it down;
  may they perish at the rebuke of your
   face!
17 But let your hand be on the man of your
   right hand,
  the son of man whom you have made
   strong for yourself!
18 Then we shall not turn back from you;
  give us life, and we will call upon your
   name!

19 Restore us, O Lord God of hosts!
  Let your face shine, that we may be
   saved!

Isaiah 28

Ah, the proud crown of the drunkards of
 Ephraim,
  and the fading flower of its glorious
   beauty,
  which is on the head of the rich valley
   of those overcome with wine!
2   Behold, the Lord has one who is mighty
   and strong;
  like a storm of hail, a destroying
   tempest,
 like a storm of mighty, overflowing
   waters,
  he casts down to the earth with his
   hand.

3   The proud crown of the drunkards of
   Ephraim
  will be trodden underfoot;
4   and the fading flower of its glorious
   beauty,
  which is on the head of the rich valley,
 will be like a first-ripe fig before the
   summer:
  when someone sees it, he swallows it
  as soon as it is in his hand.

5   In that day the Lord of hosts will be a
   crown of glory,[2]
  and a diadem of beauty, to the
   remnant of his people,
6   and a spirit of justice to him who sits in
   judgment,
  and strength to those who turn back
   the battle at the gate.

7   These also reel with wine
  and stagger with strong drink;
 the priest and the prophet reel with
   strong drink,
  they are swallowed by[3] wine,
  they stagger with strong drink,
 they reel in vision,
  they stumble in giving judgment.
8   For all tables are full of filthy vomit,
  with no space left.

9   "To whom will he teach knowledge,
  and to whom will he explain the
   message?
 Those who are weaned from the milk,
  those taken from the breast?
10 For it is precept upon precept, precept
   upon precept,
  line upon line, line upon line,
  here a little, there a little."

11 For by people of strange lips
  and with a foreign tongue
 the Lord will speak to this people,
12   to whom he has said,
 "This is rest;
  give rest to the weary;
 and this is repose";
  yet they would not hear.
13 And the word of the Lord will be to them
 precept upon precept, precept upon
   precept,
  line upon line, line upon line,
  here a little, there a little,

[1] That is, the Euphrates [2] The Hebrew words for *glory* and *hosts* sound alike [3] Or *confused by*

that they may go, and fall backward,
   and be broken, and snared, and taken.

14 Therefore hear the word of the LORD,
   you scoffers,
   who rule this people in Jerusalem!
15 Because you have said, "We have made a
   covenant with death,
   and with Sheol we have an
   agreement,
   when the overwhelming whip passes
   through
   it will not come to us,
   for we have made lies our refuge,
   and in falsehood we have taken
   shelter";
16 therefore thus says the Lord GOD,
   "Behold, I am the one who has laid[1] as a
   foundation in Zion,
   a stone, a tested stone,
   a precious cornerstone, of a sure
   foundation:
   'Whoever believes will not be in
   haste.'
17 And I will make justice the line,
   and righteousness the plumb line;
   and hail will sweep away the refuge of
   lies,
   and waters will overwhelm the
   shelter."
18 Then your covenant with death will be
   annulled,
   and your agreement with Sheol will
   not stand;
   when the overwhelming scourge passes
   through,
   you will be beaten down by it.
19 As often as it passes through it will take
   you;
   for morning by morning it will pass
   through,
   by day and by night;
   and it will be sheer terror to understand
   the message.
20 For the bed is too short to stretch oneself
   on,
   and the covering too narrow to wrap
   oneself in.
21 For the LORD will rise up as on Mount
   Perazim;
   as in the Valley of Gibeon he will be
   roused;

to do his deed—strange is his deed!
   and to work his work—alien is his
   work!
22 Now therefore do not scoff,
   lest your bonds be made strong;
   for I have heard a decree of destruction
   from the Lord GOD of hosts against
   the whole land.

23 Give ear, and hear my voice;
   give attention, and hear my speech.
24 Does he who plows for sowing plow
   continually?
   Does he continually open and harrow
   his ground?
25 When he has leveled its surface,
   does he not scatter dill, sow cumin,
   and put in wheat in rows
   and barley in its proper place,
   and emmer[2] as the border?
26 For he is rightly instructed;
   his God teaches him.

27 Dill is not threshed with a threshing
   sledge,
   nor is a cart wheel rolled over cumin,
   but dill is beaten out with a stick,
   and cumin with a rod.
28 Does one crush grain for bread?
   No, he does not thresh it forever;[3]
   when he drives his cart wheel over it
   with his horses, he does not crush it.
29 This also comes from the LORD of hosts;
   he is wonderful in counsel
   and excellent in wisdom.

2 John 1

The elder to the elect lady and her children, whom I love in truth, and not only I, but also all who know the truth, [2]because of the truth that abides in us and will be with us forever:

[3]Grace, mercy, and peace will be with us, from God the Father and from Jesus Christ the Father's Son, in truth and love.

[4]I rejoiced greatly to find some of your children walking in the truth, just as we were commanded by the Father. [5]And now I ask you, dear lady—not as though I were writing you a new commandment, but the one we have had from the beginning—that we love one another. [6]And this is love, that we walk

[1] Dead Sea Scroll *I am laying*   [2] A type of wheat   [3] Or *Grain is crushed for bread; he will surely thresh it, but not forever*

according to his commandments; this is the commandment, just as you have heard from the beginning, so that you should walk in it. [7] For many deceivers have gone out into the world, those who do not confess the coming of Jesus Christ in the flesh. Such a one is the deceiver and the antichrist. [8] Watch yourselves, so that you may not lose what we[1] have worked for, but may win a full reward. [9] Everyone who goes on ahead and does not abide in the teaching of Christ, does not have God. Whoever abides in the teaching has both the Father and the Son. [10] If anyone comes to you and does not bring this teaching, do not receive him into your house or give him any greeting, [11] for whoever greets him takes part in his wicked works.

[12] Though I have much to write to you, I would rather not use paper and ink. Instead I hope to come to you and talk face to face, so that our joy may be complete.

[13] The children of your elect sister greet you.

MAY 28

Deuteronomy 1

These are the words that Moses spoke to all Israel beyond the Jordan in the wilderness, in the Arabah opposite Suph, between Paran and Tophel, Laban, Hazeroth, and Dizahab. [2] It is eleven days' journey from Horeb by the way of Mount Seir to Kadesh-barnea. [3] In the fortieth year, on the first day of the eleventh month, Moses spoke to the people of Israel according to all that the LORD had given him in commandment to them, [4] after he had defeated Sihon the king of the Amorites, who lived in Heshbon, and Og the king of Bashan, who lived in Ashtaroth and in Edrei. [5] Beyond the Jordan, in the land of Moab, Moses undertook to explain this law, saying, [6] "The LORD our God said to us in Horeb, 'You have stayed long enough at this mountain. [7] Turn and take your journey, and go to the hill country of the Amorites and to all their neighbors in the Arabah, in the hill country and in the lowland and in the Negeb and by the seacoast, the land of the Canaanites, and Lebanon, as far as the great river, the river Euphrates. [8] See, I have set the land before you. Go in and take possession of the land that the LORD swore to your fathers, to Abraham, to Isaac, and to Jacob, to give to them and to their offspring after them.'

[9] "At that time I said to you, 'I am not able to bear you by myself. [10] The LORD your God has multiplied you, and behold, you are today as numerous as the stars of heaven. [11] May the LORD, the God of your fathers, make you a thousand times as many as you are and bless you, as he has promised you! [12] How can I bear by myself the weight and burden of you and your strife? [13] Choose for your tribes wise, understanding, and experienced men, and I will appoint them as your heads.' [14] And you answered me, 'The thing that you have spoken is good for us to do.' [15] So I took the heads of your tribes, wise and experienced men, and set them as heads over you, commanders of thousands, commanders of hundreds, commanders of fifties, commanders of tens, and officers, throughout your tribes. [16] And I charged your judges at that time, 'Hear the cases between your brothers, and judge righteously between a man and his brother or the alien who is with him. [17] You shall not be partial in judgment. You shall hear the small and the great alike. You shall not be intimidated by anyone, for the judgment is God's. And the case that is too hard for you, you shall bring to me, and I will hear it.' [18] And I commanded you at that time all the things that you should do.

[19] "Then we set out from Horeb and went through all that great and terrifying wilderness that you saw, on the way to the hill country of the Amorites, as the LORD our God commanded us. And we came to

Kadesh-barnea. ²⁰And I said to you, 'You have come to the hill country of the Amorites, which the Lord our God is giving us. ²¹See, the Lord your God has set the land before you. Go up, take possession, as the Lord, the God of your fathers, has told you. Do not fear or be dismayed.' ²²Then all of you came near me and said, 'Let us send men before us, that they may explore the land for us and bring us word again of the way by which we must go up and the cities into which we shall come.' ²³The thing seemed good to me, and I took twelve men from you, one man from each tribe. ²⁴And they turned and went up into the hill country, and came to the Valley of Eshcol and spied it out. ²⁵And they took in their hands some of the fruit of the land and brought it down to us, and brought us word again and said, 'It is a good land that the Lord our God is giving us.'

²⁶"Yet you would not go up, but rebelled against the command of the Lord your God. ²⁷And you murmured in your tents and said, 'Because the Lord hated us he has brought us out of the land of Egypt, to give us into the hand of the Amorites, to destroy us. ²⁸Where are we going up? Our brothers have made our hearts melt, saying, "The people are greater and taller than we. The cities are great and fortified up to heaven. And besides, we have seen the sons of the Anakim there."' ²⁹Then I said to you, 'Do not be in dread or afraid of them. ³⁰The Lord your God who goes before you will himself fight for you, just as he did for you in Egypt before your eyes, ³¹and in the wilderness, where you have seen how the Lord your God carried you, as a man carries his son, all the way that you went until you came to this place.' ³²Yet in spite of this word you did not believe the Lord your God, ³³who went before you in the way to seek you out a place to pitch your tents, in fire by night and in the cloud by day, to show you by what way you should go.

³⁴"And the Lord heard your words and was angered, and he swore, ³⁵'Not one of these men of this evil generation shall see the good land that I swore to give to your fathers, ³⁶except Caleb the son of Jephunneh. He shall see it, and to him and to his children I will give the land on which he has trodden, because he has wholly followed the Lord!'

³⁷Even with me the Lord was angry on your account and said, 'You also shall not go in there. ³⁸Joshua the son of Nun, who stands before you, he shall enter. Encourage him, for he shall cause Israel to inherit it. ³⁹And as for your little ones, who you said would become a prey, and your children, who today have no knowledge of good or evil, they shall go in there. And to them I will give it, and they shall possess it. ⁴⁰But as for you, turn, and journey into the wilderness in the direction of the Red Sea.'

⁴¹"Then you answered me, 'We have sinned against the Lord. We ourselves will go up and fight, just as the Lord our God commanded us.' And every one of you fastened on his weapons of war and thought it easy to go up into the hill country. ⁴²And the Lord said to me, 'Say to them, Do not go up or fight, for I am not in your midst, lest you be defeated before your enemies.' ⁴³So I spoke to you, and you would not listen; but you rebelled against the command of the Lord and presumptuously went up into the hill country. ⁴⁴Then the Amorites who lived in that hill country came out against you and chased you as bees do and beat you down in Seir as far as Hormah. ⁴⁵And you returned and wept before the Lord, but the Lord did not listen to your voice or give ear to you. ⁴⁶So you remained at Kadesh many days, the days that you remained there.

Psalm 81–82

To the choirmaster: according to The Gittith.[1] Of Asaph.

Sing aloud to God our strength;
shout for joy to the God of Jacob!
2 Raise a song; sound the tambourine,
   the sweet lyre with the harp.
3 Blow the trumpet at the new moon,
   at the full moon, on our feast day.
4 For it is a statute for Israel,
   a rule[2] of the God of Jacob.
5 He made it a decree in Joseph
   when he went out over[3] the land of
   Egypt.
   I hear a language I had not known:
6 "I relieved your[4] shoulder of the burden;
   your hands were freed from the
   basket.

[1] Probably a musical or liturgical term [2] Or just decree [3] Or against [4] Hebrew his; also next line

7 In distress you called, and I delivered
   you;
   I answered you in the secret place of
      thunder;
   I tested you at the waters of Meribah.
                                    Selah
8 Hear, O my people, while I admonish
   you!
   O Israel, if you would but listen to me!
9 There shall be no strange god among
   you;
   you shall not bow down to a foreign
      god.
10 I am the LORD your God,
   who brought you up out of the land of
      Egypt.
   Open your mouth wide, and I will fill
      it.
11 "But my people did not listen to my
   voice;
   Israel would not submit to me.
12 So I gave them over to their stubborn
   hearts,
   to follow their own counsels.
13 Oh, that my people would listen to me,
   that Israel would walk in my ways!
14 I would soon subdue their enemies
   and turn my hand against their foes.
15 Those who hate the LORD would cringe
   toward him,
   and their fate would last forever.
16 But he would feed you[1] with the finest
   of the wheat,
   and with honey from the rock I would
      satisfy you."

A PSALM OF ASAPH.

God has taken his place in the divine
   council;
   in the midst of the gods he holds
      judgment:
2 "How long will you judge unjustly
   and show partiality to the wicked?
                                    Selah
3 Give justice to the weak and the
   fatherless;
   maintain the right of the afflicted and
      the destitute.
4 Rescue the weak and the needy;
   deliver them from the hand of the
      wicked."

5 They have neither knowledge nor
   understanding,
   they walk about in darkness;
   all the foundations of the earth are
      shaken.
6 I said, "You are gods,
   sons of the Most High, all of you;
7 nevertheless, like men you shall die,
   and fall like any prince."[2]
8 Arise, O God, judge the earth;
   for you shall inherit all the nations!

───────── *Isaiah 29* ─────────

Ah, Ariel, Ariel,
   the city where David encamped!
   Add year to year;
   let the feasts run their round.
2 Yet I will distress Ariel,
   and there shall be moaning and
      lamentation,
   and she shall be to me like an Ariel.[3]
3 And I will encamp against you all
      around,
   and will besiege you with towers
   and I will raise siegeworks against you.
4 And you will be brought low; from the
      earth you shall speak,
   and from the dust your speech will be
      bowed down;
   your voice shall come from the ground
      like the voice of a ghost,
   and from the dust your speech shall
      whisper.
5 But the multitude of your foreign foes
      shall be like small dust,
   and the multitude of the ruthless like
      passing chaff.
   And in an instant, suddenly,
6 you will be visited by the LORD of hosts
   with thunder and with earthquake and
      great noise,
   with whirlwind and tempest, and the
      flame of a devouring fire.
7 And the multitude of all the nations that
      fight against Ariel,
   all that fight against her and her
      stronghold and distress her,
   shall be like a dream, a vision of the
      night.

[1] That is, Israel; Hebrew *him* [2] Or *fall as one man, O princes* [3] *Ariel* could mean *lion of God*, or *hero* (2 Samuel 23:20), or *altar hearth* (Ezekiel 43:15–16)

8 As when a hungry man dreams, and
          behold, he is eating
     and awakes with his hunger not
          satisfied,
     or as when a thirsty man dreams, and
          behold, he is drinking
     and awakes faint, with his thirst not
          quenched,
     so shall the multitude of all the
          nations be
     that fight against Mount Zion.

9 Astonish yourselves[1] and be astonished;
          blind yourselves and be blind!
     Be drunk, but not with wine;
          stagger, but not with strong drink!

10 For the Lord has poured out upon you
          a spirit of deep sleep,
     and has closed your eyes (the prophets),
          and covered your heads (the seers).

11 And the vision of all this has become to you like the words of a book that is sealed. When men give it to one who can read, saying, "Read this," he says, "I cannot, for it is sealed." 12 And when they give the book to one who cannot read, saying, "Read this," he says, "I cannot read."

13   And the Lord said:
     "Because this people draw near with
          their mouth
     and honor me with their lips,
          while their hearts are far from me,
     and their fear of me is a commandment
          taught by men,

14   therefore, behold, I will again
          do wonderful things with this people,
          with wonder upon wonder;
     and the wisdom of their wise men shall
          perish,
     and the discernment of their
          discerning men shall be hidden."

15   Ah, you who hide deep from the Lord
          your counsel,
     whose deeds are in the dark,
          and who say, "Who sees us? Who
          knows us?"

16   You turn things upside down!
     Shall the potter be regarded as the clay,
     that the thing made should say of its
          maker,
     "He did not make me";

or the thing formed say of him who
          formed it,
     "He has no understanding"?

17   Is it not yet a very little while
          until Lebanon shall be turned into a
          fruitful field,
     and the fruitful field shall be regarded
          as a forest?

18   In that day the deaf shall hear
          the words of a book,
     and out of their gloom and darkness
          the eyes of the blind shall see.

19   The meek shall obtain fresh joy in the
          Lord,
     and the poor among mankind shall
          exult in the Holy One of Israel.

20   For the ruthless shall come to nothing
          and the scoffer cease,
     and all who watch to do evil shall be
          cut off,

21   who by a word make a man out to be an
          offender,
     and lay a snare for him who reproves
          in the gate,
     and with an empty plea turn aside
          him who is in the right.

22 Therefore thus says the Lord, who redeemed Abraham, concerning the house of Jacob:

     "Jacob shall no more be ashamed,
          no more shall his face grow pale.

23   For when he sees his children,
          the work of my hands, in his midst,
          they will sanctify my name;
     they will sanctify the Holy One of Jacob
          and will stand in awe of the God of
          Israel.

24   And those who go astray in spirit will
          come to understanding,
     and those who murmur will accept
          instruction."

3 John 1

The elder to the beloved Gaius, whom I love in truth. 2 Beloved, I pray that all may go well with you and that you may be in good health, as it goes well with your soul. 3 For I rejoiced greatly when the brothers[2] came and testified to your truth,

---

[1] Or Linger awhile [2] Or brothers and sisters. The plural Greek word adelphoi (translated "brothers") refers to siblings in a family. In New Testament usage, depending on the context, adelphoi may refer either to men or to both men and women who are siblings (brothers and sisters) in God's family, the church; also verses 5, 10

as indeed you are walking in the truth. ⁴I have no greater joy than to hear that my children are walking in the truth.

⁵Beloved, it is a faithful thing you do in all your efforts for these brothers, strangers as they are, ⁶who testified to your love before the church. You will do well to send them on their journey in a manner worthy of God. ⁷For they have gone out for the sake of the name, accepting nothing from the Gentiles. ⁸Therefore we ought to support people like these, that we may be fellow workers for the truth.

⁹I have written something to the church, but Diotrephes, who likes to put himself first, does not acknowledge our authority. ¹⁰So if I come, I will bring up what he is doing, talking wicked nonsense against us. And not content with that, he refuses to welcome the brothers, and also stops those who want to and puts them out of the church.

¹¹Beloved, do not imitate evil but imitate good. Whoever does good is from God; whoever does evil has not seen God. ¹²Demetrius has received a good testimony from everyone, and from the truth itself. We also add our testimony, and you know that our testimony is true.

¹³I had much to write to you, but I would rather not write with pen and ink. ¹⁴I hope to see you soon, and we will talk face to face.

¹⁵Peace be to you. The friends greet you. Greet the friends, each by name.

MAY 29

Deuteronomy 2

¹"Then we turned and journeyed into the wilderness in the direction of the Red Sea, as the Lord told me. And for many days we traveled around Mount Seir. ²Then the Lord said to me, ³'You have been traveling around this mountain country long enough. Turn northward ⁴and command the people, "You are about to pass through the territory of your brothers, the people of Esau, who live in Seir; and they will be afraid of you. So be very careful. ⁵Do not contend with them, for I will not give you any of their land, no, not so much as for the sole of the foot to tread on, because I have given Mount Seir to Esau as a possession. ⁶You shall purchase food from them with money, that you may eat, and you shall also buy water from them with money, that you may drink. ⁷For the Lord your God has blessed you in all the work of your hands. He knows your going through this great wilderness. These forty years the Lord your God has been with you. You have lacked nothing."' ⁸So we went on, away from our brothers, the people of Esau, who live in Seir, away from the Arabah road from Elath and Ezion-geber.

"And we turned and went in the direction of the wilderness of Moab. ⁹And the Lord said to me, 'Do not harass Moab or contend with them in battle, for I will not give you any of their land for a possession, because I have given Ar to the people of Lot for a possession.' ¹⁰(The Emim formerly lived there, a people great and many, and tall as the Anakim. ¹¹Like the Anakim they are also counted as Rephaim, but the Moabites call them Emim. ¹²The Horites also lived in Seir formerly, but the people of Esau dispossessed them and destroyed them from before them and settled in their place, as Israel did to the land of their possession, which the Lord gave to them.) ¹³'Now rise up and go over the brook Zered.' So we went over the brook Zered. ¹⁴And the time from our leaving Kadesh-barnea until we crossed the brook Zered was thirty-eight years, until the entire generation, that is, the men of war, had perished from the camp, as the Lord had sworn to them. ¹⁵For indeed the hand of the Lord was against them, to destroy them from the camp, until they had perished.

¹⁶"So as soon as all the men of war had perished and were dead from among the people,

[17]the LORD said to me, [18]'Today you are to cross the border of Moab at Ar. [19]And when you approach the territory of the people of Ammon, do not harass them or contend with them, for I will not give you any of the land of the people of Ammon as a possession, because I have given it to the sons of Lot for a possession.' [20](It is also counted as a land of Rephaim. Rephaim formerly lived there—but the Ammonites call them Zamzummim— [21]a people great and many, and tall as the Anakim; but the LORD destroyed them before the Ammonites,[1] and they dispossessed them and settled in their place, [22]as he did for the people of Esau, who live in Seir, when he destroyed the Horites before them and they dispossessed them and settled in their place even to this day. [23]As for the Avvim, who lived in villages as far as Gaza, the Caphtorim, who came from Caphtor, destroyed them and settled in their place.) [24]'Rise up, set out on your journey and go over the Valley of the Arnon. Behold, I have given into your hand Sihon the Amorite, king of Heshbon, and his land. Begin to take possession, and contend with him in battle. [25]This day I will begin to put the dread and fear of you on the peoples who are under the whole heaven, who shall hear the report of you and shall tremble and be in anguish because of you.'

[26]"So I sent messengers from the wilderness of Kedemoth to Sihon the king of Heshbon, with words of peace, saying, [27]'Let me pass through your land. I will go only by the road; I will turn aside neither to the right nor to the left. [28]You shall sell me food for money, that I may eat, and give me water for money, that I may drink. Only let me pass through on foot, [29]as the sons of Esau who live in Seir and the Moabites who live in Ar did for me, until I go over the Jordan into the land that the LORD our God is giving to us.' [30]But Sihon the king of Heshbon would not let us pass by him, for the LORD your God hardened his spirit and made his heart obstinate, that he might give him into your hand, as he is this day. [31]And the LORD said to me, 'Behold, I have begun to give Sihon and his land over to you. Begin to take possession, that you may occupy his land.' [32]Then Sihon came out against us, he and all his people, to battle at Jahaz. [33]And the LORD our God gave him over to us, and we defeated him and his sons and all his people. [34]And we

captured all his cities at that time and devoted to destruction[2] every city, men, women, and children. We left no survivors. [35]Only the livestock we took as spoil for ourselves, with the plunder of the cities that we captured. [36]From Aroer, which is on the edge of the Valley of the Arnon, and from the city that is in the valley, as far as Gilead, there was not a city too high for us. The LORD our God gave all into our hands. [37]Only to the land of the sons of Ammon you did not draw near, that is, to all the banks of the river Jabbok and the cities of the hill country, whatever the LORD our God had forbidden us.

--------- Psalm 83–84 ---------

A Song. A Psalm of Asaph.

O God, do not keep silence;
  do not hold your peace or be still, O God!
2 For behold, your enemies make an
      uproar;
    those who hate you have raised their
      heads.
3 They lay crafty plans against your
      people;
    they consult together against your
      treasured ones.
4 They say, "Come, let us wipe them out as
      a nation;
    let the name of Israel be remembered
      no more!"
5 For they conspire with one accord;
    against you they make a covenant—
6 the tents of Edom and the Ishmaelites,
    Moab and the Hagrites,
7 Gebal and Ammon and Amalek,
    Philistia with the inhabitants of Tyre;
8 Asshur also has joined them;
    they are the strong arm of the
      children of Lot.   *Selah*

9 Do to them as you did to Midian,
    as to Sisera and Jabin at the river
      Kishon,
10 who were destroyed at En-dor,
    who became dung for the ground.
11 Make their nobles like Oreb and Zeeb,
    all their princes like Zebah and
      Zalmunna,
12 who said, "Let us take possession for
      ourselves
    of the pastures of God."

---

[1] Hebrew *them* [2] That is, set apart (devoted) as an offering to the Lord (for destruction)

13 O my God, make them like whirling
    dust,[1]
  like chaff before the wind.
14 As fire consumes the forest,
  as the flame sets the mountains
    ablaze,
15 so may you pursue them with your
    tempest
  and terrify them with your hurricane!
16 Fill their faces with shame,
  that they may seek your name,
    O LORD.
17 Let them be put to shame and dismayed
    forever;
  let them perish in disgrace,
18 that they may know that you alone,
  whose name is the LORD,
  are the Most High over all the earth.

TO THE CHOIRMASTER: ACCORDING TO THE
GITTITH.[2] A PSALM OF THE SONS OF KORAH.

How lovely is your dwelling place,
  O LORD of hosts!
2 My soul longs, yes, faints
  for the courts of the LORD;
  my heart and flesh sing for joy
  to the living God.
3 Even the sparrow finds a home,
  and the swallow a nest for herself,
  where she may lay her young,
  at your altars, O LORD of hosts,
  my King and my God.
4 Blessed are those who dwell in your
    house,
  ever singing your praise!   *Selah*
5 Blessed are those whose strength is in
    you,
  in whose heart are the highways to
    Zion.[3]
6 As they go through the Valley of Baca
  they make it a place of springs;
  the early rain also covers it with
    pools.
7 They go from strength to strength;
  each one appears before God in Zion.
8 O LORD God of hosts, hear my prayer;
  give ear, O God of Jacob!   *Selah*
9 Behold our shield, O God;
  look on the face of your anointed!

10 For a day in your courts is better
  than a thousand elsewhere.
  I would rather be a doorkeeper in the
    house of my God
  than dwell in the tents of wickedness.
11 For the LORD God is a sun and shield;
  the LORD bestows favor and honor.
  No good thing does he withhold
  from those who walk uprightly.
12 O LORD of hosts,
  blessed is the one who trusts in you!

Isaiah 30

"Ah, stubborn children," declares the
  LORD,
  "who carry out a plan, but not mine,
  and who make an alliance,[4] but not of
    my Spirit,
  that they may add sin to sin;
2 who set out to go down to Egypt,
  without asking for my direction,
  to take refuge in the protection of
    Pharaoh
  and to seek shelter in the shadow of
    Egypt!
3 Therefore shall the protection of
    Pharaoh turn to your shame,
  and the shelter in the shadow of Egypt
    to your humiliation.
4 For though his officials are at Zoan
  and his envoys reach Hanes,
5 everyone comes to shame
  through a people that cannot profit
    them,
  that brings neither help nor profit,
  but shame and disgrace."

6 An oracle on the beasts of the Negeb.

  Through a land of trouble and anguish,
  from where come the lioness and the
    lion,
  the adder and the flying fiery serpent,
  they carry their riches on the backs of
    donkeys,
  and their treasures on the humps of
    camels,
  to a people that cannot profit them.
7 Egypt's help is worthless and empty;
  therefore I have called her
  "Rahab who sits still."

[1] Or *like a tumbleweed* [2] Probably a musical or liturgical term [3] Hebrew lacks *to Zion* [4] Hebrew *who weave a web*

8 And now, go, write it before them on a
   tablet
      and inscribe it in a book,
   that it may be for the time to come
      as a witness forever.[1]
9 For they are a rebellious people,
      lying children,
   children unwilling to hear
      the instruction of the LORD;
10 who say to the seers, "Do not see,"
      and to the prophets, "Do not prophesy
         to us what is right;
   speak to us smooth things,
      prophesy illusions,
11 leave the way, turn aside from the path,
      let us hear no more about the Holy
         One of Israel."

12 Therefore thus says the Holy One of
   Israel,
   "Because you despise this word
      and trust in oppression and
         perverseness
      and rely on them,
13 therefore this iniquity shall be to you
      like a breach in a high wall, bulging
         out, and about to collapse,
      whose breaking comes suddenly, in an
         instant;
14 and its breaking is like that of a potter's
      vessel
   that is smashed so ruthlessly
      that among its fragments not a shard is
         found
      with which to take fire from the hearth,
      or to dip up water out of the cistern."

15 For thus said the Lord GOD, the Holy
      One of Israel,
   "In returning[2] and rest you shall be saved;
      in quietness and in trust shall be your
         strength."
   But you were unwilling, 16 and you said,
   "No! We will flee upon horses";
      therefore you shall flee away;
   and, "We will ride upon swift steeds";
      therefore your pursuers shall be swift.
17 A thousand shall flee at the threat of one;
      at the threat of five you shall flee,
   till you are left
      like a flagstaff on the top of a
         mountain,
      like a signal on a hill.

18 Therefore the LORD waits to be gracious
      to you,
   and therefore he exalts himself to
      show mercy to you.
   For the LORD is a God of justice;
      blessed are all those who wait for him.

19 For a people shall dwell in Zion, in Jerusalem; you shall weep no more. He will surely be gracious to you at the sound of your cry. As soon as he hears it, he answers you. 20 And though the Lord give you the bread of adversity and the water of affliction, yet your Teacher will not hide himself anymore, but your eyes shall see your Teacher. 21 And your ears shall hear a word behind you, saying, "This is the way, walk in it," when you turn to the right or when you turn to the left. 22 Then you will defile your carved idols overlaid with silver and your gold-plated metal images. You will scatter them as unclean things. You will say to them, "Be gone!"

23 And he will give rain for the seed with which you sow the ground, and bread, the produce of the ground, which will be rich and plenteous. In that day your livestock will graze in large pastures, 24 and the oxen and the donkeys that work the ground will eat seasoned fodder, which has been winnowed with shovel and fork. 25 And on every lofty mountain and every high hill there will be brooks running with water, in the day of the great slaughter, when the towers fall. 26 Moreover, the light of the moon will be as the light of the sun, and the light of the sun will be sevenfold, as the light of seven days, in the day when the LORD binds up the brokenness of his people, and heals the wounds inflicted by his blow.

27 Behold, the name of the LORD comes
      from afar,
      burning with his anger, and in thick
         rising smoke;[3]
   his lips are full of fury,
      and his tongue is like a devouring fire;
28 his breath is like an overflowing stream
      that reaches up to the neck;
   to sift the nations with the sieve of
      destruction,
      and to place on the jaws of the peoples
         a bridle that leads astray.

29 You shall have a song as in the night when a holy feast is kept, and gladness of heart, as

[1] Some Hebrew manuscripts, Syriac, Targum, Vulgate, and Greek versions; Masoretic Text *forever and ever* [2] Or *repentance* [3] Hebrew *in weight of uplifted clouds*

when one sets out to the sound of the flute to go to the mountain of the Lord, to the Rock of Israel. [30]And the Lord will cause his majestic voice to be heard and the descending blow of his arm to be seen, in furious anger and a flame of devouring fire, with a cloudburst and storm and hailstones. [31]The Assyrians will be terror-stricken at the voice of the Lord, when he strikes with his rod. [32]And every stroke of the appointed staff that the Lord lays on them will be to the sound of tambourines and lyres. Battling with brandished arm, he will fight with them. [33]For a burning place[1] has long been prepared; indeed, for the king it is made ready, its pyre made deep and wide, with fire and wood in abundance; the breath of the Lord, like a stream of sulfur, kindles it.

Jude 1

Jude, a servant[2] of Jesus Christ and brother of James,

To those who are called, beloved in God the Father and kept for[3] Jesus Christ:

[2]May mercy, peace, and love be multiplied to you.

[3]Beloved, although I was very eager to write to you about our common salvation, I found it necessary to write appealing to you to contend for the faith that was once for all delivered to the saints. [4]For certain people have crept in unnoticed who long ago were designated for this condemnation, ungodly people, who pervert the grace of our God into sensuality and deny our only Master and Lord, Jesus Christ.

[5]Now I want to remind you, although you once fully knew it, that Jesus, who saved[4] a people out of the land of Egypt, afterward destroyed those who did not believe. [6]And the angels who did not stay within their own position of authority, but left their proper dwelling, he has kept in eternal chains under gloomy darkness until the judgment of the great day— [7]just as Sodom and Gomorrah and the surrounding cities, which likewise indulged in sexual immorality and pursued unnatural desire,[5] serve as an example by undergoing a punishment of eternal fire.

[8]Yet in like manner these people also, relying on their dreams, defile the flesh, reject authority, and blaspheme the glorious ones. [9]But when the archangel Michael, contending

with the devil, was disputing about the body of Moses, he did not presume to pronounce a blasphemous judgment, but said, "The Lord rebuke you." [10]But these people blaspheme all that they do not understand, and they are destroyed by all that they, like unreasoning animals, understand instinctively. [11]Woe to them! For they walked in the way of Cain and abandoned themselves for the sake of gain to Balaam's error and perished in Korah's rebellion. [12]These are hidden reefs[6] at your love feasts, as they feast with you without fear, shepherds feeding themselves; waterless clouds, swept along by winds; fruitless trees in late autumn, twice dead, uprooted; [13]wild waves of the sea, casting up the foam of their own shame; wandering stars, for whom the gloom of utter darkness has been reserved forever.

[14]It was also about these that Enoch, the seventh from Adam, prophesied, saying, "Behold, the Lord comes with ten thousands of his holy ones, [15]to execute judgment on all and to convict all the ungodly of all their deeds of ungodliness that they have committed in such an ungodly way, and of all the harsh things that ungodly sinners have spoken against him." [16]These are grumblers, malcontents, following their own sinful desires; they are loud-mouthed boasters, showing favoritism to gain advantage.

[17]But you must remember, beloved, the predictions of the apostles of our Lord Jesus Christ. [18]They[7] said to you, "In the last time there will be scoffers, following their own ungodly passions." [19]It is these who cause divisions, worldly people, devoid of the Spirit. [20]But you, beloved, building yourselves up in your most holy faith and praying in the Holy Spirit, [21]keep yourselves in the love of God, waiting for the mercy of our Lord Jesus Christ that leads to eternal life. [22]And have mercy on those who doubt; [23]save others by snatching them out of the fire; to others show mercy with fear, hating even the garment[8] stained by the flesh.

[24]Now to him who is able to keep you from stumbling and to present you blameless before the presence of his glory with great joy, [25]to the only God, our Savior, through Jesus Christ our Lord, be glory, majesty, dominion, and authority, before all time and now and forever. Amen.

[1] Or For Topheth [2] Or slave (for the contextual rendering of the Greek word doulos, see Preface) [3] Or by [4] Some manuscripts although you fully knew it, that the Lord who once saved [5] Greek other flesh [6] Or are blemishes [7] Or Christ, because they [8] Greek chiton, a long garment worn under the cloak next to the skin

MAY 30

Deuteronomy 3

"Then we turned and went up the way to Bashan. And Og the king of Bashan came out against us, he and all his people, to battle at Edrei. [2]But the LORD said to me, 'Do not fear him, for I have given him and all his people and his land into your hand. And you shall do to him as you did to Sihon the king of the Amorites, who lived at Heshbon.' [3]So the LORD our God gave into our hand Og also, the king of Bashan, and all his people, and we struck him down until he had no survivor left. [4]And we took all his cities at that time—there was not a city that we did not take from them—sixty cities, the whole region of Argob, the kingdom of Og in Bashan. [5]All these were cities fortified with high walls, gates, and bars, besides very many unwalled villages. [6]And we devoted them to destruction,[1] as we did to Sihon the king of Heshbon, devoting to destruction every city, men, women, and children. [7]But all the livestock and the spoil of the cities we took as our plunder. [8]So we took the land at that time out of the hand of the two kings of the Amorites who were beyond the Jordan, from the Valley of the Arnon to Mount Hermon [9](the Sidonians call Hermon Sirion, while the Amorites call it Senir), [10]all the cities of the tableland and all Gilead and all Bashan, as far as Salecah and Edrei, cities of the kingdom of Og in Bashan. [11](For only Og the king of Bashan was left of the remnant of the Rephaim. Behold, his bed was a bed of iron. Is it not in Rabbah of the Ammonites? Nine cubits[2] was its length, and four cubits its breadth, according to the common cubit.[3])

[12]"When we took possession of this land at that time, I gave to the Reubenites and the Gadites the territory beginning at Aroer, which is on the edge of the Valley of the Arnon, and half the hill country of Gilead with its cities. [13]The rest of Gilead, and all Bashan, the kingdom of Og, that is, all the region of Argob, I gave to the half-tribe of Manasseh. (All that portion of Bashan is called the land of Rephaim. [14]Jair the Manassite took all the region of Argob, that is, Bashan, as far as the border of the Geshurites and the Maacathites, and called the villages after his own name, Havvoth-jair, as it is to this day.) [15]To Machir I gave Gilead, [16]and to the Reubenites and the Gadites I gave the territory from Gilead as far as the Valley of the Arnon, with the middle of the valley as a border, as far over as the river Jabbok, the border of the Ammonites; [17]the Arabah also, with the Jordan as the border, from Chinnereth as far as the Sea of the Arabah, the Salt Sea, under the slopes of Pisgah on the east.

[18]"And I commanded you at that time, saying, 'The LORD your God has given you this land to possess. All your men of valor shall cross over armed before your brothers, the people of Israel. [19]Only your wives, your little ones, and your livestock (I know that you have much livestock) shall remain in the cities that I have given you, [20]until the LORD gives rest to your brothers, as to you, and they also occupy the land that the LORD your God gives them beyond the Jordan. Then each of you may return to his possession which I have given you.' [21]And I commanded Joshua at that time, 'Your eyes have seen all that the LORD your God has done to these two kings. So will the LORD do to all the kingdoms into which you are crossing. [22]You shall not fear them, for it is the LORD your God who fights for you.'

[23]"And I pleaded with the LORD at that time, saying, [24]'O Lord GOD, you have only begun to show your servant your greatness and your mighty hand. For what god is there in heaven or on earth who can do such works and mighty acts as yours? [25]Please let me go over and see the good land beyond the Jordan, that good hill country and Lebanon.' [26]But the LORD was angry with me because of you and would not listen to me. And the LORD said to me, 'Enough from you; do not speak to me of this matter again. [27]Go up to the top

---

[1] That is, set apart (devoted) as an offering to the Lord (for destruction); twice in this verse [2] A *cubit* was about 18 inches or 45 centimeters [3] Hebrew *cubit of a man*

of Pisgah and lift up your eyes westward and northward and southward and eastward, and look at it with your eyes, for you shall not go over this Jordan. ²⁸ But charge Joshua, and encourage and strengthen him, for he shall go over at the head of this people, and he shall put them in possession of the land that you shall see.' ²⁹ So we remained in the valley opposite Beth-peor.

Psalm 85

TO THE CHOIRMASTER. A PSALM OF THE SONS
OF KORAH.

LORD, you were favorable to your land;
 you restored the fortunes of Jacob.
2   You forgave the iniquity of your people;
     you covered all their sin.   *Selah*
3   You withdrew all your wrath;
     you turned from your hot anger.

4   Restore us again, O God of our salvation,
     and put away your indignation toward
         us!
5   Will you be angry with us forever?
     Will you prolong your anger to all
         generations?
6   Will you not revive us again,
     that your people may rejoice in you?
7   Show us your steadfast love, O LORD,
     and grant us your salvation.

8   Let me hear what God the LORD will
         speak,
     for he will speak peace to his people,
         to his saints;
     but let them not turn back to folly.
9   Surely his salvation is near to those who
         fear him,
     that glory may dwell in our land.

10   Steadfast love and faithfulness meet;
     righteousness and peace kiss each
         other.
11   Faithfulness springs up from the
         ground,
     and righteousness looks down from
         the sky.
12   Yes, the LORD will give what is good,
     and our land will yield its increase.
13   Righteousness will go before him
     and make his footsteps a way.

Isaiah 31

Woe to those who go down to Egypt for
     help
     and rely on horses,
who trust in chariots because they are
     many
     and in horsemen because they are
         very strong,
but do not look to the Holy One of Israel
     or consult the LORD!
2   And yet he is wise and brings disaster;
     he does not call back his words,
but will arise against the house of the
     evildoers
     and against the helpers of those who
         work iniquity.
3   The Egyptians are man, and not God,
     and their horses are flesh, and not
         spirit.
When the LORD stretches out his hand,
     the helper will stumble, and he who is
         helped will fall,
     and they will all perish together.

4   For thus the LORD said to me,
"As a lion or a young lion growls over his
     prey,
     and when a band of shepherds is
         called out against him
he is not terrified by their shouting
     or daunted at their noise,
so the LORD of hosts will come down
     to fight¹ on Mount Zion and on its hill.
5   Like birds hovering, so the LORD of
         hosts
     will protect Jerusalem;
he will protect and deliver it;
     he will spare and rescue it."

⁶ Turn to him from whom people² have deeply revolted, O children of Israel. ⁷ For in that day everyone shall cast away his idols of silver and his idols of gold, which your hands have sinfully made for you.

8   "And the Assyrian shall fall by a sword,
         not of man;
     and a sword, not of man, shall devour
         him;
and he shall flee from the sword,
     and his young men shall be put to
         forced labor.

¹ The Hebrew words for *hosts* and *to fight* sound alike   ² Hebrew *they*

9   His rock shall pass away in terror,
        and his officers desert the standard in
            panic,"
    declares the LORD, whose fire is in Zion,
        and whose furnace is in Jerusalem.

Revelation 1

The revelation of Jesus Christ, which God gave him to show to his servants[1] the things that must soon take place. He made it known by sending his angel to his servant[2] John, ²who bore witness to the word of God and to the testimony of Jesus Christ, even to all that he saw. ³Blessed is the one who reads aloud the words of this prophecy, and blessed are those who hear, and who keep what is written in it, for the time is near.

⁴John to the seven churches that are in Asia:
    Grace to you and peace from him who is and who was and who is to come, and from the seven spirits who are before his throne, ⁵and from Jesus Christ the faithful witness, the firstborn of the dead, and the ruler of kings on earth.
    To him who loves us and has freed us from our sins by his blood ⁶and made us a kingdom, priests to his God and Father, to him be glory and dominion forever and ever. Amen. ⁷Behold, he is coming with the clouds, and every eye will see him, even those who pierced him, and all tribes of the earth will wail[3] on account of him. Even so. Amen.

⁸"I am the Alpha and the Omega," says the Lord God, "who is and who was and who is to come, the Almighty."

⁹I, John, your brother and partner in the tribulation and the kingdom and the patient endurance that are in Jesus, was on the island called Patmos on account of the word of God and the testimony of Jesus. ¹⁰I was in the Spirit on the Lord's day, and I heard behind me a loud voice like a trumpet ¹¹saying, "Write what you see in a book and send it to the seven churches, to Ephesus and to Smyrna and to Pergamum and to Thyatira and to Sardis and to Philadelphia and to Laodicea."

¹²Then I turned to see the voice that was speaking to me, and on turning I saw seven golden lampstands, ¹³and in the midst of the lampstands one like a son of man, clothed with a long robe and with a golden sash around his chest. ¹⁴The hairs of his head were white, like white wool, like snow. His eyes were like a flame of fire, ¹⁵his feet were like burnished bronze, refined in a furnace, and his voice was like the roar of many waters. ¹⁶In his right hand he held seven stars, from his mouth came a sharp two-edged sword, and his face was like the sun shining in full strength.

¹⁷When I saw him, I fell at his feet as though dead. But he laid his right hand on me, saying, "Fear not, I am the first and the last, ¹⁸and the living one. I died, and behold I am alive forevermore, and I have the keys of Death and Hades. ¹⁹Write therefore the things that you have seen, those that are and those that are to take place after this. ²⁰As for the mystery of the seven stars that you saw in my right hand, and the seven golden lampstands, the seven stars are the angels of the seven churches, and the seven lampstands are the seven churches.

M A Y   3 1

Deuteronomy 4

"And now, O Israel, listen to the statutes and the rules[4] that I am teaching you, and do them, that you may live, and go in and take possession of the land that the LORD, the God of your fathers, is giving you. ²You shall not add to the word that I command you, nor take from it, that you may keep the commandments of the LORD your God that I command you. ³Your eyes have seen what the LORD did at Baal-peor, for the LORD your God destroyed from among you

[1] Greek bondservants [2] Greek bondservant [3] Or mourn [4] Or just decrees; also verses 5, 8, 14, 45

all the men who followed the Baal of Peor. ⁴But you who held fast to the Lᴏʀᴅ your God are all alive today. ⁵See, I have taught you statutes and rules, as the Lᴏʀᴅ my God commanded me, that you should do them in the land that you are entering to take possession of it. ⁶Keep them and do them, for that will be your wisdom and your understanding in the sight of the peoples, who, when they hear all these statutes, will say, 'Surely this great nation is a wise and understanding people.' ⁷For what great nation is there that has a god so near to it as the Lᴏʀᴅ our God is to us, whenever we call upon him? ⁸And what great nation is there, that has statutes and rules so righteous as all this law that I set before you today?

⁹"Only take care, and keep your soul diligently, lest you forget the things that your eyes have seen, and lest they depart from your heart all the days of your life. Make them known to your children and your children's children— ¹⁰how on the day that you stood before the Lᴏʀᴅ your God at Horeb, the Lᴏʀᴅ said to me, 'Gather the people to me, that I may let them hear my words, so that they may learn to fear me all the days that they live on the earth, and that they may teach their children so.' ¹¹And you came near and stood at the foot of the mountain, while the mountain burned with fire to the heart of heaven, wrapped in darkness, cloud, and gloom. ¹²Then the Lᴏʀᴅ spoke to you out of the midst of the fire. You heard the sound of words, but saw no form; there was only a voice. ¹³And he declared to you his covenant, which he commanded you to perform, that is, the Ten Commandments,¹ and he wrote them on two tablets of stone. ¹⁴And the Lᴏʀᴅ commanded me at that time to teach you statutes and rules, that you might do them in the land that you are going over to possess.

¹⁵"Therefore watch yourselves very carefully. Since you saw no form on the day that the Lᴏʀᴅ spoke to you at Horeb out of the midst of the fire, ¹⁶beware lest you act corruptly by making a carved image for yourselves, in the form of any figure, the likeness of male or female, ¹⁷the likeness of any animal that is on the earth, the likeness of any winged bird that flies in the air, ¹⁸the likeness of anything that creeps on the ground, the likeness of any fish that is in the water under the earth. ¹⁹And beware lest you raise your eyes to heaven, and when you see

the sun and the moon and the stars, all the host of heaven, you be drawn away and bow down to them and serve them, things that the Lᴏʀᴅ your God has allotted to all the peoples under the whole heaven. ²⁰But the Lᴏʀᴅ has taken you and brought you out of the iron furnace, out of Egypt, to be a people of his own inheritance, as you are this day. ²¹Furthermore, the Lᴏʀᴅ was angry with me because of you, and he swore that I should not cross the Jordan, and that I should not enter the good land that the Lᴏʀᴅ your God is giving you for an inheritance. ²²For I must die in this land; I must not go over the Jordan. But you shall go over and take possession of that good land. ²³Take care, lest you forget the covenant of the Lᴏʀᴅ your God, which he made with you, and make a carved image, the form of anything that the Lᴏʀᴅ your God has forbidden you. ²⁴For the Lᴏʀᴅ your God is a consuming fire, a jealous God.

²⁵"When you father children and children's children, and have grown old in the land, if you act corruptly by making a carved image in the form of anything, and by doing what is evil in the sight of the Lᴏʀᴅ your God, so as to provoke him to anger, ²⁶I call heaven and earth to witness against you today, that you will soon utterly perish from the land that you are going over the Jordan to possess. You will not live long in it, but will be utterly destroyed. ²⁷And the Lᴏʀᴅ will scatter you among the peoples, and you will be left few in number among the nations where the Lᴏʀᴅ will drive you. ²⁸And there you will serve gods of wood and stone, the work of human hands, that neither see, nor hear, nor eat, nor smell. ²⁹But from there you will seek the Lᴏʀᴅ your God and you will find him, if you search after him with all your heart and with all your soul. ³⁰When you are in tribulation, and all these things come upon you in the latter days, you will return to the Lᴏʀᴅ your God and obey his voice. ³¹For the Lᴏʀᴅ your God is a merciful God. He will not leave you or destroy you or forget the covenant with your fathers that he swore to them.

³²"For ask now of the days that are past, which were before you, since the day that God created man on the earth, and ask from one end of heaven to the other, whether such a great thing as this has ever happened or was ever heard of. ³³Did any people ever hear the voice of a god speaking out of the midst of the fire,

¹ Hebrew *words*

as you have heard, and still live? [34]Or has any god ever attempted to go and take a nation for himself from the midst of another nation, by trials, by signs, by wonders, and by war, by a mighty hand and an outstretched arm, and by great deeds of terror, all of which the LORD your God did for you in Egypt before your eyes? [35]To you it was shown, that you might know that the LORD is God; there is no other besides him. [36]Out of heaven he let you hear his voice, that he might discipline you. And on earth he let you see his great fire, and you heard his words out of the midst of the fire. [37]And because he loved your fathers and chose their offspring after them[1] and brought you out of Egypt with his own presence, by his great power, [38]driving out before you nations greater and mightier than you, to bring you in, to give you their land for an inheritance, as it is this day, [39]know therefore today, and lay it to your heart, that the LORD is God in heaven above and on the earth beneath; there is no other. [40]Therefore you shall keep his statutes and his commandments, which I command you today, that it may go well with you and with your children after you, and that you may prolong your days in the land that the LORD your God is giving you for all time."

[41]Then Moses set apart three cities in the east beyond the Jordan, [42]that the manslayer might flee there, anyone who kills his neighbor unintentionally, without being at enmity with him in time past; he may flee to one of these cities and save his life: [43]Bezer in the wilderness on the tableland for the Reubenites, Ramoth in Gilead for the Gadites, and Golan in Bashan for the Manassites.

[44]This is the law that Moses set before the people of Israel. [45]These are the testimonies, the statutes, and the rules, which Moses spoke to the people of Israel when they came out of Egypt, [46]beyond the Jordan in the valley opposite Beth-peor, in the land of Sihon the king of the Amorites, who lived at Heshbon, whom Moses and the people of Israel defeated when they came out of Egypt. [47]And they took possession of his land and the land of Og, the king of Bashan, the two kings of the Amorites, who lived to the east beyond the Jordan; [48]from Aroer, which is on the edge of the Valley of the Arnon, as far as Mount Sirion[2] (that is, Hermon), [49]together with all the Arabah on the east side of the Jordan as far as the Sea of the Arabah, under the slopes of Pisgah.

Psalm 86–87

A PRAYER OF DAVID.

Incline your ear, O LORD, and answer me,
　　for I am poor and needy.
[2]　Preserve my life, for I am godly;
　　　　save your servant, who trusts in you—
　　　　　　you are my God.
[3]　Be gracious to me, O Lord,
　　　　for to you do I cry all the day.
[4]　Gladden the soul of your servant,
　　　　for to you, O Lord, do I lift up my soul.
[5]　For you, O Lord, are good and forgiving,
　　　　abounding in steadfast love to all who
　　　　　　call upon you.
[6]　Give ear, O LORD, to my prayer;
　　　　listen to my plea for grace.
[7]　In the day of my trouble I call upon you,
　　　　for you answer me.

[8]　There is none like you among the gods,
　　　　O Lord,
　　　　nor are there any works like yours.
[9]　All the nations you have made shall
　　　　come
　　　　and worship before you, O Lord,
　　　　and shall glorify your name.
[10]　For you are great and do wondrous
　　　　things;
　　　　you alone are God.
[11]　Teach me your way, O LORD,
　　　　that I may walk in your truth;
　　　　unite my heart to fear your name.
[12]　I give thanks to you, O Lord my God,
　　　　with my whole heart,
　　　　and I will glorify your name forever.
[13]　For great is your steadfast love toward
　　　　me;
　　　　you have delivered my soul from the
　　　　　　depths of Sheol.

[14]　O God, insolent men have risen up
　　　　against me;
　　　　a band of ruthless men seeks my life,
　　　　and they do not set you before them.
[15]　But you, O Lord, are a God merciful and
　　　　gracious,
　　　　slow to anger and abounding in
　　　　　　steadfast love and faithfulness.

---

[1] Hebrew *his offspring after him*　[2] Syriac; Hebrew *Sion*

16 Turn to me and be gracious to me;
　　give your strength to your servant,
　　and save the son of your maidservant.
17 Show me a sign of your favor,
　　that those who hate me may see and
　　　be put to shame
　　because you, Lord, have helped me
　　　and comforted me.

A Psalm of the Sons of Korah. A Song.

O n the holy mount stands the city he
　founded;
2 　　the Lord loves the gates of Zion
　　more than all the dwelling places of
　　　Jacob.
3 Glorious things of you are spoken,
　　O city of God.　　　　　　　　*Selah*

4 Among those who know me I mention
　　Rahab and Babylon;
　　behold, Philistia and Tyre, with Cush[1]—
　　"This one was born there," they say.
5 And of Zion it shall be said,
　　"This one and that one were born in
　　　her";
　　for the Most High himself will
　　　establish her.
6 The Lord records as he registers the
　　peoples,
　　"This one was born there."　　*Selah*
7 Singers and dancers alike say,
　　"All my springs are in you."

───────── *Isaiah 32* ─────────

B ehold, a king will reign in righteousness,
　and princes will rule in justice.
2 Each will be like a hiding place from the
　　wind,
　　a shelter from the storm,
　　like streams of water in a dry place,
　　like the shade of a great rock in a
　　　weary land.
3 Then the eyes of those who see will not
　　be closed,
　　and the ears of those who hear will
　　　give attention.
4 The heart of the hasty will understand
　　and know,
　　and the tongue of the stammerers will
　　　hasten to speak distinctly.

5 The fool will no more be called noble,
　　nor the scoundrel said to be honorable.
6 For the fool speaks folly,
　　and his heart is busy with iniquity,
　　to practice ungodliness,
　　　to utter error concerning the Lord,
　　to leave the craving of the hungry
　　　unsatisfied,
　　and to deprive the thirsty of drink.
7 As for the scoundrel—his devices are
　　evil;
　　he plans wicked schemes
　　to ruin the poor with lying words,
　　　even when the plea of the needy is
　　　right.
8 But he who is noble plans noble things,
　　and on noble things he stands.

9 Rise up, you women who are at ease,
　　hear my voice;
　　you complacent daughters, give ear to
　　　my speech.
10 In little more than a year
　　you will shudder, you complacent
　　　women;
　　for the grape harvest fails,
　　　the fruit harvest will not come.
11 Tremble, you women who are at ease,
　　shudder, you complacent ones;
　　strip, and make yourselves bare,
　　and tie sackcloth around your waist.
12 Beat your breasts for the pleasant fields,
　　for the fruitful vine,
13 for the soil of my people
　　growing up in thorns and briers,
　　yes, for all the joyous houses
　　in the exultant city.
14 For the palace is forsaken,
　　the populous city deserted;
　　the hill and the watchtower
　　will become dens forever,
　　a joy of wild donkeys,
　　a pasture of flocks;
15 until the Spirit is poured upon us from
　　on high,
　　and the wilderness becomes a fruitful
　　　field,
　　and the fruitful field is deemed a
　　　forest.
16 Then justice will dwell in the wilderness,
　　and righteousness abide in the fruitful
　　　field.

[1] Probably *Nubia*

17   And the effect of righteousness will be
        peace,
      and the result of righteousness,
        quietness and trust[1] forever.
18   My people will abide in a peaceful
        habitation,
      in secure dwellings, and in quiet
        resting places.
19   And it will hail when the forest falls
        down,
      and the city will be utterly laid low.
20   Happy are you who sow beside all
        waters,
      who let the feet of the ox and the
        donkey range free.

Revelation 2

"To the angel of the church in Ephesus write: 'The words of him who holds the seven stars in his right hand, who walks among the seven golden lampstands.

2 "'I know your works, your toil and your patient endurance, and how you cannot bear with those who are evil, but have tested those who call themselves apostles and are not, and found them to be false. 3 I know you are enduring patiently and bearing up for my name's sake, and you have not grown weary. 4 But I have this against you, that you have abandoned the love you had at first. 5 Remember therefore from where you have fallen; repent, and do the works you did at first. If not, I will come to you and remove your lampstand from its place, unless you repent. 6 Yet this you have: you hate the works of the Nicolaitans, which I also hate. 7 He who has an ear, let him hear what the Spirit says to the churches. To the one who conquers I will grant to eat of the tree of life, which is in the paradise of God.'

8 "And to the angel of the church in Smyrna write: 'The words of the first and the last, who died and came to life.

9 "'I know your tribulation and your poverty (but you are rich) and the slander[2] of those who say that they are Jews and are not, but are a synagogue of Satan. 10 Do not fear what you are about to suffer. Behold, the devil is about to throw some of you into prison, that you may be tested, and for ten days you will have tribulation. Be faithful unto death, and I will give you the crown of life. 11 He who has an ear, let

him hear what the Spirit says to the churches. The one who conquers will not be hurt by the second death.'

12 "And to the angel of the church in Pergamum write: 'The words of him who has the sharp two-edged sword.

13 "'I know where you dwell, where Satan's throne is. Yet you hold fast my name, and you did not deny my faith[3] even in the days of Antipas my faithful witness, who was killed among you, where Satan dwells. 14 But I have a few things against you: you have some there who hold the teaching of Balaam, who taught Balak to put a stumbling block before the sons of Israel, so that they might eat food sacrificed to idols and practice sexual immorality. 15 So also you have some who hold the teaching of the Nicolaitans. 16 Therefore repent. If not, I will come to you soon and war against them with the sword of my mouth. 17 He who has an ear, let him hear what the Spirit says to the churches. To the one who conquers I will give some of the hidden manna, and I will give him a white stone, with a new name written on the stone that no one knows except the one who receives it.'

18 "And to the angel of the church in Thyatira write: 'The words of the Son of God, who has eyes like a flame of fire, and whose feet are like burnished bronze.

19 "'I know your works, your love and faith and service and patient endurance, and that your latter works exceed the first. 20 But I have this against you, that you tolerate that woman Jezebel, who calls herself a prophetess and is teaching and seducing my servants[4] to practice sexual immorality and to eat food sacrificed to idols. 21 I gave her time to repent, but she refuses to repent of her sexual immorality. 22 Behold, I will throw her onto a sickbed, and those who commit adultery with her I will throw into great tribulation, unless they repent of her works, 23 and I will strike her children dead. And all the churches will know that I am he who searches mind and heart, and I will give to each of you according to your works. 24 But to the rest of you in Thyatira, who do not hold this teaching, who have not learned what some call the deep things of Satan, to you I say, I do not lay on you any other burden. 25 Only hold fast what you have until I come. 26 The one who conquers

[1] Or security [2] Greek blasphemy [3] Or your faith in me [4] Greek bondservants

and who keeps my works until the end, to him I will give authority over the nations, [27] and he will rule them with a rod of iron, as when earthen pots are broken in pieces, even as I myself have received authority from my Father. [28] And I will give him the morning star. [29] He who has an ear, let him hear what the Spirit says to the churches.'

JUNE 1

Deuteronomy 5

And Moses summoned all Israel and said to them, "Hear, O Israel, the statutes and the rules that I speak in your hearing today, and you shall learn them and be careful to do them. [2]The Lord our God made a covenant with us in Horeb. [3]Not with our fathers did the Lord make this covenant, but with us, who are all of us here alive today. [4]The Lord spoke with you face to face at the mountain, out of the midst of the fire, [5]while I stood between the Lord and you at that time, to declare to you the word of the Lord. For you were afraid because of the fire, and you did not go up into the mountain. He said:

[6]"'I am the Lord your God, who brought you out of the land of Egypt, out of the house of slavery.

[7]"'You shall have no other gods before[1] me.

[8]"'You shall not make for yourself a carved image, or any likeness of anything that is in heaven above, or that is on the earth beneath, or that is in the water under the earth. [9]You shall not bow down to them or serve them; for I the Lord your God am a jealous God, visiting the iniquity of the fathers on the children to the third and fourth generation of those who hate me, [10]but showing steadfast love to thousands[2] of those who love me and keep my commandments.

[11]"'You shall not take the name of the Lord your God in vain, for the Lord will not hold him guiltless who takes his name in vain.

[12]"'Observe the Sabbath day, to keep it holy, as the Lord your God commanded you. [13]Six days you shall labor and do all your work, [14]but the seventh day is a Sabbath to the Lord your God. On it you shall not do any work, you or your son or your daughter or your male servant or your female servant, or your ox or your donkey or any of your livestock, or the sojourner who is within your gates, that your male servant and your female servant may rest as well as you. [15]You shall remember that you were a slave[3] in the land of Egypt, and the Lord your God brought you out from there with a mighty hand and an outstretched arm. Therefore the Lord your God commanded you to keep the Sabbath day.

[16]"'Honor your father and your mother, as the Lord your God commanded you, that your days may be long, and that it may go well with you in the land that the Lord your God is giving you.

[17]"'You shall not murder.[4]

[18]"'And you shall not commit adultery.

[19]"'And you shall not steal.

[20]"'And you shall not bear false witness against your neighbor.

[21]"'And you shall not covet your neighbor's wife. And you shall not desire your neighbor's house, his field, or his male servant, or his female servant, his ox, or his donkey, or anything that is your neighbor's.'

[22]"These words the Lord spoke to all your assembly at the mountain out of the midst of the fire, the cloud, and the thick darkness, with a loud voice; and he added no more. And he wrote them on two tablets of stone and gave them to me. [23]And as soon as you heard the voice out of the midst of the darkness, while the mountain was burning with fire, you came near to me, all the heads of your tribes, and your elders. [24]And you said, 'Behold, the Lord our God has shown us his glory and greatness, and we have heard his voice out of the midst of the fire. This day we have seen God speak with man, and man still live. [25]Now therefore why should we die? For this great fire will consume us. If we hear the voice of the Lord our God any more, we shall die. [26]For who is there of all flesh, that has heard the voice of the living God speaking out of the midst of fire as we have, and has still lived? [27]Go near and hear all that the Lord our God will say, and speak to us all that the Lord our God will speak to you, and we will hear and do it.'

[28]"And the Lord heard your words, when you spoke to me. And the Lord said to me,

[1] Or *besides* [2] Or *to the thousandth generation* [3] Or *servant* [4] The Hebrew word also covers causing human death through carelessness or negligence

'I have heard the words of this people, which they have spoken to you. They are right in all that they have spoken. ²⁹Oh that they had such a heart as this always, to fear me and to keep all my commandments, that it might go well with them and with their descendants[1] forever! ³⁰Go and say to them, "Return to your tents." ³¹But you, stand here by me, and I will tell you the whole commandment and the statutes and the rules that you shall teach them, that they may do them in the land that I am giving them to possess.' ³²You shall be careful therefore to do as the Lord your God has commanded you. You shall not turn aside to the right hand or to the left. ³³You shall walk in all the way that the Lord your God has commanded you, that you may live, and that it may go well with you, and that you may live long in the land that you shall possess.

Psalm 88

A Song. A Psalm of the Sons of Korah. To the choirmaster: according to Mahalath Leannoth. A Maskil[2] of Heman the Ezrahite.

O Lord, God of my salvation;
   I cry out day and night before you.
2 Let my prayer come before you;
   incline your ear to my cry!

3 For my soul is full of troubles,
   and my life draws near to Sheol.
4 I am counted among those who go
     down to the pit;
   I am a man who has no strength,
5 like one set loose among the dead,
   like the slain that lie in the grave,
like those whom you remember no more,
   for they are cut off from your hand.
6 You have put me in the depths of the pit,
   in the regions dark and deep.
7 Your wrath lies heavy upon me,
   and you overwhelm me with all your
     waves.   *Selah*

8 You have caused my companions to
     shun me;
   you have made me a horror[3] to them.
I am shut in so that I cannot escape;
9   my eye grows dim through sorrow.
Every day I call upon you, O Lord;
   I spread out my hands to you.

10 Do you work wonders for the dead?
   Do the departed rise up to praise you?
     Selah
11 Is your steadfast love declared in the
     grave,
   or your faithfulness in Abaddon?
12 Are your wonders known in the
     darkness,
   or your righteousness in the land of
     forgetfulness?
13 But I, O Lord, cry to you;
   in the morning my prayer comes
     before you.
14 O Lord, why do you cast my soul away?
   Why do you hide your face from me?
15 Afflicted and close to death from my
     youth up,
   I suffer your terrors; I am helpless.[4]
16 Your wrath has swept over me;
   your dreadful assaults destroy me.
17 They surround me like a flood all day
     long;
   they close in on me together.
18 You have caused my beloved and my
     friend to shun me;
   my companions have become
     darkness.[5]

Isaiah 33

Ah, you destroyer,
   who yourself have not been destroyed,
you traitor,
   whom none has betrayed!
When you have ceased to destroy,
   you will be destroyed;
and when you have finished betraying,
   they will betray you.

2 O Lord, be gracious to us; we wait for
     you.
Be our arm every morning,
   our salvation in the time of trouble.
3 At the tumultuous noise peoples flee;
   when you lift yourself up, nations are
     scattered,
4 and your spoil is gathered as the
     caterpillar gathers;
   as locusts leap, it is leapt upon.

[1] Or sons [2] Probably musical or liturgical terms [3] Or an abomination [4] The meaning of the Hebrew word is uncertain [5] Or darkness has become my only companion

⁵ The Lord is exalted, for he dwells on
  high;
  he will fill Zion with justice and
  righteousness,
⁶ and he will be the stability of your
  times,
  abundance of salvation, wisdom, and
  knowledge;
  the fear of the Lord is Zion's[1]
  treasure.

⁷ Behold, their heroes cry in the streets;
  the envoys of peace weep bitterly.
⁸ The highways lie waste;
  the traveler ceases.
  Covenants are broken;
  cities[2] are despised;
  there is no regard for man.
⁹ The land mourns and languishes;
  Lebanon is confounded and withers
  away;
  Sharon is like a desert,
  and Bashan and Carmel shake off
  their leaves.
¹⁰ "Now I will arise," says the Lord,
  "now I will lift myself up;
  now I will be exalted.
¹¹ You conceive chaff; you give birth to
  stubble;
  your breath is a fire that will consume
  you.
¹² And the peoples will be as if burned to
  lime,
  like thorns cut down, that are burned
  in the fire."

¹³ Hear, you who are far off, what I have
  done;
  and you who are near, acknowledge
  my might.
¹⁴ The sinners in Zion are afraid;
  trembling has seized the godless:
  "Who among us can dwell with the
  consuming fire?
  Who among us can dwell with
  everlasting burnings?"
¹⁵ He who walks righteously and speaks
  uprightly,
  who despises the gain of
  oppressions,

who shakes his hands, lest they hold a
  bribe,
  who stops his ears from hearing of
  bloodshed
  and shuts his eyes from looking on
  evil,
¹⁶ he will dwell on the heights;
  his place of defense will be the
  fortresses of rocks;
  his bread will be given him; his water
  will be sure.

¹⁷ Your eyes will behold the king in his
  beauty;
  they will see a land that stretches afar.
¹⁸ Your heart will muse on the terror:
  "Where is he who counted, where is he
  who weighed the tribute?
  Where is he who counted the
  towers?"
¹⁹ You will see no more the insolent
  people,
  the people of an obscure speech that
  you cannot comprehend,
  stammering in a tongue that you
  cannot understand.
²⁰ Behold Zion, the city of our appointed
  feasts!
  Your eyes will see Jerusalem,
  an untroubled habitation, an
  immovable tent,
  whose stakes will never be plucked up,
  nor will any of its cords be broken.
²¹ But there the Lord in majesty will be
  for us
  a place of broad rivers and streams,
  where no galley with oars can go,
  nor majestic ship can pass.
²² For the Lord is our judge; the Lord is
  our lawgiver;
  the Lord is our king; he will save us.

²³ Your cords hang loose;
  they cannot hold the mast firm in its
  place
  or keep the sail spread out.
  Then prey and spoil in abundance will
  be divided;
  even the lame will take the prey.
²⁴ And no inhabitant will say, "I am sick";
  the people who dwell there will be
  forgiven their iniquity.

¹ Hebrew *his* ² Masoretic Text; Dead Sea Scroll *witnesses*

Revelation 3

"And to the angel of the church in Sardis write: 'The words of him who has the seven spirits of God and the seven stars.

"'I know your works. You have the reputation of being alive, but you are dead. ²Wake up, and strengthen what remains and is about to die, for I have not found your works complete in the sight of my God. ³Remember, then, what you received and heard. Keep it, and repent. If you will not wake up, I will come like a thief, and you will not know at what hour I will come against you. ⁴Yet you have still a few names in Sardis, people who have not soiled their garments, and they will walk with me in white, for they are worthy. ⁵The one who conquers will be clothed thus in white garments, and I will never blot his name out of the book of life. I will confess his name before my Father and before his angels. ⁶He who has an ear, let him hear what the Spirit says to the churches.'

⁷"And to the angel of the church in Philadelphia write: 'The words of the holy one, the true one, who has the key of David, who opens and no one will shut, who shuts and no one opens.

⁸"'I know your works. Behold, I have set before you an open door, which no one is able to shut. I know that you have but little power, and yet you have kept my word and have not denied my name. ⁹Behold, I will make those of the synagogue of Satan who say that they are Jews and are not, but lie—behold, I will make them come and bow down before your feet, and they will learn that I have loved you. ¹⁰Because you have kept my word

about patient endurance, I will keep you from the hour of trial that is coming on the whole world, to try those who dwell on the earth. ¹¹I am coming soon. Hold fast what you have, so that no one may seize your crown. ¹²The one who conquers, I will make him a pillar in the temple of my God. Never shall he go out of it, and I will write on him the name of my God, and the name of the city of my God, the new Jerusalem, which comes down from my God out of heaven, and my own new name. ¹³He who has an ear, let him hear what the Spirit says to the churches.'

¹⁴"And to the angel of the church in Laodicea write: 'The words of the Amen, the faithful and true witness, the beginning of God's creation.

¹⁵"'I know your works: you are neither cold nor hot. Would that you were either cold or hot! ¹⁶So, because you are lukewarm, and neither hot nor cold, I will spit you out of my mouth. ¹⁷For you say, I am rich, I have prospered, and I need nothing, not realizing that you are wretched, pitiable, poor, blind, and naked. ¹⁸I counsel you to buy from me gold refined by fire, so that you may be rich, and white garments so that you may clothe yourself and the shame of your nakedness may not be seen, and salve to anoint your eyes, so that you may see. ¹⁹Those whom I love, I reprove and discipline, so be zealous and repent. ²⁰Behold, I stand at the door and knock. If anyone hears my voice and opens the door, I will come in to him and eat with him, and he with me. ²¹The one who conquers, I will grant him to sit with me on my throne, as I also conquered and sat down with my Father on his throne. ²²He who has an ear, let him hear what the Spirit says to the churches.'"

JUNE 2

Deuteronomy 6

"Now this is the commandment—the statutes and the rules¹—that the Lord your God commanded me to teach you, that you may do them in the land to which you are going

over, to possess it, ²that you may fear the Lord your God, you and your son and your son's son, by keeping all his statutes and his commandments, which I command you, all the days of

¹ Or just decrees; also verse 20

your life, and that your days may be long. ³Hear therefore, O Israel, and be careful to do them, that it may go well with you, and that you may multiply greatly, as the LORD, the God of your fathers, has promised you, in a land flowing with milk and honey.

⁴"Hear, O Israel: The LORD our God, the LORD is one.¹ ⁵You shall love the LORD your God with all your heart and with all your soul and with all your might. ⁶And these words that I command you today shall be on your heart. ⁷You shall teach them diligently to your children, and shall talk of them when you sit in your house, and when you walk by the way, and when you lie down, and when you rise. ⁸You shall bind them as a sign on your hand, and they shall be as frontlets between your eyes. ⁹You shall write them on the doorposts of your house and on your gates.

¹⁰"And when the LORD your God brings you into the land that he swore to your fathers, to Abraham, to Isaac, and to Jacob, to give you—with great and good cities that you did not build, ¹¹and houses full of all good things that you did not fill, and cisterns that you did not dig, and vineyards and olive trees that you did not plant—and when you eat and are full, ¹²then take care lest you forget the LORD, who brought you out of the land of Egypt, out of the house of slavery. ¹³It is the LORD your God you shall fear. Him you shall serve and by his name you shall swear. ¹⁴You shall not go after other gods, the gods of the peoples who are around you— ¹⁵for the LORD your God in your midst is a jealous God—lest the anger of the LORD your God be kindled against you, and he destroy you from off the face of the earth.

¹⁶"You shall not put the LORD your God to the test, as you tested him at Massah. ¹⁷You shall diligently keep the commandments of the LORD your God, and his testimonies and his statutes, which he has commanded you. ¹⁸And you shall do what is right and good in the sight of the LORD, that it may go well with you, and that you may go in and take possession of the good land that the LORD swore to give to your fathers ¹⁹by thrusting out all your enemies from before you, as the LORD has promised.

²⁰"When your son asks you in time to come, 'What is the meaning of the testimonies and the statutes and the rules that the LORD our God has commanded you?' ²¹then you shall

say to your son, 'We were Pharaoh's slaves in Egypt. And the LORD brought us out of Egypt with a mighty hand. ²²And the LORD showed signs and wonders, great and grievous, against Egypt and against Pharaoh and all his household, before our eyes. ²³And he brought us out from there, that he might bring us in and give us the land that he swore to give to our fathers. ²⁴And the LORD commanded us to do all these statutes, to fear the LORD our God, for our good always, that he might preserve us alive, as we are this day. ²⁵And it will be righteousness for us, if we are careful to do all this commandment before the LORD our God, as he has commanded us.'

--------- *Psalm 89* ---------

A MASKIL² OF ETHAN THE EZRAHITE.

I will sing of the steadfast love of the LORD, forever;
    with my mouth I will make
      known your faithfulness to all
      generations.
2 For I said, "Steadfast love will be built up forever;
    in the heavens you will establish your
    faithfulness."
3 You have said, "I have made a covenant
      with my chosen one;
    I have sworn to David my servant:
4 'I will establish your offspring forever,
    and build your throne for all
      generations.'"   *Selah*

5 Let the heavens praise your wonders,
    O LORD,
    your faithfulness in the assembly of
      the holy ones!
6 For who in the skies can be compared to
      the LORD?
    Who among the heavenly beings³ is
      like the LORD,
7 a God greatly to be feared in the council
      of the holy ones,
    and awesome above all who are
      around him?
8 O LORD God of hosts,
    who is mighty as you are, O LORD,
    with your faithfulness all around you?
9 You rule the raging of the sea;
    when its waves rise, you still them.

---

¹ Or *The LORD our God is one LORD*; or *The LORD is our God, the LORD is one*; or *The LORD is our God, the LORD alone* ² Probably a musical or liturgical term ³ Hebrew *the sons of God*, or *the sons of might*

10   You crushed Rahab like a carcass;
       you scattered your enemies with your
         mighty arm.
11   The heavens are yours; the earth also is
         yours;
       the world and all that is in it, you have
         founded them.
12   The north and the south, you have
         created them;
       Tabor and Hermon joyously praise
         your name.
13   You have a mighty arm;
       strong is your hand, high your right
         hand.
14   Righteousness and justice are the
         foundation of your throne;
       steadfast love and faithfulness go
         before you.
15   Blessed are the people who know the
         festal shout,
       who walk, O LORD, in the light of your
         face,
16   who exult in your name all the day
       and in your righteousness are
         exalted.
17   For you are the glory of their strength;
       by your favor our horn is exalted.
18   For our shield belongs to the LORD,
       our king to the Holy One of Israel.

19   Of old you spoke in a vision to your
         godly one,[1] and said:
       "I have granted help to one who is
         mighty;
       I have exalted one chosen from the
         people.
20   I have found David, my servant;
       with my holy oil I have anointed
         him,
21   so that my hand shall be established
         with him;
       my arm also shall strengthen him.
22   The enemy shall not outwit him;
       the wicked shall not humble him.
23   I will crush his foes before him
       and strike down those who hate him.
24   My faithfulness and my steadfast love
         shall be with him,
       and in my name shall his horn be
         exalted.
25   I will set his hand on the sea
       and his right hand on the rivers.

26   He shall cry to me, 'You are my Father,
         my God, and the Rock of my
         salvation.'
27   And I will make him the firstborn,
       the highest of the kings of the earth.
28   My steadfast love I will keep for him
         forever,
       and my covenant will stand firm[2] for
         him.
29   I will establish his offspring forever
       and his throne as the days of the
         heavens.
30   If his children forsake my law
       and do not walk according to my
         rules,[3]
31   if they violate my statutes
       and do not keep my commandments,
32   then I will punish their transgression
         with the rod
       and their iniquity with stripes,
33   but I will not remove from him my
         steadfast love
       or be false to my faithfulness.
34   I will not violate my covenant
       or alter the word that went forth from
         my lips.
35   Once for all I have sworn by my
         holiness;
       I will not lie to David.
36   His offspring shall endure forever,
       his throne as long as the sun before
         me.
37   Like the moon it shall be established
         forever,
       a faithful witness in the skies."   Selah
38   But now you have cast off and rejected;
       you are full of wrath against your
         anointed.
39   You have renounced the covenant with
         your servant;
       you have defiled his crown in the
         dust.
40   You have breached all his walls;
       you have laid his strongholds in ruins.
41   All who pass by plunder him;
       he has become the scorn of his
         neighbors.
42   You have exalted the right hand of his
         foes;
       you have made all his enemies
         rejoice.

[1] Some Hebrew manuscripts godly ones [2] Or will remain faithful [3] Or my just decrees

43 You have also turned back the edge of
 his sword,
 and you have not made him stand in
 battle.
44 You have made his splendor to cease
 and cast his throne to the ground.
45 You have cut short the days of his youth;
 you have covered him with shame.
        Selah

46 How long, O Lord? Will you hide
  yourself forever?
 How long will your wrath burn like
  fire?
47 Remember how short my time is!
 For what vanity you have created all
  the children of man!
48 What man can live and never see
  death?
 Who can deliver his soul from the
  power of Sheol?   *Selah*

49 Lord, where is your steadfast love of old,
 which by your faithfulness you swore
  to David?
50 Remember, O Lord, how your servants
  are mocked,
 and how I bear in my heart the
  insults[1] of all the many nations,
51 with which your enemies mock,
  O Lord,
 with which they mock the footsteps of
  your anointed.

52 Blessed be the Lord forever!
  Amen and Amen.

Isaiah 34

Draw near, O nations, to hear,
 and give attention, O peoples!
 Let the earth hear, and all that fills it;
  the world, and all that comes from it.
2 For the Lord is enraged against all the
  nations,
 and furious against all their host;
 he has devoted them to destruction,[2]
  has given them over for slaughter.
3 Their slain shall be cast out,
 and the stench of their corpses shall
  rise;
 the mountains shall flow with their
  blood.

4 All the host of heaven shall rot away,
 and the skies roll up like a scroll.
 All their host shall fall,
  as leaves fall from the vine,
  like leaves falling from the fig tree.

5 For my sword has drunk its fill in the
  heavens;
 behold, it descends for judgment
  upon Edom,
 upon the people I have devoted to
  destruction.
6 The Lord has a sword; it is sated with
  blood;
 it is gorged with fat,
 with the blood of lambs and goats,
 with the fat of the kidneys of rams.
 For the Lord has a sacrifice in Bozrah,
  a great slaughter in the land of Edom.
7 Wild oxen shall fall with them,
 and young steers with the mighty
  bulls.
 Their land shall drink its fill of blood,
  and their soil shall be gorged with
  fat.

8 For the Lord has a day of vengeance,
 a year of recompense for the cause of
  Zion.
9 And the streams of Edom[3] shall be
  turned into pitch,
 and her soil into sulfur;
  her land shall become burning pitch.
10 Night and day it shall not be quenched;
 its smoke shall go up forever.
 From generation to generation it shall
  lie waste;
 none shall pass through it forever and
  ever.
11 But the hawk and the porcupine[4] shall
  possess it,
 the owl and the raven shall dwell in it.
 He shall stretch the line of confusion[5]
  over it,
 and the plumb line of emptiness.
12 Its nobles—there is no one there to call
  it a kingdom,
 and all its princes shall be nothing.

13 Thorns shall grow over its strongholds,
  nettles and thistles in its fortresses.
 It shall be the haunt of jackals,
  an abode for ostriches.[6]

[1] Hebrew lacks *the insults* [2] That is, set apart (devoted) as an offering to the Lord (for destruction); also verse 5 [3] Hebrew *her streams* [4] The identity of the animals rendered *hawk* and *porcupine* is uncertain [5] Hebrew *formlessness* [6] Or *owls*

14   And wild animals shall meet with
       hyenas;
     the wild goat shall cry to his fellow;
   indeed, there the night bird[1] settles
     and finds for herself a resting place.

15   There the owl nests and lays
     and hatches and gathers her young in
       her shadow;
   indeed, there the hawks are gathered,
     each one with her mate.

16   Seek and read from the book of the LORD:
   Not one of these shall be missing;
     none shall be without her mate.
   For the mouth of the LORD has
       commanded,
     and his Spirit has gathered them.

17   He has cast the lot for them;
     his hand has portioned it out to them
       with the line;
   they shall possess it forever;
     from generation to generation they
       shall dwell in it.

─────── **Revelation 4** ───────

After this I looked, and behold, a door standing open in heaven! And the first voice, which I had heard speaking to me like a trumpet, said, "Come up here, and I will show you what must take place after this." [2] At once I was in the Spirit, and behold, a throne stood in heaven, with one seated on the throne. [3] And he who sat there had the appearance of jasper and carnelian, and around the throne was a rainbow that had the appearance of an emerald.

[4] Around the throne were twenty-four thrones, and seated on the thrones were twenty-four elders, clothed in white garments, with golden crowns on their heads. [5] From the throne came flashes of lightning, and rumblings[2] and peals of thunder, and before the throne were burning seven torches of fire, which are the seven spirits of God, [6] and before the throne there was as it were a sea of glass, like crystal.

And around the throne, on each side of the throne, are four living creatures, full of eyes in front and behind: [7] the first living creature like a lion, the second living creature like an ox, the third living creature with the face of a man, and the fourth living creature like an eagle in flight. [8] And the four living creatures, each of them with six wings, are full of eyes all around and within, and day and night they never cease to say,

   "Holy, holy, holy, is the Lord God
     Almighty,
   who was and is and is to come!"

[9] And whenever the living creatures give glory and honor and thanks to him who is seated on the throne, who lives forever and ever, [10] the twenty-four elders fall down before him who is seated on the throne and worship him who lives forever and ever. They cast their crowns before the throne, saying,

11   "Worthy are you, our Lord and God,
     to receive glory and honor and power,
   for you created all things,
     and by your will they existed and were
       created."

JUNE 3

─────── *Deuteronomy 7* ───────

"When the LORD your God brings you into the land that you are entering to take possession of it, and clears away many nations before you, the Hittites, the Girgashites, the Amorites, the Canaanites, the Perizzites, the Hivites, and the Jebusites, seven nations more numerous and mightier than you, [2] and when the LORD your God gives them over to you, and you defeat them, then you must devote them to complete destruction.[3] You shall make no covenant with them and show no mercy to them. [3] You shall not intermarry with them,

[1] Identity uncertain [2] Or *voices, or sounds* [3] That is, set apart (devote) as an offering to the Lord (for destruction)

giving your daughters to their sons or taking their daughters for your sons, [4]for they would turn away your sons from following me, to serve other gods. Then the anger of the LORD would be kindled against you, and he would destroy you quickly. [5]But thus shall you deal with them: you shall break down their altars and dash in pieces their pillars and chop down their Asherim and burn their carved images with fire.

[6]"For you are a people holy to the LORD your God. The LORD your God has chosen you to be a people for his treasured possession, out of all the peoples who are on the face of the earth. [7]It was not because you were more in number than any other people that the LORD set his love on you and chose you, for you were the fewest of all peoples, [8]but it is because the LORD loves you and is keeping the oath that he swore to your fathers, that the LORD has brought you out with a mighty hand and redeemed you from the house of slavery, from the hand of Pharaoh king of Egypt. [9]Know therefore that the LORD your God is God, the faithful God who keeps covenant and steadfast love with those who love him and keep his commandments, to a thousand generations, [10]and repays to their face those who hate him, by destroying them. He will not be slack with one who hates him. He will repay him to his face. [11]You shall therefore be careful to do the commandment and the statutes and the rules that I command you today.

[12]"And because you listen to these rules and keep and do them, the LORD your God will keep with you the covenant and the steadfast love that he swore to your fathers. [13]He will love you, bless you, and multiply you. He will also bless the fruit of your womb and the fruit of your ground, your grain and your wine and your oil, the increase of your herds and the young of your flock, in the land that he swore to your fathers to give you. [14]You shall be blessed above all peoples. There shall not be male or female barren among you or among your livestock. [15]And the LORD will take away from you all sickness, and none of the evil diseases of Egypt, which you knew, will he inflict on you, but he will lay them on all who hate you. [16]And you shall consume all the peoples that the LORD your God will give over to you. Your eye shall not pity them,

neither shall you serve their gods, for that would be a snare to you.

[17]"If you say in your heart, 'These nations are greater than I. How can I dispossess them?' [18]you shall not be afraid of them but you shall remember what the LORD your God did to Pharaoh and to all Egypt, [19]the great trials that your eyes saw, the signs, the wonders, the mighty hand, and the outstretched arm, by which the LORD your God brought you out. So will the LORD your God do to all the peoples of whom you are afraid. [20]Moreover, the LORD your God will send hornets among them, until those who are left and hide themselves from you are destroyed. [21]You shall not be in dread of them, for the LORD your God is in your midst, a great and awesome God. [22]The LORD your God will clear away these nations before you little by little. You may not make an end of them at once,[1] lest the wild beasts grow too numerous for you. [23]But the LORD your God will give them over to you and throw them into great confusion, until they are destroyed. [24]And he will give their kings into your hand, and you shall make their name perish from under heaven. No one shall be able to stand against you until you have destroyed them. [25]The carved images of their gods you shall burn with fire. You shall not covet the silver or the gold that is on them or take it for yourselves, lest you be ensnared by it, for it is an abomination to the LORD your God. [26]And you shall not bring an abominable thing into your house and become devoted to destruction[2] like it. You shall utterly detest and abhor it, for it is devoted to destruction.

────────── *Psalm 90* ──────────

A PRAYER OF MOSES, THE MAN OF GOD.

Lord, you have been our dwelling place[3]
in all generations.
[2]　Before the mountains were brought
　　　forth,
　　　or ever you had formed the earth and
　　　　the world,
　　　from everlasting to everlasting you
　　　　are God.
[3]　You return man to dust
　　　and say, "Return, O children of
　　　man!"[4]

---

[1] Or *quickly* [2] That is, set apart (devoted) as an offering to the Lord (for destruction); twice in this verse [3] Some Hebrew manuscripts (compare Septuagint) *our refuge* [4] Or *of Adam*

4   For a thousand years in your sight
        are but as yesterday when it is past,
        or as a watch in the night.

5   You sweep them away as with a flood;
        they are like a dream,
        like grass that is renewed in the
            morning:
6   in the morning it flourishes and is
        renewed;
        in the evening it fades and withers.

7   For we are brought to an end by your
        anger;
        by your wrath we are dismayed.
8   You have set our iniquities before you,
        our secret sins in the light of your
            presence.
9   For all our days pass away under your
        wrath;
        we bring our years to an end like a
            sigh.
10 The years of our life are seventy,
        or even by reason of strength eighty;
        yet their span[1] is but toil and trouble;
        they are soon gone, and we fly away.
11 Who considers the power of your
        anger,
        and your wrath according to the fear
            of you?

12 So teach us to number our days
        that we may get a heart of wisdom.
13 Return, O LORD! How long?
        Have pity on your servants!
14 Satisfy us in the morning with your
        steadfast love,
        that we may rejoice and be glad all our
            days.
15 Make us glad for as many days as you
        have afflicted us,
        and for as many years as we have seen
            evil.
16 Let your work be shown to your
        servants,
        and your glorious power to their
            children.
17 Let the favor[2] of the Lord our God be
        upon us,
        and establish the work of our hands
            upon us;
        yes, establish the work of our hands!

Isaiah 35

The wilderness and the dry land shall be
    glad;
        the desert shall rejoice and blossom
            like the crocus;
2   it shall blossom abundantly
        and rejoice with joy and singing.
    The glory of Lebanon shall be given to it,
        the majesty of Carmel and Sharon.
    They shall see the glory of the LORD,
        the majesty of our God.

3   Strengthen the weak hands,
        and make firm the feeble knees.
4   Say to those who have an anxious heart,
        "Be strong; fear not!
    Behold, your God
        will come with vengeance,
    with the recompense of God.
        He will come and save you."

5   Then the eyes of the blind shall be
        opened,
        and the ears of the deaf unstopped;
6   then shall the lame man leap like a deer,
        and the tongue of the mute sing for joy.
    For waters break forth in the wilderness,
        and streams in the desert;
7   the burning sand shall become a pool,
        and the thirsty ground springs of
            water;
    in the haunt of jackals, where they lie
        down,
        the grass shall become reeds and
            rushes.

8   And a highway shall be there,
        and it shall be called the Way of
            Holiness;
    the unclean shall not pass over it.
        It shall belong to those who walk on
            the way;
        even if they are fools, they shall not go
            astray.[3]
9   No lion shall be there,
        nor shall any ravenous beast come up
            on it;
    they shall not be found there,
        but the redeemed shall walk there.
10 And the ransomed of the LORD shall
        return
        and come to Zion with singing;

[1] Or pride [2] Or beauty [3] Or if they are fools, they shall not wander in it

everlasting joy shall be upon their heads;
　　they shall obtain gladness and joy,
　　and sorrow and sighing shall flee
　　　away.

Revelation 5

Then I saw in the right hand of him who was seated on the throne a scroll written within and on the back, sealed with seven seals. [2]And I saw a mighty angel proclaiming with a loud voice, "Who is worthy to open the scroll and break its seals?" [3]And no one in heaven or on earth or under the earth was able to open the scroll or to look into it, [4]and I began to weep loudly because no one was found worthy to open the scroll or to look into it. [5]And one of the elders said to me, "Weep no more; behold, the Lion of the tribe of Judah, the Root of David, has conquered, so that he can open the scroll and its seven seals."

[6]And between the throne and the four living creatures and among the elders I saw a Lamb standing, as though it had been slain, with seven horns and with seven eyes, which are the seven spirits of God sent out into all the earth. [7]And he went and took the scroll from the right hand of him who was seated on the throne. [8]And when he had taken the scroll, the four living creatures and the twenty-four elders fell down before the Lamb, each holding a harp, and golden bowls full of incense, which are the prayers of the saints. [9]And they sang a new song, saying,

"Worthy are you to take the scroll
　　and to open its seals,
　for you were slain, and by your blood
　　you ransomed people for God
　from every tribe and language and
　　people and nation,
[10]　and you have made them a kingdom
　　and priests to our God,
　　and they shall reign on the earth."

[11]Then I looked, and I heard around the throne and the living creatures and the elders the voice of many angels, numbering myriads of myriads and thousands of thousands, [12]saying with a loud voice,

"Worthy is the Lamb who was slain,
　to receive power and wealth and wisdom
　　and might
　and honor and glory and blessing!"

[13]And I heard every creature in heaven and on earth and under the earth and in the sea, and all that is in them, saying,

"To him who sits on the throne and to
　　the Lamb
　be blessing and honor and glory and
　　might forever and ever!"

[14]And the four living creatures said, "Amen!" and the elders fell down and worshiped.

JUNE 4

Deuteronomy 8

"The whole commandment that I command you today you shall be careful to do, that you may live and multiply, and go in and possess the land that the LORD swore to give to your fathers. [2]And you shall remember the whole way that the LORD your God has led you these forty years in the wilderness, that he might humble you, testing you to know what was in your heart, whether you would keep his commandments or not. [3]And he humbled you and let you hunger and fed you with manna, which you did not know, nor did your fathers know, that he might make you know that man does not live by bread alone, but man lives by every word[1] that comes from the mouth of the LORD. [4]Your clothing did not wear out on you and your foot did not swell these forty years. [5]Know then in your heart that, as a man

[1] Hebrew by all

disciplines his son, the LORD your God disciplines you. **6** So you shall keep the commandments of the LORD your God by walking in his ways and by fearing him. **7** For the LORD your God is bringing you into a good land, a land of brooks of water, of fountains and springs, flowing out in the valleys and hills, **8** a land of wheat and barley, of vines and fig trees and pomegranates, a land of olive trees and honey, **9** a land in which you will eat bread without scarcity, in which you will lack nothing, a land whose stones are iron, and out of whose hills you can dig copper. **10** And you shall eat and be full, and you shall bless the LORD your God for the good land he has given you.

11 "Take care lest you forget the LORD your God by not keeping his commandments and his rules and his statutes, which I command you today, **12** lest, when you have eaten and are full and have built good houses and live in them, **13** and when your herds and flocks multiply and your silver and gold is multiplied and all that you have is multiplied, **14** then your heart be lifted up, and you forget the LORD your God, who brought you out of the land of Egypt, out of the house of slavery, **15** who led you through the great and terrifying wilderness, with its fiery serpents and scorpions and thirsty ground where there was no water, who brought you water out of the flinty rock, **16** who fed you in the wilderness with manna that your fathers did not know, that he might humble you and test you, to do you good in the end. **17** Beware lest you say in your heart, 'My power and the might of my hand have gotten me this wealth.' **18** You shall remember the LORD your God, for it is he who gives you power to get wealth, that he may confirm his covenant that he swore to your fathers, as it is this day. **19** And if you forget the LORD your God and go after other gods and serve them and worship them, I solemnly warn you today that you shall surely perish. **20** Like the nations that the LORD makes to perish before you, so shall you perish, because you would not obey the voice of the LORD your God.

Psalm 91

He who dwells in the shelter of the Most High
    will abide in the shadow of the
        Almighty.

2 I will say[1] to the LORD, "My refuge and
        my fortress,
    my God, in whom I trust."
3 For he will deliver you from the snare of
        the fowler
    and from the deadly pestilence.
4 He will cover you with his pinions,
    and under his wings you will find
        refuge;
    his faithfulness is a shield and
        buckler.
5 You will not fear the terror of the
        night,
    nor the arrow that flies by day,
6 nor the pestilence that stalks in
        darkness,
    nor the destruction that wastes at
        noonday.
7 A thousand may fall at your side,
    ten thousand at your right hand,
    but it will not come near you.
8 You will only look with your eyes
    and see the recompense of the
        wicked.
9 Because you have made the LORD your
        dwelling place—
    the Most High, who is my refuge[2]—
10 no evil shall be allowed to befall you,
    no plague come near your tent.
11 For he will command his angels
        concerning you
    to guard you in all your ways.
12 On their hands they will bear you up,
    lest you strike your foot against a
        stone.
13 You will tread on the lion and the
        adder;
    the young lion and the serpent you
        will trample underfoot.
14 "Because he holds fast to me in love, I will
        deliver him;
    I will protect him, because he knows
        my name.
15 When he calls to me, I will answer him;
    I will be with him in trouble;
    I will rescue him and honor him.
16 With long life I will satisfy him
    and show him my salvation."

[1] Septuagint *He will say* [2] Or *For you, O LORD, are my refuge! You have made the Most High your dwelling place*

Isaiah 36

In the fourteenth year of King Hezekiah, Sennacherib king of Assyria came up against all the fortified cities of Judah and took them. ²And the king of Assyria sent the Rabshakeh[1] from Lachish to King Hezekiah at Jerusalem, with a great army. And he stood by the conduit of the upper pool on the highway to the Washer's Field. ³And there came out to him Eliakim the son of Hilkiah, who was over the household, and Shebna the secretary, and Joah the son of Asaph, the recorder.

⁴And the Rabshakeh said to them, "Say to Hezekiah, 'Thus says the great king, the king of Assyria: On what do you rest this trust of yours? ⁵Do you think that mere words are strategy and power for war? In whom do you now trust, that you have rebelled against me? ⁶Behold, you are trusting in Egypt, that broken reed of a staff, which will pierce the hand of any man who leans on it. Such is Pharaoh king of Egypt to all who trust in him. ⁷But if you say to me, "We trust in the LORD our God," is it not he whose high places and altars Hezekiah has removed, saying to Judah and to Jerusalem, "You shall worship before this altar"? ⁸Come now, make a wager with my master the king of Assyria: I will give you two thousand horses, if you are able on your part to set riders on them. ⁹How then can you repulse a single captain among the least of my master's servants, when you trust in Egypt for chariots and for horsemen? ¹⁰Moreover, is it without the LORD that I have come up against this land to destroy it? The LORD said to me, Go up against this land and destroy it.'"

¹¹Then Eliakim, Shebna, and Joah said to the Rabshakeh, "Please speak to your servants in Aramaic, for we understand it. Do not speak to us in the language of Judah within the hearing of the people who are on the wall." ¹²But the Rabshakeh said, "Has my master sent me to speak these words to your master and to you, and not to the men sitting on the wall, who are doomed with you to eat their own dung and drink their own urine?"

¹³Then the Rabshakeh stood and called out in a loud voice in the language of Judah: "Hear the words of the great king, the king of Assyria! ¹⁴Thus says the king: 'Do not let Hezekiah deceive you, for he will not be able to deliver you. ¹⁵Do not let Hezekiah make you trust in the LORD by saying, "The LORD will surely deliver us. This city will not be given into the hand of the king of Assyria." ¹⁶Do not listen to Hezekiah. For thus says the king of Assyria: Make your peace with me[2] and come out to me. Then each one of you will eat of his own vine, and each one of his own fig tree, and each one of you will drink the water of his own cistern, ¹⁷until I come and take you away to a land like your own land, a land of grain and wine, a land of bread and vineyards. ¹⁸Beware lest Hezekiah mislead you by saying, "The LORD will deliver us." Has any of the gods of the nations delivered his land out of the hand of the king of Assyria? ¹⁹Where are the gods of Hamath and Arpad? Where are the gods of Sepharvaim? Have they delivered Samaria out of my hand? ²⁰Who among all the gods of these lands have delivered their lands out of my hand, that the LORD should deliver Jerusalem out of my hand?'"

²¹But they were silent and answered him not a word, for the king's command was, "Do not answer him." ²²Then Eliakim the son of Hilkiah, who was over the household, and Shebna the secretary, and Joah the son of Asaph, the recorder, came to Hezekiah with their clothes torn, and told him the words of the Rabshakeh.

Revelation 6

Now I watched when the Lamb opened one of the seven seals, and I heard one of the four living creatures say with a voice like thunder, "Come!" ²And I looked, and behold, a white horse! And its rider had a bow, and a crown was given to him, and he came out conquering, and to conquer.

³When he opened the second seal, I heard the second living creature say, "Come!" ⁴And out came another horse, bright red. Its rider was permitted to take peace from the earth, so that people should slay one another, and he was given a great sword.

⁵When he opened the third seal, I heard the third living creature say, "Come!" And I looked, and behold, a black horse! And its rider had a pair of scales in his hand. ⁶And I heard what seemed to be a voice in the midst of the four living creatures, saying, "A quart[3] of wheat for a denarius,[4] and three quarts of barley for a denarius, and do not harm the oil and wine!"

⁷When he opened the fourth seal, I heard the

---

[1] *Rabshakeh* is the title of a high-ranking Assyrian military officer [2] Hebrew *Make a blessing with me* [3] Greek *choinix*, a dry measure equal to about a quart [4] A *denarius* was a day's wage for a laborer

voice of the fourth living creature say, "Come!" [8]And I looked, and behold, a pale horse! And its rider's name was Death, and Hades followed him. And they were given authority over a fourth of the earth, to kill with sword and with famine and with pestilence and by wild beasts of the earth.

[9]When he opened the fifth seal, I saw under the altar the souls of those who had been slain for the word of God and for the witness they had borne. [10]They cried out with a loud voice, "O Sovereign Lord, holy and true, how long before you will judge and avenge our blood on those who dwell on the earth?" [11]Then they were each given a white robe and told to rest a little longer, until the number of their fellow servants[1] and their brothers[2] should be complete, who were to be killed as they themselves had been.

[12]When he opened the sixth seal, I looked, and behold, there was a great earthquake, and the sun became black as sackcloth, the full moon became like blood, [13]and the stars of the sky fell to the earth as the fig tree sheds its winter fruit when shaken by a gale. [14]The sky vanished like a scroll that is being rolled up, and every mountain and island was removed from its place. [15]Then the kings of the earth and the great ones and the generals and the rich and the powerful, and everyone, slave[3] and free, hid themselves in the caves and among the rocks of the mountains, [16]calling to the mountains and rocks, "Fall on us and hide us from the face of him who is seated on the throne, and from the wrath of the Lamb, [17]for the great day of their wrath has come, and who can stand?"

JUNE 5

Deuteronomy 9

"Hear, O Israel: you are to cross over the Jordan today, to go in to dispossess nations greater and mightier than you, cities great and fortified up to heaven, [2]a people great and tall, the sons of the Anakim, whom you know, and of whom you have heard it said, 'Who can stand before the sons of Anak?' [3]Know therefore today that he who goes over before you as a consuming fire is the Lord your God. He will destroy them and subdue them before you. So you shall drive them out and make them perish quickly, as the Lord has promised you.

[4]"Do not say in your heart, after the Lord your God has thrust them out before you, 'It is because of my righteousness that the Lord has brought me in to possess this land,' whereas it is because of the wickedness of these nations that the Lord is driving them out before you. [5]Not because of your righteousness or the uprightness of your heart are you going in to possess their land, but because of the wickedness of these nations the Lord your God is

driving them out from before you, and that he may confirm the word that the Lord swore to your fathers, to Abraham, to Isaac, and to Jacob.

[6]"Know, therefore, that the Lord your God is not giving you this good land to possess because of your righteousness, for you are a stubborn people. [7]Remember and do not forget how you provoked the Lord your God to wrath in the wilderness. From the day you came out of the land of Egypt until you came to this place, you have been rebellious against the Lord. [8]Even at Horeb you provoked the Lord to wrath, and the Lord was so angry with you that he was ready to destroy you. [9]When I went up the mountain to receive the tablets of stone, the tablets of the covenant that the Lord made with you, I remained on the mountain forty days and forty nights. I neither ate bread nor drank water. [10]And the Lord gave me the two tablets of stone written with the finger of God, and on them were all the words that the Lord had spoken with you on the mountain out of the midst of the fire on the day of the assembly.

[1] Greek *fellow bondservants* [2] Or *brothers and sisters.* The plural Greek word *adelphoi* (translated "brothers") refers to siblings in a family. In New Testament usage, depending on the context, *adelphoi* may refer either to men or to both men and women who are siblings (brothers and sisters) in God's family, the church [3] Or *servant;* Greek *bondservant*

[11]And at the end of forty days and forty nights the LORD gave me the two tablets of stone, the tablets of the covenant. [12]Then the LORD said to me, 'Arise, go down quickly from here, for your people whom you have brought from Egypt have acted corruptly. They have turned aside quickly out of the way that I commanded them; they have made themselves a metal image.'

[13]"Furthermore, the LORD said to me, 'I have seen this people, and behold, it is a stubborn people. [14]Let me alone, that I may destroy them and blot out their name from under heaven. And I will make of you a nation mightier and greater than they.' [15]So I turned and came down from the mountain, and the mountain was burning with fire. And the two tablets of the covenant were in my two hands. [16]And I looked, and behold, you had sinned against the LORD your God. You had made yourselves a golden[1] calf. You had turned aside quickly from the way that the LORD had commanded you. [17]So I took hold of the two tablets and threw them out of my two hands and broke them before your eyes. [18]Then I lay prostrate before the LORD as before, forty days and forty nights. I neither ate bread nor drank water, because of all the sin that you had committed, in doing what was evil in the sight of the LORD to provoke him to anger. [19]For I was afraid of the anger and hot displeasure that the LORD bore against you, so that he was ready to destroy you. But the LORD listened to me that time also. [20]And the LORD was so angry with Aaron that he was ready to destroy him. And I prayed for Aaron also at the same time. [21]Then I took the sinful thing, the calf that you had made, and burned it with fire and crushed it, grinding it very small, until it was as fine as dust. And I threw the dust of it into the brook that ran down from the mountain.

[22]"At Taberah also, and at Massah and at Kibroth-hattaavah you provoked the LORD to wrath. [23]And when the LORD sent you from Kadesh-barnea, saying, 'Go up and take possession of the land that I have given you,' then you rebelled against the commandment of the LORD your God and did not believe him or obey his voice. [24]You have been rebellious against the LORD from the day that I knew you.

[25]"So I lay prostrate before the LORD for these forty days and forty nights, because the LORD had said he would destroy you. [26]And I prayed to the LORD, 'O Lord GOD, do not destroy your people and your heritage, whom you have redeemed through your greatness, whom you have brought out of Egypt with a mighty hand. [27]Remember your servants, Abraham, Isaac, and Jacob. Do not regard the stubbornness of this people, or their wickedness or their sin, [28]lest the land from which you brought us say, "Because the LORD was not able to bring them into the land that he promised them, and because he hated them, he has brought them out to put them to death in the wilderness." [29]For they are your people and your heritage, whom you brought out by your great power and by your outstretched arm.'

Psalm 92–93

A PSALM. A SONG FOR THE SABBATH.

It is good to give thanks to the LORD,
  to sing praises to your name, O Most High;
2   to declare your steadfast love in the
      morning,
    and your faithfulness by night,
3   to the music of the lute and the harp,
    to the melody of the lyre.
4   For you, O LORD, have made me glad by
      your work;
    at the works of your hands I sing for
      joy.

5   How great are your works, O LORD!
    Your thoughts are very deep!
6   The stupid man cannot know;
    the fool cannot understand this:
7   that though the wicked sprout like grass
    and all evildoers flourish,
    they are doomed to destruction forever;
8   but you, O LORD, are on high forever.
9   For behold, your enemies, O LORD,
    for behold, your enemies shall perish;
    all evildoers shall be scattered.

10 But you have exalted my horn like that
      of the wild ox;
    you have poured over me[2] fresh oil.
11 My eyes have seen the downfall of my
      enemies;
    my ears have heard the doom of my
      evil assailants.

12 The righteous flourish like the palm tree
    and grow like a cedar in Lebanon.

[1] Hebrew *cast metal* [2] Compare Syriac; the meaning of the Hebrew is uncertain

13   They are planted in the house of the
      LORD;
         they flourish in the courts of our God.
14   They still bear fruit in old age;
         they are ever full of sap and green,
15   to declare that the LORD is upright;
         he is my rock, and there is no
            unrighteousness in him.

The LORD reigns; he is robed in majesty;
   the LORD is robed; he has put on strength
      as his belt.
      Yes, the world is established; it shall
         never be moved.
2   Your throne is established from of old;
         you are from everlasting.

3   The floods have lifted up, O LORD,
         the floods have lifted up their voice;
         the floods lift up their roaring.
4   Mightier than the thunders of many
            waters,
         mightier than the waves of the sea,
         the LORD on high is mighty!

5   Your decrees are very trustworthy;
         holiness befits your house,
         O LORD, forevermore.

Isaiah 37

As soon as King Hezekiah heard it, he tore his clothes and covered himself with sackcloth and went into the house of the LORD. ²And he sent Eliakim, who was over the household, and Shebna the secretary, and the senior priests, covered with sackcloth, to the prophet Isaiah the son of Amoz. ³They said to him, "Thus says Hezekiah, 'This day is a day of distress, of rebuke, and of disgrace; children have come to the point of birth, and there is no strength to bring them forth. ⁴It may be that the LORD your God will hear the words of the Rabshakeh, whom his master the king of Assyria has sent to mock the living God, and will rebuke the words that the LORD your God has heard; therefore lift up your prayer for the remnant that is left.'"

⁵When the servants of King Hezekiah came to Isaiah, ⁶Isaiah said to them, "Say to your master, 'Thus says the LORD: Do not be afraid because of the words that you have heard, with which the young men of the king of Assyria have reviled me. ⁷Behold, I will put a spirit in him, so that he shall hear a rumor and return to his own land, and I will make him fall by the sword in his own land.'"

⁸The Rabshakeh returned, and found the king of Assyria fighting against Libnah, for he had heard that the king had left Lachish. ⁹Now the king heard concerning Tirhakah king of Cush,¹ "He has set out to fight against you." And when he heard it, he sent messengers to Hezekiah, saying, ¹⁰"Thus shall you speak to Hezekiah king of Judah: 'Do not let your God in whom you trust deceive you by promising that Jerusalem will not be given into the hand of the king of Assyria. ¹¹Behold, you have heard what the kings of Assyria have done to all lands, devoting them to destruction. And shall you be delivered? ¹²Have the gods of the nations delivered them, the nations that my fathers destroyed, Gozan, Haran, Rezeph, and the people of Eden who were in Telassar? ¹³Where is the king of Hamath, the king of Arpad, the king of the city of Sepharvaim, the king of Hena, or the king of Ivvah?'"

¹⁴Hezekiah received the letter from the hand of the messengers, and read it; and Hezekiah went up to the house of the LORD, and spread it before the LORD. ¹⁵And Hezekiah prayed to the LORD: ¹⁶"O LORD of hosts, God of Israel, enthroned above the cherubim, you are the God, you alone, of all the kingdoms of the earth; you have made heaven and earth. ¹⁷Incline your ear, O LORD, and hear; open your eyes, O LORD, and see; and hear all the words of Sennacherib, which he has sent to mock the living God. ¹⁸Truly, O LORD, the kings of Assyria have laid waste all the nations and their lands, ¹⁹and have cast their gods into the fire. For they were no gods, but the work of men's hands, wood and stone. Therefore they were destroyed. ²⁰So now, O LORD our God, save us from his hand, that all the kingdoms of the earth may know that you alone are the LORD."

²¹Then Isaiah the son of Amoz sent to Hezekiah, saying, "Thus says the LORD, the God of Israel: Because you have prayed to me concerning Sennacherib king of Assyria, ²²this is the word that the LORD has spoken concerning him:

¹ Probably *Nubia*

"'She despises you, she scorns you—
  the virgin daughter of Zion;
she wags her head behind you—
  the daughter of Jerusalem.
23 "'Whom have you mocked and reviled?
  Against whom have you raised your
    voice
  and lifted your eyes to the heights?
  Against the Holy One of Israel!
24 By your servants you have mocked the
    Lord,
  and you have said, With my many
    chariots
I have gone up the heights of the
    mountains,
  to the far recesses of Lebanon,
  to cut down its tallest cedars,
    its choicest cypresses,
  to come to its remotest height,
    its most fruitful forest.
25   I dug wells
  and drank waters,
  to dry up with the sole of my foot
    all the streams of Egypt.

26 "'Have you not heard
  that I determined it long ago?
I planned from days of old
  what now I bring to pass,
that you should make fortified cities
  crash into heaps of ruins,
27   while their inhabitants, shorn of
    strength,
    are dismayed and confounded,
  and have become like plants of the field
    and like tender grass,
  like grass on the housetops,
    blighted[1] before it is grown.
28 "'I know your sitting down
    and your going out and coming in,
    and your raging against me.
29   Because you have raged against me
    and your complacency has come to
      my ears,
  I will put my hook in your nose
    and my bit in your mouth,
  and I will turn you back on the way
    by which you came.'

30 "And this shall be the sign for you: this year you shall eat what grows of itself, and in the second year what springs from that. Then in the third year sow and reap, and plant vineyards, and eat their fruit. 31And the surviving remnant of the house of Judah shall again take root downward and bear fruit upward. 32For out of Jerusalem shall go a remnant, and out of Mount Zion a band of survivors. The zeal of the LORD of hosts will do this.

33"Therefore thus says the LORD concerning the king of Assyria: He shall not come into this city or shoot an arrow there or come before it with a shield or cast up a siege mound against it. 34By the way that he came, by the same he shall return, and he shall not come into this city, declares the LORD. 35For I will defend this city to save it, for my own sake and for the sake of my servant David."

36And the angel of the LORD went out and struck down 185,000 in the camp of the Assyrians. And when people arose early in the morning, behold, these were all dead bodies. 37Then Sennacherib king of Assyria departed and returned home and lived at Nineveh. 38And as he was worshiping in the house of Nisroch his god, Adrammelech and Sharezer, his sons, struck him down with the sword. And after they escaped into the land of Ararat, Esarhaddon his son reigned in his place.

--------- *Revelation 7* ---------

After this I saw four angels standing at the four corners of the earth, holding back the four winds of the earth, that no wind might blow on earth or sea or against any tree. 2Then I saw another angel ascending from the rising of the sun, with the seal of the living God, and he called with a loud voice to the four angels who had been given power to harm earth and sea, 3saying, "Do not harm the earth or the sea or the trees, until we have sealed the servants[2] of our God on their foreheads." 4And I heard the number of the sealed, 144,000, sealed from every tribe of the sons of Israel:

5   12,000 from the tribe of Judah were
      sealed,
  12,000 from the tribe of Reuben,
  12,000 from the tribe of Gad,
6   12,000 from the tribe of Asher,
  12,000 from the tribe of Naphtali,
  12,000 from the tribe of Manasseh,
7   12,000 from the tribe of Simeon,

---

[1] Some Hebrew manuscripts and 2 Kings 19:26; most Hebrew manuscripts *like a field* [2] Greek *bondservants*

12,000 from the tribe of Levi,

12,000 from the tribe of Issachar,

8   12,000 from the tribe of Zebulun,

12,000 from the tribe of Joseph,

12,000 from the tribe of Benjamin were
    sealed.

[9] After this I looked, and behold, a great multitude that no one could number, from every nation, from all tribes and peoples and languages, standing before the throne and before the Lamb, clothed in white robes, with palm branches in their hands, [10] and crying out with a loud voice, "Salvation belongs to our God who sits on the throne, and to the Lamb!" [11] And all the angels were standing around the throne and around the elders and the four living creatures, and they fell on their faces before the throne and worshiped God, [12] saying, "Amen! Blessing and glory and wisdom and thanksgiving and honor and power and might be to our God forever and ever! Amen."

[13] Then one of the elders addressed me,

saying, "Who are these, clothed in white robes, and from where have they come?" [14] I said to him, "Sir, you know." And he said to me, "These are the ones coming out of the great tribulation. They have washed their robes and made them white in the blood of the Lamb.

15   "Therefore they are before the throne of
        God,
      and serve him day and night in his
        temple;
      and he who sits on the throne will
        shelter them with his presence.
16   They shall hunger no more, neither
        thirst anymore;
      the sun shall not strike them,
        nor any scorching heat.
17   For the Lamb in the midst of the throne
        will be their shepherd,
      and he will guide them to springs of
        living water,
      and God will wipe away every tear from
        their eyes."

JUNE 6

Deuteronomy 10

"At that time the Lord said to me, 'Cut for yourself two tablets of stone like the first, and come up to me on the mountain and make an ark of wood. [2] And I will write on the tablets the words that were on the first tablets that you broke, and you shall put them in the ark.' [3] So I made an ark of acacia wood, and cut two tablets of stone like the first, and went up the mountain with the two tablets in my hand. [4] And he wrote on the tablets, in the same writing as before, the Ten Commandments[1] that the Lord had spoken to you on the mountain out of the midst of the fire on the day of the assembly. And the Lord gave them to me. [5] Then I turned and came down from the mountain and put the tablets in the ark that I had made. And there they are, as the Lord commanded me."

[6] (The people of Israel journeyed from Beeroth Bene-jaakan[2] to Moserah. There Aaron

died, and there he was buried. And his son Eleazar ministered as priest in his place. [7] From there they journeyed to Gudgodah, and from Gudgodah to Jotbathah, a land with brooks of water. [8] At that time the Lord set apart the tribe of Levi to carry the ark of the covenant of the Lord to stand before the Lord to minister to him and to bless in his name, to this day. [9] Therefore Levi has no portion or inheritance with his brothers. The Lord is his inheritance, as the Lord your God said to him.)

[10] "I myself stayed on the mountain, as at the first time, forty days and forty nights, and the Lord listened to me that time also. The Lord was unwilling to destroy you. [11] And the Lord said to me, 'Arise, go on your journey at the head of the people, so that they may go in and possess the land, which I swore to their fathers to give them.'

---

[1] Hebrew *words* [2] Or *the wells of the Bene-jaakan*

¹²"And now, Israel, what does the Lord your God require of you, but to fear the Lord your God, to walk in all his ways, to love him, to serve the Lord your God with all your heart and with all your soul, ¹³and to keep the commandments and statutes of the Lord, which I am commanding you today for your good? ¹⁴Behold, to the Lord your God belong heaven and the heaven of heavens, the earth with all that is in it. ¹⁵Yet the Lord set his heart in love on your fathers and chose their offspring after them, you above all peoples, as you are this day. ¹⁶Circumcise therefore the foreskin of your heart, and be no longer stubborn. ¹⁷For the Lord your God is God of gods and Lord of lords, the great, the mighty, and the awesome God, who is not partial and takes no bribe. ¹⁸He executes justice for the fatherless and the widow, and loves the sojourner, giving him food and clothing. ¹⁹Love the sojourner, therefore, for you were sojourners in the land of Egypt. ²⁰You shall fear the Lord your God. You shall serve him and hold fast to him, and by his name you shall swear. ²¹He is your praise. He is your God, who has done for you these great and terrifying things that your eyes have seen. ²²Your fathers went down to Egypt seventy persons, and now the Lord your God has made you as numerous as the stars of heaven.

Psalm 94

O Lord, God of vengeance,
   O God of vengeance, shine forth!
² Rise up, O judge of the earth;
   repay to the proud what they deserve!
³ O Lord, how long shall the wicked,
   how long shall the wicked exult?
⁴ They pour out their arrogant words;
   all the evildoers boast.
⁵ They crush your people, O Lord,
   and afflict your heritage.
⁶ They kill the widow and the sojourner,
   and murder the fatherless;
⁷ and they say, "The Lord does not see;
   the God of Jacob does not perceive."
⁸ Understand, O dullest of the people!
   Fools, when will you be wise?
⁹ He who planted the ear, does he not
   hear?
   He who formed the eye, does he not see?

¹⁰ He who disciplines the nations, does he
   not rebuke?
   He who teaches man knowledge—
¹¹ the Lord—knows the thoughts of
   man,
   that they are but a breath.¹

¹² Blessed is the man whom you discipline,
   O Lord,
   and whom you teach out of your law,
¹³ to give him rest from days of trouble,
   until a pit is dug for the wicked.
¹⁴ For the Lord will not forsake his people;
   he will not abandon his heritage;
¹⁵ for justice will return to the righteous,
   and all the upright in heart will follow
   it.

¹⁶ Who rises up for me against the wicked?
   Who stands up for me against
   evildoers?
¹⁷ If the Lord had not been my help,
   my soul would soon have lived in the
   land of silence.
¹⁸ When I thought, "My foot slips,"
   your steadfast love, O Lord, held me
   up.
¹⁹ When the cares of my heart are many,
   your consolations cheer my soul.
²⁰ Can wicked rulers be allied with you,
   those who frame injustice by statute?
²¹ They band together against the life of
   the righteous
   and condemn the innocent to death.²
²² But the Lord has become my
   stronghold,
   and my God the rock of my refuge.
²³ He will bring back on them their
   iniquity
   and wipe them out for their
   wickedness;
   the Lord our God will wipe them out.

Isaiah 38

In those days Hezekiah became sick and was at the point of death. And Isaiah the prophet the son of Amoz came to him, and said to him, "Thus says the Lord: Set your house in order, for you shall die, you shall not recover."³ ²Then Hezekiah turned his face to the wall and prayed to the Lord, ³and said, "Please, O Lord, remember how I have walked before you in

¹ Septuagint *they are futile* ² Hebrew *condemn innocent blood* ³ Or *live*; also verses 9, 21

faithfulness and with a whole heart, and have done what is good in your sight." And Hezekiah wept bitterly.

⁴Then the word of the LORD came to Isaiah: ⁵"Go and say to Hezekiah, Thus says the LORD, the God of David your father: I have heard your prayer; I have seen your tears. Behold, I will add fifteen years to your life.¹ ⁶I will deliver you and this city out of the hand of the king of Assyria, and will defend this city.

⁷"This shall be the sign to you from the LORD, that the LORD will do this thing that he has promised: ⁸Behold, I will make the shadow cast by the declining sun on the dial of Ahaz turn back ten steps." So the sun turned back on the dial the ten steps by which it had declined.²

⁹A writing of Hezekiah king of Judah, after he had been sick and had recovered from his sickness:

10   I said, In the middle³ of my days
        I must depart;
      I am consigned to the gates of Sheol
        for the rest of my years.
11   I said, I shall not see the LORD,
        the LORD in the land of the living;
      I shall look on man no more
        among the inhabitants of the world.
12   My dwelling is plucked up and removed
        from me
        like a shepherd's tent;
      like a weaver I have rolled up my life;
        he cuts me off from the loom;
      from day to night you bring me to an
        end;
13   I calmed myself⁴ until morning;
      like a lion he breaks all my bones;
        from day to night you bring me to an
        end.
14   Like a swallow or a crane I chirp;
        I moan like a dove.
      My eyes are weary with looking
        upward.
      O Lord, I am oppressed; be my pledge
        of safety!
15   What shall I say? For he has spoken to
        me,
        and he himself has done it.
      I walk slowly all my years
        because of the bitterness of my soul.

16   O Lord, by these things men live,
        and in all these is the life of my spirit.
      Oh restore me to health and make me
        live!
17   Behold, it was for my welfare
        that I had great bitterness;
      but in love you have delivered my life
        from the pit of destruction,
      for you have cast all my sins
        behind your back.
18   For Sheol does not thank you;
        death does not praise you;
      those who go down to the pit do not
        hope
        for your faithfulness.
19   The living, the living, he thanks you,
        as I do this day;
      the father makes known to the children
        your faithfulness.

20   The LORD will save me,
        and we will play my music on stringed
        instruments
      all the days of our lives,
        at the house of the LORD.

²¹Now Isaiah had said, "Let them take a cake of figs and apply it to the boil, that he may recover." ²²Hezekiah also had said, "What is the sign that I shall go up to the house of the LORD?"

──────── *Revelation 8* ────────

When the Lamb opened the seventh seal, there was silence in heaven for about half an hour. ²Then I saw the seven angels who stand before God, and seven trumpets were given to them. ³And another angel came and stood at the altar with a golden censer, and he was given much incense to offer with the prayers of all the saints on the golden altar before the throne, ⁴and the smoke of the incense, with the prayers of the saints, rose before God from the hand of the angel. ⁵Then the angel took the censer and filled it with fire from the altar and threw it on the earth, and there were peals of thunder, rumblings,⁵ flashes of lightning, and an earthquake.

⁶Now the seven angels who had the seven trumpets prepared to blow them.

⁷The first angel blew his trumpet, and there followed hail and fire, mixed with blood, and

---

¹ Hebrew *to your days* ² The meaning of the Hebrew verse is uncertain ³ Or *In the quiet* ⁴ Or (with Targum) *I cried for help* ⁵ Or *voices, or sounds*

these were thrown upon the earth. And a third of the earth was burned up, and a third of the trees were burned up, and all green grass was burned up.

⁸The second angel blew his trumpet, and something like a great mountain, burning with fire, was thrown into the sea, and a third of the sea became blood. ⁹A third of the living creatures in the sea died, and a third of the ships were destroyed.

¹⁰The third angel blew his trumpet, and a great star fell from heaven, blazing like a torch, and it fell on a third of the rivers and on the springs of water. ¹¹The name of the star

is Wormwood.¹ A third of the waters became wormwood, and many people died from the water, because it had been made bitter.

¹²The fourth angel blew his trumpet, and a third of the sun was struck, and a third of the moon, and a third of the stars, so that a third of their light might be darkened, and a third of the day might be kept from shining, and likewise a third of the night.

¹³Then I looked, and I heard an eagle crying with a loud voice as it flew directly overhead, "Woe, woe, woe to those who dwell on the earth, at the blasts of the other trumpets that the three angels are about to blow!"

JUNE 7

Deuteronomy 11

"You shall therefore love the LORD your God and keep his charge, his statutes, his rules, and his commandments always. ²And consider today (since I am not speaking to your children who have not known or seen it), consider the discipline² of the LORD your God, his greatness, his mighty hand and his outstretched arm, ³his signs and his deeds that he did in Egypt to Pharaoh the king of Egypt and to all his land, ⁴and what he did to the army of Egypt, to their horses and to their chariots, how he made the water of the Red Sea flow over them as they pursued after you, and how the LORD has destroyed them to this day, ⁵and what he did to you in the wilderness, until you came to this place, ⁶and what he did to Dathan and Abiram the sons of Eliab, son of Reuben, how the earth opened its mouth and swallowed them up, with their households, their tents, and every living thing that followed them, in the midst of all Israel. ⁷For your eyes have seen all the great work of the LORD that he did.

⁸"You shall therefore keep the whole commandment that I command you today, that you may be strong, and go in and take possession of the land that you are going over to possess, ⁹and that you may live long in the land that

the LORD swore to your fathers to give to them and to their offspring, a land flowing with milk and honey. ¹⁰For the land that you are entering to take possession of it is not like the land of Egypt, from which you have come, where you sowed your seed and irrigated it,³ like a garden of vegetables. ¹¹But the land that you are going over to possess is a land of hills and valleys, which drinks water by the rain from heaven, ¹²a land that the LORD your God cares for. The eyes of the LORD your God are always upon it, from the beginning of the year to the end of the year.

¹³"And if you will indeed obey my commandments that I command you today, to love the LORD your God, and to serve him with all your heart and with all your soul, ¹⁴he⁴ will give the rain for your land in its season, the early rain and the later rain, that you may gather in your grain and your wine and your oil. ¹⁵And he will give grass in your fields for your livestock, and you shall eat and be full. ¹⁶Take care lest your heart be deceived, and you turn aside and serve other gods and worship them; ¹⁷then the anger of the LORD will be kindled against you, and he will shut up the heavens, so that there will be no rain, and the land will yield no fruit, and

¹ Wormwood is the name of a plant and of the bitter-tasting extract derived from it ² Or instruction ³ Hebrew watered it with your feet ⁴ Samaritan, Septuagint, Vulgate; Hebrew I; also verse 15

you will perish quickly off the good land that the LORD is giving you.

18 "You shall therefore lay up these words of mine in your heart and in your soul, and you shall bind them as a sign on your hand, and they shall be as frontlets between your eyes. 19 You shall teach them to your children, talking of them when you are sitting in your house, and when you are walking by the way, and when you lie down, and when you rise. 20 You shall write them on the doorposts of your house and on your gates, 21 that your days and the days of your children may be multiplied in the land that the LORD swore to your fathers to give them, as long as the heavens are above the earth. 22 For if you will be careful to do all this commandment that I command you to do, loving the LORD your God, walking in all his ways, and holding fast to him, 23 then the LORD will drive out all these nations before you, and you will dispossess nations greater and mightier than you. 24 Every place on which the sole of your foot treads shall be yours. Your territory shall be from the wilderness to[1] the Lebanon and from the River, the river Euphrates, to the western sea. 25 No one shall be able to stand against you. The LORD your God will lay the fear of you and the dread of you on all the land that you shall tread, as he promised you.

26 "See, I am setting before you today a blessing and a curse: 27 the blessing, if you obey the commandments of the LORD your God, which I command you today, 28 and the curse, if you do not obey the commandments of the LORD your God, but turn aside from the way that I am commanding you today, to go after other gods that you have not known. 29 And when the LORD your God brings you into the land that you are entering to take possession of it, you shall set the blessing on Mount Gerizim and the curse on Mount Ebal. 30 Are they not beyond the Jordan, west of the road, toward the going down of the sun, in the land of the Canaanites who live in the Arabah, opposite Gilgal, beside the oak[2] of Moreh? 31 For you are to cross over the Jordan to go in to take possession of the land that the LORD your God is giving you. And when you possess it and live in it, 32 you shall be careful to do all the statutes and the rules that I am setting before you today.

1 Hebrew *and* 2 Septuagint, Syriac; see Genesis 12:6. Hebrew *oaks*, or *terebinths*

Psalm 95–96

Oh come, let us sing to the LORD;
   let us make a joyful noise to the rock of
      our salvation!
2 Let us come into his presence with
      thanksgiving;
   let us make a joyful noise to him with
      songs of praise!
3 For the LORD is a great God,
   and a great King above all gods.
4 In his hand are the depths of the earth;
   the heights of the mountains are his
      also.
5 The sea is his, for he made it,
   and his hands formed the dry land.

6 Oh come, let us worship and bow
      down;
   let us kneel before the LORD, our
      Maker!
7 For he is our God,
   and we are the people of his pasture,
   and the sheep of his hand.
Today, if you hear his voice,
8   do not harden your hearts, as at
      Meribah,
   as on the day at Massah in the
      wilderness,
9 when your fathers put me to the test
   and put me to the proof, though they
      had seen my work.
10 For forty years I loathed that generation
   and said, "They are a people who go
      astray in their heart,
   and they have not known my ways."
11 Therefore I swore in my wrath,
   "They shall not enter my rest."

Oh sing to the LORD a new song;
   sing to the LORD, all the earth!
2 Sing to the LORD, bless his name;
   tell of his salvation from day to day.
3 Declare his glory among the nations,
   his marvelous works among all the
      peoples!
4 For great is the LORD, and greatly to be
      praised;
   he is to be feared above all gods.
5 For all the gods of the peoples are
      worthless idols,
   but the LORD made the heavens.

⁶ Splendor and majesty are before him;
  strength and beauty are in his
  sanctuary.

⁷ Ascribe to the LORD, O families of the
  peoples,
  ascribe to the LORD glory and
  strength!
⁸ Ascribe to the LORD the glory due his
  name;
  bring an offering, and come into his
  courts!
⁹ Worship the LORD in the splendor of
  holiness;¹
  tremble before him, all the earth!

¹⁰ Say among the nations, "The LORD
  reigns!
  Yes, the world is established; it shall
  never be moved;
  he will judge the peoples with equity."
¹¹ Let the heavens be glad, and let the
  earth rejoice;
  let the sea roar, and all that fills it;
¹²   let the field exult, and everything in it!
  Then shall all the trees of the forest sing
  for joy
¹³   before the LORD, for he comes,
  for he comes to judge the earth.
  He will judge the world in
  righteousness,
  and the peoples in his faithfulness.

Isaiah 39

At that time Merodach-baladan the son of Baladan, king of Babylon, sent envoys with letters and a present to Hezekiah, for he heard that he had been sick and had recovered. ²And Hezekiah welcomed them gladly. And he showed them his treasure house, the silver, the gold, the spices, the precious oil, his whole armory, all that was found in his storehouses. There was nothing in his house or in all his realm that Hezekiah did not show them. ³Then Isaiah the prophet came to King Hezekiah, and said to him, "What did these men say? And from where did they come to you?" Hezekiah said, "They have come to me from a far country, from Babylon." ⁴He said, "What have they seen in your house?" Hezekiah answered, "They have seen all that is in my house. There is nothing in my storehouses that I did not show them."

⁵Then Isaiah said to Hezekiah, "Hear the word of the LORD of hosts: ⁶Behold, the days are coming, when all that is in your house, and that which your fathers have stored up till this day, shall be carried to Babylon. Nothing shall be left, says the LORD. ⁷And some of your own sons, who will come from you, whom you will father, shall be taken away, and they shall be eunuchs in the palace of the king of Babylon." ⁸Then Hezekiah said to Isaiah, "The word of the LORD that you have spoken is good." For he thought, "There will be peace and security in my days."

Revelation 9

And the fifth angel blew his trumpet, and I saw a star fallen from heaven to earth, and he was given the key to the shaft of the bottomless pit.² ²He opened the shaft of the bottomless pit, and from the shaft rose smoke like the smoke of a great furnace, and the sun and the air were darkened with the smoke from the shaft. ³Then from the smoke came locusts on the earth, and they were given power like the power of scorpions of the earth. ⁴They were told not to harm the grass of the earth or any green plant or any tree, but only those people who do not have the seal of God on their foreheads. ⁵They were allowed to torment them for five months, but not to kill them, and their torment was like the torment of a scorpion when it stings someone. ⁶And in those days people will seek death and will not find it. They will long to die, but death will flee from them.

⁷In appearance the locusts were like horses prepared for battle: on their heads were what looked like crowns of gold; their faces were like human faces, ⁸their hair like women's hair, and their teeth like lions' teeth; ⁹they had breastplates like breastplates of iron, and the noise of their wings was like the noise of many chariots with horses rushing into battle. ¹⁰They have tails and stings like scorpions, and their power to hurt people for five months is in their tails. ¹¹They have as king over them the angel of the bottomless pit. His name in Hebrew is Abaddon, and in Greek he is called Apollyon.³

¹²The first woe has passed; behold, two woes are still to come.

---

¹ Or *in holy attire* ² Greek *the abyss*; also verses 2, 11 ³ *Abaddon* means *destruction*; *Apollyon* means *destroyer*

¹³Then the sixth angel blew his trumpet, and I heard a voice from the four horns of the golden altar before God, ¹⁴saying to the sixth angel who had the trumpet, "Release the four angels who are bound at the great river Euphrates." ¹⁵So the four angels, who had been prepared for the hour, the day, the month, and the year, were released to kill a third of mankind. ¹⁶The number of mounted troops was twice ten thousand times ten thousand; I heard their number. ¹⁷And this is how I saw the horses in my vision and those who rode them: they wore breastplates the color of fire and of sapphire[1] and of sulfur, and the heads of the horses were like lions' heads, and fire and smoke and sulfur came out of their mouths. ¹⁸By these three plagues a third of mankind was killed, by the fire and smoke and sulfur coming out of their mouths. ¹⁹For the power of the horses is in their mouths and in their tails, for their tails are like serpents with heads, and by means of them they wound.

²⁰The rest of mankind, who were not killed by these plagues, did not repent of the works of their hands nor give up worshiping demons and idols of gold and silver and bronze and stone and wood, which cannot see or hear or walk, ²¹nor did they repent of their murders or their sorceries or their sexual immorality or their thefts.

JUNE 8

Deuteronomy 12

"These are the statutes and rules that you shall be careful to do in the land that the LORD, the God of your fathers, has given you to possess, all the days that you live on the earth. ²You shall surely destroy all the places where the nations whom you shall dispossess served their gods, on the high mountains and on the hills and under every green tree. ³You shall tear down their altars and dash in pieces their pillars and burn their Asherim with fire. You shall chop down the carved images of their gods and destroy their name out of that place. ⁴You shall not worship the LORD your God in that way. ⁵But you shall seek the place that the LORD your God will choose out of all your tribes to put his name and make his habitation[2] there. There you shall go, ⁶and there you shall bring your burnt offerings and your sacrifices, your tithes and the contribution that you present, your vow offerings, your freewill offerings, and the firstborn of your herd and of your flock. ⁷And there you shall eat before the LORD your God, and you shall rejoice, you and your households, in all that you undertake, in which the LORD your God has blessed you.

⁸"You shall not do according to all that we are doing here today, everyone doing whatever is right in his own eyes, ⁹for you have not as yet come to the rest and to the inheritance that the LORD your God is giving you. ¹⁰But when you go over the Jordan and live in the land that the LORD your God is giving you to inherit, and when he gives you rest from all your enemies around, so that you live in safety, ¹¹then to the place that the LORD your God will choose, to make his name dwell there, there you shall bring all that I command you: your burnt offerings and your sacrifices, your tithes and the contribution that you present, and all your finest vow offerings that you vow to the LORD. ¹²And you shall rejoice before the LORD your God, you and your sons and your daughters, your male servants and your female servants, and the Levite that is within your towns, since he has no portion or inheritance with you. ¹³Take care that you do not offer your burnt offerings at any place that you see, ¹⁴but at the place that the LORD will choose in one of your tribes, there you shall offer your burnt offerings, and there you shall do all that I am commanding you.

¹⁵"However, you may slaughter and eat

---

[1] Greek hyacinth [2] Or name as its habitation

meat within any of your towns, as much as you desire, according to the blessing of the Lord your God that he has given you. The unclean and the clean may eat of it, as of the gazelle and as of the deer. ¹⁶Only you shall not eat the blood; you shall pour it out on the earth like water. ¹⁷You may not eat within your towns the tithe of your grain or of your wine or of your oil, or the firstborn of your herd or of your flock, or any of your vow offerings that you vow, or your freewill offerings or the contribution that you present, ¹⁸but you shall eat them before the Lord your God in the place that the Lord your God will choose, you and your son and your daughter, your male servant and your female servant, and the Levite who is within your towns. And you shall rejoice before the Lord your God in all that you undertake. ¹⁹Take care that you do not neglect the Levite as long as you live in your land.

²⁰"When the Lord your God enlarges your territory, as he has promised you, and you say, 'I will eat meat,' because you crave meat, you may eat meat whenever you desire. ²¹If the place that the Lord your God will choose to put his name there is too far from you, then you may kill any of your herd or your flock, which the Lord has given you, as I have commanded you, and you may eat within your towns whenever you desire. ²²Just as the gazelle or the deer is eaten, so you may eat of it. The unclean and the clean alike may eat of it. ²³Only be sure that you do not eat the blood, for the blood is the life, and you shall not eat the life with the flesh. ²⁴You shall not eat it; you shall pour it out on the earth like water. ²⁵You shall not eat it, that all may go well with you and with your children after you, when you do what is right in the sight of the Lord. ²⁶But the holy things that are due from you, and your vow offerings, you shall take, and you shall go to the place that the Lord will choose, ²⁷and offer your burnt offerings, the flesh and the blood, on the altar of the Lord your God. The blood of your sacrifices shall be poured out on the altar of the Lord your God, but the flesh you may eat. ²⁸Be careful to obey all these words that I command you, that it may go well with you and with your children after you forever, when you do what is good and right in the sight of the Lord your God.

²⁹"When the Lord your God cuts off before you the nations whom you go in to dispossess,

and you dispossess them and dwell in their land, ³⁰take care that you be not ensnared to follow them, after they have been destroyed before you, and that you do not inquire about their gods, saying, 'How did these nations serve their gods?—that I also may do the same.' ³¹You shall not worship the Lord your God in that way, for every abominable thing that the Lord hates they have done for their gods, for they even burn their sons and their daughters in the fire to their gods.

³²¹ "Everything that I command you, you shall be careful to do. You shall not add to it or take from it.

───────── *Psalm 97–98* ─────────

The Lord reigns, let the earth rejoice;
 let the many coastlands be glad!
2 Clouds and thick darkness are all
   around him;
   righteousness and justice are the
   foundation of his throne.
3 Fire goes before him
   and burns up his adversaries all
   around.
4 His lightnings light up the world;
   the earth sees and trembles.
5 The mountains melt like wax before the
   Lord,
   before the Lord of all the earth.

6 The heavens proclaim his righteousness,
   and all the peoples see his glory.
7 All worshipers of images are put to
   shame,
   who make their boast in worthless
   idols;
   worship him, all you gods!

8 Zion hears and is glad,
   and the daughters of Judah rejoice,
   because of your judgments, O Lord.
9 For you, O Lord, are most high over all
   the earth;
   you are exalted far above all gods.

10 O you who love the Lord, hate evil!
   He preserves the lives of his saints;
   he delivers them from the hand of the
   wicked.
11 Light is sown² for the righteous,
   and joy for the upright in heart.

¹ Ch 13:1 in Hebrew ² Most Hebrew manuscripts; one Hebrew manuscript, Septuagint, Syriac, Jerome *Light dawns*

12 Rejoice in the LORD, O you righteous,
    and give thanks to his holy name!

A PSALM.

Oh sing to the LORD a new song,
    for he has done marvelous things!
His right hand and his holy arm
    have worked salvation for him.
2   The LORD has made known his salvation;
    he has revealed his righteousness in
        the sight of the nations.
3   He has remembered his steadfast love
        and faithfulness
    to the house of Israel.
All the ends of the earth have seen
    the salvation of our God.

4   Make a joyful noise to the LORD, all the
        earth;
    break forth into joyous song and sing
        praises!
5   Sing praises to the LORD with the lyre,
    with the lyre and the sound of
        melody!
6   With trumpets and the sound of the
        horn
    make a joyful noise before the King,
        the LORD!

7   Let the sea roar, and all that fills it;
    the world and those who dwell in it!
8   Let the rivers clap their hands;
    let the hills sing for joy together
9   before the LORD, for he comes
        to judge the earth.
He will judge the world with
        righteousness,
    and the peoples with equity.

Isaiah 40

Comfort, comfort my people, says your
    God.
2   Speak tenderly to Jerusalem,
        and cry to her
    that her warfare[1] is ended,
        that her iniquity is pardoned,
    that she has received from the LORD's
        hand
        double for all her sins.

3   A voice cries:[2]

"In the wilderness prepare the way of the
    LORD;
    make straight in the desert a highway
        for our God.
4   Every valley shall be lifted up,
    and every mountain and hill be made
        low;
    the uneven ground shall become level,
        and the rough places a plain.
5   And the glory of the LORD shall be
        revealed,
    and all flesh shall see it together,
        for the mouth of the LORD has
        spoken."

6   A voice says, "Cry!"
    And I said,[3] "What shall I cry?"
All flesh is grass,
    and all its beauty[4] is like the flower of
        the field.
7   The grass withers, the flower fades
    when the breath of the LORD blows on
        it;
    surely the people are grass.
8   The grass withers, the flower fades,
    but the word of our God will stand
        forever.

9   Go on up to a high mountain,
        O Zion, herald of good news;[5]
    lift up your voice with strength,
        O Jerusalem, herald of good news;[6]
    lift it up, fear not;
    say to the cities of Judah,
        "Behold your God!"
10 Behold, the Lord GOD comes with might,
        and his arm rules for him;
    behold, his reward is with him,
        and his recompense before him.
11 He will tend his flock like a shepherd;
        he will gather the lambs in his arms;
    he will carry them in his bosom,
        and gently lead those that are with
        young.
12 Who has measured the waters in the
        hollow of his hand
    and marked off the heavens with a
        span,
    enclosed the dust of the earth in a
        measure
    and weighed the mountains in scales
        and the hills in a balance?

[1] Or hardship [2] Or A voice of one crying [3] Revocalization based on Dead Sea Scroll, Septuagint, Vulgate; Masoretic Text And someone says [4] Or all its constancy [5] Or O herald of good news to Zion [6] Or O herald of good news to Jerusalem

¹³ Who has measured¹ the Spirit of the
LORD,
  or what man shows him his counsel?
¹⁴ Whom did he consult,
  and who made him understand?
Who taught him the path of justice,
  and taught him knowledge,
  and showed him the way of
    understanding?
¹⁵ Behold, the nations are like a drop from
    a bucket,
  and are accounted as the dust on the
    scales;
  behold, he takes up the coastlands like
    fine dust.
¹⁶ Lebanon would not suffice for fuel,
  nor are its beasts enough for a burnt
    offering.
¹⁷ All the nations are as nothing before
    him,
  they are accounted by him as less than
    nothing and emptiness.

¹⁸ To whom then will you liken God,
  or what likeness compare with him?
¹⁹ An idol! A craftsman casts it,
  and a goldsmith overlays it with gold
  and casts for it silver chains.
²⁰ He who is too impoverished for an
    offering
  chooses wood² that will not rot;
  he seeks out a skillful craftsman
  to set up an idol that will not move.

²¹ Do you not know? Do you not hear?
  Has it not been told you from the
    beginning?
  Have you not understood from the
    foundations of the earth?
²² It is he who sits above the circle of the
    earth,
  and its inhabitants are like
    grasshoppers;
  who stretches out the heavens like a
    curtain,
  and spreads them like a tent to dwell in;
²³ who brings princes to nothing,
  and makes the rulers of the earth as
    emptiness.

²⁴ Scarcely are they planted, scarcely sown,
  scarcely has their stem taken root in
    the earth,

when he blows on them, and they
  wither,
  and the tempest carries them off like
    stubble.

²⁵ To whom then will you compare me,
  that I should be like him? says the
    Holy One.
²⁶ Lift up your eyes on high and see:
  who created these?
He who brings out their host by number,
  calling them all by name,
by the greatness of his might,
  and because he is strong in power
  not one is missing.

²⁷ Why do you say, O Jacob,
  and speak, O Israel,
"My way is hidden from the LORD,
  and my right is disregarded by my
    God"?
²⁸ Have you not known? Have you not
    heard?
The LORD is the everlasting God,
  the Creator of the ends of the earth.
He does not faint or grow weary;
  his understanding is unsearchable.
²⁹ He gives power to the faint,
  and to him who has no might he
    increases strength.
³⁰ Even youths shall faint and be weary,
  and young men shall fall exhausted;
³¹ but they who wait for the LORD shall
    renew their strength;
  they shall mount up with wings like
    eagles;
  they shall run and not be weary;
  they shall walk and not faint.

Revelation 10

Then I saw another mighty angel coming
down from heaven, wrapped in a cloud,
with a rainbow over his head, and his face was
like the sun, and his legs like pillars of fire. ²He
had a little scroll open in his hand. And he set
his right foot on the sea, and his left foot on
the land, ³and called out with a loud voice, like
a lion roaring. When he called out, the seven
thunders sounded. ⁴And when the seven
thunders had sounded, I was about to write,
but I heard a voice from heaven saying, "Seal
up what the seven thunders have said, and do

¹ Or has directed ² Or He chooses valuable wood

not write it down." [5]And the angel whom I saw standing on the sea and on the land raised his right hand to heaven [6]and swore by him who lives forever and ever, who created heaven and what is in it, the earth and what is in it, and the sea and what is in it, that there would be no more delay, [7]but that in the days of the trumpet call to be sounded by the seventh angel, the mystery of God would be fulfilled, just as he announced to his servants[1] the prophets.

[8]Then the voice that I had heard from heaven spoke to me again, saying, "Go, take the scroll that is open in the hand of the angel who is standing on the sea and on the land." [9]So I went to the angel and told him to give me the little scroll. And he said to me, "Take and eat it; it will make your stomach bitter, but in your mouth it will be sweet as honey." [10]And I took the little scroll from the hand of the angel and ate it. It was sweet as honey in my mouth, but when I had eaten it my stomach was made bitter. [11]And I was told, "You must again prophesy about many peoples and nations and languages and kings."

JUNE 9

Deuteronomy 13–14

"If a prophet or a dreamer of dreams arises among you and gives you a sign or a wonder, [2]and the sign or wonder that he tells you comes to pass, and if he says, 'Let us go after other gods,' which you have not known, 'and let us serve them,' [3]you shall not listen to the words of that prophet or that dreamer of dreams. For the LORD your God is testing you, to know whether you love the LORD your God with all your heart and with all your soul. [4]You shall walk after the LORD your God and fear him and keep his commandments and obey his voice, and you shall serve him and hold fast to him. [5]But that prophet or that dreamer of dreams shall be put to death, because he has taught rebellion against the LORD your God, who brought you out of the land of Egypt and redeemed you out of the house of slavery, to make you leave the way in which the LORD your God commanded you to walk. So you shall purge the evil[2] from your midst.

[6]"If your brother, the son of your mother, or your son or your daughter or the wife you embrace[3] or your friend who is as your own soul entices you secretly, saying, 'Let us go and serve other gods,' which neither you nor your fathers have known, [7]some of the gods of the peoples who are around you, whether near you or far off from you, from the one end of the earth to the other, [8]you shall not yield to him or listen to him, nor shall your eye pity him, nor shall you spare him, nor shall you conceal him. [9]But you shall kill him. Your hand shall be first against him to put him to death, and afterward the hand of all the people. [10]You shall stone him to death with stones, because he sought to draw you away from the LORD your God, who brought you out of the land of Egypt, out of the house of slavery. [11]And all Israel shall hear and fear and never again do any such wickedness as this among you.

[12]"If you hear in one of your cities, which the LORD your God is giving you to dwell there, [13]that certain worthless fellows have gone out among you and have drawn away the inhabitants of their city, saying, 'Let us go and serve other gods,' which you have not known, [14]then you shall inquire and make search and ask diligently. And behold, if it be true and certain that such an abomination has been done among you, [15]you shall surely put the inhabitants of that city to the sword, devoting it to destruction,[4] all who are in it and its cattle, with the edge of the sword. [16]You shall gather all its spoil into the midst of its open square and burn the city and all its spoil with fire, as a whole burnt offering to the LORD your God. It shall be a heap forever. It shall not be built

[1] Greek bondservants [2] Or evil person [3] Hebrew the wife of your bosom [4] That is, setting apart (devoting) as an offering to the Lord (for destruction)

again. **17**None of the devoted things shall stick to your hand, that the LORD may turn from the fierceness of his anger and show you mercy and have compassion on you and multiply you, as he swore to your fathers, **18**if you obey the voice of the LORD your God, keeping all his commandments that I am commanding you today, and doing what is right in the sight of the LORD your God.

14:1"You are the sons of the LORD your God. You shall not cut yourselves or make any baldness on your foreheads for the dead. **2**For you are a people holy to the LORD your God, and the LORD has chosen you to be a people for his treasured possession, out of all the peoples who are on the face of the earth.

3"You shall not eat any abomination. **4**These are the animals you may eat: the ox, the sheep, the goat, **5**the deer, the gazelle, the roebuck, the wild goat, the ibex,[1] the antelope, and the mountain sheep. **6**Every animal that parts the hoof and has the hoof cloven in two and chews the cud, among the animals, you may eat. **7**Yet of those that chew the cud or have the hoof cloven you shall not eat these: the camel, the hare, and the rock badger, because they chew the cud but do not part the hoof, are unclean for you. **8**And the pig, because it parts the hoof but does not chew the cud, is unclean for you. Their flesh you shall not eat, and their carcasses you shall not touch.

9"Of all that are in the waters you may eat these: whatever has fins and scales you may eat. **10**And whatever does not have fins and scales you shall not eat; it is unclean for you.

11"You may eat all clean birds. **12**But these are the ones that you shall not eat: the eagle,[2] the bearded vulture, the black vulture, **13**the kite, the falcon of any kind; **14**every raven of any kind; **15**the ostrich, the nighthawk, the sea gull, the hawk of any kind; **16**the little owl and the short-eared owl, the barn owl **17**and the tawny owl, the carrion vulture and the cormorant, **18**the stork, the heron of any kind; the hoopoe and the bat. **19**And all winged insects are unclean for you; they shall not be eaten. **20**All clean winged things you may eat.

21"You shall not eat anything that has died naturally. You may give it to the sojourner who is within your towns, that he may eat it, or you may sell it to a foreigner. For you are a people holy to the LORD your God.

"You shall not boil a young goat in its mother's milk.

22"You shall tithe all the yield of your seed that comes from the field year by year. **23**And before the LORD your God, in the place that he will choose, to make his name dwell there, you shall eat the tithe of your grain, of your wine, and of your oil, and the firstborn of your herd and flock, that you may learn to fear the LORD your God always. **24**And if the way is too long for you, so that you are not able to carry the tithe, when the LORD your God blesses you, because the place is too far from you, which the LORD your God chooses, to set his name there, **25**then you shall turn it into money and bind up the money in your hand and go to the place that the LORD your God chooses **26**and spend the money for whatever you desire—oxen or sheep or wine or strong drink, whatever your appetite craves. And you shall eat there before the LORD your God and rejoice, you and your household. **27**And you shall not neglect the Levite who is within your towns, for he has no portion or inheritance with you.

28"At the end of every three years you shall bring out all the tithe of your produce in the same year and lay it up within your towns. **29**And the Levite, because he has no portion or inheritance with you, and the sojourner, the fatherless, and the widow, who are within your towns, shall come and eat and be filled, that the LORD your God may bless you in all the work of your hands that you do.

Psalm 99–101

The LORD reigns; let the peoples tremble!
  He sits enthroned upon the cherubim; let
    the earth quake!
2 The LORD is great in Zion;
    he is exalted over all the peoples.
3 Let them praise your great and awesome
      name!
    Holy is he!
4 The King in his might loves justice.[3]
    You have established equity;
  you have executed justice
    and righteousness in Jacob.
5 Exalt the LORD our God;
    worship at his footstool!
    Holy is he!

[1] Or addax [2] The identity of many of these birds is uncertain [3] Or The might of the King loves justice

6 Moses and Aaron were among his
    priests,
   Samuel also was among those who
    called upon his name.
   They called to the LORD, and he
    answered them.
7 In the pillar of the cloud he spoke to
    them;
   they kept his testimonies
    and the statute that he gave them.

8 O LORD our God, you answered them;
   you were a forgiving God to them,
    but an avenger of their wrongdoings.
9 Exalt the LORD our God,
   and worship at his holy mountain;
    for the LORD our God is holy!

A PSALM FOR GIVING THANKS.

M ake a joyful noise to the LORD, all the
    earth!
2   Serve the LORD with gladness!
    Come into his presence with singing!

3 Know that the LORD, he is God!
   It is he who made us, and we are his;[1]
   we are his people, and the sheep of his
    pasture.

4 Enter his gates with thanksgiving,
   and his courts with praise!
   Give thanks to him; bless his name!

5 For the LORD is good;
   his steadfast love endures forever,
   and his faithfulness to all generations.

A PSALM OF DAVID.

I will sing of steadfast love and justice;
   to you, O LORD, I will make music.
2   I will ponder the way that is blameless.
    Oh when will you come to me?
    I will walk with integrity of heart
     within my house;
3   I will not set before my eyes
     anything that is worthless.
    I hate the work of those who fall away;
     it shall not cling to me.
4   A perverse heart shall be far from me;
     I will know nothing of evil.

5   Whoever slanders his neighbor secretly
     I will destroy.

   Whoever has a haughty look and an
     arrogant heart
    I will not endure.
6   I will look with favor on the faithful in
     the land,
    that they may dwell with me;
   he who walks in the way that is
     blameless
    shall minister to me.
7   No one who practices deceit
     shall dwell in my house;
   no one who utters lies
     shall continue before my eyes.
8   Morning by morning I will destroy
     all the wicked in the land,
   cutting off all the evildoers
    from the city of the LORD.

─────── *Isaiah 41* ───────

L isten to me in silence, O coastlands;
   let the peoples renew their strength;
    let them approach, then let them speak;
    let us together draw near for
     judgment.
2   Who stirred up one from the east
     whom victory meets at every step?[2]
   He gives up nations before him,
    so that he tramples kings underfoot;
   he makes them like dust with his
     sword,
    like driven stubble with his bow.
3   He pursues them and passes on safely,
    by paths his feet have not trod.
4   Who has performed and done this,
    calling the generations from the
     beginning?
   I, the LORD, the first,
    and with the last; I am he.
5   The coastlands have seen and are afraid;
    the ends of the earth tremble;
    they have drawn near and come.
6   Everyone helps his neighbor
    and says to his brother, "Be strong!"
7   The craftsman strengthens the
     goldsmith,
    and he who smooths with the hammer
     him who strikes the anvil,

─────────────────────────

[1] Or *and not we ourselves*   [2] Or *whom righteousness calls to follow?*

saying of the soldering, "It is good";
and they strengthen it with nails so
that it cannot be moved.
8 But you, Israel, my servant,
Jacob, whom I have chosen,
the offspring of Abraham, my friend;
9 you whom I took from the ends of the
earth,
and called from its farthest corners,
saying to you, "You are my servant,
I have chosen you and not cast you
off";
10 fear not, for I am with you;
be not dismayed, for I am your God;
I will strengthen you, I will help you,
I will uphold you with my righteous
right hand.
11 Behold, all who are incensed against you
shall be put to shame and
confounded;
those who strive against you
shall be as nothing and shall perish.
12 You shall seek those who contend with
you,
but you shall not find them;
those who war against you
shall be as nothing at all.
13 For I, the LORD your God,
hold your right hand;
it is I who say to you, "Fear not,
I am the one who helps you."
14 Fear not, you worm Jacob,
you men of Israel!
I am the one who helps you, declares
the LORD;
your Redeemer is the Holy One of
Israel.
15 Behold, I make of you a threshing
sledge,
new, sharp, and having teeth;
you shall thresh the mountains and
crush them,
and you shall make the hills like chaff;
16 you shall winnow them, and the wind
shall carry them away,
and the tempest shall scatter them.
And you shall rejoice in the LORD;
in the Holy One of Israel you shall
glory.

17 When the poor and needy seek water,
and there is none,
and their tongue is parched with
thirst,
I the LORD will answer them;
I the God of Israel will not forsake
them.
18 I will open rivers on the bare heights,
and fountains in the midst of the
valleys.
I will make the wilderness a pool of
water,
and the dry land springs of water.
19 I will put in the wilderness the cedar,
the acacia, the myrtle, and the olive.
I will set in the desert the cypress,
the plane and the pine together,
20 that they may see and know,
may consider and understand
together,
that the hand of the LORD has done this,
the Holy One of Israel has created it.
21 Set forth your case, says the LORD;
bring your proofs, says the King of
Jacob.
22 Let them bring them, and tell us
what is to happen.
Tell us the former things, what they are,
that we may consider them,
that we may know their outcome;
or declare to us the things to come.
23 Tell us what is to come hereafter,
that we may know that you are gods;
do good, or do harm,
that we may be dismayed and
terrified.[1]
24 Behold, you are nothing,
and your work is less than nothing;
an abomination is he who chooses
you.
25 I stirred up one from the north, and he
has come,
from the rising of the sun, and he
shall call upon my name;
he shall trample on rulers as on mortar,
as the potter treads clay.
26 Who declared it from the beginning,
that we might know,
and beforehand, that we might say,
"He is right"?

[1] Or that we may both be dismayed and see

> There was none who declared it, none
>   who proclaimed,
>   none who heard your words.
> 27 I was the first to say[1] to Zion, "Behold,
>   here they are!"
>   and I give to Jerusalem a herald of
>   good news.
> 28 But when I look, there is no one;
>   among these there is no counselor
>   who, when I ask, gives an answer.
> 29 Behold, they are all a delusion;
>   their works are nothing;
>   their metal images are empty wind.

Revelation 11

Then I was given a measuring rod like a staff, and I was told, "Rise and measure the temple of God and the altar and those who worship there, ²but do not measure the court outside the temple; leave that out, for it is given over to the nations, and they will trample the holy city for forty-two months. ³And I will grant authority to my two witnesses, and they will prophesy for 1,260 days, clothed in sackcloth."

⁴These are the two olive trees and the two lampstands that stand before the Lord of the earth. ⁵And if anyone would harm them, fire pours from their mouth and consumes their foes. If anyone would harm them, this is how he is doomed to be killed. ⁶They have the power to shut the sky, that no rain may fall during the days of their prophesying, and they have power over the waters to turn them into blood and to strike the earth with every kind of plague, as often as they desire. ⁷And when they have finished their testimony, the beast that rises from the bottomless pit[2] will make war on them and conquer them and kill them, ⁸and their dead bodies will lie in the street of the great city that symbolically[3] is called Sodom and Egypt, where their Lord was crucified. ⁹For three and a half days some from the peoples and tribes and languages and nations will gaze at their dead bodies and refuse to let them be placed in a tomb, ¹⁰and those who dwell on the earth will rejoice over them and make merry and exchange presents, because these two prophets had been a torment to those who dwell on the earth. ¹¹But after the three and a half days a breath of life from God entered them, and they stood up on their feet, and great fear fell on those who saw them. ¹²Then they heard a loud voice from heaven saying to them, "Come up here!" And they went up to heaven in a cloud, and their enemies watched them. ¹³And at that hour there was a great earthquake, and a tenth of the city fell. Seven thousand people were killed in the earthquake, and the rest were terrified and gave glory to the God of heaven.

¹⁴The second woe has passed; behold, the third woe is soon to come.

¹⁵Then the seventh angel blew his trumpet, and there were loud voices in heaven, saying, "The kingdom of the world has become the kingdom of our Lord and of his Christ, and he shall reign forever and ever." ¹⁶And the twenty-four elders who sit on their thrones before God fell on their faces and worshiped God, ¹⁷saying,

> "We give thanks to you, Lord God
>   Almighty,
>   who is and who was,
>   for you have taken your great power
>   and begun to reign.
> 18 The nations raged,
>   but your wrath came,
>   and the time for the dead to be judged,
>   and for rewarding your servants,[4] the
>   prophets and saints,
>   and those who fear your name,
>   both small and great,
>   and for destroying the destroyers of the
>   earth."

¹⁹Then God's temple in heaven was opened, and the ark of his covenant was seen within his temple. There were flashes of lightning, rumblings,[5] peals of thunder, an earthquake, and heavy hail.

---

[1] Or Formerly I said [2] Or the abyss [3] Greek spiritually [4] Greek bondservants [5] Or voices, or sounds

JUNE 10

Deuteronomy 15

"At the end of every seven years you shall grant a release. [2]And this is the manner of the release: every creditor shall release what he has lent to his neighbor. He shall not exact it of his neighbor, his brother, because the LORD's release has been proclaimed. [3]Of a foreigner you may exact it, but whatever of yours is with your brother your hand shall release. [4]But there will be no poor among you; for the LORD will bless you in the land that the LORD your God is giving you for an inheritance to possess— [5]if only you will strictly obey the voice of the LORD your God, being careful to do all this commandment that I command you today. [6]For the LORD your God will bless you, as he promised you, and you shall lend to many nations, but you shall not borrow, and you shall rule over many nations, but they shall not rule over you.

[7]"If among you, one of your brothers should become poor, in any of your towns within your land that the LORD your God is giving you, you shall not harden your heart or shut your hand against your poor brother, [8]but you shall open your hand to him and lend him sufficient for his need, whatever it may be. [9]Take care lest there be an unworthy thought in your heart and you say, 'The seventh year, the year of release is near,' and your eye look grudgingly[1] on your poor brother, and you give him nothing, and he cry to the LORD against you, and you be guilty of sin. [10]You shall give to him freely, and your heart shall not be grudging when you give to him, because for this the LORD your God will bless you in all your work and in all that you undertake. [11]For there will never cease to be poor in the land. Therefore I command you, 'You shall open wide your hand to your brother, to the needy and to the poor, in your land.'

[12]"If your brother, a Hebrew man or a Hebrew woman, is sold[2] to you, he shall serve you six years, and in the seventh year you shall let him go free from you. [13]And when you let him go free from you, you shall not let him go empty-handed. [14]You shall furnish him liberally out of your flock, out of your threshing floor, and out of your winepress. As the LORD your God has blessed you, you shall give to him. [15]You shall remember that you were a slave in the land of Egypt, and the LORD your God redeemed you; therefore I command you this today. [16]But if he says to you, 'I will not go out from you,' because he loves you and your household, since he is well-off with you, [17]then you shall take an awl, and put it through his ear into the door, and he shall be your slave[3] forever. And to your female slave[4] you shall do the same. [18]It shall not seem hard to you when you let him go free from you, for at half the cost of a hired worker he has served you six years. So the LORD your God will bless you in all that you do.

[19]"All the firstborn males that are born of your herd and flock you shall dedicate to the LORD your God. You shall do no work with the firstborn of your herd, nor shear the firstborn of your flock. [20]You shall eat it, you and your household, before the LORD your God year by year at the place that the LORD will choose. [21]But if it has any blemish, if it is lame or blind or has any serious blemish whatever, you shall not sacrifice it to the LORD your God. [22]You shall eat it within your towns. The unclean and the clean alike may eat it, as though it were a gazelle or a deer. [23]Only you shall not eat its blood; you shall pour it out on the ground like water.

Psalm 102

A PRAYER OF ONE AFFLICTED, WHEN HE IS FAINT
AND POURS OUT HIS COMPLAINT BEFORE THE LORD.

Hear my prayer, O LORD;
  let my cry come to you!
[2] Do not hide your face from me
      in the day of my distress!
  Incline your ear to me;
      answer me speedily in the day when I
      call!

[3] For my days pass away like smoke,
      and my bones burn like a furnace.

---

[1] Or *be evil*; also verse 10 [2] Or *sells himself* [3] Or *servant*; the Hebrew term *'ebed* designates a range of social and economic roles (see Preface) [4] Or *servant*

4 My heart is struck down like grass and
    has withered;
  I forget to eat my bread.
5 Because of my loud groaning
  my bones cling to my flesh.
6 I am like a desert owl of the wilderness,
  like an owl[1] of the waste places;
7 I lie awake;
  I am like a lonely sparrow on the
    housetop.
8 All the day my enemies taunt me;
    those who deride me use my name for
    a curse.
9 For I eat ashes like bread
  and mingle tears with my drink,
10 because of your indignation and anger;
  for you have taken me up and thrown
    me down.
11 My days are like an evening shadow;
  I wither away like grass.

12 But you, O LORD, are enthroned forever;
    you are remembered throughout all
    generations.
13 You will arise and have pity on Zion;
  it is the time to favor her;
  the appointed time has come.
14 For your servants hold her stones dear
  and have pity on her dust.
15 Nations will fear the name of the LORD,
  and all the kings of the earth will fear
    your glory.
16 For the LORD builds up Zion;
  he appears in his glory;
17 he regards the prayer of the destitute
  and does not despise their prayer.

18 Let this be recorded for a generation to
    come,
  so that a people yet to be created may
    praise the LORD:
19 that he looked down from his holy
    height;
  from heaven the LORD looked at the
    earth,
20 to hear the groans of the prisoners,
  to set free those who were doomed to
    die,
21 that they may declare in Zion the name
    of the LORD,
  and in Jerusalem his praise,
22 when peoples gather together,
  and kingdoms, to worship the LORD.

23 He has broken my strength in
    midcourse;
  he has shortened my days.
24 "O my God," I say, "take me not away
  in the midst of my days—
  you whose years endure
    throughout all generations!"

25 Of old you laid the foundation of the
    earth,
  and the heavens are the work of your
    hands.
26 They will perish, but you will remain;
  they will all wear out like a garment.
  You will change them like a robe, and
    they will pass away,
27 but you are the same, and your years
    have no end.
28 The children of your servants shall dwell
    secure;
  their offspring shall be established
    before you.

Isaiah 42

Behold my servant, whom I uphold,
  my chosen, in whom my soul delights;
  I have put my Spirit upon him;
  he will bring forth justice to the
    nations.
2 He will not cry aloud or lift up his voice,
  or make it heard in the street;
3 a bruised reed he will not break,
  and a faintly burning wick he will not
    quench;
  he will faithfully bring forth justice.
4 He will not grow faint or be
    discouraged[2]
  till he has established justice in the
    earth;
  and the coastlands wait for his law.

5 Thus says God, the LORD,
  who created the heavens and
    stretched them out,
  who spread out the earth and what
    comes from it,
  who gives breath to the people on it
  and spirit to those who walk in it:
6 "I am the LORD; I have called you[3] in
    righteousness;
  I will take you by the hand and keep
    you;

---

[1] The precise identity of these birds is uncertain [2] Or *bruised* [3] The Hebrew for *you* is singular; four times in this verse

I will give you as a covenant for the
people,
a light for the nations,
7   to open the eyes that are blind,
to bring out the prisoners from the
dungeon,
from the prison those who sit in
darkness.
8   I am the LORD; that is my name;
my glory I give to no other,
nor my praise to carved idols.
9   Behold, the former things have come to
pass,
and new things I now declare;
before they spring forth
I tell you of them."

10   Sing to the LORD a new song,
his praise from the end of the earth,
you who go down to the sea, and all that
fills it,
the coastlands and their inhabitants.
11   Let the desert and its cities lift up their
voice,
the villages that Kedar inhabits;
let the habitants of Sela sing for joy,
let them shout from the top of the
mountains.
12   Let them give glory to the LORD,
and declare his praise in the
coastlands.
13   The LORD goes out like a mighty man,
like a man of war he stirs up his zeal;
he cries out, he shouts aloud,
he shows himself mighty against his
foes.

14   For a long time I have held my peace;
I have kept still and restrained myself;
now I will cry out like a woman in labor;
I will gasp and pant.
15   I will lay waste mountains and hills,
and dry up all their vegetation;
I will turn the rivers into islands,[1]
and dry up the pools.
16   And I will lead the blind
in a way that they do not know,
in paths that they have not known
I will guide them.
I will turn the darkness before them into
light,
the rough places into level ground.

These are the things I do,
and I do not forsake them.
17   They are turned back and utterly put to
shame,
who trust in carved idols,
who say to metal images,
"You are our gods."

18   Hear, you deaf,
and look, you blind, that you may see!
19   Who is blind but my servant,
or deaf as my messenger whom I send?
Who is blind as my dedicated one,[2]
or blind as the servant of the LORD?
20   He sees many things, but does not
observe them;
his ears are open, but he does not hear.
21   The LORD was pleased, for his
righteousness' sake,
to magnify his law and make it
glorious.
22   But this is a people plundered and
looted;
they are all of them trapped in holes
and hidden in prisons;
they have become plunder with none to
rescue,
spoil with none to say, "Restore!"
23   Who among you will give ear to this,
will attend and listen for the time to
come?
24   Who gave up Jacob to the looter,
and Israel to the plunderers?
Was it not the LORD, against whom we
have sinned,
in whose ways they would not walk,
and whose law they would not obey?
25   So he poured on him the heat of his
anger
and the might of battle;
it set him on fire all around, but he did
not understand;
it burned him up, but he did not take
it to heart.

Revelation 12

And a great sign appeared in heaven: a
woman clothed with the sun, with the
moon under her feet, and on her head a crown
of twelve stars. [2]She was pregnant and was crying out in birth pains and the agony of giving

---

[1] Or into coastlands [2] Or as the one at peace with me

birth. ³And another sign appeared in heaven: behold, a great red dragon, with seven heads and ten horns, and on his heads seven diadems. ⁴His tail swept down a third of the stars of heaven and cast them to the earth. And the dragon stood before the woman who was about to give birth, so that when she bore her child he might devour it. ⁵She gave birth to a male child, one who is to rule all the nations with a rod of iron, but her child was caught up to God and to his throne, ⁶and the woman fled into the wilderness, where she has a place prepared by God, in which she is to be nourished for 1,260 days.

⁷Now war arose in heaven, Michael and his angels fighting against the dragon. And the dragon and his angels fought back, ⁸but he was defeated, and there was no longer any place for them in heaven. ⁹And the great dragon was thrown down, that ancient serpent, who is called the devil and Satan, the deceiver of the whole world—he was thrown down to the earth, and his angels were thrown down with him. ¹⁰And I heard a loud voice in heaven, saying, "Now the salvation and the power and the kingdom of our God and the authority of his Christ have come, for the accuser of our brothers[1] has been thrown down, who accuses them day and night before our God. ¹¹And they have conquered him by the blood of the Lamb and by the word of their testimony, for they loved not their lives even unto death. ¹²Therefore, rejoice, O heavens and you who dwell in them! But woe to you, O earth and sea, for the devil has come down to you in great wrath, because he knows that his time is short!"

¹³And when the dragon saw that he had been thrown down to the earth, he pursued the woman who had given birth to the male child. ¹⁴But the woman was given the two wings of the great eagle so that she might fly from the serpent into the wilderness, to the place where she is to be nourished for a time, and times, and half a time. ¹⁵The serpent poured water like a river out of his mouth after the woman, to sweep her away with a flood. ¹⁶But the earth came to the help of the woman, and the earth opened its mouth and swallowed the river that the dragon had poured from his mouth. ¹⁷Then the dragon became furious with the woman and went off to make war on the rest of her offspring, on those who keep the commandments of God and hold to the testimony of Jesus. And he stood[2] on the sand of the sea.

JUNE 11

Deuteronomy 16

"Observe the month of Abib and keep the Passover to the LORD your God, for in the month of Abib the LORD your God brought you out of Egypt by night. ²And you shall offer the Passover sacrifice to the LORD your God, from the flock or the herd, at the place that the LORD will choose, to make his name dwell there. ³You shall eat no leavened bread with it. Seven days you shall eat it with unleavened bread, the bread of affliction—for you came out of the land of Egypt in haste—that all the days of your life you may remember the day when you came out of the land of Egypt. ⁴No leaven shall be seen with you in all your territory for seven days, nor shall any of the flesh that you sacrifice on the evening of the first day remain all night until morning. ⁵You may not offer the Passover sacrifice within any of your towns that the LORD your God is giving you, ⁶but at the place that the LORD your God will choose, to make his name dwell in it, there you shall offer the Passover sacrifice, in the evening at sunset, at the time you came out of Egypt. ⁷And you shall cook it and eat it at the place that the LORD your God will choose. And in the morning you shall turn and go to your tents. ⁸For six days you shall eat unleavened bread, and on the seventh day there shall be a

¹ Or brothers and sisters ² Some manuscripts And I stood, connecting the sentence with 13:1

solemn assembly to the LORD your God. You shall do no work on it.

⁹"You shall count seven weeks. Begin to count the seven weeks from the time the sickle is first put to the standing grain. ¹⁰Then you shall keep the Feast of Weeks to the LORD your God with the tribute of a freewill offering from your hand, which you shall give as the LORD your God blesses you. ¹¹And you shall rejoice before the LORD your God, you and your son and your daughter, your male servant and your female servant, the Levite who is within your towns, the sojourner, the fatherless, and the widow who are among you, at the place that the LORD your God will choose, to make his name dwell there. ¹²You shall remember that you were a slave in Egypt; and you shall be careful to observe these statutes.

¹³"You shall keep the Feast of Booths seven days, when you have gathered in the produce from your threshing floor and your winepress. ¹⁴You shall rejoice in your feast, you and your son and your daughter, your male servant and your female servant, the Levite, the sojourner, the fatherless, and the widow who are within your towns. ¹⁵For seven days you shall keep the feast to the LORD your God at the place that the LORD will choose, because the LORD your God will bless you in all your produce and in all the work of your hands, so that you will be altogether joyful.

¹⁶"Three times a year all your males shall appear before the LORD your God at the place that he will choose: at the Feast of Unleavened Bread, at the Feast of Weeks, and at the Feast of Booths. They shall not appear before the LORD empty-handed. ¹⁷Every man shall give as he is able, according to the blessing of the LORD your God that he has given you.

¹⁸"You shall appoint judges and officers in all your towns that the LORD your God is giving you, according to your tribes, and they shall judge the people with righteous judgment. ¹⁹You shall not pervert justice. You shall not show partiality, and you shall not accept a bribe, for a bribe blinds the eyes of the wise and subverts the cause of the righteous. ²⁰Justice, and only justice, you shall follow, that you may live and inherit the land that the LORD your God is giving you.

²¹"You shall not plant any tree as an Asherah beside the altar of the LORD your God that you shall make. ²²And you shall not set up a pillar, which the LORD your God hates.

Psalm 103

OF DAVID.

Bless the LORD, O my soul,
and all that is within me,
bless his holy name!
2 Bless the LORD, O my soul,
and forget not all his benefits,
3 who forgives all your iniquity,
who heals all your diseases,
4 who redeems your life from the pit,
who crowns you with steadfast love
and mercy,
5 who satisfies you with good
so that your youth is renewed like the
eagle's.

6 The LORD works righteousness
and justice for all who are oppressed.
7 He made known his ways to Moses,
his acts to the people of Israel.
8 The LORD is merciful and gracious,
slow to anger and abounding in
steadfast love.
9 He will not always chide,
nor will he keep his anger forever.
10 He does not deal with us according to
our sins,
nor repay us according to our
iniquities.
11 For as high as the heavens are above the
earth,
so great is his steadfast love toward
those who fear him;
12 as far as the east is from the west,
so far does he remove our
transgressions from us.
13 As a father shows compassion to his
children,
so the LORD shows compassion to
those who fear him.
14 For he knows our frame;¹
he remembers that we are dust.

15 As for man, his days are like grass;
he flourishes like a flower of the field;
16 for the wind passes over it, and it is
gone,
and its place knows it no more.

¹ Or knows how we are formed

17 But the steadfast love of the LORD is from
     everlasting to everlasting on those
     who fear him,
   and his righteousness to children's
     children,
18 to those who keep his covenant
   and remember to do his
     commandments.
19 The LORD has established his throne in
     the heavens,
   and his kingdom rules over all.

20 Bless the LORD, O you his angels,
   you mighty ones who do his word,
   obeying the voice of his word!
21 Bless the LORD, all his hosts,
   his ministers, who do his will!
22 Bless the LORD, all his works,
   in all places of his dominion.
   Bless the LORD, O my soul!

------ *Isaiah 43* ------

But now thus says the LORD,
he who created you, O Jacob,
   he who formed you, O Israel:
"Fear not, for I have redeemed you;
   I have called you by name, you are
     mine.
2 When you pass through the waters, I will
     be with you;
   and through the rivers, they shall not
     overwhelm you;
   when you walk through fire you shall
     not be burned,
   and the flame shall not consume you.
3 For I am the LORD your God,
   the Holy One of Israel, your Savior.
   I give Egypt as your ransom,
     Cush and Seba in exchange for you.
4 Because you are precious in my eyes,
     and honored, and I love you,
   I give men in return for you,
     peoples in exchange for your life.
5 Fear not, for I am with you;
   I will bring your offspring from the east,
     and from the west I will gather you.
6 I will say to the north, Give up,
     and to the south, Do not withhold;
   bring my sons from afar
     and my daughters from the end of the
     earth,

7 everyone who is called by my name,
     whom I created for my glory,
     whom I formed and made."

8 Bring out the people who are blind, yet
     have eyes,
   who are deaf, yet have ears!
9 All the nations gather together,
     and the peoples assemble.
   Who among them can declare this,
     and show us the former things?
   Let them bring their witnesses to prove
     them right,
     and let them hear and say, It is true.
10 "You are my witnesses," declares the
     LORD,
   "and my servant whom I have chosen,
   that you may know and believe me
     and understand that I am he.
   Before me no god was formed,
     nor shall there be any after me.
11 I, I am the LORD,
     and besides me there is no savior.
12 I declared and saved and proclaimed,
     when there was no strange god
       among you;
   and you are my witnesses," declares
     the LORD, "and I am God.
13 Also henceforth I am he;
   there is none who can deliver from
     my hand;
   I work, and who can turn it back?"

14 Thus says the LORD,
     your Redeemer, the Holy One of
       Israel:
   "For your sake I send to Babylon
     and bring them all down as fugitives,
   even the Chaldeans, in the ships in
       which they rejoice.
15 I am the LORD, your Holy One,
     the Creator of Israel, your King."
16 Thus says the LORD,
     who makes a way in the sea,
     a path in the mighty waters,
17 who brings forth chariot and horse,
     army and warrior;
   they lie down, they cannot rise,
     they are extinguished, quenched like
       a wick:
18 "Remember not the former things,
     nor consider the things of old.

¹⁹ Behold, I am doing a new thing;
    now it springs forth, do you not
       perceive it?
  I will make a way in the wilderness
    and rivers in the desert.
²⁰ The wild beasts will honor me,
    the jackals and the ostriches,
  for I give water in the wilderness,
    rivers in the desert,
  to give drink to my chosen people,
²¹   the people whom I formed for myself
  that they might declare my praise.

²² "Yet you did not call upon me, O Jacob;
    but you have been weary of me,
      O Israel!
²³ You have not brought me your sheep for
      burnt offerings,
    or honored me with your sacrifices.
  I have not burdened you with offerings,
    or wearied you with frankincense.
²⁴ You have not bought me sweet cane
      with money,
    or satisfied me with the fat of your
      sacrifices.
  But you have burdened me with your
      sins;
  you have wearied me with your
      iniquities.

²⁵ "I, I am he
    who blots out your transgressions for
      my own sake,
  and I will not remember your sins.
²⁶ Put me in remembrance; let us argue
      together;
    set forth your case, that you may be
      proved right.
²⁷ Your first father sinned,
    and your mediators transgressed
      against me.
²⁸ Therefore I will profane the princes of
      the sanctuary,
  and deliver Jacob to utter destruction
  and Israel to reviling.

Revelation 13

And I saw a beast rising out of the sea, with ten horns and seven heads, with ten diadems on its horns and blasphemous names on its heads. ²And the beast that I saw was like a leopard; its feet were like a bear's, and its mouth was like a lion's mouth. And to it the dragon gave his power and his throne and great authority. ³One of its heads seemed to have a mortal wound, but its mortal wound was healed, and the whole earth marveled as they followed the beast. ⁴And they worshiped the dragon, for he had given his authority to the beast, and they worshiped the beast, saying, "Who is like the beast, and who can fight against it?"

⁵And the beast was given a mouth uttering haughty and blasphemous words, and it was allowed to exercise authority for forty-two months. ⁶It opened its mouth to utter blasphemies against God, blaspheming his name and his dwelling,[1] that is, those who dwell in heaven. ⁷Also it was allowed to make war on the saints and to conquer them.[2] And authority was given it over every tribe and people and language and nation, ⁸and all who dwell on earth will worship it, everyone whose name has not been written before the foundation of the world in the book of life of the Lamb who was slain. ⁹If anyone has an ear, let him hear:

¹⁰   If anyone is to be taken captive,
    to captivity he goes;
  if anyone is to be slain with the sword,
    with the sword must he be slain.

Here is a call for the endurance and faith of the saints.

¹¹Then I saw another beast rising out of the earth. It had two horns like a lamb and it spoke like a dragon. ¹²It exercises all the authority of the first beast in its presence,[3] and makes the earth and its inhabitants worship the first beast, whose mortal wound was healed. ¹³It performs great signs, even making fire come down from heaven to earth in front of people, ¹⁴and by the signs that it is allowed to work in the presence of[4] the beast it deceives those who dwell on earth, telling them to make an image for the beast that was wounded by the sword and yet lived. ¹⁵And it was allowed to give breath to the image of the beast, so that the image of the beast might even speak and might cause those who would not worship the image of the beast to be slain. ¹⁶Also it causes all, both small and great, both rich and poor, both free and slave,[5] to be marked on the right hand or the forehead, ¹⁷so that no one can buy or sell unless he has the mark, that is, the name of the beast or the

¹ Or *tabernacle* ² Some manuscripts omit this sentence ³ Or *on its behalf* ⁴ Or *on behalf of* ⁵ Greek *bondservant*

number of its name. [18]This calls for wisdom: let the one who has understanding calculate the number of the beast, for it is the number of a man, and his number is 666.[1]

JUNE 12

Deuteronomy 17

"You shall not sacrifice to the LORD your God an ox or a sheep in which is a blemish, any defect whatever, for that is an abomination to the LORD your God.

[2]"If there is found among you, within any of your towns that the LORD your God is giving you, a man or woman who does what is evil in the sight of the LORD your God, in transgressing his covenant, [3]and has gone and served other gods and worshiped them, or the sun or the moon or any of the host of heaven, which I have forbidden, [4]and it is told you and you hear of it, then you shall inquire diligently, and if it is true and certain that such an abomination has been done in Israel, [5]then you shall bring out to your gates that man or woman who has done this evil thing, and you shall stone that man or woman to death with stones. [6]On the evidence of two witnesses or of three witnesses the one who is to die shall be put to death; a person shall not be put to death on the evidence of one witness. [7]The hand of the witnesses shall be first against him to put him to death, and afterward the hand of all the people. So you shall purge[2] the evil[3] from your midst.

[8]"If any case arises requiring decision between one kind of homicide and another, one kind of legal right and another, or one kind of assault and another, any case within your towns that is too difficult for you, then you shall arise and go up to the place that the LORD your God will choose. [9]And you shall come to the Levitical priests and to the judge who is in office in those days, and you shall consult them, and they shall declare to you the decision. [10]Then you shall do according to what they declare to you from that place that the LORD will choose. And you shall be careful to do according to all that they direct you.

[11]According to the instructions that they give you, and according to the decision which they pronounce to you, you shall do. You shall not turn aside from the verdict that they declare to you, either to the right hand or to the left. [12]The man who acts presumptuously by not obeying the priest who stands to minister there before the LORD your God, or the judge, that man shall die. So you shall purge the evil from Israel. [13]And all the people shall hear and fear and not act presumptuously again.

[14]"When you come to the land that the LORD your God is giving you, and you possess it and dwell in it and then say, 'I will set a king over me, like all the nations that are around me,' [15]you may indeed set a king over you whom the LORD your God will choose. One from among your brothers you shall set as king over you. You may not put a foreigner over you, who is not your brother. [16]Only he must not acquire many horses for himself or cause the people to return to Egypt in order to acquire many horses, since the LORD has said to you, 'You shall never return that way again.' [17]And he shall not acquire many wives for himself, lest his heart turn away, nor shall he acquire for himself excessive silver and gold.

[18]"And when he sits on the throne of his kingdom, he shall write for himself in a book a copy of this law, approved by[4] the Levitical priests. [19]And it shall be with him, and he shall read in it all the days of his life, that he may learn to fear the LORD his God by keeping all the words of this law and these statutes, and doing them, [20]that his heart may not be lifted up above his brothers, and that he may not turn aside from the commandment, either to the right hand or to the left, so that he may continue long in his kingdom, he and his children, in Israel.

---

[1] Some manuscripts *616* [2] Septuagint *drive out*; also verse 12 [3] Or *evil person*; also verse 12 [4] Hebrew *from before*

Psalm 104

Bless the LORD, O my soul!
O LORD my God, you are very great!
You are clothed with splendor and
majesty,
2 covering yourself with light as with a
garment,
stretching out the heavens like a tent.
3 He lays the beams of his chambers on
the waters;
he makes the clouds his chariot;
he rides on the wings of the wind;
4 he makes his messengers winds,
his ministers a flaming fire.

5 He set the earth on its foundations,
so that it should never be moved.
6 You covered it with the deep as with a
garment;
the waters stood above the mountains.
7 At your rebuke they fled;
at the sound of your thunder they
took to flight.
8 The mountains rose, the valleys sank
down
to the place that you appointed for
them.
9 You set a boundary that they may not
pass,
so that they might not again cover the
earth.

10 You make springs gush forth in the
valleys;
they flow between the hills;
11 they give drink to every beast of the
field;
the wild donkeys quench their thirst.
12 Beside them the birds of the heavens
dwell;
they sing among the branches.
13 From your lofty abode you water the
mountains;
the earth is satisfied with the fruit of
your work.

14 You cause the grass to grow for the
livestock
and plants for man to cultivate,
that he may bring forth food from the
earth
15 and wine to gladden the heart of man,
oil to make his face shine
and bread to strengthen man's heart.

16 The trees of the LORD are watered
abundantly,
the cedars of Lebanon that he
planted.
17 In them the birds build their nests;
the stork has her home in the fir
trees.
18 The high mountains are for the wild
goats;
the rocks are a refuge for the rock
badgers.

19 He made the moon to mark the
seasons;[1]
the sun knows its time for setting.
20 You make darkness, and it is night,
when all the beasts of the forest creep
about.
21 The young lions roar for their prey,
seeking their food from God.
22 When the sun rises, they steal away
and lie down in their dens.
23 Man goes out to his work
and to his labor until the evening.

24 O LORD, how manifold are your works!
In wisdom have you made them all;
the earth is full of your creatures.
25 Here is the sea, great and wide,
which teems with creatures
innumerable,
living things both small and great.
26 There go the ships,
and Leviathan, which you formed to
play in it.[2]

27 These all look to you,
to give them their food in due season.
28 When you give it to them, they gather it
up;
when you open your hand, they are
filled with good things.
29 When you hide your face, they are
dismayed;
when you take away their breath, they
die
and return to their dust.
30 When you send forth your Spirit,[3] they
are created,
and you renew the face of the ground.

[1] Or the appointed times (compare Genesis 1:14) [2] Or you formed to play with [3] Or breath

³¹ May the glory of the LORD endure
forever;
may the LORD rejoice in his works,
³² who looks on the earth and it trembles,
who touches the mountains and they
smoke!
³³ I will sing to the LORD as long as I live;
I will sing praise to my God while I
have being.
³⁴ May my meditation be pleasing to him,
for I rejoice in the LORD.
³⁵ Let sinners be consumed from the earth,
and let the wicked be no more!
Bless the LORD, O my soul!
Praise the LORD!

Isaiah 44

"But now hear, O Jacob my servant,
Israel whom I have chosen!
² Thus says the LORD who made you,
who formed you from the womb and
will help you:
Fear not, O Jacob my servant,
Jeshurun whom I have chosen.
³ For I will pour water on the thirsty land,
and streams on the dry ground;
I will pour my Spirit upon your
offspring,
and my blessing on your descendants.
⁴ They shall spring up among the grass
like willows by flowing streams.
⁵ This one will say, 'I am the LORD's,'
another will call on the name of Jacob,
and another will write on his hand, 'The
LORD's,'
and name himself by the name of
Israel."

⁶ Thus says the LORD, the King of Israel
and his Redeemer, the LORD of hosts:
"I am the first and I am the last;
besides me there is no god.
⁷ Who is like me? Let him proclaim it.[1]
Let him declare and set it before me,
since I appointed an ancient people.
Let them declare what is to come, and
what will happen.
⁸ Fear not, nor be afraid;
have I not told you from of old and
declared it?
And you are my witnesses!

Is there a God besides me?
There is no Rock; I know not any."

⁹ All who fashion idols are nothing, and the
things they delight in do not profit. Their witnesses
neither see nor know, that they may be
put to shame. ¹⁰ Who fashions a god or casts
an idol that is profitable for nothing? ¹¹ Behold,
all his companions shall be put to shame, and
the craftsmen are only human. Let them all
assemble, let them stand forth. They shall be
terrified; they shall be put to shame together.
¹² The ironsmith takes a cutting tool and
works it over the coals. He fashions it with
hammers and works it with his strong arm.
He becomes hungry, and his strength fails; he
drinks no water and is faint. ¹³ The carpenter
stretches a line; he marks it out with a pencil.
He shapes it with planes and marks it with a
compass. He shapes it into the figure of a man,
with the beauty of a man, to dwell in a house.
¹⁴ He cuts down cedars, or he chooses a cypress
tree or an oak and lets it grow strong among
the trees of the forest. He plants a cedar and the
rain nourishes it. ¹⁵ Then it becomes fuel for a
man. He takes a part of it and warms himself;
he kindles a fire and bakes bread. Also he makes
a god and worships it; he makes it an idol and
falls down before it. ¹⁶ Half of it he burns in the
fire. Over the half he eats meat; he roasts it and
is satisfied. Also he warms himself and says,
"Aha, I am warm, I have seen the fire!" ¹⁷ And
the rest of it he makes into a god, his idol, and
falls down to it and worships it. He prays to it
and says, "Deliver me, for you are my god!"
¹⁸ They know not, nor do they discern, for he
has shut their eyes, so that they cannot see, and
their hearts, so that they cannot understand.
¹⁹ No one considers, nor is there knowledge or
discernment to say, "Half of it I burned in the
fire; I also baked bread on its coals; I roasted
meat and have eaten. And shall I make the rest
of it an abomination? Shall I fall down before a
block of wood?" ²⁰ He feeds on ashes; a deluded
heart has led him astray, and he cannot deliver
himself or say, "Is there not a lie in my right
hand?"

²¹ Remember these things, O Jacob,
and Israel, for you are my servant;
I formed you; you are my servant;
O Israel, you will not be forgotten by
me.

---

[1] Or Who like me can proclaim it?

²² I have blotted out your transgressions
    like a cloud
    and your sins like mist;
    return to me, for I have redeemed you.

²³ Sing, O heavens, for the LORD has done it;
    shout, O depths of the earth;
    break forth into singing, O mountains,
      O forest, and every tree in it!
    For the LORD has redeemed Jacob,
    and will be glorified[1] in Israel.

²⁴ Thus says the LORD, your Redeemer,
    who formed you from the womb:
    "I am the LORD, who made all things,
    who alone stretched out the heavens,
    who spread out the earth by myself,
²⁵ who frustrates the signs of liars
    and makes fools of diviners,
    who turns wise men back
    and makes their knowledge foolish,
²⁶ who confirms the word of his servant
    and fulfills the counsel of his
      messengers,
    who says of Jerusalem, 'She shall be
      inhabited,'
    and of the cities of Judah, 'They shall
      be built,
    and I will raise up their ruins';
²⁷ who says to the deep, 'Be dry;
    I will dry up your rivers';
²⁸ who says of Cyrus, 'He is my shepherd,
    and he shall fulfill all my purpose';
    saying of Jerusalem, 'She shall be built,'
    and of the temple, 'Your foundation
      shall be laid.'"

Revelation 14

Then I looked, and behold, on Mount Zion stood the Lamb, and with him 144,000 who had his name and his Father's name written on their foreheads. ²And I heard a voice from heaven like the roar of many waters and like the sound of loud thunder. The voice I heard was like the sound of harpists playing on their harps, ³ and they were singing a new song before the throne and before the four living creatures and before the elders. No one could learn that song except the 144,000 who had been redeemed from the earth. ⁴It is these who have not defiled themselves with women, for they are virgins. It is these who follow the Lamb

wherever he goes. These have been redeemed from mankind as firstfruits for God and the Lamb, ⁵ and in their mouth no lie was found, for they are blameless.

⁶Then I saw another angel flying directly overhead, with an eternal gospel to proclaim to those who dwell on earth, to every nation and tribe and language and people. ⁷And he said with a loud voice, "Fear God and give him glory, because the hour of his judgment has come, and worship him who made heaven and earth, the sea and the springs of water."

⁸Another angel, a second, followed, saying, "Fallen, fallen is Babylon the great, she who made all nations drink the wine of the passion[2] of her sexual immorality."

⁹And another angel, a third, followed them, saying with a loud voice, "If anyone worships the beast and its image and receives a mark on his forehead or on his hand, ¹⁰he also will drink the wine of God's wrath, poured full strength into the cup of his anger, and he will be tormented with fire and sulfur in the presence of the holy angels and in the presence of the Lamb. ¹¹And the smoke of their torment goes up forever and ever, and they have no rest, day or night, these worshipers of the beast and its image, and whoever receives the mark of its name."

¹²Here is a call for the endurance of the saints, those who keep the commandments of God and their faith in Jesus.[3]

¹³And I heard a voice from heaven saying, "Write this: Blessed are the dead who die in the Lord from now on." "Blessed indeed," says the Spirit, "that they may rest from their labors, for their deeds follow them!"

¹⁴Then I looked, and behold, a white cloud, and seated on the cloud one like a son of man, with a golden crown on his head, and a sharp sickle in his hand. ¹⁵And another angel came out of the temple, calling with a loud voice to him who sat on the cloud, "Put in your sickle, and reap, for the hour to reap has come, for the harvest of the earth is fully ripe." ¹⁶So he who sat on the cloud swung his sickle across the earth, and the earth was reaped.

¹⁷Then another angel came out of the temple in heaven, and he too had a sharp sickle. ¹⁸And another angel came out from the altar, the angel who has authority over the fire, and he called with a loud voice to the one who had the sharp sickle, "Put in your sickle and gather

¹ Or will display his beauty ² Or wrath ³ Greek and the faith of Jesus

the clusters from the vine of the earth, for its grapes are ripe." ¹⁹ So the angel swung his sickle across the earth and gathered the grape harvest of the earth and threw it into the great winepress of the wrath of God. ²⁰ And the winepress was trodden outside the city, and blood flowed from the winepress, as high as a horse's bridle, for 1,600 stadia.¹

JUNE 13

Deuteronomy 18

"The Levitical priests, all the tribe of Levi, shall have no portion or inheritance with Israel. They shall eat the LORD's food offerings² as their³ inheritance. ²They shall have no inheritance among their brothers; the LORD is their inheritance, as he promised them. ³And this shall be the priests' due from the people, from those offering a sacrifice, whether an ox or a sheep: they shall give to the priest the shoulder and the two cheeks and the stomach. ⁴The firstfruits of your grain, of your wine and of your oil, and the first fleece of your sheep, you shall give him. ⁵For the LORD your God has chosen him out of all your tribes to stand and minister in the name of the LORD, him and his sons for all time.

⁶"And if a Levite comes from any of your towns out of all Israel, where he lives—and he may come when he desires⁴—to the place that the LORD will choose, ⁷and ministers in the name of the LORD his God, like all his fellow Levites who stand to minister there before the LORD, ⁸then he may have equal portions to eat, besides what he receives from the sale of his patrimony.⁵

⁹"When you come into the land that the LORD your God is giving you, you shall not learn to follow the abominable practices of those nations. ¹⁰There shall not be found among you anyone who burns his son or his daughter as an offering,⁶ anyone who practices divination or tells fortunes or interprets omens, or a sorcerer ¹¹or a charmer or a medium or a necromancer or one who inquires of the dead, ¹²for whoever does these things is an abomination to the LORD. And because of these abominations the LORD your God is driving them out

before you. ¹³You shall be blameless before the LORD your God, ¹⁴for these nations, which you are about to dispossess, listen to fortune-tellers and to diviners. But as for you, the LORD your God has not allowed you to do this.

¹⁵"The LORD your God will raise up for you a prophet like me from among you, from your brothers—it is to him you shall listen— ¹⁶just as you desired of the LORD your God at Horeb on the day of the assembly, when you said, 'Let me not hear again the voice of the LORD my God or see this great fire any more, lest I die.' ¹⁷And the LORD said to me, 'They are right in what they have spoken. ¹⁸I will raise up for them a prophet like you from among their brothers. And I will put my words in his mouth, and he shall speak to them all that I command him. ¹⁹And whoever will not listen to my words that he shall speak in my name, I myself will require it of him. ²⁰But the prophet who presumes to speak a word in my name that I have not commanded him to speak, or⁷ who speaks in the name of other gods, that same prophet shall die.' ²¹And if you say in your heart, 'How may we know the word that the LORD has not spoken?'— ²²when a prophet speaks in the name of the LORD, if the word does not come to pass or come true, that is a word that the LORD has not spoken; the prophet has spoken it presumptuously. You need not be afraid of him.

Psalm 105

Oh give thanks to the LORD; call upon his name;
    make known his deeds among the peoples!

---

¹ About 184 miles; a *stadion* was about 607 feet or 185 meters ² Or *the offerings by fire to the LORD* ³ Hebrew *his* ⁴ Or *lives—if he comes enthusiastically* ⁵ The meaning of the Hebrew is uncertain ⁶ Hebrew *makes his son or his daughter pass through the fire* ⁷ Or *and*

2 Sing to him, sing praises to him;
    tell of all his wondrous works!
3 Glory in his holy name;
    let the hearts of those who seek the
      LORD rejoice!
4 Seek the LORD and his strength;
    seek his presence continually!
5 Remember the wondrous works that he
      has done,
    his miracles, and the judgments he
      uttered,
6 O offspring of Abraham, his servant,
    children of Jacob, his chosen ones!

7 He is the LORD our God;
    his judgments are in all the earth.
8 He remembers his covenant forever,
    the word that he commanded, for a
      thousand generations,
9 the covenant that he made with
      Abraham,
    his sworn promise to Isaac,
10 which he confirmed to Jacob as a
      statute,
    to Israel as an everlasting covenant,
11 saying, "To you I will give the land of
      Canaan
    as your portion for an inheritance."

12 When they were few in number,
    of little account, and sojourners in it,
13 wandering from nation to nation,
    from one kingdom to another people,
14 he allowed no one to oppress them;
    he rebuked kings on their account,
15 saying, "Touch not my anointed ones,
    do my prophets no harm!"

16 When he summoned a famine on the
      land
    and broke all supply[1] of bread,
17 he had sent a man ahead of them,
    Joseph, who was sold as a slave.
18 His feet were hurt with fetters;
    his neck was put in a collar of iron;
19 until what he had said came to pass,
    the word of the LORD tested him.
20 The king sent and released him;
    the ruler of the peoples set him free;
21 he made him lord of his house
    and ruler of all his possessions,
22 to bind[2] his princes at his pleasure
    and to teach his elders wisdom.

23 Then Israel came to Egypt;
    Jacob sojourned in the land of Ham.
24 And the LORD made his people very
      fruitful
    and made them stronger than their
      foes.
25 He turned their hearts to hate his
      people,
    to deal craftily with his servants.

26 He sent Moses, his servant,
    and Aaron, whom he had chosen.
27 They performed his signs among them
    and miracles in the land of Ham.
28 He sent darkness, and made the land
      dark;
    they did not rebel[3] against his words.
29 He turned their waters into blood
    and caused their fish to die.
30 Their land swarmed with frogs,
    even in the chambers of their kings.
31 He spoke, and there came swarms of
      flies,
    and gnats throughout their country.
32 He gave them hail for rain,
    and fiery lightning bolts through their
      land.
33 He struck down their vines and fig
      trees,
    and shattered the trees of their
      country.
34 He spoke, and the locusts came,
    young locusts without number,
35 which devoured all the vegetation in
      their land
    and ate up the fruit of their ground.
36 He struck down all the firstborn in their
      land,
    the firstfruits of all their strength.

37 Then he brought out Israel with silver
      and gold,
    and there was none among his tribes
      who stumbled.
38 Egypt was glad when they departed,
    for dread of them had fallen upon it.

39 He spread a cloud for a covering,
    and fire to give light by night.
40 They asked, and he brought quail,
    and gave them bread from heaven in
      abundance.

[1] Hebrew *staff* [2] Septuagint, Syriac, Jerome *instruct* [3] Septuagint, Syriac omit *not*

41 He opened the rock, and water gushed
          out;
      it flowed through the desert like a
          river.
42 For he remembered his holy promise,
      and Abraham, his servant.
43 So he brought his people out with joy,
      his chosen ones with singing.
44 And he gave them the lands of the
          nations,
      and they took possession of the fruit
          of the peoples' toil,
45 that they might keep his statutes
      and observe his laws.
      Praise the LORD!

Isaiah 45

Thus says the LORD to his anointed, to
 Cyrus,
      whose right hand I have grasped,
   to subdue nations before him
      and to loose the belts of kings,
   to open doors before him
      that gates may not be closed:
2 "I will go before you
      and level the exalted places,[1]
   I will break in pieces the doors of
          bronze
      and cut through the bars of iron,
3 I will give you the treasures of darkness
      and the hoards in secret places,
   that you may know that it is I, the
          LORD,
      the God of Israel, who call you by your
          name.
4 For the sake of my servant Jacob,
      and Israel my chosen,
   I call you by your name,
      I name you, though you do not know
          me.
5 I am the LORD, and there is no other,
      besides me there is no God;
   I equip you, though you do not know
          me,
6 that people may know, from the rising of
          the sun
      and from the west, that there is none
          besides me;
   I am the LORD, and there is no other.

7 I form light and create darkness,
      I make well-being and create
          calamity,
   I am the LORD, who does all these
          things.
8 "Shower, O heavens, from above,
      and let the clouds rain down
          righteousness;
   let the earth open, that salvation and
          righteousness may bear fruit;
   let the earth cause them both to
          sprout;
      I the LORD have created it.
9 "Woe to him who strives with him who
          formed him,
      a pot among earthen pots!
   Does the clay say to him who forms it,
      'What are you making?'
      or 'Your work has no handles'?
10 Woe to him who says to a father, 'What
          are you begetting?'
      or to a woman, 'With what are you in
          labor?'"
11 Thus says the LORD,
      the Holy One of Israel, and the one
          who formed him:
   "Ask me of things to come;
      will you command me concerning
          my children and the work of my
          hands?[2]
12 I made the earth
      and created man on it;
   it was my hands that stretched out the
          heavens,
      and I commanded all their host.
13 I have stirred him up in righteousness,
      and I will make all his ways level;
   he shall build my city
      and set my exiles free,
   not for price or reward,"
      says the LORD of hosts.
14 Thus says the LORD:
   "The wealth of Egypt and the
          merchandise of Cush,
      and the Sabeans, men of stature,
   shall come over to you and be yours;
      they shall follow you;
      they shall come over in chains and
          bow down to you.

---

[1] Masoretic Text; Dead Sea Scroll, Septuagint *level the mountains* [2] A slight emendation yields *will you question me about my children, or command me concerning the work of my hands?*

They will plead with you, saying:
'Surely God is in you, and there is no
other,
no god besides him.'"

15 Truly, you are a God who hides himself,
O God of Israel, the Savior.
16 All of them are put to shame and
confounded;
the makers of idols go in confusion
together.
17 But Israel is saved by the LORD
with everlasting salvation;
you shall not be put to shame or
confounded
to all eternity.

18 For thus says the LORD,
who created the heavens
(he is God!),
who formed the earth and made it
(he established it;
he did not create it empty,
he formed it to be inhabited!):
"I am the LORD, and there is no other.
19 I did not speak in secret,
in a land of darkness;
I did not say to the offspring of Jacob,
'Seek me in vain.'[1]
I the LORD speak the truth;
I declare what is right.

20 "Assemble yourselves and come;
draw near together,
you survivors of the nations!
They have no knowledge
who carry about their wooden idols,
and keep on praying to a god
that cannot save.
21 Declare and present your case;
let them take counsel together!
Who told this long ago?
Who declared it of old?
Was it not I, the LORD?
And there is no other god besides
me,
a righteous God and a Savior;
there is none besides me.

22 "Turn to me and be saved,
all the ends of the earth!
For I am God, and there is no other.

23 By myself I have sworn;
from my mouth has gone out in
righteousness
a word that shall not return:
'To me every knee shall bow,
every tongue shall swear allegiance.'[2]
24 "Only in the LORD, it shall be said of me,
are righteousness and strength;
to him shall come and be ashamed
all who were incensed against him.
25 In the LORD all the offspring of Israel
shall be justified and shall glory."

Revelation 15

Then I saw another sign in heaven, great and
amazing, seven angels with seven plagues,
which are the last, for with them the wrath of
God is finished. [2]And I saw what appeared to be a sea of
glass mingled with fire—and also those who
had conquered the beast and its image and the
number of its name, standing beside the sea of
glass with harps of God in their hands. [3]And
they sing the song of Moses, the servant[3] of
God, and the song of the Lamb, saying,

"Great and amazing are your deeds,
O Lord God the Almighty!
Just and true are your ways,
O King of the nations![4]
[4] Who will not fear, O Lord,
and glorify your name?
For you alone are holy.
All nations will come
and worship you,
for your righteous acts have been
revealed."

[5]After this I looked, and the sanctuary of the
tent[5] of witness in heaven was opened, [6]and
out of the sanctuary came the seven angels
with the seven plagues, clothed in pure, bright
linen, with golden sashes around their chests.
[7]And one of the four living creatures gave to
the seven angels seven golden bowls full of
the wrath of God who lives forever and ever,
[8]and the sanctuary was filled with smoke from
the glory of God and from his power, and no
one could enter the sanctuary until the seven
plagues of the seven angels were finished.

[1] Hebrew in emptiness [2] Septuagint every tongue shall confess to God [3] Greek bondservant [4] Some manuscripts the ages [5] Or tabernacle

JUNE 14

Deuteronomy 19

"When the Lord your God cuts off the nations whose land the Lord your God is giving you, and you dispossess them and dwell in their cities and in their houses, ²you shall set apart three cities for yourselves in the land that the Lord your God is giving you to possess. ³You shall measure the distances¹ and divide into three parts the area of the land that the Lord your God gives you as a possession, so that any manslayer can flee to them. ⁴"This is the provision for the manslayer, who by fleeing there may save his life. If anyone kills his neighbor unintentionally without having hated him in the past— ⁵as when someone goes into the forest with his neighbor to cut wood, and his hand swings the axe to cut down a tree, and the head slips from the handle and strikes his neighbor so that he dies—he may flee to one of these cities and live, ⁶lest the avenger of blood in hot anger pursue the manslayer and overtake him, because the way is long, and strike him fatally, though the man did not deserve to die, since he had not hated his neighbor in the past. ⁷Therefore I command you, You shall set apart three cities. ⁸And if the Lord your God enlarges your territory, as he has sworn to your fathers, and gives you all the land that he promised to give to your fathers— ⁹provided you are careful to keep all this commandment, which I command you today, by loving the Lord your God and by walking ever in his ways—then you shall add three other cities to these three, ¹⁰lest innocent blood be shed in your land that the Lord your God is giving you for an inheritance, and so the guilt of bloodshed be upon you.

¹¹"But if anyone hates his neighbor and lies in wait for him and attacks him and strikes him fatally so that he dies, and he flees into one of these cities, ¹²then the elders of his city shall send and take him from there, and hand him over to the avenger of blood, so that he may die. ¹³Your eye shall not pity him, but you shall purge the guilt of innocent blood² from Israel, so that it may be well with you.

¹⁴"You shall not move your neighbor's landmark, which the men of old have set, in the inheritance that you will hold in the land that the Lord your God is giving you to possess.

¹⁵"A single witness shall not suffice against a person for any crime or for any wrong in connection with any offense that he has committed. Only on the evidence of two witnesses or of three witnesses shall a charge be established. ¹⁶If a malicious witness arises to accuse a person of wrongdoing, ¹⁷then both parties to the dispute shall appear before the Lord, before the priests and the judges who are in office in those days. ¹⁸The judges shall inquire diligently, and if the witness is a false witness and has accused his brother falsely, ¹⁹then you shall do to him as he had meant to do to his brother. So you shall purge the evil³ from your midst. ²⁰And the rest shall hear and fear, and shall never again commit any such evil among you. ²¹Your eye shall not pity. It shall be life for life, eye for eye, tooth for tooth, hand for hand, foot for foot.

Psalm 106

Praise the Lord!
Oh give thanks to the Lord, for he is good,
for his steadfast love endures forever!
2 Who can utter the mighty deeds of the Lord,
or declare all his praise?
3 Blessed are they who observe justice,
who do righteousness at all times!

4 Remember me, O Lord, when you show favor to your people;
help me when you save them,⁴
5 that I may look upon the prosperity of your chosen ones,
that I may rejoice in the gladness of your nation,
that I may glory with your inheritance.

¹ Hebrew road ² Or the blood of the innocent ³ Or evil person ⁴ Or Remember me, O Lord, with the favor you show to your people; help me with your salvation

⁶ Both we and our fathers have sinned;
  we have committed iniquity; we have
    done wickedness.
⁷ Our fathers, when they were in Egypt,
  did not consider your wondrous works;
  they did not remember the abundance
    of your steadfast love,
  but rebelled by the sea, at the Red Sea.
⁸ Yet he saved them for his name's sake,
  that he might make known his
    mighty power.
⁹ He rebuked the Red Sea, and it became
    dry,
  and he led them through the deep as
    through a desert.
¹⁰ So he saved them from the hand of the
    foe
  and redeemed them from the power
    of the enemy.
¹¹ And the waters covered their adversaries;
  not one of them was left.
¹² Then they believed his words;
  they sang his praise.

¹³ But they soon forgot his works;
  they did not wait for his counsel.
¹⁴ But they had a wanton craving in the
    wilderness,
  and put God to the test in the desert;
¹⁵ he gave them what they asked,
  but sent a wasting disease among
    them.

¹⁶ When men in the camp were jealous of
    Moses
  and Aaron, the holy one of the Lord,
¹⁷ the earth opened and swallowed up
    Dathan,
  and covered the company of Abiram.
¹⁸ Fire also broke out in their company;
  the flame burned up the wicked.

¹⁹ They made a calf in Horeb
  and worshiped a metal image.
²⁰ They exchanged the glory of God[1]
  for the image of an ox that eats grass.
²¹ They forgot God, their Savior,
  who had done great things in Egypt,
²² wondrous works in the land of Ham,
  and awesome deeds by the Red Sea.
²³ Therefore he said he would destroy
    them—
  had not Moses, his chosen one,

stood in the breach before him,
  to turn away his wrath from
    destroying them.
²⁴ Then they despised the pleasant land,
  having no faith in his promise.
²⁵ They murmured in their tents,
  and did not obey the voice of the Lord.
²⁶ Therefore he raised his hand and swore
    to them
  that he would make them fall in the
    wilderness,
²⁷ and would make their offspring fall
    among the nations,
  scattering them among the lands.

²⁸ Then they yoked themselves to the Baal
    of Peor,
  and ate sacrifices offered to the dead;
²⁹ they provoked the Lord to anger with
    their deeds,
  and a plague broke out among them.
³⁰ Then Phinehas stood up and intervened,
  and the plague was stayed.
³¹ And that was counted to him as
    righteousness
  from generation to generation forever.

³² They angered him at the waters of
    Meribah,
  and it went ill with Moses on their
    account,
³³ for they made his spirit bitter,[2]
  and he spoke rashly with his lips.

³⁴ They did not destroy the peoples,
  as the Lord commanded them,
³⁵ but they mixed with the nations
  and learned to do as they did.
³⁶ They served their idols,
  which became a snare to them.
³⁷ They sacrificed their sons
  and their daughters to the demons;
³⁸ they poured out innocent blood,
  the blood of their sons and daughters,
  whom they sacrificed to the idols of
    Canaan,
  and the land was polluted with blood.
³⁹ Thus they became unclean by their acts,
  and played the whore in their deeds.

⁴⁰ Then the anger of the Lord was kindled
    against his people,
  and he abhorred his heritage;

[1] Hebrew *exchanged their glory* [2] Or *they rebelled against God's Spirit*

⁴¹ he gave them into the hand of the
        nations,
    so that those who hated them ruled
        over them.
⁴² Their enemies oppressed them,
    and they were brought into subjection
        under their power.
⁴³ Many times he delivered them,
    but they were rebellious in their
        purposes
    and were brought low through their
        iniquity.
⁴⁴ Nevertheless, he looked upon their
        distress,
    when he heard their cry.
⁴⁵ For their sake he remembered his
        covenant,
    and relented according to the
        abundance of his steadfast love.
⁴⁶ He caused them to be pitied
    by all those who held them captive.
⁴⁷ Save us, O LORD our God,
    and gather us from among the
        nations,
    that we may give thanks to your holy
        name
    and glory in your praise.
⁴⁸ Blessed be the LORD, the God of Israel,
    from everlasting to everlasting!
    And let all the people say, "Amen!"
    Praise the LORD!

Isaiah 46

Bel bows down; Nebo stoops;
    their idols are on beasts and livestock;
    these things you carry are borne
    as burdens on weary beasts.
² They stoop; they bow down together;
    they cannot save the burden,
    but themselves go into captivity.

³ "Listen to me, O house of Jacob,
    all the remnant of the house of Israel,
    who have been borne by me from before
        your birth,
    carried from the womb;
⁴ even to your old age I am he,
    and to gray hairs I will carry you.

I have made, and I will bear;
    I will carry and will save.
⁵ "To whom will you liken me and make
        me equal,
    and compare me, that we may be
        alike?
⁶ Those who lavish gold from the purse,
    and weigh out silver in the scales,
    hire a goldsmith, and he makes it into a
        god;
    then they fall down and worship!
⁷ They lift it to their shoulders, they carry
        it,
    they set it in its place, and it stands
        there;
    it cannot move from its place.
    If one cries to it, it does not answer
    or save him from his trouble.

⁸ "Remember this and stand firm,
    recall it to mind, you transgressors,
⁹   remember the former things of old;
    for I am God, and there is no other;
    I am God, and there is none like me,
¹⁰ declaring the end from the beginning
    and from ancient times things not yet
        done,
    saying, 'My counsel shall stand,
    and I will accomplish all my purpose,'
¹¹ calling a bird of prey from the east,
    the man of my counsel from a far
        country.
    I have spoken, and I will bring it to pass;
    I have purposed, and I will do it.

¹² "Listen to me, you stubborn of heart,
    you who are far from righteousness:
¹³ I bring near my righteousness; it is not
        far off,
    and my salvation will not delay;
    I will put salvation in Zion,
    for Israel my glory."

Revelation 16

Then I heard a loud voice from the temple tell-ing the seven angels, "Go and pour out on the earth the seven bowls of the wrath of God." ²So the first angel went and poured out his bowl on the earth, and harmful and painful sores came upon the people who bore the mark of the beast and worshiped its image.

[3] The second angel poured out his bowl into the sea, and it became like the blood of a corpse, and every living thing died that was in the sea.

[4] The third angel poured out his bowl into the rivers and the springs of water, and they became blood. [5] And I heard the angel in charge of the waters[1] say,

> "Just are you, O Holy One, who is and
>   who was,
>   for you brought these judgments.
> [6]   For they have shed the blood of saints
>   and prophets,
>   and you have given them blood to
>   drink.
> It is what they deserve!"

[7] And I heard the altar saying,

> "Yes, Lord God the Almighty,
>   true and just are your judgments!"

[8] The fourth angel poured out his bowl on the sun, and it was allowed to scorch people with fire. [9] They were scorched by the fierce heat, and they cursed[2] the name of God who had power over these plagues. They did not repent and give him glory. [10] The fifth angel poured out his bowl on the throne of the beast, and its kingdom was plunged into darkness. People gnawed their tongues in anguish [11] and cursed the God of heaven for their pain and sores. They did not repent of their deeds.

[12] The sixth angel poured out his bowl on the great river Euphrates, and its water was dried up, to prepare the way for the kings from the east. [13] And I saw, coming out of the mouth of the dragon and out of the mouth of the beast and out of the mouth of the false prophet, three unclean spirits like frogs. [14] For they are demonic spirits, performing signs, who go abroad to the kings of the whole world, to assemble them for battle on the great day of God the Almighty. [15] ("Behold, I am coming like a thief! Blessed is the one who stays awake, keeping his garments on, that he may not go about naked and be seen exposed!") [16] And they assembled them at the place that in Hebrew is called Armageddon.

[17] The seventh angel poured out his bowl into the air, and a loud voice came out of the temple, from the throne, saying, "It is done!" [18] And there were flashes of lightning, rumblings,[3] peals of thunder, and a great earthquake such as there had never been since man was on the earth, so great was that earthquake. [19] The great city was split into three parts, and the cities of the nations fell, and God remembered Babylon the great, to make her drain the cup of the wine of the fury of his wrath. [20] And every island fled away, and no mountains were to be found. [21] And great hailstones, about one hundred pounds[4] each, fell from heaven on people; and they cursed God for the plague of the hail, because the plague was so severe.

JUNE 15

Deuteronomy 20

[1] "When you go out to war against your enemies, and see horses and chariots and an army larger than your own, you shall not be afraid of them, for the LORD your God is with you, who brought you up out of the land of Egypt. [2] And when you draw near to the battle, the priest shall come forward and speak to the people [3] and shall say to them, 'Hear, O Israel, today you are drawing near for battle against your enemies: let not your heart faint. Do not fear or panic or be in dread of them, [4] for the LORD your God is he who goes with you to fight for you against your enemies, to give you the victory.' [5] Then the officers shall speak to the people, saying, 'Is there any man who has built a new house and has not dedicated it? Let him go back to his house, lest he die in the battle and another man dedicate it. [6] And is there

---

[1] Greek *angel of the waters*　[2] Greek *blasphemed; also verses 11, 21*　[3] Or *voices, or sounds*　[4] Greek *a talent in weight*

any man who has planted a vineyard and has not enjoyed its fruit? Let him go back to his house, lest he die in the battle and another man enjoy its fruit. [7]And is there any man who has betrothed a wife and has not taken her? Let him go back to his house, lest he die in the battle and another man take her.' [8]And the officers shall speak further to the people, and say, 'Is there any man who is fearful and fainthearted? Let him go back to his house, lest he make the heart of his fellows melt like his own.' [9]And when the officers have finished speaking to the people, then commanders shall be appointed at the head of the people.

[10]"When you draw near to a city to fight against it, offer terms of peace to it. [11]And if it responds to you peaceably and it opens to you, then all the people who are found in it shall do forced labor for you and shall serve you. [12]But if it makes no peace with you, but makes war against you, then you shall besiege it. [13]And when the LORD your God gives it into your hand, you shall put all its males to the sword, [14]but the women and the little ones, the livestock, and everything else in the city, all its spoil, you shall take as plunder for yourselves. And you shall enjoy the spoil of your enemies, which the LORD your God has given you. [15]Thus you shall do to all the cities that are very far from you, which are not cities of the nations here. [16]But in the cities of these peoples that the LORD your God is giving you for an inheritance, you shall save alive nothing that breathes, [17]but you shall devote them to complete destruction,[1] the Hittites and the Amorites, the Canaanites and the Perizzites, the Hivites and the Jebusites, as the LORD your God has commanded, [18]that they may not teach you to do according to all their abominable practices that they have done for their gods, and so you sin against the LORD your God.

[19]"When you besiege a city for a long time, making war against it in order to take it, you shall not destroy its trees by wielding an axe against them. You may eat from them, but you shall not cut them down. Are the trees in the field human, that they should be besieged by you? [20]Only the trees that you know are not trees for food you may destroy and cut down, that you may build siegeworks against the city that makes war with you, until it falls.

Psalm 107

Oh give thanks to the LORD, for he is good, for his steadfast love endures forever!
[2] Let the redeemed of the LORD say so, whom he has redeemed from trouble[2]
[3] and gathered in from the lands, from the east and from the west, from the north and from the south.

[4] Some wandered in desert wastes, finding no way to a city to dwell in;
[5] hungry and thirsty, their soul fainted within them.
[6] Then they cried to the LORD in their trouble, and he delivered them from their distress.
[7] He led them by a straight way till they reached a city to dwell in.
[8] Let them thank the LORD for his steadfast love, for his wondrous works to the children of man!
[9] For he satisfies the longing soul, and the hungry soul he fills with good things.

[10] Some sat in darkness and in the shadow of death, prisoners in affliction and in irons,
[11] for they had rebelled against the words of God, and spurned the counsel of the Most High.
[12] So he bowed their hearts down with hard labor; they fell down, with none to help.
[13] Then they cried to the LORD in their trouble, and he delivered them from their distress.
[14] He brought them out of darkness and the shadow of death, and burst their bonds apart.
[15] Let them thank the LORD for his steadfast love, for his wondrous works to the children of man!
[16] For he shatters the doors of bronze and cuts in two the bars of iron.

[1] That is, set apart (devote) as an offering to the Lord (for destruction) [2] Or *from the hand of the foe*

17 Some were fools through their sinful
    ways,
    and because of their iniquities
        suffered affliction;
18 they loathed any kind of food,
    and they drew near to the gates of
        death.
19 Then they cried to the LORD in their
        trouble,
    and he delivered them from their
        distress.
20 He sent out his word and healed them,
    and delivered them from their
        destruction.
21 Let them thank the LORD for his
        steadfast love,
    for his wondrous works to the
        children of man!
22 And let them offer sacrifices of
        thanksgiving,
    and tell of his deeds in songs of joy!

23 Some went down to the sea in ships,
    doing business on the great waters;
24 they saw the deeds of the LORD,
    his wondrous works in the deep.
25 For he commanded and raised the
        stormy wind,
    which lifted up the waves of the sea.
26 They mounted up to heaven; they went
        down to the depths;
    their courage melted away in their evil
        plight;
27 they reeled and staggered like drunken
        men
    and were at their wits' end.[1]
28 Then they cried to the LORD in their
        trouble,
    and he delivered them from their
        distress.
29 He made the storm be still,
    and the waves of the sea were
        hushed.
30 Then they were glad that the waters[2]
        were quiet,
    and he brought them to their desired
        haven.
31 Let them thank the LORD for his
        steadfast love,
    for his wondrous works to the
        children of man!

32 Let them extol him in the congregation
        of the people,
    and praise him in the assembly of the
        elders.
33 He turns rivers into a desert,
    springs of water into thirsty ground,
34 a fruitful land into a salty waste,
    because of the evil of its inhabitants.
35 He turns a desert into pools of water,
    a parched land into springs of water.
36 And there he lets the hungry dwell,
    and they establish a city to live in;
37 they sow fields and plant vineyards
    and get a fruitful yield.
38 By his blessing they multiply greatly,
    and he does not let their livestock
        diminish.

39 When they are diminished and brought
        low
    through oppression, evil, and sorrow,
40 he pours contempt on princes
    and makes them wander in trackless
        wastes;
41 but he raises up the needy out of
        affliction
    and makes their families like flocks.
42 The upright see it and are glad,
    and all wickedness shuts its mouth.

43 Whoever is wise, let him attend to these
        things;
    let them consider the steadfast love of
        the LORD.

—————— *Isaiah 47* ——————

Come down and sit in the dust,
    O virgin daughter of Babylon;
    sit on the ground without a throne,
        O daughter of the Chaldeans!
For you shall no more be called
    tender and delicate.
2 Take the millstones and grind flour,
    put off your veil,
    strip off your robe, uncover your legs,
        pass through the rivers.
3 Your nakedness shall be uncovered,
    and your disgrace shall be seen.
I will take vengeance,
    and I will spare no one.

[1] Hebrew *and all their wisdom was swallowed up* [2] Hebrew *they*

⁴   Our Redeemer—the LORD of hosts is his
        name—
      is the Holy One of Israel.

⁵   Sit in silence, and go into darkness,
        O daughter of the Chaldeans;
      for you shall no more be called
        the mistress of kingdoms.
⁶   I was angry with my people;
      I profaned my heritage;
      I gave them into your hand;
        you showed them no mercy;
      on the aged you made your yoke
        exceedingly heavy.
⁷   You said, "I shall be mistress forever,"
        so that you did not lay these things to
          heart
        or remember their end.

⁸   Now therefore hear this, you lover of
        pleasures,
      who sit securely,
      who say in your heart,
        "I am, and there is no one besides me;
      I shall not sit as a widow
        or know the loss of children":
⁹   These two things shall come to you
        in a moment, in one day;
      the loss of children and widowhood
        shall come upon you in full measure,
      in spite of your many sorceries
        and the great power of your
          enchantments.

¹⁰   You felt secure in your wickedness,
        you said, "No one sees me";
      your wisdom and your knowledge led
        you astray,
      and you said in your heart,
        "I am, and there is no one besides me."
¹¹   But evil shall come upon you,
        which you will not know how to
          charm away;
      disaster shall fall upon you,
        for which you will not be able to atone;
      and ruin shall come upon you suddenly,
        of which you know nothing.

¹²   Stand fast in your enchantments
        and your many sorceries,
      with which you have labored from
        your youth;
      perhaps you may be able to succeed;
        perhaps you may inspire terror.

¹³   You are wearied with your many
        counsels;
      let them stand forth and save you,
      those who divide the heavens,
        who gaze at the stars,
      who at the new moons make known
        what shall come upon you.

¹⁴   Behold, they are like stubble;
        the fire consumes them;
      they cannot deliver themselves
        from the power of the flame.
      No coal for warming oneself is this,
        no fire to sit before!
¹⁵   Such to you are those with whom you
        have labored,
      who have done business with you
        from your youth;
      they wander about, each in his own
        direction;
      there is no one to save you.

Revelation 17

Then one of the seven angels who had the seven bowls came and said to me, "Come, I will show you the judgment of the great prostitute who is seated on many waters, ²with whom the kings of the earth have committed sexual immorality, and with the wine of whose sexual immorality the dwellers on earth have become drunk." ³And he carried me away in the Spirit into a wilderness, and I saw a woman sitting on a scarlet beast that was full of blasphemous names, and it had seven heads and ten horns. ⁴The woman was arrayed in purple and scarlet, and adorned with gold and jewels and pearls, holding in her hand a golden cup full of abominations and the impurities of her sexual immorality. ⁵And on her forehead was written a name of mystery: "Babylon the great, mother of prostitutes and of earth's abominations." ⁶And I saw the woman, drunk with the blood of the saints, the blood of the martyrs of Jesus.¹

When I saw her, I marveled greatly. ⁷But the angel said to me, "Why do you marvel? I will tell you the mystery of the woman, and of the beast with seven heads and ten horns that carries her. ⁸The beast that you saw was, and is not, and is about to rise from the bottomless pit² and go to destruction. And the dwellers

¹ Greek *the witnesses to Jesus* ² Greek *the abyss*

on earth whose names have not been written in the book of life from the foundation of the world will marvel to see the beast, because it was and is not and is to come. [9]This calls for a mind with wisdom: the seven heads are seven mountains on which the woman is seated; [10]they are also seven kings, five of whom have fallen, one is, the other has not yet come, and when he does come he must remain only a little while. [11]As for the beast that was and is not, it is an eighth but it belongs to the seven, and it goes to destruction. [12]And the ten horns that you saw are ten kings who have not yet received royal power, but they are to receive authority as kings for one hour, together with the beast. [13]These are of one mind, and they hand over their power and authority to the beast. [14]They will make war on the Lamb, and the Lamb will conquer them, for he is Lord of lords and King of kings, and those with him are called and chosen and faithful."

[15]And the angel[1] said to me, "The waters that you saw, where the prostitute is seated, are peoples and multitudes and nations and languages. [16]And the ten horns that you saw, they and the beast will hate the prostitute. They will make her desolate and naked, and devour her flesh and burn her up with fire, [17]for God has put it into their hearts to carry out his purpose by being of one mind and handing over their royal power to the beast, until the words of God are fulfilled. [18]And the woman that you saw is the great city that has dominion over the kings of the earth."

JUNE 16

Deuteronomy 21

"If in the land that the LORD your God is giving you to possess someone is found slain, lying in the open country, and it is not known who killed him, [2]then your elders and your judges shall come out, and they shall measure the distance to the surrounding cities. [3]And the elders of the city that is nearest to the slain man shall take a heifer that has never been worked and that has not pulled in a yoke. [4]And the elders of that city shall bring the heifer down to a valley with running water, which is neither plowed nor sown, and shall break the heifer's neck there in the valley. [5]Then the priests, the sons of Levi, shall come forward, for the LORD your God has chosen them to minister to him and to bless in the name of the LORD, and by their word every dispute and every assault shall be settled. [6]And all the elders of that city nearest to the slain man shall wash their hands over the heifer whose neck was broken in the valley, [7]and they shall testify, 'Our hands did not shed this blood, nor did our eyes see it shed. [8]Accept atonement, O LORD, for your people Israel, whom you have redeemed, and do not set the guilt of innocent blood in the midst of your people Israel, so that their blood guilt be atoned for.' [9]So you shall purge the guilt of innocent blood from your midst, when you do what is right in the sight of the LORD.

[10]"When you go out to war against your enemies, and the LORD your God gives them into your hand and you take them captive, [11]and you see among the captives a beautiful woman, and you desire to take her to be your wife, [12]and you bring her home to your house, she shall shave her head and pare her nails. [13]And she shall take off the clothes in which she was captured and shall remain in your house and lament her father and her mother a full month. After that you may go in to her and be her husband, and she shall be your wife. [14]But if you no longer delight in her, you shall let her go where she wants. But you shall not sell her for money, nor shall you treat her as a slave, since you have humiliated her.

[15]"If a man has two wives, the one loved and the other unloved, and both the loved and the unloved have borne him children, and if the

[1] Greek he

firstborn son belongs to the unloved,[1] [16]then on the day when he assigns his possessions as an inheritance to his sons, he may not treat the son of the loved as the firstborn in preference to the son of the unloved, who is the firstborn, [17]but he shall acknowledge the firstborn, the son of the unloved, by giving him a double portion of all that he has, for he is the firstfruits of his strength. The right of the firstborn is his.

[18]"If a man has a stubborn and rebellious son who will not obey the voice of his father or the voice of his mother, and, though they discipline him, will not listen to them, [19]then his father and his mother shall take hold of him and bring him out to the elders of his city at the gate of the place where he lives, [20]and they shall say to the elders of his city, 'This our son is stubborn and rebellious; he will not obey our voice; he is a glutton and a drunkard.' [21]Then all the men of the city shall stone him to death with stones. So you shall purge the evil from your midst, and all Israel shall hear, and fear.

[22]"And if a man has committed a crime punishable by death and he is put to death, and you hang him on a tree, [23]his body shall not remain all night on the tree, but you shall bury him the same day, for a hanged man is cursed by God. You shall not defile your land that the LORD your God is giving you for an inheritance.

--------- *Psalm 108–109* ---------

A Song. A Psalm of David.

M y heart is steadfast, O God!
   I will sing and make melody with all my
     being![2]
[2] Awake, O harp and lyre!
     I will awake the dawn!
[3] I will give thanks to you, O LORD, among
     the peoples;
     I will sing praises to you among the
     nations.
[4] For your steadfast love is great above the
     heavens;
     your faithfulness reaches to the clouds.

[5] Be exalted, O God, above the heavens!
     Let your glory be over all the earth!
[6] That your beloved ones may be
     delivered,
     give salvation by your right hand and
     answer me!

[7] God has promised in his holiness:[3]
     "With exultation I will divide up
       Shechem
     and portion out the Valley of Succoth.
[8] Gilead is mine; Manasseh is mine;
     Ephraim is my helmet,
     Judah my scepter.
[9] Moab is my washbasin;
     upon Edom I cast my shoe;
     over Philistia I shout in triumph."

[10] Who will bring me to the fortified city?
     Who will lead me to Edom?
[11] Have you not rejected us, O God?
     You do not go out, O God, with our
      armies.
[12] Oh grant us help against the foe,
     for vain is the salvation of man!
[13] With God we shall do valiantly;
     it is he who will tread down our foes.

To the choirmaster. A Psalm of David.

B e not silent, O God of my praise!
  [2]For wicked and deceitful mouths are
     opened against me,
     speaking against me with lying
      tongues.
[3] They encircle me with words of hate,
     and attack me without cause.
[4] In return for my love they accuse me,
     but I give myself to prayer.[4]
[5] So they reward me evil for good,
     and hatred for my love.

[6] Appoint a wicked man against him;
     let an accuser stand at his right hand.
[7] When he is tried, let him come forth
      guilty;
     let his prayer be counted as sin!
[8] May his days be few;
     may another take his office!
[9] May his children be fatherless
     and his wife a widow!
[10] May his children wander about and beg,
     seeking food far from the ruins they
      inhabit!
[11] May the creditor seize all that he has;
     may strangers plunder the fruits of his
      toil!
[12] Let there be none to extend kindness to
      him,
     nor any to pity his fatherless children!

[1] Or *hated*; also verses 16, 17 [2] Hebrew *with my glory* [3] Or *sanctuary* [4] Hebrew *but I am prayer*

13 May his posterity be cut off;
   may his name be blotted out in the
   second generation!
14 May the iniquity of his fathers be
   remembered before the LORD,
   and let not the sin of his mother be
   blotted out!
15 Let them be before the LORD continually,
   that he may cut off the memory of
   them from the earth!

16 For he did not remember to show
   kindness,
   but pursued the poor and needy
   and the brokenhearted, to put them to
   death.
17 He loved to curse; let curses come[1] upon
   him!
   He did not delight in blessing; may it
   be far[2] from him!
18 He clothed himself with cursing as his
   coat;
   may it soak[3] into his body like water,
   like oil into his bones!
19 May it be like a garment that he wraps
   around him,
   like a belt that he puts on every day!
20 May this be the reward of my accusers
   from the LORD,
   of those who speak evil against my
   life!

21 But you, O GOD my Lord,
   deal on my behalf for your name's
   sake;
   because your steadfast love is good,
   deliver me!
22 For I am poor and needy,
   and my heart is stricken within me.
23 I am gone like a shadow at evening;
   I am shaken off like a locust.
24 My knees are weak through fasting;
   my body has become gaunt, with no
   fat.
25 I am an object of scorn to my accusers;
   when they see me, they wag their
   heads.

26 Help me, O LORD my God!
   Save me according to your steadfast
   love!
27 Let them know that this is your hand;
   you, O LORD, have done it!

28 Let them curse, but you will bless!
   They arise and are put to shame, but
   your servant will be glad!
29 May my accusers be clothed with
   dishonor;
   may they be wrapped in their own
   shame as in a cloak!

30 With my mouth I will give great thanks
   to the LORD;
   I will praise him in the midst of the
   throng.
31 For he stands at the right hand of the
   needy one,
   to save him from those who condemn
   his soul to death.

─────── *Isaiah 48* ───────

Hear this, O house of Jacob,
   who are called by the name of Israel,
   and who came from the waters of
   Judah,
   who swear by the name of the LORD
   and confess the God of Israel,
   but not in truth or right.
2 For they call themselves after the holy
   city,
   and stay themselves on the God of
   Israel;
   the LORD of hosts is his name.

3 "The former things I declared of old;
   they went out from my mouth, and I
   announced them;
   then suddenly I did them, and they
   came to pass.
4 Because I know that you are obstinate,
   and your neck is an iron sinew
   and your forehead brass,
5 I declared them to you from of old,
   before they came to pass I announced
   them to you,
   lest you should say, 'My idol did them,
   my carved image and my metal image
   commanded them.'

6 "You have heard; now see all this;
   and will you not declare it?
   From this time forth I announce to you
   new things,
   hidden things that you have not
   known.

[1] Revocalization; Masoretic Text *curses have come* [2] Revocalization; Masoretic Text *it is far* [3] Revocalization; Masoretic Text *it has soaked*

7 They are created now, not long ago;
  before today you have never heard of
    them,
  lest you should say, 'Behold, I knew
    them.'
8 You have never heard, you have never
    known,
  from of old your ear has not been
    opened.
  For I knew that you would surely deal
    treacherously,
  and that from before birth you were
    called a rebel.

9 "For my name's sake I defer my anger,
  for the sake of my praise I restrain it
    for you,
  that I may not cut you off.
10 Behold, I have refined you, but not as
    silver;
  I have tried[1] you in the furnace of
    affliction.
11 For my own sake, for my own sake, I do
    it,
  for how should my name[2] be
    profaned?
  My glory I will not give to another.

12 "Listen to me, O Jacob,
  and Israel, whom I called!
  I am he; I am the first,
  and I am the last.
13 My hand laid the foundation of the
    earth,
  and my right hand spread out the
    heavens;
  when I call to them,
  they stand forth together.

14 "Assemble, all of you, and listen!
  Who among them has declared these
    things?
  The LORD loves him;
  he shall perform his purpose on
    Babylon,
  and his arm shall be against the
    Chaldeans.
15 I, even I, have spoken and called him;
  I have brought him, and he will
    prosper in his way.
16 Draw near to me, hear this:
  from the beginning I have not spoken
    in secret,
  from the time it came to be I have
    been there."
  And now the Lord GOD has sent me, and
    his Spirit.

17 Thus says the LORD,
  your Redeemer, the Holy One of Israel:
  "I am the LORD your God,
  who teaches you to profit,
  who leads you in the way you should
    go.
18 Oh that you had paid attention to my
    commandments!
  Then your peace would have been like
    a river,
  and your righteousness like the waves
    of the sea;
19 your offspring would have been like the
    sand,
  and your descendants like its grains;
  their name would never be cut off
  or destroyed from before me."

20 Go out from Babylon, flee from Chaldea,
  declare this with a shout of joy,
    proclaim it,
  send it out to the end of the earth;
  say, "The LORD has redeemed his
    servant Jacob!"
21 They did not thirst when he led them
    through the deserts;
  he made water flow for them from the
    rock;
  he split the rock and the water gushed
    out.

22 "There is no peace," says the LORD, "for
    the wicked."

Revelation 18

After this I saw another angel coming down
from heaven, having great authority, and
the earth was made bright with his glory. ² And
he called out with a mighty voice,

"Fallen, fallen is Babylon the great!
  She has become a dwelling place for
    demons,
  a haunt for every unclean spirit,
  a haunt for every unclean bird,
  a haunt for every unclean and
    detestable beast.

---

[1] Or I have chosen [2] Hebrew lacks my name

³ For all nations have drunk[1]
    the wine of the passion of her sexual
      immorality,
  and the kings of the earth have
      committed immorality with her,
  and the merchants of the earth have
      grown rich from the power of her
      luxurious living."

⁴ Then I heard another voice from heaven
saying,

  "Come out of her, my people,
    lest you take part in her sins,
  lest you share in her plagues;
⁵ for her sins are heaped high as heaven,
    and God has remembered her
      iniquities.
⁶ Pay her back as she herself has paid back
      others,
  and repay her double for her deeds;
  mix a double portion for her in the
      cup she mixed.
⁷ As she glorified herself and lived in
      luxury,
  so give her a like measure of torment
      and mourning,
  since in her heart she says,
  'I sit as a queen,
  I am no widow,
  and mourning I shall never see.'
⁸ For this reason her plagues will come in
      a single day,
  death and mourning and famine,
  and she will be burned up with fire;
    for mighty is the Lord God who has
      judged her."

⁹ And the kings of the earth, who committed
sexual immorality and lived in luxury with her,
will weep and wail over her when they see the
smoke of her burning. ¹⁰ They will stand far off,
in fear of her torment, and say,

  "Alas! Alas! You great city,
    you mighty city, Babylon!
  For in a single hour your judgment has
      come."

¹¹ And the merchants of the earth weep and
mourn for her, since no one buys their cargo
anymore, ¹² cargo of gold, silver, jewels, pearls,
fine linen, purple cloth, silk, scarlet cloth, all
kinds of scented wood, all kinds of articles

of ivory, all kinds of articles of costly wood,
bronze, iron and marble, ¹³ cinnamon, spice,
incense, myrrh, frankincense, wine, oil, fine
flour, wheat, cattle and sheep, horses and chariots, and slaves, that is, human souls.[2]

¹⁴ "The fruit for which your soul longed
    has gone from you,
  and all your delicacies and your
      splendors
  are lost to you,
    never to be found again!"

¹⁵ The merchants of these wares, who gained
wealth from her, will stand far off, in fear of her
torment, weeping and mourning aloud,

¹⁶ "Alas, alas, for the great city
    that was clothed in fine linen,
      in purple and scarlet,
    adorned with gold,
      with jewels, and with pearls!
¹⁷ For in a single hour all this wealth has
      been laid waste."

And all shipmasters and seafaring men, sailors and all whose trade is on the sea, stood far
off ¹⁸ and cried out as they saw the smoke of
her burning,

"What city was like the great city?"

¹⁹ And they threw dust on their heads as they
wept and mourned, crying out,

  "Alas, alas, for the great city
    where all who had ships at sea
    grew rich by her wealth!
  For in a single hour she has been laid
      waste.
²⁰ Rejoice over her, O heaven,
    and you saints and apostles and
      prophets,
  for God has given judgment for you
      against her!"

²¹ Then a mighty angel took up a stone like
a great millstone and threw it into the sea,
saying,

  "So will Babylon the great city be thrown
    down with violence,
  and will be found no more;
²² and the sound of harpists and musicians,
    of flute players and trumpeters,
  will be heard in you no more,

---

¹ Some manuscripts *fallen by* ² Or *and slaves, and human lives*

and a craftsman of any craft
  will be found in you no more,
and the sound of the mill
  will be heard in you no more,
23 and the light of a lamp
  will shine in you no more,
and the voice of bridegroom and bride
  will be heard in you no more,

for your merchants were the great ones
  of the earth,
and all nations were deceived by your
  sorcery.
24 And in her was found the blood of
  prophets and of saints,
and of all who have been slain on
  earth."

JUNE 17

Deuteronomy 22

"You shall not see your brother's ox or his sheep going astray and ignore them. You shall take them back to your brother. ²And if he does not live near you and you do not know who he is, you shall bring it home to your house, and it shall stay with you until your brother seeks it. Then you shall restore it to him. ³And you shall do the same with his donkey or with his garment, or with any lost thing of your brother's, which he loses and you find; you may not ignore it. ⁴You shall not see your brother's donkey or his ox fallen down by the way and ignore them. You shall help him to lift them up again.

⁵"A woman shall not wear a man's garment, nor shall a man put on a woman's cloak, for whoever does these things is an abomination to the LORD your God.

⁶"If you come across a bird's nest in any tree or on the ground, with young ones or eggs and the mother sitting on the young or on the eggs, you shall not take the mother with the young. ⁷You shall let the mother go, but the young you may take for yourself, that it may go well with you, and that you may live long.

⁸"When you build a new house, you shall make a parapet for your roof, that you may not bring the guilt of blood upon your house, if anyone should fall from it.

⁹"You shall not sow your vineyard with two kinds of seed, lest the whole yield be forfeited,¹ the crop that you have sown and the yield of the vineyard. ¹⁰You shall not plow with an ox and a donkey together. ¹¹You shall not wear cloth of wool and linen mixed together.

¹²"You shall make yourself tassels on the four corners of the garment with which you cover yourself.

¹³"If any man takes a wife and goes in to her and then hates her ¹⁴and accuses her of misconduct and brings a bad name upon her, saying, 'I took this woman, and when I came near her, I did not find in her evidence of virginity,' ¹⁵then the father of the young woman and her mother shall take and bring out the evidence of her virginity to the elders of the city in the gate. ¹⁶And the father of the young woman shall say to the elders, 'I gave my daughter to this man to marry, and he hates her; ¹⁷and behold, he has accused her of misconduct, saying, "I did not find in your daughter evidence of virginity." And yet this is the evidence of my daughter's virginity.' And they shall spread the cloak before the elders of the city. ¹⁸Then the elders of that city shall take the man and whip² him, ¹⁹and they shall fine him a hundred shekels³ of silver and give them to the father of the young woman, because he has brought a bad name upon a virgin⁴ of Israel. And she shall be his wife. He may not divorce her all his days. ²⁰But if the thing is true, that evidence of virginity was not found in the young woman, ²¹then they shall bring out the young woman to the door of her father's house, and the men of her city shall stone her to death with stones, because

¹ Hebrew *become holy* ² Or *discipline* ³ A *shekel* was about 2/5 ounce or 11 grams ⁴ Or *girl of marriageable age*

she has done an outrageous thing in Israel by whoring in her father's house. So you shall purge the evil from your midst.

²² "If a man is found lying with the wife of another man, both of them shall die, the man who lay with the woman, and the woman. So you shall purge the evil from Israel.

²³ "If there is a betrothed virgin, and a man meets her in the city and lies with her, ²⁴ then you shall bring them both out to the gate of that city, and you shall stone them to death with stones, the young woman because she did not cry for help though she was in the city, and the man because he violated his neighbor's wife. So you shall purge the evil from your midst.

²⁵ "But if in the open country a man meets a young woman who is betrothed, and the man seizes her and lies with her, then only the man who lay with her shall die. ²⁶ But you shall do nothing to the young woman; she has committed no offense punishable by death. For this case is like that of a man attacking and murdering his neighbor, ²⁷ because he met her in the open country, and though the betrothed young woman cried for help there was no one to rescue her.

²⁸ "If a man meets a virgin who is not betrothed, and seizes her and lies with her, and they are found, ²⁹ then the man who lay with her shall give to the father of the young woman fifty shekels of silver, and she shall be his wife, because he has violated her. He may not divorce her all his days.

³⁰ ¹ "A man shall not take his father's wife, so that he does not uncover his father's nakedness.²

---------- *Psalm 110–111*³ ----------

A PSALM OF DAVID.

The LORD says to my Lord:
   "Sit at my right hand,
     until I make your enemies your
      footstool."

² The LORD sends forth from Zion
     your mighty scepter.
     Rule in the midst of your enemies!
³ Your people will offer themselves freely
     on the day of your power,⁴
     in holy garments;⁵
   from the womb of the morning,
     the dew of your youth will be yours.⁶

⁴ The LORD has sworn
     and will not change his mind,
   "You are a priest forever
     after the order of Melchizedek."
⁵ The Lord is at your right hand;
     he will shatter kings on the day of his
      wrath.
⁶ He will execute judgment among the
     nations,
     filling them with corpses;
   he will shatter chiefs⁷
     over the wide earth.
⁷ He will drink from the brook by the
     way;
     therefore he will lift up his head.

Praise the LORD!
I will give thanks to the LORD with my
     whole heart,
     in the company of the upright, in the
      congregation.
² Great are the works of the LORD,
     studied by all who delight in them.
³ Full of splendor and majesty is his
     work,
     and his righteousness endures
      forever.
⁴ He has caused his wondrous works to be
     remembered;
     the LORD is gracious and merciful.
⁵ He provides food for those who fear him;
     he remembers his covenant forever.
⁶ He has shown his people the power of
     his works,
     in giving them the inheritance of the
      nations.
⁷ The works of his hands are faithful and
     just;
     all his precepts are trustworthy;
⁸ they are established forever and ever,
     to be performed with faithfulness and
      uprightness.
⁹ He sent redemption to his people;
     he has commanded his covenant
      forever.
     Holy and awesome is his name!
¹⁰ The fear of the LORD is the beginning of
     wisdom;
     all those who practice it have a good
      understanding.
     His praise endures forever!

¹ Ch 23:1 in Hebrew ² Hebrew *uncover his father's skirt* ³ This psalm is an acrostic poem, each line beginning with the successive letters of the Hebrew alphabet ⁴ Or *on the day you lead your forces* ⁵ Masoretic Text; some Hebrew manuscripts and Jerome *on the holy mountains* ⁶ The meaning of the Hebrew is uncertain ⁷ Or *the head*

Isaiah 49

Listen to me, O coastlands,
  and give attention, you peoples from afar.
The LORD called me from the womb,
  from the body of my mother he
    named my name.
2 He made my mouth like a sharp sword;
  in the shadow of his hand he hid me;
he made me a polished arrow;
  in his quiver he hid me away.
3 And he said to me, "You are my servant,
  Israel, in whom I will be glorified."[1]
4 But I said, "I have labored in vain;
  I have spent my strength for nothing
    and vanity;
yet surely my right is with the LORD,
  and my recompense with my God."

5 And now the LORD says,
  he who formed me from the womb to
    be his servant,
to bring Jacob back to him;
  and that Israel might be gathered to
    him—
for I am honored in the eyes of the LORD,
  and my God has become my
    strength—
6 he says:
"It is too light a thing that you should be
    my servant
  to raise up the tribes of Jacob
    and to bring back the preserved of
      Israel;
I will make you as a light for the nations,
  that my salvation may reach to the
    end of the earth."

7 Thus says the LORD,
  the Redeemer of Israel and his Holy
    One,
to one deeply despised, abhorred by the
    nation,
  the servant of rulers:
"Kings shall see and arise;
  princes, and they shall prostrate
    themselves;
because of the LORD, who is faithful,
  the Holy One of Israel, who has
    chosen you."

8 Thus says the LORD:

"In a time of favor I have answered you;
  in a day of salvation I have helped
    you;
I will keep you and give you
  as a covenant to the people,
to establish the land,
  to apportion the desolate heritages,
9 saying to the prisoners, 'Come out,'
  to those who are in darkness, 'Appear.'
They shall feed along the ways;
  on all bare heights shall be their
    pasture;
10 they shall not hunger or thirst,
  neither scorching wind nor sun shall
    strike them,
for he who has pity on them will lead
    them,
  and by springs of water will guide
    them.
11 And I will make all my mountains a
    road,
  and my highways shall be raised up.
12 Behold, these shall come from afar,
  and behold, these from the north and
    from the west,[2]
  and these from the land of Syene."[3]

13 Sing for joy, O heavens, and exult,
    O earth;
  break forth, O mountains, into
    singing!
For the LORD has comforted his people
  and will have compassion on his
    afflicted.

14 But Zion said, "The LORD has forsaken
    me;
  my Lord has forgotten me."

15 "Can a woman forget her nursing child,
  that she should have no compassion
    on the son of her womb?
Even these may forget,
  yet I will not forget you.
16 Behold, I have engraved you on the
    palms of my hands;
  your walls are continually before me.
17 Your builders make haste;[4]
  your destroyers and those who laid
    you waste go out from you.
18 Lift up your eyes around and see;
  they all gather, they come to you.

[1] Or *I will display my beauty* [2] Hebrew *from the sea* [3] Dead Sea Scroll; Masoretic Text *Sinim* [4] Dead Sea Scroll; Masoretic Text *Your children make haste*

As I live, declares the LORD,
  you shall put them all on as an
    ornament;
  you shall bind them on as a bride does.

19 "Surely your waste and your desolate
    places
  and your devastated land—
surely now you will be too narrow for
    your inhabitants,
  and those who swallowed you up will
    be far away.
20 The children of your bereavement
    will yet say in your ears:
'The place is too narrow for me;
  make room for me to dwell in.'
21 Then you will say in your heart:
  'Who has borne me these?
I was bereaved and barren,
  exiled and put away,
  but who has brought up these?
Behold, I was left alone;
  from where have these come?'"

22 Thus says the Lord GOD:
"Behold, I will lift up my hand to the
    nations,
  and raise my signal to the peoples;
and they shall bring your sons in their
    arms,[1]
  and your daughters shall be carried on
    their shoulders.
23 Kings shall be your foster fathers,
  and their queens your nursing
    mothers.
With their faces to the ground they shall
    bow down to you,
  and lick the dust of your feet.
Then you will know that I am the LORD;
  those who wait for me shall not be put
    to shame."

24 Can the prey be taken from the mighty,
  or the captives of a tyrant[2] be
    rescued?
25 For thus says the LORD:
"Even the captives of the mighty shall be
    taken,
  and the prey of the tyrant be rescued,
for I will contend with those who
  contend with you,
  and I will save your children.

26   I will make your oppressors eat their
    own flesh,
  and they shall be drunk with their
    own blood as with wine.
Then all flesh shall know
  that I am the LORD your Savior,
  and your Redeemer, the Mighty One
    of Jacob."

Revelation 19

After this I heard what seemed to be the loud voice of a great multitude in heaven, crying out,

  "Hallelujah!
  Salvation and glory and power belong to
    our God,
2   for his judgments are true and just;
for he has judged the great prostitute
  who corrupted the earth with her
    immorality,
  and has avenged on her the blood of his
    servants."[3]

3 Once more they cried out,

  "Hallelujah!
  The smoke from her goes up forever and
    ever."

4 And the twenty-four elders and the four living creatures fell down and worshiped God who was seated on the throne, saying, "Amen. Hallelujah!" 5 And from the throne came a voice saying,

  "Praise our God,
  all you his servants,
you who fear him,
  small and great."

6 Then I heard what seemed to be the voice of a great multitude, like the roar of many waters and like the sound of mighty peals of thunder, crying out,

  "Hallelujah!
  For the Lord our God
    the Almighty reigns.
7   Let us rejoice and exult
    and give him the glory,
for the marriage of the Lamb has come,
  and his Bride has made herself ready;

---

[1] Hebrew *in their bosom* [2] Dead Sea Scroll, Syriac, Vulgate (see also verse 25); Masoretic Text *of a righteous man* [3] Greek *bondservants*; also verse 5

8   it was granted her to clothe herself
      with fine linen, bright and pure"—

for the fine linen is the righteous deeds of the saints.

[9]And the angel said[1] to me, "Write this: Blessed are those who are invited to the marriage supper of the Lamb." And he said to me, "These are the true words of God." [10]Then I fell down at his feet to worship him, but he said to me, "You must not do that! I am a fellow servant[2] with you and your brothers who hold to the testimony of Jesus. Worship God." For the testimony of Jesus is the spirit of prophecy.

[11]Then I saw heaven opened, and behold, a white horse! The one sitting on it is called Faithful and True, and in righteousness he judges and makes war. [12]His eyes are like a flame of fire, and on his head are many diadems, and he has a name written that no one knows but himself. [13]He is clothed in a robe dipped in[3] blood, and the name by which he is called is The Word of God. [14]And the armies of heaven, arrayed in fine linen, white and pure, were following him on white horses. [15]From his mouth comes a sharp sword with which to strike down the nations, and he will rule them with a rod of iron. He will tread the winepress of the fury of the wrath of God the Almighty. [16]On his robe and on his thigh he has a name written, King of kings and Lord of lords.

[17]Then I saw an angel standing in the sun, and with a loud voice he called to all the birds that fly directly overhead, "Come, gather for the great supper of God, [18]to eat the flesh of kings, the flesh of captains, the flesh of mighty men, the flesh of horses and their riders, and the flesh of all men, both free and slave,[4] both small and great." [19]And I saw the beast and the kings of the earth with their armies gathered to make war against him who was sitting on the horse and against his army. [20]And the beast was captured, and with it the false prophet who in its presence[5] had done the signs by which he deceived those who had received the mark of the beast and those who worshiped its image. These two were thrown alive into the lake of fire that burns with sulfur. [21]And the rest were slain by the sword that came from the mouth of him who was sitting on the horse, and all the birds were gorged with their flesh.

JUNE 18

Deuteronomy 23

"No one whose testicles are crushed or whose male organ is cut off shall enter the assembly of the Lord.

[2]"No one born of a forbidden union may enter the assembly of the Lord. Even to the tenth generation, none of his descendants may enter the assembly of the Lord.

[3]"No Ammonite or Moabite may enter the assembly of the Lord. Even to the tenth generation, none of them may enter the assembly of the Lord forever, [4]because they did not meet you with bread and with water on the way, when you came out of Egypt, and because they hired against you Balaam the son of Beor from Pethor of Mesopotamia, to curse you. [5]But the Lord your God would not listen to Balaam; instead the Lord your God turned the curse into a blessing for you, because the Lord your God loved you. [6]You shall not seek their peace or their prosperity all your days forever.

[7]"You shall not abhor an Edomite, for he is your brother. You shall not abhor an Egyptian, because you were a sojourner in his land. [8]Children born to them in the third generation may enter the assembly of the Lord.

[9]"When you are encamped against your enemies, then you shall keep yourself from every evil thing.

[10]"If any man among you becomes unclean because of a nocturnal emission, then he shall

---

[1] Greek he said [2] Greek fellow bondservant [3] Some manuscripts sprinkled with [4] Greek bondservant [5] Or on its behalf

go outside the camp. He shall not come inside the camp, [11] but when evening comes, he shall bathe himself in water, and as the sun sets, he may come inside the camp.

[12] "You shall have a place outside the camp, and you shall go out to it. [13] And you shall have a trowel with your tools, and when you sit down outside, you shall dig a hole with it and turn back and cover up your excrement. [14] Because the LORD your God walks in the midst of your camp, to deliver you and to give up your enemies before you, therefore your camp must be holy, so that he may not see anything indecent among you and turn away from you.

[15] "You shall not give up to his master a slave[1] who has escaped from his master to you. [16] He shall dwell with you, in your midst, in the place that he shall choose within one of your towns, wherever it suits him. You shall not wrong him.

[17] "None of the daughters of Israel shall be a cult prostitute, and none of the sons of Israel shall be a cult prostitute. [18] You shall not bring the fee of a prostitute or the wages of a dog[2] into the house of the LORD your God in payment for any vow, for both of these are an abomination to the LORD your God.

[19] "You shall not charge interest on loans to your brother, interest on money, interest on food, interest on anything that is lent for interest. [20] You may charge a foreigner interest, but you may not charge your brother interest, that the LORD your God may bless you in all that you undertake in the land that you are entering to take possession of it.

[21] "If you make a vow to the LORD your God, you shall not delay fulfilling it, for the LORD your God will surely require it of you, and you will be guilty of sin. [22] But if you refrain from vowing, you will not be guilty of sin. [23] You shall be careful to do what has passed your lips, for you have voluntarily vowed to the LORD your God what you have promised with your mouth.

[24] "If you go into your neighbor's vineyard, you may eat your fill of grapes, as many as you wish, but you shall not put any in your bag. [25] If you go into your neighbor's standing grain, you may pluck the ears with your hand, but you shall not put a sickle to your neighbor's standing grain.

Psalm 112[3]–113

Praise the LORD!
Blessed is the man who fears the LORD,
who greatly delights in his
commandments!
2 His offspring will be mighty in the land;
the generation of the upright will be
blessed.
3 Wealth and riches are in his house,
and his righteousness endures
forever.
4 Light dawns in the darkness for the
upright;
he is gracious, merciful, and
righteous.
5 It is well with the man who deals
generously and lends;
who conducts his affairs with justice.
6 For the righteous will never be moved;
he will be remembered forever.
7 He is not afraid of bad news;
his heart is firm, trusting in the LORD.
8 His heart is steady; he will not be afraid,
until he looks in triumph on his
adversaries.
9 He has distributed freely; he has given to
the poor;
his righteousness endures forever;
his horn is exalted in honor.
10 The wicked man sees it and is angry;
he gnashes his teeth and melts away;
the desire of the wicked will perish!

Praise the LORD!
Praise, O servants of the LORD,
praise the name of the LORD!
2 Blessed be the name of the LORD
from this time forth and forevermore!
3 From the rising of the sun to its setting,
the name of the LORD is to be praised!
4 The LORD is high above all nations,
and his glory above the heavens!
5 Who is like the LORD our God,
who is seated on high,
6 who looks far down
on the heavens and the earth?
7 He raises the poor from the dust
and lifts the needy from the ash heap,
8 to make them sit with princes,
with the princes of his people.

[1] Or *servant*; the Hebrew term *'ebed* designates a range of social and economic roles (see Preface) [2] Or *male prostitute* [3] This psalm is an acrostic poem, each line beginning with the successive letters of the Hebrew alphabet

9   He gives the barren woman a home,
     making her the joyous mother of
       children.
     Praise the LORD!

Isaiah 50

Thus says the LORD:
    "Where is your mother's certificate of
      divorce,
    with which I sent her away?
  Or which of my creditors is it
    to whom I have sold you?
  Behold, for your iniquities you were sold,
    and for your transgressions your
      mother was sent away.
2 Why, when I came, was there no man;
    why, when I called, was there no one
      to answer?
  Is my hand shortened, that it cannot
      redeem?
  Or have I no power to deliver?
  Behold, by my rebuke I dry up the sea,
    I make the rivers a desert;
  their fish stink for lack of water
    and die of thirst.
3 I clothe the heavens with blackness
    and make sackcloth their covering."

4 The Lord GOD has given me
    the tongue of those who are taught,
  that I may know how to sustain with a
      word
    him who is weary.
  Morning by morning he awakens;
    he awakens my ear
  to hear as those who are taught.
5 The Lord GOD has opened my ear,
    and I was not rebellious;
  I turned not backward.
6 I gave my back to those who strike,
    and my cheeks to those who pull out
      the beard;
  I hid not my face
    from disgrace and spitting.

7 But the Lord GOD helps me;
    therefore I have not been disgraced;
  therefore I have set my face like a flint,
    and I know that I shall not be put to
      shame.
8 He who vindicates me is near.

    Who will contend with me?
    Let us stand up together.
  Who is my adversary?
    Let him come near to me.
9 Behold, the Lord GOD helps me;
    who will declare me guilty?
  Behold, all of them will wear out like a
      garment;
    the moth will eat them up.
10 Who among you fears the LORD
    and obeys the voice of his servant?
  Let him who walks in darkness
    and has no light
  trust in the name of the LORD
    and rely on his God.
11 Behold, all you who kindle a fire,
    who equip yourselves with burning
      torches!
  Walk by the light of your fire,
    and by the torches that you have
      kindled!
  This you have from my hand:
    you shall lie down in torment.

Revelation 20

Then I saw an angel coming down from heaven, holding in his hand the key to the bottomless pit[1] and a great chain. 2 And he seized the dragon, that ancient serpent, who is the devil and Satan, and bound him for a thousand years, 3 and threw him into the pit, and shut it and sealed it over him, so that he might not deceive the nations any longer, until the thousand years were ended. After that he must be released for a little while.

4 Then I saw thrones, and seated on them were those to whom the authority to judge was committed. Also I saw the souls of those who had been beheaded for the testimony of Jesus and for the word of God, and those who had not worshiped the beast or its image and had not received its mark on their foreheads or their hands. They came to life and reigned with Christ for a thousand years. 5 The rest of the dead did not come to life until the thousand years were ended. This is the first resurrection. 6 Blessed and holy is the one who shares in the first resurrection! Over such the second death has no power, but they will be priests of God

---

1 Greek *the abyss*; also verse 3

and of Christ, and they will reign with him for a thousand years.

⁷And when the thousand years are ended, Satan will be released from his prison ⁸and will come out to deceive the nations that are at the four corners of the earth, Gog and Magog, to gather them for battle; their number is like the sand of the sea. ⁹And they marched up over the broad plain of the earth and surrounded the camp of the saints and the beloved city, but fire came down from heaven¹ and consumed them, ¹⁰and the devil who had deceived them was thrown into the lake of fire and sulfur where the beast and the false prophet were, and they will be tormented day and night forever and ever.

¹¹Then I saw a great white throne and him who was seated on it. From his presence earth and sky fled away, and no place was found for them. ¹²And I saw the dead, great and small, standing before the throne, and books were opened. Then another book was opened, which is the book of life. And the dead were judged by what was written in the books, according to what they had done. ¹³And the sea gave up the dead who were in it, Death and Hades gave up the dead who were in them, and they were judged, each one of them, according to what they had done. ¹⁴Then Death and Hades were thrown into the lake of fire. This is the second death, the lake of fire. ¹⁵And if anyone's name was not found written in the book of life, he was thrown into the lake of fire.

JUNE 19

Deuteronomy 24

"When a man takes a wife and marries her, if then she finds no favor in his eyes because he has found some indecency in her, and he writes her a certificate of divorce and puts it in her hand and sends her out of his house, and she departs out of his house, ²and if she goes and becomes another man's wife, ³and the latter man hates her and writes her a certificate of divorce and puts it in her hand and sends her out of his house, or if the latter man dies, who took her to be his wife, ⁴then her former husband, who sent her away, may not take her again to be his wife, after she has been defiled, for that is an abomination before the LORD. And you shall not bring sin upon the land that the LORD your God is giving you for an inheritance.

⁵"When a man is newly married, he shall not go out with the army or be liable for any other public duty. He shall be free at home one year to be happy with his wife whom he has taken.

⁶"No one shall take a mill or an upper millstone in pledge, for that would be taking a life in pledge.

⁷"If a man is found stealing one of his brothers of the people of Israel, and if he treats him as a slave or sells him, then that thief shall die. So you shall purge the evil from your midst.

⁸"Take care, in a case of leprous² disease, to be very careful to do according to all that the Levitical priests shall direct you. As I commanded them, so you shall be careful to do. ⁹Remember what the LORD your God did to Miriam on the way as you came out of Egypt.

¹⁰"When you make your neighbor a loan of any sort, you shall not go into his house to collect his pledge. ¹¹You shall stand outside, and the man to whom you make the loan shall bring the pledge out to you. ¹²And if he is a poor man, you shall not sleep in his pledge. ¹³You shall restore to him the pledge as the sun sets, that he may sleep in his cloak and bless you. And it shall be righteousness for you before the LORD your God.

¹⁴"You shall not oppress a hired worker who is poor and needy, whether he is one of your brothers or one of the sojourners who are in your land within your towns. ¹⁵You shall give

¹ Some manuscripts *from God, out of heaven*, or *out of heaven from God* ² *Leprosy* was a term for several skin diseases; see Leviticus 13

him his wages on the same day, before the sun sets (for he is poor and counts on it), lest he cry against you to the LORD, and you be guilty of sin.

[16] "Fathers shall not be put to death because of their children, nor shall children be put to death because of their fathers. Each one shall be put to death for his own sin.

[17] "You shall not pervert the justice due to the sojourner or to the fatherless, or take a widow's garment in pledge, [18] but you shall remember that you were a slave in Egypt and the LORD your God redeemed you from there; therefore I command you to do this.

[19] "When you reap your harvest in your field and forget a sheaf in the field, you shall not go back to get it. It shall be for the sojourner, the fatherless, and the widow, that the LORD your God may bless you in all the work of your hands. [20] When you beat your olive trees, you shall not go over them again. It shall be for the sojourner, the fatherless, and the widow. [21] When you gather the grapes of your vineyard, you shall not strip it afterward. It shall be for the sojourner, the fatherless, and the widow. [22] You shall remember that you were a slave in the land of Egypt; therefore I command you to do this.

Psalm 114–115

When Israel went out from Egypt,
  the house of Jacob from a people of
    strange language,
[2] Judah became his sanctuary,
  Israel his dominion.

[3] The sea looked and fled;
  Jordan turned back.
[4] The mountains skipped like rams,
  the hills like lambs.

[5] What ails you, O sea, that you flee?
  O Jordan, that you turn back?
[6] O mountains, that you skip like rams?
  O hills, like lambs?

[7] Tremble, O earth, at the presence of the
    Lord,
  at the presence of the God of Jacob,
[8] who turns the rock into a pool of water,
  the flint into a spring of water.

Not to us, O LORD, not to us, but to your
  name give glory,
  for the sake of your steadfast love and
    your faithfulness!

[2] Why should the nations say,
  "Where is their God?"
[3] Our God is in the heavens;
  he does all that he pleases.

[4] Their idols are silver and gold,
  the work of human hands.
[5] They have mouths, but do not speak;
  eyes, but do not see.
[6] They have ears, but do not hear;
  noses, but do not smell.
[7] They have hands, but do not feel;
  feet, but do not walk;
  and they do not make a sound in their
    throat.
[8] Those who make them become like
    them;
  so do all who trust in them.

[9] O Israel,[1] trust in the LORD!
  He is their help and their shield.
[10] O house of Aaron, trust in the LORD!
  He is their help and their shield.
[11] You who fear the LORD, trust in the
    LORD!
  He is their help and their shield.

[12] The LORD has remembered us; he will
    bless us;
  he will bless the house of Israel;
  he will bless the house of Aaron;
[13] he will bless those who fear the LORD,
  both the small and the great.

[14] May the LORD give you increase,
  you and your children!
[15] May you be blessed by the LORD,
  who made heaven and earth!

[16] The heavens are the LORD's heavens,
  but the earth he has given to the
    children of man.
[17] The dead do not praise the LORD,
  nor do any who go down into silence.
[18] But we will bless the LORD
  from this time forth and
    forevermore.
Praise the LORD!

[1] Masoretic Text; many Hebrew manuscripts, Septuagint, Syriac O house of Israel

Isaiah 51

"Listen to me, you who pursue
righteousness,
you who seek the Lord:
look to the rock from which you were
hewn,
and to the quarry from which you
were dug.
2 Look to Abraham your father
and to Sarah who bore you;
for he was but one when I called him,
that I might bless him and multiply
him.
3 For the Lord comforts Zion;
he comforts all her waste places
and makes her wilderness like Eden,
her desert like the garden of the
Lord;
joy and gladness will be found in her,
thanksgiving and the voice of song.
4 "Give attention to me, my people,
and give ear to me, my nation;
for a law[1] will go out from me,
and I will set my justice for a light to
the peoples.
5 My righteousness draws near,
my salvation has gone out,
and my arms will judge the peoples;
the coastlands hope for me,
and for my arm they wait.
6 Lift up your eyes to the heavens,
and look at the earth beneath;
for the heavens vanish like smoke,
the earth will wear out like a garment,
and they who dwell in it will die in like
manner;[2]
but my salvation will be forever,
and my righteousness will never be
dismayed.
7 "Listen to me, you who know
righteousness,
the people in whose heart is my law;
fear not the reproach of man,
nor be dismayed at their revilings.
8 For the moth will eat them up like a
garment,
and the worm will eat them like wool;
but my righteousness will be forever,
and my salvation to all generations."

9 Awake, awake, put on strength,
O arm of the Lord;
awake, as in days of old,
the generations of long ago.
Was it not you who cut Rahab in pieces,
who pierced the dragon?
10 Was it not you who dried up the sea,
the waters of the great deep,
who made the depths of the sea a way
for the redeemed to pass over?
11 And the ransomed of the Lord shall
return
and come to Zion with singing;
everlasting joy shall be upon their heads;
they shall obtain gladness and joy,
and sorrow and sighing shall flee away.
12 "I, I am he who comforts you;
who are you that you are afraid of
man who dies,
of the son of man who is made like
grass,
13 and have forgotten the Lord, your
Maker,
who stretched out the heavens
and laid the foundations of the earth,
and you fear continually all the day
because of the wrath of the oppressor,
when he sets himself to destroy?
And where is the wrath of the
oppressor?
14 He who is bowed down shall speedily be
released;
he shall not die and go down to the pit,
neither shall his bread be lacking.
15 I am the Lord your God,
who stirs up the sea so that its waves
roar—
the Lord of hosts is his name.
16 And I have put my words in your mouth
and covered you in the shadow of my
hand,
establishing[3] the heavens
and laying the foundations of the
earth,
and saying to Zion, 'You are my
people.'"
17 Wake yourself, wake yourself,
stand up, O Jerusalem,
you who have drunk from the hand of
the Lord
the cup of his wrath,

[1] Or for teaching; also verse 7   [2] Or will die like gnats   [3] Or planting

who have drunk to the dregs
 the bowl, the cup of staggering.
18 There is none to guide her
 among all the sons she has borne;
there is none to take her by the hand
 among all the sons she has brought up.
19 These two things have happened to
  you—
 who will console you?—
devastation and destruction, famine and
  sword;
 who will comfort you?[1]
20 Your sons have fainted;
 they lie at the head of every street
 like an antelope in a net;
they are full of the wrath of the LORD,
 the rebuke of your God.

21 Therefore hear this, you who are
  afflicted,
 who are drunk, but not with wine:
22 Thus says your Lord, the LORD,
 your God who pleads the cause of his
  people:
"Behold, I have taken from your hand the
  cup of staggering;
the bowl of my wrath you shall drink no
  more;
23 and I will put it into the hand of your
  tormentors,
 who have said to you,
'Bow down, that we may pass over';
and you have made your back like the
  ground
 and like the street for them to pass
  over."

Revelation 21

Then I saw a new heaven and a new earth, for the first heaven and the first earth had passed away, and the sea was no more. ²And I saw the holy city, new Jerusalem, coming down out of heaven from God, prepared as a bride adorned for her husband. ³And I heard a loud voice from the throne saying, "Behold, the dwelling place[2] of God is with man. He will dwell with them, and they will be his people,[3] and God himself will be with them as their God.[4] ⁴He will wipe away every tear from their eyes, and death shall be no more, neither shall there be mourning, nor crying, nor pain

anymore, for the former things have passed away."

⁵And he who was seated on the throne said, "Behold, I am making all things new." Also he said, "Write this down, for these words are trustworthy and true." ⁶And he said to me, "It is done! I am the Alpha and the Omega, the beginning and the end. To the thirsty I will give from the spring of the water of life without payment. ⁷The one who conquers will have this heritage, and I will be his God and he will be my son. ⁸But as for the cowardly, the faithless, the detestable, as for murderers, the sexually immoral, sorcerers, idolaters, and all liars, their portion will be in the lake that burns with fire and sulfur, which is the second death."

⁹Then came one of the seven angels who had the seven bowls full of the seven last plagues and spoke to me, saying, "Come, I will show you the Bride, the wife of the Lamb." ¹⁰And he carried me away in the Spirit to a great, high mountain, and showed me the holy city Jerusalem coming down out of heaven from God, ¹¹having the glory of God, its radiance like a most rare jewel, like a jasper, clear as crystal. ¹²It had a great, high wall, with twelve gates, and at the gates twelve angels, and on the gates the names of the twelve tribes of the sons of Israel were inscribed— ¹³on the east three gates, on the north three gates, on the south three gates, and on the west three gates. ¹⁴And the wall of the city had twelve foundations, and on them were the twelve names of the twelve apostles of the Lamb.

¹⁵And the one who spoke with me had a measuring rod of gold to measure the city and its gates and walls. ¹⁶The city lies foursquare, its length the same as its width. And he measured the city with his rod, 12,000 stadia.[5] Its length and width and height are equal. ¹⁷He also measured its wall, 144 cubits[6] by human measurement, which is also an angel's measurement. ¹⁸The wall was built of jasper, while the city was pure gold, like clear glass. ¹⁹The foundations of the wall of the city were adorned with every kind of jewel. The first was jasper, the second sapphire, the third agate, the fourth emerald, ²⁰the fifth onyx, the sixth carnelian, the seventh chrysolite, the eighth beryl, the ninth topaz, the tenth chrysoprase, the eleventh jacinth, the twelfth amethyst.

[1] Dead Sea Scroll, Septuagint, Syriac, Vulgate; Masoretic Text *how shall I comfort you* [2] Or *tabernacle* [3] Some manuscripts *peoples* [4] Some manuscripts omit *as their God*
[5] About 1,380 miles; a *stadion* was about 607 feet or 185 meters [6] A *cubit* was about 18 inches or 45 centimeters

²¹And the twelve gates were twelve pearls, each of the gates made of a single pearl, and the street of the city was pure gold, like transparent glass.

²²And I saw no temple in the city, for its temple is the Lord God the Almighty and the Lamb. ²³And the city has no need of sun or moon to shine on it, for the glory of God gives it light, and its lamp is the Lamb. ²⁴By its light will the nations walk, and the kings of the earth will bring their glory into it, ²⁵and its gates will never be shut by day—and there will be no night there. ²⁶They will bring into it the glory and the honor of the nations. ²⁷But nothing unclean will ever enter it, nor anyone who does what is detestable or false, but only those who are written in the Lamb's book of life.

JUNE 20

Deuteronomy 25

"If there is a dispute between men and they come into court and the judges decide between them, acquitting the innocent and condemning the guilty, ²then if the guilty man deserves to be beaten, the judge shall cause him to lie down and be beaten in his presence with a number of stripes in proportion to his offense. ³Forty stripes may be given him, but not more, lest, if one should go on to beat him with more stripes than these, your brother be degraded in your sight.

⁴"You shall not muzzle an ox when it is treading out the grain.

⁵"If brothers dwell together, and one of them dies and has no son, the wife of the dead man shall not be married outside the family to a stranger. Her husband's brother shall go in to her and take her as his wife and perform the duty of a husband's brother to her. ⁶And the first son whom she bears shall succeed to the name of his dead brother, that his name may not be blotted out of Israel. ⁷And if the man does not wish to take his brother's wife, then his brother's wife shall go up to the gate to the elders and say, 'My husband's brother refuses to perpetuate his brother's name in Israel; he will not perform the duty of a husband's brother to me.' ⁸Then the elders of his city shall call him and speak to him, and if he persists, saying, 'I do not wish to take her,' ⁹then his brother's wife shall go up to him in the presence of the elders and pull his sandal off his foot and spit in his face. And she shall answer and say, 'So shall it be done to the man who does not build up his brother's house.' ¹⁰And the name of his house¹ shall be called in Israel, 'The house of him who had his sandal pulled off.'

¹¹"When men fight with one another and the wife of the one draws near to rescue her husband from the hand of him who is beating him and puts out her hand and seizes him by the private parts, ¹²then you shall cut off her hand. Your eye shall have no pity.

¹³"You shall not have in your bag two kinds of weights, a large and a small. ¹⁴You shall not have in your house two kinds of measures, a large and a small. ¹⁵A full and fair² weight you shall have, a full and fair measure you shall have, that your days may be long in the land that the Lᴏʀᴅ your God is giving you. ¹⁶For all who do such things, all who act dishonestly, are an abomination to the Lᴏʀᴅ your God.

¹⁷"Remember what Amalek did to you on the way as you came out of Egypt, ¹⁸how he attacked you on the way when you were faint and weary, and cut off your tail, those who were lagging behind you, and he did not fear God. ¹⁹Therefore when the Lᴏʀᴅ your God has given you rest from all your enemies around you, in the land that the Lᴏʀᴅ your God is giving you for an inheritance to possess, you shall blot out the memory of Amalek from under heaven; you shall not forget.

¹ Hebrew *its name* ² Or *just*, or *righteous*; twice in this verse

Psalm 116

I love the LORD, because he has heard
my voice and my pleas for mercy.
2 Because he inclined his ear to me,
   therefore I will call on him as long as
   I live.
3 The snares of death encompassed me;
   the pangs of Sheol laid hold on me;
   I suffered distress and anguish.
4 Then I called on the name of the LORD:
   "O LORD, I pray, deliver my soul!"

5 Gracious is the LORD, and righteous;
   our God is merciful.
6 The LORD preserves the simple;
   when I was brought low, he saved me.
7 Return, O my soul, to your rest;
   for the LORD has dealt bountifully
   with you.

8 For you have delivered my soul from
   death,
   my eyes from tears,
   my feet from stumbling;
9 I will walk before the LORD
   in the land of the living.

10 I believed, even when[1] I spoke:
   "I am greatly afflicted";
11 I said in my alarm,
   "All mankind are liars."

12 What shall I render to the LORD
   for all his benefits to me?
13 I will lift up the cup of salvation
   and call on the name of the LORD,
14 I will pay my vows to the LORD
   in the presence of all his people.

15 Precious in the sight of the LORD
   is the death of his saints.
16 O LORD, I am your servant;
   I am your servant, the son of your
   maidservant.
   You have loosed my bonds.
17 I will offer to you the sacrifice of
   thanksgiving
   and call on the name of the LORD.
18 I will pay my vows to the LORD
   in the presence of all his people,
19 in the courts of the house of the LORD,
   in your midst, O Jerusalem.
   Praise the LORD!

Isaiah 52

Awake, awake,
   put on your strength, O Zion;
   put on your beautiful garments,
   O Jerusalem, the holy city;
for there shall no more come into you
   the uncircumcised and the unclean.
2 Shake yourself from the dust and arise;
   be seated, O Jerusalem;
loose the bonds from your neck,
   O captive daughter of Zion.

3 For thus says the LORD: "You were sold for nothing, and you shall be redeemed without money." 4 For thus says the Lord GOD: "My people went down at the first into Egypt to sojourn there, and the Assyrian oppressed them for nothing.[2] 5 Now therefore what have I here," declares the LORD, "seeing that my people are taken away for nothing? Their rulers wail," declares the LORD, "and continually all the day my name is despised. 6 Therefore my people shall know my name. Therefore in that day they shall know that it is I who speak; here I am."

7 How beautiful upon the mountains
   are the feet of him who brings good
   news,
who publishes peace, who brings good
   news of happiness,
who publishes salvation,
who says to Zion, "Your God reigns."
8 The voice of your watchmen—they lift
   up their voice;
   together they sing for joy;
for eye to eye they see
   the return of the LORD to Zion.
9 Break forth together into singing,
   you waste places of Jerusalem,
for the LORD has comforted his people;
   he has redeemed Jerusalem.
10 The LORD has bared his holy arm
   before the eyes of all the nations,
and all the ends of the earth shall see
   the salvation of our God.
11 Depart, depart, go out from there;
   touch no unclean thing;
go out from the midst of her; purify
   yourselves,
   you who bear the vessels of the LORD.

[1] Or believed, indeed; Septuagint believed, therefore   [2] Or the Assyrian has oppressed them of late

¹² For you shall not go out in haste,
    and you shall not go in flight,
for the LORD will go before you,
    and the God of Israel will be your rear
      guard.

¹³ Behold, my servant shall act wisely;[1]
    he shall be high and lifted up,
    and shall be exalted.
¹⁴ As many were astonished at you—
    his appearance was so marred, beyond
      human semblance,
    and his form beyond that of the
      children of mankind—
¹⁵ so shall he sprinkle[2] many nations;
    kings shall shut their mouths because
      of him;
for that which has not been told them
      they see,
and that which they have not heard
      they understand.

Revelation 22

Then the angel[3] showed me the river of the water of life, bright as crystal, flowing from the throne of God and of the Lamb ²through the middle of the street of the city; also, on either side of the river, the tree of life[4] with its twelve kinds of fruit, yielding its fruit each month. The leaves of the tree were for the healing of the nations. ³No longer will there be anything accursed, but the throne of God and of the Lamb will be in it, and his servants[5] will worship him. ⁴They will see his face, and his name will be on their foreheads. ⁵And night will be no more. They will need no light of lamp or sun, for the Lord God will be their light, and they will reign forever and ever.

⁶And he said to me, "These words are trustworthy and true. And the Lord, the God of the spirits of the prophets, has sent his angel to show his servants what must soon take place."

⁷ "And behold, I am coming soon. Blessed is the one who keeps the words of the prophecy of this book."

⁸I, John, am the one who heard and saw these things. And when I heard and saw them, I fell down to worship at the feet of the angel who showed them to me, ⁹but he said to me, "You must not do that! I am a fellow servant[6] with you and your brothers the prophets, and with those who keep the words of this book. Worship God."

¹⁰And he said to me, "Do not seal up the words of the prophecy of this book, for the time is near. ¹¹Let the evildoer still do evil, and the filthy still be filthy, and the righteous still do right, and the holy still be holy."

¹² "Behold, I am coming soon, bringing my recompense with me, to repay each one for what he has done. ¹³I am the Alpha and the Omega, the first and the last, the beginning and the end."

¹⁴Blessed are those who wash their robes,[7] so that they may have the right to the tree of life and that they may enter the city by the gates. ¹⁵Outside are the dogs and sorcerers and the sexually immoral and murderers and idolaters, and everyone who loves and practices falsehood.

¹⁶ "I, Jesus, have sent my angel to testify to you about these things for the churches. I am the root and the descendant of David, the bright morning star."

¹⁷The Spirit and the Bride say, "Come." And let the one who hears say, "Come." And let the one who is thirsty come; let the one who desires take the water of life without price.

¹⁸I warn everyone who hears the words of the prophecy of this book: if anyone adds to them, God will add to him the plagues described in this book, ¹⁹and if anyone takes away from the words of the book of this prophecy, God will take away his share in the tree of life and in the holy city, which are described in this book.

²⁰He who testifies to these things says, "Surely I am coming soon." Amen. Come, Lord Jesus!

²¹The grace of the Lord Jesus be with all.[8] Amen.

---

[1] Or shall prosper [2] Or startle [3] Greek he [4] Or the Lamb. In the midst of the street of the city, and on either side of the river, was the tree of life [5] Greek bondservants; also verse 6 [6] Greek fellow bondservant [7] Some manuscripts do his commandments [8] Some manuscripts all the saints

JUNE 21

Deuteronomy 26

"When you come into the land that the LORD your God is giving you for an inheritance and have taken possession of it and live in it, ²you shall take some of the first of all the fruit of the ground, which you harvest from your land that the LORD your God is giving you, and you shall put it in a basket, and you shall go to the place that the LORD your God will choose, to make his name to dwell there. ³And you shall go to the priest who is in office at that time and say to him, 'I declare today to the LORD your God that I have come into the land that the LORD swore to our fathers to give us.' ⁴Then the priest shall take the basket from your hand and set it down before the altar of the LORD your God.

⁵"And you shall make response before the LORD your God, 'A wandering Aramean was my father. And he went down into Egypt and sojourned there, few in number, and there he became a nation, great, mighty, and populous. ⁶And the Egyptians treated us harshly and humiliated us and laid on us hard labor. ⁷Then we cried to the LORD, the God of our fathers, and the LORD heard our voice and saw our affliction, our toil, and our oppression. ⁸And the LORD brought us out of Egypt with a mighty hand and an outstretched arm, with great deeds of terror,[1] with signs and wonders. ⁹And he brought us into this place and gave us this land, a land flowing with milk and honey. ¹⁰And behold, now I bring the first of the fruit of the ground, which you, O LORD, have given me.' And you shall set it down before the LORD your God and worship before the LORD your God. ¹¹And you shall rejoice in all the good that the LORD your God has given to you and to your house, you, and the Levite, and the sojourner who is among you.

¹²"When you have finished paying all the tithe of your produce in the third year, which is the year of tithing, giving it to the Levite,

the sojourner, the fatherless, and the widow, so that they may eat within your towns and be filled, ¹³then you shall say before the LORD your God, 'I have removed the sacred portion out of my house, and moreover, I have given it to the Levite, the sojourner, the fatherless, and the widow, according to all your commandment that you have commanded me. I have not transgressed any of your commandments, nor have I forgotten them. ¹⁴I have not eaten of the tithe while I was mourning, or removed any of it while I was unclean, or offered any of it to the dead. I have obeyed the voice of the LORD my God. I have done according to all that you have commanded me. ¹⁵Look down from your holy habitation, from heaven, and bless your people Israel and the ground that you have given us, as you swore to our fathers, a land flowing with milk and honey.'

¹⁶"This day the LORD your God commands you to do these statutes and rules. You shall therefore be careful to do them with all your heart and with all your soul. ¹⁷You have declared today that the LORD is your God, and that you will walk in his ways, and keep his statutes and his commandments and his rules, and will obey his voice. ¹⁸And the LORD has declared today that you are a people for his treasured possession, as he has promised you, and that you are to keep all his commandments, ¹⁹and that he will set you in praise and in fame and in honor high above all nations that he has made, and that you shall be a people holy to the LORD your God, as he promised."

Psalm 117–118

Praise the LORD, all nations!
Extol him, all peoples!
² For great is his steadfast love toward us,
and the faithfulness of the LORD
endures forever.
Praise the LORD!

[1] Hebrew *with great terror*

Oh give thanks to the LORD, for he is good;
for his steadfast love endures forever!

2 Let Israel say,
"His steadfast love endures forever."
3 Let the house of Aaron say,
"His steadfast love endures forever."
4 Let those who fear the LORD say,
"His steadfast love endures forever."

5 Out of my distress I called on the LORD;
the LORD answered me and set me
free.
6 The LORD is on my side; I will not fear.
What can man do to me?
7 The LORD is on my side as my helper;
I shall look in triumph on those who
hate me.

8 It is better to take refuge in the LORD
than to trust in man.
9 It is better to take refuge in the LORD
than to trust in princes.

10 All nations surrounded me;
in the name of the LORD I cut them off!
11 They surrounded me, surrounded me on
every side;
in the name of the LORD I cut them off!
12 They surrounded me like bees;
they went out like a fire among
thorns;
in the name of the LORD I cut them off!
13 I was pushed hard,[1] so that I was falling,
but the LORD helped me.
14 The LORD is my strength and my song;
he has become my salvation.
15 Glad songs of salvation
are in the tents of the righteous:
"The right hand of the LORD does
valiantly,
16 the right hand of the LORD exalts,
the right hand of the LORD does
valiantly!"
17 I shall not die, but I shall live,
and recount the deeds of the LORD.
18 The LORD has disciplined me severely,
but he has not given me over to death.
19 Open to me the gates of righteousness,
that I may enter through them
and give thanks to the LORD.

20 This is the gate of the LORD;
the righteous shall enter through it.
21 I thank you that you have answered me
and have become my salvation.
22 The stone that the builders rejected
has become the cornerstone.[2]
23 This is the LORD's doing;
it is marvelous in our eyes.
24 This is the day that the LORD has made;
let us rejoice and be glad in it.
25 Save us, we pray, O LORD!
O LORD, we pray, give us success!

26 Blessed is he who comes in the name of
the LORD!
We bless you from the house of the
LORD.
27 The LORD is God,
and he has made his light to shine
upon us.
Bind the festal sacrifice with cords,
up to the horns of the altar!
28 You are my God, and I will give thanks
to you;
you are my God; I will extol you.
29 Oh give thanks to the LORD, for he is
good;
for his steadfast love endures
forever!

Isaiah 53

Who has believed what he has heard
from us?[3]
And to whom has the arm of the LORD
been revealed?
2 For he grew up before him like a young
plant,
and like a root out of dry ground;
he had no form or majesty that we
should look at him,
and no beauty that we should desire
him.
3 He was despised and rejected[4] by men;
a man of sorrows,[5] and acquainted
with[6] grief;[7]
and as one from whom men hide their
faces[8]
he was despised, and we esteemed
him not.

[1] Hebrew You (that is, the enemy) pushed me hard [2] Hebrew the head of the corner [3] Or Who has believed what we have heard? [4] Or forsaken [5] Or pains; also verse 4 [6] Or and knowing
[7] Or sickness; also verse 4 [8] Or as one who hides his face from us

4 Surely he has borne our griefs
   and carried our sorrows;
yet we esteemed him stricken,
   smitten by God, and afflicted.
5 But he was pierced for our
   transgressions;
he was crushed for our iniquities;
upon him was the chastisement that
   brought us peace,
and with his wounds we are healed.
6 All we like sheep have gone astray;
   we have turned—every one—to his
    own way;
and the Lord has laid on him
   the iniquity of us all.

7 He was oppressed, and he was afflicted,
   yet he opened not his mouth;
like a lamb that is led to the slaughter,
   and like a sheep that before its
    shearers is silent,
so he opened not his mouth.
8 By oppression and judgment he was
   taken away;
and as for his generation, who
   considered
that he was cut off out of the land of the
   living,
stricken for the transgression of my
   people?
9 And they made his grave with the
   wicked
and with a rich man in his death,
although he had done no violence,
and there was no deceit in his mouth.

10 Yet it was the will of the Lord to crush
   him;
he has put him to grief;[1]
when his soul makes[2] an offering for
   guilt,
he shall see his offspring; he shall
   prolong his days;
the will of the Lord shall prosper in his
   hand.
11 Out of the anguish of his soul he shall
   see[3] and be satisfied;
by his knowledge shall the righteous
   one, my servant,
make many to be accounted
   righteous,
and he shall bear their iniquities.

12 Therefore I will divide him a portion
   with the many,[4]
and he shall divide the spoil with the
   strong,[5]
because he poured out his soul to death
   and was numbered with the
   transgressors;
yet he bore the sin of many,
   and makes intercession for the
   transgressors.

——————— *Matthew 1* ———————

The book of the genealogy of Jesus Christ, the son of David, the son of Abraham.

²Abraham was the father of Isaac, and Isaac the father of Jacob, and Jacob the father of Judah and his brothers, ³and Judah the father of Perez and Zerah by Tamar, and Perez the father of Hezron, and Hezron the father of Ram,[6] ⁴and Ram the father of Amminadab, and Amminadab the father of Nahshon, and Nahshon the father of Salmon, ⁵and Salmon the father of Boaz by Rahab, and Boaz the father of Obed by Ruth, and Obed the father of Jesse, ⁶and Jesse the father of David the king.

And David was the father of Solomon by the wife of Uriah, ⁷and Solomon the father of Rehoboam, and Rehoboam the father of Abijah, and Abijah the father of Asaph,[7] ⁸and Asaph the father of Jehoshaphat, and Jehoshaphat the father of Joram, and Joram the father of Uzziah, ⁹and Uzziah the father of Jotham, and Jotham the father of Ahaz, and Ahaz the father of Hezekiah, ¹⁰and Hezekiah the father of Manasseh, and Manasseh the father of Amos,[8] and Amos the father of Josiah, ¹¹and Josiah the father of Jechoniah and his brothers, at the time of the deportation to Babylon.

¹²And after the deportation to Babylon: Jechoniah was the father of Shealtiel,[9] and Shealtiel the father of Zerubbabel, ¹³and Zerubbabel the father of Abiud, and Abiud the father of Eliakim, and Eliakim the father of Azor, ¹⁴and Azor the father of Zadok, and Zadok the father of Achim, and Achim the father of Eliud, ¹⁵and Eliud the father of Eleazar, and Eleazar the father of Matthan, and Matthan the father of Jacob, ¹⁶and Jacob the father of Joseph the husband of Mary, of whom Jesus was born, who is called Christ.

[1] Or *he has made him sick*   [2] Or *when you make his soul*   [3] Masoretic Text; Dead Sea Scroll *he shall see light*   [4] Or *with the great*   [5] Or *with the numerous*   [6] Greek *Aram*; also verse 4
[7] *Asaph* is probably an alternate spelling of *Asa*; some manuscripts *Asa*; also verse 8   [8] *Amos* is probably an alternate spelling of *Amon*; some manuscripts *Amon*; twice in this verse
[9] Greek *Salathiel*; twice in this verse

[17]So all the generations from Abraham to David were fourteen generations, and from David to the deportation to Babylon fourteen generations, and from the deportation to Babylon to the Christ fourteen generations.

[18]Now the birth of Jesus Christ[1] took place in this way. When his mother Mary had been betrothed[2] to Joseph, before they came together she was found to be with child from the Holy Spirit. [19]And her husband Joseph, being a just man and unwilling to put her to shame, resolved to divorce her quietly. [20]But as he considered these things, behold, an angel of the Lord appeared to him in a dream, saying, "Joseph, son of David, do not fear to take Mary as your wife, for that which is conceived in her is from the Holy Spirit. [21]She will bear a son, and you shall call his name Jesus, for he will save his people from their sins." [22]All this took place to fulfill what the Lord had spoken by the prophet:

[23]   "Behold, the virgin shall conceive and
        bear a son,
      and they shall call his name
        Immanuel"

(which means, God with us). [24]When Joseph woke from sleep, he did as the angel of the Lord commanded him: he took his wife, [25]but knew her not until she had given birth to a son. And he called his name Jesus.

JUNE 22

Deuteronomy 27:1–28:19

Now Moses and the elders of Israel commanded the people, saying, "Keep the whole commandment that I command you today. [2]And on the day you cross over the Jordan to the land that the Lord your God is giving you, you shall set up large stones and plaster them with plaster. [3]And you shall write on them all the words of this law, when you cross over to enter the land that the Lord your God is giving you, a land flowing with milk and honey, as the Lord, the God of your fathers, has promised you. [4]And when you have crossed over the Jordan, you shall set up these stones, concerning which I command you today, on Mount Ebal, and you shall plaster them with plaster. [5]And there you shall build an altar to the Lord your God, an altar of stones. You shall wield no iron tool on them; [6]you shall build an altar to the Lord your God of uncut[3] stones. And you shall offer burnt offerings on it to the Lord your God, [7]and you shall sacrifice peace offerings and shall eat there, and you shall rejoice before the Lord your God. [8]And you shall write on the stones all the words of this law very plainly."

[9]Then Moses and the Levitical priests said to all Israel, "Keep silence and hear, O Israel: this day you have become the people of the Lord your God. [10]You shall therefore obey the voice of the Lord your God, keeping his commandments and his statutes, which I command you today."

[11]That day Moses charged the people, saying, [12]"When you have crossed over the Jordan, these shall stand on Mount Gerizim to bless the people: Simeon, Levi, Judah, Issachar, Joseph, and Benjamin. [13]And these shall stand on Mount Ebal for the curse: Reuben, Gad, Asher, Zebulun, Dan, and Naphtali. [14]And the Levites shall declare to all the men of Israel in a loud voice:

[15]"'Cursed be the man who makes a carved or cast metal image, an abomination to the Lord, a thing made by the hands of a craftsman, and sets it up in secret.' And all the people shall answer and say, 'Amen.'

[16]"'Cursed be anyone who dishonors his father or his mother.' And all the people shall say, 'Amen.'

[17]"'Cursed be anyone who moves his neighbor's landmark.' And all the people shall say, 'Amen.'

[18]"'Cursed be anyone who misleads a blind

man on the road.' And all the people shall say, 'Amen.'

19 "'Cursed be anyone who perverts the justice due to the sojourner, the fatherless, and the widow.' And all the people shall say, 'Amen.'

20 "'Cursed be anyone who lies with his father's wife, because he has uncovered his father's nakedness.'[1] And all the people shall say, 'Amen.'

21 "'Cursed be anyone who lies with any kind of animal.' And all the people shall say, 'Amen.'

22 "'Cursed be anyone who lies with his sister, whether the daughter of his father or the daughter of his mother.' And all the people shall say, 'Amen.'

23 "'Cursed be anyone who lies with his mother-in-law.' And all the people shall say, 'Amen.'

24 "'Cursed be anyone who strikes down his neighbor in secret.' And all the people shall say, 'Amen.'

25 "'Cursed be anyone who takes a bribe to shed innocent blood.' And all the people shall say, 'Amen.'

26 "'Cursed be anyone who does not confirm the words of this law by doing them.' And all the people shall say, 'Amen.'

28:1 "And if you faithfully obey the voice of the LORD your God, being careful to do all his commandments that I command you today, the LORD your God will set you high above all the nations of the earth. ²And all these blessings shall come upon you and overtake you, if you obey the voice of the LORD your God. ³Blessed shall you be in the city, and blessed shall you be in the field. ⁴Blessed shall be the fruit of your womb and the fruit of your ground and the fruit of your cattle, the increase of your herds and the young of your flock. ⁵Blessed shall be your basket and your kneading bowl. ⁶Blessed shall you be when you come in, and blessed shall you be when you go out.

7 "The LORD will cause your enemies who rise against you to be defeated before you. They shall come out against you one way and flee before you seven ways. ⁸The LORD will command the blessing on you in your barns and in all that you undertake. And he will bless you in the land that the LORD your God is giving you. ⁹The LORD will establish you as a people holy to himself, as he has sworn to you, if you keep the commandments of the LORD your God

and walk in his ways. ¹⁰And all the peoples of the earth shall see that you are called by the name of the LORD, and they shall be afraid of you. ¹¹And the LORD will make you abound in prosperity, in the fruit of your womb and in the fruit of your livestock and in the fruit of your ground, within the land that the LORD swore to your fathers to give you. ¹²The LORD will open to you his good treasury, the heavens, to give the rain to your land in its season and to bless all the work of your hands. And you shall lend to many nations, but you shall not borrow. ¹³And the LORD will make you the head and not the tail, and you shall only go up and not down, if you obey the commandments of the LORD your God, which I command you today, being careful to do them, ¹⁴and if you do not turn aside from any of the words that I command you today, to the right hand or to the left, to go after other gods to serve them.

15 "But if you will not obey the voice of the LORD your God or be careful to do all his commandments and his statutes that I command you today, then all these curses shall come upon you and overtake you. ¹⁶Cursed shall you be in the city, and cursed shall you be in the field. ¹⁷Cursed shall be your basket and your kneading bowl. ¹⁸Cursed shall be the fruit of your womb and the fruit of your ground, the increase of your herds and the young of your flock. ¹⁹Cursed shall you be when you come in, and cursed shall you be when you go out.

Psalm 119:1²–24

ALEPH

Blessed are those whose way is blameless,
who walk in the law of the LORD!
2   Blessed are those who keep his
testimonies,
who seek him with their whole heart,
3   who also do no wrong,
but walk in his ways!
4   You have commanded your precepts
to be kept diligently.
5   Oh that my ways may be steadfast
in keeping your statutes!
6   Then I shall not be put to shame,
having my eyes fixed on all your
commandments.
7   I will praise you with an upright heart,
when I learn your righteous rules.³

---

¹ Hebrew *uncovered his father's skirt* ² This psalm is an acrostic poem of twenty-two stanzas, following the letters of the Hebrew alphabet; within a stanza, each verse begins with the same Hebrew letter ³ Or *your just and righteous decrees*; also verses 62, 106, 160, 164

8   I will keep your statutes;
     do not utterly forsake me!

BETH

9   How can a young man keep his way
     pure?
     By guarding it according to your
     word.
10   With my whole heart I seek you;
     let me not wander from your
     commandments!
11   I have stored up your word in my heart,
     that I might not sin against you.
12   Blessed are you, O LORD;
     teach me your statutes!
13   With my lips I declare
     all the rules[1] of your mouth.
14   In the way of your testimonies I delight
     as much as in all riches.
15   I will meditate on your precepts
     and fix my eyes on your ways.
16   I will delight in your statutes;
     I will not forget your word.

GIMEL

17   Deal bountifully with your servant,
     that I may live and keep your word.
18   Open my eyes, that I may behold
     wondrous things out of your law.
19   I am a sojourner on the earth;
     hide not your commandments from
     me!
20   My soul is consumed with longing
     for your rules[2] at all times.
21   You rebuke the insolent, accursed ones,
     who wander from your
     commandments.
22   Take away from me scorn and
     contempt,
     for I have kept your testimonies.
23   Even though princes sit plotting against
     me,
     your servant will meditate on your
     statutes.
24   Your testimonies are my delight;
     they are my counselors.

Isaiah 54

"Sing, O barren one, who did not bear;
  break forth into singing and cry aloud,
  you who have not been in labor!
For the children of the desolate one will
    be more
    than the children of her who is
    married," says the LORD.
2   "Enlarge the place of your tent,
     and let the curtains of your
     habitations be stretched out;
    do not hold back; lengthen your cords
     and strengthen your stakes.
3   For you will spread abroad to the right
     and to the left,
    and your offspring will possess the
     nations
    and will people the desolate cities.

4   "Fear not, for you will not be ashamed;
     be not confounded, for you will not be
     disgraced;
    for you will forget the shame of your
     youth,
    and the reproach of your widowhood
     you will remember no more.
5   For your Maker is your husband,
     the LORD of hosts is his name;
    and the Holy One of Israel is your
     Redeemer,
    the God of the whole earth he is
     called.
6   For the LORD has called you
     like a wife deserted and grieved in
     spirit,
    like a wife of youth when she is cast
     off,
    says your God.
7   For a brief moment I deserted you,
     but with great compassion I will
     gather you.
8   In overflowing anger for a moment
     I hid my face from you,
    but with everlasting love I will have
     compassion on you,"
    says the LORD, your Redeemer.
9   "This is like the days of Noah[3] to me:
     as I swore that the waters of Noah
     should no more go over the earth,
    so I have sworn that I will not be angry
     with you,
    and will not rebuke you.
10   For the mountains may depart
     and the hills be removed,

---

[1] Or all the just decrees [2] Or your just decrees; also verses 30, 39, 43, 52, 75, 102, 108, 137, 156, 175 [3] Some manuscripts For this is as the waters of Noah

but my steadfast love shall not depart
from you,
and my covenant of peace shall not be
removed,"
says the LORD, who has compassion
on you.

11 "O afflicted one, storm-tossed and not
comforted,
behold, I will set your stones in
antimony,
and lay your foundations with
sapphires.[1]
12 I will make your pinnacles of agate,[2]
your gates of carbuncles,[3]
and all your wall of precious stones.
13 All your children shall be taught by the
LORD,
and great shall be the peace of your
children.
14 In righteousness you shall be
established;
you shall be far from oppression, for
you shall not fear;
and from terror, for it shall not come
near you.
15 If anyone stirs up strife,
it is not from me;
whoever stirs up strife with you
shall fall because of you.
16 Behold, I have created the smith
who blows the fire of coals
and produces a weapon for its
purpose.
I have also created the ravager to
destroy;
17 no weapon that is fashioned against
you shall succeed,
and you shall refute every tongue that
rises against you in judgment.
This is the heritage of the servants of the
LORD
and their vindication[4] from me,
declares the LORD."

—————— *Matthew 2* ——————

N ow after Jesus was born in Bethlehem
of Judea in the days of Herod the king,
behold, wise men[5] from the east came to Jerusalem, [2]saying, "Where is he who has been born
king of the Jews? For we saw his star when it

rose[6] and have come to worship him." [3]When
Herod the king heard this, he was troubled,
and all Jerusalem with him; [4]and assembling
all the chief priests and scribes of the people,
he inquired of them where the Christ was to be
born. [5]They told him, "In Bethlehem of Judea,
for so it is written by the prophet:

6   "'And you, O Bethlehem, in the land of
Judah,
are by no means least among the
rulers of Judah;
for from you shall come a ruler
who will shepherd my people Israel.'"

[7]Then Herod summoned the wise men
secretly and ascertained from them what time
the star had appeared. [8]And he sent them to
Bethlehem, saying, "Go and search diligently
for the child, and when you have found him,
bring me word, that I too may come and worship him." [9]After listening to the king, they
went on their way. And behold, the star that
they had seen when it rose went before them
until it came to rest over the place where the
child was. [10]When they saw the star, they
rejoiced exceedingly with great joy. [11]And
going into the house they saw the child with
Mary his mother, and they fell down and worshiped him. Then, opening their treasures, they
offered him gifts, gold and frankincense and
myrrh. [12]And being warned in a dream not to
return to Herod, they departed to their own
country by another way.

[13]Now when they had departed, behold, an
angel of the Lord appeared to Joseph in a dream
and said, "Rise, take the child and his mother,
and flee to Egypt, and remain there until I tell
you, for Herod is about to search for the child,
to destroy him." [14]And he rose and took the
child and his mother by night and departed
to Egypt [15]and remained there until the death
of Herod. This was to fulfill what the Lord had
spoken by the prophet, "Out of Egypt I called
my son."

[16]Then Herod, when he saw that he had
been tricked by the wise men, became furious,
and he sent and killed all the male children in
Bethlehem and in all that region who were two
years old or under, according to the time that
he had ascertained from the wise men. [17]Then
was fulfilled what was spoken by the prophet
Jeremiah:

[1] Or *lapis lazuli*   [2] Or *jasper, or ruby*   [3] Or *crystal*   [4] Or *righteousness*   [5] Greek *magi*; also verses 7, 16   [6] Or *in the east*; also verse 9

18   "A voice was heard in Ramah,
>   weeping and loud lamentation,
>   Rachel weeping for her children;
>   she refused to be comforted, because
>   they are no more."

19 But when Herod died, behold, an angel of the Lord appeared in a dream to Joseph in Egypt, 20 saying, "Rise, take the child and his mother and go to the land of Israel, for those who sought the child's life are dead." 21 And he rose and took the child and his mother and went to the land of Israel. 22 But when he heard that Archelaus was reigning over Judea in place of his father Herod, he was afraid to go there, and being warned in a dream he withdrew to the district of Galilee. 23 And he went and lived in a city called Nazareth, so that what was spoken by the prophets might be fulfilled, that he would be called a Nazarene.

JUNE 23

Deuteronomy 28:20–68

"The LORD will send on you curses, confusion, and frustration in all that you undertake to do, until you are destroyed and perish quickly on account of the evil of your deeds, because you have forsaken me. 21 The LORD will make the pestilence stick to you until he has consumed you off the land that you are entering to take possession of it. 22 The LORD will strike you with wasting disease and with fever, inflammation and fiery heat, and with drought[1] and with blight and with mildew. They shall pursue you until you perish. 23 And the heavens over your head shall be bronze, and the earth under you shall be iron. 24 The LORD will make the rain of your land powder. From heaven dust shall come down on you until you are destroyed.

25 "The LORD will cause you to be defeated before your enemies. You shall go out one way against them and flee seven ways before them. And you shall be a horror to all the kingdoms of the earth. 26 And your dead body shall be food for all birds of the air and for the beasts of the earth, and there shall be no one to frighten them away. 27 The LORD will strike you with the boils of Egypt, and with tumors and scabs and itch, of which you cannot be healed. 28 The LORD will strike you with madness and blindness and confusion of mind, 29 and you shall grope at noonday, as the blind grope in darkness, and you shall not prosper in your ways.[2]

And you shall be only oppressed and robbed continually, and there shall be no one to help you. 30 You shall betroth a wife, but another man shall ravish her. You shall build a house, but you shall not dwell in it. You shall plant a vineyard, but you shall not enjoy its fruit. 31 Your ox shall be slaughtered before your eyes, but you shall not eat any of it. Your donkey shall be seized before your face, but shall not be restored to you. Your sheep shall be given to your enemies, but there shall be no one to help you. 32 Your sons and your daughters shall be given to another people, while your eyes look on and fail with longing for them all day long, but you shall be helpless. 33 A nation that you have not known shall eat up the fruit of your ground and of all your labors, and you shall be only oppressed and crushed continually, 34 so that you are driven mad by the sights that your eyes see. 35 The LORD will strike you on the knees and on the legs with grievous boils of which you cannot be healed, from the sole of your foot to the crown of your head.

36 "The LORD will bring you and your king whom you set over you to a nation that neither you nor your fathers have known. And there you shall serve other gods of wood and stone. 37 And you shall become a horror, a proverb, and a byword among all the peoples where the LORD will lead you away. 38 You shall carry much seed into the field and shall gather in

[1] Or sword [2] Or shall not succeed in finding your ways

little, for the locust shall consume it. [39]You shall plant vineyards and dress them, but you shall neither drink of the wine nor gather the grapes, for the worm shall eat them. [40]You shall have olive trees throughout all your territory, but you shall not anoint yourself with the oil, for your olives shall drop off. [41]You shall father sons and daughters, but they shall not be yours, for they shall go into captivity. [42]The cricket[1] shall possess all your trees and the fruit of your ground. [43]The sojourner who is among you shall rise higher and higher above you, and you shall come down lower and lower. [44]He shall lend to you, and you shall not lend to him. He shall be the head, and you shall be the tail.

[45]"All these curses shall come upon you and pursue you and overtake you till you are destroyed, because you did not obey the voice of the LORD your God, to keep his commandments and his statutes that he commanded you. [46]They shall be a sign and a wonder against you and your offspring forever. [47]Because you did not serve the LORD your God with joyfulness and gladness of heart, because of the abundance of all things, [48]therefore you shall serve your enemies whom the LORD will send against you, in hunger and thirst, in nakedness, and lacking everything. And he will put a yoke of iron on your neck until he has destroyed you. [49]The LORD will bring a nation against you from far away, from the end of the earth, swooping down like the eagle, a nation whose language you do not understand, [50]a hard-faced nation who shall not respect the old or show mercy to the young. [51]It shall eat the offspring of your cattle and the fruit of your ground, until you are destroyed; it also shall not leave you grain, wine, or oil, the increase of your herds or the young of your flock, until they have caused you to perish. [52]"They shall besiege you in all your towns, until your high and fortified walls, in which you trusted, come down throughout all your land. And they shall besiege you in all your towns throughout all your land, which the LORD your God has given you. [53]And you shall eat the fruit of your womb, the flesh of your sons and daughters, whom the LORD your God has given you, in the siege and in the distress with which your enemies shall distress you. [54]The man who is the most tender and refined among you will begrudge food to his brother,

to the wife he embraces,[2] and to the last of the children whom he has left, [55]so that he will not give to any of them any of the flesh of his children whom he is eating, because he has nothing else left, in the siege and in the distress with which your enemy shall distress you in all your towns. [56]The most tender and refined woman among you, who would not venture to set the sole of her foot on the ground because she is so delicate and tender, will begrudge to the husband she embraces,[3] to her son and to her daughter, [57]her afterbirth that comes out from between her feet and her children whom she bears, because lacking everything she will eat them secretly, in the siege and in the distress with which your enemy shall distress you in your towns.

[58]"If you are not careful to do all the words of this law that are written in this book, that you may fear this glorious and awesome name, the LORD your God, [59]then the LORD will bring on you and your offspring extraordinary afflictions, afflictions severe and lasting, and sicknesses grievous and lasting. [60]And he will bring upon you again all the diseases of Egypt, of which you were afraid, and they shall cling to you. [61]Every sickness also and every affliction that is not recorded in the book of this law, the LORD will bring upon you, until you are destroyed. [62]Whereas you were as numerous as the stars of heaven, you shall be left few in number, because you did not obey the voice of the LORD your God. [63]And as the LORD took delight in doing you good and multiplying you, so the LORD will take delight in bringing ruin upon you and destroying you. And you shall be plucked off the land that you are entering to take possession of it.

[64]"And the LORD will scatter you among all peoples, from one end of the earth to the other, and there you shall serve other gods of wood and stone, which neither you nor your fathers have known. [65]And among these nations you shall find no respite, and there shall be no resting place for the sole of your foot, but the LORD will give you there a trembling heart and failing eyes and a languishing soul. [66]Your life shall hang in doubt before you. Night and day you shall be in dread and have no assurance of your life. [67]In the morning you shall say, 'If only it were evening!' and at evening you shall say, 'If only it were morning!' because of the dread that

---

[1] Identity uncertain   [2] Hebrew *the wife of his bosom*   [3] Hebrew *the husband of her bosom*

your heart shall feel, and the sights that your eyes shall see. [68]And the LORD will bring you back in ships to Egypt, a journey that I promised that you should never make again; and there you shall offer yourselves for sale to your enemies as male and female slaves, but there will be no buyer."

Psalm 119:25–48

DALETH
My soul clings to the dust;
give me life according to your word!
[26] When I told of my ways, you answered me;
teach me your statutes!
[27] Make me understand the way of your precepts,
and I will meditate on your wondrous works.
[28] My soul melts away for sorrow;
strengthen me according to your word!
[29] Put false ways far from me
and graciously teach me your law!
[30] I have chosen the way of faithfulness;
I set your rules before me.
[31] I cling to your testimonies, O LORD;
let me not be put to shame!
[32] I will run in the way of your commandments
when you enlarge my heart![1]

HE
[33] Teach me, O LORD, the way of your statutes;
and I will keep it to the end.[2]
[34] Give me understanding, that I may keep your law
and observe it with my whole heart.
[35] Lead me in the path of your commandments,
for I delight in it.
[36] Incline my heart to your testimonies,
and not to selfish gain!
[37] Turn my eyes from looking at worthless things;
and give me life in your ways.
[38] Confirm to your servant your promise,
that you may be feared.
[39] Turn away the reproach that I dread,
for your rules are good.

[40] Behold, I long for your precepts;
in your righteousness give me life!

WAW
[41] Let your steadfast love come to me, O LORD,
your salvation according to your promise;
[42] then shall I have an answer for him who taunts me,
for I trust in your word.
[43] And take not the word of truth utterly out of my mouth,
for my hope is in your rules.
[44] I will keep your law continually,
forever and ever,
[45] and I shall walk in a wide place,
for I have sought your precepts.
[46] I will also speak of your testimonies before kings
and shall not be put to shame,
[47] for I find my delight in your commandments,
which I love.
[48] I will lift up my hands toward your commandments, which I love,
and I will meditate on your statutes.

Isaiah 55

"Come, everyone who thirsts,
come to the waters;
and he who has no money,
come, buy and eat!
Come, buy wine and milk
without money and without price.
[2] Why do you spend your money for that which is not bread,
and your labor for that which does not satisfy?
Listen diligently to me, and eat what is good,
and delight yourselves in rich food.
[3] Incline your ear, and come to me;
hear, that your soul may live;
and I will make with you an everlasting covenant,
my steadfast, sure love for David.
[4] Behold, I made him a witness to the peoples,
a leader and commander for the peoples.

[1] Or for you set my heart free [2] Or keep it as my reward

⁵ Behold, you shall call a nation that you
do not know,
and a nation that did not know you
shall run to you,
because of the LORD your God, and of
the Holy One of Israel,
for he has glorified you.

⁶ "Seek the LORD while he may be found;
call upon him while he is near;
⁷ let the wicked forsake his way,
and the unrighteous man his
thoughts;
let him return to the LORD, that he may
have compassion on him,
and to our God, for he will abundantly
pardon.
⁸ For my thoughts are not your thoughts,
neither are your ways my ways,
declares the LORD.
⁹ For as the heavens are higher than the
earth,
so are my ways higher than your ways
and my thoughts than your thoughts.

¹⁰ "For as the rain and the snow come down
from heaven
and do not return there but water the
earth,
making it bring forth and sprout,
giving seed to the sower and bread to
the eater,
¹¹ so shall my word be that goes out from
my mouth;
it shall not return to me empty,
but it shall accomplish that which I
purpose,
and shall succeed in the thing for
which I sent it.
¹² "For you shall go out in joy
and be led forth in peace;
the mountains and the hills before you
shall break forth into singing,
and all the trees of the field shall clap
their hands.
¹³ Instead of the thorn shall come up the
cypress;
instead of the brier shall come up the
myrtle;
and it shall make a name for the LORD,
an everlasting sign that shall not be
cut off."

Matthew 3

In those days John the Baptist came preaching in the wilderness of Judea, ²"Repent, for the kingdom of heaven is at hand." ³For this is he who was spoken of by the prophet Isaiah when he said,

"The voice of one crying in the
wilderness:
'Prepare¹ the way of the Lord;
make his paths straight.'"

⁴Now John wore a garment of camel's hair and a leather belt around his waist, and his food was locusts and wild honey. ⁵Then Jerusalem and all Judea and all the region about the Jordan were going out to him, ⁶and they were baptized by him in the river Jordan, confessing their sins.

⁷But when he saw many of the Pharisees and Sadducees coming to his baptism, he said to them, "You brood of vipers! Who warned you to flee from the wrath to come? ⁸Bear fruit in keeping with repentance. ⁹And do not presume to say to yourselves, 'We have Abraham as our father,' for I tell you, God is able from these stones to raise up children for Abraham. ¹⁰Even now the axe is laid to the root of the trees. Every tree therefore that does not bear good fruit is cut down and thrown into the fire.

¹¹"I baptize you with water for repentance, but he who is coming after me is mightier than I, whose sandals I am not worthy to carry. He will baptize you with the Holy Spirit and fire. ¹²His winnowing fork is in his hand, and he will clear his threshing floor and gather his wheat into the barn, but the chaff he will burn with unquenchable fire."

¹³Then Jesus came from Galilee to the Jordan to John, to be baptized by him. ¹⁴John would have prevented him, saying, "I need to be baptized by you, and do you come to me?" ¹⁵But Jesus answered him, "Let it be so now, for thus it is fitting for us to fulfill all righteousness." Then he consented. ¹⁶And when Jesus was baptized, immediately he went up from the water, and behold, the heavens were opened to him,² and he saw the Spirit of God descending like a dove and coming to rest on him; ¹⁷and behold, a voice from heaven said, "This is my beloved Son,³ with whom I am well pleased."

¹ Or crying: Prepare in the wilderness ² Some manuscripts omit to him ³ Or my Son, my (or the) Beloved

JUNE 24

Deuteronomy 29[1]

These are the words of the covenant that the LORD commanded Moses to make with the people of Israel in the land of Moab, besides the covenant that he had made with them at Horeb.

[2] And Moses summoned all Israel and said to them: "You have seen all that the LORD did before your eyes in the land of Egypt, to Pharaoh and to all his servants and to all his land, [3] the great trials that your eyes saw, the signs, and those great wonders. [4] But to this day the LORD has not given you a heart to understand or eyes to see or ears to hear. [5] I have led you forty years in the wilderness. Your clothes have not worn out on you, and your sandals have not worn off your feet. [6] You have not eaten bread, and you have not drunk wine or strong drink, that you may know that I am the LORD your God. [7] And when you came to this place, Sihon the king of Heshbon and Og the king of Bashan came out against us to battle, but we defeated them. [8] We took their land and gave it for an inheritance to the Reubenites, the Gadites, and the half-tribe of the Manassites. [9] Therefore keep the words of this covenant and do them, that you may prosper[3] in all that you do.

[10] "You are standing today all of you before the LORD your God: the heads of your tribes,[4] your elders, and your officers, all the men of Israel, [11] your little ones, your wives, and the sojourner who is in your camp, from the one who chops your wood to the one who draws your water, [12] so that you may enter into the sworn covenant of the LORD your God, which the LORD your God is making with you today, [13] that he may establish you today as his people, and that he may be your God, as he promised you, and as he swore to your fathers, to Abraham, to Isaac, and to Jacob. [14] It is not with you alone that I am making this sworn covenant, [15] but with whoever is standing here with us today before the LORD our God, and with whoever is not here with us today.

[16] "You know how we lived in the land of Egypt, and how we came through the midst of the nations through which you passed. [17] And you have seen their detestable things, their idols of wood and stone, of silver and gold, which were among them. [18] Beware lest there be among you a man or woman or clan or tribe whose heart is turning away today from the LORD our God to go and serve the gods of those nations. Beware lest there be among you a root bearing poisonous and bitter fruit, [19] one who, when he hears the words of this sworn covenant, blesses himself in his heart, saying, 'I shall be safe, though I walk in the stubbornness of my heart.' This will lead to the sweeping away of moist and dry alike. [20] The LORD will not be willing to forgive him, but rather the anger of the LORD and his jealousy will smoke against that man, and the curses written in this book will settle upon him, and the LORD will blot out his name from under heaven. [21] And the LORD will single him out from all the tribes of Israel for calamity, in accordance with all the curses of the covenant written in this Book of the Law. [22] And the next generation, your children who rise up after you, and the foreigner who comes from a far land, will say, when they see the afflictions of that land and the sicknesses with which the LORD has made it sick— [23] the whole land burned out with brimstone and salt, nothing sown and nothing growing, where no plant can sprout, an overthrow like that of Sodom and Gomorrah, Admah, and Zeboiim, which the LORD overthrew in his anger and wrath— [24] all the nations will say, 'Why has the LORD done thus to this land? What caused the heat of this great anger?' [25] Then people will say, 'It is because they abandoned the covenant of the LORD, the God of their fathers, which he made with them when he brought them out of the land of Egypt, [26] and went and served other gods and worshiped them, gods whom they had not known and whom he had not allotted to them. [27] Therefore the anger of the LORD

---

[1] Ch 28:69 in Hebrew [2] Ch 29:1 in Hebrew [3] Or *deal wisely* [4] Septuagint, Syriac; Hebrew *your heads, your tribes*

was kindled against this land, bringing upon it all the curses written in this book, [28] and the LORD uprooted them from their land in anger and fury and great wrath, and cast them into another land, as they are this day.'

[29] "The secret things belong to the LORD our God, but the things that are revealed belong to us and to our children forever, that we may do all the words of this law.

——————— *Psalm 119:49–72* ———————

ZAYIN

Remember your word to your servant,
    in which you have made me hope.
[50] This is my comfort in my affliction,
    that your promise gives me life.
[51] The insolent utterly deride me,
    but I do not turn away from your law.
[52] When I think of your rules from of old,
    I take comfort, O LORD.
[53] Hot indignation seizes me because of
    the wicked,
    who forsake your law.
[54] Your statutes have been my songs
    in the house of my sojourning.
[55] I remember your name in the night,
    O LORD,
    and keep your law.
[56] This blessing has fallen to me,
    that I have kept your precepts.

HETH

[57] The LORD is my portion;
    I promise to keep your words.
[58] I entreat your favor with all my heart;
    be gracious to me according to your
    promise.
[59] When I think on my ways,
    I turn my feet to your testimonies;
[60] I hasten and do not delay
    to keep your commandments.
[61] Though the cords of the wicked ensnare
    me,
    I do not forget your law.
[62] At midnight I rise to praise you,
    because of your righteous rules.
[63] I am a companion of all who fear you,
    of those who keep your precepts.
[64] The earth, O LORD, is full of your
    steadfast love;
    teach me your statutes!

TETH

[65] You have dealt well with your servant,
    O LORD, according to your word.
[66] Teach me good judgment and
    knowledge,
    for I believe in your commandments.
[67] Before I was afflicted I went astray,
    but now I keep your word.
[68] You are good and do good;
    teach me your statutes.
[69] The insolent smear me with lies,
    but with my whole heart I keep your
    precepts;
[70] their heart is unfeeling like fat,
    but I delight in your law.
[71] It is good for me that I was afflicted,
    that I might learn your statutes.
[72] The law of your mouth is better to me
    than thousands of gold and silver
    pieces.

——————— *Isaiah 56* ———————

Thus says the LORD:
    "Keep justice, and do righteousness,
    for soon my salvation will come,
    and my righteousness be revealed.
[2] Blessed is the man who does this,
    and the son of man who holds it fast,
    who keeps the Sabbath, not profaning
    it,
    and keeps his hand from doing any
    evil."

[3] Let not the foreigner who has joined
    himself to the LORD say,
    "The LORD will surely separate me
    from his people";
    and let not the eunuch say,
    "Behold, I am a dry tree."
[4] For thus says the LORD:
    "To the eunuchs who keep my Sabbaths,
    who choose the things that please
    me
    and hold fast my covenant,
[5] I will give in my house and within my
    walls
    a monument and a name
    better than sons and daughters;
    I will give them an everlasting name
    that shall not be cut off.

6 "And the foreigners who join themselves
        to the LORD,
    to minister to him, to love the name of
        the LORD,
    and to be his servants,
    everyone who keeps the Sabbath and
        does not profane it,
    and holds fast my covenant—
7 these I will bring to my holy mountain,
    and make them joyful in my house of
        prayer;
    their burnt offerings and their
        sacrifices
    will be accepted on my altar;
    for my house shall be called a house of
        prayer
    for all peoples."
8 The Lord GOD,
    who gathers the outcasts of Israel,
        declares,
    "I will gather yet others to him
        besides those already gathered."

9 All you beasts of the field, come to
        devour—
    all you beasts in the forest.
10 His watchmen are blind;
    they are all without knowledge;
    they are all silent dogs;
        they cannot bark,
    dreaming, lying down,
        loving to slumber.
11 The dogs have a mighty appetite;
        they never have enough.
    But they are shepherds who have no
        understanding;
    they have all turned to their own way,
        each to his own gain, one and all.
12 "Come," they say, "let me get wine;
    let us fill ourselves with strong drink;
    and tomorrow will be like this day,
        great beyond measure."

Matthew 4

Then Jesus was led up by the Spirit into
the wilderness to be tempted by the devil.
² And after fasting forty days and forty nights,
he was hungry. ³ And the tempter came and said
to him, "If you are the Son of God, command
these stones to become loaves of bread." ⁴ But
he answered, "It is written,

"'Man shall not live by bread alone,
    but by every word that comes from
        the mouth of God.'"

⁵ Then the devil took him to the holy city and set
him on the pinnacle of the temple ⁶ and said to
him, "If you are the Son of God, throw yourself
down, for it is written,

"'He will command his angels concerning
    you,'

and

"'On their hands they will bear you up,
    lest you strike your foot against a
        stone.'"

⁷ Jesus said to him, "Again it is written, 'You
shall not put the Lord your God to the test.'"
⁸ Again, the devil took him to a very high mountain and showed him all the kingdoms of the
world and their glory. ⁹ And he said to him, "All
these I will give you, if you will fall down and
worship me." ¹⁰ Then Jesus said to him, "Be
gone, Satan! For it is written,

"'You shall worship the Lord your God
    and him only shall you serve.'"

¹¹ Then the devil left him, and behold, angels
came and were ministering to him.
¹² Now when he heard that John had been
arrested, he withdrew into Galilee. ¹³ And leaving Nazareth he went and lived in Capernaum
by the sea, in the territory of Zebulun and
Naphtali, ¹⁴ so that what was spoken by the
prophet Isaiah might be fulfilled:

15 "The land of Zebulun and the land of
        Naphtali,
    the way of the sea, beyond the Jordan,
        Galilee of the Gentiles—
16 the people dwelling in darkness
    have seen a great light,
    and for those dwelling in the region and
        shadow of death,
    on them a light has dawned."

¹⁷ From that time Jesus began to preach, saying, "Repent, for the kingdom of heaven is at
hand."
¹⁸ While walking by the Sea of Galilee, he
saw two brothers, Simon (who is called Peter)
and Andrew his brother, casting a net into the
sea, for they were fishermen. ¹⁹ And he said to

them, "Follow me, and I will make you fishers of men."[1] [20]Immediately they left their nets and followed him. [21]And going on from there he saw two other brothers, James the son of Zebedee and John his brother, in the boat with Zebedee their father, mending their nets, and he called them. [22]Immediately they left the boat and their father and followed him.

[23]And he went throughout all Galilee, teaching in their synagogues and proclaiming the gospel of the kingdom and healing every disease and every affliction among the people. [24]So his fame spread throughout all Syria, and they brought him all the sick, those afflicted with various diseases and pains, those oppressed by demons, epileptics, and paralytics, and he healed them. [25]And great crowds followed him from Galilee and the Decapolis, and from Jerusalem and Judea, and from beyond the Jordan.

JUNE 25

Deuteronomy 30

"And when all these things come upon you, the blessing and the curse, which I have set before you, and you call them to mind among all the nations where the LORD your God has driven you, [2]and return to the LORD your God, you and your children, and obey his voice in all that I command you today, with all your heart and with all your soul, [3]then the LORD your God will restore your fortunes and have mercy on you, and he will gather you again from all the peoples where the LORD your God has scattered you. [4]If your outcasts are in the uttermost parts of heaven, from there the LORD your God will gather you, and from there he will take you. [5]And the LORD your God will bring you into the land that your fathers possessed, that you may possess it. And he will make you more prosperous and numerous than your fathers. [6]And the LORD your God will circumcise your heart and the heart of your offspring, so that you will love the LORD your God with all your heart and with all your soul, that you may live. [7]And the LORD your God will put all these curses on your foes and enemies who persecuted you. [8]And you shall again obey the voice of the LORD and keep all his commandments that I command you today. [9]The LORD your God will make you abundantly prosperous in all the work of your hand, in the fruit of your womb and in the fruit of your cattle and in the fruit of your ground. For the LORD will again take delight in prospering you, as he took delight in your fathers, [10]when you obey the voice of the LORD your God, to keep his commandments and his statutes that are written in this Book of the Law, when you turn to the LORD your God with all your heart and with all your soul.

[11]"For this commandment that I command you today is not too hard for you, neither is it far off. [12]It is not in heaven, that you should say, 'Who will ascend to heaven for us and bring it to us, that we may hear it and do it?' [13]Neither is it beyond the sea, that you should say, 'Who will go over the sea for us and bring it to us, that we may hear it and do it?' [14]But the word is very near you. It is in your mouth and in your heart, so that you can do it.

[15]"See, I have set before you today life and good, death and evil. [16]If you obey the commandments of the LORD your God[2] that I command you today, by loving the LORD your God, by walking in his ways, and by keeping his commandments and his statutes and his rules,[3] then you shall live and multiply, and the LORD your God will bless you in the land that you are entering to take possession of it. [17]But if your heart turns away, and you will not hear, but are drawn away to worship other gods and serve them, [18]I declare to you today, that you shall surely perish. You shall not live long in the land that you are going over the Jordan to

---

[1] The Greek word *anthropoi* refers here to both men and women [2] Septuagint; Hebrew lacks *If you obey the commandments of the LORD your God* [3] Or *his just decrees*

enter and possess. [19] I call heaven and earth to witness against you today, that I have set before you life and death, blessing and curse. Therefore choose life, that you and your offspring may live, [20] loving the LORD your God, obeying his voice and holding fast to him, for he is your life and length of days, that you may dwell in the land that the LORD swore to your fathers, to Abraham, to Isaac, and to Jacob, to give them."

Psalm 119:73–96

YODH

[73] Your hands have made and fashioned me;
　　give me understanding that I may learn
　　　your commandments.
[74] Those who fear you shall see me and
　　　rejoice,
　　because I have hoped in your word.
[75] I know, O LORD, that your rules are
　　　righteous,
　　and that in faithfulness you have
　　　afflicted me.
[76] Let your steadfast love comfort me
　　according to your promise to your
　　　servant.
[77] Let your mercy come to me, that I may
　　　live;
　　for your law is my delight.
[78] Let the insolent be put to shame,
　　because they have wronged me with
　　　falsehood;
　　as for me, I will meditate on your
　　　precepts.
[79] Let those who fear you turn to me,
　　that they may know your testimonies.
[80] May my heart be blameless in your
　　　statutes,
　　that I may not be put to shame!

KAPH

[81] My soul longs for your salvation;
　　I hope in your word.
[82] My eyes long for your promise;
　　I ask, "When will you comfort me?"
[83] For I have become like a wineskin in the
　　　smoke,
　　yet I have not forgotten your statutes.
[84] How long must your servant endure?[1]
　　When will you judge those who
　　　persecute me?

[85] The insolent have dug pitfalls for me;
　　they do not live according to your law.
[86] All your commandments are sure;
　　they persecute me with falsehood;
　　　help me!
[87] They have almost made an end of me on
　　　earth,
　　but I have not forsaken your precepts.
[88] In your steadfast love give me life,
　　that I may keep the testimonies of
　　　your mouth.

LAMEDH

[89] Forever, O LORD, your word
　　is firmly fixed in the heavens.
[90] Your faithfulness endures to all
　　　generations;
　　you have established the earth, and it
　　　stands fast.
[91] By your appointment they stand this day,
　　for all things are your servants.
[92] If your law had not been my delight,
　　I would have perished in my affliction.
[93] I will never forget your precepts,
　　for by them you have given me life.
[94] I am yours; save me,
　　for I have sought your precepts.
[95] The wicked lie in wait to destroy me,
　　but I consider your testimonies.
[96] I have seen a limit to all perfection,
　　but your commandment is
　　　exceedingly broad.

Isaiah 57

The righteous man perishes,
　and no one lays it to heart;
　devout men are taken away,
　　while no one understands.
For the righteous man is taken away
　　from calamity;
[2] 　he enters into peace;
they rest in their beds
　who walk in their uprightness.
[3] But you, draw near,
　sons of the sorceress,
　offspring of the adulterer and the
　　loose woman.
[4] Whom are you mocking?
　Against whom do you open your
　　mouth wide
　and stick out your tongue?

[1] Hebrew *How many are the days of your servant?*

Are you not children of transgression,
   the offspring of deceit,
5 you who burn with lust among the oaks,[1]
     under every green tree,
who slaughter your children in the
     valleys,
     under the clefts of the rocks?
6 Among the smooth stones of the valley
     is your portion;
   they, they, are your lot;
to them you have poured out a drink
     offering,
     you have brought a grain offering.
     Shall I relent for these things?
7 On a high and lofty mountain
     you have set your bed,
     and there you went up to offer
     sacrifice.
8 Behind the door and the doorpost
     you have set up your memorial;
for, deserting me, you have uncovered
     your bed,
     you have gone up to it,
     you have made it wide;
and you have made a covenant for
     yourself with them,
     you have loved their bed,
     you have looked on nakedness.[2]
9 You journeyed to the king with oil
     and multiplied your perfumes;
you sent your envoys far off,
     and sent down even to Sheol.
10 You were wearied with the length of
     your way,
   but you did not say, "It is hopeless";
you found new life for your strength,
     and so you were not faint.[3]
11 Whom did you dread and fear,
    so that you lied,
and did not remember me,
    did not lay it to heart?
Have I not held my peace, even for a
     long time,
    and you do not fear me?
12 I will declare your righteousness and
     your deeds,
    but they will not profit you.
13 When you cry out, let your collection of
     idols deliver you!
    The wind will carry them all off,
    a breath will take them away.

But he who takes refuge in me shall
     possess the land
     and shall inherit my holy mountain.
14 And it shall be said,
"Build up, build up, prepare the way,
     remove every obstruction from my
     people's way."
15 For thus says the One who is high and
     lifted up,
   who inhabits eternity, whose name is
     Holy:
"I dwell in the high and holy place,
   and also with him who is of a contrite
     and lowly spirit,
to revive the spirit of the lowly,
   and to revive the heart of the contrite.
16 For I will not contend forever,
    nor will I always be angry;
for the spirit would grow faint before
     me,
    and the breath of life that I made.
17 Because of the iniquity of his unjust gain
    I was angry,
   I struck him; I hid my face and was
     angry,
   but he went on backsliding in the way
     of his own heart.
18 I have seen his ways, but I will heal him;
   I will lead him and restore comfort to
     him and his mourners,
19   creating the fruit of the lips.
Peace, peace, to the far and to the near,"
     says the LORD,
   "and I will heal him.
20 But the wicked are like the tossing sea;
    for it cannot be quiet,
    and its waters toss up mire and dirt.
21 There is no peace," says my God, "for the
     wicked."

—————— *Matthew 5* ——————

Seeing the crowds, he went up on the mountain, and when he sat down, his disciples
came to him. [2] And he opened his mouth and taught them,
saying:

[3] "Blessed are the poor in spirit, for theirs is
the kingdom of heaven.

[4] "Blessed are those who mourn, for they
shall be comforted.

---

[1] Or *among the terebinths* [2] Or *on a monument* (see 56:5); Hebrew *on a hand* [3] Hebrew *and so you were not sick*

5 "Blessed are the meek, for they shall inherit the earth.

6 "Blessed are those who hunger and thirst for righteousness, for they shall be satisfied.

7 "Blessed are the merciful, for they shall receive mercy.

8 "Blessed are the pure in heart, for they shall see God.

9 "Blessed are the peacemakers, for they shall be called sons[1] of God.

10 "Blessed are those who are persecuted for righteousness' sake, for theirs is the kingdom of heaven.

11 "Blessed are you when others revile you and persecute you and utter all kinds of evil against you falsely on my account. 12 Rejoice and be glad, for your reward is great in heaven, for so they persecuted the prophets who were before you.

13 "You are the salt of the earth, but if salt has lost its taste, how shall its saltiness be restored? It is no longer good for anything except to be thrown out and trampled under people's feet.

14 "You are the light of the world. A city set on a hill cannot be hidden. 15 Nor do people light a lamp and put it under a basket, but on a stand, and it gives light to all in the house. 16 In the same way, let your light shine before others, so that[2] they may see your good works and give glory to your Father who is in heaven.

17 "Do not think that I have come to abolish the Law or the Prophets; I have not come to abolish them but to fulfill them. 18 For truly, I say to you, until heaven and earth pass away, not an iota, not a dot, will pass from the Law until all is accomplished. 19 Therefore whoever relaxes one of the least of these commandments and teaches others to do the same will be called least in the kingdom of heaven, but whoever does them and teaches them will be called great in the kingdom of heaven. 20 For I tell you, unless your righteousness exceeds that of the scribes and Pharisees, you will never enter the kingdom of heaven.

21 "You have heard that it was said to those of old, 'You shall not murder; and whoever murders will be liable to judgment.' 22 But I say to you that everyone who is angry with his brother[3] will be liable to judgment; whoever insults[4] his brother will be liable to the council; and whoever says, 'You fool!' will be liable to the hell[5] of fire. 23 So if you are offering your gift at the altar and there remember that your brother has something against you, 24 leave your gift there before the altar and go. First be reconciled to your brother, and then come and offer your gift. 25 Come to terms quickly with your accuser while you are going with him to court, lest your accuser hand you over to the judge, and the judge to the guard, and you be put in prison. 26 Truly, I say to you, you will never get out until you have paid the last penny.[6]

27 "You have heard that it was said, 'You shall not commit adultery.' 28 But I say to you that everyone who looks at a woman with lustful intent has already committed adultery with her in his heart. 29 If your right eye causes you to sin, tear it out and throw it away. For it is better that you lose one of your members than that your whole body be thrown into hell. 30 And if your right hand causes you to sin, cut it off and throw it away. For it is better that you lose one of your members than that your whole body go into hell.

31 "It was also said, 'Whoever divorces his wife, let him give her a certificate of divorce.' 32 But I say to you that everyone who divorces his wife, except on the ground of sexual immorality, makes her commit adultery, and whoever marries a divorced woman commits adultery.

33 "Again you have heard that it was said to those of old, 'You shall not swear falsely, but shall perform to the Lord what you have sworn.' 34 But I say to you, Do not take an oath at all, either by heaven, for it is the throne of God, 35 or by the earth, for it is his footstool, or by Jerusalem, for it is the city of the great King. 36 And do not take an oath by your head, for you cannot make one hair white or black. 37 Let what you say be simply 'Yes' or 'No'; anything more than this comes from evil.[7]

38 "You have heard that it was said, 'An eye for an eye and a tooth for a tooth.' 39 But I say to you, Do not resist the one who is evil. But if anyone slaps you on the right cheek, turn to him the other also. 40 And if anyone would sue you and take your tunic,[8] let him have your cloak as well. 41 And if anyone forces you to go one mile, go with him two miles. 42 Give to the one who begs from you, and do not refuse the one who would borrow from you.

[1] Greek huioi; see Preface [2] Or house. [16] Let your light so shine before others that [3] Some manuscripts insert without cause [4] Greek says Raca to (a term of abuse) [5] Greek Gehenna; also verses 29, 30 [6] Greek kodrantes, Roman copper coin (Latin quadrans) worth about 1/64 of a denarius (which was a day's wage for a laborer) [7] Or the evil one [8] Greek chiton, a long garment worn under the cloak next to the skin

[43] "You have heard that it was said, 'You shall love your neighbor and hate your enemy.' [44] But I say to you, Love your enemies and pray for those who persecute you, [45] so that you may be sons of your Father who is in heaven. For he makes his sun rise on the evil and on the good, and sends rain on the just and on the unjust. [46] For if you love those who love you, what reward do you have? Do not even the tax collectors do the same? [47] And if you greet only your brothers,[1] what more are you doing than others? Do not even the Gentiles do the same? [48] You therefore must be perfect, as your heavenly Father is perfect.

JUNE 26

Deuteronomy 31

So Moses continued to speak these words to all Israel. [2] And he said to them, "I am 120 years old today. I am no longer able to go out and come in. The LORD has said to me, 'You shall not go over this Jordan.' [3] The LORD your God himself will go over before you. He will destroy these nations before you, so that you shall dispossess them, and Joshua will go over at your head, as the LORD has spoken. [4] And the LORD will do to them as he did to Sihon and Og, the kings of the Amorites, and to their land, when he destroyed them. [5] And the LORD will give them over to you, and you shall do to them according to the whole commandment that I have commanded you. [6] Be strong and courageous. Do not fear or be in dread of them, for it is the LORD your God who goes with you. He will not leave you or forsake you."

[7] Then Moses summoned Joshua and said to him in the sight of all Israel, "Be strong and courageous, for you shall go with this people into the land that the LORD has sworn to their fathers to give them, and you shall put them in possession of it. [8] It is the LORD who goes before you. He will be with you; he will not leave you or forsake you. Do not fear or be dismayed."

[9] Then Moses wrote this law and gave it to the priests, the sons of Levi, who carried the ark of the covenant of the LORD, and to all the elders of Israel. [10] And Moses commanded them, "At the end of every seven years, at the set time in the year of release, at the Feast of Booths, [11] when all Israel comes to appear before the LORD your God at the place that he will choose, you shall read this law before all Israel in their hearing. [12] Assemble the people, men, women, and little ones, and the sojourner within your towns, that they may hear and learn to fear the LORD your God, and be careful to do all the words of this law, [13] and that their children, who have not known it, may hear and learn to fear the LORD your God, as long as you live in the land that you are going over the Jordan to possess."

[14] And the LORD said to Moses, "Behold, the days approach when you must die. Call Joshua and present yourselves in the tent of meeting, that I may commission him." And Moses and Joshua went and presented themselves in the tent of meeting. [15] And the LORD appeared in the tent in a pillar of cloud. And the pillar of cloud stood over the entrance of the tent.

[16] And the LORD said to Moses, "Behold, you are about to lie down with your fathers. Then this people will rise and whore after the foreign gods among them in the land that they are entering, and they will forsake me and break my covenant that I have made with them. [17] Then my anger will be kindled against them in that day, and I will forsake them and hide my face from them, and they will be devoured. And many evils and troubles will come upon them, so that they will say in that day, 'Have not these evils come upon us because our God is not among us?' [18] And I will surely hide my face in that day because of all the evil that they have done, because they have turned to other gods. [19] "Now therefore write this song and teach it to the people of Israel. Put it in their mouths,

---

[1] Or *brothers and sisters*. The plural Greek word *adelphoi* (translated "brothers") refers to siblings in a family. In New Testament usage, depending on the context, *adelphoi* may refer either to *brothers* or to *brothers and sisters*

that this song may be a witness for me against the people of Israel. [20]For when I have brought them into the land flowing with milk and honey, which I swore to give to their fathers, and they have eaten and are full and grown fat, they will turn to other gods and serve them, and despise me and break my covenant. [21]And when many evils and troubles have come upon them, this song shall confront them as a witness (for it will live unforgotten in the mouths of their offspring). For I know what they are inclined to do even today, before I have brought them into the land that I swore to give." [22]So Moses wrote this song the same day and taught it to the people of Israel.

[23]And the LORD[1] commissioned Joshua the son of Nun and said, "Be strong and courageous, for you shall bring the people of Israel into the land that I swore to give them. I will be with you."

[24]When Moses had finished writing the words of this law in a book to the very end, [25]Moses commanded the Levites who carried the ark of the covenant of the LORD, [26]"Take this Book of the Law and put it by the side of the ark of the covenant of the LORD your God, that it may be there for a witness against you. [27]For I know how rebellious and stubborn you are. Behold, even today while I am yet alive with you, you have been rebellious against the LORD. How much more after my death! [28]Assemble to me all the elders of your tribes and your officers, that I may speak these words in their ears and call heaven and earth to witness against them. [29]For I know that after my death you will surely act corruptly and turn aside from the way that I have commanded you. And in the days to come evil will befall you, because you will do what is evil in the sight of the LORD, provoking him to anger through the work of your hands."

[30]Then Moses spoke the words of this song until they were finished, in the ears of all the assembly of Israel:

Psalm 119:97–120

MEM
Oh how I love your law!
　It is my meditation all the day.
[98]　Your commandment makes me wiser
　　　than my enemies,
　for it is ever with me.

[99]　I have more understanding than all my
　　　teachers,
　for your testimonies are my
　　　meditation.
[100]　I understand more than the aged,[2]
　for I keep your precepts.
[101]　I hold back my feet from every evil way,
　in order to keep your word.
[102]　I do not turn aside from your rules,
　for you have taught me.
[103]　How sweet are your words to my taste,
　sweeter than honey to my mouth!
[104]　Through your precepts I get
　　　understanding;
　therefore I hate every false way.

NUN
[105]　Your word is a lamp to my feet
　and a light to my path.
[106]　I have sworn an oath and confirmed it,
　to keep your righteous rules.
[107]　I am severely afflicted;
　give me life, O LORD, according to
　　　your word!
[108]　Accept my freewill offerings of praise,
　　　O LORD,
　and teach me your rules.
[109]　I hold my life in my hand continually,
　but I do not forget your law.
[110]　The wicked have laid a snare for me,
　but I do not stray from your precepts.
[111]　Your testimonies are my heritage
　　　forever,
　for they are the joy of my heart.
[112]　I incline my heart to perform your
　　　statutes
　forever, to the end.[3]

SAMEKH
[113]　I hate the double-minded,
　but I love your law.
[114]　You are my hiding place and my shield;
　I hope in your word.
[115]　Depart from me, you evildoers,
　that I may keep the commandments
　　　of my God.
[116]　Uphold me according to your promise,
　　　that I may live,
　and let me not be put to shame in my
　　　hope!
[117]　Hold me up, that I may be safe
　and have regard for your statutes
　　　continually!

---
[1] Hebrew he　[2] Or the elders　[3] Or statutes; the reward is eternal

118 You spurn all who go astray from your
statutes,
for their cunning is in vain.
119 All the wicked of the earth you discard
like dross,
therefore I love your testimonies.
120 My flesh trembles for fear of you,
and I am afraid of your judgments.

Isaiah 58

"Cry aloud; do not hold back;
lift up your voice like a trumpet;
declare to my people their transgression,
to the house of Jacob their sins.
2 Yet they seek me daily
and delight to know my ways,
as if they were a nation that did
righteousness
and did not forsake the judgment of
their God;
they ask of me righteous judgments;
they delight to draw near to God.
3 'Why have we fasted, and you see it not?
Why have we humbled ourselves, and
you take no knowledge of it?'
Behold, in the day of your fast you seek
your own pleasure,[1]
and oppress all your workers.
4 Behold, you fast only to quarrel and to
fight
and to hit with a wicked fist.
Fasting like yours this day
will not make your voice to be heard
on high.
5 Is such the fast that I choose,
a day for a person to humble himself?
Is it to bow down his head like a reed,
and to spread sackcloth and ashes
under him?
Will you call this a fast,
and a day acceptable to the LORD?
6 "Is not this the fast that I choose:
to loose the bonds of wickedness,
to undo the straps of the yoke,
to let the oppressed[2] go free,
and to break every yoke?
7 Is it not to share your bread with the
hungry
and bring the homeless poor into your
house;

when you see the naked, to cover him,
and not to hide yourself from your
own flesh?
8 Then shall your light break forth like the
dawn,
and your healing shall spring up
speedily;
your righteousness shall go before you;
the glory of the LORD shall be your
rear guard.
9 Then you shall call, and the LORD will
answer;
you shall cry, and he will say, 'Here I
am.'
If you take away the yoke from your
midst,
the pointing of the finger, and
speaking wickedness,
10 if you pour yourself out for the hungry
and satisfy the desire of the afflicted,
then shall your light rise in the darkness
and your gloom be as the noonday.
11 And the LORD will guide you continually
and satisfy your desire in scorched
places
and make your bones strong;
and you shall be like a watered garden,
like a spring of water,
whose waters do not fail.
12 And your ancient ruins shall be rebuilt;
you shall raise up the foundations of
many generations;
you shall be called the repairer of the
breach,
the restorer of streets to dwell in.
13 "If you turn back your foot from the
Sabbath,
from doing your pleasure[3] on my holy
day,
and call the Sabbath a delight
and the holy day of the LORD
honorable;
if you honor it, not going your own ways,
or seeking your own pleasure,[4] or
talking idly;[5]
14 then you shall take delight in the LORD,
and I will make you ride on the
heights of the earth;[6]
I will feed you with the heritage of Jacob
your father,
for the mouth of the LORD has spoken."

[1] Or pursue your own business [2] Or bruised [3] Or business [4] Or pursuing your own business [5] Hebrew or speaking a word [6] Or of the land

Matthew 6

"Beware of practicing your righteousness before other people in order to be seen by them, for then you will have no reward from your Father who is in heaven.

[2] "Thus, when you give to the needy, sound no trumpet before you, as the hypocrites do in the synagogues and in the streets, that they may be praised by others. Truly, I say to you, they have received their reward. [3] But when you give to the needy, do not let your left hand know what your right hand is doing, [4] so that your giving may be in secret. And your Father who sees in secret will reward you.

[5] "And when you pray, you must not be like the hypocrites. For they love to stand and pray in the synagogues and at the street corners, that they may be seen by others. Truly, I say to you, they have received their reward. [6] But when you pray, go into your room and shut the door and pray to your Father who is in secret. And your Father who sees in secret will reward you.

[7] "And when you pray, do not heap up empty phrases as the Gentiles do, for they think that they will be heard for their many words. [8] Do not be like them, for your Father knows what you need before you ask him. [9] Pray then like this:

> "Our Father in heaven,
> hallowed be your name.[1]
> [10] Your kingdom come,
> your will be done,[2]
> on earth as it is in heaven.
> [11] Give us this day our daily bread,[3]
> [12] and forgive us our debts,
> as we also have forgiven our debtors.
> [13] And lead us not into temptation,
> but deliver us from evil.[4]

[14] For if you forgive others their trespasses, your heavenly Father will also forgive you, [15] but if you do not forgive others their trespasses, neither will your Father forgive your trespasses.

[16] "And when you fast, do not look gloomy like the hypocrites, for they disfigure their faces that their fasting may be seen by others. Truly, I say to you, they have received their reward. [17] But when you fast, anoint your head and wash your face, [18] that your fasting may not be seen by others but by your Father who is in secret. And your Father who sees in secret will reward you.

[19] "Do not lay up for yourselves treasures on earth, where moth and rust[5] destroy and where thieves break in and steal, [20] but lay up for yourselves treasures in heaven, where neither moth nor rust destroys and where thieves do not break in and steal. [21] For where your treasure is, there your heart will be also.

[22] "The eye is the lamp of the body. So, if your eye is healthy, your whole body will be full of light, [23] but if your eye is bad, your whole body will be full of darkness. If then the light in you is darkness, how great is the darkness!

[24] "No one can serve two masters, for either he will hate the one and love the other, or he will be devoted to the one and despise the other. You cannot serve God and money.[6]

[25] "Therefore I tell you, do not be anxious about your life, what you will eat or what you will drink, nor about your body, what you will put on. Is not life more than food, and the body more than clothing? [26] Look at the birds of the air: they neither sow nor reap nor gather into barns, and yet your heavenly Father feeds them. Are you not of more value than they? [27] And which of you by being anxious can add a single hour to his span of life?[7] [28] And why are you anxious about clothing? Consider the lilies of the field, how they grow: they neither toil nor spin, [29] yet I tell you, even Solomon in all his glory was not arrayed like one of these. [30] But if God so clothes the grass of the field, which today is alive and tomorrow is thrown into the oven, will he not much more clothe you, O you of little faith? [31] Therefore do not be anxious, saying, 'What shall we eat?' or 'What shall we drink?' or 'What shall we wear?' [32] For the Gentiles seek after all these things, and your heavenly Father knows that you need them all. [33] But seek first the kingdom of God and his righteousness, and all these things will be added to you.

[34] "Therefore do not be anxious about tomorrow, for tomorrow will be anxious for itself. Sufficient for the day is its own trouble.

---

[1] Or *Let your name be kept holy*, or *Let your name be treated with reverence* [2] Or *Let your kingdom come, let your will be done* [3] Or *our bread for tomorrow* [4] Or *the evil one*; some manuscripts add *For yours is the kingdom and the power and the glory, forever. Amen.* [5] Or *worm*; also verse 20 [6] Greek *mammon*, a Semitic word for money or possessions [7] Or *a single cubit to his stature*; a cubit was about 18 inches or 45 centimeters

JUNE 27

Deuteronomy 32

"Give ear, O heavens, and I will speak,
and let the earth hear the words of my
mouth.

2 May my teaching drop as the rain,
my speech distill as the dew,
like gentle rain upon the tender grass,
and like showers upon the herb.

3 For I will proclaim the name of the LORD;
ascribe greatness to our God!

4 "The Rock, his work is perfect,
for all his ways are justice.
A God of faithfulness and without
iniquity,
just and upright is he.

5 They have dealt corruptly with him;
they are no longer his children
because they are blemished;
they are a crooked and twisted
generation.

6 Do you thus repay the LORD,
you foolish and senseless people?
Is not he your father, who created you,
who made you and established you?

7 Remember the days of old;
consider the years of many
generations;
ask your father, and he will show you,
your elders, and they will tell you.

8 When the Most High gave to the nations
their inheritance,
when he divided mankind,
he fixed the borders[1] of the peoples
according to the number of the sons
of God.[2]

9 But the LORD's portion is his people,
Jacob his allotted heritage.

10 "He found him in a desert land,
and in the howling waste of the
wilderness;
he encircled him, he cared for him,
he kept him as the apple of his eye.

11 Like an eagle that stirs up its nest,
that flutters over its young,

spreading out its wings, catching them,
bearing them on its pinions,

12 the LORD alone guided him,
no foreign god was with him.

13 He made him ride on the high places of
the land,
and he ate the produce of the field,
and he suckled him with honey out of
the rock,
and oil out of the flinty rock.

14 Curds from the herd, and milk from the
flock,
with fat[3] of lambs,
rams of Bashan and goats,
with the very finest[4] of the wheat—
and you drank foaming wine made
from the blood of the grape.

15 "But Jeshurun grew fat, and kicked;
you grew fat, stout, and sleek;
then he forsook God who made him
and scoffed at the Rock of his
salvation.

16 They stirred him to jealousy with
strange gods;
with abominations they provoked him
to anger.

17 They sacrificed to demons that were no
gods,
to gods they had never known,
to new gods that had come recently,
whom your fathers had never
dreaded.

18 You were unmindful of the Rock that
bore[5] you,
and you forgot the God who gave you
birth.

19 "The LORD saw it and spurned them,
because of the provocation of his sons
and his daughters.

20 And he said, 'I will hide my face from
them;
I will see what their end will be,

---

[1] Or *territories*   [2] Compare Dead Sea Scroll, Septuagint; Masoretic Text *sons of Israel*   [3] That is, with the best   [4] Hebrew *with the kidney fat*   [5] Or *fathered*

for they are a perverse generation,
 children in whom is no faithfulness.
21 They have made me jealous with what is
  no god;
 they have provoked me to anger with
  their idols.
So I will make them jealous with those
  who are no people;
 I will provoke them to anger with a
  foolish nation.
22 For a fire is kindled by my anger,
 and it burns to the depths of Sheol,
devours the earth and its increase,
 and sets on fire the foundations of the
  mountains.

23 "'And I will heap disasters upon them;
 I will spend my arrows on them;
24 they shall be wasted with hunger,
 and devoured by plague
 and poisonous pestilence;
I will send the teeth of beasts against
  them,
 with the venom of things that crawl in
  the dust.
25 Outdoors the sword shall bereave,
 and indoors terror,
for young man and woman alike,
 the nursing child with the man of
  gray hairs.
26 I would have said, "I will cut them to
  pieces;
 I will wipe them from human
  memory,"
27 had I not feared provocation by the
  enemy,
 lest their adversaries should
  misunderstand,
lest they should say, "Our hand is
  triumphant,
 it was not the LORD who did all this."'
28 "For they are a nation void of counsel,
 and there is no understanding in them.
29 If they were wise, they would
  understand this;
 they would discern their latter end!
30 How could one have chased a thousand,
 and two have put ten thousand to
  flight,
unless their Rock had sold them,
 and the LORD had given them up?

31 For their rock is not as our Rock;
 our enemies are by themselves.
32 For their vine comes from the vine of
  Sodom
 and from the fields of Gomorrah;
their grapes are grapes of poison;
 their clusters are bitter;
33 their wine is the poison of serpents
 and the cruel venom of asps.
34 "'Is not this laid up in store with me,
 sealed up in my treasuries?
35 Vengeance is mine, and recompense,[1]
 for the time when their foot shall slip;
for the day of their calamity is at hand,
 and their doom comes swiftly.'
36 For the LORD will vindicate[2] his people
 and have compassion on his servants,
when he sees that their power is gone
 and there is none remaining, bond or
  free.
37 Then he will say, 'Where are their gods,
 the rock in which they took refuge,
38 who ate the fat of their sacrifices
 and drank the wine of their drink
  offering?
Let them rise up and help you;
 let them be your protection!
39 "'See now that I, even I, am he,
 and there is no god beside me;
I kill and I make alive;
 I wound and I heal;
 and there is none that can deliver out
  of my hand.
40 For I lift up my hand to heaven
 and swear, As I live forever,
41 if I sharpen my flashing sword[3]
 and my hand takes hold on judgment,
I will take vengeance on my adversaries
 and will repay those who hate me.
42 I will make my arrows drunk with blood,
 and my sword shall devour flesh—
with the blood of the slain and the
  captives,
 from the long-haired heads of the
  enemy.'
43 "Rejoice with him, O heavens;[4]
 bow down to him, all gods,[5]
for he avenges the blood of his children[6]
 and takes vengeance on his
  adversaries.

He repays those who hate him[1]
and cleanses[2] his people's land."[3]

[44] Moses came and recited all the words of this song in the hearing of the people, he and Joshua[4] the son of Nun. [45] And when Moses had finished speaking all these words to all Israel, [46] he said to them, "Take to heart all the words by which I am warning you today, that you may command them to your children, that they may be careful to do all the words of this law. [47] For it is no empty word for you, but your very life, and by this word you shall live long in the land that you are going over the Jordan to possess."

[48] That very day the LORD spoke to Moses, [49] "Go up this mountain of the Abarim, Mount Nebo, which is in the land of Moab, opposite Jericho, and view the land of Canaan, which I am giving to the people of Israel for a possession. [50] And die on the mountain which you go up, and be gathered to your people, as Aaron your brother died in Mount Hor and was gathered to his people, [51] because you broke faith with me in the midst of the people of Israel at the waters of Meribah-kadesh, in the wilderness of Zin, and because you did not treat me as holy in the midst of the people of Israel. [52] For you shall see the land before you, but you shall not go there, into the land that I am giving to the people of Israel."

--------- *Psalm 119:121–144* ---------

AYIN

I have done what is just and right;
     do not leave me to my oppressors.
[122] Give your servant a pledge of good;
     let not the insolent oppress me.
[123] My eyes long for your salvation
     and for the fulfillment of your
          righteous promise.
[124] Deal with your servant according to your
          steadfast love,
     and teach me your statutes.
[125] I am your servant; give me
          understanding,
     that I may know your testimonies!
[126] It is time for the LORD to act,
     for your law has been broken.
[127] Therefore I love your commandments
     above gold, above fine gold.

[128] Therefore I consider all your precepts to
          be right;
     I hate every false way.

PE

[129] Your testimonies are wonderful;
     therefore my soul keeps them.
[130] The unfolding of your words gives light;
     it imparts understanding to the
          simple.
[131] I open my mouth and pant,
     because I long for your
          commandments.
[132] Turn to me and be gracious to me,
     as is your way with those who love
          your name.
[133] Keep steady my steps according to your
          promise,
     and let no iniquity get dominion over
          me.
[134] Redeem me from man's oppression,
     that I may keep your precepts.
[135] Make your face shine upon your servant,
     and teach me your statutes.
[136] My eyes shed streams of tears,
     because people do not keep your law.

TSADHE

[137] Righteous are you, O LORD,
     and right are your rules.
[138] You have appointed your testimonies in
          righteousness
     and in all faithfulness.
[139] My zeal consumes me,
     because my foes forget your words.
[140] Your promise is well tried,
     and your servant loves it.
[141] I am small and despised,
     yet I do not forget your precepts.
[142] Your righteousness is righteous forever,
     and your law is true.
[143] Trouble and anguish have found me out,
     but your commandments are my
          delight.
[144] Your testimonies are righteous forever;
     give me understanding that I may live.

--------- *Isaiah 59* ---------

Behold, the LORD's hand is not shortened,
     that it cannot save,
          or his ear dull, that it cannot hear;

---

[1] Dead Sea Scroll, Septuagint; Masoretic Text lacks *He repays those who hate him* [2] Or *atones for* [3] Septuagint, Vulgate; Hebrew *his land his people* [4] Septuagint, Syriac, Vulgate; Hebrew *Hoshea*

² but your iniquities have made a
　　separation
　　between you and your God,
　and your sins have hidden his face from
　　you
　　so that he does not hear.
³ For your hands are defiled with blood
　　and your fingers with iniquity;
　your lips have spoken lies;
　　your tongue mutters wickedness.
⁴ No one enters suit justly;
　　no one goes to law honestly;
　they rely on empty pleas, they speak lies,
　　they conceive mischief and give birth
　　　to iniquity.
⁵ They hatch adders' eggs;
　　they weave the spider's web;
　he who eats their eggs dies,
　　and from one that is crushed a viper is
　　　hatched.
⁶ Their webs will not serve as clothing;
　　men will not cover themselves with
　　　what they make.
　Their works are works of iniquity,
　　and deeds of violence are in their
　　　hands.
⁷ Their feet run to evil,
　　and they are swift to shed innocent
　　　blood;
　their thoughts are thoughts of iniquity;
　　desolation and destruction are in their
　　　highways.
⁸ The way of peace they do not know,
　　and there is no justice in their paths;
　they have made their roads crooked;
　　no one who treads on them knows
　　　peace.
⁹ Therefore justice is far from us,
　　and righteousness does not overtake
　　　us;
　we hope for light, and behold, darkness,
　　and for brightness, but we walk in
　　　gloom.
¹⁰ We grope for the wall like the blind;
　　we grope like those who have no eyes;
　we stumble at noon as in the twilight,
　　among those in full vigor we are like
　　　dead men.
¹¹ We all growl like bears;
　　we moan and moan like doves;

we hope for justice, but there is none;
　for salvation, but it is far from us.
¹² For our transgressions are multiplied
　　before you,
　　and our sins testify against us;
　for our transgressions are with us,
　　and we know our iniquities:
¹³ transgressing, and denying the LORD,
　　and turning back from following our
　　　God,
　speaking oppression and revolt,
　　conceiving and uttering from the
　　　heart lying words.
¹⁴ Justice is turned back,
　　and righteousness stands far away;
　for truth has stumbled in the public
　　　squares,
　　and uprightness cannot enter.
¹⁵ Truth is lacking,
　　and he who departs from evil makes
　　　himself a prey.

The LORD saw it, and it displeased him[1]
　　that there was no justice.
¹⁶ He saw that there was no man,
　　and wondered that there was no one
　　　to intercede;
　then his own arm brought him
　　　salvation,
　　and his righteousness upheld him.
¹⁷ He put on righteousness as a
　　　breastplate,
　　and a helmet of salvation on his head;
　he put on garments of vengeance for
　　　clothing,
　　and wrapped himself in zeal as a cloak.
¹⁸ According to their deeds, so will he repay,
　　wrath to his adversaries, repayment to
　　　his enemies;
　to the coastlands he will render
　　　repayment.
¹⁹ So they shall fear the name of the LORD
　　from the west,
　　and his glory from the rising of the
　　　sun;
　for he will come like a rushing stream,[2]
　　which the wind of the LORD drives.

²⁰ "And a Redeemer will come to Zion,
　　to those in Jacob who turn from
　　　transgression," declares the LORD.
²¹ "And as for me, this is my covenant with

---

[1] Hebrew *and it was evil in his eyes*　[2] Hebrew *a narrow river*

them," says the LORD: "My Spirit that is upon you, and my words that I have put in your mouth, shall not depart out of your mouth, or out of the mouth of your offspring, or out of the mouth of your children's offspring," says the LORD, "from this time forth and forevermore."

Matthew 7

"Judge not, that you be not judged. [2] For with the judgment you pronounce you will be judged, and with the measure you use it will be measured to you. [3] Why do you see the speck that is in your brother's eye, but do not notice the log that is in your own eye? [4] Or how can you say to your brother, 'Let me take the speck out of your eye,' when there is the log in your own eye? [5] You hypocrite, first take the log out of your own eye, and then you will see clearly to take the speck out of your brother's eye.

[6] "Do not give dogs what is holy, and do not throw your pearls before pigs, lest they trample them underfoot and turn to attack you.

[7] "Ask, and it will be given to you; seek, and you will find; knock, and it will be opened to you. [8] For everyone who asks receives, and the one who seeks finds, and to the one who knocks it will be opened. [9] Or which one of you, if his son asks him for bread, will give him a stone? [10] Or if he asks for a fish, will give him a serpent? [11] If you then, who are evil, know how to give good gifts to your children, how much more will your Father who is in heaven give good things to those who ask him!

[12] "So whatever you wish that others would do to you, do also to them, for this is the Law and the Prophets.

[13] "Enter by the narrow gate. For the gate is wide and the way is easy[1] that leads to destruction, and those who enter by it are many. [14] For the gate is narrow and the way is hard that leads to life, and those who find it are few.

[15] "Beware of false prophets, who come to you in sheep's clothing but inwardly are ravenous wolves. [16] You will recognize them by their fruits. Are grapes gathered from thornbushes, or figs from thistles? [17] So, every healthy tree bears good fruit, but the diseased tree bears bad fruit. [18] A healthy tree cannot bear bad fruit, nor can a diseased tree bear good fruit. [19] Every tree that does not bear good fruit is cut down and thrown into the fire. [20] Thus you will recognize them by their fruits.

[21] "Not everyone who says to me, 'Lord, Lord,' will enter the kingdom of heaven, but the one who does the will of my Father who is in heaven. [22] On that day many will say to me, 'Lord, Lord, did we not prophesy in your name, and cast out demons in your name, and do many mighty works in your name?' [23] And then will I declare to them, 'I never knew you; depart from me, you workers of lawlessness.'

[24] "Everyone then who hears these words of mine and does them will be like a wise man who built his house on the rock. [25] And the rain fell, and the floods came, and the winds blew and beat on that house, but it did not fall, because it had been founded on the rock. [26] And everyone who hears these words of mine and does not do them will be like a foolish man who built his house on the sand. [27] And the rain fell, and the floods came, and the winds blew and beat against that house, and it fell, and great was the fall of it."

[28] And when Jesus finished these sayings, the crowds were astonished at his teaching, [29] for he was teaching them as one who had authority, and not as their scribes.

[1] Some manuscripts *For the way is wide and easy*

JUNE 28

Deuteronomy 33–34

This is the blessing with which Moses the man of God blessed the people of Israel before his death. ²He said,

"The LORD came from Sinai
    and dawned from Seir upon us;[1]
    he shone forth from Mount Paran;
    he came from the ten thousands of holy
        ones,
    with flaming fire[2] at his right hand.
³ Yes, he loved his people,[3]
    all his holy ones were in his[4] hand;
    so they followed[5] in your steps,
    receiving direction from you,
⁴ when Moses commanded us a law,
    as a possession for the assembly of
        Jacob.
⁵ Thus the LORD[6] became king in
        Jeshurun,
    when the heads of the people were
        gathered,
    all the tribes of Israel together.

⁶ "Let Reuben live, and not die,
    but let his men be few."

⁷And this he said of Judah:

"Hear, O LORD, the voice of Judah,
    and bring him in to his people.
With your hands contend[7] for him,
    and be a help against his
        adversaries."

⁸And of Levi he said,

"Give to Levi[8] your Thummim,
    and your Urim to your godly one,
    whom you tested at Massah,
    with whom you quarreled at the
        waters of Meribah;
⁹ who said of his father and mother,
    'I regard them not';
he disowned his brothers
    and ignored his children.
For they observed your word
    and kept your covenant.

¹⁰ They shall teach Jacob your rules
    and Israel your law;
they shall put incense before you
    and whole burnt offerings on your
        altar.
¹¹ Bless, O LORD, his substance,
    and accept the work of his hands;
crush the loins of his adversaries,
    of those who hate him, that they rise
        not again."

¹²Of Benjamin he said,

"The beloved of the LORD dwells in safety.
The High God[9] surrounds him all day
        long,
    and dwells between his shoulders."

¹³And of Joseph he said,

"Blessed by the LORD be his land,
    with the choicest gifts of heaven
        above,[10]
    and of the deep that crouches
        beneath,
¹⁴ with the choicest fruits of the sun
    and the rich yield of the months,
¹⁵ with the finest produce of the ancient
        mountains
    and the abundance of the everlasting
        hills,
¹⁶ with the best gifts of the earth and its
        fullness
    and the favor of him who dwells in the
        bush.
May these rest on the head of Joseph,
    on the pate of him who is prince
        among his brothers.
¹⁷ A firstborn bull[11]—he has majesty,
    and his horns are the horns of a wild
        ox;
with them he shall gore the peoples,
    all of them, to the ends of the earth;
they are the ten thousands of Ephraim,
    and they are the thousands of
        Manasseh."

---

[1] Septuagint, Syriac, Vulgate; Hebrew *them* [2] The meaning of the Hebrew word is uncertain [3] Septuagint; Hebrew *peoples* [4] Hebrew *your* [5] The meaning of the Hebrew word is uncertain [6] Hebrew *Thus he* [7] Probable reading; Hebrew *With his hands he contended* [8] Dead Sea Scroll, Septuagint; Masoretic Text lacks *Give to Levi* [9] Septuagint; Hebrew *dwells in safety by him. He* [10] Two Hebrew manuscripts and Targum; Hebrew *with the dew* [11] Dead Sea Scroll, Septuagint, Samaritan; Masoretic Text *His firstborn bull*

¹⁸And of Zebulun he said,

> "Rejoice, Zebulun, in your going out,
>> and Issachar, in your tents.
> ¹⁹ They shall call peoples to their
>> mountain;
>> there they offer right sacrifices;
> for they draw from the abundance of the
>> seas
> and the hidden treasures of the sand."

²⁰And of Gad he said,

> "Blessed be he who enlarges Gad!
>> Gad crouches like a lion;
> he tears off arm and scalp.
> ²¹ He chose the best of the land for himself,
>> for there a commander's portion was
>> reserved;
> and he came with the heads of the
>> people,
> with Israel he executed the justice of
>> the LORD,
> and his judgments for Israel."

²²And of Dan he said,

> "Dan is a lion's cub
>> that leaps from Bashan."

²³And of Naphtali he said,

> "O Naphtali, sated with favor,
>> and full of the blessing of the LORD,
>> possess the lake¹ and the south."

²⁴And of Asher he said,

> "Most blessed of sons be Asher;
>> let him be the favorite of his brothers,
>> and let him dip his foot in oil.
> ²⁵ Your bars shall be iron and bronze,
>> and as your days, so shall your
>> strength be.
> ²⁶ "There is none like God, O Jeshurun,
>> who rides through the heavens to
>> your help,
>> through the skies in his majesty.
> ²⁷ The eternal God is your dwelling place,²
>> and underneath are the everlasting
>> arms.³
> And he thrust out the enemy before you
>> and said, 'Destroy.'
> ²⁸ So Israel lived in safety,
>> Jacob lived alone,⁴

> in a land of grain and wine,
>> whose heavens drop down dew.
> ²⁹ Happy are you, O Israel! Who is like you,
>> a people saved by the LORD,
> the shield of your help,
>> and the sword of your triumph!
> Your enemies shall come fawning to you,
>> and you shall tread upon their backs."

^{34:1}Then Moses went up from the plains of Moab to Mount Nebo, to the top of Pisgah, which is opposite Jericho. And the LORD showed him all the land, Gilead as far as Dan, ²all Naphtali, the land of Ephraim and Manasseh, all the land of Judah as far as the western sea, ³the Negeb, and the Plain, that is, the Valley of Jericho the city of palm trees, as far as Zoar. ⁴And the LORD said to him, "This is the land of which I swore to Abraham, to Isaac, and to Jacob, 'I will give it to your offspring.' I have let you see it with your eyes, but you shall not go over there." ⁵So Moses the servant of the LORD died there in the land of Moab, according to the word of the LORD, ⁶and he buried him in the valley in the land of Moab opposite Beth-peor; but no one knows the place of his burial to this day. ⁷Moses was 120 years old when he died. His eye was undimmed, and his vigor unabated. ⁸And the people of Israel wept for Moses in the plains of Moab thirty days. Then the days of weeping and mourning for Moses were ended.

⁹And Joshua the son of Nun was full of the spirit of wisdom, for Moses had laid his hands on him. So the people of Israel obeyed him and did as the LORD had commanded Moses. ¹⁰And there has not arisen a prophet since in Israel like Moses, whom the LORD knew face to face, ¹¹none like him for all the signs and the wonders that the LORD sent him to do in the land of Egypt, to Pharaoh and to all his servants and to all his land, ¹²and for all the mighty power and all the great deeds of terror that Moses did in the sight of all Israel.

Psalm 119:145–176

QOPH

With my whole heart I cry; answer me,
> O LORD!
> I will keep your statutes.
> ¹⁴⁶ I call to you; save me,
>> that I may observe your testimonies.

¹ Or west ² Or a dwelling place ³ Revocalization of verse 27 yields He subdues the ancient gods, and shatters the forces of old ⁴ Hebrew the abode of Jacob was alone

147   I rise before dawn and cry for help;
     I hope in your words.
148   My eyes are awake before the watches of
     the night,
     that I may meditate on your promise.
149   Hear my voice according to your
     steadfast love;
     O Lord, according to your justice give
     me life.
150   They draw near who persecute me with
     evil purpose;
     they are far from your law.
151   But you are near, O Lord,
     and all your commandments are true.
152   Long have I known from your
     testimonies
     that you have founded them forever.

Resh

153   Look on my affliction and deliver me,
     for I do not forget your law.
154   Plead my cause and redeem me;
     give me life according to your
     promise!
155   Salvation is far from the wicked,
     for they do not seek your statutes.
156   Great is your mercy, O Lord;
     give me life according to your rules.
157   Many are my persecutors and my
     adversaries,
     but I do not swerve from your
     testimonies.
158   I look at the faithless with disgust,
     because they do not keep your
     commands.
159   Consider how I love your precepts!
     Give me life according to your
     steadfast love.
160   The sum of your word is truth,
     and every one of your righteous rules
     endures forever.

Sin and Shin

161   Princes persecute me without cause,
     but my heart stands in awe of your
     words.
162   I rejoice at your word
     like one who finds great spoil.
163   I hate and abhor falsehood,
     but I love your law.
164   Seven times a day I praise you
     for your righteous rules.

165   Great peace have those who love your
     law;
     nothing can make them stumble.
166   I hope for your salvation, O Lord,
     and I do your commandments.
167   My soul keeps your testimonies;
     I love them exceedingly.
168   I keep your precepts and testimonies,
     for all my ways are before you.

Taw

169   Let my cry come before you, O Lord;
     give me understanding according to
     your word!
170   Let my plea come before you;
     deliver me according to your word.
171   My lips will pour forth praise,
     for you teach me your statutes.
172   My tongue will sing of your word,
     for all your commandments are right.
173   Let your hand be ready to help me,
     for I have chosen your precepts.
174   I long for your salvation, O Lord,
     and your law is my delight.
175   Let my soul live and praise you,
     and let your rules help me.
176   I have gone astray like a lost sheep; seek
     your servant,
     for I do not forget your
     commandments.

Isaiah 60

Arise, shine, for your light has come,
     and the glory of the Lord has risen
     upon you.
2   For behold, darkness shall cover the
     earth,
     and thick darkness the peoples;
     but the Lord will arise upon you,
     and his glory will be seen upon you.
3   And nations shall come to your light,
     and kings to the brightness of your
     rising.

4   Lift up your eyes all around, and see;
     they all gather together, they come to
     you;
     your sons shall come from afar,
     and your daughters shall be carried on
     the hip.
5   Then you shall see and be radiant;
     your heart shall thrill and exult,[1]

---

[1] Hebrew *your heart shall tremble and grow wide*

because the abundance of the sea shall
    be turned to you,
  the wealth of the nations shall come
    to you.
6 A multitude of camels shall cover you,
  the young camels of Midian and
    Ephah;
  all those from Sheba shall come.
They shall bring gold and frankincense,
  and shall bring good news, the praises
    of the LORD.
7 All the flocks of Kedar shall be gathered
    to you;
  the rams of Nebaioth shall minister to
    you;
they shall come up with acceptance on
    my altar,
  and I will beautify my beautiful
    house.

8 Who are these that fly like a cloud,
  and like doves to their windows?
9 For the coastlands shall hope for me,
  the ships of Tarshish first,
to bring your children from afar,
  their silver and gold with them,
for the name of the LORD your God,
  and for the Holy One of Israel,
  because he has made you beautiful.

10 Foreigners shall build up your walls,
  and their kings shall minister to you;
for in my wrath I struck you,
  but in my favor I have had mercy on
    you.
11 Your gates shall be open continually;
  day and night they shall not be shut,
that people may bring to you the wealth
    of the nations,
  with their kings led in procession.
12 For the nation and kingdom
  that will not serve you shall perish;
  those nations shall be utterly laid
    waste.
13 The glory of Lebanon shall come to
    you,
  the cypress, the plane, and the pine,
to beautify the place of my sanctuary,
  and I will make the place of my feet
    glorious.
14 The sons of those who afflicted you
  shall come bending low to you,

and all who despised you
  shall bow down at your feet;
they shall call you the City of the LORD,
  the Zion of the Holy One of Israel.

15 Whereas you have been forsaken and
    hated,
  with no one passing through,
I will make you majestic forever,
  a joy from age to age.
16 You shall suck the milk of nations;
  you shall nurse at the breast of kings;
and you shall know that I, the LORD, am
    your Savior
  and your Redeemer, the Mighty One
    of Jacob.

17 Instead of bronze I will bring gold,
  and instead of iron I will bring silver;
instead of wood, bronze,
  instead of stones, iron.
I will make your overseers peace
  and your taskmasters righteousness.
18 Violence shall no more be heard in your
    land,
  devastation or destruction within your
    borders;
you shall call your walls Salvation,
  and your gates Praise.

19 The sun shall be no more
  your light by day,
nor for brightness shall the moon
  give you light;[1]
but the LORD will be your everlasting
    light,
  and your God will be your glory.[2]
20 Your sun shall no more go down,
  nor your moon withdraw itself;
for the LORD will be your everlasting
    light,
  and your days of mourning shall be
    ended.
21 Your people shall all be righteous;
  they shall possess the land forever,
the branch of my planting, the work of
    my hands,
  that I might be glorified.[3]
22 The least one shall become a clan,
  and the smallest one a mighty
    nation;
I am the LORD;
  in its time I will hasten it.

[1] Masoretic Text; Dead Sea Scroll, Septuagint, Targum add *by night* [2] Or *your beauty* [3] Or *that I might display my beauty*

—————— *Matthew 8* ——————

When he came down from the mountain, great crowds followed him. [2]And behold, a leper[1] came to him and knelt before him, saying, "Lord, if you will, you can make me clean." [3]And Jesus[2] stretched out his hand and touched him, saying, "I will; be clean." And immediately his leprosy was cleansed. [4]And Jesus said to him, "See that you say nothing to anyone, but go, show yourself to the priest and offer the gift that Moses commanded, for a proof to them."

[5]When he had entered Capernaum, a centurion came forward to him, appealing to him, [6]"Lord, my servant is lying paralyzed at home, suffering terribly." [7]And he said to him, "I will come and heal him." [8]But the centurion replied, "Lord, I am not worthy to have you come under my roof, but only say the word, and my servant will be healed. [9]For I too am a man under authority, with soldiers under me. And I say to one, 'Go,' and he goes, and to another, 'Còme,' and he comes, and to my servant,[3] 'Do this,' and he does it." [10]When Jesus heard this, he marveled and said to those who followed him, "Truly, I tell you, with no one in Israel[4] have I found such faith. [11]I tell you, many will come from east and west and recline at table with Abraham, Isaac, and Jacob in the kingdom of heaven, [12]while the sons of the kingdom will be thrown into the outer darkness. In that place there will be weeping and gnashing of teeth." [13]And to the centurion Jesus said, "Go; let it be done for you as you have believed." And the servant was healed at that very moment.

[14]And when Jesus entered Peter's house, he saw his mother-in-law lying sick with a fever. [15]He touched her hand, and the fever left her, and she rose and began to serve him. [16]That evening they brought to him many who were oppressed by demons, and he cast out the spirits with a word and healed all who were sick. [17]This was to fulfill what was spoken by the prophet Isaiah: "He took our illnesses and bore our diseases."

[18]Now when Jesus saw a crowd around him, he gave orders to go over to the other side. [19]And a scribe came up and said to him, "Teacher, I will follow you wherever you go." [20]And Jesus said to him, "Foxes have holes, and birds of the air have nests, but the Son of Man has nowhere to lay his head." [21]Another of the disciples said to him, "Lord, let me first go and bury my father." [22]And Jesus said to him, "Follow me, and leave the dead to bury their own dead."

[23]And when he got into the boat, his disciples followed him. [24]And behold, there arose a great storm on the sea, so that the boat was being swamped by the waves; but he was asleep. [25]And they went and woke him, saying, "Save us, Lord; we are perishing." [26]And he said to them, "Why are you afraid, O you of little faith?" Then he rose and rebuked the winds and the sea, and there was a great calm. [27]And the men marveled, saying, "What sort of man is this, that even winds and sea obey him?"

[28]And when he came to the other side, to the country of the Gadarenes,[5] two demon-possessed[6] men met him, coming out of the tombs, so fierce that no one could pass that way. [29]And behold, they cried out, "What have you to do with us, O Son of God? Have you come here to torment us before the time?" [30]Now a herd of many pigs was feeding at some distance from them. [31]And the demons begged him, saying, "If you cast us out, send us away into the herd of pigs." [32]And he said to them, "Go." So they came out and went into the pigs, and behold, the whole herd rushed down the steep bank into the sea and drowned in the waters. [33]The herdsmen fled, and going into the city they told everything, especially what had happened to the demon-possessed men. [34]And behold, all the city came out to meet Jesus, and when they saw him, they begged him to leave their region.

---

[1] *Leprosy* was a term for several skin diseases; see Leviticus 13 [2] Greek *he* [3] Greek *bondservant* [4] Some manuscripts *not even in Israel* [5] Some manuscripts *Gergesenes*; some *Gerasenes* [6] Greek *daimonizomai*; also verse 33; elsewhere rendered *oppressed by demons*

JUNE 29

Joshua 1

After the death of Moses the servant of the LORD, the LORD said to Joshua the son of Nun, Moses' assistant, [2]"Moses my servant is dead. Now therefore arise, go over this Jordan, you and all this people, into the land that I am giving to them, to the people of Israel. [3]Every place that the sole of your foot will tread upon I have given to you, just as I promised to Moses. [4]From the wilderness and this Lebanon as far as the great river, the river Euphrates, all the land of the Hittites to the Great Sea toward the going down of the sun shall be your territory. [5]No man shall be able to stand before you all the days of your life. Just as I was with Moses, so I will be with you. I will not leave you or forsake you. [6]Be strong and courageous, for you shall cause this people to inherit the land that I swore to their fathers to give them. [7]Only be strong and very courageous, being careful to do according to all the law that Moses my servant commanded you. Do not turn from it to the right hand or to the left, that you may have good success[1] wherever you go. [8]This Book of the Law shall not depart from your mouth, but you shall meditate on it day and night, so that you may be careful to do according to all that is written in it. For then you will make your way prosperous, and then you will have good success. [9]Have I not commanded you? Be strong and courageous. Do not be frightened, and do not be dismayed, for the LORD your God is with you wherever you go."

[10]And Joshua commanded the officers of the people, [11]"Pass through the midst of the camp and command the people, 'Prepare your provisions, for within three days you are to pass over this Jordan to go in to take possession of the land that the LORD your God is giving you to possess.'"

[12]And to the Reubenites, the Gadites, and the half-tribe of Manasseh Joshua said, [13]"Remember the word that Moses the servant of the LORD commanded you, saying,

'The LORD your God is providing you a place of rest and will give you this land.' [14]Your wives, your little ones, and your livestock shall remain in the land that Moses gave you beyond the Jordan, but all the men of valor among you shall pass over armed before your brothers and shall help them, [15]until the LORD gives rest to your brothers as he has to you, and they also take possession of the land that the LORD your God is giving them. Then you shall return to the land of your possession and shall possess it, the land that Moses the servant of the LORD gave you beyond the Jordan toward the sunrise."

[16]And they answered Joshua, "All that you have commanded us we will do, and wherever you send us we will go. [17]Just as we obeyed Moses in all things, so we will obey you. Only may the LORD your God be with you, as he was with Moses! [18]Whoever rebels against your commandment and disobeys your words, whatever you command him, shall be put to death. Only be strong and courageous."

Psalm 120–122

A SONG OF ASCENTS.

In my distress I called to the LORD,
   and he answered me.
[2] Deliver me, O LORD,
     from lying lips,
     from a deceitful tongue.

[3] What shall be given to you,
     and what more shall be done to you,
     you deceitful tongue?
[4] A warrior's sharp arrows,
     with glowing coals of the broom tree!

[5] Woe to me, that I sojourn in Meshech,
     that I dwell among the tents of Kedar!
[6] Too long have I had my dwelling
     among those who hate peace.
[7] I am for peace,
     but when I speak, they are for war!

[1] Or may act wisely

A Song of Ascents.

I lift up my eyes to the hills.
  From where does my help come?
2 My help comes from the Lord,
   who made heaven and earth.

3 He will not let your foot be moved;
   he who keeps you will not slumber.
4 Behold, he who keeps Israel
   will neither slumber nor sleep.

5 The Lord is your keeper;
     the Lord is your shade on your right
       hand.
6 The sun shall not strike you by day,
     nor the moon by night.

7 The Lord will keep you from all evil;
   he will keep your life.
8 The Lord will keep
     your going out and your coming in
     from this time forth and forevermore.

A Song of Ascents. Of David.

I was glad when they said to me,
  "Let us go to the house of the Lord!"
2 Our feet have been standing
     within your gates, O Jerusalem!

3 Jerusalem—built as a city
     that is bound firmly together,
4 to which the tribes go up,
     the tribes of the Lord,
   as was decreed for[1] Israel,
     to give thanks to the name of the Lord.
5 There thrones for judgment were set,
     the thrones of the house of David.

6 Pray for the peace of Jerusalem!
     "May they be secure who love you!
7 Peace be within your walls
     and security within your towers!"
8 For my brothers and companions' sake
     I will say, "Peace be within you!"
9 For the sake of the house of the Lord
     our God,
   I will seek your good.

Isaiah 61

The Spirit of the Lord God is upon me,
  because the Lord has anointed me
to bring good news to the poor;[2]

he has sent me to bind up the
     brokenhearted,
to proclaim liberty to the captives,
     and the opening of the prison to those
       who are bound;[3]
2 to proclaim the year of the Lord's favor,
     and the day of vengeance of our God;
   to comfort all who mourn;
3 to grant to those who mourn in Zion—
     to give them a beautiful headdress
       instead of ashes,
   the oil of gladness instead of mourning,
     the garment of praise instead of a faint
       spirit;
   that they may be called oaks of
     righteousness,
     the planting of the Lord, that he may
       be glorified.[4]
4 They shall build up the ancient ruins;
     they shall raise up the former
       devastations;
   they shall repair the ruined cities,
     the devastations of many generations.

5 Strangers shall stand and tend your
     flocks;
   foreigners shall be your plowmen and
     vinedressers;
6 but you shall be called the priests of the
     Lord;
     they shall speak of you as the
       ministers of our God;
   you shall eat the wealth of the nations,
     and in their glory you shall boast.
7 Instead of your shame there shall be a
     double portion;
     instead of dishonor they shall rejoice
       in their lot;
   therefore in their land they shall possess
     a double portion;
     they shall have everlasting joy.

8 For I the Lord love justice;
     I hate robbery and wrong;[5]
   I will faithfully give them their
     recompense,
   and I will make an everlasting
     covenant with them.
9 Their offspring shall be known among
     the nations,
   and their descendants in the midst of
     the peoples;

[1] Or as a testimony for [2] Or afflicted [3] Or the opening [of the eyes] to those who are blind; Septuagint and recovery of sight to the blind [4] Or that he may display his beauty [5] Or robbery with a burnt offering

all who see them shall acknowledge
    them,
  that they are an offspring the LORD
    has blessed.
10   I will greatly rejoice in the LORD;
    my soul shall exult in my God,
  for he has clothed me with the garments
    of salvation;
  he has covered me with the robe of
    righteousness,
  as a bridegroom decks himself like a
    priest with a beautiful headdress,
  and as a bride adorns herself with her
    jewels.
11   For as the earth brings forth its sprouts,
    and as a garden causes what is sown
      in it to sprout up,
  so the Lord GOD will cause
    righteousness and praise
    to sprout up before all the nations.

Matthew 9

And getting into a boat he crossed over and came to his own city. [2]And behold, some people brought to him a paralytic, lying on a bed. And when Jesus saw their faith, he said to the paralytic, "Take heart, my son; your sins are forgiven." [3]And behold, some of the scribes said to themselves, "This man is blaspheming." [4]But Jesus, knowing[1] their thoughts, said, "Why do you think evil in your hearts? [5]For which is easier, to say, 'Your sins are forgiven,' or to say, 'Rise and walk'? [6]But that you may know that the Son of Man has authority on earth to forgive sins"—he then said to the paralytic—"Rise, pick up your bed and go home." [7]And he rose and went home. [8]When the crowds saw it, they were afraid, and they glorified God, who had given such authority to men.

[9]As Jesus passed on from there, he saw a man called Matthew sitting at the tax booth, and he said to him, "Follow me." And he rose and followed him.

[10]And as Jesus[2] reclined at table in the house, behold, many tax collectors and sinners came and were reclining with Jesus and his disciples. [11]And when the Pharisees saw this, they said to his disciples, "Why does your teacher eat with tax collectors and sinners?" [12]But when he heard it, he said, "Those who are well have no need of a physician, but those who are sick. [13]Go and learn what this means, 'I desire mercy, and not sacrifice.' For I came not to call the righteous, but sinners."

[14]Then the disciples of John came to him, saying, "Why do we and the Pharisees fast,[3] but your disciples do not fast?" [15]And Jesus said to them, "Can the wedding guests mourn as long as the bridegroom is with them? The days will come when the bridegroom is taken away from them, and then they will fast. [16]No one puts a piece of unshrunk cloth on an old garment, for the patch tears away from the garment, and a worse tear is made. [17]Neither is new wine put into old wineskins. If it is, the skins burst and the wine is spilled and the skins are destroyed. But new wine is put into fresh wineskins, and so both are preserved."

[18]While he was saying these things to them, behold, a ruler came in and knelt before him, saying, "My daughter has just died, but come and lay your hand on her, and she will live." [19]And Jesus rose and followed him, with his disciples. [20]And behold, a woman who had suffered from a discharge of blood for twelve years came up behind him and touched the fringe of his garment, [21]for she said to herself, "If I only touch his garment, I will be made well." [22]Jesus turned, and seeing her he said, "Take heart, daughter; your faith has made you well." And instantly[4] the woman was made well. [23]And when Jesus came to the ruler's house and saw the flute players and the crowd making a commotion, [24]he said, "Go away, for the girl is not dead but sleeping." And they laughed at him. [25]But when the crowd had been put outside, he went in and took her by the hand, and the girl arose. [26]And the report of this went through all that district.

[27]And as Jesus passed on from there, two blind men followed him, crying aloud, "Have mercy on us, Son of David." [28]When he entered the house, the blind men came to him, and Jesus said to them, "Do you believe that I am able to do this?" They said to him, "Yes, Lord." [29]Then he touched their eyes, saying, "According to your faith be it done to you." [30]And their eyes were opened. And Jesus sternly warned them, "See that no one knows about it." [31]But they went away and spread his fame through all that district.

[32]As they were going away, behold, a

[1] Some manuscripts *perceiving*   [2] Greek *he*   [3] Some manuscripts add *much*, or *often*   [4] Greek *from that hour*

demon-oppressed man who was mute was brought to him. ³³And when the demon had been cast out, the mute man spoke. And the crowds marveled, saying, "Never was anything like this seen in Israel." ³⁴But the Pharisees said, "He casts out demons by the prince of demons."

³⁵And Jesus went throughout all the cities and villages, teaching in their synagogues and proclaiming the gospel of the kingdom and healing every disease and every affliction. ³⁶When he saw the crowds, he had compassion for them, because they were harassed and helpless, like sheep without a shepherd. ³⁷Then he said to his disciples, "The harvest is plentiful, but the laborers are few; ³⁸therefore pray earnestly to the Lord of the harvest to send out laborers into his harvest."

JUNE 30

Joshua 2

And Joshua the son of Nun sent¹ two men secretly from Shittim as spies, saying, "Go, view the land, especially Jericho." And they went and came into the house of a prostitute whose name was Rahab and lodged there. ²And it was told to the king of Jericho, "Behold, men of Israel have come here tonight to search out the land." ³Then the king of Jericho sent to Rahab, saying, "Bring out the men who have come to you, who entered your house, for they have come to search out all the land." ⁴But the woman had taken the two men and hidden them. And she said, "True, the men came to me, but I did not know where they were from. ⁵And when the gate was about to be closed at dark, the men went out. I do not know where the men went. Pursue them quickly, for you will overtake them." ⁶But she had brought them up to the roof and hid them with the stalks of flax that she had laid in order on the roof. ⁷So the men pursued after them on the way to the Jordan as far as the fords. And the gate was shut as soon as the pursuers had gone out.

⁸Before the men² lay down, she came up to them on the roof ⁹and said to the men, "I know that the Lord has given you the land, and that the fear of you has fallen upon us, and that all the inhabitants of the land melt away before you. ¹⁰For we have heard how the Lord dried up the water of the Red Sea before you when you came out of Egypt, and what you did to the two kings of the Amorites who were beyond the Jordan, to Sihon and Og, whom you devoted to destruction.³ ¹¹And as soon as we heard it, our hearts melted, and there was no spirit left in any man because of you, for the Lord your God, he is God in the heavens above and on the earth beneath. ¹²Now then, please swear to me by the Lord that, as I have dealt kindly with you, you also will deal kindly with my father's house, and give me a sure sign ¹³that you will save alive my father and mother, my brothers and sisters, and all who belong to them, and deliver our lives from death." ¹⁴And the men said to her, "Our life for yours even to death! If you do not tell this business of ours, then when the Lord gives us the land we will deal kindly and faithfully with you."

¹⁵Then she let them down by a rope through the window, for her house was built into the city wall, so that she lived in the wall. ¹⁶And she said⁴ to them, "Go into the hills, or the pursuers will encounter you, and hide there three days until the pursuers have returned. Then afterward you may go your way." ¹⁷The men said to her, "We will be guiltless with respect to this oath of yours that you have made us swear. ¹⁸Behold, when we come into the land, you shall tie this scarlet cord in the window through which you let us down, and you shall gather into your house your father and mother, your brothers, and all your father's household. ¹⁹Then if anyone goes out of the doors of your house into the street, his blood shall be on his

¹ Or had sent ² Hebrew they ³ That is, set apart (devoted) as an offering to the Lord (for destruction) ⁴ Or had said

own head, and we shall be guiltless. But if a hand is laid on anyone who is with you in the house, his blood shall be on our head. ²⁰But if you tell this business of ours, then we shall be guiltless with respect to your oath that you have made us swear." ²¹And she said, "According to your words, so be it." Then she sent them away, and they departed. And she tied the scarlet cord in the window.

²²They departed and went into the hills and remained there three days until the pursuers returned, and the pursuers searched all along the way and found nothing. ²³Then the two men returned. They came down from the hills and passed over and came to Joshua the son of Nun, and they told him all that had happened to them. ²⁴And they said to Joshua, "Truly the LORD has given all the land into our hands. And also, all the inhabitants of the land melt away because of us."

――――― *Psalm 123–125* ―――――

A SONG OF ASCENTS.

To you I lift up my eyes,
  O you who are enthroned in the heavens!
² Behold, as the eyes of servants
    look to the hand of their master,
  as the eyes of a maidservant
    to the hand of her mistress,
  so our eyes look to the LORD our God,
    till he has mercy upon us.

³ Have mercy upon us, O LORD, have
    mercy upon us,
  for we have had more than enough of
    contempt.
⁴ Our soul has had more than enough
    of the scorn of those who are at ease,
    of the contempt of the proud.

A SONG OF ASCENTS. OF DAVID.

If it had not been the LORD who was on our
  side—
    let Israel now say—
² if it had not been the LORD who was on
    our side
  when people rose up against us,
³ then they would have swallowed us up
    alive,
  when their anger was kindled against
    us;

⁴ then the flood would have swept us
    away,
  the torrent would have gone over us;
⁵ then over us would have gone
    the raging waters.

⁶ Blessed be the LORD,
  who has not given us
    as prey to their teeth!
⁷ We have escaped like a bird
    from the snare of the fowlers;
  the snare is broken,
    and we have escaped!

⁸ Our help is in the name of the LORD,
  who made heaven and earth.

A SONG OF ASCENTS.

Those who trust in the LORD are like
  Mount Zion,
    which cannot be moved, but abides
      forever.
² As the mountains surround Jerusalem,
    so the LORD surrounds his people,
  from this time forth and forevermore.
³ For the scepter of wickedness shall not
    rest
  on the land allotted to the righteous,
    lest the righteous stretch out
      their hands to do wrong.
⁴ Do good, O LORD, to those who are
    good,
  and to those who are upright in their
    hearts!
⁵ But those who turn aside to their
    crooked ways
  the LORD will lead away with
    evildoers!
    Peace be upon Israel!

――――― *Isaiah 62* ―――――

For Zion's sake I will not keep silent,
  and for Jerusalem's sake I will not be quiet,
  until her righteousness goes forth as
    brightness,
  and her salvation as a burning torch.
² The nations shall see your
    righteousness,
  and all the kings your glory,
  and you shall be called by a new name
    that the mouth of the LORD will give.

³ You shall be a crown of beauty in the
hand of the LORD,
and a royal diadem in the hand of
your God.
⁴ You shall no more be termed Forsaken,[1]
and your land shall no more be
termed Desolate,[2]
but you shall be called My Delight Is in
Her,[3]
and your land Married;[4]
for the LORD delights in you,
and your land shall be married.
⁵ For as a young man marries a young
woman,
so shall your sons marry you,
and as the bridegroom rejoices over the
bride,
so shall your God rejoice over you.
⁶ On your walls, O Jerusalem,
I have set watchmen;
all the day and all the night
they shall never be silent.
You who put the LORD in
remembrance,
take no rest,
⁷ and give him no rest
until he establishes Jerusalem
and makes it a praise in the earth.
⁸ The LORD has sworn by his right hand
and by his mighty arm:
"I will not again give your grain
to be food for your enemies,
and foreigners shall not drink your
wine
for which you have labored;
⁹ but those who garner it shall eat it
and praise the LORD,
and those who gather it shall drink it
in the courts of my sanctuary."[5]

¹⁰ Go through, go through the gates;
prepare the way for the people;
build up, build up the highway;
clear it of stones;
lift up a signal over the peoples.
¹¹ Behold, the LORD has proclaimed
to the end of the earth:
Say to the daughter of Zion,
"Behold, your salvation comes;
behold, his reward is with him,
and his recompense before him."

¹² And they shall be called The Holy People,
The Redeemed of the LORD;
and you shall be called Sought Out,
A City Not Forsaken.

Matthew 10

And he called to him his twelve disciples and gave them authority over unclean spirits, to cast them out, and to heal every disease and every affliction. ²The names of the twelve apostles are these: first, Simon, who is called Peter, and Andrew his brother; James the son of Zebedee, and John his brother; ³Philip and Bartholomew; Thomas and Matthew the tax collector; James the son of Alphaeus, and Thaddaeus;[6] ⁴Simon the Zealot,[7] and Judas Iscariot, who betrayed him.

⁵These twelve Jesus sent out, instructing them, "Go nowhere among the Gentiles and enter no town of the Samaritans, ⁶but go rather to the lost sheep of the house of Israel. ⁷And proclaim as you go, saying, 'The kingdom of heaven is at hand.' ⁸Heal the sick, raise the dead, cleanse lepers,[8] cast out demons. You received without paying; give without pay. ⁹Acquire no gold or silver or copper for your belts, ¹⁰no bag for your journey, or two tunics[9] or sandals or a staff, for the laborer deserves his food. ¹¹And whatever town or village you enter, find out who is worthy in it and stay there until you depart. ¹²As you enter the house, greet it. ¹³And if the house is worthy, let your peace come upon it, but if it is not worthy, let your peace return to you. ¹⁴And if anyone will not receive you or listen to your words, shake off the dust from your feet when you leave that house or town. ¹⁵Truly, I say to you, it will be more bearable on the day of judgment for the land of Sodom and Gomorrah than for that town.

¹⁶"Behold, I am sending you out as sheep in the midst of wolves, so be wise as serpents and innocent as doves. ¹⁷Beware of men, for they will deliver you over to courts and flog you in their synagogues, ¹⁸and you will be dragged before governors and kings for my sake, to bear witness before them and the Gentiles. ¹⁹When they deliver you over, do not be anxious how you are to speak or what you are to say, for what you are to say will be given to you in that hour. ²⁰For it is not you who speak, but the Spirit of your Father speaking through you. ²¹Brother

will deliver brother over to death, and the father his child, and children will rise against parents and have them put to death, [22] and you will be hated by all for my name's sake. But the one who endures to the end will be saved. [23] When they persecute you in one town, flee to the next, for truly, I say to you, you will not have gone through all the towns of Israel before the Son of Man comes.

[24] "A disciple is not above his teacher, nor a servant[1] above his master. [25] It is enough for the disciple to be like his teacher, and the servant like his master. If they have called the master of the house Beelzebul, how much more will they malign[2] those of his household.

[26] "So have no fear of them, for nothing is covered that will not be revealed, or hidden that will not be known. [27] What I tell you in the dark, say in the light, and what you hear whispered, proclaim on the housetops. [28] And do not fear those who kill the body but cannot kill the soul. Rather fear him who can destroy both soul and body in hell.[3] [29] Are not two sparrows sold for a penny?[4] And not one of them will fall to the ground apart from your Father. [30] But even the hairs of your head are all numbered. [31] Fear not, therefore; you are of more value than many sparrows. [32] So everyone who acknowledges me before men, I also will acknowledge before my Father who is in heaven, [33] but whoever denies me before men, I also will deny before my Father who is in heaven.

[34] "Do not think that I have come to bring peace to the earth. I have not come to bring peace, but a sword. [35] For I have come to set a man against his father, and a daughter against her mother, and a daughter-in-law against her mother-in-law. [36] And a person's enemies will be those of his own household. [37] Whoever loves father or mother more than me is not worthy of me, and whoever loves son or daughter more than me is not worthy of me. [38] And whoever does not take his cross and follow me is not worthy of me. [39] Whoever finds his life will lose it, and whoever loses his life for my sake will find it.

[40] "Whoever receives you receives me, and whoever receives me receives him who sent me. [41] The one who receives a prophet because he is a prophet will receive a prophet's reward, and the one who receives a righteous person because he is a righteous person will receive a righteous person's reward. [42] And whoever gives one of these little ones even a cup of cold water because he is a disciple, truly, I say to you, he will by no means lose his reward."

[1] Greek bondservant; also verse 25 [2] Greek lacks will they malign [3] Greek Gehenna [4] Greek assarion, Roman copper coin (Latin quadrans) worth about 1/16 of a denarius (which was a day's wage for a laborer)

JULY 1

Joshua 3

Then Joshua rose early in the morning and they set out from Shittim. And they came to the Jordan, he and all the people of Israel, and lodged there before they passed over. ²At the end of three days the officers went through the camp ³and commanded the people, "As soon as you see the ark of the covenant of the LORD your God being carried by the Levitical priests, then you shall set out from your place and follow it. ⁴Yet there shall be a distance between you and it, about 2,000 cubits[1] in length. Do not come near it, in order that you may know the way you shall go, for you have not passed this way before." ⁵Then Joshua said to the people, "Consecrate yourselves, for tomorrow the LORD will do wonders among you." ⁶And Joshua said to the priests, "Take up the ark of the covenant and pass on before the people." So they took up the ark of the covenant and went before the people.

⁷The LORD said to Joshua, "Today I will begin to exalt you in the sight of all Israel, that they may know that, as I was with Moses, so I will be with you. ⁸And as for you, command the priests who bear the ark of the covenant, 'When you come to the brink of the waters of the Jordan, you shall stand still in the Jordan.'" ⁹And Joshua said to the people of Israel, "Come here and listen to the words of the LORD your God." ¹⁰And Joshua said, "Here is how you shall know that the living God is among you and that he will without fail drive out from before you the Canaanites, the Hittites, the Hivites, the Perizzites, the Girgashites, the Amorites, and the Jebusites. ¹¹Behold, the ark of the covenant of the Lord of all the earth[2] is passing over before you into the Jordan. ¹²Now therefore take twelve men from the tribes of Israel, from each tribe a man. ¹³And when the soles of the feet of the priests bearing the ark of the LORD, the Lord of all the earth, shall rest in the waters of the Jordan, the waters of the Jordan shall be cut off from flowing, and the waters coming down from above shall stand in one heap."

¹⁴So when the people set out from their tents to pass over the Jordan with the priests bearing the ark of the covenant before the people, ¹⁵and as soon as those bearing the ark had come as far as the Jordan, and the feet of the priests bearing the ark were dipped in the brink of the water (now the Jordan overflows all its banks throughout the time of harvest), ¹⁶the waters coming down from above stood and rose up in a heap very far away, at Adam, the city that is beside Zarethan, and those flowing down toward the Sea of the Arabah, the Salt Sea, were completely cut off. And the people passed over opposite Jericho. ¹⁷Now the priests bearing the ark of the covenant of the LORD stood firmly on dry ground in the midst of the Jordan, and all Israel was passing over on dry ground until all the nation finished passing over the Jordan.

Psalm 126–128

A Song of Ascents.

When the LORD restored the fortunes of Zion,
    we were like those who dream.
2 Then our mouth was filled with laughter,
    and our tongue with shouts of joy;
then they said among the nations,
    "The LORD has done great things for
      them."
3 The LORD has done great things for us;
    we are glad.

4 Restore our fortunes, O LORD,
    like streams in the Negeb!
5 Those who sow in tears
    shall reap with shouts of joy!
6 He who goes out weeping,
    bearing the seed for sowing,
shall come home with shouts of joy,
    bringing his sheaves with him.

[1] A *cubit* was about 18 inches or 45 centimeters [2] Hebrew *the ark of the covenant, the Lord of all the earth*

A Song of Ascents. Of Solomon.

U nless the LORD builds the house,
those who build it labor in vain.
Unless the LORD watches over the city,
the watchman stays awake in vain.
2 It is in vain that you rise up early
and go late to rest,
eating the bread of anxious toil;
for he gives to his beloved sleep.

3 Behold, children are a heritage from the
LORD,
the fruit of the womb a reward.
4 Like arrows in the hand of a warrior
are the children[1] of one's youth.
5 Blessed is the man
who fills his quiver with them!
He shall not be put to shame
when he speaks with his enemies in
the gate.[2]

A Song of Ascents.

B lessed is everyone who fears the LORD,
who walks in his ways!
2 You shall eat the fruit of the labor of
your hands;
you shall be blessed, and it shall be
well with you.

3 Your wife will be like a fruitful vine
within your house;
your children will be like olive shoots
around your table.
4 Behold, thus shall the man be blessed
who fears the LORD.

5 The LORD bless you from Zion!
May you see the prosperity of
Jerusalem
all the days of your life!
6 May you see your children's children!
Peace be upon Israel!

Isaiah 63

W ho is this who comes from Edom,
in crimsoned garments from Bozrah,
he who is splendid in his apparel,
marching in the greatness of his
strength?
"It is I, speaking in righteousness,
mighty to save."

2 Why is your apparel red,
and your garments like his who treads
in the winepress?

3 "I have trodden the winepress alone,
and from the peoples no one was with
me;
I trod them in my anger
and trampled them in my wrath;
their lifeblood[3] spattered on my
garments,
and stained all my apparel.
4 For the day of vengeance was in my
heart,
and my year of redemption[4] had
come.
5 I looked, but there was no one to help;
I was appalled, but there was no one to
uphold;
so my own arm brought me salvation,
and my wrath upheld me.
6 I trampled down the peoples in my
anger;
I made them drunk in my wrath,
and I poured out their lifeblood on the
earth."

7 I will recount the steadfast love of the
LORD,
the praises of the LORD,
according to all that the LORD has
granted us,
and the great goodness to the house
of Israel
that he has granted them according to
his compassion,
according to the abundance of his
steadfast love.
8 For he said, "Surely they are my people,
children who will not deal falsely."
And he became their Savior.
9 In all their affliction he was afflicted,[5]
and the angel of his presence saved
them;
in his love and in his pity he redeemed
them;
he lifted them up and carried them all
the days of old.

10 But they rebelled
and grieved his Holy Spirit;
therefore he turned to be their enemy,
and himself fought against them.

[1] Or sons [2] Or They shall not be put to shame when they speak with their enemies in the gate [3] Or their juice; also verse 6 [4] Or the year of my redeemed [5] Or he did not afflict

11 Then he remembered the days of old,
    of Moses and his people.[1]
Where is he who brought them up out
    of the sea
    with the shepherds of his flock?
Where is he who put in the midst of
    them
    his Holy Spirit,
12 who caused his glorious arm
    to go at the right hand of Moses,
who divided the waters before them
    to make for himself an everlasting
    name,
13 who led them through the depths?
Like a horse in the desert,
    they did not stumble.
14 Like livestock that go down into the
    valley,
    the Spirit of the LORD gave them
    rest.
So you led your people,
    to make for yourself a glorious name.

15 Look down from heaven and see,
    from your holy and beautiful[2]
    habitation.
Where are your zeal and your might?
    The stirring of your inner parts and
    your compassion
    are held back from me.
16 For you are our Father,
    though Abraham does not know us,
    and Israel does not acknowledge us;
    you, O LORD, are our Father,
    our Redeemer from of old is your
    name.
17 O LORD, why do you make us wander
    from your ways
    and harden our heart, so that we fear
    you not?
Return for the sake of your servants,
    the tribes of your heritage.
18 Your holy people held possession for a
    little while;[3]
    our adversaries have trampled down
    your sanctuary.
19 We have become like those over whom
    you have never ruled,
    like those who are not called by your
    name.

W hen Jesus had finished instructing his twelve disciples, he went on from there to teach and preach in their cities.

2 Now when John heard in prison about the deeds of the Christ, he sent word by his disciples **3** and said to him, "Are you the one who is to come, or shall we look for another?" **4** And Jesus answered them, "Go and tell John what you hear and see: **5** the blind receive their sight and the lame walk, lepers[4] are cleansed and the deaf hear, and the dead are raised up, and the poor have good news preached to them. **6** And blessed is the one who is not offended by me."

7 As they went away, Jesus began to speak to the crowds concerning John: "What did you go out into the wilderness to see? A reed shaken by the wind? **8** What then did you go out to see? A man[5] dressed in soft clothing? Behold, those who wear soft clothing are in kings' houses. **9** What then did you go out to see? A prophet?[6] Yes, I tell you, and more than a prophet. **10** This is he of whom it is written,

"'Behold, I send my messenger before
    your face,
    who will prepare your way before you.'

11 Truly, I say to you, among those born of women there has arisen no one greater than John the Baptist. Yet the one who is least in the kingdom of heaven is greater than he. **12** From the days of John the Baptist until now the kingdom of heaven has suffered violence,[7] and the violent take it by force. **13** For all the Prophets and the Law prophesied until John, **14** and if you are willing to accept it, he is Elijah who is to come. **15** He who has ears to hear,[8] let him hear.

16 "But to what shall I compare this generation? It is like children sitting in the marketplaces and calling to their playmates,

17 "'We played the flute for you, and you did
    not dance;
    we sang a dirge, and you did not
    mourn.'

18 For John came neither eating nor drinking, and they say, 'He has a demon.' **19** The Son of Man came eating and drinking, and they say,

---

[1] Or Then his people remembered the days of old, of Moses [2] Or holy and glorious [3] Or They have dispossessed your holy people for a little while [4] Leprosy was a term for several skin diseases; see Leviticus 13 [5] Or Why then did you go out? To see a man. . . [6] Some manuscripts Why then did you go out? To see a prophet? [7] Or has been coming violently [8] Some manuscripts omit to hear

'Look at him! A glutton and a drunkard, a friend of tax collectors and sinners!' Yet wisdom is justified by her deeds."[1]

[20] Then he began to denounce the cities where most of his mighty works had been done, because they did not repent. [21] "Woe to you, Chorazin! Woe to you, Bethsaida! For if the mighty works done in you had been done in Tyre and Sidon, they would have repented long ago in sackcloth and ashes. [22] But I tell you, it will be more bearable on the day of judgment for Tyre and Sidon than for you. [23] And you, Capernaum, will you be exalted to heaven? You will be brought down to Hades. For if the mighty works done in you had been done in Sodom, it would have remained until this day. [24] But I tell you that it will be more tolerable on the day of judgment for the land of Sodom than for you."

[25] At that time Jesus declared, "I thank you, Father, Lord of heaven and earth, that you have hidden these things from the wise and understanding and revealed them to little children; [26] yes, Father, for such was your gracious will.[2] [27] All things have been handed over to me by my Father, and no one knows the Son except the Father, and no one knows the Father except the Son and anyone to whom the Son chooses to reveal him. [28] Come to me, all who labor and are heavy laden, and I will give you rest. [29] Take my yoke upon you, and learn from me, for I am gentle and lowly in heart, and you will find rest for your souls. [30] For my yoke is easy, and my burden is light."

JULY 2

Joshua 4

When all the nation had finished passing over the Jordan, the LORD said to Joshua, [2] "Take twelve men from the people, from each tribe a man, [3] and command them, saying, 'Take twelve stones from here out of the midst of the Jordan, from the very place where the priests' feet stood firmly, and bring them over with you and lay them down in the place where you lodge tonight.'" [4] Then Joshua called the twelve men from the people of Israel, whom he had appointed, a man from each tribe. [5] And Joshua said to them, "Pass on before the ark of the LORD your God into the midst of the Jordan, and take up each of you a stone upon his shoulder, according to the number of the tribes of the people of Israel, [6] that this may be a sign among you. When your children ask in time to come, 'What do those stones mean to you?' [7] then you shall tell them that the waters of the Jordan were cut off before the ark of the covenant of the LORD. When it passed over the Jordan, the waters of the Jordan were cut off. So these stones shall be to the people of Israel a memorial forever."

[8] And the people of Israel did just as Joshua commanded and took up twelve stones out of the midst of the Jordan, according to the number of the tribes of the people of Israel, just as the LORD told Joshua. And they carried them over with them to the place where they lodged and laid them down[3] there. [9] And Joshua set up[4] twelve stones in the midst of the Jordan, in the place where the feet of the priests bearing the ark of the covenant had stood; and they are there to this day. [10] For the priests bearing the ark stood in the midst of the Jordan until everything was finished that the LORD commanded Joshua to tell the people, according to all that Moses had commanded Joshua.

The people passed over in haste. [11] And when all the people had finished passing over, the ark of the LORD and the priests passed over before the people. [12] The sons of Reuben and the sons of Gad and the half-tribe of Manasseh passed over armed before the people of Israel, as Moses had told them. [13] About 40,000 ready for war passed over before the LORD for battle, to the plains of Jericho. [14] On that day the LORD

---

[1] Some manuscripts *children* (compare Luke 7:35)   [2] Or *for so it pleased you well*   [3] Or *to rest*   [4] Or *Joshua had set up*

exalted Joshua in the sight of all Israel, and they stood in awe of him just as they had stood in awe of Moses, all the days of his life.

15And the LORD said to Joshua, 16"Command the priests bearing the ark of the testimony to come up out of the Jordan." 17So Joshua commanded the priests, "Come up out of the Jordan." 18And when the priests bearing the ark of the covenant of the LORD came up from the midst of the Jordan, and the soles of the priests' feet were lifted up on dry ground, the waters of the Jordan returned to their place and over-flowed all its banks, as before.

19The people came up out of the Jordan on the tenth day of the first month, and they encamped at Gilgal on the east border of Jericho. 20And those twelve stones, which they took out of the Jordan, Joshua set up at Gilgal. 21And he said to the people of Israel, "When your children ask their fathers in times to come, 'What do these stones mean?' 22then you shall let your children know, 'Israel passed over this Jordan on dry ground.' 23For the LORD your God dried up the waters of the Jordan for you until you passed over, as the LORD your God did to the Red Sea, which he dried up for us until we passed over, 24so that all the peoples of the earth may know that the hand of the LORD is mighty, that you may fear the LORD your God forever."[1]

Psalm 129–131

A SONG OF ASCENTS.

"Greatly[2] have they afflicted me from my youth"—
  let Israel now say—
2 "Greatly have they afflicted me from my
    youth,
  yet they have not prevailed against me.
3 The plowers plowed upon my back;
  they made long their furrows."
4 The LORD is righteous;
  he has cut the cords of the wicked.
5 May all who hate Zion
  be put to shame and turned backward!
6 Let them be like the grass on the
    housetops,
  which withers before it grows up,
7 with which the reaper does not fill his
    hand
  nor the binder of sheaves his arms,

8 nor do those who pass by say,
  "The blessing of the LORD be upon you!
  We bless you in the name of the
  LORD!"

A SONG OF ASCENTS.

Out of the depths I cry to you, O LORD!
2 O Lord, hear my voice!
  Let your ears be attentive
    to the voice of my pleas for mercy!
3 If you, O LORD, should mark iniquities,
  O Lord, who could stand?
4 But with you there is forgiveness,
  that you may be feared.

5 I wait for the LORD, my soul waits,
  and in his word I hope;
6 my soul waits for the Lord
  more than watchmen for the
    morning,
  more than watchmen for the
    morning.

7 O Israel, hope in the LORD!
  For with the LORD there is steadfast
    love,
  and with him is plentiful redemption.
8 And he will redeem Israel
  from all his iniquities.

A SONG OF ASCENTS. OF DAVID.

O LORD, my heart is not lifted up;
  my eyes are not raised too high;
  I do not occupy myself with things
    too great and too marvelous for me.
2 But I have calmed and quieted my soul,
  like a weaned child with its mother;
  like a weaned child is my soul within
    me.
3 O Israel, hope in the LORD
  from this time forth and
    forevermore.

Isaiah 64

Oh that you would rend the heavens and
    come down,
  that the mountains might quake at
    your presence—
23 as when fire kindles brushwood
  and the fire causes water to boil—

[1] Or all the days [2] Or Often; also verse 2 [3] Ch 64:1 in Hebrew

to make your name known to your
adversaries,
and that the nations might tremble at
your presence!

3 When you did awesome things that we
did not look for,
you came down, the mountains
quaked at your presence.

4 From of old no one has heard
or perceived by the ear,
no eye has seen a God besides you,
who acts for those who wait for him.

5 You meet him who joyfully works
righteousness,
those who remember you in your ways.
Behold, you were angry, and we sinned;
in our sins we have been a long time,
and shall we be saved?[1]

6 We have all become like one who is
unclean,
and all our righteous deeds are like a
polluted garment.
We all fade like a leaf,
and our iniquities, like the wind, take
us away.

7 There is no one who calls upon your
name,
who rouses himself to take hold of you;
for you have hidden your face from us,
and have made us melt in[2] the hand of
our iniquities.

8 But now, O LORD, you are our Father;
we are the clay, and you are our potter;
we are all the work of your hand.

9 Be not so terribly angry, O LORD,
and remember not iniquity forever.
Behold, please look, we are all your
people.

10 Your holy cities have become a
wilderness;
Zion has become a wilderness,
Jerusalem a desolation.

11 Our holy and beautiful[3] house,
where our fathers praised you,
has been burned by fire,
and all our pleasant places have
become ruins.

12 Will you restrain yourself at these
things, O LORD?
Will you keep silent, and afflict us so
terribly?

Matthew 12

At that time Jesus went through the grain-fields on the Sabbath. His disciples were hungry, and they began to pluck heads of grain and to eat. [2]But when the Pharisees saw it, they said to him, "Look, your disciples are doing what is not lawful to do on the Sabbath." [3]He said to them, "Have you not read what David did when he was hungry, and those who were with him: [4]how he entered the house of God and ate the bread of the Presence, which it was not lawful for him to eat nor for those who were with him, but only for the priests? [5]Or have you not read in the Law how on the Sabbath the priests in the temple profane the Sabbath and are guiltless? [6]I tell you, something greater than the temple is here. [7]And if you had known what this means, 'I desire mercy, and not sacrifice,' you would not have condemned the guiltless. [8]For the Son of Man is lord of the Sabbath."

[9]He went on from there and entered their synagogue. [10]And a man was there with a withered hand. And they asked him, "Is it lawful to heal on the Sabbath?"—so that they might accuse him. [11]He said to them, "Which one of you who has a sheep, if it falls into a pit on the Sabbath, will not take hold of it and lift it out? [12]Of how much more value is a man than a sheep! So it is lawful to do good on the Sabbath." [13]Then he said to the man, "Stretch out your hand." And the man stretched it out, and it was restored, healthy like the other. [14]But the Pharisees went out and conspired against him, how to destroy him.

[15]Jesus, aware of this, withdrew from there. And many followed him, and he healed them all [16]and ordered them not to make him known. [17]This was to fulfill what was spoken by the prophet Isaiah:

18 "Behold, my servant whom I have
chosen,
my beloved with whom my soul is
well pleased.
I will put my Spirit upon him,
and he will proclaim justice to the
Gentiles.

19 He will not quarrel or cry aloud,
nor will anyone hear his voice in the
streets;

[1] Or in your ways is continuance, that we might be saved   [2] Masoretic Text; Septuagint, Syriac, Targum have delivered us into   [3] Or holy and glorious

20 a bruised reed he will not break,
    and a smoldering wick he will not
      quench,
    until he brings justice to victory;
21   and in his name the Gentiles will
      hope."

22 Then a demon-oppressed man who was blind and mute was brought to him, and he healed him, so that the man spoke and saw. **23** And all the people were amazed, and said, "Can this be the Son of David?" **24** But when the Pharisees heard it, they said, "It is only by Beelzebul, the prince of demons, that this man casts out demons." **25** Knowing their thoughts, he said to them, "Every kingdom divided against itself is laid waste, and no city or house divided against itself will stand. **26** And if Satan casts out Satan, he is divided against himself. How then will his kingdom stand? **27** And if I cast out demons by Beelzebul, by whom do your sons cast them out? Therefore they will be your judges. **28** But if it is by the Spirit of God that I cast out demons, then the kingdom of God has come upon you. **29** Or how can someone enter a strong man's house and plunder his goods, unless he first binds the strong man? Then indeed he may plunder his house. **30** Whoever is not with me is against me, and whoever does not gather with me scatters. **31** Therefore I tell you, every sin and blasphemy will be forgiven people, but the blasphemy against the Spirit will not be forgiven. **32** And whoever speaks a word against the Son of Man will be forgiven, but whoever speaks against the Holy Spirit will not be forgiven, either in this age or in the age to come.

33 "Either make the tree good and its fruit good, or make the tree bad and its fruit bad, for the tree is known by its fruit. **34** You brood of vipers! How can you speak good, when you are evil? For out of the abundance of the heart the mouth speaks. **35** The good person out of his good treasure brings forth good, and the evil person out of his evil treasure brings forth evil. **36** I tell you, on the day of judgment people will give account for every careless word they speak, **37** for by your words you will be justified, and by your words you will be condemned."

38 Then some of the scribes and Pharisees answered him, saying, "Teacher, we wish to see a sign from you." **39** But he answered them, "An evil and adulterous generation seeks for a sign, but no sign will be given to it except the sign of the prophet Jonah. **40** For just as Jonah was three days and three nights in the belly of the great fish, so will the Son of Man be three days and three nights in the heart of the earth. **41** The men of Nineveh will rise up at the judgment with this generation and condemn it, for they repented at the preaching of Jonah, and behold, something greater than Jonah is here. **42** The queen of the South will rise up at the judgment with this generation and condemn it, for she came from the ends of the earth to hear the wisdom of Solomon, and behold, something greater than Solomon is here.

43 "When the unclean spirit has gone out of a person, it passes through waterless places seeking rest, but finds none. **44** Then it says, 'I will return to my house from which I came.' And when it comes, it finds the house empty, swept, and put in order. **45** Then it goes and brings with it seven other spirits more evil than itself, and they enter and dwell there, and the last state of that person is worse than the first. So also will it be with this evil generation."

46 While he was still speaking to the people, behold, his mother and his brothers stood outside, asking to speak to him.[1] **48** But he replied to the man who told him, "Who is my mother, and who are my brothers?" **49** And stretching out his hand toward his disciples, he said, "Here are my mother and my brothers! **50** For whoever does the will of my Father in heaven is my brother and sister and mother."

---

[1] Some manuscripts insert verse 47: *Someone told him, "Your mother and your brothers are standing outside, asking to speak to you"*

JULY 3

Joshua 5:1–6:5

As soon as all the kings of the Amorites who were beyond the Jordan to the west, and all the kings of the Canaanites who were by the sea, heard that the LORD had dried up the waters of the Jordan for the people of Israel until they had crossed over, their hearts melted and there was no longer any spirit in them because of the people of Israel.

²At that time the LORD said to Joshua, "Make flint knives and circumcise the sons of Israel a second time." ³So Joshua made flint knives and circumcised the sons of Israel at Gibeath-haaraloth.¹ ⁴And this is the reason why Joshua circumcised them: all the males of the people who came out of Egypt, all the men of war, had died in the wilderness on the way after they had come out of Egypt. ⁵Though all the people who came out had been circumcised, yet all the people who were born on the way in the wilderness after they had come out of Egypt had not been circumcised. ⁶For the people of Israel walked forty years in the wilderness, until all the nation, the men of war who came out of Egypt, perished, because they did not obey the voice of the LORD; the LORD swore to them that he would not let them see the land that the LORD had sworn to their fathers to give to us, a land flowing with milk and honey. ⁷So it was their children, whom he raised up in their place, that Joshua circumcised. For they were uncircumcised, because they had not been circumcised on the way.

⁸When the circumcising of the whole nation was finished, they remained in their places in the camp until they were healed. ⁹And the LORD said to Joshua, "Today I have rolled away the reproach of Egypt from you." And so the name of that place is called Gilgal² to this day.

¹⁰While the people of Israel were encamped at Gilgal, they kept the Passover on the fourteenth day of the month in the evening on the plains of Jericho. ¹¹And the day after the Passover, on that very day, they ate of the produce of the land, unleavened cakes and parched grain. ¹²And the manna ceased the day after they ate of the produce of the land. And there was no longer manna for the people of Israel, but they ate of the fruit of the land of Canaan that year.

¹³When Joshua was by Jericho, he lifted up his eyes and looked, and behold, a man was standing before him with his drawn sword in his hand. And Joshua went to him and said to him, "Are you for us, or for our adversaries?" ¹⁴And he said, "No; but I am the commander of the army of the LORD. Now I have come." And Joshua fell on his face to the earth and worshiped and said to him, "What does my lord say to his servant?" ¹⁵And the commander of the LORD's army said to Joshua, "Take off your sandals from your feet, for the place where you are standing is holy." And Joshua did so.

⁶:¹Now Jericho was shut up inside and outside because of the people of Israel. None went out, and none came in. ²And the LORD said to Joshua, "See, I have given Jericho into your hand, with its king and mighty men of valor. ³You shall march around the city, all the men of war going around the city once. Thus shall you do for six days. ⁴Seven priests shall bear seven trumpets of rams' horns before the ark. On the seventh day you shall march around the city seven times, and the priests shall blow the trumpets. ⁵And when they make a long blast with the ram's horn, when you hear the sound of the trumpet, then all the people shall shout with a great shout, and the wall of the city will fall down flat,³ and the people shall go up, everyone straight before him."

Psalm 132–134

A SONG OF ASCENTS.

Remember, O LORD, in David's favor,
    all the hardships he endured,
2 how he swore to the LORD
    and vowed to the Mighty One of Jacob,

¹ *Gibeath-haaraloth* means *the hill of the foreskins* ² *Gilgal* sounds like the Hebrew for *to roll* ³ Hebrew *under itself*; also verse 20

3 "I will not enter my house
    or get into my bed,
4 I will not give sleep to my eyes
    or slumber to my eyelids,
5 until I find a place for the Lord,
    a dwelling place for the Mighty One of
        Jacob."

6 Behold, we heard of it in Ephrathah;
    we found it in the fields of Jaar.
7 "Let us go to his dwelling place;
    let us worship at his footstool!"

8 Arise, O Lord, and go to your resting
        place,
    you and the ark of your might.
9 Let your priests be clothed with
        righteousness,
    and let your saints shout for joy.
10 For the sake of your servant David,
    do not turn away the face of your
        anointed one.

11 The Lord swore to David a sure oath
    from which he will not turn back:
    "One of the sons of your body[1]
    I will set on your throne.
12 If your sons keep my covenant
    and my testimonies that I shall teach
        them,
    their sons also forever
    shall sit on your throne."

13 For the Lord has chosen Zion;
    he has desired it for his dwelling place:
14 "This is my resting place forever;
    here I will dwell, for I have desired it.
15 I will abundantly bless her provisions;
    I will satisfy her poor with bread.
16 Her priests I will clothe with salvation,
    and her saints will shout for joy.
17 There I will make a horn to sprout for
        David;
    I have prepared a lamp for my
        anointed.
18 His enemies I will clothe with shame,
    but on him his crown will shine."

A Song of Ascents. Of David.

B ehold, how good and pleasant it is
    when brothers dwell in unity![2]
2 It is like the precious oil on the head,
    running down on the beard,

on the beard of Aaron,
    running down on the collar of his
        robes!
3 It is like the dew of Hermon,
    which falls on the mountains of
        Zion!
For there the Lord has commanded the
        blessing,
    life forevermore.

A Song of Ascents.

C ome, bless the Lord, all you servants of
    the Lord,
    who stand by night in the house of
        the Lord!
2 Lift up your hands to the holy place
    and bless the Lord!

3 May the Lord bless you from Zion,
    he who made heaven and earth!

─────────── Isaiah 65 ───────────

I was ready to be sought by those who did
    not ask for me;
    I was ready to be found by those who
        did not seek me.
I said, "Here I am, here I am,"
    to a nation that was not called by[3] my
        name.
2 I spread out my hands all the day
    to a rebellious people,
who walk in a way that is not good,
    following their own devices;
3 a people who provoke me
    to my face continually,
sacrificing in gardens
    and making offerings on bricks;
4 who sit in tombs,
    and spend the night in secret places;
who eat pig's flesh,
    and broth of tainted meat is in their
        vessels;
5 who say, "Keep to yourself,
    do not come near me, for I am too
        holy for you."
These are a smoke in my nostrils,
    a fire that burns all the day.
6 Behold, it is written before me:
    "I will not keep silent, but I will repay;

---

[1] Hebrew of your fruit of the womb [2] Or dwell together [3] Or that did not call upon

I will indeed repay into their lap
7   both your iniquities and your fathers'
         iniquities together,
                                    says the LORD;
   because they made offerings on the
         mountains
   and insulted me on the hills,
   I will measure into their lap
         payment for their former deeds."[1]

8 Thus says the LORD:
   "As the new wine is found in the cluster,
      and they say, 'Do not destroy it,
      for there is a blessing in it,'
   so I will do for my servants' sake,
      and not destroy them all.
9 I will bring forth offspring from Jacob,
      and from Judah possessors of my
         mountains;
   my chosen shall possess it,
      and my servants shall dwell there.
10 Sharon shall become a pasture for
         flocks,
      and the Valley of Achor a place for
         herds to lie down,
   for my people who have sought me.
11 But you who forsake the LORD,
      who forget my holy mountain,
   who set a table for Fortune
      and fill cups of mixed wine for
         Destiny,
12 I will destine you to the sword,
      and all of you shall bow down to the
         slaughter,
   because, when I called, you did not
         answer;
      when I spoke, you did not listen,
   but you did what was evil in my eyes
      and chose what I did not delight in."

13 Therefore thus says the Lord GOD:
   "Behold, my servants shall eat,
      but you shall be hungry;
   behold, my servants shall drink,
      but you shall be thirsty;
   behold, my servants shall rejoice,
      but you shall be put to shame;
14 behold, my servants shall sing for
         gladness of heart,
      but you shall cry out for pain of heart
      and shall wail for breaking of spirit.

15 You shall leave your name to my chosen
         for a curse,
      and the Lord GOD will put you to
         death,
   but his servants he will call by another
         name.
16 So that he who blesses himself in the
         land
      shall bless himself by the God of truth,
   and he who takes an oath in the land
      shall swear by the God of truth;
   because the former troubles are
         forgotten
      and are hidden from my eyes.

17 "For behold, I create new heavens
      and a new earth,
   and the former things shall not be
         remembered
      or come into mind.
18 But be glad and rejoice forever
      in that which I create;
   for behold, I create Jerusalem to be a
         joy,
      and her people to be a gladness.
19 I will rejoice in Jerusalem
      and be glad in my people;
   no more shall be heard in it the sound of
         weeping
      and the cry of distress.
20 No more shall there be in it
      an infant who lives but a few days,
      or an old man who does not fill out
         his days,
   for the young man shall die a hundred
         years old,
      and the sinner a hundred years old
         shall be accursed.
21 They shall build houses and inhabit
         them;
      they shall plant vineyards and eat
         their fruit.
22 They shall not build and another
         inhabit;
      they shall not plant and another eat;
   for like the days of a tree shall the days
         of my people be,
      and my chosen shall long enjoy[2] the
         work of their hands.
23 They shall not labor in vain
      or bear children for calamity,[3]

---

[1] Or I will first measure their payment into their lap   [2] Hebrew shall wear out   [3] Or for sudden terror

for they shall be the offspring of the
    blessed of the LORD,
    and their descendants with them.
24 Before they call I will answer;
    while they are yet speaking I will
    hear.
25 The wolf and the lamb shall graze
    together;
    the lion shall eat straw like the ox,
    and dust shall be the serpent's food.
They shall not hurt or destroy
    in all my holy mountain,"
               says the LORD.

Matthew 13

That same day Jesus went out of the house and sat beside the sea. ²And great crowds gathered about him, so that he got into a boat and sat down. And the whole crowd stood on the beach. ³And he told them many things in parables, saying: "A sower went out to sow. ⁴And as he sowed, some seeds fell along the path, and the birds came and devoured them. ⁵Other seeds fell on rocky ground, where they did not have much soil, and immediately they sprang up, since they had no depth of soil, ⁶but when the sun rose they were scorched. And since they had no root, they withered away. ⁷Other seeds fell among thorns, and the thorns grew up and choked them. ⁸Other seeds fell on good soil and produced grain, some a hundredfold, some sixty, some thirty. ⁹He who has ears,¹ let him hear."

¹⁰Then the disciples came and said to him, "Why do you speak to them in parables?" ¹¹And he answered them, "To you it has been given to know the secrets of the kingdom of heaven, but to them it has not been given. ¹²For to the one who has, more will be given, and he will have an abundance, but from the one who has not, even what he has will be taken away. ¹³This is why I speak to them in parables, because seeing they do not see, and hearing they do not hear, nor do they understand. ¹⁴Indeed, in their case the prophecy of Isaiah is fulfilled that says:

" "'You will indeed hear but never
    understand,
    and you will indeed see but never
    perceive."

15   For this people's heart has grown dull,
    and with their ears they can barely
    hear,
    and their eyes they have closed,
    lest they should see with their eyes
    and hear with their ears
    and understand with their heart
    and turn, and I would heal them.'

¹⁶But blessed are your eyes, for they see, and your ears, for they hear. ¹⁷For truly, I say to you, many prophets and righteous people longed to see what you see, and did not see it, and to hear what you hear, and did not hear it.

¹⁸"Hear then the parable of the sower: ¹⁹When anyone hears the word of the kingdom and does not understand it, the evil one comes and snatches away what has been sown in his heart. This is what was sown along the path. ²⁰As for what was sown on rocky ground, this is the one who hears the word and immediately receives it with joy, ²¹yet he has no root in himself, but endures for a while, and when tribulation or persecution arises on account of the word, immediately he falls away.² ²²As for what was sown among thorns, this is the one who hears the word, but the cares of the world and the deceitfulness of riches choke the word, and it proves unfruitful. ²³As for what was sown on good soil, this is the one who hears the word and understands it. He indeed bears fruit and yields, in one case a hundredfold, in another sixty, and in another thirty."

²⁴He put another parable before them, saying, "The kingdom of heaven may be compared to a man who sowed good seed in his field, ²⁵but while his men were sleeping, his enemy came and sowed weeds³ among the wheat and went away. ²⁶So when the plants came up and bore grain, then the weeds appeared also. ²⁷And the servants⁴ of the master of the house came and said to him, 'Master, did you not sow good seed in your field? How then does it have weeds?' ²⁸He said to them, 'An enemy has done this.' So the servants said to him, 'Then do you want us to go and gather them?' ²⁹But he said, 'No, lest in gathering the weeds you root up the wheat along with them. ³⁰Let both grow together until the harvest, and at harvest time I will tell the reapers, Gather the weeds first and bind them in bundles to be burned, but gather the wheat into my barn.'"

¹ Some manuscripts add here and in verse 43 *to hear* ² Or *stumbles* ³ Probably *darnel*, a wheat-like weed ⁴ Greek *bondservants*; also verse 28

[31] He put another parable before them, saying, "The kingdom of heaven is like a grain of mustard seed that a man took and sowed in his field. [32] It is the smallest of all seeds, but when it has grown it is larger than all the garden plants and becomes a tree, so that the birds of the air come and make nests in its branches."

[33] He told them another parable. "The kingdom of heaven is like leaven that a woman took and hid in three measures of flour, till it was all leavened."

[34] All these things Jesus said to the crowds in parables; indeed, he said nothing to them without a parable. [35] This was to fulfill what was spoken by the prophet:[1]

> "I will open my mouth in parables;
>   I will utter what has been hidden since the foundation of the world."

[36] Then he left the crowds and went into the house. And his disciples came to him, saying, "Explain to us the parable of the weeds of the field." [37] He answered, "The one who sows the good seed is the Son of Man. [38] The field is the world, and the good seed is the sons of the kingdom. The weeds are the sons of the evil one, [39] and the enemy who sowed them is the devil. The harvest is the end of the age, and the reapers are angels. [40] Just as the weeds are gathered and burned with fire, so will it be at the end of the age. [41] The Son of Man will send his angels, and they will gather out of his kingdom all causes of sin and all law-breakers, [42] and throw them into the fiery furnace. In that place there will be weeping and gnashing of teeth. [43] Then the righteous will shine like the sun in the kingdom of their Father. He who has ears, let him hear.

[44] "The kingdom of heaven is like treasure hidden in a field, which a man found and covered up. Then in his joy he goes and sells all that he has and buys that field.

[45] "Again, the kingdom of heaven is like a merchant in search of fine pearls, [46] who, on finding one pearl of great value, went and sold all that he had and bought it.

[47] "Again, the kingdom of heaven is like a net that was thrown into the sea and gathered fish of every kind. [48] When it was full, men drew it ashore and sat down and sorted the good into containers but threw away the bad. [49] So it will be at the end of the age. The angels will come out and separate the evil from the righteous [50] and throw them into the fiery furnace. In that place there will be weeping and gnashing of teeth.

[51] "Have you understood all these things?" They said to him, "Yes." [52] And he said to them, "Therefore every scribe who has been trained for the kingdom of heaven is like a master of a house, who brings out of his treasure what is new and what is old."

[53] And when Jesus had finished these parables, he went away from there, [54] and coming to his hometown he taught them in their synagogue, so that they were astonished, and said, "Where did this man get this wisdom and these mighty works? [55] Is not this the carpenter's son? Is not his mother called Mary? And are not his brothers James and Joseph and Simon and Judas? [56] And are not all his sisters with us? Where then did this man get all these things?" [57] And they took offense at him. But Jesus said to them, "A prophet is not without honor except in his hometown and in his own household." [58] And he did not do many mighty works there, because of their unbelief.

---

[1] Some manuscripts *Isaiah the prophet*

JULY 4

Joshua 6:6–27

So Joshua the son of Nun called the priests and said to them, "Take up the ark of the covenant and let seven priests bear seven trumpets of rams' horns before the ark of the LORD." [7] And he said to the people, "Go forward. March around the city and let the armed men pass on before the ark of the LORD."

[8] And just as Joshua had commanded the people, the seven priests bearing the seven trumpets of rams' horns before the LORD went forward, blowing the trumpets, with the ark of the covenant of the LORD following them. [9] The armed men were walking before the priests who were blowing the trumpets, and the rear guard was walking after the ark, while the trumpets blew continually. [10] But Joshua commanded the people, "You shall not shout or make your voice heard, neither shall any word go out of your mouth, until the day I tell you to shout. Then you shall shout." [11] So he caused the ark of the LORD to circle the city, going about it once. And they came into the camp and spent the night in the camp.

[12] Then Joshua rose early in the morning, and the priests took up the ark of the LORD. [13] And the seven priests bearing the seven trumpets of rams' horns before the ark of the LORD walked on, and they blew the trumpets continually. And the armed men were walking before them, and the rear guard was walking after the ark of the LORD, while the trumpets blew continually. [14] And the second day they marched around the city once, and returned into the camp. So they did for six days.

[15] On the seventh day they rose early, at the dawn of day, and marched around the city in the same manner seven times. It was only on that day that they marched around the city seven times. [16] And at the seventh time, when the priests had blown the trumpets, Joshua said to the people, "Shout, for the LORD has given you the city. [17] And the city and all that is within it shall be devoted to the LORD for destruction.[1] Only Rahab the prostitute and all who are with her in her house shall live, because she hid the messengers whom we sent. [18] But you, keep yourselves from the things devoted to destruction, lest when you have devoted them you take any of the devoted things and make the camp of Israel a thing for destruction and bring trouble upon it. [19] But all silver and gold, and every vessel of bronze and iron, are holy to the LORD; they shall go into the treasury of the LORD." [20] So the people shouted, and the trumpets were blown. As soon as the people heard the sound of the trumpet, the people shouted a great shout, and the wall fell down flat, so that the people went up into the city, every man straight before him, and they captured the city. [21] Then they devoted all in the city to destruction, both men and women, young and old, oxen, sheep, and donkeys, with the edge of the sword.

[22] But to the two men who had spied out the land, Joshua said, "Go into the prostitute's house and bring out from there the woman and all who belong to her, as you swore to her." [23] So the young men who had been spies went in and brought out Rahab and her father and mother and brothers and all who belonged to her. And they brought all her relatives and put them outside the camp of Israel. [24] And they burned the city with fire, and everything in it. Only the silver and gold, and the vessels of bronze and of iron, they put into the treasury of the house of the LORD. [25] But Rahab the prostitute and her father's household and all who belonged to her, Joshua saved alive. And she has lived in Israel to this day, because she hid the messengers whom Joshua sent to spy out Jericho.

[26] Joshua laid an oath on them at that time, saying, "Cursed before the LORD be the man who rises up and rebuilds this city, Jericho.

"At the cost of his firstborn shall he
  lay its foundation,
and at the cost of his youngest son
  shall he set up its gates."

[1] That is, set apart (devoted) as an offering to the Lord (for destruction); also verses 18, 21

²⁷ So the LORD was with Joshua, and his fame was in all the land.

─────── *Psalm 135–136* ───────

Praise the LORD!
Praise the name of the LORD,
  give praise, O servants of the LORD,
² who stand in the house of the LORD,
  in the courts of the house of our God!
³ Praise the LORD, for the LORD is good;
  sing to his name, for it is pleasant!¹
⁴ For the LORD has chosen Jacob for himself,
  Israel as his own possession.

⁵ For I know that the LORD is great,
  and that our Lord is above all gods.
⁶ Whatever the LORD pleases, he does,
  in heaven and on earth,
  in the seas and all deeps.
⁷ He it is who makes the clouds rise at the end of the earth,
  who makes lightnings for the rain
  and brings forth the wind from his storehouses.

⁸ He it was who struck down the firstborn of Egypt,
  both of man and of beast;
⁹ who in your midst, O Egypt,
  sent signs and wonders
  against Pharaoh and all his servants;
¹⁰ who struck down many nations
  and killed mighty kings,
¹¹ Sihon, king of the Amorites,
  and Og, king of Bashan,
  and all the kingdoms of Canaan,
¹² and gave their land as a heritage,
  a heritage to his people Israel.

¹³ Your name, O LORD, endures forever,
  your renown,² O LORD, throughout all ages.
¹⁴ For the LORD will vindicate his people
  and have compassion on his servants.

¹⁵ The idols of the nations are silver and gold,
  the work of human hands.
¹⁶ They have mouths, but do not speak;
  they have eyes, but do not see;
¹⁷ they have ears, but do not hear,
  nor is there any breath in their mouths.
¹⁸ Those who make them become like them,
  so do all who trust in them.

¹⁹ O house of Israel, bless the LORD!
  O house of Aaron, bless the LORD!
²⁰ O house of Levi, bless the LORD!
  You who fear the LORD, bless the LORD!
²¹ Blessed be the LORD from Zion,
  he who dwells in Jerusalem!
Praise the LORD!

Give thanks to the LORD, for he is good,
  for his steadfast love endures forever.
² Give thanks to the God of gods,
  for his steadfast love endures forever.
³ Give thanks to the Lord of lords,
  for his steadfast love endures forever;

⁴ to him who alone does great wonders,
  for his steadfast love endures forever;
⁵ to him who by understanding made the heavens,
  for his steadfast love endures forever;
⁶ to him who spread out the earth above the waters,
  for his steadfast love endures forever;
⁷ to him who made the great lights,
  for his steadfast love endures forever;
⁸ the sun to rule over the day,
  for his steadfast love endures forever;
⁹ the moon and stars to rule over the night,
  for his steadfast love endures forever;

¹⁰ to him who struck down the firstborn of Egypt,
  for his steadfast love endures forever;
¹¹ and brought Israel out from among them,
  for his steadfast love endures forever;
¹² with a strong hand and an outstretched arm,
  for his steadfast love endures forever;
¹³ to him who divided the Red Sea in two,
  for his steadfast love endures forever;
¹⁴ and made Israel pass through the midst of it,
  for his steadfast love endures forever;

¹ Or *for he is beautiful* ² Or *remembrance*

15 but overthrew[1] Pharaoh and his host in
 the Red Sea,
  for his steadfast love endures forever;
16 to him who led his people through the
 wilderness,
  for his steadfast love endures forever;
17 to him who struck down great kings,
  for his steadfast love endures forever;
18 and killed mighty kings,
  for his steadfast love endures forever;
19 Sihon, king of the Amorites,
  for his steadfast love endures forever;
20 and Og, king of Bashan,
  for his steadfast love endures forever;
21 and gave their land as a heritage,
  for his steadfast love endures forever;
22 a heritage to Israel his servant,
  for his steadfast love endures forever.

23 It is he who remembered us in our low
 estate,
  for his steadfast love endures forever;
24 and rescued us from our foes,
  for his steadfast love endures forever;
25 he who gives food to all flesh,
  for his steadfast love endures forever.
26 Give thanks to the God of heaven,
  for his steadfast love endures forever.

Isaiah 66

Thus says the LORD:
"Heaven is my throne,
 and the earth is my footstool;
what is the house that you would build
 for me,
and what is the place of my rest?
2 All these things my hand has made,
 and so all these things came to be,
   declares the LORD.
But this is the one to whom I will look:
 he who is humble and contrite in
 spirit
and trembles at my word.

3 "He who slaughters an ox is like one who
 kills a man;
he who sacrifices a lamb, like one who
 breaks a dog's neck;
he who presents a grain offering, like
 one who offers pig's blood;

he who makes a memorial offering of
 frankincense, like one who blesses
 an idol.
These have chosen their own ways,
 and their soul delights in their
 abominations;
4 I also will choose harsh treatment for
 them
 and bring their fears upon them,
because when I called, no one answered,
 when I spoke, they did not listen;
but they did what was evil in my eyes
 and chose that in which I did not
 delight."

5 Hear the word of the LORD,
 you who tremble at his word:
"Your brothers who hate you
 and cast you out for my name's sake
have said, 'Let the LORD be glorified,
 that we may see your joy';
but it is they who shall be put to
 shame.
6 "The sound of an uproar from the city!
 A sound from the temple!
The sound of the LORD,
 rendering recompense to his enemies!

7 "Before she was in labor
 she gave birth;
before her pain came upon her
 she delivered a son.
8 Who has heard such a thing?
 Who has seen such things?
Shall a land be born in one day?
 Shall a nation be brought forth in one
 moment?
For as soon as Zion was in labor
 she brought forth her children.
9 Shall I bring to the point of birth and not
 cause to bring forth?"
 says the LORD;
"shall I, who cause to bring forth, shut
 the womb?"
 says your God.

10 "Rejoice with Jerusalem, and be glad for
 her,
 all you who love her;
rejoice with her in joy,
 all you who mourn over her;
11 that you may nurse and be satisfied
 from her consoling breast;

[1] Hebrew shook off

that you may drink deeply with delight
from her glorious abundance."[1]

12   For thus says the LORD:
"Behold, I will extend peace to her like a
river,
and the glory of the nations like an
overflowing stream;
and you shall nurse, you shall be carried
upon her hip,
and bounced upon her knees.
13   As one whom his mother comforts,
so I will comfort you;
you shall be comforted in Jerusalem.
14   You shall see, and your heart shall
rejoice;
your bones shall flourish like the grass;
and the hand of the LORD shall be
known to his servants,
and he shall show his indignation
against his enemies.
15   "For behold, the LORD will come in fire,
and his chariots like the whirlwind,
to render his anger in fury,
and his rebuke with flames of fire.
16   For by fire will the LORD enter into
judgment,
and by his sword, with all flesh;
and those slain by the LORD shall be
many.

17 "Those who sanctify and purify themselves to go into the gardens, following one in
the midst, eating pig's flesh and the abomination and mice, shall come to an end together,
declares the LORD.
18 "For I know[2] their works and their thoughts,
and the time is coming[3] to gather all nations
and tongues. And they shall come and shall see
my glory, 19 and I will set a sign among them.
And from them I will send survivors to the
nations, to Tarshish, Pul, and Lud, who draw
the bow, to Tubal and Javan, to the coastlands
far away, that have not heard my fame or seen
my glory. And they shall declare my glory
among the nations. 20 And they shall bring all
your brothers from all the nations as an offering to the LORD, on horses and in chariots and
in litters and on mules and on dromedaries, to
my holy mountain Jerusalem, says the LORD,
just as the Israelites bring their grain offering in
a clean vessel to the house of the LORD. 21 And

some of them also I will take for priests and for
Levites, says the LORD.

22   "For as the new heavens and the new
earth
that I make
shall remain before me, says the LORD,
so shall your offspring and your name
remain.
23   From new moon to new moon,
and from Sabbath to Sabbath,
all flesh shall come to worship before me,
declares the LORD.

24 "And they shall go out and look on the
dead bodies of the men who have rebelled
against me. For their worm shall not die, their
fire shall not be quenched, and they shall be an
abhorrence to all flesh."

──────── *Matthew 14* ────────

At that time Herod the tetrarch heard about
the fame of Jesus, 2 and he said to his servants, "This is John the Baptist. He has been
raised from the dead; that is why these miraculous powers are at work in him." 3 For Herod
had seized John and bound him and put him
in prison for the sake of Herodias, his brother
Philip's wife,[4] 4 because John had been saying
to him, "It is not lawful for you to have her."
5 And though he wanted to put him to death,
he feared the people, because they held him
to be a prophet. 6 But when Herod's birthday
came, the daughter of Herodias danced before
the company and pleased Herod, 7 so that he
promised with an oath to give her whatever she
might ask. 8 Prompted by her mother, she said,
"Give me the head of John the Baptist here on a
platter." 9 And the king was sorry, but because
of his oaths and his guests he commanded it
to be given. 10 He sent and had John beheaded
in the prison, 11 and his head was brought on
a platter and given to the girl, and she brought
it to her mother. 12 And his disciples came and
took the body and buried it, and they went and
told Jesus.
13 Now when Jesus heard this, he withdrew
from there in a boat to a desolate place by himself. But when the crowds heard it, they followed
him on foot from the towns. 14 When he went
ashore he saw a great crowd, and he had compassion on them and healed their sick. 15 Now

1 Or *breast* 2 Septuagint, Syriac; Hebrew lacks *know* 3 Hebrew *and it is coming* 4 Some manuscripts *his brother's wife*

when it was evening, the disciples came to him and said, "This is a desolate place, and the day is now over; send the crowds away to go into the villages and buy food for themselves." [16]But Jesus said, "They need not go away; you give them something to eat." [17]They said to him, "We have only five loaves here and two fish." [18]And he said, "Bring them here to me." [19]Then he ordered the crowds to sit down on the grass, and taking the five loaves and the two fish, he looked up to heaven and said a blessing. Then he broke the loaves and gave them to the disciples, and the disciples gave them to the crowds. [20]And they all ate and were satisfied. And they took up twelve baskets full of the broken pieces left over. [21]And those who ate were about five thousand men, besides women and children.

[22]Immediately he made the disciples get into the boat and go before him to the other side, while he dismissed the crowds. [23]And after he had dismissed the crowds, he went up on the mountain by himself to pray. When evening came, he was there alone, [24]but the boat by this time was a long way[1] from the land,[2] beaten by the waves, for the wind was against them.

[25]And in the fourth watch of the night he came to them, walking on the sea. [26]But when the disciples saw him walking on the sea, they were terrified, and said, "It is a ghost!" and they cried out in fear. [27]But immediately Jesus spoke to them, saying, "Take heart; it is I. Do not be afraid."

[28]And Peter answered him, "Lord, if it is you, command me to come to you on the water." [29]He said, "Come." So Peter got out of the boat and walked on the water and came to Jesus. [30]But when he saw the wind,[3] he was afraid, and beginning to sink he cried out, "Lord, save me." [31]Jesus immediately reached out his hand and took hold of him, saying to him, "O you of little faith, why did you doubt?" [32]And when they got into the boat, the wind ceased. [33]And those in the boat worshiped him, saying, "Truly you are the Son of God."

[34]And when they had crossed over, they came to land at Gennesaret. [35]And when the men of that place recognized him, they sent around to all that region and brought to him all who were sick [36]and implored him that they might only touch the fringe of his garment. And as many as touched it were made well.

JULY 5

Joshua 7

But the people of Israel broke faith in regard to the devoted things, for Achan the son of Carmi, son of Zabdi, son of Zerah, of the tribe of Judah, took some of the devoted things. And the anger of the LORD burned against the people of Israel.

[2]Joshua sent men from Jericho to Ai, which is near Beth-aven, east of Bethel, and said to them, "Go up and spy out the land." And the men went up and spied out Ai. [3]And they returned to Joshua and said to him, "Do not have all the people go up, but let about two or three thousand men go up and attack Ai. Do not make the whole people toil up there, for they are few." [4]So about three thousand men went up there from the people. And they fled

before the men of Ai, [5]and the men of Ai killed about thirty-six of their men and chased them before the gate as far as Shebarim and struck them at the descent. And the hearts of the people melted and became as water.

[6]Then Joshua tore his clothes and fell to the earth on his face before the ark of the LORD until the evening, he and the elders of Israel. And they put dust on their heads. [7]And Joshua said, "Alas, O Lord GOD, why have you brought this people over the Jordan at all, to give us into the hands of the Amorites, to destroy us? Would that we had been content to dwell beyond the Jordan! [8]O Lord, what can I say, when Israel has turned their backs before their enemies! [9]For the Canaanites and all the inhabitants of the

[1] Greek many stadia, a stadion was about 607 feet or 185 meters [2] Some manuscripts was out on the sea [3] Some manuscripts strong wind

land will hear of it and will surround us and cut off our name from the earth. And what will you do for your great name?"

[10] The LORD said to Joshua, "Get up! Why have you fallen on your face? [11] Israel has sinned; they have transgressed my covenant that I commanded them; they have taken some of the devoted things; they have stolen and lied and put them among their own belongings. [12] Therefore the people of Israel cannot stand before their enemies. They turn their backs before their enemies, because they have become devoted for destruction.[1] I will be with you no more, unless you destroy the devoted things from among you. [13] Get up! Consecrate the people and say, 'Consecrate yourselves for tomorrow; for thus says the LORD, God of Israel, "There are devoted things in your midst, O Israel. You cannot stand before your enemies until you take away the devoted things from among you." [14] In the morning therefore you shall be brought near by your tribes. And the tribe that the LORD takes by lot shall come near by clans. And the clan that the LORD takes shall come near by households. And the household that the LORD takes shall come near man by man. [15] And he who is taken with the devoted things shall be burned with fire, he and all that he has, because he has transgressed the covenant of the LORD, and because he has done an outrageous thing in Israel.'"

[16] So Joshua rose early in the morning and brought Israel near tribe by tribe, and the tribe of Judah was taken. [17] And he brought near the clans of Judah, and the clan of the Zerahites was taken. And he brought near the clan of the Zerahites man by man, and Zabdi was taken. [18] And he brought near his household man by man, and Achan the son of Carmi, son of Zabdi, son of Zerah, of the tribe of Judah, was taken. [19] Then Joshua said to Achan, "My son, give glory to the LORD God of Israel and give praise[2] to him. And tell me now what you have done; do not hide it from me." [20] And Achan answered Joshua, "Truly I have sinned against the LORD God of Israel, and this is what I did: [21] when I saw among the spoil a beautiful cloak from Shinar, and 200 shekels of silver, and a bar of gold weighing 50 shekels,[3] then I coveted them and took them. And see, they are hidden in the earth inside my tent, with the silver underneath."

[22] So Joshua sent messengers, and they ran to the tent; and behold, it was hidden in his tent with the silver underneath. [23] And they took them out of the tent and brought them to Joshua and to all the people of Israel. And they laid them down before the LORD. [24] And Joshua and all Israel with him took Achan the son of Zerah, and the silver and the cloak and the bar of gold, and his sons and daughters and his oxen and donkeys and sheep and his tent and all that he had. And they brought them up to the Valley of Achor. [25] And Joshua said, "Why did you bring trouble on us? The LORD brings trouble on you today." And all Israel stoned him with stones. They burned them with fire and stoned them with stones. [26] And they raised over him a great heap of stones that remains to this day. Then the LORD turned from his burning anger. Therefore, to this day the name of that place is called the Valley of Achor.[4]

Psalm 137–138

By the waters of Babylon,
  there we sat down and wept,
    when we remembered Zion.
[2] On the willows[5] there
  we hung up our lyres.
[3] For there our captors
    required of us songs,
  and our tormentors, mirth, saying,
    "Sing us one of the songs of Zion!"

[4] How shall we sing the LORD's song
  in a foreign land?
[5] If I forget you, O Jerusalem,
  let my right hand forget its skill!
[6] Let my tongue stick to the roof of my
    mouth,
  if I do not remember you,
  if I do not set Jerusalem
    above my highest joy!

[7] Remember, O LORD, against the
    Edomites
  the day of Jerusalem,
  how they said, "Lay it bare, lay it bare,
    down to its foundations!"
[8] O daughter of Babylon, doomed to be
    destroyed,
  blessed shall he be who repays you
    with what you have done to us!

[1] That is, set apart (devoted) as an offering to the Lord (for destruction) [2] Or and make confession [3] A shekel was about 2/5 ounce or 11 grams [4] Achor means trouble [5] Or poplars

9 Blessed shall he be who takes your little
    ones
    and dashes them against the rock!

OF DAVID.

I give you thanks, O LORD, with my whole
heart;
    before the gods I sing your praise;
2 I bow down toward your holy temple
    and give thanks to your name for
        your steadfast love and your
        faithfulness,
    for you have exalted above all things
        your name and your word.[1]
3 On the day I called, you answered me;
    my strength of soul you increased.[2]
4 All the kings of the earth shall give you
        thanks, O LORD,
    for they have heard the words of your
        mouth,
5 and they shall sing of the ways of the
        LORD,
    for great is the glory of the LORD.
6 For though the LORD is high, he regards
        the lowly,
    but the haughty he knows from afar.
7 Though I walk in the midst of trouble,
    you preserve my life;
    you stretch out your hand against the
        wrath of my enemies,
    and your right hand delivers me.
8 The LORD will fulfill his purpose for me;
    your steadfast love, O LORD, endures
        forever.
    Do not forsake the work of your hands.

─────── *Jeremiah 1* ───────

The words of Jeremiah, the son of Hilkiah,
one of the priests who were in Anathoth
in the land of Benjamin, ² to whom the word of
the LORD came in the days of Josiah the son
of Amon, king of Judah, in the thirteenth year
of his reign. ³ It came also in the days of Jehoiakim the son of Josiah, king of Judah, and until
the end of the eleventh year of Zedekiah, the
son of Josiah, king of Judah, until the captivity
of Jerusalem in the fifth month.
    ⁴ Now the word of the LORD came to me,
saying,

5 "Before I formed you in the womb I knew
        you,
    and before you were born I consecrated
        you;
    I appointed you a prophet to the
        nations."

⁶ Then I said, "Ah, Lord GOD! Behold, I do not
know how to speak, for I am only a youth." ⁷ But
the LORD said to me,

    "Do not say, 'I am only a youth';
    for to all to whom I send you, you shall
        go,
    and whatever I command you, you shall
        speak.
8 Do not be afraid of them,
    for I am with you to deliver you,
                        declares the LORD."

⁹ Then the LORD put out his hand and touched
my mouth. And the LORD said to me,

    "Behold, I have put my words in your
        mouth.
10 See, I have set you this day over nations
        and over kingdoms,
    to pluck up and to break down,
    to destroy and to overthrow,
    to build and to plant."

¹¹ And the word of the LORD came to me, saying, "Jeremiah, what do you see?" And I said,
"I see an almond[3] branch." ¹² Then the LORD
said to me, "You have seen well, for I am watching over my word to perform it."
    ¹³ The word of the LORD came to me a sec-
ond time, saying, "What do you see?" And I
said, "I see a boiling pot, facing away from
the north." ¹⁴ Then the LORD said to me, "Out
of the north disaster[4] shall be let loose upon
all the inhabitants of the land. ¹⁵ For behold,
I am calling all the tribes of the kingdoms of
the north, declares the LORD, and they shall
come, and every one shall set his throne at the
entrance of the gates of Jerusalem, against all
its walls all around and against all the cities
of Judah. ¹⁶ And I will declare my judgments
against them, for all their evil in forsaking me.
They have made offerings to other gods and
worshiped the works of their own hands. ¹⁷ But
you, dress yourself for work;[5] arise, and say to
them everything that I command you. Do not
be dismayed by them, lest I dismay you before

─────────────────────────────

[1] Or *you have exalted your word above all your name* [2] Hebrew *you made me bold in my soul with strength* [3] *Almond* sounds like the Hebrew for *watching* (compare verse 12)
[4] The Hebrew word can mean *evil, harm,* or *disaster,* depending on the context; so throughout Jeremiah [5] Hebrew *gird up your loins*

them. [18]And I, behold, I make you this day a fortified city, an iron pillar, and bronze walls, against the whole land, against the kings of Judah, its officials, its priests, and the people of the land. [19]They will fight against you, but they shall not prevail against you, for I am with you, declares the Lord, to deliver you."

Matthew 15

Then Pharisees and scribes came to Jesus from Jerusalem and said, [2]"Why do your disciples break the tradition of the elders? For they do not wash their hands when they eat." [3]He answered them, "And why do you break the commandment of God for the sake of your tradition? [4]For God commanded, 'Honor your father and your mother,' and, 'Whoever reviles father or mother must surely die.' [5]But you say, 'If anyone tells his father or his mother, "What you would have gained from me is given to God,"[1] [6]he need not honor his father.' So for the sake of your tradition you have made void the word[2] of God. [7]You hypocrites! Well did Isaiah prophesy of you, when he said:

[8]   "'This people honors me with their lips,
       but their heart is far from me;
[9]   in vain do they worship me,
       teaching as doctrines
          the commandments of men.'"

[10]And he called the people to him and said to them, "Hear and understand: [11]it is not what goes into the mouth that defiles a person, but what comes out of the mouth; this defiles a person." [12]Then the disciples came and said to him, "Do you know that the Pharisees were offended when they heard this saying?" [13]He answered, "Every plant that my heavenly Father has not planted will be rooted up. [14]Let them alone; they are blind guides.[3] And if the blind lead the blind, both will fall into a pit." [15]But Peter said to him, "Explain the parable to us." [16]And he said, "Are you also still without understanding? [17]Do you not see that whatever goes into the mouth passes into the stomach and is expelled?[4] [18]But what comes out of the mouth proceeds from the heart, and this defiles a person. [19]For out of the heart come evil thoughts, murder, adultery, sexual immorality, theft, false witness, slander. [20]These are what defile

a person. But to eat with unwashed hands does not defile anyone."

[21]And Jesus went away from there and withdrew to the district of Tyre and Sidon. [22]And behold, a Canaanite woman from that region came out and was crying, "Have mercy on me, O Lord, Son of David; my daughter is severely oppressed by a demon." [23]But he did not answer her a word. And his disciples came and begged him, saying, "Send her away, for she is crying out after us." [24]He answered, "I was sent only to the lost sheep of the house of Israel." [25]But she came and knelt before him, saying, "Lord, help me." [26]And he answered, "It is not right to take the children's bread and throw it to the dogs." [27]She said, "Yes, Lord, yet even the dogs eat the crumbs that fall from their masters' table." [28]Then Jesus answered her, "O woman, great is your faith! Be it done for you as you desire." And her daughter was healed instantly.[5]

[29]Jesus went on from there and walked beside the Sea of Galilee. And he went up on the mountain and sat down there. [30]And great crowds came to him, bringing with them the lame, the blind, the crippled, the mute, and many others, and they put them at his feet, and he healed them, [31]so that the crowd wondered, when they saw the mute speaking, the crippled healthy, the lame walking, and the blind seeing. And they glorified the God of Israel.

[32]Then Jesus called his disciples to him and said, "I have compassion on the crowd because they have been with me now three days and have nothing to eat. And I am unwilling to send them away hungry, lest they faint on the way." [33]And the disciples said to him, "Where are we to get enough bread in such a desolate place to feed so great a crowd?" [34]And Jesus said to them, "How many loaves do you have?" They said, "Seven, and a few small fish." [35]And directing the crowd to sit down on the ground, [36]he took the seven loaves and the fish, and having given thanks he broke them and gave them to the disciples, and the disciples gave them to the crowds. [37]And they all ate and were satisfied. And they took up seven baskets full of the broken pieces left over. [38]Those who ate were four thousand men, besides women and children. [39]And after sending away the crowds, he got into the boat and went to the region of Magadan.

---

[1] Or is an offering [2] Some manuscripts law [3] Some manuscripts add of the blind [4] Greek is expelled into the latrine [5] Greek from that hour

JULY 6

Joshua 8

And the Lord said to Joshua, "Do not fear and do not be dismayed. Take all the fighting men with you, and arise, go up to Ai. See, I have given into your hand the king of Ai, and his people, his city, and his land. ²And you shall do to Ai and its king as you did to Jericho and its king. Only its spoil and its livestock you shall take as plunder for yourselves. Lay an ambush against the city, behind it."

³So Joshua and all the fighting men arose to go up to Ai. And Joshua chose 30,000 mighty men of valor and sent them out by night. ⁴And he commanded them, "Behold, you shall lie in ambush against the city, behind it. Do not go very far from the city, but all of you remain ready. ⁵And I and all the people who are with me will approach the city. And when they come out against us just as before, we shall flee before them. ⁶And they will come out after us, until we have drawn them away from the city. For they will say, 'They are fleeing from us, just as before.' So we will flee before them. ⁷Then you shall rise up from the ambush and seize the city, for the Lord your God will give it into your hand. ⁸And as soon as you have taken the city, you shall set the city on fire. You shall do according to the word of the Lord. See, I have commanded you." ⁹So Joshua sent them out. And they went to the place of ambush and lay between Bethel and Ai, to the west of Ai, but Joshua spent that night among the people.

¹⁰Joshua arose early in the morning and mustered the people and went up, he and the elders of Israel, before the people to Ai. ¹¹And all the fighting men who were with him went up and drew near before the city and encamped on the north side of Ai, with a ravine between them and Ai. ¹²He took about 5,000 men and set them in ambush between Bethel and Ai, to the west of the city. ¹³So they stationed the forces, the main encampment that was north of the city and its rear guard west of the city. But Joshua spent that night in the valley. ¹⁴And as soon as the king of Ai saw this, he and all his people, the men of the city, hurried and went out early to the appointed place[1] toward the Arabah to meet Israel in battle. But he did not know that there was an ambush against him behind the city. ¹⁵And Joshua and all Israel pretended to be beaten before them and fled in the direction of the wilderness. ¹⁶So all the people who were in the city were called together to pursue them, and as they pursued Joshua they were drawn away from the city. ¹⁷Not a man was left in Ai or Bethel who did not go out after Israel. They left the city open and pursued Israel.

¹⁸Then the Lord said to Joshua, "Stretch out the javelin that is in your hand toward Ai, for I will give it into your hand." And Joshua stretched out the javelin that was in his hand toward the city. ¹⁹And the men in the ambush rose quickly out of their place, and as soon as he had stretched out his hand, they ran and entered the city and captured it. And they hurried to set the city on fire. ²⁰So when the men of Ai looked back, behold, the smoke of the city went up to heaven, and they had no power to flee this way or that, for the people who fled to the wilderness turned back against the pursuers. ²¹And when Joshua and all Israel saw that the ambush had captured the city, and that the smoke of the city went up, then they turned back and struck down the men of Ai. ²²And the others came out from the city against them, so they were in the midst of Israel, some on this side, and some on that side. And Israel struck them down, until there was left none that survived or escaped. ²³But the king of Ai they took alive, and brought him near to Joshua.

²⁴When Israel had finished killing all the inhabitants of Ai in the open wilderness where they pursued them, and all of them to the very last had fallen by the edge of the sword, all Israel returned to Ai and struck it down with the edge of the sword. ²⁵And all who fell that day, both men and women, were 12,000, all the people of Ai. ²⁶But Joshua did not draw back

¹ Hebrew *appointed time*

his hand with which he stretched out the javelin until he had devoted all the inhabitants of Ai to destruction.[1] ²⁷Only the livestock and the spoil of that city Israel took as their plunder, according to the word of the LORD that he commanded Joshua. ²⁸So Joshua burned Ai and made it forever a heap of ruins, as it is to this day. ²⁹And he hanged the king of Ai on a tree until evening. And at sunset Joshua commanded, and they took his body down from the tree and threw it at the entrance of the gate of the city and raised over it a great heap of stones, which stands there to this day.

³⁰At that time Joshua built an altar to the LORD, the God of Israel, on Mount Ebal, ³¹just as Moses the servant of the LORD had commanded the people of Israel, as it is written in the Book of the Law of Moses, "an altar of uncut stones, upon which no man has wielded an iron tool." And they offered on it burnt offerings to the LORD and sacrificed peace offerings. ³²And there, in the presence of the people of Israel, he wrote on the stones a copy of the law of Moses, which he had written. ³³And all Israel, sojourner as well as native born, with their elders and officers and their judges, stood on opposite sides of the ark before the Levitical priests who carried the ark of the covenant of the LORD, half of them in front of Mount Gerizim and half of them in front of Mount Ebal, just as Moses the servant of the LORD had commanded at the first, to bless the people of Israel. ³⁴And afterward he read all the words of the law, the blessing and the curse, according to all that is written in the Book of the Law. ³⁵There was not a word of all that Moses commanded that Joshua did not read before all the assembly of Israel, and the women, and the little ones, and the sojourners who lived[2] among them.

Psalm 139

To the choirmaster. A Psalm of David.

O LORD, you have searched me and known me!
² You know when I sit down and when I rise up;
you discern my thoughts from afar.
³ You search out my path and my lying down
and are acquainted with all my ways.

⁴ Even before a word is on my tongue,
behold, O LORD, you know it altogether.
⁵ You hem me in, behind and before,
and lay your hand upon me.
⁶ Such knowledge is too wonderful for me;
it is high; I cannot attain it.

⁷ Where shall I go from your Spirit?
Or where shall I flee from your presence?
⁸ If I ascend to heaven, you are there!
If I make my bed in Sheol, you are there!
⁹ If I take the wings of the morning
and dwell in the uttermost parts of the sea,
¹⁰ even there your hand shall lead me,
and your right hand shall hold me.
¹¹ If I say, "Surely the darkness shall cover me,
and the light about me be night,"
¹² even the darkness is not dark to you;
the night is bright as the day,
for darkness is as light with you.

¹³ For you formed my inward parts;
you knitted me together in my mother's womb.
¹⁴ I praise you, for I am fearfully and wonderfully made.[3]
Wonderful are your works;
my soul knows it very well.
¹⁵ My frame was not hidden from you,
when I was being made in secret,
intricately woven in the depths of the earth.
¹⁶ Your eyes saw my unformed substance;
in your book were written, every one of them,
the days that were formed for me,
when as yet there was none of them.
¹⁷ How precious to me are your thoughts, O God!
How vast is the sum of them!
¹⁸ If I would count them, they are more than the sand.
I awake, and I am still with you.

¹⁹ Oh that you would slay the wicked, O God!
O men of blood, depart from me!

¹ That is, set apart (devoted) as an offering to the Lord (for destruction) ² Or traveled ³ Or for I am fearfully set apart

20 They speak against you with malicious
    intent;
       your enemies take your name in
       vain.[1]
21 Do I not hate those who hate you,
       O LORD?
    And do I not loathe those who rise up
       against you?
22 I hate them with complete hatred;
    I count them my enemies.
23 Search me, O God, and know my heart!
    Try me and know my thoughts![2]
24 And see if there be any grievous way in
       me,
    and lead me in the way everlasting![3]

Jeremiah 2

The word of the LORD came to me, saying,
2 "Go and proclaim in the hearing of Jerusalem, Thus says the LORD,

"I remember the devotion of your youth,
    your love as a bride,
   how you followed me in the wilderness,
    in a land not sown.
3 Israel was holy to the LORD,
    the firstfruits of his harvest.
   All who ate of it incurred guilt;
    disaster came upon them,
                   declares the LORD."

4 Hear the word of the LORD, O house of
Jacob, and all the clans of the house of Israel.
5 Thus says the LORD:

"What wrong did your fathers find
    in me
   that they went far from me,
   and went after worthlessness, and
    became worthless?
6 They did not say, 'Where is the LORD
    who brought us up from the land of
    Egypt,
   who led us in the wilderness,
    in a land of deserts and pits,
   in a land of drought and deep
    darkness,
   in a land that none passes through,
    where no man dwells?'
7 And I brought you into a plentiful land
    to enjoy its fruits and its good things.

   But when you came in, you defiled my
    land
   and made my heritage an
    abomination.
8 The priests did not say, 'Where is the
    LORD?'
   Those who handle the law did not
    know me;
   the shepherds[4] transgressed against me;
   the prophets prophesied by Baal
   and went after things that do not
    profit.

9 "Therefore I still contend with you,
                   declares the LORD,
   and with your children's children I
    will contend.
10 For cross to the coasts of Cyprus and see,
    or send to Kedar and examine with
    care;
   see if there has been such a thing.
11 Has a nation changed its gods,
    even though they are no gods?
   But my people have changed their glory
    for that which does not profit.
12 Be appalled, O heavens, at this;
    be shocked, be utterly desolate,
                   declares the LORD,
13 for my people have committed two evils:
   they have forsaken me,
    the fountain of living waters,
   and hewed out cisterns for themselves,
    broken cisterns that can hold no water.

14 "Is Israel a slave? Is he a homeborn
    servant?
   Why then has he become a prey?
15 The lions have roared against him;
    they have roared loudly.
   They have made his land a waste;
    his cities are in ruins, without
    inhabitant.
16 Moreover, the men of Memphis and
    Tahpanhes
   have shaved[5] the crown of your head.
17 Have you not brought this upon yourself
    by forsaking the LORD your God,
    when he led you in the way?
18 And now what do you gain by going to
    Egypt
   to drink the waters of the Nile?
   Or what do you gain by going to Assyria
    to drink the waters of the Euphrates?[6]

---

[1] Hebrew lacks *your name* [2] Or *cares* [3] Or *in the ancient way* (compare Jeremiah 6:16) [4] Or *rulers* [5] Hebrew *grazed* [6] Hebrew *the River*

¹⁹ Your evil will chastise you,
    and your apostasy will reprove you.
Know and see that it is evil and bitter
    for you to forsake the LORD your God;
    the fear of me is not in you,
        declares the Lord GOD of hosts.

²⁰ "For long ago I broke your yoke
    and burst your bonds;
    but you said, 'I will not serve.'
Yes, on every high hill
    and under every green tree
    you bowed down like a whore.

²¹ Yet I planted you a choice vine,
    wholly of pure seed.
How then have you turned degenerate
    and become a wild vine?

²² Though you wash yourself with lye
    and use much soap,
    the stain of your guilt is still before me,
        declares the Lord GOD.

²³ How can you say, 'I am not unclean,
    I have not gone after the Baals'?
Look at your way in the valley;
    know what you have done—
a restless young camel running here
      and there,

²⁴ a wild donkey used to the wilderness,
    in her heat sniffing the wind!
    Who can restrain her lust?
None who seek her need weary
      themselves;
    in her month they will find her.

²⁵ Keep your feet from going unshod
    and your throat from thirst.
But you said, 'It is hopeless,
    for I have loved foreigners,
    and after them I will go.'

²⁶ "As a thief is shamed when caught,
    so the house of Israel shall be shamed:
they, their kings, their officials,
    their priests, and their prophets,

²⁷ who say to a tree, 'You are my father,'
    and to a stone, 'You gave me birth.'
For they have turned their back to me,
    and not their face.
But in the time of their trouble they say,
    'Arise and save us!'

²⁸ But where are your gods
    that you made for yourself?
Let them arise, if they can save you,
    in your time of trouble;

for as many as your cities
    are your gods, O Judah.

²⁹ "Why do you contend with me?
    You have all transgressed against me,
        declares the LORD.

³⁰ In vain have I struck your children;
    they took no correction;
your own sword devoured your prophets
    like a ravening lion.

³¹ And you, O generation, behold the word
    of the LORD.
Have I been a wilderness to Israel,
    or a land of thick darkness?
Why then do my people say, 'We are free,
    we will come no more to you'?

³² Can a virgin forget her ornaments,
    or a bride her attire?
Yet my people have forgotten me
    days without number.

³³ "How well you direct your course
    to seek love!
So that even to wicked women
    you have taught your ways.

³⁴ Also on your skirts is found
    the lifeblood of the guiltless poor;
you did not find them breaking in.
    Yet in spite of all these things

³⁵ you say, 'I am innocent;
    surely his anger has turned from me.'
Behold, I will bring you to judgment
    for saying, 'I have not sinned.'

³⁶ How much you go about,
    changing your way!
You shall be put to shame by Egypt
    as you were put to shame by Assyria.

³⁷ From it too you will come away
    with your hands on your head,
for the LORD has rejected those in whom
    you trust,
    and you will not prosper by them.

Matthew 16

And the Pharisees and Sadducees came, and to test him they asked him to show them a sign from heaven. ²He answered them,[1] "When it is evening, you say, 'It will be fair weather, for the sky is red.' ³And in the morning, 'It will be stormy today, for the sky is red and threatening.' You know how to interpret the appearance of the sky, but you cannot interpret the signs of

---

¹ Some manuscripts omit the following words to the end of verse 3

the times. ⁴An evil and adulterous generation seeks for a sign, but no sign will be given to it except the sign of Jonah." So he left them and departed.

⁵When the disciples reached the other side, they had forgotten to bring any bread. ⁶Jesus said to them, "Watch and beware of the leaven of the Pharisees and Sadducees." ⁷And they began discussing it among themselves, saying, "We brought no bread." ⁸But Jesus, aware of this, said, "O you of little faith, why are you discussing among yourselves the fact that you have no bread? ⁹Do you not yet perceive? Do you not remember the five loaves for the five thousand, and how many baskets you gathered? ¹⁰Or the seven loaves for the four thousand, and how many baskets you gathered? ¹¹How is it that you fail to understand that I did not speak about bread? Beware of the leaven of the Pharisees and Sadducees." ¹²Then they understood that he did not tell them to beware of the leaven of bread, but of the teaching of the Pharisees and Sadducees.

¹³Now when Jesus came into the district of Caesarea Philippi, he asked his disciples, "Who do people say that the Son of Man is?" ¹⁴And they said, "Some say John the Baptist, others say Elijah, and others Jeremiah or one of the prophets." ¹⁵He said to them, "But who do you say that I am?" ¹⁶Simon Peter replied, "You are the Christ, the Son of the living God." ¹⁷And Jesus answered him, "Blessed are you, Simon Bar-Jonah! For flesh and blood has not revealed this to you, but my Father who is in heaven. ¹⁸And I tell you, you are Peter, and on this rock¹ I will build my church, and the gates of hell² shall not prevail against it. ¹⁹I will give you the keys of the kingdom of heaven, and whatever you bind on earth shall be bound in heaven, and whatever you loose on earth shall be loosed³ in heaven." ²⁰Then he strictly charged the disciples to tell no one that he was the Christ.

²¹From that time Jesus began to show his disciples that he must go to Jerusalem and suffer many things from the elders and chief priests and scribes, and be killed, and on the third day be raised. ²²And Peter took him aside and began to rebuke him, saying, "Far be it from you, Lord!⁴ This shall never happen to you." ²³But he turned and said to Peter, "Get behind me, Satan! You are a hindrance⁵ to me. For you are not setting your mind on the things of God, but on the things of man."

²⁴Then Jesus told his disciples, "If anyone would come after me, let him deny himself and take up his cross and follow me. ²⁵For whoever would save his life⁶ will lose it, but whoever loses his life for my sake will find it. ²⁶For what will it profit a man if he gains the whole world and forfeits his soul? Or what shall a man give in return for his soul? ²⁷For the Son of Man is going to come with his angels in the glory of his Father, and then he will repay each person according to what he has done. ²⁸Truly, I say to you, there are some standing here who will not taste death until they see the Son of Man coming in his kingdom."

JULY 7

Joshua 9

As soon as all the kings who were beyond the Jordan in the hill country and in the lowland all along the coast of the Great Sea toward Lebanon, the Hittites, the Amorites, the Canaanites, the Perizzites, the Hivites, and the Jebusites, heard of this, ²they gathered together as one to fight against Joshua and Israel.

³But when the inhabitants of Gibeon heard what Joshua had done to Jericho and to Ai, ⁴they on their part acted with cunning and went and made ready provisions and took worn-out sacks for their donkeys, and wineskins, worn-out and torn and mended, ⁵with worn-out, patched sandals on their feet, and worn-out clothes. And

¹ The Greek words for *Peter* and *rock* sound similar ² Greek *the gates of Hades* ³ Or *shall have been bound. . . shall have been loosed* ⁴ Or "[May God be] *merciful to you, Lord!*" ⁵ Greek *stumbling block* ⁶ The same Greek word can mean either *soul* or *life*, depending on the context; twice in this verse and twice in verse 26

all their provisions were dry and crumbly. ⁶And they went to Joshua in the camp at Gilgal and said to him and to the men of Israel, "We have come from a distant country, so now make a covenant with us." ⁷But the men of Israel said to the Hivites, "Perhaps you live among us; then how can we make a covenant with you?" ⁸They said to Joshua, "We are your servants." And Joshua said to them, "Who are you? And where do you come from?" ⁹They said to him, "From a very distant country your servants have come, because of the name of the LORD your God. For we have heard a report of him, and all that he did in Egypt, ¹⁰and all that he did to the two kings of the Amorites who were beyond the Jordan, to Sihon the king of Heshbon, and to Og king of Bashan, who lived in Ashtaroth. ¹¹So our elders and all the inhabitants of our country said to us, 'Take provisions in your hand for the journey and go to meet them and say to them, "We are your servants. Come now, make a covenant with us."' ¹²Here is our bread. It was still warm when we took it from our houses as our food for the journey on the day we set out to come to you, but now, behold, it is dry and crumbly. ¹³These wineskins were new when we filled them, and behold, they have burst. And these garments and sandals of ours are worn out from the very long journey." ¹⁴So the men took some of their provisions, but did not ask counsel from the LORD. ¹⁵And Joshua made peace with them and made a covenant with them, to let them live, and the leaders of the congregation swore to them.

¹⁶At the end of three days after they had made a covenant with them, they heard that they were their neighbors and that they lived among them. ¹⁷And the people of Israel set out and reached their cities on the third day. Now their cities were Gibeon, Chephirah, Beeroth, and Kiriath-jearim. ¹⁸But the people of Israel did not attack them, because the leaders of the congregation had sworn to them by the LORD, the God of Israel. Then all the congregation murmured against the leaders. ¹⁹But all the leaders said to all the congregation, "We have sworn to them by the LORD, the God of Israel, and now we may not touch them. ²⁰This we will do to them: let them live, lest wrath be upon us, because of the oath that we swore to them." ²¹And the leaders said to them, "Let them live." So they became cutters of wood

and drawers of water for all the congregation, just as the leaders had said of them.

²²Joshua summoned them, and he said to them, "Why did you deceive us, saying, 'We are very far from you,' when you dwell among us? ²³Now therefore you are cursed, and some of you shall never be anything but servants, cutters of wood and drawers of water for the house of my God." ²⁴They answered Joshua, "Because it was told to your servants for a certainty that the LORD your God had commanded his servant Moses to give you all the land and to destroy all the inhabitants of the land from before you—so we feared greatly for our lives because of you and did this thing. ²⁵And now, behold, we are in your hand. Whatever seems good and right in your sight to do to us, do it." ²⁶So he did this to them and delivered them out of the hand of the people of Israel, and they did not kill them. ²⁷But Joshua made them that day cutters of wood and drawers of water for the congregation and for the altar of the LORD, to this day, in the place that he should choose.

Psalm 140–141

TO THE CHOIRMASTER. A PSALM OF DAVID.

Deliver me, O LORD, from evil men;
preserve me from violent men,
2 who plan evil things in their heart
and stir up wars continually.
3 They make their tongue sharp as a
serpent's,
and under their lips is the venom of
asps. *Selah*

4 Guard me, O LORD, from the hands of
the wicked;
preserve me from violent men,
who have planned to trip up my feet.
5 The arrogant have hidden a trap for me,
and with cords they have spread a net;¹
beside the way they have set snares for
me. *Selah*

6 I say to the LORD, You are my God;
give ear to the voice of my pleas for
mercy, O LORD!
7 O LORD, my Lord, the strength of my
salvation,
you have covered my head in the day
of battle.

¹ Or *they have spread cords as a net*

8 Grant not, O Lord, the desires of the
  wicked;
    do not further their[1] evil plot, or they
    will be exalted!   *Selah*

9 As for the head of those who surround
  me,
    let the mischief of their lips
    overwhelm them!

10 Let burning coals fall upon them!
   Let them be cast into fire,
   into miry pits, no more to rise!

11 Let not the slanderer be established in
   the land;
     let evil hunt down the violent man
     speedily!

12 I know that the Lord will maintain the
   cause of the afflicted,
     and will execute justice for the
     needy.

13 Surely the righteous shall give thanks to
   your name;
     the upright shall dwell in your
     presence.

A Psalm of David.

O Lord, I call upon you; hasten to me!
  Give ear to my voice when I call to you!

2 Let my prayer be counted as incense
  before you,
    and the lifting up of my hands as the
    evening sacrifice!

3 Set a guard, O Lord, over my mouth;
    keep watch over the door of my lips!

4 Do not let my heart incline to any evil,
    to busy myself with wicked deeds
  in company with men who work
    iniquity,
    and let me not eat of their delicacies!

5 Let a righteous man strike me—it is a
  kindness;
    let him rebuke me—it is oil for my
    head;
    let my head not refuse it.
  Yet my prayer is continually against
    their evil deeds.

6 When their judges are thrown over the
  cliff,[2]
    then they shall hear my words, for
    they are pleasant.

7 As when one plows and breaks up the
  earth,
    so shall our bones be scattered at the
    mouth of Sheol.[3]

8 But my eyes are toward you, O God, my
  Lord;
    in you I seek refuge; leave me not
    defenseless![4]

9 Keep me from the trap that they have
  laid for me
    and from the snares of evildoers!

10 Let the wicked fall into their own nets,
   while I pass by safely.

Jeremiah 3

"If[5] a man divorces his wife
  and she goes from him
    and becomes another man's wife,
    will he return to her?
  Would not that land be greatly polluted?
  You have played the whore with many
    lovers;
    and would you return to me?
                  declares the Lord.

2 Lift up your eyes to the bare heights,
    and see!
    Where have you not been ravished?
  By the waysides you have sat awaiting
    lovers
    like an Arab in the wilderness.
  You have polluted the land
    with your vile whoredom.

3 Therefore the showers have been
    withheld,
    and the spring rain has not come;
  yet you have the forehead of a whore;
    you refuse to be ashamed.

4 Have you not just now called to me,
    'My father, you are the friend of my
    youth—

5 will he be angry forever,
    will he be indignant to the end?'
  Behold, you have spoken,
    but you have done all the evil that you
    could."

6 The Lord said to me in the days of King
Josiah: "Have you seen what she did, that
faithless one, Israel, how she went up on every
high hill and under every green tree, and there
played the whore? 7 And I thought, 'After she

[1] Hebrew *his* [2] Or *When their judges fall into the hands of the Rock* [3] The meaning of the Hebrew in verses 6, 7 is uncertain [4] Hebrew *refuge; do not pour out my life!* [5] Septuagint, Syriac; Hebrew *Saying, "If*

has done all this she will return to me,' but she did not return, and her treacherous sister Judah saw it. [8] She saw that for all the adulteries of that faithless one, Israel, I had sent her away with a decree of divorce. Yet her treacherous sister Judah did not fear, but she too went and played the whore. [9] Because she took her whoredom lightly, she polluted the land, committing adultery with stone and tree. [10] Yet for all this her treacherous sister Judah did not return to me with her whole heart, but in pretense, declares the LORD."

[11] And the LORD said to me, "Faithless Israel has shown herself more righteous than treacherous Judah. [12] Go, and proclaim these words toward the north, and say,

> "'Return, faithless Israel,
> >   declares the LORD.
> I will not look on you in anger,
> > for I am merciful,
> >   declares the LORD;
> I will not be angry forever.
> [13]   Only acknowledge your guilt,
> > that you rebelled against the LORD
> > > your God
> and scattered your favors among
> > > foreigners under every green tree,
> and that you have not obeyed my
> > > voice,
> >   declares the LORD.
> [14]   Return, O faithless children,
> >   declares the LORD;
> > for I am your master;
> I will take you, one from a city and two
> > > from a family,
> and I will bring you to Zion.

[15] "'And I will give you shepherds after my own heart, who will feed you with knowledge and understanding. [16] And when you have multiplied and been fruitful in the land, in those days, declares the LORD, they shall no more say, "The ark of the covenant of the LORD." It shall not come to mind or be remembered or missed; it shall not be made again. [17] At that time Jerusalem shall be called the throne of the LORD, and all nations shall gather to it, to the presence of the LORD in Jerusalem, and they shall no more stubbornly follow their own evil heart. [18] In those days the house of Judah shall join the house of Israel, and together they shall come from the land of the north to the land that I gave your fathers for a heritage.

> [19] "'I said,
> > How I would set you among my sons,
> > and give you a pleasant land,
> > > a heritage most beautiful of all
> > > > nations.
> > And I thought you would call me, My
> > > Father,
> > > and would not turn from following me.
> [20] Surely, as a treacherous wife leaves her
> > > husband,
> > > so have you been treacherous to me,
> > > > O house of Israel,
> > > >   declares the LORD.'"

> [21] A voice on the bare heights is heard,
> > the weeping and pleading of Israel's
> > > sons
> because they have perverted their way;
> > they have forgotten the LORD their
> > > God.
> [22] "Return, O faithless sons;
> > I will heal your faithlessness."
> "Behold, we come to you,
> > for you are the LORD our God.
> [23] Truly the hills are a delusion,
> > the orgies[1] on the mountains.
> Truly in the LORD our God
> > is the salvation of Israel.

[24] "But from our youth the shameful thing has devoured all for which our fathers labored, their flocks and their herds, their sons and their daughters. [25] Let us lie down in our shame, and let our dishonor cover us. For we have sinned against the LORD our God, we and our fathers, from our youth even to this day, and we have not obeyed the voice of the LORD our God."

Matthew 17

And after six days Jesus took with him Peter and James, and John his brother, and led them up a high mountain by themselves. [2] And he was transfigured before them, and his face shone like the sun, and his clothes became white as light. [3] And behold, there appeared to them Moses and Elijah, talking with him. [4] And Peter said to Jesus, "Lord, it is good that we are here. If you wish, I will

---

[1] Hebrew *commotion*

make three tents here, one for you and one for Moses and one for Elijah." [5] He was still speaking when, behold, a bright cloud overshadowed them, and a voice from the cloud said, "This is my beloved Son,[1] with whom I am well pleased; listen to him." [6] When the disciples heard this, they fell on their faces and were terrified. [7] But Jesus came and touched them, saying, "Rise, and have no fear." [8] And when they lifted up their eyes, they saw no one but Jesus only.

[9] And as they were coming down the mountain, Jesus commanded them, "Tell no one the vision, until the Son of Man is raised from the dead." [10] And the disciples asked him, "Then why do the scribes say that first Elijah must come?" [11] He answered, "Elijah does come, and he will restore all things. [12] But I tell you that Elijah has already come, and they did not recognize him, but did to him whatever they pleased. So also the Son of Man will certainly suffer at their hands." [13] Then the disciples understood that he was speaking to them of John the Baptist.

[14] And when they came to the crowd, a man came up to him and, kneeling before him, [15] said, "Lord, have mercy on my son, for he is an epileptic and he suffers terribly. For often he falls into the fire, and often into the water. [16] And I brought him to your disciples, and they could not heal him." [17] And Jesus answered,

"O faithless and twisted generation, how long am I to be with you? How long am I to bear with you? Bring him here to me." [18] And Jesus rebuked the demon,[2] and it[3] came out of him, and the boy was healed instantly.[4] [19] Then the disciples came to Jesus privately and said, "Why could we not cast it out?" [20] He said to them, "Because of your little faith. For truly, I say to you, if you have faith like a grain of mustard seed, you will say to this mountain, 'Move from here to there,' and it will move, and nothing will be impossible for you."[5]

[22] As they were gathering[6] in Galilee, Jesus said to them, "The Son of Man is about to be delivered into the hands of men, [23] and they will kill him, and he will be raised on the third day." And they were greatly distressed.

[24] When they came to Capernaum, the collectors of the two-drachma tax went up to Peter and said, "Does your teacher not pay the tax?" [25] He said, "Yes." And when he came into the house, Jesus spoke to him first, saying, "What do you think, Simon? From whom do kings of the earth take toll or tax? From their sons or from others?" [26] And when he said, "From others," Jesus said to him, "Then the sons are free. [27] However, not to give offense to them, go to the sea and cast a hook and take the first fish that comes up, and when you open its mouth you will find a shekel.[7] Take that and give it to them for me and for yourself."

JULY 8

Joshua 10

As soon as Adoni-zedek, king of Jerusalem, heard how Joshua had captured Ai and had devoted it to destruction,[8] doing to Ai and its king as he had done to Jericho and its king, and how the inhabitants of Gibeon had made peace with Israel and were among them, [2] he[9] feared greatly, because Gibeon was a great city, like one of the royal cities, and because it was greater than Ai, and all its men were warriors. [3] So Adoni-zedek king of Jerusalem sent to Hoham king of Hebron, to Piram king of Jarmuth, to Japhia king of Lachish, and to Debir king of Eglon, saying, [4] "Come up to me and help me, and let us strike Gibeon. For it has made peace with Joshua and with the people of Israel." [5] Then the five kings of the Amorites, the king of Jerusalem, the king of Hebron, the king of Jarmuth, the king of Lachish, and the

[1] Or my Son, my (or the) Beloved [2] Greek it [3] Greek the demon [4] Greek from that hour [5] Some manuscripts insert verse 21: But this kind never comes out except by prayer and fasting [6] Some manuscripts remained [7] Greek stater, a silver coin worth four drachmas or approximately one shekel [8] That is, set apart (devoted) as an offering to the Lord (for destruction); also verses 28, 35, 37, 39, 40 [9] One Hebrew manuscript, Vulgate (compare Syriac); most Hebrew manuscripts they

king of Eglon, gathered their forces and went up with all their armies and encamped against Gibeon and made war against it.

[6]And the men of Gibeon sent to Joshua at the camp in Gilgal, saying, "Do not relax your hand from your servants. Come up to us quickly and save us and help us, for all the kings of the Amorites who dwell in the hill country are gathered against us." [7]So Joshua went up from Gilgal, he and all the people of war with him, and all the mighty men of valor. [8]And the LORD said to Joshua, "Do not fear them, for I have given them into your hands. Not a man of them shall stand before you." [9]So Joshua came upon them suddenly, having marched up all night from Gilgal. [10]And the LORD threw them into a panic before Israel, who[1] struck them with a great blow at Gibeon and chased them by the way of the ascent of Beth-horon and struck them as far as Azekah and Makkedah. [11]And as they fled before Israel, while they were going down the ascent of Beth-horon, the LORD threw down large stones from heaven on them as far as Azekah, and they died. There were more who died because of the hailstones than the sons of Israel killed with the sword.

[12]At that time Joshua spoke to the LORD in the day when the LORD gave the Amorites over to the sons of Israel, and he said in the sight of Israel,

> "Sun, stand still at Gibeon,
>   and moon, in the Valley of Aijalon."
> [13]   And the sun stood still, and the moon
>   stopped,
>   until the nation took vengeance on
>   their enemies.

Is this not written in the Book of Jashar? The sun stopped in the midst of heaven and did not hurry to set for about a whole day. [14]There has been no day like it before or since, when the LORD heeded the voice of a man, for the LORD fought for Israel.

[15]So Joshua returned, and all Israel with him, to the camp at Gilgal.

[16]These five kings fled and hid themselves in the cave at Makkedah. [17]And it was told to Joshua, "The five kings have been found, hidden in the cave at Makkedah." [18]And Joshua said, "Roll large stones against the mouth of the cave and set men by it to guard them, [19]but do not stay there yourselves. Pursue your enemies;

attack their rear guard. Do not let them enter their cities, for the LORD your God has given them into your hand." [20]When Joshua and the sons of Israel had finished striking them with a great blow until they were wiped out, and when the remnant that remained of them had entered into the fortified cities, [21]then all the people returned safe to Joshua in the camp at Makkedah. Not a man moved his tongue against any of the people of Israel.

[22]Then Joshua said, "Open the mouth of the cave and bring those five kings out to me from the cave." [23]And they did so, and brought those five kings out to him from the cave, the king of Jerusalem, the king of Hebron, the king of Jarmuth, the king of Lachish, and the king of Eglon. [24]And when they brought those kings out to Joshua, Joshua summoned all the men of Israel and said to the chiefs of the men of war who had gone with him, "Come near; put your feet on the necks of these kings." Then they came near and put their feet on their necks. [25]And Joshua said to them, "Do not be afraid or dismayed; be strong and courageous. For thus the LORD will do to all your enemies against whom you fight." [26]And afterward Joshua struck them and put them to death, and he hanged them on five trees. And they hung on the trees until evening. [27]But at the time of the going down of the sun, Joshua commanded, and they took them down from the trees and threw them into the cave where they had hidden themselves, and they set large stones against the mouth of the cave, which remain to this very day.

[28]As for Makkedah, Joshua captured it on that day and struck it, and its king, with the edge of the sword. He devoted to destruction every person in it; he left none remaining. And he did to the king of Makkedah just as he had done to the king of Jericho.

[29]Then Joshua and all Israel with him passed on from Makkedah to Libnah and fought against Libnah. [30]And the LORD gave it also and its king into the hand of Israel. And he struck it with the edge of the sword, and every person in it; he left none remaining in it. And he did to its king as he had done to the king of Jericho.

[31]Then Joshua and all Israel with him passed on from Libnah to Lachish and laid siege to it and fought against it. [32]And the LORD gave Lachish into the hand of Israel, and he captured

---

[1] Or and he

it on the second day and struck it with the edge of the sword, and every person in it, as he had done to Libnah. ³³Then Horam king of Gezer came up to help Lachish. And Joshua struck him and his people, until he left none remaining.

³⁴Then Joshua and all Israel with him passed on from Lachish to Eglon. And they laid siege to it and fought against it. ³⁵And they captured it on that day, and struck it with the edge of the sword. And he devoted every person in it to destruction that day, as he had done to Lachish. ³⁶Then Joshua and all Israel with him went up from Eglon to Hebron. And they fought against it ³⁷and captured it and struck it with the edge of the sword, and its king and its towns, and every person in it. He left none remaining, as he had done to Eglon, and devoted it to destruction and every person in it. ³⁸Then Joshua and all Israel with him turned back to Debir and fought against it ³⁹and he captured it with its king and all its towns. And they struck them with the edge of the sword and devoted to destruction every person in it; he left none remaining. Just as he had done to Hebron and to Libnah and its king, so he did to Debir and to its king.

⁴⁰So Joshua struck the whole land, the hill country and the Negeb and the lowland and the slopes, and all their kings. He left none remaining, but devoted to destruction all that breathed, just as the LORD God of Israel commanded. ⁴¹And Joshua struck them from Kadesh-barnea as far as Gaza, and all the country of Goshen, as far as Gibeon. ⁴²And Joshua captured all these kings and their land at one time, because the LORD God of Israel fought for Israel. ⁴³Then Joshua returned, and all Israel with him, to the camp at Gilgal.

———— *Psalm 142–143* ————

A MASKIL[1] OF DAVID, WHEN HE WAS IN THE CAVE. A PRAYER.

With my voice I cry out to the LORD;
  with my voice I plead for mercy to the
    LORD.
2   I pour out my complaint before him;
    I tell my trouble before him.
3   When my spirit faints within me,
    you know my way!

[1] Probably a musical or liturgical term

In the path where I walk
  they have hidden a trap for me.
4   Look to the right and see:
    there is none who takes notice of me;
  no refuge remains to me;
    no one cares for my soul.
5   I cry to you, O LORD;
    I say, "You are my refuge,
    my portion in the land of the living."
6   Attend to my cry,
    for I am brought very low!
  Deliver me from my persecutors,
    for they are too strong for me!
7   Bring me out of prison,
    that I may give thanks to your name!
  The righteous will surround me,
    for you will deal bountifully with me.

A PSALM OF DAVID.

Hear my prayer, O LORD;
  give ear to my pleas for mercy!
    In your faithfulness answer me, in
      your righteousness!
2   Enter not into judgment with your
      servant,
    for no one living is righteous before
      you.
3   For the enemy has pursued my soul;
    he has crushed my life to the ground;
    he has made me sit in darkness like
      those long dead.
4   Therefore my spirit faints within me;
    my heart within me is appalled.
5   I remember the days of old;
    I meditate on all that you have done;
    I ponder the work of your hands.
6   I stretch out my hands to you;
    my soul thirsts for you like a parched
      land.   *Selah*
7   Answer me quickly, O LORD!
    My spirit fails!
  Hide not your face from me,
    lest I be like those who go down to the
      pit.
8   Let me hear in the morning of your
      steadfast love,
    for in you I trust.
  Make me know the way I should go,
    for to you I lift up my soul.

9 Deliver me from my enemies, O LORD!
I have fled to you for refuge.[1]
10 Teach me to do your will,
for you are my God!
Let your good Spirit lead me
on level ground!

11 For your name's sake, O LORD, preserve
my life!
In your righteousness bring my soul
out of trouble!
12 And in your steadfast love you will cut
off my enemies,
and you will destroy all the
adversaries of my soul,
for I am your servant.

─────── *Jeremiah 4* ───────

"If you return, O Israel,
                    declares the LORD,
to me you should return.
If you remove your detestable things
from my presence,
and do not waver,
2 and if you swear, 'As the LORD lives,'
in truth, in justice, and in
righteousness,
then nations shall bless themselves in
him,
and in him shall they glory."

3 For thus says the LORD to the men of Judah
and Jerusalem:

"Break up your fallow ground,
and sow not among thorns.
4 Circumcise yourselves to the LORD;
remove the foreskin of your hearts,
O men of Judah and inhabitants of
Jerusalem;
lest my wrath go forth like fire,
and burn with none to quench it,
because of the evil of your deeds."

5 Declare in Judah, and proclaim in Jerusalem,
and say,

"Blow the trumpet through the land;
cry aloud and say,
'Assemble, and let us go
into the fortified cities!'
6 Raise a standard toward Zion,
flee for safety, stay not,

for I bring disaster from the north,
and great destruction.
7 A lion has gone up from his thicket,
a destroyer of nations has set out;
he has gone out from his place
to make your land a waste;
your cities will be ruins
without inhabitant.
8 For this put on sackcloth,
lament and wail,
for the fierce anger of the LORD
has not turned back from us."

9 "In that day, declares the LORD, courage shall fail both king and officials. The priests shall be appalled and the prophets astounded." 10 Then I said, "Ah, Lord GOD, surely you have utterly deceived this people and Jerusalem, saying, 'It shall be well with you,' whereas the sword has reached their very life."

11 At that time it will be said to this people and to Jerusalem, "A hot wind from the bare heights in the desert toward the daughter of my people, not to winnow or cleanse, 12 a wind too full for this comes for me. Now it is I who speak in judgment upon them."

13 Behold, he comes up like clouds;
his chariots like the whirlwind;
his horses are swifter than eagles—
woe to us, for we are ruined!
14 O Jerusalem, wash your heart from evil,
that you may be saved.
How long shall your wicked thoughts
lodge within you?
15 For a voice declares from Dan
and proclaims trouble from Mount
Ephraim.
16 Warn the nations that he is coming;
announce to Jerusalem,
"Besiegers come from a distant land;
they shout against the cities of
Judah.
17 Like keepers of a field are they against
her all around,
because she has rebelled against me,
declares the LORD.
18 Your ways and your deeds
have brought this upon you.
This is your doom, and it is bitter;
it has reached your very heart."

[1] One Hebrew manuscript, Septuagint; most Hebrew manuscripts *To you I have covered*

19 My anguish, my anguish! I writhe in
  pain!
  Oh the walls of my heart!
  My heart is beating wildly;
  I cannot keep silent,
  for I hear the sound of the trumpet,
  the alarm of war.
20 Crash follows hard on crash;
  the whole land is laid waste.
  Suddenly my tents are laid waste,
  my curtains in a moment.
21 How long must I see the standard
  and hear the sound of the trumpet?

22 "For my people are foolish;
  they know me not;
  they are stupid children;
  they have no understanding.
  They are 'wise'—in doing evil!
  But how to do good they know not."

23 I looked on the earth, and behold, it was
    without form and void;
    and to the heavens, and they had no
    light.
24 I looked on the mountains, and behold,
    they were quaking,
    and all the hills moved to and fro.
25 I looked, and behold, there was no
    man,
    and all the birds of the air had fled.
26 I looked, and behold, the fruitful land
    was a desert,
    and all its cities were laid in ruins
    before the LORD, before his fierce
    anger.

27 For thus says the LORD, "The whole land
shall be a desolation; yet I will not make a
full end.

28 "For this the earth shall mourn,
  and the heavens above be dark;
  for I have spoken; I have purposed;
  I have not relented, nor will I turn
  back."

29 At the noise of horseman and archer
  every city takes to flight;
  they enter thickets; they climb among
  rocks;
  all the cities are forsaken,
  and no man dwells in them.

30 And you, O desolate one,
  what do you mean that you dress in
  scarlet,
  that you adorn yourself with
  ornaments of gold,
  that you enlarge your eyes with paint?
  In vain you beautify yourself.
  Your lovers despise you;
  they seek your life.
31 For I heard a cry as of a woman in labor,
  anguish as of one giving birth to her
  first child,
  the cry of the daughter of Zion gasping
  for breath,
  stretching out her hands,
  "Woe is me! I am fainting before
  murderers."

Matthew 18

At that time the disciples came to Jesus, say-ing, "Who is the greatest in the kingdom of heaven?" **2** And calling to him a child, he put him in the midst of them **3** and said, "Truly, I say to you, unless you turn and become like children, you will never enter the kingdom of heaven. **4** Whoever humbles himself like this child is the greatest in the kingdom of heaven.

5 "Whoever receives one such child in my name receives me, **6** but whoever causes one of these little ones who believe in me to sin,[1] it would be better for him to have a great millstone fastened around his neck and to be drowned in the depth of the sea.

7 "Woe to the world for temptations to sin![2] For it is necessary that temptations come, but woe to the one by whom the temptation comes! **8** And if your hand or your foot causes you to sin, cut it off and throw it away. It is better for you to enter life crippled or lame than with two hands or two feet to be thrown into the eter-nal fire. **9** And if your eye causes you to sin, tear it out and throw it away. It is better for you to enter life with one eye than with two eyes to be thrown into the hell[3] of fire.

10 "See that you do not despise one of these little ones. For I tell you that in heaven their angels always see the face of my Father who is in heaven.[4] **12** What do you think? If a man has a hundred sheep, and one of them has gone astray, does he not leave the ninety-nine on the mountains and go in search of the one

---

[1] Greek *causes. . . to stumble; also verses 8, 9* [2] Greek *stumbling blocks* [3] Greek *Gehenna* [4] Some manuscripts add verse 11: *For the Son of Man came to save the lost*

that went astray? [13]And if he finds it, truly, I say to you, he rejoices over it more than over the ninety-nine that never went astray. [14]So it is not the will of my[1] Father who is in heaven that one of these little ones should perish.

[15]"If your brother sins against you, go and tell him his fault, between you and him alone. If he listens to you, you have gained your brother. [16]But if he does not listen, take one or two others along with you, that every charge may be established by the evidence of two or three witnesses. [17]If he refuses to listen to them, tell it to the church. And if he refuses to listen even to the church, let him be to you as a Gentile and a tax collector. [18]Truly, I say to you, whatever you bind on earth shall be bound in heaven, and whatever you loose on earth shall be loosed[2] in heaven. [19]Again I say to you, if two of you agree on earth about anything they ask, it will be done for them by my Father in heaven. [20]For where two or three are gathered in my name, there am I among them."

[21]Then Peter came up and said to him, "Lord, how often will my brother sin against me, and I forgive him? As many as seven times?" [22]Jesus said to him, "I do not say to you seven times, but seventy-seven times.

[23]"Therefore the kingdom of heaven may be compared to a king who wished to settle accounts with his servants.[3] [24]When he began to settle, one was brought to him who owed him ten thousand talents.[4] [25]And since he could not pay, his master ordered him to be sold, with his wife and children and all that he had, and payment to be made. [26]So the servant[5] fell on his knees, imploring him, 'Have patience with me, and I will pay you everything.' [27]And out of pity for him, the master of that servant released him and forgave him the debt. [28]But when that same servant went out, he found one of his fellow servants who owed him a hundred denarii,[6] and seizing him, he began to choke him, saying, 'Pay what you owe.' [29]So his fellow servant fell down and pleaded with him, 'Have patience with me, and I will pay you.' [30]He refused and went and put him in prison until he should pay the debt. [31]When his fellow servants saw what had taken place, they were greatly distressed, and they went and reported to their master all that had taken place. [32]Then his master summoned him and said to him, 'You wicked servant! I forgave you all that debt because you pleaded with me. [33]And should not you have had mercy on your fellow servant, as I had mercy on you?' [34]And in anger his master delivered him to the jailers,[7] until he should pay all his debt. [35]So also my heavenly Father will do to every one of you, if you do not forgive your brother from your heart."

JULY 9

Joshua 11

When Jabin, king of Hazor, heard of this, he sent to Jobab king of Madon, and to the king of Shimron, and to the king of Achshaph, [2]and to the kings who were in the northern hill country, and in the Arabah south of Chinneroth, and in the lowland, and in Naphoth-dor on the west, [3]to the Canaanites in the east and the west, the Amorites, the Hittites, the Perizzites, and the Jebusites in the hill country, and the Hivites under Hermon in the land of Mizpah. [4]And they came out with all their troops, a great horde, in number like the sand that is on the seashore, with very many horses and chariots. [5]And all these kings joined their forces and came and encamped together at the waters of Merom to fight against Israel.

[6]And the LORD said to Joshua, "Do not be afraid of them, for tomorrow at this time I will give over all of them, slain, to Israel. You shall hamstring their horses and burn their chariots with fire." [7]So Joshua and all his warriors came suddenly against them by the waters of

[1] Some manuscripts *your* [2] Or *shall have been bound. . . shall have been loosed* [3] Greek *bondservants*; also verses 28, 31 [4] A *talent* was a monetary unit worth about twenty years' wages for a laborer [5] Greek *bondservant*; also verses 27, 28, 29, 32, 33 [6] A *denarius* was a day's wage for a laborer [7] Greek *torturers*

Merom and fell upon them. ⁸And the Lord gave them into the hand of Israel, who struck them and chased them as far as Great Sidon and Misrephoth-maim, and eastward as far as the Valley of Mizpeh. And they struck them until he left none remaining. ⁹And Joshua did to them just as the Lord said to him: he hamstrung their horses and burned their chariots with fire.

¹⁰And Joshua turned back at that time and captured Hazor and struck its king with the sword, for Hazor formerly was the head of all those kingdoms. ¹¹And they struck with the sword all who were in it, devoting them to destruction;[1] there was none left that breathed. And he burned Hazor with fire. ¹²And all the cities of those kings, and all their kings, Joshua captured, and struck them with the edge of the sword, devoting them to destruction, just as Moses the servant of the Lord had commanded. ¹³But none of the cities that stood on mounds did Israel burn, except Hazor alone; that Joshua burned. ¹⁴And all the spoil of these cities and the livestock, the people of Israel took for their plunder. But every person they struck with the edge of the sword until they had destroyed them, and they did not leave any who breathed. ¹⁵Just as the Lord had commanded Moses his servant, so Moses commanded Joshua, and so Joshua did. He left nothing undone of all that the Lord had commanded Moses.

¹⁶So Joshua took all that land, the hill country and all the Negeb and all the land of Goshen and the lowland and the Arabah and the hill country of Israel and its lowland ¹⁷from Mount Halak, which rises toward Seir, as far as Baalgad in the Valley of Lebanon below Mount Hermon. And he captured all their kings and struck them and put them to death. ¹⁸Joshua made war a long time with all those kings. ¹⁹There was not a city that made peace with the people of Israel except the Hivites, the inhabitants of Gibeon. They took them all in battle. ²⁰For it was the Lord's doing to harden their hearts that they should come against Israel in battle, in order that they should be devoted to destruction and should receive no mercy but be destroyed, just as the Lord commanded Moses.

²¹And Joshua came at that time and cut off the Anakim from the hill country, from Hebron, from Debir, from Anab, and from all the hill country of Judah, and from all the hill country of Israel. Joshua devoted them to destruction with their cities. ²²There was none of the Anakim left in the land of the people of Israel. Only in Gaza, in Gath, and in Ashdod did some remain. ²³So Joshua took the whole land, according to all that the Lord had spoken to Moses. And Joshua gave it for an inheritance to Israel according to their tribal allotments. And the land had rest from war.

Psalm 144

Of David.

B lessed be the Lord, my rock,
who trains my hands for war,
and my fingers for battle;
2 he is my steadfast love and my fortress,
my stronghold and my deliverer,
my shield and he in whom I take
refuge,
who subdues peoples[2] under me.

3 O Lord, what is man that you regard
him,
or the son of man that you think of
him?
4 Man is like a breath;
his days are like a passing shadow.

5 Bow your heavens, O Lord, and come
down!
Touch the mountains so that they
smoke!
6 Flash forth the lightning and scatter
them;
send out your arrows and rout them!
7 Stretch out your hand from on high;
rescue me and deliver me from the
many waters,
from the hand of foreigners,
8 whose mouths speak lies
and whose right hand is a right hand
of falsehood.

9 I will sing a new song to you, O God;
upon a ten-stringed harp I will play to
you,
10 who gives victory to kings,
who rescues David his servant from
the cruel sword.
11 Rescue me and deliver me
from the hand of foreigners,

---

[1] That is, setting apart (devoting) as an offering to the Lord (for destruction); also verses 12, 20, 21 [2] Many Hebrew manuscripts, Dead Sea Scroll, Jerome, Syriac, Aquila; most Hebrew manuscripts *subdues my people*

whose mouths speak lies
and whose right hand is a right hand
of falsehood.
12 May our sons in their youth
be like plants full grown,
our daughters like corner pillars
cut for the structure of a palace;
13 may our granaries be full,
providing all kinds of produce;
may our sheep bring forth thousands
and ten thousands in our fields;
14 may our cattle be heavy with young,
suffering no mishap or failure in
bearing;[1]
may there be no cry of distress in our
streets!
15 Blessed are the people to whom such
blessings fall!
Blessed are the people whose God is
the LORD!

Jeremiah 5

Run to and fro through the streets of
Jerusalem,
look and take note!
Search her squares to see
if you can find a man,
one who does justice
and seeks truth,
that I may pardon her.
2 Though they say, "As the LORD lives,"
yet they swear falsely.
3 O LORD, do not your eyes look for truth?
You have struck them down,
but they felt no anguish;
you have consumed them,
but they refused to take correction.
They have made their faces harder than
rock;
they have refused to repent.
4 Then I said, "These are only the poor;
they have no sense;
for they do not know the way of the
LORD,
the justice of their God.
5 I will go to the great
and will speak to them,
for they know the way of the LORD,
the justice of their God."

But they all alike had broken the yoke;
they had burst the bonds.
6 Therefore a lion from the forest shall
strike them down;
a wolf from the desert shall devastate
them.
A leopard is watching their cities;
everyone who goes out of them shall
be torn in pieces,
because their transgressions are many,
their apostasies are great.
7 "How can I pardon you?
Your children have forsaken me
and have sworn by those who are no
gods.
When I fed them to the full,
they committed adultery
and trooped to the houses of whores.
8 They were well-fed, lusty stallions,
each neighing for his neighbor's wife.
9 Shall I not punish them for these things?
declares the LORD;
and shall I not avenge myself
on a nation such as this?
10 "Go up through her vine rows and
destroy,
but make not a full end;
strip away her branches,
for they are not the LORD's.
11 For the house of Israel and the house of
Judah
have been utterly treacherous to me,
declares the LORD.
12 They have spoken falsely of the LORD
and have said, 'He will do nothing;
no disaster will come upon us,
nor shall we see sword or famine.
13 The prophets will become wind;
the word is not in them.
Thus shall it be done to them!'"
14 Therefore thus says the LORD, the God
of hosts:
"Because you have spoken this word,
behold, I am making my words in your
mouth a fire,
and this people wood, and the fire
shall consume them.
15 Behold, I am bringing against you
a nation from afar, O house of Israel,
declares the LORD.

[1] Hebrew with no breaking in or going out

It is an enduring nation;
   it is an ancient nation,
a nation whose language you do not
   know,
   nor can you understand what they say.
16 Their quiver is like an open tomb;
   they are all mighty warriors.
17 They shall eat up your harvest and your
   food;
   they shall eat up your sons and your
     daughters;
   they shall eat up your flocks and your
     herds;
   they shall eat up your vines and your
     fig trees;
   your fortified cities in which you trust
   they shall beat down with the sword."

18 "But even in those days, declares the LORD, I will not make a full end of you. 19 And when your people say, 'Why has the LORD our God done all these things to us?' you shall say to them, 'As you have forsaken me and served foreign gods in your land, so you shall serve foreigners in a land that is not yours.'"

20 Declare this in the house of Jacob;
   proclaim it in Judah:
21 "Hear this, O foolish and senseless
     people,
   who have eyes, but see not,
   who have ears, but hear not.
22 Do you not fear me? declares the LORD.
   Do you not tremble before me?
I placed the sand as the boundary for
     the sea,
   a perpetual barrier that it cannot pass;
though the waves toss, they cannot
     prevail;
   though they roar, they cannot pass
     over it.
23 But this people has a stubborn and
     rebellious heart;
   they have turned aside and gone away.
24 They do not say in their hearts,
   'Let us fear the LORD our God,
who gives the rain in its season,
   the autumn rain and the spring rain,
and keeps for us
   the weeks appointed for the harvest.'
25 Your iniquities have turned these away,
   and your sins have kept good from
     you.

26 For wicked men are found among my
     people;
   they lurk like fowlers lying in wait.[1]
They set a trap;
   they catch men.
27 Like a cage full of birds,
   their houses are full of deceit;
therefore they have become great and
     rich;
28   they have grown fat and sleek.
They know no bounds in deeds of evil;
   they judge not with justice
the cause of the fatherless, to make it
     prosper,
   and they do not defend the rights of
     the needy.
29 Shall I not punish them for these things?
               declares the LORD,
   and shall I not avenge myself
   on a nation such as this?"

30 An appalling and horrible thing
   has happened in the land:
31   the prophets prophesy falsely,
   and the priests rule at their direction;
my people love to have it so,
   but what will you do when the end
     comes?

Matthew 19

Now when Jesus had finished these sayings, he went away from Galilee and entered the region of Judea beyond the Jordan. 2 And large crowds followed him, and he healed them there.

3 And Pharisees came up to him and tested him by asking, "Is it lawful to divorce one's wife for any cause?" 4 He answered, "Have you not read that he who created them from the beginning made them male and female, 5 and said, 'Therefore a man shall leave his father and his mother and hold fast to his wife, and the two shall become one flesh'? 6 So they are no longer two but one flesh. What therefore God has joined together, let not man separate." 7 They said to him, "Why then did Moses command one to give a certificate of divorce and to send her away?" 8 He said to them, "Because of your hardness of heart Moses allowed you to divorce your wives, but from the beginning it was not so. 9 And I say to you: whoever divorces

his wife, except for sexual immorality, and marries another, commits adultery."[1]

[10] The disciples said to him, "If such is the case of a man with his wife, it is better not to marry." [11] But he said to them, "Not everyone can receive this saying, but only those to whom it is given. [12] For there are eunuchs who have been so from birth, and there are eunuchs who have been made eunuchs by men, and there are eunuchs who have made themselves eunuchs for the sake of the kingdom of heaven. Let the one who is able to receive this receive it."

[13] Then children were brought to him that he might lay his hands on them and pray. The disciples rebuked the people, [14] but Jesus said, "Let the little children come to me and do not hinder them, for to such belongs the kingdom of heaven." [15] And he laid his hands on them and went away.

[16] And behold, a man came up to him, saying, "Teacher, what good deed must I do to have eternal life?" [17] And he said to him, "Why do you ask me about what is good? There is only one who is good. If you would enter life, keep the commandments." [18] He said to him, "Which ones?" And Jesus said, "You shall not murder, You shall not commit adultery, You shall not steal, You shall not bear false witness, [19] Honor your father and mother, and, You shall love your neighbor as yourself." [20] The young man said to him, "All these I have kept. What do I still lack?" [21] Jesus said to him, "If you would be perfect, go, sell what you possess and give to the poor, and you will have treasure in heaven; and come, follow me." [22] When the young man heard this he went away sorrowful, for he had great possessions.

[23] And Jesus said to his disciples, "Truly, I say to you, only with difficulty will a rich person enter the kingdom of heaven. [24] Again I tell you, it is easier for a camel to go through the eye of a needle than for a rich person to enter the kingdom of God." [25] When the disciples heard this, they were greatly astonished, saying, "Who then can be saved?" [26] But Jesus looked at them and said, "With man this is impossible, but with God all things are possible." [27] Then Peter said in reply, "See, we have left everything and followed you. What then will we have?" [28] Jesus said to them, "Truly, I say to you, in the new world,[2] when the Son of Man will sit on his glorious throne, you who have followed me will also sit on twelve thrones, judging the twelve tribes of Israel. [29] And everyone who has left houses or brothers or sisters or father or mother or children or lands, for my name's sake, will receive a hundredfold[3] and will inherit eternal life. [30] But many who are first will be last, and the last first.

JULY 10

Joshua 12–13

Now these are the kings of the land whom the people of Israel defeated and took possession of their land beyond the Jordan toward the sunrise, from the Valley of the Arnon to Mount Hermon, with all the Arabah eastward: [2] Sihon king of the Amorites who lived at Heshbon and ruled from Aroer, which is on the edge of the Valley of the Arnon, and from the middle of the valley as far as the river Jabbok, the boundary of the Ammonites, that is, half of Gilead, [3] and the Arabah to the Sea of Chinneroth eastward, and in the direction of Beth-jeshimoth, to the Sea of the Arabah, the Salt Sea, southward to the foot of the slopes of Pisgah; [4] and Og[4] king of Bashan, one of the remnant of the Rephaim, who lived at Ashtaroth and at Edrei [5] and ruled over Mount Hermon and Salecah and all Bashan to the boundary of the Geshurites and the Maacathites, and over half of Gilead to the boundary of Sihon king of Heshbon. [6] Moses, the servant of the LORD, and the people of Israel defeated them. And Moses

[1] Some manuscripts add *and whoever marries a divorced woman commits adultery*; other manuscripts *except for sexual immorality, makes her commit adultery, and whoever marries a divorced woman commits adultery* [2] Greek *in the regeneration* [3] Some manuscripts *manifold* [4] Septuagint; Hebrew *the boundary of Og*

the servant of the LORD gave their land for a possession to the Reubenites and the Gadites and the half-tribe of Manasseh.

⁷And these are the kings of the land whom Joshua and the people of Israel defeated on the west side of the Jordan, from Baal-gad in the Valley of Lebanon to Mount Halak, that rises toward Seir (and Joshua gave their land to the tribes of Israel as a possession according to their allotments, ⁸in the hill country, in the lowland, in the Arabah, in the slopes, in the wilderness, and in the Negeb, the land of the Hittites, the Amorites, the Canaanites, the Perizzites, the Hivites, and the Jebusites): ⁹the king of Jericho, one; the king of Ai, which is beside Bethel, one; ¹⁰the king of Jerusalem, one; the king of Hebron, one; ¹¹the king of Jarmuth, one; the king of Lachish, one; ¹²the king of Eglon, one; the king of Gezer, one; ¹³the king of Debir, one; the king of Geder, one; ¹⁴the king of Hormah, one; the king of Arad, one; ¹⁵the king of Libnah, one; the king of Adullam, one; ¹⁶the king of Makkedah, one; the king of Bethel, one; ¹⁷the king of Tappuah, one; the king of Hepher, one; ¹⁸the king of Aphek, one; the king of Lasharon, one; ¹⁹the king of Madon, one; the king of Hazor, one; ²⁰the king of Shimron-meron, one; the king of Achshaph, one; ²¹the king of Taanach, one; the king of Megiddo, one; ²²the king of Kedesh, one; the king of Jokneam in Carmel, one; ²³the king of Dor in Naphath-dor, one; the king of Goiim in Galilee,¹ one; ²⁴the king of Tirzah, one: in all, thirty-one kings.

¹³:¹ Now Joshua was old and advanced in years, and the LORD said to him, "You are old and advanced in years, and there remains yet very much land to possess. ²This is the land that yet remains: all the regions of the Philistines, and all those of the Geshurites ³(from the Shihor, which is east of Egypt, northward to the boundary of Ekron, it is counted as Canaanite; there are five rulers of the Philistines, those of Gaza, Ashdod, Ashkelon, Gath, and Ekron), and those of the Avvim, ⁴in the south, all the land of the Canaanites, and Mearah that belongs to the Sidonians, to Aphek, to the boundary of the Amorites, ⁵and the land of the Gebalites, and all Lebanon, toward the sunrise, from Baal-gad below Mount Hermon to Lebo-hamath, ⁶all the inhabitants of the hill country from Lebanon to Misrephoth-maim, even all the Sidonians.

I myself will drive them out from before the people of Israel. Only allot the land to Israel for an inheritance, as I have commanded you. ⁷Now therefore divide this land for an inheritance to the nine tribes and half the tribe of Manasseh."

⁸With the other half of the tribe of Manasseh² the Reubenites and the Gadites received their inheritance, which Moses gave them, beyond the Jordan eastward, as Moses the servant of the LORD gave them: ⁹from Aroer, which is on the edge of the Valley of the Arnon, and the city that is in the middle of the valley, and all the tableland of Medeba as far as Dibon; ¹⁰and all the cities of Sihon king of the Amorites, who reigned in Heshbon, as far as the boundary of the Ammonites; ¹¹and Gilead, and the region of the Geshurites and Maacathites, and all Mount Hermon, and all Bashan to Salecah; ¹²all the kingdom of Og in Bashan, who reigned in Ashtaroth and in Edrei (he alone was left of the remnant of the Rephaim); these Moses had struck and driven out. ¹³Yet the people of Israel did not drive out the Geshurites or the Maacathites, but Geshur and Maacath dwell in the midst of Israel to this day.

¹⁴To the tribe of Levi alone Moses gave no inheritance. The offerings by fire to the LORD God of Israel are their inheritance, as he said to him.

¹⁵And Moses gave an inheritance to the tribe of the people of Reuben according to their clans. ¹⁶So their territory was from Aroer, which is on the edge of the Valley of the Arnon, and the city that is in the middle of the valley, and all the tableland by Medeba; ¹⁷with Heshbon, and all its cities that are in the tableland; Dibon, and Bamoth-baal, and Beth-baal-meon, ¹⁸and Jahaz, and Kedemoth, and Mephaath, ¹⁹and Kiriathaim, and Sibmah, and Zereth-shahar on the hill of the valley, ²⁰and Beth-peor, and the slopes of Pisgah, and Beth-jeshimoth, ²¹that is, all the cities of the tableland, and all the kingdom of Sihon king of the Amorites, who reigned in Heshbon, whom Moses defeated with the leaders of Midian, Evi and Rekem and Zur and Hur and Reba, the princes of Sihon, who lived in the land. ²²Balaam also, the son of Beor, the one who practiced divination, was killed with the sword by the people of Israel among the rest of their slain. ²³And the border of the people of Reuben was the Jordan as a boundary. This was the inheritance of the

¹ Septuagint; Hebrew *Gilgal* ² Hebrew *With it*

people of Reuben, according to their clans with their cities and villages.

²⁴ Moses gave an inheritance also to the tribe of Gad, to the people of Gad, according to their clans. ²⁵ Their territory was Jazer, and all the cities of Gilead, and half the land of the Ammonites, to Aroer, which is east of Rabbah, ²⁶ and from Heshbon to Ramath-mizpeh and Betonim, and from Mahanaim to the territory of Debir,[1] ²⁷ and in the valley Beth-haram, Beth-nimrah, Succoth, and Zaphon, the rest of the kingdom of Sihon king of Heshbon, having the Jordan as a boundary, to the lower end of the Sea of Chinnereth, eastward beyond the Jordan. ²⁸ This is the inheritance of the people of Gad according to their clans, with their cities and villages.

²⁹ And Moses gave an inheritance to the half-tribe of Manasseh. It was allotted to the half-tribe of the people of Manasseh according to their clans. ³⁰ Their region extended from Mahanaim, through all Bashan, the whole kingdom of Og king of Bashan, and all the towns of Jair, which are in Bashan, sixty cities, ³¹ and half Gilead, and Ashtaroth, and Edrei, the cities of the kingdom of Og in Bashan. These were allotted to the people of Machir the son of Manasseh for the half of the people of Machir according to their clans.

³² These are the inheritances that Moses distributed in the plains of Moab, beyond the Jordan east of Jericho. ³³ But to the tribe of Levi Moses gave no inheritance; the LORD God of Israel is their inheritance, just as he said to them.

Psalm 145[2]

A SONG OF PRAISE. OF DAVID.

I will extol you, my God and King,
    and bless your name forever and ever.
2   Every day I will bless you
    and praise your name forever and ever.
3   Great is the LORD, and greatly to be praised,
    and his greatness is unsearchable.
4   One generation shall commend your works to another,
    and shall declare your mighty acts.
5   On the glorious splendor of your majesty,
    and on your wondrous works, I will meditate.

6   They shall speak of the might of your awesome deeds,
    and I will declare your greatness.
7   They shall pour forth the fame of your abundant goodness
    and shall sing aloud of your righteousness.

8   The LORD is gracious and merciful,
    slow to anger and abounding in steadfast love.
9   The LORD is good to all,
    and his mercy is over all that he has made.

10 All your works shall give thanks to you, O LORD,
    and all your saints shall bless you!
11 They shall speak of the glory of your kingdom
    and tell of your power,
12 to make known to the children of man your[3] mighty deeds,
    and the glorious splendor of your kingdom.
13 Your kingdom is an everlasting kingdom,
    and your dominion endures throughout all generations.

[The LORD is faithful in all his words
    and kind in all his works.][4]
14 The LORD upholds all who are falling
    and raises up all who are bowed down.
15 The eyes of all look to you,
    and you give them their food in due season.
16 You open your hand;
    you satisfy the desire of every living thing.
17 The LORD is righteous in all his ways
    and kind in all his works.
18 The LORD is near to all who call on him,
    to all who call on him in truth.
19 He fulfills the desire of those who fear him;
    he also hears their cry and saves them.
20 The LORD preserves all who love him,
    but all the wicked he will destroy.

21 My mouth will speak the praise of the LORD,
    and let all flesh bless his holy name forever and ever.

---

[1] Septuagint, Syriac, Vulgate; Hebrew *Lidebir* [2] This psalm is an acrostic poem, each verse beginning with the successive letters of the Hebrew alphabet [3] Hebrew *his*; also next line [4] These two lines are supplied by one Hebrew manuscript, Septuagint, Syriac (compare Dead Sea Scroll)

--------- *Jeremiah 6* ---------

Flee for safety, O people of Benjamin,
   from the midst of Jerusalem!
     Blow the trumpet in Tekoa,
        and raise a signal on Beth-haccherem,
     for disaster looms out of the north,
     and great destruction.
2 The lovely and delicately bred I will
       destroy,
     the daughter of Zion.[1]
3 Shepherds with their flocks shall come
       against her;
     they shall pitch their tents around her;
     they shall pasture, each in his place.
4 "Prepare war against her;
     arise, and let us attack at noon!
   Woe to us, for the day declines,
     for the shadows of evening lengthen!
5 Arise, and let us attack by night
     and destroy her palaces!"

6 For thus says the Lord of hosts:
  "Cut down her trees;
     cast up a siege mound against
       Jerusalem.
   This is the city that must be punished;
     there is nothing but oppression
       within her.
7 As a well keeps its water fresh,
     so she keeps fresh her evil;
   violence and destruction are heard
     within her;
     sickness and wounds are ever before
       me.
8 Be warned, O Jerusalem,
     lest I turn from you in disgust,
   lest I make you a desolation,
     an uninhabited land."

9 Thus says the Lord of hosts:
  "They shall glean thoroughly as a vine
     the remnant of Israel;
   like a grape gatherer pass your hand
     again
     over its branches."
10 To whom shall I speak and give warning,
     that they may hear?
   Behold, their ears are uncircumcised,
     they cannot listen;
   behold, the word of the Lord is to them
     an object of scorn;
     they take no pleasure in it.

11 Therefore I am full of the wrath of the
     Lord;
     I am weary of holding it in.
  "Pour it out upon the children in the
     street,
     and upon the gatherings of young
       men, also;
   both husband and wife shall be taken,
     the elderly and the very aged.
12 Their houses shall be turned over to
     others,
     their fields and wives together,
   for I will stretch out my hand
     against the inhabitants of the land,"
                declares the Lord.
13 "For from the least to the greatest of
     them,
     everyone is greedy for unjust gain;
   and from prophet to priest,
     everyone deals falsely.
14 They have healed the wound of my
     people lightly,
     saying, 'Peace, peace,'
     when there is no peace.
15 Were they ashamed when they
     committed abomination?
     No, they were not at all ashamed;
     they did not know how to blush.
   Therefore they shall fall among those
     who fall;
     at the time that I punish them, they
       shall be overthrown,"
                says the Lord.

16 Thus says the Lord:
  "Stand by the roads, and look,
     and ask for the ancient paths,
   where the good way is; and walk in it,
     and find rest for your souls.
   But they said, 'We will not walk in it.'
17 I set watchmen over you, saying,
     'Pay attention to the sound of the
       trumpet!'
   But they said, 'We will not pay
     attention.'
18 Therefore hear, O nations,
     and know, O congregation, what will
     happen to them.
19 Hear, O earth; behold, I am bringing
     disaster upon this people,
     the fruit of their devices,

[1] Or *I have likened the daughter of Zion to the loveliest pasture*

because they have not paid attention to
my words;
and as for my law, they have rejected it.

20 What use to me is frankincense that
comes from Sheba,
or sweet cane from a distant land?
Your burnt offerings are not acceptable,
nor your sacrifices pleasing to me.

21 Therefore thus says the LORD:
'Behold, I will lay before this people
stumbling blocks against which they
shall stumble;
fathers and sons together,
neighbor and friend shall perish.'"

22 Thus says the LORD:
"Behold, a people is coming from the
north country,
a great nation is stirring from the
farthest parts of the earth.

23 They lay hold on bow and javelin;
they are cruel and have no mercy;
the sound of them is like the roaring
sea;
they ride on horses,
set in array as a man for battle,
against you, O daughter of Zion!"

24 We have heard the report of it;
our hands fall helpless;
anguish has taken hold of us,
pain as of a woman in labor.

25 Go not out into the field,
nor walk on the road,
for the enemy has a sword;
terror is on every side.

26 O daughter of my people, put on
sackcloth,
and roll in ashes;
make mourning as for an only son,
most bitter lamentation,
for suddenly the destroyer
will come upon us.

27 "I have made you a tester of metals
among my people,
that you may know and test their ways.

28 They are all stubbornly rebellious,
going about with slanders;
they are bronze and iron;
all of them act corruptly.

29 The bellows blow fiercely;
the lead is consumed by the fire;

in vain the refining goes on,
for the wicked are not removed.

30 Rejected silver they are called,
for the LORD has rejected them."

--- *Matthew 20* ---

"For the kingdom of heaven is like a master of a house who went out early in the morning to hire laborers for his vineyard. [2]After agreeing with the laborers for a denarius[1] a day, he sent them into his vineyard. [3]And going out about the third hour he saw others standing idle in the marketplace, [4]and to them he said, 'You go into the vineyard too, and whatever is right I will give you.' [5]So they went. Going out again about the sixth hour and the ninth hour, he did the same. [6]And about the eleventh hour he went out and found others standing. And he said to them, 'Why do you stand here idle all day?' [7]They said to him, 'Because no one has hired us.' He said to them, 'You go into the vineyard too.' [8]And when evening came, the owner of the vineyard said to his foreman, 'Call the laborers and pay them their wages, beginning with the last, up to the first.' [9]And when those hired about the eleventh hour came, each of them received a denarius. [10]Now when those hired first came, they thought they would receive more, but each of them also received a denarius. [11]And on receiving it they grumbled at the master of the house, [12]saying, 'These last worked only one hour, and you have made them equal to us who have borne the burden of the day and the scorching heat.' [13]But he replied to one of them, 'Friend, I am doing you no wrong. Did you not agree with me for a denarius? [14]Take what belongs to you and go. I choose to give to this last worker as I give to you. [15]Am I not allowed to do what I choose with what belongs to me? Or do you begrudge my generosity?'[2] [16]So the last will be first, and the first last."

[17]And as Jesus was going up to Jerusalem, he took the twelve disciples aside, and on the way he said to them, [18]"See, we are going up to Jerusalem. And the Son of Man will be delivered over to the chief priests and scribes, and they will condemn him to death [19]and deliver him over to the Gentiles to be mocked and flogged and crucified, and he will be raised on the third day."

---

[1] A *denarius* was a day's wage for a laborer   [2] Or *is your eye bad because I am good?*

²⁰Then the mother of the sons of Zebedee came up to him with her sons, and kneeling before him she asked him for something. ²¹And he said to her, "What do you want?" She said to him, "Say that these two sons of mine are to sit, one at your right hand and one at your left, in your kingdom." ²²Jesus answered, "You do not know what you are asking. Are you able to drink the cup that I am to drink?" They said to him, "We are able." ²³He said to them, "You will drink my cup, but to sit at my right hand and at my left is not mine to grant, but it is for those for whom it has been prepared by my Father." ²⁴And when the ten heard it, they were indignant at the two brothers. ²⁵But Jesus called them to him and said, "You know that the rulers of the Gentiles lord it over them, and their great ones exercise authority over them. ²⁶It shall not be so among you. But whoever would be great among you must be your servant,¹ ²⁷and whoever would be first among you must be your slave,² ²⁸even as the Son of Man came not to be served but to serve, and to give his life as a ransom for many."

²⁹And as they went out of Jericho, a great crowd followed him. ³⁰And behold, there were two blind men sitting by the roadside, and when they heard that Jesus was passing by, they cried out, "Lord,³ have mercy on us, Son of David!" ³¹The crowd rebuked them, telling them to be silent, but they cried out all the more, "Lord, have mercy on us, Son of David!" ³²And stopping, Jesus called them and said, "What do you want me to do for you?" ³³They said to him, "Lord, let our eyes be opened." ³⁴And Jesus in pity touched their eyes, and immediately they recovered their sight and followed him.

JULY 11

Joshua 14–15

These are the inheritances that the people of Israel received in the land of Canaan, which Eleazar the priest and Joshua the son of Nun and the heads of the fathers' houses of the tribes of the people of Israel gave them to inherit. ²Their inheritance was by lot, just as the LORD had commanded by the hand of Moses for the nine and one-half tribes. ³For Moses had given an inheritance to the two and one-half tribes beyond the Jordan, but to the Levites he gave no inheritance among them. ⁴For the people of Joseph were two tribes, Manasseh and Ephraim. And no portion was given to the Levites in the land, but only cities to dwell in, with their pasturelands for their livestock and their substance. ⁵The people of Israel did as the LORD commanded Moses; they allotted the land.

⁶Then the people of Judah came to Joshua at Gilgal. And Caleb the son of Jephunneh the Kenizzite said to him, "You know what the LORD said to Moses the man of God in Kadesh-barnea concerning you and me. ⁷I was forty years old when Moses the servant of the LORD sent me from Kadesh-barnea to spy out the land, and I brought him word again as it was in my heart. ⁸But my brothers who went up with me made the heart of the people melt; yet I wholly followed the LORD my God. ⁹And Moses swore on that day, saying, 'Surely the land on which your foot has trodden shall be an inheritance for you and your children forever, because you have wholly followed the LORD my God.' ¹⁰And now, behold, the LORD has kept me alive, just as he said, these forty-five years since the time that the LORD spoke this word to Moses, while Israel walked in the wilderness. And now, behold, I am this day eighty-five years old. ¹¹I am still as strong today as I was in the day that Moses sent me; my strength now is as my strength was then, for war and for going and coming. ¹²So now give me this hill country of which the LORD spoke on that day, for you heard on that day how the Anakim were there, with great

¹ Greek *diakonos* ² Greek *bondservant* (*doulos*) ³ Some manuscripts omit *Lord*

fortified cities. It may be that the LORD will be with me, and I shall drive them out just as the LORD said."

[13] Then Joshua blessed him, and he gave Hebron to Caleb the son of Jephunneh for an inheritance. [14] Therefore Hebron became the inheritance of Caleb the son of Jephunneh the Kenizzite to this day, because he wholly followed the LORD, the God of Israel. [15] Now the name of Hebron formerly was Kiriath-arba.[1] (Arba[2] was the greatest man among the Anakim.) And the land had rest from war.

[15:1] The allotment for the tribe of the people of Judah according to their clans reached southward to the boundary of Edom, to the wilderness of Zin at the farthest south. [2] And their south boundary ran from the end of the Salt Sea, from the bay that faces southward. [3] It goes out southward of the ascent of Akrabbim, passes along to Zin, and goes up south of Kadesh-barnea, along by Hezron, up to Addar, turns about to Karka, [4] passes along to Azmon, goes out by the Brook of Egypt, and comes to its end at the sea. This shall be your south boundary. [5] And the east boundary is the Salt Sea, to the mouth of the Jordan. And the boundary on the north side runs from the bay of the sea at the mouth of the Jordan. [6] And the boundary goes up to Beth-hoglah and passes along north of Beth-arabah. And the boundary goes up to the stone of Bohan the son of Reuben. [7] And the boundary goes up to Debir from the Valley of Achor, and so northward, turning toward Gilgal, which is opposite the ascent of Adummim, which is on the south side of the valley. And the boundary passes along to the waters of En-shemesh and ends at En-rogel. [8] Then the boundary goes up by the Valley of the Son of Hinnom at the southern shoulder of the Jebusite (that is, Jerusalem). And the boundary goes up to the top of the mountain that lies over against the Valley of Hinnom, on the west, at the northern end of the Valley of Rephaim. [9] Then the boundary extends from the top of the mountain to the spring of the waters of Nephtoah, and from there to the cities of Mount Ephron. Then the boundary bends around to Baalah (that is, Kiriath-jearim). [10] And the boundary circles west of Baalah to Mount Seir, passes along to the northern shoulder of Mount Jearim (that is, Chesalon), and goes down to Beth-shemesh and passes along by Timnah. [11] The boundary goes out to the shoulder of the hill north of Ekron, then the boundary bends around to Shikkeron and passes along to Mount Baalah and goes out to Jabneel. Then the boundary comes to an end at the sea. [12] And the west boundary was the Great Sea with its coastline. This is the boundary around the people of Judah according to their clans.

[13] According to the commandment of the LORD to Joshua, he gave to Caleb the son of Jephunneh a portion among the people of Judah, Kiriath-arba, that is, Hebron (Arba was the father of Anak). [14] And Caleb drove out from there the three sons of Anak, Sheshai and Ahiman and Talmai, the descendants of Anak. [15] And he went up from there against the inhabitants of Debir. Now the name of Debir formerly was Kiriath-sepher. [16] And Caleb said, "Whoever strikes Kiriath-sepher and captures it, to him will I give Achsah my daughter as wife." [17] And Othniel the son of Kenaz, the brother of Caleb, captured it. And he gave him Achsah his daughter as wife. [18] When she came to him, she urged him to ask her father for a field. And she got off her donkey, and Caleb said to her, "What do you want?" [19] She said to him, "Give me a blessing. Since you have given me the land of the Negeb, give me also springs of water." And he gave her the upper springs and the lower springs.

[20] This is the inheritance of the tribe of the people of Judah according to their clans. [21] The cities belonging to the tribe of the people of Judah in the extreme south, toward the boundary of Edom, were Kabzeel, Eder, Jagur, [22] Kinah, Dimonah, Adadah, [23] Kedesh, Hazor, Ithnan, [24] Ziph, Telem, Bealoth, [25] Hazor-hadattah, Kerioth-hezron (that is, Hazor), [26] Amam, Shema, Moladah, [27] Hazar-gaddah, Heshmon, Beth-pelet, [28] Hazar-shual, Beersheba, Biziothiah, [29] Baalah, Iim, Ezem, [30] Eltolad, Chesil, Hormah, [31] Ziklag, Madmannah, Sansannah, [32] Lebaoth, Shilhim, Ain, and Rimmon: in all, twenty-nine cities with their villages.

[33] And in the lowland, Eshtaol, Zorah, Ashnah, [34] Zanoah, En-gannim, Tappuah, Enam, [35] Jarmuth, Adullam, Socoh, Azekah, [36] Shaaraim, Adithaim, Gederah, Gederothaim: fourteen cities with their villages.

[37] Zenan, Hadashah, Migdal-gad, [38] Dilean, Mizpeh, Joktheel, [39] Lachish, Bozkath, Eglon,

---

[1] *Kiriath-arba* means *the city of Arba* [2] Hebrew *He*

⁴⁰Cabbon, Lahmam, Chitlish, ⁴¹Gederoth, Beth-dagon, Naamah, and Makkedah: sixteen cities with their villages.

⁴²Libnah, Ether, Ashan, ⁴³Iphtah, Ashnah, Nezib, ⁴⁴Keilah, Achzib, and Mareshah: nine cities with their villages.

⁴⁵Ekron, with its towns and its villages; ⁴⁶from Ekron to the sea, all that were by the side of Ashdod, with their villages.

⁴⁷Ashdod, its towns and its villages; Gaza, its towns and its villages; to the Brook of Egypt, and the Great Sea with its coastline.

⁴⁸And in the hill country, Shamir, Jattir, Socoh, ⁴⁹Dannah, Kiriath-sannah (that is, Debir), ⁵⁰Anab, Eshtemoh, Anim, ⁵¹Goshen, Holon, and Giloh: eleven cities with their villages.

⁵²Arab, Dumah, Eshan, ⁵³Janim, Beth-tappuah, Aphekah, ⁵⁴Humtah, Kiriath-arba (that is, Hebron), and Zior: nine cities with their villages.

⁵⁵Maon, Carmel, Ziph, Juttah, ⁵⁶Jezreel, Jokdeam, Zanoah, ⁵⁷Kain, Gibeah, and Timnah: ten cities with their villages.

⁵⁸Halhul, Beth-zur, Gedor, ⁵⁹Maarath, Beth-anoth, and Eltekon: six cities with their villages.

⁶⁰Kiriath-baal (that is, Kiriath-jearim), and Rabbah: two cities with their villages.

⁶¹In the wilderness, Beth-arabah, Middin, Secacah, ⁶²Nibshan, the City of Salt, and En-gedi: six cities with their villages.

⁶³But the Jebusites, the inhabitants of Jerusalem, the people of Judah could not drive out, so the Jebusites dwell with the people of Judah at Jerusalem to this day.

—— *Psalm 146–147* ——

Praise the LORD!
Praise the LORD, O my soul!
2   I will praise the LORD as long as I live;
        I will sing praises to my God while I
            have my being.

3   Put not your trust in princes,
        in a son of man, in whom there is no
            salvation.
4   When his breath departs, he returns to
            the earth;
        on that very day his plans perish.

5   Blessed is he whose help is the God of
            Jacob,
        whose hope is in the LORD his God,

6   who made heaven and earth,
        the sea, and all that is in them,
    who keeps faith forever;
7   who executes justice for the
            oppressed,
        who gives food to the hungry.

    The LORD sets the prisoners free;
8   the LORD opens the eyes of the blind.
    The LORD lifts up those who are bowed
            down;
        the LORD loves the righteous.
9   The LORD watches over the sojourners;
        he upholds the widow and the
            fatherless,
        but the way of the wicked he brings to
            ruin.

10 The LORD will reign forever,
        your God, O Zion, to all generations.
    Praise the LORD!

Praise the LORD!
For it is good to sing praises to our God;
    for it is pleasant,¹ and a song of praise
        is fitting.
2   The LORD builds up Jerusalem;
        he gathers the outcasts of Israel.
3   He heals the brokenhearted
        and binds up their wounds.
4   He determines the number of the stars;
        he gives to all of them their names.
5   Great is our Lord, and abundant in
            power;
        his understanding is beyond measure.
6   The LORD lifts up the humble;²
        he casts the wicked to the ground.

7   Sing to the LORD with thanksgiving;
        make melody to our God on the lyre!
8   He covers the heavens with clouds;
        he prepares rain for the earth;
        he makes grass grow on the hills.
9   He gives to the beasts their food,
        and to the young ravens that cry.
10 His delight is not in the strength of the
            horse,
        nor his pleasure in the legs of a man,
11 but the LORD takes pleasure in those
            who fear him,
        in those who hope in his steadfast love.

12 Praise the LORD, O Jerusalem!
        Praise your God, O Zion!

¹ Or *for he is beautiful*   ² Or *afflicted*

¹³ For he strengthens the bars of your gates;
    he blesses your children within you.
¹⁴ He makes peace in your borders;
    he fills you with the finest of the
        wheat.
¹⁵ He sends out his command to the earth;
    his word runs swiftly.
¹⁶ He gives snow like wool;
    he scatters frost like ashes.
¹⁷ He hurls down his crystals of ice like
        crumbs;
    who can stand before his cold?
¹⁸ He sends out his word, and melts them;
    he makes his wind blow and the
        waters flow.
¹⁹ He declares his word to Jacob,
    his statutes and rules[1] to Israel.
²⁰ He has not dealt thus with any other
        nation;
    they do not know his rules.[2]
    Praise the Lord!

Jeremiah 7

The word that came to Jeremiah from the Lord: ² "Stand in the gate of the Lord's house, and proclaim there this word, and say, Hear the word of the Lord, all you men of Judah who enter these gates to worship the Lord. ³ Thus says the Lord of hosts, the God of Israel: Amend your ways and your deeds, and I will let you dwell in this place. ⁴ Do not trust in these deceptive words: 'This is the temple of the Lord, the temple of the Lord, the temple of the Lord.'

⁵ "For if you truly amend your ways and your deeds, if you truly execute justice one with another, ⁶ if you do not oppress the sojourner, the fatherless, or the widow, or shed innocent blood in this place, and if you do not go after other gods to your own harm, ⁷ then I will let you dwell in this place, in the land that I gave of old to your fathers forever.

⁸ "Behold, you trust in deceptive words to no avail. ⁹ Will you steal, murder, commit adultery, swear falsely, make offerings to Baal, and go after other gods that you have not known, ¹⁰ and then come and stand before me in this house, which is called by my name, and say, 'We are delivered!'—only to go on doing all these abominations? ¹¹ Has this house, which is called by my name, become a den of robbers

in your eyes? Behold, I myself have seen it, declares the Lord. ¹² Go now to my place that was in Shiloh, where I made my name dwell at first, and see what I did to it because of the evil of my people Israel. ¹³ And now, because you have done all these things, declares the Lord, and when I spoke to you persistently you did not listen, and when I called you, you did not answer, ¹⁴ therefore I will do to the house that is called by my name, and in which you trust, and to the place that I gave to you and to your fathers, as I did to Shiloh. ¹⁵ And I will cast you out of my sight, as I cast out all your kinsmen, all the offspring of Ephraim.

¹⁶ "As for you, do not pray for this people, or lift up a cry or prayer for them, and do not intercede with me, for I will not hear you. ¹⁷ Do you not see what they are doing in the cities of Judah and in the streets of Jerusalem? ¹⁸ The children gather wood, the fathers kindle fire, and the women knead dough, to make cakes for the queen of heaven. And they pour out drink offerings to other gods, to provoke me to anger. ¹⁹ Is it I whom they provoke? declares the Lord. Is it not themselves, to their own shame? ²⁰ Therefore thus says the Lord God: Behold, my anger and my wrath will be poured out on this place, upon man and beast, upon the trees of the field and the fruit of the ground; it will burn and not be quenched."

²¹ Thus says the Lord of hosts, the God of Israel: "Add your burnt offerings to your sacrifices, and eat the flesh. ²² For in the day that I brought them out of the land of Egypt, I did not speak to your fathers or command them concerning burnt offerings and sacrifices. ²³ But this command I gave them: 'Obey my voice, and I will be your God, and you shall be my people. And walk in all the way that I command you, that it may be well with you.' ²⁴ But they did not obey or incline their ear, but walked in their own counsels and the stubbornness of their evil hearts, and went backward and not forward. ²⁵ From the day that your fathers came out of the land of Egypt to this day, I have persistently sent all my servants the prophets to them, day after day. ²⁶ Yet they did not listen to me or incline their ear, but stiffened their neck. They did worse than their fathers.

²⁷ "So you shall speak all these words to them, but they will not listen to you. You shall call to them, but they will not answer you. ²⁸ And you

¹ Or and just decrees ² Or his just decrees

shall say to them, 'This is the nation that did not obey the voice of the LORD their God, and did not accept discipline; truth has perished; it is cut off from their lips.

29 "'Cut off your hair and cast it away;
      raise a lamentation on the bare heights,
   for the LORD has rejected and forsaken
      the generation of his wrath.'

30 "For the sons of Judah have done evil in my sight, declares the LORD. They have set their detestable things in the house that is called by my name, to defile it. 31 And they have built the high places of Topheth, which is in the Valley of the Son of Hinnom, to burn their sons and their daughters in the fire, which I did not command, nor did it come into my mind. 32 Therefore, behold, the days are coming, declares the LORD, when it will no more be called Topheth, or the Valley of the Son of Hinnom, but the Valley of Slaughter; for they will bury in Topheth, because there is no room elsewhere. 33 And the dead bodies of this people will be food for the birds of the air, and for the beasts of the earth, and none will frighten them away. 34 And I will silence in the cities of Judah and in the streets of Jerusalem the voice of mirth and the voice of gladness, the voice of the bridegroom and the voice of the bride, for the land shall become a waste.

Matthew 21

Now when they drew near to Jerusalem and came to Bethphage, to the Mount of Olives, then Jesus sent two disciples, 2 saying to them, "Go into the village in front of you, and immediately you will find a donkey tied, and a colt with her. Untie them and bring them to me. 3 If anyone says anything to you, you shall say, 'The Lord needs them,' and he will send them at once." 4 This took place to fulfill what was spoken by the prophet, saying,

5   "Say to the daughter of Zion,
       'Behold, your king is coming to you,
         humble, and mounted on a donkey,
         on a colt,[1] the foal of a beast of
            burden.'"

6 The disciples went and did as Jesus had directed them. 7 They brought the donkey and

the colt and put on them their cloaks, and he sat on them. 8 Most of the crowd spread their cloaks on the road, and others cut branches from the trees and spread them on the road. 9 And the crowds that went before him and that followed him were shouting, "Hosanna to the Son of David! Blessed is he who comes in the name of the Lord! Hosanna in the highest!" 10 And when he entered Jerusalem, the whole city was stirred up, saying, "Who is this?" 11 And the crowds said, "This is the prophet Jesus, from Nazareth of Galilee."

12 And Jesus entered the temple[2] and drove out all who sold and bought in the temple, and he overturned the tables of the money-changers and the seats of those who sold pigeons. 13 He said to them, "It is written, 'My house shall be called a house of prayer,' but you make it a den of robbers."

14 And the blind and the lame came to him in the temple, and he healed them. 15 But when the chief priests and the scribes saw the wonderful things that he did, and the children crying out in the temple, "Hosanna to the Son of David!" they were indignant, 16 and they said to him, "Do you hear what these are saying?" And Jesus said to them, "Yes; have you never read,

   "'Out of the mouth of infants and nursing
         babies
      you have prepared praise'?"

17 And leaving them, he went out of the city to Bethany and lodged there.

18 In the morning, as he was returning to the city, he became hungry. 19 And seeing a fig tree by the wayside, he went to it and found nothing on it but only leaves. And he said to it, "May no fruit ever come from you again!" And the fig tree withered at once.

20 When the disciples saw it, they marveled, saying, "How did the fig tree wither at once?" 21 And Jesus answered them, "Truly, I say to you, if you have faith and do not doubt, you will not only do what has been done to the fig tree, but even if you say to this mountain, 'Be taken up and thrown into the sea,' it will happen. 22 And whatever you ask in prayer, you will receive, if you have faith."

23 And when he entered the temple, the chief priests and the elders of the people came up to him as he was teaching, and said, "By what authority are you doing these things, and who

[1] Or donkey, and on a colt, [2] Some manuscripts add of God

gave you this authority?" ²⁴Jesus answered them, "I also will ask you one question, and if you tell me the answer, then I also will tell you by what authority I do these things. ²⁵The baptism of John, from where did it come? From heaven or from man?" And they discussed it among themselves, saying, "If we say, 'From heaven,' he will say to us, 'Why then did you not believe him?' ²⁶But if we say, 'From man,' we are afraid of the crowd, for they all hold that John was a prophet." ²⁷So they answered Jesus, "We do not know." And he said to them, "Neither will I tell you by what authority I do these things.

²⁸"What do you think? A man had two sons. And he went to the first and said, 'Son, go and work in the vineyard today.' ²⁹And he answered, 'I will not,' but afterward he changed his mind and went. ³⁰And he went to the other son and said the same. And he answered, 'I go, sir,' but did not go. ³¹Which of the two did the will of his father?" They said, "The first." Jesus said to them, "Truly, I say to you, the tax collectors and the prostitutes go into the kingdom of God before you. ³²For John came to you in the way of righteousness, and you did not believe him, but the tax collectors and the prostitutes believed him. And even when you saw it, you did not afterward change your minds and believe him.

³³"Hear another parable. There was a master of a house who planted a vineyard and put a fence around it and dug a winepress in it and built a tower and leased it to tenants, and went into another country. ³⁴When the season for fruit drew near, he sent his servants[1] to the tenants to get his fruit. ³⁵And the tenants took his servants and beat one, killed another, and stoned another. ³⁶Again he sent other servants, more than the first. And they did the same to them. ³⁷Finally he sent his son to them, saying, 'They will respect my son.' ³⁸But when the tenants saw the son, they said to themselves, 'This is the heir. Come, let us kill him and have his inheritance.' ³⁹And they took him and threw him out of the vineyard and killed him. ⁴⁰When therefore the owner of the vineyard comes, what will he do to those tenants?" ⁴¹They said to him, "He will put those wretches to a miserable death and let out the vineyard to other tenants who will give him the fruits in their seasons."

⁴²Jesus said to them, "Have you never read in the Scriptures:

" 'The stone that the builders rejected
　　has become the cornerstone;[2]
this was the Lord's doing,
　　and it is marvelous in our eyes'?

⁴³Therefore I tell you, the kingdom of God will be taken away from you and given to a people producing its fruits. ⁴⁴And the one who falls on this stone will be broken to pieces; and when it falls on anyone, it will crush him."[3]

⁴⁵When the chief priests and the Pharisees heard his parables, they perceived that he was speaking about them. ⁴⁶And although they were seeking to arrest him, they feared the crowds, because they held him to be a prophet.

JULY 12

Joshua 16–17

The allotment of the people of Joseph went from the Jordan by Jericho, east of the waters of Jericho, into the wilderness, going up from Jericho into the hill country to Bethel. ²Then going from Bethel to Luz, it passes along to Ataroth, the territory of the Archites. ³Then it goes down westward to the territory of the Japhletites, as far as the territory of Lower Beth-horon, then to Gezer, and it ends at the sea.

⁴The people of Joseph, Manasseh and Ephraim, received their inheritance. ⁵The territory of the people of Ephraim by their clans was as follows: the boundary of their inheritance on the east was Ataroth-addar as

[1] Greek bondservants; also verses 35, 36 [2] Greek the head of the corner [3] Some manuscripts omit verse 44

far as Upper Beth-horon, [6] and the boundary goes from there to the sea. On the north is Michmethath. Then on the east the boundary turns around toward Taanath-shiloh and passes along beyond it on the east to Janoah, [7] then it goes down from Janoah to Ataroth and to Naarah, and touches Jericho, ending at the Jordan. [8] From Tappuah the boundary goes westward to the brook Kanah and ends at the sea. Such is the inheritance of the tribe of the people of Ephraim by their clans, [9] together with the towns that were set apart for the people of Ephraim within the inheritance of the Manassites, all those towns with their villages. [10] However, they did not drive out the Canaanites who lived in Gezer, so the Canaanites have lived in the midst of Ephraim to this day but have been made to do forced labor.

[17:1] Then allotment was made to the people of Manasseh, for he was the firstborn of Joseph. To Machir the firstborn of Manasseh, the father of Gilead, were allotted Gilead and Bashan, because he was a man of war. [2] And allotments were made to the rest of the people of Manasseh by their clans, Abiezer, Helek, Asriel, Shechem, Hepher, and Shemida. These were the male descendants of Manasseh the son of Joseph, by their clans.

[3] Now Zelophehad the son of Hepher, son of Gilead, son of Machir, son of Manasseh, had no sons, but only daughters, and these are the names of his daughters: Mahlah, Noah, Hoglah, Milcah, and Tirzah. [4] They approached Eleazar the priest and Joshua the son of Nun and the leaders and said, "The LORD commanded Moses to give us an inheritance along with our brothers." So according to the mouth of the LORD he gave them an inheritance among the brothers of their father. [5] Thus there fell to Manasseh ten portions, besides the land of Gilead and Bashan, which is on the other side of the Jordan, [6] because the daughters of Manasseh received an inheritance along with his sons. The land of Gilead was allotted to the rest of the people of Manasseh.

[7] The territory of Manasseh reached from Asher to Michmethath, which is east of Shechem. Then the boundary goes along southward to the inhabitants of En-tappuah. [8] The land of Tappuah belonged to Manasseh, but the town of Tappuah on the boundary of Manasseh belonged to the people of Ephraim. [9] Then the boundary went down to the brook Kanah. These cities, to the south of the brook, among the cities of Manasseh, belong to Ephraim. Then the boundary of Manasseh goes on the north side of the brook and ends at the sea, [10] the land to the south being Ephraim's and that to the north being Manasseh's, with the sea forming its boundary. On the north Asher is reached, and on the east Issachar. [11] Also in Issachar and in Asher Manasseh had Beth-shean and its villages, and Ibleam and its villages, and the inhabitants of Dor and its villages, and the inhabitants of En-dor and its villages, and the inhabitants of Taanach and its villages, and the inhabitants of Megiddo and its villages; the third is Naphath.[1] [12] Yet the people of Manasseh could not take possession of those cities, but the Canaanites persisted in dwelling in that land. [13] Now when the people of Israel grew strong, they put the Canaanites to forced labor, but did not utterly drive them out.

[14] Then the people of Joseph spoke to Joshua, saying, "Why have you given me but one lot and one portion as an inheritance, although I am a numerous people, since all along the LORD has blessed me?" [15] And Joshua said to them, "If you are a numerous people, go up by yourselves to the forest, and there clear ground for yourselves in the land of the Perizzites and the Rephaim, since the hill country of Ephraim is too narrow for you." [16] The people of Joseph said, "The hill country is not enough for us. Yet all the Canaanites who dwell in the plain have chariots of iron, both those in Beth-shean and its villages and those in the Valley of Jezreel." [17] Then Joshua said to the house of Joseph, to Ephraim and Manasseh, "You are a numerous people and have great power. You shall not have one allotment only, [18] but the hill country shall be yours, for though it is a forest, you shall clear it and possess it to its farthest borders. For you shall drive out the Canaanites, though they have chariots of iron, and though they are strong."

—————— *Psalm 148* ——————

Praise the LORD!
  Praise the LORD from the heavens;
    praise him in the heights!
[2]   Praise him, all his angels;
    praise him, all his hosts!

[1] The meaning of the Hebrew is uncertain

3 Praise him, sun and moon,
   praise him, all you shining stars!
4 Praise him, you highest heavens,
   and you waters above the heavens!
5 Let them praise the name of the LORD!
     For he commanded and they were
       created.
6 And he established them forever and
     ever;
   he gave a decree, and it shall not pass
     away.[1]
7 Praise the LORD from the earth,
     you great sea creatures and all deeps,
8 fire and hail, snow and mist,
     stormy wind fulfilling his word!
9 Mountains and all hills,
     fruit trees and all cedars!
10 Beasts and all livestock,
     creeping things and flying birds!
11 Kings of the earth and all peoples,
     princes and all rulers of the earth!
12 Young men and maidens together,
     old men and children!
13 Let them praise the name of the LORD,
     for his name alone is exalted;
     his majesty is above earth and heaven.
14 He has raised up a horn for his people,
     praise for all his saints,
     for the people of Israel who are near
       to him.
   Praise the LORD!

Jeremiah 8

"At that time, declares the LORD, the bones of the kings of Judah, the bones of its officials, the bones of the priests, the bones of the prophets, and the bones of the inhabitants of Jerusalem shall be brought out of their tombs. ²And they shall be spread before the sun and the moon and all the host of heaven, which they have loved and served, which they have gone after, and which they have sought and worshiped. And they shall not be gathered or buried. They shall be as dung on the surface of the ground. ³Death shall be preferred to life by all the remnant that remains of this evil family in all the places where I have driven them, declares the LORD of hosts.

4 "You shall say to them, Thus says the
     LORD:
   When men fall, do they not rise again?
     If one turns away, does he not return?
5 Why then has this people turned away
     in perpetual backsliding?
   They hold fast to deceit;
     they refuse to return.
6 I have paid attention and listened,
     but they have not spoken rightly;
   no man relents of his evil,
     saying, 'What have I done?'
   Everyone turns to his own course,
     like a horse plunging headlong into
       battle.
7 Even the stork in the heavens
     knows her times,
   and the turtledove, swallow, and crane[2]
     keep the time of their coming,
   but my people know not
     the rules[3] of the LORD.

8 "How can you say, 'We are wise,
     and the law of the LORD is with us'?
   But behold, the lying pen of the scribes
     has made it into a lie.
9 The wise men shall be put to shame;
     they shall be dismayed and taken;
   behold, they have rejected the word of
       the LORD,
     so what wisdom is in them?
10 Therefore I will give their wives to
       others
     and their fields to conquerors,
   because from the least to the greatest
     everyone is greedy for unjust gain;
   from prophet to priest,
     everyone deals falsely.
11 They have healed the wound of my
       people lightly,
     saying, 'Peace, peace,'
       when there is no peace.
12 Were they ashamed when they
       committed abomination?
   No, they were not at all ashamed;
     they did not know how to blush.
   Therefore they shall fall among the
       fallen;
     when I punish them, they shall be
       overthrown,
       says the LORD.

---

[1] Or it shall not be transgressed   [2] The meaning of the Hebrew word is uncertain   [3] Or just decrees

13 When I would gather them, declares the
  LORD,
    there are no grapes on the vine,
      nor figs on the fig tree;
    even the leaves are withered,
      and what I gave them has passed away
        from them."[1]

14 Why do we sit still?
  Gather together; let us go into the
    fortified cities
      and perish there,
  for the LORD our God has doomed us to
    perish
      and has given us poisoned water to
        drink,
  because we have sinned against the
    LORD.

15 We looked for peace, but no good came;
  for a time of healing, but behold,
    terror.

16 "The snorting of their horses is heard
    from Dan;
  at the sound of the neighing of their
    stallions
      the whole land quakes.
  They come and devour the land and all
    that fills it,
  the city and those who dwell in it.

17 For behold, I am sending among you
    serpents,
  adders that cannot be charmed,
  and they shall bite you,"
                    declares the LORD.

18 My joy is gone; grief is upon me;[2]
  my heart is sick within me.

19 Behold, the cry of the daughter of my
    people
  from the length and breadth of the
    land:
"Is the LORD not in Zion?
  Is her King not in her?"
"Why have they provoked me to anger
  with their carved images
  and with their foreign idols?"

20 "The harvest is past, the summer is ended,
  and we are not saved."

21 For the wound of the daughter of my
    people is my heart wounded;
  I mourn, and dismay has taken hold
    on me.

22 Is there no balm in Gilead?
    Is there no physician there?
  Why then has the health of the daughter
      of my people
    not been restored?

Matthew 22

And again Jesus spoke to them in parables, saying, [2]"The kingdom of heaven may be compared to a king who gave a wedding feast for his son, [3]and sent his servants[3] to call those who were invited to the wedding feast, but they would not come. [4]Again he sent other servants, saying, 'Tell those who are invited, "See, I have prepared my dinner, my oxen and my fat calves have been slaughtered, and everything is ready. Come to the wedding feast."' [5]But they paid no attention and went off, one to his farm, another to his business, [6]while the rest seized his servants, treated them shamefully, and killed them. [7]The king was angry, and he sent his troops and destroyed those murderers and burned their city. [8]Then he said to his servants, 'The wedding feast is ready, but those invited were not worthy. [9]Go therefore to the main roads and invite to the wedding feast as many as you find.' [10]And those servants went out into the roads and gathered all whom they found, both bad and good. So the wedding hall was filled with guests.

[11]"But when the king came in to look at the guests, he saw there a man who had no wedding garment. [12]And he said to him, 'Friend, how did you get in here without a wedding garment?' And he was speechless. [13]Then the king said to the attendants, 'Bind him hand and foot and cast him into the outer darkness. In that place there will be weeping and gnashing of teeth.' [14]For many are called, but few are chosen."

[15]Then the Pharisees went and plotted how to entangle him in his words. [16]And they sent their disciples to him, along with the Herodians, saying, "Teacher, we know that you are true and teach the way of God truthfully, and you do not care about anyone's opinion, for you are not swayed by appearances.[4] [17]Tell us, then, what you think. Is it lawful to pay taxes to Caesar, or not?" [18]But Jesus, aware of their malice, said, "Why put me to the test, you hypocrites? [19]Show me the coin for the tax."

---

[1] The meaning of the Hebrew is uncertain [2] Compare Septuagint; the meaning of the Hebrew is uncertain [3] Greek *bondservants*; also verses 4, 6, 8, 10 [4] Greek *for you do not look at people's faces*

And they brought him a denarius.[1] [20]And Jesus said to them, "Whose likeness and inscription is this?" [21]They said, "Caesar's." Then he said to them, "Therefore render to Caesar the things that are Caesar's, and to God the things that are God's." [22]When they heard it, they marveled. And they left him and went away.

[23]The same day Sadducees came to him, who say that there is no resurrection, and they asked him a question, [24]saying, "Teacher, Moses said, 'If a man dies having no children, his brother must marry the widow and raise up offspring for his brother.' [25]Now there were seven brothers among us. The first married and died, and having no offspring left his wife to his brother. [26]So too the second and third, down to the seventh. [27]After them all, the woman died. [28]In the resurrection, therefore, of the seven, whose wife will she be? For they all had her."

[29]But Jesus answered them, "You are wrong, because you know neither the Scriptures nor the power of God. [30]For in the resurrection they neither marry nor are given in marriage, but are like angels in heaven. [31]And as for the resurrection of the dead, have you not read what was said to you by God: [32]'I am the God of Abraham, and the God of Isaac, and the God of Jacob'? He is not God of the dead, but of the living." [33]And when the crowd heard it, they were astonished at his teaching.

[34]But when the Pharisees heard that he had silenced the Sadducees, they gathered together. [35]And one of them, a lawyer, asked him a question to test him. [36]"Teacher, which is the great commandment in the Law?" [37]And he said to him, "You shall love the Lord your God with all your heart and with all your soul and with all your mind. [38]This is the great and first commandment. [39]And a second is like it: You shall love your neighbor as yourself. [40]On these two commandments depend all the Law and the Prophets."

[41]Now while the Pharisees were gathered together, Jesus asked them a question, [42]saying, "What do you think about the Christ? Whose son is he?" They said to him, "The son of David." [43]He said to them, "How is it then that David, in the Spirit, calls him Lord, saying,

[44] "'The Lord said to my Lord,
  "Sit at my right hand,
    until I put your enemies under your feet"'?

[45]If then David calls him Lord, how is he his son?" [46]And no one was able to answer him a word, nor from that day did anyone dare to ask him any more questions.

JULY 13

Joshua 18–19

Then the whole congregation of the people of Israel assembled at Shiloh and set up the tent of meeting there. The land lay subdued before them.

[2]There remained among the people of Israel seven tribes whose inheritance had not yet been apportioned. [3]So Joshua said to the people of Israel, "How long will you put off going in to take possession of the land, which the LORD, the God of your fathers, has given you? [4]Provide three men from each tribe, and I will send them out that they may set out and go up and down the land. They shall write a description of it with a view to their inheritances, and then come to me. [5]They shall divide it into seven portions. Judah shall continue in his territory on the south, and the house of Joseph shall continue in their territory on the north. [6]And you shall describe the land in seven divisions and bring the description here to me. And I will cast lots for you here before the LORD our God. [7]The Levites have no portion among you, for the priesthood of the LORD is their heritage. And Gad and Reuben and half the tribe

[1] A denarius was a day's wage for a laborer

of Manasseh have received their inheritance beyond the Jordan eastward, which Moses the servant of the LORD gave them."

⁸So the men arose and went, and Joshua charged those who went to write the description of the land, saying, "Go up and down in the land and write a description and return to me. And I will cast lots for you here before the LORD in Shiloh." ⁹So the men went and passed up and down in the land and wrote in a book a description of it by towns in seven divisions. Then they came to Joshua to the camp at Shiloh, ¹⁰and Joshua cast lots for them in Shiloh before the LORD. And there Joshua apportioned the land to the people of Israel, to each his portion.

¹¹The lot of the tribe of the people of Benjamin according to its clans came up, and the territory allotted to it fell between the people of Judah and the people of Joseph. ¹²On the north side their boundary began at the Jordan. Then the boundary goes up to the shoulder north of Jericho, then up through the hill country westward, and it ends at the wilderness of Beth-aven. ¹³From there the boundary passes along southward in the direction of Luz, to the shoulder of Luz (that is, Bethel), then the boundary goes down to Ataroth-addar, on the mountain that lies south of Lower Beth-horon. ¹⁴Then the boundary goes in another direction, turning on the western side southward from the mountain that lies to the south, opposite Beth-horon, and it ends at Kiriath-baal (that is, Kiriath-jearim), a city belonging to the people of Judah. This forms the western side. ¹⁵And the southern side begins at the outskirts of Kiriath-jearim. And the boundary goes from there to Ephron,[1] to the spring of the waters of Nephtoah. ¹⁶Then the boundary goes down to the border of the mountain that overlooks the Valley of the Son of Hinnom, which is at the north end of the Valley of Rephaim. And it then goes down the Valley of Hinnom, south of the shoulder of the Jebusites, and downward to En-rogel. ¹⁷Then it bends in a northerly direction going on to En-shemesh, and from there goes to Geliloth, which is opposite the ascent of Adummim. Then it goes down to the stone of Bohan the son of Reuben, ¹⁸and passing on to the north of the shoulder of Beth-arabah[2] it goes down to the Arabah. ¹⁹Then the boundary passes on to the north of the shoulder of Beth-hoglah.

And the boundary ends at the northern bay of the Salt Sea, at the south end of the Jordan: this is the southern border. ²⁰The Jordan forms its boundary on the eastern side. This is the inheritance of the people of Benjamin, according to their clans, boundary by boundary all around.

²¹Now the cities of the tribe of the people of Benjamin according to their clans were Jericho, Beth-hoglah, Emek-keziz, ²²Beth-arabah, Zemaraim, Bethel, ²³Avvim, Parah, Ophrah, ²⁴Chephar-ammoni, Ophni, Geba—twelve cities with their villages: ²⁵Gibeon, Ramah, Beeroth, ²⁶Mizpeh, Chephirah, Mozah, ²⁷Rekem, Irpeel, Taralah, ²⁸Zela, Haeleph, Jebus[3] (that is, Jerusalem), Gibeah[4] and Kiriath-jearim[5]—fourteen cities with their villages. This is the inheritance of the people of Benjamin according to its clans.

¹⁹:¹The second lot came out for Simeon, for the tribe of the people of Simeon, according to their clans, and their inheritance was in the midst of the inheritance of the people of Judah. ²And they had for their inheritance Beersheba, Sheba, Moladah, ³Hazar-shual, Balah, Ezem, ⁴Eltolad, Bethul, Hormah, ⁵Ziklag, Beth-marcaboth, Hazar-susah, ⁶Beth-lebaoth, and Sharuhen—thirteen cities with their villages; ⁷Ain, Rimmon, Ether, and Ashan—four cities with their villages, ⁸together with all the villages around these cities as far as Baalath-beer, Ramah of the Negeb. This was the inheritance of the tribe of the people of Simeon according to their clans. ⁹The inheritance of the people of Simeon formed part of the territory of the people of Judah. Because the portion of the people of Judah was too large for them, the people of Simeon obtained an inheritance in the midst of their inheritance.

¹⁰The third lot came up for the people of Zebulun, according to their clans. And the territory of their inheritance reached as far as Sarid. ¹¹Then their boundary goes up westward and on to Mareal and touches Dabbesheth, then the brook that is east of Jokneam. ¹²From Sarid it goes in the other direction eastward toward the sunrise to the boundary of Chisloth-tabor. From there it goes to Daberath, then up to Japhia. ¹³From there it passes along on the east toward the sunrise to Gath-hepher, to Eth-kazin, and going on to Rimmon it bends toward Neah, ¹⁴then on the north the boundary turns

---

[1] See 15:9; Hebrew *westward* [2] Septuagint; Hebrew *to the shoulder over against the Arabah* [3] Septuagint, Syriac, Vulgate; Hebrew *the Jebusite* [4] Hebrew *Gibeath* [5] Septuagint; Hebrew *Kiriath*

about to Hannathon, and it ends at the Valley of Iphtahel; [15] and Kattath, Nahalal, Shimron, Idalah, and Bethlehem—twelve cities with their villages. [16] This is the inheritance of the people of Zebulun, according to their clans—these cities with their villages.

[17] The fourth lot came out for Issachar, for the people of Issachar, according to their clans. [18] Their territory included Jezreel, Chesulloth, Shunem, [19] Hapharaim, Shion, Anaharath, [20] Rabbith, Kishion, Ebez, [21] Remeth, En-gannim, En-haddah, Beth-pazzez. [22] The boundary also touches Tabor, Shahazumah, and Beth-shemesh, and its boundary ends at the Jordan—sixteen cities with their villages. [23] This is the inheritance of the tribe of the people of Issachar, according to their clans—the cities with their villages.

[24] The fifth lot came out for the tribe of the people of Asher according to their clans. [25] Their territory included Helkath, Hali, Beten, Achshaph, [26] Allammelech, Amad, and Mishal. On the west it touches Carmel and Shihor-libnath, [27] then it turns eastward, it goes to Beth-dagon, and touches Zebulun and the Valley of Iphtahel northward to Beth-emek and Neiel. Then it continues in the north to Cabul, [28] Ebron, Rehob, Hammon, Kanah, as far as Sidon the Great. [29] Then the boundary turns to Ramah, reaching to the fortified city of Tyre. Then the boundary turns to Hosah, and it ends at the sea; Mahalab,[1] Achzib, [30] Ummah, Aphek and Rehob—twenty-two cities with their villages. [31] This is the inheritance of the tribe of the people of Asher according to their clans—these cities with their villages.

[32] The sixth lot came out for the people of Naphtali, for the people of Naphtali, according to their clans. [33] And their boundary ran from Heleph, from the oak in Zaanannim, and Adami-nekeb, and Jabneel, as far as Lakkum, and it ended at the Jordan. [34] Then the boundary turns westward to Aznoth-tabor and goes from there to Hukkok, touching Zebulun at the south and Asher on the west and Judah on the east at the Jordan. [35] The fortified cities are Ziddim, Zer, Hammath, Rakkath, Chinnereth, [36] Adamah, Ramah, Hazor, [37] Kedesh, Edrei, En-hazor, [38] Yiron, Migdal-el, Horem, Beth-anath, and Beth-shemesh—nineteen cities with their villages. [39] This is the inheritance of

the tribe of the people of Naphtali according to their clans—the cities with their villages.

[40] The seventh lot came out for the tribe of the people of Dan, according to their clans. [41] And the territory of its inheritance included Zorah, Eshtaol, Ir-shemesh, [42] Shaalabbin, Aijalon, Ithlah, [43] Elon, Timnah, Ekron, [44] Eltekeh, Gibbethon, Baalath, [45] Jehud, Bene-berak, Gath-rimmon, [46] and Me-jarkon and Rakkon with the territory over against Joppa. [47] When the territory of the people of Dan was lost to them, the people of Dan went up and fought against Leshem, and after capturing it and striking it with the sword they took possession of it and settled in it, calling Leshem, Dan, after the name of Dan their ancestor. [48] This is the inheritance of the tribe of the people of Dan, according to their clans—these cities with their villages.

[49] When they had finished distributing the several territories of the land as inheritances, the people of Israel gave an inheritance among them to Joshua the son of Nun. [50] By command of the LORD they gave him the city that he asked, Timnath-serah in the hill country of Ephraim. And he rebuilt the city and settled in it.

[51] These are the inheritances that Eleazar the priest and Joshua the son of Nun and the heads of the fathers' houses of the tribes of the people of Israel distributed by lot at Shiloh before the LORD, at the entrance of the tent of meeting. So they finished dividing the land.

─────── *Psalm 149–150* ───────

Praise the LORD!
  Sing to the LORD a new song,
      his praise in the assembly of the godly!
2 Let Israel be glad in his Maker;
      let the children of Zion rejoice in their
        King!
3 Let them praise his name with dancing,
      making melody to him with
        tambourine and lyre!
4 For the LORD takes pleasure in his
        people;
      he adorns the humble with salvation.
5 Let the godly exult in glory;
      let them sing for joy on their beds.
6 Let the high praises of God be in their
        throats
      and two-edged swords in their hands,

[1] Compare Septuagint; Hebrew *Mehebel*

7 to execute vengeance on the nations
   and punishments on the peoples,
8 to bind their kings with chains
   and their nobles with fetters of iron,
9 to execute on them the judgment
    written!
   This is honor for all his godly ones.
   Praise the LORD!

Praise the LORD!
Praise God in his sanctuary;
   praise him in his mighty heavens![1]
2 Praise him for his mighty deeds;
   praise him according to his excellent
    greatness!
3 Praise him with trumpet sound;
   praise him with lute and harp!
4 Praise him with tambourine and dance;
   praise him with strings and pipe!
5 Praise him with sounding cymbals;
   praise him with loud clashing
    cymbals!
6 Let everything that has breath praise the
   LORD!
   Praise the LORD!

Jeremiah 9[2]

Oh that my head were waters,
   and my eyes a fountain of tears,
   that I might weep day and night
    for the slain of the daughter of my
     people!
23 Oh that I had in the desert
   a travelers' lodging place,
   that I might leave my people
    and go away from them!
   For they are all adulterers,
    a company of treacherous men.
3 They bend their tongue like a bow;
   falsehood and not truth has grown
    strong[4] in the land;
   for they proceed from evil to evil,
    and they do not know me, declares
     the LORD.
4 Let everyone beware of his neighbor,
   and put no trust in any brother,
   for every brother is a deceiver,
    and every neighbor goes about as a
     slanderer.

5 Everyone deceives his neighbor,
   and no one speaks the truth;
   they have taught their tongue to speak
    lies;
   they weary themselves committing
    iniquity.
6 Heaping oppression upon oppression,
   and deceit upon deceit,
   they refuse to know me, declares the
    LORD.

7 Therefore thus says the LORD of hosts:
"Behold, I will refine them and test them,
   for what else can I do, because of my
    people?
8 Their tongue is a deadly arrow;
   it speaks deceitfully;
with his mouth each speaks peace to his
    neighbor,
   but in his heart he plans an ambush
    for him.
9 Shall I not punish them for these things?
   declares the LORD,
   and shall I not avenge myself
    on a nation such as this?

10 "I will take up weeping and wailing for
    the mountains,
   and a lamentation for the pastures of
    the wilderness,
because they are laid waste so that no
    one passes through,
   and the lowing of cattle is not heard;
both the birds of the air and the beasts
    have fled and are gone.
11 I will make Jerusalem a heap of ruins,
   a lair of jackals,
and I will make the cities of Judah a
    desolation,
   without inhabitant."

12 Who is the man so wise that he can understand this? To whom has the mouth of the LORD spoken, that he may declare it? Why is the land ruined and laid waste like a wilderness, so that no one passes through? 13 And the LORD says: "Because they have forsaken my law that I set before them, and have not obeyed my voice or walked in accord with it, 14 but have stubbornly followed their own hearts and have gone after the Baals, as their fathers taught them. 15 Therefore thus says the LORD of hosts, the God of Israel: Behold, I will

---

[1] Hebrew *expanse* (compare Genesis 1:6–8) [2] Ch 8:23 in Hebrew [3] Ch 9:1 in Hebrew [4] Septuagint; Hebrew *and not for truth they have grown strong*

feed this people with bitter food, and give them poisonous water to drink. **¹⁶**I will scatter them among the nations whom neither they nor their fathers have known, and I will send the sword after them, until I have consumed them."

17   Thus says the LORD of hosts:
    "Consider, and call for the mourning
        women to come;
      send for the skillful women to come;
18   let them make haste and raise a wailing
        over us,
      that our eyes may run down with tears
      and our eyelids flow with water.
19   For a sound of wailing is heard from Zion:
    'How we are ruined!
    We are utterly shamed,
    because we have left the land,
      because they have cast down our
        dwellings.'"

20   Hear, O women, the word of the LORD,
      and let your ear receive the word of
        his mouth;
    teach to your daughters a lament,
      and each to her neighbor a dirge.
21   For death has come up into our windows;
      it has entered our palaces,
    cutting off the children from the streets
      and the young men from the squares.
22   Speak: "Thus declares the LORD,
    'The dead bodies of men shall fall
      like dung upon the open field,
    like sheaves after the reaper,
      and none shall gather them.'"

²³Thus says the LORD: "Let not the wise man boast in his wisdom, let not the mighty man boast in his might, let not the rich man boast in his riches, **²⁴**but let him who boasts boast in this, that he understands and knows me, that I am the LORD who practices steadfast love, justice, and righteousness in the earth. For in these things I delight, declares the LORD."

²⁵"Behold, the days are coming, declares the LORD, when I will punish all those who are circumcised merely in the flesh— **²⁶**Egypt, Judah, Edom, the sons of Ammon, Moab, and all who dwell in the desert who cut the corners of their hair, for all these nations are uncircumcised, and all the house of Israel are uncircumcised in heart."

Matthew 23

Then Jesus said to the crowds and to his disciples, **²**"The scribes and the Pharisees sit on Moses' seat, **³**so do and observe whatever they tell you, but not the works they do. For they preach, but do not practice. **⁴**They tie up heavy burdens, hard to bear,[1] and lay them on people's shoulders, but they themselves are not willing to move them with their finger. **⁵**They do all their deeds to be seen by others. For they make their phylacteries broad and their fringes long, **⁶**and they love the place of honor at feasts and the best seats in the synagogues **⁷**and greetings in the marketplaces and being called rabbi[2] by others. **⁸**But you are not to be called rabbi, for you have one teacher, and you are all brothers.[3] **⁹**And call no man your father on earth, for you have one Father, who is in heaven. **¹⁰**Neither be called instructors, for you have one instructor, the Christ. **¹¹**The greatest among you shall be your servant. **¹²**Whoever exalts himself will be humbled, and whoever humbles himself will be exalted.

¹³"But woe to you, scribes and Pharisees, hypocrites! For you shut the kingdom of heaven in people's faces. For you neither enter yourselves nor allow those who would enter to go in.[4] **¹⁵**Woe to you, scribes and Pharisees, hypocrites! For you travel across sea and land to make a single proselyte, and when he becomes a proselyte, you make him twice as much a child of hell[5] as yourselves.

¹⁶"Woe to you, blind guides, who say, 'If anyone swears by the temple, it is nothing, but if anyone swears by the gold of the temple, he is bound by his oath.' **¹⁷**You blind fools! For which is greater, the gold or the temple that has made the gold sacred? **¹⁸**And you say, 'If anyone swears by the altar, it is nothing, but if anyone swears by the gift that is on the altar, he is bound by his oath.' **¹⁹**You blind men! For which is greater, the gift or the altar that makes the gift sacred? **²⁰**So whoever swears by the altar swears by it and by everything on it. **²¹**And whoever swears by the temple swears by it and by him who dwells in it. **²²**And whoever swears by heaven swears by the throne of God and by him who sits upon it.

²³"Woe to you, scribes and Pharisees, hypocrites! For you tithe mint and dill and cumin,

[1] Some manuscripts omit *hard to bear* [2] *Rabbi* means *my teacher*, or *my master*; also verse 8 [3] Or *brothers and sisters* [4] Some manuscripts add here (or after verse 12) verse 14: *Woe to you, scribes and Pharisees, hypocrites! For you devour widows' houses and for a pretense you make long prayers; therefore you will receive the greater condemnation* [5] Greek *Gehenna*; also verse 33

and have neglected the weightier matters of the law: justice and mercy and faithfulness. These you ought to have done, without neglecting the others. ²⁴You blind guides, straining out a gnat and swallowing a camel!

²⁵"Woe to you, scribes and Pharisees, hypocrites! For you clean the outside of the cup and the plate, but inside they are full of greed and self-indulgence. ²⁶You blind Pharisee! First clean the inside of the cup and the plate, that the outside also may be clean.

²⁷"Woe to you, scribes and Pharisees, hypocrites! For you are like whitewashed tombs, which outwardly appear beautiful, but within are full of dead people's bones and all uncleanness. ²⁸So you also outwardly appear righteous to others, but within you are full of hypocrisy and lawlessness.

²⁹"Woe to you, scribes and Pharisees, hypocrites! For you build the tombs of the prophets and decorate the monuments of the righteous, ³⁰saying, 'If we had lived in the days of our fathers, we would not have taken part with them in shedding the blood of the prophets.'

³¹Thus you witness against yourselves that you are sons of those who murdered the prophets. ³²Fill up, then, the measure of your fathers. ³³You serpents, you brood of vipers, how are you to escape being sentenced to hell? ³⁴Therefore I send you prophets and wise men and scribes, some of whom you will kill and crucify, and some you will flog in your synagogues and persecute from town to town, ³⁵so that on you may come all the righteous blood shed on earth, from the blood of righteous Abel to the blood of Zechariah the son of Barachiah,¹ whom you murdered between the sanctuary and the altar. ³⁶Truly, I say to you, all these things will come upon this generation.

³⁷"O Jerusalem, Jerusalem, the city that kills the prophets and stones those who are sent to it! How often would I have gathered your children together as a hen gathers her brood under her wings, and you were not willing! ³⁸See, your house is left to you desolate. ³⁹For I tell you, you will not see me again, until you say, 'Blessed is he who comes in the name of the Lord.'"

JULY 14

—— Joshua 20–21 ——

Then the LORD said to Joshua, ²"Say to the people of Israel, 'Appoint the cities of refuge, of which I spoke to you through Moses, ³that the manslayer who strikes any person without intent or unknowingly may flee there. They shall be for you a refuge from the avenger of blood. ⁴He shall flee to one of these cities and shall stand at the entrance of the gate of the city and explain his case to the elders of that city. Then they shall take him into the city and give him a place, and he shall remain with them. ⁵And if the avenger of blood pursues him, they shall not give up the manslayer into his hand, because he struck his neighbor unknowingly, and did not hate him in the past. ⁶And he shall remain in that city until he has stood before the congregation for judgment,

until the death of him who is high priest at the time. Then the manslayer may return to his own town and his own home, to the town from which he fled.'"

⁷So they set apart Kedesh in Galilee in the hill country of Naphtali, and Shechem in the hill country of Ephraim, and Kiriath-arba (that is, Hebron) in the hill country of Judah. ⁸And beyond the Jordan east of Jericho, they appointed Bezer in the wilderness on the tableland, from the tribe of Reuben, and Ramoth in Gilead, from the tribe of Gad, and Golan in Bashan, from the tribe of Manasseh. ⁹These were the cities designated for all the people of Israel and for the stranger sojourning among them, that anyone who killed a person without intent could flee there, so that he might not

¹ Some manuscripts omit *the son of Barachiah*

die by the hand of the avenger of blood, till he stood before the congregation.

21:1 Then the heads of the fathers' houses of the Levites came to Eleazar the priest and to Joshua the son of Nun and to the heads of the fathers' houses of the tribes of the people of Israel. **2** And they said to them at Shiloh in the land of Canaan, "The LORD commanded through Moses that we be given cities to dwell in, along with their pasturelands for our livestock." **3** So by command of the LORD the people of Israel gave to the Levites the following cities and pasturelands out of their inheritance.

4 The lot came out for the clans of the Kohathites. So those Levites who were descendants of Aaron the priest received by lot from the tribes of Judah, Simeon, and Benjamin, thirteen cities.

5 And the rest of the Kohathites received by lot from the clans of the tribe of Ephraim, from the tribe of Dan and the half-tribe of Manasseh, ten cities.

6 The Gershonites received by lot from the clans of the tribe of Issachar, from the tribe of Asher, from the tribe of Naphtali, and from the half-tribe of Manasseh in Bashan, thirteen cities.

7 The Merarites according to their clans received from the tribe of Reuben, the tribe of Gad, and the tribe of Zebulun, twelve cities.

8 These cities and their pasturelands the people of Israel gave by lot to the Levites, as the LORD had commanded through Moses.

9 Out of the tribe of the people of Judah and the tribe of the people of Simeon they gave the following cities mentioned by name, **10** which went to the descendants of Aaron, one of the clans of the Kohathites who belonged to the people of Levi; since the lot fell to them first. **11** They gave them Kiriath-arba (Arba being the father of Anak), that is Hebron, in the hill country of Judah, along with the pasturelands around it. **12** But the fields of the city and its villages had been given to Caleb the son of Jephunneh as his possession.

13 And to the descendants of Aaron the priest they gave Hebron, the city of refuge for the manslayer, with its pasturelands, Libnah with its pasturelands, **14** Jattir with its pasturelands, Eshtemoa with its pasturelands, **15** Holon with its pasturelands, Debir with its pasturelands, **16** Ain with its pasturelands, Juttah with its pasturelands, Beth-shemesh with its pasturelands—nine cities out of these two tribes; **17** then out of the tribe of Benjamin, Gibeon with its pasturelands, Geba with its pasturelands, **18** Anathoth with its pasturelands, and Almon with its pasturelands—four cities. **19** The cities of the descendants of Aaron, the priests, were in all thirteen cities with their pasturelands.

20 As to the rest of the Kohathites belonging to the Kohathite clans of the Levites, the cities allotted to them were out of the tribe of Ephraim. **21** To them were given Shechem, the city of refuge for the manslayer, with its pasturelands in the hill country of Ephraim, Gezer with its pasturelands, **22** Kibzaim with its pasturelands, Beth-horon with its pasturelands—four cities; **23** and out of the tribe of Dan, Elteke with its pasturelands, Gibbethon with its pasturelands, **24** Aijalon with its pasturelands, Gath-rimmon with its pasturelands—four cities; **25** and out of the half-tribe of Manasseh, Taanach with its pasturelands, and Gath-rimmon with its pasturelands—two cities. **26** The cities of the clans of the rest of the Kohathites were ten in all with their pasturelands.

27 And to the Gershonites, one of the clans of the Levites, were given out of the half-tribe of Manasseh, Golan in Bashan with its pasturelands, the city of refuge for the manslayer, and Beeshterah with its pasturelands—two cities; **28** and out of the tribe of Issachar, Kishion with its pasturelands, Daberath with its pasturelands, **29** Jarmuth with its pasturelands, En-gannim with its pasturelands—four cities; **30** and out of the tribe of Asher, Mishal with its pasturelands, Abdon with its pasturelands, **31** Helkath with its pasturelands, and Rehob with its pasturelands—four cities; **32** and out of the tribe of Naphtali, Kedesh in Galilee with its pasturelands, the city of refuge for the manslayer, Hammoth-dor with its pasturelands, and Kartan with its pasturelands—three cities. **33** The cities of the several clans of the Gershonites were in all thirteen cities with their pasturelands.

34 And to the rest of the Levites, the Merarite clans, were given out of the tribe of Zebulun, Jokneam with its pasturelands, Kartah with its pasturelands, **35** Dimnah with its pasturelands, Nahalal with its pasturelands—four cities; **36** and out of the tribe of Reuben, Bezer with its pasturelands, Jahaz with its pasturelands, **37** Kedemoth with its pasturelands, and

Mephaath with its pasturelands—four cities; [38] and out of the tribe of Gad, Ramoth in Gilead with its pasturelands, the city of refuge for the manslayer, Mahanaim with its pasturelands, [39] Heshbon with its pasturelands, Jazer with its pasturelands—four cities in all. [40] As for the cities of the several Merarite clans, that is, the remainder of the clans of the Levites, those allotted to them were in all twelve cities.

[41] The cities of the Levites in the midst of the possession of the people of Israel were in all forty-eight cities with their pasturelands. [42] These cities each had its pasturelands around it. So it was with all these cities.

[43] Thus the LORD gave to Israel all the land that he swore to give to their fathers. And they took possession of it, and they settled there. [44] And the LORD gave them rest on every side just as he had sworn to their fathers. Not one of all their enemies had withstood them, for the LORD had given all their enemies into their hands. [45] Not one word of all the good promises that the LORD had made to the house of Israel had failed; all came to pass.

Acts 1

In the first book, O Theophilus, I have dealt with all that Jesus began to do and teach, [2] until the day when he was taken up, after he had given commands through the Holy Spirit to the apostles whom he had chosen. [3] He presented himself alive to them after his suffering by many proofs, appearing to them during forty days and speaking about the kingdom of God.

[4] And while staying[1] with them he ordered them not to depart from Jerusalem, but to wait for the promise of the Father, which, he said, "you heard from me; [5] for John baptized with water, but you will be baptized with[2] the Holy Spirit not many days from now."

[6] So when they had come together, they asked him, "Lord, will you at this time restore the kingdom to Israel?" [7] He said to them, "It is not for you to know times or seasons that the Father has fixed by his own authority. [8] But you will receive power when the Holy Spirit has come upon you, and you will be my witnesses in Jerusalem and in all Judea and Samaria, and to the end of the earth." [9] And when he had said these things, as they were looking on, he was lifted up, and a cloud took him out of their sight.

[10] And while they were gazing into heaven as he went, behold, two men stood by them in white robes, [11] and said, "Men of Galilee, why do you stand looking into heaven? This Jesus, who was taken up from you into heaven, will come in the same way as you saw him go into heaven."

[12] Then they returned to Jerusalem from the mount called Olivet, which is near Jerusalem, a Sabbath day's journey away. [13] And when they had entered, they went up to the upper room, where they were staying, Peter and John and James and Andrew, Philip and Thomas, Bartholomew and Matthew, James the son of Alphaeus and Simon the Zealot and Judas the son of James. [14] All these with one accord were devoting themselves to prayer, together with the women and Mary the mother of Jesus, and his brothers.[3]

[15] In those days Peter stood up among the brothers (the company of persons was in all about 120) and said, [16] "Brothers, the Scripture had to be fulfilled, which the Holy Spirit spoke beforehand by the mouth of David concerning Judas, who became a guide to those who arrested Jesus. [17] For he was numbered among us and was allotted his share in this ministry." [18] (Now this man acquired a field with the reward of his wickedness, and falling headlong[4] he burst open in the middle and all his bowels gushed out. [19] And it became known to all the inhabitants of Jerusalem, so that the field was called in their own language Akeldama, that is, Field of Blood.) [20] "For it is written in the Book of Psalms,

" 'May his camp become desolate,
    and let there be no one to dwell in it';

and

" 'Let another take his office.'

[21] So one of the men who have accompanied us during all the time that the Lord Jesus went in and out among us, [22] beginning from the baptism of John until the day when he was taken up from us—one of these men must become with us a witness to his resurrection." [23] And they put forward two, Joseph called Barsabbas, who was also called Justus, and Matthias. [24] And they prayed and said, "You, Lord, who know the hearts of all, show which one of these two you have chosen [25] to take the place in this ministry and apostleship from which Judas turned aside

---

[1] Or eating [2] Or in [3] Or brothers and sisters. The plural Greek word adelphoi (translated "brothers") refers to siblings in a family. In New Testament usage, depending on the context, adelphoi may refer either to men or to both men and women who are siblings (brothers and sisters) in God's family, the church; also verse 15 [4] Or swelling up

to go to his own place." ²⁶And they cast lots for them, and the lot fell on Matthias, and he was numbered with the eleven apostles.

──────── *Jeremiah 10* ────────

Hear the word that the Lord speaks to you, O house of Israel. ²Thus says the Lord:

"Learn not the way of the nations,
    nor be dismayed at the signs of the
      heavens
    because the nations are dismayed at
      them,
³ for the customs of the peoples are
    vanity.[1]
A tree from the forest is cut down
    and worked with an axe by the hands
      of a craftsman.
⁴ They decorate it with silver and gold;
    they fasten it with hammer and nails
    so that it cannot move.
⁵ Their idols[2] are like scarecrows in a
    cucumber field,
    and they cannot speak;
they have to be carried,
    for they cannot walk.
Do not be afraid of them,
    for they cannot do evil,
    neither is it in them to do good."

⁶ There is none like you, O Lord;
    you are great, and your name is great
      in might.
⁷ Who would not fear you, O King of the
      nations?
    For this is your due;
for among all the wise ones of the
      nations
    and in all their kingdoms
there is none like you.
⁸ They are both stupid and foolish;
    the instruction of idols is but wood!
⁹ Beaten silver is brought from Tarshish,
    and gold from Uphaz.
They are the work of the craftsman and
      of the hands of the goldsmith;
    their clothing is violet and purple;
    they are all the work of skilled men.
¹⁰ But the Lord is the true God;
    he is the living God and the
      everlasting King.

At his wrath the earth quakes,
    and the nations cannot endure his
      indignation.

¹¹ Thus shall you say to them: "The gods who did not make the heavens and the earth shall perish from the earth and from under the heavens."[3]

¹² It is he who made the earth by his power,
    who established the world by his
      wisdom,
    and by his understanding stretched
      out the heavens.
¹³ When he utters his voice, there is a
      tumult of waters in the heavens,
    and he makes the mist rise from the
      ends of the earth.
He makes lightning for the rain,
    and he brings forth the wind from his
      storehouses.
¹⁴ Every man is stupid and without
      knowledge;
    every goldsmith is put to shame by his
      idols,
for his images are false,
    and there is no breath in them.
¹⁵ They are worthless, a work of delusion;
    at the time of their punishment they
      shall perish.
¹⁶ Not like these is he who is the portion of
      Jacob,
    for he is the one who formed all
      things,
and Israel is the tribe of his inheritance;
    the Lord of hosts is his name.

¹⁷ Gather up your bundle from the ground,
    O you who dwell under siege!
¹⁸ For thus says the Lord:
"Behold, I am slinging out the
      inhabitants of the land
    at this time,
and I will bring distress on them,
    that they may feel it."

¹⁹ Woe is me because of my hurt!
    My wound is grievous.
But I said, "Truly this is an affliction,
    and I must bear it."
²⁰ My tent is destroyed,
    and all my cords are broken;
my children have gone from me,
    and they are not;

---

[1] Or *vapor, or mist* [2] Hebrew *They* [3] This verse is in Aramaic

there is no one to spread my tent again
　　and to set up my curtains.
²¹ For the shepherds are stupid
　　and do not inquire of the LORD;
　　therefore they have not prospered,
　　and all their flock is scattered.
²² A voice, a rumor! Behold, it comes!—
　　a great commotion out of the north
　　　country
　to make the cities of Judah a desolation,
　　a lair of jackals.
²³ I know, O LORD, that the way of man is
　　　not in himself,
　　that it is not in man who walks to
　　　direct his steps.
²⁴ Correct me, O LORD, but in justice;
　　not in your anger, lest you bring me to
　　　nothing.
²⁵ Pour out your wrath on the nations that
　　　know you not,
　　and on the peoples that call not on
　　　your name,
　for they have devoured Jacob;
　　they have devoured him and
　　　consumed him,
　　and have laid waste his habitation.

—————— Matthew 24 ——————

Jesus left the temple and was going away, when his disciples came to point out to him the buildings of the temple. ²But he answered them, "You see all these, do you not? Truly, I say to you, there will not be left here one stone upon another that will not be thrown down."

³As he sat on the Mount of Olives, the disciples came to him privately, saying, "Tell us, when will these things be, and what will be the sign of your coming and of the end of the age?" ⁴And Jesus answered them, "See that no one leads you astray. ⁵For many will come in my name, saying, 'I am the Christ,' and they will lead many astray. ⁶And you will hear of wars and rumors of wars. See that you are not alarmed, for this must take place, but the end is not yet. ⁷For nation will rise against nation, and kingdom against kingdom, and there will be famines and earthquakes in various places. ⁸All these are but the beginning of the birth pains.

⁹"Then they will deliver you up to tribulation and put you to death, and you will be hated by all nations for my name's sake. ¹⁰And then many will fall away¹ and betray one another and hate one another. ¹¹And many false prophets will arise and lead many astray. ¹²And because lawlessness will be increased, the love of many will grow cold. ¹³But the one who endures to the end will be saved. ¹⁴And this gospel of the kingdom will be proclaimed throughout the whole world as a testimony to all nations, and then the end will come.

¹⁵"So when you see the abomination of desolation spoken of by the prophet Daniel, standing in the holy place (let the reader understand), ¹⁶then let those who are in Judea flee to the mountains. ¹⁷Let the one who is on the housetop not go down to take what is in his house, ¹⁸and let the one who is in the field not turn back to take his cloak. ¹⁹And alas for women who are pregnant and for those who are nursing infants in those days! ²⁰Pray that your flight may not be in winter or on a Sabbath. ²¹For then there will be great tribulation, such as has not been from the beginning of the world until now, no, and never will be. ²²And if those days had not been cut short, no human being would be saved. But for the sake of the elect those days will be cut short. ²³Then if anyone says to you, 'Look, here is the Christ!' or 'There he is!' do not believe it. ²⁴For false christs and false prophets will arise and perform great signs and wonders, so as to lead astray, if possible, even the elect. ²⁵See, I have told you beforehand. ²⁶So, if they say to you, 'Look, he is in the wilderness,' do not go out. If they say, 'Look, he is in the inner rooms,' do not believe it. ²⁷For as the lightning comes from the east and shines as far as the west, so will be the coming of the Son of Man. ²⁸Wherever the corpse is, there the vultures will gather.

²⁹"Immediately after the tribulation of those days the sun will be darkened, and the moon will not give its light, and the stars will fall from heaven, and the powers of the heavens will be shaken. ³⁰Then will appear in heaven the sign of the Son of Man, and then all the tribes of the earth will mourn, and they will see the Son of Man coming on the clouds of heaven with power and great glory. ³¹And he will send out his angels with a loud trumpet call, and they will gather his elect from the four winds, from one end of heaven to the other.

¹ Or *stumble*

[32] "From the fig tree learn its lesson: as soon as its branch becomes tender and puts out its leaves, you know that summer is near. [33] So also, when you see all these things, you know that he is near, at the very gates. [34] Truly, I say to you, this generation will not pass away until all these things take place. [35] Heaven and earth will pass away, but my words will not pass away.

[36] "But concerning that day and hour no one knows, not even the angels of heaven, nor the Son,[1] but the Father only. [37] For as were the days of Noah, so will be the coming of the Son of Man. [38] For as in those days before the flood they were eating and drinking, marrying and giving in marriage, until the day when Noah entered the ark, [39] and they were unaware until the flood came and swept them all away, so will be the coming of the Son of Man. [40] Then two men will be in the field; one will be taken and one left. [41] Two women will be grinding at the mill; one will be taken and one left. [42] Therefore, stay awake, for you do not know on what day your Lord is coming. [43] But know this, that if the master of the house had known in what part of the night the thief was coming, he would have stayed awake and would not have let his house be broken into. [44] Therefore you also must be ready, for the Son of Man is coming at an hour you do not expect.

[45] "Who then is the faithful and wise servant,[2] whom his master has set over his household, to give them their food at the proper time? [46] Blessed is that servant whom his master will find so doing when he comes. [47] Truly, I say to you, he will set him over all his possessions. [48] But if that wicked servant says to himself, 'My master is delayed,' [49] and begins to beat his fellow servants[3] and eats and drinks with drunkards, [50] the master of that servant will come on a day when he does not expect him and at an hour he does not know [51] and will cut him in pieces and put him with the hypocrites. In that place there will be weeping and gnashing of teeth.

JULY 15

Joshua 22

At that time Joshua summoned the Reubenites and the Gadites and the half-tribe of Manasseh, [2] and said to them, "You have kept all that Moses the servant of the LORD commanded you and have obeyed my voice in all that I have commanded you. [3] You have not forsaken your brothers these many days, down to this day, but have been careful to keep the charge of the LORD your God. [4] And now the LORD your God has given rest to your brothers, as he promised them. Therefore turn and go to your tents in the land where your possession lies, which Moses the servant of the LORD gave you on the other side of the Jordan. [5] Only be very careful to observe the commandment and the law that Moses the servant of the LORD commanded you, to love the LORD your God, and to walk in all his ways and to keep his commandments and to cling to him and to serve him with all your heart and with all your soul." [6] So Joshua blessed them and sent them away, and they went to their tents.

[7] Now to the one half of the tribe of Manasseh Moses had given a possession in Bashan, but to the other half Joshua had given a possession beside their brothers in the land west of the Jordan. And when Joshua sent them away to their homes and blessed them, [8] he said to them, "Go back to your tents with much wealth and with very much livestock, with silver, gold, bronze, and iron, and with much clothing. Divide the spoil of your enemies with your brothers." [9] So the people of Reuben and the people of Gad and the half-tribe of Manasseh returned home, parting from the people of Israel at Shiloh, which is in the land of Canaan, to go to the land of Gilead, their own land of which they had possessed

[1] Some manuscripts omit nor the Son   [2] Greek bondservant; also verses 46, 48, 50   [3] Greek bondservants

themselves by command of the Lord through Moses.

¹⁰And when they came to the region of the Jordan that is in the land of Canaan, the people of Reuben and the people of Gad and the half-tribe of Manasseh built there an altar by the Jordan, an altar of imposing size. ¹¹And the people of Israel heard it said, "Behold, the people of Reuben and the people of Gad and the half-tribe of Manasseh have built the altar at the frontier of the land of Canaan, in the region about the Jordan, on the side that belongs to the people of Israel." ¹²And when the people of Israel heard of it, the whole assembly of the people of Israel gathered at Shiloh to make war against them.

¹³Then the people of Israel sent to the people of Reuben and the people of Gad and the half-tribe of Manasseh, in the land of Gilead, Phinehas the son of Eleazar the priest, ¹⁴and with him ten chiefs, one from each of the tribal families of Israel, every one of them the head of a family among the clans of Israel. ¹⁵And they came to the people of Reuben, the people of Gad, and the half-tribe of Manasseh, in the land of Gilead, and they said to them, ¹⁶"Thus says the whole congregation of the Lord, 'What is this breach of faith that you have committed against the God of Israel in turning away this day from following the Lord by building yourselves an altar this day in rebellion against the Lord? ¹⁷Have we not had enough of the sin at Peor from which even yet we have not cleansed ourselves, and for which there came a plague upon the congregation of the Lord, ¹⁸that you too must turn away this day from following the Lord? And if you too rebel against the Lord today then tomorrow he will be angry with the whole congregation of Israel. ¹⁹But now, if the land of your possession is unclean, pass over into the Lord's land where the Lord's tabernacle stands, and take for yourselves a possession among us. Only do not rebel against the Lord or make us as rebels by building for yourselves an altar other than the altar of the Lord our God. ²⁰Did not Achan the son of Zerah break faith in the matter of the devoted things, and wrath fell upon all the congregation of Israel? And he did not perish alone for his iniquity.'"

²¹Then the people of Reuben, the people of Gad, and the half-tribe of Manasseh said in answer to the heads of the families of Israel, ²²"The Mighty One, God, the Lord! The Mighty One, God, the Lord! He knows; and let Israel itself know! If it was in rebellion or in breach of faith against the Lord, do not spare us today ²³for building an altar to turn away from following the Lord. Or if we did so to offer burnt offerings or grain offerings or peace offerings on it, may the Lord himself take vengeance. ²⁴No, but we did it from fear that in time to come your children might say to our children, 'What have you to do with the Lord, the God of Israel? ²⁵For the Lord has made the Jordan a boundary between us and you, you people of Reuben and people of Gad. You have no portion in the Lord.' So your children might make our children cease to worship the Lord. ²⁶Therefore we said, 'Let us now build an altar, not for burnt offering, nor for sacrifice, ²⁷but to be a witness between us and you, and between our generations after us, that we do perform the service of the Lord in his presence with our burnt offerings and sacrifices and peace offerings, so your children will not say to our children in time to come, "You have no portion in the Lord."' ²⁸And we thought, 'If this should be said to us or to our descendants in time to come, we should say, "Behold, the copy of the altar of the Lord, which our fathers made, not for burnt offerings, nor for sacrifice, but to be a witness between us and you."' ²⁹Far be it from us that we should rebel against the Lord and turn away this day from following the Lord by building an altar for burnt offering, grain offering, or sacrifice, other than the altar of the Lord our God that stands before his tabernacle!"

³⁰When Phinehas the priest and the chiefs of the congregation, the heads of the families of Israel who were with him, heard the words that the people of Reuben and the people of Gad and the people of Manasseh spoke, it was good in their eyes. ³¹And Phinehas the son of Eleazar the priest said to the people of Reuben and the people of Gad and the people of Manasseh, "Today we know that the Lord is in our midst, because you have not committed this breach of faith against the Lord. Now you have delivered the people of Israel from the hand of the Lord."

³²Then Phinehas the son of Eleazar the priest, and the chiefs, returned from the people

of Reuben and the people of Gad in the land of Gilead to the land of Canaan, to the people of Israel, and brought back word to them. ³³And the report was good in the eyes of the people of Israel. And the people of Israel blessed God and spoke no more of making war against them to destroy the land where the people of Reuben and the people of Gad were settled. ³⁴The people of Reuben and the people of Gad called the altar Witness, "For," they said, "it is a witness between us that the LORD is God."

--------- Acts 2 ---------

When the day of Pentecost arrived, they were all together in one place. ²And suddenly there came from heaven a sound like a mighty rushing wind, and it filled the entire house where they were sitting. ³And divided tongues as of fire appeared to them and rested[1] on each one of them. ⁴And they were all filled with the Holy Spirit and began to speak in other tongues as the Spirit gave them utterance.

⁵ Now there were dwelling in Jerusalem Jews, devout men from every nation under heaven. ⁶And at this sound the multitude came together, and they were bewildered, because each one was hearing them speak in his own language. ⁷And they were amazed and astonished, saying, "Are not all these who are speaking Galileans? ⁸And how is it that we hear, each of us in his own native language? ⁹Parthians and Medes and Elamites and residents of Mesopotamia, Judea and Cappadocia, Pontus and Asia, ¹⁰Phrygia and Pamphylia, Egypt and the parts of Libya belonging to Cyrene, and visitors from Rome, ¹¹both Jews and proselytes, Cretans and Arabians—we hear them telling in our own tongues the mighty works of God." ¹²And all were amazed and perplexed, saying to one another, "What does this mean?" ¹³But others mocking said, "They are filled with new wine."

¹⁴But Peter, standing with the eleven, lifted up his voice and addressed them: "Men of Judea and all who dwell in Jerusalem, let this be known to you, and give ear to my words. ¹⁵For these people are not drunk, as you suppose, since it is only the third hour of the day.[2] ¹⁶But this is what was uttered through the prophet Joel:

¹⁷ "'And in the last days it shall be, God declares,
    that I will pour out my Spirit on all flesh,
    and your sons and your daughters shall prophesy,
      and your young men shall see visions,
      and your old men shall dream dreams;
¹⁸ even on my male servants[3] and female servants
    in those days I will pour out my Spirit,
      and they shall prophesy.
¹⁹ And I will show wonders in the heavens above
    and signs on the earth below,
    blood, and fire, and vapor of smoke;
²⁰ the sun shall be turned to darkness
    and the moon to blood,
    before the day of the Lord comes, the great and magnificent day.
²¹ And it shall come to pass that everyone who calls upon the name of the Lord shall be saved.'

²²"Men of Israel, hear these words: Jesus of Nazareth, a man attested to you by God with mighty works and wonders and signs that God did through him in your midst, as you yourselves know— ²³this Jesus,[4] delivered up according to the definite plan and foreknowledge of God, you crucified and killed by the hands of lawless men. ²⁴God raised him up, loosing the pangs of death, because it was not possible for him to be held by it. ²⁵For David says concerning him,

" 'I saw the Lord always before me,
    for he is at my right hand that I may not be shaken;
²⁶ therefore my heart was glad, and my tongue rejoiced;
    my flesh also will dwell in hope.
²⁷ For you will not abandon my soul to Hades,
    or let your Holy One see corruption.
²⁸ You have made known to me the paths of life;
    you will make me full of gladness with your presence.'

²⁹"Brothers, I may say to you with confidence about the patriarch David that he both died and was buried, and his tomb is with us

---

[1] Or And tongues as of fire appeared to them, distributed among them, and rested   [2] That is, 9 A.M.   [3] Greek bondservants; twice in this verse   [4] Greek this one

to this day. [30] Being therefore a prophet, and knowing that God had sworn with an oath to him that he would set one of his descendants on his throne, [31] he foresaw and spoke about the resurrection of the Christ, that he was not abandoned to Hades, nor did his flesh see corruption. [32] This Jesus God raised up, and of that we all are witnesses. [33] Being therefore exalted at the right hand of God, and having received from the Father the promise of the Holy Spirit, he has poured out this that you yourselves are seeing and hearing. [34] For David did not ascend into the heavens, but he himself says,

" 'The Lord said to my Lord,
"Sit at my right hand,
[35]　　until I make your enemies your
　　　　footstool." '

[36] Let all the house of Israel therefore know for certain that God has made him both Lord and Christ, this Jesus whom you crucified."

[37] Now when they heard this they were cut to the heart, and said to Peter and the rest of the apostles, "Brothers, what shall we do?" [38] And Peter said to them, "Repent and be baptized every one of you in the name of Jesus Christ for the forgiveness of your sins, and you will receive the gift of the Holy Spirit. [39] For the promise is for you and for your children and for all who are far off, everyone whom the Lord our God calls to himself." [40] And with many other words he bore witness and continued to exhort them, saying, "Save yourselves from this crooked generation." [41] So those who received his word were baptized, and there were added that day about three thousand souls.

[42] And they devoted themselves to the apostles' teaching and the fellowship, to the breaking of bread and the prayers. [43] And awe[1] came upon every soul, and many wonders and signs were being done through the apostles. [44] And all who believed were together and had all things in common. [45] And they were selling their possessions and belongings and distributing the proceeds to all, as any had need. [46] And day by day, attending the temple together and breaking bread in their homes, they received their food with glad and generous hearts, [47] praising God and having favor with all the people. And the Lord added to their number day by day those who were being saved.

[1] Or fear

Jeremiah 11

The word that came to Jeremiah from the Lord: [2] "Hear the words of this covenant, and speak to the men of Judah and the inhabitants of Jerusalem. [3] You shall say to them, Thus says the Lord, the God of Israel: Cursed be the man who does not hear the words of this covenant [4] that I commanded your fathers when I brought them out of the land of Egypt, from the iron furnace, saying, Listen to my voice, and do all that I command you. So shall you be my people, and I will be your God, [5] that I may confirm the oath that I swore to your fathers, to give them a land flowing with milk and honey, as at this day." Then I answered, "So be it, Lord."

[6] And the Lord said to me, "Proclaim all these words in the cities of Judah and in the streets of Jerusalem: Hear the words of this covenant and do them. [7] For I solemnly warned your fathers when I brought them up out of the land of Egypt, warning them persistently, even to this day, saying, Obey my voice. [8] Yet they did not obey or incline their ear, but everyone walked in the stubbornness of his evil heart. Therefore I brought upon them all the words of this covenant, which I commanded them to do, but they did not."

[9] Again the Lord said to me, "A conspiracy exists among the men of Judah and the inhabitants of Jerusalem. [10] They have turned back to the iniquities of their forefathers, who refused to hear my words. They have gone after other gods to serve them. The house of Israel and the house of Judah have broken my covenant that I made with their fathers. [11] Therefore, thus says the Lord, Behold, I am bringing disaster upon them that they cannot escape. Though they cry to me, I will not listen to them. [12] Then the cities of Judah and the inhabitants of Jerusalem will go and cry to the gods to whom they make offerings, but they cannot save them in the time of their trouble. [13] For your gods have become as many as your cities, O Judah, and as many as the streets of Jerusalem are the altars you have set up to shame, altars to make offerings to Baal.

[14] "Therefore do not pray for this people, or lift up a cry or prayer on their behalf, for I will not listen when they call to me in the time of their trouble. [15] What right has my beloved in my house, when she has done many vile deeds?

Can even sacrificial flesh avert your doom? Can you then exult? [16] The LORD once called you 'a green olive tree, beautiful with good fruit.' But with the roar of a great tempest he will set fire to it, and its branches will be consumed. [17] The LORD of hosts, who planted you, has decreed disaster against you, because of the evil that the house of Israel and the house of Judah have done, provoking me to anger by making offerings to Baal."

[18] The LORD made it known to me and I knew;
then you showed me their deeds.
[19] But I was like a gentle lamb
led to the slaughter.
I did not know it was against me
they devised schemes, saying,
"Let us destroy the tree with its fruit,
let us cut him off from the land of the living,
that his name be remembered no more."
[20] But, O LORD of hosts, who judges righteously,
who tests the heart and the mind,
let me see your vengeance upon them,
for to you have I committed my cause.

[21] Therefore thus says the LORD concerning the men of Anathoth, who seek your life, and say, "Do not prophesy in the name of the LORD, or you will die by our hand"— [22] therefore thus says the LORD of hosts: "Behold, I will punish them. The young men shall die by the sword, their sons and their daughters shall die by famine, [23] and none of them shall be left. For I will bring disaster upon the men of Anathoth, the year of their punishment."

Matthew 25

[1] "Then the kingdom of heaven will be like ten virgins who took their lamps[1] and went to meet the bridegroom.[2] [2] Five of them were foolish, and five were wise. [3] For when the foolish took their lamps, they took no oil with them, [4] but the wise took flasks of oil with their lamps. [5] As the bridegroom was delayed, they all became drowsy and slept. [6] But at midnight there was a cry, 'Here is the bridegroom! Come out to meet him.' [7] Then all those virgins rose and trimmed their lamps. [8] And the foolish said to the wise, 'Give us some of your oil, for our lamps are going out.' [9] But the wise answered, saying, 'Since there will not be enough for us and for you, go rather to the dealers and buy for yourselves.' [10] And while they were going to buy, the bridegroom came, and those who were ready went in with him to the marriage feast, and the door was shut. [11] Afterward the other virgins came also, saying, 'Lord, lord, open to us.' [12] But he answered, 'Truly, I say to you, I do not know you.' [13] Watch therefore, for you know neither the day nor the hour.

[14] "For it will be like a man going on a journey, who called his servants[3] and entrusted to them his property. [15] To one he gave five talents,[4] to another two, to another one, to each according to his ability. Then he went away. [16] He who had received the five talents went at once and traded with them, and he made five talents more. [17] So also he who had the two talents made two talents more. [18] But he who had received the one talent went and dug in the ground and hid his master's money. [19] Now after a long time the master of those servants came and settled accounts with them. [20] And he who had received the five talents came forward, bringing five talents more, saying, 'Master, you delivered to me five talents; here I have made five talents more.' [21] His master said to him, 'Well done, good and faithful servant.[5] You have been faithful over a little; I will set you over much. Enter into the joy of your master.' [22] And he also who had the two talents came forward, saying, 'Master, you delivered to me two talents; here I have made two talents more.' [23] His master said to him, 'Well done, good and faithful servant. You have been faithful over a little; I will set you over much. Enter into the joy of your master.' [24] He also who had received the one talent came forward, saying, 'Master, I knew you to be a hard man, reaping where you did not sow, and gathering where you scattered no seed, [25] so I was afraid, and I went and hid your talent in the ground. Here you have what is yours.' [26] But his master answered him, 'You wicked and slothful servant! You knew that I reap where I have not sown and gather where I scattered no seed? [27] Then you ought to have invested my money with the bankers, and at my coming I should have received what was my own with interest. [28] So take the talent from him and give it to him who has the ten

----

[1] Or torches   [2] Some manuscripts add *and the bride*   [3] Greek *bondservants*; also verse 19   [4] A *talent* was a monetary unit worth about twenty years' wages for a laborer   [5] Greek *bondservant*; also verses 23, 26, 30

talents. [29]For to everyone who has will more be given, and he will have an abundance. But from the one who has not, even what he has will be taken away. [30]And cast the worthless servant into the outer darkness. In that place there will be weeping and gnashing of teeth.'

[31]"When the Son of Man comes in his glory, and all the angels with him, then he will sit on his glorious throne. [32]Before him will be gathered all the nations, and he will separate people one from another as a shepherd separates the sheep from the goats. [33]And he will place the sheep on his right, but the goats on the left. [34]Then the King will say to those on his right, 'Come, you who are blessed by my Father, inherit the kingdom prepared for you from the foundation of the world. [35]For I was hungry and you gave me food, I was thirsty and you gave me drink, I was a stranger and you welcomed me, [36]I was naked and you clothed me, I was sick and you visited me, I was in prison and you came to me.' [37]Then the righteous will answer him, saying, 'Lord, when did we see you hungry and feed you, or thirsty and give you drink? [38]And when did we see you a stranger and welcome you, or naked and clothe you? [39]And when did we see you sick or in prison and visit you?' [40]And the King will answer them, 'Truly, I say to you, as you did it to one of the least of these my brothers,[1] you did it to me.'

[41]"Then he will say to those on his left, 'Depart from me, you cursed, into the eternal fire prepared for the devil and his angels. [42]For I was hungry and you gave me no food, I was thirsty and you gave me no drink, [43]I was a stranger and you did not welcome me, naked and you did not clothe me, sick and in prison and you did not visit me.' [44]Then they also will answer, saying, 'Lord, when did we see you hungry or thirsty or a stranger or naked or sick or in prison, and did not minister to you?' [45]Then he will answer them, saying, 'Truly, I say to you, as you did not do it to one of the least of these, you did not do it to me.' [46]And these will go away into eternal punishment, but the righteous into eternal life."

JULY 16

Joshua 23

A long time afterward, when the LORD had given rest to Israel from all their surrounding enemies, and Joshua was old and well advanced in years, [2]Joshua summoned all Israel, its elders and heads, its judges and officers, and said to them, "I am now old and well advanced in years. [3]And you have seen all that the LORD your God has done to all these nations for your sake, for it is the LORD your God who has fought for you. [4]Behold, I have allotted to you as an inheritance for your tribes those nations that remain, along with all the nations that I have already cut off, from the Jordan to the Great Sea in the west. [5]The LORD your God will push them back before you and drive them out of your sight. And you shall possess their land, just as the LORD your God promised you. [6]Therefore, be very strong to keep and to do all that is written in the Book of the Law of Moses, turning aside from it neither to the right hand nor to the left, [7]that you may not mix with these nations remaining among you or make mention of the names of their gods or swear by them or serve them or bow down to them, [8]but you shall cling to the LORD your God just as you have done to this day. [9]For the LORD has driven out before you great and strong nations. And as for you, no man has been able to stand before you to this day. [10]One man of you puts to flight a thousand, since it is the LORD your God who fights for you, just as he promised you. [11]Be very careful, therefore, to love the LORD your God. [12]For if you turn back and cling to the remnant of these nations remaining among you and make marriages with them, so that you associate with them and they with

[1] Or brothers and sisters

you, [13]know for certain that the LORD your God will no longer drive out these nations before you, but they shall be a snare and a trap for you, a whip on your sides and thorns in your eyes, until you perish from off this good ground that the LORD your God has given you.

[14]"And now I am about to go the way of all the earth, and you know in your hearts and souls, all of you, that not one word has failed of all the good things[1] that the LORD your God promised concerning you. All have come to pass for you; not one of them has failed. [15]But just as all the good things that the LORD your God promised concerning you have been fulfilled for you, so the LORD will bring upon you all the evil things, until he has destroyed you from off this good land that the LORD your God has given you, [16]if you transgress the covenant of the LORD your God, which he commanded you, and go and serve other gods and bow down to them. Then the anger of the LORD will be kindled against you, and you shall perish quickly from off the good land that he has given to you."

Acts 3

Now Peter and John were going up to the temple at the hour of prayer, the ninth hour.[2] [2]And a man lame from birth was being carried, whom they laid daily at the gate of the temple that is called the Beautiful Gate to ask alms of those entering the temple. [3]Seeing Peter and John about to go into the temple, he asked to receive alms. [4]And Peter directed his gaze at him, as did John, and said, "Look at us." [5]And he fixed his attention on them, expecting to receive something from them. [6]But Peter said, "I have no silver and gold, but what I do have I give to you. In the name of Jesus Christ of Nazareth, rise up and walk!" [7]And he took him by the right hand and raised him up, and immediately his feet and ankles were made strong. [8]And leaping up he stood and began to walk, and entered the temple with them, walking and leaping and praising God. [9]And all the people saw him walking and praising God, [10]and recognized him as the one who sat at the Beautiful Gate of the temple, asking for alms. And they were filled with wonder and amazement at what had happened to him.

[11]While he clung to Peter and John, all the people, utterly astounded, ran together to them in the portico called Solomon's. [12]And when Peter saw it he addressed the people: "Men of Israel, why do you wonder at this, or why do you stare at us, as though by our own power or piety we have made him walk? [13]The God of Abraham, the God of Isaac, and the God of Jacob, the God of our fathers, glorified his servant[3] Jesus, whom you delivered over and denied in the presence of Pilate, when he had decided to release him. [14]But you denied the Holy and Righteous One, and asked for a murderer to be granted to you, [15]and you killed the Author of life, whom God raised from the dead. To this we are witnesses. [16]And his name—by faith in his name—has made this man strong whom you see and know, and the faith that is through Jesus[4] has given the man this perfect health in the presence of you all.

[17]"And now, brothers, I know that you acted in ignorance, as did also your rulers. [18]But what God foretold by the mouth of all the prophets, that his Christ would suffer, he thus fulfilled. [19]Repent therefore, and turn back, that your sins may be blotted out, [20]that times of refreshing may come from the presence of the Lord, and that he may send the Christ appointed for you, Jesus, [21]whom heaven must receive until the time for restoring all the things about which God spoke by the mouth of his holy prophets long ago. [22]Moses said, 'The Lord God will raise up for you a prophet like me from your brothers. You shall listen to him in whatever he tells you. [23]And it shall be that every soul who does not listen to that prophet shall be destroyed from the people.' [24]And all the prophets who have spoken, from Samuel and those who came after him, also proclaimed these days. [25]You are the sons of the prophets and of the covenant that God made with your fathers, saying to Abraham, 'And in your offspring shall all the families of the earth be blessed.' [26]God, having raised up his servant, sent him to you first, to bless you by turning every one of you from your wickedness."

Jeremiah 12

Righteous are you, O LORD, when I complain to you; yet I would plead my case before you.

Why does the way of the wicked
    prosper?
Why do all who are treacherous
    thrive?
2 You plant them, and they take root;
    they grow and produce fruit;
you are near in their mouth
    and far from their heart.
3 But you, O Lord, know me;
    you see me, and test my heart toward
    you.
Pull them out like sheep for the
    slaughter,
    and set them apart for the day of
    slaughter.
4 How long will the land mourn
    and the grass of every field wither?
For the evil of those who dwell in it
    the beasts and the birds are swept
    away,
    because they said, "He will not see our
    latter end."

5 "If you have raced with men on foot, and
    they have wearied you,
    how will you compete with horses?
And if in a safe land you are so
    trusting,
    what will you do in the thicket of the
    Jordan?
6 For even your brothers and the house of
    your father,
    even they have dealt treacherously
    with you;
    they are in full cry after you;
do not believe them,
    though they speak friendly words to
    you."

7 "I have forsaken my house;
    I have abandoned my heritage;
I have given the beloved of my soul
    into the hands of her enemies.
8 My heritage has become to me
    like a lion in the forest;
she has lifted up her voice against me;
    therefore I hate her.
9 Is my heritage to me like a hyena's lair?
    Are the birds of prey against her all
    around?
Go, assemble all the wild beasts;
    bring them to devour.

10 Many shepherds have destroyed my
    vineyard;
    they have trampled down my portion;
they have made my pleasant portion
    a desolate wilderness.
11 They have made it a desolation;
    desolate, it mourns to me.
The whole land is made desolate,
    but no man lays it to heart.
12 Upon all the bare heights in the desert
    destroyers have come,
for the sword of the Lord devours
    from one end of the land to the other;
    no flesh has peace.
13 They have sown wheat and have reaped
    thorns;
    they have tired themselves out but
    profit nothing.
They shall be ashamed of their[1] harvests
    because of the fierce anger of the
    Lord."

14 Thus says the Lord concerning all my evil neighbors who touch the heritage that I have given my people Israel to inherit: "Behold, I will pluck them up from their land, and I will pluck up the house of Judah from among them. 15 And after I have plucked them up, I will again have compassion on them, and I will bring them again each to his heritage and each to his land. 16 And it shall come to pass, if they will diligently learn the ways of my people, to swear by my name, 'As the Lord lives,' even as they taught my people to swear by Baal, then they shall be built up in the midst of my people. 17 But if any nation will not listen, then I will utterly pluck it up and destroy it, declares the Lord."

Matthew 26

When Jesus had finished all these sayings, he said to his disciples, 2 "You know that after two days the Passover is coming, and the Son of Man will be delivered up to be crucified." 3 Then the chief priests and the elders of the people gathered in the palace of the high priest, whose name was Caiaphas, 4 and plotted together in order to arrest Jesus by stealth and kill him. 5 But they said, "Not during the feast, lest there be an uproar among the people."

6 Now when Jesus was at Bethany in the house of Simon the leper,[2] 7 a woman came up

---

[1] Hebrew your [2] Leprosy was a term for several skin diseases; see Leviticus 13

to him with an alabaster flask of very expensive ointment, and she poured it on his head as he reclined at table. [8]And when the disciples saw it, they were indignant, saying, "Why this waste? [9]For this could have been sold for a large sum and given to the poor." [10]But Jesus, aware of this, said to them, "Why do you trouble the woman? For she has done a beautiful thing to me. [11]For you always have the poor with you, but you will not always have me. [12]In pouring this ointment on my body, she has done it to prepare me for burial. [13]Truly, I say to you, wherever this gospel is proclaimed in the whole world, what she has done will also be told in memory of her."

[14]Then one of the twelve, whose name was Judas Iscariot, went to the chief priests [15]and said, "What will you give me if I deliver him over to you?" And they paid him thirty pieces of silver. [16]And from that moment he sought an opportunity to betray him.

[17]Now on the first day of Unleavened Bread the disciples came to Jesus, saying, "Where will you have us prepare for you to eat the Passover?" [18]He said, "Go into the city to a certain man and say to him, 'The Teacher says, My time is at hand. I will keep the Passover at your house with my disciples.'" [19]And the disciples did as Jesus had directed them, and they prepared the Passover.

[20]When it was evening, he reclined at table with the twelve.[1] [21]And as they were eating, he said, "Truly, I say to you, one of you will betray me." [22]And they were very sorrowful and began to say to him one after another, "Is it I, Lord?" [23]He answered, "He who has dipped his hand in the dish with me will betray me. [24]The Son of Man goes as it is written of him, but woe to that man by whom the Son of Man is betrayed! It would have been better for that man if he had not been born." [25]Judas, who would betray him, answered, "Is it I, Rabbi?" He said to him, "You have said so."

[26]Now as they were eating, Jesus took bread, and after blessing it broke it and gave it to the disciples, and said, "Take, eat; this is my body." [27]And he took a cup, and when he had given thanks he gave it to them, saying, "Drink of it, all of you, [28]for this is my blood of the[2] covenant, which is poured out for many for the forgiveness of sins. [29]I tell you I will not drink again of this fruit of the vine until that day when I drink it new with you in my Father's kingdom."

[30]And when they had sung a hymn, they went out to the Mount of Olives. [31]Then Jesus said to them, "You will all fall away because of me this night. For it is written, 'I will strike the shepherd, and the sheep of the flock will be scattered.' [32]But after I am raised up, I will go before you to Galilee." [33]Peter answered him, "Though they all fall away because of you, I will never fall away." [34]Jesus said to him, "Truly, I tell you, this very night, before the rooster crows, you will deny me three times." [35]Peter said to him, "Even if I must die with you, I will not deny you!" And all the disciples said the same.

[36]Then Jesus went with them to a place called Gethsemane, and he said to his disciples, "Sit here, while I go over there and pray." [37]And taking with him Peter and the two sons of Zebedee, he began to be sorrowful and troubled. [38]Then he said to them, "My soul is very sorrowful, even to death; remain here, and watch[3] with me." [39]And going a little farther he fell on his face and prayed, saying, "My Father, if it be possible, let this cup pass from me; nevertheless, not as I will, but as you will." [40]And he came to the disciples and found them sleeping. And he said to Peter, "So, could you not watch with me one hour? [41]Watch and pray that you may not enter into temptation. The spirit indeed is willing, but the flesh is weak." [42]Again, for the second time, he went away and prayed, "My Father, if this cannot pass unless I drink it, your will be done." [43]And again he came and found them sleeping, for their eyes were heavy. [44]So, leaving them again, he went away and prayed for the third time, saying the same words again. [45]Then he came to the disciples and said to them, "Sleep and take your rest later on.[4] See, the hour is at hand, and the Son of Man is betrayed into the hands of sinners. [46]Rise, let us be going; see, my betrayer is at hand."

[47]While he was still speaking, Judas came, one of the twelve, and with him a great crowd with swords and clubs, from the chief priests and the elders of the people. [48]Now the betrayer had given them a sign, saying, "The one I will kiss is the man; seize him." [49]And he came up to Jesus at once and said, "Greetings, Rabbi!" And he kissed him. [50]Jesus said to him, "Friend, do what you came to do."[5] Then they came up

---

[1] Some manuscripts add *disciples* [2] Some manuscripts insert *new* [3] Or *keep awake; also verses 40, 41* [4] Or *Are you still sleeping and taking your rest?* [5] Or *Friend, why are you here?*

and laid hands on Jesus and seized him. [51]And behold, one of those who were with Jesus stretched out his hand and drew his sword and struck the servant[1] of the high priest and cut off his ear. [52]Then Jesus said to him, "Put your sword back into its place. For all who take the sword will perish by the sword. [53]Do you think that I cannot appeal to my Father, and he will at once send me more than twelve legions of angels? [54]But how then should the Scriptures be fulfilled, that it must be so?" [55]At that hour Jesus said to the crowds, "Have you come out as against a robber, with swords and clubs to capture me? Day after day I sat in the temple teaching, and you did not seize me. [56]But all this has taken place that the Scriptures of the prophets might be fulfilled." Then all the disciples left him and fled.

[57]Then those who had seized Jesus led him to Caiaphas the high priest, where the scribes and the elders had gathered. [58]And Peter was following him at a distance, as far as the courtyard of the high priest, and going inside he sat with the guards to see the end. [59]Now the chief priests and the whole council[2] were seeking false testimony against Jesus that they might put him to death, [60]but they found none, though many false witnesses came forward. At last two came forward [61]and said, "This man said, 'I am able to destroy the temple of God, and to rebuild it in three days.'" [62]And the high priest stood up and said, "Have you no answer to make? What is it that these men testify against you?"[3] [63]But Jesus remained silent. And the high priest said to him, "I adjure you by the living God, tell us if you are the Christ, the Son of God." [64]Jesus said to him, "You have said so. But I tell you, from now on you will see the Son of Man seated at the right hand of Power and coming on the clouds of heaven." [65]Then the high priest tore his robes and said, "He has uttered blasphemy. What further witnesses do we need? You have now heard his blasphemy. [66]What is your judgment?" They answered, "He deserves death." [67]Then they spit in his face and struck him. And some slapped him, [68]saying, "Prophesy to us, you Christ! Who is it that struck you?"

[69]Now Peter was sitting outside in the courtyard. And a servant girl came up to him and said, "You also were with Jesus the Galilean." [70]But he denied it before them all, saying, "I do not know what you mean." [71]And when he went out to the entrance, another servant girl saw him, and she said to the bystanders, "This man was with Jesus of Nazareth." [72]And again he denied it with an oath: "I do not know the man." [73]After a little while the bystanders came up and said to Peter, "Certainly you too are one of them, for your accent betrays you." [74]Then he began to invoke a curse on himself and to swear, "I do not know the man." And immediately the rooster crowed. [75]And Peter remembered the saying of Jesus, "Before the rooster crows, you will deny me three times." And he went out and wept bitterly.

J U L Y 1 7

— Joshua 24 —

Joshua gathered all the tribes of Israel to Shechem and summoned the elders, the heads, the judges, and the officers of Israel. And they presented themselves before God. [2]And Joshua said to all the people, "Thus says the Lord, the God of Israel, 'Long ago, your fathers lived beyond the Euphrates,[4] Terah, the father of Abraham and of Nahor; and they served other gods. [3]Then I took your father Abraham from beyond the River and led him through all the land of Canaan, and made his offspring many. I gave him Isaac. [4]And to Isaac I gave Jacob and Esau. And I gave Esau the hill country of Seir to possess, but Jacob and his children went down to Egypt. [5]And I sent Moses and Aaron, and I plagued Egypt with

---

[1] Greek bondservant [2] Greek Sanhedrin [3] Or Have you no answer to what these men testify against you? [4] Hebrew the River

what I did in the midst of it, and afterward I brought you out. ⁶" 'Then I brought your fathers out of Egypt, and you came to the sea. And the Egyptians pursued your fathers with chariots and horsemen to the Red Sea. ⁷And when they cried to the LORD, he put darkness between you and the Egyptians and made the sea come upon them and cover them; and your eyes saw what I did in Egypt. And you lived in the wilderness a long time. ⁸Then I brought you to the land of the Amorites, who lived on the other side of the Jordan. They fought with you, and I gave them into your hand, and you took possession of their land, and I destroyed them before you. ⁹Then Balak the son of Zippor, king of Moab, arose and fought against Israel. And he sent and invited Balaam the son of Beor to curse you, ¹⁰but I would not listen to Balaam. Indeed, he blessed you. So I delivered you out of his hand. ¹¹And you went over the Jordan and came to Jericho, and the leaders of Jericho fought against you, and also the Amorites, the Perizzites, the Canaanites, the Hittites, the Girgashites, the Hivites, and the Jebusites. And I gave them into your hand. ¹²And I sent the hornet before you, which drove them out before you, the two kings of the Amorites; it was not by your sword or by your bow. ¹³I gave you a land on which you had not labored and cities that you had not built, and you dwell in them. You eat the fruit of vineyards and olive orchards that you did not plant.'

¹⁴"Now therefore fear the LORD and serve him in sincerity and in faithfulness. Put away the gods that your fathers served beyond the River and in Egypt, and serve the LORD. ¹⁵And if it is evil in your eyes to serve the LORD, choose this day whom you will serve, whether the gods your fathers served in the region beyond the River, or the gods of the Amorites in whose land you dwell. But as for me and my house, we will serve the LORD."

¹⁶Then the people answered, "Far be it from us that we should forsake the LORD to serve other gods, ¹⁷for it is the LORD our God who brought us and our fathers up from the land of Egypt, out of the house of slavery, and who did those great signs in our sight and preserved us in all the way that we went, and among all the peoples through whom we passed. ¹⁸And the LORD drove out before us all the peoples, the Amorites who lived in the land. Therefore we also will serve the LORD, for he is our God."

¹⁹But Joshua said to the people, "You are not able to serve the LORD, for he is a holy God. He is a jealous God; he will not forgive your transgressions or your sins. ²⁰If you forsake the LORD and serve foreign gods, then he will turn and do you harm and consume you, after having done you good." ²¹And the people said to Joshua, "No, but we will serve the LORD." ²²Then Joshua said to the people, "You are witnesses against yourselves that you have chosen the LORD, to serve him." And they said, "We are witnesses." ²³He said, "Then put away the foreign gods that are among you, and incline your heart to the LORD, the God of Israel." ²⁴And the people said to Joshua, "The LORD our God we will serve, and his voice we will obey." ²⁵So Joshua made a covenant with the people that day, and put in place statutes and rules for them at Shechem. ²⁶And Joshua wrote these words in the Book of the Law of God. And he took a large stone and set it up there under the terebinth that was by the sanctuary of the LORD. ²⁷And Joshua said to all the people, "Behold, this stone shall be a witness against us, for it has heard all the words of the LORD that he spoke to us. Therefore it shall be a witness against you, lest you deal falsely with your God." ²⁸So Joshua sent the people away, every man to his inheritance.

²⁹After these things Joshua the son of Nun, the servant of the LORD, died, being 110 years old. ³⁰And they buried him in his own inheritance at Timnath-serah, which is in the hill country of Ephraim, north of the mountain of Gaash.

³¹Israel served the LORD all the days of Joshua, and all the days of the elders who outlived Joshua and had known all the work that the LORD did for Israel.

³²As for the bones of Joseph, which the people of Israel brought up from Egypt, they buried them at Shechem, in the piece of land that Jacob bought from the sons of Hamor the father of Shechem for a hundred pieces of money.[1] It became an inheritance of the descendants of Joseph.

³³And Eleazar the son of Aaron died, and they buried him at Gibeah, the town of Phinehas his son, which had been given him in the hill country of Ephraim.

[1] Hebrew *for a hundred qesitah*; a unit of money of unknown value

Acts 4

And as they were speaking to the people, the priests and the captain of the temple and the Sadducees came upon them, [2] greatly annoyed because they were teaching the people and proclaiming in Jesus the resurrection from the dead. [3] And they arrested them and put them in custody until the next day, for it was already evening. [4] But many of those who had heard the word believed, and the number of the men came to about five thousand.

[5] On the next day their rulers and elders and scribes gathered together in Jerusalem, [6] with Annas the high priest and Caiaphas and John and Alexander, and all who were of the high-priestly family. [7] And when they had set them in the midst, they inquired, "By what power or by what name did you do this?" [8] Then Peter, filled with the Holy Spirit, said to them, "Rulers of the people and elders, [9] if we are being examined today concerning a good deed done to a crippled man, by what means this man has been healed, [10] let it be known to all of you and to all the people of Israel that by the name of Jesus Christ of Nazareth, whom you crucified, whom God raised from the dead—by him this man is standing before you well. [11] This Jesus[1] is the stone that was rejected by you, the builders, which has become the cornerstone.[2] [12] And there is salvation in no one else, for there is no other name under heaven given among men[3] by which we must be saved."

[13] Now when they saw the boldness of Peter and John, and perceived that they were uneducated, common men, they were astonished. And they recognized that they had been with Jesus. [14] But seeing the man who was healed standing beside them, they had nothing to say in opposition. [15] But when they had commanded them to leave the council, they conferred with one another, [16] saying, "What shall we do with these men? For that a notable sign has been performed through them is evident to all the inhabitants of Jerusalem, and we cannot deny it. [17] But in order that it may spread no further among the people, let us warn them to speak no more to anyone in this name." [18] So they called them and charged them not to speak or teach at all in the name of Jesus. [19] But Peter and John answered them, "Whether it is right in the sight of God to listen to you rather than

to God, you must judge, [20] for we cannot but speak of what we have seen and heard." [21] And when they had further threatened them, they let them go, finding no way to punish them, because of the people, for all were praising God for what had happened. [22] For the man on whom this sign of healing was performed was more than forty years old.

[23] When they were released, they went to their friends and reported what the chief priests and the elders had said to them. [24] And when they heard it, they lifted their voices together to God and said, "Sovereign Lord, who made the heaven and the earth and the sea and everything in them, [25] who through the mouth of our father David, your servant,[4] said by the Holy Spirit,

"'Why did the Gentiles rage,
and the peoples plot in vain?
[26]   The kings of the earth set themselves,
and the rulers were gathered together,
against the Lord and against his
Anointed'[5]—

[27] for truly in this city there were gathered together against your holy servant Jesus, whom you anointed, both Herod and Pontius Pilate, along with the Gentiles and the peoples of Israel, [28] to do whatever your hand and your plan had predestined to take place. [29] And now, Lord, look upon their threats and grant to your servants[6] to continue to speak your word with all boldness, [30] while you stretch out your hand to heal, and signs and wonders are performed through the name of your holy servant Jesus." [31] And when they had prayed, the place in which they were gathered together was shaken, and they were all filled with the Holy Spirit and continued to speak the word of God with boldness.

[32] Now the full number of those who believed were of one heart and soul, and no one said that any of the things that belonged to him was his own, but they had everything in common. [33] And with great power the apostles were giving their testimony to the resurrection of the Lord Jesus, and great grace was upon them all. [34] There was not a needy person among them, for as many as were owners of lands or houses sold them and brought the proceeds of what was sold [35] and laid it at the apostles' feet, and it was distributed to each as any had

need. ³⁶Thus Joseph, who was also called by the apostles Barnabas (which means son of encouragement), a Levite, a native of Cyprus, ³⁷sold a field that belonged to him and brought the money and laid it at the apostles' feet.

Jeremiah 13

Thus says the LORD to me, "Go and buy a linen loincloth and put it around your waist, and do not dip it in water." ²So I bought a loincloth according to the word of the LORD, and put it around my waist. ³And the word of the LORD came to me a second time, ⁴"Take the loincloth that you have bought, which is around your waist, and arise, go to the Euphrates and hide it there in a cleft of the rock." ⁵So I went and hid it by the Euphrates, as the LORD commanded me. ⁶And after many days the LORD said to me, "Arise, go to the Euphrates, and take from there the loincloth that I commanded you to hide there." ⁷Then I went to the Euphrates, and dug, and I took the loincloth from the place where I had hidden it. And behold, the loincloth was spoiled; it was good for nothing.

⁸Then the word of the LORD came to me: ⁹"Thus says the LORD: Even so will I spoil the pride of Judah and the great pride of Jerusalem. ¹⁰This evil people, who refuse to hear my words, who stubbornly follow their own heart and have gone after other gods to serve them and worship them, shall be like this loincloth, which is good for nothing. ¹¹For as the loincloth clings to the waist of a man, so I made the whole house of Israel and the whole house of Judah cling to me, declares the LORD, that they might be for me a people, a name, a praise, and a glory, but they would not listen.

¹²"You shall speak to them this word: 'Thus says the LORD, the God of Israel, "Every jar shall be filled with wine." ' And they will say to you, 'Do we not indeed know that every jar will be filled with wine?' ¹³Then you shall say to them, 'Thus says the LORD: Behold, I will fill with drunkenness all the inhabitants of this land: the kings who sit on David's throne, the priests, the prophets, and all the inhabitants of Jerusalem. ¹⁴And I will dash them one against another, fathers and sons together, declares the LORD. I will not pity or spare or have compassion, that I should not destroy them.' "

¹⁵ Hear and give ear; be not proud,
  for the LORD has spoken.
¹⁶ Give glory to the LORD your God
  before he brings darkness,
before your feet stumble
  on the twilight mountains,
and while you look for light
  he turns it into gloom
  and makes it deep darkness.
¹⁷ But if you will not listen,
  my soul will weep in secret for your pride;
my eyes will weep bitterly and run down with tears,
  because the LORD's flock has been taken captive.

¹⁸ Say to the king and the queen mother:
  "Take a lowly seat,
for your beautiful crown
  has come down from your head."
¹⁹ The cities of the Negeb are shut up,
  with none to open them;
all Judah is taken into exile,
  wholly taken into exile.

²⁰ "Lift up your eyes and see
  those who come from the north.
Where is the flock that was given you,
  your beautiful flock?
²¹ What will you say when they set as head
  over you
those whom you yourself have taught
  to be friends to you?
Will not pangs take hold of you
  like those of a woman in labor?
²² And if you say in your heart,
  'Why have these things come upon me?'
it is for the greatness of your iniquity
  that your skirts are lifted up
  and you suffer violence.
²³ Can the Ethiopian change his skin
  or the leopard his spots?
Then also you can do good
  who are accustomed to do evil.
²⁴ I will scatter you¹ like chaff
  driven by the wind from the desert.
²⁵ This is your lot,
  the portion I have measured out to you, declares the LORD,
because you have forgotten me
  and trusted in lies.

¹ Hebrew them

26 I myself will lift up your skirts over your
face,
and your shame will be seen.
27 I have seen your abominations,
your adulteries and neighings, your
lewd whorings,
on the hills in the field.
Woe to you, O Jerusalem!
How long will it be before you are
made clean?"

Matthew 27

When morning came, all the chief priests and the elders of the people took counsel against Jesus to put him to death. ²And they bound him and led him away and delivered him over to Pilate the governor.

³Then when Judas, his betrayer, saw that Jesus[1] was condemned, he changed his mind and brought back the thirty pieces of silver to the chief priests and the elders, ⁴saying, "I have sinned by betraying innocent blood." They said, "What is that to us? See to it yourself." ⁵And throwing down the pieces of silver into the temple, he departed, and he went and hanged himself. ⁶But the chief priests, taking the pieces of silver, said, "It is not lawful to put them into the treasury, since it is blood money." ⁷So they took counsel and bought with them the potter's field as a burial place for strangers. ⁸Therefore that field has been called the Field of Blood to this day. ⁹Then was fulfilled what had been spoken by the prophet Jeremiah, saying, "And they took the thirty pieces of silver, the price of him on whom a price had been set by some of the sons of Israel, ¹⁰and they gave them for the potter's field, as the Lord directed me."

¹¹Now Jesus stood before the governor, and the governor asked him, "Are you the King of the Jews?" Jesus said, "You have said so." ¹²But when he was accused by the chief priests and elders, he gave no answer. ¹³Then Pilate said to him, "Do you not hear how many things they testify against you?" ¹⁴But he gave no answer, not even to a single charge, so that the governor was greatly amazed.

¹⁵Now at the feast the governor was accustomed to release for the crowd any one prisoner whom they wanted. ¹⁶And they had then a notorious prisoner called Barabbas. ¹⁷So when they had gathered, Pilate said to them, "Whom do you want me to release for you: Barabbas, or Jesus who is called Christ?" ¹⁸For he knew that it was out of envy that they had delivered him up. ¹⁹Besides, while he was sitting on the judgment seat, his wife sent word to him, "Have nothing to do with that righteous man, for I have suffered much because of him today in a dream." ²⁰Now the chief priests and the elders persuaded the crowd to ask for Barabbas and destroy Jesus. ²¹The governor again said to them, "Which of the two do you want me to release for you?" And they said, "Barabbas." ²²Pilate said to them, "Then what shall I do with Jesus who is called Christ?" They all said, "Let him be crucified!" ²³And he said, "Why, what evil has he done?" But they shouted all the more, "Let him be crucified!"

²⁴So when Pilate saw that he was gaining nothing, but rather that a riot was beginning, he took water and washed his hands before the crowd, saying, "I am innocent of this man's blood;[2] see to it yourselves." ²⁵And all the people answered, "His blood be on us and on our children!" ²⁶Then he released for them Barabbas, and having scourged[3] Jesus, delivered him to be crucified.

²⁷Then the soldiers of the governor took Jesus into the governor's headquarters,[4] and they gathered the whole battalion[5] before him. ²⁸And they stripped him and put a scarlet robe on him, ²⁹and twisting together a crown of thorns, they put it on his head and put a reed in his right hand. And kneeling before him, they mocked him, saying, "Hail, King of the Jews!" ³⁰And they spit on him and took the reed and struck him on the head. ³¹And when they had mocked him, they stripped him of the robe and put his own clothes on him and led him away to crucify him.

³²As they went out, they found a man of Cyrene, Simon by name. They compelled this man to carry his cross. ³³And when they came to a place called Golgotha (which means Place of a Skull), ³⁴they offered him wine to drink, mixed with gall, but when he tasted it, he would not drink it. ³⁵And when they had crucified him, they divided his garments among them by casting lots. ³⁶Then they sat down and kept watch over him there. ³⁷And over his head they put the charge against him, which read, "This is Jesus, the King of the Jews." ³⁸Then two robbers were crucified with him, one on the right

---

[1] Greek he [2] Some manuscripts this righteous blood, or this righteous man's blood [3] A Roman judicial penalty, consisting of a severe beating with a multi-lashed whip containing imbedded pieces of bone and metal [4] Greek the praetorium [5] Greek cohort; a tenth of a Roman legion, usually about 600 men

10,000 of them at Bezek. [5]They found Adoni-bezek at Bezek and fought against him and defeated the Canaanites and the Perizzites. [6]Adoni-bezek fled, but they pursued him and caught him and cut off his thumbs and his big toes. [7]And Adoni-bezek said, "Seventy kings with their thumbs and their big toes cut off used to pick up scraps under my table. As I have done, so God has repaid me." And they brought him to Jerusalem, and he died there.

[8]And the men of Judah fought against Jerusalem and captured it and struck it with the edge of the sword and set the city on fire. [9]And afterward the men of Judah went down to fight against the Canaanites who lived in the hill country, in the Negeb, and in the low-land. [10]And Judah went against the Canaanites who lived in Hebron (now the name of Hebron was formerly Kiriath-arba), and they defeated Sheshai and Ahiman and Talmai.

[11]From there they went against the inhabitants of Debir. The name of Debir was formerly Kiriath-sepher. [12]And Caleb said, "He who attacks Kiriath-sepher and captures it, I will give him Achsah my daughter for a wife." [13]And Othniel the son of Kenaz, Caleb's younger brother, captured it. And he gave him Achsah his daughter for a wife. [14]When she came to him, she urged him to ask her father for a field. And she dismounted from her donkey, and Caleb said to her, "What do you want?" [15]She said to him, "Give me a blessing. Since you have set me in the land of the Negeb, give me also springs of water." And Caleb gave her the upper springs and the lower springs.

[16]And the descendants of the Kenite, Moses' father-in-law, went up with the people of Judah from the city of palms into the wilderness of Judah, which lies in the Negeb near Arad, and they went and settled with the people. [17]And Judah went with Simeon his brother, and they defeated the Canaanites who inhabited Zephath and devoted it to destruction. So the name of the city was called Hormah.[1] [18]Judah also captured Gaza with its territory, and Ashkelon with its territory, and Ekron with its territory. [19]And the LORD was with Judah, and he took possession of the hill country, but he could not drive out the inhabitants of the plain because they had chariots of iron. [20]And Hebron was given to Caleb, as Moses had said. And he drove out from it the three sons of Anak. [21]But the people of Benjamin did not drive out the Jebusites who lived in Jerusalem, so the Jebusites have lived with the people of Benjamin in Jerusalem to this day.

[22]The house of Joseph also went up against Bethel, and the LORD was with them. [23]And the house of Joseph scouted out Bethel. (Now the name of the city was formerly Luz.) [24]And the spies saw a man coming out of the city, and they said to him, "Please show us the way into the city, and we will deal kindly with you." [25]And he showed them the way into the city. And they struck the city with the edge of the sword, but they let the man and all his family go. [26]And the man went to the land of the Hittites and built a city and called its name Luz. That is its name to this day.

[27]Manasseh did not drive out the inhabitants of Beth-shean and its villages, or Taanach and its villages, or the inhabitants of Dor and its villages, or the inhabitants of Ibleam and its villages, or the inhabitants of Megiddo and its villages, for the Canaanites persisted in dwelling in that land. [28]When Israel grew strong, they put the Canaanites to forced labor, but did not drive them out completely.

[29]And Ephraim did not drive out the Canaanites who lived in Gezer, so the Canaanites lived in Gezer among them.

[30]Zebulun did not drive out the inhabitants of Kitron, or the inhabitants of Nahalol, so the Canaanites lived among them, but became subject to forced labor.

[31]Asher did not drive out the inhabitants of Acco, or the inhabitants of Sidon or of Ahlab or of Achzib or of Helbah or of Aphik or of Rehob, [32]so the Asherites lived among the Canaanites, the inhabitants of the land, for they did not drive them out.

[33]Naphtali did not drive out the inhabitants of Beth-shemesh, or the inhabitants of Beth-anath, so they lived among the Canaanites, the inhabitants of the land. Nevertheless, the inhabitants of Beth-shemesh and of Beth-anath became subject to forced labor for them.

[34]The Amorites pressed the people of Dan back into the hill country, for they did not allow them to come down to the plain. [35]The Amorites persisted in dwelling in Mount Heres, in Aijalon, and in Shaalbim, but the hand of the house of Joseph rested heavily on them, and they became subject to forced labor. [36]And the

[1] Hormah means utter destruction

border of the Amorites ran from the ascent of Akrabbim, from Sela and upward.

Acts 5

B ut a man named Ananias, with his wife Sapphira, sold a piece of property, [2] and with his wife's knowledge he kept back for himself some of the proceeds and brought only a part of it and laid it at the apostles' feet. [3] But Peter said, "Ananias, why has Satan filled your heart to lie to the Holy Spirit and to keep back for yourself part of the proceeds of the land? [4] While it remained unsold, did it not remain your own? And after it was sold, was it not at your disposal? Why is it that you have contrived this deed in your heart? You have not lied to man but to God." [5] When Ananias heard these words, he fell down and breathed his last. And great fear came upon all who heard of it. [6] The young men rose and wrapped him up and carried him out and buried him.

[7] After an interval of about three hours his wife came in, not knowing what had happened. [8] And Peter said to her, "Tell me whether you[1] sold the land for so much." And she said, "Yes, for so much." [9] But Peter said to her, "How is it that you have agreed together to test the Spirit of the Lord? Behold, the feet of those who have buried your husband are at the door, and they will carry you out." [10] Immediately she fell down at his feet and breathed her last. When the young men came in they found her dead, and they carried her out and buried her beside her husband. [11] And great fear came upon the whole church and upon all who heard of these things.

[12] Now many signs and wonders were regularly done among the people by the hands of the apostles. And they were all together in Solomon's Portico. [13] None of the rest dared join them, but the people held them in high esteem. [14] And more than ever believers were added to the Lord, multitudes of both men and women, [15] so that they even carried out the sick into the streets and laid them on cots and mats, that as Peter came by at least his shadow might fall on some of them. [16] The people also gathered from the towns around Jerusalem, bringing the sick and those afflicted with unclean spirits, and they were all healed.

[17] But the high priest rose up, and all who were with him (that is, the party of the Sad-

ducees), and filled with jealousy [18] they arrested the apostles and put them in the public prison. [19] But during the night an angel of the Lord opened the prison doors and brought them out, and said, [20] "Go and stand in the temple and speak to the people all the words of this Life." [21] And when they heard this, they entered the temple at daybreak and began to teach.

Now when the high priest came, and those who were with him, they called together the council, all the senate of the people of Israel, and sent to the prison to have them brought. [22] But when the officers came, they did not find them in the prison, so they returned and reported, [23] "We found the prison securely locked and the guards standing at the doors, but when we opened them we found no one inside." [24] Now when the captain of the temple and the chief priests heard these words, they were greatly perplexed about them, wondering what this would come to. [25] And someone came and told them, "Look! The men whom you put in prison are standing in the temple and teaching the people." [26] Then the captain with the officers went and brought them, but not by force, for they were afraid of being stoned by the people.

[27] And when they had brought them, they set them before the council. And the high priest questioned them, [28] saying, "We strictly charged you not to teach in this name, yet here you have filled Jerusalem with your teaching, and you intend to bring this man's blood upon us." [29] But Peter and the apostles answered, "We must obey God rather than men. [30] The God of our fathers raised Jesus, whom you killed by hanging him on a tree. [31] God exalted him at his right hand as Leader and Savior, to give repentance to Israel and forgiveness of sins. [32] And we are witnesses to these things, and so is the Holy Spirit, whom God has given to those who obey him."

[33] When they heard this, they were enraged and wanted to kill them. [34] But a Pharisee in the council named Gamaliel, a teacher of the law held in honor by all the people, stood up and gave orders to put the men outside for a little while. [35] And he said to them, "Men of Israel, take care what you are about to do with these men. [36] For before these days Theudas rose up, claiming to be somebody, and a number of men, about four hundred, joined him. He was

---

[1] The Greek for you is plural here

killed, and all who followed him were dispersed and came to nothing. ³⁷After him Judas the Galilean rose up in the days of the census and drew away some of the people after him. He too perished, and all who followed him were scattered. ³⁸So in the present case I tell you, keep away from these men and let them alone, for if this plan or this undertaking is of man, it will fail; ³⁹but if it is of God, you will not be able to overthrow them. You might even be found opposing God!" So they took his advice, ⁴⁰and when they had called in the apostles, they beat them and charged them not to speak in the name of Jesus, and let them go. ⁴¹Then they left the presence of the council, rejoicing that they were counted worthy to suffer dishonor for the name. ⁴²And every day, in the temple and from house to house, they did not cease teaching and preaching that the Christ is Jesus.

Jeremiah 14

The word of the LORD that came to Jeremiah concerning the drought:

² "Judah mourns,
     and her gates languish;
  her people lament on the ground,
     and the cry of Jerusalem goes up.
³   Her nobles send their servants for water;
     they come to the cisterns;
  they find no water;
     they return with their vessels empty;
  they are ashamed and confounded
     and cover their heads.
⁴   Because of the ground that is dismayed,
     since there is no rain on the land,
  the farmers are ashamed;
     they cover their heads.
⁵   Even the doe in the field forsakes her
        newborn fawn
     because there is no grass.
⁶   The wild donkeys stand on the bare
        heights;
     they pant for air like jackals;
  their eyes fail
     because there is no vegetation.

⁷ "Though our iniquities testify against us,
     act, O LORD, for your name's sake;
  for our backslidings are many;
     we have sinned against you.

⁸   O you hope of Israel,
     its savior in time of trouble,
  why should you be like a stranger in the
        land,
     like a traveler who turns aside to tarry
        for a night?
⁹   Why should you be like a man confused,
     like a mighty warrior who cannot
        save?
  Yet you, O LORD, are in the midst of us,
     and we are called by your name;
     do not leave us."

¹⁰   Thus says the LORD concerning this
        people:
  "They have loved to wander thus;
     they have not restrained their feet;
  therefore the LORD does not accept
        them;
     now he will remember their iniquity
     and punish their sins."

¹¹The LORD said to me: "Do not pray for the welfare of this people. ¹²Though they fast, I will not hear their cry, and though they offer burnt offering and grain offering, I will not accept them. But I will consume them by the sword, by famine, and by pestilence." ¹³Then I said: "Ah, Lord GOD, behold, the prophets say to them, 'You shall not see the sword, nor shall you have famine, but I will give you assured peace in this place.'" ¹⁴And the LORD said to me: "The prophets are prophesying lies in my name. I did not send them, nor did I command them or speak to them. They are prophesying to you a lying vision, worthless divination, and the deceit of their own minds. ¹⁵Therefore thus says the LORD concerning the prophets who prophesy in my name although I did not send them, and who say, 'Sword and famine shall not come upon this land': By sword and famine those prophets shall be consumed. ¹⁶And the people to whom they prophesy shall be cast out in the streets of Jerusalem, victims of famine and sword, with none to bury them—them, their wives, their sons, and their daughters. For I will pour out their evil upon them.

¹⁷ "You shall say to them this word:
  'Let my eyes run down with tears night
        and day,
     and let them not cease,

for the virgin daughter of my people is
    shattered with a great wound,
  with a very grievous blow.
18 If I go out into the field,
    behold, those pierced by the sword!
  And if I enter the city,
    behold, the diseases of famine!
  For both prophet and priest ply their
    trade through the land
  and have no knowledge.'"

19 Have you utterly rejected Judah?
    Does your soul loathe Zion?
  Why have you struck us down
    so that there is no healing for us?
  We looked for peace, but no good came;
    for a time of healing, but behold,
    terror.
20 We acknowledge our wickedness,
    O Lord,
  and the iniquity of our fathers,
    for we have sinned against you.
21 Do not spurn us, for your name's sake;
    do not dishonor your glorious throne;
  remember and do not break your
    covenant with us.
22 Are there any among the false gods of
    the nations that can bring rain?
  Or can the heavens give showers?
  Are you not he, O Lord our God?
  We set our hope on you,
    for you do all these things.

———— *Matthew 28* ————

Now after the Sabbath, toward the dawn of the first day of the week, Mary Magdalene and the other Mary went to see the tomb. ²And behold, there was a great earthquake, for an angel of the Lord descended from heaven and came and rolled back the stone and sat on it. ³His appearance was like lightning, and his clothing white as snow. ⁴And for fear of him the guards trembled and became like dead men. ⁵But the angel said to the women, "Do not be afraid, for I know that you seek Jesus who was crucified. ⁶He is not here, for he has risen, as he said. Come, see the place where he[1] lay. ⁷Then go quickly and tell his disciples that he has risen from the dead, and behold, he is going before you to Galilee; there you will see him. See, I have told you." ⁸So they departed quickly from the tomb with fear and great joy, and ran to tell his disciples. ⁹And behold, Jesus met them and said, "Greetings!" And they came up and took hold of his feet and worshiped him. ¹⁰Then Jesus said to them, "Do not be afraid; go and tell my brothers to go to Galilee, and there they will see me."

¹¹While they were going, behold, some of the guard went into the city and told the chief priests all that had taken place. ¹²And when they had assembled with the elders and taken counsel, they gave a sufficient sum of money to the soldiers ¹³and said, "Tell people, 'His disciples came by night and stole him away while we were asleep.' ¹⁴And if this comes to the governor's ears, we will satisfy him and keep you out of trouble." ¹⁵So they took the money and did as they were directed. And this story has been spread among the Jews to this day.

¹⁶Now the eleven disciples went to Galilee, to the mountain to which Jesus had directed them. ¹⁷And when they saw him they worshiped him, but some doubted. ¹⁸And Jesus came and said to them, "All authority in heaven and on earth has been given to me. ¹⁹Go therefore and make disciples of all nations, baptizing them in[2] the name of the Father and of the Son and of the Holy Spirit, ²⁰teaching them to observe all that I have commanded you. And behold, I am with you always, to the end of the age."

---

[1] Some manuscripts *the Lord* [2] Or *into*

JULY 19

Judges 2

Now the angel of the LORD went up from Gilgal to Bochim. And he said, "I brought you up from Egypt and brought you into the land that I swore to give to your fathers. I said, 'I will never break my covenant with you, ²and you shall make no covenant with the inhabitants of this land; you shall break down their altars.' But you have not obeyed my voice. What is this you have done? ³So now I say, I will not drive them out before you, but they shall become thorns in your sides, and their gods shall be a snare to you." ⁴As soon as the angel of the LORD spoke these words to all the people of Israel, the people lifted up their voices and wept. ⁵And they called the name of that place Bochim.¹ And they sacrificed there to the LORD.

⁶When Joshua dismissed the people, the people of Israel went each to his inheritance to take possession of the land. ⁷And the people served the LORD all the days of Joshua, and all the days of the elders who outlived Joshua, who had seen all the great work that the LORD had done for Israel. ⁸And Joshua the son of Nun, the servant of the LORD, died at the age of 110 years. ⁹And they buried him within the boundaries of his inheritance in Timnath-heres, in the hill country of Ephraim, north of the mountain of Gaash. ¹⁰And all that generation also were gathered to their fathers. And there arose another generation after them who did not know the LORD or the work that he had done for Israel.

¹¹And the people of Israel did what was evil in the sight of the LORD and served the Baals. ¹²And they abandoned the LORD, the God of their fathers, who had brought them out of the land of Egypt. They went after other gods, from among the gods of the peoples who were around them, and bowed down to them. And they provoked the LORD to anger. ¹³They abandoned the LORD and served the Baals and the Ashtaroth. ¹⁴So the anger of the LORD was kindled against Israel, and he gave them over to plunderers, who plundered them. And he sold them into the hand of their surrounding enemies, so that they could no longer withstand their enemies. ¹⁵Whenever they marched out, the hand of the LORD was against them for harm, as the LORD had warned, and as the LORD had sworn to them. And they were in terrible distress.

¹⁶Then the LORD raised up judges, who saved them out of the hand of those who plundered them. ¹⁷Yet they did not listen to their judges, for they whored after other gods and bowed down to them. They soon turned aside from the way in which their fathers had walked, who had obeyed the commandments of the LORD, and they did not do so. ¹⁸Whenever the LORD raised up judges for them, the LORD was with the judge, and he saved them from the hand of their enemies all the days of the judge. For the LORD was moved to pity by their groaning because of those who afflicted and oppressed them. ¹⁹But whenever the judge died, they turned back and were more corrupt than their fathers, going after other gods, serving them and bowing down to them. They did not drop any of their practices or their stubborn ways. ²⁰So the anger of the LORD was kindled against Israel, and he said, "Because this people have transgressed my covenant that I commanded their fathers and have not obeyed my voice, ²¹I will no longer drive out before them any of the nations that Joshua left when he died, ²²in order to test Israel by them, whether they will take care to walk in the way of the LORD as their fathers did, or not." ²³So the LORD left those nations, not driving them out quickly, and he did not give them into the hand of Joshua.

Acts 6

Now in these days when the disciples were increasing in number, a complaint by the Hellenists² arose against the Hebrews because

¹ *Bochim* means *weepers* ² That is, Greek-speaking Jews

their widows were being neglected in the daily distribution. ²And the twelve summoned the full number of the disciples and said, "It is not right that we should give up preaching the word of God to serve tables. ³Therefore, brothers,¹ pick out from among you seven men of good repute, full of the Spirit and of wisdom, whom we will appoint to this duty. ⁴But we will devote ourselves to prayer and to the ministry of the word." ⁵And what they said pleased the whole gathering, and they chose Stephen, a man full of faith and of the Holy Spirit, and Philip, and Prochorus, and Nicanor, and Timon, and Parmenas, and Nicolaus, a proselyte of Antioch. ⁶These they set before the apostles, and they prayed and laid their hands on them.

⁷And the word of God continued to increase, and the number of the disciples multiplied greatly in Jerusalem, and a great many of the priests became obedient to the faith.

⁸And Stephen, full of grace and power, was doing great wonders and signs among the people. ⁹Then some of those who belonged to the synagogue of the Freedmen (as it was called), and of the Cyrenians, and of the Alexandrians, and of those from Cilicia and Asia, rose up and disputed with Stephen. ¹⁰But they could not withstand the wisdom and the Spirit with which he was speaking. ¹¹Then they secretly instigated men who said, "We have heard him speak blasphemous words against Moses and God." ¹²And they stirred up the people and the elders and the scribes, and they came upon him and seized him and brought him before the council, ¹³and they set up false witnesses who said, "This man never ceases to speak words against this holy place and the law, ¹⁴for we have heard him say that this Jesus of Nazareth will destroy this place and will change the customs that Moses delivered to us." ¹⁵And gazing at him, all who sat in the council saw that his face was like the face of an angel.

──────── *Jeremiah 15* ────────

Then the LORD said to me, "Though Moses and Samuel stood before me, yet my heart would not turn toward this people. Send them out of my sight, and let them go! ²And when they ask you, 'Where shall we go?' you shall say to them, 'Thus says the LORD:

" 'Those who are for pestilence, to pestilence,
    and those who are for the sword, to the sword;
those who are for famine, to famine,
    and those who are for captivity, to captivity.'

³I will appoint over them four kinds of destroyers, declares the LORD: the sword to kill, the dogs to tear, and the birds of the air and the beasts of the earth to devour and destroy. ⁴And I will make them a horror to all the kingdoms of the earth because of what Manasseh the son of Hezekiah, king of Judah, did in Jerusalem.

5 "Who will have pity on you, O Jerusalem,
      or who will grieve for you?
   Who will turn aside
      to ask about your welfare?
6 You have rejected me, declares the LORD;
      you keep going backward,
   so I have stretched out my hand against you and destroyed you—
      I am weary of relenting.
7 I have winnowed them with a winnowing fork
      in the gates of the land;
   I have bereaved them; I have destroyed my people;
      they did not turn from their ways.
8 I have made their widows more in number
      than the sand of the seas;
   I have brought against the mothers of young men
      a destroyer at noonday;
   I have made anguish and terror fall upon them suddenly.
9 She who bore seven has grown feeble;
      she has fainted away;
   her sun went down while it was yet day;
      she has been shamed and disgraced.
   And the rest of them I will give to the sword
      before their enemies,
         declares the LORD."

¹⁰Woe is me, my mother, that you bore me, a man of strife and contention to the whole land! I have not lent, nor have I borrowed, yet all of them curse me. ¹¹The LORD said, "Have I not² set you free for their good? Have I not pleaded

───
¹ Or *brothers and sisters* ² The meaning of the Hebrew is uncertain

for you before the enemy in the time of trouble and in the time of distress? ¹²Can one break iron, iron from the north, and bronze?

¹³"Your wealth and your treasures I will give as spoil, without price, for all your sins, throughout all your territory. ¹⁴I will make you serve your enemies in a land that you do not know, for in my anger a fire is kindled that shall burn forever."

15   O Lord, you know;
     remember me and visit me,
     and take vengeance for me on my
      persecutors.
     In your forbearance take me not away;
     know that for your sake I bear
      reproach.
16   Your words were found, and I ate them,
     and your words became to me a joy
     and the delight of my heart,
     for I am called by your name,
     O Lord, God of hosts.
17   I did not sit in the company of revelers,
     nor did I rejoice;
     I sat alone, because your hand was upon
      me,
     for you had filled me with
      indignation.
18   Why is my pain unceasing,
     my wound incurable,
     refusing to be healed?
     Will you be to me like a deceitful brook,
     like waters that fail?
19   Therefore thus says the Lord:
     "If you return, I will restore you,
     and you shall stand before me.
     If you utter what is precious, and not
      what is worthless,
     you shall be as my mouth.
     They shall turn to you,
     but you shall not turn to them.
20   And I will make you to this people
     a fortified wall of bronze;
     they will fight against you,
     but they shall not prevail over you,
     for I am with you
     to save you and deliver you,
          declares the Lord.
21   I will deliver you out of the hand of the
     wicked,
     and redeem you from the grasp of the
     ruthless."

Mark 1

The beginning of the gospel of Jesus Christ, the Son of God.¹ ²As it is written in Isaiah the prophet,²

"Behold, I send my messenger before
   your face,
   who will prepare your way,
3   the voice of one crying in the
    wilderness:
   'Prepare³ the way of the Lord,
   make his paths straight,'"

⁴John appeared, baptizing in the wilderness and proclaiming a baptism of repentance for the forgiveness of sins. ⁵And all the country of Judea and all Jerusalem were going out to him and were being baptized by him in the river Jordan, confessing their sins. ⁶Now John was clothed with camel's hair and wore a leather belt around his waist and ate locusts and wild honey. ⁷And he preached, saying, "After me comes he who is mightier than I, the strap of whose sandals I am not worthy to stoop down and untie. ⁸I have baptized you with water, but he will baptize you with the Holy Spirit."

⁹In those days Jesus came from Nazareth of Galilee and was baptized by John in the Jordan. ¹⁰And when he came up out of the water, immediately he saw the heavens being torn open and the Spirit descending on him like a dove. ¹¹And a voice came from heaven, "You are my beloved Son;⁴ with you I am well pleased."

¹²The Spirit immediately drove him out into the wilderness. ¹³And he was in the wilderness forty days, being tempted by Satan. And he was with the wild animals, and the angels were ministering to him.

¹⁴Now after John was arrested, Jesus came into Galilee, proclaiming the gospel of God, ¹⁵and saying, "The time is fulfilled, and the kingdom of God is at hand; repent and believe in the gospel."

¹⁶Passing alongside the Sea of Galilee, he saw Simon and Andrew the brother of Simon casting a net into the sea, for they were fishermen. ¹⁷And Jesus said to them, "Follow me, and I will make you become fishers of men."⁵ ¹⁸And immediately they left their nets and followed him. ¹⁹And going on a little farther, he saw James the son of Zebedee and John his brother, who were in their boat mending the

¹ Some manuscripts omit *the Son of God* ² Some manuscripts *in the prophets* ³ Or *crying: Prepare in the wilderness* ⁴ Or *my Son, my* (or *the*) *Beloved* ⁵ The Greek word *anthropoi* refers here to both men and women

nets. [20]And immediately he called them, and they left their father Zebedee in the boat with the hired servants and followed him.

[21]And they went into Capernaum, and immediately on the Sabbath he entered the synagogue and was teaching. [22]And they were astonished at his teaching, for he taught them as one who had authority, and not as the scribes. [23]And immediately there was in their synagogue a man with an unclean spirit. And he cried out, [24]"What have you to do with us, Jesus of Nazareth? Have you come to destroy us? I know who you are—the Holy One of God." [25]But Jesus rebuked him, saying, "Be silent, and come out of him!" [26]And the unclean spirit, convulsing him and crying out with a loud voice, came out of him. [27]And they were all amazed, so that they questioned among themselves, saying, "What is this? A new teaching with authority! He commands even the unclean spirits, and they obey him." [28]And at once his fame spread everywhere throughout all the surrounding region of Galilee.

[29]And immediately he[1] left the synagogue and entered the house of Simon and Andrew, with James and John. [30]Now Simon's mother-in-law lay ill with a fever, and immediately they told him about her. [31]And he came and took her by the hand and lifted her up, and the fever left her, and she began to serve them.

[32]That evening at sundown they brought to him all who were sick or oppressed by demons. [33]And the whole city was gathered together at the door. [34]And he healed many who were sick with various diseases, and cast out many demons. And he would not permit the demons to speak, because they knew him.

[35]And rising very early in the morning, while it was still dark, he departed and went out to a desolate place, and there he prayed. [36]And Simon and those who were with him searched for him, [37]and they found him and said to him, "Everyone is looking for you." [38]And he said to them, "Let us go on to the next towns, that I may preach there also, for that is why I came out." [39]And he went throughout all Galilee, preaching in their synagogues and casting out demons.

[40]And a leper[2] came to him, imploring him, and kneeling said to him, "If you will, you can make me clean." [41]Moved with pity, he stretched out his hand and touched him and said to him, "I will; be clean." [42]And immediately the leprosy left him, and he was made clean. [43]And Jesus[3] sternly charged him and sent him away at once, [44]and said to him, "See that you say nothing to anyone, but go, show yourself to the priest and offer for your cleansing what Moses commanded, for a proof to them." [45]But he went out and began to talk freely about it, and to spread the news, so that Jesus could no longer openly enter a town, but was out in desolate places, and people were coming to him from every quarter.

JULY 20

Judges 3

Now these are the nations that the Lord left, to test Israel by them, that is, all in Israel who had not experienced all the wars in Canaan. [2]It was only in order that the generations of the people of Israel might know war, to teach war to those who had not known it before. [3]These are the nations: the five lords of the Philistines and all the Canaanites and the Sidonians and the Hivites who lived on Mount Lebanon, from Mount Baal-hermon as far as Lebo-hamath. [4]They were for the testing of Israel, to know whether Israel would obey the commandments of the Lord, which he commanded their fathers by the hand of Moses. [5]So the people of Israel lived among the Canaanites, the Hittites, the Amorites, the Perizzites, the Hivites, and the Jebusites. [6]And their daughters they took to themselves for wives, and their

---

[1] Some manuscripts *they*   [2] *Leprosy* was a term for several skin diseases; see Leviticus 13   [3] Greek *he*; also verse 45

own daughters they gave to their sons, and they served their gods.

⁷And the people of Israel did what was evil in the sight of the LORD. They forgot the LORD their God and served the Baals and the Asheroth. ⁸Therefore the anger of the LORD was kindled against Israel, and he sold them into the hand of Cushan-rishathaim king of Mesopotamia. And the people of Israel served Cushan-rishathaim eight years. ⁹But when the people of Israel cried out to the LORD, the LORD raised up a deliverer for the people of Israel, who saved them, Othniel the son of Kenaz, Caleb's younger brother. ¹⁰The Spirit of the LORD was upon him, and he judged Israel. He went out to war, and the LORD gave Cushan-rishathaim king of Mesopotamia into his hand. And his hand prevailed over Cushan-rishathaim. ¹¹So the land had rest forty years. Then Othniel the son of Kenaz died.

¹²And the people of Israel again did what was evil in the sight of the LORD, and the LORD strengthened Eglon the king of Moab against Israel, because they had done what was evil in the sight of the LORD. ¹³He gathered to himself the Ammonites and the Amalekites, and went and defeated Israel. And they took possession of the city of palms. ¹⁴And the people of Israel served Eglon the king of Moab eighteen years.

¹⁵Then the people of Israel cried out to the LORD, and the LORD raised up for them a deliverer, Ehud, the son of Gera, the Benjaminite, a left-handed man. The people of Israel sent tribute by him to Eglon the king of Moab. ¹⁶And Ehud made for himself a sword with two edges, a cubit¹ in length, and he bound it on his right thigh under his clothes. ¹⁷And he presented the tribute to Eglon king of Moab. Now Eglon was a very fat man. ¹⁸And when Ehud had finished presenting the tribute, he sent away the people who carried the tribute. ¹⁹But he himself turned back at the idols near Gilgal and said, "I have a secret message for you, O king." And he commanded, "Silence." And all his attendants went out from his presence. ²⁰And Ehud came to him as he was sitting alone in his cool roof chamber. And Ehud said, "I have a message from God for you." And he arose from his seat. ²¹And Ehud reached with his left hand, took the sword from his right thigh, and thrust it into his belly. ²²And the hilt also went in after

the blade, and the fat closed over the blade, for he did not pull the sword out of his belly; and the dung came out. ²³Then Ehud went out into the porch² and closed the doors of the roof chamber behind him and locked them.

²⁴When he had gone, the servants came, and when they saw that the doors of the roof chamber were locked, they thought, "Surely he is relieving himself in the closet of the cool chamber." ²⁵And they waited till they were embarrassed. But when he still did not open the doors of the roof chamber, they took the key and opened them, and there lay their lord dead on the floor.

²⁶Ehud escaped while they delayed, and he passed beyond the idols and escaped to Seirah. ²⁷When he arrived, he sounded the trumpet in the hill country of Ephraim. Then the people of Israel went down with him from the hill country, and he was their leader. ²⁸And he said to them, "Follow after me, for the LORD has given your enemies the Moabites into your hand." So they went down after him and seized the fords of the Jordan against the Moabites and did not allow anyone to pass over. ²⁹And they killed at that time about 10,000 of the Moabites, all strong, able-bodied men; not a man escaped. ³⁰So Moab was subdued that day under the hand of Israel. And the land had rest for eighty years.

³¹After him was Shamgar the son of Anath, who killed 600 of the Philistines with an oxgoad, and he also saved Israel.

Acts 7

And the high priest said, "Are these things so?" ²And Stephen said:

"Brothers and fathers, hear me. The God of glory appeared to our father Abraham when he was in Mesopotamia, before he lived in Haran, ³and said to him, 'Go out from your land and from your kindred and go into the land that I will show you.' ⁴Then he went out from the land of the Chaldeans and lived in Haran. And after his father died, God removed him from there into this land in which you are now living. ⁵Yet he gave him no inheritance in it, not even a foot's length, but promised to give it to him as a possession and to his offspring after him, though he had no child. ⁶And God spoke to this effect—that his offspring would be

¹ A *cubit* was about 18 inches or 45 centimeters ² The meaning of the Hebrew word is uncertain

sojourners in a land belonging to others, who would enslave them and afflict them four hundred years. [7]'But I will judge the nation that they serve,' said God, 'and after that they shall come out and worship me in this place.' [8]And he gave him the covenant of circumcision. And so Abraham became the father of Isaac, and circumcised him on the eighth day, and Isaac became the father of Jacob, and Jacob of the twelve patriarchs.

[9]"And the patriarchs, jealous of Joseph, sold him into Egypt; but God was with him [10]and rescued him out of all his afflictions and gave him favor and wisdom before Pharaoh, king of Egypt, who made him ruler over Egypt and over all his household. [11]Now there came a famine throughout all Egypt and Canaan, and great affliction, and our fathers could find no food. [12]But when Jacob heard that there was grain in Egypt, he sent out our fathers on their first visit. [13]And on the second visit Joseph made himself known to his brothers, and Joseph's family became known to Pharaoh. [14]And Joseph sent and summoned Jacob his father and all his kindred, seventy-five persons in all. [15]And Jacob went down into Egypt, and he died, he and our fathers, [16]and they were carried back to Shechem and laid in the tomb that Abraham had bought for a sum of silver from the sons of Hamor in Shechem.

[17]"But as the time of the promise drew near, which God had granted to Abraham, the people increased and multiplied in Egypt [18]until there arose over Egypt another king who did not know Joseph. [19]He dealt shrewdly with our race and forced our fathers to expose their infants, so that they would not be kept alive. [20]At this time Moses was born; and he was beautiful in God's sight. And he was brought up for three months in his father's house, [21]and when he was exposed, Pharaoh's daughter adopted him and brought him up as her own son. [22]And Moses was instructed in all the wisdom of the Egyptians, and he was mighty in his words and deeds.

[23]"When he was forty years old, it came into his heart to visit his brothers, the children of Israel. [24]And seeing one of them being wronged, he defended the oppressed man and avenged him by striking down the Egyptian. [25]He supposed that his brothers would understand that God was giving them salvation by his hand, but they did not understand. [26]And on the following day he appeared to them as they were quarreling and tried to reconcile them, saying, 'Men, you are brothers. Why do you wrong each other?' [27]But the man who was wronging his neighbor thrust him aside, saying, 'Who made you a ruler and a judge over us? [28]Do you want to kill me as you killed the Egyptian yesterday?' [29]At this retort Moses fled and became an exile in the land of Midian, where he became the father of two sons.

[30]"Now when forty years had passed, an angel appeared to him in the wilderness of Mount Sinai, in a flame of fire in a bush. [31]When Moses saw it, he was amazed at the sight, and as he drew near to look, there came the voice of the Lord: [32]'I am the God of your fathers, the God of Abraham and of Isaac and of Jacob.' And Moses trembled and did not dare to look. [33]Then the Lord said to him, 'Take off the sandals from your feet, for the place where you are standing is holy ground. [34]I have surely seen the affliction of my people who are in Egypt, and have heard their groaning, and I have come down to deliver them. And now come, I will send you to Egypt.'

[35]"This Moses, whom they rejected, saying, 'Who made you a ruler and a judge?'—this man God sent as both ruler and redeemer by the hand of the angel who appeared to him in the bush. [36]This man led them out, performing wonders and signs in Egypt and at the Red Sea and in the wilderness for forty years. [37]This is the Moses who said to the Israelites, 'God will raise up for you a prophet like me from your brothers.' [38]This is the one who was in the congregation in the wilderness with the angel who spoke to him at Mount Sinai, and with our fathers. He received living oracles to give to us. [39]Our fathers refused to obey him, but thrust him aside, and in their hearts they turned to Egypt, [40]saying to Aaron, 'Make for us gods who will go before us. As for this Moses who led us out from the land of Egypt, we do not know what has become of him.' [41]And they made a calf in those days, and offered a sacrifice to the idol and were rejoicing in the works of their hands. [42]But God turned away and gave them over to worship the host of heaven, as it is written in the book of the prophets:

"'Did you bring to me slain beasts and
    sacrifices,
    during the forty years in the
    wilderness, O house of Israel?
⁴³ You took up the tent of Moloch
    and the star of your god Rephan,
    the images that you made to worship;
    and I will send you into exile beyond
    Babylon.'

⁴⁴"Our fathers had the tent of witness in the wilderness, just as he who spoke to Moses directed him to make it, according to the pattern that he had seen. ⁴⁵Our fathers in turn brought it in with Joshua when they dispossessed the nations that God drove out before our fathers. So it was until the days of David, ⁴⁶who found favor in the sight of God and asked to find a dwelling place for the God of Jacob.[1] ⁴⁷But it was Solomon who built a house for him. ⁴⁸Yet the Most High does not dwell in houses made by hands, as the prophet says,

⁴⁹ "'Heaven is my throne,
    and the earth is my footstool.
 What kind of house will you build for
    me, says the Lord,
    or what is the place of my rest?
⁵⁰   Did not my hand make all these things?'

⁵¹"You stiff-necked people, uncircumcised in heart and ears, you always resist the Holy Spirit. As your fathers did, so do you. ⁵²Which of the prophets did your fathers not persecute? And they killed those who announced beforehand the coming of the Righteous One, whom you have now betrayed and murdered, ⁵³you who received the law as delivered by angels and did not keep it."

⁵⁴Now when they heard these things they were enraged, and they ground their teeth at him. ⁵⁵But he, full of the Holy Spirit, gazed into heaven and saw the glory of God, and Jesus standing at the right hand of God. ⁵⁶And he said, "Behold, I see the heavens opened, and the Son of Man standing at the right hand of God." ⁵⁷But they cried out with a loud voice and stopped their ears and rushed together[2] at him. ⁵⁸Then they cast him out of the city and stoned him. And the witnesses laid down their garments at the feet of a young man named Saul. ⁵⁹And as they were stoning Stephen, he called out, "Lord Jesus, receive my spirit." ⁶⁰And

falling to his knees he cried out with a loud voice, "Lord, do not hold this sin against them." And when he had said this, he fell asleep.

Jeremiah 16

The word of the LORD came to me: ²"You shall not take a wife, nor shall you have sons or daughters in this place. ³For thus says the LORD concerning the sons and daughters who are born in this place, and concerning the mothers who bore them and the fathers who fathered them in this land: ⁴They shall die of deadly diseases. They shall not be lamented, nor shall they be buried. They shall be as dung on the surface of the ground. They shall perish by the sword and by famine, and their dead bodies shall be food for the birds of the air and for the beasts of the earth.

⁵"For thus says the LORD: Do not enter the house of mourning, or go to lament or grieve for them, for I have taken away my peace from this people, my steadfast love and mercy, declares the LORD. ⁶Both great and small shall die in this land. They shall not be buried, and no one shall lament for them or cut himself or make himself bald for them. ⁷No one shall break bread for the mourner, to comfort him for the dead, nor shall anyone give him the cup of consolation to drink for his father or his mother. ⁸You shall not go into the house of feasting to sit with them, to eat and drink. ⁹For thus says the LORD of hosts, the God of Israel: Behold, I will silence in this place, before your eyes and in your days, the voice of mirth and the voice of gladness, the voice of the bridegroom and the voice of the bride.

¹⁰"And when you tell this people all these words, and they say to you, 'Why has the LORD pronounced all this great evil against us? What is our iniquity? What is the sin that we have committed against the LORD our God?' ¹¹then you shall say to them: 'Because your fathers have forsaken me, declares the LORD, and have gone after other gods and have served and worshiped them, and have forsaken me and have not kept my law, ¹²and because you have done worse than your fathers, for behold, every one of you follows his stubborn, evil will, refusing to listen to me. ¹³Therefore I will hurl you out of this land into a land that neither you nor your fathers have known, and there you shall serve

[1] Some manuscripts for the house of Jacob [2] Or rushed with one mind

other gods day and night, for I will show you no favor.'

¹⁴"Therefore, behold, the days are coming, declares the LORD, when it shall no longer be said, 'As the LORD lives who brought up the people of Israel out of the land of Egypt,' ¹⁵but 'As the LORD lives who brought up the people of Israel out of the north country and out of all the countries where he had driven them.' For I will bring them back to their own land that I gave to their fathers.

¹⁶"Behold, I am sending for many fishers, declares the LORD, and they shall catch them. And afterward I will send for many hunters, and they shall hunt them from every mountain and every hill, and out of the clefts of the rocks. ¹⁷For my eyes are on all their ways. They are not hidden from me, nor is their iniquity concealed from my eyes. ¹⁸But first I will doubly repay their iniquity and their sin, because they have polluted my land with the carcasses of their detestable idols, and have filled my inheritance with their abominations."

¹⁹　O LORD, my strength and my
　　　　stronghold,
　　my refuge in the day of trouble,
　to you shall the nations come
　　　from the ends of the earth and say:
　"Our fathers have inherited nothing but
　　　　lies,
　　worthless things in which there is no
　　　　profit.
²⁰　Can man make for himself gods?
　　Such are not gods!"

²¹"Therefore, behold, I will make them know, this once I will make them know my power and my might, and they shall know that my name is the LORD."

───────── *Mark 2* ─────────

A nd when he returned to Capernaum after some days, it was reported that he was at home. ²And many were gathered together, so that there was no more room, not even at the door. And he was preaching the word to them. ³And they came, bringing to him a paralytic carried by four men. ⁴And when they could not get near him because of the crowd, they removed the roof above him, and when they had made an opening, they let down the bed on which the paralytic lay. ⁵And when Jesus saw their faith, he said to the paralytic, "Son, your sins are forgiven." ⁶Now some of the scribes were sitting there, questioning in their hearts, ⁷"Why does this man speak like that? He is blaspheming! Who can forgive sins but God alone?" ⁸And immediately Jesus, perceiving in his spirit that they thus questioned within themselves, said to them, "Why do you question these things in your hearts? ⁹Which is easier, to say to the paralytic, 'Your sins are forgiven,' or to say, 'Rise, take up your bed and walk'? ¹⁰But that you may know that the Son of Man has authority on earth to forgive sins"—he said to the paralytic— ¹¹"I say to you, rise, pick up your bed, and go home." ¹²And he rose and immediately picked up his bed and went out before them all, so that they were all amazed and glorified God, saying, "We never saw anything like this!"

¹³He went out again beside the sea, and all the crowd was coming to him, and he was teaching them. ¹⁴And as he passed by, he saw Levi the son of Alphaeus sitting at the tax booth, and he said to him, "Follow me." And he rose and followed him.

¹⁵And as he reclined at table in his house, many tax collectors and sinners were reclining with Jesus and his disciples, for there were many who followed him. ¹⁶And the scribes of¹ the Pharisees, when they saw that he was eating with sinners and tax collectors, said to his disciples, "Why does he eat² with tax collectors and sinners?" ¹⁷And when Jesus heard it, he said to them, "Those who are well have no need of a physician, but those who are sick. I came not to call the righteous, but sinners."

¹⁸Now John's disciples and the Pharisees were fasting. And people came and said to him, "Why do John's disciples and the disciples of the Pharisees fast, but your disciples do not fast?" ¹⁹And Jesus said to them, "Can the wedding guests fast while the bridegroom is with them? As long as they have the bridegroom with them, they cannot fast. ²⁰The days will come when the bridegroom is taken away from them, and then they will fast in that day. ²¹No one sews a piece of unshrunk cloth on an old garment. If he does, the patch tears away from it, the new from the old, and a worse tear is made. ²²And no one puts new wine into old wineskins. If he does, the wine will burst the

---

¹ Some manuscripts *and*　² Some manuscripts add *and drink*

skins—and the wine is destroyed, and so are the skins. But new wine is for fresh wineskins."[1]

²³ One Sabbath he was going through the grainfields, and as they made their way, his disciples began to pluck heads of grain. ²⁴ And the Pharisees were saying to him, "Look, why are they doing what is not lawful on the Sabbath?" ²⁵ And he said to them, "Have you never read what David did, when he was in need and was hungry, he and those who were with him: ²⁶ how he entered the house of God, in the time of[2] Abiathar the high priest, and ate the bread of the Presence, which it is not lawful for any but the priests to eat, and also gave it to those who were with him?" ²⁷ And he said to them, "The Sabbath was made for man, not man for the Sabbath. ²⁸ So the Son of Man is lord even of the Sabbath."

JULY 21

Judges 4

And the people of Israel again did what was evil in the sight of the LORD after Ehud died. ² And the LORD sold them into the hand of Jabin king of Canaan, who reigned in Hazor. The commander of his army was Sisera, who lived in Harosheth-hagoyim. ³ Then the people of Israel cried out to the LORD for help, for he had 900 chariots of iron and he oppressed the people of Israel cruelly for twenty years.

⁴ Now Deborah, a prophetess, the wife of Lappidoth, was judging Israel at that time. ⁵ She used to sit under the palm of Deborah between Ramah and Bethel in the hill country of Ephraim, and the people of Israel came up to her for judgment. ⁶ She sent and summoned Barak the son of Abinoam from Kedesh-naphtali and said to him, "Has not the LORD, the God of Israel, commanded you, 'Go, gather your men at Mount Tabor, taking 10,000 from the people of Naphtali and the people of Zebulun. ⁷ And I will draw out Sisera, the general of Jabin's army, to meet you by the river Kishon with his chariots and his troops, and I will give him into your hand'?" ⁸ Barak said to her, "If you will go with me, I will go, but if you will not go with me, I will not go." ⁹ And she said, "I will surely go with you. Nevertheless, the road on which you are going will not lead to your glory, for the LORD will sell Sisera into the hand of a woman." Then Deborah arose and went with Barak to Kedesh. ¹⁰ And Barak called out Zebulun and Naphtali to Kedesh. And 10,000 men went up at his heels, and Deborah went up with him.

¹¹ Now Heber the Kenite had separated from the Kenites, the descendants of Hobab the father-in-law of Moses, and had pitched his tent as far away as the oak in Zaanannim, which is near Kedesh.

¹² When Sisera was told that Barak the son of Abinoam had gone up to Mount Tabor, ¹³ Sisera called out all his chariots, 900 chariots of iron, and all the men who were with him, from Harosheth-hagoyim to the river Kishon. ¹⁴ And Deborah said to Barak, "Up! For this is the day in which the LORD has given Sisera into your hand. Does not the LORD go out before you?" So Barak went down from Mount Tabor with 10,000 men following him. ¹⁵ And the LORD routed Sisera and all his chariots and all his army before Barak by the edge of the sword. And Sisera got down from his chariot and fled away on foot. ¹⁶ And Barak pursued the chariots and the army to Harosheth-hagoyim, and all the army of Sisera fell by the edge of the sword; not a man was left.

¹⁷ But Sisera fled away on foot to the tent of Jael, the wife of Heber the Kenite, for there was peace between Jabin the king of Hazor and the house of Heber the Kenite. ¹⁸ And Jael came out to meet Sisera and said to him, "Turn aside, my lord; turn aside to me; do not be afraid." So he turned aside to her into the tent, and she covered him with a rug. ¹⁹ And he said to her,

[1] Some manuscripts omit *But new wine is for fresh wineskins* [2] Or *in the passage about*

"Please give me a little water to drink, for I am thirsty." So she opened a skin of milk and gave him a drink and covered him. [20]And he said to her, "Stand at the opening of the tent, and if any man comes and asks you, 'Is anyone here?' say, 'No.' " [21]But Jael the wife of Heber took a tent peg, and took a hammer in her hand. Then she went softly to him and drove the peg into his temple until it went down into the ground while he was lying fast asleep from weariness. So he died. [22]And behold, as Barak was pursuing Sisera, Jael went out to meet him and said to him, "Come, and I will show you the man whom you are seeking." So he went in to her tent, and there lay Sisera dead, with the tent peg in his temple.

[23]So on that day God subdued Jabin the king of Canaan before the people of Israel. [24]And the hand of the people of Israel pressed harder and harder against Jabin the king of Canaan, until they destroyed Jabin king of Canaan.

Acts 8

A nd Saul approved of his execution. And there arose on that day a great persecution against the church in Jerusalem, and they were all scattered throughout the regions of Judea and Samaria, except the apostles. [2]Devout men buried Stephen and made great lamentation over him. [3]But Saul was ravaging the church, and entering house after house, he dragged off men and women and committed them to prison.

[4]Now those who were scattered went about preaching the word. [5]Philip went down to the city[1] of Samaria and proclaimed to them the Christ. [6]And the crowds with one accord paid attention to what was being said by Philip when they heard him and saw the signs that he did. [7]For unclean spirits, crying out with a loud voice, came out of many who had them, and many who were paralyzed or lame were healed. [8]So there was much joy in that city.

[9]But there was a man named Simon, who had previously practiced magic in the city and amazed the people of Samaria, saying that he himself was somebody great. [10]They all paid attention to him, from the least to the greatest, saying, "This man is the power of God that is called Great." [11]And they paid attention to him because for a long time he had amazed them

with his magic. [12]But when they believed Philip as he preached good news about the kingdom of God and the name of Jesus Christ, they were baptized, both men and women. [13]Even Simon himself believed, and after being baptized he continued with Philip. And seeing signs and great miracles[2] performed, he was amazed.

[14]Now when the apostles at Jerusalem heard that Samaria had received the word of God, they sent to them Peter and John, [15]who came down and prayed for them that they might receive the Holy Spirit, [16]for he had not yet fallen on any of them, but they had only been baptized in the name of the Lord Jesus. [17]Then they laid their hands on them and they received the Holy Spirit. [18]Now when Simon saw that the Spirit was given through the laying on of the apostles' hands, he offered them money, [19]saying, "Give me this power also, so that anyone on whom I lay my hands may receive the Holy Spirit." [20]But Peter said to him, "May your silver perish with you, because you thought you could obtain the gift of God with money! [21]You have neither part nor lot in this matter, for your heart is not right before God. [22]Repent, therefore, of this wickedness of yours, and pray to the Lord that, if possible, the intent of your heart may be forgiven you. [23]For I see that you are in the gall[3] of bitterness and in the bond of iniquity." [24]And Simon answered, "Pray for me to the Lord, that nothing of what you have said may come upon me."

[25]Now when they had testified and spoken the word of the Lord, they returned to Jerusalem, preaching the gospel to many villages of the Samaritans.

[26]Now an angel of the Lord said to Philip, "Rise and go toward the south[4] to the road that goes down from Jerusalem to Gaza." This is a desert place. [27]And he rose and went. And there was an Ethiopian, a eunuch, a court official of Candace, queen of the Ethiopians, who was in charge of all her treasure. He had come to Jerusalem to worship [28]and was returning, seated in his chariot, and he was reading the prophet Isaiah. [29]And the Spirit said to Philip, "Go over and join this chariot." [30]So Philip ran to him and heard him reading Isaiah the prophet and asked, "Do you understand what you are reading?" [31]And he said, "How can I, unless someone guides me?" And he invited Philip to come up and sit with him. [32]Now the

[1] Some manuscripts *a city*   [2] Greek *works of power*   [3] That is, a bitter fluid secreted by the liver; bile   [4] Or *go at about noon*

passage of the Scripture that he was reading was this:

> "Like a sheep he was led to the slaughter
>   and like a lamb before its shearer is
>   silent,
>   so he opens not his mouth.
> 33 In his humiliation justice was denied
>   him.
>   Who can describe his generation?
>   For his life is taken away from the earth."

34 And the eunuch said to Philip, "About whom, I ask you, does the prophet say this, about himself or about someone else?" 35 Then Philip opened his mouth, and beginning with this Scripture he told him the good news about Jesus. 36 And as they were going along the road they came to some water, and the eunuch said, "See, here is water! What prevents me from being baptized?"[1] 38 And he commanded the chariot to stop, and they both went down into the water, Philip and the eunuch, and he baptized him. 39 And when they came up out of the water, the Spirit of the Lord carried Philip away, and the eunuch saw him no more, and went on his way rejoicing. 40 But Philip found himself at Azotus, and as he passed through he preached the gospel to all the towns until he came to Caesarea.

Jeremiah 17

"The sin of Judah is written with a pen of iron; with a point of diamond it is engraved on the tablet of their heart, and on the horns of their altars, 2 while their children remember their altars and their Asherim, beside every green tree and on the high hills, 3 on the mountains in the open country. Your wealth and all your treasures I will give for spoil as the price of your high places for sin throughout all your territory. 4 You shall loosen your hand from your heritage that I gave to you, and I will make you serve your enemies in a land that you do not know, for in my anger a fire is kindled that shall burn forever."

> 5 Thus says the Lord:
>   "Cursed is the man who trusts in man
>   and makes flesh his strength,[2]
>   whose heart turns away from the
>   Lord.

> 6 He is like a shrub in the desert,
>   and shall not see any good come.
>   He shall dwell in the parched places of
>   the wilderness,
>   in an uninhabited salt land.
> 7 "Blessed is the man who trusts in the
>   Lord,
>   whose trust is the Lord.
> 8 He is like a tree planted by water,
>   that sends out its roots by the stream,
>   and does not fear when heat comes,
>   for its leaves remain green,
>   and is not anxious in the year of
>   drought,
>   for it does not cease to bear fruit."

> 9 The heart is deceitful above all things,
>   and desperately sick;
>   who can understand it?
> 10 "I the Lord search the heart
>   and test the mind,[3]
>   to give every man according to his ways,
>   according to the fruit of his deeds."

> 11 Like the partridge that gathers a brood
>   that she did not hatch,
>   so is he who gets riches but not by
>   justice;
>   in the midst of his days they will leave
>   him,
>   and at his end he will be a fool.

> 12 A glorious throne set on high from the
>   beginning
>   is the place of our sanctuary.
> 13 O Lord, the hope of Israel,
>   all who forsake you shall be put to
>   shame;
>   those who turn away from you[4] shall be
>   written in the earth,
>   for they have forsaken the Lord, the
>   fountain of living water.

> 14 Heal me, O Lord, and I shall be healed;
>   save me, and I shall be saved,
>   for you are my praise.
> 15 Behold, they say to me,
>   "Where is the word of the Lord?
>   Let it come!"
> 16 I have not run away from being your
>   shepherd,
>   nor have I desired the day of sickness.

---

[1] Some manuscripts add all or most of verse 37: And Philip said, "If you believe with all your heart, you may." And he replied, "I believe that Jesus Christ is the Son of God." [2] Hebrew arm [3] Hebrew kidneys [4] Hebrew me

You know what came out of my lips;
    it was before your face.
17 Be not a terror to me;
    you are my refuge in the day of
      disaster.
18 Let those be put to shame who
      persecute me,
    but let me not be put to shame;
  let them be dismayed,
    but let me not be dismayed;
  bring upon them the day of disaster;
    destroy them with double
      destruction!

¹⁹Thus said the LORD to me: "Go and stand in the People's Gate, by which the kings of Judah enter and by which they go out, and in all the gates of Jerusalem, ²⁰and say: 'Hear the word of the LORD, you kings of Judah, and all Judah, and all the inhabitants of Jerusalem, who enter by these gates. ²¹Thus says the LORD: Take care for the sake of your lives, and do not bear a burden on the Sabbath day or bring it in by the gates of Jerusalem. ²²And do not carry a burden out of your houses on the Sabbath or do any work, but keep the Sabbath day holy, as I commanded your fathers. ²³Yet they did not listen or incline their ear, but stiffened their neck, that they might not hear and receive instruction.

²⁴"'But if you listen to me, declares the LORD, and bring in no burden by the gates of this city on the Sabbath day, but keep the Sabbath day holy and do no work on it, ²⁵then there shall enter by the gates of this city kings and princes who sit on the throne of David, riding in chariots and on horses, they and their officials, the men of Judah and the inhabitants of Jerusalem. And this city shall be inhabited forever. ²⁶And people shall come from the cities of Judah and the places around Jerusalem, from the land of Benjamin, from the Shephelah, from the hill country, and from the Negeb, bringing burnt offerings and sacrifices, grain offerings and frankincense, and bringing thank offerings to the house of the LORD. ²⁷But if you do not listen to me, to keep the Sabbath day holy, and not to bear a burden and enter by the gates of Jerusalem on the Sabbath day, then I will kindle a fire in its gates, and it shall devour the palaces of Jerusalem and shall not be quenched.'"

---------------------------- *Mark 3* ----------------------------

Again he entered the synagogue, and a man was there with a withered hand. ²And they watched Jesus,¹ to see whether he would heal him on the Sabbath, so that they might accuse him. ³And he said to the man with the withered hand, "Come here." ⁴And he said to them, "Is it lawful on the Sabbath to do good or to do harm, to save life or to kill?" But they were silent. ⁵And he looked around at them with anger, grieved at their hardness of heart, and said to the man, "Stretch out your hand." He stretched it out, and his hand was restored. ⁶The Pharisees went out and immediately held counsel with the Herodians against him, how to destroy him.

⁷Jesus withdrew with his disciples to the sea, and a great crowd followed, from Galilee and Judea ⁸and Jerusalem and Idumea and from beyond the Jordan and from around Tyre and Sidon. When the great crowd heard all that he was doing, they came to him. ⁹And he told his disciples to have a boat ready for him because of the crowd, lest they crush him, ¹⁰for he had healed many, so that all who had diseases pressed around him to touch him. ¹¹And whenever the unclean spirits saw him, they fell down before him and cried out, "You are the Son of God." ¹²And he strictly ordered them not to make him known.

¹³And he went up on the mountain and called to him those whom he desired, and they came to him. ¹⁴And he appointed twelve (whom he also named apostles) so that they might be with him and he might send them out to preach ¹⁵and have authority to cast out demons. ¹⁶He appointed the twelve: Simon (to whom he gave the name Peter); ¹⁷James the son of Zebedee and John the brother of James (to whom he gave the name Boanerges, that is, Sons of Thunder); ¹⁸Andrew, and Philip, and Bartholomew, and Matthew, and Thomas, and James the son of Alphaeus, and Thaddaeus, and Simon the Zealot,² ¹⁹and Judas Iscariot, who betrayed him.

²⁰Then he went home, and the crowd gathered again, so that they could not even eat. ²¹And when his family heard it, they went out to seize him, for they were saying, "He is out of his mind."

²²And the scribes who came down from Jerusalem were saying, "He is possessed by

---

¹ Greek *him* ² Greek *kananaios*, meaning *zealot*

Beelzebul," and "by the prince of demons he casts out the demons." [23]And he called them to him and said to them in parables, "How can Satan cast out Satan? [24]If a kingdom is divided against itself, that kingdom cannot stand. [25]And if a house is divided against itself, that house will not be able to stand. [26]And if Satan has risen up against himself and is divided, he cannot stand, but is coming to an end. [27]But no one can enter a strong man's house and plunder his goods, unless he first binds the strong man. Then indeed he may plunder his house.

[28]"Truly, I say to you, all sins will be forgiven the children of man, and whatever blasphemies they utter, [29]but whoever blasphemes against the Holy Spirit never has forgiveness, but is guilty of an eternal sin"— [30]for they were saying, "He has an unclean spirit."

[31]And his mother and his brothers came, and standing outside they sent to him and called him. [32]And a crowd was sitting around him, and they said to him, "Your mother and your brothers[1] are outside, seeking you." [33]And he answered them, "Who are my mother and my brothers?" [34]And looking about at those who sat around him, he said, "Here are my mother and my brothers! [35]For whoever does the will of God, he is my brother and sister and mother."

JULY 22

Judges 5

Then sang Deborah and Barak the son of Abinoam on that day:

[2]   "That the leaders took the lead in Israel,
        that the people offered themselves
            willingly,
        bless the LORD!

[3]   "Hear, O kings; give ear, O princes;
        to the LORD I will sing;
        I will make melody to the LORD, the
            God of Israel.

[4]   "LORD, when you went out from Seir,
        when you marched from the region of
            Edom,
        the earth trembled
        and the heavens dropped,
        yes, the clouds dropped water.

[5]   The mountains quaked before the
            LORD,
        even Sinai before the LORD, the God of
            Israel.

[6]   "In the days of Shamgar, son of Anath,
        in the days of Jael, the highways were
            abandoned,
        and travelers kept to the byways.

[7]   The villagers ceased in Israel;
        they ceased to be until I arose;
        I, Deborah, arose as a mother in Israel.

[8]   When new gods were chosen,
        then war was in the gates.
        Was shield or spear to be seen
        among forty thousand in Israel?

[9]   My heart goes out to the commanders of
            Israel
        who offered themselves willingly
            among the people.
        Bless the LORD.

[10]   "Tell of it, you who ride on white
            donkeys,
        you who sit on rich carpets[2]
        and you who walk by the way.

[11]   To the sound of musicians[3] at the
            watering places,
        there they repeat the righteous
            triumphs of the LORD,
        the righteous triumphs of his villagers
            in Israel.

    "Then down to the gates marched the
        people of the LORD.

[12]   "Awake, awake, Deborah!
        Awake, awake, break out in a song!

[1] Other early manuscripts add *and your sisters* [2] The meaning of the Hebrew word is uncertain; it may connote *saddle blankets* [3] Or *archers*; the meaning of the Hebrew word is uncertain

Arise, Barak, lead away your captives,
  O son of Abinoam.
13 Then down marched the remnant of the
    noble;
  the people of the LORD marched down
    for me against the mighty.
14 From Ephraim their root they marched
    down into the valley,[1]
  following you, Benjamin, with your
    kinsmen;
  from Machir marched down the
    commanders,
  and from Zebulun those who bear the
    lieutenant's[2] staff;
15 the princes of Issachar came with
    Deborah,
  and Issachar faithful to Barak;
  into the valley they rushed at his heels.
  Among the clans of Reuben
    there were great searchings of heart.
16 Why did you sit still among the
    sheepfolds,
  to hear the whistling for the flocks?
  Among the clans of Reuben
    there were great searchings of heart.
17 Gilead stayed beyond the Jordan;
  and Dan, why did he stay with the
    ships?
  Asher sat still at the coast of the sea,
    staying by his landings.
18 Zebulun is a people who risked their
    lives to the death;
  Naphtali, too, on the heights of the
    field.

19 "The kings came, they fought;
  then fought the kings of Canaan,
  at Taanach, by the waters of Megiddo;
    they got no spoils of silver.
20 From heaven the stars fought,
  from their courses they fought against
    Sisera.
21 The torrent Kishon swept them away,
  the ancient torrent, the torrent
    Kishon.
  March on, my soul, with might!

22 "Then loud beat the horses' hoofs
  with the galloping, galloping of his
    steeds.

23 "Curse Meroz, says the angel of the LORD,
  curse its inhabitants thoroughly,

because they did not come to the help of
    the LORD,
  to the help of the LORD against the
    mighty.

24 "Most blessed of women be Jael,
  the wife of Heber the Kenite,
  of tent-dwelling women most blessed.
25 He asked for water and she gave him
    milk;
  she brought him curds in a noble's
    bowl.
26 She sent her hand to the tent peg
  and her right hand to the workmen's
    mallet;
  she struck Sisera;
    she crushed his head;
    she shattered and pierced his temple.
27 Between her feet
    he sank, he fell, he lay still;
  between her feet
    he sank, he fell;
  where he sank,
    there he fell—dead.

28 "Out of the window she peered,
  the mother of Sisera wailed through
    the lattice:
  'Why is his chariot so long in coming?
  Why tarry the hoofbeats of his
    chariots?'
29 Her wisest princesses answer,
  indeed, she answers herself,
30 'Have they not found and divided the
    spoil?—
  A womb or two for every man;
  spoil of dyed materials for Sisera,
  spoil of dyed materials embroidered,
  two pieces of dyed work embroidered
    for the neck as spoil?'

31 "So may all your enemies perish, O LORD!
  But your friends be like the sun as he
    rises in his might."

And the land had rest for forty years.

———————— *Acts 9* ————————

But Saul, still breathing threats and murder
against the disciples of the Lord, went to
the high priest [2] and asked him for letters to the
synagogues at Damascus, so that if he found

[1] Septuagint; Hebrew in Amalek [2] Hebrew commander's

any belonging to the Way, men or women, he might bring them bound to Jerusalem. ³Now as he went on his way, he approached Damascus, and suddenly a light from heaven shone around him. ⁴And falling to the ground he heard a voice saying to him, "Saul, Saul, why are you persecuting me?" ⁵And he said, "Who are you, Lord?" And he said, "I am Jesus, whom you are persecuting. ⁶But rise and enter the city, and you will be told what you are to do." ⁷The men who were traveling with him stood speechless, hearing the voice but seeing no one. ⁸Saul rose from the ground, and although his eyes were opened, he saw nothing. So they led him by the hand and brought him into Damascus. ⁹And for three days he was without sight, and neither ate nor drank.

¹⁰Now there was a disciple at Damascus named Ananias. The Lord said to him in a vision, "Ananias." And he said, "Here I am, Lord." ¹¹And the Lord said to him, "Rise and go to the street called Straight, and at the house of Judas look for a man of Tarsus named Saul, for behold, he is praying, ¹²and he has seen in a vision a man named Ananias come in and lay his hands on him so that he might regain his sight." ¹³But Ananias answered, "Lord, I have heard from many about this man, how much evil he has done to your saints at Jerusalem. ¹⁴And here he has authority from the chief priests to bind all who call on your name." ¹⁵But the Lord said to him, "Go, for he is a chosen instrument of mine to carry my name before the Gentiles and kings and the children of Israel. ¹⁶For I will show him how much he must suffer for the sake of my name." ¹⁷So Ananias departed and entered the house. And laying his hands on him he said, "Brother Saul, the Lord Jesus who appeared to you on the road by which you came has sent me so that you may regain your sight and be filled with the Holy Spirit." ¹⁸And immediately something like scales fell from his eyes, and he regained his sight. Then he rose and was baptized; ¹⁹and taking food, he was strengthened.

For some days he was with the disciples at Damascus. ²⁰And immediately he proclaimed Jesus in the synagogues, saying, "He is the Son of God." ²¹And all who heard him were amazed and said, "Is not this the man who made havoc in Jerusalem of those who called upon this name? And has he not come here for this

purpose, to bring them bound before the chief priests?" ²²But Saul increased all the more in strength, and confounded the Jews who lived in Damascus by proving that Jesus was the Christ.

²³When many days had passed, the Jews¹ plotted to kill him, ²⁴but their plot became known to Saul. They were watching the gates day and night in order to kill him, ²⁵but his disciples took him by night and let him down through an opening in the wall,² lowering him in a basket.

²⁶And when he had come to Jerusalem, he attempted to join the disciples. And they were all afraid of him, for they did not believe that he was a disciple. ²⁷But Barnabas took him and brought him to the apostles and declared to them how on the road he had seen the Lord, who spoke to him, and how at Damascus he had preached boldly in the name of Jesus. ²⁸So he went in and out among them at Jerusalem, preaching boldly in the name of the Lord. ²⁹And he spoke and disputed against the Hellenists.³ But they were seeking to kill him. ³⁰And when the brothers learned this, they brought him down to Caesarea and sent him off to Tarsus.

³¹So the church throughout all Judea and Galilee and Samaria had peace and was being built up. And walking in the fear of the Lord and in the comfort of the Holy Spirit, it multiplied.

³²Now as Peter went here and there among them all, he came down also to the saints who lived at Lydda. ³³There he found a man named Aeneas, bedridden for eight years, who was paralyzed. ³⁴And Peter said to him, "Aeneas, Jesus Christ heals you; rise and make your bed." And immediately he rose. ³⁵And all the residents of Lydda and Sharon saw him, and they turned to the Lord.

³⁶Now there was in Joppa a disciple named Tabitha, which, translated, means Dorcas.⁴ She was full of good works and acts of charity. ³⁷In those days she became ill and died, and when they had washed her, they laid her in an upper room. ³⁸Since Lydda was near Joppa, the disciples, hearing that Peter was there, sent two men to him, urging him, "Please come to us without delay." ³⁹So Peter rose and went with them. And when he arrived, they took him to the upper room. All the widows stood beside him weeping and showing tunics⁵ and other garments that Dorcas made while she was with them. ⁴⁰But Peter put them all outside, and knelt down and

prayed; and turning to the body he said, "Tabitha, arise." And she opened her eyes, and when she saw Peter she sat up. ⁴¹And he gave her his hand and raised her up. Then calling the saints and widows, he presented her alive. ⁴²And it became known throughout all Joppa, and many believed in the Lord. ⁴³And he stayed in Joppa for many days with one Simon, a tanner.

Jeremiah 18

The word that came to Jeremiah from the Lord: ²"Arise, and go down to the potter's house, and there I will let you hear my words." ³So I went down to the potter's house, and there he was working at his wheel. ⁴And the vessel he was making of clay was spoiled in the potter's hand, and he reworked it into another vessel, as it seemed good to the potter to do.

⁵Then the word of the Lord came to me: ⁶"O house of Israel, can I not do with you as this potter has done? declares the Lord. Behold, like the clay in the potter's hand, so are you in my hand, O house of Israel. ⁷If at any time I declare concerning a nation or a kingdom, that I will pluck up and break down and destroy it, ⁸and if that nation, concerning which I have spoken, turns from its evil, I will relent of the disaster that I intended to do to it. ⁹And if at any time I declare concerning a nation or a kingdom that I will build and plant it, ¹⁰and if it does evil in my sight, not listening to my voice, then I will relent of the good that I had intended to do to it. ¹¹Now, therefore, say to the men of Judah and the inhabitants of Jerusalem: 'Thus says the Lord, Behold, I am shaping disaster against you and devising a plan against you. Return, every one from his evil way, and amend your ways and your deeds.'

¹²"But they say, 'That is in vain! We will follow our own plans, and will every one act according to the stubbornness of his evil heart.'

¹³ "Therefore thus says the Lord:
Ask among the nations,
   Who has heard the like of this?
The virgin Israel
   has done a very horrible thing.
¹⁴ Does the snow of Lebanon leave
   the crags of Sirion?¹
Do the mountain waters run dry,²
   the cold flowing streams?

¹⁵ But my people have forgotten me;
   they make offerings to false gods;
they made them stumble in their ways,
   in the ancient roads,
and to walk into side roads,
   not the highway,
¹⁶ making their land a horror,
   a thing to be hissed at forever.
Everyone who passes by it is horrified
   and shakes his head.
¹⁷ Like the east wind I will scatter them
   before the enemy.
I will show them my back, not my face,
   in the day of their calamity."

¹⁸Then they said, "Come, let us make plots against Jeremiah, for the law shall not perish from the priest, nor counsel from the wise, nor the word from the prophet. Come, let us strike him with the tongue, and let us not pay attention to any of his words."

¹⁹ Hear me, O Lord,
   and listen to the voice of my
      adversaries.
²⁰ Should good be repaid with evil?
   Yet they have dug a pit for my life.
Remember how I stood before you
   to speak good for them,
   to turn away your wrath from them.
²¹ Therefore deliver up their children to
      famine;
   give them over to the power of the
      sword;
let their wives become childless and
      widowed.
May their men meet death by
      pestilence,
   their youths be struck down by the
      sword in battle.
²² May a cry be heard from their houses,
   when you bring the plunderer
      suddenly upon them!
For they have dug a pit to take me
   and laid snares for my feet.
²³ Yet you, O Lord, know
   all their plotting to kill me.
Forgive not their iniquity,
   nor blot out their sin from your
      sight.
Let them be overthrown before you;
   deal with them in the time of your
      anger.

¹ Hebrew of the field ² Hebrew Are foreign waters plucked up

Mark 4

Again he began to teach beside the sea. And a very large crowd gathered about him, so that he got into a boat and sat in it on the sea, and the whole crowd was beside the sea on the land. ²And he was teaching them many things in parables, and in his teaching he said to them: ³"Listen! Behold, a sower went out to sow. ⁴And as he sowed, some seed fell along the path, and the birds came and devoured it. ⁵Other seed fell on rocky ground, where it did not have much soil, and immediately it sprang up, since it had no depth of soil. ⁶And when the sun rose, it was scorched, and since it had no root, it withered away. ⁷Other seed fell among thorns, and the thorns grew up and choked it, and it yielded no grain. ⁸And other seeds fell into good soil and produced grain, growing up and increasing and yielding thirtyfold and sixtyfold and a hundredfold." ⁹And he said, "He who has ears to hear, let him hear."

¹⁰And when he was alone, those around him with the twelve asked him about the parables. ¹¹And he said to them, "To you has been given the secret of the kingdom of God, but for those outside everything is in parables, ¹²so that

"they may indeed see but not perceive,
    and may indeed hear but not
        understand,
    lest they should turn and be forgiven."

¹³And he said to them, "Do you not understand this parable? How then will you understand all the parables? ¹⁴The sower sows the word. ¹⁵And these are the ones along the path, where the word is sown: when they hear, Satan immediately comes and takes away the word that is sown in them. ¹⁶And these are the ones sown on rocky ground: the ones who, when they hear the word, immediately receive it with joy. ¹⁷And they have no root in themselves, but endure for a while; then, when tribulation or persecution arises on account of the word, immediately they fall away.[1] ¹⁸And others are the ones sown among thorns. They are those who hear the word, ¹⁹but the cares of the world and the deceitfulness of riches and the desires for other things enter in and choke the word, and it proves unfruitful. ²⁰But those that were sown on the good soil are the ones who hear the word and accept it

and bear fruit, thirtyfold and sixtyfold and a hundredfold."

²¹And he said to them, "Is a lamp brought in to be put under a basket, or under a bed, and not on a stand? ²²For nothing is hidden except to be made manifest; nor is anything secret except to come to light. ²³If anyone has ears to hear, let him hear." ²⁴And he said to them, "Pay attention to what you hear: with the measure you use, it will be measured to you, and still more will be added to you. ²⁵For to the one who has, more will be given, and from the one who has not, even what he has will be taken away."

²⁶And he said, "The kingdom of God is as if a man should scatter seed on the ground. ²⁷He sleeps and rises night and day, and the seed sprouts and grows; he knows not how. ²⁸The earth produces by itself, first the blade, then the ear, then the full grain in the ear. ²⁹But when the grain is ripe, at once he puts in the sickle, because the harvest has come."

³⁰And he said, "With what can we compare the kingdom of God, or what parable shall we use for it? ³¹It is like a grain of mustard seed, which, when sown on the ground, is the smallest of all the seeds on earth, ³²yet when it is sown it grows up and becomes larger than all the garden plants and puts out large branches, so that the birds of the air can make nests in its shade."

³³With many such parables he spoke the word to them, as they were able to hear it. ³⁴He did not speak to them without a parable, but privately to his own disciples he explained everything.

³⁵On that day, when evening had come, he said to them, "Let us go across to the other side." ³⁶And leaving the crowd, they took him with them in the boat, just as he was. And other boats were with him. ³⁷And a great windstorm arose, and the waves were breaking into the boat, so that the boat was already filling. ³⁸But he was in the stern, asleep on the cushion. And they woke him and said to him, "Teacher, do you not care that we are perishing?" ³⁹And he awoke and rebuked the wind and said to the sea, "Peace! Be still!" And the wind ceased, and there was a great calm. ⁴⁰He said to them, "Why are you so afraid? Have you still no faith?" ⁴¹And they were filled with great fear and said to one another, "Who then is this, that even the wind and the sea obey him?"

---

[1] Or stumble

JULY 23

Judges 6

The people of Israel did what was evil in the sight of the Lord, and the Lord gave them into the hand of Midian seven years. ²And the hand of Midian overpowered Israel, and because of Midian the people of Israel made for themselves the dens that are in the mountains and the caves and the strongholds. ³For whenever the Israelites planted crops, the Midianites and the Amalekites and the people of the East would come up against them. ⁴They would encamp against them and devour the produce of the land, as far as Gaza, and leave no sustenance in Israel and no sheep or ox or donkey. ⁵For they would come up with their livestock and their tents; they would come like locusts in number—both they and their camels could not be counted—so that they laid waste the land as they came in. ⁶And Israel was brought very low because of Midian. And the people of Israel cried out for help to the Lord.

⁷When the people of Israel cried out to the Lord on account of the Midianites, ⁸the Lord sent a prophet to the people of Israel. And he said to them, "Thus says the Lord, the God of Israel: I led you up from Egypt and brought you out of the house of slavery. ⁹And I delivered you from the hand of the Egyptians and from the hand of all who oppressed you, and drove them out before you and gave you their land. ¹⁰And I said to you, 'I am the Lord your God; you shall not fear the gods of the Amorites in whose land you dwell.' But you have not obeyed my voice."

¹¹Now the angel of the Lord came and sat under the terebinth at Ophrah, which belonged to Joash the Abiezrite, while his son Gideon was beating out wheat in the winepress to hide it from the Midianites. ¹²And the angel of the Lord appeared to him and said to him, "The Lord is with you, O mighty man of valor." ¹³And Gideon said to him, "Please, sir,¹ if the Lord is with us, why then has all this happened to us? And where are all his wonderful deeds that our fathers recounted to us, saying, 'Did not the Lord bring us up from Egypt?' But now the

Lord has forsaken us and given us into the hand of Midian." ¹⁴And the Lord² turned to him and said, "Go in this might of yours and save Israel from the hand of Midian; do not I send you?" ¹⁵And he said to him, "Please, Lord, how can I save Israel? Behold, my clan is the weakest in Manasseh, and I am the least in my father's house." ¹⁶And the Lord said to him, "But I will be with you, and you shall strike the Midianites as one man." ¹⁷And he said to him, "If now I have found favor in your eyes, then show me a sign that it is you who speak with me. ¹⁸Please do not depart from here until I come to you and bring out my present and set it before you." And he said, "I will stay till you return."

¹⁹So Gideon went into his house and prepared a young goat and unleavened cakes from an ephah³ of flour. The meat he put in a basket, and the broth he put in a pot, and brought them to him under the terebinth and presented them. ²⁰And the angel of God said to him, "Take the meat and the unleavened cakes, and put them on this rock, and pour the broth over them." And he did so. ²¹Then the angel of the Lord reached out the tip of the staff that was in his hand and touched the meat and the unleavened cakes. And fire sprang up from the rock and consumed the meat and the unleavened cakes. And the angel of the Lord vanished from his sight. ²²Then Gideon perceived that he was the angel of the Lord. And Gideon said, "Alas, O Lord God! For now I have seen the angel of the Lord face to face." ²³But the Lord said to him, "Peace be to you. Do not fear; you shall not die." ²⁴Then Gideon built an altar there to the Lord and called it, The Lord Is Peace. To this day it still stands at Ophrah, which belongs to the Abiezrites.

²⁵That night the Lord said to him, "Take your father's bull, and the second bull seven years old, and pull down the altar of Baal that your father has, and cut down the Asherah that is beside it ²⁶and build an altar to the Lord your God on the top of the stronghold here, with

¹ Or Please, my Lord ² Septuagint the angel of the Lord; also verse 16 ³ An ephah was about 3/5 bushel or 22 liters

stones laid in due order. Then take the second bull and offer it as a burnt offering with the wood of the Asherah that you shall cut down." ²⁷So Gideon took ten men of his servants and did as the LORD had told him. But because he was too afraid of his family and the men of the town to do it by day, he did it by night.

²⁸When the men of the town rose early in the morning, behold, the altar of Baal was broken down, and the Asherah beside it was cut down, and the second bull was offered on the altar that had been built. ²⁹And they said to one another, "Who has done this thing?" And after they had searched and inquired, they said, "Gideon the son of Joash has done this thing." ³⁰Then the men of the town said to Joash, "Bring out your son, that he may die, for he has broken down the altar of Baal and cut down the Asherah beside it." ³¹But Joash said to all who stood against him, "Will you contend for Baal? Or will you save him? Whoever contends for him shall be put to death by morning. If he is a god, let him contend for himself, because his altar has been broken down." ³²Therefore on that day Gideon¹ was called Jerubbaal, that is to say, "Let Baal contend against him," because he broke down his altar.

³³Now all the Midianites and the Amalekites and the people of the East came together, and they crossed the Jordan and encamped in the Valley of Jezreel. ³⁴But the Spirit of the LORD clothed Gideon, and he sounded the trumpet, and the Abiezrites were called out to follow him. ³⁵And he sent messengers throughout all Manasseh, and they too were called out to follow him. And he sent messengers to Asher, Zebulun, and Naphtali, and they went up to meet them.

³⁶Then Gideon said to God, "If you will save Israel by my hand, as you have said, ³⁷behold, I am laying a fleece of wool on the threshing floor. If there is dew on the fleece alone, and it is dry on all the ground, then I shall know that you will save Israel by my hand, as you have said." ³⁸And it was so. When he rose early next morning and squeezed the fleece, he wrung enough dew from the fleece to fill a bowl with water. ³⁹Then Gideon said to God, "Let not your anger burn against me; let me speak just once more. Please let me test just once more with the fleece. Please let it be dry on the fleece only, and on all the ground let there be dew." ⁴⁰And God

did so that night; and it was dry on the fleece only, and on all the ground there was dew.

Acts 10

At Caesarea there was a man named Cornelius, a centurion of what was known as the Italian Cohort, ²a devout man who feared God with all his household, gave alms generously to the people, and prayed continually to God. ³About the ninth hour of the day² he saw clearly in a vision an angel of God come in and say to him, "Cornelius." ⁴And he stared at him in terror and said, "What is it, Lord?" And he said to him, "Your prayers and your alms have ascended as a memorial before God. ⁵And now send men to Joppa and bring one Simon who is called Peter. ⁶He is lodging with one Simon, a tanner, whose house is by the sea." ⁷When the angel who spoke to him had departed, he called two of his servants and a devout soldier from among those who attended him, ⁸and having related everything to them, he sent them to Joppa.

⁹The next day, as they were on their journey and approaching the city, Peter went up on the housetop about the sixth hour³ to pray. ¹⁰And he became hungry and wanted something to eat, but while they were preparing it, he fell into a trance ¹¹and saw the heavens opened and something like a great sheet descending, being let down by its four corners upon the earth. ¹²In it were all kinds of animals and reptiles and birds of the air. ¹³And there came a voice to him: "Rise, Peter; kill and eat." ¹⁴But Peter said, "By no means, Lord; for I have never eaten anything that is common or unclean." ¹⁵And the voice came to him again a second time, "What God has made clean, do not call common." ¹⁶This happened three times, and the thing was taken up at once to heaven.

¹⁷Now while Peter was inwardly perplexed as to what the vision that he had seen might mean, behold, the men who were sent by Cornelius, having made inquiry for Simon's house, stood at the gate ¹⁸and called out to ask whether Simon who was called Peter was lodging there. ¹⁹And while Peter was pondering the vision, the Spirit said to him, "Behold, three men are looking for you. ²⁰Rise and go down and accompany them without hesitation,⁴ for I have sent them." ²¹And Peter went

¹ Hebrew *he* ² That is, 3 P.M. ³ That is, noon ⁴ Or *accompany them, making no distinction*

down to the men and said, "I am the one you are looking for. What is the reason for your coming?" [22]And they said, "Cornelius, a centurion, an upright and God-fearing man, who is well spoken of by the whole Jewish nation, was directed by a holy angel to send for you to come to his house and to hear what you have to say." [23]So he invited them in to be his guests.

The next day he rose and went away with them, and some of the brothers from Joppa accompanied him. [24]And on the following day they entered Caesarea. Cornelius was expecting them and had called together his relatives and close friends. [25]When Peter entered, Cornelius met him and fell down at his feet and worshiped him. [26]But Peter lifted him up, saying, "Stand up; I too am a man." [27]And as he talked with him, he went in and found many persons gathered. [28]And he said to them, "You yourselves know how unlawful it is for a Jew to associate with or to visit anyone of another nation, but God has shown me that I should not call any person common or unclean. [29]So when I was sent for, I came without objection. I ask then why you sent for me."

[30]And Cornelius said, "Four days ago, about this hour, I was praying in my house at the ninth hour,[1] and behold, a man stood before me in bright clothing [31]and said, 'Cornelius, your prayer has been heard and your alms have been remembered before God. [32]Send therefore to Joppa and ask for Simon who is called Peter. He is lodging in the house of Simon, a tanner, by the sea.' [33]So I sent for you at once, and you have been kind enough to come. Now therefore we are all here in the presence of God to hear all that you have been commanded by the Lord."

[34]So Peter opened his mouth and said: "Truly I understand that God shows no partiality, [35]but in every nation anyone who fears him and does what is right is acceptable to him. [36]As for the word that he sent to Israel, preaching good news of peace through Jesus Christ (he is Lord of all), [37]you yourselves know what happened throughout all Judea, beginning from Galilee after the baptism that John proclaimed: [38]how God anointed Jesus of Nazareth with the Holy Spirit and with power. He went about doing good and healing all who were oppressed by the devil, for God was with him. [39]And we are witnesses of all that he did both in the country of the Jews and in Jerusalem. They put him

to death by hanging him on a tree, [40]but God raised him on the third day and made him to appear, [41]not to all the people but to us who had been chosen by God as witnesses, who ate and drank with him after he rose from the dead. [42]And he commanded us to preach to the people and to testify that he is the one appointed by God to be judge of the living and the dead. [43]To him all the prophets bear witness that everyone who believes in him receives forgiveness of sins through his name."

[44]While Peter was still saying these things, the Holy Spirit fell on all who heard the word. [45]And the believers from among the circumcised who had come with Peter were amazed, because the gift of the Holy Spirit was poured out even on the Gentiles. [46]For they were hearing them speaking in tongues and extolling God. Then Peter declared, [47]"Can anyone withhold water for baptizing these people, who have received the Holy Spirit just as we have?" [48]And he commanded them to be baptized in the name of Jesus Christ. Then they asked him to remain for some days.

Jeremiah 19

Thus says the LORD, "Go, buy a potter's earthenware flask, and take some of the elders of the people and some of the elders of the priests, [2]and go out to the Valley of the Son of Hinnom at the entry of the Potsherd Gate, and proclaim there the words that I tell you. [3]You shall say, 'Hear the word of the LORD, O kings of Judah and inhabitants of Jerusalem. Thus says the LORD of hosts, the God of Israel: Behold, I am bringing such disaster upon this place that the ears of everyone who hears of it will tingle. [4]Because the people have forsaken me and have profaned this place by making offerings in it to other gods whom neither they nor their fathers nor the kings of Judah have known; and because they have filled this place with the blood of innocents, [5]and have built the high places of Baal to burn their sons in the fire as burnt offerings to Baal, which I did not command or decree, nor did it come into my mind— [6]therefore, behold, days are coming, declares the LORD, when this place shall no more be called Topheth, or the Valley of the Son of Hinnom, but the Valley of Slaughter. [7]And in this place I will make void the plans of Judah

[1] That is, 3 P.M.

and Jerusalem, and will cause their people to fall by the sword before their enemies, and by the hand of those who seek their life. I will give their dead bodies for food to the birds of the air and to the beasts of the earth. ⁸And I will make this city a horror, a thing to be hissed at. Everyone who passes by it will be horrified and will hiss because of all its wounds. ⁹And I will make them eat the flesh of their sons and their daughters, and everyone shall eat the flesh of his neighbor in the siege and in the distress, with which their enemies and those who seek their life afflict them.'

¹⁰"Then you shall break the flask in the sight of the men who go with you, ¹¹and shall say to them, 'Thus says the LORD of hosts: So will I break this people and this city, as one breaks a potter's vessel, so that it can never be mended. Men shall bury in Topheth because there will be no place else to bury. ¹²Thus will I do to this place, declares the LORD, and to its inhabitants, making this city like Topheth. ¹³The houses of Jerusalem and the houses of the kings of Judah—all the houses on whose roofs offerings have been offered to all the host of heaven, and drink offerings have been poured out to other gods—shall be defiled like the place of Topheth.'"

¹⁴Then Jeremiah came from Topheth, where the LORD had sent him to prophesy, and he stood in the court of the LORD's house and said to all the people: ¹⁵"Thus says the LORD of hosts, the God of Israel, behold, I am bringing upon this city and upon all its towns all the disaster that I have pronounced against it, because they have stiffened their neck, refusing to hear my words."

Mark 5

They came to the other side of the sea, to the country of the Gerasenes.¹ ²And when Jesus² had stepped out of the boat, immediately there met him out of the tombs a man with an unclean spirit. ³He lived among the tombs. And no one could bind him anymore, not even with a chain, ⁴for he had often been bound with shackles and chains, but he wrenched the chains apart, and he broke the shackles in pieces. No one had the strength to subdue him. ⁵Night and day among the tombs and on the mountains he was always crying out and

cutting himself with stones. ⁶And when he saw Jesus from afar, he ran and fell down before him. ⁷And crying out with a loud voice, he said, "What have you to do with me, Jesus, Son of the Most High God? I adjure you by God, do not torment me." ⁸For he was saying to him, "Come out of the man, you unclean spirit!" ⁹And Jesus asked him, "What is your name?" He replied, "My name is Legion, for we are many." ¹⁰And he begged him earnestly not to send them out of the country. ¹¹Now a great herd of pigs was feeding there on the hillside, ¹²and they begged him, saying, "Send us to the pigs; let us enter them." ¹³So he gave them permission. And the unclean spirits came out and entered the pigs; and the herd, numbering about two thousand, rushed down the steep bank into the sea and drowned in the sea.

¹⁴The herdsmen fled and told it in the city and in the country. And people came to see what it was that had happened. ¹⁵And they came to Jesus and saw the demon-possessed³ man, the one who had had the legion, sitting there, clothed and in his right mind, and they were afraid. ¹⁶And those who had seen it described to them what had happened to the demon-possessed man and to the pigs. ¹⁷And they began to beg Jesus⁴ to depart from their region. ¹⁸As he was getting into the boat, the man who had been possessed with demons begged him that he might be with him. ¹⁹And he did not permit him but said to him, "Go home to your friends and tell them how much the Lord has done for you, and how he has had mercy on you." ²⁰And he went away and began to proclaim in the Decapolis how much Jesus had done for him, and everyone marveled.

²¹And when Jesus had crossed again in the boat to the other side, a great crowd gathered about him, and he was beside the sea. ²²Then came one of the rulers of the synagogue, Jairus by name, and seeing him, he fell at his feet ²³and implored him earnestly, saying, "My little daughter is at the point of death. Come and lay your hands on her, so that she may be made well and live." ²⁴And he went with him.

And a great crowd followed him and thronged about him. ²⁵And there was a woman who had had a discharge of blood for twelve years, ²⁶and who had suffered much under many physicians, and had spent all that she had, and was no better but rather grew worse. ²⁷She had heard the

---

¹ Some manuscripts *Gergesenes*; some *Gadarenes* ² Greek *he*; also verse 9 ³ Greek *daimonizomai*; also verses 16, 18; elsewhere rendered *oppressed by demons* ⁴ Greek *him*

reports about Jesus and came up behind him in the crowd and touched his garment. ²⁸For she said, "If I touch even his garments, I will be made well." ²⁹And immediately the flow of blood dried up, and she felt in her body that she was healed of her disease. ³⁰And Jesus, perceiving in himself that power had gone out from him, immediately turned about in the crowd and said, "Who touched my garments?" ³¹And his disciples said to him, "You see the crowd pressing around you, and yet you say, 'Who touched me?'" ³²And he looked around to see who had done it. ³³But the woman, knowing what had happened to her, came in fear and trembling and fell down before him and told him the whole truth. ³⁴And he said to her, "Daughter, your faith has made you well; go in peace, and be healed of your disease."

³⁵While he was still speaking, there came from the ruler's house some who said, "Your daughter is dead. Why trouble the Teacher any further?" ³⁶But overhearing[1] what they said, Jesus said to the ruler of the synagogue, "Do not fear, only believe." ³⁷And he allowed no one to follow him except Peter and James and John the brother of James. ³⁸They came to the house of the ruler of the synagogue, and Jesus[2] saw a commotion, people weeping and wailing loudly. ³⁹And when he had entered, he said to them, "Why are you making a commotion and weeping? The child is not dead but sleeping." ⁴⁰And they laughed at him. But he put them all outside and took the child's father and mother and those who were with him and went in where the child was. ⁴¹Taking her by the hand he said to her, "Talitha cumi," which means, "Little girl, I say to you, arise." ⁴²And immediately the girl got up and began walking (for she was twelve years of age), and they were immediately overcome with amazement. ⁴³And he strictly charged them that no one should know this, and told them to give her something to eat.

JULY 24

Judges 7

Then Jerubbaal (that is, Gideon) and all the people who were with him rose early and encamped beside the spring of Harod. And the camp of Midian was north of them, by the hill of Moreh, in the valley.

²The LORD said to Gideon, "The people with you are too many for me to give the Midianites into their hand, lest Israel boast over me, saying, 'My own hand has saved me.' ³Now therefore proclaim in the ears of the people, saying, 'Whoever is fearful and trembling, let him return home and hurry away from Mount Gilead.'" Then 22,000 of the people returned, and 10,000 remained.

⁴And the LORD said to Gideon, "The people are still too many. Take them down to the water, and I will test them for you there, and anyone of whom I say to you, 'This one shall go with you,' shall go with you, and anyone of whom I say to you, 'This one shall not go with you,' shall

not go." ⁵So he brought the people down to the water. And the LORD said to Gideon, "Every one who laps the water with his tongue, as a dog laps, you shall set by himself. Likewise, every one who kneels down to drink." ⁶And the number of those who lapped, putting their hands to their mouths, was 300 men, but all the rest of the people knelt down to drink water. ⁷And the LORD said to Gideon, "With the 300 men who lapped I will save you and give the Midianites into your hand, and let all the others go every man to his home." ⁸So the people took provisions in their hands, and their trumpets. And he sent all the rest of Israel every man to his tent, but retained the 300 men. And the camp of Midian was below him in the valley.

⁹That same night the LORD said to him, "Arise, go down against the camp, for I have given it into your hand. ¹⁰But if you are afraid to go down, go down to the camp with Purah

your servant. [11]And you shall hear what they say, and afterward your hands shall be strengthened to go down against the camp." Then he went down with Purah his servant to the outposts of the armed men who were in the camp. [12]And the Midianites and the Amalekites and all the people of the East lay along the valley like locusts in abundance, and their camels were without number, as the sand that is on the seashore in abundance. [13]When Gideon came, behold, a man was telling a dream to his comrade. And he said, "Behold, I dreamed a dream, and behold, a cake of barley bread tumbled into the camp of Midian and came to the tent and struck it so that it fell and turned it upside down, so that the tent lay flat." [14]And his comrade answered, "This is no other than the sword of Gideon the son of Joash, a man of Israel; God has given into his hand Midian and all the camp."

[15]As soon as Gideon heard the telling of the dream and its interpretation, he worshiped. And he returned to the camp of Israel and said, "Arise, for the LORD has given the host of Midian into your hand." [16]And he divided the 300 men into three companies and put trumpets into the hands of all of them and empty jars, with torches inside the jars. [17]And he said to them, "Look at me, and do likewise. When I come to the outskirts of the camp, do as I do. [18]When I blow the trumpet, I and all who are with me, then blow the trumpets also on every side of all the camp and shout, 'For the LORD and for Gideon.'"

[19]So Gideon and the hundred men who were with him came to the outskirts of the camp at the beginning of the middle watch, when they had just set the watch. And they blew the trumpets and smashed the jars that were in their hands. [20]Then the three companies blew the trumpets and broke the jars. They held in their left hands the torches, and in their right hands the trumpets to blow. And they cried out, "A sword for the LORD and for Gideon!" [21]Every man stood in his place around the camp, and all the army ran. They cried out and fled. [22]When they blew the 300 trumpets, the LORD set every man's sword against his comrade and against all the army. And the army fled as far as Bethshittah toward Zererah,[1] as far as the border of Abel-meholah, by Tabbath. [23]And the men of Israel were called out from Naphtali and from

Asher and from all Manasseh, and they pursued after Midian.

[24]Gideon sent messengers throughout all the hill country of Ephraim, saying, "Come down against the Midianites and capture the waters against them, as far as Beth-barah, and also the Jordan." So all the men of Ephraim were called out, and they captured the waters as far as Beth-barah, and also the Jordan. [25]And they captured the two princes of Midian, Oreb and Zeeb. They killed Oreb at the rock of Oreb, and Zeeb they killed at the winepress of Zeeb. Then they pursued Midian, and they brought the heads of Oreb and Zeeb to Gideon across the Jordan.

Acts 11

[N]ow the apostles and the brothers[2] who were throughout Judea heard that the Gentiles also had received the word of God. [2]So when Peter went up to Jerusalem, the circumcision party[3] criticized him, saying, [3]"You went to uncircumcised men and ate with them." [4]But Peter began and explained it to them in order: [5]"I was in the city of Joppa praying, and in a trance I saw a vision, something like a great sheet descending, being let down from heaven by its four corners, and it came down to me. [6]Looking at it closely, I observed animals and beasts of prey and reptiles and birds of the air. [7]And I heard a voice saying to me, 'Rise, Peter; kill and eat.' [8]But I said, 'By no means, Lord; for nothing common or unclean has ever entered my mouth.' [9]But the voice answered a second time from heaven, 'What God has made clean, do not call common.' [10]This happened three times, and all was drawn up again into heaven. [11]And behold, at that very moment three men arrived at the house in which we were, sent to me from Caesarea. [12]And the Spirit told me to go with them, making no distinction. These six brothers also accompanied me, and we entered the man's house. [13]And he told us how he had seen the angel stand in his house and say, 'Send to Joppa and bring Simon who is called Peter; [14]he will declare to you a message by which you will be saved, you and all your household.' [15]As I began to speak, the Holy Spirit fell on them just as on us at the beginning. [16]And I remembered the word of the Lord, how he said, 'John baptized with water, but you will be baptized with the Holy Spirit.' [17]If then God gave

[1] Some Hebrew manuscripts Zeredah [2] Or brothers and sisters [3] Or Jerusalem, those of the circumcision

the same gift to them as he gave to us when we believed in the Lord Jesus Christ, who was I that I could stand in God's way?" [18] When they heard these things they fell silent. And they glorified God, saying, "Then to the Gentiles also God has granted repentance that leads to life."

[19] Now those who were scattered because of the persecution that arose over Stephen traveled as far as Phoenicia and Cyprus and Antioch, speaking the word to no one except Jews. [20] But there were some of them, men of Cyprus and Cyrene, who on coming to Antioch spoke to the Hellenists[1] also, preaching the Lord Jesus. [21] And the hand of the Lord was with them, and a great number who believed turned to the Lord. [22] The report of this came to the ears of the church in Jerusalem, and they sent Barnabas to Antioch. [23] When he came and saw the grace of God, he was glad, and he exhorted them all to remain faithful to the Lord with steadfast purpose, [24] for he was a good man, full of the Holy Spirit and of faith. And a great many people were added to the Lord. [25] So Barnabas went to Tarsus to look for Saul, [26] and when he had found him, he brought him to Antioch. For a whole year they met with the church and taught a great many people. And in Antioch the disciples were first called Christians.

[27] Now in these days prophets came down from Jerusalem to Antioch. [28] And one of them named Agabus stood up and foretold by the Spirit that there would be a great famine over all the world (this took place in the days of Claudius). [29] So the disciples determined, every one according to his ability, to send relief to the brothers[2] living in Judea. [30] And they did so, sending it to the elders by the hand of Barnabas and Saul.

--- *Jeremiah 20* ---

N ow Pashhur the priest, the son of Immer, who was chief officer in the house of the Lord, heard Jeremiah prophesying these things. [2] Then Pashhur beat Jeremiah the prophet, and put him in the stocks that were in the upper Benjamin Gate of the house of the Lord. [3] The next day, when Pashhur released Jeremiah from the stocks, Jeremiah said to him, "The Lord does not call your name Pashhur, but Terror on Every Side. [4] For thus says the

Lord: Behold, I will make you a terror to yourself and to all your friends. They shall fall by the sword of their enemies while you look on. And I will give all Judah into the hand of the king of Babylon. He shall carry them captive to Babylon, and shall strike them down with the sword. [5] Moreover, I will give all the wealth of the city, all its gains, all its prized belongings, and all the treasures of the kings of Judah into the hand of their enemies, who shall plunder them and seize them and carry them to Babylon. [6] And you, Pashhur, and all who dwell in your house, shall go into captivity. To Babylon you shall go, and there you shall die, and there you shall be buried, you and all your friends, to whom you have prophesied falsely."

[7]   O Lord, you have deceived me,
            and I was deceived;
        you are stronger than I,
            and you have prevailed.
        I have become a laughingstock all the
            day;
            everyone mocks me.
[8]   For whenever I speak, I cry out,
            I shout, "Violence and destruction!"
        For the word of the Lord has become
            for me
        a reproach and derision all day long.
[9]   If I say, "I will not mention him,
            or speak any more in his name,"
        there is in my heart as it were a burning
            fire
            shut up in my bones,
        and I am weary with holding it in,
            and I cannot.
[10]   For I hear many whispering.
            Terror is on every side!
        "Denounce him! Let us denounce him!"
            say all my close friends,
            watching for my fall.
        "Perhaps he will be deceived;
            then we can overcome him
            and take our revenge on him."
[11]   But the Lord is with me as a dread
            warrior;
        therefore my persecutors will stumble;
            they will not overcome me.
        They will be greatly shamed,
            for they will not succeed.
        Their eternal dishonor
            will never be forgotten.

[1] Or Greeks (that is, Greek-speaking non-Jews) [2] Or brothers and sisters

12   O LORD of hosts, who tests the righteous,
     who sees the heart and the mind,[1]
   let me see your vengeance upon them,
     for to you have I committed my cause.

13   Sing to the LORD;
     praise the LORD!
   For he has delivered the life of the needy
     from the hand of evildoers.

14   Cursed be the day
     on which I was born!
   The day when my mother bore me,
     let it not be blessed!

15   Cursed be the man who brought the
     news to my father,
   "A son is born to you,"
     making him very glad.

16   Let that man be like the cities
     that the LORD overthrew without pity;
   let him hear a cry in the morning
     and an alarm at noon,

17   because he did not kill me in the womb;
     so my mother would have been my
     grave,
   and her womb forever great.

18   Why did I come out from the womb
     to see toil and sorrow,
   and spend my days in shame?

Mark 6

He went away from there and came to his hometown, and his disciples followed him. [2] And on the Sabbath he began to teach in the synagogue, and many who heard him were astonished, saying, "Where did this man get these things? What is the wisdom given to him? How are such mighty works done by his hands? [3] Is not this the carpenter, the son of Mary and brother of James and Joses and Judas and Simon? And are not his sisters here with us?" And they took offense at him. [4] And Jesus said to them, "A prophet is not without honor, except in his hometown and among his relatives and in his own household." [5] And he could do no mighty work there, except that he laid his hands on a few sick people and healed them. [6] And he marveled because of their unbelief.

And he went about among the villages teaching.

[7] And he called the twelve and began to send them out two by two, and gave them authority over the unclean spirits. [8] He charged them to take nothing for their journey except a staff— no bread, no bag, no money in their belts— [9] but to wear sandals and not put on two tunics.[2] [10] And he said to them, "Whenever you enter a house, stay there until you depart from there. [11] And if any place will not receive you and they will not listen to you, when you leave, shake off the dust that is on your feet as a testimony against them." [12] So they went out and proclaimed that people should repent. [13] And they cast out many demons and anointed with oil many who were sick and healed them.

[14] King Herod heard of it, for Jesus'[3] name had become known. Some[4] said, "John the Baptist[5] has been raised from the dead. That is why these miraculous powers are at work in him." [15] But others said, "He is Elijah." And others said, "He is a prophet, like one of the prophets of old." [16] But when Herod heard of it, he said, "John, whom I beheaded, has been raised." [17] For it was Herod who had sent and seized John and bound him in prison for the sake of Herodias, his brother Philip's wife, because he had married her. [18] For John had been saying to Herod, "It is not lawful for you to have your brother's wife." [19] And Herodias had a grudge against him and wanted to put him to death. But she could not, [20] for Herod feared John, knowing that he was a righteous and holy man, and he kept him safe. When he heard him, he was greatly perplexed, and yet he heard him gladly.

[21] But an opportunity came when Herod on his birthday gave a banquet for his nobles and military commanders and the leading men of Galilee. [22] For when Herodias's daughter came in and danced, she pleased Herod and his guests. And the king said to the girl, "Ask me for whatever you wish, and I will give it to you." [23] And he vowed to her, "Whatever you ask me, I will give you, up to half of my kingdom." [24] And she went out and said to her mother, "For what should I ask?" And she said, "The head of John the Baptist." [25] And she came in immediately with haste to the king and asked, saying, "I want you to give me at once the head of John the Baptist on a platter." [26] And the king was exceedingly sorry, but because of his oaths and his guests he did not want to break his word to her. [27] And immediately the king sent an executioner with orders to bring John's[6] head.

---

[1] Hebrew *kidneys*   [2] Greek *chiton*, a long garment worn under the cloak next to the skin   [3] Greek *his*   [4] Some manuscripts *He*   [5] Greek *baptizer*; also verse 24   [6] Greek *his*

He went and beheaded him in the prison [28] and brought his head on a platter and gave it to the girl, and the girl gave it to her mother. [29] When his disciples heard of it, they came and took his body and laid it in a tomb.

[30] The apostles returned to Jesus and told him all that they had done and taught. [31] And he said to them, "Come away by yourselves to a desolate place and rest a while." For many were coming and going, and they had no leisure even to eat. [32] And they went away in the boat to a desolate place by themselves. [33] Now many saw them going and recognized them, and they ran there on foot from all the towns and got there ahead of them. [34] When he went ashore he saw a great crowd, and he had compassion on them, because they were like sheep without a shepherd. And he began to teach them many things. [35] And when it grew late, his disciples came to him and said, "This is a desolate place, and the hour is now late. [36] Send them away to go into the surrounding countryside and villages and buy themselves something to eat." [37] But he answered them, "You give them something to eat." And they said to him, "Shall we go and buy two hundred denarii[1] worth of bread and give it to them to eat?" [38] And he said to them, "How many loaves do you have? Go and see." And when they had found out, they said, "Five, and two fish." [39] Then he commanded them all to sit down in groups on the green grass. [40] So they sat down in groups, by hundreds and by fifties. [41] And taking the five loaves and the two fish he looked up to heaven and said a blessing and broke the loaves and gave them to the disciples to set before the people. And he divided the two fish among them all. [42] And they all ate and were satisfied. [43] And they took up twelve baskets full of broken pieces and of the fish. [44] And those who ate the loaves were five thousand men.

[45] Immediately he made his disciples get into the boat and go before him to the other side, to Bethsaida, while he dismissed the crowd. [46] And after he had taken leave of them, he went up on the mountain to pray. [47] And when evening came, the boat was out on the sea, and he was alone on the land. [48] And he saw that they were making headway painfully, for the wind was against them. And about the fourth watch of the night[2] he came to them, walking on the sea. He meant to pass by them, [49] but when they saw him walking on the sea they thought it was a ghost, and cried out, [50] for they all saw him and were terrified. But immediately he spoke to them and said, "Take heart; it is I. Do not be afraid." [51] And he got into the boat with them, and the wind ceased. And they were utterly astounded, [52] for they did not understand about the loaves, but their hearts were hardened.

[53] When they had crossed over, they came to land at Gennesaret and moored to the shore. [54] And when they got out of the boat, the people immediately recognized him [55] and ran about the whole region and began to bring the sick people on their beds to wherever they heard he was. [56] And wherever he came, in villages, cities, or countryside, they laid the sick in the marketplaces and implored him that they might touch even the fringe of his garment. And as many as touched it were made well.

JULY 25

Judges 8

Then the men of Ephraim said to him, "What is this that you have done to us, not to call us when you went to fight against Midian?" And they accused him fiercely. [2] And he said to them, "What have I done now in comparison with you? Is not the gleaning of the grapes of Ephraim better than the grape harvest of Abiezer? [3] God has given into your hands the princes of Midian, Oreb and Zeeb. What have I been able to do in comparison with you?" Then their anger[3] against him subsided when he said this.

[1] A *denarius* was a day's wage for a laborer [2] That is, between 3 A.M. and 6 A.M. [3] Hebrew *their spirit*

⁴And Gideon came to the Jordan and crossed over, he and the 300 men who were with him, exhausted yet pursuing. ⁵So he said to the men of Succoth, "Please give loaves of bread to the people who follow me, for they are exhausted, and I am pursuing after Zebah and Zalmunna, the kings of Midian." ⁶And the officials of Succoth said, "Are the hands of Zebah and Zalmunna already in your hand, that we should give bread to your army?" ⁷So Gideon said, "Well then, when the LORD has given Zebah and Zalmunna into my hand, I will flail your flesh with the thorns of the wilderness and with briers." ⁸And from there he went up to Penuel, and spoke to them in the same way, and the men of Penuel answered him as the men of Succoth had answered. ⁹And he said to the men of Penuel, "When I come again in peace, I will break down this tower."

¹⁰Now Zebah and Zalmunna were in Karkor with their army, about 15,000 men, all who were left of all the army of the people of the East, for there had fallen 120,000 men who drew the sword. ¹¹And Gideon went up by the way of the tent dwellers east of Nobah and Jogbehah and attacked the army, for the army felt secure. ¹²And Zebah and Zalmunna fled, and he pursued them and captured the two kings of Midian, Zebah and Zalmunna, and he threw all the army into a panic.

¹³Then Gideon the son of Joash returned from the battle by the ascent of Heres. ¹⁴And he captured a young man of Succoth and questioned him. And he wrote down for him the officials and elders of Succoth, seventy-seven men. ¹⁵And he came to the men of Succoth and said, "Behold Zebah and Zalmunna, about whom you taunted me, saying, 'Are the hands of Zebah and Zalmunna already in your hand, that we should give bread to your men who are exhausted?'" ¹⁶And he took the elders of the city, and he took thorns of the wilderness and briers and with them taught the men of Succoth a lesson. ¹⁷And he broke down the tower of Penuel and killed the men of the city.

¹⁸Then he said to Zebah and Zalmunna, "Where are the men whom you killed at Tabor?" They answered, "As you are, so were they. Every one of them resembled the son of a king." ¹⁹And he said, "They were my brothers, the sons of my mother. As the LORD lives, if you had saved them alive, I would not kill you."

²⁰So he said to Jether his firstborn, "Rise and kill them!" But the young man did not draw his sword, for he was afraid, because he was still a young man. ²¹Then Zebah and Zalmunna said, "Rise yourself and fall upon us, for as the man is, so is his strength." And Gideon arose and killed Zebah and Zalmunna, and he took the crescent ornaments that were on the necks of their camels.

²²Then the men of Israel said to Gideon, "Rule over us, you and your son and your grandson also, for you have saved us from the hand of Midian." ²³Gideon said to them, "I will not rule over you, and my son will not rule over you; the LORD will rule over you." ²⁴And Gideon said to them, "Let me make a request of you: every one of you give me the earrings from his spoil." (For they had golden earrings, because they were Ishmaelites.) ²⁵And they answered, "We will willingly give them." And they spread a cloak, and every man threw in it the earrings of his spoil. ²⁶And the weight of the golden earrings that he requested was 1,700 shekels[1] of gold, besides the crescent ornaments and the pendants and the purple garments worn by the kings of Midian, and besides the collars that were around the necks of their camels. ²⁷And Gideon made an ephod of it and put it in his city, in Ophrah. And all Israel whored after it there, and it became a snare to Gideon and to his family. ²⁸So Midian was subdued before the people of Israel, and they raised their heads no more. And the land had rest forty years in the days of Gideon.

²⁹Jerubbaal the son of Joash went and lived in his own house. ³⁰Now Gideon had seventy sons, his own offspring,[2] for he had many wives. ³¹And his concubine who was in Shechem also bore him a son, and he called his name Abimelech. ³²And Gideon the son of Joash died in a good old age and was buried in the tomb of Joash his father, at Ophrah of the Abiezrites.

³³As soon as Gideon died, the people of Israel turned again and whored after the Baals and made Baal-berith their god. ³⁴And the people of Israel did not remember the LORD their God, who had delivered them from the hand of all their enemies on every side, ³⁵and they did not show steadfast love to the family of Jerubbaal (that is, Gideon) in return for all the good that he had done to Israel.

---

[1] A shekel was about 2/5 ounce or 11 grams [2] Hebrew *who came from his own loins*

Acts 12

About that time Herod the king laid violent hands on some who belonged to the church. [2] He killed James the brother of John with the sword, [3] and when he saw that it pleased the Jews, he proceeded to arrest Peter also. This was during the days of Unleavened Bread. [4] And when he had seized him, he put him in prison, delivering him over to four squads of soldiers to guard him, intending after the Passover to bring him out to the people. [5] So Peter was kept in prison, but earnest prayer for him was made to God by the church.

[6] Now when Herod was about to bring him out, on that very night, Peter was sleeping between two soldiers, bound with two chains, and sentries before the door were guarding the prison. [7] And behold, an angel of the Lord stood next to him, and a light shone in the cell. He struck Peter on the side and woke him, saying, "Get up quickly." And the chains fell off his hands. [8] And the angel said to him, "Dress yourself and put on your sandals." And he did so. And he said to him, "Wrap your cloak around you and follow me." [9] And he went out and followed him. He did not know that what was being done by the angel was real, but thought he was seeing a vision. [10] When they had passed the first and the second guard, they came to the iron gate leading into the city. It opened for them of its own accord, and they went out and went along one street, and immediately the angel left him. [11] When Peter came to himself, he said, "Now I am sure that the Lord has sent his angel and rescued me from the hand of Herod and from all that the Jewish people were expecting."

[12] When he realized this, he went to the house of Mary, the mother of John whose other name was Mark, where many were gathered together and were praying. [13] And when he knocked at the door of the gateway, a servant girl named Rhoda came to answer. [14] Recognizing Peter's voice, in her joy she did not open the gate but ran in and reported that Peter was standing at the gate. [15] They said to her, "You are out of your mind." But she kept insisting that it was so, and they kept saying, "It is his angel!" [16] But Peter continued knocking, and when they opened, they saw him and were amazed. [17] But motioning to them with his hand to be silent, he described to them how the Lord had brought him out of the prison. And he said, "Tell these things to James and to the brothers."[1] Then he departed and went to another place.

[18] Now when day came, there was no little disturbance among the soldiers over what had become of Peter. [19] And after Herod searched for him and did not find him, he examined the sentries and ordered that they should be put to death. Then he went down from Judea to Caesarea and spent time there.

[20] Now Herod was angry with the people of Tyre and Sidon, and they came to him with one accord, and having persuaded Blastus, the king's chamberlain,[2] they asked for peace, because their country depended on the king's country for food. [21] On an appointed day Herod put on his royal robes, took his seat upon the throne, and delivered an oration to them. [22] And the people were shouting, "The voice of a god, and not of a man!" [23] Immediately an angel of the Lord struck him down, because he did not give God the glory, and he was eaten by worms and breathed his last.

[24] But the word of God increased and multiplied.

[25] And Barnabas and Saul returned from[3] Jerusalem when they had completed their service, bringing with them John, whose other name was Mark.

Jeremiah 21

This is the word that came to Jeremiah from the LORD, when King Zedekiah sent to him Pashhur the son of Malchiah and Zephaniah the priest, the son of Maaseiah, saying, [2] "Inquire of the LORD for us, for Nebuchadnezzar[4] king of Babylon is making war against us. Perhaps the LORD will deal with us according to all his wonderful deeds and will make him withdraw from us."

[3] Then Jeremiah said to them: "Thus you shall say to Zedekiah, [4] 'Thus says the LORD, the God of Israel: Behold, I will turn back the weapons of war that are in your hands and with which you are fighting against the king of Babylon and against the Chaldeans who are besieging you outside the walls. And I will bring them together into the midst of this city. [5] I myself will fight against you with outstretched hand and strong arm, in anger and in fury and in

---

[1] Or brothers and sisters   [2] That is, trusted personal attendant   [3] Some manuscripts to   [4] Hebrew Nebuchadrezzar, an alternate spelling of Nebuchadnezzar (king of Babylon) occurring frequently from Jeremiah 21–52; this latter spelling is used throughout Jeremiah for consistency

great wrath. [6] And I will strike down the inhabitants of this city, both man and beast. They shall die of a great pestilence. [7] Afterward, declares the LORD, I will give Zedekiah king of Judah and his servants and the people in this city who survive the pestilence, sword, and famine into the hand of Nebuchadnezzar king of Babylon and into the hand of their enemies, into the hand of those who seek their lives. He shall strike them down with the edge of the sword. He shall not pity them or spare them or have compassion.'

[8] "And to this people you shall say: 'Thus says the LORD: Behold, I set before you the way of life and the way of death. [9] He who stays in this city shall die by the sword, by famine, and by pestilence, but he who goes out and surrenders to the Chaldeans who are besieging you shall live and shall have his life as a prize of war. [10] For I have set my face against this city for harm and not for good, declares the LORD: it shall be given into the hand of the king of Babylon, and he shall burn it with fire.'

[11] "And to the house of the king of Judah say, 'Hear the word of the LORD, [12] O house of David! Thus says the LORD:

" 'Execute justice in the morning,
      and deliver from the hand of the
         oppressor
      him who has been robbed,
   lest my wrath go forth like fire,
      and burn with none to quench it,
      because of your evil deeds.' "

[13]   "Behold, I am against you, O inhabitant
         of the valley,
      O rock of the plain,
                        declares the LORD;
   you who say, 'Who shall come down
         against us,
      or who shall enter our habitations?'
[14]   I will punish you according to the fruit
         of your deeds,
                        declares the LORD;
   I will kindle a fire in her forest,
      and it shall devour all that is around
         her."

------------------------------ *Mark 7* ------------------------------

N ow when the Pharisees gathered to him, with some of the scribes who had come from Jerusalem, [2] they saw that some of his disciples ate with hands that were defiled, that is, unwashed. [3] (For the Pharisees and all the Jews do not eat unless they wash their hands properly,[1] holding to the tradition of the elders, [4] and when they come from the marketplace, they do not eat unless they wash.[2] And there are many other traditions that they observe, such as the washing of cups and pots and copper vessels and dining couches.[3]) [5] And the Pharisees and the scribes asked him, "Why do your disciples not walk according to the tradition of the elders, but eat with defiled hands?" [6] And he said to them, "Well did Isaiah prophesy of you hypocrites, as it is written,

   " 'This people honors me with their lips,
         but their heart is far from me;
[7]   in vain do they worship me,
         teaching as doctrines the
            commandments of men.'

[8] You leave the commandment of God and hold to the tradition of men."

[9] And he said to them, "You have a fine way of rejecting the commandment of God in order to establish your tradition! [10] For Moses said, 'Honor your father and your mother'; and, 'Whoever reviles father or mother must surely die.' [11] But you say, 'If a man tells his father or his mother, "Whatever you would have gained from me is Corban"' (that is, given to God)[4]— [12] then you no longer permit him to do anything for his father or mother, [13] thus making void the word of God by your tradition that you have handed down. And many such things you do."

[14] And he called the people to him again and said to them, "Hear me, all of you, and understand: [15] There is nothing outside a person that by going into him can defile him, but the things that come out of a person are what defile him."[5] [17] And when he had entered the house and left the people, his disciples asked him about the parable. [18] And he said to them, "Then are you also without understanding? Do you not see that whatever goes into a person from outside cannot defile him, [19] since it enters not his heart but his stomach, and is expelled?"[6] (Thus he declared all foods clean.) [20] And he said, "What comes out of a person is what defiles him. [21] For from within, out of the heart of man, come evil thoughts, sexual immorality, theft, murder, adultery, [22] coveting, wickedness,

---

[1] Greek *unless they wash the hands with a fist*, probably indicating a kind of ceremonial washing [2] Greek *unless they baptize*; some manuscripts *unless they purify themselves*
[3] Some manuscripts omit *and dining couches* [4] Or *an offering* [5] Some manuscripts add verse 16: *If anyone has ears to hear, let him hear* [6] Greek *goes out into the latrine*

deceit, sensuality, envy, slander, pride, foolishness. ²³All these evil things come from within, and they defile a person."

²⁴And from there he arose and went away to the region of Tyre and Sidon.¹ And he entered a house and did not want anyone to know, yet he could not be hidden. ²⁵But immediately a woman whose little daughter had an unclean spirit heard of him and came and fell down at his feet. ²⁶Now the woman was a Gentile, a Syrophoenician by birth. And she begged him to cast the demon out of her daughter. ²⁷And he said to her, "Let the children be fed first, for it is not right to take the children's bread and throw it to the dogs." ²⁸But she answered him, "Yes, Lord; yet even the dogs under the table eat the children's crumbs." ²⁹And he said to her, "For this statement you may go your way; the demon has left your daughter." ³⁰And she

went home and found the child lying in bed and the demon gone.

³¹Then he returned from the region of Tyre and went through Sidon to the Sea of Galilee, in the region of the Decapolis. ³²And they brought to him a man who was deaf and had a speech impediment, and they begged him to lay his hand on him. ³³And taking him aside from the crowd privately, he put his fingers into his ears, and after spitting touched his tongue. ³⁴And looking up to heaven, he sighed and said to him, "Ephphatha," that is, "Be opened." ³⁵And his ears were opened, his tongue was released, and he spoke plainly. ³⁶And Jesus² charged them to tell no one. But the more he charged them, the more zealously they proclaimed it. ³⁷And they were astonished beyond measure, saying, "He has done all things well. He even makes the deaf hear and the mute speak."

JULY 26

Judges 9

Now Abimelech the son of Jerubbaal went to Shechem to his mother's relatives and said to them and to the whole clan of his mother's family, ²"Say in the ears of all the leaders of Shechem, 'Which is better for you, that all seventy of the sons of Jerubbaal rule over you, or that one rule over you?' Remember also that I am your bone and your flesh." ³And his mother's relatives spoke all these words on his behalf in the ears of all the leaders of Shechem, and their hearts inclined to follow Abimelech, for they said, "He is our brother." ⁴And they gave him seventy pieces of silver out of the house of Baal-berith with which Abimelech hired worthless and reckless fellows, who followed him. ⁵And he went to his father's house at Ophrah and killed his brothers the sons of Jerubbaal, seventy men, on one stone. But Jotham the youngest son of Jerubbaal was left, for he hid himself. ⁶And all the leaders of Shechem came together, and all Beth-millo, and they went and made

Abimelech king, by the oak of the pillar at Shechem.

⁷When it was told to Jotham, he went and stood on top of Mount Gerizim and cried aloud and said to them, "Listen to me, you leaders of Shechem, that God may listen to you. ⁸The trees once went out to anoint a king over them, and they said to the olive tree, 'Reign over us.' ⁹But the olive tree said to them, 'Shall I leave my abundance, by which gods and men are honored, and go hold sway over the trees?' ¹⁰And the trees said to the fig tree, 'You come and reign over us.' ¹¹But the fig tree said to them, 'Shall I leave my sweetness and my good fruit and go hold sway over the trees?' ¹²And the trees said to the vine, 'You come and reign over us.' ¹³But the vine said to them, 'Shall I leave my wine that cheers God and men and go hold sway over the trees?' ¹⁴Then all the trees said to the bramble, 'You come and reign over us.' ¹⁵And the bramble said to the trees, 'If in good faith you are anointing me king over you,

¹ Some manuscripts omit and Sidon ² Greek he

then come and take refuge in my shade, but if not, let fire come out of the bramble and devour the cedars of Lebanon.'

16 "Now therefore, if you acted in good faith and integrity when you made Abimelech king, and if you have dealt well with Jerubbaal and his house and have done to him as his deeds deserved— 17 for my father fought for you and risked his life and delivered you from the hand of Midian, 18 and you have risen up against my father's house this day and have killed his sons, seventy men on one stone, and have made Abimelech, the son of his female servant, king over the leaders of Shechem, because he is your relative— 19 if you then have acted in good faith and integrity with Jerubbaal and with his house this day, then rejoice in Abimelech, and let him also rejoice in you. 20 But if not, let fire come out from Abimelech and devour the leaders of Shechem and Beth-millo; and let fire come out from the leaders of Shechem and from Beth-millo and devour Abimelech." 21 And Jotham ran away and fled and went to Beer and lived there, because of Abimelech his brother.

22 Abimelech ruled over Israel three years. 23 And God sent an evil spirit between Abimelech and the leaders of Shechem, and the leaders of Shechem dealt treacherously with Abimelech, 24 that the violence done to the seventy sons of Jerubbaal might come, and their blood be laid on Abimelech their brother, who killed them, and on the men of Shechem, who strengthened his hands to kill his brothers. 25 And the leaders of Shechem put men in ambush against him on the mountaintops, and they robbed all who passed by them along that way. And it was told to Abimelech.

26 And Gaal the son of Ebed moved into Shechem with his relatives, and the leaders of Shechem put confidence in him. 27 And they went out into the field and gathered the grapes from their vineyards and trod them and held a festival; and they went into the house of their god and ate and drank and reviled Abimelech. 28 And Gaal the son of Ebed said, "Who is Abimelech, and who are we of Shechem, that we should serve him? Is he not the son of Jerubbaal, and is not Zebul his officer? Serve the men of Hamor the father of Shechem; but why should we serve him? 29 Would that this people were under my hand! Then I would remove Abimelech. I would say[1] to Abimelech, 'Increase your army, and come out.'"

30 When Zebul the ruler of the city heard the words of Gaal the son of Ebed, his anger was kindled. 31 And he sent messengers to Abimelech secretly,[2] saying, "Behold, Gaal the son of Ebed and his relatives have come to Shechem, and they are stirring up[3] the city against you. 32 Now therefore, go by night, you and the people who are with you, and set an ambush in the field. 33 Then in the morning, as soon as the sun is up, rise early and rush upon the city. And when he and the people who are with him come out against you, you may do to them as your hand finds to do."

34 So Abimelech and all the men who were with him rose up by night and set an ambush against Shechem in four companies. 35 And Gaal the son of Ebed went out and stood in the entrance of the gate of the city, and Abimelech and the people who were with him rose from the ambush. 36 And when Gaal saw the people, he said to Zebul, "Look, people are coming down from the mountaintops!" And Zebul said to him, "You mistake[4] the shadow of the mountains for men." 37 Gaal spoke again and said, "Look, people are coming down from the center of the land, and one company is coming from the direction of the Diviners' Oak." 38 Then Zebul said to him, "Where is your mouth now, you who said, 'Who is Abimelech, that we should serve him?' Are not these the people whom you despised? Go out now and fight with them." 39 And Gaal went out at the head of the leaders of Shechem and fought with Abimelech. 40 And Abimelech chased him, and he fled before him. And many fell wounded, up to the entrance of the gate. 41 And Abimelech lived at Arumah, and Zebul drove out Gaal and his relatives, so that they could not dwell at Shechem.

42 On the following day, the people went out into the field, and Abimelech was told. 43 He took his people and divided them into three companies and set an ambush in the fields. And he looked and saw the people coming out of the city. So he rose against them and killed them. 44 Abimelech and the company that was with him rushed forward and stood at the entrance of the gate of the city, while the two companies rushed upon all who were in the field and killed them. 45 And Abimelech fought

1 Septuagint; Hebrew and he said 2 Or at Tormah 3 Hebrew besieging, or closing up 4 Hebrew You see

against the city all that day. He captured the city and killed the people who were in it, and he razed the city and sowed it with salt.

[46] When all the leaders of the Tower of Shechem heard of it, they entered the stronghold of the house of El-berith. [47] Abimelech was told that all the leaders of the Tower of Shechem were gathered together. [48] And Abimelech went up to Mount Zalmon, he and all the people who were with him. And Abimelech took an axe in his hand and cut down a bundle of brushwood and took it up and laid it on his shoulder. And he said to the men who were with him, "What you have seen me do, hurry and do as I have done." [49] So every one of the people cut down his bundle and following Abimelech put it against the stronghold, and they set the stronghold on fire over them, so that all the people of the Tower of Shechem also died, about 1,000 men and women.

[50] Then Abimelech went to Thebez and encamped against Thebez and captured it. [51] But there was a strong tower within the city, and all the men and women and all the leaders of the city fled to it and shut themselves in, and they went up to the roof of the tower. [52] And Abimelech came to the tower and fought against it and drew near to the door of the tower to burn it with fire. [53] And a certain woman threw an upper millstone on Abimelech's head and crushed his skull. [54] Then he called quickly to the young man his armor-bearer and said to him, "Draw your sword and kill me, lest they say of me, 'A woman killed him.'" And his young man thrust him through, and he died. [55] And when the men of Israel saw that Abimelech was dead, everyone departed to his home. [56] Thus God returned the evil of Abimelech, which he committed against his father in killing his seventy brothers. [57] And God also made all the evil of the men of Shechem return on their heads, and upon them came the curse of Jotham the son of Jerubbaal.

Acts 13

Now there were in the church at Antioch prophets and teachers, Barnabas, Simeon who was called Niger,[1] Lucius of Cyrene, Manaen a lifelong friend of Herod the tetrarch, and Saul. [2] While they were worshiping the Lord and fasting, the Holy Spirit said, "Set apart for me Barnabas and Saul for the work to which I have called them." [3] Then after fasting and praying they laid their hands on them and sent them off.

[4] So, being sent out by the Holy Spirit, they went down to Seleucia, and from there they sailed to Cyprus. [5] When they arrived at Salamis, they proclaimed the word of God in the synagogues of the Jews. And they had John to assist them. [6] When they had gone through the whole island as far as Paphos, they came upon a certain magician, a Jewish false prophet named Bar-Jesus. [7] He was with the proconsul, Sergius Paulus, a man of intelligence, who summoned Barnabas and Saul and sought to hear the word of God. [8] But Elymas the magician (for that is the meaning of his name) opposed them, seeking to turn the proconsul away from the faith. [9] But Saul, who was also called Paul, filled with the Holy Spirit, looked intently at him [10] and said, "You son of the devil, you enemy of all righteousness, full of all deceit and villainy, will you not stop making crooked the straight paths of the Lord? [11] And now, behold, the hand of the Lord is upon you, and you will be blind and unable to see the sun for a time." Immediately mist and darkness fell upon him, and he went about seeking people to lead him by the hand. [12] Then the proconsul believed, when he saw what had occurred, for he was astonished at the teaching of the Lord.

[13] Now Paul and his companions set sail from Paphos and came to Perga in Pamphylia. And John left them and returned to Jerusalem, [14] but they went on from Perga and came to Antioch in Pisidia. And on the Sabbath day they went into the synagogue and sat down. [15] After the reading from the Law and the Prophets, the rulers of the synagogue sent a message to them, saying, "Brothers, if you have any word of encouragement for the people, say it." [16] So Paul stood up, and motioning with his hand said:

"Men of Israel and you who fear God, listen. [17] The God of this people Israel chose our fathers and made the people great during their stay in the land of Egypt, and with uplifted arm he led them out of it. [18] And for about forty years he put up with[2] them in the wilderness. [19] And after destroying seven nations in the land of Canaan, he gave them their land as an inheritance. [20] All this took

[1] Niger is a Latin word meaning *black*, or *dark* [2] Some manuscripts *he carried* (compare Deuteronomy 1:31)

about 450 years. And after that he gave them judges until Samuel the prophet. ²¹Then they asked for a king, and God gave them Saul the son of Kish, a man of the tribe of Benjamin, for forty years. ²²And when he had removed him, he raised up David to be their king, of whom he testified and said, 'I have found in David the son of Jesse a man after my heart, who will do all my will.' ²³Of this man's offspring God has brought to Israel a Savior, Jesus, as he promised. ²⁴Before his coming, John had proclaimed a baptism of repentance to all the people of Israel. ²⁵And as John was finishing his course, he said, 'What do you suppose that I am? I am not he. No, but behold, after me one is coming, the sandals of whose feet I am not worthy to untie.'

²⁶"Brothers, sons of the family of Abraham, and those among you who fear God, to us has been sent the message of this salvation. ²⁷For those who live in Jerusalem and their rulers, because they did not recognize him nor understand the utterances of the prophets, which are read every Sabbath, fulfilled them by condemning him. ²⁸And though they found in him no guilt worthy of death, they asked Pilate to have him executed. ²⁹And when they had carried out all that was written of him, they took him down from the tree and laid him in a tomb. ³⁰But God raised him from the dead, ³¹and for many days he appeared to those who had come up with him from Galilee to Jerusalem, who are now his witnesses to the people. ³²And we bring you the good news that what God promised to the fathers, ³³this he has fulfilled to us their children by raising Jesus, as also it is written in the second Psalm,

" 'You are my Son,
    today I have begotten you.'

³⁴And as for the fact that he raised him from the dead, no more to return to corruption, he has spoken in this way,

" 'I will give you the holy and sure
    blessings of David.'

³⁵Therefore he says also in another psalm,

" 'You will not let your Holy One see
    corruption.'

³⁶For David, after he had served the purpose of God in his own generation, fell asleep and

was laid with his fathers and saw corruption, ³⁷but he whom God raised up did not see corruption. ³⁸Let it be known to you therefore, brothers, that through this man forgiveness of sins is proclaimed to you, ³⁹and by him everyone who believes is freed[1] from everything from which you could not be freed by the law of Moses. ⁴⁰Beware, therefore, lest what is said in the Prophets should come about:

⁴¹ " 'Look, you scoffers,
        be astounded and perish;
    for I am doing a work in your days,
        a work that you will not believe, even
            if one tells it to you.' "

⁴²As they went out, the people begged that these things might be told them the next Sabbath. ⁴³And after the meeting of the synagogue broke up, many Jews and devout converts to Judaism followed Paul and Barnabas, who, as they spoke with them, urged them to continue in the grace of God.

⁴⁴The next Sabbath almost the whole city gathered to hear the word of the Lord. ⁴⁵But when the Jews saw the crowds, they were filled with jealousy and began to contradict what was spoken by Paul, reviling him. ⁴⁶And Paul and Barnabas spoke out boldly, saying, "It was necessary that the word of God be spoken first to you. Since you thrust it aside and judge yourselves unworthy of eternal life, behold, we are turning to the Gentiles. ⁴⁷For so the Lord has commanded us, saying,

" 'I have made you a light for the
        Gentiles,
    that you may bring salvation to the
        ends of the earth.' "

⁴⁸And when the Gentiles heard this, they began rejoicing and glorifying the word of the Lord, and as many as were appointed to eternal life believed. ⁴⁹And the word of the Lord was spreading throughout the whole region. ⁵⁰But the Jews[2] incited the devout women of high standing and the leading men of the city, stirred up persecution against Paul and Barnabas, and drove them out of their district. ⁵¹But they shook off the dust from their feet against them and went to Iconium. ⁵²And the disciples were filled with joy and with the Holy Spirit.

[1] Greek justified; twice in this verse [2] Greek Ioudaioi probably refers here to Jewish religious leaders, and others under their influence, in that time

Jeremiah 22

Thus says the LORD: "Go down to the house of the king of Judah and speak there this word, ²and say, 'Hear the word of the LORD, O king of Judah, who sits on the throne of David, you, and your servants, and your people who enter these gates. ³Thus says the LORD: Do justice and righteousness, and deliver from the hand of the oppressor him who has been robbed. And do no wrong or violence to the resident alien, the fatherless, and the widow, nor shed innocent blood in this place. ⁴For if you will indeed obey this word, then there shall enter the gates of this house kings who sit on the throne of David, riding in chariots and on horses, they and their servants and their people. ⁵But if you will not obey these words, I swear by myself, declares the LORD, that this house shall become a desolation. ⁶For thus says the LORD concerning the house of the king of Judah:

"'You are like Gilead to me,
   like the summit of Lebanon,
yet surely I will make you a desert,
   an uninhabited city.¹
7   I will prepare destroyers against you,
     each with his weapons,
   and they shall cut down your choicest
       cedars
     and cast them into the fire.

8 "'And many nations will pass by this city, and every man will say to his neighbor, "Why has the LORD dealt thus with this great city?" ⁹And they will answer, "Because they have forsaken the covenant of the LORD their God and worshiped other gods and served them."'"

10   Weep not for him who is dead,
       nor grieve for him,
     but weep bitterly for him who goes
         away,
       for he shall return no more
       to see his native land.

¹¹For thus says the LORD concerning Shallum the son of Josiah, king of Judah, who reigned instead of Josiah his father, and who went away from this place: "He shall return here no more, ¹²but in the place where they have carried him captive, there shall he die, and he shall never see this land again."

13 "Woe to him who builds his house by
       unrighteousness,
     and his upper rooms by injustice,
   who makes his neighbor serve him for
       nothing
     and does not give him his wages,
14   who says, 'I will build myself a great
       house
     with spacious upper rooms,'
   who cuts out windows for it,
     paneling it with cedar
     and painting it with vermilion.
15   Do you think you are a king
     because you compete in cedar?
   Did not your father eat and drink
     and do justice and righteousness?
     Then it was well with him.
16   He judged the cause of the poor and
       needy;
     then it was well.
   Is not this to know me?
     declares the LORD.
17   But you have eyes and heart
     only for your dishonest gain,
   for shedding innocent blood,
     and for practicing oppression and
       violence."

¹⁸Therefore thus says the LORD concerning Jehoiakim the son of Josiah, king of Judah:

"They shall not lament for him, saying,
   'Ah, my brother!' or 'Ah, sister!'
They shall not lament for him, saying,
   'Ah, lord!' or 'Ah, his majesty!'
19   With the burial of a donkey he shall be
       buried,
     dragged and dumped beyond the
       gates of Jerusalem."

20 "Go up to Lebanon, and cry out,
     and lift up your voice in Bashan;
   cry out from Abarim,
     for all your lovers are destroyed.
21   I spoke to you in your prosperity,
     but you said, 'I will not listen.'
   This has been your way from your
       youth,
     that you have not obeyed my voice.
22   The wind shall shepherd all your
       shepherds,
     and your lovers shall go into
       captivity;

¹ Hebrew cities

then you will be ashamed and
confounded
because of all your evil.
23 O inhabitant of Lebanon,
nested among the cedars,
how you will be pitied when pangs come
upon you,
pain as of a woman in labor!"

24 "As I live, declares the Lord, though
Coniah the son of Jehoiakim, king of Judah,
were the signet ring on my right hand, yet I
would tear you off 25 and give you into the hand
of those who seek your life, into the hand of
those of whom you are afraid, even into the
hand of Nebuchadnezzar king of Babylon and
into the hand of the Chaldeans. 26 I will hurl
you and the mother who bore you into another
country, where you were not born, and there
you shall die. 27 But to the land to which they
will long to return, there they shall not return."

28 Is this man Coniah a despised, broken
pot,
a vessel no one cares for?
Why are he and his children hurled and
cast
into a land that they do not know?
29 O land, land, land,
hear the word of the Lord!
30 Thus says the Lord:
"Write this man down as childless,
a man who shall not succeed in his
days,
for none of his offspring shall succeed
in sitting on the throne of David
and ruling again in Judah."

Mark 8

In those days, when again a great crowd had
gathered, and they had nothing to eat, he
called his disciples to him and said to them,
2 "I have compassion on the crowd, because
they have been with me now three days and
have nothing to eat. 3 And if I send them away
hungry to their homes, they will faint on the
way. And some of them have come from far
away." 4 And his disciples answered him, "How
can one feed these people with bread here in
this desolate place?" 5 And he asked them, "How
many loaves do you have?" They said, "Seven."
6 And he directed the crowd to sit down on the
ground. And he took the seven loaves, and having given thanks, he broke them and gave them
to his disciples to set before the people; and
they set them before the crowd. 7 And they had
a few small fish. And having blessed them, he
said that these also should be set before them.
8 And they ate and were satisfied. And they took
up the broken pieces left over, seven baskets
full. 9 And there were about four thousand people. And he sent them away. 10 And immediately
he got into the boat with his disciples and went
to the district of Dalmanutha.¹

11 The Pharisees came and began to argue
with him, seeking from him a sign from heaven
to test him. 12 And he sighed deeply in his spirit
and said, "Why does this generation seek a
sign? Truly, I say to you, no sign will be given
to this generation." 13 And he left them, got into
the boat again, and went to the other side.

14 Now they had forgotten to bring bread, and
they had only one loaf with them in the boat.
15 And he cautioned them, saying, "Watch out;
beware of the leaven of the Pharisees and the
leaven of Herod."² 16 And they began discussing with one another the fact that they had
no bread. 17 And Jesus, aware of this, said to
them, "Why are you discussing the fact that
you have no bread? Do you not yet perceive
or understand? Are your hearts hardened?
18 Having eyes do you not see, and having ears
do you not hear? And do you not remember?
19 When I broke the five loaves for the five thousand, how many baskets full of broken pieces
did you take up?" They said to him, "Twelve."
20 "And the seven for the four thousand, how
many baskets full of broken pieces did you take
up?" And they said to him, "Seven." 21 And he
said to them, "Do you not yet understand?"

22 And they came to Bethsaida. And some
people brought to him a blind man and begged
him to touch him. 23 And he took the blind man
by the hand and led him out of the village, and
when he had spit on his eyes and laid his hands
on him, he asked him, "Do you see anything?"
24 And he looked up and said, "I see people, but
they look like trees, walking." 25 Then Jesus³ laid
his hands on his eyes again; and he opened his
eyes, his sight was restored, and he saw everything clearly. 26 And he sent him to his home,
saying, "Do not even enter the village."

27 And Jesus went on with his disciples to the
villages of Caesarea Philippi. And on the way

¹ Some manuscripts *Magadan*, or *Magdala* ² Some manuscripts *the Herodians* ³ Greek *he*

he asked his disciples, "Who do people say that I am?" [28]And they told him, "John the Baptist; and others say, Elijah; and others, one of the prophets." [29]And he asked them, "But who do you say that I am?" Peter answered him, "You are the Christ." [30]And he strictly charged them to tell no one about him.

[31]And he began to teach them that the Son of Man must suffer many things and be rejected by the elders and the chief priests and the scribes and be killed, and after three days rise again. [32]And he said this plainly. And Peter took him aside and began to rebuke him. [33]But turning and seeing his disciples, he rebuked Peter and said, "Get behind me, Satan! For you are not setting your mind on the things of God, but on the things of man."

[34]And calling the crowd to him with his disciples, he said to them, "If anyone would come after me, let him deny himself and take up his cross and follow me. [35]For whoever would save his life[1] will lose it, but whoever loses his life for my sake and the gospel's will save it. [36]For what does it profit a man to gain the whole world and forfeit his soul? [37]For what can a man give in return for his soul? [38]For whoever is ashamed of me and of my words in this adulterous and sinful generation, of him will the Son of Man also be ashamed when he comes in the glory of his Father with the holy angels."

JULY 27

Judges 10:1–11:11

After Abimelech there arose to save Israel Tola the son of Puah, son of Dodo, a man of Issachar, and he lived at Shamir in the hill country of Ephraim. [2]And he judged Israel twenty-three years. Then he died and was buried at Shamir.

[3]After him arose Jair the Gileadite, who judged Israel twenty-two years. [4]And he had thirty sons who rode on thirty donkeys, and they had thirty cities, called Havvoth-jair to this day, which are in the land of Gilead. [5]And Jair died and was buried in Kamon.

[6]The people of Israel again did what was evil in the sight of the LORD and served the Baals and the Ashtaroth, the gods of Syria, the gods of Sidon, the gods of Moab, the gods of the Ammonites, and the gods of the Philistines. And they forsook the LORD and did not serve him. [7]So the anger of the LORD was kindled against Israel, and he sold them into the hand of the Philistines and into the hand of the Ammonites, [8]and they crushed and oppressed the people of Israel that year. For eighteen years they oppressed all the people of Israel who were beyond the Jordan in the land of the Amorites, which is in Gilead. [9]And the Ammonites crossed the Jordan to fight also against Judah and against Benjamin and against the house of Ephraim, so that Israel was severely distressed.

[10]And the people of Israel cried out to the LORD, saying, "We have sinned against you, because we have forsaken our God and have served the Baals." [11]And the LORD said to the people of Israel, "Did I not save you from the Egyptians and from the Amorites, from the Ammonites and from the Philistines? [12]The Sidonians also, and the Amalekites and the Maonites oppressed you, and you cried out to me, and I saved you out of their hand. [13]Yet you have forsaken me and served other gods; therefore I will save you no more. [14]Go and cry out to the gods whom you have chosen; let them save you in the time of your distress." [15]And the people of Israel said to the LORD, "We have sinned; do to us whatever seems good to you. Only please deliver us this day." [16]So they put away the foreign gods from among them and served the LORD, and he became impatient over the misery of Israel.

[17]Then the Ammonites were called to arms, and they encamped in Gilead. And the people

[1] The same Greek word can mean either *soul* or *life*, depending on the context; twice in this verse and once in verse 36 and once in verse 37

of Israel came together, and they encamped at Mizpah. [18]And the people, the leaders of Gilead, said one to another, "Who is the man who will begin to fight against the Ammonites? He shall be head over all the inhabitants of Gilead."

[11:1]Now Jephthah the Gileadite was a mighty warrior, but he was the son of a prostitute. Gilead was the father of Jephthah. [2]And Gilead's wife also bore him sons. And when his wife's sons grew up, they drove Jephthah out and said to him, "You shall not have an inheritance in our father's house, for you are the son of another woman." [3]Then Jephthah fled from his brothers and lived in the land of Tob, and worthless fellows collected around Jephthah and went out with him.

[4]After a time the Ammonites made war against Israel. [5]And when the Ammonites made war against Israel, the elders of Gilead went to bring Jephthah from the land of Tob. [6]And they said to Jephthah, "Come and be our leader, that we may fight against the Ammonites." [7]But Jephthah said to the elders of Gilead, "Did you not hate me and drive me out of my father's house? Why have you come to me now when you are in distress?" [8]And the elders of Gilead said to Jephthah, "That is why we have turned to you now, that you may go with us and fight against the Ammonites and be our head over all the inhabitants of Gilead." [9]Jephthah said to the elders of Gilead, "If you bring me home again to fight against the Ammonites, and the LORD gives them over to me, I will be your head." [10]And the elders of Gilead said to Jephthah, "The LORD will be witness between us, if we do not do as you say." [11]So Jephthah went with the elders of Gilead, and the people made him head and leader over them. And Jephthah spoke all his words before the LORD at Mizpah.

Acts 14

Now at Iconium they entered together into the Jewish synagogue and spoke in such a way that a great number of both Jews and Greeks believed. [2]But the unbelieving Jews stirred up the Gentiles and poisoned their minds against the brothers.[1] [3]So they remained for a long time, speaking boldly for the Lord, who bore witness to the word of his grace, granting signs and wonders to be done by their hands. [4]But the people of the city were divided; some sided with the Jews and some with the apostles. [5]When an attempt was made by both Gentiles and Jews, with their rulers, to mistreat them and to stone them, [6]they learned of it and fled to Lystra and Derbe, cities of Lycaonia, and to the surrounding country, [7]and there they continued to preach the gospel.

[8]Now at Lystra there was a man sitting who could not use his feet. He was crippled from birth and had never walked. [9]He listened to Paul speaking. And Paul, looking intently at him and seeing that he had faith to be made well,[2] [10]said in a loud voice, "Stand upright on your feet." And he sprang up and began walking. [11]And when the crowds saw what Paul had done, they lifted up their voices, saying in Lycaonian, "The gods have come down to us in the likeness of men!" [12]Barnabas they called Zeus, and Paul, Hermes, because he was the chief speaker. [13]And the priest of Zeus, whose temple was at the entrance to the city, brought oxen and garlands to the gates and wanted to offer sacrifice with the crowds. [14]But when the apostles Barnabas and Paul heard of it, they tore their garments and rushed out into the crowd, crying out, [15]"Men, why are you doing these things? We also are men, of like nature with you, and we bring you good news, that you should turn from these vain things to a living God, who made the heaven and the earth and the sea and all that is in them. [16]In past generations he allowed all the nations to walk in their own ways. [17]Yet he did not leave himself without witness, for he did good by giving you rains from heaven and fruitful seasons, satisfying your hearts with food and gladness." [18]Even with these words they scarcely restrained the people from offering sacrifice to them.

[19]But Jews came from Antioch and Iconium, and having persuaded the crowds, they stoned Paul and dragged him out of the city, supposing that he was dead. [20]But when the disciples gathered about him, he rose up and entered the city, and on the next day he went on with Barnabas to Derbe. [21]When they had preached the gospel to that city and had made many disciples, they returned to Lystra and to Iconium and to Antioch, [22]strengthening the souls of the disciples, encouraging them to continue in the faith, and saying that through many

[1] Or brothers and sisters [2] Or be saved

tribulations we must enter the kingdom of God. ²³And when they had appointed elders for them in every church, with prayer and fasting they committed them to the Lord in whom they had believed.

²⁴Then they passed through Pisidia and came to Pamphylia. ²⁵And when they had spoken the word in Perga, they went down to Attalia, ²⁶and from there they sailed to Antioch, where they had been commended to the grace of God for the work that they had fulfilled. ²⁷And when they arrived and gathered the church together, they declared all that God had done with them, and how he had opened a door of faith to the Gentiles. ²⁸And they remained no little time with the disciples.

Jeremiah 23

"Woe to the shepherds who destroy and scatter the sheep of my pasture!" declares the LORD. ²Therefore thus says the LORD, the God of Israel, concerning the shepherds who care for my people: "You have scattered my flock and have driven them away, and you have not attended to them. Behold, I will attend to you for your evil deeds, declares the LORD. ³Then I will gather the remnant of my flock out of all the countries where I have driven them, and I will bring them back to their fold, and they shall be fruitful and multiply. ⁴I will set shepherds over them who will care for them, and they shall fear no more, nor be dismayed, neither shall any be missing, declares the LORD.

⁵"Behold, the days are coming, declares the LORD, when I will raise up for David a righteous Branch, and he shall reign as king and deal wisely, and shall execute justice and righteousness in the land. ⁶In his days Judah will be saved, and Israel will dwell securely. And this is the name by which he will be called: 'The LORD is our righteousness.'

⁷"Therefore, behold, the days are coming, declares the LORD, when they shall no longer say, 'As the LORD lives who brought up the people of Israel out of the land of Egypt,' ⁸but 'As the LORD lives who brought up and led the offspring of the house of Israel out of the north country and out of all the countries where he¹ had driven them.' Then they shall dwell in their own land."

⁹Concerning the prophets:

My heart is broken within me;
   all my bones shake;
I am like a drunken man,
   like a man overcome by wine,
because of the LORD
   and because of his holy words.
¹⁰ For the land is full of adulterers;
   because of the curse the land mourns,
   and the pastures of the wilderness are
     dried up.
Their course is evil,
   and their might is not right.
¹¹ "Both prophet and priest are ungodly;
   even in my house I have found their
     evil,
               declares the LORD.
¹² Therefore their way shall be to them
   like slippery paths in the darkness,
   into which they shall be driven and
     fall,
for I will bring disaster upon them
   in the year of their punishment,
               declares the LORD.
¹³ In the prophets of Samaria
   I saw an unsavory thing:
they prophesied by Baal
   and led my people Israel astray.
¹⁴ But in the prophets of Jerusalem
   I have seen a horrible thing:
they commit adultery and walk in lies;
   they strengthen the hands of
     evildoers,
   so that no one turns from his evil;
all of them have become like Sodom to
     me,
   and its inhabitants like Gomorrah."
¹⁵ Therefore thus says the LORD of hosts
     concerning the prophets:
"Behold, I will feed them with bitter food
   and give them poisoned water to drink,
for from the prophets of Jerusalem
   ungodliness has gone out into all the
     land."

¹⁶Thus says the LORD of hosts: "Do not listen to the words of the prophets who prophesy to you, filling you with vain hopes. They speak visions of their own minds, not from the mouth of the LORD. ¹⁷They say continually to those who despise the word of the LORD, 'It shall be well with you'; and to everyone who stubbornly

---

¹ Septuagint; Hebrew *I*

follows his own heart, they say, 'No disaster shall come upon you.'"

18 For who among them has stood in the
          council of the LORD
       to see and to hear his word,
          or who has paid attention to his word
          and listened?
19 Behold, the storm of the LORD!
       Wrath has gone forth,
    a whirling tempest;
       it will burst upon the head of the
          wicked.
20 The anger of the LORD will not turn back
       until he has executed and
          accomplished
       the intents of his heart.
    In the latter days you will understand it
       clearly.
21 "I did not send the prophets,
       yet they ran;
    I did not speak to them,
       yet they prophesied.
22 But if they had stood in my council,
       then they would have proclaimed my
          words to my people,
    and they would have turned them from
          their evil way,
       and from the evil of their deeds.

23 "Am I a God at hand, declares the LORD, and not a God far away? 24 Can a man hide himself in secret places so that I cannot see him? declares the LORD. Do I not fill heaven and earth? declares the LORD. 25 I have heard what the prophets have said who prophesy lies in my name, saying, 'I have dreamed, I have dreamed!' 26 How long shall there be lies in the heart of the prophets who prophesy lies, and who prophesy the deceit of their own heart, 27 who think to make my people forget my name by their dreams that they tell one another, even as their fathers forgot my name for Baal? 28 Let the prophet who has a dream tell the dream, but let him who has my word speak my word faithfully. What has straw in common with wheat? declares the LORD. 29 Is not my word like fire, declares the LORD, and like a hammer that breaks the rock in pieces? 30 Therefore, behold, I am against the prophets, declares the LORD, who steal my words from one another. 31 Behold, I am against the prophets, declares the LORD, who use their tongues and declare, 'declares the LORD.' 32 Behold, I am against those who prophesy lying dreams, declares the LORD, and who tell them and lead my people astray by their lies and their recklessness, when I did not send them or charge them. So they do not profit this people at all, declares the LORD.

33 "When one of this people, or a prophet or a priest asks you, 'What is the burden of the LORD?' you shall say to them, 'You are the burden,[1] and I will cast you off, declares the LORD.' 34 And as for the prophet, priest, or one of the people who says, 'The burden of the LORD,' I will punish that man and his household. 35 Thus shall you say, every one to his neighbor and every one to his brother, 'What has the LORD answered?' or 'What has the LORD spoken?' 36 But 'the burden of the LORD' you shall mention no more, for the burden is every man's own word, and you pervert the words of the living God, the LORD of hosts, our God. 37 Thus you shall say to the prophet, 'What has the LORD answered you?' or 'What has the LORD spoken?' 38 But if you say, 'The burden of the LORD,' thus says the LORD, 'Because you have said these words, "The burden of the LORD," when I sent to you, saying, "You shall not say, 'The burden of the LORD,'" 39 therefore, behold, I will surely lift you up and cast you away from my presence, you and the city that I gave to you and your fathers. 40 And I will bring upon you everlasting reproach and perpetual shame, which shall not be forgotten.'"

Mark 9

And he said to them, "Truly, I say to you, there are some standing here who will not taste death until they see the kingdom of God after it has come with power."

2 And after six days Jesus took with him Peter and James and John, and led them up a high mountain by themselves. And he was transfigured before them, 3 and his clothes became radiant, intensely white, as no one[2] on earth could bleach them. 4 And there appeared to them Elijah with Moses, and they were talking with Jesus. 5 And Peter said to Jesus, "Rabbi,[3] it is good that we are here. Let us make three tents, one for you and one for Moses and one for Elijah." 6 For he did not know what to say,

1 Septuagint, Vulgate; Hebrew What burden? 2 Greek launderer (gnapheus) 3 Rabbi means my teacher, or my master

for they were terrified. [7]And a cloud overshadowed them, and a voice came out of the cloud, "This is my beloved Son;[1] listen to him." [8]And suddenly, looking around, they no longer saw anyone with them but Jesus only.

[9]And as they were coming down the mountain, he charged them to tell no one what they had seen, until the Son of Man had risen from the dead. [10]So they kept the matter to themselves, questioning what this rising from the dead might mean. [11]And they asked him, "Why do the scribes say that first Elijah must come?" [12]And he said to them, "Elijah does come first to restore all things. And how is it written of the Son of Man that he should suffer many things and be treated with contempt? [13]But I tell you that Elijah has come, and they did to him whatever they pleased, as it is written of him."

[14]And when they came to the disciples, they saw a great crowd around them, and scribes arguing with them. [15]And immediately all the crowd, when they saw him, were greatly amazed and ran up to him and greeted him. [16]And he asked them, "What are you arguing about with them?" [17]And someone from the crowd answered him, "Teacher, I brought my son to you, for he has a spirit that makes him mute. [18]And whenever it seizes him, it throws him down, and he foams and grinds his teeth and becomes rigid. So I asked your disciples to cast it out, and they were not able." [19]And he answered them, "O faithless generation, how long am I to be with you? How long am I to bear with you? Bring him to me." [20]And they brought the boy to him. And when the spirit saw him, immediately it convulsed the boy, and he fell on the ground and rolled about, foaming at the mouth. [21]And Jesus asked his father, "How long has this been happening to him?" And he said, "From childhood. [22]And it has often cast him into fire and into water, to destroy him. But if you can do anything, have compassion on us and help us." [23]And Jesus said to him, "'If you can'! All things are possible for one who believes." [24]Immediately the father of the child cried out[2] and said, "I believe; help my unbelief!" [25]And when Jesus saw that a crowd came running together, he rebuked the unclean spirit, saying to it, "You mute and deaf spirit, I command you, come out of him and never enter him again." [26]And after crying out

and convulsing him terribly, it came out, and the boy was like a corpse, so that most of them said, "He is dead." [27]But Jesus took him by the hand and lifted him up, and he arose. [28]And when he had entered the house, his disciples asked him privately, "Why could we not cast it out?" [29]And he said to them, "This kind cannot be driven out by anything but prayer."[3]

[30]They went on from there and passed through Galilee. And he did not want anyone to know, [31]for he was teaching his disciples, saying to them, "The Son of Man is going to be delivered into the hands of men, and they will kill him. And when he is killed, after three days he will rise." [32]But they did not understand the saying, and were afraid to ask him.

[33]And they came to Capernaum. And when he was in the house he asked them, "What were you discussing on the way?" [34]But they kept silent, for on the way they had argued with one another about who was the greatest. [35]And he sat down and called the twelve. And he said to them, "If anyone would be first, he must be last of all and servant of all." [36]And he took a child and put him in the midst of them, and taking him in his arms, he said to them, [37]"Whoever receives one such child in my name receives me, and whoever receives me, receives not me but him who sent me."

[38]John said to him, "Teacher, we saw someone casting out demons in your name,[4] and we tried to stop him, because he was not following us." [39]But Jesus said, "Do not stop him, for no one who does a mighty work in my name will be able soon afterward to speak evil of me. [40]For the one who is not against us is for us. [41]For truly, I say to you, whoever gives you a cup of water to drink because you belong to Christ will by no means lose his reward.

[42]"Whoever causes one of these little ones who believe in me to sin,[5] it would be better for him if a great millstone were hung around his neck and he were thrown into the sea. [43]And if your hand causes you to sin, cut it off. It is better for you to enter life crippled than with two hands to go to hell,[6] to the unquenchable fire.[7] [45]And if your foot causes you to sin, cut it off. It is better for you to enter life lame than with two feet to be thrown into hell. [47]And if your eye causes you to sin, tear it out. It is better for you to enter the kingdom of God with one eye than with two eyes to be thrown into hell,

⁴⁸'where their worm does not die and the fire is not quenched.' ⁴⁹For everyone will be salted with fire.¹ ⁵⁰Salt is good, but if the salt has lost its saltiness, how will you make it salty again? Have salt in yourselves, and be at peace with one another."

JULY 28

Judges 11:12–40

Then Jephthah sent messengers to the king of the Ammonites and said, "What do you have against me, that you have come to me to fight against my land?" ¹³And the king of the Ammonites answered the messengers of Jephthah, "Because Israel on coming up from Egypt took away my land, from the Arnon to the Jabbok and to the Jordan; now therefore restore it peaceably." ¹⁴Jephthah again sent messengers to the king of the Ammonites ¹⁵and said to him, "Thus says Jephthah: Israel did not take away the land of Moab or the land of the Ammonites, ¹⁶but when they came up from Egypt, Israel went through the wilderness to the Red Sea and came to Kadesh. ¹⁷Israel then sent messengers to the king of Edom, saying, 'Please let us pass through your land,' but the king of Edom would not listen. And they sent also to the king of Moab, but he would not consent. So Israel remained at Kadesh.

¹⁸"Then they journeyed through the wilderness and went around the land of Edom and the land of Moab and arrived on the east side of the land of Moab and camped on the other side of the Arnon. But they did not enter the territory of Moab, for the Arnon was the boundary of Moab. ¹⁹Israel then sent messengers to Sihon king of the Amorites, king of Heshbon, and Israel said to him, 'Please let us pass through your land to our country,' ²⁰but Sihon did not trust Israel to pass through his territory, so Sihon gathered all his people together and encamped at Jahaz and fought with Israel. ²¹And the LORD, the God of Israel, gave Sihon and all his people into the hand of Israel, and they defeated them. So Israel took possession of all the land of the Amorites, who inhabited that country. ²²And they took possession of all the territory of the Amorites from the Arnon to the Jabbok and from the wilderness to the Jordan. ²³So then the LORD, the God of Israel, dispossessed the Amorites from before his people Israel; and are you to take possession of them? ²⁴Will you not possess what Chemosh your god gives you to possess? And all that the LORD our God has dispossessed before us, we will possess. ²⁵Now are you any better than Balak the son of Zippor, king of Moab? Did he ever contend against Israel, or did he ever go to war with them? ²⁶While Israel lived in Heshbon and its villages, and in Aroer and its villages, and in all the cities that are on the banks of the Arnon, 300 years, why did you not deliver them within that time? ²⁷I therefore have not sinned against you, and you do me wrong by making war on me. The LORD, the Judge, decide this day between the people of Israel and the people of Ammon." ²⁸But the king of the Ammonites did not listen to the words of Jephthah that he sent to him.

²⁹Then the Spirit of the LORD was upon Jephthah, and he passed through Gilead and Manasseh and passed on to Mizpah of Gilead, and from Mizpah of Gilead he passed on to the Ammonites. ³⁰And Jephthah made a vow to the LORD and said, "If you will give the Ammonites into my hand, ³¹then whatever² comes out from the doors of my house to meet me when I return in peace from the Ammonites shall be the LORD's, and I will offer it³ up for a burnt offering." ³²So Jephthah crossed over to the Ammonites to fight against them, and the LORD gave them into his hand. ³³And he struck them from Aroer to the neighborhood of Minnith, twenty cities, and as far as Abel-keramim, with

---

¹ Some manuscripts add *and every sacrifice will be salted with salt* ² Or *whoever* ³ Or *him*

a great blow. So the Ammonites were subdued before the people of Israel.

³⁴ Then Jephthah came to his home at Mizpah. And behold, his daughter came out to meet him with tambourines and with dances. She was his only child; besides her he had neither son nor daughter. ³⁵ And as soon as he saw her, he tore his clothes and said, "Alas, my daughter! You have brought me very low, and you have become the cause of great trouble to me. For I have opened my mouth to the LORD, and I cannot take back my vow." ³⁶ And she said to him, "My father, you have opened your mouth to the LORD; do to me according to what has gone out of your mouth, now that the LORD has avenged you on your enemies, on the Ammonites." ³⁷ So she said to her father, "Let this thing be done for me: leave me alone two months, that I may go up and down on the mountains and weep for my virginity, I and my companions." ³⁸ So he said, "Go." Then he sent her away for two months, and she departed, she and her companions, and wept for her virginity on the mountains. ³⁹ And at the end of two months, she returned to her father, who did with her according to his vow that he had made. She had never known a man, and it became a custom in Israel ⁴⁰ that the daughters of Israel went year by year to lament the daughter of Jephthah the Gileadite four days in the year.

Acts 15

^But some men came down from Judea and were teaching the brothers, "Unless you are circumcised according to the custom of Moses, you cannot be saved." ² And after Paul and Barnabas had no small dissension and debate with them, Paul and Barnabas and some of the others were appointed to go up to Jerusalem to the apostles and the elders about this question. ³ So, being sent on their way by the church, they passed through both Phoenicia and Samaria, describing in detail the conversion of the Gentiles, and brought great joy to all the brothers.¹ ⁴ When they came to Jerusalem, they were welcomed by the church and the apostles and the elders, and they declared all that God had done with them. ⁵ But some believers who belonged to the party of the Pharisees rose up and said, "It

is necessary to circumcise them and to order them to keep the law of Moses."

⁶ The apostles and the elders were gathered together to consider this matter. ⁷ And after there had been much debate, Peter stood up and said to them, "Brothers, you know that in the early days God made a choice among you, that by my mouth the Gentiles should hear the word of the gospel and believe. ⁸ And God, who knows the heart, bore witness to them, by giving them the Holy Spirit just as he did to us, ⁹ and he made no distinction between us and them, having cleansed their hearts by faith. ¹⁰ Now, therefore, why are you putting God to the test by placing a yoke on the neck of the disciples that neither our fathers nor we have been able to bear? ¹¹ But we believe that we will be saved through the grace of the Lord Jesus, just as they will."

¹² And all the assembly fell silent, and they listened to Barnabas and Paul as they related what signs and wonders God had done through them among the Gentiles. ¹³ After they finished speaking, James replied, "Brothers, listen to me. ¹⁴ Simeon has related how God first visited the Gentiles, to take from them a people for his name. ¹⁵ And with this the words of the prophets agree, just as it is written,

¹⁶　"'After this I will return,
　　and I will rebuild the tent of David that
　　　　has fallen;
　　I will rebuild its ruins,
　　　　and I will restore it,
¹⁷　　that the remnant² of mankind may seek
　　　　the Lord,
　　and all the Gentiles who are called by
　　　　my name,
　　　says the Lord, who makes these things
　　　　¹⁸ known from of old.'

¹⁹ Therefore my judgment is that we should not trouble those of the Gentiles who turn to God, ²⁰ but should write to them to abstain from the things polluted by idols, and from sexual immorality, and from what has been strangled, and from blood. ²¹ For from ancient generations Moses has had in every city those who proclaim him, for he is read every Sabbath in the synagogues."

²² Then it seemed good to the apostles and the elders, with the whole church, to choose men from among them and send them to

---

¹ Or brothers and sisters; also verse 22　² Or rest

Antioch with Paul and Barnabas. They sent Judas called Barsabbas, and Silas, leading men among the brothers, [23] with the following letter: "The brothers, both the apostles and the elders, to the brothers[1] who are of the Gentiles in Antioch and Syria and Cilicia, greetings. [24] Since we have heard that some persons have gone out from us and troubled you[2] with words, unsettling your minds, although we gave them no instructions, [25] it has seemed good to us, having come to one accord, to choose men and send them to you with our beloved Barnabas and Paul, [26] men who have risked their lives for the name of our Lord Jesus Christ. [27] We have therefore sent Judas and Silas, who themselves will tell you the same things by word of mouth. [28] For it has seemed good to the Holy Spirit and to us to lay on you no greater burden than these requirements: [29] that you abstain from what has been sacrificed to idols, and from blood, and from what has been strangled, and from sexual immorality. If you keep yourselves from these, you will do well. Farewell."

[30] So when they were sent off, they went down to Antioch, and having gathered the congregation together, they delivered the letter. [31] And when they had read it, they rejoiced because of its encouragement. [32] And Judas and Silas, who were themselves prophets, encouraged and strengthened the brothers with many words. [33] And after they had spent some time, they were sent off in peace by the brothers to those who had sent them.[3] [35] But Paul and Barnabas remained in Antioch, teaching and preaching the word of the Lord, with many others also.

[36] And after some days Paul said to Barnabas, "Let us return and visit the brothers in every city where we proclaimed the word of the Lord, and see how they are." [37] Now Barnabas wanted to take with them John called Mark. [38] But Paul thought best not to take with them one who had withdrawn from them in Pamphylia and had not gone with them to the work. [39] And there arose a sharp disagreement, so that they separated from each other. Barnabas took Mark with him and sailed away to Cyprus, [40] but Paul chose Silas and departed, having been commended by the brothers to the grace of the Lord. [41] And he went through Syria and Cilicia, strengthening the churches.

Jeremiah 24

After Nebuchadnezzar king of Babylon had taken into exile from Jerusalem Jeconiah the son of Jehoiakim, king of Judah, together with the officials of Judah, the craftsmen, and the metal workers, and had brought them to Babylon, the LORD showed me this vision: behold, two baskets of figs placed before the temple of the LORD. [2] One basket had very good figs, like first-ripe figs, but the other basket had very bad figs, so bad that they could not be eaten. [3] And the LORD said to me, "What do you see, Jeremiah?" I said, "Figs, the good figs very good, and the bad figs very bad, so bad that they cannot be eaten."

[4] Then the word of the LORD came to me: [5] "Thus says the LORD, the God of Israel: Like these good figs, so I will regard as good the exiles from Judah, whom I have sent away from this place to the land of the Chaldeans. [6] I will set my eyes on them for good, and I will bring them back to this land. I will build them up, and not tear them down; I will plant them, and not pluck them up. [7] I will give them a heart to know that I am the LORD, and they shall be my people and I will be their God, for they shall return to me with their whole heart.

[8] "But thus says the LORD: Like the bad figs that are so bad they cannot be eaten, so will I treat Zedekiah the king of Judah, his officials, the remnant of Jerusalem who remain in this land, and those who dwell in the land of Egypt. [9] I will make them a horror[4] to all the kingdoms of the earth, to be a reproach, a byword, a taunt, and a curse in all the places where I shall drive them. [10] And I will send sword, famine, and pestilence upon them, until they shall be utterly destroyed from the land that I gave to them and their fathers."

Mark 10

And he left there and went to the region of Judea and beyond the Jordan, and crowds gathered to him again. And again, as was his custom, he taught them.

[2] And Pharisees came up and in order to test him asked, "Is it lawful for a man to divorce his wife?" [3] He answered them, "What did Moses command you?" [4] They said, "Moses allowed a man to write a certificate of divorce and to send

[1] Or brothers and sisters; also verses 32, 33, 36 [2] Some manuscripts some persons from us have troubled you [3] Some manuscripts insert verse 34: But it seemed good to Silas to remain there [4] Compare Septuagint; Hebrew horror for evil

her away." [5]And Jesus said to them, "Because of your hardness of heart he wrote you this commandment. [6]But from the beginning of creation, 'God made them male and female.' [7]'Therefore a man shall leave his father and mother and hold fast to his wife,[1] [8]and the two shall become one flesh.' So they are no longer two but one flesh. [9]What therefore God has joined together, let not man separate."

[10]And in the house the disciples asked him again about this matter. [11]And he said to them, "Whoever divorces his wife and marries another commits adultery against her, [12]and if she divorces her husband and marries another, she commits adultery."

[13]And they were bringing children to him that he might touch them, and the disciples rebuked them. [14]But when Jesus saw it, he was indignant and said to them, "Let the children come to me; do not hinder them, for to such belongs the kingdom of God. [15]Truly, I say to you, whoever does not receive the kingdom of God like a child shall not enter it." [16]And he took them in his arms and blessed them, laying his hands on them.

[17]And as he was setting out on his journey, a man ran up and knelt before him and asked him, "Good Teacher, what must I do to inherit eternal life?" [18]And Jesus said to him, "Why do you call me good? No one is good except God alone. [19]You know the commandments: 'Do not murder, Do not commit adultery, Do not steal, Do not bear false witness, Do not defraud, Honor your father and mother.'" [20]And he said to him, "Teacher, all these I have kept from my youth." [21]And Jesus, looking at him, loved him, and said to him, "You lack one thing: go, sell all that you have and give to the poor, and you will have treasure in heaven; and come, follow me." [22]Disheartened by the saying, he went away sorrowful, for he had great possessions.

[23]And Jesus looked around and said to his disciples, "How difficult it will be for those who have wealth to enter the kingdom of God!" [24]And the disciples were amazed at his words. But Jesus said to them again, "Children, how difficult it is[2] to enter the kingdom of God! [25]It is easier for a camel to go through the eye of a needle than for a rich person to enter the kingdom of God." [26]And they were exceedingly astonished, and said to him,[3] "Then who can be saved?" [27]Jesus looked at them and said, "With

man it is impossible, but not with God. For all things are possible with God." [28]Peter began to say to him, "See, we have left everything and followed you." [29]Jesus said, "Truly, I say to you, there is no one who has left house or brothers or sisters or mother or father or children or lands, for my sake and for the gospel, [30]who will not receive a hundredfold now in this time, houses and brothers and sisters and mothers and children and lands, with persecutions, and in the age to come eternal life. [31]But many who are first will be last, and the last first."

[32]And they were on the road, going up to Jerusalem, and Jesus was walking ahead of them. And they were amazed, and those who followed were afraid. And taking the twelve again, he began to tell them what was to happen to him, [33]saying, "See, we are going up to Jerusalem, and the Son of Man will be delivered over to the chief priests and the scribes, and they will condemn him to death and deliver him over to the Gentiles. [34]And they will mock him and spit on him, and flog him and kill him. And after three days he will rise."

[35]And James and John, the sons of Zebedee, came up to him and said to him, "Teacher, we want you to do for us whatever we ask of you." [36]And he said to them, "What do you want me to do for you?" [37]And they said to him, "Grant us to sit, one at your right hand and one at your left, in your glory." [38]Jesus said to them, "You do not know what you are asking. Are you able to drink the cup that I drink, or to be baptized with the baptism with which I am baptized?" [39]And they said to him, "We are able." And Jesus said to them, "The cup that I drink you will drink, and with the baptism with which I am baptized, you will be baptized, [40]but to sit at my right hand or at my left is not mine to grant, but it is for those for whom it has been prepared." [41]And when the ten heard it, they began to be indignant at James and John. [42]And Jesus called them to him and said to them, "You know that those who are considered rulers of the Gentiles lord it over them, and their great ones exercise authority over them. [43]But it shall not be so among you. But whoever would be great among you must be your servant,[4] [44]and whoever would be first among you must be slave[5] of all. [45]For even the Son of Man came not to be served but to serve, and to give his life as a ransom for many."

[1] Some manuscripts omit *and hold fast to his wife* [2] Some manuscripts add *for those who trust in riches* [3] Some manuscripts *to one another* [4] Greek *diakonos* [5] Greek *bondservant* (*doulos*)

⁴⁶And they came to Jericho. And as he was leaving Jericho with his disciples and a great crowd, Bartimaeus, a blind beggar, the son of Timaeus, was sitting by the roadside. ⁴⁷And when he heard that it was Jesus of Nazareth, he began to cry out and say, "Jesus, Son of David, have mercy on me!" ⁴⁸And many rebuked him, telling him to be silent. But he cried out all the more, "Son of David, have mercy on me!" ⁴⁹And Jesus stopped and said, "Call him." And they called the blind man, saying to him, "Take heart. Get up; he is calling you." ⁵⁰And throwing off his cloak, he sprang up and came to Jesus. ⁵¹And Jesus said to him, "What do you want me to do for you?" And the blind man said to him, "Rabbi, let me recover my sight." ⁵²And Jesus said to him, "Go your way; your faith has made you well." And immediately he recovered his sight and followed him on the way.

JULY 29

Judges 12

The men of Ephraim were called to arms, and they crossed to Zaphon and said to Jephthah, "Why did you cross over to fight against the Ammonites and did not call us to go with you? We will burn your house over you with fire." ²And Jephthah said to them, "I and my people had a great dispute with the Ammonites, and when I called you, you did not save me from their hand. ³And when I saw that you would not save me, I took my life in my hand and crossed over against the Ammonites, and the LORD gave them into my hand. Why then have you come up to me this day to fight against me?" ⁴Then Jephthah gathered all the men of Gilead and fought with Ephraim. And the men of Gilead struck Ephraim, because they said, "You are fugitives of Ephraim, you Gileadites, in the midst of Ephraim and Manasseh." ⁵And the Gileadites captured the fords of the Jordan against the Ephraimites. And when any of the fugitives of Ephraim said, "Let me go over," the men of Gilead said to him, "Are you an Ephraimite?" When he said, "No," ⁶they said to him, "Then say Shibboleth," and he said, "Sibboleth," for he could not pronounce it right. Then they seized him and slaughtered him at the fords of the Jordan. At that time 42,000 of the Ephraimites fell.

⁷Jephthah judged Israel six years. Then Jephthah the Gileadite died and was buried in his city in Gilead.[1]

⁸After him Ibzan of Bethlehem judged Israel. ⁹He had thirty sons, and thirty daughters he gave in marriage outside his clan, and thirty daughters he brought in from outside for his sons. And he judged Israel seven years. ¹⁰Then Ibzan died and was buried at Bethlehem.

¹¹After him Elon the Zebulunite judged Israel, and he judged Israel ten years. ¹²Then Elon the Zebulunite died and was buried at Aijalon in the land of Zebulun.

¹³After him Abdon the son of Hillel the Pirathonite judged Israel. ¹⁴He had forty sons and thirty grandsons, who rode on seventy donkeys, and he judged Israel eight years. ¹⁵Then Abdon the son of Hillel the Pirathonite died and was buried at Pirathon in the land of Ephraim, in the hill country of the Amalekites.

Acts 16

Paul[2] came also to Derbe and to Lystra. A disciple was there, named Timothy, the son of a Jewish woman who was a believer, but his father was a Greek. ²He was well spoken of by the brothers[3] at Lystra and Iconium. ³Paul wanted Timothy to accompany him, and he took him and circumcised him because of the Jews who were in those places, for they all knew that his father was a Greek. ⁴As they went on their way through the cities, they delivered to them for observance the decisions that had

¹ Septuagint; Hebrew *in the cities of Gilead* ² Greek *He* ³ Or *brothers and sisters*; also verse 40

been reached by the apostles and elders who were in Jerusalem. [5]So the churches were strengthened in the faith, and they increased in numbers daily.

[6]And they went through the region of Phrygia and Galatia, having been forbidden by the Holy Spirit to speak the word in Asia. [7]And when they had come up to Mysia, they attempted to go into Bithynia, but the Spirit of Jesus did not allow them. [8]So, passing by Mysia, they went down to Troas. [9]And a vision appeared to Paul in the night: a man of Macedonia was standing there, urging him and saying, "Come over to Macedonia and help us." [10]And when Paul[1] had seen the vision, immediately we sought to go on into Macedonia, concluding that God had called us to preach the gospel to them.

[11]So, setting sail from Troas, we made a direct voyage to Samothrace, and the following day to Neapolis, [12]and from there to Philippi, which is a leading city of the[2] district of Macedonia and a Roman colony. We remained in this city some days. [13]And on the Sabbath day we went outside the gate to the riverside, where we supposed there was a place of prayer, and we sat down and spoke to the women who had come together. [14]One who heard us was a woman named Lydia, from the city of Thyatira, a seller of purple goods, who was a worshiper of God. The Lord opened her heart to pay attention to what was said by Paul. [15]And after she was baptized, and her household as well, she urged us, saying, "If you have judged me to be faithful to the Lord, come to my house and stay." And she prevailed upon us.

[16]As we were going to the place of prayer, we were met by a slave girl who had a spirit of divination and brought her owners much gain by fortune-telling. [17]She followed Paul and us, crying out, "These men are servants[3] of the Most High God, who proclaim to you the way of salvation." [18]And this she kept doing for many days. Paul, having become greatly annoyed, turned and said to the spirit, "I command you in the name of Jesus Christ to come out of her." And it came out that very hour.

[19]But when her owners saw that their hope of gain was gone, they seized Paul and Silas and dragged them into the marketplace before the rulers. [20]And when they had brought them to the magistrates, they said, "These men are

Jews, and they are disturbing our city. [21]They advocate customs that are not lawful for us as Romans to accept or practice." [22]The crowd joined in attacking them, and the magistrates tore the garments off them and gave orders to beat them with rods. [23]And when they had inflicted many blows upon them, they threw them into prison, ordering the jailer to keep them safely. [24]Having received this order, he put them into the inner prison and fastened their feet in the stocks.

[25]About midnight Paul and Silas were praying and singing hymns to God, and the prisoners were listening to them, [26]and suddenly there was a great earthquake, so that the foundations of the prison were shaken. And immediately all the doors were opened, and everyone's bonds were unfastened. [27]When the jailer woke and saw that the prison doors were open, he drew his sword and was about to kill himself, supposing that the prisoners had escaped. [28]But Paul cried with a loud voice, "Do not harm yourself, for we are all here." [29]And the jailer[4] called for lights and rushed in, and trembling with fear he fell down before Paul and Silas. [30]Then he brought them out and said, "Sirs, what must I do to be saved?" [31]And they said, "Believe in the Lord Jesus, and you will be saved, you and your household." [32]And they spoke the word of the Lord to him and to all who were in his house. [33]And he took them the same hour of the night and washed their wounds; and he was baptized at once, he and all his family. [34]Then he brought them up into his house and set food before them. And he rejoiced along with his entire household that he had believed in God.

[35]But when it was day, the magistrates sent the police, saying, "Let those men go." [36]And the jailer reported these words to Paul, saying, "The magistrates have sent to let you go. Therefore come out now and go in peace." [37]But Paul said to them, "They have beaten us publicly, uncondemned, men who are Roman citizens, and have thrown us into prison; and do they now throw us out secretly? No! Let them come themselves and take us out." [38]The police reported these words to the magistrates, and they were afraid when they heard that they were Roman citizens. [39]So they came and apologized to them. And they took them out and asked them to leave the city. [40]So they went

[1] Greek he [2] Or that [3] Greek bondservants [4] Greek he

out of the prison and visited Lydia. And when they had seen the brothers, they encouraged them and departed.

―――――――― *Jeremiah 25* ――――――――

The word that came to Jeremiah concerning all the people of Judah, in the fourth year of Jehoiakim the son of Josiah, king of Judah (that was the first year of Nebuchadnezzar king of Babylon), ²which Jeremiah the prophet spoke to all the people of Judah and all the inhabitants of Jerusalem: ³"For twenty-three years, from the thirteenth year of Josiah the son of Amon, king of Judah, to this day, the word of the LORD has come to me, and I have spoken persistently to you, but you have not listened. ⁴You have neither listened nor inclined your ears to hear, although the LORD persistently sent to you all his servants the prophets, ⁵saying, 'Turn now, every one of you, from his evil way and evil deeds, and dwell upon the land that the LORD has given to you and your fathers from of old and forever. ⁶Do not go after other gods to serve and worship them, or provoke me to anger with the work of your hands. Then I will do you no harm.' ⁷Yet you have not listened to me, declares the LORD, that you might provoke me to anger with the work of your hands to your own harm.

⁸"Therefore thus says the LORD of hosts: Because you have not obeyed my words, ⁹behold, I will send for all the tribes of the north, declares the LORD, and for Nebuchadnezzar the king of Babylon, my servant, and I will bring them against this land and its inhabitants, and against all these surrounding nations. I will devote them to destruction, and make them a horror, a hissing, and an everlasting desolation. ¹⁰Moreover, I will banish from them the voice of mirth and the voice of gladness, the voice of the bridegroom and the voice of the bride, the grinding of the millstones and the light of the lamp. ¹¹This whole land shall become a ruin and a waste, and these nations shall serve the king of Babylon seventy years. ¹²Then after seventy years are completed, I will punish the king of Babylon and that nation, the land of the Chaldeans, for their iniquity, declares the LORD, making the land an everlasting waste. ¹³I will bring upon that land all the words that I have uttered against it, everything written in

this book, which Jeremiah prophesied against all the nations. ¹⁴For many nations and great kings shall make slaves even of them, and I will recompense them according to their deeds and the work of their hands."

¹⁵Thus the LORD, the God of Israel, said to me: "Take from my hand this cup of the wine of wrath, and make all the nations to whom I send you drink it. ¹⁶They shall drink and stagger and be crazed because of the sword that I am sending among them."

¹⁷So I took the cup from the LORD's hand, and made all the nations to whom the LORD sent me drink it: ¹⁸Jerusalem and the cities of Judah, its kings and officials, to make them a desolation and a waste, a hissing and a curse, as at this day; ¹⁹Pharaoh king of Egypt, his servants, his officials, all his people, ²⁰and all the mixed tribes among them; all the kings of the land of Uz and all the kings of the land of the Philistines (Ashkelon, Gaza, Ekron, and the remnant of Ashdod); ²¹Edom, Moab, and the sons of Ammon; ²²all the kings of Tyre, all the kings of Sidon, and the kings of the coastland across the sea; ²³Dedan, Tema, Buz, and all who cut the corners of their hair; ²⁴all the kings of Arabia and all the kings of the mixed tribes who dwell in the desert; ²⁵all the kings of Zimri, all the kings of Elam, and all the kings of Media; ²⁶all the kings of the north, far and near, one after another, and all the kingdoms of the world that are on the face of the earth. And after them the king of Babylon[1] shall drink.

²⁷"Then you shall say to them, 'Thus says the LORD of hosts, the God of Israel: Drink, be drunk and vomit, fall and rise no more, because of the sword that I am sending among you.'

²⁸"And if they refuse to accept the cup from your hand to drink, then you shall say to them, 'Thus says the LORD of hosts: You must drink! ²⁹For behold, I begin to work disaster at the city that is called by my name, and shall you go unpunished? You shall not go unpunished, for I am summoning a sword against all the inhabitants of the earth, declares the LORD of hosts.'

³⁰"You, therefore, shall prophesy against them all these words, and say to them:

" 'The LORD will roar from on high,
    and from his holy habitation utter his
        voice;

―――――――――――――――――――――――
[1] Hebrew *Sheshach*, a code name for Babylon

he will roar mightily against his fold,
> and shout, like those who tread grapes,
> against all the inhabitants of the earth.

31 The clamor will resound to the ends of
> the earth,
>> for the LORD has an indictment
>> against the nations;
> he is entering into judgment with all
>> flesh,
> and the wicked he will put to the
>> sword,
>>>> declares the LORD.'

32 "Thus says the LORD of hosts:
> Behold, disaster is going forth
>> from nation to nation,
> and a great tempest is stirring
>> from the farthest parts of the earth!

33 "And those pierced by the LORD on that day shall extend from one end of the earth to the other. They shall not be lamented, or gathered, or buried; they shall be dung on the surface of the ground.

34 "Wail, you shepherds, and cry out,
>> and roll in ashes, you lords of the flock,
> for the days of your slaughter and
>> dispersion have come,
> and you shall fall like a choice vessel.

35 No refuge will remain for the shepherds,
>> nor escape for the lords of the flock.

36 A voice—the cry of the shepherds,
>> and the wail of the lords of the flock!
> For the LORD is laying waste their
>> pasture,

37 and the peaceful folds are devastated
>> because of the fierce anger of the
>> LORD.

38 Like a lion he has left his lair,
>> for their land has become a waste
> because of the sword of the oppressor,
>> and because of his fierce anger."

Mark 11

Now when they drew near to Jerusalem, to Bethphage and Bethany, at the Mount of Olives, Jesus[1] sent two of his disciples [2]and said to them, "Go into the village in front of you, and immediately as you enter it you will find a colt tied, on which no one has ever sat. Untie it and bring it. [3]If anyone says to you, 'Why are you doing this?' say, 'The Lord has need of it and will send it back here immediately.'" [4]And they went away and found a colt tied at a door outside in the street, and they untied it. [5]And some of those standing there said to them, "What are you doing, untying the colt?" [6]And they told them what Jesus had said, and they let them go. [7]And they brought the colt to Jesus and threw their cloaks on it, and he sat on it. [8]And many spread their cloaks on the road, and others spread leafy branches that they had cut from the fields. [9]And those who went before and those who followed were shouting, "Hosanna! Blessed is he who comes in the name of the Lord! [10]Blessed is the coming kingdom of our father David! Hosanna in the highest!"

[11]And he entered Jerusalem and went into the temple. And when he had looked around at everything, as it was already late, he went out to Bethany with the twelve.

[12]On the following day, when they came from Bethany, he was hungry. [13]And seeing in the distance a fig tree in leaf, he went to see if he could find anything on it. When he came to it, he found nothing but leaves, for it was not the season for figs. [14]And he said to it, "May no one ever eat fruit from you again." And his disciples heard it.

[15]And they came to Jerusalem. And he entered the temple and began to drive out those who sold and those who bought in the temple, and he overturned the tables of the money-changers and the seats of those who sold pigeons. [16]And he would not allow anyone to carry anything through the temple. [17]And he was teaching them and saying to them, "Is it not written, 'My house shall be called a house of prayer for all the nations'? But you have made it a den of robbers." [18]And the chief priests and the scribes heard it and were seeking a way to destroy him, for they feared him, because all the crowd was astonished at his teaching. [19]And when evening came they[2] went out of the city.

[20]As they passed by in the morning, they saw the fig tree withered away to its roots. [21]And Peter remembered and said to him, "Rabbi, look! The fig tree that you cursed has withered." [22]And Jesus answered them, "Have faith in God. [23]Truly, I say to you, whoever says to this mountain, 'Be taken up and thrown into the sea,' and does not doubt in his heart, but

[1] Greek he [2] Some manuscripts he

believes that what he says will come to pass, it will be done for him. **24**Therefore I tell you, whatever you ask in prayer, believe that you have received[1] it, and it will be yours. **25**And whenever you stand praying, forgive, if you have anything against anyone, so that your Father also who is in heaven may forgive you your trespasses."[2]

27And they came again to Jerusalem. And as he was walking in the temple, the chief priests and the scribes and the elders came to him, **28**and they said to him, "By what authority are you doing these things, or who gave you this authority to do them?" **29**Jesus said to them, "I will ask you one question; answer me, and I will tell you by what authority I do these things. **30**Was the baptism of John from heaven or from man? Answer me." **31**And they discussed it with one another, saying, "If we say, 'From heaven,' he will say, 'Why then did you not believe him?' **32**But shall we say, 'From man'?"—they were afraid of the people, for they all held that John really was a prophet. **33**So they answered Jesus, "We do not know." And Jesus said to them, "Neither will I tell you by what authority I do these things."

JULY 30

Judges 13

And the people of Israel again did what was evil in the sight of the LORD, so the LORD gave them into the hand of the Philistines for forty years.

2There was a certain man of Zorah, of the tribe of the Danites, whose name was Manoah. And his wife was barren and had no children. **3**And the angel of the LORD appeared to the woman and said to her, "Behold, you are barren and have not borne children, but you shall conceive and bear a son. **4**Therefore be careful and drink no wine or strong drink, and eat nothing unclean, **5**for behold, you shall conceive and bear a son. No razor shall come upon his head, for the child shall be a Nazirite to God from the womb, and he shall begin to save Israel from the hand of the Philistines." **6**Then the woman came and told her husband, "A man of God came to me, and his appearance was like the appearance of the angel of God, very awesome. I did not ask him where he was from, and he did not tell me his name, **7**but he said to me, 'Behold, you shall conceive and bear a son. So then drink no wine or strong drink, and eat nothing unclean, for the child shall be a Nazirite to God from the womb to the day of his death.'"

8Then Manoah prayed to the LORD and said, "O Lord, please let the man of God whom you sent come again to us and teach us what we are to do with the child who will be born." **9**And God listened to the voice of Manoah, and the angel of God came again to the woman as she sat in the field. But Manoah her husband was not with her. **10**So the woman ran quickly and told her husband, "Behold, the man who came to me the other day has appeared to me." **11**And Manoah arose and went after his wife and came to the man and said to him, "Are you the man who spoke to this woman?" And he said, "I am." **12**And Manoah said, "Now when your words come true, what is to be the child's manner of life, and what is his mission?" **13**And the angel of the LORD said to Manoah, "Of all that I said to the woman let her be careful. **14**She may not eat of anything that comes from the vine, neither let her drink wine or strong drink, or eat any unclean thing. All that I commanded her let her observe."

15Manoah said to the angel of the LORD, "Please let us detain you and prepare a young goat for you." **16**And the angel of the LORD said to Manoah, "If you detain me, I will not eat of your food. But if you prepare a burnt offering, then offer it to the LORD." (For Manoah did not know that he was the angel of the LORD.) **17**And

Manoah said to the angel of the LORD, "What is your name, so that, when your words come true, we may honor you?" [18] And the angel of the LORD said to him, "Why do you ask my name, seeing it is wonderful?" [19] So Manoah took the young goat with the grain offering, and offered it on the rock to the LORD, to the one who works[1] wonders, and Manoah and his wife were watching. [20] And when the flame went up toward heaven from the altar, the angel of the LORD went up in the flame of the altar. Now Manoah and his wife were watching, and they fell on their faces to the ground.

[21] The angel of the LORD appeared no more to Manoah and to his wife. Then Manoah knew that he was the angel of the LORD. [22] And Manoah said to his wife, "We shall surely die, for we have seen God." [23] But his wife said to him, "If the LORD had meant to kill us, he would not have accepted a burnt offering and a grain offering at our hands, or shown us all these things, or now announced to us such things as these." [24] And the woman bore a son and called his name Samson. And the young man grew, and the LORD blessed him. [25] And the Spirit of the LORD began to stir him in Mahaneh-dan, between Zorah and Eshtaol.

Acts 17

N ow when they had passed through Amphipolis and Apollonia, they came to Thessalonica, where there was a synagogue of the Jews. [2] And Paul went in, as was his custom, and on three Sabbath days he reasoned with them from the Scriptures, [3] explaining and proving that it was necessary for the Christ to suffer and to rise from the dead, and saying, "This Jesus, whom I proclaim to you, is the Christ." [4] And some of them were persuaded and joined Paul and Silas, as did a great many of the devout Greeks and not a few of the leading women. [5] But the Jews[2] were jealous, and taking some wicked men of the rabble, they formed a mob, set the city in an uproar, and attacked the house of Jason, seeking to bring them out to the crowd. [6] And when they could not find them, they dragged Jason and some of the brothers before the city authorities, shouting, "These men who have turned the world upside down have come here also, [7] and Jason has received them, and they are all acting

against the decrees of Caesar, saying that there is another king, Jesus." [8] And the people and the city authorities were disturbed when they heard these things. [9] And when they had taken money as security from Jason and the rest, they let them go.

[10] The brothers[3] immediately sent Paul and Silas away by night to Berea, and when they arrived they went into the Jewish synagogue. [11] Now these Jews were more noble than those in Thessalonica; they received the word with all eagerness, examining the Scriptures daily to see if these things were so. [12] Many of them therefore believed, with not a few Greek women of high standing as well as men. [13] But when the Jews from Thessalonica learned that the word of God was proclaimed by Paul at Berea also, they came there too, agitating and stirring up the crowds. [14] Then the brothers immediately sent Paul off on his way to the sea, but Silas and Timothy remained there. [15] Those who conducted Paul brought him as far as Athens, and after receiving a command for Silas and Timothy to come to him as soon as possible, they departed.

[16] Now while Paul was waiting for them at Athens, his spirit was provoked within him as he saw that the city was full of idols. [17] So he reasoned in the synagogue with the Jews and the devout persons, and in the marketplace every day with those who happened to be there. [18] Some of the Epicurean and Stoic philosophers also conversed with him. And some said, "What does this babbler wish to say?" Others said, "He seems to be a preacher of foreign divinities"—because he was preaching Jesus and the resurrection. [19] And they took him and brought him to the Areopagus, saying, "May we know what this new teaching is that you are presenting? [20] For you bring some strange things to our ears. We wish to know therefore what these things mean." [21] Now all the Athenians and the foreigners who lived there would spend their time in nothing except telling or hearing something new.

[22] So Paul, standing in the midst of the Areopagus, said: "Men of Athens, I perceive that in every way you are very religious. [23] For as I passed along and observed the objects of your worship, I found also an altar with this inscription, 'To the unknown god.' What therefore you worship as unknown, this I proclaim to

---

[1] Septuagint, Vulgate; Hebrew LORD, and working [2] Greek Ioudaioi probably refers here to Jewish religious leaders, and others under their influence, in that time; also verse 13 [3] Or brothers and sisters; also verse 14

you. [24]The God who made the world and everything in it, being Lord of heaven and earth, does not live in temples made by man,[1] [25]nor is he served by human hands, as though he needed anything, since he himself gives to all mankind life and breath and everything. [26]And he made from one man every nation of mankind to live on all the face of the earth, having determined allotted periods and the boundaries of their dwelling place, [27]that they should seek God, and perhaps feel their way toward him and find him. Yet he is actually not far from each one of us, [28]for

"'In him we live and move and have our being';[2]

as even some of your own poets have said,

"'For we are indeed his offspring.'[3]

[29]Being then God's offspring, we ought not to think that the divine being is like gold or silver or stone, an image formed by the art and imagination of man. [30]The times of ignorance God overlooked, but now he commands all people everywhere to repent, [31]because he has fixed a day on which he will judge the world in righteousness by a man whom he has appointed; and of this he has given assurance to all by raising him from the dead."

[32]Now when they heard of the resurrection of the dead, some mocked. But others said, "We will hear you again about this." [33]So Paul went out from their midst. [34]But some men joined him and believed, among whom also were Dionysius the Areopagite and a woman named Damaris and others with them.

Jeremiah 26

In the beginning of the reign of Jehoiakim the son of Josiah, king of Judah, this word came from the LORD: [2]"Thus says the LORD: Stand in the court of the LORD's house, and speak to all the cities of Judah that come to worship in the house of the LORD all the words that I command you to speak to them; do not hold back a word. [3]It may be they will listen, and every one turn from his evil way, that I may relent of the disaster that I intend to do to them because of their evil deeds. [4]You shall say to them, 'Thus says the LORD: If you will not listen to me, to

walk in my law that I have set before you, [5]and to listen to the words of my servants the prophets whom I send to you urgently, though you have not listened, [6]then I will make this house like Shiloh, and I will make this city a curse for all the nations of the earth.'"

[7]The priests and the prophets and all the people heard Jeremiah speaking these words in the house of the LORD. [8]And when Jeremiah had finished speaking all that the LORD had commanded him to speak to all the people, then the priests and the prophets and all the people laid hold of him, saying, "You shall die! [9]Why have you prophesied in the name of the LORD, saying, 'This house shall be like Shiloh, and this city shall be desolate, without inhabitant'?" And all the people gathered around Jeremiah in the house of the LORD.

[10]When the officials of Judah heard these things, they came up from the king's house to the house of the LORD and took their seat in the entry of the New Gate of the house of the LORD. [11]Then the priests and the prophets said to the officials and to all the people, "This man deserves the sentence of death, because he has prophesied against this city, as you have heard with your own ears."

[12]Then Jeremiah spoke to all the officials and all the people, saying, "The LORD sent me to prophesy against this house and this city all the words you have heard. [13]Now therefore mend your ways and your deeds, and obey the voice of the LORD your God, and the LORD will relent of the disaster that he has pronounced against you. [14]But as for me, behold, I am in your hands. Do with me as seems good and right to you. [15]Only know for certain that if you put me to death, you will bring innocent blood upon yourselves and upon this city and its inhabitants, for in truth the LORD sent me to you to speak all these words in your ears."

[16]Then the officials and all the people said to the priests and the prophets, "This man does not deserve the sentence of death, for he has spoken to us in the name of the LORD our God." [17]And certain of the elders of the land arose and spoke to all the assembled people, saying, [18]"Micah of Moresheth prophesied in the days of Hezekiah king of Judah, and said to all the people of Judah: 'Thus says the LORD of hosts,

---

[1] Greek *made by hands* [2] Probably from Epimenides of Crete [3] From Aratus's poem "Phainomena"

" 'Zion shall be plowed as a field;
  Jerusalem shall become a heap of
    ruins,
  and the mountain of the house a
    wooded height.'

[19] Did Hezekiah king of Judah and all Judah put him to death? Did he not fear the LORD and entreat the favor of the LORD, and did not the LORD relent of the disaster that he had pronounced against them? But we are about to bring great disaster upon ourselves."

[20] There was another man who prophesied in the name of the LORD, Uriah the son of Shemaiah from Kiriath-jearim. He prophesied against this city and against this land in words like those of Jeremiah. [21] And when King Jehoiakim, with all his warriors and all the officials, heard his words, the king sought to put him to death. But when Uriah heard of it, he was afraid and fled and escaped to Egypt. [22] Then King Jehoiakim sent to Egypt certain men, Elnathan the son of Achbor and others with him, [23] and they took Uriah from Egypt and brought him to King Jehoiakim, who struck him down with the sword and dumped his dead body into the burial place of the common people.

[24] But the hand of Ahikam the son of Shaphan was with Jeremiah so that he was not given over to the people to be put to death.

--- Mark 12 ---

And he began to speak to them in parables. "A man planted a vineyard and put a fence around it and dug a pit for the winepress and built a tower, and leased it to tenants and went into another country. [2] When the season came, he sent a servant[1] to the tenants to get from them some of the fruit of the vineyard. [3] And they took him and beat him and sent him away empty-handed. [4] Again he sent to them another servant, and they struck him on the head and treated him shamefully. [5] And he sent another, and him they killed. And so with many others: some they beat, and some they killed. [6] He had still one other, a beloved son. Finally he sent him to them, saying, 'They will respect my son.' [7] But those tenants said to one another, 'This is the heir. Come, let us kill him, and the inheritance will be ours.' [8] And they took him

and killed him and threw him out of the vineyard. [9] What will the owner of the vineyard do? He will come and destroy the tenants and give the vineyard to others. [10] Have you not read this Scripture:

" 'The stone that the builders rejected
    has become the cornerstone;[2]
[11] this was the Lord's doing,
    and it is marvelous in our eyes'?"

[12] And they were seeking to arrest him but feared the people, for they perceived that he had told the parable against them. So they left him and went away.

[13] And they sent to him some of the Pharisees and some of the Herodians, to trap him in his talk. [14] And they came and said to him, "Teacher, we know that you are true and do not care about anyone's opinion. For you are not swayed by appearances,[3] but truly teach the way of God. Is it lawful to pay taxes to Caesar, or not? Should we pay them, or should we not?" [15] But, knowing their hypocrisy, he said to them, "Why put me to the test? Bring me a denarius[4] and let me look at it." [16] And they brought one. And he said to them, "Whose likeness and inscription is this?" They said to him, "Caesar's." [17] Jesus said to them, "Render to Caesar the things that are Caesar's, and to God the things that are God's." And they marveled at him.

[18] And Sadducees came to him, who say that there is no resurrection. And they asked him a question, saying, [19] "Teacher, Moses wrote for us that if a man's brother dies and leaves a wife, but leaves no child, the man[5] must take the widow and raise up offspring for his brother. [20] There were seven brothers; the first took a wife, and when he died left no offspring. [21] And the second took her, and died, leaving no offspring. And the third likewise. [22] And the seven left no offspring. Last of all the woman also died. [23] In the resurrection, when they rise again, whose wife will she be? For the seven had her as wife."

[24] Jesus said to them, "Is this not the reason you are wrong, because you know neither the Scriptures nor the power of God? [25] For when they rise from the dead, they neither marry nor are given in marriage, but are like angels in heaven. [26] And as for the dead being raised, have you not read in the book of Moses, in the passage about the bush, how God spoke to

[1] Greek bondservant; also verse 4 [2] Greek the head of the corner [3] Greek you do not look at people's faces [4] A denarius was a day's wage for a laborer [5] Greek his brother

him, saying, 'I am the God of Abraham, and the God of Isaac, and the God of Jacob'? [27] He is not God of the dead, but of the living. You are quite wrong."

[28] And one of the scribes came up and heard them disputing with one another, and seeing that he answered them well, asked him, "Which commandment is the most important of all?" [29] Jesus answered, "The most important is, 'Hear, O Israel: The Lord our God, the Lord is one. [30] And you shall love the Lord your God with all your heart and with all your soul and with all your mind and with all your strength.' [31] The second is this: 'You shall love your neighbor as yourself.' There is no other commandment greater than these." [32] And the scribe said to him, "You are right, Teacher. You have truly said that he is one, and there is no other besides him. [33] And to love him with all the heart and with all the understanding and with all the strength, and to love one's neighbor as oneself, is much more than all whole burnt offerings and sacrifices." [34] And when Jesus saw that he answered wisely, he said to him, "You are not far from the kingdom of God." And after that no one dared to ask him any more questions.

[35] And as Jesus taught in the temple, he said, "How can the scribes say that the Christ is the son of David? [36] David himself, in the Holy Spirit, declared,

"'The Lord said to my Lord,
"Sit at my right hand,
    until I put your enemies under your
        feet."'

[37] David himself calls him Lord. So how is he his son?" And the great throng heard him gladly.

[38] And in his teaching he said, "Beware of the scribes, who like to walk around in long robes and like greetings in the marketplaces [39] and have the best seats in the synagogues and the places of honor at feasts, [40] who devour widows' houses and for a pretense make long prayers. They will receive the greater condemnation."

[41] And he sat down opposite the treasury and watched the people putting money into the offering box. Many rich people put in large sums. [42] And a poor widow came and put in two small copper coins, which make a penny.[1] [43] And he called his disciples to him and said to them, "Truly, I say to you, this poor widow has put in more than all those who are contributing to the offering box. [44] For they all contributed out of their abundance, but she out of her poverty has put in everything she had, all she had to live on."

JULY 31

Judges 14

Samson went down to Timnah, and at Timnah he saw one of the daughters of the Philistines. [2] Then he came up and told his father and mother, "I saw one of the daughters of the Philistines at Timnah. Now get her for me as my wife." [3] But his father and mother said to him, "Is there not a woman among the daughters of your relatives, or among all our people, that you must go to take a wife from the uncircumcised Philistines?" But Samson said to his father, "Get her for me, for she is right in my eyes."

[4] His father and mother did not know that it was from the LORD, for he was seeking an opportunity against the Philistines. At that time the Philistines ruled over Israel.

[5] Then Samson went down with his father and mother to Timnah, and they came to the vineyards of Timnah. And behold, a young lion came toward him roaring. [6] Then the Spirit of the LORD rushed upon him, and although he had nothing in his hand, he tore the lion in pieces as one tears a young goat. But he did not tell his father or his mother what he had done. [7] Then he went down and talked with the woman, and she was right in Samson's eyes.

[1] Greek two lepta, which make a kodrantes; a kodrantes (Latin quadrans) was a Roman copper coin worth about 1/64 of a denarius (which was a day's wage for a laborer)

[8]After some days he returned to take her. And he turned aside to see the carcass of the lion, and behold, there was a swarm of bees in the body of the lion, and honey. [9]He scraped it out into his hands and went on, eating as he went. And he came to his father and mother and gave some to them, and they ate. But he did not tell them that he had scraped the honey from the carcass of the lion.

[10]His father went down to the woman, and Samson prepared a feast there, for so the young men used to do. [11]As soon as the people saw him, they brought thirty companions to be with him. [12]And Samson said to them, "Let me now put a riddle to you. If you can tell me what it is, within the seven days of the feast, and find it out, then I will give you thirty linen garments and thirty changes of clothes, [13]but if you cannot tell me what it is, then you shall give me thirty linen garments and thirty changes of clothes." And they said to him, "Put your riddle, that we may hear it." [14]And he said to them,

> "Out of the eater came something to eat.
> Out of the strong came something sweet."

And in three days they could not solve the riddle. [15]On the fourth[1] day they said to Samson's wife, "Entice your husband to tell us what the riddle is, lest we burn you and your father's house with fire. Have you invited us here to impoverish us?" [16]And Samson's wife wept over him and said, "You only hate me; you do not love me. You have put a riddle to my people, and you have not told me what it is." And he said to her, "Behold, I have not told my father nor my mother, and shall I tell you?" [17]She wept before him the seven days that their feast lasted, and on the seventh day he told her, because she pressed him hard. Then she told the riddle to her people. [18]And the men of the city said to him on the seventh day before the sun went down,

> "What is sweeter than honey?
> What is stronger than a lion?"

And he said to them,

> "If you had not plowed with my heifer,
> you would not have found out my riddle."

[19]And the Spirit of the Lord rushed upon him, and he went down to Ashkelon and struck

down thirty men of the town and took their spoil and gave the garments to those who had told the riddle. In hot anger he went back to his father's house. [20]And Samson's wife was given to his companion, who had been his best man.

Acts 18

After this Paul[2] left Athens and went to Corinth. [2]And he found a Jew named Aquila, a native of Pontus, recently come from Italy with his wife Priscilla, because Claudius had commanded all the Jews to leave Rome. And he went to see them, [3]and because he was of the same trade he stayed with them and worked, for they were tentmakers by trade. [4]And he reasoned in the synagogue every Sabbath, and tried to persuade Jews and Greeks.

[5]When Silas and Timothy arrived from Macedonia, Paul was occupied with the word, testifying to the Jews that the Christ was Jesus. [6]And when they opposed and reviled him, he shook out his garments and said to them, "Your blood be on your own heads! I am innocent. From now on I will go to the Gentiles." [7]And he left there and went to the house of a man named Titius Justus, a worshiper of God. His house was next door to the synagogue. [8]Crispus, the ruler of the synagogue, believed in the Lord, together with his entire household. And many of the Corinthians hearing Paul believed and were baptized. [9]And the Lord said to Paul one night in a vision, "Do not be afraid, but go on speaking and do not be silent, [10]for I am with you, and no one will attack you to harm you, for I have many in this city who are my people." [11]And he stayed a year and six months, teaching the word of God among them.

[12]But when Gallio was proconsul of Achaia, the Jews[3] made a united attack on Paul and brought him before the tribunal, [13]saying, "This man is persuading people to worship God contrary to the law." [14]But when Paul was about to open his mouth, Gallio said to the Jews, "If it were a matter of wrongdoing or vicious crime, O Jews, I would have reason to accept your complaint. [15]But since it is a matter of questions about words and names and your own law, see to it yourselves. I refuse to be a judge of these things." [16]And he drove

---

[1] Septuagint, Syriac; Hebrew *seventh* [2] Greek *he* [3] Greek *Ioudaioi* probably refers here to Jewish religious leaders, and others under their influence, in that time; also verses 14 (twice), 28

them from the tribunal. [17]And they all seized Sosthenes, the ruler of the synagogue, and beat him in front of the tribunal. But Gallio paid no attention to any of this.

[18]After this, Paul stayed many days longer and then took leave of the brothers[1] and set sail for Syria, and with him Priscilla and Aquila. At Cenchreae he had cut his hair, for he was under a vow. [19]And they came to Ephesus, and he left them there, but he himself went into the synagogue and reasoned with the Jews. [20]When they asked him to stay for a longer period, he declined. [21]But on taking leave of them he said, "I will return to you if God wills," and he set sail from Ephesus.

[22]When he had landed at Caesarea, he went up and greeted the church, and then went down to Antioch. [23]After spending some time there, he departed and went from one place to the next through the region of Galatia and Phrygia, strengthening all the disciples.

[24]Now a Jew named Apollos, a native of Alexandria, came to Ephesus. He was an eloquent man, competent in the Scriptures. [25]He had been instructed in the way of the Lord. And being fervent in spirit,[2] he spoke and taught accurately the things concerning Jesus, though he knew only the baptism of John. [26]He began to speak boldly in the synagogue, but when Priscilla and Aquila heard him, they took him aside and explained to him the way of God more accurately. [27]And when he wished to cross to Achaia, the brothers encouraged him and wrote to the disciples to welcome him. When he arrived, he greatly helped those who through grace had believed, [28]for he powerfully refuted the Jews in public, showing by the Scriptures that the Christ was Jesus.

Jeremiah 27

In the beginning of the reign of Zedekiah[3] the son of Josiah, king of Judah, this word came to Jeremiah from the LORD. [2]Thus the LORD said to me: "Make yourself straps and yoke-bars, and put them on your neck. [3]Send word[4] to the king of Edom, the king of Moab, the king of the sons of Ammon, the king of Tyre, and the king of Sidon by the hand of the envoys who have come to Jerusalem to Zedekiah king of Judah. [4]Give them this charge for their masters: 'Thus says the LORD

of hosts, the God of Israel: This is what you shall say to your masters: [5]"It is I who by my great power and my outstretched arm have made the earth, with the men and animals that are on the earth, and I give it to whomever it seems right to me. [6]Now I have given all these lands into the hand of Nebuchadnezzar, the king of Babylon, my servant, and I have given him also the beasts of the field to serve him. [7]All the nations shall serve him and his son and his grandson, until the time of his own land comes. Then many nations and great kings shall make him their slave.

[8]"'"But if any nation or kingdom will not serve this Nebuchadnezzar king of Babylon, and put its neck under the yoke of the king of Babylon, I will punish that nation with the sword, with famine, and with pestilence, declares the LORD, until I have consumed it by his hand. [9]So do not listen to your prophets, your diviners, your dreamers, your fortune-tellers, or your sorcerers, who are saying to you, 'You shall not serve the king of Babylon.' [10]For it is a lie that they are prophesying to you, with the result that you will be removed far from your land, and I will drive you out, and you will perish. [11]But any nation that will bring its neck under the yoke of the king of Babylon and serve him, I will leave on its own land, to work it and dwell there, declares the LORD."'"

[12]To Zedekiah king of Judah I spoke in like manner: "Bring your necks under the yoke of the king of Babylon, and serve him and his people and live. [13]Why will you and your people die by the sword, by famine, and by pestilence, as the LORD has spoken concerning any nation that will not serve the king of Babylon? [14]Do not listen to the words of the prophets who are saying to you, 'You shall not serve the king of Babylon,' for it is a lie that they are prophesying to you. [15]I have not sent them, declares the LORD, but they are prophesying falsely in my name, with the result that I will drive you out and you will perish, you and the prophets who are prophesying to you."

[16]Then I spoke to the priests and to all this people, saying, "Thus says the LORD: Do not listen to the words of your prophets who are prophesying to you, saying, 'Behold, the vessels of the LORD's house will now shortly be brought back from Babylon,' for it is a lie that they are prophesying to you. [17]Do not listen

[1] Or brothers and sisters; also verse 27 [2] Or in the Spirit [3] Or Jehoiakim [4] Hebrew Send them

to them; serve the king of Babylon and live. Why should this city become a desolation? [18] If they are prophets, and if the word of the LORD is with them, then let them intercede with the LORD of hosts, that the vessels that are left in the house of the LORD, in the house of the king of Judah, and in Jerusalem may not go to Babylon. [19] For thus says the LORD of hosts concerning the pillars, the sea, the stands, and the rest of the vessels that are left in this city, [20] which Nebuchadnezzar king of Babylon did not take away, when he took into exile from Jerusalem to Babylon Jeconiah the son of Jehoiakim, king of Judah, and all the nobles of Judah and Jerusalem— [21] thus says the LORD of hosts, the God of Israel, concerning the vessels that are left in the house of the LORD, in the house of the king of Judah, and in Jerusalem: [22] They shall be carried to Babylon and remain there until the day when I visit them, declares the LORD. Then I will bring them back and restore them to this place."

Mark 13

And as he came out of the temple, one of his disciples said to him, "Look, Teacher, what wonderful stones and what wonderful buildings!" [2] And Jesus said to him, "Do you see these great buildings? There will not be left here one stone upon another that will not be thrown down."

[3] And as he sat on the Mount of Olives opposite the temple, Peter and James and John and Andrew asked him privately, [4] "Tell us, when will these things be, and what will be the sign when all these things are about to be accomplished?" [5] And Jesus began to say to them, "See that no one leads you astray. [6] Many will come in my name, saying, 'I am he!' and they will lead many astray. [7] And when you hear of wars and rumors of wars, do not be alarmed. This must take place, but the end is not yet. [8] For nation will rise against nation, and kingdom against kingdom. There will be earthquakes in various places; there will be famines. These are but the beginning of the birth pains.

[9] "But be on your guard. For they will deliver you over to councils, and you will be beaten in synagogues, and you will stand before governors and kings for my sake, to bear witness before them. [10] And the gospel must first be proclaimed to all nations. [11] And when they bring you to trial and deliver you over, do not be anxious beforehand what you are to say, but say whatever is given you in that hour, for it is not you who speak, but the Holy Spirit. [12] And brother will deliver brother over to death, and the father his child, and children will rise against parents and have them put to death. [13] And you will be hated by all for my name's sake. But the one who endures to the end will be saved.

[14] "But when you see the abomination of desolation standing where he ought not to be (let the reader understand), then let those who are in Judea flee to the mountains. [15] Let the one who is on the housetop not go down, nor enter his house, to take anything out, [16] and let the one who is in the field not turn back to take his cloak. [17] And alas for women who are pregnant and for those who are nursing infants in those days! [18] Pray that it may not happen in winter. [19] For in those days there will be such tribulation as has not been from the beginning of the creation that God created until now, and never will be. [20] And if the Lord had not cut short the days, no human being would be saved. But for the sake of the elect, whom he chose, he shortened the days. [21] And then if anyone says to you, 'Look, here is the Christ!' or 'Look, there he is!' do not believe it. [22] For false christs and false prophets will arise and perform signs and wonders, to lead astray, if possible, the elect. [23] But be on guard; I have told you all things beforehand.

[24] "But in those days, after that tribulation, the sun will be darkened, and the moon will not give its light, [25] and the stars will be falling from heaven, and the powers in the heavens will be shaken. [26] And then they will see the Son of Man coming in clouds with great power and glory. [27] And then he will send out the angels and gather his elect from the four winds, from the ends of the earth to the ends of heaven.

[28] "From the fig tree learn its lesson: as soon as its branch becomes tender and puts out its leaves, you know that summer is near. [29] So also, when you see these things taking place, you know that he is near, at the very gates. [30] Truly, I say to you, this generation will not pass away until all these things take place. [31] Heaven and earth will pass away, but my words will not pass away.

[32] "But concerning that day or that hour, no one knows, not even the angels in heaven, nor the Son, but only the Father. [33] Be on guard, keep awake.[1] For you do not know when the time will come. [34] It is like a man going on a journey, when he leaves home and puts his servants[2] in charge, each with his work, and commands the doorkeeper to stay awake. [35] Therefore stay awake—for you do not know when the master of the house will come, in the evening, or at midnight, or when the rooster crows,[3] or in the morning— [36] lest he come suddenly and find you asleep. [37] And what I say to you I say to all: Stay awake."

---

[1] Some manuscripts add *and pray* [2] Greek *bondservants* [3] That is, the third watch of the night, between midnight and 3 A.M.

AUGUST 1

Judges 15

After some days, at the time of wheat harvest, Samson went to visit his wife with a young goat. And he said, "I will go in to my wife in the chamber." But her father would not allow him to go in. ²And her father said, "I really thought that you utterly hated her, so I gave her to your companion. Is not her younger sister more beautiful than she? Please take her instead." ³And Samson said to them, "This time I shall be innocent in regard to the Philistines, when I do them harm." ⁴So Samson went and caught 300 foxes and took torches. And he turned them tail to tail and put a torch between each pair of tails. ⁵And when he had set fire to the torches, he let the foxes go into the standing grain of the Philistines and set fire to the stacked grain and the standing grain, as well as the olive orchards. ⁶Then the Philistines said, "Who has done this?" And they said, "Samson, the son-in-law of the Timnite, because he has taken his wife and given her to his companion." And the Philistines came up and burned her and her father with fire. ⁷And Samson said to them, "If this is what you do, I swear I will be avenged on you, and after that I will quit." ⁸And he struck them hip and thigh with a great blow, and he went down and stayed in the cleft of the rock of Etam.

⁹Then the Philistines came up and encamped in Judah and made a raid on Lehi. ¹⁰And the men of Judah said, "Why have you come up against us?" They said, "We have come up to bind Samson, to do to him as he did to us." ¹¹Then 3,000 men of Judah went down to the cleft of the rock of Etam, and said to Samson, "Do you not know that the Philistines are rulers over us? What then is this that you have done to us?" And he said to them, "As they did to me, so have I done to them." ¹²And they said to him, "We have come down to bind you, that we may give you into the hands of the Philistines." And Samson said to them, "Swear to me that you will not attack me yourselves." ¹³They said to him, "No; we will only bind you and give you

into their hands. We will surely not kill you." So they bound him with two new ropes and brought him up from the rock.

¹⁴When he came to Lehi, the Philistines came shouting to meet him. Then the Spirit of the LORD rushed upon him, and the ropes that were on his arms became as flax that has caught fire, and his bonds melted off his hands. ¹⁵And he found a fresh jawbone of a donkey, and put out his hand and took it, and with it he struck 1,000 men. ¹⁶And Samson said,

"With the jawbone of a donkey,
    heaps upon heaps,
  with the jawbone of a donkey
    have I struck down a thousand men."

¹⁷As soon as he had finished speaking, he threw away the jawbone out of his hand. And that place was called Ramath-lehi.¹

¹⁸And he was very thirsty, and he called upon the LORD and said, "You have granted this great salvation by the hand of your servant, and shall I now die of thirst and fall into the hands of the uncircumcised?" ¹⁹And God split open the hollow place that is at Lehi, and water came out from it. And when he drank, his spirit returned, and he revived. Therefore the name of it was called En-hakkore;² it is at Lehi to this day. ²⁰And he judged Israel in the days of the Philistines twenty years.

Acts 19

And it happened that while Apollos was at Corinth, Paul passed through the inland³ country and came to Ephesus. There he found some disciples. ²And he said to them, "Did you receive the Holy Spirit when you believed?" And they said, "No, we have not even heard that there is a Holy Spirit." ³And he said, "Into what then were you baptized?" They said, "Into John's baptism." ⁴And Paul said, "John baptized with the baptism of repentance, telling the people to believe in the one who was to come after

¹ Ramath-lehi means the hill of the jawbone ² En-hakkore means the spring of him who called ³ Greek upper (that is, highland)

him, that is, Jesus." [5]On hearing this, they were baptized in[1] the name of the Lord Jesus. [6]And when Paul had laid his hands on them, the Holy Spirit came on them, and they began speaking in tongues and prophesying. [7]There were about twelve men in all.

[8]And he entered the synagogue and for three months spoke boldly, reasoning and persuading them about the kingdom of God. [9]But when some became stubborn and continued in unbelief, speaking evil of the Way before the congregation, he withdrew from them and took the disciples with him, reasoning daily in the hall of Tyrannus.[2] [10]This continued for two years, so that all the residents of Asia heard the word of the Lord, both Jews and Greeks.

[11]And God was doing extraordinary miracles by the hands of Paul, [12]so that even handkerchiefs or aprons that had touched his skin were carried away to the sick, and their diseases left them and the evil spirits came out of them. [13]Then some of the itinerant Jewish exorcists undertook to invoke the name of the Lord Jesus over those who had evil spirits, saying, "I adjure you by the Jesus whom Paul proclaims." [14]Seven sons of a Jewish high priest named Sceva were doing this. [15]But the evil spirit answered them, "Jesus I know, and Paul I recognize, but who are you?" [16]And the man in whom was the evil spirit leaped on them, mastered all[3] of them and overpowered them, so that they fled out of that house naked and wounded. [17]And this became known to all the residents of Ephesus, both Jews and Greeks. And fear fell upon them all, and the name of the Lord Jesus was extolled. [18]Also many of those who were now believers came, confessing and divulging their practices. [19]And a number of those who had practiced magic arts brought their books together and burned them in the sight of all. And they counted the value of them and found it came to fifty thousand pieces of silver. [20]So the word of the Lord continued to increase and prevail mightily.

[21]Now after these events Paul resolved in the Spirit to pass through Macedonia and Achaia and go to Jerusalem, saying, "After I have been there, I must also see Rome." [22]And having sent into Macedonia two of his helpers, Timothy and Erastus, he himself stayed in Asia for a while.

[23]About that time there arose no little disturbance concerning the Way. [24]For a man named Demetrius, a silversmith, who made silver shrines of Artemis, brought no little business to the craftsmen. [25]These he gathered together, with the workmen in similar trades, and said, "Men, you know that from this business we have our wealth. [26]And you see and hear that not only in Ephesus but in almost all of Asia this Paul has persuaded and turned away a great many people, saying that gods made with hands are not gods. [27]And there is danger not only that this trade of ours may come into disrepute but also that the temple of the great goddess Artemis may be counted as nothing, and that she may even be deposed from her magnificence, she whom all Asia and the world worship."

[28]When they heard this they were enraged and were crying out, "Great is Artemis of the Ephesians!" [29]So the city was filled with the confusion, and they rushed together into the theater, dragging with them Gaius and Aristarchus, Macedonians who were Paul's companions in travel. [30]But when Paul wished to go in among the crowd, the disciples would not let him. [31]And even some of the Asiarchs,[4] who were friends of his, sent to him and were urging him not to venture into the theater. [32]Now some cried out one thing, some another, for the assembly was in confusion, and most of them did not know why they had come together. [33]Some of the crowd prompted Alexander, whom the Jews had put forward. And Alexander, motioning with his hand, wanted to make a defense to the crowd. [34]But when they recognized that he was a Jew, for about two hours they all cried out with one voice, "Great is Artemis of the Ephesians!"

[35]And when the town clerk had quieted the crowd, he said, "Men of Ephesus, who is there who does not know that the city of the Ephesians is temple keeper of the great Artemis, and of the sacred stone that fell from the sky?[5] [36]Seeing then that these things cannot be denied, you ought to be quiet and do nothing rash. [37]For you have brought these men here who are neither sacrilegious nor blasphemers of our goddess. [38]If therefore Demetrius and the craftsmen with him have a complaint against anyone, the courts are open, and there are proconsuls. Let them bring charges against one another. [39]But if you seek anything further,[6] it shall be settled in the regular assembly.

---

[1] Or into [2] Some manuscripts add *from the fifth hour to the tenth* (that is, from 11 A.M. to 4 P.M.) [3] Or *both* [4] That is, high-ranking officers of the province of Asia [5] The meaning of the Greek is uncertain [6] Some manuscripts *seek about other matters*

⁴⁰For we really are in danger of being charged with rioting today, since there is no cause that we can give to justify this commotion." ⁴¹And when he had said these things, he dismissed the assembly.

Jeremiah 28

In that same year, at the beginning of the reign of Zedekiah king of Judah, in the fifth month of the fourth year, Hananiah the son of Azzur, the prophet from Gibeon, spoke to me in the house of the LORD, in the presence of the priests and all the people, saying, ²"Thus says the LORD of hosts, the God of Israel: I have broken the yoke of the king of Babylon. ³Within two years I will bring back to this place all the vessels of the LORD's house, which Nebuchadnezzar king of Babylon took away from this place and carried to Babylon. ⁴I will also bring back to this place Jeconiah the son of Jehoiakim, king of Judah, and all the exiles from Judah who went to Babylon, declares the LORD, for I will break the yoke of the king of Babylon."

⁵Then the prophet Jeremiah spoke to Hananiah the prophet in the presence of the priests and all the people who were standing in the house of the LORD, ⁶and the prophet Jeremiah said, "Amen! May the LORD do so; may the LORD make the words that you have prophesied come true, and bring back to this place from Babylon the vessels of the house of the LORD, and all the exiles. ⁷Yet hear now this word that I speak in your hearing and in the hearing of all the people. ⁸The prophets who preceded you and me from ancient times prophesied war, famine, and pestilence against many countries and great kingdoms. ⁹As for the prophet who prophesies peace, when the word of that prophet comes to pass, then it will be known that the LORD has truly sent the prophet."

¹⁰Then the prophet Hananiah took the yoke-bars from the neck of Jeremiah the prophet and broke them. ¹¹And Hananiah spoke in the presence of all the people, saying, "Thus says the LORD: Even so will I break the yoke of Nebuchadnezzar king of Babylon from the neck of all the nations within two years." But Jeremiah the prophet went his way.

¹²Sometime after the prophet Hananiah had broken the yoke-bars from off the neck of Jeremiah the prophet, the word of the LORD came to Jeremiah: ¹³"Go, tell Hananiah, 'Thus says the LORD: You have broken wooden bars, but you have made in their place bars of iron. ¹⁴For thus says the LORD of hosts, the God of Israel: I have put upon the neck of all these nations an iron yoke to serve Nebuchadnezzar king of Babylon, and they shall serve him, for I have given to him even the beasts of the field.'" ¹⁵And Jeremiah the prophet said to the prophet Hananiah, "Listen, Hananiah, the LORD has not sent you, and you have made this people trust in a lie. ¹⁶Therefore thus says the LORD: 'Behold, I will remove you from the face of the earth. This year you shall die, because you have uttered rebellion against the LORD.'"

¹⁷In that same year, in the seventh month, the prophet Hananiah died.

Mark 14

It was now two days before the Passover and the Feast of Unleavened Bread. And the chief priests and the scribes were seeking how to arrest him by stealth and kill him, ²for they said, "Not during the feast, lest there be an uproar from the people."

³And while he was at Bethany in the house of Simon the leper,[1] as he was reclining at table, a woman came with an alabaster flask of ointment of pure nard, very costly, and she broke the flask and poured it over his head. ⁴There were some who said to themselves indignantly, "Why was the ointment wasted like that? ⁵For this ointment could have been sold for more than three hundred denarii[2] and given to the poor." And they scolded her. ⁶But Jesus said, "Leave her alone. Why do you trouble her? She has done a beautiful thing to me. ⁷For you always have the poor with you, and whenever you want, you can do good for them. But you will not always have me. ⁸She has done what she could; she has anointed my body beforehand for burial. ⁹And truly, I say to you, wherever the gospel is proclaimed in the whole world, what she has done will be told in memory of her."

¹⁰Then Judas Iscariot, who was one of the twelve, went to the chief priests in order to betray him to them. ¹¹And when they heard it, they were glad and promised to give him money. And he sought an opportunity to betray him.

[1] Leprosy was a term for several skin diseases; see Leviticus 13 [2] A denarius was a day's wage for a laborer

[12]And on the first day of Unleavened Bread, when they sacrificed the Passover lamb, his disciples said to him, "Where will you have us go and prepare for you to eat the Passover?" [13]And he sent two of his disciples and said to them, "Go into the city, and a man carrying a jar of water will meet you. Follow him, [14]and wherever he enters, say to the master of the house, 'The Teacher says, Where is my guest room, where I may eat the Passover with my disciples?' [15]And he will show you a large upper room furnished and ready; there prepare for us." [16]And the disciples set out and went to the city and found it just as he had told them, and they prepared the Passover.

[17]And when it was evening, he came with the twelve. [18]And as they were reclining at table and eating, Jesus said, "Truly, I say to you, one of you will betray me, one who is eating with me." [19]They began to be sorrowful and to say to him one after another, "Is it I?" [20]He said to them, "It is one of the twelve, one who is dipping bread into the dish with me. [21]For the Son of Man goes as it is written of him, but woe to that man by whom the Son of Man is betrayed! It would have been better for that man if he had not been born."

[22]And as they were eating, he took bread, and after blessing it broke it and gave it to them, and said, "Take; this is my body." [23]And he took a cup, and when he had given thanks he gave it to them, and they all drank of it. [24]And he said to them, "This is my blood of the[1] covenant, which is poured out for many. [25]Truly, I say to you, I will not drink again of the fruit of the vine until that day when I drink it new in the kingdom of God."

[26]And when they had sung a hymn, they went out to the Mount of Olives. [27]And Jesus said to them, "You will all fall away, for it is written, 'I will strike the shepherd, and the sheep will be scattered.' [28]But after I am raised up, I will go before you to Galilee." [29]Peter said to him, "Even though they all fall away, I will not." [30]And Jesus said to him, "Truly, I tell you, this very night, before the rooster crows twice, you will deny me three times." [31]But he said emphatically, "If I must die with you, I will not deny you." And they all said the same.

[32]And they went to a place called Gethsemane. And he said to his disciples, "Sit here while I pray." [33]And he took with him Peter and James and John, and began to be greatly distressed and troubled. [34]And he said to them, "My soul is very sorrowful, even to death. Remain here and watch."[2] [35]And going a little farther, he fell on the ground and prayed that, if it were possible, the hour might pass from him. [36]And he said, "Abba, Father, all things are possible for you. Remove this cup from me. Yet not what I will, but what you will." [37]And he came and found them sleeping, and he said to Peter, "Simon, are you asleep? Could you not watch one hour? [38]Watch and pray that you may not enter into temptation. The spirit indeed is willing, but the flesh is weak." [39]And again he went away and prayed, saying the same words. [40]And again he came and found them sleeping, for their eyes were very heavy, and they did not know what to answer him. [41]And he came the third time and said to them, "Are you still sleeping and taking your rest? It is enough; the hour has come. The Son of Man is betrayed into the hands of sinners. [42]Rise, let us be going; see, my betrayer is at hand."

[43]And immediately, while he was still speaking, Judas came, one of the twelve, and with him a crowd with swords and clubs, from the chief priests and the scribes and the elders. [44]Now the betrayer had given them a sign, saying, "The one I will kiss is the man. Seize him and lead him away under guard." [45]And when he came, he went up to him at once and said, "Rabbi!" And he kissed him. [46]And they laid hands on him and seized him. [47]But one of those who stood by drew his sword and struck the servant[3] of the high priest and cut off his ear. [48]And Jesus said to them, "Have you come out as against a robber, with swords and clubs to capture me? [49]Day after day I was with you in the temple teaching, and you did not seize me. But let the Scriptures be fulfilled." [50]And they all left him and fled.

[51]And a young man followed him, with nothing but a linen cloth about his body. And they seized him, [52]but he left the linen cloth and ran away naked.

[53]And they led Jesus to the high priest. And all the chief priests and the elders and the scribes came together. [54]And Peter had followed him at a distance, right into the courtyard of the high priest. And he was sitting with the guards and warming himself at the fire. [55]Now the chief priests and the whole council[4]

---

[1] Some manuscripts insert *new* [2] Or *keep awake*; also verses 37, 38 [3] Greek *bondservant* [4] Greek *Sanhedrin*

were seeking testimony against Jesus to put him to death, but they found none. [56]For many bore false witness against him, but their testimony did not agree. [57]And some stood up and bore false witness against him, saying, [58]"We heard him say, 'I will destroy this temple that is made with hands, and in three days I will build another, not made with hands.'" [59]Yet even about this their testimony did not agree. [60]And the high priest stood up in the midst and asked Jesus, "Have you no answer to make? What is it that these men testify against you?"[1] [61]But he remained silent and made no answer. Again the high priest asked him, "Are you the Christ, the Son of the Blessed?" [62]And Jesus said, "I am, and you will see the Son of Man seated at the right hand of Power, and coming with the clouds of heaven." [63]And the high priest tore his garments and said, "What further witnesses do we need? [64]You have heard his blasphemy. What is your decision?" And they all condemned him as deserving death. [65]And some began to spit on him

and to cover his face and to strike him, saying to him, "Prophesy!" And the guards received him with blows.

[66]And as Peter was below in the courtyard, one of the servant girls of the high priest came, [67]and seeing Peter warming himself, she looked at him and said, "You also were with the Nazarene, Jesus." [68]But he denied it, saying, "I neither know nor understand what you mean." And he went out into the gateway[2] and the rooster crowed.[3] [69]And the servant girl saw him and began again to say to the bystanders, "This man is one of them." [70]But again he denied it. And after a little while the bystanders again said to Peter, "Certainly you are one of them, for you are a Galilean." [71]But he began to invoke a curse on himself and to swear, "I do not know this man of whom you speak." [72]And immediately the rooster crowed a second time. And Peter remembered how Jesus had said to him, "Before the rooster crows twice, you will deny me three times." And he broke down and wept.[4]

AUGUST 2

Judges 16

Samson went to Gaza, and there he saw a prostitute, and he went in to her. [2]The Gazites were told, "Samson has come here." And they surrounded the place and set an ambush for him all night at the gate of the city. They kept quiet all night, saying, "Let us wait till the light of the morning; then we will kill him." [3]But Samson lay till midnight, and at midnight he arose and took hold of the doors of the gate of the city and the two posts, and pulled them up, bar and all, and put them on his shoulders and carried them to the top of the hill that is in front of Hebron.

[4]After this he loved a woman in the Valley of Sorek, whose name was Delilah. [5]And the lords of the Philistines came up to her and said to her, "Seduce him, and see where his great strength lies, and by what means we may overpower

him, that we may bind him to humble him. And we will each give you 1,100 pieces of silver." [6]So Delilah said to Samson, "Please tell me where your great strength lies, and how you might be bound, that one could subdue you."

[7]Samson said to her, "If they bind me with seven fresh bowstrings that have not been dried, then I shall become weak and be like any other man." [8]Then the lords of the Philistines brought up to her seven fresh bowstrings that had not been dried, and she bound him with them. [9]Now she had men lying in ambush in an inner chamber. And she said to him, "The Philistines are upon you, Samson!" But he snapped the bowstrings, as a thread of flax snaps when it touches the fire. So the secret of his strength was not known.

[10]Then Delilah said to Samson, "Behold, you

have mocked me and told me lies. Please tell me how you might be bound." [11] And he said to her, "If they bind me with new ropes that have not been used, then I shall become weak and be like any other man." [12] So Delilah took new ropes and bound him with them and said to him, "The Philistines are upon you, Samson!" And the men lying in ambush were in an inner chamber. But he snapped the ropes off his arms like a thread.

[13] Then Delilah said to Samson, "Until now you have mocked me and told me lies. Tell me how you might be bound." And he said to her, "If you weave the seven locks of my head with the web and fasten it tight with the pin, then I shall become weak and be like any other man." [14] So while he slept, Delilah took the seven locks of his head and wove them into the web.[1] And she made them tight with the pin and said to him, "The Philistines are upon you, Samson!" But he awoke from his sleep and pulled away the pin, the loom, and the web.

[15] And she said to him, "How can you say, 'I love you,' when your heart is not with me? You have mocked me these three times, and you have not told me where your great strength lies." [16] And when she pressed him hard with her words day after day, and urged him, his soul was vexed to death. [17] And he told her all his heart, and said to her, "A razor has never come upon my head, for I have been a Nazirite to God from my mother's womb. If my head is shaved, then my strength will leave me, and I shall become weak and be like any other man."

[18] When Delilah saw that he had told her all his heart, she sent and called the lords of the Philistines, saying, "Come up again, for he has told me all his heart." Then the lords of the Philistines came up to her and brought the money in their hands. [19] She made him sleep on her knees. And she called a man and had him shave off the seven locks of his head. Then she began to torment him, and his strength left him. [20] And she said, "The Philistines are upon you, Samson!" And he awoke from his sleep and said, "I will go out as at other times and shake myself free." But he did not know that the LORD had left him. [21] And the Philistines seized him and gouged out his eyes and brought him down to Gaza and bound him with bronze shackles. And he ground at the mill in the prison. [22] But

the hair of his head began to grow again after it had been shaved.

[23] Now the lords of the Philistines gathered to offer a great sacrifice to Dagon their god and to rejoice, and they said, "Our god has given Samson our enemy into our hand." [24] And when the people saw him, they praised their god. For they said, "Our god has given our enemy into our hand, the ravager of our country, who has killed many of us."[2] [25] And when their hearts were merry, they said, "Call Samson, that he may entertain us." So they called Samson out of the prison, and he entertained them. They made him stand between the pillars. [26] And Samson said to the young man who held him by the hand, "Let me feel the pillars on which the house rests, that I may lean against them." [27] Now the house was full of men and women. All the lords of the Philistines were there, and on the roof there were about 3,000 men and women, who looked on while Samson entertained.

[28] Then Samson called to the LORD and said, "O Lord GOD, please remember me and please strengthen me only this once, O God, that I may be avenged on the Philistines for my two eyes." [29] And Samson grasped the two middle pillars on which the house rested, and he leaned his weight against them, his right hand on the one and his left hand on the other. [30] And Samson said, "Let me die with the Philistines." Then he bowed with all his strength, and the house fell upon the lords and upon all the people who were in it. So the dead whom he killed at his death were more than those whom he had killed during his life. [31] Then his brothers and all his family came down and took him and brought him up and buried him between Zorah and Eshtaol in the tomb of Manoah his father. He had judged Israel twenty years.

Acts 20

After the uproar ceased, Paul sent for the disciples, and after encouraging them, he said farewell and departed for Macedonia. [2] When he had gone through those regions and had given them much encouragement, he came to Greece. [3] There he spent three months, and when a plot was made against him by the Jews[3] as he was about to set sail for Syria, he decided to return through Macedonia. [4] Sopater

[1] Compare Septuagint; Hebrew lacks *and fasten it tight. . . into the web* [2] Or *who has multiplied our slain* [3] Greek *Ioudaioi* probably refers here to Jewish religious leaders, and others under their influence, in that time; also verse 19

the Berean, son of Pyrrhus, accompanied him; and of the Thessalonians, Aristarchus and Secundus; and Gaius of Derbe, and Timothy; and the Asians, Tychicus and Trophimus. [5] These went on ahead and were waiting for us at Troas, [6] but we sailed away from Philippi after the days of Unleavened Bread, and in five days we came to them at Troas, where we stayed for seven days.

[7] On the first day of the week, when we were gathered together to break bread, Paul talked with them, intending to depart on the next day, and he prolonged his speech until midnight. [8] There were many lamps in the upper room where we were gathered. [9] And a young man named Eutychus, sitting at the window, sank into a deep sleep as Paul talked still longer. And being overcome by sleep, he fell down from the third story and was taken up dead. [10] But Paul went down and bent over him, and taking him in his arms, said, "Do not be alarmed, for his life is in him." [11] And when Paul had gone up and had broken bread and eaten, he conversed with them a long while, until daybreak, and so departed. [12] And they took the youth away alive, and were not a little comforted.

[13] But going ahead to the ship, we set sail for Assos, intending to take Paul aboard there, for so he had arranged, intending himself to go by land. [14] And when he met us at Assos, we took him on board and went to Mitylene. [15] And sailing from there we came the following day opposite Chios; the next day we touched at Samos; and[1] the day after that we went to Miletus. [16] For Paul had decided to sail past Ephesus, so that he might not have to spend time in Asia, for he was hastening to be at Jerusalem, if possible, on the day of Pentecost.

[17] Now from Miletus he sent to Ephesus and called the elders of the church to come to him. [18] And when they came to him, he said to them:

"You yourselves know how I lived among you the whole time from the first day that I set foot in Asia, [19] serving the Lord with all humility and with tears and with trials that happened to me through the plots of the Jews; [20] how I did not shrink from declaring to you anything that was profitable, and teaching you in public and from house to house, [21] testifying both to Jews and to Greeks of repentance toward God and of faith in our Lord Jesus Christ. [22] And now, behold, I am going to Jerusalem, constrained by[2] the

Spirit, not knowing what will happen to me there, [23] except that the Holy Spirit testifies to me in every city that imprisonment and afflictions await me. [24] But I do not account my life of any value nor as precious to myself, if only I may finish my course and the ministry that I received from the Lord Jesus, to testify to the gospel of the grace of God. [25] And now, behold, I know that none of you among whom I have gone about proclaiming the kingdom will see my face again. [26] Therefore I testify to you this day that I am innocent of the blood of all, [27] for I did not shrink from declaring to you the whole counsel of God. [28] Pay careful attention to yourselves and to all the flock, in which the Holy Spirit has made you overseers, to care for the church of God,[3] which he obtained with his own blood.[4] [29] I know that after my departure fierce wolves will come in among you, not sparing the flock; [30] and from among your own selves will arise men speaking twisted things, to draw away the disciples after them. [31] Therefore be alert, remembering that for three years I did not cease night or day to admonish every one with tears. [32] And now I commend you to God and to the word of his grace, which is able to build you up and to give you the inheritance among all those who are sanctified. [33] I coveted no one's silver or gold or apparel. [34] You yourselves know that these hands ministered to my necessities and to those who were with me. [35] In all things I have shown you that by working hard in this way we must help the weak and remember the words of the Lord Jesus, how he himself said, 'It is more blessed to give than to receive.'"

[36] And when he had said these things, he knelt down and prayed with them all. [37] And there was much weeping on the part of all; they embraced Paul and kissed him, [38] being sorrowful most of all because of the word he had spoken, that they would not see his face again. And they accompanied him to the ship.

--------- Jeremiah 29 ---------

These are the words of the letter that Jeremiah the prophet sent from Jerusalem to the surviving elders of the exiles, and to the priests, the prophets, and all the people, whom Nebuchadnezzar had taken into exile from Jerusalem to Babylon. [2] This was after King Jeconiah and the queen mother, the eunuchs,

[1] Some manuscripts add after remaining at Trogyllium [2] Or bound in [3] Some manuscripts of the Lord [4] Or with the blood of his Own

the officials of Judah and Jerusalem, the crafts-men, and the metal workers had departed from Jerusalem. [3] The letter was sent by the hand of Elasah the son of Shaphan and Gemariah the son of Hilkiah, whom Zedekiah king of Judah sent to Babylon to Nebuchadnezzar king of Babylon. It said: [4] "Thus says the LORD of hosts, the God of Israel, to all the exiles whom I have sent into exile from Jerusalem to Babylon: [5] Build houses and live in them; plant gardens and eat their produce. [6] Take wives and have sons and daughters; take wives for your sons, and give your daughters in marriage, that they may bear sons and daughters; multiply there, and do not decrease. [7] But seek the welfare of the city where I have sent you into exile, and pray to the LORD on its behalf, for in its welfare you will find your welfare. [8] For thus says the LORD of hosts, the God of Israel: Do not let your prophets and your diviners who are among you deceive you, and do not listen to the dreams that they dream,[1] [9] for it is a lie that they are prophesying to you in my name; I did not send them, declares the LORD.

[10] "For thus says the LORD: When seventy years are completed for Babylon, I will visit you, and I will fulfill to you my promise and bring you back to this place. [11] For I know the plans I have for you, declares the LORD, plans for welfare[2] and not for evil, to give you a future and a hope. [12] Then you will call upon me and come and pray to me, and I will hear you. [13] You will seek me and find me, when you seek me with all your heart. [14] I will be found by you, declares the LORD, and I will restore your for-tunes and gather you from all the nations and all the places where I have driven you, declares the LORD, and I will bring you back to the place from which I sent you into exile.

[15] "Because you have said, 'The LORD has raised up prophets for us in Babylon,' [16] thus says the LORD concerning the king who sits on the throne of David, and concerning all the people who dwell in this city, your kins-men who did not go out with you into exile: [17] 'Thus says the LORD of hosts, behold, I am sending on them sword, famine, and pesti-lence, and I will make them like vile figs that are so rotten they cannot be eaten. [18] I will pursue them with sword, famine, and pesti-lence, and will make them a horror to all the kingdoms of the earth, to be a curse, a terror, a

hissing, and a reproach among all the nations where I have driven them, [19] because they did not pay attention to my words, declares the LORD, that I persistently sent to you by my ser-vants the prophets, but you would not listen, declares the LORD.' [20] Hear the word of the LORD, all you exiles whom I sent away from Jerusalem to Babylon: [21] 'Thus says the LORD of hosts, the God of Israel, concerning Ahab the son of Kolaiah and Zedekiah the son of Maaseiah, who are prophesying a lie to you in my name: Behold, I will deliver them into the hand of Nebuchadnezzar king of Babylon, and he shall strike them down before your eyes. [22] Because of them this curse shall be used by all the exiles from Judah in Babylon: "The LORD make you like Zedekiah and Ahab, whom the king of Babylon roasted in the fire," [23] because they have done an outrageous thing in Israel, they have committed adultery with their neighbors' wives, and they have spoken in my name lying words that I did not com-mand them. I am the one who knows, and I am witness, declares the LORD.' "

[24] To Shemaiah of Nehelam you shall say: [25] "Thus says the LORD of hosts, the God of Israel: You have sent letters in your name to all the people who are in Jerusalem, and to Zephaniah the son of Maaseiah the priest, and to all the priests, saying, [26] 'The LORD has made you priest instead of Jehoiada the priest, to have charge in the house of the LORD over every madman who prophesies, to put him in the stocks and neck irons. [27] Now why have you not rebuked Jeremiah of Anathoth who is prophesying to you? [28] For he has sent to us in Babylon, saying, "Your exile will be long; build houses and live in them, and plant gardens and eat their produce." ' "

[29] Zephaniah the priest read this letter in the hearing of Jeremiah the prophet. [30] Then the word of the LORD came to Jeremiah: [31] "Send to all the exiles, saying, 'Thus says the LORD concerning Shemaiah of Nehelam: Because Shemaiah had prophesied to you when I did not send him, and has made you trust in a lie, [32] therefore thus says the LORD: Behold, I will punish Shemaiah of Nehelam and his descen-dants. He shall not have anyone living among this people, and he shall not see the good that I will do to my people, declares the LORD, for he has spoken rebellion against the LORD.' "

[1] Hebrew *your dreams, which you cause to dream* [2] Or *peace*

Mark 15

And as soon as it was morning, the chief priests held a consultation with the elders and scribes and the whole council. And they bound Jesus and led him away and delivered him over to Pilate. ²And Pilate asked him, "Are you the King of the Jews?" And he answered him, "You have said so." ³And the chief priests accused him of many things. ⁴And Pilate again asked him, "Have you no answer to make? See how many charges they bring against you." ⁵But Jesus made no further answer, so that Pilate was amazed.

⁶Now at the feast he used to release for them one prisoner for whom they asked. ⁷And among the rebels in prison, who had committed murder in the insurrection, there was a man called Barabbas. ⁸And the crowd came up and began to ask Pilate to do as he usually did for them. ⁹And he answered them, saying, "Do you want me to release for you the King of the Jews?" ¹⁰For he perceived that it was out of envy that the chief priests had delivered him up. ¹¹But the chief priests stirred up the crowd to have him release for them Barabbas instead. ¹²And Pilate again said to them, "Then what shall I do with the man you call the King of the Jews?" ¹³And they cried out again, "Crucify him." ¹⁴And Pilate said to them, "Why, what evil has he done?" But they shouted all the more, "Crucify him." ¹⁵So Pilate, wishing to satisfy the crowd, released for them Barabbas, and having scourged[1] Jesus, he delivered him to be crucified.

¹⁶And the soldiers led him away inside the palace (that is, the governor's headquarters),[2] and they called together the whole battalion.[3] ¹⁷And they clothed him in a purple cloak, and twisting together a crown of thorns, they put it on him. ¹⁸And they began to salute him, "Hail, King of the Jews!" ¹⁹And they were striking his head with a reed and spitting on him and kneeling down in homage to him. ²⁰And when they had mocked him, they stripped him of the purple cloak and put his own clothes on him. And they led him out to crucify him.

²¹And they compelled a passerby, Simon of Cyrene, who was coming in from the country, the father of Alexander and Rufus, to carry his cross. ²²And they brought him to the place called Golgotha (which means Place of a Skull). ²³And they offered him wine mixed with myrrh, but he did not take it. ²⁴And they crucified him and divided his garments among them, casting lots for them, to decide what each should take. ²⁵And it was the third hour[4] when they crucified him. ²⁶And the inscription of the charge against him read, "The King of the Jews." ²⁷And with him they crucified two robbers, one on his right and one on his left.[5] ²⁹And those who passed by derided him, wagging their heads and saying, "Aha! You who would destroy the temple and rebuild it in three days, ³⁰save yourself, and come down from the cross!" ³¹So also the chief priests with the scribes mocked him to one another, saying, "He saved others; he cannot save himself. ³²Let the Christ, the King of Israel, come down now from the cross that we may see and believe." Those who were crucified with him also reviled him.

³³And when the sixth hour[6] had come, there was darkness over the whole land until the ninth hour.[7] ³⁴And at the ninth hour Jesus cried with a loud voice, "Eloi, Eloi, lema sabachthani?" which means, "My God, my God, why have you forsaken me?" ³⁵And some of the bystanders hearing it said, "Behold, he is calling Elijah." ³⁶And someone ran and filled a sponge with sour wine, put it on a reed and gave it to him to drink, saying, "Wait, let us see whether Elijah will come to take him down." ³⁷And Jesus uttered a loud cry and breathed his last. ³⁸And the curtain of the temple was torn in two, from top to bottom. ³⁹And when the centurion, who stood facing him, saw that in this way he[8] breathed his last, he said, "Truly this man was the Son[9] of God!"

⁴⁰There were also women looking on from a distance, among whom were Mary Magdalene, and Mary the mother of James the younger and of Joses, and Salome. ⁴¹When he was in Galilee, they followed him and ministered to him, and there were also many other women who came up with him to Jerusalem.

⁴²And when evening had come, since it was the day of Preparation, that is, the day before the Sabbath, ⁴³Joseph of Arimathea, a respected member of the council, who was also himself looking for the kingdom of God, took courage and went to Pilate and asked for the body of Jesus. ⁴⁴Pilate was surprised to hear that he should have already died.[10] And summoning

---

[1] A Roman judicial penalty, consisting of a severe beating with a multi-lashed whip containing imbedded pieces of bone and metal [2] Greek *the praetorium* [3] Greek *cohort*; a tenth of a Roman legion, usually about 600 men [4] That is, 9 A.M. [5] Some manuscripts insert verse 28: *And the Scripture was fulfilled that says, "He was numbered with the transgressors"* [6] That is, noon [7] That is, 3 P.M. [8] Some manuscripts insert *cried out and* [9] Or *a son* [10] Or *Pilate wondered whether he had already died*

the centurion, he asked him whether he was already dead. [45]And when he learned from the centurion that he was dead, he granted the corpse to Joseph. [46]And Joseph[1] bought a linen shroud, and taking him down, wrapped him in the linen shroud and laid him in a tomb that had been cut out of the rock. And he rolled a stone against the entrance of the tomb. [47]Mary Magdalene and Mary the mother of Joses saw where he was laid.

AUGUST 3

Judges 17

There was a man of the hill country of Ephraim, whose name was Micah. [2]And he said to his mother, "The 1,100 pieces of silver that were taken from you, about which you uttered a curse, and also spoke it in my ears, behold, the silver is with me; I took it." And his mother said, "Blessed be my son by the LORD." [3]And he restored the 1,100 pieces of silver to his mother. And his mother said, "I dedicate the silver to the LORD from my hand for my son, to make a carved image and a metal image. Now therefore I will restore it to you." [4]So when he restored the money to his mother, his mother took 200 pieces of silver and gave it to the silversmith, who made it into a carved image and a metal image. And it was in the house of Micah. [5]And the man Micah had a shrine, and he made an ephod and household gods, and ordained[2] one of his sons, who became his priest. [6]In those days there was no king in Israel. Everyone did what was right in his own eyes.

[7]Now there was a young man of Bethlehem in Judah, of the family of Judah, who was a Levite, and he sojourned there. [8]And the man departed from the town of Bethlehem in Judah to sojourn where he could find a place. And as he journeyed, he came to the hill country of Ephraim to the house of Micah. [9]And Micah said to him, "Where do you come from?" And he said to him, "I am a Levite of Bethlehem in Judah, and I am going to sojourn where I may find a place." [10]And Micah said to him, "Stay with me, and be to me a father and a priest, and I will give you ten pieces of silver a year and a suit of clothes and your living." And the Levite went in. [11]And the Levite was content to dwell with the man, and the young man became to him like one of his sons. [12]And Micah ordained the Levite, and the young man became his priest, and was in the house of Micah. [13]Then Micah said, "Now I know that the LORD will prosper me, because I have a Levite as priest."

Acts 21

And when we had parted from them and set sail, we came by a straight course to Cos, and the next day to Rhodes, and from there to Patara.[3] [2]And having found a ship crossing to Phoenicia, we went aboard and set sail. [3]When we had come in sight of Cyprus, leaving it on the left we sailed to Syria and landed at Tyre, for there the ship was to unload its cargo. [4]And having sought out the disciples, we stayed there for seven days. And through the Spirit they were telling Paul not to go on to Jerusalem. [5]When our days there were ended, we departed and went on our journey, and they all, with wives and children, accompanied us until we were outside the city. And kneeling down on the beach, we prayed [6]and said farewell to one another. Then we went on board the ship, and they returned home.

[7]When we had finished the voyage from Tyre, we arrived at Ptolemais, and we greeted the brothers[4] and stayed with them for one day. [8]On the next day we departed and came to Caesarea, and we entered the house of Philip the evangelist, who was one of the seven, and stayed with him. [9]He had four unmarried daughters, who prophesied. [10]While we were staying for many days, a prophet named

Agabus came down from Judea. ¹¹And coming to us, he took Paul's belt and bound his own feet and hands and said, "Thus says the Holy Spirit, 'This is how the Jews¹ at Jerusalem will bind the man who owns this belt and deliver him into the hands of the Gentiles.'" ¹²When we heard this, we and the people there urged him not to go up to Jerusalem. ¹³Then Paul answered, "What are you doing, weeping and breaking my heart? For I am ready not only to be imprisoned but even to die in Jerusalem for the name of the Lord Jesus." ¹⁴And since he would not be persuaded, we ceased and said, "Let the will of the Lord be done."

¹⁵After these days we got ready and went up to Jerusalem. ¹⁶And some of the disciples from Caesarea went with us, bringing us to the house of Mnason of Cyprus, an early disciple, with whom we should lodge.

¹⁷When we had come to Jerusalem, the brothers received us gladly. ¹⁸On the following day Paul went in with us to James, and all the elders were present. ¹⁹After greeting them, he related one by one the things that God had done among the Gentiles through his ministry. ²⁰And when they heard it, they glorified God. And they said to him, "You see, brother, how many thousands there are among the Jews of those who have believed. They are all zealous for the law, ²¹and they have been told about you that you teach all the Jews who are among the Gentiles to forsake Moses, telling them not to circumcise their children or walk according to our customs. ²²What then is to be done? They will certainly hear that you have come. ²³Do therefore what we tell you. We have four men who are under a vow; ²⁴take these men and purify yourself along with them and pay their expenses, so that they may shave their heads. Thus all will know that there is nothing in what they have been told about you, but that you yourself also live in observance of the law. ²⁵But as for the Gentiles who have believed, we have sent a letter with our judgment that they should abstain from what has been sacrificed to idols, and from blood, and from what has been strangled,² and from sexual immorality." ²⁶Then Paul took the men, and the next day he purified himself along with them and went into the temple, giving notice when the days of purification would be fulfilled and the offering presented for each one of them.

²⁷When the seven days were almost completed, the Jews from Asia, seeing him in the temple, stirred up the whole crowd and laid hands on him, ²⁸crying out, "Men of Israel, help! This is the man who is teaching everyone everywhere against the people and the law and this place. Moreover, he even brought Greeks into the temple and has defiled this holy place." ²⁹For they had previously seen Trophimus the Ephesian with him in the city, and they supposed that Paul had brought him into the temple. ³⁰Then all the city was stirred up, and the people ran together. They seized Paul and dragged him out of the temple, and at once the gates were shut. ³¹And as they were seeking to kill him, word came to the tribune of the cohort that all Jerusalem was in confusion. ³²He at once took soldiers and centurions and ran down to them. And when they saw the tribune and the soldiers, they stopped beating Paul. ³³Then the tribune came up and arrested him and ordered him to be bound with two chains. He inquired who he was and what he had done. ³⁴Some in the crowd were shouting one thing, some another. And as he could not learn the facts because of the uproar, he ordered him to be brought into the barracks. ³⁵And when he came to the steps, he was actually carried by the soldiers because of the violence of the crowd, ³⁶for the mob of the people followed, crying out, "Away with him!"

³⁷As Paul was about to be brought into the barracks, he said to the tribune, "May I say something to you?" And he said, "Do you know Greek? ³⁸Are you not the Egyptian, then, who recently stirred up a revolt and led the four thousand men of the Assassins out into the wilderness?" ³⁹Paul replied, "I am a Jew, from Tarsus in Cilicia, a citizen of no obscure city. I beg you, permit me to speak to the people." ⁴⁰And when he had given him permission, Paul, standing on the steps, motioned with his hand to the people. And when there was a great hush, he addressed them in the Hebrew language,³ saying:

Jeremiah 30–31

The word that came to Jeremiah from the LORD: ²"Thus says the LORD, the God of Israel: Write in a book all the words that I have spoken to you. ³For behold, days are coming,

---

¹ Greek *Ioudaioi* probably refers here to Jewish religious leaders, and others under their influence, in that time ² Some manuscripts omit *and from what has been strangled* ³ Or the Hebrew dialect (probably Aramaic)

declares the LORD, when I will restore the fortunes of my people, Israel and Judah, says the LORD, and I will bring them back to the land that I gave to their fathers, and they shall take possession of it."

⁴ These are the words that the LORD spoke concerning Israel and Judah:

⁵　"Thus says the LORD:
　　We have heard a cry of panic,
　　　of terror, and no peace.
⁶　Ask now, and see,
　　　can a man bear a child?
　　Why then do I see every man
　　　with his hands on his stomach like a
　　　　woman in labor?
　　Why has every face turned pale?
⁷　Alas! That day is so great
　　　there is none like it;
　　it is a time of distress for Jacob;
　　　yet he shall be saved out of it.

⁸ "And it shall come to pass in that day, declares the LORD of hosts, that I will break his yoke from off your neck, and I will burst your bonds, and foreigners shall no more make a servant of him.[1] ⁹ But they shall serve the LORD their God and David their king, whom I will raise up for them.

¹⁰　"Then fear not, O Jacob my servant,
　　　declares the LORD,
　　　nor be dismayed, O Israel;
　　for behold, I will save you from far away,
　　　and your offspring from the land of
　　　　their captivity.
　　Jacob shall return and have quiet and
　　　ease,
　　　and none shall make him afraid.
¹¹　For I am with you to save you,
　　　　　　　declares the LORD;
　　I will make a full end of all the nations
　　　among whom I scattered you,
　　　but of you I will not make a full end.
　　I will discipline you in just measure,
　　　and I will by no means leave you
　　　　unpunished.
¹²　"For thus says the LORD:
　　Your hurt is incurable,
　　　and your wound is grievous.
¹³　There is none to uphold your cause,
　　　no medicine for your wound,
　　　no healing for you.

¹⁴　All your lovers have forgotten you;
　　　they care nothing for you;
　　for I have dealt you the blow of an enemy,
　　　the punishment of a merciless foe,
　　because your guilt is great,
　　　because your sins are flagrant.
¹⁵　Why do you cry out over your hurt?
　　　Your pain is incurable.
　　Because your guilt is great,
　　　because your sins are flagrant,
　　　I have done these things to you.
¹⁶　Therefore all who devour you shall be
　　　devoured,
　　　and all your foes, every one of them,
　　　shall go into captivity;
　　those who plunder you shall be
　　　plundered,
　　　and all who prey on you I will make a
　　　　prey.
¹⁷　For I will restore health to you,
　　　and your wounds I will heal,
　　　　　　　　　　declares the LORD,
　　because they have called you an outcast:
　　　'It is Zion, for whom no one cares!'

¹⁸　"Thus says the LORD:
　　Behold, I will restore the fortunes of the
　　　tents of Jacob
　　　and have compassion on his dwellings;
　　the city shall be rebuilt on its mound,
　　　and the palace shall stand where it
　　　　used to be.
¹⁹　Out of them shall come songs of
　　　thanksgiving,
　　　and the voices of those who celebrate.
　　I will multiply them, and they shall not
　　　be few;
　　　I will make them honored, and they
　　　　shall not be small.
²⁰　Their children shall be as they were of
　　　old,
　　　and their congregation shall be
　　　　established before me,
　　　and I will punish all who oppress them.
²¹　Their prince shall be one of themselves;
　　　their ruler shall come out from their
　　　　midst;
　　I will make him draw near, and he shall
　　　approach me,
　　　for who would dare of himself to
　　　　approach me?
　　　　　　　　　　declares the LORD.

[1] Or serve him

22 And you shall be my people,
     and I will be your God."

23 Behold the storm of the LORD!
     Wrath has gone forth,
     a whirling tempest;
       it will burst upon the head of the
         wicked.
24 The fierce anger of the LORD will not
     turn back
       until he has executed and
         accomplished
       the intentions of his mind.
     In the latter days you will understand
       this.

31:1 "At that time, declares the LORD, I will be
the God of all the clans of Israel, and they shall
be my people."

2   Thus says the LORD:
     "The people who survived the sword
       found grace in the wilderness;
     when Israel sought for rest,
3   the LORD appeared to him[1] from far
         away.
     I have loved you with an everlasting love;
       therefore I have continued my
         faithfulness to you.
4   Again I will build you, and you shall be
         built,
       O virgin Israel!
     Again you shall adorn yourself with
       tambourines
     and shall go forth in the dance of the
       merrymakers.
5   Again you shall plant vineyards
       on the mountains of Samaria;
     the planters shall plant
       and shall enjoy the fruit.
6   For there shall be a day when watchmen
       will call
     in the hill country of Ephraim:
     'Arise, and let us go up to Zion,
       to the LORD our God.'"

7   For thus says the LORD:
     "Sing aloud with gladness for Jacob,
       and raise shouts for the chief of the
         nations;
     proclaim, give praise, and say,
     'O LORD, save your people,
       the remnant of Israel.'

8   Behold, I will bring them from the north
         country
       and gather them from the farthest
         parts of the earth,
     among them the blind and the lame,
       the pregnant woman and she who is
         in labor, together;
     a great company, they shall return
       here.
9   With weeping they shall come,
       and with pleas for mercy I will lead
         them back,
     I will make them walk by brooks of
       water,
       in a straight path in which they shall
         not stumble,
     for I am a father to Israel,
       and Ephraim is my firstborn.

10   "Hear the word of the LORD, O nations,
       and declare it in the coastlands far
         away;
     say, 'He who scattered Israel will gather
       him,
       and will keep him as a shepherd keeps
         his flock.'
11   For the LORD has ransomed Jacob
       and has redeemed him from hands
         too strong for him.
12   They shall come and sing aloud on the
         height of Zion,
       and they shall be radiant over the
         goodness of the LORD,
     over the grain, the wine, and the oil,
       and over the young of the flock and
         the herd;
     their life shall be like a watered garden,
       and they shall languish no more.
13   Then shall the young women rejoice in
         the dance,
       and the young men and the old shall
         be merry.
     I will turn their mourning into joy;
       I will comfort them, and give them
         gladness for sorrow.
14   I will feast the soul of the priests with
         abundance,
       and my people shall be satisfied with
         my goodness,
                         declares the LORD."

15   Thus says the LORD:

---

[1] Septuagint; Hebrew me

"A voice is heard in Ramah,
    lamentation and bitter weeping.
Rachel is weeping for her children;
    she refuses to be comforted for her
        children,
    because they are no more."

16 Thus says the LORD:
"Keep your voice from weeping,
    and your eyes from tears,
for there is a reward for your work,
                declares the LORD,
and they shall come back from the
    land of the enemy.
17 There is hope for your future,
                declares the LORD,
and your children shall come back to
    their own country.
18 I have heard Ephraim grieving,
'You have disciplined me, and I was
    disciplined,
    like an untrained calf;
bring me back that I may be restored,
    for you are the LORD my God.
19 For after I had turned away, I relented,
    and after I was instructed, I struck my
        thigh;
I was ashamed, and I was confounded,
    because I bore the disgrace of my
        youth.'
20 Is Ephraim my dear son?
    Is he my darling child?
For as often as I speak against him,
    I do remember him still.
Therefore my heart[1] yearns for him;
    I will surely have mercy on him,
                declares the LORD.

21 "Set up road markers for yourself;
    make yourself guideposts;
consider well the highway,
    the road by which you went.
Return, O virgin Israel,
    return to these your cities.
22 How long will you waver,
    O faithless daughter?
For the LORD has created a new thing on
    the earth:
    a woman encircles a man."

23 Thus says the LORD of hosts, the God of Israel: "Once more they shall use these words

in the land of Judah and in its cities, when I restore their fortunes:

"'The LORD bless you, O habitation of
    righteousness,
    O holy hill!'

24 And Judah and all its cities shall dwell there together, and the farmers and those who wander with their flocks. 25 For I will satisfy the weary soul, and every languishing soul I will replenish."

26 At this I awoke and looked, and my sleep was pleasant to me.

27 "Behold, the days are coming, declares the LORD, when I will sow the house of Israel and the house of Judah with the seed of man and the seed of beast. 28 And it shall come to pass that as I have watched over them to pluck up and break down, to overthrow, destroy, and bring harm, so I will watch over them to build and to plant, declares the LORD. 29 In those days they shall no longer say:

"'The fathers have eaten sour grapes,
    and the children's teeth are set on
        edge.'

30 But everyone shall die for his own iniquity. Each man who eats sour grapes, his teeth shall be set on edge.

31 "Behold, the days are coming, declares the LORD, when I will make a new covenant with the house of Israel and the house of Judah, 32 not like the covenant that I made with their fathers on the day when I took them by the hand to bring them out of the land of Egypt, my covenant that they broke, though I was their husband, declares the LORD. 33 For this is the covenant that I will make with the house of Israel after those days, declares the LORD: I will put my law within them, and I will write it on their hearts. And I will be their God, and they shall be my people. 34 And no longer shall each one teach his neighbor and each his brother, saying, 'Know the LORD,' for they shall all know me, from the least of them to the greatest, declares the LORD. For I will forgive their iniquity, and I will remember their sin no more."

35 Thus says the LORD,
    who gives the sun for light by day
    and the fixed order of the moon and
        the stars for light by night,

[1] Hebrew bowels

who stirs up the sea so that its waves
    roar—
  the LORD of hosts is his name:
[36] "If this fixed order departs
  from before me, declares the LORD,
  then shall the offspring of Israel cease
    from being a nation before me
      forever."

[37]   Thus says the LORD:
  "If the heavens above can be measured,
    and the foundations of the earth
      below can be explored,
  then I will cast off all the offspring of
    Israel
  for all that they have done,
              declares the LORD."

[38] "Behold, the days are coming, declares the LORD, when the city shall be rebuilt for the LORD from the Tower of Hananel to the Corner Gate. [39] And the measuring line shall go out farther, straight to the hill Gareb, and shall then turn to Goah. [40] The whole valley of the dead bodies and the ashes, and all the fields as far as the brook Kidron, to the corner of the Horse Gate toward the east, shall be sacred to the LORD. It shall not be plucked up or overthrown anymore forever."

--------------------- Mark 16 ---------------------

When the Sabbath was past, Mary Magdalene, Mary the mother of James, and Salome bought spices, so that they might go and anoint him. [2] And very early on the first day of the week, when the sun had risen, they went to the tomb. [3] And they were saying to one another, "Who will roll away the stone for us from the entrance of the tomb?" [4] And looking up, they saw that the stone had been rolled back—it was very large. [5] And entering the tomb, they saw a young man sitting on the right side, dressed in a white robe, and they were alarmed. [6] And he said to them, "Do not

be alarmed. You seek Jesus of Nazareth, who was crucified. He has risen; he is not here. See the place where they laid him. [7] But go, tell his disciples and Peter that he is going before you to Galilee. There you will see him, just as he told you." [8] And they went out and fled from the tomb, for trembling and astonishment had seized them, and they said nothing to anyone, for they were afraid.

[SOME OF THE EARLIEST MANUSCRIPTS
DO NOT INCLUDE 16:9–20.][1]

[9] [[Now when he rose early on the first day of the week, he appeared first to Mary Magdalene, from whom he had cast out seven demons. [10] She went and told those who had been with him, as they mourned and wept. [11] But when they heard that he was alive and had been seen by her, they would not believe it.

[12] After these things he appeared in another form to two of them, as they were walking into the country. [13] And they went back and told the rest, but they did not believe them.

[14] Afterward he appeared to the eleven themselves as they were reclining at table, and he rebuked them for their unbelief and hardness of heart, because they had not believed those who saw him after he had risen. [15] And he said to them, "Go into all the world and proclaim the gospel to the whole creation. [16] Whoever believes and is baptized will be saved, but whoever does not believe will be condemned. [17] And these signs will accompany those who believe: in my name they will cast out demons; they will speak in new tongues; [18] they will pick up serpents with their hands; and if they drink any deadly poison, it will not hurt them; they will lay their hands on the sick, and they will recover."

[19] So then the Lord Jesus, after he had spoken to them, was taken up into heaven and sat down at the right hand of God. [20] And they went out and preached everywhere, while the Lord worked with them and confirmed the message by accompanying signs.]]

---

[1] Some manuscripts end the book with 16:8; others include verses 9–20 immediately after verse 8. At least one manuscript inserts additional material after verse 14; some manuscripts include after verse 8 the following: *But they reported briefly to Peter and those with him all that they had been told. And after this, Jesus himself sent out by means of them, from east to west, the sacred and imperishable proclamation of eternal salvation.* These manuscripts then continue with verses 9–20

AUGUST 4

Judges 18

In those days there was no king in Israel. And in those days the tribe of the people of Dan was seeking for itself an inheritance to dwell in, for until then no inheritance among the tribes of Israel had fallen to them. [2] So the people of Dan sent five able men from the whole number of their tribe, from Zorah and from Eshtaol, to spy out the land and to explore it. And they said to them, "Go and explore the land." And they came to the hill country of Ephraim, to the house of Micah, and lodged there. [3] When they were by the house of Micah, they recognized the voice of the young Levite. And they turned aside and said to him, "Who brought you here? What are you doing in this place? What is your business here?" [4] And he said to them, "This is how Micah dealt with me: he has hired me, and I have become his priest." [5] And they said to him, "Inquire of God, please, that we may know whether the journey on which we are setting out will succeed." [6] And the priest said to them, "Go in peace. The journey on which you go is under the eye of the Lord."

[7] Then the five men departed and came to Laish and saw the people who were there, how they lived in security, after the manner of the Sidonians, quiet and unsuspecting, lacking[1] nothing that is in the earth and possessing wealth, and how they were far from the Sidonians and had no dealings with anyone. [8] And when they came to their brothers at Zorah and Eshtaol, their brothers said to them, "What do you report?" [9] They said, "Arise, and let us go up against them, for we have seen the land, and behold, it is very good. And will you do nothing? Do not be slow to go, to enter in and possess the land. [10] As soon as you go, you will come to an unsuspecting people. The land is spacious, for God has given it into your hands, a place where there is no lack of anything that is in the earth."

[11] So 600 men of the tribe of Dan, armed with weapons of war, set out from Zorah and Eshtaol, [12] and went up and encamped at Kiriath-jearim in Judah. On this account that place is called Mahaneh-dan[2] to this day; behold, it is west of Kiriath-jearim. [13] And they passed on from there to the hill country of Ephraim, and came to the house of Micah.

[14] Then the five men who had gone to scout out the country of Laish said to their brothers, "Do you know that in these houses there are an ephod, household gods, a carved image, and a metal image? Now therefore consider what you will do." [15] And they turned aside there and came to the house of the young Levite, at the home of Micah, and asked him about his welfare. [16] Now the 600 men of the Danites, armed with their weapons of war, stood by the entrance of the gate. [17] And the five men who had gone to scout out the land went up and entered and took the carved image, the ephod, the household gods, and the metal image, while the priest stood by the entrance of the gate with the 600 men armed with weapons of war. [18] And when these went into Micah's house and took the carved image, the ephod, the household gods, and the metal image, the priest said to them, "What are you doing?" [19] And they said to him, "Keep quiet; put your hand on your mouth and come with us and be to us a father and a priest. Is it better for you to be priest to the house of one man, or to be priest to a tribe and clan in Israel?" [20] And the priest's heart was glad. He took the ephod and the household gods and the carved image and went along with the people.

[21] So they turned and departed, putting the little ones and the livestock and the goods in front of them. [22] When they had gone a distance from the home of Micah, the men who were in the houses near Micah's house were called out, and they overtook the people of Dan. [23] And they shouted to the people of Dan, who turned around and said to Micah, "What is the matter with you, that you come with such a company?" [24] And he said, "You take my gods that I made and the priest, and go away, and what have I

---

[1] Compare 18:10; the meaning of the Hebrew word is uncertain   [2] *Mahaneh-dan* means *camp of Dan*

left? How then do you ask me, 'What is the matter with you?'" **25**And the people of Dan said to him, "Do not let your voice be heard among us, lest angry fellows fall upon you, and you lose your life with the lives of your household." **26**Then the people of Dan went their way. And when Micah saw that they were too strong for him, he turned and went back to his home.

27But the people of Dan took what Micah had made, and the priest who belonged to him, and they came to Laish, to a people quiet and unsuspecting, and struck them with the edge of the sword and burned the city with fire. **28**And there was no deliverer because it was far from Sidon, and they had no dealings with anyone. It was in the valley that belongs to Beth-rehob. Then they rebuilt the city and lived in it. **29**And they named the city Dan, after the name of Dan their ancestor, who was born to Israel; but the name of the city was Laish at the first. **30**And the people of Dan set up the carved image for themselves, and Jonathan the son of Gershom, son of Moses,[1] and his sons were priests to the tribe of the Danites until the day of the captivity of the land. **31**So they set up Micah's carved image that he made, as long as the house of God was at Shiloh.

Acts 22

"Brothers and fathers, hear the defense that I now make before you."

2And when they heard that he was addressing them in the Hebrew language,[2] they became even more quiet. And he said:

3"I am a Jew, born in Tarsus in Cilicia, but brought up in this city, educated at the feet of Gamaliel[3] according to the strict manner of the law of our fathers, being zealous for God as all of you are this day. **4**I persecuted this Way to the death, binding and delivering to prison both men and women, **5**as the high priest and the whole council of elders can bear me witness. From them I received letters to the brothers, and I journeyed toward Damascus to take those also who were there and bring them in bonds to Jerusalem to be punished.

6"As I was on my way and drew near to Damascus, about noon a great light from heaven suddenly shone around me. **7**And I fell to the ground and heard a voice saying to me, 'Saul, Saul, why are you persecuting me?' **8**And

I answered, 'Who are you, Lord?' And he said to me, 'I am Jesus of Nazareth, whom you are persecuting.' **9**Now those who were with me saw the light but did not understand[4] the voice of the one who was speaking to me. **10**And I said, 'What shall I do, Lord?' And the Lord said to me, 'Rise, and go into Damascus, and there you will be told all that is appointed for you to do.' **11**And since I could not see because of the brightness of that light, I was led by the hand by those who were with me, and came into Damascus.

12"And one Ananias, a devout man according to the law, well spoken of by all the Jews who lived there, **13**came to me, and standing by me said to me, 'Brother Saul, receive your sight.' And at that very hour I received my sight and saw him. **14**And he said, 'The God of our fathers appointed you to know his will, to see the Righteous One and to hear a voice from his mouth; **15**for you will be a witness for him to everyone of what you have seen and heard. **16**And now why do you wait? Rise and be baptized and wash away your sins, calling on his name.'

17"When I had returned to Jerusalem and was praying in the temple, I fell into a trance **18**and saw him saying to me, 'Make haste and get out of Jerusalem quickly, because they will not accept your testimony about me.' **19**And I said, 'Lord, they themselves know that in one synagogue after another I imprisoned and beat those who believed in you. **20**And when the blood of Stephen your witness was being shed, I myself was standing by and approving and watching over the garments of those who killed him.' **21**And he said to me, 'Go, for I will send you far away to the Gentiles.'"

22Up to this word they listened to him. Then they raised their voices and said, "Away with such a fellow from the earth! For he should not be allowed to live." **23**And as they were shouting and throwing off their cloaks and flinging dust into the air, **24**the tribune ordered him to be brought into the barracks, saying that he should be examined by flogging, to find out why they were shouting against him like this. **25**But when they had stretched him out for the whips,[5] Paul said to the centurion who was standing by, "Is it lawful for you to flog a man who is a Roman citizen and uncondemned?" **26**When the centurion heard this, he went to the tribune and said to him, "What are you

---

[1] Or *Manasseh* [2] Or *the Hebrew dialect (probably Aramaic)* [3] Or *city at the feet of Gamaliel, educated* [4] Or *hear with understanding* [5] Or *when they had tied him up with leather strips*

about to do? For this man is a Roman citizen." ²⁷So the tribune came and said to him, "Tell me, are you a Roman citizen?" And he said, "Yes." ²⁸The tribune answered, "I bought this citizenship for a large sum." Paul said, "But I am a citizen by birth." ²⁹So those who were about to examine him withdrew from him immediately, and the tribune also was afraid, for he realized that Paul was a Roman citizen and that he had bound him.

³⁰But on the next day, desiring to know the real reason why he was being accused by the Jews, he unbound him and commanded the chief priests and all the council to meet, and he brought Paul down and set him before them.

Jeremiah 32

The word that came to Jeremiah from the LORD in the tenth year of Zedekiah king of Judah, which was the eighteenth year of Nebuchadnezzar. ²At that time the army of the king of Babylon was besieging Jerusalem, and Jeremiah the prophet was shut up in the court of the guard that was in the palace of the king of Judah. ³For Zedekiah king of Judah had imprisoned him, saying, "Why do you prophesy and say, 'Thus says the LORD: Behold, I am giving this city into the hand of the king of Babylon, and he shall capture it; ⁴Zedekiah king of Judah shall not escape out of the hand of the Chaldeans, but shall surely be given into the hand of the king of Babylon, and shall speak with him face to face and see him eye to eye. ⁵And he shall take Zedekiah to Babylon, and there he shall remain until I visit him, declares the LORD. Though you fight against the Chaldeans, you shall not succeed'?"

⁶Jeremiah said, "The word of the LORD came to me: ⁷Behold, Hanamel the son of Shallum your uncle will come to you and say, 'Buy my field that is at Anathoth, for the right of redemption by purchase is yours.' ⁸Then Hanamel my cousin came to me in the court of the guard, in accordance with the word of the LORD, and said to me, 'Buy my field that is at Anathoth in the land of Benjamin, for the right of possession and redemption is yours; buy it for yourself.' Then I knew that this was the word of the LORD.

⁹"And I bought the field at Anathoth from Hanamel my cousin, and weighed out the money to him, seventeen shekels of silver. ¹⁰I signed the deed, sealed it, got witnesses, and weighed the money on scales. ¹¹Then I took the sealed deed of purchase, containing the terms and conditions and the open copy. ¹²And I gave the deed of purchase to Baruch the son of Neriah son of Mahseiah, in the presence of Hanamel my cousin, in the presence of the witnesses who signed the deed of purchase, and in the presence of all the Judeans who were sitting in the court of the guard. ¹³I charged Baruch in their presence, saying, ¹⁴'Thus says the LORD of hosts, the God of Israel: Take these deeds, both this sealed deed of purchase and this open deed, and put them in an earthenware vessel, that they may last for a long time. ¹⁵For thus says the LORD of hosts, the God of Israel: Houses and fields and vineyards shall again be bought in this land.'

¹⁶"After I had given the deed of purchase to Baruch the son of Neriah, I prayed to the LORD, saying: ¹⁷'Ah, Lord GOD! It is you who have made the heavens and the earth by your great power and by your outstretched arm! Nothing is too hard for you. ¹⁸You show steadfast love to thousands, but you repay the guilt of fathers to their children after them, O great and mighty God, whose name is the LORD of hosts, ¹⁹great in counsel and mighty in deed, whose eyes are open to all the ways of the children of man, rewarding each one according to his ways and according to the fruit of his deeds. ²⁰You have shown signs and wonders in the land of Egypt, and to this day in Israel and among all mankind, and have made a name for yourself, as at this day. ²¹You brought your people Israel out of the land of Egypt with signs and wonders, with a strong hand and outstretched arm, and with great terror. ²²And you gave them this land, which you swore to their fathers to give them, a land flowing with milk and honey. ²³And they entered and took possession of it. But they did not obey your voice or walk in your law. They did nothing of all you commanded them to do. Therefore you have made all this disaster come upon them. ²⁴Behold, the siege mounds have come up to the city to take it, and because of sword and famine and pestilence the city is given into the hands of the Chaldeans who are fighting against it. What you spoke has come to pass, and behold, you see it. ²⁵Yet you, O Lord GOD, have said to me, "Buy the field for money

and get witnesses"—though the city is given into the hands of the Chaldeans.'"

²⁶The word of the LORD came to Jeremiah: ²⁷"Behold, I am the LORD, the God of all flesh. Is anything too hard for me? ²⁸Therefore, thus says the LORD: Behold, I am giving this city into the hands of the Chaldeans and into the hand of Nebuchadnezzar king of Babylon, and he shall capture it. ²⁹The Chaldeans who are fighting against this city shall come and set this city on fire and burn it, with the houses on whose roofs offerings have been made to Baal and drink offerings have been poured out to other gods, to provoke me to anger. ³⁰For the children of Israel and the children of Judah have done nothing but evil in my sight from their youth. The children of Israel have done nothing but provoke me to anger by the work of their hands, declares the LORD. ³¹This city has aroused my anger and wrath, from the day it was built to this day, so that I will remove it from my sight ³²because of all the evil of the children of Israel and the children of Judah that they did to provoke me to anger—their kings and their officials, their priests and their prophets, the men of Judah and the inhabitants of Jerusalem. ³³They have turned to me their back and not their face. And though I have taught them persistently, they have not listened to receive instruction. ³⁴They set up their abominations in the house that is called by my name, to defile it. ³⁵They built the high places of Baal in the Valley of the Son of Hinnom, to offer up their sons and daughters to Molech, though I did not command them, nor did it enter into my mind, that they should do this abomination, to cause Judah to sin.

³⁶"Now therefore thus says the LORD, the God of Israel, concerning this city of which you say, 'It is given into the hand of the king of Babylon by sword, by famine, and by pestilence': ³⁷Behold, I will gather them from all the countries to which I drove them in my anger and my wrath and in great indignation. I will bring them back to this place, and I will make them dwell in safety. ³⁸And they shall be my people, and I will be their God. ³⁹I will give them one heart and one way, that they may fear me forever, for their own good and the good of their children after them. ⁴⁰I will make with them an everlasting covenant, that I will not turn away from doing good to them. And I will put the fear of me in their hearts, that they may not turn from me. ⁴¹I will rejoice in doing them good, and I will plant them in this land in faithfulness, with all my heart and all my soul.

⁴²"For thus says the LORD: Just as I have brought all this great disaster upon this people, so I will bring upon them all the good that I promise them. ⁴³Fields shall be bought in this land of which you are saying, 'It is a desolation, without man or beast; it is given into the hand of the Chaldeans.' ⁴⁴Fields shall be bought for money, and deeds shall be signed and sealed and witnessed, in the land of Benjamin, in the places about Jerusalem, and in the cities of Judah, in the cities of the hill country, in the cities of the Shephelah, and in the cities of the Negeb; for I will restore their fortunes, declares the LORD."

Psalm 1–2

Blessed is the man[1]
  who walks not in the counsel of the
     wicked,
  nor stands in the way of sinners,
     nor sits in the seat of scoffers;
2 but his delight is in the law[2] of the LORD,
     and on his law he meditates day and
       night.

3 He is like a tree
     planted by streams of water
  that yields its fruit in its season,
     and its leaf does not wither.
  In all that he does, he prospers.
4 The wicked are not so,
     but are like chaff that the wind drives
       away.

5 Therefore the wicked will not stand in
       the judgment,
     nor sinners in the congregation of the
       righteous;
6 for the LORD knows the way of the
       righteous,
     but the way of the wicked will perish.

Why do the nations rage[3]
  and the peoples plot in vain?
2 The kings of the earth set themselves,
     and the rulers take counsel together,
  against the LORD and against his
     Anointed, saying,

[1] The singular Hebrew word for *man* (ish) is used here to portray a representative example of a godly person; see Preface [2] Or *instruction* [3] Or *nations noisily assemble*

³ "Let us burst their bonds apart
 and cast away their cords from us."
⁴ He who sits in the heavens laughs;
 the Lord holds them in derision.
⁵ Then he will speak to them in his wrath,
 and terrify them in his fury, saying,
⁶ "As for me, I have set my King
 on Zion, my holy hill."

⁷ I will tell of the decree:
 The Lord said to me, "You are my Son;
 today I have begotten you.
⁸ Ask of me, and I will make the nations
 your heritage,

 and the ends of the earth your
  possession.
⁹ You shall break¹ them with a rod of iron
 and dash them in pieces like a potter's
  vessel."

¹⁰ Now therefore, O kings, be wise;
 be warned, O rulers of the earth.
¹¹ Serve the Lord with fear,
 and rejoice with trembling.
¹² Kiss the Son,
 lest he be angry, and you perish in the
  way,
 for his wrath is quickly kindled.
 Blessed are all who take refuge in him.

AUGUST 5

Judges 19

In those days, when there was no king in Israel, a certain Levite was sojourning in the remote parts of the hill country of Ephraim, who took to himself a concubine from Bethlehem in Judah. ²And his concubine was unfaithful to² him, and she went away from him to her father's house at Bethlehem in Judah, and was there some four months. ³Then her husband arose and went after her, to speak kindly to her and bring her back. He had with him his servant and a couple of donkeys. And she brought him into her father's house. And when the girl's father saw him, he came with joy to meet him. ⁴And his father-in-law, the girl's father, made him stay, and he remained with him three days. So they ate and drank and spent the night there. ⁵And on the fourth day they arose early in the morning, and he prepared to go, but the girl's father said to his son-in-law, "Strengthen your heart with a morsel of bread, and after that you may go." ⁶So the two of them sat and ate and drank together. And the girl's father said to the man, "Be pleased to spend the night, and let your heart be merry." ⁷And when the man rose up to go, his father-in-law pressed him, till he spent the night there again. ⁸And on the fifth day he arose early in

the morning to depart. And the girl's father said, "Strengthen your heart and wait until the day declines." So they ate, both of them. ⁹And when the man and his concubine and his servant rose up to depart, his father-in-law, the girl's father, said to him, "Behold, now the day has waned toward evening. Please, spend the night. Behold, the day draws to its close. Lodge here and let your heart be merry, and tomorrow you shall arise early in the morning for your journey, and go home."

¹⁰But the man would not spend the night. He rose up and departed and arrived opposite Jebus (that is, Jerusalem). He had with him a couple of saddled donkeys, and his concubine was with him. ¹¹When they were near Jebus, the day was nearly over, and the servant said to his master, "Come now, let us turn aside to this city of the Jebusites and spend the night in it." ¹²And his master said to him, "We will not turn aside into the city of foreigners, who do not belong to the people of Israel, but we will pass on to Gibeah." ¹³And he said to his young man, "Come and let us draw near to one of these places and spend the night at Gibeah or at Ramah." ¹⁴So they passed on and went their way. And the sun went down on them

¹ Revocalization yields (compare Septuagint) *You shall rule* ² Septuagint, Old Latin *became angry with*

near Gibeah, which belongs to Benjamin, [15]and they turned aside there, to go in and spend the night at Gibeah. And he went in and sat down in the open square of the city, for no one took them into his house to spend the night.

[16]And behold, an old man was coming from his work in the field at evening. The man was from the hill country of Ephraim, and he was sojourning in Gibeah. The men of the place were Benjaminites. [17]And he lifted up his eyes and saw the traveler in the open square of the city. And the old man said, "Where are you going? And where do you come from?" [18]And he said to him, "We are passing from Bethlehem in Judah to the remote parts of the hill country of Ephraim, from which I come. I went to Bethlehem in Judah, and I am going to the house of the Lord,[1] but no one has taken me into his house. [19]We have straw and feed for our donkeys, with bread and wine for me and your female servant and the young man with your servants. There is no lack of anything." [20]And the old man said, "Peace be to you; I will care for all your wants. Only, do not spend the night in the square." [21]So he brought him into his house and gave the donkeys feed. And they washed their feet, and ate and drank.

[22]As they were making their hearts merry, behold, the men of the city, worthless fellows, surrounded the house, beating on the door. And they said to the old man, the master of the house, "Bring out the man who came into your house, that we may know him." [23]And the man, the master of the house, went out to them and said to them, "No, my brothers, do not act so wickedly; since this man has come into my house, do not do this vile thing. [24]Behold, here are my virgin daughter and his concubine. Let me bring them out now. Violate them and do with them what seems good to you, but against this man do not do this outrageous thing." [25]But the men would not listen to him. So the man seized his concubine and made her go out to them. And they knew her and abused her all night until the morning. And as the dawn began to break, they let her go. [26]And as morning appeared, the woman came and fell down at the door of the man's house where her master was, until it was light.

[27]And her master rose up in the morning, and when he opened the doors of the house

and went out to go on his way, behold, there was his concubine lying at the door of the house, with her hands on the threshold. [28]He said to her, "Get up, let us be going." But there was no answer. Then he put her on the donkey, and the man rose up and went away to his home. [29]And when he entered his house, he took a knife, and taking hold of his concubine he divided her, limb by limb, into twelve pieces, and sent her throughout all the territory of Israel. [30]And all who saw it said, "Such a thing has never happened or been seen from the day that the people of Israel came up out of the land of Egypt until this day; consider it, take counsel, and speak."

Acts 23

And looking intently at the council, Paul said, "Brothers, I have lived my life before God in all good conscience up to this day." [2]And the high priest Ananias commanded those who stood by him to strike him on the mouth. [3]Then Paul said to him, "God is going to strike you, you whitewashed wall! Are you sitting to judge me according to the law, and yet contrary to the law you order me to be struck?" [4]Those who stood by said, "Would you revile God's high priest?" [5]And Paul said, "I did not know, brothers, that he was the high priest, for it is written, 'You shall not speak evil of a ruler of your people.'"

[6]Now when Paul perceived that one part were Sadducees and the other Pharisees, he cried out in the council, "Brothers, I am a Pharisee, a son of Pharisees. It is with respect to the hope and the resurrection of the dead that I am on trial." [7]And when he had said this, a dissension arose between the Pharisees and the Sadducees, and the assembly was divided. [8]For the Sadducees say that there is no resurrection, nor angel, nor spirit, but the Pharisees acknowledge them all. [9]Then a great clamor arose, and some of the scribes of the Pharisees' party stood up and contended sharply, "We find nothing wrong in this man. What if a spirit or an angel spoke to him?" [10]And when the dissension became violent, the tribune, afraid that Paul would be torn to pieces by them, commanded the soldiers to go down and take him away from among them by force and bring him into the barracks.

[1] Septuagint *my home*; compare verse 29

¹¹The following night the Lord stood by him and said, "Take courage, for as you have testified to the facts about me in Jerusalem, so you must testify also in Rome."

¹²When it was day, the Jews made a plot and bound themselves by an oath neither to eat nor drink till they had killed Paul. ¹³There were more than forty who made this conspiracy. ¹⁴They went to the chief priests and elders and said, "We have strictly bound ourselves by an oath to taste no food till we have killed Paul. ¹⁵Now therefore you, along with the council, give notice to the tribune to bring him down to you, as though you were going to determine his case more exactly. And we are ready to kill him before he comes near."

¹⁶Now the son of Paul's sister heard of their ambush, so he went and entered the barracks and told Paul. ¹⁷Paul called one of the centurions and said, "Take this young man to the tribune, for he has something to tell him." ¹⁸So he took him and brought him to the tribune and said, "Paul the prisoner called me and asked me to bring this young man to you, as he has something to say to you." ¹⁹The tribune took him by the hand, and going aside asked him privately, "What is it that you have to tell me?" ²⁰And he said, "The Jews have agreed to ask you to bring Paul down to the council tomorrow, as though they were going to inquire somewhat more closely about him. ²¹But do not be persuaded by them, for more than forty of their men are lying in ambush for him, who have bound themselves by an oath neither to eat nor drink till they have killed him. And now they are ready, waiting for your consent." ²²So the tribune dismissed the young man, charging him, "Tell no one that you have informed me of these things."

²³Then he called two of the centurions and said, "Get ready two hundred soldiers, with seventy horsemen and two hundred spearmen to go as far as Caesarea at the third hour of the night.¹ ²⁴Also provide mounts for Paul to ride and bring him safely to Felix the governor." ²⁵And he wrote a letter to this effect:

²⁶"Claudius Lysias, to his Excellency the governor Felix, greetings. ²⁷This man was seized by the Jews and was about to be killed by them when I came upon them with the soldiers and rescued him, having learned that he was a Roman citizen. ²⁸And desiring to know the charge for which they were accusing him, I brought him down to their council. ²⁹I found that he was being accused about questions of their law, but charged with nothing deserving death or imprisonment. ³⁰And when it was disclosed to me that there would be a plot against the man, I sent him to you at once, ordering his accusers also to state before you what they have against him."

³¹So the soldiers, according to their instructions, took Paul and brought him by night to Antipatris. ³²And on the next day they returned to the barracks, letting the horsemen go on with him. ³³When they had come to Caesarea and delivered the letter to the governor, they presented Paul also before him. ³⁴On reading the letter, he asked what province he was from. And when he learned that he was from Cilicia, ³⁵he said, "I will give you a hearing when your accusers arrive." And he commanded him to be guarded in Herod's praetorium.

Jeremiah 33

The word of the LORD came to Jeremiah a second time, while he was still shut up in the court of the guard: ²"Thus says the LORD who made the earth,² the LORD who formed it to establish it—the LORD is his name: ³Call to me and I will answer you, and will tell you great and hidden things that you have not known. ⁴For thus says the LORD, the God of Israel, concerning the houses of this city and the houses of the kings of Judah that were torn down to make a defense against the siege mounds and against the sword: ⁵They are coming in to fight against the Chaldeans and to fill them³ with the dead bodies of men whom I shall strike down in my anger and my wrath, for I have hidden my face from this city because of all their evil. ⁶Behold, I will bring to it health and healing, and I will heal them and reveal to them abundance of prosperity and security. ⁷I will restore the fortunes of Judah and the fortunes of Israel, and rebuild them as they were at first. ⁸I will cleanse them from all the guilt of their sin against me, and I will forgive all the guilt of their sin and rebellion against me. ⁹And this city⁴ shall be to me a name of joy, a praise and a glory before all the nations of the earth who shall hear of all the

¹ That is, 9 P.M. ² Septuagint; Hebrew *it* ³ That is, the torn-down houses ⁴ Hebrew *And it*

good that I do for them. They shall fear and tremble because of all the good and all the prosperity I provide for it.

¹⁰"Thus says the LORD: In this place of which you say, 'It is a waste without man or beast,' in the cities of Judah and the streets of Jerusalem that are desolate, without man or inhabitant or beast, there shall be heard again ¹¹the voice of mirth and the voice of gladness, the voice of the bridegroom and the voice of the bride, the voices of those who sing, as they bring thank offerings to the house of the LORD:

"'Give thanks to the LORD of hosts,
    for the LORD is good,
    for his steadfast love endures
        forever!'

For I will restore the fortunes of the land as at first, says the LORD.

¹²"Thus says the LORD of hosts: In this place that is waste, without man or beast, and in all of its cities, there shall again be habitations of shepherds resting their flocks. ¹³In the cities of the hill country, in the cities of the Shephelah, and in the cities of the Negeb, in the land of Benjamin, the places about Jerusalem, and in the cities of Judah, flocks shall again pass under the hands of the one who counts them, says the LORD.

¹⁴"Behold, the days are coming, declares the LORD, when I will fulfill the promise I made to the house of Israel and the house of Judah. ¹⁵In those days and at that time I will cause a righteous Branch to spring up for David, and he shall execute justice and righteousness in the land. ¹⁶In those days Judah will be saved, and Jerusalem will dwell securely. And this is the name by which it will be called: 'The LORD is our righteousness.'

¹⁷"For thus says the LORD: David shall never lack a man to sit on the throne of the house of Israel, ¹⁸and the Levitical priests shall never lack a man in my presence to offer burnt offerings, to burn grain offerings, and to make sacrifices forever."

¹⁹The word of the LORD came to Jeremiah: ²⁰"Thus says the LORD: If you can break my covenant with the day and my covenant with the night, so that day and night will not come at their appointed time, ²¹then also my covenant with David my servant may be broken, so that he shall not have a son to reign on his throne,

and my covenant with the Levitical priests my ministers. ²²As the host of heaven cannot be numbered and the sands of the sea cannot be measured, so I will multiply the offspring of David my servant, and the Levitical priests who minister to me."

²³The word of the LORD came to Jeremiah: ²⁴"Have you not observed that these people are saying, 'The LORD has rejected the two clans that he chose'? Thus they have despised my people so that they are no longer a nation in their sight. ²⁵Thus says the LORD: If I have not established my covenant with day and night and the fixed order of heaven and earth, ²⁶then I will reject the offspring of Jacob and David my servant and will not choose one of his offspring to rule over the offspring of Abraham, Isaac, and Jacob. For I will restore their fortunes and will have mercy on them."

--- Psalm 3–4 ---

A PSALM OF DAVID, WHEN HE FLED FROM ABSALOM HIS SON.

O LORD, how many are my foes!
    Many are rising against me;
² many are saying of my soul,
        there is no salvation for him in God.
                                    Selah[1]

³ But you, O LORD, are a shield about
        me,
    my glory, and the lifter of my head.
⁴ I cried aloud to the LORD,
    and he answered me from his holy
        hill.   *Selah*

⁵ I lay down and slept;
    I woke again, for the LORD sustained
        me.
⁶ I will not be afraid of many thousands of
        people
    who have set themselves against me
        all around.

⁷ Arise, O LORD!
    Save me, O my God!
For you strike all my enemies on the
        cheek;
    you break the teeth of the wicked.

⁸ Salvation belongs to the LORD;
    your blessing be on your people!
                                    Selah

[1] The meaning of the Hebrew word *Selah*, used frequently in the Psalms, is uncertain. It may be a musical or liturgical direction

To the choirmaster: with stringed instruments. A Psalm of David.

Answer me when I call, O God of my righteousness!
  You have given me relief when I was
    in distress.
  Be gracious to me and hear my
    prayer!

2 O men,[1] how long shall my honor be
    turned into shame?
  How long will you love vain words and
    seek after lies?   *Selah*

3 But know that the LORD has set apart
    the godly for himself;
  the LORD hears when I call to him.

4 Be angry,[2] and do not sin;
  ponder in your own hearts on your
    beds, and be silent.   *Selah*
5 Offer right sacrifices,
  and put your trust in the LORD.

6 There are many who say, "Who will
    show us some good?
  Lift up the light of your face upon us,
    O LORD!"
7 You have put more joy in my heart
  than they have when their grain and
    wine abound.

8 In peace I will both lie down and sleep;
  for you alone, O LORD, make me dwell
    in safety.

AUGUST 6

Judges 20

Then all the people of Israel came out, from Dan to Beersheba, including the land of Gilead, and the congregation assembled as one man to the LORD at Mizpah. ²And the chiefs of all the people, of all the tribes of Israel, presented themselves in the assembly of the people of God, 400,000 men on foot that drew the sword. ³(Now the people of Benjamin heard that the people of Israel had gone up to Mizpah.) And the people of Israel said, "Tell us, how did this evil happen?" ⁴And the Levite, the husband of the woman who was murdered, answered and said, "I came to Gibeah that belongs to Benjamin, I and my concubine, to spend the night. ⁵And the leaders of Gibeah rose against me and surrounded the house against me by night. They meant to kill me, and they violated my concubine, and she is dead. ⁶So I took hold of my concubine and cut her in pieces and sent her throughout all the country of the inheritance of Israel, for they have committed abomination and outrage in Israel. ⁷Behold, you people of Israel, all of you, give your advice and counsel here."

⁸And all the people arose as one man, saying, "None of us will go to his tent, and none of us will return to his house. ⁹But now this is what we will do to Gibeah: we will go up against it by lot, ¹⁰and we will take ten men of a hundred throughout all the tribes of Israel, and a hundred of a thousand, and a thousand of ten thousand, to bring provisions for the people, that when they come they may repay Gibeah of Benjamin, for all the outrage that they have committed in Israel." ¹¹So all the men of Israel gathered against the city, united as one man.

¹²And the tribes of Israel sent men through all the tribe of Benjamin, saying, "What evil is this that has taken place among you? ¹³Now therefore give up the men, the worthless fellows in Gibeah, that we may put them to death and purge evil from Israel." But the Benjaminites would not listen to the voice of their brothers, the people of Israel. ¹⁴Then the people of Benjamin came together out of the cities to Gibeah to go out to battle against the people of Israel. ¹⁵And the people of Benjamin mustered out of their cities on that day 26,000 men who drew the sword, besides the inhabitants of Gibeah, who mustered 700

[1] Or *O men of rank* [2] Or *Be agitated*

chosen men. ¹⁶Among all these were 700 chosen men who were left-handed; every one could sling a stone at a hair and not miss. ¹⁷And the men of Israel, apart from Benjamin, mustered 400,000 men who drew the sword; all these were men of war.

¹⁸The people of Israel arose and went up to Bethel and inquired of God, "Who shall go up first for us to fight against the people of Benjamin?" And the LORD said, "Judah shall go up first."

¹⁹Then the people of Israel rose in the morning and encamped against Gibeah. ²⁰And the men of Israel went out to fight against Benjamin, and the men of Israel drew up the battle line against them at Gibeah. ²¹The people of Benjamin came out of Gibeah and destroyed on that day 22,000 men of the Israelites. ²²But the people, the men of Israel, took courage, and again formed the battle line in the same place where they had formed it on the first day. ²³And the people of Israel went up and wept before the LORD until the evening. And they inquired of the LORD, "Shall we again draw near to fight against our brothers, the people of Benjamin?" And the LORD said, "Go up against them."

²⁴So the people of Israel came near against the people of Benjamin the second day. ²⁵And Benjamin went against them out of Gibeah the second day, and destroyed 18,000 men of the people of Israel. All these were men who drew the sword. ²⁶Then all the people of Israel, the whole army, went up and came to Bethel and wept. They sat there before the LORD and fasted that day until evening, and offered burnt offerings and peace offerings before the LORD. ²⁷And the people of Israel inquired of the LORD (for the ark of the covenant of God was there in those days, ²⁸and Phinehas the son of Eleazar, son of Aaron, ministered before it in those days), saying, "Shall we go out once more to battle against our brothers, the people of Benjamin, or shall we cease?" And the LORD said, "Go up, for tomorrow I will give them into your hand."

²⁹So Israel set men in ambush around Gibeah. ³⁰And the people of Israel went up against the people of Benjamin on the third day and set themselves in array against Gibeah, as at other times. ³¹And the people of Benjamin went out against the people and were drawn away from the city. And as at other times they began to strike and kill some of the people in the highways, one of which goes up to Bethel and the other to Gibeah, and in the open country, about thirty men of Israel. ³²And the people of Benjamin said, "They are routed before us, as at the first." But the people of Israel said, "Let us flee and draw them away from the city to the highways." ³³And all the men of Israel rose up out of their place and set themselves in array at Baal-tamar, and the men of Israel who were in ambush rushed out of their place from Maareh-geba.¹ ³⁴And there came against Gibeah 10,000 chosen men out of all Israel, and the battle was hard, but the Benjaminites did not know that disaster was close upon them. ³⁵And the LORD defeated Benjamin before Israel, and the people of Israel destroyed 25,100 men of Benjamin that day. All these were men who drew the sword. ³⁶So the people of Benjamin saw that they were defeated.

The men of Israel gave ground to Benjamin, because they trusted the men in ambush whom they had set against Gibeah. ³⁷Then the men in ambush hurried and rushed against Gibeah; the men in ambush moved out and struck all the city with the edge of the sword. ³⁸Now the appointed signal between the men of Israel and the men in the main ambush was that when they made a great cloud of smoke rise up out of the city ³⁹the men of Israel should turn in battle. Now Benjamin had begun to strike and kill about thirty men of Israel. They said, "Surely they are defeated before us, as in the first battle." ⁴⁰But when the signal began to rise out of the city in a column of smoke, the Benjaminites looked behind them, and behold, the whole of the city went up in smoke to heaven. ⁴¹Then the men of Israel turned, and the men of Benjamin were dismayed, for they saw that disaster was close upon them. ⁴²Therefore they turned their backs before the men of Israel in the direction of the wilderness, but the battle overtook them. And those who came out of the cities were destroying them in their midst. ⁴³Surrounding the Benjaminites, they pursued them and trod them down from Nohah² as far as opposite Gibeah on the east. ⁴⁴Eighteen thousand men of Benjamin fell, all of them men of valor. ⁴⁵And they turned and fled toward the wilderness to the rock of Rimmon. Five thousand men of them were cut down in the highways. And they were pursued hard to Gidom, and 2,000

¹ Some Septuagint manuscripts *place west of Geba* ² Septuagint; Hebrew [at their] *resting place*

men of them were struck down. [46]So all who fell that day of Benjamin were 25,000 men who drew the sword, all of them men of valor. [47]But 600 men turned and fled toward the wilderness to the rock of Rimmon and remained at the rock of Rimmon four months. [48]And the men of Israel turned back against the people of Benjamin and struck them with the edge of the sword, the city, men and beasts and all that they found. And all the towns that they found they set on fire.

Acts 24

And after five days the high priest Ananias came down with some elders and a spokesman, one Tertullus. They laid before the governor their case against Paul. [2]And when he had been summoned, Tertullus began to accuse him, saying:

"Since through you we enjoy much peace, and since by your foresight, most excellent Felix, reforms are being made for this nation, [3]in every way and everywhere we accept this with all gratitude. [4]But, to detain[1] you no further, I beg you in your kindness to hear us briefly. [5]For we have found this man a plague, one who stirs up riots among all the Jews throughout the world and is a ringleader of the sect of the Nazarenes. [6]He even tried to profane the temple, but we seized him.[2] [8]By examining him yourself you will be able to find out from him about everything of which we accuse him."

[9]The Jews also joined in the charge, affirming that all these things were so.

[10]And when the governor had nodded to him to speak, Paul replied:

"Knowing that for many years you have been a judge over this nation, I cheerfully make my defense. [11]You can verify that it is not more than twelve days since I went up to worship in Jerusalem, [12]and they did not find me disputing with anyone or stirring up a crowd, either in the temple or in the synagogues or in the city. [13]Neither can they prove to you what they now bring up against me. [14]But this I confess to you, that according to the Way, which they call a sect, I worship the God of our fathers, believing everything laid down by the Law and written in the Prophets, [15]having a hope in God, which these men themselves accept, that there will be a resurrection of both the just and the unjust.

[16]So I always take pains to have a clear conscience toward both God and man. [17]Now after several years I came to bring alms to my nation and to present offerings. [18]While I was doing this, they found me purified in the temple, without any crowd or tumult. But some Jews from Asia— [19]they ought to be here before you and to make an accusation, should they have anything against me. [20]Or else let these men themselves say what wrongdoing they found when I stood before the council, [21]other than this one thing that I cried out while standing among them: 'It is with respect to the resurrection of the dead that I am on trial before you this day.'"

[22]But Felix, having a rather accurate knowledge of the Way, put them off, saying, "When Lysias the tribune comes down, I will decide your case." [23]Then he gave orders to the centurion that he should be kept in custody but have some liberty, and that none of his friends should be prevented from attending to his needs.

[24]After some days Felix came with his wife Drusilla, who was Jewish, and he sent for Paul and heard him speak about faith in Christ Jesus. [25]And as he reasoned about righteousness and self-control and the coming judgment, Felix was alarmed and said, "Go away for the present. When I get an opportunity I will summon you." [26]At the same time he hoped that money would be given him by Paul. So he sent for him often and conversed with him. [27]When two years had elapsed, Felix was succeeded by Porcius Festus. And desiring to do the Jews a favor, Felix left Paul in prison.

Jeremiah 34

The word that came to Jeremiah from the LORD, when Nebuchadnezzar king of Babylon and all his army and all the kingdoms of the earth under his dominion and all the peoples were fighting against Jerusalem and all of its cities: [2]"Thus says the LORD, the God of Israel: Go and speak to Zedekiah king of Judah and say to him, 'Thus says the LORD: Behold, I am giving this city into the hand of the king of Babylon, and he shall burn it with fire. [3]You shall not escape from his hand but shall surely be captured and delivered into his hand. You shall see the king of Babylon eye to eye and speak with him face to face. And you shall go

---

[1] Or *weary* [2] Some manuscripts add *and we would have judged him according to our law.* [7]But the chief captain Lysias came and with great violence took him out of our hands, [8]commanding his accusers to come before you.

to Babylon.' **4**Yet hear the word of the Lord, O Zedekiah king of Judah! Thus says the Lord concerning you: 'You shall not die by the sword. **5**You shall die in peace. And as spices were burned for your fathers, the former kings who were before you, so people shall burn spices for you and lament for you, saying, "Alas, lord!"' For I have spoken the word, declares the Lord."

6Then Jeremiah the prophet spoke all these words to Zedekiah king of Judah, in Jerusalem, **7**when the army of the king of Babylon was fighting against Jerusalem and against all the cities of Judah that were left, Lachish and Azekah, for these were the only fortified cities of Judah that remained.

8The word that came to Jeremiah from the Lord, after King Zedekiah had made a covenant with all the people in Jerusalem to make a proclamation of liberty to them, **9**that everyone should set free his Hebrew slaves, male and female, so that no one should enslave a Jew, his brother. **10**And they obeyed, all the officials and all the people who had entered into the covenant that everyone would set free his slave, male or female, so that they would not be enslaved again. They obeyed and set them free. **11**But afterward they turned around and took back the male and female slaves they had set free, and brought them into subjection as slaves. **12**The word of the Lord came to Jeremiah from the Lord: **13**"Thus says the Lord, the God of Israel: I myself made a covenant with your fathers when I brought them out of the land of Egypt, out of the house of slavery, saying, **14**'At the end of seven years each of you must set free the fellow Hebrew who has been sold to you and has served you six years; you must set him free from your service.' But your fathers did not listen to me or incline their ears to me. **15**You recently repented and did what was right in my eyes by proclaiming liberty, each to his neighbor, and you made a covenant before me in the house that is called by my name, **16**but then you turned around and profaned my name when each of you took back his male and female slaves, whom you had set free according to their desire, and you brought them into subjection to be your slaves.

17"Therefore, thus says the Lord: You have not obeyed me by proclaiming liberty, every one to his brother and to his neighbor; behold, I proclaim to you liberty to the sword, to pestilence, and to famine, declares the Lord. I will make you a horror to all the kingdoms of the earth. **18**And the men who transgressed my covenant and did not keep the terms of the covenant that they made before me, I will make them like[1] the calf that they cut in two and passed between its parts— **19**the officials of Judah, the officials of Jerusalem, the eunuchs, the priests, and all the people of the land who passed between the parts of the calf. **20**And I will give them into the hand of their enemies and into the hand of those who seek their lives. Their dead bodies shall be food for the birds of the air and the beasts of the earth. **21**And Zedekiah king of Judah and his officials I will give into the hand of their enemies and into the hand of those who seek their lives, into the hand of the army of the king of Babylon which has withdrawn from you. **22**Behold, I will command, declares the Lord, and will bring them back to this city. And they will fight against it and take it and burn it with fire. I will make the cities of Judah a desolation without inhabitant."

Psalm 5–6

To the choirmaster: for the flutes. A Psalm of David.

G ive ear to my words, O Lord;
consider my groaning.
2　Give attention to the sound of my cry,
　　my King and my God,
　　for to you do I pray.
3　O Lord, in the morning you hear my
　　　voice;
　　in the morning I prepare a sacrifice for
　　　you[2] and watch.

4　For you are not a God who delights in
　　　wickedness;
　　evil may not dwell with you.
5　The boastful shall not stand before your
　　　eyes;
　　you hate all evildoers.
6　You destroy those who speak lies;
　　the Lord abhors the bloodthirsty and
　　　deceitful man.

7　But I, through the abundance of your
　　　steadfast love,
　　will enter your house.
　　I will bow down toward your holy temple
　　in the fear of you.

---

[1] Hebrew lacks *them like* [2] Or *I direct my prayer to you*

8   Lead me, O LORD, in your righteousness
     because of my enemies;
     make your way straight before me.
9   For there is no truth in their mouth;
     their inmost self is destruction;
   their throat is an open grave;
     they flatter with their tongue.
10   Make them bear their guilt, O God;
     let them fall by their own counsels;
   because of the abundance of their
     transgressions cast them out,
   for they have rebelled against you.

11   But let all who take refuge in you rejoice;
     let them ever sing for joy,
   and spread your protection over them,
     that those who love your name may
     exult in you.
12   For you bless the righteous, O LORD;
     you cover him with favor as with a
     shield.

TO THE CHOIRMASTER: WITH STRINGED
INSTRUMENTS; ACCORDING TO THE SHEMINITH.[1]
A PSALM OF DAVID.

O LORD, rebuke me not in your anger,
   nor discipline me in your wrath.

2   Be gracious to me, O LORD, for I am
     languishing;
   heal me, O LORD, for my bones are
     troubled.
3   My soul also is greatly troubled.
     But you, O LORD—how long?
4   Turn, O LORD, deliver my life;
     save me for the sake of your steadfast
     love.
5   For in death there is no remembrance of
     you;
   in Sheol who will give you praise?
6   I am weary with my moaning;
     every night I flood my bed with tears;
   I drench my couch with my weeping.
7   My eye wastes away because of grief;
     it grows weak because of all my foes.

8   Depart from me, all you workers of evil,
     for the LORD has heard the sound of
     my weeping.
9   The LORD has heard my plea;
     the LORD accepts my prayer.
10   All my enemies shall be ashamed and
     greatly troubled;
   they shall turn back and be put to
     shame in a moment.

[1] Probably a musical or liturgical term

AUGUST 7

Judges 21

Now the men of Israel had sworn at Mizpah, "No one of us shall give his daughter in marriage to Benjamin." [2] And the people came to Bethel and sat there till evening before God, and they lifted up their voices and wept bitterly. [3] And they said, "O LORD, the God of Israel, why has this happened in Israel, that today there should be one tribe lacking in Israel?" [4] And the next day the people rose early and built there an altar and offered burnt offerings and peace offerings. [5] And the people of Israel said, "Which of all the tribes of Israel did not come up in the assembly to the LORD?" For they had taken a great oath concerning him who did not come up to the LORD to Mizpah, saying, "He shall surely be put to death." [6] And the people of Israel had compassion for Benjamin their brother and said, "One tribe is cut off from Israel this day. [7] What shall we do for wives for those who are left, since we have sworn by the LORD that we will not give them any of our daughters for wives?"

[8] And they said, "What one is there of the tribes of Israel that did not come up to the LORD to Mizpah?" And behold, no one had come to the camp from Jabesh-gilead, to the assembly. [9] For when the people were mustered, behold, not one of the inhabitants of

Jabesh-gilead was there. [10]So the congregation sent 12,000 of their bravest men there and commanded them, "Go and strike the inhabitants of Jabesh-gilead with the edge of the sword; also the women and the little ones. [11]This is what you shall do: every male and every woman that has lain with a male you shall devote to destruction." [12]And they found among the inhabitants of Jabesh-gilead 400 young virgins who had not known a man by lying with him, and they brought them to the camp at Shiloh, which is in the land of Canaan.

[13]Then the whole congregation sent word to the people of Benjamin who were at the rock of Rimmon and proclaimed peace to them. [14]And Benjamin returned at that time. And they gave them the women whom they had saved alive of the women of Jabesh-gilead, but they were not enough for them. [15]And the people had compassion on Benjamin because the LORD had made a breach in the tribes of Israel.

[16]Then the elders of the congregation said, "What shall we do for wives for those who are left, since the women are destroyed out of Benjamin?" [17]And they said, "There must be an inheritance for the survivors of Benjamin, that a tribe not be blotted out from Israel. [18]Yet we cannot give them wives from our daughters." For the people of Israel had sworn, "Cursed be he who gives a wife to Benjamin." [19]So they said, "Behold, there is the yearly feast of the LORD at Shiloh, which is north of Bethel, on the east of the highway that goes up from Bethel to Shechem, and south of Lebonah." [20]And they commanded the people of Benjamin, saying, "Go and lie in ambush in the vineyards [21]and watch. If the daughters of Shiloh come out to dance in the dances, then come out of the vineyards and snatch each man his wife from the daughters of Shiloh, and go to the land of Benjamin. [22]And when their fathers or their brothers come to complain to us, we will say to them, 'Grant them graciously to us, because we did not take for each man of them his wife in battle, neither did you give them to them, else you would now be guilty.'" [23]And the people of Benjamin did so and took their wives, according to their number, from the dancers whom they carried off. Then they went and returned to their inheritance and rebuilt the towns and lived in them. [24]And the people of Israel departed from there at that time, every man to his tribe and family, and they went out from there every man to his inheritance.

[25]In those days there was no king in Israel. Everyone did what was right in his own eyes.

Acts 25

Now three days after Festus had arrived in the province, he went up to Jerusalem from Caesarea. [2]And the chief priests and the principal men of the Jews laid out their case against Paul, and they urged him, [3]asking as a favor against Paul[1] that he summon him to Jerusalem—because they were planning an ambush to kill him on the way. [4]Festus replied that Paul was being kept at Caesarea and that he himself intended to go there shortly. [5]"So," said he, "let the men of authority among you go down with me, and if there is anything wrong about the man, let them bring charges against him."

[6]After he stayed among them not more than eight or ten days, he went down to Caesarea. And the next day he took his seat on the tribunal and ordered Paul to be brought. [7]When he had arrived, the Jews who had come down from Jerusalem stood around him, bringing many and serious charges against him that they could not prove. [8]Paul argued in his defense, "Neither against the law of the Jews, nor against the temple, nor against Caesar have I committed any offense." [9]But Festus, wishing to do the Jews a favor, said to Paul, "Do you wish to go up to Jerusalem and there be tried on these charges before me?" [10]But Paul said, "I am standing before Caesar's tribunal, where I ought to be tried. To the Jews I have done no wrong, as you yourself know very well. [11]If then I am a wrongdoer and have committed anything for which I deserve to die, I do not seek to escape death. But if there is nothing to their charges against me, no one can give me up to them. I appeal to Caesar." [12]Then Festus, when he had conferred with his council, answered, "To Caesar you have appealed; to Caesar you shall go."

[13]Now when some days had passed, Agrippa the king and Bernice arrived at Caesarea and greeted Festus. [14]And as they stayed there many days, Festus laid Paul's case before the king, saying, "There is a man left prisoner by Felix, [15]and when I was at Jerusalem, the chief priests and the elders of the Jews laid out their

[1] Greek him

case against him, asking for a sentence of condemnation against him. ¹⁶I answered them that it was not the custom of the Romans to give up anyone before the accused met the accusers face to face and had opportunity to make his defense concerning the charge laid against him. ¹⁷So when they came together here, I made no delay, but on the next day took my seat on the tribunal and ordered the man to be brought. ¹⁸When the accusers stood up, they brought no charge in his case of such evils as I supposed. ¹⁹Rather they had certain points of dispute with him about their own religion and about a certain Jesus, who was dead, but whom Paul asserted to be alive. ²⁰Being at a loss how to investigate these questions, I asked whether he wanted to go to Jerusalem and be tried there regarding them. ²¹But when Paul had appealed to be kept in custody for the decision of the emperor, I ordered him to be held until I could send him to Caesar." ²²Then Agrippa said to Festus, "I would like to hear the man myself." "Tomorrow," said he, "you will hear him."

²³So on the next day Agrippa and Bernice came with great pomp, and they entered the audience hall with the military tribunes and the prominent men of the city. Then, at the command of Festus, Paul was brought in. ²⁴And Festus said, "King Agrippa and all who are present with us, you see this man about whom the whole Jewish people petitioned me, both in Jerusalem and here, shouting that he ought not to live any longer. ²⁵But I found that he had done nothing deserving death. And as he himself appealed to the emperor, I decided to go ahead and send him. ²⁶But I have nothing definite to write to my lord about him. Therefore I have brought him before you all, and especially before you, King Agrippa, so that, after we have examined him, I may have something to write. ²⁷For it seems to me unreasonable, in sending a prisoner, not to indicate the charges against him."

Jeremiah 35

The word that came to Jeremiah from the LORD in the days of Jehoiakim the son of Josiah, king of Judah: ²"Go to the house of the Rechabites and speak with them and bring them to the house of the LORD, into one of the chambers; then offer them wine to drink."

³So I took Jaazaniah the son of Jeremiah, son of Habazziniah and his brothers and all his sons and the whole house of the Rechabites. ⁴I brought them to the house of the LORD into the chamber of the sons of Hanan the son of Igdaliah, the man of God, which was near the chamber of the officials, above the chamber of Maaseiah the son of Shallum, keeper of the threshold. ⁵Then I set before the Rechabites pitchers full of wine, and cups, and I said to them, "Drink wine." ⁶But they answered, "We will drink no wine, for Jonadab the son of Rechab, our father, commanded us, 'You shall not drink wine, neither you nor your sons forever. ⁷You shall not build a house; you shall not sow seed; you shall not plant or have a vineyard; but you shall live in tents all your days, that you may live many days in the land where you sojourn.' ⁸We have obeyed the voice of Jonadab the son of Rechab, our father, in all that he commanded us, to drink no wine all our days, ourselves, our wives, our sons, or our daughters, ⁹and not to build houses to dwell in. We have no vineyard or field or seed, ¹⁰but we have lived in tents and have obeyed and done all that Jonadab our father commanded us. ¹¹But when Nebuchadnezzar king of Babylon came up against the land, we said, 'Come, and let us go to Jerusalem for fear of the army of the Chaldeans and the army of the Syrians.' So we are living in Jerusalem."

¹²Then the word of the LORD came to Jeremiah: ¹³"Thus says the LORD of hosts, the God of Israel: Go and say to the people of Judah and the inhabitants of Jerusalem, Will you not receive instruction and listen to my words? declares the LORD. ¹⁴The command that Jonadab the son of Rechab gave to his sons, to drink no wine, has been kept, and they drink none to this day, for they have obeyed their father's command. I have spoken to you persistently, but you have not listened to me. ¹⁵I have sent to you all my servants the prophets, sending them persistently, saying, 'Turn now every one of you from his evil way, and amend your deeds, and do not go after other gods to serve them, and then you shall dwell in the land that I gave to you and your fathers.' But you did not incline your ear or listen to me. ¹⁶The sons of Jonadab the son of Rechab have kept the command that their father gave them, but this people has not obeyed me. ¹⁷Therefore,

thus says the LORD, the God of hosts, the God of Israel: Behold, I am bringing upon Judah and all the inhabitants of Jerusalem all the disaster that I have pronounced against them, because I have spoken to them and they have not listened, I have called to them and they have not answered."

[18]But to the house of the Rechabites Jeremiah said, "Thus says the LORD of hosts, the God of Israel: Because you have obeyed the command of Jonadab your father and kept all his precepts and done all that he commanded you, [19]therefore thus says the LORD of hosts, the God of Israel: Jonadab the son of Rechab shall never lack a man to stand before me."

Psalm 7–8

A SHIGGAION[1] OF DAVID, WHICH HE SANG TO THE LORD CONCERNING THE WORDS OF CUSH, A BENJAMINITE.

O LORD my God, in you do I take refuge;
    save me from all my pursuers and
        deliver me,
[2] lest like a lion they tear my soul apart,
    rending it in pieces, with none to
        deliver.

[3] O LORD my God, if I have done this,
    if there is wrong in my hands,
[4] if I have repaid my friend[2] with evil
    or plundered my enemy without
        cause,
[5] let the enemy pursue my soul and
        overtake it,
    and let him trample my life to the
        ground
    and lay my glory in the dust. *Selah*

[6] Arise, O LORD, in your anger;
    lift yourself up against the fury of my
        enemies;
    awake for me; you have appointed a
        judgment.
[7] Let the assembly of the peoples be
        gathered about you;
    over it return on high.
[8] The LORD judges the peoples;
    judge me, O LORD, according to my
        righteousness
    and according to the integrity that is
        in me.

[9] Oh, let the evil of the wicked come to an
        end,
    and may you establish the righteous—
    you who test the minds and hearts,[3]
        O righteous God!
[10] My shield is with God,
    who saves the upright in heart.
[11] God is a righteous judge,
    and a God who feels indignation every
        day.

[12] If a man[4] does not repent, God[5] will
        whet his sword;
    he has bent and readied his bow;
[13] he has prepared for him his deadly
        weapons,
    making his arrows fiery shafts.
[14] Behold, the wicked man conceives evil
    and is pregnant with mischief
    and gives birth to lies.
[15] He makes a pit, digging it out,
    and falls into the hole that he has
        made.
[16] His mischief returns upon his own
        head,
    and on his own skull his violence
        descends.

[17] I will give to the LORD the thanks due to
        his righteousness,
    and I will sing praise to the name of
        the LORD, the Most High.

TO THE CHOIRMASTER: ACCORDING TO THE GITTITH.[6] A PSALM OF DAVID.

O LORD, our Lord,
    how majestic is your name in all the
        earth!
You have set your glory above the
        heavens.
[2] Out of the mouth of babies and
        infants,
you have established strength because
        of your foes,
    to still the enemy and the avenger.

[3] When I look at your heavens, the work
        of your fingers,
    the moon and the stars, which you
        have set in place,
[4] what is man that you are mindful of him,
    and the son of man that you care for
        him?

---

[1] Probably a musical or liturgical term [2] Hebrew *the one at peace with me* [3] Hebrew *the hearts and kidneys* [4] Hebrew *he* [5] Hebrew *he* [6] Probably a musical or liturgical term

5 Yet you have made him a little lower
than the heavenly beings[1]
and crowned him with glory and honor.
6 You have given him dominion over the
works of your hands;
you have put all things under his feet,
7 all sheep and oxen,
and also the beasts of the field,
8 the birds of the heavens, and the fish of
the sea,
whatever passes along the paths of
the seas.
9 O Lord, our Lord,
how majestic is your name in all the
earth!

AUGUST 8

Ruth 1

In the days when the judges ruled there was a famine in the land, and a man of Bethlehem in Judah went to sojourn in the country of Moab, he and his wife and his two sons. ²The name of the man was Elimelech and the name of his wife Naomi, and the names of his two sons were Mahlon and Chilion. They were Ephrathites from Bethlehem in Judah. They went into the country of Moab and remained there. ³But Elimelech, the husband of Naomi, died, and she was left with her two sons. ⁴These took Moabite wives; the name of the one was Orpah and the name of the other Ruth. They lived there about ten years, ⁵and both Mahlon and Chilion died, so that the woman was left without her two sons and her husband.

⁶Then she arose with her daughters-in-law to return from the country of Moab, for she had heard in the fields of Moab that the Lord had visited his people and given them food. ⁷So she set out from the place where she was with her two daughters-in-law, and they went on the way to return to the land of Judah. ⁸But Naomi said to her two daughters-in-law, "Go, return each of you to her mother's house. May the Lord deal kindly with you, as you have dealt with the dead and with me. ⁹The Lord grant that you may find rest, each of you in the house of her husband!" Then she kissed them, and they lifted up their voices and wept. ¹⁰And they said to her, "No, we will return with you to your people." ¹¹But Naomi said, "Turn back, my daughters; why will you go with me? Have I yet sons in my womb that they may become your husbands? ¹²Turn back, my daughters; go your way, for I am too old to have a husband. If I should say I have hope, even if I should have a husband this night and should bear sons, ¹³would you therefore wait till they were grown? Would you therefore refrain from marrying? No, my daughters, for it is exceedingly bitter to me for your sake that the hand of the Lord has gone out against me." ¹⁴Then they lifted up their voices and wept again. And Orpah kissed her mother-in-law, but Ruth clung to her.

¹⁵And she said, "See, your sister-in-law has gone back to her people and to her gods; return after your sister-in-law." ¹⁶But Ruth said, "Do not urge me to leave you or to return from following you. For where you go I will go, and where you lodge I will lodge. Your people shall be my people, and your God my God. ¹⁷Where you die I will die, and there will I be buried. May the Lord do so to me and more also if anything but death parts me from you." ¹⁸And when Naomi saw that she was determined to go with her, she said no more.

¹⁹So the two of them went on until they came to Bethlehem. And when they came to Bethlehem, the whole town was stirred because of them. And the women said, "Is this Naomi?" ²⁰She said to them, "Do not call me Naomi;[2] call me Mara,[3] for the Almighty has dealt very bitterly with me. ²¹I went away full, and the Lord has brought me back empty. Why call me Naomi, when the Lord

---

[1] Or than God; Septuagint than the angels [2] Naomi means pleasant [3] Mara means bitter

has testified against me and the Almighty has brought calamity upon me?"

²²So Naomi returned, and Ruth the Moabite her daughter-in-law with her, who returned from the country of Moab. And they came to Bethlehem at the beginning of barley harvest.

Acts 26

So Agrippa said to Paul, "You have permission to speak for yourself." Then Paul stretched out his hand and made his defense: ²"I consider myself fortunate that it is before you, King Agrippa, I am going to make my defense today against all the accusations of the Jews, ³especially because you are familiar with all the customs and controversies of the Jews. Therefore I beg you to listen to me patiently. ⁴"My manner of life from my youth, spent from the beginning among my own nation and in Jerusalem, is known by all the Jews. ⁵They have known for a long time, if they are willing to testify, that according to the strictest party of our religion I have lived as a Pharisee. ⁶And now I stand here on trial because of my hope in the promise made by God to our fathers, ⁷to which our twelve tribes hope to attain, as they earnestly worship night and day. And for this hope I am accused by Jews, O king! ⁸Why is it thought incredible by any of you that God raises the dead?

⁹"I myself was convinced that I ought to do many things in opposing the name of Jesus of Nazareth. ¹⁰And I did so in Jerusalem. I not only locked up many of the saints in prison after receiving authority from the chief priests, but when they were put to death I cast my vote against them. ¹¹And I punished them often in all the synagogues and tried to make them blaspheme, and in raging fury against them I persecuted them even to foreign cities.

¹²"In this connection I journeyed to Damascus with the authority and commission of the chief priests. ¹³At midday, O king, I saw on the way a light from heaven, brighter than the sun, that shone around me and those who journeyed with me. ¹⁴And when we had all fallen to the ground, I heard a voice saying to me in the Hebrew language,¹ 'Saul, Saul, why are you persecuting me? It is hard for you to kick against the goads.' ¹⁵And I said, 'Who are you, Lord?' And the Lord said, 'I am

Jesus whom you are persecuting. ¹⁶But rise and stand upon your feet, for I have appeared to you for this purpose, to appoint you as a servant and witness to the things in which you have seen me and to those in which I will appear to you, ¹⁷delivering you from your people and from the Gentiles—to whom I am sending you ¹⁸to open their eyes, so that they may turn from darkness to light and from the power of Satan to God, that they may receive forgiveness of sins and a place among those who are sanctified by faith in me.'

¹⁹"Therefore, O King Agrippa, I was not disobedient to the heavenly vision, ²⁰but declared first to those in Damascus, then in Jerusalem and throughout all the region of Judea, and also to the Gentiles, that they should repent and turn to God, performing deeds in keeping with their repentance. ²¹For this reason the Jews seized me in the temple and tried to kill me. ²²To this day I have had the help that comes from God, and so I stand here testifying both to small and great, saying nothing but what the prophets and Moses said would come to pass: ²³that the Christ must suffer and that, by being the first to rise from the dead, he would proclaim light both to our people and to the Gentiles."

²⁴And as he was saying these things in his defense, Festus said with a loud voice, "Paul, you are out of your mind; your great learning is driving you out of your mind." ²⁵But Paul said, "I am not out of my mind, most excellent Festus, but I am speaking true and rational words. ²⁶For the king knows about these things, and to him I speak boldly. For I am persuaded that none of these things has escaped his notice, for this has not been done in a corner. ²⁷King Agrippa, do you believe the prophets? I know that you believe." ²⁸And Agrippa said to Paul, "In a short time would you persuade me to be a Christian?"² ²⁹And Paul said, "Whether short or long, I would to God that not only you but also all who hear me this day might become such as I am—except for these chains."

³⁰Then the king rose, and the governor and Bernice and those who were sitting with them. ³¹And when they had withdrawn, they said to one another, "This man is doing nothing to deserve death or imprisonment." ³²And Agrippa said to Festus, "This man could have been set free if he had not appealed to Caesar."

¹ Or the Hebrew dialect (probably Aramaic) ² Or In a short time you would persuade me to act like a Christian!

Jeremiah 36, 45

In the fourth year of Jehoiakim the son of Josiah, king of Judah, this word came to Jeremiah from the LORD: ²"Take a scroll and write on it all the words that I have spoken to you against Israel and Judah and all the nations, from the day I spoke to you, from the days of Josiah until today. ³It may be that the house of Judah will hear all the disaster that I intend to do to them, so that every one may turn from his evil way, and that I may forgive their iniquity and their sin."

⁴Then Jeremiah called Baruch the son of Neriah, and Baruch wrote on a scroll at the dictation of Jeremiah all the words of the LORD that he had spoken to him. ⁵And Jeremiah ordered Baruch, saying, "I am banned from going to the house of the LORD, ⁶so you are to go, and on a day of fasting in the hearing of all the people in the LORD's house you shall read the words of the LORD from the scroll that you have written at my dictation. You shall read them also in the hearing of all the men of Judah who come out of their cities. ⁷It may be that their plea for mercy will come before the LORD, and that every one will turn from his evil way, for great is the anger and wrath that the LORD has pronounced against this people." ⁸And Baruch the son of Neriah did all that Jeremiah the prophet ordered him about reading from the scroll the words of the LORD in the LORD's house.

⁹In the fifth year of Jehoiakim the son of Josiah, king of Judah, in the ninth month, all the people in Jerusalem and all the people who came from the cities of Judah to Jerusalem proclaimed a fast before the LORD. ¹⁰Then, in the hearing of all the people, Baruch read the words of Jeremiah from the scroll, in the house of the LORD, in the chamber of Gemariah the son of Shaphan the secretary, which was in the upper court, at the entry of the New Gate of the LORD's house.

¹¹When Micaiah the son of Gemariah, son of Shaphan, heard all the words of the LORD from the scroll, ¹²he went down to the king's house, into the secretary's chamber, and all the officials were sitting there: Elishama the secretary, Delaiah the son of Shemaiah, Elnathan the son of Achbor, Gemariah the son of Shaphan, Zedekiah the son of Hananiah,

and all the officials. ¹³And Micaiah told them all the words that he had heard, when Baruch read the scroll in the hearing of the people. ¹⁴Then all the officials sent Jehudi the son of Nethaniah, son of Shelemiah, son of Cushi, to say to Baruch, "Take in your hand the scroll that you read in the hearing of the people, and come." So Baruch the son of Neriah took the scroll in his hand and came to them. ¹⁵And they said to him, "Sit down and read it." So Baruch read it to them. ¹⁶When they heard all the words, they turned one to another in fear. And they said to Baruch, "We must report all these words to the king." ¹⁷Then they asked Baruch, "Tell us, please, how did you write all these words? Was it at his dictation?" ¹⁸Baruch answered them, "He dictated all these words to me, while I wrote them with ink on the scroll." ¹⁹Then the officials said to Baruch, "Go and hide, you and Jeremiah, and let no one know where you are."

²⁰So they went into the court to the king, having put the scroll in the chamber of Elishama the secretary, and they reported all the words to the king. ²¹Then the king sent Jehudi to get the scroll, and he took it from the chamber of Elishama the secretary. And Jehudi read it to the king and all the officials who stood beside the king. ²²It was the ninth month, and the king was sitting in the winter house, and there was a fire burning in the fire pot before him. ²³As Jehudi read three or four columns, the king would cut them off with a knife and throw them into the fire in the fire pot, until the entire scroll was consumed in the fire that was in the fire pot. ²⁴Yet neither the king nor any of his servants who heard all these words was afraid, nor did they tear their garments. ²⁵Even when Elnathan and Delaiah and Gemariah urged the king not to burn the scroll, he would not listen to them. ²⁶And the king commanded Jerahmeel the king's son and Seraiah the son of Azriel and Shelemiah the son of Abdeel to seize Baruch the secretary and Jeremiah the prophet, but the LORD hid them.

²⁷Now after the king had burned the scroll with the words that Baruch wrote at Jeremiah's dictation, the word of the LORD came to Jeremiah: ²⁸"Take another scroll and write on it all the former words that were in the first scroll, which Jehoiakim the

king of Judah has burned. [29]And concerning Jehoiakim king of Judah you shall say, 'Thus says the LORD, You have burned this scroll, saying, "Why have you written in it that the king of Babylon will certainly come and destroy this land, and will cut off from it man and beast?" [30]Therefore thus says the LORD concerning Jehoiakim king of Judah: He shall have none to sit on the throne of David, and his dead body shall be cast out to the heat by day and the frost by night. [31]And I will punish him and his offspring and his servants for their iniquity. I will bring upon them and upon the inhabitants of Jerusalem and upon the people of Judah all the disaster that I have pronounced against them, but they would not hear.'"

[32]Then Jeremiah took another scroll and gave it to Baruch the scribe, the son of Neriah, who wrote on it at the dictation of Jeremiah all the words of the scroll that Jehoiakim king of Judah had burned in the fire. And many similar words were added to them.

[45:1]The word that Jeremiah the prophet spoke to Baruch the son of Neriah, when he wrote these words in a book at the dictation of Jeremiah, in the fourth year of Jehoiakim the son of Josiah, king of Judah: [2]"Thus says the LORD, the God of Israel, to you, O Baruch: [3]You said, 'Woe is me! For the LORD has added sorrow to my pain. I am weary with my groaning, and I find no rest.' [4]Thus shall you say to him, Thus says the LORD: Behold, what I have built I am breaking down, and what I have planted I am plucking up—that is, the whole land. [5]And do you seek great things for yourself? Seek them not, for behold, I am bringing disaster upon all flesh, declares the LORD. But I will give you your life as a prize of war in all places to which you may go."

Psalm 9[1]

TO THE CHOIRMASTER: ACCORDING TO
MUTH-LABBEN.[2] A PSALM OF DAVID.

I will give thanks to the LORD with my
  whole heart;
    I will recount all of your wonderful
      deeds.
[2] I will be glad and exult in you;
    I will sing praise to your name, O Most
      High.

[3] When my enemies turn back,
    they stumble and perish before[3] your
      presence.
[4] For you have maintained my just
      cause;
    you have sat on the throne, giving
      righteous judgment.

[5] You have rebuked the nations; you have
      made the wicked perish;
    you have blotted out their name
      forever and ever.
[6] The enemy came to an end in
      everlasting ruins;
    their cities you rooted out;
    the very memory of them has
      perished.

[7] But the LORD sits enthroned forever;
    he has established his throne for
      justice,
[8] and he judges the world with
      righteousness;
    he judges the peoples with
      uprightness.

[9] The LORD is a stronghold for the
      oppressed,
    a stronghold in times of trouble.
[10] And those who know your name put
      their trust in you,
    for you, O LORD, have not forsaken
      those who seek you.

[11] Sing praises to the LORD, who sits
      enthroned in Zion!
    Tell among the peoples his deeds!
[12] For he who avenges blood is mindful of
      them;
    he does not forget the cry of the
      afflicted.

[13] Be gracious to me, O LORD!
    See my affliction from those who hate
      me,
    O you who lift me up from the gates of
      death,
[14] that I may recount all your praises,
    that in the gates of the daughter of
      Zion
    I may rejoice in your salvation.

[15] The nations have sunk in the pit that
      they made;

---

[1] Psalms 9 and 10 together follow an acrostic pattern, each stanza beginning with the successive letters of the Hebrew alphabet. In the Septuagint they form one psalm [2] Probably a musical or liturgical term [3] Or *because of*

in the net that they hid, their own foot
   has been caught.
¹⁶ The LORD has made himself known; he
   has executed judgment;
the wicked are snared in the work of
   their own hands.   *Higgaion.*[1] *Selah*

¹⁷ The wicked shall return to Sheol,
   all the nations that forget God.

¹⁸ For the needy shall not always be
   forgotten,
   and the hope of the poor shall not
   perish forever.

¹⁹ Arise, O LORD! Let not man prevail;
   let the nations be judged before you!
²⁰ Put them in fear, O LORD!
   Let the nations know that they are but
   men!   *Selah*

AUGUST 9

Ruth 2

Now Naomi had a relative of her husband's, a worthy man of the clan of Elimelech, whose name was Boaz. ²And Ruth the Moabite said to Naomi, "Let me go to the field and glean among the ears of grain after him in whose sight I shall find favor." And she said to her, "Go, my daughter." ³So she set out and went and gleaned in the field after the reapers, and she happened to come to the part of the field belonging to Boaz, who was of the clan of Elimelech. ⁴And behold, Boaz came from Bethlehem. And he said to the reapers, "The LORD be with you!" And they answered, "The LORD bless you." ⁵Then Boaz said to his young man who was in charge of the reapers, "Whose young woman is this?" ⁶And the servant who was in charge of the reapers answered, "She is the young Moabite woman, who came back with Naomi from the country of Moab. ⁷She said, 'Please let me glean and gather among the sheaves after the reapers.' So she came, and she has continued from early morning until now, except for a short rest."[2]

⁸Then Boaz said to Ruth, "Now, listen, my daughter, do not go to glean in another field or leave this one, but keep close to my young women. ⁹Let your eyes be on the field that they are reaping, and go after them. Have I not charged the young men not to touch you? And when you are thirsty, go to the vessels and drink what the young men have drawn." ¹⁰Then she fell on her face, bowing to the ground, and said

to him, "Why have I found favor in your eyes, that you should take notice of me, since I am a foreigner?" ¹¹But Boaz answered her, "All that you have done for your mother-in-law since the death of your husband has been fully told to me, and how you left your father and mother and your native land and came to a people that you did not know before. ¹²The LORD repay you for what you have done, and a full reward be given you by the LORD, the God of Israel, under whose wings you have come to take refuge!" ¹³Then she said, "I have found favor in your eyes, my lord, for you have comforted me and spoken kindly to your servant, though I am not one of your servants."

¹⁴And at mealtime Boaz said to her, "Come here and eat some bread and dip your morsel in the wine." So she sat beside the reapers, and he passed to her roasted grain. And she ate until she was satisfied, and she had some left over. ¹⁵When she rose to glean, Boaz instructed his young men, saying, "Let her glean even among the sheaves, and do not reproach her. ¹⁶And also pull out some from the bundles for her and leave it for her to glean, and do not rebuke her."

¹⁷So she gleaned in the field until evening. Then she beat out what she had gleaned, and it was about an *ephah*[3] of barley. ¹⁸And she took it up and went into the city. Her mother-in-law saw what she had gleaned. She also brought out and gave her what food she had left over after being satisfied. ¹⁹And her mother-in-law said

---

[1] Probably a musical or liturgical term [2] Compare Septuagint, Vulgate; the meaning of the Hebrew phrase is uncertain [3] An *ephah* was about 3/5 bushel or 22 liters

to her, "Where did you glean today? And where have you worked? Blessed be the man who took notice of you." So she told her mother-in-law with whom she had worked and said, "The man's name with whom I worked today is Boaz." ²⁰And Naomi said to her daughter-in-law, "May he be blessed by the LORD, whose kindness has not forsaken the living or the dead!" Naomi also said to her, "The man is a close relative of ours, one of our redeemers." ²¹And Ruth the Moabite said, "Besides, he said to me, 'You shall keep close by my young men until they have finished all my harvest.'" ²²And Naomi said to Ruth, her daughter-in-law, "It is good, my daughter, that you go out with his young women, lest in another field you be assaulted." ²³So she kept close to the young women of Boaz, gleaning until the end of the barley and wheat harvests. And she lived with her mother-in-law.

Acts 27

A nd when it was decided that we should sail for Italy, they delivered Paul and some other prisoners to a centurion of the Augustan Cohort named Julius. ²And embarking in a ship of Adramyttium, which was about to sail to the ports along the coast of Asia, we put to sea, accompanied by Aristarchus, a Macedonian from Thessalonica. ³The next day we put in at Sidon. And Julius treated Paul kindly and gave him leave to go to his friends and be cared for. ⁴And putting out to sea from there we sailed under the lee of Cyprus, because the winds were against us. ⁵And when we had sailed across the open sea along the coast of Cilicia and Pamphylia, we came to Myra in Lycia. ⁶There the centurion found a ship of Alexandria sailing for Italy and put us on board. ⁷We sailed slowly for a number of days and arrived with difficulty off Cnidus, and as the wind did not allow us to go farther, we sailed under the lee of Crete off Salmone. ⁸Coasting along it with difficulty, we came to a place called Fair Havens, near which was the city of Lasea.

⁹Since much time had passed, and the voyage was now dangerous because even the Fast¹ was already over, Paul advised them, ¹⁰saying, "Sirs, I perceive that the voyage will be with injury and much loss, not only of the cargo and the ship, but also of our lives." ¹¹But the centurion paid more attention to the pilot and to the owner of the ship than to what Paul said. ¹²And because the harbor was not suitable to spend the winter in, the majority decided to put out to sea from there, on the chance that somehow they could reach Phoenix, a harbor of Crete, facing both southwest and northwest, and spend the winter there.

¹³Now when the south wind blew gently, supposing that they had obtained their purpose, they weighed anchor and sailed along Crete, close to the shore. ¹⁴But soon a tempestuous wind, called the northeaster, struck down from the land. ¹⁵And when the ship was caught and could not face the wind, we gave way to it and were driven along. ¹⁶Running under the lee of a small island called Cauda,² we managed with difficulty to secure the ship's boat. ¹⁷After hoisting it up, they used supports to undergird the ship. Then, fearing that they would run aground on the Syrtis, they lowered the gear,³ and thus they were driven along. ¹⁸Since we were violently storm-tossed, they began the next day to jettison the cargo. ¹⁹And on the third day they threw the ship's tackle overboard with their own hands. ²⁰When neither sun nor stars appeared for many days, and no small tempest lay on us, all hope of our being saved was at last abandoned.

²¹Since they had been without food for a long time, Paul stood up among them and said, "Men, you should have listened to me and not have set sail from Crete and incurred this injury and loss. ²²Yet now I urge you to take heart, for there will be no loss of life among you, but only of the ship. ²³For this very night there stood before me an angel of the God to whom I belong and whom I worship, ²⁴and he said, 'Do not be afraid, Paul; you must stand before Caesar. And behold, God has granted you all those who sail with you.' ²⁵So take heart, men, for I have faith in God that it will be exactly as I have been told. ²⁶But we must run aground on some island."

²⁷When the fourteenth night had come, as we were being driven across the Adriatic Sea, about midnight the sailors suspected that they were nearing land. ²⁸So they took a sounding and found twenty fathoms.⁴ A little farther on they took a sounding again and found fifteen fathoms.⁵ ²⁹And fearing that we might run on the rocks, they let down four anchors from the stern and prayed for day to come. ³⁰And as the

¹ That is, the Day of Atonement ² Some manuscripts *Clauda* ³ That is, the sea-anchor (or possibly the mainsail) ⁴ About 120 feet; a fathom (Greek *orguia*) was about 6 feet or 2 meters ⁵ About 90 feet (see previous note)

sailors were seeking to escape from the ship, and had lowered the ship's boat into the sea under pretense of laying out anchors from the bow, [31]Paul said to the centurion and the soldiers, "Unless these men stay in the ship, you cannot be saved." [32]Then the soldiers cut away the ropes of the ship's boat and let it go.

[33]As day was about to dawn, Paul urged them all to take some food, saying, "Today is the fourteenth day that you have continued in suspense and without food, having taken nothing. [34]Therefore I urge you to take some food. For it will give you strength,[1] for not a hair is to perish from the head of any of you." [35]And when he had said these things, he took bread, and giving thanks to God in the presence of all he broke it and began to eat. [36]Then they all were encouraged and ate some food themselves. [37](We were in all 276[2] persons in the ship.) [38]And when they had eaten enough, they lightened the ship, throwing out the wheat into the sea.

[39]Now when it was day, they did not recognize the land, but they noticed a bay with a beach, on which they planned if possible to run the ship ashore. [40]So they cast off the anchors and left them in the sea, at the same time loosening the ropes that tied the rudders. Then hoisting the foresail to the wind they made for the beach. [41]But striking a reef,[3] they ran the vessel aground. The bow stuck and remained immovable, and the stern was being broken up by the surf. [42]The soldiers' plan was to kill the prisoners, lest any should swim away and escape. [43]But the centurion, wishing to save Paul, kept them from carrying out their plan. He ordered those who could swim to jump overboard first and make for the land, [44]and the rest on planks or on pieces of the ship. And so it was that all were brought safely to land.

Jeremiah 37

Zedekiah the son of Josiah, whom Nebuchadnezzar king of Babylon made king in the land of Judah, reigned instead of Coniah the son of Jehoiakim. [2]But neither he nor his servants nor the people of the land listened to the words of the LORD that he spoke through Jeremiah the prophet.

[3]King Zedekiah sent Jehucal the son of Shelemiah, and Zephaniah the priest, the son of Maaseiah, to Jeremiah the prophet, saying, "Please pray for us to the LORD our God." [4]Now Jeremiah was still going in and out among the people, for he had not yet been put in prison. [5]The army of Pharaoh had come out of Egypt. And when the Chaldeans who were besieging Jerusalem heard news about them, they withdrew from Jerusalem.

[6]Then the word of the LORD came to Jeremiah the prophet: [7]"Thus says the LORD, God of Israel: Thus shall you say to the king of Judah who sent you to me to inquire of me, 'Behold, Pharaoh's army that came to help you is about to return to Egypt, to its own land. [8]And the Chaldeans shall come back and fight against this city. They shall capture it and burn it with fire. [9]Thus says the LORD, Do not deceive yourselves, saying, "The Chaldeans will surely go away from us," for they will not go away. [10]For even if you should defeat the whole army of Chaldeans who are fighting against you, and there remained of them only wounded men, every man in his tent, they would rise up and burn this city with fire.'"

[11]Now when the Chaldean army had withdrawn from Jerusalem at the approach of Pharaoh's army, [12]Jeremiah set out from Jerusalem to go to the land of Benjamin to receive his portion there among the people. [13]When he was at the Benjamin Gate, a sentry there named Irijah the son of Shelemiah, son of Hananiah, seized Jeremiah the prophet, saying, "You are deserting to the Chaldeans." [14]And Jeremiah said, "It is a lie; I am not deserting to the Chaldeans." But Irijah would not listen to him, and seized Jeremiah and brought him to the officials. [15]And the officials were enraged at Jeremiah, and they beat him and imprisoned him in the house of Jonathan the secretary, for it had been made a prison.

[16]When Jeremiah had come to the dungeon cells and remained there many days, [17]King Zedekiah sent for him and received him. The king questioned him secretly in his house and said, "Is there any word from the LORD?" Jeremiah said, "There is." Then he said, "You shall be delivered into the hand of the king of Babylon." [18]Jeremiah also said to King Zedekiah, "What wrong have I done to you or your servants or this people, that you have put me in prison? [19]Where are your prophets who prophesied to you, saying, 'The king of Babylon

---

[1] Or For it is for your deliverance　[2] Some manuscripts seventy-six, or about seventy-six　[3] Or sandbank, or crosscurrent; Greek place between two seas

will not come against you and against this land"? ²⁰Now hear, please, O my lord the king: let my humble plea come before you and do not send me back to the house of Jonathan the secretary, lest I die there." ²¹So King Zedekiah gave orders, and they committed Jeremiah to the court of the guard. And a loaf of bread was given him daily from the bakers' street, until all the bread of the city was gone. So Jeremiah remained in the court of the guard.

——————— *Psalm 10* ———————

W hy, O LORD, do you stand far away?
　　Why do you hide yourself in times of
　　　trouble?

² 　In arrogance the wicked hotly pursue
　　　the poor;
　　　let them be caught in the schemes
　　　　that they have devised.
³ 　For the wicked boasts of the desires of
　　　his soul,
　　　and the one greedy for gain curses¹
　　　　and renounces the LORD.
⁴ 　In the pride of his face² the wicked does
　　　not seek him;³
　　　all his thoughts are, "There is no
　　　　God."
⁵ 　His ways prosper at all times;
　　　your judgments are on high, out of his
　　　　sight;
　　　as for all his foes, he puffs at them.
⁶ 　He says in his heart, "I shall not be
　　　moved;
　　　throughout all generations I shall not
　　　　meet adversity."
⁷ 　His mouth is filled with cursing and
　　　deceit and oppression;
　　　under his tongue are mischief and
　　　　iniquity.

⁸ 　He sits in ambush in the villages;
　　　in hiding places he murders the
　　　　innocent.
　　His eyes stealthily watch for the
　　　helpless;
⁹ 　he lurks in ambush like a lion in his
　　　thicket;
　　he lurks that he may seize the poor;
　　　he seizes the poor when he draws him
　　　　into his net.
¹⁰ 　The helpless are crushed, sink down,
　　　and fall by his might.
¹¹ 　He says in his heart, "God has forgotten,
　　　he has hidden his face, he will never
　　　　see it."

¹² 　Arise, O LORD; O God, lift up your hand;
　　　forget not the afflicted.
¹³ 　Why does the wicked renounce God
　　　and say in his heart, "You will not call
　　　　to account"?
¹⁴ 　But you do see, for you note mischief
　　　and vexation,
　　　that you may take it into your hands;
　　to you the helpless commits himself;
　　　you have been the helper of the
　　　　fatherless.
¹⁵ 　Break the arm of the wicked and
　　　evildoer;
　　　call his wickedness to account till you
　　　　find none.

¹⁶ 　The LORD is king forever and ever;
　　　the nations perish from his land.
¹⁷ 　O LORD, you hear the desire of the
　　　afflicted;
　　　you will strengthen their heart; you
　　　　will incline your ear
¹⁸ 　to do justice to the fatherless and the
　　　oppressed,
　　　so that man who is of the earth may
　　　　strike terror no more.

¹ Or *and he blesses the one greedy for gain*　² Or *of his anger*　³ Or *the wicked says,* "He will not call to account"

AUGUST 10

Ruth 3–4

Then Naomi her mother-in-law said to her, "My daughter, should I not seek rest for you, that it may be well with you? ²Is not Boaz our relative, with whose young women you were? See, he is winnowing barley tonight at the threshing floor. ³Wash therefore and anoint yourself, and put on your cloak and go down to the threshing floor, but do not make yourself known to the man until he has finished eating and drinking. ⁴But when he lies down, observe the place where he lies. Then go and uncover his feet and lie down, and he will tell you what to do." ⁵And she replied, "All that you say I will do."

⁶So she went down to the threshing floor and did just as her mother-in-law had commanded her. ⁷And when Boaz had eaten and drunk, and his heart was merry, he went to lie down at the end of the heap of grain. Then she came softly and uncovered his feet and lay down. ⁸At midnight the man was startled and turned over, and behold, a woman lay at his feet! ⁹He said, "Who are you?" And she answered, "I am Ruth, your servant. Spread your wings¹ over your servant, for you are a redeemer." ¹⁰And he said, "May you be blessed by the LORD, my daughter. You have made this last kindness greater than the first in that you have not gone after young men, whether poor or rich. ¹¹And now, my daughter, do not fear. I will do for you all that you ask, for all my fellow townsmen know that you are a worthy woman. ¹²And now it is true that I am a redeemer. Yet there is a redeemer nearer than I. ¹³Remain tonight, and in the morning, if he will redeem you, good; let him do it. But if he is not willing to redeem you, then, as the LORD lives, I will redeem you. Lie down until the morning."

¹⁴So she lay at his feet until the morning, but arose before one could recognize another. And he said, "Let it not be known that the woman came to the threshing floor." ¹⁵And he said, "Bring the garment you are wearing and hold it out." So she held it, and he measured out six measures of barley and put it on her. Then she went into the city. ¹⁶And when she came to her mother-in-law, she said, "How did you fare, my daughter?" Then she told her all that the man had done for her, ¹⁷saying, "These six measures of barley he gave to me, for he said to me, 'You must not go back empty-handed to your mother-in-law.'" ¹⁸She replied, "Wait, my daughter, until you learn how the matter turns out, for the man will not rest but will settle the matter today."

⁴:¹Now Boaz had gone up to the gate and sat down there. And behold, the redeemer, of whom Boaz had spoken, came by. So Boaz said, "Turn aside, friend; sit down here." And he turned aside and sat down. ²And he took ten men of the elders of the city and said, "Sit down here." So they sat down. ³Then he said to the redeemer, "Naomi, who has come back from the country of Moab, is selling the parcel of land that belonged to our relative Elimelech. ⁴So I thought I would tell you of it and say, 'Buy it in the presence of those sitting here and in the presence of the elders of my people.' If you will redeem it, redeem it. But if you² will not, tell me, that I may know, for there is no one besides you to redeem it, and I come after you." And he said, "I will redeem it." ⁵Then Boaz said, "The day you buy the field from the hand of Naomi, you also acquire Ruth³ the Moabite, the widow of the dead, in order to perpetuate the name of the dead in his inheritance." ⁶Then the redeemer said, "I cannot redeem it for myself, lest I impair my own inheritance. Take my right of redemption yourself, for I cannot redeem it."

⁷Now this was the custom in former times in Israel concerning redeeming and exchanging: to confirm a transaction, the one drew off his sandal and gave it to the other, and this was the manner of attesting in Israel. ⁸So when the redeemer said to Boaz, "Buy it for yourself," he drew off his sandal. ⁹Then Boaz said to the elders and all the people, "You are witnesses this day that I have bought from the hand of Naomi all that belonged to Elimelech and all

---

¹ Compare 2:12; the word for *wings* can also mean *corners of a garment*   ² Hebrew *he*   ³ Masoretic Text *you also buy it from Ruth*

that belonged to Chilion and to Mahlon. [10]Also Ruth the Moabite, the widow of Mahlon, I have bought to be my wife, to perpetuate the name of the dead in his inheritance, that the name of the dead may not be cut off from among his brothers and from the gate of his native place. You are witnesses this day." [11]Then all the people who were at the gate and the elders said, "We are witnesses. May the LORD make the woman, who is coming into your house, like Rachel and Leah, who together built up the house of Israel. May you act worthily in Ephrathah and be renowned in Bethlehem, [12]and may your house be like the house of Perez, whom Tamar bore to Judah, because of the offspring that the LORD will give you by this young woman."

[13]So Boaz took Ruth, and she became his wife. And he went in to her, and the LORD gave her conception, and she bore a son. [14]Then the women said to Naomi, "Blessed be the LORD, who has not left you this day without a redeemer, and may his name be renowned in Israel! [15]He shall be to you a restorer of life and a nourisher of your old age, for your daughter-in-law who loves you, who is more to you than seven sons, has given birth to him." [16]Then Naomi took the child and laid him on her lap and became his nurse. [17]And the women of the neighborhood gave him a name, saying, "A son has been born to Naomi." They named him Obed. He was the father of Jesse, the father of David.

[18]Now these are the generations of Perez: Perez fathered Hezron, [19]Hezron fathered Ram, Ram fathered Amminadab, [20]Amminadab fathered Nahshon, Nahshon fathered Salmon, [21]Salmon fathered Boaz, Boaz fathered Obed, [22]Obed fathered Jesse, and Jesse fathered David.

Acts 28

After we were brought safely through, we then learned that the island was called Malta. [2]The native people[1] showed us unusual kindness, for they kindled a fire and welcomed us all, because it had begun to rain and was cold. [3]When Paul had gathered a bundle of sticks and put them on the fire, a viper came out because of the heat and fastened on his hand. [4]When the native people saw the creature hanging from his hand, they said to one another, "No doubt this man is a murderer.

Though he has escaped from the sea, Justice[2] has not allowed him to live." [5]He, however, shook off the creature into the fire and suffered no harm. [6]They were waiting for him to swell up or suddenly fall down dead. But when they had waited a long time and saw no misfortune come to him, they changed their minds and said that he was a god.

[7]Now in the neighborhood of that place were lands belonging to the chief man of the island, named Publius, who received us and entertained us hospitably for three days. [8]It happened that the father of Publius lay sick with fever and dysentery. And Paul visited him and prayed, and putting his hands on him healed him. [9]And when this had taken place, the rest of the people on the island who had diseases also came and were cured. [10]They also honored us greatly,[3] and when we were about to sail, they put on board whatever we needed.

[11]After three months we set sail in a ship that had wintered in the island, a ship of Alexandria, with the twin gods[4] as a figurehead. [12]Putting in at Syracuse, we stayed there for three days. [13]And from there we made a circuit and arrived at Rhegium. And after one day a south wind sprang up, and on the second day we came to Puteoli. [14]There we found brothers[5] and were invited to stay with them for seven days. And so we came to Rome. [15]And the brothers there, when they heard about us, came as far as the Forum of Appius and Three Taverns to meet us. On seeing them, Paul thanked God and took courage. [16]And when we came into Rome, Paul was allowed to stay by himself, with the soldier who guarded him.

[17]After three days he called together the local leaders of the Jews, and when they had gathered, he said to them, "Brothers, though I had done nothing against our people or the customs of our fathers, yet I was delivered as a prisoner from Jerusalem into the hands of the Romans. [18]When they had examined me, they wished to set me at liberty, because there was no reason for the death penalty in my case. [19]But because the Jews objected, I was compelled to appeal to Caesar—though I had no charge to bring against my nation. [20]For this reason, therefore, I have asked to see you and speak with you, since it is because of the hope of Israel that I am wearing this chain." [21]And they said to him, "We have received no letters

---

[1] Greek *barbaroi* (that is, non–Greek speakers); also verse 4   [2] Or *justice*   [3] Greek *honored us with many honors*   [4] That is, the Greek gods Castor and Pollux   [5] Or *brothers and sisters*; also verses 15, 21

from Judea about you, and none of the brothers coming here has reported or spoken any evil about you. ²²But we desire to hear from you what your views are, for with regard to this sect we know that everywhere it is spoken against."

²³When they had appointed a day for him, they came to him at his lodging in greater numbers. From morning till evening he expounded to them, testifying to the kingdom of God and trying to convince them about Jesus both from the Law of Moses and from the Prophets. ²⁴And some were convinced by what he said, but others disbelieved. ²⁵And disagreeing among themselves, they departed after Paul had made one statement: "The Holy Spirit was right in saying to your fathers through Isaiah the prophet:

²⁶ " 'Go to this people, and say,
    "You will indeed hear but never
        understand,
      and you will indeed see but never
        perceive."
²⁷   For this people's heart has grown dull,
      and with their ears they can barely
        hear,
    and their eyes they have closed;
  lest they should see with their eyes
      and hear with their ears
  and understand with their heart
      and turn, and I would heal them.'

²⁸Therefore let it be known to you that this salvation of God has been sent to the Gentiles; they will listen."[1]

³⁰He lived there two whole years at his own expense,[2] and welcomed all who came to him, ³¹proclaiming the kingdom of God and teaching about the Lord Jesus Christ with all boldness and without hindrance.

Jeremiah 38

Now Shephatiah the son of Mattan, Gedaliah the son of Pashhur, Jucal the son of Shelemiah, and Pashhur the son of Malchiah heard the words that Jeremiah was saying to all the people, ²"Thus says the LORD: He who stays in this city shall die by the sword, by famine, and by pestilence, but he who goes out to the Chaldeans shall live. He shall have his life as a prize of war, and live. ³Thus says the LORD: This city shall surely be given into the hand of

the army of the king of Babylon and be taken." ⁴Then the officials said to the king, "Let this man be put to death, for he is weakening the hands of the soldiers who are left in this city, and the hands of all the people, by speaking such words to them. For this man is not seeking the welfare of this people, but their harm." ⁵King Zedekiah said, "Behold, he is in your hands, for the king can do nothing against you." ⁶So they took Jeremiah and cast him into the cistern of Malchiah, the king's son, which was in the court of the guard, letting Jeremiah down by ropes. And there was no water in the cistern, but only mud, and Jeremiah sank in the mud.

⁷When Ebed-melech the Ethiopian, a eunuch who was in the king's house, heard that they had put Jeremiah into the cistern—the king was sitting in the Benjamin Gate— ⁸Ebed-melech went from the king's house and said to the king, ⁹"My lord the king, these men have done evil in all that they did to Jeremiah the prophet by casting him into the cistern, and he will die there of hunger, for there is no bread left in the city." ¹⁰Then the king commanded Ebed-melech the Ethiopian, "Take thirty men with you from here, and lift Jeremiah the prophet out of the cistern before he dies." ¹¹So Ebed-melech took the men with him and went to the house of the king, to a wardrobe in the storehouse, and took from there old rags and worn-out clothes, which he let down to Jeremiah in the cistern by ropes. ¹²Then Ebed-melech the Ethiopian said to Jeremiah, "Put the rags and clothes between your armpits and the ropes." Jeremiah did so. ¹³Then they drew Jeremiah up with ropes and lifted him out of the cistern. And Jeremiah remained in the court of the guard.

¹⁴King Zedekiah sent for Jeremiah the prophet and received him at the third entrance of the temple of the LORD. The king said to Jeremiah, "I will ask you a question; hide nothing from me." ¹⁵Jeremiah said to Zedekiah, "If I tell you, will you not surely put me to death? And if I give you counsel, you will not listen to me." ¹⁶Then King Zedekiah swore secretly to Jeremiah, "As the LORD lives, who made our souls, I will not put you to death or deliver you into the hand of these men who seek your life."

¹⁷Then Jeremiah said to Zedekiah, "Thus says the LORD, the God of hosts, the God of Israel: If you will surrender to the officials of the king

---

[1] Some manuscripts add verse 29: And when he had said these words, the Jews departed, having much dispute among themselves   [2] Or in his own hired dwelling

of Babylon, then your life shall be spared, and this city shall not be burned with fire, and you and your house shall live. [18]But if you do not surrender to the officials of the king of Babylon, then this city shall be given into the hand of the Chaldeans, and they shall burn it with fire, and you shall not escape from their hand." [19]King Zedekiah said to Jeremiah, "I am afraid of the Judeans who have deserted to the Chaldeans, lest I be handed over to them and they deal cruelly with me." [20]Jeremiah said, "You shall not be given to them. Obey now the voice of the LORD in what I say to you, and it shall be well with you, and your life shall be spared. [21]But if you refuse to surrender, this is the vision which the LORD has shown to me: [22]Behold, all the women left in the house of the king of Judah were being led out to the officials of the king of Babylon and were saying,

"'Your trusted friends have deceived you
        and prevailed against you;
    now that your feet are sunk in the mud,
        they turn away from you.'

[23]All your wives and your sons shall be led out to the Chaldeans, and you yourself shall not escape from their hand, but shall be seized by the king of Babylon, and this city shall be burned with fire."

[24]Then Zedekiah said to Jeremiah, "Let no one know of these words, and you shall not die. [25]If the officials hear that I have spoken with you and come to you and say to you, 'Tell us what you said to the king and what the king said to you; hide nothing from us and we will not put you to death,' [26]then you shall say to them, 'I made a humble plea to the king that he would not send me back to the house of Jonathan to die there.'" [27]Then all the officials came to Jeremiah and asked him, and he answered them as the king had instructed him. So they stopped speaking with him, for the conversation had not been overheard. [28]And Jeremiah remained in the court of the guard until the day that Jerusalem was taken.

─────── **Psalm 11–12** ───────

To the choirmaster. Of David.

In the LORD I take refuge;
    how can you say to my soul,
    "Flee like a bird to your mountain,

[2] for behold, the wicked bend the bow;
        they have fitted their arrow to the
            string
        to shoot in the dark at the upright in
            heart;
[3] if the foundations are destroyed,
        what can the righteous do?"[1]

[4] The LORD is in his holy temple;
        the LORD's throne is in heaven;
        his eyes see, his eyelids test the
            children of man.
[5] The LORD tests the righteous,
        but his soul hates the wicked and the
            one who loves violence.
[6] Let him rain coals on the wicked;
        fire and sulfur and a scorching wind
            shall be the portion of their cup.
[7] For the LORD is righteous;
    he loves righteous deeds;
        the upright shall behold his face.

To the choirmaster: according to The
Sheminith.[2] A Psalm of David.

Save, O LORD, for the godly one is gone;
    for the faithful have vanished from
            among the children of man.
[2] Everyone utters lies to his neighbor;
        with flattering lips and a double heart
            they speak.

[3] May the LORD cut off all flattering lips,
        the tongue that makes great boasts,
[4] those who say, "With our tongue we will
            prevail,
        our lips are with us; who is master
            over us?"

[5] "Because the poor are plundered, because
            the needy groan,
        I will now arise," says the LORD;
        "I will place him in the safety for which
            he longs."
[6] The words of the LORD are pure words,
        like silver refined in a furnace on the
            ground,
        purified seven times.

[7] You, O LORD, will keep them;
        you will guard us[3] from this
            generation forever.
[8] On every side the wicked prowl,
        as vileness is exalted among the
            children of man.

[1] Or for the foundations will be destroyed; what has the righteous done? [2] Probably a musical or liturgical term [3] Or guard him

AUGUST 11

1 Samuel 1

There was a certain man of Ramathaim-zophim of the hill country of Ephraim whose name was Elkanah the son of Jeroham, son of Elihu, son of Tohu, son of Zuph, an Ephrathite. [2] He had two wives. The name of the one was Hannah, and the name of the other, Peninnah. And Peninnah had children, but Hannah had no children.

[3] Now this man used to go up year by year from his city to worship and to sacrifice to the LORD of hosts at Shiloh, where the two sons of Eli, Hophni and Phinehas, were priests of the LORD. [4] On the day when Elkanah sacrificed, he would give portions to Peninnah his wife and to all her sons and daughters. [5] But to Hannah he gave a double portion, because he loved her, though the LORD had closed her womb.[1] [6] And her rival used to provoke her grievously to irritate her, because the LORD had closed her womb. [7] So it went on year by year. As often as she went up to the house of the LORD, she used to provoke her. Therefore Hannah wept and would not eat. [8] And Elkanah, her husband, said to her, "Hannah, why do you weep? And why do you not eat? And why is your heart sad? Am I not more to you than ten sons?"

[9] After they had eaten and drunk in Shiloh, Hannah rose. Now Eli the priest was sitting on the seat beside the doorpost of the temple of the LORD. [10] She was deeply distressed and prayed to the LORD and wept bitterly. [11] And she vowed a vow and said, "O LORD of hosts, if you will indeed look on the affliction of your servant and remember me and not forget your servant, but will give to your servant a son, then I will give him to the LORD all the days of his life, and no razor shall touch his head."

[12] As she continued praying before the LORD, Eli observed her mouth. [13] Hannah was speaking in her heart; only her lips moved, and her voice was not heard. Therefore Eli took her to be a drunken woman. [14] And Eli said to her, "How long will you go on being drunk? Put your wine away from you." [15] But Hannah answered, "No, my lord, I am a woman troubled in spirit. I have drunk neither wine nor strong drink, but I have been pouring out my soul before the LORD. [16] Do not regard your servant as a worthless woman, for all along I have been speaking out of my great anxiety and vexation." [17] Then Eli answered, "Go in peace, and the God of Israel grant your petition that you have made to him." [18] And she said, "Let your servant find favor in your eyes." Then the woman went her way and ate, and her face was no longer sad.

[19] They rose early in the morning and worshiped before the LORD; then they went back to their house at Ramah. And Elkanah knew Hannah his wife, and the LORD remembered her. [20] And in due time Hannah conceived and bore a son, and she called his name Samuel, for she said, "I have asked for him from the LORD."[2]

[21] The man Elkanah and all his house went up to offer to the LORD the yearly sacrifice and to pay his vow. [22] But Hannah did not go up, for she said to her husband, "As soon as the child is weaned, I will bring him, so that he may appear in the presence of the LORD and dwell there forever." [23] Elkanah her husband said to her, "Do what seems best to you; wait until you have weaned him; only, may the LORD establish his word." So the woman remained and nursed her son until she weaned him. [24] And when she had weaned him, she took him up with her, along with a three-year-old bull,[3] an ephah[4] of flour, and a skin of wine, and she brought him to the house of the LORD at Shiloh. And the child was young. [25] Then they slaughtered the bull, and they brought the child to Eli. [26] And she said, "Oh, my lord! As you live, my lord, I am the woman who was standing here in your presence, praying to the LORD. [27] For this child I prayed, and the LORD has granted me my petition that I made to him. [28] Therefore I have lent him to the LORD. As long as he lives, he is lent to the LORD."

And he worshiped the LORD there.

[1] Syriac; the meaning of the Hebrew is uncertain. Septuagint *And, although he loved Hannah, he would give Hannah only one portion, because the LORD had closed her womb* [2] *Samuel* sounds like the Hebrew for *heard of God* [3] Dead Sea Scroll, Septuagint, Syriac; Masoretic Text *three bulls* [4] An ephah was about 3/5 bushel or 22 liters

Romans 1

Paul, a servant[1] of Christ Jesus, called to be an apostle, set apart for the gospel of God, [2] which he promised beforehand through his prophets in the holy Scriptures, [3] concerning his Son, who was descended from David[2] according to the flesh [4] and was declared to be the Son of God in power according to the Spirit of holiness by his resurrection from the dead, Jesus Christ our Lord, [5] through whom we have received grace and apostleship to bring about the obedience of faith for the sake of his name among all the nations, [6] including you who are called to belong to Jesus Christ,

[7] To all those in Rome who are loved by God and called to be saints:

Grace to you and peace from God our Father and the Lord Jesus Christ.

[8] First, I thank my God through Jesus Christ for all of you, because your faith is proclaimed in all the world. [9] For God is my witness, whom I serve with my spirit in the gospel of his Son, that without ceasing I mention you [10] always in my prayers, asking that somehow by God's will I may now at last succeed in coming to you. [11] For I long to see you, that I may impart to you some spiritual gift to strengthen you— [12] that is, that we may be mutually encouraged by each other's faith, both yours and mine. [13] I do not want you to be unaware, brothers,[3] that I have often intended to come to you (but thus far have been prevented), in order that I may reap some harvest among you as well as among the rest of the Gentiles. [14] I am under obligation both to Greeks and to barbarians,[4] both to the wise and to the foolish. [15] So I am eager to preach the gospel to you also who are in Rome.

[16] For I am not ashamed of the gospel, for it is the power of God for salvation to everyone who believes, to the Jew first and also to the Greek. [17] For in it the righteousness of God is revealed from faith for faith,[5] as it is written, "The righteous shall live by faith."[6]

[18] For the wrath of God is revealed from heaven against all ungodliness and unrighteousness of men, who by their unrighteousness suppress the truth. [19] For what can be known about God is plain to them, because God has shown it to them. [20] For his invisible attributes, namely, his eternal power and divine nature, have been clearly perceived, ever since the creation of the world,[7] in the things that have been made. So they are without excuse. [21] For although they knew God, they did not honor him as God or give thanks to him, but they became futile in their thinking, and their foolish hearts were darkened. [22] Claiming to be wise, they became fools, [23] and exchanged the glory of the immortal God for images resembling mortal man and birds and animals and creeping things.

[24] Therefore God gave them up in the lusts of their hearts to impurity, to the dishonoring of their bodies among themselves, [25] because they exchanged the truth about God for a lie and worshiped and served the creature rather than the Creator, who is blessed forever! Amen.

[26] For this reason God gave them up to dishonorable passions. For their women exchanged natural relations for those that are contrary to nature; [27] and the men likewise gave up natural relations with women and were consumed with passion for one another, men committing shameless acts with men and receiving in themselves the due penalty for their error.

[28] And since they did not see fit to acknowledge God, God gave them up to a debased mind to do what ought not to be done. [29] They were filled with all manner of unrighteousness, evil, covetousness, malice. They are full of envy, murder, strife, deceit, maliciousness. They are gossips, [30] slanderers, haters of God, insolent, haughty, boastful, inventors of evil, disobedient to parents, [31] foolish, faithless, heartless, ruthless. [32] Though they know God's righteous decree that those who practice such things deserve to die, they not only do them but give approval to those who practice them.

Jeremiah 39

In the ninth year of Zedekiah king of Judah, in the tenth month, Nebuchadnezzar king of Babylon and all his army came against Jerusalem and besieged it. [2] In the eleventh year of Zedekiah, in the fourth month, on the ninth day of the month, a breach was made in the city. [3] Then all the officials of the king of Babylon came and sat in the middle gate: Nergal-sarezer of Samgar, Nebu-sar-sekim the Rab-saris,

[1] Or slave (for the contextual rendering of the Greek word doulos, see Preface) [2] Or who came from the offspring of David [3] Or brothers and sisters. The plural Greek word adelphoi (translated "brothers") refers to siblings in a family. In New Testament usage, depending on the context, adelphoi may refer either to men or to both men and women who are siblings (brothers and sisters) in God's family, the church [4] That is, non-Greeks [5] Or beginning and ending in faith [6] Or The one who by faith is righteous shall live [7] Or clearly perceived from the creation of the world

Nergal-sar-ezer the Rab-mag, with all the rest of the officers of the king of Babylon. ⁴When Zedekiah king of Judah and all the soldiers saw them, they fled, going out of the city at night by way of the king's garden through the gate between the two walls; and they went toward the Arabah. ⁵But the army of the Chaldeans pursued them and overtook Zedekiah in the plains of Jericho. And when they had taken him, they brought him up to Nebuchadnezzar king of Babylon, at Riblah, in the land of Hamath; and he passed sentence on him. ⁶The king of Babylon slaughtered the sons of Zedekiah at Riblah before his eyes, and the king of Babylon slaughtered all the nobles of Judah. ⁷He put out the eyes of Zedekiah and bound him in chains to take him to Babylon. ⁸The Chaldeans burned the king's house and the house of the people, and broke down the walls of Jerusalem. ⁹Then Nebuzaradan, the captain of the guard, carried into exile to Babylon the rest of the people who were left in the city, those who had deserted to him, and the people who remained. ¹⁰Nebuzaradan, the captain of the guard, left in the land of Judah some of the poor people who owned nothing, and gave them vineyards and fields at the same time.

¹¹Nebuchadnezzar king of Babylon gave command concerning Jeremiah through Nebuzaradan, the captain of the guard, saying, ¹²"Take him, look after him well, and do him no harm, but deal with him as he tells you." ¹³So Nebuzaradan the captain of the guard, Nebushazban the Rab-saris, Nergal-sar-ezer the Rab-mag, and all the chief officers of the king of Babylon ¹⁴sent and took Jeremiah from the court of the guard. They entrusted him to Gedaliah the son of Ahikam, son of Shaphan, that he should take him home. So he lived among the people.

¹⁵The word of the LORD came to Jeremiah while he was shut up in the court of the guard: ¹⁶"Go, and say to Ebed-melech the Ethiopian, 'Thus says the LORD of hosts, the God of Israel: Behold, I will fulfill my words against this city for harm and not for good, and they shall be accomplished before you on that day. ¹⁷But I will deliver you on that day, declares the LORD, and you shall not be given into the hand of the men of whom you are afraid. ¹⁸For I will surely save you, and you shall not fall by the sword, but you shall have your life as a prize of war,

because you have put your trust in me, declares the LORD.'"

Psalm 13–14

To the choirmaster. A Psalm of David.

How long, O LORD? Will you forget me forever?
How long will you hide your face from me?
2 How long must I take counsel in my soul and have sorrow in my heart all the day?
How long shall my enemy be exalted over me?
3 Consider and answer me, O LORD my God;
light up my eyes, lest I sleep the sleep of death,
4 lest my enemy say, "I have prevailed over him,"
lest my foes rejoice because I am shaken.
5 But I have trusted in your steadfast love; my heart shall rejoice in your salvation.
6 I will sing to the LORD, because he has dealt bountifully with me.

To the choirmaster. Of David.

The fool says in his heart, "There is no God."
They are corrupt, they do abominable deeds,
there is none who does good.
2 The LORD looks down from heaven on the children of man,
to see if there are any who understand,[1]
who seek after God.
3 They have all turned aside; together they have become corrupt;
there is none who does good,
not even one.
4 Have they no knowledge, all the evildoers
who eat up my people as they eat bread
and do not call upon the LORD?

[1] Or that act wisely

5 There they are in great terror,
　　for God is with the generation of the
　　　righteous.
6 You would shame the plans of the poor,
　　but[1] the LORD is his refuge.

7 Oh, that salvation for Israel would come
　　out of Zion!
　When the LORD restores the fortunes
　　of his people,
　let Jacob rejoice, let Israel be glad.

AUGUST 12

1 Samuel 2

And Hannah prayed and said,

　"My heart exults in the LORD;
　　my horn is exalted in the LORD.
　My mouth derides my enemies,
　　because I rejoice in your salvation.

2 "There is none holy like the LORD:
　　for there is none besides you;
　　there is no rock like our God.
3 Talk no more so very proudly,
　　let not arrogance come from your
　　　mouth;
　for the LORD is a God of knowledge,
　　and by him actions are weighed.
4 The bows of the mighty are broken,
　　but the feeble bind on strength.
5 Those who were full have hired
　　themselves out for bread,
　　but those who were hungry have
　　　ceased to hunger.
　The barren has borne seven,
　　but she who has many children is
　　　forlorn.
6 The LORD kills and brings to life;
　　he brings down to Sheol and raises
　　　up.
7 The LORD makes poor and makes rich;
　　he brings low and he exalts.
8 He raises up the poor from the dust;
　　he lifts the needy from the ash heap
　to make them sit with princes
　　and inherit a seat of honor.
　For the pillars of the earth are the
　　LORD's,
　　and on them he has set the world.

9 "He will guard the feet of his faithful ones,
　　but the wicked shall be cut off in
　　　darkness,
　for not by might shall a man prevail.
10 The adversaries of the LORD shall be
　　broken to pieces;
　　against them he will thunder in
　　　heaven.
　The LORD will judge the ends of the
　　earth;
　　he will give strength to his king
　　and exalt the horn of his anointed."

[11] Then Elkanah went home to Ramah. And the boy[2] was ministering to the LORD in the presence of Eli the priest.

[12] Now the sons of Eli were worthless men. They did not know the LORD. [13] The custom of the priests with the people was that when any man offered sacrifice, the priest's servant would come, while the meat was boiling, with a three-pronged fork in his hand, [14] and he would thrust it into the pan or kettle or cauldron or pot. All that the fork brought up the priest would take for himself. This is what they did at Shiloh to all the Israelites who came there. [15] Moreover, before the fat was burned, the priest's servant would come and say to the man who was sacrificing, "Give meat for the priest to roast, for he will not accept boiled meat from you but only raw." [16] And if the man said to him, "Let them burn the fat first, and then take as much as you wish," he would say, "No, you must give it now, and if not, I will take it by force." [17] Thus the sin of the young men was very great in the sight of the LORD, for the men treated the offering of the LORD with contempt.

[1] Or for　[2] Hebrew *na'ar* can be rendered *boy* (2:11, 18, 21, 26; 3:1, 8), *servant* (2:13, 15), or *young man* (2:17), depending on the context

[18] Samuel was ministering before the LORD, a boy clothed with a linen ephod. [19] And his mother used to make for him a little robe and take it to him each year when she went up with her husband to offer the yearly sacrifice. [20] Then Eli would bless Elkanah and his wife, and say, "May the LORD give you children by this woman for the petition she asked of the LORD." So then they would return to their home.

[21] Indeed the LORD visited Hannah, and she conceived and bore three sons and two daughters. And the boy Samuel grew in the presence of the LORD.

[22] Now Eli was very old, and he kept hearing all that his sons were doing to all Israel, and how they lay with the women who were serving at the entrance to the tent of meeting. [23] And he said to them, "Why do you do such things? For I hear of your evil dealings from all these people. [24] No, my sons; it is no good report that I hear the people of the LORD spreading abroad. [25] If someone sins against a man, God will mediate for him, but if someone sins against the LORD, who can intercede for him?" But they would not listen to the voice of their father, for it was the will of the LORD to put them to death.

[26] Now the boy Samuel continued to grow both in stature and in favor with the LORD and also with man.

[27] And there came a man of God to Eli and said to him, "Thus says the LORD, 'Did I indeed reveal myself to the house of your father when they were in Egypt subject to the house of Pharaoh? [28] Did I choose him out of all the tribes of Israel to be my priest, to go up to my altar, to burn incense, to wear an ephod before me? I gave to the house of your father all my offerings by fire from the people of Israel. [29] Why then do you scorn[1] my sacrifices and my offerings that I commanded for my dwelling, and honor your sons above me by fattening yourselves on the choicest parts of every offering of my people Israel?' [30] Therefore the LORD, the God of Israel, declares: 'I promised that your house and the house of your father should go in and out before me forever,' but now the LORD declares: 'Far be it from me, for those who honor me I will honor, and those who despise me shall be lightly esteemed. [31] Behold, the days are coming when I will cut off your strength and the strength of your father's house, so that there will not be an old man in your house.

[32] Then in distress you will look with envious eye on all the prosperity that shall be bestowed on Israel, and there shall not be an old man in your house forever. [33] The only one of you whom I shall not cut off from my altar shall be spared to weep his[2] eyes out to grieve his heart, and all the descendants[3] of your house shall die by the sword of men.[4] [34] And this that shall come upon your two sons, Hophni and Phinehas, shall be the sign to you: both of them shall die on the same day. [35] And I will raise up for myself a faithful priest, who shall do according to what is in my heart and in my mind. And I will build him a sure house, and he shall go in and out before my anointed forever. [36] And everyone who is left in your house shall come to implore him for a piece of silver or a loaf of bread and shall say, "Please put me in one of the priests' places, that I may eat a morsel of bread." '"

Romans 2

Therefore you have no excuse, O man, every one of you who judges. For in passing judgment on another you condemn yourself, because you, the judge, practice the very same things. [2] We know that the judgment of God rightly falls on those who practice such things. [3] Do you suppose, O man—you who judge those who practice such things and yet do them yourself—that you will escape the judgment of God? [4] Or do you presume on the riches of his kindness and forbearance and patience, not knowing that God's kindness is meant to lead you to repentance? [5] But because of your hard and impenitent heart you are storing up wrath for yourself on the day of wrath when God's righteous judgment will be revealed.

[6] He will render to each one according to his works: [7] to those who by patience in well-doing seek for glory and honor and immortality, he will give eternal life; [8] but for those who are self-seeking[5] and do not obey the truth, but obey unrighteousness, there will be wrath and fury. [9] There will be tribulation and distress for every human being who does evil, the Jew first and also the Greek, [10] but glory and honor and peace for everyone who does good, the Jew first and also the Greek. [11] For God shows no partiality.

[12] For all who have sinned without the law will also perish without the law, and all who

---

[1] Hebrew *kick at* [2] Septuagint; Hebrew *your*; twice in this verse [3] Hebrew *increase* [4] Septuagint; Hebrew *die as men* [5] Or *contentious*

have sinned under the law will be judged by the law. [13] For it is not the hearers of the law who are righteous before God, but the doers of the law who will be justified. [14] For when Gentiles, who do not have the law, by nature do what the law requires, they are a law to themselves, even though they do not have the law. [15] They show that the work of the law is written on their hearts, while their conscience also bears witness, and their conflicting thoughts accuse or even excuse them [16] on that day when, according to my gospel, God judges the secrets of men by Christ Jesus.

[17] But if you call yourself a Jew and rely on the law and boast in God [18] and know his will and approve what is excellent, because you are instructed from the law; [19] and if you are sure that you yourself are a guide to the blind, a light to those who are in darkness, [20] an instructor of the foolish, a teacher of children, having in the law the embodiment of knowledge and truth— [21] you then who teach others, do you not teach yourself? While you preach against stealing, do you steal? [22] You who say that one must not commit adultery, do you commit adultery? You who abhor idols, do you rob temples? [23] You who boast in the law dishonor God by breaking the law. [24] For, as it is written, "The name of God is blasphemed among the Gentiles because of you."

[25] For circumcision indeed is of value if you obey the law, but if you break the law, your circumcision becomes uncircumcision. [26] So, if a man who is uncircumcised keeps the precepts of the law, will not his uncircumcision be regarded[1] as circumcision? [27] Then he who is physically[2] uncircumcised but keeps the law will condemn you who have the written code[3] and circumcision but break the law. [28] For no one is a Jew who is merely one outwardly, nor is circumcision outward and physical. [29] But a Jew is one inwardly, and circumcision is a matter of the heart, by the Spirit, not by the letter. His praise is not from man but from God.

Jeremiah 40

The word that came to Jeremiah from the LORD after Nebuzaradan the captain of the guard had let him go from Ramah, when he took him bound in chains along with all the captives of Jerusalem and Judah who were being exiled to Babylon. [2] The captain of the guard took Jeremiah and said to him, "The LORD your God pronounced this disaster against this place. [3] The LORD has brought it about, and has done as he said. Because you sinned against the LORD and did not obey his voice, this thing has come upon you. [4] Now, behold, I release you today from the chains on your hands. If it seems good to you to come with me to Babylon, come, and I will look after you well, but if it seems wrong to you to come with me to Babylon, do not come. See, the whole land is before you; go wherever you think it good and right to go. [5] If you remain,[4] then return to Gedaliah the son of Ahikam, son of Shaphan, whom the king of Babylon appointed governor of the cities of Judah, and dwell with him among the people. Or go wherever you think it right to go." So the captain of the guard gave him an allowance of food and a present, and let him go. [6] Then Jeremiah went to Gedaliah the son of Ahikam, at Mizpah, and lived with him among the people who were left in the land.

[7] When all the captains of the forces in the open country and their men heard that the king of Babylon had appointed Gedaliah the son of Ahikam governor in the land and had committed to him men, women, and children, those of the poorest of the land who had not been taken into exile to Babylon, [8] they went to Gedaliah at Mizpah—Ishmael the son of Nethaniah, Johanan the son of Kareah, Seraiah the son of Tanhumeth, the sons of Ephai the Netophathite, Jezaniah the son of the Maacathite, they and their men. [9] Gedaliah the son of Ahikam, son of Shaphan, swore to them and their men, saying, "Do not be afraid to serve the Chaldeans. Dwell in the land and serve the king of Babylon, and it shall be well with you. [10] As for me, I will dwell at Mizpah, to represent you before the Chaldeans who will come to us. But as for you, gather wine and summer fruits and oil, and store them in your vessels, and dwell in your cities that you have taken." [11] Likewise, when all the Judeans who were in Moab and among the Ammonites and in Edom and in other lands heard that the king of Babylon had left a remnant in Judah and had appointed Gedaliah the son of Ahikam, son of Shaphan, as governor over them, [12] then all the Judeans returned from all the places to

[1] Or counted [2] Or is by nature [3] Or the letter. [4] Syriac; the meaning of the Hebrew phrase is uncertain

which they had been driven and came to the land of Judah, to Gedaliah at Mizpah. And they gathered wine and summer fruits in great abundance.

¹³ Now Johanan the son of Kareah and all the leaders of the forces in the open country came to Gedaliah at Mizpah ¹⁴ and said to him, "Do you know that Baalis the king of the Ammonites has sent Ishmael the son of Nethaniah to take your life?" But Gedaliah the son of Ahikam would not believe them. ¹⁵ Then Johanan the son of Kareah spoke secretly to Gedaliah at Mizpah, "Please let me go and strike down Ishmael the son of Nethaniah, and no one will know it. Why should he take your life, so that all the Judeans who are gathered about you would be scattered, and the remnant of Judah would perish?" ¹⁶ But Gedaliah the son of Ahikam said to Johanan the son of Kareah, "You shall not do this thing, for you are speaking falsely of Ishmael."

——— *Psalm 15–16* ———

A PSALM OF DAVID.

O LORD, who shall sojourn in your tent?
  Who shall dwell on your holy hill?
² He who walks blamelessly and does
      what is right
    and speaks truth in his heart;
³ who does not slander with his tongue
    and does no evil to his neighbor,
    nor takes up a reproach against his
      friend;
⁴ in whose eyes a vile person is despised,
    but who honors those who fear the
      LORD;
  who swears to his own hurt and does
      not change;
⁵ who does not put out his money at
      interest

and does not take a bribe against the
      innocent.
He who does these things shall never be
      moved.

A MIKTAM¹ OF DAVID.

Preserve me, O God, for in you I take refuge.
  ² I say to the LORD, "You are my Lord;
    I have no good apart from you."

³   As for the saints in the land, they are the
        excellent ones,
      in whom is all my delight.²

⁴   The sorrows of those who run after³
        another god shall multiply;
      their drink offerings of blood I will not
        pour out
      or take their names on my lips.

⁵   The LORD is my chosen portion and my
        cup;
      you hold my lot.
⁶   The lines have fallen for me in pleasant
        places;
      indeed, I have a beautiful inheritance.

⁷   I bless the LORD who gives me counsel;
      in the night also my heart instructs
        me.⁴
⁸   I have set the LORD always before me;
      because he is at my right hand, I shall
        not be shaken.

⁹   Therefore my heart is glad, and my
        whole being⁵ rejoices;
      my flesh also dwells secure.
¹⁰ For you will not abandon my soul to
        Sheol,
      or let your holy one see corruption.⁶

¹¹ You make known to me the path of life;
      in your presence there is fullness of joy;
      at your right hand are pleasures
        forevermore.

---

¹ Probably a musical or liturgical term ² Or *To the saints in the land, the excellent in whom is all my delight, I say:* ³ Or *who acquire* ⁴ Hebrew *my kidneys instruct me* ⁵ Hebrew *my glory*
⁶ Or *see the pit*

AUGUST 13

1 Samuel 3

Now the boy Samuel was ministering to the Lord in the presence of Eli. And the word of the Lord was rare in those days; there was no frequent vision.

²At that time Eli, whose eyesight had begun to grow dim so that he could not see, was lying down in his own place. ³The lamp of God had not yet gone out, and Samuel was lying down in the temple of the Lord, where the ark of God was.

⁴Then the Lord called Samuel, and he said, "Here I am!" ⁵and ran to Eli and said, "Here I am, for you called me." But he said, "I did not call; lie down again." So he went and lay down.

⁶And the Lord called again, "Samuel!" and Samuel arose and went to Eli and said, "Here I am, for you called me." But he said, "I did not call, my son; lie down again." ⁷Now Samuel did not yet know the Lord, and the word of the Lord had not yet been revealed to him.

⁸And the Lord called Samuel again the third time. And he arose and went to Eli and said, "Here I am, for you called me." Then Eli perceived that the Lord was calling the boy. ⁹Therefore Eli said to Samuel, "Go, lie down, and if he calls you, you shall say, 'Speak, Lord, for your servant hears.'" So Samuel went and lay down in his place.

¹⁰And the Lord came and stood, calling as at other times, "Samuel! Samuel!" And Samuel said, "Speak, for your servant hears." ¹¹Then the Lord said to Samuel, "Behold, I am about to do a thing in Israel at which the two ears of everyone who hears it will tingle. ¹²On that day I will fulfill against Eli all that I have spoken concerning his house, from beginning to end. ¹³And I declare to him that I am about to punish his house forever, for the iniquity that he knew, because his sons were blaspheming God,[1] and he did not restrain them. ¹⁴Therefore I swear to the house of Eli that the iniquity of Eli's house shall not be atoned for by sacrifice or offering forever."

¹⁵Samuel lay until morning; then he opened the doors of the house of the Lord. And Samuel was afraid to tell the vision to Eli. ¹⁶But Eli called Samuel and said, "Samuel, my son." And he said, "Here I am." ¹⁷And Eli said, "What was it that he told you? Do not hide it from me. May God do so to you and more also if you hide anything from me of all that he told you." ¹⁸So Samuel told him everything and hid nothing from him. And he said, "It is the Lord. Let him do what seems good to him."

¹⁹And Samuel grew, and the Lord was with him and let none of his words fall to the ground. ²⁰And all Israel from Dan to Beersheba knew that Samuel was established as a prophet of the Lord. ²¹And the Lord appeared again at Shiloh, for the Lord revealed himself to Samuel at Shiloh by the word of the Lord.

Romans 3

Then what advantage has the Jew? Or what is the value of circumcision? ²Much in every way. To begin with, the Jews were entrusted with the oracles of God. ³What if some were unfaithful? Does their faithlessness nullify the faithfulness of God? ⁴By no means! Let God be true though every one were a liar, as it is written,

"That you may be justified in your words, and prevail when you are judged."

⁵But if our unrighteousness serves to show the righteousness of God, what shall we say? That God is unrighteous to inflict wrath on us? (I speak in a human way.) ⁶By no means! For then how could God judge the world? ⁷But if through my lie God's truth abounds to his glory, why am I still being condemned as a sinner? ⁸And why not do evil that good may come?—as some people slanderously charge us with saying. Their condemnation is just.

⁹What then? Are we Jews[2] any better off?[3] No, not at all. For we have already charged that all, both Jews and Greeks, are under sin, ¹⁰as it is written:

[1] Or blaspheming for themselves [2] Greek Are we [3] Or at any disadvantage?

"None is righteous, no, not one;
11   no one understands;
       no one seeks for God.
12   All have turned aside; together they
       have become worthless;
       no one does good,
       not even one."
13   "Their throat is an open grave;
       they use their tongues to deceive."
     "The venom of asps is under their lips."
14   "Their mouth is full of curses and
       bitterness."
15   "Their feet are swift to shed blood;
16   in their paths are ruin and misery,
17   and the way of peace they have not
       known."
18   "There is no fear of God before their
       eyes."

19 Now we know that whatever the law says it speaks to those who are under the law, so that every mouth may be stopped, and the whole world may be held accountable to God. 20 For by works of the law no human being[1] will be justified in his sight, since through the law comes knowledge of sin.

21 But now the righteousness of God has been manifested apart from the law, although the Law and the Prophets bear witness to it— 22 the righteousness of God through faith in Jesus Christ for all who believe. For there is no distinction: 23 for all have sinned and fall short of the glory of God, 24 and are justified by his grace as a gift, through the redemption that is in Christ Jesus, 25 whom God put forward as a propitiation by his blood, to be received by faith. This was to show God's righteousness, because in his divine forbearance he had passed over former sins. 26 It was to show his righteousness at the present time, so that he might be just and the justifier of the one who has faith in Jesus.

27 Then what becomes of our boasting? It is excluded. By what kind of law? By a law of works? No, but by the law of faith. 28 For we hold that one is justified by faith apart from works of the law. 29 Or is God the God of Jews only? Is he not the God of Gentiles also? Yes, of Gentiles also, 30 since God is one—who will justify the circumcised by faith and the uncircumcised through faith. 31 Do we then overthrow the law by this faith? By no means! On the contrary, we uphold the law.

--------- *Jeremiah 41* ---------

In the seventh month, Ishmael the son of Nethaniah, son of Elishama, of the royal family, one of the chief officers of the king, came with ten men to Gedaliah the son of Ahikam, at Mizpah. As they ate bread together there at Mizpah, 2 Ishmael the son of Nethaniah and the ten men with him rose up and struck down Gedaliah the son of Ahikam, son of Shaphan, with the sword, and killed him, whom the king of Babylon had appointed governor in the land. 3 Ishmael also struck down all the Judeans who were with Gedaliah at Mizpah, and the Chaldean soldiers who happened to be there.

4 On the day after the murder of Gedaliah, before anyone knew of it, 5 eighty men arrived from Shechem and Shiloh and Samaria, with their beards shaved and their clothes torn, and their bodies gashed, bringing grain offerings and incense to present at the temple of the LORD. 6 And Ishmael the son of Nethaniah came out from Mizpah to meet them, weeping as he came. As he met them, he said to them, "Come in to Gedaliah the son of Ahikam." 7 When they came into the city, Ishmael the son of Nethaniah and the men with him slaughtered them and cast them into a cistern. 8 But there were ten men among them who said to Ishmael, "Do not put us to death, for we have stores of wheat, barley, oil, and honey hidden in the fields." So he refrained and did not put them to death with their companions.

9 Now the cistern into which Ishmael had thrown all the bodies of the men whom he had struck down along with[2] Gedaliah was the large cistern that King Asa had made for defense against Baasha king of Israel; Ishmael the son of Nethaniah filled it with the slain. 10 Then Ishmael took captive all the rest of the people who were in Mizpah, the king's daughters and all the people who were left at Mizpah, whom Nebuzaradan, the captain of the guard, had committed to Gedaliah the son of Ahikam. Ishmael the son of Nethaniah took them captive and set out to cross over to the Ammonites.

11 But when Johanan the son of Kareah and all the leaders of the forces with him heard of all the evil that Ishmael the son of Nethaniah had done, 12 they took all their men and went to fight against Ishmael the son of Nethaniah. They came upon him at the great pool that is

---

[1] Greek *flesh* [2] Hebrew *by the hand of*

in Gibeon. [13]And when all the people who were with Ishmael saw Johanan the son of Kareah and all the leaders of the forces with him, they rejoiced. [14]So all the people whom Ishmael had carried away captive from Mizpah turned around and came back, and went to Johanan the son of Kareah. [15]But Ishmael the son of Nethaniah escaped from Johanan with eight men, and went to the Ammonites. [16]Then Johanan the son of Kareah and all the leaders of the forces with him took from Mizpah all the rest of the people whom he had recovered from Ishmael the son of Nethaniah, after he had struck down Gedaliah the son of Ahikam—soldiers, women, children, and eunuchs, whom Johanan brought back from Gibeon. [17]And they went and stayed at Geruth Chimham near Bethlehem, intending to go to Egypt [18]because of the Chaldeans. For they were afraid of them, because Ishmael the son of Nethaniah had struck down Gedaliah the son of Ahikam, whom the king of Babylon had made governor over the land.

Psalm 17

A Prayer of David.

Hear a just cause, O Lord; attend to my cry!
 Give ear to my prayer from lips free of
  deceit!
[2] From your presence let my vindication
  come!
  Let your eyes behold the right!

[3] You have tried my heart, you have
   visited me by night,
  you have tested me, and you will find
   nothing;
  I have purposed that my mouth will
   not transgress.
[4] With regard to the works of man, by the
   word of your lips
  I have avoided the ways of the violent.

[5] My steps have held fast to your paths;
  my feet have not slipped.

[6] I call upon you, for you will answer me,
   O God;
  incline your ear to me; hear my
   words.
[7] Wondrously show[1] your steadfast love,
  O Savior of those who seek refuge
  from their adversaries at your right
   hand.

[8] Keep me as the apple of your eye;
  hide me in the shadow of your
   wings,
[9] from the wicked who do me violence,
  my deadly enemies who surround
   me.

[10] They close their hearts to pity;
  with their mouths they speak
   arrogantly.
[11] They have now surrounded our steps;
  they set their eyes to cast us to the
   ground.
[12] He is like a lion eager to tear,
  as a young lion lurking in ambush.

[13] Arise, O Lord! Confront him, subdue
   him!
  Deliver my soul from the wicked by
   your sword,
[14] from men by your hand, O Lord,
  from men of the world whose portion
   is in this life.[2]
  You fill their womb with treasure;[3]
  they are satisfied with children,
  and they leave their abundance to
   their infants.

[15] As for me, I shall behold your face in
   righteousness;
  when I awake, I shall be satisfied with
   your likeness.

---

[1] Or Distinguish me by   [2] Or from men whose portion in life is of the world   [3] Or As for your treasured ones, you fill their womb

AUGUST 14

1 Samuel 4

And the word of Samuel came to all Israel. Now Israel went out to battle against the Philistines. They encamped at Ebenezer, and the Philistines encamped at Aphek. ²The Philistines drew up in line against Israel, and when the battle spread, Israel was defeated before the Philistines, who killed about four thousand men on the field of battle. ³And when the people came to the camp, the elders of Israel said, "Why has the LORD defeated us today before the Philistines? Let us bring the ark of the covenant of the LORD here from Shiloh, that it¹ may come among us and save us from the power of our enemies." ⁴So the people sent to Shiloh and brought from there the ark of the covenant of the LORD of hosts, who is enthroned on the cherubim. And the two sons of Eli, Hophni and Phinehas, were there with the ark of the covenant of God.

⁵As soon as the ark of the covenant of the LORD came into the camp, all Israel gave a mighty shout, so that the earth resounded. ⁶And when the Philistines heard the noise of the shouting, they said, "What does this great shouting in the camp of the Hebrews mean?" And when they learned that the ark of the LORD had come to the camp, ⁷the Philistines were afraid, for they said, "A god has come into the camp." And they said, "Woe to us! For nothing like this has happened before. ⁸Woe to us! Who can deliver us from the power of these mighty gods? These are the gods who struck the Egyptians with every sort of plague in the wilderness. ⁹Take courage, and be men, O Philistines, lest you become slaves to the Hebrews as they have been to you; be men and fight."

¹⁰So the Philistines fought, and Israel was defeated, and they fled, every man to his home. And there was a very great slaughter, for thirty thousand foot soldiers of Israel fell. ¹¹And the ark of God was captured, and the two sons of Eli, Hophni and Phinehas, died.

¹²A man of Benjamin ran from the battle line and came to Shiloh the same day, with his clothes torn and with dirt on his head. ¹³When he arrived, Eli was sitting on his seat by the road watching, for his heart trembled for the ark of God. And when the man came into the city and told the news, all the city cried out. ¹⁴When Eli heard the sound of the outcry, he said, "What is this uproar?" Then the man hurried and came and told Eli. ¹⁵Now Eli was ninety-eight years old and his eyes were set so that he could not see. ¹⁶And the man said to Eli, "I am he who has come from the battle; I fled from the battle today." And he said, "How did it go, my son?" ¹⁷He who brought the news answered and said, "Israel has fled before the Philistines, and there has also been a great defeat among the people. Your two sons also, Hophni and Phinehas, are dead, and the ark of God has been captured." ¹⁸As soon as he mentioned the ark of God, Eli fell over backward from his seat by the side of the gate, and his neck was broken and he died, for the man was old and heavy. He had judged Israel forty years.

¹⁹Now his daughter-in-law, the wife of Phinehas, was pregnant, about to give birth. And when she heard the news that the ark of God was captured, and that her father-in-law and her husband were dead, she bowed and gave birth, for her pains came upon her. ²⁰And about the time of her death the women attending her said to her, "Do not be afraid, for you have borne a son." But she did not answer or pay attention. ²¹And she named the child Ichabod, saying, "The glory has departed² from Israel!" because the ark of God had been captured and because of her father-in-law and her husband. ²²And she said, "The glory has departed from Israel, for the ark of God has been captured."

Romans 4

What then shall we say was gained by³ Abraham, our forefather according to the flesh? ²For if Abraham was justified by

¹ Or he ² Or gone into exile; also verse 22 ³ Some manuscripts say about

works, he has something to boast about, but not before God. [3]For what does the Scripture say? "Abraham believed God, and it was counted to him as righteousness." [4]Now to the one who works, his wages are not counted as a gift but as his due. [5]And to the one who does not work but believes in[1] him who justifies the ungodly, his faith is counted as righteousness, [6]just as David also speaks of the blessing of the one to whom God counts righteousness apart from works:

[7]   "Blessed are those whose lawless deeds
        are forgiven,
     and whose sins are covered;
[8]   blessed is the man against whom the
        Lord will not count his sin."

[9]Is this blessing then only for the circumcised, or also for the uncircumcised? For we say that faith was counted to Abraham as righteousness. [10]How then was it counted to him? Was it before or after he had been circumcised? It was not after, but before he was circumcised. [11]He received the sign of circumcision as a seal of the righteousness that he had by faith while he was still uncircumcised. The purpose was to make him the father of all who believe without being circumcised, so that righteousness would be counted to them as well, [12]and to make him the father of the circumcised who are not merely circumcised but who also walk in the footsteps of the faith that our father Abraham had before he was circumcised.

[13]For the promise to Abraham and his offspring that he would be heir of the world did not come through the law but through the righteousness of faith. [14]For if it is the adherents of the law who are to be the heirs, faith is null and the promise is void. [15]For the law brings wrath, but where there is no law there is no transgression.

[16]That is why it depends on faith, in order that the promise may rest on grace and be guaranteed to all his offspring—not only to the adherent of the law but also to the one who shares the faith of Abraham, who is the father of us all, [17]as it is written, "I have made you the father of many nations"—in the presence of the God in whom he believed, who gives life to the dead and calls into existence the things that do not exist. [18]In hope he believed against hope, that he should become the father of many nations, as he had been told, "So shall your offspring be." [19]He did not weaken in faith when he considered his own body, which was as good as dead (since he was about a hundred years old), or when he considered the barrenness[2] of Sarah's womb. [20]No unbelief made him waver concerning the promise of God, but he grew strong in his faith as he gave glory to God, [21]fully convinced that God was able to do what he had promised. [22]That is why his faith was "counted to him as righteousness." [23]But the words "it was counted to him" were not written for his sake alone, [24]but for ours also. It will be counted to us who believe in him who raised from the dead Jesus our Lord, [25]who was delivered up for our trespasses and raised for our justification.

——————— *Jeremiah 42* ———————

Then all the commanders of the forces, and Johanan the son of Kareah and Jezaniah the son of Hoshaiah, and all the people from the least to the greatest, came near [2]and said to Jeremiah the prophet, "Let our plea for mercy come before you, and pray to the LORD your God for us, for all this remnant—because we are left with but a few, as your eyes see us— [3]that the LORD your God may show us the way we should go, and the thing that we should do." [4]Jeremiah the prophet said to them, "I have heard you. Behold, I will pray to the LORD your God according to your request, and whatever the LORD answers you I will tell you. I will keep nothing back from you." [5]Then they said to Jeremiah, "May the LORD be a true and faithful witness against us if we do not act according to all the word with which the LORD your God sends you to us. [6]Whether it is good or bad, we will obey the voice of the LORD our God to whom we are sending you, that it may be well with us when we obey the voice of the LORD our God."

[7]At the end of ten days the word of the LORD came to Jeremiah. [8]Then he summoned Johanan the son of Kareah and all the commanders of the forces who were with him, and all the people from the least to the greatest, [9]and said to them, "Thus says the LORD, the God of Israel, to whom you sent me to present your plea for mercy before him: [10]If you will remain in this land, then I will build you up and not pull you down; I will plant you, and not pluck you up; for I relent of the disaster that I did to you. [11]Do not fear the king of Babylon, of whom you are afraid. Do not fear him, declares

---

[1] Or *but trusts*; compare verse 24 [2] Greek *deadness*

the Lord, for I am with you, to save you and to deliver you from his hand. ¹²I will grant you mercy, that he may have mercy on you and let you remain in your own land. ¹³But if you say, 'We will not remain in this land,' disobeying the voice of the Lord your God ¹⁴and saying, 'No, we will go to the land of Egypt, where we shall not see war or hear the sound of the trumpet or be hungry for bread, and we will dwell there,' ¹⁵then hear the word of the Lord, O remnant of Judah. Thus says the Lord of hosts, the God of Israel: If you set your faces to enter Egypt and go to live there, ¹⁶then the sword that you fear shall overtake you there in the land of Egypt, and the famine of which you are afraid shall follow close after you to Egypt, and there you shall die. ¹⁷All the men who set their faces to go to Egypt to live there shall die by the sword, by famine, and by pestilence. They shall have no remnant or survivor from the disaster that I will bring upon them.

¹⁸"For thus says the Lord of hosts, the God of Israel: As my anger and my wrath were poured out on the inhabitants of Jerusalem, so my wrath will be poured out on you when you go to Egypt. You shall become an execration, a horror, a curse, and a taunt. You shall see this place no more. ¹⁹The Lord has said to you, O remnant of Judah, 'Do not go to Egypt.' Know for a certainty that I have warned you this day ²⁰that you have gone astray at the cost of your lives. For you sent me to the Lord your God, saying, 'Pray for us to the Lord our God, and whatever the Lord our God says declare to us and we will do it.' ²¹And I have this day declared it to you, but you have not obeyed the voice of the Lord your God in anything that he sent me to tell you. ²²Now therefore know for a certainty that you shall die by the sword, by famine, and by pestilence in the place where you desire to go to live."

Psalm 18

TO THE CHOIRMASTER. A PSALM OF DAVID, THE SERVANT OF THE LORD, WHO ADDRESSED THE WORDS OF THIS SONG TO THE LORD ON THE DAY WHEN THE LORD RESCUED HIM FROM THE HAND OF ALL HIS ENEMIES, AND FROM THE HAND OF SAUL. HE SAID:

I love you, O Lord, my strength.
² The Lord is my rock and my fortress and
my deliverer,

my God, my rock, in whom I take
refuge,
my shield, and the horn of my
salvation, my stronghold.
³ I call upon the Lord, who is worthy to
be praised,
and I am saved from my enemies.

⁴ The cords of death encompassed me;
the torrents of destruction assailed
me;¹
⁵ the cords of Sheol entangled me;
the snares of death confronted me.

⁶ In my distress I called upon the Lord;
to my God I cried for help.
From his temple he heard my voice,
and my cry to him reached his ears.

⁷ Then the earth reeled and rocked;
the foundations also of the mountains
trembled
and quaked, because he was angry.
⁸ Smoke went up from his nostrils,²
and devouring fire from his mouth;
glowing coals flamed forth from
him.
⁹ He bowed the heavens and came down;
thick darkness was under his feet.
¹⁰ He rode on a cherub and flew;
he came swiftly on the wings of the
wind.
¹¹ He made darkness his covering, his
canopy around him,
thick clouds dark with water.
¹² Out of the brightness before him
hailstones and coals of fire broke
through his clouds.
¹³ The Lord also thundered in the
heavens,
and the Most High uttered his voice,
hailstones and coals of fire.
¹⁴ And he sent out his arrows and
scattered them;
he flashed forth lightnings and routed
them.
¹⁵ Then the channels of the sea were
seen,
and the foundations of the world were
laid bare
at your rebuke, O Lord,
at the blast of the breath of your
nostrils.

¹ Or terrified me ² Or in his wrath

16 He sent from on high, he took me;
    he drew me out of many waters.
17 He rescued me from my strong enemy
    and from those who hated me,
    for they were too mighty for me.
18 They confronted me in the day of my
       calamity,
    but the LORD was my support.
19 He brought me out into a broad place;
    he rescued me, because he delighted
       in me.

20 The LORD dealt with me according to
       my righteousness;
    according to the cleanness of my
       hands he rewarded me.
21 For I have kept the ways of the LORD,
    and have not wickedly departed from
       my God.
22 For all his rules[1] were before me,
    and his statutes I did not put away
       from me.
23 I was blameless before him,
    and I kept myself from my guilt.
24 So the LORD has rewarded me according
       to my righteousness,
    according to the cleanness of my
       hands in his sight.

25 With the merciful you show yourself
       merciful;
    with the blameless man you show
       yourself blameless;
26 with the purified you show yourself
       pure;
    and with the crooked you make
       yourself seem tortuous.
27 For you save a humble people,
    but the haughty eyes you bring
       down.
28 For it is you who light my lamp;
    the LORD my God lightens my
       darkness.
29 For by you I can run against a troop,
    and by my God I can leap over a wall.
30 This God—his way is perfect;[2]
    the word of the LORD proves true;
    he is a shield for all those who take
       refuge in him.
31 For who is God, but the LORD?
    And who is a rock, except our God?—

32 the God who equipped me with strength
    and made my way blameless.
33 He made my feet like the feet of a deer
    and set me secure on the heights.
34 He trains my hands for war,
    so that my arms can bend a bow of
       bronze.
35 You have given me the shield of your
       salvation,
    and your right hand supported me,
    and your gentleness made me great.
36 You gave a wide place for my steps
       under me,
    and my feet did not slip.
37 I pursued my enemies and overtook
       them,
    and did not turn back till they were
       consumed.
38 I thrust them through, so that they were
       not able to rise;
    they fell under my feet.
39 For you equipped me with strength for
       the battle;
    you made those who rise against me
       sink under me.
40 You made my enemies turn their backs
       to me,[3]
    and those who hated me I destroyed.
41 They cried for help, but there was none
       to save;
    they cried to the LORD, but he did not
       answer them.
42 I beat them fine as dust before the
       wind;
    I cast them out like the mire of the
       streets.

43 You delivered me from strife with the
       people;
    you made me the head of the nations;
    people whom I had not known served
       me.
44 As soon as they heard of me they
       obeyed me;
    foreigners came cringing to me.
45 Foreigners lost heart
    and came trembling out of their
       fortresses.

46 The LORD lives, and blessed be my rock,
    and exalted be the God of my
       salvation—

[1] Or just decrees [2] Or blameless [3] Or You gave me my enemies' necks

47 the God who gave me vengeance
and subdued peoples under me,
48 who delivered me from my enemies;
yes, you exalted me above those who
rose against me;
you rescued me from the man of
violence.

49 For this I will praise you, O LORD, among
the nations,
and sing to your name.
50 Great salvation he brings to his king,
and shows steadfast love to his
anointed,
to David and his offspring forever.

AUGUST 15

1 Samuel 5–6

When the Philistines captured the ark of God, they brought it from Ebenezer to Ashdod. ²Then the Philistines took the ark of God and brought it into the house of Dagon and set it up beside Dagon. ³And when the people of Ashdod rose early the next day, behold, Dagon had fallen face downward on the ground before the ark of the LORD. So they took Dagon and put him back in his place. ⁴But when they rose early on the next morning, behold, Dagon had fallen face downward on the ground before the ark of the LORD, and the head of Dagon and both his hands were lying cut off on the threshold. Only the trunk of Dagon was left to him. ⁵This is why the priests of Dagon and all who enter the house of Dagon do not tread on the threshold of Dagon in Ashdod to this day.

⁶The hand of the LORD was heavy against the people of Ashdod, and he terrified and afflicted them with tumors, both Ashdod and its territory. ⁷And when the men of Ashdod saw how things were, they said, "The ark of the God of Israel must not remain with us, for his hand is hard against us and against Dagon our god." ⁸So they sent and gathered together all the lords of the Philistines and said, "What shall we do with the ark of the God of Israel?" They answered, "Let the ark of the God of Israel be brought around to Gath." So they brought the ark of the God of Israel there. ⁹But after they had brought it around, the hand of the LORD was against the city, causing a very great panic, and he afflicted the men of the city, both young and old, so that tumors broke out on them. ¹⁰So

they sent the ark of God to Ekron. But as soon as the ark of God came to Ekron, the people of Ekron cried out, "They have brought around to us the ark of the God of Israel to kill us and our people." ¹¹They sent therefore and gathered together all the lords of the Philistines and said, "Send away the ark of the God of Israel, and let it return to its own place, that it may not kill us and our people." For there was a deathly panic throughout the whole city. The hand of God was very heavy there. ¹²The men who did not die were struck with tumors, and the cry of the city went up to heaven.

⁶:¹The ark of the LORD was in the country of the Philistines seven months. ²And the Philistines called for the priests and the diviners and said, "What shall we do with the ark of the LORD? Tell us with what we shall send it to its place." ³They said, "If you send away the ark of the God of Israel, do not send it empty, but by all means return him a guilt offering. Then you will be healed, and it will be known to you why his hand does not turn away from you." ⁴And they said, "What is the guilt offering that we shall return to him?" They answered, "Five golden tumors and five golden mice, according to the number of the lords of the Philistines, for the same plague was on all of you and on your lords. ⁵So you must make images of your tumors and images of your mice that ravage the land, and give glory to the God of Israel. Perhaps he will lighten his hand from off you and your gods and your land. ⁶Why should you harden your hearts as the Egyptians and

Pharaoh hardened their hearts? After he had dealt severely with them, did they not send the people away, and they departed? ⁷Now then, take and prepare a new cart and two milk cows on which there has never come a yoke, and yoke the cows to the cart, but take their calves home, away from them. ⁸And take the ark of the Lord and place it on the cart and put in a box at its side the figures of gold, which you are returning to him as a guilt offering. Then send it off and let it go its way ⁹and watch. If it goes up on the way to its own land, to Beth-shemesh, then it is he who has done us this great harm, but if not, then we shall know that it is not his hand that struck us; it happened to us by coincidence."

¹⁰The men did so, and took two milk cows and yoked them to the cart and shut up their calves at home. ¹¹And they put the ark of the Lord on the cart and the box with the golden mice and the images of their tumors. ¹²And the cows went straight in the direction of Beth-shemesh along one highway, lowing as they went. They turned neither to the right nor to the left, and the lords of the Philistines went after them as far as the border of Beth-shemesh. ¹³Now the people of Beth-shemesh were reaping their wheat harvest in the valley. And when they lifted up their eyes and saw the ark, they rejoiced to see it. ¹⁴The cart came into the field of Joshua of Beth-shemesh and stopped there. A great stone was there. And they split up the wood of the cart and offered the cows as a burnt offering to the Lord. ¹⁵And the Levites took down the ark of the Lord and the box that was beside it, in which were the golden figures, and set them upon the great stone. And the men of Beth-shemesh offered burnt offerings and sacrificed sacrifices on that day to the Lord. ¹⁶And when the five lords of the Philistines saw it, they returned that day to Ekron.

¹⁷These are the golden tumors that the Philistines returned as a guilt offering to the Lord: one for Ashdod, one for Gaza, one for Ashkelon, one for Gath, one for Ekron, ¹⁸and the golden mice, according to the number of all the cities of the Philistines belonging to the five lords, both fortified cities and unwalled villages. The great stone beside which they set down the ark of the Lord is a witness to this day in the field of Joshua of Beth-shemesh.

¹⁹And he struck some of the men of Beth-shemesh, because they looked upon the ark of the Lord. He struck seventy men of them,[1] and the people mourned because the Lord had struck the people with a great blow. ²⁰Then the men of Beth-shemesh said, "Who is able to stand before the Lord, this holy God? And to whom shall he go up away from us?" ²¹So they sent messengers to the inhabitants of Kiriath-jearim, saying, "The Philistines have returned the ark of the Lord. Come down and take it up to you."

Romans 5

Therefore, since we have been justified by faith, we[2] have peace with God through our Lord Jesus Christ. ²Through him we have also obtained access by faith[3] into this grace in which we stand, and we[4] rejoice[5] in hope of the glory of God. ³Not only that, but we rejoice in our sufferings, knowing that suffering produces endurance, ⁴and endurance produces character, and character produces hope, ⁵and hope does not put us to shame, because God's love has been poured into our hearts through the Holy Spirit who has been given to us.

⁶For while we were still weak, at the right time Christ died for the ungodly. ⁷For one will scarcely die for a righteous person—though perhaps for a good person one would dare even to die— ⁸but God shows his love for us in that while we were still sinners, Christ died for us. ⁹Since, therefore, we have now been justified by his blood, much more shall we be saved by him from the wrath of God. ¹⁰For if while we were enemies we were reconciled to God by the death of his Son, much more, now that we are reconciled, shall we be saved by his life. ¹¹More than that, we also rejoice in God through our Lord Jesus Christ, through whom we have now received reconciliation.

¹²Therefore, just as sin came into the world through one man, and death through sin, and so death spread to all men[6] because all sinned— ¹³for sin indeed was in the world before the law was given, but sin is not counted where there is no law. ¹⁴Yet death reigned from Adam to Moses, even over those whose sinning was not like the transgression of Adam, who was a type of the one who was to come.

¹⁵But the free gift is not like the trespass.

[1] Most Hebrew manuscripts *struck of the people seventy men, fifty thousand men* [2] Some manuscripts *let us* [3] Some manuscripts omit *by faith* [4] Or *let us*; also verse 3 [5] Or *boast*; also verses 3, 11 [6] The Greek word *anthropoi* refers here to both men and women; also twice in verse 18

For if many died through one man's trespass, much more have the grace of God and the free gift by the grace of that one man Jesus Christ abounded for many. [16]And the free gift is not like the result of that one man's sin. For the judgment following one trespass brought condemnation, but the free gift following many trespasses brought justification. [17]For if, because of one man's trespass, death reigned through that one man, much more will those who receive the abundance of grace and the free gift of righteousness reign in life through the one man Jesus Christ.

[18]Therefore, as one trespass[1] led to condemnation for all men, so one act of righteousness[2] leads to justification and life for all men. [19]For as by the one man's disobedience the many were made sinners, so by the one man's obedience the many will be made righteous. [20]Now the law came in to increase the trespass, but where sin increased, grace abounded all the more, [21]so that, as sin reigned in death, grace also might reign through righteousness leading to eternal life through Jesus Christ our Lord.

Jeremiah 43

When Jeremiah finished speaking to all the people all these words of the LORD their God, with which the LORD their God had sent him to them, [2]Azariah the son of Hoshaiah and Johanan the son of Kareah and all the insolent men said to Jeremiah, "You are telling a lie. The LORD our God did not send you to say, 'Do not go to Egypt to live there,' [3]but Baruch the son of Neriah has set you against us, to deliver us into the hand of the Chaldeans, that they may kill us or take us into exile in Babylon." [4]So Johanan the son of Kareah and all the commanders of the forces and all the people did not obey the voice of the LORD, to remain in the land of Judah. [5]But Johanan the son of Kareah and all the commanders of the forces took all the remnant of Judah who had returned to live in the land of Judah from all the nations to which they had been driven— [6]the men, the women, the children, the princesses, and every person whom Nebuzaradan the captain of the guard had left with Gedaliah the son of Ahikam, son of Shaphan; also Jeremiah the prophet and Baruch the son of Neriah. [7]And they came into the land of Egypt,

for they did not obey the voice of the LORD. And they arrived at Tahpanhes.

[8]Then the word of the LORD came to Jeremiah in Tahpanhes: [9]"Take in your hands large stones and hide them in the mortar in the pavement that is at the entrance to Pharaoh's palace in Tahpanhes, in the sight of the men of Judah, [10]and say to them, 'Thus says the LORD of hosts, the God of Israel: Behold, I will send and take Nebuchadnezzar the king of Babylon, my servant, and I will set his throne above these stones that I have hidden, and he will spread his royal canopy over them. [11]He shall come and strike the land of Egypt, giving over to the pestilence those who are doomed to the pestilence, to captivity those who are doomed to captivity, and to the sword those who are doomed to the sword. [12]I shall kindle a fire in the temples of the gods of Egypt, and he shall burn them and carry them away captive. And he shall clean the land of Egypt as a shepherd cleans his cloak of vermin, and he shall go away from there in peace. [13]He shall break the obelisks of Heliopolis, which is in the land of Egypt, and the temples of the gods of Egypt he shall burn with fire.'"

Psalm 19

To the choirmaster. A Psalm of David.

The heavens declare the glory of God,
  and the sky above[3] proclaims his
    handiwork.
[2] Day to day pours out speech,
    and night to night reveals
      knowledge.
[3] There is no speech, nor are there words,
    whose voice is not heard.
[4] Their voice[4] goes out through all the
      earth,
    and their words to the end of the
      world.
  In them he has set a tent for the sun,
[5]   which comes out like a bridegroom
      leaving his chamber,
    and, like a strong man, runs its course
      with joy.
[6] Its rising is from the end of the
      heavens,
    and its circuit to the end of them,
    and there is nothing hidden from its
      heat.

---

[1] Or the trespass of one [2] Or the act of righteousness of one [3] Hebrew the expanse; compare Genesis 1:6–8 [4] Or Their measuring line

7 The law of the LORD is perfect,[1]
   reviving the soul;
   the testimony of the LORD is sure,
   making wise the simple;
8 the precepts of the LORD are right,
   rejoicing the heart;
   the commandment of the LORD is pure,
   enlightening the eyes;
9 the fear of the LORD is clean,
   enduring forever;
   the rules[2] of the LORD are true,
   and righteous altogether.
10 More to be desired are they than gold,
   even much fine gold;
   sweeter also than honey
   and drippings of the honeycomb.

11 Moreover, by them is your servant
   warned;
   in keeping them there is great reward.
12 Who can discern his errors?
   Declare me innocent from hidden
   faults.
13 Keep back your servant also from
   presumptuous sins;
   let them not have dominion over me!
   Then I shall be blameless,
   and innocent of great transgression.

14 Let the words of my mouth and the
   meditation of my heart
   be acceptable in your sight,
   O LORD, my rock and my redeemer.

AUGUST 16

1 Samuel 7–8

And the men of Kiriath-jearim came and took up the ark of the LORD and brought it to the house of Abinadab on the hill. And they consecrated his son Eleazar to have charge of the ark of the LORD. ²From the day that the ark was lodged at Kiriath-jearim, a long time passed, some twenty years, and all the house of Israel lamented after the LORD.

³And Samuel said to all the house of Israel, "If you are returning to the LORD with all your heart, then put away the foreign gods and the Ashtaroth from among you and direct your heart to the LORD and serve him only, and he will deliver you out of the hand of the Philistines." ⁴So the people of Israel put away the Baals and the Ashtaroth, and they served the LORD only.

⁵Then Samuel said, "Gather all Israel at Mizpah, and I will pray to the LORD for you." ⁶So they gathered at Mizpah and drew water and poured it out before the LORD and fasted on that day and said there, "We have sinned against the LORD." And Samuel judged the people of Israel at Mizpah. ⁷Now when the Philistines heard that the people of Israel had gathered at Mizpah, the lords of the Philistines went up against Israel. And when the people of Israel heard of it, they were afraid of the Philistines. ⁸And the people of Israel said to Samuel, "Do not cease to cry out to the LORD our God for us, that he may save us from the hand of the Philistines." ⁹So Samuel took a nursing lamb and offered it as a whole burnt offering to the LORD. And Samuel cried out to the LORD for Israel, and the LORD answered him. ¹⁰As Samuel was offering up the burnt offering, the Philistines drew near to attack Israel. But the LORD thundered with a mighty sound that day against the Philistines and threw them into confusion, and they were defeated before Israel. ¹¹And the men of Israel went out from Mizpah and pursued the Philistines and struck them, as far as below Beth-car.

¹²Then Samuel took a stone and set it up between Mizpah and Shen[3] and called its name Ebenezer;[4] for he said, "Till now the LORD has helped us." ¹³So the Philistines were subdued and did not again enter the territory of Israel. And the hand of the LORD was against the Philistines all the days of Samuel. ¹⁴The cities

¹ Or blameless ² Or just decrees ³ Hebrew; Septuagint, Syriac Jeshanah ⁴ Ebenezer means stone of help

that the Philistines had taken from Israel were restored to Israel, from Ekron to Gath, and Israel delivered their territory from the hand of the Philistines. There was peace also between Israel and the Amorites. ¹⁵ Samuel judged Israel all the days of his life. ¹⁶ And he went on a circuit year by year to Bethel, Gilgal, and Mizpah. And he judged Israel in all these places. ¹⁷ Then he would return to Ramah, for his home was there, and there also he judged Israel. And he built there an altar to the Lord.

⁸:¹ When Samuel became old, he made his sons judges over Israel. ² The name of his first-born son was Joel, and the name of his second, Abijah; they were judges in Beersheba. ³ Yet his sons did not walk in his ways but turned aside after gain. They took bribes and perverted justice.

⁴ Then all the elders of Israel gathered together and came to Samuel at Ramah ⁵ and said to him, "Behold, you are old and your sons do not walk in your ways. Now appoint for us a king to judge us like all the nations." ⁶ But the thing displeased Samuel when they said, "Give us a king to judge us." And Samuel prayed to the Lord. ⁷ And the Lord said to Samuel, "Obey the voice of the people in all that they say to you, for they have not rejected you, but they have rejected me from being king over them. ⁸ According to all the deeds that they have done, from the day I brought them up out of Egypt even to this day, forsaking me and serving other gods, so they are also doing to you. ⁹ Now then, obey their voice; only you shall solemnly warn them and show them the ways of the king who shall reign over them."

¹⁰ So Samuel told all the words of the Lord to the people who were asking for a king from him. ¹¹ He said, "These will be the ways of the king who will reign over you: he will take your sons and appoint them to his chariots and to be his horsemen and to run before his chariots. ¹² And he will appoint for himself commanders of thousands and commanders of fifties, and some to plow his ground and to reap his harvest, and to make his implements of war and the equipment of his chariots. ¹³ He will take your daughters to be perfumers and cooks and bakers. ¹⁴ He will take the best of your fields and vineyards and olive orchards and give them to his servants. ¹⁵ He will take the tenth of your

grain and of your vineyards and give it to his officers and to his servants. ¹⁶ He will take your male servants and female servants and the best of your young men[1] and your donkeys, and put them to his work. ¹⁷ He will take the tenth of your flocks, and you shall be his slaves. ¹⁸ And in that day you will cry out because of your king, whom you have chosen for yourselves, but the Lord will not answer you in that day."

¹⁹ But the people refused to obey the voice of Samuel. And they said, "No! But there shall be a king over us, ²⁰ that we also may be like all the nations, and that our king may judge us and go out before us and fight our battles." ²¹ And when Samuel had heard all the words of the people, he repeated them in the ears of the Lord. ²² And the Lord said to Samuel, "Obey their voice and make them a king." Samuel then said to the men of Israel, "Go every man to his city."

Romans 6

What shall we say then? Are we to continue in sin that grace may abound? ² By no means! How can we who died to sin still live in it? ³ Do you not know that all of us who have been baptized into Christ Jesus were baptized into his death? ⁴ We were buried therefore with him by baptism into death, in order that, just as Christ was raised from the dead by the glory of the Father, we too might walk in newness of life.

⁵ For if we have been united with him in a death like his, we shall certainly be united with him in a resurrection like his. ⁶ We know that our old self[2] was crucified with him in order that the body of sin might be brought to nothing, so that we would no longer be enslaved to sin. ⁷ For one who has died has been set free[3] from sin. ⁸ Now if we have died with Christ, we believe that we will also live with him. ⁹ We know that Christ, being raised from the dead, will never die again; death no longer has dominion over him. ¹⁰ For the death he died he died to sin, once for all, but the life he lives he lives to God. ¹¹ So you also must consider yourselves dead to sin and alive to God in Christ Jesus.

¹² Let not sin therefore reign in your mortal body, to make you obey its passions. ¹³ Do not present your members to sin as instruments for

[1] Septuagint cattle [2] Greek man [3] Greek has been justified

unrighteousness, but present yourselves to God as those who have been brought from death to life, and your members to God as instruments for righteousness. ¹⁴For sin will have no dominion over you, since you are not under law but under grace.

¹⁵What then? Are we to sin because we are not under law but under grace? By no means! ¹⁶Do you not know that if you present yourselves to anyone as obedient slaves,¹ you are slaves of the one whom you obey, either of sin, which leads to death, or of obedience, which leads to righteousness? ¹⁷But thanks be to God, that you who were once slaves of sin have become obedient from the heart to the standard of teaching to which you were committed, ¹⁸and, having been set free from sin, have become slaves of righteousness. ¹⁹I am speaking in human terms, because of your natural limitations. For just as you once presented your members as slaves to impurity and to lawlessness leading to more lawlessness, so now present your members as slaves to righteousness leading to sanctification.

²⁰For when you were slaves of sin, you were free in regard to righteousness. ²¹But what fruit were you getting at that time from the things of which you are now ashamed? For the end of those things is death. ²²But now that you have been set free from sin and have become slaves of God, the fruit you get leads to sanctification and its end, eternal life. ²³For the wages of sin is death, but the free gift of God is eternal life in Christ Jesus our Lord.

──────── *Jeremiah 44* ────────

The word that came to Jeremiah concerning all the Judeans who lived in the land of Egypt, at Migdol, at Tahpanhes, at Memphis, and in the land of Pathros, ²"Thus says the LORD of hosts, the God of Israel: You have seen all the disaster that I brought upon Jerusalem and upon all the cities of Judah. Behold, this day they are a desolation, and no one dwells in them, ³because of the evil that they committed, provoking me to anger, in that they went to make offerings and serve other gods that they knew not, neither they, nor you, nor your fathers. ⁴Yet I persistently sent to you all my servants the prophets, saying, 'Oh, do not do this abomination that I

hate!' ⁵But they did not listen or incline their ear, to turn from their evil and make no offerings to other gods. ⁶Therefore my wrath and my anger were poured out and kindled in the cities of Judah and in the streets of Jerusalem, and they became a waste and a desolation, as at this day. ⁷And now thus says the LORD God of hosts, the God of Israel: Why do you commit this great evil against yourselves, to cut off from you man and woman, infant and child, from the midst of Judah, leaving you no remnant? ⁸Why do you provoke me to anger with the works of your hands, making offerings to other gods in the land of Egypt where you have come to live, so that you may be cut off and become a curse and a taunt among all the nations of the earth? ⁹Have you forgotten the evil of your fathers, the evil of the kings of Judah, the evil of their² wives, your own evil, and the evil of your wives, which they committed in the land of Judah and in the streets of Jerusalem? ¹⁰They have not humbled themselves even to this day, nor have they feared, nor walked in my law and my statutes that I set before you and before your fathers.

¹¹"Therefore thus says the LORD of hosts, the God of Israel: Behold, I will set my face against you for harm, to cut off all Judah. ¹²I will take the remnant of Judah who have set their faces to come to the land of Egypt to live, and they shall all be consumed. In the land of Egypt they shall fall; by the sword and by famine they shall be consumed. From the least to the greatest, they shall die by the sword and by famine, and they shall become an oath, a horror, a curse, and a taunt. ¹³I will punish those who dwell in the land of Egypt, as I have punished Jerusalem, with the sword, with famine, and with pestilence, ¹⁴so that none of the remnant of Judah who have come to live in the land of Egypt shall escape or survive or return to the land of Judah, to which they desire to return to dwell there. For they shall not return, except some fugitives."

¹⁵Then all the men who knew that their wives had made offerings to other gods, and all the women who stood by, a great assembly, all the people who lived in Pathros in the land of Egypt, answered Jeremiah: ¹⁶"As for the word that you have spoken to us in the name of the LORD, we will not listen to you. ¹⁷But we will do everything that we have vowed, make offerings to the queen of heaven and pour out

drink offerings to her, as we did, both we and our fathers, our kings and our officials, in the cities of Judah and in the streets of Jerusalem. For then we had plenty of food, and prospered, and saw no disaster. [18] But since we left off making offerings to the queen of heaven and pouring out drink offerings to her, we have lacked everything and have been consumed by the sword and by famine." [19] And the women said,[1] "When we made offerings to the queen of heaven and poured out drink offerings to her, was it without our husbands' approval that we made cakes for her bearing her image and poured out drink offerings to her?"

[20] Then Jeremiah said to all the people, men and women, all the people who had given him this answer: [21] "As for the offerings that you offered in the cities of Judah and in the streets of Jerusalem, you and your fathers, your kings and your officials, and the people of the land, did not the LORD remember them? Did it not come into his mind? [22] The LORD could no longer bear your evil deeds and the abominations that you committed. Therefore your land has become a desolation and a waste and a curse, without inhabitant, as it is this day. [23] It is because you made offerings and because you sinned against the LORD and did not obey the voice of the LORD or walk in his law and in his statutes and in his testimonies that this disaster has happened to you, as at this day."

[24] Jeremiah said to all the people and all the women, "Hear the word of the LORD, all you of Judah who are in the land of Egypt. [25] Thus says the LORD of hosts, the God of Israel: You and your wives have declared with your mouths, and have fulfilled it with your hands, saying, 'We will surely perform our vows that we have made, to make offerings to the queen of heaven and to pour out drink offerings to her.' Then confirm your vows and perform your vows! [26] Therefore hear the word of the LORD, all you of Judah who dwell in the land of Egypt: Behold, I have sworn by my great name, says the LORD, that my name shall no more be invoked by the mouth of any man of Judah in all the land of Egypt, saying, 'As the Lord GOD lives.' [27] Behold, I am watching over them for disaster and not for good. All the men of Judah who are in the land of Egypt shall be consumed by the sword and by famine, until there is an end of them. [28] And those who

escape the sword shall return from the land of Egypt to the land of Judah, few in number; and all the remnant of Judah, who came to the land of Egypt to live, shall know whose word will stand, mine or theirs. [29] This shall be the sign to you, declares the LORD, that I will punish you in this place, in order that you may know that my words will surely stand against you for harm: [30] Thus says the LORD, Behold, I will give Pharaoh Hophra king of Egypt into the hand of his enemies and into the hand of those who seek his life, as I gave Zedekiah king of Judah into the hand of Nebuchadnezzar king of Babylon, who was his enemy and sought his life."

Psalm 20–21

To the choirmaster. A Psalm of David.

M ay the LORD answer you in the day of trouble!
      May the name of the God of Jacob
        protect you!
2   May he send you help from the
        sanctuary
      and give you support from Zion!
3   May he remember all your offerings
      and regard with favor your burnt
        sacrifices!   *Selah*

4   May he grant you your heart's desire
      and fulfill all your plans!
5   May we shout for joy over your
        salvation,
      and in the name of our God set up our
        banners!
      May the LORD fulfill all your petitions!

6   Now I know that the LORD saves his
        anointed;
      he will answer him from his holy
        heaven
      with the saving might of his right
        hand.
7   Some trust in chariots and some in
        horses,
      but we trust in the name of the LORD
        our God.
8   They collapse and fall,
      but we rise and stand upright.

9   O LORD, save the king!
      May he answer us when we call.

[1] Compare Syriac; Hebrew lacks *And the women said*

To the choirmaster. A Psalm of David.

O LORD, in your strength the king rejoices,
　　and in your salvation how greatly he
　　　exults!
2 You have given him his heart's desire
　　and have not withheld the request of
　　　his lips. 　　　　　　　　*Selah*
3 For you meet him with rich blessings;
　　you set a crown of fine gold upon his
　　　head.
4 He asked life of you; you gave it to him,
　　length of days forever and ever.
5 His glory is great through your salvation;
　　splendor and majesty you bestow on
　　　him.
6 For you make him most blessed forever;[1]
　　you make him glad with the joy of
　　　your presence.
7 For the king trusts in the LORD,
　　and through the steadfast love of the
　　　Most High he shall not be moved.

8 Your hand will find out all your
　　enemies;
　　your right hand will find out those
　　　who hate you.
9 You will make them as a blazing oven
　　when you appear.
The LORD will swallow them up in his
　　wrath,
　　and fire will consume them.
10 You will destroy their descendants from
　　the earth,
　　and their offspring from among the
　　　children of man.
11 Though they plan evil against you,
　　though they devise mischief, they will
　　　not succeed.
12 For you will put them to flight;
　　you will aim at their faces with your
　　　bows.
13 Be exalted, O LORD, in your strength!
　　We will sing and praise your power.

AUGUST 17

1 Samuel 9

There was a man of Benjamin whose name was Kish, the son of Abiel, son of Zeror, son of Becorath, son of Aphiah, a Benjaminite, a man of wealth. ²And he had a son whose name was Saul, a handsome young man. There was not a man among the people of Israel more handsome than he. From his shoulders upward he was taller than any of the people.

³ Now the donkeys of Kish, Saul's father, were lost. So Kish said to Saul his son, "Take one of the young men with you, and arise, go and look for the donkeys." ⁴And he passed through the hill country of Ephraim and passed through the land of Shalishah, but they did not find them. And they passed through the land of Shaalim, but they were not there. Then they passed through the land of Benjamin, but did not find them.

⁵ When they came to the land of Zuph, Saul said to his servant² who was with him, "Come, let us go back, lest my father cease to care about the donkeys and become anxious about us." ⁶But he said to him, "Behold, there is a man of God in this city, and he is a man who is held in honor; all that he says comes true. So now let us go there. Perhaps he can tell us the way we should go." ⁷Then Saul said to his servant, "But if we go, what can we bring the man? For the bread in our sacks is gone, and there is no present to bring to the man of God. What do we have?" ⁸The servant answered Saul again, "Here, I have with me a quarter of a shekel³ of silver, and I will give it to the man of God to tell us our way." ⁹(Formerly in Israel, when a man went to inquire of God, he said, "Come, let us go to the seer," for today's "prophet" was formerly called a seer.) ¹⁰And Saul said to his servant, "Well said; come, let us go." So they went to the city where the man of God was.

---

¹ Or *make him a source of blessing forever* ² Hebrew *young man*; also verses 7, 8, 10, 27 ³ A *shekel* was about 2/5 ounce or 11 grams

¹¹As they went up the hill to the city, they met young women coming out to draw water and said to them, "Is the seer here?" ¹²They answered, "He is; behold, he is just ahead of you. Hurry. He has come just now to the city, because the people have a sacrifice today on the high place. ¹³As soon as you enter the city you will find him, before he goes up to the high place to eat. For the people will not eat till he comes, since he must bless the sacrifice; afterward those who are invited will eat. Now go up, for you will meet him immediately." ¹⁴So they went up to the city. As they were entering the city, they saw Samuel coming out toward them on his way up to the high place.

¹⁵Now the day before Saul came, the Lord had revealed to Samuel: ¹⁶"Tomorrow about this time I will send to you a man from the land of Benjamin, and you shall anoint him to be prince¹ over my people Israel. He shall save my people from the hand of the Philistines. For I have seen² my people, because their cry has come to me." ¹⁷When Samuel saw Saul, the Lord told him, "Here is the man of whom I spoke to you! He it is who shall restrain my people." ¹⁸Then Saul approached Samuel in the gate and said, "Tell me where is the house of the seer?" ¹⁹Samuel answered Saul, "I am the seer. Go up before me to the high place, for today you shall eat with me, and in the morning I will let you go and will tell you all that is on your mind. ²⁰As for your donkeys that were lost three days ago, do not set your mind on them, for they have been found. And for whom is all that is desirable in Israel? Is it not for you and for all your father's house?" ²¹Saul answered, "Am I not a Benjaminite, from the least of the tribes of Israel? And is not my clan the humblest of all the clans of the tribe of Benjamin? Why then have you spoken to me in this way?"

²²Then Samuel took Saul and his young man and brought them into the hall and gave them a place at the head of those who had been invited, who were about thirty persons. ²³And Samuel said to the cook, "Bring the portion I gave you, of which I said to you, 'Put it aside.'" ²⁴So the cook took up the leg and what was on it and set them before Saul. And Samuel said, "See, what was kept is set before you. Eat, because it was kept for you until the hour appointed, that you might eat with the guests."³

So Saul ate with Samuel that day. ²⁵And when they came down from the high place into the city, a bed was spread for Saul⁴ on the roof, and he lay down to sleep. ²⁶Then at the break of dawn⁵ Samuel called to Saul on the roof, "Up, that I may send you on your way." So Saul arose, and both he and Samuel went out into the street.

²⁷As they were going down to the outskirts of the city, Samuel said to Saul, "Tell the servant to pass on before us, and when he has passed on, stop here yourself for a while, that I may make known to you the word of God."

Romans 7

Or do you not know, brothers⁶—for I am speaking to those who know the law—that the law is binding on a person only as long as he lives? ²For a married woman is bound by law to her husband while he lives, but if her husband dies she is released from the law of marriage.⁷ ³Accordingly, she will be called an adulteress if she lives with another man while her husband is alive. But if her husband dies, she is free from that law, and if she marries another man she is not an adulteress.

⁴Likewise, my brothers, you also have died to the law through the body of Christ, so that you may belong to another, to him who has been raised from the dead, in order that we may bear fruit for God. ⁵For while we were living in the flesh, our sinful passions, aroused by the law, were at work in our members to bear fruit for death. ⁶But now we are released from the law, having died to that which held us captive, so that we serve in the new way of the Spirit and not in the old way of the written code.⁸

⁷What then shall we say? That the law is sin? By no means! Yet if it had not been for the law, I would not have known sin. For I would not have known what it is to covet if the law had not said, "You shall not covet." ⁸But sin, seizing an opportunity through the commandment, produced in me all kinds of covetousness. For apart from the law, sin lies dead. ⁹I was once alive apart from the law, but when the commandment came, sin came alive and I died. ¹⁰The very commandment that promised life proved to be death to me. ¹¹For sin, seizing an opportunity through the commandment, deceived me and through it killed me. ¹²So the

law is holy, and the commandment is holy and righteous and good.

¹³ Did that which is good, then, bring death to me? By no means! It was sin, producing death in me through what is good, in order that sin might be shown to be sin, and through the commandment might become sinful beyond measure. ¹⁴ For we know that the law is spiritual, but I am of the flesh, sold under sin. ¹⁵ For I do not understand my own actions. For I do not do what I want, but I do the very thing I hate. ¹⁶ Now if I do what I do not want, I agree with the law, that it is good. ¹⁷ So now it is no longer I who do it, but sin that dwells within me. ¹⁸ For I know that nothing good dwells in me, that is, in my flesh. For I have the desire to do what is right, but not the ability to carry it out. ¹⁹ For I do not do the good I want, but the evil I do not want is what I keep on doing. ²⁰ Now if I do what I do not want, it is no longer I who do it, but sin that dwells within me.

²¹ So I find it to be a law that when I want to do right, evil lies close at hand. ²² For I delight in the law of God, in my inner being, ²³ but I see in my members another law waging war against the law of my mind and making me captive to the law of sin that dwells in my members. ²⁴ Wretched man that I am! Who will deliver me from this body of death? ²⁵ Thanks be to God through Jesus Christ our Lord! So then, I myself serve the law of God with my mind, but with my flesh I serve the law of sin.

───────── *Jeremiah 46* ─────────

The word of the LORD that came to Jeremiah the prophet concerning the nations.

²About Egypt. Concerning the army of Pharaoh Neco, king of Egypt, which was by the river Euphrates at Carchemish and which Nebuchadnezzar king of Babylon defeated in the fourth year of Jehoiakim the son of Josiah, king of Judah:

3   "Prepare buckler and shield,
       and advance for battle!
4   Harness the horses;
       mount, O horsemen!
    Take your stations with your helmets,
       polish your spears,
       put on your armor!

5   Why have I seen it?
    They are dismayed
       and have turned backward.
    Their warriors are beaten down
       and have fled in haste;
    they look not back—
       terror on every side!
                        declares the LORD.

6   "The swift cannot flee away,
       nor the warrior escape;
    in the north by the river Euphrates
       they have stumbled and fallen.

7   "Who is this, rising like the Nile,
       like rivers whose waters surge?
8   Egypt rises like the Nile,
       like rivers whose waters surge.
    He said, 'I will rise, I will cover the
       earth,
       I will destroy cities and their
          inhabitants.'
9   Advance, O horses,
       and rage, O chariots!
    Let the warriors go out:
       men of Cush and Put who handle the
          shield,
       men of Lud, skilled in handling the
          bow.
10 That day is the day of the Lord GOD of
       hosts,
       a day of vengeance,
       to avenge himself on his foes.
    The sword shall devour and be sated
       and drink its fill of their blood.
    For the Lord GOD of hosts holds a
       sacrifice
       in the north country by the river
          Euphrates.
11 Go up to Gilead, and take balm,
       O virgin daughter of Egypt!
    In vain you have used many medicines;
       there is no healing for you.
12 The nations have heard of your shame,
       and the earth is full of your cry;
    for warrior has stumbled against
       warrior;
       they have both fallen together."

¹³ The word that the LORD spoke to Jeremiah the prophet about the coming of Nebuchadnezzar king of Babylon to strike the land of Egypt:

14 "Declare in Egypt, and proclaim in
      Migdol;
   proclaim in Memphis and
      Tahpanhes;
   say, 'Stand ready and be prepared,
      for the sword shall devour around
         you.'
15 Why are your mighty ones face down?
      They do not stand[1]
   because the LORD thrust them down.
16 He made many stumble, and they fell,
      and they said one to another,
   'Arise, and let us go back to our own
         people
      and to the land of our birth,
   because of the sword of the
         oppressor.'
17 Call the name of Pharaoh, king of
      Egypt,
   'Noisy one who lets the hour go by.'

18 "As I live, declares the King,
      whose name is the LORD of hosts,
   like Tabor among the mountains
      and like Carmel by the sea, shall one
         come.
19 Prepare yourselves baggage for exile,
      O inhabitants of Egypt!
   For Memphis shall become a waste,
      a ruin, without inhabitant.

20 "A beautiful heifer is Egypt,
      but a biting fly from the north has
         come upon her.
21 Even her hired soldiers in her midst
      are like fattened calves;
   yes, they have turned and fled together;
      they did not stand,
   for the day of their calamity has come
         upon them,
      the time of their punishment.

22 "She makes a sound like a serpent
         gliding away;
   for her enemies march in force
      and come against her with axes
         like those who fell trees.
23 They shall cut down her forest,
                     declares the LORD,
      though it is impenetrable,
   because they are more numerous than
         locusts;
      they are without number.

24 The daughter of Egypt shall be put to
      shame;
   she shall be delivered into the hand of
      a people from the north."

25 The LORD of hosts, the God of Israel, said: "Behold, I am bringing punishment upon Amon of Thebes, and Pharaoh and Egypt and her gods and her kings, upon Pharaoh and those who trust in him. 26 I will deliver them into the hand of those who seek their life, into the hand of Nebuchadnezzar king of Babylon and his officers. Afterward Egypt shall be inhabited as in the days of old, declares the LORD.

27 "But fear not, O Jacob my servant,
      nor be dismayed, O Israel,
   for behold, I will save you from far
      away,
   and your offspring from the land of
      their captivity.
   Jacob shall return and have quiet and
      ease,
      and none shall make him afraid.
28 Fear not, O Jacob my servant,
                     declares the LORD,
      for I am with you.
   I will make a full end of all the nations
      to which I have driven you,
      but of you I will not make a full end.
   I will discipline you in just measure,
      and I will by no means leave you
         unpunished."

--------- *Psalm 22* ---------

TO THE CHOIRMASTER: ACCORDING TO THE DOE OF
THE DAWN. A PSALM OF DAVID.

My God, my God, why have you forsaken
   me?
   Why are you so far from saving me,
      from the words of my groaning?
2 O my God, I cry by day, but you do not
      answer,
   and by night, but I find no rest.

3 Yet you are holy,
      enthroned on the praises[2] of Israel.
4 In you our fathers trusted;
      they trusted, and you delivered them.
5 To you they cried and were rescued;
      in you they trusted and were not put
         to shame.

[1] Hebrew *He does not stand* [2] Or *dwelling in the praises*

6 But I am a worm and not a man,
  scorned by mankind and despised by
    the people.
7 All who see me mock me;
  they make mouths at me; they wag
    their heads;
8 "He trusts in the LORD; let him deliver
    him;
  let him rescue him, for he delights in
    him!"
9 Yet you are he who took me from the
    womb;
  you made me trust you at my mother's
    breasts.
10 On you was I cast from my birth,
  and from my mother's womb you
    have been my God.
11 Be not far from me,
  for trouble is near,
  and there is none to help.
12 Many bulls encompass me;
  strong bulls of Bashan surround me;
13 they open wide their mouths at me,
  like a ravening and roaring lion.
14 I am poured out like water,
  and all my bones are out of joint;
  my heart is like wax;
  it is melted within my breast;
15 my strength is dried up like a potsherd,
  and my tongue sticks to my jaws;
  you lay me in the dust of death.
16 For dogs encompass me;
  a company of evildoers encircles me;
  they have pierced my hands and
    feet[1]—
17 I can count all my bones—
  they stare and gloat over me;
18 they divide my garments among them,
  and for my clothing they cast lots.
19 But you, O LORD, do not be far off!
  O you my help, come quickly to my
    aid!

20 Deliver my soul from the sword,
  my precious life from the power of the
    dog!
21 Save me from the mouth of the lion!
  You have rescued[2] me from the horns of
    the wild oxen!
22 I will tell of your name to my brothers;
  in the midst of the congregation I will
    praise you:
23 You who fear the LORD, praise him!
  All you offspring of Jacob, glorify him,
  and stand in awe of him, all you
    offspring of Israel!
24 For he has not despised or abhorred
  the affliction of the afflicted,
  and he has not hidden his face from him,
  but has heard, when he cried to him.
25 From you comes my praise in the great
    congregation;
  my vows I will perform before those
    who fear him.
26 The afflicted[3] shall eat and be satisfied;
  those who seek him shall praise the
    LORD!
  May your hearts live forever!
27 All the ends of the earth shall remember
  and turn to the LORD,
  and all the families of the nations
  shall worship before you.
28 For kingship belongs to the LORD,
  and he rules over the nations.
29 All the prosperous of the earth eat and
    worship;
  before him shall bow all who go down
    to the dust,
  even the one who could not keep
    himself alive.
30 Posterity shall serve him;
  it shall be told of the Lord to the
    coming generation;
31 they shall come and proclaim his
  righteousness to a people yet
    unborn,
  that he has done it.

[1] Some Hebrew manuscripts, Septuagint, Vulgate, Syriac; most Hebrew manuscripts *like a lion* [they are at] *my hands and feet* [2] Hebrew *answered* [3] Or *The meek*

AUGUST 18

1 Samuel 10

Then Samuel took a flask of oil and poured it on his head and kissed him and said, "Has not the LORD anointed you to be prince[1] over his people Israel? And you shall reign over the people of the LORD and you will save them from the hand of their surrounding enemies. And this shall be the sign to you that the LORD has anointed you to be prince[2] over his heritage. ²When you depart from me today, you will meet two men by Rachel's tomb in the territory of Benjamin at Zelzah, and they will say to you, 'The donkeys that you went to seek are found, and now your father has ceased to care about the donkeys and is anxious about you, saying, "What shall I do about my son?"' ³Then you shall go on from there farther and come to the oak of Tabor. Three men going up to God at Bethel will meet you there, one carrying three young goats, another carrying three loaves of bread, and another carrying a skin of wine. ⁴And they will greet you and give you two loaves of bread, which you shall accept from their hand. ⁵After that you shall come to Gibeath-elohim,[3] where there is a garrison of the Philistines. And there, as soon as you come to the city, you will meet a group of prophets coming down from the high place with harp, tambourine, flute, and lyre before them, prophesying. ⁶Then the Spirit of the LORD will rush upon you, and you will prophesy with them and be turned into another man. ⁷Now when these signs meet you, do what your hand finds to do, for God is with you. ⁸Then go down before me to Gilgal. And behold, I am coming down to you to offer burnt offerings and to sacrifice peace offerings. Seven days you shall wait, until I come to you and show you what you shall do."

⁹When he turned his back to leave Samuel, God gave him another heart. And all these signs came to pass that day. ¹⁰When they came to Gibeah,[4] behold, a group of prophets met him, and the Spirit of God rushed upon him, and he prophesied among them. ¹¹And when all who knew him previously saw how he prophesied with the prophets, the people said to one another, "What has come over the son of Kish? Is Saul also among the prophets?" ¹²And a man of the place answered, "And who is their father?" Therefore it became a proverb, "Is Saul also among the prophets?" ¹³When he had finished prophesying, he came to the high place.

¹⁴Saul's uncle said to him and to his servant, "Where did you go?" And he said, "To seek the donkeys. And when we saw they were not to be found, we went to Samuel." ¹⁵And Saul's uncle said, "Please tell me what Samuel said to you." ¹⁶And Saul said to his uncle, "He told us plainly that the donkeys had been found." But about the matter of the kingdom, of which Samuel had spoken, he did not tell him anything.

¹⁷Now Samuel called the people together to the LORD at Mizpah. ¹⁸And he said to the people of Israel, "Thus says the LORD, the God of Israel, 'I brought up Israel out of Egypt, and I delivered you from the hand of the Egyptians and from the hand of all the kingdoms that were oppressing you.' ¹⁹But today you have rejected your God, who saves you from all your calamities and your distresses, and you have said to him, 'Set a king over us.' Now therefore present yourselves before the LORD by your tribes and by your thousands."

²⁰Then Samuel brought all the tribes of Israel near, and the tribe of Benjamin was taken by lot. ²¹He brought the tribe of Benjamin near by its clans, and the clan of the Matrites was taken by lot;[5] and Saul the son of Kish was taken by lot. But when they sought him, he could not be found. ²²So they inquired again of the LORD, "Is there a man still to come?" and the LORD said, "Behold, he has hidden himself among the baggage." ²³Then they ran and took him from there. And when he stood among the people, he was taller than any of the people from his shoulders upward. ²⁴And Samuel said to all the people, "Do you see him whom the LORD has chosen? There is none like him among all the people." And all the people shouted, "Long live the king!"

---

[1] Or leader [2] Septuagint; Hebrew lacks *over his people Israel? And you shall. . . . to be prince* [3] *Gibeath-elohim* means *the hill of God* [4] *Gibeah* means *the hill* [5] Septuagint adds *finally he brought the family of the Matrites near, man by man*

25 Then Samuel told the people the rights and duties of the kingship, and he wrote them in a book and laid it up before the LORD. Then Samuel sent all the people away, each one to his home. 26 Saul also went to his home at Gibeah, and with him went men of valor whose hearts God had touched. 27 But some worthless fellows said, "How can this man save us?" And they despised him and brought him no present. But he held his peace.

Romans 8

There is therefore now no condemnation for those who are in Christ Jesus.[1] 2 For the law of the Spirit of life has set you[2] free in Christ Jesus from the law of sin and death. 3 For God has done what the law, weakened by the flesh, could not do. By sending his own Son in the likeness of sinful flesh and for sin,[3] he condemned sin in the flesh, 4 in order that the righteous requirement of the law might be fulfilled in us, who walk not according to the flesh but according to the Spirit. 5 For those who live according to the flesh set their minds on the things of the flesh, but those who live according to the Spirit set their minds on the things of the Spirit. 6 For to set the mind on the flesh is death, but to set the mind on the Spirit is life and peace. 7 For the mind that is set on the flesh is hostile to God, for it does not submit to God's law; indeed, it cannot. 8 Those who are in the flesh cannot please God.

9 You, however, are not in the flesh but in the Spirit, if in fact the Spirit of God dwells in you. Anyone who does not have the Spirit of Christ does not belong to him. 10 But if Christ is in you, although the body is dead because of sin, the Spirit is life because of righteousness. 11 If the Spirit of him who raised Jesus from the dead dwells in you, he who raised Christ Jesus[4] from the dead will also give life to your mortal bodies through his Spirit who dwells in you.

12 So then, brothers,[5] we are debtors, not to the flesh, to live according to the flesh. 13 For if you live according to the flesh you will die, but if by the Spirit you put to death the deeds of the body, you will live. 14 For all who are led by the Spirit of God are sons[6] of God. 15 For you did not receive the spirit of slavery to fall back into fear, but you have received the Spirit of adoption as sons, by whom we cry, "Abba! Father!" 16 The Spirit himself bears witness with our spirit that we are children of God, 17 and if children, then heirs—heirs of God and fellow heirs with Christ, provided we suffer with him in order that we may also be glorified with him.

18 For I consider that the sufferings of this present time are not worth comparing with the glory that is to be revealed to us. 19 For the creation waits with eager longing for the revealing of the sons of God. 20 For the creation was subjected to futility, not willingly, but because of him who subjected it, in hope 21 that the creation itself will be set free from its bondage to corruption and obtain the freedom of the glory of the children of God. 22 For we know that the whole creation has been groaning together in the pains of childbirth until now. 23 And not only the creation, but we ourselves, who have the firstfruits of the Spirit, groan inwardly as we wait eagerly for adoption as sons, the redemption of our bodies. 24 For in this hope we were saved. Now hope that is seen is not hope. For who hopes for what he sees? 25 But if we hope for what we do not see, we wait for it with patience.

26 Likewise the Spirit helps us in our weakness. For we do not know what to pray for as we ought, but the Spirit himself intercedes for us with groanings too deep for words. 27 And he who searches hearts knows what is the mind of the Spirit, because[7] the Spirit intercedes for the saints according to the will of God. 28 And we know that for those who love God all things work together for good,[8] for those who are called according to his purpose. 29 For those whom he foreknew he also predestined to be conformed to the image of his Son, in order that he might be the firstborn among many brothers. 30 And those whom he predestined he also called, and those whom he called he also justified, and those whom he justified he also glorified.

31 What then shall we say to these things? If God is for us, who can be[9] against us? 32 He who did not spare his own Son but gave him up for us all, how will he not also with him graciously give us all things? 33 Who shall bring any charge against God's elect? It is God who justifies. 34 Who is to condemn? Christ Jesus is the one

---

[1] Some manuscripts add *who walk not according to the flesh (but according to the Spirit)* [2] Some manuscripts *me* [3] Or *and as a sin offering* [4] Some manuscripts lack *Jesus* [5] Or *brothers and sisters; also verse 29* [6] See discussion on "sons" in the Preface [7] Or *that* [8] Some manuscripts *God works all things together for good,* or *God works in all things for the good* [9] Or *who is*

who died—more than that, who was raised—who is at the right hand of God, who indeed is interceding for us.[1] [35]Who shall separate us from the love of Christ? Shall tribulation, or distress, or persecution, or famine, or nakedness, or danger, or sword? [36]As it is written,

> "For your sake we are being killed all the
> day long;
>   we are regarded as sheep to be
>   slaughtered."

[37]No, in all these things we are more than conquerors through him who loved us. [38]For I am sure that neither death nor life, nor angels nor rulers, nor things present nor things to come, nor powers, [39]nor height nor depth, nor anything else in all creation, will be able to separate us from the love of God in Christ Jesus our Lord.

Jeremiah 47

The word of the LORD that came to Jeremiah the prophet concerning the Philistines, before Pharaoh struck down Gaza.

[2]   "Thus says the LORD:
   Behold, waters are rising out of the
       north,
       and shall become an overflowing
          torrent;
   they shall overflow the land and all that
       fills it,
       the city and those who dwell in it.
   Men shall cry out,
       and every inhabitant of the land shall
          wail.
[3]   At the noise of the stamping of the hoofs
       of his stallions,
       at the rushing of his chariots, at the
          rumbling of their wheels,
   the fathers look not back to their children,
       so feeble are their hands,
[4]   because of the day that is coming to
       destroy
       all the Philistines,
   to cut off from Tyre and Sidon
       every helper that remains.
   For the LORD is destroying the Philistines,
       the remnant of the coastland of
          Caphtor.
[5]   Baldness has come upon Gaza;
       Ashkelon has perished.

O remnant of their valley,
       how long will you gash yourselves?
[6]   Ah, sword of the LORD!
       How long till you are quiet?
   Put yourself into your scabbard;
       rest and be still!
[7]   How can it[2] be quiet
       when the LORD has given it a charge?
   Against Ashkelon and against the
          seashore
       he has appointed it."

Psalm 23–24

A PSALM OF DAVID.

The LORD is my shepherd; I shall not want.
   [2]He makes me lie down in green pastures.
   He leads me beside still waters.[3]
[3]   He restores my soul.
   He leads me in paths of righteousness[4]
       for his name's sake.

[4]   Even though I walk through the valley of
       the shadow of death,[5]
       I will fear no evil,
   for you are with me;
       your rod and your staff,
       they comfort me.

[5]   You prepare a table before me
       in the presence of my enemies;
   you anoint my head with oil;
       my cup overflows.
[6]   Surely[6] goodness and mercy[7] shall
          follow me
       all the days of my life,
   and I shall dwell[8] in the house of the LORD
       forever.[9]

A PSALM OF DAVID.

The earth is the LORD's and the fullness
       thereof,[10]
       the world and those who dwell
          therein,
[2]   for he has founded it upon the seas
       and established it upon the rivers.

[3]   Who shall ascend the hill of the LORD?
       And who shall stand in his holy place?
[4]   He who has clean hands and a pure heart,
       who does not lift up his soul to what is
          false
       and does not swear deceitfully.

---

[1] Or *Is it Christ Jesus who died. . . for us?* [2] Septuagint, Vulgate; Hebrew *you* [3] Hebrew *beside waters of rest* [4] Or *in right paths* [5] Or *the valley of deep darkness* [6] Or *Only* [7] Or *steadfast love* [8] Or *shall return to dwell* [9] Hebrew *for length of days* [10] Or *and all that fills it*

5   He will receive blessing from the LORD
        and righteousness from the God of his
        salvation.
6   Such is the generation of those who
        seek him,
    who seek the face of the God of Jacob.[1]
                                            Selah

7   Lift up your heads, O gates!
    And be lifted up, O ancient doors,

    that the King of glory may come in.
8   Who is this King of glory?
    The LORD, strong and mighty,
        the LORD, mighty in battle!
9   Lift up your heads, O gates!
    And lift them up, O ancient doors,
        that the King of glory may come in.
10 Who is this King of glory?
    The LORD of hosts,
        he is the King of glory!   *Selah*

AUGUST 19

1 Samuel 11

Then Nahash the Ammonite went up and besieged Jabesh-gilead, and all the men of Jabesh said to Nahash, "Make a treaty with us, and we will serve you." ²But Nahash the Ammonite said to them, "On this condition I will make a treaty with you, that I gouge out all your right eyes, and thus bring disgrace on all Israel." ³The elders of Jabesh said to him, "Give us seven days' respite that we may send messengers through all the territory of Israel. Then, if there is no one to save us, we will give ourselves up to you." ⁴When the messengers came to Gibeah of Saul, they reported the matter in the ears of the people, and all the people wept aloud.

⁵Now, behold, Saul was coming from the field behind the oxen. And Saul said, "What is wrong with the people, that they are weeping?" So they told him the news of the men of Jabesh. ⁶And the Spirit of God rushed upon Saul when he heard these words, and his anger was greatly kindled. ⁷He took a yoke of oxen and cut them in pieces and sent them throughout all the territory of Israel by the hand of the messengers, saying, "Whoever does not come out after Saul and Samuel, so shall it be done to his oxen!" Then the dread of the LORD fell upon the people, and they came out as one man. ⁸When he mustered them at Bezek, the people of Israel were three hundred thousand, and the men of Judah thirty thousand. ⁹And they said to the

messengers who had come, "Thus shall you say to the men of Jabesh-gilead: 'Tomorrow, by the time the sun is hot, you shall have salvation.'" When the messengers came and told the men of Jabesh, they were glad. ¹⁰Therefore the men of Jabesh said, "Tomorrow we will give ourselves up to you, and you may do to us whatever seems good to you." ¹¹And the next day Saul put the people in three companies. And they came into the midst of the camp in the morning watch and struck down the Ammonites until the heat of the day. And those who survived were scattered, so that no two of them were left together.

¹²Then the people said to Samuel, "Who is it that said, 'Shall Saul reign over us?' Bring the men, that we may put them to death." ¹³But Saul said, "Not a man shall be put to death this day, for today the LORD has worked salvation in Israel." ¹⁴Then Samuel said to the people, "Come, let us go to Gilgal and there renew the kingdom." ¹⁵So all the people went to Gilgal, and there they made Saul king before the LORD in Gilgal. There they sacrificed peace offerings before the LORD, and there Saul and all the men of Israel rejoiced greatly.

Romans 9

I am speaking the truth in Christ—I am not lying; my conscience bears me witness in the Holy Spirit— ²that I have great sorrow and

---

[1] Septuagint, Syriac, and two Hebrew manuscripts; Masoretic Text *Jacob, who seek your face*

unceasing anguish in my heart. ³For I could wish that I myself were accursed and cut off from Christ for the sake of my brothers,[1] my kinsmen according to the flesh. ⁴They are Israelites, and to them belong the adoption, the glory, the covenants, the giving of the law, the worship, and the promises. ⁵To them belong the patriarchs, and from their race, according to the flesh, is the Christ, who is God over all, blessed forever. Amen.

⁶But it is not as though the word of God has failed. For not all who are descended from Israel belong to Israel, ⁷and not all are children of Abraham because they are his offspring, but "Through Isaac shall your offspring be named." ⁸This means that it is not the children of the flesh who are the children of God, but the children of the promise are counted as offspring. ⁹For this is what the promise said: "About this time next year I will return, and Sarah shall have a son." ¹⁰And not only so, but also when Rebekah had conceived children by one man, our forefather Isaac, ¹¹though they were not yet born and had done nothing either good or bad—in order that God's purpose of election might continue, not because of works but because of him who calls— ¹²she was told, "The older will serve the younger." ¹³As it is written, "Jacob I loved, but Esau I hated."

¹⁴What shall we say then? Is there injustice on God's part? By no means! ¹⁵For he says to Moses, "I will have mercy on whom I have mercy, and I will have compassion on whom I have compassion." ¹⁶So then it depends not on human will or exertion,[2] but on God, who has mercy. ¹⁷For the Scripture says to Pharaoh, "For this very purpose I have raised you up, that I might show my power in you, and that my name might be proclaimed in all the earth." ¹⁸So then he has mercy on whomever he wills, and he hardens whomever he wills.

¹⁹You will say to me then, "Why does he still find fault? For who can resist his will?" ²⁰But who are you, O man, to answer back to God? Will what is molded say to its molder, "Why have you made me like this?" ²¹Has the potter no right over the clay, to make out of the same lump one vessel for honorable use and another for dishonorable use? ²²What if God, desiring to show his wrath and to make known his power, has endured with much patience

vessels of wrath prepared for destruction, ²³in order to make known the riches of his glory for vessels of mercy, which he has prepared beforehand for glory— ²⁴even us whom he has called, not from the Jews only but also from the Gentiles? ²⁵As indeed he says in Hosea,

> "Those who were not my people I will call
>   'my people,'
>   and her who was not beloved I will call
>   'beloved.'"
> ²⁶ "And in the very place where it was said
>   to them, 'You are not my people,'
>   there they will be called 'sons of the
>   living God.'"

²⁷And Isaiah cries out concerning Israel: "Though the number of the sons of Israel[3] be as the sand of the sea, only a remnant of them will be saved, ²⁸for the Lord will carry out his sentence upon the earth fully and without delay." ²⁹And as Isaiah predicted,

> "If the Lord of hosts had not left us
>   offspring,
>   we would have been like Sodom
>   and become like Gomorrah."

³⁰What shall we say, then? That Gentiles who did not pursue righteousness have attained it, that is, a righteousness that is by faith; ³¹but that Israel who pursued a law that would lead to righteousness[4] did not succeed in reaching that law. ³²Why? Because they did not pursue it by faith, but as if it were based on works. They have stumbled over the stumbling stone, ³³as it is written,

> "Behold, I am laying in Zion a stone of
>   stumbling, and a rock of offense;
>   and whoever believes in him will not
>   be put to shame."

Jeremiah 48

Concerning Moab.
Thus says the LORD of hosts, the God of Israel:

> "Woe to Nebo, for it is laid waste!
>   Kiriathaim is put to shame, it is taken;
>   the fortress is put to shame and broken
>   down;
> ²   the renown of Moab is no more.

---

¹ Or brothers and sisters ² Greek not of him who wills or runs ³ Or children of Israel ⁴ Greek a law of righteousness

In Heshbon they planned disaster
    against her:
'Come, let us cut her off from being a
    nation!'
You also, O Madmen, shall be brought to
    silence;
    the sword shall pursue you.

3 "A voice! A cry from Horonaim,
    'Desolation and great destruction!'
4 Moab is destroyed;
    her little ones have made a cry.
5 For at the ascent of Luhith
    they go up weeping;[1]
for at the descent of Horonaim
    they have heard the distressed cry[2] of
    destruction.
6 Flee! Save yourselves!
    You will be like a juniper in the
    desert!
7 For, because you trusted in your works
    and your treasures,
    you also shall be taken;
and Chemosh shall go into exile
    with his priests and his officials.
8 The destroyer shall come upon every city,
    and no city shall escape;
the valley shall perish,
    and the plain shall be destroyed,
    as the LORD has spoken.
9 "Give wings to Moab,
    for she would fly away;
her cities shall become a desolation,
    with no inhabitant in them.

10 "Cursed is he who does the work of the LORD with slackness, and cursed is he who keeps back his sword from bloodshed.

11 "Moab has been at ease from his youth
    and has settled on his dregs;
he has not been emptied from vessel to
    vessel,
    nor has he gone into exile;
so his taste remains in him,
    and his scent is not changed.

12 "Therefore, behold, the days are coming, declares the LORD, when I shall send to him pourers who will pour him, and empty his vessels and break his[3] jars in pieces. 13 Then Moab shall be ashamed of Chemosh, as the house of Israel was ashamed of Bethel, their confidence.

14 "How do you say, 'We are heroes
    and mighty men of war'?
15 The destroyer of Moab and his cities has
    come up,
and the choicest of his young men
    have gone down to slaughter,
declares the King, whose name is the
    LORD of hosts.
16 The calamity of Moab is near at hand,
    and his affliction hastens swiftly.
17 Grieve for him, all you who are around
    him,
    and all who know his name;
say, 'How the mighty scepter is broken,
    the glorious staff.'
18 "Come down from your glory,
    and sit on the parched ground,
    O inhabitant of Dibon!
For the destroyer of Moab has come up
    against you;
    he has destroyed your strongholds.
19 Stand by the way and watch,
    O inhabitant of Aroer!
Ask him who flees and her who
    escapes;
    say, 'What has happened?'
20 Moab is put to shame, for it is broken;
    wail and cry!
Tell it beside the Arnon,
    that Moab is laid waste.

21 "Judgment has come upon the tableland, upon Holon, and Jahzah, and Mephaath, 22 and Dibon, and Nebo, and Beth-diblathaim, 23 and Kiriathaim, and Beth-gamul, and Beth-meon, 24 and Kerioth, and Bozrah, and all the cities of the land of Moab, far and near. 25 The horn of Moab is cut off, and his arm is broken, declares the LORD.

26 "Make him drunk, because he magnified himself against the LORD, so that Moab shall wallow in his vomit, and he too shall be held in derision. 27 Was not Israel a derision to you? Was he found among thieves, that whenever you spoke of him you wagged your head?

28 "Leave the cities, and dwell in the rock,
    O inhabitants of Moab!
Be like the dove that nests
    in the sides of the mouth of a gorge.
29 We have heard of the pride of Moab—
    he is very proud—

---

[1] Hebrew *weeping goes up with weeping*   [2] Septuagint (compare Isaiah 15:5) *heard the cry*   [3] Septuagint, Aquila; Hebrew *their*

of his loftiness, his pride, and his
    arrogance,
  and the haughtiness of his heart.
30 I know his insolence, declares the LORD;
  his boasts are false,
  his deeds are false.
31 Therefore I wail for Moab;
  I cry out for all Moab;
  for the men of Kir-hareseth I mourn.
32 More than for Jazer I weep for you,
  O vine of Sibmah!
Your branches passed over the sea,
  reached to the Sea of Jazer;
on your summer fruits and your grapes
  the destroyer has fallen.
33 Gladness and joy have been taken away
  from the fruitful land of Moab;
I have made the wine cease from the
  winepresses;
  no one treads them with shouts of
    joy;
  the shouting is not the shout of joy.

34 "From the outcry at Heshbon even to Elealeh, as far as Jahaz they utter their voice, from Zoar to Horonaim and Eglath-shelishiyah. For the waters of Nimrim also have become desolate. 35 And I will bring to an end in Moab, declares the LORD, him who offers sacrifice in the high place and makes offerings to his god. 36 Therefore my heart moans for Moab like a flute, and my heart moans like a flute for the men of Kir-hareseth. Therefore the riches they gained have perished.

37 "For every head is shaved and every beard cut off. On all the hands are gashes, and around the waist is sackcloth. 38 On all the housetops of Moab and in the squares there is nothing but lamentation, for I have broken Moab like a vessel for which no one cares, declares the LORD. 39 How it is broken! How they wail! How Moab has turned his back in shame! So Moab has become a derision and a horror to all that are around him."

40 For thus says the LORD:
"Behold, one shall fly swiftly like an
  eagle
  and spread his wings against Moab;
41 the cities shall be taken
  and the strongholds seized.
The heart of the warriors of Moab shall
  be in that day

like the heart of a woman in her birth
  pains;
42 Moab shall be destroyed and be no
  longer a people,
  because he magnified himself against
    the LORD.
43 Terror, pit, and snare
  are before you, O inhabitant of Moab!
      declares the LORD.
44 He who flees from the terror
  shall fall into the pit,
and he who climbs out of the pit
  shall be caught in the snare.
For I will bring these things upon
  Moab,
  the year of their punishment,
      declares the LORD.
45 "In the shadow of Heshbon
  fugitives stop without strength,
for fire came out from Heshbon,
  flame from the house of Sihon;
it has destroyed the forehead of Moab,
  the crown of the sons of tumult.
46 Woe to you, O Moab!
  The people of Chemosh are undone,
for your sons have been taken captive,
  and your daughters into captivity.
47 Yet I will restore the fortunes of Moab
  in the latter days, declares the LORD."
Thus far is the judgment on Moab.

Psalm 25[1]

OF DAVID.

To you, O LORD, I lift up my soul.
 2 O my God, in you I trust;
  let me not be put to shame;
  let not my enemies exult over me.
3 Indeed, none who wait for you shall be
  put to shame;
  they shall be ashamed who are
    wantonly treacherous.

4 Make me to know your ways, O LORD;
  teach me your paths.
5 Lead me in your truth and teach me,
  for you are the God of my salvation;
  for you I wait all the day long.

6 Remember your mercy, O LORD, and
  your steadfast love,
  for they have been from of old.

[1] This psalm is an acrostic poem, each verse beginning with the successive letters of the Hebrew alphabet

7 Remember not the sins of my youth or
my transgressions;
according to your steadfast love
remember me,
for the sake of your goodness,
O Lord!

8 Good and upright is the Lord;
therefore he instructs sinners in the
way.
9 He leads the humble in what is right,
and teaches the humble his way.
10 All the paths of the Lord are steadfast
love and faithfulness,
for those who keep his covenant and
his testimonies.

11 For your name's sake, O Lord,
pardon my guilt, for it is great.
12 Who is the man who fears the Lord?
Him will he instruct in the way that he
should choose.
13 His soul shall abide in well-being,
and his offspring shall inherit the
land.

14 The friendship[1] of the Lord is for those
who fear him,
and he makes known to them his
covenant.
15 My eyes are ever toward the Lord,
for he will pluck my feet out of the net.
16 Turn to me and be gracious to me,
for I am lonely and afflicted.
17 The troubles of my heart are enlarged;
bring me out of my distresses.
18 Consider my affliction and my trouble,
and forgive all my sins.
19 Consider how many are my foes,
and with what violent hatred they
hate me.
20 Oh, guard my soul, and deliver me!
Let me not be put to shame, for I take
refuge in you.
21 May integrity and uprightness preserve
me,
for I wait for you.
22 Redeem Israel, O God,
out of all his troubles.

AUGUST 20

1 Samuel 12

And Samuel said to all Israel, "Behold, I have obeyed your voice in all that you have said to me and have made a king over you. 2 And now, behold, the king walks before you, and I am old and gray; and behold, my sons are with you. I have walked before you from my youth until this day. 3 Here I am; testify against me before the Lord and before his anointed. Whose ox have I taken? Or whose donkey have I taken? Or whom have I defrauded? Whom have I oppressed? Or from whose hand have I taken a bribe to blind my eyes with it? Testify against me[2] and I will restore it to you." 4 They said, "You have not defrauded us or oppressed us or taken anything from any man's hand." 5 And he said to them, "The Lord is witness against you, and his anointed is witness this day, that

you have not found anything in my hand." And they said, "He is witness."

6 And Samuel said to the people, "The Lord is witness,[3] who appointed Moses and Aaron and brought your fathers up out of the land of Egypt. 7 Now therefore stand still that I may plead with you before the Lord concerning all the righteous deeds of the Lord that he performed for you and for your fathers. 8 When Jacob went into Egypt, and the Egyptians oppressed them,[4] then your fathers cried out to the Lord and the Lord sent Moses and Aaron, who brought your fathers out of Egypt and made them dwell in this place. 9 But they forgot the Lord their God. And he sold them into the hand of Sisera, commander of the army of Hazor,[5] and into the hand of the Philistines,

[1] Or The secret counsel   [2] Septuagint; Hebrew lacks Testify against me   [3] Septuagint; Hebrew lacks is witness   [4] Septuagint; Hebrew lacks and the Egyptians oppressed them   [5] Septuagint the army of Jabin king of Hazor

and into the hand of the king of Moab. And they fought against them. [10]And they cried out to the LORD and said, 'We have sinned, because we have forsaken the LORD and have served the Baals and the Ashtaroth. But now deliver us out of the hand of our enemies, that we may serve you.' [11]And the LORD sent Jerubbaal and Barak[1] and Jephthah and Samuel and delivered you out of the hand of your enemies on every side, and you lived in safety. [12]And when you saw that Nahash the king of the Ammonites came against you, you said to me, 'No, but a king shall reign over us,' when the LORD your God was your king. [13]And now behold the king whom you have chosen, for whom you have asked; behold, the LORD has set a king over you. [14]If you will fear the LORD and serve him and obey his voice and not rebel against the commandment of the LORD, and if both you and the king who reigns over you will follow the LORD your God, it will be well. [15]But if you will not obey the voice of the LORD, but rebel against the commandment of the LORD, then the hand of the LORD will be against you and your king.[2] [16]Now therefore stand still and see this great thing that the LORD will do before your eyes. [17]Is it not wheat harvest today? I will call upon the LORD, that he may send thunder and rain. And you shall know and see that your wickedness is great, which you have done in the sight of the LORD, in asking for yourselves a king." [18]So Samuel called upon the LORD, and the LORD sent thunder and rain that day, and all the people greatly feared the LORD and Samuel.

[19]And all the people said to Samuel, "Pray for your servants to the LORD your God, that we may not die, for we have added to all our sins this evil, to ask for ourselves a king." [20]And Samuel said to the people, "Do not be afraid; you have done all this evil. Yet do not turn aside from following the LORD, but serve the LORD with all your heart. [21]And do not turn aside after empty things that cannot profit or deliver, for they are empty. [22]For the LORD will not forsake his people, for his great name's sake, because it has pleased the LORD to make you a people for himself. [23]Moreover, as for me, far be it from me that I should sin against the LORD by ceasing to pray for you, and I will instruct you in the good and the right way. [24]Only fear the LORD and serve him faithfully with all your heart. For consider what great things he has done for you. [25]But if you still do wickedly, you shall be swept away, both you and your king."

Romans 10

Brothers,[3] my heart's desire and prayer to God for them is that they may be saved. [2]For I bear them witness that they have a zeal for God, but not according to knowledge. [3]For, being ignorant of the righteousness of God, and seeking to establish their own, they did not submit to God's righteousness. [4]For Christ is the end of the law for righteousness to everyone who believes.[4]

[5]For Moses writes about the righteousness that is based on the law, that the person who does the commandments shall live by them. [6]But the righteousness based on faith says, "Do not say in your heart, 'Who will ascend into heaven?'" (that is, to bring Christ down) [7]"or 'Who will descend into the abyss?'" (that is, to bring Christ up from the dead). [8]But what does it say? "The word is near you, in your mouth and in your heart" (that is, the word of faith that we proclaim); [9]because, if you confess with your mouth that Jesus is Lord and believe in your heart that God raised him from the dead, you will be saved. [10]For with the heart one believes and is justified, and with the mouth one confesses and is saved. [11]For the Scripture says, "Everyone who believes in him will not be put to shame." [12]For there is no distinction between Jew and Greek; for the same Lord is Lord of all, bestowing his riches on all who call on him. [13]For "everyone who calls on the name of the Lord will be saved."

[14]How then will they call on him in whom they have not believed? And how are they to believe in him of whom they have never heard?[5] And how are they to hear without someone preaching? [15]And how are they to preach unless they are sent? As it is written, "How beautiful are the feet of those who preach the good news!" [16]But they have not all obeyed the gospel. For Isaiah says, "Lord, who has believed what he has heard from us?" [17]So faith comes from hearing, and hearing through the word of Christ.

[18]But I ask, have they not heard? Indeed they have, for

---

[1] Septuagint, Syriac; Hebrew *Bedan*   [2] Septuagint; Hebrew *fathers*   [3] Or *Brothers and sisters*   [4] Or *end of the law, that everyone who believes may be justified*   [5] Or *him whom they have never heard*

"Their voice has gone out to all the earth,
and their words to the ends of the
world."

19 But I ask, did Israel not understand? First
Moses says,

"I will make you jealous of those who are
not a nation;
with a foolish nation I will make you
angry."

20 Then Isaiah is so bold as to say,

"I have been found by those who did not
seek me;
I have shown myself to those who did
not ask for me."

21 But of Israel he says, "All day long I have held
out my hands to a disobedient and contrary
people."

Jeremiah 49

Concerning the Ammonites.
Thus says the LORD:

"Has Israel no sons?
Has he no heir?
Why then has Milcom dispossessed Gad,
and his people settled in its cities?
2 Therefore, behold, the days are coming,
declares the LORD,
when I will cause the battle cry to be
heard
against Rabbah of the Ammonites;
it shall become a desolate mound,
and its villages shall be burned with
fire;
then Israel shall dispossess those who
dispossessed him,
says the LORD.
3 "Wail, O Heshbon, for Ai is laid waste!
Cry out, O daughters of Rabbah!
Put on sackcloth,
lament, and run to and fro among the
hedges!
For Milcom shall go into exile,
with his priests and his officials.
4 Why do you boast of your valleys,[1]
O faithless daughter,
who trusted in her treasures, saying,
'Who will come against me?'

[1] Hebrew *boast of your valleys, your valley flows*

5 Behold, I will bring terror upon you,
declares the Lord GOD of hosts,
from all who are around you,
and you shall be driven out, every man
straight before him,
with none to gather the fugitives.

6 "But afterward I will restore the fortunes of
the Ammonites, declares the LORD."
7 Concerning Edom.
Thus says the LORD of hosts:

"Is wisdom no more in Teman?
Has counsel perished from the
prudent?
Has their wisdom vanished?
8 Flee, turn back, dwell in the depths,
O inhabitants of Dedan!
For I will bring the calamity of Esau
upon him,
the time when I punish him.
9 If grape gatherers came to you,
would they not leave gleanings?
If thieves came by night,
would they not destroy only enough
for themselves?
10 But I have stripped Esau bare;
I have uncovered his hiding places,
and he is not able to conceal himself.
His children are destroyed, and his
brothers,
and his neighbors; and he is no
more.
11 Leave your fatherless children; I will
keep them alive;
and let your widows trust in me."

12 For thus says the LORD: "If those who did
not deserve to drink the cup must drink it, will
you go unpunished? You shall not go unpunished, but you must drink. **13** For I have sworn
by myself, declares the LORD, that Bozrah shall
become a horror, a taunt, a waste, and a curse,
and all her cities shall be perpetual wastes."

14 I have heard a message from the LORD,
and an envoy has been sent among
the nations:
"Gather yourselves together and come
against her,
and rise up for battle!
15 For behold, I will make you small among
the nations,
despised among mankind.

¹⁶ The horror you inspire has deceived you,
    and the pride of your heart,
you who live in the clefts of the rock,[1]
    who hold the height of the hill.
Though you make your nest as high as
    the eagle's,
    I will bring you down from there,
                declares the LORD.

¹⁷ "Edom shall become a horror. Everyone who passes by it will be horrified and will hiss because of all its disasters. ¹⁸As when Sodom and Gomorrah and their neighboring cities were overthrown, says the LORD, no man shall dwell there, no man shall sojourn in her. ¹⁹Behold, like a lion coming up from the jungle of the Jordan against a perennial pasture, I will suddenly make him[2] run away from her. And I will appoint over her whomever I choose. For who is like me? Who will summon me? What shepherd can stand before me? ²⁰Therefore hear the plan that the LORD has made against Edom and the purposes that he has formed against the inhabitants of Teman: Even the little ones of the flock shall be dragged away. Surely their fold shall be appalled at their fate. ²¹At the sound of their fall the earth shall tremble; the sound of their cry shall be heard at the Red Sea. ²²Behold, one shall mount up and fly swiftly like an eagle and spread his wings against Bozrah, and the heart of the warriors of Edom shall be in that day like the heart of a woman in her birth pains."

²³ Concerning Damascus:

"Hamath and Arpad are confounded,
    for they have heard bad news;
they melt in fear,
    they are troubled like the sea that
        cannot be quiet.
²⁴ Damascus has become feeble, she
      turned to flee,
    and panic seized her;
anguish and sorrows have taken hold of
    her,
    as of a woman in labor.
²⁵ How is the famous city not forsaken,
    the city of my joy?
²⁶ Therefore her young men shall fall in
      her squares,
    and all her soldiers shall be destroyed
      in that day,
            declares the LORD of hosts.

²⁷ And I will kindle a fire in the wall of
      Damascus,
    and it shall devour the strongholds of
      Ben-hadad."

²⁸ Concerning Kedar and the kingdoms of Hazor that Nebuchadnezzar king of Babylon struck down.

Thus says the LORD:
"Rise up, advance against Kedar!
    Destroy the people of the east!
²⁹ Their tents and their flocks shall be
      taken,
    their curtains and all their goods;
their camels shall be led away from them,
    and men shall cry to them: 'Terror on
      every side!'
³⁰ Flee, wander far away, dwell in the depths,
    O inhabitants of Hazor!
             declares the LORD.
For Nebuchadnezzar king of Babylon
    has made a plan against you
    and formed a purpose against you.

³¹ "Rise up, advance against a nation at ease,
    that dwells securely,
            declares the LORD,
that has no gates or bars,
    that dwells alone.
³² Their camels shall become plunder,
    their herds of livestock a spoil.
I will scatter to every wind
    those who cut the corners of their hair,
and I will bring their calamity
    from every side of them,
            declares the LORD.
³³ Hazor shall become a haunt of jackals,
    an everlasting waste;
no man shall dwell there;
    no man shall sojourn in her."

³⁴ The word of the LORD that came to Jeremiah the prophet concerning Elam, in the beginning of the reign of Zedekiah king of Judah. ³⁵Thus says the LORD of hosts: "Behold, I will break the bow of Elam, the mainstay of their might. ³⁶And I will bring upon Elam the four winds from the four quarters of heaven. And I will scatter them to all those winds, and there shall be no nation to which those driven out of Elam shall not come. ³⁷I will terrify Elam before their enemies and before those who seek their life. I will bring disaster upon them, my fierce

¹ Or *of Sela* ² Septuagint, Syriac *them*

anger, declares the LORD. I will send the sword after them, until I have consumed them, **38** and I will set my throne in Elam and destroy their king and officials, declares the LORD. **39** "But in the latter days I will restore the fortunes of Elam, declares the LORD."

—————— *Psalm 26–27* ——————

OF DAVID.

Vindicate me, O LORD,
   for I have walked in my integrity,
   and I have trusted in the LORD
      without wavering.
2 Prove me, O LORD, and try me;
   test my heart and my mind.[1]
3 For your steadfast love is before my eyes,
   and I walk in your faithfulness.

4 I do not sit with men of falsehood,
   nor do I consort with hypocrites.
5 I hate the assembly of evildoers,
   and I will not sit with the wicked.

6 I wash my hands in innocence
   and go around your altar, O LORD,
7 proclaiming thanksgiving aloud,
   and telling all your wondrous deeds.

8 O LORD, I love the habitation of your
      house
   and the place where your glory dwells.
9 Do not sweep my soul away with sinners,
   nor my life with bloodthirsty men,
10 in whose hands are evil devices,
   and whose right hands are full of
      bribes.

11 But as for me, I shall walk in my integrity;
   redeem me, and be gracious to me.
12 My foot stands on level ground;
   in the great assembly I will bless the
      LORD.

OF DAVID.

The LORD is my light and my salvation;
   whom shall I fear?
   The LORD is the stronghold[2] of my life;
      of whom shall I be afraid?

2 When evildoers assail me
   to eat up my flesh,
my adversaries and foes,
   it is they who stumble and fall.

3 Though an army encamp against me,
   my heart shall not fear;
though war arise against me,
   yet[3] I will be confident.

4 One thing have I asked of the LORD,
   that will I seek after:
that I may dwell in the house of the
      LORD
   all the days of my life,
to gaze upon the beauty of the LORD
   and to inquire[4] in his temple.

5 For he will hide me in his shelter
   in the day of trouble;
he will conceal me under the cover of
      his tent;
   he will lift me high upon a rock.

6 And now my head shall be lifted up
   above my enemies all around me,
and I will offer in his tent
   sacrifices with shouts of joy;
I will sing and make melody to the LORD.

7 Hear, O LORD, when I cry aloud;
   be gracious to me and answer me!
8 You have said, "Seek[5] my face."
My heart says to you,
   "Your face, LORD, do I seek."[6]
9 Hide not your face from me.
Turn not your servant away in anger,
   O you who have been my help.
Cast me not off; forsake me not,
   O God of my salvation!
10 For my father and my mother have
      forsaken me,
   but the LORD will take me in.

11 Teach me your way, O LORD,
   and lead me on a level path
   because of my enemies.
12 Give me not up to the will of my
      adversaries;
for false witnesses have risen against
      me,
   and they breathe out violence.

13 I believe[7] that I shall look upon the
      goodness of the LORD
   in the land of the living!
14 Wait for the LORD;
   be strong, and let your heart take
      courage;
wait for the LORD!

[1] Hebrew *test my kidneys and my heart* [2] Or *refuge* [3] Or *in this* [4] Or *meditate* [5] The command (*seek*) is addressed to more than one person [6] The meaning of the Hebrew verse is uncertain [7] Other Hebrew manuscripts *Oh! Had I not believed*

AUGUST 21

1 Samuel 13

Saul lived for one year and then became king, and when he had reigned for two years over Israel,[1] [2] Saul chose three thousand men of Israel. Two thousand were with Saul in Michmash and the hill country of Bethel, and a thousand were with Jonathan in Gibeah of Benjamin. The rest of the people he sent home, every man to his tent. [3] Jonathan defeated the garrison of the Philistines that was at Geba, and the Philistines heard of it. And Saul blew the trumpet throughout all the land, saying, "Let the Hebrews hear." [4] And all Israel heard it said that Saul had defeated the garrison of the Philistines, and also that Israel had become a stench to the Philistines. And the people were called out to join Saul at Gilgal.

[5] And the Philistines mustered to fight with Israel, thirty thousand chariots and six thousand horsemen and troops like the sand on the seashore in multitude. They came up and encamped in Michmash, to the east of Beth-aven. [6] When the men of Israel saw that they were in trouble (for the people were hard pressed), the people hid themselves in caves and in holes and in rocks and in tombs and in cisterns, [7] and some Hebrews crossed the fords of the Jordan to the land of Gad and Gilead. Saul was still at Gilgal, and all the people followed him trembling.

[8] He waited seven days, the time appointed by Samuel. But Samuel did not come to Gilgal, and the people were scattering from him. [9] So Saul said, "Bring the burnt offering here to me, and the peace offerings." And he offered the burnt offering. [10] As soon as he had finished offering the burnt offering, behold, Samuel came. And Saul went out to meet him and greet him. [11] Samuel said, "What have you done?" And Saul said, "When I saw that the people were scattering from me, and that you did not come within the days appointed, and that the Philistines had mustered at Michmash, [12] I said, 'Now the Philistines will come down against me at Gilgal, and I have not sought the favor of the LORD.' So I forced myself, and offered the burnt offering." [13] And Samuel said to Saul, "You have done foolishly. You have not kept the command of the LORD your God, with which he commanded you. For then the LORD would have established your kingdom over Israel forever. [14] But now your kingdom shall not continue. The LORD has sought out a man after his own heart, and the LORD has commanded him to be prince[2] over his people, because you have not kept what the LORD commanded you." [15] And Samuel arose and went up from Gilgal. The rest of the people went up after Saul to meet the army; they went up from Gilgal[3] to Gibeah of Benjamin.

And Saul numbered the people who were present with him, about six hundred men. [16] And Saul and Jonathan his son and the people who were present with them stayed in Geba of Benjamin, but the Philistines encamped in Michmash. [17] And raiders came out of the camp of the Philistines in three companies. One company turned toward Ophrah, to the land of Shual; [18] another company turned toward Beth-horon; and another company turned toward the border that looks down on the Valley of Zeboim toward the wilderness.

[19] Now there was no blacksmith to be found throughout all the land of Israel, for the Philistines said, "Lest the Hebrews make themselves swords or spears." [20] But every one of the Israelites went down to the Philistines to sharpen his plowshare, his mattock, his axe, or his sickle,[4] [21] and the charge was two-thirds of a shekel[5] for the plowshares and for the mattocks, and a third of a shekel[6] for sharpening the axes and for setting the goads.[7] [22] So on the day of the battle there was neither sword nor spear found in the hand of any of the people with Saul and Jonathan, but Saul and Jonathan his son had them. [23] And the garrison of the Philistines went out to the pass of Michmash.

[1] Hebrew *Saul was one year old when he became king, and he reigned two years over Israel* (see 1 Samuel 10:6); some Greek manuscripts give Saul's age when he began to reign as thirty years   [2] Or *leader*   [3] Septuagint; Hebrew lacks *The rest of the people. . . from Gilgal*   [4] Septuagint; Hebrew *plowshare*   [5] Hebrew *was a pim*   [6] A *shekel* was about 2/5 ounce or 11 grams   [7] The meaning of the Hebrew verse is uncertain

Romans 11

I ask, then, has God rejected his people? By no means! For I myself am an Israelite, a descendant of Abraham,[1] a member of the tribe of Benjamin. [2]God has not rejected his people whom he foreknew. Do you not know what the Scripture says of Elijah, how he appeals to God against Israel? [3]"Lord, they have killed your prophets, they have demolished your altars, and I alone am left, and they seek my life." [4]But what is God's reply to him? "I have kept for myself seven thousand men who have not bowed the knee to Baal." [5]So too at the present time there is a remnant, chosen by grace. [6]But if it is by grace, it is no longer on the basis of works; otherwise grace would no longer be grace.

[7]What then? Israel failed to obtain what it was seeking. The elect obtained it, but the rest were hardened, [8]as it is written,

"God gave them a spirit of stupor,
  eyes that would not see
  and ears that would not hear,
  down to this very day."

[9]And David says,

"Let their table become a snare and a trap,
  a stumbling block and a retribution
    for them;
[10] let their eyes be darkened so that they
      cannot see,
  and bend their backs forever."

[11]So I ask, did they stumble in order that they might fall? By no means! Rather through their trespass salvation has come to the Gentiles, so as to make Israel jealous. [12]Now if their trespass means riches for the world, and if their failure means riches for the Gentiles, how much more will their full inclusion[2] mean!

[13]Now I am speaking to you Gentiles. Inasmuch then as I am an apostle to the Gentiles, I magnify my ministry [14]in order somehow to make my fellow Jews jealous, and thus save some of them. [15]For if their rejection means the reconciliation of the world, what will their acceptance mean but life from the dead? [16]If the dough offered as firstfruits is holy, so is the whole lump, and if the root is holy, so are the branches.

[17]But if some of the branches were broken off, and you, although a wild olive shoot, were grafted in among the others and now share in the nourishing root[3] of the olive tree, [18]do not be arrogant toward the branches. If you are, remember it is not you who support the root, but the root that supports you. [19]Then you will say, "Branches were broken off so that I might be grafted in." [20]That is true. They were broken off because of their unbelief, but you stand fast through faith. So do not become proud, but fear. [21]For if God did not spare the natural branches, neither will he spare you. [22]Note then the kindness and the severity of God: severity toward those who have fallen, but God's kindness to you, provided you continue in his kindness. Otherwise you too will be cut off. [23]And even they, if they do not continue in their unbelief, will be grafted in, for God has the power to graft them in again. [24]For if you were cut from what is by nature a wild olive tree, and grafted, contrary to nature, into a cultivated olive tree, how much more will these, the natural branches, be grafted back into their own olive tree.

[25]Lest you be wise in your own sight, I do not want you to be unaware of this mystery, brothers:[4] a partial hardening has come upon Israel, until the fullness of the Gentiles has come in. [26]And in this way all Israel will be saved, as it is written,

"The Deliverer will come from Zion,
  he will banish ungodliness from
    Jacob";
[27] "and this will be my covenant with them
    when I take away their sins."

[28]As regards the gospel, they are enemies for your sake. But as regards election, they are beloved for the sake of their forefathers. [29]For the gifts and the calling of God are irrevocable. [30]For just as you were at one time disobedient to God but now have received mercy because of their disobedience, [31]so they too have now been disobedient in order that by the mercy shown to you they also may now[5] receive mercy. [32]For God has consigned all to disobedience, that he may have mercy on all.

[33]Oh, the depth of the riches and wisdom and knowledge of God! How unsearchable are his judgments and how inscrutable his ways!

[34] "For who has known the mind of the Lord,
    or who has been his counselor?"

[1] Or one of the offspring of Abraham [2] Greek their fullness [3] Greek root of richness; some manuscripts richness [4] Or brothers and sisters [5] Some manuscripts omit now

35 "Or who has given a gift to him
that he might be repaid?"

36 For from him and through him and to him
are all things. To him be glory forever. Amen.

──────── *Jeremiah 50* ────────

The word that the LORD spoke concerning Babylon, concerning the land of the
Chaldeans, by Jeremiah the prophet:

2 "Declare among the nations and
proclaim,
set up a banner and proclaim,
conceal it not, and say:
'Babylon is taken,
Bel is put to shame,
Merodach is dismayed.
Her images are put to shame,
her idols are dismayed.'

3 "For out of the north a nation has come up
against her, which shall make her land a desolation, and none shall dwell in it; both man and
beast shall flee away.

4 "In those days and in that time, declares
the LORD, the people of Israel and the people
of Judah shall come together, weeping as they
come, and they shall seek the LORD their God.
5 They shall ask the way to Zion, with faces
turned toward it, saying, 'Come, let us join ourselves to the LORD in an everlasting covenant
that will never be forgotten.'

6 "My people have been lost sheep. Their
shepherds have led them astray, turning them
away on the mountains. From mountain to hill
they have gone. They have forgotten their fold.
7 All who found them have devoured them, and
their enemies have said, 'We are not guilty, for
they have sinned against the LORD, their habitation of righteousness, the LORD, the hope of
their fathers.'

8 "Flee from the midst of Babylon, and go out
of the land of the Chaldeans, and be as male
goats before the flock. 9 For behold, I am stirring up and bringing against Babylon a gathering of great nations, from the north country.
And they shall array themselves against her.
From there she shall be taken. Their arrows
are like a skilled warrior who does not return

empty-handed. 10 Chaldea shall be plundered;
all who plunder her shall be sated, declares
the LORD.

11 "Though you rejoice, though you exult,
O plunderers of my heritage,
though you frolic like a heifer in the
pasture,
and neigh like stallions,
12 your mother shall be utterly shamed,
and she who bore you shall be
disgraced.
Behold, she shall be the last of the
nations,
a wilderness, a dry land, and a desert.
13 Because of the wrath of the LORD she
shall not be inhabited
but shall be an utter desolation;
everyone who passes by Babylon shall
be appalled,
and hiss because of all her wounds.
14 Set yourselves in array against Babylon
all around,
all you who bend the bow;
shoot at her, spare no arrows,
for she has sinned against the LORD.
15 Raise a shout against her all around;
she has surrendered;
her bulwarks have fallen;
her walls are thrown down.
For this is the vengeance of the LORD:
take vengeance on her;
do to her as she has done.
16 Cut off from Babylon the sower,
and the one who handles the sickle in
time of harvest;
because of the sword of the oppressor,
every one shall turn to his own
people,
and every one shall flee to his own
land.

17 "Israel is a hunted sheep driven away
by lions. First the king of Assyria devoured
him, and now at last Nebuchadnezzar king of
Babylon has gnawed his bones. 18 Therefore,
thus says the LORD of hosts, the God of Israel:
Behold, I am bringing punishment on the
king of Babylon and his land, as I punished
the king of Assyria. 19 I will restore Israel to
his pasture, and he shall feed on Carmel and
in Bashan, and his desire shall be satisfied on
the hills of Ephraim and in Gilead. 20 In those

days and in that time, declares the LORD, iniquity shall be sought in Israel, and there shall be none, and sin in Judah, and none shall be found, for I will pardon those whom I leave as a remnant.

21 "Go up against the land of Merathaim,[1]
    and against the inhabitants of Pekod.[2]
Kill, and devote them to destruction,[3]
            declares the LORD,
    and do all that I have commanded
        you.
22 The noise of battle is in the land,
    and great destruction!
23 How the hammer of the whole earth
    is cut down and broken!
How Babylon has become
    a horror among the nations!
24 I set a snare for you and you were taken,
        O Babylon,
    and you did not know it;
you were found and caught,
    because you opposed the LORD.
25 The LORD has opened his armory
    and brought out the weapons of his
        wrath,
for the Lord GOD of hosts has a work
        to do
    in the land of the Chaldeans.
26 Come against her from every quarter;
    open her granaries;
pile her up like heaps of grain, and
        devote her to destruction;
    let nothing be left of her.
27 Kill all her bulls;
    let them go down to the slaughter.
Woe to them, for their day has come,
    the time of their punishment.

28 "A voice! They flee and escape from the land of Babylon, to declare in Zion the vengeance of the LORD our God, vengeance for his temple.

29 "Summon archers against Babylon, all those who bend the bow. Encamp around her; let no one escape. Repay her according to her deeds; do to her according to all that she has done. For she has proudly defied the LORD, the Holy One of Israel. 30 Therefore her young men shall fall in her squares, and all her soldiers shall be destroyed on that day, declares the LORD.

31 "Behold, I am against you, O proud one,
    declares the Lord GOD of hosts,
for your day has come,
    the time when I will punish you.
32 The proud one shall stumble and fall,
    with none to raise him up,
and I will kindle a fire in his cities,
    and it will devour all that is around
        him.

33 "Thus says the LORD of hosts: The people of Israel are oppressed, and the people of Judah with them. All who took them captive have held them fast; they refuse to let them go. 34 Their Redeemer is strong; the LORD of hosts is his name. He will surely plead their cause, that he may give rest to the earth, but unrest to the inhabitants of Babylon.

35 "A sword against the Chaldeans, declares
        the LORD,
    and against the inhabitants of
        Babylon,
    and against her officials and her wise
        men!
36 A sword against the diviners,
    that they may become fools!
A sword against her warriors,
    that they may be destroyed!
37 A sword against her horses and against
        her chariots,
    and against all the foreign troops in
        her midst,
    that they may become women!
A sword against all her treasures,
    that they may be plundered!
38 A drought against her waters,
    that they may be dried up!
For it is a land of images,
    and they are mad over idols.

39 "Therefore wild beasts shall dwell with hyenas in Babylon, and ostriches shall dwell in her. She shall never again have people, nor be inhabited for all generations. 40 As when God overthrew Sodom and Gomorrah and their neighboring cities, declares the LORD, so no man shall dwell there, and no son of man shall sojourn in her.

41 "Behold, a people comes from the north;
    a mighty nation and many kings
    are stirring from the farthest parts of
        the earth.

[1] Merathaim means double rebellion [2] Pekod means punishment [3] That is, set apart (devote) as an offering to the Lord (for destruction)

42 They lay hold of bow and spear;
  they are cruel and have no mercy.
The sound of them is like the roaring of
    the sea;
  they ride on horses,
arrayed as a man for battle
  against you, O daughter of Babylon!

43 "The king of Babylon heard the report of
    them,
  and his hands fell helpless;
anguish seized him,
  pain as of a woman in labor.

44 "Behold, like a lion coming up from the thicket of the Jordan against a perennial pasture, I will suddenly make them run away from her, and I will appoint over her whomever I choose. For who is like me? Who will summon me? What shepherd can stand before me? 45 Therefore hear the plan that the LORD has made against Babylon, and the purposes that he has formed against the land of the Chaldeans: Surely the little ones of their flock shall be dragged away; surely their fold shall be appalled at their fate. 46 At the sound of the capture of Babylon the earth shall tremble, and her cry shall be heard among the nations."

———— *Psalm 28–29* ————

OF DAVID.

To you, O LORD, I call;
  my rock, be not deaf to me,
lest, if you be silent to me,
  I become like those who go down to
    the pit.
2 Hear the voice of my pleas for mercy,
  when I cry to you for help,
when I lift up my hands
  toward your most holy sanctuary.[1]

3 Do not drag me off with the wicked,
  with the workers of evil,
who speak peace with their neighbors
  while evil is in their hearts.
4 Give to them according to their work
  and according to the evil of their
    deeds;
give to them according to the work of
    their hands;
  render them their due reward.

5 Because they do not regard the works of
    the LORD
  or the work of his hands,
he will tear them down and build them
    up no more.

6 Blessed be the LORD!
  For he has heard the voice of my pleas
    for mercy.
7 The LORD is my strength and my shield;
  in him my heart trusts, and I am
    helped;
my heart exults,
  and with my song I give thanks to him.

8 The LORD is the strength of his people;[2]
  he is the saving refuge of his anointed.
9 Oh, save your people and bless your
    heritage!
  Be their shepherd and carry them
    forever.

A PSALM OF DAVID.

Ascribe to the LORD, O heavenly beings,[3]
  ascribe to the LORD glory and strength.
2 Ascribe to the LORD the glory due his
    name;
  worship the LORD in the splendor of
    holiness.[4]

3 The voice of the LORD is over the waters;
  the God of glory thunders,
  the LORD, over many waters.
4 The voice of the LORD is powerful;
  the voice of the LORD is full of
    majesty.

5 The voice of the LORD breaks the cedars;
  the LORD breaks the cedars of
    Lebanon.
6 He makes Lebanon to skip like a calf,
  and Sirion like a young wild ox.

7 The voice of the LORD flashes forth
    flames of fire.
8 The voice of the LORD shakes the
    wilderness;
  the LORD shakes the wilderness of
    Kadesh.

9 The voice of the LORD makes the deer
    give birth[5]
  and strips the forests bare,
  and in his temple all cry, "Glory!"

[1] Hebrew *your innermost sanctuary* [2] Some Hebrew manuscripts, Septuagint, Syriac; most Hebrew manuscripts *is their strength* [3] Hebrew *sons of God*, or *sons of might* [4] Or *in holy attire* [5] Revocalization yields *makes the oaks to shake*

10 The LORD sits enthroned over the flood;
the LORD sits enthroned as king
forever.

11 May the LORD give strength to his people!
May the LORD bless[1] his people with
peace!

AUGUST 22

—— *1 Samuel 14* ——

One day Jonathan the son of Saul said to the young man who carried his armor, "Come, let us go over to the Philistine garrison on the other side." But he did not tell his father. **2**Saul was staying in the outskirts of Gibeah in the pomegranate cave[2] at Migron. The people who were with him were about six hundred men, **3**including Ahijah the son of Ahitub, Ichabod's brother, son of Phinehas, son of Eli, the priest of the LORD in Shiloh, wearing an ephod. And the people did not know that Jonathan had gone. **4**Within the passes, by which Jonathan sought to go over to the Philistine garrison, there was a rocky crag on the one side and a rocky crag on the other side. The name of the one was Bozez, and the name of the other Seneh. **5**The one crag rose on the north in front of Michmash, and the other on the south in front of Geba.

6Jonathan said to the young man who carried his armor, "Come, let us go over to the garrison of these uncircumcised. It may be that the LORD will work for us, for nothing can hinder the LORD from saving by many or by few." **7**And his armor-bearer said to him, "Do all that is in your heart. Do as you wish.[3] Behold, I am with you heart and soul." **8**Then Jonathan said, "Behold, we will cross over to the men, and we will show ourselves to them. **9**If they say to us, 'Wait until we come to you,' then we will stand still in our place, and we will not go up to them. **10**But if they say, 'Come up to us,' then we will go up, for the LORD has given them into our hand. And this shall be the sign to us." **11**So both of them showed themselves to the garrison of the Philistines. And the Philistines said, "Look, Hebrews are coming out of the holes where they have hidden themselves." **12**And the men of the garrison hailed Jonathan and his armor-bearer and said, "Come up to us, and we will show you a thing." And Jonathan said to his armor-bearer, "Come up after me, for the LORD has given them into the hand of Israel." **13**Then Jonathan climbed up on his hands and feet, and his armor-bearer after him. And they fell before Jonathan, and his armor-bearer killed them after him. **14**And that first strike, which Jonathan and his armor-bearer made, killed about twenty men within as it were half a furrow's length in an acre[4] of land. **15**And there was a panic in the camp, in the field, and among all the people. The garrison and even the raiders trembled, the earth quaked, and it became a very great panic.[5]

16And the watchmen of Saul in Gibeah of Benjamin looked, and behold, the multitude was dispersing here and there.[6] **17**Then Saul said to the people who were with him, "Count and see who has gone from us." And when they had counted, behold, Jonathan and his armor-bearer were not there. **18**So Saul said to Ahijah, "Bring the ark of God here." For the ark of God went at that time with the people[7] of Israel. **19**Now while Saul was talking to the priest, the tumult in the camp of the Philistines increased more and more. So Saul said to the priest, "Withdraw your hand." **20**Then Saul and all the people who were with him rallied and went into the battle. And behold, every Philistine's sword was against his fellow, and there was very great confusion. **21**Now the Hebrews who had been with the Philistines before that time and who had gone up with them into the camp, even they also turned to be with the Israelites who were with Saul and Jonathan. **22**Likewise, when all the men of Israel who had hidden themselves in the hill

---

[1] Or The LORD will give. . . The LORD will bless [2] Or under the pomegranate [tree] [3] Septuagint Do all that your mind inclines to [4] Hebrew a yoke [5] Or became a panic from God
[6] Septuagint; Hebrew they went here and there [7] Hebrew; Septuagint "Bring the ephod." For at that time he wore the ephod before the people

country of Ephraim heard that the Philistines were fleeing, they too followed hard after them in the battle. [23] So the LORD saved Israel that day. And the battle passed beyond Beth-aven.

[24] And the men of Israel had been hard pressed that day, so Saul had laid an oath on the people, saying, "Cursed be the man who eats food until it is evening and I am avenged on my enemies." So none of the people had tasted food. [25] Now when all the people[1] came to the forest, behold, there was honey on the ground. [26] And when the people entered the forest, behold, the honey was dropping, but no one put his hand to his mouth, for the people feared the oath. [27] But Jonathan had not heard his father charge the people with the oath, so he put out the tip of the staff that was in his hand and dipped it in the honeycomb and put his hand to his mouth, and his eyes became bright. [28] Then one of the people said, "Your father strictly charged the people with an oath, saying, 'Cursed be the man who eats food this day.'" And the people were faint. [29] Then Jonathan said, "My father has troubled the land. See how my eyes have become bright because I tasted a little of this honey. [30] How much better if the people had eaten freely today of the spoil of their enemies that they found. For now the defeat among the Philistines has not been great."

[31] They struck down the Philistines that day from Michmash to Aijalon. And the people were very faint. [32] The people pounced on the spoil and took sheep and oxen and calves and slaughtered them on the ground. And the people ate them with the blood. [33] Then they told Saul, "Behold, the people are sinning against the LORD by eating with the blood." And he said, "You have dealt treacherously; roll a great stone to me here."[2] [34] And Saul said, "Disperse yourselves among the people and say to them, 'Let every man bring his ox or his sheep and slaughter them here and eat, and do not sin against the LORD by eating with the blood.'" So every one of the people brought his ox with him that night and they slaughtered them there. [35] And Saul built an altar to the LORD; it was the first altar that he built to the LORD.

[36] Then Saul said, "Let us go down after the Philistines by night and plunder them until the morning light; let us not leave a man of them." And they said, "Do whatever seems good to you." But the priest said, "Let us draw near to God here." [37] And Saul inquired of God, "Shall I go down after the Philistines? Will you give them into the hand of Israel?" But he did not answer him that day. [38] And Saul said, "Come here, all you leaders of the people, and know and see how this sin has arisen today. [39] For as the LORD lives who saves Israel, though it be in Jonathan my son, he shall surely die." But there was not a man among all the people who answered him. [40] Then he said to all Israel, "You shall be on one side, and I and Jonathan my son will be on the other side." And the people said to Saul, "Do what seems good to you." [41] Therefore Saul said, "O LORD God of Israel, why have you not answered your servant this day? If this guilt is in me or in Jonathan my son, O LORD, God of Israel, give Urim. But if this guilt is in your people Israel, give Thummim."[3] And Jonathan and Saul were taken, but the people escaped. [42] Then Saul said, "Cast the lot between me and my son Jonathan." And Jonathan was taken.

[43] Then Saul said to Jonathan, "Tell me what you have done." And Jonathan told him, "I tasted a little honey with the tip of the staff that was in my hand. Here I am; I will die." [44] And Saul said, "God do so to me and more also; you shall surely die, Jonathan." [45] Then the people said to Saul, "Shall Jonathan die, who has worked this great salvation in Israel? Far from it! As the LORD lives, there shall not one hair of his head fall to the ground, for he has worked with God this day." So the people ransomed Jonathan, so that he did not die. [46] Then Saul went up from pursuing the Philistines, and the Philistines went to their own place.

[47] When Saul had taken the kingship over Israel, he fought against all his enemies on every side, against Moab, against the Ammonites, against Edom, against the kings of Zobah, and against the Philistines. Wherever he turned he routed them. [48] And he did valiantly and struck the Amalekites and delivered Israel out of the hands of those who plundered them.

[49] Now the sons of Saul were Jonathan, Ishvi, and Malchi-shua. And the names of his two daughters were these: the name of the firstborn was Merab, and the name of the younger Michal. [50] And the name of Saul's wife was Ahinoam the daughter of Ahimaaz. And the name of the commander of his army was Abner the son of Ner, Saul's uncle. [51] Kish was

[1] Hebrew *land* [2] Septuagint; Hebrew *this day* [3] Vulgate and Septuagint; Hebrew *Therefore Saul said to the LORD, the God of Israel, "Give Thummim."*

the father of Saul, and Ner the father of Abner was the son of Abiel.

[52] There was hard fighting against the Philistines all the days of Saul. And when Saul saw any strong man, or any valiant man, he attached him to himself.

Romans 12

I appeal to you therefore, brothers,[1] by the mercies of God, to present your bodies as a living sacrifice, holy and acceptable to God, which is your spiritual worship.[2] [2] Do not be conformed to this world,[3] but be transformed by the renewal of your mind, that by testing you may discern what is the will of God, what is good and acceptable and perfect.[4]

[3] For by the grace given to me I say to everyone among you not to think of himself more highly than he ought to think, but to think with sober judgment, each according to the measure of faith that God has assigned. [4] For as in one body we have many members,[5] and the members do not all have the same function, [5] so we, though many, are one body in Christ, and individually members one of another. [6] Having gifts that differ according to the grace given to us, let us use them: if prophecy, in proportion to our faith; [7] if service, in our serving; the one who teaches, in his teaching; [8] the one who exhorts, in his exhortation; the one who contributes, in generosity; the one who leads,[6] with zeal; the one who does acts of mercy, with cheerfulness.

[9] Let love be genuine. Abhor what is evil; hold fast to what is good. [10] Love one another with brotherly affection. Outdo one another in showing honor. [11] Do not be slothful in zeal, be fervent in spirit,[7] serve the Lord. [12] Rejoice in hope, be patient in tribulation, be constant in prayer. [13] Contribute to the needs of the saints and seek to show hospitality.

[14] Bless those who persecute you; bless and do not curse them. [15] Rejoice with those who rejoice, weep with those who weep. [16] Live in harmony with one another. Do not be haughty, but associate with the lowly.[8] Never be wise in your own sight. [17] Repay no one evil for evil, but give thought to do what is honorable in the sight of all. [18] If possible, so far as it depends on you, live peaceably with all. [19] Beloved, never avenge yourselves, but leave it[9] to the wrath of God, for it is written, "Vengeance is mine, I will repay, says the Lord." [20] To the contrary, "if your enemy is hungry, feed him; if he is thirsty, give him something to drink; for by so doing you will heap burning coals on his head." [21] Do not be overcome by evil, but overcome evil with good.

Jeremiah 51

Thus says the LORD:
"Behold, I will stir up the spirit of a
   destroyer
  against Babylon,
  against the inhabitants of
   Leb-kamai,[10]
[2] and I will send to Babylon winnowers,
  and they shall winnow her,
  and they shall empty her land,
   when they come against her from
    every side
  on the day of trouble.
[3] Let not the archer bend his bow,
  and let him not stand up in his armor.
  Spare not her young men;
   devote to destruction[11] all her army.
[4] They shall fall down slain in the land of
   the Chaldeans,
  and wounded in her streets.
[5] For Israel and Judah have not been
   forsaken
  by their God, the LORD of hosts,
  but the land of the Chaldeans[12] is full of
   guilt
  against the Holy One of Israel.
[6] "Flee from the midst of Babylon;
  let every one save his life!
  Be not cut off in her punishment,
  for this is the time of the LORD's
   vengeance,
  the repayment he is rendering her.
[7] Babylon was a golden cup in the LORD's
   hand,
  making all the earth drunken;
  the nations drank of her wine;
  therefore the nations went mad.
[8] Suddenly Babylon has fallen and been
   broken;
  wail for her!
  Take balm for her pain;
  perhaps she may be healed.
[9] We would have healed Babylon,
  but she was not healed.

[1] Or brothers and sisters [2] Or your rational service [3] Greek age [4] Or what is the good and acceptable and perfect will of God [5] Greek parts; also verse 5 [6] Or gives aid [7] Or fervent in the Spirit [8] Or give yourselves to humble tasks [9] Greek give place [10] A code name for Chaldea [11] That is, set apart (devote) as an offering to the Lord (for destruction) [12] Hebrew their land

Forsake her, and let us go
  each to his own country,
for her judgment has reached up to
    heaven
  and has been lifted up even to the
    skies.
¹⁰ The LORD has brought about our
    vindication;
  come, let us declare in Zion
    the work of the LORD our God.

¹¹ "Sharpen the arrows!
    Take up the shields!

The LORD has stirred up the spirit of the kings
of the Medes, because his purpose concerning
Babylon is to destroy it, for that is the vengeance
of the LORD, the vengeance for his temple.

¹² "Set up a standard against the walls of
    Babylon;
  make the watch strong;
  set up watchmen;
    prepare the ambushes;
  for the LORD has both planned and done
    what he spoke concerning the
    inhabitants of Babylon.
¹³ O you who dwell by many waters,
    rich in treasures,
  your end has come;
    the thread of your life is cut.
¹⁴ The LORD of hosts has sworn by himself:
  Surely I will fill you with men, as many
    as locusts,
  and they shall raise the shout of
    victory over you.

¹⁵ "It is he who made the earth by his power,
  who established the world by his
    wisdom,
  and by his understanding stretched out
    the heavens.
¹⁶ When he utters his voice there is a
    tumult of waters in the heavens,
  and he makes the mist rise from the
    ends of the earth.
  He makes lightning for the rain,
    and he brings forth the wind from his
    storehouses.
¹⁷ Every man is stupid and without
    knowledge;
  every goldsmith is put to shame by his
    idols,

for his images are false,
    and there is no breath in them.
¹⁸ They are worthless, a work of delusion;
  at the time of their punishment they
    shall perish.
¹⁹ Not like these is he who is the portion of
    Jacob,
  for he is the one who formed all
    things,
  and Israel is the tribe of his inheritance;
    the LORD of hosts is his name.

²⁰ "You are my hammer and weapon of
    war:
  with you I break nations in pieces;
    with you I destroy kingdoms;
²¹ with you I break in pieces the horse and
    his rider;
  with you I break in pieces the chariot
    and the charioteer;
²² with you I break in pieces man and
    woman;
  with you I break in pieces the old man
    and the youth;
  with you I break in pieces the young
    man and the young woman;
²³ with you I break in pieces the
    shepherd and his flock;
  with you I break in pieces the farmer
    and his team;
  with you I break in pieces governors
    and commanders.

²⁴ "I will repay Babylon and all the inhabitants of Chaldea before your very eyes for all
the evil that they have done in Zion, declares
the LORD.

²⁵ "Behold, I am against you, O destroying
    mountain,
            declares the LORD,
  which destroys the whole earth;
  I will stretch out my hand against you,
    and roll you down from the crags,
    and make you a burnt mountain.
²⁶ No stone shall be taken from you for a
    corner
  and no stone for a foundation,
  but you shall be a perpetual waste,
    declares the LORD.

²⁷ "Set up a standard on the earth;
  blow the trumpet among the nations;

prepare the nations for war against her;
  summon against her the kingdoms,
  Ararat, Minni, and Ashkenaz;
appoint a marshal against her;
  bring up horses like bristling locusts.
28 Prepare the nations for war against her,
  the kings of the Medes, with their
    governors and deputies,
  and every land under their dominion.
29 The land trembles and writhes in pain,
  for the Lord's purposes against
    Babylon stand,
to make the land of Babylon a
  desolation,
  without inhabitant.
30 The warriors of Babylon have ceased
    fighting;
  they remain in their strongholds;
their strength has failed;
  they have become women;
her dwellings are on fire;
  her bars are broken.
31 One runner runs to meet another,
  and one messenger to meet another,
to tell the king of Babylon
  that his city is taken on every side;
32 the fords have been seized,
  the marshes are burned with fire,
  and the soldiers are in panic.
33 For thus says the Lord of hosts, the God
    of Israel:
The daughter of Babylon is like a
    threshing floor
  at the time when it is trodden;
yet a little while
  and the time of her harvest will come."

34 "Nebuchadnezzar the king of Babylon
    has devoured me;
  he has crushed me;
he has made me an empty vessel;
  he has swallowed me like a monster;
he has filled his stomach with my
    delicacies;
  he has rinsed me out.[1]
35 The violence done to me and to my
    kinsmen be upon Babylon,"
  let the inhabitant of Zion say.
"My blood be upon the inhabitants of
    Chaldea,"
  let Jerusalem say.
36 Therefore thus says the Lord:

"Behold, I will plead your cause
  and take vengeance for you.
I will dry up her sea
  and make her fountain dry,
37 and Babylon shall become a heap of
    ruins,
  the haunt of jackals,
a horror and a hissing,
  without inhabitant.
38 "They shall roar together like lions;
  they shall growl like lions' cubs.
39 While they are inflamed I will prepare
    them a feast
  and make them drunk, that they may
    become merry,
then sleep a perpetual sleep
  and not wake, declares the Lord.
40 I will bring them down like lambs to the
    slaughter,
  like rams and male goats.

41 "How Babylon[2] is taken,
  the praise of the whole earth seized!
How Babylon has become
  a horror among the nations!
42 The sea has come up on Babylon;
  she is covered with its tumultuous
    waves.
43 Her cities have become a horror,
  a land of drought and a desert,
a land in which no one dwells,
  and through which no son of man
    passes.
44 And I will punish Bel in Babylon,
  and take out of his mouth what he has
    swallowed.
The nations shall no longer flow to him;
  the wall of Babylon has fallen.

45 "Go out of the midst of her, my people!
  Let every one save his life
  from the fierce anger of the Lord!
46 Let not your heart faint, and be not
    fearful
  at the report heard in the land,
when a report comes in one year
  and afterward a report in another year,
and violence is in the land,
  and ruler is against ruler.

47 "Therefore, behold, the days are coming
  when I will punish the images of
    Babylon;

[1] Or he has expelled me   [2] Hebrew Sheshach, a code name for Babylon

her whole land shall be put to shame,
   and all her slain shall fall in the midst
     of her.
48 Then the heavens and the earth,
   and all that is in them,
shall sing for joy over Babylon,
   for the destroyers shall come against
     them out of the north,
          declares the LORD.
49 Babylon must fall for the slain of Israel,
   just as for Babylon have fallen the
     slain of all the earth.

50 "You who have escaped from the sword,
   go, do not stand still!
Remember the LORD from far away,
   and let Jerusalem come into your
     mind:
51 'We are put to shame, for we have heard
   reproach;
   dishonor has covered our face,
for foreigners have come
   into the holy places of the LORD's
     house.'
52 "Therefore, behold, the days are coming,
   declares the LORD,
   when I will execute judgment upon
     her images,
and through all her land
   the wounded shall groan.
53 Though Babylon should mount up to
     heaven,
   and though she should fortify her
     strong height,
yet destroyers would come from me
   against her,
   declares the LORD.

54 "A voice! A cry from Babylon!
   The noise of great destruction from
     the land of the Chaldeans!
55 For the LORD is laying Babylon waste
   and stilling her mighty voice.
Their waves roar like many waters;
   the noise of their voice is raised,
56 for a destroyer has come upon her,
   upon Babylon;
her warriors are taken;
   their bows are broken in pieces,
for the LORD is a God of recompense;
   he will surely repay.

57 I will make drunk her officials and her
     wise men,
   her governors, her commanders, and
     her warriors;
they shall sleep a perpetual sleep and
     not wake,
   declares the King, whose name is the
     LORD of hosts.

58 "Thus says the LORD of hosts:
The broad wall of Babylon
   shall be leveled to the ground,
and her high gates
   shall be burned with fire.
The peoples labor for nothing,
   and the nations weary themselves
     only for fire."

59 The word that Jeremiah the prophet commanded Seraiah the son of Neriah, son of Mahseiah, when he went with Zedekiah king of Judah to Babylon, in the fourth year of his reign. Seraiah was the quartermaster. 60 Jeremiah wrote in a book all the disaster that should come upon Babylon, all these words that are written concerning Babylon. 61 And Jeremiah said to Seraiah: "When you come to Babylon, see that you read all these words, 62 and say, 'O LORD, you have said concerning this place that you will cut it off, so that nothing shall dwell in it, neither man nor beast, and it shall be desolate forever.' 63 When you finish reading this book, tie a stone to it and cast it into the midst of the Euphrates, 64 and say, 'Thus shall Babylon sink, to rise no more, because of the disaster that I am bringing upon her, and they shall become exhausted.'"

Thus far are the words of Jeremiah.

Psalm 30

A PSALM OF DAVID. A SONG AT THE DEDICATION OF THE TEMPLE.

I will extol you, O LORD, for you have drawn
  me up
   and have not let my foes rejoice over
     me.
2 O LORD my God, I cried to you for help,
   and you have healed me.
3 O LORD, you have brought up my soul
   from Sheol;
   you restored me to life from among
     those who go down to the pit.[1]

---

[1] Or to life, that I should not go down to the pit

4 Sing praises to the LORD, O you his saints,
  and give thanks to his holy name.[1]
5 For his anger is but for a moment,
  and his favor is for a lifetime.[2]
  Weeping may tarry for the night,
  but joy comes with the morning.
6 As for me, I said in my prosperity,
  "I shall never be moved."
7 By your favor, O LORD,
  you made my mountain stand strong;
  you hid your face;
  I was dismayed.
8 To you, O LORD, I cry,
  and to the Lord I plead for mercy:

9 "What profit is there in my death,[3]
  if I go down to the pit?[4]
  Will the dust praise you?
  Will it tell of your faithfulness?
10 Hear, O LORD, and be merciful to me!
  O LORD, be my helper!"
11 You have turned for me my mourning
  into dancing;
  you have loosed my sackcloth
  and clothed me with gladness,
12 that my glory may sing your praise and
  not be silent.
  O LORD my God, I will give thanks to
  you forever!

AUGUST 23

1 Samuel 15

And Samuel said to Saul, "The LORD sent me to anoint you king over his people Israel; now therefore listen to the words of the LORD. [2]Thus says the LORD of hosts, 'I have noted what Amalek did to Israel in opposing them on the way when they came up out of Egypt. [3]Now go and strike Amalek and devote to destruction[5] all that they have. Do not spare them, but kill both man and woman, child and infant, ox and sheep, camel and donkey.'"

[4]So Saul summoned the people and numbered them in Telaim, two hundred thousand men on foot, and ten thousand men of Judah. [5]And Saul came to the city of Amalek and lay in wait in the valley. [6]Then Saul said to the Kenites, "Go, depart; go down from among the Amalekites, lest I destroy you with them. For you showed kindness to all the people of Israel when they came up out of Egypt." So the Kenites departed from among the Amalekites. [7]And Saul defeated the Amalekites from Havilah as far as Shur, which is east of Egypt. [8]And he took Agag the king of the Amalekites alive and devoted to destruction all the people with the edge of the sword. [9]But Saul and the people spared Agag and the best of the sheep

and of the oxen and of the fattened calves[6] and the lambs, and all that was good, and would not utterly destroy them. All that was despised and worthless they devoted to destruction.

[10]The word of the LORD came to Samuel: [11]"I regret[7] that I have made Saul king, for he has turned back from following me and has not performed my commandments." And Samuel was angry, and he cried to the LORD all night. [12]And Samuel rose early to meet Saul in the morning. And it was told Samuel, "Saul came to Carmel, and behold, he set up a monument for himself and turned and passed on and went down to Gilgal." [13]And Samuel came to Saul, and Saul said to him, "Blessed be you to the LORD. I have performed the commandment of the LORD." [14]And Samuel said, "What then is this bleating of the sheep in my ears and the lowing of the oxen that I hear?" [15]Saul said, "They have brought them from the Amalekites, for the people spared the best of the sheep and of the oxen to sacrifice to the LORD your God, and the rest we have devoted to destruction." [16]Then Samuel said to Saul, "Stop! I will tell you what the LORD said to me this night." And he said to him, "Speak."

[1] Hebrew to the memorial of his holiness (see Exodus 3:15) [2] Or and in his favor is life [3] Hebrew in my blood [4] Or to corruption [5] That is, set apart (devote) as an offering to the Lord (for destruction); also verses 8, 9, 15, 18, 20, 21 [6] The meaning of the Hebrew term is uncertain [7] See also verses 29, 35

[17]And Samuel said, "Though you are little in your own eyes, are you not the head of the tribes of Israel? The LORD anointed you king over Israel. [18]And the LORD sent you on a mission and said, 'Go, devote to destruction the sinners, the Amalekites, and fight against them until they are consumed.' [19]Why then did you not obey the voice of the LORD? Why did you pounce on the spoil and do what was evil in the sight of the LORD?" [20]And Saul said to Samuel, "I have obeyed the voice of the LORD. I have gone on the mission on which the LORD sent me. I have brought Agag the king of Amalek, and I have devoted the Amalekites to destruction. [21]But the people took of the spoil, sheep and oxen, the best of the things devoted to destruction, to sacrifice to the LORD your God in Gilgal." [22]And Samuel said,

> "Has the LORD as great delight in burnt
>   offerings and sacrifices,
>   as in obeying the voice of the LORD?
> Behold, to obey is better than sacrifice,
>   and to listen than the fat of rams.
> [23] For rebellion is as the sin of divination,
>   and presumption is as iniquity and
>   idolatry.
> Because you have rejected the word of
>   the LORD,
>   he has also rejected you from being
>   king."

[24]Saul said to Samuel, "I have sinned, for I have transgressed the commandment of the LORD and your words, because I feared the people and obeyed their voice. [25]Now therefore, please pardon my sin and return with me that I may bow before the LORD." [26]And Samuel said to Saul, "I will not return with you. For you have rejected the word of the LORD, and the LORD has rejected you from being king over Israel." [27]As Samuel turned to go away, Saul seized the skirt of his robe, and it tore. [28]And Samuel said to him, "The LORD has torn the kingdom of Israel from you this day and has given it to a neighbor of yours, who is better than you. [29]And also the Glory of Israel will not lie or have regret, for he is not a man, that he should have regret." [30]Then he said, "I have sinned; yet honor me now before the elders of my people and before Israel, and return with me, that I may bow before the LORD your God."

[31]So Samuel turned back after Saul, and Saul bowed before the LORD.

[32]Then Samuel said, "Bring here to me Agag the king of the Amalekites." And Agag came to him cheerfully.[1] Agag said, "Surely the bitterness of death is past." [33]And Samuel said, "As your sword has made women childless, so shall your mother be childless among women." And Samuel hacked Agag to pieces before the LORD in Gilgal.

[34]Then Samuel went to Ramah, and Saul went up to his house in Gibeah of Saul. [35]And Samuel did not see Saul again until the day of his death, but Samuel grieved over Saul. And the LORD regretted that he had made Saul king over Israel.

─────── *Romans 13* ───────

L et every person be subject to the governing authorities. For there is no authority except from God, and those that exist have been instituted by God. [2]Therefore whoever resists the authorities resists what God has appointed, and those who resist will incur judgment. [3]For rulers are not a terror to good conduct, but to bad. Would you have no fear of the one who is in authority? Then do what is good, and you will receive his approval, [4]for he is God's servant for your good. But if you do wrong, be afraid, for he does not bear the sword in vain. For he is the servant of God, an avenger who carries out God's wrath on the wrongdoer. [5]Therefore one must be in subjection, not only to avoid God's wrath but also for the sake of conscience. [6]For because of this you also pay taxes, for the authorities are ministers of God, attending to this very thing. [7]Pay to all what is owed to them: taxes to whom taxes are owed, revenue to whom revenue is owed, respect to whom respect is owed, honor to whom honor is owed.

[8]Owe no one anything, except to love each other, for the one who loves another has fulfilled the law. [9]For the commandments, "You shall not commit adultery, You shall not murder, You shall not steal, You shall not covet," and any other commandment, are summed up in this word: "You shall love your neighbor as yourself." [10]Love does no wrong to a neighbor; therefore love is the fulfilling of the law.

[11]Besides this you know the time, that the

---

[1] Or *haltingly* (compare Septuagint); the Hebrew is uncertain

hour has come for you to wake from sleep. For salvation is nearer to us now than when we first believed. [12] The night is far gone; the day is at hand. So then let us cast off the works of darkness and put on the armor of light. [13] Let us walk properly as in the daytime, not in orgies and drunkenness, not in sexual immorality and sensuality, not in quarreling and jealousy. [14] But put on the Lord Jesus Christ, and make no provision for the flesh, to gratify its desires.

———— *Jeremiah 52* ————

Zedekiah was twenty-one years old when he became king, and he reigned eleven years in Jerusalem. His mother's name was Hamutal the daughter of Jeremiah of Libnah. [2] And he did what was evil in the sight of the LORD, according to all that Jehoiakim had done. [3] For because of the anger of the LORD it came to the point in Jerusalem and Judah that he cast them out from his presence.

And Zedekiah rebelled against the king of Babylon. [4] And in the ninth year of his reign, in the tenth month, on the tenth day of the month, Nebuchadnezzar king of Babylon came with all his army against Jerusalem, and laid siege to it. And they built siegeworks all around it. [5] So the city was besieged till the eleventh year of King Zedekiah. [6] On the ninth day of the fourth month the famine was so severe in the city that there was no food for the people of the land. [7] Then a breach was made in the city, and all the men of war fled and went out from the city by night by the way of a gate between the two walls, by the king's garden, and the Chaldeans were around the city. And they went in the direction of the Arabah. [8] But the army of the Chaldeans pursued the king and overtook Zedekiah in the plains of Jericho, and all his army was scattered from him. [9] Then they captured the king and brought him up to the king of Babylon at Riblah in the land of Hamath, and he passed sentence on him. [10] The king of Babylon slaughtered the sons of Zedekiah before his eyes, and also slaughtered all the officials of Judah at Riblah. [11] He put out the eyes of Zedekiah, and bound him in chains, and the king of Babylon took him to Babylon, and put him in prison till the day of his death.

[12] In the fifth month, on the tenth day of the month—that was the nineteenth year of King Nebuchadnezzar, king of Babylon— Nebuzaradan the captain of the bodyguard, who served the king of Babylon, entered Jerusalem. [13] And he burned the house of the LORD, and the king's house and all the houses of Jerusalem; every great house he burned down. [14] And all the army of the Chaldeans, who were with the captain of the guard, broke down all the walls around Jerusalem. [15] And Nebuzaradan the captain of the guard carried away captive some of the poorest of the people and the rest of the people who were left in the city and the deserters who had deserted to the king of Babylon, together with the rest of the artisans. [16] But Nebuzaradan the captain of the guard left some of the poorest of the land to be vinedressers and plowmen.

[17] And the pillars of bronze that were in the house of the LORD, and the stands and the bronze sea that were in the house of the LORD, the Chaldeans broke in pieces, and carried all the bronze to Babylon. [18] And they took away the pots and the shovels and the snuffers and the basins and the dishes for incense and all the vessels of bronze used in the temple service; [19] also the small bowls and the fire pans and the basins and the pots and the lampstands and the dishes for incense and the bowls for drink offerings. What was of gold the captain of the guard took away as gold, and what was of silver, as silver. [20] As for the two pillars, the one sea, the twelve bronze bulls that were under the sea,[1] and the stands, which Solomon the king had made for the house of the LORD, the bronze of all these things was beyond weight. [21] As for the pillars, the height of the one pillar was eighteen cubits,[2] its circumference was twelve cubits, and its thickness was four fingers, and it was hollow. [22] On it was a capital of bronze. The height of the one capital was five cubits. A network and pomegranates, all of bronze, were around the capital. And the second pillar had the same, with pomegranates. [23] There were ninety-six pomegranates on the sides; all the pomegranates were a hundred upon the network all around.

[24] And the captain of the guard took Seraiah the chief priest, and Zephaniah the second priest and the three keepers of the threshold; [25] and from the city he took an officer who had been in command of the men of war, and seven men of the king's council, who were found in

[1] Hebrew lacks *the sea*   [2] A *cubit* was about 18 inches or 45 centimeters

the city; and the secretary of the commander of the army, who mustered the people of the land; and sixty men of the people of the land, who were found in the midst of the city. ²⁶And Nebuzaradan the captain of the guard took them and brought them to the king of Babylon at Riblah. ²⁷And the king of Babylon struck them down and put them to death at Riblah in the land of Hamath. So Judah was taken into exile out of its land.

²⁸This is the number of the people whom Nebuchadnezzar carried away captive: in the seventh year, 3,023 Judeans; ²⁹in the eighteenth year of Nebuchadnezzar he carried away captive from Jerusalem 832 persons; ³⁰in the twenty-third year of Nebuchadnezzar, Nebuzaradan the captain of the guard carried away captive of the Judeans 745 persons; all the persons were 4,600.

³¹And in the thirty-seventh year of the exile of Jehoiachin king of Judah, in the twelfth month, on the twenty-fifth day of the month, Evil-merodach king of Babylon, in the year that he began to reign, graciously freed[1] Jehoiachin king of Judah and brought him out of prison. ³²And he spoke kindly to him and gave him a seat above the seats of the kings who were with him in Babylon. ³³So Jehoiachin put off his prison garments. And every day of his life he dined regularly at the king's table, ³⁴and for his allowance, a regular allowance was given him by the king, according to his daily needs, until the day of his death, as long as he lived.

Psalm 31

To the choirmaster. A Psalm of David.

In you, O Lord, do I take refuge;
  let me never be put to shame;
    in your righteousness deliver me!
² Incline your ear to me;
    rescue me speedily!
  Be a rock of refuge for me,
    a strong fortress to save me!

³ For you are my rock and my fortress;
    and for your name's sake you lead me
      and guide me;
⁴ you take me out of the net they have
    hidden for me,
  for you are my refuge.

⁵ Into your hand I commit my spirit;
  you have redeemed me, O Lord,
    faithful God.

⁶ I hate[2] those who pay regard to
    worthless idols,
  but I trust in the Lord.
⁷ I will rejoice and be glad in your
    steadfast love,
  because you have seen my affliction;
  you have known the distress of my
    soul,
⁸ and you have not delivered me into the
    hand of the enemy;
  you have set my feet in a broad place.

⁹ Be gracious to me, O Lord, for I am in
    distress;
  my eye is wasted from grief;
    my soul and my body also.
¹⁰ For my life is spent with sorrow,
    and my years with sighing;
  my strength fails because of my
    iniquity,
    and my bones waste away.

¹¹ Because of all my adversaries I have
    become a reproach,
  especially to my neighbors,
  and an object of dread to my
    acquaintances;
  those who see me in the street flee
    from me.
¹² I have been forgotten like one who is
    dead;
  I have become like a broken vessel.
¹³ For I hear the whispering of many—
    terror on every side!—
  as they scheme together against me,
    as they plot to take my life.

¹⁴ But I trust in you, O Lord;
  I say, "You are my God."
¹⁵ My times are in your hand;
  rescue me from the hand of
    my enemies and from my
    persecutors!
¹⁶ Make your face shine on your servant;
  save me in your steadfast love!
¹⁷ O Lord, let me not be put to shame,
    for I call upon you;
  let the wicked be put to shame;
    let them go silently to Sheol.

¹ Hebrew *king, lifted up the head of*   ² Masoretic Text; one Hebrew manuscript, Septuagint, Syriac, Jerome *You hate*

18 Let the lying lips be mute,
   which speak insolently against the
      righteous
   in pride and contempt.
19 Oh, how abundant is your goodness,
   which you have stored up for those
      who fear you
   and worked for those who take refuge in
      you,
   in the sight of the children of
      mankind!
20 In the cover of your presence you hide
      them
   from the plots of men;
   you store them in your shelter
   from the strife of tongues.

21 Blessed be the LORD,
   for he has wondrously shown his
      steadfast love to me
   when I was in a besieged city.
22 I had said in my alarm,[1]
   "I am cut off from your sight."
   But you heard the voice of my pleas for
      mercy
   when I cried to you for help.
23 Love the LORD, all you his saints!
   The LORD preserves the faithful
   but abundantly repays the one who
      acts in pride.
24 Be strong, and let your heart take
      courage,
   all you who wait for the LORD!

AUGUST 24

1 Samuel 16

The LORD said to Samuel, "How long will you grieve over Saul, since I have rejected him from being king over Israel? Fill your horn with oil, and go. I will send you to Jesse the Bethlehemite, for I have provided for myself a king among his sons." ²And Samuel said, "How can I go? If Saul hears it, he will kill me." And the LORD said, "Take a heifer with you and say, 'I have come to sacrifice to the LORD.' ³And invite Jesse to the sacrifice, and I will show you what you shall do. And you shall anoint for me him whom I declare to you." ⁴Samuel did what the LORD commanded and came to Bethlehem. The elders of the city came to meet him trembling and said, "Do you come peaceably?" ⁵And he said, "Peaceably; I have come to sacrifice to the LORD. Consecrate yourselves, and come with me to the sacrifice." And he consecrated Jesse and his sons and invited them to the sacrifice.

⁶When they came, he looked on Eliab and thought, "Surely the LORD's anointed is before him." ⁷But the LORD said to Samuel, "Do not look on his appearance or on the height of his stature, because I have rejected him. For the LORD sees not as man sees: man looks on the outward appearance, but the LORD looks on the heart." ⁸Then Jesse called Abinadab and made him pass before Samuel. And he said, "Neither has the LORD chosen this one." ⁹Then Jesse made Shammah pass by. And he said, "Neither has the LORD chosen this one." ¹⁰And Jesse made seven of his sons pass before Samuel. And Samuel said to Jesse, "The LORD has not chosen these." ¹¹Then Samuel said to Jesse, "Are all your sons here?" And he said, "There remains yet the youngest,[2] but behold, he is keeping the sheep." And Samuel said to Jesse, "Send and get him, for we will not sit down till he comes here." ¹²And he sent and brought him in. Now he was ruddy and had beautiful eyes and was handsome. And the LORD said, "Arise, anoint him, for this is he." ¹³Then Samuel took the horn of oil and anointed him in the midst of his brothers. And the Spirit of the LORD rushed upon David from that day forward. And Samuel rose up and went to Ramah.

¹⁴Now the Spirit of the LORD departed from Saul, and a harmful spirit from the LORD tormented him. ¹⁵And Saul's servants said to him,

¹ Or *in my haste* ² Or *smallest*

"Behold now, a harmful spirit from God is tormenting you. [16]Let our lord now command your servants who are before you to seek out a man who is skillful in playing the lyre, and when the harmful spirit from God is upon you, he will play it, and you will be well." [17]So Saul said to his servants, "Provide for me a man who can play well and bring him to me." [18]One of the young men answered, "Behold, I have seen a son of Jesse the Bethlehemite, who is skillful in playing, a man of valor, a man of war, prudent in speech, and a man of good presence, and the LORD is with him." [19]Therefore Saul sent messengers to Jesse and said, "Send me David your son, who is with the sheep." [20]And Jesse took a donkey laden with bread and a skin of wine and a young goat and sent them by David his son to Saul. [21]And David came to Saul and entered his service. And Saul loved him greatly, and he became his armor-bearer. [22]And Saul sent to Jesse, saying, "Let David remain in my service, for he has found favor in my sight." [23]And whenever the harmful spirit from God was upon Saul, David took the lyre and played it with his hand. So Saul was refreshed and was well, and the harmful spirit departed from him.

Romans 14

As for the one who is weak in faith, welcome him, but not to quarrel over opinions. [2]One person believes he may eat anything, while the weak person eats only vegetables. [3]Let not the one who eats despise the one who abstains, and let not the one who abstains pass judgment on the one who eats, for God has welcomed him. [4]Who are you to pass judgment on the servant of another? It is before his own master[1] that he stands or falls. And he will be upheld, for the Lord is able to make him stand. [5]One person esteems one day as better than another, while another esteems all days alike. Each one should be fully convinced in his own mind. [6]The one who observes the day, observes it in honor of the Lord. The one who eats, eats in honor of the Lord, since he gives thanks to God, while the one who abstains, abstains in honor of the Lord and gives thanks to God. [7]For none of us lives to himself, and none of us dies to himself. [8]For if we live, we live to the Lord, and if we die, we die to the Lord. So then,

whether we live or whether we die, we are the Lord's. [9]For to this end Christ died and lived again, that he might be Lord both of the dead and of the living.

[10]Why do you pass judgment on your brother? Or you, why do you despise your brother? For we will all stand before the judgment seat of God; [11]for it is written,

"As I live, says the Lord, every knee shall
        bow to me,
    and every tongue shall confess[2] to
        God."

[12]So then each of us will give an account of himself to God.

[13]Therefore let us not pass judgment on one another any longer, but rather decide never to put a stumbling block or hindrance in the way of a brother. [14]I know and am persuaded in the Lord Jesus that nothing is unclean in itself, but it is unclean for anyone who thinks it unclean. [15]For if your brother is grieved by what you eat, you are no longer walking in love. By what you eat, do not destroy the one for whom Christ died. [16]So do not let what you regard as good be spoken of as evil. [17]For the kingdom of God is not a matter of eating and drinking but of righteousness and peace and joy in the Holy Spirit. [18]Whoever thus serves Christ is acceptable to God and approved by men. [19]So then let us pursue what makes for peace and for mutual upbuilding.

[20]Do not, for the sake of food, destroy the work of God. Everything is indeed clean, but it is wrong for anyone to make another stumble by what he eats. [21]It is good not to eat meat or drink wine or do anything that causes your brother to stumble.[3] [22]The faith that you have, keep between yourself and God. Blessed is the one who has no reason to pass judgment on himself for what he approves. [23]But whoever has doubts is condemned if he eats, because the eating is not from faith. For whatever does not proceed from faith is sin.[4]

Lamentations 1

How lonely sits the city
    that was full of people!
How like a widow has she become,
    she who was great among the
        nations!

[1]Or lord [2]Or shall give praise [3]Some manuscripts add or be hindered or be weakened [4]Some manuscripts insert here 16:25–27

She who was a princess among the
    provinces
  has become a slave.

2 She weeps bitterly in the night,
     with tears on her cheeks;
   among all her lovers
     she has none to comfort her;
   all her friends have dealt treacherously
     with her;
     they have become her enemies.

3 Judah has gone into exile because of
     affliction
     and hard servitude;
   she dwells now among the nations,
     but finds no resting place;
   her pursuers have all overtaken her
     in the midst of her distress.[1]

4 The roads to Zion mourn,
     for none come to the festival;
   all her gates are desolate;
     her priests groan;
   her virgins have been afflicted,[2]
     and she herself suffers bitterly.

5 Her foes have become the head;
     her enemies prosper,
   because the LORD has afflicted her
     for the multitude of her
       transgressions;
   her children have gone away,
     captives before the foe.

6 From the daughter of Zion
     all her majesty has departed.
   Her princes have become like deer
     that find no pasture;
   they fled without strength
     before the pursuer.

7 Jerusalem remembers
     in the days of her affliction and
       wandering
   all the precious things
     that were hers from days of old.
   When her people fell into the hand of
       the foe,
     and there was none to help her,
   her foes gloated over her;
     they mocked at her downfall.

8 Jerusalem sinned grievously;
     therefore she became filthy;

all who honored her despise her,
  for they have seen her nakedness;
she herself groans
  and turns her face away.

9 Her uncleanness was in her skirts;
     she took no thought of her future;[3]
   therefore her fall is terrible;
     she has no comforter.
   "O LORD, behold my affliction,
     for the enemy has triumphed!"

10 The enemy has stretched out his hands
      over all her precious things;
    for she has seen the nations
      enter her sanctuary,
    those whom you forbade
      to enter your congregation.

11 All her people groan
      as they search for bread;
    they trade their treasures for food
      to revive their strength.
    "Look, O LORD, and see,
      for I am despised."

12 "Is it nothing to you, all you who pass by?
      Look and see
    if there is any sorrow like my sorrow,
      which was brought upon me,
    which the LORD inflicted
      on the day of his fierce anger.

13 "From on high he sent fire;
      into my bones[4] he made it descend;
    he spread a net for my feet;
      he turned me back;
    he has left me stunned,
      faint all the day long.

14 "My transgressions were bound[5] into a
        yoke;
      by his hand they were fastened
        together;
    they were set upon my neck;
      he caused my strength to fail;
    the Lord gave me into the hands
      of those whom I cannot withstand.

15 "The Lord rejected
      all my mighty men in my midst;
    he summoned an assembly against me
      to crush my young men;
    the Lord has trodden as in a winepress
      the virgin daughter of Judah.

[1] Or in the narrow passes [2] Septuagint, Old Latin dragged away [3] Or end [4] Septuagint; Hebrew bones and [5] The meaning of the Hebrew is uncertain

16 "For these things I weep;
      my eyes flow with tears;
   for a comforter is far from me,
      one to revive my spirit;
   my children are desolate,
      for the enemy has prevailed."

17 Zion stretches out her hands,
      but there is none to comfort her;
   the LORD has commanded against
         Jacob
      that his neighbors should be his
         foes;
   Jerusalem has become
      a filthy thing among them.

18 "The LORD is in the right,
      for I have rebelled against his word;
   but hear, all you peoples,
      and see my suffering;
   my young women and my young men
      have gone into captivity.

19 "I called to my lovers,
      but they deceived me;
   my priests and elders
      perished in the city,
   while they sought food
      to revive their strength.

20 "Look, O LORD, for I am in distress;
      my stomach churns;
   my heart is wrung within me,
      because I have been very rebellious.
   In the street the sword bereaves;
      in the house it is like death.

21 "They heard[1] my groaning,
      yet there is no one to comfort me.
   All my enemies have heard of my
         trouble;
      they are glad that you have done it.
   You have brought[2] the day you
         announced;
      now let them be as I am.

22 "Let all their evildoing come before you,
      and deal with them
   as you have dealt with me
      because of all my transgressions;
   for my groans are many,
      and my heart is faint."

Psalm 32

A MASKIL[3] OF DAVID.

Blessed is the one whose transgression is
      forgiven,
      whose sin is covered.
2   Blessed is the man against whom the
         LORD counts no iniquity,
      and in whose spirit there is no deceit.

3   For when I kept silent, my bones wasted
         away
      through my groaning all day long.
4   For day and night your hand was heavy
         upon me;
      my strength was dried up[4] as by the
         heat of summer.   Selah

5   I acknowledged my sin to you,
      and I did not cover my iniquity;
   I said, "I will confess my transgressions
         to the LORD,"
      and you forgave the iniquity of my
         sin.   Selah

6   Therefore let everyone who is godly
      offer prayer to you at a time when you
         may be found;
   surely in the rush of great waters,
      they shall not reach him.
7   You are a hiding place for me;
      you preserve me from trouble;
      you surround me with shouts of
         deliverance.   Selah

8   I will instruct you and teach you in the
         way you should go;
      I will counsel you with my eye upon
         you.
9   Be not like a horse or a mule, without
         understanding,
      which must be curbed with bit and
         bridle,
      or it will not stay near you.

10   Many are the sorrows of the wicked,
      but steadfast love surrounds the one
         who trusts in the LORD.
11   Be glad in the LORD, and rejoice,
         O righteous,
      and shout for joy, all you upright in
         heart!

---

[1] Septuagint, Syriac *Hear* [2] Syriac *Bring* [3] Probably a musical or liturgical term [4] Hebrew *my vitality was changed*

AUGUST 25

1 Samuel 17

Now the Philistines gathered their armies for battle. And they were gathered at Socoh, which belongs to Judah, and encamped between Socoh and Azekah, in Ephes-dammim. ²And Saul and the men of Israel were gathered, and encamped in the Valley of Elah, and drew up in line of battle against the Philistines. ³And the Philistines stood on the mountain on the one side, and Israel stood on the mountain on the other side, with a valley between them. ⁴And there came out from the camp of the Philistines a champion named Goliath of Gath, whose height was six¹ cubits² and a span. ⁵He had a helmet of bronze on his head, and he was armed with a coat of mail, and the weight of the coat was five thousand shekels³ of bronze. ⁶And he had bronze armor on his legs, and a javelin of bronze slung between his shoulders. ⁷The shaft of his spear was like a weaver's beam, and his spear's head weighed six hundred shekels of iron. And his shield-bearer went before him. ⁸He stood and shouted to the ranks of Israel, "Why have you come out to draw up for battle? Am I not a Philistine, and are you not servants of Saul? Choose a man for yourselves, and let him come down to me. ⁹If he is able to fight with me and kill me, then we will be your servants. But if I prevail against him and kill him, then you shall be our servants and serve us." ¹⁰And the Philistine said, "I defy the ranks of Israel this day. Give me a man, that we may fight together." ¹¹When Saul and all Israel heard these words of the Philistine, they were dismayed and greatly afraid.

¹²Now David was the son of an Ephrathite of Bethlehem in Judah, named Jesse, who had eight sons. In the days of Saul the man was already old and advanced in years.⁴ ¹³The three oldest sons of Jesse had followed Saul to the battle. And the names of his three sons who went to the battle were Eliab the firstborn, and next to him Abinadab, and the third Shammah. ¹⁴David was the youngest. The three eldest followed Saul, ¹⁵but David went back and forth from Saul to feed his father's sheep at Bethlehem. ¹⁶For forty days the Philistine came forward and took his stand, morning and evening.

¹⁷And Jesse said to David his son, "Take for your brothers an ephah⁵ of this parched grain, and these ten loaves, and carry them quickly to the camp to your brothers. ¹⁸Also take these ten cheeses to the commander of their thousand. See if your brothers are well, and bring some token from them."

¹⁹Now Saul and they and all the men of Israel were in the Valley of Elah, fighting with the Philistines. ²⁰And David rose early in the morning and left the sheep with a keeper and took the provisions and went, as Jesse had commanded him. And he came to the encampment as the host was going out to the battle line, shouting the war cry. ²¹And Israel and the Philistines drew up for battle, army against army. ²²And David left the things in charge of the keeper of the baggage and ran to the ranks and went and greeted his brothers. ²³As he talked with them, behold, the champion, the Philistine of Gath, Goliath by name, came up out of the ranks of the Philistines and spoke the same words as before. And David heard him.

²⁴All the men of Israel, when they saw the man, fled from him and were much afraid. ²⁵And the men of Israel said, "Have you seen this man who has come up? Surely he has come up to defy Israel. And the king will enrich the man who kills him with great riches and will give him his daughter and make his father's house free in Israel." ²⁶And David said to the men who stood by him, "What shall be done for the man who kills this Philistine and takes away the reproach from Israel? For who is this uncircumcised Philistine, that he should defy the armies of the living God?" ²⁷And the people answered him in the same way, "So shall it be done to the man who kills him."

²⁸Now Eliab his eldest brother heard when he spoke to the men. And Eliab's anger was kindled against David, and he said, "Why have

---

¹ Hebrew; Septuagint, Dead Sea Scroll and Josephus *four* ² A *cubit* was about 18 inches or 45 centimeters ³ A *shekel* was about 2/5 ounce or 11 grams ⁴ Septuagint, Syriac; Hebrew *advanced among men* ⁵ An *ephah* was about 3/5 bushel or 22 liters

you come down? And with whom have you left those few sheep in the wilderness? I know your presumption and the evil of your heart, for you have come down to see the battle." ²⁹And David said, "What have I done now? Was it not but a word?" ³⁰And he turned away from him toward another, and spoke in the same way, and the people answered him again as before.

³¹When the words that David spoke were heard, they repeated them before Saul, and he sent for him. ³²And David said to Saul, "Let no man's heart fail because of him. Your servant will go and fight with this Philistine." ³³And Saul said to David, "You are not able to go against this Philistine to fight with him, for you are but a youth, and he has been a man of war from his youth." ³⁴But David said to Saul, "Your servant used to keep sheep for his father. And when there came a lion, or a bear, and took a lamb from the flock, ³⁵I went after him and struck him and delivered it out of his mouth. And if he arose against me, I caught him by his beard and struck him and killed him. ³⁶Your servant has struck down both lions and bears, and this uncircumcised Philistine shall be like one of them, for he has defied the armies of the living God." ³⁷And David said, "The LORD who delivered me from the paw of the lion and from the paw of the bear will deliver me from the hand of this Philistine." And Saul said to David, "Go, and the LORD be with you!"

³⁸Then Saul clothed David with his armor. He put a helmet of bronze on his head and clothed him with a coat of mail, ³⁹and David strapped his sword over his armor. And he tried in vain to go, for he had not tested them. Then David said to Saul, "I cannot go with these, for I have not tested them." So David put them off. ⁴⁰Then he took his staff in his hand and chose five smooth stones from the brook and put them in his shepherd's pouch. His sling was in his hand, and he approached the Philistine.

⁴¹And the Philistine moved forward and came near to David, with his shield-bearer in front of him. ⁴²And when the Philistine looked and saw David, he disdained him, for he was but a youth, ruddy and handsome in appearance. ⁴³And the Philistine said to David, "Am I a dog, that you come to me with sticks?" And the Philistine cursed David by his gods. ⁴⁴The Philistine said to David, "Come to me, and I will give your flesh to the birds of the air and to the

beasts of the field." ⁴⁵Then David said to the Philistine, "You come to me with a sword and with a spear and with a javelin, but I come to you in the name of the LORD of hosts, the God of the armies of Israel, whom you have defied. ⁴⁶This day the LORD will deliver you into my hand, and I will strike you down and cut off your head. And I will give the dead bodies of the host of the Philistines this day to the birds of the air and to the wild beasts of the earth, that all the earth may know that there is a God in Israel, ⁴⁷and that all this assembly may know that the LORD saves not with sword and spear. For the battle is the LORD's, and he will give you into our hand."

⁴⁸When the Philistine arose and came and drew near to meet David, David ran quickly toward the battle line to meet the Philistine. ⁴⁹And David put his hand in his bag and took out a stone and slung it and struck the Philistine on his forehead. The stone sank into his forehead, and he fell on his face to the ground.

⁵⁰So David prevailed over the Philistine with a sling and with a stone, and struck the Philistine and killed him. There was no sword in the hand of David. ⁵¹Then David ran and stood over the Philistine and took his sword and drew it out of its sheath and killed him and cut off his head with it. When the Philistines saw that their champion was dead, they fled. ⁵²And the men of Israel and Judah rose with a shout and pursued the Philistines as far as Gath¹ and the gates of Ekron, so that the wounded Philistines fell on the way from Shaaraim as far as Gath and Ekron. ⁵³And the people of Israel came back from chasing the Philistines, and they plundered their camp. ⁵⁴And David took the head of the Philistine and brought it to Jerusalem, but he put his armor in his tent.

⁵⁵As soon as Saul saw David go out against the Philistine, he said to Abner, the commander of the army, "Abner, whose son is this youth?" And Abner said, "As your soul lives, O king, I do not know." ⁵⁶And the king said, "Inquire whose son the boy is." ⁵⁷And as soon as David returned from the striking down of the Philistine, Abner took him, and brought him before Saul with the head of the Philistine in his hand. ⁵⁸And Saul said to him, "Whose son are you, young man?" And David answered, "I am the son of your servant Jesse the Bethlehemite."

¹ Septuagint; Hebrew *Gai*

——————— *Romans 15* ———————

We who are strong have an obligation to bear with the failings of the weak, and not to please ourselves. [2] Let each of us please his neighbor for his good, to build him up. [3] For Christ did not please himself, but as it is written, "The reproaches of those who reproached you fell on me." [4] For whatever was written in former days was written for our instruction, that through endurance and through the encouragement of the Scriptures we might have hope. [5] May the God of endurance and encouragement grant you to live in such harmony with one another, in accord with Christ Jesus, [6] that together you may with one voice glorify the God and Father of our Lord Jesus Christ. [7] Therefore welcome one another as Christ has welcomed you, for the glory of God.

[8] For I tell you that Christ became a servant to the circumcised to show God's truthfulness, in order to confirm the promises given to the patriarchs, [9] and in order that the Gentiles might glorify God for his mercy. As it is written,

> "Therefore I will praise you among the
>   Gentiles,
>   and sing to your name."

[10] And again it is said,

> "Rejoice, O Gentiles, with his people."

[11] And again,

> "Praise the Lord, all you Gentiles,
>   and let all the peoples extol him."

[12] And again Isaiah says,

> "The root of Jesse will come,
>   even he who arises to rule the
>   Gentiles;
> in him will the Gentiles hope."

[13] May the God of hope fill you with all joy and peace in believing, so that by the power of the Holy Spirit you may abound in hope.

[14] I myself am satisfied about you, my brothers,[1] that you yourselves are full of goodness, filled with all knowledge and able to instruct one another. [15] But on some points I have written to you very boldly by way of reminder, because of the grace given me by God [16] to be a minister of Christ Jesus to the Gentiles in the priestly service of the gospel of God, so that the offering of the Gentiles may be acceptable, sanctified by the Holy Spirit. [17] In Christ Jesus, then, I have reason to be proud of my work for God. [18] For I will not venture to speak of anything except what Christ has accomplished through me to bring the Gentiles to obedience—by word and deed, [19] by the power of signs and wonders, by the power of the Spirit of God—so that from Jerusalem and all the way around to Illyricum I have fulfilled the ministry of the gospel of Christ; [20] and thus I make it my ambition to preach the gospel, not where Christ has already been named, lest I build on someone else's foundation, [21] but as it is written,

> "Those who have never been told of him
>   will see,
>   and those who have never heard will
>   understand."

[22] This is the reason why I have so often been hindered from coming to you. [23] But now, since I no longer have any room for work in these regions, and since I have longed for many years to come to you, [24] I hope to see you in passing as I go to Spain, and to be helped on my journey there by you, once I have enjoyed your company for a while. [25] At present, however, I am going to Jerusalem bringing aid to the saints. [26] For Macedonia and Achaia have been pleased to make some contribution for the poor among the saints at Jerusalem. [27] For they were pleased to do it, and indeed they owe it to them. For if the Gentiles have come to share in their spiritual blessings, they ought also to be of service to them in material blessings. [28] When therefore I have completed this and have delivered to them what has been collected,[2] I will leave for Spain by way of you. [29] I know that when I come to you I will come in the fullness of the blessing[3] of Christ.

[30] I appeal to you, brothers, by our Lord Jesus Christ and by the love of the Spirit, to strive together with me in your prayers to God on my behalf, [31] that I may be delivered from the unbelievers in Judea, and that my service for Jerusalem may be acceptable to the saints, [32] so that by God's will I may come to you with joy and be refreshed in your company. [33] May the God of peace be with you all. Amen.

[1] Or *brothers and sisters*; also verse 30 [2] Greek *sealed to them this fruit* [3] Some manuscripts insert *of the gospel*

Lamentations 2

How the Lord in his anger
has set the daughter of Zion under a
cloud!
He has cast down from heaven to earth
the splendor of Israel;
he has not remembered his footstool
in the day of his anger.

2 The Lord has swallowed up without
mercy
all the habitations of Jacob;
in his wrath he has broken down
the strongholds of the daughter of
Judah;
he has brought down to the ground in
dishonor
the kingdom and its rulers.

3 He has cut down in fierce anger
all the might of Israel;
he has withdrawn from them his right
hand
in the face of the enemy;
he has burned like a flaming fire in
Jacob,
consuming all around.

4 He has bent his bow like an enemy,
with his right hand set like a foe;
and he has killed all who were delightful
in our eyes
in the tent of the daughter of Zion;
he has poured out his fury like fire.

5 The Lord has become like an enemy;
he has swallowed up Israel;
he has swallowed up all its palaces;
he has laid in ruins its strongholds,
and he has multiplied in the daughter of
Judah
mourning and lamentation.

6 He has laid waste his booth like a
garden,
laid in ruins his meeting place;
the LORD has made Zion forget
festival and Sabbath,
and in his fierce indignation has
spurned king and priest.

7 The Lord has scorned his altar,
disowned his sanctuary;

he has delivered into the hand of the
enemy
the walls of her palaces;
they raised a clamor in the house of the
LORD
as on the day of festival.

8 The LORD determined to lay in ruins
the wall of the daughter of Zion;
he stretched out the measuring line;
he did not restrain his hand from
destroying;
he caused rampart and wall to lament;
they languished together.

9 Her gates have sunk into the ground;
he has ruined and broken her bars;
her king and princes are among the
nations;
the law is no more,
and her prophets find
no vision from the LORD.

10 The elders of the daughter of Zion
sit on the ground in silence;
they have thrown dust on their heads
and put on sackcloth;
the young women of Jerusalem
have bowed their heads to the
ground.

11 My eyes are spent with weeping;
my stomach churns;
my bile is poured out to the ground
because of the destruction of the
daughter of my people,
because infants and babies faint
in the streets of the city.

12 They cry to their mothers,
"Where is bread and wine?"
as they faint like a wounded man
in the streets of the city,
as their life is poured out
on their mothers' bosom.

13 What can I say for you, to what compare
you,
O daughter of Jerusalem?
What can I liken to you, that I may
comfort you,
O virgin daughter of Zion?
For your ruin is vast as the sea;
who can heal you?

14 Your prophets have seen for you
　　false and deceptive visions;
　they have not exposed your iniquity
　　to restore your fortunes,
　but have seen for you oracles
　　that are false and misleading.

15 All who pass along the way
　　clap their hands at you;
　they hiss and wag their heads
　　at the daughter of Jerusalem:
　"Is this the city that was called
　　the perfection of beauty,
　　the joy of all the earth?"

16 All your enemies
　　rail against you;
　they hiss, they gnash their teeth,
　　they cry: "We have swallowed her!
　Ah, this is the day we longed for;
　　now we have it; we see it!"

17 The LORD has done what he purposed;
　　he has carried out his word,
　which he commanded long ago;
　　he has thrown down without pity;
　he has made the enemy rejoice over you
　　and exalted the might of your foes.

18 Their heart cried to the Lord.
　　O wall of the daughter of Zion,
　let tears stream down like a torrent
　　day and night!
　Give yourself no rest,
　　your eyes no respite!

19 "Arise, cry out in the night,
　　at the beginning of the night watches!
　Pour out your heart like water
　　before the presence of the Lord!
　Lift your hands to him
　　for the lives of your children,
　who faint for hunger
　　at the head of every street."

20 Look, O LORD, and see!
　　With whom have you dealt thus?
　Should women eat the fruit of their
　　womb,
　　the children of their tender care?
　Should priest and prophet be killed
　　in the sanctuary of the Lord?

21 In the dust of the streets
　　lie the young and the old;

my young women and my young men
　　have fallen by the sword;
　you have killed them in the day of your
　　anger,
　　slaughtering without pity.

22 You summoned as if to a festival day
　　my terrors on every side,
　and on the day of the anger of the LORD
　　no one escaped or survived;
　those whom I held and raised
　　my enemy destroyed.

Psalm 33

Shout for joy in the LORD, O you righteous!
　Praise befits the upright.
2 　Give thanks to the LORD with the lyre;
　　make melody to him with the harp of
　　ten strings!
3 　Sing to him a new song;
　　play skillfully on the strings, with loud
　　shouts.

4 　For the word of the LORD is upright,
　　and all his work is done in faithfulness.
5 　He loves righteousness and justice;
　　the earth is full of the steadfast love of
　　the LORD.

6 　By the word of the LORD the heavens
　　were made,
　　and by the breath of his mouth all
　　their host.
7 　He gathers the waters of the sea as a
　　heap;
　　he puts the deeps in storehouses.

8 　Let all the earth fear the LORD;
　　let all the inhabitants of the world
　　stand in awe of him!
9 　For he spoke, and it came to be;
　　he commanded, and it stood firm.

10 　The LORD brings the counsel of the
　　nations to nothing;
　　he frustrates the plans of the peoples.
11 　The counsel of the LORD stands forever,
　　the plans of his heart to all
　　generations.
12 　Blessed is the nation whose God is the
　　LORD,
　　the people whom he has chosen as his
　　heritage!

13 The Lord looks down from heaven;
   he sees all the children of man;
14 from where he sits enthroned he looks
   out
   on all the inhabitants of the earth,
15 he who fashions the hearts of them all
   and observes all their deeds.
16 The king is not saved by his great army;
   a warrior is not delivered by his great
   strength.
17 The war horse is a false hope for
   salvation,
   and by its great might it cannot
   rescue.

18 Behold, the eye of the Lord is on those
   who fear him,
   on those who hope in his steadfast
   love,
19 that he may deliver their soul from death
   and keep them alive in famine.

20 Our soul waits for the Lord;
   he is our help and our shield.
21 For our heart is glad in him,
   because we trust in his holy name.
22 Let your steadfast love, O Lord, be upon
   us,
   even as we hope in you.

AUGUST 26

1 Samuel 18

As soon as he had finished speaking to Saul, the soul of Jonathan was knit to the soul of David, and Jonathan loved him as his own soul. ²And Saul took him that day and would not let him return to his father's house. ³Then Jonathan made a covenant with David, because he loved him as his own soul. ⁴And Jonathan stripped himself of the robe that was on him and gave it to David, and his armor, and even his sword and his bow and his belt. ⁵And David went out and was successful wherever Saul sent him, so that Saul set him over the men of war. And this was good in the sight of all the people and also in the sight of Saul's servants.

⁶As they were coming home, when David returned from striking down the Philistine, the women came out of all the cities of Israel, singing and dancing, to meet King Saul, with tambourines, with songs of joy, and with musical instruments.[1] ⁷And the women sang to one another as they celebrated,

"Saul has struck down his thousands,
   and David his ten thousands."

⁸And Saul was very angry, and this saying displeased him. He said, "They have ascribed to David ten thousands, and to me they have ascribed thousands, and what more can he have but the kingdom?" ⁹And Saul eyed David from that day on.

¹⁰The next day a harmful spirit from God rushed upon Saul, and he raved within his house while David was playing the lyre, as he did day by day. Saul had his spear in his hand. ¹¹And Saul hurled the spear, for he thought, "I will pin David to the wall." But David evaded him twice.

¹²Saul was afraid of David because the Lord was with him but had departed from Saul. ¹³So Saul removed him from his presence and made him a commander of a thousand. And he went out and came in before the people. ¹⁴And David had success in all his undertakings, for the Lord was with him. ¹⁵And when Saul saw that he had great success, he stood in fearful awe of him. ¹⁶But all Israel and Judah loved David, for he went out and came in before them.

¹⁷Then Saul said to David, "Here is my elder daughter Merab. I will give her to you for a wife. Only be valiant for me and fight the Lord's battles." For Saul thought, "Let not my hand be against him, but let the hand of the Philistines be against him." ¹⁸And David said to Saul, "Who am I, and who are my relatives, my

---

¹ Or triangles, or three-stringed instruments

father's clan in Israel, that I should be son-in-law to the king?" [19]But at the time when Merab, Saul's daughter, should have been given to David, she was given to Adriel the Meholathite for a wife.

[20]Now Saul's daughter Michal loved David. And they told Saul, and the thing pleased him. [21]Saul thought, "Let me give her to him, that she may be a snare for him and that the hand of the Philistines may be against him." Therefore Saul said to David a second time,[1] "You shall now be my son-in-law." [22]And Saul commanded his servants, "Speak to David in private and say, 'Behold, the king has delight in you, and all his servants love you. Now then become the king's son-in-law.'" [23]And Saul's servants spoke those words in the ears of David. And David said, "Does it seem to you a little thing to become the king's son-in-law, since I am a poor man and have no reputation?" [24]And the servants of Saul told him, "Thus and so did David speak." [25]Then Saul said, "Thus shall you say to David, 'The king desires no bride-price except a hundred foreskins of the Philistines, that he may be avenged of the king's enemies.'" Now Saul thought to make David fall by the hand of the Philistines. [26]And when his servants told David these words, it pleased David well to be the king's son-in-law. Before the time had expired, [27]David arose and went, along with his men, and killed two hundred of the Philistines. And David brought their foreskins, which were given in full number to the king, that he might become the king's son-in-law. And Saul gave him his daughter Michal for a wife. [28]But when Saul saw and knew that the LORD was with David, and that Michal, Saul's daughter, loved him, [29]Saul was even more afraid of David. So Saul was David's enemy continually.

[30]Then the commanders of the Philistines came out to battle, and as often as they came out David had more success than all the servants of Saul, so that his name was highly esteemed.

Romans 16

I commend to you our sister Phoebe, a servant[2] of the church at Cenchreae, [2]that you may welcome her in the Lord in a way worthy of the saints, and help her in whatever she may need from you, for she has been a patron of many and of myself as well.

[3]Greet Prisca and Aquila, my fellow workers in Christ Jesus, [4]who risked their necks for my life, to whom not only I give thanks but all the churches of the Gentiles give thanks as well. [5]Greet also the church in their house. Greet my beloved Epaenetus, who was the first convert[3] to Christ in Asia. [6]Greet Mary, who has worked hard for you. [7]Greet Andronicus and Junia,[4] my kinsmen and my fellow prisoners. They are well known to the apostles,[5] and they were in Christ before me. [8]Greet Ampliatus, my beloved in the Lord. [9]Greet Urbanus, our fellow worker in Christ, and my beloved Stachys. [10]Greet Apelles, who is approved in Christ. Greet those who belong to the family of Aristobulus. [11]Greet my kinsman Herodion. Greet those in the Lord who belong to the family of Narcissus. [12]Greet those workers in the Lord, Tryphaena and Tryphosa. Greet the beloved Persis, who has worked hard in the Lord. [13]Greet Rufus, chosen in the Lord; also his mother, who has been a mother to me as well. [14]Greet Asyncritus, Phlegon, Hermes, Patrobas, Hermas, and the brothers[6] who are with them. [15]Greet Philologus, Julia, Nereus and his sister, and Olympas, and all the saints who are with them. [16]Greet one another with a holy kiss. All the churches of Christ greet you.

[17]I appeal to you, brothers, to watch out for those who cause divisions and create obstacles contrary to the doctrine that you have been taught; avoid them. [18]For such persons do not serve our Lord Christ, but their own appetites,[7] and by smooth talk and flattery they deceive the hearts of the naive. [19]For your obedience is known to all, so that I rejoice over you, but I want you to be wise as to what is good and innocent as to what is evil. [20]The God of peace will soon crush Satan under your feet. The grace of our Lord Jesus Christ be with you.

[21]Timothy, my fellow worker, greets you; so do Lucius and Jason and Sosipater, my kinsmen.

[22]I Tertius, who wrote this letter, greet you in the Lord.

[23]Gaius, who is host to me and to the whole church, greets you. Erastus, the city treasurer, and our brother Quartus, greet you.[8]

[25]Now to him who is able to strengthen you according to my gospel and the preaching of Jesus Christ, according to the revelation of the mystery that was kept secret for long ages [26]but has now been disclosed and through the

[1] Hebrew by two [2] Or deaconess [3] Greek firstfruit [4] Or Junias [5] Or messengers [6] Or brothers and sisters; also verse 17 [7] Greek their own belly [8] Some manuscripts insert verse 24: The grace of our Lord Jesus Christ be with you all. Amen.

prophetic writings has been made known to all nations, according to the command of the eternal God, to bring about the obedience of faith— [27] to the only wise God be glory forevermore through Jesus Christ! Amen.

Lamentations 3

I am the man who has seen affliction
   under the rod of his wrath;
2   he has driven and brought me
     into darkness without any light;
3   surely against me he turns his hand
     again and again the whole day long.
4   He has made my flesh and my skin
     waste away;
     he has broken my bones;
5   he has besieged and enveloped me
     with bitterness and tribulation;
6   he has made me dwell in darkness
     like the dead of long ago.

7   He has walled me about so that I cannot
     escape;
     he has made my chains heavy;
8   though I call and cry for help,
     he shuts out my prayer;
9   he has blocked my ways with blocks of
     stones;
     he has made my paths crooked.

10 He is a bear lying in wait for me,
     a lion in hiding;
11 he turned aside my steps and tore me to
     pieces;
     he has made me desolate;
12 he bent his bow and set me
     as a target for his arrow.

13 He drove into my kidneys
     the arrows of his quiver;
14 I have become the laughingstock of all
     peoples,
     the object of their taunts all day long.
15 He has filled me with bitterness;
     he has sated me with wormwood.

16 He has made my teeth grind on gravel,
     and made me cower in ashes;
17 my soul is bereft of peace;
     I have forgotten what happiness[1] is;
18 so I say, "My endurance has perished;
     so has my hope from the LORD."

19 Remember my affliction and my
     wanderings,
     the wormwood and the gall!
20 My soul continually remembers it
     and is bowed down within me.
21 But this I call to mind,
     and therefore I have hope:

22 The steadfast love of the LORD never
     ceases;[2]
     his mercies never come to an end;
23 they are new every morning;
     great is your faithfulness.
24 "The LORD is my portion," says my soul,
     "therefore I will hope in him."

25 The LORD is good to those who wait for
     him,
     to the soul who seeks him.
26 It is good that one should wait quietly
     for the salvation of the LORD.
27 It is good for a man that he bear
     the yoke in his youth.

28 Let him sit alone in silence
     when it is laid on him;
29 let him put his mouth in the dust—
     there may yet be hope;
30 let him give his cheek to the one who
     strikes,
     and let him be filled with insults.

31 For the Lord will not
     cast off forever,
32 but, though he cause grief, he will have
     compassion
     according to the abundance of his
     steadfast love;
33 for he does not afflict from his heart
     or grieve the children of men.

34 To crush underfoot
     all the prisoners of the earth,
35 to deny a man justice
     in the presence of the Most High,
36 to subvert a man in his lawsuit,
     the Lord does not approve.

37 Who has spoken and it came to pass,
     unless the Lord has commanded it?
38 Is it not from the mouth of the Most
     High
     that good and bad come?

[1] Hebrew good [2] Syriac, Targum; Hebrew *Because of the steadfast love of the LORD, we are not cut off*

³⁹ Why should a living man complain,
   a man, about the punishment of his
     sins?
⁴⁰ Let us test and examine our ways,
   and return to the LORD!
⁴¹ Let us lift up our hearts and hands
   to God in heaven:
⁴² "We have transgressed and rebelled,
   and you have not forgiven.

⁴³ "You have wrapped yourself with anger
    and pursued us,
   killing without pity;
⁴⁴ you have wrapped yourself with a cloud
   so that no prayer can pass through.
⁴⁵ You have made us scum and garbage
   among the peoples.

⁴⁶ "All our enemies
   open their mouths against us;
⁴⁷ panic and pitfall have come upon us,
   devastation and destruction;
⁴⁸ my eyes flow with rivers of tears
   because of the destruction of the
     daughter of my people.

⁴⁹ "My eyes will flow without ceasing,
   without respite,
⁵⁰ until the LORD from heaven
   looks down and sees;
⁵¹ my eyes cause me grief
   at the fate of all the daughters of my
     city.

⁵² "I have been hunted like a bird
   by those who were my enemies
    without cause;
⁵³ they flung me alive into the pit
   and cast stones on me;
⁵⁴ water closed over my head;
   I said, 'I am lost.'

⁵⁵ "I called on your name, O LORD,
   from the depths of the pit;
⁵⁶ you heard my plea, 'Do not close
   your ear to my cry for help!'
⁵⁷ You came near when I called on you;
   you said, 'Do not fear!'

⁵⁸ "You have taken up my cause, O Lord;
   you have redeemed my life.
⁵⁹ You have seen the wrong done to me,
   O LORD;
   judge my cause.

⁶⁰ You have seen all their vengeance,
   all their plots against me.

⁶¹ "You have heard their taunts, O LORD,
   all their plots against me.
⁶² The lips and thoughts of my assailants
   are against me all the day long.
⁶³ Behold their sitting and their rising;
   I am the object of their taunts.

⁶⁴ "You will repay them,[1] O LORD,
   according to the work of their hands.
⁶⁵ You will give them[2] dullness of heart;
   your curse will be[3] on them.
⁶⁶ You will pursue them[4] in anger and
   destroy them
   from under your heavens, O LORD."[5]

Psalm 34[6]

OF DAVID, WHEN HE CHANGED HIS BEHAVIOR
BEFORE ABIMELECH, SO THAT HE DROVE HIM OUT,
AND HE WENT AWAY.

I will bless the LORD at all times;
  his praise shall continually be in my mouth.
² My soul makes its boast in the LORD;
   let the humble hear and be glad.
³ Oh, magnify the LORD with me,
   and let us exalt his name together!

⁴ I sought the LORD, and he answered me
   and delivered me from all my fears.
⁵ Those who look to him are radiant,
   and their faces shall never be
     ashamed.
⁶ This poor man cried, and the LORD
   heard him
   and saved him out of all his troubles.
⁷ The angel of the LORD encamps
   around those who fear him, and
     delivers them.

⁸ Oh, taste and see that the LORD is good!
   Blessed is the man who takes refuge
    in him!
⁹ Oh, fear the LORD, you his saints,
   for those who fear him have no lack!
¹⁰ The young lions suffer want and hunger;
   but those who seek the LORD lack no
    good thing.

¹¹ Come, O children, listen to me;
   I will teach you the fear of the LORD.

[1] Or *Repay them* [2] Or *Give them* [3] Or *place your curse* [4] Or *Pursue them* [5] Syriac (compare Septuagint, Vulgate); Hebrew *the heavens of the LORD* [6] This psalm is an acrostic poem, each verse beginning with the successive letters of the Hebrew alphabet

12 What man is there who desires life
    and loves many days, that he may see
        good?
13 Keep your tongue from evil
    and your lips from speaking deceit.
14 Turn away from evil and do good;
    seek peace and pursue it.
15 The eyes of the LORD are toward the
        righteous
    and his ears toward their cry.
16 The face of the LORD is against those
        who do evil,
    to cut off the memory of them from
        the earth.
17 When the righteous cry for help, the
    LORD hears

    and delivers them out of all their
        troubles.
18 The LORD is near to the brokenhearted
    and saves the crushed in spirit.
19 Many are the afflictions of the righteous,
    but the LORD delivers him out of them
        all.
20 He keeps all his bones;
    not one of them is broken.
21 Affliction will slay the wicked,
    and those who hate the righteous will
        be condemned.
22 The LORD redeems the life of his
        servants;
    none of those who take refuge in him
        will be condemned.

AUGUST 27

1 Samuel 19

And Saul spoke to Jonathan his son and to all his servants, that they should kill David. But Jonathan, Saul's son, delighted much in David. ²And Jonathan told David, "Saul my father seeks to kill you. Therefore be on your guard in the morning. Stay in a secret place and hide yourself. ³And I will go out and stand beside my father in the field where you are, and I will speak to my father about you. And if I learn anything I will tell you." ⁴And Jonathan spoke well of David to Saul his father and said to him, "Let not the king sin against his servant David, because he has not sinned against you, and because his deeds have brought good to you. ⁵For he took his life in his hand and he struck down the Philistine, and the LORD worked a great salvation for all Israel. You saw it, and rejoiced. Why then will you sin against innocent blood by killing David without cause?" ⁶And Saul listened to the voice of Jonathan. Saul swore, "As the LORD lives, he shall not be put to death." ⁷And Jonathan called David, and Jonathan reported to him all these things. And Jonathan brought David to Saul, and he was in his presence as before.

⁸And there was war again. And David went out and fought with the Philistines and struck them with a great blow, so that they fled before him. ⁹Then a harmful spirit from the LORD came upon Saul, as he sat in his house with his spear in his hand. And David was playing the lyre. ¹⁰And Saul sought to pin David to the wall with the spear, but he eluded Saul, so that he struck the spear into the wall. And David fled and escaped that night.

¹¹Saul sent messengers to David's house to watch him, that he might kill him in the morning. But Michal, David's wife, told him, "If you do not escape with your life tonight, tomorrow you will be killed." ¹²So Michal let David down through the window, and he fled away and escaped. ¹³Michal took an image[1] and laid it on the bed and put a pillow of goats' hair at its head and covered it with the clothes. ¹⁴And when Saul sent messengers to take David, she said, "He is sick." ¹⁵Then Saul sent the messengers to see David, saying, "Bring him up to me in the bed, that I may kill him." ¹⁶And when the messengers came in, behold, the image was in the bed, with the pillow of goats' hair

---

[1] Or *a household god*

at its head. [17]Saul said to Michal, "Why have you deceived me thus and let my enemy go, so that he has escaped?" And Michal answered Saul, "He said to me, 'Let me go. Why should I kill you?'"

[18]Now David fled and escaped, and he came to Samuel at Ramah and told him all that Saul had done to him. And he and Samuel went and lived at Naioth. [19]And it was told Saul, "Behold, David is at Naioth in Ramah." [20]Then Saul sent messengers to take David, and when they saw the company of the prophets prophesying, and Samuel standing as head over them, the Spirit of God came upon the messengers of Saul, and they also prophesied. [21]When it was told Saul, he sent other messengers, and they also prophesied. And Saul sent messengers again the third time, and they also prophesied. [22]Then he himself went to Ramah and came to the great well that is in Secu. And he asked, "Where are Samuel and David?" And one said, "Behold, they are at Naioth in Ramah." [23]And he went there to Naioth in Ramah. And the Spirit of God came upon him also, and as he went he prophesied until he came to Naioth in Ramah. [24]And he too stripped off his clothes, and he too prophesied before Samuel and lay naked all that day and all that night. Thus it is said, "Is Saul also among the prophets?"

1 Corinthians 1

Paul, called by the will of God to be an apostle of Christ Jesus, and our brother Sosthenes,

[2]To the church of God that is in Corinth, to those sanctified in Christ Jesus, called to be saints together with all those who in every place call upon the name of our Lord Jesus Christ, both their Lord and ours:

[3]Grace to you and peace from God our Father and the Lord Jesus Christ.

[4]I give thanks to my God always for you because of the grace of God that was given you in Christ Jesus, [5]that in every way you were enriched in him in all speech and all knowledge— [6]even as the testimony about Christ was confirmed among you— [7]so that you are not lacking in any gift, as you wait for the revealing of our Lord Jesus Christ, [8]who will sustain you to the end, guiltless in the day of our Lord Jesus Christ. [9]God is faithful, by whom you

were called into the fellowship of his Son, Jesus Christ our Lord.

[10]I appeal to you, brothers,[1] by the name of our Lord Jesus Christ, that all of you agree, and that there be no divisions among you, but that you be united in the same mind and the same judgment. [11]For it has been reported to me by Chloe's people that there is quarreling among you, my brothers. [12]What I mean is that each one of you says, "I follow Paul," or "I follow Apollos," or "I follow Cephas," or "I follow Christ." [13]Is Christ divided? Was Paul crucified for you? Or were you baptized in the name of Paul? [14]I thank God that I baptized none of you except Crispus and Gaius, [15]so that no one may say that you were baptized in my name. [16](I did baptize also the household of Stephanas. Beyond that, I do not know whether I baptized anyone else.) [17]For Christ did not send me to baptize but to preach the gospel, and not with words of eloquent wisdom, lest the cross of Christ be emptied of its power.

[18]For the word of the cross is folly to those who are perishing, but to us who are being saved it is the power of God. [19]For it is written,

"I will destroy the wisdom of the wise,
　and the discernment of the discerning
　　I will thwart."

[20]Where is the one who is wise? Where is the scribe? Where is the debater of this age? Has not God made foolish the wisdom of the world? [21]For since, in the wisdom of God, the world did not know God through wisdom, it pleased God through the folly of what we preach[2] to save those who believe. [22]For Jews demand signs and Greeks seek wisdom, [23]but we preach Christ crucified, a stumbling block to Jews and folly to Gentiles, [24]but to those who are called, both Jews and Greeks, Christ the power of God and the wisdom of God. [25]For the foolishness of God is wiser than men, and the weakness of God is stronger than men.

[26]For consider your calling, brothers: not many of you were wise according to worldly standards,[3] not many were powerful, not many were of noble birth. [27]But God chose what is foolish in the world to shame the wise; God chose what is weak in the world to shame the strong; [28]God chose what is low and despised in the world, even things that are not,

[1] Or brothers and sisters. The plural Greek word adelphoi (translated "brothers") refers to siblings in a family. In New Testament usage, depending on the context, adelphoi may refer either to men or to both men and women who are siblings (brothers and sisters) in God's family, the church; also verses 11, 26 [2] Or the folly of preaching [3] Greek according to the flesh

to bring to nothing things that are, [29] so that no human being[1] might boast in the presence of God. [30] And because of him[2] you are in Christ Jesus, who became to us wisdom from God, righteousness and sanctification and redemption, [31] so that, as it is written, "Let the one who boasts, boast in the Lord."

Lamentations 4

How the gold has grown dim,
   how the pure gold is changed!
The holy stones lie scattered
   at the head of every street.

2   The precious sons of Zion,
   worth their weight in fine gold,
how they are regarded as earthen pots,
   the work of a potter's hands!

3   Even jackals offer the breast;
   they nurse their young,
but the daughter of my people has
    become cruel,
   like the ostriches in the wilderness.

4   The tongue of the nursing infant sticks
   to the roof of its mouth for thirst;
the children beg for food,
   but no one gives to them.

5   Those who once feasted on delicacies
   perish in the streets;
those who were brought up in purple
   embrace ash heaps.

6   For the chastisement[3] of the daughter of
    my people has been greater
   than the punishment[4] of Sodom,
which was overthrown in a moment,
   and no hands were wrung for her.[5]

7   Her princes were purer than snow,
   whiter than milk;
their bodies were more ruddy than coral,
   the beauty of their form[6] was like
    sapphire.[7]

8   Now their face is blacker than soot;
   they are not recognized in the streets;
their skin has shriveled on their bones;
   it has become as dry as wood.

9   Happier were the victims of the sword
   than the victims of hunger,
who wasted away, pierced
   by lack of the fruits of the field.

10   The hands of compassionate women
   have boiled their own children;
they became their food
   during the destruction of the daughter
    of my people.

11   The LORD gave full vent to his wrath;
   he poured out his hot anger,
and he kindled a fire in Zion
   that consumed its foundations.

12   The kings of the earth did not believe,
   nor any of the inhabitants of the
    world,
that foe or enemy could enter
   the gates of Jerusalem.

13   This was for the sins of her prophets
   and the iniquities of her priests,
who shed in the midst of her
   the blood of the righteous.

14   They wandered, blind, through the
    streets;
   they were so defiled with blood
that no one was able to touch
   their garments.

15   "Away! Unclean!" people cried at them.
   "Away! Away! Do not touch!"
So they became fugitives and wanderers;
   people said among the nations,
   "They shall stay with us no longer."

16   The LORD himself[8] has scattered them;
   he will regard them no more;
no honor was shown to the priests,
   no favor to the elders.

17   Our eyes failed, ever watching
   vainly for help;
in our watching we watched
   for a nation which could not save.

18   They dogged our steps
   so that we could not walk in our
    streets;
our end drew near; our days were
    numbered,
   for our end had come.

19   Our pursuers were swifter
   than the eagles in the heavens;

---

[1] Greek *no flesh* [2] Greek *And from him* [3] Or *iniquity* [4] Or *sin* [5] The meaning of the Hebrew is uncertain [6] The meaning of the Hebrew is uncertain [7] Hebrew *lapis lazuli* [8] Hebrew *The face of the LORD*

they chased us on the mountains;
   they lay in wait for us in the
      wilderness.

20 The breath of our nostrils, the Lord's
      anointed,
   was captured in their pits,
 of whom we said, "Under his shadow
     we shall live among the nations."

21 Rejoice and be glad, O daughter of Edom,
   you who dwell in the land of Uz;
 but to you also the cup shall pass;
   you shall become drunk and strip
     yourself bare.

22 The punishment of your iniquity, O
     daughter of Zion, is accomplished;
   he will keep you in exile no longer;[1]
 but your iniquity, O daughter of Edom,
    he will punish;
 he will uncover your sins.

Psalm 35

Of David.

Contend, O Lord, with those who contend
  with me;
   fight against those who fight against
     me!
2   Take hold of shield and buckler
   and rise for my help!
3   Draw the spear and javelin[2]
   against my pursuers!
Say to my soul,
  "I am your salvation!"

4 Let them be put to shame and dishonor
   who seek after my life!
 Let them be turned back and
    disappointed
   who devise evil against me!
5 Let them be like chaff before the wind,
   with the angel of the Lord driving
     them away!
6 Let their way be dark and slippery,
   with the angel of the Lord pursuing
    them!
7 For without cause they hid their net for
    me;
 without cause they dug a pit for my
   life.[3]

8 Let destruction come upon him when
   he does not know it!
 And let the net that he hid ensnare
    him;
   let him fall into it—to his
     destruction!

9 Then my soul will rejoice in the Lord,
   exulting in his salvation.
10 All my bones shall say,
  "O Lord, who is like you,
 delivering the poor
   from him who is too strong for him,
   the poor and needy from him who
     robs him?"

11 Malicious[4] witnesses rise up;
   they ask me of things that I do not
     know.
12 They repay me evil for good;
   my soul is bereft.[5]
13 But I, when they were sick—
   I wore sackcloth;
   I afflicted myself with fasting;
 I prayed with head bowed[6] on my
    chest.
14 I went about as though I grieved for
     my friend or my brother;
 as one who laments his mother,
   I bowed down in mourning.

15 But at my stumbling they rejoiced and
     gathered;
   they gathered together against me;
 wretches whom I did not know
   tore at me without ceasing;
16 like profane mockers at a feast,[7]
   they gnash at me with their teeth.

17 How long, O Lord, will you look on?
   Rescue me from their destruction,
   my precious life from the lions!
18 I will thank you in the great
     congregation;
 in the mighty throng I will praise you.

19 Let not those rejoice over me
   who are wrongfully my foes,
 and let not those wink the eye
   who hate me without cause.
20 For they do not speak peace,
   but against those who are quiet in the
     land
   they devise words of deceit.

---

[1] Or he will not exile you again [2] Or and close the way [3] The word pit is transposed from the preceding line; Hebrew For without cause they hid the pit of their net for me; without cause they dug for my life [4] Or Violent [5] Hebrew it is bereavement to my soul [6] Or my prayer shall turn back [7] The meaning of the Hebrew phrase is uncertain

21 They open wide their mouths against
        me;
    they say, "Aha, Aha!
    Our eyes have seen it!"

22 You have seen, O LORD; be not silent!
    O Lord, be not far from me!

23 Awake and rouse yourself for my
        vindication,
    for my cause, my God and my Lord!

24 Vindicate me, O LORD, my God,
        according to your righteousness,
    and let them not rejoice over me!

25 Let them not say in their hearts,
    "Aha, our heart's desire!"
    Let them not say, "We have swallowed
        him up."

26 Let them be put to shame and
        disappointed altogether
    who rejoice at my calamity!
    Let them be clothed with shame and
        dishonor
    who magnify themselves against me!

27 Let those who delight in my
        righteousness
    shout for joy and be glad
    and say evermore,
    "Great is the LORD,
        who delights in the welfare of his
            servant!"

28 Then my tongue shall tell of your
        righteousness
    and of your praise all the day long.

AUGUST 28

1 Samuel 20

Then David fled from Naioth in Ramah and came and said before Jonathan, "What have I done? What is my guilt? And what is my sin before your father, that he seeks my life?" ²And he said to him, "Far from it! You shall not die. Behold, my father does nothing either great or small without disclosing it to me. And why should my father hide this from me? It is not so." ³But David vowed again, saying, "Your father knows well that I have found favor in your eyes, and he thinks, 'Do not let Jonathan know this, lest he be grieved.' But truly, as the LORD lives and as your soul lives, there is but a step between me and death." ⁴Then Jonathan said to David, "Whatever you say, I will do for you." ⁵David said to Jonathan, "Behold, tomorrow is the new moon, and I should not fail to sit at table with the king. But let me go, that I may hide myself in the field till the third day at evening. ⁶If your father misses me at all, then say, 'David earnestly asked leave of me to run to Bethlehem his city, for there is a yearly sacrifice there for all the clan.' ⁷If he says, 'Good!' it will be well with your servant, but if he is angry, then know that harm is determined by him. ⁸Therefore deal kindly with your servant, for you have brought your servant into a covenant of the LORD with you. But if there is guilt in me, kill me yourself, for why should you bring me to your father?" ⁹And Jonathan said, "Far be it from you! If I knew that it was determined by my father that harm should come to you, would I not tell you?" ¹⁰Then David said to Jonathan, "Who will tell me if your father answers you roughly?" ¹¹And Jonathan said to David, "Come, let us go out into the field." So they both went out into the field.

¹²And Jonathan said to David, "The LORD, the God of Israel, be witness![1] When I have sounded out my father, about this time tomorrow, or the third day, behold, if he is well disposed toward David, shall I not then send and disclose it to you? ¹³But should it please my father to do you harm, the LORD do so to Jonathan and more also if I do not disclose it to you and send you away, that you may go in safety. May the LORD be with you, as he has been with my father. ¹⁴If I am still alive, show me the steadfast love of the LORD, that I may not die; ¹⁵and do not cut off[2] your steadfast love from my house forever,

---

¹ Hebrew lacks *be witness* ² Or *but if I die, do not cut off*

when the Lord cuts off every one of the enemies of David from the face of the earth." ¹⁶And Jonathan made a covenant with the house of David, saying, "May¹ the Lord take vengeance on David's enemies." ¹⁷And Jonathan made David swear again by his love for him, for he loved him as he loved his own soul.

¹⁸Then Jonathan said to him, "Tomorrow is the new moon, and you will be missed, because your seat will be empty. ¹⁹On the third day go down quickly to the place where you hid yourself when the matter was in hand, and remain beside the stone heap.² ²⁰And I will shoot three arrows to the side of it, as though I shot at a mark. ²¹And behold, I will send the boy, saying, 'Go, find the arrows.' If I say to the boy, 'Look, the arrows are on this side of you, take them,' then you are to come, for, as the Lord lives, it is safe for you and there is no danger. ²²But if I say to the youth, 'Look, the arrows are beyond you,' then go, for the Lord has sent you away. ²³And as for the matter of which you and I have spoken, behold, the Lord is between you and me forever."

²⁴So David hid himself in the field. And when the new moon came, the king sat down to eat food. ²⁵The king sat on his seat, as at other times, on the seat by the wall. Jonathan sat opposite,³ and Abner sat by Saul's side, but David's place was empty. ²⁶Yet Saul did not say anything that day, for he thought, "Something has happened to him. He is not clean; surely he is not clean." ²⁷But on the second day, the day after the new moon, David's place was empty. And Saul said to Jonathan his son, "Why has not the son of Jesse come to the meal, either yesterday or today?" ²⁸Jonathan answered Saul, "David earnestly asked leave of me to go to Bethlehem. ²⁹He said, 'Let me go, for our clan holds a sacrifice in the city, and my brother has commanded me to be there. So now, if I have found favor in your eyes, let me get away and see my brothers.' For this reason he has not come to the king's table." ³⁰Then Saul's anger was kindled against Jonathan, and he said to him, "You son of a perverse, rebellious woman, do I not know that you have chosen the son of Jesse to your own shame, and to the shame of your mother's nakedness? ³¹For as long as the son of Jesse lives on the earth, neither you nor your kingdom shall be

established. Therefore send and bring him to me, for he shall surely die." ³²Then Jonathan answered Saul his father, "Why should he be put to death? What has he done?" ³³But Saul hurled his spear at him to strike him. So Jonathan knew that his father was determined to put David to death. ³⁴And Jonathan rose from the table in fierce anger and ate no food the second day of the month, for he was grieved for David, because his father had disgraced him.

³⁵In the morning Jonathan went out into the field to the appointment with David, and with him a little boy. ³⁶And he said to his boy, "Run and find the arrows that I shoot." As the boy ran, he shot an arrow beyond him. ³⁷And when the boy came to the place of the arrow that Jonathan had shot, Jonathan called after the boy and said, "Is not the arrow beyond you?" ³⁸And Jonathan called after the boy, "Hurry! Be quick! Do not stay!" So Jonathan's boy gathered up the arrows and came to his master. ³⁹But the boy knew nothing. Only Jonathan and David knew the matter. ⁴⁰And Jonathan gave his weapons to his boy and said to him, "Go and carry them to the city." ⁴¹And as soon as the boy had gone, David rose from beside the stone heap⁴ and fell on his face to the ground and bowed three times. And they kissed one another and wept with one another, David weeping the most. ⁴²Then Jonathan said to David, "Go in peace, because we have sworn both of us in the name of the Lord, saying, 'The Lord shall be between me and you, and between my offspring and your offspring, forever.'" And he rose and departed, and Jonathan went into the city.⁵

1 Corinthians 2

And I, when I came to you, brothers,⁶ did not come proclaiming to you the testimony⁷ of God with lofty speech or wisdom. ²For I decided to know nothing among you except Jesus Christ and him crucified. ³And I was with you in weakness and in fear and much trembling, ⁴and my speech and my message were not in plausible words of wisdom, but in demonstration of the Spirit and of power, ⁵so that your faith might not rest in the wisdom of men⁸ but in the power of God.

⁶Yet among the mature we do impart wisdom, although it is not a wisdom of this age

or of the rulers of this age, who are doomed to pass away. [7]But we impart a secret and hidden wisdom of God, which God decreed before the ages for our glory. [8]None of the rulers of this age understood this, for if they had, they would not have crucified the Lord of glory. [9]But, as it is written,

> "What no eye has seen, nor ear heard,
>   nor the heart of man imagined,
> what God has prepared for those who
>   love him"—

[10]these things God has revealed to us through the Spirit. For the Spirit searches everything, even the depths of God. [11]For who knows a person's thoughts except the spirit of that person, which is in him? So also no one comprehends the thoughts of God except the Spirit of God. [12]Now we have received not the spirit of the world, but the Spirit who is from God, that we might understand the things freely given us by God. [13]And we impart this in words not taught by human wisdom but taught by the Spirit, interpreting spiritual truths to those who are spiritual.[1]

[14]The natural person does not accept the things of the Spirit of God, for they are folly to him, and he is not able to understand them because they are spiritually discerned. [15]The spiritual person judges all things, but is himself to be judged by no one. [16]"For who has understood the mind of the Lord so as to instruct him?" But we have the mind of Christ.

------- *Lamentations 5* -------

Remember, O LORD, what has befallen us;
  look, and see our disgrace!
[2] Our inheritance has been turned over to
      strangers,
    our homes to foreigners.
[3] We have become orphans, fatherless;
    our mothers are like widows.
[4] We must pay for the water we drink;
    the wood we get must be bought.
[5] Our pursuers are at our necks;[2]
    we are weary; we are given no rest.
[6] We have given the hand to Egypt, and to
      Assyria,
    to get bread enough.
[7] Our fathers sinned, and are no more;
    and we bear their iniquities.

[8] Slaves rule over us;
    there is none to deliver us from their
      hand.
[9] We get our bread at the peril of our lives,
    because of the sword in the wilderness.
[10] Our skin is hot as an oven
    with the burning heat of famine.
[11] Women are raped in Zion,
    young women in the towns of Judah.
[12] Princes are hung up by their hands;
    no respect is shown to the elders.
[13] Young men are compelled to grind at
      the mill,
    and boys stagger under loads of wood.
[14] The old men have left the city gate,
    the young men their music.
[15] The joy of our hearts has ceased;
    our dancing has been turned to
      mourning.
[16] The crown has fallen from our head;
    woe to us, for we have sinned!
[17] For this our heart has become sick,
    for these things our eyes have grown
      dim,
[18] for Mount Zion which lies desolate;
    jackals prowl over it.
[19] But you, O LORD, reign forever;
    your throne endures to all generations.
[20] Why do you forget us forever,
    why do you forsake us for so many
      days?
[21] Restore us to yourself, O LORD, that we
      may be restored!
    Renew our days as of old—
[22] unless you have utterly rejected us,
    and you remain exceedingly angry
      with us.

------- *Psalm 36* -------

TO THE CHOIRMASTER. OF DAVID, THE SERVANT OF THE LORD.

Transgression speaks to the wicked
  deep in his heart;[3]
    there is no fear of God
    before his eyes.
[2] For he flatters himself in his own eyes
    that his iniquity cannot be found out
      and hated.
[3] The words of his mouth are trouble and
      deceit;
    he has ceased to act wisely and do good.

---

[1] Or *interpreting spiritual truths in spiritual language, or comparing spiritual things with spiritual* [2] Symmachus *With a yoke on our necks* [3] Some Hebrew manuscripts, Syriac, Jerome (compare Septuagint); most Hebrew manuscripts *in my heart*

4 He plots trouble while on his bed;
  he sets himself in a way that is not
    good;
  he does not reject evil.
5 Your steadfast love, O LORD, extends to
    the heavens,
  your faithfulness to the clouds.
6 Your righteousness is like the
    mountains of God;
  your judgments are like the great deep;
  man and beast you save, O LORD.
7 How precious is your steadfast love,
    O God!
  The children of mankind take refuge
    in the shadow of your wings.

8 They feast on the abundance of your
    house,
  and you give them drink from the
    river of your delights.
9 For with you is the fountain of life;
  in your light do we see light.
10 Oh, continue your steadfast love to those
    who know you,
  and your righteousness to the upright
    of heart!
11 Let not the foot of arrogance come upon
    me,
  nor the hand of the wicked drive me
    away.
12 There the evildoers lie fallen;
  they are thrust down, unable to rise.

AUGUST 29

1 Samuel 21¹–22

Then David came to Nob to Ahimelech the priest. And Ahimelech came to meet David trembling and said to him, "Why are you alone, and no one with you?" ²And David said to Ahimelech the priest, "The king has charged me with a matter and said to me, 'Let no one know anything of the matter about which I send you, and with which I have charged you.' I have made an appointment with the young men for such and such a place. ³Now then, what do you have on hand? Give me five loaves of bread, or whatever is here." ⁴And the priest answered David, "I have no common bread on hand, but there is holy bread—if the young men have kept themselves from women." ⁵And David answered the priest, "Truly women have been kept from us as always when I go on an expedition. The vessels of the young men are holy even when it is an ordinary journey. How much more today will their vessels be holy?" ⁶So the priest gave him the holy bread, for there was no bread there but the bread of the Presence, which is removed from before the LORD, to be replaced by hot bread on the day it is taken away.

⁷Now a certain man of the servants of Saul was there that day, detained before the LORD. His name was Doeg the Edomite, the chief of Saul's herdsmen. ⁸Then David said to Ahimelech, "Then have you not here a spear or a sword at hand? For I have brought neither my sword nor my weapons with me, because the king's business required haste." ⁹And the priest said, "The sword of Goliath the Philistine, whom you struck down in the Valley of Elah, behold, it is here wrapped in a cloth behind the ephod. If you will take that, take it, for there is none but that here." And David said, "There is none like that; give it to me."

¹⁰And David rose and fled that day from Saul and went to Achish the king of Gath. ¹¹And the servants of Achish said to him, "Is not this David the king of the land? Did they not sing to one another of him in dances,

'Saul has struck down his thousands,
  and David his ten thousands'?"

¹²And David took these words to heart and was much afraid of Achish the king of Gath. ¹³So

¹ Ch 21:2 in Hebrew

he changed his behavior before them and pretended to be insane in their hands and made marks on the doors of the gate and let his spittle run down his beard. [14]Then Achish said to his servants, "Behold, you see the man is mad. Why then have you brought him to me? [15]Do I lack madmen, that you have brought this fellow to behave as a madman in my presence? Shall this fellow come into my house?"

[22:1]David departed from there and escaped to the cave of Adullam. And when his brothers and all his father's house heard it, they went down there to him. [2]And everyone who was in distress, and everyone who was in debt, and everyone who was bitter in soul,[1] gathered to him. And he became commander over them. And there were with him about four hundred men.

[3]And David went from there to Mizpeh of Moab. And he said to the king of Moab, "Please let my father and my mother stay[2] with you, till I know what God will do for me." [4]And he left them with the king of Moab, and they stayed with him all the time that David was in the stronghold. [5]Then the prophet Gad said to David, "Do not remain in the stronghold; depart, and go into the land of Judah." So David departed and went into the forest of Hereth.

[6]Now Saul heard that David was discovered, and the men who were with him. Saul was sitting at Gibeah under the tamarisk tree on the height with his spear in his hand, and all his servants were standing about him. [7]And Saul said to his servants who stood about him, "Hear now, people of Benjamin; will the son of Jesse give every one of you fields and vineyards, will he make you all commanders of thousands and commanders of hundreds, [8]that all of you have conspired against me? No one discloses to me when my son makes a covenant with the son of Jesse. None of you is sorry for me or discloses to me that my son has stirred up my servant against me, to lie in wait, as at this day." [9]Then answered Doeg the Edomite, who stood by the servants of Saul, "I saw the son of Jesse coming to Nob, to Ahimelech the son of Ahitub, [10]and he inquired of the LORD for him and gave him provisions and gave him the sword of Goliath the Philistine." [11]Then the king sent to summon Ahimelech the priest, the son of Ahitub, and all his father's house, the priests who were at Nob, and all of them came to the king. [12]And Saul said, "Hear

now, son of Ahitub." And he answered, "Here I am, my lord." [13]And Saul said to him, "Why have you conspired against me, you and the son of Jesse, in that you have given him bread and a sword and have inquired of God for him, so that he has risen against me, to lie in wait, as at this day?" [14]Then Ahimelech answered the king, "And who among all your servants is so faithful as David, who is the king's son-in-law, and captain over[3] your bodyguard, and honored in your house? [15]Is today the first time that I have inquired of God for him? No! Let not the king impute anything to his servant or to all the house of my father, for your servant has known nothing of all this, much or little." [16]And the king said, "You shall surely die, Ahimelech, you and all your father's house." [17]And the king said to the guard who stood about him, "Turn and kill the priests of the LORD, because their hand also is with David, and they knew that he fled and did not disclose it to me." But the servants of the king would not put out their hand to strike the priests of the LORD. [18]Then the king said to Doeg, "You turn and strike the priests." And Doeg the Edomite turned and struck down the priests, and he killed on that day eighty-five persons who wore the linen ephod. [19]And Nob, the city of the priests, he put to the sword; both man and woman, child and infant, ox, donkey and sheep, he put to the sword.

[20]But one of the sons of Ahimelech the son of Ahitub, named Abiathar, escaped and fled after David. [21]And Abiathar told David that Saul had killed the priests of the LORD. [22]And David said to Abiathar, "I knew on that day, when Doeg the Edomite was there, that he would surely tell Saul. I have occasioned the death of all the persons of your father's house. [23]Stay with me; do not be afraid, for he who seeks my life seeks your life. With me you shall be in safekeeping."

1 Corinthians 3

But I, brothers,[4] could not address you as spiritual people, but as people of the flesh, as infants in Christ. [2]I fed you with milk, not solid food, for you were not ready for it. And even now you are not yet ready, [3]for you are still of the flesh. For while there is jealousy and strife among you, are you not of the flesh and behaving only in a human way? [4]For when one says, "I follow Paul," and another, "I follow Apollos," are you not being merely human?

⁵What then is Apollos? What is Paul? Servants through whom you believed, as the Lord assigned to each. ⁶I planted, Apollos watered, but God gave the growth. ⁷So neither he who plants nor he who waters is anything, but only God who gives the growth. ⁸He who plants and he who waters are one, and each will receive his wages according to his labor. ⁹For we are God's fellow workers. You are God's field, God's building.

¹⁰According to the grace of God given to me, like a skilled master builder I laid a foundation, and someone else is building upon it. Let each one take care how he builds upon it. ¹¹For no one can lay a foundation other than that which is laid, which is Jesus Christ. ¹²Now if anyone builds on the foundation with gold, silver, precious stones, wood, hay, straw— ¹³each one's work will become manifest, for the Day will disclose it, because it will be revealed by fire, and the fire will test what sort of work each one has done. ¹⁴If the work that anyone has built on the foundation survives, he will receive a reward. ¹⁵If anyone's work is burned up, he will suffer loss, though he himself will be saved, but only as through fire.

¹⁶Do you not know that you[1] are God's temple and that God's Spirit dwells in you? ¹⁷If anyone destroys God's temple, God will destroy him. For God's temple is holy, and you are that temple.

¹⁸Let no one deceive himself. If anyone among you thinks that he is wise in this age, let him become a fool that he may become wise. ¹⁹For the wisdom of this world is folly with God. For it is written, "He catches the wise in their craftiness," ²⁰and again, "The Lord knows the thoughts of the wise, that they are futile." ²¹So let no one boast in men. For all things are yours, ²²whether Paul or Apollos or Cephas or the world or life or death or the present or the future—all are yours, ²³and you are Christ's, and Christ is God's.

Ezekiel 1

In the thirtieth year, in the fourth month, on the fifth day of the month, as I was among the exiles by the Chebar canal, the heavens were opened, and I saw visions of God.[2] ²On the fifth day of the month (it was the fifth year of the exile of King Jehoiachin), ³the word of the LORD came to Ezekiel the priest, the son of Buzi, in the land of the Chaldeans by the Chebar canal, and the hand of the LORD was upon him there.

⁴As I looked, behold, a stormy wind came out of the north, and a great cloud, with brightness around it, and fire flashing forth continually, and in the midst of the fire, as it were gleaming metal.[3] ⁵And from the midst of it came the likeness of four living creatures. And this was their appearance: they had a human likeness, ⁶but each had four faces, and each of them had four wings. ⁷Their legs were straight, and the soles of their feet were like the sole of a calf's foot. And they sparkled like burnished bronze. ⁸Under their wings on their four sides they had human hands. And the four had their faces and their wings thus: ⁹their wings touched one another. Each one of them went straight forward, without turning as they went. ¹⁰As for the likeness of their faces, each had a human face. The four had the face of a lion on the right side, the four had the face of an ox on the left side, and the four had the face of an eagle. ¹¹Such were their faces. And their wings were spread out above. Each creature had two wings, each of which touched the wing of another, while two covered their bodies. ¹²And each went straight forward. Wherever the spirit[4] would go, they went, without turning as they went. ¹³As for the likeness of the living creatures, their appearance was like burning coals of fire, like the appearance of torches moving to and fro among the living creatures. And the fire was bright, and out of the fire went forth lightning. ¹⁴And the living creatures darted to and fro, like the appearance of a flash of lightning.

¹⁵Now as I looked at the living creatures, I saw a wheel on the earth beside the living creatures, one for each of the four of them.[5] ¹⁶As for the appearance of the wheels and their construction: their appearance was like the gleaming of beryl. And the four had the same likeness, their appearance and construction being as it were a wheel within a wheel. ¹⁷When they went, they went in any of their four directions[6] without turning as they went. ¹⁸And their rims were tall and awesome, and the rims of all four were full of eyes all around. ¹⁹And when the living creatures went, the

---

¹ The Greek for *you* is plural in verses 16 and 17   ² Or *from God*   ³ Or *amber*; also verse 27   ⁴ Or *Spirit*; also twice in verse 20 and once in verse 21   ⁵ Hebrew *of their faces*   ⁶ Hebrew *on their four sides*

wheels went beside them; and when the living creatures rose from the earth, the wheels rose. [20]Wherever the spirit wanted to go, they went, and the wheels rose along with them, for the spirit of the living creatures[1] was in the wheels. [21]When those went, these went; and when those stood, these stood; and when those rose from the earth, the wheels rose along with them, for the spirit of the living creatures was in the wheels. [22]Over the heads of the living creatures there was the likeness of an expanse, shining like awe-inspiring crystal, spread out above their heads. [23]And under the expanse their wings were stretched out straight, one toward another. And each creature had two wings covering its body. [24]And when they went, I heard the sound of their wings like the sound of many waters, like the sound of the Almighty, a sound of tumult like the sound of an army. When they stood still, they let down their wings. [25]And there came a voice from above the expanse over their heads. When they stood still, they let down their wings.

[26]And above the expanse over their heads there was the likeness of a throne, in appearance like sapphire;[2] and seated above the likeness of a throne was a likeness with a human appearance. [27]And upward from what had the appearance of his waist I saw as it were gleaming metal, like the appearance of fire enclosed all around. And downward from what had the appearance of his waist I saw as it were the appearance of fire, and there was brightness around him.[3] [28]Like the appearance of the bow that is in the cloud on the day of rain, so was the appearance of the brightness all around.

Such was the appearance of the likeness of the glory of the LORD. And when I saw it, I fell on my face, and I heard the voice of one speaking.

Psalm 37[4]

OF DAVID.

Fret not yourself because of evildoers;
be not envious of wrongdoers!
[2]   For they will soon fade like the grass
and wither like the green herb.

[3]   Trust in the LORD, and do good;
dwell in the land and befriend
faithfulness.[5]

[4]   Delight yourself in the LORD,
and he will give you the desires of
your heart.
[5]   Commit your way to the LORD;
trust in him, and he will act.
[6]   He will bring forth your righteousness
as the light,
and your justice as the noonday.

[7]   Be still before the LORD and wait
patiently for him;
fret not yourself over the one who
prospers in his way,
over the man who carries out evil
devices!
[8]   Refrain from anger, and forsake wrath!
Fret not yourself; it tends only to evil.
[9]   For the evildoers shall be cut off,
but those who wait for the LORD shall
inherit the land.

[10]   In just a little while, the wicked will be
no more;
though you look carefully at his place,
he will not be there.
[11]   But the meek shall inherit the land
and delight themselves in abundant
peace.

[12]   The wicked plots against the righteous
and gnashes his teeth at him,
[13]   but the Lord laughs at the wicked,
for he sees that his day is coming.
[14]   The wicked draw the sword and bend
their bows
to bring down the poor and needy,
to slay those whose way is upright;
[15]   their sword shall enter their own heart,
and their bows shall be broken.

[16]   Better is the little that the righteous has
than the abundance of many wicked.
[17]   For the arms of the wicked shall be
broken,
but the LORD upholds the righteous.
[18]   The LORD knows the days of the
blameless,
and their heritage will remain forever;
[19]   they are not put to shame in evil times;
in the days of famine they have
abundance.

[1] Or the spirit of life; also verse 21   [2] Or lapis lazuli   [3] Or it   [4] This psalm is an acrostic poem, each stanza beginning with the successive letters of the Hebrew alphabet   [5] Or and feed on faithfulness, or and find safe pasture

20 But the wicked will perish;
    the enemies of the LORD are like the
       glory of the pastures;
    they vanish—like smoke they vanish
       away.
21 The wicked borrows but does not pay
       back,
    but the righteous is generous and
       gives;
22 for those blessed by the LORD[1] shall
       inherit the land,
    but those cursed by him shall be cut
       off.
23 The steps of a man are established by
       the LORD,
    when he delights in his way;
24 though he fall, he shall not be cast
       headlong,
    for the LORD upholds his hand.
25 I have been young, and now am old,
    yet I have not seen the righteous
       forsaken
    or his children begging for bread.
26 He is ever lending generously,
    and his children become a blessing.
27 Turn away from evil and do good;
    so shall you dwell forever.
28 For the LORD loves justice;
    he will not forsake his saints.
    They are preserved forever,
    but the children of the wicked shall be
       cut off.
29 The righteous shall inherit the land
    and dwell upon it forever.
30 The mouth of the righteous utters
       wisdom,
    and his tongue speaks justice.

31 The law of his God is in his heart;
    his steps do not slip.
32 The wicked watches for the righteous
    and seeks to put him to death.
33 The LORD will not abandon him to his
       power
    or let him be condemned when he is
       brought to trial.
34 Wait for the LORD and keep his way,
    and he will exalt you to inherit the
       land;
    you will look on when the wicked are
       cut off.
35 I have seen a wicked, ruthless man,
    spreading himself like a green laurel
       tree.[2]
36 But he passed away,[3] and behold, he was
       no more;
    though I sought him, he could not be
       found.
37 Mark the blameless and behold the
       upright,
    for there is a future for the man of
       peace.
38 But transgressors shall be altogether
       destroyed;
    the future of the wicked shall be cut
       off.
39 The salvation of the righteous is from
       the LORD;
    he is their stronghold in the time of
       trouble.
40 The LORD helps them and delivers
       them;
    he delivers them from the wicked and
       saves them,
    because they take refuge in him.

[1] Hebrew by him   [2] The identity of this tree is uncertain   [3] Or But one passed by

AUGUST 30

1 Samuel 23

Now they told David, "Behold, the Philistines are fighting against Keilah and are robbing the threshing floors." ²Therefore David inquired of the Lord, "Shall I go and attack these Philistines?" And the Lord said to David, "Go and attack the Philistines and save Keilah." ³But David's men said to him, "Behold, we are afraid here in Judah; how much more then if we go to Keilah against the armies of the Philistines?" ⁴Then David inquired of the Lord again. And the Lord answered him, "Arise, go down to Keilah, for I will give the Philistines into your hand." ⁵And David and his men went to Keilah and fought with the Philistines and brought away their livestock and struck them with a great blow. So David saved the inhabitants of Keilah.

⁶When Abiathar the son of Ahimelech had fled to David to Keilah, he had come down with an ephod in his hand. ⁷Now it was told Saul that David had come to Keilah. And Saul said, "God has given him into my hand, for he has shut himself in by entering a town that has gates and bars." ⁸And Saul summoned all the people to war, to go down to Keilah, to besiege David and his men. ⁹David knew that Saul was plotting harm against him. And he said to Abiathar the priest, "Bring the ephod here." ¹⁰Then David said, "O Lord, the God of Israel, your servant has surely heard that Saul seeks to come to Keilah, to destroy the city on my account. ¹¹Will the men of Keilah surrender me into his hand? Will Saul come down, as your servant has heard? O Lord, the God of Israel, please tell your servant." And the Lord said, "He will come down." ¹²Then David said, "Will the men of Keilah surrender me and my men into the hand of Saul?" And the Lord said, "They will surrender you." ¹³Then David and his men, who were about six hundred, arose and departed from Keilah, and they went wherever they could go. When Saul was told that David had escaped from Keilah, he gave up the expedition. ¹⁴And David remained in the strongholds in the wilderness, in the hill country of the wilderness of Ziph. And Saul sought him every day, but God did not give him into his hand.

¹⁵David saw that Saul had come out to seek his life. David was in the wilderness of Ziph at Horesh. ¹⁶And Jonathan, Saul's son, rose and went to David at Horesh, and strengthened his hand in God. ¹⁷And he said to him, "Do not fear, for the hand of Saul my father shall not find you. You shall be king over Israel, and I shall be next to you. Saul my father also knows this." ¹⁸And the two of them made a covenant before the Lord. David remained at Horesh, and Jonathan went home.

¹⁹Then the Ziphites went up to Saul at Gibeah, saying, "Is not David hiding among us in the strongholds at Horesh, on the hill of Hachilah, which is south of Jeshimon? ²⁰Now come down, O king, according to all your heart's desire to come down, and our part shall be to surrender him into the king's hand." ²¹And Saul said, "May you be blessed by the Lord, for you have had compassion on me. ²²Go, make yet more sure. Know and see the place where his foot is, and who has seen him there, for it is told me that he is very cunning. ²³See therefore and take note of all the lurking places where he hides, and come back to me with sure information. Then I will go with you. And if he is in the land, I will search him out among all the thousands of Judah." ²⁴And they arose and went to Ziph ahead of Saul.

Now David and his men were in the wilderness of Maon, in the Arabah to the south of Jeshimon. ²⁵And Saul and his men went to seek him. And David was told, so he went down to the rock and lived in the wilderness of Maon. And when Saul heard that, he pursued after David in the wilderness of Maon. ²⁶Saul went on one side of the mountain, and David and his men on the other side of the mountain. And David was hurrying to get away from Saul.

As Saul and his men were closing in on David and his men to capture them, ²⁷ a messenger came to Saul, saying, "Hurry and come, for the Philistines have made a raid against the land." ²⁸ So Saul returned from pursuing after David and went against the Philistines. Therefore that place was called the Rock of Escape.¹ ²⁹² And David went up from there and lived in the strongholds of Engedi.

---

1 Corinthians 4

This is how one should regard us, as servants of Christ and stewards of the mysteries of God. ²Moreover, it is required of stewards that they be found faithful. ³But with me it is a very small thing that I should be judged by you or by any human court. In fact, I do not even judge myself. ⁴For I am not aware of anything against myself, but I am not thereby acquitted. It is the Lord who judges me. ⁵Therefore do not pronounce judgment before the time, before the Lord comes, who will bring to light the things now hidden in darkness and will disclose the purposes of the heart. Then each one will receive his commendation from God.

⁶I have applied all these things to myself and Apollos for your benefit, brothers,³ that you may learn by us not to go beyond what is written, that none of you may be puffed up in favor of one against another. ⁷For who sees anything different in you? What do you have that you did not receive? If then you received it, why do you boast as if you did not receive it?

⁸Already you have all you want! Already you have become rich! Without us you have become kings! And would that you did reign, so that we might share the rule with you! ⁹For I think that God has exhibited us apostles as last of all, like men sentenced to death, because we have become a spectacle to the world, to angels, and to men. ¹⁰We are fools for Christ's sake, but you are wise in Christ. We are weak, but you are strong. You are held in honor, but we in disrepute. ¹¹To the present hour we hunger and thirst, we are poorly dressed and buffeted and homeless, ¹²and we labor, working with our own hands. When reviled, we bless; when persecuted, we endure; ¹³when slandered, we entreat. We have become, and are still, like the scum of the world, the refuse of all things.

¹⁴I do not write these things to make you ashamed, but to admonish you as my beloved children. ¹⁵For though you have countless⁴ guides in Christ, you do not have many fathers. For I became your father in Christ Jesus through the gospel. ¹⁶I urge you, then, be imitators of me. ¹⁷That is why I sent⁵ you Timothy, my beloved and faithful child in the Lord, to remind you of my ways in Christ,⁶ as I teach them everywhere in every church. ¹⁸Some are arrogant, as though I were not coming to you. ¹⁹But I will come to you soon, if the Lord wills, and I will find out not the talk of these arrogant people but their power. ²⁰For the kingdom of God does not consist in talk but in power. ²¹What do you wish? Shall I come to you with a rod, or with love in a spirit of gentleness?

Ezekiel 2

And he said to me, "Son of man,⁷ stand on your feet, and I will speak with you." ²And as he spoke to me, the Spirit entered into me and set me on my feet, and I heard him speaking to me. ³And he said to me, "Son of man, I send you to the people of Israel, to nations of rebels, who have rebelled against me. They and their fathers have transgressed against me to this very day. ⁴The descendants also are impudent and stubborn: I send you to them, and you shall say to them, 'Thus says the Lord GOD.' ⁵And whether they hear or refuse to hear (for they are a rebellious house) they will know that a prophet has been among them. ⁶And you, son of man, be not afraid of them, nor be afraid of their words, though briers and thorns are with you and you sit on scorpions.⁸ Be not afraid of their words, nor be dismayed at their looks, for they are a rebellious house. ⁷And you shall speak my words to them, whether they hear or refuse to hear, for they are a rebellious house.

⁸"But you, son of man, hear what I say to you. Be not rebellious like that rebellious house; open your mouth and eat what I give you." ⁹And when I looked, behold, a hand was stretched out to me, and behold, a scroll of a book was in it. ¹⁰And he spread it before me. And it had writing on the front and on the back, and there were written on it words of lamentation and mourning and woe.

---

¹ Or Rock of Divisions ² Ch 24:1 in Hebrew ³ Or brothers and sisters ⁴ Greek you have ten thousand ⁵ Or am sending ⁶ Some manuscripts add Jesus ⁷ Or Son of Adam; so throughout Ezekiel ⁸ Or on scorpion plants

——— *Psalm 38* ———

A PSALM OF DAVID, FOR THE MEMORIAL OFFERING.

O LORD, rebuke me not in your anger,
    nor discipline me in your wrath!
2 For your arrows have sunk into me,
    and your hand has come down on me.

3 There is no soundness in my flesh
    because of your indignation;
  there is no health in my bones
    because of my sin.
4 For my iniquities have gone over my
    head;
  like a heavy burden, they are too
    heavy for me.

5 My wounds stink and fester
    because of my foolishness,
6 I am utterly bowed down and prostrate;
    all the day I go about mourning.
7 For my sides are filled with burning,
    and there is no soundness in my flesh.
8 I am feeble and crushed;
    I groan because of the tumult of my
    heart.

9 O Lord, all my longing is before you;
    my sighing is not hidden from you.
10 My heart throbs; my strength fails me,
    and the light of my eyes—it also has
    gone from me.
11 My friends and companions stand aloof
    from my plague,
  and my nearest kin stand far off.

12 Those who seek my life lay their snares;
    those who seek my hurt speak of ruin
    and meditate treachery all day long.

13 But I am like a deaf man; I do not hear,
    like a mute man who does not open
    his mouth.
14 I have become like a man who does not
    hear,
  and in whose mouth are no rebukes.

15 But for you, O LORD, do I wait;
    it is you, O Lord my God, who will
    answer.
16 For I said, "Only let them not rejoice
    over me,
  who boast against me when my foot
    slips!"

17 For I am ready to fall,
    and my pain is ever before me.
18 I confess my iniquity;
    I am sorry for my sin.
19 But my foes are vigorous, they are
    mighty,
  and many are those who hate me
    wrongfully.
20 Those who render me evil for good
    accuse me because I follow after
    good.

21 Do not forsake me, O LORD!
    O my God, be not far from me!
22 Make haste to help me,
    O Lord, my salvation!

AUGUST 31

——— *1 Samuel 24*[1] ———

When Saul returned from following the Philistines, he was told, "Behold, David is in the wilderness of Engedi." 2 Then Saul took three thousand chosen men out of all Israel and went to seek David and his men in front of the Wildgoats' Rocks. 3 And he came to the sheepfolds by the way, where there was a cave, and Saul went in to relieve himself.[2] Now David and his men were sitting in the innermost parts of the cave. 4 And the men of David said to him, "Here is the day of which the LORD said to you, 'Behold, I will give your enemy into your hand, and you shall do to him as it shall seem good to you.'" Then David arose and stealthily cut off a corner of Saul's robe. 5 And afterward David's heart struck him, because he had cut off a corner

[1] Ch 24:2 in Hebrew   [2] Hebrew *cover his feet*

of Saul's robe. [6]He said to his men, "The LORD forbid that I should do this thing to my lord, the LORD's anointed, to put out my hand against him, seeing he is the LORD's anointed." [7]So David persuaded his men with these words and did not permit them to attack Saul. And Saul rose up and left the cave and went on his way.

[8]Afterward David also arose and went out of the cave, and called after Saul, "My lord the king!" And when Saul looked behind him, David bowed with his face to the earth and paid homage. [9]And David said to Saul, "Why do you listen to the words of men who say, 'Behold, David seeks your harm'? [10]Behold, this day your eyes have seen how the LORD gave you today into my hand in the cave. And some told me to kill you, but I spared you.[1] I said, 'I will not put out my hand against my lord, for he is the LORD's anointed.' [11]See, my father, see the corner of your robe in my hand. For by the fact that I cut off the corner of your robe and did not kill you, you may know and see that there is no wrong or treason in my hands. I have not sinned against you, though you hunt my life to take it. [12]May the LORD judge between me and you, may the LORD avenge me against you, but my hand shall not be against you. [13]As the proverb of the ancients says, 'Out of the wicked comes wickedness.' But my hand shall not be against you. [14]After whom has the king of Israel come out? After whom do you pursue? After a dead dog! After a flea! [15]May the LORD therefore be judge and give sentence between me and you, and see to it and plead my cause and deliver me from your hand."

[16]As soon as David had finished speaking these words to Saul, Saul said, "Is this your voice, my son David?" And Saul lifted up his voice and wept. [17]He said to David, "You are more righteous than I, for you have repaid me good, whereas I have repaid you evil. [18]And you have declared this day how you have dealt well with me, in that you did not kill me when the LORD put me into your hands. [19]For if a man finds his enemy, will he let him go away safe? So may the LORD reward you with good for what you have done to me this day. [20]And now, behold, I know that you shall surely be king, and that the kingdom of Israel shall be established in your hand. [21]Swear to me therefore by the LORD that you will not cut off my offspring after me, and that you will not destroy my name

out of my father's house." [22]And David swore this to Saul. Then Saul went home, but David and his men went up to the stronghold.

1 Corinthians 5

It is actually reported that there is sexual immorality among you, and of a kind that is not tolerated even among pagans, for a man has his father's wife. [2]And you are arrogant! Ought you not rather to mourn? Let him who has done this be removed from among you.

[3]For though absent in body, I am present in spirit; and as if present, I have already pronounced judgment on the one who did such a thing. [4]When you are assembled in the name of the Lord Jesus and my spirit is present, with the power of our Lord Jesus, [5]you are to deliver this man to Satan for the destruction of the flesh, so that his spirit may be saved in the day of the Lord.[2]

[6]Your boasting is not good. Do you not know that a little leaven leavens the whole lump? [7]Cleanse out the old leaven that you may be a new lump, as you really are unleavened. For Christ, our Passover lamb, has been sacrificed. [8]Let us therefore celebrate the festival, not with the old leaven, the leaven of malice and evil, but with the unleavened bread of sincerity and truth.

[9]I wrote to you in my letter not to associate with sexually immoral people— [10]not at all meaning the sexually immoral of this world, or the greedy and swindlers, or idolaters, since then you would need to go out of the world. [11]But now I am writing to you not to associate with anyone who bears the name of brother if he is guilty of sexual immorality or greed, or is an idolater, reviler, drunkard, or swindler—not even to eat with such a one. [12]For what have I to do with judging outsiders? Is it not those inside the church[3] whom you are to judge? [13]God judges[4] those outside. "Purge the evil person from among you."

Ezekiel 3

And he said to me, "Son of man, eat whatever you find here. Eat this scroll, and go, speak to the house of Israel." [2]So I opened my mouth, and he gave me this scroll to eat. [3]And

[1] Septuagint, Syriac, Targum; Hebrew it [my eye] spared you [2] Some manuscripts add Jesus [3] Greek those inside [4] Or will judge

he said to me, "Son of man, feed your belly with this scroll that I give you and fill your stomach with it." Then I ate it, and it was in my mouth as sweet as honey.

⁴And he said to me, "Son of man, go to the house of Israel and speak with my words to them. ⁵For you are not sent to a people of foreign speech and a hard language, but to the house of Israel— ⁶not to many peoples of foreign speech and a hard language, whose words you cannot understand. Surely, if I sent you to such, they would listen to you. ⁷But the house of Israel will not be willing to listen to you, for they are not willing to listen to me: because all the house of Israel have a hard forehead and a stubborn heart. ⁸Behold, I have made your face as hard as their faces, and your forehead as hard as their foreheads. ⁹Like emery harder than flint have I made your forehead. Fear them not, nor be dismayed at their looks, for they are a rebellious house." ¹⁰Moreover, he said to me, "Son of man, all my words that I shall speak to you receive in your heart, and hear with your ears. ¹¹And go to the exiles, to your people, and speak to them and say to them, 'Thus says the Lord GOD,' whether they hear or refuse to hear."

¹²Then the Spirit[1] lifted me up, and I heard behind me the voice[2] of a great earthquake: "Blessed be the glory of the LORD from its place!" ¹³It was the sound of the wings of the living creatures as they touched one another, and the sound of the wheels beside them, and the sound of a great earthquake. ¹⁴The Spirit lifted me up and took me away, and I went in bitterness in the heat of my spirit, the hand of the LORD being strong upon me. ¹⁵And I came to the exiles at Tel-abib, who were dwelling by the Chebar canal, and I sat where they were dwelling.[3] And I sat there overwhelmed among them seven days.

¹⁶And at the end of seven days, the word of the LORD came to me: ¹⁷"Son of man, I have made you a watchman for the house of Israel. Whenever you hear a word from my mouth, you shall give them warning from me. ¹⁸If I say to the wicked, 'You shall surely die,' and you give him no warning, nor speak to warn the wicked from his wicked way, in order to save his life, that wicked person shall die for[4] his iniquity, but his blood I will require at your hand. ¹⁹But if you warn the wicked, and he does not turn from his wickedness, or from

his wicked way, he shall die for his iniquity, but you will have delivered your soul. ²⁰Again, if a righteous person turns from his righteousness and commits injustice, and I lay a stumbling block before him, he shall die. Because you have not warned him, he shall die for his sin, and his righteous deeds that he has done shall not be remembered, but his blood I will require at your hand. ²¹But if you warn the righteous person not to sin, and he does not sin, he shall surely live, because he took warning, and you will have delivered your soul."

²²And the hand of the LORD was upon me there. And he said to me, "Arise, go out into the valley,[5] and there I will speak with you." ²³So I arose and went out into the valley, and behold, the glory of the LORD stood there, like the glory that I had seen by the Chebar canal, and I fell on my face. ²⁴But the Spirit entered into me and set me on my feet, and he spoke with me and said to me, "Go, shut yourself within your house. ²⁵And you, O son of man, behold, cords will be placed upon you, and you shall be bound with them, so that you cannot go out among the people. ²⁶And I will make your tongue cling to the roof of your mouth, so that you shall be mute and unable to reprove them, for they are a rebellious house. ²⁷But when I speak with you, I will open your mouth, and you shall say to them, 'Thus says the Lord GOD.' He who will hear, let him hear; and he who will refuse to hear, let him refuse, for they are a rebellious house.

Psalm 39

TO THE CHOIRMASTER: TO JEDUTHUN.
A PSALM OF DAVID.

I said, "I will guard my ways,
that I may not sin with my tongue;
   I will guard my mouth with a muzzle,
     so long as the wicked are in my
      presence."
2   I was mute and silent;
   I held my peace to no avail,
and my distress grew worse.
3   My heart became hot within me.
As I mused, the fire burned;
   then I spoke with my tongue:

4   "O LORD, make me know my end
   and what is the measure of my days;
let me know how fleeting I am!

¹ Or the wind; also verse 14 ² Or sound ³ Or Chebar, and to where they dwelt ⁴ Or in; also verses 19, 20 ⁵ Or plain; also verse 23

5 Behold, you have made my days a few
   handbreadths,
   and my lifetime is as nothing before
   you.
   Surely all mankind stands as a mere
   breath!   *Selah*

6 Surely a man goes about as a
   shadow!
   Surely for nothing[1] they are in turmoil;
   man heaps up wealth and does not
   know who will gather!

7 "And now, O Lord, for what do I wait?
   My hope is in you.
8 Deliver me from all my transgressions.
   Do not make me the scorn of the fool!
9 I am mute; I do not open my mouth,
   for it is you who have done it.

10 Remove your stroke from me;
   I am spent by the hostility of your
   hand.
11 When you discipline a man
   with rebukes for sin,
   you consume like a moth what is dear to
   him;
   surely all mankind is a mere breath!
                              Selah

12 "Hear my prayer, O LORD,
   and give ear to my cry;
   hold not your peace at my tears!
   For I am a sojourner with you,
   a guest, like all my fathers.
13 Look away from me, that I may smile
   again,
   before I depart and am no more!"

[1] Hebrew *Surely as a breath*

SEPTEMBER 1

1 Samuel 25

Now Samuel died. And all Israel assembled and mourned for him, and they buried him in his house at Ramah.

Then David rose and went down to the wilderness of Paran. ² And there was a man in Maon whose business was in Carmel. The man was very rich; he had three thousand sheep and a thousand goats. He was shearing his sheep in Carmel. ³ Now the name of the man was Nabal, and the name of his wife Abigail. The woman was discerning and beautiful, but the man was harsh and badly behaved; he was a Calebite. ⁴ David heard in the wilderness that Nabal was shearing his sheep. ⁵ So David sent ten young men. And David said to the young men, "Go up to Carmel, and go to Nabal and greet him in my name. ⁶ And thus you shall greet him: 'Peace be to you, and peace be to your house, and peace be to all that you have. ⁷ I hear that you have shearers. Now your shepherds have been with us, and we did them no harm, and they missed nothing all the time they were in Carmel. ⁸ Ask your young men, and they will tell you. Therefore let my young men find favor in your eyes, for we come on a feast day. Please give whatever you have at hand to your servants and to your son David.'"

⁹ When David's young men came, they said all this to Nabal in the name of David, and then they waited. ¹⁰ And Nabal answered David's servants, "Who is David? Who is the son of Jesse? There are many servants these days who are breaking away from their masters. ¹¹ Shall I take my bread and my water and my meat that I have killed for my shearers and give it to men who come from I do not know where?" ¹² So David's young men turned away and came back and told him all this. ¹³ And David said to his men, "Every man strap on his sword!" And every man of them strapped on his sword. David also strapped on his sword. And about four hundred men went up after David, while two hundred remained with the baggage.

¹⁴ But one of the young men told Abigail, Nabal's wife, "Behold, David sent messengers out of the wilderness to greet our master, and he railed at them. ¹⁵ Yet the men were very good to us, and we suffered no harm, and we did not miss anything when we were in the fields, as long as we went with them. ¹⁶ They were a wall to us both by night and by day, all the while we were with them keeping the sheep. ¹⁷ Now therefore know this and consider what you should do, for harm is determined against our master and against all his house, and he is such a worthless man that one cannot speak to him."

¹⁸ Then Abigail made haste and took two hundred loaves and two skins of wine and five sheep already prepared and five seahs[1] of parched grain and a hundred clusters of raisins and two hundred cakes of figs, and laid them on donkeys. ¹⁹ And she said to her young men, "Go on before me; behold, I come after you." But she did not tell her husband Nabal. ²⁰ And as she rode on the donkey and came down under cover of the mountain, behold, David and his men came down toward her, and she met them. ²¹ Now David had said, "Surely in vain have I guarded all that this fellow has in the wilderness, so that nothing was missed of all that belonged to him, and he has returned me evil for good. ²² God do so to the enemies of David[2] and more also, if by morning I leave so much as one male of all who belong to him."

²³ When Abigail saw David, she hurried and got down from the donkey and fell before David on her face and bowed to the ground. ²⁴ She fell at his feet and said, "On me alone, my lord, be the guilt. Please let your servant speak in your ears, and hear the words of your servant. ²⁵ Let not my lord regard this worthless fellow, Nabal, for as his name is, so is he. Nabal[3] is his name, and folly is with him. But I your servant did not see the young men of my lord, whom you sent. ²⁶ Now then, my lord, as the LORD lives, and as your soul lives, because the LORD has restrained you from bloodguilt and from saving with your own hand, now

[1] A seah was about 7 quarts or 7.3 liters [2] Septuagint to David [3] Nabal means fool

then let your enemies and those who seek to do evil to my lord be as Nabal. [27]And now let this present that your servant has brought to my lord be given to the young men who follow my lord. [28]Please forgive the trespass of your servant. For the LORD will certainly make my lord a sure house, because my lord is fighting the battles of the LORD, and evil shall not be found in you so long as you live. [29]If men rise up to pursue you and to seek your life, the life of my lord shall be bound in the bundle of the living in the care of the LORD your God. And the lives of your enemies he shall sling out as from the hollow of a sling. [30]And when the LORD has done to my lord according to all the good that he has spoken concerning you and has appointed you prince[1] over Israel, [31]my lord shall have no cause of grief or pangs of conscience for having shed blood without cause or for my lord working salvation himself. And when the LORD has dealt well with my lord, then remember your servant."

[32]And David said to Abigail, "Blessed be the LORD, the God of Israel, who sent you this day to meet me! [33]Blessed be your discretion, and blessed be you, who have kept me this day from bloodguilt and from working salvation with my own hand! [34]For as surely as the LORD, the God of Israel, lives, who has restrained me from hurting you, unless you had hurried and come to meet me, truly by morning there had not been left to Nabal so much as one male." [35]Then David received from her hand what she had brought him. And he said to her, "Go up in peace to your house. See, I have obeyed your voice, and I have granted your petition."

[36]And Abigail came to Nabal, and behold, he was holding a feast in his house, like the feast of a king. And Nabal's heart was merry within him, for he was very drunk. So she told him nothing at all until the morning light. [37]In the morning, when the wine had gone out of Nabal, his wife told him these things, and his heart died within him, and he became as a stone. [38]And about ten days later the LORD struck Nabal, and he died.

[39]When David heard that Nabal was dead, he said, "Blessed be the LORD who has avenged the insult I received at the hand of Nabal, and has kept back his servant from wrongdoing. The LORD has returned the evil of Nabal on his own head." Then David sent and spoke to Abigail,

to take her as his wife. [40]When the servants of David came to Abigail at Carmel, they said to her, "David has sent us to you to take you to him as his wife." [41]And she rose and bowed with her face to the ground and said, "Behold, your handmaid is a servant to wash the feet of the servants of my lord." [42]And Abigail hurried and rose and mounted a donkey, and her five young women attended her. She followed the messengers of David and became his wife.

[43]David also took Ahinoam of Jezreel, and both of them became his wives. [44]Saul had given Michal his daughter, David's wife, to Palti the son of Laish, who was of Gallim.

--------- *1 Corinthians 6* ---------

When one of you has a grievance against another, does he dare go to law before the unrighteous instead of the saints? [2]Or do you not know that the saints will judge the world? And if the world is to be judged by you, are you incompetent to try trivial cases? [3]Do you not know that we are to judge angels? How much more, then, matters pertaining to this life! [4]So if you have such cases, why do you lay them before those who have no standing in the church? [5]I say this to your shame. Can it be that there is no one among you wise enough to settle a dispute between the brothers, [6]but brother goes to law against brother, and that before unbelievers? [7]To have lawsuits at all with one another is already a defeat for you. Why not rather suffer wrong? Why not rather be defrauded? [8]But you yourselves wrong and defraud—even your own brothers![2]

[9]Or do you not know that the unrighteous[3] will not inherit the kingdom of God? Do not be deceived: neither the sexually immoral, nor idolaters, nor adulterers, nor men who practice homosexuality,[4] [10]nor thieves, nor the greedy, nor drunkards, nor revilers, nor swindlers will inherit the kingdom of God. [11]And such were some of you. But you were washed, you were sanctified, you were justified in the name of the Lord Jesus Christ and by the Spirit of our God.

[12]"All things are lawful for me," but not all things are helpful. "All things are lawful for me," but I will not be dominated by anything. [13]"Food is meant for the stomach and the stomach for food"—and God will destroy both one and the other. The body is not meant for sexual

---

[1] Or leader   [2] Or brothers and sisters   [3] Or wrongdoers   [4] The two Greek terms translated by this phrase refer to the passive and active partners in consensual homosexual acts

immorality, but for the Lord, and the Lord for the body. [14]And God raised the Lord and will also raise us up by his power. [15]Do you not know that your bodies are members of Christ? Shall I then take the members of Christ and make them members of a prostitute? Never! [16]Or do you not know that he who is joined[1] to a prostitute becomes one body with her? For, as it is written, "The two will become one flesh." [17]But he who is joined to the Lord becomes one spirit with him. [18]Flee from sexual immorality. Every other sin[2] a person commits is outside the body, but the sexually immoral person sins against his own body. [19]Or do you not know that your body is a temple of the Holy Spirit within you, whom you have from God? You are not your own, [20]for you were bought with a price. So glorify God in your body.

Ezekiel 4

"And you, son of man, take a brick and lay it before you, and engrave on it a city, even Jerusalem. [2]And put siegeworks against it, and build a siege wall against it, and cast up a mound against it. Set camps also against it, and plant battering rams against it all around. [3]And you, take an iron griddle, and place it as an iron wall between you and the city; and set your face toward it, and let it be in a state of siege, and press the siege against it. This is a sign for the house of Israel.

[4]"Then lie on your left side, and place the punishment[3] of the house of Israel upon it. For the number of the days that you lie on it, you shall bear their punishment. [5]For I assign to you a number of days, 390 days, equal to the number of the years of their punishment. So long shall you bear the punishment of the house of Israel. [6]And when you have completed these, you shall lie down a second time, but on your right side, and bear the punishment of the house of Judah. Forty days I assign you, a day for each year. [7]And you shall set your face toward the siege of Jerusalem, with your arm bared, and you shall prophesy against the city. [8]And behold, I will place cords upon you, so that you cannot turn from one side to the other, till you have completed the days of your siege.

[9]"And you, take wheat and barley, beans and lentils, millet and emmer,[4] and put them into a single vessel and make your bread from them. During the number of days that you lie on your side, 390 days, you shall eat it. [10]And your food that you eat shall be by weight, twenty shekels[5] a day; from day to day[6] you shall eat it. [11]And water you shall drink by measure, the sixth part of a hin;[7] from day to day you shall drink. [12]And you shall eat it as a barley cake, baking it in their sight on human dung." [13]And the LORD said, "Thus shall the people of Israel eat their bread unclean, among the nations where I will drive them." [14]Then I said, "Ah, Lord GOD! Behold, I have never defiled myself.[8] From my youth up till now I have never eaten what died of itself or was torn by beasts, nor has tainted meat come into my mouth." [15]Then he said to me, "See, I assign to you cow's dung instead of human dung, on which you may prepare your bread." [16]Moreover, he said to me, "Son of man, behold, I will break the supply[9] of bread in Jerusalem. They shall eat bread by weight and with anxiety, and they shall drink water by measure and in dismay. [17]I will do this that they may lack bread and water, and look at one another in dismay, and rot away because of their punishment.

Psalm 40–41

To the choirmaster. A Psalm of David.

I waited patiently for the LORD;
  he inclined to me and heard my cry.
[2]   He drew me up from the pit of
        destruction,
     out of the miry bog,
  and set my feet upon a rock,
     making my steps secure.
[3]   He put a new song in my mouth,
     a song of praise to our God.
  Many will see and fear,
     and put their trust in the LORD.

[4]   Blessed is the man who makes
     the LORD his trust,
  who does not turn to the proud,
     to those who go astray after a lie!
[5]   You have multiplied, O LORD my God,
     your wondrous deeds and your
        thoughts toward us;
     none can compare with you!
  I will proclaim and tell of them,
     yet they are more than can be told.

[1] Or who holds fast (compare Genesis 2:24 and Deuteronomy 10:20); also verse 17 [2] Or Every sin [3] Or iniquity; also verses 5, 6, 17 [4] A type of wheat [5] A shekel was about 2/5 ounce or 11 grams [6] Or at a set time daily; also verse 11 [7] A hin was about 4 quarts or 3.5 liters [8] Hebrew my soul (or throat) has never been made unclean [9] Hebrew staff

6 In sacrifice and offering you have not
　　delighted,
　but you have given me an open ear.[1]
　Burnt offering and sin offering
　　you have not required.
7 Then I said, "Behold, I have come;
　in the scroll of the book it is written of
　　me:
8 I delight to do your will, O my God;
　your law is within my heart."

9 I have told the glad news of deliverance[2]
　　in the great congregation;
　behold, I have not restrained my lips,
　　as you know, O LORD.
10 I have not hidden your deliverance
　　within my heart;
　I have spoken of your faithfulness and
　　your salvation;
　I have not concealed your steadfast love
　　and your faithfulness
　from the great congregation.

11 As for you, O LORD, you will not
　　restrain
　　your mercy from me;
　your steadfast love and your faithfulness
　　will
　　ever preserve me!
12 For evils have encompassed me
　　beyond number;
　my iniquities have overtaken me,
　　and I cannot see;
　they are more than the hairs of my
　　head;
　my heart fails me.

13 Be pleased, O LORD, to deliver me!
　O LORD, make haste to help me!
14 Let those be put to shame and
　　disappointed altogether
　who seek to snatch away my life;
　let those be turned back and brought to
　　dishonor
　who delight in my hurt!
15 Let those be appalled because of their
　　shame
　who say to me, "Aha, Aha!"

16 But may all who seek you
　　rejoice and be glad in you;
　may those who love your salvation
　　say continually, "Great is the LORD!"

17 As for me, I am poor and needy,
　　but the Lord takes thought for me.
　You are my help and my deliverer;
　　do not delay, O my God!

To the choirmaster. A Psalm of David.

Blessed is the one who considers the poor![3]
　In the day of trouble the LORD delivers
　　him;
2 the LORD protects him and keeps him
　　alive;
　he is called blessed in the land;
　you do not give him up to the will of
　　his enemies.
3 The LORD sustains him on his sickbed;
　in his illness you restore him to full
　　health.[4]

4 As for me, I said, "O LORD, be gracious
　　to me;
　heal me,[5] for I have sinned against
　　you!"
5 My enemies say of me in malice,
　"When will he die, and his name
　　perish?"
6 And when one comes to see me, he
　　utters empty words,
　while his heart gathers iniquity;
　when he goes out, he tells it abroad.
7 All who hate me whisper together about
　　me;
　they imagine the worst for me.[6]
8 They say, "A deadly thing is poured out[7]
　　on him;
　he will not rise again from where he
　　lies."
9 Even my close friend in whom I trusted,
　who ate my bread, has lifted his heel
　　against me.
10 But you, O LORD, be gracious to me,
　and raise me up, that I may repay them!

11 By this I know that you delight in me:
　my enemy will not shout in triumph
　　over me.
12 But you have upheld me because of my
　　integrity,
　and set me in your presence forever.
13 Blessed be the LORD, the God of Israel,
　from everlasting to everlasting!
　　Amen and Amen.

---

[1] Hebrew ears you have dug for me [2] Hebrew righteousness; also verse 10 [3] Or weak [4] Hebrew you turn all his bed [5] Hebrew my soul [6] Or they devise evil against me [7] Or has fastened

SEPTEMBER 2

1 Samuel 26

Then the Ziphites came to Saul at Gibeah, saying, "Is not David hiding himself on the hill of Hachilah, which is on the east of Jeshimon?" ²So Saul arose and went down to the wilderness of Ziph with three thousand chosen men of Israel to seek David in the wilderness of Ziph. ³And Saul encamped on the hill of Hachilah, which is beside the road on the east of Jeshimon. But David remained in the wilderness. When he saw that Saul came after him into the wilderness, ⁴David sent out spies and learned that Saul had indeed come. ⁵Then David rose and came to the place where Saul had encamped. And David saw the place where Saul lay, with Abner the son of Ner, the commander of his army. Saul was lying within the encampment, while the army was encamped around him.

⁶Then David said to Ahimelech the Hittite, and to Joab's brother Abishai the son of Zeruiah, "Who will go down with me into the camp to Saul?" And Abishai said, "I will go down with you." ⁷So David and Abishai went to the army by night. And there lay Saul sleeping within the encampment, with his spear stuck in the ground at his head, and Abner and the army lay around him. ⁸Then Abishai said to David, "God has given your enemy into your hand this day. Now please let me pin him to the earth with one stroke of the spear, and I will not strike him twice." ⁹But David said to Abishai, "Do not destroy him, for who can put out his hand against the LORD's anointed and be guiltless?" ¹⁰And David said, "As the LORD lives, the LORD will strike him, or his day will come to die, or he will go down into battle and perish. ¹¹The LORD forbid that I should put out my hand against the LORD's anointed. But take now the spear that is at his head and the jar of water, and let us go." ¹²So David took the spear and the jar of water from Saul's head, and they went away. No man saw it or knew it, nor did any awake, for they were all asleep, because a deep sleep from the LORD had fallen upon them.

¹³Then David went over to the other side and stood far off on the top of the hill, with a great space between them. ¹⁴And David called to the army, and to Abner the son of Ner, saying, "Will you not answer, Abner?" Then Abner answered, "Who are you who calls to the king?" ¹⁵And David said to Abner, "Are you not a man? Who is like you in Israel? Why then have you not kept watch over your lord the king? For one of the people came in to destroy the king your lord. ¹⁶This thing that you have done is not good. As the LORD lives, you deserve to die, because you have not kept watch over your lord, the LORD's anointed. And now see where the king's spear is and the jar of water that was at his head."

¹⁷Saul recognized David's voice and said, "Is this your voice, my son David?" And David said, "It is my voice, my lord, O king." ¹⁸And he said, "Why does my lord pursue after his servant? For what have I done? What evil is on my hands? ¹⁹Now therefore let my lord the king hear the words of his servant. If it is the LORD who has stirred you up against me, may he accept an offering, but if it is men, may they be cursed before the LORD, for they have driven me out this day that I should have no share in the heritage of the LORD, saying, 'Go, serve other gods.' ²⁰Now therefore, let not my blood fall to the earth away from the presence of the LORD, for the king of Israel has come out to seek a single flea like one who hunts a partridge in the mountains."

²¹Then Saul said, "I have sinned. Return, my son David, for I will no more do you harm, because my life was precious in your eyes this day. Behold, I have acted foolishly, and have made a great mistake." ²²And David answered and said, "Here is the spear, O king! Let one of the young men come over and take it. ²³The LORD rewards every man for his righteousness and his faithfulness, for the LORD gave you into my hand today, and I would not put out my hand against the LORD's anointed. ²⁴Behold, as your life was precious this day in my sight, so may my life be precious in the sight of the LORD, and may he deliver me out of all

tribulation." [25] Then Saul said to David, "Blessed be you, my son David! You will do many things and will succeed in them." So David went his way, and Saul returned to his place.

---

1 Corinthians 7

Now concerning the matters about which you wrote: "It is good for a man not to have sexual relations with a woman." [2] But because of the temptation to sexual immorality, each man should have his own wife and each woman her own husband. [3] The husband should give to his wife her conjugal rights, and likewise the wife to her husband. [4] For the wife does not have authority over her own body, but the husband does. Likewise the husband does not have authority over his own body, but the wife does. [5] Do not deprive one another, except perhaps by agreement for a limited time, that you may devote yourselves to prayer; but then come together again, so that Satan may not tempt you because of your lack of self-control.

[6] Now as a concession, not a command, I say this.[1] [7] I wish that all were as I myself am. But each has his own gift from God, one of one kind and one of another.

[8] To the unmarried and the widows I say that it is good for them to remain single as I am. [9] But if they cannot exercise self-control, they should marry. For it is better to marry than to burn with passion.

[10] To the married I give this charge (not I, but the Lord): the wife should not separate from her husband [11] (but if she does, she should remain unmarried or else be reconciled to her husband), and the husband should not divorce his wife. [12] To the rest I say (I, not the Lord) that if any brother has a wife who is an unbeliever, and she consents to live with him, he should not divorce her. [13] If any woman has a husband who is an unbeliever, and he consents to live with her, she should not divorce him. [14] For the unbelieving husband is made holy because of his wife, and the unbelieving wife is made holy because of her husband. Otherwise your children would be unclean, but as it is, they are holy. [15] But if the unbelieving partner separates, let it be so. In such cases the brother or sister is not enslaved. God has called you[2] to peace. [16] For how do you know, wife, whether you will save your husband? Or how do you know, husband, whether you will save your wife?

[17] Only let each person lead the life[3] that the Lord has assigned to him, and to which God has called him. This is my rule in all the churches. [18] Was anyone at the time of his call already circumcised? Let him not seek to remove the marks of circumcision. Was anyone at the time of his call uncircumcised? Let him not seek circumcision. [19] For neither circumcision counts for anything nor uncircumcision, but keeping the commandments of God. [20] Each one should remain in the condition in which he was called. [21] Were you a bondservant[4] when called? Do not be concerned about it. (But if you can gain your freedom, avail yourself of the opportunity.) [22] For he who was called in the Lord as a bondservant is a freedman of the Lord. Likewise he who was free when called is a bondservant of Christ. [23] You were bought with a price; do not become bondservants[5] of men. [24] So, brothers,[6] in whatever condition each was called, there let him remain with God.

[25] Now concerning[7] the betrothed,[8] I have no command from the Lord, but I give my judgment as one who by the Lord's mercy is trustworthy. [26] I think that in view of the present[9] distress it is good for a person to remain as he is. [27] Are you bound to a wife? Do not seek to be free. Are you free from a wife? Do not seek a wife. [28] But if you do marry, you have not sinned, and if a betrothed woman[10] marries, she has not sinned. Yet those who marry will have worldly troubles, and I would spare you that. [29] This is what I mean, brothers: the appointed time has grown very short. From now on, let those who have wives live as though they had none, [30] and those who mourn as though they were not mourning, and those who rejoice as though they were not rejoicing, and those who buy as though they had no goods, [31] and those who deal with the world as though they had no dealings with it. For the present form of this world is passing away.

[32] I want you to be free from anxieties. The unmarried man is anxious about the things of the Lord, how to please the Lord. [33] But the married man is anxious about worldly things, how to please his wife, [34] and his interests are divided. And the unmarried or betrothed woman is anxious about the things of the Lord, how to be holy in body and spirit. But

---

[1] Or I say this: [2] Some manuscripts us [3] Or each person walk in the way [4] Or slave; also twice in verse 22 (for the contextual rendering of the Greek word doulos, see Preface) [5] Or slaves (for the contextual rendering of the Greek word doulos, see Preface) [6] Or brothers and sisters; also verse 29 [7] The expression Now concerning introduces a reply to a question in the Corinthians' letter; see 7:1 [8] Greek virgins [9] Or impending [10] Greek virgin; also verse 34

the married woman is anxious about worldly things, how to please her husband. [35]I say this for your own benefit, not to lay any restraint upon you, but to promote good order and to secure your undivided devotion to the Lord.

[36]If anyone thinks that he is not behaving properly toward his betrothed,[1] if his[2] passions are strong, and it has to be, let him do as he wishes: let them marry—it is no sin. [37]But whoever is firmly established in his heart, being under no necessity but having his desire under control, and has determined this in his heart, to keep her as his betrothed, he will do well. [38]So then he who marries his betrothed does well, and he who refrains from marriage will do even better.

[39]A wife is bound to her husband as long as he lives. But if her husband dies, she is free to be married to whom she wishes, only in the Lord. [40]Yet in my judgment she is happier if she remains as she is. And I think that I too have the Spirit of God.

Ezekiel 5

"And you, O son of man, take a sharp sword. Use it as a barber's razor and pass it over your head and your beard. Then take balances for weighing and divide the hair. [2]A third part you shall burn in the fire in the midst of the city, when the days of the siege are completed. And a third part you shall take and strike with the sword all around the city. And a third part you shall scatter to the wind, and I will unsheathe the sword after them. [3]And you shall take from these a small number and bind them in the skirts of your robe. [4]And of these again you shall take some and cast them into the midst of the fire and burn them in the fire. From there a fire will come out into all the house of Israel.

[5]"Thus says the Lord GOD: This is Jerusalem. I have set her in the center of the nations, with countries all around her. [6]And she has rebelled against my rules by doing wickedness more than the nations, and against my statutes more than the countries all around her; for they have rejected my rules and have not walked in my statutes. [7]Therefore thus says the Lord GOD: Because you are more turbulent than the nations that are all around you, and have not walked in my statutes or obeyed my rules, and

have not[3] even acted according to the rules of the nations that are all around you, [8]therefore thus says the Lord GOD: Behold, I, even I, am against you. And I will execute judgments[4] in your midst in the sight of the nations. [9]And because of all your abominations I will do with you what I have never yet done, and the like of which I will never do again. [10]Therefore fathers shall eat their sons in your midst, and sons shall eat their fathers. And I will execute judgments on you, and any of you who survive I will scatter to all the winds. [11]Therefore, as I live, declares the Lord GOD, surely, because you have defiled my sanctuary with all your detestable things and with all your abominations, therefore I will withdraw.[5] My eye will not spare, and I will have no pity. [12]A third part of you shall die of pestilence and be consumed with famine in your midst; a third part shall fall by the sword all around you; and a third part I will scatter to all the winds and will unsheathe the sword after them.

[13]"Thus shall my anger spend itself, and I will vent my fury upon them and satisfy myself. And they shall know that I am the LORD—that I have spoken in my jealousy—when I spend my fury upon them. [14]Moreover, I will make you a desolation and an object of reproach among the nations all around you and in the sight of all who pass by. [15]You shall be[6] a reproach and a taunt, a warning and a horror, to the nations all around you, when I execute judgments on you in anger and fury, and with furious rebukes—I am the LORD; I have spoken— [16]when I send against you[7] the deadly arrows of famine, arrows for destruction, which I will send to destroy you, and when I bring more and more famine upon you and break your supply[8] of bread. [17]I will send famine and wild beasts against you, and they will rob you of your children. Pestilence and blood shall pass through you, and I will bring the sword upon you. I am the LORD; I have spoken."

Psalm 42–43

TO THE CHOIRMASTER. A MASKIL[9] OF THE SONS OF KORAH.

As a deer pants for flowing streams,
so pants my soul for you, O God.
[2] My soul thirsts for God,
      for the living God.

When shall I come and appear before
    God?[1]

3 My tears have been my food
        day and night,
    while they say to me all the day long,
        "Where is your God?"

4 These things I remember,
        as I pour out my soul:
    how I would go with the throng
    and lead them in procession to the
        house of God
    with glad shouts and songs of praise,
        a multitude keeping festival.

5 Why are you cast down, O my soul,
        and why are you in turmoil within me?
    Hope in God; for I shall again praise him,
    my salvation[2] 6and my God.

    My soul is cast down within me;
        therefore I remember you
    from the land of Jordan and of Hermon,
        from Mount Mizar.

7 Deep calls to deep
        at the roar of your waterfalls;
    all your breakers and your waves
        have gone over me.

8 By day the LORD commands his
        steadfast love,
    and at night his song is with me,
        a prayer to the God of my life.

9 I say to God, my rock:
        "Why have you forgotten me?
    Why do I go mourning
        because of the oppression of the
        enemy?"

10 As with a deadly wound in my bones,
        my adversaries taunt me,
    while they say to me all the day long,
        "Where is your God?"

11 Why are you cast down, O my soul,
        and why are you in turmoil within me?
    Hope in God; for I shall again praise
        him,
    my salvation and my God.

V indicate me, O God, and defend my cause
        against an ungodly people,
    from the deceitful and unjust man
        deliver me!

2 For you are the God in whom I take
        refuge;
    why have you rejected me?
    Why do I go about mourning
        because of the oppression of the
        enemy?

3 Send out your light and your truth;
        let them lead me;
    let them bring me to your holy hill
        and to your dwelling!

4 Then I will go to the altar of God,
        to God my exceeding joy,
    and I will praise you with the lyre,
        O God, my God.

5 Why are you cast down, O my soul,
        and why are you in turmoil within me?
    Hope in God; for I shall again praise
        him,
    my salvation and my God.

SEPTEMBER 3

1 Samuel 27

Then David said in his heart, "Now I shall perish one day by the hand of Saul. There is nothing better for me than that I should escape to the land of the Philistines. Then Saul will despair of seeking me any longer within the borders of Israel, and I shall escape out of his hand." [2]So David arose and went over, he and the six hundred men who were with him, to Achish the son of Maoch, king of Gath. [3]And David lived with Achish at Gath, he and his men, every man with his household, and David with his two wives, Ahinoam of Jezreel, and

[1] Revocalization yields and see the face of God [2] Hebrew the salvation of my face; also verse 11 and 43:5

Abigail of Carmel, Nabal's widow. ⁴And when it was told Saul that David had fled to Gath, he no longer sought him.

⁵Then David said to Achish, "If I have found favor in your eyes, let a place be given me in one of the country towns, that I may dwell there. For why should your servant dwell in the royal city with you?" ⁶So that day Achish gave him Ziklag. Therefore Ziklag has belonged to the kings of Judah to this day. ⁷And the number of the days that David lived in the country of the Philistines was a year and four months.

⁸Now David and his men went up and made raids against the Geshurites, the Girzites, and the Amalekites, for these were the inhabitants of the land from of old, as far as Shur, to the land of Egypt. ⁹And David would strike the land and would leave neither man nor woman alive, but would take away the sheep, the oxen, the donkeys, the camels, and the garments, and come back to Achish. ¹⁰When Achish asked, "Where have you made a raid today?" David would say, "Against the Negeb of Judah," or, "Against the Negeb of the Jerahmeelites," or, "Against the Negeb of the Kenites." ¹¹And David would leave neither man nor woman alive to bring news to Gath, thinking, "lest they should tell about us and say, 'So David has done.'" Such was his custom all the while he lived in the country of the Philistines. ¹²And Achish trusted David, thinking, "He has made himself an utter stench to his people Israel; therefore he shall always be my servant."

1 Corinthians 8

Now concerning¹ food offered to idols: we know that "all of us possess knowledge." This "knowledge" puffs up, but love builds up. ²If anyone imagines that he knows something, he does not yet know as he ought to know. ³But if anyone loves God, he is known by God.²

⁴Therefore, as to the eating of food offered to idols, we know that "an idol has no real existence," and that "there is no God but one." ⁵For although there may be so-called gods in heaven or on earth—as indeed there are many "gods" and many "lords"— ⁶yet for us there is one God, the Father, from whom are all things and for whom we exist, and one Lord, Jesus Christ, through whom are all things and through whom we exist.

⁷However, not all possess this knowledge. But some, through former association with idols, eat food as really offered to an idol, and their conscience, being weak, is defiled. ⁸Food will not commend us to God. We are no worse off if we do not eat, and no better off if we do. ⁹But take care that this right of yours does not somehow become a stumbling block to the weak. ¹⁰For if anyone sees you who have knowledge eating³ in an idol's temple, will he not be encouraged,⁴ if his conscience is weak, to eat food offered to idols? ¹¹And so by your knowledge this weak person is destroyed, the brother for whom Christ died. ¹²Thus, sinning against your brothers⁵ and wounding their conscience when it is weak, you sin against Christ. ¹³Therefore, if food makes my brother stumble, I will never eat meat, lest I make my brother stumble.

Ezekiel 6

The word of the LORD came to me: ²"Son of man, set your face toward the mountains of Israel, and prophesy against them, ³and say, You mountains of Israel, hear the word of the Lord GOD! Thus says the Lord GOD to the mountains and the hills, to the ravines and the valleys: Behold, I, even I, will bring a sword upon you, and I will destroy your high places. ⁴Your altars shall become desolate, and your incense altars shall be broken, and I will cast down your slain before your idols. ⁵And I will lay the dead bodies of the people of Israel before their idols, and I will scatter your bones around your altars. ⁶Wherever you dwell, the cities shall be waste and the high places ruined, so that your altars will be waste and ruined,⁶ your idols broken and destroyed, your incense altars cut down, and your works wiped out. ⁷And the slain shall fall in your midst, and you shall know that I am the LORD.

⁸"Yet I will leave some of you alive. When you have among the nations some who escape the sword, and when you are scattered through the countries, ⁹then those of you who escape will remember me among the nations where they are carried captive, how I have been broken over their whoring heart that has departed from me and over their eyes that go whoring after their idols. And they will be loathsome in their own sight for the evils that they have committed, for all their abominations. ¹⁰And

¹ The expression *Now concerning* introduces a reply to a question in the Corinthians' letter; see 7:1 ² Greek *him* ³ Greek *reclining at table* ⁴ Or *fortified*; Greek *built up* ⁵ Or *brothers and sisters* ⁶ Or *punished*

they shall know that I am the LORD. I have not said in vain that I would do this evil to them."

[11] Thus says the Lord GOD: "Clap your hands and stamp your foot and say, Alas, because of all the evil abominations of the house of Israel, for they shall fall by the sword, by famine, and by pestilence. [12] He who is far off shall die of pestilence, and he who is near shall fall by the sword, and he who is left and is preserved shall die of famine. Thus I will spend my fury upon them. [13] And you shall know that I am the LORD, when their slain lie among their idols around their altars, on every high hill, on all the mountaintops, under every green tree, and under every leafy oak, wherever they offered pleasing aroma to all their idols. [14] And I will stretch out my hand against them and make the land desolate and waste, in all their dwelling places, from the wilderness to Riblah.[1] Then they will know that I am the LORD."

Psalm 44

To the choirmaster. A Maskil[2] of the Sons of Korah.

O God, we have heard with our ears,
  our fathers have told us,
  what deeds you performed in their days,
    in the days of old:
[2] you with your own hand drove out the nations,
  but them you planted;
  you afflicted the peoples,
  but them you set free;
[3] for not by their own sword did they win the land,
  nor did their own arm save them,
  but your right hand and your arm,
  and the light of your face,
  for you delighted in them.

[4] You are my King, O God;
  ordain salvation for Jacob!
[5] Through you we push down our foes;
  through your name we tread down
    those who rise up against us.
[6] For not in my bow do I trust,
  nor can my sword save me.
[7] But you have saved us from our foes
  and have put to shame those who hate us.

[8] In God we have boasted continually,
  and we will give thanks to your name forever. *Selah*

[9] But you have rejected us and disgraced us
  and have not gone out with our armies.
[10] You have made us turn back from the foe,
  and those who hate us have gotten spoil.
[11] You have made us like sheep for slaughter
  and have scattered us among the nations.
[12] You have sold your people for a trifle,
  demanding no high price for them.
[13] You have made us the taunt of our neighbors,
  the derision and scorn of those around us.
[14] You have made us a byword among the nations,
  a laughingstock[3] among the peoples.
[15] All day long my disgrace is before me,
  and shame has covered my face
[16] at the sound of the taunter and reviler,
  at the sight of the enemy and the avenger.

[17] All this has come upon us,
  though we have not forgotten you,
  and we have not been false to your covenant.
[18] Our heart has not turned back,
  nor have our steps departed from your way;
[19] yet you have broken us in the place of jackals
  and covered us with the shadow of death.
[20] If we had forgotten the name of our God
  or spread out our hands to a foreign god,
[21] would not God discover this?
  For he knows the secrets of the heart.
[22] Yet for your sake we are killed all the day long;
  we are regarded as sheep to be slaughtered.

[1] Some Hebrew manuscripts; most Hebrew manuscripts *Diblah* [2] Probably a musical or liturgical term [3] Hebrew *a shaking of the head*

23 Awake! Why are you sleeping, O Lord?
  Rouse yourself! Do not reject us
    forever!
24 Why do you hide your face?
  Why do you forget our affliction and
    oppression?

25 For our soul is bowed down to the
    dust;
  our belly clings to the ground.
26 Rise up; come to our help!
  Redeem us for the sake of your
    steadfast love!

SEPTEMBER 4

1 Samuel 28

In those days the Philistines gathered their forces for war, to fight against Israel. And Achish said to David, "Understand that you and your men are to go out with me in the army." ²David said to Achish, "Very well, you shall know what your servant can do." And Achish said to David, "Very well, I will make you my bodyguard for life."

³Now Samuel had died, and all Israel had mourned for him and buried him in Ramah, his own city. And Saul had put the mediums and the necromancers out of the land. ⁴The Philistines assembled and came and encamped at Shunem. And Saul gathered all Israel, and they encamped at Gilboa. ⁵When Saul saw the army of the Philistines, he was afraid, and his heart trembled greatly. ⁶And when Saul inquired of the LORD, the LORD did not answer him, either by dreams, or by Urim, or by prophets. ⁷Then Saul said to his servants, "Seek out for me a woman who is a medium, that I may go to her and inquire of her." And his servants said to him, "Behold, there is a medium at En-dor."

⁸So Saul disguised himself and put on other garments and went, he and two men with him. And they came to the woman by night. And he said, "Divine for me by a spirit and bring up for me whomever I shall name to you." ⁹The woman said to him, "Surely you know what Saul has done, how he has cut off the mediums and the necromancers from the land. Why then are you laying a trap for my life to bring about my death?" ¹⁰But Saul swore to her by the LORD, "As the LORD lives, no punishment shall come upon you for this thing." ¹¹Then the woman said, "Whom shall I bring up for you?" He said, "Bring up Samuel for me." ¹²When the woman saw Samuel, she cried out with a loud voice. And the woman said to Saul, "Why have you deceived me? You are Saul." ¹³The king said to her, "Do not be afraid. What do you see?" And the woman said to Saul, "I see a god coming up out of the earth." ¹⁴He said to her, "What is his appearance?" And she said, "An old man is coming up, and he is wrapped in a robe." And Saul knew that it was Samuel, and he bowed with his face to the ground and paid homage.

¹⁵Then Samuel said to Saul, "Why have you disturbed me by bringing me up?" Saul answered, "I am in great distress, for the Philistines are warring against me, and God has turned away from me and answers me no more, either by prophets or by dreams. Therefore I have summoned you to tell me what I shall do." ¹⁶And Samuel said, "Why then do you ask me, since the LORD has turned from you and become your enemy? ¹⁷The LORD has done to you as he spoke by me, for the LORD has torn the kingdom out of your hand and given it to your neighbor, David. ¹⁸Because you did not obey the voice of the LORD and did not carry out his fierce wrath against Amalek, therefore the LORD has done this thing to you this day. ¹⁹Moreover, the LORD will give Israel also with you into the hand of the Philistines, and tomorrow you and your sons shall be with me. The LORD will give the army of Israel also into the hand of the Philistines."

²⁰Then Saul fell at once full length on the

ground, filled with fear because of the words of Samuel. And there was no strength in him, for he had eaten nothing all day and all night. ²¹And the woman came to Saul, and when she saw that he was terrified, she said to him, "Behold, your servant has obeyed you. I have taken my life in my hand and have listened to what you have said to me. ²²Now therefore, you also obey your servant. Let me set a morsel of bread before you; and eat, that you may have strength when you go on your way." ²³He refused and said, "I will not eat." But his servants, together with the woman, urged him, and he listened to their words. So he arose from the earth and sat on the bed. ²⁴Now the woman had a fattened calf in the house, and she quickly killed it, and she took flour and kneaded it and baked unleavened bread of it, ²⁵and she put it before Saul and his servants, and they ate. Then they rose and went away that night.

1 Corinthians 9

Am I not free? Am I not an apostle? Have I not seen Jesus our Lord? Are not you my workmanship in the Lord? ²If to others I am not an apostle, at least I am to you, for you are the seal of my apostleship in the Lord.

³This is my defense to those who would examine me. ⁴Do we not have the right to eat and drink? ⁵Do we not have the right to take along a believing wife,¹ as do the other apostles and the brothers of the Lord and Cephas? ⁶Or is it only Barnabas and I who have no right to refrain from working for a living? ⁷Who serves as a soldier at his own expense? Who plants a vineyard without eating any of its fruit? Or who tends a flock without getting some of the milk?

⁸Do I say these things on human authority? Does not the Law say the same? ⁹For it is written in the Law of Moses, "You shall not muzzle an ox when it treads out the grain." Is it for oxen that God is concerned? ¹⁰Does he not certainly speak for our sake? It was written for our sake, because the plowman should plow in hope and the thresher thresh in hope of sharing in the crop. ¹¹If we have sown spiritual things among you, is it too much if we reap material things from you? ¹²If others share this rightful claim on you, do not we even more?

Nevertheless, we have not made use of this right, but we endure anything rather than put an obstacle in the way of the gospel of Christ. ¹³Do you not know that those who are employed in the temple service get their food from the temple, and those who serve at the altar share in the sacrificial offerings? ¹⁴In the same way, the Lord commanded that those who proclaim the gospel should get their living by the gospel.

¹⁵But I have made no use of any of these rights, nor am I writing these things to secure any such provision. For I would rather die than have anyone deprive me of my ground for boasting. ¹⁶For if I preach the gospel, that gives me no ground for boasting. For necessity is laid upon me. Woe to me if I do not preach the gospel! ¹⁷For if I do this of my own will, I have a reward, but if not of my own will, I am still entrusted with a stewardship. ¹⁸What then is my reward? That in my preaching I may present the gospel free of charge, so as not to make full use of my right in the gospel.

¹⁹For though I am free from all, I have made myself a servant to all, that I might win more of them. ²⁰To the Jews I became as a Jew, in order to win Jews. To those under the law I became as one under the law (though not being myself under the law) that I might win those under the law. ²¹To those outside the law I became as one outside the law (not being outside the law of God but under the law of Christ) that I might win those outside the law. ²²To the weak I became weak, that I might win the weak. I have become all things to all people, that by all means I might save some. ²³I do it all for the sake of the gospel, that I may share with them in its blessings.

²⁴Do you not know that in a race all the runners run, but only one receives the prize? So run that you may obtain it. ²⁵Every athlete exercises self-control in all things. They do it to receive a perishable wreath, but we an imperishable. ²⁶So I do not run aimlessly; I do not box as one beating the air. ²⁷But I discipline my body and keep it under control,² lest after preaching to others I myself should be disqualified.

Ezekiel 7

The word of the LORD came to me: ²"And you, O son of man, thus says the Lord GOD to the land of Israel: An end! The end has come upon the four corners of the land.³ ³Now the

¹ Greek a sister as wife ² Greek I pummel my body and make it a slave ³ Or earth

end is upon you, and I will send my anger upon you; I will judge you according to your ways, and I will punish you for all your abominations. [4]And my eye will not spare you, nor will I have pity, but I will punish you for your ways, while your abominations are in your midst. Then you will know that I am the LORD.

[5]"Thus says the Lord GOD: Disaster after disaster![1] Behold, it comes. [6]An end has come; the end has come; it has awakened against you. Behold, it comes. [7]Your doom[2] has come to you, O inhabitant of the land. The time has come; the day is near, a day of tumult, and not of joyful shouting on the mountains. [8]Now I will soon pour out my wrath upon you, and spend my anger against you, and judge you according to your ways, and I will punish you for all your abominations. [9]And my eye will not spare, nor will I have pity. I will punish you according to your ways, while your abominations are in your midst. Then you will know that I am the LORD, who strikes.

[10]"Behold, the day! Behold, it comes! Your doom has come; the rod has blossomed; pride has budded. [11]Violence has grown up into a rod of wickedness. None of them shall remain, nor their abundance, nor their wealth; neither shall there be preeminence among them.[3] [12]The time has come; the day has arrived. Let not the buyer rejoice, nor the seller mourn, for wrath is upon all their multitude.[4] [13]For the seller shall not return to what he has sold, while they live. For the vision concerns all their multitude; it shall not turn back; and because of his iniquity, none can maintain his life.[5]

[14]"They have blown the trumpet and made everything ready, but none goes to battle, for my wrath is upon all their multitude. [15]The sword is without; pestilence and famine are within. He who is in the field dies by the sword, and him who is in the city famine and pestilence devour. [16]And if any survivors escape, they will be on the mountains, like doves of the valleys, all of them moaning, each one over his iniquity. [17]All hands are feeble, and all knees turn to water. [18]They put on sackcloth, and horror covers them. Shame is on all faces, and baldness on all their heads. [19]They cast their silver into the streets, and their gold is like an unclean thing. Their silver and gold are not able to deliver them in the day of the wrath of the LORD. They cannot satisfy their hunger or fill their stomachs with it. For it was the stumbling block of their iniquity. [20]His beautiful ornament they used for pride, and they made their abominable images and their detestable things of it. Therefore I make it an unclean thing to them. [21]And I will give it into the hands of foreigners for prey, and to the wicked of the earth for spoil, and they shall profane it. [22]I will turn my face from them, and they shall profane my treasured[6] place. Robbers shall enter and profane it.

[23]"Forge a chain![7] For the land is full of bloody crimes and the city is full of violence. [24]I will bring the worst of the nations to take possession of their houses. I will put an end to the pride of the strong, and their holy places[8] shall be profaned. [25]When anguish comes, they will seek peace, but there shall be none. [26]Disaster comes upon disaster; rumor follows rumor. They seek a vision from the prophet, while the law[9] perishes from the priest and counsel from the elders. [27]The king mourns, the prince is wrapped in despair, and the hands of the people of the land are paralyzed by terror. According to their way I will do to them, and according to their judgments I will judge them, and they shall know that I am the LORD."

Psalm 45

TO THE CHOIRMASTER: ACCORDING TO LILIES. A MASKIL[10] OF THE SONS OF KORAH; A LOVE SONG.

My heart overflows with a pleasing theme;
　　I address my verses to the king;
　　my tongue is like the pen of a ready scribe.

[2]　You are the most handsome of the sons of men;
　　grace is poured upon your lips;
　　therefore God has blessed you forever.
[3]　Gird your sword on your thigh,
　　　O mighty one,
　　in your splendor and majesty!

[4]　In your majesty ride out victoriously
　　for the cause of truth and meekness and righteousness;
　　let your right hand teach you awesome deeds!

[1] Some Hebrew manuscripts (compare Syriac, Targum); most Hebrew manuscripts Disaster! A unique disaster! [2] The meaning of the Hebrew word is uncertain; also verse 10 [3] The meaning of this last Hebrew sentence is uncertain [4] Or abundance; also verses 13, 14 [5] The meaning of this last Hebrew sentence is uncertain [6] Or secret [7] Probably refers to an instrument of captivity [8] By revocalization (compare Septuagint); Hebrew and those who sanctify them [9] Or instruction [10] Probably a musical or liturgical term

5   Your arrows are sharp
      in the heart of the king's enemies;
      the peoples fall under you.

6   Your throne, O God, is forever and ever.
      The scepter of your kingdom is a
        scepter of uprightness;
7   you have loved righteousness and
      hated wickedness.
      Therefore God, your God, has anointed
        you
      with the oil of gladness beyond your
        companions;
8   your robes are all fragrant with myrrh
      and aloes and cassia.
      From ivory palaces stringed instruments
      make you glad;
9   daughters of kings are among your
      ladies of honor;
      at your right hand stands the queen in
      gold of Ophir.

10   Hear, O daughter, and consider, and
      incline your ear:
      forget your people and your father's
      house,

11   and the king will desire your beauty.
      Since he is your lord, bow to him.
12   The people[1] of Tyre will seek your
        favor with gifts,
      the richest of the people.[2]

13   All glorious is the princess in her
        chamber, with robes interwoven
        with gold.
14   In many-colored robes she is led to the
        king,
      with her virgin companions following
        behind her.
15   With joy and gladness they are led
        along
      as they enter the palace of the king.

16   In place of your fathers shall be your
        sons;
      you will make them princes in all the
        earth.
17   I will cause your name to be
        remembered in all generations;
      therefore nations will praise you
        forever and ever.

SEPTEMBER 5

1 Samuel 29–30

Now the Philistines had gathered all their forces at Aphek. And the Israelites were encamped by the spring that is in Jezreel. [2]As the lords of the Philistines were passing on by hundreds and by thousands, and David and his men were passing on in the rear with Achish, [3]the commanders of the Philistines said, "What are these Hebrews doing here?" And Achish said to the commanders of the Philistines, "Is this not David, the servant of Saul, king of Israel, who has been with me now for days and years, and since he deserted to me I have found no fault in him to this day." [4]But the commanders of the Philistines were angry with him. And the commanders of the Philistines said to him, "Send the man back, that he may return to the place to which you have assigned him. He shall not go down with us to battle, lest in the battle he become an adversary to us. For how could this fellow reconcile himself to his lord? Would it not be with the heads of the men here? [5]Is not this David, of whom they sing to one another in dances,

'Saul has struck down his thousands,
   and David his ten thousands'?"

[6]Then Achish called David and said to him, "As the LORD lives, you have been honest, and to me it seems right that you should march out and in with me in the campaign. For I have found nothing wrong in you from the day of your coming to me to this day. Nevertheless,

[1] Hebrew *daughter* [2] Or *The daughter of Tyre is here with gifts, the richest of people seek your favor*

the lords do not approve of you. [7] So go back now; and go peaceably, that you may not displease the lords of the Philistines." [8] And David said to Achish, "But what have I done? What have you found in your servant from the day I entered your service until now, that I may not go and fight against the enemies of my lord the king?" [9] And Achish answered David and said, "I know that you are as blameless in my sight as an angel of God. Nevertheless, the commanders of the Philistines have said, 'He shall not go up with us to the battle.' [10] Now then rise early in the morning with the servants of your lord who came with you, and start early in the morning, and depart as soon as you have light." [11] So David set out with his men early in the morning to return to the land of the Philistines. But the Philistines went up to Jezreel.

[30:1] Now when David and his men came to Ziklag on the third day, the Amalekites had made a raid against the Negeb and against Ziklag. They had overcome Ziklag and burned it with fire [2] and taken captive the women and all[1] who were in it, both small and great. They killed no one, but carried them off and went their way. [3] And when David and his men came to the city, they found it burned with fire, and their wives and sons and daughters taken captive. [4] Then David and the people who were with him raised their voices and wept until they had no more strength to weep. [5] David's two wives also had been taken captive, Ahinoam of Jezreel and Abigail the widow of Nabal of Carmel. [6] And David was greatly distressed, for the people spoke of stoning him, because all the people were bitter in soul,[2] each for his sons and daughters. But David strengthened himself in the LORD his God.

[7] And David said to Abiathar the priest, the son of Ahimelech, "Bring me the ephod." So Abiathar brought the ephod to David. [8] And David inquired of the LORD, "Shall I pursue after this band? Shall I overtake them?" He answered him, "Pursue, for you shall surely overtake and shall surely rescue." [9] So David set out, and the six hundred men who were with him, and they came to the brook Besor, where those who were left behind stayed. [10] But David pursued, he and four hundred men. Two hundred stayed behind, who were too exhausted to cross the brook Besor.

[11] They found an Egyptian in the open country and brought him to David. And they gave him bread and he ate. They gave him water to drink, [12] and they gave him a piece of a cake of figs and two clusters of raisins. And when he had eaten, his spirit revived, for he had not eaten bread or drunk water for three days and three nights. [13] And David said to him, "To whom do you belong? And where are you from?" He said, "I am a young man of Egypt, servant to an Amalekite, and my master left me behind because I fell sick three days ago. [14] We had made a raid against the Negeb of the Cherethites and against that which belongs to Judah and against the Negeb of Caleb, and we burned Ziklag with fire." [15] And David said to him, "Will you take me down to this band?" And he said, "Swear to me by God that you will not kill me or deliver me into the hands of my master, and I will take you down to this band."

[16] And when he had taken him down, behold, they were spread abroad over all the land, eating and drinking and dancing, because of all the great spoil they had taken from the land of the Philistines and from the land of Judah. [17] And David struck them down from twilight until the evening of the next day, and not a man of them escaped, except four hundred young men, who mounted camels and fled. [18] David recovered all that the Amalekites had taken, and David rescued his two wives. [19] Nothing was missing, whether small or great, sons or daughters, spoil or anything that had been taken. David brought back all. [20] David also captured all the flocks and herds, and the people drove the livestock before him,[3] and said, "This is David's spoil."

[21] Then David came to the two hundred men who had been too exhausted to follow David, and who had been left at the brook Besor. And they went out to meet David and to meet the people who were with him. And when David came near to the people he greeted them. [22] Then all the wicked and worthless fellows among the men who had gone with David said, "Because they did not go with us, we will not give them any of the spoil that we have recovered, except that each man may lead away his wife and children, and depart." [23] But David said, "You shall not do so, my brothers, with what the LORD has given us. He has preserved us and given into our hand the band that came against us. [24] Who would listen to you in this

[1] Septuagint; Hebrew lacks *and all* [2] Compare 22:2 [3] The meaning of the Hebrew clause is uncertain

matter? For as his share is who goes down into the battle, so shall his share be who stays by the baggage. They shall share alike." ²⁵And he made it a statute and a rule for Israel from that day forward to this day.

²⁶When David came to Ziklag, he sent part of the spoil to his friends, the elders of Judah, saying, "Here is a present for you from the spoil of the enemies of the LORD." ²⁷It was for those in Bethel, in Ramoth of the Negeb, in Jattir, ²⁸in Aroer, in Siphmoth, in Eshtemoa, ²⁹in Racal, in the cities of the Jerahmeelites, in the cities of the Kenites, ³⁰in Hormah, in Bor-ashan, in Athach, ³¹in Hebron, for all the places where David and his men had roamed.

----- *1 Corinthians 10* -----

For I do not want you to be unaware, brothers,¹ that our fathers were all under the cloud, and all passed through the sea, ²and all were baptized into Moses in the cloud and in the sea, ³and all ate the same spiritual food, ⁴and all drank the same spiritual drink. For they drank from the spiritual Rock that followed them, and the Rock was Christ. ⁵Nevertheless, with most of them God was not pleased, for they were overthrown² in the wilderness.

⁶Now these things took place as examples for us, that we might not desire evil as they did. ⁷Do not be idolaters as some of them were; as it is written, "The people sat down to eat and drink and rose up to play." ⁸We must not indulge in sexual immorality as some of them did, and twenty-three thousand fell in a single day. ⁹We must not put Christ³ to the test, as some of them did and were destroyed by serpents, ¹⁰nor grumble, as some of them did and were destroyed by the Destroyer. ¹¹Now these things happened to them as an example, but they were written down for our instruction, on whom the end of the ages has come. ¹²Therefore let anyone who thinks that he stands take heed lest he fall. ¹³No temptation has overtaken you that is not common to man. God is faithful, and he will not let you be tempted beyond your ability, but with the temptation he will also provide the way of escape, that you may be able to endure it.

¹⁴Therefore, my beloved, flee from idolatry. ¹⁵I speak as to sensible people; judge for yourselves what I say. ¹⁶The cup of blessing that we bless, is it not a participation in the blood of Christ? The bread that we break, is it not a participation in the body of Christ? ¹⁷Because there is one bread, we who are many are one body, for we all partake of the one bread. ¹⁸Consider the people of Israel:⁴ are not those who eat the sacrifices participants in the altar? ¹⁹What do I imply then? That food offered to idols is anything, or that an idol is anything? ²⁰No, I imply that what pagans sacrifice they offer to demons and not to God. I do not want you to be participants with demons. ²¹You cannot drink the cup of the Lord and the cup of demons. You cannot partake of the table of the Lord and the table of demons. ²²Shall we provoke the Lord to jealousy? Are we stronger than he?

²³"All things are lawful," but not all things are helpful. "All things are lawful," but not all things build up. ²⁴Let no one seek his own good, but the good of his neighbor. ²⁵Eat whatever is sold in the meat market without raising any question on the ground of conscience. ²⁶For "the earth is the Lord's, and the fullness thereof." ²⁷If one of the unbelievers invites you to dinner and you are disposed to go, eat whatever is set before you without raising any question on the ground of conscience. ²⁸But if someone says to you, "This has been offered in sacrifice," then do not eat it, for the sake of the one who informed you, and for the sake of conscience— ²⁹I do not mean your conscience, but his. For why should my liberty be determined by someone else's conscience? ³⁰If I partake with thankfulness, why am I denounced because of that for which I give thanks?

³¹So, whether you eat or drink, or whatever you do, do all to the glory of God. ³²Give no offense to Jews or to Greeks or to the church of God, ³³just as I try to please everyone in everything I do, not seeking my own advantage, but that of many, that they may be saved.

----- *Ezekiel 8* -----

In the sixth year, in the sixth month, on the fifth day of the month, as I sat in my house, with the elders of Judah sitting before me, the hand of the Lord GOD fell upon me there. ²Then I looked, and behold, a form that had the appearance of a man.⁵ Below what appeared to

---

¹ Or *brothers and sisters* ² Or *were laid low* ³ Some manuscripts *the Lord* ⁴ Greek *Consider Israel according to the flesh* ⁵ By revocalization (compare Septuagint); Hebrew *of fire*

be his waist was fire, and above his waist was something like the appearance of brightness, like gleaming metal.[1] [3]He put out the form of a hand and took me by a lock of my head, and the Spirit lifted me up between earth and heaven and brought me in visions of God to Jerusalem, to the entrance of the gateway of the inner court that faces north, where was the seat of the image of jealousy, which provokes to jealousy. [4]And behold, the glory of the God of Israel was there, like the vision that I saw in the valley.

[5]Then he said to me, "Son of man, lift up your eyes now toward the north." So I lifted up my eyes toward the north, and behold, north of the altar gate, in the entrance, was this image of jealousy. [6]And he said to me, "Son of man, do you see what they are doing, the great abominations that the house of Israel are committing here, to drive me far from my sanctuary? But you will see still greater abominations."

[7]And he brought me to the entrance of the court, and when I looked, behold, there was a hole in the wall. [8]Then he said to me, "Son of man, dig in the wall." So I dug in the wall, and behold, there was an entrance. [9]And he said to me, "Go in, and see the vile abominations that they are committing here." [10]So I went in and saw. And there, engraved on the wall all around, was every form of creeping things and loathsome beasts, and all the idols of the house of Israel. [11]And before them stood seventy men of the elders of the house of Israel, with Jaazaniah the son of Shaphan standing among them. Each had his censer in his hand, and the smoke of the cloud of incense went up. [12]Then he said to me, "Son of man, have you seen what the elders of the house of Israel are doing in the dark, each in his room of pictures? For they say, 'The LORD does not see us, the LORD has forsaken the land.'" [13]He said also to me, "You will see still greater abominations that they commit."

[14]Then he brought me to the entrance of the north gate of the house of the LORD, and behold, there sat women weeping for Tammuz. [15]Then he said to me, "Have you seen this, O son of man? You will see still greater abominations than these."

[16]And he brought me into the inner court of the house of the LORD. And behold, at the entrance of the temple of the LORD, between the porch and the altar, were about twenty-five men, with their backs to the temple of the LORD, and their faces toward the east, worshiping the sun toward the east. [17]Then he said to me, "Have you seen this, O son of man? Is it too light a thing for the house of Judah to commit the abominations that they commit here, that they should fill the land with violence and provoke me still further to anger? Behold, they put the branch to their[2] nose. [18]Therefore I will act in wrath. My eye will not spare, nor will I have pity. And though they cry in my ears with a loud voice, I will not hear them."

Psalm 46–47

To the choirmaster. Of the Sons of Korah. According to Alamoth.[3] A Song.

God is our refuge and strength,
    a very present[4] help in trouble.
[2] Therefore we will not fear though the
      earth gives way,
   though the mountains be moved into
      the heart of the sea,
[3] though its waters roar and foam,
   though the mountains tremble at its
      swelling.   *Selah*

[4] There is a river whose streams make
      glad the city of God,
   the holy habitation of the Most High.
[5] God is in the midst of her; she shall not
      be moved;
   God will help her when morning
      dawns.
[6] The nations rage, the kingdoms totter;
   he utters his voice, the earth melts.
[7] The LORD of hosts is with us;
   the God of Jacob is our fortress.   *Selah*

[8] Come, behold the works of the LORD,
   how he has brought desolations on
      the earth.
[9] He makes wars cease to the end of the
      earth;
   he breaks the bow and shatters the
      spear;
   he burns the chariots with fire.
[10] "Be still, and know that I am God.
   I will be exalted among the nations,
   I will be exalted in the earth!"
[11] The LORD of hosts is with us;
   the God of Jacob is our fortress.   *Selah*

[1] Or *amber* [2] Or *my* [3] Probably a musical or liturgical term [4] Or *well proved*

To the choirmaster. A Psalm of the Sons
of Korah.

C lap your hands, all peoples!
   Shout to God with loud songs of joy!
2   For the Lord, the Most High, is to be
      feared,
      a great king over all the earth.
3   He subdued peoples under us,
      and nations under our feet.
4   He chose our heritage for us,
      the pride of Jacob whom he loves.
                              Selah

5   God has gone up with a shout,
      the Lord with the sound of a trumpet.
6   Sing praises to God, sing praises!
      Sing praises to our King, sing praises!
7   For God is the King of all the earth;
      sing praises with a psalm![1]
8   God reigns over the nations;
      God sits on his holy throne.
9   The princes of the peoples gather
      as the people of the God of Abraham.
      For the shields of the earth belong to God;
      he is highly exalted!

SEPTEMBER 6

1 Samuel 31

Now the Philistines were fighting against Israel, and the men of Israel fled before the Philistines and fell slain on Mount Gilboa. ²And the Philistines overtook Saul and his sons, and the Philistines struck down Jonathan and Abinadab and Malchi-shua, the sons of Saul. ³The battle pressed hard against Saul, and the archers found him, and he was badly wounded by the archers. ⁴Then Saul said to his armor-bearer, "Draw your sword, and thrust me through with it, lest these uncircumcised come and thrust me through, and mistreat me." But his armor-bearer would not, for he feared greatly. Therefore Saul took his own sword and fell upon it. ⁵And when his armor-bearer saw that Saul was dead, he also fell upon his sword and died with him. ⁶Thus Saul died, and his three sons, and his armor-bearer, and all his men, on the same day together. ⁷And when the men of Israel who were on the other side of the valley and those beyond the Jordan saw that the men of Israel had fled and that Saul and his sons were dead, they abandoned their cities and fled. And the Philistines came and lived in them.

⁸The next day, when the Philistines came to strip the slain, they found Saul and his three sons fallen on Mount Gilboa. ⁹So they cut off his head and stripped off his armor and sent messengers throughout the land of the Philistines, to carry the good news to the house of their idols and to the people. ¹⁰They put his armor in the temple of Ashtaroth, and they fastened his body to the wall of Beth-shan. ¹¹But when the inhabitants of Jabesh-gilead heard what the Philistines had done to Saul, ¹²all the valiant men arose and went all night and took the body of Saul and the bodies of his sons from the wall of Beth-shan, and they came to Jabesh and burned them there. ¹³And they took their bones and buried them under the tamarisk tree in Jabesh and fasted seven days.

1 Corinthians 11

Be imitators of me, as I am of Christ. ²Now I commend you because you remember me in everything and maintain the traditions even as I delivered them to you. ³But I want you to understand that the head of every man is Christ, the head of a wife[2] is her husband, and the head of Christ is God. ⁴Every man who prays or prophesies with his head covered dishonors his head, ⁵but every wife[3] who prays or prophesies with her head uncovered dishonors her head, since it is the same as if her head were shaven. ⁶For if a wife will not cover her head, then she should cut her hair short. But

---

[1] Hebrew *maskil* [2] Greek *gunē*. This term may refer to a *woman* or a *wife*, depending on the context [3] In verses 5–13, the Greek word *gunē* is translated *wife* in verses that deal with wearing a veil, a sign of being married in first-century culture

since it is disgraceful for a wife to cut off her hair or shave her head, let her cover her head. [7] For a man ought not to cover his head, since he is the image and glory of God, but woman is the glory of man. [8] For man was not made from woman, but woman from man. [9] Neither was man created for woman, but woman for man. [10] That is why a wife ought to have a symbol of authority on her head, because of the angels.[1] [11] Nevertheless, in the Lord woman is not independent of man nor man of woman; [12] for as woman was made from man, so man is now born of woman. And all things are from God. [13] Judge for yourselves: is it proper for a wife to pray to God with her head uncovered? [14] Does not nature itself teach you that if a man wears long hair it is a disgrace for him, [15] but if a woman has long hair, it is her glory? For her hair is given to her for a covering. [16] If anyone is inclined to be contentious, we have no such practice, nor do the churches of God.

[17] But in the following instructions I do not commend you, because when you come together it is not for the better but for the worse. [18] For, in the first place, when you come together as a church, I hear that there are divisions among you. And I believe it in part,[2] [19] for there must be factions among you in order that those who are genuine among you may be recognized. [20] When you come together, it is not the Lord's supper that you eat. [21] For in eating, each one goes ahead with his own meal. One goes hungry, another gets drunk. [22] What! Do you not have houses to eat and drink in? Or do you despise the church of God and humiliate those who have nothing? What shall I say to you? Shall I commend you in this? No, I will not.

[23] For I received from the Lord what I also delivered to you, that the Lord Jesus on the night when he was betrayed took bread, [24] and when he had given thanks, he broke it, and said, "This is my body which is for[3] you. Do this in remembrance of me."[4] [25] In the same way also he took the cup, after supper, saying, "This cup is the new covenant in my blood. Do this, as often as you drink it, in remembrance of me." [26] For as often as you eat this bread and drink the cup, you proclaim the Lord's death until he comes.

[27] Whoever, therefore, eats the bread or drinks the cup of the Lord in an unworthy manner will be guilty concerning the body and blood of the Lord. [28] Let a person examine himself, then, and so eat of the bread and drink of the cup. [29] For anyone who eats and drinks without discerning the body eats and drinks judgment on himself. [30] That is why many of you are weak and ill, and some have died.[5] [31] But if we judged[6] ourselves truly, we would not be judged. [32] But when we are judged by the Lord, we are disciplined[7] so that we may not be condemned along with the world.

[33] So then, my brothers,[8] when you come together to eat, wait for[9] one another— [34] if anyone is hungry, let him eat at home—so that when you come together it will not be for judgment. About the other things I will give directions when I come.

--- *Ezekiel 9* ---

Then he cried in my ears with a loud voice, saying, "Bring near the executioners of the city, each with his destroying weapon in his hand." [2] And behold, six men came from the direction of the upper gate, which faces north, each with his weapon for slaughter in his hand, and with them was a man clothed in linen, with a writing case at his waist. And they went in and stood beside the bronze altar.

[3] Now the glory of the God of Israel had gone up from the cherub on which it rested to the threshold of the house. And he called to the man clothed in linen, who had the writing case at his waist. [4] And the Lord said to him, "Pass through the city, through Jerusalem, and put a mark on the foreheads of the men who sigh and groan over all the abominations that are committed in it." [5] And to the others he said in my hearing, "Pass through the city after him, and strike. Your eye shall not spare, and you shall show no pity. [6] Kill old men outright, young men and maidens, little children and women, but touch no one on whom is the mark. And begin at my sanctuary." So they began with the elders who were before the house. [7] Then he said to them, "Defile the house, and fill the courts with the slain. Go out." So they went out and struck in the city. [8] And while they were striking, and I was left alone, I fell upon my face, and cried, "Ah, Lord God! Will you destroy all the remnant of Israel in the outpouring of your wrath on Jerusalem?"

[9] Then he said to me, "The guilt of the house

[1] Or *messengers*, that is, people sent to observe and report [2] Or *I believe a certain report* [3] Some manuscripts *broken for* [4] Or *as my memorial*; also verse 25 [5] Greek *have fallen asleep* (as in 15:6, 20) [6] Or *discerned* [7] Or *when we are judged we are being disciplined by the Lord* [8] Or *brothers and sisters* [9] Or *share with*

of Israel and Judah is exceedingly great. The land is full of blood, and the city full of injustice. For they say, 'The Lord has forsaken the land, and the Lord does not see.' ¹⁰As for me, my eye will not spare, nor will I have pity; I will bring their deeds upon their heads."

¹¹And behold, the man clothed in linen, with the writing case at his waist, brought back word, saying, "I have done as you commanded me."

Psalm 48

A Song. A Psalm of the Sons of Korah.

Great is the Lord and greatly to be praised
    in the city of our God!
  His holy mountain, ²beautiful in
      elevation,
    is the joy of all the earth,
  Mount Zion, in the far north,
    the city of the great King.
³ Within her citadels God
    has made himself known as a fortress.

⁴ For behold, the kings assembled;
    they came on together.
⁵ As soon as they saw it, they were
      astounded;
  they were in panic; they took to flight.

⁶ Trembling took hold of them there,
    anguish as of a woman in labor.
⁷ By the east wind you shattered
    the ships of Tarshish.
⁸ As we have heard, so have we seen
    in the city of the Lord of hosts,
  in the city of our God,
    which God will establish forever.
                                    Selah

⁹ We have thought on your steadfast love,
      O God,
    in the midst of your temple.
¹⁰ As your name, O God,
    so your praise reaches to the ends of
      the earth.
  Your right hand is filled with
      righteousness.
¹¹   Let Mount Zion be glad!
  Let the daughters of Judah rejoice
    because of your judgments!

¹² Walk about Zion, go around her,
      number her towers,
¹³   consider well her ramparts,
    go through her citadels,
  that you may tell the next generation
¹⁴   that this is God,
  our God forever and ever.
  He will guide us forever.[1]

SEPTEMBER 7

---
2 Samuel 1

After the death of Saul, when David had returned from striking down the Amalekites, David remained two days in Ziklag. ²And on the third day, behold, a man came from Saul's camp, with his clothes torn and dirt on his head. And when he came to David, he fell to the ground and paid homage. ³David said to him, "Where do you come from?" And he said to him, "I have escaped from the camp of Israel." ⁴And David said to him, "How did it go? Tell me." And he answered, "The people fled from the battle, and also many of the people have fallen and are dead, and Saul and his son Jonathan are also dead." ⁵Then David said to the young man who told him, "How do you know that Saul and his son Jonathan are dead?" ⁶And the young man who told him said, "By chance I happened to be on Mount Gilboa, and there was Saul leaning on his spear, and behold, the chariots and the horsemen were close upon him. ⁷And when he looked behind him, he saw me, and called to me. And I answered, 'Here I am.' ⁸And he said to me, 'Who are you?' I answered him, 'I am an Amalekite.' ⁹And he

[1] Septuagint; another reading is (compare Jerome, Syriac) He will guide us beyond death

said to me, 'Stand beside me and kill me, for anguish has seized me, and yet my life still lingers.' ¹⁰ So I stood beside him and killed him, because I was sure that he could not live after he had fallen. And I took the crown that was on his head and the armlet that was on his arm, and I have brought them here to my lord."

¹¹ Then David took hold of his clothes and tore them, and so did all the men who were with him. ¹² And they mourned and wept and fasted until evening for Saul and for Jonathan his son and for the people of the LORD and for the house of Israel, because they had fallen by the sword. ¹³ And David said to the young man who told him, "Where do you come from?" And he answered, "I am the son of a sojourner, an Amalekite." ¹⁴ David said to him, "How is it you were not afraid to put out your hand to destroy the LORD's anointed?" ¹⁵ Then David called one of the young men and said, "Go, execute him." And he struck him down so that he died. ¹⁶ And David said to him, "Your blood be on your head, for your own mouth has testified against you, saying, 'I have killed the LORD's anointed.'"

¹⁷ And David lamented with this lamentation over Saul and Jonathan his son, ¹⁸ and he said it[1] should be taught to the people of Judah; behold, it is written in the Book of Jashar.[2] He said:

¹⁹　　"Your glory, O Israel, is slain on your high
　　　　places!
　　　How the mighty have fallen!
²⁰　　Tell it not in Gath,
　　　　publish it not in the streets of
　　　　　Ashkelon,
　　　lest the daughters of the Philistines
　　　　rejoice,
　　　lest the daughters of the
　　　　uncircumcised exult.

²¹　　"You mountains of Gilboa,
　　　　let there be no dew or rain upon you,
　　　　nor fields of offerings![3]
　　　For there the shield of the mighty was
　　　　defiled,
　　　　the shield of Saul, not anointed with
　　　　　oil.

²²　　"From the blood of the slain,
　　　　from the fat of the mighty,
　　　the bow of Jonathan turned not back,
　　　　and the sword of Saul returned not
　　　　　empty.

²³　　"Saul and Jonathan, beloved and lovely!
　　　　In life and in death they were not
　　　　　divided;
　　　they were swifter than eagles;
　　　　they were stronger than lions.

²⁴　　"You daughters of Israel, weep over Saul,
　　　　who clothed you luxuriously in
　　　　　scarlet,
　　　who put ornaments of gold on your
　　　　apparel.

²⁵　　"How the mighty have fallen
　　　　in the midst of the battle!

　　　"Jonathan lies slain on your high places.
²⁶　　I am distressed for you, my brother
　　　　Jonathan;
　　　very pleasant have you been to me;
　　　　your love to me was extraordinary,
　　　　surpassing the love of women.

²⁷　　"How the mighty have fallen,
　　　　and the weapons of war perished!"

1 Corinthians 12

Now concerning[4] spiritual gifts,[5] brothers,[6] I do not want you to be uninformed. ² You know that when you were pagans you were led astray to mute idols, however you were led. ³ Therefore I want you to understand that no one speaking in the Spirit of God ever says "Jesus is accursed!" and no one can say "Jesus is Lord" except in the Holy Spirit.

⁴ Now there are varieties of gifts, but the same Spirit; ⁵ and there are varieties of service, but the same Lord; ⁶ and there are varieties of activities, but it is the same God who empowers them all in everyone. ⁷ To each is given the manifestation of the Spirit for the common good. ⁸ For to one is given through the Spirit the utterance of wisdom, and to another the utterance of knowledge according to the same Spirit, ⁹ to another faith by the same Spirit, to another gifts of healing by the one Spirit, ¹⁰ to another the working of miracles, to another prophecy, to another the ability to distinguish between spirits, to another various kinds of tongues, to another the interpretation of tongues. ¹¹ All these are empowered by one and the same Spirit, who apportions to each one individually as he wills.

[1] Septuagint; Hebrew *the Bow*, which may be the name of the lament's tune　[2] Or *of the upright*　[3] Septuagint *firstfruits*　[4] The expression *Now concerning* introduces a reply to a question in the Corinthians' letter; see 7:1　[5] Or *spiritual persons*　[6] Or *brothers and sisters*

[12] For just as the body is one and has many members, and all the members of the body, though many, are one body, so it is with Christ. [13] For in one Spirit we were all baptized into one body—Jews or Greeks, slaves[1] or free—and all were made to drink of one Spirit.

[14] For the body does not consist of one member but of many. [15] If the foot should say, "Because I am not a hand, I do not belong to the body," that would not make it any less a part of the body. [16] And if the ear should say, "Because I am not an eye, I do not belong to the body," that would not make it any less a part of the body. [17] If the whole body were an eye, where would be the sense of hearing? If the whole body were an ear, where would be the sense of smell? [18] But as it is, God arranged the members in the body, each one of them, as he chose. [19] If all were a single member, where would the body be? [20] As it is, there are many parts,[2] yet one body.

[21] The eye cannot say to the hand, "I have no need of you," nor again the head to the feet, "I have no need of you." [22] On the contrary, the parts of the body that seem to be weaker are indispensable, [23] and on those parts of the body that we think less honorable we bestow the greater honor, and our unpresentable parts are treated with greater modesty, [24] which our more presentable parts do not require. But God has so composed the body, giving greater honor to the part that lacked it, [25] that there may be no division in the body, but that the members may have the same care for one another. [26] If one member suffers, all suffer together; if one member is honored, all rejoice together.

[27] Now you are the body of Christ and individually members of it. [28] And God has appointed in the church first apostles, second prophets, third teachers, then miracles, then gifts of healing, helping, administrating, and various kinds of tongues. [29] Are all apostles? Are all prophets? Are all teachers? Do all work miracles? [30] Do all possess gifts of healing? Do all speak with tongues? Do all interpret? [31] But earnestly desire the higher gifts.

And I will show you a still more excellent way.

Ezekiel 10

Then I looked, and behold, on the expanse that was over the heads of the cherubim there appeared above them something like a sapphire,[3] in appearance like a throne. [2] And he said to the man clothed in linen, "Go in among the whirling wheels underneath the cherubim. Fill your hands with burning coals from between the cherubim, and scatter them over the city."

And he went in before my eyes. [3] Now the cherubim were standing on the south side of the house, when the man went in, and a cloud filled the inner court. [4] And the glory of the LORD went up from the cherub to the threshold of the house, and the house was filled with the cloud, and the court was filled with the brightness of the glory of the LORD. [5] And the sound of the wings of the cherubim was heard as far as the outer court, like the voice of God Almighty when he speaks.

[6] And when he commanded the man clothed in linen, "Take fire from between the whirling wheels, from between the cherubim," he went in and stood beside a wheel. [7] And a cherub stretched out his hand from between the cherubim to the fire that was between the cherubim, and took some of it and put it into the hands of the man clothed in linen, who took it and went out. [8] The cherubim appeared to have the form of a human hand under their wings.

[9] And I looked, and behold, there were four wheels beside the cherubim, one beside each cherub, and the appearance of the wheels was like sparkling beryl. [10] And as for their appearance, the four had the same likeness, as if a wheel were within a wheel. [11] When they went, they went in any of their four directions[4] without turning as they went, but in whatever direction the front wheel[5] faced, the others followed without turning as they went. [12] And their whole body, their rims, and their spokes, their wings,[6] and the wheels were full of eyes all around—the wheels that the four of them had. [13] As for the wheels, they were called in my hearing "the whirling wheels." [14] And every one had four faces: the first face was the face of the cherub, and the second face was a human face, and the third the face of a lion, and the fourth the face of an eagle.

[15] And the cherubim mounted up. These were the living creatures that I saw by the Chebar canal. [16] And when the cherubim went, the wheels went beside them. And when the cherubim lifted up their wings to mount up from the earth, the wheels did not turn from beside

[1] Or servants; Greek bondservants [2] Or members; also verse 22 [3] Or lapis lazuli [4] Hebrew to their four sides [5] Hebrew the head [6] Or their whole body, their backs, their hands, and their wings

them. [17]When they stood still, these stood still, and when they mounted up, these mounted up with them, for the spirit of the living creatures[1] was in them.

[18]Then the glory of the LORD went out from the threshold of the house, and stood over the cherubim. [19]And the cherubim lifted up their wings and mounted up from the earth before my eyes as they went out, with the wheels beside them. And they stood at the entrance of the east gate of the house of the LORD, and the glory of the God of Israel was over them.

[20]These were the living creatures that I saw underneath the God of Israel by the Chebar canal; and I knew that they were cherubim. [21]Each had four faces, and each four wings, and underneath their wings the likeness of human hands. [22]And as for the likeness of their faces, they were the same faces whose appearance I had seen by the Chebar canal. Each one of them went straight forward.

Psalm 49

To the choirmaster. A Psalm of the Sons of Korah.

Hear this, all peoples!
Give ear, all inhabitants of the world,
[2] both low and high,
rich and poor together!
[3] My mouth shall speak wisdom;
the meditation of my heart shall be understanding.
[4] I will incline my ear to a proverb;
I will solve my riddle to the music of the lyre.

[5] Why should I fear in times of trouble,
when the iniquity of those who cheat me surrounds me,
[6] those who trust in their wealth
and boast of the abundance of their riches?
[7] Truly no man can ransom another,
or give to God the price of his life,

[8] for the ransom of their life is costly
and can never suffice,
[9] that he should live on forever
and never see the pit.

[10] For he sees that even the wise die;
the fool and the stupid alike must perish
and leave their wealth to others.
[11] Their graves are their homes forever,[2]
their dwelling places to all generations,
though they called lands by their own names.
[12] Man in his pomp will not remain;
he is like the beasts that perish.

[13] This is the path of those who have foolish confidence;
yet after them people approve of their boasts.[3] *Selah*
[14] Like sheep they are appointed for Sheol;
death shall be their shepherd,
and the upright shall rule over them in the morning.
Their form shall be consumed in Sheol, with no place to dwell.
[15] But God will ransom my soul from the power of Sheol,
for he will receive me. *Selah*

[16] Be not afraid when a man becomes rich,
when the glory of his house increases.
[17] For when he dies he will carry nothing away;
his glory will not go down after him.
[18] For though, while he lives, he counts himself blessed
—and though you get praise when you do well for yourself—
[19] his soul will go to the generation of his fathers,
who will never again see light.
[20] Man in his pomp yet without understanding is like the beasts that perish.

[1] Or spirit of life [2] Septuagint, Syriac, Targum; Hebrew Their inward thought was that their homes were forever [3] Or and of those after them who approve of their boasts

SEPTEMBER 8

2 Samuel 2

After this David inquired of the LORD, "Shall I go up into any of the cities of Judah?" And the LORD said to him, "Go up." David said, "To which shall I go up?" And he said, "To Hebron." ²So David went up there, and his two wives also, Ahinoam of Jezreel and Abigail the widow of Nabal of Carmel. ³And David brought up his men who were with him, everyone with his household, and they lived in the towns of Hebron. ⁴And the men of Judah came, and there they anointed David king over the house of Judah.

When they told David, "It was the men of Jabesh-gilead who buried Saul," ⁵David sent messengers to the men of Jabesh-gilead and said to them, "May you be blessed by the LORD, because you showed this loyalty to Saul your lord and buried him. ⁶Now may the LORD show steadfast love and faithfulness to you, And I will do good to you because you have done this thing. ⁷Now therefore let your hands be strong, and be valiant, for Saul your lord is dead, and the house of Judah has anointed me king over them."

⁸But Abner the son of Ner, commander of Saul's army, took Ish-bosheth the son of Saul and brought him over to Mahanaim, ⁹and he made him king over Gilead and the Ashurites and Jezreel and Ephraim and Benjamin and all Israel. ¹⁰Ish-bosheth, Saul's son, was forty years old when he began to reign over Israel, and he reigned two years. But the house of Judah followed David. ¹¹And the time that David was king in Hebron over the house of Judah was seven years and six months.

¹²Abner the son of Ner, and the servants of Ish-bosheth the son of Saul, went out from Mahanaim to Gibeon. ¹³And Joab the son of Zeruiah and the servants of David went out and met them at the pool of Gibeon. And they sat down, the one on the one side of the pool, and the other on the other side of the pool. ¹⁴And Abner said to Joab, "Let the young men arise and compete before us." And Joab said, "Let them arise." ¹⁵Then they arose and passed over by number, twelve for Benjamin and Ish-bosheth the son of Saul, and twelve of the servants of David. ¹⁶And each caught his opponent by the head and thrust his sword in his opponent's side, so they fell down together. Therefore that place was called Helkath-hazzurim,[1] which is at Gibeon. ¹⁷And the battle was very fierce that day. And Abner and the men of Israel were beaten before the servants of David.

¹⁸And the three sons of Zeruiah were there, Joab, Abishai, and Asahel. Now Asahel was as swift of foot as a wild gazelle. ¹⁹And Asahel pursued Abner, and as he went, he turned neither to the right hand nor to the left from following Abner. ²⁰Then Abner looked behind him and said, "Is it you, Asahel?" And he answered, "It is I." ²¹Abner said to him, "Turn aside to your right hand or to your left, and seize one of the young men and take his spoil." But Asahel would not turn aside from following him. ²²And Abner said again to Asahel, "Turn aside from following me. Why should I strike you to the ground? How then could I lift up my face to your brother Joab?" ²³But he refused to turn aside. Therefore Abner struck him in the stomach with the butt of his spear, so that the spear came out at his back. And he fell there and died where he was. And all who came to the place where Asahel had fallen and died, stood still.

²⁴But Joab and Abishai pursued Abner. And as the sun was going down they came to the hill of Ammah, which lies before Giah on the way to the wilderness of Gibeon. ²⁵And the people of Benjamin gathered themselves together behind Abner and became one group and took their stand on the top of a hill. ²⁶Then Abner called to Joab, "Shall the sword devour forever? Do you not know that the end will be bitter? How long will it be before you tell your people to turn from the pursuit of their brothers?" ²⁷And Joab said,

[1] Helkath-hazzurim means the field of sword-edges

"As God lives, if you had not spoken, surely the men would not have given up the pursuit of their brothers until the morning." [28] So Joab blew the trumpet, and all the men stopped and pursued Israel no more, nor did they fight anymore.

[29] And Abner and his men went all that night through the Arabah. They crossed the Jordan, and marching the whole morning, they came to Mahanaim. [30] Joab returned from the pursuit of Abner. And when he had gathered all the people together, there were missing from David's servants nineteen men besides Asahel. [31] But the servants of David had struck down of Benjamin 360 of Abner's men. [32] And they took up Asahel and buried him in the tomb of his father, which was at Bethlehem. And Joab and his men marched all night, and the day broke upon them at Hebron.

1 Corinthians 13

If I speak in the tongues of men and of angels, but have not love, I am a noisy gong or a clanging cymbal. [2] And if I have prophetic powers, and understand all mysteries and all knowledge, and if I have all faith, so as to remove mountains, but have not love, I am nothing. [3] If I give away all I have, and if I deliver up my body to be burned,[1] but have not love, I gain nothing.

[4] Love is patient and kind; love does not envy or boast; it is not arrogant [5] or rude. It does not insist on its own way; it is not irritable or resentful;[2] [6] it does not rejoice at wrongdoing, but rejoices with the truth. [7] Love bears all things, believes all things, hopes all things, endures all things.

[8] Love never ends. As for prophecies, they will pass away; as for tongues, they will cease; as for knowledge, it will pass away. [9] For we know in part and we prophesy in part, [10] but when the perfect comes, the partial will pass away. [11] When I was a child, I spoke like a child, I thought like a child, I reasoned like a child. When I became a man, I gave up childish ways. [12] For now we see in a mirror dimly, but then face to face. Now I know in part; then I shall know fully, even as I have been fully known.

[13] So now faith, hope, and love abide, these three; but the greatest of these is love.

Ezekiel 11

The Spirit lifted me up and brought me to the east gate of the house of the LORD, which faces east. And behold, at the entrance of the gateway there were twenty-five men. And I saw among them Jaazaniah the son of Azzur, and Pelatiah the son of Benaiah, princes of the people. [2] And he said to me, "Son of man, these are the men who devise iniquity and who give wicked counsel in this city; [3] who say, 'The time is not near[3] to build houses. This city is the cauldron, and we are the meat.' [4] Therefore prophesy against them, prophesy, O son of man."

[5] And the Spirit of the LORD fell upon me, and he said to me, "Say, Thus says the LORD: So you think, O house of Israel. For I know the things that come into your mind. [6] You have multiplied your slain in this city and have filled its streets with the slain. [7] Therefore thus says the Lord GOD: Your slain whom you have laid in the midst of it, they are the meat, and this city is the cauldron, but you shall be brought out of the midst of it. [8] You have feared the sword, and I will bring the sword upon you, declares the Lord GOD. [9] And I will bring you out of the midst of it, and give you into the hands of foreigners, and execute judgments upon you. [10] You shall fall by the sword. I will judge you at the border of Israel, and you shall know that I am the LORD. [11] This city shall not be your cauldron, nor shall you be the meat in the midst of it. I will judge you at the border of Israel, [12] and you shall know that I am the LORD. For you have not walked in my statutes, nor obeyed my rules, but have acted according to the rules of the nations that are around you."

[13] And it came to pass, while I was prophesying, that Pelatiah the son of Benaiah died. Then I fell down on my face and cried out with a loud voice and said, "Ah, Lord GOD! Will you make a full end of the remnant of Israel?"

[14] And the word of the LORD came to me: [15] "Son of man, your brothers, even your brothers, your kinsmen,[4] the whole house of Israel, all of them, are those of whom the inhabitants of Jerusalem have said, 'Go far from the LORD; to us this land is given for a possession.' [16] Therefore say, 'Thus says the Lord GOD: Though I removed them far off among the nations, and though I scattered them among the countries, yet I have been a sanctuary to

[1] Some manuscripts deliver up my body [to death] that I may boast [2] Greek irritable and does not count up wrongdoing [3] Or Is not the time near...? [4] Hebrew the men of your redemption

them for a while[1] in the countries where they have gone.' [17]Therefore say, 'Thus says the Lord GOD: I will gather you from the peoples and assemble you out of the countries where you have been scattered, and I will give you the land of Israel.' [18]And when they come there, they will remove from it all its detestable things and all its abominations. [19]And I will give them one heart, and a new spirit I will put within them. I will remove the heart of stone from their flesh and give them a heart of flesh, [20]that they may walk in my statutes and keep my rules and obey them. And they shall be my people, and I will be their God. [21]But as for those whose heart goes after their detestable things and their abominations, I will[2] bring their deeds upon their own heads, declares the Lord GOD."

[22]Then the cherubim lifted up their wings, with the wheels beside them, and the glory of the God of Israel was over them. [23]And the glory of the LORD went up from the midst of the city and stood on the mountain that is on the east side of the city. [24]And the Spirit lifted me up and brought me in the vision by the Spirit of God into Chaldea, to the exiles. Then the vision that I had seen went up from me. [25]And I told the exiles all the things that the LORD had shown me.

Psalm 50

A PSALM OF ASAPH.

The Mighty One, God the LORD,
  speaks and summons the earth
    from the rising of the sun to its
      setting.
[2] Out of Zion, the perfection of beauty,
    God shines forth.

[3] Our God comes; he does not keep
      silence;[3]
    before him is a devouring fire,
    around him a mighty tempest.
[4] He calls to the heavens above
    and to the earth, that he may judge his
      people:
[5] "Gather to me my faithful ones,
    who made a covenant with me by
      sacrifice!"
[6] The heavens declare his righteousness,
    for God himself is judge!   *Selah*

[7] "Hear, O my people, and I will speak;
    O Israel, I will testify against you.
    I am God, your God.
[8] Not for your sacrifices do I rebuke you;
    your burnt offerings are continually
      before me.
[9] I will not accept a bull from your house
    or goats from your folds.
[10] For every beast of the forest is mine,
    the cattle on a thousand hills.
[11] I know all the birds of the hills,
    and all that moves in the field is mine.

[12] "If I were hungry, I would not tell you,
    for the world and its fullness are mine.
[13] Do I eat the flesh of bulls
    or drink the blood of goats?
[14] Offer to God a sacrifice of thanksgiving,[4]
    and perform your vows to the Most
      High,
[15] and call upon me in the day of trouble;
    I will deliver you, and you shall glorify
      me."

[16] But to the wicked God says:
    "What right have you to recite my
      statutes
    or take my covenant on your lips?
[17] For you hate discipline,
    and you cast my words behind you.
[18] If you see a thief, you are pleased with
      him,
    and you keep company with
      adulterers.

[19] "You give your mouth free rein for evil,
    and your tongue frames deceit.
[20] You sit and speak against your brother;
    you slander your own mother's son.
[21] These things you have done, and I have
      been silent;
    you thought that I[5] was one like
      yourself.
    But now I rebuke you and lay the charge
      before you.

[22] "Mark this, then, you who forget God,
    lest I tear you apart, and there be none
      to deliver!
[23] The one who offers thanksgiving as his
      sacrifice glorifies me;
    to one who orders his way rightly
    I will show the salvation of God!"

[1] Or *in small measure* [2] Hebrew *To the heart of their detestable things and their abominations their heart goes; I will* [3] Or *May our God come, and not keep silence* [4] Or *Make thanksgiving your sacrifice to God* [5] Or *that the I AM*

SEPTEMBER 9

2 Samuel 3

There was a long war between the house of Saul and the house of David. And David grew stronger and stronger, while the house of Saul became weaker and weaker.

²And sons were born to David at Hebron: his firstborn was Amnon, of Ahinoam of Jezreel; ³and his second, Chileab, of Abigail the widow of Nabal of Carmel; and the third, Absalom the son of Maacah the daughter of Talmai king of Geshur; ⁴and the fourth, Adonijah the son of Haggith; and the fifth, Shephatiah the son of Abital; ⁵and the sixth, Ithream, of Eglah, David's wife. These were born to David in Hebron.

⁶While there was war between the house of Saul and the house of David, Abner was making himself strong in the house of Saul. ⁷Now Saul had a concubine whose name was Rizpah, the daughter of Aiah. And Ish-bosheth said to Abner, "Why have you gone in to my father's concubine?" ⁸Then Abner was very angry over the words of Ish-bosheth and said, "Am I a dog's head of Judah? To this day I keep showing steadfast love to the house of Saul your father, to his brothers, and to his friends, and have not given you into the hand of David. And yet you charge me today with a fault concerning a woman. ⁹God do so to Abner and more also, if I do not accomplish for David what the LORD has sworn to him, ¹⁰to transfer the kingdom from the house of Saul and set up the throne of David over Israel and over Judah, from Dan to Beersheba." ¹¹And Ish-bosheth could not answer Abner another word, because he feared him.

¹²And Abner sent messengers to David on his behalf,¹ saying, "To whom does the land belong? Make your covenant with me, and behold, my hand shall be with you to bring over all Israel to you." ¹³And he said, "Good; I will make a covenant with you. But one thing I require of you; that is, you shall not see my face unless you first bring Michal, Saul's daughter, when you come to see my face." ¹⁴Then David sent messengers to Ish-bosheth, Saul's son, saying, "Give me my wife Michal, for whom I paid the bridal price of a hundred foreskins of the Philistines." ¹⁵And Ish-bosheth sent and took her from her husband Paltiel the son of Laish. ¹⁶But her husband went with her, weeping after her all the way to Bahurim. Then Abner said to him, "Go, return." And he returned.

¹⁷And Abner conferred with the elders of Israel, saying, "For some time past you have been seeking David as king over you. ¹⁸Now then bring it about, for the LORD has promised David, saying, 'By the hand of my servant David I will save my people Israel from the hand of the Philistines, and from the hand of all their enemies.'" ¹⁹Abner also spoke to Benjamin. And then Abner went to tell David at Hebron all that Israel and the whole house of Benjamin thought good to do.

²⁰When Abner came with twenty men to David at Hebron, David made a feast for Abner and the men who were with him. ²¹And Abner said to David, "I will arise and go and will gather all Israel to my lord the king, that they may make a covenant with you, and that you may reign over all that your heart desires." So David sent Abner away, and he went in peace.

²²Just then the servants of David arrived with Joab from a raid, bringing much spoil with them. But Abner was not with David at Hebron, for he had sent him away, and he had gone in peace. ²³When Joab and all the army that was with him came, it was told Joab, "Abner the son of Ner came to the king, and he has let him go, and he has gone in peace." ²⁴Then Joab went to the king and said, "What have you done? Behold, Abner came to you. Why is it that you have sent him away, so that he is gone? ²⁵You know that Abner the son of Ner came to deceive you and to know your going out and your coming in, and to know all that you are doing."

²⁶When Joab came out from David's presence, he sent messengers after Abner, and they brought him back from the cistern of Sirah. But David did not know about it. ²⁷And when

¹ Or *where he was*; Septuagint *at Hebron*

Abner returned to Hebron, Joab took him aside into the midst of the gate to speak with him privately, and there he struck him in the stomach, so that he died, for the blood of Asahel his brother. [28]Afterward, when David heard of it, he said, "I and my kingdom are forever guiltless before the LORD for the blood of Abner the son of Ner. [29]May it fall upon the head of Joab and upon all his father's house, and may the house of Joab never be without one who has a discharge or who is leprous or who holds a spindle or who falls by the sword or who lacks bread!" [30]So Joab and Abishai his brother killed Abner, because he had put their brother Asahel to death in the battle at Gibeon.

[31]Then David said to Joab and to all the people who were with him, "Tear your clothes and put on sackcloth and mourn before Abner." And King David followed the bier. [32]They buried Abner at Hebron. And the king lifted up his voice and wept at the grave of Abner, and all the people wept. [33]And the king lamented for Abner, saying,

> "Should Abner die as a fool dies?
> [34]   Your hands were not bound;
>   your feet were not fettered;
>   as one falls before the wicked
>   you have fallen."

And all the people wept again over him. [35]Then all the people came to persuade David to eat bread while it was yet day. But David swore, saying, "God do so to me and more also, if I taste bread or anything else till the sun goes down!" [36]And all the people took notice of it, and it pleased them, as everything that the king did pleased all the people. [37]So all the people and all Israel understood that day that it had not been the king's will to put to death Abner the son of Ner. [38]And the king said to his servants, "Do you not know that a prince and a great man has fallen this day in Israel? [39]And I was gentle today, though anointed king. These men, the sons of Zeruiah, are more severe than I. The LORD repay the evildoer according to his wickedness!"

--------- *1 Corinthians 14* ---------

P ursue love, and earnestly desire the spiritual gifts, especially that you may prophesy. [2]For one who speaks in a tongue speaks not to men but to God; for no one understands him, but he utters mysteries in the Spirit. [3]On the other hand, the one who prophesies speaks to people for their upbuilding and encouragement and consolation. [4]The one who speaks in a tongue builds up himself, but the one who prophesies builds up the church. [5]Now I want you all to speak in tongues, but even more to prophesy. The one who prophesies is greater than the one who speaks in tongues, unless someone interprets, so that the church may be built up.

[6]Now, brothers,[1] if I come to you speaking in tongues, how will I benefit you unless I bring you some revelation or knowledge or prophecy or teaching? [7]If even lifeless instruments, such as the flute or the harp, do not give distinct notes, how will anyone know what is played? [8]And if the bugle gives an indistinct sound, who will get ready for battle? [9]So with yourselves, if with your tongue you utter speech that is not intelligible, how will anyone know what is said? For you will be speaking into the air. [10]There are doubtless many different languages in the world, and none is without meaning, [11]but if I do not know the meaning of the language, I will be a foreigner to the speaker and the speaker a foreigner to me. [12]So with yourselves, since you are eager for manifestations of the Spirit, strive to excel in building up the church.

[13]Therefore, one who speaks in a tongue should pray that he may interpret. [14]For if I pray in a tongue, my spirit prays but my mind is unfruitful. [15]What am I to do? I will pray with my spirit, but I will pray with my mind also; I will sing praise with my spirit, but I will sing with my mind also. [16]Otherwise, if you give thanks with your spirit, how can anyone in the position of an outsider[2] say "Amen" to your thanksgiving when he does not know what you are saying? [17]For you may be giving thanks well enough, but the other person is not being built up. [18]I thank God that I speak in tongues more than all of you. [19]Nevertheless, in church I would rather speak five words with my mind in order to instruct others, than ten thousand words in a tongue.

[20]Brothers, do not be children in your thinking. Be infants in evil, but in your thinking be mature. [21]In the Law it is written, "By people of strange tongues and by the lips of foreigners will I speak to this people, and even then they will not listen to me, says the Lord." [22]Thus

---

[1] Or *brothers and sisters; also verses 20, 26, 39*   [2] Or *of him that is without gifts*

tongues are a sign not for believers but for unbelievers, while prophecy is a sign[1] not for unbelievers but for believers. ²³If, therefore, the whole church comes together and all speak in tongues, and outsiders or unbelievers enter, will they not say that you are out of your minds? ²⁴But if all prophesy, and an unbeliever or outsider enters, he is convicted by all, he is called to account by all, ²⁵the secrets of his heart are disclosed, and so, falling on his face, he will worship God and declare that God is really among you.

²⁶What then, brothers? When you come together, each one has a hymn, a lesson, a revelation, a tongue, or an interpretation. Let all things be done for building up. ²⁷If any speak in a tongue, let there be only two or at most three, and each in turn, and let someone interpret. ²⁸But if there is no one to interpret, let each of them keep silent in church and speak to himself and to God. ²⁹Let two or three prophets speak, and let the others weigh what is said. ³⁰If a revelation is made to another sitting there, let the first be silent. ³¹For you can all prophesy one by one, so that all may learn and all be encouraged, ³²and the spirits of prophets are subject to prophets. ³³For God is not a God of confusion but of peace.

As in all the churches of the saints, ³⁴the women should keep silent in the churches. For they are not permitted to speak, but should be in submission, as the Law also says. ³⁵If there is anything they desire to learn, let them ask their husbands at home. For it is shameful for a woman to speak in church.

³⁶Or was it from you that the word of God came? Or are you the only ones it has reached? ³⁷If anyone thinks that he is a prophet, or spiritual, he should acknowledge that the things I am writing to you are a command of the Lord. ³⁸If anyone does not recognize this, he is not recognized. ³⁹So, my brothers, earnestly desire to prophesy, and do not forbid speaking in tongues. ⁴⁰But all things should be done decently and in order.

Ezekiel 12

The word of the LORD came to me: ²"Son of man, you dwell in the midst of a rebellious house, who have eyes to see, but see not, who have ears to hear, but hear not, for they are a

rebellious house. ³As for you, son of man, prepare for yourself an exile's baggage, and go into exile by day in their sight. You shall go like an exile from your place to another place in their sight. Perhaps they will understand, though[2] they are a rebellious house. ⁴You shall bring out your baggage by day in their sight, as baggage for exile, and you shall go out yourself at evening in their sight, as those do who must go into exile. ⁵In their sight dig through the wall, and bring your baggage out through it. ⁶In their sight you shall lift the baggage upon your shoulder and carry it out at dusk. You shall cover your face that you may not see the land, for I have made you a sign for the house of Israel."

⁷And I did as I was commanded. I brought out my baggage by day, as baggage for exile, and in the evening I dug through the wall with my own hands. I brought out my baggage at dusk, carrying it on my shoulder in their sight. ⁸In the morning the word of the LORD came to me: ⁹"Son of man, has not the house of Israel, the rebellious house, said to you, 'What are you doing?' ¹⁰Say to them, 'Thus says the Lord GOD: This oracle concerns[3] the prince in Jerusalem and all the house of Israel who are in it.'[4] ¹¹Say, 'I am a sign for you: as I have done, so shall it be done to them. They shall go into exile, into captivity.' ¹²And the prince who is among them shall lift his baggage upon his shoulder at dusk, and shall go out. They shall dig through the wall to bring him out through it. He shall cover his face, that he may not see the land with his eyes. ¹³And I will spread my net over him, and he shall be taken in my snare. And I will bring him to Babylon, the land of the Chaldeans, yet he shall not see it, and he shall die there. ¹⁴And I will scatter toward every wind all who are around him, his helpers and all his troops, and I will unsheathe the sword after them. ¹⁵And they shall know that I am the LORD, when I disperse them among the nations and scatter them among the countries. ¹⁶But I will let a few of them escape from the sword, from famine and pestilence, that they may declare all their abominations among the nations where they go, and may know that I am the LORD."

¹⁷And the word of the LORD came to me: ¹⁸"Son of man, eat your bread with quaking, and drink water with trembling and with anxiety. ¹⁹And say to the people of the land, Thus

[1] Greek lacks a sign   [2] Or will see that   [3] Or This burden is   [4] Hebrew in the midst of them

says the Lord GOD concerning the inhabitants of Jerusalem in the land of Israel: They shall eat their bread with anxiety, and drink water in dismay. In this way her land will be stripped of all it contains, on account of the violence of all those who dwell in it. [20]And the inhabited cities shall be laid waste, and the land shall become a desolation; and you shall know that I am the LORD."

[21]And the word of the LORD came to me: [22]"Son of man, what is this proverb that you[1] have about the land of Israel, saying, 'The days grow long, and every vision comes to nothing'? [23]Tell them therefore, 'Thus says the Lord GOD: I will put an end to this proverb, and they shall no more use it as a proverb in Israel.' But say to them, The days are near, and the fulfillment[2] of every vision. [24]For there shall be no more any false vision or flattering divination within the house of Israel. [25]For I am the LORD; I will speak the word that I will speak, and it will be performed. It will no longer be delayed, but in your days, O rebellious house, I will speak the word and perform it, declares the Lord GOD."

[26]And the word of the LORD came to me: [27]"Son of man, behold, they of the house of Israel say, 'The vision that he sees is for many days from now, and he prophesies of times far off.' [28]Therefore say to them, Thus says the Lord GOD: None of my words will be delayed any longer, but the word that I speak will be performed, declares the Lord GOD."

--------- *Psalm 51* ---------

TO THE CHOIRMASTER. A PSALM OF DAVID, WHEN NATHAN THE PROPHET WENT TO HIM, AFTER HE HAD GONE IN TO BATHSHEBA.

Have mercy on me,[3] O God,
according to your steadfast love;
according to your abundant mercy
blot out my transgressions.
[2] Wash me thoroughly from my iniquity,
and cleanse me from my sin!

[3] For I know my transgressions,
and my sin is ever before me.
[4] Against you, you only, have I sinned
and done what is evil in your sight,

so that you may be justified in your words
and blameless in your judgment.
[5] Behold, I was brought forth in iniquity,
and in sin did my mother conceive me.
[6] Behold, you delight in truth in the inward being,
and you teach me wisdom in the secret heart.

[7] Purge me with hyssop, and I shall be clean;
wash me, and I shall be whiter than snow.
[8] Let me hear joy and gladness;
let the bones that you have broken rejoice.
[9] Hide your face from my sins,
and blot out all my iniquities.
[10] Create in me a clean heart, O God,
and renew a right[4] spirit within me.
[11] Cast me not away from your presence,
and take not your Holy Spirit from me.
[12] Restore to me the joy of your salvation,
and uphold me with a willing spirit.

[13] Then I will teach transgressors your ways,
and sinners will return to you.
[14] Deliver me from bloodguiltiness, O God,
O God of my salvation,
and my tongue will sing aloud of your righteousness.
[15] O Lord, open my lips,
and my mouth will declare your praise.
[16] For you will not delight in sacrifice, or I would give it;
you will not be pleased with a burnt offering.
[17] The sacrifices of God are a broken spirit;
a broken and contrite heart, O God,
you will not despise.

[18] Do good to Zion in your good pleasure;
build up the walls of Jerusalem;
[19] then will you delight in right sacrifices,
in burnt offerings and whole burnt offerings;
then bulls will be offered on your altar.

---

[1] The Hebrew for *you* is plural [2] Hebrew *word* [3] Or *Be gracious to me* [4] Or *steadfast*

SEPTEMBER 10

---
2 Samuel 4–5

When Ish-bosheth, Saul's son, heard that Abner had died at Hebron, his courage failed, and all Israel was dismayed. ²Now Saul's son had two men who were captains of raiding bands; the name of the one was Baanah, and the name of the other Rechab, sons of Rimmon a man of Benjamin from Beeroth (for Beeroth also is counted part of Benjamin; ³the Beerothites fled to Gittaim and have been sojourners there to this day).

⁴Jonathan, the son of Saul, had a son who was crippled in his feet. He was five years old when the news about Saul and Jonathan came from Jezreel, and his nurse took him up and fled, and as she fled in her haste, he fell and became lame. And his name was Mephibosheth.

⁵Now the sons of Rimmon the Beerothite, Rechab and Baanah, set out, and about the heat of the day they came to the house of Ish-bosheth as he was taking his noonday rest. ⁶And they came into the midst of the house as if to get wheat, and they stabbed him in the stomach. Then Rechab and Baanah his brother escaped.¹ ⁷When they came into the house, as he lay on his bed in his bedroom, they struck him and put him to death and beheaded him. They took his head and went by the way of the Arabah all night, ⁸and brought the head of Ish-bosheth to David at Hebron. And they said to the king, "Here is the head of Ish-bosheth, the son of Saul, your enemy, who sought your life. The LORD has avenged my lord the king this day on Saul and on his offspring." ⁹But David answered Rechab and Baanah his brother, the sons of Rimmon the Beerothite, "As the LORD lives, who has redeemed my life out of every adversity, ¹⁰when one told me, 'Behold, Saul is dead,' and thought he was bringing good news, I seized him and killed him at Ziklag, which was the reward I gave him for his news. ¹¹How much more, when wicked men have killed a righteous man in his own house on his bed, shall I not now require his blood at your hand and destroy you from the earth?" ¹²And

David commanded his young men, and they killed them and cut off their hands and feet and hanged them beside the pool at Hebron. But they took the head of Ish-bosheth and buried it in the tomb of Abner at Hebron.

⁵:¹Then all the tribes of Israel came to David at Hebron and said, "Behold, we are your bone and flesh. ²In times past, when Saul was king over us, it was you who led out and brought in Israel. And the LORD said to you, 'You shall be shepherd of my people Israel, and you shall be prince² over Israel.'" ³So all the elders of Israel came to the king at Hebron, and King David made a covenant with them at Hebron before the LORD, and they anointed David king over Israel. ⁴David was thirty years old when he began to reign, and he reigned forty years. ⁵At Hebron he reigned over Judah seven years and six months, and at Jerusalem he reigned over all Israel and Judah thirty-three years.³

⁶And the king and his men went to Jerusalem against the Jebusites, the inhabitants of the land, who said to David, "You will not come in here, but the blind and the lame will ward you off"—thinking, "David cannot come in here." ⁷Nevertheless, David took the stronghold of Zion, that is, the city of David. ⁸And David said on that day, "Whoever would strike the Jebusites, let him get up the water shaft to attack 'the lame and the blind,' who are hated by David's soul." Therefore it is said, "The blind and the lame shall not come into the house." ⁹And David lived in the stronghold and called it the city of David. And David built the city all around from the Millo inward. ¹⁰And David became greater and greater, for the LORD, the God of hosts, was with him.

¹¹And Hiram king of Tyre sent messengers to David, and cedar trees, also carpenters and masons who built David a house. ¹²And David knew that the LORD had established him king over Israel, and that he had exalted his kingdom for the sake of his people Israel.

¹³And David took more concubines and wives

¹ Septuagint *And behold, the doorkeeper of the house had been cleaning wheat, but she grew drowsy and slept. So Rechab and Baanah his brother slipped in* ² Or *leader* ³ Dead Sea Scroll lacks verses 4–5

from Jerusalem, after he came from Hebron, and more sons and daughters were born to David. [14]And these are the names of those who were born to him in Jerusalem: Shammua, Shobab, Nathan, Solomon, [15]Ibhar, Elishua, Nepheg, Japhia, [16]Elishama, Eliada, and Eliphelet.

[17]When the Philistines heard that David had been anointed king over Israel, all the Philistines went up to search for David. But David heard of it and went down to the stronghold. [18]Now the Philistines had come and spread out in the Valley of Rephaim. [19]And David inquired of the LORD, "Shall I go up against the Philistines? Will you give them into my hand?" And the LORD said to David, "Go up, for I will certainly give the Philistines into your hand." [20]And David came to Baal-perazim, and David defeated them there. And he said, "The LORD has broken through my enemies before me like a breaking flood." Therefore the name of that place is called Baal-perazim.[1] [21]And the Philistines left their idols there, and David and his men carried them away.

[22]And the Philistines came up yet again and spread out in the Valley of Rephaim. [23]And when David inquired of the LORD, he said, "You shall not go up; go around to their rear, and come against them opposite the balsam trees. [24]And when you hear the sound of marching in the tops of the balsam trees, then rouse yourself, for then the LORD has gone out before you to strike down the army of the Philistines." [25]And David did as the LORD commanded him, and struck down the Philistines from Geba to Gezer.

---

1 Corinthians 15

Now I would remind you, brothers,[2] of the gospel I preached to you, which you received, in which you stand, [2]and by which you are being saved, if you hold fast to the word I preached to you—unless you believed in vain. [3]For I delivered to you as of first importance what I also received: that Christ died for our sins in accordance with the Scriptures, [4]that he was buried, that he was raised on the third day in accordance with the Scriptures, [5]and that he appeared to Cephas, then to the twelve. [6]Then he appeared to more than five hundred brothers at one time, most of whom are still alive, though some have fallen asleep. [7]Then he appeared to James, then to all the apostles. [8]Last of all, as to one untimely born, he appeared also to me. [9]For I am the least of the apostles, unworthy to be called an apostle, because I persecuted the church of God. [10]But by the grace of God I am what I am, and his grace toward me was not in vain. On the contrary, I worked harder than any of them, though it was not I, but the grace of God that is with me. [11]Whether then it was I or they, so we preach and so you believed.

[12]Now if Christ is proclaimed as raised from the dead, how can some of you say that there is no resurrection of the dead? [13]But if there is no resurrection of the dead, then not even Christ has been raised. [14]And if Christ has not been raised, then our preaching is in vain and your faith is in vain. [15]We are even found to be misrepresenting God, because we testified about God that he raised Christ, whom he did not raise if it is true that the dead are not raised. [16]For if the dead are not raised, not even Christ has been raised. [17]And if Christ has not been raised, your faith is futile and you are still in your sins. [18]Then those also who have fallen asleep in Christ have perished. [19]If in Christ we have hope[3] in this life only, we are of all people most to be pitied.

[20]But in fact Christ has been raised from the dead, the firstfruits of those who have fallen asleep. [21]For as by a man came death, by a man has come also the resurrection of the dead. [22]For as in Adam all die, so also in Christ shall all be made alive. [23]But each in his own order: Christ the firstfruits, then at his coming those who belong to Christ. [24]Then comes the end, when he delivers the kingdom to God the Father after destroying every rule and every authority and power. [25]For he must reign until he has put all his enemies under his feet. [26]The last enemy to be destroyed is death. [27]For "God[4] has put all things in subjection under his feet." But when it says, "all things are put in subjection," it is plain that he is excepted who put all things in subjection under him. [28]When all things are subjected to him, then the Son himself will also be subjected to him who put all things in subjection under him, that God may be all in all.

[29]Otherwise, what do people mean by being baptized on behalf of the dead? If the dead are not raised at all, why are people baptized on their behalf? [30]Why are we in danger every

---

[1] Baal-perazim means lord of bursting through   [2] Or brothers and sisters; also verses 6, 31, 50, 58   [3] Or we have hoped   [4] Greek he

hour? [31] I protest, brothers, by my pride in you, which I have in Christ Jesus our Lord, I die every day! [32] What do I gain if, humanly speaking, I fought with beasts at Ephesus? If the dead are not raised, "Let us eat and drink, for tomorrow we die." [33] Do not be deceived: "Bad company ruins good morals."[1] [34] Wake up from your drunken stupor, as is right, and do not go on sinning. For some have no knowledge of God. I say this to your shame.

[35] But someone will ask, "How are the dead raised? With what kind of body do they come?" [36] You foolish person! What you sow does not come to life unless it dies. [37] And what you sow is not the body that is to be, but a bare kernel, perhaps of wheat or of some other grain. [38] But God gives it a body as he has chosen, and to each kind of seed its own body. [39] For not all flesh is the same, but there is one kind for humans, another for animals, another for birds, and another for fish. [40] There are heavenly bodies and earthly bodies, but the glory of the heavenly is of one kind, and the glory of the earthly is of another. [41] There is one glory of the sun, and another glory of the moon, and another glory of the stars; for star differs from star in glory.

[42] So is it with the resurrection of the dead. What is sown is perishable; what is raised is imperishable. [43] It is sown in dishonor; it is raised in glory. It is sown in weakness; it is raised in power. [44] It is sown a natural body; it is raised a spiritual body. If there is a natural body, there is also a spiritual body. [45] Thus it is written, "The first man Adam became a living being";[2] the last Adam became a life-giving spirit. [46] But it is not the spiritual that is first but the natural, and then the spiritual. [47] The first man was from the earth, a man of dust; the second man is from heaven. [48] As was the man of dust, so also are those who are of the dust, and as is the man of heaven, so also are those who are of heaven. [49] Just as we have borne the image of the man of dust, we shall[3] also bear the image of the man of heaven.

[50] I tell you this, brothers: flesh and blood cannot inherit the kingdom of God, nor does the perishable inherit the imperishable. [51] Behold! I tell you a mystery. We shall not all sleep, but we shall all be changed, [52] in a moment, in the twinkling of an eye, at the last trumpet. For the trumpet will sound, and the dead will be raised imperishable, and we shall be changed. [53] For this perishable body must put on the imperishable, and this mortal body must put on immortality. [54] When the perishable puts on the imperishable, and the mortal puts on immortality, then shall come to pass the saying that is written:

> "Death is swallowed up in victory."
> [55] "O death, where is your victory?
> O death, where is your sting?"

[56] The sting of death is sin, and the power of sin is the law. [57] But thanks be to God, who gives us the victory through our Lord Jesus Christ.

[58] Therefore, my beloved brothers, be steadfast, immovable, always abounding in the work of the Lord, knowing that in the Lord your labor is not in vain.

Ezekiel 13

The word of the Lord came to me: [2] "Son of man, prophesy against the prophets of Israel, who are prophesying, and say to those who prophesy from their own hearts: 'Hear the word of the Lord!' [3] Thus says the Lord God, Woe to the foolish prophets who follow their own spirit, and have seen nothing! [4] Your prophets have been like jackals among ruins, O Israel. [5] You have not gone up into the breaches, or built up a wall for the house of Israel, that it might stand in battle in the day of the Lord. [6] They have seen false visions and lying divinations. They say, 'Declares the Lord,' when the Lord has not sent them, and yet they expect him to fulfill their word. [7] Have you not seen a false vision and uttered a lying divination, whenever you have said, 'Declares the Lord,' although I have not spoken?"

[8] Therefore thus says the Lord God: "Because you have uttered falsehood and seen lying visions, therefore behold, I am against you, declares the Lord God. [9] My hand will be against the prophets who see false visions and who give lying divinations. They shall not be in the council of my people, nor be enrolled in the register of the house of Israel, nor shall they enter the land of Israel. And you shall know that I am the Lord God. [10] Precisely because they have misled my people, saying, 'Peace,' when there is no peace, and because, when the people build a wall, these prophets smear

---

[1] Probably from Menander's comedy *Thais*   [2] Greek *a living soul*   [3] Some manuscripts *let us*

it with whitewash,[1] [11]say to those who smear it with whitewash that it shall fall! There will be a deluge of rain, and you, O great hailstones, will fall, and a stormy wind break out. [12]And when the wall falls, will it not be said to you, 'Where is the coating with which you smeared it?' [13]Therefore thus says the Lord GOD: I will make a stormy wind break out in my wrath, and there shall be a deluge of rain in my anger, and great hailstones in wrath to make a full end. [14]And I will break down the wall that you have smeared with whitewash, and bring it down to the ground, so that its foundation will be laid bare. When it falls, you shall perish in the midst of it, and you shall know that I am the LORD. [15]Thus will I spend my wrath upon the wall and upon those who have smeared it with whitewash, and I will say to you, The wall is no more, nor those who smeared it, [16]the prophets of Israel who prophesied concerning Jerusalem and saw visions of peace for her, when there was no peace, declares the Lord GOD.

[17]"And you, son of man, set your face against the daughters of your people, who prophesy out of their own hearts. Prophesy against them [18]and say, Thus says the Lord GOD: Woe to the women who sew magic bands upon all wrists, and make veils for the heads of persons of every stature, in the hunt for souls! Will you hunt down souls belonging to my people and keep your own souls alive? [19]You have profaned me among my people for handfuls of barley and for pieces of bread, putting to death souls who should not die and keeping alive souls who should not live, by your lying to my people, who listen to lies.

[20]"Therefore thus says the Lord GOD: Behold, I am against your magic bands with which you hunt the souls like birds, and I will tear them from your arms, and I will let the souls whom you hunt go free, the souls like birds. [21]Your veils also I will tear off and deliver my people out of your hand, and they shall be no more in your hand as prey, and you shall know that I am the LORD. [22]Because you have disheartened the righteous falsely, although I have not grieved him, and you have encouraged the wicked, that he should not turn from his evil way to save his life, [23]therefore you shall no more see false visions nor practice divination. I will deliver my people out of your hand. And you shall know that I am the LORD."

Psalm 52–54

To the choirmaster. A Maskil[2] of David, when Doeg, the Edomite, came and told Saul, "David has come to the house of Ahimelech."

Why do you boast of evil, O mighty man?
    The steadfast love of God endures all
      the day.
[2] Your tongue plots destruction,
    like a sharp razor, you worker of deceit.
[3] You love evil more than good,
    and lying more than speaking what is
      right.   Selah
[4] You love all words that devour,
    O deceitful tongue.

[5] But God will break you down forever;
    he will snatch and tear you from your
      tent;
    he will uproot you from the land of
      the living.   Selah
[6] The righteous shall see and fear,
    and shall laugh at him, saying,
[7] "See the man who would not make
    God his refuge,
but trusted in the abundance of his riches
    and sought refuge in his own
      destruction!"[3]

[8] But I am like a green olive tree
    in the house of God.
    I trust in the steadfast love of God
    forever and ever.
[9] I will thank you forever,
    because you have done it.
    I will wait for your name, for it is good,
    in the presence of the godly.

To the choirmaster: according to Mahalath. A Maskil[4] of David.

The fool says in his heart, "There is no God."
    They are corrupt, doing abominable
      iniquity;
    there is none who does good.

[2] God looks down from heaven
    on the children of man
    to see if there are any who understand,[5]
    who seek after God.

[3] They have all fallen away;
    together they have become corrupt;
    there is none who does good,
      not even one.

[1] Or plaster; also verses 11, 14, 15   [2] Probably a musical or liturgical term   [3] Or in his work of destruction   [4] Probably musical or liturgical terms   [5] Or who act wisely

4 Have those who work evil no knowledge,
who eat up my people as they eat bread,
and do not call upon God?

5 There they are, in great terror,
where there is no terror!
For God scatters the bones of him who
encamps against you;
you put them to shame, for God has
rejected them.

6 Oh, that salvation for Israel would come
out of Zion!
When God restores the fortunes of his
people,
let Jacob rejoice, let Israel be glad.

To the choirmaster: with stringed
instruments. A Maskil[1] of David, when the
Ziphites went and told Saul, "Is not David
hiding among us?"

O God, save me by your name,
and vindicate me by your might.

2 O God, hear my prayer;
give ear to the words of my mouth.

3 For strangers[2] have risen against me;
ruthless men seek my life;
they do not set God before
themselves.   *Selah*

4 Behold, God is my helper;
the Lord is the upholder of my life.

5 He will return the evil to my enemies;
in your faithfulness put an end to
them.

6 With a freewill offering I will sacrifice to
you;
I will give thanks to your name,
O Lord, for it is good.

7 For he has delivered me from every
trouble,
and my eye has looked in triumph on
my enemies.

SEPTEMBER 11

2 Samuel 6

David again gathered all the chosen men of Israel, thirty thousand. ²And David arose and went with all the people who were with him from Baale-judah to bring up from there the ark of God, which is called by the name of the Lord of hosts who sits enthroned on the cherubim. ³And they carried the ark of God on a new cart and brought it out of the house of Abinadab, which was on the hill. And Uzzah and Ahio,[3] the sons of Abinadab, were driving the new cart,[4] ⁴with the ark of God, and Ahio went before the ark. ⁵And David and all the house of Israel were celebrating before the Lord, with songs[5] and lyres and harps and tambourines and castanets and cymbals. ⁶And when they came to the threshing floor of Nacon, Uzzah put out his hand to the ark of God and took hold of it, for the oxen stumbled. ⁷And the anger of the Lord was kindled against Uzzah, and God struck him down there because of his error, and he died there beside the ark of God. ⁸And David was angry because the Lord had broken out against Uzzah. And that place is called Perez-uzzah[6] to this day. ⁹And David was afraid of the Lord that day, and he said, "How can the ark of the Lord come to me?" ¹⁰So David was not willing to take the ark of the Lord into the city of David. But David took it aside to the house of Obed-edom the Gittite. ¹¹And the ark of the Lord remained in the house of Obed-edom the Gittite three months, and the Lord blessed Obed-edom and all his household.

¹²And it was told King David, "The Lord has blessed the household of Obed-edom and all that belongs to him, because of the ark of God." So David went and brought up the ark of God from the house of Obed-edom to the city of

---

[1] Probably a musical or liturgical term [2] Some Hebrew manuscripts and Targum *insolent men* (compare Psalm 86:14) [3] Or *and his brother*; also verse 4 [4] Compare Septuagint; Hebrew *the new cart, and brought it out of the house of Abinadab, which was on the hill* [5] Septuagint, 1 Chronicles 13:8; Hebrew *fir trees* [6] *Perez-uzzah* means *the breaking out against Uzzah*

David with rejoicing. ¹³And when those who bore the ark of the LORD had gone six steps, he sacrificed an ox and a fattened animal. ¹⁴And David danced before the LORD with all his might. And David was wearing a linen ephod. ¹⁵So David and all the house of Israel brought up the ark of the LORD with shouting and with the sound of the horn.

¹⁶As the ark of the LORD came into the city of David, Michal the daughter of Saul looked out of the window and saw King David leaping and dancing before the LORD, and she despised him in her heart. ¹⁷And they brought in the ark of the LORD and set it in its place, inside the tent that David had pitched for it. And David offered burnt offerings and peace offerings before the LORD. ¹⁸And when David had finished offering the burnt offerings and the peace offerings, he blessed the people in the name of the LORD of hosts ¹⁹and distributed among all the people, the whole multitude of Israel, both men and women, a cake of bread, a portion of meat,¹ and a cake of raisins to each one. Then all the people departed, each to his house.

²⁰And David returned to bless his household. But Michal the daughter of Saul came out to meet David and said, "How the king of Israel honored himself today, uncovering himself today before the eyes of his servants' female servants, as one of the vulgar fellows shamelessly uncovers himself!" ²¹And David said to Michal, "It was before the LORD, who chose me above your father and above all his house, to appoint me as prince² over Israel, the people of the LORD—and I will celebrate before the LORD. ²²I will make myself yet more contemptible than this, and I will be abased in your³ eyes. But by the female servants of whom you have spoken, by them I shall be held in honor." ²³And Michal the daughter of Saul had no child to the day of her death.

1 Corinthians 16

Now concerning⁴ the collection for the saints: as I directed the churches of Galatia, so you also are to do. ²On the first day of every week, each of you is to put something aside and store it up, as he may prosper, so that there will be no collecting when I come. ³And when I arrive, I will send those whom you accredit by letter to carry your gift to Jerusalem.

⁴If it seems advisable that I should go also, they will accompany me. ⁵I will visit you after passing through Macedonia, for I intend to pass through Macedonia, ⁶and perhaps I will stay with you or even spend the winter, so that you may help me on my journey, wherever I go. ⁷For I do not want to see you now just in passing. I hope to spend some time with you, if the Lord permits. ⁸But I will stay in Ephesus until Pentecost, ⁹for a wide door for effective work has opened to me, and there are many adversaries.

¹⁰When Timothy comes, see that you put him at ease among you, for he is doing the work of the Lord, as I am. ¹¹So let no one despise him. Help him on his way in peace, that he may return to me, for I am expecting him with the brothers. ¹²Now concerning our brother Apollos, I strongly urged him to visit you with the other brothers, but it was not at all his will⁵ to come now. He will come when he has opportunity.

¹³Be watchful, stand firm in the faith, act like men, be strong. ¹⁴Let all that you do be done in love.

¹⁵Now I urge you, brothers⁶—you know that the household⁷ of Stephanas were the first converts in Achaia, and that they have devoted themselves to the service of the saints— ¹⁶be subject to such as these, and to every fellow worker and laborer. ¹⁷I rejoice at the coming of Stephanas and Fortunatus and Achaicus, because they have made up for your absence, ¹⁸for they refreshed my spirit as well as yours. Give recognition to such people.

¹⁹The churches of Asia send you greetings. Aquila and Prisca, together with the church in their house, send you hearty greetings in the Lord. ²⁰All the brothers send you greetings. Greet one another with a holy kiss.

²¹I, Paul, write this greeting with my own hand. ²²If anyone has no love for the Lord, let him be accursed. Our Lord, come!⁸ ²³The grace of the Lord Jesus be with you. ²⁴My love be with you all in Christ Jesus. Amen.

Ezekiel 14

Then certain of the elders of Israel came to me and sat before me. ²And the word of the LORD came to me: ³"Son of man, these men have taken their idols into their hearts,

¹ Vulgate; the meaning of the Hebrew term is uncertain ² Or leader ³ Septuagint; Hebrew my ⁴ The expression Now concerning introduces a reply to a question in the Corinthians' letter; see 7:1; also verse 12 ⁵ Or God's will for him ⁶ Or brothers and sisters; also verse 20 ⁷ Greek house ⁸ Greek Maranatha (a transliteration of Aramaic)

and set the stumbling block of their iniquity before their faces. Should I indeed let myself be consulted by them? [4]Therefore speak to them and say to them, Thus says the Lord GOD: Any one of the house of Israel who takes his idols into his heart and sets the stumbling block of his iniquity before his face, and yet comes to the prophet, I the LORD will answer him as he comes with the multitude of his idols, [5]that I may lay hold of the hearts of the house of Israel, who are all estranged from me through their idols.

[6]"Therefore say to the house of Israel, Thus says the Lord GOD: Repent and turn away from your idols, and turn away your faces from all your abominations. [7]For any one of the house of Israel, or of the strangers who sojourn in Israel, who separates himself from me, taking his idols into his heart and putting the stumbling block of his iniquity before his face, and yet comes to a prophet to consult me through him, I the LORD will answer him myself. [8]And I will set my face against that man; I will make him a sign and a byword and cut him off from the midst of my people, and you shall know that I am the LORD. [9]And if the prophet is deceived and speaks a word, I, the LORD, have deceived that prophet, and I will stretch out my hand against him and will destroy him from the midst of my people Israel. [10]And they shall bear their punishment[1]—the punishment of the prophet and the punishment of the inquirer shall be alike— [11]that the house of Israel may no more go astray from me, nor defile themselves anymore with all their transgressions, but that they may be my people and I may be their God, declares the Lord GOD."

[12]And the word of the LORD came to me: [13]"Son of man, when a land sins against me by acting faithlessly, and I stretch out my hand against it and break its supply[2] of bread and send famine upon it, and cut off from it man and beast, [14]even if these three men, Noah, Daniel, and Job, were in it, they would deliver but their own lives by their righteousness, declares the Lord GOD.

[15]"If I cause wild beasts to pass through the land, and they ravage it, and it be made desolate, so that no one may pass through because of the beasts, [16]even if these three men were in it, as I live, declares the Lord GOD, they would deliver neither sons nor daughters. They alone

would be delivered, but the land would be desolate.

[17]"Or if I bring a sword upon that land and say, Let a sword pass through the land, and I cut off from it man and beast, [18]though these three men were in it, as I live, declares the Lord GOD, they would deliver neither sons nor daughters, but they alone would be delivered.

[19]"Or if I send a pestilence into that land and pour out my wrath upon it with blood, to cut off from it man and beast, [20]even if Noah, Daniel, and Job were in it, as I live, declares the Lord GOD, they would deliver neither son nor daughter. They would deliver but their own lives by their righteousness.

[21]"For thus says the Lord GOD: How much more when I send upon Jerusalem my four disastrous acts of judgment, sword, famine, wild beasts, and pestilence, to cut off from it man and beast! [22]But behold, some survivors will be left in it, sons and daughters who will be brought out; behold, when they come out to you, and you see their ways and their deeds, you will be consoled for the disaster that I have brought upon Jerusalem, for all that I have brought upon it. [23]They will console you, when you see their ways and their deeds, and you shall know that I have not done without cause all that I have done in it, declares the Lord GOD."

Psalm 55

TO THE CHOIRMASTER: WITH STRINGED INSTRUMENTS. A MASKIL[3] OF DAVID.

Give ear to my prayer, O God,
and hide not yourself from my plea for mercy!
2　Attend to me, and answer me;
　　I am restless in my complaint and I moan,
3　because of the noise of the enemy,
　　because of the oppression of the wicked.
　For they drop trouble upon me,
　　and in anger they bear a grudge against me.

4　My heart is in anguish within me;
　　the terrors of death have fallen upon me.
5　Fear and trembling come upon me,
　　and horror overwhelms me.

[1] Or *iniquity*; three times in this verse　[2] Hebrew *staff*　[3] Probably a musical or liturgical term

6 And I say, "Oh, that I had wings like a
    dove!
  I would fly away and be at rest;
7 yes, I would wander far away;
  I would lodge in the wilderness;   *Selah*
8 I would hurry to find a shelter
    from the raging wind and tempest."

9 Destroy, O Lord, divide their tongues;
    for I see violence and strife in the city.
10 Day and night they go around it
    on its walls,
  and iniquity and trouble are within it;
11 ruin is in its midst;
  oppression and fraud
    do not depart from its marketplace.

12 For it is not an enemy who taunts me—
    then I could bear it;
  it is not an adversary who deals
      insolently with me—
    then I could hide from him.
13 But it is you, a man, my equal,
  my companion, my familiar friend.
14 We used to take sweet counsel together;
  within God's house we walked in the
      throng.
15 Let death steal over them;
  let them go down to Sheol alive;
    for evil is in their dwelling place and
      in their heart.

16 But I call to God,
    and the LORD will save me.
17 Evening and morning and at noon
    I utter my complaint and moan,
    and he hears my voice.
18 He redeems my soul in safety
    from the battle that I wage,
    for many are arrayed against me.
19 God will give ear and humble them,
    he who is enthroned from of old, *Selah*
  because they do not change
    and do not fear God.

20 My companion[1] stretched out his hand
      against his friends;
    he violated his covenant.
21 His speech was smooth as butter,
    yet war was in his heart;
  his words were softer than oil,
    yet they were drawn swords.

22 Cast your burden on the LORD,
    and he will sustain you;
  he will never permit
    the righteous to be moved.

23 But you, O God, will cast them down
    into the pit of destruction;
  men of blood and treachery
    shall not live out half their days.
  But I will trust in you.

S E P T E M B E R   1 2

2 Samuel 7

Now when the king lived in his house and the LORD had given him rest from all his surrounding enemies, [2]the king said to Nathan the prophet, "See now, I dwell in a house of cedar, but the ark of God dwells in a tent." [3]And Nathan said to the king, "Go, do all that is in your heart, for the LORD is with you."

[4]But that same night the word of the LORD came to Nathan, [5]"Go and tell my servant David, 'Thus says the LORD: Would you build me a house to dwell in? [6]I have not lived in a house since the day I brought up the people of Israel from Egypt to this day, but I have been moving about in a tent for my dwelling. [7]In all places where I have moved with all the people of Israel, did I speak a word with any of the judges[2] of Israel, whom I commanded to shepherd my people Israel, saying, "Why have you not built me a house of cedar?"' [8]Now, therefore, thus you shall say to my servant David, 'Thus says the LORD of hosts, I took you from the pasture, from following the sheep, that you

---

[1] Hebrew *He* [2] Compare 1 Chronicles 17:6; Hebrew *tribes*

should be prince[1] over my people Israel. [9]And I have been with you wherever you went and have cut off all your enemies from before you. And I will make for you a great name, like the name of the great ones of the earth. [10]And I will appoint a place for my people Israel and will plant them, so that they may dwell in their own place and be disturbed no more. And violent men shall afflict them no more, as formerly, [11]from the time that I appointed judges over my people Israel. And I will give you rest from all your enemies. Moreover, the LORD declares to you that the LORD will make you a house. [12]When your days are fulfilled and you lie down with your fathers, I will raise up your offspring after you, who shall come from your body, and I will establish his kingdom. [13]He shall build a house for my name, and I will establish the throne of his kingdom forever. [14]I will be to him a father, and he shall be to me a son. When he commits iniquity, I will discipline him with the rod of men, with the stripes of the sons of men, [15]but my steadfast love will not depart from him, as I took it from Saul, whom I put away from before you. [16]And your house and your kingdom shall be made sure forever before me.[2] Your throne shall be established forever.'" [17]In accordance with all these words, and in accordance with all this vision, Nathan spoke to David.

[18]Then King David went in and sat before the LORD and said, "Who am I, O Lord GOD, and what is my house, that you have brought me thus far? [19]And yet this was a small thing in your eyes, O Lord GOD. You have spoken also of your servant's house for a great while to come, and this is instruction for mankind, O Lord GOD! [20]And what more can David say to you? For you know your servant, O Lord GOD! [21]Because of your promise, and according to your own heart, you have brought about all this greatness, to make your servant know it. [22]Therefore you are great, O LORD God. For there is none like you, and there is no God besides you, according to all that we have heard with our ears. [23]And who is like your people Israel, the one nation on earth whom God went to redeem to be his people, making himself a name and doing for them[3] great and awesome things by driving out[4] before your people, whom you redeemed for yourself from Egypt,

a nation and its gods? [24]And you established for yourself your people Israel to be your people forever. And you, O LORD, became their God. [25]And now, O LORD God, confirm forever the word that you have spoken concerning your servant and concerning his house, and do as you have spoken. [26]And your name will be magnified forever, saying, 'The LORD of hosts is God over Israel,' and the house of your servant David will be established before you. [27]For you, O LORD of hosts, the God of Israel, have made this revelation to your servant, saying, 'I will build you a house.' Therefore your servant has found courage to pray this prayer to you. [28]And now, O Lord GOD, you are God, and your words are true, and you have promised this good thing to your servant. [29]Now therefore may it please you to bless the house of your servant, so that it may continue forever before you. For you, O Lord GOD, have spoken, and with your blessing shall the house of your servant be blessed forever."

2 Corinthians 1

Paul, an apostle of Christ Jesus by the will of God, and Timothy our brother,

To the church of God that is at Corinth, with all the saints who are in the whole of Achaia:

[2]Grace to you and peace from God our Father and the Lord Jesus Christ.

[3]Blessed be the God and Father of our Lord Jesus Christ, the Father of mercies and God of all comfort, [4]who comforts us in all our affliction, so that we may be able to comfort those who are in any affliction, with the comfort with which we ourselves are comforted by God. [5]For as we share abundantly in Christ's sufferings, so through Christ we share abundantly in comfort too.[5] [6]If we are afflicted, it is for your comfort and salvation; and if we are comforted, it is for your comfort, which you experience when you patiently endure the same sufferings that we suffer. [7]Our hope for you is unshaken, for we know that as you share in our sufferings, you will also share in our comfort.

[8]For we do not want you to be unaware, brothers,[6] of the affliction we experienced in Asia. For we were so utterly burdened beyond our strength that we despaired of life itself. [9]Indeed, we felt that we had received the sentence of death. But that was to make us rely not

---

[1] Or leader [2] Septuagint; Hebrew *you* [3] With a few Targums, Vulgate, Syriac; Hebrew *you* [4] Septuagint (compare 1 Chronicles 17:21); Hebrew *for your land* [5] Or *For as the sufferings of Christ abound for us, so also our comfort abounds through Christ* [6] Or *brothers and sisters*. The plural Greek word *adelphoi* (translated "brothers") refers to siblings in a family. In New Testament usage, depending on the context, *adelphoi* may refer either to men or to both men and women who are siblings (brothers and sisters) in God's family, the church

on ourselves but on God who raises the dead. [10] He delivered us from such a deadly peril, and he will deliver us. On him we have set our hope that he will deliver us again. [11] You also must help us by prayer, so that many will give thanks on our behalf for the blessing granted us through the prayers of many.

[12] For our boast is this, the testimony of our conscience, that we behaved in the world with simplicity[1] and godly sincerity, not by earthly wisdom but by the grace of God, and supremely so toward you. [13] For we are not writing to you anything other than what you read and understand and I hope you will fully understand— [14] just as you did partially understand us—that on the day of our Lord Jesus you will boast of us as we will boast of you.

[15] Because I was sure of this, I wanted to come to you first, so that you might have a second experience of grace. [16] I wanted to visit you on my way to Macedonia, and to come back to you from Macedonia and have you send me on my way to Judea. [17] Was I vacillating when I wanted to do this? Do I make my plans according to the flesh, ready to say "Yes, yes" and "No, no" at the same time? [18] As surely as God is faithful, our word to you has not been Yes and No. [19] For the Son of God, Jesus Christ, whom we proclaimed among you, Silvanus and Timothy and I, was not Yes and No, but in him it is always Yes. [20] For all the promises of God find their Yes in him. That is why it is through him that we utter our Amen to God for his glory. [21] And it is God who establishes us with you in Christ, and has anointed us, [22] and who has also put his seal on us and given us his Spirit in our hearts as a guarantee.[2]

[23] But I call God to witness against me—it was to spare you that I refrained from coming again to Corinth. [24] Not that we lord it over your faith, but we work with you for your joy, for you stand firm in your faith.

Ezekiel 15

And the word of the Lord came to me: [2] "Son of man, how does the wood of the vine surpass any wood, the vine branch that is among the trees of the forest? [3] Is wood taken from it to make anything? Do people take a peg from it to hang any vessel on it? [4] Behold, it is given to the fire for fuel. When the fire has consumed both ends of it, and the middle of it is charred, is it useful for anything? [5] Behold, when it was whole, it was used for nothing. How much less, when the fire has consumed it and it is charred, can it ever be used for anything! [6] Therefore thus says the Lord God: Like the wood of the vine among the trees of the forest, which I have given to the fire for fuel, so have I given up the inhabitants of Jerusalem. [7] And I will set my face against them. Though they escape from the fire, the fire shall yet consume them, and you will know that I am the Lord, when I set my face against them. [8] And I will make the land desolate, because they have acted faithlessly, declares the Lord God."

Psalm 56–57

To the choirmaster: according to The Dove on Far-off Terebinths. A Miktam[3] of David, when the Philistines seized him in Gath.

Be gracious to me, O God, for man tramples on me;
   all day long an attacker oppresses me;
[2] my enemies trample on me all day long,
   for many attack me proudly.
[3] When I am afraid,
   I put my trust in you.
[4] In God, whose word I praise,
   in God I trust; I shall not be afraid.
   What can flesh do to me?

[5] All day long they injure my cause;[4]
   all their thoughts are against me for evil.
[6] They stir up strife, they lurk;
   they watch my steps,
   as they have waited for my life.
[7] For their crime will they escape?
   In wrath cast down the peoples, O God!

[8] You have kept count of my tossings;[5]
   put my tears in your bottle.
   Are they not in your book?
[9] Then my enemies will turn back
   in the day when I call.
   This I know, that[6] God is for me.
[10] In God, whose word I praise,
   in the Lord, whose word I praise,
[11] in God I trust; I shall not be afraid.
   What can man do to me?

---

[1] Some manuscripts *holiness* [2] Or *down payment* [3] Probably a musical or liturgical term [4] Or *they twist my words* [5] Or *wanderings* [6] Or *because*

¹² I must perform my vows to you, O God;
   I will render thank offerings to you.
¹³ For you have delivered my soul from
       death,
   yes, my feet from falling,
   that I may walk before God
       in the light of life.

To the choirmaster: according to Do Not
Destroy. A Miktam[1] of David, when he fled
from Saul, in the cave.

Be merciful to me, O God, be merciful to me,
for in you my soul takes refuge;
   in the shadow of your wings I will take
       refuge,
   till the storms of destruction pass by.
² I cry out to God Most High,
   to God who fulfills his purpose for me.
³ He will send from heaven and save me;
   he will put to shame him who
       tramples on me.   *Selah*
   God will send out his steadfast love and
       his faithfulness!

⁴ My soul is in the midst of lions;
   I lie down amid fiery beasts—
the children of man, whose teeth are
       spears and arrows,
   whose tongues are sharp swords.

⁵ Be exalted, O God, above the heavens!
   Let your glory be over all the earth!

⁶ They set a net for my steps;
   my soul was bowed down.
   They dug a pit in my way,
       but they have fallen into it
           themselves.   *Selah*
⁷ My heart is steadfast, O God,
   my heart is steadfast!
   I will sing and make melody!
⁸ Awake, my glory![2]
   Awake, O harp and lyre!
   I will awake the dawn!
⁹ I will give thanks to you, O Lord, among
       the peoples;
   I will sing praises to you among the
       nations.
¹⁰ For your steadfast love is great to the
       heavens,
   your faithfulness to the clouds.

¹¹ Be exalted, O God, above the heavens!
   Let your glory be over all the earth!

SEPTEMBER 13

2 Samuel 8–9

After this David defeated the Philistines and subdued them, and David took Metheg-ammah out of the hand of the Philistines. ²And he defeated Moab and he measured them with a line, making them lie down on the ground. Two lines he measured to be put to death, and one full line to be spared. And the Moabites became servants to David and brought tribute.

³ David also defeated Hadadezer the son of Rehob, king of Zobah, as he went to restore his power at the river Euphrates. ⁴And David took from him 1,700 horsemen, and 20,000 foot soldiers. And David hamstrung all the chariot horses but left enough for 100 chariots. ⁵And when the Syrians of Damascus came to help Hadadezer king of Zobah, David struck down 22,000 men of the Syrians. ⁶Then David put garrisons in Aram of Damascus, and the Syrians became servants to David and brought tribute. And the LORD gave victory to David wherever he went. ⁷And David took the shields of gold that were carried by the servants of Hadadezer and brought them to Jerusalem. ⁸And from Betah and from Berothai, cities of Hadadezer, King David took very much bronze.

⁹ When Toi king of Hamath heard that David had defeated the whole army of Hadadezer, ¹⁰Toi sent his son Joram to King David, to ask about his health and to bless him because he

[1] Probably a musical or liturgical term [2] Or *my whole being*

had fought against Hadadezer and defeated him, for Hadadezer had often been at war with Toi. And Joram brought with him articles of silver, of gold, and of bronze. ¹¹These also King David dedicated to the LORD, together with the silver and gold that he dedicated from all the nations he subdued, ¹²from Edom, Moab, the Ammonites, the Philistines, Amalek, and from the spoil of Hadadezer the son of Rehob, king of Zobah.

¹³And David made a name for himself when he returned from striking down 18,000 Edomites in the Valley of Salt. ¹⁴Then he put garrisons in Edom; throughout all Edom he put garrisons, and all the Edomites became David's servants. And the LORD gave victory to David wherever he went.

¹⁵So David reigned over all Israel. And David administered justice and equity to all his people. ¹⁶Joab the son of Zeruiah was over the army, and Jehoshaphat the son of Ahilud was recorder, ¹⁷and Zadok the son of Ahitub and Ahimelech the son of Abiathar were priests, and Seraiah was secretary, ¹⁸and Benaiah the son of Jehoiada was over[1] the Cherethites and the Pelethites, and David's sons were priests.

⁹:¹And David said, "Is there still anyone left of the house of Saul, that I may show him kindness for Jonathan's sake?" ²Now there was a servant of the house of Saul whose name was Ziba, and they called him to David. And the king said to him, "Are you Ziba?" And he said, "I am your servant." ³And the king said, "Is there not still someone of the house of Saul, that I may show the kindness of God to him?" Ziba said to the king, "There is still a son of Jonathan; he is crippled in his feet." ⁴The king said to him, "Where is he?" And Ziba said to the king, "He is in the house of Machir the son of Ammiel, at Lo-debar." ⁵Then King David sent and brought him from the house of Machir the son of Ammiel, at Lo-debar. ⁶And Mephibosheth the son of Jonathan, son of Saul, came to David and fell on his face and paid homage. And David said, "Mephibosheth!" And he answered, "Behold, I am your servant." ⁷And David said to him, "Do not fear, for I will show you kindness for the sake of your father Jonathan, and I will restore to you all the land of Saul your father, and you shall eat at my table always." ⁸And he paid homage and said, "What

is your servant, that you should show regard for a dead dog such as I?"

⁹Then the king called Ziba, Saul's servant, and said to him, "All that belonged to Saul and to all his house I have given to your master's grandson. ¹⁰And you and your sons and your servants shall till the land for him and shall bring in the produce, that your master's grandson may have bread to eat. But Mephibosheth your master's grandson shall always eat at my table." Now Ziba had fifteen sons and twenty servants. ¹¹Then Ziba said to the king, "According to all that my lord the king commands his servant, so will your servant do." So Mephibosheth ate at David's[2] table, like one of the king's sons. ¹²And Mephibosheth had a young son, whose name was Mica. And all who lived in Ziba's house became Mephibosheth's servants. ¹³So Mephibosheth lived in Jerusalem, for he ate always at the king's table. Now he was lame in both his feet.

——— *2 Corinthians 2* ———

For I made up my mind not to make another painful visit to you. ²For if I cause you pain, who is there to make me glad but the one whom I have pained? ³And I wrote as I did, so that when I came I might not suffer pain from those who should have made me rejoice, for I felt sure of all of you, that my joy would be the joy of you all. ⁴For I wrote to you out of much affliction and anguish of heart and with many tears, not to cause you pain but to let you know the abundant love that I have for you.

⁵Now if anyone has caused pain, he has caused it not to me, but in some measure—not to put it too severely—to all of you. ⁶For such a one, this punishment by the majority is enough, ⁷so you should rather turn to forgive and comfort him, or he may be overwhelmed by excessive sorrow. ⁸So I beg you to reaffirm your love for him. ⁹For this is why I wrote, that I might test you and know whether you are obedient in everything. ¹⁰Anyone whom you forgive, I also forgive. Indeed, what I have forgiven, if I have forgiven anything, has been for your sake in the presence of Christ, ¹¹so that we would not be outwitted by Satan; for we are not ignorant of his designs.

¹²When I came to Troas to preach the gospel of Christ, even though a door was opened

---

¹ Compare 20:23, 1 Chronicles 18:17, Syriac, Targum, Vulgate; Hebrew lacks *was over* ² Septuagint; Hebrew *my*

for me in the Lord, ¹³my spirit was not at rest because I did not find my brother Titus there. So I took leave of them and went on to Macedonia.

¹⁴But thanks be to God, who in Christ always leads us in triumphal procession, and through us spreads the fragrance of the knowledge of him everywhere. ¹⁵For we are the aroma of Christ to God among those who are being saved and among those who are perishing, ¹⁶to one a fragrance from death to death, to the other a fragrance from life to life. Who is sufficient for these things? ¹⁷For we are not, like so many, peddlers of God's word, but as men of sincerity, as commissioned by God, in the sight of God we speak in Christ.

Ezekiel 16

Again the word of the LORD came to me: ²"Son of man, make known to Jerusalem her abominations, ³and say, Thus says the Lord GOD to Jerusalem: Your origin and your birth are of the land of the Canaanites; your father was an Amorite and your mother a Hittite. ⁴And as for your birth, on the day you were born your cord was not cut, nor were you washed with water to cleanse you, nor rubbed with salt, nor wrapped in swaddling cloths. ⁵No eye pitied you, to do any of these things to you out of compassion for you, but you were cast out on the open field, for you were abhorred, on the day that you were born.

⁶"And when I passed by you and saw you wallowing in your blood, I said to you in your blood, 'Live!' I said to you in your blood, 'Live!' ⁷I made you flourish like a plant of the field. And you grew up and became tall and arrived at full adornment. Your breasts were formed, and your hair had grown; yet you were naked and bare.

⁸"When I passed by you again and saw you, behold, you were at the age for love, and I spread the corner of my garment over you and covered your nakedness; I made my vow to you and entered into a covenant with you, declares the Lord GOD, and you became mine. ⁹Then I bathed you with water and washed off your blood from you and anointed you with oil. ¹⁰I clothed you also with embroidered cloth and shod you with fine leather. I wrapped you in fine linen and covered you with silk.¹ ¹¹And I adorned you with ornaments and put bracelets on your wrists and a chain on your neck. ¹²And I put a ring on your nose and earrings in your ears and a beautiful crown on your head. ¹³Thus you were adorned with gold and silver, and your clothing was of fine linen and silk and embroidered cloth. You ate fine flour and honey and oil. You grew exceedingly beautiful and advanced to royalty. ¹⁴And your renown went forth among the nations because of your beauty, for it was perfect through the splendor that I had bestowed on you, declares the Lord GOD.

¹⁵"But you trusted in your beauty and played the whore² because of your renown and lavished your whorings³ on any passerby; your beauty⁴ became his. ¹⁶You took some of your garments and made for yourself colorful shrines, and on them played the whore. The like has never been, nor ever shall be.⁵ ¹⁷You also took your beautiful jewels of my gold and of my silver, which I had given you, and made for yourself images of men, and with them played the whore. ¹⁸And you took your embroidered garments to cover them, and set my oil and my incense before them. ¹⁹Also my bread that I gave you—I fed you with fine flour and oil and honey—you set before them for a pleasing aroma; and so it was, declares the Lord GOD. ²⁰And you took your sons and your daughters, whom you had borne to me, and these you sacrificed to them to be devoured. Were your whorings so small a matter ²¹that you slaughtered my children and delivered them up as an offering by fire to them? ²²And in all your abominations and your whorings you did not remember the days of your youth, when you were naked and bare, wallowing in your blood.

²³"And after all your wickedness (woe, woe to you! declares the Lord GOD), ²⁴you built yourself a vaulted chamber and made yourself a lofty place in every square. ²⁵At the head of every street you built your lofty place and made your beauty an abomination, offering yourself⁶ to any passerby and multiplying your whoring. ²⁶You also played the whore with the Egyptians, your lustful neighbors, multiplying your whoring, to provoke me to anger. ²⁷Behold, therefore, I stretched out my hand against you and diminished your allotted portion and delivered you to the greed of your enemies, the daughters of the Philistines, who were ashamed of your lewd behavior. ²⁸You played the whore also with the Assyrians, because you were not satisfied; yes,

you played the whore with them, and still you were not satisfied. [29] You multiplied your whoring also with the trading land of Chaldea, and even with this you were not satisfied.

[30] "How sick is your heart,[1] declares the Lord GOD, because you did all these things, the deeds of a brazen prostitute, [31] building your vaulted chamber at the head of every street, and making your lofty place in every square. Yet you were not like a prostitute, because you scorned payment. [32] Adulterous wife, who receives strangers instead of her husband! [33] Men give gifts to all prostitutes, but you gave your gifts to all your lovers, bribing them to come to you from every side with your whorings. [34] So you were different from other women in your whorings. No one solicited you to play the whore, and you gave payment, while no payment was given to you; therefore you were different.

[35] "Therefore, O prostitute, hear the word of the LORD: [36] Thus says the Lord GOD, Because your lust was poured out and your nakedness uncovered in your whorings with your lovers, and with all your abominable idols, and because of the blood of your children that you gave to them, [37] therefore, behold, I will gather all your lovers with whom you took pleasure, all those you loved and all those you hated. I will gather them against you from every side and will uncover your nakedness to them, that they may see all your nakedness. [38] And I will judge you as women who commit adultery and shed blood are judged, and bring upon you the blood of wrath and jealousy. [39] And I will give you into their hands, and they shall throw down your vaulted chamber and break down your lofty places. They shall strip you of your clothes and take your beautiful jewels and leave you naked and bare. [40] They shall bring up a crowd against you, and they shall stone you and cut you to pieces with their swords. [41] And they shall burn your houses and execute judgments upon you in the sight of many women. I will make you stop playing the whore, and you shall also give payment no more. [42] So will I satisfy my wrath on you, and my jealousy shall depart from you. I will be calm and will no more be angry. [43] Because you have not remembered the days of your youth, but have enraged me with all these things, therefore, behold, I have returned your deeds upon your head, declares the Lord GOD. Have you not committed lewdness in addition to all your abominations?

[44] "Behold, everyone who uses proverbs will use this proverb about you: 'Like mother, like daughter.' [45] You are the daughter of your mother, who loathed her husband and her children; and you are the sister of your sisters, who loathed their husbands and their children. Your mother was a Hittite and your father an Amorite. [46] And your elder sister is Samaria, who lived with her daughters to the north of you; and your younger sister, who lived to the south of you, is Sodom with her daughters. [47] Not only did you walk in their ways and do according to their abominations; within a very little time you were more corrupt than they in all your ways. [48] As I live, declares the Lord GOD, your sister Sodom and her daughters have not done as you and your daughters have done. [49] Behold, this was the guilt of your sister Sodom: she and her daughters had pride, excess of food, and prosperous ease, but did not aid the poor and needy. [50] They were haughty and did an abomination before me. So I removed them, when I saw it. [51] Samaria has not committed half your sins. You have committed more abominations than they, and have made your sisters appear righteous by all the abominations that you have committed. [52] Bear your disgrace, you also, for you have intervened on behalf of your sisters. Because of your sins in which you acted more abominably than they, they are more in the right than you. So be ashamed, you also, and bear your disgrace, for you have made your sisters appear righteous.

[53] "I will restore their fortunes, both the fortunes of Sodom and her daughters, and the fortunes of Samaria and her daughters, and I will restore your own fortunes in their midst, [54] that you may bear your disgrace and be ashamed of all that you have done, becoming a consolation to them. [55] As for your sisters, Sodom and her daughters shall return to their former state, and Samaria and her daughters shall return to their former state, and you and your daughters shall return to your former state. [56] Was not your sister Sodom a byword in your mouth in the day of your pride, [57] before your wickedness was uncovered? Now you have become an object of reproach for the daughters of Syria[2] and all those around her, and for the daughters of the Philistines, those all around who despise you.

---

[1] Revocalization yields *How I am filled with anger against you* [2] Some manuscripts (compare Syriac) *of Edom*

[58] You bear the penalty of your lewdness and your abominations, declares the LORD.

[59] "For thus says the Lord GOD: I will deal with you as you have done, you who have despised the oath in breaking the covenant, [60] yet I will remember my covenant with you in the days of your youth, and I will establish for you an everlasting covenant. [61] Then you will remember your ways and be ashamed when you take your sisters, both your elder and your younger, and I give them to you as daughters, but not on account of[1] the covenant with you. [62] I will establish my covenant with you, and you shall know that I am the LORD, [63] that you may remember and be confounded, and never open your mouth again because of your shame, when I atone for you for all that you have done, declares the Lord GOD."

Psalm 58–59

To the choirmaster: according to Do Not Destroy. A Miktam[2] of David.

[1] Do you indeed decree what is right, you gods?[3]
Do you judge the children of man uprightly?
[2] No, in your hearts you devise wrongs;
your hands deal out violence on earth.

[3] The wicked are estranged from the womb;
they go astray from birth, speaking lies.
[4] They have venom like the venom of a serpent,
like the deaf adder that stops its ear,
[5] so that it does not hear the voice of charmers
or of the cunning enchanter.

[6] O God, break the teeth in their mouths;
tear out the fangs of the young lions, O LORD!
[7] Let them vanish like water that runs away;
when he aims his arrows, let them be blunted.
[8] Let them be like the snail that dissolves into slime,
like the stillborn child who never sees the sun.

[9] Sooner than your pots can feel the heat of thorns,
whether green or ablaze, may he sweep them away![4]

[10] The righteous will rejoice when he sees the vengeance;
he will bathe his feet in the blood of the wicked.
[11] Mankind will say, "Surely there is a reward for the righteous;
surely there is a God who judges on earth."

To the choirmaster: according to Do Not Destroy. A Miktam[5] of David, when Saul sent men to watch his house in order to kill him.

[1] Deliver me from my enemies, O my God;
protect me from those who rise up against me;
[2] deliver me from those who work evil,
and save me from bloodthirsty men.

[3] For behold, they lie in wait for my life;
fierce men stir up strife against me.
For no transgression or sin of mine, O LORD,
[4] for no fault of mine, they run and make ready.
Awake, come to meet me, and see!
[5] You, LORD God of hosts, are God of Israel.
Rouse yourself to punish all the nations;
spare none of those who treacherously plot evil.   *Selah*

[6] Each evening they come back,
howling like dogs
and prowling about the city.
[7] There they are, bellowing with their mouths
with swords in their lips—
for "Who," they think,[6] "will hear us?"

[8] But you, O LORD, laugh at them;
you hold all the nations in derision.
[9] O my Strength, I will watch for you,
for you, O God, are my fortress.
[10] My God in his steadfast love[7] will meet me;
God will let me look in triumph on my enemies.

---

[1] Or *not apart from*   [2] Probably a musical or liturgical term   [3] Or *you mighty lords* (by revocalization; Hebrew *in silence*)   [4] The meaning of the Hebrew verse is uncertain   [5] Probably a musical or liturgical term   [6] Hebrew lacks *they think*   [7] Or *The God who shows me steadfast love*

11 Kill them not, lest my people forget;
   make them totter[1] by your power and
      bring them down,
   O Lord, our shield!
12 For the sin of their mouths, the words of
      their lips,
   let them be trapped in their pride.
   For the cursing and lies that they utter,
13 consume them in wrath;
   consume them till they are no more,
   that they may know that God rules over
      Jacob
   to the ends of the earth.   *Selah*

14 Each evening they come back,
   howling like dogs
   and prowling about the city.
15 They wander about for food
   and growl if they do not get their fill.
16 But I will sing of your strength;
   I will sing aloud of your steadfast love
      in the morning.
   For you have been to me a fortress
   and a refuge in the day of my distress.
17 O my Strength, I will sing praises to you,
   for you, O God, are my fortress,
   the God who shows me steadfast love.

SEPTEMBER 14

2 Samuel 10

After this the king of the Ammonites died, and Hanun his son reigned in his place. ²And David said, "I will deal loyally[2] with Hanun the son of Nahash, as his father dealt loyally with me." So David sent by his servants to console him concerning his father. And David's servants came into the land of the Ammonites. ³But the princes of the Ammonites said to Hanun their lord, "Do you think, because David has sent comforters to you, that he is honoring your father? Has not David sent his servants to you to search the city and to spy it out and to overthrow it?" ⁴So Hanun took David's servants and shaved off half the beard of each and cut off their garments in the middle, at their hips, and sent them away. ⁵When it was told David, he sent to meet them, for the men were greatly ashamed. And the king said, "Remain at Jericho until your beards have grown and then return."

⁶When the Ammonites saw that they had become a stench to David, the Ammonites sent and hired the Syrians of Beth-rehob, and the Syrians of Zobah, 20,000 foot soldiers, and the king of Maacah with 1,000 men, and the men of Tob, 12,000 men. ⁷And when David heard of it, he sent Joab and all the host of the mighty men. ⁸And the Ammonites came out and drew up in battle array at the entrance of the gate, and the Syrians of Zobah and of Rehob and the men of Tob and Maacah were by themselves in the open country.

⁹When Joab saw that the battle was set against him both in front and in the rear, he chose some of the best men of Israel and arrayed them against the Syrians. ¹⁰The rest of his men he put in the charge of Abishai his brother, and he arrayed them against the Ammonites. ¹¹And he said, "If the Syrians are too strong for me, then you shall help me, but if the Ammonites are too strong for you, then I will come and help you. ¹²Be of good courage, and let us be courageous for our people, and for the cities of our God, and may the Lord do what seems good to him." ¹³So Joab and the people who were with him drew near to battle against the Syrians, and they fled before him. ¹⁴And when the Ammonites saw that the Syrians fled, they likewise fled before Abishai and entered the city. Then Joab returned from fighting against the Ammonites and came to Jerusalem.

¹⁵But when the Syrians saw that they had been defeated by Israel, they gathered themselves together. ¹⁶And Hadadezer sent and brought out the Syrians who were beyond the

---

[1] Or *wander*   [2] Or *kindly*; twice in this verse

Euphrates.[1] They came to Helam, with Shobach the commander of the army of Hadadezer at their head. [17] And when it was told David, he gathered all Israel together and crossed the Jordan and came to Helam. The Syrians arrayed themselves against David and fought with him. [18] And the Syrians fled before Israel, and David killed of the Syrians the men of 700 chariots, and 40,000 horsemen, and wounded Shobach the commander of their army, so that he died there. [19] And when all the kings who were servants of Hadadezer saw that they had been defeated by Israel, they made peace with Israel and became subject to them. So the Syrians were afraid to save the Ammonites anymore.

2 Corinthians 3

Are we beginning to commend ourselves again? Or do we need, as some do, letters of recommendation to you, or from you? [2] You yourselves are our letter of recommendation, written on our[2] hearts, to be known and read by all. [3] And you show that you are a letter from Christ delivered by us, written not with ink but with the Spirit of the living God, not on tablets of stone but on tablets of human hearts.[3]

[4] Such is the confidence that we have through Christ toward God. [5] Not that we are sufficient in ourselves to claim anything as coming from us, but our sufficiency is from God, [6] who has made us sufficient to be ministers of a new covenant, not of the letter but of the Spirit. For the letter kills, but the Spirit gives life.

[7] Now if the ministry of death, carved in letters on stone, came with such glory that the Israelites could not gaze at Moses' face because of its glory, which was being brought to an end, [8] will not the ministry of the Spirit have even more glory? [9] For if there was glory in the ministry of condemnation, the ministry of righteousness must far exceed it in glory. [10] Indeed, in this case, what once had glory has come to have no glory at all, because of the glory that surpasses it. [11] For if what was being brought to an end came with glory, much more will what is permanent have glory.

[12] Since we have such a hope, we are very bold, [13] not like Moses, who would put a veil over his face so that the Israelites might not gaze at the outcome of what was being brought to an end. [14] But their minds were hardened. For to this day, when they read the old covenant, that same veil remains unlifted, because only through Christ is it taken away. [15] Yes, to this day whenever Moses is read a veil lies over their hearts. [16] But when one[4] turns to the Lord, the veil is removed. [17] Now the Lord[5] is the Spirit, and where the Spirit of the Lord is, there is freedom. [18] And we all, with unveiled face, beholding the glory of the Lord,[6] are being transformed into the same image from one degree of glory to another. For this comes from the Lord who is the Spirit.

Ezekiel 17

The word of the LORD came to me: [2] "Son of man, propound a riddle, and speak a parable to the house of Israel; [3] say, Thus says the Lord GOD: A great eagle with great wings and long pinions, rich in plumage of many colors, came to Lebanon and took the top of the cedar. [4] He broke off the topmost of its young twigs and carried it to a land of trade and set it in a city of merchants. [5] Then he took of the seed of the land and planted it in fertile soil.[7] He placed it beside abundant waters. He set it like a willow twig, [6] and it sprouted and became a low spreading vine, and its branches turned toward him, and its roots remained where it stood. So it became a vine and produced branches and put out boughs.

[7] "And there was another great eagle with great wings and much plumage, and behold, this vine bent its roots toward him and shot forth its branches toward him from the bed where it was planted, that he might water it. [8] It had been planted on good soil by abundant waters, that it might produce branches and bear fruit and become a noble vine.

[9] "Say, Thus says the Lord GOD: Will it thrive? Will he not pull up its roots and cut off its fruit, so that it withers, so that all its fresh sprouting leaves wither? It will not take a strong arm or many people to pull it from its roots. [10] Behold, it is planted; will it thrive? Will it not utterly wither when the east wind strikes it—wither away on the bed where it sprouted?"

[11] Then the word of the LORD came to me: [12] "Say now to the rebellious house, Do

[1] Hebrew the River [2] Some manuscripts your [3] Greek fleshly hearts [4] Greek he [5] Or this Lord [6] Or reflecting the glory of the Lord [7] Hebrew in a field of seed

you not know what these things mean? Tell them, behold, the king of Babylon came to Jerusalem, and took her king and her princes and brought them to him to Babylon. [13]And he took one of the royal offspring[1] and made a covenant with him, putting him under oath (the chief men of the land he had taken away), [14]that the kingdom might be humble and not lift itself up, and keep his covenant that it might stand. [15]But he rebelled against him by sending his ambassadors to Egypt, that they might give him horses and a large army. Will he thrive? Can one escape who does such things? Can he break the covenant and yet escape?

[16]"As I live, declares the Lord GOD, surely in the place where the king dwells who made him king, whose oath he despised, and whose covenant with him he broke, in Babylon he shall die. [17]Pharaoh with his mighty army and great company will not help him in war, when mounds are cast up and siege walls built to cut off many lives. [18]He despised the oath in breaking the covenant, and behold, he gave his hand and did all these things; he shall not escape. [19]Therefore thus says the Lord GOD: As I live, surely it is my oath that he despised, and my covenant that he broke. I will return it upon his head. [20]I will spread my net over him, and he shall be taken in my snare, and I will bring him to Babylon and enter into judgment with him there for the treachery he has committed against me. [21]And all the pick[2] of his troops shall fall by the sword, and the survivors shall be scattered to every wind, and you shall know that I am the LORD; I have spoken."

[22]Thus says the Lord GOD: "I myself will take a sprig from the lofty top of the cedar and will set it out. I will break off from the topmost of its young twigs a tender one, and I myself will plant it on a high and lofty mountain. [23]On the mountain height of Israel will I plant it, that it may bear branches and produce fruit and become a noble cedar. And under it will dwell every kind of bird; in the shade of its branches birds of every sort will nest. [24]And all the trees of the field shall know that I am the LORD; I bring low the high tree, and make high the low tree, dry up the green tree, and make the dry tree flourish. I am the LORD; I have spoken, and I will do it."

Psalm 60–61

To the choirmaster: according to Shushan Eduth. A Miktam[3] of David; for instruction; when he strove with Aram-naharaim and with Aram-zobah, and when Joab on his return struck down twelve thousand of Edom in the Valley of Salt.

O God, you have rejected us, broken our defenses;
  you have been angry; oh, restore us.
[2] You have made the land to quake; you have torn it open;
  repair its breaches, for it totters.
[3] You have made your people see hard things;
  you have given us wine to drink that made us stagger.

[4] You have set up a banner for those who fear you,
  that they may flee to it from the bow.[4]
    Selah
[5] That your beloved ones may be delivered,
  give salvation by your right hand and answer us!

[6] God has spoken in his holiness:[5]
  "With exultation I will divide up Shechem
  and portion out the Vale of Succoth.
[7] Gilead is mine; Manasseh is mine;
  Ephraim is my helmet;
  Judah is my scepter.
[8] Moab is my washbasin;
  upon Edom I cast my shoe;
  over Philistia I shout in triumph."[6]

[9] Who will bring me to the fortified city?
  Who will lead me to Edom?
[10] Have you not rejected us, O God?
  You do not go forth, O God, with our armies.
[11] Oh, grant us help against the foe,
  for vain is the salvation of man!
[12] With God we shall do valiantly;
  it is he who will tread down our foes.

To the choirmaster: with stringed instruments. Of David.

Hear my cry, O God,
  listen to my prayer;
[2] from the end of the earth I call to you
  when my heart is faint.

Lead me to the rock
    that is higher than I,
³ for you have been my refuge,
    a strong tower against the enemy.

⁴ Let me dwell in your tent forever!
    Let me take refuge under the shelter
       of your wings!   *Selah*
⁵ For you, O God, have heard my vows;
    you have given me the heritage of
       those who fear your name.

⁶ Prolong the life of the king;
    may his years endure to all
       generations!
⁷ May he be enthroned forever before
    God;
    appoint steadfast love and faithfulness
       to watch over him!

⁸ So will I ever sing praises to your
    name,
    as I perform my vows day after day.

SEPTEMBER 15

2 Samuel 11

In the spring of the year, the time when kings go out to battle, David sent Joab, and his servants with him, and all Israel. And they ravaged the Ammonites and besieged Rabbah. But David remained at Jerusalem.

²It happened, late one afternoon, when David arose from his couch and was walking on the roof of the king's house, that he saw from the roof a woman bathing; and the woman was very beautiful. ³And David sent and inquired about the woman. And one said, "Is not this Bathsheba, the daughter of Eliam, the wife of Uriah the Hittite?" ⁴So David sent messengers and took her, and she came to him, and he lay with her. (Now she had been purifying herself from her uncleanness.) Then she returned to her house. ⁵And the woman conceived, and she sent and told David, "I am pregnant."

⁶So David sent word to Joab, "Send me Uriah the Hittite." And Joab sent Uriah to David. ⁷When Uriah came to him, David asked how Joab was doing and how the people were doing and how the war was going. ⁸Then David said to Uriah, "Go down to your house and wash your feet." And Uriah went out of the king's house, and there followed him a present from the king. ⁹But Uriah slept at the door of the king's house with all the servants of his lord, and did not go down to his house. ¹⁰When they told David, "Uriah did not go down to his house," David said to Uriah, "Have you not come from

a journey? Why did you not go down to your house?" ¹¹Uriah said to David, "The ark and Israel and Judah dwell in booths, and my lord Joab and the servants of my lord are camping in the open field. Shall I then go to my house, to eat and to drink and to lie with my wife? As you live, and as your soul lives, I will not do this thing." ¹²Then David said to Uriah, "Remain here today also, and tomorrow I will send you back." So Uriah remained in Jerusalem that day and the next. ¹³And David invited him, and he ate in his presence and drank, so that he made him drunk. And in the evening he went out to lie on his couch with the servants of his lord, but he did not go down to his house.

¹⁴In the morning David wrote a letter to Joab and sent it by the hand of Uriah. ¹⁵In the letter he wrote, "Set Uriah in the forefront of the hardest fighting, and then draw back from him, that he may be struck down, and die." ¹⁶And as Joab was besieging the city, he assigned Uriah to the place where he knew there were valiant men. ¹⁷And the men of the city came out and fought with Joab, and some of the servants of David among the people fell. Uriah the Hittite also died. ¹⁸Then Joab sent and told David all the news about the fighting. ¹⁹And he instructed the messenger, "When you have finished telling all the news about the fighting to the king, ²⁰then, if the king's anger rises, and if he says to you, 'Why did you go so near the

city to fight? Did you not know that they would shoot from the wall? [21] Who killed Abimelech the son of Jerubbesheth? Did not a woman cast an upper millstone on him from the wall, so that he died at Thebez? Why did you go so near the wall?' then you shall say, 'Your servant Uriah the Hittite is dead also.'"

[22] So the messenger went and came and told David all that Joab had sent him to tell. [23] The messenger said to David, "The men gained an advantage over us and came out against us in the field, but we drove them back to the entrance of the gate. [24] Then the archers shot at your servants from the wall. Some of the king's servants are dead, and your servant Uriah the Hittite is dead also." [25] David said to the messenger, "Thus shall you say to Joab, 'Do not let this matter displease you, for the sword devours now one and now another. Strengthen your attack against the city and overthrow it.' And encourage him."

[26] When the wife of Uriah heard that Uriah her husband was dead, she lamented over her husband. [27] And when the mourning was over, David sent and brought her to his house, and she became his wife and bore him a son. But the thing that David had done displeased the LORD.

2 Corinthians 4

Therefore, having this ministry by the mercy of God,[1] we do not lose heart. [2] But we have renounced disgraceful, underhanded ways. We refuse to practice[2] cunning or to tamper with God's word, but by the open statement of the truth we would commend ourselves to everyone's conscience in the sight of God. [3] And even if our gospel is veiled, it is veiled to those who are perishing. [4] In their case the god of this world has blinded the minds of the unbelievers, to keep them from seeing the light of the gospel of the glory of Christ, who is the image of God. [5] For what we proclaim is not ourselves, but Jesus Christ as Lord, with ourselves as your servants[3] for Jesus' sake. [6] For God, who said, "Let light shine out of darkness," has shone in our hearts to give the light of the knowledge of the glory of God in the face of Jesus Christ. [7] But we have this treasure in jars of clay, to show that the surpassing power belongs to God and not to us. [8] We are afflicted in every way, but not crushed; perplexed, but not driven to

despair; [9] persecuted, but not forsaken; struck down, but not destroyed; [10] always carrying in the body the death of Jesus, so that the life of Jesus may also be manifested in our bodies. [11] For we who live are always being given over to death for Jesus' sake, so that the life of Jesus also may be manifested in our mortal flesh. [12] So death is at work in us, but life in you.

[13] Since we have the same spirit of faith according to what has been written, "I believed, and so I spoke," we also believe, and so we also speak, [14] knowing that he who raised the Lord Jesus will raise us also with Jesus and bring us with you into his presence. [15] For it is all for your sake, so that as grace extends to more and more people it may increase thanksgiving, to the glory of God.

[16] So we do not lose heart. Though our outer self[4] is wasting away, our inner self is being renewed day by day. [17] For this light momentary affliction is preparing for us an eternal weight of glory beyond all comparison, [18] as we look not to the things that are seen but to the things that are unseen. For the things that are seen are transient, but the things that are unseen are eternal.

Ezekiel 18

The word of the LORD came to me: [2] "What do you[5] mean by repeating this proverb concerning the land of Israel, 'The fathers have eaten sour grapes, and the children's teeth are set on edge'? [3] As I live, declares the Lord GOD, this proverb shall no more be used by you in Israel. [4] Behold, all souls are mine; the soul of the father as well as the soul of the son is mine: the soul who sins shall die.

[5] "If a man is righteous and does what is just and right— [6] if he does not eat upon the mountains or lift up his eyes to the idols of the house of Israel, does not defile his neighbor's wife or approach a woman in her time of menstrual impurity, [7] does not oppress anyone, but restores to the debtor his pledge, commits no robbery, gives his bread to the hungry and covers the naked with a garment, [8] does not lend at interest or take any profit,[6] withholds his hand from injustice, executes true justice between man and man, [9] walks in my statutes, and keeps my rules by acting faithfully—he is righteous; he shall surely live, declares the Lord GOD.

---

[1] Greek *as we have received mercy* [2] Greek *to walk in* [3] Greek *bondservants* [4] Greek *man* [5] The Hebrew for *you* is plural [6] That is, profit that comes from charging interest to the poor; also verses 13, 17 (compare Leviticus 25:36)

[10] "If he fathers a son who is violent, a shedder of blood, who does any of these things [11](though he himself did none of these things), who even eats upon the mountains, defiles his neighbor's wife, [12]oppresses the poor and needy, commits robbery, does not restore the pledge, lifts up his eyes to the idols, commits abomination, [13]lends at interest, and takes profit; shall he then live? He shall not live. He has done all these abominations; he shall surely die; his blood shall be upon himself.

[14]"Now suppose this man fathers a son who sees all the sins that his father has done; he sees, and does not do likewise: [15]he does not eat upon the mountains or lift up his eyes to the idols of the house of Israel, does not defile his neighbor's wife, [16]does not oppress anyone, exacts no pledge, commits no robbery, but gives his bread to the hungry and covers the naked with a garment, [17]withholds his hand from iniquity,[1] takes no interest or profit, obeys my rules, and walks in my statutes; he shall not die for his father's iniquity; he shall surely live. [18]As for his father, because he practiced extortion, robbed his brother, and did what is not good among his people, behold, he shall die for his iniquity.

[19]"Yet you say, 'Why should not the son suffer for the iniquity of the father?' When the son has done what is just and right, and has been careful to observe all my statutes, he shall surely live. [20]The soul who sins shall die. The son shall not suffer for the iniquity of the father, nor the father suffer for the iniquity of the son. The righteousness of the righteous shall be upon himself, and the wickedness of the wicked shall be upon himself.

[21]"But if a wicked person turns away from all his sins that he has committed and keeps all my statutes and does what is just and right, he shall surely live; he shall not die. [22]None of the transgressions that he has committed shall be remembered against him; for the righteousness that he has done he shall live. [23]Have I any pleasure in the death of the wicked, declares the Lord GOD, and not rather that he should turn from his way and live? [24]But when a righteous person turns away from his righteousness and does injustice and does the same abominations that the wicked person does, shall he live? None of the righteous deeds that he has done shall be remembered; for the treachery of which he is guilty and the sin he has committed, for them he shall die.

[25]"Yet you say, 'The way of the Lord is not just.' Hear now, O house of Israel: Is my way not just? Is it not your ways that are not just? [26]When a righteous person turns away from his righteousness and does injustice, he shall die for it; for the injustice that he has done he shall die. [27]Again, when a wicked person turns away from the wickedness he has committed and does what is just and right, he shall save his life. [28]Because he considered and turned away from all the transgressions that he had committed, he shall surely live; he shall not die. [29]Yet the house of Israel says, 'The way of the Lord is not just.' O house of Israel, are my ways not just? Is it not your ways that are not just?

[30]"Therefore I will judge you, O house of Israel, every one according to his ways, declares the Lord GOD. Repent and turn from all your transgressions, lest iniquity be your ruin.[2] [31]Cast away from you all the transgressions that you have committed, and make yourselves a new heart and a new spirit! Why will you die, O house of Israel? [32]For I have no pleasure in the death of anyone, declares the Lord GOD; so turn, and live."

Psalm 62–63

To the choirmaster: according to Jeduthun. A Psalm of David.

For God alone my soul waits in silence;
    from him comes my salvation.
2   He alone is my rock and my salvation,
      my fortress; I shall not be greatly
      shaken.

3   How long will all of you attack a man
      to batter him,
    like a leaning wall, a tottering fence?
4   They only plan to thrust him down from
      his high position.
    They take pleasure in falsehood.
    They bless with their mouths,
      but inwardly they curse.   *Selah*

5   For God alone, O my soul, wait in
      silence,
    for my hope is from him.
6   He only is my rock and my salvation,
      my fortress; I shall not be shaken.

---

[1] Septuagint; Hebrew *from the poor* [2] Or *lest iniquity be your stumbling block*

⁷ On God rests my salvation and my glory;
    my mighty rock, my refuge is God.

⁸ Trust in him at all times, O people;
    pour out your heart before him;
    God is a refuge for us.   *Selah*

⁹ Those of low estate are but a breath;
    those of high estate are a delusion;
    in the balances they go up;
    they are together lighter than a
      breath.

¹⁰ Put no trust in extortion;
    set no vain hopes on robbery;
    if riches increase, set not your heart
      on them.

¹¹ Once God has spoken;
    twice have I heard this:
    that power belongs to God,

¹² and that to you, O Lord, belongs
      steadfast love.
For you will render to a man
    according to his work.

A PSALM OF DAVID, WHEN HE WAS IN THE
WILDERNESS OF JUDAH.

O God, you are my God; earnestly I seek
  you;
    my soul thirsts for you;
    my flesh faints for you,
      as in a dry and weary land where there
      is no water.

² So I have looked upon you in the
      sanctuary,
    beholding your power and glory.

³ Because your steadfast love is better
      than life,
    my lips will praise you.

⁴ So I will bless you as long as I live;
    in your name I will lift up my hands.

⁵ My soul will be satisfied as with fat and
      rich food,
    and my mouth will praise you with
      joyful lips,

⁶ when I remember you upon my bed,
    and meditate on you in the watches of
      the night;

⁷ for you have been my help,
    and in the shadow of your wings I will
      sing for joy.

⁸ My soul clings to you;
    your right hand upholds me.

⁹ But those who seek to destroy my life
    shall go down into the depths of the
      earth;

¹⁰ they shall be given over to the power of
      the sword;
    they shall be a portion for jackals.

¹¹ But the king shall rejoice in God;
    all who swear by him shall exult,
    for the mouths of liars will be stopped.

SEPTEMBER 16

2 Samuel 12

And the LORD sent Nathan to David. He came to him and said to him, "There were two men in a certain city, the one rich and the other poor. ²The rich man had very many flocks and herds, ³but the poor man had nothing but one little ewe lamb, which he had bought. And he brought it up, and it grew up with him and with his children. It used to eat of his morsel and drink from his cup and lie in his arms,¹ and it was like a daughter to him. ⁴Now there came a traveler to the rich man, and he was unwilling to take one of his own flock or herd to prepare for the guest who had come to him, but he took the poor man's lamb and prepared it for the man who had come to him." ⁵Then David's anger was greatly kindled against the man, and he said to Nathan, "As the LORD lives, the man who has done this deserves to die, ⁶and he shall restore the lamb fourfold, because he did this thing, and because he had no pity."

¹ Hebrew *bosom*; also verse 8

[7]Nathan said to David, "You are the man! Thus says the Lord, the God of Israel, 'I anointed you king over Israel, and I delivered you out of the hand of Saul. [8]And I gave you your master's house and your master's wives into your arms and gave you the house of Israel and of Judah. And if this were too little, I would add to you as much more. [9]Why have you despised the word of the Lord, to do what is evil in his sight? You have struck down Uriah the Hittite with the sword and have taken his wife to be your wife and have killed him with the sword of the Ammonites. [10]Now therefore the sword shall never depart from your house, because you have despised me and have taken the wife of Uriah the Hittite to be your wife.' [11]Thus says the Lord, 'Behold, I will raise up evil against you out of your own house. And I will take your wives before your eyes and give them to your neighbor, and he shall lie with your wives in the sight of this sun. [12]For you did it secretly, but I will do this thing before all Israel and before the sun.'" [13]David said to Nathan, "I have sinned against the Lord." And Nathan said to David, "The Lord also has put away your sin; you shall not die. [14]Nevertheless, because by this deed you have utterly scorned the Lord,[1] the child who is born to you shall die." [15]Then Nathan went to his house.

And the Lord afflicted the child that Uriah's wife bore to David, and he became sick. [16]David therefore sought God on behalf of the child. And David fasted and went in and lay all night on the ground. [17]And the elders of his house stood beside him, to raise him from the ground, but he would not, nor did he eat food with them. [18]On the seventh day the child died. And the servants of David were afraid to tell him that the child was dead, for they said, "Behold, while the child was yet alive, we spoke to him, and he did not listen to us. How then can we say to him the child is dead? He may do himself some harm." [19]But when David saw that his servants were whispering together, David understood that the child was dead. And David said to his servants, "Is the child dead?" They said, "He is dead." [20]Then David arose from the earth and washed and anointed himself and changed his clothes. And he went into the house of the Lord and worshiped. He then went to his own house. And when he asked, they set food before him, and he ate. [21]Then his servants said to him, "What is this thing that you have done? You fasted and wept for the child while he was alive; but when the child died, you arose and ate food." [22]He said, "While the child was still alive, I fasted and wept, for I said, 'Who knows whether the Lord will be gracious to me, that the child may live?' [23]But now he is dead. Why should I fast? Can I bring him back again? I shall go to him, but he will not return to me."

[24]Then David comforted his wife, Bathsheba, and went in to her and lay with her, and she bore a son, and he called his name Solomon. And the Lord loved him [25]and sent a message by Nathan the prophet. So he called his name Jedidiah,[2] because of the Lord.

[26]Now Joab fought against Rabbah of the Ammonites and took the royal city. [27]And Joab sent messengers to David and said, "I have fought against Rabbah; moreover, I have taken the city of waters. [28]Now then gather the rest of the people together and encamp against the city and take it, lest I take the city and it be called by my name." [29]So David gathered all the people together and went to Rabbah and fought against it and took it. [30]And he took the crown of their king from his head. The weight of it was a talent[3] of gold, and in it was a precious stone, and it was placed on David's head. And he brought out the spoil of the city, a very great amount. [31]And he brought out the people who were in it and set them to labor with saws and iron picks and iron axes and made them toil at[4] the brick kilns. And thus he did to all the cities of the Ammonites. Then David and all the people returned to Jerusalem.

2 Corinthians 5

For we know that if the tent that is our earthly home is destroyed, we have a building from God, a house not made with hands, eternal in the heavens. [2]For in this tent we groan, longing to put on our heavenly dwelling, [3]if indeed by putting it on[5] we may not be found naked. [4]For while we are still in this tent, we groan, being burdened—not that we would be unclothed, but that we would be further clothed, so that what is mortal may be swallowed up by life. [5]He who has prepared us for this very thing is God, who has given us the Spirit as a guarantee.

---

[1] Masoretic Text *the enemies of the Lord*; Dead Sea Scroll *the word of the Lord* [2] *Jedidiah* means *beloved of the Lord* [3] A talent was about 75 pounds or 34 kilograms [4] Hebrew *pass through* [5] Some manuscripts *putting it off*

⁶ So we are always of good courage. We know that while we are at home in the body we are away from the Lord, ⁷ for we walk by faith, not by sight. ⁸ Yes, we are of good courage, and we would rather be away from the body and at home with the Lord. ⁹ So whether we are at home or away, we make it our aim to please him. ¹⁰ For we must all appear before the judgment seat of Christ, so that each one may receive what is due for what he has done in the body, whether good or evil.

¹¹ Therefore, knowing the fear of the Lord, we persuade others. But what we are is known to God, and I hope it is known also to your conscience. ¹² We are not commending ourselves to you again but giving you cause to boast about us, so that you may be able to answer those who boast about outward appearance and not about what is in the heart. ¹³ For if we are beside ourselves, it is for God; if we are in our right mind, it is for you. ¹⁴ For the love of Christ controls us, because we have concluded this: that one has died for all, therefore all have died; ¹⁵ and he died for all, that those who live might no longer live for themselves but for him who for their sake died and was raised.

¹⁶ From now on, therefore, we regard no one according to the flesh. Even though we once regarded Christ according to the flesh, we regard him thus no longer. ¹⁷ Therefore, if anyone is in Christ, he is a new creation.¹ The old has passed away; behold, the new has come. ¹⁸ All this is from God, who through Christ reconciled us to himself and gave us the ministry of reconciliation; ¹⁹ that is, in Christ God was reconciling² the world to himself, not counting their trespasses against them, and entrusting to us the message of reconciliation. ²⁰ Therefore, we are ambassadors for Christ, God making his appeal through us. We implore you on behalf of Christ, be reconciled to God. ²¹ For our sake he made him to be sin who knew no sin, so that in him we might become the righteousness of God.

--- Ezekiel 19 ---

And you, take up a lamentation for the princes of Israel, ² and say:

What was your mother? A lioness!
  Among lions she crouched;
in the midst of young lions
  she reared her cubs.
³ And she brought up one of her cubs;
  he became a young lion,
and he learned to catch prey;
  he devoured men.
⁴ The nations heard about him;
  he was caught in their pit,
and they brought him with hooks
  to the land of Egypt.
⁵ When she saw that she waited in vain,
  that her hope was lost,
she took another of her cubs
  and made him a young lion.
⁶ He prowled among the lions;
  he became a young lion,
and he learned to catch prey;
  he devoured men,
⁷ and seized³ their widows.
  He laid waste their cities,
and the land was appalled and all who
      were in it
  at the sound of his roaring.
⁸ Then the nations set against him
  from provinces on every side;
they spread their net over him;
  he was taken in their pit.
⁹ With hooks they put him in a cage⁴
  and brought him to the king of
      Babylon;
  they brought him into custody,
that his voice should no more be heard
  on the mountains of Israel.

¹⁰ Your mother was like a vine in a
      vineyard⁵
  planted by the water,
fruitful and full of branches
  by reason of abundant water.
¹¹ Its strong stems became
  rulers' scepters;
it towered aloft
  among the thick boughs;⁶
it was seen in its height
  with the mass of its branches.
¹² But the vine was plucked up in fury,
  cast down to the ground;
the east wind dried up its fruit;
  they were stripped off and withered.
As for its strong stem,
  fire consumed it.

¹ Or creature ² Or God was in Christ, reconciling ³ Hebrew knew ⁴ Or in a wooden collar ⁵ Some Hebrew manuscripts; most Hebrew manuscripts in your blood ⁶ Or the clouds

13 Now it is planted in the wilderness,
   in a dry and thirsty land.
14 And fire has gone out from the stem of
   its shoots,
   has consumed its fruit,
   so that there remains in it no strong
   stem,
   no scepter for ruling.

This is a lamentation and has become a lamentation.

───── Psalm 64–65 ─────

To the choirmaster. A Psalm of David.

Hear my voice, O God, in my complaint;
 preserve my life from dread of the
 enemy.
2 Hide me from the secret plots of the
   wicked,
   from the throng of evildoers,
3 who whet their tongues like swords,
   who aim bitter words like arrows,
4 shooting from ambush at the
   blameless,
   shooting at him suddenly and without
   fear.
5 They hold fast to their evil purpose;
   they talk of laying snares secretly,
thinking, "Who can see them?"
6 They search out injustice,
saying, "We have accomplished a
   diligent search."
   For the inward mind and heart of a
   man are deep.

7 But God shoots his arrow at them;
   they are wounded suddenly.
8 They are brought to ruin, with their own
   tongues turned against them;
   all who see them will wag their
   heads.
9 Then all mankind fears;
   they tell what God has brought about
   and ponder what he has done.

10 Let the righteous one rejoice in the
    LORD
    and take refuge in him!
    Let all the upright in heart exult!

To the choirmaster. A Psalm of David. A Song.

Praise is due to you,[1] O God, in Zion,
 and to you shall vows be performed.
2 O you who hear prayer,
   to you shall all flesh come.
3 When iniquities prevail against me,
   you atone for our transgressions.
4 Blessed is the one you choose and bring
   near,
   to dwell in your courts!
We shall be satisfied with the goodness
   of your house,
   the holiness of your temple!

5 By awesome deeds you answer us with
   righteousness,
   O God of our salvation,
the hope of all the ends of the earth
   and of the farthest seas;
6 the one who by his strength established
   the mountains,
   being girded with might;
7 who stills the roaring of the seas,
   the roaring of their waves,
   the tumult of the peoples,
8 so that those who dwell at the ends of
   the earth are in awe at your signs.
You make the going out of the morning
   and the evening to shout for joy.

9 You visit the earth and water it;[2]
   you greatly enrich it;
the river of God is full of water;
   you provide their grain,
   for so you have prepared it.
10 You water its furrows abundantly,
    settling its ridges,
softening it with showers,
   and blessing its growth.
11 You crown the year with your bounty;
   your wagon tracks overflow with
   abundance.
12 The pastures of the wilderness overflow,
   the hills gird themselves with joy,
13 the meadows clothe themselves with
   flocks,
   the valleys deck themselves with
   grain,
   they shout and sing together for joy.

[1] Or Praise waits for you in silence [2] Or and make it overflow

SEPTEMBER 17

2 Samuel 13

Now Absalom, David's son, had a beautiful sister, whose name was Tamar. And after a time Amnon, David's son, loved her. ²And Amnon was so tormented that he made himself ill because of his sister Tamar, for she was a virgin, and it seemed impossible to Amnon to do anything to her. ³But Amnon had a friend, whose name was Jonadab, the son of Shimeah, David's brother. And Jonadab was a very crafty man. ⁴And he said to him, "O son of the king, why are you so haggard morning after morning? Will you not tell me?" Amnon said to him, "I love Tamar, my brother Absalom's sister." ⁵Jonadab said to him, "Lie down on your bed and pretend to be ill. And when your father comes to see you, say to him, 'Let my sister Tamar come and give me bread to eat, and prepare the food in my sight, that I may see it and eat it from her hand.'" ⁶So Amnon lay down and pretended to be ill. And when the king came to see him, Amnon said to the king, "Please let my sister Tamar come and make a couple of cakes in my sight, that I may eat from her hand."

⁷Then David sent home to Tamar, saying, "Go to your brother Amnon's house and prepare food for him." ⁸So Tamar went to her brother Amnon's house, where he was lying down. And she took dough and kneaded it and made cakes in his sight and baked the cakes. ⁹And she took the pan and emptied it out before him, but he refused to eat. And Amnon said, "Send out everyone from me." So everyone went out from him. ¹⁰Then Amnon said to Tamar, "Bring the food into the chamber, that I may eat from your hand." And Tamar took the cakes she had made and brought them into the chamber to Amnon her brother. ¹¹But when she brought them near him to eat, he took hold of her and said to her, "Come, lie with me, my sister." ¹²She answered him, "No, my brother, do not violate¹ me, for such a thing is not done in Israel; do not do this outrageous thing. ¹³As for me, where could I carry my shame? And as for you, you would be

as one of the outrageous fools in Israel. Now therefore, please speak to the king, for he will not withhold me from you." ¹⁴But he would not listen to her, and being stronger than she, he violated her and lay with her.

¹⁵Then Amnon hated her with very great hatred, so that the hatred with which he hated her was greater than the love with which he had loved her. And Amnon said to her, "Get up! Go!" ¹⁶But she said to him, "No, my brother, for this wrong in sending me away is greater than the other that you did to me."² But he would not listen to her. ¹⁷He called the young man who served him and said, "Put this woman out of my presence and bolt the door after her." ¹⁸Now she was wearing a long robe³ with sleeves, for thus were the virgin daughters of the king dressed. So his servant put her out and bolted the door after her. ¹⁹And Tamar put ashes on her head and tore the long robe that she wore. And she laid her hand on her head and went away, crying aloud as she went.

²⁰And her brother Absalom said to her, "Has Amnon your brother been with you? Now hold your peace, my sister. He is your brother; do not take this to heart." So Tamar lived, a desolate woman, in her brother Absalom's house. ²¹When King David heard of all these things, he was very angry.⁴ ²²But Absalom spoke to Amnon neither good nor bad, for Absalom hated Amnon, because he had violated his sister Tamar.

²³After two full years Absalom had sheepshearers at Baal-hazor, which is near Ephraim, and Absalom invited all the king's sons. ²⁴And Absalom came to the king and said, "Behold, your servant has sheepshearers. Please let the king and his servants go with your servant." ²⁵But the king said to Absalom, "No, my son, let us not all go, lest we be burdensome to you." He pressed him, but he would not go but gave him his blessing. ²⁶Then Absalom said, "If not, please let my brother Amnon go with us." And the king said to him, "Why should he go with

¹ Or humiliate; also verses 14, 22, 32 ² Compare Septuagint, Vulgate; the meaning of the Hebrew is uncertain ³ Or a robe of many colors (compare Genesis 37:3); also verse 19
⁴ Dead Sea Scroll, Septuagint add But he would not punish his son Amnon, because he loved him, since he was his firstborn

you?" ²⁷But Absalom pressed him until he let Amnon and all the king's sons go with him. ²⁸Then Absalom commanded his servants, "Mark when Amnon's heart is merry with wine, and when I say to you, 'Strike Amnon,' then kill him. Do not fear; have I not commanded you? Be courageous and be valiant." ²⁹So the servants of Absalom did to Amnon as Absalom had commanded. Then all the king's sons arose, and each mounted his mule and fled.

³⁰While they were on the way, news came to David, "Absalom has struck down all the king's sons, and not one of them is left." ³¹Then the king arose and tore his garments and lay on the earth. And all his servants who were standing by tore their garments. ³²But Jonadab the son of Shimeah, David's brother, said, "Let not my lord suppose that they have killed all the young men, the king's sons, for Amnon alone is dead. For by the command of Absalom this has been determined from the day he violated his sister Tamar. ³³Now therefore let not my lord the king so take it to heart as to suppose that all the king's sons are dead, for Amnon alone is dead."

³⁴But Absalom fled. And the young man who kept the watch lifted up his eyes and looked, and behold, many people were coming from the road behind him[1] by the side of the mountain. ³⁵And Jonadab said to the king, "Behold, the king's sons have come; as your servant said, so it has come about." ³⁶And as soon as he had finished speaking, behold, the king's sons came and lifted up their voice and wept. And the king also and all his servants wept very bitterly.

³⁷But Absalom fled and went to Talmai the son of Ammihud, king of Geshur. And David mourned for his son day after day. ³⁸So Absalom fled and went to Geshur, and was there three years. ³⁹And the spirit of the king[2] longed to go out[3] to Absalom, because he was comforted about Amnon, since he was dead.

2 Corinthians 6

Working together with him, then, we appeal to you not to receive the grace of God in vain. ²For he says,

"In a favorable time I listened to you,
    and in a day of salvation I have helped
    you."

Behold, now is the favorable time; behold, now is the day of salvation. ³We put no obstacle in anyone's way, so that no fault may be found with our ministry, ⁴but as servants of God we commend ourselves in every way: by great endurance, in afflictions, hardships, calamities, ⁵beatings, imprisonments, riots, labors, sleepless nights, hunger; ⁶by purity, knowledge, patience, kindness, the Holy Spirit, genuine love; ⁷by truthful speech, and the power of God; with the weapons of righteousness for the right hand and for the left; ⁸through honor and dishonor, through slander and praise. We are treated as impostors, and yet are true; ⁹as unknown, and yet well known; as dying, and behold, we live; as punished, and yet not killed; ¹⁰as sorrowful, yet always rejoicing; as poor, yet making many rich; as having nothing, yet possessing everything.

¹¹We have spoken freely to you,[4] Corinthians; our heart is wide open. ¹²You are not restricted by us, but you are restricted in your own affections. ¹³In return (I speak as to children) widen your hearts also.

¹⁴Do not be unequally yoked with unbelievers. For what partnership has righteousness with lawlessness? Or what fellowship has light with darkness? ¹⁵What accord has Christ with Belial?[5] Or what portion does a believer share with an unbeliever? ¹⁶What agreement has the temple of God with idols? For we are the temple of the living God; as God said,

"I will make my dwelling among them
        and walk among them,
    and I will be their God,
        and they shall be my people.
¹⁷   Therefore go out from their midst,
        and be separate from them, says the
        Lord,
    and touch no unclean thing;
        then I will welcome you,
¹⁸   and I will be a father to you,
        and you shall be sons and daughters
        to me,
    says the Lord Almighty."

Ezekiel 20

In the seventh year, in the fifth month, on the tenth day of the month, certain of the elders of Israel came to inquire of the LORD, and sat before me. ²And the word of the LORD came to me: [3]"Son of man, speak to the elders of Israel, and say to them, Thus says the Lord GOD, Is it to inquire of me that you come? As I live, declares the Lord GOD, I will not be inquired of by you. [4]Will you judge them, son of man, will you judge them? Let them know the abominations of their fathers, [5]and say to them, Thus says the Lord GOD: On the day when I chose Israel, I swore[1] to the offspring of the house of Jacob, making myself known to them in the land of Egypt; I swore to them, saying, I am the LORD your God. [6]On that day I swore to them that I would bring them out of the land of Egypt into a land that I had searched out for them, a land flowing with milk and honey, the most glorious of all lands. [7]And I said to them, Cast away the detestable things your eyes feast on, every one of you, and do not defile yourselves with the idols of Egypt; I am the LORD your God. [8]But they rebelled against me and were not willing to listen to me. None of them cast away the detestable things their eyes feasted on, nor did they forsake the idols of Egypt.

"Then I said I would pour out my wrath upon them and spend my anger against them in the midst of the land of Egypt. [9]But I acted for the sake of my name, that it should not be profaned in the sight of the nations among whom they lived, in whose sight I made myself known to them in bringing them out of the land of Egypt. [10]So I led them out of the land of Egypt and brought them into the wilderness. [11]I gave them my statutes and made known to them my rules, by which, if a person does them, he shall live. [12]Moreover, I gave them my Sabbaths, as a sign between me and them, that they might know that I am the LORD who sanctifies them. [13]But the house of Israel rebelled against me in the wilderness. They did not walk in my statutes but rejected my rules, by which, if a person does them, he shall live; and my Sabbaths they greatly profaned.

"Then I said I would pour out my wrath upon them in the wilderness, to make a full end of them. [14]But I acted for the sake of my name, that it should not be profaned in the sight of the nations, in whose sight I had brought them out. [15]Moreover, I swore to them in the wilderness that I would not bring them into the land that I had given them, a land flowing with milk and honey, the most glorious of all lands, [16]because they rejected my rules and did not walk in my statutes, and profaned my Sabbaths; for their heart went after their idols. [17]Nevertheless, my eye spared them, and I did not destroy them or make a full end of them in the wilderness.

[18]"And I said to their children in the wilderness, Do not walk in the statutes of your fathers, nor keep their rules, nor defile yourselves with their idols. [19]I am the LORD your God; walk in my statutes, and be careful to obey my rules, [20]and keep my Sabbaths holy that they may be a sign between me and you, that you may know that I am the LORD your God. [21]But the children rebelled against me. They did not walk in my statutes and were not careful to obey my rules, by which, if a person does them, he shall live; they profaned my Sabbaths.

"Then I said I would pour out my wrath upon them and spend my anger against them in the wilderness. [22]But I withheld my hand and acted for the sake of my name, that it should not be profaned in the sight of the nations, in whose sight I had brought them out. [23]Moreover, I swore to them in the wilderness that I would scatter them among the nations and disperse them through the countries, [24]because they had not obeyed my rules, but had rejected my statutes and profaned my Sabbaths, and their eyes were set on their fathers' idols. [25]Moreover, I gave them statutes that were not good and rules by which they could not have life, [26]and I defiled them through their very gifts in their offering up all their firstborn, that I might devastate them. I did it that they might know that I am the LORD.

[27]"Therefore, son of man, speak to the house of Israel and say to them, Thus says the Lord GOD: In this also your fathers blasphemed me, by dealing treacherously with me. [28]For when I had brought them into the land that I swore to give them, then wherever they saw any high hill or any leafy tree, there they offered their sacrifices and there they presented the provocation of their offering; there they sent up their pleasing aromas, and there they poured out their drink offerings. [29](I said to them, What is the high place to which you go? So its name is called Bamah[2] to this day.)

[30]"Therefore say to the house of Israel, Thus says the Lord GOD: Will you defile yourselves after the manner of your fathers and go whoring after their detestable things? [31]When you present your gifts and offer up your children in

[1] Hebrew *I lifted my hand*; twice in this verse; also verses 6, 15, 23, 28, 42   [2] *Bamah* means *high place*

fire,[1] you defile yourselves with all your idols to this day. And shall I be inquired of by you, O house of Israel? As I live, declares the Lord GOD, I will not be inquired of by you.

[32] "What is in your mind shall never happen—the thought, 'Let us be like the nations, like the tribes of the countries, and worship wood and stone.'

[33] "As I live, declares the Lord GOD, surely with a mighty hand and an outstretched arm and with wrath poured out I will be king over you. [34] I will bring you out from the peoples and gather you out of the countries where you are scattered, with a mighty hand and an outstretched arm, and with wrath poured out. [35] And I will bring you into the wilderness of the peoples, and there I will enter into judgment with you face to face. [36] As I entered into judgment with your fathers in the wilderness of the land of Egypt, so I will enter into judgment with you, declares the Lord GOD. [37] I will make you pass under the rod, and I will bring you into the bond of the covenant. [38] I will purge out the rebels from among you, and those who transgress against me. I will bring them out of the land where they sojourn, but they shall not enter the land of Israel. Then you will know that I am the LORD.

[39] "As for you, O house of Israel, thus says the Lord GOD: Go serve every one of you his idols, now and hereafter, if you will not listen to me; but my holy name you shall no more profane with your gifts and your idols.

[40] "For on my holy mountain, the mountain height of Israel, declares the Lord GOD, there all the house of Israel, all of them, shall serve me in the land. There I will accept them, and there I will require your contributions and the choicest of your gifts, with all your sacred offerings. [41] As a pleasing aroma I will accept you, when I bring you out from the peoples and gather you out of the countries where you have been scattered. And I will manifest my holiness among you in the sight of the nations. [42] And you shall know that I am the LORD, when I bring you into the land of Israel, the country that I swore to give to your fathers. [43] And there you shall remember your ways and all your deeds with which you have defiled yourselves, and you shall loathe yourselves for all the evils that you have committed. [44] And you shall know that I am the LORD, when I deal with you for my name's sake,

not according to your evil ways, nor according to your corrupt deeds, O house of Israel, declares the Lord GOD."

[45] [2] And the word of the LORD came to me: [46] "Son of man, set your face toward the southland;[3] preach against the south, and prophesy against the forest land in the Negeb. [47] Say to the forest of the Negeb, Hear the word of the LORD: Thus says the Lord GOD, Behold, I will kindle a fire in you, and it shall devour every green tree in you and every dry tree. The blazing flame shall not be quenched, and all faces from south to north shall be scorched by it. [48] All flesh shall see that I the LORD have kindled it; it shall not be quenched." [49] Then I said, "Ah, Lord GOD! They are saying of me, 'Is he not a maker of parables?'"

Psalm 66–67

To the choirmaster. A Song. A Psalm.

Shout for joy to God, all the earth;
[2] sing the glory of his name;
    give to him glorious praise!
[3] Say to God, "How awesome are your deeds!
    So great is your power that your
        enemies come cringing to you.
[4] All the earth worships you
    and sings praises to you;
    they sing praises to your name." *Selah*

[5] Come and see what God has done:
    he is awesome in his deeds toward the
        children of man.
[6] He turned the sea into dry land;
    they passed through the river on foot.
There did we rejoice in him,
[7]   who rules by his might forever,
whose eyes keep watch on the nations—
    let not the rebellious exalt themselves.
        Selah

[8] Bless our God, O peoples;
    let the sound of his praise be heard,
[9] who has kept our soul among the living
    and has not let our feet slip.
[10] For you, O God, have tested us;
    you have tried us as silver is tried.
[11] You brought us into the net;
    you laid a crushing burden on our
        backs;

---

[1] Hebrew *and make your children pass through the fire* [2] Ch 21:1 in Hebrew [3] Or *toward Teman*

[12] you let men ride over our heads;
we went through fire and through
water;
yet you have brought us out to a place of
abundance.
[13] I will come into your house with burnt
offerings;
I will perform my vows to you,
[14] that which my lips uttered
and my mouth promised when I was
in trouble.
[15] I will offer to you burnt offerings of
fattened animals,
with the smoke of the sacrifice of rams;
I will make an offering of bulls and
goats.   *Selah*
[16] Come and hear, all you who fear God,
and I will tell what he has done for my
soul.
[17] I cried to him with my mouth,
and high praise was on[1] my tongue.[2]
[18] If I had cherished iniquity in my heart,
the Lord would not have listened.
[19] But truly God has listened;
he has attended to the voice of my
prayer.

[20] Blessed be God,
because he has not rejected my
prayer
or removed his steadfast love from
me!

TO THE CHOIRMASTER: WITH STRINGED
INSTRUMENTS. A PSALM. A SONG.

May God be gracious to us and bless us
and make his face to shine upon us,   *Selah*
[2] that your way may be known on earth,
your saving power among all nations.
[3] Let the peoples praise you, O God;
let all the peoples praise you!

[4] Let the nations be glad and sing for joy,
for you judge the peoples with equity
and guide the nations upon earth.   *Selah*
[5] Let the peoples praise you, O God;
let all the peoples praise you!

[6] The earth has yielded its increase;
God, our God, shall bless us.
[7] God shall bless us;
let all the ends of the earth fear him!

SEPTEMBER 18

2 Samuel 14

Now Joab the son of Zeruiah knew that the king's heart went out to Absalom. [2] And Joab sent to Tekoa and brought from there a wise woman and said to her, "Pretend to be a mourner and put on mourning garments. Do not anoint yourself with oil, but behave like a woman who has been mourning many days for the dead. [3] Go to the king and speak thus to him." So Joab put the words in her mouth.

[4] When the woman of Tekoa came to the king, she fell on her face to the ground and paid homage and said, "Save me, O king." [5] And the king said to her, "What is your trouble?" She answered, "Alas, I am a widow; my husband is dead. [6] And your servant had two sons, and they quarreled with one another in the field. There was no one to separate them, and one struck the other and killed him. [7] And now the whole clan has risen against your servant, and they say, 'Give up the man who struck his brother, that we may put him to death for the life of his brother whom he killed.' And so they would destroy the heir also. Thus they would quench my coal that is left and leave to my husband neither name nor remnant on the face of the earth."

[8] Then the king said to the woman, "Go to your house, and I will give orders concerning you." [9] And the woman of Tekoa said to the king,

[1] Hebrew *under* [2] Or *and he was exalted with my tongue*

"On me be the guilt, my lord the king, and on my father's house; let the king and his throne be guiltless." ¹⁰The king said, "If anyone says anything to you, bring him to me, and he shall never touch you again." ¹¹Then she said, "Please let the king invoke the LORD your God, that the avenger of blood kill no more, and my son be not destroyed." He said, "As the LORD lives, not one hair of your son shall fall to the ground."

¹²Then the woman said, "Please let your servant speak a word to my lord the king." He said, "Speak." ¹³And the woman said, "Why then have you planned such a thing against the people of God? For in giving this decision the king convicts himself, inasmuch as the king does not bring his banished one home again. ¹⁴We must all die; we are like water spilled on the ground, which cannot be gathered up again. But God will not take away life, and he devises means so that the banished one will not remain an outcast. ¹⁵Now I have come to say this to my lord the king because the people have made me afraid, and your servant thought, 'I will speak to the king; it may be that the king will perform the request of his servant. ¹⁶For the king will hear and deliver his servant from the hand of the man who would destroy me and my son together from the heritage of God.' ¹⁷And your servant thought, 'The word of my lord the king will set me at rest,' for my lord the king is like the angel of God to discern good and evil. The LORD your God be with you!"

¹⁸Then the king answered the woman, "Do not hide from me anything I ask you." And the woman said, "Let my lord the king speak." ¹⁹The king said, "Is the hand of Joab with you in all this?" The woman answered and said, "As surely as you live, my lord the king, one cannot turn to the right hand or to the left from anything that my lord the king has said. It was your servant Joab who commanded me; it was he who put all these words in the mouth of your servant. ²⁰In order to change the course of things your servant Joab did this. But my lord has wisdom like the wisdom of the angel of God to know all things that are on the earth."

²¹Then the king said to Joab, "Behold now, I grant this; go, bring back the young man Absalom." ²²And Joab fell on his face to the ground and paid homage and blessed the king. And Joab said, "Today your servant knows that I have found favor in your sight, my lord the

king, in that the king has granted the request of his servant." ²³So Joab arose and went to Geshur and brought Absalom to Jerusalem. ²⁴And the king said, "Let him dwell apart in his own house; he is not to come into my presence." So Absalom lived apart in his own house and did not come into the king's presence.

²⁵Now in all Israel there was no one so much to be praised for his handsome appearance as Absalom. From the sole of his foot to the crown of his head there was no blemish in him. ²⁶And when he cut the hair of his head (for at the end of every year he used to cut it; when it was heavy on him, he cut it), he weighed the hair of his head, two hundred shekels[1] by the king's weight. ²⁷There were born to Absalom three sons, and one daughter whose name was Tamar. She was a beautiful woman.

²⁸So Absalom lived two full years in Jerusalem, without coming into the king's presence. ²⁹Then Absalom sent for Joab, to send him to the king, but Joab would not come to him. And he sent a second time, but Joab would not come. ³⁰Then he said to his servants, "See, Joab's field is next to mine, and he has barley there; go and set it on fire." So Absalom's servants set the field on fire.[2] ³¹Then Joab arose and went to Absalom at his house and said to him, "Why have your servants set my field on fire?" ³²Absalom answered Joab, "Behold, I sent word to you, 'Come here, that I may send you to the king, to ask, "Why have I come from Geshur? It would be better for me to be there still." Now therefore let me go into the presence of the king, and if there is guilt in me, let him put me to death.'" ³³Then Joab went to the king and told him, and he summoned Absalom. So he came to the king and bowed himself on his face to the ground before the king, and the king kissed Absalom.

2 Corinthians 7

Since we have these promises, beloved, let us cleanse ourselves from every defilement of body[3] and spirit, bringing holiness to completion in the fear of God.

²Make room in your hearts[4] for us. We have wronged no one, we have corrupted no one, we have taken advantage of no one. ³I do not say this to condemn you, for I said before that you are in our hearts, to die together and to

---

[1] A shekel was about 2/5 ounce or 11 grams [2] Septuagint, Dead Sea Scroll add *So Joab's servants came to him with their clothes torn, and they said to him, "The servants of Absalom have set your field on fire."* [3] Greek *flesh* [4] Greek lacks *in your hearts*

live together. [4]I am acting with great boldness toward you; I have great pride in you; I am filled with comfort. In all our affliction, I am overflowing with joy.

[5]For even when we came into Macedonia, our bodies had no rest, but we were afflicted at every turn—fighting without and fear within. [6]But God, who comforts the downcast, comforted us by the coming of Titus, [7]and not only by his coming but also by the comfort with which he was comforted by you, as he told us of your longing, your mourning, your zeal for me, so that I rejoiced still more. [8]For even if I made you grieve with my letter, I do not regret it—though I did regret it, for I see that that letter grieved you, though only for a while. [9]As it is, I rejoice, not because you were grieved, but because you were grieved into repenting. For you felt a godly grief, so that you suffered no loss through us.

[10]For godly grief produces a repentance that leads to salvation without regret, whereas worldly grief produces death. [11]For see what earnestness this godly grief has produced in you, but also what eagerness to clear yourselves, what indignation, what fear, what longing, what zeal, what punishment! At every point you have proved yourselves innocent in the matter. [12]So although I wrote to you, it was not for the sake of the one who did the wrong, nor for the sake of the one who suffered the wrong, but in order that your earnestness for us might be revealed to you in the sight of God. [13]Therefore we are comforted.

And besides our own comfort, we rejoiced still more at the joy of Titus, because his spirit has been refreshed by you all. [14]For whatever boasts I made to him about you, I was not put to shame. But just as everything we said to you was true, so also our boasting before Titus has proved true. [15]And his affection for you is even greater, as he remembers the obedience of you all, how you received him with fear and trembling. [16]I rejoice, because I have complete confidence in you.

Ezekiel 21[1]

[1]The word of the LORD came to me: [2]"Son of man, set your face toward Jerusalem and preach against the sanctuaries.[2] Prophesy against the land of Israel [3]and say to the land of Israel, Thus says the LORD: Behold, I am against you and will draw my sword from its sheath and will cut off from you both righteous and wicked. [4]Because I will cut off from you both righteous and wicked, therefore my sword shall be drawn from its sheath against all flesh from south to north. [5]And all flesh shall know that I am the LORD. I have drawn my sword from its sheath; it shall not be sheathed again.

[6]"As for you, son of man, groan; with breaking heart and bitter grief, groan before their eyes. [7]And when they say to you, 'Why do you groan?' you shall say, 'Because of the news that it is coming. Every heart will melt, and all hands will be feeble; every spirit will faint, and all knees will be weak as water. Behold, it is coming, and it will be fulfilled,'" declares the Lord GOD.

[8]And the word of the LORD came to me: [9]"Son of man, prophesy and say, Thus says the Lord, say:

"A sword, a sword is sharpened
    and also polished,
10   sharpened for slaughter,
    polished to flash like lightning!

(Or shall we rejoice? You have despised the rod, my son, with everything of wood.)[3] [11]So the sword is given to be polished, that it may be grasped in the hand. It is sharpened and polished to be given into the hand of the slayer. [12]Cry out and wail, son of man, for it is against my people. It is against all the princes of Israel. They are delivered over to the sword with my people. Strike therefore upon your thigh. [13]For it will not be a testing—what could it do if you despise the rod?"[4] declares the Lord GOD.

[14]"As for you, son of man, prophesy. Clap your hands and let the sword come down twice, yes, three times,[5] the sword for those to be slain. It is the sword for the great slaughter, which surrounds them, [15]that their hearts may melt, and many stumble.[6] At all their gates I have given the glittering sword. Ah, it is made like lightning; it is taken up[7] for slaughter. [16]Cut sharply to the right; set yourself to the left, wherever your face is directed. [17]I also will clap my hands, and I will satisfy my fury; I the LORD have spoken."

[18]The word of the LORD came to me again:

19 "As for you, son of man, mark two ways for the sword of the king of Babylon to come. Both of them shall come from the same land. And make a signpost; make it at the head of the way to a city. **20** Mark a way for the sword to come to Rabbah of the Ammonites and to Judah, into Jerusalem the fortified. **21** For the king of Babylon stands at the parting of the way, at the head of the two ways, to use divination. He shakes the arrows; he consults the teraphim;[1] he looks at the liver. **22** Into his right hand comes the divination for Jerusalem, to set battering rams, to open the mouth with murder, to lift up the voice with shouting, to set battering rams against the gates, to cast up mounds, to build siege towers. **23** But to them it will seem like a false divination. They have sworn solemn oaths, but he brings their guilt to remembrance, that they may be taken.

24 "Therefore thus says the Lord GOD: Because you have made your guilt to be remembered, in that your transgressions are uncovered, so that in all your deeds your sins appear—because you have come to remembrance, you shall be taken in hand. **25** And you, O profane[2] wicked one, prince of Israel, whose day has come, the time of your final punishment, **26** thus says the Lord GOD: Remove the turban and take off the crown. Things shall not remain as they are. Exalt that which is low, and bring low that which is exalted. **27** A ruin, ruin, ruin I will make it. This also shall not be, until he comes, the one to whom judgment belongs, and I will give it to him.

28 "And you, son of man, prophesy, and say, Thus says the Lord GOD concerning the Ammonites and concerning their reproach; say, A sword, a sword is drawn for the slaughter. It is polished to consume and to flash like lightning— **29** while they see for you false visions, while they divine lies for you—to place you on the necks of the profane wicked, whose day has come, the time of their final punishment. **30** Return it to its sheath. In the place where you were created, in the land of your origin, I will judge you. **31** And I will pour out my indignation upon you; I will blow upon you with the fire of my wrath, and I will deliver you into the hands of brutish men, skillful to destroy. **32** You shall be fuel for the fire. Your blood shall be in the midst of the land. You shall be no more remembered, for I the LORD have spoken."

Psalm 68

TO THE CHOIRMASTER. A PSALM OF DAVID. A SONG.

God shall arise, his enemies shall be scattered;
    and those who hate him shall flee
      before him!
2 As smoke is driven away, so you shall
    drive them away;
    as wax melts before fire,
    so the wicked shall perish before God!
3 But the righteous shall be glad;
    they shall exult before God;
    they shall be jubilant with joy!

4 Sing to God, sing praises to his name;
    lift up a song to him who rides
      through the deserts;
his name is the LORD;
    exult before him!
5 Father of the fatherless and protector of
    widows
    is God in his holy habitation.
6 God settles the solitary in a home;
    he leads out the prisoners to
      prosperity,
    but the rebellious dwell in a parched
      land.

7 O God, when you went out before your
    people,
    when you marched through the
      wilderness,　　　　　　　*Selah*
8 the earth quaked, the heavens poured
    down rain,
    before God, the One of Sinai,
    before God, the God of Israel.
9 Rain in abundance, O God, you shed
    abroad;
    you restored your inheritance as it
      languished;
10 your flock[3] found a dwelling in it;
    in your goodness, O God, you
      provided for the needy.

11 The Lord gives the word;
    the women who announce the news
      are a great host:
12 "The kings of the armies—they flee,
    they flee!"
The women at home divide the spoil—
13   though you men lie among the
      sheepfolds—

---

[1] Or *household idols*　[2] Or *slain; also verse 29*　[3] Or *your congregation*

the wings of a dove covered with silver,
its pinions with shimmering gold.
14 When the Almighty scatters kings there,
let snow fall on Zalmon.
15 O mountain of God, mountain of
Bashan;
O many-peaked[1] mountain, mountain
of Bashan!
16 Why do you look with hatred, O many-
peaked mountain,
at the mount that God desired for his
abode,
yes, where the LORD will dwell
forever?
17 The chariots of God are twice ten
thousand,
thousands upon thousands;
the Lord is among them; Sinai is now
in the sanctuary.
18 You ascended on high,
leading a host of captives in your
train
and receiving gifts among men,
even among the rebellious, that the
LORD God may dwell there.
19 Blessed be the Lord,
who daily bears us up;
God is our salvation.   Selah
20 Our God is a God of salvation,
and to GOD, the Lord, belong
deliverances from death.
21 But God will strike the heads of his
enemies,
the hairy crown of him who walks in
his guilty ways.
22 The Lord said,
"I will bring them back from Bashan,
I will bring them back from the depths
of the sea,
23 that you may strike your feet in their
blood,
that the tongues of your dogs may
have their portion from the foe."

24 Your procession is[2] seen, O God,
the procession of my God, my King,
into the sanctuary—
25 the singers in front, the musicians last,
between them virgins playing
tambourines:
26 "Bless God in the great congregation,
the LORD, O you[3] who are of Israel's
fountain!"
27 There is Benjamin, the least of them, in
the lead,
the princes of Judah in their throng,
the princes of Zebulun, the princes of
Naphtali.
28 Summon your power, O God,[4]
the power, O God, by which you have
worked for us.
29 Because of your temple at Jerusalem
kings shall bear gifts to you.
30 Rebuke the beasts that dwell among the
reeds,
the herd of bulls with the calves of the
peoples.
Trample underfoot those who lust after
tribute;
scatter the peoples who delight in war.[5]
31 Nobles shall come from Egypt;
Cush shall hasten to stretch out her
hands to God.
32 O kingdoms of the earth, sing to God;
sing praises to the Lord,   Selah
33 to him who rides in the heavens, the
ancient heavens;
behold, he sends out his voice, his
mighty voice.
34 Ascribe power to God,
whose majesty is over Israel,
and whose power is in the skies.
35 Awesome is God from his[6] sanctuary;
the God of Israel—he is the one who
gives power and strength to his
people.
Blessed be God!

[1] Or hunch-backed; also verse 16 [2] Or has been [3] The Hebrew for you is plural here [4] By revocalization (compare Septuagint); Hebrew Your God has summoned your power
[5] The meaning of the Hebrew verse is uncertain [6] Septuagint; Hebrew your

SEPTEMBER 19

2 Samuel 15

After this Absalom got himself a chariot and horses, and fifty men to run before him. [2]And Absalom used to rise early and stand beside the way of the gate. And when any man had a dispute to come before the king for judgment, Absalom would call to him and say, "From what city are you?" And when he said, "Your servant is of such and such a tribe in Israel," [3]Absalom would say to him, "See, your claims are good and right, but there is no man designated by the king to hear you." [4]Then Absalom would say, "Oh that I were judge in the land! Then every man with a dispute or cause might come to me, and I would give him justice." [5]And whenever a man came near to pay homage to him, he would put out his hand and take hold of him and kiss him. [6]Thus Absalom did to all of Israel who came to the king for judgment. So Absalom stole the hearts of the men of Israel.

[7]And at the end of four[1] years Absalom said to the king, "Please let me go and pay my vow, which I have vowed to the LORD, in Hebron. [8]For your servant vowed a vow while I lived at Geshur in Aram, saying, 'If the LORD will indeed bring me back to Jerusalem, then I will offer worship to[2] the LORD.' " [9]The king said to him, "Go in peace." So he arose and went to Hebron. [10]But Absalom sent secret messengers throughout all the tribes of Israel, saying, "As soon as you hear the sound of the trumpet, then say, 'Absalom is king at Hebron!' " [11]With Absalom went two hundred men from Jerusalem who were invited guests, and they went in their innocence and knew nothing. [12]And while Absalom was offering the sacrifices, he sent for[3] Ahithophel the Gilonite, David's counselor, from his city Giloh. And the conspiracy grew strong, and the people with Absalom kept increasing.

[13]And a messenger came to David, saying, "The hearts of the men of Israel have gone after Absalom." [14]Then David said to all his servants who were with him at Jerusalem, "Arise, and let us flee, or else there will be no escape for us from Absalom. Go quickly, lest he overtake us

quickly and bring down ruin on us and strike the city with the edge of the sword." [15]And the king's servants said to the king, "Behold, your servants are ready to do whatever my lord the king decides." [16]So the king went out, and all his household after him. And the king left ten concubines to keep the house. [17]And the king went out, and all the people after him. And they halted at the last house.

[18]And all his servants passed by him, and all the Cherethites, and all the Pelethites, and all the six hundred Gittites who had followed him from Gath, passed on before the king. [19]Then the king said to Ittai the Gittite, "Why do you also go with us? Go back and stay with the king, for you are a foreigner and also an exile from your home. [20]You came only yesterday, and shall I today make you wander about with us, since I go I know not where? Go back and take your brothers with you, and may the LORD show[4] steadfast love and faithfulness to you." [21]But Ittai answered the king, "As the LORD lives, and as my lord the king lives, wherever my lord the king shall be, whether for death or for life, there also will your servant be." [22]And David said to Ittai, "Go then, pass on." So Ittai the Gittite passed on with all his men and all the little ones who were with him. [23]And all the land wept aloud as all the people passed by, and the king crossed the brook Kidron, and all the people passed on toward the wilderness.

[24]And Abiathar came up, and behold, Zadok came also with all the Levites, bearing the ark of the covenant of God. And they set down the ark of God until the people had all passed out of the city. [25]Then the king said to Zadok, "Carry the ark of God back into the city. If I find favor in the eyes of the LORD, he will bring me back and let me see both it and his dwelling place. [26]But if he says, 'I have no pleasure in you,' behold, here I am, let him do to me what seems good to him." [27]The king also said to Zadok the priest, "Are you not a seer? Go back[5] to the city in peace, with your two sons, Ahimaaz your

[1] Septuagint, Syriac; Hebrew *forty* [2] Or *will serve* [3] Or *sent* [4] Septuagint; Hebrew lacks *may the LORD show* [5] Septuagint *The king also said to Zadok the priest, "Look, go back*

son, and Jonathan the son of Abiathar. ²⁸See, I will wait at the fords of the wilderness until word comes from you to inform me." ²⁹So Zadok and Abiathar carried the ark of God back to Jerusalem, and they remained there.

³⁰But David went up the ascent of the Mount of Olives, weeping as he went, barefoot and with his head covered. And all the people who were with him covered their heads, and they went up, weeping as they went. ³¹And it was told David, "Ahithophel is among the conspirators with Absalom." And David said, "O Lord, please turn the counsel of Ahithophel into foolishness."

³²While David was coming to the summit, where God was worshiped, behold, Hushai the Archite came to meet him with his coat torn and dirt on his head. ³³David said to him, "If you go on with me, you will be a burden to me. ³⁴But if you return to the city and say to Absalom, 'I will be your servant, O king; as I have been your father's servant in time past, so now I will be your servant,' then you will defeat for me the counsel of Ahithophel. ³⁵Are not Zadok and Abiathar the priests with you there? So whatever you hear from the king's house, tell it to Zadok and Abiathar the priests. ³⁶Behold, their two sons are with them there, Ahimaaz, Zadok's son, and Jonathan, Abiathar's son, and by them you shall send to me everything you hear." ³⁷So Hushai, David's friend, came into the city, just as Absalom was entering Jerusalem.

2 Corinthians 8

We want you to know, brothers,¹ about the grace of God that has been given among the churches of Macedonia, ²for in a severe test of affliction, their abundance of joy and their extreme poverty have overflowed in a wealth of generosity on their part. ³For they gave according to their means, as I can testify, and beyond their means, of their own accord, ⁴begging us earnestly for the favor² of taking part in the relief of the saints— ⁵and this, not as we expected, but they gave themselves first to the Lord and then by the will of God to us. ⁶Accordingly, we urged Titus that as he had started, so he should complete among you this act of grace. ⁷But as you excel in everything—in faith, in speech, in knowledge, in all earnestness, and in our love for you³—see that you excel in this act of grace also.

⁸I say this not as a command, but to prove by the earnestness of others that your love also is genuine. ⁹For you know the grace of our Lord Jesus Christ, that though he was rich, yet for your sake he became poor, so that you by his poverty might become rich. ¹⁰And in this matter I give my judgment: this benefits you, who a year ago started not only to do this work but also to desire to do it. ¹¹So now finish doing it as well, so that your readiness in desiring it may be matched by your completing it out of what you have. ¹²For if the readiness is there, it is acceptable according to what a person has, not according to what he does not have. ¹³For I do not mean that others should be eased and you burdened, but that as a matter of fairness ¹⁴your abundance at the present time should supply their need, so that their abundance may supply your need, that there may be fairness. ¹⁵As it is written, "Whoever gathered much had nothing left over, and whoever gathered little had no lack."

¹⁶But thanks be to God, who put into the heart of Titus the same earnest care I have for you. ¹⁷For he not only accepted our appeal, but being himself very earnest he is going⁴ to you of his own accord. ¹⁸With him we are sending⁵ the brother who is famous among all the churches for his preaching of the gospel. ¹⁹And not only that, but he has been appointed by the churches to travel with us as we carry out this act of grace that is being ministered by us, for the glory of the Lord himself and to show our good will. ²⁰We take this course so that no one should blame us about this generous gift that is being administered by us, ²¹for we aim at what is honorable not only in the Lord's sight but also in the sight of man. ²²And with them we are sending our brother whom we have often tested and found earnest in many matters, but who is now more earnest than ever because of his great confidence in you. ²³As for Titus, he is my partner and fellow worker for your benefit. And as for our brothers, they are messengers⁶ of the churches, the glory of Christ. ²⁴So give proof before the churches of your love and of our boasting about you to these men.

Ezekiel 22

And the word of the Lord came to me, saying, ²"And you, son of man, will you judge, will you judge the bloody city? Then declare to

¹ Or brothers and sisters ² The Greek word charis can mean favor or grace or thanks, depending on the context ³ Some manuscripts in your love for us ⁴ Or he went ⁵ Or we sent; also verse 22 ⁶ Greek apostles

her all her abominations. ³You shall say, Thus says the Lord GOD: A city that sheds blood in her midst, so that her time may come, and that makes idols to defile herself! ⁴You have become guilty by the blood that you have shed, and defiled by the idols that you have made, and you have brought your days near, the appointed time of¹ your years has come. Therefore I have made you a reproach to the nations, and a mockery to all the countries. ⁵Those who are near and those who are far from you will mock you; your name is defiled; you are full of tumult.

⁶"Behold, the princes of Israel in you, every one according to his power, have been bent on shedding blood. ⁷Father and mother are treated with contempt in you; the sojourner suffers extortion in your midst; the fatherless and the widow are wronged in you. ⁸You have despised my holy things and profaned my Sabbaths. ⁹There are men in you who slander to shed blood, and people in you who eat on the mountains; they commit lewdness in your midst. ¹⁰In you men uncover their fathers' nakedness; in you they violate women who are unclean in their menstrual impurity. ¹¹One commits abomination with his neighbor's wife; another lewdly defiles his daughter-in-law; another in you violates his sister, his father's daughter. ¹²In you they take bribes to shed blood; you take interest and profit² and make gain of your neighbors by extortion; but me you have forgotten, declares the Lord GOD.

¹³"Behold, I strike my hand at the dishonest gain that you have made, and at the blood that has been in your midst. ¹⁴Can your courage endure, or can your hands be strong, in the days that I shall deal with you? I the LORD have spoken, and I will do it. ¹⁵I will scatter you among the nations and disperse you through the countries, and I will consume your uncleanness out of you. ¹⁶And you shall be profaned by your own doing in the sight of the nations, and you shall know that I am the LORD."

¹⁷And the word of the LORD came to me: ¹⁸"Son of man, the house of Israel has become dross to me; all of them are bronze and tin and iron and lead in the furnace; they are dross of silver. ¹⁹Therefore thus says the Lord GOD: Because you have all become dross, therefore, behold, I will gather you into the midst of Jerusalem. ²⁰As one gathers silver and bronze and iron and lead and tin into a furnace, to blow the fire on it in order to melt it, so I will gather you in my anger and in my wrath, and I will put you in and melt you. ²¹I will gather you and blow on you with the fire of my wrath, and you shall be melted in the midst of it. ²²As silver is melted in a furnace, so you shall be melted in the midst of it, and you shall know that I am the LORD; I have poured out my wrath upon you."

²³And the word of the LORD came to me: ²⁴"Son of man, say to her, You are a land that is not cleansed or rained upon in the day of indignation. ²⁵The conspiracy of her prophets in her midst is like a roaring lion tearing the prey; they have devoured human lives; they have taken treasure and precious things; they have made many widows in her midst. ²⁶Her priests have done violence to my law and have profaned my holy things. They have made no distinction between the holy and the common, neither have they taught the difference between the unclean and the clean, and they have disregarded my Sabbaths, so that I am profaned among them. ²⁷Her princes in her midst are like wolves tearing the prey, shedding blood, destroying lives to get dishonest gain. ²⁸And her prophets have smeared whitewash for them, seeing false visions and divining lies for them, saying, 'Thus says the Lord GOD,' when the LORD has not spoken. ²⁹The people of the land have practiced extortion and committed robbery. They have oppressed the poor and needy, and have extorted from the sojourner without justice. ³⁰And I sought for a man among them who should build up the wall and stand in the breach before me for the land, that I should not destroy it, but I found none. ³¹Therefore I have poured out my indignation upon them. I have consumed them with the fire of my wrath. I have returned their way upon their heads, declares the Lord GOD."

Psalm 69

TO THE CHOIRMASTER: ACCORDING TO LILIES.
OF DAVID.

Save me, O God!
 For the waters have come up to my neck.³
² I sink in deep mire,
     where there is no foothold;
   I have come into deep waters,
     and the flood sweeps over me.

¹ Some Hebrew manuscripts, Septuagint, Syriac, Vulgate, Targum; most Hebrew manuscripts *until* ² That is, profit that comes from charging interest to the poor (compare Leviticus 25:36) ³ Or *waters threaten my life*

3 I am weary with my crying out;
   my throat is parched.
My eyes grow dim
   with waiting for my God.

4 More in number than the hairs of my
   head
   are those who hate me without cause;
mighty are those who would destroy me,
   those who attack me with lies.
What I did not steal
   must I now restore?

5 O God, you know my folly;
   the wrongs I have done are not hidden
   from you.

6 Let not those who hope in you be put to
   shame through me,
   O Lord GOD of hosts;
let not those who seek you be brought to
   dishonor through me,
   O God of Israel.

7 For it is for your sake that I have borne
   reproach,
   that dishonor has covered my face.

8 I have become a stranger to my brothers,
   an alien to my mother's sons.

9 For zeal for your house has consumed
   me,
   and the reproaches of those who
   reproach you have fallen on me.

10 When I wept and humbled[1] my soul
   with fasting,
   it became my reproach.

11 When I made sackcloth my clothing,
   I became a byword to them.

12 I am the talk of those who sit in the gate,
   and the drunkards make songs about
   me.

13 But as for me, my prayer is to you,
   O LORD.
   At an acceptable time, O God,
in the abundance of your steadfast
   love answer in your saving
   faithfulness.

14 Deliver me
   from sinking in the mire;
let me be delivered from my enemies
   and from the deep waters.

15 Let not the flood sweep over me,
   or the deep swallow me up,
   or the pit close its mouth over me.

16 Answer me, O LORD, for your steadfast
   love is good;
according to your abundant mercy,
   turn to me.

17 Hide not your face from your servant;
   for I am in distress; make haste to
   answer me.

18 Draw near to my soul, redeem me;
   ransom me because of my enemies!

19 You know my reproach,
   and my shame and my dishonor;
   my foes are all known to you.

20 Reproaches have broken my heart,
   so that I am in despair.
I looked for pity, but there was none,
   and for comforters, but I found none.

21 They gave me poison for food,
   and for my thirst they gave me sour
   wine to drink.

22 Let their own table before them become
   a snare;
   and when they are at peace, let it
   become a trap.[2]

23 Let their eyes be darkened, so that they
   cannot see,
   and make their loins tremble
   continually.

24 Pour out your indignation upon them,
   and let your burning anger overtake
   them.

25 May their camp be a desolation;
   let no one dwell in their tents.

26 For they persecute him whom you have
   struck down,
   and they recount the pain of those you
   have wounded.

27 Add to them punishment upon
   punishment;
   may they have no acquittal from you.[3]

28 Let them be blotted out of the book of
   the living;
   let them not be enrolled among the
   righteous.

29 But I am afflicted and in pain;
   let your salvation, O God, set me on
   high!

30 I will praise the name of God with a
   song;
   I will magnify him with thanksgiving.

[1] Hebrew lacks and humbled [2] Hebrew; a slight revocalization yields (compare Septuagint, Syriac, Jerome) a snare, and retribution and a trap [3] Hebrew may they not come into your righteousness

31   This will please the LORD more than
        an ox
     or a bull with horns and hoofs.
32   When the humble see it they will be
        glad;
     you who seek God, let your hearts
        revive.
33   For the LORD hears the needy
     and does not despise his own people
        who are prisoners.

34   Let heaven and earth praise him,
     the seas and everything that moves in
        them.
35   For God will save Zion
     and build up the cities of Judah,
     and people shall dwell there and possess
        it;
36   the offspring of his servants shall
        inherit it,
     and those who love his name shall
        dwell in it.

SEPTEMBER 20

2 Samuel 16

When David had passed a little beyond the summit, Ziba the servant of Mephibosheth met him, with a couple of donkeys saddled, bearing two hundred loaves of bread, a hundred bunches of raisins, a hundred of summer fruits, and a skin of wine. ²And the king said to Ziba, "Why have you brought these?" Ziba answered, "The donkeys are for the king's household to ride on, the bread and summer fruit for the young men to eat, and the wine for those who faint in the wilderness to drink." ³And the king said, "And where is your master's son?" Ziba said to the king, "Behold, he remains in Jerusalem, for he said, 'Today the house of Israel will give me back the kingdom of my father.'" ⁴Then the king said to Ziba, "Behold, all that belonged to Mephibosheth is now yours." And Ziba said, "I pay homage; let me ever find favor in your sight, my lord the king."

⁵When King David came to Bahurim, there came out a man of the family of the house of Saul, whose name was Shimei, the son of Gera, and as he came he cursed continually. ⁶And he threw stones at David and at all the servants of King David, and all the people and all the mighty men were on his right hand and on his left. ⁷And Shimei said as he cursed, "Get out, get out, you man of blood, you worthless man! ⁸The LORD has avenged on you all the blood

of the house of Saul, in whose place you have reigned, and the LORD has given the kingdom into the hand of your son Absalom. See, your evil is on you, for you are a man of blood."

⁹Then Abishai the son of Zeruiah said to the king, "Why should this dead dog curse my lord the king? Let me go over and take off his head." ¹⁰But the king said, "What have I to do with you, you sons of Zeruiah? If he is cursing because the LORD has said to him, 'Curse David,' who then shall say, 'Why have you done so?'" ¹¹And David said to Abishai and to all his servants, "Behold, my own son seeks my life; how much more now may this Benjaminite! Leave him alone, and let him curse, for the LORD has told him to. ¹²It may be that the LORD will look on the wrong done to me,[1] and that the LORD will repay me with good for his cursing today." ¹³So David and his men went on the road, while Shimei went along on the hillside opposite him and cursed as he went and threw stones at him and flung dust. ¹⁴And the king, and all the people who were with him, arrived weary at the Jordan.[2] And there he refreshed himself.

¹⁵Now Absalom and all the people, the men of Israel, came to Jerusalem, and Ahithophel with him. ¹⁶And when Hushai the Archite, David's friend, came to Absalom, Hushai said to Absalom, "Long live the king! Long live the king!" ¹⁷And Absalom said to Hushai, "Is this

---

[1] Septuagint, Vulgate *will look upon my affliction*   [2] Septuagint; Hebrew lacks *at the Jordan*

your loyalty to your friend? Why did you not go with your friend?" [18]And Hushai said to Absalom, "No, for whom the LORD and this people and all the men of Israel have chosen, his I will be, and with him I will remain. [19]And again, whom should I serve? Should it not be his son? As I have served your father, so I will serve you."

[20]Then Absalom said to Ahithophel, "Give your counsel. What shall we do?" [21]Ahithophel said to Absalom, "Go in to your father's concubines, whom he has left to keep the house, and all Israel will hear that you have made yourself a stench to your father, and the hands of all who are with you will be strengthened." [22]So they pitched a tent for Absalom on the roof. And Absalom went in to his father's concubines in the sight of all Israel. [23]Now in those days the counsel that Ahithophel gave was as if one consulted the word of God; so was all the counsel of Ahithophel esteemed, both by David and by Absalom.

──────── 2 Corinthians 9 ────────

Now it is superfluous for me to write to you about the ministry for the saints, [2]for I know your readiness, of which I boast about you to the people of Macedonia, saying that Achaia has been ready since last year. And your zeal has stirred up most of them. [3]But I am sending[1] the brothers so that our boasting about you may not prove empty in this matter, so that you may be ready, as I said you would be. [4]Otherwise, if some Macedonians come with me and find that you are not ready, we would be humiliated—to say nothing of you—for being so confident. [5]So I thought it necessary to urge the brothers to go on ahead to you and arrange in advance for the gift[2] you have promised, so that it may be ready as a willing gift, not as an exaction.[3]

[6]The point is this: whoever sows sparingly will also reap sparingly, and whoever sows bountifully[4] will also reap bountifully. [7]Each one must give as he has decided in his heart, not reluctantly or under compulsion, for God loves a cheerful giver. [8]And God is able to make all grace abound to you, so that having all sufficiency[5] in all things at all times, you may abound in every good work. [9]As it is written,

"He has distributed freely, he has given to the poor;
    his righteousness endures forever."

[10]He who supplies seed to the sower and bread for food will supply and multiply your seed for sowing and increase the harvest of your righteousness. [11]You will be enriched in every way to be generous in every way, which through us will produce thanksgiving to God. [12]For the ministry of this service is not only supplying the needs of the saints but is also overflowing in many thanksgivings to God. [13]By their approval of this service, they[6] will glorify God because of your submission that comes from your confession of the gospel of Christ, and the generosity of your contribution for them and for all others, [14]while they long for you and pray for you, because of the surpassing grace of God upon you. [15]Thanks be to God for his inexpressible gift!

──────── Ezekiel 23 ────────

The word of the LORD came to me: [2]"Son of man, there were two women, the daughters of one mother. [3]They played the whore in Egypt; they played the whore in their youth; there their breasts were pressed and their virgin bosoms[7] handled. [4]Oholah was the name of the elder and Oholibah the name of her sister. They became mine, and they bore sons and daughters. As for their names, Oholah is Samaria, and Oholibah is Jerusalem.

[5]"Oholah played the whore while she was mine, and she lusted after her lovers the Assyrians, warriors [6]clothed in purple, governors and commanders, all of them desirable young men, horsemen riding on horses. [7]She bestowed her whoring upon them, the choicest men of Assyria all of them, and she defiled herself with all the idols of everyone after whom she lusted. [8]She did not give up her whoring that she had begun in Egypt; for in her youth men had lain with her and handled her virgin bosom and poured out their whoring lust upon her. [9]Therefore I delivered her into the hands of her lovers, into the hands of the Assyrians, after whom she lusted. [10]These uncovered her nakedness; they seized her sons and her daughters; and as for her, they killed her with the sword; and she became a byword among

[1] Or I have sent [2] Greek blessing; twice in this verse [3] Or a gift expecting something in return; Greek greed [4] Greek with blessings; twice in this verse [5] Or all contentment [6] Or you
[7] Hebrew nipples; also verses 8, 21

women, when judgment had been executed on her.

11 "Her sister Oholibah saw this, and she became more corrupt than her sister[1] in her lust and in her whoring, which was worse than that of her sister. 12 She lusted after the Assyrians, governors and commanders, warriors clothed in full armor, horsemen riding on horses, all of them desirable young men. 13 And I saw that she was defiled; they both took the same way. 14 But she carried her whoring further. She saw men portrayed on the wall, the images of the Chaldeans portrayed in vermilion, 15 wearing belts on their waists, with flowing turbans on their heads, all of them having the appearance of officers, a likeness of Babylonians whose native land was Chaldea. 16 When she saw them, she lusted after them and sent messengers to them in Chaldea. 17 And the Babylonians came to her into the bed of love, and they defiled her with their whoring lust. And after she was defiled by them, she turned from them in disgust. 18 When she carried on her whoring so openly and flaunted her nakedness, I turned in disgust from her, as I had turned in disgust from her sister. 19 Yet she increased her whoring, remembering the days of her youth, when she played the whore in the land of Egypt 20 and lusted after her lovers there, whose members were like those of donkeys, and whose issue was like that of horses. 21 Thus you longed for the lewdness of your youth, when the Egyptians handled your bosom and pressed[2] your young breasts."

22 Therefore, O Oholibah, thus says the Lord GOD: "Behold, I will stir up against you your lovers from whom you turned in disgust, and I will bring them against you from every side: 23 the Babylonians and all the Chaldeans, Pekod and Shoa and Koa, and all the Assyrians with them, desirable young men, governors and commanders all of them, officers and men of renown, all of them riding on horses. 24 And they shall come against you from the north[3] with chariots and wagons and a host of peoples. They shall set themselves against you on every side with buckler, shield, and helmet; and I will commit the judgment to them, and they shall judge you according to their judgments. 25 And I will direct my jealousy against you, that they may deal with you in fury. They shall cut off your nose and your ears, and your survivors shall fall by the sword. They shall seize your sons and your daughters, and your survivors shall be devoured by fire. 26 They shall also strip you of your clothes and take away your beautiful jewels. 27 Thus I will put an end to your lewdness and your whoring begun in the land of Egypt, so that you shall not lift up your eyes to them or remember Egypt anymore.

28 "For thus says the Lord GOD: Behold, I will deliver you into the hands of those whom you hate, into the hands of those from whom you turned in disgust, 29 and they shall deal with you in hatred and take away all the fruit of your labor and leave you naked and bare, and the nakedness of your whoring shall be uncovered. Your lewdness and your whoring 30 have brought this upon you, because you played the whore with the nations and defiled yourself with their idols. 31 You have gone the way of your sister; therefore I will give her cup into your hand. 32 Thus says the Lord GOD:

> "You shall drink your sister's cup
>   that is deep and large;
> you shall be laughed at and held in
>   derision,
>   for it contains much;
> 33 you will be filled with drunkenness and
>   sorrow.
> A cup of horror and desolation,
>   the cup of your sister Samaria;
> 34 you shall drink it and drain it out,
>   and gnaw its shards,
>   and tear your breasts;

for I have spoken, declares the Lord GOD. 35 Therefore thus says the Lord GOD: Because you have forgotten me and cast me behind your back, you yourself must bear the consequences of your lewdness and whoring."

36 The LORD said to me: "Son of man, will you judge Oholah and Oholibah? Declare to them their abominations. 37 For they have committed adultery, and blood is on their hands. With their idols they have committed adultery, and they have even offered up[4] to them for food the children whom they had borne to me. 38 Moreover, this they have done to me: they have defiled my sanctuary on the same day and profaned my Sabbaths. 39 For when they had slaughtered their children in sacrifice to their idols, on the same day they came into my sanctuary to profane it. And behold, this is what they did in my house. 40 They even sent for men to come

from afar, to whom a messenger was sent; and behold, they came. For them you bathed yourself, painted your eyes, and adorned yourself with ornaments. [41]You sat on a stately couch, with a table spread before it on which you had placed my incense and my oil. [42]The sound of a carefree multitude was with her; and with men of the common sort, drunkards[1] were brought from the wilderness; and they put bracelets on the hands of the women, and beautiful crowns on their heads.

[43]"Then I said of her who was worn out by adultery, Now they will continue to use her for a whore, even her![2] [44]For they have gone in to her, as men go in to a prostitute. Thus they went in to Oholah and to Oholibah, lewd women! [45]But righteous men shall pass judgment on them with the sentence of adulteresses, and with the sentence of women who shed blood, because they are adulteresses, and blood is on their hands."

[46]For thus says the Lord God: "Bring up a vast host against them, and make them an object of terror and a plunder. [47]And the host shall stone them and cut them down with their swords. They shall kill their sons and their daughters, and burn up their houses. [48]Thus will I put an end to lewdness in the land, that all women may take warning and not commit lewdness as you have done. [49]And they shall return your lewdness upon you, and you shall bear the penalty for your sinful idolatry, and you shall know that I am the Lord God."

Psalm 70–71

To the choirmaster. Of David, for the memorial offering.

Make haste, O God, to deliver me!
  O Lord, make haste to help me!
[2] Let them be put to shame and confusion
    who seek my life!
  Let them be turned back and brought to dishonor
    who delight in my hurt!
[3] Let them turn back because of their shame
    who say, "Aha, Aha!"

[4] May all who seek you
  rejoice and be glad in you!

May those who love your salvation
  say evermore, "God is great!"
[5] But I am poor and needy;
  hasten to me, O God!
You are my help and my deliverer;
  O Lord, do not delay!

In you, O Lord, do I take refuge;
  let me never be put to shame!
[2] In your righteousness deliver me and rescue me;
  incline your ear to me, and save me!
[3] Be to me a rock of refuge,
  to which I may continually come;
you have given the command to save me,
  for you are my rock and my fortress.

[4] Rescue me, O my God, from the hand of the wicked,
  from the grasp of the unjust and cruel man.
[5] For you, O Lord, are my hope,
  my trust, O Lord, from my youth.
[6] Upon you I have leaned from before my birth;
  you are he who took me from my mother's womb.
My praise is continually of you.

[7] I have been as a portent to many,
  but you are my strong refuge.
[8] My mouth is filled with your praise,
  and with your glory all the day.
[9] Do not cast me off in the time of old age;
  forsake me not when my strength is spent.
[10] For my enemies speak concerning me;
  those who watch for my life consult together
[11] and say, "God has forsaken him;
  pursue and seize him,
  for there is none to deliver him."

[12] O God, be not far from me;
  O my God, make haste to help me!
[13] May my accusers be put to shame and consumed;
  with scorn and disgrace may they be covered
  who seek my hurt.
[14] But I will hope continually
  and will praise you yet more and more.

---

[1] Or Sabeans [2] The meaning of the Hebrew verse is uncertain

15 My mouth will tell of your righteous acts,
    of your deeds of salvation all the day,
    for their number is past my knowledge.
16 With the mighty deeds of the Lord GOD
    I will come;
    I will remind them of your
    righteousness, yours alone.

17 O God, from my youth you have taught
    me,
    and I still proclaim your wondrous
    deeds.
18 So even to old age and gray hairs,
    O God, do not forsake me,
    until I proclaim your might to another
    generation,
    your power to all those to come.
19 Your righteousness, O God,
    reaches the high heavens.
    You who have done great things,
    O God, who is like you?

20 You who have made me see many
    troubles and calamities
    will revive me again;
    from the depths of the earth
    you will bring me up again.
21 You will increase my greatness
    and comfort me again.

22 I will also praise you with the harp
    for your faithfulness, O my God;
    I will sing praises to you with the lyre,
    O Holy One of Israel.
23 My lips will shout for joy,
    when I sing praises to you;
    my soul also, which you have
    redeemed.
24 And my tongue will talk of your
    righteous help all the day long,
    for they have been put to shame and
    disappointed
    who sought to do me hurt.

SEPTEMBER 21

2 Samuel 17

Moreover, Ahithophel said to Absalom, "Let me choose twelve thousand men, and I will arise and pursue David tonight. ²I will come upon him while he is weary and discouraged and throw him into a panic, and all the people who are with him will flee. I will strike down only the king, ³and I will bring all the people back to you as a bride comes home to her husband. You seek the life of only one man,¹ and all the people will be at peace." ⁴And the advice seemed right in the eyes of Absalom and all the elders of Israel.

⁵ Then Absalom said, "Call Hushai the Archite also, and let us hear what he has to say." ⁶And when Hushai came to Absalom, Absalom said to him, "Thus has Ahithophel spoken; shall we do as he says? If not, you speak." ⁷Then Hushai said to Absalom, "This time the counsel that Ahithophel has given is not good." ⁸Hushai said, "You know that your father and his men are mighty men, and that

they are enraged,² like a bear robbed of her cubs in the field. Besides, your father is expert in war; he will not spend the night with the people. ⁹Behold, even now he has hidden himself in one of the pits or in some other place. And as soon as some of the people fall³ at the first attack, whoever hears it will say, 'There has been a slaughter among the people who follow Absalom.' ¹⁰Then even the valiant man, whose heart is like the heart of a lion, will utterly melt with fear, for all Israel knows that your father is a mighty man, and that those who are with him are valiant men. ¹¹But my counsel is that all Israel be gathered to you, from Dan to Beersheba, as the sand by the sea for multitude, and that you go to battle in person. ¹²So we shall come upon him in some place where he is to be found, and we shall light upon him as the dew falls on the ground, and of him and all the men with him not one will be left. ¹³If he withdraws into a city, then

¹ Septuagint; Hebrew *back to you*. Like the return of the whole is the man whom you seek ² Hebrew *bitter of soul* ³ Or *And as he falls on them*

all Israel will bring ropes to that city, and we shall drag it into the valley, until not even a pebble is to be found there." [14]And Absalom and all the men of Israel said, "The counsel of Hushai the Archite is better than the counsel of Ahithophel." For the LORD had ordained[1] to defeat the good counsel of Ahithophel, so that the LORD might bring harm upon Absalom.

[15]Then Hushai said to Zadok and Abiathar the priests, "Thus and so did Ahithophel counsel Absalom and the elders of Israel, and thus and so have I counseled. [16]Now therefore send quickly and tell David, 'Do not stay tonight at the fords of the wilderness, but by all means pass over, lest the king and all the people who are with him be swallowed up.'" [17]Now Jonathan and Ahimaaz were waiting at En-rogel. A female servant was to go and tell them, and they were to go and tell King David, for they were not to be seen entering the city. [18]But a young man saw them and told Absalom. So both of them went away quickly and came to the house of a man at Bahurim, who had a well in his courtyard. And they went down into it. [19]And the woman took and spread a covering over the well's mouth and scattered grain on it, and nothing was known of it. [20]When Absalom's servants came to the woman at the house, they said, "Where are Ahimaaz and Jonathan?" And the woman said to them, "They have gone over the brook[2] of water." And when they had sought and could not find them, they returned to Jerusalem.

[21]After they had gone, the men came up out of the well, and went and told King David. They said to David, "Arise, and go quickly over the water, for thus and so has Ahithophel counseled against you." [22]Then David arose, and all the people who were with him, and they crossed the Jordan. By daybreak not one was left who had not crossed the Jordan.

[23]When Ahithophel saw that his counsel was not followed, he saddled his donkey and went off home to his own city. He set his house in order and hanged himself, and he died and was buried in the tomb of his father.

[24]Then David came to Mahanaim. And Absalom crossed the Jordan with all the men of Israel. [25]Now Absalom had set Amasa over the army instead of Joab. Amasa was the son of a man named Ithra the Ishmaelite,[3] who had married Abigal the daughter of Nahash, sister of Zeruiah, Joab's mother. [26]And Israel and Absalom encamped in the land of Gilead.

[27]When David came to Mahanaim, Shobi the son of Nahash from Rabbah of the Ammonites, and Machir the son of Ammiel from Lo-debar, and Barzillai the Gileadite from Rogelim, [28]brought beds, basins, and earthen vessels, wheat, barley, flour, parched grain, beans and lentils,[4] [29]honey and curds and sheep and cheese from the herd, for David and the people with him to eat, for they said, "The people are hungry and weary and thirsty in the wilderness."

─────── *2 Corinthians 10* ───────

I, Paul, myself entreat you, by the meekness and gentleness of Christ—I who am humble when face to face with you, but bold toward you when I am away!— [2]I beg of you that when I am present I may not have to show boldness with such confidence as I count on showing against some who suspect us of walking according to the flesh. [3]For though we walk in the flesh, we are not waging war according to the flesh. [4]For the weapons of our warfare are not of the flesh but have divine power to destroy strongholds. [5]We destroy arguments and every lofty opinion raised against the knowledge of God, and take every thought captive to obey Christ, [6]being ready to punish every disobedience, when your obedience is complete.

[7]Look at what is before your eyes. If anyone is confident that he is Christ's, let him remind himself that just as he is Christ's, so also are we. [8]For even if I boast a little too much of our authority, which the Lord gave for building you up and not for destroying you, I will not be ashamed. [9]I do not want to appear to be frightening you with my letters. [10]For they say, "His letters are weighty and strong, but his bodily presence is weak, and his speech of no account." [11]Let such a person understand that what we say by letter when absent, we do when present. [12]Not that we dare to classify or compare ourselves with some of those who are commending themselves. But when they measure themselves by one another and compare themselves with one another, they are without understanding.

[13]But we will not boast beyond limits, but will boast only with regard to the area of

[1] Hebrew *commanded*   [2] The meaning of the Hebrew word is uncertain   [3] Compare 1 Chronicles 2:17; Hebrew *Israelite*   [4] Hebrew adds *and parched grain*

influence God assigned to us, to reach even to you. ¹⁴For we are not overextending ourselves, as though we did not reach you. For we were the first to come all the way to you with the gospel of Christ. ¹⁵We do not boast beyond limit in the labors of others. But our hope is that as your faith increases, our area of influence among you may be greatly enlarged, ¹⁶so that we may preach the gospel in lands beyond you, without boasting of work already done in another's area of influence. ¹⁷"Let the one who boasts, boast in the Lord." ¹⁸For it is not the one who commends himself who is approved, but the one whom the Lord commends.

Ezekiel 24

In the ninth year, in the tenth month, on the tenth day of the month, the word of the Lᴏʀᴅ came to me: ²"Son of man, write down the name of this day, this very day. The king of Babylon has laid siege to Jerusalem this very day. ³And utter a parable to the rebellious house and say to them, Thus says the Lord Gᴏᴅ:

"Set on the pot, set it on;
    pour in water also;
⁴   put in it the pieces of meat,
      all the good pieces, the thigh and the
        shoulder;
    fill it with choice bones.
⁵   Take the choicest one of the flock;
      pile the logs¹ under it;
    boil it well;
      seethe also its bones in it.

⁶"Therefore thus says the Lord Gᴏᴅ: Woe to the bloody city, to the pot whose corrosion is in it, and whose corrosion has not gone out of it! Take out of it piece after piece, without making any choice.² ⁷For the blood she has shed is in her midst; she put it on the bare rock; she did not pour it out on the ground to cover it with dust. ⁸To rouse my wrath, to take vengeance, I have set on the bare rock the blood she has shed, that it may not be covered. ⁹Therefore thus says the Lord Gᴏᴅ: Woe to the bloody city! I also will make the pile great. ¹⁰Heap on the logs, kindle the fire, boil the meat well, mix in the spices,³ and let the bones be burned up. ¹¹Then set it empty upon the coals, that it may become hot, and its copper may burn, that its uncleanness may be melted in it, its corrosion

consumed. ¹²She has wearied herself with toil;⁴ its abundant corrosion does not go out of it. Into the fire with its corrosion! ¹³On account of your unclean lewdness, because I would have cleansed you and you were not cleansed from your uncleanness, you shall not be cleansed anymore till I have satisfied my fury upon you. ¹⁴I am the Lᴏʀᴅ. I have spoken; it shall come to pass; I will do it. I will not go back; I will not spare; I will not relent; according to your ways and your deeds you will be judged, declares the Lord Gᴏᴅ."

¹⁵The word of the Lᴏʀᴅ came to me: ¹⁶"Son of man, behold, I am about to take the delight of your eyes away from you at a stroke; yet you shall not mourn or weep, nor shall your tears run down. ¹⁷Sigh, but not aloud; make no mourning for the dead. Bind on your turban, and put your shoes on your feet; do not cover your lips, nor eat the bread of men." ¹⁸So I spoke to the people in the morning, and at evening my wife died. And on the next morning I did as I was commanded.

¹⁹And the people said to me, "Will you not tell us what these things mean for us, that you are acting thus?" ²⁰Then I said to them, "The word of the Lᴏʀᴅ came to me: ²¹'Say to the house of Israel, Thus says the Lord Gᴏᴅ: Behold, I will profane my sanctuary, the pride of your power, the delight of your eyes, and the yearning of your soul, and your sons and your daughters whom you left behind shall fall by the sword. ²²And you shall do as I have done; you shall not cover your lips, nor eat the bread of men. ²³Your turbans shall be on your heads and your shoes on your feet; you shall not mourn or weep, but you shall rot away in your iniquities and groan to one another. ²⁴Thus shall Ezekiel be to you a sign; according to all that he has done you shall do. When this comes, then you will know that I am the Lord Gᴏᴅ.'

²⁵"As for you, son of man, surely on the day when I take from them their stronghold, their joy and glory, the delight of their eyes and their soul's desire, and also their sons and daughters, ²⁶on that day a fugitive will come to you to report to you the news. ²⁷On that day your mouth will be opened to the fugitive, and you shall speak and be no longer mute. So you will be a sign to them, and they will know that I am the Lᴏʀᴅ."

¹ Compare verse 10; Hebrew *the bones* ² Hebrew *no lot has fallen upon it* ³ Or *empty out the broth* ⁴ The meaning of the Hebrew is uncertain

—————— *Psalm 72* ——————

OF SOLOMON.

G ive the king your justice, O God,
  and your righteousness to the royal son!
2 May he judge your people with
      righteousness,
    and your poor with justice!
3 Let the mountains bear prosperity for
      the people,
    and the hills, in righteousness!
4 May he defend the cause of the poor of
      the people,
    give deliverance to the children of the
      needy,
    and crush the oppressor!

5 May they fear you[1] while the sun
      endures,
    and as long as the moon, throughout
      all generations!
6 May he be like rain that falls on the
      mown grass,
    like showers that water the earth!
7 In his days may the righteous flourish,
    and peace abound, till the moon be no
      more!
8 May he have dominion from sea to sea,
    and from the River[2] to the ends of the
      earth!
9 May desert tribes bow down before him,
    and his enemies lick the dust!
10 May the kings of Tarshish and of the
      coastlands
    render him tribute;
    may the kings of Sheba and Seba
      bring gifts!

11 May all kings fall down before him,
    all nations serve him!
12 For he delivers the needy when he calls,
    the poor and him who has no helper.
13 He has pity on the weak and the needy,
    and saves the lives of the needy.
14 From oppression and violence he
      redeems their life,
    and precious is their blood in his
      sight.

15 Long may he live;
    may gold of Sheba be given to him!
  May prayer be made for him
      continually,
    and blessings invoked for him all the
      day!
16 May there be abundance of grain in the
      land;
    on the tops of the mountains may it
      wave;
  may its fruit be like Lebanon;
  and may people blossom in the cities
    like the grass of the field!
17 May his name endure forever,
    his fame continue as long as the sun!
  May people be blessed in him,
    all nations call him blessed!

18 Blessed be the LORD, the God of Israel,
    who alone does wondrous things.
19 Blessed be his glorious name forever;
    may the whole earth be filled with his
      glory!
        Amen and Amen!

20 The prayers of David, the son of Jesse,
    are ended.

SEPTEMBER 22

—————— *2 Samuel 18* ——————

T hen David mustered the men who were
  with him and set over them commanders
of thousands and commanders of hundreds.
2 And David sent out the army, one third under
the command of Joab, one third under the
command of Abishai the son of Zeruiah, Joab's
brother, and one third under the command of
Ittai the Gittite. And the king said to the men,

[1] Septuagint *He shall endure* [2] That is, the Euphrates

"I myself will also go out with you." ³But the men said, "You shall not go out. For if we flee, they will not care about us. If half of us die, they will not care about us. But you are worth ten thousand of us. Therefore it is better that you send us help from the city." ⁴The king said to them, "Whatever seems best to you I will do." So the king stood at the side of the gate, while all the army marched out by hundreds and by thousands. ⁵And the king ordered Joab and Abishai and Ittai, "Deal gently for my sake with the young man Absalom." And all the people heard when the king gave orders to all the commanders about Absalom.

⁶So the army went out into the field against Israel, and the battle was fought in the forest of Ephraim. ⁷And the men of Israel were defeated there by the servants of David, and the loss there was great on that day, twenty thousand men. ⁸The battle spread over the face of all the country, and the forest devoured more people that day than the sword.

⁹And Absalom happened to meet the servants of David. Absalom was riding on his mule, and the mule went under the thick branches of a great oak,¹ and his head caught fast in the oak, and he was suspended between heaven and earth, while the mule that was under him went on. ¹⁰And a certain man saw it and told Joab, "Behold, I saw Absalom hanging in an oak." ¹¹Joab said to the man who told him, "What, you saw him! Why then did you not strike him there to the ground? I would have been glad to give you ten pieces of silver and a belt." ¹²But the man said to Joab, "Even if I felt in my hand the weight of a thousand pieces of silver, I would not reach out my hand against the king's son, for in our hearing the king commanded you and Abishai and Ittai, 'For my sake protect the young man Absalom.' ¹³On the other hand, if I had dealt treacherously against his life² (and there is nothing hidden from the king), then you yourself would have stood aloof." ¹⁴Joab said, "I will not waste time like this with you." And he took three javelins in his hand and thrust them into the heart of Absalom while he was still alive in the oak. ¹⁵And ten young men, Joab's armor-bearers, surrounded Absalom and struck him and killed him.

¹⁶Then Joab blew the trumpet, and the troops came back from pursuing Israel, for Joab restrained them. ¹⁷And they took Absalom and threw him into a great pit in the forest and raised over him a very great heap of stones. And all Israel fled every one to his own home. ¹⁸Now Absalom in his lifetime had taken and set up for himself the pillar that is in the King's Valley, for he said, "I have no son to keep my name in remembrance." He called the pillar after his own name, and it is called Absalom's monument³ to this day.

¹⁹Then Ahimaaz the son of Zadok said, "Let me run and carry news to the king that the Lord has delivered him from the hand of his enemies." ²⁰And Joab said to him, "You are not to carry news today. You may carry news another day, but today you shall carry no news, because the king's son is dead." ²¹Then Joab said to the Cushite, "Go, tell the king what you have seen." The Cushite bowed before Joab, and ran. ²²Then Ahimaaz the son of Zadok said again to Joab, "Come what may, let me also run after the Cushite." And Joab said, "Why will you run, my son, seeing that you will have no reward for the news?" ²³"Come what may," he said, "I will run." So he said to him, "Run." Then Ahimaaz ran by the way of the plain, and outran the Cushite.

²⁴Now David was sitting between the two gates, and the watchman went up to the roof of the gate by the wall, and when he lifted up his eyes and looked, he saw a man running alone. ²⁵The watchman called out and told the king. And the king said, "If he is alone, there is news in his mouth." And he drew nearer and nearer. ²⁶The watchman saw another man running. And the watchman called to the gate and said, "See, another man running alone!" The king said, "He also brings news." ²⁷The watchman said, "I think the running of the first is like the running of Ahimaaz the son of Zadok." And the king said, "He is a good man and comes with good news."

²⁸Then Ahimaaz cried out to the king, "All is well." And he bowed before the king with his face to the earth and said, "Blessed be the Lord your God, who has delivered up the men who raised their hand against my lord the king." ²⁹And the king said, "Is it well with the young man Absalom?" Ahimaaz answered, "When Joab sent the king's servant, your servant, I saw a great commotion, but I do not know what it was." ³⁰And the king said, "Turn

¹ Or terebinth; also verses 10, 14　² Or at the risk of my life　³ Or Absalom's hand

aside and stand here." So he turned aside and stood still.

³¹And behold, the Cushite came, and the Cushite said, "Good news for my lord the king! For the Lᴏʀᴅ has delivered you this day from the hand of all who rose up against you." ³²The king said to the Cushite, "Is it well with the young man Absalom?" And the Cushite answered, "May the enemies of my lord the king and all who rise up against you for evil be like that young man." ³³¹And the king was deeply moved and went up to the chamber over the gate and wept. And as he went, he said, "O my son Absalom, my son, my son Absalom! Would I had died instead of you, O Absalom, my son, my son!"

─────── *2 Corinthians 11* ───────

I wish you would bear with me in a little foolishness. Do bear with me! ²For I feel a divine jealousy for you, since I betrothed you to one husband, to present you as a pure virgin to Christ. ³But I am afraid that as the serpent deceived Eve by his cunning, your thoughts will be led astray from a sincere and pure devotion to Christ. ⁴For if someone comes and proclaims another Jesus than the one we proclaimed, or if you receive a different spirit from the one you received, or if you accept a different gospel from the one you accepted, you put up with it readily enough. ⁵Indeed, I consider that I am not in the least inferior to these super-apostles. ⁶Even if I am unskilled in speaking, I am not so in knowledge; indeed, in every way we have made this plain to you in all things.

⁷Or did I commit a sin in humbling myself so that you might be exalted, because I preached God's gospel to you free of charge? ⁸I robbed other churches by accepting support from them in order to serve you. ⁹And when I was with you and was in need, I did not burden anyone, for the brothers who came from Macedonia supplied my need. So I refrained and will refrain from burdening you in any way. ¹⁰As the truth of Christ is in me, this boasting of mine will not be silenced in the regions of Achaia. ¹¹And why? Because I do not love you? God knows I do!

¹²And what I am doing I will continue to do, in order to undermine the claim of those who would like to claim that in their boasted mission they work on the same terms as we do. ¹³For such men are false apostles, deceitful workmen, disguising themselves as apostles of Christ. ¹⁴And no wonder, for even Satan disguises himself as an angel of light. ¹⁵So it is no surprise if his servants, also, disguise themselves as servants of righteousness. Their end will correspond to their deeds.

¹⁶I repeat, let no one think me foolish. But even if you do, accept me as a fool, so that I too may boast a little. ¹⁷What I am saying with this boastful confidence, I say not as the Lord would² but as a fool. ¹⁸Since many boast according to the flesh, I too will boast. ¹⁹For you gladly bear with fools, being wise yourselves! ²⁰For you bear it if someone makes slaves of you, or devours you, or takes advantage of you, or puts on airs, or strikes you in the face. ²¹To my shame, I must say, we were too weak for that!

But whatever anyone else dares to boast of—I am speaking as a fool—I also dare to boast of that. ²²Are they Hebrews? So am I. Are they Israelites? So am I. Are they offspring of Abraham? So am I. ²³Are they servants of Christ? I am a better one—I am talking like a madman—with far greater labors, far more imprisonments, with countless beatings, and often near death. ²⁴Five times I received at the hands of the Jews the forty lashes less one. ²⁵Three times I was beaten with rods. Once I was stoned. Three times I was shipwrecked; a night and a day I was adrift at sea; ²⁶on frequent journeys, in danger from rivers, danger from robbers, danger from my own people, danger from Gentiles, danger in the city, danger in the wilderness, danger at sea, danger from false brothers; ²⁷in toil and hardship, through many a sleepless night, in hunger and thirst, often without food,³ in cold and exposure. ²⁸And, apart from other things, there is the daily pressure on me of my anxiety for all the churches. ²⁹Who is weak, and I am not weak? Who is made to fall, and I am not indignant?

³⁰If I must boast, I will boast of the things that show my weakness. ³¹The God and Father of the Lord Jesus, he who is blessed forever, knows that I am not lying. ³²At Damascus, the governor under King Aretas was guarding the city of Damascus in order to seize me, ³³but I was let down in a basket through a window in the wall and escaped his hands.

¹ Ch 19:1 in Hebrew ² Greek *not according to the Lord* ³ Or *often in fasting*

Ezekiel 25

The word of the Lord came to me: ²"Son of man, set your face toward the Ammonites and prophesy against them. ³Say to the Ammonites, Hear the word of the Lord God: Thus says the Lord God, Because you said, 'Aha!' over my sanctuary when it was profaned, and over the land of Israel when it was made desolate, and over the house of Judah when they went into exile, ⁴therefore behold, I am handing you over to the people of the East for a possession, and they shall set their encampments among you and make their dwellings in your midst. They shall eat your fruit, and they shall drink your milk. ⁵I will make Rabbah a pasture for camels and Ammon¹ a fold for flocks. Then you will know that I am the Lord. ⁶For thus says the Lord God: Because you have clapped your hands and stamped your feet and rejoiced with all the malice within your soul against the land of Israel, ⁷therefore, behold, I have stretched out my hand against you, and will hand you over as plunder to the nations. And I will cut you off from the peoples and will make you perish out of the countries; I will destroy you. Then you will know that I am the Lord.

⁸"Thus says the Lord God: Because Moab and Seir² said, 'Behold, the house of Judah is like all the other nations,' ⁹therefore I will lay open the flank of Moab from the cities, from its cities on its frontier, the glory of the country, Beth-jeshimoth, Baal-meon, and Kiriathaim. ¹⁰I will give it along with the Ammonites to the people of the East as a possession, that the Ammonites may be remembered no more among the nations, ¹¹and I will execute judgments upon Moab. Then they will know that I am the Lord.

¹²"Thus says the Lord God: Because Edom acted revengefully against the house of Judah and has grievously offended in taking vengeance on them, ¹³therefore thus says the Lord God, I will stretch out my hand against Edom and cut off from it man and beast. And I will make it desolate; from Teman even to Dedan they shall fall by the sword. ¹⁴And I will lay my vengeance upon Edom by the hand of my people Israel, and they shall do in Edom according to my anger and according to my wrath, and they shall know my vengeance, declares the Lord God.

¹⁵"Thus says the Lord God: Because the Philistines acted revengefully and took vengeance with malice of soul to destroy in never-ending enmity, ¹⁶therefore thus says the Lord God, Behold, I will stretch out my hand against the Philistines, and I will cut off the Cherethites and destroy the rest of the seacoast. ¹⁷I will execute great vengeance on them with wrathful rebukes. Then they will know that I am the Lord, when I lay my vengeance upon them."

Psalm 73

A Psalm of Asaph.

Truly God is good to Israel,
  to those who are pure in heart.
2 But as for me, my feet had almost stumbled,
    my steps had nearly slipped.
3 For I was envious of the arrogant
    when I saw the prosperity of the wicked.

4 For they have no pangs until death;
    their bodies are fat and sleek.
5 They are not in trouble as others are;
    they are not stricken like the rest of mankind.
6 Therefore pride is their necklace;
    violence covers them as a garment.
7 Their eyes swell out through fatness;
    their hearts overflow with follies.
8 They scoff and speak with malice;
    loftily they threaten oppression.
9 They set their mouths against the heavens,
    and their tongue struts through the earth.
10 Therefore his people turn back to them,
    and find no fault in them.³
11 And they say, "How can God know?
    Is there knowledge in the Most High?"
12 Behold, these are the wicked;
    always at ease, they increase in riches.
13 All in vain have I kept my heart clean
    and washed my hands in innocence.
14 For all the day long I have been stricken
    and rebuked every morning.
15 If I had said, "I will speak thus,"
    I would have betrayed the generation
      of your children.

¹ Hebrew *and the Ammonites* ² Septuagint lacks *and Seir* ³ Probable reading; Hebrew *the waters of a full cup are drained by them*

16 But when I thought how to understand
    this,
    it seemed to me a wearisome task,
17 until I went into the sanctuary of God;
    then I discerned their end.

18 Truly you set them in slippery places;
    you make them fall to ruin.
19 How they are destroyed in a moment,
    swept away utterly by terrors!
20 Like a dream when one awakes,
    O Lord, when you rouse yourself, you
        despise them as phantoms.
21 When my soul was embittered,
    when I was pricked in heart,
22 I was brutish and ignorant;
    I was like a beast toward you.

23 Nevertheless, I am continually with you;
    you hold my right hand.
24 You guide me with your counsel,
    and afterward you will receive me to
        glory.
25 Whom have I in heaven but you?
    And there is nothing on earth that I
        desire besides you.
26 My flesh and my heart may fail,
    but God is the strength[1] of my heart
        and my portion forever.
27 For behold, those who are far from you
        shall perish;
    you put an end to everyone who is
        unfaithful to you.
28 But for me it is good to be near God;
    I have made the Lord GOD my refuge,
    that I may tell of all your works.

SEPTEMBER 23

2 Samuel 19

It was told Joab, "Behold, the king is weeping and mourning for Absalom." ²So the victory that day was turned into mourning for all the people, for the people heard that day, "The king is grieving for his son." ³And the people stole into the city that day as people steal in who are ashamed when they flee in battle. ⁴The king covered his face, and the king cried with a loud voice, "O my son Absalom, O Absalom, my son, my son!" ⁵Then Joab came into the house to the king and said, "You have today covered with shame the faces of all your servants, who have this day saved your life and the lives of your sons and your daughters and the lives of your wives and your concubines, ⁶because you love those who hate you and hate those who love you. For you have made it clear today that commanders and servants are nothing to you, for today I know that if Absalom were alive and all of us were dead today, then you would be pleased. ⁷Now therefore arise, go out and speak kindly to your servants, for I swear by the LORD, if you do not go, not a man will stay with you

this night, and this will be worse for you than all the evil that has come upon you from your youth until now." ⁸Then the king arose and took his seat in the gate. And the people were all told, "Behold, the king is sitting in the gate." And all the people came before the king.

Now Israel had fled every man to his own home. ⁹And all the people were arguing throughout all the tribes of Israel, saying, "The king delivered us from the hand of our enemies and saved us from the hand of the Philistines, and now he has fled out of the land from Absalom. ¹⁰But Absalom, whom we anointed over us, is dead in battle. Now therefore why do you say nothing about bringing the king back?"

¹¹And King David sent this message to Zadok and Abiathar the priests: "Say to the elders of Judah, 'Why should you be the last to bring the king back to his house, when the word of all Israel has come to the king?[2] ¹²You are my brothers; you are my bone and my flesh. Why then should you be the last to bring back the king?' ¹³And say to Amasa, 'Are you not

[1] Hebrew rock [2] Septuagint; Hebrew to the king, to his house

my bone and my flesh? God do so to me and more also, if you are not commander of my army from now on in place of Joab.'" ¹⁴And he swayed the heart of all the men of Judah as one man, so that they sent word to the king, "Return, both you and all your servants." ¹⁵So the king came back to the Jordan, and Judah came to Gilgal to meet the king and to bring the king over the Jordan.

¹⁶And Shimei the son of Gera, the Benjaminite, from Bahurim, hurried to come down with the men of Judah to meet King David. ¹⁷And with him were a thousand men from Benjamin. And Ziba the servant of the house of Saul, with his fifteen sons and his twenty servants, rushed down to the Jordan before the king, ¹⁸and they crossed the ford to bring over the king's household and to do his pleasure. And Shimei the son of Gera fell down before the king, as he was about to cross the Jordan, ¹⁹and said to the king, "Let not my lord hold me guilty or remember how your servant did wrong on the day my lord the king left Jerusalem. Do not let the king take it to heart. ²⁰For your servant knows that I have sinned. Therefore, behold, I have come this day, the first of all the house of Joseph to come down to meet my lord the king." ²¹Abishai the son of Zeruiah answered, "Shall not Shimei be put to death for this, because he cursed the LORD's anointed?" ²²But David said, "What have I to do with you, you sons of Zeruiah, that you should this day be as an adversary to me? Shall anyone be put to death in Israel this day? For do I not know that I am this day king over Israel?" ²³And the king said to Shimei, "You shall not die." And the king gave him his oath.

²⁴And Mephibosheth the son of Saul came down to meet the king. He had neither taken care of his feet nor trimmed his beard nor washed his clothes, from the day the king departed until the day he came back in safety. ²⁵And when he came to Jerusalem to meet the king, the king said to him, "Why did you not go with me, Mephibosheth?" ²⁶He answered, "My lord, O king, my servant deceived me, for your servant said to him, 'I will saddle a donkey for myself,¹ that I may ride on it and go with the king.' For your servant is lame. ²⁷He has slandered your servant to my lord the king. But my lord the king is like the angel of God; do therefore what seems good to you. ²⁸For

all my father's house were but men doomed to death before my lord the king, but you set your servant among those who eat at your table. What further right have I, then, to cry to the king?" ²⁹And the king said to him, "Why speak any more of your affairs? I have decided: you and Ziba shall divide the land." ³⁰And Mephibosheth said to the king, "Oh, let him take it all, since my lord the king has come safely home."

³¹Now Barzillai the Gileadite had come down from Rogelim, and he went on with the king to the Jordan, to escort him over the Jordan. ³²Barzillai was a very aged man, eighty years old. He had provided the king with food while he stayed at Mahanaim, for he was a very wealthy man. ³³And the king said to Barzillai, "Come over with me, and I will provide for you with me in Jerusalem." ³⁴But Barzillai said to the king, "How many years have I still to live, that I should go up with the king to Jerusalem? ³⁵I am this day eighty years old. Can I discern what is pleasant and what is not? Can your servant taste what he eats or what he drinks? Can I still listen to the voice of singing men and singing women? Why then should your servant be an added burden to my lord the king? ³⁶Your servant will go a little way over the Jordan with the king. Why should the king repay me with such a reward? ³⁷Please let your servant return, that I may die in my own city near the grave of my father and my mother. But here is your servant Chimham. Let him go over with my lord the king, and do for him whatever seems good to you." ³⁸And the king answered, "Chimham shall go over with me, and I will do for him whatever seems good to you, and all that you desire of me I will do for you." ³⁹Then all the people went over the Jordan, and the king went over. And the king kissed Barzillai and blessed him, and he returned to his own home. ⁴⁰The king went on to Gilgal, and Chimham went on with him. All the people of Judah, and also half the people of Israel, brought the king on his way.

⁴¹Then all the men of Israel came to the king and said to the king, "Why have our brothers the men of Judah stolen you away and brought the king and his household over the Jordan, and all David's men with him?" ⁴²All the men of Judah answered the men of Israel, "Because the king is our close relative. Why then are

¹ Septuagint, Syriac, Vulgate *Saddle a donkey for me*

you angry over this matter? Have we eaten at all at the king's expense? Or has he given us any gift?" ⁴³And the men of Israel answered the men of Judah, "We have ten shares in the king, and in David also we have more than you. Why then did you despise us? Were we not the first to speak of bringing back our king?" But the words of the men of Judah were fiercer than the words of the men of Israel.

2 Corinthians 12

I must go on boasting. Though there is nothing to be gained by it, I will go on to visions and revelations of the Lord. ²I know a man in Christ who fourteen years ago was caught up to the third heaven—whether in the body or out of the body I do not know, God knows. ³And I know that this man was caught up into paradise—whether in the body or out of the body I do not know, God knows— ⁴and he heard things that cannot be told, which man may not utter. ⁵On behalf of this man I will boast, but on my own behalf I will not boast, except of my weaknesses— ⁶though if I should wish to boast, I would not be a fool, for I would be speaking the truth; but I refrain from it, so that no one may think more of me than he sees in me or hears from me. ⁷So to keep me from becoming conceited because of the surpassing greatness of the revelations,¹ a thorn was given me in the flesh, a messenger of Satan to harass me, to keep me from becoming conceited. ⁸Three times I pleaded with the Lord about this, that it should leave me. ⁹But he said to me, "My grace is sufficient for you, for my power is made perfect in weakness." Therefore I will boast all the more gladly of my weaknesses, so that the power of Christ may rest upon me. ¹⁰For the sake of Christ, then, I am content with weaknesses, insults, hardships, persecutions, and calamities. For when I am weak, then I am strong.

¹¹I have been a fool! You forced me to it, for I ought to have been commended by you. For I was not at all inferior to these super-apostles, even though I am nothing. ¹²The signs of a true apostle were performed among you with utmost patience, with signs and wonders and mighty works. ¹³For in what were you less favored than the rest of the churches, except that I myself did not burden you? Forgive me this wrong!

¹⁴Here for the third time I am ready to come to you. And I will not be a burden, for I seek not what is yours but you. For children are not obligated to save up for their parents, but parents for their children. ¹⁵I will most gladly spend and be spent for your souls. If I love you more, am I to be loved less? ¹⁶But granting that I myself did not burden you, I was crafty, you say, and got the better of you by deceit. ¹⁷Did I take advantage of you through any of those whom I sent to you? ¹⁸I urged Titus to go, and sent the brother with him. Did Titus take advantage of you? Did we not act in the same spirit? Did we not take the same steps?

¹⁹Have you been thinking all along that we have been defending ourselves to you? It is in the sight of God that we have been speaking in Christ, and all for your upbuilding, beloved. ²⁰For I fear that perhaps when I come I may find you not as I wish, and that you may find me not as you wish—that perhaps there may be quarreling, jealousy, anger, hostility, slander, gossip, conceit, and disorder. ²¹I fear that when I come again my God may humble me before you, and I may have to mourn over many of those who sinned earlier and have not repented of the impurity, sexual immorality, and sensuality that they have practiced.

Ezekiel 26

In the eleventh year, on the first day of the month, the word of the LORD came to me: ²"Son of man, because Tyre said concerning Jerusalem, 'Aha, the gate of the peoples is broken; it has swung open to me. I shall be replenished, now that she is laid waste,' ³therefore thus says the Lord GOD: Behold, I am against you, O Tyre, and will bring up many nations against you, as the sea brings up its waves. ⁴They shall destroy the walls of Tyre and break down her towers, and I will scrape her soil from her and make her a bare rock. ⁵She shall be in the midst of the sea a place for the spreading of nets, for I have spoken, declares the Lord GOD. And she shall become plunder for the nations, ⁶and her daughters on the mainland shall be killed by the sword. Then they will know that I am the LORD.

⁷"For thus says the Lord GOD: Behold, I will bring against Tyre from the north Nebuchadnezzar² king of Babylon, king of kings,

¹ Or hears from me, even because of the surpassing greatness of the revelations. So to keep me from becoming conceited ² Hebrew Nebuchadrezzar; so throughout Ezekiel

with horses and chariots, and with horsemen and a host of many soldiers. [8]He will kill with the sword your daughters on the mainland. He will set up a siege wall against you and throw up a mound against you, and raise a roof of shields against you. [9]He will direct the shock of his battering rams against your walls, and with his axes he will break down your towers. [10]His horses will be so many that their dust will cover you. Your walls will shake at the noise of the horsemen and wagons and chariots, when he enters your gates as men enter a city that has been breached. [11]With the hoofs of his horses he will trample all your streets. He will kill your people with the sword, and your mighty pillars will fall to the ground. [12]They will plunder your riches and loot your merchandise. They will break down your walls and destroy your pleasant houses. Your stones and timber and soil they will cast into the midst of the waters. [13]And I will stop the music of your songs, and the sound of your lyres shall be heard no more. [14]I will make you a bare rock. You shall be a place for the spreading of nets. You shall never be rebuilt, for I am the LORD; I have spoken, declares the Lord GOD.

[15]"Thus says the Lord GOD to Tyre: Will not the coastlands shake at the sound of your fall, when the wounded groan, when slaughter is made in your midst? [16]Then all the princes of the sea will step down from their thrones and remove their robes and strip off their embroidered garments. They will clothe themselves with trembling; they will sit on the ground and tremble every moment and be appalled at you. [17]And they will raise a lamentation over you and say to you,

" 'How you have perished,
    you who were inhabited from the seas,
O city renowned,
    who was mighty on the sea;
    she and her inhabitants imposed their terror
    on all her inhabitants!
[18] Now the coastlands tremble
    on the day of your fall,
and the coastlands that are on the sea
    are dismayed at your passing.'

[19]"For thus says the Lord GOD: When I make you a city laid waste, like the cities that are not inhabited, when I bring up the deep over you, and the great waters cover you, [20]then I will make you go down with those who go down to the pit, to the people of old, and I will make you to dwell in the world below, among ruins from of old, with those who go down to the pit, so that you will not be inhabited; but I will set beauty in the land of the living. [21]I will bring you to a dreadful end, and you shall be no more. Though you be sought for, you will never be found again, declares the Lord GOD."

Psalm 74

A MASKIL[1] OF ASAPH.

O God, why do you cast us off forever?
    Why does your anger smoke against the sheep of your pasture?
[2] Remember your congregation, which you have purchased of old,
    which you have redeemed to be the tribe of your heritage!
    Remember Mount Zion, where you have dwelt.
[3] Direct your steps to the perpetual ruins;
    the enemy has destroyed everything in the sanctuary!

[4] Your foes have roared in the midst of your meeting place;
    they set up their own signs for signs.
[5] They were like those who swing axes in a forest of trees.[2]
[6] And all its carved wood
    they broke down with hatchets and hammers.
[7] They set your sanctuary on fire;
    they profaned the dwelling place of your name,
    bringing it down to the ground.
[8] They said to themselves, "We will utterly subdue them";
    they burned all the meeting places of God in the land.

[9] We do not see our signs;
    there is no longer any prophet,
    and there is none among us who knows how long.
[10] How long, O God, is the foe to scoff?
    Is the enemy to revile your name forever?

[1] Probably a musical or liturgical term [2] The meaning of the Hebrew is uncertain

11 Why do you hold back your hand, your
   right hand?
   Take it from the fold of your garment[1]
   and destroy them!

12 Yet God my King is from of old,
   working salvation in the midst of the
   earth.

13 You divided the sea by your might;
   you broke the heads of the sea
   monsters[2] on the waters.

14 You crushed the heads of Leviathan;
   you gave him as food for the creatures
   of the wilderness.

15 You split open springs and brooks;
   you dried up ever-flowing streams.

16 Yours is the day, yours also the night;
   you have established the heavenly
   lights and the sun.

17 You have fixed all the boundaries of the
   earth;
   you have made summer and winter.

18 Remember this, O Lord, how the enemy
   scoffs,
   and a foolish people reviles your name.

19 Do not deliver the soul of your dove to
   the wild beasts;
   do not forget the life of your poor
   forever.

20 Have regard for the covenant,
   for the dark places of the land are full
   of the habitations of violence.

21 Let not the downtrodden turn back in
   shame;
   let the poor and needy praise your
   name.

22 Arise, O God, defend your cause;
   remember how the foolish scoff at you
   all the day!

23 Do not forget the clamor of your foes,
   the uproar of those who rise against
   you, which goes up continually!

S E P T E M B E R   2 4

2 Samuel 20

Now there happened to be there a worthless man, whose name was Sheba, the son of Bichri, a Benjaminite. And he blew the trumpet and said,

"We have no portion in David,
and we have no inheritance in the son
   of Jesse;
every man to his tents, O Israel!"

² So all the men of Israel withdrew from David and followed Sheba the son of Bichri. But the men of Judah followed their king steadfastly from the Jordan to Jerusalem.

³ And David came to his house at Jerusalem. And the king took the ten concubines whom he had left to care for the house and put them in a house under guard and provided for them, but did not go in to them. So they were shut up until the day of their death, living as if in widowhood.

⁴ Then the king said to Amasa, "Call the men of Judah together to me within three days, and be here yourself." ⁵ So Amasa went to summon Judah, but he delayed beyond the set time that had been appointed him. ⁶ And David said to Abishai, "Now Sheba the son of Bichri will do us more harm than Absalom. Take your lord's servants and pursue him, lest he get himself to fortified cities and escape from us."[3] ⁷ And there went out after him Joab's men and the Cherethites and the Pelethites, and all the mighty men. They went out from Jerusalem to pursue Sheba the son of Bichri. ⁸ When they were at the great stone that is in Gibeon, Amasa came to meet them. Now Joab was wearing a soldier's garment, and over it was a belt with a sword in its sheath fastened on his thigh, and as he went forward it fell out. ⁹ And Joab said to Amasa, "Is it well with you, my brother?" And Joab took Amasa by the beard with his right hand to kiss him. ¹⁰ But Amasa did not observe

---

[1] Hebrew *from your bosom* [2] Or *the great sea creatures* [3] Hebrew *and snatch away our eyes*

the sword that was in Joab's hand. So Joab struck him with it in the stomach and spilled his entrails to the ground without striking a second blow, and he died.

Then Joab and Abishai his brother pursued Sheba the son of Bichri. [11]And one of Joab's young men took his stand by Amasa and said, "Whoever favors Joab, and whoever is for David, let him follow Joab." [12]And Amasa lay wallowing in his blood in the highway. And anyone who came by, seeing him, stopped. And when the man saw that all the people stopped, he carried Amasa out of the highway into the field and threw a garment over him. [13]When he was taken out of the highway, all the people went on after Joab to pursue Sheba the son of Bichri.

[14]And Sheba passed through all the tribes of Israel to Abel of Beth-maacah,[1] and all the Bichrites[2] assembled and followed him in. [15]And all the men who were with Joab came and besieged him in Abel of Beth-maacah. They cast up a mound against the city, and it stood against the rampart, and they were battering the wall to throw it down. [16]Then a wise woman called from the city, "Listen! Listen! Tell Joab, 'Come here, that I may speak to you.'" [17]And he came near her, and the woman said, "Are you Joab?" He answered, "I am." Then she said to him, "Listen to the words of your servant." And he answered, "I am listening." [18]Then she said, "They used to say in former times, 'Let them but ask counsel at Abel,' and so they settled a matter. [19]I am one of those who are peaceable and faithful in Israel. You seek to destroy a city that is a mother in Israel. Why will you swallow up the heritage of the LORD?" [20]Joab answered, "Far be it from me, far be it, that I should swallow up or destroy! [21]That is not true. But a man of the hill country of Ephraim, called Sheba the son of Bichri, has lifted up his hand against King David. Give up him alone, and I will withdraw from the city." And the woman said to Joab, "Behold, his head shall be thrown to you over the wall." [22]Then the woman went to all the people in her wisdom. And they cut off the head of Sheba the son of Bichri and threw it out to Joab. So he blew the trumpet, and they dispersed from the city, every man to his home. And Joab returned to Jerusalem to the king.

[23]Now Joab was in command of all the army of Israel; and Benaiah the son of Jehoiada was in command of the Cherethites and the Pelethites; [24]and Adoram was in charge of the forced labor; and Jehoshaphat the son of Ahilud was the recorder; [25]and Sheva was secretary; and Zadok and Abiathar were priests; [26]and Ira the Jairite was also David's priest.

2 Corinthians 13

This is the third time I am coming to you. Every charge must be established by the evidence of two or three witnesses. [2]I warned those who sinned before and all the others, and I warn them now while absent, as I did when present on my second visit, that if I come again I will not spare them— [3]since you seek proof that Christ is speaking in me. He is not weak in dealing with you, but is powerful among you. [4]For he was crucified in weakness, but lives by the power of God. For we also are weak in him, but in dealing with you we will live with him by the power of God.

[5]Examine yourselves, to see whether you are in the faith. Test yourselves. Or do you not realize this about yourselves, that Jesus Christ is in you?—unless indeed you fail to meet the test! [6]I hope you will find out that we have not failed the test. [7]But we pray to God that you may not do wrong—not that we may appear to have met the test, but that you may do what is right, though we may seem to have failed. [8]For we cannot do anything against the truth, but only for the truth. [9]For we are glad when we are weak and you are strong. Your restoration is what we pray for. [10]For this reason I write these things while I am away from you, that when I come I may not have to be severe in my use of the authority that the Lord has given me for building up and not for tearing down.

[11]Finally, brothers,[3] rejoice. Aim for restoration, comfort one another,[4] agree with one another, live in peace; and the God of love and peace will be with you. [12]Greet one another with a holy kiss. [13]All the saints greet you.

[14]The grace of the Lord Jesus Christ and the love of God and the fellowship of the Holy Spirit be with you all.

Ezekiel 27

The word of the LORD came to me: [2]"Now you, son of man, raise a lamentation over Tyre, [3]and say to Tyre, who dwells at the entrances to the sea, merchant of the peoples to many coastlands, thus says the Lord GOD:

> "O Tyre, you have said,
>> 'I am perfect in beauty.'

4 Your borders are in the heart of the seas;
>> your builders made perfect your beauty.

5 They made all your planks
>> of fir trees from Senir;
> they took a cedar from Lebanon
>> to make a mast for you.

6 Of oaks of Bashan
>> they made your oars;
> they made your deck of pines
>> from the coasts of Cyprus,
>> inlaid with ivory.

7 Of fine embroidered linen from Egypt
>> was your sail,
>> serving as your banner;
> blue and purple from the coasts of
>> Elishah
>> was your awning.

8 The inhabitants of Sidon and Arvad
>> were your rowers;
> your skilled men, O Tyre, were in you;
>> they were your pilots.

9 The elders of Gebal and her skilled men
>> were in you,
>> caulking your seams;
> all the ships of the sea with their
>> mariners were in you
>> to barter for your wares.

10 "Persia and Lud and Put were in your army as your men of war. They hung the shield and helmet in you; they gave you splendor. 11 Men of Arvad and Helech were on your walls all around, and men of Gamad were in your towers. They hung their shields on your walls all around; they made perfect your beauty. 12 "Tarshish did business with you because of your great wealth of every kind; silver, iron, tin, and lead they exchanged for your wares. 13 Javan, Tubal, and Meshech traded with you; they exchanged human beings and vessels of bronze for your merchandise. 14 From Beth-togarmah they exchanged horses, war horses, and mules for your wares. 15 The men of Dedan[1] traded with you. Many coastlands were your own special markets; they brought you in payment ivory tusks and ebony. 16 Syria did business with you because of your abundant goods; they exchanged for your wares emeralds, purple, embroidered work, fine linen, coral, and ruby. 17 Judah and the land of Israel traded with you; they exchanged for your merchandise wheat of Minnith, meal,[2] honey, oil, and balm. 18 Damascus did business with you for your abundant goods, because of your great wealth of every kind; wine of Helbon and wool of Sahar 19 and casks of wine[3] from Uzal they exchanged for your wares; wrought iron, cassia, and calamus were bartered for your merchandise. 20 Dedan traded with you in saddlecloths for riding. 21 Arabia and all the princes of Kedar were your favored dealers in lambs, rams, and goats; in these they did business with you. 22 The traders of Sheba and Raamah traded with you; they exchanged for your wares the best of all kinds of spices and all precious stones and gold. 23 Haran, Canneh, Eden, traders of Sheba, Asshur, and Chilmad traded with you. 24 In your market these traded with you in choice garments, in clothes of blue and embroidered work, and in carpets of colored material, bound with cords and made secure. 25 The ships of Tarshish traveled for you with your merchandise. So you were filled and heavily laden in the heart of the seas.

26 "Your rowers have brought you out
>> into the high seas.
> The east wind has wrecked you
>> in the heart of the seas.

27 Your riches, your wares, your
>> merchandise,
> your mariners and your pilots,
> your caulkers, your dealers in
>> merchandise,
> and all your men of war who are in
>> you,
> with all your crew
>> that is in your midst,
> sink into the heart of the seas
>> on the day of your fall.

28 At the sound of the cry of your pilots
>> the countryside shakes,

29 and down from their ships
>> come all who handle the oar.
> The mariners and all the pilots of the sea
>> stand on the land

30 and shout aloud over you
>> and cry out bitterly.
> They cast dust on their heads
>> and wallow in ashes;

---

[1] Hebrew; Septuagint *Rhodes*   [2] The meaning of the Hebrew word is unknown   [3] Probable reading; Hebrew *wool of Sahar, Vedan, and Javan*

³¹ they make themselves bald for you
    and put sackcloth on their waist,
and they weep over you in bitterness of
    soul,
    with bitter mourning.
³² In their wailing they raise a lamentation
    for you
    and lament over you:
'Who is like Tyre,
    like one destroyed in the midst of the
    sea?
³³ When your wares came from the seas,
    you satisfied many peoples;
with your abundant wealth and
    merchandise
    you enriched the kings of the earth.
³⁴ Now you are wrecked by the seas,
    in the depths of the waters;
your merchandise and all your crew in
    your midst
    have sunk with you.
³⁵ All the inhabitants of the coastlands
    are appalled at you,
and the hair of their kings bristles with
    horror;
    their faces are convulsed.
³⁶ The merchants among the peoples hiss
    at you;
you have come to a dreadful end
    and shall be no more forever.'"

Psalm 75–76

To the choirmaster: according to Do Not
Destroy. A Psalm of Asaph. A Song.

We give thanks to you, O God;
    we give thanks, for your name is near.
We[1] recount your wondrous deeds.

² "At the set time that I appoint
    I will judge with equity.
³ When the earth totters, and all its
    inhabitants,
    it is I who keep steady its pillars.   *Selah*
⁴ I say to the boastful, 'Do not boast,'
    and to the wicked, 'Do not lift up your
    horn;
⁵ do not lift up your horn on high,
    or speak with haughty neck.'"

⁶ For not from the east or from the west
    and not from the wilderness comes
    lifting up,
⁷ but it is God who executes judgment,
    putting down one and lifting up
    another.
⁸ For in the hand of the Lord there is a cup
    with foaming wine, well mixed,
and he pours out from it,
    and all the wicked of the earth
    shall drain it down to the dregs.

⁹ But I will declare it forever;
    I will sing praises to the God of Jacob.
¹⁰ All the horns of the wicked I will cut off,
    but the horns of the righteous shall be
    lifted up.

To the choirmaster: with stringed
instruments. A Psalm of Asaph. A Song.

In Judah God is known;
    his name is great in Israel.
² His abode has been established in Salem,
    his dwelling place in Zion.
³ There he broke the flashing arrows,
    the shield, the sword, and the
    weapons of war.   *Selah*

⁴ Glorious are you, more majestic
    than the mountains full of prey.
⁵ The stouthearted were stripped of their
    spoil;
    they sank into sleep;
all the men of war
    were unable to use their hands.
⁶ At your rebuke, O God of Jacob,
    both rider and horse lay stunned.

⁷ But you, you are to be feared!
    Who can stand before you
    when once your anger is roused?
⁸ From the heavens you uttered judgment;
    the earth feared and was still,
⁹ when God arose to establish judgment,
    to save all the humble of the earth.   *Selah*

¹⁰ Surely the wrath of man shall praise you;
    the remnant[2] of wrath you will put on
    like a belt.
¹¹ Make your vows to the Lord your God
    and perform them;
    let all around him bring gifts
    to him who is to be feared,
¹² who cuts off the spirit of princes,
    who is to be feared by the kings of the
    earth.

[1] Hebrew *They* [2] Or *extremity*

SEPTEMBER 25

2 Samuel 21

Now there was a famine in the days of David for three years, year after year. And David sought the face of the LORD. And the LORD said, "There is bloodguilt on Saul and on his house, because he put the Gibeonites to death." ² So the king called the Gibeonites and spoke to them. Now the Gibeonites were not of the people of Israel but of the remnant of the Amorites. Although the people of Israel had sworn to spare them, Saul had sought to strike them down in his zeal for the people of Israel and Judah. ³ And David said to the Gibeonites, "What shall I do for you? And how shall I make atonement, that you may bless the heritage of the LORD?" ⁴ The Gibeonites said to him, "It is not a matter of silver or gold between us and Saul or his house; neither is it for us to put any man to death in Israel." And he said, "What do you say that I shall do for you?" ⁵ They said to the king, "The man who consumed us and planned to destroy us, so that we should have no place in all the territory of Israel, ⁶ let seven of his sons be given to us, so that we may hang them before the LORD at Gibeah of Saul, the chosen of the LORD." And the king said, "I will give them."

⁷ But the king spared Mephibosheth, the son of Saul's son Jonathan, because of the oath of the LORD that was between them, between David and Jonathan the son of Saul. ⁸ The king took the two sons of Rizpah the daughter of Aiah, whom she bore to Saul, Armoni and Mephibosheth; and the five sons of Merab[1] the daughter of Saul, whom she bore to Adriel the son of Barzillai the Meholathite; ⁹ and he gave them into the hands of the Gibeonites, and they hanged them on the mountain before the LORD, and the seven of them perished together. They were put to death in the first days of harvest, at the beginning of barley harvest.

¹⁰ Then Rizpah the daughter of Aiah took sackcloth and spread it for herself on the rock, from the beginning of harvest until rain fell upon them from the heavens. And she did not allow the birds of the air to come upon them by day, or the beasts of the field by night. ¹¹ When David was told what Rizpah the daughter of Aiah, the concubine of Saul, had done, ¹² David went and took the bones of Saul and the bones of his son Jonathan from the men of Jabesh-gilead, who had stolen them from the public square of Beth-shan, where the Philistines had hanged them, on the day the Philistines killed Saul on Gilboa. ¹³ And he brought up from there the bones of Saul and the bones of his son Jonathan; and they gathered the bones of those who were hanged. ¹⁴ And they buried the bones of Saul and his son Jonathan in the land of Benjamin in Zela, in the tomb of Kish his father. And they did all that the king commanded. And after that God responded to the plea for the land.

¹⁵ There was war again between the Philistines and Israel, and David went down together with his servants, and they fought against the Philistines. And David grew weary. ¹⁶ And Ishbi-benob, one of the descendants of the giants, whose spear weighed three hundred shekels[2] of bronze, and who was armed with a new sword, thought to kill David. ¹⁷ But Abishai the son of Zeruiah came to his aid and attacked the Philistine and killed him. Then David's men swore to him, "You shall no longer go out with us to battle, lest you quench the lamp of Israel."

¹⁸ After this there was again war with the Philistines at Gob. Then Sibbecai the Hushathite struck down Saph, who was one of the descendants of the giants. ¹⁹ And there was again war with the Philistines at Gob, and Elhanan the son of Jaare-oregim, the Bethlehemite, struck down Goliath the Gittite, the shaft of whose spear was like a weaver's beam.[3] ²⁰ And there was again war at Gath, where there was a man of great stature, who had six fingers on each hand, and six toes on each foot, twenty-four in number, and he also was descended from the giants. ²¹ And when he taunted Israel, Jonathan the son of Shimei, David's brother, struck him down.

[1] Two Hebrew manuscripts, Septuagint; most Hebrew manuscripts *Michal* [2] A *shekel* was about 2/5 ounce or 11 grams [3] Contrast 1 Chronicles 20:5, which may preserve the original reading

²²These four were descended from the giants in Gath, and they fell by the hand of David and by the hand of his servants.

Galatians 1

Paul, an apostle—not from men nor through man, but through Jesus Christ and God the Father, who raised him from the dead— ²and all the brothers¹ who are with me,

To the churches of Galatia:

³Grace to you and peace from God our Father and the Lord Jesus Christ, ⁴who gave himself for our sins to deliver us from the present evil age, according to the will of our God and Father, ⁵to whom be the glory forever and ever. Amen.

⁶I am astonished that you are so quickly deserting him who called you in the grace of Christ and are turning to a different gospel— ⁷not that there is another one, but there are some who trouble you and want to distort the gospel of Christ. ⁸But even if we or an angel from heaven should preach to you a gospel contrary to the one we preached to you, let him be accursed. ⁹As we have said before, so now I say again: If anyone is preaching to you a gospel contrary to the one you received, let him be accursed.

¹⁰For am I now seeking the approval of man, or of God? Or am I trying to please man? If I were still trying to please man, I would not be a servant² of Christ.

¹¹For I would have you know, brothers, that the gospel that was preached by me is not man's gospel.³ ¹²For I did not receive it from any man, nor was I taught it, but I received it through a revelation of Jesus Christ. ¹³For you have heard of my former life in Judaism, how I persecuted the church of God violently and tried to destroy it. ¹⁴And I was advancing in Judaism beyond many of my own age among my people, so extremely zealous was I for the traditions of my fathers. ¹⁵But when he who had set me apart before I was born,⁴ and who called me by his grace, ¹⁶was pleased to reveal his Son to⁵ me, in order that I might preach him among the Gentiles, I did not immediately consult with anyone;⁶ ¹⁷nor did I go up to Jerusalem to those who were apostles before me, but I went away into Arabia, and returned again to Damascus.

¹⁸Then after three years I went up to Jerusalem to visit Cephas and remained with him fifteen days. ¹⁹But I saw none of the other apostles except James the Lord's brother. ²⁰(In what I am writing to you, before God, I do not lie!) ²¹Then I went into the regions of Syria and Cilicia. ²²And I was still unknown in person to the churches of Judea that are in Christ. ²³They only were hearing it said, "He who used to persecute us is now preaching the faith he once tried to destroy." ²⁴And they glorified God because of me.

Ezekiel 28

The word of the LORD came to me: ²"Son of man, say to the prince of Tyre, Thus says the Lord GOD:

> "Because your heart is proud,
>   and you have said, 'I am a god,
> I sit in the seat of the gods,
>   in the heart of the seas,'
> yet you are but a man, and no god,
>   though you make your heart like the
>   heart of a god—
> ³ you are indeed wiser than Daniel;
>   no secret is hidden from you;
> ⁴ by your wisdom and your
>   understanding
>   you have made wealth for yourself,
> and have gathered gold and silver
>   into your treasuries;
> ⁵ by your great wisdom in your trade
>   you have increased your wealth,
>   and your heart has become proud in
>   your wealth—
> ⁶ therefore thus says the Lord GOD:
> Because you make your heart
>   like the heart of a god,
> ⁷ therefore, behold, I will bring foreigners
>   upon you,
>   the most ruthless of the nations;
> and they shall draw their swords against
>   the beauty of your wisdom
>   and defile your splendor.
> ⁸ They shall thrust you down into the pit,
>   and you shall die the death of the slain
>   in the heart of the seas.
> ⁹ Will you still say, 'I am a god,'
>   in the presence of those who kill you,

---

¹ Or brothers and sisters. The plural Greek word adelphoi (translated "brothers") refers to siblings in a family. In New Testament usage, depending on the context, adelphoi may refer either to men or to both men and women who are siblings (brothers and sisters) in God's family, the church; also verse 11 ² Or slave; Greek bondservant ³ Greek not according to man ⁴ Greek set me apart from my mother's womb ⁵ Greek in ⁶ Greek with flesh and blood

though you are but a man, and no god,
in the hands of those who slay you?
10 You shall die the death of the
uncircumcised
by the hand of foreigners;
for I have spoken, declares the Lord
GOD."

11 Moreover, the word of the LORD came to me: 12 "Son of man, raise a lamentation over the king of Tyre, and say to him, Thus says the Lord GOD:

"You were the signet of perfection,[1]
full of wisdom and perfect in beauty.
13 You were in Eden, the garden of God;
every precious stone was your
covering,
sardius, topaz, and diamond,
beryl, onyx, and jasper,
sapphire,[2] emerald, and carbuncle;
and crafted in gold were your settings
and your engravings.[3]
On the day that you were created
they were prepared.
14 You were an anointed guardian cherub.
I placed you;[4] you were on the holy
mountain of God;
in the midst of the stones of fire you
walked.
15 You were blameless in your ways
from the day you were created,
till unrighteousness was found in you.
16 In the abundance of your trade
you were filled with violence in your
midst, and you sinned;
so I cast you as a profane thing from the
mountain of God,
and I destroyed you,[5] O guardian
cherub,
from the midst of the stones of fire.
17 Your heart was proud because of your
beauty;
you corrupted your wisdom for the
sake of your splendor.
I cast you to the ground;
I exposed you before kings,
to feast their eyes on you.
18 By the multitude of your iniquities,
in the unrighteousness of your trade
you profaned your sanctuaries;
so I brought fire out from your midst;
it consumed you,

and I turned you to ashes on the earth
in the sight of all who saw you.
19 All who know you among the peoples
are appalled at you;
you have come to a dreadful end
and shall be no more forever."

20 The word of the LORD came to me: 21 "Son of man, set your face toward Sidon, and prophesy against her 22 and say, Thus says the Lord GOD:

"Behold, I am against you, O Sidon,
and I will manifest my glory in your
midst.
And they shall know that I am the LORD
when I execute judgments in her
and manifest my holiness in her;
23 for I will send pestilence into her,
and blood into her streets;
and the slain shall fall in her midst,
by the sword that is against her on
every side.
Then they will know that I am the LORD.

24 "And for the house of Israel there shall be no more a brier to prick or a thorn to hurt them among all their neighbors who have treated them with contempt. Then they will know that I am the Lord GOD. 25 "Thus says the Lord GOD: When I gather the house of Israel from the peoples among whom they are scattered, and manifest my holiness in them in the sight of the nations, then they shall dwell in their own land that I gave to my servant Jacob. 26 And they shall dwell securely in it, and they shall build houses and plant vineyards. They shall dwell securely, when I execute judgments upon all their neighbors who have treated them with contempt. Then they will know that I am the LORD their God."

─────────── *Psalm 77* ───────────

TO THE CHOIRMASTER: ACCORDING TO JEDUTHUN.
A PSALM OF ASAPH.

I cry aloud to God,
aloud to God, and he will hear me.
2 In the day of my trouble I seek the Lord;
in the night my hand is stretched out
without wearying;
my soul refuses to be comforted.
3 When I remember God, I moan;
when I meditate, my spirit faints. *Selah*

[1] The meaning of the Hebrew phrase is uncertain [2] Or *lapis lazuli* [3] The meaning of the Hebrew phrase is uncertain [4] The meaning of the Hebrew phrase is uncertain [5] Or *banished you*

⁴ You hold my eyelids open;
    I am so troubled that I cannot speak.
⁵ I consider the days of old,
    the years long ago.
⁶ I said,[1] "Let me remember my song in
        the night;
    let me meditate in my heart."
    Then my spirit made a diligent search:
⁷ "Will the Lord spurn forever,
    and never again be favorable?
⁸ Has his steadfast love forever ceased?
    Are his promises at an end for all
        time?
⁹ Has God forgotten to be gracious?
    Has he in anger shut up his
        compassion?"   *Selah*
¹⁰ Then I said, "I will appeal to this,
    to the years of the right hand of the
        Most High."[2]
¹¹ I will remember the deeds of the LORD;
    yes, I will remember your wonders of
        old.
¹² I will ponder all your work,
    and meditate on your mighty deeds.

¹³ Your way, O God, is holy.
    What god is great like our God?
¹⁴ You are the God who works wonders;
    you have made known your might
        among the peoples.
¹⁵ You with your arm redeemed your
        people,
    the children of Jacob and Joseph.
                            Selah

¹⁶ When the waters saw you, O God,
    when the waters saw you, they were
        afraid;
    indeed, the deep trembled.
¹⁷ The clouds poured out water;
    the skies gave forth thunder;
    your arrows flashed on every side.
¹⁸ The crash of your thunder was in the
        whirlwind;
    your lightnings lighted up the world;
    the earth trembled and shook.
¹⁹ Your way was through the sea,
    your path through the great waters;
    yet your footprints were unseen.[3]
²⁰ You led your people like a flock
    by the hand of Moses and Aaron.

SEPTEMBER 26

— 2 Samuel 22 —

And David spoke to the LORD the words of this song on the day when the LORD delivered him from the hand of all his enemies, and from the hand of Saul. ²He said,

"The LORD is my rock and my fortress
    and my deliverer,
³ my[4] God, my rock, in whom I take
    refuge,
my shield, and the horn of my salvation,
    my stronghold and my refuge,
    my savior; you save me from
        violence.
⁴ I call upon the LORD, who is worthy to
        be praised,
    and I am saved from my enemies.

⁵ "For the waves of death encompassed me,
    the torrents of destruction assailed me;[5]
⁶ the cords of Sheol entangled me;
    the snares of death confronted me.

⁷ "In my distress I called upon the LORD;
    to my God I called.
From his temple he heard my voice,
    and my cry came to his ears.

⁸ "Then the earth reeled and rocked;
    the foundations of the heavens
        trembled
    and quaked, because he was angry.
⁹ Smoke went up from his nostrils,[6]
    and devouring fire from his mouth;
    glowing coals flamed forth from him.

---

[1] Hebrew lacks *I said* [2] Or *This is my grief: that the right hand of the Most High has changed* [3] Hebrew *unknown* [4] Septuagint (compare Psalm 18:2); Hebrew lacks *my* [5] Or *terrified me*
[6] Or *in his wrath*

10 He bowed the heavens and came down;
    thick darkness was under his feet.

11 He rode on a cherub and flew;
    he was seen on the wings of the wind.

12 He made darkness around him his
    canopy,
    thick clouds, a gathering of water.

13 Out of the brightness before him
    coals of fire flamed forth.

14 The Lord thundered from heaven,
    and the Most High uttered his voice.

15 And he sent out arrows and scattered
    them;
    lightning, and routed them.

16 Then the channels of the sea were seen;
    the foundations of the world were laid
    bare,
    at the rebuke of the Lord,
    at the blast of the breath of his
    nostrils.

17 "He sent from on high, he took me;
    he drew me out of many waters.

18 He rescued me from my strong enemy,
    from those who hated me,
    for they were too mighty for me.

19 They confronted me in the day of my
    calamity,
    but the Lord was my support.

20 He brought me out into a broad place;
    he rescued me, because he delighted
    in me.

21 "The Lord dealt with me according to
    my righteousness;
    according to the cleanness of my
    hands he rewarded me.

22 For I have kept the ways of the Lord
    and have not wickedly departed from
    my God.

23 For all his rules were before me,
    and from his statutes I did not turn
    aside.

24 I was blameless before him,
    and I kept myself from guilt.

25 And the Lord has rewarded me
    according to my righteousness,
    according to my cleanness in his sight.

26 "With the merciful you show yourself
    merciful;
    with the blameless man you show
    yourself blameless;

27 with the purified you deal purely,
    and with the crooked you make
    yourself seem tortuous.

28 You save a humble people,
    but your eyes are on the haughty to
    bring them down.

29 For you are my lamp, O Lord,
    and my God lightens my darkness.

30 For by you I can run against a troop,
    and by my God I can leap over a wall.

31 This God—his way is perfect;
    the word of the Lord proves true;
    he is a shield for all those who take
    refuge in him.

32 "For who is God, but the Lord?
    And who is a rock, except our God?

33 This God is my strong refuge
    and has made my[1] way blameless.[2]

34 He made my feet like the feet of a deer
    and set me secure on the heights.

35 He trains my hands for war,
    so that my arms can bend a bow of
    bronze.

36 You have given me the shield of your
    salvation,
    and your gentleness made me great.

37 You gave a wide place for my steps
    under me,
    and my feet[3] did not slip;

38 I pursued my enemies and destroyed
    them,
    and did not turn back until they were
    consumed.

39 I consumed them; I thrust them
    through, so that they did not rise;
    they fell under my feet.

40 For you equipped me with strength for
    the battle;
    you made those who rise against me
    sink under me.

41 You made my enemies turn their backs
    to me,[4]
    those who hated me, and I destroyed
    them.

42 They looked, but there was none to
    save;
    they cried to the Lord, but he did not
    answer them.

43 I beat them fine as the dust of the earth;
    I crushed them and stamped them
    down like the mire of the streets.

[1] Or his; also verse 34 [2] Compare Psalm 18:32; Hebrew he has blamelessly set my way free, or he has made my way spring up blamelessly [3] Hebrew ankles [4] Or You gave me my enemies' necks

44 "You delivered me from strife with my
  people;[1]
    you kept me as the head of the nations;
    people whom I had not known served
      me.
45 Foreigners came cringing to me;
    as soon as they heard of me, they
      obeyed me.
46 Foreigners lost heart
    and came trembling[2] out of their
      fortresses.

47 "The LORD lives, and blessed be my rock,
    and exalted be my God, the rock of my
      salvation,
48 the God who gave me vengeance
    and brought down peoples under me,
49 who brought me out from my enemies;
    you exalted me above those who rose
      against me;
    you delivered me from men of violence.

50 "For this I will praise you, O LORD, among
    the nations,
    and sing praises to your name.
51 Great salvation he brings[3] to his king,
    and shows steadfast love to his
      anointed,
    to David and his offspring forever."

Galatians 2

Then after fourteen years I went up again to Jerusalem with Barnabas, taking Titus along with me. [2] I went up because of a revelation and set before them (though privately before those who seemed influential) the gospel that I proclaim among the Gentiles, in order to make sure I was not running or had not run in vain. [3] But even Titus, who was with me, was not forced to be circumcised, though he was a Greek. [4] Yet because of false brothers secretly brought in—who slipped in to spy out our freedom that we have in Christ Jesus, so that they might bring us into slavery— [5] to them we did not yield in submission even for a moment, so that the truth of the gospel might be preserved for you. [6] And from those who seemed to be influential (what they were makes no difference to me; God shows no partiality)—those, I say, who seemed influential added nothing to me. [7] On the contrary, when they saw that I had been entrusted with the gospel to the uncircumcised, just as Peter had been entrusted with the gospel to the circumcised [8] (for he who worked through Peter for his apostolic ministry to the circumcised worked also through me for mine to the Gentiles), [9] and when James and Cephas and John, who seemed to be pillars, perceived the grace that was given to me, they gave the right hand of fellowship to Barnabas and me, that we should go to the Gentiles and they to the circumcised. [10] Only, they asked us to remember the poor, the very thing I was eager to do.

[11] But when Cephas came to Antioch, I opposed him to his face, because he stood condemned. [12] For before certain men came from James, he was eating with the Gentiles; but when they came he drew back and separated himself, fearing the circumcision party.[4] [13] And the rest of the Jews acted hypocritically along with him, so that even Barnabas was led astray by their hypocrisy. [14] But when I saw that their conduct was not in step with the truth of the gospel, I said to Cephas before them all, "If you, though a Jew, live like a Gentile and not like a Jew, how can you force the Gentiles to live like Jews?"

[15] We ourselves are Jews by birth and not Gentile sinners; [16] yet we know that a person is not justified[5] by works of the law but through faith in Jesus Christ, so we also have believed in Christ Jesus, in order to be justified by faith in Christ and not by works of the law, because by works of the law no one will be justified.

[17] But if, in our endeavor to be justified in Christ, we too were found to be sinners, is Christ then a servant of sin? Certainly not! [18] For if I rebuild what I tore down, I prove myself to be a transgressor. [19] For through the law I died to the law, so that I might live to God. [20] I have been crucified with Christ. It is no longer I who live, but Christ who lives in me. And the life I now live in the flesh I live by faith in the Son of God, who loved me and gave himself for me. [21] I do not nullify the grace of God, for if righteousness[6] were through the law, then Christ died for no purpose.

Ezekiel 29

In the tenth year, in the tenth month, on the twelfth day of the month, the word of the LORD came to me: [2] "Son of man, set your face against Pharaoh king of Egypt, and prophesy against him and against all Egypt; ³ speak, and say, Thus says the Lord GOD:

> "Behold, I am against you,
>> Pharaoh king of Egypt,
> the great dragon that lies
>> in the midst of his streams,
> that says, 'My Nile is my own;
>> I made it for myself.'
> ⁴ I will put hooks in your jaws,
>> and make the fish of your streams
>>> stick to your scales;
> and I will draw you up out of the midst
>> of your streams,
> with all the fish of your streams
>> that stick to your scales.
> ⁵ And I will cast you out into the
>> wilderness,
> you and all the fish of your streams;
> you shall fall on the open field,
>> and not be brought together or
>>> gathered.
> To the beasts of the earth and to the
>> birds of the heavens
> I give you as food.

⁶ Then all the inhabitants of Egypt shall know that I am the LORD.

"Because you¹ have been a staff of reed to the house of Israel, ⁷ when they grasped you with the hand, you broke and tore all their shoulders; and when they leaned on you, you broke and made all their loins to shake.² ⁸ Therefore thus says the Lord GOD: Behold, I will bring a sword upon you, and will cut off from you man and beast, ⁹ and the land of Egypt shall be a desolation and a waste. Then they will know that I am the LORD.

"Because you³ said, 'The Nile is mine, and I made it,' ¹⁰ therefore, behold, I am against you and against your streams, and I will make the land of Egypt an utter waste and desolation, from Migdol to Syene, as far as the border of Cush. ¹¹ No foot of man shall pass through it, and no foot of beast shall pass through it; it shall be uninhabited forty years. ¹² And I will make the land of Egypt a desolation in the midst of desolated countries, and her cities shall be a desolation forty years among cities that are laid waste. I will scatter the Egyptians among the nations, and disperse them through the countries.

¹³ "For thus says the Lord GOD: At the end of forty years I will gather the Egyptians from the peoples among whom they were scattered, ¹⁴ and I will restore the fortunes of Egypt and bring them back to the land of Pathros, the land of their origin, and there they shall be a lowly kingdom. ¹⁵ It shall be the most lowly of the kingdoms, and never again exalt itself above the nations. And I will make them so small that they will never again rule over the nations. ¹⁶ And it shall never again be the reliance of the house of Israel, recalling their iniquity, when they turn to them for aid. Then they will know that I am the Lord GOD."

¹⁷ In the twenty-seventh year, in the first month, on the first day of the month, the word of the LORD came to me: ¹⁸ "Son of man, Nebuchadnezzar king of Babylon made his army labor hard against Tyre. Every head was made bald, and every shoulder was rubbed bare, yet neither he nor his army got anything from Tyre to pay for the labor that he had performed against her. ¹⁹ Therefore thus says the Lord GOD: Behold, I will give the land of Egypt to Nebuchadnezzar king of Babylon; and he shall carry off its wealth⁴ and despoil it and plunder it; and it shall be the wages for his army. ²⁰ I have given him the land of Egypt as his payment for which he labored, because they worked for me, declares the Lord GOD.

²¹ "On that day I will cause a horn to spring up for the house of Israel, and I will open your lips among them. Then they will know that I am the LORD."

Psalm 78:1–37

A MASKIL⁵ OF ASAPH.

> Give ear, O my people, to my teaching;
> incline your ears to the words of my
>> mouth!
> ² I will open my mouth in a parable;
>> I will utter dark sayings from of old,
> ³ things that we have heard and known,
>> that our fathers have told us.
> ⁴ We will not hide them from their
>> children,
> but tell to the coming generation
> the glorious deeds of the LORD, and his
>> might,
> and the wonders that he has done.

---

¹ Hebrew *they*   ² Syriac (compare Psalm 69:23); Hebrew *to stand*   ³ Hebrew *he*   ⁴ Or *multitude*   ⁵ Probably a musical or liturgical term

5 He established a testimony in Jacob
   and appointed a law in Israel,
which he commanded our fathers
   to teach to their children,
6 that the next generation might know
   them,
   the children yet unborn,
and arise and tell them to their children,
7   so that they should set their hope in
      God
   and not forget the works of God,
   but keep his commandments;
8 and that they should not be like their
      fathers,
   a stubborn and rebellious generation,
a generation whose heart was not
      steadfast,
   whose spirit was not faithful to God.

9 The Ephraimites, armed with[1] the bow,
   turned back on the day of battle.
10 They did not keep God's covenant,
   but refused to walk according to his
      law.
11 They forgot his works
   and the wonders that he had shown
      them.
12 In the sight of their fathers he
      performed wonders
   in the land of Egypt, in the fields of
      Zoan.
13 He divided the sea and let them pass
      through it,
   and made the waters stand like a
      heap.
14 In the daytime he led them with a
      cloud,
   and all the night with a fiery light.
15 He split rocks in the wilderness
   and gave them drink abundantly as
      from the deep.
16 He made streams come out of the rock
   and caused waters to flow down like
      rivers.
17 Yet they sinned still more against him,
   rebelling against the Most High in the
      desert.
18 They tested God in their heart
   by demanding the food they craved.
19 They spoke against God, saying,
   "Can God spread a table in the
      wilderness?

20 He struck the rock so that water gushed
      out
   and streams overflowed.
Can he also give bread
   or provide meat for his people?"

21 Therefore, when the Lord heard, he was
      full of wrath;
   a fire was kindled against Jacob;
   his anger rose against Israel,
22 because they did not believe in God
   and did not trust his saving power.
23 Yet he commanded the skies above
   and opened the doors of heaven,
24 and he rained down on them manna to
      eat
   and gave them the grain of heaven.
25 Man ate of the bread of the angels;
   he sent them food in abundance.
26 He caused the east wind to blow in the
      heavens,
   and by his power he led out the south
      wind;
27 he rained meat on them like dust,
   winged birds like the sand of the seas;
28 he let them fall in the midst of their
      camp,
   all around their dwellings.
29 And they ate and were well filled,
   for he gave them what they craved.
30 But before they had satisfied their
      craving,
   while the food was still in their mouths,
31 the anger of God rose against them,
   and he killed the strongest of them
   and laid low the young men of Israel.

32 In spite of all this, they still sinned;
   despite his wonders, they did not
      believe.
33 So he made their days vanish like[2] a
      breath,[3]
   and their years in terror.
34 When he killed them, they sought him;
   they repented and sought God
      earnestly.
35 They remembered that God was their
      rock,
   the Most High God their redeemer.
36 But they flattered him with their mouths;
   they lied to him with their tongues.
37 Their heart was not steadfast toward him;
   they were not faithful to his covenant.

[1] Hebrew *armed and shooting* [2] Hebrew *in* [3] Or *vapor*

SEPTEMBER 27

2 Samuel 23

Now these are the last words of David:

The oracle of David, the son of Jesse,
　the oracle of the man who was raised
　　on high,
the anointed of the God of Jacob,
　the sweet psalmist of Israel:[1]

2 "The Spirit of the LORD speaks by me;
　his word is on my tongue.
3 The God of Israel has spoken;
　the Rock of Israel has said to me:
When one rules justly over men,
　ruling in the fear of God,
4 he dawns on them like the morning
　　light,
like the sun shining forth on a
　　cloudless morning,
like rain[2] that makes grass to sprout
　from the earth.

5 "For does not my house stand so with
　　God?
For he has made with me an
　　everlasting covenant,
ordered in all things and secure.
For will he not cause to prosper
　all my help and my desire?
6 But worthless men[3] are all like thorns
　that are thrown away,
for they cannot be taken with the
　　hand;
7 but the man who touches them
arms himself with iron and the shaft
　of a spear,
and they are utterly consumed with
　fire."[4]

8 These are the names of the mighty men whom David had: Josheb-basshebeth a Tahchemonite; he was chief of the three.[5] He wielded his spear[6] against eight hundred whom he killed at one time. 9 And next to him among the three mighty men was Eleazar the son of Dodo, son of Ahohi. He was with David when they defied the Philistines who were gathered there for battle, and the men of Israel withdrew. 10 He rose and struck down the Philistines until his hand was weary, and his hand clung to the sword. And the LORD brought about a great victory that day, and the men returned after him only to strip the slain.

11 And next to him was Shammah, the son of Agee the Hararite. The Philistines gathered together at Lehi, where there was a plot of ground full of lentils, and the men fled from the Philistines. 12 But he took his stand in the midst of the plot and defended it and struck down the Philistines, and the LORD worked a great victory.

13 And three of the thirty chief men went down and came about harvest time to David at the cave of Adullam, when a band of Philistines was encamped in the Valley of Rephaim. 14 David was then in the stronghold, and the garrison of the Philistines was then at Bethlehem. 15 And David said longingly, "Oh, that someone would give me water to drink from the well of Bethlehem that is by the gate!" 16 Then the three mighty men broke through the camp of the Philistines and drew water out of the well of Bethlehem that was by the gate and carried and brought it to David. But he would not drink of it. He poured it out to the LORD 17 and said, "Far be it from me, O LORD, that I should do this. Shall I drink the blood of the men who went at the risk of their lives?" Therefore he would not drink it. These things the three mighty men did.

18 Now Abishai, the brother of Joab, the son of Zeruiah, was chief of the thirty.[7] And he wielded his spear against three hundred men[8] and killed them and won a name beside the three. 19 He was the most renowned of the thirty[9] and became their commander, but he did not attain to the three.

20 And Benaiah the son of Jehoiada was a valiant man[10] of Kabzeel, a doer of great deeds. He

---

[1] Or the favorite of the songs of Israel [2] Hebrew from rain [3] Hebrew worthlessness [4] Hebrew consumed with fire in the sitting [5] Or of the captains [6] Compare 1 Chronicles 11:11; the meaning of the Hebrew expression is uncertain [7] Two Hebrew manuscripts, Syriac; most Hebrew manuscripts three [8] Or slain ones [9] Compare 1 Chronicles 11:25; Hebrew Was he the most renowned of the three? [10] Or the son of Ishhai

struck down two ariels[1] of Moab. He also went down and struck down a lion in a pit on a day when snow had fallen. [21]And he struck down an Egyptian, a handsome man. The Egyptian had a spear in his hand, but Benaiah went down to him with a staff and snatched the spear out of the Egyptian's hand and killed him with his own spear. [22]These things did Benaiah the son of Jehoiada, and won a name beside the three mighty men. [23]He was renowned among the thirty, but he did not attain to the three. And David set him over his bodyguard.

[24]Asahel the brother of Joab was one of the thirty; Elhanan the son of Dodo of Bethlehem, [25]Shammah of Harod, Elika of Harod, [26]Helez the Paltite, Ira the son of Ikkesh of Tekoa, [27]Abiezer of Anathoth, Mebunnai the Hushathite, [28]Zalmon the Ahohite, Maharai of Netophah, [29]Heleb the son of Baanah of Netophah, Ittai the son of Ribai of Gibeah of the people of Benjamin, [30]Benaiah of Pirathon, Hiddai of the brooks of Gaash, [31]Abialbon the Arbathite, Azmaveth of Bahurim, [32]Eliahba the Shaalbonite, the sons of Jashen, Jonathan, [33]Shammah the Hararite, Ahiam the son of Sharar the Hararite, [34]Eliphelet the son of Ahasbai of Maacah, Eliam the son of Ahithophel of Gilo, [35]Hezro[2] of Carmel, Paarai the Arbite, [36]Igal the son of Nathan of Zobah, Bani the Gadite, [37]Zelek the Ammonite, Naharai of Beeroth, the armor-bearer of Joab the son of Zeruiah, [38]Ira the Ithrite, Gareb the Ithrite, [39]Uriah the Hittite: thirty-seven in all.

─── *Galatians 3* ───

O foolish Galatians! Who has bewitched you? It was before your eyes that Jesus Christ was publicly portrayed as crucified. [2]Let me ask you only this: Did you receive the Spirit by works of the law or by hearing with faith? [3]Are you so foolish? Having begun by the Spirit, are you now being perfected by[3] the flesh? [4]Did you suffer[4] so many things in vain—if indeed it was in vain? [5]Does he who supplies the Spirit to you and works miracles among you do so by works of the law, or by hearing with faith— [6]just as Abraham "believed God, and it was counted to him as righteousness"?

[7]Know then that it is those of faith who are the sons of Abraham. [8]And the Scripture, foreseeing that God would justify[5] the Gentiles by faith, preached the gospel beforehand to Abraham, saying, "In you shall all the nations be blessed." [9]So then, those who are of faith are blessed along with Abraham, the man of faith.

[10]For all who rely on works of the law are under a curse; for it is written, "Cursed be everyone who does not abide by all things written in the Book of the Law, and do them." [11]Now it is evident that no one is justified before God by the law, for "The righteous shall live by faith."[6] [12]But the law is not of faith, rather "The one who does them shall live by them." [13]Christ redeemed us from the curse of the law by becoming a curse for us—for it is written, "Cursed is everyone who is hanged on a tree"— [14]so that in Christ Jesus the blessing of Abraham might come to the Gentiles, so that we might receive the promised Spirit[7] through faith.

[15]To give a human example, brothers:[8] even with a man-made covenant, no one annuls it or adds to it once it has been ratified. [16]Now the promises were made to Abraham and to his offspring. It does not say, "And to offsprings," referring to many, but referring to one, "And to your offspring," who is Christ. [17]This is what I mean: the law, which came 430 years afterward, does not annul a covenant previously ratified by God, so as to make the promise void. [18]For if the inheritance comes by the law, it no longer comes by promise; but God gave it to Abraham by a promise.

[19]Why then the law? It was added because of transgressions, until the offspring should come to whom the promise had been made, and it was put in place through angels by an intermediary. [20]Now an intermediary implies more than one, but God is one.

[21]Is the law then contrary to the promises of God? Certainly not! For if a law had been given that could give life, then righteousness would indeed be by the law. [22]But the Scripture imprisoned everything under sin, so that the promise by faith in Jesus Christ might be given to those who believe.

[23]Now before faith came, we were held captive under the law, imprisoned until the coming faith would be revealed. [24]So then, the law was our guardian until Christ came, in order that we might be justified by faith. [25]But now that faith has come, we are no longer under a guardian, [26]for in Christ Jesus you are all sons of God, through faith. [27]For as many of

[1] The meaning of the word *ariel* is unknown [2] Or *Hezrai* [3] Or *now ending with* [4] Or *experience* [5] Or *count righteous; also verses 11, 24* [6] Or *The one who by faith is righteous will live*
[7] Greek *receive the promise of the Spirit* [8] Or *brothers and sisters*

you as were baptized into Christ have put on Christ. ²⁸ There is neither Jew nor Greek, there is neither slave[1] nor free, there is no male and female, for you are all one in Christ Jesus. ²⁹ And if you are Christ's, then you are Abraham's offspring, heirs according to promise.

Ezekiel 30

The word of the LORD came to me: ² "Son of man, prophesy, and say, Thus says the Lord GOD:

"Wail, 'Alas for the day!'
3   For the day is near,
       the day of the LORD is near;
   it will be a day of clouds,
       a time of doom for[2] the nations.
4 A sword shall come upon Egypt,
       and anguish shall be in Cush,
   when the slain fall in Egypt,
       and her wealth[3] is carried away,
       and her foundations are torn down.

⁵ Cush, and Put, and Lud, and all Arabia, and Libya,[4] and the people of the land that is in league,[5] shall fall with them by the sword.

6   "Thus says the LORD:
    Those who support Egypt shall fall,
        and her proud might shall come down;
    from Migdol to Syene
        they shall fall within her by the sword,
    declares the Lord GOD.
7   And they shall be desolated in the midst
        of desolated countries,
        and their cities shall be in the midst of
            cities that are laid waste.
8   Then they will know that I am the LORD,
        when I have set fire to Egypt,
        and all her helpers are broken.

⁹ "On that day messengers shall go out from me in ships to terrify the unsuspecting people of Cush, and anguish shall come upon them on the day of Egypt's doom;[6] for, behold, it comes!
¹⁰ "Thus says the Lord GOD:

"I will put an end to the wealth of Egypt,
    by the hand of Nebuchadnezzar king
        of Babylon.
11 He and his people with him, the most
        ruthless of nations,
        shall be brought in to destroy the land,

and they shall draw their swords against
        Egypt
    and fill the land with the slain.
12 And I will dry up the Nile
    and will sell the land into the hand of
        evildoers;
   I will bring desolation upon the land
        and everything in it,
    by the hand of foreigners;
   I am the LORD; I have spoken.

¹³ "Thus says the Lord GOD:

"I will destroy the idols
    and put an end to the images in
        Memphis;
   there shall no longer be a prince from
        the land of Egypt;
   so I will put fear in the land of Egypt.
14 I will make Pathros a desolation
    and will set fire to Zoan
    and will execute judgments on
        Thebes.
15 And I will pour out my wrath on
        Pelusium,
    the stronghold of Egypt,
    and cut off the multitude[7] of Thebes.
16 And I will set fire to Egypt;
    Pelusium shall be in great agony;
   Thebes shall be breached,
    and Memphis shall face enemies[8] by
        day.
17 The young men of On and of Pi-beseth
        shall fall by the sword,
    and the women[9] shall go into
        captivity.
18 At Tehaphnehes the day shall be dark,
    when I break there the yoke bars of
        Egypt,
   and her proud might shall come to an
        end in her;
    she shall be covered by a cloud,
    and her daughters shall go into
        captivity.
19 Thus I will execute judgments on Egypt.
    Then they will know that I am the
        LORD."

²⁰ In the eleventh year, in the first month, on the seventh day of the month, the word of the LORD came to me: ²¹ "Son of man, I have broken the arm of Pharaoh king of Egypt, and behold, it has not been bound up, to heal it by binding

[1] Greek bondservant [2] Hebrew lacks doom for [3] Or multitude; also verse 10 [4] With Septuagint; Hebrew Cub [5] Hebrew and the sons of the land of the covenant [6] Hebrew the day of Egypt [7] Or wealth [8] Or distress [9] Or the cities; Hebrew they

it with a bandage, so that it may become strong to wield the sword. ²²Therefore thus says the Lord God: Behold, I am against Pharaoh king of Egypt and will break his arms, both the strong arm and the one that was broken, and I will make the sword fall from his hand. ²³I will scatter the Egyptians among the nations and disperse them through the countries. ²⁴And I will strengthen the arms of the king of Babylon and put my sword in his hand, but I will break the arms of Pharaoh, and he will groan before him like a man mortally wounded. ²⁵I will strengthen the arms of the king of Babylon, but the arms of Pharaoh shall fall. Then they shall know that I am the Lord, when I put my sword into the hand of the king of Babylon and he stretches it out against the land of Egypt. ²⁶And I will scatter the Egyptians among the nations and disperse them throughout the countries. Then they will know that I am the Lord."

─────── *Psalm 78:38–72* ───────

Yet he, being compassionate,
　atoned for their iniquity
　　and did not destroy them;
　he restrained his anger often
　　and did not stir up all his wrath.
³⁹ He remembered that they were but
　　flesh,
　　a wind that passes and comes not
　　again.
⁴⁰ How often they rebelled against him in
　　the wilderness
　　and grieved him in the desert!
⁴¹ They tested God again and again
　　and provoked the Holy One of Israel.
⁴² They did not remember his power[1]
　　or the day when he redeemed them
　　from the foe,
⁴³ when he performed his signs in Egypt
　　and his marvels in the fields of Zoan.
⁴⁴ He turned their rivers to blood,
　　so that they could not drink of their
　　streams.
⁴⁵ He sent among them swarms of flies,
　　which devoured them,
　　and frogs, which destroyed them.
⁴⁶ He gave their crops to the destroying
　　locust
　　and the fruit of their labor to the
　　locust.

⁴⁷ He destroyed their vines with hail
　　and their sycamores with frost.
⁴⁸ He gave over their cattle to the hail
　　and their flocks to thunderbolts.
⁴⁹ He let loose on them his burning anger,
　　wrath, indignation, and distress,
　　a company of destroying angels.
⁵⁰ He made a path for his anger;
　　he did not spare them from death,
　　but gave their lives over to the
　　plague.
⁵¹ He struck down every firstborn in
　　Egypt,
　　the firstfruits of their strength in the
　　tents of Ham.
⁵² Then he led out his people like sheep
　　and guided them in the wilderness
　　like a flock.
⁵³ He led them in safety, so that they were
　　not afraid,
　　but the sea overwhelmed their
　　enemies.
⁵⁴ And he brought them to his holy land,
　　to the mountain which his right hand
　　had won.
⁵⁵ He drove out nations before them;
　　he apportioned them for a possession
　　and settled the tribes of Israel in their
　　tents.
⁵⁶ Yet they tested and rebelled against the
　　Most High God
　　and did not keep his testimonies,
⁵⁷ but turned away and acted treacherously
　　like their fathers;
　　they twisted like a deceitful bow.
⁵⁸ For they provoked him to anger with
　　their high places;
　　they moved him to jealousy with their
　　idols.
⁵⁹ When God heard, he was full of wrath,
　　and he utterly rejected Israel.
⁶⁰ He forsook his dwelling at Shiloh,
　　the tent where he dwelt among
　　mankind,
⁶¹ and delivered his power to captivity,
　　his glory to the hand of the foe.
⁶² He gave his people over to the sword
　　and vented his wrath on his heritage.
⁶³ Fire devoured their young men,
　　and their young women had no
　　marriage song.

[1] Hebrew *hand*

64 Their priests fell by the sword,
      and their widows made no
      lamentation.
65 Then the Lord awoke as from sleep,
      like a strong man shouting because of
      wine.
66 And he put his adversaries to rout;
      he put them to everlasting shame.
67 He rejected the tent of Joseph;
      he did not choose the tribe of
      Ephraim,
68 but he chose the tribe of Judah,
      Mount Zion, which he loves.

69 He built his sanctuary like the high
      heavens,
      like the earth, which he has founded
      forever.
70 He chose David his servant
      and took him from the sheepfolds;
71 from following the nursing ewes he
      brought him
      to shepherd Jacob his people,
      Israel his inheritance.
72 With upright heart he shepherded them
      and guided them with his skillful
      hand.

SEPTEMBER 28

2 Samuel 24

Again the anger of the Lord was kindled against Israel, and he incited David against them, saying, "Go, number Israel and Judah." ²So the king said to Joab, the commander of the army,¹ who was with him, "Go through all the tribes of Israel, from Dan to Beersheba, and number the people, that I may know the number of the people." ³But Joab said to the king, "May the Lord your God add to the people a hundred times as many as they are, while the eyes of my lord the king still see it, but why does my lord the king delight in this thing?" ⁴But the king's word prevailed against Joab and the commanders of the army. So Joab and the commanders of the army went out from the presence of the king to number the people of Israel. ⁵They crossed the Jordan and began from Aroer,² and from the city that is in the middle of the valley, toward Gad and on to Jazer. ⁶Then they came to Gilead, and to Kadesh in the land of the Hittites;³ and they came to Dan, and from Dan⁴ they went around to Sidon, ⁷and came to the fortress of Tyre and to all the cities of the Hivites and Canaanites; and they went out to the Negeb of Judah at Beersheba. ⁸So when they had gone through all the land, they came to Jerusalem at the end of nine months and twenty days. ⁹And Joab gave the sum of the

numbering of the people to the king: in Israel there were 800,000 valiant men who drew the sword, and the men of Judah were 500,000.

¹⁰But David's heart struck him after he had numbered the people. And David said to the Lord, "I have sinned greatly in what I have done. But now, O Lord, please take away the iniquity of your servant, for I have done very foolishly." ¹¹And when David arose in the morning, the word of the Lord came to the prophet Gad, David's seer, saying, ¹²"Go and say to David, 'Thus says the Lord, Three things I offer⁵ you. Choose one of them, that I may do it to you.'" ¹³So Gad came to David and told him, and said to him, "Shall three⁶ years of famine come to you in your land? Or will you flee three months before your foes while they pursue you? Or shall there be three days' pestilence in your land? Now consider, and decide what answer I shall return to him who sent me." ¹⁴Then David said to Gad, "I am in great distress. Let us fall into the hand of the Lord, for his mercy is great; but let me not fall into the hand of man."

¹⁵So the Lord sent a pestilence on Israel from the morning until the appointed time. And there died of the people from Dan to Beersheba 70,000 men. ¹⁶And when the angel

¹ Septuagint to Joab and the commanders of the army ² Septuagint; Hebrew encamped in Aroer ³ Septuagint; Hebrew to the land of Tahtim-hodshi ⁴ Septuagint; Hebrew they came to Dan-jaan and ⁵ Or hold over ⁶ Compare 1 Chronicles 21:12, Septuagint; Hebrew seven

stretched out his hand toward Jerusalem to destroy it, the LORD relented from the calamity and said to the angel who was working destruction among the people, "It is enough; now stay your hand." And the angel of the LORD was by the threshing floor of Araunah the Jebusite. ¹⁷Then David spoke to the LORD when he saw the angel who was striking the people, and said, "Behold, I have sinned, and I have done wickedly. But these sheep, what have they done? Please let your hand be against me and against my father's house."

¹⁸And Gad came that day to David and said to him, "Go up, raise an altar to the LORD on the threshing floor of Araunah the Jebusite." ¹⁹So David went up at Gad's word, as the LORD commanded. ²⁰And when Araunah looked down, he saw the king and his servants coming on toward him. And Araunah went out and paid homage to the king with his face to the ground. ²¹And Araunah said, "Why has my lord the king come to his servant?" David said, "To buy the threshing floor from you, in order to build an altar to the LORD, that the plague may be averted from the people." ²²Then Araunah said to David, "Let my lord the king take and offer up what seems good to him. Here are the oxen for the burnt offering and the threshing sledges and the yokes of the oxen for the wood. ²³All this, O king, Araunah gives to the king." And Araunah said to the king, "May the LORD your God accept you." ²⁴But the king said to Araunah, "No, but I will buy it from you for a price. I will not offer burnt offerings to the LORD my God that cost me nothing." So David bought the threshing floor and the oxen for fifty shekels[1] of silver. ²⁵And David built there an altar to the LORD and offered burnt offerings and peace offerings. So the LORD responded to the plea for the land, and the plague was averted from Israel.

Galatians 4

I mean that the heir, as long as he is a child, is no different from a slave,[2] though he is the owner of everything, ²but he is under guardians and managers until the date set by his father. ³In the same way we also, when we were children, were enslaved to the elementary principles[3] of the world. ⁴But when the fullness of time had come, God sent forth his Son, born of

woman, born under the law, ⁵to redeem those who were under the law, so that we might receive adoption as sons. ⁶And because you are sons, God has sent the Spirit of his Son into our hearts, crying, "Abba! Father!" ⁷So you are no longer a slave, but a son, and if a son, then an heir through God.

⁸Formerly, when you did not know God, you were enslaved to those that by nature are not gods. ⁹But now that you have come to know God, or rather to be known by God, how can you turn back again to the weak and worthless elementary principles of the world, whose slaves you want to be once more? ¹⁰You observe days and months and seasons and years! ¹¹I am afraid I may have labored over you in vain.

¹²Brothers,[4] I entreat you, become as I am, for I also have become as you are. You did me no wrong. ¹³You know it was because of a bodily ailment that I preached the gospel to you at first, ¹⁴and though my condition was a trial to you, you did not scorn or despise me, but received me as an angel of God, as Christ Jesus. ¹⁵What then has become of your blessedness? For I testify to you that, if possible, you would have gouged out your eyes and given them to me. ¹⁶Have I then become your enemy by telling you the truth?[5] ¹⁷They make much of you, but for no good purpose. They want to shut you out, that you may make much of them. ¹⁸It is always good to be made much of for a good purpose, and not only when I am present with you, ¹⁹my little children, for whom I am again in the anguish of childbirth until Christ is formed in you! ²⁰I wish I could be present with you now and change my tone, for I am perplexed about you.

²¹Tell me, you who desire to be under the law, do you not listen to the law? ²²For it is written that Abraham had two sons, one by a slave woman and one by a free woman. ²³But the son of the slave was born according to the flesh, while the son of the free woman was born through promise. ²⁴Now this may be interpreted allegorically: these women are two covenants. One is from Mount Sinai, bearing children for slavery; she is Hagar. ²⁵Now Hagar is Mount Sinai in Arabia;[6] she corresponds to the present Jerusalem, for she is in slavery with her children. ²⁶But the Jerusalem above is free, and she is our mother. ²⁷For it is written,

---

[1] A shekel was about 2/5 ounce or 11 grams [2] Greek bondservant; also verse 7 [3] Or elemental spirits; also verse 9 [4] Or Brothers and sisters; also verses 28, 31 [5] Or by dealing truthfully with you [6] Some manuscripts For Sinai is a mountain in Arabia

"Rejoice, O barren one who does not
        bear;
    break forth and cry aloud, you who
        are not in labor!
    For the children of the desolate one will
        be more
    than those of the one who has a
        husband."

[28]Now you,[1] brothers, like Isaac, are children of promise. [29]But just as at that time he who was born according to the flesh persecuted him who was born according to the Spirit, so also it is now. [30]But what does the Scripture say? "Cast out the slave woman and her son, for the son of the slave woman shall not inherit with the son of the free woman." [31]So, brothers, we are not children of the slave but of the free woman.

--------- *Ezekiel 31* ---------

In the eleventh year, in the third month, on the first day of the month, the word of the LORD came to me: [2]"Son of man, say to Pharaoh king of Egypt and to his multitude:

    "Whom are you like in your greatness?
[3]   Behold, Assyria was a cedar in
            Lebanon,
        with beautiful branches and forest
            shade,
        and of towering height,
            its top among the clouds.[2]
[4]   The waters nourished it;
            the deep made it grow tall,
        making its rivers flow
            around the place of its planting,
        sending forth its streams
            to all the trees of the field.
[5]   So it towered high
            above all the trees of the field;
        its boughs grew large
            and its branches long
            from abundant water in its shoots.
[6]   All the birds of the heavens
            made their nests in its boughs;
        under its branches all the beasts of the
            field
            gave birth to their young,
        and under its shadow
            lived all great nations.
[7]   It was beautiful in its greatness,
            in the length of its branches;

    for its roots went down
        to abundant waters.
[8]   The cedars in the garden of God could
            not rival it,
        nor the fir trees equal its boughs;
        neither were the plane trees
            like its branches;
        no tree in the garden of God
            was its equal in beauty.
[9]   I made it beautiful
            in the mass of its branches,
        and all the trees of Eden envied it,
            that were in the garden of God.

[10]"Therefore thus says the Lord GOD: Because it[3] towered high and set its top among the clouds, and its heart was proud of its height, [11]I will give it into the hand of a mighty one of the nations. He shall surely deal with it as its wickedness deserves. I have cast it out. [12]Foreigners, the most ruthless of nations, have cut it down and left it. On the mountains and in all the valleys its branches have fallen, and its boughs have been broken in all the ravines of the land, and all the peoples of the earth have gone away from its shadow and left it. [13]On its fallen trunk dwell all the birds of the heavens, and on its branches are all the beasts of the field. [14]All this is in order that no trees by the waters may grow to towering height or set their tops among the clouds, and that no trees that drink water may reach up to them in height. For they are all given over to death, to the world below, among the children of man,[4] with those who go down to the pit.

[15]"Thus says the Lord GOD: On the day the cedar[5] went down to Sheol I caused mourning; I closed the deep over it, and restrained its rivers, and many waters were stopped. I clothed Lebanon in gloom for it, and all the trees of the field fainted because of it. [16]I made the nations quake at the sound of its fall, when I cast it down to Sheol with those who go down to the pit. And all the trees of Eden, the choice and best of Lebanon, all that drink water, were comforted in the world below. [17]They also went down to Sheol with it, to those who are slain by the sword; yes, those who were its arm, who lived under its shadow among the nations.

[18]"Whom are you thus like in glory and in greatness among the trees of Eden? You shall be brought down with the trees of Eden to the

[1] Some manuscripts *we* [2] Or *its top went through the thick boughs*; also verses 10, 14 [3] Syriac, Vulgate; Hebrew *you* [4] Or *of Adam* [5] Hebrew *it*

world below. You shall lie among the uncircumcised, with those who are slain by the sword.

"This is Pharaoh and all his multitude, declares the Lord God."

Psalm 79

A Psalm of Asaph.

O God, the nations have come into your inheritance;
　　they have defiled your holy temple;
　　they have laid Jerusalem in ruins.
2　They have given the bodies of your servants
　　to the birds of the heavens for food,
　　the flesh of your faithful to the beasts of the earth.
3　They have poured out their blood like water
　　all around Jerusalem,
　　and there was no one to bury them.
4　We have become a taunt to our neighbors,
　　mocked and derided by those around us.

5　How long, O Lord? Will you be angry forever?
　　Will your jealousy burn like fire?
6　Pour out your anger on the nations
　　that do not know you,
and on the kingdoms
　　that do not call upon your name!

7　For they have devoured Jacob
　　and laid waste his habitation.
8　Do not remember against us our former iniquities;[1]
　　let your compassion come speedily to meet us,
　　for we are brought very low.
9　Help us, O God of our salvation,
　　for the glory of your name;
deliver us, and atone for our sins,
　　for your name's sake!
10　Why should the nations say,
　　"Where is their God?"
Let the avenging of the outpoured blood
　　of your servants
　　be known among the nations before our eyes!
11　Let the groans of the prisoners come before you;
　　according to your great power,
　　preserve those doomed to die!
12　Return sevenfold into the lap of our neighbors
　　the taunts with which they have taunted you, O Lord!
13　But we your people, the sheep of your pasture,
　　will give thanks to you forever;
　　from generation to generation we will recount your praise.

SEPTEMBER 29

---

1 Kings 1

Now King David was old and advanced in years. And although they covered him with clothes, he could not get warm. ²Therefore his servants said to him, "Let a young woman be sought for my lord the king, and let her wait on the king and be in his service. Let her lie in your arms,[2] that my lord the king may be warm." ³So they sought for a beautiful young woman throughout all the territory of Israel, and found Abishag the Shunammite, and brought her to the king. ⁴The young woman was very beautiful, and she was of service to the king and attended to him, but the king knew her not.

⁵Now Adonijah the son of Haggith exalted himself, saying, "I will be king." And he prepared for himself chariots and horsemen, and fifty men to run before him. ⁶His father had never at any time displeased him by asking,

---

¹ Or the iniquities of former generations ² Or in your bosom

"Why have you done thus and so?" He was also a very handsome man, and he was born next after Absalom. [7]He conferred with Joab the son of Zeruiah and with Abiathar the priest. And they followed Adonijah and helped him. [8]But Zadok the priest and Benaiah the son of Jehoiada and Nathan the prophet and Shimei and Rei and David's mighty men were not with Adonijah.

[9]Adonijah sacrificed sheep, oxen, and fattened cattle by the Serpent's Stone, which is beside En-rogel, and he invited all his brothers, the king's sons, and all the royal officials of Judah, [10]but he did not invite Nathan the prophet or Benaiah or the mighty men or Solomon his brother.

[11]Then Nathan said to Bathsheba the mother of Solomon, "Have you not heard that Adonijah the son of Haggith has become king and David our lord does not know it? [12]Now therefore come, let me give you advice, that you may save your own life and the life of your son Solomon. [13]Go in at once to King David, and say to him, 'Did you not, my lord the king, swear to your servant, saying, "Solomon your son shall reign after me, and he shall sit on my throne"? Why then is Adonijah king?' [14]Then while you are still speaking with the king, I also will come in after you and confirm[1] your words."

[15]So Bathsheba went to the king in his chamber (now the king was very old, and Abishag the Shunammite was attending to the king). [16]Bathsheba bowed and paid homage to the king, and the king said, "What do you desire?" [17]She said to him, "My lord, you swore to your servant by the LORD your God, saying, 'Solomon your son shall reign after me, and he shall sit on my throne.' [18]And now, behold, Adonijah is king, although you, my lord the king, do not know it. [19]He has sacrificed oxen, fattened cattle, and sheep in abundance, and has invited all the sons of the king, Abiathar the priest, and Joab the commander of the army, but Solomon your servant he has not invited. [20]And now, my lord the king, the eyes of all Israel are on you, to tell them who shall sit on the throne of my lord the king after him. [21]Otherwise it will come to pass, when my lord the king sleeps with his fathers, that I and my son Solomon will be counted offenders."

[22]While she was still speaking with the king, Nathan the prophet came in. [23]And they told

the king, "Here is Nathan the prophet." And when he came in before the king, he bowed before the king, with his face to the ground. [24]And Nathan said, "My lord the king, have you said, 'Adonijah shall reign after me, and he shall sit on my throne'? [25]For he has gone down this day and has sacrificed oxen, fattened cattle, and sheep in abundance, and has invited all the king's sons, the commanders[2] of the army, and Abiathar the priest. And behold, they are eating and drinking before him, and saying, 'Long live King Adonijah!' [26]But me, your servant, and Zadok the priest, and Benaiah the son of Jehoiada, and your servant Solomon he has not invited. [27]Has this thing been brought about by my lord the king and you have not told your servants who should sit on the throne of my lord the king after him?"

[28]Then King David answered, "Call Bathsheba to me." So she came into the king's presence and stood before the king. [29]And the king swore, saying, "As the LORD lives, who has redeemed my soul out of every adversity, [30]as I swore to you by the LORD, the God of Israel, saying, 'Solomon your son shall reign after me, and he shall sit on my throne in my place,' even so will I do this day." [31]Then Bathsheba bowed with her face to the ground and paid homage to the king and said, "May my lord King David live forever!"

[32]King David said, "Call to me Zadok the priest, Nathan the prophet, and Benaiah the son of Jehoiada." So they came before the king. [33]And the king said to them, "Take with you the servants of your lord and have Solomon my son ride on my own mule, and bring him down to Gihon. [34]And let Zadok the priest and Nathan the prophet there anoint him king over Israel. Then blow the trumpet and say, 'Long live King Solomon!' [35]You shall then come up after him, and he shall come and sit on my throne, for he shall be king in my place. And I have appointed him to be ruler over Israel and over Judah." [36]And Benaiah the son of Jehoiada answered the king, "Amen! May the LORD, the God of my lord the king, say so. [37]As the LORD has been with my lord the king, even so may he be with Solomon, and make his throne greater than the throne of my lord King David."

[38]So Zadok the priest, Nathan the prophet, and Benaiah the son of Jehoiada, and the Cherethites and the Pelethites went down and

[1] Or expand on [2] Hebrew; Septuagint *Joab the commander*

had Solomon ride on King David's mule and brought him to Gihon. [39]There Zadok the priest took the horn of oil from the tent and anointed Solomon. Then they blew the trumpet, and all the people said, "Long live King Solomon!" [40]And all the people went up after him, playing on pipes, and rejoicing with great joy, so that the earth was split by their noise.

[41]Adonijah and all the guests who were with him heard it as they finished feasting. And when Joab heard the sound of the trumpet, he said, "What does this uproar in the city mean?" [42]While he was still speaking, behold, Jonathan the son of Abiathar the priest came. And Adonijah said, "Come in, for you are a worthy man and bring good news." [43]Jonathan answered Adonijah, "No, for our lord King David has made Solomon king, [44]and the king has sent with him Zadok the priest, Nathan the prophet, and Benaiah the son of Jehoiada, and the Cherethites and the Pelethites. And they had him ride on the king's mule. [45]And Zadok the priest and Nathan the prophet have anointed him king at Gihon, and they have gone up from there rejoicing, so that the city is in an uproar. This is the noise that you have heard. [46]Solomon sits on the royal throne. [47]Moreover, the king's servants came to congratulate our lord King David, saying, 'May your God make the name of Solomon more famous than yours, and make his throne greater than your throne.' And the king bowed himself on the bed. [48]And the king also said, 'Blessed be the LORD, the God of Israel, who has granted someone[1] to sit on my throne this day, my own eyes seeing it.'"

[49]Then all the guests of Adonijah trembled and rose, and each went his own way. [50]And Adonijah feared Solomon. So he arose and went and took hold of the horns of the altar. [51]Then it was told Solomon, "Behold, Adonijah fears King Solomon, for behold, he has laid hold of the horns of the altar, saying, 'Let King Solomon swear to me first that he will not put his servant to death with the sword.'" [52]And Solomon said, "If he will show himself a worthy man, not one of his hairs shall fall to the earth, but if wickedness is found in him, he shall die." [53]So King Solomon sent, and they brought him down from the altar. And he came and paid homage to King Solomon, and Solomon said to him, "Go to your house."

Galatians 5

For freedom Christ has set us free; stand firm therefore, and do not submit again to a yoke of slavery. [2]Look: I, Paul, say to you that if you accept circumcision, Christ will be of no advantage to you. [3]I testify again to every man who accepts circumcision that he is obligated to keep the whole law. [4]You are severed from Christ, you who would be justified[2] by the law; you have fallen away from grace. [5]For through the Spirit, by faith, we ourselves eagerly wait for the hope of righteousness. [6]For in Christ Jesus neither circumcision nor uncircumcision counts for anything, but only faith working through love.

[7]You were running well. Who hindered you from obeying the truth? [8]This persuasion is not from him who calls you. [9]A little leaven leavens the whole lump. [10]I have confidence in the Lord that you will take no other view, and the one who is troubling you will bear the penalty, whoever he is. [11]But if I, brothers,[3] still preach[4] circumcision, why am I still being persecuted? In that case the offense of the cross has been removed. [12]I wish those who unsettle you would emasculate themselves!

[13]For you were called to freedom, brothers. Only do not use your freedom as an opportunity for the flesh, but through love serve one another. [14]For the whole law is fulfilled in one word: "You shall love your neighbor as yourself." [15]But if you bite and devour one another, watch out that you are not consumed by one another.

[16]But I say, walk by the Spirit, and you will not gratify the desires of the flesh. [17]For the desires of the flesh are against the Spirit, and the desires of the Spirit are against the flesh, for these are opposed to each other, to keep you from doing the things you want to do. [18]But if you are led by the Spirit, you are not under the law. [19]Now the works of the flesh are evident: sexual immorality, impurity, sensuality, [20]idolatry, sorcery, enmity, strife, jealousy, fits of anger, rivalries, dissensions, divisions, [21]envy,[5] drunkenness, orgies, and things like these. I warn you, as I warned you before, that those who do such things will not inherit the kingdom of God. [22]But the fruit of the Spirit is love, joy, peace, patience, kindness, goodness, faithfulness, [23]gentleness, self-control; against

such things there is no law. ²⁴And those who belong to Christ Jesus have crucified the flesh with its passions and desires.

²⁵If we live by the Spirit, let us also keep in step with the Spirit. ²⁶Let us not become conceited, provoking one another, envying one another.

Ezekiel 32

In the twelfth year, in the twelfth month, on the first day of the month, the word of the LORD came to me: ²"Son of man, raise a lamentation over Pharaoh king of Egypt and say to him:

"You consider yourself a lion of the nations,
    but you are like a dragon in the seas;
you burst forth in your rivers,
    trouble the waters with your feet,
    and foul their rivers.
³ Thus says the Lord GOD:
    I will throw my net over you
    with a host of many peoples,
    and they will haul you up in my
        dragnet.
⁴ And I will cast you on the ground;
    on the open field I will fling you,
and will cause all the birds of the
        heavens to settle on you,
    and I will gorge the beasts of the
        whole earth with you.
⁵ I will strew your flesh upon the
        mountains
    and fill the valleys with your carcass.¹
⁶ I will drench the land even to the
        mountains
    with your flowing blood,
    and the ravines will be full of you.
⁷ When I blot you out, I will cover the
        heavens
    and make their stars dark;
I will cover the sun with a cloud,
    and the moon shall not give its light.
⁸ All the bright lights of heaven
    will I make dark over you,
    and put darkness on your land,
                declares the Lord GOD.

⁹"I will trouble the hearts of many peoples, when I bring your destruction among the nations, into the countries that you have not known. ¹⁰I will make many peoples appalled

at you, and the hair of their kings shall bristle with horror because of you, when I brandish my sword before them. They shall tremble every moment, every one for his own life, on the day of your downfall.

¹¹"For thus says the Lord GOD: The sword of the king of Babylon shall come upon you. ¹²I will cause your multitude to fall by the swords of mighty ones, all of them most ruthless of nations.

"They shall bring to ruin the pride of
        Egypt,
    and all its multitude² shall perish.
¹³   I will destroy all its beasts
        from beside many waters;
    and no foot of man shall trouble them
        anymore,
    nor shall the hoofs of beasts trouble
        them.
¹⁴   Then I will make their waters clear,
        and cause their rivers to run like oil,
                declares the Lord GOD.
¹⁵   When I make the land of Egypt
        desolate,
    and when the land is desolate of all
        that fills it,
    when I strike down all who dwell in it,
        then they will know that I am the
        LORD.

¹⁶This is a lamentation that shall be chanted; the daughters of the nations shall chant it; over Egypt, and over all her multitude, shall they chant it, declares the Lord GOD."

¹⁷In the twelfth year, in the twelfth month,³ on the fifteenth day of the month, the word of the LORD came to me: ¹⁸"Son of man, wail over the multitude of Egypt, and send them down, her and the daughters of majestic nations, to the world below, to those who have gone down to the pit:

¹⁹   'Whom do you surpass in beauty?
        Go down and be laid to rest with the
        uncircumcised.'

²⁰They shall fall amid those who are slain by the sword. Egypt⁴ is delivered to the sword; drag her away, and all her multitudes. ²¹The mighty chiefs shall speak of them, with their helpers, out of the midst of Sheol: 'They have come down, they lie still, the uncircumcised, slain by the sword.'

---

¹ Hebrew your height ² Or wealth ³ Hebrew lacks in the twelfth month ⁴ Hebrew She

22 "Assyria is there, and all her company, its graves all around it, all of them slain, fallen by the sword, 23 whose graves are set in the uttermost parts of the pit; and her company is all around her grave, all of them slain, fallen by the sword, who spread terror in the land of the living.

24 "Elam is there, and all her multitude around her grave; all of them slain, fallen by the sword, who went down uncircumcised into the world below, who spread their terror in the land of the living; and they bear their shame with those who go down to the pit. 25 They have made her a bed among the slain with all her multitude, her graves all around it, all of them uncircumcised, slain by the sword; for terror of them was spread in the land of the living, and they bear their shame with those who go down to the pit; they are placed among the slain.

26 "Meshech-Tubal is there, and all her multitude, her graves all around it, all of them uncircumcised, slain by the sword; for they spread their terror in the land of the living. 27 And they do not lie with the mighty, the fallen from among the uncircumcised, who went down to Sheol with their weapons of war, whose swords were laid under their heads, and whose iniquities are upon their bones; for the terror of the mighty men was in the land of the living. 28 But as for you, you shall be broken and lie among the uncircumcised, with those who are slain by the sword.

29 "Edom is there, her kings and all her princes, who for all their might are laid with those who are killed by the sword; they lie with the uncircumcised, with those who go down to the pit.

30 "The princes of the north are there, all of them, and all the Sidonians, who have gone down in shame with the slain, for all the terror that they caused by their might; they lie uncircumcised with those who are slain by the sword, and bear their shame with those who go down to the pit.

31 "When Pharaoh sees them, he will be comforted for all his multitude, Pharaoh and all his army, slain by the sword, declares the Lord GOD. 32 For I spread terror in the land of the living; and he shall be laid to rest among the uncircumcised, with those who are slain by the sword, Pharaoh and all his multitude, declares the Lord GOD."

1 Or Turn us again; also verses 7, 19   2 That is, the Euphrates

Psalm 80

TO THE CHOIRMASTER: ACCORDING TO LILIES. A TESTIMONY. OF ASAPH, A PSALM.

Give ear, O Shepherd of Israel,
    you who lead Joseph like a flock.
  You who are enthroned upon the
      cherubim, shine forth.
2   Before Ephraim and Benjamin and
      Manasseh,
  stir up your might
    and come to save us!

3 Restore us,[1] O God;
    let your face shine, that we may be
      saved!

4 O LORD God of hosts,
    how long will you be angry with your
      people's prayers?
5 You have fed them with the bread of
      tears
    and given them tears to drink in full
      measure.
6 You make us an object of contention for
      our neighbors,
    and our enemies laugh among
      themselves.

7 Restore us, O God of hosts;
    let your face shine, that we may be
      saved!

8 You brought a vine out of Egypt;
    you drove out the nations and planted
      it.
9 You cleared the ground for it;
    it took deep root and filled the land.
10 The mountains were covered with its
      shade,
    the mighty cedars with its branches.
11 It sent out its branches to the sea
    and its shoots to the River.[2]
12 Why then have you broken down its
      walls,
    so that all who pass along the way
      pluck its fruit?
13 The boar from the forest ravages it,
    and all that move in the field feed on it.

14 Turn again, O God of hosts!
    Look down from heaven, and see;
  have regard for this vine,
15   the stock that your right hand planted,

and for the son whom you made
    strong for yourself.
16 They have burned it with fire; they have
    cut it down;
    may they perish at the rebuke of your
    face!
17 But let your hand be on the man of your
    right hand,

the son of man whom you have made
    strong for yourself!
18 Then we shall not turn back from you;
    give us life, and we will call upon your
    name!
19 Restore us, O LORD God of hosts!
    Let your face shine, that we may be
    saved!

SEPTEMBER 30

1 Kings 2

When David's time to die drew near, he commanded Solomon his son, saying, ²"I am about to go the way of all the earth. Be strong, and show yourself a man, ³and keep the charge of the LORD your God, walking in his ways and keeping his statutes, his commandments, his rules, and his testimonies, as it is written in the Law of Moses, that you may prosper in all that you do and wherever you turn, ⁴that the LORD may establish his word that he spoke concerning me, saying, 'If your sons pay close attention to their way, to walk before me in faithfulness with all their heart and with all their soul, you shall not lack¹ a man on the throne of Israel.'

⁵"Moreover, you also know what Joab the son of Zeruiah did to me, how he dealt with the two commanders of the armies of Israel, Abner the son of Ner, and Amasa the son of Jether, whom he killed, avenging² in time of peace for blood that had been shed in war, and putting the blood of war³ on the belt around his⁴ waist and on the sandals on his feet. ⁶Act therefore according to your wisdom, but do not let his gray head go down to Sheol in peace. ⁷But deal loyally with the sons of Barzillai the Gileadite, and let them be among those who eat at your table, for with such loyalty⁵ they met me when I fled from Absalom your brother. ⁸And there is also with you Shimei the son of Gera, the Benjaminite from Bahurim, who cursed me with a grievous curse on the day when I went to Mahanaim. But when he came down to meet

me at the Jordan, I swore to him by the LORD, saying, 'I will not put you to death with the sword.' ⁹Now therefore do not hold him guiltless, for you are a wise man. You will know what you ought to do to him, and you shall bring his gray head down with blood to Sheol."

¹⁰Then David slept with his fathers and was buried in the city of David. ¹¹And the time that David reigned over Israel was forty years. He reigned seven years in Hebron and thirty-three years in Jerusalem. ¹²So Solomon sat on the throne of David his father, and his kingdom was firmly established.

¹³Then Adonijah the son of Haggith came to Bathsheba the mother of Solomon. And she said, "Do you come peacefully?" He said, "Peacefully." ¹⁴Then he said, "I have something to say to you." She said, "Speak." ¹⁵He said, "You know that the kingdom was mine, and that all Israel fully expected me to reign. However, the kingdom has turned about and become my brother's, for it was his from the LORD. ¹⁶And now I have one request to make of you; do not refuse me." She said to him, "Speak." ¹⁷And he said, "Please ask King Solomon—he will not refuse you—to give me Abishag the Shunammite as my wife." ¹⁸Bathsheba said, "Very well; I will speak for you to the king."

¹⁹So Bathsheba went to King Solomon to speak to him on behalf of Adonijah. And the king rose to meet her and bowed down to her. Then he sat on his throne and had a seat brought for the king's mother, and she sat on his

¹ Hebrew *there shall not be cut off for you* ² Septuagint; Hebrew *placing* ³ Septuagint *innocent blood* ⁴ Septuagint *my*; twice in this verse ⁵ Or *steadfast love*

right. ²⁰Then she said, "I have one small request to make of you; do not refuse me." And the king said to her, "Make your request, my mother, for I will not refuse you." ²¹She said, "Let Abishag the Shunammite be given to Adonijah your brother as his wife." ²²King Solomon answered his mother, "And why do you ask Abishag the Shunammite for Adonijah? Ask for him the kingdom also, for he is my older brother, and on his side are Abiathar¹ the priest and Joab the son of Zeruiah." ²³Then King Solomon swore by the Lord, saying, "God do so to me and more also if this word does not cost Adonijah his life! ²⁴Now therefore as the Lord lives, who has established me and placed me on the throne of David my father, and who has made me a house, as he promised, Adonijah shall be put to death today." ²⁵So King Solomon sent Benaiah the son of Jehoiada, and he struck him down, and he died.

²⁶And to Abiathar the priest the king said, "Go to Anathoth, to your estate, for you deserve death. But I will not at this time put you to death, because you carried the ark of the Lord God before David my father, and because you shared in all my father's affliction." ²⁷So Solomon expelled Abiathar from being priest to the Lord, thus fulfilling the word of the Lord that he had spoken concerning the house of Eli in Shiloh.

²⁸When the news came to Joab—for Joab had supported Adonijah although he had not supported Absalom—Joab fled to the tent of the Lord and caught hold of the horns of the altar. ²⁹And when it was told King Solomon, "Joab has fled to the tent of the Lord, and behold, he is beside the altar," Solomon sent Benaiah the son of Jehoiada, saying, "Go, strike him down." ³⁰So Benaiah came to the tent of the Lord and said to him, "The king commands, 'Come out.'" But he said, "No, I will die here." Then Benaiah brought the king word again, saying, "Thus said Joab, and thus he answered me." ³¹The king replied to him, "Do as he has said, strike him down and bury him, and thus take away from me and from my father's house the guilt for the blood that Joab shed without cause. ³²The Lord will bring back his bloody deeds on his own head, because, without the knowledge of my father David, he attacked and killed with the sword two men more righteous and better than himself, Abner the son of Ner, commander

of the army of Israel, and Amasa the son of Jether, commander of the army of Judah. ³³So shall their blood come back on the head of Joab and on the head of his descendants forever. But for David and for his descendants and for his house and for his throne there shall be peace from the Lord forevermore." ³⁴Then Benaiah the son of Jehoiada went up and struck him down and put him to death. And he was buried in his own house in the wilderness. ³⁵The king put Benaiah the son of Jehoiada over the army in place of Joab, and the king put Zadok the priest in the place of Abiathar.

³⁶Then the king sent and summoned Shimei and said to him, "Build yourself a house in Jerusalem and dwell there, and do not go out from there to any place whatever. ³⁷For on the day you go out and cross the brook Kidron, know for certain that you shall die. Your blood shall be on your own head." ³⁸And Shimei said to the king, "What you say is good; as my lord the king has said, so will your servant do." So Shimei lived in Jerusalem many days.

³⁹But it happened at the end of three years that two of Shimei's servants ran away to Achish, son of Maacah, king of Gath. And when it was told Shimei, "Behold, your servants are in Gath," ⁴⁰Shimei arose and saddled a donkey and went to Gath to Achish to seek his servants. Shimei went and brought his servants from Gath. ⁴¹And when Solomon was told that Shimei had gone from Jerusalem to Gath and returned, ⁴²the king sent and summoned Shimei and said to him, "Did I not make you swear by the Lord and solemnly warn you, saying, 'Know for certain that on the day you go out and go to any place whatever, you shall die'? And you said to me, 'What you say is good; I will obey.' ⁴³Why then have you not kept your oath to the Lord and the commandment with which I commanded you?" ⁴⁴The king also said to Shimei, "You know in your own heart all the harm that you did to David my father. So the Lord will bring back your harm on your own head. ⁴⁵But King Solomon shall be blessed, and the throne of David shall be established before the Lord forever." ⁴⁶Then the king commanded Benaiah the son of Jehoiada, and he went out and struck him down, and he died.

So the kingdom was established in the hand of Solomon.

¹ Septuagint, Syriac, Vulgate; Hebrew *and for him and for Abiathar*

--- Galatians 6 ---

Brothers,[1] if anyone is caught in any transgression, you who are spiritual should restore him in a spirit of gentleness. Keep watch on yourself, lest you too be tempted. [2] Bear one another's burdens, and so fulfill the law of Christ. [3] For if anyone thinks he is something, when he is nothing, he deceives himself. [4] But let each one test his own work, and then his reason to boast will be in himself alone and not in his neighbor. [5] For each will have to bear his own load.

[6] Let the one who is taught the word share all good things with the one who teaches. [7] Do not be deceived: God is not mocked, for whatever one sows, that will he also reap. [8] For the one who sows to his own flesh will from the flesh reap corruption, but the one who sows to the Spirit will from the Spirit reap eternal life. [9] And let us not grow weary of doing good, for in due season we will reap, if we do not give up. [10] So then, as we have opportunity, let us do good to everyone, and especially to those who are of the household of faith.

[11] See with what large letters I am writing to you with my own hand. [12] It is those who want to make a good showing in the flesh who would force you to be circumcised, and only in order that they may not be persecuted for the cross of Christ. [13] For even those who are circumcised do not themselves keep the law, but they desire to have you circumcised that they may boast in your flesh. [14] But far be it from me to boast except in the cross of our Lord Jesus Christ, by which[2] the world has been crucified to me, and I to the world. [15] For neither circumcision counts for anything, nor uncircumcision, but a new creation. [16] And as for all who walk by this rule, peace and mercy be upon them, and upon the Israel of God.

[17] From now on let no one cause me trouble, for I bear on my body the marks of Jesus.

[18] The grace of our Lord Jesus Christ be with your spirit, brothers. Amen.

--- Ezekiel 33 ---

The word of the LORD came to me: [2] "Son of man, speak to your people and say to them, If I bring the sword upon a land, and the people of the land take a man from among them, and make him their watchman, [3] and if he sees the sword coming upon the land and blows the trumpet and warns the people, [4] then if anyone who hears the sound of the trumpet does not take warning, and the sword comes and takes him away, his blood shall be upon his own head. [5] He heard the sound of the trumpet and did not take warning; his blood shall be upon himself. But if he had taken warning, he would have saved his life. [6] But if the watchman sees the sword coming and does not blow the trumpet, so that the people are not warned, and the sword comes and takes any one of them, that person is taken away in his iniquity, but his blood I will require at the watchman's hand.

[7] "So you, son of man, I have made a watchman for the house of Israel. Whenever you hear a word from my mouth, you shall give them warning from me. [8] If I say to the wicked, O wicked one, you shall surely die, and you do not speak to warn the wicked to turn from his way, that wicked person shall die in his iniquity, but his blood I will require at your hand. [9] But if you warn the wicked to turn from his way, and he does not turn from his way, that person shall die in his iniquity, but you will have delivered your soul.

[10] "And you, son of man, say to the house of Israel, Thus have you said: 'Surely our transgressions and our sins are upon us, and we rot away because of them. How then can we live?' [11] Say to them, As I live, declares the Lord GOD, I have no pleasure in the death of the wicked, but that the wicked turn from his way and live; turn back, turn back from your evil ways, for why will you die, O house of Israel?

[12] "And you, son of man, say to your people, The righteousness of the righteous shall not deliver him when he transgresses, and as for the wickedness of the wicked, he shall not fall by it when he turns from his wickedness, and the righteous shall not be able to live by his righteousness[3] when he sins. [13] Though I say to the righteous that he shall surely live, yet if he trusts in his righteousness and does injustice, none of his righteous deeds shall be remembered, but in his injustice that he has done he shall die. [14] Again, though I say to the wicked, 'You shall surely die,' yet if he turns from his sin and does what is just and right, [15] if the wicked restores the pledge, gives back what he

---

[1] Or *Brothers and sisters;* also verse 18 [2] Or *through whom* [3] Hebrew *by it*

has taken by robbery, and walks in the statutes of life, not doing injustice, he shall surely live; he shall not die. [16]None of the sins that he has committed shall be remembered against him. He has done what is just and right; he shall surely live.

[17]"Yet your people say, 'The way of the Lord is not just,' when it is their own way that is not just. [18]When the righteous turns from his righteousness and does injustice, he shall die for it. [19]And when the wicked turns from his wickedness and does what is just and right, he shall live by this. [20]Yet you say, 'The way of the Lord is not just.' O house of Israel, I will judge each of you according to his ways."

[21]In the twelfth year of our exile, in the tenth month, on the fifth day of the month, a fugitive from Jerusalem came to me and said, "The city has been struck down." [22]Now the hand of the LORD had been upon me the evening before the fugitive came; and he had opened my mouth by the time the man came to me in the morning, so my mouth was opened, and I was no longer mute.

[23]The word of the LORD came to me: [24]"Son of man, the inhabitants of these waste places in the land of Israel keep saying, 'Abraham was only one man, yet he got possession of the land; but we are many; the land is surely given us to possess.' [25]Therefore say to them, Thus says the Lord GOD: You eat flesh with the blood and lift up your eyes to your idols and shed blood; shall you then possess the land? [26]You rely on the sword, you commit abominations, and each of you defiles his neighbor's wife; shall you then possess the land? [27]Say this to them, Thus says the Lord GOD: As I live, surely those who are in the waste places shall fall by the sword, and whoever is in the open field I will give to the beasts to be devoured, and those who are in strongholds and in caves shall die by pestilence. [28]And I will make the land a desolation and a waste, and her proud might shall come to an end, and the mountains of Israel shall be so desolate that none will pass through. [29]Then they will know that I am the LORD, when I have made the land a desolation and a waste because of all their abominations that they have committed.

[30]"As for you, son of man, your people who talk together about you by the walls and at the doors of the houses, say to one another,

each to his brother, 'Come, and hear what the word is that comes from the LORD.' [31]And they come to you as people come, and they sit before you as my people, and they hear what you say but they will not do it; for with lustful talk in their mouths they act; their heart is set on their gain. [32]And behold, you are to them like one who sings lustful songs with a beautiful voice and plays[1] well on an instrument, for they hear what you say, but they will not do it. [33]When this comes—and come it will!—then they will know that a prophet has been among them."

Psalm 81–82

TO THE CHOIRMASTER: ACCORDING TO THE GITTITH.[2] OF ASAPH.

Sing aloud to God our strength;
　shout for joy to the God of Jacob!
2　Raise a song; sound the tambourine,
　　the sweet lyre with the harp.
3　Blow the trumpet at the new moon,
　　at the full moon, on our feast day.

4　For it is a statute for Israel,
　　a rule[3] of the God of Jacob.
5　He made it a decree in Joseph
　　when he went out over[4] the land of
　　　Egypt.
　I hear a language I had not known:
6　"I relieved your[5] shoulder of the burden;
　　your hands were freed from the
　　　basket.
7　In distress you called, and I delivered
　　　you;
　　I answered you in the secret place of
　　　thunder;
　　I tested you at the waters of Meribah.
　　　　　　　　　　　　　　　　Selah
8　Hear, O my people, while I admonish
　　　you!
　　O Israel, if you would but listen to me!
9　There shall be no strange god among
　　　you;
　　you shall not bow down to a foreign
　　　god.
10　I am the LORD your God,
　　who brought you up out of the land of
　　　Egypt.
　　Open your mouth wide, and I will fill
　　　it.

[1] Hebrew *like the singing of lustful songs with a beautiful voice and one who plays*　[2] Probably a musical or liturgical term　[3] Or *just decree*　[4] Or *against*　[5] Hebrew *his*; also next line

11 "But my people did not listen to my voice;
   Israel would not submit to me.
12 So I gave them over to their stubborn
      hearts,
   to follow their own counsels.
13 Oh, that my people would listen to me,
   that Israel would walk in my ways!
14 I would soon subdue their enemies
   and turn my hand against their foes.
15 Those who hate the Lord would cringe
      toward him,
   and their fate would last forever.
16 But he would feed you[1] with the finest
      of the wheat,
   and with honey from the rock I would
      satisfy you."

A Psalm of Asaph.

G od has taken his place in the divine
   council;
   in the midst of the gods he holds
      judgment:

2 "How long will you judge unjustly
   and show partiality to the wicked?   *Selah*
3 Give justice to the weak and the fatherless;
   maintain the right of the afflicted and
      the destitute.
4 Rescue the weak and the needy;
   deliver them from the hand of the
      wicked."
5 They have neither knowledge nor
      understanding,
   they walk about in darkness;
   all the foundations of the earth are
      shaken.

6 I said, "You are gods,
   sons of the Most High, all of you;
7 nevertheless, like men you shall die,
   and fall like any prince."[2]
8 Arise, O God, judge the earth;
   for you shall inherit all the nations!

---

[1] That is, Israel; Hebrew *him* [2] Or *fall as one man, O princes*

OCTOBER 1

1 Kings 3

Solomon made a marriage alliance with Pharaoh king of Egypt. He took Pharaoh's daughter and brought her into the city of David until he had finished building his own house and the house of the LORD and the wall around Jerusalem. ²The people were sacrificing at the high places, however, because no house had yet been built for the name of the LORD.

³Solomon loved the LORD, walking in the statutes of David his father, only he sacrificed and made offerings at the high places. ⁴And the king went to Gibeon to sacrifice there, for that was the great high place. Solomon used to offer a thousand burnt offerings on that altar. ⁵At Gibeon the LORD appeared to Solomon in a dream by night, and God said, "Ask what I shall give you." ⁶And Solomon said, "You have shown great and steadfast love to your servant David my father, because he walked before you in faithfulness, in righteousness, and in uprightness of heart toward you. And you have kept for him this great and steadfast love and have given him a son to sit on his throne this day. ⁷And now, O LORD my God, you have made your servant king in place of David my father, although I am but a little child. I do not know how to go out or come in. ⁸And your servant is in the midst of your people whom you have chosen, a great people, too many to be numbered or counted for multitude. ⁹Give your servant therefore an understanding mind to govern your people, that I may discern between good and evil, for who is able to govern this your great people?"

¹⁰It pleased the Lord that Solomon had asked this. ¹¹And God said to him, "Because you have asked this, and have not asked for yourself long life or riches or the life of your enemies, but have asked for yourself understanding to discern what is right, ¹²behold, I now do according to your word. Behold, I give you a wise and discerning mind, so that none like you has been before you and none like you shall arise after you. ¹³I give you also what you have not asked, both riches and honor, so that no other king shall compare with you, all your days. ¹⁴And if you will walk in my ways, keeping my statutes and my commandments, as your father David walked, then I will lengthen your days."

¹⁵And Solomon awoke, and behold, it was a dream. Then he came to Jerusalem and stood before the ark of the covenant of the Lord, and offered up burnt offerings and peace offerings, and made a feast for all his servants.

¹⁶Then two prostitutes came to the king and stood before him. ¹⁷The one woman said, "Oh, my lord, this woman and I live in the same house, and I gave birth to a child while she was in the house. ¹⁸Then on the third day after I gave birth, this woman also gave birth. And we were alone. There was no one else with us in the house; only we two were in the house. ¹⁹And this woman's son died in the night, because she lay on him. ²⁰And she arose at midnight and took my son from beside me, while your servant slept, and laid him at her breast, and laid her dead son at my breast. ²¹When I rose in the morning to nurse my child, behold, he was dead. But when I looked at him closely in the morning, behold, he was not the child that I had borne." ²²But the other woman said, "No, the living child is mine, and the dead child is yours." The first said, "No, the dead child is yours, and the living child is mine." Thus they spoke before the king.

²³Then the king said, "The one says, 'This is my son that is alive, and your son is dead'; and the other says, 'No; but your son is dead, and my son is the living one.'" ²⁴And the king said, "Bring me a sword." So a sword was brought before the king. ²⁵And the king said, "Divide the living child in two, and give half to the one and half to the other." ²⁶Then the woman whose son was alive said to the king, because her heart yearned for her son, "Oh, my lord, give her the living child, and by no means put him to death." But the other said, "He shall be neither mine nor yours; divide him." ²⁷Then

the king answered and said, "Give the living child to the first woman, and by no means put him to death; she is his mother." [28]And all Israel heard of the judgment that the king had rendered, and they stood in awe of the king, because they perceived that the wisdom of God was in him to do justice.

———————— *Ephesians 1* ————————

Paul, an apostle of Christ Jesus by the will of God,

To the saints who are in Ephesus, and are faithful[1] in Christ Jesus:

[2]Grace to you and peace from God our Father and the Lord Jesus Christ.

[3]Blessed be the God and Father of our Lord Jesus Christ, who has blessed us in Christ with every spiritual blessing in the heavenly places, [4]even as he chose us in him before the foundation of the world, that we should be holy and blameless before him. In love [5]he predestined us[2] for adoption as sons through Jesus Christ, according to the purpose of his will, [6]to the praise of his glorious grace, with which he has blessed us in the Beloved. [7]In him we have redemption through his blood, the forgiveness of our trespasses, according to the riches of his grace, [8]which he lavished upon us, in all wisdom and insight [9]making known[3] to us the mystery of his will, according to his purpose, which he set forth in Christ [10]as a plan for the fullness of time, to unite all things in him, things in heaven and things on earth.

[11]In him we have obtained an inheritance, having been predestined according to the purpose of him who works all things according to the counsel of his will, [12]so that we who were the first to hope in Christ might be to the praise of his glory. [13]In him you also, when you heard the word of truth, the gospel of your salvation, and believed in him, were sealed with the promised Holy Spirit, [14]who is the guarantee[4] of our inheritance until we acquire possession of it,[5] to the praise of his glory.

[15]For this reason, because I have heard of your faith in the Lord Jesus and your love[6] toward all the saints, [16]I do not cease to give thanks for you, remembering you in my prayers, [17]that the God of our Lord Jesus Christ, the Father of glory, may give you the Spirit of wisdom and of revelation in the knowledge of him, [18]having the eyes of your hearts enlightened, that you may know what is the hope to which he has called you, what are the riches of his glorious inheritance in the saints, [19]and what is the immeasurable greatness of his power toward us who believe, according to the working of his great might [20]that he worked in Christ when he raised him from the dead and seated him at his right hand in the heavenly places, [21]far above all rule and authority and power and dominion, and above every name that is named, not only in this age but also in the one to come. [22]And he put all things under his feet and gave him as head over all things to the church, [23]which is his body, the fullness of him who fills all in all.

———————— *Ezekiel 34* ————————

The word of the LORD came to me: [2]"Son of man, prophesy against the shepherds of Israel; prophesy, and say to them, even to the shepherds, Thus says the Lord GOD: Ah, shepherds of Israel who have been feeding yourselves! Should not shepherds feed the sheep? [3]You eat the fat, you clothe yourselves with the wool, you slaughter the fat ones, but you do not feed the sheep. [4]The weak you have not strengthened, the sick you have not healed, the injured you have not bound up, the strayed you have not brought back, the lost you have not sought, and with force and harshness you have ruled them. [5]So they were scattered, because there was no shepherd, and they became food for all the wild beasts. [6]My sheep were scattered; they wandered over all the mountains and on every high hill. My sheep were scattered over all the face of the earth, with none to search or seek for them.

[7]"Therefore, you shepherds, hear the word of the LORD: [8]As I live, declares the Lord GOD, surely because my sheep have become a prey, and my sheep have become food for all the wild beasts, since there was no shepherd, and because my shepherds have not searched for my sheep, but the shepherds have fed themselves, and have not fed my sheep, [9]therefore, you shepherds, hear the word of the LORD: [10]Thus says the Lord GOD, Behold, I am against the shepherds, and I will require my sheep at their hand and put a stop to their feeding the sheep. No longer shall the

[1] Some manuscripts *saints who are also faithful* (omitting *in Ephesus*) [2] Or *before him in love, having predestined us* [3] Or *he lavished upon us in all wisdom and insight, making known*. . . [4] Or *down payment* [5] Or *until God redeems his possession* [6] Some manuscripts omit *your love*

shepherds feed themselves. I will rescue my sheep from their mouths, that they may not be food for them.

[11] "For thus says the Lord God: Behold, I, I myself will search for my sheep and will seek them out. [12]As a shepherd seeks out his flock when he is among his sheep that have been scattered, so will I seek out my sheep, and I will rescue them from all places where they have been scattered on a day of clouds and thick darkness. [13]And I will bring them out from the peoples and gather them from the countries, and will bring them into their own land. And I will feed them on the mountains of Israel, by the ravines, and in all the inhabited places of the country. [14]I will feed them with good pasture, and on the mountain heights of Israel shall be their grazing land. There they shall lie down in good grazing land, and on rich pasture they shall feed on the mountains of Israel. [15]I myself will be the shepherd of my sheep, and I myself will make them lie down, declares the Lord God. [16]I will seek the lost, and I will bring back the strayed, and I will bind up the injured, and I will strengthen the weak, and the fat and the strong I will destroy.[1] I will feed them in justice.

[17]"As for you, my flock, thus says the Lord God: Behold, I judge between sheep and sheep, between rams and male goats. [18]Is it not enough for you to feed on the good pasture, that you must tread down with your feet the rest of your pasture; and to drink of clear water, that you must muddy the rest of the water with your feet? [19]And must my sheep eat what you have trodden with your feet, and drink what you have muddied with your feet?

[20]"Therefore, thus says the Lord God to them: Behold, I, I myself will judge between the fat sheep and the lean sheep. [21]Because you push with side and shoulder, and thrust at all the weak with your horns, till you have scattered them abroad, [22]I will rescue[2] my flock; they shall no longer be a prey. And I will judge between sheep and sheep. [23]And I will set up over them one shepherd, my servant David, and he shall feed them: he shall feed them and be their shepherd. [24]And I, the Lord, will be their God, and my servant David shall be prince among them. I am the Lord; I have spoken.

[25]"I will make with them a covenant of peace and banish wild beasts from the land, so that they may dwell securely in the wilderness and sleep in the woods. [26]And I will make them and the places all around my hill a blessing, and I will send down the showers in their season; they shall be showers of blessing. [27]And the trees of the field shall yield their fruit, and the earth shall yield its increase, and they shall be secure in their land. And they shall know that I am the Lord, when I break the bars of their yoke, and deliver them from the hand of those who enslaved them. [28]They shall no more be a prey to the nations, nor shall the beasts of the land devour them. They shall dwell securely, and none shall make them afraid. [29]And I will provide for them renowned plantations so that they shall no more be consumed with hunger in the land, and no longer suffer the reproach of the nations. [30]And they shall know that I am the Lord their God with them, and that they, the house of Israel, are my people, declares the Lord God. [31]And you are my sheep, human sheep of my pasture, and I am your God, declares the Lord God."

─────── *Psalm 83–84* ───────

A Song. A Psalm of Asaph.

O God, do not keep silence;
   do not hold your peace or be still,
      O God!
[2] For behold, your enemies make an
         uproar;
      those who hate you have raised their
         heads.
[3] They lay crafty plans against your
         people;
      they consult together against your
         treasured ones.
[4] They say, "Come, let us wipe them out as
         a nation;
      let the name of Israel be remembered
         no more!"
[5] For they conspire with one accord;
      against you they make a covenant—
[6] the tents of Edom and the Ishmaelites,
      Moab and the Hagrites,
[7] Gebal and Ammon and Amalek,
      Philistia with the inhabitants of Tyre;
[8] Asshur also has joined them;
      they are the strong arm of the children
         of Lot.   *Selah*

[1] Septuagint, Syriac, Vulgate *I will watch over* [2] Or *save*

9 Do to them as you did to Midian,
   as to Sisera and Jabin at the river
      Kishon,
10 who were destroyed at En-dor,
   who became dung for the ground.
11 Make their nobles like Oreb and Zeeb,
   all their princes like Zebah and
      Zalmunna,
12 who said, "Let us take possession for
      ourselves
   of the pastures of God."

13 O my God, make them like whirling
      dust,[1]
   like chaff before the wind.
14 As fire consumes the forest,
   as the flame sets the mountains
      ablaze,
15 so may you pursue them with your
      tempest
   and terrify them with your hurricane!
16 Fill their faces with shame,
   that they may seek your name,
      O LORD.
17 Let them be put to shame and dismayed
      forever;
   let them perish in disgrace,
18 that they may know that you alone,
   whose name is the LORD,
   are the Most High over all the earth.

TO THE CHOIRMASTER: ACCORDING TO THE
GITTITH.[2] A PSALM OF THE SONS OF KORAH.

How lovely is your dwelling place,
   O LORD of hosts!
2 My soul longs, yes, faints
   for the courts of the LORD;

my heart and flesh sing for joy
   to the living God.
3 Even the sparrow finds a home,
   and the swallow a nest for herself,
      where she may lay her young,
   at your altars, O LORD of hosts,
      my King and my God.
4 Blessed are those who dwell in your
      house,
   ever singing your praise!   *Selah*
5 Blessed are those whose strength is in
      you,
   in whose heart are the highways to
      Zion.[3]
6 As they go through the Valley of Baca
   they make it a place of springs;
   the early rain also covers it with
      pools.
7 They go from strength to strength;
   each one appears before God in Zion.
8 O LORD God of hosts, hear my prayer;
   give ear, O God of Jacob!   *Selah*
9 Behold our shield, O God;
   look on the face of your anointed!
10 For a day in your courts is better
      than a thousand elsewhere.
   I would rather be a doorkeeper in the
      house of my God
   than dwell in the tents of wickedness.
11 For the LORD God is a sun and shield;
   the LORD bestows favor and honor.
   No good thing does he withhold
      from those who walk uprightly.
12 O LORD of hosts,
   blessed is the one who trusts in you!

OCTOBER 2

1 Kings 4–5

King Solomon was king over all Israel, [2]and these were his high officials: Azariah the son of Zadok was the priest; [3]Eli-horeph and Ahijah the sons of Shisha were secretaries; Jehoshaphat the son of Ahilud was recorder; [4]Benaiah the son of Jehoiada was in command of the army; Zadok and Abiathar were priests; [5]Azariah the son of

[1] Or *like a tumbleweed* [2] Probably a musical or liturgical term [3] Hebrew lacks *to Zion*

Nathan was over the officers; Zabud the son of Nathan was priest and king's friend; [6]Ahishar was in charge of the palace; and Adoniram the son of Abda was in charge of the forced labor.

[7] Solomon had twelve officers over all Israel, who provided food for the king and his household. Each man had to make provision for one month in the year. [8]These were their names: Ben-hur, in the hill country of Ephraim; [9]Ben-deker, in Makaz, Shaalbim, Beth-shemesh, and Elonbeth-hanan; [10]Ben-hesed, in Arubboth (to him belonged Socoh and all the land of Hepher); [11]Ben-abinadab, in all Naphath-dor (he had Taphath the daughter of Solomon as his wife); [12]Baana the son of Ahilud, in Taanach, Megiddo, and all Beth-shean that is beside Zarethan below Jezreel, and from Beth-shean to Abel-meholah, as far as the other side of Jokmeam; [13]Ben-geber, in Ramoth-gilead (he had the villages of Jair the son of Manasseh, which are in Gilead, and he had the region of Argob, which is in Bashan, sixty great cities with walls and bronze bars); [14]Ahinadab the son of Iddo, in Mahanaim; [15]Ahimaaz, in Naphtali (he had taken Basemath the daughter of Solomon as his wife); [16]Baana the son of Hushai, in Asher and Bealoth; [17]Jehoshaphat the son of Paruah, in Issachar; [18]Shimei the son of Ela, in Benjamin; [19]Geber the son of Uri, in the land of Gilead, the country of Sihon king of the Amorites and of Og king of Bashan. And there was one governor who was over the land.

[20]Judah and Israel were as many as the sand by the sea. They ate and drank and were happy. [21][1] Solomon ruled over all the kingdoms from the Euphrates[2] to the land of the Philistines and to the border of Egypt. They brought tribute and served Solomon all the days of his life.

[22] Solomon's provision for one day was thirty cors[3] of fine flour and sixty cors of meal, [23]ten fat oxen, and twenty pasture-fed cattle, a hundred sheep, besides deer, gazelles, roebucks, and fattened fowl. [24]For he had dominion over all the region west of the Euphrates[4] from Tiphsah to Gaza, over all the kings west of the Euphrates. And he had peace on all sides around him. [25]And Judah and Israel lived in safety, from Dan even to Beersheba, every man under his vine and under his fig tree, all the days of Solomon. [26]Solomon also had 40,000[5] stalls of horses for his chariots, and 12,000 horsemen. [27]And those officers supplied provisions for King Solomon, and for all who came to King Solomon's table, each one in his month. They let nothing be lacking. [28]Barley also and straw for the horses and swift steeds they brought to the place where it was required, each according to his duty.

[29]And God gave Solomon wisdom and understanding beyond measure, and breadth of mind like the sand on the seashore, [30]so that Solomon's wisdom surpassed the wisdom of all the people of the east and all the wisdom of Egypt. [31]For he was wiser than all other men, wiser than Ethan the Ezrahite, and Heman, Calcol, and Darda, the sons of Mahol, and his fame was in all the surrounding nations. [32]He also spoke 3,000 proverbs, and his songs were 1,005. [33]He spoke of trees, from the cedar that is in Lebanon to the hyssop that grows out of the wall. He spoke also of beasts, and of birds, and of reptiles, and of fish. [34]And people of all nations came to hear the wisdom of Solomon, and from all the kings of the earth, who had heard of his wisdom.

[5:16] Now Hiram king of Tyre sent his servants to Solomon when he heard that they had anointed him king in place of his father, for Hiram always loved David. [2]And Solomon sent word to Hiram, [3]"You know that David my father could not build a house for the name of the Lord his God because of the warfare with which his enemies surrounded him, until the Lord put them under the soles of his feet. [4]But now the Lord my God has given me rest on every side. There is neither adversary nor misfortune. [5]And so I intend to build a house for the name of the Lord my God, as the Lord said to David my father, 'Your son, whom I will set on your throne in your place, shall build the house for my name.' [6]Now therefore command that cedars of Lebanon be cut for me. And my servants will join your servants, and I will pay you for your servants such wages as you set, for you know that there is no one among us who knows how to cut timber like the Sidonians."

[7]As soon as Hiram heard the words of Solomon, he rejoiced greatly and said, "Blessed be the Lord this day, who has given to David a wise son to be over this great people." [8]And

[1] Ch 5:1 in Hebrew [2] Hebrew *the River* [3] A cor was about 6 bushels or 220 liters [4] Hebrew *the River*; twice in this verse [5] Hebrew; one Hebrew manuscript (see 2 Chron. 9:25 and Septuagint of 1 Kings 10:26) *4,000* [6] Ch 5:15 in Hebrew

Hiram sent to Solomon, saying, "I have heard the message that you have sent to me. I am ready to do all you desire in the matter of cedar and cypress timber. ⁹My servants shall bring it down to the sea from Lebanon, and I will make it into rafts to go by sea to the place you direct. And I will have them broken up there, and you shall receive it. And you shall meet my wishes by providing food for my household." ¹⁰So Hiram supplied Solomon with all the timber of cedar and cypress that he desired, ¹¹while Solomon gave Hiram 20,000 cors¹ of wheat as food for his household, and 20,000² cors of beaten oil. Solomon gave this to Hiram year by year. ¹²And the LORD gave Solomon wisdom, as he promised him. And there was peace between Hiram and Solomon, and the two of them made a treaty.

¹³King Solomon drafted forced labor out of all Israel, and the draft numbered 30,000 men. ¹⁴And he sent them to Lebanon, 10,000 a month in shifts. They would be a month in Lebanon and two months at home. Adoniram was in charge of the draft. ¹⁵Solomon also had 70,000 burden-bearers and 80,000 stonecutters in the hill country, ¹⁶besides Solomon's 3,300 chief officers who were over the work, who had charge of the people who carried on the work. ¹⁷At the king's command they quarried out great, costly stones in order to lay the foundation of the house with dressed stones. ¹⁸So Solomon's builders and Hiram's builders and the men of Gebal did the cutting and prepared the timber and the stone to build the house.

--- *Ephesians 2* ---

And you were dead in the trespasses and sins ²in which you once walked, following the course of this world, following the prince of the power of the air, the spirit that is now at work in the sons of disobedience— ³among whom we all once lived in the passions of our flesh, carrying out the desires of the body³ and the mind, and were by nature children of wrath, like the rest of mankind.⁴ ⁴But⁵ God, being rich in mercy, because of the great love with which he loved us, ⁵even when we were dead in our trespasses, made us alive together with Christ—by grace you have been saved— ⁶and raised us up with him and

seated us with him in the heavenly places in Christ Jesus, ⁷so that in the coming ages he might show the immeasurable riches of his grace in kindness toward us in Christ Jesus. ⁸For by grace you have been saved through faith. And this is not your own doing; it is the gift of God, ⁹not a result of works, so that no one may boast. ¹⁰For we are his workmanship, created in Christ Jesus for good works, which God prepared beforehand, that we should walk in them.

¹¹Therefore remember that at one time you Gentiles in the flesh, called "the uncircumcision" by what is called the circumcision, which is made in the flesh by hands— ¹²remember that you were at that time separated from Christ, alienated from the commonwealth of Israel and strangers to the covenants of promise, having no hope and without God in the world. ¹³But now in Christ Jesus you who once were far off have been brought near by the blood of Christ. ¹⁴For he himself is our peace, who has made us both one and has broken down in his flesh the dividing wall of hostility ¹⁵by abolishing the law of commandments expressed in ordinances, that he might create in himself one new man in place of the two, so making peace, ¹⁶and might reconcile us both to God in one body through the cross, thereby killing the hostility. ¹⁷And he came and preached peace to you who were far off and peace to those who were near. ¹⁸For through him we both have access in one Spirit to the Father. ¹⁹So then you are no longer strangers and aliens,⁶ but you are fellow citizens with the saints and members of the household of God, ²⁰built on the foundation of the apostles and prophets, Christ Jesus himself being the cornerstone, ²¹in whom the whole structure, being joined together, grows into a holy temple in the Lord. ²²In him you also are being built together into a dwelling place for God by⁷ the Spirit.

--- *Ezekiel 35* ---

The word of the LORD came to me: ²"Son of man, set your face against Mount Seir, and prophesy against it, ³and say to it, Thus says the Lord GOD: Behold, I am against you, Mount Seir, and I will stretch out my hand against you, and I will make you a desolation and a

¹ A cor was about 6 bushels or 220 liters ² Septuagint; Hebrew *twenty* ³ Greek *flesh* ⁴ Greek *like the rest* ⁵ Or *And* ⁶ Or *sojourners* ⁷ Or *in*

waste. [4]I will lay your cities waste, and you shall become a desolation, and you shall know that I am the LORD. [5]Because you cherished perpetual enmity and gave over the people of Israel to the power of the sword at the time of their calamity, at the time of their final punishment, [6]therefore, as I live, declares the Lord GOD, I will prepare you for blood, and blood shall pursue you; because you did not hate bloodshed, therefore blood shall pursue you. [7]I will make Mount Seir a waste and a desolation, and I will cut off from it all who come and go. [8]And I will fill its mountains with the slain. On your hills and in your valleys and in all your ravines those slain with the sword shall fall. [9]I will make you a perpetual desolation, and your cities shall not be inhabited. Then you will know that I am the LORD.

[10]"Because you said, 'These two nations and these two countries shall be mine, and we will take possession of them'—although the LORD was there— [11]therefore, as I live, declares the Lord GOD, I will deal with you according to the anger and envy that you showed because of your hatred against them. And I will make myself known among them, when I judge you. [12]And you shall know that I am the LORD.

"I have heard all the revilings that you uttered against the mountains of Israel, saying, 'They are laid desolate; they are given us to devour.' [13]And you magnified yourselves against me with your mouth, and multiplied your words against me; I heard it. [14]Thus says the Lord GOD: While the whole earth rejoices, I will make you desolate. [15]As you rejoiced over the inheritance of the house of Israel, because it was desolate, so I will deal with you; you shall be desolate, Mount Seir, and all Edom, all of it. Then they will know that I am the LORD.

Psalm 85

TO THE CHOIRMASTER. A PSALM OF THE SONS OF KORAH.

LORD, you were favorable to your land;
　you restored the fortunes of Jacob.
[2]　You forgave the iniquity of your people;
　　you covered all their sin.　　　*Selah*
[3]　You withdrew all your wrath;
　　you turned from your hot anger.

[4]　Restore us again, O God of our salvation,
　　and put away your indignation toward
　　　us!
[5]　Will you be angry with us forever?
　　Will you prolong your anger to all
　　　generations?
[6]　Will you not revive us again,
　　that your people may rejoice in you?
[7]　Show us your steadfast love, O LORD,
　　and grant us your salvation.

[8]　Let me hear what God the LORD will
　　　speak,
　　for he will speak peace to his people,
　　　to his saints;
　　but let them not turn back to folly.
[9]　Surely his salvation is near to those who
　　　fear him,
　　that glory may dwell in our land.

[10]　Steadfast love and faithfulness meet;
　　righteousness and peace kiss each
　　　other.
[11]　Faithfulness springs up from the ground,
　　and righteousness looks down from
　　　the sky.
[12]　Yes, the LORD will give what is good,
　　and our land will yield its increase.
[13]　Righteousness will go before him
　　and make his footsteps a way.

OCTOBER 3

1 Kings 6

In the four hundred and eightieth year after the people of Israel came out of the land of Egypt, in the fourth year of Solomon's reign over Israel, in the month of Ziv, which is the second month, he began to build the house of the LORD. [2] The house that King Solomon built for the LORD was sixty cubits[1] long, twenty cubits wide, and thirty cubits high. [3] The vestibule in front of the nave of the house was twenty cubits long, equal to the width of the house, and ten cubits deep in front of the house. [4] And he made for the house windows with recessed frames.[2] [5] He also built a structure[3] against the wall of the house, running around the walls of the house, both the nave and the inner sanctuary. And he made side chambers all around. [6] The lowest story[4] was five cubits broad, the middle one was six cubits broad, and the third was seven cubits broad. For around the outside of the house he made offsets on the wall in order that the supporting beams should not be inserted into the walls of the house.

[7] When the house was built, it was with stone prepared at the quarry, so that neither hammer nor axe nor any tool of iron was heard in the house while it was being built.

[8] The entrance for the lowest[5] story was on the south side of the house, and one went up by stairs to the middle story, and from the middle story to the third. [9] So he built the house and finished it, and he made the ceiling of the house of beams and planks of cedar. [10] He built the structure against the whole house, five cubits high, and it was joined to the house with timbers of cedar.

[11] Now the word of the LORD came to Solomon, [12] "Concerning this house that you are building, if you will walk in my statutes and obey my rules and keep all my commandments and walk in them, then I will establish my word with you, which I spoke to David your father. [13] And I will dwell among the children of Israel and will not forsake my people Israel."

[14] So Solomon built the house and finished it.

[15] He lined the walls of the house on the inside with boards of cedar. From the floor of the house to the walls of the ceiling, he covered them on the inside with wood, and he covered the floor of the house with boards of cypress. [16] He built twenty cubits of the rear of the house with boards of cedar from the floor to the walls, and he built this within as an inner sanctuary, as the Most Holy Place. [17] The house, that is, the nave in front of the inner sanctuary, was forty cubits long. [18] The cedar within the house was carved in the form of gourds and open flowers. All was cedar; no stone was seen. [19] The inner sanctuary he prepared in the innermost part of the house, to set there the ark of the covenant of the LORD. [20] The inner sanctuary[6] was twenty cubits long, twenty cubits wide, and twenty cubits high, and he overlaid it with pure gold. He also overlaid[7] an altar of cedar. [21] And Solomon overlaid the inside of the house with pure gold, and he drew chains of gold across, in front of the inner sanctuary, and overlaid it with gold. [22] And he overlaid the whole house with gold, until all the house was finished. Also the whole altar that belonged to the inner sanctuary he overlaid with gold.

[23] In the inner sanctuary he made two cherubim of olivewood, each ten cubits high. [24] Five cubits was the length of one wing of the cherub, and five cubits the length of the other wing of the cherub; it was ten cubits from the tip of one wing to the tip of the other. [25] The other cherub also measured ten cubits; both cherubim had the same measure and the same form. [26] The height of one cherub was ten cubits, and so was that of the other cherub. [27] He put the cherubim in the innermost part of the house. And the wings of the cherubim were spread out so that a wing of one touched the one wall, and a wing of the other cherub touched the other wall; their other wings touched each other in the middle of the house. [28] And he overlaid the cherubim with gold.

[29] Around all the walls of the house he carved

---

[1] A cubit was about 18 inches or 45 centimeters [2] Or blocked lattice windows [3] Or platform; also verse 10 [4] Septuagint; Hebrew structure, or platform [5] Septuagint, Targum; Hebrew middle [6] Vulgate; Hebrew and before the inner sanctuary [7] Septuagint made

engraved figures of cherubim and palm trees and open flowers, in the inner and outer rooms. [30]The floor of the house he overlaid with gold in the inner and outer rooms.

[31]For the entrance to the inner sanctuary he made doors of olivewood; the lintel and the doorposts were five-sided.[1] [32]He covered the two doors of olivewood with carvings of cherubim, palm trees, and open flowers. He overlaid them with gold and spread gold on the cherubim and on the palm trees.

[33]So also he made for the entrance to the nave doorposts of olivewood, in the form of a square, [34]and two doors of cypress wood. The two leaves of the one door were folding, and the two leaves of the other door were folding. [35]On them he carved cherubim and palm trees and open flowers, and he overlaid them with gold evenly applied on the carved work. [36]He built the inner court with three courses of cut stone and one course of cedar beams.

[37]In the fourth year the foundation of the house of the LORD was laid, in the month of Ziv. [38]And in the eleventh year, in the month of Bul, which is the eighth month, the house was finished in all its parts, and according to all its specifications. He was seven years in building it.

Ephesians 3

For this reason I, Paul, a prisoner for Christ Jesus on behalf of you Gentiles— [2]assuming that you have heard of the stewardship of God's grace that was given to me for you, [3]how the mystery was made known to me by revelation, as I have written briefly. [4]When you read this, you can perceive my insight into the mystery of Christ, [5]which was not made known to the sons of men in other generations as it has now been revealed to his holy apostles and prophets by the Spirit. [6]This mystery is[2] that the Gentiles are fellow heirs, members of the same body, and partakers of the promise in Christ Jesus through the gospel.

[7]Of this gospel I was made a minister according to the gift of God's grace, which was given me by the working of his power. [8]To me, though I am the very least of all the saints, this grace was given, to preach to the Gentiles the unsearchable riches of Christ, [9]and to bring to light for everyone what is the plan of

the mystery hidden for ages in[3] God who created all things, [10]so that through the church the manifold wisdom of God might now be made known to the rulers and authorities in the heavenly places. [11]This was according to the eternal purpose that he has realized in Christ Jesus our Lord, [12]in whom we have boldness and access with confidence through our faith in him. [13]So I ask you not to lose heart over what I am suffering for you, which is your glory.

[14]For this reason I bow my knees before the Father, [15]from whom every family[4] in heaven and on earth is named, [16]that according to the riches of his glory he may grant you to be strengthened with power through his Spirit in your inner being, [17]so that Christ may dwell in your hearts through faith—that you, being rooted and grounded in love, [18]may have strength to comprehend with all the saints what is the breadth and length and height and depth, [19]and to know the love of Christ that surpasses knowledge, that you may be filled with all the fullness of God.

[20]Now to him who is able to do far more abundantly than all that we ask or think, according to the power at work within us, [21]to him be glory in the church and in Christ Jesus throughout all generations, forever and ever. Amen.

Ezekiel 36

"And you, son of man, prophesy to the mountains of Israel, and say, O mountains of Israel, hear the word of the LORD. [2]Thus says the Lord GOD: Because the enemy said of you, 'Aha!' and, 'The ancient heights have become our possession,' [3]therefore prophesy, and say, Thus says the Lord GOD: Precisely because they made you desolate and crushed you from all sides, so that you became the possession of the rest of the nations, and you became the talk and evil gossip of the people, [4]therefore, O mountains of Israel, hear the word of the Lord GOD: Thus says the Lord GOD to the mountains and the hills, the ravines and the valleys, the desolate wastes and the deserted cities, which have become a prey and derision to the rest of the nations all around, [5]therefore thus says the Lord GOD: Surely I have spoken in my hot jealousy against the rest of the nations and against all Edom, who gave my land to themselves as a possession with wholehearted

---

[1] The meaning of the Hebrew phrase is uncertain   [2] The words *This mystery is* are inferred from verse 4   [3] Or *by*   [4] Or *fatherhood*; the Greek word *patria* is closely related to the word for *Father* in verse 14

joy and utter contempt, that they might make its pasturelands a prey. [6]Therefore prophesy concerning the land of Israel, and say to the mountains and hills, to the ravines and valleys, Thus says the Lord GOD: Behold, I have spoken in my jealous wrath, because you have suffered the reproach of the nations. [7]Therefore thus says the Lord GOD: I swear that the nations that are all around you shall themselves suffer reproach.

[8]"But you, O mountains of Israel, shall shoot forth your branches and yield your fruit to my people Israel, for they will soon come home. [9]For behold, I am for you, and I will turn to you, and you shall be tilled and sown. [10]And I will multiply people on you, the whole house of Israel, all of it. The cities shall be inhabited and the waste places rebuilt. [11]And I will multiply on you man and beast, and they shall multiply and be fruitful. And I will cause you to be inhabited as in your former times, and will do more good to you than ever before. Then you will know that I am the LORD. [12]I will let people walk on you, even my people Israel. And they shall possess you, and you shall be their inheritance, and you shall no longer bereave them of children. [13]Thus says the Lord GOD: Because they say to you, 'You devour people, and you bereave your nation of children,' [14]therefore you shall no longer devour people and no longer bereave your nation of children, declares the Lord GOD. [15]And I will not let you hear anymore the reproach of the nations, and you shall no longer bear the disgrace of the peoples and no longer cause your nation to stumble, declares the Lord GOD."

[16]The word of the LORD came to me: [17]"Son of man, when the house of Israel lived in their own land, they defiled it by their ways and their deeds. Their ways before me were like the uncleanness of a woman in her menstrual impurity. [18]So I poured out my wrath upon them for the blood that they had shed in the land, for the idols with which they had defiled it. [19]I scattered them among the nations, and they were dispersed through the countries. In accordance with their ways and their deeds I judged them. [20]But when they came to the nations, wherever they came, they profaned my holy name, in that people said of them, 'These are the people of the LORD, and yet they had to go out of his land.' [21]But I had concern for my holy name, which the house of Israel had profaned among the nations to which they came.

[22]"Therefore say to the house of Israel, Thus says the Lord GOD: It is not for your sake, O house of Israel, that I am about to act, but for the sake of my holy name, which you have profaned among the nations to which you came. [23]And I will vindicate the holiness of my great name, which has been profaned among the nations, and which you have profaned among them. And the nations will know that I am the LORD, declares the Lord GOD, when through you I vindicate my holiness before their eyes. [24]I will take you from the nations and gather you from all the countries and bring you into your own land. [25]I will sprinkle clean water on you, and you shall be clean from all your uncleannesses, and from all your idols I will cleanse you. [26]And I will give you a new heart, and a new spirit I will put within you. And I will remove the heart of stone from your flesh and give you a heart of flesh. [27]And I will put my Spirit within you, and cause you to walk in my statutes and be careful to obey my rules.[1] [28]You shall dwell in the land that I gave to your fathers, and you shall be my people, and I will be your God. [29]And I will deliver you from all your uncleannesses. And I will summon the grain and make it abundant and lay no famine upon you. [30]I will make the fruit of the tree and the increase of the field abundant, that you may never again suffer the disgrace of famine among the nations. [31]Then you will remember your evil ways, and your deeds that were not good, and you will loathe yourselves for your iniquities and your abominations. [32]It is not for your sake that I will act, declares the Lord GOD; let that be known to you. Be ashamed and confounded for your ways, O house of Israel.

[33]"Thus says the Lord GOD: On the day that I cleanse you from all your iniquities, I will cause the cities to be inhabited, and the waste places shall be rebuilt. [34]And the land that was desolate shall be tilled, instead of being the desolation that it was in the sight of all who passed by. [35]And they will say, 'This land that was desolate has become like the garden of Eden, and the waste and desolate and ruined cities are now fortified and inhabited.' [36]Then the nations that are left all around you shall know that I am the LORD; I have rebuilt the ruined places

[1] Or my just decrees

and replanted that which was desolate. I am the LORD; I have spoken, and I will do it.

[37] "Thus says the Lord GOD: This also I will let the house of Israel ask me to do for them: to increase their people like a flock. [38] Like the flock for sacrifices,[1] like the flock at Jerusalem during her appointed feasts, so shall the waste cities be filled with flocks of people. Then they will know that I am the LORD."

Psalm 86

A PRAYER OF DAVID.

Incline your ear, O LORD, and answer me,
    for I am poor and needy.
[2]   Preserve my life, for I am godly;
      save your servant, who trusts in you—
        you are my God.
[3]   Be gracious to me, O Lord,
      for to you do I cry all the day.
[4]   Gladden the soul of your servant,
      for to you, O Lord, do I lift up my soul.
[5]   For you, O Lord, are good and forgiving,
      abounding in steadfast love to all who
        call upon you.
[6]   Give ear, O LORD, to my prayer;
      listen to my plea for grace.
[7]   In the day of my trouble I call upon you,
      for you answer me.

[8]   There is none like you among the gods,
      O Lord,
      nor are there any works like yours.

[9]   All the nations you have made shall come
      and worship before you, O Lord,
      and shall glorify your name.
[10]   For you are great and do wondrous
      things;
      you alone are God.
[11]   Teach me your way, O LORD,
      that I may walk in your truth;
      unite my heart to fear your name.
[12]   I give thanks to you, O Lord my God,
      with my whole heart,
      and I will glorify your name forever.
[13]   For great is your steadfast love toward
      me;
      you have delivered my soul from the
        depths of Sheol.

[14]   O God, insolent men have risen up
      against me;
      a band of ruthless men seeks my life,
      and they do not set you before them.
[15]   But you, O Lord, are a God merciful and
      gracious,
      slow to anger and abounding in
        steadfast love and faithfulness.
[16]   Turn to me and be gracious to me;
      give your strength to your servant,
      and save the son of your maidservant.
[17]   Show me a sign of your favor,
      that those who hate me may see and
        be put to shame
      because you, LORD, have helped me
      and comforted me.

OCTOBER 4

1 Kings 7

Solomon was building his own house thirteen years, and he finished his entire house. [2] He built the House of the Forest of Lebanon. Its length was a hundred cubits[2] and its breadth fifty cubits and its height thirty cubits, and it was built on four[3] rows of cedar pillars, with cedar beams on the pillars. [3] And it was covered with cedar above the chambers that were on the forty-five pillars, fifteen in each row. [4] There were window frames in three rows, and window opposite window in three tiers. [5] All the doorways and windows[4] had square frames, and window was opposite window in three tiers.

[6] And he made the Hall of Pillars; its length was fifty cubits, and its breadth thirty cubits. There was a porch in front with pillars, and a canopy in front of them.

[1] Hebrew *flock of holy things* [2] A *cubit* was about 18 inches or 45 centimeters [3] Septuagint *three* [4] Septuagint; Hebrew *posts*

[7]And he made the Hall of the Throne where he was to pronounce judgment, even the Hall of Judgment. It was finished with cedar from floor to rafters.[1]

[8]His own house where he was to dwell, in the other court back of the hall, was of like workmanship. Solomon also made a house like this hall for Pharaoh's daughter whom he had taken in marriage.

[9]All these were made of costly stones, cut according to measure, sawed with saws, back and front, even from the foundation to the coping, and from the outside to the great court. [10]The foundation was of costly stones, huge stones, stones of eight and ten cubits. [11]And above were costly stones, cut according to measurement, and cedar. [12]The great court had three courses of cut stone all around, and a course of cedar beams; so had the inner court of the house of the LORD and the vestibule of the house.

[13]And King Solomon sent and brought Hiram from Tyre. [14]He was the son of a widow of the tribe of Naphtali, and his father was a man of Tyre, a worker in bronze. And he was full of wisdom, understanding, and skill for making any work in bronze. He came to King Solomon and did all his work.

[15]He cast two pillars of bronze. Eighteen cubits was the height of one pillar, and a line of twelve cubits measured its circumference. It was hollow, and its thickness was four fingers. The second pillar was the same.[2] [16]He also made two capitals of cast bronze to set on the tops of the pillars. The height of the one capital was five cubits, and the height of the other capital was five cubits. [17]There were lattices of checker work with wreaths of chain work for the capitals on the tops of the pillars, a lattice[3] for the one capital and a lattice for the other capital. [18]Likewise he made pomegranates[4] in two rows around the one latticework to cover the capital that was on the top of the pillar, and he did the same with the other capital. [19]Now the capitals that were on the tops of the pillars in the vestibule were of lily-work, four cubits. [20]The capitals were on the two pillars and also above the rounded projection which was beside the latticework. There were two hundred pomegranates in two rows all around, and so with the other capital. [21]He set up the pillars at the vestibule of the temple. He set up the pillar on

the south and called its name Jachin, and he set up the pillar on the north and called its name Boaz. [22]And on the tops of the pillars was lily-work. Thus the work of the pillars was finished.

[23]Then he made the sea of cast metal. It was round, ten cubits from brim to brim, and five cubits high, and a line of thirty cubits measured its circumference. [24]Under its brim were gourds, for ten cubits, compassing the sea all around. The gourds were in two rows, cast with it when it was cast. [25]It stood on twelve oxen, three facing north, three facing west, three facing south, and three facing east. The sea was set on them, and all their rear parts were inward. [26]Its thickness was a handbreadth,[5] and its brim was made like the brim of a cup, like the flower of a lily. It held two thousand baths.[6]

[27]He also made the ten stands of bronze. Each stand was four cubits long, four cubits wide, and three cubits high. [28]This was the construction of the stands: they had panels, and the panels were set in the frames, [29]and on the panels that were set in the frames were lions, oxen, and cherubim. On the frames, both above and below the lions and oxen, there were wreaths of beveled work. [30]Moreover, each stand had four bronze wheels and axles of bronze, and at the four corners were supports for a basin. The supports were cast with wreaths at the side of each. [31]Its opening was within a crown that projected upward one cubit. Its opening was round, as a pedestal is made, a cubit and a half deep. At its opening there were carvings, and its panels were square, not round. [32]And the four wheels were underneath the panels. The axles of the wheels were of one piece with the stands, and the height of a wheel was a cubit and a half. [33]The wheels were made like a chariot wheel; their axles, their rims, their spokes, and their hubs were all cast. [34]There were four supports at the four corners of each stand. The supports were of one piece with the stands. [35]And on the top of the stand there was a round band half a cubit high; and on the top of the stand its stays and its panels were of one piece with it. [36]And on the surfaces of its stays and on its panels, he carved cherubim, lions, and palm trees, according to the space of each, with wreaths all around. [37]After this manner he made the ten stands. All of them were cast alike, of the same measure and the same form.

[1] Syriac, Vulgate; Hebrew floor [2] Targum, Syriac (compare Septuagint and Jeremiah 52:21); Hebrew fingers. And a line of twelve cubits measured the circumference of the second pillar [3] Septuagint; Hebrew seven; twice in this verse [4] Two manuscripts (compare Septuagint); Hebrew pillars [5] A handbreadth was about 3 inches or 7.5 centimeters [6] A bath was about 6 gallons or 22 liters

38And he made ten basins of bronze. Each basin held forty baths, each basin measured four cubits, and there was a basin for each of the ten stands. **39**And he set the stands, five on the south side of the house, and five on the north side of the house. And he set the sea at the southeast corner of the house.

40Hiram also made the pots, the shovels, and the basins. So Hiram finished all the work that he did for King Solomon on the house of the Lord: **41**the two pillars, the two bowls of the capitals that were on the tops of the pillars, and the two latticeworks to cover the two bowls of the capitals that were on the tops of the pillars; **42**and the four hundred pomegranates for the two latticeworks, two rows of pomegranates for each latticework, to cover the two bowls of the capitals that were on the pillars; **43**the ten stands, and the ten basins on the stands; **44**and the one sea, and the twelve oxen underneath the sea.

45Now the pots, the shovels, and the basins, all these vessels in the house of the Lord, which Hiram made for King Solomon, were of burnished bronze. **46**In the plain of the Jordan the king cast them, in the clay ground between Succoth and Zarethan. **47**And Solomon left all the vessels unweighed, because there were so many of them; the weight of the bronze was not ascertained.

48So Solomon made all the vessels that were in the house of the Lord: the golden altar, the golden table for the bread of the Presence, **49**the lampstands of pure gold, five on the south side and five on the north, before the inner sanctuary; the flowers, the lamps, and the tongs, of gold; **50**the cups, snuffers, basins, dishes for incense, and fire pans, of pure gold; and the sockets of gold, for the doors of the innermost part of the house, the Most Holy Place, and for the doors of the nave of the temple.

51Thus all the work that King Solomon did on the house of the Lord was finished. And Solomon brought in the things that David his father had dedicated, the silver, the gold, and the vessels, and stored them in the treasuries of the house of the Lord.

―――――― *Ephesians 4* ――――――

I therefore, a prisoner for the Lord, urge you to walk in a manner worthy of the calling to which you have been called, **2**with all humility and gentleness, with patience, bearing with one another in love, **3**eager to maintain the unity of the Spirit in the bond of peace. **4**There is one body and one Spirit—just as you were called to the one hope that belongs to your call— **5**one Lord, one faith, one baptism, **6**one God and Father of all, who is over all and through all and in all. **7**But grace was given to each one of us according to the measure of Christ's gift. **8**Therefore it says,

"When he ascended on high he led a host of captives,
    and he gave gifts to men."[1]

9(In saying, "He ascended," what does it mean but that he had also descended into the lower regions, the earth?[2] **10**He who descended is the one who also ascended far above all the heavens, that he might fill all things.) **11**And he gave the apostles, the prophets, the evangelists, the shepherds[3] and teachers,[4] **12**to equip the saints for the work of ministry, for building up the body of Christ, **13**until we all attain to the unity of the faith and of the knowledge of the Son of God, to mature manhood,[5] to the measure of the stature of the fullness of Christ, **14**so that we may no longer be children, tossed to and fro by the waves and carried about by every wind of doctrine, by human cunning, by craftiness in deceitful schemes. **15**Rather, speaking the truth in love, we are to grow up in every way into him who is the head, into Christ, **16**from whom the whole body, joined and held together by every joint with which it is equipped, when each part is working properly, makes the body grow so that it builds itself up in love.

17Now this I say and testify in the Lord, that you must no longer walk as the Gentiles do, in the futility of their minds. **18**They are darkened in their understanding, alienated from the life of God because of the ignorance that is in them, due to their hardness of heart. **19**They have become callous and have given themselves up to sensuality, greedy to practice every kind of impurity. **20**But that is not the way you learned Christ!— **21**assuming that you have heard about him and were taught in him, as the truth is in Jesus, **22**to put off your old self,[6] which belongs to your former manner of life and is corrupt through deceitful desires, **23**and to be renewed in the spirit of your minds, **24**and to put on the new self,

―――――――――――――――――――――――

[1] The Greek word *anthropoi* can refer to both men and women   [2] Or *the lower parts of the earth?*   [3] Or *pastors*   [4] Or *the shepherd-teachers*   [5] Greek *to a full-grown man*   [6] Greek *man; also verse 24*

created after the likeness of God in true righ-teousness and holiness.

²⁵Therefore, having put away falsehood, let each one of you speak the truth with his neighbor, for we are members one of another. ²⁶Be angry and do not sin; do not let the sun go down on your anger, ²⁷and give no opportunity to the devil. ²⁸Let the thief no longer steal, but rather let him labor, doing honest work with his own hands, so that he may have something to share with anyone in need. ²⁹Let no corrupting talk come out of your mouths, but only such as is good for building up, as fits the occasion, that it may give grace to those who hear. ³⁰And do not grieve the Holy Spirit of God, by whom you were sealed for the day of redemption. ³¹Let all bitterness and wrath and anger and clamor and slander be put away from you, along with all malice. ³²Be kind to one another, tenderhearted, forgiving one another, as God in Christ forgave you.

Ezekiel 37

The hand of the Lord was upon me, and he brought me out in the Spirit of the Lord and set me down in the middle of the valley;¹ it was full of bones. ²And he led me around among them, and behold, there were very many on the surface of the valley, and behold, they were very dry. ³And he said to me, "Son of man, can these bones live?" And I answered, "O Lord God, you know." ⁴Then he said to me, "Prophesy over these bones, and say to them, O dry bones, hear the word of the Lord. ⁵Thus says the Lord God to these bones: Behold, I will cause breath² to enter you, and you shall live. ⁶And I will lay sinews upon you, and will cause flesh to come upon you, and cover you with skin, and put breath in you, and you shall live, and you shall know that I am the Lord."

⁷So I prophesied as I was commanded. And as I prophesied, there was a sound, and behold, a rattling,³ and the bones came together, bone to its bone. ⁸And I looked, and behold, there were sinews on them, and flesh had come upon them, and skin had covered them. But there was no breath in them. ⁹Then he said to me, "Prophesy to the breath; prophesy, son of man, and say to the breath, Thus says the Lord God: Come from the four winds, O breath, and breathe on these slain, that they may live."

¹⁰So I prophesied as he commanded me, and the breath came into them, and they lived and stood on their feet, an exceedingly great army. ¹¹Then he said to me, "Son of man, these bones are the whole house of Israel. Behold, they say, 'Our bones are dried up, and our hope is lost; we are indeed cut off.' ¹²Therefore prophesy, and say to them, Thus says the Lord God: Behold, I will open your graves and raise you from your graves, O my people. And I will bring you into the land of Israel. ¹³And you shall know that I am the Lord, when I open your graves, and raise you from your graves, O my people. ¹⁴And I will put my Spirit within you, and you shall live, and I will place you in your own land. Then you shall know that I am the Lord; I have spoken, and I will do it, declares the Lord."

¹⁵The word of the Lord came to me: ¹⁶"Son of man, take a stick⁴ and write on it, 'For Judah, and the people of Israel associated with him'; then take another stick and write on it, 'For Joseph (the stick of Ephraim) and all the house of Israel associated with him.' ¹⁷And join them one to another into one stick, that they may become one in your hand. ¹⁸And when your people say to you, 'Will you not tell us what you mean by these?' ¹⁹say to them, Thus says the Lord God: Behold, I am about to take the stick of Joseph (that is in the hand of Ephraim) and the tribes of Israel associated with him. And I will join with it the stick of Judah,⁵ and make them one stick, that they may be one in my hand. ²⁰When the sticks on which you write are in your hand before their eyes, ²¹then say to them, Thus says the Lord God: Behold, I will take the people of Israel from the nations among which they have gone, and will gather them from all around, and bring them to their own land. ²²And I will make them one nation in the land, on the mountains of Israel. And one king shall be king over them all, and they shall be no longer two nations, and no longer divided into two kingdoms. ²³They shall not defile themselves anymore with their idols and their detestable things, or with any of their transgressions. But I will save them from all the backslidings⁶ in which they have sinned, and will cleanse them; and they shall be my people, and I will be their God.

²⁴"My servant David shall be king over them, and they shall all have one shepherd. They shall

¹ Or plain; also verse 2 ² Or spirit; also verses 6, 9, 10 ³ Or an earthquake (compare 3:12, 13) ⁴ Or one piece of wood; also verses 17, 19, 20 ⁵ Hebrew And I will place them on it, the stick of Judah ⁶ Many Hebrew manuscripts; other Hebrew manuscripts dwellings

walk in my rules and be careful to obey my statutes. [25] They shall dwell in the land that I gave to my servant Jacob, where your fathers lived. They and their children and their children's children shall dwell there forever, and David my servant shall be their prince forever. [26] I will make a covenant of peace with them. It shall be an everlasting covenant with them. And I will set them in their land[1] and multiply them, and will set my sanctuary in their midst forevermore. [27] My dwelling place shall be with them, and I will be their God, and they shall be my people. [28] Then the nations will know that I am the LORD who sanctifies Israel, when my sanctuary is in their midst forevermore."

Psalm 87–88

A PSALM OF THE SONS OF KORAH. A SONG.

On the holy mount stands the city he founded;
[2]   the LORD loves the gates of Zion
       more than all the dwelling places of
       Jacob.
[3]   Glorious things of you are spoken,
       O city of God.   *Selah*

[4]   Among those who know me I mention
       Rahab and Babylon;
       behold, Philistia and Tyre, with Cush[2]—
       "This one was born there," they say.
[5]   And of Zion it shall be said,
       "This one and that one were born in
       her";
       for the Most High himself will
       establish her.
[6]   The LORD records as he registers the
       peoples,
       "This one was born there."   *Selah*

[7]   Singers and dancers alike say,
       "All my springs are in you."

A SONG. A PSALM OF THE SONS OF KORAH. TO THE CHOIRMASTER: ACCORDING TO MAHALATH LEANNOTH. A MASKIL[3] OF HEMAN THE EZRAHITE.

O LORD, God of my salvation;
   I cry out day and night before you.
[2]   Let my prayer come before you;
      incline your ear to my cry!

[3] For my soul is full of troubles,
     and my life draws near to Sheol.
[4] I am counted among those who go
       down to the pit;
     I am a man who has no strength,
[5] like one set loose among the dead,
     like the slain that lie in the grave,
     like those whom you remember no more,
     for they are cut off from your hand.
[6] You have put me in the depths of the pit,
     in the regions dark and deep.
[7] Your wrath lies heavy upon me,
     and you overwhelm me with all your
       waves.   *Selah*

[8] You have caused my companions to
       shun me;
     you have made me a horror[4] to them.
     I am shut in so that I cannot escape;
[9]   my eye grows dim through sorrow.
     Every day I call upon you, O LORD;
     I spread out my hands to you.
[10] Do you work wonders for the dead?
     Do the departed rise up to praise you?
                                  Selah
[11] Is your steadfast love declared in the
       grave,
     or your faithfulness in Abaddon?
[12] Are your wonders known in the
       darkness,
     or your righteousness in the land of
       forgetfulness?

[13] But I, O LORD, cry to you;
     in the morning my prayer comes
       before you.
[14] O LORD, why do you cast my soul away?
     Why do you hide your face from me?
[15] Afflicted and close to death from my
       youth up,
     I suffer your terrors; I am helpless.[5]
[16] Your wrath has swept over me;
     your dreadful assaults destroy me.
[17] They surround me like a flood all day
       long;
     they close in on me together.
[18] You have caused my beloved and my
       friend to shun me;
     my companions have become
       darkness.[6]

---

[1] Hebrew lacks *in their land*   [2] Probably *Nubia*   [3] Probably musical or liturgical terms   [4] Or *an abomination*   [5] The meaning of the Hebrew word is uncertain   [6] Or *darkness has become my only companion*

OCTOBER 5

1 Kings 8

Then Solomon assembled the elders of Israel and all the heads of the tribes, the leaders of the fathers' houses of the people of Israel, before King Solomon in Jerusalem, to bring up the ark of the covenant of the LORD out of the city of David, which is Zion. ²And all the men of Israel assembled to King Solomon at the feast in the month Ethanim, which is the seventh month. ³And all the elders of Israel came, and the priests took up the ark. ⁴And they brought up the ark of the LORD, the tent of meeting, and all the holy vessels that were in the tent; the priests and the Levites brought them up. ⁵And King Solomon and all the congregation of Israel, who had assembled before him, were with him before the ark, sacrificing so many sheep and oxen that they could not be counted or numbered. ⁶Then the priests brought the ark of the covenant of the LORD to its place in the inner sanctuary of the house, in the Most Holy Place, underneath the wings of the cherubim. ⁷For the cherubim spread out their wings over the place of the ark, so that the cherubim overshadowed the ark and its poles. ⁸And the poles were so long that the ends of the poles were seen from the Holy Place before the inner sanctuary; but they could not be seen from outside. And they are there to this day. ⁹There was nothing in the ark except the two tablets of stone that Moses put there at Horeb, where the LORD made a covenant with the people of Israel, when they came out of the land of Egypt. ¹⁰And when the priests came out of the Holy Place, a cloud filled the house of the LORD, ¹¹so that the priests could not stand to minister because of the cloud, for the glory of the LORD filled the house of the LORD.

¹²Then Solomon said, "The LORD¹ has said that he would dwell in thick darkness. ¹³I have indeed built you an exalted house, a place for you to dwell in forever." ¹⁴Then the king turned around and blessed all the assembly of Israel, while all the assembly of Israel stood. ¹⁵And he said, "Blessed be the LORD, the God of Israel, who with his hand has fulfilled what he promised with his mouth to David my father, saying, ¹⁶'Since the day that I brought my people Israel out of Egypt, I chose no city out of all the tribes of Israel in which to build a house, that my name might be there. But I chose David to be over my people Israel.' ¹⁷Now it was in the heart of David my father to build a house for the name of the LORD, the God of Israel. ¹⁸But the LORD said to David my father, 'Whereas it was in your heart to build a house for my name, you did well that it was in your heart. ¹⁹Nevertheless, you shall not build the house, but your son who shall be born to you shall build the house for my name.' ²⁰Now the LORD has fulfilled his promise that he made. For I have risen in the place of David my father, and sit on the throne of Israel, as the LORD promised, and I have built the house for the name of the LORD, the God of Israel. ²¹And there I have provided a place for the ark, in which is the covenant of the LORD that he made with our fathers, when he brought them out of the land of Egypt."

²²Then Solomon stood before the altar of the LORD in the presence of all the assembly of Israel and spread out his hands toward heaven, ²³and said, "O LORD, God of Israel, there is no God like you, in heaven above or on earth beneath, keeping covenant and showing steadfast love to your servants who walk before you with all their heart; ²⁴you have kept with your servant David my father what you declared to him. You spoke with your mouth, and with your hand have fulfilled it this day. ²⁵Now therefore, O LORD, God of Israel, keep for your servant David my father what you have promised him, saying, 'You shall not lack a man to sit before me on the throne of Israel, if only your sons pay close attention to their way, to walk before me as you have walked before me.' ²⁶Now therefore, O God of Israel, let your word be confirmed, which you have spoken to your servant David my father.

²⁷"But will God indeed dwell on the earth?

---

¹ Septuagint *The LORD has set the sun in the heavens, but*

Behold, heaven and the highest heaven cannot contain you; how much less this house that I have built! ²⁸ Yet have regard to the prayer of your servant and to his plea, O Lᴏʀᴅ my God, listening to the cry and to the prayer that your servant prays before you this day, ²⁹ that your eyes may be open night and day toward this house, the place of which you have said, 'My name shall be there,' that you may listen to the prayer that your servant offers toward this place. ³⁰ And listen to the plea of your servant and of your people Israel, when they pray toward this place. And listen in heaven your dwelling place, and when you hear, forgive.

³¹ "If a man sins against his neighbor and is made to take an oath and comes and swears his oath before your altar in this house, ³² then hear in heaven and act and judge your servants, condemning the guilty by bringing his conduct on his own head, and vindicating the righteous by rewarding him according to his righteousness.

³³ "When your people Israel are defeated before the enemy because they have sinned against you, and if they turn again to you and acknowledge your name and pray and plead with you in this house, ³⁴ then hear in heaven and forgive the sin of your people Israel and bring them again to the land that you gave to their fathers.

³⁵ "When heaven is shut up and there is no rain because they have sinned against you, if they pray toward this place and acknowledge your name and turn from their sin, when you afflict them, ³⁶ then hear in heaven and forgive the sin of your servants, your people Israel, when you teach them the good way in which they should walk, and grant rain upon your land, which you have given to your people as an inheritance.

³⁷ "If there is famine in the land, if there is pestilence or blight or mildew or locust or caterpillar, if their enemy besieges them in the land at their gates,¹ whatever plague, whatever sickness there is, ³⁸ whatever prayer, whatever plea is made by any man or by all your people Israel, each knowing the affliction of his own heart and stretching out his hands toward this house, ³⁹ then hear in heaven your dwelling place and forgive and act and render to each whose heart you know, according to all his ways (for you, you only, know the hearts of all the children of mankind), ⁴⁰ that they may fear you

all the days that they live in the land that you gave to our fathers.

⁴¹ "Likewise, when a foreigner, who is not of your people Israel, comes from a far country for your name's sake ⁴² (for they shall hear of your great name and your mighty hand, and of your outstretched arm), when he comes and prays toward this house, ⁴³ hear in heaven your dwelling place and do according to all for which the foreigner calls to you, in order that all the peoples of the earth may know your name and fear you, as do your people Israel, and that they may know that this house that I have built is called by your name.

⁴⁴ "If your people go out to battle against their enemy, by whatever way you shall send them, and they pray to the Lᴏʀᴅ toward the city that you have chosen and the house that I have built for your name, ⁴⁵ then hear in heaven their prayer and their plea, and maintain their cause.

⁴⁶ "If they sin against you—for there is no one who does not sin—and you are angry with them and give them to an enemy, so that they are carried away captive to the land of the enemy, far off or near, ⁴⁷ yet if they turn their heart in the land to which they have been carried captive, and repent and plead with you in the land of their captors, saying, 'We have sinned and have acted perversely and wickedly,' ⁴⁸ if they repent with all their mind and with all their heart in the land of their enemies, who carried them captive, and pray to you toward their land, which you gave to their fathers, the city that you have chosen, and the house that I have built for your name, ⁴⁹ then hear in heaven your dwelling place their prayer and their plea, and maintain their cause ⁵⁰ and forgive your people who have sinned against you, and all their transgressions that they have committed against you, and grant them compassion in the sight of those who carried them captive, that they may have compassion on them ⁵¹ (for they are your people, and your heritage, which you brought out of Egypt, from the midst of the iron furnace). ⁵² Let your eyes be open to the plea of your servant and to the plea of your people Israel, giving ear to them whenever they call to you. ⁵³ For you separated them from among all the peoples of the earth to be your heritage, as you declared through Moses your servant, when you brought our fathers out of Egypt, O Lord Gᴏᴅ."

⁵⁴ Now as Solomon finished offering all this

¹ Septuagint, Syriac *in any of their cities*

prayer and plea to the Lord, he arose from before the altar of the Lord, where he had knelt with hands outstretched toward heaven. [55]And he stood and blessed all the assembly of Israel with a loud voice, saying, [56]"Blessed be the Lord who has given rest to his people Israel, according to all that he promised. Not one word has failed of all his good promise, which he spoke by Moses his servant. [57]The Lord our God be with us, as he was with our fathers. May he not leave us or forsake us, [58]that he may incline our hearts to him, to walk in all his ways and to keep his commandments, his statutes, and his rules, which he commanded our fathers. [59]Let these words of mine, with which I have pleaded before the Lord, be near to the Lord our God day and night, and may he maintain the cause of his servant and the cause of his people Israel, as each day requires, [60]that all the peoples of the earth may know that the Lord is God; there is no other. [61]Let your heart therefore be wholly true to the Lord our God, walking in his statutes and keeping his commandments, as at this day."

[62]Then the king, and all Israel with him, offered sacrifice before the Lord. [63]Solomon offered as peace offerings to the Lord 22,000 oxen and 120,000 sheep. So the king and all the people of Israel dedicated the house of the Lord. [64]The same day the king consecrated the middle of the court that was before the house of the Lord, for there he offered the burnt offering and the grain offering and the fat pieces of the peace offerings, because the bronze altar that was before the Lord was too small to receive the burnt offering and the grain offering and the fat pieces of the peace offerings.

[65]So Solomon held the feast at that time, and all Israel with him, a great assembly, from Lebo-hamath to the Brook of Egypt, before the Lord our God, seven days.[1] [66]On the eighth day he sent the people away, and they blessed the king and went to their homes joyful and glad of heart for all the goodness that the Lord had shown to David his servant and to Israel his people.

--------- Ephesians 5 ---------

Therefore be imitators of God, as beloved children. [2]And walk in love, as Christ loved us and gave himself up for us, a fragrant offering and sacrifice to God.

[3]But sexual immorality and all impurity or covetousness must not even be named among you, as is proper among saints. [4]Let there be no filthiness nor foolish talk nor crude joking, which are out of place, but instead let there be thanksgiving. [5]For you may be sure of this, that everyone who is sexually immoral or impure, or who is covetous (that is, an idolater), has no inheritance in the kingdom of Christ and God. [6]Let no one deceive you with empty words, for because of these things the wrath of God comes upon the sons of disobedience. [7]Therefore do not become partners with them; [8]for at one time you were darkness, but now you are light in the Lord. Walk as children of light [9](for the fruit of light is found in all that is good and right and true), [10]and try to discern what is pleasing to the Lord. [11]Take no part in the unfruitful works of darkness, but instead expose them. [12]For it is shameful even to speak of the things that they do in secret. [13]But when anything is exposed by the light, it becomes visible, [14]for anything that becomes visible is light. Therefore it says,

"Awake, O sleeper,
    and arise from the dead,
    and Christ will shine on you."

[15]Look carefully then how you walk, not as unwise but as wise, [16]making the best use of the time, because the days are evil. [17]Therefore do not be foolish, but understand what the will of the Lord is. [18]And do not get drunk with wine, for that is debauchery, but be filled with the Spirit, [19]addressing one another in psalms and hymns and spiritual songs, singing and making melody to the Lord with your heart, [20]giving thanks always and for everything to God the Father in the name of our Lord Jesus Christ, [21]submitting to one another out of reverence for Christ.

[22]Wives, submit to your own husbands, as to the Lord. [23]For the husband is the head of the wife even as Christ is the head of the church, his body, and is himself its Savior. [24]Now as the church submits to Christ, so also wives should submit in everything to their husbands.

[25]Husbands, love your wives, as Christ loved the church and gave himself up for her, [26]that he might sanctify her, having cleansed her by the washing of water with the word, [27]so that he might present the church to himself in

---

[1] Septuagint; Hebrew *seven days and seven days, fourteen days*

splendor, without spot or wrinkle or any such thing, that she might be holy and without blemish.[1] [28]In the same way husbands should love their wives as their own bodies. He who loves his wife loves himself. [29]For no one ever hated his own flesh, but nourishes and cherishes it, just as Christ does the church, [30]because we are members of his body. [31]"Therefore a man shall leave his father and mother and hold fast to his wife, and the two shall become one flesh." [32]This mystery is profound, and I am saying that it refers to Christ and the church. [33]However, let each one of you love his wife as himself, and let the wife see that she respects her husband.

―――――― *Ezekiel 38* ――――――

The word of the LORD came to me: [2]"Son of man, set your face toward Gog, of the land of Magog, the chief prince of Meshech[2] and Tubal, and prophesy against him [3]and say, Thus says the Lord GOD: Behold, I am against you, O Gog, chief prince of Meshech[3] and Tubal. [4]And I will turn you about and put hooks into your jaws, and I will bring you out, and all your army, horses and horsemen, all of them clothed in full armor, a great host, all of them with buckler and shield, wielding swords. [5]Persia, Cush, and Put are with them, all of them with shield and helmet; [6]Gomer and all his hordes; Beth-togarmah from the uttermost parts of the north with all his hordes—many peoples are with you.

[7]"Be ready and keep ready, you and all your hosts that are assembled about you, and be a guard for them. [8]After many days you will be mustered. In the latter years you will go against the land that is restored from war, the land whose people were gathered from many peoples upon the mountains of Israel, which had been a continual waste. Its people were brought out from the peoples and now dwell securely, all of them. [9]You will advance, coming on like a storm. You will be like a cloud covering the land, you and all your hordes, and many peoples with you.

[10]"Thus says the Lord GOD: On that day, thoughts will come into your mind, and you will devise an evil scheme [11]and say, 'I will go up against the land of unwalled villages. I will fall upon the quiet people who dwell securely, all of them dwelling without walls, and having no bars or gates,' [12]to seize spoil and carry off plunder, to turn your hand against the waste places that are now inhabited, and the people who were gathered from the nations, who have acquired livestock and goods, who dwell at the center of the earth. [13]Sheba and Dedan and the merchants of Tarshish and all its leaders[4] will say to you, 'Have you come to seize spoil? Have you assembled your hosts to carry off plunder, to carry away silver and gold, to take away livestock and goods, to seize great spoil?'

[14]"Therefore, son of man, prophesy, and say to Gog, Thus says the Lord GOD: On that day when my people Israel are dwelling securely, will you not know it? [15]You will come from your place out of the uttermost parts of the north, you and many peoples with you, all of them riding on horses, a great host, a mighty army. [16]You will come up against my people Israel, like a cloud covering the land. In the latter days I will bring you against my land, that the nations may know me, when through you, O Gog, I vindicate my holiness before their eyes.

[17]"Thus says the Lord GOD: Are you he of whom I spoke in former days by my servants the prophets of Israel, who in those days prophesied for years that I would bring you against them? [18]But on that day, the day that Gog shall come against the land of Israel, declares the Lord GOD, my wrath will be roused in my anger. [19]For in my jealousy and in my blazing wrath I declare, On that day there shall be a great earthquake in the land of Israel. [20]The fish of the sea and the birds of the heavens and the beasts of the field and all creeping things that creep on the ground, and all the people who are on the face of the earth, shall quake at my presence. And the mountains shall be thrown down, and the cliffs shall fall, and every wall shall tumble to the ground. [21]I will summon a sword against Gog[5] on all my mountains, declares the Lord GOD. Every man's sword will be against his brother. [22]With pestilence and bloodshed I will enter into judgment with him, and I will rain upon him and his hordes and the many peoples who are with him torrential rains and hailstones, fire and sulfur. [23]So I will show my greatness and my holiness and make myself known in the eyes of many nations. Then they will know that I am the LORD.

―――――――――――――――――――――――――――――――――
[1] Or holy and blameless [2] Or Magog, the prince of Rosh, Meshech [3] Or Gog, prince of Rosh, Meshech [4] Hebrew young lions [5] Hebrew against him

Psalm 89

A Maskil[1] of Ethan the Ezrahite.

I will sing of the steadfast love of the Lord,
forever;
    with my mouth I will make
      known your faithfulness to all
      generations.

2 For I said, "Steadfast love will be built up
    forever;
    in the heavens you will establish your
      faithfulness."

3 You have said, "I have made a covenant
    with my chosen one;
    I have sworn to David my servant:

4 'I will establish your offspring forever,
    and build your throne for all
      generations.'"   *Selah*

5 Let the heavens praise your wonders,
    O Lord,
    your faithfulness in the assembly of
      the holy ones!

6 For who in the skies can be compared to
    the Lord?
    Who among the heavenly beings[2] is
      like the Lord,

7 a God greatly to be feared in the council
    of the holy ones,
    and awesome above all who are
      around him?

8 O Lord God of hosts,
    who is mighty as you are, O Lord,
    with your faithfulness all around
      you?

9 You rule the raging of the sea;
    when its waves rise, you still them.

10 You crushed Rahab like a carcass;
    you scattered your enemies with your
      mighty arm.

11 The heavens are yours; the earth also is
    yours;
    the world and all that is in it, you have
      founded them.

12 The north and the south, you have
    created them;
    Tabor and Hermon joyously praise
      your name.

13 You have a mighty arm;
    strong is your hand, high your right
      hand.

14 Righteousness and justice are the
    foundation of your throne;
    steadfast love and faithfulness go
      before you.

15 Blessed are the people who know the
    festal shout,
    who walk, O Lord, in the light of your
      face,

16 who exult in your name all the day
    and in your righteousness are exalted.

17 For you are the glory of their strength;
    by your favor our horn is exalted.

18 For our shield belongs to the Lord,
    our king to the Holy One of Israel.

19 Of old you spoke in a vision to your
    godly one,[3] and said:
    "I have granted help to one who is
      mighty;
    I have exalted one chosen from the
      people.

20 I have found David, my servant;
    with my holy oil I have anointed him,

21 so that my hand shall be established
    with him;
    my arm also shall strengthen him.

22 The enemy shall not outwit him;
    the wicked shall not humble him.

23 I will crush his foes before him
    and strike down those who hate him.

24 My faithfulness and my steadfast love
    shall be with him,
    and in my name shall his horn be
      exalted.

25 I will set his hand on the sea
    and his right hand on the rivers.

26 He shall cry to me, 'You are my Father,
    my God, and the Rock of my
      salvation.'

27 And I will make him the firstborn,
    the highest of the kings of the earth.

28 My steadfast love I will keep for him
    forever,
    and my covenant will stand firm[4] for
      him.

29 I will establish his offspring forever
    and his throne as the days of the
      heavens.

30 If his children forsake my law
    and do not walk according to my rules,[5]

31 if they violate my statutes
    and do not keep my commandments,

---

[1] Probably a musical or liturgical term   [2] Hebrew *the sons of God, or the sons of might*   [3] Some Hebrew manuscripts *godly ones*   [4] Or *will remain faithful*   [5] Or *my just decrees*

32 then I will punish their transgression
with the rod
and their iniquity with stripes,
33 but I will not remove from him my
steadfast love
or be false to my faithfulness.
34 I will not violate my covenant
or alter the word that went forth from
my lips.
35 Once for all I have sworn by my
holiness;
I will not lie to David.
36 His offspring shall endure forever,
his throne as long as the sun before me.
37 Like the moon it shall be established
forever,
a faithful witness in the skies." *Selah*

38 But now you have cast off and rejected;
you are full of wrath against your
anointed.
39 You have renounced the covenant with
your servant;
you have defiled his crown in the
dust.
40 You have breached all his walls;
you have laid his strongholds in ruins.
41 All who pass by plunder him;
he has become the scorn of his
neighbors.
42 You have exalted the right hand of his
foes;
you have made all his enemies rejoice.

43 You have also turned back the edge of
his sword,
and you have not made him stand in
battle.
44 You have made his splendor to cease
and cast his throne to the ground.
45 You have cut short the days of his youth;
you have covered him with shame. *Selah*

46 How long, O Lord? Will you hide
yourself forever?
How long will your wrath burn like
fire?
47 Remember how short my time is!
For what vanity you have created all
the children of man!
48 What man can live and never see death?
Who can deliver his soul from the
power of Sheol? *Selah*
49 Lord, where is your steadfast love of old,
which by your faithfulness you swore
to David?
50 Remember, O Lord, how your servants
are mocked,
and how I bear in my heart the
insults[1] of all the many nations,
51 with which your enemies mock, O Lord,
with which they mock the footsteps of
your anointed.

52 Blessed be the Lord forever!
Amen and Amen.

OCTOBER 6

1 Kings 9

As soon as Solomon had finished building the house of the Lord and the king's house and all that Solomon desired to build, ²the Lord appeared to Solomon a second time, as he had appeared to him at Gibeon. ³And the Lord said to him, "I have heard your prayer and your plea, which you have made before me. I have consecrated this house that you have built, by putting my name there forever. My eyes and my heart will be there for all time. ⁴And as for you, if you will walk before me, as David your father walked, with integrity of heart and uprightness, doing according to all that I have commanded you, and keeping my statutes and my rules, ⁵then I will establish your royal throne over Israel forever, as I promised David your father, saying, 'You shall not lack a man on the throne of Israel.' ⁶But if you turn aside from following

[1] Hebrew lacks *the insults*

me, you or your children, and do not keep my commandments and my statutes that I have set before you, but go and serve other gods and worship them, [7] then I will cut off Israel from the land that I have given them, and the house that I have consecrated for my name I will cast out of my sight, and Israel will become a proverb and a byword among all peoples. [8] And this house will become a heap of ruins.[1] Everyone passing by it will be astonished and will hiss, and they will say, 'Why has the LORD done thus to this land and to this house?' [9] Then they will say, 'Because they abandoned the LORD their God who brought their fathers out of the land of Egypt and laid hold on other gods and worshiped them and served them. Therefore the LORD has brought all this disaster on them.'"

[10] At the end of twenty years, in which Solomon had built the two houses, the house of the LORD and the king's house, [11] and Hiram king of Tyre had supplied Solomon with cedar and cypress timber and gold, as much as he desired, King Solomon gave to Hiram twenty cities in the land of Galilee. [12] But when Hiram came from Tyre to see the cities that Solomon had given him, they did not please him. [13] Therefore he said, "What kind of cities are these that you have given me, my brother?" So they are called the land of Cabul to this day. [14] Hiram had sent to the king 120 talents[2] of gold.

[15] And this is the account of the forced labor that King Solomon drafted to build the house of the LORD and his own house and the Millo and the wall of Jerusalem and Hazor and Megiddo and Gezer [16] (Pharaoh king of Egypt had gone up and captured Gezer and burned it with fire, and had killed the Canaanites who lived in the city, and had given it as dowry to his daughter, Solomon's wife; [17] so Solomon rebuilt Gezer) and Lower Beth-horon [18] and Baalath and Tamar in the wilderness, in the land of Judah,[3] [19] and all the store cities that Solomon had, and the cities for his chariots, and the cities for his horsemen, and whatever Solomon desired to build in Jerusalem, in Lebanon, and in all the land of his dominion. [20] All the people who were left of the Amorites, the Hittites, the Perizzites, the Hivites, and the Jebusites, who were not of the people of Israel— [21] their descendants who were left after them in the land, whom the people of Israel were unable to devote to destruction[4]—these Solomon drafted to be slaves, and so they are to this day. [22] But of the people of Israel Solomon made no slaves. They were the soldiers, they were his officials, his commanders, his captains, his chariot commanders and his horsemen.

[23] These were the chief officers who were over Solomon's work: 550 who had charge of the people who carried on the work.

[24] But Pharaoh's daughter went up from the city of David to her own house that Solomon had built for her. Then he built the Millo.

[25] Three times a year Solomon used to offer up burnt offerings and peace offerings on the altar that he built to the LORD, making offerings with it[5] before the LORD. So he finished the house.

[26] King Solomon built a fleet of ships at Ezion-geber, which is near Eloth on the shore of the Red Sea, in the land of Edom. [27] And Hiram sent with the fleet his servants, seamen who were familiar with the sea, together with the servants of Solomon. [28] And they went to Ophir and brought from there gold, 420 talents, and they brought it to King Solomon.

───── *Ephesians 6* ─────

Children, obey your parents in the Lord, for this is right. [2] "Honor your father and mother" (this is the first commandment with a promise), [3] "that it may go well with you and that you may live long in the land." [4] Fathers, do not provoke your children to anger, but bring them up in the discipline and instruction of the Lord.

[5] Bondservants,[6] obey your earthly masters[7] with fear and trembling, with a sincere heart, as you would Christ, [6] not by the way of eye-service, as people-pleasers, but as bondservants of Christ, doing the will of God from the heart, [7] rendering service with a good will as to the Lord and not to man, [8] knowing that whatever good anyone does, this he will receive back from the Lord, whether he is a bondservant[8] or is free. [9] Masters, do the same to them, and stop your threatening, knowing that he who is both their Master[9] and yours is in heaven, and that there is no partiality with him.

[10] Finally, be strong in the Lord and in the strength of his might. [11] Put on the whole armor

[1] Syriac, Old Latin; Hebrew *will become high* [2] A talent was about 75 pounds or 34 kilograms [3] Hebrew lacks *of Judah* [4] That is, set apart (devote) as an offering to the Lord (for destruction) [5] Septuagint lacks *with it* [6] Or *slaves*; also verse 6 (for the contextual rendering of the Greek word *doulos*, see Preface) [7] Or *your masters according to the flesh* [8] Or *slave* (for the contextual rendering of the Greek word *doulos*, see Preface) [9] Greek *Lord*

of God, that you may be able to stand against the schemes of the devil. [12]For we do not wrestle against flesh and blood, but against the rulers, against the authorities, against the cosmic powers over this present darkness, against the spiritual forces of evil in the heavenly places. [13]Therefore take up the whole armor of God, that you may be able to withstand in the evil day, and having done all, to stand firm. [14]Stand therefore, having fastened on the belt of truth, and having put on the breastplate of righteousness, [15]and, as shoes for your feet, having put on the readiness given by the gospel of peace. [16]In all circumstances take up the shield of faith, with which you can extinguish all the flaming darts of the evil one; [17]and take the helmet of salvation, and the sword of the Spirit, which is the word of God, [18]praying at all times in the Spirit, with all prayer and supplication. To that end keep alert with all perseverance, making supplication for all the saints, [19]and also for me, that words may be given to me in opening my mouth boldly to proclaim the mystery of the gospel, [20]for which I am an ambassador in chains, that I may declare it boldly, as I ought to speak.

[21]So that you also may know how I am and what I am doing, Tychicus the beloved brother and faithful minister in the Lord will tell you everything. [22]I have sent him to you for this very purpose, that you may know how we are, and that he may encourage your hearts.

[23]Peace be to the brothers,[1] and love with faith, from God the Father and the Lord Jesus Christ. [24]Grace be with all who love our Lord Jesus Christ with love incorruptible.

Ezekiel 39

[1]"And you, son of man, prophesy against Gog and say, Thus says the Lord GOD: Behold, I am against you, O Gog, chief prince of Meshech[2] and Tubal. [2]And I will turn you about and drive you forward, and bring you up from the uttermost parts of the north, and lead you against the mountains of Israel. [3]Then I will strike your bow from your left hand, and will make your arrows drop out of your right hand. [4]You shall fall on the mountains of Israel, you and all your hordes and the peoples who are with you. I will give you to birds of prey of every sort and to the beasts of the field to be

devoured. [5]You shall fall in the open field, for I have spoken, declares the Lord GOD. [6]I will send fire on Magog and on those who dwell securely in the coastlands, and they shall know that I am the LORD.

[7]"And my holy name I will make known in the midst of my people Israel, and I will not let my holy name be profaned anymore. And the nations shall know that I am the LORD, the Holy One in Israel. [8]Behold, it is coming and it will be brought about, declares the Lord GOD. That is the day of which I have spoken.

[9]"Then those who dwell in the cities of Israel will go out and make fires of the weapons and burn them, shields and bucklers, bow and arrows, clubs[3] and spears; and they will make fires of them for seven years, [10]so that they will not need to take wood out of the field or cut down any out of the forests, for they will make their fires of the weapons. They will seize the spoil of those who despoiled them, and plunder those who plundered them, declares the Lord GOD.

[11]"On that day I will give to Gog a place for burial in Israel, the Valley of the Travelers, east of the sea. It will block the travelers, for there Gog and all his multitude will be buried. It will be called the Valley of Hamon-gog.[4] [12]For seven months the house of Israel will be burying them, in order to cleanse the land. [13]All the people of the land will bury them, and it will bring them renown on the day that I show my glory, declares the Lord GOD. [14]They will set apart men to travel through the land regularly and bury those travelers remaining on the face of the land, so as to cleanse it. At[5] the end of seven months they will make their search. [15]And when these travel through the land and anyone sees a human bone, then he shall set up a sign by it, till the buriers have buried it in the Valley of Hamon-gog. [16](Hamonah[6] is also the name of the city.) Thus shall they cleanse the land.

[17]"As for you, son of man, thus says the Lord GOD: Speak to the birds of every sort and to all beasts of the field, 'Assemble and come, gather from all around to the sacrificial feast that I am preparing for you, a great sacrificial feast on the mountains of Israel, and you shall eat flesh and drink blood. [18]You shall eat the flesh of the mighty, and drink the blood of the princes of the earth—of rams, of lambs, and of he-goats, of bulls, all of them fat beasts of Bashan. [19]And

---

[1] Or brothers and sisters [2] Or Gog, prince of Rosh, Meshech [3] Or javelins [4] Hamon-gog means the multitude of Gog [5] Or Until [6] Hamonah means multitude

you shall eat fat till you are filled, and drink blood till you are drunk, at the sacrificial feast that I am preparing for you. ²⁰And you shall be filled at my table with horses and charioteers, with mighty men and all kinds of warriors,' declares the Lord GOD.

²¹"And I will set my glory among the nations, and all the nations shall see my judgment that I have executed, and my hand that I have laid on them. ²²The house of Israel shall know that I am the LORD their God, from that day forward. ²³And the nations shall know that the house of Israel went into captivity for their iniquity, because they dealt so treacherously with me that I hid my face from them and gave them into the hand of their adversaries, and they all fell by the sword. ²⁴I dealt with them according to their uncleanness and their transgressions, and hid my face from them.

²⁵"Therefore thus says the Lord GOD: Now I will restore the fortunes of Jacob and have mercy on the whole house of Israel, and I will be jealous for my holy name. ²⁶They shall forget their shame and all the treachery they have practiced against me, when they dwell securely in their land with none to make them afraid, ²⁷when I have brought them back from the peoples and gathered them from their enemies' lands, and through them have vindicated my holiness in the sight of many nations. ²⁸Then they shall know that I am the LORD their God, because I sent them into exile among the nations and then assembled them into their own land. I will leave none of them remaining among the nations anymore. ²⁹And I will not hide my face anymore from them, when I pour out my Spirit upon the house of Israel, declares the Lord GOD."

Psalm 90

A PRAYER OF MOSES, THE MAN OF GOD.

Lord, you have been our dwelling place¹
in all generations.
2   Before the mountains were brought
forth,
or ever you had formed the earth and
the world,
from everlasting to everlasting you
are God.

3   You return man to dust
and say, "Return, O children of man!"²
4   For a thousand years in your sight
are but as yesterday when it is past,
or as a watch in the night.

5   You sweep them away as with a flood;
they are like a dream,
like grass that is renewed in the
morning:
6   in the morning it flourishes and is
renewed;
in the evening it fades and withers.

7   For we are brought to an end by your
anger;
by your wrath we are dismayed.
8   You have set our iniquities before you,
our secret sins in the light of your
presence.

9   For all our days pass away under your
wrath;
we bring our years to an end like a sigh.
10   The years of our life are seventy,
or even by reason of strength eighty;
yet their span³ is but toil and trouble;
they are soon gone, and we fly away.
11   Who considers the power of your anger,
and your wrath according to the fear
of you?

12   So teach us to number our days
that we may get a heart of wisdom.
13   Return, O LORD! How long?
Have pity on your servants!
14   Satisfy us in the morning with your
steadfast love,
that we may rejoice and be glad all our
days.
15   Make us glad for as many days as you
have afflicted us,
and for as many years as we have seen
evil.
16   Let your work be shown to your servants,
and your glorious power to their
children.
17   Let the favor⁴ of the Lord our God be
upon us,
and establish the work of our hands
upon us;
yes, establish the work of our hands!

¹ Some Hebrew manuscripts (compare Septuagint) *our refuge* ² Or *of Adam* ³ Or *pride* ⁴ Or *beauty*

OCTOBER 7

1 Kings 10

Now when the queen of Sheba heard of the fame of Solomon concerning the name of the LORD, she came to test him with hard questions. ²She came to Jerusalem with a very great retinue, with camels bearing spices and very much gold and precious stones. And when she came to Solomon, she told him all that was on her mind. ³And Solomon answered all her questions; there was nothing hidden from the king that he could not explain to her. ⁴And when the queen of Sheba had seen all the wisdom of Solomon, the house that he had built, ⁵the food of his table, the seating of his officials, and the attendance of his servants, their clothing, his cupbearers, and his burnt offerings that he offered at the house of the LORD, there was no more breath in her.

⁶And she said to the king, "The report was true that I heard in my own land of your words and of your wisdom, ⁷but I did not believe the reports until I came and my own eyes had seen it. And behold, the half was not told me. Your wisdom and prosperity surpass the report that I heard. ⁸Happy are your men! Happy are your servants, who continually stand before you and hear your wisdom! ⁹Blessed be the LORD your God, who has delighted in you and set you on the throne of Israel! Because the LORD loved Israel forever, he has made you king, that you may execute justice and righteousness." ¹⁰Then she gave the king 120 talents¹ of gold, and a very great quantity of spices and precious stones. Never again came such an abundance of spices as these that the queen of Sheba gave to King Solomon.

¹¹Moreover, the fleet of Hiram, which brought gold from Ophir, brought from Ophir a very great amount of almug wood and precious stones. ¹²And the king made of the almug wood supports for the house of the LORD and for the king's house, also lyres and harps for the singers. No such almug wood has come or been seen to this day.

¹³And King Solomon gave to the queen of Sheba all that she desired, whatever she asked besides what was given her by the bounty of King Solomon. So she turned and went back to her own land with her servants.

¹⁴Now the weight of gold that came to Solomon in one year was 666 talents of gold, ¹⁵besides that which came from the explorers and from the business of the merchants, and from all the kings of the west and from the governors of the land. ¹⁶King Solomon made 200 large shields of beaten gold; 600 shekels² of gold went into each shield. ¹⁷And he made 300 shields of beaten gold; three minas³ of gold went into each shield. And the king put them in the House of the Forest of Lebanon. ¹⁸The king also made a great ivory throne and overlaid it with the finest gold. ¹⁹The throne had six steps, and the throne had a round top,⁴ and on each side of the seat were armrests and two lions standing beside the armrests, ²⁰while twelve lions stood there, one on each end of a step on the six steps. The like of it was never made in any kingdom. ²¹All King Solomon's drinking vessels were of gold, and all the vessels of the House of the Forest of Lebanon were of pure gold. None were of silver; silver was not considered as anything in the days of Solomon. ²²For the king had a fleet of ships of Tarshish at sea with the fleet of Hiram. Once every three years the fleet of ships of Tarshish used to come bringing gold, silver, ivory, apes, and peacocks.⁵

²³Thus King Solomon excelled all the kings of the earth in riches and in wisdom. ²⁴And the whole earth sought the presence of Solomon to hear his wisdom, which God had put into his mind. ²⁵Every one of them brought his present, articles of silver and gold, garments, myrrh, spices, horses, and mules, so much year by year.

²⁶And Solomon gathered together chariots and horsemen. He had 1,400 chariots and 12,000 horsemen, whom he stationed in the chariot cities and with the king in Jerusalem. ²⁷And the king made silver as common in Jerusalem as stone, and he made cedar as

¹ A talent was about 75 pounds or 34 kilograms ² A shekel was about 2/5 ounce or 11 grams ³ A mina was about 1 1/4 pounds or 0.6 kilogram ⁴ Or and at the back of the throne was a calf's head ⁵ Or baboons

plentiful as the sycamore of the Shephelah. [28]And Solomon's import of horses was from Egypt and Kue, and the king's traders received them from Kue at a price. [29]A chariot could be imported from Egypt for 600 shekels of silver and a horse for 150, and so through the king's traders they were exported to all the kings of the Hittites and the kings of Syria.

Philippians 1

Paul and Timothy, servants[1] of Christ Jesus, To all the saints in Christ Jesus who are at Philippi, with the overseers[2] and deacons:[3]

[2]Grace to you and peace from God our Father and the Lord Jesus Christ.

[3]I thank my God in all my remembrance of you, [4]always in every prayer of mine for you all making my prayer with joy, [5]because of your partnership in the gospel from the first day until now. [6]And I am sure of this, that he who began a good work in you will bring it to completion at the day of Jesus Christ. [7]It is right for me to feel this way about you all, because I hold you in my heart, for you are all partakers with me of grace,[4] both in my imprisonment and in the defense and confirmation of the gospel. [8]For God is my witness, how I yearn for you all with the affection of Christ Jesus. [9]And it is my prayer that your love may abound more and more, with knowledge and all discernment, [10]so that you may approve what is excellent, and so be pure and blameless for the day of Christ, [11]filled with the fruit of righteousness that comes through Jesus Christ, to the glory and praise of God.

[12]I want you to know, brothers,[5] that what has happened to me has really served to advance the gospel, [13]so that it has become known throughout the whole imperial guard[6] and to all the rest that my imprisonment is for Christ. [14]And most of the brothers, having become confident in the Lord by my imprisonment, are much more bold to speak the word[7] without fear.

[15]Some indeed preach Christ from envy and rivalry, but others from good will. [16]The latter do it out of love, knowing that I am put here for the defense of the gospel. [17]The former proclaim Christ out of selfish ambition, not sincerely but thinking to afflict me in my imprisonment. [18]What then? Only that in every way, whether in pretense or in truth, Christ is proclaimed, and in that I rejoice.

Yes, and I will rejoice, [19]for I know that through your prayers and the help of the Spirit of Jesus Christ this will turn out for my deliverance, [20]as it is my eager expectation and hope that I will not be at all ashamed, but that with full courage now as always Christ will be honored in my body, whether by life or by death. [21]For to me to live is Christ, and to die is gain. [22]If I am to live in the flesh, that means fruitful labor for me. Yet which I shall choose I cannot tell. [23]I am hard pressed between the two. My desire is to depart and be with Christ, for that is far better. [24]But to remain in the flesh is more necessary on your account. [25]Convinced of this, I know that I will remain and continue with you all, for your progress and joy in the faith, [26]so that in me you may have ample cause to glory in Christ Jesus, because of my coming to you again.

[27]Only let your manner of life be worthy[8] of the gospel of Christ, so that whether I come and see you or am absent, I may hear of you that you are standing firm in one spirit, with one mind striving side by side for the faith of the gospel, [28]and not frightened in anything by your opponents. This is a clear sign to them of their destruction, but of your salvation, and that from God. [29]For it has been granted to you that for the sake of Christ you should not only believe in him but also suffer for his sake, [30]engaged in the same conflict that you saw I had and now hear that I still have.

Ezekiel 40

In the twenty-fifth year of our exile, at the beginning of the year, on the tenth day of the month, in the fourteenth year after the city was struck down, on that very day, the hand of the LORD was upon me, and he brought me to the city.[9] [2]In visions of God he brought me to the land of Israel, and set me down on a very high mountain, on which was a structure like a city to the south. [3]When he brought me there, behold, there was a man whose appearance was like bronze, with a linen cord and a measuring reed in his hand. And he was standing in the gateway. **4**And the man said to me, "Son of man, look with your eyes, and hear with your ears, and set your heart upon all that I shall show you, for you were brought here in order that I might show it to you. Declare all that you see to the house of Israel."

5And behold, there was a wall all around the outside of the temple area, and the length of the measuring reed in the man's hand was six long cubits, each being a cubit and a handbreadth[1] in length. So he measured the thickness of the wall, one reed; and the height, one reed. **6**Then he went into the gateway facing east, going up its steps, and measured the threshold of the gate, one reed deep.[2] **7**And the side rooms, one reed long and one reed broad; and the space between the side rooms, five cubits; and the threshold of the gate by the vestibule of the gate at the inner end, one reed. **8**Then he measured the vestibule of the gateway, on the inside, one reed. **9**Then he measured the vestibule of the gateway, eight cubits; and its jambs, two cubits; and the vestibule of the gate was at the inner end. **10**And there were three side rooms on either side of the east gate. The three were of the same size, and the jambs on either side were of the same size. **11**Then he measured the width of the opening of the gateway, ten cubits; and the length of the gateway, thirteen cubits. **12**There was a barrier before the side rooms, one cubit on either side. And the side rooms were six cubits on either side. **13**Then he measured the gate from the ceiling of the one side room to the ceiling of the other, a breadth of twenty-five cubits; the openings faced each other. **14**He measured also the vestibule, twenty cubits. And around the vestibule of the gateway was the court.[3] **15**From the front of the gate at the entrance to the front of the inner vestibule of the gate was fifty cubits. **16**And the gateway had windows all around, narrowing inwards toward the side rooms and toward their jambs, and likewise the vestibule had windows all around inside, and on the jambs were palm trees.

17Then he brought me into the outer court. And behold, there were chambers and a pavement, all around the court. Thirty chambers faced the pavement. **18**And the pavement ran along the side of the gates, corresponding to the length of the gates. This was the lower pavement. **19**Then he measured the distance from the inner front of the lower gate to the outer front of the inner court,[4] a hundred cubits on the east side and on the north side.[5]

20As for the gate that faced toward the north, belonging to the outer court, he measured its length and its breadth. **21**Its side rooms, three on either side, and its jambs and its vestibule were of the same size as those of the first gate. Its length was fifty cubits, and its breadth twenty-five cubits. **22**And its windows, its vestibule, and its palm trees were of the same size as those of the gate that faced toward the east. And by seven steps people would go up to it, and find its vestibule before them. **23**And opposite the gate on the north, as on the east, was a gate to the inner court. And he measured from gate to gate, a hundred cubits.

24And he led me toward the south, and behold, there was a gate on the south. And he measured its jambs and its vestibule; they had the same size as the others. **25**Both it and its vestibule had windows all around, like the windows of the others. Its length was fifty cubits, and its breadth twenty-five cubits. **26**And there were seven steps leading up to it, and its vestibule was before them, and it had palm trees on its jambs, one on either side. **27**And there was a gate on the south of the inner court. And he measured from gate to gate toward the south, a hundred cubits.

28Then he brought me to the inner court through the south gate, and he measured the south gate. It was of the same size as the others. **29**Its side rooms, its jambs, and its vestibule were of the same size as the others, and both it and its vestibule had windows all around. Its length was fifty cubits, and its breadth twenty-five cubits. **30**And there were vestibules all around, twenty-five cubits long and five cubits broad. **31**Its vestibule faced the outer court, and palm trees were on its jambs, and its stairway had eight steps.

32Then he brought me to the inner court on the east side, and he measured the gate. It was of the same size as the others. **33**Its side rooms, its jambs, and its vestibule were of the same size as the others, and both it and its vestibule had windows all around. Its length was fifty cubits, and its breadth twenty-five cubits. **34**Its vestibule faced the outer court, and it had palm trees

[1] A cubit was about 18 inches or 45 centimeters; a *handbreadth* was about 3 inches or 7.5 centimeters [2] Hebrew *deep, and one threshold, one reed deep* [3] Text uncertain; Hebrew *And he made the jambs sixty cubits, and to the jamb of the court was the gateway all around* [4] Hebrew *distance from before the low gate before the inner court to the outside* [5] Or *cubits. So far the eastern gate; now to the northern gate.*

on its jambs, on either side, and its stairway had eight steps.

³⁵Then he brought me to the north gate, and he measured it. It had the same size as the others. ³⁶Its side rooms, its jambs, and its vestibule were of the same size as the others,¹ and it had windows all around. Its length was fifty cubits, and its breadth twenty-five cubits. ³⁷Its vestibule² faced the outer court, and it had palm trees on its jambs, on either side, and its stairway had eight steps.

³⁸There was a chamber with its door in the vestibule of the gate,³ where the burnt offering was to be washed. ³⁹And in the vestibule of the gate were two tables on either side, on which the burnt offering and the sin offering and the guilt offering were to be slaughtered. ⁴⁰And off to the side, on the outside as one goes up to the entrance of the north gate, were two tables; and off to the other side of the vestibule of the gate were two tables. ⁴¹Four tables were on either side of the gate, eight tables, on which to slaughter. ⁴²And there were four tables of hewn stone for the burnt offering, a cubit and a half long, and a cubit and a half broad, and one cubit high, on which the instruments were to be laid with which the burnt offerings and the sacrifices were slaughtered. ⁴³And hooks,⁴ a handbreadth long, were fastened all around within. And on the tables the flesh of the offering was to be laid.

⁴⁴On the outside of the inner gateway there were two chambers⁵ in the inner court, one⁶ at the side of the north gate facing south, the other at the side of the south⁷ gate facing north. ⁴⁵And he said to me, "This chamber that faces south is for the priests who have charge of the temple, ⁴⁶and the chamber that faces north is for the priests who have charge of the altar. These are the sons of Zadok, who alone⁸ among the sons of Levi may come near to the LORD to minister to him." ⁴⁷And he measured the court, a hundred cubits long and a hundred cubits broad, a square. And the altar was in front of the temple.

⁴⁸Then he brought me to the vestibule of the temple and measured the jambs of the vestibule, five cubits on either side. And the breadth of the gate was fourteen cubits, and the sidewalls of the gate⁹ were three cubits on

either side. ⁴⁹The length of the vestibule was twenty cubits, and the breadth twelve¹⁰ cubits, and people would go up to it by ten steps.¹¹ And there were pillars beside the jambs, one on either side.

Psalm 91

He who dwells in the shelter of the Most High
  will abide in the shadow of the Almighty.
² I will say¹² to the LORD, "My refuge and my fortress,
  my God, in whom I trust."

³ For he will deliver you from the snare of the fowler
  and from the deadly pestilence.
⁴ He will cover you with his pinions,
  and under his wings you will find refuge;
  his faithfulness is a shield and buckler.
⁵ You will not fear the terror of the night,
  nor the arrow that flies by day,
⁶ nor the pestilence that stalks in darkness,
  nor the destruction that wastes at noonday.

⁷ A thousand may fall at your side,
  ten thousand at your right hand,
  but it will not come near you.
⁸ You will only look with your eyes
  and see the recompense of the wicked.

⁹ Because you have made the LORD your dwelling place—
  the Most High, who is my refuge¹³—
¹⁰ no evil shall be allowed to befall you,
  no plague come near your tent.

¹¹ For he will command his angels concerning you
  to guard you in all your ways.
¹² On their hands they will bear you up,
  lest you strike your foot against a stone.
¹³ You will tread on the lion and the adder;
  the young lion and the serpent you will trample underfoot.

¹ One manuscript (compare verses 29 and 33); most manuscripts lack were of the same size as the others ² Septuagint, Vulgate (compare verses 26, 31, 34); Hebrew jambs ³ Hebrew at the jambs, the gates ⁴ Or shelves ⁵ Septuagint; Hebrew were chambers for singers ⁶ Hebrew lacks one ⁷ Septuagint; Hebrew east ⁸ Hebrew lacks alone ⁹ Septuagint; Hebrew lacks was fourteen cubits, and the sidewalls of the gate ¹⁰ Septuagint; Hebrew eleven ¹¹ Septuagint; Hebrew and by steps that would go up to it ¹² Septuagint He will say ¹³ Or For you, O LORD, are my refuge! You have made the Most High your dwelling place

14   "Because he holds fast to me in love, I
      will deliver him;
     I will protect him, because he knows
      my name.
15   When he calls to me, I will answer him;

     I will be with him in trouble;
      I will rescue him and honor him.
16   With long life I will satisfy him
      and show him my salvation."

OCTOBER 8

1 Kings 11

Now King Solomon loved many foreign women, along with the daughter of Pharaoh: Moabite, Ammonite, Edomite, Sidonian, and Hittite women, ²from the nations concerning which the LORD had said to the people of Israel, "You shall not enter into marriage with them, neither shall they with you, for surely they will turn away your heart after their gods." Solomon clung to these in love. ³He had 700 wives, who were princesses, and 300 concubines. And his wives turned away his heart. ⁴For when Solomon was old his wives turned away his heart after other gods, and his heart was not wholly true to the LORD his God, as was the heart of David his father. ⁵For Solomon went after Ashtoreth the goddess of the Sidonians, and after Milcom the abomination of the Ammonites. ⁶So Solomon did what was evil in the sight of the LORD and did not wholly follow the LORD, as David his father had done. ⁷Then Solomon built a high place for Chemosh the abomination of Moab, and for Molech the abomination of the Ammonites, on the mountain east of Jerusalem. ⁸And so he did for all his foreign wives, who made offerings and sacrificed to their gods.

⁹And the LORD was angry with Solomon, because his heart had turned away from the LORD, the God of Israel, who had appeared to him twice ¹⁰and had commanded him concerning this thing, that he should not go after other gods. But he did not keep what the LORD commanded. ¹¹Therefore the LORD said to Solomon, "Since this has been your practice and you have not kept my covenant and my statutes that I have commanded you, I will

surely tear the kingdom from you and will give it to your servant. ¹²Yet for the sake of David your father I will not do it in your days, but I will tear it out of the hand of your son. ¹³However, I will not tear away all the kingdom, but I will give one tribe to your son, for the sake of David my servant and for the sake of Jerusalem that I have chosen."

¹⁴And the LORD raised up an adversary against Solomon, Hadad the Edomite. He was of the royal house in Edom. ¹⁵For when David was in Edom, and Joab the commander of the army went up to bury the slain, he struck down every male in Edom ¹⁶(for Joab and all Israel remained there six months, until he had cut off every male in Edom). ¹⁷But Hadad fled to Egypt, together with certain Edomites of his father's servants, Hadad still being a little child. ¹⁸They set out from Midian and came to Paran and took men with them from Paran and came to Egypt, to Pharaoh king of Egypt, who gave him a house and assigned him an allowance of food and gave him land. ¹⁹And Hadad found great favor in the sight of Pharaoh, so that he gave him in marriage the sister of his own wife, the sister of Tahpenes the queen. ²⁰And the sister of Tahpenes bore him Genubath his son, whom Tahpenes weaned in Pharaoh's house. And Genubath was in Pharaoh's house among the sons of Pharaoh. ²¹But when Hadad heard in Egypt that David slept with his fathers and that Joab the commander of the army was dead, Hadad said to Pharaoh, "Let me depart, that I may go to my own country." ²²But Pharaoh said to him, "What have you lacked with me that you are now seeking to go to your own

country?" And he said to him, "Only let me depart."

²³God also raised up as an adversary to him, Rezon the son of Eliada, who had fled from his master Hadadezer king of Zobah. ²⁴And he gathered men about him and became leader of a marauding band, after the killing by David. And they went to Damascus and lived there and made him king in Damascus. ²⁵He was an adversary of Israel all the days of Solomon, doing harm as Hadad did. And he loathed Israel and reigned over Syria.

²⁶Jeroboam the son of Nebat, an Ephraimite of Zeredah, a servant of Solomon, whose mother's name was Zeruah, a widow, also lifted up his hand against the king. ²⁷And this was the reason why he lifted up his hand against the king. Solomon built the Millo, and closed up the breach of the city of David his father. ²⁸The man Jeroboam was very able, and when Solomon saw that the young man was industrious he gave him charge over all the forced labor of the house of Joseph. ²⁹And at that time, when Jeroboam went out of Jerusalem, the prophet Ahijah the Shilonite found him on the road. Now Ahijah had dressed himself in a new garment, and the two of them were alone in the open country. ³⁰Then Ahijah laid hold of the new garment that was on him, and tore it into twelve pieces. ³¹And he said to Jeroboam, "Take for yourself ten pieces, for thus says the LORD, the God of Israel, 'Behold, I am about to tear the kingdom from the hand of Solomon and will give you ten tribes ³²(but he shall have one tribe, for the sake of my servant David and for the sake of Jerusalem, the city that I have chosen out of all the tribes of Israel), ³³because they have¹ forsaken me and worshiped Ashtoreth the goddess of the Sidonians, Chemosh the god of Moab, and Milcom the god of the Ammonites, and they have not walked in my ways, doing what is right in my sight and keeping my statutes and my rules, as David his father did. ³⁴Nevertheless, I will not take the whole kingdom out of his hand, but I will make him ruler all the days of his life, for the sake of David my servant whom I chose, who kept my commandments and my statutes. ³⁵But I will take the kingdom out of his son's hand and will give it to you, ten tribes. ³⁶Yet to his son I will give one tribe, that David my servant may always have a lamp before me

in Jerusalem, the city where I have chosen to put my name. ³⁷And I will take you, and you shall reign over all that your soul desires, and you shall be king over Israel. ³⁸And if you will listen to all that I command you, and will walk in my ways, and do what is right in my eyes by keeping my statutes and my commandments, as David my servant did, I will be with you and will build you a sure house, as I built for David, and I will give Israel to you. ³⁹And I will afflict the offspring of David because of this, but not forever.' " ⁴⁰Solomon sought therefore to kill Jeroboam. But Jeroboam arose and fled into Egypt, to Shishak king of Egypt, and was in Egypt until the death of Solomon.

⁴¹Now the rest of the acts of Solomon, and all that he did, and his wisdom, are they not written in the Book of the Acts of Solomon? ⁴²And the time that Solomon reigned in Jerusalem over all Israel was forty years. ⁴³And Solomon slept with his fathers and was buried in the city of David his father. And Rehoboam his son reigned in his place.

Philippians 2

So if there is any encouragement in Christ, any comfort from love, any participation in the Spirit, any affection and sympathy, ²complete my joy by being of the same mind, having the same love, being in full accord and of one mind. ³Do nothing from selfish ambition or conceit, but in humility count others more significant than yourselves. ⁴Let each of you look not only to his own interests, but also to the interests of others. ⁵Have this mind among yourselves, which is yours in Christ Jesus,² ⁶who, though he was in the form of God, did not count equality with God a thing to be grasped, ⁷but emptied himself, by taking the form of a servant,³ being born in the likeness of men. ⁸And being found in human form, he humbled himself by becoming obedient to the point of death, even death on a cross. ⁹Therefore God has highly exalted him and bestowed on him the name that is above every name, ¹⁰so that at the name of Jesus every knee should bow, in heaven and on earth and under the earth, ¹¹and every tongue confess that Jesus Christ is Lord, to the glory of God the Father.

¹²Therefore, my beloved, as you have always obeyed, so now, not only as in my presence but

---

¹ Septuagint, Syriac, Vulgate *he has*; twice in this verse ² Or *which was also in Christ Jesus* ³ Greek *bondservant*

much more in my absence, work out your own salvation with fear and trembling, [13]for it is God who works in you, both to will and to work for his good pleasure.

[14]Do all things without grumbling or disputing, [15]that you may be blameless and innocent, children of God without blemish in the midst of a crooked and twisted generation, among whom you shine as lights in the world, [16]holding fast to the word of life, so that in the day of Christ I may be proud that I did not run in vain or labor in vain. [17]Even if I am to be poured out as a drink offering upon the sacrificial offering of your faith, I am glad and rejoice with you all. [18]Likewise you also should be glad and rejoice with me.

[19]I hope in the Lord Jesus to send Timothy to you soon, so that I too may be cheered by news of you. [20]For I have no one like him, who will be genuinely concerned for your welfare. [21]For they all seek their own interests, not those of Jesus Christ. [22]But you know Timothy's[1] proven worth, how as a son[2] with a father he has served with me in the gospel. [23]I hope therefore to send him just as soon as I see how it will go with me, [24]and I trust in the Lord that shortly I myself will come also.

[25]I have thought it necessary to send to you Epaphroditus my brother and fellow worker and fellow soldier, and your messenger and minister to my need, [26]for he has been longing for you all and has been distressed because you heard that he was ill. [27]Indeed he was ill, near to death. But God had mercy on him, and not only on him but on me also, lest I should have sorrow upon sorrow. [28]I am the more eager to send him, therefore, that you may rejoice at seeing him again, and that I may be less anxious. [29]So receive him in the Lord with all joy, and honor such men, [30]for he nearly died for the work of Christ, risking his life to complete what was lacking in your service to me.

Ezekiel 41

Then he brought me to the nave and measured the jambs. On each side six cubits[3] was the breadth of the jambs.[4] [2]And the breadth of the entrance was ten cubits, and the sidewalls of the entrance were five cubits on either side. And he measured the length of the nave,[5] forty cubits, and its breadth, twenty

cubits. [3]Then he went into the inner room and measured the jambs of the entrance, two cubits; and the entrance, six cubits; and the sidewalls on either side[6] of the entrance, seven cubits. [4]And he measured the length of the room, twenty cubits, and its breadth, twenty cubits, across the nave. And he said to me, "This is the Most Holy Place."

[5]Then he measured the wall of the temple, six cubits thick, and the breadth of the side chambers, four cubits, all around the temple. [6]And the side chambers were in three stories, one over another, thirty in each story. There were offsets[7] all around the wall of the temple to serve as supports for the side chambers, so that they should not be supported by the wall of the temple. [7]And it became broader as it wound upward to the side chambers, because the temple was enclosed upward all around the temple. Thus the temple had a broad area upward, and so one went up from the lowest story to the top story through the middle story. [8]I saw also that the temple had a raised platform all around; the foundations of the side chambers measured a full reed of six long cubits. [9]The thickness of the outer wall of the side chambers was five cubits. The free space between the side chambers of the temple and the [10]other chambers was a breadth of twenty cubits all around the temple on every side. [11]And the doors of the side chambers opened on the free space, one door toward the north, and another door toward the south. And the breadth of the free space was five cubits all around.

[12]The building that was facing the separate yard on the west side was seventy cubits broad, and the wall of the building was five cubits thick all around, and its length ninety cubits. [13]Then he measured the temple, a hundred cubits long; and the yard and the building with its walls, a hundred cubits long; [14]also the breadth of the east front of the temple and the yard, a hundred cubits.

[15]Then he measured the length of the building facing the yard that was at the back and its galleries[8] on either side, a hundred cubits.

The inside of the nave and the vestibules of the court, [16]the thresholds and the narrow windows and the galleries all around the three of them, opposite the threshold, were paneled with wood all around, from the floor up to the windows (now the windows were covered),

---

[1] Greek *his* [2] Greek *child* [3] A *cubit* was about 18 inches or 45 centimeters [4] Compare Septuagint; Hebrew *tent* [5] Hebrew *its length* [6] Septuagint; Hebrew *and the breadth*
[7] Septuagint, compare 1 Kings 6:6; the meaning of the Hebrew word is uncertain [8] The meaning of the Hebrew term is unknown; also verse 16

[17] to the space above the door, even to the inner room, and on the outside. And on all the walls all around, inside and outside, was a measured pattern.[1] [18] It was carved of cherubim and palm trees, a palm tree between cherub and cherub. Every cherub had two faces: [19] a human face toward the palm tree on the one side, and the face of a young lion toward the palm tree on the other side. They were carved on the whole temple all around. [20] From the floor to above the door, cherubim and palm trees were carved; similarly the wall of the nave.

[21] The doorposts of the nave were squared, and in front of the Holy Place was something resembling [22] an altar of wood, three cubits high, two cubits long, and two cubits broad.[2] Its corners, its base,[3] and its walls were of wood. He said to me, "This is the table that is before the LORD." [23] The nave and the Holy Place had each a double door. [24] The double doors had two leaves apiece, two swinging leaves for each door. [25] And on the doors of the nave were carved cherubim and palm trees, such as were carved on the walls. And there was a canopy[4] of wood in front of the vestibule outside. [26] And there were narrow windows and palm trees on either side, on the sidewalls of the vestibule, the side chambers of the temple, and the canopies.

Psalm 92–93

A PSALM. A SONG FOR THE SABBATH.

It is good to give thanks to the LORD,
    to sing praises to your name, O Most High;
[2]   to declare your steadfast love in the
        morning,
    and your faithfulness by night,
[3]   to the music of the lute and the harp,
    to the melody of the lyre.
[4]   For you, O LORD, have made me glad by
        your work;
    at the works of your hands I sing for
        joy.

[5]   How great are your works, O LORD!
    Your thoughts are very deep!
[6]   The stupid man cannot know;
    the fool cannot understand this:
[7]   that though the wicked sprout like grass
        and all evildoers flourish,
    they are doomed to destruction forever;
[8]   but you, O LORD, are on high forever.
[9]   For behold, your enemies, O LORD,
        for behold, your enemies shall perish;
    all evildoers shall be scattered.

[10]   But you have exalted my horn like that
        of the wild ox;
    you have poured over me[5] fresh oil.
[11]   My eyes have seen the downfall of my
        enemies;
    my ears have heard the doom of my
        evil assailants.

[12]   The righteous flourish like the palm tree
        and grow like a cedar in Lebanon.
[13]   They are planted in the house of the
        LORD;
    they flourish in the courts of our God.
[14]   They still bear fruit in old age;
    they are ever full of sap and green,
[15]   to declare that the LORD is upright;
    he is my rock, and there is no
        unrighteousness in him.

The LORD reigns; he is robed in majesty;
    the LORD is robed; he has put on strength
        as his belt.
Yes, the world is established; it shall
        never be moved.
[2]   Your throne is established from of old;
    you are from everlasting.

[3]   The floods have lifted up, O LORD,
    the floods have lifted up their voice;
    the floods lift up their roaring.
[4]   Mightier than the thunders of many
        waters,
    mightier than the waves of the sea,
    the LORD on high is mighty!

[5]   Your decrees are very trustworthy;
    holiness befits your house,
    O LORD, forevermore.

[1] Hebrew were measurements [2] Septuagint; Hebrew lacks two cubits broad [3] Septuagint; Hebrew length [4] The meaning of the Hebrew word is unknown; also verse 26 [5] Compare Syriac; the meaning of the Hebrew is uncertain

OCTOBER 9

1 Kings 12

Rehoboam went to Shechem, for all Israel had come to Shechem to make him king. ²And as soon as Jeroboam the son of Nebat heard of it (for he was still in Egypt, where he had fled from King Solomon), then Jeroboam returned from[1] Egypt. ³And they sent and called him, and Jeroboam and all the assembly of Israel came and said to Rehoboam, ⁴"Your father made our yoke heavy. Now therefore lighten the hard service of your father and his heavy yoke on us, and we will serve you." ⁵He said to them, "Go away for three days, then come again to me." So the people went away.

⁶Then King Rehoboam took counsel with the old men, who had stood before Solomon his father while he was yet alive, saying, "How do you advise me to answer this people?" ⁷And they said to him, "If you will be a servant to this people today and serve them, and speak good words to them when you answer them, then they will be your servants forever." ⁸But he abandoned the counsel that the old men gave him and took counsel with the young men who had grown up with him and stood before him. ⁹And he said to them, "What do you advise that we answer this people who have said to me, 'Lighten the yoke that your father put on us'?" ¹⁰And the young men who had grown up with him said to him, "Thus shall you speak to this people who said to you, 'Your father made our yoke heavy, but you lighten it for us,' thus shall you say to them, 'My little finger is thicker than my father's thighs. ¹¹And now, whereas my father laid on you a heavy yoke, I will add to your yoke. My father disciplined you with whips, but I will discipline you with scorpions.'"

¹²So Jeroboam and all the people came to Rehoboam the third day, as the king said, "Come to me again the third day." ¹³And the king answered the people harshly, and forsaking the counsel that the old men had given him, ¹⁴he spoke to them according to the counsel of the young men, saying, "My father made your yoke heavy, but I will add to your yoke. My father

disciplined you with whips, but I will discipline you with scorpions." ¹⁵So the king did not listen to the people, for it was a turn of affairs brought about by the LORD that he might fulfill his word, which the LORD spoke by Ahijah the Shilonite to Jeroboam the son of Nebat.

¹⁶And when all Israel saw that the king did not listen to them, the people answered the king, "What portion do we have in David? We have no inheritance in the son of Jesse. To your tents, O Israel! Look now to your own house, David." So Israel went to their tents. ¹⁷But Rehoboam reigned over the people of Israel who lived in the cities of Judah. ¹⁸Then King Rehoboam sent Adoram, who was taskmaster over the forced labor, and all Israel stoned him to death with stones. And King Rehoboam hurried to mount his chariot to flee to Jerusalem. ¹⁹So Israel has been in rebellion against the house of David to this day. ²⁰And when all Israel heard that Jeroboam had returned, they sent and called him to the assembly and made him king over all Israel. There was none that followed the house of David but the tribe of Judah only.

²¹When Rehoboam came to Jerusalem, he assembled all the house of Judah and the tribe of Benjamin, 180,000 chosen warriors, to fight against the house of Israel, to restore the kingdom to Rehoboam the son of Solomon. ²²But the word of God came to Shemaiah the man of God: ²³"Say to Rehoboam the son of Solomon, king of Judah, and to all the house of Judah and Benjamin, and to the rest of the people, ²⁴'Thus says the LORD, You shall not go up or fight against your relatives the people of Israel. Every man return to his home, for this thing is from me.'" So they listened to the word of the LORD and went home again, according to the word of the LORD.

²⁵Then Jeroboam built Shechem in the hill country of Ephraim and lived there. And he went out from there and built Penuel. ²⁶And Jeroboam said in his heart, "Now the kingdom

[1] Septuagint, Vulgate (compare 2 Chronicles 10:2); Hebrew *lived in*

will turn back to the house of David. **²⁷**If this people go up to offer sacrifices in the temple of the LORD at Jerusalem, then the heart of this people will turn again to their lord, to Rehoboam king of Judah, and they will kill me and return to Rehoboam king of Judah." **²⁸**So the king took counsel and made two calves of gold. And he said to the people, "You have gone up to Jerusalem long enough. Behold your gods, O Israel, who brought you up out of the land of Egypt." **²⁹**And he set one in Bethel, and the other he put in Dan. **³⁰**Then this thing became a sin, for the people went as far as Dan to be before one.¹ **³¹**He also made temples on high places and appointed priests from among all the people, who were not of the Levites. **³²**And Jeroboam appointed a feast on the fifteenth day of the eighth month like the feast that was in Judah, and he offered sacrifices on the altar. So he did in Bethel, sacrificing to the calves that he made. And he placed in Bethel the priests of the high places that he had made. **³³**He went up to the altar that he had made in Bethel on the fifteenth day in the eighth month, in the month that he had devised from his own heart. And he instituted a feast for the people of Israel and went up to the altar to make offerings.

Philippians 3

Finally, my brothers,² rejoice in the Lord. To write the same things to you is no trouble to me and is safe for you.

²Look out for the dogs, look out for the evildoers, look out for those who mutilate the flesh. **³**For we are the circumcision, who worship by the Spirit of God³ and glory in Christ Jesus and put no confidence in the flesh— **⁴**though I myself have reason for confidence in the flesh also. If anyone else thinks he has reason for confidence in the flesh, I have more: **⁵**circumcised on the eighth day, of the people of Israel, of the tribe of Benjamin, a Hebrew of Hebrews; as to the law, a Pharisee; **⁶**as to zeal, a persecutor of the church; as to righteousness under the law,⁴ blameless. **⁷**But whatever gain I had, I counted as loss for the sake of Christ. **⁸**Indeed, I count everything as loss because of the surpassing worth of knowing Christ Jesus my Lord. For his sake I have suffered the loss of all things and count them as rubbish, in order

that I may gain Christ **⁹**and be found in him, not having a righteousness of my own that comes from the law, but that which comes through faith in Christ, the righteousness from God that depends on faith— **¹⁰**that I may know him and the power of his resurrection, and may share his sufferings, becoming like him in his death, **¹¹**that by any means possible I may attain the resurrection from the dead.

¹²Not that I have already obtained this or am already perfect, but I press on to make it my own, because Christ Jesus has made me his own. **¹³**Brothers, I do not consider that I have made it my own. But one thing I do: forgetting what lies behind and straining forward to what lies ahead, **¹⁴**I press on toward the goal for the prize of the upward call of God in Christ Jesus. **¹⁵**Let those of us who are mature think this way, and if in anything you think otherwise, God will reveal that also to you. **¹⁶**Only let us hold true to what we have attained.

¹⁷Brothers, join in imitating me, and keep your eyes on those who walk according to the example you have in us. **¹⁸**For many, of whom I have often told you and now tell you even with tears, walk as enemies of the cross of Christ. **¹⁹**Their end is destruction, their god is their belly, and they glory in their shame, with minds set on earthly things. **²⁰**But our citizenship is in heaven, and from it we await a Savior, the Lord Jesus Christ, **²¹**who will transform our lowly body to be like his glorious body, by the power that enables him even to subject all things to himself.

Ezekiel 42

Then he led me out into the outer court, toward the north, and he brought me to the chambers that were opposite the separate yard and opposite the building on the north. **²**The length of the building whose door faced north was a hundred cubits,⁵ and the breadth fifty cubits. **³**Facing the twenty cubits that belonged to the inner court, and facing the pavement that belonged to the outer court, was gallery⁶ against gallery in three stories. **⁴**And before the chambers was a passage inward, ten cubits wide and a hundred cubits long,⁷ and their doors were on the north. **⁵**Now the upper chambers were narrower, for the galleries took more away from them than from the

¹ Septuagint *went to the one at Bethel and to the other as far as Dan* ² Or *brothers and sisters; also verses 13, 17* ³ Some manuscripts *God in spirit* ⁴ Greek *in the law* ⁵ A cubit was about 18 inches or 45 centimeters ⁶ The meaning of the Hebrew word is unknown; also verse 5 ⁷ Septuagint, Syriac; Hebrew *and a way of one cubit*

lower and middle chambers of the building. [6] For they were in three stories, and they had no pillars like the pillars of the courts. Thus the upper chambers were set back from the ground more than the lower and the middle ones. [7] And there was a wall outside parallel to the chambers, toward the outer court, opposite the chambers, fifty cubits long. [8] For the chambers on the outer court were fifty cubits long, while those opposite the nave[1] were a hundred cubits long. [9] Below these chambers was an entrance on the east side, as one enters them from the outer court.

[10] In the thickness of the wall of the court, on the south[2] also, opposite the yard and opposite the building, there were chambers [11] with a passage in front of them. They were similar to the chambers on the north, of the same length and breadth, with the same exits[3] and arrangements and doors, [12] as were the entrances of the chambers on the south. There was an entrance at the beginning of the passage, the passage before the corresponding wall on the east as one enters them.[4]

[13] Then he said to me, "The north chambers and the south chambers opposite the yard are the holy chambers, where the priests who approach the LORD shall eat the most holy offerings. There they shall put the most holy offerings—the grain offering, the sin offering, and the guilt offering—for the place is holy. [14] When the priests enter the Holy Place, they shall not go out of it into the outer court without laying there the garments in which they minister, for these are holy. They shall put on other garments before they go near to that which is for the people."

[15] Now when he had finished measuring the interior of the temple area, he led me out by the gate that faced east, and measured the temple area all around. [16] He measured the east side with the measuring reed, 500 cubits by the measuring reed all around. [17] He measured the north side, 500 cubits by the measuring reed all around. [18] He measured the south side, 500 cubits by the measuring reed. [19] Then he turned to the west side and measured, 500 cubits by the measuring reed. [20] He measured it on the four sides. It had a wall around it, 500 cubits long and 500 cubits broad, to make a separation between the holy and the common.

Psalm 94

O LORD, God of vengeance,
  O God of vengeance, shine forth!
[2] Rise up, O judge of the earth;
  repay to the proud what they deserve!
[3] O LORD, how long shall the wicked,
  how long shall the wicked exult?
[4] They pour out their arrogant words;
  all the evildoers boast.
[5] They crush your people, O LORD,
  and afflict your heritage.
[6] They kill the widow and the sojourner,
  and murder the fatherless;
[7] and they say, "The LORD does not see;
  the God of Jacob does not perceive."

[8] Understand, O dullest of the people!
  Fools, when will you be wise?
[9] He who planted the ear, does he not
    hear?
He who formed the eye, does he not see?
[10] He who disciplines the nations, does he
    not rebuke?
He who teaches man knowledge—
[11]   the LORD—knows the thoughts of
    man,
  that they are but a breath.[5]

[12] Blessed is the man whom you discipline,
  O LORD,
  and whom you teach out of your law,
[13] to give him rest from days of trouble,
  until a pit is dug for the wicked.
[14] For the LORD will not forsake his people;
  he will not abandon his heritage;
[15] for justice will return to the righteous,
  and all the upright in heart will follow
    it.

[16] Who rises up for me against the wicked?
  Who stands up for me against
    evildoers?
[17] If the LORD had not been my help,
  my soul would soon have lived in the
    land of silence.
[18] When I thought, "My foot slips,"
  your steadfast love, O LORD, held me
    up.
[19] When the cares of my heart are many,
  your consolations cheer my soul.
[20] Can wicked rulers be allied with you,
  those who frame injustice by statute?

[1] Or temple [2] Septuagint; Hebrew east [3] Hebrew and all their exits [4] The meaning of the Hebrew verse is uncertain [5] Septuagint they are futile

21   They band together against the life of
          the righteous
       and condemn the innocent to death.[1]
22   But the Lord has become my stronghold,
       and my God the rock of my refuge.

23   He will bring back on them their
          iniquity
       and wipe them out for their
          wickedness;
       the Lord our God will wipe them out.

OCTOBER 10

1 Kings 13

And behold, a man of God came out of Judah by the word of the Lord to Bethel. Jeroboam was standing by the altar to make offerings. ²And the man cried against the altar by the word of the Lord and said, "O altar, altar, thus says the Lord: 'Behold, a son shall be born to the house of David, Josiah by name, and he shall sacrifice on you the priests of the high places who make offerings on you, and human bones shall be burned on you.'" ³And he gave a sign the same day, saying, "This is the sign that the Lord has spoken: 'Behold, the altar shall be torn down, and the ashes that are on it shall be poured out.'" ⁴And when the king heard the saying of the man of God, which he cried against the altar at Bethel, Jeroboam stretched out his hand from the altar, saying, "Seize him." And his hand, which he stretched out against him, dried up, so that he could not draw it back to himself. ⁵The altar also was torn down, and the ashes poured out from the altar, according to the sign that the man of God had given by the word of the Lord. ⁶And the king said to the man of God, "Entreat now the favor of the Lord your God, and pray for me, that my hand may be restored to me." And the man of God entreated the Lord, and the king's hand was restored to him and became as it was before. ⁷And the king said to the man of God, "Come home with me, and refresh yourself, and I will give you a reward." ⁸And the man of God said to the king, "If you give me half your house, I will not go in with you. And I will not eat bread or drink water in this place, ⁹for so was it commanded me by the word of the Lord, saying, 'You shall neither eat bread nor drink water

nor return by the way that you came.'" ¹⁰So he went another way and did not return by the way that he came to Bethel.

¹¹Now an old prophet lived in Bethel. And his sons[2] came and told him all that the man of God had done that day in Bethel. They also told to their father the words that he had spoken to the king. ¹²And their father said to them, "Which way did he go?" And his sons showed him the way that the man of God who came from Judah had gone. ¹³And he said to his sons, "Saddle the donkey for me." So they saddled the donkey for him and he mounted it. ¹⁴And he went after the man of God and found him sitting under an oak. And he said to him, "Are you the man of God who came from Judah?" And he said, "I am." ¹⁵Then he said to him, "Come home with me and eat bread." ¹⁶And he said, "I may not return with you, or go in with you, neither will I eat bread nor drink water with you in this place, ¹⁷for it was said to me by the word of the Lord, 'You shall neither eat bread nor drink water there, nor return by the way that you came.'" ¹⁸And he said to him, "I also am a prophet as you are, and an angel spoke to me by the word of the Lord, saying, 'Bring him back with you into your house that he may eat bread and drink water.'" But he lied to him. ¹⁹So he went back with him and ate bread in his house and drank water.

²⁰And as they sat at the table, the word of the Lord came to the prophet who had brought him back. ²¹And he cried to the man of God who came from Judah, "Thus says the Lord, 'Because you have disobeyed the word of the Lord and have not kept the command that the

---

[1] Hebrew condemn innocent blood   [2] Septuagint, Syriac, Vulgate; Hebrew son

LORD your God commanded you, [22] but have come back and have eaten bread and drunk water in the place of which he said to you, "Eat no bread and drink no water," your body shall not come to the tomb of your fathers.'" [23] And after he had eaten bread and drunk, he saddled the donkey for the prophet whom he had brought back. [24] And as he went away a lion met him on the road and killed him. And his body was thrown in the road, and the donkey stood beside it; the lion also stood beside the body. [25] And behold, men passed by and saw the body thrown in the road and the lion standing by the body. And they came and told it in the city where the old prophet lived.

[26] And when the prophet who had brought him back from the way heard of it, he said, "It is the man of God who disobeyed the word of the LORD; therefore the LORD has given him to the lion, which has torn him and killed him, according to the word that the LORD spoke to him." [27] And he said to his sons, "Saddle the donkey for me." And they saddled it. [28] And he went and found his body thrown in the road, and the donkey and the lion standing beside the body. The lion had not eaten the body or torn the donkey. [29] And the prophet took up the body of the man of God and laid it on the donkey and brought it back to the city[1] to mourn and to bury him. [30] And he laid the body in his own grave. And they mourned over him, saying, "Alas, my brother!" [31] And after he had buried him, he said to his sons, "When I die, bury me in the grave in which the man of God is buried; lay my bones beside his bones. [32] For the saying that he called out by the word of the LORD against the altar in Bethel and against all the houses of the high places that are in the cities of Samaria shall surely come to pass."

[33] After this thing Jeroboam did not turn from his evil way, but made priests for the high places again from among all the people. Any who would, he ordained to be priests of the high places. [34] And this thing became sin to the house of Jeroboam, so as to cut it off and to destroy it from the face of the earth.

Philippians 4

Therefore, my brothers,[2] whom I love and long for, my joy and crown, stand firm thus in the Lord, my beloved.

[2] I entreat Euodia and I entreat Syntyche to agree in the Lord. [3] Yes, I ask you also, true companion,[3] help these women, who have labored side by side with me in the gospel together with Clement and the rest of my fellow workers, whose names are in the book of life.

[4] Rejoice in the Lord always; again I will say, rejoice. [5] Let your reasonableness be known to everyone. The Lord is at hand; [6] do not be anxious about anything, but in everything by prayer and supplication with thanksgiving let your requests be made known to God. [7] And the peace of God, which surpasses all understanding, will guard your hearts and your minds in Christ Jesus.

[8] Finally, brothers, whatever is true, whatever is honorable, whatever is just, whatever is pure, whatever is lovely, whatever is commendable, if there is any excellence, if there is anything worthy of praise, think about these things. [9] What you have learned and received and heard and seen in me—practice these things, and the God of peace will be with you.

[10] I rejoiced in the Lord greatly that now at length you have revived your concern for me. You were indeed concerned for me, but you had no opportunity. [11] Not that I am speaking of being in need, for I have learned in whatever situation I am to be content. [12] I know how to be brought low, and I know how to abound. In any and every circumstance, I have learned the secret of facing plenty and hunger, abundance and need. [13] I can do all things through him who strengthens me.

[14] Yet it was kind of you to share[4] my trouble. [15] And you Philippians yourselves know that in the beginning of the gospel, when I left Macedonia, no church entered into partnership with me in giving and receiving, except you only. [16] Even in Thessalonica you sent me help for my needs once and again. [17] Not that I seek the gift, but I seek the fruit that increases to your credit.[5] [18] I have received full payment, and more. I am well supplied, having received from Epaphroditus the gifts you sent, a fragrant offering, a sacrifice acceptable and pleasing to God. [19] And my God will supply every need of yours according to his riches in glory in Christ Jesus. [20] To our God and Father be glory forever and ever. Amen.

[21] Greet every saint in Christ Jesus. The brothers who are with me greet you. [22] All the

---

[1] Septuagint; Hebrew *he came to the city of the old prophet* [2] Or *brothers and sisters*; also verses 8, 21 [3] Or *loyal Syzygus*; Greek *true yokefellow* [4] Or *have fellowship in* [5] Or *I seek the profit that accrues to your account*

saints greet you, especially those of Caesar's household.

²³The grace of the Lord Jesus Christ be with your spirit.

———— *Ezekiel 43* ————

Then he led me to the gate, the gate facing east. ²And behold, the glory of the God of Israel was coming from the east. And the sound of his coming was like the sound of many waters, and the earth shone with his glory. ³And the vision I saw was just like the vision that I had seen when he[1] came to destroy the city, and just like the vision that I had seen by the Chebar canal. And I fell on my face. ⁴As the glory of the LORD entered the temple by the gate facing east, ⁵the Spirit lifted me up and brought me into the inner court; and behold, the glory of the LORD filled the temple.

⁶While the man was standing beside me, I heard one speaking to me out of the temple, ⁷and he said to me, "Son of man, this is the place of my throne and the place of the soles of my feet, where I will dwell in the midst of the people of Israel forever. And the house of Israel shall no more defile my holy name, neither they, nor their kings, by their whoring and by the dead bodies[2] of their kings at their high places,[3] ⁸by setting their threshold by my threshold and their doorposts beside my doorposts, with only a wall between me and them. They have defiled my holy name by their abominations that they have committed, so I have consumed them in my anger. ⁹Now let them put away their whoring and the dead bodies of their kings far from me, and I will dwell in their midst forever.

¹⁰"As for you, son of man, describe to the house of Israel the temple, that they may be ashamed of their iniquities; and they shall measure the plan. ¹¹And if they are ashamed of all that they have done, make known to them the design of the temple, its arrangement, its exits and its entrances, that is, its whole design; and make known to them as well all its statutes and its whole design and all its laws, and write it down in their sight, so that they may observe all its laws and all its statutes and carry them out. ¹²This is the law of the temple: the whole territory on the top of the mountain all around shall be most holy. Behold, this is the law of the temple.

¹³"These are the measurements of the altar by cubits (the cubit being a cubit and a handbreadth):[4] its base shall be one cubit high[5] and one cubit broad, with a rim of one span[6] around its edge. And this shall be the height of the altar: ¹⁴from the base on the ground to the lower ledge, two cubits, with a breadth of one cubit; and from the smaller ledge to the larger ledge, four cubits, with a breadth of one cubit; ¹⁵and the altar hearth, four cubits; and from the altar hearth projecting upward, four horns. ¹⁶The altar hearth shall be square, twelve cubits long by twelve broad. ¹⁷The ledge also shall be square, fourteen cubits long by fourteen broad, with a rim around it half a cubit broad, and its base one cubit all around. The steps of the altar shall face east."

¹⁸And he said to me, "Son of man, thus says the Lord GOD: These are the ordinances for the altar: On the day when it is erected for offering burnt offerings upon it and for throwing blood against it, ¹⁹you shall give to the Levitical priests of the family of Zadok, who draw near to me to minister to me, declares the Lord GOD, a bull from the herd for a sin offering. ²⁰And you shall take some of its blood and put it on the four horns of the altar and on the four corners of the ledge and upon the rim all around. Thus you shall purify the altar and make atonement for it. ²¹You shall also take the bull of the sin offering, and it shall be burned in the appointed place belonging to the temple, outside the sacred area. ²²And on the second day you shall offer a male goat without blemish for a sin offering; and the altar shall be purified, as it was purified with the bull. ²³When you have finished purifying it, you shall offer a bull from the herd without blemish and a ram from the flock without blemish. ²⁴You shall present them before the LORD, and the priests shall sprinkle salt on them and offer them up as a burnt offering to the LORD. ²⁵For seven days you shall provide daily a male goat for a sin offering; also, a bull from the herd and a ram from the flock, without blemish, shall be provided. ²⁶Seven days shall they make atonement for the altar and cleanse it, and so consecrate it.[7] ²⁷And when they have completed these days, then from the eighth day onward the priests shall offer on the altar your burnt offerings and your peace offerings, and I will accept you, declares the Lord GOD."

---

[1] Some Hebrew manuscripts and Vulgate; most Hebrew manuscripts *when I* [2] Or *the monuments*; also verse 9 [3] Or *at their deaths* [4] A *cubit* was about 18 inches or 45 centimeters; a *handbreadth* was about 3 inches or 7.5 centimeters [5] Or *its gutter shall be one cubit deep* [6] A *span* was about 9 inches or 22 centimeters [7] Hebrew *fill its hand*

—————— *Psalm 95–96* ——————

Oh come, let us sing to the LORD;
let us make a joyful noise to the rock of
our salvation!
2 Let us come into his presence with
thanksgiving;
let us make a joyful noise to him with
songs of praise!
3 For the LORD is a great God,
and a great King above all gods.
4 In his hand are the depths of the earth;
the heights of the mountains are his
also.
5 The sea is his, for he made it,
and his hands formed the dry land.

6 Oh come, let us worship and bow down;
let us kneel before the LORD, our
Maker!
7 For he is our God,
and we are the people of his pasture,
and the sheep of his hand.
Today, if you hear his voice,
8 do not harden your hearts, as at
Meribah,
as on the day at Massah in the
wilderness,
9 when your fathers put me to the test
and put me to the proof, though they
had seen my work.
10 For forty years I loathed that generation
and said, "They are a people who go
astray in their heart,
and they have not known my ways."
11 Therefore I swore in my wrath,
"They shall not enter my rest."

Oh sing to the LORD a new song;
sing to the LORD, all the earth!
2 Sing to the LORD, bless his name;
tell of his salvation from day to day.

3 Declare his glory among the nations,
his marvelous works among all the
peoples!
4 For great is the LORD, and greatly to be
praised;
he is to be feared above all gods.
5 For all the gods of the peoples are
worthless idols,
but the LORD made the heavens.
6 Splendor and majesty are before him;
strength and beauty are in his
sanctuary.

7 Ascribe to the LORD, O families of the
peoples,
ascribe to the LORD glory and
strength!
8 Ascribe to the LORD the glory due his
name;
bring an offering, and come into his
courts!
9 Worship the LORD in the splendor of
holiness;[1]
tremble before him, all the earth!

10 Say among the nations, "The LORD
reigns!
Yes, the world is established; it shall
never be moved;
he will judge the peoples with equity."
11 Let the heavens be glad, and let the
earth rejoice;
let the sea roar, and all that fills it;
12 let the field exult, and everything in
it!
Then shall all the trees of the forest sing
for joy
13 before the LORD, for he comes,
for he comes to judge the earth.
He will judge the world in
righteousness,
and the peoples in his faithfulness.

[1] Or *in holy attire*

OCTOBER 11

1 Kings 14

At that time Abijah the son of Jeroboam fell sick. [2]And Jeroboam said to his wife, "Arise, and disguise yourself, that it not be known that you are the wife of Jeroboam, and go to Shiloh. Behold, Ahijah the prophet is there, who said of me that I should be king over this people. [3]Take with you ten loaves, some cakes, and a jar of honey, and go to him. He will tell you what shall happen to the child."

[4]Jeroboam's wife did so. She arose and went to Shiloh and came to the house of Ahijah. Now Ahijah could not see, for his eyes were dim because of his age. [5]And the LORD said to Ahijah, "Behold, the wife of Jeroboam is coming to inquire of you concerning her son, for he is sick. Thus and thus shall you say to her."

When she came, she pretended to be another woman. [6]But when Ahijah heard the sound of her feet, as she came in at the door, he said, "Come in, wife of Jeroboam. Why do you pretend to be another? For I am charged with unbearable news for you. [7]Go, tell Jeroboam, 'Thus says the LORD, the God of Israel: "Because I exalted you from among the people and made you leader over my people Israel [8]and tore the kingdom away from the house of David and gave it to you, and yet you have not been like my servant David, who kept my commandments and followed me with all his heart, doing only that which was right in my eyes, [9]but you have done evil above all who were before you and have gone and made for yourself other gods and metal images, provoking me to anger, and have cast me behind your back, [10]therefore behold, I will bring harm upon the house of Jeroboam and will cut off from Jeroboam every male, both bond and free in Israel, and will burn up the house of Jeroboam, as a man burns up dung until it is all gone. [11]Anyone belonging to Jeroboam who dies in the city the dogs shall eat, and anyone who dies in the open country the birds of the heavens shall eat, for the LORD has spoken it."' [12]Arise therefore, go to your house. When your feet enter the city, the child shall die. [13]And all Israel shall mourn for him and bury him, for he only of Jeroboam shall come to the grave, because in him there is found something pleasing to the LORD, the God of Israel, in the house of Jeroboam. [14]Moreover, the LORD will raise up for himself a king over Israel who shall cut off the house of Jeroboam today. And henceforth, [15]the LORD will strike Israel as a reed is shaken in the water, and root up Israel out of this good land that he gave to their fathers and scatter them beyond the Euphrates,[1] because they have made their Asherim, provoking the LORD to anger. [16]And he will give Israel up because of the sins of Jeroboam, which he sinned and made Israel to sin."

[17]Then Jeroboam's wife arose and departed and came to Tirzah. And as she came to the threshold of the house, the child died. [18]And all Israel buried him and mourned for him, according to the word of the LORD, which he spoke by his servant Ahijah the prophet.

[19]Now the rest of the acts of Jeroboam, how he warred and how he reigned, behold, they are written in the Book of the Chronicles of the Kings of Israel. [20]And the time that Jeroboam reigned was twenty-two years. And he slept with his fathers, and Nadab his son reigned in his place.

[21]Now Rehoboam the son of Solomon reigned in Judah. Rehoboam was forty-one years old when he began to reign, and he reigned seventeen years in Jerusalem, the city that the LORD had chosen out of all the tribes of Israel, to put his name there. His mother's name was Naamah the Ammonite. [22]And Judah did what was evil in the sight of the LORD, and they provoked him to jealousy with their sins that they committed, more than all that their fathers had done. [23]For they also built for themselves high places and pillars and Asherim on every high hill and under every green tree, [24]and there were also male cult prostitutes in the land. They did according

---

[1] Hebrew *the River*

to all the abominations of the nations that the Lord drove out before the people of Israel. ²⁵In the fifth year of King Rehoboam, Shishak king of Egypt came up against Jerusalem. ²⁶He took away the treasures of the house of the Lord and the treasures of the king's house. He took away everything. He also took away all the shields of gold that Solomon had made, ²⁷and King Rehoboam made in their place shields of bronze, and committed them to the hands of the officers of the guard, who kept the door of the king's house. ²⁸And as often as the king went into the house of the Lord, the guard carried them and brought them back to the guardroom.

²⁹Now the rest of the acts of Rehoboam and all that he did, are they not written in the Book of the Chronicles of the Kings of Judah? ³⁰And there was war between Rehoboam and Jeroboam continually. ³¹And Rehoboam slept with his fathers and was buried with his fathers in the city of David. His mother's name was Naamah the Ammonite. And Abijam his son reigned in his place.

Colossians 1

Paul, an apostle of Christ Jesus by the will of God, and Timothy our brother,

²To the saints and faithful brothers[1] in Christ at Colossae:

Grace to you and peace from God our Father.

³We always thank God, the Father of our Lord Jesus Christ, when we pray for you, ⁴since we heard of your faith in Christ Jesus and of the love that you have for all the saints, ⁵because of the hope laid up for you in heaven. Of this you have heard before in the word of the truth, the gospel, ⁶which has come to you, as indeed in the whole world it is bearing fruit and increasing—as it also does among you, since the day you heard it and understood the grace of God in truth, ⁷just as you learned it from Epaphras our beloved fellow servant.[2] He is a faithful minister of Christ on your[3] behalf ⁸and has made known to us your love in the Spirit.

⁹And so, from the day we heard, we have not ceased to pray for you, asking that you may be filled with the knowledge of his will in all spiritual wisdom and understanding, ¹⁰so as to walk in a manner worthy of the Lord, fully

pleasing to him, bearing fruit in every good work and increasing in the knowledge of God. ¹¹May you be strengthened with all power, according to his glorious might, for all endurance and patience with joy, ¹²giving thanks[4] to the Father, who has qualified you[5] to share in the inheritance of the saints in light. ¹³He has delivered us from the domain of darkness and transferred us to the kingdom of his beloved Son, ¹⁴in whom we have redemption, the forgiveness of sins.

¹⁵He is the image of the invisible God, the firstborn of all creation. ¹⁶For by[6] him all things were created, in heaven and on earth, visible and invisible, whether thrones or dominions or rulers or authorities—all things were created through him and for him. ¹⁷And he is before all things, and in him all things hold together. ¹⁸And he is the head of the body, the church. He is the beginning, the firstborn from the dead, that in everything he might be preeminent. ¹⁹For in him all the fullness of God was pleased to dwell, ²⁰and through him to reconcile to himself all things, whether on earth or in heaven, making peace by the blood of his cross.

²¹And you, who once were alienated and hostile in mind, doing evil deeds, ²²he has now reconciled in his body of flesh by his death, in order to present you holy and blameless and above reproach before him, ²³if indeed you continue in the faith, stable and steadfast, not shifting from the hope of the gospel that you heard, which has been proclaimed in all creation[7] under heaven, and of which I, Paul, became a minister.

²⁴Now I rejoice in my sufferings for your sake, and in my flesh I am filling up what is lacking in Christ's afflictions for the sake of his body, that is, the church, ²⁵of which I became a minister according to the stewardship from God that was given to me for you, to make the word of God fully known, ²⁶the mystery hidden for ages and generations but now revealed to his saints. ²⁷To them God chose to make known how great among the Gentiles are the riches of the glory of this mystery, which is Christ in you, the hope of glory. ²⁸Him we proclaim, warning everyone and teaching everyone with all wisdom, that we may present everyone mature in Christ. ²⁹For this I toil, struggling with all his energy that he powerfully works within me.

¹ Or brothers and sisters. The plural Greek word adelphoi (translated "brothers") refers to siblings in a family. In New Testament usage, depending on the context, adelphoi may refer either to men or to both men and women who are siblings (brothers and sisters) in God's family, the church ² Greek fellow bondservant ³ Some manuscripts our ⁴ Or patience, with joy giving thanks ⁵ Some manuscripts us ⁶ That is, by means of; or in ⁷ Or to every creature

--------- *Ezekiel 44* ---------

Then he brought me back to the outer gate of the sanctuary, which faces east. And it was shut. ²And the LORD said to me, "This gate shall remain shut; it shall not be opened, and no one shall enter by it, for the LORD, the God of Israel, has entered by it. Therefore it shall remain shut. ³Only the prince may sit in it to eat bread before the LORD. He shall enter by way of the vestibule of the gate, and shall go out by the same way."

⁴Then he brought me by way of the north gate to the front of the temple, and I looked, and behold, the glory of the LORD filled the temple of the LORD. And I fell on my face. ⁵And the LORD said to me, "Son of man, mark well, see with your eyes, and hear with your ears all that I shall tell you concerning all the statutes of the temple of the LORD and all its laws. And mark well the entrance to the temple and all the exits from the sanctuary. ⁶And say to the rebellious house,[1] to the house of Israel, Thus says the Lord GOD: O house of Israel, enough of all your abominations, ⁷in admitting foreigners, uncircumcised in heart and flesh, to be in my sanctuary, profaning my temple, when you offer to me my food, the fat and the blood. You[2] have broken my covenant, in addition to all your abominations. ⁸And you have not kept charge of my holy things, but you have set others to keep my charge for you in my sanctuary.

⁹"Thus says the Lord GOD: No foreigner, uncircumcised in heart and flesh, of all the foreigners who are among the people of Israel, shall enter my sanctuary. ¹⁰But the Levites who went far from me, going astray from me after their idols when Israel went astray, shall bear their punishment.[3] ¹¹They shall be ministers in my sanctuary, having oversight at the gates of the temple and ministering in the temple. They shall slaughter the burnt offering and the sacrifice for the people, and they shall stand before the people, to minister to them. ¹²Because they ministered to them before their idols and became a stumbling block of iniquity to the house of Israel, therefore I have sworn concerning them, declares the Lord GOD, and they shall bear their punishment. ¹³They shall not come near to me, to serve me as priest, nor come near any of my holy things and the things that are most holy, but they shall bear their shame and the abominations that they have committed. ¹⁴Yet I will appoint them to keep charge of the temple, to do all its service and all that is to be done in it.

¹⁵"But the Levitical priests, the sons of Zadok, who kept the charge of my sanctuary when the people of Israel went astray from me, shall come near to me to minister to me. And they shall stand before me to offer me the fat and the blood, declares the Lord GOD. ¹⁶They shall enter my sanctuary, and they shall approach my table, to minister to me, and they shall keep my charge. ¹⁷When they enter the gates of the inner court, they shall wear linen garments. They shall have nothing of wool on them, while they minister at the gates of the inner court, and within. ¹⁸They shall have linen turbans on their heads, and linen undergarments around their waists. They shall not bind themselves with anything that causes sweat. ¹⁹And when they go out into the outer court to the people, they shall put off the garments in which they have been ministering and lay them in the holy chambers. And they shall put on other garments, lest they transmit holiness to the people with their garments. ²⁰They shall not shave their heads or let their locks grow long; they shall surely trim the hair of their heads. ²¹No priest shall drink wine when he enters the inner court. ²²They shall not marry a widow or a divorced woman, but only virgins of the offspring of the house of Israel, or a widow who is the widow of a priest. ²³They shall teach my people the difference between the holy and the common, and show them how to distinguish between the unclean and the clean. ²⁴In a dispute, they shall act as judges, and they shall judge it according to my judgments. They shall keep my laws and my statutes in all my appointed feasts, and they shall keep my Sabbaths holy. ²⁵They shall not defile themselves by going near to a dead person. However, for father or mother, for son or daughter, for brother or unmarried sister they may defile themselves. ²⁶After he[4] has become clean, they shall count seven days for him. ²⁷And on the day that he goes into the Holy Place, into the inner court, to minister in the Holy Place, he shall offer his sin offering, declares the Lord GOD.

²⁸"This shall be their inheritance: I am their inheritance: and you shall give them no possession in Israel; I am their possession. ²⁹They

---

¹ Septuagint; Hebrew lacks *house* ² Septuagint, Syriac, Vulgate; Hebrew *They* ³ Or *iniquity*; also verse 12 ⁴ That is, a priest

shall eat the grain offering, the sin offering, and the guilt offering, and every devoted thing in Israel shall be theirs. ³⁰And the first of all the firstfruits of all kinds, and every offering of all kinds from all your offerings, shall belong to the priests. You shall also give to the priests the first of your dough, that a blessing may rest on your house. ³¹The priests shall not eat of anything, whether bird or beast, that has died of itself or is torn by wild animals.

Psalm 97–98

The LORD reigns, let the earth rejoice;
   let the many coastlands be glad!
2   Clouds and thick darkness are all
         around him;
      righteousness and justice are the
         foundation of his throne.
3   Fire goes before him
      and burns up his adversaries all
         around.
4   His lightnings light up the world;
      the earth sees and trembles.
5   The mountains melt like wax before the
         LORD,
      before the Lord of all the earth.
6   The heavens proclaim his
         righteousness,
      and all the peoples see his glory.
7   All worshipers of images are put to
         shame,
      who make their boast in worthless
         idols;
      worship him, all you gods!
8   Zion hears and is glad,
      and the daughters of Judah rejoice,
      because of your judgments, O LORD.
9   For you, O LORD, are most high over all
         the earth;
      you are exalted far above all gods.

10   O you who love the LORD, hate evil!
      He preserves the lives of his saints;
      he delivers them from the hand of the
         wicked.
11   Light is sown¹ for the righteous,
      and joy for the upright in heart.
12   Rejoice in the LORD, O you righteous,
      and give thanks to his holy name!

A PSALM.

Oh sing to the LORD a new song,
   for he has done marvelous things!
   His right hand and his holy arm
      have worked salvation for him.
2   The LORD has made known his salvation;
      he has revealed his righteousness in
         the sight of the nations.
3   He has remembered his steadfast love
         and faithfulness
      to the house of Israel.
   All the ends of the earth have seen
      the salvation of our God.

4   Make a joyful noise to the LORD, all the
         earth;
      break forth into joyous song and sing
         praises!
5   Sing praises to the LORD with the lyre,
      with the lyre and the sound of
         melody!
6   With trumpets and the sound of the horn
      make a joyful noise before the King,
         the LORD!

7   Let the sea roar, and all that fills it;
      the world and those who dwell in it!
8   Let the rivers clap their hands;
      let the hills sing for joy together
9   before the LORD, for he comes
      to judge the earth.
   He will judge the world with
         righteousness,
      and the peoples with equity.

¹ Most Hebrew manuscripts; one Hebrew manuscript, Septuagint, Syriac, Jerome *Light dawns*

OCTOBER 12

1 Kings 15

Now in the eighteenth year of King Jeroboam the son of Nebat, Abijam began to reign over Judah. ²He reigned for three years in Jerusalem. His mother's name was Maacah the daughter of Abishalom. ³And he walked in all the sins that his father did before him, and his heart was not wholly true to the LORD his God, as the heart of David his father. ⁴Nevertheless, for David's sake the LORD his God gave him a lamp in Jerusalem, setting up his son after him, and establishing Jerusalem, ⁵because David did what was right in the eyes of the LORD and did not turn aside from anything that he commanded him all the days of his life, except in the matter of Uriah the Hittite. ⁶Now there was war between Rehoboam and Jeroboam all the days of his life. ⁷The rest of the acts of Abijam and all that he did, are they not written in the Book of the Chronicles of the Kings of Judah? And there was war between Abijam and Jeroboam. ⁸And Abijam slept with his fathers, and they buried him in the city of David. And Asa his son reigned in his place.

⁹In the twentieth year of Jeroboam king of Israel, Asa began to reign over Judah, ¹⁰and he reigned forty-one years in Jerusalem. His mother's name was Maacah the daughter of Abishalom. ¹¹And Asa did what was right in the eyes of the LORD, as David his father had done. ¹²He put away the male cult prostitutes out of the land and removed all the idols that his fathers had made. ¹³He also removed Maacah his mother from being queen mother because she had made an abominable image for Asherah. And Asa cut down her image and burned it at the brook Kidron. ¹⁴But the high places were not taken away. Nevertheless, the heart of Asa was wholly true to the LORD all his days. ¹⁵And he brought into the house of the LORD the sacred gifts of his father and his own sacred gifts, silver, and gold, and vessels.

¹⁶And there was war between Asa and Baasha king of Israel all their days. ¹⁷Baasha king of Israel went up against Judah and built Ramah, that he might permit no one to go out or come in to Asa king of Judah. ¹⁸Then Asa took all the silver and the gold that were left in the treasures of the house of the LORD and the treasures of the king's house and gave them into the hands of his servants. And King Asa sent them to Ben-hadad the son of Tabrimmon, the son of Hezion, king of Syria, who lived in Damascus, saying, ¹⁹"Let there be a covenant¹ between me and you, as there was between my father and your father. Behold, I am sending to you a present of silver and gold. Go, break your covenant with Baasha king of Israel, that he may withdraw from me." ²⁰And Ben-hadad listened to King Asa and sent the commanders of his armies against the cities of Israel and conquered Ijon, Dan, Abel-beth-maacah, and all Chinneroth, with all the land of Naphtali. ²¹And when Baasha heard of it, he stopped building Ramah, and he lived in Tirzah. ²²Then King Asa made a proclamation to all Judah, none was exempt, and they carried away the stones of Ramah and its timber, with which Baasha had been building, and with them King Asa built Geba of Benjamin and Mizpah. ²³Now the rest of all the acts of Asa, all his might, and all that he did, and the cities that he built, are they not written in the Book of the Chronicles of the Kings of Judah? But in his old age he was diseased in his feet. ²⁴And Asa slept with his fathers and was buried with his fathers in the city of David his father, and Jehoshaphat his son reigned in his place.

²⁵Nadab the son of Jeroboam began to reign over Israel in the second year of Asa king of Judah, and he reigned over Israel two years. ²⁶He did what was evil in the sight of the LORD and walked in the way of his father, and in his sin which he made Israel to sin.

²⁷Baasha the son of Ahijah, of the house of Issachar, conspired against him. And Baasha struck him down at Gibbethon, which belonged to the Philistines, for Nadab and all Israel were laying siege to Gibbethon. ²⁸So Baasha killed

¹ Or treaty; twice in this verse

him in the third year of Asa king of Judah and reigned in his place. ²⁹And as soon as he was king, he killed all the house of Jeroboam. He left to the house of Jeroboam not one that breathed, until he had destroyed it, according to the word of the LORD that he spoke by his servant Ahijah the Shilonite. ³⁰It was for the sins of Jeroboam that he sinned and that he made Israel to sin, and because of the anger to which he provoked the LORD, the God of Israel.

³¹Now the rest of the acts of Nadab and all that he did, are they not written in the Book of the Chronicles of the Kings of Israel? ³²And there was war between Asa and Baasha king of Israel all their days.

³³In the third year of Asa king of Judah, Baasha the son of Ahijah began to reign over all Israel at Tirzah, and he reigned twenty-four years. ³⁴He did what was evil in the sight of the LORD and walked in the way of Jeroboam and in his sin which he made Israel to sin.

Colossians 2

For I want you to know how great a struggle I have for you and for those at Laodicea and for all who have not seen me face to face, ²that their hearts may be encouraged, being knit together in love, to reach all the riches of full assurance of understanding and the knowledge of God's mystery, which is Christ, ³in whom are hidden all the treasures of wisdom and knowledge. ⁴I say this in order that no one may delude you with plausible arguments. ⁵For though I am absent in body, yet I am with you in spirit, rejoicing to see your good order and the firmness of your faith in Christ.

⁶Therefore, as you received Christ Jesus the Lord, so walk in him, ⁷rooted and built up in him and established in the faith, just as you were taught, abounding in thanksgiving.

⁸See to it that no one takes you captive by philosophy and empty deceit, according to human tradition, according to the elemental spirits[1] of the world, and not according to Christ. ⁹For in him the whole fullness of deity dwells bodily, ¹⁰and you have been filled in him, who is the head of all rule and authority. ¹¹In him also you were circumcised with a circumcision made without hands, by putting off the body of the flesh, by the circumcision of Christ, ¹²having been buried with him in baptism, in

which you were also raised with him through faith in the powerful working of God, who raised him from the dead. ¹³And you, who were dead in your trespasses and the uncircumcision of your flesh, God made alive together with him, having forgiven us all our trespasses, ¹⁴by canceling the record of debt that stood against us with its legal demands. This he set aside, nailing it to the cross. ¹⁵He disarmed the rulers and authorities[2] and put them to open shame, by triumphing over them in him.[3]

¹⁶Therefore let no one pass judgment on you in questions of food and drink, or with regard to a festival or a new moon or a Sabbath. ¹⁷These are a shadow of the things to come, but the substance belongs to Christ. ¹⁸Let no one disqualify you, insisting on asceticism and worship of angels, going on in detail about visions,[4] puffed up without reason by his sensuous mind, ¹⁹and not holding fast to the Head, from whom the whole body, nourished and knit together through its joints and ligaments, grows with a growth that is from God.

²⁰If with Christ you died to the elemental spirits of the world, why, as if you were still alive in the world, do you submit to regulations— ²¹"Do not handle, Do not taste, Do not touch" ²²(referring to things that all perish as they are used)— according to human precepts and teachings? ²³These have indeed an appearance of wisdom in promoting self-made religion and asceticism and severity to the body, but they are of no value in stopping the indulgence of the flesh.

Ezekiel 45

"When you allot the land as an inheritance, you shall set apart for the LORD a portion of the land as a holy district, 25,000 cubits[5] long and 20,000[6] cubits broad. It shall be holy throughout its whole extent. ²Of this a square plot of 500 by 500 cubits shall be for the sanctuary, with fifty cubits for an open space around it. ³And from this measured district you shall measure off a section 25,000 cubits long and 10,000 broad, in which shall be the sanctuary, the Most Holy Place. ⁴It shall be the holy portion of the land. It shall be for the priests, who minister in the sanctuary and approach the LORD to minister to him, and it shall be a place for their houses and a holy place for the sanctuary. ⁵Another section, 25,000 cubits long

[1] Or *elementary principles*; also verse 20 [2] Probably demonic rulers and authorities [3] Or *in it* (that is, the cross) [4] Or *about the things he has seen* [5] A cubit was about 18 inches or 45 centimeters [6] Septuagint; Hebrew *ten*

and 10,000 cubits broad, shall be for the Levites who minister at the temple, as their possession for cities to live in.[1]

⁶"Alongside the portion set apart as the holy district you shall assign for the property of the city an area 5,000 cubits broad and 25,000 cubits long. It shall belong to the whole house of Israel.

⁷"And to the prince shall belong the land on both sides of the holy district and the property of the city, alongside the holy district and the property of the city, on the west and on the east, corresponding in length to one of the tribal portions, and extending from the western to the eastern boundary ⁸of the land. It is to be his property in Israel. And my princes shall no more oppress my people, but they shall let the house of Israel have the land according to their tribes. ⁹"Thus says the Lord GOD: Enough, O princes of Israel! Put away violence and oppression, and execute justice and righteousness. Cease your evictions of my people, declares the Lord GOD.

¹⁰"You shall have just balances, a just ephah, and a just bath.[2] ¹¹The ephah and the bath shall be of the same measure, the bath containing one tenth of a homer,[3] and the ephah one tenth of a homer; the homer shall be the standard measure. ¹²The shekel shall be twenty gerahs;[4] twenty shekels plus twenty-five shekels plus fifteen shekels shall be your mina.[5]

¹³"This is the offering that you shall make: one sixth of an ephah from each homer of wheat, and one sixth of an ephah from each homer of barley, ¹⁴and as the fixed portion of oil, measured in baths, one tenth of a bath from each cor[6] (the cor, like the homer, contains ten baths).[7] ¹⁵And one sheep from every flock of two hundred, from the watering places of Israel for grain offering, burnt offering, and peace offerings, to make atonement for them, declares the Lord GOD. ¹⁶All the people of the land shall be obliged to give this offering to the prince in Israel. ¹⁷It shall be the prince's duty to furnish the burnt offerings, grain offerings, and drink offerings, at the feasts, the new moons, and the Sabbaths, all the appointed feasts of the house of Israel: he shall provide the sin offerings, grain offerings, burnt offerings, and peace offerings, to make atonement on behalf of the house of Israel.

¹⁸"Thus says the Lord GOD: In the first month,

on the first day of the month, you shall take a bull from the herd without blemish, and purify the sanctuary. ¹⁹The priest shall take some of the blood of the sin offering and put it on the doorposts of the temple, the four corners of the ledge of the altar, and the posts of the gate of the inner court. ²⁰You shall do the same on the seventh day of the month for anyone who has sinned through error or ignorance; so you shall make atonement for the temple.

²¹"In the first month, on the fourteenth day of the month, you shall celebrate the Feast of the Passover, and for seven days unleavened bread shall be eaten. ²²On that day the prince shall provide for himself and all the people of the land a young bull for a sin offering. ²³And on the seven days of the festival he shall provide as a burnt offering to the LORD seven young bulls and seven rams without blemish, on each of the seven days; and a male goat daily for a sin offering. ²⁴And he shall provide as a grain offering an ephah for each bull, an ephah for each ram, and a hin[8] of oil to each ephah. ²⁵In the seventh month, on the fifteenth day of the month and for the seven days of the feast, he shall make the same provision for sin offerings, burnt offerings, and grain offerings, and for the oil.

Psalm 99–101

The LORD reigns; let the peoples tremble!
He sits enthroned upon the cherubim; let
the earth quake!
2 The LORD is great in Zion;
he is exalted over all the peoples.
3 Let them praise your great and awesome
name!
Holy is he!
4 The King in his might loves justice.[9]
You have established equity;
you have executed justice
and righteousness in Jacob.
5 Exalt the LORD our God;
worship at his footstool!
Holy is he!

6 Moses and Aaron were among his priests,
Samuel also was among those who
called upon his name.
They called to the LORD, and he
answered them.

¹ Septuagint; Hebrew as their possession, twenty chambers ² An ephah was about 3/5 of a bushel or 22 liters; a bath was about 6 gallons or 22 liters ³ A homer was about 6 bushels or 220 liters ⁴ A shekel was about 2/5 ounce or 11 grams; a gerah was about 1/50 ounce or 0.6 gram ⁵ A mina was about 1 1/4 pounds or 0.6 kilogram ⁶ A cor was about 6 bushels or 220 liters ⁷ See Vulgate; Hebrew (ten baths are a homer, for ten baths are a homer) ⁸ A hin was about 4 quarts or 3.5 liters ⁹ Or The might of the King loves justice

7 In the pillar of the cloud he spoke to them;
  they kept his testimonies
  and the statute that he gave them.

8 O LORD our God, you answered them;
  you were a forgiving God to them,
  but an avenger of their wrongdoings.

9 Exalt the LORD our God,
  and worship at his holy mountain;
  for the LORD our God is holy!

A PSALM FOR GIVING THANKS.

Make a joyful noise to the LORD, all the
earth!
2 Serve the LORD with gladness!
  Come into his presence with singing!

3 Know that the LORD, he is God!
  It is he who made us, and we are his;[1]
  we are his people, and the sheep of his
  pasture.

4 Enter his gates with thanksgiving,
  and his courts with praise!
  Give thanks to him; bless his name!

5 For the LORD is good;
  his steadfast love endures forever,
  and his faithfulness to all generations.

A PSALM OF DAVID.

I will sing of steadfast love and justice;
to you, O LORD, I will make music.

2 I will ponder the way that is blameless.
  Oh when will you come to me?
  I will walk with integrity of heart
  within my house;

3 I will not set before my eyes
  anything that is worthless.
  I hate the work of those who fall away;
  it shall not cling to me.

4 A perverse heart shall be far from me;
  I will know nothing of evil.

5 Whoever slanders his neighbor secretly
  I will destroy.
  Whoever has a haughty look and an
  arrogant heart
  I will not endure.

6 I will look with favor on the faithful in
  the land,
  that they may dwell with me;
  he who walks in the way that is
  blameless
  shall minister to me.

7 No one who practices deceit
  shall dwell in my house;
  no one who utters lies
  shall continue before my eyes.

8 Morning by morning I will destroy
  all the wicked in the land,
  cutting off all the evildoers
  from the city of the LORD.

OCTOBER 13

1 Kings 16

And the word of the LORD came to Jehu the son of Hanani against Baasha, saying, 2 "Since I exalted you out of the dust and made you leader over my people Israel, and you have walked in the way of Jeroboam and have made my people Israel to sin, provoking me to anger with their sins, 3 behold, I will utterly sweep away Baasha and his house, and I will make your house like the house of Jeroboam the son of Nebat. 4 Anyone belonging to Baasha who dies in the city the dogs shall eat, and anyone of his who dies in the field the birds of the heavens shall eat."

5 Now the rest of the acts of Baasha and what he did, and his might, are they not written in the Book of the Chronicles of the Kings of Israel? 6 And Baasha slept with his fathers and was buried at Tirzah, and Elah his son reigned in his place. 7 Moreover, the word of the LORD came by the prophet Jehu the son of Hanani

[1] Or and not we ourselves

against Baasha and his house, both because of all the evil that he did in the sight of the Lord, provoking him to anger with the work of his hands, in being like the house of Jeroboam, and also because he destroyed it.

[8] In the twenty-sixth year of Asa king of Judah, Elah the son of Baasha began to reign over Israel in Tirzah, and he reigned two years. [9] But his servant Zimri, commander of half his chariots, conspired against him. When he was at Tirzah, drinking himself drunk in the house of Arza, who was over the household in Tirzah, [10] Zimri came in and struck him down and killed him, in the twenty-seventh year of Asa king of Judah, and reigned in his place.

[11] When he began to reign, as soon as he had seated himself on his throne, he struck down all the house of Baasha. He did not leave him a single male of his relatives or his friends. [12] Thus Zimri destroyed all the house of Baasha, according to the word of the Lord, which he spoke against Baasha by Jehu the prophet, [13] for all the sins of Baasha and the sins of Elah his son, which they sinned and which they made Israel to sin, provoking the Lord God of Israel to anger with their idols. [14] Now the rest of the acts of Elah and all that he did, are they not written in the Book of the Chronicles of the Kings of Israel?

[15] In the twenty-seventh year of Asa king of Judah, Zimri reigned seven days in Tirzah. Now the troops were encamped against Gibbethon, which belonged to the Philistines, [16] and the troops who were encamped heard it said, "Zimri has conspired, and he has killed the king." Therefore all Israel made Omri, the commander of the army, king over Israel that day in the camp. [17] So Omri went up from Gibbethon, and all Israel with him, and they besieged Tirzah. [18] And when Zimri saw that the city was taken, he went into the citadel of the king's house and burned the king's house over him with fire and died, [19] because of his sins that he committed, doing evil in the sight of the Lord, walking in the way of Jeroboam, and for his sin which he committed, making Israel to sin. [20] Now the rest of the acts of Zimri, and the conspiracy that he made, are they not written in the Book of the Chronicles of the Kings of Israel?

[21] Then the people of Israel were divided into two parts. Half of the people followed Tibni the son of Ginath, to make him king, and half followed Omri. [22] But the people who followed Omri overcame the people who followed Tibni the son of Ginath. So Tibni died, and Omri became king. [23] In the thirty-first year of Asa king of Judah, Omri began to reign over Israel, and he reigned for twelve years; six years he reigned in Tirzah. [24] He bought the hill of Samaria from Shemer for two talents[1] of silver, and he fortified the hill and called the name of the city that he built Samaria, after the name of Shemer, the owner of the hill.

[25] Omri did what was evil in the sight of the Lord, and did more evil than all who were before him. [26] For he walked in all the way of Jeroboam the son of Nebat, and in the sins that he made Israel to sin, provoking the Lord, the God of Israel, to anger by their idols. [27] Now the rest of the acts of Omri that he did, and the might that he showed, are they not written in the Book of the Chronicles of the Kings of Israel? [28] And Omri slept with his fathers and was buried in Samaria, and Ahab his son reigned in his place.

[29] In the thirty-eighth year of Asa king of Judah, Ahab the son of Omri began to reign over Israel, and Ahab the son of Omri reigned over Israel in Samaria twenty-two years. [30] And Ahab the son of Omri did evil in the sight of the Lord, more than all who were before him. [31] And as if it had been a light thing for him to walk in the sins of Jeroboam the son of Nebat, he took for his wife Jezebel the daughter of Ethbaal king of the Sidonians, and went and served Baal and worshiped him. [32] He erected an altar for Baal in the house of Baal, which he built in Samaria. [33] And Ahab made an Asherah. Ahab did more to provoke the Lord, the God of Israel, to anger than all the kings of Israel who were before him. [34] In his days Hiel of Bethel built Jericho. He laid its foundation at the cost of Abiram his firstborn, and set up its gates at the cost of his youngest son Segub, according to the word of the Lord, which he spoke by Joshua the son of Nun.

Colossians 3

If then you have been raised with Christ, seek the things that are above, where Christ is, seated at the right hand of God. [2] Set your

---

[1] A *talent* was about 75 pounds or 34 kilograms

minds on things that are above, not on things that are on earth. ³For you have died, and your life is hidden with Christ in God. ⁴When Christ who is your¹ life appears, then you also will appear with him in glory.

⁵Put to death therefore what is earthly in you:² sexual immorality, impurity, passion, evil desire, and covetousness, which is idolatry. ⁶On account of these the wrath of God is coming.³ ⁷In these you too once walked, when you were living in them. ⁸But now you must put them all away: anger, wrath, malice, slander, and obscene talk from your mouth. ⁹Do not lie to one another, seeing that you have put off the old self⁴ with its practices ¹⁰and have put on the new self, which is being renewed in knowledge after the image of its creator. ¹¹Here there is not Greek and Jew, circumcised and uncircumcised, barbarian, Scythian, slave,⁵ free; but Christ is all, and in all.

¹²Put on then, as God's chosen ones, holy and beloved, compassionate hearts, kindness, humility, meekness, and patience, ¹³bearing with one another and, if one has a complaint against another, forgiving each other; as the Lord has forgiven you, so you also must forgive. ¹⁴And above all these put on love, which binds everything together in perfect harmony. ¹⁵And let the peace of Christ rule in your hearts, to which indeed you were called in one body. And be thankful. ¹⁶Let the word of Christ dwell in you richly, teaching and admonishing one another in all wisdom, singing psalms and hymns and spiritual songs, with thankfulness in your hearts to God. ¹⁷And whatever you do, in word or deed, do everything in the name of the Lord Jesus, giving thanks to God the Father through him.

¹⁸Wives, submit to your husbands, as is fitting in the Lord. ¹⁹Husbands, love your wives, and do not be harsh with them. ²⁰Children, obey your parents in everything, for this pleases the Lord. ²¹Fathers, do not provoke your children, lest they become discouraged. ²²Bondservants,⁶ obey in everything those who are your earthly masters,⁷ not by way of eye-service, as people-pleasers, but with sincerity of heart, fearing the Lord. ²³Whatever you do, work heartily, as for the Lord and not for men, ²⁴knowing that from the Lord you will receive the inheritance as your reward. You are serving

the Lord Christ. ²⁵For the wrongdoer will be paid back for the wrong he has done, and there is no partiality.

Ezekiel 46

"Thus says the Lord GOD: The gate of the inner court that faces east shall be shut on the six working days, but on the Sabbath day it shall be opened, and on the day of the new moon it shall be opened. ²The prince shall enter by the vestibule of the gate from outside, and shall take his stand by the post of the gate. The priests shall offer his burnt offering and his peace offerings, and he shall worship at the threshold of the gate. Then he shall go out, but the gate shall not be shut until evening. ³The people of the land shall bow down at the entrance of that gate before the LORD on the Sabbaths and on the new moons. ⁴The burnt offering that the prince offers to the LORD on the Sabbath day shall be six lambs without blemish and a ram without blemish. ⁵And the grain offering with the ram shall be an ephah,⁸ and the grain offering with the lambs shall be as much as he is able, together with a hin⁹ of oil to each ephah. ⁶On the day of the new moon he shall offer a bull from the herd without blemish, and six lambs and a ram, which shall be without blemish. ⁷As a grain offering he shall provide an ephah with the bull and an ephah with the ram, and with the lambs as much as he is able, together with a hin of oil to each ephah. ⁸When the prince enters, he shall enter by the vestibule of the gate, and he shall go out by the same way.

⁹"When the people of the land come before the LORD at the appointed feasts, he who enters by the north gate to worship shall go out by the south gate, and he who enters by the south gate shall go out by the north gate: no one shall return by way of the gate by which he entered, but each shall go out straight ahead. ¹⁰When they enter, the prince shall enter with them, and when they go out, he shall go out.

¹¹"At the feasts and the appointed festivals, the grain offering with a young bull shall be an ephah, and with a ram an ephah, and with the lambs as much as one is able to give, together with a hin of oil to an ephah. ¹²When the prince provides a freewill offering, either a

¹ Some manuscripts *our* ² Greek *therefore your members that are on the earth* ³ Some manuscripts add *upon the sons of disobedience* ⁴ Greek *man;* also as supplied in verse 10 ⁵ Greek *bondservant* ⁶ Or *Slaves;* also 4:1 (for the contextual rendering of the Greek word *doulos,* see Preface) ⁷ Or *your masters according to the flesh* ⁸ An *ephah* was about 3/5 bushel or 22 liters ⁹ A *hin* was about 4 quarts or 3.5 liters

burnt offering or peace offerings as a freewill offering to the LORD, the gate facing east shall be opened for him. And he shall offer his burnt offering or his peace offerings as he does on the Sabbath day. Then he shall go out, and after he has gone out the gate shall be shut.

¹³ "You shall provide a lamb a year old without blemish for a burnt offering to the LORD daily; morning by morning you shall provide it. ¹⁴ And you shall provide a grain offering with it morning by morning, one sixth of an ephah, and one third of a hin of oil to moisten the flour, as a grain offering to the LORD. This is a perpetual statute. ¹⁵ Thus the lamb and the meal offering and the oil shall be provided, morning by morning, for a regular burnt offering.

¹⁶ "Thus says the Lord GOD: If the prince makes a gift to any of his sons as his inheritance, it shall belong to his sons. It is their property by inheritance. ¹⁷ But if he makes a gift out of his inheritance to one of his servants, it shall be his to the year of liberty. Then it shall revert to the prince; surely it is his inheritance—it shall belong to his sons. ¹⁸ The prince shall not take any of the inheritance of the people, thrusting them out of their property. He shall give his sons their inheritance out of his own property, so that none of my people shall be scattered from his property."

¹⁹ Then he brought me through the entrance, which was at the side of the gate, to the north row of the holy chambers for the priests, and behold, a place was there at the extreme western end of them. ²⁰ And he said to me, "This is the place where the priests shall boil the guilt offering and the sin offering, and where they shall bake the grain offering, in order not to bring them out into the outer court and so transmit holiness to the people."

²¹ Then he brought me out to the outer court and led me around to the four corners of the court. And behold, in each corner of the court there was another court— ²² in the four corners of the court were small¹ courts, forty cubits² long and thirty broad; the four were of the same size. ²³ On the inside, around each of the four courts was a row of masonry, with hearths made at the bottom of the rows all around. ²⁴ Then he said to me, "These are the kitchens where those who minister at the temple shall boil the sacrifices of the people."

——————— *Psalm 102* ———————

A PRAYER OF ONE AFFLICTED, WHEN HE IS FAINT AND POURS OUT HIS COMPLAINT BEFORE THE LORD.

Hear my prayer, O LORD;
   let my cry come to you!
2 Do not hide your face from me
   in the day of my distress!
Incline your ear to me;
   answer me speedily in the day when
     I call!

3 For my days pass away like smoke,
   and my bones burn like a furnace.
4 My heart is struck down like grass and
     has withered;
   I forget to eat my bread.
5 Because of my loud groaning
   my bones cling to my flesh.
6 I am like a desert owl of the
     wilderness,
   like an owl³ of the waste places;
7 I lie awake;
   I am like a lonely sparrow on the
     housetop.
8 All the day my enemies taunt me;
   those who deride me use my name for
     a curse.
9 For I eat ashes like bread
   and mingle tears with my drink,
10 because of your indignation and anger;
   for you have taken me up and thrown
     me down.
11 My days are like an evening shadow;
   I wither away like grass.

12 But you, O LORD, are enthroned
     forever;
   you are remembered throughout all
     generations.
13 You will arise and have pity on Zion;
   it is the time to favor her;
   the appointed time has come.
14 For your servants hold her stones dear
   and have pity on her dust.
15 Nations will fear the name of the LORD,
   and all the kings of the earth will fear
     your glory.
16 For the LORD builds up Zion;
   he appears in his glory;
17 he regards the prayer of the destitute
   and does not despise their prayer.

¹ Septuagint, Syriac, Vulgate; the meaning of the Hebrew word is uncertain ² A *cubit* was about 18 inches or 45 centimeters ³ The precise identity of these birds is uncertain

18 Let this be recorded for a generation to
come,
so that a people yet to be created may
praise the LORD:
19 that he looked down from his holy
height;
from heaven the LORD looked at the
earth,
20 to hear the groans of the prisoners,
to set free those who were doomed to
die,
21 that they may declare in Zion the name
of the LORD,
and in Jerusalem his praise,
22 when peoples gather together,
and kingdoms, to worship the LORD.

23 He has broken my strength in midcourse;
he has shortened my days.

24 "O my God," I say, "take me not away
in the midst of my days—
you whose years endure
throughout all generations!"

25 Of old you laid the foundation of the
earth,
and the heavens are the work of your
hands.
26 They will perish, but you will remain;
they will all wear out like a garment.
You will change them like a robe, and
they will pass away,
27 but you are the same, and your years
have no end.
28 The children of your servants shall dwell
secure;
their offspring shall be established
before you.

OCTOBER 14

1 Kings 17

Now Elijah the Tishbite, of Tishbe[1] in Gilead, said to Ahab, "As the LORD, the God of Israel, lives, before whom I stand, there shall be neither dew nor rain these years, except by my word." ²And the word of the LORD came to him: ³"Depart from here and turn eastward and hide yourself by the brook Cherith, which is east of the Jordan. ⁴You shall drink from the brook, and I have commanded the ravens to feed you there." ⁵So he went and did according to the word of the LORD. He went and lived by the brook Cherith that is east of the Jordan. ⁶And the ravens brought him bread and meat in the morning, and bread and meat in the evening, and he drank from the brook. ⁷And after a while the brook dried up, because there was no rain in the land.

⁸Then the word of the LORD came to him, ⁹"Arise, go to Zarephath, which belongs to Sidon, and dwell there. Behold, I have commanded a widow there to feed you." ¹⁰So he arose and went to Zarephath. And when he came to the gate of the city, behold, a widow was there gathering sticks. And he called to her and said, "Bring me a little water in a vessel, that I may drink." ¹¹And as she was going to bring it, he called to her and said, "Bring me a morsel of bread in your hand." ¹²And she said, "As the LORD your God lives, I have nothing baked, only a handful of flour in a jar and a little oil in a jug. And now I am gathering a couple of sticks that I may go in and prepare it for myself and my son, that we may eat it and die." ¹³And Elijah said to her, "Do not fear; go and do as you have said. But first make me a little cake of it and bring it to me, and afterward make something for yourself and your son. ¹⁴For thus says the LORD, the God of Israel, 'The jar of flour shall not be spent, and the jug of oil shall not be empty, until the day that the LORD sends rain upon the earth.'" ¹⁵And she went and did as Elijah said. And she and he and her household ate for many days. ¹⁶The jar of flour was not spent, neither did the jug of oil become empty, according to the word of the LORD that he spoke by Elijah.

¹ Septuagint; Hebrew *of the settlers*

[17]After this the son of the woman, the mistress of the house, became ill. And his illness was so severe that there was no breath left in him. [18]And she said to Elijah, "What have you against me, O man of God? You have come to me to bring my sin to remembrance and to cause the death of my son!" [19]And he said to her, "Give me your son." And he took him from her arms and carried him up into the upper chamber where he lodged, and laid him on his own bed. [20]And he cried to the LORD, "O LORD my God, have you brought calamity even upon the widow with whom I sojourn, by killing her son?" [21]Then he stretched himself upon the child three times and cried to the LORD, "O LORD my God, let this child's life[1] come into him again." [22]And the LORD listened to the voice of Elijah. And the life of the child came into him again, and he revived. [23]And Elijah took the child and brought him down from the upper chamber into the house and delivered him to his mother. And Elijah said, "See, your son lives." [24]And the woman said to Elijah, "Now I know that you are a man of God, and that the word of the LORD in your mouth is truth."

Colossians 4

Masters, treat your bondservants justly and fairly, knowing that you also have a Master in heaven.

[2]Continue steadfastly in prayer, being watchful in it with thanksgiving. [3]At the same time, pray also for us, that God may open to us a door for the word, to declare the mystery of Christ, on account of which I am in prison— [4]that I may make it clear, which is how I ought to speak.

[5]Walk in wisdom toward outsiders, making the best use of the time. [6]Let your speech always be gracious, seasoned with salt, so that you may know how you ought to answer each person.

[7]Tychicus will tell you all about my activities. He is a beloved brother and faithful minister and fellow servant[2] in the Lord. [8]I have sent him to you for this very purpose, that you may know how we are and that he may encourage your hearts, [9]and with him Onesimus, our faithful and beloved brother, who is one of you. They will tell you of everything that has taken place here.

[10]Aristarchus my fellow prisoner greets you, and Mark the cousin of Barnabas (concerning whom you have received instructions—if he comes to you, welcome him), [11]and Jesus who is called Justus. These are the only men of the circumcision among my fellow workers for the kingdom of God, and they have been a comfort to me. [12]Epaphras, who is one of you, a servant of Christ Jesus, greets you, always struggling on your behalf in his prayers, that you may stand mature and fully assured in all the will of God. [13]For I bear him witness that he has worked hard for you and for those in Laodicea and in Hierapolis. [14]Luke the beloved physician greets you, as does Demas. [15]Give my greetings to the brothers[3] at Laodicea, and to Nympha and the church in her house. [16]And when this letter has been read among you, have it also read in the church of the Laodiceans; and see that you also read the letter from Laodicea. [17]And say to Archippus, "See that you fulfill the ministry that you have received in the Lord."

[18]I, Paul, write this greeting with my own hand. Remember my chains. Grace be with you.

Ezekiel 47

Then he brought me back to the door of the temple, and behold, water was issuing from below the threshold of the temple toward the east (for the temple faced east). The water was flowing down from below the south end of the threshold of the temple, south of the altar. [2]Then he brought me out by way of the north gate and led me around on the outside to the outer gate that faces toward the east; and behold, the water was trickling out on the south side.

[3]Going on eastward with a measuring line in his hand, the man measured a thousand cubits,[4] and then led me through the water, and it was ankle-deep. [4]Again he measured a thousand, and led me through the water, and it was knee-deep. Again he measured a thousand, and led me through the water, and it was waist-deep. [5]Again he measured a thousand, and it was a river that I could not pass through, for the water had risen. It was deep enough to swim in, a river that could not be passed through. [6]And he said to me, "Son of man, have you seen this?"

Then he led me back to the bank of the river. [7]As I went back, I saw on the bank of the river very many trees on the one side and on the other. [8]And he said to me, "This water flows

[1] Or soul; also verse 22 [2] Greek fellow bondservant; also verse 12 [3] Or brothers and sisters [4] A cubit was about 18 inches or 45 centimeters

toward the eastern region and goes down into the Arabah, and enters the sea;[1] when the water flows into the sea, the water will become fresh.[2] [9] And wherever the river goes,[3] every living creature that swarms will live, and there will be very many fish. For this water goes there, that the waters of the sea[4] may become fresh; so everything will live where the river goes. [10] Fishermen will stand beside the sea. From Engedi to Eneglaim it will be a place for the spreading of nets. Its fish will be of very many kinds, like the fish of the Great Sea.[5] [11] But its swamps and marshes will not become fresh; they are to be left for salt. [12] And on the banks, on both sides of the river, there will grow all kinds of trees for food. Their leaves will not wither, nor their fruit fail, but they will bear fresh fruit every month, because the water for them flows from the sanctuary. Their fruit will be for food, and their leaves for healing."

[13] Thus says the Lord God: "This is the boundary[6] by which you shall divide the land for inheritance among the twelve tribes of Israel. Joseph shall have two portions. [14] And you shall divide equally what I swore to give to your fathers. This land shall fall to you as your inheritance.

[15] "This shall be the boundary of the land: On the north side, from the Great Sea by way of Hethlon to Lebo-hamath, and on to Zedad,[7] [16] Berothah, Sibraim (which lies on the border between Damascus and Hamath), as far as Hazer-hatticon, which is on the border of Hauran. [17] So the boundary shall run from the sea to Hazar-enan, which is on the northern border of Damascus, with the border of Hamath to the north.[8] This shall be the north side.[9]

[18] "On the east side, the boundary shall run between Hauran and Damascus; along the Jordan between Gilead and the land of Israel; to the eastern sea and as far as Tamar.[10] This shall be the east side.

[19] "On the south side, it shall run from Tamar as far as the waters of Meribah-kadesh, from there along the Brook of Egypt[11] to the Great Sea. This shall be the south side.

[20] "On the west side, the Great Sea shall be the boundary to a point opposite Lebo-hamath. This shall be the west side.

[21] "So you shall divide this land among you according to the tribes of Israel. [22] You shall allot it as an inheritance for yourselves and for the sojourners who reside among you and have had children among you. They shall be to you as native-born children of Israel. With you they shall be allotted an inheritance among the tribes of Israel. [23] In whatever tribe the sojourner resides, there you shall assign him his inheritance, declares the Lord God.

Psalm 103

Of David.

B less the Lord, O my soul,
  and all that is within me,
    bless his holy name!
2   Bless the Lord, O my soul,
    and forget not all his benefits,
3   who forgives all your iniquity,
    who heals all your diseases,
4   who redeems your life from the pit,
    who crowns you with steadfast love
      and mercy,
5   who satisfies you with good
    so that your youth is renewed like the
      eagle's.

6   The Lord works righteousness
    and justice for all who are oppressed.
7   He made known his ways to Moses,
    his acts to the people of Israel.
8   The Lord is merciful and gracious,
    slow to anger and abounding in
      steadfast love.
9   He will not always chide,
    nor will he keep his anger forever.
10   He does not deal with us according to
      our sins,
    nor repay us according to our iniquities.
11   For as high as the heavens are above the
      earth,
    so great is his steadfast love toward
      those who fear him;
12   as far as the east is from the west,
    so far does he remove our
      transgressions from us.
13   As a father shows compassion to his
      children,
    so the Lord shows compassion to
      those who fear him.
14   For he knows our frame;[12]
    he remembers that we are dust.

---

[1] That is, the Dead Sea [2] Hebrew *will be healed*; also verses 9, 11 [3] Septuagint, Syriac, Vulgate, Targum; Hebrew *the two rivers go* [4] Hebrew lacks *the waters of the sea* [5] That is, the Mediterranean Sea; also verses 15, 19, 20 [6] Probable reading; Hebrew *The valley of the boundary* [7] Septuagint; Hebrew *the entrance of Zedad, Hamath* [8] The meaning of the Hebrew is uncertain [9] Probable reading; Hebrew *and as for the north side* [10] Compare Syriac; Hebrew *to the eastern sea you shall measure* [11] Hebrew lacks *of Egypt* [12] Or *knows how we are formed*

15 As for man, his days are like grass;
    he flourishes like a flower of the field;
16 for the wind passes over it, and it is gone,
    and its place knows it no more.
17 But the steadfast love of the LORD is from
    everlasting to everlasting on those
    who fear him,
    and his righteousness to children's
    children,
18 to those who keep his covenant
    and remember to do his
    commandments.

19 The LORD has established his throne in
    the heavens,
    and his kingdom rules over all.
20 Bless the LORD, O you his angels,
    you mighty ones who do his word,
    obeying the voice of his word!
21 Bless the LORD, all his hosts,
    his ministers, who do his will!
22 Bless the LORD, all his works,
    in all places of his dominion.
    Bless the LORD, O my soul!

OCTOBER 15

1 Kings 18

After many days the word of the LORD came to Elijah, in the third year, saying, "Go, show yourself to Ahab, and I will send rain upon the earth." ²So Elijah went to show himself to Ahab. Now the famine was severe in Samaria. ³And Ahab called Obadiah, who was over the household. (Now Obadiah feared the LORD greatly, ⁴and when Jezebel cut off the prophets of the LORD, Obadiah took a hundred prophets and hid them by fifties in a cave and fed them with bread and water.) ⁵And Ahab said to Obadiah, "Go through the land to all the springs of water and to all the valleys. Perhaps we may find grass and save the horses and mules alive, and not lose some of the animals." ⁶So they divided the land between them to pass through it. Ahab went in one direction by himself, and Obadiah went in another direction by himself.

⁷And as Obadiah was on the way, behold, Elijah met him. And Obadiah recognized him and fell on his face and said, "Is it you, my lord Elijah?" ⁸And he answered him, "It is I. Go, tell your lord, 'Behold, Elijah is here.'" ⁹And he said, "How have I sinned, that you would give your servant into the hand of Ahab, to kill me? ¹⁰As the LORD your God lives, there is no nation or kingdom where my lord has not sent to seek you. And when they would say, 'He is not here,' he would take an oath of the kingdom or nation, that they had not found you. ¹¹And now you say, 'Go, tell your lord, "Behold, Elijah is here."' ¹²And as soon as I have gone from you, the Spirit of the LORD will carry you I know not where. And so, when I come and tell Ahab and he cannot find you, he will kill me, although I your servant have feared the LORD from my youth. ¹³Has it not been told my lord what I did when Jezebel killed the prophets of the LORD, how I hid a hundred men of the LORD's prophets by fifties in a cave and fed them with bread and water? ¹⁴And now you say, 'Go, tell your lord, "Behold, Elijah is here"'; and he will kill me." ¹⁵And Elijah said, "As the LORD of hosts lives, before whom I stand, I will surely show myself to him today." ¹⁶So Obadiah went to meet Ahab, and told him. And Ahab went to meet Elijah.

¹⁷When Ahab saw Elijah, Ahab said to him, "Is it you, you troubler of Israel?" ¹⁸And he answered, "I have not troubled Israel, but you have, and your father's house, because you have abandoned the commandments of the LORD and followed the Baals. ¹⁹Now therefore send and gather all Israel to me at Mount Carmel, and the 450 prophets of Baal and the 400 prophets of Asherah, who eat at Jezebel's table."

²⁰So Ahab sent to all the people of Israel and gathered the prophets together at Mount Carmel. ²¹And Elijah came near to all the people and said, "How long will you go limping between two different opinions? If the LORD is God, follow him; but if Baal, then follow him." And the people did not answer him a word. ²²Then Elijah said to the people, "I, even I only, am left a prophet of the LORD, but Baal's prophets are 450 men. ²³Let two bulls be given to us, and let them choose one bull for themselves and cut it in pieces and lay it on the wood, but put no fire to it. And I will prepare the other bull and lay it on the wood and put no fire to it. ²⁴And you call upon the name of your god, and I will call upon the name of the LORD, and the God who answers by fire, he is God." And all the people answered, "It is well spoken." ²⁵Then Elijah said to the prophets of Baal, "Choose for yourselves one bull and prepare it first, for you are many, and call upon the name of your god, but put no fire to it." ²⁶And they took the bull that was given them, and they prepared it and called upon the name of Baal from morning until noon, saying, "O Baal, answer us!" But there was no voice, and no one answered. And they limped around the altar that they had made. ²⁷And at noon Elijah mocked them, saying, "Cry aloud, for he is a god. Either he is musing, or he is relieving himself, or he is on a journey, or perhaps he is asleep and must be awakened." ²⁸And they cried aloud and cut themselves after their custom with swords and lances, until the blood gushed out upon them. ²⁹And as midday passed, they raved on until the time of the offering of the oblation, but there was no voice. No one answered; no one paid attention.

³⁰Then Elijah said to all the people, "Come near to me." And all the people came near to him. And he repaired the altar of the LORD that had been thrown down. ³¹Elijah took twelve stones, according to the number of the tribes of the sons of Jacob, to whom the word of the LORD came, saying, "Israel shall be your name," ³²and with the stones he built an altar in the name of the LORD. And he made a trench about the altar, as great as would contain two seahs[1] of seed. ³³And he put the wood in order and cut the bull in pieces and laid it on the wood. And he said, "Fill four jars with water and pour it on the burnt offering and on the wood." ³⁴And he said, "Do it a second time." And they did it a second time. And he said, "Do it a third time." And they did it a third time. ³⁵And the water ran around the altar and filled the trench also with water.

³⁶And at the time of the offering of the oblation, Elijah the prophet came near and said, "O LORD, God of Abraham, Isaac, and Israel, let it be known this day that you are God in Israel, and that I am your servant, and that I have done all these things at your word. ³⁷Answer me, O LORD, answer me, that this people may know that you, O LORD, are God, and that you have turned their hearts back." ³⁸Then the fire of the LORD fell and consumed the burnt offering and the wood and the stones and the dust, and licked up the water that was in the trench. ³⁹And when all the people saw it, they fell on their faces and said, "The LORD, he is God; the LORD, he is God." ⁴⁰And Elijah said to them, "Seize the prophets of Baal; let not one of them escape." And they seized them. And Elijah brought them down to the brook Kishon and slaughtered them there.

⁴¹And Elijah said to Ahab, "Go up, eat and drink, for there is a sound of the rushing of rain." ⁴²So Ahab went up to eat and to drink. And Elijah went up to the top of Mount Carmel. And he bowed himself down on the earth and put his face between his knees. ⁴³And he said to his servant, "Go up now, look toward the sea." And he went up and looked and said, "There is nothing." And he said, "Go again," seven times. ⁴⁴And at the seventh time he said, "Behold, a little cloud like a man's hand is rising from the sea." And he said, "Go up, say to Ahab, 'Prepare your chariot and go down, lest the rain stop you.'" ⁴⁵And in a little while the heavens grew black with clouds and wind, and there was a great rain. And Ahab rode and went to Jezreel. ⁴⁶And the hand of the LORD was on Elijah, and he gathered up his garment and ran before Ahab to the entrance of Jezreel.

1 Thessalonians 1

Paul, Silvanus, and Timothy,

To the church of the Thessalonians in God the Father and the Lord Jesus Christ:

Grace to you and peace.

²We give thanks to God always for all of you, constantly[2] mentioning you in our prayers, ³remembering before our God and Father your

---

[1] A *seah* was about 7 quarts or 7.3 liters [2] Or *without ceasing*

work of faith and labor of love and steadfastness of hope in our Lord Jesus Christ. ⁴For we know, brothers¹ loved by God, that he has chosen you, ⁵because our gospel came to you not only in word, but also in power and in the Holy Spirit and with full conviction. You know what kind of men we proved to be among you for your sake. ⁶And you became imitators of us and of the Lord, for you received the word in much affliction, with the joy of the Holy Spirit, ⁷so that you became an example to all the believers in Macedonia and in Achaia. ⁸For not only has the word of the Lord sounded forth from you in Macedonia and Achaia, but your faith in God has gone forth everywhere, so that we need not say anything. ⁹For they themselves report concerning us the kind of reception we had among you, and how you turned to God from idols to serve the living and true God, ¹⁰and to wait for his Son from heaven, whom he raised from the dead, Jesus who delivers us from the wrath to come.

Ezekiel 48

¹"These are the names of the tribes: Beginning at the northern extreme, beside the way of Hethlon to Lebo-hamath, as far as Hazar-enan (which is on the northern border of Damascus over against Hamath), and² extending from the east side to the west,³ Dan, one portion. ²Adjoining the territory of Dan, from the east side to the west, Asher, one portion. ³Adjoining the territory of Asher, from the east side to the west, Naphtali, one portion. ⁴Adjoining the territory of Naphtali, from the east side to the west, Manasseh, one portion. ⁵Adjoining the territory of Manasseh, from the east side to the west, Ephraim, one portion. ⁶Adjoining the territory of Ephraim, from the east side to the west, Reuben, one portion. ⁷Adjoining the territory of Reuben, from the east side to the west, Judah, one portion.

⁸"Adjoining the territory of Judah, from the east side to the west, shall be the portion which you shall set apart, 25,000 cubits⁴ in breadth, and in length equal to one of the tribal portions, from the east side to the west, with the sanctuary in the midst of it. ⁹The portion that you shall set apart for the LORD shall be 25,000 cubits in length, and 20,000⁵

in breadth. ¹⁰These shall be the allotments of the holy portion: the priests shall have an allotment measuring 25,000 cubits on the northern side, 10,000 cubits in breadth on the western side, 10,000 in breadth on the eastern side, and 25,000 in length on the southern side, with the sanctuary of the LORD in the midst of it. ¹¹This shall be for the consecrated priests, the sons of Zadok, who kept my charge, who did not go astray when the people of Israel went astray, as the Levites did. ¹²And it shall belong to them as a special portion from the holy portion of the land, a most holy place, adjoining the territory of the Levites. ¹³And alongside the territory of the priests, the Levites shall have an allotment 25,000 cubits in length and 10,000 in breadth. The whole length shall be 25,000 cubits and the breadth 20,000.⁶ ¹⁴They shall not sell or exchange any of it. They shall not alienate this choice portion of the land, for it is holy to the LORD.

¹⁵"The remainder, 5,000 cubits in breadth and 25,000 in length, shall be for common use for the city, for dwellings and for open country. In the midst of it shall be the city, ¹⁶and these shall be its measurements: the north side 4,500 cubits, the south side 4,500, the east side 4,500, and the west side 4,500. ¹⁷And the city shall have open land: on the north 250 cubits, on the south 250, on the east 250, and on the west 250. ¹⁸The remainder of the length alongside the holy portion shall be 10,000 cubits to the east, and 10,000 to the west, and it shall be alongside the holy portion. Its produce shall be food for the workers of the city. ¹⁹And the workers of the city, from all the tribes of Israel, shall till it. ²⁰The whole portion that you shall set apart shall be 25,000 cubits square, that is, the holy portion together with the property of the city.

²¹"What remains on both sides of the holy portion and of the property of the city shall belong to the prince. Extending from the 25,000 cubits of the holy portion to the east border, and westward from the 25,000 cubits to the west border, parallel to the tribal portions, it shall belong to the prince. The holy portion with the sanctuary of the temple shall be in its midst. ²²It shall be separate from the property of the Levites and the property of the city, which are in the midst of that which belongs

to the prince. The portion of the prince shall lie between the territory of Judah and the territory of Benjamin.

²³ "As for the rest of the tribes: from the east side to the west, Benjamin, one portion. ²⁴ Adjoining the territory of Benjamin, from the east side to the west, Simeon, one portion. ²⁵ Adjoining the territory of Simeon, from the east side to the west, Issachar, one portion. ²⁶ Adjoining the territory of Issachar, from the east side to the west, Zebulun, one portion. ²⁷ Adjoining the territory of Zebulun, from the east side to the west, Gad, one portion. ²⁸ And adjoining the territory of Gad to the south, the boundary shall run from Tamar to the waters of Meribah-kadesh, from there along the Brook of Egypt¹ to the Great Sea.² ²⁹ This is the land that you shall allot as an inheritance among the tribes of Israel, and these are their portions, declares the Lord God.

³⁰ "These shall be the exits of the city: On the north side, which is to be 4,500 cubits by measure, ³¹ three gates, the gate of Reuben, the gate of Judah, and the gate of Levi, the gates of the city being named after the tribes of Israel. ³² On the east side, which is to be 4,500 cubits, three gates, the gate of Joseph, the gate of Benjamin, and the gate of Dan. ³³ On the south side, which is to be 4,500 cubits by measure, three gates, the gate of Simeon, the gate of Issachar, and the gate of Zebulun. ³⁴ On the west side, which is to be 4,500 cubits, three gates,³ the gate of Gad, the gate of Asher, and the gate of Naphtali. ³⁵ The circumference of the city shall be 18,000 cubits. And the name of the city from that time on shall be, The Lord Is There."

Psalm 104

Bless the Lord, O my soul!
  O Lord my God, you are very great!
    You are clothed with splendor and
      majesty,
²   covering yourself with light as with a
      garment,
    stretching out the heavens like a tent.
³   He lays the beams of his chambers on
      the waters;
    he makes the clouds his chariot;
    he rides on the wings of the wind;
⁴   he makes his messengers winds,
    his ministers a flaming fire.

5   He set the earth on its foundations,
    so that it should never be moved.
6   You covered it with the deep as with a
      garment;
    the waters stood above the mountains.
7   At your rebuke they fled;
    at the sound of your thunder they
      took to flight.
8   The mountains rose, the valleys sank
      down
    to the place that you appointed for
      them.
9   You set a boundary that they may not
      pass,
    so that they might not again cover the
      earth.

10   You make springs gush forth in the
      valleys;
    they flow between the hills;
11   they give drink to every beast of the field;
    the wild donkeys quench their thirst.
12   Beside them the birds of the heavens
      dwell;
    they sing among the branches.
13   From your lofty abode you water the
      mountains;
    the earth is satisfied with the fruit of
      your work.

14   You cause the grass to grow for the
      livestock
    and plants for man to cultivate,
  that he may bring forth food from the
      earth
15   and wine to gladden the heart of man,
    oil to make his face shine
    and bread to strengthen man's heart.

16   The trees of the Lord are watered
      abundantly,
    the cedars of Lebanon that he planted.
17   In them the birds build their nests;
    the stork has her home in the fir trees.
18   The high mountains are for the wild
      goats;
    the rocks are a refuge for the rock
      badgers.

19   He made the moon to mark the seasons;⁴
    the sun knows its time for setting.
20   You make darkness, and it is night,
    when all the beasts of the forest creep
      about.

¹ Hebrew lacks *of Egypt* ² That is, the Mediterranean Sea ³ One Hebrew manuscript, Syriac (compare Septuagint); most Hebrew manuscripts *their gates three* ⁴ Or *the appointed times* (compare Genesis 1:14)

21 The young lions roar for their prey,
     seeking their food from God.
22 When the sun rises, they steal away
     and lie down in their dens.
23 Man goes out to his work
     and to his labor until the evening.

24 O Lord, how manifold are your works!
     In wisdom have you made them all;
     the earth is full of your creatures.
25 Here is the sea, great and wide,
     which teems with creatures
          innumerable,
     living things both small and great.
26 There go the ships,
     and Leviathan, which you formed to
          play in it.[1]

27 These all look to you,
     to give them their food in due season.
28 When you give it to them, they gather it
          up;
     when you open your hand, they are
          filled with good things.

29 When you hide your face, they are
          dismayed;
     when you take away their breath, they
          die
     and return to their dust.
30 When you send forth your Spirit,[2] they
          are created,
     and you renew the face of the ground.

31 May the glory of the Lord endure
          forever;
     may the Lord rejoice in his works,
32 who looks on the earth and it trembles,
     who touches the mountains and they
          smoke!
33 I will sing to the Lord as long as I live;
     I will sing praise to my God while I
          have being.
34 May my meditation be pleasing to him,
     for I rejoice in the Lord.
35 Let sinners be consumed from the earth,
     and let the wicked be no more!
     Bless the Lord, O my soul!
     Praise the Lord!

OCTOBER 16

1 Kings 19

Ahab told Jezebel all that Elijah had done, and how he had killed all the prophets with the sword. [2]Then Jezebel sent a messenger to Elijah, saying, "So may the gods do to me and more also, if I do not make your life as the life of one of them by this time tomorrow." [3]Then he was afraid, and he arose and ran for his life and came to Beersheba, which belongs to Judah, and left his servant there.

[4]But he himself went a day's journey into the wilderness and came and sat down under a broom tree. And he asked that he might die, saying, "It is enough; now, O Lord, take away my life, for I am no better than my fathers." [5]And he lay down and slept under a broom tree. And behold, an angel touched him and said to him, "Arise and eat." [6]And he looked, and behold, there was at his head a cake baked on hot stones and a jar of water. And he ate and drank and lay down again. [7]And the angel of the Lord came again a second time and touched him and said, "Arise and eat, for the journey is too great for you." [8]And he arose and ate and drank, and went in the strength of that food forty days and forty nights to Horeb, the mount of God.

[9]There he came to a cave and lodged in it. And behold, the word of the Lord came to him, and he said to him, "What are you doing here, Elijah?" [10]He said, "I have been very jealous for the Lord, the God of hosts. For the people of Israel have forsaken your covenant, thrown down your altars, and killed your prophets with the sword, and I, even I only, am left, and they seek my life, to take it away." [11]And he said, "Go out and stand on the mount before the Lord."

[1] Or you formed to play with [2] Or breath

And behold, the LORD passed by, and a great and strong wind tore the mountains and broke in pieces the rocks before the LORD, but the LORD was not in the wind. And after the wind an earthquake, but the LORD was not in the earthquake. ¹²And after the earthquake a fire, but the LORD was not in the fire. And after the fire the sound of a low whisper.¹ ¹³And when Elijah heard it, he wrapped his face in his cloak and went out and stood at the entrance of the cave. And behold, there came a voice to him and said, "What are you doing here, Elijah?" ¹⁴He said, "I have been very jealous for the LORD, the God of hosts. For the people of Israel have forsaken your covenant, thrown down your altars, and killed your prophets with the sword, and I, even I only, am left, and they seek my life, to take it away." ¹⁵And the LORD said to him, "Go, return on your way to the wilderness of Damascus. And when you arrive, you shall anoint Hazael to be king over Syria. ¹⁶And Jehu the son of Nimshi you shall anoint to be king over Israel, and Elisha the son of Shaphat of Abel-meholah you shall anoint to be prophet in your place. ¹⁷And the one who escapes from the sword of Hazael shall Jehu put to death, and the one who escapes from the sword of Jehu shall Elisha put to death. ¹⁸Yet I will leave seven thousand in Israel, all the knees that have not bowed to Baal, and every mouth that has not kissed him."

¹⁹So he departed from there and found Elisha the son of Shaphat, who was plowing with twelve yoke of oxen in front of him, and he was with the twelfth. Elijah passed by him and cast his cloak upon him. ²⁰And he left the oxen and ran after Elijah and said, "Let me kiss my father and my mother, and then I will follow you." And he said to him, "Go back again, for what have I done to you?" ²¹And he returned from following him and took the yoke of oxen and sacrificed them and boiled their flesh with the yokes of the oxen and gave it to the people, and they ate. Then he arose and went after Elijah and assisted him.

1 Thessalonians 2

For you yourselves know, brothers,² that our coming to you was not in vain. ²But though we had already suffered and been shamefully treated at Philippi, as you know, we had boldness in our God to declare to you the gospel of God in the midst of much conflict. ³For our appeal does not spring from error or impurity or any attempt to deceive, ⁴but just as we have been approved by God to be entrusted with the gospel, so we speak, not to please man, but to please God who tests our hearts. ⁵For we never came with words of flattery,³ as you know, nor with a pretext for greed—God is witness. ⁶Nor did we seek glory from people, whether from you or from others, though we could have made demands as apostles of Christ. ⁷But we were gentle⁴ among you, like a nursing mother taking care of her own children. ⁸So, being affectionately desirous of you, we were ready to share with you not only the gospel of God but also our own selves, because you had become very dear to us.

⁹For you remember, brothers, our labor and toil: we worked night and day, that we might not be a burden to any of you, while we proclaimed to you the gospel of God. ¹⁰You are witnesses, and God also, how holy and righteous and blameless was our conduct toward you believers. ¹¹For you know how, like a father with his children, ¹²we exhorted each one of you and encouraged you and charged you to walk in a manner worthy of God, who calls you into his own kingdom and glory.

¹³And we also thank God constantly⁵ for this, that when you received the word of God, which you heard from us, you accepted it not as the word of men⁶ but as what it really is, the word of God, which is at work in you believers. ¹⁴For you, brothers, became imitators of the churches of God in Christ Jesus that are in Judea. For you suffered the same things from your own countrymen as they did from the Jews,⁷ ¹⁵who killed both the Lord Jesus and the prophets, and drove us out, and displease God and oppose all mankind ¹⁶by hindering us from speaking to the Gentiles that they might be saved—so as always to fill up the measure of their sins. But wrath has come upon them at last!⁸

¹⁷But since we were torn away from you, brothers, for a short time, in person not in heart, we endeavored the more eagerly and with great desire to see you face to face, ¹⁸because we wanted to come to you—I, Paul, again and again—but Satan hindered us. ¹⁹For

¹ Or a sound, a thin silence ² Or brothers and sisters; also verses 9, 14, 17 ³ Or with a flattering speech ⁴ Some manuscripts infants ⁵ Or without ceasing ⁶ The Greek word anthropoi can refer to both men and women ⁷ The Greek word Ioudaioi can refer to Jewish religious leaders and others under their influence, who opposed the Christian faith in that time ⁸ Or completely, or forever

what is our hope or joy or crown of boasting before our Lord Jesus at his coming? Is it not you? ²⁰For you are our glory and joy.

Daniel 1

In the third year of the reign of Jehoiakim king of Judah, Nebuchadnezzar king of Babylon came to Jerusalem and besieged it. ²And the Lord gave Jehoiakim king of Judah into his hand, with some of the vessels of the house of God. And he brought them to the land of Shinar, to the house of his god, and placed the vessels in the treasury of his god. ³Then the king commanded Ashpenaz, his chief eunuch, to bring some of the people of Israel, both of the royal family¹ and of the nobility, ⁴youths without blemish, of good appearance and skillful in all wisdom, endowed with knowledge, understanding learning, and competent to stand in the king's palace, and to teach them the literature and language of the Chaldeans. ⁵The king assigned them a daily portion of the food that the king ate, and of the wine that he drank. They were to be educated for three years, and at the end of that time they were to stand before the king. ⁶Among these were Daniel, Hananiah, Mishael, and Azariah of the tribe of Judah. ⁷And the chief of the eunuchs gave them names: Daniel he called Belteshazzar, Hananiah he called Shadrach, Mishael he called Meshach, and Azariah he called Abednego.

⁸But Daniel resolved that he would not defile himself with the king's food, or with the wine that he drank. Therefore he asked the chief of the eunuchs to allow him not to defile himself. ⁹And God gave Daniel favor and compassion in the sight of the chief of the eunuchs, ¹⁰and the chief of the eunuchs said to Daniel, "I fear my lord the king, who assigned your food and your drink; for why should he see that you were in worse condition than the youths who are of your own age? So you would endanger my head with the king." ¹¹Then Daniel said to the steward whom the chief of the eunuchs had assigned over Daniel, Hananiah, Mishael, and Azariah, ¹²"Test your servants for ten days; let us be given vegetables to eat and water to drink. ¹³Then let our appearance and the appearance of the youths who eat the king's food be observed by you, and deal with your servants according to what you see." ¹⁴So he listened

¹ Hebrew of the seed of the kingdom

to them in this matter, and tested them for ten days. ¹⁵At the end of ten days it was seen that they were better in appearance and fatter in flesh than all the youths who ate the king's food. ¹⁶So the steward took away their food and the wine they were to drink, and gave them vegetables.

¹⁷As for these four youths, God gave them learning and skill in all literature and wisdom, and Daniel had understanding in all visions and dreams. ¹⁸At the end of the time, when the king had commanded that they should be brought in, the chief of the eunuchs brought them in before Nebuchadnezzar. ¹⁹And the king spoke with them, and among all of them none was found like Daniel, Hananiah, Mishael, and Azariah. Therefore they stood before the king. ²⁰And in every matter of wisdom and understanding about which the king inquired of them, he found them ten times better than all the magicians and enchanters that were in all his kingdom. ²¹And Daniel was there until the first year of King Cyrus.

Psalm 105

Oh give thanks to the Lord; call upon his name;
  make known his deeds among the peoples!
2 Sing to him, sing praises to him;
  tell of all his wondrous works!
3 Glory in his holy name;
  let the hearts of those who seek the Lord rejoice!
4 Seek the Lord and his strength;
  seek his presence continually!
5 Remember the wondrous works that he has done,
  his miracles, and the judgments he uttered,
6 O offspring of Abraham, his servant, children of Jacob, his chosen ones!
7 He is the Lord our God;
  his judgments are in all the earth.
8 He remembers his covenant forever, the word that he commanded, for a thousand generations,
9 the covenant that he made with Abraham, his sworn promise to Isaac,

10 which he confirmed to Jacob as a statute,
   to Israel as an everlasting covenant,

11 saying, "To you I will give the land of Canaan
   as your portion for an inheritance."

12 When they were few in number,
   of little account, and sojourners in it,

13 wandering from nation to nation,
   from one kingdom to another people,

14 he allowed no one to oppress them;
   he rebuked kings on their account,

15 saying, "Touch not my anointed ones,
   do my prophets no harm!"

16 When he summoned a famine on the land
   and broke all supply[1] of bread,

17 he had sent a man ahead of them,
   Joseph, who was sold as a slave.

18 His feet were hurt with fetters;
   his neck was put in a collar of iron;

19 until what he had said came to pass,
   the word of the LORD tested him.

20 The king sent and released him;
   the ruler of the peoples set him free;

21 he made him lord of his house
   and ruler of all his possessions,

22 to bind[2] his princes at his pleasure
   and to teach his elders wisdom.

23 Then Israel came to Egypt;
   Jacob sojourned in the land of Ham.

24 And the LORD made his people very fruitful
   and made them stronger than their foes.

25 He turned their hearts to hate his people,
   to deal craftily with his servants.

26 He sent Moses, his servant,
   and Aaron, whom he had chosen.

27 They performed his signs among them
   and miracles in the land of Ham.

28 He sent darkness, and made the land dark;
   they did not rebel[3] against his words.

29 He turned their waters into blood
   and caused their fish to die.

30 Their land swarmed with frogs,
   even in the chambers of their kings.

31 He spoke, and there came swarms of flies,
   and gnats throughout their country.

32 He gave them hail for rain,
   and fiery lightning bolts through their land.

33 He struck down their vines and fig trees,
   and shattered the trees of their country.

34 He spoke, and the locusts came,
   young locusts without number,

35 which devoured all the vegetation in their land
   and ate up the fruit of their ground.

36 He struck down all the firstborn in their land,
   the firstfruits of all their strength.

37 Then he brought out Israel with silver and gold,
   and there was none among his tribes who stumbled.

38 Egypt was glad when they departed,
   for dread of them had fallen upon it.

39 He spread a cloud for a covering,
   and fire to give light by night.

40 They asked, and he brought quail,
   and gave them bread from heaven in abundance.

41 He opened the rock, and water gushed out;
   it flowed through the desert like a river.

42 For he remembered his holy promise,
   and Abraham, his servant.

43 So he brought his people out with joy,
   his chosen ones with singing.

44 And he gave them the lands of the nations,
   and they took possession of the fruit of the peoples' toil,

45 that they might keep his statutes
   and observe his laws.
   Praise the LORD!

[1] Hebrew *staff* [2] Septuagint, Syriac, Jerome *instruct* [3] Septuagint, Syriac omit *not*

OCTOBER 17

1 Kings 20

Ben-hadad the king of Syria gathered all his army together. Thirty-two kings were with him, and horses and chariots. And he went up and closed in on Samaria and fought against it. ²And he sent messengers into the city to Ahab king of Israel and said to him, "Thus says Ben-hadad: ³ 'Your silver and your gold are mine; your best wives and children also are mine.' " ⁴And the king of Israel answered, "As you say, my lord, O king, I am yours, and all that I have." ⁵The messengers came again and said, "Thus says Ben-hadad: 'I sent to you, saying, "Deliver to me your silver and your gold, your wives and your children." ⁶Nevertheless I will send my servants to you tomorrow about this time, and they shall search your house and the houses of your servants and lay hands on whatever pleases you and take it away.' " ⁷Then the king of Israel called all the elders of the land and said, "Mark, now, and see how this man is seeking trouble, for he sent to me for my wives and my children, and for my silver and my gold, and I did not refuse him." ⁸And all the elders and all the people said to him, "Do not listen or consent." ⁹So he said to the messengers of Ben-hadad, "Tell my lord the king, 'All that you first demanded of your servant I will do, but this thing I cannot do.' " And the messengers departed and brought him word again. ¹⁰Ben-hadad sent to him and said, "The gods do so to me and more also, if the dust of Samaria shall suffice for handfuls for all the people who follow me." ¹¹And the king of Israel answered, "Tell him, 'Let not him who straps on his armor boast himself as he who takes it off.' " ¹²When Ben-hadad heard this message as he was drinking with the kings in the booths, he said to his men, "Take your positions." And they took their positions against the city.

¹³And behold, a prophet came near to Ahab king of Israel and said, "Thus says the LORD, Have you seen all this great multitude? Behold, I will give it into your hand this day, and you shall know that I am the LORD." ¹⁴And Ahab said, "By whom?" He said, "Thus says the LORD, By the servants of the governors of the districts." Then he said, "Who shall begin the battle?" He answered, "You." ¹⁵Then he mustered the servants of the governors of the districts, and they were 232. And after them he mustered all the people of Israel, seven thousand.

¹⁶And they went out at noon, while Ben-hadad was drinking himself drunk in the booths, he and the thirty-two kings who helped him. ¹⁷The servants of the governors of the districts went out first. And Ben-hadad sent out scouts, and they reported to him, "Men are coming out from Samaria." ¹⁸He said, "If they have come out for peace, take them alive. Or if they have come out for war, take them alive."

¹⁹So these went out of the city, the servants of the governors of the districts and the army that followed them. ²⁰And each struck down his man. The Syrians fled, and Israel pursued them, but Ben-hadad king of Syria escaped on a horse with horsemen. ²¹And the king of Israel went out and struck the horses and chariots, and struck the Syrians with a great blow.

²²Then the prophet came near to the king of Israel and said to him, "Come, strengthen yourself, and consider well what you have to do, for in the spring the king of Syria will come up against you."

²³And the servants of the king of Syria said to him, "Their gods are gods of the hills, and so they were stronger than we. But let us fight against them in the plain, and surely we shall be stronger than they. ²⁴And do this: remove the kings, each from his post, and put commanders in their places, ²⁵and muster an army like the army that you have lost, horse for horse, and chariot for chariot. Then we will fight against them in the plain, and surely we shall be stronger than they." And he listened to their voice and did so.

²⁶In the spring, Ben-hadad mustered the Syrians and went up to Aphek to fight against Israel. ²⁷And the people of Israel were mustered

and were provisioned and went against them. The people of Israel encamped before them like two little flocks of goats, but the Syrians filled the country. [28]And a man of God came near and said to the king of Israel, "Thus says the LORD, 'Because the Syrians have said, "The LORD is a god of the hills but he is not a god of the valleys," therefore I will give all this great multitude into your hand, and you shall know that I am the LORD.'" [29]And they encamped opposite one another seven days. Then on the seventh day the battle was joined. And the people of Israel struck down of the Syrians 100,000 foot soldiers in one day. [30]And the rest fled into the city of Aphek, and the wall fell upon 27,000 men who were left.

Ben-hadad also fled and entered an inner chamber in the city. [31]And his servants said to him, "Behold now, we have heard that the kings of the house of Israel are merciful kings. Let us put sackcloth around our waists and ropes on our heads and go out to the king of Israel. Perhaps he will spare your life." [32]So they tied sackcloth around their waists and put ropes on their heads and went to the king of Israel and said, "Your servant Ben-hadad says, 'Please, let me live.'" And he said, "Does he still live? He is my brother." [33]Now the men were watching for a sign, and they quickly took it up from him and said, "Yes, your brother Ben-hadad." Then he said, "Go and bring him." Then Ben-hadad came out to him, and he caused him to come up into the chariot. [34]And Ben-hadad said to him, "The cities that my father took from your father I will restore, and you may establish bazaars for yourself in Damascus, as my father did in Samaria." And Ahab said, "I will let you go on these terms." So he made a covenant with him and let him go.

[35]And a certain man of the sons of the prophets said to his fellow at the command of the LORD, "Strike me, please." But the man refused to strike him. [36]Then he said to him, "Because you have not obeyed the voice of the LORD, behold, as soon as you have gone from me, a lion shall strike you down." And as soon as he had departed from him, a lion met him and struck him down. [37]Then he found another man and said, "Strike me, please." And the man struck him—struck him and wounded him. [38]So the prophet departed and waited for the king by the way, disguising himself with a bandage over his eyes. [39]And as the king passed, he cried to the king and said, "Your servant went out into the midst of the battle, and behold, a soldier turned and brought a man to me and said, 'Guard this man; if by any means he is missing, your life shall be for his life, or else you shall pay a talent[1] of silver.' [40]And as your servant was busy here and there, he was gone." The king of Israel said to him, "So shall your judgment be; you yourself have decided it." [41]Then he hurried to take the bandage away from his eyes, and the king of Israel recognized him as one of the prophets. [42]And he said to him, "Thus says the LORD, 'Because you have let go out of your hand the man whom I had devoted to destruction,[2] therefore your life shall be for his life, and your people for his people.'" [43]And the king of Israel went to his house vexed and sullen and came to Samaria.

1 Thessalonians 3

Therefore when we could bear it no longer, we were willing to be left behind at Athens alone, [2]and we sent Timothy, our brother and God's coworker[3] in the gospel of Christ, to establish and exhort you in your faith, [3]that no one be moved by these afflictions. For you yourselves know that we are destined for this. [4]For when we were with you, we kept telling you beforehand that we were to suffer affliction, just as it has come to pass, and just as you know. [5]For this reason, when I could bear it no longer, I sent to learn about your faith, for fear that somehow the tempter had tempted you and our labor would be in vain.

[6]But now that Timothy has come to us from you, and has brought us the good news of your faith and love and reported that you always remember us kindly and long to see us, as we long to see you— [7]for this reason, brothers,[4] in all our distress and affliction we have been comforted about you through your faith. [8]For now we live, if you are standing fast in the Lord. [9]For what thanksgiving can we return to God for you, for all the joy that we feel for your sake before our God, [10]as we pray most earnestly night and day that we may see you face to face and supply what is lacking in your faith?

[11]Now may our God and Father himself, and our Lord Jesus, direct our way to you, [12]and may the Lord make you increase and abound in love

[1] A *talent* was about 75 pounds or 34 kilograms [2] That is, set apart (devoted) as an offering to the Lord (for destruction) [3] Some manuscripts *servant* [4] Or *brothers and sisters*

for one another and for all, as we do for you, [13] so that he may establish your hearts blameless in holiness before our God and Father, at the coming of our Lord Jesus with all his saints.

Daniel 2

In the second year of the reign of Nebuchadnezzar, Nebuchadnezzar had dreams; his spirit was troubled, and his sleep left him. [2] Then the king commanded that the magicians, the enchanters, the sorcerers, and the Chaldeans be summoned to tell the king his dreams. So they came in and stood before the king. [3] And the king said to them, "I had a dream, and my spirit is troubled to know the dream." [4] Then the Chaldeans said to the king in Aramaic,[1] "O king, live forever! Tell your servants the dream, and we will show the interpretation." [5] The king answered and said to the Chaldeans, "The word from me is firm: if you do not make known to me the dream and its interpretation, you shall be torn limb from limb, and your houses shall be laid in ruins. [6] But if you show the dream and its interpretation, you shall receive from me gifts and rewards and great honor. Therefore show me the dream and its interpretation." [7] They answered a second time and said, "Let the king tell his servants the dream, and we will show its interpretation." [8] The king answered and said, "I know with certainty that you are trying to gain time, because you see that the word from me is firm— [9] if you do not make the dream known to me, there is but one sentence for you. You have agreed to speak lying and corrupt words before me till the times change. Therefore tell me the dream, and I shall know that you can show me its interpretation." [10] The Chaldeans answered the king and said, "There is not a man on earth who can meet the king's demand, for no great and powerful king has asked such a thing of any magician or enchanter or Chaldean. [11] The thing that the king asks is difficult, and no one can show it to the king except the gods, whose dwelling is not with flesh."

[12] Because of this the king was angry and very furious, and commanded that all the wise men of Babylon be destroyed. [13] So the decree went out, and the wise men were about to be killed; and they sought Daniel and his companions, to kill them. [14] Then Daniel replied with prudence and discretion to Arioch, the captain of the king's guard, who had gone out to kill the wise men of Babylon. [15] He declared[2] to Arioch, the king's captain, "Why is the decree of the king so urgent?" Then Arioch made the matter known to Daniel. [16] And Daniel went in and requested the king to appoint him a time, that he might show the interpretation to the king.

[17] Then Daniel went to his house and made the matter known to Hananiah, Mishael, and Azariah, his companions, [18] and told them to seek mercy from the God of heaven concerning this mystery, so that Daniel and his companions might not be destroyed with the rest of the wise men of Babylon. [19] Then the mystery was revealed to Daniel in a vision of the night. Then Daniel blessed the God of heaven. [20] Daniel answered and said:

> "Blessed be the name of God forever and
>   ever,
>   to whom belong wisdom and might.
> [21] He changes times and seasons;
>   he removes kings and sets up kings;
>   he gives wisdom to the wise
>   and knowledge to those who have
>   understanding;
> [22] he reveals deep and hidden things;
>   he knows what is in the darkness,
>   and the light dwells with him.
> [23] To you, O God of my fathers,
>   I give thanks and praise,
> for you have given me wisdom and
>   might,
>   and have now made known to me
>   what we asked of you,
>   for you have made known to us the
>   king's matter."

[24] Therefore Daniel went in to Arioch, whom the king had appointed to destroy the wise men of Babylon. He went and said thus to him: "Do not destroy the wise men of Babylon; bring me in before the king, and I will show the king the interpretation."

[25] Then Arioch brought in Daniel before the king in haste and said thus to him: "I have found among the exiles from Judah a man who will make known to the king the interpretation." [26] The king declared to Daniel, whose name was Belteshazzar, "Are you able to make known to me the dream that I have seen and its interpretation?" [27] Daniel answered the king

---

[1] The text from this point to the end of chapter 7 is in Aramaic [2] Aramaic *answered and said*; also verse 26

and said, "No wise men, enchanters, magicians, or astrologers can show to the king the mystery that the king has asked, [28]but there is a God in heaven who reveals mysteries, and he has made known to King Nebuchadnezzar what will be in the latter days. Your dream and the visions of your head as you lay in bed are these: [29]To you, O king, as you lay in bed came thoughts of what would be after this, and he who reveals mysteries made known to you what is to be. [30]But as for me, this mystery has been revealed to me, not because of any wisdom that I have more than all the living, but in order that the interpretation may be made known to the king, and that you may know the thoughts of your mind.

[31]"You saw, O king, and behold, a great image. This image, mighty and of exceeding brightness, stood before you, and its appearance was frightening. [32]The head of this image was of fine gold, its chest and arms of silver, its middle and thighs of bronze, [33]its legs of iron, its feet partly of iron and partly of clay. [34]As you looked, a stone was cut out by no human hand, and it struck the image on its feet of iron and clay, and broke them in pieces. [35]Then the iron, the clay, the bronze, the silver, and the gold, all together were broken in pieces, and became like the chaff of the summer threshing floors; and the wind carried them away, so that not a trace of them could be found. But the stone that struck the image became a great mountain and filled the whole earth.

[36]"This was the dream. Now we will tell the king its interpretation. [37]You, O king, the king of kings, to whom the God of heaven has given the kingdom, the power, and the might, and the glory, [38]and into whose hand he has given, wherever they dwell, the children of man, the beasts of the field, and the birds of the heavens, making you rule over them all—you are the head of gold. [39]Another kingdom inferior to you shall arise after you, and yet a third kingdom of bronze, which shall rule over all the earth. [40]And there shall be a fourth kingdom, strong as iron, because iron breaks to pieces and shatters all things. And like iron that crushes, it shall break and crush all these. [41]And as you saw the feet and toes, partly of potter's clay and partly of iron, it shall be a divided kingdom, but some of the firmness of iron shall be in it, just as you saw iron mixed with the soft clay. [42]And as the toes of the feet were partly iron and partly clay, so the kingdom shall be partly strong and partly brittle. [43]As you saw the iron mixed with soft clay, so they will mix with one another in marriage,[1] but they will not hold together, just as iron does not mix with clay. [44]And in the days of those kings the God of heaven will set up a kingdom that shall never be destroyed, nor shall the kingdom be left to another people. It shall break in pieces all these kingdoms and bring them to an end, and it shall stand forever, [45]just as you saw that a stone was cut from a mountain by no human hand, and that it broke in pieces the iron, the bronze, the clay, the silver, and the gold. A great God has made known to the king what shall be after this. The dream is certain, and its interpretation sure."

[46]Then King Nebuchadnezzar fell upon his face and paid homage to Daniel, and commanded that an offering and incense be offered up to him. [47]The king answered and said to Daniel, "Truly, your God is God of gods and Lord of kings, and a revealer of mysteries, for you have been able to reveal this mystery." [48]Then the king gave Daniel high honors and many great gifts, and made him ruler over the whole province of Babylon and chief prefect over all the wise men of Babylon. [49]Daniel made a request of the king, and he appointed Shadrach, Meshach, and Abednego over the affairs of the province of Babylon. But Daniel remained at the king's court.

Psalm 106

Praise the LORD!
  Oh give thanks to the LORD, for he is good,
    for his steadfast love endures forever!
2 Who can utter the mighty deeds of the LORD,
    or declare all his praise?
3 Blessed are they who observe justice,
    who do righteousness at all times!

4 Remember me, O LORD, when you show
      favor to your people;
    help me when you save them,[2]
5 that I may look upon the prosperity of
      your chosen ones,
    that I may rejoice in the gladness of
      your nation,
    that I may glory with your inheritance.

[1] Aramaic by the seed of men [2] Or Remember me, O LORD, with the favor you show to your people; help me with your salvation

6 Both we and our fathers have sinned;
  we have committed iniquity; we have
    done wickedness.
7 Our fathers, when they were in Egypt,
    did not consider your wondrous
      works;
  they did not remember the abundance
    of your steadfast love,
    but rebelled by the sea, at the Red
      Sea.
8 Yet he saved them for his name's sake,
    that he might make known his
      mighty power.
9 He rebuked the Red Sea, and it became
    dry,
  and he led them through the deep as
    through a desert.
10 So he saved them from the hand of the
    foe
  and redeemed them from the power
    of the enemy.
11 And the waters covered their
      adversaries;
  not one of them was left.
12 Then they believed his words;
  they sang his praise.
13 But they soon forgot his works;
  they did not wait for his counsel.
14 But they had a wanton craving in the
    wilderness,
  and put God to the test in the desert;
15 he gave them what they asked,
  but sent a wasting disease among
    them.
16 When men in the camp were jealous of
    Moses
  and Aaron, the holy one of the LORD,
17 the earth opened and swallowed up
    Dathan,
  and covered the company of Abiram.
18 Fire also broke out in their company;
  the flame burned up the wicked.
19 They made a calf in Horeb
  and worshiped a metal image.
20 They exchanged the glory of God[1]
  for the image of an ox that eats grass.
21 They forgot God, their Savior,
  who had done great things in Egypt,
22 wondrous works in the land of Ham,
  and awesome deeds by the Red Sea.

23 Therefore he said he would destroy
      them—
  had not Moses, his chosen one,
stood in the breach before him,
  to turn away his wrath from
    destroying them.
24 Then they despised the pleasant land,
  having no faith in his promise.
25 They murmured in their tents,
  and did not obey the voice of the
    LORD.
26 Therefore he raised his hand and swore
    to them
  that he would make them fall in the
    wilderness,
27 and would make their offspring fall
    among the nations,
  scattering them among the lands.
28 Then they yoked themselves to the Baal
    of Peor,
  and ate sacrifices offered to the dead;
29 they provoked the LORD to anger with
    their deeds,
  and a plague broke out among them.
30 Then Phinehas stood up and intervened,
  and the plague was stayed.
31 And that was counted to him as
    righteousness
  from generation to generation forever.
32 They angered him at the waters of
    Meribah,
  and it went ill with Moses on their
    account,
33 for they made his spirit bitter,[2]
  and he spoke rashly with his lips.
34 They did not destroy the peoples,
  as the LORD commanded them,
35 but they mixed with the nations
  and learned to do as they did.
36 They served their idols,
  which became a snare to them.
37 They sacrificed their sons
  and their daughters to the demons;
38 they poured out innocent blood,
  the blood of their sons and daughters,
whom they sacrificed to the idols of
    Canaan,
  and the land was polluted with blood.
39 Thus they became unclean by their acts,
  and played the whore in their deeds.

[1] Hebrew *exchanged their glory* [2] Or *they rebelled against God's Spirit*

40 Then the anger of the LORD was kindled
      against his people,
   and he abhorred his heritage;
41 he gave them into the hand of the nations,
      so that those who hated them ruled
         over them.
42 Their enemies oppressed them,
      and they were brought into subjection
         under their power.
43 Many times he delivered them,
      but they were rebellious in their
         purposes
   and were brought low through their
      iniquity.
44 Nevertheless, he looked upon their
      distress,
   when he heard their cry.

45 For their sake he remembered his
      covenant,
   and relented according to the
      abundance of his steadfast love.
46 He caused them to be pitied
      by all those who held them captive.

47 Save us, O LORD our God,
      and gather us from among the
         nations,
   that we may give thanks to your holy
      name
   and glory in your praise.

48 Blessed be the LORD, the God of Israel,
      from everlasting to everlasting!
   And let all the people say, "Amen!"
      Praise the LORD!

OCTOBER 18

1 Kings 21

Now Naboth the Jezreelite had a vineyard in Jezreel, beside the palace of Ahab king of Samaria. ²And after this Ahab said to Naboth, "Give me your vineyard, that I may have it for a vegetable garden, because it is near my house, and I will give you a better vineyard for it; or, if it seems good to you, I will give you its value in money." ³But Naboth said to Ahab, "The LORD forbid that I should give you the inheritance of my fathers." ⁴And Ahab went into his house vexed and sullen because of what Naboth the Jezreelite had said to him, for he had said, "I will not give you the inheritance of my fathers." And he lay down on his bed and turned away his face and would eat no food.

⁵But Jezebel his wife came to him and said to him, "Why is your spirit so vexed that you eat no food?" ⁶And he said to her, "Because I spoke to Naboth the Jezreelite and said to him, 'Give me your vineyard for money, or else, if it please you, I will give you another vineyard for it.' And he answered, 'I will not give you my vineyard.'" ⁷And Jezebel his wife said to him, "Do you now govern Israel? Arise and eat bread and let your heart be cheerful; I will give you the vineyard of Naboth the Jezreelite."

⁸So she wrote letters in Ahab's name and sealed them with his seal, and she sent the letters to the elders and the leaders who lived with Naboth in his city. ⁹And she wrote in the letters, "Proclaim a fast, and set Naboth at the head of the people. ¹⁰And set two worthless men opposite him, and let them bring a charge against him, saying, 'You have cursed[1] God and the king.' Then take him out and stone him to death." ¹¹And the men of his city, the elders and the leaders who lived in his city, did as Jezebel had sent word to them. As it was written in the letters that she had sent to them, ¹²they proclaimed a fast and set Naboth at the head of the people. ¹³And the two worthless men came in and sat opposite him. And the worthless men brought a charge against Naboth in the presence of the people, saying, "Naboth cursed God and the king." So they took him outside the city and stoned him to death with stones. ¹⁴Then they sent to Jezebel, saying, "Naboth has been stoned; he is dead."

---

[1] Hebrew *blessed*; also verse 13

¹⁵As soon as Jezebel heard that Naboth had been stoned and was dead, Jezebel said to Ahab, "Arise, take possession of the vineyard of Naboth the Jezreelite, which he refused to give you for money, for Naboth is not alive, but dead." ¹⁶And as soon as Ahab heard that Naboth was dead, Ahab arose to go down to the vineyard of Naboth the Jezreelite, to take possession of it.

¹⁷Then the word of the LORD came to Elijah the Tishbite, saying, ¹⁸"Arise, go down to meet Ahab king of Israel, who is in Samaria; behold, he is in the vineyard of Naboth, where he has gone to take possession. ¹⁹And you shall say to him, 'Thus says the LORD, "Have you killed and also taken possession?"' And you shall say to him, 'Thus says the LORD: "In the place where dogs licked up the blood of Naboth shall dogs lick your own blood."'"

²⁰Ahab said to Elijah, "Have you found me, O my enemy?" He answered, "I have found you, because you have sold yourself to do what is evil in the sight of the LORD. ²¹Behold, I will bring disaster upon you. I will utterly burn you up, and will cut off from Ahab every male, bond or free, in Israel. ²²And I will make your house like the house of Jeroboam the son of Nebat, and like the house of Baasha the son of Ahijah, for the anger to which you have provoked me, and because you have made Israel to sin. ²³And of Jezebel the LORD also said, 'The dogs shall eat Jezebel within the walls of Jezreel.' ²⁴Anyone belonging to Ahab who dies in the city the dogs shall eat, and anyone of his who dies in the open country the birds of the heavens shall eat."

²⁵(There was none who sold himself to do what was evil in the sight of the LORD like Ahab, whom Jezebel his wife incited. ²⁶He acted very abominably in going after idols, as the Amorites had done, whom the LORD cast out before the people of Israel.)

²⁷And when Ahab heard those words, he tore his clothes and put sackcloth on his flesh and fasted and lay in sackcloth and went about dejectedly. ²⁸And the word of the LORD came to Elijah the Tishbite, saying, ²⁹"Have you seen how Ahab has humbled himself before me? Because he has humbled himself before me, I will not bring the disaster in his days; but in his son's days I will bring the disaster upon his house."

1 Thessalonians 4

Finally, then, brothers,[1] we ask and urge you in the Lord Jesus, that as you received from us how you ought to walk and to please God, just as you are doing, that you do so more and more. ²For you know what instructions we gave you through the Lord Jesus. ³For this is the will of God, your sanctification:[2] that you abstain from sexual immorality; ⁴that each one of you know how to control his own body[3] in holiness and honor, ⁵not in the passion of lust like the Gentiles who do not know God; ⁶that no one transgress and wrong his brother in this matter, because the Lord is an avenger in all these things, as we told you beforehand and solemnly warned you. ⁷For God has not called us for impurity, but in holiness. ⁸Therefore whoever disregards this, disregards not man but God, who gives his Holy Spirit to you.

⁹Now concerning brotherly love you have no need for anyone to write to you, for you yourselves have been taught by God to love one another, ¹⁰for that indeed is what you are doing to all the brothers throughout Macedonia. But we urge you, brothers, to do this more and more, ¹¹and to aspire to live quietly, and to mind your own affairs, and to work with your hands, as we instructed you, ¹²so that you may walk properly before outsiders and be dependent on no one.

¹³But we do not want you to be uninformed, brothers, about those who are asleep, that you may not grieve as others do who have no hope. ¹⁴For since we believe that Jesus died and rose again, even so, through Jesus, God will bring with him those who have fallen asleep. ¹⁵For this we declare to you by a word from the Lord,[4] that we who are alive, who are left until the coming of the Lord, will not precede those who have fallen asleep. ¹⁶For the Lord himself will descend from heaven with a cry of command, with the voice of an archangel, and with the sound of the trumpet of God. And the dead in Christ will rise first. ¹⁷Then we who are alive, who are left, will be caught up together with them in the clouds to meet the Lord in the air, and so we will always be with the Lord. ¹⁸Therefore encourage one another with these words.

---

[1] Or brothers and sisters; also verses 10, 13 [2] Or your holiness [3] Or how to take a wife for himself; Greek how to possess his own vessel [4] Or by the word of the Lord

Daniel 3

King Nebuchadnezzar made an image of gold, whose height was sixty cubits[1] and its breadth six cubits. He set it up on the plain of Dura, in the province of Babylon. [2]Then King Nebuchadnezzar sent to gather the satraps, the prefects, and the governors, the counselors, the treasurers, the justices, the magistrates, and all the officials of the provinces to come to the dedication of the image that King Nebuchadnezzar had set up. [3]Then the satraps, the prefects, and the governors, the counselors, the treasurers, the justices, the magistrates, and all the officials of the provinces gathered for the dedication of the image that King Nebuchadnezzar had set up. And they stood before the image that Nebuchadnezzar had set up. [4]And the herald proclaimed aloud, "You are commanded, O peoples, nations, and languages, [5]that when you hear the sound of the horn, pipe, lyre, trigon, harp, bagpipe, and every kind of music, you are to fall down and worship the golden image that King Nebuchadnezzar has set up. [6]And whoever does not fall down and worship shall immediately be cast into a burning fiery furnace." [7]Therefore, as soon as all the peoples heard the sound of the horn, pipe, lyre, trigon, harp, bagpipe, and every kind of music, all the peoples, nations, and languages fell down and worshiped the golden image that King Nebuchadnezzar had set up.

[8]Therefore at that time certain Chaldeans came forward and maliciously accused the Jews. [9]They declared[2] to King Nebuchadnezzar, "O king, live forever! [10]You, O king, have made a decree, that every man who hears the sound of the horn, pipe, lyre, trigon, harp, bagpipe, and every kind of music, shall fall down and worship the golden image. [11]And whoever does not fall down and worship shall be cast into a burning fiery furnace. [12]There are certain Jews whom you have appointed over the affairs of the province of Babylon: Shadrach, Meshach, and Abednego. These men, O king, pay no attention to you; they do not serve your gods or worship the golden image that you have set up."

[13]Then Nebuchadnezzar in furious rage commanded that Shadrach, Meshach, and Abednego be brought. So they brought these men before the king. [14]Nebuchadnezzar answered and said to them, "Is it true, O Shadrach, Meshach, and Abednego, that you do not serve my gods or worship the golden image that I have set up? [15]Now if you are ready when you hear the sound of the horn, pipe, lyre, trigon, harp, bagpipe, and every kind of music, to fall down and worship the image that I have made, well and good.[3] But if you do not worship, you shall immediately be cast into a burning fiery furnace. And who is the god who will deliver you out of my hands?"

[16]Shadrach, Meshach, and Abednego answered and said to the king, "O Nebuchadnezzar, we have no need to answer you in this matter. [17]If this be so, our God whom we serve is able to deliver us from the burning fiery furnace, and he will deliver us out of your hand, O king.[4] [18]But if not, be it known to you, O king, that we will not serve your gods or worship the golden image that you have set up."

[19]Then Nebuchadnezzar was filled with fury, and the expression of his face was changed against Shadrach, Meshach, and Abednego. He ordered the furnace heated seven times more than it was usually heated. [20]And he ordered some of the mighty men of his army to bind Shadrach, Meshach, and Abednego, and to cast them into the burning fiery furnace. [21]Then these men were bound in their cloaks, their tunics,[5] their hats, and their other garments, and they were thrown into the burning fiery furnace. [22]Because the king's order was urgent and the furnace overheated, the flame of the fire killed those men who took up Shadrach, Meshach, and Abednego. [23]And these three men, Shadrach, Meshach, and Abednego, fell bound into the burning fiery furnace.

[24]Then King Nebuchadnezzar was astonished and rose up in haste. He declared to his counselors, "Did we not cast three men bound into the fire?" They answered and said to the king, "True, O king." [25]He answered and said, "But I see four men unbound, walking in the midst of the fire, and they are not hurt; and the appearance of the fourth is like a son of the gods."

[26]Then Nebuchadnezzar came near to the door of the burning fiery furnace; he declared, "Shadrach, Meshach, and Abednego, servants of the Most High God, come out, and come here!" Then Shadrach, Meshach, and Abednego came out from the fire. [27]And the satraps, the prefects, the governors, and the king's counselors

[1] A cubit was about 18 inches or 45 centimeters [2] Aramaic answered and said; also verses 24, 26 [3] Aramaic lacks well and good [4] Or If our God whom we serve is able to deliver us, he will deliver us from the burning fiery furnace and out of your hand, O king. [5] The meaning of the Aramaic words rendered cloaks and tunics is uncertain; also verse 27

gathered together and saw that the fire had not had any power over the bodies of those men. The hair of their heads was not singed, their cloaks were not harmed, and no smell of fire had come upon them. ²⁸Nebuchadnezzar answered and said, "Blessed be the God of Shadrach, Meshach, and Abednego, who has sent his angel and delivered his servants, who trusted in him, and set aside[1] the king's command, and yielded up their bodies rather than serve and worship any god except their own God. ²⁹Therefore I make a decree: Any people, nation, or language that speaks anything against the God of Shadrach, Meshach, and Abednego shall be torn limb from limb, and their houses laid in ruins, for there is no other god who is able to rescue in this way." ³⁰Then the king promoted Shadrach, Meshach, and Abednego in the province of Babylon.

──────── Psalm 107 ────────

Oh give thanks to the LORD, for he is good,
    for his steadfast love endures forever!
2   Let the redeemed of the LORD say so,
        whom he has redeemed from
            trouble[2]
3   and gathered in from the lands,
        from the east and from the west,
        from the north and from the south.

4   Some wandered in desert wastes,
        finding no way to a city to dwell in;
5   hungry and thirsty,
        their soul fainted within them.
6   Then they cried to the LORD in their
            trouble,
        and he delivered them from their
            distress.
7   He led them by a straight way
        till they reached a city to dwell in.
8   Let them thank the LORD for his
            steadfast love,
        for his wondrous works to the
            children of man!
9   For he satisfies the longing soul,
        and the hungry soul he fills with good
            things.
10 Some sat in darkness and in the shadow
            of death,
        prisoners in affliction and in irons,

11 for they had rebelled against the words
            of God,
        and spurned the counsel of the Most
            High.
12 So he bowed their hearts down with
            hard labor;
        they fell down, with none to help.
13 Then they cried to the LORD in their
            trouble,
        and he delivered them from their
            distress.
14 He brought them out of darkness and
            the shadow of death,
        and burst their bonds apart.
15 Let them thank the LORD for his
            steadfast love,
        for his wondrous works to the
            children of man!
16 For he shatters the doors of bronze
        and cuts in two the bars of iron.

17 Some were fools through their sinful
            ways,
        and because of their iniquities
            suffered affliction;
18 they loathed any kind of food,
        and they drew near to the gates of
            death.
19 Then they cried to the LORD in their
            trouble,
        and he delivered them from their
            distress.
20 He sent out his word and healed them,
        and delivered them from their
            destruction.
21 Let them thank the LORD for his
            steadfast love,
        for his wondrous works to the
            children of man!
22 And let them offer sacrifices of
            thanksgiving,
        and tell of his deeds in songs of joy!

23 Some went down to the sea in ships,
        doing business on the great waters;
24 they saw the deeds of the LORD,
        his wondrous works in the deep.
25 For he commanded and raised the
            stormy wind,
        which lifted up the waves of the sea.

[1] Aramaic and changed [2] Or from the hand of the foe

26 They mounted up to heaven; they went
    down to the depths;
    their courage melted away in their evil
      plight;
27 they reeled and staggered like drunken
    men
    and were at their wits' end.¹
28 Then they cried to the LORD in their
    trouble,
    and he delivered them from their
      distress.
29 He made the storm be still,
    and the waves of the sea were hushed.
30 Then they were glad that the waters²
    were quiet,
    and he brought them to their desired
      haven.
31 Let them thank the LORD for his
    steadfast love,
    for his wondrous works to the
      children of man!
32 Let them extol him in the congregation
    of the people,
    and praise him in the assembly of the
      elders.
33 He turns rivers into a desert,
    springs of water into thirsty ground,
34 a fruitful land into a salty waste,
    because of the evil of its inhabitants.
35 He turns a desert into pools of water,
    a parched land into springs of water.
36 And there he lets the hungry dwell,
    and they establish a city to live in;
37 they sow fields and plant vineyards
    and get a fruitful yield.
38 By his blessing they multiply greatly,
    and he does not let their livestock
      diminish.
39 When they are diminished and brought
    low
    through oppression, evil, and sorrow,
40 he pours contempt on princes
    and makes them wander in trackless
      wastes;
41 but he raises up the needy out of
    affliction
    and makes their families like flocks.
42 The upright see it and are glad,
    and all wickedness shuts its mouth.
43 Whoever is wise, let him attend to these
    things;
    let them consider the steadfast love of
      the LORD.

OCTOBER 19

1 Kings 22

For three years Syria and Israel continued without war. ²But in the third year Jehoshaphat the king of Judah came down to the king of Israel. ³And the king of Israel said to his servants, "Do you know that Ramoth-gilead belongs to us, and we keep quiet and do not take it out of the hand of the king of Syria?" ⁴And he said to Jehoshaphat, "Will you go with me to battle at Ramoth-gilead?" And Jehoshaphat said to the king of Israel, "I am as you are, my people as your people, my horses as your horses."

⁵And Jehoshaphat said to the king of Israel, "Inquire first for the word of the LORD."

⁶Then the king of Israel gathered the prophets together, about four hundred men, and said to them, "Shall I go to battle against Ramoth-gilead, or shall I refrain?" And they said, "Go up, for the Lord will give it into the hand of the king." ⁷But Jehoshaphat said, "Is there not here another prophet of the LORD of whom we may inquire?" ⁸And the king of Israel said to Jehoshaphat, "There is yet one man by whom we may inquire of the LORD, Micaiah the son of Imlah, but I hate him, for he never prophesies good concerning me, but evil." And Jehoshaphat said, "Let not the king say so." ⁹Then the king of Israel summoned

¹ Hebrew *and all their wisdom was swallowed up* ² Hebrew *they*

an officer and said, "Bring quickly Micaiah the son of Imlah." [10] Now the king of Israel and Jehoshaphat the king of Judah were sitting on their thrones, arrayed in their robes, at the threshing floor at the entrance of the gate of Samaria, and all the prophets were prophesying before them. [11] And Zedekiah the son of Chenaanah made for himself horns of iron and said, "Thus says the LORD, 'With these you shall push the Syrians until they are destroyed.'" [12] And all the prophets prophesied so and said, "Go up to Ramoth-gilead and triumph; the LORD will give it into the hand of the king."

[13] And the messenger who went to summon Micaiah said to him, "Behold, the words of the prophets with one accord are favorable to the king. Let your word be like the word of one of them, and speak favorably." [14] But Micaiah said, "As the LORD lives, what the LORD says to me, that I will speak." [15] And when he had come to the king, the king said to him, "Micaiah, shall we go to Ramoth-gilead to battle, or shall we refrain?" And he answered him, "Go up and triumph; the LORD will give it into the hand of the king." [16] But the king said to him, "How many times shall I make you swear that you speak to me nothing but the truth in the name of the LORD?" [17] And he said, "I saw all Israel scattered on the mountains, as sheep that have no shepherd. And the LORD said, 'These have no master; let each return to his home in peace.'" [18] And the king of Israel said to Jehoshaphat, "Did I not tell you that he would not prophesy good concerning me, but evil?" [19] And Micaiah said, "Therefore hear the word of the LORD: I saw the LORD sitting on his throne, and all the host of heaven standing beside him on his right hand and on his left; [20] and the LORD said, 'Who will entice Ahab, that he may go up and fall at Ramoth-gilead?' And one said one thing, and another said another. [21] Then a spirit came forward and stood before the LORD, saying, 'I will entice him.' [22] And the LORD said to him, 'By what means?' And he said, 'I will go out, and will be a lying spirit in the mouth of all his prophets.' And he said, 'You are to entice him, and you shall succeed; go out and do so.' [23] Now therefore behold, the LORD has put a lying spirit in the mouth of all these your prophets; the LORD has declared disaster for you."

[24] Then Zedekiah the son of Chenaanah came near and struck Micaiah on the cheek and said, "How did the Spirit of the LORD go from me to speak to you?" [25] And Micaiah said, "Behold, you shall see on that day when you go into an inner chamber to hide yourself." [26] And the king of Israel said, "Seize Micaiah, and take him back to Amon the governor of the city and to Joash the king's son, [27] and say, 'Thus says the king, "Put this fellow in prison and feed him meager rations of bread and water, until I come in peace."'" [28] And Micaiah said, "If you return in peace, the LORD has not spoken by me." And he said, "Hear, all you peoples!"

[29] So the king of Israel and Jehoshaphat the king of Judah went up to Ramoth-gilead. [30] And the king of Israel said to Jehoshaphat, "I will disguise myself and go into battle, but you wear your robes." And the king of Israel disguised himself and went into battle. [31] Now the king of Syria had commanded the thirty-two captains of his chariots, "Fight with neither small nor great, but only with the king of Israel." [32] And when the captains of the chariots saw Jehoshaphat, they said, "It is surely the king of Israel." So they turned to fight against him. And Jehoshaphat cried out. [33] And when the captains of the chariots saw that it was not the king of Israel, they turned back from pursuing him. [34] But a certain man drew his bow at random[1] and struck the king of Israel between the scale armor and the breastplate. Therefore he said to the driver of his chariot, "Turn around and carry me out of the battle, for I am wounded." [35] And the battle continued that day, and the king was propped up in his chariot facing the Syrians, until at evening he died. And the blood of the wound flowed into the bottom of the chariot. [36] And about sunset a cry went through the army, "Every man to his city, and every man to his country!"

[37] So the king died, and was brought to Samaria. And they buried the king in Samaria. [38] And they washed the chariot by the pool of Samaria, and the dogs licked up his blood, and the prostitutes washed themselves in it, according to the word of the LORD that he had spoken. [39] Now the rest of the acts of Ahab and all that he did, and the ivory house that he built and all the cities that he built, are they not written in the Book of the Chronicles of the Kings of Israel? [40] So Ahab slept with his fathers, and Ahaziah his son reigned in his place.

[41] Jehoshaphat the son of Asa began to reign

[1] Hebrew *in his innocence*

over Judah in the fourth year of Ahab king of Israel. ⁴²Jehoshaphat was thirty-five years old when he began to reign, and he reigned twenty-five years in Jerusalem. His mother's name was Azubah the daughter of Shilhi. ⁴³He walked in all the way of Asa his father. He did not turn aside from it, doing what was right in the sight of the LORD. Yet the high places were not taken away, and the people still sacrificed and made offerings on the high places. ⁴⁴Jehoshaphat also made peace with the king of Israel.

⁴⁵Now the rest of the acts of Jehoshaphat, and his might that he showed, and how he warred, are they not written in the Book of the Chronicles of the Kings of Judah? ⁴⁶And from the land he exterminated the remnant of the male cult prostitutes who remained in the days of his father Asa.

⁴⁷There was no king in Edom; a deputy was king. ⁴⁸Jehoshaphat made ships of Tarshish to go to Ophir for gold, but they did not go, for the ships were wrecked at Ezion-geber. ⁴⁹Then Ahaziah the son of Ahab said to Jehoshaphat, "Let my servants go with your servants in the ships," but Jehoshaphat was not willing. ⁵⁰And Jehoshaphat slept with his fathers and was buried with his fathers in the city of David his father, and Jehoram his son reigned in his place.

⁵¹Ahaziah the son of Ahab began to reign over Israel in Samaria in the seventeenth year of Jehoshaphat king of Judah, and he reigned two years over Israel. ⁵²He did what was evil in the sight of the LORD and walked in the way of his father and in the way of his mother and in the way of Jeroboam the son of Nebat, who made Israel to sin. ⁵³He served Baal and worshiped him and provoked the LORD, the God of Israel, to anger in every way that his father had done.

---

1 Thessalonians 5

N ow concerning the times and the seasons, brothers,[1] you have no need to have anything written to you. ²For you yourselves are fully aware that the day of the Lord will come like a thief in the night. ³While people are saying, "There is peace and security," then sudden destruction will come upon them as labor pains come upon a pregnant woman, and they will not escape. ⁴But you are not in darkness, brothers, for that day to surprise you like a

thief. ⁵For you are all children[2] of light, children of the day. We are not of the night or of the darkness. ⁶So then let us not sleep, as others do, but let us keep awake and be sober. ⁷For those who sleep, sleep at night, and those who get drunk, are drunk at night. ⁸But since we belong to the day, let us be sober, having put on the breastplate of faith and love, and for a helmet the hope of salvation. ⁹For God has not destined us for wrath, but to obtain salvation through our Lord Jesus Christ, ¹⁰who died for us so that whether we are awake or asleep we might live with him. ¹¹Therefore encourage one another and build one another up, just as you are doing.

¹²We ask you, brothers, to respect those who labor among you and are over you in the Lord and admonish you, ¹³and to esteem them very highly in love because of their work. Be at peace among yourselves. ¹⁴And we urge you, brothers, admonish the idle,[3] encourage the fainthearted, help the weak, be patient with them all. ¹⁵See that no one repays anyone evil for evil, but always seek to do good to one another and to everyone. ¹⁶Rejoice always, ¹⁷pray without ceasing, ¹⁸give thanks in all circumstances; for this is the will of God in Christ Jesus for you. ¹⁹Do not quench the Spirit. ²⁰Do not despise prophecies, ²¹but test everything; hold fast what is good. ²²Abstain from every form of evil.

²³Now may the God of peace himself sanctify you completely, and may your whole spirit and soul and body be kept blameless at the coming of our Lord Jesus Christ. ²⁴He who calls you is faithful; he will surely do it.

²⁵Brothers, pray for us.

²⁶Greet all the brothers with a holy kiss.

²⁷I put you under oath before the Lord to have this letter read to all the brothers.

²⁸The grace of our Lord Jesus Christ be with you.

Daniel 4[4]

K ing Nebuchadnezzar to all peoples, nations, and languages, that dwell in all the earth: Peace be multiplied to you! ²It has seemed good to me to show the signs and wonders that the Most High God has done for me.

³   How great are his signs,
        how mighty his wonders!

---

¹ Or brothers and sisters; also verses 4, 12, 14, 25, 26, 27 ² Or sons; twice in this verse ³ Or disorderly, or undisciplined ⁴ Ch 3:31 in Aramaic

His kingdom is an everlasting kingdom,
and his dominion endures from
generation to generation.

⁴ ¹ I, Nebuchadnezzar, was at ease in my house and prospering in my palace. ⁵I saw a dream that made me afraid. As I lay in bed the fancies and the visions of my head alarmed me. ⁶So I made a decree that all the wise men of Babylon should be brought before me, that they might make known to me the interpretation of the dream. ⁷Then the magicians, the enchanters, the Chaldeans, and the astrologers came in, and I told them the dream, but they could not make known to me its interpretation. ⁸At last Daniel came in before me—he who was named Belteshazzar after the name of my god, and in whom is the spirit of the holy gods²—and I told him the dream, saying, ⁹"O Belteshazzar, chief of the magicians, because I know that the spirit of the holy gods is in you and that no mystery is too difficult for you, tell me the visions of my dream that I saw and their interpretation. ¹⁰The visions of my head as I lay in bed were these: I saw, and behold, a tree in the midst of the earth, and its height was great. ¹¹The tree grew and became strong, and its top reached to heaven, and it was visible to the end of the whole earth. ¹²Its leaves were beautiful and its fruit abundant, and in it was food for all. The beasts of the field found shade under it, and the birds of the heavens lived in its branches, and all flesh was fed from it.

¹³"I saw in the visions of my head as I lay in bed, and behold, a watcher, a holy one, came down from heaven. ¹⁴He proclaimed aloud and said thus: 'Chop down the tree and lop off its branches, strip off its leaves and scatter its fruit. Let the beasts flee from under it and the birds from its branches. ¹⁵But leave the stump of its roots in the earth, bound with a band of iron and bronze, amid the tender grass of the field. Let him be wet with the dew of heaven. Let his portion be with the beasts in the grass of the earth. ¹⁶Let his mind be changed from a man's, and let a beast's mind be given to him; and let seven periods of time pass over him. ¹⁷The sentence is by the decree of the watchers, the decision by the word of the holy ones, to the end that the living may know that the Most High rules the kingdom of men and gives it to whom he will and sets over it the lowliest

of men.' ¹⁸This dream I, King Nebuchadnezzar, saw. And you, O Belteshazzar, tell me the interpretation, because all the wise men of my kingdom are not able to make known to me the interpretation, but you are able, for the spirit of the holy gods is in you."

¹⁹Then Daniel, whose name was Belteshazzar, was dismayed for a while, and his thoughts alarmed him. The king answered and said, "Belteshazzar, let not the dream or the interpretation alarm you." Belteshazzar answered and said, "My lord, may the dream be for those who hate you and its interpretation for your enemies! ²⁰The tree you saw, which grew and became strong, so that its top reached to heaven, and it was visible to the end of the whole earth, ²¹whose leaves were beautiful and its fruit abundant, and in which was food for all, under which beasts of the field found shade, and in whose branches the birds of the heavens lived— ²²it is you, O king, who have grown and become strong. Your greatness has grown and reaches to heaven, and your dominion to the ends of the earth. ²³And because the king saw a watcher, a holy one, coming down from heaven and saying, 'Chop down the tree and destroy it, but leave the stump of its roots in the earth, bound with a band of iron and bronze, in the tender grass of the field, and let him be wet with the dew of heaven, and let his portion be with the beasts of the field, till seven periods of time pass over him,' ²⁴this is the interpretation, O king: It is a decree of the Most High, which has come upon my lord the king, ²⁵that you shall be driven from among men, and your dwelling shall be with the beasts of the field. You shall be made to eat grass like an ox, and you shall be wet with the dew of heaven, and seven periods of time shall pass over you, till you know that the Most High rules the kingdom of men and gives it to whom he will. ²⁶And as it was commanded to leave the stump of the roots of the tree, your kingdom shall be confirmed for you from the time that you know that Heaven rules. ²⁷Therefore, O king, let my counsel be acceptable to you: break off your sins by practicing righteousness, and your iniquities by showing mercy to the oppressed, that there may perhaps be a lengthening of your prosperity."

²⁸All this came upon King Nebuchadnezzar. ²⁹At the end of twelve months he was walking on the roof of the royal palace of Babylon, ³⁰and

¹ Ch 4:1 in Aramaic ² Or *Spirit of the holy God*; also verses 9, 18

the king answered and said, "Is not this great Babylon, which I have built by my mighty power as a royal residence and for the glory of my majesty?" [31] While the words were still in the king's mouth, there fell a voice from heaven, "O King Nebuchadnezzar, to you it is spoken: The kingdom has departed from you, [32] and you shall be driven from among men, and your dwelling shall be with the beasts of the field. And you shall be made to eat grass like an ox, and seven periods of time shall pass over you, until you know that the Most High rules the kingdom of men and gives it to whom he will." [33] Immediately the word was fulfilled against Nebuchadnezzar. He was driven from among men and ate grass like an ox, and his body was wet with the dew of heaven till his hair grew as long as eagles' feathers, and his nails were like birds' claws.

[34] At the end of the days I, Nebuchadnezzar, lifted my eyes to heaven, and my reason returned to me, and I blessed the Most High, and praised and honored him who lives forever,

> for his dominion is an everlasting dominion,
> and his kingdom endures from generation to generation;
> [35] all the inhabitants of the earth are accounted as nothing,
> and he does according to his will among the host of heaven
> and among the inhabitants of the earth;
> and none can stay his hand
> or say to him, "What have you done?"

[36] At the same time my reason returned to me, and for the glory of my kingdom, my majesty and splendor returned to me. My counselors and my lords sought me, and I was established in my kingdom, and still more greatness was added to me. [37] Now I, Nebuchadnezzar, praise and extol and honor the King of heaven, for all his works are right and his ways are just; and those who walk in pride he is able to humble.

--------- *Psalm 108–109* ---------

A Song. A Psalm of David.

My heart is steadfast, O God!
I will sing and make melody with all my being![1]

[2] Awake, O harp and lyre!
I will awake the dawn!
[3] I will give thanks to you, O Lord, among the peoples;
I will sing praises to you among the nations.
[4] For your steadfast love is great above the heavens;
your faithfulness reaches to the clouds.

[5] Be exalted, O God, above the heavens!
Let your glory be over all the earth!
[6] That your beloved ones may be delivered,
give salvation by your right hand and answer me!

[7] God has promised in his holiness:[2]
"With exultation I will divide up Shechem
and portion out the Valley of Succoth.
[8] Gilead is mine; Manasseh is mine;
Ephraim is my helmet,
Judah my scepter.
[9] Moab is my washbasin;
upon Edom I cast my shoe;
over Philistia I shout in triumph."

[10] Who will bring me to the fortified city?
Who will lead me to Edom?
[11] Have you not rejected us, O God?
You do not go out, O God, with our armies.
[12] Oh grant us help against the foe,
for vain is the salvation of man!
[13] With God we shall do valiantly;
it is he who will tread down our foes.

To the choirmaster. A Psalm of David.

Be not silent, O God of my praise!
[2] For wicked and deceitful mouths are opened against me,
speaking against me with lying tongues.
[3] They encircle me with words of hate,
and attack me without cause.
[4] In return for my love they accuse me,
but I give myself to prayer.[3]
[5] So they reward me evil for good,
and hatred for my love.

[6] Appoint a wicked man against him;
let an accuser stand at his right hand.

[1] Hebrew *with my glory* [2] Or *sanctuary* [3] Hebrew *but I am prayer*

7 When he is tried, let him come forth
guilty;
     let his prayer be counted as sin!
8 May his days be few;
     may another take his office!
9 May his children be fatherless
     and his wife a widow!
10 May his children wander about and
beg,
     seeking food far from the ruins they
inhabit!
11 May the creditor seize all that he has;
     may strangers plunder the fruits of his
toil!
12 Let there be none to extend kindness to
him,
     nor any to pity his fatherless
children!
13 May his posterity be cut off;
     may his name be blotted out in the
second generation!
14 May the iniquity of his fathers be
remembered before the Lord,
     and let not the sin of his mother be
blotted out!
15 Let them be before the Lord
continually,
     that he may cut off the memory of
them from the earth!
16 For he did not remember to show
kindness,
     but pursued the poor and needy
     and the brokenhearted, to put them to
death.
17 He loved to curse; let curses come[1] upon
him!
     He did not delight in blessing; may it
be far[2] from him!
18 He clothed himself with cursing as his
coat;
     may it soak[3] into his body like water,
     like oil into his bones!

19 May it be like a garment that he wraps
around him,
     like a belt that he puts on every day!
20 May this be the reward of my accusers
from the Lord,
     of those who speak evil against my life!

21 But you, O God my Lord,
     deal on my behalf for your name's
sake;
     because your steadfast love is good,
deliver me!
22 For I am poor and needy,
     and my heart is stricken within me.
23 I am gone like a shadow at evening;
     I am shaken off like a locust.
24 My knees are weak through fasting;
     my body has become gaunt, with no
fat.
25 I am an object of scorn to my accusers;
     when they see me, they wag their
heads.

26 Help me, O Lord my God!
     Save me according to your steadfast
love!
27 Let them know that this is your hand;
     you, O Lord, have done it!
28 Let them curse, but you will bless!
     They arise and are put to shame, but
your servant will be glad!
29 May my accusers be clothed with
dishonor;
     may they be wrapped in their own
shame as in a cloak!

30 With my mouth I will give great thanks
to the Lord;
     I will praise him in the midst of the
throng.
31 For he stands at the right hand of the
needy one,
     to save him from those who condemn
his soul to death.

---

[1] Revocalization; Masoretic Text *curses have come*   [2] Revocalization; Masoretic Text *it is far*   [3] Revocalization; Masoretic Text *it has soaked*

OCTOBER 20

2 Kings 1

After the death of Ahab, Moab rebelled against Israel.

²Now Ahaziah fell through the lattice in his upper chamber in Samaria, and lay sick; so he sent messengers, telling them, "Go, inquire of Baal-zebub, the god of Ekron, whether I shall recover from this sickness." ³But the angel of the Lord said to Elijah the Tishbite, "Arise, go up to meet the messengers of the king of Samaria, and say to them, 'Is it because there is no God in Israel that you are going to inquire of Baal-zebub, the god of Ekron? ⁴Now therefore thus says the Lord, You shall not come down from the bed to which you have gone up, but you shall surely die.'" So Elijah went.

⁵The messengers returned to the king, and he said to them, "Why have you returned?" ⁶And they said to him, "There came a man to meet us, and said to us, 'Go back to the king who sent you, and say to him, Thus says the Lord, Is it because there is no God in Israel that you are sending to inquire of Baal-zebub, the god of Ekron? Therefore you shall not come down from the bed to which you have gone up, but you shall surely die.'" ⁷He said to them, "What kind of man was he who came to meet you and told you these things?" ⁸They answered him, "He wore a garment of hair, with a belt of leather about his waist." And he said, "It is Elijah the Tishbite."

⁹Then the king sent to him a captain of fifty men with his fifty. He went up to Elijah, who was sitting on the top of a hill, and said to him, "O man of God, the king says, 'Come down.'" ¹⁰But Elijah answered the captain of fifty, "If I am a man of God, let fire come down from heaven and consume you and your fifty." Then fire came down from heaven and consumed him and his fifty.

¹¹Again the king sent to him another captain of fifty men with his fifty. And he answered and said to him, "O man of God, this is the king's order, 'Come down quickly!'" ¹²But Elijah answered them, "If I am a man of God, let fire come down from heaven and consume you and your fifty." Then the fire of God came down from heaven and consumed him and his fifty.

¹³Again the king sent the captain of a third fifty with his fifty. And the third captain of fifty went up and came and fell on his knees before Elijah and entreated him, "O man of God, please let my life, and the life of these fifty servants of yours, be precious in your sight. ¹⁴Behold, fire came down from heaven and consumed the two former captains of fifty men with their fifties, but now let my life be precious in your sight." ¹⁵Then the angel of the Lord said to Elijah, "Go down with him; do not be afraid of him." So he arose and went down with him to the king ¹⁶and said to him, "Thus says the Lord, 'Because you have sent messengers to inquire of Baal-zebub, the god of Ekron—is it because there is no God in Israel to inquire of his word?—therefore you shall not come down from the bed to which you have gone up, but you shall surely die.'"

¹⁷So he died according to the word of the Lord that Elijah had spoken. Jehoram became king in his place in the second year of Jehoram the son of Jehoshaphat, king of Judah, because Ahaziah had no son. ¹⁸Now the rest of the acts of Ahaziah that he did, are they not written in the Book of the Chronicles of the Kings of Israel?

2 Thessalonians 1

Paul, Silvanus, and Timothy,

To the church of the Thessalonians in God our Father and the Lord Jesus Christ:

²Grace to you and peace from God our Father and the Lord Jesus Christ.

³We ought always to give thanks to God for you, brothers,[1] as is right, because your faith is growing abundantly, and the love of every one of you for one another is increasing. ⁴Therefore we ourselves boast about you in the churches of God for your steadfastness and faith in all your persecutions and in the afflictions that you are enduring.

⁵This is evidence of the righteous judgment

[1] Or brothers and sisters. The plural Greek word adelphoi (translated "brothers") refers to siblings in a family. In New Testament usage, depending on the context, adelphoi may refer either to men or to both men and women who are siblings (brothers and sisters) in God's family, the church

of God, that you may be considered worthy of the kingdom of God, for which you are also suffering— ⁶since indeed God considers it just to repay with affliction those who afflict you, ⁷and to grant relief to you who are afflicted as well as to us, when the Lord Jesus is revealed from heaven with his mighty angels ⁸in flaming fire, inflicting vengeance on those who do not know God and on those who do not obey the gospel of our Lord Jesus. ⁹They will suffer the punishment of eternal destruction, away from¹ the presence of the Lord and from the glory of his might, ¹⁰when he comes on that day to be glorified in his saints, and to be marveled at among all who have believed, because our testimony to you was believed. ¹¹To this end we always pray for you, that our God may make you worthy of his calling and may fulfill every resolve for good and every work of faith by his power, ¹²so that the name of our Lord Jesus may be glorified in you, and you in him, according to the grace of our God and the Lord Jesus Christ.

────────── *Daniel 5* ──────────

King Belshazzar made a great feast for a thousand of his lords and drank wine in front of the thousand.

²Belshazzar, when he tasted the wine, commanded that the vessels of gold and of silver that Nebuchadnezzar his father² had taken out of the temple in Jerusalem be brought, that the king and his lords, his wives, and his concubines might drink from them. ³Then they brought in the golden vessels that had been taken out of the temple, the house of God in Jerusalem, and the king and his lords, his wives, and his concubines drank from them. ⁴They drank wine and praised the gods of gold and silver, bronze, iron, wood, and stone.

⁵Immediately the fingers of a human hand appeared and wrote on the plaster of the wall of the king's palace, opposite the lampstand. And the king saw the hand as it wrote. ⁶Then the king's color changed, and his thoughts alarmed him; his limbs gave way, and his knees knocked together. ⁷The king called loudly to bring in the enchanters, the Chaldeans, and the astrologers. The king declared³ to the wise men of Babylon, "Whoever reads this writing, and shows me its interpretation, shall be clothed with purple and have a chain of gold around his neck and shall

be the third ruler in the kingdom." ⁸Then all the king's wise men came in, but they could not read the writing or make known to the king the interpretation. ⁹Then King Belshazzar was greatly alarmed, and his color changed, and his lords were perplexed.

¹⁰The queen,⁴ because of the words of the king and his lords, came into the banqueting hall, and the queen declared, "O king, live forever! Let not your thoughts alarm you or your color change. ¹¹There is a man in your kingdom in whom is the spirit of the holy gods.⁵ In the days of your father, light and understanding and wisdom like the wisdom of the gods were found in him, and King Nebuchadnezzar, your father—your father the king—made him chief of the magicians, enchanters, Chaldeans, and astrologers, ¹²because an excellent spirit, knowledge, and understanding to interpret dreams, explain riddles, and solve problems were found in this Daniel, whom the king named Belteshazzar. Now let Daniel be called, and he will show the interpretation."

¹³Then Daniel was brought in before the king. The king answered and said to Daniel, "You are that Daniel, one of the exiles of Judah, whom the king my father brought from Judah. ¹⁴I have heard of you that the spirit of the gods⁶ is in you, and that light and understanding and excellent wisdom are found in you. ¹⁵Now the wise men, the enchanters, have been brought in before me to read this writing and make known to me its interpretation, but they could not show the interpretation of the matter. ¹⁶But I have heard that you can give interpretations and solve problems. Now if you can read the writing and make known to me its interpretation, you shall be clothed with purple and have a chain of gold around your neck and shall be the third ruler in the kingdom."

¹⁷Then Daniel answered and said before the king, "Let your gifts be for yourself, and give your rewards to another. Nevertheless, I will read the writing to the king and make known to him the interpretation. ¹⁸O king, the Most High God gave Nebuchadnezzar your father kingship and greatness and glory and majesty. ¹⁹And because of the greatness that he gave him, all peoples, nations, and languages trembled and feared before him. Whom he would, he killed, and whom he would, he kept alive; whom he would, he raised up, and whom he

would, he humbled. **²⁰**But when his heart was lifted up and his spirit was hardened so that he dealt proudly, he was brought down from his kingly throne, and his glory was taken from him. **²¹**He was driven from among the children of mankind, and his mind was made like that of a beast, and his dwelling was with the wild donkeys. He was fed grass like an ox, and his body was wet with the dew of heaven, until he knew that the Most High God rules the kingdom of mankind and sets over it whom he will. **²²**And you his son,[1] Belshazzar, have not humbled your heart, though you knew all this, **²³**but you have lifted up yourself against the Lord of heaven. And the vessels of his house have been brought in before you, and you and your lords, your wives, and your concubines have drunk wine from them. And you have praised the gods of silver and gold, of bronze, iron, wood, and stone, which do not see or hear or know, but the God in whose hand is your breath, and whose are all your ways, you have not honored.

²⁴"Then from his presence the hand was sent, and this writing was inscribed. **²⁵**And this is the writing that was inscribed: MENE, MENE, TEKEL, and PARSIN. **²⁶**This is the interpretation of the matter: MENE, God has numbered[2] the days of your kingdom and brought it to an end; **²⁷**TEKEL, you have been weighed[3] in the balances and found wanting; **²⁸**PERES, your kingdom is divided and given to the Medes and Persians."[4]

²⁹Then Belshazzar gave the command, and Daniel was clothed with purple, a chain of gold was put around his neck, and a proclamation was made about him, that he should be the third ruler in the kingdom.

³⁰That very night Belshazzar the Chaldean king was killed. **³¹**[5]And Darius the Mede received the kingdom, being about sixty-two years old.

Psalm 110–111[6]

A PSALM OF DAVID.

The LORD says to my Lord:
  "Sit at my right hand,
    until I make your enemies your footstool."
2 The LORD sends forth from Zion
    your mighty scepter.
    Rule in the midst of your enemies!
3 Your people will offer themselves freely
    on the day of your power,[7]

in holy garments;[8]
from the womb of the morning,
  the dew of your youth will be yours.[9]
4 The LORD has sworn
  and will not change his mind,
"You are a priest forever
  after the order of Melchizedek."

5 The Lord is at your right hand;
  he will shatter kings on the day of his wrath.
6 He will execute judgment among the nations,
  filling them with corpses;
he will shatter chiefs[10]
  over the wide earth.
7 He will drink from the brook by the way;
  therefore he will lift up his head.

Praise the LORD!
  I will give thanks to the LORD with my whole heart,
    in the company of the upright, in the congregation.
2 Great are the works of the LORD,
    studied by all who delight in them.
3 Full of splendor and majesty is his work,
    and his righteousness endures forever.
4 He has caused his wondrous works to be remembered;
    the LORD is gracious and merciful.
5 He provides food for those who fear him;
    he remembers his covenant forever.
6 He has shown his people the power of his works,
    in giving them the inheritance of the nations.
7 The works of his hands are faithful and just;
    all his precepts are trustworthy;
8 they are established forever and ever,
    to be performed with faithfulness and uprightness.
9 He sent redemption to his people;
    he has commanded his covenant forever.
    Holy and awesome is his name!
10 The fear of the LORD is the beginning of wisdom;
    all those who practice it have a good understanding.
    His praise endures forever!

---

[1] Or *successor* [2] MENE sounds like the Aramaic for *numbered* [3] TEKEL sounds like the Aramaic for *weighed* [4] PERES (the singular of *Parsin*) sounds like the Aramaic for *divided* and for *Persia* [5] Ch 6:1 in Aramaic [6] This psalm is an acrostic poem, each line beginning with the successive letters of the Hebrew alphabet [7] Or *on the day you lead your forces* [8] Masoretic Text; some Hebrew manuscripts and Jerome *on the holy mountains* [9] The meaning of the Hebrew is uncertain [10] Or *the head*

OCTOBER 21

2 Kings 2

Now when the LORD was about to take Elijah up to heaven by a whirlwind, Elijah and Elisha were on their way from Gilgal. ²And Elijah said to Elisha, "Please stay here, for the LORD has sent me as far as Bethel." But Elisha said, "As the LORD lives, and as you yourself live, I will not leave you." So they went down to Bethel. ³And the sons of the prophets who were in Bethel came out to Elisha and said to him, "Do you know that today the LORD will take away your master from over you?" And he said, "Yes, I know it; keep quiet."

⁴Elijah said to him, "Elisha, please stay here, for the LORD has sent me to Jericho." But he said, "As the LORD lives, and as you yourself live, I will not leave you." So they came to Jericho. ⁵The sons of the prophets who were at Jericho drew near to Elisha and said to him, "Do you know that today the LORD will take away your master from over you?" And he answered, "Yes, I know it; keep quiet."

⁶Then Elijah said to him, "Please stay here, for the LORD has sent me to the Jordan." But he said, "As the LORD lives, and as you yourself live, I will not leave you." So the two of them went on. ⁷Fifty men of the sons of the prophets also went and stood at some distance from them, as they both were standing by the Jordan. ⁸Then Elijah took his cloak and rolled it up and struck the water, and the water was parted to the one side and to the other, till the two of them could go over on dry ground.

⁹When they had crossed, Elijah said to Elisha, "Ask what I shall do for you, before I am taken from you." And Elisha said, "Please let there be a double portion of your spirit on me." ¹⁰And he said, "You have asked a hard thing; yet, if you see me as I am being taken from you, it shall be so for you, but if you do not see me, it shall not be so." ¹¹And as they still went on and talked, behold, chariots of fire and horses of fire separated the two of them. And Elijah went up by a whirlwind into

heaven. ¹²And Elisha saw it and he cried, "My father, my father! The chariots of Israel and its horsemen!" And he saw him no more.

Then he took hold of his own clothes and tore them in two pieces. ¹³And he took up the cloak of Elijah that had fallen from him and went back and stood on the bank of the Jordan. ¹⁴Then he took the cloak of Elijah that had fallen from him and struck the water, saying, "Where is the LORD, the God of Elijah?" And when he had struck the water, the water was parted to the one side and to the other, and Elisha went over.

¹⁵Now when the sons of the prophets who were at Jericho saw him opposite them, they said, "The spirit of Elijah rests on Elisha." And they came to meet him and bowed to the ground before him. ¹⁶And they said to him, "Behold now, there are with your servants fifty strong men. Please let them go and seek your master. It may be that the Spirit of the LORD has caught him up and cast him upon some mountain or into some valley." And he said, "You shall not send." ¹⁷But when they urged him till he was ashamed, he said, "Send." They sent therefore fifty men. And for three days they sought him but did not find him. ¹⁸And they came back to him while he was staying at Jericho, and he said to them, "Did I not say to you, 'Do not go'?"

¹⁹Now the men of the city said to Elisha, "Behold, the situation of this city is pleasant, as my lord sees, but the water is bad, and the land is unfruitful." ²⁰He said, "Bring me a new bowl, and put salt in it." So they brought it to him. ²¹Then he went to the spring of water and threw salt in it and said, "Thus says the LORD, I have healed this water; from now on neither death nor miscarriage shall come from it." ²²So the water has been healed to this day, according to the word that Elisha spoke.

²³He went up from there to Bethel, and while he was going up on the way, some small boys came out of the city and jeered at him, saying,

"Go up, you baldhead! Go up, you baldhead!" [24]And he turned around, and when he saw them, he cursed them in the name of the LORD. And two she-bears came out of the woods and tore forty-two of the boys. [25]From there he went on to Mount Carmel, and from there he returned to Samaria.

2 Thessalonians 2

[N]ow concerning the coming of our Lord Jesus Christ and our being gathered together to him, we ask you, brothers,[1] [2]not to be quickly shaken in mind or alarmed, either by a spirit or a spoken word, or a letter seeming to be from us, to the effect that the day of the Lord has come. [3]Let no one deceive you in any way. For that day will not come, unless the rebellion comes first, and the man of lawlessness[2] is revealed, the son of destruction,[3] [4]who opposes and exalts himself against every so-called god or object of worship, so that he takes his seat in the temple of God, proclaiming himself to be God. [5]Do you not remember that when I was still with you I told you these things? [6]And you know what is restraining him now so that he may be revealed in his time. [7]For the mystery of lawlessness is already at work. Only he who now restrains it will do so until he is out of the way. [8]And then the lawless one will be revealed, whom the Lord Jesus will kill with the breath of his mouth and bring to nothing by the appearance of his coming. [9]The coming of the lawless one is by the activity of Satan with all power and false signs and wonders, [10]and with all wicked deception for those who are perishing, because they refused to love the truth and so be saved. [11]Therefore God sends them a strong delusion, so that they may believe what is false, [12]in order that all may be condemned who did not believe the truth but had pleasure in unrighteousness.

[13]But we ought always to give thanks to God for you, brothers beloved by the Lord, because God chose you as the firstfruits[4] to be saved, through sanctification by the Spirit and belief in the truth. [14]To this he called you through our gospel, so that you may obtain the glory of our Lord Jesus Christ. [15]So then, brothers, stand firm and hold to the traditions that you were taught by us, either by our spoken word or by our letter.

[16]Now may our Lord Jesus Christ himself, and God our Father, who loved us and gave us eternal comfort and good hope through grace, [17]comfort your hearts and establish them in every good work and word.

Daniel 6

[I]t pleased Darius to set over the kingdom 120 satraps, to be throughout the whole kingdom; [2]and over them three high officials, of whom Daniel was one, to whom these satraps should give account, so that the king might suffer no loss. [3]Then this Daniel became distinguished above all the other high officials and satraps, because an excellent spirit was in him. And the king planned to set him over the whole kingdom. [4]Then the high officials and the satraps sought to find a ground for complaint against Daniel with regard to the kingdom, but they could find no ground for complaint or any fault, because he was faithful, and no error or fault was found in him. [5]Then these men said, "We shall not find any ground for complaint against this Daniel unless we find it in connection with the law of his God."

[6]Then these high officials and satraps came by agreement[5] to the king and said to him, "O King Darius, live forever! [7]All the high officials of the kingdom, the prefects and the satraps, the counselors and the governors are agreed that the king should establish an ordinance and enforce an injunction, that whoever makes petition to any god or man for thirty days, except to you, O king, shall be cast into the den of lions. [8]Now, O king, establish the injunction and sign the document, so that it cannot be changed, according to the law of the Medes and the Persians, which cannot be revoked." [9]Therefore King Darius signed the document and injunction.

[10]When Daniel knew that the document had been signed, he went to his house where he had windows in his upper chamber open toward Jerusalem. He got down on his knees three times a day and prayed and gave thanks before his God, as he had done previously. [11]Then these men came by agreement and found Daniel making petition and plea before his God. [12]Then they came near and said before the king, concerning the injunction, "O king! Did you not sign an injunction, that anyone

who makes petition to any god or man within thirty days except to you, O king, shall be cast into the den of lions?" The king answered and said, "The thing stands fast, according to the law of the Medes and Persians, which cannot be revoked." ¹³Then they answered and said before the king, "Daniel, who is one of the exiles from Judah, pays no attention to you, O king, or the injunction you have signed, but makes his petition three times a day."

¹⁴Then the king, when he heard these words, was much distressed and set his mind to deliver Daniel. And he labored till the sun went down to rescue him. ¹⁵Then these men came by agreement to the king and said to the king, "Know, O king, that it is a law of the Medes and Persians that no injunction or ordinance that the king establishes can be changed."

¹⁶Then the king commanded, and Daniel was brought and cast into the den of lions. The king declared¹ to Daniel, "May your God, whom you serve continually, deliver you!" ¹⁷And a stone was brought and laid on the mouth of the den, and the king sealed it with his own signet and with the signet of his lords, that nothing might be changed concerning Daniel. ¹⁸Then the king went to his palace and spent the night fasting; no diversions were brought to him, and sleep fled from him.

¹⁹Then, at break of day, the king arose and went in haste to the den of lions. ²⁰As he came near to the den where Daniel was, he cried out in a tone of anguish. The king declared to Daniel, "O Daniel, servant of the living God, has your God, whom you serve continually, been able to deliver you from the lions?" ²¹Then Daniel said to the king, "O king, live forever! ²²My God sent his angel and shut the lions' mouths, and they have not harmed me, because I was found blameless before him; and also before you, O king, I have done no harm." ²³Then the king was exceedingly glad, and commanded that Daniel be taken up out of the den. So Daniel was taken up out of the den, and no kind of harm was found on him, because he had trusted in his God. ²⁴And the king commanded, and those men who had maliciously accused Daniel were brought and cast into the den of lions—they, their children, and their wives. And before they reached the bottom of the den, the lions overpowered them and broke all their bones in pieces.

²⁵Then King Darius wrote to all the peoples, nations, and languages that dwell in all the earth: "Peace be multiplied to you. ²⁶I make a decree, that in all my royal dominion people are to tremble and fear before the God of Daniel,

for he is the living God,
    enduring forever;
his kingdom shall never be destroyed,
    and his dominion shall be to the end.
²⁷ He delivers and rescues;
    he works signs and wonders
    in heaven and on earth,
he who has saved Daniel
    from the power of the lions."

²⁸So this Daniel prospered during the reign of Darius and the reign of Cyrus the Persian.

——— *Psalm 112²–113* ———

Praise the LORD!
    Blessed is the man who fears the LORD,
        who greatly delights in his
            commandments!
² His offspring will be mighty in the land;
    the generation of the upright will be
        blessed.
³ Wealth and riches are in his house,
    and his righteousness endures
        forever.
⁴ Light dawns in the darkness for the
        upright;
    he is gracious, merciful, and
        righteous.
⁵ It is well with the man who deals
        generously and lends;
    who conducts his affairs with justice.
⁶ For the righteous will never be moved;
    he will be remembered forever.
⁷ He is not afraid of bad news;
    his heart is firm, trusting in the LORD.
⁸ His heart is steady; he will not be afraid,
    until he looks in triumph on his
        adversaries.
⁹ He has distributed freely; he has given to
        the poor;
    his righteousness endures forever;
    his horn is exalted in honor.
¹⁰ The wicked man sees it and is angry;
    he gnashes his teeth and melts away;
    the desire of the wicked will perish!

¹ Aramaic *answered and said*; also verse 20 ² This psalm is an acrostic poem, each line beginning with the successive letters of the Hebrew alphabet

Praise the LORD!
Praise, O servants of the LORD,
   praise the name of the LORD!

2 Blessed be the name of the LORD
   from this time forth and
     forevermore!
3 From the rising of the sun to its setting,
   the name of the LORD is to be
     praised!

4 The LORD is high above all nations,
   and his glory above the heavens!

5 Who is like the LORD our God,
   who is seated on high,
6 who looks far down
   on the heavens and the earth?
7 He raises the poor from the dust
   and lifts the needy from the ash heap,
8 to make them sit with princes,
   with the princes of his people.
9 He gives the barren woman a home,
   making her the joyous mother of
     children.
Praise the LORD!

OCTOBER 22

2 Kings 3

In the eighteenth year of Jehoshaphat king of Judah, Jehoram the son of Ahab became king over Israel in Samaria, and he reigned twelve years. ²He did what was evil in the sight of the LORD, though not like his father and mother, for he put away the pillar of Baal that his father had made. ³Nevertheless, he clung to the sin of Jeroboam the son of Nebat, which he made Israel to sin; he did not depart from it.

⁴Now Mesha king of Moab was a sheep breeder, and he had to deliver to the king of Israel 100,000 lambs and the wool of 100,000 rams. ⁵But when Ahab died, the king of Moab rebelled against the king of Israel. ⁶So King Jehoram marched out of Samaria at that time and mustered all Israel. ⁷And he went and sent word to Jehoshaphat king of Judah, "The king of Moab has rebelled against me. Will you go with me to battle against Moab?" And he said, "I will go. I am as you are, my people as your people, my horses as your horses." ⁸Then he said, "By which way shall we march?" Jehoram answered, "By the way of the wilderness of Edom."

⁹So the king of Israel went with the king of Judah and the king of Edom. And when they had made a circuitous march of seven days, there was no water for the army or for the animals that followed them. ¹⁰Then the king of Israel said, "Alas! The LORD has called these three kings to give them into the hand of Moab." ¹¹And Jehoshaphat said, "Is there no prophet of the LORD here, through whom we may inquire of the LORD?" Then one of the king of Israel's servants answered, "Elisha the son of Shaphat is here, who poured water on the hands of Elijah." ¹²And Jehoshaphat said, "The word of the LORD is with him." So the king of Israel and Jehoshaphat and the king of Edom went down to him.

¹³And Elisha said to the king of Israel, "What have I to do with you? Go to the prophets of your father and to the prophets of your mother." But the king of Israel said to him, "No; it is the LORD who has called these three kings to give them into the hand of Moab." ¹⁴And Elisha said, "As the LORD of hosts lives, before whom I stand, were it not that I have regard for Jehoshaphat the king of Judah, I would neither look at you nor see you. ¹⁵But now bring me a musician." And when the musician played, the hand of the LORD came upon him. ¹⁶And he said, "Thus says the LORD, 'I will make this dry streambed full of pools.' ¹⁷For thus says the LORD, 'You shall not see wind or rain, but that streambed shall be filled with water, so that you shall drink, you, your livestock, and your animals.' ¹⁸This is a light thing in the sight of the LORD. He will also give the Moabites into your

hand, [19] and you shall attack every fortified city and every choice city, and shall fell every good tree and stop up all springs of water and ruin every good piece of land with stones." [20] The next morning, about the time of offering the sacrifice, behold, water came from the direction of Edom, till the country was filled with water.

[21] When all the Moabites heard that the kings had come up to fight against them, all who were able to put on armor, from the youngest to the oldest, were called out and were drawn up at the border. [22] And when they rose early in the morning and the sun shone on the water, the Moabites saw the water opposite them as red as blood. [23] And they said, "This is blood; the kings have surely fought together and struck one another down. Now then, Moab, to the spoil!" [24] But when they came to the camp of Israel, the Israelites rose and struck the Moabites, till they fled before them. And they went forward, striking the Moabites as they went.[1] [25] And they overthrew the cities, and on every good piece of land every man threw a stone until it was covered. They stopped every spring of water and felled all the good trees, till only its stones were left in Kir-hareseth, and the slingers surrounded and attacked it. [26] When the king of Moab saw that the battle was going against him, he took with him 700 swordsmen to break through, opposite the king of Edom, but they could not. [27] Then he took his oldest son who was to reign in his place and offered him for a burnt offering on the wall. And there came great wrath against Israel. And they withdrew from him and returned to their own land.

2 Thessalonians 3

Finally, brothers,[2] pray for us, that the word of the Lord may speed ahead and be honored,[3] as happened among you, [2] and that we may be delivered from wicked and evil men. For not all have faith. [3] But the Lord is faithful. He will establish you and guard you against the evil one.[4] [4] And we have confidence in the Lord about you, that you are doing and will do the things that we command. [5] May the Lord direct your hearts to the love of God and to the steadfastness of Christ.

[6] Now we command you, brothers, in the name of our Lord Jesus Christ, that you keep away from any brother who is walking in idleness and not in accord with the tradition that you received from us. [7] For you yourselves know how you ought to imitate us, because we were not idle when we were with you, [8] nor did we eat anyone's bread without paying for it, but with toil and labor we worked night and day, that we might not be a burden to any of you. [9] It was not because we do not have that right, but to give you in ourselves an example to imitate. [10] For even when we were with you, we would give you this command: If anyone is not willing to work, let him not eat. [11] For we hear that some among you walk in idleness, not busy at work, but busybodies. [12] Now such persons we command and encourage in the Lord Jesus Christ to do their work quietly and to earn their own living.[5]

[13] As for you, brothers, do not grow weary in doing good. [14] If anyone does not obey what we say in this letter, take note of that person, and have nothing to do with him, that he may be ashamed. [15] Do not regard him as an enemy, but warn him as a brother.

[16] Now may the Lord of peace himself give you peace at all times in every way. The Lord be with you all.

[17] I, Paul, write this greeting with my own hand. This is the sign of genuineness in every letter of mine; it is the way I write. [18] The grace of our Lord Jesus Christ be with you all.

Daniel 7

In the first year of Belshazzar king of Babylon, Daniel saw a dream and visions of his head as he lay in his bed. Then he wrote down the dream and told the sum of the matter. [2] Daniel declared,[6] "I saw in my vision by night, and behold, the four winds of heaven were stirring up the great sea. [3] And four great beasts came up out of the sea, different from one another. [4] The first was like a lion and had eagles' wings. Then as I looked its wings were plucked off, and it was lifted up from the ground and made to stand on two feet like a man, and the mind of a man was given to it. [5] And behold, another beast, a second one, like a bear. It was raised up on one side. It had three ribs in its mouth between its teeth; and it was told, 'Arise, devour much flesh.' [6] After this I looked, and behold, another, like a leopard, with four wings of a bird on its back. And the beast had four heads, and dominion was given to it. [7] After this I saw in the night visions, and behold, a fourth beast, terrifying and dreadful and exceedingly strong. It had great iron teeth; it devoured and broke in pieces and stamped what was left with its feet. It was different from all the beasts that were before it, and it had ten horns. [8]I considered the horns, and behold, there came up among them another horn, a little one, before which three of the first horns were plucked up by the roots. And behold, in this horn were eyes like the eyes of a man, and a mouth speaking great things.

[9]"As I looked,

> thrones were placed,
>   and the Ancient of Days took his seat;
> his clothing was white as snow,
>   and the hair of his head like pure wool;
> his throne was fiery flames;
>   its wheels were burning fire.
> [10] A stream of fire issued
>   and came out from before him;
> a thousand thousands served him,
>   and ten thousand times ten thousand
>   stood before him;
> the court sat in judgment,
>   and the books were opened.

[11]"I looked then because of the sound of the great words that the horn was speaking. And as I looked, the beast was killed, and its body destroyed and given over to be burned with fire. [12]As for the rest of the beasts, their dominion was taken away, but their lives were prolonged for a season and a time.

[13]"I saw in the night visions,

> and behold, with the clouds of heaven
>   there came one like a son of man,
> and he came to the Ancient of Days
>   and was presented before him.
> [14] And to him was given dominion
>   and glory and a kingdom,
> that all peoples, nations, and languages
>   should serve him;
> his dominion is an everlasting dominion,
>   which shall not pass away,
> and his kingdom one
>   that shall not be destroyed.

[15]"As for me, Daniel, my spirit within me[1] was anxious, and the visions of my head alarmed me. [16]I approached one of those who stood there and asked him the truth concerning all this. So he told me and made known to me

the interpretation of the things. [17]'These four great beasts are four kings who shall arise out of the earth. [18]But the saints of the Most High shall receive the kingdom and possess the kingdom forever, forever and ever.'

[19]"Then I desired to know the truth about the fourth beast, which was different from all the rest, exceedingly terrifying, with its teeth of iron and claws of bronze, and which devoured and broke in pieces and stamped what was left with its feet, [20]and about the ten horns that were on its head, and the other horn that came up and before which three of them fell, the horn that had eyes and a mouth that spoke great things, and that seemed greater than its companions. [21]As I looked, this horn made war with the saints and prevailed over them, [22]until the Ancient of Days came, and judgment was given for the saints of the Most High, and the time came when the saints possessed the kingdom.

[23]"Thus he said: 'As for the fourth beast,

> there shall be a fourth kingdom on earth,
>   which shall be different from all the
>   kingdoms,
> and it shall devour the whole earth,
>   and trample it down, and break it to
>   pieces.
> [24] As for the ten horns,
>   out of this kingdom ten kings shall arise,
>   and another shall arise after them;
> he shall be different from the former
>   ones,
>   and shall put down three kings.
> [25] He shall speak words against the Most
>   High,
>   and shall wear out the saints of the
>   Most High,
>   and shall think to change the times
>   and the law;
> and they shall be given into his hand
>   for a time, times, and half a time.
> [26] But the court shall sit in judgment,
>   and his dominion shall be taken away,
>   to be consumed and destroyed to the
>   end.
> [27] And the kingdom and the dominion
>   and the greatness of the kingdoms
>   under the whole heaven
>   shall be given to the people of the
>   saints of the Most High;

[1] Aramaic within its sheath

his kingdom shall be an everlasting
　　kingdom,
and all dominions shall serve and
　　obey him.'[1]

28 "Here is the end of the matter. As for me,
Daniel, my thoughts greatly alarmed me, and
my color changed, but I kept the matter in my
heart."

────────── *Psalm 114–115* ──────────

When Israel went out from Egypt,
　　the house of Jacob from a people of
　　　strange language,
2　Judah became his sanctuary,
　　Israel his dominion.

3　The sea looked and fled;
　　Jordan turned back.
4　The mountains skipped like rams,
　　the hills like lambs.

5　What ails you, O sea, that you flee?
　　O Jordan, that you turn back?
6　O mountains, that you skip like rams?
　　O hills, like lambs?

7　Tremble, O earth, at the presence of the
　　　Lord,
　　at the presence of the God of Jacob,
8　who turns the rock into a pool of water,
　　the flint into a spring of water.

Not to us, O Lord, not to us, but to your
　　name give glory,
　　for the sake of your steadfast love and
　　　your faithfulness!

2　Why should the nations say,
　　"Where is their God?"
3　Our God is in the heavens;
　　he does all that he pleases.

4　Their idols are silver and gold,
　　the work of human hands.
5　They have mouths, but do not speak;
　　eyes, but do not see.
6　They have ears, but do not hear;
　　noses, but do not smell.
7　They have hands, but do not feel;
　　feet, but do not walk;
　　and they do not make a sound in their
　　　throat.
8　Those who make them become like
　　　them;
　　so do all who trust in them.

9　O Israel,[2] trust in the Lord!
　　He is their help and their shield.
10　O house of Aaron, trust in the Lord!
　　He is their help and their shield.
11　You who fear the Lord, trust in the
　　　Lord!
　　He is their help and their shield.

12　The Lord has remembered us; he will
　　　bless us;
　　he will bless the house of Israel;
　　he will bless the house of Aaron;
13　he will bless those who fear the Lord,
　　both the small and the great.

14　May the Lord give you increase,
　　you and your children!
15　May you be blessed by the Lord,
　　who made heaven and earth!

16　The heavens are the Lord's heavens,
　　but the earth he has given to the
　　　children of man.
17　The dead do not praise the Lord,
　　nor do any who go down into silence.
18　But we will bless the Lord
　　from this time forth and
　　　forevermore.
Praise the Lord!

---

[1] Or their kingdom shall be an everlasting kingdom, and all dominions shall serve and obey them [2] Masoretic Text; many Hebrew manuscripts, Septuagint, Syriac O house of Israel

OCTOBER 23

2 Kings 4

Now the wife of one of the sons of the prophets cried to Elisha, "Your servant my husband is dead, and you know that your servant feared the LORD, but the creditor has come to take my two children to be his slaves." ²And Elisha said to her, "What shall I do for you? Tell me; what have you in the house?" And she said, "Your servant has nothing in the house except a jar of oil." ³Then he said, "Go outside, borrow vessels from all your neighbors, empty vessels and not too few. ⁴Then go in and shut the door behind yourself and your sons and pour into all these vessels. And when one is full, set it aside." ⁵So she went from him and shut the door behind herself and her sons. And as she poured they brought the vessels to her. ⁶When the vessels were full, she said to her son, "Bring me another vessel." And he said to her, "There is not another." Then the oil stopped flowing. ⁷She came and told the man of God, and he said, "Go, sell the oil and pay your debts, and you and your sons can live on the rest."

⁸One day Elisha went on to Shunem, where a wealthy woman lived, who urged him to eat some food. So whenever he passed that way, he would turn in there to eat food. ⁹And she said to her husband, "Behold now, I know that this is a holy man of God who is continually passing our way. ¹⁰Let us make a small room on the roof with walls and put there for him a bed, a table, a chair, and a lamp, so that whenever he comes to us, he can go in there."

¹¹One day he came there, and he turned into the chamber and rested there. ¹²And he said to Gehazi his servant, "Call this Shunammite." When he had called her, she stood before him. ¹³And he said to him, "Say now to her, 'See, you have taken all this trouble for us; what is to be done for you? Would you have a word spoken on your behalf to the king or to the commander of the army?'" She answered, "I dwell among my own people." ¹⁴And he said, "What then is to be done for her?" Gehazi answered, "Well, she has no son, and her husband is old." ¹⁵He said, "Call her." And when he had called her, she stood in the doorway. ¹⁶And he said, "At this season, about this time next year, you shall embrace a son." And she said, "No, my lord, O man of God; do not lie to your servant." ¹⁷But the woman conceived, and she bore a son about that time the following spring, as Elisha had said to her.

¹⁸When the child had grown, he went out one day to his father among the reapers. ¹⁹And he said to his father, "Oh, my head, my head!" The father said to his servant, "Carry him to his mother." ²⁰And when he had lifted him and brought him to his mother, the child sat on her lap till noon, and then he died. ²¹And she went up and laid him on the bed of the man of God and shut the door behind him and went out. ²²Then she called to her husband and said, "Send me one of the servants and one of the donkeys, that I may quickly go to the man of God and come back again." ²³And he said, "Why will you go to him today? It is neither new moon nor Sabbath." She said, "All is well." ²⁴Then she saddled the donkey, and she said to her servant, "Urge the animal on; do not slacken the pace for me unless I tell you." ²⁵So she set out and came to the man of God at Mount Carmel.

When the man of God saw her coming, he said to Gehazi his servant, "Look, there is the Shunammite. ²⁶Run at once to meet her and say to her, 'Is all well with you? Is all well with your husband? Is all well with the child?'" And she answered, "All is well." ²⁷And when she came to the mountain to the man of God, she caught hold of his feet. And Gehazi came to push her away. But the man of God said, "Leave her alone, for she is in bitter distress, and the LORD has hidden it from me and has not told me." ²⁸Then she said, "Did I ask my lord for a son? Did I not say, 'Do not deceive me?'" ²⁹He said to Gehazi, "Tie up your garment and take my staff in your hand and go. If you meet anyone, do not greet him, and if anyone greets you, do not reply. And lay my staff on the face of the child." ³⁰Then the mother of the child said, "As the LORD lives and as you yourself live, I will not leave you." So he arose and followed her. ³¹Gehazi went on ahead and laid the staff on the face of the child, but there was no sound or sign of life. Therefore he returned to meet him and told him, "The child has not awakened."

³²When Elisha came into the house, he saw the child lying dead on his bed. ³³So he went in and shut the door behind the two of them and prayed to the LORD. ³⁴Then he went up and lay on the child, putting his mouth on his mouth, his eyes on his eyes, and his hands on his hands. And as he stretched himself upon him, the flesh of the child became warm. ³⁵Then he got up again and walked once back and forth in the house, and went up and stretched himself upon him. The child sneezed seven times, and the child opened his eyes. ³⁶Then he summoned Gehazi and said, "Call this Shunammite." So he called her. And when she came to him, he said, "Pick up your son." ³⁷She came and fell at his feet, bowing to the ground. Then she picked up her son and went out.

³⁸And Elisha came again to Gilgal when there was a famine in the land. And as the sons of the prophets were sitting before him, he said to his servant, "Set on the large pot, and boil stew for the sons of the prophets." ³⁹One of them went out into the field to gather herbs, and found a wild vine and gathered from it his lap full of wild gourds, and came and cut them up into the pot of stew, not knowing what they were. ⁴⁰And they poured out some for the men to eat. But while they were eating of the stew, they cried out, "O man of God, there is death in the pot!" And they could not eat it. ⁴¹He said, "Then bring flour." And he threw it into the pot and said, "Pour some out for the men, that they may eat." And there was no harm in the pot.

⁴²A man came from Baal-shalishah, bringing the man of God bread of the firstfruits, twenty loaves of barley and fresh ears of grain in his sack. And Elisha said, "Give to the men, that they may eat." ⁴³But his servant said, "How can I set this before a hundred men?" So he repeated, "Give them to the men, that they may eat, for thus says the LORD, 'They shall eat and have some left.'" ⁴⁴So he set it before them. And they ate and had some left, according to the word of the LORD.

1 Timothy 1

Paul, an apostle of Christ Jesus by command of God our Savior and of Christ Jesus our hope,

²To Timothy, my true child in the faith:

Grace, mercy, and peace from God the Father and Christ Jesus our Lord.

³As I urged you when I was going to Macedonia, remain at Ephesus so that you may charge certain persons not to teach any different doctrine, ⁴nor to devote themselves to myths and endless genealogies, which promote speculations rather than the stewardship[1] from God that is by faith. ⁵The aim of our charge is love that issues from a pure heart and a good conscience and a sincere faith. ⁶Certain persons, by swerving from these, have wandered away into vain discussion, ⁷desiring to be teachers of the law, without understanding either what they are saying or the things about which they make confident assertions.

⁸Now we know that the law is good, if one uses it lawfully, ⁹understanding this, that the law is not laid down for the just but for the lawless and disobedient, for the ungodly and sinners, for the unholy and profane, for those who strike their fathers and mothers, for murderers, ¹⁰the sexually immoral, men who practice homosexuality, enslavers,[2] liars, perjurers, and whatever else is contrary to sound[3] doctrine, ¹¹in accordance with the gospel of the glory of the blessed God with which I have been entrusted.

¹²I thank him who has given me strength, Christ Jesus our Lord, because he judged me faithful, appointing me to his service, ¹³though formerly I was a blasphemer, persecutor, and insolent opponent. But I received mercy because I had acted ignorantly in unbelief, ¹⁴and the grace of our Lord overflowed for me with the faith and love that are in Christ Jesus. ¹⁵The saying is trustworthy and deserving of full acceptance, that Christ Jesus came into the world to save sinners, of whom I am the foremost. ¹⁶But I received mercy for this reason, that in me, as the foremost, Jesus Christ might display his perfect patience as an example to those who were to believe in him for eternal life. ¹⁷To the King of the ages, immortal, invisible, the only God, be honor and glory forever and ever.[4] Amen.

¹⁸This charge I entrust to you, Timothy, my

---

¹ Or good order ² That is, those who take someone captive in order to sell him into slavery ³ Or healthy ⁴ Greek to the ages of ages

child, in accordance with the prophecies previously made about you, that by them you may wage the good warfare, [19] holding faith and a good conscience. By rejecting this, some have made shipwreck of their faith, [20] among whom are Hymenaeus and Alexander, whom I have handed over to Satan that they may learn not to blaspheme.

Daniel 8

In the third year of the reign of King Belshazzar a vision appeared to me, Daniel, after that which appeared to me at the first. [2] And I saw in the vision; and when I saw, I was in Susa the citadel, which is in the province of Elam. And I saw in the vision, and I was at the Ulai canal. [3] I raised my eyes and saw, and behold, a ram standing on the bank of the canal. It had two horns, and both horns were high, but one was higher than the other, and the higher one came up last. [4] I saw the ram charging westward and northward and southward. No beast could stand before him, and there was no one who could rescue from his power. He did as he pleased and became great.

[5] As I was considering, behold, a male goat came from the west across the face of the whole earth, without touching the ground. And the goat had a conspicuous horn between his eyes. [6] He came to the ram with the two horns, which I had seen standing on the bank of the canal, and he ran at him in his powerful wrath. [7] I saw him come close to the ram, and he was enraged against him and struck the ram and broke his two horns. And the ram had no power to stand before him, but he cast him down to the ground and trampled on him. And there was no one who could rescue the ram from his power. [8] Then the goat became exceedingly great, but when he was strong, the great horn was broken, and instead of it there came up four conspicuous horns toward the four winds of heaven.

[9] Out of one of them came a little horn, which grew exceedingly great toward the south, toward the east, and toward the glorious land. [10] It grew great, even to the host of heaven. And some of the host and some[1] of the stars it threw down to the ground and trampled on them. [11] It became great, even as great as the Prince of the host. And the regular burnt offering was taken away from him, and the place

of his sanctuary was overthrown. [12] And a host will be given over to it together with the regular burnt offering because of transgression,[2] and it will throw truth to the ground, and it will act and prosper. [13] Then I heard a holy one speaking, and another holy one said to the one who spoke, "For how long is the vision concerning the regular burnt offering, the transgression that makes desolate, and the giving over of the sanctuary and host to be trampled underfoot?" [14] And he said to me,[3] "For 2,300 evenings and mornings. Then the sanctuary shall be restored to its rightful state."

[15] When I, Daniel, had seen the vision, I sought to understand it. And behold, there stood before me one having the appearance of a man. [16] And I heard a man's voice between the banks of the Ulai, and it called, "Gabriel, make this man understand the vision." [17] So he came near where I stood. And when he came, I was frightened and fell on my face. But he said to me, "Understand, O son of man, that the vision is for the time of the end."

[18] And when he had spoken to me, I fell into a deep sleep with my face to the ground. But he touched me and made me stand up. [19] He said, "Behold, I will make known to you what shall be at the latter end of the indignation, for it refers to the appointed time of the end. [20] As for the ram that you saw with the two horns, these are the kings of Media and Persia. [21] And the goat[4] is the king of Greece. And the great horn between his eyes is the first king. [22] As for the horn that was broken, in place of which four others arose, four kingdoms shall arise from his[5] nation, but not with his power. [23] And at the latter end of their kingdom, when the transgressors have reached their limit, a king of bold face, one who understands riddles, shall arise. [24] His power shall be great—but not by his own power; and he shall cause fearful destruction and shall succeed in what he does, and destroy mighty men and the people who are the saints. [25] By his cunning he shall make deceit prosper under his hand, and in his own mind he shall become great. Without warning he shall destroy many. And he shall even rise up against the Prince of princes, and he shall be broken—but by no human hand. [26] The vision of the evenings and the mornings that has been told is true, but seal up the vision, for it refers to many days from now."

[1] Or host, that is, some　[2] Or in an act of rebellion　[3] Hebrew; Septuagint, Theodotion, Vulgate to him　[4] Or the shaggy goat　[5] Theodotion, Septuagint, Vulgate; Hebrew the

[27]And I, Daniel, was overcome and lay sick for some days. Then I rose and went about the king's business, but I was appalled by the vision and did not understand it.

——————— *Psalm 116* ———————

I love the LORD, because he has heard
  my voice and my pleas for mercy.
2 Because he inclined his ear to me,
     therefore I will call on him as long as I
       live.
3 The snares of death encompassed me;
     the pangs of Sheol laid hold on me;
     I suffered distress and anguish.
4 Then I called on the name of the LORD:
     "O LORD, I pray, deliver my soul!"

5 Gracious is the LORD, and righteous;
     our God is merciful.
6 The LORD preserves the simple;
     when I was brought low, he saved me.
7 Return, O my soul, to your rest;
     for the LORD has dealt bountifully
       with you.

8 For you have delivered my soul from
       death,
     my eyes from tears,
     my feet from stumbling;
9 I will walk before the LORD
     in the land of the living.

10 I believed, even when[1] I spoke:
      "I am greatly afflicted";
11 I said in my alarm,
      "All mankind are liars."

12 What shall I render to the LORD
      for all his benefits to me?
13 I will lift up the cup of salvation
      and call on the name of the LORD,
14 I will pay my vows to the LORD
      in the presence of all his people.

15 Precious in the sight of the LORD
      is the death of his saints.
16 O LORD, I am your servant;
      I am your servant, the son of your
        maidservant.
      You have loosed my bonds.
17 I will offer to you the sacrifice of
        thanksgiving
      and call on the name of the LORD.
18 I will pay my vows to the LORD
      in the presence of all his people,
19 in the courts of the house of the LORD,
      in your midst, O Jerusalem.
    Praise the LORD!

OCTOBER 24

——————— *2 Kings 5* ———————

N aaman, commander of the army of the king of Syria, was a great man with his master and in high favor, because by him the LORD had given victory to Syria. He was a mighty man of valor, but he was a leper.[2] 2Now the Syrians on one of their raids had carried off a little girl from the land of Israel, and she worked in the service of Naaman's wife. 3She said to her mistress, "Would that my lord were with the prophet who is in Samaria! He would cure him of his leprosy." 4So Naaman went in and told his lord, "Thus and so spoke the girl from the land of Israel."

5And the king of Syria said, "Go now, and I will send a letter to the king of Israel."

So he went, taking with him ten talents of silver, six thousand shekels[3] of gold, and ten changes of clothing. 6And he brought the letter to the king of Israel, which read, "When this letter reaches you, know that I have sent to you Naaman my servant, that you may cure him of his leprosy." 7And when the king of Israel read the letter, he tore his clothes and said, "Am I God, to kill and to make alive, that this man sends word to me to cure a man of his leprosy?

[1] Or *believed, indeed; Septuagint believed, therefore* [2] *Leprosy* was a term for several skin diseases; see Leviticus 13 [3] A *talent* was about 75 pounds or 34 kilograms; a *shekel* was about 2/5 ounce or 11 grams

Only consider, and see how he is seeking a quarrel with me."

[8] But when Elisha the man of God heard that the king of Israel had torn his clothes, he sent to the king, saying, "Why have you torn your clothes? Let him come now to me, that he may know that there is a prophet in Israel." [9] So Naaman came with his horses and chariots and stood at the door of Elisha's house. [10] And Elisha sent a messenger to him, saying, "Go and wash in the Jordan seven times, and your flesh shall be restored, and you shall be clean." [11] But Naaman was angry and went away, saying, "Behold, I thought that he would surely come out to me and stand and call upon the name of the LORD his God, and wave his hand over the place and cure the leper. [12] Are not Abana[1] and Pharpar, the rivers of Damascus, better than all the waters of Israel? Could I not wash in them and be clean?" So he turned and went away in a rage. [13] But his servants came near and said to him, "My father, it is a great word the prophet has spoken to you; will you not do it? Has he actually said to you, 'Wash, and be clean'?" [14] So he went down and dipped himself seven times in the Jordan, according to the word of the man of God, and his flesh was restored like the flesh of a little child, and he was clean.

[15] Then he returned to the man of God, he and all his company, and he came and stood before him. And he said, "Behold, I know that there is no God in all the earth but in Israel; so accept now a present from your servant." [16] But he said, "As the LORD lives, before whom I stand, I will receive none." And he urged him to take it, but he refused. [17] Then Naaman said, "If not, please let there be given to your servant two mule loads of earth, for from now on your servant will not offer burnt offering or sacrifice to any god but the LORD. [18] In this matter may the LORD pardon your servant: when my master goes into the house of Rimmon to worship there, leaning on my arm, and I bow myself in the house of Rimmon, when I bow myself in the house of Rimmon, the LORD pardon your servant in this matter." [19] He said to him, "Go in peace."

But when Naaman had gone from him a short distance, [20] Gehazi, the servant of Elisha the man of God, said, "See, my master has spared this Naaman the Syrian, in not accepting from his hand what he brought. As the LORD lives, I will run after him and get something from him." [21] So Gehazi followed Naaman. And when Naaman saw someone running after him, he got down from the chariot to meet him and said, "Is all well?" [22] And he said, "All is well. My master has sent me to say, 'There have just now come to me from the hill country of Ephraim two young men of the sons of the prophets. Please give them a talent of silver and two changes of clothing.'" [23] And Naaman said, "Be pleased to accept two talents." And he urged him and tied up two talents of silver in two bags, with two changes of clothing, and laid them on two of his servants. And they carried them before Gehazi. [24] And when he came to the hill, he took them from their hand and put them in the house, and he sent the men away, and they departed. [25] He went in and stood before his master, and Elisha said to him, "Where have you been, Gehazi?" And he said, "Your servant went nowhere." [26] But he said to him, "Did not my heart go when the man turned from his chariot to meet you? Was it a time to accept money and garments, olive orchards and vineyards, sheep and oxen, male servants and female servants? [27] Therefore the leprosy of Naaman shall cling to you and to your descendants forever." So he went out from his presence a leper, like snow.

1 Timothy 2

First of all, then, I urge that supplications, prayers, intercessions, and thanksgivings be made for all people, [2] for kings and all who are in high positions, that we may lead a peaceful and quiet life, godly and dignified in every way. [3] This is good, and it is pleasing in the sight of God our Savior, [4] who desires all people to be saved and to come to the knowledge of the truth. [5] For there is one God, and there is one mediator between God and men, the man[2] Christ Jesus, [6] who gave himself as a ransom for all, which is the testimony given at the proper time. [7] For this I was appointed a preacher and an apostle (I am telling the truth, I am not lying), a teacher of the Gentiles in faith and truth.

[8] I desire then that in every place the men should pray, lifting holy hands without anger or quarreling; [9] likewise also that women should adorn themselves in respectable apparel, with

[1] Or Amana [2] men and man render the same Greek word that is translated people in verses 1 and 4

modesty and self-control, not with braided hair and gold or pearls or costly attire, [10]but with what is proper for women who profess godliness—with good works. [11]Let a woman learn quietly with all submissiveness. [12]I do not permit a woman to teach or to exercise authority over a man; rather, she is to remain quiet. [13]For Adam was formed first, then Eve; [14]and Adam was not deceived, but the woman was deceived and became a transgressor. [15]Yet she will be saved through childbearing—if they continue in faith and love and holiness, with self-control.

Daniel 9

In the first year of Darius the son of Ahasuerus, by descent a Mede, who was made king over the realm of the Chaldeans— [2]in the first year of his reign, I, Daniel, perceived in the books the number of years that, according to the word of the LORD to Jeremiah the prophet, must pass before the end of the desolations of Jerusalem, namely, seventy years.

[3]Then I turned my face to the Lord God, seeking him by prayer and pleas for mercy with fasting and sackcloth and ashes. [4]I prayed to the LORD my God and made confession, saying, "O Lord, the great and awesome God, who keeps covenant and steadfast love with those who love him and keep his commandments, [5]we have sinned and done wrong and acted wickedly and rebelled, turning aside from your commandments and rules. [6]We have not listened to your servants the prophets, who spoke in your name to our kings, our princes, and our fathers, and to all the people of the land. [7]To you, O Lord, belongs righteousness, but to us open shame, as at this day, to the men of Judah, to the inhabitants of Jerusalem, and to all Israel, those who are near and those who are far away, in all the lands to which you have driven them, because of the treachery that they have committed against you. [8]To us, O LORD, belongs open shame, to our kings, to our princes, and to our fathers, because we have sinned against you. [9]To the Lord our God belong mercy and forgiveness, for we have rebelled against him [10]and have not obeyed the voice of the LORD our God by walking in his laws, which he set before us by his servants the prophets. [11]All Israel has transgressed your law and turned aside, refusing to obey your voice. And the curse and oath that are written in the Law of Moses the servant of God have been poured out upon us, because we have sinned against him. [12]He has confirmed his words, which he spoke against us and against our rulers who ruled us,[1] by bringing upon us a great calamity. For under the whole heaven there has not been done anything like what has been done against Jerusalem. [13]As it is written in the Law of Moses, all this calamity has come upon us; yet we have not entreated the favor of the LORD our God, turning from our iniquities and gaining insight by your truth. [14]Therefore the LORD has kept ready the calamity and has brought it upon us, for the LORD our God is righteous in all the works that he has done, and we have not obeyed his voice. [15]And now, O Lord our God, who brought your people out of the land of Egypt with a mighty hand, and have made a name for yourself, as at this day, we have sinned, we have done wickedly.

[16]"O Lord, according to all your righteous acts, let your anger and your wrath turn away from your city Jerusalem, your holy hill, because for our sins, and for the iniquities of our fathers, Jerusalem and your people have become a byword among all who are around us. [17]Now therefore, O our God, listen to the prayer of your servant and to his pleas for mercy, and for your own sake, O Lord,[2] make your face to shine upon your sanctuary, which is desolate. [18]O my God, incline your ear and hear. Open your eyes and see our desolations, and the city that is called by your name. For we do not present our pleas before you because of our righteousness, but because of your great mercy. [19]O Lord, hear; O Lord, forgive. O Lord, pay attention and act. Delay not, for your own sake, O my God, because your city and your people are called by your name."

[20]While I was speaking and praying, confessing my sin and the sin of my people Israel, and presenting my plea before the LORD my God for the holy hill of my God, [21]while I was speaking in prayer, the man Gabriel, whom I had seen in the vision at the first, came to me in swift flight at the time of the evening sacrifice. [22]He made me understand, speaking with me and saying, "O Daniel, I have now come out to give you insight and understanding. [23]At the beginning of your pleas for mercy a word went out, and I have come to tell it to you, for you are

[1] Or our judges who judged us [2] Hebrew for the Lord's sake

greatly loved. Therefore consider the word and understand the vision.

²⁴ "Seventy weeks[1] are decreed about your people and your holy city, to finish the transgression, to put an end to sin, and to atone for iniquity, to bring in everlasting righteousness, to seal both vision and prophet, and to anoint a most holy place.[2] ²⁵ Know therefore and understand that from the going out of the word to restore and build Jerusalem to the coming of an anointed one, a prince, there shall be seven weeks. Then for sixty-two weeks it shall be built again[3] with squares and moat, but in a troubled time. ²⁶ And after the sixty-two weeks, an anointed one shall be cut off and shall have nothing. And the people of the prince who is to come shall destroy the city and the sanctuary. Its[4] end shall come with a flood, and to the end there shall be war. Desolations are decreed. ²⁷ And he shall make a strong covenant with many for one week,[5] and for half of the week he shall put an end to sacrifice and offering. And on the wing of abominations shall come one who makes desolate, until the decreed end is poured out on the desolator."

Psalm 117–118

P raise the LORD, all nations!
  Extol him, all peoples!
² For great is his steadfast love toward us,
    and the faithfulness of the LORD
      endures forever.
  Praise the LORD!

O h give thanks to the LORD, for he is good;
  for his steadfast love endures forever!

² Let Israel say,
    "His steadfast love endures forever."
³ Let the house of Aaron say,
    "His steadfast love endures forever."
⁴ Let those who fear the LORD say,
    "His steadfast love endures forever."

⁵ Out of my distress I called on the LORD;
    the LORD answered me and set me free.
⁶ The LORD is on my side; I will not fear.
    What can man do to me?
⁷ The LORD is on my side as my helper;
    I shall look in triumph on those who
      hate me.

⁸ It is better to take refuge in the LORD
    than to trust in man.
⁹ It is better to take refuge in the LORD
    than to trust in princes.
¹⁰ All nations surrounded me;
    in the name of the LORD I cut them off!
¹¹ They surrounded me, surrounded me on
      every side;
    in the name of the LORD I cut them off!
¹² They surrounded me like bees;
    they went out like a fire among
      thorns;
    in the name of the LORD I cut them off!
¹³ I was pushed hard,[6] so that I was falling,
    but the LORD helped me.
¹⁴ The LORD is my strength and my song;
    he has become my salvation.
¹⁵ Glad songs of salvation
    are in the tents of the righteous:
  "The right hand of the LORD does
      valiantly,
¹⁶ the right hand of the LORD exalts,
    the right hand of the LORD does
      valiantly!"
¹⁷ I shall not die, but I shall live,
    and recount the deeds of the LORD.
¹⁸ The LORD has disciplined me severely,
    but he has not given me over to
      death.
¹⁹ Open to me the gates of righteousness,
    that I may enter through them
    and give thanks to the LORD.
²⁰ This is the gate of the LORD;
    the righteous shall enter through it.
²¹ I thank you that you have answered me
    and have become my salvation.
²² The stone that the builders rejected
    has become the cornerstone.[7]
²³ This is the LORD's doing;
    it is marvelous in our eyes.
²⁴ This is the day that the LORD has made;
    let us rejoice and be glad in it.
²⁵ Save us, we pray, O LORD!
    O LORD, we pray, give us success!
²⁶ Blessed is he who comes in the name of
      the LORD!
    We bless you from the house of the
      LORD.

¹ Or sevens; also twice in verse 25 and once in verse 26 ² Or thing, or one ³ Or there shall be seven weeks and sixty-two weeks. It shall be built again ⁴ Or His ⁵ Or seven; twice in this verse ⁶ Hebrew You (that is, the enemy) pushed me hard ⁷ Hebrew the head of the corner

27 The LORD is God,
    and he has made his light to shine
        upon us.
    Bind the festal sacrifice with cords,
        up to the horns of the altar!

28 You are my God, and I will give thanks
        to you;
    you are my God; I will extol you.
29 Oh give thanks to the LORD, for he is good;
    for his steadfast love endures forever!

OCTOBER 25

2 Kings 6

Now the sons of the prophets said to Elisha, "See, the place where we dwell under your charge is too small for us. ²Let us go to the Jordan and each of us get there a log, and let us make a place for us to dwell there." And he answered, "Go." ³Then one of them said, "Be pleased to go with your servants." And he answered, "I will go." ⁴So he went with them. And when they came to the Jordan, they cut down trees. ⁵But as one was felling a log, his axe head fell into the water, and he cried out, "Alas, my master! It was borrowed." ⁶Then the man of God said, "Where did it fall?" When he showed him the place, he cut off a stick and threw it in there and made the iron float. ⁷And he said, "Take it up." So he reached out his hand and took it.

⁸Once when the king of Syria was warring against Israel, he took counsel with his servants, saying, "At such and such a place shall be my camp." ⁹But the man of God sent word to the king of Israel, "Beware that you do not pass this place, for the Syrians are going down there." ¹⁰And the king of Israel sent to the place about which the man of God told him. Thus he used to warn him, so that he saved himself there more than once or twice.

¹¹And the mind of the king of Syria was greatly troubled because of this thing, and he called his servants and said to them, "Will you not show me who of us is for the king of Israel?" ¹²And one of his servants said, "None, my lord, O king; but Elisha, the prophet who is in Israel, tells the king of Israel the words that you speak in your bedroom." ¹³And he said, "Go and see where he is, that I may send and seize him." It

was told him, "Behold, he is in Dothan." ¹⁴So he sent there horses and chariots and a great army, and they came by night and surrounded the city.

¹⁵When the servant of the man of God rose early in the morning and went out, behold, an army with horses and chariots was all around the city. And the servant said, "Alas, my master! What shall we do?" ¹⁶He said, "Do not be afraid, for those who are with us are more than those who are with them." ¹⁷Then Elisha prayed and said, "O LORD, please open his eyes that he may see." So the LORD opened the eyes of the young man, and he saw, and behold, the mountain was full of horses and chariots of fire all around Elisha. ¹⁸And when the Syrians came down against him, Elisha prayed to the LORD and said, "Please strike this people with blindness." So he struck them with blindness in accordance with the prayer of Elisha. ¹⁹And Elisha said to them, "This is not the way, and this is not the city. Follow me, and I will bring you to the man whom you seek." And he led them to Samaria.

²⁰As soon as they entered Samaria, Elisha said, "O LORD, open the eyes of these men, that they may see." So the LORD opened their eyes and they saw, and behold, they were in the midst of Samaria. ²¹As soon as the king of Israel saw them, he said to Elisha, "My father, shall I strike them down? Shall I strike them down?" ²²He answered, "You shall not strike them down. Would you strike down those whom you have taken captive with your sword and with your bow? Set bread and water before them, that they may eat and drink and go to

their master." ²³So he prepared for them a great feast, and when they had eaten and drunk, he sent them away, and they went to their master. And the Syrians did not come again on raids into the land of Israel.

²⁴Afterward Ben-hadad king of Syria mustered his entire army and went up and besieged Samaria. ²⁵And there was a great famine in Samaria, as they besieged it, until a donkey's head was sold for eighty shekels of silver, and the fourth part of a kab¹ of dove's dung for five shekels of silver. ²⁶Now as the king of Israel was passing by on the wall, a woman cried out to him, saying, "Help, my lord, O king!" ²⁷And he said, "If the LORD will not help you, how shall I help you? From the threshing floor, or from the winepress?" ²⁸And the king asked her, "What is your trouble?" She answered, "This woman said to me, 'Give your son, that we may eat him today, and we will eat my son tomorrow.' ²⁹So we boiled my son and ate him. And on the next day I said to her, 'Give your son, that we may eat him.' But she has hidden her son." ³⁰When the king heard the words of the woman, he tore his clothes—now he was passing by on the wall—and the people looked, and behold, he had sackcloth beneath on his body— ³¹and he said, "May God do so to me and more also, if the head of Elisha the son of Shaphat remains on his shoulders today."

³²Elisha was sitting in his house, and the elders were sitting with him. Now the king had dispatched a man from his presence, but before the messenger arrived Elisha said to the elders, "Do you see how this murderer has sent to take off my head? Look, when the messenger comes, shut the door and hold the door fast against him. Is not the sound of his master's feet behind him?" ³³And while he was still speaking with them, the messenger came down to him and said, "This trouble is from the LORD! Why should I wait for the LORD any longer?"

1 Timothy 3

The saying is trustworthy: If anyone aspires to the office of overseer, he desires a noble task. ²Therefore an overseer² must be above reproach, the husband of one wife,³ sober-minded, self-controlled, respectable, hospitable, able to teach, ³not a drunkard, not violent but gentle, not quarrelsome, not a lover of money. ⁴He must manage his own household well, with all dignity keeping his children submissive, ⁵for if someone does not know how to manage his own household, how will he care for God's church? ⁶He must not be a recent convert, or he may become puffed up with conceit and fall into the condemnation of the devil. ⁷Moreover, he must be well thought of by outsiders, so that he may not fall into disgrace, into a snare of the devil.

⁸Deacons likewise must be dignified, not double-tongued,⁴ not addicted to much wine, not greedy for dishonest gain. ⁹They must hold the mystery of the faith with a clear conscience. ¹⁰And let them also be tested first; then let them serve as deacons if they prove themselves blameless. ¹¹Their wives likewise must⁵ be dignified, not slanderers, but sober-minded, faithful in all things. ¹²Let deacons each be the husband of one wife, managing their children and their own households well. ¹³For those who serve well as deacons gain a good standing for themselves and also great confidence in the faith that is in Christ Jesus.

¹⁴I hope to come to you soon, but I am writing these things to you so that, ¹⁵if I delay, you may know how one ought to behave in the household of God, which is the church of the living God, a pillar and buttress of the truth. ¹⁶Great indeed, we confess, is the mystery of godliness:

He⁶ was manifested in the flesh,
    vindicated⁷ by the Spirit,⁸
    seen by angels,
proclaimed among the nations,
    believed on in the world,
    taken up in glory.

Daniel 10

In the third year of Cyrus king of Persia a word was revealed to Daniel, who was named Belteshazzar. And the word was true, and it was a great conflict.⁹ And he understood the word and had understanding of the vision.

²In those days I, Daniel, was mourning for three weeks. ³I ate no delicacies, no meat or wine entered my mouth, nor did I anoint myself at all, for the full three weeks. ⁴On the twenty-fourth day of the first month, as I was standing

¹ A shekel was about 2/5 ounce or 11 grams; a kab was about 1 quart or 1 liter ² Or bishop; Greek episkopos; a similar term occurs in verse 1 ³ Or a man of one woman; also verse 12 ⁴ Or devious in speech ⁵ Or Wives, likewise, must, or Women, likewise, must ⁶ Greek Who; some manuscripts God; others Which ⁷ Or justified ⁸ Or vindicated in spirit ⁹ Or and it was about a great conflict

on the bank of the great river (that is, the Tigris) [5] I lifted up my eyes and looked, and behold, a man clothed in linen, with a belt of fine gold from Uphaz around his waist. [6] His body was like beryl, his face like the appearance of lightning, his eyes like flaming torches, his arms and legs like the gleam of burnished bronze, and the sound of his words like the sound of a multitude. [7] And I, Daniel, alone saw the vision, for the men who were with me did not see the vision, but a great trembling fell upon them, and they fled to hide themselves. [8] So I was left alone and saw this great vision, and no strength was left in me. My radiant appearance was fearfully changed,[1] and I retained no strength. [9] Then I heard the sound of his words, and as I heard the sound of his words, I fell on my face in deep sleep with my face to the ground.

[10] And behold, a hand touched me and set me trembling on my hands and knees. [11] And he said to me, "O Daniel, man greatly loved, understand the words that I speak to you, and stand upright, for now I have been sent to you." And when he had spoken this word to me, I stood up trembling. [12] Then he said to me, "Fear not, Daniel, for from the first day that you set your heart to understand and humbled yourself before your God, your words have been heard, and I have come because of your words. [13] The prince of the kingdom of Persia withstood me twenty-one days, but Michael, one of the chief princes, came to help me, for I was left there with the kings of Persia, [14] and came to make you understand what is to happen to your people in the latter days. For the vision is for days yet to come."

[15] When he had spoken to me according to these words, I turned my face toward the ground and was mute. [16] And behold, one in the likeness of the children of man touched my lips. Then I opened my mouth and spoke. I said to him who stood before me, "O my lord, by reason of the vision pains have come upon me, and I retain no strength. [17] How can my lord's servant talk with my lord? For now no strength remains in me, and no breath is left in me."

[18] Again one having the appearance of a man touched me and strengthened me. [19] And he said, "O man greatly loved, fear not, peace be with you; be strong and of good courage." And as he spoke to me, I was strengthened and said, "Let my lord speak, for you have strengthened me." [20] Then he said, "Do you know why I have

come to you? But now I will return to fight against the prince of Persia; and when I go out, behold, the prince of Greece will come. [21] But I will tell you what is inscribed in the book of truth: there is none who contends by my side against these except Michael, your prince.

Psalm 119:1[2]–24

Aleph

Blessed are those whose way is blameless, who walk in the law of the Lord!
[2] Blessed are those who keep his testimonies,
who seek him with their whole heart,
[3] who also do no wrong,
but walk in his ways!
[4] You have commanded your precepts
to be kept diligently.
[5] Oh that my ways may be steadfast
in keeping your statutes!
[6] Then I shall not be put to shame,
having my eyes fixed on all your commandments.
[7] I will praise you with an upright heart,
when I learn your righteous rules.[3]
[8] I will keep your statutes;
do not utterly forsake me!

Beth

[9] How can a young man keep his way pure?
By guarding it according to your word.
[10] With my whole heart I seek you;
let me not wander from your commandments!
[11] I have stored up your word in my heart,
that I might not sin against you.
[12] Blessed are you, O Lord;
teach me your statutes!
[13] With my lips I declare
all the rules[4] of your mouth.
[14] In the way of your testimonies I delight
as much as in all riches.
[15] I will meditate on your precepts
and fix my eyes on your ways.
[16] I will delight in your statutes;
I will not forget your word.

Gimel

[17] Deal bountifully with your servant,
that I may live and keep your word.
[18] Open my eyes, that I may behold
wondrous things out of your law.

[1] Hebrew *My splendor was changed to ruin* [2] This psalm is an acrostic poem of twenty-two stanzas, following the letters of the Hebrew alphabet; within a stanza, each verse begins with the same Hebrew letter [3] Or *your just and righteous decrees; also verses 62, 106, 160, 164* [4] Or *all the just decrees*

19 I am a sojourner on the earth;
    hide not your commandments from
        me!
20 My soul is consumed with longing
    for your rules¹ at all times.
21 You rebuke the insolent, accursed ones,
    who wander from your
        commandments.

22 Take away from me scorn and contempt,
    for I have kept your testimonies.
23 Even though princes sit plotting against
        me,
    your servant will meditate on your
        statutes.
24 Your testimonies are my delight;
    they are my counselors.

OCTOBER 26

2 Kings 7

But Elisha said, "Hear the word of the LORD: thus says the LORD, Tomorrow about this time a seah² of fine flour shall be sold for a shekel,³ and two seahs of barley for a shekel, at the gate of Samaria." ²Then the captain on whose hand the king leaned said to the man of God, "If the LORD himself should make windows in heaven, could this thing be?" But he said, "You shall see it with your own eyes, but you shall not eat of it."

³Now there were four men who were lepers⁴ at the entrance to the gate. And they said to one another, "Why are we sitting here until we die? ⁴If we say, 'Let us enter the city,' the famine is in the city, and we shall die there. And if we sit here, we die also. So now come, let us go over to the camp of the Syrians. If they spare our lives we shall live, and if they kill us we shall but die." ⁵So they arose at twilight to go to the camp of the Syrians. But when they came to the edge of the camp of the Syrians, behold, there was no one there. ⁶For the Lord had made the army of the Syrians hear the sound of chariots and of horses, the sound of a great army, so that they said to one another, "Behold, the king of Israel has hired against us the kings of the Hittites and the kings of Egypt to come against us." ⁷So they fled away in the twilight and abandoned their tents, their horses, and their donkeys, leaving the camp as it was, and fled for their lives. ⁸And when these lepers came to the edge of the camp, they went into a tent and ate and drank, and they carried off silver and gold and

clothing and went and hid them. Then they came back and entered another tent and carried off things from it and went and hid them. ⁹Then they said to one another, "We are not doing right. This day is a day of good news. If we are silent and wait until the morning light, punishment will overtake us. Now therefore come; let us go and tell the king's household." ¹⁰So they came and called to the gatekeepers of the city and told them, "We came to the camp of the Syrians, and behold, there was no one to be seen or heard there, nothing but the horses tied and the donkeys tied and the tents as they were." ¹¹Then the gatekeepers called out, and it was told within the king's household. ¹²And the king rose in the night and said to his servants, "I will tell you what the Syrians have done to us. They know that we are hungry. Therefore they have gone out of the camp to hide themselves in the open country, thinking, 'When they come out of the city, we shall take them alive and get into the city.'" ¹³And one of his servants said, "Let some men take five of the remaining horses, seeing that those who are left here will fare like the whole multitude of Israel who have already perished. Let us send and see." ¹⁴So they took two horsemen, and the king sent them after the army of the Syrians, saying, "Go and see." ¹⁵So they went after them as far as the Jordan, and behold, all the way was littered with garments and equipment that the Syrians had thrown away in their haste. And the messengers returned and told the king.

¹ Or *your just decrees*; also verses 30, 39, 43, 52, 75, 102, 108, 137, 156, 175   ² A *seah* was about 7 quarts or 7.3 liters   ³ A *shekel* was about 2/5 ounce or 11 grams   ⁴ *Leprosy* was a term for several skin diseases; see Leviticus 13

[16] Then the people went out and plundered the camp of the Syrians. So a seah of fine flour was sold for a shekel, and two seahs of barley for a shekel, according to the word of the LORD. [17] Now the king had appointed the captain on whose hand he leaned to have charge of the gate. And the people trampled him in the gate, so that he died, as the man of God had said when the king came down to him. [18] For when the man of God had said to the king, "Two seahs of barley shall be sold for a shekel, and a seah of fine flour for a shekel, about this time tomorrow in the gate of Samaria," [19] the captain had answered the man of God, "If the LORD himself should make windows in heaven, could such a thing be?" And he had said, "You shall see it with your own eyes, but you shall not eat of it." [20] And so it happened to him, for the people trampled him in the gate and he died.

1 Timothy 4

Now the Spirit expressly says that in later times some will depart from the faith by devoting themselves to deceitful spirits and teachings of demons, [2] through the insincerity of liars whose consciences are seared, [3] who forbid marriage and require abstinence from foods that God created to be received with thanksgiving by those who believe and know the truth. [4] For everything created by God is good, and nothing is to be rejected if it is received with thanksgiving, [5] for it is made holy by the word of God and prayer.

[6] If you put these things before the brothers,[1] you will be a good servant of Christ Jesus, being trained in the words of the faith and of the good doctrine that you have followed. [7] Have nothing to do with irreverent, silly myths. Rather train yourself for godliness; [8] for while bodily training is of some value, godliness is of value in every way, as it holds promise for the present life and also for the life to come. [9] The saying is trustworthy and deserving of full acceptance. [10] For to this end we toil and strive,[2] because we have our hope set on the living God, who is the Savior of all people, especially of those who believe.

[11] Command and teach these things. [12] Let no one despise you for your youth, but set the believers an example in speech, in conduct, in love, in faith, in purity. [13] Until I come, devote yourself to the public reading of Scripture, to exhortation, to teaching. [14] Do not neglect the gift you have, which was given you by prophecy when the council of elders laid their hands on you. [15] Practice these things, immerse yourself in them,[3] so that all may see your progress. [16] Keep a close watch on yourself and on the teaching. Persist in this, for by so doing you will save both yourself and your hearers.

Daniel 11

"And as for me, in the first year of Darius the Mede, I stood up to confirm and strengthen him.

[2] "And now I will show you the truth. Behold, three more kings shall arise in Persia, and a fourth shall be far richer than all of them. And when he has become strong through his riches, he shall stir up all against the kingdom of Greece. [3] Then a mighty king shall arise, who shall rule with great dominion and do as he wills. [4] And as soon as he has arisen, his kingdom shall be broken and divided toward the four winds of heaven, but not to his posterity, nor according to the authority with which he ruled, for his kingdom shall be plucked up and go to others besides these.

[5] "Then the king of the south shall be strong, but one of his princes shall be stronger than he and shall rule, and his authority shall be a great authority. [6] After some years they shall make an alliance, and the daughter of the king of the south shall come to the king of the north to make an agreement. But she shall not retain the strength of her arm, and he and his arm shall not endure, but she shall be given up, and her attendants, he who fathered her, and he who supported[4] her in those times.

[7] "And from a branch from her roots one shall arise in his place. He shall come against the army and enter the fortress of the king of the north, and he shall deal with them and shall prevail. [8] He shall also carry off to Egypt their gods with their metal images and their precious vessels of silver and gold, and for some years he shall refrain from attacking the king of the north. [9] Then the latter shall come into the realm of the king of the south but shall return to his own land.

[10] "His sons shall wage war and assemble a multitude of great forces, which shall keep

coming and overflow and pass through, and again shall carry the war as far as his fortress. [11] Then the king of the south, moved with rage, shall come out and fight against the king of the north. And he shall raise a great multitude, but it shall be given into his hand. [12] And when the multitude is taken away, his heart shall be exalted, and he shall cast down tens of thousands, but he shall not prevail. [13] For the king of the north shall again raise a multitude, greater than the first. And after some years[1] he shall come on with a great army and abundant supplies.

[14] "In those times many shall rise against the king of the south, and the violent among your own people shall lift themselves up in order to fulfill the vision, but they shall fail. [15] Then the king of the north shall come and throw up siegeworks and take a well-fortified city. And the forces of the south shall not stand, or even his best troops, for there shall be no strength to stand. [16] But he who comes against him shall do as he wills, and none shall stand before him. And he shall stand in the glorious land, with destruction in his hand. [17] He shall set his face to come with the strength of his whole kingdom, and he shall bring terms of an agreement and perform them. He shall give him the daughter of women to destroy the kingdom,[2] but it shall not stand or be to his advantage. [18] Afterward he shall turn his face to the coastlands and shall capture many of them, but a commander shall put an end to his insolence. Indeed,[3] he shall turn his insolence back upon him. [19] Then he shall turn his face back toward the fortresses of his own land, but he shall stumble and fall, and shall not be found.

[20] "Then shall arise in his place one who shall send an exactor of tribute for the glory of the kingdom. But within a few days he shall be broken, neither in anger nor in battle. [21] In his place shall arise a contemptible person to whom royal majesty has not been given. He shall come in without warning and obtain the kingdom by flatteries. [22] Armies shall be utterly swept away before him and broken, even the prince of the covenant. [23] And from the time that an alliance is made with him he shall act deceitfully, and he shall become strong with a small people. [24] Without warning he shall come into the richest parts[4] of the province, and he shall do what neither his fathers nor his fathers' fathers have done, scattering among them plunder, spoil, and goods. He shall devise plans against strongholds, but only for a time. [25] And he shall stir up his power and his heart against the king of the south with a great army. And the king of the south shall wage war with an exceedingly great and mighty army, but he shall not stand, for plots shall be devised against him. [26] Even those who eat his food shall break him. His army shall be swept away, and many shall fall down slain. [27] And as for the two kings, their hearts shall be bent on doing evil. They shall speak lies at the same table, but to no avail, for the end is yet to be at the time appointed. [28] And he shall return to his land with great wealth, but his heart shall be set against the holy covenant. And he shall work his will and return to his own land.

[29] "At the time appointed he shall return and come into the south, but it shall not be this time as it was before. [30] For ships of Kittim shall come against him, and he shall be afraid and withdraw, and shall turn back and be enraged and take action against the holy covenant. He shall turn back and pay attention to those who forsake the holy covenant. [31] Forces from him shall appear and profane the temple and fortress, and shall take away the regular burnt offering. And they shall set up the abomination that makes desolate. [32] He shall seduce with flattery those who violate the covenant, but the people who know their God shall stand firm and take action. [33] And the wise among the people shall make many understand, though for some days they shall stumble by sword and flame, by captivity and plunder. [34] When they stumble, they shall receive a little help. And many shall join themselves to them with flattery, [35] and some of the wise shall stumble, so that they may be refined, purified, and made white, until the time of the end, for it still awaits the appointed time.

[36] "And the king shall do as he wills. He shall exalt himself and magnify himself above every god, and shall speak astonishing things against the God of gods. He shall prosper till the indignation is accomplished; for what is decreed shall be done. [37] He shall pay no attention to the gods of his fathers, or to the one beloved by women. He shall not pay attention to any other god, for he shall magnify himself above all. [38] He shall honor the god of fortresses instead of these.

---

[1] Hebrew *at the end of the times* [2] Hebrew *her, or it* [3] The meaning of the Hebrew is uncertain [4] Or *among the richest men*

A god whom his fathers did not know he shall honor with gold and silver, with precious stones and costly gifts. [39]He shall deal with the strongest fortresses with the help of a foreign god. Those who acknowledge him he shall load with honor. He shall make them rulers over many and shall divide the land for a price.[1]

[40]"At the time of the end, the king of the south shall attack[2] him, but the king of the north shall rush upon him like a whirlwind, with chariots and horsemen, and with many ships. And he shall come into countries and shall overflow and pass through. [41]He shall come into the glorious land. And tens of thousands shall fall, but these shall be delivered out of his hand: Edom and Moab and the main part of the Ammonites. [42]He shall stretch out his hand against the countries, and the land of Egypt shall not escape. [43]He shall become ruler of the treasures of gold and of silver, and all the precious things of Egypt, and the Libyans and the Cushites shall follow in his train. [44]But news from the east and the north shall alarm him, and he shall go out with great fury to destroy and devote many to destruction. [45]And he shall pitch his palatial tents between the sea and the glorious holy mountain. Yet he shall come to his end, with none to help him.

Psalm 119:25–48

DALETH

My soul clings to the dust;
give me life according to your word!
[26] When I told of my ways, you answered me;
teach me your statutes!
[27] Make me understand the way of your precepts,
and I will meditate on your wondrous works.
[28] My soul melts away for sorrow;
strengthen me according to your word!
[29] Put false ways far from me
and graciously teach me your law!
[30] I have chosen the way of faithfulness;
I set your rules before me.
[31] I cling to your testimonies, O LORD;
let me not be put to shame!

[32] I will run in the way of your commandments
when you enlarge my heart![3]

HE

[33] Teach me, O LORD, the way of your statutes;
and I will keep it to the end.[4]
[34] Give me understanding, that I may keep your law
and observe it with my whole heart.
[35] Lead me in the path of your commandments,
for I delight in it.
[36] Incline my heart to your testimonies,
and not to selfish gain!
[37] Turn my eyes from looking at worthless things;
and give me life in your ways.
[38] Confirm to your servant your promise,
that you may be feared.
[39] Turn away the reproach that I dread,
for your rules are good.
[40] Behold, I long for your precepts;
in your righteousness give me life!

WAW

[41] Let your steadfast love come to me, O LORD,
your salvation according to your promise;
[42] then shall I have an answer for him who taunts me,
for I trust in your word.
[43] And take not the word of truth utterly out of my mouth,
for my hope is in your rules.
[44] I will keep your law continually,
forever and ever,
[45] and I shall walk in a wide place,
for I have sought your precepts.
[46] I will also speak of your testimonies before kings
and shall not be put to shame,
[47] for I find my delight in your commandments,
which I love.
[48] I will lift up my hands toward your commandments, which I love,
and I will meditate on your statutes.

[1] Or land as payment [2] Hebrew thrust at [3] Or for you set my heart free [4] Or keep it as my reward

OCTOBER 27

2 Kings 8

Now Elisha had said to the woman whose son he had restored to life, "Arise, and depart with your household, and sojourn wherever you can, for the LORD has called for a famine, and it will come upon the land for seven years." ²So the woman arose and did according to the word of the man of God. She went with her household and sojourned in the land of the Philistines seven years. ³And at the end of the seven years, when the woman returned from the land of the Philistines, she went to appeal to the king for her house and her land. ⁴Now the king was talking with Gehazi the servant of the man of God, saying, "Tell me all the great things that Elisha has done." ⁵And while he was telling the king how Elisha had restored the dead to life, behold, the woman whose son he had restored to life appealed to the king for her house and her land. And Gehazi said, "My lord, O king, here is the woman, and here is her son whom Elisha restored to life." ⁶And when the king asked the woman, she told him. So the king appointed an official for her, saying, "Restore all that was hers, together with all the produce of the fields from the day that she left the land until now."

⁷Now Elisha came to Damascus. Ben-hadad the king of Syria was sick. And when it was told him, "The man of God has come here," ⁸the king said to Hazael, "Take a present with you and go to meet the man of God, and inquire of the LORD through him, saying, 'Shall I recover from this sickness?'" ⁹So Hazael went to meet him, and took a present with him, all kinds of goods of Damascus, forty camels' loads. When he came and stood before him, he said, "Your son Ben-hadad king of Syria has sent me to you, saying, 'Shall I recover from this sickness?'" ¹⁰And Elisha said to him, "Go, say to him, 'You shall certainly recover,' but[1] the LORD has shown me that he shall certainly die." ¹¹And he fixed his gaze and stared at him, until he was embarrassed. And the man of God wept. ¹²And Hazael said, "Why does my lord weep?"

He answered, "Because I know the evil that you will do to the people of Israel. You will set on fire their fortresses, and you will kill their young men with the sword and dash in pieces their little ones and rip open their pregnant women." ¹³And Hazael said, "What is your servant, who is but a dog, that he should do this great thing?" Elisha answered, "The LORD has shown me that you are to be king over Syria." ¹⁴Then he departed from Elisha and came to his master, who said to him, "What did Elisha say to you?" And he answered, "He told me that you would certainly recover." ¹⁵But the next day he took the bed cloth[2] and dipped it in water and spread it over his face, till he died. And Hazael became king in his place.

¹⁶In the fifth year of Joram the son of Ahab, king of Israel, when Jehoshaphat was king of Judah,[3] Jehoram the son of Jehoshaphat, king of Judah, began to reign. ¹⁷He was thirty-two years old when he became king, and he reigned eight years in Jerusalem. ¹⁸And he walked in the way of the kings of Israel, as the house of Ahab had done, for the daughter of Ahab was his wife. And he did what was evil in the sight of the LORD. ¹⁹Yet the LORD was not willing to destroy Judah, for the sake of David his servant, since he promised to give a lamp to him and to his sons forever.

²⁰In his days Edom revolted from the rule of Judah and set up a king of their own. ²¹Then Joram[4] passed over to Zair with all his chariots and rose by night, and he and his chariot commanders struck the Edomites who had surrounded him, but his army fled home. ²²So Edom revolted from the rule of Judah to this day. Then Libnah revolted at the same time. ²³Now the rest of the acts of Joram, and all that he did, are they not written in the Book of the Chronicles of the Kings of Judah? ²⁴So Joram slept with his fathers and was buried with his fathers in the city of David, and Ahaziah his son reigned in his place. ²⁵In the twelfth year of Joram the son of Ahab,

[1] Some manuscripts say, 'You shall certainly not recover,' for   [2] The meaning of the Hebrew is uncertain   [3] Septuagint, Syriac lack when Jehoshaphat was king of Judah   [4] Joram is an alternate spelling of Jehoram (the son of Jehoshaphat) as in verse 16; also verses 23, 24

king of Israel, Ahaziah the son of Jehoram, king of Judah, began to reign. [26]Ahaziah was twenty-two years old when he began to reign, and he reigned one year in Jerusalem. His mother's name was Athaliah; she was a granddaughter of Omri king of Israel. [27]He also walked in the way of the house of Ahab and did what was evil in the sight of the LORD, as the house of Ahab had done, for he was son-in-law to the house of Ahab.

[28]He went with Joram the son of Ahab to make war against Hazael king of Syria at Ramoth-gilead, and the Syrians wounded Joram. [29]And King Joram returned to be healed in Jezreel of the wounds that the Syrians had given him at Ramah, when he fought against Hazael king of Syria. And Ahaziah the son of Jehoram king of Judah went down to see Joram the son of Ahab in Jezreel, because he was sick.

---

1 Timothy 5

Do not rebuke an older man but encourage him as you would a father, younger men as brothers, [2]older women as mothers, younger women as sisters, in all purity.

[3]Honor widows who are truly widows. [4]But if a widow has children or grandchildren, let them first learn to show godliness to their own household and to make some return to their parents, for this is pleasing in the sight of God. [5]She who is truly a widow, left all alone, has set her hope on God and continues in supplications and prayers night and day, [6]but she who is self-indulgent is dead even while she lives. [7]Command these things as well, so that they may be without reproach. [8]But if anyone does not provide for his relatives, and especially for members of his household, he has denied the faith and is worse than an unbeliever.

[9]Let a widow be enrolled if she is not less than sixty years of age, having been the wife of one husband,[1] [10]and having a reputation for good works: if she has brought up children, has shown hospitality, has washed the feet of the saints, has cared for the afflicted, and has devoted herself to every good work. [11]But refuse to enroll younger widows, for when their passions draw them away from Christ, they desire to marry [12]and so incur condemnation for having abandoned their former faith. [13]Besides that, they learn to be idlers, going about from house to house, and not only idlers, but also gossips and busybodies, saying what they should not. [14]So I would have younger widows marry, bear children, manage their households, and give the adversary no occasion for slander. [15]For some have already strayed after Satan. [16]If any believing woman has relatives who are widows, let her care for them. Let the church not be burdened, so that it may care for those who are truly widows.

[17]Let the elders who rule well be considered worthy of double honor, especially those who labor in preaching and teaching. [18]For the Scripture says, "You shall not muzzle an ox when it treads out the grain," and, "The laborer deserves his wages." [19]Do not admit a charge against an elder except on the evidence of two or three witnesses. [20]As for those who persist in sin, rebuke them in the presence of all, so that the rest may stand in fear. [21]In the presence of God and of Christ Jesus and of the elect angels I charge you to keep these rules without prejudging, doing nothing from partiality. [22]Do not be hasty in the laying on of hands, nor take part in the sins of others; keep yourself pure. [23](No longer drink only water, but use a little wine for the sake of your stomach and your frequent ailments.) [24]The sins of some people are conspicuous, going before them to judgment, but the sins of others appear later. [25]So also good works are conspicuous, and even those that are not cannot remain hidden.

Daniel 12

"At that time shall arise Michael, the great prince who has charge of your people. And there shall be a time of trouble, such as never has been since there was a nation till that time. But at that time your people shall be delivered, everyone whose name shall be found written in the book. [2]And many of those who sleep in the dust of the earth shall awake, some to everlasting life, and some to shame and everlasting contempt. [3]And those who are wise shall shine like the brightness of the sky above;[2] and those who turn many to righteousness, like the stars forever and ever. [4]But you, Daniel, shut up the words and seal the book, until the time of the end. Many shall run to and fro, and knowledge shall increase."

[1] Or a woman of one man [2] Hebrew the expanse; compare Genesis 1:6–8

⁵Then I, Daniel, looked, and behold, two others stood, one on this bank of the stream and one on that bank of the stream. ⁶And someone said to the man clothed in linen, who was above the waters of the stream,¹ "How long shall it be till the end of these wonders?" ⁷And I heard the man clothed in linen, who was above the waters of the stream; he raised his right hand and his left hand toward heaven and swore by him who lives forever that it would be for a time, times, and half a time, and that when the shattering of the power of the holy people comes to an end all these things would be finished. ⁸I heard, but I did not understand. Then I said, "O my lord, what shall be the outcome of these things?" ⁹He said, "Go your way, Daniel, for the words are shut up and sealed until the time of the end. ¹⁰Many shall purify themselves and make themselves white and be refined, but the wicked shall act wickedly. And none of the wicked shall understand, but those who are wise shall understand. ¹¹And from the time that the regular burnt offering is taken away and the abomination that makes desolate is set up, there shall be 1,290 days. ¹²Blessed is he who waits and arrives at the 1,335 days. ¹³But go your way till the end. And you shall rest and shall stand in your allotted place at the end of the days."

Psalm 119:49–72

ZAYIN

Remember your word to your servant,
  in which you have made me hope.
⁵⁰ This is my comfort in my affliction,
    that your promise gives me life.
⁵¹ The insolent utterly deride me,
    but I do not turn away from your law.
⁵² When I think of your rules from of old,
    I take comfort, O LORD.
⁵³ Hot indignation seizes me because of
      the wicked,
    who forsake your law.
⁵⁴ Your statutes have been my songs
    in the house of my sojourning.

⁵⁵ I remember your name in the night,
    O LORD,
  and keep your law.
⁵⁶ This blessing has fallen to me,
    that I have kept your precepts.

HETH

⁵⁷ The LORD is my portion;
    I promise to keep your words.
⁵⁸ I entreat your favor with all my heart;
    be gracious to me according to your
      promise.
⁵⁹ When I think on my ways,
    I turn my feet to your testimonies;
⁶⁰ I hasten and do not delay
    to keep your commandments.
⁶¹ Though the cords of the wicked ensnare
      me,
    I do not forget your law.
⁶² At midnight I rise to praise you,
    because of your righteous rules.
⁶³ I am a companion of all who fear you,
    of those who keep your precepts.
⁶⁴ The earth, O LORD, is full of your
      steadfast love;
    teach me your statutes!

TETH

⁶⁵ You have dealt well with your servant,
    O LORD, according to your word.
⁶⁶ Teach me good judgment and
      knowledge,
    for I believe in your commandments.
⁶⁷ Before I was afflicted I went astray,
    but now I keep your word.
⁶⁸ You are good and do good;
    teach me your statutes.
⁶⁹ The insolent smear me with lies,
    but with my whole heart I keep your
      precepts;
⁷⁰ their heart is unfeeling like fat,
    but I delight in your law.
⁷¹ It is good for me that I was afflicted,
    that I might learn your statutes.
⁷² The law of your mouth is better to me
    than thousands of gold and silver
      pieces.

---

¹ Or *who was upstream*; also verse 7

OCTOBER 28

2 Kings 9

Then Elisha the prophet called one of the sons of the prophets and said to him, "Tie up your garments, and take this flask of oil in your hand, and go to Ramoth-gilead. ²And when you arrive, look there for Jehu the son of Jehoshaphat, son of Nimshi. And go in and have him rise from among his fellows, and lead him to an inner chamber. ³Then take the flask of oil and pour it on his head and say, 'Thus says the Lord, I anoint you king over Israel.' Then open the door and flee; do not linger."

⁴So the young man, the servant of the prophet, went to Ramoth-gilead. ⁵And when he came, behold, the commanders of the army were in council. And he said, "I have a word for you, O commander." And Jehu said, "To which of us all?" And he said, "To you, O commander." ⁶So he arose and went into the house. And the young man poured the oil on his head, saying to him, "Thus says the Lord, the God of Israel, I anoint you king over the people of the Lord, over Israel. ⁷And you shall strike down the house of Ahab your master, so that I may avenge on Jezebel the blood of my servants the prophets, and the blood of all the servants of the Lord. ⁸For the whole house of Ahab shall perish, and I will cut off from Ahab every male, bond or free, in Israel. ⁹And I will make the house of Ahab like the house of Jeroboam the son of Nebat, and like the house of Baasha the son of Ahijah. ¹⁰And the dogs shall eat Jezebel in the territory of Jezreel, and none shall bury her." Then he opened the door and fled.

¹¹When Jehu came out to the servants of his master, they said to him, "Is all well? Why did this mad fellow come to you?" And he said to them, "You know the fellow and his talk." ¹²And they said, "That is not true; tell us now." And he said, "Thus and so he spoke to me, saying, 'Thus says the Lord, I anoint you king over Israel.'" ¹³Then in haste every man of them took his garment and put it under him on the bare[1] steps, and they blew the trumpet and proclaimed, "Jehu is king."

¹⁴Thus Jehu the son of Jehoshaphat the son of Nimshi conspired against Joram. (Now Joram with all Israel had been on guard at Ramoth-gilead against Hazael king of Syria, ¹⁵but King Joram had returned to be healed in Jezreel of the wounds that the Syrians had given him, when he fought with Hazael king of Syria.) So Jehu said, "If this is your decision, then let no one slip out of the city to go and tell the news in Jezreel." ¹⁶Then Jehu mounted his chariot and went to Jezreel, for Joram lay there. And Ahaziah king of Judah had come down to visit Joram.

¹⁷Now the watchman was standing on the tower in Jezreel, and he saw the company of Jehu as he came and said, "I see a company." And Joram said, "Take a horseman and send to meet them, and let him say, 'Is it peace?'" ¹⁸So a man on horseback went to meet him and said, "Thus says the king, 'Is it peace?'" And Jehu said, "What do you have to do with peace? Turn around and ride behind me." And the watchman reported, saying, "The messenger reached them, but he is not coming back." ¹⁹Then he sent out a second horseman, who came to them and said, "Thus the king has said, 'Is it peace?'" And Jehu answered, "What do you have to do with peace? Turn around and ride behind me." ²⁰Again the watchman reported, "He reached them, but he is not coming back. And the driving is like the driving of Jehu the son of Nimshi, for he drives furiously."

²¹Joram said, "Make ready." And they made ready his chariot. Then Joram king of Israel and Ahaziah king of Judah set out, each in his chariot, and went to meet Jehu, and met him at the property of Naboth the Jezreelite. ²²And when Joram saw Jehu, he said, "Is it peace, Jehu?" He answered, "What peace can there be, so long as the whorings and the sorceries of your mother Jezebel are so many?" ²³Then Joram reined about and fled, saying to Ahaziah, "Treachery, O Ahaziah!" ²⁴And Jehu drew his bow with his full strength, and shot Joram between the shoulders, so that the arrow

[1] The meaning of the Hebrew word is uncertain

pierced his heart, and he sank in his chariot. [25]Jehu said to Bidkar his aide, "Take him up and throw him on the plot of ground belonging to Naboth the Jezreelite. For remember, when you and I rode side by side behind Ahab his father, how the LORD made this pronouncement against him: [26]'As surely as I saw yesterday the blood of Naboth and the blood of his sons—declares the LORD—I will repay you on this plot of ground.' Now therefore take him up and throw him on the plot of ground, in accordance with the word of the LORD." [27]When Ahaziah the king of Judah saw this, he fled in the direction of Beth-haggan. And Jehu pursued him and said, "Shoot him also." And they shot him[1] in the chariot at the ascent of Gur, which is by Ibleam. And he fled to Megiddo and died there. [28]His servants carried him in a chariot to Jerusalem, and buried him in his tomb with his fathers in the city of David.

[29]In the eleventh year of Joram the son of Ahab, Ahaziah began to reign over Judah.

[30]When Jehu came to Jezreel, Jezebel heard of it. And she painted her eyes and adorned her head and looked out of the window. [31]And as Jehu entered the gate, she said, "Is it peace, you Zimri, murderer of your master?" [32]And he lifted up his face to the window and said, "Who is on my side? Who?" Two or three eunuchs looked out at him. [33]He said, "Throw her down." So they threw her down. And some of her blood spattered on the wall and on the horses, and they trampled on her. [34]Then he went in and ate and drank. And he said, "See now to this cursed woman and bury her, for she is a king's daughter." [35]But when they went to bury her, they found no more of her than the skull and the feet and the palms of her hands. [36]When they came back and told him, he said, "This is the word of the LORD, which he spoke by his servant Elijah the Tishbite: 'In the territory of Jezreel the dogs shall eat the flesh of Jezebel, [37]and the corpse of Jezebel shall be as dung on the face of the field in the territory of Jezreel, so that no one can say, This is Jezebel.'"

1 Timothy 6

Let all who are under a yoke as bondservants[2] regard their own masters as worthy of all honor, so that the name of God and the teaching may not be reviled. [2]Those who have

believing masters must not be disrespectful on the ground that they are brothers; rather they must serve all the better since those who benefit by their good service are believers and beloved.

Teach and urge these things. [3]If anyone teaches a different doctrine and does not agree with the sound[3] words of our Lord Jesus Christ and the teaching that accords with godliness, [4]he is puffed up with conceit and understands nothing. He has an unhealthy craving for controversy and for quarrels about words, which produce envy, dissension, slander, evil suspicions, [5]and constant friction among people who are depraved in mind and deprived of the truth, imagining that godliness is a means of gain. [6]But godliness with contentment is great gain, [7]for we brought nothing into the world, and[4] we cannot take anything out of the world. [8]But if we have food and clothing, with these we will be content. [9]But those who desire to be rich fall into temptation, into a snare, into many senseless and harmful desires that plunge people into ruin and destruction. [10]For the love of money is a root of all kinds of evils. It is through this craving that some have wandered away from the faith and pierced themselves with many pangs.

[11]But as for you, O man of God, flee these things. Pursue righteousness, godliness, faith, love, steadfastness, gentleness. [12]Fight the good fight of the faith. Take hold of the eternal life to which you were called and about which you made the good confession in the presence of many witnesses. [13]I charge you in the presence of God, who gives life to all things, and of Christ Jesus, who in his testimony before[5] Pontius Pilate made the good confession, [14]to keep the commandment unstained and free from reproach until the appearing of our Lord Jesus Christ, [15]which he will display at the proper time—he who is the blessed and only Sovereign, the King of kings and Lord of lords, [16]who alone has immortality, who dwells in unapproachable light, whom no one has ever seen or can see. To him be honor and eternal dominion. Amen.

[17]As for the rich in this present age, charge them not to be haughty, nor to set their hopes on the uncertainty of riches, but on God, who richly provides us with everything to enjoy. [18]They are to do good, to be rich in good works, to be generous and ready to share, [19]thus

[1] Syriac, Vulgate (compare Septuagint); Hebrew lacks *and they shot him*   [2] Or *slaves* (for the contextual rendering of the Greek word *doulos*, see Preface)   [3] Or *healthy*   [4] Greek *for;* some manuscripts insert [it is] *certain* [that]   [5] Or *in the time of*

storing up treasure for themselves as a good foundation for the future, so that they may take hold of that which is truly life. ²⁰O Timothy, guard the deposit entrusted to you. Avoid the irreverent babble and contradictions of what is falsely called "knowledge," ²¹for by professing it some have swerved from the faith.

Grace be with you.[1]

Hosea 1

The word of the LORD that came to Hosea, the son of Beeri, in the days of Uzziah, Jotham, Ahaz, and Hezekiah, kings of Judah, and in the days of Jeroboam the son of Joash, king of Israel.

²When the LORD first spoke through Hosea, the LORD said to Hosea, "Go, take to yourself a wife of whoredom and have children of whoredom, for the land commits great whoredom by forsaking the LORD." ³So he went and took Gomer, the daughter of Diblaim, and she conceived and bore him a son.

⁴And the LORD said to him, "Call his name Jezreel, for in just a little while I will punish the house of Jehu for the blood of Jezreel, and I will put an end to the kingdom of the house of Israel. ⁵And on that day I will break the bow of Israel in the Valley of Jezreel."

⁶She conceived again and bore a daughter. And the LORD said to him, "Call her name No Mercy,[2] for I will no more have mercy on the house of Israel, to forgive them at all. ⁷But I will have mercy on the house of Judah, and I will save them by the LORD their God. I will not save them by bow or by sword or by war or by horses or by horsemen."

⁸When she had weaned No Mercy, she conceived and bore a son. ⁹And the LORD said, "Call his name Not My People,[3] for you are not my people, and I am not your God."[4]

¹⁰[5] Yet the number of the children of Israel shall be like the sand of the sea, which cannot be measured or numbered. And in the place where it was said to them, "You are not my people," it shall be said to them, "Children[6] of the living God." ¹¹And the children of Judah and the children of Israel shall be gathered together, and they shall appoint for themselves one head. And they shall go up from the land, for great shall be the day of Jezreel.

Psalm 119:73–96

YODH

Your hands have made and fashioned me;
  give me understanding that I may learn
    your commandments.
⁷⁴ Those who fear you shall see me and
    rejoice,
  because I have hoped in your word.
⁷⁵ I know, O LORD, that your rules are
    righteous,
  and that in faithfulness you have
    afflicted me.
⁷⁶ Let your steadfast love comfort me
  according to your promise to your
    servant.
⁷⁷ Let your mercy come to me, that I may
    live;
  for your law is my delight.
⁷⁸ Let the insolent be put to shame,
  because they have wronged me with
    falsehood;
  as for me, I will meditate on your
    precepts.
⁷⁹ Let those who fear you turn to me,
  that they may know your testimonies.
⁸⁰ May my heart be blameless in your
    statutes,
  that I may not be put to shame!

KAPH

⁸¹ My soul longs for your salvation;
  I hope in your word.
⁸² My eyes long for your promise;
  I ask, "When will you comfort me?"
⁸³ For I have become like a wineskin in the
    smoke,
  yet I have not forgotten your statutes.
⁸⁴ How long must your servant endure?[7]
  When will you judge those who
    persecute me?
⁸⁵ The insolent have dug pitfalls for me;
  they do not live according to your law.
⁸⁶ All your commandments are sure;
  they persecute me with falsehood;
    help me!
⁸⁷ They have almost made an end of me on
    earth,
  but I have not forsaken your precepts.
⁸⁸ In your steadfast love give me life,
  that I may keep the testimonies of
    your mouth.

¹ The Greek for you is plural ² Hebrew Lo-ruhama, which means she has not received mercy ³ Hebrew Lo-ammi, which means not my people ⁴ Hebrew I am not yours ⁵ Ch 2:1 in Hebrew ⁶ Or Sons ⁷ Hebrew How many are the days of your servant?

LAMEDH
89 Forever, O LORD, your word
    is firmly fixed in the heavens.
90 Your faithfulness endures to all
    generations;
    you have established the earth, and it
    stands fast.
91 By your appointment they stand this
    day,
    for all things are your servants.
92 If your law had not been my delight,

    I would have perished in my
      affliction.
93 I will never forget your precepts,
    for by them you have given me life.
94 I am yours; save me,
    for I have sought your precepts.
95 The wicked lie in wait to destroy me,
    but I consider your testimonies.
96 I have seen a limit to all perfection,
    but your commandment is
      exceedingly broad.

OCTOBER 29

2 Kings 10

Now Ahab had seventy sons in Samaria. So Jehu wrote letters and sent them to Samaria, to the rulers of the city,[1] to the elders, and to the guardians of the sons[2] of Ahab, saying, **2** "Now then, as soon as this letter comes to you, seeing your master's sons are with you, and there are with you chariots and horses, fortified cities also, and weapons, **3** select the best and fittest of your master's sons and set him on his father's throne and fight for your master's house." **4** But they were exceedingly afraid and said, "Behold, the two kings could not stand before him. How then can we stand?" **5** So he who was over the palace, and he who was over the city, together with the elders and the guardians, sent to Jehu, saying, "We are your servants, and we will do all that you tell us. We will not make anyone king. Do whatever is good in your eyes." **6** Then he wrote to them a second letter, saying, "If you are on my side, and if you are ready to obey me, take the heads of your master's sons and come to me at Jezreel tomorrow at this time." Now the king's sons, seventy persons, were with the great men of the city, who were bringing them up. **7** And as soon as the letter came to them, they took the king's sons and slaughtered them, seventy persons, and put their heads in baskets and sent them to him at Jezreel. **8** When the messenger came and told him, "They have brought the heads of the king's

sons," he said, "Lay them in two heaps at the entrance of the gate until the morning." **9** Then in the morning, when he went out, he stood and said to all the people, "You are innocent. It was I who conspired against my master and killed him, but who struck down all these? **10** Know then that there shall fall to the earth nothing of the word of the LORD, which the LORD spoke concerning the house of Ahab, for the LORD has done what he said by his servant Elijah." **11** So Jehu struck down all who remained of the house of Ahab in Jezreel, all his great men and his close friends and his priests, until he left him none remaining.

12 Then he set out and went to Samaria. On the way, when he was at Beth-eked of the Shepherds, **13** Jehu met the relatives of Ahaziah king of Judah, and he said, "Who are you?" And they answered, "We are the relatives of Ahaziah, and we came down to visit the royal princes and the sons of the queen mother." **14** He said, "Take them alive." And they took them alive and slaughtered them at the pit of Beth-eked, forty-two persons, and he spared none of them.

15 And when he departed from there, he met Jehonadab the son of Rechab coming to meet him. And he greeted him and said to him, "Is your heart true to my heart as mine is to yours?" And Jehonadab answered, "It is." Jehu

[1] Septuagint, Vulgate; Hebrew *rulers of Jezreel* [2] Hebrew lacks *of the sons*

said,[1] "If it is, give me your hand." So he gave him his hand. And Jehu took him up with him into the chariot. [16]And he said, "Come with me, and see my zeal for the LORD." So he[2] had him ride in his chariot. [17]And when he came to Samaria, he struck down all who remained to Ahab in Samaria, till he had wiped them out, according to the word of the LORD that he spoke to Elijah.

[18]Then Jehu assembled all the people and said to them, "Ahab served Baal a little, but Jehu will serve him much. [19]Now therefore call to me all the prophets of Baal, all his worshipers and all his priests. Let none be missing, for I have a great sacrifice to offer to Baal. Whoever is missing shall not live." But Jehu did it with cunning in order to destroy the worshipers of Baal. [20]And Jehu ordered, "Sanctify a solemn assembly for Baal." So they proclaimed it. [21]And Jehu sent throughout all Israel, and all the worshipers of Baal came, so that there was not a man left who did not come. And they entered the house of Baal, and the house of Baal was filled from one end to the other. [22]He said to him who was in charge of the wardrobe, "Bring out the vestments for all the worshipers of Baal." So he brought out the vestments for them. [23]Then Jehu went into the house of Baal with Jehonadab the son of Rechab, and he said to the worshipers of Baal, "Search, and see that there is no servant of the LORD here among you, but only the worshipers of Baal." [24]Then they[3] went in to offer sacrifices and burnt offerings.

Now Jehu had stationed eighty men outside and said, "The man who allows any of those whom I give into your hands to escape shall forfeit his life." [25]So as soon as he had made an end of offering the burnt offering, Jehu said to the guard and to the officers, "Go in and strike them down; let not a man escape." So when they put them to the sword, the guard and the officers cast them out and went into the inner room of the house of Baal, [26]and they brought out the pillar that was in the house of Baal and burned it. [27]And they demolished the pillar of Baal, and demolished the house of Baal, and made it a latrine to this day.

[28]Thus Jehu wiped out Baal from Israel. [29]But Jehu did not turn aside from the sins of Jeroboam the son of Nebat, which he made Israel to sin—that is, the golden calves that were in Bethel and in Dan. [30]And the LORD said to Jehu, "Because you have done well in carrying out what is right in my eyes, and have done to the house of Ahab according to all that was in my heart, your sons of the fourth generation shall sit on the throne of Israel." [31]But Jehu was not careful to walk in the law of the LORD, the God of Israel, with all his heart. He did not turn from the sins of Jeroboam, which he made Israel to sin.

[32]In those days the LORD began to cut off parts of Israel. Hazael defeated them throughout the territory of Israel: [33]from the Jordan eastward, all the land of Gilead, the Gadites, and the Reubenites, and the Manassites, from Aroer, which is by the Valley of the Arnon, that is, Gilead and Bashan. [34]Now the rest of the acts of Jehu and all that he did, and all his might, are they not written in the Book of the Chronicles of the Kings of Israel? [35]So Jehu slept with his fathers, and they buried him in Samaria. And Jehoahaz his son reigned in his place. [36]The time that Jehu reigned over Israel in Samaria was twenty-eight years.

2 Timothy 1

Paul, an apostle of Christ Jesus by the will of God according to the promise of the life that is in Christ Jesus,

[2]To Timothy, my beloved child:

Grace, mercy, and peace from God the Father and Christ Jesus our Lord.

[3]I thank God whom I serve, as did my ancestors, with a clear conscience, as I remember you constantly in my prayers night and day. [4]As I remember your tears, I long to see you, that I may be filled with joy. [5]I am reminded of your sincere faith, a faith that dwelt first in your grandmother Lois and your mother Eunice and now, I am sure, dwells in you as well. [6]For this reason I remind you to fan into flame the gift of God, which is in you through the laying on of my hands, [7]for God gave us a spirit not of fear but of power and love and self-control.

[8]Therefore do not be ashamed of the testimony about our Lord, nor of me his prisoner, but share in suffering for the gospel by the power of God, [9]who saved us and called us to[4] a holy calling, not because of our works but because of his own purpose and grace, which he

[1] Septuagint; Hebrew lacks *Jehu said* [2] Septuagint, Syriac, Targum; Hebrew *they* [3] Septuagint *he* (compare verse 25) [4] Or *with*

gave us in Christ Jesus before the ages began,[1] [10]and which now has been manifested through the appearing of our Savior Christ Jesus, who abolished death and brought life and immortality to light through the gospel, [11]for which I was appointed a preacher and apostle and teacher, [12]which is why I suffer as I do. But I am not ashamed, for I know whom I have believed, and I am convinced that he is able to guard until that Day what has been entrusted to me.[2] [13]Follow the pattern of the sound[3] words that you have heard from me, in the faith and love that are in Christ Jesus. [14]By the Holy Spirit who dwells within us, guard the good deposit entrusted to you.

[15]You are aware that all who are in Asia turned away from me, among whom are Phygelus and Hermogenes. [16]May the Lord grant mercy to the household of Onesiphorus, for he often refreshed me and was not ashamed of my chains, [17]but when he arrived in Rome he searched for me earnestly and found me— [18]may the Lord grant him to find mercy from the Lord on that Day!—and you well know all the service he rendered at Ephesus.

Hosea 2[4]

Say to your brothers, "You are my people,"[5] and to your sisters, "You have received mercy."[6]

[2] "Plead with your mother, plead—
    for she is not my wife,
    and I am not her husband—
  that she put away her whoring from her
      face,
    and her adultery from between her
      breasts;
[3] lest I strip her naked
    and make her as in the day she was
      born,
  and make her like a wilderness,
    and make her like a parched land,
    and kill her with thirst.
[4]   Upon her children also I will have no
      mercy,
    because they are children of
      whoredom.
[5]   For their mother has played the whore;
    she who conceived them has acted
      shamefully.

For she said, 'I will go after my lovers,
  who give me my bread and my water,
  my wool and my flax, my oil and my
    drink.'
[6] Therefore I will hedge up her[7] way with
    thorns,
  and I will build a wall against her,
    so that she cannot find her paths.
[7] She shall pursue her lovers
  but not overtake them,
  and she shall seek them
  but shall not find them.
Then she shall say,
  'I will go and return to my first
    husband,
  for it was better for me then than
    now.'
[8] And she did not know
  that it was I who gave her
  the grain, the wine, and the oil,
  and who lavished on her silver and
    gold,
  which they used for Baal.
[9] Therefore I will take back
  my grain in its time,
  and my wine in its season,
  and I will take away my wool and my
    flax,
  which were to cover her nakedness.
[10] Now I will uncover her lewdness
  in the sight of her lovers,
  and no one shall rescue her out of my
    hand.
[11] And I will put an end to all her mirth,
  her feasts, her new moons, her
    Sabbaths,
  and all her appointed feasts.
[12] And I will lay waste her vines and her fig
    trees,
  of which she said,
  'These are my wages,
  which my lovers have given me.'
I will make them a forest,
  and the beasts of the field shall devour
    them.
[13] And I will punish her for the feast days
    of the Baals
  when she burned offerings to them
  and adorned herself with her ring and
    jewelry,
  and went after her lovers
  and forgot me, declares the LORD.

---

[1] Greek before times eternal [2] Or what I have entrusted to him; Greek my deposit [3] Or healthy [4] Ch 2:3 in Hebrew [5] Hebrew ammi, which means my people [6] Hebrew ruhama, which means she has received mercy [7] Hebrew your

¹⁴ "Therefore, behold, I will allure her,
    and bring her into the wilderness,
    and speak tenderly to her.
¹⁵ And there I will give her her vineyards
    and make the Valley of Achor[1] a door
      of hope.
    And there she shall answer as in the
      days of her youth,
      as at the time when she came out of
        the land of Egypt.

¹⁶ "And in that day, declares the Lord, you will call me 'My Husband,' and no longer will you call me 'My Baal.' ¹⁷ For I will remove the names of the Baals from her mouth, and they shall be remembered by name no more. ¹⁸ And I will make for them a covenant on that day with the beasts of the field, the birds of the heavens, and the creeping things of the ground. And I will abolish[2] the bow, the sword, and war from the land, and I will make you lie down in safety. ¹⁹ And I will betroth you to me forever. I will betroth you to me in righteousness and in justice, in steadfast love and in mercy. ²⁰ I will betroth you to me in faithfulness. And you shall know the Lord.

²¹ "And in that day I will answer, declares
      the Lord,
    I will answer the heavens,
    and they shall answer the earth,
²²   and the earth shall answer the grain, the
      wine, and the oil,
    and they shall answer Jezreel,[3]
²³   and I will sow her for myself in the land.
    And I will have mercy on No Mercy,[4]
    and I will say to Not My People,[5] 'You
      are my people';
    and he shall say, 'You are my God.'"

―――――― Psalm 119:97–120 ――――――

MEM

Oh how I love your law!
    It is my meditation all the day.
⁹⁸ Your commandment makes me wiser
      than my enemies,
    for it is ever with me.
⁹⁹ I have more understanding than all my
      teachers,
    for your testimonies are my meditation.
¹⁰⁰ I understand more than the aged,[6]
    for I keep your precepts.

¹⁰¹ I hold back my feet from every evil way,
    in order to keep your word.
¹⁰² I do not turn aside from your rules,
    for you have taught me.
¹⁰³ How sweet are your words to my taste,
    sweeter than honey to my mouth!
¹⁰⁴ Through your precepts I get
      understanding;
    therefore I hate every false way.

NUN

¹⁰⁵ Your word is a lamp to my feet
    and a light to my path.
¹⁰⁶ I have sworn an oath and confirmed it,
    to keep your righteous rules.
¹⁰⁷ I am severely afflicted;
    give me life, O Lord, according to
      your word!
¹⁰⁸ Accept my freewill offerings of praise,
    O Lord,
    and teach me your rules.
¹⁰⁹ I hold my life in my hand continually,
    but I do not forget your law.
¹¹⁰ The wicked have laid a snare for me,
    but I do not stray from your precepts.
¹¹¹ Your testimonies are my heritage forever,
    for they are the joy of my heart.
¹¹² I incline my heart to perform your statutes
    forever, to the end.[7]

SAMEKH

¹¹³ I hate the double-minded,
    but I love your law.
¹¹⁴ You are my hiding place and my shield;
    I hope in your word.
¹¹⁵ Depart from me, you evildoers,
    that I may keep the commandments
      of my God.
¹¹⁶ Uphold me according to your promise,
    that I may live,
    and let me not be put to shame in my
      hope!
¹¹⁷ Hold me up, that I may be safe
    and have regard for your statutes
      continually!
¹¹⁸ You spurn all who go astray from your
      statutes,
    for their cunning is in vain.
¹¹⁹ All the wicked of the earth you discard
      like dross,
    therefore I love your testimonies.
¹²⁰ My flesh trembles for fear of you,
    and I am afraid of your judgments.

---

[1] Achor means *trouble*; compare Joshua 7:26   [2] Hebrew *break*   [3] *Jezreel* means *God will sow*   [4] Hebrew *Lo-ruhama*   [5] Hebrew *Lo-ammi*   [6] Or *the elders*   [7] Or *statutes; the reward is eternal*

OCTOBER 30

---
2 Kings 11–12

Now when Athaliah the mother of Ahaziah saw that her son was dead, she arose and destroyed all the royal family. ²But Jehosheba, the daughter of King Joram, sister of Ahaziah, took Joash the son of Ahaziah and stole him away from among the king's sons who were being put to death, and she put¹ him and his nurse in a bedroom. Thus they² hid him from Athaliah, so that he was not put to death. ³And he remained with her six years, hidden in the house of the LORD, while Athaliah reigned over the land.

⁴But in the seventh year Jehoiada sent and brought the captains of the Carites and of the guards, and had them come to him in the house of the LORD. And he made a covenant with them and put them under oath in the house of the LORD, and he showed them the king's son. ⁵And he commanded them, "This is the thing that you shall do: one third of you, those who come off duty on the Sabbath and guard the king's house ⁶(another third being at the gate Sur and a third at the gate behind the guards) shall guard the palace.³ ⁷And the two divisions of you, which come on duty in force on the Sabbath and guard the house of the LORD on behalf of the king, ⁸shall surround the king, each with his weapons in his hand. And whoever approaches the ranks is to be put to death. Be with the king when he goes out and when he comes in."

⁹The captains did according to all that Jehoiada the priest commanded, and they each brought his men who were to go off duty on the Sabbath, with those who were to come on duty on the Sabbath, and came to Jehoiada the priest. ¹⁰And the priest gave to the captains the spears and shields that had been King David's, which were in the house of the LORD. ¹¹And the guards stood, every man with his weapons in his hand, from the south side of the house to the north side of the house, around the altar and the house on behalf of the king. ¹²Then he brought out the king's son and put the crown

on him and gave him the testimony. And they proclaimed him king and anointed him, and they clapped their hands and said, "Long live the king!"

¹³When Athaliah heard the noise of the guard and of the people, she went into the house of the LORD to the people. ¹⁴And when she looked, there was the king standing by the pillar, according to the custom, and the captains and the trumpeters beside the king, and all the people of the land rejoicing and blowing trumpets. And Athaliah tore her clothes and cried, "Treason! Treason!" ¹⁵Then Jehoiada the priest commanded the captains who were set over the army, "Bring her out between the ranks, and put to death with the sword anyone who follows her." For the priest said, "Let her not be put to death in the house of the LORD." ¹⁶So they laid hands on her; and she went through the horses' entrance to the king's house, and there she was put to death.

¹⁷And Jehoiada made a covenant between the LORD and the king and people, that they should be the LORD's people, and also between the king and the people. ¹⁸Then all the people of the land went to the house of Baal and tore it down; his altars and his images they broke in pieces, and they killed Mattan the priest of Baal before the altars. And the priest posted watchmen over the house of the LORD. ¹⁹And he took the captains, the Carites, the guards, and all the people of the land, and they brought the king down from the house of the LORD, marching through the gate of the guards to the king's house. And he took his seat on the throne of the kings. ²⁰So all the people of the land rejoiced, and the city was quiet after Athaliah had been put to death with the sword at the king's house.

²¹⁴ Jehoash⁵ was seven years old when he began to reign.

¹²:¹ In the seventh year of Jehu, Jehoash⁶ began to reign, and he reigned forty years in Jerusalem. His mother's name was Zibiah

---

¹ Compare 2 Chronicles 22:11; Hebrew lacks *and she put* ² Septuagint, Syriac, Vulgate (compare 2 Chronicles 22:11) *she* ³ The meaning of the Hebrew word is uncertain ⁴ Ch 12:1 in Hebrew ⁵ *Jehoash* is an alternate spelling of *Joash* (son of Ahaziah) as in verse 2 ⁶ *Jehoash* is an alternate spelling of *Joash* (son of Ahaziah) as in 11:2; also verses 2, 4, 6, 7, 18

of Beersheba. ²And Jehoash did what was right in the eyes of the LORD all his days, because Jehoiada the priest instructed him. ³Nevertheless, the high places were not taken away; the people continued to sacrifice and make offerings on the high places.

⁴Jehoash said to the priests, "All the money of the holy things that is brought into the house of the LORD, the money for which each man is assessed—the money from the assessment of persons—and the money that a man's heart prompts him to bring into the house of the LORD, ⁵let the priests take, each from his donor, and let them repair the house wherever any need of repairs is discovered." ⁶But by the twenty-third year of King Jehoash, the priests had made no repairs on the house. ⁷Therefore King Jehoash summoned Jehoiada the priest and the other priests and said to them, "Why are you not repairing the house? Now therefore take no more money from your donors, but hand it over for the repair of the house." ⁸So the priests agreed that they should take no more money from the people, and that they should not repair the house.

⁹Then Jehoiada the priest took a chest and bored a hole in the lid of it and set it beside the altar on the right side as one entered the house of the LORD. And the priests who guarded the threshold put in it all the money that was brought into the house of the LORD. ¹⁰And whenever they saw that there was much money in the chest, the king's secretary and the high priest came up and they bagged and counted the money that was found in the house of the LORD. ¹¹Then they would give the money that was weighed out into the hands of the workmen who had the oversight of the house of the LORD. And they paid it out to the carpenters and the builders who worked on the house of the LORD, ¹²and to the masons and the stonecutters, as well as to buy timber and quarried stone for making repairs on the house of the LORD, and for any outlay for the repairs of the house. ¹³But there were not made for the house of the LORD basins of silver, snuffers, bowls, trumpets, or any vessels of gold, or of silver, from the money that was brought into the house of the LORD, ¹⁴for that was given to the workmen who were repairing the house of the LORD with it. ¹⁵And they did not ask for an accounting from the men into whose

hand they delivered the money to pay out to the workmen, for they dealt honestly. ¹⁶The money from the guilt offerings and the money from the sin offerings was not brought into the house of the LORD; it belonged to the priests.

¹⁷At that time Hazael king of Syria went up and fought against Gath and took it. But when Hazael set his face to go up against Jerusalem, ¹⁸Jehoash king of Judah took all the sacred gifts that Jehoshaphat and Jehoram and Ahaziah his fathers, the kings of Judah, had dedicated, and his own sacred gifts, and all the gold that was found in the treasuries of the house of the LORD and of the king's house, and sent these to Hazael king of Syria. Then Hazael went away from Jerusalem.

¹⁹Now the rest of the acts of Joash and all that he did, are they not written in the Book of the Chronicles of the Kings of Judah? ²⁰His servants arose and made a conspiracy and struck down Joash in the house of Millo, on the way that goes down to Silla. ²¹It was Jozacar the son of Shimeath and Jehozabad the son of Shomer, his servants, who struck him down, so that he died. And they buried him with his fathers in the city of David, and Amaziah his son reigned in his place.

2 Timothy 2

You then, my child, be strengthened by the grace that is in Christ Jesus, ²and what you have heard from me in the presence of many witnesses entrust to faithful men[1] who will be able to teach others also. ³Share in suffering as a good soldier of Christ Jesus. ⁴No soldier gets entangled in civilian pursuits, since his aim is to please the one who enlisted him. ⁵An athlete is not crowned unless he competes according to the rules. ⁶It is the hard-working farmer who ought to have the first share of the crops. ⁷Think over what I say, for the Lord will give you understanding in everything.

⁸Remember Jesus Christ, risen from the dead, the offspring of David, as preached in my gospel, ⁹for which I am suffering, bound with chains as a criminal. But the word of God is not bound! ¹⁰Therefore I endure everything for the sake of the elect, that they also may obtain the salvation that is in Christ Jesus with eternal glory. ¹¹The saying is trustworthy, for:

---

[1] The Greek word *anthropoi* can refer to both men and women, depending on the context

If we have died with him, we will also
    live with him;
[12] if we endure, we will also reign with him;
    if we deny him, he also will deny us;
[13] if we are faithless, he remains faithful—
for he cannot deny himself.

[14] Remind them of these things, and charge them before God[1] not to quarrel about words, which does no good, but only ruins the hearers. [15] Do your best to present yourself to God as one approved,[2] a worker who has no need to be ashamed, rightly handling the word of truth. [16] But avoid irreverent babble, for it will lead people into more and more ungodliness, [17] and their talk will spread like gangrene. Among them are Hymenaeus and Philetus, [18] who have swerved from the truth, saying that the resurrection has already happened. They are upsetting the faith of some. [19] But God's firm foundation stands, bearing this seal: "The Lord knows those who are his," and, "Let everyone who names the name of the Lord depart from iniquity."

[20] Now in a great house there are not only vessels of gold and silver but also of wood and clay, some for honorable use, some for dishonorable. [21] Therefore, if anyone cleanses himself from what is dishonorable,[3] he will be a vessel for honorable use, set apart as holy, useful to the master of the house, ready for every good work.

[22] So flee youthful passions and pursue righteousness, faith, love, and peace, along with those who call on the Lord from a pure heart. [23] Have nothing to do with foolish, ignorant controversies; you know that they breed quarrels. [24] And the Lord's servant[4] must not be quarrelsome but kind to everyone, able to teach, patiently enduring evil, [25] correcting his opponents with gentleness. God may perhaps grant them repentance leading to a knowledge of the truth, [26] and they may come to their senses and escape from the snare of the devil, after being captured by him to do his will.

Hosea 3–4

And the LORD said to me, "Go again, love a woman who is loved by another man and is an adulteress, even as the LORD loves the children of Israel, though they turn to other gods and love cakes of raisins." [2] So I bought her for fifteen shekels of silver and a homer and a lethech[5] of barley. [3] And I said to her, "You must dwell as mine for many days. You shall not play the whore, or belong to another man; so will I also be to you." [4] For the children of Israel shall dwell many days without king or prince, without sacrifice or pillar, without ephod or household gods. [5] Afterward the children of Israel shall return and seek the LORD their God, and David their king, and they shall come in fear to the LORD and to his goodness in the latter days.

[4:1] Hear the word of the LORD, O children
    of Israel,
  for the LORD has a controversy with
    the inhabitants of the land.
There is no faithfulness or steadfast
    love,
  and no knowledge of God in the land;
[2] there is swearing, lying, murder,
    stealing, and committing adultery;
  they break all bounds, and bloodshed
    follows bloodshed.
[3] Therefore the land mourns,
    and all who dwell in it languish,
and also the beasts of the field
    and the birds of the heavens,
    and even the fish of the sea are taken
    away.

[4] Yet let no one contend,
    and let none accuse,
  for with you is my contention,
    O priest.[6]
[5] You shall stumble by day;
    the prophet also shall stumble with
      you by night;
  and I will destroy your mother.
[6] My people are destroyed for lack of
    knowledge;
  because you have rejected knowledge,
  I reject you from being a priest to me.
And since you have forgotten the law of
    your God,
  I also will forget your children.

[7] The more they increased,
    the more they sinned against me;
  I will change their glory into shame.
[8] They feed on the sin[7] of my people;
    they are greedy for their iniquity.

[1] Some manuscripts the Lord [2] That is, one approved after being tested [3] Greek from these things [4] Greek bondservant [5] A shekel was about 2/5 ounce or 11 grams; a homer was about 6 bushels or 220 liters; a lethech was about 3 bushels or 110 liters [6] Or for your people are like those who contend with the priest [7] Or sin offering

9   And it shall be like people, like priest;
     I will punish them for their ways
     and repay them for their deeds.

10   They shall eat, but not be satisfied;
     they shall play the whore, but not
       multiply,
   because they have forsaken the LORD
     to cherish [11] whoredom, wine, and
       new wine,
     which take away the understanding.

12   My people inquire of a piece of wood,
     and their walking staff gives them
       oracles.
   For a spirit of whoredom has led them
     astray,
     and they have left their God to play
       the whore.

13   They sacrifice on the tops of the
       mountains
     and burn offerings on the hills,
   under oak, poplar, and terebinth,
     because their shade is good.
   Therefore your daughters play the
       whore,
     and your brides commit adultery.

14   I will not punish your daughters when
       they play the whore,
     nor your brides when they commit
       adultery;
   for the men themselves go aside with
       prostitutes
     and sacrifice with cult prostitutes,
   and a people without understanding
     shall come to ruin.

15   Though you play the whore, O Israel,
     let not Judah become guilty.
   Enter not into Gilgal,
     nor go up to Beth-aven,
     and swear not, "As the LORD lives."

16   Like a stubborn heifer,
     Israel is stubborn;
   can the LORD now feed them
     like a lamb in a broad pasture?

17   Ephraim is joined to idols;
     leave him alone.

18   When their drink is gone, they give
       themselves to whoring;
     their rulers[1] dearly love shame.

19   A wind has wrapped them[2] in its wings,
     and they shall be ashamed because of
       their sacrifices.

--- *Psalm 119:121–144* ---

AYIN

I have done what is just and right;
   do not leave me to my oppressors.

122   Give your servant a pledge of good;
     let not the insolent oppress me.

123   My eyes long for your salvation
     and for the fulfillment of your
       righteous promise.

124   Deal with your servant according to your
       steadfast love,
     and teach me your statutes.

125   I am your servant; give me
       understanding,
     that I may know your testimonies!

126   It is time for the LORD to act,
     for your law has been broken.

127   Therefore I love your commandments
     above gold, above fine gold.

128   Therefore I consider all your precepts to
       be right;
     I hate every false way.

PE

129   Your testimonies are wonderful;
     therefore my soul keeps them.

130   The unfolding of your words gives light;
     it imparts understanding to the
       simple.

131   I open my mouth and pant,
     because I long for your
       commandments.

132   Turn to me and be gracious to me,
     as is your way with those who love
       your name.

133   Keep steady my steps according to your
       promise,
     and let no iniquity get dominion over
       me.

134   Redeem me from man's oppression,
     that I may keep your precepts.

135   Make your face shine upon your servant,
     and teach me your statutes.

136   My eyes shed streams of tears,
     because people do not keep your law.

TSADHE

137   Righteous are you, O LORD,
     and right are your rules.

138   You have appointed your testimonies in
       righteousness
     and in all faithfulness.

[1] Hebrew *shields* [2] Hebrew *her*

139 My zeal consumes me,
   because my foes forget your words.
140 Your promise is well tried,
   and your servant loves it.
141 I am small and despised,
   yet I do not forget your precepts.
142 Your righteousness is righteous forever,

   and your law is true.
143 Trouble and anguish have found me out,
   but your commandments are my
   delight.
144 Your testimonies are righteous forever;
   give me understanding that I may
   live.

OCTOBER 31

2 Kings 13

In the twenty-third year of Joash the son of Ahaziah, king of Judah, Jehoahaz the son of Jehu began to reign over Israel in Samaria, and he reigned seventeen years. ²He did what was evil in the sight of the LORD and followed the sins of Jeroboam the son of Nebat, which he made Israel to sin; he did not depart from them. ³And the anger of the LORD was kindled against Israel, and he gave them continually into the hand of Hazael king of Syria and into the hand of Ben-hadad the son of Hazael. ⁴Then Jehoahaz sought the favor of the LORD, and the LORD listened to him, for he saw the oppression of Israel, how the king of Syria oppressed them. ⁵(Therefore the LORD gave Israel a savior, so that they escaped from the hand of the Syrians, and the people of Israel lived in their homes as formerly. ⁶Nevertheless, they did not depart from the sins of the house of Jeroboam, which he made Israel to sin, but walked[1] in them; and the Asherah also remained in Samaria.) ⁷For there was not left to Jehoahaz an army of more than fifty horsemen and ten chariots and ten thousand footmen, for the king of Syria had destroyed them and made them like the dust at threshing. ⁸Now the rest of the acts of Jehoahaz and all that he did, and his might, are they not written in the Book of the Chronicles of the Kings of Israel? ⁹So Jehoahaz slept with his fathers, and they buried him in Samaria, and Joash his son reigned in his place.

¹⁰In the thirty-seventh year of Joash king of Judah, Jehoash[2] the son of Jehoahaz began to reign over Israel in Samaria, and he reigned

sixteen years. ¹¹He also did what was evil in the sight of the LORD. He did not depart from all the sins of Jeroboam the son of Nebat, which he made Israel to sin, but he walked in them. ¹²Now the rest of the acts of Joash and all that he did, and the might with which he fought against Amaziah king of Judah, are they not written in the Book of the Chronicles of the Kings of Israel? ¹³So Joash slept with his fathers, and Jeroboam sat on his throne. And Joash was buried in Samaria with the kings of Israel.

¹⁴Now when Elisha had fallen sick with the illness of which he was to die, Joash king of Israel went down to him and wept before him, crying, "My father, my father! The chariots of Israel and its horsemen!" ¹⁵And Elisha said to him, "Take a bow and arrows." So he took a bow and arrows. ¹⁶Then he said to the king of Israel, "Draw the bow," and he drew it. And Elisha laid his hands on the king's hands. ¹⁷And he said, "Open the window eastward," and he opened it. Then Elisha said, "Shoot," and he shot. And he said, "The LORD's arrow of victory, the arrow of victory over Syria! For you shall fight the Syrians in Aphek until you have made an end of them." ¹⁸And he said, "Take the arrows," and he took them. And he said to the king of Israel, "Strike the ground with them." And he struck three times and stopped. ¹⁹Then the man of God was angry with him and said, "You should have struck five or six times; then you would have struck down Syria until you had made an end of it, but now you will strike down Syria only three times."

¹ Septuagint, Syriac, Targum, Vulgate; Hebrew *he walked* ² *Jehoash* is an alternate spelling of *Joash* (son of Jehoahaz) as in verses 9, 12–14; also verse 25

²⁰So Elisha died, and they buried him. Now bands of Moabites used to invade the land in the spring of the year. ²¹And as a man was being buried, behold, a marauding band was seen and the man was thrown into the grave of Elisha, and as soon as the man touched the bones of Elisha, he revived and stood on his feet.

²²Now Hazael king of Syria oppressed Israel all the days of Jehoahaz. ²³But the LORD was gracious to them and had compassion on them, and he turned toward them, because of his covenant with Abraham, Isaac, and Jacob, and would not destroy them, nor has he cast them from his presence until now.

²⁴When Hazael king of Syria died, Ben-hadad his son became king in his place. ²⁵Then Jehoash the son of Jehoahaz took again from Ben-hadad the son of Hazael the cities that he had taken from Jehoahaz his father in war. Three times Joash defeated him and recovered the cities of Israel.

2 Timothy 3

But understand this, that in the last days there will come times of difficulty. ²For people will be lovers of self, lovers of money, proud, arrogant, abusive, disobedient to their parents, ungrateful, unholy, ³heartless, unappeasable, slanderous, without self-control, brutal, not loving good, ⁴treacherous, reckless, swollen with conceit, lovers of pleasure rather than lovers of God, ⁵having the appearance of godliness, but denying its power. Avoid such people. ⁶For among them are those who creep into households and capture weak women, burdened with sins and led astray by various passions, ⁷always learning and never able to arrive at a knowledge of the truth. ⁸Just as Jannes and Jambres opposed Moses, so these men also oppose the truth, men corrupted in mind and disqualified regarding the faith. ⁹But they will not get very far, for their folly will be plain to all, as was that of those two men.

¹⁰You, however, have followed my teaching, my conduct, my aim in life, my faith, my patience, my love, my steadfastness, ¹¹my persecutions and sufferings that happened to me at Antioch, at Iconium, and at Lystra—which persecutions I endured; yet from them all the Lord rescued me. ¹²Indeed, all who desire to live a godly life in Christ Jesus will be persecuted,

¹³while evil people and impostors will go on from bad to worse, deceiving and being deceived. ¹⁴But as for you, continue in what you have learned and have firmly believed, knowing from whom¹ you learned it ¹⁵and how from childhood you have been acquainted with the sacred writings, which are able to make you wise for salvation through faith in Christ Jesus. ¹⁶All Scripture is breathed out by God and profitable for teaching, for reproof, for correction, and for training in righteousness, ¹⁷that the man of God² may be complete, equipped for every good work.

Hosea 5–6

Hear this, O priests!
Pay attention, O house of Israel!
Give ear, O house of the king!
 For the judgment is for you;
 for you have been a snare at Mizpah
 and a net spread upon Tabor.
² And the revolters have gone deep into slaughter,
 but I will discipline all of them.
³ I know Ephraim,
 and Israel is not hidden from me;
 for now, O Ephraim, you have played the whore;
 Israel is defiled.
⁴ Their deeds do not permit them
 to return to their God.
 For the spirit of whoredom is within them,
 and they know not the LORD.
⁵ The pride of Israel testifies to his face;³
 Israel and Ephraim shall stumble in his guilt;
 Judah also shall stumble with them.
⁶ With their flocks and herds they shall go to seek the LORD,
 but they will not find him;
 he has withdrawn from them.
⁷ They have dealt faithlessly with the LORD;
 for they have borne alien children.
 Now the new moon shall devour them with their fields.
⁸ Blow the horn in Gibeah,
 the trumpet in Ramah.

¹ The Greek for *whom* is plural ² That is, a messenger of God (the phrase echoes a common Old Testament expression) ³ Or in *his presence*

Sound the alarm at Beth-aven;
  we follow you,[1] O Benjamin!
9 Ephraim shall become a desolation
  in the day of punishment;
among the tribes of Israel
  I make known what is sure.
10 The princes of Judah have become
  like those who move the landmark;
upon them I will pour out
  my wrath like water.
11 Ephraim is oppressed, crushed in
    judgment,
because he was determined to go after
  filth.[2]
12 But I am like a moth to Ephraim,
  and like dry rot to the house of Judah.

13 When Ephraim saw his sickness,
  and Judah his wound,
then Ephraim went to Assyria,
  and sent to the great king.[3]
But he is not able to cure you
  or heal your wound.
14 For I will be like a lion to Ephraim,
  and like a young lion to the house of
    Judah.
I, even I, will tear and go away;
  I will carry off, and no one shall
    rescue.
15 I will return again to my place,
  until they acknowledge their guilt and
    seek my face,
  and in their distress earnestly seek me.

6:1 "Come, let us return to the LORD;
  for he has torn us, that he may heal us;
  he has struck us down, and he will
    bind us up.
2 After two days he will revive us;
  on the third day he will raise us up,
  that we may live before him.
3 Let us know; let us press on to know the
    LORD;
  his going out is sure as the dawn;
he will come to us as the showers,
  as the spring rains that water the
    earth."

4 What shall I do with you, O Ephraim?
  What shall I do with you, O Judah?
Your love is like a morning cloud,
  like the dew that goes early away.

5 Therefore I have hewn them by the
    prophets;
  I have slain them by the words of my
    mouth,
  and my judgment goes forth as the
    light.
6 For I desire steadfast love[4] and not
    sacrifice,
  the knowledge of God rather than
    burnt offerings.

7 But like Adam they transgressed the
    covenant;
  there they dealt faithlessly with me.
8 Gilead is a city of evildoers,
  tracked with blood.
9 As robbers lie in wait for a man,
  so the priests band together;
they murder on the way to Shechem;
  they commit villainy.
10 In the house of Israel I have seen a
    horrible thing;
  Ephraim's whoredom is there; Israel is
    defiled.

11 For you also, O Judah, a harvest is
    appointed,
  when I restore the fortunes of my
    people.

Psalm 119:145–176

QOPH

145 With my whole heart I cry; answer me,
  O LORD!
  I will keep your statutes.
146 I call to you; save me,
  that I may observe your testimonies.
147 I rise before dawn and cry for help;
  I hope in your words.
148 My eyes are awake before the watches of
    the night,
  that I may meditate on your promise.
149 Hear my voice according to your
    steadfast love;
  O LORD, according to your justice give
    me life.
150 They draw near who persecute me with
    evil purpose;
  they are far from your law.
151 But you are near, O LORD,
  and all your commandments are true.

[1] Or after you [2] Or to follow human precepts [3] Or to King Jareb [4] Septuagint mercy

152 Long have I known from your
    testimonies
   that you have founded them forever.

RESH

153 Look on my affliction and deliver me,
   for I do not forget your law.
154 Plead my cause and redeem me;
   give me life according to your
     promise!
155 Salvation is far from the wicked,
   for they do not seek your statutes.
156 Great is your mercy, O LORD;
   give me life according to your rules.
157 Many are my persecutors and my
    adversaries,
   but I do not swerve from your
     testimonies.
158 I look at the faithless with disgust,
   because they do not keep your
     commands.
159 Consider how I love your precepts!
   Give me life according to your
     steadfast love.
160 The sum of your word is truth,
   and every one of your righteous rules
     endures forever.

SIN AND SHIN

161 Princes persecute me without cause,
   but my heart stands in awe of your
     words.
162 I rejoice at your word
   like one who finds great spoil.

163 I hate and abhor falsehood,
   but I love your law.
164 Seven times a day I praise you
   for your righteous rules.
165 Great peace have those who love your
    law;
   nothing can make them stumble.
166 I hope for your salvation, O LORD,
   and I do your commandments.
167 My soul keeps your testimonies;
   I love them exceedingly.
168 I keep your precepts and testimonies,
   for all my ways are before you.

TAW

169 Let my cry come before you, O LORD;
   give me understanding according to
     your word!
170 Let my plea come before you;
   deliver me according to your word.
171 My lips will pour forth praise,
   for you teach me your statutes.
172 My tongue will sing of your word,
   for all your commandments are right.
173 Let your hand be ready to help me,
   for I have chosen your precepts.
174 I long for your salvation, O LORD,
   and your law is my delight.
175 Let my soul live and praise you,
   and let your rules help me.
176 I have gone astray like a lost sheep; seek
    your servant,
   for I do not forget your
     commandments.

NOVEMBER 1

2 Kings 14

In the second year of Joash the son of Joahaz, king of Israel, Amaziah the son of Joash, king of Judah, began to reign. [2]He was twenty-five years old when he began to reign, and he reigned twenty-nine years in Jerusalem. His mother's name was Jehoaddin of Jerusalem. [3]And he did what was right in the eyes of the LORD, yet not like David his father. He did in all things as Joash his father had done. [4]But the high places were not removed; the people still sacrificed and made offerings on the high places. [5]And as soon as the royal power was firmly in his hand, he struck down his servants who had struck down the king his father. [6]But he did not put to death the children of the murderers, according to what is written in the Book of the Law of Moses, where the LORD commanded, "Fathers shall not be put to death because of their children, nor shall children be put to death because of their fathers. But each one shall die for his own sin."

[7]He struck down ten thousand Edomites in the Valley of Salt and took Sela by storm, and called it Joktheel, which is its name to this day.

[8]Then Amaziah sent messengers to Jehoash[1] the son of Jehoahaz, son of Jehu, king of Israel, saying, "Come, let us look one another in the face." [9]And Jehoash king of Israel sent word to Amaziah king of Judah, "A thistle on Lebanon sent to a cedar on Lebanon, saying, 'Give your daughter to my son for a wife,' and a wild beast of Lebanon passed by and trampled down the thistle. [10]You have indeed struck down Edom, and your heart has lifted you up. Be content with your glory, and stay at home, for why should you provoke trouble so that you fall, you and Judah with you?"

[11]But Amaziah would not listen. So Jehoash king of Israel went up, and he and Amaziah king of Judah faced one another in battle at Beth-shemesh, which belongs to Judah. [12]And Judah was defeated by Israel, and every man fled to his home. [13]And Jehoash king of Israel captured Amaziah king of Judah, the son of Jehoash, son of Ahaziah, at Beth-shemesh, and came to Jerusalem and broke down the wall of Jerusalem for four hundred cubits,[2] from the Ephraim Gate to the Corner Gate. [14]And he seized all the gold and silver, and all the vessels that were found in the house of the LORD and in the treasuries of the king's house, also hostages, and he returned to Samaria.

[15]Now the rest of the acts of Jehoash that he did, and his might, and how he fought with Amaziah king of Judah, are they not written in the Book of the Chronicles of the Kings of Israel? [16]And Jehoash slept with his fathers and was buried in Samaria with the kings of Israel, and Jeroboam his son reigned in his place.

[17]Amaziah the son of Joash, king of Judah, lived fifteen years after the death of Jehoash son of Jehoahaz, king of Israel. [18]Now the rest of the deeds of Amaziah, are they not written in the Book of the Chronicles of the Kings of Judah? [19]And they made a conspiracy against him in Jerusalem, and he fled to Lachish. But they sent after him to Lachish and put him to death there. [20]And they brought him on horses; and he was buried in Jerusalem with his fathers in the city of David. [21]And all the people of Judah took Azariah, who was sixteen years old, and made him king instead of his father Amaziah. [22]He built Elath and restored it to Judah, after the king slept with his fathers.

[23]In the fifteenth year of Amaziah the son of Joash, king of Judah, Jeroboam the son of Joash, king of Israel, began to reign in Samaria, and he reigned forty-one years. [24]And he did what was evil in the sight of the LORD. He did not depart from all the sins of Jeroboam the son of Nebat, which he made Israel to sin. [25]He restored the border of Israel from Lebo-hamath as far as the Sea of the Arabah, according to the word of the LORD, the God of Israel, which he spoke by his servant Jonah the son of Amittai, the prophet, who was from Gath-hepher. [26]For the LORD saw that the affliction of Israel was

---

[1] *Jehoash* is an alternate spelling of *Joash* (son of Jehoahaz) as in 13:9, 12–14; also verses 9, 11–16   [2] A *cubit* was about 18 inches or 45 centimeters

very bitter, for there was none left, bond or free, and there was none to help Israel. [27] But the LORD had not said that he would blot out the name of Israel from under heaven, so he saved them by the hand of Jeroboam the son of Joash.

[28] Now the rest of the acts of Jeroboam and all that he did, and his might, how he fought, and how he restored Damascus and Hamath to Judah in Israel, are they not written in the Book of the Chronicles of the Kings of Israel? [29] And Jeroboam slept with his fathers, the kings of Israel, and Zechariah his son reigned in his place.

2 Timothy 4

I charge you in the presence of God and of Christ Jesus, who is to judge the living and the dead, and by his appearing and his kingdom: [2] preach the word; be ready in season and out of season; reprove, rebuke, and exhort, with complete patience and teaching. [3] For the time is coming when people will not endure sound[1] teaching, but having itching ears they will accumulate for themselves teachers to suit their own passions, [4] and will turn away from listening to the truth and wander off into myths. [5] As for you, always be sober-minded, endure suffering, do the work of an evangelist, fulfill your ministry.

[6] For I am already being poured out as a drink offering, and the time of my departure has come. [7] I have fought the good fight, I have finished the race, I have kept the faith. [8] Henceforth there is laid up for me the crown of righteousness, which the Lord, the righteous judge, will award to me on that Day, and not only to me but also to all who have loved his appearing.

[9] Do your best to come to me soon. [10] For Demas, in love with this present world, has deserted me and gone to Thessalonica. Crescens has gone to Galatia,[2] Titus to Dalmatia. [11] Luke alone is with me. Get Mark and bring him with you, for he is very useful to me for ministry. [12] Tychicus I have sent to Ephesus. [13] When you come, bring the cloak that I left with Carpus at Troas, also the books, and above all the parchments. [14] Alexander the coppersmith did me great harm; the Lord will repay him according to his deeds. [15] Beware

of him yourself, for he strongly opposed our message. [16] At my first defense no one came to stand by me, but all deserted me. May it not be charged against them! [17] But the Lord stood by me and strengthened me, so that through me the message might be fully proclaimed and all the Gentiles might hear it. So I was rescued from the lion's mouth. [18] The Lord will rescue me from every evil deed and bring me safely into his heavenly kingdom. To him be the glory forever and ever. Amen.

[19] Greet Prisca and Aquila, and the household of Onesiphorus. [20] Erastus remained at Corinth, and I left Trophimus, who was ill, at Miletus. [21] Do your best to come before winter. Eubulus sends greetings to you, as do Pudens and Linus and Claudia and all the brothers.[3]

[22] The Lord be with your spirit. Grace be with you.[4]

Hosea 7

When I would heal Israel,
  the iniquity of Ephraim is revealed,
    and the evil deeds of Samaria;
for they deal falsely;
  the thief breaks in,
    and the bandits raid outside.
2 But they do not consider
    that I remember all their evil.
  Now their deeds surround them;
    they are before my face.
3 By their evil they make the king glad,
    and the princes by their treachery.
4 They are all adulterers;
    they are like a heated oven
  whose baker ceases to stir the fire,
    from the kneading of the dough
      until it is leavened.
5 On the day of our king, the princes
    became sick with the heat of wine;
  he stretched out his hand with
      mockers.
6 For with hearts like an oven they
      approach their intrigue;
  all night their anger smolders;
    in the morning it blazes like a flaming
      fire.
7 All of them are hot as an oven,
    and they devour their rulers.
  All their kings have fallen,
    and none of them calls upon me.

---

[1] Or healthy [2] Some manuscripts Gaul [3] Or brothers and sisters. The plural Greek word adelphoi (translated "brothers") refers to siblings in a family. In New Testament usage, depending on the context, adelphoi may refer either to men or to both men and women who are siblings (brothers and sisters) in God's family, the church [4] The Greek for you is plural

8 Ephraim mixes himself with the
peoples;
Ephraim is a cake not turned.
9 Strangers devour his strength,
and he knows it not;
gray hairs are sprinkled upon him,
and he knows it not.
10 The pride of Israel testifies to his face;[1]
yet they do not return to the LORD
their God,
nor seek him, for all this.

11 Ephraim is like a dove,
silly and without sense,
calling to Egypt, going to Assyria.
12 As they go, I will spread over them my
net;
I will bring them down like birds of
the heavens;
I will discipline them according to the
report made to their congregation.
13 Woe to them, for they have strayed from
me!
Destruction to them, for they have
rebelled against me!
I would redeem them,
but they speak lies against me.
14 They do not cry to me from the heart,
but they wail upon their beds;
for grain and wine they gash
themselves;
they rebel against me.
15 Although I trained and strengthened
their arms,
yet they devise evil against me.
16 They return, but not upward;[2]
they are like a treacherous bow;
their princes shall fall by the sword
because of the insolence of their
tongue.
This shall be their derision in the land of
Egypt.

Psalm 120–122

A SONG OF ASCENTS.

I n my distress I called to the LORD,
and he answered me.
2 Deliver me, O LORD,
from lying lips,
from a deceitful tongue.

3 What shall be given to you,
and what more shall be done to you,
you deceitful tongue?
4 A warrior's sharp arrows,
with glowing coals of the broom tree!

5 Woe to me, that I sojourn in Meshech,
that I dwell among the tents of Kedar!
6 Too long have I had my dwelling
among those who hate peace.
7 I am for peace,
but when I speak, they are for war!

A SONG OF ASCENTS.

I lift up my eyes to the hills.
From where does my help come?
2 My help comes from the LORD,
who made heaven and earth.
3 He will not let your foot be moved;
he who keeps you will not slumber.
4 Behold, he who keeps Israel
will neither slumber nor sleep.

5 The LORD is your keeper;
the LORD is your shade on your right
hand.
6 The sun shall not strike you by day,
nor the moon by night.

7 The LORD will keep you from all evil;
he will keep your life.
8 The LORD will keep
your going out and your coming in
from this time forth and forevermore.

A SONG OF ASCENTS. OF DAVID.

I was glad when they said to me,
"Let us go to the house of the LORD!"
2 Our feet have been standing
within your gates, O Jerusalem!

3 Jerusalem—built as a city
that is bound firmly together,
4 to which the tribes go up,
the tribes of the LORD,
as was decreed for[3] Israel,
to give thanks to the name of the
LORD.
5 There thrones for judgment were set,
the thrones of the house of David.

6 Pray for the peace of Jerusalem!
"May they be secure who love you!

[1] Or in his presence [2] Or to the Most High [3] Or as a testimony for

⁷ Peace be within your walls
  and security within your towers!"
⁸ For my brothers and companions' sake
  I will say, "Peace be within you!"

⁹ For the sake of the house of the LORD
  our God,
  I will seek your good.

NOVEMBER 2

2 Kings 15

In the twenty-seventh year of Jeroboam king of Israel, Azariah the son of Amaziah, king of Judah, began to reign. ²He was sixteen years old when he began to reign, and he reigned fifty-two years in Jerusalem. His mother's name was Jecoliah of Jerusalem. ³And he did what was right in the eyes of the LORD, according to all that his father Amaziah had done. ⁴Nevertheless, the high places were not taken away. The people still sacrificed and made offerings on the high places. ⁵And the LORD touched the king, so that he was a leper[1] to the day of his death, and he lived in a separate house.[2] And Jotham the king's son was over the household, governing the people of the land. ⁶Now the rest of the acts of Azariah, and all that he did, are they not written in the Book of the Chronicles of the Kings of Judah? ⁷And Azariah slept with his fathers, and they buried him with his fathers in the city of David, and Jotham his son reigned in his place.

⁸In the thirty-eighth year of Azariah king of Judah, Zechariah the son of Jeroboam reigned over Israel in Samaria six months. ⁹And he did what was evil in the sight of the LORD, as his fathers had done. He did not depart from the sins of Jeroboam the son of Nebat, which he made Israel to sin. ¹⁰Shallum the son of Jabesh conspired against him and struck him down at Ibleam and put him to death and reigned in his place. ¹¹Now the rest of the deeds of Zechariah, behold, they are written in the Book of the Chronicles of the Kings of Israel. ¹²(This was the promise of the LORD that he gave to Jehu, "Your sons shall sit on the throne of Israel to the fourth generation." And so it came to pass.)

¹³Shallum the son of Jabesh began to reign in the thirty-ninth year of Uzziah[3] king of Judah, and he reigned one month in Samaria. ¹⁴Then Menahem the son of Gadi came up from Tirzah and came to Samaria, and he struck down Shallum the son of Jabesh in Samaria and put him to death and reigned in his place. ¹⁵Now the rest of the deeds of Shallum, and the conspiracy that he made, behold, they are written in the Book of the Chronicles of the Kings of Israel. ¹⁶At that time Menahem sacked Tiphsah and all who were in it and its territory from Tirzah on, because they did not open it to him. Therefore he sacked it, and he ripped open all the women in it who were pregnant.

¹⁷In the thirty-ninth year of Azariah king of Judah, Menahem the son of Gadi began to reign over Israel, and he reigned ten years in Samaria. ¹⁸And he did what was evil in the sight of the LORD. He did not depart all his days from all the sins of Jeroboam the son of Nebat, which he made Israel to sin. ¹⁹Pul[4] the king of Assyria came against the land, and Menahem gave Pul a thousand talents[5] of silver, that he might help him to confirm his hold on the royal power. ²⁰Menahem exacted the money from Israel, that is, from all the wealthy men, fifty shekels[6] of silver from every man, to give to the king of Assyria. So the king of Assyria turned back and did not stay there in the land. ²¹Now the rest of the deeds of Menahem and all that he did, are they not written in the Book of the Chronicles of the Kings of Israel? ²²And Menahem slept with his fathers, and Pekahiah his son reigned in his place.

---

[1] *Leprosy* was a term for several skin diseases; see Leviticus 13   [2] The meaning of the Hebrew word is uncertain   [3] Another name for *Azariah*   [4] Another name for *Tiglath-pileser III* (compare verse 29)   [5] A *talent* was about 75 pounds or 34 kilograms   [6] A *shekel* was about 2/5 ounce or 11 grams

²³In the fiftieth year of Azariah king of Judah, Pekahiah the son of Menahem began to reign over Israel in Samaria, and he reigned two years. ²⁴And he did what was evil in the sight of the LORD. He did not turn away from the sins of Jeroboam the son of Nebat, which he made Israel to sin. ²⁵And Pekah the son of Remaliah, his captain, conspired against him with fifty men of the people of Gilead, and struck him down in Samaria, in the citadel of the king's house with Argob and Arieh; he put him to death and reigned in his place. ²⁶Now the rest of the deeds of Pekahiah and all that he did, behold, they are written in the Book of the Chronicles of the Kings of Israel.

²⁷In the fifty-second year of Azariah king of Judah, Pekah the son of Remaliah began to reign over Israel in Samaria, and he reigned twenty years. ²⁸And he did what was evil in the sight of the LORD. He did not depart from the sins of Jeroboam the son of Nebat, which he made Israel to sin.

²⁹In the days of Pekah king of Israel, Tiglath-pileser king of Assyria came and captured Ijon, Abel-beth-maacah, Janoah, Kedesh, Hazor, Gilead, and Galilee, all the land of Naphtali, and he carried the people captive to Assyria. ³⁰Then Hoshea the son of Elah made a conspiracy against Pekah the son of Remaliah and struck him down and put him to death and reigned in his place, in the twentieth year of Jotham the son of Uzziah. ³¹Now the rest of the acts of Pekah and all that he did, behold, they are written in the Book of the Chronicles of the Kings of Israel.

³²In the second year of Pekah the son of Remaliah, king of Israel, Jotham the son of Uzziah, king of Judah, began to reign. ³³He was twenty-five years old when he began to reign, and he reigned sixteen years in Jerusalem. His mother's name was Jerusha the daughter of Zadok. ³⁴And he did what was right in the eyes of the LORD, according to all that his father Uzziah had done. ³⁵Nevertheless, the high places were not removed. The people still sacrificed and made offerings on the high places. He built the upper gate of the house of the LORD. ³⁶Now the rest of the acts of Jotham and all that he did, are they not written in the Book of the Chronicles of the Kings of Judah? ³⁷In those days the LORD began to send Rezin the king of Syria and Pekah the son of Remaliah

against Judah. ³⁸Jotham slept with his fathers and was buried with his fathers in the city of David his father, and Ahaz his son reigned in his place.

Titus 1

Paul, a servant¹ of God and an apostle of Jesus Christ, for the sake of the faith of God's elect and their knowledge of the truth, which accords with godliness, ²in hope of eternal life, which God, who never lies, promised before the ages began² ³and at the proper time manifested in his word through the preaching with which I have been entrusted by the command of God our Savior;

⁴To Titus, my true child in a common faith:

Grace and peace from God the Father and Christ Jesus our Savior.

⁵This is why I left you in Crete, so that you might put what remained into order, and appoint elders in every town as I directed you— ⁶if anyone is above reproach, the husband of one wife,³ and his children are believers⁴ and not open to the charge of debauchery or insubordination. ⁷For an overseer,⁵ as God's steward, must be above reproach. He must not be arrogant or quick-tempered or a drunkard or violent or greedy for gain, ⁸but hospitable, a lover of good, self-controlled, upright, holy, and disciplined. ⁹He must hold firm to the trustworthy word as taught, so that he may be able to give instruction in sound⁶ doctrine and also to rebuke those who contradict it.

¹⁰For there are many who are insubordinate, empty talkers and deceivers, especially those of the circumcision party.⁷ ¹¹They must be silenced, since they are upsetting whole families by teaching for shameful gain what they ought not to teach. ¹²One of the Cretans,⁸ a prophet of their own, said, "Cretans are always liars, evil beasts, lazy gluttons."⁹ ¹³This testimony is true. Therefore rebuke them sharply, that they may be sound in the faith, ¹⁴not devoting themselves to Jewish myths and the commands of people who turn away from the truth. ¹⁵To the pure, all things are pure, but to the defiled and unbelieving, nothing is pure; but both their minds and their consciences are defiled. ¹⁶They profess to know God, but they deny him by their works. They are detestable, disobedient, unfit for any good work.

---

¹ Or slave (for the contextual rendering of the Greek word doulos, see Preface) ² Greek before times eternal ³ Or a man of one woman ⁴ Or are faithful ⁵ Or bishop; Greek episkopos ⁶ Or healthy; also verse 13 ⁷ Or especially those of the circumcision ⁸ Greek One of them ⁹ Probably from Epimenides of Crete

Hosea 8

Set the trumpet to your lips!
　One like a vulture is over the house of the
　　Lord,
　　because they have transgressed my
　　　covenant
　　　and rebelled against my law.
2　To me they cry,
　　"My God, we—Israel—know you."
3　Israel has spurned the good;
　　the enemy shall pursue him.

4　They made kings, but not through me.
　　They set up princes, but I knew it not.
　　With their silver and gold they made
　　　idols
　　　for their own destruction.
5　I have[1] spurned your calf, O Samaria.
　　My anger burns against them.
　　How long will they be incapable of
　　　innocence?
6　For it is from Israel;
　　a craftsman made it;
　　　it is not God.
　　The calf of Samaria
　　　shall be broken to pieces.[2]

7　For they sow the wind,
　　and they shall reap the whirlwind.
　　The standing grain has no heads;
　　　it shall yield no flour;
　　if it were to yield,
　　　strangers would devour it.
8　Israel is swallowed up;
　　already they are among the nations
　　　as a useless vessel.
9　For they have gone up to Assyria,
　　a wild donkey wandering alone;
　　　Ephraim has hired lovers.
10　Though they hire allies among the
　　　nations,
　　　I will soon gather them up.
　　And the king and princes shall soon
　　　writhe
　　　because of the tribute.
11　Because Ephraim has multiplied altars
　　　for sinning,
　　they have become to him altars for
　　　sinning.
12　Were I to write for him my laws by the
　　　ten thousands,

they would be regarded as a strange
　　thing.
13　As for my sacrificial offerings,
　　they sacrifice meat and eat it,
　　but the Lord does not accept them.
　　Now he will remember their iniquity
　　　and punish their sins;
　　they shall return to Egypt.
14　For Israel has forgotten his Maker
　　　and built palaces,
　　and Judah has multiplied fortified
　　　cities;
　　so I will send a fire upon his cities,
　　　and it shall devour her strongholds.

Psalm 123–125

A Song of Ascents.

To you I lift up my eyes,
　O you who are enthroned in the
　　heavens!
2　Behold, as the eyes of servants
　　look to the hand of their master,
　　as the eyes of a maidservant
　　　to the hand of her mistress,
　　so our eyes look to the Lord our God,
　　　till he has mercy upon us.
3　Have mercy upon us, O Lord, have
　　　mercy upon us,
　　for we have had more than enough of
　　　contempt.
4　Our soul has had more than enough
　　of the scorn of those who are at ease,
　　of the contempt of the proud.

A Song of Ascents. Of David.

If it had not been the Lord who was on our
　side—
　　let Israel now say—
2　if it had not been the Lord who was on
　　our side
　　when people rose up against us,
3　then they would have swallowed us up
　　alive,
　　when their anger was kindled against
　　　us;
4　then the flood would have swept us
　　away,
　　the torrent would have gone over us;
5　then over us would have gone
　　the raging waters.

---

[1] Hebrew He has　[2] Or shall go up in flames

6   Blessed be the LORD,
       who has not given us
       as prey to their teeth!
7   We have escaped like a bird
       from the snare of the fowlers;
    the snare is broken,
       and we have escaped!
8   Our help is in the name of the LORD,
       who made heaven and earth.

A SONG OF ASCENTS.

Those who trust in the LORD are like
    Mount Zion,
       which cannot be moved, but abides
          forever.

2   As the mountains surround Jerusalem,
       so the LORD surrounds his people,
       from this time forth and forevermore.
3   For the scepter of wickedness shall not
          rest
       on the land allotted to the righteous,
    lest the righteous stretch out
       their hands to do wrong.
4   Do good, O LORD, to those who are good,
       and to those who are upright in their
          hearts!
5   But those who turn aside to their
          crooked ways
       the LORD will lead away with
          evildoers!
       Peace be upon Israel!

NOVEMBER 3

2 Kings 16

In the seventeenth year of Pekah the son of Remaliah, Ahaz the son of Jotham, king of Judah, began to reign. ²Ahaz was twenty years old when he began to reign, and he reigned sixteen years in Jerusalem. And he did not do what was right in the eyes of the LORD his God, as his father David had done, ³but he walked in the way of the kings of Israel. He even burned his son as an offering,¹ according to the despicable practices of the nations whom the LORD drove out before the people of Israel. ⁴And he sacrificed and made offerings on the high places and on the hills and under every green tree.

⁵Then Rezin king of Syria and Pekah the son of Remaliah, king of Israel, came up to wage war on Jerusalem, and they besieged Ahaz but could not conquer him. ⁶At that time Rezin the king of Syria recovered Elath for Syria and drove the men of Judah from Elath, and the Edomites came to Elath, where they dwell to this day. ⁷So Ahaz sent messengers to Tiglath-pileser king of Assyria, saying, "I am your servant and your son. Come up and rescue me from the hand of the king of Syria and from the hand of the king of Israel, who are attacking

me." ⁸Ahaz also took the silver and gold that was found in the house of the LORD and in the treasures of the king's house and sent a present to the king of Assyria. ⁹And the king of Assyria listened to him. The king of Assyria marched up against Damascus and took it, carrying its people captive to Kir, and he killed Rezin.

¹⁰When King Ahaz went to Damascus to meet Tiglath-pileser king of Assyria, he saw the altar that was at Damascus. And King Ahaz sent to Uriah the priest a model of the altar, and its pattern, exact in all its details. ¹¹And Uriah the priest built the altar; in accordance with all that King Ahaz had sent from Damascus, so Uriah the priest made it, before King Ahaz arrived from Damascus. ¹²And when the king came from Damascus, the king viewed the altar. Then the king drew near to the altar and went up on it ¹³and burned his burnt offering and his grain offering and poured his drink offering and threw the blood of his peace offerings on the altar. ¹⁴And the bronze altar that was before the LORD he removed from the front of the house, from the place between his altar and the house of the LORD, and put it on

¹ Or made his son pass through the fire

the north side of his altar. [15]And King Ahaz commanded Uriah the priest, saying, "On the great altar burn the morning burnt offering and the evening grain offering and the king's burnt offering and his grain offering, with the burnt offering of all the people of the land, and their grain offering and their drink offering. And throw on it all the blood of the burnt offering and all the blood of the sacrifice, but the bronze altar shall be for me to inquire by." [16]Uriah the priest did all this, as King Ahaz commanded.

[17]And King Ahaz cut off the frames of the stands and removed the basin from them, and he took down the sea[1] from off the bronze oxen that were under it and put it on a stone pedestal. [18]And the covered way for the Sabbath that had been built inside the house and the outer entrance for the king he caused to go around the house of the LORD, because of the king of Assyria. [19]Now the rest of the acts of Ahaz that he did, are they not written in the Book of the Chronicles of the Kings of Judah? [20]And Ahaz slept with his fathers and was buried with his fathers in the city of David, and Hezekiah his son reigned in his place.

Titus 2

But as for you, teach what accords with sound[2] doctrine. [2]Older men are to be sober-minded, dignified, self-controlled, sound in faith, in love, and in steadfastness. [3]Older women likewise are to be reverent in behavior, not slanderers or slaves to much wine. They are to teach what is good, [4]and so train the young women to love their husbands and children, [5]to be self-controlled, pure, working at home, kind, and submissive to their own husbands, that the word of God may not be reviled. [6]Likewise, urge the younger men to be self-controlled. [7]Show yourself in all respects to be a model of good works, and in your teaching show integrity, dignity, [8]and sound speech that cannot be condemned, so that an opponent may be put to shame, having nothing evil to say about us. [9]Bondservants[3] are to be submissive to their own masters in everything; they are to be well-pleasing, not argumentative, [10]not pilfering, but showing all good faith, so that in everything they may adorn the doctrine of God our Savior.

[11]For the grace of God has appeared, bringing salvation for all people, [12]training us to renounce ungodliness and worldly passions, and to live self-controlled, upright, and godly lives in the present age, [13]waiting for our blessed hope, the appearing of the glory of our great God and Savior Jesus Christ, [14]who gave himself for us to redeem us from all lawlessness and to purify for himself a people for his own possession who are zealous for good works.

[15]Declare these things; exhort and rebuke with all authority. Let no one disregard you.

Hosea 9

Rejoice not, O Israel!
  Exult not like the peoples;
    for you have played the whore, forsaking
      your God.
    You have loved a prostitute's wages
    on all threshing floors.
[2] Threshing floor and wine vat shall not
      feed them,
    and the new wine shall fail them.
[3] They shall not remain in the land of the
      LORD,
    but Ephraim shall return to Egypt,
    and they shall eat unclean food in
      Assyria.

[4] They shall not pour drink offerings of
      wine to the LORD,
    and their sacrifices shall not please
      him.
  It shall be like mourners' bread to
      them;
    all who eat of it shall be defiled;
  for their bread shall be for their hunger
      only;
    it shall not come to the house of the
      LORD.

[5] What will you do on the day of the
      appointed festival,
    and on the day of the feast of the
      LORD?
[6] For behold, they are going away from
      destruction;
    but Egypt shall gather them;
    Memphis shall bury them.
  Nettles shall possess their precious
      things of silver;
    thorns shall be in their tents.

---

[1] Compare 1 Kings 7:23 [2] Or *healthy*; also verses 2, 8 [3] Or *Slaves* (for the contextual rendering of the Greek word *doulos*, see Preface)

7 The days of punishment have come;
   the days of recompense have come;
   Israel shall know it.
The prophet is a fool;
   the man of the spirit is mad,
because of your great iniquity
   and great hatred.
8 The prophet is the watchman of
      Ephraim with my God;
   yet a fowler's snare is on all his ways,
   and hatred in the house of his God.
9 They have deeply corrupted themselves
      as in the days of Gibeah:
   he will remember their iniquity;
   he will punish their sins.

10 Like grapes in the wilderness,
      I found Israel.
Like the first fruit on the fig tree
      in its first season,
   I saw your fathers.
But they came to Baal-peor
      and consecrated themselves to the
         thing of shame,
      and became detestable like the thing
         they loved.
11 Ephraim's glory shall fly away like a
      bird—
   no birth, no pregnancy, no conception!
12 Even if they bring up children,
   I will bereave them till none is left.
Woe to them
   when I depart from them!
13 Ephraim, as I have seen, was like a
      young palm[1] planted in a meadow;
   but Ephraim must lead his children
      out to slaughter.[2]
14 Give them, O LORD—
   what will you give?
Give them a miscarrying womb
   and dry breasts.
15 Every evil of theirs is in Gilgal;
   there I began to hate them.
Because of the wickedness of their
      deeds
   I will drive them out of my house.
I will love them no more;
   all their princes are rebels.
16 Ephraim is stricken;
   their root is dried up;
   they shall bear no fruit.

Even though they give birth,
   I will put their beloved children to
      death.
17 My God will reject them
   because they have not listened to him;
   they shall be wanderers among the
      nations.

——————— *Psalm 126–128* ———————

A SONG OF ASCENTS.

When the LORD restored the fortunes of
      Zion,
   we were like those who dream.
2 Then our mouth was filled with
         laughter,
   and our tongue with shouts of joy;
then they said among the nations,
   "The LORD has done great things for
         them."
3 The LORD has done great things for us;
   we are glad.

4 Restore our fortunes, O LORD,
   like streams in the Negeb!
5 Those who sow in tears
   shall reap with shouts of joy!
6 He who goes out weeping,
   bearing the seed for sowing,
shall come home with shouts of joy,
   bringing his sheaves with him.

A SONG OF ASCENTS. OF SOLOMON.

Unless the LORD builds the house,
   those who build it labor in vain.
Unless the LORD watches over the city,
   the watchman stays awake in vain.
2 It is in vain that you rise up early
   and go late to rest,
eating the bread of anxious toil;
   for he gives to his beloved sleep.

3 Behold, children are a heritage from the
      LORD,
   the fruit of the womb a reward.
4 Like arrows in the hand of a warrior
   are the children[3] of one's youth.
5 Blessed is the man
   who fills his quiver with them!
He shall not be put to shame
   when he speaks with his enemies in
      the gate.[4]

[1] Or like Tyre [2] Hebrew to him who slaughters [3] Or sons [4] Or They shall not be put to shame when they speak with their enemies in the gate

A Song of Ascents.

B lessed is everyone who fears the LORD,
who walks in his ways!
2   You shall eat the fruit of the labor of
        your hands;
    you shall be blessed, and it shall be
        well with you.

3   Your wife will be like a fruitful vine
        within your house;

your children will be like olive shoots
        around your table.
4   Behold, thus shall the man be blessed
        who fears the LORD.

5   The LORD bless you from Zion!
    May you see the prosperity of Jerusalem
        all the days of your life!

6   May you see your children's children!
        Peace be upon Israel!

NOVEMBER 4

---

2 Kings 17

In the twelfth year of Ahaz king of Judah, Hoshea the son of Elah began to reign in Samaria over Israel, and he reigned nine years. ²And he did what was evil in the sight of the LORD, yet not as the kings of Israel who were before him. ³Against him came up Shalmaneser king of Assyria. And Hoshea became his vassal and paid him tribute. ⁴But the king of Assyria found treachery in Hoshea, for he had sent messengers to So, king of Egypt, and offered no tribute to the king of Assyria, as he had done year by year. Therefore the king of Assyria shut him up and bound him in prison. ⁵Then the king of Assyria invaded all the land and came to Samaria, and for three years he besieged it.

⁶In the ninth year of Hoshea, the king of Assyria captured Samaria, and he carried the Israelites away to Assyria and placed them in Halah, and on the Habor, the river of Gozan, and in the cities of the Medes.

⁷And this occurred because the people of Israel had sinned against the LORD their God, who had brought them up out of the land of Egypt from under the hand of Pharaoh king of Egypt, and had feared other gods ⁸and walked in the customs of the nations whom the LORD drove out before the people of Israel, and in the customs that the kings of Israel had practiced. ⁹And the people of Israel did secretly against the LORD their God things that were not right. They built for themselves high places

in all their towns, from watchtower to fortified city. ¹⁰They set up for themselves pillars and Asherim on every high hill and under every green tree, ¹¹and there they made offerings on all the high places, as the nations did whom the LORD carried away before them. And they did wicked things, provoking the LORD to anger, ¹²and they served idols, of which the LORD had said to them, "You shall not do this." ¹³Yet the LORD warned Israel and Judah by every prophet and every seer, saying, "Turn from your evil ways and keep my commandments and my statutes, in accordance with all the Law that I commanded your fathers, and that I sent to you by my servants the prophets."

¹⁴But they would not listen, but were stubborn, as their fathers had been, who did not believe in the LORD their God. ¹⁵They despised his statutes and his covenant that he made with their fathers and the warnings that he gave them. They went after false idols and became false, and they followed the nations that were around them, concerning whom the LORD had commanded them that they should not do like them. ¹⁶And they abandoned all the commandments of the LORD their God, and made for themselves metal images of two calves; and they made an Asherah and worshiped all the host of heaven and served Baal. ¹⁷And they burned their sons and their daughters as offerings[1] and used divination and omens and sold

¹ Or made their sons and their daughters pass through the fire

themselves to do evil in the sight of the LORD, provoking him to anger. [18]Therefore the LORD was very angry with Israel and removed them out of his sight. None was left but the tribe of Judah only.

[19]Judah also did not keep the commandments of the LORD their God, but walked in the customs that Israel had introduced. [20]And the LORD rejected all the descendants of Israel and afflicted them and gave them into the hand of plunderers, until he had cast them out of his sight.

[21]When he had torn Israel from the house of David, they made Jeroboam the son of Nebat king. And Jeroboam drove Israel from following the LORD and made them commit great sin. [22]The people of Israel walked in all the sins that Jeroboam did. They did not depart from them, [23]until the LORD removed Israel out of his sight, as he had spoken by all his servants the prophets. So Israel was exiled from their own land to Assyria until this day.

[24]And the king of Assyria brought people from Babylon, Cuthah, Avva, Hamath, and Sepharvaim, and placed them in the cities of Samaria instead of the people of Israel. And they took possession of Samaria and lived in its cities. [25]And at the beginning of their dwelling there, they did not fear the LORD. Therefore the LORD sent lions among them, which killed some of them. [26]So the king of Assyria was told, "The nations that you have carried away and placed in the cities of Samaria do not know the law of the god of the land. Therefore he has sent lions among them, and behold, they are killing them, because they do not know the law of the god of the land." [27]Then the king of Assyria commanded, "Send there one of the priests whom you carried away from there, and let him[1] go and dwell there and teach them the law of the god of the land." [28]So one of the priests whom they had carried away from Samaria came and lived in Bethel and taught them how they should fear the LORD.

[29]But every nation still made gods of its own and put them in the shrines of the high places that the Samaritans had made, every nation in the cities in which they lived. [30]The men of Babylon made Succoth-benoth, the men of Cuth made Nergal, the men of Hamath made Ashima, [31]and the Avvites made Nibhaz and Tartak; and the Sepharvites burned their children in the fire to Adrammelech and Anammelech, the gods of Sepharvaim. [32]They also feared the LORD and appointed from among themselves all sorts of people as priests of the high places, who sacrificed for them in the shrines of the high places. [33]So they feared the LORD but also served their own gods, after the manner of the nations from among whom they had been carried away.

[34]To this day they do according to the former manner. They do not fear the LORD, and they do not follow the statutes or the rules or the law or the commandment that the LORD commanded the children of Jacob, whom he named Israel. [35]The LORD made a covenant with them and commanded them, "You shall not fear other gods or bow yourselves to them or serve them or sacrifice to them, [36]but you shall fear the LORD, who brought you out of the land of Egypt with great power and with an outstretched arm. You shall bow yourselves to him, and to him you shall sacrifice. [37]And the statutes and the rules and the law and the commandment that he wrote for you, you shall always be careful to do. You shall not fear other gods, [38]and you shall not forget the covenant that I have made with you. You shall not fear other gods, [39]but you shall fear the LORD your God, and he will deliver you out of the hand of all your enemies." [40]However, they would not listen, but they did according to their former manner.

[41]So these nations feared the LORD and also served their carved images. Their children did likewise, and their children's children—as their fathers did, so they do to this day.

Titus 3

Remind them to be submissive to rulers and authorities, to be obedient, to be ready for every good work, [2]to speak evil of no one, to avoid quarreling, to be gentle, and to show perfect courtesy toward all people. [3]For we ourselves were once foolish, disobedient, led astray, slaves to various passions and pleasures, passing our days in malice and envy, hated by others and hating one another. [4]But when the goodness and loving kindness of God our Savior appeared, [5]he saved us, not because of works done by us in righteousness, but according to his own mercy, by the washing of regeneration and renewal of the Holy Spirit, [6]whom

---

[1] Syriac, Vulgate; Hebrew *them*

he poured out on us richly through Jesus Christ our Savior, [7] so that being justified by his grace we might become heirs according to the hope of eternal life. [8] The saying is trustworthy, and I want you to insist on these things, so that those who have believed in God may be careful to devote themselves to good works. These things are excellent and profitable for people. [9] But avoid foolish controversies, genealogies, dissensions, and quarrels about the law, for they are unprofitable and worthless. [10] As for a person who stirs up division, after warning him once and then twice, have nothing more to do with him, [11] knowing that such a person is warped and sinful; he is self-condemned.

[12] When I send Artemas or Tychicus to you, do your best to come to me at Nicopolis, for I have decided to spend the winter there. [13] Do your best to speed Zenas the lawyer and Apollos on their way; see that they lack nothing. [14] And let our people learn to devote themselves to good works, so as to help cases of urgent need, and not be unfruitful.

[15] All who are with me send greetings to you. Greet those who love us in the faith.

Grace be with you all.

Hosea 10

Israel is a luxuriant vine
  that yields its fruit.
    The more his fruit increased,
      the more altars he built;
    as his country improved,
      he improved his pillars.
[2] Their heart is false;
    now they must bear their guilt.
  The LORD[1] will break down their altars
    and destroy their pillars.

[3] For now they will say:
  "We have no king,
  for we do not fear the LORD;
    and a king—what could he do for us?"
[4] They utter mere words;
    with empty oaths they make
      covenants;
  so judgment springs up like poisonous
      weeds
    in the furrows of the field.
[5] The inhabitants of Samaria tremble
    for the calf[2] of Beth-aven.

Its people mourn for it, and so do its
      idolatrous priests—
    those who rejoiced over it and over its
      glory—
  for it has departed[3] from them.
[6] The thing itself shall be carried to
      Assyria
    as tribute to the great king.[4]
  Ephraim shall be put to shame,
    and Israel shall be ashamed of his
      idol.[5]

[7] Samaria's king shall perish
    like a twig on the face of the waters.
[8] The high places of Aven, the sin of
      Israel,
    shall be destroyed.
  Thorn and thistle shall grow up
    on their altars,
  and they shall say to the mountains,
      "Cover us,"
    and to the hills, "Fall on us."

[9] From the days of Gibeah, you have
      sinned, O Israel;
    there they have continued.
  Shall not the war against the unjust[6]
    overtake them in Gibeah?
[10] When I please, I will discipline them,
    and nations shall be gathered against
      them
  when they are bound up for their
    double iniquity.

[11] Ephraim was a trained calf
    that loved to thresh,
    and I spared her fair neck;
  but I will put Ephraim to the yoke;
    Judah must plow;
    Jacob must harrow for himself.
[12] Sow for yourselves righteousness;
    reap steadfast love;
  break up your fallow ground,
  for it is the time to seek the LORD,
    that he may come and rain
      righteousness upon you.

[13] You have plowed iniquity;
    you have reaped injustice;
    you have eaten the fruit of lies.
  Because you have trusted in your own
      way
    and in the multitude of your
      warriors,

14 therefore the tumult of war shall arise
      among your people,
   and all your fortresses shall be
      destroyed,
   as Shalman destroyed Beth-arbel on the
      day of battle;
   mothers were dashed in pieces with
      their children.
15 Thus it shall be done to you, O Bethel,
   because of your great evil.
   At dawn the king of Israel
      shall be utterly cut off.

─────── *Psalm 129–131* ───────

A SONG OF ASCENTS.

"Greatly[1] have they afflicted me from my
   youth"—
      let Israel now say—
2 "Greatly have they afflicted me from my
      youth,
   yet they have not prevailed against me.
3 The plowers plowed upon my back;
   they made long their furrows."
4 The LORD is righteous;
   he has cut the cords of the wicked.
5 May all who hate Zion
   be put to shame and turned backward!
6 Let them be like the grass on the
      housetops,
   which withers before it grows up,
7 with which the reaper does not fill his
      hand
      nor the binder of sheaves his arms,
8 nor do those who pass by say,
   "The blessing of the LORD be upon you!
   We bless you in the name of the LORD!"

A SONG OF ASCENTS.

Out of the depths I cry to you, O LORD!
   2 O Lord, hear my voice!
   Let your ears be attentive
      to the voice of my pleas for mercy!

3 If you, O LORD, should mark iniquities,
   O Lord, who could stand?
4 But with you there is forgiveness,
   that you may be feared.

5 I wait for the LORD, my soul waits,
   and in his word I hope;
6 my soul waits for the Lord
   more than watchmen for the
      morning,
   more than watchmen for the
      morning.

7 O Israel, hope in the LORD!
   For with the LORD there is steadfast
      love,
   and with him is plentiful redemption.
8 And he will redeem Israel
   from all his iniquities.

A SONG OF ASCENTS. OF DAVID.

O LORD, my heart is not lifted up;
   my eyes are not raised too high;
   I do not occupy myself with things
      too great and too marvelous for me.
2 But I have calmed and quieted my soul,
   like a weaned child with its mother;
   like a weaned child is my soul within
      me.

3 O Israel, hope in the LORD
   from this time forth and forevermore.

---

[1] Or *Often;* also verse 2

NOVEMBER 5

2 Kings 18

In the third year of Hoshea son of Elah, king of Israel, Hezekiah the son of Ahaz, king of Judah, began to reign. ²He was twenty-five years old when he began to reign, and he reigned twenty-nine years in Jerusalem. His mother's name was Abi the daughter of Zechariah. ³And he did what was right in the eyes of the LORD, according to all that David his father had done. ⁴He removed the high places and broke the pillars and cut down the Asherah. And he broke in pieces the bronze serpent that Moses had made, for until those days the people of Israel had made offerings to it (it was called Nehushtan).[1] ⁵He trusted in the LORD, the God of Israel, so that there was none like him among all the kings of Judah after him, nor among those who were before him. ⁶For he held fast to the LORD. He did not depart from following him, but kept the commandments that the LORD commanded Moses. ⁷And the LORD was with him; wherever he went out, he prospered. He rebelled against the king of Assyria and would not serve him. ⁸He struck down the Philistines as far as Gaza and its territory, from watchtower to fortified city.

⁹In the fourth year of King Hezekiah, which was the seventh year of Hoshea son of Elah, king of Israel, Shalmaneser king of Assyria came up against Samaria and besieged it, ¹⁰and at the end of three years he took it. In the sixth year of Hezekiah, which was the ninth year of Hoshea king of Israel, Samaria was taken. ¹¹The king of Assyria carried the Israelites away to Assyria and put them in Halah, and on the Habor, the river of Gozan, and in the cities of the Medes, ¹²because they did not obey the voice of the LORD their God but transgressed his covenant, even all that Moses the servant of the LORD commanded. They neither listened nor obeyed.

¹³In the fourteenth year of King Hezekiah, Sennacherib king of Assyria came up against all the fortified cities of Judah and took them.

¹⁴And Hezekiah king of Judah sent to the king of Assyria at Lachish, saying, "I have done wrong; withdraw from me. Whatever you impose on me I will bear." And the king of Assyria required of Hezekiah king of Judah three hundred talents[2] of silver and thirty talents of gold. ¹⁵And Hezekiah gave him all the silver that was found in the house of the LORD and in the treasuries of the king's house. ¹⁶At that time Hezekiah stripped the gold from the doors of the temple of the LORD and from the doorposts that Hezekiah king of Judah had overlaid and gave it to the king of Assyria. ¹⁷And the king of Assyria sent the Tartan, the Rab-saris, and the Rabshakeh with a great army from Lachish to King Hezekiah at Jerusalem. And they went up and came to Jerusalem. When they arrived, they came and stood by the conduit of the upper pool, which is on the highway to the Washer's Field. ¹⁸And when they called for the king, there came out to them Eliakim the son of Hilkiah, who was over the household, and Shebnah the secretary, and Joah the son of Asaph, the recorder.

¹⁹And the Rabshakeh said to them, "Say to Hezekiah, 'Thus says the great king, the king of Assyria: On what do you rest this trust of yours? ²⁰Do you think that mere words are strategy and power for war? In whom do you now trust, that you have rebelled against me? ²¹Behold, you are trusting now in Egypt, that broken reed of a staff, which will pierce the hand of any man who leans on it. Such is Pharaoh king of Egypt to all who trust in him. ²²But if you say to me, "We trust in the LORD our God," is it not he whose high places and altars Hezekiah has removed, saying to Judah and to Jerusalem, "You shall worship before this altar in Jerusalem"? ²³Come now, make a wager with my master the king of Assyria: I will give you two thousand horses, if you are able on your part to set riders on them. ²⁴How then can you repulse a single captain among the least of my master's servants, when you trust in Egypt for

---

[1] Nehushtan sounds like the Hebrew for both bronze and serpent [2] A talent was about 75 pounds or 34 kilograms

chariots and for horsemen? [25]Moreover, is it without the LORD that I have come up against this place to destroy it? The LORD said to me, Go up against this land, and destroy it.'"

[26]Then Eliakim the son of Hilkiah, and Shebnah, and Joah, said to the Rabshakeh, "Please speak to your servants in Aramaic, for we understand it. Do not speak to us in the language of Judah within the hearing of the people who are on the wall." [27]But the Rabshakeh said to them, "Has my master sent me to speak these words to your master and to you, and not to the men sitting on the wall, who are doomed with you to eat their own dung and to drink their own urine?"

[28]Then the Rabshakeh stood and called out in a loud voice in the language of Judah: "Hear the word of the great king, the king of Assyria! [29]Thus says the king: 'Do not let Hezekiah deceive you, for he will not be able to deliver you out of my[1] hand. [30]Do not let Hezekiah make you trust in the LORD by saying, The LORD will surely deliver us, and this city will not be given into the hand of the king of Assyria.' [31]Do not listen to Hezekiah, for thus says the king of Assyria: 'Make your peace with me[2] and come out to me. Then each one of you will eat of his own vine, and each one of his own fig tree, and each one of you will drink the water of his own cistern, [32]until I come and take you away to a land like your own land, a land of grain and wine, a land of bread and vineyards, a land of olive trees and honey, that you may live, and not die. And do not listen to Hezekiah when he misleads you by saying, "The LORD will deliver us." [33]Has any of the gods of the nations ever delivered his land out of the hand of the king of Assyria? [34]Where are the gods of Hamath and Arpad? Where are the gods of Sepharvaim, Hena, and Ivvah? Have they delivered Samaria out of my hand? [35]Who among all the gods of the lands have delivered their lands out of my hand, that the LORD should deliver Jerusalem out of my hand?'"

[36]But the people were silent and answered him not a word, for the king's command was, "Do not answer him." [37]Then Eliakim the son of Hilkiah, who was over the household, and Shebna the secretary, and Joah the son of Asaph, the recorder, came to Hezekiah with their clothes torn and told him the words of the Rabshakeh.

Philemon 1

Paul, a prisoner for Christ Jesus, and Timothy our brother,

To Philemon our beloved fellow worker [2]and Apphia our sister and Archippus our fellow soldier, and the church in your house:

[3]Grace to you and peace from God our Father and the Lord Jesus Christ.

[4]I thank my God always when I remember you in my prayers, [5]because I hear of your love and of the faith that you have toward the Lord Jesus and for all the saints, [6]and I pray that the sharing of your faith may become effective for the full knowledge of every good thing that is in us for the sake of Christ.[3] [7]For I have derived much joy and comfort from your love, my brother, because the hearts of the saints have been refreshed through you.

[8]Accordingly, though I am bold enough in Christ to command you to do what is required, [9]yet for love's sake I prefer to appeal to you—I, Paul, an old man and now a prisoner also for Christ Jesus— [10]I appeal to you for my child, Onesimus,[4] whose father I became in my imprisonment. [11](Formerly he was useless to you, but now he is indeed useful to you and to me.) [12]I am sending him back to you, sending my very heart. [13]I would have been glad to keep him with me, in order that he might serve me on your behalf during my imprisonment for the gospel, [14]but I preferred to do nothing without your consent in order that your goodness might not be by compulsion but of your own accord. [15]For this perhaps is why he was parted from you for a while, that you might have him back forever, [16]no longer as a bondservant[5] but more than a bondservant, as a beloved brother—especially to me, but how much more to you, both in the flesh and in the Lord.

[17]So if you consider me your partner, receive him as you would receive me. [18]If he has wronged you at all, or owes you anything, charge that to my account. [19]I, Paul, write this with my own hand: I will repay it—to say nothing of your owing me even your own self. [20]Yes, brother, I want some benefit from you in the Lord. Refresh my heart in Christ.

[21]Confident of your obedience, I write to you, knowing that you will do even more than I say. [22]At the same time, prepare a guest room for

[1] Hebrew *his* [2] Hebrew *Make a blessing with me* [3] Or *for Christ's service* [4] *Onesimus* means *useful* (see verse 11) or *beneficial* (see verse 20) [5] Or *slave*; twice in this verse (for the contextual rendering of the Greek word *doulos*, see Preface)

me, for I am hoping that through your prayers I will be graciously given to you.

²³ Epaphras, my fellow prisoner in Christ Jesus, sends greetings to you, ²⁴ and so do Mark, Aristarchus, Demas, and Luke, my fellow workers.

²⁵ The grace of the Lord Jesus Christ be with your spirit.

Hosea 11

When Israel was a child, I loved him,
  and out of Egypt I called my son.
2   The more they were called,
    the more they went away;
  they kept sacrificing to the Baals
    and burning offerings to idols.

3   Yet it was I who taught Ephraim to walk;
    I took them up by their arms,
    but they did not know that I healed
      them.
4   I led them with cords of kindness,¹
    with the bands of love,
  and I became to them as one who eases
      the yoke on their jaws,
    and I bent down to them and fed
      them.

5   They shall not² return to the land of
    Egypt,
  but Assyria shall be their king,
    because they have refused to return to
      me.
6   The sword shall rage against their cities,
    consume the bars of their gates,
  and devour them because of their own
      counsels.
7   My people are bent on turning away
    from me,
  and though they call out to the Most
      High,
  he shall not raise them up at all.

8   How can I give you up, O Ephraim?
    How can I hand you over, O Israel?
  How can I make you like Admah?
    How can I treat you like Zeboiim?
  My heart recoils within me;
    my compassion grows warm and
      tender.
9   I will not execute my burning anger;
    I will not again destroy Ephraim;

for I am God and not a man,
  the Holy One in your midst,
  and I will not come in wrath.³
10   They shall go after the LORD;
    he will roar like a lion;
  when he roars,
    his children shall come trembling
      from the west;
11   they shall come trembling like birds
    from Egypt,
    and like doves from the land of
      Assyria,
  and I will return them to their homes,
    declares the LORD.
12⁴   Ephraim has surrounded me with lies,
    and the house of Israel with deceit,
  but Judah still walks with God
    and is faithful to the Holy One.

Psalm 132–134

A SONG OF ASCENTS.

Remember, O LORD, in David's favor,
  all the hardships he endured,
2   how he swore to the LORD
    and vowed to the Mighty One of
      Jacob,
3   "I will not enter my house
    or get into my bed,
4   I will not give sleep to my eyes
    or slumber to my eyelids,
5   until I find a place for the LORD,
    a dwelling place for the Mighty One of
      Jacob."

6   Behold, we heard of it in Ephrathah;
    we found it in the fields of Jaar.
7   "Let us go to his dwelling place;
    let us worship at his footstool!"

8   Arise, O LORD, and go to your resting
    place,
  you and the ark of your might.
9   Let your priests be clothed with
    righteousness,
  and let your saints shout for joy.
10   For the sake of your servant David,
    do not turn away the face of your
      anointed one.

11   The LORD swore to David a sure oath
    from which he will not turn back:

¹ Or humaneness; Hebrew man ² Or surely ³ Or into the city ⁴ Ch 12:1 in Hebrew

"One of the sons of your body[1]
    I will set on your throne.
12 If your sons keep my covenant
        and my testimonies that I shall teach
            them,
    their sons also forever
        shall sit on your throne."

13 For the LORD has chosen Zion;
        he has desired it for his dwelling
            place:
14 "This is my resting place forever;
        here I will dwell, for I have desired it.
15 I will abundantly bless her provisions;
        I will satisfy her poor with bread.
16 Her priests I will clothe with salvation,
        and her saints will shout for joy.
17 There I will make a horn to sprout for
            David;
        I have prepared a lamp for my
            anointed.
18 His enemies I will clothe with shame,
        but on him his crown will shine."

A SONG OF ASCENTS. OF DAVID.

Behold, how good and pleasant it is
    when brothers dwell in unity![2]
2   It is like the precious oil on the head,
        running down on the beard,
    on the beard of Aaron,
        running down on the collar of his robes!
3   It is like the dew of Hermon,
        which falls on the mountains of Zion!
    For there the LORD has commanded the
            blessing,
        life forevermore.

A SONG OF ASCENTS.

Come, bless the LORD, all you servants of
    the LORD,
        who stand by night in the house of
            the LORD!
2   Lift up your hands to the holy place
        and bless the LORD!
3   May the LORD bless you from Zion,
        he who made heaven and earth!

NOVEMBER 6

2 Kings 19

As soon as King Hezekiah heard it, he tore his clothes and covered himself with sackcloth and went into the house of the LORD. ²And he sent Eliakim, who was over the household, and Shebna the secretary, and the senior priests, covered with sackcloth, to the prophet Isaiah the son of Amoz. ³They said to him, "Thus says Hezekiah, This day is a day of distress, of rebuke, and of disgrace; children have come to the point of birth, and there is no strength to bring them forth. ⁴It may be that the LORD your God heard all the words of the Rabshakeh, whom his master the king of Assyria has sent to mock the living God, and will rebuke the words that the LORD your God has heard; therefore lift up your prayer for the remnant that is left." ⁵When the servants of King Hezekiah came to Isaiah, ⁶Isaiah said to them, "Say to your master, 'Thus says the LORD: Do not be afraid because of the words that you have heard, with which the servants of the king of Assyria have reviled me. ⁷Behold, I will put a spirit in him, so that he shall hear a rumor and return to his own land, and I will make him fall by the sword in his own land.'"

⁸The Rabshakeh returned, and found the king of Assyria fighting against Libnah, for he heard that the king had left Lachish. ⁹Now the king heard concerning Tirhakah king of Cush, "Behold, he has set out to fight against you." So he sent messengers again to Hezekiah, saying, ¹⁰"Thus shall you speak to Hezekiah king of Judah: 'Do not let your God in whom you trust deceive you by promising that Jerusalem will not be given into the hand of the king of Assyria. ¹¹Behold, you have heard what the

---

[1] Hebrew *of your fruit of the womb*   [2] Or *dwell together*

kings of Assyria have done to all lands, devoting them to destruction. And shall you be delivered? [12]Have the gods of the nations delivered them, the nations that my fathers destroyed, Gozan, Haran, Rezeph, and the people of Eden who were in Telassar? [13]Where is the king of Hamath, the king of Arpad, the king of the city of Sepharvaim, the king of Hena, or the king of Ivvah?'"

[14]Hezekiah received the letter from the hand of the messengers and read it; and Hezekiah went up to the house of the LORD and spread it before the LORD. [15]And Hezekiah prayed before the LORD and said: "O LORD, the God of Israel, enthroned above the cherubim, you are the God, you alone, of all the kingdoms of the earth; you have made heaven and earth. [16]Incline your ear, O LORD, and hear; open your eyes, O LORD, and see; and hear the words of Sennacherib, which he has sent to mock the living God. [17]Truly, O LORD, the kings of Assyria have laid waste the nations and their lands [18]and have cast their gods into the fire, for they were not gods, but the work of men's hands, wood and stone. Therefore they were destroyed. [19]So now, O LORD our God, save us, please, from his hand, that all the kingdoms of the earth may know that you, O LORD, are God alone."

[20]Then Isaiah the son of Amoz sent to Hezekiah, saying, "Thus says the LORD, the God of Israel: Your prayer to me about Sennacherib king of Assyria I have heard. [21]This is the word that the LORD has spoken concerning him:

"She despises you, she scorns you—
　　the virgin daughter of Zion;
she wags her head behind you—
　　the daughter of Jerusalem.

[22]　"Whom have you mocked and reviled?
　　Against whom have you raised your
　　　　voice
　and lifted your eyes to the heights?
　　Against the Holy One of Israel!
[23]　By your messengers you have mocked
　　　　the Lord,
　and you have said, 'With my many
　　　　chariots
　I have gone up the heights of the
　　　　mountains,
　　to the far recesses of Lebanon;

I felled its tallest cedars,
　　its choicest cypresses;
I entered its farthest lodging place,
　　its most fruitful forest.
[24]　I dug wells
　　and drank foreign waters,
　and I dried up with the sole of my foot
　　all the streams of Egypt.'

[25]　"Have you not heard
　　that I determined it long ago?
　I planned from days of old
　　what now I bring to pass,
　that you should turn fortified cities
　　into heaps of ruins,
[26]　while their inhabitants, shorn of strength,
　　are dismayed and confounded,
　and have become like plants of the field
　　and like tender grass,
　like grass on the housetops,
　　blighted before it is grown.

[27]　"But I know your sitting down
　　and your going out and coming in,
　　and your raging against me.
[28]　Because you have raged against me
　　and your complacency has come into
　　　　my ears,
　I will put my hook in your nose
　　and my bit in your mouth,
　and I will turn you back on the way
　　by which you came.

[29]"And this shall be the sign for you: this year eat what grows of itself, and in the second year what springs of the same. Then in the third year sow and reap and plant vineyards, and eat their fruit. [30]And the surviving remnant of the house of Judah shall again take root downward and bear fruit upward. [31]For out of Jerusalem shall go a remnant, and out of Mount Zion a band of survivors. The zeal of the LORD will do this.

[32]"Therefore thus says the LORD concerning the king of Assyria: He shall not come into this city or shoot an arrow there, or come before it with a shield or cast up a siege mound against it. [33]By the way that he came, by the same he shall return, and he shall not come into this city, declares the LORD. [34]For I will defend this city to save it, for my own sake and for the sake of my servant David."

[35]And that night the angel of the LORD went

out and struck down 185,000 in the camp of the Assyrians. And when people arose early in the morning, behold, these were all dead bodies. ³⁶Then Sennacherib king of Assyria departed and went home and lived at Nineveh. ³⁷And as he was worshiping in the house of Nisroch his god, Adrammelech and Sharezer, his sons, struck him down with the sword and escaped into the land of Ararat. And Esarhaddon his son reigned in his place.

Hebrews 1

Long ago, at many times and in many ways, God spoke to our fathers by the prophets, ²but in these last days he has spoken to us by his Son, whom he appointed the heir of all things, through whom also he created the world. ³He is the radiance of the glory of God and the exact imprint of his nature, and he upholds the universe by the word of his power. After making purification for sins, he sat down at the right hand of the Majesty on high, ⁴having become as much superior to angels as the name he has inherited is more excellent than theirs.

⁵For to which of the angels did God ever say,

"You are my Son,
today I have begotten you"?

Or again,

"I will be to him a father,
and he shall be to me a son"?

⁶And again, when he brings the firstborn into the world, he says,

"Let all God's angels worship him."

⁷Of the angels he says,

"He makes his angels winds,
and his ministers a flame of fire."

⁸But of the Son he says,

"Your throne, O God, is forever and ever,
the scepter of uprightness is the
scepter of your kingdom.
⁹You have loved righteousness and hated
wickedness;
therefore God, your God, has anointed
you
with the oil of gladness beyond your
companions."

¹⁰And,

"You, Lord, laid the foundation of the
earth in the beginning,
and the heavens are the work of your
hands;
¹¹they will perish, but you remain;
they will all wear out like a garment,
¹²like a robe you will roll them up,
like a garment they will be changed.¹
But you are the same,
and your years will have no end."

¹³And to which of the angels has he ever said,

"Sit at my right hand
until I make your enemies a footstool
for your feet"?

¹⁴Are they not all ministering spirits sent out to serve for the sake of those who are to inherit salvation?

Hosea 12

Ephraim feeds on the wind
and pursues the east wind all day long;
they multiply falsehood and violence;
they make a covenant with Assyria,
and oil is carried to Egypt.

² The LORD has an indictment against
Judah
and will punish Jacob according to his
ways;
he will repay him according to his
deeds.
³ In the womb he took his brother by the
heel,
and in his manhood he strove with
God.
⁴ He strove with the angel and prevailed;
he wept and sought his favor.
He met God² at Bethel,
and there God spoke with us—
⁵ the LORD, the God of hosts,
the LORD is his memorial name:
⁶ "So you, by the help of your God, return,
hold fast to love and justice,
and wait continually for your God."

⁷ A merchant, in whose hands are false
balances,
he loves to oppress.

¹ Some manuscripts omit *like a garment* ² Hebrew *him*

8 Ephraim has said, "Ah, but I am rich;
I have found wealth for myself;
in all my labors they cannot find in me
iniquity or sin."
9 I am the LORD your God
from the land of Egypt;
I will again make you dwell in tents,
as in the days of the appointed feast.
10 I spoke to the prophets;
it was I who multiplied visions,
and through the prophets gave
parables.
11 If there is iniquity in Gilead,
they shall surely come to nothing:
in Gilgal they sacrifice bulls;
their altars also are like stone heaps
on the furrows of the field.
12 Jacob fled to the land of Aram;
there Israel served for a wife,
and for a wife he guarded sheep.
13 By a prophet the LORD brought Israel up
from Egypt,
and by a prophet he was guarded.
14 Ephraim has given bitter provocation;
so his Lord will leave his bloodguilt on
him
and will repay him for his disgraceful
deeds.

—— Psalm 135–136 ——

Praise the LORD!
Praise the name of the LORD,
give praise, O servants of the LORD,
2 who stand in the house of the LORD,
in the courts of the house of our God!
3 Praise the LORD, for the LORD is good;
sing to his name, for it is pleasant![1]
4 For the LORD has chosen Jacob for
himself,
Israel as his own possession.
5 For I know that the LORD is great,
and that our Lord is above all gods.
6 Whatever the LORD pleases, he does,
in heaven and on earth,
in the seas and all deeps.
7 He it is who makes the clouds rise at the
end of the earth,
who makes lightnings for the rain
and brings forth the wind from his
storehouses.

8 He it was who struck down the firstborn
of Egypt,
both of man and of beast;
9 who in your midst, O Egypt,
sent signs and wonders
against Pharaoh and all his servants;
10 who struck down many nations
and killed mighty kings,
11 Sihon, king of the Amorites,
and Og, king of Bashan,
and all the kingdoms of Canaan,
12 and gave their land as a heritage,
a heritage to his people Israel.
13 Your name, O LORD, endures forever,
your renown,[2] O LORD, throughout all
ages.
14 For the LORD will vindicate his people
and have compassion on his servants.
15 The idols of the nations are silver and
gold,
the work of human hands.
16 They have mouths, but do not speak;
they have eyes, but do not see;
17 they have ears, but do not hear,
nor is there any breath in their
mouths.
18 Those who make them become like
them,
so do all who trust in them.
19 O house of Israel, bless the LORD!
O house of Aaron, bless the LORD!
20 O house of Levi, bless the LORD!
You who fear the LORD, bless the
LORD!
21 Blessed be the LORD from Zion,
he who dwells in Jerusalem!
Praise the LORD!

Give thanks to the LORD, for he is good,
for his steadfast love endures forever.
2 Give thanks to the God of gods,
for his steadfast love endures forever.
3 Give thanks to the Lord of lords,
for his steadfast love endures forever;
4 to him who alone does great wonders,
for his steadfast love endures forever;
5 to him who by understanding made the
heavens,
for his steadfast love endures forever;

[1] Or for he is beautiful [2] Or remembrance

6 to him who spread out the earth above
   the waters,
      for his steadfast love endures forever;
7 to him who made the great lights,
      for his steadfast love endures forever;
8 the sun to rule over the day,
      for his steadfast love endures forever;
9 the moon and stars to rule over the night,
      for his steadfast love endures forever;
10 to him who struck down the firstborn of
    Egypt,
      for his steadfast love endures forever;
11 and brought Israel out from among them,
      for his steadfast love endures forever;
12 with a strong hand and an outstretched
    arm,
      for his steadfast love endures forever;
13 to him who divided the Red Sea in two,
      for his steadfast love endures forever;
14 and made Israel pass through the midst
    of it,
      for his steadfast love endures forever;
15 but overthrew[1] Pharaoh and his host in
    the Red Sea,
      for his steadfast love endures forever;
16 to him who led his people through the
    wilderness,
      for his steadfast love endures forever;
17 to him who struck down great kings,
      for his steadfast love endures forever;
18 and killed mighty kings,
      for his steadfast love endures forever;
19 Sihon, king of the Amorites,
      for his steadfast love endures forever;
20 and Og, king of Bashan,
      for his steadfast love endures forever;
21 and gave their land as a heritage,
      for his steadfast love endures forever;
22 a heritage to Israel his servant,
      for his steadfast love endures forever.
23 It is he who remembered us in our low
    estate,
      for his steadfast love endures forever;
24 and rescued us from our foes,
      for his steadfast love endures forever;
25 he who gives food to all flesh,
      for his steadfast love endures forever.
26 Give thanks to the God of heaven,
      for his steadfast love endures forever.

NOVEMBER 7

2 Kings 20

In those days Hezekiah became sick and was at the point of death. And Isaiah the prophet the son of Amoz came to him and said to him, "Thus says the Lord, 'Set your house in order, for you shall die; you shall not recover.'" ²Then Hezekiah turned his face to the wall and prayed to the Lord, saying, ³ "Now, O Lord, please remember how I have walked before you in faithfulness and with a whole heart, and have done what is good in your sight." And Hezekiah wept bitterly. ⁴And before Isaiah had gone out of the middle court, the word of the Lord came to him: ⁵ "Turn back, and say to Hezekiah the leader of my people, Thus says the Lord, the God of David your father: I have heard your prayer; I have seen your tears. Behold, I will heal you. On the third day you shall go up to the house of the Lord, ⁶and I will add fifteen years to your life. I will deliver you and this city out of the hand of the king of Assyria, and I will defend this city for my own sake and for my servant David's sake." ⁷And Isaiah said, "Bring a cake of figs. And let them take and lay it on the boil, that he may recover."

⁸And Hezekiah said to Isaiah, "What shall be the sign that the Lord will heal me, and that I shall go up to the house of the Lord on the third day?" ⁹And Isaiah said, "This shall be the sign to you from the Lord, that the Lord will do the thing that he has promised: shall the shadow go forward ten steps, or go back ten steps?" ¹⁰And Hezekiah answered, "It is an

---

[1] Hebrew shook off

easy thing for the shadow to lengthen ten steps. Rather let the shadow go back ten steps." ¹¹And Isaiah the prophet called to the LORD, and he brought the shadow back ten steps, by which it had gone down on the steps of Ahaz.

¹²At that time Merodach-baladan the son of Baladan, king of Babylon, sent envoys with letters and a present to Hezekiah, for he heard that Hezekiah had been sick. ¹³And Hezekiah welcomed them, and he showed them all his treasure house, the silver, the gold, the spices, the precious oil, his armory, all that was found in his storehouses. There was nothing in his house or in all his realm that Hezekiah did not show them. ¹⁴Then Isaiah the prophet came to King Hezekiah, and said to him, "What did these men say? And from where did they come to you?" And Hezekiah said, "They have come from a far country, from Babylon." ¹⁵He said, "What have they seen in your house?" And Hezekiah answered, "They have seen all that is in my house; there is nothing in my storehouses that I did not show them."

¹⁶Then Isaiah said to Hezekiah, "Hear the word of the LORD: ¹⁷Behold, the days are coming, when all that is in your house, and that which your fathers have stored up till this day, shall be carried to Babylon. Nothing shall be left, says the LORD. ¹⁸And some of your own sons, who shall be born to you, shall be taken away, and they shall be eunuchs in the palace of the king of Babylon." ¹⁹Then Hezekiah said to Isaiah, "The word of the LORD that you have spoken is good." For he thought, "Why not, if there will be peace and security in my days?"

²⁰The rest of the deeds of Hezekiah and all his might and how he made the pool and the conduit and brought water into the city, are they not written in the Book of the Chronicles of the Kings of Judah? ²¹And Hezekiah slept with his fathers, and Manasseh his son reigned in his place.

Hebrews 2

Therefore we must pay much closer attention to what we have heard, lest we drift away from it. ²For since the message declared by angels proved to be reliable, and every transgression or disobedience received a just retribution, ³how shall we escape if we neglect such a great salvation? It was declared at first by the Lord, and it was attested to us by those who heard, ⁴while God also bore witness by signs and wonders and various miracles and by gifts of the Holy Spirit distributed according to his will.

⁵For it was not to angels that God subjected the world to come, of which we are speaking. ⁶It has been testified somewhere,

"What is man, that you are mindful of him,
    or the son of man, that you care for him?
⁷ You made him for a little while lower than the angels;
    you have crowned him with glory and honor,¹
⁸ putting everything in subjection under his feet."

Now in putting everything in subjection to him, he left nothing outside his control. At present, we do not yet see everything in subjection to him. ⁹But we see him who for a little while was made lower than the angels, namely Jesus, crowned with glory and honor because of the suffering of death, so that by the grace of God he might taste death for everyone.

¹⁰For it was fitting that he, for whom and by whom all things exist, in bringing many sons to glory, should make the founder of their salvation perfect through suffering. ¹¹For he who sanctifies and those who are sanctified all have one source.² That is why he is not ashamed to call them brothers,³ ¹²saying,

"I will tell of your name to my brothers;
    in the midst of the congregation I will sing your praise."

¹³And again,

"I will put my trust in him."

And again,

"Behold, I and the children God has given me."

¹⁴Since therefore the children share in flesh and blood, he himself likewise partook of the same things, that through death he might destroy the one who has the power of death, that is, the devil, ¹⁵and deliver all those who through fear of death were subject to lifelong

¹ Some manuscripts insert *and set him over the works of your hands* ² Greek *all are of one* ³ Or *brothers and sisters.* The plural Greek word *adelphoi* (translated "brothers") refers to siblings in a family. In New Testament usage, depending on the context, *adelphoi* may refer either to men or to both men and women who are siblings (brothers and sisters) in God's family, the church; also verse 12

slavery. [16] For surely it is not angels that he helps, but he helps the offspring of Abraham. [17] Therefore he had to be made like his brothers in every respect, so that he might become a merciful and faithful high priest in the service of God, to make propitiation for the sins of the people. [18] For because he himself has suffered when tempted, he is able to help those who are being tempted.

Hosea 13

When Ephraim spoke, there was trembling;
>he was exalted in Israel,
>>but he incurred guilt through Baal and died.
[2] And now they sin more and more,
>and make for themselves metal images,
>idols skillfully made of their silver,
>>all of them the work of craftsmen.
>It is said of them,
>>"Those who offer human sacrifice kiss calves!"
[3] Therefore they shall be like the morning mist
>or like the dew that goes early away,
>like the chaff that swirls from the threshing floor
>>or like smoke from a window.

[4] But I am the LORD your God
>from the land of Egypt;
>you know no God but me,
>>and besides me there is no savior.
[5] It was I who knew you in the wilderness,
>in the land of drought;
[6] but when they had grazed,[1] they became full,
>>they were filled, and their heart was lifted up;
>>therefore they forgot me.
[7] So I am to them like a lion;
>like a leopard I will lurk beside the way.
[8] I will fall upon them like a bear robbed of her cubs;
>I will tear open their breast,
>and there I will devour them like a lion,
>>as a wild beast would rip them open.

[9] He destroys[2] you, O Israel,
>for you are against me, against your helper.

[10] Where now is your king, to save you in all your cities?
>Where are all your rulers—
>those of whom you said,
>>"Give me a king and princes"?
[11] I gave you a king in my anger,
>and I took him away in my wrath.

[12] The iniquity of Ephraim is bound up;
>his sin is kept in store.
[13] The pangs of childbirth come for him,
>but he is an unwise son,
>for at the right time he does not present himself
>>at the opening of the womb.

[14] Shall I ransom them from the power of Sheol?
>Shall I redeem them from Death?
>O Death, where are your plagues?
>O Sheol, where is your sting?
>>Compassion is hidden from my eyes.

[15] Though he may flourish among his brothers,
>the east wind, the wind of the LORD,
>>shall come,
>rising from the wilderness,
>and his fountain shall dry up;
>his spring shall be parched;
>it shall strip his treasury
>of every precious thing.
[16] [3] Samaria shall bear her guilt,
>because she has rebelled against her God;
>they shall fall by the sword;
>their little ones shall be dashed in pieces,
>and their pregnant women ripped open.

Psalm 137–138

By the waters of Babylon,
>there we sat down and wept,
>>when we remembered Zion.
[2] On the willows[4] there
>we hung up our lyres.
[3] For there our captors
>required of us songs,
>and our tormentors, mirth, saying,
>"Sing us one of the songs of Zion!"

---

[1] Hebrew according to their pasture   [2] Or I will destroy   [3] Ch 14:1 in Hebrew   [4] Or poplars

4 How shall we sing the Lord's song
    in a foreign land?
5 If I forget you, O Jerusalem,
    let my right hand forget its skill!
6 Let my tongue stick to the roof of my
    mouth,
    if I do not remember you,
    if I do not set Jerusalem
    above my highest joy!

7 Remember, O Lord, against the Edomites
    the day of Jerusalem,
    how they said, "Lay it bare, lay it bare,
    down to its foundations!"
8 O daughter of Babylon, doomed to be
    destroyed,
    blessed shall he be who repays you
    with what you have done to us!
9 Blessed shall he be who takes your little
    ones
    and dashes them against the rock!

Of David.

I give you thanks, O Lord, with my whole
heart;
    before the gods I sing your praise;
2 I bow down toward your holy temple

    and give thanks to your name for your
    steadfast love and your faithfulness,
    for you have exalted above all things
    your name and your word.[1]
3 On the day I called, you answered me;
    my strength of soul you increased.[2]

4 All the kings of the earth shall give you
    thanks, O Lord,
    for they have heard the words of your
    mouth,
5 and they shall sing of the ways of the
    Lord,
    for great is the glory of the Lord.
6 For though the Lord is high, he regards
    the lowly,
    but the haughty he knows from afar.

7 Though I walk in the midst of trouble,
    you preserve my life;
    you stretch out your hand against the
    wrath of my enemies,
    and your right hand delivers me.
8 The Lord will fulfill his purpose for me;
    your steadfast love, O Lord, endures
    forever.
    Do not forsake the work of your hands.

NOVEMBER 8

2 Kings 21

Manasseh was twelve years old when he began to reign, and he reigned fifty-five years in Jerusalem. His mother's name was Hephzibah. ²And he did what was evil in the sight of the Lord, according to the despicable practices of the nations whom the Lord drove out before the people of Israel. ³For he rebuilt the high places that Hezekiah his father had destroyed, and he erected altars for Baal and made an Asherah, as Ahab king of Israel had done, and worshiped all the host of heaven and served them. ⁴And he built altars in the house of the Lord, of which the Lord had said, "In Jerusalem will I put my name." ⁵And he built altars for all the host of heaven in the two courts of the house of the Lord. ⁶And he burned his son as an offering[3] and used fortune-telling and omens and dealt with mediums and with necromancers. He did much evil in the sight of the Lord, provoking him to anger. ⁷And the carved image of Asherah that he had made he set in the house of which the Lord said to David and to Solomon his son, "In this house, and in Jerusalem, which I have chosen out of all the tribes of Israel, I will put my name forever. ⁸And I will not cause the feet of Israel to wander anymore out of the land that I gave to their fathers, if only they will be careful to do according to all

[1] Or you have exalted your word above all your name   [2] Hebrew you made me bold in my soul with strength   [3] Hebrew made his son pass through the fire

that I have commanded them, and according to all the Law that my servant Moses commanded them." [9]But they did not listen, and Manasseh led them astray to do more evil than the nations had done whom the LORD destroyed before the people of Israel.

[10]And the LORD said by his servants the prophets, [11]"Because Manasseh king of Judah has committed these abominations and has done things more evil than all that the Amorites did, who were before him, and has made Judah also to sin with his idols, [12]therefore thus says the LORD, the God of Israel: Behold, I am bringing upon Jerusalem and Judah such disaster[1] that the ears of everyone who hears of it will tingle. [13]And I will stretch over Jerusalem the measuring line of Samaria, and the plumb line of the house of Ahab, and I will wipe Jerusalem as one wipes a dish, wiping it and turning it upside down. [14]And I will forsake the remnant of my heritage and give them into the hand of their enemies, and they shall become a prey and a spoil to all their enemies, [15]because they have done what is evil in my sight and have provoked me to anger, since the day their fathers came out of Egypt, even to this day."

[16]Moreover, Manasseh shed very much innocent blood, till he had filled Jerusalem from one end to another, besides the sin that he made Judah to sin so that they did what was evil in the sight of the LORD.

[17]Now the rest of the acts of Manasseh and all that he did, and the sin that he committed, are they not written in the Book of the Chronicles of the Kings of Judah? [18]And Manasseh slept with his fathers and was buried in the garden of his house, in the garden of Uzza, and Amon his son reigned in his place.

[19]Amon was twenty-two years old when he began to reign, and he reigned two years in Jerusalem. His mother's name was Meshullemeth the daughter of Haruz of Jotbah. [20]And he did what was evil in the sight of the LORD, as Manasseh his father had done. [21]He walked in all the way in which his father walked and served the idols that his father served and worshiped them. [22]He abandoned the LORD, the God of his fathers, and did not walk in the way of the LORD. [23]And the servants of Amon conspired against him and put the king to death in his house. [24]But the people of the land struck down all those who had conspired against King Amon, and the people of the land made Josiah his son king in his place. [25]Now the rest of the acts of Amon that he did, are they not written in the Book of the Chronicles of the Kings of Judah? [26]And he was buried in his tomb in the garden of Uzza, and Josiah his son reigned in his place.

Hebrews 3

Therefore, holy brothers,[2] you who share in a heavenly calling, consider Jesus, the apostle and high priest of our confession, [2]who was faithful to him who appointed him, just as Moses also was faithful in all God's[3] house. [3]For Jesus has been counted worthy of more glory than Moses—as much more glory as the builder of a house has more honor than the house itself. [4](For every house is built by someone, but the builder of all things is God.) [5]Now Moses was faithful in all God's house as a servant, to testify to the things that were to be spoken later, [6]but Christ is faithful over God's house as a son. And we are his house if indeed we hold fast our confidence and our boasting in our hope.[4]

[7]Therefore, as the Holy Spirit says,

"Today, if you hear his voice,
[8]   do not harden your hearts as in the rebellion,
   on the day of testing in the wilderness,
[9]   where your fathers put me to the test
   and saw my works for forty years.
[10]   Therefore I was provoked with that generation,
and said, 'They always go astray in their heart;
   they have not known my ways.'
[11]   As I swore in my wrath,
   'They shall not enter my rest.'"

[12]Take care, brothers, lest there be in any of you an evil, unbelieving heart, leading you to fall away from the living God. [13]But exhort one another every day, as long as it is called "today," that none of you may be hardened by the deceitfulness of sin. [14]For we have come to share in Christ, if indeed we hold our original confidence firm to the end. [15]As it is said,

"Today, if you hear his voice,
   do not harden your hearts as in the rebellion."

---

[1] Or *evil* [2] Or *brothers and sisters*; also verse 12 [3] Greek *his*; also verses 5, 6 [4] Some manuscripts insert *firm to the end*

16 For who were those who heard and yet rebelled? Was it not all those who left Egypt led by Moses? 17 And with whom was he provoked for forty years? Was it not with those who sinned, whose bodies fell in the wilderness? 18 And to whom did he swear that they would not enter his rest, but to those who were disobedient? 19 So we see that they were unable to enter because of unbelief.

Hosea 14

Return, O Israel, to the LORD your God,
   for you have stumbled because of your
    iniquity.
2 Take with you words
   and return to the LORD;
say to him,
   "Take away all iniquity;
accept what is good,
   and we will pay with bulls
   the vows[1] of our lips.
3 Assyria shall not save us;
   we will not ride on horses;
and we will say no more, 'Our God,'
   to the work of our hands.
In you the orphan finds mercy."

4 I will heal their apostasy;
   I will love them freely,
   for my anger has turned from them.
5 I will be like the dew to Israel;
   he shall blossom like the lily;
   he shall take root like the trees of
    Lebanon;
6 his shoots shall spread out;
   his beauty shall be like the olive,
   and his fragrance like Lebanon.
7 They shall return and dwell beneath my[2]
    shadow;
they shall flourish like the grain;
they shall blossom like the vine;
   their fame shall be like the wine of
    Lebanon.
8 O Ephraim, what have I to do with
    idols?
   It is I who answer and look after you.[3]
I am like an evergreen cypress;
   from me comes your fruit.

9 Whoever is wise, let him understand
   these things;

whoever is discerning, let him know
   them;
for the ways of the LORD are right,
   and the upright walk in them,
but transgressors stumble in them.

Psalm 139

TO THE CHOIRMASTER. A PSALM OF DAVID.

O LORD, you have searched me and known
   me!
2 You know when I sit down and when I
    rise up;
   you discern my thoughts from afar.
3 You search out my path and my lying
    down
   and are acquainted with all my ways.
4 Even before a word is on my tongue,
   behold, O LORD, you know it
    altogether.
5 You hem me in, behind and before,
   and lay your hand upon me.
6 Such knowledge is too wonderful for me;
   it is high; I cannot attain it.

7 Where shall I go from your Spirit?
   Or where shall I flee from your
    presence?
8 If I ascend to heaven, you are there!
   If I make my bed in Sheol, you are there!
9 If I take the wings of the morning
   and dwell in the uttermost parts of the
    sea,
10 even there your hand shall lead me,
   and your right hand shall hold me.
11 If I say, "Surely the darkness shall cover
    me,
   and the light about me be night,"
12 even the darkness is not dark to you;
   the night is bright as the day,
   for darkness is as light with you.

13 For you formed my inward parts;
   you knitted me together in my
    mother's womb.
14 I praise you, for I am fearfully and
    wonderfully made.[4]
Wonderful are your works;
   my soul knows it very well.
15 My frame was not hidden from you,
   when I was being made in secret,
   intricately woven in the depths of the
    earth.

---

[1] Septuagint, Syriac pay the fruit [2] Hebrew his [3] Hebrew him [4] Or for I am fearfully set apart

16 Your eyes saw my unformed substance;
in your book were written, every one of
them,
the days that were formed for me,
when as yet there was none of them.

17 How precious to me are your thoughts,
O God!
How vast is the sum of them!

18 If I would count them, they are more
than the sand.
I awake, and I am still with you.

19 Oh that you would slay the wicked,
O God!
O men of blood, depart from me!

20 They speak against you with malicious
intent;
your enemies take your name in
vain.[1]

21 Do I not hate those who hate you,
O LORD?
And do I not loathe those who rise up
against you?

22 I hate them with complete hatred;
I count them my enemies.

23 Search me, O God, and know my heart!
Try me and know my thoughts![2]

24 And see if there be any grievous way in
me,
and lead me in the way everlasting![3]

NOVEMBER 9

2 Kings 22

Josiah was eight years old when he began to reign, and he reigned thirty-one years in Jerusalem. His mother's name was Jedidah the daughter of Adaiah of Bozkath. **2**And he did what was right in the eyes of the LORD and walked in all the way of David his father, and he did not turn aside to the right or to the left.

3In the eighteenth year of King Josiah, the king sent Shaphan the son of Azaliah, son of Meshullam, the secretary, to the house of the LORD, saying, **4**"Go up to Hilkiah the high priest, that he may count the money that has been brought into the house of the LORD, which the keepers of the threshold have collected from the people. **5**And let it be given into the hand of the workmen who have the oversight of the house of the LORD, and let them give it to the workmen who are at the house of the LORD, repairing the house **6**(that is, to the carpenters, and to the builders, and to the masons), and let them use it for buying timber and quarried stone to repair the house. **7**But no accounting shall be asked from them for the money that is delivered into their hand, for they deal honestly."

8And Hilkiah the high priest said to Shaphan the secretary, "I have found the Book of the Law in the house of the LORD." And Hilkiah gave the book to Shaphan, and he read it. **9**And Shaphan the secretary came to the king, and reported to the king, "Your servants have emptied out the money that was found in the house and have delivered it into the hand of the workmen who have the oversight of the house of the LORD." **10**Then Shaphan the secretary told the king, "Hilkiah the priest has given me a book." And Shaphan read it before the king.

11When the king heard the words of the Book of the Law, he tore his clothes. **12**And the king commanded Hilkiah the priest, and Ahikam the son of Shaphan, and Achbor the son of Micaiah, and Shaphan the secretary, and Asaiah the king's servant, saying, **13**"Go, inquire of the LORD for me, and for the people, and for all Judah, concerning the words of this book that has been found. For great is the wrath of the LORD that is kindled against us, because our fathers have not obeyed the words of this book, to do according to all that is written concerning us."

14So Hilkiah the priest, and Ahikam, and Achbor, and Shaphan, and Asaiah went to

Huldah the prophetess, the wife of Shallum the son of Tikvah, son of Harhas, keeper of the wardrobe (now she lived in Jerusalem in the Second Quarter), and they talked with her. [15]And she said to them, "Thus says the LORD, the God of Israel: 'Tell the man who sent you to me, [16]Thus says the LORD, Behold, I will bring disaster upon this place and upon its inhabitants, all the words of the book that the king of Judah has read. [17]Because they have forsaken me and have made offerings to other gods, that they might provoke me to anger with all the work of their hands, therefore my wrath will be kindled against this place, and it will not be quenched. [18]But to the king of Judah, who sent you to inquire of the LORD, thus shall you say to him, Thus says the LORD, the God of Israel: Regarding the words that you have heard, [19]because your heart was penitent, and you humbled yourself before the LORD, when you heard how I spoke against this place and against its inhabitants, that they should become a desolation and a curse, and you have torn your clothes and wept before me, I also have heard you, declares the LORD. [20]Therefore, behold, I will gather you to your fathers, and you shall be gathered to your grave in peace, and your eyes shall not see all the disaster that I will bring upon this place.'" And they brought back word to the king.

--------- Hebrews 4 ---------

Therefore, while the promise of entering his rest still stands, let us fear lest any of you should seem to have failed to reach it. [2]For good news came to us just as to them, but the message they heard did not benefit them, because they were not united by faith with those who listened.[1] [3]For we who have believed enter that rest, as he has said,

"As I swore in my wrath,
'They shall not enter my rest,'"

although his works were finished from the foundation of the world. [4]For he has somewhere spoken of the seventh day in this way: "And God rested on the seventh day from all his works." [5]And again in this passage he said,

"They shall not enter my rest."

[6]Since therefore it remains for some to enter it, and those who formerly received the good news failed to enter because of disobedience, [7]again he appoints a certain day, "Today," saying through David so long afterward, in the words already quoted,

"Today, if you hear his voice,
do not harden your hearts."

[8]For if Joshua had given them rest, God[2] would not have spoken of another day later on. [9]So then, there remains a Sabbath rest for the people of God, [10]for whoever has entered God's rest has also rested from his works as God did from his.

[11]Let us therefore strive to enter that rest, so that no one may fall by the same sort of disobedience. [12]For the word of God is living and active, sharper than any two-edged sword, piercing to the division of soul and of spirit, of joints and of marrow, and discerning the thoughts and intentions of the heart. [13]And no creature is hidden from his sight, but all are naked and exposed to the eyes of him to whom we must give account.

[14]Since then we have a great high priest who has passed through the heavens, Jesus, the Son of God, let us hold fast our confession. [15]For we do not have a high priest who is unable to sympathize with our weaknesses, but one who in every respect has been tempted as we are, yet without sin. [16]Let us then with confidence draw near to the throne of grace, that we may receive mercy and find grace to help in time of need.

--------- Joel 1 ---------

The word of the LORD that came to Joel, the son of Pethuel:

[2]   Hear this, you elders;
        give ear, all inhabitants of the land!
    Has such a thing happened in your days,
        or in the days of your fathers?
[3]   Tell your children of it,
        and let your children tell their
            children,
        and their children to another
            generation.

[4]   What the cutting locust left,
        the swarming locust has eaten.

[1] Some manuscripts *it did not meet with faith in the hearers* [2] Greek *he*

What the swarming locust left,
  the hopping locust has eaten,
and what the hopping locust left,
  the destroying locust has eaten.

5 Awake, you drunkards, and weep,
    and wail, all you drinkers of wine,
  because of the sweet wine,
    for it is cut off from your mouth.
6 For a nation has come up against my
      land,
    powerful and beyond number;
  its teeth are lions' teeth,
    and it has the fangs of a lioness.
7 It has laid waste my vine
    and splintered my fig tree;
  it has stripped off their bark and thrown
      it down;
    their branches are made white.

8 Lament like a virgin[1] wearing sackcloth
    for the bridegroom of her youth.
9 The grain offering and the drink
      offering are cut off
    from the house of the LORD.
  The priests mourn,
    the ministers of the LORD.
10 The fields are destroyed,
    the ground mourns,
  because the grain is destroyed,
    the wine dries up,
    the oil languishes.

11 Be ashamed,[2] O tillers of the soil;
    wail, O vinedressers,
  for the wheat and the barley,
    because the harvest of the field has
      perished.
12 The vine dries up;
    the fig tree languishes.
  Pomegranate, palm, and apple,
    all the trees of the field are dried up,
  and gladness dries up
    from the children of man.

13 Put on sackcloth and lament, O priests;
    wail, O ministers of the altar.
  Go in, pass the night in sackcloth,
    O ministers of my God!
  Because grain offering and drink
      offering
    are withheld from the house of your
      God.

14 Consecrate a fast;
    call a solemn assembly.
  Gather the elders
    and all the inhabitants of the land
  to the house of the LORD your God,
    and cry out to the LORD.

15 Alas for the day!
  For the day of the LORD is near,
    and as destruction from the Almighty[3]
      it comes.
16 Is not the food cut off
    before our eyes,
  joy and gladness
    from the house of our God?

17 The seed shrivels under the clods;[4]
    the storehouses are desolate;
  the granaries are torn down
    because the grain has dried up.
18 How the beasts groan!
    The herds of cattle are perplexed
  because there is no pasture for them;
    even the flocks of sheep suffer.[5]

19 To you, O LORD, I call.
  For fire has devoured
    the pastures of the wilderness,
  and flame has burned
    all the trees of the field.
20 Even the beasts of the field pant for you
    because the water brooks are dried
      up,
  and fire has devoured
    the pastures of the wilderness.

———— Psalm 140–141 ————

TO THE CHOIRMASTER. A PSALM OF DAVID.

Deliver me, O LORD, from evil men;
  preserve me from violent men,
2   who plan evil things in their heart
    and stir up wars continually.
3   They make their tongue sharp as a
        serpent's,
    and under their lips is the venom of
        asps.   Selah

4 Guard me, O LORD, from the hands of
      the wicked;
  preserve me from violent men,
    who have planned to trip up my feet.

[1] Or young woman [2] The Hebrew words for dry up and be ashamed in verses 10–12, 17 sound alike [3] Destruction sounds like the Hebrew for Almighty [4] The meaning of the Hebrew line is uncertain [5] Or are made desolate

5 The arrogant have hidden a trap for
     me,
   and with cords they have spread a
     net;[1]
   beside the way they have set snares for
     me.   *Selah*

6 I say to the LORD, You are my God;
   give ear to the voice of my pleas for
     mercy, O LORD!
7 O LORD, my Lord, the strength of my
     salvation,
   you have covered my head in the day
     of battle.
8 Grant not, O LORD, the desires of the
     wicked;
   do not further their[2] evil plot, or they
     will be exalted!   *Selah*
9 As for the head of those who surround
     me,
   let the mischief of their lips
     overwhelm them!
10 Let burning coals fall upon them!
   Let them be cast into fire,
   into miry pits, no more to rise!
11 Let not the slanderer be established in
     the land;
   let evil hunt down the violent man
     speedily!

12 I know that the LORD will maintain the
     cause of the afflicted,
   and will execute justice for the
     needy.
13 Surely the righteous shall give thanks to
     your name;
   the upright shall dwell in your
     presence.

A PSALM OF DAVID.

O LORD, I call upon you; hasten to me!
   Give ear to my voice when I call to you!
2 Let my prayer be counted as incense
     before you,
   and the lifting up of my hands as the
     evening sacrifice!
3 Set a guard, O LORD, over my mouth;
   keep watch over the door of my lips!
4 Do not let my heart incline to any evil,
   to busy myself with wicked deeds
   in company with men who work iniquity,
   and let me not eat of their delicacies!

5 Let a righteous man strike me—it is a
     kindness;
   let him rebuke me—it is oil for my
     head;
   let my head not refuse it.
Yet my prayer is continually against
     their evil deeds.
6 When their judges are thrown over the
     cliff,[3]
   then they shall hear my words, for
     they are pleasant.
7 As when one plows and breaks up the
     earth,
   so shall our bones be scattered at the
     mouth of Sheol.[4]

8 But my eyes are toward you, O GOD, my
     Lord;
   in you I seek refuge; leave me not
     defenseless![5]
9 Keep me from the trap that they have
     laid for me
   and from the snares of evildoers!
10 Let the wicked fall into their own nets,
   while I pass by safely.

---

[1] Or *they have spread cords as a net* [2] Hebrew *his* [3] Or *When their judges fall into the hands of the Rock* [4] The meaning of the Hebrew in verses 6, 7 is uncertain [5] Hebrew *refuge; do not pour out my life!*

NOVEMBER 10

2 Kings 23

Then the king sent, and all the elders of Judah and Jerusalem were gathered to him. ²And the king went up to the house of the Lord, and with him all the men of Judah and all the inhabitants of Jerusalem and the priests and the prophets, all the people, both small and great. And he read in their hearing all the words of the Book of the Covenant that had been found in the house of the Lord. ³And the king stood by the pillar and made a covenant before the Lord, to walk after the Lord and to keep his commandments and his testimonies and his statutes with all his heart and all his soul, to perform the words of this covenant that were written in this book. And all the people joined in the covenant.

⁴And the king commanded Hilkiah the high priest and the priests of the second order and the keepers of the threshold to bring out of the temple of the Lord all the vessels made for Baal, for Asherah, and for all the host of heaven. He burned them outside Jerusalem in the fields of the Kidron and carried their ashes to Bethel. ⁵And he deposed the priests whom the kings of Judah had ordained to make offerings in the high places at the cities of Judah and around Jerusalem; those also who burned incense to Baal, to the sun and the moon and the constellations and all the host of the heavens. ⁶And he brought out the Asherah from the house of the Lord, outside Jerusalem, to the brook Kidron, and burned it at the brook Kidron and beat it to dust and cast the dust of it upon the graves of the common people. ⁷And he broke down the houses of the male cult prostitutes who were in the house of the Lord, where the women wove hangings for the Asherah. ⁸And he brought all the priests out of the cities of Judah, and defiled the high places where the priests had made offerings, from Geba to Beersheba. And he broke down the high places of the gates that were at the entrance of the gate of Joshua the governor of the city, which were on one's left at the gate of the city. ⁹However, the priests of the high places did not come up to the altar of the Lord in Jerusalem, but they ate unleavened bread among their brothers. ¹⁰And he defiled Topheth, which is in the Valley of the Son of Hinnom, that no one might burn his son or his daughter as an offering to Molech.¹ ¹¹And he removed the horses that the kings of Judah had dedicated to the sun, at the entrance to the house of the Lord, by the chamber of Nathan-melech the chamberlain, which was in the precincts.² And he burned the chariots of the sun with fire. ¹²And the altars on the roof of the upper chamber of Ahaz, which the kings of Judah had made, and the altars that Manasseh had made in the two courts of the house of the Lord, he pulled down and broke in pieces³ and cast the dust of them into the brook Kidron. ¹³And the king defiled the high places that were east of Jerusalem, to the south of the mount of corruption, which Solomon the king of Israel had built for Ashtoreth the abomination of the Sidonians, and for Chemosh the abomination of Moab, and for Milcom the abomination of the Ammonites. ¹⁴And he broke in pieces the pillars and cut down the Asherim and filled their places with the bones of men.

¹⁵Moreover, the altar at Bethel, the high place erected by Jeroboam the son of Nebat, who made Israel to sin, that altar with the high place he pulled down and burned,⁴ reducing it to dust. He also burned the Asherah. ¹⁶And as Josiah turned, he saw the tombs there on the mount. And he sent and took the bones out of the tombs and burned them on the altar and defiled it, according to the word of the Lord that the man of God proclaimed, who had predicted these things. ¹⁷Then he said, "What is that monument that I see?" And the men of the city told him, "It is the tomb of the man of God who came from Judah and predicted⁵ these things that you have done against the altar at Bethel." ¹⁸And he said, "Let him be; let no man move his bones." So they let his bones alone, with the bones of the prophet who came

¹ Hebrew *might cause his son or daughter to pass through the fire for Molech* ² The meaning of the Hebrew word is uncertain ³ Hebrew *pieces from there* ⁴ Septuagint *broke in pieces its stones* ⁵ Hebrew *called*

out of Samaria. ¹⁹And Josiah removed all the shrines also of the high places that were in the cities of Samaria, which kings of Israel had made, provoking the LORD to anger. He did to them according to all that he had done at Bethel. ²⁰And he sacrificed all the priests of the high places who were there, on the altars, and burned human bones on them. Then he returned to Jerusalem.

²¹And the king commanded all the people, "Keep the Passover to the LORD your God, as it is written in this Book of the Covenant." ²²For no such Passover had been kept since the days of the judges who judged Israel, or during all the days of the kings of Israel or of the kings of Judah. ²³But in the eighteenth year of King Josiah this Passover was kept to the LORD in Jerusalem.

²⁴Moreover, Josiah put away the mediums and the necromancers and the household gods and the idols and all the abominations that were seen in the land of Judah and in Jerusalem, that he might establish the words of the law that were written in the book that Hilkiah the priest found in the house of the LORD. ²⁵Before him there was no king like him, who turned to the LORD with all his heart and with all his soul and with all his might, according to all the Law of Moses, nor did any like him arise after him.

²⁶Still the LORD did not turn from the burning of his great wrath, by which his anger was kindled against Judah, because of all the provocations with which Manasseh had provoked him. ²⁷And the LORD said, "I will remove Judah also out of my sight, as I have removed Israel, and I will cast off this city that I have chosen, Jerusalem, and the house of which I said, My name shall be there."

²⁸Now the rest of the acts of Josiah and all that he did, are they not written in the Book of the Chronicles of the Kings of Judah? ²⁹In his days Pharaoh Neco king of Egypt went up to the king of Assyria to the river Euphrates. King Josiah went to meet him, and Pharaoh Neco killed him at Megiddo, as soon as he saw him. ³⁰And his servants carried him dead in a chariot from Megiddo and brought him to Jerusalem and buried him in his own tomb. And the people of the land took Jehoahaz the son of Josiah, and anointed him, and made him king in his father's place.

³¹Jehoahaz was twenty-three years old when he began to reign, and he reigned three months in Jerusalem. His mother's name was Hamutal the daughter of Jeremiah of Libnah. ³²And he did what was evil in the sight of the LORD, according to all that his fathers had done. ³³And Pharaoh Neco put him in bonds at Riblah in the land of Hamath, that he might not reign in Jerusalem, and laid on the land a tribute of a hundred talents¹ of silver and a talent of gold. ³⁴And Pharaoh Neco made Eliakim the son of Josiah king in the place of Josiah his father, and changed his name to Jehoiakim. But he took Jehoahaz away, and he came to Egypt and died there. ³⁵And Jehoiakim gave the silver and the gold to Pharaoh, but he taxed the land to give the money according to the command of Pharaoh. He exacted the silver and the gold of the people of the land, from everyone according to his assessment, to give it to Pharaoh Neco.

³⁶Jehoiakim was twenty-five years old when he began to reign, and he reigned eleven years in Jerusalem. His mother's name was Zebidah the daughter of Pedaiah of Rumah. ³⁷And he did what was evil in the sight of the LORD, according to all that his fathers had done.

Hebrews 5

For every high priest chosen from among men is appointed to act on behalf of men in relation to God, to offer gifts and sacrifices for sins. ²He can deal gently with the ignorant and wayward, since he himself is beset with weakness. ³Because of this he is obligated to offer sacrifice for his own sins just as he does for those of the people. ⁴And no one takes this honor for himself, but only when called by God, just as Aaron was.

⁵So also Christ did not exalt himself to be made a high priest, but was appointed by him who said to him,

"You are my Son,
today I have begotten you";

⁶as he says also in another place,

"You are a priest forever,
after the order of Melchizedek."

⁷In the days of his flesh, Jesus² offered up prayers and supplications, with loud cries and

¹ A talent was about 75 pounds or 34 kilograms   ² Greek *he*

tears, to him who was able to save him from death, and he was heard because of his reverence. ⁸Although he was a son, he learned obedience through what he suffered. ⁹And being made perfect, he became the source of eternal salvation to all who obey him, ¹⁰being designated by God a high priest after the order of Melchizedek.

¹¹About this we have much to say, and it is hard to explain, since you have become dull of hearing. ¹²For though by this time you ought to be teachers, you need someone to teach you again the basic principles of the oracles of God. You need milk, not solid food, ¹³for everyone who lives on milk is unskilled in the word of righteousness, since he is a child. ¹⁴But solid food is for the mature, for those who have their powers of discernment trained by constant practice to distinguish good from evil.

Joel 2

Blow a trumpet in Zion;
sound an alarm on my holy mountain!
Let all the inhabitants of the land
tremble,
for the day of the LORD is coming; it is
near,
2 a day of darkness and gloom,
a day of clouds and thick darkness!
Like blackness there is spread upon the
mountains
a great and powerful people;
their like has never been before,
nor will be again after them
through the years of all generations.

3 Fire devours before them,
and behind them a flame burns.
The land is like the garden of Eden
before them,
but behind them a desolate
wilderness,
and nothing escapes them.

4 Their appearance is like the appearance
of horses,
and like war horses they run.
5 As with the rumbling of chariots,
they leap on the tops of the
mountains,
like the crackling of a flame of fire
devouring the stubble,

like a powerful army
drawn up for battle.
6 Before them peoples are in anguish;
all faces grow pale.
7 Like warriors they charge;
like soldiers they scale the wall.
They march each on his way;
they do not swerve from their paths.
8 They do not jostle one another;
each marches in his path;
they burst through the weapons
and are not halted.
9 They leap upon the city,
they run upon the walls,
they climb up into the houses,
they enter through the windows like a
thief.
10 The earth quakes before them;
the heavens tremble.
The sun and the moon are darkened,
and the stars withdraw their shining.
11 The LORD utters his voice
before his army,
for his camp is exceedingly great;
he who executes his word is powerful.
For the day of the LORD is great and very
awesome;
who can endure it?

12 "Yet even now," declares the LORD,
"return to me with all your heart,
with fasting, with weeping, and with
mourning;
13 and rend your hearts and not your
garments."
Return to the LORD your God,
for he is gracious and merciful,
slow to anger, and abounding in
steadfast love;
and he relents over disaster.
14 Who knows whether he will not turn
and relent,
and leave a blessing behind him,
a grain offering and a drink offering
for the LORD your God?

15 Blow the trumpet in Zion;
consecrate a fast;
call a solemn assembly;
16 gather the people.
Consecrate the congregation;
assemble the elders;

gather the children,
  even nursing infants.
Let the bridegroom leave his room,
  and the bride her chamber.

17 Between the vestibule and the altar
  let the priests, the ministers of the
    Lord, weep
and say, "Spare your people, O Lord,
  and make not your heritage a
    reproach,
  a byword among the nations.[1]
Why should they say among the
  peoples,
'Where is their God?'"

18 Then the Lord became jealous for his
  land
  and had pity on his people.
19 The Lord answered and said to his
  people,
"Behold, I am sending to you
  grain, wine, and oil,
  and you will be satisfied;
and I will no more make you
  a reproach among the nations.

20 "I will remove the northerner far from
  you,
  and drive him into a parched and
    desolate land,
his vanguard[2] into the eastern sea,
  and his rear guard[3] into the western
    sea;
the stench and foul smell of him will rise,
  for he has done great things.

21 "Fear not, O land;
  be glad and rejoice,
  for the Lord has done great things!
22 Fear not, you beasts of the field,
  for the pastures of the wilderness are
    green;
the tree bears its fruit;
  the fig tree and vine give their full
    yield.

23 "Be glad, O children of Zion,
  and rejoice in the Lord your God,
for he has given the early rain for your
  vindication;
he has poured down for you abundant
  rain,
the early and the latter rain, as before.

24 "The threshing floors shall be full of grain;
  the vats shall overflow with wine and
    oil.
25 I will restore[4] to you the years
  that the swarming locust has eaten,
the hopper, the destroyer, and the cutter,
  my great army, which I sent among
    you.

26 "You shall eat in plenty and be satisfied,
  and praise the name of the Lord your
    God,
  who has dealt wondrously with you.
And my people shall never again be put
  to shame.
27 You shall know that I am in the midst of
  Israel,
  and that I am the Lord your God and
    there is none else.
And my people shall never again be put
  to shame.

28 [5] "And it shall come to pass afterward,
  that I will pour out my Spirit on all
    flesh;
your sons and your daughters shall
  prophesy,
  your old men shall dream dreams,
  and your young men shall see visions.
29 Even on the male and female servants
  in those days I will pour out my Spirit.

30 "And I will show wonders in the heavens and on the earth, blood and fire and columns of smoke. [31]The sun shall be turned to darkness, and the moon to blood, before the great and awesome day of the Lord comes. [32]And it shall come to pass that everyone who calls on the name of the Lord shall be saved. For in Mount Zion and in Jerusalem there shall be those who escape, as the Lord has said, and among the survivors shall be those whom the Lord calls.

Psalm 142

A Maskil[6] of David, when he was in the cave. A Prayer.

With my voice I cry out to the Lord;
  with my voice I plead for mercy to the
    Lord.
2 I pour out my complaint before him;
  I tell my trouble before him.
3 When my spirit faints within me,

[1] Or reproach, that the nations should rule over them [2] Hebrew face [3] Hebrew his end [4] Or pay back [5] Ch 3:1 in Hebrew [6] Probably a musical or liturgical term

you know my way!
 In the path where I walk
  they have hidden a trap for me.
⁴ Look to the right and see:
  there is none who takes notice of me;
 no refuge remains to me;
  no one cares for my soul.
⁵ I cry to you, O Lᴏʀᴅ;
  I say, "You are my refuge,

my portion in the land of the living."
⁶ Attend to my cry,
  for I am brought very low!
 Deliver me from my persecutors,
  for they are too strong for me!
⁷ Bring me out of prison,
  that I may give thanks to your name!
 The righteous will surround me,
  for you will deal bountifully with me.

NOVEMBER 11

2 Kings 24

In his days, Nebuchadnezzar king of Babylon came up, and Jehoiakim became his servant for three years. Then he turned and rebelled against him. ²And the Lᴏʀᴅ sent against him bands of the Chaldeans and bands of the Syrians and bands of the Moabites and bands of the Ammonites, and sent them against Judah to destroy it, according to the word of the Lᴏʀᴅ that he spoke by his servants the prophets. ³Surely this came upon Judah at the command of the Lᴏʀᴅ, to remove them out of his sight, for the sins of Manasseh, according to all that he had done, ⁴and also for the innocent blood that he had shed. For he filled Jerusalem with innocent blood, and the Lᴏʀᴅ would not pardon. ⁵Now the rest of the deeds of Jehoiakim and all that he did, are they not written in the Book of the Chronicles of the Kings of Judah? ⁶So Jehoiakim slept with his fathers, and Jehoiachin his son reigned in his place. ⁷And the king of Egypt did not come again out of his land, for the king of Babylon had taken all that belonged to the king of Egypt from the Brook of Egypt to the river Euphrates.

⁸Jehoiachin was eighteen years old when he became king, and he reigned three months in Jerusalem. His mother's name was Nehushta the daughter of Elnathan of Jerusalem. ⁹And he did what was evil in the sight of the Lᴏʀᴅ, according to all that his father had done.

¹⁰At that time the servants of Nebuchadnezzar king of Babylon came up to Jerusalem, and the city was besieged. ¹¹And Nebuchadnezzar king of Babylon came to the city while his servants were besieging it, ¹²and Jehoiachin the king of Judah gave himself up to the king of Babylon, himself and his mother and his servants and his officials and his palace officials. The king of Babylon took him prisoner in the eighth year of his reign ¹³and carried off all the treasures of the house of the Lᴏʀᴅ and the treasures of the king's house, and cut in pieces all the vessels of gold in the temple of the Lᴏʀᴅ, which Solomon king of Israel had made, as the Lᴏʀᴅ had foretold. ¹⁴He carried away all Jerusalem and all the officials and all the mighty men of valor, 10,000 captives, and all the craftsmen and the smiths. None remained, except the poorest people of the land. ¹⁵And he carried away Jehoiachin to Babylon. The king's mother, the king's wives, his officials, and the chief men of the land he took into captivity from Jerusalem to Babylon. ¹⁶And the king of Babylon brought captive to Babylon all the men of valor, 7,000, and the craftsmen and the metal workers, 1,000, all of them strong and fit for war. ¹⁷And the king of Babylon made Mattaniah, Jehoiachin's uncle, king in his place, and changed his name to Zedekiah.

¹⁸Zedekiah was twenty-one years old when he became king, and he reigned eleven years in Jerusalem. His mother's name was Hamutal the daughter of Jeremiah of Libnah. ¹⁹And he did what was evil in the sight of the Lᴏʀᴅ,

according to all that Jehoiakim had done. ²⁰ For because of the anger of the Lord it came to the point in Jerusalem and Judah that he cast them out from his presence.

And Zedekiah rebelled against the king of Babylon.

Hebrews 6

Therefore let us leave the elementary doctrine of Christ and go on to maturity, not laying again a foundation of repentance from dead works and of faith toward God, ² and of instruction about washings,¹ the laying on of hands, the resurrection of the dead, and eternal judgment. ³ And this we will do if God permits. ⁴ For it is impossible, in the case of those who have once been enlightened, who have tasted the heavenly gift, and have shared in the Holy Spirit, ⁵ and have tasted the goodness of the word of God and the powers of the age to come, ⁶ and then have fallen away, to restore them again to repentance, since they are crucifying once again the Son of God to their own harm and holding him up to contempt. ⁷ For land that has drunk the rain that often falls on it, and produces a crop useful to those for whose sake it is cultivated, receives a blessing from God. ⁸ But if it bears thorns and thistles, it is worthless and near to being cursed, and its end is to be burned.

⁹ Though we speak in this way, yet in your case, beloved, we feel sure of better things— things that belong to salvation. ¹⁰ For God is not unjust so as to overlook your work and the love that you have shown for his name in serving the saints, as you still do. ¹¹ And we desire each one of you to show the same earnestness to have the full assurance of hope until the end, ¹² so that you may not be sluggish, but imitators of those who through faith and patience inherit the promises.

¹³ For when God made a promise to Abraham, since he had no one greater by whom to swear, he swore by himself, ¹⁴ saying, "Surely I will bless you and multiply you." ¹⁵ And thus Abraham,² having patiently waited, obtained the promise. ¹⁶ For people swear by something greater than themselves, and in all their disputes an oath is final for confirmation. ¹⁷ So when God desired to show more convincingly to the heirs of the promise the unchangeable character of his purpose, he guaranteed it with an oath, ¹⁸ so that by two unchangeable things, in which it is impossible for God to lie, we who have fled for refuge might have strong encouragement to hold fast to the hope set before us. ¹⁹ We have this as a sure and steadfast anchor of the soul, a hope that enters into the inner place behind the curtain, ²⁰ where Jesus has gone as a forerunner on our behalf, having become a high priest forever after the order of Melchizedek.

Joel 3³

"For behold, in those days and at that time, when I restore the fortunes of Judah and Jerusalem, ² I will gather all the nations and bring them down to the Valley of Jehoshaphat. And I will enter into judgment with them there, on behalf of my people and my heritage Israel, because they have scattered them among the nations and have divided up my land, ³ and have cast lots for my people, and have traded a boy for a prostitute, and have sold a girl for wine and have drunk it.

⁴ "What are you to me, O Tyre and Sidon, and all the regions of Philistia? Are you paying me back for something? If you are paying me back, I will return your payment on your own head swiftly and speedily. ⁵ For you have taken my silver and my gold, and have carried my rich treasures into your temples.⁴ ⁶ You have sold the people of Judah and Jerusalem to the Greeks in order to remove them far from their own border. ⁷ Behold, I will stir them up from the place to which you have sold them, and I will return your payment on your own head. ⁸ I will sell your sons and your daughters into the hand of the people of Judah, and they will sell them to the Sabeans, to a nation far away, for the Lord has spoken."

⁹ Proclaim this among the nations:
   Consecrate for war;⁵
     stir up the mighty men.
   Let all the men of war draw near;
     let them come up.
¹⁰ Beat your plowshares into swords,
     and your pruning hooks into spears;
     let the weak say, "I am a warrior."

¹¹ Hasten and come,
     all you surrounding nations,
     and gather yourselves there.
   Bring down your warriors, O Lord.

¹ Or baptisms (that is, cleansing rites) ² Greek he ³ Ch 4:1 in Hebrew ⁴ Or palaces ⁵ Or Consecrate a war

¹² Let the nations stir themselves up
    and come up to the Valley of
        Jehoshaphat;
  for there I will sit to judge
    all the surrounding nations.

¹³ Put in the sickle,
    for the harvest is ripe.
  Go in, tread,
    for the winepress is full.
  The vats overflow,
    for their evil is great.

¹⁴ Multitudes, multitudes,
    in the valley of decision!
  For the day of the LORD is near
    in the valley of decision.

¹⁵ The sun and the moon are darkened,
    and the stars withdraw their shining.

¹⁶ The LORD roars from Zion,
    and utters his voice from Jerusalem,
    and the heavens and the earth quake.
  But the LORD is a refuge to his people,
    a stronghold to the people of Israel.

¹⁷ "So you shall know that I am the LORD
    your God,
  who dwells in Zion, my holy
    mountain.
  And Jerusalem shall be holy,
    and strangers shall never again pass
      through it.

¹⁸ "And in that day
  the mountains shall drip sweet wine,
    and the hills shall flow with milk,
  and all the streambeds of Judah
    shall flow with water;
  and a fountain shall come forth from
    the house of the LORD
    and water the Valley of Shittim.

¹⁹ "Egypt shall become a desolation
    and Edom a desolate wilderness,
  for the violence done to the people of
    Judah,
  because they have shed innocent
    blood in their land.

²⁰ But Judah shall be inhabited forever,
    and Jerusalem to all generations.

²¹ I will avenge their blood,
    blood I have not avenged,[1]
  for the LORD dwells in Zion."

Psalm 143

A PSALM OF DAVID.

Hear my prayer, O LORD;
  give ear to my pleas for mercy!
    In your faithfulness answer me, in
      your righteousness!

² Enter not into judgment with your
    servant,
  for no one living is righteous before
    you.

³ For the enemy has pursued my soul;
    he has crushed my life to the ground;
    he has made me sit in darkness like
      those long dead.

⁴ Therefore my spirit faints within me;
    my heart within me is appalled.

⁵ I remember the days of old;
    I meditate on all that you have done;
    I ponder the work of your hands.

⁶ I stretch out my hands to you;
    my soul thirsts for you like a parched
      land.   *Selah*

⁷ Answer me quickly, O LORD!
    My spirit fails!
  Hide not your face from me,
    lest I be like those who go down to the
      pit.

⁸ Let me hear in the morning of your
    steadfast love,
  for in you I trust.
  Make me know the way I should go,
    for to you I lift up my soul.

⁹ Deliver me from my enemies, O LORD!
    I have fled to you for refuge.[2]

¹⁰ Teach me to do your will,
    for you are my God!
  Let your good Spirit lead me
    on level ground!

¹¹ For your name's sake, O LORD, preserve
    my life!
  In your righteousness bring my soul
    out of trouble!

¹² And in your steadfast love you will cut
    off my enemies,
  and you will destroy all the
    adversaries of my soul,
  for I am your servant.

---

[1] Or *I will acquit their bloodguilt that I have not acquitted* [2] One Hebrew manuscript, Septuagint; most Hebrew manuscripts *To you I have covered*

NOVEMBER 12

2 Kings 25

And in the ninth year of his reign, in the tenth month, on the tenth day of the month, Nebuchadnezzar king of Babylon came with all his army against Jerusalem and laid siege to it. And they built siegeworks all around it. ² So the city was besieged till the eleventh year of King Zedekiah. ³ On the ninth day of the fourth month the famine was so severe in the city that there was no food for the people of the land. ⁴ Then a breach was made in the city, and all the men of war fled by night by the way of the gate between the two walls, by the king's garden, and the Chaldeans were around the city. And they went in the direction of the Arabah. ⁵ But the army of the Chaldeans pursued the king and overtook him in the plains of Jericho, and all his army was scattered from him. ⁶ Then they captured the king and brought him up to the king of Babylon at Riblah, and they passed sentence on him. ⁷ They slaughtered the sons of Zedekiah before his eyes, and put out the eyes of Zedekiah and bound him in chains and took him to Babylon.

⁸ In the fifth month, on the seventh day of the month—that was the nineteenth year of King Nebuchadnezzar, king of Babylon—Nebuzaradan, the captain of the bodyguard, a servant of the king of Babylon, came to Jerusalem. ⁹ And he burned the house of the LORD and the king's house and all the houses of Jerusalem; every great house he burned down. ¹⁰ And all the army of the Chaldeans, who were with the captain of the guard, broke down the walls around Jerusalem. ¹¹ And the rest of the people who were left in the city and the deserters who had deserted to the king of Babylon, together with the rest of the multitude, Nebuzaradan the captain of the guard carried into exile. ¹² But the captain of the guard left some of the poorest of the land to be vinedressers and plowmen.

¹³ And the pillars of bronze that were in the house of the LORD, and the stands and the bronze sea that were in the house of the LORD, the Chaldeans broke in pieces and carried the bronze to Babylon. ¹⁴ And they took away the pots and the shovels and the snuffers and the dishes for incense and all the vessels of bronze used in the temple service, ¹⁵ the fire pans also and the bowls. What was of gold the captain of the guard took away as gold, and what was of silver, as silver. ¹⁶ As for the two pillars, the one sea, and the stands that Solomon had made for the house of the LORD, the bronze of all these vessels was beyond weight. ¹⁷ The height of the one pillar was eighteen cubits,[1] and on it was a capital of bronze. The height of the capital was three cubits. A latticework and pomegranates, all of bronze, were all around the capital. And the second pillar had the same, with the latticework.

¹⁸ And the captain of the guard took Seraiah the chief priest and Zephaniah the second priest and the three keepers of the threshold; ¹⁹ and from the city he took an officer who had been in command of the men of war, and five men of the king's council who were found in the city; and the secretary of the commander of the army, who mustered the people of the land; and sixty men of the people of the land, who were found in the city. ²⁰ And Nebuzaradan the captain of the guard took them and brought them to the king of Babylon at Riblah. ²¹ And the king of Babylon struck them down and put them to death at Riblah in the land of Hamath. So Judah was taken into exile out of its land.

²² And over the people who remained in the land of Judah, whom Nebuchadnezzar king of Babylon had left, he appointed Gedaliah the son of Ahikam, son of Shaphan, governor. ²³ Now when all the captains and their men heard that the king of Babylon had appointed Gedaliah governor, they came with their men to Gedaliah at Mizpah, namely, Ishmael the son of Nethaniah, and Johanan the son of Kareah, and Seraiah the son of Tanhumeth the Netophathite, and Jaazaniah the son of the Maacathite. ²⁴ And Gedaliah swore to them and their men, saying, "Do not be afraid because of the Chaldean

---

[1] A cubit was about 18 inches or 45 centimeters

officials. Live in the land and serve the king of Babylon, and it shall be well with you." ²⁵But in the seventh month, Ishmael the son of Nethaniah, son of Elishama, of the royal family, came with ten men and struck down Gedaliah and put him to death along with the Jews and the Chaldeans who were with him at Mizpah. ²⁶Then all the people, both small and great, and the captains of the forces arose and went to Egypt, for they were afraid of the Chaldeans.

²⁷And in the thirty-seventh year of the exile of Jehoiachin king of Judah, in the twelfth month, on the twenty-seventh day of the month, Evil-merodach king of Babylon, in the year that he began to reign, graciously freed¹ Jehoiachin king of Judah from prison. ²⁸And he spoke kindly to him and gave him a seat above the seats of the kings who were with him in Babylon. ²⁹So Jehoiachin put off his prison garments. And every day of his life he dined regularly at the king's table, ³⁰and for his allowance, a regular allowance was given him by the king, according to his daily needs, as long as he lived.

──── Hebrews 7 ────

For this Melchizedek, king of Salem, priest of the Most High God, met Abraham returning from the slaughter of the kings and blessed him, ²and to him Abraham apportioned a tenth part of everything. He is first, by translation of his name, king of righteousness, and then he is also king of Salem, that is, king of peace. ³He is without father or mother or genealogy, having neither beginning of days nor end of life, but resembling the Son of God he continues a priest forever.

⁴See how great this man was to whom Abraham the patriarch gave a tenth of the spoils! ⁵And those descendants of Levi who receive the priestly office have a commandment in the law to take tithes from the people, that is, from their brothers,² though these also are descended from Abraham. ⁶But this man who does not have his descent from them received tithes from Abraham and blessed him who had the promises. ⁷It is beyond dispute that the inferior is blessed by the superior. ⁸In the one case tithes are received by mortal men, but in the other case, by one of whom it is testified that he lives. ⁹One might even say that Levi himself, who receives tithes, paid tithes through

Abraham, ¹⁰for he was still in the loins of his ancestor when Melchizedek met him.

¹¹Now if perfection had been attainable through the Levitical priesthood (for under it the people received the law), what further need would there have been for another priest to arise after the order of Melchizedek, rather than one named after the order of Aaron? ¹²For when there is a change in the priesthood, there is necessarily a change in the law as well. ¹³For the one of whom these things are spoken belonged to another tribe, from which no one has ever served at the altar. ¹⁴For it is evident that our Lord was descended from Judah, and in connection with that tribe Moses said nothing about priests.

¹⁵This becomes even more evident when another priest arises in the likeness of Melchizedek, ¹⁶who has become a priest, not on the basis of a legal requirement concerning bodily descent, but by the power of an indestructible life. ¹⁷For it is witnessed of him,

> "You are a priest forever,
>   after the order of Melchizedek."

¹⁸For on the one hand, a former commandment is set aside because of its weakness and uselessness ¹⁹(for the law made nothing perfect); but on the other hand, a better hope is introduced, through which we draw near to God. ²⁰And it was not without an oath. For those who formerly became priests were made such without an oath, ²¹but this one was made a priest with an oath by the one who said to him:

> "The Lord has sworn
>   and will not change his mind,
>   'You are a priest forever.'"

²²This makes Jesus the guarantor of a better covenant.

²³The former priests were many in number, because they were prevented by death from continuing in office, ²⁴but he holds his priesthood permanently, because he continues forever. ²⁵Consequently, he is able to save to the uttermost³ those who draw near to God through him, since he always lives to make intercession for them.

²⁶For it was indeed fitting that we should have such a high priest, holy, innocent, unstained, separated from sinners, and exalted above the heavens. ²⁷He has no need, like those

¹ Hebrew reign, lifted up the head of ² Or brothers and sisters ³ That is, completely; or at all times

high priests, to offer sacrifices daily, first for his own sins and then for those of the people, since he did this once for all when he offered up himself. ²⁸For the law appoints men in their weakness as high priests, but the word of the oath, which came later than the law, appoints a Son who has been made perfect forever.

─────── Amos 1 ───────

The words of Amos, who was among the shepherds¹ of Tekoa, which he saw concerning Israel in the days of Uzziah king of Judah and in the days of Jeroboam the son of Joash, king of Israel, two years² before the earthquake.
²And he said:

"The LORD roars from Zion
    and utters his voice from Jerusalem;
the pastures of the shepherds mourn,
    and the top of Carmel withers."

³Thus says the LORD:

"For three transgressions of Damascus,
    and for four, I will not revoke the
        punishment,³
because they have threshed Gilead
    with threshing sledges of iron.
⁴ So I will send a fire upon the house of
        Hazael,
    and it shall devour the strongholds of
        Ben-hadad.
⁵ I will break the gate-bar of Damascus,
    and cut off the inhabitants from the
        Valley of Aven,⁴
and him who holds the scepter from
        Beth-eden;
and the people of Syria shall go into
    exile to Kir,"
                    says the LORD.

⁶Thus says the LORD:

"For three transgressions of Gaza,
    and for four, I will not revoke the
        punishment,
because they carried into exile a whole
        people
    to deliver them up to Edom.
⁷ So I will send a fire upon the wall of
        Gaza,
    and it shall devour her strongholds."

⁸ I will cut off the inhabitants from
        Ashdod,
    and him who holds the scepter from
        Ashkelon;
I will turn my hand against Ekron,
    and the remnant of the Philistines
        shall perish,"
                    says the Lord GOD.

⁹Thus says the LORD:

"For three transgressions of Tyre,
    and for four, I will not revoke the
        punishment,
because they delivered up a whole
        people to Edom,
    and did not remember the covenant of
        brotherhood.
¹⁰ So I will send a fire upon the wall of
        Tyre,
    and it shall devour her strongholds."

¹¹Thus says the LORD:

"For three transgressions of Edom,
    and for four, I will not revoke the
        punishment,
because he pursued his brother with the
        sword
    and cast off all pity,
and his anger tore perpetually,
    and he kept his wrath forever.
¹² So I will send a fire upon Teman,
    and it shall devour the strongholds of
        Bozrah."

¹³Thus says the LORD:

"For three transgressions of the
        Ammonites,
    and for four, I will not revoke the
        punishment,
because they have ripped open pregnant
        women in Gilead,
    that they might enlarge their border.
¹⁴ So I will kindle a fire in the wall of
        Rabbah,
    and it shall devour her strongholds,
with shouting on the day of battle,
    with a tempest in the day of the
        whirlwind;
¹⁵ and their king shall go into exile,
    he and his princes⁵ together,"
                    says the LORD.

──────────── *Psalm 144* ────────────

OF DAVID.

Blessed be the LORD, my rock,
who trains my hands for war,
and my fingers for battle;

2   he is my steadfast love and my fortress,
my stronghold and my deliverer,
my shield and he in whom I take refuge,
who subdues peoples[1] under me.

3   O LORD, what is man that you regard him,
or the son of man that you think of
him?

4   Man is like a breath;
his days are like a passing shadow.

5   Bow your heavens, O LORD, and come
down!
Touch the mountains so that they
smoke!

6   Flash forth the lightning and scatter them;
send out your arrows and rout them!

7   Stretch out your hand from on high;
rescue me and deliver me from the
many waters,
from the hand of foreigners,

8   whose mouths speak lies
and whose right hand is a right hand
of falsehood.

9   I will sing a new song to you, O God;
upon a ten-stringed harp I will play to
you,

10   who gives victory to kings,
who rescues David his servant from
the cruel sword.

11   Rescue me and deliver me
from the hand of foreigners,
whose mouths speak lies
and whose right hand is a right hand
of falsehood.

12   May our sons in their youth
be like plants full grown,
our daughters like corner pillars
cut for the structure of a palace;

13   may our granaries be full,
providing all kinds of produce;
may our sheep bring forth thousands
and ten thousands in our fields;

14   may our cattle be heavy with young,
suffering no mishap or failure in
bearing;[2]
may there be no cry of distress in our
streets!

15   Blessed are the people to whom such
blessings fall!
Blessed are the people whose God is
the LORD!

NOVEMBER 13

──────────── *1 Chronicles 1[3]–2* ────────────

Adam, Seth, Enosh; [2]Kenan, Mahalalel, Jared; [3]Enoch, Methuselah, Lamech; [4]Noah,
Shem, Ham, and Japheth.
   [5]The sons of Japheth: Gomer, Magog, Madai,
Javan, Tubal, Meshech, and Tiras. [6]The sons of
Gomer: Ashkenaz, Riphath,[4] and Togarmah.
[7]The sons of Javan: Elishah, Tarshish, Kittim,
and Rodanim.
   [8]The sons of Ham: Cush, Egypt, Put, and
Canaan. [9]The sons of Cush: Seba, Havilah,
Sabta, Raama, and Sabteca. The sons of Raamah: Sheba and Dedan. [10]Cush fathered

Nimrod. He was the first on earth to be a
mighty man.[5]
   [11]Egypt fathered Ludim, Anamim, Lehabim,
Naphtuhim, [12]Pathrusim, Casluhim (from
whom the Philistines came), and Caphtorim.
   [13]Canaan fathered Sidon his firstborn and
Heth, [14]and the Jebusites, the Amorites, the
Girgashites, [15]the Hivites, the Arkites, the
Sinites, [16]the Arvadites, the Zemarites, and
the Hamathites.
   [17]The sons of Shem: Elam, Asshur, Arpachshad, Lud, and Aram. And the sons of Aram:[6]

[1] Many Hebrew manuscripts, Dead Sea Scroll, Jerome, Syriac, Aquila; most Hebrew manuscripts *subdues my people* [2] Hebrew *with no breaking in or going out* [3] Many names in these
genealogies are spelled differently in other biblical books [4] Septuagint; Hebrew *Diphath* [5] Or *He began to be a mighty man on the earth* [6] Septuagint; Hebrew lacks *And the sons
of Aram*

Uz, Hul, Gether, and Meshech. [18]Arpachshad fathered Shelah, and Shelah fathered Eber. [19]To Eber were born two sons: the name of the one was Peleg[1] (for in his days the earth was divided), and his brother's name was Joktan. [20]Joktan fathered Almodad, Sheleph, Hazarmaveth, Jerah, [21]Hadoram, Uzal, Diklah, [22]Obal,[2] Abimael, Sheba, [23]Ophir, Havilah, and Jobab; all these were the sons of Joktan.

[24]Shem, Arpachshad, Shelah; [25]Eber, Peleg, Reu; [26]Serug, Nahor, Terah; [27]Abram, that is, Abraham.

[28]The sons of Abraham: Isaac and Ishmael. [29]These are their genealogies: the firstborn of Ishmael, Nebaioth, and Kedar, Adbeel, Mibsam, [30]Mishma, Dumah, Massa, Hadad, Tema, [31]Jetur, Naphish, and Kedemah. These are the sons of Ishmael. [32]The sons of Keturah, Abraham's concubine: she bore Zimran, Jokshan, Medan, Midian, Ishbak, and Shuah. The sons of Jokshan: Sheba and Dedan. [33]The sons of Midian: Ephah, Epher, Hanoch, Abida, and Eldaah. All these were the descendants of Keturah.

[34]Abraham fathered Isaac. The sons of Isaac: Esau and Israel. [35]The sons of Esau: Eliphaz, Reuel, Jeush, Jalam, and Korah. [36]The sons of Eliphaz: Teman, Omar, Zepho, Gatam, Kenaz, and of Timna,[3] Amalek. [37]The sons of Reuel: Nahath, Zerah, Shammah, and Mizzah.

[38]The sons of Seir: Lotan, Shobal, Zibeon, Anah, Dishon, Ezer, and Dishan. [39]The sons of Lotan: Hori and Hemam;[4] and Lotan's sister was Timna. [40]The sons of Shobal: Alvan,[5] Manahath, Ebal, Shepho,[6] and Onam. The sons of Zibeon: Aiah and Anah. [41]The son[7] of Anah: Dishon. The sons of Dishon: Hemdan,[8] Eshban, Ithran, and Cheran. [42]The sons of Ezer: Bilhan, Zaavan, and Akan.[9] The sons of Dishan: Uz and Aran.

[43]These are the kings who reigned in the land of Edom before any king reigned over the people of Israel: Bela the son of Beor, the name of his city being Dinhabah. [44]Bela died, and Jobab the son of Zerah of Bozrah reigned in his place. [45]Jobab died, and Husham of the land of the Temanites reigned in his place. [46]Husham died, and Hadad the son of Bedad, who defeated Midian in the country of Moab, reigned in his place, the name of his city being Avith. [47]Hadad died, and Samlah of Masrekah reigned in his place. [48]Samlah died, and Shaul of Rehoboth on the Euphrates[10] reigned in his

place. [49]Shaul died, and Baal-hanan, the son of Achbor, reigned in his place. [50]Baal-hanan died, and Hadad reigned in his place, the name of his city being Pai; and his wife's name was Mehetabel, the daughter of Matred, the daughter of Mezahab. [51]And Hadad died.

The chiefs of Edom were: chiefs Timna, Alvah, Jetheth, [52]Oholibamah, Elah, Pinon, [53]Kenaz, Teman, Mibzar, [54]Magdiel, and Iram; these are the chiefs of Edom.

[2:1]These are the sons of Israel: Reuben, Simeon, Levi, Judah, Issachar, Zebulun, [2]Dan, Joseph, Benjamin, Naphtali, Gad, and Asher. [3]The sons of Judah: Er, Onan and Shelah; these three Bath-shua the Canaanite bore to him. Now Er, Judah's firstborn, was evil in the sight of the LORD, and he put him to death. [4]His daughter-in-law Tamar also bore him Perez and Zerah. Judah had five sons in all.

[5]The sons of Perez: Hezron and Hamul. [6]The sons of Zerah: Zimri, Ethan, Heman, Calcol, and Dara, five in all. [7]The son[11] of Carmi: Achan, the troubler of Israel, who broke faith in the matter of the devoted thing; [8]and Ethan's son was Azariah.

[9]The sons of Hezron that were born to him: Jerahmeel, Ram, and Chelubai. [10]Ram fathered Amminadab, and Amminadab fathered Nahshon, prince of the sons of Judah. [11]Nahshon fathered Salmon,[12] Salmon fathered Boaz, [12]Boaz fathered Obed, Obed fathered Jesse. [13]Jesse fathered Eliab his firstborn, Abinadab the second, Shimea the third, [14]Nethanel the fourth, Raddai the fifth, [15]Ozem the sixth, David the seventh. [16]And their sisters were Zeruiah and Abigail. The sons of Zeruiah: Abishai, Joab, and Asahel, three. [17]Abigail bore Amasa, and the father of Amasa was Jether the Ishmaelite.

[18]Caleb the son of Hezron fathered children by his wife Azubah, and by Jerioth; and these were her sons: Jesher, Shobab, and Ardon. [19]When Azubah died, Caleb married Ephrath, who bore him Hur. [20]Hur fathered Uri, and Uri fathered Bezalel.

[21]Afterward Hezron went in to the daughter of Machir the father of Gilead, whom he married when he was sixty years old, and she bore him Segub. [22]And Segub fathered Jair, who had twenty-three cities in the land of Gilead. [23]But Geshur and Aram took from them Havvoth-jair, Kenath, and its villages, sixty towns. All

---

[1] Peleg means division [2] Septuagint, Syriac (compare Genesis 10:28); Hebrew Ebal [3] Septuagint (compare Genesis 36:12); Hebrew lacks and of [4] Septuagint (compare Genesis 36:22); Hebrew Homam [5] Septuagint (compare Genesis 36:23); Hebrew Alian [6] Septuagint (compare Genesis 36:23); Hebrew Shephi [7] Hebrew sons [8] Septuagint (compare Genesis 36:26); Hebrew Hamran [9] Septuagint (compare Genesis 36:27); Hebrew Jaakan [10] Hebrew the River [11] Hebrew sons [12] Septuagint (compare Ruth 4:21); Hebrew Salma

these were descendants of Machir, the father of Gilead. ²⁴After the death of Hezron, Caleb went in to Ephrathah,¹ the wife of Hezron his father, and she bore him Ashhur, the father of Tekoa.

²⁵The sons of Jerahmeel, the firstborn of Hezron: Ram, his firstborn, Bunah, Oren, Ozem, and Ahijah. ²⁶Jerahmeel also had another wife, whose name was Atarah; she was the mother of Onam. ²⁷The sons of Ram, the firstborn of Jerahmeel: Maaz, Jamin, and Eker. ²⁸The sons of Onam: Shammai and Jada. The sons of Shammai: Nadab and Abishur. ²⁹The name of Abishur's wife was Abihail, and she bore him Ahban and Molid. ³⁰The sons of Nadab: Seled and Appaim; and Seled died childless. ³¹The son² of Appaim: Ishi. The son of Ishi: Sheshan. The son of Sheshan: Ahlai. ³²The sons of Jada, Shammai's brother: Jether and Jonathan; and Jether died childless. ³³The sons of Jonathan: Peleth and Zaza. These were the descendants of Jerahmeel. ³⁴Now Sheshan had no sons, only daughters, but Sheshan had an Egyptian slave whose name was Jarha. ³⁵So Sheshan gave his daughter in marriage to Jarha his slave, and she bore him Attai. ³⁶Attai fathered Nathan, and Nathan fathered Zabad. ³⁷Zabad fathered Ephlal, and Ephlal fathered Obed. ³⁸Obed fathered Jehu, and Jehu fathered Azariah. ³⁹Azariah fathered Helez, and Helez fathered Eleasah. ⁴⁰Eleasah fathered Sismai, and Sismai fathered Shallum. ⁴¹Shallum fathered Jekamiah, and Jekamiah fathered Elishama.

⁴²The sons of Caleb the brother of Jerahmeel: Mareshah³ his firstborn, who fathered Ziph. The son⁴ of Mareshah: Hebron.⁵ ⁴³The sons of Hebron: Korah, Tappuah, Rekem and Shema. ⁴⁴Shema fathered Raham, the father of Jorkeam; and Rekem fathered Shammai. ⁴⁵The son of Shammai: Maon; and Maon fathered Beth-zur. ⁴⁶Ephah also, Caleb's concubine, bore Haran, Moza, and Gazez; and Haran fathered Gazez. ⁴⁷The sons of Jahdai: Regem, Jotham, Geshan, Pelet, Ephah, and Shaaph. ⁴⁸Maacah, Caleb's concubine, bore Sheber and Tirhanah. ⁴⁹She also bore Shaaph the father of Madmannah, Sheva the father of Machbenah and the father of Gibea; and the daughter of Caleb was Achsah. ⁵⁰These were the descendants of Caleb.

The sons⁶ of Hur the firstborn of Ephrathah: Shobal the father of Kiriath-jearim, ⁵¹Salma, the father of Bethlehem, and Hareph the father of Beth-gader. ⁵²Shobal the father of Kiriath-jearim had other sons: Haroeh, half of the Menuhoth. ⁵³And the clans of Kiriath-jearim: the Ithrites, the Puthites, the Shumathites, and the Mishraites; from these came the Zorathites and the Eshtaolites. ⁵⁴The sons of Salma: Bethlehem, the Netophathites, Atroth-beth-joab and half of the Manahathites, the Zorites. ⁵⁵The clans also of the scribes who lived at Jabez: the Tirathites, the Shimeathites and the Sucathites. These are the Kenites who came from Hammath, the father of the house of Rechab.

Hebrews 8

Now the point in what we are saying is this: we have such a high priest, one who is seated at the right hand of the throne of the Majesty in heaven, ²a minister in the holy places, in the true tent⁷ that the Lord set up, not man. ³For every high priest is appointed to offer gifts and sacrifices; thus it is necessary for this priest also to have something to offer. ⁴Now if he were on earth, he would not be a priest at all, since there are priests who offer gifts according to the law. ⁵They serve a copy and shadow of the heavenly things. For when Moses was about to erect the tent, he was instructed by God, saying, "See that you make everything according to the pattern that was shown you on the mountain." ⁶But as it is, Christ⁸ has obtained a ministry that is as much more excellent than the old as the covenant he mediates is better, since it is enacted on better promises. ⁷For if that first covenant had been faultless, there would have been no occasion to look for a second.

⁸For he finds fault with them when he says:⁹

> "Behold, the days are coming, declares the Lord,
>   when I will establish a new covenant
>   with the house of Israel
>   and with the house of Judah,
> ⁹ not like the covenant that I made with their fathers
>   on the day when I took them by the hand to bring them out of the land of Egypt.
> For they did not continue in my covenant,
>   and so I showed no concern for them, declares the Lord.

¹ Septuagint, Vulgate; Hebrew *in Caleb Ephrathah* ² Hebrew *sons*; three times in this verse ³ Septuagint; Hebrew *Mesha* ⁴ Hebrew *sons* ⁵ Hebrew *the father of Hebron* ⁶ Septuagint, Vulgate; Hebrew *son* ⁷ Or *tabernacle; also verse 5* ⁸ Greek *he* ⁹ Some manuscripts *For finding fault with it he says to them*

10 For this is the covenant that I will make
      with the house of Israel
   after those days, declares the Lord:
   I will put my laws into their minds,
      and write them on their hearts,
   and I will be their God,
      and they shall be my people.
11 And they shall not teach, each one his
      neighbor
   and each one his brother, saying,
      'Know the Lord,'
   for they shall all know me,
      from the least of them to the
         greatest.
12 For I will be merciful toward their
      iniquities,
   and I will remember their sins no
      more."

13 In speaking of a new covenant, he makes the first one obsolete. And what is becoming obsolete and growing old is ready to vanish away.

────────── *Amos 2* ──────────

Thus says the LORD:

   "For three transgressions of Moab,
      and for four, I will not revoke the
         punishment,[1]
   because he burned to lime
      the bones of the king of Edom.
2 So I will send a fire upon Moab,
      and it shall devour the strongholds of
         Kerioth,
   and Moab shall die amid uproar,
      amid shouting and the sound of the
         trumpet;
3 I will cut off the ruler from its midst,
      and will kill all its princes[2] with him,"
                    says the LORD.

4 Thus says the LORD:

   "For three transgressions of Judah,
      and for four, I will not revoke the
         punishment,
   because they have rejected the law of
      the LORD,
      and have not kept his statutes,
   but their lies have led them astray,
      those after which their fathers
         walked.

5 So I will send a fire upon Judah,
      and it shall devour the strongholds of
         Jerusalem."

6 Thus says the LORD:

   "For three transgressions of Israel,
      and for four, I will not revoke the
         punishment,
   because they sell the righteous for silver,
      and the needy for a pair of sandals—
7 those who trample the head of the poor
         into the dust of the earth
      and turn aside the way of the afflicted;
   a man and his father go in to the same
         girl,
      so that my holy name is profaned;
8 they lay themselves down beside every
         altar
      on garments taken in pledge,
   and in the house of their God they drink
      the wine of those who have been
         fined.

9 "Yet it was I who destroyed the Amorite
         before them,
      whose height was like the height of
         the cedars
      and who was as strong as the oaks;
   I destroyed his fruit above
      and his roots beneath.
10 Also it was I who brought you up out of
         the land of Egypt
      and led you forty years in the
         wilderness,
      to possess the land of the Amorite.
11 And I raised up some of your sons for
         prophets,
      and some of your young men for
         Nazirites.
   Is it not indeed so, O people of Israel?"
                    declares the LORD.

12 "But you made the Nazirites drink wine,
      and commanded the prophets,
      saying, 'You shall not prophesy.'
13 "Behold, I will press you down in your
         place,
      as a cart full of sheaves presses down.
14 Flight shall perish from the swift,
      and the strong shall not retain his
         strength,
      nor shall the mighty save his life;

[1] Hebrew *I will not turn it back*; also verses 4, 6   [2] Or *officials*

15 he who handles the bow shall not stand,
  and he who is swift of foot shall not
    save himself,
  nor shall he who rides the horse save
    his life;
16 and he who is stout of heart among the
    mighty
  shall flee away naked in that day,"
        declares the LORD.

────── *Psalm 145*[1] ──────

A SONG OF PRAISE. OF DAVID.

I will extol you, my God and King,
  and bless your name forever and ever.
2 Every day I will bless you
  and praise your name forever and ever.
3 Great is the LORD, and greatly to be
    praised,
  and his greatness is unsearchable.

4 One generation shall commend your
    works to another,
  and shall declare your mighty acts.
5 On the glorious splendor of your majesty,
  and on your wondrous works, I will
    meditate.
6 They shall speak of the might of your
    awesome deeds,
  and I will declare your greatness.
7 They shall pour forth the fame of your
    abundant goodness
  and shall sing aloud of your
    righteousness.

8 The LORD is gracious and merciful,
  slow to anger and abounding in
    steadfast love.
9 The LORD is good to all,
  and his mercy is over all that he has
    made.

10 All your works shall give thanks to you,
    O LORD,
  and all your saints shall bless you!
11 They shall speak of the glory of your
    kingdom
  and tell of your power,
12 to make known to the children of man
    your[2] mighty deeds,
  and the glorious splendor of your
    kingdom.
13 Your kingdom is an everlasting
    kingdom,
  and your dominion endures
    throughout all generations.

[The LORD is faithful in all his words
  and kind in all his works.][3]
14 The LORD upholds all who are falling
  and raises up all who are bowed
    down.
15 The eyes of all look to you,
  and you give them their food in due
    season.
16 You open your hand;
  you satisfy the desire of every living
    thing.
17 The LORD is righteous in all his ways
  and kind in all his works.
18 The LORD is near to all who call on him,
  to all who call on him in truth.
19 He fulfills the desire of those who fear
    him;
  he also hears their cry and saves
    them.
20 The LORD preserves all who love him,
  but all the wicked he will destroy.

21 My mouth will speak the praise of the
    LORD,
  and let all flesh bless his holy name
    forever and ever.

---

[1] This psalm is an acrostic poem, each verse beginning with the successive letters of the Hebrew alphabet [2] Hebrew *his*; also next line [3] These two lines are supplied by one Hebrew manuscript, Septuagint, Syriac (compare Dead Sea Scroll)

NOVEMBER 14

--------- *1 Chronicles 3–4* ---------

These are the sons of David who were born to him in Hebron: the firstborn, Amnon, by Ahinoam the Jezreelite; the second, Daniel, by Abigail the Carmelite, ²the third, Absalom, whose mother was Maacah, the daughter of Talmai, king of Geshur; the fourth, Adonijah, whose mother was Haggith; ³the fifth, Shephatiah, by Abital; the sixth, Ithream, by his wife Eglah; ⁴six were born to him in Hebron, where he reigned for seven years and six months. And he reigned thirty-three years in Jerusalem. ⁵These were born to him in Jerusalem: Shimea, Shobab, Nathan and Solomon, four by Bath-shua, the daughter of Ammiel; ⁶then Ibhar, Elishama, Eliphelet, ⁷Nogah, Nepheg, Japhia, ⁸Elishama, Eliada, and Eliphelet, nine. ⁹All these were David's sons, besides the sons of the concubines, and Tamar was their sister.

¹⁰The son of Solomon was Rehoboam, Abijah his son, Asa his son, Jehoshaphat his son, ¹¹Joram his son, Ahaziah his son, Joash his son, ¹²Amaziah his son, Azariah his son, Jotham his son, ¹³Ahaz his son, Hezekiah his son, Manasseh his son, ¹⁴Amon his son, Josiah his son. ¹⁵The sons of Josiah: Johanan the firstborn, the second Jehoiakim, the third Zedekiah, the fourth Shallum. ¹⁶The descendants of Jehoiakim: Jeconiah his son, Zedekiah his son; ¹⁷and the sons of Jeconiah, the captive: Shealtiel his son, ¹⁸Malchiram, Pedaiah, Shenazzar, Jekamiah, Hoshama and Nedabiah; ¹⁹and the sons of Pedaiah: Zerubbabel and Shimei; and the sons of Zerubbabel: Meshullam and Hananiah, and Shelomith was their sister; ²⁰and Hashubah, Ohel, Berechiah, Hasadiah, and Jushab-hesed, five. ²¹The sons of Hananiah: Pelatiah and Jeshaiah, his son¹ Rephaiah, his son Arnan, his son Obadiah, his son Shecaniah. ²²The son² of Shecaniah: Shemaiah. And the sons of Shemaiah: Hattush, Igal, Bariah, Neariah, and Shaphat, six. ²³The sons of Neariah: Elioenai, Hizkiah, and Azrikam, three. ²⁴The sons of

Elioenai: Hodaviah, Eliashib, Pelaiah, Akkub, Johanan, Delaiah, and Anani, seven.

⁴:¹The sons of Judah: Perez, Hezron, Carmi, Hur, and Shobal. ²Reaiah the son of Shobal fathered Jahath, and Jahath fathered Ahumai and Lahad. These were the clans of the Zorathites. ³These were the sons³ of Etam: Jezreel, Ishma, and Idbash; and the name of their sister was Hazzelelponi, ⁴and Penuel fathered Gedor, and Ezer fathered Hushah. These were the sons of Hur, the firstborn of Ephrathah, the father of Bethlehem. ⁵Ashhur, the father of Tekoa, had two wives, Helah and Naarah; ⁶Naarah bore him Ahuzzam, Hepher, Temeni, and Haahashtari. These were the sons of Naarah. ⁷The sons of Helah: Zereth, Izhar, and Ethnan. ⁸Koz fathered Anub, Zobebah, and the clans of Aharhel, the son of Harum. ⁹Jabez was more honorable than his brothers; and his mother called his name Jabez, saying, "Because I bore him in pain."⁴ ¹⁰Jabez called upon the God of Israel, saying, "Oh that you would bless me and enlarge my border, and that your hand might be with me, and that you would keep me from harm⁵ so that it might not bring me pain!" And God granted what he asked. ¹¹Chelub, the brother of Shuhah, fathered Mehir, who fathered Eshton. ¹²Eshton fathered Beth-rapha, Paseah, and Tehinnah, the father of Ir-nahash. These are the men of Recah. ¹³The sons of Kenaz: Othniel and Seraiah; and the sons of Othniel: Hathath and Meonothai.⁶ ¹⁴Meonothai fathered Ophrah; and Seraiah fathered Joab, the father of Ge-harashim,⁷ so-called because they were craftsmen. ¹⁵The sons of Caleb the son of Jephunneh: Iru, Elah, and Naam; and the son⁸ of Elah: Kenaz. ¹⁶The sons of Jehallelel: Ziph, Ziphah, Tiria, and Asarel. ¹⁷The sons of Ezrah: Jether, Mered, Epher, and Jalon. These are the sons of Bithiah, the daughter of Pharaoh, whom Mered married;⁹ and she conceived and bore¹⁰ Miriam, Shammai, and Ishbah, the father of Eshtemoa. ¹⁸And his Judahite wife bore Jered the father of Gedor, Heber the father of Soco,

¹ Septuagint (compare Syriac, Vulgate); Hebrew *sons of;* four times in this verse ² Hebrew *sons* ³ Septuagint (compare Vulgate); Hebrew *father* ⁴ *Jabez* sounds like the Hebrew for *pain* ⁵ Or *evil* ⁶ Septuagint, Vulgate; Hebrew lacks *Meonothai* ⁷ *Ge-harashim* means *valley of craftsmen* ⁸ Hebrew *sons* ⁹ The clause *These are. . . married* is transposed from verse 18 ¹⁰ Hebrew lacks *and bore*

and Jekuthiel the father of Zanoah. [19] The sons of the wife of Hodiah, the sister of Naham, were the fathers of Keilah the Garmite and Eshtemoa the Maacathite. [20] The sons of Shimon: Amnon, Rinnah, Ben-hanan, and Tilon. The sons of Ishi: Zoheth and Ben-zoheth. [21] The sons of Shelah the son of Judah: Er the father of Lecah, Laadah the father of Mareshah, and the clans of the house of linen workers at Beth-ashbea; [22] and Jokim, and the men of Cozeba, and Joash, and Saraph, who ruled in Moab and returned to Lehem[1] (now the records[2] are ancient). [23] These were the potters who were inhabitants of Netaim and Gederah. They lived there in the king's service.

[24] The sons of Simeon: Nemuel, Jamin, Jarib, Zerah, Shaul; [25] Shallum was his son, Mibsam his son, Mishma his son. [26] The sons of Mishma: Hammuel his son, Zaccur his son, Shimei his son. [27] Shimei had sixteen sons and six daughters; but his brothers did not have many children, nor did all their clan multiply like the men of Judah. [28] They lived in Beersheba, Moladah, Hazar-shual, [29] Bilhah, Ezem, Tolad, [30] Bethuel, Hormah, Ziklag, [31] Beth-marcaboth, Hazar-susim, Beth-biri, and Shaaraim. These were their cities until David reigned. [32] And their villages were Etam, Ain, Rimmon, Tochen, and Ashan, five cities, [33] along with all their villages that were around these cities as far as Baal. These were their settlements, and they kept a genealogical record.

[34] Meshobab, Jamlech, Joshah the son of Amaziah, [35] Joel, Jehu the son of Joshibiah, son of Seraiah, son of Asiel, [36] Elioenai, Jaakobah, Jeshohaiah, Asaiah, Adiel, Jesimiel, Benaiah, [37] Ziza the son of Shiphi, son of Allon, son of Jedaiah, son of Shimri, son of Shemaiah— [38] these mentioned by name were princes in their clans, and their fathers' houses increased greatly. [39] They journeyed to the entrance of Gedor, to the east side of the valley, to seek pasture for their flocks, [40] where they found rich, good pasture, and the land was very broad, quiet, and peaceful, for the former inhabitants there belonged to Ham. [41] These, registered by name, came in the days of Hezekiah, king of Judah, and destroyed their tents and the Meunites who were found there, and marked them for destruction to this day, and settled in their place, because there was pasture there

for their flocks. [42] And some of them, five hundred men of the Simeonites, went to Mount Seir, having as their leaders Pelatiah, Neariah, Rephaiah, and Uzziel, the sons of Ishi. [43] And they defeated the remnant of the Amalekites who had escaped, and they have lived there to this day.

Hebrews 9

Now even the first covenant had regulations for worship and an earthly place of holiness. [2] For a tent[3] was prepared, the first section, in which were the lampstand and the table and the bread of the Presence.[4] It is called the Holy Place. [3] Behind the second curtain was a second section[5] called the Most Holy Place, [4] having the golden altar of incense and the ark of the covenant covered on all sides with gold, in which was a golden urn holding the manna, and Aaron's staff that budded, and the tablets of the covenant. [5] Above it were the cherubim of glory overshadowing the mercy seat. Of these things we cannot now speak in detail.

[6] These preparations having thus been made, the priests go regularly into the first section, performing their ritual duties, [7] but into the second only the high priest goes, and he but once a year, and not without taking blood, which he offers for himself and for the unintentional sins of the people. [8] By this the Holy Spirit indicates that the way into the holy places is not yet opened as long as the first section is still standing [9] (which is symbolic for the present age).[6] According to this arrangement, gifts and sacrifices are offered that cannot perfect the conscience of the worshiper, [10] but deal only with food and drink and various washings, regulations for the body imposed until the time of reformation.

[11] But when Christ appeared as a high priest of the good things that have come,[7] then through the greater and more perfect tent (not made with hands, that is, not of this creation) [12] he entered once for all into the holy places, not by means of the blood of goats and calves but by means of his own blood, thus securing an eternal redemption. [13] For if the blood of goats and bulls, and the sprinkling of defiled persons with the ashes of a heifer, sanctify[8] for the purification of the flesh, [14] how much more will the blood of Christ, who through the

[1] Vulgate (compare Septuagint); Hebrew and Jashubi-lahem   [2] Or matters   [3] Or tabernacle; also verses 11, 21   [4] Greek the presentation of the loaves   [5] Greek tent; also verses 6, 8
[6] Or which is symbolic for the age then present   [7] Some manuscripts good things to come   [8] Or For if the sprinkling of defiled persons with the blood of goats and bulls and with the ashes of a heifer sanctifies

eternal Spirit offered himself without blemish to God, purify our[1] conscience from dead works to serve the living God.

[15]Therefore he is the mediator of a new covenant, so that those who are called may receive the promised eternal inheritance, since a death has occurred that redeems them from the transgressions committed under the first covenant.[2] [16]For where a will is involved, the death of the one who made it must be established. [17]For a will takes effect only at death, since it is not in force as long as the one who made it is alive. [18]Therefore not even the first covenant was inaugurated without blood. [19]For when every commandment of the law had been declared by Moses to all the people, he took the blood of calves and goats, with water and scarlet wool and hyssop, and sprinkled both the book itself and all the people, [20]saying, "This is the blood of the covenant that God commanded for you." [21]And in the same way he sprinkled with the blood both the tent and all the vessels used in worship. [22]Indeed, under the law almost everything is purified with blood, and without the shedding of blood there is no forgiveness of sins.

[23]Thus it was necessary for the copies of the heavenly things to be purified with these rites, but the heavenly things themselves with better sacrifices than these. [24]For Christ has entered, not into holy places made with hands, which are copies of the true things, but into heaven itself, now to appear in the presence of God on our behalf. [25]Nor was it to offer himself repeatedly, as the high priest enters the holy places every year with blood not his own, [26]for then he would have had to suffer repeatedly since the foundation of the world. But as it is, he has appeared once for all at the end of the ages to put away sin by the sacrifice of himself. [27]And just as it is appointed for man to die once, and after that comes judgment, [28]so Christ, having been offered once to bear the sins of many, will appear a second time, not to deal with sin but to save those who are eagerly waiting for him.

Amos 3

Hear this word that the LORD has spoken against you, O people of Israel, against the whole family that I brought up out of the land of Egypt:

[2] "You only have I known
　　of all the families of the earth;
　therefore I will punish you
　　for all your iniquities.

[3] "Do two walk together,
　　unless they have agreed to meet?
[4] Does a lion roar in the forest,
　　when he has no prey?
　Does a young lion cry out from his den,
　　if he has taken nothing?
[5] Does a bird fall in a snare on the earth,
　　when there is no trap for it?
　Does a snare spring up from the
　　ground,
　　when it has taken nothing?
[6] Is a trumpet blown in a city,
　　and the people are not afraid?
　Does disaster come to a city,
　　unless the LORD has done it?

[7] "For the Lord GOD does nothing
　　without revealing his secret
　　to his servants the prophets.
[8] The lion has roared;
　　who will not fear?
　The Lord GOD has spoken;
　　who can but prophesy?"

[9] Proclaim to the strongholds in Ashdod
　　and to the strongholds in the land of
　　　Egypt,
　and say, "Assemble yourselves on the
　　mountains of Samaria,
　　and see the great tumults within
　　　her,
　　and the oppressed in her midst."
[10] "They do not know how to do right,"
　　declares the LORD,
　"those who store up violence and
　　robbery in their strongholds."

[11]Therefore thus says the Lord GOD:

"An adversary shall surround the land
　　and bring down[3] your defenses from
　　　you,
　　and your strongholds shall be
　　　plundered."

[12]Thus says the LORD: "As the shepherd rescues from the mouth of the lion two legs, or a piece of an ear, so shall the people of Israel who dwell in Samaria be rescued, with the corner of a couch and part[4] of a bed.

[1] Some manuscripts your [2] The Greek word means both *covenant* and *will*; also verses 16, 17 [3] Hebrew *An adversary, one who surrounds the land—he shall bring down* [4] The meaning of the Hebrew word is uncertain

13 "Hear, and testify against the house of
 Jacob,"
 declares the Lord GOD, the God of hosts,
14 "that on the day I punish Israel for his
 transgressions,
 I will punish the altars of Bethel,
 and the horns of the altar shall be cut off
 and fall to the ground.
15 I will strike the winter house along with
 the summer house,
 and the houses of ivory shall perish,
 and the great houses¹ shall come to an
 end,"
 declares the LORD.

Psalm 146–147

Praise the LORD!
 Praise the LORD, O my soul!
2 I will praise the LORD as long as I live;
 I will sing praises to my God while I
 have my being.

3 Put not your trust in princes,
 in a son of man, in whom there is no
 salvation.
4 When his breath departs, he returns to
 the earth;
 on that very day his plans perish.

5 Blessed is he whose help is the God of
 Jacob,
 whose hope is in the LORD his God,
6 who made heaven and earth,
 the sea, and all that is in them,
 who keeps faith forever;
7 who executes justice for the oppressed,
 who gives food to the hungry.

The LORD sets the prisoners free;
8 the LORD opens the eyes of the blind.
 The LORD lifts up those who are bowed
 down;
 the LORD loves the righteous.
9 The LORD watches over the sojourners;
 he upholds the widow and the
 fatherless,
 but the way of the wicked he brings to
 ruin.

10 The LORD will reign forever,
 your God, O Zion, to all generations.
 Praise the LORD!

Praise the LORD!
 For it is good to sing praises to our God;
 for it is pleasant,² and a song of praise
 is fitting.
2 The LORD builds up Jerusalem;
 he gathers the outcasts of Israel.
3 He heals the brokenhearted
 and binds up their wounds.
4 He determines the number of the stars;
 he gives to all of them their names.
5 Great is our Lord, and abundant in
 power;
 his understanding is beyond measure.
6 The LORD lifts up the humble;³
 he casts the wicked to the ground.

7 Sing to the LORD with thanksgiving;
 make melody to our God on the lyre!
8 He covers the heavens with clouds;
 he prepares rain for the earth;
 he makes grass grow on the hills.
9 He gives to the beasts their food,
 and to the young ravens that cry.
10 His delight is not in the strength of the
 horse,
 nor his pleasure in the legs of a man,
11 but the LORD takes pleasure in those
 who fear him,
 in those who hope in his steadfast love.

12 Praise the LORD, O Jerusalem!
 Praise your God, O Zion!
13 For he strengthens the bars of your gates;
 he blesses your children within you.
14 He makes peace in your borders;
 he fills you with the finest of the
 wheat.
15 He sends out his command to the earth;
 his word runs swiftly.
16 He gives snow like wool;
 he scatters frost like ashes.
17 He hurls down his crystals of ice like
 crumbs;
 who can stand before his cold?
18 He sends out his word, and melts them;
 he makes his wind blow and the
 waters flow.
19 He declares his word to Jacob,
 his statutes and rules⁴ to Israel.
20 He has not dealt thus with any other
 nation;
 they do not know his rules.⁵
 Praise the LORD!

¹ Or and many houses ² Or for he is beautiful ³ Or afflicted ⁴ Or and just decrees ⁵ Or his just decrees

NOVEMBER 15

1 Chronicles 5–6

The sons of Reuben the firstborn of Israel (for he was the firstborn, but because he defiled his father's couch, his birthright was given to the sons of Joseph the son of Israel, so that he could not be enrolled as the oldest son; ²though Judah became strong among his brothers and a chief came from him, yet the birthright belonged to Joseph), ³the sons of Reuben, the firstborn of Israel: Hanoch, Pallu, Hezron, and Carmi. ⁴The sons of Joel: Shemaiah his son, Gog his son, Shimei his son, ⁵Micah his son, Reaiah his son, Baal his son, ⁶Beerah his son, whom Tiglath-pileser¹ king of Assyria carried away into exile; he was a chief of the Reubenites. ⁷And his kinsmen by their clans, when the genealogy of their generations was recorded: the chief, Jeiel, and Zechariah, ⁸and Bela the son of Azaz, son of Shema, son of Joel, who lived in Aroer, as far as Nebo and Baal-meon. ⁹He also lived to the east as far as the entrance of the desert this side of the Euphrates, because their livestock had multiplied in the land of Gilead. ¹⁰And in the days of Saul they waged war against the Hagrites, who fell into their hand. And they lived in their tents throughout all the region east of Gilead.

¹¹The sons of Gad lived over against them in the land of Bashan as far as Salecah: ¹²Joel the chief, Shapham the second, Janai, and Shaphat in Bashan. ¹³And their kinsmen according to their fathers' houses: Michael, Meshullam, Sheba, Jorai, Jacan, Zia and Eber, seven. ¹⁴These were the sons of Abihail the son of Huri, son of Jaroah, son of Gilead, son of Michael, son of Jeshishai, son of Jahdo, son of Buz. ¹⁵Ahi the son of Abdiel, son of Guni, was chief in their fathers' houses, ¹⁶and they lived in Gilead, in Bashan and in its towns, and in all the pasturelands of Sharon to their limits. ¹⁷All of these were recorded in genealogies in the days of Jotham king of Judah, and in the days of Jeroboam king of Israel.

¹⁸The Reubenites, the Gadites, and the half-tribe of Manasseh had valiant men who carried shield and sword, and drew the bow, expert in war, 44,760, able to go to war. ¹⁹They waged war against the Hagrites, Jetur, Naphish, and Nodab. ²⁰And when they prevailed² over them, the Hagrites and all who were with them were given into their hands, for they cried out to God in the battle, and he granted their urgent plea because they trusted in him. ²¹They carried off their livestock: 50,000 of their camels, 250,000 sheep, 2,000 donkeys, and 100,000 men alive. ²²For many fell, because the war was of God. And they lived in their place until the exile.

²³The members of the half-tribe of Manasseh lived in the land. They were very numerous from Bashan to Baal-hermon, Senir, and Mount Hermon. ²⁴These were the heads of their fathers' houses: Epher,³ Ishi, Eliel, Azriel, Jeremiah, Hodaviah, and Jahdiel, mighty warriors, famous men, heads of their fathers' houses. ²⁵But they broke faith with the God of their fathers, and whored after the gods of the peoples of the land, whom God had destroyed before them. ²⁶So the God of Israel stirred up the spirit of Pul king of Assyria, the spirit of Tiglath-pileser king of Assyria, and he took them into exile, namely, the Reubenites, the Gadites, and the half-tribe of Manasseh, and brought them to Halah, Habor, Hara, and the river Gozan, to this day.

⁶:¹⁴The sons of Levi: Gershon, Kohath, and Merari. ²The sons of Kohath: Amram, Izhar, Hebron, and Uzziel. ³The children of Amram: Aaron, Moses, and Miriam. The sons of Aaron: Nadab, Abihu, Eleazar, and Ithamar. ⁴Eleazar fathered Phinehas, Phinehas fathered Abishua, ⁵Abishua fathered Bukki, Bukki fathered Uzzi, ⁶Uzzi fathered Zerahiah, Zerahiah fathered Meraioth, ⁷Meraioth fathered Amariah, Amariah fathered Ahitub, ⁸Ahitub fathered Zadok, Zadok fathered Ahimaaz, ⁹Ahimaaz fathered Azariah, Azariah fathered Johanan, ¹⁰and Johanan fathered Azariah (it was he who served as priest in the house that Solomon built in Jerusalem). ¹¹Azariah fathered Amariah,

¹ Hebrew *Tilgath-pilneser*; also verse 26 ² Or *they were helped to prevail* ³ Septuagint, Vulgate; Hebrew *and Epher* ⁴ Ch 5:27 in Hebrew

Amariah fathered Ahitub, [12]Ahitub fathered Zadok, Zadok fathered Shallum, [13]Shallum fathered Hilkiah, Hilkiah fathered Azariah, [14]Azariah fathered Seraiah, Seraiah fathered Jehozadak; [15]and Jehozadak went into exile when the LORD sent Judah and Jerusalem into exile by the hand of Nebuchadnezzar.

[16][1] The sons of Levi: Gershom, Kohath, and Merari. [17]And these are the names of the sons of Gershom: Libni and Shimei. [18]The sons of Kohath: Amram, Izhar, Hebron and Uzziel. [19]The sons of Merari: Mahli and Mushi. These are the clans of the Levites according to their fathers. [20]Of Gershom: Libni his son, Jahath his son, Zimmah his son, [21]Joah his son, Iddo his son, Zerah his son, Jeatherai his son. [22]The sons of Kohath: Amminadab his son, Korah his son, Assir his son, [23]Elkanah his son, Ebiasaph his son, Assir his son, [24]Tahath his son, Uriel his son, Uzziah his son, and Shaul his son. [25]The sons of Elkanah: Amasai and Ahimoth, [26]Elkanah his son, Zophai his son, Nahath his son, [27]Eliab his son, Jeroham his son, Elkanah his son. [28]The sons of Samuel: Joel[2] his first-born, the second Abijah.[3] [29]The sons of Merari: Mahli, Libni his son, Shimei his son, Uzzah his son, [30]Shimea his son, Haggiah his son, and Asaiah his son.

[31]These are the men whom David put in charge of the service of song in the house of the LORD after the ark rested there. [32]They ministered with song before the tabernacle of the tent of meeting until Solomon built the house of the LORD in Jerusalem, and they performed their service according to their order. [33]These are the men who served and their sons. Of the sons of the Kohathites: Heman the singer the son of Joel, son of Samuel, [34]son of Elkanah, son of Jeroham, son of Eliel, son of Toah, [35]son of Zuph, son of Elkanah, son of Mahath, son of Amasai, [36]son of Elkanah, son of Joel, son of Azariah, son of Zephaniah, [37]son of Tahath, son of Assir, son of Ebiasaph, son of Korah, [38]son of Izhar, son of Kohath, son of Levi, son of Israel; [39]and his brother Asaph, who stood on his right hand, namely, Asaph the son of Berechiah, son of Shimea, [40]son of Michael, son of Baaseiah, son of Malchijah, [41]son of Ethni, son of Zerah, son of Adaiah, [42]son of Ethan, son of Zimmah, son of Shimei, [43]son of Jahath, son of Gershom, son of Levi. [44]On the left hand were their brothers, the sons of Merari: Ethan the son of Kishi, son of Abdi, son of Malluch, [45]son of Hashabiah, son of Amaziah, son of Hilkiah, [46]son of Amzi, son of Bani, son of Shemer, [47]son of Mahli, son of Mushi, son of Merari, son of Levi. [48]And their brothers the Levites were appointed for all the service of the tabernacle of the house of God.

[49]But Aaron and his sons made offerings on the altar of burnt offering and on the altar of incense for all the work of the Most Holy Place, and to make atonement for Israel, according to all that Moses the servant of God had commanded. [50]These are the sons of Aaron: Eleazar his son, Phinehas his son, Abishua his son, [51]Bukki his son, Uzzi his son, Zerahiah his son, [52]Meraioth his son, Amariah his son, Ahitub his son, [53]Zadok his son, Ahimaaz his son.

[54]These are their dwelling places according to their settlements within their borders: to the sons of Aaron of the clans of Kohathites, for theirs was the first lot, [55]to them they gave Hebron in the land of Judah and its surrounding pasturelands, [56]but the fields of the city and its villages they gave to Caleb the son of Jephunneh. [57]To the sons of Aaron they gave the cities of refuge: Hebron, Libnah with its pasturelands, Jattir, Eshtemoa with its pasturelands, [58]Hilen with its pasturelands, Debir with its pasturelands, [59]Ashan with its pasturelands, and Beth-shemesh with its pasturelands; [60]and from the tribe of Benjamin, Gibeon,[4] Geba with its pasturelands, Alemeth with its pasturelands, and Anathoth with its pasturelands. All their cities throughout their clans were thirteen.

[61]To the rest of the Kohathites were given by lot out of the clan of the tribe, out of the half-tribe, the half of Manasseh, ten cities. [62]To the Gershomites according to their clans were allotted thirteen cities out of the tribes of Issachar, Asher, Naphtali and Manasseh in Bashan. [63]To the Merarites according to their clans were allotted twelve cities out of the tribes of Reuben, Gad, and Zebulun. [64]So the people of Israel gave the Levites the cities with their pasturelands. [65]They gave by lot out of the tribes of Judah, Simeon, and Benjamin these cities that are mentioned by name.

[66]And some of the clans of the sons of Kohath had cities of their territory out of the tribe of Ephraim. [67]They were given the cities of refuge: Shechem with its pasturelands in the hill country of Ephraim, Gezer with its pasturelands,

[1] Ch 6:1 in Hebrew [2] Septuagint, Syriac (compare verse 33 and 1 Samuel 8:2); Hebrew lacks *Joel* [3] Hebrew *and Abijah* [4] Septuagint, Syriac (compare Joshua 21:17); Hebrew lacks *Gibeon*

⁶⁸Jokmeam with its pasturelands, Beth-horon with its pasturelands, ⁶⁹Aijalon with its pasturelands, Gath-rimmon with its pasturelands, ⁷⁰and out of the half-tribe of Manasseh, Aner with its pasturelands, and Bileam with its pasturelands, for the rest of the clans of the Kohathites.

⁷¹To the Gershomites were given out of the clan of the half-tribe of Manasseh: Golan in Bashan with its pasturelands and Ashtaroth with its pasturelands; ⁷²and out of the tribe of Issachar: Kedesh with its pasturelands, Daberath with its pasturelands, ⁷³Ramoth with its pasturelands, and Anem with its pasturelands; ⁷⁴out of the tribe of Asher: Mashal with its pasturelands, Abdon with its pasturelands, ⁷⁵Hukok with its pasturelands, and Rehob with its pasturelands; ⁷⁶and out of the tribe of Naphtali: Kedesh in Galilee with its pasturelands, Hammon with its pasturelands, and Kiriathaim with its pasturelands. ⁷⁷To the rest of the Merarites were allotted out of the tribe of Zebulun: Rimmono with its pasturelands, Tabor with its pasturelands, ⁷⁸and beyond the Jordan at Jericho, on the east side of the Jordan, out of the tribe of Reuben: Bezer in the wilderness with its pasturelands, Jahzah with its pasturelands, ⁷⁹Kedemoth with its pasturelands, and Mephaath with its pasturelands; ⁸⁰and out of the tribe of Gad: Ramoth in Gilead with its pasturelands, Mahanaim with its pasturelands, ⁸¹Heshbon with its pasturelands, and Jazer with its pasturelands.

Hebrews 10

For since the law has but a shadow of the good things to come instead of the true form of these realities, it can never, by the same sacrifices that are continually offered every year, make perfect those who draw near. ²Otherwise, would they not have ceased to be offered, since the worshipers, having once been cleansed, would no longer have any consciousness of sins? ³But in these sacrifices there is a reminder of sins every year. ⁴For it is impossible for the blood of bulls and goats to take away sins.

⁵Consequently, when Christ¹ came into the world, he said,

"Sacrifices and offerings you have not desired,
    but a body have you prepared for me;

⁶ in burnt offerings and sin offerings
    you have taken no pleasure.
⁷ Then I said, 'Behold, I have come to do your will, O God,
    as it is written of me in the scroll of the book.'"

⁸When he said above, "You have neither desired nor taken pleasure in sacrifices and offerings and burnt offerings and sin offerings" (these are offered according to the law), ⁹then he added, "Behold, I have come to do your will." He does away with the first in order to establish the second. ¹⁰And by that will we have been sanctified through the offering of the body of Jesus Christ once for all.

¹¹And every priest stands daily at his service, offering repeatedly the same sacrifices, which can never take away sins. ¹²But when Christ² had offered for all time a single sacrifice for sins, he sat down at the right hand of God, ¹³waiting from that time until his enemies should be made a footstool for his feet. ¹⁴For by a single offering he has perfected for all time those who are being sanctified.

¹⁵And the Holy Spirit also bears witness to us; for after saying,

¹⁶ "This is the covenant that I will make with them
    after those days, declares the Lord:
I will put my laws on their hearts,
    and write them on their minds,"

¹⁷then he adds,

"I will remember their sins and their
    lawless deeds no more."

¹⁸Where there is forgiveness of these, there is no longer any offering for sin.

¹⁹Therefore, brothers,³ since we have confidence to enter the holy places by the blood of Jesus, ²⁰by the new and living way that he opened for us through the curtain, that is, through his flesh, ²¹and since we have a great priest over the house of God, ²²let us draw near with a true heart in full assurance of faith, with our hearts sprinkled clean from an evil conscience and our bodies washed with pure water. ²³Let us hold fast the confession of our hope without wavering, for he who promised is faithful. ²⁴And let us consider how to stir up one another to love and good works, ²⁵not

¹ Greek he ² Greek this one ³ Or brothers and sisters

neglecting to meet together, as is the habit of some, but encouraging one another, and all the more as you see the Day drawing near.

²⁶For if we go on sinning deliberately after receiving the knowledge of the truth, there no longer remains a sacrifice for sins, ²⁷but a fearful expectation of judgment, and a fury of fire that will consume the adversaries. ²⁸Anyone who has set aside the law of Moses dies without mercy on the evidence of two or three witnesses. ²⁹How much worse punishment, do you think, will be deserved by the one who has trampled underfoot the Son of God, and has profaned the blood of the covenant by which he was sanctified, and has outraged the Spirit of grace? ³⁰For we know him who said, "Vengeance is mine; I will repay." And again, "The Lord will judge his people." ³¹It is a fearful thing to fall into the hands of the living God.

³²But recall the former days when, after you were enlightened, you endured a hard struggle with sufferings, ³³sometimes being publicly exposed to reproach and affliction, and sometimes being partners with those so treated. ³⁴For you had compassion on those in prison, and you joyfully accepted the plundering of your property, since you knew that you yourselves had a better possession and an abiding one. ³⁵Therefore do not throw away your confidence, which has a great reward. ³⁶For you have need of endurance, so that when you have done the will of God you may receive what is promised. ³⁷For,

"Yet a little while,
  and the coming one will come and
    will not delay;
³⁸ but my righteous one shall live by faith,
    and if he shrinks back,
  my soul has no pleasure in him."

³⁹But we are not of those who shrink back and are destroyed, but of those who have faith and preserve their souls.

—————— *Amos 4* ——————

"Hear this word, you cows of Bashan,
  who are on the mountain of Samaria,
who oppress the poor, who crush the
    needy,
  who say to your husbands, 'Bring, that
    we may drink!'

2 The Lord GOD has sworn by his
    holiness
  that, behold, the days are coming
    upon you,
when they shall take you away with
    hooks,
  even the last of you with fishhooks.
3 And you shall go out through the
    breaches,
  each one straight ahead;
  and you shall be cast out into
    Harmon,"
                declares the LORD.

4 "Come to Bethel, and transgress;
  to Gilgal, and multiply transgression;
bring your sacrifices every morning,
  your tithes every three days;
5 offer a sacrifice of thanksgiving of that
    which is leavened,
  and proclaim freewill offerings,
    publish them;
for so you love to do, O people of
    Israel!"
              declares the Lord GOD.

6 "I gave you cleanness of teeth in all your
    cities,
  and lack of bread in all your places,
yet you did not return to me,"
                declares the LORD.

7 "I also withheld the rain from you
  when there were yet three months to
    the harvest;
I would send rain on one city,
  and send no rain on another city;
one field would have rain,
  and the field on which it did not rain
    would wither;
8 so two or three cities would wander to
    another city
  to drink water, and would not be
    satisfied;
yet you did not return to me,"
                declares the LORD.

9 "I struck you with blight and mildew;
  your many gardens and your
    vineyards,
  your fig trees and your olive trees the
    locust devoured;
yet you did not return to me,"
                declares the LORD.

10 "I sent among you a pestilence after the
manner of Egypt;
  I killed your young men with the
sword,
  and carried away your horses,[1]
    and I made the stench of your camp
go up into your nostrils;
  yet you did not return to me,"
               declares the LORD.

11 "I overthrew some of you,
  as when God overthrew Sodom and
Gomorrah,
  and you were as a brand[2] plucked out
of the burning;
  yet you did not return to me,"
               declares the LORD.

12 "Therefore thus I will do to you, O Israel;
  because I will do this to you,
  prepare to meet your God, O Israel!"

13 For behold, he who forms the
      mountains and creates the wind,
  and declares to man what is his
thought,
  who makes the morning darkness,
  and treads on the heights of the
earth—
  the LORD, the God of hosts, is his name!

———— *Psalm 148–150* ————

P raise the LORD!
  Praise the LORD from the heavens;
    praise him in the heights!
2   Praise him, all his angels;
    praise him, all his hosts!

3   Praise him, sun and moon,
    praise him, all you shining stars!
4   Praise him, you highest heavens,
    and you waters above the heavens!

5   Let them praise the name of the LORD!
    For he commanded and they were
created.
6   And he established them forever and
ever;
    he gave a decree, and it shall not pass
away.[3]

7   Praise the LORD from the earth,
    you great sea creatures and all deeps,

8   fire and hail, snow and mist,
    stormy wind fulfilling his word!
9   Mountains and all hills,
    fruit trees and all cedars!
10 Beasts and all livestock,
    creeping things and flying birds!
11 Kings of the earth and all peoples,
    princes and all rulers of the earth!
12 Young men and maidens together,
    old men and children!

13 Let them praise the name of the LORD,
    for his name alone is exalted;
    his majesty is above earth and heaven.
14 He has raised up a horn for his people,
    praise for all his saints,
    for the people of Israel who are near
to him.
  Praise the LORD!

P raise the LORD!
  Sing to the LORD a new song,
    his praise in the assembly of the godly!
2   Let Israel be glad in his Maker;
    let the children of Zion rejoice in their
King!
3   Let them praise his name with dancing,
    making melody to him with
tambourine and lyre!
4   For the LORD takes pleasure in his people;
    he adorns the humble with salvation.
5   Let the godly exult in glory;
    let them sing for joy on their beds.
6   Let the high praises of God be in their
throats
    and two-edged swords in their hands,
7   to execute vengeance on the nations
    and punishments on the peoples,
8   to bind their kings with chains
    and their nobles with fetters of iron,
9   to execute on them the judgment
written!
  This is honor for all his godly ones.
  Praise the LORD!

P raise the LORD!
  Praise God in his sanctuary;
    praise him in his mighty heavens![4]
2   Praise him for his mighty deeds;
    praise him according to his excellent
greatness!

---

[1] Hebrew *along with the captivity of your horses*   [2] That is, a burning stick   [3] Or *it shall not be transgressed*   [4] Hebrew *expanse* (compare Genesis 1:6–8)

3 Praise him with trumpet sound;
  praise him with lute and harp!
4 Praise him with tambourine and
  dance;
  praise him with strings and pipe!

5 Praise him with sounding cymbals;
  praise him with loud clashing cymbals!
6 Let everything that has breath praise the
  Lord!
  Praise the Lord!

NOVEMBER 16

1 Chronicles 7–8

The sons[1] of Issachar: Tola, Puah, Jashub, and Shimron, four. [2] The sons of Tola: Uzzi, Rephaiah, Jeriel, Jahmai, Ibsam, and Shemuel, heads of their fathers' houses, namely of Tola, mighty warriors of their generations, their number in the days of David being 22,600. [3] The son[2] of Uzzi: Izrahiah. And the sons of Izrahiah: Michael, Obadiah, Joel, and Isshiah, all five of them were chief men. [4] And along with them, by their generations, according to their fathers' houses, were units of the army for war, 36,000, for they had many wives and sons. [5] Their kinsmen belonging to all the clans of Issachar were in all 87,000 mighty warriors, enrolled by genealogy.

[6] The sons of Benjamin: Bela, Becher, and Jediael, three. [7] The sons of Bela: Ezbon, Uzzi, Uzziel, Jerimoth, and Iri, five, heads of fathers' houses, mighty warriors. And their enrollment by genealogies was 22,034. [8] The sons of Becher: Zemirah, Joash, Eliezer, Elioenai, Omri, Jeremoth, Abijah, Anathoth, and Alemeth. All these were the sons of Becher. [9] And their enrollment by genealogies, according to their generations, as heads of their fathers' houses, mighty warriors, was 20,200. [10] The son of Jediael: Bilhan. And the sons of Bilhan: Jeush, Benjamin, Ehud, Chenaanah, Zethan, Tarshish, and Ahishahar. [11] All these were the sons of Jediael according to the heads of their fathers' houses, mighty warriors, 17,200, able to go to war. [12] And Shuppim and Huppim were the sons of Ir, Hushim the son of Aher.

[13] The sons of Naphtali: Jahziel, Guni, Jezer and Shallum, the descendants of Bilhah.

[14] The sons of Manasseh: Asriel, whom his Aramean concubine bore; she bore Machir the father of Gilead. [15] And Machir took a wife for Huppim and for Shuppim. The name of his sister was Maacah. And the name of the second was Zelophehad, and Zelophehad had daughters. [16] And Maacah the wife of Machir bore a son, and she called his name Peresh; and the name of his brother was Sheresh; and his sons were Ulam and Rakem. [17] The son of Ulam: Bedan. These were the sons of Gilead the son of Machir, son of Manasseh. [18] And his sister Hammolecheth bore Ishhod, Abiezer and Mahlah. [19] The sons of Shemida were Ahian, Shechem, Likhi, and Aniam.

[20] The sons of Ephraim: Shuthelah, and Bered his son, Tahath his son, Eleadah his son, Tahath his son, [21] Zabad his son, Shuthelah his son, and Ezer and Elead, whom the men of Gath who were born in the land killed, because they came down to raid their livestock. [22] And Ephraim their father mourned many days, and his brothers came to comfort him. [23] And Ephraim went in to his wife, and she conceived and bore a son. And he called his name Beriah, because disaster had befallen his house.[3] [24] His daughter was Sheerah, who built both Lower and Upper Beth-horon, and Uzzen-sheerah. [25] Rephah was his son, Resheph his son, Telah his son, Tahan his son, [26] Ladan his son, Ammihud his son, Elishama his son, [27] Nun[4] his son, Joshua his son. [28] Their possessions and settlements were Bethel and its towns, and to the east Naaran, and to the west Gezer and its towns, Shechem and its towns, and Ayyah and its towns; [29] also in possession of the Manassites, Beth-shean and its towns, Taanach and its towns, Megiddo

[1] Syriac (compare Vulgate); Hebrew *And to the sons* [2] Hebrew *sons*; also verses 10, 12, 17 [3] *Beriah* sounds like the Hebrew for *disaster* [4] Hebrew *Non*

and its towns, Dor and its towns. In these lived the sons of Joseph the son of Israel.

[30] The sons of Asher: Imnah, Ishvah, Ishvi, Beriah, and their sister Serah. [31] The sons of Beriah: Heber, and Malchiel, who fathered Birzaith. [32] Heber fathered Japhlet, Shomer, Hotham, and their sister Shua. [33] The sons of Japhlet: Pasach, Bimhal, and Ashvath. These are the sons of Japhlet. [34] The sons of Shemer his brother: Rohgah, Jehubbah, and Aram. [35] The sons of Helem his brother: Zophah, Imna, Shelesh, and Amal. [36] The sons of Zophah: Suah, Harnepher, Shual, Beri, Imrah. [37] Bezer, Hod, Shamma, Shilshah, Ithran, and Beera. [38] The sons of Jether: Jephunneh, Pispa, and Ara. [39] The sons of Ulla: Arah, Hanniel, and Rizia. [40] All of these were men of Asher, heads of fathers' houses, approved, mighty warriors, chiefs of the princes. Their number enrolled by genealogies, for service in war, was 26,000 men.

[8:1] Benjamin fathered Bela his firstborn, Ashbel the second, Aharah the third, [2] Nohah the fourth, and Rapha the fifth. [3] And Bela had sons: Addar, Gera, Abihud, [4] Abishua, Naaman, Ahoah, [5] Gera, Shephuphan, and Huram. [6] These are the sons of Ehud (they were heads of fathers' houses of the inhabitants of Geba, and they were carried into exile to Manahath): [7] Naaman,[1] Ahijah, and Gera, that is, Heglam,[2] who fathered Uzza and Ahihud. [8] And Shaharaim fathered sons in the country of Moab after he had sent away Hushim and Baara his wives. [9] He fathered sons by Hodesh his wife: Jobab, Zibia, Mesha, Malcam, [10] Jeuz, Sachia, and Mirmah. These were his sons, heads of fathers' houses. [11] He also fathered sons by Hushim: Abitub and Elpaal. [12] The sons of Elpaal: Eber, Misham, and Shemed, who built Ono and Lod with its towns, [13] and Beriah and Shema (they were heads of fathers' houses of the inhabitants of Aijalon, who caused the inhabitants of Gath to flee); [14] and Ahio, Shashak, and Jeremoth. [15] Zebadiah, Arad, Eder, [16] Michael, Ishpah, and Joha were sons of Beriah. [17] Zebadiah, Meshullam, Hizki, Heber, [18] Ishmerai, Izliah, and Jobab were the sons of Elpaal. [19] Jakim, Zichri, Zabdi, [20] Elienai, Zillethai, Eliel, [21] Adaiah, Beraiah, and Shimrath were the sons of Shimei. [22] Ishpan, Eber, Eliel, [23] Abdon, Zichri, Hanan, [24] Hananiah, Elam, Anthothijah, [25] Iphdeiah, and Penuel were the sons of Shashak. [26] Shamsherai, Shehariah,

Athaliah, [27] Jaareshiah, Elijah, and Zichri were the sons of Jeroham. [28] These were the heads of fathers' houses, according to their generations, chief men. These lived in Jerusalem.

[29] Jeiel[3] the father of Gibeon lived in Gibeon, and the name of his wife was Maacah. [30] His firstborn son: Abdon, then Zur, Kish, Baal, Nadab, [31] Gedor, Ahio, Zecher, [32] and Mikloth (he fathered Shimeah). Now these also lived opposite their kinsmen in Jerusalem, with their kinsmen. [33] Ner was the father of Kish, Kish of Saul, Saul of Jonathan, Malchi-shua, Abinadab and Eshbaal; [34] and the son of Jonathan was Merib-baal; and Merib-baal was the father of Micah. [35] The sons of Micah: Pithon, Melech, Tarea, and Ahaz. [36] Ahaz fathered Jehoaddah, and Jehoaddah fathered Alemeth, Azmaveth, and Zimri. Zimri fathered Moza. [37] Moza fathered Binea; Raphah was his son, Eleasah his son, Azel his son. [38] Azel had six sons, and these are their names: Azrikam, Bocheru, Ishmael, Sheariah, Obadiah, and Hanan. All these were the sons of Azel. [39] The sons of Eshek his brother: Ulam his firstborn, Jeush the second, and Eliphelet the third. [40] The sons of Ulam were men who were mighty warriors, bowmen, having many sons and grandsons, 150. All these were Benjaminites.

Hebrews 11

N ow faith is the assurance of things hoped for, the conviction of things not seen. [2] For by it the people of old received their commendation. [3] By faith we understand that the universe was created by the word of God, so that what is seen was not made out of things that are visible.

[4] By faith Abel offered to God a more acceptable sacrifice than Cain, through which he was commended as righteous, God commending him by accepting his gifts. And through his faith, though he died, he still speaks. [5] By faith Enoch was taken up so that he should not see death, and he was not found, because God had taken him. Now before he was taken he was commended as having pleased God. [6] And without faith it is impossible to please him, for whoever would draw near to God must believe that he exists and that he rewards those who seek him. [7] By faith Noah, being warned by God concerning events as yet unseen, in reverent

---

[1] Hebrew and Naaman   [2] Or he carried them into exile   [3] Compare 9:35; Hebrew lacks Jeiel

fear constructed an ark for the saving of his household. By this he condemned the world and became an heir of the righteousness that comes by faith.

[8] By faith Abraham obeyed when he was called to go out to a place that he was to receive as an inheritance. And he went out, not knowing where he was going. [9] By faith he went to live in the land of promise, as in a foreign land, living in tents with Isaac and Jacob, heirs with him of the same promise. [10] For he was looking forward to the city that has foundations, whose designer and builder is God. [11] By faith Sarah herself received power to conceive, even when she was past the age, since she considered him faithful who had promised. [12] Therefore from one man, and him as good as dead, were born descendants as many as the stars of heaven and as many as the innumerable grains of sand by the seashore.

[13] These all died in faith, not having received the things promised, but having seen them and greeted them from afar, and having acknowledged that they were strangers and exiles on the earth. [14] For people who speak thus make it clear that they are seeking a homeland. [15] If they had been thinking of that land from which they had gone out, they would have had opportunity to return. [16] But as it is, they desire a better country, that is, a heavenly one. Therefore God is not ashamed to be called their God, for he has prepared for them a city.

[17] By faith Abraham, when he was tested, offered up Isaac, and he who had received the promises was in the act of offering up his only son, [18] of whom it was said, "Through Isaac shall your offspring be named." [19] He considered that God was able even to raise him from the dead, from which, figuratively speaking, he did receive him back. [20] By faith Isaac invoked future blessings on Jacob and Esau. [21] By faith Jacob, when dying, blessed each of the sons of Joseph, bowing in worship over the head of his staff. [22] By faith Joseph, at the end of his life, made mention of the exodus of the Israelites and gave directions concerning his bones.

[23] By faith Moses, when he was born, was hidden for three months by his parents, because they saw that the child was beautiful, and they were not afraid of the king's edict. [24] By faith Moses, when he was grown up, refused to be called the son of Pharaoh's daughter, [25] choosing rather to be mistreated with the people of God than to enjoy the fleeting pleasures of sin. [26] He considered the reproach of Christ greater wealth than the treasures of Egypt, for he was looking to the reward. [27] By faith he left Egypt, not being afraid of the anger of the king, for he endured as seeing him who is invisible. [28] By faith he kept the Passover and sprinkled the blood, so that the Destroyer of the firstborn might not touch them.

[29] By faith the people crossed the Red Sea as on dry land, but the Egyptians, when they attempted to do the same, were drowned. [30] By faith the walls of Jericho fell down after they had been encircled for seven days. [31] By faith Rahab the prostitute did not perish with those who were disobedient, because she had given a friendly welcome to the spies.

[32] And what more shall I say? For time would fail me to tell of Gideon, Barak, Samson, Jephthah, of David and Samuel and the prophets— [33] who through faith conquered kingdoms, enforced justice, obtained promises, stopped the mouths of lions, [34] quenched the power of fire, escaped the edge of the sword, were made strong out of weakness, became mighty in war, put foreign armies to flight. [35] Women received back their dead by resurrection. Some were tortured, refusing to accept release, so that they might rise again to a better life. [36] Others suffered mocking and flogging, and even chains and imprisonment. [37] They were stoned, they were sawn in two,[1] they were killed with the sword. They went about in skins of sheep and goats, destitute, afflicted, mistreated— [38] of whom the world was not worthy—wandering about in deserts and mountains, and in dens and caves of the earth.

[39] And all these, though commended through their faith, did not receive what was promised, [40] since God had provided something better for us, that apart from us they should not be made perfect.

——————— *Amos 5* ———————

Hear this word that I take up over you in lamentation, O house of Israel:

2   "Fallen, no more to rise,
         is the virgin Israel;

---
[1] Some manuscripts add *they were tempted*

forsaken on her land,
with none to raise her up."

³For thus says the Lord GOD:

"The city that went out a thousand
shall have a hundred left,
and that which went out a hundred
shall have ten left
to the house of Israel."

⁴For thus says the LORD to the house of Israel:

"Seek me and live;
⁵   but do not seek Bethel,
and do not enter into Gilgal
or cross over to Beersheba;
for Gilgal shall surely go into exile,
and Bethel shall come to nothing."

⁶   Seek the LORD and live,
lest he break out like fire in the house
of Joseph,
and it devour, with none to quench it
for Bethel,
⁷   O you who turn justice to wormwood¹
and cast down righteousness to the
earth!
⁸   He who made the Pleiades and Orion,
and turns deep darkness into the
morning
and darkens the day into night,
who calls for the waters of the sea
and pours them out on the surface of
the earth,
the LORD is his name;
⁹   who makes destruction flash forth
against the strong,
so that destruction comes upon the
fortress.
¹⁰   They hate him who reproves in the gate,
and they abhor him who speaks the
truth.
¹¹   Therefore because you trample on² the
poor
and you exact taxes of grain from him,
you have built houses of hewn stone,
but you shall not dwell in them;
you have planted pleasant vineyards,
but you shall not drink their wine.
¹²   For I know how many are your
transgressions
and how great are your sins—

you who afflict the righteous, who take
a bribe,
and turn aside the needy in the gate.
¹³   Therefore he who is prudent will keep
silent in such a time,
for it is an evil time.

¹⁴   Seek good, and not evil,
that you may live;
and so the LORD, the God of hosts, will
be with you,
as you have said.
¹⁵   Hate evil, and love good,
and establish justice in the gate;
it may be that the LORD, the God of hosts,
will be gracious to the remnant of
Joseph.

¹⁶Therefore thus says the LORD, the God of
hosts, the Lord:

"In all the squares there shall be wailing,
and in all the streets they shall say,
'Alas! Alas!'
They shall call the farmers to mourning
and to wailing those who are skilled in
lamentation,
¹⁷   and in all vineyards there shall be wailing,
for I will pass through your midst,"
says the LORD.

¹⁸   Woe to you who desire the day of the
LORD!
Why would you have the day of the
LORD?
It is darkness, and not light,
¹⁹   as if a man fled from a lion,
and a bear met him,
or went into the house and leaned his
hand against the wall,
and a serpent bit him.
²⁰   Is not the day of the LORD darkness, and
not light,
and gloom with no brightness in it?

²¹   "I hate, I despise your feasts,
and I take no delight in your solemn
assemblies.
²²   Even though you offer me your burnt
offerings and grain offerings,
I will not accept them;
and the peace offerings of your fattened
animals,
I will not look upon them.

¹ Or to bitter fruit ² Or you tax

²³ Take away from me the noise of your
songs;
to the melody of your harps I will not
listen.
²⁴ But let justice roll down like waters,
and righteousness like an ever-
flowing stream.

²⁵ "Did you bring to me sacrifices and offerings during the forty years in the wilderness,
O house of Israel? ²⁶ You shall take up Sikkuth
your king, and Kiyyun your star-god—your
images that you made for yourselves, ²⁷ and
I will send you into exile beyond Damascus,"
says the LORD, whose name is the God of hosts.

Luke 1:1–38

Inasmuch as many have undertaken to compile a narrative of the things that have been
accomplished among us, ² just as those who
from the beginning were eyewitnesses and
ministers of the word have delivered them
to us, ³ it seemed good to me also, having followed all things closely for some time past, to
write an orderly account for you, most excellent Theophilus, ⁴ that you may have certainty
concerning the things you have been taught.

⁵ In the days of Herod, king of Judea, there
was a priest named Zechariah,¹ of the division
of Abijah. And he had a wife from the daughters of Aaron, and her name was Elizabeth.
⁶ And they were both righteous before God,
walking blamelessly in all the commandments
and statutes of the Lord. ⁷ But they had no child,
because Elizabeth was barren, and both were
advanced in years.

⁸ Now while he was serving as priest before
God when his division was on duty, ⁹ according to the custom of the priesthood, he was
chosen by lot to enter the temple of the Lord
and burn incense. ¹⁰ And the whole multitude
of the people were praying outside at the hour
of incense. ¹¹ And there appeared to him an
angel of the Lord standing on the right side of
the altar of incense. ¹² And Zechariah was troubled when he saw him, and fear fell upon him.
¹³ But the angel said to him, "Do not be afraid,
Zechariah, for your prayer has been heard, and
your wife Elizabeth will bear you a son, and you
shall call his name John. ¹⁴ And you will have
joy and gladness, and many will rejoice at his

birth, ¹⁵ for he will be great before the Lord.
And he must not drink wine or strong drink,
and he will be filled with the Holy Spirit, even
from his mother's womb. ¹⁶ And he will turn
many of the children of Israel to the Lord their
God, ¹⁷ and he will go before him in the spirit
and power of Elijah, to turn the hearts of the
fathers to the children, and the disobedient to
the wisdom of the just, to make ready for the
Lord a people prepared."

¹⁸ And Zechariah said to the angel, "How
shall I know this? For I am an old man, and
my wife is advanced in years." ¹⁹ And the angel
answered him, "I am Gabriel. I stand in the
presence of God, and I was sent to speak to you
and to bring you this good news. ²⁰ And behold,
you will be silent and unable to speak until the
day that these things take place, because you
did not believe my words, which will be fulfilled in their time." ²¹ And the people were
waiting for Zechariah, and they were wondering at his delay in the temple. ²² And when he
came out, he was unable to speak to them, and
they realized that he had seen a vision in the
temple. And he kept making signs to them and
remained mute. ²³ And when his time of service
was ended, he went to his home.

²⁴ After these days his wife Elizabeth conceived, and for five months she kept herself
hidden, saying, ²⁵ "Thus the Lord has done for
me in the days when he looked on me, to take
away my reproach among people."

²⁶ In the sixth month the angel Gabriel
was sent from God to a city of Galilee named
Nazareth, ²⁷ to a virgin betrothed² to a man
whose name was Joseph, of the house of David.
And the virgin's name was Mary. ²⁸ And he
came to her and said, "Greetings, O favored one,
the Lord is with you!"³ ²⁹ But she was greatly
troubled at the saying, and tried to discern what
sort of greeting this might be. ³⁰ And the angel
said to her, "Do not be afraid, Mary, for you have
found favor with God. ³¹ And behold, you will
conceive in your womb and bear a son, and you
shall call his name Jesus. ³² He will be great and
will be called the Son of the Most High. And
the Lord God will give to him the throne of his
father David, ³³ and he will reign over the house
of Jacob forever, and of his kingdom there will
be no end."

³⁴ And Mary said to the angel, "How will this
be, since I am a virgin?"⁴

¹ Greek Zacharias ² That is, legally pledged to be married ³ Some manuscripts add Blessed are you among women! ⁴ Greek since I do not know a man

[35]And the angel answered her, "The Holy Spirit will come upon you, and the power of the Most High will overshadow you; therefore the child to be born[1] will be called holy—the Son of God. [36]And behold, your relative Elizabeth in her old age has also conceived a son, and this is the sixth month with her who was called barren. [37]For nothing will be impossible with God." [38]And Mary said, "Behold, I am the servant[2] of the Lord; let it be to me according to your word." And the angel departed from her.

NOVEMBER 17

1 Chronicles 9–10

So all Israel was recorded in genealogies, and these are written in the Book of the Kings of Israel. And Judah was taken into exile in Babylon because of their breach of faith. [2]Now the first to dwell again in their possessions in their cities were Israel, the priests, the Levites, and the temple servants. [3]And some of the people of Judah, Benjamin, Ephraim, and Manasseh lived in Jerusalem: [4]Uthai the son of Ammihud, son of Omri, son of Imri, son of Bani, from the sons of Perez the son of Judah. [5]And of the Shilonites: Asaiah the firstborn, and his sons. [6]Of the sons of Zerah: Jeuel and their kinsmen, 690. [7]Of the Benjaminites: Sallu the son of Meshullam, son of Hodaviah, son of Hassenuah, [8]Ibneiah the son of Jeroham, Elah the son of Uzzi, son of Michri, and Meshullam the son of Shephatiah, son of Reuel, son of Ibnijah; [9]and their kinsmen according to their generations, 956. All these were heads of fathers' houses according to their fathers' houses.

[10]Of the priests: Jedaiah, Jehoiarib, Jachin, [11]and Azariah the son of Hilkiah, son of Meshullam, son of Zadok, son of Meraioth, son of Ahitub, the chief officer of the house of God; [12]and Adaiah the son of Jeroham, son of Pashhur, son of Malchijah, and Maasai the son of Adiel, son of Jahzerah, son of Meshullam, son of Meshillemith, son of Immer; [13]besides their kinsmen, heads of their fathers' houses, 1,760, mighty men for the work of the service of the house of God.

[14]Of the Levites: Shemaiah the son of Hasshub, son of Azrikam, son of Hashabiah, of the sons of Merari; [15]and Bakbakkar, Heresh, Galal and Mattaniah the son of Mica, son of Zichri, son of Asaph; [16]and Obadiah the son of Shemaiah, son of Galal, son of Jeduthun, and Berechiah the son of Asa, son of Elkanah, who lived in the villages of the Netophathites.

[17]The gatekeepers were Shallum, Akkub, Talmon, Ahiman, and their kinsmen (Shallum was the chief); [18]until then they were in the king's gate on the east side as the gatekeepers of the camps of the Levites. [19]Shallum the son of Kore, son of Ebiasaph, son of Korah, and his kinsmen of his fathers' house, the Korahites, were in charge of the work of the service, keepers of the thresholds of the tent, as their fathers had been in charge of the camp of the LORD, keepers of the entrance. [20]And Phinehas the son of Eleazar was the chief officer over them in time past; the LORD was with him. [21]Zechariah the son of Meshelemiah was gatekeeper at the entrance of the tent of meeting. [22]All these, who were chosen as gatekeepers at the thresholds, were 212. They were enrolled by genealogies in their villages. David and Samuel the seer established them in their office of trust. [23]So they and their sons were in charge of the gates of the house of the LORD, that is, the house of the tent, as guards. [24]The gatekeepers were on the four sides, east, west, north, and south. [25]And their kinsmen who were in their villages were obligated to come in every seven days, in turn, to be with these, [26]for the four chief gatekeepers, who were Levites, were entrusted to be over the chambers and the treasures of the house of God. [27]And they

lodged around the house of God, for on them lay the duty of watching, and they had charge of opening it every morning. ²⁸Some of them had charge of the utensils of service, for they were required to count them when they were brought in and taken out. ²⁹Others of them were appointed over the furniture and over all the holy utensils, also over the fine flour, the wine, the oil, the incense, and the spices. ³⁰Others, of the sons of the priests, prepared the mixing of the spices, ³¹and Mattithiah, one of the Levites, the firstborn of Shallum the Korahite, was entrusted with making the flat cakes. ³²Also some of their kinsmen of the Kohathites had charge of the showbread, to prepare it every Sabbath.

³³Now these, the singers, the heads of fathers' houses of the Levites, were in the chambers of the temple free from other service, for they were on duty day and night. ³⁴These were heads of fathers' houses of the Levites, according to their generations, leaders. These lived in Jerusalem.

³⁵In Gibeon lived the father of Gibeon, Jeiel, and the name of his wife was Maacah, ³⁶and his firstborn son Abdon, then Zur, Kish, Baal, Ner, Nadab, ³⁷Gedor, Ahio, Zechariah, and Mikloth; ³⁸and Mikloth was the father of Shimeam; and these also lived opposite their kinsmen in Jerusalem, with their kinsmen. ³⁹Ner fathered Kish, Kish fathered Saul, Saul fathered Jonathan, Malchi-shua, Abinadab, and Eshbaal. ⁴⁰And the son of Jonathan was Merib-baal, and Merib-baal fathered Micah. ⁴¹The sons of Micah: Pithon, Melech, Tahrea, and Ahaz.¹ ⁴²And Ahaz fathered Jarah, and Jarah fathered Alemeth, Azmaveth, and Zimri. And Zimri fathered Moza. ⁴³Moza fathered Binea, and Rephaiah was his son, Eleasah his son, Azel his son. ⁴⁴Azel had six sons and these are their names: Azrikam, Bocheru, Ishmael, Sheariah, Obadiah, and Hanan; these were the sons of Azel.

¹⁰:¹Now the Philistines fought against Israel, and the men of Israel fled before the Philistines and fell slain on Mount Gilboa. ²And the Philistines overtook Saul and his sons, and the Philistines struck down Jonathan and Abinadab and Malchi-shua, the sons of Saul. ³The battle pressed hard against Saul, and the archers found him, and he was wounded by the archers. ⁴Then Saul said to his armor-bearer, "Draw your sword and thrust me through with it, lest these uncircumcised come and mistreat

me." But his armor-bearer would not, for he feared greatly. Therefore Saul took his own sword and fell upon it. ⁵And when his armor-bearer saw that Saul was dead, he also fell upon his sword and died. ⁶Thus Saul died; he and his three sons and all his house died together. ⁷And when all the men of Israel who were in the valley saw that the army² had fled and that Saul and his sons were dead, they abandoned their cities and fled, and the Philistines came and lived in them.

⁸The next day, when the Philistines came to strip the slain, they found Saul and his sons fallen on Mount Gilboa. ⁹And they stripped him and took his head and his armor, and sent messengers throughout the land of the Philistines to carry the good news to their idols and to the people. ¹⁰And they put his armor in the temple of their gods and fastened his head in the temple of Dagon. ¹¹But when all Jabesh-gilead heard all that the Philistines had done to Saul, ¹²all the valiant men arose and took away the body of Saul and the bodies of his sons, and brought them to Jabesh. And they buried their bones under the oak in Jabesh and fasted seven days.

¹³So Saul died for his breach of faith. He broke faith with the LORD in that he did not keep the command of the LORD, and also consulted a medium, seeking guidance. ¹⁴He did not seek guidance from the LORD. Therefore the LORD put him to death and turned the kingdom over to David the son of Jesse.

Hebrews 12

Therefore, since we are surrounded by so great a cloud of witnesses, let us also lay aside every weight, and sin which clings so closely, and let us run with endurance the race that is set before us, ²looking to Jesus, the founder and perfecter of our faith, who for the joy that was set before him endured the cross, despising the shame, and is seated at the right hand of the throne of God.

³Consider him who endured from sinners such hostility against himself, so that you may not grow weary or fainthearted. ⁴In your struggle against sin you have not yet resisted to the point of shedding your blood. ⁵And have you forgotten the exhortation that addresses you as sons?

¹ Compare 8:35; Hebrew lacks *and Ahaz* ² Hebrew *they*

"My son, do not regard lightly the
    discipline of the Lord,
    nor be weary when reproved by him.
[6] For the Lord disciplines the one he loves,
    and chastises every son whom he
    receives."

[7] It is for discipline that you have to endure. God is treating you as sons. For what son is there whom his father does not discipline? [8] If you are left without discipline, in which all have participated, then you are illegitimate children and not sons. [9] Besides this, we have had earthly fathers who disciplined us and we respected them. Shall we not much more be subject to the Father of spirits and live? [10] For they disciplined us for a short time as it seemed best to them, but he disciplines us for our good, that we may share his holiness. [11] For the moment all discipline seems painful rather than pleasant, but later it yields the peaceful fruit of righteousness to those who have been trained by it.

[12] Therefore lift your drooping hands and strengthen your weak knees, [13] and make straight paths for your feet, so that what is lame may not be put out of joint but rather be healed. [14] Strive for peace with everyone, and for the holiness without which no one will see the Lord. [15] See to it that no one fails to obtain the grace of God; that no "root of bitterness" springs up and causes trouble, and by it many become defiled; [16] that no one is sexually immoral or unholy like Esau, who sold his birthright for a single meal. [17] For you know that afterward, when he desired to inherit the blessing, he was rejected, for he found no chance to repent, though he sought it with tears.

[18] For you have not come to what may be touched, a blazing fire and darkness and gloom and a tempest [19] and the sound of a trumpet and a voice whose words made the hearers beg that no further messages be spoken to them. [20] For they could not endure the order that was given, "If even a beast touches the mountain, it shall be stoned." [21] Indeed, so terrifying was the sight that Moses said, "I tremble with fear." [22] But you have come to Mount Zion and to the city of the living God, the heavenly Jerusalem, and to innumerable angels in festal gathering, [23] and to the assembly[1] of the firstborn who are enrolled in heaven, and to God, the judge of all, and to the spirits of the righteous made perfect,

[24] and to Jesus, the mediator of a new covenant, and to the sprinkled blood that speaks a better word than the blood of Abel.

[25] See that you do not refuse him who is speaking. For if they did not escape when they refused him who warned them on earth, much less will we escape if we reject him who warns from heaven. [26] At that time his voice shook the earth, but now he has promised, "Yet once more I will shake not only the earth but also the heavens." [27] This phrase, "Yet once more," indicates the removal of things that are shaken—that is, things that have been made—in order that the things that cannot be shaken may remain. [28] Therefore let us be grateful for receiving a kingdom that cannot be shaken, and thus let us offer to God acceptable worship, with reverence and awe, [29] for our God is a consuming fire.

Amos 6

1 "Woe to those who are at ease in Zion,
    and to those who feel secure on the
        mountain of Samaria,
the notable men of the first of the
        nations,
to whom the house of Israel comes!
2   Pass over to Calneh, and see,
    and from there go to Hamath the
        great;
    then go down to Gath of the Philistines.
Are you better than these kingdoms?
    Or is their territory greater than your
        territory,
3   O you who put far away the day of
        disaster
    and bring near the seat of violence?

4   "Woe to those who lie on beds of ivory
    and stretch themselves out on their
        couches,
and eat lambs from the flock
    and calves from the midst of the stall,
5   who sing idle songs to the sound of the
        harp
    and like David invent for themselves
        instruments of music,
6   who drink wine in bowls
    and anoint themselves with the finest
        oils,
    but are not grieved over the ruin of
        Joseph!

[1] Or church

7   Therefore they shall now be the first of
        those who go into exile,
        and the revelry of those who stretch
        themselves out shall pass away."

[8] The Lord GOD has sworn by himself, declares
the LORD, the God of hosts:

"I abhor the pride of Jacob
    and hate his strongholds,
    and I will deliver up the city and all
        that is in it."

[9] And if ten men remain in one house, they
shall die. [10] And when one's relative, the one
who anoints him for burial, shall take him up
to bring the bones out of the house, and shall
say to him who is in the innermost parts of the
house, "Is there still anyone with you?" he shall
say, "No"; and he shall say, "Silence! We must
not mention the name of the LORD."

11 For behold, the LORD commands,
        and the great house shall be struck
            down into fragments,
        and the little house into bits.
12 Do horses run on rocks?
        Does one plow there[1] with oxen?
        But you have turned justice into poison
        and the fruit of righteousness into
            wormwood[2]—
13 you who rejoice in Lo-debar,[3]
        who say, "Have we not by our own
            strength
        captured Karnaim[4] for ourselves?"
14 "For behold, I will raise up against you a
        nation,
        O house of Israel," declares the LORD,
        the God of hosts;
"and they shall oppress you from
        Lebo-hamath
    to the Brook of the Arabah."

-------- *Luke 1:39–80* --------

In those days Mary arose and went with haste
into the hill country, to a town in Judah, [40] and
she entered the house of Zechariah and greeted
Elizabeth. [41] And when Elizabeth heard the
greeting of Mary, the baby leaped in her womb.
And Elizabeth was filled with the Holy Spirit,
[42] and she exclaimed with a loud cry, "Blessed
are you among women, and blessed is the fruit

of your womb! [43] And why is this granted to me
that the mother of my Lord should come to me?
[44] For behold, when the sound of your greeting
came to my ears, the baby in my womb leaped
for joy. [45] And blessed is she who believed that
there would be[5] a fulfillment of what was spoken to her from the Lord."

[46] And Mary said,

"My soul magnifies the Lord,
47   and my spirit rejoices in God my
            Savior,
48 for he has looked on the humble estate
            of his servant.
        For behold, from now on all
            generations will call me blessed;
49 for he who is mighty has done great
            things for me,
        and holy is his name.
50 And his mercy is for those who fear him
            from generation to generation.
51 He has shown strength with his arm;
        he has scattered the proud in the
            thoughts of their hearts;
52 he has brought down the mighty from
            their thrones
        and exalted those of humble estate;
53 he has filled the hungry with good
            things,
        and the rich he has sent away empty.
54 He has helped his servant Israel,
        in remembrance of his mercy,
55 as he spoke to our fathers,
        to Abraham and to his offspring
            forever."

[56] And Mary remained with her about three
months and returned to her home.

[57] Now the time came for Elizabeth to give
birth, and she bore a son. [58] And her neighbors and relatives heard that the Lord had
shown great mercy to her, and they rejoiced
with her. [59] And on the eighth day they came
to circumcise the child. And they would have
called him Zechariah after his father, [60] but his
mother answered, "No; he shall be called John."
[61] And they said to her, "None of your relatives
is called by this name." [62] And they made signs
to his father, inquiring what he wanted him to
be called. [63] And he asked for a writing tablet
and wrote, "His name is John." And they all
wondered. [64] And immediately his mouth was
opened and his tongue loosed, and he spoke,

-----
[1] Or *the sea* [2] Or *into bitter fruit* [3] *Lo-debar* means *nothing* [4] *Karnaim* means *horns* (a symbol of strength) [5] Or *believed, for there will be*

blessing God. ⁶⁵And fear came on all their neighbors. And all these things were talked about through all the hill country of Judea, ⁶⁶and all who heard them laid them up in their hearts, saying, "What then will this child be?" For the hand of the Lord was with him.

⁶⁷And his father Zechariah was filled with the Holy Spirit and prophesied, saying,

68 "Blessed be the Lord God of Israel,
    for he has visited and redeemed his
        people
69 and has raised up a horn of salvation
        for us
    in the house of his servant David,
70 as he spoke by the mouth of his holy
        prophets from of old,
71 that we should be saved from our
        enemies
    and from the hand of all who hate us;
72 to show the mercy promised to our
        fathers
    and to remember his holy covenant,

73 the oath that he swore to our father
        Abraham, to grant us
74 that we, being delivered from the
        hand of our enemies,
    might serve him without fear,
75 in holiness and righteousness before
        him all our days.
76 And you, child, will be called the
        prophet of the Most High;
    for you will go before the Lord to
        prepare his ways,
77 to give knowledge of salvation to his
        people
    in the forgiveness of their sins,
78 because of the tender mercy of our God,
    whereby the sunrise shall visit us¹
        from on high
79 to give light to those who sit in darkness
        and in the shadow of death,
    to guide our feet into the way of peace."

⁸⁰And the child grew and became strong in spirit, and he was in the wilderness until the day of his public appearance to Israel.

NOVEMBER 18

1 Chronicles 11–12

Then all Israel gathered together to David at Hebron and said, "Behold, we are your bone and flesh. ²In times past, even when Saul was king, it was you who led out and brought in Israel. And the LORD your God said to you, 'You shall be shepherd of my people Israel, and you shall be prince over my people Israel.'" ³So all the elders of Israel came to the king at Hebron, and David made a covenant with them at Hebron before the LORD. And they anointed David king over Israel, according to the word of the LORD by Samuel.

⁴And David and all Israel went to Jerusalem, that is, Jebus, where the Jebusites were, the inhabitants of the land. ⁵The inhabitants of Jebus said to David, "You will not come in here." Nevertheless, David took the stronghold of Zion, that is, the city of David. ⁶David said, "Whoever strikes the Jebusites first shall be chief and commander." And Joab the son of Zeruiah went up first, so he became chief. ⁷And David lived in the stronghold; therefore it was called the city of David. ⁸And he built the city all around from the Millo in complete circuit, and Joab repaired the rest of the city. ⁹And David became greater and greater, for the LORD of hosts was with him.

¹⁰Now these are the chiefs of David's mighty men, who gave him strong support in his kingdom, together with all Israel, to make him king, according to the word of the LORD concerning Israel. ¹¹This is an account of David's mighty men: Jashobeam, a Hachmonite, was chief of the three.² He wielded his spear against 300 whom he killed at one time. ¹²And next to him among the three mighty

¹ Or when the sunrise shall dawn upon us; some manuscripts since the sunrise has visited us ² Compare 2 Samuel 23:8; Hebrew thirty, or captains

men was Eleazar the son of Dodo, the Ahohite. [13]He was with David at Pas-dammim when the Philistines were gathered there for battle. There was a plot of ground full of barley, and the men fled from the Philistines. [14]But he took his[1] stand in the midst of the plot and defended it and killed the Philistines. And the LORD saved them by a great victory.

[15]Three of the thirty chief men went down to the rock to David at the cave of Adullam, when the army of Philistines was encamped in the Valley of Rephaim. [16]David was then in the stronghold, and the garrison of the Philistines was then at Bethlehem. [17]And David said longingly, "Oh that someone would give me water to drink from the well of Bethlehem that is by the gate!" [18]Then the three mighty men broke through the camp of the Philistines and drew water out of the well of Bethlehem that was by the gate and took it and brought it to David. But David would not drink it. He poured it out to the LORD [19]and said, "Far be it from me before my God that I should do this. Shall I drink the lifeblood of these men? For at the risk of their lives they brought it." Therefore he would not drink it. These things did the three mighty men.

[20]Now Abishai, the brother of Joab, was chief of the thirty.[2] And he wielded his spear against 300 men and killed them and won a name beside the three. [21]He was the most renowned[3] of the thirty[4] and became their commander, but he did not attain to the three.

[22]And Benaiah the son of Jehoiada was a valiant man[5] of Kabzeel, a doer of great deeds. He struck down two heroes of Moab. He also went down and struck down a lion in a pit on a day when snow had fallen. [23]And he struck down an Egyptian, a man of great stature, five cubits[6] tall. The Egyptian had in his hand a spear like a weaver's beam, but Benaiah went down to him with a staff and snatched the spear out of the Egyptian's hand and killed him with his own spear. [24]These things did Benaiah the son of Jehoiada and won a name beside the three mighty men. [25]He was renowned among the thirty, but he did not attain to the three. And David set him over his bodyguard.

[26]The mighty men were Asahel the brother of Joab, Elhanan the son of Dodo of Bethlehem, [27]Shammoth of Harod,[7] Helez the Pelonite, [28]Ira the son of Ikkesh of Tekoa, Abiezer of Anathoth, [29]Sibbecai the Hushathite, Ilai the Ahohite, [30]Maharai of Netophah, Heled the son of Baanah of Netophah, [31]Ithai the son of Ribai of Gibeah of the people of Benjamin, Benaiah of Pirathon, [32]Hurai of the brooks of Gaash, Abiel the Arbathite, [33]Azmaveth of Baharum, Eliahba the Shaalbonite, [34]Hashem[8] the Gizonite, Jonathan the son of Shagee the Hararite, [35]Ahiam the son of Sachar the Hararite, Eliphal the son of Ur, [36]Hepher the Mecherathite, Ahijah the Pelonite, [37]Hezro of Carmel, Naarai the son of Ezbai, [38]Joel the brother of Nathan, Mibhar the son of Hagri, [39]Zelek the Ammonite, Naharai of Beeroth, the armor-bearer of Joab the son of Zeruiah, [40]Ira the Ithrite, Gareb the Ithrite, [41]Uriah the Hittite, Zabad the son of Ahlai, [42]Adina the son of Shiza the Reubenite, a leader of the Reubenites, and thirty with him, [43]Hanan the son of Maacah, and Joshaphat the Mithnite, [44]Uzzia the Ashterathite, Shama and Jeiel the sons of Hotham the Aroerite, [45]Jediael the son of Shimri, and Joha his brother, the Tizite, [46]Eliel the Mahavite, and Jeribai, and Joshaviah, the sons of Elnaam, and Ithmah the Moabite, [47]Eliel, and Obed, and Jaasiel the Mezobaite.

[12:1]Now these are the men who came to David at Ziklag, while he could not move about freely because of Saul the son of Kish. And they were among the mighty men who helped him in war. [2]They were bowmen and could shoot arrows and sling stones with either the right or the left hand; they were Benjaminites, Saul's kinsmen. [3]The chief was Ahiezer, then Joash, both sons of Shemaah of Gibeah; also Jeziel and Pelet, the sons of Azmaveth; Beracah, Jehu of Anathoth, [4]Ishmaiah of Gibeon, a mighty man among the thirty and a leader over the thirty; Jeremiah,[9] Jahaziel, Johanan, Jozabad of Gederah, [5]Eluzai,[10] Jerimoth, Bealiah, Shemariah, Shephatiah the Haruphite; [6]Elkanah, Isshiah, Azarel, Joezer, and Jashobeam, the Korahites; [7]And Joelah and Zebadiah, the sons of Jeroham of Gedor.

[8]From the Gadites there went over to David at the stronghold in the wilderness mighty and experienced warriors, expert with shield and spear, whose faces were like the faces of lions and who were swift as gazelles upon the mountains: [9]Ezer the chief, Obadiah second, Eliab third, [10]Mishmannah fourth, Jeremiah fifth, [11]Attai sixth, Eliel seventh, [12]Johanan eighth, Elzabad

---

[1] Compare 2 Samuel 23:12; Hebrew *they. . . their* [2] Syriac; Hebrew *three* [3] Compare 2 Samuel 23:19; Hebrew *more renowned among the two* [4] Syriac; Hebrew *three* [5] Syriac; Hebrew *the son of a valiant man* [6] A cubit was about 18 inches or 45 centimeters [7] Compare 2 Samuel 23:25; Hebrew *the Harorite* [8] Compare Septuagint and 2 Samuel 23:32; Hebrew *the sons of Hashem* [9] Hebrew verse 5 [10] Hebrew verse 6

ninth, [13]Jeremiah tenth, Machbannai eleventh. [14]These Gadites were officers of the army; the least was a match for a hundred men and the greatest for a thousand. [15]These are the men who crossed the Jordan in the first month, when it was overflowing all its banks, and put to flight all those in the valleys, to the east and to the west.

[16]And some of the men of Benjamin and Judah came to the stronghold to David. [17]David went out to meet them and said to them, "If you have come to me in friendship to help me, my heart will be joined to you; but if to betray me to my adversaries, although there is no wrong in my hands, then may the God of our fathers see and rebuke you." [18]Then the Spirit clothed Amasai, chief of the thirty, and he said,

"We are yours, O David,
     and with you, O son of Jesse!
Peace, peace to you,
     and peace to your helpers!
For your God helps you."

Then David received them and made them officers of his troops.

[19]Some of the men of Manasseh deserted to David when he came with the Philistines for the battle against Saul. (Yet he did not help them, for the rulers of the Philistines took counsel and sent him away, saying, "At peril to our heads he will desert to his master Saul.") [20]As he went to Ziklag, these men of Manasseh deserted to him: Adnah, Jozabad, Jediael, Michael, Jozabad, Elihu, and Zillethai, chiefs of thousands in Manasseh. [21]They helped David against the band of raiders, for they were all mighty men of valor and were commanders in the army. [22]For from day to day men came to David to help him, until there was a great army, like an army of God.

[23]These are the numbers of the divisions of the armed troops who came to David in Hebron to turn the kingdom of Saul over to him, according to the word of the LORD. [24]The men of Judah bearing shield and spear were 6,800 armed troops. [25]Of the Simeonites, mighty men of valor for war, 7,100. [26]Of the Levites 4,600. [27]The prince Jehoiada, of the house of Aaron, and with him 3,700. [28]Zadok, a young man mighty in valor, and twenty-two commanders from his own fathers' house. [29]Of the Benjaminites, the kinsmen of Saul, 3,000, of whom the majority had to that point kept their allegiance to the house of Saul. [30]Of the Ephraimites 20,800, mighty men of valor, famous men in their fathers' houses. [31]Of the half-tribe of Manasseh 18,000, who were expressly named to come and make David king. [32]Of Issachar, men who had understanding of the times, to know what Israel ought to do, 200 chiefs, and all their kinsmen under their command. [33]Of Zebulun 50,000 seasoned troops, equipped for battle with all the weapons of war, to help David[1] with singleness of purpose. [34]Of Naphtali 1,000 commanders with whom were 37,000 men armed with shield and spear. [35]Of the Danites 28,600 men equipped for battle. [36]Of Asher 40,000 seasoned troops ready for battle. [37]Of the Reubenites and Gadites and the half-tribe of Manasseh from beyond the Jordan, 120,000 men armed with all the weapons of war.

[38]All these, men of war, arrayed in battle order, came to Hebron with a whole heart to make David king over all Israel. Likewise, all the rest of Israel were of a single mind to make David king. [39]And they were there with David for three days, eating and drinking, for their brothers had made preparation for them. [40]And also their relatives, from as far as Issachar and Zebulun and Naphtali, came bringing food on donkeys and on camels and on mules and on oxen, abundant provisions of flour, cakes of figs, clusters of raisins, and wine and oil, oxen and sheep, for there was joy in Israel.

Hebrews 13

Let brotherly love continue. [2]Do not neglect to show hospitality to strangers, for thereby some have entertained angels unawares. [3]Remember those who are in prison, as though in prison with them, and those who are mistreated, since you also are in the body. [4]Let marriage be held in honor among all, and let the marriage bed be undefiled, for God will judge the sexually immoral and adulterous. [5]Keep your life free from love of money, and be content with what you have, for he has said, "I will never leave you nor forsake you." [6]So we can confidently say,

"The Lord is my helper;
     I will not fear;
what can man do to me?"

[7]Remember your leaders, those who spoke to you the word of God. Consider the outcome of their way of life, and imitate their faith.

[1] Septuagint; Hebrew lacks *David*

⁸Jesus Christ is the same yesterday and today and forever. ⁹Do not be led away by diverse and strange teachings, for it is good for the heart to be strengthened by grace, not by foods, which have not benefited those devoted to them. ¹⁰We have an altar from which those who serve the tent have no right to eat. ¹¹For the bodies of those animals whose blood is brought into the holy places by the high priest as a sacrifice for sin are burned outside the camp. ¹²So Jesus also suffered outside the gate in order to sanctify the people through his own blood. ¹³Therefore let us go to him outside the camp and bear the reproach he endured. ¹⁴For here we have no lasting city, but we seek the city that is to come. ¹⁵Through him then let us continually offer up a sacrifice of praise to God, that is, the fruit of lips that acknowledge his name. ¹⁶Do not neglect to do good and to share what you have, for such sacrifices are pleasing to God.

¹⁷Obey your leaders and submit to them, for they are keeping watch over your souls, as those who will have to give an account. Let them do this with joy and not with groaning, for that would be of no advantage to you.

¹⁸Pray for us, for we are sure that we have a clear conscience, desiring to act honorably in all things. ¹⁹I urge you the more earnestly to do this in order that I may be restored to you the sooner.

²⁰Now may the God of peace who brought again from the dead our Lord Jesus, the great shepherd of the sheep, by the blood of the eternal covenant, ²¹equip you with everything good that you may do his will, working in us[1] that which is pleasing in his sight, through Jesus Christ, to whom be glory forever and ever. Amen.

²²I appeal to you, brothers,[2] bear with my word of exhortation, for I have written to you briefly. ²³You should know that our brother Timothy has been released, with whom I shall see you if he comes soon. ²⁴Greet all your leaders and all the saints. Those who come from Italy send you greetings. ²⁵Grace be with all of you.

Amos 7

This is what the Lord GOD showed me: behold, he was forming locusts when the latter growth was just beginning to sprout, and behold, it was the latter growth after the king's mowings. ²When they had finished eating the grass of the land, I said,

"O Lord GOD, please forgive!
  How can Jacob stand?
  He is so small!"
³ The LORD relented concerning this:
  "It shall not be," said the LORD.

⁴This is what the Lord GOD showed me: behold, the Lord GOD was calling for a judgment by fire, and it devoured the great deep and was eating up the land. ⁵Then I said,

"O Lord GOD, please cease!
  How can Jacob stand?
  He is so small!"
⁶ The LORD relented concerning this:
  "This also shall not be," said the Lord GOD.

⁷This is what he showed me: behold, the Lord was standing beside a wall built with a plumb line, with a plumb line in his hand. ⁸And the LORD said to me, "Amos, what do you see?" And I said, "A plumb line." Then the Lord said,

"Behold, I am setting a plumb line
  in the midst of my people Israel;
  I will never again pass by them;
⁹ the high places of Isaac shall be made desolate,
  and the sanctuaries of Israel shall be laid waste,
  and I will rise against the house of Jeroboam with the sword."

¹⁰Then Amaziah the priest of Bethel sent to Jeroboam king of Israel, saying, "Amos has conspired against you in the midst of the house of Israel. The land is not able to bear all his words. ¹¹For thus Amos has said,

"'Jeroboam shall die by the sword,
  and Israel must go into exile away from his land.'"

¹²And Amaziah said to Amos, "O seer, go, flee away to the land of Judah, and eat bread there, and prophesy there, ¹³but never again prophesy at Bethel, for it is the king's sanctuary, and it is a temple of the kingdom."

¹⁴Then Amos answered and said to Amaziah, "I was[3] no prophet, nor a prophet's son, but I was a herdsman and a dresser of sycamore figs. ¹⁵But the LORD took me from following the flock, and the LORD said to me, 'Go, prophesy

[1] Some manuscripts you   [2] Or brothers and sisters   [3] Or am; twice in this verse

to my people Israel.' ¹⁶Now therefore hear the word of the LORD.

> "You say, 'Do not prophesy against Israel,
> and do not preach against the house
> of Isaac.'

¹⁷Therefore thus says the LORD:

> "'Your wife shall be a prostitute in the city,
> and your sons and your daughters
> shall fall by the sword,
> and your land shall be divided up with
> a measuring line;
> you yourself shall die in an unclean land,
> and Israel shall surely go into exile
> away from its land.'"

―――――― Luke 2 ――――――

In those days a decree went out from Caesar Augustus that all the world should be registered. ²This was the first registration when¹ Quirinius was governor of Syria. ³And all went to be registered, each to his own town. ⁴And Joseph also went up from Galilee, from the town of Nazareth, to Judea, to the city of David, which is called Bethlehem, because he was of the house and lineage of David, ⁵to be registered with Mary, his betrothed,² who was with child. ⁶And while they were there, the time came for her to give birth. ⁷And she gave birth to her firstborn son and wrapped him in swaddling cloths and laid him in a manger, because there was no place for them in the inn.

⁸And in the same region there were shepherds out in the field, keeping watch over their flock by night. ⁹And an angel of the Lord appeared to them, and the glory of the Lord shone around them, and they were filled with great fear. ¹⁰And the angel said to them, "Fear not, for behold, I bring you good news of great joy that will be for all the people. ¹¹For unto you is born this day in the city of David a Savior, who is Christ the Lord. ¹²And this will be a sign for you: you will find a baby wrapped in swaddling cloths and lying in a manger." ¹³And suddenly there was with the angel a multitude of the heavenly host praising God and saying,

¹⁴ "Glory to God in the highest,
> and on earth peace among those with
> whom he is pleased!"³

¹⁵When the angels went away from them into heaven, the shepherds said to one another, "Let us go over to Bethlehem and see this thing that has happened, which the Lord has made known to us." ¹⁶And they went with haste and found Mary and Joseph, and the baby lying in a manger. ¹⁷And when they saw it, they made known the saying that had been told them concerning this child. ¹⁸And all who heard it wondered at what the shepherds told them. ¹⁹But Mary treasured up all these things, pondering them in her heart. ²⁰And the shepherds returned, glorifying and praising God for all they had heard and seen, as it had been told them.

²¹And at the end of eight days, when he was circumcised, he was called Jesus, the name given by the angel before he was conceived in the womb.

²²And when the time came for their purification according to the Law of Moses, they brought him up to Jerusalem to present him to the Lord ²³(as it is written in the Law of the Lord, "Every male who first opens the womb shall be called holy to the Lord") ²⁴and to offer a sacrifice according to what is said in the Law of the Lord, "a pair of turtledoves, or two young pigeons." ²⁵Now there was a man in Jerusalem, whose name was Simeon, and this man was righteous and devout, waiting for the consolation of Israel, and the Holy Spirit was upon him. ²⁶And it had been revealed to him by the Holy Spirit that he would not see death before he had seen the Lord's Christ. ²⁷And he came in the Spirit into the temple, and when the parents brought in the child Jesus, to do for him according to the custom of the Law, ²⁸he took him up in his arms and blessed God and said,

²⁹ "Lord, now you are letting your servant⁴
> depart in peace,
> according to your word;
³⁰ for my eyes have seen your salvation
³¹ that you have prepared in the
> presence of all peoples,
³² a light for revelation to the Gentiles,
> and for glory to your people Israel."

³³And his father and his mother marveled at what was said about him. ³⁴And Simeon blessed them and said to Mary his mother, "Behold, this child is appointed for the fall and rising of many in Israel, and for a sign that is opposed ³⁵(and a sword will pierce through

¹ Or This was the registration before ² That is, one legally pledged to be married ³ Some manuscripts peace, good will among men ⁴ Greek bondservant

your own soul also), so that thoughts from many hearts may be revealed."

36And there was a prophetess, Anna, the daughter of Phanuel, of the tribe of Asher. She was advanced in years, having lived with her husband seven years from when she was a virgin, **37**and then as a widow until she was eighty-four.[1] She did not depart from the temple, worshiping with fasting and prayer night and day. **38**And coming up at that very hour she began to give thanks to God and to speak of him to all who were waiting for the redemption of Jerusalem.

39And when they had performed everything according to the Law of the Lord, they returned into Galilee, to their own town of Nazareth. **40**And the child grew and became strong, filled with wisdom. And the favor of God was upon him.

41Now his parents went to Jerusalem every year at the Feast of the Passover. **42**And when he was twelve years old, they went up according to custom. **43**And when the feast was ended, as they were returning, the boy Jesus stayed behind in Jerusalem. His parents did not know it, **44**but supposing him to be in the group they went a day's journey, but then they began to search for him among their relatives and acquaintances, **45**and when they did not find him, they returned to Jerusalem, searching for him. **46**After three days they found him in the temple, sitting among the teachers, listening to them and asking them questions. **47**And all who heard him were amazed at his understanding and his answers. **48**And when his parents[2] saw him, they were astonished. And his mother said to him, "Son, why have you treated us so? Behold, your father and I have been searching for you in great distress." **49**And he said to them, "Why were you looking for me? Did you not know that I must be in my Father's house?"[3] **50**And they did not understand the saying that he spoke to them. **51**And he went down with them and came to Nazareth and was submissive to them. And his mother treasured up all these things in her heart.

52And Jesus increased in wisdom and in stature[4] and in favor with God and man.

NOVEMBER 19

1 Chronicles 13–14

David consulted with the commanders of thousands and of hundreds, with every leader. **2**And David said to all the assembly of Israel, "If it seems good to you and from the LORD our God, let us send abroad to our brothers who remain in all the lands of Israel, as well as to the priests and Levites in the cities that have pasturelands, that they may be gathered to us. **3**Then let us bring again the ark of our God to us, for we did not seek it[5] in the days of Saul." **4**All the assembly agreed to do so, for the thing was right in the eyes of all the people. **5**So David assembled all Israel from the Nile[6] of Egypt to Lebo-hamath, to bring the ark of God from Kiriath-jearim. **6**And David and all Israel went up to Baalah, that is, to Kiriath-jearim that belongs to Judah, to bring up from there the ark of God, which is called by the name of the LORD who sits enthroned above the cherubim. **7**And they carried the ark of God on a new cart, from the house of Abinadab, and Uzzah and Ahio[7] were driving the cart. **8**And David and all Israel were celebrating before God with all their might, with song and lyres and harps and tambourines and cymbals and trumpets.

9And when they came to the threshing floor of Chidon, Uzzah put out his hand to take hold of the ark, for the oxen stumbled. **10**And the anger of the LORD was kindled against Uzzah, and he struck him down because he put out his hand to the ark, and he died there before God. **11**And David was angry because the LORD had broken out against Uzzah. And that place is called Perez-uzza[8] to this day. **12**And David was

[1] Or as a widow for eighty-four years [2] Greek they [3] Or about my Father's business [4] Or years [5] Or him [6] Hebrew Shihor [7] Or and his brother [8] Perez-uzza means the breaking out against Uzzah

afraid of God that day, and he said, "How can I bring the ark of God home to me?" ¹³So David did not take the ark home into the city of David, but took it aside to the house of Obed-edom the Gittite. ¹⁴And the ark of God remained with the household of Obed-edom in his house three months. And the LORD blessed the household of Obed-edom and all that he had.

¹⁴:¹And Hiram king of Tyre sent messengers to David, and cedar trees, also masons and carpenters to build a house for him. ²And David knew that the LORD had established him as king over Israel, and that his kingdom was highly exalted for the sake of his people Israel. ³And David took more wives in Jerusalem, and David fathered more sons and daughters. ⁴These are the names of the children born to him in Jerusalem: Shammua, Shobab, Nathan, Solomon, ⁵Ibhar, Elishua, Elpelet, ⁶Nogah, Nepheg, Japhia, ⁷Elishama, Beeliada and Eliphelet.

⁸When the Philistines heard that David had been anointed king over all Israel, all the Philistines went up to search for David. But David heard of it and went out against them. ⁹Now the Philistines had come and made a raid in the Valley of Rephaim. ¹⁰And David inquired of God, "Shall I go up against the Philistines? Will you give them into my hand?" And the LORD said to him, "Go up, and I will give them into your hand." ¹¹And he went up to Baal-perazim, and David struck them down there. And David said, "God has broken through¹ my enemies by my hand, like a bursting flood." Therefore the name of that place is called Baal-perazim. ¹²And they left their gods there, and David gave command, and they were burned.

¹³And the Philistines yet again made a raid in the valley. ¹⁴And when David again inquired of God, God said to him, "You shall not go up after them; go around and come against them opposite the balsam trees. ¹⁵And when you hear the sound of marching in the tops of the balsam trees, then go out to battle, for God has gone out before you to strike down the army of the Philistines." ¹⁶And David did as God commanded him, and they struck down the Philistine army from Gibeon to Gezer. ¹⁷And the fame of David went out into all lands, and the LORD brought the fear of him upon all nations.

James 1

James, a servant² of God and of the Lord Jesus Christ,

To the twelve tribes in the Dispersion:

Greetings.

²Count it all joy, my brothers,³ when you meet trials of various kinds, ³for you know that the testing of your faith produces steadfastness. ⁴And let steadfastness have its full effect, that you may be perfect and complete, lacking in nothing.

⁵If any of you lacks wisdom, let him ask God, who gives generously to all without reproach, and it will be given him. ⁶But let him ask in faith, with no doubting, for the one who doubts is like a wave of the sea that is driven and tossed by the wind. ⁷For that person must not suppose that he will receive anything from the Lord; ⁸he is a double-minded man, unstable in all his ways.

⁹Let the lowly brother boast in his exaltation, ¹⁰and the rich in his humiliation, because like a flower of the grass⁴ he will pass away. ¹¹For the sun rises with its scorching heat and withers the grass; its flower falls, and its beauty perishes. So also will the rich man fade away in the midst of his pursuits.

¹²Blessed is the man who remains steadfast under trial, for when he has stood the test he will receive the crown of life, which God has promised to those who love him. ¹³Let no one say when he is tempted, "I am being tempted by God," for God cannot be tempted with evil, and he himself tempts no one. ¹⁴But each person is tempted when he is lured and enticed by his own desire. ¹⁵Then desire when it has conceived gives birth to sin, and sin when it is fully grown brings forth death.

¹⁶Do not be deceived, my beloved brothers. ¹⁷Every good gift and every perfect gift is from above, coming down from the Father of lights with whom there is no variation or shadow due to change.⁵ ¹⁸Of his own will he brought us forth by the word of truth, that we should be a kind of firstfruits of his creatures.

¹⁹Know this, my beloved brothers: let every person be quick to hear, slow to speak, slow to anger; ²⁰for the anger of man does not produce the righteousness of God. ²¹Therefore put away all filthiness and rampant wickedness and

¹ Baal-perazim means Lord of breaking through ² Or slave (for the contextual rendering of the Greek word doulos, see Preface) ³ Or brothers and sisters. The plural Greek word adelphoi (translated "brothers") refers to siblings in a family. In New Testament usage, depending on the context, adelphoi may refer either to men or to both men and women who are siblings (brothers and sisters) in God's family, the church; also verses 16, 19 ⁴ Or a wild flower ⁵ Some manuscripts variation due to a shadow of turning

receive with meekness the implanted word, which is able to save your souls. ²²But be doers of the word, and not hearers only, deceiving yourselves. ²³For if anyone is a hearer of the word and not a doer, he is like a man who looks intently at his natural face in a mirror. ²⁴For he looks at himself and goes away and at once forgets what he was like. ²⁵But the one who looks into the perfect law, the law of liberty, and perseveres, being no hearer who forgets but a doer who acts, he will be blessed in his doing.

²⁶If anyone thinks he is religious and does not bridle his tongue but deceives his heart, this person's religion is worthless. ²⁷Religion that is pure and undefiled before God, the Father, is this: to visit orphans and widows in their affliction, and to keep oneself unstained from the world.

Amos 8

This is what the Lord GOD showed me: behold, a basket of summer fruit. ²And he said, "Amos, what do you see?" And I said, "A basket of summer fruit." Then the LORD said to me,

"The end¹ has come upon my people Israel;
    I will never again pass by them.
³ The songs of the temple² shall become wailings³ in that day,"
            declares the Lord GOD.
"So many dead bodies!"
"They are thrown everywhere!"
"Silence!"

⁴ Hear this, you who trample on the needy
    and bring the poor of the land to an end,
⁵ saying, "When will the new moon be over,
    that we may sell grain?
And the Sabbath,
    that we may offer wheat for sale,
that we may make the ephah small and the shekel⁴ great
    and deal deceitfully with false balances,
⁶ that we may buy the poor for silver
    and the needy for a pair of sandals
    and sell the chaff of the wheat?"

⁷ The LORD has sworn by the pride of Jacob:
"Surely I will never forget any of their deeds.
⁸ Shall not the land tremble on this account,
    and everyone mourn who dwells in it,
and all of it rise like the Nile,
    and be tossed about and sink again,
    like the Nile of Egypt?"

⁹ "And on that day," declares the Lord GOD,
    "I will make the sun go down at noon
    and darken the earth in broad daylight.
¹⁰ I will turn your feasts into mourning
    and all your songs into lamentation;
I will bring sackcloth on every waist
    and baldness on every head;
I will make it like the mourning for an only son
    and the end of it like a bitter day.

¹¹ "Behold, the days are coming," declares the Lord GOD,
    "when I will send a famine on the land—
not a famine of bread, nor a thirst for water,
    but of hearing the words of the LORD.
¹² They shall wander from sea to sea,
    and from north to east;
they shall run to and fro, to seek the word of the LORD,
    but they shall not find it.
¹³ "In that day the lovely virgins and the young men
    shall faint for thirst.
¹⁴ Those who swear by the Guilt of Samaria,
    and say, 'As your god lives, O Dan,'
    and, 'As the Way of Beersheba lives,'
    they shall fall, and never rise again."

Luke 3

In the fifteenth year of the reign of Tiberius Caesar, Pontius Pilate being governor of Judea, and Herod being tetrarch of Galilee, and his brother Philip tetrarch of the region of Ituraea and Trachonitis, and Lysanias tetrarch of Abilene, ²during the high priesthood of Annas and Caiaphas, the word of God came to John the son of Zechariah in the wilderness.

¹ The Hebrew words for *end* and *summer fruit* sound alike ² Or *palace* ³ Or *The singing women of the palace shall wail* ⁴ An *ephah* was about 3/5 bushel or 22 liters; a *shekel* was about 2/5 ounce or 11 grams

[3] And he went into all the region around the Jordan, proclaiming a baptism of repentance for the forgiveness of sins. [4] As it is written in the book of the words of Isaiah the prophet,

> "The voice of one crying in the
> wilderness:
> 'Prepare the way of the Lord,[1]
> make his paths straight.
> [5] Every valley shall be filled,
> and every mountain and hill shall be
> made low,
> and the crooked shall become straight,
> and the rough places shall become
> level ways,
> [6] and all flesh shall see the salvation of
> God.'"

[7] He said therefore to the crowds that came out to be baptized by him, "You brood of vipers! Who warned you to flee from the wrath to come? [8] Bear fruits in keeping with repentance. And do not begin to say to yourselves, 'We have Abraham as our father.' For I tell you, God is able from these stones to raise up children for Abraham. [9] Even now the axe is laid to the root of the trees. Every tree therefore that does not bear good fruit is cut down and thrown into the fire."

[10] And the crowds asked him, "What then shall we do?" [11] And he answered them, "Whoever has two tunics[2] is to share with him who has none, and whoever has food is to do likewise." [12] Tax collectors also came to be baptized and said to him, "Teacher, what shall we do?" [13] And he said to them, "Collect no more than you are authorized to do." [14] Soldiers also asked him, "And we, what shall we do?" And he said to them, "Do not extort money from anyone by threats or by false accusation, and be content with your wages."

[15] As the people were in expectation, and all were questioning in their hearts concerning John, whether he might be the Christ, [16] John answered them all, saying, "I baptize you with water, but he who is mightier than I is coming, the strap of whose sandals I am not worthy to untie. He will baptize you with the Holy Spirit and fire. [17] His winnowing fork is in his hand, to clear his threshing floor and to gather the wheat into his barn, but the chaff he will burn with unquenchable fire."

[18] So with many other exhortations he preached good news to the people. [19] But Herod the tetrarch, who had been reproved by him for Herodias, his brother's wife, and for all the evil things that Herod had done, [20] added this to them all, that he locked up John in prison.

[21] Now when all the people were baptized, and when Jesus also had been baptized and was praying, the heavens were opened, [22] and the Holy Spirit descended on him in bodily form, like a dove; and a voice came from heaven, "You are my beloved Son;[3] with you I am well pleased."[4]

[23] Jesus, when he began his ministry, was about thirty years of age, being the son (as was supposed) of Joseph, the son of Heli, [24] the son of Matthat, the son of Levi, the son of Melchi, the son of Jannai, the son of Joseph, [25] the son of Mattathias, the son of Amos, the son of Nahum, the son of Esli, the son of Naggai, [26] the son of Maath, the son of Mattathias, the son of Semein, the son of Josech, the son of Joda, [27] the son of Joanan, the son of Rhesa, the son of Zerubbabel, the son of Shealtiel,[5] the son of Neri, [28] the son of Melchi, the son of Addi, the son of Cosam, the son of Elmadam, the son of Er, [29] the son of Joshua, the son of Eliezer, the son of Jorim, the son of Matthat, the son of Levi, [30] the son of Simeon, the son of Judah, the son of Joseph, the son of Jonam, the son of Eliakim, [31] the son of Melea, the son of Menna, the son of Mattatha, the son of Nathan, the son of David, [32] the son of Jesse, the son of Obed, the son of Boaz, the son of Sala, the son of Nahshon, [33] the son of Amminadab, the son of Admin, the son of Arni, the son of Hezron, the son of Perez, the son of Judah, [34] the son of Jacob, the son of Isaac, the son of Abraham, the son of Terah, the son of Nahor, [35] the son of Serug, the son of Reu, the son of Peleg, the son of Eber, the son of Shelah, [36] the son of Cainan, the son of Arphaxad, the son of Shem, the son of Noah, the son of Lamech, [37] the son of Methuselah, the son of Enoch, the son of Jared, the son of Mahalaleel, the son of Cainan, [38] the son of Enos, the son of Seth, the son of Adam, the son of God.

---

[1] Or crying, *Prepare in the wilderness the way of the Lord* [2] Greek *chiton*, a long garment worn under the cloak next to the skin [3] Or *my Son, my* (or *the*) *Beloved* [4] Some manuscripts *beloved Son; today I have begotten you* [5] Greek *Salathiel*

NOVEMBER 20

1 Chronicles 15

David[1] built houses for himself in the city of David. And he prepared a place for the ark of God and pitched a tent for it. ²Then David said that no one but the Levites may carry the ark of God, for the LORD had chosen them to carry the ark of the LORD and to minister to him forever. ³And David assembled all Israel at Jerusalem to bring up the ark of the LORD to its place, which he had prepared for it. ⁴And David gathered together the sons of Aaron and the Levites: ⁵of the sons of Kohath, Uriel the chief, with 120 of his brothers; ⁶of the sons of Merari, Asaiah the chief, with 220 of his brothers; ⁷of the sons of Gershom, Joel the chief, with 130 of his brothers; ⁸of the sons of Elizaphan, Shemaiah the chief, with 200 of his brothers; ⁹of the sons of Hebron, Eliel the chief, with 80 of his brothers; ¹⁰of the sons of Uzziel, Amminadab the chief, with 112 of his brothers. ¹¹Then David summoned the priests Zadok and Abiathar, and the Levites Uriel, Asaiah, Joel, Shemaiah, Eliel, and Amminadab, ¹²and said to them, "You are the heads of the fathers' houses of the Levites. Consecrate yourselves, you and your brothers, so that you may bring up the ark of the LORD, the God of Israel, to the place that I have prepared for it. ¹³Because you did not carry it the first time, the LORD our God broke out against us, because we did not seek him according to the rule." ¹⁴So the priests and the Levites consecrated themselves to bring up the ark of the LORD, the God of Israel. ¹⁵And the Levites carried the ark of God on their shoulders with the poles, as Moses had commanded according to the word of the LORD.

¹⁶David also commanded the chiefs of the Levites to appoint their brothers as the singers who should play loudly on musical instruments, on harps and lyres and cymbals, to raise sounds of joy. ¹⁷So the Levites appointed Heman the son of Joel; and of his brothers Asaph the son of Berechiah; and of the sons of Merari, their brothers, Ethan the son of Kushaiah; ¹⁸and with them their brothers of the second order, Zechariah, Jaaziel, Shemiramoth, Jehiel, Unni, Eliab, Benaiah, Maaseiah, Mattithiah, Eliphelehu, and Mikneiah, and the gatekeepers Obed-edom and Jeiel. ¹⁹The singers, Heman, Asaph, and Ethan, were to sound bronze cymbals; ²⁰Zechariah, Aziel, Shemiramoth, Jehiel, Unni, Eliab, Maaseiah, and Benaiah were to play harps according to Alamoth; ²¹but Mattithiah, Eliphelehu, Mikneiah, Obed-edom, Jeiel, and Azaziah were to lead with lyres according to the Sheminith. ²²Chenaniah, leader of the Levites in music, should direct the music, for he understood it. ²³Berechiah and Elkanah were to be gatekeepers for the ark. ²⁴Shebaniah, Joshaphat, Nethanel, Amasai, Zechariah, Benaiah, and Eliezer, the priests, should blow the trumpets before the ark of God. Obed-edom and Jehiah were to be gatekeepers for the ark.

²⁵So David and the elders of Israel and the commanders of thousands went to bring up the ark of the covenant of the LORD from the house of Obed-edom with rejoicing. ²⁶And because God helped the Levites who were carrying the ark of the covenant of the LORD, they sacrificed seven bulls and seven rams. ²⁷David was clothed with a robe of fine linen, as also were all the Levites who were carrying the ark, and the singers and Chenaniah the leader of the music of the singers. And David wore a linen ephod. ²⁸So all Israel brought up the ark of the covenant of the LORD with shouting, to the sound of the horn, trumpets, and cymbals, and made loud music on harps and lyres.

²⁹And as the ark of the covenant of the LORD came to the city of David, Michal the daughter of Saul looked out of the window and saw King David dancing and celebrating, and she despised him in her heart.

James 2

My brothers,[2] show no partiality as you hold the faith in our Lord Jesus Christ, the Lord of glory. ²For if a man wearing a gold

---

¹ Hebrew *He* ² Or *brothers and sisters*; also verses 5, 14

ring and fine clothing comes into your assembly, and a poor man in shabby clothing also comes in, ³and if you pay attention to the one who wears the fine clothing and say, "You sit here in a good place," while you say to the poor man, "You stand over there," or, "Sit down at my feet," ⁴have you not then made distinctions among yourselves and become judges with evil thoughts? ⁵Listen, my beloved brothers, has not God chosen those who are poor in the world to be rich in faith and heirs of the kingdom, which he has promised to those who love him? ⁶But you have dishonored the poor man. Are not the rich the ones who oppress you, and the ones who drag you into court? ⁷Are they not the ones who blaspheme the honorable name by which you were called?

⁸If you really fulfill the royal law according to the Scripture, "You shall love your neighbor as yourself," you are doing well. ⁹But if you show partiality, you are committing sin and are convicted by the law as transgressors. ¹⁰For whoever keeps the whole law but fails in one point has become accountable for all of it. ¹¹For he who said, "Do not commit adultery," also said, "Do not murder." If you do not commit adultery but do murder, you have become a transgressor of the law. ¹²So speak and so act as those who are to be judged under the law of liberty. ¹³For judgment is without mercy to one who has shown no mercy. Mercy triumphs over judgment.

¹⁴What good is it, my brothers, if someone says he has faith but does not have works? Can that faith save him? ¹⁵If a brother or sister is poorly clothed and lacking in daily food, ¹⁶and one of you says to them, "Go in peace, be warmed and filled," without giving them the things needed for the body, what good[1] is that? ¹⁷So also faith by itself, if it does not have works, is dead.

¹⁸But someone will say, "You have faith and I have works." Show me your faith apart from your works, and I will show you my faith by my works. ¹⁹You believe that God is one; you do well. Even the demons believe—and shudder! ²⁰Do you want to be shown, you foolish person, that faith apart from works is useless? ²¹Was not Abraham our father justified by works when he offered up his son Isaac on the altar? ²²You see that faith was active along with his works, and faith was completed by his works; ²³and the Scripture was fulfilled that says, "Abraham believed God, and it was counted to him as righteousness"—and he was called a friend of God. ²⁴You see that a person is justified by works and not by faith alone. ²⁵And in the same way was not also Rahab the prostitute justified by works when she received the messengers and sent them out by another way? ²⁶For as the body apart from the spirit is dead, so also faith apart from works is dead.

Amos 9

I saw the Lord standing beside[2] the altar, and he said:

"Strike the capitals until the thresholds shake,
  and shatter them on the heads of all the people;[3]
and those who are left of them I will kill with the sword;
  not one of them shall flee away;
  not one of them shall escape.

2   "If they dig into Sheol,
      from there shall my hand take them;
    if they climb up to heaven,
      from there I will bring them down.
3   If they hide themselves on the top of Carmel,
      from there I will search them out and take them;
    and if they hide from my sight at the bottom of the sea,
      there I will command the serpent, and it shall bite them.
4   And if they go into captivity before their enemies,
      there I will command the sword, and it shall kill them;
    and I will fix my eyes upon them
      for evil and not for good."

5   The Lord GOD of hosts,
    he who touches the earth and it melts,
      and all who dwell in it mourn,
    and all of it rises like the Nile,
      and sinks again, like the Nile of Egypt;
6   who builds his upper chambers in the heavens
      and founds his vault upon the earth;

---

[1] Or benefit [2] Or on [3] Hebrew all of them

who calls for the waters of the sea
  and pours them out upon the surface
    of the earth—
  the LORD is his name.
7 "Are you not like the Cushites to me,
    O people of Israel?" declares the
      LORD.
  "Did I not bring up Israel from the land of
      Egypt,
    and the Philistines from Caphtor and
    the Syrians from Kir?
8 Behold, the eyes of the Lord GOD are
      upon the sinful kingdom,
    and I will destroy it from the surface
      of the ground,
    except that I will not utterly destroy
      the house of Jacob,"
                          declares the LORD.
9 "For behold, I will command,
    and shake the house of Israel among
      all the nations
    as one shakes with a sieve,
    but no pebble shall fall to the earth.
10 All the sinners of my people shall die by
      the sword,
    who say, 'Disaster shall not overtake or
      meet us.'
11 "In that day I will raise up
    the booth of David that is fallen
  and repair its breaches,
    and raise up its ruins
    and rebuild it as in the days of old,
12 that they may possess the remnant of
      Edom
    and all the nations who are called by
      my name,"[1]
    declares the LORD who does this.
13 "Behold, the days are coming," declares
      the LORD,
  "when the plowman shall overtake the
      reaper
    and the treader of grapes him who
      sows the seed;
  the mountains shall drip sweet wine,
    and all the hills shall flow with it.
14 I will restore the fortunes of my people
      Israel,
    and they shall rebuild the ruined cities
      and inhabit them;

they shall plant vineyards and drink
      their wine,
    and they shall make gardens and eat
      their fruit.
15 I will plant them on their land,
    and they shall never again be
      uprooted
    out of the land that I have given them,"
            says the LORD your God.

Luke 4

And Jesus, full of the Holy Spirit, returned from the Jordan and was led by the Spirit in the wilderness [2] for forty days, being tempted by the devil. And he ate nothing during those days. And when they were ended, he was hungry. [3] The devil said to him, "If you are the Son of God, command this stone to become bread." [4] And Jesus answered him, "It is written, 'Man shall not live by bread alone.'" [5] And the devil took him up and showed him all the kingdoms of the world in a moment of time, [6] and said to him, "To you I will give all this authority and their glory, for it has been delivered to me, and I give it to whom I will. [7] If you, then, will worship me, it will all be yours." [8] And Jesus answered him, "It is written,

"'You shall worship the Lord your God,
    and him only shall you serve.'"

[9] And he took him to Jerusalem and set him on the pinnacle of the temple and said to him, "If you are the Son of God, throw yourself down from here, [10] for it is written,

"'He will command his angels concerning
      you,
    to guard you,'

[11] and

"'On their hands they will bear you up,
    lest you strike your foot against a
      stone.'"

[12] And Jesus answered him, "It is said, 'You shall not put the Lord your God to the test.'" [13] And when the devil had ended every temptation, he departed from him until an opportune time.
[14] And Jesus returned in the power of the Spirit to Galilee, and a report about him went out through all the surrounding country. [15] And

---

[1] Hebrew; Septuagint (compare Acts 15:17) that the remnant of mankind and all the nations who are called by my name may seek the Lord

he taught in their synagogues, being glorified by all.

[16]And he came to Nazareth, where he had been brought up. And as was his custom, he went to the synagogue on the Sabbath day, and he stood up to read. [17]And the scroll of the prophet Isaiah was given to him. He unrolled the scroll and found the place where it was written,

[18]   "The Spirit of the Lord is upon me,
       because he has anointed me
         to proclaim good news to the poor.
       He has sent me to proclaim liberty to the
         captives
       and recovering of sight to the blind,
       to set at liberty those who are
         oppressed,
[19]   to proclaim the year of the Lord's favor."

[20]And he rolled up the scroll and gave it back to the attendant and sat down. And the eyes of all in the synagogue were fixed on him. [21]And he began to say to them, "Today this Scripture has been fulfilled in your hearing." [22]And all spoke well of him and marveled at the gracious words that were coming from his mouth. And they said, "Is not this Joseph's son?" [23]And he said to them, "Doubtless you will quote to me this proverb, 'Physician, heal yourself.' What we have heard you did at Capernaum, do here in your hometown as well." [24]And he said, "Truly, I say to you, no prophet is acceptable in his hometown. [25]But in truth, I tell you, there were many widows in Israel in the days of Elijah, when the heavens were shut up three years and six months, and a great famine came over all the land, [26]and Elijah was sent to none of them but only to Zarephath, in the land of Sidon, to a woman who was a widow. [27]And there were many lepers[1] in Israel in the time of the prophet Elisha, and none of them was cleansed, but only Naaman the Syrian." [28]When they heard these things, all in the synagogue were filled with wrath. [29]And they rose up and drove him out of the town and brought him to the brow of the hill on which their town was built, so that they could throw him down the cliff. [30]But passing through their midst, he went away.

[31]And he went down to Capernaum, a city of Galilee. And he was teaching them on the Sabbath, [32]and they were astonished at his teaching, for his word possessed authority. [33]And in the synagogue there was a man who had the spirit of an unclean demon, and he cried out with a loud voice, [34]"Ha![2] What have you to do with us, Jesus of Nazareth? Have you come to destroy us? I know who you are—the Holy One of God." [35]But Jesus rebuked him, saying, "Be silent and come out of him!" And when the demon had thrown him down in their midst, he came out of him, having done him no harm. [36]And they were all amazed and said to one another, "What is this word? For with authority and power he commands the unclean spirits, and they come out!" [37]And reports about him went out into every place in the surrounding region.

[38]And he arose and left the synagogue and entered Simon's house. Now Simon's mother-in-law was ill with a high fever, and they appealed to him on her behalf. [39]And he stood over her and rebuked the fever, and it left her, and immediately she rose and began to serve them.

[40]Now when the sun was setting, all those who had any who were sick with various diseases brought them to him, and he laid his hands on every one of them and healed them. [41]And demons also came out of many, crying, "You are the Son of God!" But he rebuked them and would not allow them to speak, because they knew that he was the Christ.

[42]And when it was day, he departed and went into a desolate place. And the people sought him and came to him, and would have kept him from leaving them, [43]but he said to them, "I must preach the good news of the kingdom of God to the other towns as well; for I was sent for this purpose." [44]And he was preaching in the synagogues of Judea.[3]

[1] *Leprosy* was a term for several skin diseases; see Leviticus 13 [2] Or *Leave us alone* [3] Some manuscripts *Galilee*

NOVEMBER 21

1 Chronicles 16

And they brought in the ark of God and set it inside the tent that David had pitched for it, and they offered burnt offerings and peace offerings before God. ²And when David had finished offering the burnt offerings and the peace offerings, he blessed the people in the name of the LORD ³and distributed to all Israel, both men and women, to each a loaf of bread, a portion of meat,[1] and a cake of raisins.

⁴Then he appointed some of the Levites as ministers before the ark of the LORD, to invoke, to thank, and to praise the LORD, the God of Israel. ⁵Asaph was the chief, and second to him were Zechariah, Jeiel, Shemiramoth, Jehiel, Mattithiah, Eliab, Benaiah, Obed-edom, and Jeiel, who were to play harps and lyres; Asaph was to sound the cymbals, ⁶and Benaiah and Jahaziel the priests were to blow trumpets regularly before the ark of the covenant of God. ⁷Then on that day David first appointed that thanksgiving be sung to the LORD by Asaph and his brothers.

8   Oh give thanks to the LORD; call upon
          his name;
        make known his deeds among the
          peoples!
9   Sing to him, sing praises to him;
        tell of all his wondrous works!
10   Glory in his holy name;
        let the hearts of those who seek the
          LORD rejoice!
11   Seek the LORD and his strength;
        seek his presence continually!
12   Remember the wondrous works that he
          has done,
        his miracles and the judgments he
          uttered,
13   O offspring of Israel his servant,
        children of Jacob, his chosen ones!
14   He is the LORD our God;
        his judgments are in all the earth.
15   Remember his covenant forever,

        the word that he commanded, for a
          thousand generations,
16   the covenant that he made with
          Abraham,
        his sworn promise to Isaac,
17   which he confirmed to Jacob as a
          statute,
        to Israel as an everlasting covenant,
18   saying, "To you I will give the land of
          Canaan,
        as your portion for an inheritance."

19   When you were few in number,
        of little account, and sojourners in it,
20   wandering from nation to nation,
        from one kingdom to another
          people,
21   he allowed no one to oppress them;
        he rebuked kings on their account,
22   saying, "Touch not my anointed ones,
        do my prophets no harm!"

23   Sing to the LORD, all the earth!
        Tell of his salvation from day to day.
24   Declare his glory among the nations,
        his marvelous works among all the
          peoples!
25   For great is the LORD, and greatly to be
          praised,
        and he is to be feared above all gods.
26   For all the gods of the peoples are
          worthless idols,
        but the LORD made the heavens.
27   Splendor and majesty are before him;
        strength and joy are in his place.

28   Ascribe to the LORD, O families of the
          peoples,
        ascribe to the LORD glory and
          strength!
29   Ascribe to the LORD the glory due his
          name;
        bring an offering and come before
          him!
      Worship the LORD in the splendor of
          holiness;[2]

---

[1] Compare Septuagint, Syriac, Vulgate; the meaning of the Hebrew is uncertain   [2] Or *in holy attire*

30   tremble before him, all the earth;
      yes, the world is established; it shall
        never be moved.
31   Let the heavens be glad, and let the
        earth rejoice,
      and let them say among the nations,
        "The LORD reigns!"
32   Let the sea roar, and all that fills it;
      let the field exult, and everything in
        it!
33   Then shall the trees of the forest sing for
        joy
      before the LORD, for he comes to
        judge the earth.
34   Oh give thanks to the LORD, for he is
        good;
      for his steadfast love endures
        forever!

35 Say also:

    "Save us, O God of our salvation,
      and gather and deliver us from among
        the nations,
    that we may give thanks to your holy
        name
      and glory in your praise.
36   Blessed be the LORD, the God of Israel,
      from everlasting to everlasting!"

Then all the people said, "Amen!" and praised
the LORD.

37 So David left Asaph and his brothers there
before the ark of the covenant of the LORD to
minister regularly before the ark as each day
required, 38 and also Obed-edom and his[1] sixty-
eight brothers, while Obed-edom, the son of
Jeduthun, and Hosah were to be gatekeepers.
39 And he left Zadok the priest and his brothers
the priests before the tabernacle of the LORD
in the high place that was at Gibeon 40 to offer
burnt offerings to the LORD on the altar of
burnt offering regularly morning and evening,
to do all that is written in the Law of the LORD
that he commanded Israel. 41 With them were
Heman and Jeduthun and the rest of those
chosen and expressly named to give thanks to
the LORD, for his steadfast love endures forever. 42 Heman and Jeduthun had trumpets
and cymbals for the music and instruments
for sacred song. The sons of Jeduthun were
appointed to the gate.
43 Then all the people departed each to

his house, and David went home to bless his
household.

——————— *James 3* ———————

Not many of you should become teachers, my brothers, for you know that we
who teach will be judged with greater strictness. 2 For we all stumble in many ways. And
if anyone does not stumble in what he says,
he is a perfect man, able also to bridle his
whole body. 3 If we put bits into the mouths
of horses so that they obey us, we guide their
whole bodies as well. 4 Look at the ships also:
though they are so large and are driven by
strong winds, they are guided by a very small
rudder wherever the will of the pilot directs.
5 So also the tongue is a small member, yet it
boasts of great things.

How great a forest is set ablaze by such a
small fire! 6 And the tongue is a fire, a world
of unrighteousness. The tongue is set among
our members, staining the whole body, setting
on fire the entire course of life,[2] and set on
fire by hell.[3] 7 For every kind of beast and bird,
of reptile and sea creature, can be tamed and
has been tamed by mankind, 8 but no human
being can tame the tongue. It is a restless evil,
full of deadly poison. 9 With it we bless our
Lord and Father, and with it we curse people
who are made in the likeness of God. 10 From
the same mouth come blessing and cursing.
My brothers,[4] these things ought not to be
so. 11 Does a spring pour forth from the same
opening both fresh and salt water? 12 Can a fig
tree, my brothers, bear olives, or a grapevine
produce figs? Neither can a salt pond yield
fresh water.

13 Who is wise and understanding among
you? By his good conduct let him show his
works in the meekness of wisdom. 14 But if
you have bitter jealousy and selfish ambition
in your hearts, do not boast and be false to the
truth. 15 This is not the wisdom that comes
down from above, but is earthly, unspiritual,
demonic. 16 For where jealousy and selfish
ambition exist, there will be disorder and every
vile practice. 17 But the wisdom from above is
first pure, then peaceable, gentle, open to reason, full of mercy and good fruits, impartial
and sincere. 18 And a harvest of righteousness
is sown in peace by those who make peace.

[1] Hebrew *their* [2] Or *wheel of birth* [3] Greek *Gehenna* [4] Or *brothers and sisters; also verse 12*

Obadiah 1

The vision of Obadiah.

Thus says the Lord GOD concerning
  Edom:
We have heard a report from the LORD,
  and a messenger has been sent among
    the nations:
"Rise up! Let us rise against her for
    battle!"
2 Behold, I will make you small among
    the nations;
  you shall be utterly despised.[1]
3 The pride of your heart has deceived
    you,
  you who live in the clefts of the rock,[2]
    in your lofty dwelling,
  who say in your heart,
    "Who will bring me down to the
      ground?"
4 Though you soar aloft like the eagle,
    though your nest is set among the
      stars,
  from there I will bring you down,
          declares the LORD.

5 If thieves came to you,
    if plunderers came by night—
  how you have been destroyed!—
  would they not steal only enough for
    themselves?
  If grape gatherers came to you,
    would they not leave gleanings?
6 How Esau has been pillaged,
    his treasures sought out!
7 All your allies have driven you to your
    border;
  those at peace with you have deceived
    you;
  they have prevailed against you;
  those who eat your bread[3] have set a
    trap beneath you—
  you have[4] no understanding.
8 Will I not on that day, declares the
    LORD,
  destroy the wise men out of Edom,
    and understanding out of Mount Esau?
9 And your mighty men shall be
    dismayed, O Teman,
  so that every man from Mount Esau
    will be cut off by slaughter.

10 Because of the violence done to your
    brother Jacob,
  shame shall cover you,
    and you shall be cut off forever.
11 On the day that you stood aloof,
  on the day that strangers carried off
    his wealth
  and foreigners entered his gates
    and cast lots for Jerusalem,
  you were like one of them.
12 But do not gloat over the day of your
    brother
  in the day of his misfortune;
  do not rejoice over the people of Judah
    in the day of their ruin;
  do not boast[5]
    in the day of distress.
13 Do not enter the gate of my people
    in the day of their calamity;
  do not gloat over his disaster
    in the day of his calamity;
  do not loot his wealth
    in the day of his calamity.
14 Do not stand at the crossroads
    to cut off his fugitives;
  do not hand over his survivors
    in the day of distress.

15 For the day of the LORD is near upon all
    the nations.
  As you have done, it shall be done to you;
    your deeds shall return on your own
      head.
16 For as you have drunk on my holy
    mountain,
  so all the nations shall drink
    continually;
  they shall drink and swallow,
    and shall be as though they had never
      been.
17 But in Mount Zion there shall be those
    who escape,
  and it shall be holy,
  and the house of Jacob shall possess
    their own possessions.
18 The house of Jacob shall be a fire,
    and the house of Joseph a flame,
    and the house of Esau stubble;
  they shall burn them and consume them,
  and there shall be no survivor for the
    house of Esau,
          for the LORD has spoken.

---

[1] Or Behold, I have made you small among the nations; you are utterly despised [2] Or Sela [3] Hebrew lacks those who eat [4] Hebrew he has [5] Hebrew do not enlarge your mouth

19 Those of the Negeb shall possess Mount
      Esau,
         and those of the Shephelah shall
            possess the land of the Philistines;
      they shall possess the land of Ephraim
            and the land of Samaria,
         and Benjamin shall possess Gilead.
20 The exiles of this host of the people of
      Israel
         shall possess the land of the
            Canaanites as far as Zarephath,
      and the exiles of Jerusalem who are in
         Sepharad
         shall possess the cities of the Negeb.
21 Saviors shall go up to Mount Zion
      to rule Mount Esau,
         and the kingdom shall be the LORD's.

Luke 5

On one occasion, while the crowd was pressing in on him to hear the word of God, he
was standing by the lake of Gennesaret, [2] and
he saw two boats by the lake, but the fishermen
had gone out of them and were washing their
nets. [3] Getting into one of the boats, which was
Simon's, he asked him to put out a little from
the land. And he sat down and taught the people from the boat. [4] And when he had finished
speaking, he said to Simon, "Put out into the
deep and let down your nets for a catch." [5] And
Simon answered, "Master, we toiled all night
and took nothing! But at your word I will let
down the nets." [6] And when they had done this,
they enclosed a large number of fish, and their
nets were breaking. [7] They signaled to their partners in the other boat to come and help them.
And they came and filled both the boats, so that
they began to sink. [8] But when Simon Peter saw
it, he fell down at Jesus' knees, saying, "Depart
from me, for I am a sinful man, O Lord." [9] For
he and all who were with him were astonished
at the catch of fish that they had taken, [10] and
so also were James and John, sons of Zebedee,
who were partners with Simon. And Jesus said
to Simon, "Do not be afraid; from now on you
will be catching men."[1] [11] And when they had
brought their boats to land, they left everything
and followed him.

[12] While he was in one of the cities, there
came a man full of leprosy.[2] And when he saw
Jesus, he fell on his face and begged him, "Lord,

if you will, you can make me clean." [13] And
Jesus[3] stretched out his hand and touched
him, saying, "I will; be clean." And immediately
the leprosy left him. [14] And he charged him to
tell no one, but "go and show yourself to the
priest, and make an offering for your cleansing, as Moses commanded, for a proof to them."
[15] But now even more the report about him
went abroad, and great crowds gathered to hear
him and to be healed of their infirmities. [16] But
he would withdraw to desolate places and pray.

[17] On one of those days, as he was teaching,
Pharisees and teachers of the law were sitting there, who had come from every village
of Galilee and Judea and from Jerusalem. And
the power of the Lord was with him to heal.[4]
[18] And behold, some men were bringing on a
bed a man who was paralyzed, and they were
seeking to bring him in and lay him before
Jesus, [19] but finding no way to bring him in,
because of the crowd, they went up on the
roof and let him down with his bed through
the tiles into the midst before Jesus. [20] And
when he saw their faith, he said, "Man, your
sins are forgiven you." [21] And the scribes and
the Pharisees began to question, saying, "Who
is this who speaks blasphemies? Who can forgive sins but God alone?" [22] When Jesus perceived their thoughts, he answered them, "Why
do you question in your hearts? [23] Which is
easier, to say, 'Your sins are forgiven you,' or to
say, 'Rise and walk'? [24] But that you may know
that the Son of Man has authority on earth
to forgive sins"—he said to the man who was
paralyzed—"I say to you, rise, pick up your bed
and go home." [25] And immediately he rose up
before them and picked up what he had been
lying on and went home, glorifying God. [26] And
amazement seized them all, and they glorified
God and were filled with awe, saying, "We have
seen extraordinary things today."

[27] After this he went out and saw a tax collector named Levi, sitting at the tax booth. And he
said to him, "Follow me." [28] And leaving everything, he rose and followed him.

[29] And Levi made him a great feast in his
house, and there was a large company of tax
collectors and others reclining at table with
them. [30] And the Pharisees and their scribes
grumbled at his disciples, saying, "Why do you
eat and drink with tax collectors and sinners?"
[31] And Jesus answered them, "Those who are

---

[1] The Greek word *anthropoi* refers here to both men and women [2] *Leprosy* was a term for several skin diseases; see Leviticus 13 [3] Greek *he* [4] Some manuscripts *was present to heal them*

well have no need of a physician, but those who are sick. [32]I have not come to call the righteous but sinners to repentance."

[33]And they said to him, "The disciples of John fast often and offer prayers, and so do the disciples of the Pharisees, but yours eat and drink." [34]And Jesus said to them, "Can you make wedding guests fast while the bridegroom is with them? [35]The days will come when the bridegroom is taken away from them, and then they will fast in those days."

[36]He also told them a parable: "No one tears a piece from a new garment and puts it on an old garment. If he does, he will tear the new, and the piece from the new will not match the old. [37]And no one puts new wine into old wineskins. If he does, the new wine will burst the skins and it will be spilled, and the skins will be destroyed. [38]But new wine must be put into fresh wineskins. [39]And no one after drinking old wine desires new, for he says, 'The old is good.'"[1]

NOVEMBER 22

1 Chronicles 17

Now when David lived in his house, David said to Nathan the prophet, "Behold, I dwell in a house of cedar, but the ark of the covenant of the LORD is under a tent." [2]And Nathan said to David, "Do all that is in your heart, for God is with you."

[3]But that same night the word of the LORD came to Nathan, [4]"Go and tell my servant David, 'Thus says the LORD: It is not you who will build me a house to dwell in. [5]For I have not lived in a house since the day I brought up Israel to this day, but I have gone from tent to tent and from dwelling to dwelling. [6]In all places where I have moved with all Israel, did I speak a word with any of the judges of Israel, whom I commanded to shepherd my people, saying, "Why have you not built me a house of cedar?"' [7]Now, therefore, thus shall you say to my servant David, 'Thus says the LORD of hosts, I took you from the pasture, from following the sheep, to be prince over my people Israel, [8]and I have been with you wherever you have gone and have cut off all your enemies from before you. And I will make for you a name, like the name of the great ones of the earth. [9]And I will appoint a place for my people Israel and will plant them, that they may dwell in their own place and be disturbed no more. And violent men shall waste them no more, as formerly, [10]from the time that I appointed judges over my people Israel. And I will subdue all your enemies. Moreover, I declare to you that the LORD will build you a house. [11]When your days are fulfilled to walk with your fathers, I will raise up your offspring after you, one of your own sons, and I will establish his kingdom. [12]He shall build a house for me, and I will establish his throne forever. [13]I will be to him a father, and he shall be to me a son. I will not take my steadfast love from him, as I took it from him who was before you, [14]but I will confirm him in my house and in my kingdom forever, and his throne shall be established forever.'" [15]In accordance with all these words, and in accordance with all this vision, Nathan spoke to David.

[16]Then King David went in and sat before the LORD and said, "Who am I, O LORD God, and what is my house, that you have brought me thus far? [17]And this was a small thing in your eyes, O God. You have also spoken of your servant's house for a great while to come, and have shown me future generations,[2] O LORD God! [18]And what more can David say to you for honoring your servant? For you know your servant. [19]For your servant's sake, O LORD, and according to your own heart, you have done all this greatness, in making known all these great things. [20]There is none like you, O LORD, and there is no God besides you, according to

all that we have heard with our ears. ²¹And who is like your people Israel, the one¹ nation on earth whom God went to redeem to be his people, making for yourself a name for great and awesome things, in driving out nations before your people whom you redeemed from Egypt? ²²And you made your people Israel to be your people forever, and you, O LORD, became their God. ²³And now, O LORD, let the word that you have spoken concerning your servant and concerning his house be established forever, and do as you have spoken, ²⁴and your name will be established and magnified forever, saying, 'The LORD of hosts, the God of Israel, is Israel's God,' and the house of your servant David will be established before you. ²⁵For you, my God, have revealed to your servant that you will build a house for him. Therefore your servant has found courage to pray before you. ²⁶And now, O LORD, you are God, and you have promised this good thing to your servant. ²⁷Now you have been pleased to bless the house of your servant, that it may continue forever before you, for it is you, O LORD, who have blessed, and it is blessed forever."

James 4

What causes quarrels and what causes fights among you? Is it not this, that your passions² are at war within you?³ ²You desire and do not have, so you murder. You covet and cannot obtain, so you fight and quarrel. You do not have, because you do not ask. ³You ask and do not receive, because you ask wrongly, to spend it on your passions. ⁴You adulterous people!⁴ Do you not know that friendship with the world is enmity with God? Therefore whoever wishes to be a friend of the world makes himself an enemy of God. ⁵Or do you suppose it is to no purpose that the Scripture says, "He yearns jealously over the spirit that he has made to dwell in us"? ⁶But he gives more grace. Therefore it says, "God opposes the proud, but gives grace to the humble." ⁷Submit yourselves therefore to God. Resist the devil, and he will flee from you. ⁸Draw near to God, and he will draw near to you. Cleanse your hands, you sinners, and purify your hearts, you double-minded. ⁹Be wretched and mourn and weep. Let your laughter be turned to mourning and

your joy to gloom. ¹⁰Humble yourselves before the Lord, and he will exalt you.

¹¹Do not speak evil against one another, brothers.⁵ The one who speaks against a brother or judges his brother, speaks evil against the law and judges the law. But if you judge the law, you are not a doer of the law but a judge. ¹²There is only one lawgiver and judge, he who is able to save and to destroy. But who are you to judge your neighbor?

¹³Come now, you who say, "Today or tomorrow we will go into such and such a town and spend a year there and trade and make a profit"— ¹⁴yet you do not know what tomorrow will bring. What is your life? For you are a mist that appears for a little time and then vanishes. ¹⁵Instead you ought to say, "If the Lord wills, we will live and do this or that." ¹⁶As it is, you boast in your arrogance. All such boasting is evil. ¹⁷So whoever knows the right thing to do and fails to do it, for him it is sin.

Jonah 1

Now the word of the LORD came to Jonah the son of Amittai, saying, ²"Arise, go to Nineveh, that great city, and call out against it, for their evil⁶ has come up before me." ³But Jonah rose to flee to Tarshish from the presence of the LORD. He went down to Joppa and found a ship going to Tarshish. So he paid the fare and went down into it, to go with them to Tarshish, away from the presence of the LORD.

⁴But the LORD hurled a great wind upon the sea, and there was a mighty tempest on the sea, so that the ship threatened to break up. ⁵Then the mariners were afraid, and each cried out to his god. And they hurled the cargo that was in the ship into the sea to lighten it for them. But Jonah had gone down into the inner part of the ship and had lain down and was fast asleep. ⁶So the captain came and said to him, "What do you mean, you sleeper? Arise, call out to your god! Perhaps the god will give a thought to us, that we may not perish."

⁷And they said to one another, "Come, let us cast lots, that we may know on whose account this evil has come upon us." So they cast lots, and the lot fell on Jonah. ⁸Then they said to him, "Tell us on whose account this evil has come upon us. What is your occupation? And where do you come from? What is your

---

¹ Septuagint, Vulgate *other* ² Greek *pleasures*; also verse 3 ³ Greek *in your members* ⁴ Greek *You adulteresses!* ⁵ Or *brothers and sisters* ⁶ The same Hebrew word can mean *evil* or *disaster*, depending on the context; so throughout Jonah

country? And of what people are you?" **9**And he said to them, "I am a Hebrew, and I fear the LORD, the God of heaven, who made the sea and the dry land." **10**Then the men were exceedingly afraid and said to him, "What is this that you have done!" For the men knew that he was fleeing from the presence of the LORD, because he had told them.

11Then they said to him, "What shall we do to you, that the sea may quiet down for us?" For the sea grew more and more tempestuous. **12**He said to them, "Pick me up and hurl me into the sea; then the sea will quiet down for you, for I know it is because of me that this great tempest has come upon you." **13**Nevertheless, the men rowed hard[1] to get back to dry land, but they could not, for the sea grew more and more tempestuous against them. **14**Therefore they called out to the LORD, "O LORD, let us not perish for this man's life, and lay not on us innocent blood, for you, O LORD, have done as it pleased you." **15**So they picked up Jonah and hurled him into the sea, and the sea ceased from its raging. **16**Then the men feared the LORD exceedingly, and they offered a sacrifice to the LORD and made vows.

17[2] And the LORD appointed[3] a great fish to swallow up Jonah. And Jonah was in the belly of the fish three days and three nights.

Luke 6

On a Sabbath,[4] while he was going through the grainfields, his disciples plucked and ate some heads of grain, rubbing them in their hands. **2**But some of the Pharisees said, "Why are you doing what is not lawful to do on the Sabbath?" **3**And Jesus answered them, "Have you not read what David did when he was hungry, he and those who were with him: **4**how he entered the house of God and took and ate the bread of the Presence, which is not lawful for any but the priests to eat, and also gave it to those with him?" **5**And he said to them, "The Son of Man is lord of the Sabbath."

6On another Sabbath, he entered the synagogue and was teaching, and a man was there whose right hand was withered. **7**And the scribes and the Pharisees watched him, to see whether he would heal on the Sabbath, so that they might find a reason to accuse him. **8**But he knew their thoughts, and he said to the man with the withered hand, "Come and stand here." And he rose and stood there. **9**And Jesus said to them, "I ask you, is it lawful on the Sabbath to do good or to do harm, to save life or to destroy it?" **10**And after looking around at them all he said to him, "Stretch out your hand." And he did so, and his hand was restored. **11**But they were filled with fury and discussed with one another what they might do to Jesus.

12In these days he went out to the mountain to pray, and all night he continued in prayer to God. **13**And when day came, he called his disciples and chose from them twelve, whom he named apostles: **14**Simon, whom he named Peter, and Andrew his brother, and James and John, and Philip, and Bartholomew, **15**and Matthew, and Thomas, and James the son of Alphaeus, and Simon who was called the Zealot, **16**and Judas the son of James, and Judas Iscariot, who became a traitor.

17And he came down with them and stood on a level place, with a great crowd of his disciples and a great multitude of people from all Judea and Jerusalem and the seacoast of Tyre and Sidon, **18**who came to hear him and to be healed of their diseases. And those who were troubled with unclean spirits were cured. **19**And all the crowd sought to touch him, for power came out from him and healed them all.

20And he lifted up his eyes on his disciples, and said:

"Blessed are you who are poor, for yours is the kingdom of God.

21"Blessed are you who are hungry now, for you shall be satisfied.

"Blessed are you who weep now, for you shall laugh.

22"Blessed are you when people hate you and when they exclude you and revile you and spurn your name as evil, on account of the Son of Man! **23**Rejoice in that day, and leap for joy, for behold, your reward is great in heaven; for so their fathers did to the prophets.

24"But woe to you who are rich, for you have received your consolation.

25"Woe to you who are full now, for you shall be hungry.

"Woe to you who laugh now, for you shall mourn and weep.

26"Woe to you, when all people speak well of you, for so their fathers did to the false prophets.

²⁷"But I say to you who hear, Love your enemies, do good to those who hate you, ²⁸bless those who curse you, pray for those who abuse you. ²⁹To one who strikes you on the cheek, offer the other also, and from one who takes away your cloak do not withhold your tunic¹ either. ³⁰Give to everyone who begs from you, and from one who takes away your goods do not demand them back. ³¹And as you wish that others would do to you, do so to them.

³²"If you love those who love you, what benefit is that to you? For even sinners love those who love them. ³³And if you do good to those who do good to you, what benefit is that to you? For even sinners do the same. ³⁴And if you lend to those from whom you expect to receive, what credit is that to you? Even sinners lend to sinners, to get back the same amount. ³⁵But love your enemies, and do good, and lend, expecting nothing in return, and your reward will be great, and you will be sons of the Most High, for he is kind to the ungrateful and the evil. ³⁶Be merciful, even as your Father is merciful.

³⁷"Judge not, and you will not be judged; condemn not, and you will not be condemned; forgive, and you will be forgiven; ³⁸give, and it will be given to you. Good measure, pressed down, shaken together, running over, will be put into your lap. For with the measure you use it will be measured back to you."

³⁹He also told them a parable: "Can a blind man lead a blind man? Will they not both fall into a pit? ⁴⁰A disciple is not above his teacher, but everyone when he is fully trained will be like his teacher. ⁴¹Why do you see the speck that is in your brother's eye, but do not notice the log that is in your own eye? ⁴²How can you say to your brother, 'Brother, let me take out the speck that is in your eye,' when you yourself do not see the log that is in your own eye? You hypocrite, first take the log out of your own eye, and then you will see clearly to take out the speck that is in your brother's eye.

⁴³"For no good tree bears bad fruit, nor again does a bad tree bear good fruit, ⁴⁴for each tree is known by its own fruit. For figs are not gathered from thornbushes, nor are grapes picked from a bramble bush. ⁴⁵The good person out of the good treasure of his heart produces good, and the evil person out of his evil treasure produces evil, for out of the abundance of the heart his mouth speaks.

⁴⁶"Why do you call me 'Lord, Lord,' and not do what I tell you? ⁴⁷Everyone who comes to me and hears my words and does them, I will show you what he is like: ⁴⁸he is like a man building a house, who dug deep and laid the foundation on the rock. And when a flood arose, the stream broke against that house and could not shake it, because it had been well built.² ⁴⁹But the one who hears and does not do them is like a man who built a house on the ground without a foundation. When the stream broke against it, immediately it fell, and the ruin of that house was great."

NOVEMBER 23

1 Chronicles 18

After this David defeated the Philistines and subdued them, and he took Gath and its villages out of the hand of the Philistines.

²And he defeated Moab, and the Moabites became servants to David and brought tribute.

³David also defeated Hadadezer king of Zobah-Hamath, as he went to set up his monument³ at the river Euphrates. ⁴And David took from him 1,000 chariots, 7,000 horsemen, and 20,000 foot soldiers. And David hamstrung all the chariot horses, but left enough for 100 chariots. ⁵And when the Syrians of Damascus came to help Hadadezer king of Zobah, David struck down 22,000 men of the Syrians. ⁶Then David put garrisons⁴ in Syria of Damascus, and the Syrians became servants to David and

---

¹ Greek *chiton*, a long garment worn under the cloak next to the skin ² Some manuscripts *founded upon the rock* ³ Hebrew *hand* ⁴ Septuagint, Vulgate, 2 Samuel 8:6 (compare Syriac); Hebrew lacks *garrisons*

brought tribute. And the LORD gave victory to David[1] wherever he went. [7]And David took the shields of gold that were carried by the servants of Hadadezer and brought them to Jerusalem. [8]And from Tibhath and from Cun, cities of Hadadezer, David took a large amount of bronze. With it Solomon made the bronze sea and the pillars and the vessels of bronze.

[9]When Tou king of Hamath heard that David had defeated the whole army of Hadadezer, king of Zobah, [10]he sent his son Hadoram to King David, to ask about his health and to bless him because he had fought against Hadadezer and defeated him; for Hadadezer had often been at war with Tou. And he sent all sorts of articles of gold, of silver, and of bronze. [11]These also King David dedicated to the LORD, together with the silver and gold that he had carried off from all the nations, from Edom, Moab, the Ammonites, the Philistines, and Amalek.

[12]And Abishai, the son of Zeruiah, killed 18,000 Edomites in the Valley of Salt. [13]Then he put garrisons in Edom, and all the Edomites became David's servants. And the LORD gave victory to David wherever he went.

[14]So David reigned over all Israel, and he administered justice and equity to all his people. [15]And Joab the son of Zeruiah was over the army; and Jehoshaphat the son of Ahilud was recorder; [16]and Zadok the son of Ahitub and Ahimelech the son of Abiathar were priests; and Shavsha was secretary; [17]and Benaiah the son of Jehoiada was over the Cherethites and the Pelethites; and David's sons were the chief officials in the service of the king.

James 5

Come now, you rich, weep and howl for the miseries that are coming upon you. [2]Your riches have rotted and your garments are moth-eaten. [3]Your gold and silver have corroded, and their corrosion will be evidence against you and will eat your flesh like fire. You have laid up treasure in the last days. [4]Behold, the wages of the laborers who mowed your fields, which you kept back by fraud, are crying out against you, and the cries of the harvesters have reached the ears of the Lord of hosts. [5]You have lived on the earth in luxury and in self-indulgence. You have fattened your hearts in a day of slaughter.

[6]You have condemned and murdered the righteous person. He does not resist you.

[7]Be patient, therefore, brothers,[2] until the coming of the Lord. See how the farmer waits for the precious fruit of the earth, being patient about it, until it receives the early and the late rains. [8]You also, be patient. Establish your hearts, for the coming of the Lord is at hand. [9]Do not grumble against one another, brothers, so that you may not be judged; behold, the Judge is standing at the door. [10]As an example of suffering and patience, brothers, take the prophets who spoke in the name of the Lord. [11]Behold, we consider those blessed who remained steadfast. You have heard of the steadfastness of Job, and you have seen the purpose of the Lord, how the Lord is compassionate and merciful.

[12]But above all, my brothers, do not swear, either by heaven or by earth or by any other oath, but let your "yes" be yes and your "no" be no, so that you may not fall under condemnation.

[13]Is anyone among you suffering? Let him pray. Is anyone cheerful? Let him sing praise. [14]Is anyone among you sick? Let him call for the elders of the church, and let them pray over him, anointing him with oil in the name of the Lord. [15]And the prayer of faith will save the one who is sick, and the Lord will raise him up. And if he has committed sins, he will be forgiven. [16]Therefore, confess your sins to one another and pray for one another, that you may be healed. The prayer of a righteous person has great power as it is working.[3] [17]Elijah was a man with a nature like ours, and he prayed fervently that it might not rain, and for three years and six months it did not rain on the earth. [18]Then he prayed again, and heaven gave rain, and the earth bore its fruit.

[19]My brothers, if anyone among you wanders from the truth and someone brings him back, [20]let him know that whoever brings back a sinner from his wandering will save his soul from death and will cover a multitude of sins.

Jonah 2

Then Jonah prayed to the LORD his God from the belly of the fish, [2]saying,

"I called out to the LORD, out of my distress,
and he answered me;

[1] Hebrew the LORD saved David; also verse 13 [2] Or brothers and sisters; also verses 9, 10, 12, 19 [3] Or The effective prayer of a righteous person has great power

out of the belly of Sheol I cried,
  and you heard my voice.
3 For you cast me into the deep,
    into the heart of the seas,
    and the flood surrounded me;
  all your waves and your billows
    passed over me.
4 Then I said, 'I am driven away
    from your sight;
  yet I shall again look
    upon your holy temple.'
5 The waters closed in over me to take my
    life;
    the deep surrounded me;
  weeds were wrapped about my head
6   at the roots of the mountains.
  I went down to the land
    whose bars closed upon me forever;
  yet you brought up my life from the pit,
    O LORD my God.
7 When my life was fainting away,
    I remembered the LORD,
  and my prayer came to you,
    into your holy temple.
8 Those who pay regard to vain idols
    forsake their hope of steadfast love.
9 But I with the voice of thanksgiving
    will sacrifice to you;
  what I have vowed I will pay.
    Salvation belongs to the LORD!"

[10]And the LORD spoke to the fish, and it vomited Jonah out upon the dry land.

——— Luke 7 ———

After he had finished all his sayings in the hearing of the people, he entered Capernaum. [2]Now a centurion had a servant[1] who was sick and at the point of death, who was highly valued by him. [3]When the centurion[2] heard about Jesus, he sent to him elders of the Jews, asking him to come and heal his servant. [4]And when they came to Jesus, they pleaded with him earnestly, saying, "He is worthy to have you do this for him, [5]for he loves our nation, and he is the one who built us our synagogue." [6]And Jesus went with them. When he was not far from the house, the centurion sent friends, saying to him, "Lord, do not trouble yourself, for I am not worthy to have you come under my roof. [7]Therefore I did not presume

to come to you. But say the word, and let my servant be healed. [8]For I too am a man set under authority, with soldiers under me: and I say to one, 'Go,' and he goes; and to another, 'Come,' and he comes; and to my servant, 'Do this,' and he does it." [9]When Jesus heard these things, he marveled at him, and turning to the crowd that followed him, said, "I tell you, not even in Israel have I found such faith." [10]And when those who had been sent returned to the house, they found the servant well.

[11]Soon afterward[3] he went to a town called Nain, and his disciples and a great crowd went with him. [12]As he drew near to the gate of the town, behold, a man who had died was being carried out, the only son of his mother, and she was a widow, and a considerable crowd from the town was with her. [13]And when the Lord saw her, he had compassion on her and said to her, "Do not weep." [14]Then he came up and touched the bier, and the bearers stood still. And he said, "Young man, I say to you, arise." [15]And the dead man sat up and began to speak, and Jesus[4] gave him to his mother. [16]Fear seized them all, and they glorified God, saying, "A great prophet has arisen among us!" and "God has visited his people!" [17]And this report about him spread through the whole of Judea and all the surrounding country.

[18]The disciples of John reported all these things to him. And John, [19]calling two of his disciples to him, sent them to the Lord, saying, "Are you the one who is to come, or shall we look for another?" [20]And when the men had come to him, they said, "John the Baptist has sent us to you, saying, 'Are you the one who is to come, or shall we look for another?'" [21]In that hour he healed many people of diseases and plagues and evil spirits, and on many who were blind he bestowed sight. [22]And he answered them, "Go and tell John what you have seen and heard: the blind receive their sight, the lame walk, lepers[5] are cleansed, and the deaf hear, the dead are raised up, the poor have good news preached to them. [23]And blessed is the one who is not offended by me."

[24]When John's messengers had gone, Jesus[6] began to speak to the crowds concerning John: "What did you go out into the wilderness to see? A reed shaken by the wind? [25]What then did you go out to see? A man dressed in soft clothing? Behold, those who are dressed in

---

[1] Greek *bondservant*; also verses 3, 8, 10   [2] Greek *he*   [3] Some manuscripts *The next day*   [4] Greek *he*   [5] *Leprosy* was a term for several skin diseases; see Leviticus 13   [6] Greek *he*

splendid clothing and live in luxury are in kings' courts. [26]What then did you go out to see? A prophet? Yes, I tell you, and more than a prophet. [27]This is he of whom it is written,

"'Behold, I send my messenger before
        your face,
    who will prepare your way before you.'

[28]I tell you, among those born of women none is greater than John. Yet the one who is least in the kingdom of God is greater than he." [29](When all the people heard this, and the tax collectors too, they declared God just,[1] having been baptized with the baptism of John, [30]but the Pharisees and the lawyers rejected the purpose of God for themselves, not having been baptized by him.) [31]"To what then shall I compare the people of this generation, and what are they like? [32]They are like children sitting in the marketplace and calling to one another,

"'We played the flute for you, and you did
        not dance;
    we sang a dirge, and you did not weep.'

[33]For John the Baptist has come eating no bread and drinking no wine, and you say, 'He has a demon.' [34]The Son of Man has come eating and drinking, and you say, 'Look at him! A glutton and a drunkard, a friend of tax collectors and sinners!' [35]Yet wisdom is justified by all her children."

[36]One of the Pharisees asked him to eat with him, and he went into the Pharisee's house and reclined at the table. [37]And behold, a woman of the city, who was a sinner, when she learned that he was reclining at table in the Pharisee's house, brought an alabaster flask of ointment, [38]and standing behind him at his feet, weeping, she began to wet his feet with her tears and wiped them with the hair of her head and kissed his feet and anointed them with the ointment. [39]Now when the Pharisee who had invited him saw this, he said to himself, "If this man were a prophet, he would have known who and what sort of woman this is who is touching him, for she is a sinner." [40]And Jesus answering said to him, "Simon, I have something to say to you." And he answered, "Say it, Teacher."

[41]"A certain moneylender had two debtors. One owed five hundred denarii, and the other fifty. [42]When they could not pay, he cancelled the debt of both. Now which of them will love him more?" [43]Simon answered, "The one, I suppose, for whom he cancelled the larger debt." And he said to him, "You have judged rightly." [44]Then turning toward the woman he said to Simon, "Do you see this woman? I entered your house; you gave me no water for my feet, but she has wet my feet with her tears and wiped them with her hair. [45]You gave me no kiss, but from the time I came in she has not ceased to kiss my feet. [46]You did not anoint my head with oil, but she has anointed my feet with ointment. [47]Therefore I tell you, her sins, which are many, are forgiven—for she loved much. But he who is forgiven little, loves little." [48]And he said to her, "Your sins are forgiven." [49]Then those who were at table with him began to say among[2] themselves, "Who is this, who even forgives sins?" [50]And he said to the woman, "Your faith has saved you; go in peace."

NOVEMBER 24

1 Chronicles 19–20

Now after this Nahash the king of the Ammonites died, and his son reigned in his place. [2]And David said, "I will deal kindly with Hanun the son of Nahash, for his father dealt kindly with me." So David sent messengers to console him concerning his father. And David's servants came to the land of the Ammonites to Hanun to console him. [3]But the princes of the Ammonites said to Hanun, "Do you think, because David has sent

[1] Greek they justified God [2] Or to

comforters to you, that he is honoring your father? Have not his servants come to you to search and to overthrow and to spy out the land?" ⁴So Hanun took David's servants and shaved them and cut off their garments in the middle, at their hips, and sent them away; ⁵and they departed. When David was told concerning the men, he sent messengers to meet them, for the men were greatly ashamed. And the king said, "Remain at Jericho until your beards have grown and then return."

⁶When the Ammonites saw that they had become a stench to David, Hanun and the Ammonites sent 1,000 talents¹ of silver to hire chariots and horsemen from Mesopotamia, from Aram-maacah, and from Zobah. ⁷They hired 32,000 chariots and the king of Maacah with his army, who came and encamped before Medeba. And the Ammonites were mustered from their cities and came to battle. ⁸When David heard of it, he sent Joab and all the army of the mighty men. ⁹And the Ammonites came out and drew up in battle array at the entrance of the city, and the kings who had come were by themselves in the open country.

¹⁰When Joab saw that the battle was set against him both in front and in the rear, he chose some of the best men of Israel and arrayed them against the Syrians. ¹¹The rest of his men he put in the charge of Abishai his brother, and they were arrayed against the Ammonites. ¹²And he said, "If the Syrians are too strong for me, then you shall help me, but if the Ammonites are too strong for you, then I will help you. ¹³Be strong, and let us use our strength for our people and for the cities of our God, and may the LORD do what seems good to him." ¹⁴So Joab and the people who were with him drew near before the Syrians for battle, and they fled before him. ¹⁵And when the Ammonites saw that the Syrians fled, they likewise fled before Abishai, Joab's brother, and entered the city. Then Joab came to Jerusalem.

¹⁶But when the Syrians saw that they had been defeated by Israel, they sent messengers and brought out the Syrians who were beyond the Euphrates,² with Shophach the commander of the army of Hadadezer at their head. ¹⁷And when it was told to David, he gathered all Israel together and crossed the Jordan and came to them and drew up his forces against them.

And when David set the battle in array against the Syrians, they fought with him. ¹⁸And the Syrians fled before Israel, and David killed of the Syrians the men of 7,000 chariots and 40,000 foot soldiers, and put to death also Shophach the commander of their army. ¹⁹And when the servants of Hadadezer saw that they had been defeated by Israel, they made peace with David and became subject to him. So the Syrians were not willing to save the Ammonites anymore.

20:1 In the spring of the year, the time when kings go out to battle, Joab led out the army and ravaged the country of the Ammonites and came and besieged Rabbah. But David remained at Jerusalem. And Joab struck down Rabbah and overthrew it. ²And David took the crown of their king from his head. He found that it weighed a talent³ of gold, and in it was a precious stone. And it was placed on David's head. And he brought out the spoil of the city, a very great amount. ³And he brought out the people who were in it and set them to labor⁴ with saws and iron picks and axes.⁵ And thus David did to all the cities of the Ammonites. Then David and all the people returned to Jerusalem.

⁴And after this there arose war with the Philistines at Gezer. Then Sibbecai the Hushathite struck down Sippai, who was one of the descendants of the giants, and the Philistines were subdued. ⁵And there was again war with the Philistines, and Elhanan the son of Jair struck down Lahmi the brother of Goliath the Gittite, the shaft of whose spear was like a weaver's beam. ⁶And there was again war at Gath, where there was a man of great stature, who had six fingers on each hand and six toes on each foot, twenty-four in number, and he also was descended from the giants. ⁷And when he taunted Israel, Jonathan the son of Shimea, David's brother, struck him down. ⁸These were descended from the giants in Gath, and they fell by the hand of David and by the hand of his servants.

1 Peter 1

Peter, an apostle of Jesus Christ,
To those who are elect exiles of the Dispersion in Pontus, Galatia, Cappadocia, Asia, and Bithynia, ²according to the foreknowledge of God the Father, in the sanctification of the

¹ A talent was about 75 pounds or 34 kilograms ² Hebrew the River ³ A talent was about 75 pounds or 34 kilograms ⁴ Compare 2 Samuel 12:31; Hebrew he sawed ⁵ Compare 2 Samuel 12:31; Hebrew saws

Spirit, for obedience to Jesus Christ and for sprinkling with his blood:

May grace and peace be multiplied to you.

[3] Blessed be the God and Father of our Lord Jesus Christ! According to his great mercy, he has caused us to be born again to a living hope through the resurrection of Jesus Christ from the dead, [4] to an inheritance that is imperishable, undefiled, and unfading, kept in heaven for you, [5] who by God's power are being guarded through faith for a salvation ready to be revealed in the last time. [6] In this you rejoice, though now for a little while, if necessary, you have been grieved by various trials, [7] so that the tested genuineness of your faith—more precious than gold that perishes though it is tested by fire—may be found to result in praise and glory and honor at the revelation of Jesus Christ. [8] Though you have not seen him, you love him. Though you do not now see him, you believe in him and rejoice with joy that is inexpressible and filled with glory, [9] obtaining the outcome of your faith, the salvation of your souls.

[10] Concerning this salvation, the prophets who prophesied about the grace that was to be yours searched and inquired carefully, [11] inquiring what person or time the Spirit of Christ in them was indicating when he predicted the sufferings of Christ and the subsequent glories. [12] It was revealed to them that they were serving not themselves but you, in the things that have now been announced to you through those who preached the good news to you by the Holy Spirit sent from heaven, things into which angels long to look.

[13] Therefore, preparing your minds for action,[1] and being sober-minded, set your hope fully on the grace that will be brought to you at the revelation of Jesus Christ. [14] As obedient children, do not be conformed to the passions of your former ignorance, [15] but as he who called you is holy, you also be holy in all your conduct, [16] since it is written, "You shall be holy, for I am holy." [17] And if you call on him as Father who judges impartially according to each one's deeds, conduct yourselves with fear throughout the time of your exile, [18] knowing that you were ransomed from the futile ways inherited from your forefathers, not with perishable things such as silver or gold, [19] but with the precious blood of Christ, like that of a lamb without blemish or spot. [20] He was foreknown

before the foundation of the world but was made manifest in the last times for the sake of you [21] who through him are believers in God, who raised him from the dead and gave him glory, so that your faith and hope are in God.

[22] Having purified your souls by your obedience to the truth for a sincere brotherly love, love one another earnestly from a pure heart, [23] since you have been born again, not of perishable seed but of imperishable, through the living and abiding word of God; [24] for

> "All flesh is like grass
>   and all its glory like the flower of grass.
> The grass withers,
>   and the flower falls,
> [25]   but the word of the Lord remains forever."

And this word is the good news that was preached to you.

Jonah 3

Then the word of the LORD came to Jonah the second time, saying, [2] "Arise, go to Nineveh, that great city, and call out against it the message that I tell you." [3] So Jonah arose and went to Nineveh, according to the word of the LORD. Now Nineveh was an exceedingly great city,[2] three days' journey in breadth.[3] [4] Jonah began to go into the city, going a day's journey. And he called out, "Yet forty days, and Nineveh shall be overthrown!" [5] And the people of Nineveh believed God. They called for a fast and put on sackcloth, from the greatest of them to the least of them.

[6] The word reached[4] the king of Nineveh, and he arose from his throne, removed his robe, covered himself with sackcloth, and sat in ashes. [7] And he issued a proclamation and published through Nineveh, "By the decree of the king and his nobles: Let neither man nor beast, herd nor flock, taste anything. Let them not feed or drink water, [8] but let man and beast be covered with sackcloth, and let them call out mightily to God. Let everyone turn from his evil way and from the violence that is in his hands. [9] Who knows? God may turn and relent and turn from his fierce anger, so that we may not perish." [10] When God saw what they did, how they turned from their evil way, God relented of the disaster that he had said he would do to them, and he did not do it.

---

[1] Greek *girding up the loins of your mind* [2] Hebrew *a great city to God* [3] Or *a visit was a three days' journey* [4] Or *had reached*

Luke 8

Soon afterward he went on through cities and villages, proclaiming and bringing the good news of the kingdom of God. And the twelve were with him, ²and also some women who had been healed of evil spirits and infirmities: Mary, called Magdalene, from whom seven demons had gone out, ³and Joanna, the wife of Chuza, Herod's household manager, and Susanna, and many others, who provided for them[1] out of their means.

⁴And when a great crowd was gathering and people from town after town came to him, he said in a parable, ⁵"A sower went out to sow his seed. And as he sowed, some fell along the path and was trampled underfoot, and the birds of the air devoured it. ⁶And some fell on the rock, and as it grew up, it withered away, because it had no moisture. ⁷And some fell among thorns, and the thorns grew up with it and choked it. ⁸And some fell into good soil and grew and yielded a hundredfold." As he said these things, he called out, "He who has ears to hear, let him hear."

⁹And when his disciples asked him what this parable meant, ¹⁰he said, "To you it has been given to know the secrets of the kingdom of God, but for others they are in parables, so that 'seeing they may not see, and hearing they may not understand.' ¹¹Now the parable is this: The seed is the word of God. ¹²The ones along the path are those who have heard; then the devil comes and takes away the word from their hearts, so that they may not believe and be saved. ¹³And the ones on the rock are those who, when they hear the word, receive it with joy. But these have no root; they believe for a while, and in time of testing fall away. ¹⁴And as for what fell among the thorns, they are those who hear, but as they go on their way they are choked by the cares and riches and pleasures of life, and their fruit does not mature. ¹⁵As for that in the good soil, they are those who, hearing the word, hold it fast in an honest and good heart, and bear fruit with patience.

¹⁶"No one after lighting a lamp covers it with a jar or puts it under a bed, but puts it on a stand, so that those who enter may see the light. ¹⁷For nothing is hidden that will not be made manifest, nor is anything secret that will not be known and come to light. ¹⁸Take care

then how you hear, for to the one who has, more will be given, and from the one who has not, even what he thinks that he has will be taken away."

¹⁹Then his mother and his brothers came to him, but they could not reach him because of the crowd. ²⁰And he was told, "Your mother and your brothers are standing outside, desiring to see you." ²¹But he answered them, "My mother and my brothers are those who hear the word of God and do it."

²²One day he got into a boat with his disciples, and he said to them, "Let us go across to the other side of the lake." So they set out, ²³and as they sailed he fell asleep. And a windstorm came down on the lake, and they were filling with water and were in danger. ²⁴And they went and woke him, saying, "Master, Master, we are perishing!" And he awoke and rebuked the wind and the raging waves, and they ceased, and there was a calm. ²⁵He said to them, "Where is your faith?" And they were afraid, and they marveled, saying to one another, "Who then is this, that he commands even winds and water, and they obey him?"

²⁶Then they sailed to the country of the Gerasenes,[2] which is opposite Galilee. ²⁷When Jesus[3] had stepped out on land, there met him a man from the city who had demons. For a long time he had worn no clothes, and he had not lived in a house but among the tombs. ²⁸When he saw Jesus, he cried out and fell down before him and said with a loud voice, "What have you to do with me, Jesus, Son of the Most High God? I beg you, do not torment me." ²⁹For he had commanded the unclean spirit to come out of the man. (For many a time it had seized him. He was kept under guard and bound with chains and shackles, but he would break the bonds and be driven by the demon into the desert.) ³⁰Jesus then asked him, "What is your name?" And he said, "Legion," for many demons had entered him. ³¹And they begged him not to command them to depart into the abyss. ³²Now a large herd of pigs was feeding there on the hillside, and they begged him to let them enter these. So he gave them permission. ³³Then the demons came out of the man and entered the pigs, and the herd rushed down the steep bank into the lake and drowned.

³⁴When the herdsmen saw what had happened, they fled and told it in the city and in

[1] Some manuscripts him   [2] Some manuscripts Gadarenes; others Gergesenes; also verse 37   [3] Greek he; also verses 38, 42

the country. ³⁵Then people went out to see what had happened, and they came to Jesus and found the man from whom the demons had gone, sitting at the feet of Jesus, clothed and in his right mind, and they were afraid. ³⁶And those who had seen it told them how the demon-possessed¹ man had been healed. ³⁷Then all the people of the surrounding country of the Gerasenes asked him to depart from them, for they were seized with great fear. So he got into the boat and returned. ³⁸The man from whom the demons had gone begged that he might be with him, but Jesus sent him away, saying, ³⁹"Return to your home, and declare how much God has done for you." And he went away, proclaiming throughout the whole city how much Jesus had done for him.

⁴⁰Now when Jesus returned, the crowd welcomed him, for they were all waiting for him. ⁴¹And there came a man named Jairus, who was a ruler of the synagogue. And falling at Jesus' feet, he implored him to come to his house, ⁴²for he had an only daughter, about twelve years of age, and she was dying.

As Jesus went, the people pressed around him. ⁴³And there was a woman who had had a discharge of blood for twelve years, and though she had spent all her living on physicians,² she could not be healed by anyone. ⁴⁴She came up behind him and touched the fringe of his garment, and immediately her discharge of blood ceased. ⁴⁵And Jesus said, "Who was it that touched me?" When all denied it, Peter³ said, "Master, the crowds surround you and are pressing in on you!" ⁴⁶But Jesus said, "Someone touched me, for I perceive that power has gone out from me." ⁴⁷And when the woman saw that she was not hidden, she came trembling, and falling down before him declared in the presence of all the people why she had touched him, and how she had been immediately healed. ⁴⁸And he said to her, "Daughter, your faith has made you well; go in peace."

⁴⁹While he was still speaking, someone from the ruler's house came and said, "Your daughter is dead; do not trouble the Teacher any more." ⁵⁰But Jesus on hearing this answered him, "Do not fear; only believe, and she will be well." ⁵¹And when he came to the house, he allowed no one to enter with him, except Peter and John and James, and the father and mother of the child. ⁵²And all were weeping and mourning for her, but he said, "Do not weep, for she is not dead but sleeping." ⁵³And they laughed at him, knowing that she was dead. ⁵⁴But taking her by the hand he called, saying, "Child, arise." ⁵⁵And her spirit returned, and she got up at once. And he directed that something should be given her to eat. ⁵⁶And her parents were amazed, but he charged them to tell no one what had happened.

NOVEMBER 25

1 Chronicles 21

Then Satan stood against Israel and incited David to number Israel. ²So David said to Joab and the commanders of the army, "Go, number Israel, from Beersheba to Dan, and bring me a report, that I may know their number." ³But Joab said, "May the LORD add to his people a hundred times as many as they are! Are they not, my lord the king, all of them my lord's servants? Why then should my lord require this? Why should it be a cause of guilt for Israel?" ⁴But the king's word prevailed against Joab. So Joab departed and went throughout all Israel and came back to Jerusalem. ⁵And Joab gave the sum of the numbering of the people to David. In all Israel there were 1,100,000 men who drew the sword, and in Judah 470,000 who drew the sword. ⁶But he did not include Levi and Benjamin in the numbering, for the king's command was abhorrent to Joab.

⁷But God was displeased with this thing, and

¹ Greek daimonizomai; elsewhere rendered oppressed by demons ² Some manuscripts omit and though she had spent all her living on physicians, ³ Some manuscripts add and those who were with him

he struck Israel. [8]And David said to God, "I have sinned greatly in that I have done this thing. But now, please take away the iniquity of your servant, for I have acted very foolishly." [9]And the LORD spoke to Gad, David's seer, saying, [10]"Go and say to David, 'Thus says the LORD, Three things I offer you; choose one of them, that I may do it to you.'" [11]So Gad came to David and said to him, "Thus says the LORD, 'Choose what you will: [12]either three years of famine, or three months of devastation by your foes while the sword of your enemies overtakes you, or else three days of the sword of the LORD, pestilence on the land, with the angel of the LORD destroying throughout all the territory of Israel.' Now decide what answer I shall return to him who sent me." [13]Then David said to Gad, "I am in great distress. Let me fall into the hand of the LORD, for his mercy is very great, but do not let me fall into the hand of man."

[14]So the LORD sent a pestilence on Israel, and 70,000 men of Israel fell. [15]And God sent the angel to Jerusalem to destroy it, but as he was about to destroy it, the LORD saw, and he relented from the calamity. And he said to the angel who was working destruction, "It is enough; now stay your hand." And the angel of the LORD was standing by the threshing floor of Ornan the Jebusite. [16]And David lifted his eyes and saw the angel of the LORD standing between earth and heaven, and in his hand a drawn sword stretched out over Jerusalem. Then David and the elders, clothed in sackcloth, fell upon their faces. [17]And David said to God, "Was it not I who gave command to number the people? It is I who have sinned and done great evil. But these sheep, what have they done? Please let your hand, O LORD my God, be against me and against my father's house. But do not let the plague be on your people."

[18]Now the angel of the LORD had commanded Gad to say to David that David should go up and raise an altar to the LORD on the threshing floor of Ornan the Jebusite. [19]So David went up at Gad's word, which he had spoken in the name of the LORD. [20]Now Ornan was threshing wheat. He turned and saw the angel, and his four sons who were with him hid themselves. [21]As David came to Ornan, Ornan looked and saw David and went out from the threshing floor and paid homage to David with his face to the ground. [22]And

David said to Ornan, "Give me the site of the threshing floor that I may build on it an altar to the LORD—give it to me at its full price—that the plague may be averted from the people." [23]Then Ornan said to David, "Take it, and let my lord the king do what seems good to him. See, I give the oxen for burnt offerings and the threshing sledges for the wood and the wheat for a grain offering; I give it all." [24]But King David said to Ornan, "No, but I will buy them for the full price. I will not take for the LORD what is yours, nor offer burnt offerings that cost me nothing." [25]So David paid Ornan 600 shekels[1] of gold by weight for the site. [26]And David built there an altar to the LORD and presented burnt offerings and peace offerings and called on the LORD, and the LORD[2] answered him with fire from heaven upon the altar of burnt offering. [27]Then the LORD commanded the angel, and he put his sword back into its sheath.

[28]At that time, when David saw that the LORD had answered him at the threshing floor of Ornan the Jebusite, he sacrificed there. [29]For the tabernacle of the LORD, which Moses had made in the wilderness, and the altar of burnt offering were at that time in the high place at Gibeon, [30]but David could not go before it to inquire of God, for he was afraid of the sword of the angel of the LORD.

---

1 Peter 2

So put away all malice and all deceit and hypocrisy and envy and all slander. [2]Like newborn infants, long for the pure spiritual milk, that by it you may grow up into salvation— [3]if indeed you have tasted that the Lord is good.

[4]As you come to him, a living stone rejected by men but in the sight of God chosen and precious, [5]you yourselves like living stones are being built up as a spiritual house, to be a holy priesthood, to offer spiritual sacrifices acceptable to God through Jesus Christ. [6]For it stands in Scripture:

"Behold, I am laying in Zion a stone,
a cornerstone chosen and precious,
and whoever believes in him will not be
put to shame."

[7]So the honor is for you who believe, but for those who do not believe,

[1] A *shekel* was about 2/5 ounce or 11 grams [2] Hebrew *he*

"The stone that the builders rejected
  has become the cornerstone,"[1]

[8]and

"A stone of stumbling,
  and a rock of offense."

They stumble because they disobey the word, as they were destined to do. [9]But you are a chosen race, a royal priesthood, a holy nation, a people for his own possession, that you may proclaim the excellencies of him who called you out of darkness into his marvelous light. [10]Once you were not a people, but now you are God's people; once you had not received mercy, but now you have received mercy. [11]Beloved, I urge you as sojourners and exiles to abstain from the passions of the flesh, which wage war against your soul. [12]Keep your conduct among the Gentiles honorable, so that when they speak against you as evildoers, they may see your good deeds and glorify God on the day of visitation.

[13]Be subject for the Lord's sake to every human institution,[2] whether it be to the emperor[3] as supreme, [14]or to governors as sent by him to punish those who do evil and to praise those who do good. [15]For this is the will of God, that by doing good you should put to silence the ignorance of foolish people. [16]Live as people who are free, not using your freedom as a cover-up for evil, but living as servants[4] of God. [17]Honor everyone. Love the brotherhood. Fear God. Honor the emperor.

[18]Servants, be subject to your masters with all respect, not only to the good and gentle but also to the unjust. [19]For this is a gracious thing, when, mindful of God, one endures sorrows while suffering unjustly. [20]For what credit is it if, when you sin and are beaten for it, you endure? But if when you do good and suffer for it you endure, this is a gracious thing in the sight of God. [21]For to this you have been called, because Christ also suffered for you, leaving you an example, so that you might follow in his steps. [22]He committed no sin, neither was deceit found in his mouth. [23]When he was reviled, he did not revile in return; when he suffered, he did not threaten, but continued entrusting himself to him who judges justly. [24]He himself bore our sins in his body on the tree, that we might die to sin and live to

righteousness. By his wounds you have been healed. [25]For you were straying like sheep, but have now returned to the Shepherd and Overseer of your souls.

Jonah 4

But it displeased Jonah exceedingly,[5] and he was angry. [2]And he prayed to the Lord and said, "O Lord, is not this what I said when I was yet in my country? That is why I made haste to flee to Tarshish; for I knew that you are a gracious God and merciful, slow to anger and abounding in steadfast love, and relenting from disaster. [3]Therefore now, O Lord, please take my life from me, for it is better for me to die than to live." [4]And the Lord said, "Do you do well to be angry?"

[5]Jonah went out of the city and sat to the east of the city and made a booth for himself there. He sat under it in the shade, till he should see what would become of the city. [6]Now the Lord God appointed a plant[6] and made it come up over Jonah, that it might be a shade over his head, to save him from his discomfort.[7] So Jonah was exceedingly glad because of the plant. [7]But when dawn came up the next day, God appointed a worm that attacked the plant, so that it withered. [8]When the sun rose, God appointed a scorching east wind, and the sun beat down on the head of Jonah so that he was faint. And he asked that he might die and said, "It is better for me to die than to live." [9]But God said to Jonah, "Do you do well to be angry for the plant?" And he said, "Yes, I do well to be angry, angry enough to die." [10]And the Lord said, "You pity the plant, for which you did not labor, nor did you make it grow, which came into being in a night and perished in a night. [11]And should not I pity Nineveh, that great city, in which there are more than 120,000 persons who do not know their right hand from their left, and also much cattle?"

Luke 9

And he called the twelve together and gave them power and authority over all demons and to cure diseases, [2]and he sent them out to proclaim the kingdom of God and to heal. [3]And he said to them, "Take nothing for your journey, no staff, nor bag, nor bread, nor money; and do not have two tunics.¹ ⁴And whatever house you enter, stay there, and from there depart. ⁵And wherever they do not receive you, when you leave that town shake off the dust from your feet as a testimony against them." ⁶And they departed and went through the villages, preaching the gospel and healing everywhere.

⁷Now Herod the tetrarch heard about all that was happening, and he was perplexed, because it was said by some that John had been raised from the dead, ⁸by some that Elijah had appeared, and by others that one of the prophets of old had risen. ⁹Herod said, "John I beheaded, but who is this about whom I hear such things?" And he sought to see him.

¹⁰On their return the apostles told him all that they had done. And he took them and withdrew apart to a town called Bethsaida. ¹¹When the crowds learned it, they followed him, and he welcomed them and spoke to them of the kingdom of God and cured those who had need of healing. ¹²Now the day began to wear away, and the twelve came and said to him, "Send the crowd away to go into the surrounding villages and countryside to find lodging and get provisions, for we are here in a desolate place." ¹³But he said to them, "You give them something to eat." They said, "We have no more than five loaves and two fish—unless we are to go and buy food for all these people." ¹⁴For there were about five thousand men. And he said to his disciples, "Have them sit down in groups of about fifty each." ¹⁵And they did so, and had them all sit down. ¹⁶And taking the five loaves and the two fish, he looked up to heaven and said a blessing over them. Then he broke the loaves and gave them to the disciples to set before the crowd. ¹⁷And they all ate and were satisfied. And what was left over was picked up, twelve baskets of broken pieces.

¹⁸Now it happened that as he was praying alone, the disciples were with him. And he asked them, "Who do the crowds say that I am?" ¹⁹And they answered, "John the Baptist. But others say, Elijah, and others, that one of the prophets of old has risen." ²⁰Then he said to them, "But who do you say that I am?" And Peter answered, "The Christ of God."

²¹And he strictly charged and commanded them to tell this to no one, ²²saying, "The Son of Man must suffer many things and be rejected by the elders and chief priests and scribes, and be killed, and on the third day be raised."

²³And he said to all, "If anyone would come after me, let him deny himself and take up his cross daily and follow me. ²⁴For whoever would save his life will lose it, but whoever loses his life for my sake will save it. ²⁵For what does it profit a man if he gains the whole world and loses or forfeits himself? ²⁶For whoever is ashamed of me and of my words, of him will the Son of Man be ashamed when he comes in his glory and the glory of the Father and of the holy angels. ²⁷But I tell you truly, there are some standing here who will not taste death until they see the kingdom of God."

²⁸Now about eight days after these sayings he took with him Peter and John and James and went up on the mountain to pray. ²⁹And as he was praying, the appearance of his face was altered, and his clothing became dazzling white. ³⁰And behold, two men were talking with him, Moses and Elijah, ³¹who appeared in glory and spoke of his departure,² which he was about to accomplish at Jerusalem. ³²Now Peter and those who were with him were heavy with sleep, but when they became fully awake they saw his glory and the two men who stood with him. ³³And as the men were parting from him, Peter said to Jesus, "Master, it is good that we are here. Let us make three tents, one for you and one for Moses and one for Elijah"— not knowing what he said. ³⁴As he was saying these things, a cloud came and overshadowed them, and they were afraid as they entered the cloud. ³⁵And a voice came out of the cloud, saying, "This is my Son, my Chosen One;³ listen to him!" ³⁶And when the voice had spoken, Jesus was found alone. And they kept silent and told no one in those days anything of what they had seen.

³⁷On the next day, when they had come down from the mountain, a great crowd met him. ³⁸And behold, a man from the crowd cried out, "Teacher, I beg you to look at my son, for he is my only child. ³⁹And behold, a spirit seizes him, and he suddenly cries out. It convulses him so that he foams at the mouth, and shatters him, and will hardly leave him. ⁴⁰And I begged your disciples to cast it out, but they could not." ⁴¹Jesus answered, "O faithless and twisted generation, how long am I to be with you and bear with you? Bring your son here."

---

¹ Greek *chiton*, a long garment worn under the cloak next to the skin ² Greek *exodus* ³ Some manuscripts *my Beloved*

[42] While he was coming, the demon threw him to the ground and convulsed him. But Jesus rebuked the unclean spirit and healed the boy, and gave him back to his father. [43] And all were astonished at the majesty of God.

But while they were all marveling at everything he was doing, Jesus[1] said to his disciples, [44] "Let these words sink into your ears: The Son of Man is about to be delivered into the hands of men." [45] But they did not understand this saying, and it was concealed from them, so that they might not perceive it. And they were afraid to ask him about this saying.

[46] An argument arose among them as to which of them was the greatest. [47] But Jesus, knowing the reasoning of their hearts, took a child and put him by his side [48] and said to them, "Whoever receives this child in my name receives me, and whoever receives me receives him who sent me. For he who is least among you all is the one who is great."

[49] John answered, "Master, we saw someone casting out demons in your name, and we tried to stop him, because he does not follow with us." [50] But Jesus said to him, "Do not stop him, for the one who is not against you is for you."

[51] When the days drew near for him to be taken up, he set his face to go to Jerusalem. [52] And he sent messengers ahead of him, who went and entered a village of the Samaritans, to make preparations for him. [53] But the people did not receive him, because his face was set toward Jerusalem. [54] And when his disciples James and John saw it, they said, "Lord, do you want us to tell fire to come down from heaven and consume them?"[2] [55] But he turned and rebuked them.[3] [56] And they went on to another village.

[57] As they were going along the road, someone said to him, "I will follow you wherever you go." [58] And Jesus said to him, "Foxes have holes, and birds of the air have nests, but the Son of Man has nowhere to lay his head." [59] To another he said, "Follow me." But he said, "Lord, let me first go and bury my father." [60] And Jesus[4] said to him, "Leave the dead to bury their own dead. But as for you, go and proclaim the kingdom of God." [61] Yet another said, "I will follow you, Lord, but let me first say farewell to those at my home." [62] Jesus said to him, "No one who puts his hand to the plow and looks back is fit for the kingdom of God."

NOVEMBER 26

1 Chronicles 22

Then David said, "Here shall be the house of the LORD God and here the altar of burnt offering for Israel."

[2] David commanded to gather together the resident aliens who were in the land of Israel, and he set stonecutters to prepare dressed stones for building the house of God. [3] David also provided great quantities of iron for nails for the doors of the gates and for clamps, as well as bronze in quantities beyond weighing, [4] and cedar timbers without number, for the Sidonians and Tyrians brought great quantities of cedar to David. [5] For David said, "Solomon my son is young and inexperienced, and the house that is to be built for the LORD must be

exceedingly magnificent, of fame and glory throughout all lands. I will therefore make preparation for it." So David provided materials in great quantity before his death.

[6] Then he called for Solomon his son and charged him to build a house for the LORD, the God of Israel. [7] David said to Solomon, "My son, I had it in my heart to build a house to the name of the LORD my God. [8] But the word of the LORD came to me, saying, 'You have shed much blood and have waged great wars. You shall not build a house to my name, because you have shed so much blood before me on the earth. [9] Behold, a son shall be born to you who shall be a man of rest. I will give him rest from

---

[1] Greek *he* [2] Some manuscripts add *as Elijah did* [3] Some manuscripts add *and he said, "You do not know what manner of spirit you are of; for the Son of Man came not to destroy people's lives but to save them"* [4] Greek *he*

all his surrounding enemies. For his name shall be Solomon, and I will give peace and quiet to Israel in his days. ¹⁰He shall build a house for my name. He shall be my son, and I will be his father, and I will establish his royal throne in Israel forever.'

¹¹"Now, my son, the LORD be with you, so that you may succeed in building the house of the LORD your God, as he has spoken concerning you. ¹²Only, may the LORD grant you discretion and understanding, that when he gives you charge over Israel you may keep the law of the LORD your God. ¹³Then you will prosper if you are careful to observe the statutes and the rules that the LORD commanded Moses for Israel. Be strong and courageous. Fear not; do not be dismayed. ¹⁴With great pains I have provided for the house of the LORD 100,000 talents¹ of gold, a million talents of silver, and bronze and iron beyond weighing, for there is so much of it; timber and stone, too, I have provided. To these you must add. ¹⁵You have an abundance of workmen: stonecutters, masons, carpenters, and all kinds of craftsmen without number, skilled in working ¹⁶gold, silver, bronze, and iron. Arise and work! The LORD be with you!"

¹⁷David also commanded all the leaders of Israel to help Solomon his son, saying, ¹⁸"Is not the LORD your God with you? And has he not given you peace on every side? For he has delivered the inhabitants of the land into my hand, and the land is subdued before the LORD and his people. ¹⁹Now set your mind and heart to seek the LORD your God. Arise and build the sanctuary of the LORD God, so that the ark of the covenant of the LORD and the holy vessels of God may be brought into a house built for the name of the LORD."

1 Peter 3

Likewise, wives, be subject to your own husbands, so that even if some do not obey the word, they may be won without a word by the conduct of their wives, ²when they see your respectful and pure conduct. ³Do not let your adorning be external—the braiding of hair and the putting on of gold jewelry, or the clothing you wear— ⁴but let your adorning be the hidden person of the heart with the imperishable beauty of a gentle and quiet spirit, which in God's sight is very precious. ⁵For this is how the

holy women who hoped in God used to adorn themselves, by submitting to their own husbands, ⁶as Sarah obeyed Abraham, calling him lord. And you are her children, if you do good and do not fear anything that is frightening.

⁷Likewise, husbands, live with your wives in an understanding way, showing honor to the woman as the weaker vessel, since they are heirs with you² of the grace of life, so that your prayers may not be hindered.

⁸Finally, all of you, have unity of mind, sympathy, brotherly love, a tender heart, and a humble mind. ⁹Do not repay evil for evil or reviling for reviling, but on the contrary, bless, for to this you were called, that you may obtain a blessing. ¹⁰For

> "Whoever desires to love life
>   and see good days,
> let him keep his tongue from evil
>   and his lips from speaking deceit;
> 11 let him turn away from evil and do good;
>   let him seek peace and pursue it.
> 12 For the eyes of the Lord are on the
>   righteous,
>   and his ears are open to their prayer.
> But the face of the Lord is against those
>   who do evil."

¹³Now who is there to harm you if you are zealous for what is good? ¹⁴But even if you should suffer for righteousness' sake, you will be blessed. Have no fear of them, nor be troubled, ¹⁵but in your hearts honor Christ the Lord as holy, always being prepared to make a defense to anyone who asks you for a reason for the hope that is in you; yet do it with gentleness and respect, ¹⁶having a good conscience, so that, when you are slandered, those who revile your good behavior in Christ may be put to shame. ¹⁷For it is better to suffer for doing good, if that should be God's will, than for doing evil.

¹⁸For Christ also suffered³ once for sins, the righteous for the unrighteous, that he might bring us to God, being put to death in the flesh but made alive in the spirit, ¹⁹in which⁴ he went and proclaimed⁵ to the spirits in prison, ²⁰because⁶ they formerly did not obey, when God's patience waited in the days of Noah, while the ark was being prepared, in which a few, that is, eight persons, were brought safely through water. ²¹Baptism, which corresponds to this, now saves you, not as a removal of dirt

¹ A talent was about 75 pounds or 34 kilograms ² Some manuscripts since you are joint heirs ³ Some manuscripts died ⁴ Or the Spirit, in whom ⁵ Or preached ⁶ Or when

from the body but as an appeal to God for a good conscience, through the resurrection of Jesus Christ, ²²who has gone into heaven and is at the right hand of God, with angels, authorities, and powers having been subjected to him.

Micah 1

The word of the Lord that came to Micah of Moresheth in the days of Jotham, Ahaz, and Hezekiah, kings of Judah, which he saw concerning Samaria and Jerusalem.

2   Hear, you peoples, all of you;[1]
     pay attention, O earth, and all that is
       in it,
   and let the Lord God be a witness
     against you,
     the Lord from his holy temple.
3   For behold, the Lord is coming out of
     his place,
   and will come down and tread upon
     the high places of the earth.
4   And the mountains will melt under him,
     and the valleys will split open,
   like wax before the fire,
     like waters poured down a steep place.
5   All this is for the transgression of Jacob
     and for the sins of the house of Israel.
   What is the transgression of Jacob?
     Is it not Samaria?
   And what is the high place of Judah?
     Is it not Jerusalem?
6   Therefore I will make Samaria a heap in
     the open country,
     a place for planting vineyards,
   and I will pour down her stones into the
     valley
     and uncover her foundations.
7   All her carved images shall be beaten to
     pieces,
   all her wages shall be burned with fire,
     and all her idols I will lay waste,
   for from the fee of a prostitute she
     gathered them,
     and to the fee of a prostitute they shall
     return.
8   For this I will lament and wail;
     I will go stripped and naked;
   I will make lamentation like the jackals,
     and mourning like the ostriches.

9   For her wound is incurable,
     and it has come to Judah;
   it has reached to the gate of my people,
     to Jerusalem.
10   Tell it not in Gath;
     weep not at all;
   in Beth-le-aphrah
     roll yourselves in the dust.
11   Pass on your way,
     inhabitants of Shaphir,
     in nakedness and shame;
   the inhabitants of Zaanan
     do not come out;
   the lamentation of Beth-ezel
     shall take away from you its standing
       place.
12   For the inhabitants of Maroth
     wait anxiously for good,
   because disaster has come down from
     the Lord
     to the gate of Jerusalem.
13   Harness the steeds to the chariots,
     inhabitants of Lachish;
   it was the beginning of sin
     to the daughter of Zion,
   for in you were found
     the transgressions of Israel.
14   Therefore you shall give parting gifts[2]
     to Moresheth-gath;
   the houses of Achzib shall be a deceitful
     thing
     to the kings of Israel.
15   I will again bring a conqueror to you,
     inhabitants of Mareshah;
   the glory of Israel
     shall come to Adullam.
16   Make yourselves bald and cut off your
     hair,
     for the children of your delight;
   make yourselves as bald as the eagle,
     for they shall go from you into exile.

Luke 10

After this the Lord appointed seventy-two[3] others and sent them on ahead of him, two by two, into every town and place where he himself was about to go. ²And he said to them, "The harvest is plentiful, but the laborers are few. Therefore pray earnestly to the Lord of the harvest to send out laborers into his harvest.

[1] Hebrew *all of them*   [2] Or *give dowry*   [3] Some manuscripts *seventy*; also verse 17

³Go your way; behold, I am sending you out as lambs in the midst of wolves. ⁴Carry no moneybag, no knapsack, no sandals, and greet no one on the road. ⁵Whatever house you enter, first say, 'Peace be to this house!' ⁶And if a son of peace is there, your peace will rest upon him. But if not, it will return to you. ⁷And remain in the same house, eating and drinking what they provide, for the laborer deserves his wages. Do not go from house to house. ⁸Whenever you enter a town and they receive you, eat what is set before you. ⁹Heal the sick in it and say to them, 'The kingdom of God has come near to you.' ¹⁰But whenever you enter a town and they do not receive you, go into its streets and say, ¹¹'Even the dust of your town that clings to our feet we wipe off against you. Nevertheless know this, that the kingdom of God has come near.' ¹²I tell you, it will be more bearable on that day for Sodom than for that town.

¹³"Woe to you, Chorazin! Woe to you, Bethsaida! For if the mighty works done in you had been done in Tyre and Sidon, they would have repented long ago, sitting in sackcloth and ashes. ¹⁴But it will be more bearable in the judgment for Tyre and Sidon than for you. ¹⁵And you, Capernaum, will you be exalted to heaven? You shall be brought down to Hades.

¹⁶"The one who hears you hears me, and the one who rejects you rejects me, and the one who rejects me rejects him who sent me."

¹⁷The seventy-two returned with joy, saying, "Lord, even the demons are subject to us in your name!" ¹⁸And he said to them, "I saw Satan fall like lightning from heaven. ¹⁹Behold, I have given you authority to tread on serpents and scorpions, and over all the power of the enemy, and nothing shall hurt you. ²⁰Nevertheless, do not rejoice in this, that the spirits are subject to you, but rejoice that your names are written in heaven."

²¹In that same hour he rejoiced in the Holy Spirit and said, "I thank you, Father, Lord of heaven and earth, that you have hidden these things from the wise and understanding and revealed them to little children; yes, Father, for such was your gracious will.[1] ²²All things have been handed over to me by my Father, and no one knows who the Son is except the Father, or who the Father is except the Son and anyone to whom the Son chooses to reveal him."

²³Then turning to the disciples he said privately, "Blessed are the eyes that see what you see! ²⁴For I tell you that many prophets and kings desired to see what you see, and did not see it, and to hear what you hear, and did not hear it."

²⁵And behold, a lawyer stood up to put him to the test, saying, "Teacher, what shall I do to inherit eternal life?" ²⁶He said to him, "What is written in the Law? How do you read it?" ²⁷And he answered, "You shall love the Lord your God with all your heart and with all your soul and with all your strength and with all your mind, and your neighbor as yourself." ²⁸And he said to him, "You have answered correctly; do this, and you will live."

²⁹But he, desiring to justify himself, said to Jesus, "And who is my neighbor?" ³⁰Jesus replied, "A man was going down from Jerusalem to Jericho, and he fell among robbers, who stripped him and beat him and departed, leaving him half dead. ³¹Now by chance a priest was going down that road, and when he saw him he passed by on the other side. ³²So likewise a Levite, when he came to the place and saw him, passed by on the other side. ³³But a Samaritan, as he journeyed, came to where he was, and when he saw him, he had compassion. ³⁴He went to him and bound up his wounds, pouring on oil and wine. Then he set him on his own animal and brought him to an inn and took care of him. ³⁵And the next day he took out two denarii[2] and gave them to the innkeeper, saying, 'Take care of him, and whatever more you spend, I will repay you when I come back.' ³⁶Which of these three, do you think, proved to be a neighbor to the man who fell among the robbers?" ³⁷He said, "The one who showed him mercy." And Jesus said to him, "You go, and do likewise."

³⁸Now as they went on their way, Jesus[3] entered a village. And a woman named Martha welcomed him into her house. ³⁹And she had a sister called Mary, who sat at the Lord's feet and listened to his teaching. ⁴⁰But Martha was distracted with much serving. And she went up to him and said, "Lord, do you not care that my sister has left me to serve alone? Tell her then to help me." ⁴¹But the Lord answered her, "Martha, Martha, you are anxious and troubled about many things, ⁴²but one thing is necessary.[4] Mary has chosen the good portion, which will not be taken away from her."

[1] Or for so it pleased you well [2] A denarius was a day's wage for a laborer [3] Greek he [4] Some manuscripts few things are necessary, or only one

NOVEMBER 27

1 Chronicles 23

When David was old and full of days, he made Solomon his son king over Israel. [2] David[1] assembled all the leaders of Israel and the priests and the Levites. [3] The Levites, thirty years old and upward, were numbered, and the total was 38,000 men. [4] "Twenty-four thousand of these," David said,[2] "shall have charge of the work in the house of the LORD, 6,000 shall be officers and judges, [5] 4,000 gatekeepers, and 4,000 shall offer praises to the LORD with the instruments that I have made for praise." [6] And David organized them in divisions corresponding to the sons of Levi: Gershon, Kohath, and Merari.

[7] The sons of Gershon[3] were Ladan and Shimei. [8] The sons of Ladan: Jehiel the chief, and Zetham, and Joel, three. [9] The sons of Shimei: Shelomoth, Haziel, and Haran, three. These were the heads of the fathers' houses of Ladan. [10] And the sons of Shimei: Jahath, Zina, and Jeush and Beriah. These four were the sons of Shimei. [11] Jahath was the chief, and Zizah the second; but Jeush and Beriah did not have many sons, therefore they became counted as a single father's house.

[12] The sons of Kohath: Amram, Izhar, Hebron, and Uzziel, four. [13] The sons of Amram: Aaron and Moses. Aaron was set apart to dedicate the most holy things, that he and his sons forever should make offerings before the LORD and minister to him and pronounce blessings in his name forever. [14] But the sons of Moses the man of God were named among the tribe of Levi. [15] The sons of Moses: Gershom and Eliezer. [16] The sons of Gershom: Shebuel the chief. [17] The sons of Eliezer: Rehabiah the chief. Eliezer had no other sons, but the sons of Rehabiah were very many. [18] The sons of Izhar: Shelomith the chief. [19] The sons of Hebron: Jeriah the chief, Amariah the second, Jahaziel the third, and Jekameam the fourth. [20] The sons of Uzziel: Micah the chief and Isshiah the second.

[21] The sons of Merari: Mahli and Mushi. The sons of Mahli: Eleazar and Kish. [22] Eleazar died having no sons, but only daughters; their kinsmen, the sons of Kish, married them. [23] The sons of Mushi: Mahli, Eder, and Jeremoth, three.

[24] These were the sons of Levi by their fathers' houses, the heads of fathers' houses as they were listed according to the number of the names of the individuals from twenty years old and upward who were to do the work for the service of the house of the LORD. [25] For David said, "The LORD, the God of Israel, has given rest to his people, and he dwells in Jerusalem forever. [26] And so the Levites no longer need to carry the tabernacle or any of the things for its service." [27] For by the last words of David the sons of Levi were numbered from twenty years old and upward. [28] For their duty was to assist the sons of Aaron for the service of the house of the LORD, having the care of the courts and the chambers, the cleansing of all that is holy, and any work for the service of the house of God. [29] Their duty was also to assist with the showbread, the flour for the grain offering, the wafers of unleavened bread, the baked offering, the offering mixed with oil, and all measures of quantity or size. [30] And they were to stand every morning, thanking and praising the LORD, and likewise at evening, [31] and whenever burnt offerings were offered to the LORD on Sabbaths, new moons, and feast days, according to the number required of them, regularly before the LORD. [32] Thus they were to keep charge of the tent of meeting and the sanctuary, and to attend the sons of Aaron, their brothers, for the service of the house of the LORD.

1 Peter 4

Since therefore Christ suffered in the flesh,[4] arm yourselves with the same way of thinking, for whoever has suffered in the flesh has ceased from sin, [2] so as to live for the rest of the time in the flesh no longer for human passions but for the will of God. [3] For the time that is past suffices for doing what the Gentiles want to do, living in sensuality, passions, drunkenness,

[1] Hebrew He [2] Hebrew lacks David said [3] Vulgate (compare Septuagint, Syriac); Hebrew to the Gershonite [4] Some manuscripts add for us; some for you

orgies, drinking parties, and lawless idolatry. [4]With respect to this they are surprised when you do not join them in the same flood of debauchery, and they malign you; [5]but they will give account to him who is ready to judge the living and the dead. [6]For this is why the gospel was preached even to those who are dead, that though judged in the flesh the way people are, they might live in the spirit the way God does.

[7]The end of all things is at hand; therefore be self-controlled and sober-minded for the sake of your prayers. [8]Above all, keep loving one another earnestly, since love covers a multitude of sins. [9]Show hospitality to one another without grumbling. [10]As each has received a gift, use it to serve one another, as good stewards of God's varied grace: [11]whoever speaks, as one who speaks oracles of God; whoever serves, as one who serves by the strength that God supplies—in order that in everything God may be glorified through Jesus Christ. To him belong glory and dominion forever and ever. Amen.

[12]Beloved, do not be surprised at the fiery trial when it comes upon you to test you, as though something strange were happening to you. [13]But rejoice insofar as you share Christ's sufferings, that you may also rejoice and be glad when his glory is revealed. [14]If you are insulted for the name of Christ, you are blessed, because the Spirit of glory[1] and of God rests upon you. [15]But let none of you suffer as a murderer or a thief or an evildoer or as a meddler. [16]Yet if anyone suffers as a Christian, let him not be ashamed, but let him glorify God in that name. [17]For it is time for judgment to begin at the household of God; and if it begins with us, what will be the outcome for those who do not obey the gospel of God? [18]And

> "If the righteous is scarcely saved,
>   what will become of the ungodly and
>   the sinner?"[2]

[19]Therefore let those who suffer according to God's will entrust their souls to a faithful Creator while doing good.

Micah 2

Woe to those who devise wickedness
    and work evil on their beds!
When the morning dawns, they perform
    it,

because it is in the power of their hand.
[2] They covet fields and seize them,
    and houses, and take them away;
they oppress a man and his house,
    a man and his inheritance.

[3] Therefore thus says the LORD:
behold, against this family I am devising
    disaster,[3]
    from which you cannot remove your
        necks,
and you shall not walk haughtily,
    for it will be a time of disaster.
[4] In that day they shall take up a taunt
        song against you
    and moan bitterly,
and say, "We are utterly ruined;
    he changes the portion of my people;
how he removes it from me!
    To an apostate he allots our fields."
[5] Therefore you will have none to cast the
        line by lot
    in the assembly of the LORD.

[6] "Do not preach"—thus they preach—
    "one should not preach of such things;
    disgrace will not overtake us."
[7] Should this be said, O house of Jacob?
    Has the LORD grown impatient?[4]
    Are these his deeds?
Do not my words do good
    to him who walks uprightly?
[8] But lately my people have risen up as an
        enemy;
you strip the rich robe from those who
        pass by trustingly
    with no thought of war.[5]
[9] The women of my people you drive out
    from their delightful houses;
from their young children you take away
    my splendor forever.
[10] Arise and go,
    for this is no place to rest,
because of uncleanness that destroys
    with a grievous destruction.
[11] If a man should go about and utter wind
        and lies,
    saying, "I will preach to you of wine
        and strong drink,"
    he would be the preacher for this
        people!
[12] I will surely assemble all of you, O Jacob;
    I will gather the remnant of Israel;

---

[1] Some manuscripts insert *and of power* [2] Greek *where will the ungodly and sinner appear?* [3] The same Hebrew word can mean *evil* or *disaster*, depending on the context [4] Hebrew *Has the spirit of the LORD grown short?* [5] Or *returning from war*

I will set them together
    like sheep in a fold,
    like a flock in its pasture,
    a noisy multitude of men.
13 He who opens the breach goes up before
    them;
    they break through and pass the gate,
    going out by it.
    Their king passes on before them,
    the LORD at their head.

Luke 11

Now Jesus[1] was praying in a certain place, and when he finished, one of his disciples said to him, "Lord, teach us to pray, as John taught his disciples." [2]And he said to them, "When you pray, say:

"Father, hallowed be your name.
    Your kingdom come.
3   Give us each day our daily bread,[2]
4   and forgive us our sins,
        for we ourselves forgive everyone who
          is indebted to us.
    And lead us not into temptation."

[5]And he said to them, "Which of you who has a friend will go to him at midnight and say to him, 'Friend, lend me three loaves, [6]for a friend of mine has arrived on a journey, and I have nothing to set before him'; [7]and he will answer from within, 'Do not bother me; the door is now shut, and my children are with me in bed. I cannot get up and give you anything'? [8]I tell you, though he will not get up and give him anything because he is his friend, yet because of his impudence[3] he will rise and give him whatever he needs. [9]And I tell you, ask, and it will be given to you; seek, and you will find; knock, and it will be opened to you. [10]For everyone who asks receives, and the one who seeks finds, and to the one who knocks it will be opened. [11]What father among you, if his son asks for[4] a fish, will instead of a fish give him a serpent; [12]or if he asks for an egg, will give him a scorpion? [13]If you then, who are evil, know how to give good gifts to your children, how much more will the heavenly Father give the Holy Spirit to those who ask him!"

[14]Now he was casting out a demon that was mute. When the demon had gone out, the mute man spoke, and the people marveled. [15]But some of them said, "He casts out demons by Beelzebul, the prince of demons," [16]while others, to test him, kept seeking from him a sign from heaven. [17]But he, knowing their thoughts, said to them, "Every kingdom divided against itself is laid waste, and a divided household falls. [18]And if Satan also is divided against himself, how will his kingdom stand? For you say that I cast out demons by Beelzebul. [19]And if I cast out demons by Beelzebul, by whom do your sons cast them out? Therefore they will be your judges. [20]But if it is by the finger of God that I cast out demons, then the kingdom of God has come upon you. [21]When a strong man, fully armed, guards his own palace, his goods are safe; [22]but when one stronger than he attacks him and overcomes him, he takes away his armor in which he trusted and divides his spoil. [23]Whoever is not with me is against me, and whoever does not gather with me scatters.

[24]"When the unclean spirit has gone out of a person, it passes through waterless places seeking rest, and finding none it says, 'I will return to my house from which I came.' [25]And when it comes, it finds the house swept and put in order. [26]Then it goes and brings seven other spirits more evil than itself, and they enter and dwell there. And the last state of that person is worse than the first."

[27]As he said these things, a woman in the crowd raised her voice and said to him, "Blessed is the womb that bore you, and the breasts at which you nursed!" [28]But he said, "Blessed rather are those who hear the word of God and keep it!"

[29]When the crowds were increasing, he began to say, "This generation is an evil generation. It seeks for a sign, but no sign will be given to it except the sign of Jonah. [30]For as Jonah became a sign to the people of Nineveh, so will the Son of Man be to this generation. [31]The queen of the South will rise up at the judgment with the men of this generation and condemn them, for she came from the ends of the earth to hear the wisdom of Solomon, and behold, something greater than Solomon is here. [32]The men of Nineveh will rise up at the judgment with this generation and condemn it, for they repented at the preaching of Jonah, and behold, something greater than Jonah is here.

[33]"No one after lighting a lamp puts it in a cellar or under a basket, but on a stand, so that

---

[1] Greek *he* [2] Or *our bread for tomorrow* [3] Or *persistence* [4] Some manuscripts insert *bread, will give him a stone; or if he asks for*

those who enter may see the light. [34]Your eye is the lamp of your body. When your eye is healthy, your whole body is full of light, but when it is bad, your body is full of darkness. [35]Therefore be careful lest the light in you be darkness. [36]If then your whole body is full of light, having no part dark, it will be wholly bright, as when a lamp with its rays gives you light."

[37]While Jesus[1] was speaking, a Pharisee asked him to dine with him, so he went in and reclined at table. [38]The Pharisee was astonished to see that he did not first wash before dinner. [39]And the Lord said to him, "Now you Pharisees cleanse the outside of the cup and of the dish, but inside you are full of greed and wickedness. [40]You fools! Did not he who made the outside make the inside also? [41]But give as alms those things that are within, and behold, everything is clean for you.

[42]"But woe to you Pharisees! For you tithe mint and rue and every herb, and neglect justice and the love of God. These you ought to have done, without neglecting the others. [43]Woe to you Pharisees! For you love the best seat in the synagogues and greetings in the marketplaces. [44]Woe to you! For you are like unmarked graves, and people walk over them without knowing it."

[45]One of the lawyers answered him, "Teacher, in saying these things you insult us also." [46]And he said, "Woe to you lawyers also! For you load people with burdens hard to bear, and you yourselves do not touch the burdens with one of your fingers. [47]Woe to you! For you build the tombs of the prophets whom your fathers killed. [48]So you are witnesses and you consent to the deeds of your fathers, for they killed them, and you build their tombs. [49]Therefore also the Wisdom of God said, 'I will send them prophets and apostles, some of whom they will kill and persecute,' [50]so that the blood of all the prophets, shed from the foundation of the world, may be charged against this generation, [51]from the blood of Abel to the blood of Zechariah, who perished between the altar and the sanctuary. Yes, I tell you, it will be required of this generation. [52]Woe to you lawyers! For you have taken away the key of knowledge. You did not enter yourselves, and you hindered those who were entering."

[53]As he went away from there, the scribes and the Pharisees began to press him hard and to provoke him to speak about many things, [54]lying in wait for him, to catch him in something he might say.

NOVEMBER 28

1 Chronicles 24–25

The divisions of the sons of Aaron were these. The sons of Aaron: Nadab, Abihu, Eleazar, and Ithamar. [2]But Nadab and Abihu died before their father and had no children, so Eleazar and Ithamar became the priests. [3]With the help of Zadok of the sons of Eleazar, and Ahimelech of the sons of Ithamar, David organized them according to the appointed duties in their service. [4]Since more chief men were found among the sons of Eleazar than among the sons of Ithamar, they organized them under sixteen heads of fathers' houses of the sons of Eleazar, and eight of the sons of

Ithamar. [5]They divided them by lot, all alike, for there were sacred officers and officers of God among both the sons of Eleazar and the sons of Ithamar. [6]And the scribe Shemaiah, the son of Nethanel, a Levite, recorded them in the presence of the king and the princes and Zadok the priest and Ahimelech the son of Abiathar and the heads of the fathers' houses of the priests and of the Levites, one father's house being chosen for Eleazar and one chosen for Ithamar.

[7]The first lot fell to Jehoiarib, the second to Jedaiah, [8]the third to Harim, the fourth to Seorim, [9]the fifth to Malchijah, the sixth to

[1] Greek he

Mijamin, [10]the seventh to Hakkoz, the eighth to Abijah, [11]the ninth to Jeshua, the tenth to Shecaniah, [12]the eleventh to Eliashib, the twelfth to Jakim, [13]the thirteenth to Huppah, the fourteenth to Jeshebeab, [14]the fifteenth to Bilgah, the sixteenth to Immer, [15]the seventeenth to Hezir, the eighteenth to Happizzez, [16]the nineteenth to Pethahiah, the twentieth to Jehezkel, [17]the twenty-first to Jachin, the twenty-second to Gamul, [18]the twenty-third to Delaiah, the twenty-fourth to Maaziah. [19]These had as their appointed duty in their service to come into the house of the LORD according to the procedure established for them by Aaron their father, as the LORD God of Israel had commanded him.

[20]And of the rest of the sons of Levi: of the sons of Amram, Shubael; of the sons of Shubael, Jehdeiah. [21]Of Rehabiah: of the sons of Rehabiah, Isshiah the chief. [22]Of the Izharites, Shelomoth; of the sons of Shelomoth, Jahath. [23]The sons of Hebron:[1] Jeriah the chief,[2] Amariah the second, Jahaziel the third, Jekameam the fourth. [24]The sons of Uzziel, Micah; of the sons of Micah, Shamir. [25]The brother of Micah, Isshiah; of the sons of Isshiah, Zechariah. [26]The sons of Merari: Mahli and Mushi. The sons of Jaaziah: Beno.[3] [27]The sons of Merari: of Jaaziah, Beno, Shoham, Zaccur, and Ibri. [28]Of Mahli: Eleazar, who had no sons. [29]Of Kish, the sons of Kish: Jerahmeel. [30]The sons of Mushi: Mahli, Eder, and Jerimoth. These were the sons of the Levites according to their fathers' houses. [31]These also, the head of each father's house and his younger brother alike, cast lots, just as their brothers the sons of Aaron, in the presence of King David, Zadok, Ahimelech, and the heads of fathers' houses of the priests and of the Levites.

[25:1]David and the chiefs of the service also set apart for the service the sons of Asaph, and of Heman, and of Jeduthun, who prophesied with lyres, with harps, and with cymbals. The list of those who did the work and of their duties was: [2]Of the sons of Asaph: Zaccur, Joseph, Nethaniah, and Asharelah, sons of Asaph, under the direction of Asaph, who prophesied under the direction of the king. [3]Of Jeduthun, the sons of Jeduthun: Gedaliah, Zeri, Jeshaiah, Shimei,[4] Hashabiah, and Mattithiah, six, under the direction of their father Jeduthun, who prophesied with the lyre in thanksgiving and praise to the LORD. [4]Of Heman, the sons of Heman: Bukkiah, Mattaniah, Uzziel, Shebuel and Jerimoth, Hananiah, Hanani, Eliathah, Giddalti, and Romamti-ezer, Joshbekashah, Mallothi, Hothir, Mahazioth. [5]All these were the sons of Heman the king's seer, according to the promise of God to exalt him, for God had given Heman fourteen sons and three daughters. [6]They were all under the direction of their father in the music in the house of the LORD with cymbals, harps, and lyres for the service of the house of God. Asaph, Jeduthun, and Heman were under the order of the king. [7]The number of them along with their brothers, who were trained in singing to the LORD, all who were skillful, was 288. [8]And they cast lots for their duties, small and great, teacher and pupil alike.

[9]The first lot fell for Asaph to Joseph; the second to Gedaliah, to him and his brothers and his sons, twelve; [10]the third to Zaccur, his sons and his brothers, twelve; [11]the fourth to Izri, his sons and his brothers, twelve; [12]the fifth to Nethaniah, his sons and his brothers, twelve; [13]the sixth to Bukkiah, his sons and his brothers, twelve; [14]the seventh to Jesharelah, his sons and his brothers, twelve; [15]the eighth to Jeshaiah, his sons and his brothers, twelve; [16]the ninth to Mattaniah, his sons and his brothers, twelve; [17]the tenth to Shimei, his sons and his brothers, twelve; [18]the eleventh to Azarel, his sons and his brothers, twelve; [19]the twelfth to Hashabiah, his sons and his brothers, twelve; [20]to the thirteenth, Shubael, his sons and his brothers, twelve; [21]to the fourteenth, Mattithiah, his sons and his brothers, twelve; [22]to the fifteenth, to Jeremoth, his sons and his brothers, twelve; [23]to the sixteenth, to Hananiah, his sons and his brothers, twelve; [24]to the seventeenth, to Joshbekashah, his sons and his brothers, twelve; [25]to the eighteenth, to Hanani, his sons and his brothers, twelve; [26]to the nineteenth, to Mallothi, his sons and his brothers, twelve; [27]to the twentieth, to Eliathah, his sons and his brothers, twelve; [28]to the twenty-first, to Hothir, his sons and his brothers, twelve; [29]to the twenty-second, to Giddalti, his sons and his brothers, twelve; [30]to the twenty-third, to Mahazioth, his sons and his brothers, twelve; [31]to the twenty-fourth, to Romamti-ezer, his sons and his brothers, twelve.

---

[1] Compare 23:19; Hebrew lacks *Hebron* [2] Compare 23:19; Hebrew lacks *the chief* [3] Or *his son*; also verse 27 [4] One Hebrew manuscript, Septuagint; most Hebrew manuscripts lack *Shimei*

1 Peter 5

So I exhort the elders among you, as a fellow elder and a witness of the sufferings of Christ, as well as a partaker in the glory that is going to be revealed: ²shepherd the flock of God that is among you, exercising oversight,[1] not under compulsion, but willingly, as God would have you;[2] not for shameful gain, but eagerly; ³not domineering over those in your charge, but being examples to the flock. ⁴And when the chief Shepherd appears, you will receive the unfading crown of glory. ⁵Likewise, you who are younger, be subject to the elders. Clothe yourselves, all of you, with humility toward one another, for "God opposes the proud but gives grace to the humble."

⁶Humble yourselves, therefore, under the mighty hand of God so that at the proper time he may exalt you, ⁷casting all your anxieties on him, because he cares for you. ⁸Be soberminded; be watchful. Your adversary the devil prowls around like a roaring lion, seeking someone to devour. ⁹Resist him, firm in your faith, knowing that the same kinds of suffering are being experienced by your brotherhood throughout the world. ¹⁰And after you have suffered a little while, the God of all grace, who has called you to his eternal glory in Christ, will himself restore, confirm, strengthen, and establish you. ¹¹To him be the dominion forever and ever. Amen.

¹²By Silvanus, a faithful brother as I regard him, I have written briefly to you, exhorting and declaring that this is the true grace of God. Stand firm in it. ¹³She who is at Babylon, who is likewise chosen, sends you greetings, and so does Mark, my son. ¹⁴Greet one another with the kiss of love.

Peace to all of you who are in Christ.

Micah 3

And I said:
Hear, you heads of Jacob
    and rulers of the house of Israel!
Is it not for you to know justice?—
²   you who hate the good and love the
        evil,
    who tear the skin from off my people[3]
        and their flesh from off their bones,

³ who eat the flesh of my people,
    and flay their skin from off them,
and break their bones in pieces
    and chop them up like meat in a pot,
    like flesh in a cauldron.

⁴ Then they will cry to the LORD,
    but he will not answer them;
he will hide his face from them at that
        time,
    because they have made their deeds
        evil.

⁵ Thus says the LORD concerning the
        prophets
    who lead my people astray,
who cry "Peace"
    when they have something to eat,
but declare war against him
    who puts nothing into their mouths.
⁶ Therefore it shall be night to you,
        without vision,
    and darkness to you, without
        divination.
The sun shall go down on the prophets,
    and the day shall be black over them;
⁷ the seers shall be disgraced,
    and the diviners put to shame;
they shall all cover their lips,
    for there is no answer from God.
⁸ But as for me, I am filled with power,
    with the Spirit of the LORD,
    and with justice and might,
to declare to Jacob his transgression
    and to Israel his sin.

⁹ Hear this, you heads of the house of
        Jacob
    and rulers of the house of Israel,
who detest justice
    and make crooked all that is straight,
¹⁰ who build Zion with blood
    and Jerusalem with iniquity.
¹¹ Its heads give judgment for a bribe;
    its priests teach for a price;
    its prophets practice divination for
        money;
yet they lean on the LORD and say,
    "Is not the LORD in the midst of us?
    No disaster shall come upon us."
¹² Therefore because of you
    Zion shall be plowed as a field;

---

[1] Some manuscripts omit *exercising oversight* [2] Some manuscripts omit *as God would have you* [3] Hebrew *from off them*

Jerusalem shall become a heap of ruins,
and the mountain of the house a
wooded height.

Luke 12

In the meantime, when so many thousands of the people had gathered together that they were trampling one another, he began to say to his disciples first, "Beware of the leaven of the Pharisees, which is hypocrisy. ²Nothing is covered up that will not be revealed, or hidden that will not be known. ³Therefore whatever you have said in the dark shall be heard in the light, and what you have whispered in private rooms shall be proclaimed on the housetops.

⁴"I tell you, my friends, do not fear those who kill the body, and after that have nothing more that they can do. ⁵But I will warn you whom to fear: fear him who, after he has killed, has authority to cast into hell.¹ Yes, I tell you, fear him! ⁶Are not five sparrows sold for two pennies?² And not one of them is forgotten before God. ⁷Why, even the hairs of your head are all numbered. Fear not; you are of more value than many sparrows.

⁸"And I tell you, everyone who acknowledges me before men, the Son of Man also will acknowledge before the angels of God, ⁹but the one who denies me before men will be denied before the angels of God. ¹⁰And everyone who speaks a word against the Son of Man will be forgiven, but the one who blasphemes against the Holy Spirit will not be forgiven. ¹¹And when they bring you before the synagogues and the rulers and the authorities, do not be anxious about how you should defend yourself or what you should say, ¹²for the Holy Spirit will teach you in that very hour what you ought to say."

¹³Someone in the crowd said to him, "Teacher, tell my brother to divide the inheritance with me." ¹⁴But he said to him, "Man, who made me a judge or arbitrator over you?" ¹⁵And he said to them, "Take care, and be on your guard against all covetousness, for one's life does not consist in the abundance of his possessions." ¹⁶And he told them a parable, saying, "The land of a rich man produced plentifully, ¹⁷and he thought to himself, 'What shall I do, for I have nowhere to store my crops?' ¹⁸And he said, 'I will do this: I will tear down my barns

and build larger ones, and there I will store all my grain and my goods. ¹⁹And I will say to my soul, "Soul, you have ample goods laid up for many years; relax, eat, drink, be merry."' ²⁰But God said to him, 'Fool! This night your soul is required of you, and the things you have prepared, whose will they be?' ²¹So is the one who lays up treasure for himself and is not rich toward God."

²²And he said to his disciples, "Therefore I tell you, do not be anxious about your life, what you will eat, nor about your body, what you will put on. ²³For life is more than food, and the body more than clothing. ²⁴Consider the ravens: they neither sow nor reap, they have neither storehouse nor barn, and yet God feeds them. Of how much more value are you than the birds! ²⁵And which of you by being anxious can add a single hour to his span of life?³ ²⁶If then you are not able to do as small a thing as that, why are you anxious about the rest? ²⁷Consider the lilies, how they grow: they neither toil nor spin,⁴ yet I tell you, even Solomon in all his glory was not arrayed like one of these. ²⁸But if God so clothes the grass, which is alive in the field today, and tomorrow is thrown into the oven, how much more will he clothe you, O you of little faith! ²⁹And do not seek what you are to eat and what you are to drink, nor be worried. ³⁰For all the nations of the world seek after these things, and your Father knows that you need them. ³¹Instead, seek his⁵ kingdom, and these things will be added to you.

³²"Fear not, little flock, for it is your Father's good pleasure to give you the kingdom. ³³Sell your possessions, and give to the needy. Provide yourselves with moneybags that do not grow old, with a treasure in the heavens that does not fail, where no thief approaches and no moth destroys. ³⁴For where your treasure is, there will your heart be also.

³⁵"Stay dressed for action⁶ and keep your lamps burning, ³⁶and be like men who are waiting for their master to come home from the wedding feast, so that they may open the door to him at once when he comes and knocks. ³⁷Blessed are those servants⁷ whom the master finds awake when he comes. Truly, I say to you, he will dress himself for service and have them recline at table, and he will come and serve them. ³⁸If he comes in the second watch,

---

¹ Greek Gehenna ² Greek two assaria; an assarion was a Roman copper coin worth about 1/16 of a denarius (which was a day's wage for a laborer) ³ Or a single cubit to his stature; a cubit was about 18 inches or 45 centimeters ⁴ Some manuscripts Consider the lilies; they neither spin nor weave ⁵ Some manuscripts God's ⁶ Greek Let your loins stay girded; compare Exodus 12:11 ⁷ Greek bondservants

or in the third, and finds them awake, blessed are those servants! [39]But know this, that if the master of the house had known at what hour the thief was coming, he[1] would not have left his house to be broken into. [40]You also must be ready, for the Son of Man is coming at an hour you do not expect."

[41]Peter said, "Lord, are you telling this parable for us or for all?" [42]And the Lord said, "Who then is the faithful and wise manager, whom his master will set over his household, to give them their portion of food at the proper time? [43]Blessed is that servant[2] whom his master will find so doing when he comes. [44]Truly, I say to you, he will set him over all his possessions. [45]But if that servant says to himself, 'My master is delayed in coming,' and begins to beat the male and female servants, and to eat and drink and get drunk, [46]the master of that servant will come on a day when he does not expect him and at an hour he does not know, and will cut him in pieces and put him with the unfaithful. [47]And that servant who knew his master's will but did not get ready or act according to his will, will receive a severe beating. [48]But the one who did not know, and did what deserved a beating, will receive a light beating. Everyone to whom much was given, of him much will be required, and from him to whom they entrusted much, they will demand the more.

[49]"I came to cast fire on the earth, and would that it were already kindled! [50]I have a baptism to be baptized with, and how great is my distress until it is accomplished! [51]Do you think that I have come to give peace on earth? No, I tell you, but rather division. [52]For from now on in one house there will be five divided, three against two and two against three. [53]They will be divided, father against son and son against father, mother against daughter and daughter against mother, mother-in-law against her daughter-in-law and daughter-in-law against mother-in-law."

[54]He also said to the crowds, "When you see a cloud rising in the west, you say at once, 'A shower is coming.' And so it happens. [55]And when you see the south wind blowing, you say, 'There will be scorching heat,' and it happens. [56]You hypocrites! You know how to interpret the appearance of earth and sky, but why do you not know how to interpret the present time?

[57]"And why do you not judge for yourselves what is right? [58]As you go with your accuser before the magistrate, make an effort to settle with him on the way, lest he drag you to the judge, and the judge hand you over to the officer, and the officer put you in prison. [59]I tell you, you will never get out until you have paid the very last penny."[3]

NOVEMBER 29

1 Chronicles 26–27

As for the divisions of the gatekeepers: of the Korahites, Meshelemiah the son of Kore, of the sons of Asaph. [2]And Meshelemiah had sons: Zechariah the firstborn, Jediael the second, Zebadiah the third, Jathniel the fourth, [3]Elam the fifth, Jehohanan the sixth, Eliehoenai the seventh. [4]And Obed-edom had sons: Shemaiah the firstborn, Jehozabad the second, Joah the third, Sachar the fourth, Nethanel the fifth, [5]Ammiel the sixth, Issachar the seventh, Peullethai the eighth, for God

blessed him. [6]Also to his son Shemaiah were sons born who were rulers in their fathers' houses, for they were men of great ability. [7]The sons of Shemaiah: Othni, Rephael, Obed and Elzabad, whose brothers were able men, Elihu and Semachiah. [8]All these were of the sons of Obed-edom with their sons and brothers, able men qualified for the service; sixty-two of Obed-edom. [9]And Meshelemiah had sons and brothers, able men, eighteen. [10]And Hosah, of the sons of Merari, had sons: Shimri the

[1] Some manuscripts add *would have stayed awake and* [2] Greek *bondservant*; also verses 45, 46, 47 [3] Greek *lepton*, a Jewish bronze or copper coin worth about 1/128 of a *denarius* (which was a day's wage for a laborer)

chief (for though he was not the firstborn, his father made him chief), ¹¹Hilkiah the second, Tebaliah the third, Zechariah the fourth: all the sons and brothers of Hosah were thirteen.

¹²These divisions of the gatekeepers, corresponding to their chief men, had duties, just as their brothers did, ministering in the house of the Lord. ¹³And they cast lots by fathers' houses, small and great alike, for their gates. ¹⁴The lot for the east fell to Shelemiah. They cast lots also for his son Zechariah, a shrewd counselor, and his lot came out for the north. ¹⁵Obed-edom's came out for the south, and to his sons was allotted the gatehouse. ¹⁶For Shuppim and Hosah it came out for the west, at the gate of Shallecheth on the road that goes up. Watch corresponded to watch. ¹⁷On the east there were six each day,¹ on the north four each day, on the south four each day, as well as two and two at the gatehouse. ¹⁸And for the colonnade² on the west there were four at the road and two at the colonnade. ¹⁹These were the divisions of the gatekeepers among the Korahites and the sons of Merari.

²⁰And of the Levites, Ahijah had charge of the treasuries of the house of God and the treasuries of the dedicated gifts. ²¹The sons of Ladan, the sons of the Gershonites belonging to Ladan, the heads of the fathers' houses belonging to Ladan the Gershonite: Jehieli.³ ²²The sons of Jehieli, Zetham, and Joel his brother, were in charge of the treasuries of the house of the Lord. ²³Of the Amramites, the Izharites, the Hebronites, and the Uzzielites— ²⁴and Shebuel the son of Gershom, son of Moses, was chief officer in charge of the treasuries. ²⁵His brothers: from Eliezer were his son Rehabiah, and his son Jeshaiah, and his son Joram, and his son Zichri, and his son Shelomoth. ²⁶This Shelomoth and his brothers were in charge of all the treasuries of the dedicated gifts that David the king and the heads of the fathers' houses and the officers of the thousands and the hundreds and the commanders of the army had dedicated. ²⁷From spoil won in battles they dedicated gifts for the maintenance of the house of the Lord. ²⁸Also all that Samuel the seer and Saul the son of Kish and Abner the son of Ner and Joab the son of Zeruiah had dedicated—all dedicated gifts were in the care of Shelomoth⁴ and his brothers.

²⁹Of the Izharites, Chenaniah and his sons were appointed to external duties for Israel, as officers and judges. ³⁰Of the Hebronites, Hashabiah and his brothers, 1,700 men of ability, had the oversight of Israel westward of the Jordan for all the work of the Lord and for the service of the king. ³¹Of the Hebronites, Jerijah was chief of the Hebronites of whatever genealogy or fathers' houses. (In the fortieth year of David's reign search was made and men of great ability among them were found at Jazer in Gilead.) ³²King David appointed him and his brothers, 2,700 men of ability, heads of fathers' houses, to have the oversight of the Reubenites, the Gadites and the half-tribe of the Manassites for everything pertaining to God and for the affairs of the king.

²⁷:¹This is the number of the people of Israel, the heads of fathers' houses, the commanders of thousands and hundreds, and their officers who served the king in all matters concerning the divisions that came and went, month after month throughout the year, each division numbering 24,000:

²Jashobeam the son of Zabdiel was in charge of the first division in the first month; in his division were 24,000. ³He was a descendant of Perez and was chief of all the commanders. He served for the first month. ⁴Dodai the Ahohite⁵ was in charge of the division of the second month; in his division were 24,000. ⁵The third commander, for the third month, was Benaiah, the son of Jehoiada the chief priest; in his division were 24,000. ⁶This is the Benaiah who was a mighty man of the thirty and in command of the thirty; Ammizabad his son was in charge of his division.⁶ ⁷Asahel the brother of Joab was fourth, for the fourth month, and his son Zebadiah after him; in his division were 24,000. ⁸The fifth commander, for the fifth month, was Shamhuth the Izrahite; in his division were 24,000. ⁹Sixth, for the sixth month, was Ira, the son of Ikkesh the Tekoite; in his division were 24,000. ¹⁰Seventh, for the seventh month, was Helez the Pelonite, of the sons of Ephraim; in his division were 24,000. ¹¹Eighth, for the eighth month, was Sibbecai the Hushathite, of the Zerahites; in his division were 24,000. ¹²Ninth, for the ninth month, was Abiezer of Anathoth, a Benjaminite; in his division were 24,000. ¹³Tenth, for the tenth month, was Maharai of Netophah, of the Zerahites; in his division were 24,000. ¹⁴Eleventh, for the

¹ Septuagint; Hebrew six Levites ² Or court; Hebrew parbar (meaning unknown); twice in this verse ³ The Hebrew of verse 21 is uncertain ⁴ Hebrew Shelomith ⁵ Septuagint; Hebrew Ahohite and his division and Mikloth the chief officer ⁶ Septuagint, Vulgate; Hebrew was his division

eleventh month, was Benaiah of Pirathon, of the sons of Ephraim; in his division were 24,000. [15]Twelfth, for the twelfth month, was Heldai the Netophathite, of Othniel; in his division were 24,000.

[16]Over the tribes of Israel, for the Reubenites, Eliezer the son of Zichri was chief officer; for the Simeonites, Shephatiah the son of Maacah; [17]for Levi, Hashabiah the son of Kemuel; for Aaron, Zadok; [18]for Judah, Elihu, one of David's brothers; for Issachar, Omri the son of Michael; [19]for Zebulun, Ishmaiah the son of Obadiah; for Naphtali, Jeremoth the son of Azriel; [20]for the Ephraimites, Hoshea the son of Azaziah; for the half-tribe of Manasseh, Joel the son of Pedaiah; [21]for the half-tribe of Manasseh in Gilead, Iddo the son of Zechariah; for Benjamin, Jaasiel the son of Abner; [22]for Dan, Azarel the son of Jeroham. These were the leaders of the tribes of Israel. [23]David did not count those below twenty years of age, for the LORD had promised to make Israel as many as the stars of heaven. [24]Joab the son of Zeruiah began to count, but did not finish. Yet wrath came upon Israel for this, and the number was not entered in the chronicles of King David.

[25]Over the king's treasuries was Azmaveth the son of Adiel; and over the treasuries in the country, in the cities, in the villages, and in the towers, was Jonathan the son of Uzziah; [26]and over those who did the work of the field for tilling the soil was Ezri the son of Chelub; [27]and over the vineyards was Shimei the Ramathite; and over the produce of the vineyards for the wine cellars was Zabdi the Shiphmite. [28]Over the olive and sycamore trees in the Shephelah was Baal-hanan the Gederite; and over the stores of oil was Joash. [29]Over the herds that pastured in Sharon was Shitrai the Sharonite; over the herds in the valleys was Shaphat the son of Adlai. [30]Over the camels was Obil the Ishmaelite; and over the donkeys was Jehdeiah the Meronothite. Over the flocks was Jaziz the Hagrite. [31]All these were stewards of King David's property.

[32]Jonathan, David's uncle, was a counselor, being a man of understanding and a scribe. He and Jehiel the son of Hachmoni attended the king's sons. [33]Ahithophel was the king's counselor, and Hushai the Archite was the king's friend. [34]Ahithophel was succeeded by Jehoiada the son of Benaiah, and Abiathar. Joab was commander of the king's army.

─────────── 2 Peter 1 ───────────

S imeon[1] Peter, a servant[2] and apostle of Jesus Christ,

To those who have obtained a faith of equal standing with ours by the righteousness of our God and Savior Jesus Christ:

[2]May grace and peace be multiplied to you in the knowledge of God and of Jesus our Lord.

[3]His divine power has granted to us all things that pertain to life and godliness, through the knowledge of him who called us to[3] his own glory and excellence,[4] [4]by which he has granted to us his precious and very great promises, so that through them you may become partakers of the divine nature, having escaped from the corruption that is in the world because of sinful desire. [5]For this very reason, make every effort to supplement your faith with virtue,[5] and virtue with knowledge, [6]and knowledge with self-control, and self-control with steadfastness, and steadfastness with godliness, [7]and godliness with brotherly affection, and brotherly affection with love. [8]For if these qualities[6] are yours and are increasing, they keep you from being ineffective or unfruitful in the knowledge of our Lord Jesus Christ. [9]For whoever lacks these qualities is so nearsighted that he is blind, having forgotten that he was cleansed from his former sins. [10]Therefore, brothers,[7] be all the more diligent to confirm your calling and election, for if you practice these qualities you will never fall. [11]For in this way there will be richly provided for you an entrance into the eternal kingdom of our Lord and Savior Jesus Christ.

[12]Therefore I intend always to remind you of these qualities, though you know them and are established in the truth that you have. [13]I think it right, as long as I am in this body,[8] to stir you up by way of reminder, [14]since I know that the putting off of my body will be soon, as our Lord Jesus Christ made clear to me. [15]And I will make every effort so that after my departure you may be able at any time to recall these things.

[16]For we did not follow cleverly devised myths when we made known to you the power and coming of our Lord Jesus Christ, but we were eyewitnesses of his majesty. [17]For when he

[1]Some manuscripts Simon [2]Or slave (for the contextual rendering of the Greek word doulos, see Preface) [3]Or by [4]Or virtue [5]Or excellence; twice in this verse [6]Greek these things; also verses 9, 10, 12 [7]Or brothers and sisters. The plural Greek word adelphoi (translated "brothers") refers to siblings in a family. In New Testament usage, depending on the context, adelphoi may refer either to men or to both men and women who are siblings (brothers and sisters) in God's family, the church [8]Greek tent; also verse 14

received honor and glory from God the Father, and the voice was borne to him by the Majestic Glory, "This is my beloved Son,[1] with whom I am well pleased," [18]we ourselves heard this very voice borne from heaven, for we were with him on the holy mountain. [19]And we have the prophetic word more fully confirmed, to which you will do well to pay attention as to a lamp shining in a dark place, until the day dawns and the morning star rises in your hearts, [20]knowing this first of all, that no prophecy of Scripture comes from someone's own interpretation. [21]For no prophecy was ever produced by the will of man, but men spoke from God as they were carried along by the Holy Spirit.

Micah 4

It shall come to pass in the latter days
that the mountain of the house of the LORD
    shall be established as the highest of the
        mountains,
    and it shall be lifted up above the hills;
and peoples shall flow to it,
[2]   and many nations shall come, and say:
"Come, let us go up to the mountain of
        the LORD,
    to the house of the God of Jacob,
that he may teach us his ways
    and that we may walk in his paths."
For out of Zion shall go forth the law,[2]
    and the word of the LORD from
        Jerusalem.
[3] He shall judge between many peoples,
    and shall decide for strong nations far
        away;
and they shall beat their swords into
        plowshares,
    and their spears into pruning hooks;
nation shall not lift up sword against
        nation,
    neither shall they learn war anymore;
[4] but they shall sit every man under his
        vine and under his fig tree,
    and no one shall make them afraid,
    for the mouth of the LORD of hosts
        has spoken.
[5] For all the peoples walk
    each in the name of its god,
but we will walk in the name of the
        LORD our God
    forever and ever.

[6] In that day, declares the LORD,
    I will assemble the lame
and gather those who have been driven
        away
    and those whom I have afflicted;
[7] and the lame I will make the remnant,
    and those who were cast off, a strong
        nation;
and the LORD will reign over them in
        Mount Zion
    from this time forth and
        forevermore.

[8] And you, O tower of the flock,
    hill of the daughter of Zion,
to you shall it come,
    the former dominion shall come,
    kingship for the daughter of
        Jerusalem.

[9] Now why do you cry aloud?
    Is there no king in you?
Has your counselor perished,
    that pain seized you like a woman in
        labor?
[10] Writhe and groan,[3] O daughter of
        Zion,
    like a woman in labor,
for now you shall go out from the city
    and dwell in the open country;
    you shall go to Babylon.
There you shall be rescued;
    there the LORD will redeem you
    from the hand of your enemies.

[11] Now many nations
    are assembled against you,
saying, "Let her be defiled,
    and let our eyes gaze upon Zion."
[12] But they do not know
    the thoughts of the LORD;
they do not understand his plan,
    that he has gathered them as sheaves
        to the threshing floor.
[13] Arise and thresh,
    O daughter of Zion,
for I will make your horn iron,
    and I will make your hoofs bronze;
you shall beat in pieces many peoples;
    and shall devote[4] their gain to the
        LORD,
    their wealth to the Lord of the whole
        earth.

[1] Or my Son, my (or the) Beloved [2] Or teaching [3] Or push [4] Hebrew devote to destruction

Luke 13

There were some present at that very time who told him about the Galileans whose blood Pilate had mingled with their sacrifices. [2]And he answered them, "Do you think that these Galileans were worse sinners than all the other Galileans, because they suffered in this way? [3]No, I tell you; but unless you repent, you will all likewise perish. [4]Or those eighteen on whom the tower in Siloam fell and killed them: do you think that they were worse offenders than all the others who lived in Jerusalem? [5]No, I tell you; but unless you repent, you will all likewise perish."

[6]And he told this parable: "A man had a fig tree planted in his vineyard, and he came seeking fruit on it and found none. [7]And he said to the vinedresser, 'Look, for three years now I have come seeking fruit on this fig tree, and I find none. Cut it down. Why should it use up the ground?' [8]And he answered him, 'Sir, let it alone this year also, until I dig around it and put on manure. [9]Then if it should bear fruit next year, well and good; but if not, you can cut it down.'"

[10]Now he was teaching in one of the synagogues on the Sabbath. [11]And behold, there was a woman who had had a disabling spirit for eighteen years. She was bent over and could not fully straighten herself. [12]When Jesus saw her, he called her over and said to her, "Woman, you are freed from your disability." [13]And he laid his hands on her, and immediately she was made straight, and she glorified God. [14]But the ruler of the synagogue, indignant because Jesus had healed on the Sabbath, said to the people, "There are six days in which work ought to be done. Come on those days and be healed, and not on the Sabbath day." [15]Then the Lord answered him, "You hypocrites! Does not each of you on the Sabbath untie his ox or his donkey from the manger and lead it away to water it? [16]And ought not this woman, a daughter of Abraham whom Satan bound for eighteen years, be loosed from this bond on the Sabbath day?" [17]As he said these things, all his adversaries were put to shame, and all the people rejoiced at all the glorious things that were done by him.

[18]He said therefore, "What is the kingdom of God like? And to what shall I compare it? [19]It is like a grain of mustard seed that a man took and sowed in his garden, and it grew and became a tree, and the birds of the air made nests in its branches."

[20]And again he said, "To what shall I compare the kingdom of God? [21]It is like leaven that a woman took and hid in three measures of flour, until it was all leavened."

[22]He went on his way through towns and villages, teaching and journeying toward Jerusalem. [23]And someone said to him, "Lord, will those who are saved be few?" And he said to them, [24]"Strive to enter through the narrow door. For many, I tell you, will seek to enter and will not be able. [25]When once the master of the house has risen and shut the door, and you begin to stand outside and to knock at the door, saying, 'Lord, open to us,' then he will answer you, 'I do not know where you come from.' [26]Then you will begin to say, 'We ate and drank in your presence, and you taught in our streets.' [27]But he will say, 'I tell you, I do not know where you come from. Depart from me, all you workers of evil!' [28]In that place there will be weeping and gnashing of teeth, when you see Abraham and Isaac and Jacob and all the prophets in the kingdom of God but you yourselves cast out. [29]And people will come from east and west, and from north and south, and recline at table in the kingdom of God. [30]And behold, some are last who will be first, and some are first who will be last."

[31]At that very hour some Pharisees came and said to him, "Get away from here, for Herod wants to kill you." [32]And he said to them, "Go and tell that fox, 'Behold, I cast out demons and perform cures today and tomorrow, and the third day I finish my course. [33]Nevertheless, I must go on my way today and tomorrow and the day following, for it cannot be that a prophet should perish away from Jerusalem.' [34]O Jerusalem, Jerusalem, the city that kills the prophets and stones those who are sent to it! How often would I have gathered your children together as a hen gathers her brood under her wings, and you were not willing! [35]Behold, your house is forsaken. And I tell you, you will not see me until you say, 'Blessed is he who comes in the name of the Lord!'"

NOVEMBER 30

1 Chronicles 28

David assembled at Jerusalem all the officials of Israel, the officials of the tribes, the officers of the divisions that served the king, the commanders of thousands, the commanders of hundreds, the stewards of all the property and livestock of the king and his sons, together with the palace officials, the mighty men and all the seasoned warriors. ²Then King David rose to his feet and said: "Hear me, my brothers and my people. I had it in my heart to build a house of rest for the ark of the covenant of the LORD and for the footstool of our God, and I made preparations for building. ³But God said to me, 'You may not build a house for my name, for you are a man of war and have shed blood.' ⁴Yet the LORD God of Israel chose me from all my father's house to be king over Israel forever. For he chose Judah as leader, and in the house of Judah my father's house, and among my father's sons he took pleasure in me to make me king over all Israel. ⁵And of all my sons (for the LORD has given me many sons) he has chosen Solomon my son to sit on the throne of the kingdom of the LORD over Israel. ⁶He said to me, 'It is Solomon your son who shall build my house and my courts, for I have chosen him to be my son, and I will be his father. ⁷I will establish his kingdom forever if he continues strong in keeping my commandments and my rules, as he is today.' ⁸Now therefore in the sight of all Israel, the assembly of the LORD, and in the hearing of our God, observe and seek out all the commandments of the LORD your God, that you may possess this good land and leave it for an inheritance to your children after you forever.

⁹"And you, Solomon my son, know the God of your father and serve him with a whole heart and with a willing mind, for the LORD searches all hearts and understands every plan and thought. If you seek him, he will be found by you, but if you forsake him, he will cast you off forever. ¹⁰Be careful now, for the LORD has chosen you to build a house for the sanctuary; be strong and do it."

¹¹Then David gave Solomon his son the plan of the vestibule of the temple,[1] and of its houses, its treasuries, its upper rooms, and its inner chambers, and of the room for the mercy seat; ¹²and the plan of all that he had in mind for the courts of the house of the LORD, all the surrounding chambers, the treasuries of the house of God, and the treasuries for dedicated gifts; ¹³for the divisions of the priests and of the Levites, and all the work of the service in the house of the LORD; for all the vessels for the service in the house of the LORD, ¹⁴the weight of gold for all golden vessels for each service, the weight of silver vessels for each service, ¹⁵the weight of the golden lampstands and their lamps, the weight of gold for each lampstand and its lamps, the weight of silver for a lampstand and its lamps, according to the use of each lampstand in the service, ¹⁶the weight of gold for each table for the showbread, the silver for the silver tables, ¹⁷and pure gold for the forks, the basins and the cups; for the golden bowls and the weight of each; for the silver bowls and the weight of each; ¹⁸for the altar of incense made of refined gold, and its weight; also his plan for the golden chariot of the cherubim that spread their wings and covered the ark of the covenant of the LORD. ¹⁹"All this he made clear to me in writing from the hand of the LORD, all the work to be done according to the plan."

²⁰Then David said to Solomon his son, "Be strong and courageous and do it. Do not be afraid and do not be dismayed, for the LORD God, even my God, is with you. He will not leave you or forsake you, until all the work for the service of the house of the LORD is finished. ²¹And behold the divisions of the priests and the Levites for all the service of the house of God; and with you in all the work will be every willing man who has skill for any kind of service; also the officers and all the people will be wholly at your command."

[1] Hebrew lacks *of the temple*

2 Peter 2

But false prophets also arose among the people, just as there will be false teachers among you, who will secretly bring in destructive heresies, even denying the Master who bought them, bringing upon themselves swift destruction. ²And many will follow their sensuality, and because of them the way of truth will be blasphemed. ³And in their greed they will exploit you with false words. Their condemnation from long ago is not idle, and their destruction is not asleep.

⁴For if God did not spare angels when they sinned, but cast them into hell¹ and committed them to chains² of gloomy darkness to be kept until the judgment; ⁵if he did not spare the ancient world, but preserved Noah, a herald of righteousness, with seven others, when he brought a flood upon the world of the ungodly; ⁶if by turning the cities of Sodom and Gomorrah to ashes he condemned them to extinction, making them an example of what is going to happen to the ungodly;³ ⁷and if he rescued righteous Lot, greatly distressed by the sensual conduct of the wicked ⁸(for as that righteous man lived among them day after day, he was tormenting his righteous soul over their lawless deeds that he saw and heard); ⁹then the Lord knows how to rescue the godly from trials,⁴ and to keep the unrighteous under punishment until the day of judgment, ¹⁰and especially those who indulge⁵ in the lust of defiling passion and despise authority.

Bold and willful, they do not tremble as they blaspheme the glorious ones, ¹¹whereas angels, though greater in might and power, do not pronounce a blasphemous judgment against them before the Lord. ¹²But these, like irrational animals, creatures of instinct, born to be caught and destroyed, blaspheming about matters of which they are ignorant, will also be destroyed in their destruction, ¹³suffering wrong as the wage for their wrongdoing. They count it pleasure to revel in the daytime. They are blots and blemishes, reveling in their deceptions,⁶ while they feast with you. ¹⁴They have eyes full of adultery, insatiable for sin. They entice unsteady souls. They have hearts trained in greed. Accursed children! ¹⁵Forsaking the right way, they have gone astray. They have followed the way of Balaam, the son of Beor, who loved gain from wrongdoing, ¹⁶but was rebuked for his own transgression; a speechless donkey spoke with human voice and restrained the prophet's madness.

¹⁷These are waterless springs and mists driven by a storm. For them the gloom of utter darkness has been reserved. ¹⁸For, speaking loud boasts of folly, they entice by sensual passions of the flesh those who are barely escaping from those who live in error. ¹⁹They promise them freedom, but they themselves are slaves⁷ of corruption. For whatever overcomes a person, to that he is enslaved. ²⁰For if, after they have escaped the defilements of the world through the knowledge of our Lord and Savior Jesus Christ, they are again entangled in them and overcome, the last state has become worse for them than the first. ²¹For it would have been better for them never to have known the way of righteousness than after knowing it to turn back from the holy commandment delivered to them. ²²What the true proverb says has happened to them: "The dog returns to its own vomit, and the sow, after washing herself, returns to wallow in the mire."

Micah 5⁸

Now muster your troops, O daughter⁹ of troops;
    siege is laid against us;
    with a rod they strike the judge of Israel
      on the cheek.
² ¹⁰ But you, O Bethlehem Ephrathah,
    who are too little to be among the
      clans of Judah,
  from you shall come forth for me
    one who is to be ruler in Israel,
  whose coming forth is from of old,
    from ancient days.
³   Therefore he shall give them up until
      the time
    when she who is in labor has given
      birth;
  then the rest of his brothers shall
      return
    to the people of Israel.
⁴   And he shall stand and shepherd his
      flock in the strength of the Lord,
  in the majesty of the name of the
      Lord his God.

¹ Greek *Tartarus* ² Some manuscripts *pits* ³ Some manuscripts *an example to those who were to be ungodly* ⁴ Or *temptations* ⁵ Greek *who go after the flesh* ⁶ Some manuscripts *love feasts* ⁷ Greek *bondservants* ⁸ Ch 4:14 in Hebrew ⁹ That is, *city* ¹⁰ Ch 5:1 in Hebrew

And they shall dwell secure, for now he
    shall be great
    to the ends of the earth.
5 And he shall be their peace.

When the Assyrian comes into our land
    and treads in our palaces,
then we will raise against him seven
    shepherds
    and eight princes of men;
6 they shall shepherd the land of Assyria
    with the sword,
    and the land of Nimrod at its
      entrances;
and he shall deliver us from the
    Assyrian
    when he comes into our land
    and treads within our border.

7 Then the remnant of Jacob shall be
    in the midst of many peoples
like dew from the LORD,
    like showers on the grass,
which delay not for a man
    nor wait for the children of man.
8 And the remnant of Jacob shall be
    among the nations,
    in the midst of many peoples,
like a lion among the beasts of the
    forest,
like a young lion among the flocks of
    sheep,
which, when it goes through, treads
    down
    and tears in pieces, and there is none
      to deliver.
9 Your hand shall be lifted up over your
    adversaries,
    and all your enemies shall be cut off.

10 And in that day, declares the LORD,
    I will cut off your horses from among
      you
    and will destroy your chariots;
11 and I will cut off the cities of your land
    and throw down all your
      strongholds;
12 and I will cut off sorceries from your
    hand,
    and you shall have no more tellers of
      fortunes;
13 and I will cut off your carved images
    and your pillars from among you,

    and you shall bow down no more
    to the work of your hands;
14 and I will root out your Asherah images
    from among you
    and destroy your cities.
15 And in anger and wrath I will execute
    vengeance
    on the nations that did not obey.

Luke 14

One Sabbath, when he went to dine at the house of a ruler of the Pharisees, they were watching him carefully. ² And behold, there was a man before him who had dropsy. ³ And Jesus responded to the lawyers and Pharisees, saying, "Is it lawful to heal on the Sabbath, or not?" ⁴ But they remained silent. Then he took him and healed him and sent him away. ⁵ And he said to them, "Which of you, having a son[1] or an ox that has fallen into a well on a Sabbath day, will not immediately pull him out?" ⁶ And they could not reply to these things.

⁷ Now he told a parable to those who were invited, when he noticed how they chose the places of honor, saying to them, ⁸ "When you are invited by someone to a wedding feast, do not sit down in a place of honor, lest someone more distinguished than you be invited by him, ⁹ and he who invited you both will come and say to you, 'Give your place to this person,' and then you will begin with shame to take the lowest place. ¹⁰ But when you are invited, go and sit in the lowest place, so that when your host comes he may say to you, 'Friend, move up higher.' Then you will be honored in the presence of all who sit at table with you. ¹¹ For everyone who exalts himself will be humbled, and he who humbles himself will be exalted."

¹² He said also to the man who had invited him, "When you give a dinner or a banquet, do not invite your friends or your brothers[2] or your relatives or rich neighbors, lest they also invite you in return and you be repaid. ¹³ But when you give a feast, invite the poor, the crippled, the lame, the blind, ¹⁴ and you will be blessed, because they cannot repay you. For you will be repaid at the resurrection of the just."

¹⁵ When one of those who reclined at table with him heard these things, he said to him, "Blessed is everyone who will eat bread in the kingdom of God!" ¹⁶ But he said to him, "A man

---

[1] Some manuscripts *a donkey* [2] Or *your brothers and sisters*. The plural Greek word *adelphoi* (translated "brothers") refers to siblings in a family. In New Testament usage, depending on the context, *adelphoi* may refer either to *brothers* or to *brothers and sisters*

once gave a great banquet and invited many. [17]And at the time for the banquet he sent his servant[1] to say to those who had been invited, 'Come, for everything is now ready.' [18]But they all alike began to make excuses. The first said to him, 'I have bought a field, and I must go out and see it. Please have me excused.' [19]And another said, 'I have bought five yoke of oxen, and I go to examine them. Please have me excused.' [20]And another said, 'I have married a wife, and therefore I cannot come.' [21]So the servant came and reported these things to his master. Then the master of the house became angry and said to his servant, 'Go out quickly to the streets and lanes of the city, and bring in the poor and crippled and blind and lame.' [22]And the servant said, 'Sir, what you commanded has been done, and still there is room.' [23]And the master said to the servant, 'Go out to the highways and hedges and compel people to come in, that my house may be filled. [24]For I tell you,[2] none of those men who were invited shall taste my banquet.'"

[25]Now great crowds accompanied him, and he turned and said to them, [26]"If anyone comes to me and does not hate his own father and mother and wife and children and brothers and sisters, yes, and even his own life, he cannot be my disciple. [27]Whoever does not bear his own cross and come after me cannot be my disciple. [28]For which of you, desiring to build a tower, does not first sit down and count the cost, whether he has enough to complete it? [29]Otherwise, when he has laid a foundation and is not able to finish, all who see it begin to mock him, [30]saying, 'This man began to build and was not able to finish.' [31]Or what king, going out to encounter another king in war, will not sit down first and deliberate whether he is able with ten thousand to meet him who comes against him with twenty thousand? [32]And if not, while the other is yet a great way off, he sends a delegation and asks for terms of peace. [33]So therefore, any one of you who does not renounce all that he has cannot be my disciple.

[34]"Salt is good, but if salt has lost its taste, how shall its saltiness be restored? [35]It is of no use either for the soil or for the manure pile. It is thrown away. He who has ears to hear, let him hear."

---

[1] Greek bondservant; also verses 21, 22, 23　[2] The Greek word for you here is plural

DECEMBER 1

1 Chronicles 29

And David the king said to all the assembly, "Solomon my son, whom alone God has chosen, is young and inexperienced, and the work is great, for the palace will not be for man but for the LORD God. ²So I have provided for the house of my God, so far as I was able, the gold for the things of gold, the silver for the things of silver, and the bronze for the things of bronze, the iron for the things of iron, and wood for the things of wood, besides great quantities of onyx and stones for setting, antimony, colored stones, all sorts of precious stones and marble. ³Moreover, in addition to all that I have provided for the holy house, I have a treasure of my own of gold and silver, and because of my devotion to the house of my God I give it to the house of my God: ⁴3,000 talents¹ of gold, of the gold of Ophir, and 7,000 talents of refined silver, for overlaying the walls of the house,² ⁵and for all the work to be done by craftsmen, gold for the things of gold and silver for the things of silver. Who then will offer willingly, consecrating himself³ today to the LORD?"

⁶Then the leaders of fathers' houses made their freewill offerings, as did also the leaders of the tribes, the commanders of thousands and of hundreds, and the officers over the king's work. ⁷They gave for the service of the house of God 5,000 talents and 10,000 darics⁴ of gold, 10,000 talents of silver, 18,000 talents of bronze and 100,000 talents of iron. ⁸And whoever had precious stones gave them to the treasury of the house of the LORD, in the care of Jehiel the Gershonite. ⁹Then the people rejoiced because they had given willingly, for with a whole heart they had offered freely to the LORD. David the king also rejoiced greatly.

¹⁰Therefore David blessed the LORD in the presence of all the assembly. And David said: "Blessed are you, O LORD, the God of Israel our father, forever and ever. ¹¹Yours, O LORD, is the greatness and the power and the glory and the victory and the majesty, for all that is in the heavens and in the earth is yours. Yours

is the kingdom, O LORD, and you are exalted as head above all. ¹²Both riches and honor come from you, and you rule over all. In your hand are power and might, and in your hand it is to make great and to give strength to all. ¹³And now we thank you, our God, and praise your glorious name.

¹⁴"But who am I, and what is my people, that we should be able thus to offer willingly? For all things come from you, and of your own have we given you. ¹⁵For we are strangers before you and sojourners, as all our fathers were. Our days on the earth are like a shadow, and there is no abiding.⁵ ¹⁶O LORD our God, all this abundance that we have provided for building you a house for your holy name comes from your hand and is all your own. ¹⁷I know, my God, that you test the heart and have pleasure in uprightness. In the uprightness of my heart I have freely offered all these things, and now I have seen your people, who are present here, offering freely and joyously to you. ¹⁸O LORD, the God of Abraham, Isaac, and Israel, our fathers, keep forever such purposes and thoughts in the hearts of your people, and direct their hearts toward you. ¹⁹Grant to Solomon my son a whole heart that he may keep your commandments, your testimonies, and your statutes, performing all, and that he may build the palace for which I have made provision."

²⁰Then David said to all the assembly, "Bless the LORD your God." And all the assembly blessed the LORD, the God of their fathers, and bowed their heads and paid homage to the LORD and to the king. ²¹And they offered sacrifices to the LORD, and on the next day offered burnt offerings to the LORD, 1,000 bulls, 1,000 rams, and 1,000 lambs, with their drink offerings, and sacrifices in abundance for all Israel. ²²And they ate and drank before the LORD on that day with great gladness.

And they made Solomon the son of David king the second time, and they anointed him as prince for the LORD, and Zadok as priest.

¹ A talent was about 75 pounds or 34 kilograms ² Septuagint; Hebrew houses ³ Or ordaining himself; Hebrew filling his hand ⁴ A daric was a coin weighing about 1/4 ounce or 8.5 grams ⁵ Septuagint, Vulgate; Hebrew hope, or prospect

²³Then Solomon sat on the throne of the LORD as king in place of David his father. And he prospered, and all Israel obeyed him. ²⁴All the leaders and the mighty men, and also all the sons of King David, pledged their allegiance to King Solomon. ²⁵And the LORD made Solomon very great in the sight of all Israel and bestowed on him such royal majesty as had not been on any king before him in Israel.

²⁶Thus David the son of Jesse reigned over all Israel. ²⁷The time that he reigned over Israel was forty years. He reigned seven years in Hebron and thirty-three years in Jerusalem. ²⁸Then he died at a good age, full of days, riches, and honor. And Solomon his son reigned in his place. ²⁹Now the acts of King David, from first to last, are written in the Chronicles of Samuel the seer, and in the Chronicles of Nathan the prophet, and in the Chronicles of Gad the seer, ³⁰with accounts of all his rule and his might and of the circumstances that came upon him and upon Israel and upon all the kingdoms of the countries.

───────── *2 Peter 3* ─────────

This is now the second letter that I am writing to you, beloved. In both of them I am stirring up your sincere mind by way of reminder, ²that you should remember the predictions of the holy prophets and the commandment of the Lord and Savior through your apostles, ³knowing this first of all, that scoffers will come in the last days with scoffing, following their own sinful desires. ⁴They will say, "Where is the promise of his coming? For ever since the fathers fell asleep, all things are continuing as they were from the beginning of creation." ⁵For they deliberately overlook this fact, that the heavens existed long ago, and the earth was formed out of water and through water by the word of God, ⁶and that by means of these the world that then existed was deluged with water and perished. ⁷But by the same word the heavens and earth that now exist are stored up for fire, being kept until the day of judgment and destruction of the ungodly.

⁸But do not overlook this one fact, beloved, that with the Lord one day is as a thousand years, and a thousand years as one day. ⁹The Lord is not slow to fulfill his promise as some

count slowness, but is patient toward you,¹ not wishing that any should perish, but that all should reach repentance. ¹⁰But the day of the Lord will come like a thief, and then the heavens will pass away with a roar, and the heavenly bodies² will be burned up and dissolved, and the earth and the works that are done on it will be exposed.³

¹¹Since all these things are thus to be dissolved, what sort of people ought you to be in lives of holiness and godliness, ¹²waiting for and hastening the coming of the day of God, because of which the heavens will be set on fire and dissolved, and the heavenly bodies will melt as they burn! ¹³But according to his promise we are waiting for new heavens and a new earth in which righteousness dwells.

¹⁴Therefore, beloved, since you are waiting for these, be diligent to be found by him without spot or blemish, and at peace. ¹⁵And count the patience of our Lord as salvation, just as our beloved brother Paul also wrote to you according to the wisdom given him, ¹⁶as he does in all his letters when he speaks in them of these matters. There are some things in them that are hard to understand, which the ignorant and unstable twist to their own destruction, as they do the other Scriptures. ¹⁷You therefore, beloved, knowing this beforehand, take care that you are not carried away with the error of lawless people and lose your own stability. ¹⁸But grow in the grace and knowledge of our Lord and Savior Jesus Christ. To him be the glory both now and to the day of eternity. Amen.

───────── *Micah 6* ─────────

Hear what the LORD says:
Arise, plead your case before the
        mountains,
    and let the hills hear your voice.
2   Hear, you mountains, the indictment of
        the LORD,
    and you enduring foundations of the
        earth,
    for the LORD has an indictment against
        his people,
    and he will contend with Israel.

3   "O my people, what have I done to you?
    How have I wearied you? Answer me!

4 For I brought you up from the land of
     Egypt
     and redeemed you from the house of
         slavery,
     and I sent before you Moses,
         Aaron, and Miriam.
5 O my people, remember what Balak
         king of Moab devised,
     and what Balaam the son of Beor
         answered him,
     and what happened from Shittim to
         Gilgal,
     that you may know the righteous acts
         of the LORD."

6 "With what shall I come before the LORD,
     and bow myself before God on high?
     Shall I come before him with burnt
         offerings,
     with calves a year old?
7 Will the LORD be pleased with[1]
         thousands of rams,
     with ten thousands of rivers of oil?
     Shall I give my firstborn for my
         transgression,
     the fruit of my body for the sin of my
         soul?"
8 He has told you, O man, what is good;
     and what does the LORD require of
         you
     but to do justice, and to love kindness,[2]
     and to walk humbly with your God?

9 The voice of the LORD cries to the city—
     and it is sound wisdom to fear your
         name:
     "Hear of the rod and of him who
         appointed it![3]
10 Can I forget any longer the treasures[4]
         of wickedness in the house of the
         wicked,
     and the scant measure that is
         accursed?
11 Shall I acquit the man with wicked scales
     and with a bag of deceitful weights?
12 Your[5] rich men are full of violence;
     your inhabitants speak lies,
     and their tongue is deceitful in their
         mouth.
13 Therefore I strike you with a grievous
         blow,
     making you desolate because of your
         sins.

14 You shall eat, but not be satisfied,
     and there shall be hunger within you;
     you shall put away, but not preserve,
     and what you preserve I will give to
         the sword.
15 You shall sow, but not reap;
     you shall tread olives, but not anoint
         yourselves with oil;
     you shall tread grapes, but not drink
         wine.
16 For you have kept the statutes of Omri,[6]
     and all the works of the house of Ahab;
     and you have walked in their counsels,
     that I may make you a desolation, and
         your[7] inhabitants a hissing;
     so you shall bear the scorn of my
         people."

Luke 15

Now the tax collectors and sinners were all drawing near to hear him. ²And the Pharisees and the scribes grumbled, saying, "This man receives sinners and eats with them."

³So he told them this parable: ⁴"What man of you, having a hundred sheep, if he has lost one of them, does not leave the ninety-nine in the open country, and go after the one that is lost, until he finds it? ⁵And when he has found it, he lays it on his shoulders, rejoicing. ⁶And when he comes home, he calls together his friends and his neighbors, saying to them, 'Rejoice with me, for I have found my sheep that was lost.' ⁷Just so, I tell you, there will be more joy in heaven over one sinner who repents than over ninety-nine righteous persons who need no repentance.

⁸"Or what woman, having ten silver coins,[8] if she loses one coin, does not light a lamp and sweep the house and seek diligently until she finds it? ⁹And when she has found it, she calls together her friends and neighbors, saying, 'Rejoice with me, for I have found the coin that I had lost.' ¹⁰Just so, I tell you, there is joy before the angels of God over one sinner who repents."

¹¹And he said, "There was a man who had two sons. ¹²And the younger of them said to his father, 'Father, give me the share of property that is coming to me.' And he divided his property between them. ¹³Not many days later, the younger son gathered all he had and took a journey into a far country, and there

---

[1] Or Will the LORD accept   [2] Or steadfast love   [3] The meaning of the Hebrew is uncertain   [4] Or Are there still treasures   [5] Hebrew whose   [6] Hebrew For the statutes of Omri are kept
[7] Hebrew its   [8] Greek ten drachmas; a drachma was a Greek coin approximately equal in value to a Roman denarius, worth about a day's wage for a laborer

he squandered his property in reckless living. [14]And when he had spent everything, a severe famine arose in that country, and he began to be in need. [15]So he went and hired himself out to[1] one of the citizens of that country, who sent him into his fields to feed pigs. [16]And he was longing to be fed with the pods that the pigs ate, and no one gave him anything.

[17]"But when he came to himself, he said, 'How many of my father's hired servants have more than enough bread, but I perish here with hunger! [18]I will arise and go to my father, and I will say to him, "Father, I have sinned against heaven and before you. [19]I am no longer worthy to be called your son. Treat me as one of your hired servants."' [20]And he arose and came to his father. But while he was still a long way off, his father saw him and felt compassion, and ran and embraced him and kissed him. [21]And the son said to him, 'Father, I have sinned against heaven and before you. I am no longer worthy to be called your son.'[2] [22]But the father said to his servants,[3] 'Bring quickly the best robe, and put it on him, and put a ring on his hand, and

shoes on his feet. [23]And bring the fattened calf and kill it, and let us eat and celebrate. [24]For this my son was dead, and is alive again; he was lost, and is found.' And they began to celebrate.

[25]"Now his older son was in the field, and as he came and drew near to the house, he heard music and dancing. [26]And he called one of the servants and asked what these things meant. [27]And he said to him, 'Your brother has come, and your father has killed the fattened calf, because he has received him back safe and sound.' [28]But he was angry and refused to go in. His father came out and entreated him, [29]but he answered his father, 'Look, these many years I have served you, and I never disobeyed your command, yet you never gave me a young goat, that I might celebrate with my friends. [30]But when this son of yours came, who has devoured your property with prostitutes, you killed the fattened calf for him!' [31]And he said to him, 'Son, you are always with me, and all that is mine is yours. [32]It was fitting to celebrate and be glad, for this your brother was dead, and is alive; he was lost, and is found.'"

DECEMBER 2

2 Chronicles 1

Solomon the son of David established himself in his kingdom, and the LORD his God was with him and made him exceedingly great.

[2]Solomon spoke to all Israel, to the commanders of thousands and of hundreds, to the judges, and to all the leaders in all Israel, the heads of fathers' houses. [3]And Solomon, and all the assembly with him, went to the high place that was at Gibeon, for the tent of meeting of God, which Moses the servant of the LORD had made in the wilderness, was there. [4](But David had brought up the ark of God from Kiriath-jearim to the place that David had prepared for it, for he had pitched a tent for it in Jerusalem.) [5]Moreover, the bronze altar that Bezalel the son of Uri, son of Hur, had made, was there before the tabernacle of the LORD. And Solomon and

the assembly sought it[4] out. [6]And Solomon went up there to the bronze altar before the LORD, which was at the tent of meeting, and offered a thousand burnt offerings on it.

[7]In that night God appeared to Solomon, and said to him, "Ask what I shall give you." [8]And Solomon said to God, "You have shown great and steadfast love to David my father, and have made me king in his place. [9]O LORD God, let your word to David my father be now fulfilled, for you have made me king over a people as numerous as the dust of the earth. [10]Give me now wisdom and knowledge to go out and come in before this people, for who can govern this people of yours, which is so great?" [11]God answered Solomon, "Because this was in your heart, and you have not asked for possessions,

[1] Greek *joined himself to*   [2] Some manuscripts add *treat me as one of your hired servants*   [3] Greek *bondservants*   [4] Or *him*

wealth, honor, or the life of those who hate you, and have not even asked for long life, but have asked for wisdom and knowledge for yourself that you may govern my people over whom I have made you king, [12] wisdom and knowledge are granted to you. I will also give you riches, possessions, and honor, such as none of the kings had who were before you, and none after you shall have the like." [13] So Solomon came from[1] the high place at Gibeon, from before the tent of meeting, to Jerusalem. And he reigned over Israel.

[14] Solomon gathered together chariots and horsemen. He had 1,400 chariots and 12,000 horsemen, whom he stationed in the chariot cities and with the king in Jerusalem. [15] And the king made silver and gold as common in Jerusalem as stone, and he made cedar as plentiful as the sycamore of the Shephelah. [16] And Solomon's import of horses was from Egypt and Kue, and the king's traders would buy them from Kue for a price. [17] They imported a chariot from Egypt for 600 shekels[2] of silver, and a horse for 150. Likewise through them these were exported to all the kings of the Hittites and the kings of Syria.

1 John 1

That which was from the beginning, which we have heard, which we have seen with our eyes, which we looked upon and have touched with our hands, concerning the word of life— [2] the life was made manifest, and we have seen it, and testify to it and proclaim to you the eternal life, which was with the Father and was made manifest to us— [3] that which we have seen and heard we proclaim also to you, so that you too may have fellowship with us; and indeed our fellowship is with the Father and with his Son Jesus Christ. [4] And we are writing these things so that our[3] joy may be complete.

[5] This is the message we have heard from him and proclaim to you, that God is light, and in him is no darkness at all. [6] If we say we have fellowship with him while we walk in darkness, we lie and do not practice the truth. [7] But if we walk in the light, as he is in the light, we have fellowship with one another, and the blood of Jesus his Son cleanses us from all sin. [8] If we say we have no sin, we deceive ourselves, and the truth is not in us. [9] If we confess our sins,

he is faithful and just to forgive us our sins and to cleanse us from all unrighteousness. [10] If we say we have not sinned, we make him a liar, and his word is not in us.

Micah 7

Woe is me! For I have become
  as when the summer fruit has been
    gathered,
  as when the grapes have been
    gleaned:
there is no cluster to eat,
  no first-ripe fig that my soul desires.
[2] The godly has perished from the earth,
  and there is no one upright among
    mankind;
they all lie in wait for blood,
  and each hunts the other with a net.
[3] Their hands are on what is evil, to do it
    well;
  the prince and the judge ask for a
    bribe,
and the great man utters the evil desire
    of his soul;
  thus they weave it together.
[4] The best of them is like a brier,
  the most upright of them a thorn
    hedge.
The day of your watchmen, of your
    punishment, has come;
  now their confusion is at hand.
[5] Put no trust in a neighbor;
  have no confidence in a friend;
guard the doors of your mouth
  from her who lies in your arms;[4]
[6] for the son treats the father with
    contempt,
  the daughter rises up against her
    mother,
the daughter-in-law against her
    mother-in-law;
  a man's enemies are the men of his
    own house.
[7] But as for me, I will look to the LORD;
  I will wait for the God of my salvation;
  my God will hear me.

[8] Rejoice not over me, O my enemy;
  when I fall, I shall rise;
when I sit in darkness,
  the LORD will be a light to me.

[1] Septuagint, Vulgate; Hebrew to [2] A *shekel* was about 2/5 ounce or 11 grams [3] Some manuscripts your [4] Hebrew *bosom*

9 I will bear the indignation of the LORD
   because I have sinned against him,
until he pleads my cause
   and executes judgment for me.
He will bring me out to the light;
   I shall look upon his vindication.
10 Then my enemy will see,
   and shame will cover her who said to
      me,
"Where is the LORD your God?"
My eyes will look upon her;
   now she will be trampled down
   like the mire of the streets.

11 A day for the building of your walls!
   In that day the boundary shall be far
      extended.
12 In that day they[1] will come to you,
   from Assyria and the cities of Egypt,
and from Egypt to the River,
   from sea to sea and from mountain to
      mountain.
13 But the earth will be desolate
   because of its inhabitants,
   for the fruit of their deeds.

14 Shepherd your people with your staff,
   the flock of your inheritance,
who dwell alone in a forest
   in the midst of a garden land;[2]
let them graze in Bashan and Gilead
   as in the days of old.
15 As in the days when you came out of the
      land of Egypt,
   I will show them[3] marvelous things.
16 The nations shall see and be ashamed of
      all their might;
they shall lay their hands on their
      mouths;
   their ears shall be deaf;
17 they shall lick the dust like a serpent,
   like the crawling things of the earth;
they shall come trembling out of their
      strongholds;
   they shall turn in dread to the LORD
      our God,
   and they shall be in fear of you.

18 Who is a God like you, pardoning
      iniquity
   and passing over transgression
   for the remnant of his inheritance?

He does not retain his anger forever,
   because he delights in steadfast love.
19 He will again have compassion on us;
   he will tread our iniquities underfoot.
You will cast all our[4] sins
   into the depths of the sea.
20 You will show faithfulness to Jacob
   and steadfast love to Abraham,
as you have sworn to our fathers
   from the days of old.

Luke 16

He also said to the disciples, "There was a rich man who had a manager, and charges were brought to him that this man was wasting his possessions. [2]And he called him and said to him, 'What is this that I hear about you? Turn in the account of your management, for you can no longer be manager.' [3]And the manager said to himself, 'What shall I do, since my master is taking the management away from me? I am not strong enough to dig, and I am ashamed to beg. [4]I have decided what to do, so that when I am removed from management, people may receive me into their houses.' [5]So, summoning his master's debtors one by one, he said to the first, 'How much do you owe my master?' [6]He said, 'A hundred measures[5] of oil.' He said to him, 'Take your bill, and sit down quickly and write fifty.' [7]Then he said to another, 'And how much do you owe?' He said, 'A hundred measures[6] of wheat.' He said to him, 'Take your bill, and write eighty.' [8]The master commended the dishonest manager for his shrewdness. For the sons of this world[7] are more shrewd in dealing with their own generation than the sons of light. [9]And I tell you, make friends for yourselves by means of unrighteous wealth,[8] so that when it fails they may receive you into the eternal dwellings.

[10]"One who is faithful in a very little is also faithful in much, and one who is dishonest in a very little is also dishonest in much. [11]If then you have not been faithful in the unrighteous wealth, who will entrust to you the true riches? [12]And if you have not been faithful in that which is another's, who will give you that which is your own? [13]No servant can serve two masters, for either he will hate the one and love the other, or he will be devoted to the one and despise the other. You cannot serve God and money."

[1] Hebrew *he* [2] Hebrew *of Carmel* [3] Hebrew *him* [4] Hebrew *their* [5] About 875 gallons or 3,200 liters [6] Between 1,000 and 1,200 bushels or 37,000 to 45,000 liters [7] Greek *age*
[8] Greek *mammon*, a Semitic word for money or possessions; also verse 11; rendered *money* in verse 13

¹⁴The Pharisees, who were lovers of money, heard all these things, and they ridiculed him. ¹⁵And he said to them, "You are those who justify yourselves before men, but God knows your hearts. For what is exalted among men is an abomination in the sight of God.

¹⁶"The Law and the Prophets were until John; since then the good news of the kingdom of God is preached, and everyone forces his way into it.¹ ¹⁷But it is easier for heaven and earth to pass away than for one dot of the Law to become void.

¹⁸"Everyone who divorces his wife and marries another commits adultery, and he who marries a woman divorced from her husband commits adultery.

¹⁹"There was a rich man who was clothed in purple and fine linen and who feasted sumptuously every day. ²⁰And at his gate was laid a poor man named Lazarus, covered with sores, ²¹who desired to be fed with what fell from the rich man's table. Moreover, even the dogs came and licked his sores. ²²The poor man died and was carried by the angels to Abraham's side.² The rich man also died and was buried, ²³and in Hades, being in torment, he lifted up his eyes and saw Abraham far off and Lazarus at his side. ²⁴And he called out, 'Father Abraham, have mercy on me, and send Lazarus to dip the end of his finger in water and cool my tongue, for I am in anguish in this flame.' ²⁵But Abraham said, 'Child, remember that you in your lifetime received your good things, and Lazarus in like manner bad things; but now he is comforted here, and you are in anguish. ²⁶And besides all this, between us and you a great chasm has been fixed, in order that those who would pass from here to you may not be able, and none may cross from there to us.' ²⁷And he said, 'Then I beg you, father, to send him to my father's house— ²⁸for I have five brothers³—so that he may warn them, lest they also come into this place of torment.' ²⁹But Abraham said, 'They have Moses and the Prophets; let them hear them.' ³⁰And he said, 'No, father Abraham, but if someone goes to them from the dead, they will repent.' ³¹He said to him, 'If they do not hear Moses and the Prophets, neither will they be convinced if someone should rise from the dead.'"

DECEMBER 3

*2 Chronicles 2*⁴

Now Solomon purposed to build a temple for the name of the LORD, and a royal palace for himself. ²⁵ And Solomon assigned 70,000 men to bear burdens and 80,000 to quarry in the hill country, and 3,600 to oversee them. ³And Solomon sent word to Hiram the king of Tyre: "As you dealt with David my father and sent him cedar to build himself a house to dwell in, so deal with me. ⁴Behold, I am about to build a house for the name of the LORD my God and dedicate it to him for the burning of incense of sweet spices before him, and for the regular arrangement of the showbread, and for burnt offerings morning and evening, on the Sabbaths and the new moons and the appointed feasts of the LORD our God, as ordained forever for Israel. ⁵The house that I am to build will be great, for our God is greater than all gods. ⁶But who is able to build him a house, since heaven, even highest heaven, cannot contain him? Who am I to build a house for him, except as a place to make offerings before him? ⁷So now send me a man skilled to work in gold, silver, bronze, and iron, and in purple, crimson, and blue fabrics, trained also in engraving, to be with the skilled workers who are with me in Judah and Jerusalem, whom David my father provided. ⁸Send me also cedar, cypress, and algum timber from Lebanon, for I know that your servants know how to cut timber in Lebanon. And my servants will be with your servants, ⁹to prepare timber for me in

¹ Or *everyone is forcefully urged into it*   ² Greek *bosom; also verse* 23   ³ Or *brothers and sisters*   ⁴ Ch 1:18 in Hebrew   ⁵ Ch 2:1 in Hebrew

abundance, for the house I am to build will be great and wonderful. [10]I will give for your servants, the woodsmen who cut timber, 20,000 cors[1] of crushed wheat, 20,000 cors of barley, 20,000 baths[2] of wine, and 20,000 baths of oil." [11]Then Hiram the king of Tyre answered in a letter that he sent to Solomon, "Because the LORD loves his people, he has made you king over them." [12]Hiram also said, "Blessed be the LORD God of Israel, who made heaven and earth, who has given King David a wise son, who has discretion and understanding, who will build a temple for the LORD and a royal palace for himself.

[13]"Now I have sent a skilled man, who has understanding, Huram-abi, [14]the son of a woman of the daughters of Dan, and his father was a man of Tyre. He is trained to work in gold, silver, bronze, iron, stone, and wood, and in purple, blue, and crimson fabrics and fine linen, and to do all sorts of engraving and execute any design that may be assigned him, with your craftsmen, the craftsmen of my lord, David your father. [15]Now therefore the wheat and barley, oil and wine, of which my lord has spoken, let him send to his servants. [16]And we will cut whatever timber you need from Lebanon and bring it to you in rafts by sea to Joppa, so that you may take it up to Jerusalem."

[17]Then Solomon counted all the resident aliens who were in the land of Israel, after the census of them that David his father had taken, and there were found 153,600. [18]Seventy thousand of them he assigned to bear burdens, 80,000 to quarry in the hill country, and 3,600 as overseers to make the people work.

---

1 John 2

My little children, I am writing these things to you so that you may not sin. But if anyone does sin, we have an advocate with the Father, Jesus Christ the righteous. [2]He is the propitiation for our sins, and not for ours only but also for the sins of the whole world. [3]And by this we know that we have come to know him, if we keep his commandments. [4]Whoever says "I know him" but does not keep his commandments is a liar, and the truth is not in him, [5]but whoever keeps his word, in him truly the love of God is perfected. By this we may know that we are in him: [6]whoever says he abides in

him ought to walk in the same way in which he walked.

[7]Beloved, I am writing you no new commandment, but an old commandment that you had from the beginning. The old commandment is the word that you have heard. [8]At the same time, it is a new commandment that I am writing to you, which is true in him and in you, because[3] the darkness is passing away and the true light is already shining. [9]Whoever says he is in the light and hates his brother is still in darkness. [10]Whoever loves his brother abides in the light, and in him[4] there is no cause for stumbling. [11]But whoever hates his brother is in the darkness and walks in the darkness, and does not know where he is going, because the darkness has blinded his eyes.

[12] I am writing to you, little children,
   because your sins are forgiven for his
      name's sake.
[13] I am writing to you, fathers,
   because you know him who is from
      the beginning.
I am writing to you, young men,
   because you have overcome the evil
      one.
I write to you, children,
   because you know the Father.
[14] I write to you, fathers,
   because you know him who is from
      the beginning.
I write to you, young men,
   because you are strong,
   and the word of God abides in you,
   and you have overcome the evil one.

[15]Do not love the world or the things in the world. If anyone loves the world, the love of the Father is not in him. [16]For all that is in the world—the desires of the flesh and the desires of the eyes and pride of life[5]—is not from the Father but is from the world. [17]And the world is passing away along with its desires, but whoever does the will of God abides forever.

[18]Children, it is the last hour, and as you have heard that antichrist is coming, so now many antichrists have come. Therefore we know that it is the last hour. [19]They went out from us, but they were not of us; for if they had been of us, they would have continued with us. But they went out, that it might become plain that they all are not of us. [20]But you have been

---

[1] A cor was about 6 bushels or 220 liters [2] A bath was about 6 gallons or 22 liters [3] Or that [4] Or it [5] Or pride in possessions

anointed by the Holy One, and you all have knowledge.[1] 21 I write to you, not because you do not know the truth, but because you know it, and because no lie is of the truth. 22 Who is the liar but he who denies that Jesus is the Christ? This is the antichrist, he who denies the Father and the Son. 23 No one who denies the Son has the Father. Whoever confesses the Son has the Father also. 24 Let what you heard from the beginning abide in you. If what you heard from the beginning abides in you, then you too will abide in the Son and in the Father. 25 And this is the promise that he made to us[2]— eternal life.

26 I write these things to you about those who are trying to deceive you. 27 But the anointing that you received from him abides in you, and you have no need that anyone should teach you. But as his anointing teaches you about everything, and is true, and is no lie—just as it has taught you, abide in him.

28 And now, little children, abide in him, so that when he appears we may have confidence and not shrink from him in shame at his coming. 29 If you know that he is righteous, you may be sure that everyone who practices righteousness has been born of him.

Nahum 1

An oracle concerning Nineveh. The book of the vision of Nahum of Elkosh.

2 The LORD is a jealous and avenging God;
the LORD is avenging and wrathful;
the LORD takes vengeance on his adversaries
and keeps wrath for his enemies.
3 The LORD is slow to anger and great in power,
and the LORD will by no means clear the guilty.
His way is in whirlwind and storm,
and the clouds are the dust of his feet.
4 He rebukes the sea and makes it dry;
he dries up all the rivers;
Bashan and Carmel wither;
the bloom of Lebanon withers.
5 The mountains quake before him;
the hills melt;
the earth heaves before him,
the world and all who dwell in it.

6 Who can stand before his indignation?
Who can endure the heat of his anger?
His wrath is poured out like fire,
and the rocks are broken into pieces by him.
7 The LORD is good,
a stronghold in the day of trouble;
he knows those who take refuge in him.
8 But with an overflowing flood
he will make a complete end of the adversaries,[3]
and will pursue his enemies into darkness.
9 What do you plot against the LORD?
He will make a complete end;
trouble will not rise up a second time.
10 For they are like entangled thorns,
like drunkards as they drink;
they are consumed like stubble fully dried.
11 From you came one
who plotted evil against the LORD,
a worthless counselor.
12 Thus says the LORD,
"Though they are at full strength and many,
they will be cut down and pass away.
Though I have afflicted you,
I will afflict you no more.
13 And now I will break his yoke from off you
and will burst your bonds apart."
14 The LORD has given commandment about you:
"No more shall your name be perpetuated;
from the house of your gods I will cut off
the carved image and the metal image.
I will make your grave, for you are vile."
15[4] Behold, upon the mountains, the feet of him
who brings good news,
who publishes peace!
Keep your feasts, O Judah;
fulfill your vows,
for never again shall the worthless pass through you;
he is utterly cut off.

[1] Some manuscripts you know everything [2] Some manuscripts you [3] Hebrew of her place [4] Ch 2:1 in Hebrew

———————— *Luke 17* ————————

And he said to his disciples, "Temptations to sin[1] are sure to come, but woe to the one through whom they come! [2]It would be better for him if a millstone were hung around his neck and he were cast into the sea than that he should cause one of these little ones to sin.[2] [3]Pay attention to yourselves! If your brother sins, rebuke him, and if he repents, forgive him, [4]and if he sins against you seven times in the day, and turns to you seven times, saying, 'I repent,' you must forgive him."

[5]The apostles said to the Lord, "Increase our faith!" [6]And the Lord said, "If you had faith like a grain of mustard seed, you could say to this mulberry tree, 'Be uprooted and planted in the sea,' and it would obey you.

[7]"Will any one of you who has a servant[3] plowing or keeping sheep say to him when he has come in from the field, 'Come at once and recline at table'? [8]Will he not rather say to him, 'Prepare supper for me, and dress properly,[4] and serve me while I eat and drink, and afterward you will eat and drink'? [9]Does he thank the servant because he did what was commanded? [10]So you also, when you have done all that you were commanded, say, 'We are unworthy servants;[5] we have only done what was our duty.'"

[11]On the way to Jerusalem he was passing along between Samaria and Galilee. [12]And as he entered a village, he was met by ten lepers,[6] who stood at a distance [13]and lifted up their voices, saying, "Jesus, Master, have mercy on us." [14]When he saw them he said to them, "Go and show yourselves to the priests." And as they went they were cleansed. [15]Then one of them, when he saw that he was healed, turned back, praising God with a loud voice; [16]and he fell on his face at Jesus' feet, giving him thanks. Now he was a Samaritan. [17]Then Jesus answered, "Were not ten cleansed? Where are the nine? [18]Was no one found to return and give praise to God except this foreigner?" [19]And he said to him, "Rise and go your way; your faith has made you well."[7]

[20]Being asked by the Pharisees when the kingdom of God would come, he answered them, "The kingdom of God is not coming in ways that can be observed, [21]nor will they say, 'Look, here it is!' or 'There!' for behold, the kingdom of God is in the midst of you."[8]

[22]And he said to the disciples, "The days are coming when you will desire to see one of the days of the Son of Man, and you will not see it. [23]And they will say to you, 'Look, there!' or 'Look, here!' Do not go out or follow them. [24]For as the lightning flashes and lights up the sky from one side to the other, so will the Son of Man be in his day.[9] [25]But first he must suffer many things and be rejected by this generation. [26]Just as it was in the days of Noah, so will it be in the days of the Son of Man. [27]They were eating and drinking and marrying and being given in marriage, until the day when Noah entered the ark, and the flood came and destroyed them all. [28]Likewise, just as it was in the days of Lot—they were eating and drinking, buying and selling, planting and building, [29]but on the day when Lot went out from Sodom, fire and sulfur rained from heaven and destroyed them all— [30]so will it be on the day when the Son of Man is revealed. [31]On that day, let the one who is on the housetop, with his goods in the house, not come down to take them away, and likewise let the one who is in the field not turn back. [32]Remember Lot's wife. [33]Whoever seeks to preserve his life will lose it, but whoever loses his life will keep it. [34]I tell you, in that night there will be two in one bed. One will be taken and the other left. [35]There will be two women grinding together. One will be taken and the other left."[10] [37]And they said to him, "Where, Lord?" He said to them, "Where the corpse[11] is, there the vultures[12] will gather."

---

[1] Greek *Stumbling blocks* [2] Greek *stumble* [3] Greek *bondservant*; also verse 9 [4] Greek *gird yourself* [5] Greek *bondservants* [6] *Leprosy* was a term for several skin diseases; see Leviticus 13 [7] Or *has saved you* [8] Or *within you, or within your grasp* [9] Some manuscripts omit *in his day* [10] Some manuscripts add verse 36: *Two men will be in the field; one will be taken and the other left* [11] Greek *body* [12] Or *eagles*

DECEMBER 4

2 Chronicles 3–4

Then Solomon began to build the house of the Lord in Jerusalem on Mount Moriah, where the Lord[1] had appeared to David his father, at the place that David had appointed, on the threshing floor of Ornan the Jebusite. [2]He began to build in the second month of the fourth year of his reign. [3]These are Solomon's measurements[2] for building the house of God: the length, in cubits[3] of the old standard, was sixty cubits, and the breadth twenty cubits. [4]The vestibule in front of the nave of the house was twenty cubits long, equal to the width of the house,[4] and its height was 120 cubits. He overlaid it on the inside with pure gold. [5]The nave he lined with cypress and covered it with fine gold and made palms and chains on it. [6]He adorned the house with settings of precious stones. The gold was gold of Parvaim. [7]So he lined the house with gold—its beams, its thresholds, its walls, and its doors—and he carved cherubim on the walls.

[8]And he made the Most Holy Place. Its length, corresponding to the breadth of the house, was twenty cubits, and its breadth was twenty cubits. He overlaid it with 600 talents[5] of fine gold. [9]The weight of gold for the nails was fifty shekels.[6] And he overlaid the upper chambers with gold.

[10]In the Most Holy Place he made two cherubim of wood[7] and overlaid[8] them with gold. [11]The wings of the cherubim together extended twenty cubits: one wing of the one, of five cubits, touched the wall of the house, and its other wing, of five cubits, touched the wing of the other cherub; [12]and of this cherub, one wing, of five cubits, touched the wall of the house, and the other wing, also of five cubits, was joined to the wing of the first cherub. [13]The wings of these cherubim extended twenty cubits. The cherubim[9] stood on their feet, facing the nave. [14]And he made the veil of blue and purple and crimson fabrics and fine linen, and he worked cherubim on it.

[15]In front of the house he made two pillars thirty-five cubits high, with a capital of five cubits on the top of each. [16]He made chains like a necklace[10] and put them on the tops of the pillars, and he made a hundred pomegranates and put them on the chains. [17]He set up the pillars in front of the temple, one on the south, the other on the north; that on the south he called Jachin, and that on the north Boaz.

[4:1]He made an altar of bronze, twenty cubits[11] long and twenty cubits wide and ten cubits high. [2]Then he made the sea of cast metal. It was round, ten cubits from brim to brim, and five cubits high, and a line of thirty cubits measured its circumference. [3]Under it were figures of gourds,[12] for ten cubits, compassing the sea all around. The gourds were in two rows, cast with it when it was cast. [4]It stood on twelve oxen, three facing north, three facing west, three facing south, and three facing east. The sea was set on them, and all their rear parts were inward. [5]Its thickness was a handbreadth.[13] And its brim was made like the brim of a cup, like the flower of a lily. It held 3,000 baths.[14] [6]He also made ten basins in which to wash, and set five on the south side, and five on the north side. In these they were to rinse off what was used for the burnt offering, and the sea was for the priests to wash in.

[7]And he made ten golden lampstands as prescribed, and set them in the temple, five on the south side and five on the north. [8]He also made ten tables and placed them in the temple, five on the south side and five on the north. And he made a hundred basins of gold. [9]He made the court of the priests and the great court and doors for the court and overlaid their doors with bronze. [10]And he set the sea at the southeast corner of the house.

[11]Hiram also made the pots, the shovels, and the basins. So Hiram finished the work that he did for King Solomon on the house of God: [12]the two pillars, the bowls, and the two

[1] Septuagint; Hebrew lacks *the Lord* [2] Syriac; Hebrew *foundations* [3] A *cubit* was about 18 inches or 45 centimeters [4] Compare 1 Kings 6:3; the meaning of the Hebrew is uncertain [5] A *talent* was about 75 pounds or 34 kilograms [6] A *shekel* was about 2/5 ounce or 11 grams [7] Septuagint; the meaning of the Hebrew is uncertain [8] Hebrew *they overlaid* [9] Hebrew *they* [10] Hebrew *chains in the inner sanctuary* [11] A *cubit* was about 18 inches or 45 centimeters [12] Compare 1 Kings 7:24; Hebrew *oxen*; twice in this verse [13] A *handbreadth* was about 3 inches or 7.5 centimeters [14] A *bath* was about 6 gallons or 22 liters

capitals on the top of the pillars; and the two latticeworks to cover the two bowls of the capitals that were on the top of the pillars; [13] and the 400 pomegranates for the two latticeworks, two rows of pomegranates for each latticework, to cover the two bowls of the capitals that were on the pillars. [14] He made the stands also, and the basins on the stands, [15] and the one sea, and the twelve oxen underneath it. [16] The pots, the shovels, the forks, and all the equipment for these Huram-abi made of burnished bronze for King Solomon for the house of the LORD. [17] In the plain of the Jordan the king cast them, in the clay ground between Succoth and Zeredah.[1] [18] Solomon made all these things in great quantities, for the weight of the bronze was not sought.

[19] So Solomon made all the vessels that were in the house of God: the golden altar, the tables for the bread of the Presence, [20] the lampstands and their lamps of pure gold to burn before the inner sanctuary, as prescribed; [21] the flowers, the lamps, and the tongs, of purest gold; [22] the snuffers, basins, dishes for incense, and fire pans, of pure gold, and the sockets[2] of the temple, for the inner doors to the Most Holy Place and for the doors of the nave of the temple were of gold.

1 John 3

See what kind of love the Father has given to us, that we should be called children of God; and so we are. The reason why the world does not know us is that it did not know him. [2] Beloved, we are God's children now, and what we will be has not yet appeared; but we know that when he appears[3] we shall be like him, because we shall see him as he is. [3] And everyone who thus hopes in him purifies himself as he is pure.

[4] Everyone who makes a practice of sinning also practices lawlessness; sin is lawlessness. [5] You know that he appeared in order to take away sins, and in him there is no sin. [6] No one who abides in him keeps on sinning; no one who keeps on sinning has either seen him or known him. [7] Little children, let no one deceive you. Whoever practices righteousness is righteous, as he is righteous. [8] Whoever makes a practice of sinning is of the devil, for the devil

has been sinning from the beginning. The reason the Son of God appeared was to destroy the works of the devil. [9] No one born of God makes a practice of sinning, for God's[4] seed abides in him, and he cannot keep on sinning because he has been born of God. [10] By this it is evident who are the children of God, and who are the children of the devil: whoever does not practice righteousness is not of God, nor is the one who does not love his brother.

[11] For this is the message that you have heard from the beginning, that we should love one another. [12] We should not be like Cain, who was of the evil one and murdered his brother. And why did he murder him? Because his own deeds were evil and his brother's righteous. [13] Do not be surprised, brothers,[5] that the world hates you. [14] We know that we have passed out of death into life, because we love the brothers. Whoever does not love abides in death. [15] Everyone who hates his brother is a murderer, and you know that no murderer has eternal life abiding in him.

[16] By this we know love, that he laid down his life for us, and we ought to lay down our lives for the brothers. [17] But if anyone has the world's goods and sees his brother in need, yet closes his heart against him, how does God's love abide in him? [18] Little children, let us not love in word or talk but in deed and in truth.

[19] By this we shall know that we are of the truth and reassure our heart before him; [20] for whenever our heart condemns us, God is greater than our heart, and he knows everything. [21] Beloved, if our heart does not condemn us, we have confidence before God; [22] and whatever we ask we receive from him, because we keep his commandments and do what pleases him. [23] And this is his commandment, that we believe in the name of his Son Jesus Christ and love one another, just as he has commanded us. [24] Whoever keeps his commandments abides in God,[6] and God[7] in him. And by this we know that he abides in us, by the Spirit whom he has given us.

Nahum 2

The scatterer has come up against you.
    Man the ramparts;
      watch the road;

---

[1] Spelled *Zarethan* in 1 Kings 7:46 [2] Compare 1 Kings 7:50; Hebrew *the entrance of the house* [3] Or *when it appears* [4] Greek *his* [5] Or *brothers and sisters*. The plural Greek word *adelphoi* (translated "brothers") refers to siblings in a family. In New Testament usage, depending on the context, *adelphoi* may refer either to men or to both men and women who are siblings (brothers and sisters) in God's family, the church; also verses 14, 16 [6] Greek *him* [7] Greek *he*

dress for battle;[1]
  collect all your strength.
2 For the LORD is restoring the majesty of Jacob
  as the majesty of Israel,
for plunderers have plundered them
  and ruined their branches.

3 The shield of his mighty men is red;
  his soldiers are clothed in scarlet.
The chariots come with flashing metal
  on the day he musters them;
  the cypress spears are brandished.
4 The chariots race madly through the streets;
  they rush to and fro through the squares;
they gleam like torches;
  they dart like lightning.
5 He remembers his officers;
  they stumble as they go,
they hasten to the wall;
  the siege tower[2] is set up.
6 The river gates are opened;
  the palace melts away;
7 its mistress[3] is stripped;[4] she is carried off,
  her slave girls lamenting,
moaning like doves
  and beating their breasts.
8 Nineveh is like a pool
  whose waters run away.[5]
"Halt! Halt!" they cry,
  but none turns back.
9 Plunder the silver,
  plunder the gold!
There is no end of the treasure
  or of the wealth of all precious things.

10 Desolate! Desolation and ruin!
  Hearts melt and knees tremble;
anguish is in all loins;
  all faces grow pale!
11 Where is the lions' den,
  the feeding place of the young lions,
where the lion and lioness went,
  where his cubs were, with none to disturb?
12 The lion tore enough for his cubs
  and strangled prey for his lionesses;
he filled his caves with prey
  and his dens with torn flesh.

13 Behold, I am against you, declares the LORD of hosts, and I will burn your[6] chariots in smoke, and the sword shall devour your young lions. I will cut off your prey from the earth, and the voice of your messengers shall no longer be heard.

Luke 18

And he told them a parable to the effect that they ought always to pray and not lose heart. [2] He said, "In a certain city there was a judge who neither feared God nor respected man. [3] And there was a widow in that city who kept coming to him and saying, 'Give me justice against my adversary.' [4] For a while he refused, but afterward he said to himself, 'Though I neither fear God nor respect man, [5] yet because this widow keeps bothering me, I will give her justice, so that she will not beat me down by her continual coming.'" [6] And the Lord said, "Hear what the unrighteous judge says. [7] And will not God give justice to his elect, who cry to him day and night? Will he delay long over them? [8] I tell you, he will give justice to them speedily. Nevertheless, when the Son of Man comes, will he find faith on earth?"

[9] He also told this parable to some who trusted in themselves that they were righteous, and treated others with contempt: [10] "Two men went up into the temple to pray, one a Pharisee and the other a tax collector. [11] The Pharisee, standing by himself, prayed[7] thus: 'God, I thank you that I am not like other men, extortioners, unjust, adulterers, or even like this tax collector. [12] I fast twice a week; I give tithes of all that I get.' [13] But the tax collector, standing far off, would not even lift up his eyes to heaven, but beat his breast, saying, 'God, be merciful to me, a sinner!' [14] I tell you, this man went down to his house justified, rather than the other. For everyone who exalts himself will be humbled, but the one who humbles himself will be exalted."

[15] Now they were bringing even infants to him that he might touch them. And when the disciples saw it, they rebuked them. [16] But Jesus called them to him, saying, "Let the children come to me, and do not hinder them, for to such belongs the kingdom of God. [17] Truly, I say to you, whoever does not receive the kingdom of God like a child shall not enter it."

[18] And a ruler asked him, "Good Teacher,

---

[1] Hebrew *gird your loins*   [2] Or *the mantelet*   [3] The meaning of the Hebrew word rendered *its mistress* is uncertain   [4] Or *exiled*   [5] Compare Septuagint; the meaning of the Hebrew is uncertain   [6] Hebrew *her*   [7] Or *standing, prayed to himself*

what must I do to inherit eternal life?" ¹⁹And Jesus said to him, "Why do you call me good? No one is good except God alone. ²⁰You know the commandments: 'Do not commit adultery, Do not murder, Do not steal, Do not bear false witness, Honor your father and mother.'" ²¹And he said, "All these I have kept from my youth." ²²When Jesus heard this, he said to him, "One thing you still lack. Sell all that you have and distribute to the poor, and you will have treasure in heaven; and come, follow me." ²³But when he heard these things, he became very sad, for he was extremely rich. ²⁴Jesus, seeing that he had become sad, said, "How difficult it is for those who have wealth to enter the kingdom of God! ²⁵For it is easier for a camel to go through the eye of a needle than for a rich person to enter the kingdom of God." ²⁶Those who heard it said, "Then who can be saved?" ²⁷But he said, "What is impossible with man is possible with God." ²⁸And Peter said, "See, we have left our homes and followed you." ²⁹And he said to them, "Truly, I say to you, there is no one who has left house or wife or brothers[1] or parents or children, for the sake of the kingdom of God, ³⁰who will not receive many times more in this time, and in the age to come eternal life."

³¹And taking the twelve, he said to them, "See, we are going up to Jerusalem, and everything that is written about the Son of Man by the prophets will be accomplished. ³²For he will be delivered over to the Gentiles and will be mocked and shamefully treated and spit upon. ³³And after flogging him, they will kill him, and on the third day he will rise." ³⁴But they understood none of these things. This saying was hidden from them, and they did not grasp what was said.

³⁵As he drew near to Jericho, a blind man was sitting by the roadside begging. ³⁶And hearing a crowd going by, he inquired what this meant. ³⁷They told him, "Jesus of Nazareth is passing by." ³⁸And he cried out, "Jesus, Son of David, have mercy on me!" ³⁹And those who were in front rebuked him, telling him to be silent. But he cried out all the more, "Son of David, have mercy on me!" ⁴⁰And Jesus stopped and commanded him to be brought to him. And when he came near, he asked him, ⁴¹"What do you want me to do for you?" He said, "Lord, let me recover my sight." ⁴²And Jesus said to him, "Recover your sight; your faith has made you well." ⁴³And immediately he recovered his sight and followed him, glorifying God. And all the people, when they saw it, gave praise to God.

DECEMBER 5

2 Chronicles 5:1–6:11

Thus all the work that Solomon did for the house of the LORD was finished. And Solomon brought in the things that David his father had dedicated, and stored the silver, the gold, and all the vessels in the treasuries of the house of God.

²Then Solomon assembled the elders of Israel and all the heads of the tribes, the leaders of the fathers' houses of the people of Israel, in Jerusalem, to bring up the ark of the covenant of the LORD out of the city of David, which is Zion. ³And all the men of Israel assembled before the king at the feast that is in the seventh month. ⁴And all the elders of Israel came, and the Levites took up the ark. ⁵And they brought up the ark, the tent of meeting, and all the holy vessels that were in the tent; the Levitical priests brought them up. ⁶And King Solomon and all the congregation of Israel, who had assembled before him, were before the ark, sacrificing so many sheep and oxen that they could not be counted or numbered. ⁷Then the priests brought the ark of the covenant of the LORD to its place, in the inner sanctuary of the house, in the Most Holy Place, underneath the wings of the cherubim. ⁸The cherubim spread out

[1] Or wife or brothers and sisters

their wings over the place of the ark, so that the cherubim made a covering above the ark and its poles. [9]And the poles were so long that the ends of the poles were seen from the Holy Place before the inner sanctuary, but they could not be seen from outside. And they are[1] there to this day. [10]There was nothing in the ark except the two tablets that Moses put there at Horeb, where the LORD made a covenant with the people of Israel, when they came out of Egypt. [11]And when the priests came out of the Holy Place (for all the priests who were present had consecrated themselves, without regard to their divisions, [12]and all the Levitical singers, Asaph, Heman, and Jeduthun, their sons and kinsmen, arrayed in fine linen, with cymbals, harps, and lyres, stood east of the altar with 120 priests who were trumpeters; [13]and it was the duty of the trumpeters and singers to make themselves heard in unison in praise and thanksgiving to the LORD), and when the song was raised, with trumpets and cymbals and other musical instruments, in praise to the LORD,

"For he is good,
    for his steadfast love endures forever,"

the house, the house of the LORD, was filled with a cloud, [14]so that the priests could not stand to minister because of the cloud, for the glory of the LORD filled the house of God.

[6:1]Then Solomon said, "The LORD has said that he would dwell in thick darkness. [2]But I have built you an exalted house, a place for you to dwell in forever." [3]Then the king turned around and blessed all the assembly of Israel, while all the assembly of Israel stood. [4]And he said, "Blessed be the LORD, the God of Israel, who with his hand has fulfilled what he promised with his mouth to David my father, saying, [5]'Since the day that I brought my people out of the land of Egypt, I chose no city out of all the tribes of Israel in which to build a house, that my name might be there, and I chose no man as prince over my people Israel; [6]but I have chosen Jerusalem that my name may be there, and I have chosen David to be over my people Israel.' [7]Now it was in the heart of David my father to build a house for the name of the LORD, the God of Israel. [8]But the LORD said to David my father, 'Whereas it was in your heart to build a house for my name, you did well that it was in your heart. [9]Nevertheless, it is not you

who shall build the house, but your son who shall be born to you shall build the house for my name.' [10]Now the LORD has fulfilled his promise that he made. For I have risen in the place of David my father and sit on the throne of Israel, as the LORD promised, and I have built the house for the name of the LORD, the God of Israel. [11]And there I have set the ark, in which is the covenant of the LORD that he made with the people of Israel."

──────── 1 John 4 ────────

Beloved, do not believe every spirit, but test the spirits to see whether they are from God, for many false prophets have gone out into the world. [2]By this you know the Spirit of God: every spirit that confesses that Jesus Christ has come in the flesh is from God, [3]and every spirit that does not confess Jesus is not from God. This is the spirit of the antichrist, which you heard was coming and now is in the world already. [4]Little children, you are from God and have overcome them, for he who is in you is greater than he who is in the world. [5]They are from the world; therefore they speak from the world, and the world listens to them. [6]We are from God. Whoever knows God listens to us; whoever is not from God does not listen to us. By this we know the Spirit of truth and the spirit of error.

[7]Beloved, let us love one another, for love is from God, and whoever loves has been born of God and knows God. [8]Anyone who does not love does not know God, because God is love. [9]In this the love of God was made manifest among us, that God sent his only Son into the world, so that we might live through him. [10]In this is love, not that we have loved God but that he loved us and sent his Son to be the propitiation for our sins. [11]Beloved, if God so loved us, we also ought to love one another. [12]No one has ever seen God; if we love one another, God abides in us and his love is perfected in us.

[13]By this we know that we abide in him and he in us, because he has given us of his Spirit. [14]And we have seen and testify that the Father has sent his Son to be the Savior of the world. [15]Whoever confesses that Jesus is the Son of God, God abides in him, and he in God. [16]So we have come to know and to believe the love that

[1] Hebrew *it is*

God has for us. God is love, and whoever abides in love abides in God, and God abides in him. [17] By this is love perfected with us, so that we may have confidence for the day of judgment, because as he is so also are we in this world. [18] There is no fear in love, but perfect love casts out fear. For fear has to do with punishment, and whoever fears has not been perfected in love. [19] We love because he first loved us. [20] If anyone says, "I love God," and hates his brother, he is a liar; for he who does not love his brother whom he has seen cannot[1] love God whom he has not seen. [21] And this commandment we have from him: whoever loves God must also love his brother.

Nahum 3

Woe to the bloody city,
  all full of lies and plunder—
  no end to the prey!
[2] The crack of the whip, and rumble of the wheel,
  galloping horse and bounding chariot!
[3] Horsemen charging,
  flashing sword and glittering spear,
hosts of slain,
  heaps of corpses,
dead bodies without end—
  they stumble over the bodies!
[4] And all for the countless whorings of the prostitute,
  graceful and of deadly charms,
who betrays nations with her whorings,
  and peoples with her charms.
[5] Behold, I am against you,
  declares the LORD of hosts,
  and will lift up your skirts over your face;
and I will make nations look at your nakedness
  and kingdoms at your shame.
[6] I will throw filth at you
  and treat you with contempt
  and make you a spectacle.
[7] And all who look at you will shrink from you and say,
  "Wasted is Nineveh; who will grieve for her?"
Where shall I seek comforters for you?

[8] Are you better than Thebes[2]
  that sat by the Nile,
with water around her,
  her rampart a sea,
  and water her wall?
[9] Cush was her strength;
  Egypt too, and that without limit;
Put and the Libyans were her[3] helpers.
[10] Yet she became an exile;
  she went into captivity;
her infants were dashed in pieces
  at the head of every street;
for her honored men lots were cast,
  and all her great men were bound in chains.
[11] You also will be drunken;
  you will go into hiding;
you will seek a refuge from the enemy.
[12] All your fortresses are like fig trees
  with first-ripe figs—
if shaken they fall
  into the mouth of the eater.
[13] Behold, your troops
  are women in your midst.
The gates of your land
  are wide open to your enemies;
  fire has devoured your bars.
[14] Draw water for the siege;
  strengthen your forts;
go into the clay;
  tread the mortar;
  take hold of the brick mold!
[15] There will the fire devour you;
  the sword will cut you off.
It will devour you like the locust.
Multiply yourselves like the locust;
  multiply like the grasshopper!
[16] You increased your merchants
  more than the stars of the heavens.
The locust spreads its wings and flies away.
[17] Your princes are like grasshoppers,
  your scribes[4] like clouds of locusts
settling on the fences
  in a day of cold—
when the sun rises, they fly away;
  no one knows where they are.
[18] Your shepherds are asleep,
  O king of Assyria;
  your nobles slumber.

[1] Some manuscripts how can he [2] Hebrew No-amon [3] Hebrew your [4] Or marshals

Your people are scattered on the
　　mountains
　　with none to gather them.
19　There is no easing your hurt;
　　your wound is grievous.
　All who hear the news about you
　　clap their hands over you.
　For upon whom has not come
　　your unceasing evil?

Luke 19

He entered Jericho and was passing through. ²And behold, there was a man named Zacchaeus. He was a chief tax collector and was rich. ³And he was seeking to see who Jesus was, but on account of the crowd he could not, because he was small in stature. ⁴So he ran on ahead and climbed up into a sycamore tree to see him, for he was about to pass that way. ⁵And when Jesus came to the place, he looked up and said to him, "Zacchaeus, hurry and come down, for I must stay at your house today." ⁶So he hurried and came down and received him joyfully. ⁷And when they saw it, they all grumbled, "He has gone in to be the guest of a man who is a sinner." ⁸And Zacchaeus stood and said to the Lord, "Behold, Lord, the half of my goods I give to the poor. And if I have defrauded anyone of anything, I restore it fourfold." ⁹And Jesus said to him, "Today salvation has come to this house, since he also is a son of Abraham. ¹⁰For the Son of Man came to seek and to save the lost."

¹¹As they heard these things, he proceeded to tell a parable, because he was near to Jerusalem, and because they supposed that the kingdom of God was to appear immediately. ¹²He said therefore, "A nobleman went into a far country to receive for himself a kingdom and then return. ¹³Calling ten of his servants,[1] he gave them ten minas,[2] and said to them, 'Engage in business until I come.' ¹⁴But his citizens hated him and sent a delegation after him, saying, 'We do not want this man to reign over us.' ¹⁵When he returned, having received the kingdom, he ordered these servants to whom he had given the money to be called to him, that he might know what they had gained by doing business. ¹⁶The first came before him, saying, 'Lord, your mina has made ten minas more.' ¹⁷And he said to him, 'Well done, good

servant![3] Because you have been faithful in a very little, you shall have authority over ten cities.' ¹⁸And the second came, saying, 'Lord, your mina has made five minas.' ¹⁹And he said to him, 'And you are to be over five cities.' ²⁰Then another came, saying, 'Lord, here is your mina, which I kept laid away in a handkerchief; ²¹for I was afraid of you, because you are a severe man. You take what you did not deposit, and reap what you did not sow.' ²²He said to him, 'I will condemn you with your own words, you wicked servant! You knew that I was a severe man, taking what I did not deposit and reaping what I did not sow? ²³Why then did you not put my money in the bank, and at my coming I might have collected it with interest?' ²⁴And he said to those who stood by, 'Take the mina from him, and give it to the one who has the ten minas.' ²⁵And they said to him, 'Lord, he has ten minas!' ²⁶'I tell you that to everyone who has, more will be given, but from the one who has not, even what he has will be taken away. ²⁷But as for these enemies of mine, who did not want me to reign over them, bring them here and slaughter them before me.'"

²⁸And when he had said these things, he went on ahead, going up to Jerusalem. ²⁹When he drew near to Bethphage and Bethany, at the mount that is called Olivet, he sent two of the disciples, ³⁰saying, "Go into the village in front of you, where on entering you will find a colt tied, on which no one has ever yet sat. Untie it and bring it here. ³¹If anyone asks you, 'Why are you untying it?' you shall say this: 'The Lord has need of it.'" ³²So those who were sent went away and found it just as he had told them. ³³And as they were untying the colt, its owners said to them, "Why are you untying the colt?" ³⁴And they said, "The Lord has need of it." ³⁵And they brought it to Jesus, and throwing their cloaks on the colt, they set Jesus on it. ³⁶And as he rode along, they spread their cloaks on the road. ³⁷As he was drawing near—already on the way down the Mount of Olives—the whole multitude of his disciples began to rejoice and praise God with a loud voice for all the mighty works that they had seen, ³⁸saying, "Blessed is the King who comes in the name of the Lord! Peace in heaven and glory in the highest!" ³⁹And some of the Pharisees in the crowd said to him, "Teacher, rebuke your disciples." ⁴⁰He

[1] Greek bondservants; also verse 15　[2] A mina was about three months' wages for a laborer　[3] Greek bondservant; also verse 22

answered, "I tell you, if these were silent, the very stones would cry out."

⁴¹And when he drew near and saw the city, he wept over it, ⁴²saying, "Would that you, even you, had known on this day the things that make for peace! But now they are hidden from your eyes. ⁴³For the days will come upon you, when your enemies will set up a barricade around you and surround you and hem you in on every side ⁴⁴and tear you down to the ground, you and your children within you. And they will not leave one stone upon another

in you, because you did not know the time of your visitation."

⁴⁵And he entered the temple and began to drive out those who sold, ⁴⁶saying to them, "It is written, 'My house shall be a house of prayer,' but you have made it a den of robbers."

⁴⁷And he was teaching daily in the temple. The chief priests and the scribes and the principal men of the people were seeking to destroy him, ⁴⁸but they did not find anything they could do, for all the people were hanging on his words.

DECEMBER 6

2 Chronicles 6:12–42

Then Solomon stood before the altar of the LORD in the presence of all the assembly of Israel and spread out his hands. ¹³Solomon had made a bronze platform five cubits¹ long, five cubits wide, and three cubits high, and had set it in the court, and he stood on it. Then he knelt on his knees in the presence of all the assembly of Israel, and spread out his hands toward heaven, ¹⁴and said, "O LORD, God of Israel, there is no God like you, in heaven or on earth, keeping covenant and showing steadfast love to your servants who walk before you with all their heart, ¹⁵who have kept with your servant David my father what you declared to him. You spoke with your mouth, and with your hand have fulfilled it this day. ¹⁶Now therefore, O LORD, God of Israel, keep for your servant David my father what you have promised him, saying, 'You shall not lack a man to sit before me on the throne of Israel, if only your sons pay close attention to their way, to walk in my law as you have walked before me.' ¹⁷Now therefore, O LORD, God of Israel, let your word be confirmed, which you have spoken to your servant David.

¹⁸"But will God indeed dwell with man on the earth? Behold, heaven and the highest heaven cannot contain you, how much less this house that I have built! ¹⁹Yet have regard

to the prayer of your servant and to his plea, O LORD my God, listening to the cry and to the prayer that your servant prays before you, ²⁰that your eyes may be open day and night toward this house, the place where you have promised to set your name, that you may listen to the prayer that your servant offers toward this place. ²¹And listen to the pleas of your servant and of your people Israel, when they pray toward this place. And listen from heaven your dwelling place, and when you hear, forgive.

²²"If a man sins against his neighbor and is made to take an oath and comes and swears his oath before your altar in this house, ²³then hear from heaven and act and judge your servants, repaying the guilty by bringing his conduct on his own head, and vindicating the righteous by rewarding him according to his righteousness.

²⁴"If your people Israel are defeated before the enemy because they have sinned against you, and they turn again and acknowledge your name and pray and plead with you in this house, ²⁵then hear from heaven and forgive the sin of your people Israel and bring them again to the land that you gave to them and to their fathers.

²⁶"When heaven is shut up and there is no rain because they have sinned against you, if they pray toward this place and acknowledge your name and turn from their sin, when you

¹ A *cubit* was about 18 inches or 45 centimeters

afflict[1] them, ²⁷then hear in heaven and forgive the sin of your servants, your people Israel, when you teach them the good way[2] in which they should walk, and grant rain upon your land, which you have given to your people as an inheritance.

²⁸"If there is famine in the land, if there is pestilence or blight or mildew or locust or caterpillar, if their enemies besiege them in the land at their gates, whatever plague, whatever sickness there is, ²⁹whatever prayer, whatever plea is made by any man or by all your people Israel, each knowing his own affliction and his own sorrow and stretching out his hands toward this house, ³⁰then hear from heaven your dwelling place and forgive and render to each whose heart you know, according to all his ways, for you, you only, know the hearts of the children of mankind, ³¹that they may fear you and walk in your ways all the days that they live in the land that you gave to our fathers.

³²"Likewise, when a foreigner, who is not of your people Israel, comes from a far country for the sake of your great name and your mighty hand and your outstretched arm, when he comes and prays toward this house, ³³hear from heaven your dwelling place and do according to all for which the foreigner calls to you, in order that all the peoples of the earth may know your name and fear you, as do your people Israel, and that they may know that this house that I have built is called by your name.

³⁴"If your people go out to battle against their enemies, by whatever way you shall send them, and they pray to you toward this city that you have chosen and the house that I have built for your name, ³⁵then hear from heaven their prayer and their plea, and maintain their cause.

³⁶"If they sin against you—for there is no one who does not sin—and you are angry with them and give them to an enemy, so that they are carried away captive to a land far or near, ³⁷yet if they turn their heart in the land to which they have been carried captive, and repent and plead with you in the land of their captivity, saying, 'We have sinned and have acted perversely and wickedly,' ³⁸if they repent with all their mind and with all their heart in the land of their captivity to which they were carried captive, and pray toward their land, which you gave to their fathers, the city that you have chosen and the house that I have built

for your name, ³⁹then hear from heaven your dwelling place their prayer and their pleas, and maintain their cause and forgive your people who have sinned against you. ⁴⁰Now, O my God, let your eyes be open and your ears attentive to the prayer of this place.

⁴¹   "And now arise, O Lᴏʀᴅ God, and go to
       your resting place,
      you and the ark of your might.
     Let your priests, O Lᴏʀᴅ God, be clothed
       with salvation,
     and let your saints rejoice in your
       goodness.
⁴²   O Lᴏʀᴅ God, do not turn away the face
       of your anointed one!
     Remember your steadfast love for
       David your servant."

1 John 5

Everyone who believes that Jesus is the Christ has been born of God, and everyone who loves the Father loves whoever has been born of him. ²By this we know that we love the children of God, when we love God and obey his commandments. ³For this is the love of God, that we keep his commandments. And his commandments are not burdensome. ⁴For everyone who has been born of God overcomes the world. And this is the victory that has overcome the world—our faith. ⁵Who is it that overcomes the world except the one who believes that Jesus is the Son of God?

⁶This is he who came by water and blood—Jesus Christ; not by the water only but by the water and the blood. And the Spirit is the one who testifies, because the Spirit is the truth. ⁷For there are three that testify: ⁸the Spirit and the water and the blood; and these three agree. ⁹If we receive the testimony of men, the testimony of God is greater, for this is the testimony of God that he has borne concerning his Son. ¹⁰Whoever believes in the Son of God has the testimony in himself. Whoever does not believe God has made him a liar, because he has not believed in the testimony that God has borne concerning his Son. ¹¹And this is the testimony, that God gave us eternal life, and this life is in his Son. ¹²Whoever has the Son has life; whoever does not have the Son of God does not have life.

---

¹ Septuagint, Vulgate; Hebrew *answer* ² Septuagint, Syriac, Vulgate (compare 1 Kings 8:36); Hebrew *toward the good way*

¹³I write these things to you who believe in the name of the Son of God that you may know that you have eternal life. ¹⁴And this is the confidence that we have toward him, that if we ask anything according to his will he hears us. ¹⁵And if we know that he hears us in whatever we ask, we know that we have the requests that we have asked of him.

¹⁶If anyone sees his brother committing a sin not leading to death, he shall ask, and God¹ will give him life—to those who commit sins that do not lead to death. There is sin that leads to death; I do not say that one should pray for that. ¹⁷All wrongdoing is sin, but there is sin that does not lead to death.

¹⁸We know that everyone who has been born of God does not keep on sinning, but he who was born of God protects him, and the evil one does not touch him.

¹⁹We know that we are from God, and the whole world lies in the power of the evil one.

²⁰And we know that the Son of God has come and has given us understanding, so that we may know him who is true; and we are in him who is true, in his Son Jesus Christ. He is the true God and eternal life. ²¹Little children, keep yourselves from idols.

Habakkuk 1

The oracle that Habakkuk the prophet saw.

2   O Lord, how long shall I cry for help,
       and you will not hear?
     Or cry to you "Violence!"
       and you will not save?
3   Why do you make me see iniquity,
       and why do you idly look at wrong?
     Destruction and violence are before me;
       strife and contention arise.
4   So the law is paralyzed,
       and justice never goes forth.
     For the wicked surround the righteous;
       so justice goes forth perverted.

5   "Look among the nations, and see;
       wonder and be astounded.
     For I am doing a work in your days
       that you would not believe if told.
6   For behold, I am raising up the
         Chaldeans,
       that bitter and hasty nation,

who march through the breadth of the
    earth,
  to seize dwellings not their own.
7   They are dreaded and fearsome;
       their justice and dignity go forth from
         themselves.
8   Their horses are swifter than leopards,
       more fierce than the evening wolves;
       their horsemen press proudly on.
     Their horsemen come from afar;
       they fly like an eagle swift to devour.
9   They all come for violence,
       all their faces forward.
     They gather captives like sand.
10   At kings they scoff,
       and at rulers they laugh.
     They laugh at every fortress,
       for they pile up earth and take it.
11   Then they sweep by like the wind and
         go on,
       guilty men, whose own might is their
         god!"

12   Are you not from everlasting,
       O Lord my God, my Holy One?
     We shall not die.
     O Lord, you have ordained them as a
         judgment,
       and you, O Rock, have established
         them for reproof.
13   You who are of purer eyes than to see
         evil
       and cannot look at wrong,
     why do you idly look at traitors
       and remain silent when the wicked
         swallows up
       the man more righteous than he?
14   You make mankind like the fish of the
         sea,
       like crawling things that have no
         ruler.
15   He² brings all of them up with a hook;
       he drags them out with his net;
     he gathers them in his dragnet;
       so he rejoices and is glad.
16   Therefore he sacrifices to his net
       and makes offerings to his dragnet;
     for by them he lives in luxury,³
       and his food is rich.
17   Is he then to keep on emptying his net
       and mercilessly killing nations
         forever?

¹ Greek *he* ² That is, the wicked foe ³ Hebrew *his portion is fat*

Luke 20

One day, as Jesus[1] was teaching the people in the temple and preaching the gospel, the chief priests and the scribes with the elders came up [2] and said to him, "Tell us by what authority you do these things, or who it is that gave you this authority." [3] He answered them, "I also will ask you a question. Now tell me, [4] was the baptism of John from heaven or from man?" [5] And they discussed it with one another, saying, "If we say, 'From heaven,' he will say, 'Why did you not believe him?' [6] But if we say, 'From man,' all the people will stone us to death, for they are convinced that John was a prophet." [7] So they answered that they did not know where it came from. [8] And Jesus said to them, "Neither will I tell you by what authority I do these things."

[9] And he began to tell the people this parable: "A man planted a vineyard and let it out to tenants and went into another country for a long while. [10] When the time came, he sent a servant[2] to the tenants, so that they would give him some of the fruit of the vineyard. But the tenants beat him and sent him away empty-handed. [11] And he sent another servant. But they also beat and treated him shamefully, and sent him away empty-handed. [12] And he sent yet a third. This one also they wounded and cast out. [13] Then the owner of the vineyard said, 'What shall I do? I will send my beloved son; perhaps they will respect him.' [14] But when the tenants saw him, they said to themselves, 'This is the heir. Let us kill him, so that the inheritance may be ours.' [15] And they threw him out of the vineyard and killed him. What then will the owner of the vineyard do to them? [16] He will come and destroy those tenants and give the vineyard to others." When they heard this, they said, "Surely not!" [17] But he looked directly at them and said, "What then is this that is written:

" 'The stone that the builders rejected
    has become the cornerstone'?[3]

[18] Everyone who falls on that stone will be broken to pieces, and when it falls on anyone, it will crush him."

[19] The scribes and the chief priests sought to lay hands on him at that very hour, for they perceived that he had told this parable against them, but they feared the people. [20] So they watched him and sent spies, who pretended to be sincere, that they might catch him in something he said, so as to deliver him up to the authority and jurisdiction of the governor. [21] So they asked him, "Teacher, we know that you speak and teach rightly, and show no partiality,[4] but truly teach the way of God. [22] Is it lawful for us to give tribute to Caesar, or not?" [23] But he perceived their craftiness, and said to them, [24] "Show me a denarius.[5] Whose likeness and inscription does it have?" They said, "Caesar's." [25] He said to them, "Then render to Caesar the things that are Caesar's, and to God the things that are God's." [26] And they were not able in the presence of the people to catch him in what he said, but marveling at his answer they became silent.

[27] There came to him some Sadducees, those who deny that there is a resurrection, [28] and they asked him a question, saying, "Teacher, Moses wrote for us that if a man's brother dies, having a wife but no children, the man[6] must take the widow and raise up offspring for his brother. [29] Now there were seven brothers. The first took a wife, and died without children. [30] And the second [31] and the third took her, and likewise all seven left no children and died. [32] Afterward the woman also died. [33] In the resurrection, therefore, whose wife will the woman be? For the seven had her as wife."

[34] And Jesus said to them, "The sons of this age marry and are given in marriage, [35] but those who are considered worthy to attain to that age and to the resurrection from the dead neither marry nor are given in marriage, [36] for they cannot die anymore, because they are equal to angels and are sons of God, being sons[7] of the resurrection. [37] But that the dead are raised, even Moses showed, in the passage about the bush, where he calls the Lord the God of Abraham and the God of Isaac and the God of Jacob. [38] Now he is not God of the dead, but of the living, for all live to him." [39] Then some of the scribes answered, "Teacher, you have spoken well." [40] For they no longer dared to ask him any question.

[41] But he said to them, "How can they say that the Christ is David's son? [42] For David himself says in the Book of Psalms,

[1] Greek he [2] Greek bondservant; also verse 11 [3] Greek the head of the corner [4] Greek and do not receive a face [5] A denarius was a day's wage for a laborer [6] Greek his brother
[7] Greek huioi; see Preface

" 'The Lord said to my Lord,
"Sit at my right hand,
43   until I make your enemies your
footstool." '
⁴⁴David thus calls him Lord, so how is he his son?"
⁴⁵And in the hearing of all the people he said to his disciples, ⁴⁶"Beware of the scribes, who like to walk around in long robes, and love greetings in the marketplaces and the best seats in the synagogues and the places of honor at feasts, ⁴⁷who devour widows' houses and for a pretense make long prayers. They will receive the greater condemnation."

DECEMBER 7

2 Chronicles 7

As soon as Solomon finished his prayer, fire came down from heaven and consumed the burnt offering and the sacrifices, and the glory of the LORD filled the temple. ²And the priests could not enter the house of the LORD, because the glory of the LORD filled the LORD's house. ³When all the people of Israel saw the fire come down and the glory of the LORD on the temple, they bowed down with their faces to the ground on the pavement and worshiped and gave thanks to the LORD, saying, "For he is good, for his steadfast love endures forever."
⁴Then the king and all the people offered sacrifice before the LORD. ⁵King Solomon offered as a sacrifice 22,000 oxen and 120,000 sheep. So the king and all the people dedicated the house of God. ⁶The priests stood at their posts; the Levites also, with the instruments for music to the LORD that King David had made for giving thanks to the LORD—for his steadfast love endures forever—whenever David offered praises by their ministry;¹ opposite them the priests sounded trumpets, and all Israel stood.
⁷And Solomon consecrated the middle of the court that was before the house of the LORD, for there he offered the burnt offering and the fat of the peace offerings, because the bronze altar Solomon had made could not hold the burnt offering and the grain offering and the fat.
⁸At that time Solomon held the feast for seven days, and all Israel with him, a very great assembly, from Lebo-hamath to the Brook of Egypt. ⁹And on the eighth day they held a solemn assembly, for they had kept the dedication of the altar seven days and the feast seven days. ¹⁰On the twenty-third day of the seventh month he sent the people away to their homes, joyful and glad of heart for the prosperity that the LORD had granted to David and to Solomon and to Israel his people.
¹¹Thus Solomon finished the house of the LORD and the king's house. All that Solomon had planned to do in the house of the LORD and in his own house he successfully accomplished. ¹²Then the LORD appeared to Solomon in the night and said to him: "I have heard your prayer and have chosen this place for myself as a house of sacrifice. ¹³When I shut up the heavens so that there is no rain, or command the locust to devour the land, or send pestilence among my people, ¹⁴if my people who are called by my name humble themselves, and pray and seek my face and turn from their wicked ways, then I will hear from heaven and will forgive their sin and heal their land. ¹⁵Now my eyes will be open and my ears attentive to the prayer that is made in this place. ¹⁶For now I have chosen and consecrated this house that my name may be there forever. My eyes and my heart will be there for all time. ¹⁷And as for you, if you will walk before me as David your father walked, doing according to all that I have commanded you and keeping my statutes and my rules, ¹⁸then I will establish your royal throne, as I covenanted with David your father, saying, 'You shall not lack a man to rule Israel.'
¹⁹"But if you² turn aside and forsake my statutes and my commandments that I have

¹ Hebrew by their hand ² The Hebrew for you is plural here

set before you, and go and serve other gods and worship them, [20]then I will pluck you[1] up from my land that I have given you, and this house that I have consecrated for my name, I will cast out of my sight, and I will make it a proverb and a byword among all peoples. [21]And at this house, which was exalted, everyone passing by will be astonished and say, 'Why has the LORD done thus to this land and to this house?' [22]Then they will say, 'Because they abandoned the LORD, the God of their fathers who brought them out of the land of Egypt, and laid hold on other gods and worshiped them and served them. Therefore he has brought all this disaster on them.'"

---
2 John 1

The elder to the elect lady and her children, whom I love in truth, and not only I, but also all who know the truth, [2]because of the truth that abides in us and will be with us forever:

[3]Grace, mercy, and peace will be with us, from God the Father and from Jesus Christ the Father's Son, in truth and love.

[4]I rejoiced greatly to find some of your children walking in the truth, just as we were commanded by the Father. [5]And now I ask you, dear lady—not as though I were writing you a new commandment, but the one we have had from the beginning—that we love one another. [6]And this is love, that we walk according to his commandments; this is the commandment, just as you have heard from the beginning, so that you should walk in it. [7]For many deceivers have gone out into the world, those who do not confess the coming of Jesus Christ in the flesh. Such a one is the deceiver and the antichrist. [8]Watch yourselves, so that you may not lose what we[2] have worked for, but may win a full reward. [9]Everyone who goes on ahead and does not abide in the teaching of Christ, does not have God. Whoever abides in the teaching has both the Father and the Son. [10]If anyone comes to you and does not bring this teaching, do not receive him into your house or give him any greeting, [11]for whoever greets him takes part in his wicked works.

[12]Though I have much to write to you, I would rather not use paper and ink. Instead I

hope to come to you and talk face to face, so that our joy may be complete.

[13]The children of your elect sister greet you.

Habakkuk 2

I will take my stand at my watchpost
and station myself on the tower,
  and look out to see what he will say to
    me,
  and what I will answer concerning my
    complaint.

[2]And the LORD answered me:

"Write the vision;
  make it plain on tablets,
  so he may run who reads it.
[3]   For still the vision awaits its appointed
    time;
  it hastens to the end—it will not lie.
If it seems slow, wait for it;
  it will surely come; it will not delay.

[4]   "Behold, his soul is puffed up; it is not
    upright within him,
  but the righteous shall live by his
    faith.[3]

[5]   "Moreover, wine[4] is a traitor,
  an arrogant man who is never at rest.[5]
His greed is as wide as Sheol;
  like death he has never enough.
He gathers for himself all nations
  and collects as his own all peoples."

[6]Shall not all these take up their taunt against him, with scoffing and riddles for him, and say,

  "Woe to him who heaps up what is not
    his own—
  for how long?—
  and loads himself with pledges!"
[7]   Will not your debtors suddenly arise,
  and those awake who will make you
    tremble?
  Then you will be spoil for them.
[8]   Because you have plundered many
    nations,
  all the remnant of the peoples shall
    plunder you,
for the blood of man and violence to the
    earth,
  to cities and all who dwell in them.

9 "Woe to him who gets evil gain for his
    house,
    to set his nest on high,
    to be safe from the reach of harm!
10 You have devised shame for your house
    by cutting off many peoples;
    you have forfeited your life.
11 For the stone will cry out from the wall,
    and the beam from the woodwork
        respond.

12 "Woe to him who builds a town with
        blood
    and founds a city on iniquity!
13 Behold, is it not from the LORD of hosts
    that peoples labor merely for fire,
    and nations weary themselves for
        nothing?
14 For the earth will be filled
    with the knowledge of the glory of the
        LORD
    as the waters cover the sea.

15 "Woe to him who makes his neighbors
        drink—
    you pour out your wrath and make
        them drunk,
    in order to gaze at their nakedness!
16 You will have your fill of shame instead
        of glory.
    Drink, yourself, and show your
        uncircumcision!
    The cup in the LORD's right hand
    will come around to you,
    and utter shame will come upon your
        glory!
17 The violence done to Lebanon will
        overwhelm you,
    as will the destruction of the beasts
        that terrified them,
    for the blood of man and violence to the
        earth,
    to cities and all who dwell in them.

18 "What profit is an idol
    when its maker has shaped it,
    a metal image, a teacher of lies?
    For its maker trusts in his own creation
    when he makes speechless idols!
19 Woe to him who says to a wooden thing,
        Awake;
    to a silent stone, Arise!
    Can this teach?

Behold, it is overlaid with gold and
        silver,
    and there is no breath at all in it.
20 But the LORD is in his holy temple;
    let all the earth keep silence before
        him."

Luke 21

Jesus[1] looked up and saw the rich putting their gifts into the offering box, [2] and he saw a poor widow put in two small copper coins.[2] [3] And he said, "Truly, I tell you, this poor widow has put in more than all of them. [4] For they all contributed out of their abundance, but she out of her poverty put in all she had to live on."

[5] And while some were speaking of the temple, how it was adorned with noble stones and offerings, he said, [6] "As for these things that you see, the days will come when there will not be left here one stone upon another that will not be thrown down." [7] And they asked him, "Teacher, when will these things be, and what will be the sign when these things are about to take place?" [8] And he said, "See that you are not led astray. For many will come in my name, saying, 'I am he!' and, 'The time is at hand!' Do not go after them. [9] And when you hear of wars and tumults, do not be terrified, for these things must first take place, but the end will not be at once."

[10] Then he said to them, "Nation will rise against nation, and kingdom against kingdom. [11] There will be great earthquakes, and in various places famines and pestilences. And there will be terrors and great signs from heaven. [12] But before all this they will lay their hands on you and persecute you, delivering you up to the synagogues and prisons, and you will be brought before kings and governors for my name's sake. [13] This will be your opportunity to bear witness. [14] Settle it therefore in your minds not to meditate beforehand how to answer, [15] for I will give you a mouth and wisdom, which none of your adversaries will be able to withstand or contradict. [16] You will be delivered up even by parents and brothers[3] and relatives and friends, and some of you they will put to death. [17] You will be hated by all for my name's sake. [18] But not a hair of your head will perish. [19] By your endurance you will gain your lives.

[20] "But when you see Jerusalem surrounded by armies, then know that its desolation has

---

[1] Greek He [2] Greek two lepta; a lepton was a Jewish bronze or copper coin worth about 1/128 of a denarius (which was a day's wage for a laborer) [3] Or parents and brothers and sisters

come near. [21] Then let those who are in Judea flee to the mountains, and let those who are inside the city depart, and let not those who are out in the country enter it, [22] for these are days of vengeance, to fulfill all that is written. [23] Alas for women who are pregnant and for those who are nursing infants in those days! For there will be great distress upon the earth and wrath against this people. [24] They will fall by the edge of the sword and be led captive among all nations, and Jerusalem will be trampled underfoot by the Gentiles, until the times of the Gentiles are fulfilled.

[25] "And there will be signs in sun and moon and stars, and on the earth distress of nations in perplexity because of the roaring of the sea and the waves, [26] people fainting with fear and with foreboding of what is coming on the world. For the powers of the heavens will be shaken. [27] And then they will see the Son of Man coming in a cloud with power and great glory. [28] Now when these things begin to take place, straighten up and raise your heads, because your redemption is drawing near."

[29] And he told them a parable: "Look at the fig tree, and all the trees. [30] As soon as they come out in leaf, you see for yourselves and know that the summer is already near. [31] So also, when you see these things taking place, you know that the kingdom of God is near. [32] Truly, I say to you, this generation will not pass away until all has taken place. [33] Heaven and earth will pass away, but my words will not pass away.

[34] "But watch yourselves lest your hearts be weighed down with dissipation and drunkenness and cares of this life, and that day come upon you suddenly like a trap. [35] For it will come upon all who dwell on the face of the whole earth. [36] But stay awake at all times, praying that you may have strength to escape all these things that are going to take place, and to stand before the Son of Man."

[37] And every day he was teaching in the temple, but at night he went out and lodged on the mount called Olivet. [38] And early in the morning all the people came to him in the temple to hear him.

DECEMBER 8

2 Chronicles 8

At the end of twenty years, in which Solomon had built the house of the LORD and his own house, [2] Solomon rebuilt the cities that Hiram had given to him, and settled the people of Israel in them.

[3] And Solomon went to Hamath-zobah and took it. [4] He built Tadmor in the wilderness and all the store cities that he built in Hamath. [5] He also built Upper Beth-horon and Lower Beth-horon, fortified cities with walls, gates, and bars, [6] and Baalath, and all the store cities that Solomon had and all the cities for his chariots and the cities for his horsemen, and whatever Solomon desired to build in Jerusalem, in Lebanon, and in all the land of his dominion. [7] All the people who were left of the Hittites, the Amorites, the Perizzites, the Hivites, and the Jebusites, who were not of Israel, [8] from their descendants who were left after them in the land, whom the people of Israel had not destroyed—these Solomon drafted as forced labor, and so they are to this day. [9] But of the people of Israel Solomon made no slaves for his work; they were soldiers, and his officers, the commanders of his chariots, and his horsemen. [10] And these were the chief officers of King Solomon, 250, who exercised authority over the people.

[11] Solomon brought Pharaoh's daughter up from the city of David to the house that he had built for her, for he said, "My wife shall not live in the house of David king of Israel, for the places to which the ark of the LORD has come are holy."

[12]Then Solomon offered up burnt offerings to the Lord on the altar of the Lord that he had built before the vestibule, [13]as the duty of each day required, offering according to the commandment of Moses for the Sabbaths, the new moons, and the three annual feasts—the Feast of Unleavened Bread, the Feast of Weeks, and the Feast of Booths. [14]According to the ruling of David his father, he appointed the divisions of the priests for their service, and the Levites for their offices of praise and ministry before the priests as the duty of each day required, and the gatekeepers in their divisions at each gate, for so David the man of God had commanded. [15]And they did not turn aside from what the king had commanded the priests and Levites concerning any matter and concerning the treasuries.

[16]Thus was accomplished all the work of Solomon from[1] the day the foundation of the house of the Lord was laid until it was finished. So the house of the Lord was completed. [17]Then Solomon went to Ezion-geber and Eloth on the shore of the sea, in the land of Edom. [18]And Hiram sent to him by the hand of his servants ships and servants familiar with the sea, and they went to Ophir together with the servants of Solomon and brought from there 450 talents[2] of gold and brought it to King Solomon.

3 John 1

The elder to the beloved Gaius, whom I love in truth. [2]Beloved, I pray that all may go well with you and that you may be in good health, as it goes well with your soul. [3]For I rejoiced greatly when the brothers[3] came and testified to your truth, as indeed you are walking in the truth. [4]I have no greater joy than to hear that my children are walking in the truth.

[5]Beloved, it is a faithful thing you do in all your efforts for these brothers, strangers as they are, [6]who testified to your love before the church. You will do well to send them on their journey in a manner worthy of God. [7]For they have gone out for the sake of the name, accepting nothing from the Gentiles. [8]Therefore we ought to support people like these, that we may be fellow workers for the truth.

[9]I have written something to the church, but Diotrephes, who likes to put himself first, does not acknowledge our authority. [10]So if I come, I will bring up what he is doing, talking wicked nonsense against us. And not content with that, he refuses to welcome the brothers, and also stops those who want to and puts them out of the church. [11]Beloved, do not imitate evil but imitate good. Whoever does good is from God; whoever does evil has not seen God. [12]Demetrius has received a good testimony from everyone, and from the truth itself. We also add our testimony, and you know that our testimony is true.

[13]I had much to write to you, but I would rather not write with pen and ink. [14]I hope to see you soon, and we will talk face to face. [15]Peace be to you. The friends greet you. Greet the friends, each by name.

Habakkuk 3

A prayer of Habakkuk the prophet, according to Shigionoth.

  [2] O Lord, I have heard the report of you,
     and your work, O Lord, do I fear.
  In the midst of the years revive it;
     in the midst of the years make it known;
     in wrath remember mercy.
  [3] God came from Teman,
     and the Holy One from Mount Paran.
                      Selah

  His splendor covered the heavens,
     and the earth was full of his praise.
  [4] His brightness was like the light;
     rays flashed from his hand;
     and there he veiled his power.
  [5] Before him went pestilence,
     and plague followed at his heels.[4]
  [6] He stood and measured the earth;
     he looked and shook the nations;
  then the eternal mountains were scattered;
     the everlasting hills sank low.
  His were the everlasting ways.
  [7] I saw the tents of Cushan in affliction;
     the curtains of the land of Midian did tremble.

---

8 Was your wrath against the rivers,
        O LORD?
    Was your anger against the rivers,
        or your indignation against the sea,
    when you rode on your horses,
        on your chariot of salvation?
9 You stripped the sheath from your bow,
        calling for many arrows.[1]   Selah
    You split the earth with rivers.
10 The mountains saw you and writhed;
        the raging waters swept on;
    the deep gave forth its voice;
        it lifted its hands on high.
11 The sun and moon stood still in their
            place
        at the light of your arrows as they
            sped,
        at the flash of your glittering spear.
12 You marched through the earth in fury;
        you threshed the nations in anger.
13 You went out for the salvation of your
            people,
        for the salvation of your anointed.
    You crushed the head of the house of
            the wicked,
        laying him bare from thigh to neck.[2]
                                             Selah
14 You pierced with his own arrows the
            heads of his warriors,
        who came like a whirlwind to scatter
            me,
        rejoicing as if to devour the poor in
            secret.
15 You trampled the sea with your horses,
        the surging of mighty waters.

16 I hear, and my body trembles;
        my lips quiver at the sound;
    rottenness enters into my bones;
        my legs tremble beneath me.
    Yet I will quietly wait for the day of
            trouble
        to come upon people who invade us.

17 Though the fig tree should not blossom,
        nor fruit be on the vines,
    the produce of the olive fail
        and the fields yield no food,
    the flock be cut off from the fold
        and there be no herd in the stalls,
18 yet I will rejoice in the LORD;
        I will take joy in the God of my
            salvation.

19 GOD, the Lord, is my strength;
        he makes my feet like the deer's;
        he makes me tread on my high places.

To the choirmaster: with stringed[3]
    instruments.

──────── Luke 22 ────────

Now the Feast of Unleavened Bread drew near, which is called the Passover. [2]And the chief priests and the scribes were seeking how to put him to death, for they feared the people. [3]Then Satan entered into Judas called Iscariot, who was of the number of the twelve. [4]He went away and conferred with the chief priests and officers how he might betray him to them. [5]And they were glad, and agreed to give him money. [6]So he consented and sought an opportunity to betray him to them in the absence of a crowd.

[7]Then came the day of Unleavened Bread, on which the Passover lamb had to be sacrificed. [8]So Jesus[4] sent Peter and John, saying, "Go and prepare the Passover for us, that we may eat it." [9]They said to him, "Where will you have us prepare it?" [10]He said to them, "Behold, when you have entered the city, a man carrying a jar of water will meet you. Follow him into the house that he enters [11]and tell the master of the house, 'The Teacher says to you, Where is the guest room, where I may eat the Passover with my disciples?' [12]And he will show you a large upper room furnished; prepare it there." [13]And they went and found it just as he had told them, and they prepared the Passover.

[14]And when the hour came, he reclined at table, and the apostles with him. [15]And he said to them, "I have earnestly desired to eat this Passover with you before I suffer. [16]For I tell you I will not eat it[5] until it is fulfilled in the kingdom of God." [17]And he took a cup, and when he had given thanks he said, "Take this, and divide it among yourselves. [18]For I tell you that from now on I will not drink of the fruit of the vine until the kingdom of God comes." [19]And he took bread, and when he had given thanks, he broke it and gave it to them, saying, "This is my body, which is given for you. Do this in remembrance of me." [20]And likewise the cup after they had eaten, saying, "This cup that is poured out

for you is the new covenant in my blood.[1] [21]But behold, the hand of him who betrays me is with me on the table. [22]For the Son of Man goes as it has been determined, but woe to that man by whom he is betrayed!" [23]And they began to question one another, which of them it could be who was going to do this.

[24]A dispute also arose among them, as to which of them was to be regarded as the greatest. [25]And he said to them, "The kings of the Gentiles exercise lordship over them, and those in authority over them are called benefactors. [26]But not so with you. Rather, let the greatest among you become as the youngest, and the leader as one who serves. [27]For who is the greater, one who reclines at table or one who serves? Is it not the one who reclines at table? But I am among you as the one who serves.

[28]"You are those who have stayed with me in my trials, [29]and I assign to you, as my Father assigned to me, a kingdom, [30]that you may eat and drink at my table in my kingdom and sit on thrones judging the twelve tribes of Israel.

[31]"Simon, Simon, behold, Satan demanded to have you,[2] that he might sift you like wheat, [32]but I have prayed for you that your faith may not fail. And when you have turned again, strengthen your brothers." [33]Peter[3] said to him, "Lord, I am ready to go with you both to prison and to death." [34]Jesus[4] said, "I tell you, Peter, the rooster will not crow this day, until you deny three times that you know me."

[35]And he said to them, "When I sent you out with no moneybag or knapsack or sandals, did you lack anything?" They said, "Nothing." [36]He said to them, "But now let the one who has a moneybag take it, and likewise a knapsack. And let the one who has no sword sell his cloak and buy one. [37]For I tell you that this Scripture must be fulfilled in me: 'And he was numbered with the transgressors.' For what is written about me has its fulfillment." [38]And they said, "Look, Lord, here are two swords." And he said to them, "It is enough."

[39]And he came out and went, as was his custom, to the Mount of Olives, and the disciples followed him. [40]And when he came to the place, he said to them, "Pray that you may not enter into temptation." [41]And he withdrew from them about a stone's throw, and knelt down and prayed, [42]saying, "Father, if you are willing, remove this cup from me.

Nevertheless, not my will, but yours, be done." [43]And there appeared to him an angel from heaven, strengthening him. [44]And being in an agony he prayed more earnestly; and his sweat became like great drops of blood falling down to the ground.[5] [45]And when he rose from prayer, he came to the disciples and found them sleeping for sorrow, [46]and he said to them, "Why are you sleeping? Rise and pray that you may not enter into temptation."

[47]While he was still speaking, there came a crowd, and the man called Judas, one of the twelve, was leading them. He drew near to Jesus to kiss him, [48]but Jesus said to him, "Judas, would you betray the Son of Man with a kiss?" [49]And when those who were around him saw what would follow, they said, "Lord, shall we strike with the sword?" [50]And one of them struck the servant[6] of the high priest and cut off his right ear. [51]But Jesus said, "No more of this!" And he touched his ear and healed him. [52]Then Jesus said to the chief priests and officers of the temple and elders, who had come out against him, "Have you come out as against a robber, with swords and clubs? [53]When I was with you day after day in the temple, you did not lay hands on me. But this is your hour, and the power of darkness."

[54]Then they seized him and led him away, bringing him into the high priest's house, and Peter was following at a distance. [55]And when they had kindled a fire in the middle of the courtyard and sat down together, Peter sat down among them. [56]Then a servant girl, seeing him as he sat in the light and looking closely at him, said, "This man also was with him." [57]But he denied it, saying, "Woman, I do not know him." [58]And a little later someone else saw him and said, "You also are one of them." But Peter said, "Man, I am not." [59]And after an interval of about an hour still another insisted, saying, "Certainly this man also was with him, for he too is a Galilean." [60]But Peter said, "Man, I do not know what you are talking about." And immediately, while he was still speaking, the rooster crowed. [61]And the Lord turned and looked at Peter. And Peter remembered the saying of the Lord, how he had said to him, "Before the rooster crows today, you will deny me three times." [62]And he went out and wept bitterly.

[63]Now the men who were holding Jesus in

[1] Some manuscripts omit, in whole or in part, verses 19b-20 (which is given. . . in my blood) [2] The Greek word for you (twice in this verse) is plural; in verse 32, all four instances are singular [3] Greek He [4] Greek He [5] Some manuscripts omit verses 43 and 44 [6] Greek bondservant

custody were mocking him as they beat him. ⁶⁴They also blindfolded him and kept asking him, "Prophesy! Who is it that struck you?" ⁶⁵And they said many other things against him, blaspheming him.

⁶⁶When day came, the assembly of the elders of the people gathered together, both chief priests and scribes. And they led him away to their council, and they said, ⁶⁷"If you are the Christ, tell us." But he said to them, "If I tell you, you will not believe, ⁶⁸and if I ask you, you will not answer. ⁶⁹But from now on the Son of Man shall be seated at the right hand of the power of God." ⁷⁰So they all said, "Are you the Son of God, then?" And he said to them, "You say that I am." ⁷¹Then they said, "What further testimony do we need? We have heard it ourselves from his own lips."

DECEMBER 9

2 Chronicles 9

Now when the queen of Sheba heard of the fame of Solomon, she came to Jerusalem to test him with hard questions, having a very great retinue and camels bearing spices and very much gold and precious stones. And when she came to Solomon, she told him all that was on her mind. ²And Solomon answered all her questions. There was nothing hidden from Solomon that he could not explain to her. ³And when the queen of Sheba had seen the wisdom of Solomon, the house that he had built, ⁴the food of his table, the seating of his officials, and the attendance of his servants, and their clothing, his cupbearers, and their clothing, and his burnt offerings that he offered at the house of the LORD, there was no more breath in her.

⁵And she said to the king, "The report was true that I heard in my own land of your words and of your wisdom, ⁶but I did not believe the¹ reports until I came and my own eyes had seen it. And behold, half the greatness of your wisdom was not told me; you surpass the report that I heard. ⁷Happy are your wives!² Happy are these your servants, who continually stand before you and hear your wisdom! ⁸Blessed be the LORD your God, who has delighted in you and set you on his throne as king for the LORD your God! Because your God loved Israel and would establish them forever, he has made you king over them, that you may execute justice and righteousness." ⁹Then she gave the king 120 talents³ of gold, and a very great quantity of spices, and precious stones. There were no spices such as those that the queen of Sheba gave to King Solomon.

¹⁰Moreover, the servants of Hiram and the servants of Solomon, who brought gold from Ophir, brought algum wood and precious stones. ¹¹And the king made from the algum wood supports for the house of the LORD and for the king's house, lyres also and harps for the singers. There never was seen the like of them before in the land of Judah.

¹²And King Solomon gave to the queen of Sheba all that she desired, whatever she asked besides what she had brought to the king. So she turned and went back to her own land with her servants.

¹³Now the weight of gold that came to Solomon in one year was 666 talents of gold, ¹⁴besides that which the explorers and merchants brought. And all the kings of Arabia and the governors of the land brought gold and silver to Solomon. ¹⁵King Solomon made 200 large shields of beaten gold; 600 shekels⁴ of beaten gold went into each shield. ¹⁶And he made 300 shields of beaten gold; 300 shekels of gold went into each shield; and the king put them in the House of the Forest of Lebanon. ¹⁷The king also made a great ivory throne and overlaid it with pure gold. ¹⁸The throne had six steps and a footstool of gold, which were attached to the throne, and on each side of the seat were armrests and two lions standing

¹ Hebrew their ² Septuagint (compare 1 Kings 10:8); Hebrew men ³ A talent was about 75 pounds or 34 kilograms ⁴ A shekel was about 2/5 ounce or 11 grams

beside the armrests, [19]while twelve lions stood there, one on each end of a step on the six steps. Nothing like it was ever made for any kingdom. [20]All King Solomon's drinking vessels were of gold, and all the vessels of the House of the Forest of Lebanon were of pure gold. Silver was not considered as anything in the days of Solomon. [21]For the king's ships went to Tarshish with the servants of Hiram. Once every three years the ships of Tarshish used to come bringing gold, silver, ivory, apes, and peacocks.[1]

[22]Thus King Solomon excelled all the kings of the earth in riches and in wisdom. [23]And all the kings of the earth sought the presence of Solomon to hear his wisdom, which God had put into his mind. [24]Every one of them brought his present, articles of silver and of gold, garments, myrrh, spices, horses, and mules, so much year by year. [25]And Solomon had 4,000 stalls for horses and chariots, and 12,000 horsemen, whom he stationed in the chariot cities and with the king in Jerusalem. [26]And he ruled over all the kings from the Euphrates[2] to the land of the Philistines and to the border of Egypt. [27]And the king made silver as common in Jerusalem as stone, and he made cedar as plentiful as the sycamore of the Shephelah. [28]And horses were imported for Solomon from Egypt and from all lands.

[29]Now the rest of the acts of Solomon, from first to last, are they not written in the history of Nathan the prophet, and in the prophecy of Ahijah the Shilonite, and in the visions of Iddo the seer concerning Jeroboam the son of Nebat? [30]Solomon reigned in Jerusalem over all Israel forty years. [31]And Solomon slept with his fathers and was buried in the city of David his father, and Rehoboam his son reigned in his place.

Jude 1

Jude, a servant[3] of Jesus Christ and brother of James,

To those who are called, beloved in God the Father and kept for[4] Jesus Christ:

[2]May mercy, peace, and love be multiplied to you.

[3]Beloved, although I was very eager to write to you about our common salvation, I found it necessary to write appealing to you to contend for the faith that was once for all delivered to the saints. [4]For certain people have crept in unnoticed who long ago were designated for this condemnation, ungodly people, who pervert the grace of our God into sensuality and deny our only Master and Lord, Jesus Christ.

[5]Now I want to remind you, although you once fully knew it, that Jesus, who saved[5] a people out of the land of Egypt, afterward destroyed those who did not believe. [6]And the angels who did not stay within their own position of authority, but left their proper dwelling, he has kept in eternal chains under gloomy darkness until the judgment of the great day— [7]just as Sodom and Gomorrah and the surrounding cities, which likewise indulged in sexual immorality and pursued unnatural desire,[6] serve as an example by undergoing a punishment of eternal fire.

[8]Yet in like manner these people also, relying on their dreams, defile the flesh, reject authority, and blaspheme the glorious ones. [9]But when the archangel Michael, contending with the devil, was disputing about the body of Moses, he did not presume to pronounce a blasphemous judgment, but said, "The Lord rebuke you." [10]But these people blaspheme all that they do not understand, and they are destroyed by all that they, like unreasoning animals, understand instinctively. [11]Woe to them! For they walked in the way of Cain and abandoned themselves for the sake of gain to Balaam's error and perished in Korah's rebellion. [12]These are hidden reefs[7] at your love feasts, as they feast with you without fear, shepherds feeding themselves; waterless clouds, swept along by winds; fruitless trees in late autumn, twice dead, uprooted; [13]wild waves of the sea, casting up the foam of their own shame; wandering stars, for whom the gloom of utter darkness has been reserved forever.

[14]It was also about these that Enoch, the seventh from Adam, prophesied, saying, "Behold, the Lord comes with ten thousands of his holy ones, [15]to execute judgment on all and to convict all the ungodly of all their deeds of ungodliness that they have committed in such an ungodly way, and of all the harsh things that ungodly sinners have spoken against him." [16]These are grumblers, malcontents, following their own sinful desires; they are loud-mouthed boasters, showing favoritism to gain advantage.

---

[1] Or baboons [2] Hebrew the River [3] Or slave (for the contextual rendering of the Greek word doulos, see Preface) [4] Or by [5] Some manuscripts although you fully knew it, that the Lord who once saved [6] Greek other flesh [7] Or are blemishes

[17]But you must remember, beloved, the predictions of the apostles of our Lord Jesus Christ. [18]They[1] said to you, "In the last time there will be scoffers, following their own ungodly passions." [19]It is these who cause divisions, worldly people, devoid of the Spirit. [20]But you, beloved, building yourselves up in your most holy faith and praying in the Holy Spirit, [21]keep yourselves in the love of God, waiting for the mercy of our Lord Jesus Christ that leads to eternal life. [22]And have mercy on those who doubt; [23]save others by snatching them out of the fire; to others show mercy with fear, hating even the garment[2] stained by the flesh.

[24]Now to him who is able to keep you from stumbling and to present you blameless before the presence of his glory with great joy, [25]to the only God, our Savior, through Jesus Christ our Lord, be glory, majesty, dominion, and authority, before all time and now and forever. Amen.

--- *Zephaniah 1* ---

The word of the Lord that came to Zephaniah the son of Cushi, son of Gedaliah, son of Amariah, son of Hezekiah, in the days of Josiah the son of Amon, king of Judah.

[2] "I will utterly sweep away everything
　　from the face of the earth," declares
　　the Lord.
[3] "I will sweep away man and beast;
　　I will sweep away the birds of the
　　　heavens
　　　and the fish of the sea,
　　and the rubble[3] with the wicked.
　　I will cut off mankind
　　from the face of the earth," declares
　　　the Lord.
[4] "I will stretch out my hand against
　　　Judah
　　and against all the inhabitants of
　　　Jerusalem;
　　and I will cut off from this place the
　　　remnant of Baal
　　and the name of the idolatrous priests
　　　along with the priests,
[5] those who bow down on the roofs
　　to the host of the heavens,
　　those who bow down and swear to the
　　　Lord
　　and yet swear by Milcom,

[6] those who have turned back from
　　　following the Lord,
　　who do not seek the Lord or inquire
　　　of him."

[7] Be silent before the Lord God!
　　For the day of the Lord is near;
　　the Lord has prepared a sacrifice
　　and consecrated his guests.
[8] And on the day of the Lord's sacrifice—
　　"I will punish the officials and the king's
　　　sons
　　and all who array themselves in
　　　foreign attire.
[9] On that day I will punish
　　everyone who leaps over the
　　　threshold,
　　and those who fill their master's[4] house
　　with violence and fraud.

[10] "On that day," declares the Lord,
　　"a cry will be heard from the Fish Gate,
　　a wail from the Second Quarter,
　　a loud crash from the hills.
[11] Wail, O inhabitants of the Mortar!
　　For all the traders[5] are no more;
　　all who weigh out silver are cut off.
[12] At that time I will search Jerusalem with
　　　lamps,
　　and I will punish the men
　　who are complacent,[6]
　　those who say in their hearts,
　　'The Lord will not do good,
　　　nor will he do ill.'
[13] Their goods shall be plundered,
　　and their houses laid waste.
　　Though they build houses,
　　　they shall not inhabit them;
　　though they plant vineyards,
　　　they shall not drink wine from
　　　　them."

[14] The great day of the Lord is near,
　　near and hastening fast;
　　the sound of the day of the Lord is
　　　bitter;
　　the mighty man cries aloud there.
[15] A day of wrath is that day,
　　a day of distress and anguish,
　　a day of ruin and devastation,
　　a day of darkness and gloom,
　　a day of clouds and thick darkness,
[16] a day of trumpet blast and battle cry

against the fortified cities
  and against the lofty battlements.
17 I will bring distress on mankind,
      so that they shall walk like the blind,
      because they have sinned against the
          LORD;
    their blood shall be poured out like dust,
      and their flesh like dung.
18 Neither their silver nor their gold
      shall be able to deliver them
      on the day of the wrath of the LORD.
    In the fire of his jealousy,
      all the earth shall be consumed;
    for a full and sudden end
      he will make of all the inhabitants of
          the earth.

--------- *Luke 23* ---------

Then the whole company of them arose and brought him before Pilate. ²And they began to accuse him, saying, "We found this man misleading our nation and forbidding us to give tribute to Caesar, and saying that he himself is Christ, a king." ³And Pilate asked him, "Are you the King of the Jews?" And he answered him, "You have said so." ⁴Then Pilate said to the chief priests and the crowds, "I find no guilt in this man." ⁵But they were urgent, saying, "He stirs up the people, teaching throughout all Judea, from Galilee even to this place."

⁶When Pilate heard this, he asked whether the man was a Galilean. ⁷And when he learned that he belonged to Herod's jurisdiction, he sent him over to Herod, who was himself in Jerusalem at that time. ⁸When Herod saw Jesus, he was very glad, for he had long desired to see him, because he had heard about him, and he was hoping to see some sign done by him. ⁹So he questioned him at some length, but he made no answer. ¹⁰The chief priests and the scribes stood by, vehemently accusing him. ¹¹And Herod with his soldiers treated him with contempt and mocked him. Then, arraying him in splendid clothing, he sent him back to Pilate. ¹²And Herod and Pilate became friends with each other that very day, for before this they had been at enmity with each other.

¹³Pilate then called together the chief priests and the rulers and the people, ¹⁴and said to them, "You brought me this man as one who

was misleading the people. And after examining him before you, behold, I did not find this man guilty of any of your charges against him. ¹⁵Neither did Herod, for he sent him back to us. Look, nothing deserving death has been done by him. ¹⁶I will therefore punish and release him."[1]

¹⁸But they all cried out together, "Away with this man, and release to us Barabbas"— ¹⁹a man who had been thrown into prison for an insurrection started in the city and for murder. ²⁰Pilate addressed them once more, desiring to release Jesus, ²¹but they kept shouting, "Crucify, crucify him!" ²²A third time he said to them, "Why, what evil has he done? I have found in him no guilt deserving death. I will therefore punish and release him." ²³But they were urgent, demanding with loud cries that he should be crucified. And their voices prevailed. ²⁴So Pilate decided that their demand should be granted. ²⁵He released the man who had been thrown into prison for insurrection and murder, for whom they asked, but he delivered Jesus over to their will.

²⁶And as they led him away, they seized one Simon of Cyrene, who was coming in from the country, and laid on him the cross, to carry it behind Jesus. ²⁷And there followed him a great multitude of the people and of women who were mourning and lamenting for him. ²⁸But turning to them Jesus said, "Daughters of Jerusalem, do not weep for me, but weep for yourselves and for your children. ²⁹For behold, the days are coming when they will say, 'Blessed are the barren and the wombs that never bore and the breasts that never nursed!' ³⁰Then they will begin to say to the mountains, 'Fall on us,' and to the hills, 'Cover us.' ³¹For if they do these things when the wood is green, what will happen when it is dry?"

³²Two others, who were criminals, were led away to be put to death with him. ³³And when they came to the place that is called The Skull, there they crucified him, and the criminals, one on his right and one on his left. ³⁴And Jesus said, "Father, forgive them, for they know not what they do."[2] And they cast lots to divide his garments. ³⁵And the people stood by, watching, but the rulers scoffed at him, saying, "He saved others; let him save himself, if he is the Christ of God, his Chosen One!" ³⁶The soldiers also mocked him, coming up and offering him sour wine ³⁷and saying, "If you are the King of the

---

[1] Here, or after verse 19, some manuscripts add verse 17: *Now he was obliged to release one man to them at the festival* [2] Some manuscripts omit the sentence *And Jesus. . . what they do*

Jews, save yourself!" ³⁸There was also an inscription over him,¹ "This is the King of the Jews."

³⁹One of the criminals who were hanged railed at him,² saying, "Are you not the Christ? Save yourself and us!" ⁴⁰But the other rebuked him, saying, "Do you not fear God, since you are under the same sentence of condemnation? ⁴¹And we indeed justly, for we are receiving the due reward of our deeds; but this man has done nothing wrong." ⁴²And he said, "Jesus, remember me when you come into your kingdom." ⁴³And he said to him, "Truly, I say to you, today you will be with me in Paradise."

⁴⁴It was now about the sixth hour,³ and there was darkness over the whole land until the ninth hour,⁴ ⁴⁵while the sun's light failed. And the curtain of the temple was torn in two. ⁴⁶Then Jesus, calling out with a loud voice, said, "Father, into your hands I commit my spirit!" And having said this he breathed his last. ⁴⁷Now when the centurion saw what had taken place, he praised God, saying, "Certainly this

man was innocent!" ⁴⁸And all the crowds that had assembled for this spectacle, when they saw what had taken place, returned home beating their breasts. ⁴⁹And all his acquaintances and the women who had followed him from Galilee stood at a distance watching these things.

⁵⁰Now there was a man named Joseph, from the Jewish town of Arimathea. He was a member of the council, a good and righteous man, ⁵¹who had not consented to their decision and action; and he was looking for the kingdom of God. ⁵²This man went to Pilate and asked for the body of Jesus. ⁵³Then he took it down and wrapped it in a linen shroud and laid him in a tomb cut in stone, where no one had ever yet been laid. ⁵⁴It was the day of Preparation, and the Sabbath was beginning.⁵ ⁵⁵The women who had come with him from Galilee followed and saw the tomb and how his body was laid. ⁵⁶Then they returned and prepared spices and ointments.

On the Sabbath they rested according to the commandment.

DECEMBER 10

2 Chronicles 10

Rehoboam went to Shechem, for all Israel had come to Shechem to make him king. ²And as soon as Jeroboam the son of Nebat heard of it (for he was in Egypt, where he had fled from King Solomon), then Jeroboam returned from Egypt. ³And they sent and called him. And Jeroboam and all Israel came and said to Rehoboam, ⁴"Your father made our yoke heavy. Now therefore lighten the hard service of your father and his heavy yoke on us, and we will serve you." ⁵He said to them, "Come to me again in three days." So the people went away.

⁶Then King Rehoboam took counsel with the old men,⁶ who had stood before Solomon his father while he was yet alive, saying, "How do you advise me to answer this people?" ⁷And they said to him, "If you will be good to this people and please them and speak good words to them, then they will be your servants

forever." ⁸But he abandoned the counsel that the old men gave him, and took counsel with the young men who had grown up with him and stood before him. ⁹And he said to them, "What do you advise that we answer this people who have said to me, 'Lighten the yoke that your father put on us'?" ¹⁰And the young men who had grown up with him said to him, "Thus shall you speak to the people who said to you, 'Your father made our yoke heavy, but you lighten it for us'; thus shall you say to them, 'My little finger is thicker than my father's thighs. ¹¹And now, whereas my father laid on you a heavy yoke, I will add to your yoke. My father disciplined you with whips, but I will discipline you with scorpions.'"

¹²So Jeroboam and all the people came to Rehoboam the third day, as the king said, "Come to me again the third day." ¹³And the

¹ Some manuscripts add in letters of Greek and Latin and Hebrew ² Or blasphemed him ³ That is, noon ⁴ That is, 3 P.M. ⁵ Greek was dawning ⁶ Or the elders; also verses 8, 13

king answered them harshly; and forsaking the counsel of the old men, [14]King Rehoboam spoke to them according to the counsel of the young men, saying, "My father made your yoke heavy, but I will add to it. My father disciplined you with whips, but I will discipline you with scorpions." [15]So the king did not listen to the people, for it was a turn of affairs brought about by God that the LORD might fulfill his word, which he spoke by Ahijah the Shilonite to Jeroboam the son of Nebat.

[16]And when all Israel saw that the king did not listen to them, the people answered the king, "What portion have we in David? We have no inheritance in the son of Jesse. Each of you to your tents, O Israel! Look now to your own house, David." So all Israel went to their tents. [17]But Rehoboam reigned over the people of Israel who lived in the cities of Judah. [18]Then King Rehoboam sent Hadoram,[1] who was taskmaster over the forced labor, and the people of Israel stoned him to death with stones. And King Rehoboam quickly mounted his chariot to flee to Jerusalem. [19]So Israel has been in rebellion against the house of David to this day.

--------- *Revelation 1* ---------

The revelation of Jesus Christ, which God gave him to show to his servants[2] the things that must soon take place. He made it known by sending his angel to his servant[3] John, [2]who bore witness to the word of God and to the testimony of Jesus Christ, even to all that he saw. [3]Blessed is the one who reads aloud the words of this prophecy, and blessed are those who hear, and who keep what is written in it, for the time is near.

[4]John to the seven churches that are in Asia:
Grace to you and peace from him who is and who was and who is to come, and from the seven spirits who are before his throne, [5]and from Jesus Christ the faithful witness, the first-born of the dead, and the ruler of kings on earth.

To him who loves us and has freed us from our sins by his blood [6]and made us a kingdom, priests to his God and Father, to him be glory and dominion forever and ever. Amen. [7]Behold, he is coming with the clouds, and every eye will see him, even those who pierced him, and all tribes of the earth will wail[4] on account of him. Even so. Amen.

[8]"I am the Alpha and the Omega," says the Lord God, "who is and who was and who is to come, the Almighty."

[9]I, John, your brother and partner in the tribulation and the kingdom and the patient endurance that are in Jesus, was on the island called Patmos on account of the word of God and the testimony of Jesus. [10]I was in the Spirit on the Lord's day, and I heard behind me a loud voice like a trumpet [11]saying, "Write what you see in a book and send it to the seven churches, to Ephesus and to Smyrna and to Pergamum and to Thyatira and to Sardis and to Philadelphia and to Laodicea."

[12]Then I turned to see the voice that was speaking to me, and on turning I saw seven golden lampstands, [13]and in the midst of the lampstands one like a son of man, clothed with a long robe and with a golden sash around his chest. [14]The hairs of his head were white, like white wool, like snow. His eyes were like a flame of fire, [15]his feet were like burnished bronze, refined in a furnace, and his voice was like the roar of many waters. [16]In his right hand he held seven stars, from his mouth came a sharp two-edged sword, and his face was like the sun shining in full strength.

[17]When I saw him, I fell at his feet as though dead. But he laid his right hand on me, saying, "Fear not, I am the first and the last, [18]and the living one. I died, and behold I am alive forevermore, and I have the keys of Death and Hades. [19]Write therefore the things that you have seen, those that are and those that are to take place after this. [20]As for the mystery of the seven stars that you saw in my right hand, and the seven golden lampstands, the seven stars are the angels of the seven churches, and the seven lampstands are the seven churches.

--------- *Zephaniah 2* ---------

Gather together, yes, gather,
O shameless nation,
[2]   before the decree takes effect[5]
     —before the day passes away like
       chaff—
before there comes upon you
   the burning anger of the LORD,
before there comes upon you
   the day of the anger of the LORD.

[1] Spelled *Adoram* in 1 Kings 12:18   [2] Greek *bondservants*   [3] Greek *bondservant*   [4] Or *mourn*   [5] Hebrew *gives birth*

3 Seek the LORD, all you humble of the
    land,
    who do his just commands;[1]
seek righteousness; seek humility;
    perhaps you may be hidden
    on the day of the anger of the LORD.

4 For Gaza shall be deserted,
    and Ashkelon shall become a
      desolation;
Ashdod's people shall be driven out at
      noon,
    and Ekron shall be uprooted.

5 Woe to you inhabitants of the seacoast,
    you nation of the Cherethites!
The word of the LORD is against you,
    O Canaan, land of the Philistines;
    and I will destroy you until no
      inhabitant is left.

6 And you, O seacoast, shall be pastures,
    with meadows[2] for shepherds
    and folds for flocks.

7 The seacoast shall become the
      possession
    of the remnant of the house of Judah,
    on which they shall graze,
and in the houses of Ashkelon
    they shall lie down at evening.
For the LORD their God will be mindful
      of them
    and restore their fortunes.

8 "I have heard the taunts of Moab
    and the revilings of the Ammonites,
how they have taunted my people
    and made boasts against their
      territory.

9 Therefore, as I live," declares the LORD
    of hosts,
    the God of Israel,
"Moab shall become like Sodom,
    and the Ammonites like Gomorrah,
a land possessed by nettles and salt pits,
    and a waste forever.
The remnant of my people shall plunder
      them,
    and the survivors of my nation shall
      possess them."

10 This shall be their lot in return for their
      pride,
    because they taunted and boasted
    against the people of the LORD of
      hosts.

11 The LORD will be awesome against them;
    for he will famish all the gods of the
      earth,
and to him shall bow down,
    each in its place,
    all the lands of the nations.

12 You also, O Cushites,
    shall be slain by my sword.

13 And he will stretch out his hand against
      the north
    and destroy Assyria,
and he will make Nineveh a desolation,
    a dry waste like the desert.

14 Herds shall lie down in her midst,
    all kinds of beasts;[3]
even the owl and the hedgehog[4]
    shall lodge in her capitals;
a voice shall hoot in the window;
    devastation will be on the threshold;
    for her cedar work will be laid bare.

15 This is the exultant city
    that lived securely,
that said in her heart,
    "I am, and there is no one else."
What a desolation she has become,
    a lair for wild beasts!
Everyone who passes by her
    hisses and shakes his fist.

Luke 24

But on the first day of the week, at early dawn, they went to the tomb, taking the spices they had prepared. [2]And they found the stone rolled away from the tomb, [3]but when they went in they did not find the body of the Lord Jesus. [4]While they were perplexed about this, behold, two men stood by them in dazzling apparel. [5]And as they were frightened and bowed their faces to the ground, the men said to them, "Why do you seek the living among the dead? [6]He is not here, but has risen. Remember how he told you, while he was still in Galilee, [7]that the Son of Man must be delivered into the hands of sinful men and be crucified and on the third day rise." [8]And they remembered his words, [9]and returning from the tomb they told all these things to the eleven and to all the rest. [10]Now it was Mary Magdalene and Joanna and Mary the mother of James and the other women with them who told these things to the apostles, [11]but these words seemed to them an idle tale, and they did not believe them. [12]But Peter rose and ran to the tomb; stooping and looking in, he saw the linen cloths by themselves; and he went home marveling at what had happened.

[13]That very day two of them were going to a village named Emmaus, about seven miles[1] from Jerusalem, [14]and they were talking with each other about all these things that had happened. [15]While they were talking and discussing together, Jesus himself drew near and went with them. [16]But their eyes were kept from recognizing him. [17]And he said to them, "What is this conversation that you are holding with each other as you walk?" And they stood still, looking sad. [18]Then one of them, named Cleopas, answered him, "Are you the only visitor to Jerusalem who does not know the things that have happened there in these days?" [19]And he said to them, "What things?" And they said to him, "Concerning Jesus of Nazareth, a man who was a prophet mighty in deed and word before God and all the people, [20]and how our chief priests and rulers delivered him up to be condemned to death, and crucified him. [21]But we had hoped that he was the one to redeem Israel. Yes, and besides all this, it is now the third day since these things happened. [22]Moreover, some women of our company amazed us. They were at the tomb early in the morning, [23]and when they did not find his body, they came back saying that they had even seen a vision of angels, who said that he was alive. [24]Some of those who were with us went to the tomb and found it just as the women had said, but him they did not see." [25]And he said to them, "O foolish ones, and slow of heart to believe all that the prophets have spoken! [26]Was it not necessary that the Christ should suffer these things and enter into his glory?" [27]And beginning with Moses and all the Prophets, he interpreted to them in all the Scriptures the things concerning himself.

[28]So they drew near to the village to which they were going. He acted as if he were going farther, [29]but they urged him strongly, saying, "Stay with us, for it is toward evening and the day is now far spent." So he went in to stay with them. [30]When he was at table with them, he took the bread and blessed and broke it and gave it to them. [31]And their eyes were opened, and they recognized him. And he vanished from their sight. [32]They said to each other, "Did not our hearts burn within us while he talked to us on the road, while he opened to us the Scriptures?" [33]And they rose that same hour and returned to Jerusalem. And they found the eleven and those who were with them gathered together, [34]saying, "The Lord has risen indeed, and has appeared to Simon!" [35]Then they told what had happened on the road, and how he was known to them in the breaking of the bread.

[36]As they were talking about these things, Jesus himself stood among them, and said to them, "Peace to you!" [37]But they were startled and frightened and thought they saw a spirit. [38]And he said to them, "Why are you troubled, and why do doubts arise in your hearts? [39]See my hands and my feet, that it is I myself. Touch me, and see. For a spirit does not have flesh and bones as you see that I have." [40]And when he had said this, he showed them his hands and his feet. [41]And while they still disbelieved for joy and were marveling, he said to them, "Have you anything here to eat?" [42]They gave him a piece of broiled fish,[2] [43]and he took it and ate before them.

[44]Then he said to them, "These are my words that I spoke to you while I was still with you, that everything written about me in the Law of Moses and the Prophets and the Psalms must be fulfilled." [45]Then he opened their minds to understand the Scriptures, [46]and said to them, "Thus it is written, that the Christ should suffer and on the third day rise from the dead, [47]and that repentance and[3] forgiveness of sins should be proclaimed in his name to all nations, beginning from Jerusalem. [48]You are witnesses of these things. [49]And behold, I am sending the promise of my Father upon you. But stay in the city until you are clothed with power from on high."

[50]Then he led them out as far as Bethany, and lifting up his hands he blessed them. [51]While he blessed them, he parted from them and was carried up into heaven. [52]And they worshiped him and returned to Jerusalem with great joy, [53]and were continually in the temple blessing God.

---

[1] Greek sixty stadia; a stadion was about 607 feet or 185 meters [2] Some manuscripts add and some honeycomb [3] Some manuscripts for

DECEMBER 11

— 2 Chronicles 11–12 —

When Rehoboam came to Jerusalem, he assembled the house of Judah and Benjamin, 180,000 chosen warriors, to fight against Israel, to restore the kingdom to Rehoboam. ²But the word of the Lord came to Shemaiah the man of God: ³"Say to Rehoboam the son of Solomon, king of Judah, and to all Israel in Judah and Benjamin, ⁴'Thus says the Lord, You shall not go up or fight against your relatives. Return every man to his home, for this thing is from me.'" So they listened to the word of the Lord and returned and did not go against Jeroboam.

⁵Rehoboam lived in Jerusalem, and he built cities for defense in Judah. ⁶He built Bethlehem, Etam, Tekoa, ⁷Beth-zur, Soco, Adullam, ⁸Gath, Mareshah, Ziph, ⁹Adoraim, Lachish, Azekah, ¹⁰Zorah, Aijalon, and Hebron, fortified cities that are in Judah and in Benjamin. ¹¹He made the fortresses strong, and put commanders in them, and stores of food, oil, and wine. ¹²And he put shields and spears in all the cities and made them very strong. So he held Judah and Benjamin.

¹³And the priests and the Levites who were in all Israel presented themselves to him from all places where they lived. ¹⁴For the Levites left their common lands and their holdings and came to Judah and Jerusalem, because Jeroboam and his sons cast them out from serving as priests of the Lord, ¹⁵and he appointed his own priests for the high places and for the goat idols and for the calves that he had made. ¹⁶And those who had set their hearts to seek the Lord God of Israel came after them from all the tribes of Israel to Jerusalem to sacrifice to the Lord, the God of their fathers. ¹⁷They strengthened the kingdom of Judah, and for three years they made Rehoboam the son of Solomon secure, for they walked for three years in the way of David and Solomon.

¹⁸Rehoboam took as wife Mahalath the daughter of Jerimoth the son of David, and of Abihail the daughter of Eliab the son of Jesse, ¹⁹and she bore him sons, Jeush, Shemariah, and Zaham. ²⁰After her he took Maacah the daughter of Absalom, who bore him Abijah, Attai, Ziza, and Shelomith. ²¹Rehoboam loved Maacah the daughter of Absalom above all his wives and concubines (he took eighteen wives and sixty concubines, and fathered twenty-eight sons and sixty daughters). ²²And Rehoboam appointed Abijah the son of Maacah as chief prince among his brothers, for he intended to make him king. ²³And he dealt wisely and distributed some of his sons through all the districts of Judah and Benjamin, in all the fortified cities, and he gave them abundant provisions and procured wives for them.[1]

¹²:¹When the rule of Rehoboam was established and he was strong, he abandoned the law of the Lord, and all Israel with him. ²In the fifth year of King Rehoboam, because they had been unfaithful to the Lord, Shishak king of Egypt came up against Jerusalem ³with 1,200 chariots and 60,000 horsemen. And the people were without number who came with him from Egypt—Libyans, Sukkiim, and Ethiopians. ⁴And he took the fortified cities of Judah and came as far as Jerusalem. ⁵Then Shemaiah the prophet came to Rehoboam and to the princes of Judah, who had gathered at Jerusalem because of Shishak, and said to them, "Thus says the Lord, 'You abandoned me, so I have abandoned you to the hand of Shishak.'" ⁶Then the princes of Israel and the king humbled themselves and said, "The Lord is righteous." ⁷When the Lord saw that they humbled themselves, the word of the Lord came to Shemaiah: "They have humbled themselves. I will not destroy them, but I will grant them some deliverance, and my wrath shall not be poured out on Jerusalem by the hand of Shishak. ⁸Nevertheless, they shall be servants to him, that they may know my service and the service of the kingdoms of the countries."

⁹So Shishak king of Egypt came up against Jerusalem. He took away the treasures of the

---

¹ Hebrew *and sought a multitude of wives*

house of the LORD and the treasures of the king's house. He took away everything. He also took away the shields of gold that Solomon had made, [10] and King Rehoboam made in their place shields of bronze and committed them to the hands of the officers of the guard, who kept the door of the king's house. [11] And as often as the king went into the house of the LORD, the guard came and carried them and brought them back to the guardroom. [12] And when he humbled himself the wrath of the LORD turned from him, so as not to make a complete destruction. Moreover, conditions were good[1] in Judah.

[13] So King Rehoboam grew strong in Jerusalem and reigned. Rehoboam was forty-one years old when he began to reign, and he reigned seventeen years in Jerusalem, the city that the LORD had chosen out of all the tribes of Israel to put his name there. His mother's name was Naamah the Ammonite. [14] And he did evil, for he did not set his heart to seek the LORD.

[15] Now the acts of Rehoboam, from first to last, are they not written in the chronicles of Shemaiah the prophet and of Iddo the seer?[2] There were continual wars between Rehoboam and Jeroboam. [16] And Rehoboam slept with his fathers and was buried in the city of David, and Abijah[3] his son reigned in his place.

Revelation 2

[1] "To the angel of the church in Ephesus write: 'The words of him who holds the seven stars in his right hand, who walks among the seven golden lampstands.

[2] "'I know your works, your toil and your patient endurance, and how you cannot bear with those who are evil, but have tested those who call themselves apostles and are not, and found them to be false. [3] I know you are enduring patiently and bearing up for my name's sake, and you have not grown weary. [4] But I have this against you, that you have abandoned the love you had at first. [5] Remember therefore from where you have fallen; repent, and do the works you did at first. If not, I will come to you and remove your lampstand from its place, unless you repent. [6] Yet this you have: you hate the works of the Nicolaitans, which I also hate. [7] He who has an ear, let him hear what the Spirit says to the churches. To the one who conquers

I will grant to eat of the tree of life, which is in the paradise of God.'

[8] "And to the angel of the church in Smyrna write: 'The words of the first and the last, who died and came to life.

[9] "'I know your tribulation and your poverty (but you are rich) and the slander[4] of those who say that they are Jews and are not, but are a synagogue of Satan. [10] Do not fear what you are about to suffer. Behold, the devil is about to throw some of you into prison, that you may be tested, and for ten days you will have tribulation. Be faithful unto death, and I will give you the crown of life. [11] He who has an ear, let him hear what the Spirit says to the churches. The one who conquers will not be hurt by the second death.'

[12] "And to the angel of the church in Pergamum write: 'The words of him who has the sharp two-edged sword.

[13] "'I know where you dwell, where Satan's throne is. Yet you hold fast my name, and you did not deny my faith[5] even in the days of Antipas my faithful witness, who was killed among you, where Satan dwells. [14] But I have a few things against you: you have some there who hold the teaching of Balaam, who taught Balak to put a stumbling block before the sons of Israel, so that they might eat food sacrificed to idols and practice sexual immorality. [15] So also you have some who hold the teaching of the Nicolaitans. [16] Therefore repent. If not, I will come to you soon and war against them with the sword of my mouth. [17] He who has an ear, let him hear what the Spirit says to the churches. To the one who conquers I will give some of the hidden manna, and I will give him a white stone, with a new name written on the stone that no one knows except the one who receives it.'

[18] "And to the angel of the church in Thyatira write: 'The words of the Son of God, who has eyes like a flame of fire, and whose feet are like burnished bronze.

[19] "'I know your works, your love and faith and service and patient endurance, and that your latter works exceed the first. [20] But I have this against you, that you tolerate that woman Jezebel, who calls herself a prophetess and is teaching and seducing my servants[6] to practice sexual immorality and to eat food sacrificed to idols. [21] I gave her time to repent, but

---

[1] Hebrew *good things were found*   [2] After *seer*, Hebrew adds *according to genealogy*   [3] Spelled *Abijam* in 1 Kings 14:31   [4] Greek *blasphemy*   [5] Or *your faith in me*   [6] Greek *bondservants*

she refuses to repent of her sexual immorality. ²²Behold, I will throw her onto a sickbed, and those who commit adultery with her I will throw into great tribulation, unless they repent of her works, ²³and I will strike her children dead. And all the churches will know that I am he who searches mind and heart, and I will give to each of you according to your works. ²⁴But to the rest of you in Thyatira, who do not hold this teaching, who have not learned what some call the deep things of Satan, to you I say, I do not lay on you any other burden. ²⁵Only hold fast what you have until I come. ²⁶The one who conquers and who keeps my works until the end, to him I will give authority over the nations, ²⁷and he will rule them with a rod of iron, as when earthen pots are broken in pieces, even as I myself have received authority from my Father. ²⁸And I will give him the morning star. ²⁹He who has an ear, let him hear what the Spirit says to the churches.'

——— *Zephaniah 3* ———

Woe to her who is rebellious and defiled,
    the oppressing city!
2 She listens to no voice;
    she accepts no correction.
   She does not trust in the LORD;
    she does not draw near to her God.

3 Her officials within her
    are roaring lions;
   her judges are evening wolves
    that leave nothing till the morning.
4 Her prophets are fickle, treacherous
        men;
   her priests profane what is holy;
    they do violence to the law.
5 The LORD within her is righteous;
    he does no injustice;
   every morning he shows forth his
        justice;
    each dawn he does not fail;
    but the unjust knows no shame.

6 "I have cut off nations;
    their battlements are in ruins;
   I have laid waste their streets
    so that no one walks in them;
   their cities have been made desolate,
    without a man, without an
        inhabitant.

7 I said, 'Surely you will fear me;
    you will accept correction.
   Then your¹ dwelling would not be cut off
    according to all that I have appointed
        against you.'²
   But all the more they were eager
    to make all their deeds corrupt.

8 "Therefore wait for me," declares the
        LORD,
    "for the day when I rise up to seize the
        prey.
   For my decision is to gather nations,
    to assemble kingdoms,
   to pour out upon them my indignation,
    all my burning anger;
   for in the fire of my jealousy
    all the earth shall be consumed.

9 "For at that time I will change the speech
        of the peoples
    to a pure speech,
   that all of them may call upon the name
        of the LORD
    and serve him with one accord.
10 From beyond the rivers of Cush
    my worshipers, the daughter of my
        dispersed ones,
    shall bring my offering.
11 "On that day you shall not be put to
        shame
    because of the deeds by which you
        have rebelled against me;
   for then I will remove from your midst
    your proudly exultant ones,
   and you shall no longer be haughty
    in my holy mountain.
12 But I will leave in your midst
    a people humble and lowly.
   They shall seek refuge in the name of
        the LORD,
13   those who are left in Israel;
   they shall do no injustice
    and speak no lies,
   nor shall there be found in their mouth
    a deceitful tongue.
   For they shall graze and lie down,
    and none shall make them afraid."

14 Sing aloud, O daughter of Zion;
    shout, O Israel!
   Rejoice and exult with all your heart,
    O daughter of Jerusalem!

¹ Hebrew *her* ² Hebrew *her*

15 The LORD has taken away the judgments
        against you;
    he has cleared away your enemies.
    The King of Israel, the LORD, is in your
        midst;
    you shall never again fear evil.
16 On that day it shall be said to Jerusalem:
    "Fear not, O Zion;
        let not your hands grow weak.
17 The LORD your God is in your midst,
        a mighty one who will save;
    he will rejoice over you with gladness;
        he will quiet you by his love;
    he will exult over you with loud singing.
18 I will gather those of you who mourn for
        the festival,
    so that you will no longer suffer
        reproach.[1]
19 Behold, at that time I will deal
        with all your oppressors.
    And I will save the lame
        and gather the outcast,
    and I will change their shame into praise
        and renown in all the earth.
20 At that time I will bring you in,
        at the time when I gather you together;
    for I will make you renowned and praised
        among all the peoples of the earth,
    when I restore your fortunes
        before your eyes," says the LORD.

——————— *John 1* ———————

In the beginning was the Word, and the Word
was with God, and the Word was God. [2]He
was in the beginning with God. [3]All things were
made through him, and without him was not
any thing made that was made. [4]In him was
life,[2] and the life was the light of men. [5]The
light shines in the darkness, and the darkness
has not overcome it.

[6]There was a man sent from God, whose
name was John. [7]He came as a witness, to bear
witness about the light, that all might believe
through him. [8]He was not the light, but came
to bear witness about the light.

[9]The true light, which gives light to everyone, was coming into the world. [10]He was in
the world, and the world was made through
him, yet the world did not know him. [11]He
came to his own,[3] and his own people[4] did not

receive him. [12]But to all who did receive him,
who believed in his name, he gave the right to
become children of God, [13]who were born, not
of blood nor of the will of the flesh nor of the
will of man, but of God.

[14]And the Word became flesh and dwelt
among us, and we have seen his glory, glory as
of the only Son from the Father, full of grace
and truth. [15](John bore witness about him, and
cried out, "This was he of whom I said, 'He who
comes after me ranks before me, because he
was before me.'") [16]For from his fullness we
have all received, grace upon grace.[5] [17]For the
law was given through Moses; grace and truth
came through Jesus Christ. [18]No one has ever
seen God; the only God,[6] who is at the Father's
side,[7] he has made him known.

[19]And this is the testimony of John, when the
Jews sent priests and Levites from Jerusalem
to ask him, "Who are you?" [20]He confessed,
and did not deny, but confessed, "I am not the
Christ." [21]And they asked him, "What then?
Are you Elijah?" He said, "I am not." "Are you
the Prophet?" And he answered, "No." [22]So
they said to him, "Who are you? We need to
give an answer to those who sent us. What do
you say about yourself?" [23]He said, "I am the
voice of one crying out in the wilderness, 'Make
straight[8] the way of the Lord,' as the prophet
Isaiah said."

[24](Now they had been sent from the Pharisees.) [25]They asked him, "Then why are you
baptizing, if you are neither the Christ, nor Elijah, nor the Prophet?" [26]John answered them,
"I baptize with water, but among you stands one
you do not know, [27]even he who comes after
me, the strap of whose sandal I am not worthy
to untie." [28]These things took place in Bethany
across the Jordan, where John was baptizing.

[29]The next day he saw Jesus coming toward
him, and said, "Behold, the Lamb of God, who
takes away the sin of the world! [30]This is he of
whom I said, 'After me comes a man who ranks
before me, because he was before me.' [31]I myself
did not know him, but for this purpose I came
baptizing with water, that he might be revealed
to Israel." [32]And John bore witness: "I saw the
Spirit descend from heaven like a dove, and it
remained on him. [33]I myself did not know him,
but he who sent me to baptize with water said
to me, 'He on whom you see the Spirit descend

---

[1] The meaning of the Hebrew is uncertain [2] Or *was not any thing made. That which has been made was life in him* [3] Greek *to his own things; that is, to his own domain, or to his own people* [4] *People* is implied in Greek [5] Or *grace in place of grace* [6] Or *the only One, who is God*; some manuscripts *the only Son* [7] Greek *in the bosom of the Father* [8] Or *crying out, 'In the wilderness make straight*

and remain, this is he who baptizes with the Holy Spirit.' [34]And I have seen and have borne witness that this is the Son of God."

[35]The next day again John was standing with two of his disciples, [36]and he looked at Jesus as he walked by and said, "Behold, the Lamb of God!" [37]The two disciples heard him say this, and they followed Jesus. [38]Jesus turned and saw them following and said to them, "What are you seeking?" And they said to him, "Rabbi" (which means Teacher), "where are you staying?" [39]He said to them, "Come and you will see." So they came and saw where he was staying, and they stayed with him that day, for it was about the tenth hour.[1] [40]One of the two who heard John speak and followed Jesus[2] was Andrew, Simon Peter's brother. [41]He first found his own brother Simon and said to him, "We have found the Messiah" (which means Christ). [42]He brought him to Jesus. Jesus looked at him and said, "You are Simon the son of John. You shall be called Cephas" (which means Peter[3]).

[43]The next day Jesus decided to go to Galilee. He found Philip and said to him, "Follow me." [44]Now Philip was from Bethsaida, the city of Andrew and Peter. [45]Philip found Nathanael and said to him, "We have found him of whom Moses in the Law and also the prophets wrote, Jesus of Nazareth, the son of Joseph." [46]Nathanael said to him, "Can anything good come out of Nazareth?" Philip said to him, "Come and see." [47]Jesus saw Nathanael coming toward him and said of him, "Behold, an Israelite indeed, in whom there is no deceit!" [48]Nathanael said to him, "How do you know me?" Jesus answered him, "Before Philip called you, when you were under the fig tree, I saw you." [49]Nathanael answered him, "Rabbi, you are the Son of God! You are the King of Israel!" [50]Jesus answered him, "Because I said to you, 'I saw you under the fig tree,' do you believe? You will see greater things than these." [51]And he said to him, "Truly, truly, I say to you,[4] you will see heaven opened, and the angels of God ascending and descending on the Son of Man."

DECEMBER 12

2 Chronicles 13

In the eighteenth year of King Jeroboam, Abijah began to reign over Judah. [2]He reigned for three years in Jerusalem. His mother's name was Micaiah[5] the daughter of Uriel of Gibeah.

Now there was war between Abijah and Jeroboam. [3]Abijah went out to battle, having an army of valiant men of war, 400,000 chosen men. And Jeroboam drew up his line of battle against him with 800,000 chosen mighty warriors. [4]Then Abijah stood up on Mount Zemaraim that is in the hill country of Ephraim and said, "Hear me, O Jeroboam and all Israel! [5]Ought you not to know that the LORD God of Israel gave the kingship over Israel forever to David and his sons by a covenant of salt? [6]Yet Jeroboam the son of Nebat, a servant of Solomon the son of David, rose up and rebelled against his lord, [7]and certain

worthless scoundrels gathered about him and defied Rehoboam the son of Solomon, when Rehoboam was young and irresolute[6] and could not withstand them.

[8]"And now you think to withstand the kingdom of the LORD in the hand of the sons of David, because you are a great multitude and have with you the golden calves that Jeroboam made you for gods. [9]Have you not driven out the priests of the LORD, the sons of Aaron, and the Levites, and made priests for yourselves like the peoples of other lands? Whoever comes for ordination[7] with a young bull or seven rams becomes a priest of what are no gods. [10]But as for us, the LORD is our God, and we have not forsaken him. We have priests ministering to the LORD who are sons of Aaron, and Levites for their service. [11]They offer to the LORD

[1] That is, about 4 P.M. [2] Greek him [3] Cephas and Peter are from the word for rock in Aramaic and Greek, respectively [4] The Greek for you is plural; twice in this verse [5] Spelled Maacah in 1 Kings 15:2 [6] Hebrew soft of heart [7] Hebrew to fill his hand

every morning and every evening burnt offerings and incense of sweet spices, set out the showbread on the table of pure gold, and care for the golden lampstand that its lamps may burn every evening. For we keep the charge of the LORD our God, but you have forsaken him. ¹²Behold, God is with us at our head, and his priests with their battle trumpets to sound the call to battle against you. O sons of Israel, do not fight against the LORD, the God of your fathers, for you cannot succeed."

¹³Jeroboam had sent an ambush around to come upon them from behind. Thus his troops[1] were in front of Judah, and the ambush was behind them. ¹⁴And when Judah looked, behold, the battle was in front of and behind them. And they cried to the LORD, and the priests blew the trumpets. ¹⁵Then the men of Judah raised the battle shout. And when the men of Judah shouted, God defeated Jeroboam and all Israel before Abijah and Judah. ¹⁶The men of Israel fled before Judah, and God gave them into their hand. ¹⁷Abijah and his people struck them with great force, so there fell slain of Israel 500,000 chosen men. ¹⁸Thus the men of Israel were subdued at that time, and the men of Judah prevailed, because they relied on the LORD, the God of their fathers. ¹⁹And Abijah pursued Jeroboam and took cities from him, Bethel with its villages and Jeshanah with its villages and Ephron[2] with its villages. ²⁰Jeroboam did not recover his power in the days of Abijah. And the LORD struck him down, and he died. ²¹But Abijah grew mighty. And he took fourteen wives and had twenty-two sons and sixteen daughters. ²²The rest of the acts of Abijah, his ways and his sayings, are written in the story of the prophet Iddo.

Revelation 3

"And to the angel of the church in Sardis write: 'The words of him who has the seven spirits of God and the seven stars.

"'I know your works. You have the reputation of being alive, but you are dead. ²Wake up, and strengthen what remains and is about to die, for I have not found your works complete in the sight of my God. ³Remember, then, what you received and heard. Keep it, and repent. If you will not wake up, I will come like a thief, and you will not know at what hour I will come

against you. ⁴Yet you have still a few names in Sardis, people who have not soiled their garments, and they will walk with me in white, for they are worthy. ⁵The one who conquers will be clothed thus in white garments, and I will never blot his name out of the book of life. I will confess his name before my Father and before his angels. ⁶He who has an ear, let him hear what the Spirit says to the churches.'

⁷"And to the angel of the church in Philadelphia write: 'The words of the holy one, the true one, who has the key of David, who opens and no one will shut, who shuts and no one opens.

⁸"'I know your works. Behold, I have set before you an open door, which no one is able to shut. I know that you have but little power, and yet you have kept my word and have not denied my name. ⁹Behold, I will make those of the synagogue of Satan who say that they are Jews and are not, but lie—behold, I will make them come and bow down before your feet, and they will learn that I have loved you. ¹⁰Because you have kept my word about patient endurance, I will keep you from the hour of trial that is coming on the whole world, to try those who dwell on the earth. ¹¹I am coming soon. Hold fast what you have, so that no one may seize your crown. ¹²The one who conquers, I will make him a pillar in the temple of my God. Never shall he go out of it, and I will write on him the name of my God, and the name of the city of my God, the new Jerusalem, which comes down from my God out of heaven, and my own new name. ¹³He who has an ear, let him hear what the Spirit says to the churches.'

¹⁴"And to the angel of the church in Laodicea write: 'The words of the Amen, the faithful and true witness, the beginning of God's creation.

¹⁵"'I know your works: you are neither cold nor hot. Would that you were either cold or hot! ¹⁶So, because you are lukewarm, and neither hot nor cold, I will spit you out of my mouth. ¹⁷For you say, I am rich, I have prospered, and I need nothing, not realizing that you are wretched, pitiable, poor, blind, and naked. ¹⁸I counsel you to buy from me gold refined by fire, so that you may be rich, and white garments so that you may clothe yourself and the shame of your nakedness may not be seen, and salve to anoint your eyes, so that you may see. ¹⁹Those whom I love, I reprove and discipline, so be zealous and repent. ²⁰Behold, I stand at the door and

[1] Hebrew they [2] Or Ephrain

knock. If anyone hears my voice and opens the door, I will come in to him and eat with him, and he with me. [21] The one who conquers, I will grant him to sit with me on my throne, as I also conquered and sat down with my Father on his throne. [22] He who has an ear, let him hear what the Spirit says to the churches.'"

Haggai 1

In the second year of Darius the king, in the sixth month, on the first day of the month, the word of the LORD came by the hand of Haggai the prophet to Zerubbabel the son of Shealtiel, governor of Judah, and to Joshua the son of Jehozadak, the high priest: [2] "Thus says the LORD of hosts: These people say the time has not yet come to rebuild the house of the LORD." [3] Then the word of the LORD came by the hand of Haggai the prophet, [4] "Is it a time for you yourselves to dwell in your paneled houses, while this house lies in ruins? [5] Now, therefore, thus says the LORD of hosts: Consider your ways. [6] You have sown much, and harvested little. You eat, but you never have enough; you drink, but you never have your fill. You clothe yourselves, but no one is warm. And he who earns wages does so to put them into a bag with holes.

[7] "Thus says the LORD of hosts: Consider your ways. [8] Go up to the hills and bring wood and build the house, that I may take pleasure in it and that I may be glorified, says the LORD. [9] You looked for much, and behold, it came to little. And when you brought it home, I blew it away. Why? declares the LORD of hosts. Because of my house that lies in ruins, while each of you busies himself with his own house. [10] Therefore the heavens above you have withheld the dew, and the earth has withheld its produce. [11] And I have called for a drought on the land and the hills, on the grain, the new wine, the oil, on what the ground brings forth, on man and beast, and on all their labors."

[12] Then Zerubbabel the son of Shealtiel, and Joshua the son of Jehozadak, the high priest, with all the remnant of the people, obeyed the voice of the LORD their God, and the words of Haggai the prophet, as the LORD their God had sent him. And the people feared the LORD. [13] Then Haggai, the messenger of the LORD, spoke to the people with the LORD's message,

"I am with you, declares the LORD." [14] And the LORD stirred up the spirit of Zerubbabel the son of Shealtiel, governor of Judah, and the spirit of Joshua the son of Jehozadak, the high priest, and the spirit of all the remnant of the people. And they came and worked on the house of the LORD of hosts, their God, [15] on the twenty-fourth day of the month, in the sixth month, in the second year of Darius the king.

John 2

On the third day there was a wedding at Cana in Galilee, and the mother of Jesus was there. [2] Jesus also was invited to the wedding with his disciples. [3] When the wine ran out, the mother of Jesus said to him, "They have no wine." [4] And Jesus said to her, "Woman, what does this have to do with me? My hour has not yet come." [5] His mother said to the servants, "Do whatever he tells you."

[6] Now there were six stone water jars there for the Jewish rites of purification, each holding twenty or thirty gallons.[1] [7] Jesus said to the servants, "Fill the jars with water." And they filled them up to the brim. [8] And he said to them, "Now draw some out and take it to the master of the feast." So they took it. [9] When the master of the feast tasted the water now become wine, and did not know where it came from (though the servants who had drawn the water knew), the master of the feast called the bridegroom [10] and said to him, "Everyone serves the good wine first, and when people have drunk freely, then the poor wine. But you have kept the good wine until now." [11] This, the first of his signs, Jesus did at Cana in Galilee, and manifested his glory. And his disciples believed in him.

[12] After this he went down to Capernaum, with his mother and his brothers[2] and his disciples, and they stayed there for a few days.

[13] The Passover of the Jews was at hand, and Jesus went up to Jerusalem. [14] In the temple he found those who were selling oxen and sheep and pigeons, and the money-changers sitting there. [15] And making a whip of cords, he drove them all out of the temple, with the sheep and oxen. And he poured out the coins of the money-changers and overturned their tables. [16] And he told those who sold the pigeons, "Take these things away; do not make my Father's house a house of trade." [17] His disciples

[1] Greek two or three measures (metrētas); a metrētēs was about 10 gallons or 35 liters [2] Or brothers and sisters. The plural Greek word adelphoi (translated "brothers") refers to siblings in a family. In New Testament usage, depending on the context, adelphoi may refer either to brothers or to brothers and sisters

remembered that it was written, "Zeal for your house will consume me."

[18] So the Jews said to him, "What sign do you show us for doing these things?" [19] Jesus answered them, "Destroy this temple, and in three days I will raise it up." [20] The Jews then said, "It has taken forty-six years to build this temple,[1] and will you raise it up in three days?" [21] But he was speaking about the temple of his body. [22] When therefore he was raised from the dead, his disciples remembered that he had said this, and they believed the Scripture and the word that Jesus had spoken.

[23] Now when he was in Jerusalem at the Passover Feast, many believed in his name when they saw the signs that he was doing. [24] But Jesus on his part did not entrust himself to them, because he knew all people [25] and needed no one to bear witness about man, for he himself knew what was in man.

DECEMBER 13

2 Chronicles 14[2]–15

Abijah slept with his fathers, and they buried him in the city of David. And Asa his son reigned in his place. In his days the land had rest for ten years. [2][3] And Asa did what was good and right in the eyes of the LORD his God. [3] He took away the foreign altars and the high places and broke down the pillars and cut down the Asherim [4] and commanded Judah to seek the LORD, the God of their fathers, and to keep the law and the commandment. [5] He also took out of all the cities of Judah the high places and the incense altars. And the kingdom had rest under him. [6] He built fortified cities in Judah, for the land had rest. He had no war in those years, for the LORD gave him peace. [7] And he said to Judah, "Let us build these cities and surround them with walls and towers, gates and bars. The land is still ours, because we have sought the LORD our God. We have sought him, and he has given us peace on every side." So they built and prospered. [8] And Asa had an army of 300,000 from Judah, armed with large shields and spears, and 280,000 men from Benjamin that carried shields and drew bows. All these were mighty men of valor.

[9] Zerah the Ethiopian came out against them with an army of a million men and 300 chariots, and came as far as Mareshah. [10] And Asa went out to meet him, and they drew up their lines of battle in the Valley of Zephathah at Mareshah. [11] And Asa cried to the LORD his God, "O LORD, there is none like you to help, between the mighty and the weak. Help us, O LORD our God, for we rely on you, and in your name we have come against this multitude. O LORD, you are our God; let not man prevail against you." [12] So the LORD defeated the Ethiopians before Asa and before Judah, and the Ethiopians fled. [13] Asa and the people who were with him pursued them as far as Gerar, and the Ethiopians fell until none remained alive, for they were broken before the LORD and his army. The men of Judah[4] carried away very much spoil. [14] And they attacked all the cities around Gerar, for the fear of the LORD was upon them. They plundered all the cities, for there was much plunder in them. [15] And they struck down the tents of those who had livestock and carried away sheep in abundance and camels. Then they returned to Jerusalem.

[15:1] The Spirit of God came upon Azariah the son of Oded, [2] and he went out to meet Asa and said to him, "Hear me, Asa, and all Judah and Benjamin: The LORD is with you while you are with him. If you seek him, he will be found by you, but if you forsake him, he will forsake you. [3] For a long time Israel was without the true God, and without a teaching priest and without law, [4] but when in their distress they turned to the LORD, the God of Israel, and sought him, he was found by them. [5] In those times there was no peace to him who went out or to him

[1] Or This temple was built forty-six years ago [2] Ch 13:23 in Hebrew [3] Ch 14:1 in Hebrew [4] Hebrew They

who came in, for great disturbances afflicted all the inhabitants of the lands. ⁶They were broken in pieces. Nation was crushed by nation and city by city, for God troubled them with every sort of distress. ⁷But you, take courage! Do not let your hands be weak, for your work shall be rewarded."

⁸As soon as Asa heard these words, the prophecy of Azariah the son of Oded, he took courage and put away the detestable idols from all the land of Judah and Benjamin and from the cities that he had taken in the hill country of Ephraim, and he repaired the altar of the LORD that was in front of the vestibule of the house of the LORD.¹ ⁹And he gathered all Judah and Benjamin, and those from Ephraim, Manasseh, and Simeon who were residing with them, for great numbers had deserted to him from Israel when they saw that the LORD his God was with him. ¹⁰They were gathered at Jerusalem in the third month of the fifteenth year of the reign of Asa. ¹¹They sacrificed to the LORD on that day from the spoil that they had brought 700 oxen and 7,000 sheep. ¹²And they entered into a covenant to seek the LORD, the God of their fathers, with all their heart and with all their soul, ¹³but that whoever would not seek the LORD, the God of Israel, should be put to death, whether young or old, man or woman. ¹⁴They swore an oath to the LORD with a loud voice and with shouting and with trumpets and with horns. ¹⁵And all Judah rejoiced over the oath, for they had sworn with all their heart and had sought him with their whole desire, and he was found by them, and the LORD gave them rest all around.

¹⁶Even Maacah, his mother, King Asa removed from being queen mother because she had made a detestable image for Asherah. Asa cut down her image, crushed it, and burned it at the brook Kidron. ¹⁷But the high places were not taken out of Israel. Nevertheless, the heart of Asa was wholly true all his days. ¹⁸And he brought into the house of God the sacred gifts of his father and his own sacred gifts, silver, and gold, and vessels. ¹⁹And there was no more war until the thirty-fifth year of the reign of Asa.

Revelation 4

After this I looked, and behold, a door standing open in heaven! And the first voice, which I had heard speaking to me like a

trumpet, said, "Come up here, and I will show you what must take place after this." ²At once I was in the Spirit, and behold, a throne stood in heaven, with one seated on the throne. ³And he who sat there had the appearance of jasper and carnelian, and around the throne was a rainbow that had the appearance of an emerald. ⁴Around the throne were twenty-four thrones, and seated on the thrones were twenty-four elders, clothed in white garments, with golden crowns on their heads. ⁵From the throne came flashes of lightning, and rumblings² and peals of thunder, and before the throne were burning seven torches of fire, which are the seven spirits of God, ⁶and before the throne there was as it were a sea of glass, like crystal.

And around the throne, on each side of the throne, are four living creatures, full of eyes in front and behind: ⁷the first living creature like a lion, the second living creature like an ox, the third living creature with the face of a man, and the fourth living creature like an eagle in flight. ⁸And the four living creatures, each of them with six wings, are full of eyes all around and within, and day and night they never cease to say,

"Holy, holy, holy, is the Lord God Almighty,
    who was and is and is to come!"

⁹And whenever the living creatures give glory and honor and thanks to him who is seated on the throne, who lives forever and ever, ¹⁰the twenty-four elders fall down before him who is seated on the throne and worship him who lives forever and ever. They cast their crowns before the throne, saying,

¹¹   "Worthy are you, our Lord and God,
    to receive glory and honor and power,
  for you created all things,
    and by your will they existed and were created."

Haggai 2

In the seventh month, on the twenty-first day of the month, the word of the LORD came by the hand of Haggai the prophet, ²"Speak now to Zerubbabel the son of Shealtiel, governor of Judah, and to Joshua the son of Jehozadak, the high priest, and to all the remnant of the

¹ Hebrew *the vestibule of the LORD* ² Or *voices, or sounds*

people, and say, [3] 'Who is left among you who saw this house in its former glory? How do you see it now? Is it not as nothing in your eyes? [4] Yet now be strong, O Zerubbabel, declares the LORD. Be strong, O Joshua, son of Jehozadak, the high priest. Be strong, all you people of the land, declares the LORD. Work, for I am with you, declares the LORD of hosts, [5] according to the covenant that I made with you when you came out of Egypt. My Spirit remains in your midst. Fear not. [6] For thus says the LORD of hosts: Yet once more, in a little while, I will shake the heavens and the earth and the sea and the dry land. [7] And I will shake all nations, so that the treasures of all nations shall come in, and I will fill this house with glory, says the LORD of hosts. [8] The silver is mine, and the gold is mine, declares the LORD of hosts. [9] The latter glory of this house shall be greater than the former, says the LORD of hosts. And in this place I will give peace, declares the LORD of hosts.' "

[10] On the twenty-fourth day of the ninth month, in the second year of Darius, the word of the LORD came by Haggai the prophet, [11] "Thus says the LORD of hosts: Ask the priests about the law: [12] 'If someone carries holy meat in the fold of his garment and touches with his fold bread or stew or wine or oil or any kind of food, does it become holy?' " The priests answered and said, "No." [13] Then Haggai said, "If someone who is unclean by contact with a dead body touches any of these, does it become unclean?" The priests answered and said, "It does become unclean." [14] Then Haggai answered and said, "So is it with this people, and with this nation before me, declares the LORD, and so with every work of their hands. And what they offer there is unclean. [15] Now then, consider from this day onward.[1] Before stone was placed upon stone in the temple of the LORD, [16] how did you fare? When[2] one came to a heap of twenty measures, there were but ten. When one came to the wine vat to draw fifty measures, there were but twenty. [17] I struck you and all the products of your toil with blight and with mildew and with hail, yet you did not turn to me, declares the LORD. [18] Consider from this day onward, from the twenty-fourth day of the ninth month. Since the day that the foundation of the LORD's temple was laid, consider: [19] Is the seed yet in the barn? Indeed, the vine, the fig tree, the pomegranate, and the olive tree have yielded nothing. But from this day on I will bless you."

[20] The word of the LORD came a second time to Haggai on the twenty-fourth day of the month, [21] "Speak to Zerubbabel, governor of Judah, saying, I am about to shake the heavens and the earth, [22] and to overthrow the throne of kingdoms. I am about to destroy the strength of the kingdoms of the nations, and overthrow the chariots and their riders. And the horses and their riders shall go down, every one by the sword of his brother. [23] On that day, declares the LORD of hosts, I will take you, O Zerubbabel my servant, the son of Shealtiel, declares the LORD, and make you like a[3] signet ring, for I have chosen you, declares the LORD of hosts."

――――― *John 3* ―――――

Now there was a man of the Pharisees named Nicodemus, a ruler of the Jews. [2] This man came to Jesus[4] by night and said to him, "Rabbi, we know that you are a teacher come from God, for no one can do these signs that you do unless God is with him." [3] Jesus answered him, "Truly, truly, I say to you, unless one is born again[5] he cannot see the kingdom of God." [4] Nicodemus said to him, "How can a man be born when he is old? Can he enter a second time into his mother's womb and be born?" [5] Jesus answered, "Truly, truly, I say to you, unless one is born of water and the Spirit, he cannot enter the kingdom of God. [6] That which is born of the flesh is flesh, and that which is born of the Spirit is spirit.[6] [7] Do not marvel that I said to you, 'You[7] must be born again.' [8] The wind[8] blows where it wishes, and you hear its sound, but you do not know where it comes from or where it goes. So it is with everyone who is born of the Spirit."

[9] Nicodemus said to him, "How can these things be?" [10] Jesus answered him, "Are you the teacher of Israel and yet you do not understand these things? [11] Truly, truly, I say to you, we speak of what we know, and bear witness to what we have seen, but you[9] do not receive our testimony. [12] If I have told you earthly things and you do not believe, how can you believe if I tell you heavenly things? [13] No one has ascended into heaven except he who descended

---

[1] Or *backward*; also verse 18   [2] Probable reading (compare Septuagint); Hebrew *LORD, since they were. When*   [3] Hebrew *the*   [4] Greek *him*   [5] Or *from above*; the Greek is purposely ambiguous and can mean both *again* and *from above*; also verse 7   [6] The same Greek word means both *wind* and *spirit*   [7] The Greek for *you* is plural here   [8] The same Greek word means both *wind* and *spirit*   [9] The Greek for *you* is plural here; also four times in verse 12

from heaven, the Son of Man.[1] [14]And as Moses lifted up the serpent in the wilderness, so must the Son of Man be lifted up, [15]that whoever believes in him may have eternal life.[2]

[16]"For God so loved the world,[3] that he gave his only Son, that whoever believes in him should not perish but have eternal life. [17]For God did not send his Son into the world to condemn the world, but in order that the world might be saved through him. [18]Whoever believes in him is not condemned, but whoever does not believe is condemned already, because he has not believed in the name of the only Son of God. [19]And this is the judgment: the light has come into the world, and people loved the darkness rather than the light because their works were evil. [20]For everyone who does wicked things hates the light and does not come to the light, lest his works should be exposed. [21]But whoever does what is true comes to the light, so that it may be clearly seen that his works have been carried out in God."

[22]After this Jesus and his disciples went into the Judean countryside, and he remained there with them and was baptizing. [23]John also was baptizing at Aenon near Salim, because water was plentiful there, and people were coming and being baptized [24](for John had not yet been put in prison).

[25]Now a discussion arose between some of John's disciples and a Jew over purification. [26]And they came to John and said to him, "Rabbi, he who was with you across the Jordan, to whom you bore witness—look, he is baptizing, and all are going to him." [27]John answered, "A person cannot receive even one thing unless it is given him from heaven. [28]You yourselves bear me witness, that I said, 'I am not the Christ, but I have been sent before him.' [29]The one who has the bride is the bridegroom. The friend of the bridegroom, who stands and hears him, rejoices greatly at the bridegroom's voice. Therefore this joy of mine is now complete. [30]He must increase, but I must decrease."[4]

[31]He who comes from above is above all. He who is of the earth belongs to the earth and speaks in an earthly way. He who comes from heaven is above all. [32]He bears witness to what he has seen and heard, yet no one receives his testimony. [33]Whoever receives his testimony sets his seal to this, that God is true. [34]For he whom God has sent utters the words of God, for he gives the Spirit without measure. [35]The Father loves the Son and has given all things into his hand. [36]Whoever believes in the Son has eternal life; whoever does not obey the Son shall not see life, but the wrath of God remains on him.

DECEMBER 14

2 Chronicles 16

In the thirty-sixth year of the reign of Asa, Baasha king of Israel went up against Judah and built Ramah, that he might permit no one to go out or come in to Asa king of Judah. [2]Then Asa took silver and gold from the treasures of the house of the LORD and the king's house and sent them to Ben-hadad king of Syria, who lived in Damascus, saying, [3]"There is a covenant[5] between me and you, as there was between my father and your father. Behold, I am sending to you silver and gold. Go, break your covenant with Baasha king of Israel, that

he may withdraw from me." [4]And Ben-hadad listened to King Asa and sent the commanders of his armies against the cities of Israel, and they conquered Ijon, Dan, Abel-maim, and all the store cities of Naphtali. [5]And when Baasha heard of it, he stopped building Ramah and let his work cease. [6]Then King Asa took all Judah, and they carried away the stones of Ramah and its timber, with which Baasha had been building, and with them he built Geba and Mizpah.

[7]At that time Hanani the seer came to Asa king of Judah and said to him, "Because

[1] Some manuscripts add *who is in heaven* [2] Some interpreters hold that the quotation ends at verse 15 [3] Or *For this is how God loved the world* [4] Some interpreters hold that the quotation continues through verse 36 [5] Or *treaty*; twice in this verse

you relied on the king of Syria, and did not rely on the LORD your God, the army of the king of Syria has escaped you. [8]Were not the Ethiopians and the Libyans a huge army with very many chariots and horsemen? Yet because you relied on the LORD, he gave them into your hand. [9]For the eyes of the LORD run to and fro throughout the whole earth, to give strong support to those whose heart is blameless[1] toward him. You have done foolishly in this, for from now on you will have wars." [10]Then Asa was angry with the seer and put him in the stocks in prison, for he was in a rage with him because of this. And Asa inflicted cruelties upon some of the people at the same time.

[11]The acts of Asa, from first to last, are written in the Book of the Kings of Judah and Israel. [12]In the thirty-ninth year of his reign Asa was diseased in his feet, and his disease became severe. Yet even in his disease he did not seek the LORD, but sought help from physicians. [13]And Asa slept with his fathers, dying in the forty-first year of his reign. [14]They buried him in the tomb that he had cut for himself in the city of David. They laid him on a bier that had been filled with various kinds of spices prepared by the perfumer's art, and they made a very great fire in his honor.

—————— *Revelation 5* ——————

Then I saw in the right hand of him who was seated on the throne a scroll written within and on the back, sealed with seven seals. [2]And I saw a mighty angel proclaiming with a loud voice, "Who is worthy to open the scroll and break its seals?" [3]And no one in heaven or on earth or under the earth was able to open the scroll or to look into it, [4]and I began to weep loudly because no one was found worthy to open the scroll or to look into it. [5]And one of the elders said to me, "Weep no more; behold, the Lion of the tribe of Judah, the Root of David, has conquered, so that he can open the scroll and its seven seals."

[6]And between the throne and the four living creatures and among the elders I saw a Lamb standing, as though it had been slain, with seven horns and with seven eyes, which are the seven spirits of God sent out into all the earth. [7]And he went and took the scroll from the right hand of him who was seated on the throne. [8]And when he had taken the scroll, the four living creatures and the twenty-four elders fell down before the Lamb, each holding a harp, and golden bowls full of incense, which are the prayers of the saints. [9]And they sang a new song, saying,

"Worthy are you to take the scroll
 and to open its seals,
for you were slain, and by your blood
 you ransomed people for God
 from every tribe and language and
  people and nation,
10 and you have made them a kingdom
  and priests to our God,
 and they shall reign on the earth."

[11]Then I looked, and I heard around the throne and the living creatures and the elders the voice of many angels, numbering myriads of myriads and thousands of thousands, [12]saying with a loud voice,

"Worthy is the Lamb who was slain,
 to receive power and wealth and wisdom
  and might
 and honor and glory and blessing!"

[13]And I heard every creature in heaven and on earth and under the earth and in the sea, and all that is in them, saying,

"To him who sits on the throne and to
  the Lamb
 be blessing and honor and glory and
  might forever and ever!"

[14]And the four living creatures said, "Amen!" and the elders fell down and worshiped.

—————— *Zechariah 1* ——————

In the eighth month, in the second year of Darius, the word of the LORD came to the prophet Zechariah, the son of Berechiah, son of Iddo, saying, [2]"The LORD was very angry with your fathers. [3]Therefore say to them, Thus declares the LORD of hosts: Return to me, says the LORD of hosts, and I will return to you, says the LORD of hosts. [4]Do not be like your fathers, to whom the former prophets cried out, 'Thus says the LORD of hosts, Return from your evil ways and from your evil deeds.' But they did not hear or pay attention to me, declares the

[1] Or *whole*

LORD. [5]Your fathers, where are they? And the prophets, do they live forever? [6]But my words and my statutes, which I commanded my servants the prophets, did they not overtake your fathers? So they repented and said, 'As the LORD of hosts purposed to deal with us for our ways and deeds, so has he dealt with us.'"

[7]On the twenty-fourth day of the eleventh month, which is the month of Shebat, in the second year of Darius, the word of the LORD came to the prophet Zechariah, the son of Berechiah, son of Iddo, saying, [8]"I saw in the night, and behold, a man riding on a red horse! He was standing among the myrtle trees in the glen, and behind him were red, sorrel, and white horses. [9]Then I said, 'What are these, my lord?' The angel who talked with me said to me, 'I will show you what they are.' [10]So the man who was standing among the myrtle trees answered, 'These are they whom the LORD has sent to patrol the earth.' [11]And they answered the angel of the LORD who was standing among the myrtle trees, and said, 'We have patrolled the earth, and behold, all the earth remains at rest.' [12]Then the angel of the LORD said, 'O LORD of hosts, how long will you have no mercy on Jerusalem and the cities of Judah, against which you have been angry these seventy years?' [13]And the LORD answered gracious and comforting words to the angel who talked with me. [14]So the angel who talked with me said to me, 'Cry out, Thus says the LORD of hosts: I am exceedingly jealous for Jerusalem and for Zion. [15]And I am exceedingly angry with the nations that are at ease; for while I was angry but a little, they furthered the disaster. [16]Therefore, thus says the LORD, I have returned to Jerusalem with mercy; my house shall be built in it, declares the LORD of hosts, and the measuring line shall be stretched out over Jerusalem. [17]Cry out again, Thus says the LORD of hosts: My cities shall again overflow with prosperity, and the LORD will again comfort Zion and again choose Jerusalem.'"

[18][1] And I lifted my eyes and saw, and behold, four horns! [19]And I said to the angel who talked with me, "What are these?" And he said to me, "These are the horns that have scattered Judah, Israel, and Jerusalem." [20]Then the LORD showed me four craftsmen. [21]And I said, "What are these coming to do?" He said, "These are the horns that scattered Judah, so that no one

raised his head. And these have come to terrify them, to cast down the horns of the nations who lifted up their horns against the land of Judah to scatter it."

John 4

Now when Jesus learned that the Pharisees had heard that Jesus was making and baptizing more disciples than John [2](although Jesus himself did not baptize, but only his disciples), [3]he left Judea and departed again for Galilee. [4]And he had to pass through Samaria. [5]So he came to a town of Samaria called Sychar, near the field that Jacob had given to his son Joseph. [6]Jacob's well was there; so Jesus, wearied as he was from his journey, was sitting beside the well. It was about the sixth hour.[2]

[7]A woman from Samaria came to draw water. Jesus said to her, "Give me a drink." [8](For his disciples had gone away into the city to buy food.) [9]The Samaritan woman said to him, "How is it that you, a Jew, ask for a drink from me, a woman of Samaria?" (For Jews have no dealings with Samaritans.) [10]Jesus answered her, "If you knew the gift of God, and who it is that is saying to you, 'Give me a drink,' you would have asked him, and he would have given you living water." [11]The woman said to him, "Sir, you have nothing to draw water with, and the well is deep. Where do you get that living water? [12]Are you greater than our father Jacob? He gave us the well and drank from it himself, as did his sons and his livestock." [13]Jesus said to her, "Everyone who drinks of this water will be thirsty again, [14]but whoever drinks of the water that I will give him will never be thirsty again.[3] The water that I will give him will become in him a spring of water welling up to eternal life." [15]The woman said to him, "Sir, give me this water, so that I will not be thirsty or have to come here to draw water."

[16]Jesus said to her, "Go, call your husband, and come here." [17]The woman answered him, "I have no husband." Jesus said to her, "You are right in saying, 'I have no husband'; [18]for you have had five husbands, and the one you now have is not your husband. What you have said is true." [19]The woman said to him, "Sir, I perceive that you are a prophet. [20]Our fathers worshiped on this mountain, but you say that in Jerusalem

[1] Ch 2:1 in Hebrew [2] That is, about noon [3] Greek *forever*

is the place where people ought to worship." ²¹Jesus said to her, "Woman, believe me, the hour is coming when neither on this mountain nor in Jerusalem will you worship the Father. ²²You worship what you do not know; we worship what we know, for salvation is from the Jews. ²³But the hour is coming, and is now here, when the true worshipers will worship the Father in spirit and truth, for the Father is seeking such people to worship him. ²⁴God is spirit, and those who worship him must worship in spirit and truth." ²⁵The woman said to him, "I know that Messiah is coming (he who is called Christ). When he comes, he will tell us all things." ²⁶Jesus said to her, "I who speak to you am he."

²⁷Just then his disciples came back. They marveled that he was talking with a woman, but no one said, "What do you seek?" or, "Why are you talking with her?" ²⁸So the woman left her water jar and went away into town and said to the people, ²⁹"Come, see a man who told me all that I ever did. Can this be the Christ?" ³⁰They went out of the town and were coming to him.

³¹Meanwhile the disciples were urging him, saying, "Rabbi, eat." ³²But he said to them, "I have food to eat that you do not know about." ³³So the disciples said to one another, "Has anyone brought him something to eat?" ³⁴Jesus said to them, "My food is to do the will of him who sent me and to accomplish his work. ³⁵Do you not say, 'There are yet four months, then comes the harvest'? Look, I tell you, lift up your eyes, and see that the fields are white for harvest. ³⁶Already the one who reaps is receiving wages and gathering fruit for eternal life, so that sower and reaper may rejoice together. ³⁷For here the saying holds true, 'One sows and another reaps.' ³⁸I sent you to reap that for which you did not labor.

Others have labored, and you have entered into their labor."

³⁹Many Samaritans from that town believed in him because of the woman's testimony, "He told me all that I ever did." ⁴⁰So when the Samaritans came to him, they asked him to stay with them, and he stayed there two days. ⁴¹And many more believed because of his word. ⁴²They said to the woman, "It is no longer because of what you said that we believe, for we have heard for ourselves, and we know that this is indeed the Savior of the world."

⁴³After the two days he departed for Galilee. ⁴⁴(For Jesus himself had testified that a prophet has no honor in his own hometown.) ⁴⁵So when he came to Galilee, the Galileans welcomed him, having seen all that he had done in Jerusalem at the feast. For they too had gone to the feast.

⁴⁶So he came again to Cana in Galilee, where he had made the water wine. And at Capernaum there was an official whose son was ill. ⁴⁷When this man heard that Jesus had come from Judea to Galilee, he went to him and asked him to come down and heal his son, for he was at the point of death. ⁴⁸So Jesus said to him, "Unless you[1] see signs and wonders you will not believe." ⁴⁹The official said to him, "Sir, come down before my child dies." ⁵⁰Jesus said to him, "Go; your son will live." The man believed the word that Jesus spoke to him and went on his way. ⁵¹As he was going down, his servants[2] met him and told him that his son was recovering. ⁵²So he asked them the hour when he began to get better, and they said to him, "Yesterday at the seventh hour[3] the fever left him." ⁵³The father knew that was the hour when Jesus had said to him, "Your son will live." And he himself believed, and all his household. ⁵⁴This was now the second sign that Jesus did when he had come from Judea to Galilee.

---

[1] The Greek for you is plural; twice in this verse   [2] Greek bondservants   [3] That is, at 1 P.M.

DECEMBER 15

2 Chronicles 17

Jehoshaphat his son reigned in his place and strengthened himself against Israel. ²He placed forces in all the fortified cities of Judah and set garrisons in the land of Judah, and in the cities of Ephraim that Asa his father had captured. ³The LORD was with Jehoshaphat, because he walked in the earlier ways of his father David. He did not seek the Baals, ⁴but sought the God of his father and walked in his commandments, and not according to the practices of Israel. ⁵Therefore the LORD established the kingdom in his hand. And all Judah brought tribute to Jehoshaphat, and he had great riches and honor. ⁶His heart was courageous in the ways of the LORD. And furthermore, he took the high places and the Asherim out of Judah.

⁷In the third year of his reign he sent his officials, Ben-hail, Obadiah, Zechariah, Nethanel, and Micaiah, to teach in the cities of Judah; ⁸and with them the Levites, Shemaiah, Nethaniah, Zebadiah, Asahel, Shemiramoth, Jehonathan, Adonijah, Tobijah, and Tobadonijah; and with these Levites, the priests Elishama and Jehoram. ⁹And they taught in Judah, having the Book of the Law of the LORD with them. They went about through all the cities of Judah and taught among the people.

¹⁰And the fear of the LORD fell upon all the kingdoms of the lands that were around Judah, and they made no war against Jehoshaphat. ¹¹Some of the Philistines brought Jehoshaphat presents and silver for tribute, and the Arabians also brought him 7,700 rams and 7,700 goats. ¹²And Jehoshaphat grew steadily greater. He built in Judah fortresses and store cities, ¹³and he had large supplies in the cities of Judah. He had soldiers, mighty men of valor, in Jerusalem. ¹⁴This was the muster of them by fathers' houses: Of Judah, the commanders of thousands: Adnah the commander, with 300,000 mighty men of valor; ¹⁵and next to him Jehohanan the commander, with 280,000; ¹⁶and next to him Amasiah the son of Zichri,

a volunteer for the service of the LORD, with 200,000 mighty men of valor. ¹⁷Of Benjamin: Eliada, a mighty man of valor, with 200,000 men armed with bow and shield; ¹⁸and next to him Jehozabad with 180,000 armed for war. ¹⁹These were in the service of the king, besides those whom the king had placed in the fortified cities throughout all Judah.

Revelation 6

Now I watched when the Lamb opened one of the seven seals, and I heard one of the four living creatures say with a voice like thunder, "Come!" ²And I looked, and behold, a white horse! And its rider had a bow, and a crown was given to him, and he came out conquering, and to conquer.

³When he opened the second seal, I heard the second living creature say, "Come!" ⁴And out came another horse, bright red. Its rider was permitted to take peace from the earth, so that people should slay one another, and he was given a great sword.

⁵When he opened the third seal, I heard the third living creature say, "Come!" And I looked, and behold, a black horse! And its rider had a pair of scales in his hand. ⁶And I heard what seemed to be a voice in the midst of the four living creatures, saying, "A quart¹ of wheat for a denarius,² and three quarts of barley for a denarius, and do not harm the oil and wine!"

⁷When he opened the fourth seal, I heard the voice of the fourth living creature say, "Come!" ⁸And I looked, and behold, a pale horse! And its rider's name was Death, and Hades followed him. And they were given authority over a fourth of the earth, to kill with sword and with famine and with pestilence and by wild beasts of the earth.

⁹When he opened the fifth seal, I saw under the altar the souls of those who had been slain for the word of God and for the witness they had borne. ¹⁰They cried out with a loud voice,

¹ Greek choinix, a dry measure equal to about a quart ² A denarius was a day's wage for a laborer

"O Sovereign Lord, holy and true, how long before you will judge and avenge our blood on those who dwell on the earth?" ¹¹Then they were each given a white robe and told to rest a little longer, until the number of their fellow servants¹ and their brothers² should be complete, who were to be killed as they themselves had been.

¹²When he opened the sixth seal, I looked, and behold, there was a great earthquake, and the sun became black as sackcloth, the full moon became like blood, ¹³and the stars of the sky fell to the earth as the fig tree sheds its winter fruit when shaken by a gale. ¹⁴The sky vanished like a scroll that is being rolled up, and every mountain and island was removed from its place. ¹⁵Then the kings of the earth and the great ones and the generals and the rich and the powerful, and everyone, slave³ and free, hid themselves in the caves and among the rocks of the mountains, ¹⁶calling to the mountains and rocks, "Fall on us and hide us from the face of him who is seated on the throne, and from the wrath of the Lamb, ¹⁷for the great day of their wrath has come, and who can stand?"

Zechariah 2⁴

And I lifted my eyes and saw, and behold, a man with a measuring line in his hand! ²Then I said, "Where are you going?" And he said to me, "To measure Jerusalem, to see what is its width and what is its length." ³And behold, the angel who talked with me came forward, and another angel came forward to meet him ⁴and said to him, "Run, say to that young man, 'Jerusalem shall be inhabited as villages without walls, because of the multitude of people and livestock in it. ⁵And I will be to her a wall of fire all around, declares the Lord, and I will be the glory in her midst.'"

⁶Up! Up! Flee from the land of the north, declares the Lord. For I have spread you abroad as the four winds of the heavens, declares the Lord. ⁷Up! Escape to Zion, you who dwell with the daughter of Babylon. ⁸For thus said the Lord of hosts, after his glory sent me⁵ to the nations who plundered you, for he who touches you touches the apple of his eye: ⁹"Behold, I will shake my hand over them, and they shall become plunder for those who served them. Then you will know that the Lord of hosts has sent me. ¹⁰Sing and rejoice, O daughter of Zion, for behold, I come and I will dwell in your midst, declares the Lord. ¹¹And many nations shall join themselves to the Lord in that day, and shall be my people. And I will dwell in your midst, and you shall know that the Lord of hosts has sent me to you. ¹²And the Lord will inherit Judah as his portion in the holy land, and will again choose Jerusalem."

¹³Be silent, all flesh, before the Lord, for he has roused himself from his holy dwelling.

John 5

After this there was a feast of the Jews, and Jesus went up to Jerusalem.

²Now there is in Jerusalem by the Sheep Gate a pool, in Aramaic⁶ called Bethesda,⁷ which has five roofed colonnades. ³In these lay a multitude of invalids—blind, lame, and paralyzed.⁸ ⁵One man was there who had been an invalid for thirty-eight years. ⁶When Jesus saw him lying there and knew that he had already been there a long time, he said to him, "Do you want to be healed?" ⁷The sick man answered him, "Sir, I have no one to put me into the pool when the water is stirred up, and while I am going another steps down before me." ⁸Jesus said to him, "Get up, take up your bed, and walk." ⁹And at once the man was healed, and he took up his bed and walked.

Now that day was the Sabbath. ¹⁰So the Jews⁹ said to the man who had been healed, "It is the Sabbath, and it is not lawful for you to take up your bed." ¹¹But he answered them, "The man who healed me, that man said to me, 'Take up your bed, and walk.'" ¹²They asked him, "Who is the man who said to you, 'Take up your bed and walk'?" ¹³Now the man who had been healed did not know who it was, for Jesus had withdrawn, as there was a crowd in the place. ¹⁴Afterward Jesus found him in the temple and said to him, "See, you are well! Sin no more, that nothing worse may happen to you." ¹⁵The man went away and told the Jews that it was Jesus who had healed him. ¹⁶And this was why the Jews were persecuting Jesus, because he was doing these things on the Sabbath. ¹⁷But

¹ Greek *fellow bondservants* ² Or *brothers and sisters.* The plural Greek word *adelphoi* (translated "brothers") refers to siblings in a family. In New Testament usage, depending on the context, *adelphoi* may refer either to men or to both men and women who are siblings (brothers and sisters) in God's family, the church ³ Or *servant;* Greek *bondservant* ⁴ Ch 2:5 in Hebrew ⁵ Or *he sent me after glory* ⁶ Or *Hebrew* ⁷ Some manuscripts *Bethsaida* ⁸ Some manuscripts insert, wholly or in part, *waiting for the moving of the water;* ⁴for an angel of the Lord went down at certain seasons into the pool, and stirred the water: whoever stepped in first after the stirring of the water was healed of whatever disease he had ⁹ The Greek word *Ioudaioi* refers specifically here to Jewish religious leaders, and others under their influence, who opposed Jesus in that time; also verses 15, 16, 18

Jesus answered them, "My Father is working until now, and I am working."

[18] This was why the Jews were seeking all the more to kill him, because not only was he breaking the Sabbath, but he was even calling God his own Father, making himself equal with God.

[19] So Jesus said to them, "Truly, truly, I say to you, the Son can do nothing of his own accord, but only what he sees the Father doing. For whatever the Father[1] does, that the Son does likewise. [20] For the Father loves the Son and shows him all that he himself is doing. And greater works than these will he show him, so that you may marvel. [21] For as the Father raises the dead and gives them life, so also the Son gives life to whom he will. [22] The Father judges no one, but has given all judgment to the Son, [23] that all may honor the Son, just as they honor the Father. Whoever does not honor the Son does not honor the Father who sent him. [24] Truly, truly, I say to you, whoever hears my word and believes him who sent me has eternal life. He does not come into judgment, but has passed from death to life.

[25] "Truly, truly, I say to you, an hour is coming, and is now here, when the dead will hear the voice of the Son of God, and those who hear will live. [26] For as the Father has life in himself, so he has granted the Son also to have life in himself. [27] And he has given him authority to execute judgment, because he is the Son of Man. [28] Do not marvel at this, for an hour is coming when all who are in the tombs will hear his voice [29] and come out, those who have done good to the resurrection of life, and those who have done evil to the resurrection of judgment.

[30] "I can do nothing on my own. As I hear, I judge, and my judgment is just, because I seek not my own will but the will of him who sent me. [31] If I alone bear witness about myself, my testimony is not true. [32] There is another who bears witness about me, and I know that the testimony that he bears about me is true. [33] You sent to John, and he has borne witness to the truth. [34] Not that the testimony that I receive is from man, but I say these things so that you may be saved. [35] He was a burning and shining lamp, and you were willing to rejoice for a while in his light. [36] But the testimony that I have is greater than that of John. For the works that the Father has given me to accomplish, the very works that I am doing, bear witness about me that the Father has sent me. [37] And the Father who sent me has himself borne witness about me. His voice you have never heard, his form you have never seen, [38] and you do not have his word abiding in you, for you do not believe the one whom he has sent. [39] You search the Scriptures because you think that in them you have eternal life; and it is they that bear witness about me, [40] yet you refuse to come to me that you may have life. [41] I do not receive glory from people. [42] But I know that you do not have the love of God within you. [43] I have come in my Father's name, and you do not receive me. If another comes in his own name, you will receive him. [44] How can you believe, when you receive glory from one another and do not seek the glory that comes from the only God? [45] Do not think that I will accuse you to the Father. There is one who accuses you: Moses, on whom you have set your hope. [46] For if you believed Moses, you would believe me; for he wrote of me. [47] But if you do not believe his writings, how will you believe my words?"

[1] Greek he

DECEMBER 16

2 Chronicles 18

Now Jehoshaphat had great riches and honor, and he made a marriage alliance with Ahab. ²After some years he went down to Ahab in Samaria. And Ahab killed an abundance of sheep and oxen for him and for the people who were with him, and induced him to go up against Ramoth-gilead. ³Ahab king of Israel said to Jehoshaphat king of Judah, "Will you go with me to Ramoth-gilead?" He answered him, "I am as you are, my people as your people. We will be with you in the war."

⁴And Jehoshaphat said to the king of Israel, "Inquire first for the word of the LORD." ⁵Then the king of Israel gathered the prophets together, four hundred men, and said to them, "Shall we go to battle against Ramoth-gilead, or shall I refrain?" And they said, "Go up, for God will give it into the hand of the king." ⁶But Jehoshaphat said, "Is there not here another prophet of the LORD of whom we may inquire?" ⁷And the king of Israel said to Jehoshaphat, "There is yet one man by whom we may inquire of the LORD, Micaiah the son of Imlah; but I hate him, for he never prophesies good concerning me, but always evil." And Jehoshaphat said, "Let not the king say so." ⁸Then the king of Israel summoned an officer and said, "Bring quickly Micaiah the son of Imlah." ⁹Now the king of Israel and Jehoshaphat the king of Judah were sitting on their thrones, arrayed in their robes. And they were sitting at the threshing floor at the entrance of the gate of Samaria, and all the prophets were prophesying before them. ¹⁰And Zedekiah the son of Chenaanah made for himself horns of iron and said, "Thus says the LORD, 'With these you shall push the Syrians until they are destroyed.'" ¹¹And all the prophets prophesied so and said, "Go up to Ramoth-gilead and triumph. The LORD will give it into the hand of the king."

¹²And the messenger who went to summon Micaiah said to him, "Behold, the words of the prophets with one accord are favorable to the king. Let your word be like the word of one of them, and speak favorably." ¹³But Micaiah said, "As the LORD lives, what my God says, that I will speak." ¹⁴And when he had come to the king, the king said to him, "Micaiah, shall we go to Ramoth-gilead to battle, or shall I refrain?" And he answered, "Go up and triumph; they will be given into your hand." ¹⁵But the king said to him, "How many times shall I make you swear that you speak to me nothing but the truth in the name of the LORD?" ¹⁶And he said, "I saw all Israel scattered on the mountains, as sheep that have no shepherd. And the LORD said, 'These have no master; let each return to his home in peace.'" ¹⁷And the king of Israel said to Jehoshaphat, "Did I not tell you that he would not prophesy good concerning me, but evil?" ¹⁸And Micaiah said, "Therefore hear the word of the LORD: I saw the LORD sitting on his throne, and all the host of heaven standing on his right hand and on his left. ¹⁹And the LORD said, 'Who will entice Ahab the king of Israel, that he may go up and fall at Ramoth-gilead?' And one said one thing, and another said another. ²⁰Then a spirit came forward and stood before the LORD, saying, 'I will entice him.' And the LORD said to him, 'By what means?' ²¹And he said, 'I will go out, and will be a lying spirit in the mouth of all his prophets.' And he said, 'You are to entice him, and you shall succeed; go out and do so.' ²²Now therefore behold, the LORD has put a lying spirit in the mouth of these your prophets. The LORD has declared disaster concerning you."

²³Then Zedekiah the son of Chenaanah came near and struck Micaiah on the cheek and said, "Which way did the Spirit of the LORD go from me to speak to you?" ²⁴And Micaiah said, "Behold, you shall see on that day when you go into an inner chamber to hide yourself." ²⁵And the king of Israel said, "Seize Micaiah and take him back to Amon the governor of the city and to Joash the king's son, ²⁶and say, 'Thus says the king, Put this fellow in prison and feed him with meager rations of bread and water until I

return in peace.'" ²⁷And Micaiah said, "If you return in peace, the LORD has not spoken by me." And he said, "Hear, all you peoples!"

²⁸So the king of Israel and Jehoshaphat the king of Judah went up to Ramoth-gilead. ²⁹And the king of Israel said to Jehoshaphat, "I will disguise myself and go into battle, but you wear your robes." And the king of Israel disguised himself, and they went into battle. ³⁰Now the king of Syria had commanded the captains of his chariots, "Fight with neither small nor great, but only with the king of Israel." ³¹As soon as the captains of the chariots saw Jehoshaphat, they said, "It is the king of Israel." So they turned to fight against him. And Jehoshaphat cried out, and the LORD helped him; God drew them away from him. ³²For as soon as the captains of the chariots saw that it was not the king of Israel, they turned back from pursuing him. ³³But a certain man drew his bow at random[1] and struck the king of Israel between the scale armor and the breastplate. Therefore he said to the driver of his chariot, "Turn around and carry me out of the battle, for I am wounded." ³⁴And the battle continued that day, and the king of Israel was propped up in his chariot facing the Syrians until evening. Then at sunset he died.

--------- Revelation 7 ---------

After this I saw four angels standing at the four corners of the earth, holding back the four winds of the earth, that no wind might blow on earth or sea or against any tree. ²Then I saw another angel ascending from the rising of the sun, with the seal of the living God, and he called with a loud voice to the four angels who had been given power to harm earth and sea, ³saying, "Do not harm the earth or the sea or the trees, until we have sealed the servants[2] of our God on their foreheads." ⁴And I heard the number of the sealed, 144,000, sealed from every tribe of the sons of Israel:

⁵   12,000 from the tribe of Judah were sealed,
    12,000 from the tribe of Reuben,
    12,000 from the tribe of Gad,
⁶   12,000 from the tribe of Asher,
    12,000 from the tribe of Naphtali,
    12,000 from the tribe of Manasseh,

⁷   12,000 from the tribe of Simeon,
    12,000 from the tribe of Levi,
    12,000 from the tribe of Issachar,
⁸   12,000 from the tribe of Zebulun,
    12,000 from the tribe of Joseph,
    12,000 from the tribe of Benjamin were sealed.

⁹After this I looked, and behold, a great multitude that no one could number, from every nation, from all tribes and peoples and languages, standing before the throne and before the Lamb, clothed in white robes, with palm branches in their hands, ¹⁰and crying out with a loud voice, "Salvation belongs to our God who sits on the throne, and to the Lamb!" ¹¹And all the angels were standing around the throne and around the elders and the four living creatures, and they fell on their faces before the throne and worshiped God, ¹²saying, "Amen! Blessing and glory and wisdom and thanksgiving and honor and power and might be to our God forever and ever! Amen."

¹³Then one of the elders addressed me, saying, "Who are these, clothed in white robes, and from where have they come?" ¹⁴I said to him, "Sir, you know." And he said to me, "These are the ones coming out of the great tribulation. They have washed their robes and made them white in the blood of the Lamb.

¹⁵   "Therefore they are before the throne of God,
        and serve him day and night in his temple;
        and he who sits on the throne will shelter them with his presence.
¹⁶   They shall hunger no more, neither thirst anymore;
        the sun shall not strike them, nor any scorching heat.
¹⁷   For the Lamb in the midst of the throne will be their shepherd,
        and he will guide them to springs of living water,
        and God will wipe away every tear from their eyes."

--------- Zechariah 3 ---------

Then he showed me Joshua the high priest standing before the angel of the LORD, and Satan[3] standing at his right hand to accuse him. [2] And the LORD said to Satan, "The LORD rebuke you, O Satan! The LORD who has chosen Jerusalem rebuke you! Is not this a brand[1] plucked from the fire?" [3] Now Joshua was standing before the angel, clothed with filthy garments. [4] And the angel said to those who were standing before him, "Remove the filthy garments from him." And to him he said, "Behold, I have taken your iniquity away from you, and I will clothe you with pure vestments." [5] And I said, "Let them put a clean turban on his head." So they put a clean turban on his head and clothed him with garments. And the angel of the LORD was standing by.

[6] And the angel of the LORD solemnly assured Joshua, [7] "Thus says the LORD of hosts: If you will walk in my ways and keep my charge, then you shall rule my house and have charge of my courts, and I will give you the right of access among those who are standing here. [8] Hear now, O Joshua the high priest, you and your friends who sit before you, for they are men who are a sign: behold, I will bring my servant the Branch. [9] For behold, on the stone that I have set before Joshua, on a single stone with seven eyes,[2] I will engrave its inscription, declares the LORD of hosts, and I will remove the iniquity of this land in a single day. [10] In that day, declares the LORD of hosts, every one of you will invite his neighbor to come under his vine and under his fig tree."

―――――― *John 6* ――――――

After this Jesus went away to the other side of the Sea of Galilee, which is the Sea of Tiberias. [2] And a large crowd was following him, because they saw the signs that he was doing on the sick. [3] Jesus went up on the mountain, and there he sat down with his disciples. [4] Now the Passover, the feast of the Jews, was at hand. [5] Lifting up his eyes, then, and seeing that a large crowd was coming toward him, Jesus said to Philip, "Where are we to buy bread, so that these people may eat?" [6] He said this to test him, for he himself knew what he would do. [7] Philip answered him, "Two hundred denarii[3] worth of bread would not be enough for each of them to get a little." [8] One of his disciples, Andrew, Simon Peter's brother, said to him, [9] "There is a boy here who has five barley loaves and two fish, but what are they for so many?" [10] Jesus

said, "Have the people sit down." Now there was much grass in the place. So the men sat down, about five thousand in number. [11] Jesus then took the loaves, and when he had given thanks, he distributed them to those who were seated. So also the fish, as much as they wanted. [12] And when they had eaten their fill, he told his disciples, "Gather up the leftover fragments, that nothing may be lost." [13] So they gathered them up and filled twelve baskets with fragments from the five barley loaves left by those who had eaten. [14] When the people saw the sign that he had done, they said, "This is indeed the Prophet who is to come into the world!"

[15] Perceiving then that they were about to come and take him by force to make him king, Jesus withdrew again to the mountain by himself.

[16] When evening came, his disciples went down to the sea, [17] got into a boat, and started across the sea to Capernaum. It was now dark, and Jesus had not yet come to them. [18] The sea became rough because a strong wind was blowing. [19] When they had rowed about three or four miles,[4] they saw Jesus walking on the sea and coming near the boat, and they were frightened. [20] But he said to them, "It is I; do not be afraid." [21] Then they were glad to take him into the boat, and immediately the boat was at the land to which they were going.

[22] On the next day the crowd that remained on the other side of the sea saw that there had been only one boat there, and that Jesus had not entered the boat with his disciples, but that his disciples had gone away alone. [23] Other boats from Tiberias came near the place where they had eaten the bread after the Lord had given thanks. [24] So when the crowd saw that Jesus was not there, nor his disciples, they themselves got into the boats and went to Capernaum, seeking Jesus.

[25] When they found him on the other side of the sea, they said to him, "Rabbi, when did you come here?" [26] Jesus answered them, "Truly, truly, I say to you, you are seeking me, not because you saw signs, but because you ate your fill of the loaves. [27] Do not work for the food that perishes, but for the food that endures to eternal life, which the Son of Man will give to you. For on him God the Father has set his seal." [28] Then they said to him, "What must we do, to be doing the works of God?" [29] Jesus

---

[1] That is, a burning stick   [2] Or *facets*   [3] A *denarius* was a day's wage for a laborer   [4] Greek *twenty-five or thirty stadia; a stadion* was about 607 feet or 185 meters

answered them, "This is the work of God, that you believe in him whom he has sent." ³⁰So they said to him, "Then what sign do you do, that we may see and believe you? What work do you perform? ³¹Our fathers ate the manna in the wilderness; as it is written, 'He gave them bread from heaven to eat.'" ³²Jesus then said to them, "Truly, truly, I say to you, it was not Moses who gave you the bread from heaven, but my Father gives you the true bread from heaven. ³³For the bread of God is he who comes down from heaven and gives life to the world." ³⁴They said to him, "Sir, give us this bread always."

³⁵Jesus said to them, "I am the bread of life; whoever comes to me shall not hunger, and whoever believes in me shall never thirst. ³⁶But I said to you that you have seen me and yet do not believe. ³⁷All that the Father gives me will come to me, and whoever comes to me I will never cast out. ³⁸For I have come down from heaven, not to do my own will but the will of him who sent me. ³⁹And this is the will of him who sent me, that I should lose nothing of all that he has given me, but raise it up on the last day. ⁴⁰For this is the will of my Father, that everyone who looks on the Son and believes in him should have eternal life, and I will raise him up on the last day."

⁴¹So the Jews grumbled about him, because he said, "I am the bread that came down from heaven." ⁴²They said, "Is not this Jesus, the son of Joseph, whose father and mother we know? How does he now say, 'I have come down from heaven'?" ⁴³Jesus answered them, "Do not grumble among yourselves. ⁴⁴No one can come to me unless the Father who sent me draws him. And I will raise him up on the last day. ⁴⁵It is written in the Prophets, 'And they will all be taught by God.' Everyone who has heard and learned from the Father comes to me— ⁴⁶not that anyone has seen the Father except he who is from God; he has seen the Father. ⁴⁷Truly, truly, I say to you, whoever believes has eternal life. ⁴⁸I am the bread of life. ⁴⁹Your fathers ate the manna in the wilderness, and they died. ⁵⁰This is the bread that comes down from heaven, so that one may eat of it and not die. ⁵¹I am the living bread that came down

from heaven. If anyone eats of this bread, he will live forever. And the bread that I will give for the life of the world is my flesh."

⁵²The Jews then disputed among themselves, saying, "How can this man give us his flesh to eat?" ⁵³So Jesus said to them, "Truly, truly, I say to you, unless you eat the flesh of the Son of Man and drink his blood, you have no life in you. ⁵⁴Whoever feeds on my flesh and drinks my blood has eternal life, and I will raise him up on the last day. ⁵⁵For my flesh is true food, and my blood is true drink. ⁵⁶Whoever feeds on my flesh and drinks my blood abides in me, and I in him. ⁵⁷As the living Father sent me, and I live because of the Father, so whoever feeds on me, he also will live because of me. ⁵⁸This is the bread that came down from heaven, not like the bread¹ the fathers ate, and died. Whoever feeds on this bread will live forever." ⁵⁹Jesus² said these things in the synagogue, as he taught at Capernaum.

⁶⁰When many of his disciples heard it, they said, "This is a hard saying; who can listen to it?" ⁶¹But Jesus, knowing in himself that his disciples were grumbling about this, said to them, "Do you take offense at this? ⁶²Then what if you were to see the Son of Man ascending to where he was before? ⁶³It is the Spirit who gives life; the flesh is no help at all. The words that I have spoken to you are spirit and life. ⁶⁴But there are some of you who do not believe." (For Jesus knew from the beginning who those were who did not believe, and who it was who would betray him.) ⁶⁵And he said, "This is why I told you that no one can come to me unless it is granted him by the Father."

⁶⁶After this many of his disciples turned back and no longer walked with him. ⁶⁷So Jesus said to the Twelve, "Do you want to go away as well?" ⁶⁸Simon Peter answered him, "Lord, to whom shall we go? You have the words of eternal life, ⁶⁹and we have believed, and have come to know, that you are the Holy One of God." ⁷⁰Jesus answered them, "Did I not choose you, the Twelve? And yet one of you is a devil." ⁷¹He spoke of Judas the son of Simon Iscariot, for he, one of the Twelve, was going to betray him.

DECEMBER 17

2 Chronicles 19–20

Jehoshaphat the king of Judah returned in safety to his house in Jerusalem. [2] But Jehu the son of Hanani the seer went out to meet him and said to King Jehoshaphat, "Should you help the wicked and love those who hate the Lord? Because of this, wrath has gone out against you from the Lord. [3] Nevertheless, some good is found in you, for you destroyed the Asheroth out of the land, and have set your heart to seek God."

[4] Jehoshaphat lived at Jerusalem. And he went out again among the people, from Beersheba to the hill country of Ephraim, and brought them back to the Lord, the God of their fathers. [5] He appointed judges in the land in all the fortified cities of Judah, city by city, [6] and said to the judges, "Consider what you do, for you judge not for man but for the Lord. He is with you in giving judgment. [7] Now then, let the fear of the Lord be upon you. Be careful what you do, for there is no injustice with the Lord our God, or partiality or taking bribes."

[8] Moreover, in Jerusalem Jehoshaphat appointed certain Levites and priests and heads of families of Israel, to give judgment for the Lord and to decide disputed cases. They had their seat at Jerusalem. [9] And he charged them: "Thus you shall do in the fear of the Lord, in faithfulness, and with your whole heart: [10] whenever a case comes to you from your brothers who live in their cities, concerning bloodshed, law or commandment, statutes or rules, then you shall warn them, that they may not incur guilt before the Lord and wrath may not come upon you and your brothers. Thus you shall do, and you will not incur guilt. [11] And behold, Amariah the chief priest is over you in all matters of the Lord; and Zebadiah the son of Ishmael, the governor of the house of Judah, in all the king's matters, and the Levites will serve you as officers. Deal courageously, and may the Lord be with the upright!"[1]

20:1 After this the Moabites and Ammonites, and with them some of the Meunites,[2] came against Jehoshaphat for battle. [2] Some men came and told Jehoshaphat, "A great multitude is coming against you from Edom,[3] from beyond the sea; and, behold, they are in Hazazon-tamar" (that is, Engedi). [3] Then Jehoshaphat was afraid and set his face to seek the Lord, and proclaimed a fast throughout all Judah. [4] And Judah assembled to seek help from the Lord; from all the cities of Judah they came to seek the Lord.

[5] And Jehoshaphat stood in the assembly of Judah and Jerusalem, in the house of the Lord, before the new court, [6] and said, "O Lord, God of our fathers, are you not God in heaven? You rule over all the kingdoms of the nations. In your hand are power and might, so that none is able to withstand you. [7] Did you not, our God, drive out the inhabitants of this land before your people Israel, and give it forever to the descendants of Abraham your friend? [8] And they have lived in it and have built for you in it a sanctuary for your name, saying, [9] 'If disaster comes upon us, the sword, judgment,[4] or pestilence, or famine, we will stand before this house and before you—for your name is in this house—and cry out to you in our affliction, and you will hear and save.' [10] And now behold, the men of Ammon and Moab and Mount Seir, whom you would not let Israel invade when they came from the land of Egypt, and whom they avoided and did not destroy— [11] behold, they reward us by coming to drive us out of your possession, which you have given us to inherit. [12] O our God, will you not execute judgment on them? For we are powerless against this great horde that is coming against us. We do not know what to do, but our eyes are on you."

[13] Meanwhile all Judah stood before the Lord, with their little ones, their wives, and their children. [14] And the Spirit of the Lord came upon Jahaziel the son of Zechariah, son of Benaiah, son of Jeiel, son of Mattaniah, a Levite of the sons of Asaph, in the midst of the assembly. [15] And he said, "Listen, all Judah and

---

[1] Hebrew *the good*   [2] Compare 26:7; Hebrew *Ammonites*   [3] One Hebrew manuscript; most Hebrew manuscripts *Aram* (Syria)   [4] Or *the sword of judgment*

inhabitants of Jerusalem and King Jehoshaphat: Thus says the LORD to you, 'Do not be afraid and do not be dismayed at this great horde, for the battle is not yours but God's. ¹⁶Tomorrow go down against them. Behold, they will come up by the ascent of Ziz. You will find them at the end of the valley, east of the wilderness of Jeruel. ¹⁷You will not need to fight in this battle. Stand firm, hold your position, and see the salvation of the LORD on your behalf, O Judah and Jerusalem.' Do not be afraid and do not be dismayed. Tomorrow go out against them, and the LORD will be with you."

¹⁸Then Jehoshaphat bowed his head with his face to the ground, and all Judah and the inhabitants of Jerusalem fell down before the LORD, worshiping the LORD. ¹⁹And the Levites, of the Kohathites and the Korahites, stood up to praise the LORD, the God of Israel, with a very loud voice.

²⁰And they rose early in the morning and went out into the wilderness of Tekoa. And when they went out, Jehoshaphat stood and said, "Hear me, Judah and inhabitants of Jerusalem! Believe in the LORD your God, and you will be established; believe his prophets, and you will succeed." ²¹And when he had taken counsel with the people, he appointed those who were to sing to the LORD and praise him in holy attire, as they went before the army, and say,

"Give thanks to the LORD,
    for his steadfast love endures forever."

²²And when they began to sing and praise, the LORD set an ambush against the men of Ammon, Moab, and Mount Seir, who had come against Judah, so that they were routed. ²³For the men of Ammon and Moab rose against the inhabitants of Mount Seir, devoting them to destruction, and when they had made an end of the inhabitants of Seir, they all helped to destroy one another.

²⁴When Judah came to the watchtower of the wilderness, they looked toward the horde, and behold, there¹ were dead bodies lying on the ground; none had escaped. ²⁵When Jehoshaphat and his people came to take their spoil, they found among them, in great numbers, goods, clothing, and precious things, which they took for themselves until they could carry no more. They were three days in taking

the spoil, it was so much. ²⁶On the fourth day they assembled in the Valley of Beracah,² for there they blessed the LORD. Therefore the name of that place has been called the Valley of Beracah to this day. ²⁷Then they returned, every man of Judah and Jerusalem, and Jehoshaphat at their head, returning to Jerusalem with joy, for the LORD had made them rejoice over their enemies. ²⁸They came to Jerusalem with harps and lyres and trumpets, to the house of the LORD. ²⁹And the fear of God came on all the kingdoms of the countries when they heard that the LORD had fought against the enemies of Israel. ³⁰So the realm of Jehoshaphat was quiet, for his God gave him rest all around.

³¹Thus Jehoshaphat reigned over Judah. He was thirty-five years old when he began to reign, and he reigned twenty-five years in Jerusalem. His mother's name was Azubah the daughter of Shilhi. ³²He walked in the way of Asa his father and did not turn aside from it, doing what was right in the sight of the LORD. ³³The high places, however, were not taken away; the people had not yet set their hearts upon the God of their fathers.

³⁴Now the rest of the acts of Jehoshaphat, from first to last, are written in the chronicles of Jehu the son of Hanani, which are recorded in the Book of the Kings of Israel.

³⁵After this Jehoshaphat king of Judah joined with Ahaziah king of Israel, who acted wickedly. ³⁶He joined him in building ships to go to Tarshish, and they built the ships in Eziongeber. ³⁷Then Eliezer the son of Dodavahu of Mareshah prophesied against Jehoshaphat, saying, "Because you have joined with Ahaziah, the LORD will destroy what you have made." And the ships were wrecked and were not able to go to Tarshish.

Revelation 8

When the Lamb opened the seventh seal, there was silence in heaven for about half an hour. ²Then I saw the seven angels who stand before God, and seven trumpets were given to them. ³And another angel came and stood at the altar with a golden censer, and he was given much incense to offer with the prayers of all the saints on the golden altar before the throne, ⁴and the smoke of the incense, with the prayers of the saints, rose

¹ Hebrew they ² Beracah means blessing

before God from the hand of the angel. [5]Then the angel took the censer and filled it with fire from the altar and threw it on the earth, and there were peals of thunder, rumblings,[1] flashes of lightning, and an earthquake.

[6]Now the seven angels who had the seven trumpets prepared to blow them.

[7]The first angel blew his trumpet, and there followed hail and fire, mixed with blood, and these were thrown upon the earth. And a third of the earth was burned up, and a third of the trees were burned up, and all green grass was burned up.

[8]The second angel blew his trumpet, and something like a great mountain, burning with fire, was thrown into the sea, and a third of the sea became blood. [9]A third of the living creatures in the sea died, and a third of the ships were destroyed.

[10]The third angel blew his trumpet, and a great star fell from heaven, blazing like a torch, and it fell on a third of the rivers and on the springs of water. [11]The name of the star is Wormwood.[2] A third of the waters became wormwood, and many people died from the water, because it had been made bitter.

[12]The fourth angel blew his trumpet, and a third of the sun was struck, and a third of the moon, and a third of the stars, so that a third of their light might be darkened, and a third of the day might be kept from shining, and likewise a third of the night.

[13]Then I looked, and I heard an eagle crying with a loud voice as it flew directly overhead, "Woe, woe, woe to those who dwell on the earth, at the blasts of the other trumpets that the three angels are about to blow!"

Zechariah 4

And the angel who talked with me came again and woke me, like a man who is awakened out of his sleep. [2]And he said to me, "What do you see?" I said, "I see, and behold, a lampstand all of gold, with a bowl on the top of it, and seven lamps on it, with seven lips on each of the lamps that are on the top of it. [3]And there are two olive trees by it, one on the right of the bowl and the other on its left." [4]And I said to the angel who talked with me, "What are these, my lord?" [5]Then the angel who talked with me answered and said to me, "Do

you not know what these are?" I said, "No, my lord." [6]Then he said to me, "This is the word of the LORD to Zerubbabel: Not by might, nor by power, but by my Spirit, says the LORD of hosts. [7]Who are you, O great mountain? Before Zerubbabel you shall become a plain. And he shall bring forward the top stone amid shouts of 'Grace, grace to it!'"

[8]Then the word of the LORD came to me, saying, [9]"The hands of Zerubbabel have laid the foundation of this house; his hands shall also complete it. Then you will know that the LORD of hosts has sent me to you. [10]For whoever has despised the day of small things shall rejoice, and shall see the plumb line in the hand of Zerubbabel.

"These seven are the eyes of the LORD, which range through the whole earth." [11]Then I said to him, "What are these two olive trees on the right and the left of the lampstand?" [12]And a second time I answered and said to him, "What are these two branches of the olive trees, which are beside the two golden pipes from which the golden oil[3] is poured out?" [13]He said to me, "Do you not know what these are?" I said, "No, my lord." [14]Then he said, "These are the two anointed ones[4] who stand by the Lord of the whole earth."

John 7:1–52

After this Jesus went about in Galilee. He would not go about in Judea, because the Jews[5] were seeking to kill him. [2]Now the Jews' Feast of Booths was at hand. [3]So his brothers[6] said to him, "Leave here and go to Judea, that your disciples also may see the works you are doing. [4]For no one works in secret if he seeks to be known openly. If you do these things, show yourself to the world." [5]For not even his brothers believed in him. [6]Jesus said to them, "My time has not yet come, but your time is always here. [7]The world cannot hate you, but it hates me because I testify about it that its works are evil. [8]You go up to the feast. I am not[7] going up to this feast, for my time has not yet fully come." [9]After saying this, he remained in Galilee.

[10]But after his brothers had gone up to the feast, then he also went up, not publicly but in private. [11]The Jews were looking for him at the feast, and saying, "Where is he?" [12]And

---

[1] Or voices, or sounds [2] Wormwood is the name of a plant and of the bitter-tasting extract derived from it [3] Hebrew lacks oil [4] Hebrew two sons of new oil [5] Or Judeans; Greek Ioudaioi probably refers here to Jewish religious leaders, and others under their influence, in that time [6] Or brothers and sisters; also verses 5, 10 [7] Some manuscripts add yet

there was much muttering about him among the people. While some said, "He is a good man," others said, "No, he is leading the people astray." [13] Yet for fear of the Jews no one spoke openly of him.

[14] About the middle of the feast Jesus went up into the temple and began teaching. [15] The Jews therefore marveled, saying, "How is it that this man has learning,[1] when he has never studied?" [16] So Jesus answered them, "My teaching is not mine, but his who sent me. [17] If anyone's will is to do God's[2] will, he will know whether the teaching is from God or whether I am speaking on my own authority. [18] The one who speaks on his own authority seeks his own glory; but the one who seeks the glory of him who sent him is true, and in him there is no falsehood. [19] Has not Moses given you the law? Yet none of you keeps the law. Why do you seek to kill me?" [20] The crowd answered, "You have a demon! Who is seeking to kill you?" [21] Jesus answered them, "I did one work, and you all marvel at it. [22] Moses gave you circumcision (not that it is from Moses, but from the fathers), and you circumcise a man on the Sabbath. [23] If on the Sabbath a man receives circumcision, so that the law of Moses may not be broken, are you angry with me because on the Sabbath I made a man's whole body well? [24] Do not judge by appearances, but judge with right judgment."

[25] Some of the people of Jerusalem therefore said, "Is not this the man whom they seek to kill? [26] And here he is, speaking openly, and they say nothing to him! Can it be that the authorities really know that this is the Christ? [27] But we know where this man comes from, and when the Christ appears, no one will know where he comes from." [28] So Jesus proclaimed, as he taught in the temple, "You know me, and you know where I come from. But I have not come of my own accord. He who sent me is true, and him you do not know. [29] I know him, for I come from him, and he sent me." [30] So they were seeking to arrest him, but no one laid a hand on him, because his hour had not yet come. [31] Yet many of the people believed in him. They said, "When the

Christ appears, will he do more signs than this man has done?"

[32] The Pharisees heard the crowd muttering these things about him, and the chief priests and Pharisees sent officers to arrest him. [33] Jesus then said, "I will be with you a little longer, and then I am going to him who sent me. [34] You will seek me and you will not find me. Where I am you cannot come." [35] The Jews said to one another, "Where does this man intend to go that we will not find him? Does he intend to go to the Dispersion among the Greeks and teach the Greeks? [36] What does he mean by saying, 'You will seek me and you will not find me,' and, 'Where I am you cannot come'?"

[37] On the last day of the feast, the great day, Jesus stood up and cried out, "If anyone thirsts, let him come to me and drink. [38] Whoever believes in me, as[3] the Scripture has said, 'Out of his heart will flow rivers of living water.'" [39] Now this he said about the Spirit, whom those who believed in him were to receive, for as yet the Spirit had not been given, because Jesus was not yet glorified.

[40] When they heard these words, some of the people said, "This really is the Prophet." [41] Others said, "This is the Christ." But some said, "Is the Christ to come from Galilee? [42] Has not the Scripture said that the Christ comes from the offspring of David, and comes from Bethlehem, the village where David was?" [43] So there was a division among the people over him. [44] Some of them wanted to arrest him, but no one laid hands on him.

[45] The officers then came to the chief priests and Pharisees, who said to them, "Why did you not bring him?" [46] The officers answered, "No one ever spoke like this man!" [47] The Pharisees answered them, "Have you also been deceived? [48] Have any of the authorities or the Pharisees believed in him? [49] But this crowd that does not know the law is accursed." [50] Nicodemus, who had gone to him before, and who was one of them, said to them, [51] "Does our law judge a man without first giving him a hearing and learning what he does?" [52] They replied, "Are you from Galilee too? Search and see that no prophet arises from Galilee."

[1] Or this man knows his letters [2] Greek his [3] Or let him come to me, and let him who believes in me drink. As

DECEMBER 18

2 Chronicles 21

Jehoshaphat slept with his fathers and was buried with his fathers in the city of David, and Jehoram his son reigned in his place. ²He had brothers, the sons of Jehoshaphat: Azariah, Jehiel, Zechariah, Azariah, Michael, and Shephatiah; all these were the sons of Jehoshaphat king of Israel.¹ ³Their father gave them great gifts of silver, gold, and valuable possessions, together with fortified cities in Judah, but he gave the kingdom to Jehoram, because he was the firstborn. ⁴When Jehoram had ascended the throne of his father and was established, he killed all his brothers with the sword, and also some of the princes of Israel. ⁵Jehoram was thirty-two years old when he became king, and he reigned eight years in Jerusalem. ⁶And he walked in the way of the kings of Israel, as the house of Ahab had done, for the daughter of Ahab was his wife. And he did what was evil in the sight of the LORD. ⁷Yet the LORD was not willing to destroy the house of David, because of the covenant that he had made with David, and since he had promised to give a lamp to him and to his sons forever.

⁸In his days Edom revolted from the rule of Judah and set up a king of their own. ⁹Then Jehoram passed over with his commanders and all his chariots, and he rose by night and struck the Edomites who had surrounded him and his chariot commanders. ¹⁰So Edom revolted from the rule of Judah to this day. At that time Libnah also revolted from his rule, because he had forsaken the LORD, the God of his fathers.

¹¹Moreover, he made high places in the hill country of Judah and led the inhabitants of Jerusalem into whoredom and made Judah go astray. ¹²And a letter came to him from Elijah the prophet, saying, "Thus says the LORD, the God of David your father, 'Because you have not walked in the ways of Jehoshaphat your father, or in the ways of Asa king of Judah, ¹³but have walked in the way of the kings of Israel and have enticed Judah and the inhabitants of Jerusalem into whoredom, as the house of Ahab led Israel into whoredom, and also you have killed your brothers, of your father's house, who were better than you, ¹⁴behold, the LORD will bring a great plague on your people, your children, your wives, and all your possessions, ¹⁵and you yourself will have a severe sickness with a disease of your bowels, until your bowels come out because of the disease, day by day.'"

¹⁶And the LORD stirred up against Jehoram the anger² of the Philistines and of the Arabians who are near the Ethiopians. ¹⁷And they came up against Judah and invaded it and carried away all the possessions they found that belonged to the king's house, and also his sons and his wives, so that no son was left to him except Jehoahaz, his youngest son. ¹⁸And after all this the LORD struck him in his bowels with an incurable disease. ¹⁹In the course of time, at the end of two years, his bowels came out because of the disease, and he died in great agony. His people made no fire in his honor, like the fires made for his fathers. ²⁰He was thirty-two years old when he began to reign, and he reigned eight years in Jerusalem. And he departed with no one's regret. They buried him in the city of David, but not in the tombs of the kings.

Revelation 9

And the fifth angel blew his trumpet, and I saw a star fallen from heaven to earth, and he was given the key to the shaft of the bottomless pit.³ ²He opened the shaft of the bottomless pit, and from the shaft rose smoke like the smoke of a great furnace, and the sun and the air were darkened with the smoke from the shaft. ³Then from the smoke came locusts on the earth, and they were given power like the power of scorpions of the earth. ⁴They were told not to harm the grass of the earth or any green plant or any tree, but only those people who do not have the seal of God on their foreheads.

¹ That is, Judah   ² Hebrew *spirit*   ³ Greek *the abyss*; also verses 2, 11

[5] They were allowed to torment them for five months, but not to kill them, and their torment was like the torment of a scorpion when it stings someone. [6] And in those days people will seek death and will not find it. They will long to die, but death will flee from them.

[7] In appearance the locusts were like horses prepared for battle: on their heads were what looked like crowns of gold; their faces were like human faces, [8] their hair like women's hair, and their teeth like lions' teeth; [9] they had breastplates like breastplates of iron, and the noise of their wings was like the noise of many chariots with horses rushing into battle. [10] They have tails and stings like scorpions, and their power to hurt people for five months is in their tails. [11] They have as king over them the angel of the bottomless pit. His name in Hebrew is Abaddon, and in Greek he is called Apollyon.[1]

[12] The first woe has passed; behold, two woes are still to come.

[13] Then the sixth angel blew his trumpet, and I heard a voice from the four horns of the golden altar before God, [14] saying to the sixth angel who had the trumpet, "Release the four angels who are bound at the great river Euphrates." [15] So the four angels, who had been prepared for the hour, the day, the month, and the year, were released to kill a third of mankind. [16] The number of mounted troops was twice ten thousand times ten thousand; I heard their number. [17] And this is how I saw the horses in my vision and those who rode them: they wore breastplates the color of fire and of sapphire[2] and of sulfur, and the heads of the horses were like lions' heads, and fire and smoke and sulfur came out of their mouths. [18] By these three plagues a third of mankind was killed, by the fire and smoke and sulfur coming out of their mouths. [19] For the power of the horses is in their mouths and in their tails, for their tails are like serpents with heads, and by means of them they wound.

[20] The rest of mankind, who were not killed by these plagues, did not repent of the works of their hands nor give up worshiping demons and idols of gold and silver and bronze and stone and wood, which cannot see or hear or walk, [21] nor did they repent of their murders or their sorceries or their sexual immorality or their thefts.

Zechariah 5

Again I lifted my eyes and saw, and behold, a flying scroll! [2] And he said to me, "What do you see?" I answered, "I see a flying scroll. Its length is twenty cubits, and its width ten cubits."[3] [3] Then he said to me, "This is the curse that goes out over the face of the whole land. For everyone who steals shall be cleaned out according to what is on one side, and everyone who swears falsely[4] shall be cleaned out according to what is on the other side. [4] I will send it out, declares the LORD of hosts, and it shall enter the house of the thief, and the house of him who swears falsely by my name. And it shall remain in his house and consume it, both timber and stones."

[5] Then the angel who talked with me came forward and said to me, "Lift your eyes and see what this is that is going out." [6] And I said, "What is it?" He said, "This is the basket[5] that is going out." And he said, "This is their iniquity[6] in all the land." [7] And behold, the leaden cover was lifted, and there was a woman sitting in the basket! [8] And he said, "This is Wickedness." And he thrust her back into the basket, and thrust down the leaden weight on its opening.

[9] Then I lifted my eyes and saw, and behold, two women coming forward! The wind was in their wings. They had wings like the wings of a stork, and they lifted up the basket between earth and heaven. [10] Then I said to the angel who talked with me, "Where are they taking the basket?" [11] He said to me, "To the land of Shinar, to build a house for it. And when this is prepared, they will set the basket down there on its base."

John 7:53–8:59

[THE EARLIEST MANUSCRIPTS DO NOT INCLUDE 7:53–8:11.][7]

[[They went each to his own house, [8:1] but Jesus went to the Mount of Olives. [2] Early in the morning he came again to the temple. All the people came to him, and he sat down and taught them. [3] The scribes and the Pharisees brought a woman who had been caught in adultery, and placing her in the midst [4] they said to him, "Teacher, this woman has been caught in the act of adultery. [5] Now in the Law Moses

---

[1] Abaddon means destruction; Apollyon means destroyer [2] Greek hyacinth [3] A cubit was about 18 inches or 45 centimeters [4] Hebrew lacks falsely (supplied from verse 4) [5] Hebrew ephah; also verses 7–11. An ephah was about 3/5 bushel or 22 liters [6] One Hebrew manuscript, Septuagint, Syriac; most Hebrew manuscripts eye [7] Some manuscripts do not include 7:53–8:11; others add the passage here or after 7:36 or after 21:25 or after Luke 21:38, with variations in the text

commanded us to stone such women. So what do you say?" **6** This they said to test him, that they might have some charge to bring against him. Jesus bent down and wrote with his finger on the ground. **7** And as they continued to ask him, he stood up and said to them, "Let him who is without sin among you be the first to throw a stone at her." **8** And once more he bent down and wrote on the ground. **9** But when they heard it, they went away one by one, beginning with the older ones, and Jesus was left alone with the woman standing before him. **10** Jesus stood up and said to her, "Woman, where are they? Has no one condemned you?" **11** She said, "No one, Lord." And Jesus said, "Neither do I condemn you; go, and from now on sin no more."]]

12 Again Jesus spoke to them, saying, "I am the light of the world. Whoever follows me will not walk in darkness, but will have the light of life." **13** So the Pharisees said to him, "You are bearing witness about yourself; your testimony is not true." **14** Jesus answered, "Even if I do bear witness about myself, my testimony is true, for I know where I came from and where I am going, but you do not know where I come from or where I am going. **15** You judge according to the flesh; I judge no one. **16** Yet even if I do judge, my judgment is true, for it is not I alone who judge, but I and the Father[1] who sent me. **17** In your Law it is written that the testimony of two people is true. **18** I am the one who bears witness about myself, and the Father who sent me bears witness about me." **19** They said to him therefore, "Where is your Father?" Jesus answered, "You know neither me nor my Father. If you knew me, you would know my Father also." **20** These words he spoke in the treasury, as he taught in the temple; but no one arrested him, because his hour had not yet come.

21 So he said to them again, "I am going away, and you will seek me, and you will die in your sin. Where I am going, you cannot come." **22** So the Jews said, "Will he kill himself, since he says, 'Where I am going, you cannot come'?" **23** He said to them, "You are from below; I am from above. You are of this world; I am not of this world. **24** I told you that you would die in your sins, for unless you believe that I am he you will die in your sins." **25** So they said to him, "Who are you?" Jesus said to them, "Just what I have been telling you from the beginning.

26 I have much to say about you and much to judge, but he who sent me is true, and I declare to the world what I have heard from him." **27** They did not understand that he had been speaking to them about the Father. **28** So Jesus said to them, "When you have lifted up the Son of Man, then you will know that I am he, and that I do nothing on my own authority, but speak just as the Father taught me. **29** And he who sent me is with me. He has not left me alone, for I always do the things that are pleasing to him." **30** As he was saying these things, many believed in him.

31 So Jesus said to the Jews who had believed him, "If you abide in my word, you are truly my disciples, **32** and you will know the truth, and the truth will set you free." **33** They answered him, "We are offspring of Abraham and have never been enslaved to anyone. How is it that you say, 'You will become free'?"

34 Jesus answered them, "Truly, truly, I say to you, everyone who practices sin is a slave[2] to sin. **35** The slave does not remain in the house forever; the son remains forever. **36** So if the Son sets you free, you will be free indeed. **37** I know that you are offspring of Abraham; yet you seek to kill me because my word finds no place in you. **38** I speak of what I have seen with my Father, and you do what you have heard from your father."

39 They answered him, "Abraham is our father." Jesus said to them, "If you were Abraham's children, you would be doing the works Abraham did, **40** but now you seek to kill me, a man who has told you the truth that I heard from God. This is not what Abraham did. **41** You are doing the works your father did." They said to him, "We were not born of sexual immorality. We have one Father—even God." **42** Jesus said to them, "If God were your Father, you would love me, for I came from God and I am here. I came not of my own accord, but he sent me. **43** Why do you not understand what I say? It is because you cannot bear to hear my word. **44** You are of your father the devil, and your will is to do your father's desires. He was a murderer from the beginning, and does not stand in the truth, because there is no truth in him. When he lies, he speaks out of his own character, for he is a liar and the father of lies. **45** But because I tell the truth, you do not believe me. **46** Which one of you convicts me of sin? If

---

[1] Some manuscripts *he*   [2] Greek *bondservant*; also verse 35

I tell the truth, why do you not believe me? ⁴⁷Whoever is of God hears the words of God. The reason why you do not hear them is that you are not of God."

⁴⁸The Jews answered him, "Are we not right in saying that you are a Samaritan and have a demon?" ⁴⁹Jesus answered, "I do not have a demon, but I honor my Father, and you dishonor me. ⁵⁰Yet I do not seek my own glory; there is One who seeks it, and he is the judge. ⁵¹Truly, truly, I say to you, if anyone keeps my word, he will never see death." ⁵²The Jews said to him, "Now we know that you have a demon! Abraham died, as did the prophets, yet you say, 'If anyone keeps my word, he will never taste death.' ⁵³Are you greater than our father Abraham, who died? And the prophets died! Who do you make yourself out to be?" ⁵⁴Jesus answered, "If I glorify myself, my glory is nothing. It is my Father who glorifies me, of whom you say, 'He is our God.'[1] ⁵⁵But you have not known him. I know him. If I were to say that I do not know him, I would be a liar like you, but I do know him and I keep his word. ⁵⁶Your father Abraham rejoiced that he would see my day. He saw it and was glad." ⁵⁷So the Jews said to him, "You are not yet fifty years old, and have you seen Abraham?"[2] ⁵⁸Jesus said to them, "Truly, truly, I say to you, before Abraham was, I am." ⁵⁹So they picked up stones to throw at him, but Jesus hid himself and went out of the temple.

DECEMBER 19

2 Chronicles 22–23

And the inhabitants of Jerusalem made Ahaziah, his youngest son, king in his place, for the band of men that came with the Arabians to the camp had killed all the older sons. So Ahaziah the son of Jehoram king of Judah reigned. ²Ahaziah was twenty-two[3] years old when he began to reign, and he reigned one year in Jerusalem. His mother's name was Athaliah, the granddaughter of Omri. ³He also walked in the ways of the house of Ahab, for his mother was his counselor in doing wickedly. ⁴He did what was evil in the sight of the LORD, as the house of Ahab had done. For after the death of his father they were his counselors, to his undoing. ⁵He even followed their counsel and went with Jehoram the son of Ahab king of Israel to make war against Hazael king of Syria at Ramoth-gilead. And the Syrians wounded Joram, ⁶and he returned to be healed in Jezreel of the wounds that he had received at Ramah, when he fought against Hazael king of Syria. And Ahaziah the son of Jehoram king of Judah went down to see Joram the son of Ahab in Jezreel, because he was wounded.

⁷But it was ordained by God that the downfall of Ahaziah should come about through his going to visit Joram. For when he came there, he went out with Jehoram to meet Jehu the son of Nimshi, whom the LORD had anointed to destroy the house of Ahab. ⁸And when Jehu was executing judgment on the house of Ahab, he met the princes of Judah and the sons of Ahaziah's brothers, who attended Ahaziah, and he killed them. ⁹He searched for Ahaziah, and he was captured while hiding in Samaria, and he was brought to Jehu and put to death. They buried him, for they said, "He is the grandson of Jehoshaphat, who sought the LORD with all his heart." And the house of Ahaziah had no one able to rule the kingdom.

¹⁰Now when Athaliah the mother of Ahaziah saw that her son was dead, she arose and destroyed all the royal family of the house of Judah. ¹¹But Jehoshabeath,[4] the daughter of the king, took Joash the son of Ahaziah and stole him away from among the king's sons who were about to be put to death, and she put him and his nurse in a bedroom. Thus Jehoshabeath, the daughter of King Jehoram and wife of Jehoiada the priest, because she was a sister of Ahaziah,

hid him¹ from Athaliah, so that she did not put him to death. ¹²And he remained with them six years, hidden in the house of God, while Athaliah reigned over the land.

²³:¹ But in the seventh year Jehoiada took courage and entered into a covenant with the commanders of hundreds, Azariah the son of Jeroham, Ishmael the son of Jehohanan, Azariah the son of Obed, Maaseiah the son of Adaiah, and Elishaphat the son of Zichri. ²And they went about through Judah and gathered the Levites from all the cities of Judah, and the heads of fathers' houses of Israel, and they came to Jerusalem. ³And all the assembly made a covenant with the king in the house of God. And Jehoiada² said to them, "Behold, the king's son! Let him reign, as the LORD spoke concerning the sons of David. ⁴This is the thing that you shall do: of you priests and Levites who come off duty on the Sabbath, one third shall be gatekeepers, ⁵and one third shall be at the king's house and one third at the Gate of the Foundation. And all the people shall be in the courts of the house of the LORD. ⁶Let no one enter the house of the LORD except the priests and ministering Levites. They may enter, for they are holy, but all the people shall keep the charge of the LORD. ⁷The Levites shall surround the king, each with his weapons in his hand. And whoever enters the house shall be put to death. Be with the king when he comes in and when he goes out."

⁸The Levites and all Judah did according to all that Jehoiada the priest commanded, and they each brought his men, who were to go off duty on the Sabbath, with those who were to come on duty on the Sabbath, for Jehoiada the priest did not dismiss the divisions. ⁹And Jehoiada the priest gave to the captains spears and the large and small shields that had been King David's, which were in the house of God. ¹⁰And he set all the people as a guard for the king, every man with his weapon in his hand, from the south side of the house to the north side of the house, around the altar and the house. ¹¹Then they brought out the king's son and put the crown on him and gave him the testimony. And they proclaimed him king, and Jehoiada and his sons anointed him, and they said, "Long live the king."

¹²When Athaliah heard the noise of the people running and praising the king, she went into the house of the LORD to the people. ¹³And when she looked, there was the king standing by his pillar at the entrance, and the captains and the trumpeters beside the king, and all the people of the land rejoicing and blowing trumpets, and the singers with their musical instruments leading in the celebration. And Athaliah tore her clothes and cried, "Treason! Treason!" ¹⁴Then Jehoiada the priest brought out the captains who were set over the army, saying to them, "Bring her out between the ranks, and anyone who follows her is to be put to death with the sword." For the priest said, "Do not put her to death in the house of the LORD." ¹⁵So they laid hands on her,³ and she went into the entrance of the horse gate of the king's house, and they put her to death there.

¹⁶And Jehoiada made a covenant between himself and all the people and the king that they should be the LORD's people. ¹⁷Then all the people went to the house of Baal and tore it down; his altars and his images they broke in pieces, and they killed Mattan the priest of Baal before the altars. ¹⁸And Jehoiada posted watchmen for the house of the LORD under the direction of the Levitical priests and the Levites whom David had organized to be in charge of the house of the LORD, to offer burnt offerings to the LORD, as it is written in the Law of Moses, with rejoicing and with singing, according to the order of David. ¹⁹He stationed the gatekeepers at the gates of the house of the LORD so that no one should enter who was in any way unclean. ²⁰And he took the captains, the nobles, the governors of the people, and all the people of the land, and they brought the king down from the house of the LORD, marching through the upper gate to the king's house. And they set the king on the royal throne. ²¹So all the people of the land rejoiced, and the city was quiet after Athaliah had been put to death with the sword.

Revelation 10

Then I saw another mighty angel coming down from heaven, wrapped in a cloud, with a rainbow over his head, and his face was like the sun, and his legs like pillars of fire. ²He had a little scroll open in his hand. And he set his right foot on the sea, and his left foot on the land, ³and called out with a loud voice, like

¹ That is, Joash ² Hebrew he ³ Or they made a passage for her

a lion roaring. When he called out, the seven thunders sounded. **4**And when the seven thunders had sounded, I was about to write, but I heard a voice from heaven saying, "Seal up what the seven thunders have said, and do not write it down." **5**And the angel whom I saw standing on the sea and on the land raised his right hand to heaven **6**and swore by him who lives forever and ever, who created heaven and what is in it, the earth and what is in it, and the sea and what is in it, that there would be no more delay, **7**but that in the days of the trumpet call to be sounded by the seventh angel, the mystery of God would be fulfilled, just as he announced to his servants[1] the prophets.

8Then the voice that I had heard from heaven spoke to me again, saying, "Go, take the scroll that is open in the hand of the angel who is standing on the sea and on the land." **9**So I went to the angel and told him to give me the little scroll. And he said to me, "Take and eat it; it will make your stomach bitter, but in your mouth it will be sweet as honey." **10**And I took the little scroll from the hand of the angel and ate it. It was sweet as honey in my mouth, but when I had eaten it my stomach was made bitter. **11**And I was told, "You must again prophesy about many peoples and nations and languages and kings."

Zechariah 6

Again I lifted my eyes and saw, and behold, four chariots came out from between two mountains. And the mountains were mountains of bronze. **2**The first chariot had red horses, the second black horses, **3**the third white horses, and the fourth chariot dappled horses—all of them strong.[2] **4**Then I answered and said to the angel who talked with me, "What are these, my lord?" **5**And the angel answered and said to me, "These are going out to the four winds of heaven, after presenting themselves before the Lord of all the earth. **6**The chariot with the black horses goes toward the north country, the white ones go after them, and the dappled ones go toward the south country." **7**When the strong horses came out, they were impatient to go and patrol the earth. And he said, "Go, patrol the earth." So they patrolled the earth. **8**Then he cried to me, "Behold, those who go toward the north country have set my Spirit at rest in the north country."

9And the word of the LORD came to me: **10**"Take from the exiles Heldai, Tobijah, and Jedaiah, who have arrived from Babylon, and go the same day to the house of Josiah, the son of Zephaniah. **11**Take from them silver and gold, and make a crown, and set it on the head of Joshua, the son of Jehozadak, the high priest. **12**And say to him, 'Thus says the LORD of hosts, "Behold, the man whose name is the Branch: for he shall branch out from his place, and he shall build the temple of the LORD. **13**It is he who shall build the temple of the LORD and shall bear royal honor, and shall sit and rule on his throne. And there shall be a priest on his throne, and the counsel of peace shall be between them both."' **14**And the crown shall be in the temple of the LORD as a reminder to Helem,[3] Tobijah, Jedaiah, and Hen the son of Zephaniah.

15"And those who are far off shall come and help to build the temple of the LORD. And you shall know that the LORD of hosts has sent me to you. And this shall come to pass, if you will diligently obey the voice of the LORD your God."

John 9

As he passed by, he saw a man blind from birth. **2**And his disciples asked him, "Rabbi, who sinned, this man or his parents, that he was born blind?" **3**Jesus answered, "It was not that this man sinned, or his parents, but that the works of God might be displayed in him. **4**We must work the works of him who sent me while it is day; night is coming, when no one can work. **5**As long as I am in the world, I am the light of the world." **6**Having said these things, he spit on the ground and made mud with the saliva. Then he anointed the man's eyes with the mud **7**and said to him, "Go, wash in the pool of Siloam" (which means Sent). So he went and washed and came back seeing.

8The neighbors and those who had seen him before as a beggar were saying, "Is this not the man who used to sit and beg?" **9**Some said, "It is he." Others said, "No, but he is like him." He kept saying, "I am the man." **10**So they said to him, "Then how were your eyes opened?" **11**He answered, "The man called Jesus made mud and anointed my eyes and said to me, 'Go to Siloam and wash.' So I went and washed and received my sight." **12**They said to him, "Where is he?" He said, "I do not know."

---

[1] Greek bondservants [2] Or and the fourth chariot strong dappled horses [3] An alternate spelling of Heldai (verse 10)

¹³They brought to the Pharisees the man who had formerly been blind. ¹⁴Now it was a Sabbath day when Jesus made the mud and opened his eyes. ¹⁵So the Pharisees again asked him how he had received his sight. And he said to them, "He put mud on my eyes, and I washed, and I see." ¹⁶Some of the Pharisees said, "This man is not from God, for he does not keep the Sabbath." But others said, "How can a man who is a sinner do such signs?" And there was a division among them. ¹⁷So they said again to the blind man, "What do you say about him, since he has opened your eyes?" He said, "He is a prophet."

¹⁸The Jews[1] did not believe that he had been blind and had received his sight, until they called the parents of the man who had received his sight ¹⁹and asked them, "Is this your son, who you say was born blind? How then does he now see?" ²⁰His parents answered, "We know that this is our son and that he was born blind. ²¹But how he now sees we do not know, nor do we know who opened his eyes. Ask him; he is of age. He will speak for himself." ²²(His parents said these things because they feared the Jews, for the Jews had already agreed that if anyone should confess Jesus[2] to be Christ, he was to be put out of the synagogue.) ²³Therefore his parents said, "He is of age; ask him."

²⁴So for the second time they called the man who had been blind and said to him, "Give glory to God. We know that this man is a sinner." ²⁵He answered, "Whether he is a sinner I do not know. One thing I do know, that though I was blind, now I see." ²⁶They said to him, "What did he do to you? How did he open your eyes?" ²⁷He answered them, "I have told you already, and you would not listen. Why do you want to hear it again? Do you also want to become his disciples?" ²⁸And they reviled him, saying, "You are his disciple, but we are disciples of Moses. ²⁹We know that God has spoken to Moses, but as for this man, we do not know where he comes from." ³⁰The man answered, "Why, this is an amazing thing! You do not know where he comes from, and yet he opened my eyes. ³¹We know that God does not listen to sinners, but if anyone is a worshiper of God and does his will, God listens to him. ³²Never since the world began has it been heard that anyone opened the eyes of a man born blind. ³³If this man were not from God, he could do nothing." ³⁴They answered him, "You were born in utter sin, and would you teach us?" And they cast him out.

³⁵Jesus heard that they had cast him out, and having found him he said, "Do you believe in the Son of Man?"[3] ³⁶He answered, "And who is he, sir, that I may believe in him?" ³⁷Jesus said to him, "You have seen him, and it is he who is speaking to you." ³⁸He said, "Lord, I believe," and he worshiped him. ³⁹Jesus said, "For judgment I came into this world, that those who do not see may see, and those who see may become blind." ⁴⁰Some of the Pharisees near him heard these things, and said to him, "Are we also blind?" ⁴¹Jesus said to them, "If you were blind, you would have no guilt;[4] but now that you say, 'We see,' your guilt remains.

DECEMBER 20

2 Chronicles 24

Joash[5] was seven years old when he began to reign, and he reigned forty years in Jerusalem. His mother's name was Zibiah of Beersheba. ²And Joash did what was right in the eyes of the LORD all the days of Jehoiada the priest. ³Jehoiada got for him two wives, and he had sons and daughters.

⁴After this Joash decided to restore the house of the LORD. ⁵And he gathered the priests and the Levites and said to them, "Go out to the cities of Judah and gather from all Israel money to repair the house of your God from year to year, and see that you act quickly." But the Levites did not act quickly. ⁶So the king summoned

Jehoiada the chief and said to him, "Why have you not required the Levites to bring in from Judah and Jerusalem the tax levied by Moses, the servant of the LORD, and the congregation of Israel for the tent of testimony?" ⁷For the sons of Athaliah, that wicked woman, had broken into the house of God, and had also used all the dedicated things of the house of the LORD for the Baals.

⁸So the king commanded, and they made a chest and set it outside the gate of the house of the LORD. ⁹And proclamation was made throughout Judah and Jerusalem to bring in for the LORD the tax that Moses the servant of God laid on Israel in the wilderness. ¹⁰And all the princes and all the people rejoiced and brought their tax and dropped it into the chest until they had finished.¹ ¹¹And whenever the chest was brought to the king's officers by the Levites, when they saw that there was much money in it, the king's secretary and the officer of the chief priest would come and empty the chest and take it and return it to its place. Thus they did day after day, and collected money in abundance. ¹²And the king and Jehoiada gave it to those who had charge of the work of the house of the LORD, and they hired masons and carpenters to restore the house of the LORD, and also workers in iron and bronze to repair the house of the LORD. ¹³So those who were engaged in the work labored, and the repairing went forward in their hands, and they restored the house of God to its proper condition and strengthened it. ¹⁴And when they had finished, they brought the rest of the money before the king and Jehoiada, and with it were made utensils for the house of the LORD, both for the service and for the burnt offerings, and dishes for incense and vessels of gold and silver. And they offered burnt offerings in the house of the LORD regularly all the days of Jehoiada.

¹⁵But Jehoiada grew old and full of days, and died. He was 130 years old at his death. ¹⁶And they buried him in the city of David among the kings, because he had done good in Israel, and toward God and his house.

¹⁷Now after the death of Jehoiada the princes of Judah came and paid homage to the king. Then the king listened to them. ¹⁸And they abandoned the house of the LORD, the God of their fathers, and served the Asherim and the idols. And wrath came upon Judah and Jerusalem for this guilt of theirs. ¹⁹Yet he sent prophets among them to bring them back to the LORD. These testified against them, but they would not pay attention.

²⁰Then the Spirit of God clothed Zechariah the son of Jehoiada the priest, and he stood above the people, and said to them, "Thus says God, 'Why do you break the commandments of the LORD, so that you cannot prosper? Because you have forsaken the LORD, he has forsaken you.'" ²¹But they conspired against him, and by command of the king they stoned him with stones in the court of the house of the LORD. ²²Thus Joash the king did not remember the kindness that Jehoiada, Zechariah's father, had shown him, but killed his son. And when he was dying, he said, "May the LORD see and avenge!"²

²³At the end of the year the army of the Syrians came up against Joash. They came to Judah and Jerusalem and destroyed all the princes of the people from among the people and sent all their spoil to the king of Damascus. ²⁴Though the army of the Syrians had come with few men, the LORD delivered into their hand a very great army, because Judah³ had forsaken the LORD, the God of their fathers. Thus they executed judgment on Joash.

²⁵When they had departed from him, leaving him severely wounded, his servants conspired against him because of the blood of the son⁴ of Jehoiada the priest, and killed him on his bed. So he died, and they buried him in the city of David, but they did not bury him in the tombs of the kings. ²⁶Those who conspired against him were Zabad the son of Shimeath the Ammonite, and Jehozabad the son of Shimrith the Moabite. ²⁷Accounts of his sons and of the many oracles against him and of the rebuilding⁵ of the house of God are written in the Story of the Book of the Kings. And Amaziah his son reigned in his place.

Revelation 11

Then I was given a measuring rod like a staff, and I was told, "Rise and measure the temple of God and the altar and those who worship there, ²but do not measure the court outside the temple; leave that out, for it is given over to the nations, and they will trample the holy city for forty-two months. ³And I will grant authority to my two witnesses, and they will prophesy for 1,260 days, clothed in sackcloth." ⁴These are the two olive trees and the two lampstands that stand before the Lord of the earth. ⁵And if anyone would harm them, fire pours from their mouth and consumes their foes. If anyone would harm them, this is how he is doomed to be killed. ⁶They have the power to shut the sky, that no rain may fall during the days of their prophesying, and they have power over the waters to turn them into blood and to strike the earth with every kind of plague, as often as they desire. ⁷And when they have finished their testimony, the beast that rises from the bottomless pit¹ will make war on them and conquer them and kill them, ⁸and their dead bodies will lie in the street of the great city that symbolically² is called Sodom and Egypt, where their Lord was crucified. ⁹For three and a half days some from the peoples and tribes and languages and nations will gaze at their dead bodies and refuse to let them be placed in a tomb, ¹⁰and those who dwell on the earth will rejoice over them and make merry and exchange presents, because these two prophets had been a torment to those who dwell on the earth. ¹¹But after the three and a half days a breath of life from God entered them, and they stood up on their feet, and great fear fell on those who saw them. ¹²Then they heard a loud voice from heaven saying to them, "Come up here!" And they went up to heaven in a cloud, and their enemies watched them. ¹³And at that hour there was a great earthquake, and a tenth of the city fell. Seven thousand people were killed in the earthquake, and the rest were terrified and gave glory to the God of heaven.

¹⁴The second woe has passed; behold, the third woe is soon to come.

¹⁵Then the seventh angel blew his trumpet, and there were loud voices in heaven, saying, "The kingdom of the world has become the kingdom of our Lord and of his Christ, and he shall reign forever and ever." ¹⁶And the twenty-four elders who sit on their thrones before God fell on their faces and worshiped God, ¹⁷saying,

"We give thanks to you, Lord God Almighty,
who is and who was,
for you have taken your great power
and begun to reign.

¹⁸The nations raged,
but your wrath came,
and the time for the dead to be judged,
and for rewarding your servants,³ the prophets and saints,
and those who fear your name,
both small and great,
and for destroying the destroyers of the earth."

¹⁹Then God's temple in heaven was opened, and the ark of his covenant was seen within his temple. There were flashes of lightning, rumblings,⁴ peals of thunder, an earthquake, and heavy hail.

Zechariah 7

In the fourth year of King Darius, the word of the LORD came to Zechariah on the fourth day of the ninth month, which is Chislev. ²Now the people of Bethel had sent Sharezer and Regem-melech and their men to entreat the favor of the LORD, ³saying to the priests of the house of the LORD of hosts and the prophets, "Should I weep and abstain in the fifth month, as I have done for so many years?"

⁴Then the word of the LORD of hosts came to me: ⁵"Say to all the people of the land and the priests, When you fasted and mourned in the fifth month and in the seventh, for these seventy years, was it for me that you fasted? ⁶And when you eat and when you drink, do you not eat for yourselves and drink for yourselves? ⁷Were not these the words that the LORD proclaimed by the former prophets, when Jerusalem was inhabited and prosperous, with her cities around her, and the South and the lowland were inhabited?"

⁸And the word of the LORD came to Zechariah, saying, ⁹"Thus says the LORD of hosts, Render true judgments, show kindness and mercy to one another, ¹⁰do not oppress the widow, the fatherless, the sojourner, or the poor, and let none of you devise evil against another in your heart." ¹¹But they refused to pay attention and turned a stubborn shoulder and stopped their ears that they might not hear.⁵ ¹²They made their hearts diamond-hard lest they should hear the law and the words that the LORD of hosts had sent by his Spirit through the

¹ Or the abyss ² Greek spiritually ³ Greek bondservants ⁴ Or voices, or sounds ⁵ Hebrew and made their ears too heavy to hear

former prophets. Therefore great anger came from the Lord of hosts. [13]"As I[1] called, and they would not hear, so they called, and I would not hear," says the Lord of hosts, [14]"and I scattered them with a whirlwind among all the nations that they had not known. Thus the land they left was desolate, so that no one went to and fro, and the pleasant land was made desolate."

John 10

[1]"Truly, truly, I say to you, he who does not enter the sheepfold by the door but climbs in by another way, that man is a thief and a robber. [2]But he who enters by the door is the shepherd of the sheep. [3]To him the gatekeeper opens. The sheep hear his voice, and he calls his own sheep by name and leads them out. [4]When he has brought out all his own, he goes before them, and the sheep follow him, for they know his voice. [5]A stranger they will not follow, but they will flee from him, for they do not know the voice of strangers." [6]This figure of speech Jesus used with them, but they did not understand what he was saying to them.

[7]So Jesus again said to them, "Truly, truly, I say to you, I am the door of the sheep. [8]All who came before me are thieves and robbers, but the sheep did not listen to them. [9]I am the door. If anyone enters by me, he will be saved and will go in and out and find pasture. [10]The thief comes only to steal and kill and destroy. I came that they may have life and have it abundantly. [11]I am the good shepherd. The good shepherd lays down his life for the sheep. [12]He who is a hired hand and not a shepherd, who does not own the sheep, sees the wolf coming and leaves the sheep and flees, and the wolf snatches them and scatters them. [13]He flees because he is a hired hand and cares nothing for the sheep. [14]I am the good shepherd. I know my own and my own know me, [15]just as the Father knows me and I know the Father; and I lay down my life for the sheep. [16]And I have other sheep that are not of this fold. I must bring them also, and they will listen to my voice. So there will be one flock, one shepherd. [17]For this reason the Father loves me, because I lay down my life that I may take it up again. [18]No one takes it from me, but I lay it down of my own accord. I have authority to lay it down, and I have authority

to take it up again. This charge I have received from my Father."

[19]There was again a division among the Jews because of these words. [20]Many of them said, "He has a demon, and is insane; why listen to him?" [21]Others said, "These are not the words of one who is oppressed by a demon. Can a demon open the eyes of the blind?"

[22]At that time the Feast of Dedication took place at Jerusalem. It was winter, [23]and Jesus was walking in the temple, in the colonnade of Solomon. [24]So the Jews gathered around him and said to him, "How long will you keep us in suspense? If you are the Christ, tell us plainly." [25]Jesus answered them, "I told you, and you do not believe. The works that I do in my Father's name bear witness about me, [26]but you do not believe because you are not among my sheep. [27]My sheep hear my voice, and I know them, and they follow me. [28]I give them eternal life, and they will never perish, and no one will snatch them out of my hand. [29]My Father, who has given them to me,[2] is greater than all, and no one is able to snatch them out of the Father's hand. [30]I and the Father are one."

[31]The Jews picked up stones again to stone him. [32]Jesus answered them, "I have shown you many good works from the Father; for which of them are you going to stone me?" [33]The Jews answered him, "It is not for a good work that we are going to stone you but for blasphemy, because you, being a man, make yourself God." [34]Jesus answered them, "Is it not written in your Law, 'I said, you are gods'? [35]If he called them gods to whom the word of God came—and Scripture cannot be broken— [36]do you say of him whom the Father consecrated and sent into the world, 'You are blaspheming,' because I said, 'I am the Son of God'? [37]If I am not doing the works of my Father, then do not believe me; [38]but if I do them, even though you do not believe me, believe the works, that you may know and understand that the Father is in me and I am in the Father." [39]Again they sought to arrest him, but he escaped from their hands.

[40]He went away again across the Jordan to the place where John had been baptizing at first, and there he remained. [41]And many came to him. And they said, "John did no sign, but everything that John said about this man was true." [42]And many believed in him there.

[1] Hebrew he [2] Some manuscripts What my Father has given to me

DECEMBER 21

2 Chronicles 25

Amaziah was twenty-five years old when he began to reign, and he reigned twenty-nine years in Jerusalem. His mother's name was Jehoaddan of Jerusalem. ²And he did what was right in the eyes of the LORD, yet not with a whole heart. ³And as soon as the royal power was firmly his, he killed his servants who had struck down the king his father. ⁴But he did not put their children to death, according to what is written in the Law, in the Book of Moses, where the LORD commanded, "Fathers shall not die because of their children, nor children die because of their fathers, but each one shall die for his own sin."

⁵Then Amaziah assembled the men of Judah and set them by fathers' houses under commanders of thousands and of hundreds for all Judah and Benjamin. He mustered those twenty years old and upward, and found that they were 300,000 choice men, fit for war, able to handle spear and shield. ⁶He hired also 100,000 mighty men of valor from Israel for 100 talents¹ of silver. ⁷But a man of God came to him and said, "O king, do not let the army of Israel go with you, for the LORD is not with Israel, with all these Ephraimites. ⁸But go, act, be strong for the battle. Why should you suppose that God will cast you down before the enemy? For God has power to help or to cast down." ⁹And Amaziah said to the man of God, "But what shall we do about the hundred talents that I have given to the army of Israel?" The man of God answered, "The LORD is able to give you much more than this." ¹⁰Then Amaziah discharged the army that had come to him from Ephraim to go home again. And they became very angry with Judah and returned home in fierce anger. ¹¹But Amaziah took courage and led out his people and went to the Valley of Salt and struck down 10,000 men of Seir. ¹²The men of Judah captured another 10,000 alive and took them to the top of a rock and threw them down from the top of the rock, and they were all dashed to pieces. ¹³But the men

of the army whom Amaziah sent back, not letting them go with him to battle, raided the cities of Judah, from Samaria to Beth-horon, and struck down 3,000 people in them and took much spoil.

¹⁴After Amaziah came from striking down the Edomites, he brought the gods of the men of Seir and set them up as his gods and worshiped them, making offerings to them. ¹⁵Therefore the LORD was angry with Amaziah and sent to him a prophet, who said to him, "Why have you sought the gods of a people who did not deliver their own people from your hand?" ¹⁶But as he was speaking, the king said to him, "Have we made you a royal counselor? Stop! Why should you be struck down?" So the prophet stopped, but said, "I know that God has determined to destroy you, because you have done this and have not listened to my counsel."

¹⁷Then Amaziah king of Judah took counsel and sent to Joash the son of Jehoahaz, son of Jehu, king of Israel, saying, "Come, let us look one another in the face." ¹⁸And Joash the king of Israel sent word to Amaziah king of Judah, "A thistle on Lebanon sent to a cedar on Lebanon, saying, 'Give your daughter to my son for a wife,' and a wild beast of Lebanon passed by and trampled down the thistle. ¹⁹You say, 'See, I² have struck down Edom,' and your heart has lifted you up in boastfulness. But now stay at home. Why should you provoke trouble so that you fall, you and Judah with you?"

²⁰But Amaziah would not listen, for it was of God, in order that he might give them into the hand of their enemies, because they had sought the gods of Edom. ²¹So Joash king of Israel went up, and he and Amaziah king of Judah faced one another in battle at Beth-shemesh, which belongs to Judah. ²²And Judah was defeated by Israel, and every man fled to his home. ²³And Joash king of Israel captured Amaziah king of Judah, the son of Joash, son of Ahaziah, at Beth-shemesh, and brought him to Jerusalem and broke down the wall of Jerusalem for 400

¹ A *talent* was about 75 pounds or 34 kilograms ² Hebrew *you*

cubits,[1] from the Ephraim Gate to the Corner Gate. [24]And he seized all the gold and silver, and all the vessels that were found in the house of God, in the care of Obed-edom. He seized also the treasuries of the king's house, also hostages, and he returned to Samaria.

[25]Amaziah the son of Joash, king of Judah, lived fifteen years after the death of Joash the son of Jehoahaz, king of Israel. [26]Now the rest of the deeds of Amaziah, from first to last, are they not written in the Book of the Kings of Judah and Israel? [27]From the time when he turned away from the LORD they made a conspiracy against him in Jerusalem, and he fled to Lachish. But they sent after him to Lachish and put him to death there. [28]And they brought him upon horses, and he was buried with his fathers in the city of David.[2]

Revelation 12

And a great sign appeared in heaven: a woman clothed with the sun, with the moon under her feet, and on her head a crown of twelve stars. [2]She was pregnant and was crying out in birth pains and the agony of giving birth. [3]And another sign appeared in heaven: behold, a great red dragon, with seven heads and ten horns, and on his heads seven diadems. [4]His tail swept down a third of the stars of heaven and cast them to the earth. And the dragon stood before the woman who was about to give birth, so that when she bore her child he might devour it. [5]She gave birth to a male child, one who is to rule all the nations with a rod of iron, but her child was caught up to God and to his throne, [6]and the woman fled into the wilderness, where she has a place prepared by God, in which she is to be nourished for 1,260 days.

[7]Now war arose in heaven, Michael and his angels fighting against the dragon. And the dragon and his angels fought back, [8]but he was defeated, and there was no longer any place for them in heaven. [9]And the great dragon was thrown down, that ancient serpent, who is called the devil and Satan, the deceiver of the whole world—he was thrown down to the earth, and his angels were thrown down with him. [10]And I heard a loud voice in heaven, saying, "Now the salvation and the power and the kingdom of our God and the authority of his Christ have come, for the accuser of our brothers[3] has been thrown down, who accuses them day and night before our God. [11]And they have conquered him by the blood of the Lamb and by the word of their testimony, for they loved not their lives even unto death. [12]Therefore, rejoice, O heavens and you who dwell in them! But woe to you, O earth and sea, for the devil has come down to you in great wrath, because he knows that his time is short!"

[13]And when the dragon saw that he had been thrown down to the earth, he pursued the woman who had given birth to the male child. [14]But the woman was given the two wings of the great eagle so that she might fly from the serpent into the wilderness, to the place where she is to be nourished for a time, and times, and half a time. [15]The serpent poured water like a river out of his mouth after the woman, to sweep her away with a flood. [16]But the earth came to the help of the woman, and the earth opened its mouth and swallowed the river that the dragon had poured from his mouth. [17]Then the dragon became furious with the woman and went off to make war on the rest of her offspring, on those who keep the commandments of God and hold to the testimony of Jesus. And he stood[4] on the sand of the sea.

Zechariah 8

And the word of the LORD of hosts came, saying, [2]"Thus says the LORD of hosts: I am jealous for Zion with great jealousy, and I am jealous for her with great wrath. [3]Thus says the LORD: I have returned to Zion and will dwell in the midst of Jerusalem, and Jerusalem shall be called the faithful city, and the mountain of the LORD of hosts, the holy mountain. [4]Thus says the LORD of hosts: Old men and old women shall again sit in the streets of Jerusalem, each with staff in hand because of great age. [5]And the streets of the city shall be full of boys and girls playing in its streets. [6]Thus says the LORD of hosts: If it is marvelous in the sight of the remnant of this people in those days, should it also be marvelous in my sight, declares the LORD of hosts? [7]Thus says the LORD of hosts: Behold, I will save my people from the east country and from the west country, [8]and I will bring them to dwell in the midst of Jerusalem. And they shall be my people, and I will be their God, in faithfulness and in righteousness."

[1] A cubit was about 18 inches or 45 centimeters [2] Hebrew of Judah [3] Or brothers and sisters [4] Some manuscripts And I stood, connecting the sentence with 13:1

[9] Thus says the LORD of hosts: "Let your hands be strong, you who in these days have been hearing these words from the mouth of the prophets who were present on the day that the foundation of the house of the LORD of hosts was laid, that the temple might be built. [10] For before those days there was no wage for man or any wage for beast, neither was there any safety from the foe for him who went out or came in, for I set every man against his neighbor. [11] But now I will not deal with the remnant of this people as in the former days, declares the LORD of hosts. [12] For there shall be a sowing of peace. The vine shall give its fruit, and the ground shall give its produce, and the heavens shall give their dew. And I will cause the remnant of this people to possess all these things. [13] And as you have been a byword of cursing among the nations, O house of Judah and house of Israel, so will I save you, and you shall be a blessing. Fear not, but let your hands be strong."

[14] For thus says the LORD of hosts: "As I purposed to bring disaster to you when your fathers provoked me to wrath, and I did not relent, says the LORD of hosts, [15] so again have I purposed in these days to bring good to Jerusalem and to the house of Judah; fear not. [16] These are the things that you shall do: Speak the truth to one another; render in your gates judgments that are true and make for peace; [17] do not devise evil in your hearts against one another, and love no false oath, for all these things I hate, declares the LORD."

[18] And the word of the LORD of hosts came to me, saying, [19] "Thus says the LORD of hosts: The fast of the fourth month and the fast of the fifth and the fast of the seventh and the fast of the tenth shall be to the house of Judah seasons of joy and gladness and cheerful feasts. Therefore love truth and peace.

[20] "Thus says the LORD of hosts: Peoples shall yet come, even the inhabitants of many cities. [21] The inhabitants of one city shall go to another, saying, 'Let us go at once to entreat the favor of the LORD and to seek the LORD of hosts; I myself am going.' [22] Many peoples and strong nations shall come to seek the LORD of hosts in Jerusalem and to entreat the favor of the LORD. [23] Thus says the LORD of hosts: In those days ten men from the nations of every tongue shall take hold of the robe of a Jew, saying, 'Let us go with you, for we have heard that God is with you.'"

John 11

Now a certain man was ill, Lazarus of Bethany, the village of Mary and her sister Martha. [2] It was Mary who anointed the Lord with ointment and wiped his feet with her hair, whose brother Lazarus was ill. [3] So the sisters sent to him, saying, "Lord, he whom you love is ill." [4] But when Jesus heard it he said, "This illness does not lead to death. It is for the glory of God, so that the Son of God may be glorified through it."

[5] Now Jesus loved Martha and her sister and Lazarus. [6] So, when he heard that Lazarus[1] was ill, he stayed two days longer in the place where he was. [7] Then after this he said to the disciples, "Let us go to Judea again." [8] The disciples said to him, "Rabbi, the Jews were just now seeking to stone you, and are you going there again?" [9] Jesus answered, "Are there not twelve hours in the day? If anyone walks in the day, he does not stumble, because he sees the light of this world. [10] But if anyone walks in the night, he stumbles, because the light is not in him." [11] After saying these things, he said to them, "Our friend Lazarus has fallen asleep, but I go to awaken him." [12] The disciples said to him, "Lord, if he has fallen asleep, he will recover." [13] Now Jesus had spoken of his death, but they thought that he meant taking rest in sleep. [14] Then Jesus told them plainly, "Lazarus has died, [15] and for your sake I am glad that I was not there, so that you may believe. But let us go to him." [16] So Thomas, called the Twin,[2] said to his fellow disciples, "Let us also go, that we may die with him."

[17] Now when Jesus came, he found that Lazarus had already been in the tomb four days. [18] Bethany was near Jerusalem, about two miles[3] off, [19] and many of the Jews had come to Martha and Mary to console them concerning their brother. [20] So when Martha heard that Jesus was coming, she went and met him, but Mary remained seated in the house. [21] Martha said to Jesus, "Lord, if you had been here, my brother would not have died. [22] But even now I know that whatever you ask from God, God will give you." [23] Jesus said to her, "Your brother will rise again." [24] Martha said to him, "I know

---

[1] Greek *he*; also verse 17   [2] Greek *Didymus*   [3] Greek *fifteen stadia*; a *stadion* was about 607 feet or 185 meters

that he will rise again in the resurrection on the last day." [25] Jesus said to her, "I am the resurrection and the life.[1] Whoever believes in me, though he die, yet shall he live, [26] and everyone who lives and believes in me shall never die. Do you believe this?" [27] She said to him, "Yes, Lord; I believe that you are the Christ, the Son of God, who is coming into the world."

[28] When she had said this, she went and called her sister Mary, saying in private, "The Teacher is here and is calling for you." [29] And when she heard it, she rose quickly and went to him. [30] Now Jesus had not yet come into the village, but was still in the place where Martha had met him. [31] When the Jews who were with her in the house, consoling her, saw Mary rise quickly and go out, they followed her, supposing that she was going to the tomb to weep there. [32] Now when Mary came to where Jesus was and saw him, she fell at his feet, saying to him, "Lord, if you had been here, my brother would not have died." [33] When Jesus saw her weeping, and the Jews who had come with her also weeping, he was deeply moved[2] in his spirit and greatly troubled. [34] And he said, "Where have you laid him?" They said to him, "Lord, come and see." [35] Jesus wept. [36] So the Jews said, "See how he loved him!" [37] But some of them said, "Could not he who opened the eyes of the blind man also have kept this man from dying?"

[38] Then Jesus, deeply moved again, came to the tomb. It was a cave, and a stone lay against it. [39] Jesus said, "Take away the stone." Martha, the sister of the dead man, said to him, "Lord, by this time there will be an odor, for he has been dead four days." [40] Jesus said to her, "Did I not tell you that if you believed you would see the glory of God?" [41] So they took away the stone. And Jesus lifted up his eyes and said, "Father, I thank you that you have heard me. [42] I knew that you always hear me, but I said this on account of the people standing around, that they may believe that you sent me." [43] When he had said these things, he cried out with a loud voice, "Lazarus, come out." [44] The man who had died came out, his hands and feet bound with linen strips, and his face wrapped with a cloth. Jesus said to them, "Unbind him, and let him go."

[45] Many of the Jews therefore, who had come with Mary and had seen what he did, believed in him, [46] but some of them went to the Pharisees and told them what Jesus had done. [47] So the chief priests and the Pharisees gathered the council and said, "What are we to do? For this man performs many signs. [48] If we let him go on like this, everyone will believe in him, and the Romans will come and take away both our place and our nation." [49] But one of them, Caiaphas, who was high priest that year, said to them, "You know nothing at all. [50] Nor do you understand that it is better for you that one man should die for the people, not that the whole nation should perish." [51] He did not say this of his own accord, but being high priest that year he prophesied that Jesus would die for the nation, [52] and not for the nation only, but also to gather into one the children of God who are scattered abroad. [53] So from that day on they made plans to put him to death.

[54] Jesus therefore no longer walked openly among the Jews, but went from there to the region near the wilderness, to a town called Ephraim, and there he stayed with the disciples.

[55] Now the Passover of the Jews was at hand, and many went up from the country to Jerusalem before the Passover to purify themselves. [56] They were looking for[3] Jesus and saying to one another as they stood in the temple, "What do you think? That he will not come to the feast at all?" [57] Now the chief priests and the Pharisees had given orders that if anyone knew where he was, he should let them know, so that they might arrest him.

[1] Some manuscripts omit *and the life* [2] Or *was indignant; also verse 38* [3] Greek *were seeking for*

DECEMBER 22

2 Chronicles 26

And all the people of Judah took Uzziah, who was sixteen years old, and made him king instead of his father Amaziah. [2] He built Eloth and restored it to Judah, after the king slept with his fathers. [3] Uzziah was sixteen years old when he began to reign, and he reigned fifty-two years in Jerusalem. His mother's name was Jecoliah of Jerusalem. [4] And he did what was right in the eyes of the LORD, according to all that his father Amaziah had done. [5] He set himself to seek God in the days of Zechariah, who instructed him in the fear of God, and as long as he sought the LORD, God made him prosper.

[6] He went out and made war against the Philistines and broke through the wall of Gath and the wall of Jabneh and the wall of Ashdod, and he built cities in the territory of Ashdod and elsewhere among the Philistines. [7] God helped him against the Philistines and against the Arabians who lived in Gurbaal and against the Meunites. [8] The Ammonites paid tribute to Uzziah, and his fame spread even to the border of Egypt, for he became very strong. [9] Moreover, Uzziah built towers in Jerusalem at the Corner Gate and at the Valley Gate and at the Angle, and fortified them. [10] And he built towers in the wilderness and cut out many cisterns, for he had large herds, both in the Shephelah and in the plain, and he had farmers and vinedressers in the hills and in the fertile lands, for he loved the soil. [11] Moreover, Uzziah had an army of soldiers, fit for war, in divisions according to the numbers in the muster made by Jeiel the secretary and Maaseiah the officer, under the direction of Hananiah, one of the king's commanders. [12] The whole number of the heads of fathers' houses of mighty men of valor was 2,600. [13] Under their command was an army of 307,500, who could make war with mighty power, to help the king against the enemy. [14] And Uzziah prepared for all the army shields, spears, helmets, coats of mail, bows, and stones for slinging. [15] In Jerusalem he made machines, invented by skillful men, to be on the towers and the corners, to shoot arrows and great stones. And his fame spread far, for he was marvelously helped, till he was strong.

[16] But when he was strong, he grew proud, to his destruction. For he was unfaithful to the LORD his God and entered the temple of the LORD to burn incense on the altar of incense. [17] But Azariah the priest went in after him, with eighty priests of the LORD who were men of valor, [18] and they withstood King Uzziah and said to him, "It is not for you, Uzziah, to burn incense to the LORD, but for the priests, the sons of Aaron, who are consecrated to burn incense. Go out of the sanctuary, for you have done wrong, and it will bring you no honor from the LORD God." [19] Then Uzziah was angry. Now he had a censer in his hand to burn incense, and when he became angry with the priests, leprosy[1] broke out on his forehead in the presence of the priests in the house of the LORD, by the altar of incense. [20] And Azariah the chief priest and all the priests looked at him, and behold, he was leprous in his forehead! And they rushed him out quickly, and he himself hurried to go out, because the LORD had struck him. [21] And King Uzziah was a leper to the day of his death, and being a leper lived in a separate house, for he was excluded from the house of the LORD. And Jotham his son was over the king's household, governing the people of the land.

[22] Now the rest of the acts of Uzziah, from first to last, Isaiah the prophet the son of Amoz wrote. [23] And Uzziah slept with his fathers, and they buried him with his fathers in the burial field that belonged to the kings, for they said, "He is a leper." And Jotham his son reigned in his place.

Revelation 13

And I saw a beast rising out of the sea, with ten horns and seven heads, with ten diadems on its horns and blasphemous names on

[1] Leprosy was a term for several skin diseases; see Leviticus 13

its heads. ²And the beast that I saw was like a leopard; its feet were like a bear's, and its mouth was like a lion's mouth. And to it the dragon gave his power and his throne and great authority. ³One of its heads seemed to have a mortal wound, but its mortal wound was healed, and the whole earth marveled as they followed the beast. ⁴And they worshiped the dragon, for he had given his authority to the beast, and they worshiped the beast, saying, "Who is like the beast, and who can fight against it?"

⁵And the beast was given a mouth uttering haughty and blasphemous words, and it was allowed to exercise authority for forty-two months. ⁶It opened its mouth to utter blasphemies against God, blaspheming his name and his dwelling,¹ that is, those who dwell in heaven. ⁷Also it was allowed to make war on the saints and to conquer them.² And authority was given it over every tribe and people and language and nation, ⁸and all who dwell on earth will worship it, everyone whose name has not been written before the foundation of the world in the book of life of the Lamb who was slain. ⁹If anyone has an ear, let him hear:

¹⁰   If anyone is to be taken captive,
          to captivity he goes;
       if anyone is to be slain with the sword,
          with the sword must he be slain.

Here is a call for the endurance and faith of the saints.

¹¹Then I saw another beast rising out of the earth. It had two horns like a lamb and it spoke like a dragon. ¹²It exercises all the authority of the first beast in its presence,³ and makes the earth and its inhabitants worship the first beast, whose mortal wound was healed. ¹³It performs great signs, even making fire come down from heaven to earth in front of people, ¹⁴and by the signs that it is allowed to work in the presence of⁴ the beast it deceives those who dwell on earth, telling them to make an image for the beast that was wounded by the sword and yet lived. ¹⁵And it was allowed to give breath to the image of the beast, so that the image of the beast might even speak and might cause those who would not worship the image of the beast to be slain. ¹⁶Also it causes all, both small and great, both rich and poor, both free and slave,⁵ to be marked on the right hand or the forehead, ¹⁷so that no one can buy or sell unless he has

the mark, that is, the name of the beast or the number of its name. ¹⁸This calls for wisdom: let the one who has understanding calculate the number of the beast, for it is the number of a man, and his number is 666.⁶

Zechariah 9

The oracle of the word of the LORD is against the land of Hadrach
      and Damascus is its resting place.
    For the LORD has an eye on mankind
      and on all the tribes of Israel,⁷
²   and on Hamath also, which borders on it,
      Tyre and Sidon, though they are very
          wise.
³   Tyre has built herself a rampart
      and heaped up silver like dust,
      and fine gold like the mud of the
          streets.
⁴   But behold, the Lord will strip her of her
          possessions
      and strike down her power on the sea,
      and she shall be devoured by fire.

⁵   Ashkelon shall see it, and be afraid;
      Gaza too, and shall writhe in anguish;
      Ekron also, because its hopes are
          confounded.
    The king shall perish from Gaza;
      Ashkelon shall be uninhabited;
⁶   a mixed people⁸ shall dwell in Ashdod,
      and I will cut off the pride of Philistia.
⁷   I will take away its blood from its
          mouth,
      and its abominations from between
          its teeth;
    it too shall be a remnant for our God;
      it shall be like a clan in Judah,
      and Ekron shall be like the Jebusites.
⁸   Then I will encamp at my house as a
          guard,
      so that none shall march to and fro;
    no oppressor shall again march over
          them,
      for now I see with my own eyes.

⁹   Rejoice greatly, O daughter of Zion!
      Shout aloud, O daughter of Jerusalem!
    Behold, your king is coming to you;
      righteous and having salvation is he,
    humble and mounted on a donkey,
      on a colt, the foal of a donkey.

¹ Or tabernacle ² Some manuscripts omit this sentence ³ Or on its behalf ⁴ Or on behalf of ⁵ Greek bondservant ⁶ Some manuscripts 616 ⁷ Or For the eye of mankind, especially of all the tribes of Israel, is toward the LORD ⁸ Or a foreign people; Hebrew a bastard

10   I will cut off the chariot from Ephraim
          and the war horse from Jerusalem;
      and the battle bow shall be cut off,
          and he shall speak peace to the
              nations;
      his rule shall be from sea to sea,
          and from the River to the ends of the
              earth.
11   As for you also, because of the blood of
          my covenant with you,
      I will set your prisoners free from the
          waterless pit.
12   Return to your stronghold, O prisoners
          of hope;
      today I declare that I will restore to
          you double.
13   For I have bent Judah as my bow;
      I have made Ephraim its arrow.
      I will stir up your sons, O Zion,
          against your sons, O Greece,
          and wield you like a warrior's sword.
14   Then the LORD will appear over them,
          and his arrow will go forth like
              lightning;
      the Lord GOD will sound the trumpet
          and will march forth in the
              whirlwinds of the south.
15   The LORD of hosts will protect them,
          and they shall devour, and tread down
              the sling stones,
      and they shall drink and roar as if drunk
          with wine,
          and be full like a bowl,
          drenched like the corners of the altar.
16   On that day the LORD their God will
          save them,
          as the flock of his people;
      for like the jewels of a crown
          they shall shine on his land.
17   For how great is his goodness, and how
          great his beauty!
      Grain shall make the young men
          flourish,
          and new wine the young women.

———————— John 12 ————————

Six days before the Passover, Jesus therefore came to Bethany, where Lazarus was,
whom Jesus had raised from the dead. ²So they
gave a dinner for him there. Martha served,
and Lazarus was one of those reclining with
him at table. ³Mary therefore took a pound¹ of
expensive ointment made from pure nard, and
anointed the feet of Jesus and wiped his feet
with her hair. The house was filled with the
fragrance of the perfume. ⁴But Judas Iscariot,
one of his disciples (he who was about to betray
him), said, ⁵"Why was this ointment not sold
for three hundred denarii² and given to the
poor?" ⁶He said this, not because he cared
about the poor, but because he was a thief,
and having charge of the moneybag he used
to help himself to what was put into it. ⁷Jesus
said, "Leave her alone, so that she may keep
it³ for the day of my burial. ⁸For the poor you
always have with you, but you do not always
have me."

⁹When the large crowd of the Jews learned
that Jesus⁴ was there, they came, not only on
account of him but also to see Lazarus, whom
he had raised from the dead. ¹⁰So the chief
priests made plans to put Lazarus to death as
well, ¹¹because on account of him many of the
Jews were going away and believing in Jesus.

¹²The next day the large crowd that had
come to the feast heard that Jesus was coming to Jerusalem. ¹³So they took branches of
palm trees and went out to meet him, crying
out, "Hosanna! Blessed is he who comes in
the name of the Lord, even the King of Israel!"
¹⁴And Jesus found a young donkey and sat on
it, just as it is written,

15   "Fear not, daughter of Zion;
          behold, your king is coming,
              sitting on a donkey's colt!"

¹⁶His disciples did not understand these things
at first, but when Jesus was glorified, then they
remembered that these things had been written
about him and had been done to him. ¹⁷The
crowd that had been with him when he called
Lazarus out of the tomb and raised him from
the dead continued to bear witness. ¹⁸The
reason why the crowd went to meet him was
that they heard he had done this sign. ¹⁹So the
Pharisees said to one another, "You see that you
are gaining nothing. Look, the world has gone
after him."

²⁰Now among those who went up to worship at the feast were some Greeks. ²¹So these
came to Philip, who was from Bethsaida in
Galilee, and asked him, "Sir, we wish to see

¹ Greek litra; a litra (or Roman pound) was equal to about 11 1/2 ounces or 327 grams ² A denarius was a day's wage for a laborer ³ Or Leave her alone; she intended to keep it
⁴ Greek he

Jesus." [22]Philip went and told Andrew; Andrew and Philip went and told Jesus. [23]And Jesus answered them, "The hour has come for the Son of Man to be glorified. [24]Truly, truly, I say to you, unless a grain of wheat falls into the earth and dies, it remains alone; but if it dies, it bears much fruit. [25]Whoever loves his life loses it, and whoever hates his life in this world will keep it for eternal life. [26]If anyone serves me, he must follow me; and where I am, there will my servant be also. If anyone serves me, the Father will honor him.

[27]"Now is my soul troubled. And what shall I say? 'Father, save me from this hour'? But for this purpose I have come to this hour. [28]Father, glorify your name." Then a voice came from heaven: "I have glorified it, and I will glorify it again." [29]The crowd that stood there and heard it said that it had thundered. Others said, "An angel has spoken to him." [30]Jesus answered, "This voice has come for your sake, not mine. [31]Now is the judgment of this world; now will the ruler of this world be cast out. [32]And I, when I am lifted up from the earth, will draw all people to myself." [33]He said this to show by what kind of death he was going to die. [34]So the crowd answered him, "We have heard from the Law that the Christ remains forever. How can you say that the Son of Man must be lifted up? Who is this Son of Man?" [35]So Jesus said to them, "The light is among you for a little while longer. Walk while you have the light, lest darkness overtake you. The one who walks in the darkness does not know where he is going. [36]While you have the light, believe in the light, that you may become sons of light."

When Jesus had said these things, he departed and hid himself from them. [37]Though he had done so many signs before them, they still did not believe in him, [38]so that the word spoken by the prophet Isaiah might be fulfilled:

> "Lord, who has believed what he heard
>   from us,
> and to whom has the arm of the Lord
>   been revealed?"

[39]Therefore they could not believe. For again Isaiah said,

[40] > "He has blinded their eyes
>   and hardened their heart,
> lest they see with their eyes,
>   and understand with their heart, and
>   turn,
> and I would heal them."

[41]Isaiah said these things because he saw his glory and spoke of him. [42]Nevertheless, many even of the authorities believed in him, but for fear of the Pharisees they did not confess it, so that they would not be put out of the synagogue; [43]for they loved the glory that comes from man more than the glory that comes from God.

[44]And Jesus cried out and said, "Whoever believes in me, believes not in me but in him who sent me. [45]And whoever sees me sees him who sent me. [46]I have come into the world as light, so that whoever believes in me may not remain in darkness. [47]If anyone hears my words and does not keep them, I do not judge him; for I did not come to judge the world but to save the world. [48]The one who rejects me and does not receive my words has a judge; the word that I have spoken will judge him on the last day. [49]For I have not spoken on my own authority, but the Father who sent me has himself given me a commandment—what to say and what to speak. [50]And I know that his commandment is eternal life. What I say, therefore, I say as the Father has told me."

DECEMBER 23

2 Chronicles 27–28

Jotham was twenty-five years old when he began to reign, and he reigned sixteen years in Jerusalem. His mother's name was Jerushah the daughter of Zadok. ²And he did what was right in the eyes of the LORD according to all that his father Uzziah had done, except he did not enter the temple of the LORD. But the people still followed corrupt practices. ³He built the upper gate of the house of the LORD and did much building on the wall of Ophel. ⁴Moreover, he built cities in the hill country of Judah, and forts and towers on the wooded hills. ⁵He fought with the king of the Ammonites and prevailed against them. And the Ammonites gave him that year 100 talents¹ of silver, and 10,000 cors² of wheat and 10,000 of barley. The Ammonites paid him the same amount in the second and the third years. ⁶So Jotham became mighty, because he ordered his ways before the LORD his God. ⁷Now the rest of the acts of Jotham, and all his wars and his ways, behold, they are written in the Book of the Kings of Israel and Judah. ⁸He was twenty-five years old when he began to reign, and he reigned sixteen years in Jerusalem. ⁹And Jotham slept with his fathers, and they buried him in the city of David, and Ahaz his son reigned in his place.

28:1 Ahaz was twenty years old when he began to reign, and he reigned sixteen years in Jerusalem. And he did not do what was right in the eyes of the LORD, as his father David had done, ²but he walked in the ways of the kings of Israel. He even made metal images for the Baals, ³and he made offerings in the Valley of the Son of Hinnom and burned his sons as an offering,³ according to the abominations of the nations whom the LORD drove out before the people of Israel. ⁴And he sacrificed and made offerings on the high places and on the hills and under every green tree.

⁵Therefore the LORD his God gave him into the hand of the king of Syria, who defeated him and took captive a great number of his people and brought them to Damascus. He was also given into the hand of the king of Israel, who struck him with great force. ⁶For Pekah the son of Remaliah killed 120,000 from Judah in one day, all of them men of valor, because they had forsaken the LORD, the God of their fathers. ⁷And Zichri, a mighty man of Ephraim, killed Maaseiah the king's son and Azrikam the commander of the palace and Elkanah the next in authority to the king.

⁸The men of Israel took captive 200,000 of their relatives, women, sons, and daughters. They also took much spoil from them and brought the spoil to Samaria. ⁹But a prophet of the LORD was there, whose name was Oded, and he went out to meet the army that came to Samaria and said to them, "Behold, because the LORD, the God of your fathers, was angry with Judah, he gave them into your hand, but you have killed them in a rage that has reached up to heaven. ¹⁰And now you intend to subjugate the people of Judah and Jerusalem, male and female, as your slaves. Have you not sins of your own against the LORD your God? ¹¹Now hear me, and send back the captives from your relatives whom you have taken, for the fierce wrath of the LORD is upon you."

¹²Certain chiefs also of the men of Ephraim, Azariah the son of Johanan, Berechiah the son of Meshillemoth, Jehizkiah the son of Shallum, and Amasa the son of Hadlai, stood up against those who were coming from the war ¹³and said to them, "You shall not bring the captives in here, for you propose to bring upon us guilt against the LORD in addition to our present sins and guilt. For our guilt is already great, and there is fierce wrath against Israel." ¹⁴So the armed men left the captives and the spoil before the princes and all the assembly. ¹⁵And the men who have been mentioned by name rose and took the captives, and with the spoil they clothed all who were naked among them. They clothed them, gave them sandals, provided them with food and drink, and anointed them, and carrying all the feeble among them

---

¹ A *talent* was about 75 pounds or 34 kilograms ² A *cor* was about 6 bushels or 220 liters ³ Hebrew *made his sons pass through the fire*

on donkeys, they brought them to their kins-folk at Jericho, the city of palm trees. Then they returned to Samaria.

¹⁶At that time King Ahaz sent to the king¹ of Assyria for help. ¹⁷For the Edomites had again invaded and defeated Judah and carried away captives. ¹⁸And the Philistines had made raids on the cities in the Shephelah and the Negeb of Judah, and had taken Beth-shemesh, Aijalon, Gederoth, Soco with its villages, Timnah with its villages, and Gimzo with its villages. And they settled there. ¹⁹For the Lᴏʀᴅ humbled Judah because of Ahaz king of Israel, for he had made Judah act sinfully² and had been very unfaithful to the Lᴏʀᴅ. ²⁰So Tiglath-pileser³ king of Assyria came against him and afflicted him instead of strengthening him. ²¹For Ahaz took a portion from the house of the Lᴏʀᴅ and the house of the king and of the princes, and gave tribute to the king of Assyria, but it did not help him.

²²In the time of his distress he became yet more faithless to the Lᴏʀᴅ—this same King Ahaz. ²³For he sacrificed to the gods of Damascus that had defeated him and said, "Because the gods of the kings of Syria helped them, I will sacrifice to them that they may help me." But they were the ruin of him and of all Israel. ²⁴And Ahaz gathered together the vessels of the house of God and cut in pieces the vessels of the house of God, and he shut up the doors of the house of the Lᴏʀᴅ, and he made himself altars in every corner of Jerusalem. ²⁵In every city of Judah he made high places to make offerings to other gods, provoking to anger the Lᴏʀᴅ, the God of his fathers. ²⁶Now the rest of his acts and all his ways, from first to last, behold, they are written in the Book of the Kings of Judah and Israel. ²⁷And Ahaz slept with his fathers, and they buried him in the city, in Jerusalem, for they did not bring him into the tombs of the kings of Israel. And Hezekiah his son reigned in his place.

Revelation 14

Then I looked, and behold, on Mount Zion stood the Lamb, and with him 144,000 who had his name and his Father's name written on their foreheads. ²And I heard a voice from heaven like the roar of many waters and like the sound of loud thunder. The voice I heard

was like the sound of harpists playing on their harps, ³and they were singing a new song before the throne and before the four living creatures and before the elders. No one could learn that song except the 144,000 who had been redeemed from the earth. ⁴It is these who have not defiled themselves with women, for they are virgins. It is these who follow the Lamb wherever he goes. These have been redeemed from mankind as firstfruits for God and the Lamb, ⁵and in their mouth no lie was found, for they are blameless.

⁶Then I saw another angel flying directly overhead, with an eternal gospel to proclaim to those who dwell on earth, to every nation and tribe and language and people. ⁷And he said with a loud voice, "Fear God and give him glory, because the hour of his judgment has come, and worship him who made heaven and earth, the sea and the springs of water."

⁸Another angel, a second, followed, saying, "Fallen, fallen is Babylon the great, she who made all nations drink the wine of the passion⁴ of her sexual immorality."

⁹And another angel, a third, followed them, saying with a loud voice, "If anyone worships the beast and its image and receives a mark on his forehead or on his hand, ¹⁰he also will drink the wine of God's wrath, poured full strength into the cup of his anger, and he will be tormented with fire and sulfur in the presence of the holy angels and in the presence of the Lamb. ¹¹And the smoke of their torment goes up forever and ever, and they have no rest, day or night, these worshipers of the beast and its image, and whoever receives the mark of its name."

¹²Here is a call for the endurance of the saints, those who keep the commandments of God and their faith in Jesus.⁵

¹³And I heard a voice from heaven saying, "Write this: Blessed are the dead who die in the Lord from now on." "Blessed indeed," says the Spirit, "that they may rest from their labors, for their deeds follow them!"

¹⁴Then I looked, and behold, a white cloud, and seated on the cloud one like a son of man, with a golden crown on his head, and a sharp sickle in his hand. ¹⁵And another angel came out of the temple, calling with a loud voice to him who sat on the cloud, "Put in your sickle, and reap, for the hour to reap has come, for the harvest of the earth is fully ripe." ¹⁶So he who

---

¹ Septuagint, Syriac, Vulgate (compare 2 Kings 16:7); Hebrew *kings* ² Or *wildly* ³ Hebrew *Tilgath-pilneser* ⁴ Or *wrath* ⁵ Greek *and the faith of Jesus*

sat on the cloud swung his sickle across the earth, and the earth was reaped.

[17] Then another angel came out of the temple in heaven, and he too had a sharp sickle. [18] And another angel came out from the altar, the angel who has authority over the fire, and he called with a loud voice to the one who had the sharp sickle, "Put in your sickle and gather the clusters from the vine of the earth, for its grapes are ripe." [19] So the angel swung his sickle across the earth and gathered the grape harvest of the earth and threw it into the great winepress of the wrath of God. [20] And the winepress was trodden outside the city, and blood flowed from the winepress, as high as a horse's bridle, for 1,600 stadia.[1]

Zechariah 10

Ask rain from the LORD
  in the season of the spring rain,
    from the LORD who makes the storm
      clouds,
      and he will give them showers of rain,
    to everyone the vegetation in the
      field.
[2] For the household gods utter nonsense,
    and the diviners see lies;
  they tell false dreams
    and give empty consolation.
  Therefore the people wander like sheep;
    they are afflicted for lack of a
      shepherd.

[3] "My anger is hot against the shepherds,
    and I will punish the leaders;[2]
  for the LORD of hosts cares for his flock,
    the house of Judah,
    and will make them like his majestic
      steed in battle.
[4] From him shall come the cornerstone,
    from him the tent peg,
  from him the battle bow,
    from him every ruler—all of them
      together.
[5] They shall be like mighty men in battle,
    trampling the foe in the mud of the
      streets;
  they shall fight because the LORD is
    with them,
    and they shall put to shame the riders
      on horses.

[6] "I will strengthen the house of Judah,
    and I will save the house of Joseph.
  I will bring them back because I have
    compassion on them,
    and they shall be as though I had not
      rejected them,
  for I am the LORD their God and I will
    answer them.
[7] Then Ephraim shall become like a
    mighty warrior,
    and their hearts shall be glad as with
      wine.
  Their children shall see it and be glad;
    their hearts shall rejoice in the LORD.

[8] "I will whistle for them and gather them
    in,
    for I have redeemed them,
    and they shall be as many as they were
      before.
[9] Though I scattered them among the
    nations,
    yet in far countries they shall
      remember me,
    and with their children they shall live
      and return.
[10] I will bring them home from the land of
    Egypt,
    and gather them from Assyria,
  and I will bring them to the land of
    Gilead and to Lebanon,
    till there is no room for them.
[11] He shall pass through the sea of troubles
    and strike down the waves of the sea,
    and all the depths of the Nile shall be
      dried up.
  The pride of Assyria shall be laid low,
    and the scepter of Egypt shall depart.
[12] I will make them strong in the LORD,
    and they shall walk in his name,"
        declares the LORD.

John 13

Now before the Feast of the Passover, when Jesus knew that his hour had come to depart out of this world to the Father, having loved his own who were in the world, he loved them to the end. [2] During supper, when the devil had already put it into the heart of Judas Iscariot, Simon's son, to betray him, [3] Jesus, knowing that the Father had given all things

[1] About 184 miles; a stadion was about 607 feet or 185 meters [2] Hebrew the male goats

into his hands, and that he had come from God and was going back to God, **4**rose from supper. He laid aside his outer garments, and taking a towel, tied it around his waist. **5**Then he poured water into a basin and began to wash the disciples' feet and to wipe them with the towel that was wrapped around him. **6**He came to Simon Peter, who said to him, "Lord, do you wash my feet?" **7**Jesus answered him, "What I am doing you do not understand now, but afterward you will understand." **8**Peter said to him, "You shall never wash my feet." Jesus answered him, "If I do not wash you, you have no share with me." **9**Simon Peter said to him, "Lord, not my feet only but also my hands and my head!" **10**Jesus said to him, "The one who has bathed does not need to wash, except for his feet,[1] but is completely clean. And you[2] are clean, but not every one of you." **11**For he knew who was to betray him; that was why he said, "Not all of you are clean."

12When he had washed their feet and put on his outer garments and resumed his place, he said to them, "Do you understand what I have done to you? **13**You call me Teacher and Lord, and you are right, for so I am. **14**If I then, your Lord and Teacher, have washed your feet, you also ought to wash one another's feet. **15**For I have given you an example, that you also should do just as I have done to you. **16**Truly, truly, I say to you, a servant[3] is not greater than his master, nor is a messenger greater than the one who sent him. **17**If you know these things, blessed are you if you do them. **18**I am not speaking of all of you; I know whom I have chosen. But the Scripture will be fulfilled,[4] 'He who ate my bread has lifted his heel against me.' **19**I am telling you this now, before it takes place, that when it does take place you may believe that I am he. **20**Truly, truly, I say to you, whoever receives the one I send receives me, and whoever receives me receives the one who sent me."

21After saying these things, Jesus was troubled in his spirit, and testified, "Truly, truly, I say to you, one of you will betray me." **22**The disciples looked at one another, uncertain of whom he spoke. **23**One of his disciples, whom Jesus loved, was reclining at table at Jesus' side,[5] **24**so Simon Peter motioned to him to ask Jesus[6] of whom he was speaking. **25**So that disciple, leaning back against Jesus, said to him, "Lord, who is it?" **26**Jesus answered, "It is he to whom I will give this morsel of bread when I have dipped it." So when he had dipped the morsel, he gave it to Judas, the son of Simon Iscariot. **27**Then after he had taken the morsel, Satan entered into him. Jesus said to him, "What you are going to do, do quickly." **28**Now no one at the table knew why he said this to him. **29**Some thought that, because Judas had the moneybag, Jesus was telling him, "Buy what we need for the feast," or that he should give something to the poor. **30**So, after receiving the morsel of bread, he immediately went out. And it was night.

31When he had gone out, Jesus said, "Now is the Son of Man glorified, and God is glorified in him. **32**If God is glorified in him, God will also glorify him in himself, and glorify him at once. **33**Little children, yet a little while I am with you. You will seek me, and just as I said to the Jews, so now I also say to you, 'Where I am going you cannot come.' **34**A new commandment I give to you, that you love one another: just as I have loved you, you also are to love one another. **35**By this all people will know that you are my disciples, if you have love for one another."

36Simon Peter said to him, "Lord, where are you going?" Jesus answered him, "Where I am going you cannot follow me now, but you will follow afterward." **37**Peter said to him, "Lord, why can I not follow you now? I will lay down my life for you." **38**Jesus answered, "Will you lay down your life for me? Truly, truly, I say to you, the rooster will not crow till you have denied me three times.

---

[1] Some manuscripts omit *except for his feet* [2] The Greek words for *you* in this verse are plural [3] Greek *bondservant* [4] Greek *But in order that the Scripture may be fulfilled* [5] Greek *in the bosom of Jesus* [6] Greek lacks *Jesus*

DECEMBER 24

2 Chronicles 29

Hezekiah began to reign when he was twenty-five years old, and he reigned twenty-nine years in Jerusalem. His mother's name was Abijah[1] the daughter of Zechariah. [2] And he did what was right in the eyes of the LORD, according to all that David his father had done.

[3] In the first year of his reign, in the first month, he opened the doors of the house of the LORD and repaired them. [4] He brought in the priests and the Levites and assembled them in the square on the east [5] and said to them, "Hear me, Levites! Now consecrate yourselves, and consecrate the house of the LORD, the God of your fathers, and carry out the filth from the Holy Place. [6] For our fathers have been unfaithful and have done what was evil in the sight of the LORD our God. They have forsaken him and have turned away their faces from the habitation of the LORD and turned their backs. [7] They also shut the doors of the vestibule and put out the lamps and have not burned incense or offered burnt offerings in the Holy Place to the God of Israel. [8] Therefore the wrath of the LORD came on Judah and Jerusalem, and he has made them an object of horror, of astonishment, and of hissing, as you see with your own eyes. [9] For behold, our fathers have fallen by the sword, and our sons and our daughters and our wives are in captivity for this. [10] Now it is in my heart to make a covenant with the LORD, the God of Israel, in order that his fierce anger may turn away from us. [11] My sons, do not now be negligent, for the LORD has chosen you to stand in his presence, to minister to him and to be his ministers and make offerings to him."

[12] Then the Levites arose, Mahath the son of Amasai, and Joel the son of Azariah, of the sons of the Kohathites; and of the sons of Merari, Kish the son of Abdi, and Azariah the son of Jehallelel; and of the Gershonites, Joah the son of Zimmah, and Eden the son of Joah; [13] and of the sons of Elizaphan, Shimri and Jeuel; and of the sons of Asaph, Zechariah and Mattaniah; [14] and of the sons of Heman, Jehuel and Shimei; and of the sons of Jeduthun, Shemaiah and Uzziel. [15] They gathered their brothers and consecrated themselves and went in as the king had commanded, by the words of the LORD, to cleanse the house of the LORD. [16] The priests went into the inner part of the house of the LORD to cleanse it, and they brought out all the uncleanness that they found in the temple of the LORD into the court of the house of the LORD. And the Levites took it and carried it out to the brook Kidron. [17] They began to consecrate on the first day of the first month, and on the eighth day of the month they came to the vestibule of the LORD. Then for eight days they consecrated the house of the LORD, and on the sixteenth day of the first month they finished. [18] Then they went in to Hezekiah the king and said, "We have cleansed all the house of the LORD, the altar of burnt offering and all its utensils, and the table for the showbread and all its utensils. [19] All the utensils that King Ahaz discarded in his reign when he was faithless, we have made ready and consecrated, and behold, they are before the altar of the LORD."

[20] Then Hezekiah the king rose early and gathered the officials of the city and went up to the house of the LORD. [21] And they brought seven bulls, seven rams, seven lambs, and seven male goats for a sin offering for the kingdom and for the sanctuary and for Judah. And he commanded the priests, the sons of Aaron, to offer them on the altar of the LORD. [22] So they slaughtered the bulls, and the priests received the blood and threw it against the altar. And they slaughtered the rams, and their blood was thrown against the altar. And they slaughtered the lambs, and their blood was thrown against the altar. [23] Then the goats for the sin offering were brought to the king and the assembly, and they laid their hands on them, [24] and

[1] Spelled *Abi* in 2 Kings 18:2

the priests slaughtered them and made a sin offering with their blood on the altar, to make atonement for all Israel. For the king commanded that the burnt offering and the sin offering should be made for all Israel.

²⁵And he stationed the Levites in the house of the Lord with cymbals, harps, and lyres, according to the commandment of David and of Gad the king's seer and of Nathan the prophet, for the commandment was from the Lord through his prophets. ²⁶The Levites stood with the instruments of David, and the priests with the trumpets. ²⁷Then Hezekiah commanded that the burnt offering be offered on the altar. And when the burnt offering began, the song to the Lord began also, and the trumpets, accompanied by the instruments of David king of Israel. ²⁸The whole assembly worshiped, and the singers sang, and the trumpeters sounded. All this continued until the burnt offering was finished. ²⁹When the offering was finished, the king and all who were present with him bowed themselves and worshiped. ³⁰And Hezekiah the king and the officials commanded the Levites to sing praises to the Lord with the words of David and of Asaph the seer. And they sang praises with gladness, and they bowed down and worshiped.

³¹Then Hezekiah said, "You have now consecrated yourselves to¹ the Lord. Come near; bring sacrifices and thank offerings to the house of the Lord." And the assembly brought sacrifices and thank offerings, and all who were of a willing heart brought burnt offerings. ³²The number of the burnt offerings that the assembly brought was 70 bulls, 100 rams, and 200 lambs; all these were for a burnt offering to the Lord. ³³And the consecrated offerings were 600 bulls and 3,000 sheep. ³⁴But the priests were too few and could not flay all the burnt offerings, so until other priests had consecrated themselves, their brothers the Levites helped them, until the work was finished—for the Levites were more upright in heart than the priests in consecrating themselves. ³⁵Besides the great number of burnt offerings, there was the fat of the peace offerings, and there were the drink offerings for the burnt offerings. Thus the service of the house of the Lord was restored. ³⁶And Hezekiah and all the people rejoiced because God had provided for the people, for the thing came about suddenly.

Revelation 15

Then I saw another sign in heaven, great and amazing, seven angels with seven plagues, which are the last, for with them the wrath of God is finished.

²And I saw what appeared to be a sea of glass mingled with fire—and also those who had conquered the beast and its image and the number of its name, standing beside the sea of glass with harps of God in their hands. ³And they sing the song of Moses, the servant² of God, and the song of the Lamb, saying,

"Great and amazing are your deeds,
    O Lord God the Almighty!
Just and true are your ways,
    O King of the nations!³
⁴ Who will not fear, O Lord,
    and glorify your name?
For you alone are holy.
    All nations will come
    and worship you,
for your righteous acts have been
    revealed."

⁵After this I looked, and the sanctuary of the tent⁴ of witness in heaven was opened, ⁶and out of the sanctuary came the seven angels with the seven plagues, clothed in pure, bright linen, with golden sashes around their chests. ⁷And one of the four living creatures gave to the seven angels seven golden bowls full of the wrath of God who lives forever and ever, ⁸and the sanctuary was filled with smoke from the glory of God and from his power, and no one could enter the sanctuary until the seven plagues of the seven angels were finished.

Zechariah 11

Open your doors, O Lebanon,
    that the fire may devour your cedars!
² Wail, O cypress, for the cedar has fallen,
    for the glorious trees are ruined!
Wail, oaks of Bashan,
    for the thick forest has been felled!
³ The sound of the wail of the shepherds,
    for their glory is ruined!

¹ Hebrew filled your hand for ² Greek bondservant ³ Some manuscripts the ages ⁴ Or tabernacle

The sound of the roar of the lions,
for the thicket of the Jordan is ruined!

4Thus said the LORD my God: "Become shepherd of the flock doomed to slaughter. **5**Those who buy them slaughter them and go unpunished, and those who sell them say, 'Blessed be the LORD, I have become rich,' and their own shepherds have no pity on them. **6**For I will no longer have pity on the inhabitants of this land, declares the LORD. Behold, I will cause each of them to fall into the hand of his neighbor, and each into the hand of his king, and they shall crush the land, and I will deliver none from their hand."

7So I became the shepherd of the flock doomed to be slaughtered by the sheep traders. And I took two staffs, one I named Favor, the other I named Union. And I tended the sheep. **8**In one month I destroyed the three shepherds. But I became impatient with them, and they also detested me. **9**So I said, "I will not be your shepherd. What is to die, let it die. What is to be destroyed, let it be destroyed. And let those who are left devour the flesh of one another." **10**And I took my staff Favor, and I broke it, annulling the covenant that I had made with all the peoples. **11**So it was annulled on that day, and the sheep traders, who were watching me, knew that it was the word of the LORD. **12**Then I said to them, "If it seems good to you, give me my wages; but if not, keep them." And they weighed out as my wages thirty pieces of silver. **13**Then the LORD said to me, "Throw it to the potter"—the lordly price at which I was priced by them. So I took the thirty pieces of silver and threw them into the house of the LORD, to the potter. **14**Then I broke my second staff Union, annulling the brotherhood between Judah and Israel.

15Then the LORD said to me, "Take once more the equipment of a foolish shepherd. **16**For behold, I am raising up in the land a shepherd who does not care for those being destroyed, or seek the young or heal the maimed or nourish the healthy, but devours the flesh of the fat ones, tearing off even their hoofs.

17   "Woe to my worthless shepherd,
who deserts the flock!
May the sword strike his arm
and his right eye!

Let his arm be wholly withered,
his right eye utterly blinded!"

John 14

"Let not your hearts be troubled. Believe in God;[1] believe also in me. **2**In my Father's house are many rooms. If it were not so, would I have told you that I go to prepare a place for you?[2] **3**And if I go and prepare a place for you, I will come again and will take you to myself, that where I am you may be also. **4**And you know the way to where I am going."[3] **5**Thomas said to him, "Lord, we do not know where you are going. How can we know the way?" **6**Jesus said to him, "I am the way, and the truth, and the life. No one comes to the Father except through me. **7**If you had known me, you would have known my Father also.[4] From now on you do know him and have seen him."

8Philip said to him, "Lord, show us the Father, and it is enough for us." **9**Jesus said to him, "Have I been with you so long, and you still do not know me, Philip? Whoever has seen me has seen the Father. How can you say, 'Show us the Father'? **10**Do you not believe that I am in the Father and the Father is in me? The words that I say to you I do not speak on my own authority, but the Father who dwells in me does his works. **11**Believe me that I am in the Father and the Father is in me, or else believe on account of the works themselves.

12"Truly, truly, I say to you, whoever believes in me will also do the works that I do; and greater works than these will he do, because I am going to the Father. **13**Whatever you ask in my name, this I will do, that the Father may be glorified in the Son. **14**If you ask me[5] anything in my name, I will do it.

15"If you love me, you will keep my commandments. **16**And I will ask the Father, and he will give you another Helper,[6] to be with you forever, **17**even the Spirit of truth, whom the world cannot receive, because it neither sees him nor knows him. You know him, for he dwells with you and will be[7] in you. **18**"I will not leave you as orphans; I will come to you. **19**Yet a little while and the world will see me no more, but you will see me. Because I live, you also will live. **20**In that day you will know that I am in my Father, and you in me, and I in

[1] Or You believe in God [2] Or In my Father's house are many rooms; if it were not so, I would have told you; for I go to prepare a place for you [3] Some manuscripts Where I am going you know, and the way you know [4] Or If you know me, you will know my Father also, or If you have known me, you will know my Father also [5] Some manuscripts omit me [6] Or Advocate, or Counselor; also 14:26; 15:26; 16:7 [7] Some manuscripts and is

you. [21] Whoever has my commandments and keeps them, he it is who loves me. And he who loves me will be loved by my Father, and I will love him and manifest myself to him." [22] Judas (not Iscariot) said to him, "Lord, how is it that you will manifest yourself to us, and not to the world?" [23] Jesus answered him, "If anyone loves me, he will keep my word, and my Father will love him, and we will come to him and make our home with him. [24] Whoever does not love me does not keep my words. And the word that you hear is not mine but the Father's who sent me.

[25] "These things I have spoken to you while I am still with you. [26] But the Helper, the Holy Spirit, whom the Father will send in my name, he will teach you all things and bring to your remembrance all that I have said to you. [27] Peace I leave with you; my peace I give to you. Not as the world gives do I give to you. Let not your hearts be troubled, neither let them be afraid. [28] You heard me say to you, 'I am going away, and I will come to you.' If you loved me, you would have rejoiced, because I am going to the Father, for the Father is greater than I. [29] And now I have told you before it takes place, so that when it does take place you may believe. [30] I will no longer talk much with you, for the ruler of this world is coming. He has no claim on me, [31] but I do as the Father has commanded me, so that the world may know that I love the Father. Rise, let us go from here.

DECEMBER 25

2 Chronicles 30

Hezekiah sent to all Israel and Judah, and wrote letters also to Ephraim and Manasseh, that they should come to the house of the Lord at Jerusalem to keep the Passover to the Lord, the God of Israel. [2] For the king and his princes and all the assembly in Jerusalem had taken counsel to keep the Passover in the second month— [3] for they could not keep it at that time because the priests had not consecrated themselves in sufficient number, nor had the people assembled in Jerusalem— [4] and the plan seemed right to the king and all the assembly. [5] So they decreed to make a proclamation throughout all Israel, from Beersheba to Dan, that the people should come and keep the Passover to the Lord, the God of Israel, at Jerusalem, for they had not kept it as often as prescribed. [6] So couriers went throughout all Israel and Judah with letters from the king and his princes, as the king had commanded, saying, "O people of Israel, return to the Lord, the God of Abraham, Isaac, and Israel, that he may turn again to the remnant of you who have escaped from the hand of the kings of Assyria. [7] Do not be like your fathers and your brothers, who were faithless to the Lord God of their fathers, so that he made them a desolation, as you see. [8] Do not now be stiff-necked as your fathers were, but yield yourselves to the Lord and come to his sanctuary, which he has consecrated forever, and serve the Lord your God, that his fierce anger may turn away from you. [9] For if you return to the Lord, your brothers and your children will find compassion with their captors and return to this land. For the Lord your God is gracious and merciful and will not turn away his face from you, if you return to him."

[10] So the couriers went from city to city through the country of Ephraim and Manasseh, and as far as Zebulun, but they laughed them to scorn and mocked them. [11] However, some men of Asher, of Manasseh, and of Zebulun humbled themselves and came to Jerusalem. [12] The hand of God was also on Judah to give them one heart to do what the king and the princes commanded by the word of the Lord.

[13] And many people came together in Jerusalem to keep the Feast of Unleavened Bread in the second month, a very great assembly.

[14]They set to work and removed the altars that were in Jerusalem, and all the altars for burning incense they took away and threw into the brook Kidron. [15]And they slaughtered the Passover lamb on the fourteenth day of the second month. And the priests and the Levites were ashamed, so that they consecrated themselves and brought burnt offerings into the house of the LORD. [16]They took their accustomed posts according to the Law of Moses the man of God. The priests threw the blood that they received from the hand of the Levites. [17]For there were many in the assembly who had not consecrated themselves. Therefore the Levites had to slaughter the Passover lamb for everyone who was not clean, to consecrate it to the LORD. [18]For a majority of the people, many of them from Ephraim, Manasseh, Issachar, and Zebulun, had not cleansed themselves, yet they ate the Passover otherwise than as prescribed. For Hezekiah had prayed for them, saying, "May the good LORD pardon everyone [19]who sets his heart to seek God, the LORD, the God of his fathers, even though not according to the sanctuary's rules of cleanness."[1] [20]And the LORD heard Hezekiah and healed the people. [21]And the people of Israel who were present at Jerusalem kept the Feast of Unleavened Bread seven days with great gladness, and the Levites and the priests praised the LORD day by day, singing with all their might[2] to the LORD. [22]And Hezekiah spoke encouragingly to all the Levites who showed good skill in the service of the LORD. So they ate the food of the festival for seven days, sacrificing peace offerings and giving thanks to the LORD, the God of their fathers.

[23]Then the whole assembly agreed together to keep the feast for another seven days. So they kept it for another seven days with gladness. [24]For Hezekiah king of Judah gave the assembly 1,000 bulls and 7,000 sheep for offerings, and the princes gave the assembly 1,000 bulls and 10,000 sheep. And the priests consecrated themselves in great numbers. [25]The whole assembly of Judah, and the priests and the Levites, and the whole assembly that came out of Israel, and the sojourners who came out of the land of Israel, and the sojourners who lived in Judah, rejoiced. [26]So there was great joy in Jerusalem, for since the time of Solomon the son of David king of Israel there had been nothing like this in Jerusalem. [27]Then the priests and the Levites arose and blessed the people, and their voice was heard, and their prayer came to his holy habitation in heaven.

Revelation 16

Then I heard a loud voice from the temple telling the seven angels, "Go and pour out on the earth the seven bowls of the wrath of God."

[2]So the first angel went and poured out his bowl on the earth, and harmful and painful sores came upon the people who bore the mark of the beast and worshiped its image.

[3]The second angel poured out his bowl into the sea, and it became like the blood of a corpse, and every living thing died that was in the sea.

[4]The third angel poured out his bowl into the rivers and the springs of water, and they became blood. [5]And I heard the angel in charge of the waters[3] say,

> "Just are you, O Holy One, who is and who was,
> for you brought these judgments.
> [6]For they have shed the blood of saints and prophets,
> and you have given them blood to drink.
> It is what they deserve!"

[7]And I heard the altar saying,

> "Yes, Lord God the Almighty,
> true and just are your judgments!"

[8]The fourth angel poured out his bowl on the sun, and it was allowed to scorch people with fire. [9]They were scorched by the fierce heat, and they cursed[4] the name of God who had power over these plagues. They did not repent and give him glory.

[10]The fifth angel poured out his bowl on the throne of the beast, and its kingdom was plunged into darkness. People gnawed their tongues in anguish [11]and cursed the God of heaven for their pain and sores. They did not repent of their deeds.

[12]The sixth angel poured out his bowl on the great river Euphrates, and its water was dried up, to prepare the way for the kings from the east. [13]And I saw, coming out of the mouth of the dragon and out of the mouth of the beast and out of the mouth of the false prophet,

---

[1] Hebrew *not according to the cleanness of holiness* [2] Compare 1 Chronicles 13:8; Hebrew *with instruments of might* [3] Greek *angel of the waters* [4] Greek *blasphemed*; also verses 11, 21

three unclean spirits like frogs. [14] For they are demonic spirits, performing signs, who go abroad to the kings of the whole world, to assemble them for battle on the great day of God the Almighty. [15] ("Behold, I am coming like a thief! Blessed is the one who stays awake, keeping his garments on, that he may not go about naked and be seen exposed!") [16] And they assembled them at the place that in Hebrew is called Armageddon.

[17] The seventh angel poured out his bowl into the air, and a loud voice came out of the temple, from the throne, saying, "It is done!" [18] And there were flashes of lightning, rumblings,[1] peals of thunder, and a great earthquake such as there had never been since man was on the earth, so great was that earthquake. [19] The great city was split into three parts, and the cities of the nations fell, and God remembered Babylon the great, to make her drain the cup of the wine of the fury of his wrath. [20] And every island fled away, and no mountains were to be found. [21] And great hailstones, about one hundred pounds[2] each, fell from heaven on people; and they cursed God for the plague of the hail, because the plague was so severe.

Zechariah 12:1–13:1

The oracle of the word of the LORD concerning Israel: Thus declares the LORD, who stretched out the heavens and founded the earth and formed the spirit of man within him: [2] "Behold, I am about to make Jerusalem a cup of staggering to all the surrounding peoples. The siege of Jerusalem will also be against Judah. [3] On that day I will make Jerusalem a heavy stone for all the peoples. All who lift it will surely hurt themselves. And all the nations of the earth will gather against it. [4] On that day, declares the LORD, I will strike every horse with panic, and its rider with madness. But for the sake of the house of Judah I will keep my eyes open, when I strike every horse of the peoples with blindness. [5] Then the clans of Judah shall say to themselves, 'The inhabitants of Jerusalem have strength through the LORD of hosts, their God.' [6] "On that day I will make the clans of Judah like a blazing pot in the midst of wood, like a flaming torch among sheaves. And they shall devour to the right and to the left all the

surrounding peoples, while Jerusalem shall again be inhabited in its place, in Jerusalem.

[7] "And the LORD will give salvation to the tents of Judah first, that the glory of the house of David and the glory of the inhabitants of Jerusalem may not surpass that of Judah. [8] On that day the LORD will protect the inhabitants of Jerusalem, so that the feeblest among them on that day shall be like David, and the house of David shall be like God, like the angel of the LORD, going before them. [9] And on that day I will seek to destroy all the nations that come against Jerusalem.

[10] "And I will pour out on the house of David and the inhabitants of Jerusalem a spirit of grace and pleas for mercy, so that, when they look on me, on him whom they have pierced, they shall mourn for him, as one mourns for an only child, and weep bitterly over him, as one weeps over a firstborn. [11] On that day the mourning in Jerusalem will be as great as the mourning for Hadad-rimmon in the plain of Megiddo. [12] The land shall mourn, each family[3] by itself: the family of the house of David by itself, and their wives by themselves; the family of the house of Nathan by itself, and their wives by themselves; [13] the family of the house of Levi by itself, and their wives by themselves; the family of the Shimeites by itself, and their wives by themselves; [14] and all the families that are left, each by itself, and their wives by themselves.

[13:1] "On that day there shall be a fountain opened for the house of David and the inhabitants of Jerusalem, to cleanse them from sin and uncleanness.

John 15

"I am the true vine, and my Father is the vinedresser. [2] Every branch in me that does not bear fruit he takes away, and every branch that does bear fruit he prunes, that it may bear more fruit. [3] Already you are clean because of the word that I have spoken to you. [4] Abide in me, and I in you. As the branch cannot bear fruit by itself, unless it abides in the vine, neither can you, unless you abide in me. [5] I am the vine; you are the branches. Whoever abides in me and I in him, he it is that bears much fruit, for apart from me you can do nothing. [6] If anyone does not abide in me he is thrown away like a branch and withers; and

[1] Or voices, or sounds [2] Greek a talent in weight [3] Or clan; also verses 13, 14

the branches are gathered, thrown into the fire, and burned. [7] If you abide in me, and my words abide in you, ask whatever you wish, and it will be done for you. [8] By this my Father is glorified, that you bear much fruit and so prove to be my disciples. [9] As the Father has loved me, so have I loved you. Abide in my love. [10] If you keep my commandments, you will abide in my love, just as I have kept my Father's commandments and abide in his love. [11] These things I have spoken to you, that my joy may be in you, and that your joy may be full.

[12] "This is my commandment, that you love one another as I have loved you. [13] Greater love has no one than this, that someone lay down his life for his friends. [14] You are my friends if you do what I command you. [15] No longer do I call you servants,[1] for the servant[2] does not know what his master is doing; but I have called you friends, for all that I have heard from my Father I have made known to you. [16] You did not choose me, but I chose you and appointed you that you should go and bear fruit and that your fruit should abide, so that whatever you ask the Father in my name, he may give it to you. [17] These things I command you, so that you will love one another.

[18] "If the world hates you, know that it has hated me before it hated you. [19] If you were of the world, the world would love you as its own; but because you are not of the world, but I chose you out of the world, therefore the world hates you. [20] Remember the word that I said to you: 'A servant is not greater than his master.' If they persecuted me, they will also persecute you. If they kept my word, they will also keep yours. [21] But all these things they will do to you on account of my name, because they do not know him who sent me. [22] If I had not come and spoken to them, they would not have been guilty of sin,[3] but now they have no excuse for their sin. [23] Whoever hates me hates my Father also. [24] If I had not done among them the works that no one else did, they would not be guilty of sin, but now they have seen and hated both me and my Father. [25] But the word that is written in their Law must be fulfilled: 'They hated me without a cause.'

[26] "But when the Helper comes, whom I will send to you from the Father, the Spirit of truth, who proceeds from the Father, he will bear witness about me. [27] And you also will bear witness, because you have been with me from the beginning.

DECEMBER 26

2 Chronicles 31

Now when all this was finished, all Israel who were present went out to the cities of Judah and broke in pieces the pillars and cut down the Asherim and broke down the high places and the altars throughout all Judah and Benjamin, and in Ephraim and Manasseh, until they had destroyed them all. Then all the people of Israel returned to their cities, every man to his possession.

[2] And Hezekiah appointed the divisions of the priests and of the Levites, division by division, each according to his service, the priests and the Levites, for burnt offerings and peace offerings, to minister in the gates of the camp of the LORD and to give thanks and praise. [3] The contribution of the king from his own possessions was for the burnt offerings: the burnt offerings of morning and evening, and the burnt offerings for the Sabbaths, the new moons, and the appointed feasts, as it is written in the Law of the LORD. [4] And he commanded the people who lived in Jerusalem to give the portion due to the priests and the Levites, that they might give themselves to the Law of the LORD. [5] As soon as the command was spread abroad, the people of Israel gave in abundance the firstfruits of grain, wine, oil, honey, and of all the produce of the field. And they brought

[1] Greek bondservants   [2] Greek bondservant; also verse 20   [3] Greek they would not have sin; also verse 24

in abundantly the tithe of everything. [6]And the people of Israel and Judah who lived in the cities of Judah also brought in the tithe of cattle and sheep, and the tithe of the dedicated things that had been dedicated to the LORD their God, and laid them in heaps. [7]In the third month they began to pile up the heaps, and finished them in the seventh month. [8]When Hezekiah and the princes came and saw the heaps, they blessed the LORD and his people Israel. [9]And Hezekiah questioned the priests and the Levites about the heaps. [10]Azariah the chief priest, who was of the house of Zadok, answered him, "Since they began to bring the contributions into the house of the LORD, we have eaten and had enough and have plenty left, for the LORD has blessed his people, so that we have this large amount left."

[11] Then Hezekiah commanded them to prepare chambers in the house of the LORD, and they prepared them. [12]And they faithfully brought in the contributions, the tithes, and the dedicated things. The chief officer in charge of them was Conaniah the Levite, with Shimei his brother as second, [13]while Jehiel, Azaziah, Nahath, Asahel, Jerimoth, Jozabad, Eliel, Ismachiah, Mahath, and Benaiah were overseers assisting Conaniah and Shimei his brother, by the appointment of Hezekiah the king and Azariah the chief officer of the house of God. [14]And Kore the son of Imnah the Levite, keeper of the east gate, was over the freewill offerings to God, to apportion the contribution reserved for the LORD and the most holy offerings. [15]Eden, Miniamin, Jeshua, Shemaiah, Amariah, and Shecaniah were faithfully assisting him in the cities of the priests, to distribute the portions to their brothers, old and young alike, by divisions, [16]except those enrolled by genealogy, males from three years old and upward—all who entered the house of the LORD as the duty of each day required—for their service according to their offices, by their divisions. [17]The enrollment of the priests was according to their fathers' houses; that of the Levites from twenty years old and upward was according to their offices, by their divisions. [18]They were enrolled with all their little children, their wives, their sons, and their daughters, the whole assembly, for they were faithful in keeping themselves holy. [19]And for the sons of Aaron, the priests, who were in the fields of common land belonging to their cities, there were men in the several cities who were designated by name to distribute portions to every male among the priests and to everyone among the Levites who was enrolled.

[20]Thus Hezekiah did throughout all Judah, and he did what was good and right and faithful before the LORD his God. [21]And every work that he undertook in the service of the house of God and in accordance with the law and the commandments, seeking his God, he did with all his heart, and prospered.

Revelation 17

Then one of the seven angels who had the seven bowls came and said to me, "Come, I will show you the judgment of the great prostitute who is seated on many waters, [2]with whom the kings of the earth have committed sexual immorality, and with the wine of whose sexual immorality the dwellers on earth have become drunk." [3]And he carried me away in the Spirit into a wilderness, and I saw a woman sitting on a scarlet beast that was full of blasphemous names, and it had seven heads and ten horns. [4]The woman was arrayed in purple and scarlet, and adorned with gold and jewels and pearls, holding in her hand a golden cup full of abominations and the impurities of her sexual immorality. [5]And on her forehead was written a name of mystery: "Babylon the great, mother of prostitutes and of earth's abominations." [6]And I saw the woman, drunk with the blood of the saints, the blood of the martyrs of Jesus.[1]

When I saw her, I marveled greatly. [7]But the angel said to me, "Why do you marvel? I will tell you the mystery of the woman, and of the beast with seven heads and ten horns that carries her. [8]The beast that you saw was, and is not, and is about to rise from the bottomless pit[2] and go to destruction. And the dwellers on earth whose names have not been written in the book of life from the foundation of the world will marvel to see the beast, because it was and is not and is to come. [9]This calls for a mind with wisdom: the seven heads are seven mountains on which the woman is seated; [10]they are also seven kings, five of whom have fallen, one is, the other has not yet come, and when he does come he must remain only a little while. [11] As for the beast that was and is not, it is an eighth but it belongs to the seven, and it goes to destruction. [12] And the ten horns that you saw are ten kings who have not yet received royal power, but they are to receive authority as kings for one hour, together with the beast. [13] These are of one mind, and they hand over their power and authority to the beast. [14] They will make war on the Lamb, and the Lamb will conquer them, for he is Lord of lords and King of kings, and those with him are called and chosen and faithful."

[15] And the angel[1] said to me, "The waters that you saw, where the prostitute is seated, are peoples and multitudes and nations and languages. [16] And the ten horns that you saw, they and the beast will hate the prostitute. They will make her desolate and naked, and devour her flesh and burn her up with fire, [17] for God has put it into their hearts to carry out his purpose by being of one mind and handing over their royal power to the beast, until the words of God are fulfilled. [18] And the woman that you saw is the great city that has dominion over the kings of the earth."

Zechariah 13:2–9

"And on that day, declares the LORD of hosts, I will cut off the names of the idols from the land, so that they shall be remembered no more. And also I will remove from the land the prophets and the spirit of uncleanness. [3] And if anyone again prophesies, his father and mother who bore him will say to him, 'You shall not live, for you speak lies in the name of the LORD.' And his father and mother who bore him shall pierce him through when he prophesies.

[4] "On that day every prophet will be ashamed of his vision when he prophesies. He will not put on a hairy cloak in order to deceive, [5] but he will say, 'I am no prophet, I am a worker of the soil, for a man sold me in my youth.'[2] [6] And if one asks him, 'What are these wounds on your back?'[3] he will say, 'The wounds I received in the house of my friends.'

[7]   "Awake, O sword, against my shepherd,
      against the man who stands next to
         me,"
            declares the LORD of hosts.

"Strike the shepherd, and the sheep will
      be scattered;
   I will turn my hand against the little
      ones.
[8]   In the whole land, declares the LORD,
      two thirds shall be cut off and perish,
      and one third shall be left alive.
[9]   And I will put this third into the fire,
      and refine them as one refines silver,
      and test them as gold is tested.
   They will call upon my name,
      and I will answer them.
   I will say, 'They are my people';
      and they will say, 'The LORD is my
         God.'"

John 16

"I have said all these things to you to keep you from falling away. [2] They will put you out of the synagogues. Indeed, the hour is coming when whoever kills you will think he is offering service to God. [3] And they will do these things because they have not known the Father, nor me. [4] But I have said these things to you, that when their hour comes you may remember that I told them to you.

"I did not say these things to you from the beginning, because I was with you. [5] But now I am going to him who sent me, and none of you asks me, 'Where are you going?' [6] But because I have said these things to you, sorrow has filled your heart. [7] Nevertheless, I tell you the truth: it is to your advantage that I go away, for if I do not go away, the Helper will not come to you. But if I go, I will send him to you. [8] And when he comes, he will convict the world concerning sin and righteousness and judgment: [9] concerning sin, because they do not believe in me; [10] concerning righteousness, because I go to the Father, and you will see me no longer; [11] concerning judgment, because the ruler of this world is judged.

[12] "I still have many things to say to you, but you cannot bear them now. [13] When the Spirit of truth comes, he will guide you into all the truth, for he will not speak on his own authority, but whatever he hears he will speak, and he will declare to you the things that are to come. [14] He will glorify me, for he will take what is mine and declare it to you. [15] All that the Father

[1] Greek he [2] Or for the land has been my possession since my youth [3] Or on your chest; Hebrew wounds between your hands

has is mine; therefore I said that he will take what is mine and declare it to you. [16]"A little while, and you will see me no longer; and again a little while, and you will see me." [17]So some of his disciples said to one another, "What is this that he says to us, 'A little while, and you will not see me, and again a little while, and you will see me'; and, 'because I am going to the Father'?" [18]So they were saying, "What does he mean by 'a little while'? We do not know what he is talking about." [19]Jesus knew that they wanted to ask him, so he said to them, "Is this what you are asking yourselves, what I meant by saying, 'A little while and you will not see me, and again a little while and you will see me'? [20]Truly, truly, I say to you, you will weep and lament, but the world will rejoice. You will be sorrowful, but your sorrow will turn into joy. [21]When a woman is giving birth, she has sorrow because her hour has come, but when she has delivered the baby, she no longer remembers the anguish, for joy that a human being has been born into the world. [22]So also you have sorrow now, but I will see you again, and your hearts will rejoice, and no one will take your joy from you. [23]In that day you will ask nothing of me. Truly, truly, I say to you, whatever you ask of the Father in my

name, he will give it to you. [24]Until now you have asked nothing in my name. Ask, and you will receive, that your joy may be full. [25]"I have said these things to you in figures of speech. The hour is coming when I will no longer speak to you in figures of speech but will tell you plainly about the Father. [26]In that day you will ask in my name, and I do not say to you that I will ask the Father on your behalf; [27]for the Father himself loves you, because you have loved me and have believed that I came from God.[1] [28]I came from the Father and have come into the world, and now I am leaving the world and going to the Father."

[29]His disciples said, "Ah, now you are speaking plainly and not using figurative speech! [30]Now we know that you know all things and do not need anyone to question you; this is why we believe that you came from God." [31]Jesus answered them, "Do you now believe? [32]Behold, the hour is coming, indeed it has come, when you will be scattered, each to his own home, and will leave me alone. Yet I am not alone, for the Father is with me. [33]I have said these things to you, that in me you may have peace. In the world you will have tribulation. But take heart; I have overcome the world."

DECEMBER 27

2 Chronicles 32

After these things and these acts of faithfulness, Sennacherib king of Assyria came and invaded Judah and encamped against the fortified cities, thinking to win them for himself. [2]And when Hezekiah saw that Sennacherib had come and intended to fight against Jerusalem, [3]he planned with his officers and his mighty men to stop the water of the springs that were outside the city; and they helped him. [4]A great many people were gathered, and they stopped all the springs and the brook that flowed through the land, saying, "Why should the kings of Assyria come

and find much water?" [5]He set to work resolutely and built up all the wall that was broken down and raised towers upon it,[2] and outside it he built another wall, and he strengthened the Millo in the city of David. He also made weapons and shields in abundance. [6]And he set combat commanders over the people and gathered them together to him in the square at the gate of the city and spoke encouragingly to them, saying, [7]"Be strong and courageous. Do not be afraid or dismayed before the king of Assyria and all the horde that is with him, for there are more with us than with him. [8]With him is an arm of flesh, but with us is the LORD our God, to help us and to fight our battles." And the people took confidence from the words of Hezekiah king of Judah.

⁹After this, Sennacherib king of Assyria, who was besieging Lachish with all his forces, sent his servants to Jerusalem to Hezekiah king of Judah and to all the people of Judah who were in Jerusalem, saying, ¹⁰"Thus says Sennacherib king of Assyria, 'On what are you trusting, that you endure the siege in Jerusalem? ¹¹Is not Hezekiah misleading you, that he may give you over to die by famine and by thirst, when he tells you, "The LORD our God will deliver us from the hand of the king of Assyria"? ¹²Has not this same Hezekiah taken away his high places and his altars and commanded Judah and Jerusalem, "Before one altar you shall worship, and on it you shall burn your sacrifices"? ¹³Do you not know what I and my fathers have done to all the peoples of other lands? Were the gods of the nations of those lands at all able to deliver their lands out of my hand? ¹⁴Who among all the gods of those nations that my fathers devoted to destruction was able to deliver his people from my hand, that your God should be able to deliver you from my hand? ¹⁵Now, therefore, do not let Hezekiah deceive you or mislead you in this fashion, and do not believe him, for no god of any nation or kingdom has been able to deliver his people from my hand or from the hand of my fathers. How much less will your God deliver you out of my hand!'"

¹⁶And his servants said still more against the LORD God and against his servant Hezekiah. ¹⁷And he wrote letters to cast contempt on the LORD, the God of Israel, and to speak against him, saying, "Like the gods of the nations of the lands who have not delivered their people from my hands, so the God of Hezekiah will not deliver his people from my hand." ¹⁸And they shouted it with a loud voice in the language of Judah to the people of Jerusalem who were on the wall, to frighten and terrify them, in order that they might take the city. ¹⁹And they spoke of the God of Jerusalem as they spoke of the gods of the peoples of the earth, which are the work of men's hands.

²⁰Then Hezekiah the king and Isaiah the prophet, the son of Amoz, prayed because of this and cried to heaven. ²¹And the LORD sent an angel, who cut off all the mighty warriors and commanders and officers in the camp of the king of Assyria. So he returned with shame of face to his own land. And when he came into the house of his god, some of his own sons struck him down there with the sword. ²²So the LORD saved Hezekiah and the inhabitants of Jerusalem from the hand of Sennacherib king of Assyria and from the hand of all his enemies, and he provided for them on every side. ²³And many brought gifts to the LORD to Jerusalem and precious things to Hezekiah king of Judah, so that he was exalted in the sight of all nations from that time onward.

²⁴In those days Hezekiah became sick and was at the point of death, and he prayed to the LORD, and he answered him and gave him a sign. ²⁵But Hezekiah did not make return according to the benefit done to him, for his heart was proud. Therefore wrath came upon him and Judah and Jerusalem. ²⁶But Hezekiah humbled himself for the pride of his heart, both he and the inhabitants of Jerusalem, so that the wrath of the LORD did not come upon them in the days of Hezekiah.

²⁷And Hezekiah had very great riches and honor, and he made for himself treasuries for silver, for gold, for precious stones, for spices, for shields, and for all kinds of costly vessels; ²⁸storehouses also for the yield of grain, wine, and oil; and stalls for all kinds of cattle, and sheepfolds. ²⁹He likewise provided cities for himself, and flocks and herds in abundance, for God had given him very great possessions. ³⁰This same Hezekiah closed the upper outlet of the waters of Gihon and directed them down to the west side of the city of David. And Hezekiah prospered in all his works. ³¹And so in the matter of the envoys of the princes of Babylon, who had been sent to him to inquire about the sign that had been done in the land, God left him to himself, in order to test him and to know all that was in his heart.

³²Now the rest of the acts of Hezekiah and his good deeds, behold, they are written in the vision of Isaiah the prophet the son of Amoz, in the Book of the Kings of Judah and Israel. ³³And Hezekiah slept with his fathers, and they buried him in the upper part of the tombs of the sons of David, and all Judah and the inhabitants of Jerusalem did him honor at his death. And Manasseh his son reigned in his place.

——————— *Revelation 18* ———————

After this I saw another angel coming down from heaven, having great authority, and the earth was made bright with his glory. [2]And he called out with a mighty voice,

"Fallen, fallen is Babylon the great!
    She has become a dwelling place for
        demons,
a haunt for every unclean spirit,
    a haunt for every unclean bird,
    a haunt for every unclean and
        detestable beast.
[3]   For all nations have drunk[1]
    the wine of the passion of her sexual
        immorality,
and the kings of the earth have
        committed immorality with her,
and the merchants of the earth have
        grown rich from the power of her
        luxurious living."

[4]Then I heard another voice from heaven saying,

"Come out of her, my people,
    lest you take part in her sins,
    lest you share in her plagues;
[5]   for her sins are heaped high as heaven,
    and God has remembered her
        iniquities.
[6]   Pay her back as she herself has paid back
        others,
    and repay her double for her deeds;
    mix a double portion for her in the
        cup she mixed.
[7]   As she glorified herself and lived in
        luxury,
    so give her a like measure of torment
        and mourning,
since in her heart she says,
    'I sit as a queen,
I am no widow,
    and mourning I shall never see.'
[8]   For this reason her plagues will come in
        a single day,
    death and mourning and famine,
and she will be burned up with fire;
    for mighty is the Lord God who has
        judged her."

[9]And the kings of the earth, who committed sexual immorality and lived in luxury with her, will weep and wail over her when they see the smoke of her burning. [10]They will stand far off, in fear of her torment, and say,

"Alas! Alas! You great city,
    you mighty city, Babylon!
For in a single hour your judgment has
        come."

[11]And the merchants of the earth weep and mourn for her, since no one buys their cargo anymore, [12]cargo of gold, silver, jewels, pearls, fine linen, purple cloth, silk, scarlet cloth, all kinds of scented wood, all kinds of articles of ivory, all kinds of articles of costly wood, bronze, iron and marble, [13]cinnamon, spice, incense, myrrh, frankincense, wine, oil, fine flour, wheat, cattle and sheep, horses and chariots, and slaves, that is, human souls.[2]

[14]   "The fruit for which your soul longed
        has gone from you,
    and all your delicacies and your
        splendors
    are lost to you,
    never to be found again!"

[15]The merchants of these wares, who gained wealth from her, will stand far off, in fear of her torment, weeping and mourning aloud,

[16]   "Alas, alas, for the great city
        that was clothed in fine linen,
            in purple and scarlet,
        adorned with gold,
            with jewels, and with pearls!
[17]   For in a single hour all this wealth has
            been laid waste."

And all shipmasters and seafaring men, sailors and all whose trade is on the sea, stood far off [18]and cried out as they saw the smoke of her burning,

"What city was like the great city?"

[19]And they threw dust on their heads as they wept and mourned, crying out,

"Alas, alas, for the great city
    where all who had ships at sea
    grew rich by her wealth!
For in a single hour she has been laid
        waste.
[20]   Rejoice over her, O heaven,
    and you saints and apostles and
        prophets,

<hr>

[1] Some manuscripts *fallen by* [2] Or *and slaves, and human lives*

for God has given judgment for you against her!"

²¹Then a mighty angel took up a stone like a great millstone and threw it into the sea, saying,

"So will Babylon the great city be thrown
down with violence,
and will be found no more;
²² and the sound of harpists and musicians,
of flute players and trumpeters,
will be heard in you no more,
and a craftsman of any craft
will be found in you no more,
and the sound of the mill
will be heard in you no more,
²³ and the light of a lamp
will shine in you no more,
and the voice of bridegroom and bride
will be heard in you no more,
for your merchants were the great ones
of the earth,
and all nations were deceived by your
sorcery.
²⁴ And in her was found the blood of
prophets and of saints,
and of all who have been slain on
earth."

Zechariah 14

Behold, a day is coming for the LORD, when the spoil taken from you will be divided in your midst. ²For I will gather all the nations against Jerusalem to battle, and the city shall be taken and the houses plundered and the women raped. Half of the city shall go out into exile, but the rest of the people shall not be cut off from the city. ³Then the LORD will go out and fight against those nations as when he fights on a day of battle. ⁴On that day his feet shall stand on the Mount of Olives that lies before Jerusalem on the east, and the Mount of Olives shall be split in two from east to west by a very wide valley, so that one half of the Mount shall move northward, and the other half southward. ⁵And you shall flee to the valley of my mountains, for the valley of the mountains shall reach to Azal. And you shall flee as you fled from the earthquake in the days of Uzziah king of Judah. Then the LORD my God will come, and all the holy ones with him.

⁶On that day there shall be no light, cold, or frost.[1] ⁷And there shall be a unique[2] day, which is known to the LORD, neither day nor night, but at evening time there shall be light.

⁸On that day living waters shall flow out from Jerusalem, half of them to the eastern sea[3] and half of them to the western sea.[4] It shall continue in summer as in winter.

⁹And the LORD will be king over all the earth. On that day the LORD will be one and his name one.

¹⁰The whole land shall be turned into a plain from Geba to Rimmon south of Jerusalem. But Jerusalem shall remain aloft on its site from the Gate of Benjamin to the place of the former gate, to the Corner Gate, and from the Tower of Hananel to the king's winepresses. ¹¹And it shall be inhabited, for there shall never again be a decree of utter destruction.[5] Jerusalem shall dwell in security.

¹²And this shall be the plague with which the LORD will strike all the peoples that wage war against Jerusalem: their flesh will rot while they are still standing on their feet, their eyes will rot in their sockets, and their tongues will rot in their mouths. ¹³And on that day a great panic from the LORD shall fall on them, so that each will seize the hand of another, and the hand of the one will be raised against the hand of the other. ¹⁴Even Judah will fight at Jerusalem. And the wealth of all the surrounding nations shall be collected, gold, silver, and garments in great abundance. ¹⁵And a plague like this plague shall fall on the horses, the mules, the camels, the donkeys, and whatever beasts may be in those camps.

¹⁶Then everyone who survives of all the nations that have come against Jerusalem shall go up year after year to worship the King, the LORD of hosts, and to keep the Feast of Booths. ¹⁷And if any of the families of the earth do not go up to Jerusalem to worship the King, the LORD of hosts, there will be no rain on them. ¹⁸And if the family of Egypt does not go up and present themselves, then on them there shall be no rain;[6] there shall be the plague with which the LORD afflicts the nations that do not go up to keep the Feast of Booths. ¹⁹This shall be the punishment to Egypt and the punishment to all the nations that do not go up to keep the Feast of Booths.

---

[1] Compare Septuagint, Syriac, Vulgate, Targum; the meaning of the Hebrew is uncertain [2] Hebrew *one* [3] That is, the Dead Sea [4] That is, the Mediterranean Sea [5] The Hebrew term rendered *decree of utter destruction* refers to things devoted (or set apart) to the Lord (or by the Lord) for destruction [6] Hebrew lacks *rain*

20And on that day there shall be inscribed on the bells of the horses, "Holy to the Lord." And the pots in the house of the Lord shall be as the bowls before the altar. **21**And every pot in Jerusalem and Judah shall be holy to the Lord of hosts, so that all who sacrifice may come and take of them and boil the meat of the sacrifice in them. And there shall no longer be a trader[1] in the house of the Lord of hosts on that day.

John 17

When Jesus had spoken these words, he lifted up his eyes to heaven, and said, "Father, the hour has come; glorify your Son that the Son may glorify you, **2**since you have given him authority over all flesh, to give eternal life to all whom you have given him. **3**And this is eternal life, that they know you the only true God, and Jesus Christ whom you have sent. **4**I glorified you on earth, having accomplished the work that you gave me to do. **5**And now, Father, glorify me in your own presence with the glory that I had with you before the world existed.

6"I have manifested your name to the people whom you gave me out of the world. Yours they were, and you gave them to me, and they have kept your word. **7**Now they know that everything that you have given me is from you. **8**For I have given them the words that you gave me, and they have received them and have come to know in truth that I came from you; and they have believed that you sent me. **9**I am praying for them. I am not praying for the world but for those whom you have given me, for they are yours. **10**All mine are yours, and yours are mine, and I am glorified in them. **11**And I am no longer in the world, but they are in the world, and I am coming to you. Holy Father, keep them

in your name, which you have given me, that they may be one, even as we are one. **12**While I was with them, I kept them in your name, which you have given me. I have guarded them, and not one of them has been lost except the son of destruction, that the Scripture might be fulfilled. **13**But now I am coming to you, and these things I speak in the world, that they may have my joy fulfilled in themselves. **14**I have given them your word, and the world has hated them because they are not of the world, just as I am not of the world. **15**I do not ask that you take them out of the world, but that you keep them from the evil one.[2] **16**They are not of the world, just as I am not of the world. **17**Sanctify them[3] in the truth; your word is truth. **18**As you sent me into the world, so I have sent them into the world. **19**And for their sake I consecrate myself,[4] that they also may be sanctified[5] in truth.

20"I do not ask for these only, but also for those who will believe in me through their word, **21**that they may all be one, just as you, Father, are in me, and I in you, that they also may be in us, so that the world may believe that you have sent me. **22**The glory that you have given me I have given to them, that they may be one even as we are one, **23**I in them and you in me, that they may become perfectly one, so that the world may know that you sent me and loved them even as you loved me. **24**Father, I desire that they also, whom you have given me, may be with me where I am, to see my glory that you have given me because you loved me before the foundation of the world. **25**O righteous Father, even though the world does not know you, I know you, and these know that you have sent me. **26**I made known to them your name, and I will continue to make it known, that the love with which you have loved me may be in them, and I in them."

---

[1] Or Canaanite [2] Or from evil [3] Greek Set them apart (for holy service to God) [4] Or I sanctify myself; or I set myself apart (for holy service to God) [5] Greek may be set apart (for holy service to God)

DECEMBER 28

2 Chronicles 33

Manasseh was twelve years old when he began to reign, and he reigned fifty-five years in Jerusalem. ²And he did what was evil in the sight of the LORD, according to the abominations of the nations whom the LORD drove out before the people of Israel. ³For he rebuilt the high places that his father Hezekiah had broken down, and he erected altars to the Baals, and made Asheroth, and worshiped all the host of heaven and served them. ⁴And he built altars in the house of the LORD, of which the LORD had said, "In Jerusalem shall my name be forever." ⁵And he built altars for all the host of heaven in the two courts of the house of the LORD. ⁶And he burned his sons as an offering in the Valley of the Son of Hinnom, and used fortune-telling and omens and sorcery, and dealt with mediums and with necromancers. He did much evil in the sight of the LORD, provoking him to anger. ⁷And the carved image of the idol that he had made he set in the house of God, of which God said to David and to Solomon his son, "In this house, and in Jerusalem, which I have chosen out of all the tribes of Israel, I will put my name forever, ⁸and I will no more remove the foot of Israel from the land that I appointed for your fathers, if only they will be careful to do all that I have commanded them, all the law, the statutes, and the rules given through Moses." ⁹Manasseh led Judah and the inhabitants of Jerusalem astray, to do more evil than the nations whom the LORD destroyed before the people of Israel.

¹⁰The LORD spoke to Manasseh and to his people, but they paid no attention. ¹¹Therefore the LORD brought upon them the commanders of the army of the king of Assyria, who captured Manasseh with hooks and bound him with chains of bronze and brought him to Babylon. ¹²And when he was in distress, he entreated the favor of the LORD his God and humbled himself greatly before the God of his fathers. ¹³He prayed to him, and God was moved by his entreaty and heard his plea and brought him

again to Jerusalem into his kingdom. Then Manasseh knew that the LORD was God.

¹⁴Afterward he built an outer wall for the city of David west of Gihon, in the valley, and for the entrance into the Fish Gate, and carried it around Ophel, and raised it to a very great height. He also put commanders of the army in all the fortified cities in Judah. ¹⁵And he took away the foreign gods and the idol from the house of the LORD, and all the altars that he had built on the mountain of the house of the LORD and in Jerusalem, and he threw them outside of the city. ¹⁶He also restored the altar of the LORD and offered on it sacrifices of peace offerings and of thanksgiving, and he commanded Judah to serve the LORD, the God of Israel. ¹⁷Nevertheless, the people still sacrificed at the high places, but only to the LORD their God.

¹⁸Now the rest of the acts of Manasseh, and his prayer to his God, and the words of the seers who spoke to him in the name of the LORD, the God of Israel, behold, they are in the Chronicles of the Kings of Israel. ¹⁹And his prayer, and how God was moved by his entreaty, and all his sin and his faithlessness, and the sites on which he built high places and set up the Asherim and the images, before he humbled himself, behold, they are written in the Chronicles of the Seers.¹ ²⁰So Manasseh slept with his fathers, and they buried him in his house, and Amon his son reigned in his place.

²¹Amon was twenty-two years old when he began to reign, and he reigned two years in Jerusalem. ²²And he did what was evil in the sight of the LORD, as Manasseh his father had done. Amon sacrificed to all the images that Manasseh his father had made, and served them. ²³And he did not humble himself before the LORD, as Manasseh his father had humbled himself, but this Amon incurred guilt more and more. ²⁴And his servants conspired against him and put him to death in his house. ²⁵But the

¹ One Hebrew manuscript, Septuagint; most Hebrew manuscripts *of Hozai*

people of the land struck down all those who had conspired against King Amon. And the people of the land made Josiah his son king in his place.

─────── **Revelation 19** ───────

After this I heard what seemed to be the loud voice of a great multitude in heaven, crying out,

> "Hallelujah!
> Salvation and glory and power belong to our God,
> 2　　for his judgments are true and just;
> for he has judged the great prostitute
> who corrupted the earth with her immorality,
> and has avenged on her the blood of his servants."[1]

[3] Once more they cried out,

> "Hallelujah!
> The smoke from her goes up forever and ever."

[4] And the twenty-four elders and the four living creatures fell down and worshiped God who was seated on the throne, saying, "Amen. Hallelujah!" [5] And from the throne came a voice saying,

> "Praise our God,
> all you his servants,
> you who fear him,
> small and great."

[6] Then I heard what seemed to be the voice of a great multitude, like the roar of many waters and like the sound of mighty peals of thunder, crying out,

> "Hallelujah!
> For the Lord our God
> the Almighty reigns.
> 7　Let us rejoice and exult
> and give him the glory,
> for the marriage of the Lamb has come,
> and his Bride has made herself ready;
> 8　it was granted her to clothe herself
> with fine linen, bright and pure"—

for the fine linen is the righteous deeds of the saints.

[9] And the angel said[2] to me, "Write this: Blessed are those who are invited to the marriage supper of the Lamb." And he said to me, "These are the true words of God." [10] Then I fell down at his feet to worship him, but he said to me, "You must not do that! I am a fellow servant[3] with you and your brothers who hold to the testimony of Jesus. Worship God." For the testimony of Jesus is the spirit of prophecy.

[11] Then I saw heaven opened, and behold, a white horse! The one sitting on it is called Faithful and True, and in righteousness he judges and makes war. [12] His eyes are like a flame of fire, and on his head are many diadems, and he has a name written that no one knows but himself. [13] He is clothed in a robe dipped in[4] blood, and the name by which he is called is The Word of God. [14] And the armies of heaven, arrayed in fine linen, white and pure, were following him on white horses. [15] From his mouth comes a sharp sword with which to strike down the nations, and he will rule them with a rod of iron. He will tread the winepress of the fury of the wrath of God the Almighty. [16] On his robe and on his thigh he has a name written, King of kings and Lord of lords.

[17] Then I saw an angel standing in the sun, and with a loud voice he called to all the birds that fly directly overhead, "Come, gather for the great supper of God, [18] to eat the flesh of kings, the flesh of captains, the flesh of mighty men, the flesh of horses and their riders, and the flesh of all men, both free and slave,[5] both small and great." [19] And I saw the beast and the kings of the earth with their armies gathered to make war against him who was sitting on the horse and against his army. [20] And the beast was captured, and with it the false prophet who in its presence[6] had done the signs by which he deceived those who had received the mark of the beast and those who worshiped its image. These two were thrown alive into the lake of fire that burns with sulfur. [21] And the rest were slain by the sword that came from the mouth of him who was sitting on the horse, and all the birds were gorged with their flesh.

─────── **Malachi 1** ───────

The oracle of the word of the Lord to Israel by Malachi.[7]

[2] "I have loved you," says the Lord. But you

---

[1] Greek bondservants; also verse 5　[2] Greek he said　[3] Greek fellow bondservant　[4] Some manuscripts sprinkled with　[5] Greek bondservant　[6] Or on its behalf　[7] Malachi means my messenger

say, "How have you loved us?" "Is not Esau Jacob's brother?" declares the LORD. "Yet I have loved Jacob ³but Esau I have hated. I have laid waste his hill country and left his heritage to jackals of the desert." ⁴If Edom says, "We are shattered but we will rebuild the ruins," the LORD of hosts says, "They may build, but I will tear down, and they will be called 'the wicked country,' and 'the people with whom the LORD is angry forever.'" ⁵Your own eyes shall see this, and you shall say, "Great is the LORD beyond the border of Israel!"

⁶"A son honors his father, and a servant his master. If then I am a father, where is my honor? And if I am a master, where is my fear? says the LORD of hosts to you, O priests, who despise my name. But you say, 'How have we despised your name?' ⁷By offering polluted food upon my altar. But you say, 'How have we polluted you?' By saying that the LORD's table may be despised. ⁸When you offer blind animals in sacrifice, is that not evil? And when you offer those that are lame or sick, is that not evil? Present that to your governor; will he accept you or show you favor? says the LORD of hosts. ⁹And now entreat the favor of God, that he may be gracious to us. With such a gift from your hand, will he show favor to any of you? says the LORD of hosts. ¹⁰Oh that there were one among you who would shut the doors, that you might not kindle fire on my altar in vain! I have no pleasure in you, says the LORD of hosts, and I will not accept an offering from your hand. ¹¹For from the rising of the sun to its setting my name will be¹ great among the nations, and in every place incense will be offered to my name, and a pure offering. For my name will be great among the nations, says the LORD of hosts. ¹²But you profane it when you say that the Lord's table is polluted, and its fruit, that is, its food may be despised. ¹³But you say, 'What a weariness this is,' and you snort at it, says the LORD of hosts. You bring what has been taken by violence or is lame or sick, and this you bring as your offering! Shall I accept that from your hand? says the LORD. ¹⁴Cursed be the cheat who has a male in his flock, and vows it, and yet sacrifices to the Lord what is blemished. For I am a great King, says the LORD of hosts, and my name will be feared among the nations.

John 18

When Jesus had spoken these words, he went out with his disciples across the brook Kidron, where there was a garden, which he and his disciples entered. ²Now Judas, who betrayed him, also knew the place, for Jesus often met there with his disciples. ³So Judas, having procured a band of soldiers and some officers from the chief priests and the Pharisees, went there with lanterns and torches and weapons. ⁴Then Jesus, knowing all that would happen to him, came forward and said to them, "Whom do you seek?" ⁵They answered him, "Jesus of Nazareth." Jesus said to them, "I am he."² Judas, who betrayed him, was standing with them. ⁶When Jesus³ said to them, "I am he," they drew back and fell to the ground. ⁷So he asked them again, "Whom do you seek?" And they said, "Jesus of Nazareth." ⁸Jesus answered, "I told you that I am he. So, if you seek me, let these men go." ⁹This was to fulfill the word that he had spoken: "Of those whom you gave me I have lost not one." ¹⁰Then Simon Peter, having a sword, drew it and struck the high priest's servant⁴ and cut off his right ear. (The servant's name was Malchus.) ¹¹So Jesus said to Peter, "Put your sword into its sheath; shall I not drink the cup that the Father has given me?"

¹²So the band of soldiers and their captain and the officers of the Jews⁵ arrested Jesus and bound him. ¹³First they led him to Annas, for he was the father-in-law of Caiaphas, who was high priest that year. ¹⁴It was Caiaphas who had advised the Jews that it would be expedient that one man should die for the people.

¹⁵Simon Peter followed Jesus, and so did another disciple. Since that disciple was known to the high priest, he entered with Jesus into the courtyard of the high priest, ¹⁶but Peter stood outside at the door. So the other disciple, who was known to the high priest, went out and spoke to the servant girl who kept watch at the door, and brought Peter in. ¹⁷The servant girl at the door said to Peter, "You also are not one of this man's disciples, are you?" He said, "I am not." ¹⁸Now the servants⁶ and officers had made a charcoal fire, because it was cold, and they were standing and warming themselves. Peter also was with them, standing and warming himself.

¹ Or is (three times in verse 11; also verse 14) ² Greek *I am*; also verses 6, 8 ³ Greek *he* ⁴ Greek *bondservant*; twice in this verse ⁵ Greek *Ioudaioi* probably refers here to Jewish religious leaders, and others under their influence, in that time; also verses 14, 31, 36, 38 ⁶ Greek *bondservants*; also verse 26

[19] The high priest then questioned Jesus about his disciples and his teaching. [20] Jesus answered him, "I have spoken openly to the world. I have always taught in synagogues and in the temple, where all Jews come together. I have said nothing in secret. [21] Why do you ask me? Ask those who have heard me what I said to them; they know what I said." [22] When he had said these things, one of the officers standing by struck Jesus with his hand, saying, "Is that how you answer the high priest?" [23] Jesus answered him, "If what I said is wrong, bear witness about the wrong; but if what I said is right, why do you strike me?" [24] Annas then sent him bound to Caiaphas the high priest.

[25] Now Simon Peter was standing and warming himself. So they said to him, "You also are not one of his disciples, are you?" He denied it and said, "I am not." [26] One of the servants of the high priest, a relative of the man whose ear Peter had cut off, asked, "Did I not see you in the garden with him?" [27] Peter again denied it, and at once a rooster crowed.

[28] Then they led Jesus from the house of Caiaphas to the governor's headquarters.[1] It was early morning. They themselves did not enter the governor's headquarters, so that they would not be defiled, but could eat the Passover. [29] So Pilate went outside to them and said, "What accusation do you bring against this man?" [30] They answered him, "If this man were not doing evil, we would not have delivered him over to you." [31] Pilate said to them, "Take him yourselves and judge him by your own law." The Jews said to him, "It is not lawful for us to put anyone to death." [32] This was to fulfill the word that Jesus had spoken to show by what kind of death he was going to die.

[33] So Pilate entered his headquarters again and called Jesus and said to him, "Are you the King of the Jews?" [34] Jesus answered, "Do you say this of your own accord, or did others say it to you about me?" [35] Pilate answered, "Am I a Jew? Your own nation and the chief priests have delivered you over to me. What have you done?" [36] Jesus answered, "My kingdom is not of this world. If my kingdom were of this world, my servants would have been fighting, that I might not be delivered over to the Jews. But my kingdom is not from the world." [37] Then Pilate said to him, "So you are a king?" Jesus answered, "You say that I am a king. For this purpose I was born and for this purpose I have come into the world—to bear witness to the truth. Everyone who is of the truth listens to my voice." [38] Pilate said to him, "What is truth?"

After he had said this, he went back outside to the Jews and told them, "I find no guilt in him. [39] But you have a custom that I should release one man for you at the Passover. So do you want me to release to you the King of the Jews?" [40] They cried out again, "Not this man, but Barabbas!" Now Barabbas was a robber.[2]

DECEMBER 29

2 Chronicles 34

Josiah was eight years old when he began to reign, and he reigned thirty-one years in Jerusalem. [2] And he did what was right in the eyes of the LORD, and walked in the ways of David his father; and he did not turn aside to the right hand or to the left. [3] For in the eighth year of his reign, while he was yet a boy, he began to seek the God of David his father, and in the twelfth year he began to purge Judah and Jerusalem of the high places, the Asherim, and the carved and the metal images. [4] And they chopped down the altars of the Baals in his presence, and he cut down the incense altars that stood above them. And he broke in pieces the Asherim and the carved and the metal images, and he made dust of them and scattered it over the graves of those who had sacrificed to them. [5] He also burned the bones of

[1] Greek the praetorium [2] Or an insurrectionist

the priests on their altars and cleansed Judah and Jerusalem. [6]And in the cities of Manasseh, Ephraim, and Simeon, and as far as Naphtali, in their ruins[1] all around, [7]he broke down the altars and beat the Asherim and the images into powder and cut down all the incense altars throughout all the land of Israel. Then he returned to Jerusalem.

[8]Now in the eighteenth year of his reign, when he had cleansed the land and the house, he sent Shaphan the son of Azaliah, and Maaseiah the governor of the city, and Joah the son of Joahaz, the recorder, to repair the house of the LORD his God. [9]They came to Hilkiah the high priest and gave him the money that had been brought into the house of God, which the Levites, the keepers of the threshold, had collected from Manasseh and Ephraim and from all the remnant of Israel and from all Judah and Benjamin and from the inhabitants of Jerusalem. [10]And they gave it to the workmen who were working in the house of the LORD. And the workmen who were working in the house of the LORD gave it for repairing and restoring the house. [11]They gave it to the carpenters and the builders to buy quarried stone, and timber for binders and beams for the buildings that the kings of Judah had let go to ruin. [12]And the men did the work faithfully. Over them were set Jahath and Obadiah the Levites, of the sons of Merari, and Zechariah and Meshullam, of the sons of the Kohathites, to have oversight. The Levites, all who were skillful with instruments of music, [13]were over the burden-bearers and directed all who did work in every kind of service, and some of the Levites were scribes and officials and gatekeepers.

[14]While they were bringing out the money that had been brought into the house of the LORD, Hilkiah the priest found the Book of the Law of the LORD given through Moses. [15]Then Hilkiah answered and said to Shaphan the secretary, "I have found the Book of the Law in the house of the LORD." And Hilkiah gave the book to Shaphan. [16]Shaphan brought the book to the king, and further reported to the king, "All that was committed to your servants they are doing. [17]They have emptied out the money that was found in the house of the LORD and have given it into the hand of the overseers and the workmen." [18]Then Shaphan the secretary told the king, "Hilkiah the priest has given me a book." And Shaphan read from it before the king.

[19]And when the king heard the words of the Law, he tore his clothes. [20]And the king commanded Hilkiah, Ahikam the son of Shaphan, Abdon the son of Micah, Shaphan the secretary, and Asaiah the king's servant, saying, [21]"Go, inquire of the LORD for me and for those who are left in Israel and in Judah, concerning the words of the book that has been found. For great is the wrath of the LORD that is poured out on us, because our fathers have not kept the word of the LORD, to do according to all that is written in this book."

[22]So Hilkiah and those whom the king had sent[2] went to Huldah the prophetess, the wife of Shallum the son of Tokhath, son of Hasrah, keeper of the wardrobe (now she lived in Jerusalem in the Second Quarter) and spoke to her to that effect. [23]And she said to them, "Thus says the LORD, the God of Israel: 'Tell the man who sent you to me, [24]Thus says the LORD, Behold, I will bring disaster upon this place and upon its inhabitants, all the curses that are written in the book that was read before the king of Judah. [25]Because they have forsaken me and have made offerings to other gods, that they might provoke me to anger with all the works of their hands, therefore my wrath will be poured out on this place and will not be quenched. [26]But to the king of Judah, who sent you to inquire of the LORD, thus shall you say to him, Thus says the LORD, the God of Israel: Regarding the words that you have heard, [27]because your heart was tender and you humbled yourself before God when you heard his words against this place and its inhabitants, and you have humbled yourself before me and have torn your clothes and wept before me, I also have heard you, declares the LORD. [28]Behold, I will gather you to your fathers, and you shall be gathered to your grave in peace, and your eyes shall not see all the disaster that I will bring upon this place and its inhabitants.'" And they brought back word to the king.

[29]Then the king sent and gathered together all the elders of Judah and Jerusalem. [30]And the king went up to the house of the LORD, with all the men of Judah and the inhabitants of Jerusalem and the priests and the Levites, all the people both great and small. And he read in their hearing all the words of the Book of

---

[1] The meaning of the Hebrew is uncertain [2] Syriac, Vulgate; Hebrew lacks *had sent*

the Covenant that had been found in the house of the Lord. [31] And the king stood in his place and made a covenant before the Lord, to walk after the Lord and to keep his commandments and his testimonies and his statutes, with all his heart and all his soul, to perform the words of the covenant that were written in this book. [32] Then he made all who were present in Jerusalem and in Benjamin join in it. And the inhabitants of Jerusalem did according to the covenant of God, the God of their fathers. [33] And Josiah took away all the abominations from all the territory that belonged to the people of Israel and made all who were present in Israel serve the Lord their God. All his days they did not turn away from following the Lord, the God of their fathers.

--------- Revelation 20 ---------

Then I saw an angel coming down from heaven, holding in his hand the key to the bottomless pit[1] and a great chain. [2] And he seized the dragon, that ancient serpent, who is the devil and Satan, and bound him for a thousand years, [3] and threw him into the pit, and shut it and sealed it over him, so that he might not deceive the nations any longer, until the thousand years were ended. After that he must be released for a little while.

[4] Then I saw thrones, and seated on them were those to whom the authority to judge was committed. Also I saw the souls of those who had been beheaded for the testimony of Jesus and for the word of God, and those who had not worshiped the beast or its image and had not received its mark on their foreheads or their hands. They came to life and reigned with Christ for a thousand years. [5] The rest of the dead did not come to life until the thousand years were ended. This is the first resurrection. [6] Blessed and holy is the one who shares in the first resurrection! Over such the second death has no power, but they will be priests of God and of Christ, and they will reign with him for a thousand years.

[7] And when the thousand years are ended, Satan will be released from his prison [8] and will come out to deceive the nations that are at the four corners of the earth, Gog and Magog, to gather them for battle; their number is like the sand of the sea. [9] And they marched up over the broad plain of the earth and surrounded the camp of the saints and the beloved city, but fire came down from heaven[2] and consumed them, [10] and the devil who had deceived them was thrown into the lake of fire and sulfur where the beast and the false prophet were, and they will be tormented day and night forever and ever.

[11] Then I saw a great white throne and him who was seated on it. From his presence earth and sky fled away, and no place was found for them. [12] And I saw the dead, great and small, standing before the throne, and books were opened. Then another book was opened, which is the book of life. And the dead were judged by what was written in the books, according to what they had done. [13] And the sea gave up the dead who were in it, Death and Hades gave up the dead who were in them, and they were judged, each one of them, according to what they had done. [14] Then Death and Hades were thrown into the lake of fire. This is the second death, the lake of fire. [15] And if anyone's name was not found written in the book of life, he was thrown into the lake of fire.

--------- Malachi 2 ---------

"And now, O priests, this command is for you. [2] If you will not listen, if you will not take it to heart to give honor to my name, says the Lord of hosts, then I will send the curse upon you and I will curse your blessings. Indeed, I have already cursed them, because you do not lay it to heart. [3] Behold, I will rebuke your offspring,[3] and spread dung on your faces, the dung of your offerings, and you shall be taken away with it.[4] [4] So shall you know that I have sent this command to you, that my covenant with Levi may stand, says the Lord of hosts. [5] My covenant with him was one of life and peace, and I gave them to him. It was a covenant of fear, and he feared me. He stood in awe of my name. [6] True instruction[5] was in his mouth, and no wrong was found on his lips. He walked with me in peace and uprightness, and he turned many from iniquity. [7] For the lips of a priest should guard knowledge, and people[6] should seek instruction from his mouth, for he is the messenger of the Lord of hosts. [8] But you have turned aside from the way. You have caused many to stumble by your instruction. You have corrupted the covenant of Levi, says

[1] Greek the abyss; also verse 3 [2] Some manuscripts from God, out of heaven, or out of heaven from God [3] Hebrew seed [4] Or to it [5] Or law; also verses 7, 8, 9 [6] Hebrew they

the LORD of hosts, [9]and so I make you despised and abased before all the people, inasmuch as you do not keep my ways but show partiality in your instruction."

[10]Have we not all one Father? Has not one God created us? Why then are we faithless to one another, profaning the covenant of our fathers? [11]Judah has been faithless, and abomination has been committed in Israel and in Jerusalem. For Judah has profaned the sanctuary of the LORD, which he loves, and has married the daughter of a foreign god. [12]May the LORD cut off from the tents of Jacob any descendant[1] of the man who does this, who brings an offering to the LORD of hosts!

[13]And this second thing you do. You cover the LORD's altar with tears, with weeping and groaning because he no longer regards the offering or accepts it with favor from your hand. [14]But you say, "Why does he not?" Because the LORD was witness between you and the wife of your youth, to whom you have been faithless, though she is your companion and your wife by covenant. [15]Did he not make them one, with a portion of the Spirit in their union?[2] And what was the one God[3] seeking?[4] Godly offspring. So guard yourselves[5] in your spirit, and let none of you be faithless to the wife of your youth. [16]"For the man who does not love his wife but divorces her,[6] says the LORD, the God of Israel, covers[7] his garment with violence, says the LORD of hosts. So guard yourselves in your spirit, and do not be faithless."

[17]You have wearied the LORD with your words. But you say, "How have we wearied him?" By saying, "Everyone who does evil is good in the sight of the LORD, and he delights in them." Or by asking, "Where is the God of justice?"

John 19

Then Pilate took Jesus and flogged him. [2]And the soldiers twisted together a crown of thorns and put it on his head and arrayed him in a purple robe. [3]They came up to him, saying, "Hail, King of the Jews!" and struck him with their hands. [4]Pilate went out again and said to them, "See, I am bringing him out to you that you may know that I find no guilt in

him." [5]So Jesus came out, wearing the crown of thorns and the purple robe. Pilate said to them, "Behold the man!" [6]When the chief priests and the officers saw him, they cried out, "Crucify him, crucify him!" Pilate said to them, "Take him yourselves and crucify him, for I find no guilt in him." [7]The Jews[8] answered him, "We have a law, and according to that law he ought to die because he has made himself the Son of God." [8]When Pilate heard this statement, he was even more afraid. [9]He entered his headquarters again and said to Jesus, "Where are you from?" But Jesus gave him no answer. [10]So Pilate said to him, "You will not speak to me? Do you not know that I have authority to release you and authority to crucify you?" [11]Jesus answered him, "You would have no authority over me at all unless it had been given you from above. Therefore he who delivered me over to you has the greater sin."

[12]From then on Pilate sought to release him, but the Jews cried out, "If you release this man, you are not Caesar's friend. Everyone who makes himself a king opposes Caesar." [13]So when Pilate heard these words, he brought Jesus out and sat down on the judgment seat at a place called The Stone Pavement, and in Aramaic[9] Gabbatha. [14]Now it was the day of Preparation of the Passover. It was about the sixth hour.[10] He said to the Jews, "Behold your King!" [15]They cried out, "Away with him, away with him, crucify him!" Pilate said to them, "Shall I crucify your King?" The chief priests answered, "We have no king but Caesar." [16]So he delivered him over to them to be crucified.

So they took Jesus, [17]and he went out, bearing his own cross, to the place called The Place of a Skull, which in Aramaic is called Golgotha. [18]There they crucified him, and with him two others, one on either side, and Jesus between them. [19]Pilate also wrote an inscription and put it on the cross. It read, "Jesus of Nazareth, the King of the Jews." [20]Many of the Jews read this inscription, for the place where Jesus was crucified was near the city, and it was written in Aramaic, in Latin, and in Greek. [21]So the chief priests of the Jews said to Pilate, "Do not write, 'The King of the Jews,' but rather, 'This man said, I am King of the Jews.'" [22]Pilate answered, "What I have written I have written."

---

[1] Hebrew *any who wakes and answers* [2] Hebrew *in it* [3] Hebrew *the one* [4] Or *And not one has done this who has a portion of the Spirit. And what was that one seeking?* [5] Or *So take care;* also verse 16 [6] Hebrew *who hates and divorces* [7] Probable meaning (compare Septuagint and Deuteronomy 24:1–4); or *"The LORD, the God of Israel, says that he hates divorce, and him who covers* [8] Greek *Ioudaioi* probably refers here to Jewish religious leaders, and others under their influence, in that time; also verses 12, 14, 31, 38 [9] Or *Hebrew;* also verses 17, 20 [10] That is, about noon

²³ When the soldiers had crucified Jesus, they took his garments and divided them into four parts, one part for each soldier; also his tunic.¹ But the tunic was seamless, woven in one piece from top to bottom, ²⁴ so they said to one another, "Let us not tear it, but cast lots for it to see whose it shall be." This was to fulfill the Scripture which says,

> "They divided my garments among them,
> and for my clothing they cast lots."

So the soldiers did these things, ²⁵ but standing by the cross of Jesus were his mother and his mother's sister, Mary the wife of Clopas, and Mary Magdalene. ²⁶ When Jesus saw his mother and the disciple whom he loved standing nearby, he said to his mother, "Woman, behold, your son!" ²⁷ Then he said to the disciple, "Behold, your mother!" And from that hour the disciple took her to his own home.

²⁸ After this, Jesus, knowing that all was now finished, said (to fulfill the Scripture), "I thirst." ²⁹ A jar full of sour wine stood there, so they put a sponge full of the sour wine on a hyssop branch and held it to his mouth. ³⁰ When Jesus had received the sour wine, he said, "It is finished," and he bowed his head and gave up his spirit.

³¹ Since it was the day of Preparation, and so that the bodies would not remain on the cross on the Sabbath (for that Sabbath was a high day), the Jews asked Pilate that their legs might be broken and that they might be taken away. ³² So the soldiers came and broke the legs of the first, and of the other who had been crucified with him. ³³ But when they came to Jesus and saw that he was already dead, they did not break his legs. ³⁴ But one of the soldiers pierced his side with a spear, and at once there came out blood and water. ³⁵ He who saw it has borne witness—his testimony is true, and he knows that he is telling the truth—that you also may believe. ³⁶ For these things took place that the Scripture might be fulfilled: "Not one of his bones will be broken." ³⁷ And again another Scripture says, "They will look on him whom they have pierced."

³⁸ After these things Joseph of Arimathea, who was a disciple of Jesus, but secretly for fear of the Jews, asked Pilate that he might take away the body of Jesus, and Pilate gave him permission. So he came and took away his body. ³⁹ Nicodemus also, who earlier had come to Jesus² by night, came bringing a mixture of myrrh and aloes, about seventy-five pounds³ in weight. ⁴⁰ So they took the body of Jesus and bound it in linen cloths with the spices, as is the burial custom of the Jews. ⁴¹ Now in the place where he was crucified there was a garden, and in the garden a new tomb in which no one had yet been laid. ⁴² So because of the Jewish day of Preparation, since the tomb was close at hand, they laid Jesus there.

DECEMBER 30

2 Chronicles 35

Josiah kept a Passover to the LORD in Jerusalem. And they slaughtered the Passover lamb on the fourteenth day of the first month. ²He appointed the priests to their offices and encouraged them in the service of the house of the LORD. ³And he said to the Levites who taught all Israel and who were holy to the LORD, "Put the holy ark in the house that Solomon the son of David, king of Israel, built. You need not carry it on your shoulders. Now serve the LORD your God and his people Israel. ⁴Prepare yourselves according to your fathers' houses by your divisions, as prescribed in the writing of David king of Israel and the document of Solomon his son. ⁵And stand in the Holy Place according to the groupings of the fathers' houses of your brothers the lay people, and according to the division of the Levites by fathers' household. ⁶And slaughter the Passover lamb, and consecrate yourselves, and prepare for your

¹ Greek chiton, a long garment worn under the cloak next to the skin ² Greek him ³ Greek one hundred litras; a litra (or Roman pound) was equal to about 11 1/2 ounces or 327 grams

brothers, to do according to the word of the LORD by Moses."

[7] Then Josiah contributed to the lay people, as Passover offerings for all who were present, lambs and young goats from the flock to the number of 30,000, and 3,000 bulls; these were from the king's possessions. [8] And his officials contributed willingly to the people, to the priests, and to the Levites. Hilkiah, Zechariah, and Jehiel, the chief officers of the house of God, gave to the priests for the Passover offerings 2,600 Passover lambs and 300 bulls. [9] Conaniah also, and Shemaiah and Nethanel his brothers, and Hashabiah and Jeiel and Jozabad, the chiefs of the Levites, gave to the Levites for the Passover offerings 5,000 lambs and young goats and 500 bulls.

[10] When the service had been prepared for, the priests stood in their place, and the Levites in their divisions according to the king's command. [11] And they slaughtered the Passover lamb, and the priests threw the blood that they received from them while the Levites flayed the sacrifices. [12] And they set aside the burnt offerings that they might distribute them according to the groupings of the fathers' houses of the lay people, to offer to the LORD, as it is written in the Book of Moses. And so they did with the bulls. [13] And they roasted the Passover lamb with fire according to the rule; and they boiled the holy offerings in pots, in cauldrons, and in pans, and carried them quickly to all the lay people. [14] And afterward they prepared for themselves and for the priests, because the priests, the sons of Aaron, were offering the burnt offerings and the fat parts until night; so the Levites prepared for themselves and for the priests, the sons of Aaron. [15] The singers, the sons of Asaph, were in their place according to the command of David, and Asaph, and Heman, and Jeduthun the king's seer; and the gatekeepers were at each gate. They did not need to depart from their service, for their brothers the Levites prepared for them.

[16] So all the service of the LORD was prepared that day, to keep the Passover and to offer burnt offerings on the altar of the LORD, according to the command of King Josiah. [17] And the people of Israel who were present kept the Passover at that time, and the Feast of Unleavened Bread seven days. [18] No Passover like it had been kept in Israel since the days of Samuel the prophet.

None of the kings of Israel had kept such a Passover as was kept by Josiah, and the priests and the Levites, and all Judah and Israel who were present, and the inhabitants of Jerusalem. [19] In the eighteenth year of the reign of Josiah this Passover was kept.

[20] After all this, when Josiah had prepared the temple, Neco king of Egypt went up to fight at Carchemish on the Euphrates, and Josiah went out to meet him. [21] But he sent envoys to him, saying, "What have we to do with each other, king of Judah? I am not coming against you this day, but against the house with which I am at war. And God has commanded me to hurry. Cease opposing God, who is with me, lest he destroy you." [22] Nevertheless, Josiah did not turn away from him, but disguised himself in order to fight with him. He did not listen to the words of Neco from the mouth of God, but came to fight in the plain of Megiddo. [23] And the archers shot King Josiah. And the king said to his servants, "Take me away, for I am badly wounded." [24] So his servants took him out of the chariot and carried him in his second chariot and brought him to Jerusalem. And he died and was buried in the tombs of his fathers. All Judah and Jerusalem mourned for Josiah. [25] Jeremiah also uttered a lament for Josiah; and all the singing men and singing women have spoken of Josiah in their laments to this day. They made these a rule in Israel; behold, they are written in the Laments. [26] Now the rest of the acts of Josiah, and his good deeds according to what is written in the Law of the LORD, [27] and his acts, first and last, behold, they are written in the Book of the Kings of Israel and Judah.

Revelation 21

Then I saw a new heaven and a new earth, for the first heaven and the first earth had passed away, and the sea was no more. [2] And I saw the holy city, new Jerusalem, coming down out of heaven from God, prepared as a bride adorned for her husband. [3] And I heard a loud voice from the throne saying, "Behold, the dwelling place[1] of God is with man. He will dwell with them, and they will be his people,[2] and God himself will be with them as their God.[3] [4] He will wipe away every tear from their eyes, and death shall be no more, neither shall there be mourning, nor crying,

---

[1] Or tabernacle [2] Some manuscripts peoples [3] Some manuscripts omit as their God

nor pain anymore, for the former things have passed away."

⁵And he who was seated on the throne said, "Behold, I am making all things new." Also he said, "Write this down, for these words are trustworthy and true." ⁶And he said to me, "It is done! I am the Alpha and the Omega, the beginning and the end. To the thirsty I will give from the spring of the water of life without payment. ⁷The one who conquers will have this heritage, and I will be his God and he will be my son. ⁸But as for the cowardly, the faithless, the detestable, as for murderers, the sexually immoral, sorcerers, idolaters, and all liars, their portion will be in the lake that burns with fire and sulfur, which is the second death."

⁹Then came one of the seven angels who had the seven bowls full of the seven last plagues and spoke to me, saying, "Come, I will show you the Bride, the wife of the Lamb." ¹⁰And he carried me away in the Spirit to a great, high mountain, and showed me the holy city Jerusalem coming down out of heaven from God, ¹¹having the glory of God, its radiance like a most rare jewel, like a jasper, clear as crystal. ¹²It had a great, high wall, with twelve gates, and at the gates twelve angels, and on the gates the names of the twelve tribes of the sons of Israel were inscribed— ¹³on the east three gates, on the north three gates, on the south three gates, and on the west three gates. ¹⁴And the wall of the city had twelve foundations, and on them were the twelve names of the twelve apostles of the Lamb.

¹⁵And the one who spoke with me had a measuring rod of gold to measure the city and its gates and walls. ¹⁶The city lies foursquare, its length the same as its width. And he measured the city with his rod, 12,000 stadia.¹ Its length and width and height are equal. ¹⁷He also measured its wall, 144 cubits² by human measurement, which is also an angel's measurement. ¹⁸The wall was built of jasper, while the city was pure gold, like clear glass. ¹⁹The foundations of the wall of the city were adorned with every kind of jewel. The first was jasper, the second sapphire, the third agate, the fourth emerald, ²⁰the fifth onyx, the sixth carnelian, the seventh chrysolite, the eighth beryl, the ninth topaz, the tenth chrysoprase, the eleventh jacinth, the twelfth amethyst. ²¹And the twelve gates were twelve pearls, each of the gates made of a single pearl, and the street of the city was pure gold, like transparent glass.

²²And I saw no temple in the city, for its temple is the Lord God the Almighty and the Lamb. ²³And the city has no need of sun or moon to shine on it, for the glory of God gives it light, and its lamp is the Lamb. ²⁴By its light will the nations walk, and the kings of the earth will bring their glory into it, ²⁵and its gates will never be shut by day—and there will be no night there. ²⁶They will bring into it the glory and the honor of the nations. ²⁷But nothing unclean will ever enter it, nor anyone who does what is detestable or false, but only those who are written in the Lamb's book of life.

───────── *Malachi 3* ─────────

"Behold, I send my messenger, and he will prepare the way before me. And the Lord whom you seek will suddenly come to his temple; and the messenger of the covenant in whom you delight, behold, he is coming, says the LORD of hosts. ²But who can endure the day of his coming, and who can stand when he appears? For he is like a refiner's fire and like fullers' soap. ³He will sit as a refiner and purifier of silver, and he will purify the sons of Levi and refine them like gold and silver, and they will bring offerings in righteousness to the LORD.³ ⁴Then the offering of Judah and Jerusalem will be pleasing to the LORD as in the days of old and as in former years.

⁵"Then I will draw near to you for judgment. I will be a swift witness against the sorcerers, against the adulterers, against those who swear falsely, against those who oppress the hired worker in his wages, the widow and the fatherless, against those who thrust aside the sojourner, and do not fear me, says the LORD of hosts.

⁶"For I the LORD do not change; therefore you, O children of Jacob, are not consumed. ⁷From the days of your fathers you have turned aside from my statutes and have not kept them. Return to me, and I will return to you, says the LORD of hosts. But you say, 'How shall we return?' ⁸Will man rob God? Yet you are robbing me. But you say, 'How have we robbed you?' In your tithes and contributions. ⁹You are cursed with a curse, for you are robbing me, the whole nation of you. ¹⁰Bring the

¹ About 1,380 miles; a *stadion* was about 607 feet or 185 meters ² A *cubit* was about 18 inches or 45 centimeters ³ Or *and they will belong to the LORD, bringers of an offering in righteousness*

full tithe into the storehouse, that there may be food in my house. And thereby put me to the test, says the LORD of hosts, if I will not open the windows of heaven for you and pour down for you a blessing until there is no more need. [11] I will rebuke the devourer[1] for you, so that it will not destroy the fruits of your soil, and your vine in the field shall not fail to bear, says the LORD of hosts. [12] Then all nations will call you blessed, for you will be a land of delight, says the LORD of hosts.

[13] "Your words have been hard against me, says the LORD. But you say, 'How have we spoken against you?' [14] You have said, 'It is vain to serve God. What is the profit of our keeping his charge or of walking as in mourning before the LORD of hosts? [15] And now we call the arrogant blessed. Evildoers not only prosper but they put God to the test and they escape.'"

[16] Then those who feared the LORD spoke with one another. The LORD paid attention and heard them, and a book of remembrance was written before him of those who feared the LORD and esteemed his name. [17] "They shall be mine, says the LORD of hosts, in the day when I make up my treasured possession, and I will spare them as a man spares his son who serves him. [18] Then once more you shall see the distinction between the righteous and the wicked, between one who serves God and one who does not serve him.

John 20

Now on the first day of the week Mary Magdalene came to the tomb early, while it was still dark, and saw that the stone had been taken away from the tomb. [2] So she ran and went to Simon Peter and the other disciple, the one whom Jesus loved, and said to them, "They have taken the Lord out of the tomb, and we do not know where they have laid him." [3] So Peter went out with the other disciple, and they were going toward the tomb. [4] Both of them were running together, but the other disciple outran Peter and reached the tomb first. [5] And stooping to look in, he saw the linen cloths lying there, but he did not go in. [6] Then Simon Peter came, following him, and went into the tomb. He saw the linen cloths lying there, [7] and the face cloth, which had been on Jesus'[2] head, not lying with the linen cloths but folded up in

a place by itself. [8] Then the other disciple, who had reached the tomb first, also went in, and he saw and believed; [9] for as yet they did not understand the Scripture, that he must rise from the dead. [10] Then the disciples went back to their homes.

[11] But Mary stood weeping outside the tomb, and as she wept she stooped to look into the tomb. [12] And she saw two angels in white, sitting where the body of Jesus had lain, one at the head and one at the feet. [13] They said to her, "Woman, why are you weeping?" She said to them, "They have taken away my Lord, and I do not know where they have laid him." [14] Having said this, she turned around and saw Jesus standing, but she did not know that it was Jesus. [15] Jesus said to her, "Woman, why are you weeping? Whom are you seeking?" Supposing him to be the gardener, she said to him, "Sir, if you have carried him away, tell me where you have laid him, and I will take him away." [16] Jesus said to her, "Mary." She turned and said to him in Aramaic,[3] "Rabboni!" (which means Teacher). [17] Jesus said to her, "Do not cling to me, for I have not yet ascended to the Father; but go to my brothers and say to them, 'I am ascending to my Father and your Father, to my God and your God.'" [18] Mary Magdalene went and announced to the disciples, "I have seen the Lord"—and that he had said these things to her.

[19] On the evening of that day, the first day of the week, the doors being locked where the disciples were for fear of the Jews,[4] Jesus came and stood among them and said to them, "Peace be with you." [20] When he had said this, he showed them his hands and his side. Then the disciples were glad when they saw the Lord. [21] Jesus said to them again, "Peace be with you. As the Father has sent me, even so I am sending you." [22] And when he had said this, he breathed on them and said to them, "Receive the Holy Spirit. [23] If you forgive the sins of any, they are forgiven them; if you withhold forgiveness from any, it is withheld."

[24] Now Thomas, one of the Twelve, called the Twin,[5] was not with them when Jesus came. [25] So the other disciples told him, "We have seen the Lord." But he said to them, "Unless I see in his hands the mark of the nails, and place my finger into the mark of the nails, and place my hand into his side, I will never believe."

[1] Probably a name for some crop-destroying pest or pests [2] Greek *his* [3] Or *Hebrew* [4] Greek *Ioudaioi* probably refers here to Jewish religious leaders, and others under their influence, in that time [5] Greek *Didymus*

26 Eight days later, his disciples were inside again, and Thomas was with them. Although the doors were locked, Jesus came and stood among them and said, "Peace be with you." **27** Then he said to Thomas, "Put your finger here, and see my hands; and put out your hand, and place it in my side. Do not disbelieve, but believe." **28** Thomas answered him, "My Lord and my God!" **29** Jesus said to him, "Have you believed because you have seen me? Blessed are those who have not seen and yet have believed."

30 Now Jesus did many other signs in the presence of the disciples, which are not written in this book; **31** but these are written so that you may believe that Jesus is the Christ, the Son of God, and that by believing you may have life in his name.

DECEMBER 31

2 Chronicles 36

The people of the land took Jehoahaz the son of Josiah and made him king in his father's place in Jerusalem. **2** Jehoahaz was twenty-three years old when he began to reign, and he reigned three months in Jerusalem. **3** Then the king of Egypt deposed him in Jerusalem and laid on the land a tribute of a hundred talents of silver and a talent[1] of gold. **4** And the king of Egypt made Eliakim his brother king over Judah and Jerusalem, and changed his name to Jehoiakim. But Neco took Jehoahaz his brother and carried him to Egypt.

5 Jehoiakim was twenty-five years old when he began to reign, and he reigned eleven years in Jerusalem. He did what was evil in the sight of the LORD his God. **6** Against him came up Nebuchadnezzar king of Babylon and bound him in chains to take him to Babylon. **7** Nebuchadnezzar also carried part of the vessels of the house of the LORD to Babylon and put them in his palace in Babylon. **8** Now the rest of the acts of Jehoiakim, and the abominations that he did, and what was found against him, behold, they are written in the Book of the Kings of Israel and Judah. And Jehoiachin his son reigned in his place.

9 Jehoiachin was eighteen[2] years old when he became king, and he reigned three months and ten days in Jerusalem. He did what was evil in the sight of the LORD. **10** In the spring of the year King Nebuchadnezzar sent and brought him to Babylon, with the precious vessels of the house of the LORD, and made his brother Zedekiah king over Judah and Jerusalem.

11 Zedekiah was twenty-one years old when he began to reign, and he reigned eleven years in Jerusalem. **12** He did what was evil in the sight of the LORD his God. He did not humble himself before Jeremiah the prophet, who spoke from the mouth of the LORD. **13** He also rebelled against King Nebuchadnezzar, who had made him swear by God. He stiffened his neck and hardened his heart against turning to the LORD, the God of Israel. **14** All the officers of the priests and the people likewise were exceedingly unfaithful, following all the abominations of the nations. And they polluted the house of the LORD that he had made holy in Jerusalem.

15 The LORD, the God of their fathers, sent persistently to them by his messengers, because he had compassion on his people and on his dwelling place. **16** But they kept mocking the messengers of God, despising his words and scoffing at his prophets, until the wrath of the LORD rose against his people, until there was no remedy. **17** Therefore he brought up against them the king of the Chaldeans, who killed their young men with the sword in the house of their sanctuary and had no compassion on young man or virgin, old man or aged. He gave them all into his hand. **18** And all the vessels of the house of God, great and small, and the treasures of the house of the LORD, and the treasures of the

[1] A *talent* was about 75 pounds or 34 kilograms [2] Septuagint (compare 2 Kings 24:8); most Hebrew manuscripts *eight*

king and of his princes, all these he brought to Babylon. ¹⁹And they burned the house of God and broke down the wall of Jerusalem and burned all its palaces with fire and destroyed all its precious vessels. ²⁰He took into exile in Babylon those who had escaped from the sword, and they became servants to him and to his sons until the establishment of the kingdom of Persia, ²¹to fulfill the word of the LORD by the mouth of Jeremiah, until the land had enjoyed its Sabbaths. All the days that it lay desolate it kept Sabbath, to fulfill seventy years.

²²Now in the first year of Cyrus king of Persia, that the word of the LORD by the mouth of Jeremiah might be fulfilled, the LORD stirred up the spirit of Cyrus king of Persia, so that he made a proclamation throughout all his kingdom and also put it in writing: ²³"Thus says Cyrus king of Persia, 'The LORD, the God of heaven, has given me all the kingdoms of the earth, and he has charged me to build him a house at Jerusalem, which is in Judah. Whoever is among you of all his people, may the LORD his God be with him. Let him go up.'"

Revelation 22

Then the angel¹ showed me the river of the water of life, bright as crystal, flowing from the throne of God and of the Lamb ²through the middle of the street of the city; also, on either side of the river, the tree of life² with its twelve kinds of fruit, yielding its fruit each month. The leaves of the tree were for the healing of the nations. ³No longer will there be anything accursed, but the throne of God and of the Lamb will be in it, and his servants³ will worship him. ⁴They will see his face, and his name will be on their foreheads. ⁵And night will be no more. They will need no light of lamp or sun, for the Lord God will be their light, and they will reign forever and ever.

⁶And he said to me, "These words are trustworthy and true. And the Lord, the God of the spirits of the prophets, has sent his angel to show his servants what must soon take place."

⁷"And behold, I am coming soon. Blessed is the one who keeps the words of the prophecy of this book."

⁸I, John, am the one who heard and saw these things. And when I heard and saw them, I fell down to worship at the feet of the angel who showed them to me, ⁹but he said to me, "You must not do that! I am a fellow servant⁴ with you and your brothers the prophets, and with those who keep the words of this book. Worship God."

¹⁰And he said to me, "Do not seal up the words of the prophecy of this book, for the time is near. ¹¹Let the evildoer still do evil, and the filthy still be filthy, and the righteous still do right, and the holy still be holy."

¹²"Behold, I am coming soon, bringing my recompense with me, to repay each one for what he has done. ¹³I am the Alpha and the Omega, the first and the last, the beginning and the end."

¹⁴Blessed are those who wash their robes,⁵ so that they may have the right to the tree of life and that they may enter the city by the gates. ¹⁵Outside are the dogs and sorcerers and the sexually immoral and murderers and idolaters, and everyone who loves and practices falsehood.

¹⁶"I, Jesus, have sent my angel to testify to you about these things for the churches. I am the root and the descendant of David, the bright morning star."

¹⁷The Spirit and the Bride say, "Come." And let the one who hears say, "Come." And let the one who is thirsty come; let the one who desires take the water of life without price.

¹⁸I warn everyone who hears the words of the prophecy of this book: if anyone adds to them, God will add to him the plagues described in this book, ¹⁹and if anyone takes away from the words of the book of this prophecy, God will take away his share in the tree of life and in the holy city, which are described in this book.

²⁰He who testifies to these things says, "Surely I am coming soon." Amen. Come, Lord Jesus!

²¹The grace of the Lord Jesus be with all.⁶ Amen.

Malachi 4⁷

"For behold, the day is coming, burning like an oven, when all the arrogant and all evildoers will be stubble. The day that is coming shall set them ablaze, says the LORD of hosts, so that it will leave them neither root nor branch. ²But for you who fear my name, the sun of righteousness shall rise with healing in its wings. You shall go out leaping like calves

---

¹ Greek he ² Or the Lamb. In the midst of the street of the city, and on either side of the river, was the tree of life ³ Greek bondservants; also verse 6 ⁴ Greek fellow bondservant
⁵ Some manuscripts do his commandments ⁶ Some manuscripts all the saints ⁷ Ch 4:1–6 is ch 3:19–24 in Hebrew

from the stall. ³And you shall tread down the wicked, for they will be ashes under the soles of your feet, on the day when I act, says the LORD of hosts.

⁴"Remember the law of my servant Moses, the statutes and rules¹ that I commanded him at Horeb for all Israel.

⁵"Behold, I will send you Elijah the prophet before the great and awesome day of the LORD comes. ⁶And he will turn the hearts of fathers to their children and the hearts of children to their fathers, lest I come and strike the land with a decree of utter destruction."²

────── *John 21* ──────

After this Jesus revealed himself again to the disciples by the Sea of Tiberias, and he revealed himself in this way. ²Simon Peter, Thomas (called the Twin), Nathanael of Cana in Galilee, the sons of Zebedee, and two others of his disciples were together. ³Simon Peter said to them, "I am going fishing." They said to him, "We will go with you." They went out and got into the boat, but that night they caught nothing.

⁴Just as day was breaking, Jesus stood on the shore; yet the disciples did not know that it was Jesus. ⁵Jesus said to them, "Children, do you have any fish?" They answered him, "No." ⁶He said to them, "Cast the net on the right side of the boat, and you will find some." So they cast it, and now they were not able to haul it in, because of the quantity of fish. ⁷That disciple whom Jesus loved therefore said to Peter, "It is the Lord!" When Simon Peter heard that it was the Lord, he put on his outer garment, for he was stripped for work, and threw himself into the sea. ⁸The other disciples came in the boat, dragging the net full of fish, for they were not far from the land, but about a hundred yards³ off.

⁹When they got out on land, they saw a charcoal fire in place, with fish laid out on it, and bread. ¹⁰Jesus said to them, "Bring some of the fish that you have just caught." ¹¹So Simon Peter went aboard and hauled the net ashore, full of large fish, 153 of them. And although there were so many, the net was not torn. ¹²Jesus said to them, "Come and have breakfast." Now none of the disciples dared ask him, "Who are you?" They knew it was the Lord. ¹³Jesus came and took the bread and gave it to them, and so with the fish. ¹⁴This was now the third time that Jesus was revealed to the disciples after he was raised from the dead.

¹⁵When they had finished breakfast, Jesus said to Simon Peter, "Simon, son of John, do you love me more than these?" He said to him, "Yes, Lord; you know that I love you." He said to him, "Feed my lambs." ¹⁶He said to him a second time, "Simon, son of John, do you love me?" He said to him, "Yes, Lord; you know that I love you." He said to him, "Tend my sheep." ¹⁷He said to him the third time, "Simon, son of John, do you love me?" Peter was grieved because he said to him the third time, "Do you love me?" and he said to him, "Lord, you know everything; you know that I love you." Jesus said to him, "Feed my sheep. ¹⁸Truly, truly, I say to you, when you were young, you used to dress yourself and walk wherever you wanted, but when you are old, you will stretch out your hands, and another will dress you and carry you where you do not want to go." ¹⁹(This he said to show by what kind of death he was to glorify God.) And after saying this he said to him, "Follow me."

²⁰Peter turned and saw the disciple whom Jesus loved following them, the one who also had leaned back against him during the supper and had said, "Lord, who is it that is going to betray you?" ²¹When Peter saw him, he said to Jesus, "Lord, what about this man?" ²²Jesus said to him, "If it is my will that he remain until I come, what is that to you? You follow me!" ²³So the saying spread abroad among the brothers⁴ that this disciple was not to die; yet Jesus did not say to him that he was not to die, but, "If it is my will that he remain until I come, what is that to you?"

²⁴This is the disciple who is bearing witness about these things, and who has written these things, and we know that his testimony is true.

²⁵Now there are also many other things that Jesus did. Were every one of them to be written, I suppose that the world itself could not contain the books that would be written.

---

¹ Or *and just decrees* ² The Hebrew term rendered *decree of utter destruction* refers to things devoted (or set apart) to the Lord (or by the Lord) for destruction ³ Greek *two hundred cubits*; a cubit was about 18 inches or 45 centimeters ⁴ Or *brothers and sisters*

WEIGHTS AND MEASURES

The following table is based on the best generally accepted information available for biblical weights, measures, and monetary units. All equivalents are approximate. Weights and measures also varied somewhat in different times and places in the ancient world. Most weights, measures, and monetary units are also explained in footnotes on the pages where they occur in the ESV text.

Biblical Unit	Approximate American and Metric Equivalents	Biblical Equivalent
bath	A *bath* was about 6 gallons or 22 liters	1 ephah
beka	A *beka* was about 1/5 ounce or 5.5 grams	10 gerahs
cor	A *cor* was about 6 bushels or 220 liters	10 ephahs
cubit	A *cubit* was about 18 inches or 45 centimeters	6 handbreadths
daric	A *daric* was a coin of about 1/4 ounce or 8.5 grams	
denarius	A *denarius* was a day's wage for a laborer	
ephah	An *ephah* was about 3/5 bushel or 22 liters	10 omers
gerah	A *gerah* was about 1/50 ounce or 0.6 gram	1/10 beka
handbreadth	A *handbreadth* was about 3 inches or 7.5 centimeters	1/6 cubit
hin	A *hin* was about 4 quarts or 3.5 liters	1/6 bath
homer	A *homer* was about 6 bushels or 220 liters	10 ephahs
kab	A *kab* was about 1 quart or 1 liter	1/22 ephah
lethech	A *lethech* was about 3 bushels or 110 liters	5 ephahs
log	A *log* was about 1/3 quart or 0.3 liter	1/72 bath
mina	A *mina* was about 1 1/4 pounds or 0.6 kilogram	50 shekels
omer	An *omer* was about 2 quarts or 2 liters	1/10 ephah
pim	A *pim* was about 1/3 ounce or 7.5 grams	2/3 shekel
seah	A *seah* was about 7 quarts or 7.3 liters	1/3 ephah
shekel	A *shekel* was about 2/5 ounce or 11 grams	2 bekas
span	A *span* was about 9 inches or 22 centimeters	3 handbreadths
stadion	A *stadion* was about 607 feet or 185 meters	
talent	A *talent* was about 75 pounds or 34 kilograms	60 minas

M'CHEYNE READING PLAN

19	Exodus 2	Luke 5	Job 19	1 Corinthians 6
20	Exodus 3	Luke 6	Job 20	1 Corinthians 7
21	Exodus 4	Luke 7	Job 21	1 Corinthians 8
22	Exodus 5	Luke 8	Job 22	1 Corinthians 9
23	Exodus 6	Luke 9	Job 23	1 Corinthians 10
24	Exodus 7	Luke 10	Job 24	1 Corinthians 11
25	Exodus 8	Luke 11	Job 25–26	1 Corinthians 12
26	Exodus 9	Luke 12	Job 27	1 Corinthians 13
27	Exodus 10	Luke 13	Job 28	1 Corinthians 14
28	Exodus 11:1–12:21	Luke 14	Job 29	1 Corinthians 15

MARCH

1	Exodus 12:22–51	Luke 15	Job 30	1 Corinthians 16
2	Exodus 13	Luke 16	Job 31	2 Corinthians 1
3	Exodus 14	Luke 17	Job 32	2 Corinthians 2
4	Exodus 15	Luke 18	Job 33	2 Corinthians 3
5	Exodus 16	Luke 19	Job 34	2 Corinthians 4
6	Exodus 17	Luke 20	Job 35	2 Corinthians 5
7	Exodus 18	Luke 21	Job 36	2 Corinthians 6
8	Exodus 19	Luke 22	Job 37	2 Corinthians 7
9	Exodus 20	Luke 23	Job 38	2 Corinthians 8
10	Exodus 21	Luke 24	Job 39	2 Corinthians 9
11	Exodus 22	John 1	Job 40	2 Corinthians 10
12	Exodus 23	John 2	Job 41	2 Corinthians 11
13	Exodus 24	John 3	Job 42	2 Corinthians 12
14	Exodus 25	John 4	Proverbs 1	2 Corinthians 13
15	Exodus 26	John 5	Proverbs 2	Galatians 1
16	Exodus 27	John 6	Proverbs 3	Galatians 2
17	Exodus 28	John 7	Proverbs 4	Galatians 3
18	Exodus 29	John 8	Proverbs 5	Galatians 4
19	Exodus 30	John 9	Proverbs 6	Galatians 5
20	Exodus 31	John 10	Proverbs 7	Galatians 6
21	Exodus 32	John 11	Proverbs 8	Ephesians 1
22	Exodus 33	John 12	Proverbs 9	Ephesians 2
23	Exodus 34	John 13	Proverbs 10	Ephesians 3
24	Exodus 35	John 14	Proverbs 11	Ephesians 4
25	Exodus 36	John 15	Proverbs 12	Ephesians 5
26	Exodus 37	John 16	Proverbs 13	Ephesians 6
27	Exodus 38	John 17	Proverbs 14	Philippians 1
28	Exodus 39	John 18	Proverbs 15	Philippians 2
29	Exodus 40	John 19	Proverbs 16	Philippians 3
30	Leviticus 1	John 20	Proverbs 17	Philippians 4
31	Leviticus 2–3	John 21	Proverbs 18	Colossians 1

APRIL

1	Leviticus 4	Psalms 1–2	Proverbs 19	Colossians 2
2	Leviticus 5	Psalms 3–4	Proverbs 20	Colossians 3
3	Leviticus 6	Psalms 5–6	Proverbs 21	Colossians 4
4	Leviticus 7	Psalms 7–8	Proverbs 22	1 Thessalonians 1
5	Leviticus 8	Psalm 9	Proverbs 23	1 Thessalonians 2
6	Leviticus 9	Psalm 10	Proverbs 24	1 Thessalonians 3
7	Leviticus 10	Psalms 11–12	Proverbs 25	1 Thessalonians 4
8	Leviticus 11–12	Psalms 13–14	Proverbs 26	1 Thessalonians 5
9	Leviticus 13	Psalms 15–16	Proverbs 27	2 Thessalonians 1
10	Leviticus 14	Psalm 17	Proverbs 28	2 Thessalonians 2
11	Leviticus 15	Psalm 18	Proverbs 29	2 Thessalonians 3
12	Leviticus 16	Psalm 19	Proverbs 30	1 Timothy 1

13	Leviticus 17	Psalms 20–21	Proverbs 31	1 Timothy 2
14	Leviticus 18	Psalm 22	Ecclesiastes 1	1 Timothy 3
15	Leviticus 19	Psalms 23–24	Ecclesiastes 2	1 Timothy 4
16	Leviticus 20	Psalm 25	Ecclesiastes 3	1 Timothy 5
17	Leviticus 21	Psalms 26–27	Ecclesiastes 4	1 Timothy 6
18	Leviticus 22	Psalms 28–29	Ecclesiastes 5	2 Timothy 1
19	Leviticus 23	Psalm 30	Ecclesiastes 6	2 Timothy 2
20	Leviticus 24	Psalm 31	Ecclesiastes 7	2 Timothy 3
21	Leviticus 25	Psalm 32	Ecclesiastes 8	2 Timothy 4
22	Leviticus 26	Psalm 33	Ecclesiastes 9	Titus 1
23	Leviticus 27	Psalm 34	Ecclesiastes 10	Titus 2
24	Numbers 1	Psalm 35	Ecclesiastes 11	Titus 3
25	Numbers 2	Psalm 36	Ecclesiastes 12	Philemon 1
26	Numbers 3	Psalm 37	Song of Solomon 1	Hebrews 1
27	Numbers 4	Psalm 38	Song of Solomon 2	Hebrews 2
28	Numbers 5	Psalm 39	Song of Solomon 3	Hebrews 3
29	Numbers 6	Psalms 40–41	Song of Solomon 4	Hebrews 4
30	Numbers 7	Psalms 42–43	Song of Solomon 5	Hebrews 5

MAY

1	Numbers 8	Psalm 44	Song of Solomon 6	Hebrews 6
2	Numbers 9	Psalm 45	Song of Solomon 7	Hebrews 7
3	Numbers 10	Psalms 46–47	Song of Solomon 8	Hebrews 8
4	Numbers 11	Psalm 48	Isaiah 1	Hebrews 9
5	Numbers 12–13	Psalm 49	Isaiah 2	Hebrews 10
6	Numbers 14	Psalm 50	Isaiah 3–4	Hebrews 11
7	Numbers 15	Psalm 51	Isaiah 5	Hebrews 12
8	Numbers 16	Psalms 52–54	Isaiah 6	Hebrews 13
9	Numbers 17–18	Psalm 55	Isaiah 7	James 1
10	Numbers 19	Psalms 56–57	Isaiah 8:1–9:7	James 2
11	Numbers 20	Psalms 58–59	Isaiah 9:8–10:4	James 3
12	Numbers 21	Psalms 60–61	Isaiah 10:5–34	James 4
13	Numbers 22	Psalms 62–63	Isaiah 11–12	James 5
14	Numbers 23	Psalms 64–65	Isaiah 13	1 Peter 1
15	Numbers 24	Psalms 66–67	Isaiah 14	1 Peter 2
16	Numbers 25	Psalm 68	Isaiah 15	1 Peter 3
17	Numbers 26	Psalm 69	Isaiah 16	1 Peter 4
18	Numbers 27	Psalms 70–71	Isaiah 17–18	1 Peter 5
19	Numbers 28	Psalm 72	Isaiah 19–20	2 Peter 1
20	Numbers 29	Psalm 73	Isaiah 21	2 Peter 2
21	Numbers 30	Psalm 74	Isaiah 22	2 Peter 3
22	Numbers 31	Psalms 75–76	Isaiah 23	1 John 1
23	Numbers 32	Psalm 77	Isaiah 24	1 John 2
24	Numbers 33	Psalm 78:1–37	Isaiah 25	1 John 3
25	Numbers 34	Psalm 78:38–72	Isaiah 26	1 John 4
26	Numbers 35	Psalm 79	Isaiah 27	1 John 5
27	Numbers 36	Psalm 80	Isaiah 28	2 John 1
28	Deuteronomy 1	Psalms 81–82	Isaiah 29	3 John 1
29	Deuteronomy 2	Psalms 83–84	Isaiah 30	Jude 1
30	Deuteronomy 3	Psalm 85	Isaiah 31	Revelation 1
31	Deuteronomy 4	Psalms 86–87	Isaiah 32	Revelation 2

JUNE

1	Deuteronomy 5	Psalm 88	Isaiah 33	Revelation 3
2	Deuteronomy 6	Psalm 89	Isaiah 34	Revelation 4
3	Deuteronomy 7	Psalm 90	Isaiah 35	Revelation 5
4	Deuteronomy 8	Psalm 91	Isaiah 36	Revelation 6
5	Deuteronomy 9	Psalms 92–93	Isaiah 37	Revelation 7
6	Deuteronomy 10	Psalm 94	Isaiah 38	Revelation 8
7	Deuteronomy 11	Psalms 95–96	Isaiah 39	Revelation 9
8	Deuteronomy 12	Psalms 97–98	Isaiah 40	Revelation 10
9	Deuteronomy 13–14	Psalms 99–101	Isaiah 41	Revelation 11
10	Deuteronomy 15	Psalm 102	Isaiah 42	Revelation 12
11	Deuteronomy 16	Psalm 103	Isaiah 43	Revelation 13
12	Deuteronomy 17	Psalm 104	Isaiah 44	Revelation 14
13	Deuteronomy 18	Psalm 105	Isaiah 45	Revelation 15
14	Deuteronomy 19	Psalm 106	Isaiah 46	Revelation 16
15	Deuteronomy 20	Psalm 107	Isaiah 47	Revelation 17
16	Deuteronomy 21	Psalms 108–109	Isaiah 48	Revelation 18
17	Deuteronomy 22	Psalms 110–111	Isaiah 49	Revelation 19
18	Deuteronomy 23	Psalms 112–113	Isaiah 50	Revelation 20
19	Deuteronomy 24	Psalms 114–115	Isaiah 51	Revelation 21
20	Deuteronomy 25	Psalm 116	Isaiah 52	Revelation 22
21	Deuteronomy 26	Psalms 117–118	Isaiah 53	Matthew 1
22	Deuteronomy 27:1–28:19	Psalm 119:1–24	Isaiah 54	Matthew 2
23	Deuteronomy 28:20–68	Psalm 119:25–48	Isaiah 55	Matthew 3
24	Deuteronomy 29	Psalm 119:49–72	Isaiah 56	Matthew 4
25	Deuteronomy 30	Psalm 119:73–96	Isaiah 57	Matthew 5
26	Deuteronomy 31	Psalm 119:97–120	Isaiah 58	Matthew 6
27	Deuteronomy 32	Psalm 119:121–144	Isaiah 59	Matthew 7
28	Deuteronomy 33–34	Psalm 119:145–176	Isaiah 60	Matthew 8
29	Joshua 1	Psalms 120–122	Isaiah 61	Matthew 9
30	Joshua 2	Psalms 123–125	Isaiah 62	Matthew 10

JULY

1	Joshua 3	Psalms 126–128	Isaiah 63	Matthew 11
2	Joshua 4	Psalms 129–131	Isaiah 64	Matthew 12
3	Joshua 5:1–6:5	Psalms 132–134	Isaiah 65	Matthew 13
4	Joshua 6:6–27	Psalms 135–136	Isaiah 66	Matthew 14
5	Joshua 7	Psalms 137–138	Jeremiah 1	Matthew 15
6	Joshua 8	Psalm 139	Jeremiah 2	Matthew 16
7	Joshua 9	Psalms 140–141	Jeremiah 3	Matthew 17
8	Joshua 10	Psalms 142–143	Jeremiah 4	Matthew 18
9	Joshua 11	Psalm 144	Jeremiah 5	Matthew 19
10	Joshua 12–13	Psalm 145	Jeremiah 6	Matthew 20
11	Joshua 14–15	Psalms 146–147	Jeremiah 7	Matthew 21
12	Joshua 16–17	Psalm 148	Jeremiah 8	Matthew 22
13	Joshua 18–19	Psalms 149–150	Jeremiah 9	Matthew 23
14	Joshua 20–21	Acts 1	Jeremiah 10	Matthew 24
15	Joshua 22	Acts 2	Jeremiah 11	Matthew 25
16	Joshua 23	Acts 3	Jeremiah 12	Matthew 26
17	Joshua 24	Acts 4	Jeremiah 13	Matthew 27
18	Judges 1	Acts 5	Jeremiah 14	Matthew 28
19	Judges 2	Acts 6	Jeremiah 15	Mark 1
20	Judges 3	Acts 7	Jeremiah 16	Mark 2
21	Judges 4	Acts 8	Jeremiah 17	Mark 3
22	Judges 5	Acts 9	Jeremiah 18	Mark 4
23	Judges 6	Acts 10	Jeremiah 19	Mark 5
24	Judges 7	Acts 11	Jeremiah 20	Mark 6

25	Judges 8	Acts 12	Jeremiah 21	Mark 7
26	Judges 9	Acts 13	Jeremiah 22	Mark 8
27	Judges 10:1–11:11	Acts 14	Jeremiah 23	Mark 9
28	Judges 11:12–40	Acts 15	Jeremiah 24	Mark 10
29	Judges 12	Acts 16	Jeremiah 25	Mark 11
30	Judges 13	Acts 17	Jeremiah 26	Mark 12
31	Judges 14	Acts 18	Jeremiah 27	Mark 13

AUGUST

1	Judges 15	Acts 19	Jeremiah 28	Mark 14
2	Judges 16	Acts 20	Jeremiah 29	Mark 15
3	Judges 17	Acts 21	Jeremiah 30–31	Mark 16
4	Judges 18	Acts 22	Jeremiah 32	Psalms 1–2
5	Judges 19	Acts 23	Jeremiah 33	Psalms 3–4
6	Judges 20	Acts 24	Jeremiah 34	Psalms 5–6
7	Judges 21	Acts 25	Jeremiah 35	Psalms 7–8
8	Ruth 1	Acts 26	Jeremiah 36, 45	Psalm 9
9	Ruth 2	Acts 27	Jeremiah 37	Psalm 10
10	Ruth 3–4	Acts 28	Jeremiah 38	Psalms 11–12
11	1 Samuel 1	Romans 1	Jeremiah 39	Psalms 13–14
12	1 Samuel 2	Romans 2	Jeremiah 40	Psalms 15–16
13	1 Samuel 3	Romans 3	Jeremiah 41	Psalm 17
14	1 Samuel 4	Romans 4	Jeremiah 42	Psalm 18
15	1 Samuel 5–6	Romans 5	Jeremiah 43	Psalm 19
16	1 Samuel 7–8	Romans 6	Jeremiah 44	Psalms 20–21
17	1 Samuel 9	Romans 7	Jeremiah 46	Psalm 22
18	1 Samuel 10	Romans 8	Jeremiah 47	Psalms 23–24
19	1 Samuel 11	Romans 9	Jeremiah 48	Psalm 25
20	1 Samuel 12	Romans 10	Jeremiah 49	Psalms 26–27
21	1 Samuel 13	Romans 11	Jeremiah 50	Psalms 28–29
22	1 Samuel 14	Romans 12	Jeremiah 51	Psalm 30
23	1 Samuel 15	Romans 13	Jeremiah 52	Psalm 31
24	1 Samuel 16	Romans 14	Lamentations 1	Psalm 32
25	1 Samuel 17	Romans 15	Lamentations 2	Psalm 33
26	1 Samuel 18	Romans 16	Lamentations 3	Psalm 34
27	1 Samuel 19	1 Corinthians 1	Lamentations 4	Psalm 35
28	1 Samuel 20	1 Corinthians 2	Lamentations 5	Psalm 36
29	1 Samuel 21–22	1 Corinthians 3	Ezekiel 1	Psalm 37
30	1 Samuel 23	1 Corinthians 4	Ezekiel 2	Psalm 38
31	1 Samuel 24	1 Corinthians 5	Ezekiel 3	Psalm 39

SEPTEMBER

1	1 Samuel 25	1 Corinthians 6	Ezekiel 4	Psalms 40–41
2	1 Samuel 26	1 Corinthians 7	Ezekiel 5	Psalms 42–43
3	1 Samuel 27	1 Corinthians 8	Ezekiel 6	Psalm 44
4	1 Samuel 28	1 Corinthians 9	Ezekiel 7	Psalm 45
5	1 Samuel 29–30	1 Corinthians 10	Ezekiel 8	Psalms 46–47
6	1 Samuel 31	1 Corinthians 11	Ezekiel 9	Psalm 48
7	2 Samuel 1	1 Corinthians 12	Ezekiel 10	Psalm 49
8	2 Samuel 2	1 Corinthians 13	Ezekiel 11	Psalm 50
9	2 Samuel 3	1 Corinthians 14	Ezekiel 12	Psalm 51
10	2 Samuel 4–5	1 Corinthians 15	Ezekiel 13	Psalms 52–54
11	2 Samuel 6	1 Corinthians 16	Ezekiel 14	Psalm 55
12	2 Samuel 7	2 Corinthians 1	Ezekiel 15	Psalms 56–57
13	2 Samuel 8–9	2 Corinthians 2	Ezekiel 16	Psalms 58–59
14	2 Samuel 10	2 Corinthians 3	Ezekiel 17	Psalms 60–61
15	2 Samuel 11	2 Corinthians 4	Ezekiel 18	Psalms 62–63

16	2 Samuel 12	2 Corinthians 5	Ezekiel 19	Psalms 64–65
17	2 Samuel 13	2 Corinthians 6	Ezekiel 20	Psalms 66–67
18	2 Samuel 14	2 Corinthians 7	Ezekiel 21	Psalm 68
19	2 Samuel 15	2 Corinthians 8	Ezekiel 22	Psalm 69
20	2 Samuel 16	2 Corinthians 9	Ezekiel 23	Psalms 70–71
21	2 Samuel 17	2 Corinthians 10	Ezekiel 24	Psalm 72
22	2 Samuel 18	2 Corinthians 11	Ezekiel 25	Psalm 73
23	2 Samuel 19	2 Corinthians 12	Ezekiel 26	Psalm 74
24	2 Samuel 20	2 Corinthians 13	Ezekiel 27	Psalms 75–76
25	2 Samuel 21	Galatians 1	Ezekiel 28	Psalm 77
26	2 Samuel 22	Galatians 2	Ezekiel 29	Psalm 78:1–37
27	2 Samuel 23	Galatians 3	Ezekiel 30	Psalm 78:38–72
28	2 Samuel 24	Galatians 4	Ezekiel 31	Psalm 79
29	1 Kings 1	Galatians 5	Ezekiel 32	Psalm 80
30	1 Kings 2	Galatians 6	Ezekiel 33	Psalms 81–82

OCTOBER

1	1 Kings 3	Ephesians 1	Ezekiel 34	Psalms 83–84
2	1 Kings 4–5	Ephesians 2	Ezekiel 35	Psalm 85
3	1 Kings 6	Ephesians 3	Ezekiel 36	Psalm 86
4	1 Kings 7	Ephesians 4	Ezekiel 37	Psalms 87–88
5	1 Kings 8	Ephesians 5	Ezekiel 38	Psalm 89
6	1 Kings 9	Ephesians 6	Ezekiel 39	Psalm 90
7	1 Kings 10	Philippians 1	Ezekiel 40	Psalm 91
8	1 Kings 11	Philippians 2	Ezekiel 41	Psalms 92–93
9	1 Kings 12	Philippians 3	Ezekiel 42	Psalm 94
10	1 Kings 13	Philippians 4	Ezekiel 43	Psalms 95–96
11	1 Kings 14	Colossians 1	Ezekiel 44	Psalms 97–98
12	1 Kings 15	Colossians 2	Ezekiel 45	Psalms 99–101
13	1 Kings 16	Colossians 3	Ezekiel 46	Psalm 102
14	1 Kings 17	Colossians 4	Ezekiel 47	Psalm 103
15	1 Kings 18	1 Thessalonians 1	Ezekiel 48	Psalm 104
16	1 Kings 19	1 Thessalonians 2	Daniel 1	Psalm 105
17	1 Kings 20	1 Thessalonians 3	Daniel 2	Psalm 106
18	1 Kings 21	1 Thessalonians 4	Daniel 3	Psalm 107
19	1 Kings 22	1 Thessalonians 5	Daniel 4	Psalms 108–109
20	2 Kings 1	2 Thessalonians 1	Daniel 5	Psalms 110–111
21	2 Kings 2	2 Thessalonians 2	Daniel 6	Psalms 112–113
22	2 Kings 3	2 Thessalonians 3	Daniel 7	Psalms 114–115
23	2 Kings 4	1 Timothy 1	Daniel 8	Psalm 116
24	2 Kings 5	1 Timothy 2	Daniel 9	Psalms 117–118
25	2 Kings 6	1 Timothy 3	Daniel 10	Psalm 119:1–24
26	2 Kings 7	1 Timothy 4	Daniel 11	Psalm 119:25–48
27	2 Kings 8	1 Timothy 5	Daniel 12	Psalm 119:49–72
28	2 Kings 9	1 Timothy 6	Hosea 1	Psalm 119:73–96
29	2 Kings 10	2 Timothy 1	Hosea 2	Psalm 119:97–120
30	2 Kings 11–12	2 Timothy 2	Hosea 3–4	Psalm 119:121–144
31	2 Kings 13	2 Timothy 3	Hosea 5–6	Psalm 119:145–176

NOVEMBER

1	2 Kings 14	2 Timothy 4	Hosea 7	Psalms 120–122
2	2 Kings 15	Titus 1	Hosea 8	Psalms 123–125
3	2 Kings 16	Titus 2	Hosea 9	Psalms 126–128
4	2 Kings 17	Titus 3	Hosea 10	Psalms 129–131
5	2 Kings 18	Philemon 1	Hosea 11	Psalms 132–134
6	2 Kings 19	Hebrews 1	Hosea 12	Psalms 135–136
7	2 Kings 20	Hebrews 2	Hosea 13	Psalms 137–138

8	2 Kings 21	Hebrews 3	Hosea 14	Psalm 139
9	2 Kings 22	Hebrews 4	Joel 1	Psalms 140–141
10	2 Kings 23	Hebrews 5	Joel 2	Psalm 142
11	2 Kings 24	Hebrews 6	Joel 3	Psalm 143
12	2 Kings 25	Hebrews 7	Amos 1	Psalm 144
13	1 Chronicles 1–2	Hebrews 8	Amos 2	Psalm 145
14	1 Chronicles 3–4	Hebrews 9	Amos 3	Psalms 146–147
15	1 Chronicles 5–6	Hebrews 10	Amos 4	Psalms 148–150
16	1 Chronicles 7–8	Hebrews 11	Amos 5	Luke 1:1–38
17	1 Chronicles 9–10	Hebrews 12	Amos 6	Luke 1:39–80
18	1 Chronicles 11–12	Hebrews 13	Amos 7	Luke 2
19	1 Chronicles 13–14	James 1	Amos 8	Luke 3
20	1 Chronicles 15	James 2	Amos 9	Luke 4
21	1 Chronicles 16	James 3	Obadiah 1	Luke 5
22	1 Chronicles 17	James 4	Jonah 1	Luke 6
23	1 Chronicles 18	James 5	Jonah 2	Luke 7
24	1 Chronicles 19–20	1 Peter 1	Jonah 3	Luke 8
25	1 Chronicles 21	1 Peter 2	Jonah 4	Luke 9
26	1 Chronicles 22	1 Peter 3	Micah 1	Luke 10
27	1 Chronicles 23	1 Peter 4	Micah 2	Luke 11
28	1 Chronicles 24–25	1 Peter 5	Micah 3	Luke 12
29	1 Chronicles 26–27	2 Peter 1	Micah 4	Luke 13
30	1 Chronicles 28	2 Peter 2	Micah 5	Luke 14

DECEMBER

1	1 Chronicles 29	2 Peter 3	Micah 6	Luke 15
2	2 Chronicles 1	1 John 1	Micah 7	Luke 16
3	2 Chronicles 2	1 John 2	Nahum 1	Luke 17
4	2 Chronicles 3–4	1 John 3	Nahum 2	Luke 18
5	2 Chronicles 5:1–6:11	1 John 4	Nahum 3	Luke 19
6	2 Chronicles 6:12–42	1 John 5	Habakkuk 1	Luke 20
7	2 Chronicles 7	2 John 1	Habakkuk 2	Luke 21
8	2 Chronicles 8	3 John 1	Habakkuk 3	Luke 22
9	2 Chronicles 9	Jude 1	Zephaniah 1	Luke 23
10	2 Chronicles 10	Revelation 1	Zephaniah 2	Luke 24
11	2 Chronicles 11–12	Revelation 2	Zephaniah 3	John 1
12	2 Chronicles 13	Revelation 3	Haggai 1	John 2
13	2 Chronicles 14–15	Revelation 4	Haggai 2	John 3
14	2 Chronicles 16	Revelation 5	Zechariah 1	John 4
15	2 Chronicles 17	Revelation 6	Zechariah 2	John 5
16	2 Chronicles 18	Revelation 7	Zechariah 3	John 6
17	2 Chronicles 19–20	Revelation 8	Zechariah 4	John 7
18	2 Chronicles 21	Revelation 9	Zechariah 5	John 8
19	2 Chronicles 22–23	Revelation 10	Zechariah 6	John 9
20	2 Chronicles 24	Revelation 11	Zechariah 7	John 10
21	2 Chronicles 25	Revelation 12	Zechariah 8	John 11
22	2 Chronicles 26	Revelation 13	Zechariah 9	John 12
23	2 Chronicles 27–28	Revelation 14	Zechariah 10	John 13
24	2 Chronicles 29	Revelation 15	Zechariah 11	John 14
25	2 Chronicles 30	Revelation 16	Zechariah 12:1–13:1	John 15
26	2 Chronicles 31	Revelation 17	Zechariah 13:2–9	John 16
27	2 Chronicles 32	Revelation 18	Zechariah 14	John 17
28	2 Chronicles 33	Revelation 19	Malachi 1	John 18
29	2 Chronicles 34	Revelation 20	Malachi 2	John 19
30	2 Chronicles 35	Revelation 21	Malachi 3	John 20
31	2 Chronicles 36	Revelation 22	Malachi 4	John 21